EU COMPETITION PROCEDURE

THIRD EDITION

EU COMPETITION PROCEDURE

THIRD EDITION

Edited by

LUIS ORTIZ BLANCO

With contributions by
LUIS ORTIZ BLANCO
KONSTANTIN JÖRGENS
RALF SAUER
CORNELIU HÖDLMAYR
MANUEL KELLERBAUER AND
MARISA TIERNO CENTELLA (PART I)
MARCOS ARAUJO BOYD AND NICOLAS VON LINGEN (PART II)
JOSÉ LUIS BUENDÍA SIERRA (PART III)
JEAN-PAUL KEPPENNE AND CARLOS URRACA CAVIEDES (PART IV)
KIERON BEAL (PART V) AND GORDON BLANKE (PART VI)

OXFORD
UNIVERSITY PRESS

OXFORD
UNIVERSITY PRESS

Great Clarendon Street, Oxford, OX2 6DP,
United Kingdom

Oxford University Press is a department of the University of Oxford.
It furthers the University's objective of excellence in research, scholarship,
and education by publishing worldwide. Oxford is a registered trade mark of
Oxford University Press in the UK and in certain other countries

© The Authors, 2013

The moral rights of the authors have been asserted

First edition published in 1996
Third edition published in 2013

Impression: 1

Published in the United States of America by Oxford University Press
198 Madison Avenue, New York, NY 10016, United States of America

British Library Cataloguing in Publication Data
Data available

Library of Congress Control Number: 2013940571

ISBN 978-0-19-964183-3

Printed in Great Britain by
CPI Group (UK) Ltd, Croydon, CR0 4YY

CONTENTS

I ANTITRUST RULES (ARTICLES 101 AND 102 TFEU)

II CONTROL OF CONCENTRATIONS
(REGULATION (EC) 139/2004)

V COMPETITION LAW AND PROCEDURE IN THE EUROPEAN ECONOMIC AREA

VI ARBITRATION

TABLE OF CASES

TABLE OF TREATIES AND AGREEMENTS

TABLE OF REGULATIONS

TABLE OF DIRECTIVES

TABLE OF NATIONAL LEGISLATION

PART I

ANTITRUST RULES
(ARTICLES 101 AND 102 TFEU)*

---

* Aaron Kahn, Oran Kiazim, Lina Barauskaite, Moritz Jakobs, and Bastian Baumann provided research assistance for the drafting of this Part.

1

THE INSTITUTIONAL FRAMEWORK

Luis Ortiz Blanco and Konstantin Jörgens

I. Sources of Procedure

A. Substantive Provisions

The basic European Union ('EU') competition provisions applicable to businesses or undertak- **1.01** ings are Articles 101 and 102 of the Treaty on the Functioning of the European Union ('TFEU'),[1] Both provisions are an important part of the EU legal order and pursue one of the main objectives of the TFEU and the Treaty on European Union ('TEU'), namely that of achieving an internal market. While Title 1 of the TEU and Part One of the TFEU only refer to the establishment of

---

[1] The 'Lisbon Treaty', which entered into force on 1 December 2009, actually consists of two separate instruments. First, there is the Treaty on European Union ('TEU'), which is conceived as a substantial amendment of the Treaty on the European Union (the Maastricht Treaty) and sets forth the objectives and principles of the EU. Secondly, there is the TFEU, which builds on the original EC Treaty, and complements the TEU with respect to the organizational and functional details. A consolidated version of the TFEU and the TEU is contained in the Official Journal ('OJ') [2010] OJ C83/1 and available at <http://eur-lex.europa.eu/en/treaties/index.htm>.

the internal market as a key objective and no longer declare that 'a system ensuring that competition... is not distorted' is one of the stated objectives of the EU,[2] a legally binding Protocol on the Internal Market and Competition which contained the previous wording was ultimately annexed to the Treaties, thus enabling the EU to take appropriate action to this end.[3]

1.02 Article 101(1) TFEU prohibits agreements and arrangements between undertakings that affect trade between Member States and which have as their object or effect the prevention, restriction, or distortion of competition within the EU.[4] Article 102 TFEU prohibits abuses of a dominant position within the internal market by one or more undertakings. Apart from various actions listed in Article 102(2) TFEU, abuses may take the form of any conduct by a dominant undertaking that appreciably distorts competition or exploits customers in the market in question. The effective enforcement of Articles 101 and 102 TFEU is recognized as an 'objective of general interest recognised by the Union'.[5]

1.03 The assessment of the effect of agreements and conduct on competition often involves a complex analysis of the facts, and the conclusions derived from these facts may differ significantly depending on the underlying economic theory and model employed. Establishing the most basic concepts in competition law, such as the relevant market, are often major challenges that require very specific data and sophisticated analytical tools.[6] Competition authorities are increasingly confronted with the need to investigate such complex cases, which require in-depth fact-finding and rigorous economic and empirical analysis.[7] Due to the increasing importance of economics in complex cases, the European Commission ('Commission') often

---

[2] This removal is understood to have been engineered mainly by France and raised concerns that the emphasis on competition law enforcement would be reduced in the face of protectionist policies by certain Member States. As a result, the European Council's Legal Service issued an opinion stating that the fact that reference to 'a system ensuring that competition in the internal market is not distorted' has been omitted from the EU's objectives does not prevent the EU legislator from acting to ensure that competition in the internal market is not distorted. It, therefore, considers that the Protocol on the Internal Market and Competition, while in conformity with the Treaty, is legally superfluous. See also MEMO/07/250 'Statement by European Commissioner for Competition Neelie Kroes on results of June 21–22 European Council—Protocol on Internal Market and Competition' of 23 June 2007. Kerse & Khan, *EC Antitrust Procedure* (6th edn, Sweet & Maxwell 2012) para 1-005, pointing out that it does not appear that the changes will make any difference to the Court's approach to the interpretation of competition law.

[3] Protocol (No 27) on the internal market and competition [2008] OJ 115/309.

[4] The importance of the objective of undistorted competition led those who drafted the EC Treaty to provide expressly, in Art 81(2) (now Art 101 (2) TFEU), that *any* agreements or decisions prohibited pursuant to that provision are to be automatically void (Case C-126/97 *Eco Swiss* [1999] ECR I-3055 para 36) unless it meets the requirements of Art 81(3) EC (now Art 101(3) TFEU). Commission Notice, Guidelines on the application of Art 81(3) [now Art 101(3) TFEU] of the Treaty [2004] OJ C101/97.

[5] See WPJ Wils, 'EU Antitrust Enforcement Powers and Procedural Rights and Guarantees: The Interplay between EU Law, National Law, the Charter of Fundamental Rights of the EU and the European Convention on Human Rights' (2011) 34(2) World Competition 189, 202, n 50, citing the rulings that follow. According to the judgment of the ECJ of 1 June 1999 in Case C-126/97 *Eco Swiss v Benetton* [1999] ECR I-3079, para 36, '[Article 101 TFEU] constitutes a fundamental provision which is essential for the accomplishment of the tasks entrusted to the [EU] and, in particular, for the functioning of the internal market'; see also Judgment of 7 January 2004 in Joined Cases C-204/00 P etc *Aalborg Portland and Others v Commission* [2004] ECR I-123, paras 53 and 54, and Opinion of Advocate General ('AG') Geelhoed of 19 January 2006 in Case C-301/04 P *Commission v SGL Carbon* [2006] ECR I-5915, para 67.

[6] See in this respect the information available at the website of the Directorate-General for Competition ('DG COMP') about the Chief Competition Economist's team, available at <http://ec.europa.eu/competition/index_en.html>. MP Schinkel, 'Forensic Economics in Competition Law Enforcement' (2007) 4(1) Journal of Competition Law and Economics 1 and Director-General at DG COMP A Italianer, 'Best Practices for Antitrust Proceedings and the Submission of Economic Evidence and the Enhanced Role of the Hearing Officer', OECD Competition Committee Meeting 18 October 2011, Paris.

[7] According to Case C-234/89 *Stergios Delimitis v Henninger Bräu AG* [1991] ECR I-935, para 44, it is for the Commission to adopt, subject to review by the General Court ('GC', formerly the Court of First Instance ('CFI')) and the ECJ, individual decisions in accordance with the procedural rules in force and to

requests substantial economic data, and parties often submit arguments based on complex economic theories or provide empirical analysis. In order to streamline the submission and assessment of such evidence, the Commission published in 2011 'Best Practices' that outline the criteria that economic and econometric analysis should fulfil and explain how they will be dealt with.[8]

The shift from the traditional approach towards a more economic-oriented assessment to **1.04** ensure quality and the key role of economic advice in enforcement and policy making has been a key objective of the Commission in recent years.[9] Further, competition law procedures often make it necessary for the public authorities to take economic policy decisions based on public interest considerations and social welfare objectives which fall outside national courts' traditional sphere of activity, as they are better placed to deal with private damages actions for breaches of antitrust rules.[10] Unlike a normal commercial dispute, where to some extent the parties can determine the rules of the game, where Articles 101 and 102 TFEU are concerned, the parties are bound by the public interest aim of these provisions with a view to guaranteeing the maintenance of a system that ensures that competition is

---

adopt exemption regulations. The performance of that task would necessarily entail complex economic assessments, in particular in order to assess whether an agreement falls under Art 101 TFEU. See also Opinion of AG Cosmas in Case C-344/98 *Masterfoods* [2000] ECR I-11369, para 54. The review of the EU Courts is in principle limited to verifying whether the relevant rules on procedure and on the statement of reasons have been complied with, whether the facts have been accurately stated, and whether there has been any manifest error of appraisal or misuse of powers, and the Courts should not substitute their own assessment for that of the Commission, thereby encroaching on the discretion enjoyed by the Commission. For example, Case 42/84 *Remia and others v Commission* [1985] ECR 2545, para 34, and Joined Cases 142/84 and 156/84 *BAT and Reynolds v Commission* [1987] ECR 4487, para 62; Case C-194/99 *Thyssen StahlAG v Commission* [2003] ECR I-10821, para 78; Case C-441/07 P EC *Commission v Alrosa* [2010] ECR I-5949, paras 67 and 68. F Cengiz, 'Judicial Review and the Rule of Law in the EU Competition Law Regime after Alrosa' (2011) 7(1) European Competition Journal 127. For more details on the aspects of judicial review, including more recent case law, see Ch 15, 'Steps Following the Adoption of a Formal Decision', para 15.32 et seq.

[8] The Best Practices on the submission of economic evidence are part of the 'Best Practices Package' that the European Commission published in October 2011. IP/11/2011 'Commission reforms antitrust procedures and expands role of Hearing Officer', 17 October 2011; see also MEMO/11/703, 'Competition: Best Practices to increase interaction with parties and enhanced role of hearing officer—frequently asked questions', 17 October 2011. For more details, see para 1.104.

[9] In 2002, the GC annulled three Commission merger decisions in four months (Case T-342/99 *Airtours v Commission* [2002] ECR II-2585; Case T-310/01 *Schneider Electric SA v Commission* [2002] ECR II-4071). This also drew attention to the issue of the burden of proof incumbent on the Commission in adopting negative decisions. In 2003, the Commission appointed a Chief Economist who is part of the Commission's DG COMP. The Chief Economist assists the Commission in evaluating the economic impact of its actions and provides independent guidance on methodological issues of economics and econometrics in the application of the EU competition rules. He contributes to individual competition cases (in particular ones involving complex economic issues and quantitative analysis), the development of general policy instruments, and assisting with cases pending before the EU Courts. The Chief Economist also coordinates the activities of the Economic Advisory Group in Competition Policy ('EAGCP'), a discussion forum on competition policy matters between academics who have a recognized reputation in the field of industrial organization. Its main purpose is to support DG COMP in improving the economic reasoning in competition policy analysis; former Director-General of DG COMP, P Lowe 'The Design of Competition Policy Institutions for the 21st Century—The Experience of the European Commission and DG Competition' (2008) 3 Competition Policy Newsletter 1, 7. See also Director-General of DG COMP, A Italianer, ' "Quantity" and "quality" in economic assessments', Speech to the Charles River Associates Annual Conference, Brussels, 7 December 2011.

[10] Commission Notice on cooperation between the Commission and the courts of the EU Member States in the application of Arts [101] and [102 TFEU] [2004] OJ C101/54 ('National Courts Cooperation Notice') para 6: 'Where an individual asks the national court to safeguard his subjective rights, national courts play a specific role in the enforcement of Arts [101] and [102 TFEU], which is different from the enforcement in the public interest by the Commission or by national competition authorities.' Case C-94/00 *Roquette Frères* [2002] ECR I-9011, para 42: 'the powers conferred on the Commission by Art 14(1) of Reg No 17 [now Art 20 of Reg 1/2003] are designed to enable it to perform its task of ensuring that the competition rules are applied in the common market, the function of those rules being to prevent competition from being distorted

not distorted.[11] Furthermore, EU competition law extends beyond the interests of any one Member State and seeks to attain specific economic objectives on a much greater scale.[12] All these features, together with the principle of limited intervention laid down in Article 103 TFEU and the principle that the Commission's administrative practice must be appropriate to the prevailing circumstances, are reflected in the rules and procedural practices according to which the Commission and the EU Courts have applied substantive competition law.[13]

B. Procedural Rules

1.05 Article 103 TFEU empowers the EU Council to adopt regulations and directives in order, in particular, to do the following:

(a) ensure compliance with the prohibitions laid down in Article 101(1) and in Article 102 TFEU by making provision for fines and periodic penalty payments;
(b) lay down detailed rules for the application of Article 101(3), taking into account the need to ensure effective supervision on the one hand, and to simplify administration to the greatest possible extent on the other;
(c) define, if need be, in the various branches of the economy, the scope of the provisions of Articles 101 and 102;
(d) define the respective functions of the Commission and the Court of Justice ('ECJ') in applying the provisions laid down in this paragraph;
(e) determine the relationship between national laws and the provisions contained in this Section or adopted pursuant to this Article.

1.06 On the basis of that provision, the Council adopted a series of regulations which define in detail the procedure applicable to competition matters, and has entrusted the application of that procedure to the Commission. The Council also authorized the Commission to adopt supplementary procedural rules.

---

to the detriment of the public interest, individual undertakings and consumers, thereby ensuring economic well-being in the Community'.

[11] See Case T-528/93 *Métropole Télévision v Commission* [1996] ECR II-649, para 118, in which the Court held that, for the purposes of an overall assessment, the EC Commission could base its decisions to grant an exemption under Art 101(3) TFEU on considerations relating to the pursuit of the public interest. See also Opinion of Advocate General Léger, in Case C-309/99 *Wouters* [2002] ECR I-1577, para 113.

[12] Case T-31/99 *ABB Asea Brown Boveri Ltd v Commission* [2002] ECR-II 1881 para 116: '[the] task [of the Commission] certainly includes the duty to investigate and punish individual infringements, but it also encompasses the duty to pursue a general policy designed to apply, in competition matters, the principles laid down by the Treaty and to guide the conduct of undertakings in the light of those principles'. See also Joined Cases T-456/05 and T-457/05 *Gütermann AG/Zwicky & Co AG v Commission* [2010] ECR II-1443, para 79.

[13] WPJ Wils, 'Should Private Antitrust Enforcement Be Encouraged' [2003] World Competition 473, 480–4 argues that if the goal of antitrust enforcement is to ensure that antitrust prohibitions are not violated, public enforcement is inherently superior to private enforcement. See also the other publications of WPJ Wils, 'The Relationship between Public Antitrust Enforcement and Private Actions for Damages' (2009) 32(1) World Competition 3; 'Discretion and Prioritisation in Public Antitrust Enforcement, in Particular EU Antitrust Enforcement' (2011) 34(3) World Competition 353. By contrast, see CA Jones, 'Private Antitrust Enforcement in Europe: A Policy Analysis and Reality Check' (2004) 27(1) World Competition 13 (arguing that private enforcement would have great value as a supplement to public enforcement and as the primary means of compensating victims of infringements whose interests are to be protected by national courts). See also on this debate A Riley, 'Beyond Leniency: Enhancing Enforcement in EC Antitrust Law' (2005) 28(3) World Competition 377, 381 et seq and Commissioner for Competition, J Almunia, 'Public Enforcement and Private Damages Actions in Antitrust European Parliament', ECON Committee Brussels, 22 September

1. General regime

On 1 May 2004, Regulation 1/2003[14] entered into force and modernized the procedural rules **1.07** contained in the First Regulation implementing Articles 81 and 82 of the Treaty, commonly known as Regulation 17.[15] Regulation 1/2003 is the result of a comprehensive reform process that the Commission started more than a decade ago with the adoption of the White Paper on modernization of the rules implementing Articles [101] and [102] TFEU.[16] The key features of this process were the following:

- The abolition of the practice of notifying business agreements to the Commission, enabling the Commission to focus its resources on the important fight against cartels and other serious violations of the antitrust rules.
- The empowerment of national competition authorities ('NCAs') and courts to apply EU antitrust rules in their entirety, so that there are multiple enforcers and therefore wider application of the EU antitrust rules.
- A more level playing field for cross-border businesses, as all competition enforcers, including NCAs and national courts, are obliged to apply EU antitrust rules to cases that affect trade between Member States.
- Close cooperation between the Commission and national competition authorities in the European Competition Network ('ECN').
- Enhanced enforcement tools for the Commission so that it is better equipped to detect and address breaches of the antitrust rules.[17]

In order to complement Regulation 1/2003, following extensive consultations the Commission **1.08** adopted the 'Modernization Package' which, with respect to procedural matters, includes the following:[18]

2011, stressing the need to protect the balance between public and private enforcement, suggesting regulation may be needed, particularly over access to evidence.

  [14] [2003] OJ L1/1.
  [15] Council Reg (EEC) 17 implementing Arts [105] and [106] [TFEU], as amended [1962] OJ 13/204 [1959–62] OJ Spec Ed 87.
  [16] White Paper on modernization of the rules implementing Articles 85 and 86 [now 101 and 102] of the EC Treaty [1999] OJ C132/1. The White Paper sought to deal with the enforcement problems which had arisen since the adoption of Reg 17 in 1962. In September 2000, the Commission presented a first proposal to amend the system of enforcement of Arts 101 and 102. See EC Commission IP/00/1064 of 27 September 2000 'Competition: Commission proposes Regulation that extensively amends system for implementing Arts [101] and [102] [TFEU]'. It went on to initiate a broad debate, in which all the interested parties—companies, associations, jurists, economists, lawyers, members of the judiciary, and national governments—were offered an opportunity to express their views, both positive and negative, to make proposals, and to look further into the issues at stake. For a more general outlook post-modernization, former Director-General of DG COMP, P Lowe, 'Setting enforcement priorities at European and national level post modernisation', Speech at VIII Treviso Conference, 22 May 2008 available at <http://ec.europa.eu/competition/speeches/>.
  [17] Communication from the Commission to the European Parliament and the Council—Report on the functioning of Regulation 1/2003 SEC(2009)574, 29 April 2009, point 2. See also E Gippini Fournier, 'The Modernisation of European Competition Law: First Experiences with Regulation 1/2003—Institutional Report' in HF Koeck and MM Karollus (eds), The Modernisation of European Competition Law—Initial Experiences with Regulation 1/2003, FIDE XXIII Congress Linz 2008—Congress Publications Vol 2 (Nomos 2008) 379 et seq.
  [18] From the outset, there had been the question of whether the notices could have a binding effect upon NCAs and national courts, M Schwela, 'Die Bindungswirkung von Bekanntmachungen and Leitlinien der Europäischen Kommission' [2004] Wirtschaft und Wettbewerb 1133; and reply of P Pohlmann, 'Keine Bindungswirkung von Bekanntmachungen und Leitlinien der Europäischen Kommission' [2005] Wirtschaft und Wettbewerb 1105. See Case T-339/04 *France Télécom SA v Commission* [2004] [2007] ECR II-521 para 77 et seq, where it was held that the Commission's notice on cooperation within the network of competition authorities ('ECN Cooperation Notice') would have no binding effect in that it would not impose an obligation on the Commission not to deal with a case which is being dealt with by an NCA. Accordingly, there

- *Commission Regulation 773/2004 of 7 April 2004 relating to the conduct of proceedings by the Commission pursuant to Articles [101] and [102] [TFEU].*[19] Regulation 773/2004 contains detailed rules regarding, in particular, the initiation of proceedings, oral statements, complaints, hearings of parties, access to the file, and the handling of confidential information in antitrust procedures conducted by the Commission. In 2008, this implementing Regulation was modified when the Commission introduced the settlement procedure in cartel cases.[20]

- *Commission Notice on cooperation within the network of competition authorities ('ECN Cooperation Notice').*[21] The ECN Cooperation Notice sets out the main pillars of cooperation between the Commission and the competition authorities of the Member States in the European Competition Network ('ECN'). It also spells out the principles for sharing case work between the members of the network. In this respect, the ECN Cooperation Notice follows the Joint Statement of the Council and the Commission, which was issued on the day when Regulation 1/2003 was adopted.[22] It provides for particular arrangements regarding the interface between exchanges of information between authorities pursuant to Articles 11(2) and (3) as well as Article 12 of Regulation 1/2003 and the operation of leniency programmes. The NCAs signed a statement in which they declared that they would abide by the principles set out in the Commission Notice.[23]

- *Commission Notice on the cooperation between the Commission and the courts of the EU Member States in the application of Articles [101] and [102] [TFEU] ('National Courts Cooperation Notice').*[24] The notice was intended to serve as a practical tool for national judges who apply Articles 101 and 102 TFEU in accordance with Regulation 1/2003. It brings together the relevant case law of the ECJ up to 2004, thus clarifying the procedural context in which national judges are operating. Particular attention is given to the situation where the national court deals with a case at the same time or after the Commission and where national judges ask the Commission for an opinion or to supply information which it holds. In addition, it created the possibility for the Commission to submit written and oral observations to the national courts in the interest of coherent application. The National Courts Cooperation Notice spells out how cooperation mechanisms work.

- *Commission Notice on the handling of complaints by the Commission under Articles [101] and [102] [TFEU].*[25] This Notice starts by providing general information on the work sharing

---

would be no such thing as a 'reallocation' decision that might be subject to challenge. The Commission's own competence to deal with individual cases of infringement at any time, irrespective of the intervention of a national authority, has been confirmed by the case law, see Ch 3 'The Role of National Competition Authorities' para 3.44 note 93 with the case law cited by E Gippini-Fournier, 'The Modernisation of European Competition Law: First Experiences with Regulation 1/2003—Institutional Report' in HF Koeck and MM Karollus (eds), The Modernisation of European Competition Law—Initial Experiences with Regulation 1/2003, FIDE XXIII Congress Linz 2008—Congress Publications Vol 2 (Nomos 2008) 375, 449–51. The modernization package with the six original notices is available at <http://europa.eu.int/comm/competition/antitrust/legislation/>.

[19] [2004] OJ L123/18.

[20] Commission Regulation (EC) No 622/2008 of 30 June 2008 amending Regulation (EC) No 773/2004, as regards the conduct of settlement procedures in cartel cases [2008] OJ L171/3.

[21] [2004] OJ C101/43.

[22] Joint Statement of the Council and the Commission on the functioning of the network of competition authorities. Council Document 15435/02 ADD 1 of 10 December 2002. See Case T-339/04 *France Télécom SA v Commission* [2004] ECR II-521, para 85 of which reiterates that the Joint Statement is political in nature and does not create legal rights or obligations. The applicant cannot therefore rely on this document with a view to procuring the annulment of an act of EU law that adversely affects it. See also more generally K Dekeyser and M Jaspers, 'A New Era of ECN Cooperation, Achievements and Challenges with Special Focus on Work in the Leniency Field' (2007) 30(1) World Competition 3; Annex to report on Competition Policy 2006, Doc SEC(2007) 860 (COM(2007) 358 final) para 313 et seq.

[23] Each NCA of the twenty-seven Member States has signed the statement regarding the ECN Cooperation Notice. The list is available on the DG COMP's website at <http://ec.europa.eu/competition/index_en.html>.

[24] [2004] OJ C101/54.

[25] [2004] OJ C101/65.

of the different enforcers and invites potential complainants to make an informed choice of the authority where they will lodge their complaint or file their claim (whether the Commission, a national court, or an NCA) in the light of the case allocation criteria. The bulk of the notice contains explanations of the Commission's assessment of complaints in the field of antitrust and the procedures applicable. The notice also includes an indicative deadline of four months, within which the Commission endeavours to inform complainants whether or not it intends to conduct a full investigation of a complaint.

• *Commission Notice on informal guidance relating to novel questions concerning Articles [101] and [102] [TFEU] that arise in individual cases (Guidance Letters).*[26] The goal of Regulation 1/2003 is to enable the Commission to concentrate its enforcement action on the detection of serious infringements. The abolition of the notification system is a crucial element in this context. However, in a limited number of cases, where a genuinely novel question concerning Articles 101 and 102 TFEU arises, it would also seem reasonable for the Commission, subject to its other enforcement priorities, to provide guidance to undertakings in writing (guidance letter). The notice sets out details about this instrument.

It should be noted that the Modernization Package did not affect the existing enabling block **1.09** exemption regulations which remain in force. Thus, Council Regulations 19/65/EEC,[27] (EEC) 2821/71,[28] (EEC) 487/2009,[29] (EEC) 1534/91,[30] or (EEC) 246/2009[31] all empower the Commission to apply Article 101(3) TFEU by Regulation to certain categories of agreements, decisions taken by associations of undertakings, and concerted practices. In the areas defined by such Regulations, the Commission has adopted and may continue to adopt 'block' exemption regulations, by which it declares Article 101(1) TFEU to be inapplicable to certain categories of agreements, decisions, and concerted practices. In addition, a number of Commission notices and guidelines remain fully applicable alongside Regulation 1/2003.[32]

Under Regulation 1/2003, the Commission is jointly competent with NCAs to apply Article **1.10** 101 and 102 TFEU, unless it initiates proceedings for the adoption of a Commission decision under Regulation 1/2003.[33] By enabling NCAs and national courts to apply Articles 101 and 102 TFEU in full, Regulation 1/2003 has removed the principal obstacles to the prosecution of infringements of Articles 101 and 102 TFEU at the Member State level.

---

[26] [2004] OJ C101/78.

[27] Council Reg (EEC) 19/65 of 2 March 1965 on the application of Art 85(3) of the Treaty to certain categories of agreements and concerted practices [1965] OJ L36/533, as amended.

[28] Council Reg (EEC) 2821/71 of 20 December 1971 on the application of Art 81(3) [now 101(3)] to certain categories of agreements, decisions and concerted practices [1971] OJ L285/46, as amended.

[29] Council Reg (EC) No 487/2009 of 25 May 2009 on the application of Art 81(3) [now 101(3)] of the Treaty to certain categories of agreements and concerted practices in the air transport sector [2009] OJ L148/1 replaced in the meantime Council Reg (EEC) 3976/87 of 14 December 1987 on the application of Art 81(3) [now 101(3)] of the Treaty to certain categories of agreements and concerted practices in the air transport sector [1987] OJ L374/9, as amended.

[30] Council Reg (EEC) 1534/91 on the application of Art 81(3) [now 101(3)] of the Treaty to certain categories of agreements, decisions and concerted practices in the insurance sector [1991] OJ L1 43/1, as amended.

[31] Council Reg (EC) No 246/2009 of 26 February 2009 on the application of Art 81(3) [now 101(3)] of the Treaty to certain categories of agreements, decisions and concerted practices between liner shipping companies also replaced in the meantime Council Reg (EEC) 479/92 [1992] OJ L55/3, as amended.

[32] An up-to-date list of the existing block exemptions is available at <http://ec.europa.eu/competition/antitrust/legislation/legislation.html>.

[33] See Art 11(6) of Reg 1/2003. However, the Commission only applies Art 11(6) of Reg 1/2003 in a limited number of special situations. For more details, E Gippini-Fournier, 'The Modernisation of European Competition Law: First Experiences with Regulation 1/2003—Institutional Report' in HF Koeck and MM Karollus (eds), The Modernisation of European Competition Law—Initial Experiences with Regulation 1/2003, FIDE XXIII Congress Linz 2008—Congress Publications Vol 2 (Nomos 2008) 375, 449–51. See Ch 3, 'The Role of National Competition Authorities', para 3.11 et seq.

On the one hand, Article 35 of Regulation 1/2003 obliges the Member States to designate the competition authority or authorities responsible for the application of Articles 101 and 102 TFEU and to take the measures necessary to empower those authorities to apply those Articles. On the other hand, the Member States remain free to organize their system of public enforcement. In this regard, Regulation 1/2003 recognizes the wide variety of public enforcement systems existing in the Member States,[34] which is acceptable as long as Member States can ensure that their NCAs have the necessary resources to be represented on the Advisory Committee,[35] provide assistance in inspections conducted by the Commission in their territory,[36] and undertake inspections requested by the Commission.[37]

1.11 Article 3(1) of Regulation 1/2003 provides that where an NCA or national court applies national competition law to agreements, decisions of undertakings, or concerted practices within the meaning of Article 101(1) TFEU which may affect trade between Member States or any abuse prohibited by Article 102 TFEU, they must apply Article 101 or 102 TFEU. When dealing with an agreement, decision, or practice within the meaning of Article 101(1) TFEU which may affect trade between Member States or an abuse prohibited by Article 102 TFEU, NCAs will thus have the choice of either applying just Articles 101 or 102 TFEU, or applying both national competition law and Articles 101 or 102 TFEU.[38] When NCAs of the Member States rule on agreements, decisions, or practices under Articles 101 or 102 TFEU which are already the subject of a Commission decision, they cannot take decisions which would run counter to that adopted by the Commission.[39] In the same vein, when national courts rule on agreements, decisions, or practices under Article 101 or 102 TFEU which are already the subject of a Commission decision, they cannot take decisions running counter to the latter.[40] The NCAs' powers to take decisions are circumscribed by Regulation 1/2003. They may require that an infringement be brought to an end, order interim measures, accept commitments, and impose fines, but they may not adopt non-infringement decisions like those the Commission may adopt under Article 10 of Regulation 1/2003.[41] The underlying idea is that the Commission and the NCAs should have parallel competences and together should form a network of authorities applying Articles 101 and 102 TFEU in close cooperation.

1.12 In fact, NCAs may have stronger powers than the Commission under Regulation 1/2003. Thus, whereas Regulation 1/2003 only empowers the Commission to impose fines on undertakings for infringements of Articles 101 and 102 TFEU, Article 5 of the Regulation also allows NCAs to impose 'any other penalty provided for in their national law', including imprisonment or criminal sanctions on natural persons. With regard to the application of national competition law, the

---

[34] Recital 35 and Art 35(2) of Reg 1/2003.

[35] Article 14 of Reg 1/2003; see Ch 3, 'The Role of the National Competition Authorities', para 3.113 et seq.

[36] Article 20(5) and (6) of Reg 1/2003; see Ch 8, 'Inspections', para 8.72.

[37] Article 22 of Reg 1/2003; see Ch 8, 'Inspections', para 8.77.

[38] In both cases, under Reg 1/2003 they will have to inform the Commission at the beginning of their proceedings pursuant to Art 11(3) and inform the Commission of their envisaged decision at the latest thirty days before its adoption in accordance with Art 11(4). E Gippini-Fournier, 'The Modernisation of European Competition Law: First Experiences with Regulation 1/2003—Institutional Report' in HF Koeck and MM Karollus (eds), The Modernisation of European Competition Law—Initial Experiences with Regulation 1/2003, FIDE XXIII Congress Linz 2008—Congress Publications Vol 2 (Nomos 2008) 375, 433. The Commission can remove the case from NCAs by opening proceedings under Art 11(6). Indeed, it follows from Art 11(6) in conjunction with Art 3(1) that an initiation of proceedings by the Commission relieves NCAs not only of their competence to apply Arts 101 or 102 TFEU, but also of their competence to apply national competition law in the same case.

[39] Article 16 of Reg 1/2003.

[40] The national court may assess whether it is necessary to stay its proceedings.

[41] Article 5 of Reg 1/2003. Case C-375/09 *Prezes Urzędu Ochrony Konkurencji i Konsumentów v Tele2 Polska sp. zoo* [now *Netia SA w Warszawie*] [2011] ECR I-3055.

obligation to apply Articles 101 and 102 TFEU does not exist where the NCAs and national courts apply national merger control rules. Nor does Regulation 1/2003 preclude the application of provisions of national law that predominantly pursue an objective different from that pursued by Articles 101 and 102 TFEU.[42] Member States can apply national legislation that protects legitimate interests other than the protection of competition in the market, provided that such legislation is compatible with general principles and other provisions of EU law.[43]

2. Special regimes

Transport

Initially, the Commission's powers under Regulation 17 to enforce the competition rules did **1.13** not apply to the transport sector, since Council Regulation 141 retroactively excluded this sector from the application of the procedural rules.[44] Over the years, however, the Council adopted rules for the application of Articles 101 and 102 TFEU to road, rail and inland waterway transport,[45] maritime transport,[46] and air transport[47] ('Council Transport Regulations').

---

[42] Article 3(3) of Reg 1/2003. See also Recital 8, which states that Reg 1/2003 does not apply to national laws which impose criminal sanctions on natural persons except to the extent that these are the means of enforcing the competition rules applying to undertakings.

[43] Recital 9 of Reg 1/2003 specifically states that legislation intended to prevent undertakings from imposing on their trading partner's terms and conditions that are unjustified, disproportionate, and without consideration could be applied by Member States.

[44] Council Reg (EEC) 141 exempting transport from the application of Council Reg 17 [1962] OJ 124/2753, as amended [1959–62] OJ Spec Ed 291. This Regulation is no longer in force. The reason for this exclusion was doubt about whether the EU competition rules were applicable to the transport sector. See, however, Joined Cases 209 to 213/84 *Ministèrepublic v Asjes (Nouvelles Fontieres)* [1986] ECR 1425, para 42, stating that the competition rules are applicable to transport; L Ortiz Blanco and B van Houtte, *EC Competition Law in the Transport Sector* (Oxford University Press 1996) ch 2.

[45] Council Reg (EC) No 169/2009 of 26 February 2009 applying rules of competition to transport by rail, road and inland waterway [2009] OJ L61/1. This regulation is a codified version of the now repealed Council Reg (EEC) 1017/68 applying rules of competition to transport by rail, road, and inland waterway [1968] OJ L175/1 [1968] OJ Spec Ed 302. Only Art 13(3) of that Regulation continues to apply to the extent specified in Art 4(1) of Reg (EC) No 169/2009 mentioned previously.

[46] Regulation 1/2003 now applies to all maritime transport services, including cabotage and international tramp services. Thus, the Commission now enjoys the same investigation and enforcement powers as regards cabotage and tramp services as in all other economic sectors. The latter was achieved through the adoption of Council Regulation (EC) No 1419/2006 of 25 September 2006 that repealed Reg (EEC) No 4056/86 laying down detailed rules for the application of Arts 85 and 86 of the Treaty on maritime transport, and amending Reg (EC) No 1/2003 as regards the extension of its scope to include cabotage and international tramp services. Consequently, as of 18 October 2006, all maritime transport services sectors had been subject to the generally applicable procedural framework. The Commission also adopted guidelines to cover all maritime sectors that are concerned by Reg 1419/2006 on the application of the competition rules to the maritime sector, namely cabotage, liner, and tramp shipping services. [2008] OJ C245/2. Regulation (EC) No 246/2009 empowers the Commission to apply Art 101(3) TFEU by regulation to certain categories of agreements, decisions and concerted practices between shipping companies relating to the joint operation of liner shipping services (consortia). The Commission used these powers to adopt Commission Reg (EC) No 906/2009 of 28 September 2009 on the application of Art 81(3) [now 101(3)] of the Treaty to certain categories of agreements, decisions, and concerted practices between liner shipping companies (consortia). See the updated legislation list at <http://ec.europa.eu/competition/sectors/transport/legislation_maritime.html>

[47] Council Reg (EEC) 3975/87 laying down the procedure for the application of the rules on competition to undertakings in the air transport sector [1987] OJ 1987 L374/1, as amended by Reg 1/2003. Council Reg (EC) 411/2004 repealed the Regulation on air transport and deleted the provision in Regulation 1/2003 which excluded from its scope air transport between the EU and third countries, with the result that all enforcement rules in Regulation 1/2003 will also apply to these routes. Council Reg (EC) No 411/2004 of 26 February 2004 repealing Reg (EEC) No 3975/87 and amending Regulations (EEC) No 3976/87 and (EC) No 1/2003, in connection with air transport between the Community and third countries [2004] L68/1. Reg (EEC) No 3976/87 was later repealed by Council Reg (EC) No 487/2009 of 25 May 2009 on the application of Art 81(3) [now 101(3)] of the Treaty to certain categories of agreements and concerted practices in the air transport sector [2009] OJ L148/1.

1.14   Regulation 1/2003 brought about a highly desirable simplification of a previously some-what confusing situation.[48] In essence, all transport sectors are now governed entirely by Regulation 1/2003.

EU Merger Control Regulation

1.15   Regulation 1/2003 does not apply to concentrations as defined in Article 3 of Regulation 139/2004,[49] except in relation to joint ventures that do not have an EU dimension and which have as their object or effect the coordination of the competitive behaviour of undertakings that remain independent.[50] Regulation 139/2004 provides for the prior notification of concentrations with an EU dimension and is particularly rigorous from the procedural point of view, laying down very strict time limits which have to be observed by the Commission. The Council Regulation is supplemented by very detailed rules on notifications and hearings.[51]

Other procedures for the application of Articles 101 and 102 TFEU

1.16   **Article 104 TFEU**   Article 104 TFEU requires Member States' authorities to apply Articles 101 (in particular paragraph 3) and 102 TFEU where the EU Council has not adopted Regulations under Article 103 TFEU giving effect to Articles 101 and 102. These powers are limited, transitional, and cease to exist on the entry into force of the implementing provisions adopted under Article 103 TFEU. While the adoption of Regulation 17 had already curtailed the scope of this provision considerably, Regulation 1/2003 and further amendments in recent years have virtually made Article 104 TFEU obsolete.[52] For example, as indicated above, in the maritime transport sector, Regulation 1/2003 now also applies to tramp vessel service and cabotage services, although it did not remove from Member States' authorities the powers derived from Article 103 to enforce Articles 101 and 102 TFEU.

1.17   **Article 105 TFEU**   Article 105(1) TFEU confers upon the Commission a general supervisory role for competition matters,[53] although Article 105(2) TFEU could be construed as limiting the effectiveness of the power granted to the Commission by stating that if the

[48] On the situation existing before Reg 1/2003, see generally L Ortiz Blanco and B van Houtte, *EC Competition Law in the Transport Sector* (Oxford University Press 1996) ch 6.

[49] Council Reg (EC) 139/2004 of 20 January 2004 on the control of concentrations between undertakings [2004] OJ L24/1. See Chs 16 and 17 of this book on EU merger control procedure.

[50] This applies also to Reg 1017/68 (land transport) and Reg 4056/86 (maritime transport). See Art 21(1) of Reg 139/2004. Note that Art 101 TFEU may be applied under Reg 139/2004 to spill-over effects between parent companies resulting from the formation of full-function joint ventures that have an EU dimension (Art 2(4)) and to restrictive covenants that comprise part of a notification, but which are not ancillary to that transaction. See Part II on merger control, Ch 16, 'General Issues. Scope of Control', para 16.78.

[51] Commission Reg (EC) 802/2004 of 7 April 2004 implementing Council Reg (EC) 139/2004 on the control of concentrations between undertakings [2004] OJ L1 33/1. See Part II on merger control, Ch 17, 'Procedures', para 17.01 et seq.

[52] C Bellamy and G Child, *European Community Law of Competition* (6th edn, Oxford University Press 2008) para 1-023, indicates that Art 104 TFEU has become otiose given that all economic sectors are now covered by the procedural rules laid down in Regulation 1/2003. See also overview in V Rose, 'Sectoral Regimes' in C Bellamy and G Child, *European Community Law of Competition* (2nd Cumulative Supplement, Oxford University Press 2012) ch 12, para 12.006 et seq.

[53] Joined Cases T-305/94 to T-307/94, T-313/94 to T-316/94, T-318/94, T-325/94, T-328/94, T-329/94, and T-335/94 *Limburgse Vinyl Maatschappij NV et al v Commission* [1999] ECR II-931, paras 148 and 149: 'The supervisory role conferred upon the Commission in competition matters includes the duty to investigate and penalise individual infringements, but it also encompasses the duty to pursue a general policy designed to apply, in competition matters, the principles laid down by the Treaty and to guide the conduct of undertakings in the light of those principles'; Opinion of AG Ruiz-Jarabo Colomer in Case C-119/97 P *Union française de l'express (Ufex), formerly Syndicat français de l'express international (SFEI), DHL International and Service CRIE v Commission* [1999] ECR I-1341, para 63; Case T-110/95 *International Express Carriers Conference (IECC) v EC Commission* [1998] ECR II-3605, para 54; Case T-54/99 *Max.mobil Telekommunikation Service GmbH v Commission* [2002] ECR-II 313, para 52; Kerse & Khan, *EC Antitrust Procedure* (6th edn, Sweet & Maxwell 2012) paras 1-068–1-070 referring to Case T-77/92 *Parker Pen v Commission* [1994] ECR II-549, para 63.

infringement is not brought to an end, the Commission may merely record it in a reasoned decision which it may publish and authorize Member States to take the measures needed to remedy the situation. Despite this, in the past the Commission has acted in a number of proceedings on the basis of Article 105, particularly those involving airline alliances.[54]

Article 4 third paragraph, second subparagraph TFEU [former Article 10, second para- **1.18** **graph EC] in connection with Articles 101 and 102 TFEU**[55]   While it is true that Articles 101 and 102 TFEU are primarily aimed at undertakings and do not cover measures adopted by Member States by legislation or regulations, Member States may require or encourage undertakings to adopt restrictive agreements or concerted practices prohibited under Article 101 TFEU or to engage in abusive practices contrary to Article 102 TFEU. For example, they may do this by imposing minimum or maximum prices for goods or services; adopting discriminatory taxation measures; imposing regulatory rules that make it difficult for undertakings to enter markets; or operating restrictive licensing regimes for particular economic activities.[56] The EU Courts have consistently held that Article 4, third paragraph, second subparagraph TFEU (former Article 10, second paragraph EC) imposes a duty on Member States not to maintain or to adopt measures which deprive these provisions of their effectiveness.[57] Member States may not enact measures enabling private undertakings to escape from the constraints imposed by Articles 101 and 102 TFEU. In the current case law, the Court

---

[54]   In particular, the Commission has investigated a number of alliance agreements between EU and US airlines regarding their compatibility under the EU competition rules. In 1996, the Commission initiated proceedings in various air alliance cases, focusing on the transatlantic routes covered by those alliances. In the absence of a specific enforcement Regulation for the application of the EU competition rules on transport between the EU and third countries, the legal basis for these proceedings was Art 105 TFEU. In 2002, the Commission decided to end its proceedings with regard to the alliance agreements between *KLM/ NorthWest* ([2002] OJ C181/6) and *Lufthansa/SAS/United* ([2002] OJ C264/5) respectively, in the latter case after the parties had proposed certain remedies addressing the competition issues identified. See also *British Airways/American Airlines* [1998] OJ C239/10. The Commission had always argued that the extension of the competition enforcement rules to include international air transport to and from the EU would afford airlines the clear benefit of a common EU-wide enforcement system which would decide the legality of their agreements under the EU competition rules based on a much less ponderous and more direct procedure than that contained in Art 105 TFEU. With air transport now being subject to the general enforcement rules under Regulation 1/2003, the Commission has investigated alliances under Art 101 TFEU (see eg more recently, IP/10/936 Antitrust: British Airways, American Airlines and Iberia commitments to ensure competition on transatlantic passenger air transport markets made legally binding, 14 July 2010; IP/12/79 Antitrust: Commission opens a probe into transatlantic joint venture between Air France-KLM, Alitalia and Delta and closes proceedings against eight members of SkyTeam airline alliance, 27 January 2012).

[55]   Article 4 sub-para 3 TFEU states as follows: 'The Member States shall take any appropriate measure, general or particular, to ensure fulfilment of the obligations arising out of the Treaties or resulting from the acts of the institutions of the Union.' R Whish, *Competition Law* (7th edn, Oxford University Press 2012) 216–22.

[56]   R Whish, *Competition Law* (7th edn, Oxford University Press 2012) 217 notes that the case law has been predominantly concerned with the liability of Member States for infringements of Art 101 by undertakings, whereas issues in relation to abusive behaviour usually arise in the context of the former Art 106(1) TFEU, applicable to public undertakings and undertakings to which Member States grant special or exclusive rights. See also J Temple Lang, 'Developments, Issues and New Remedies—The Duties of National Authorities and Courts under Article 10 of the EC Treaty' [2004] Fordham International Law Journal 1904, 1924 et seq, on the case law of the EU Courts regarding the duties of national non-judicial authorities under Art 10 EC.

[57]   Case 13/77 SA *GB-INNO-BM v Association des détaillants en tabac (ATAB)* [1977] ECR 2115 para 31; Case C-332/89 *Marchandise and others* [1991] ECR I-1027 para 22; Case C-185/91 *Bundesanstalt für den Güterverkehr v Reiff* [1993] ECR I-5801 para 14; Case C-401/92 *Criminal proceedings against Tankstation 't Heukske vof and JBE Boermans* [1992] ECR I-2199 para 16. According to former Commissioner for Competition Policy N Kroes, 'The Competition Principle as a Guideline for Legislation and State Action— the Responsibility of Politicians and the Role of Competition Authorities', 12th International Conference on Competition, Bonn, 6 June 2005, '[…] States are subject to obligations under Article [4 TFEU], combined with Articles [101] or [102], Article [4] obliges Member States to abstain from any measure that could

considers that a State measure is liable to negate the effectiveness of the competition rules in three situations:

(1) where a Member State requires, or favours, the adoption of agreements, decisions of associations of undertakings, or concerted practices contrary to Article 101 TFEU;

(2) where a Member State reinforces the effects of such conduct; and

(3) where a Member State deprives its own rules of their legislative character by delegating to private economic operators the responsibility for taking decisions affecting the economic sphere.[58]

1.19 In procedural terms, EU law does not provide for a particular procedure against Member States for not fulfilling their obligations under Article 4, third paragraph, second subparagraph in connection with Articles 101 and/or 102 TFEU. A complainant could request the Commission to direct a request to the Member State to comply with its obligations under the TFEU and, if need be, to initiate infringement proceedings against it.[59] In this case, the relationship between the complainant and the Commission is governed by the Commission Communication on relations with the complainant in respect of infringements of EU law.[60] To what extent a complainant is able to challenge a refusal to initiate proceedings before the EU Courts is subject to debate. The ECJ stated that the Commission has the right but no obligation to commence proceedings under Article 258 TFEU; it would have a discretionary power precluding the right of individuals to require it to adopt a particular position and to bring an action for annulment against its refusal to take action.[61] If the Commission considers that a Member State has failed to fulfil an obligation under the TFEU, it delivers a reasoned opinion on the matter after giving the Member State concerned the opportunity to submit its observations. If the Member State does not comply with the opinion within the time allowed, the Commission is entitled, but not obliged, to apply to the ECJ for a declaration establishing the failure to fulfil an obligation of which the Member State is accused.[62] The EU Courts are also likely to reject an action under Article 265 TFEU in respect of the

---

jeopardise the attainment of the objectives of the Treaty, one of which is to ensure that competition is not distorted. The European Court of Justice has concluded from this that Member States are prohibited from introducing State measures which may deprive Articles [101] and [102] of their useful effect [...]'. See also OECD, DAF/COMP/WP3/WD(2009)42, Roundtable on the application of antitrust law to state-owned enterprises, European Commission, 28 September 2009, <http://ec.europa.eu/competition/international/multilateral/antitrustlaw.pdf>

[58] Case 267/86 *Van Eycke v ASPA, NV* [1989] ECR 4769, para 16. The issue was whether Belgian legislation which restricts the benefit of an exemption from income tax solely to certain deposits was compatible with the EC Treaty. Case C-2/91 *Criminal proceedings against Wolf W Meng* [1993] ECR I-5751, paras 14–15; in Opinion of AG Léger Case C-35/99 *Criminal proceedings against Manuele Arduino* [2002] ECR I-1529, para 37.

[59] Article 258 TFEU: 'If the Commission considers that a Member State has failed to fulfil an obligation under this Treaty, it shall deliver a reasoned opinion on the matter after giving the *State* concerned the opportunity to submit its observations. If the State concerned does not comply with the opinion within the period laid down by the Commission, the latter may bring the matter before the Court of Justice.'

[60] Commission Communication to the European Parliament and the European Ombudsman on relations with the Complainant in respect of Infringements of Community Law COM(2002) 141 final, 20 March 2002; Commission Communication to the European Parliament and the European Council Updating the handling of relations with the complainant in respect of the application of Union law COM(2012) 154 final, 2 April 2012.

[61] Case C-87/89 *Société nationale interprofessionelle de la tomate and others v Commission* [1990] ECR I-1981, para 6.

[62] Case C-87/89 *Société nationale interprofessionelle de la tomate and others v Commission* [1990] ECR I-1981, paras 6 and 7; Case T-126/95 *Dumez v EC Commission* [1995] ECR II-2863, para 33: 'It has consistently been held that individuals are not entitled to contest a refusal by the Commission to take action under Article [265] against a Member State... The case-law of the Community judicature concerning the non-actionable nature of a refusal by the Commission to initiate the procedure under Article [265] of the Treaty is based not only on the discretionary power conferred on the Commission by Article [265] itself, but

failure to act. It would be possible to challenge a failure to take a decision or to define a position, but not the adoption of a measure different from that desired or considered necessary
by those concerned. In this context, the General Court ('GC') has noted that the action
for failure to act under Article 265 TFEU is contingent on the institution concerned being
under an obligation to act, so that its alleged failure to act is contrary to the TFEU. Yet
this is not the case here, since whether or not the procedure in question is initiated is at the
Commission's discretion.[63]

However, it is questionable whether the discretionary power of the Commission must be **1.20**
excluded from the outset from any judicial review. A refusal by the Commission to act against
a Member State contains a legal assessment, which is capable of producing legal effects within
the meaning of Article 263 TFEU. It terminates proceedings governed by a Communication
of the Commission and it may contain an assessment of the Commission on the compatibility of national law with EU law. The purpose of the legal challenge would probably not be to
oblige the Commission to initiate proceedings, since this is considered as coming within the
scope of the Commission's discretionary power,[64] but rather to annul the legal assessment of
the Commission according to which it decided not to investigate the complaint.[65]

3. Limitation periods[66]

Article 25 of Regulation 1/2003 replaced the rules formerly contained in Regulation **1.21**
2988/74,[67] which laid down limitation periods both for proceedings and for the enforcement
of sanctions under the EU competition rules. It establishes limitation periods for action on
the part of the Commission against competition law infringements: three years for provisions concerning requests for information or the conduct of inspections, and five years for all
other infringements. Article 26 of Regulation 1/2003 provides that the limitation period for
enforcing fines and periodic penalty payments is five years.[68]

---

also on the principle that, where the Commission's decision is negative, it must be appraised in the light of
the nature of the request to which it constitutes a reply...It is clear from the scheme of Article [265] of the
Treaty that the reasoned opinion is merely a preliminary stage following which an action may be brought
before the Court of Justice for failure to fulfil obligations, and cannot therefore be regarded as an act which
could form the subject-matter of proceedings for annulment. Consequently, the Commission's refusal to
initiate the Art [253] procedure also constitutes an act which is not open to challenge, and there is no need to
determine whether it was of direct and individual concern to the applicant.' See also Order in Case T-1 82/97
Smanor v Commission [1998] ECR II-271, para 27 stating that under [Art 265 TFEU] the only act which
could be refused would be a reasoned opinion, which itself cannot form the subject matter of proceedings
for annulment.

[63] Case T-126/95 *Dumez v Commission* [1995] ECR II-2863, paras 43–4.

[64] Case C-317/92 *EC Commission v Germany* [1994] ECR I-2039, para 4; Case C-212/98 *Commission v
Ireland* [1999] ECR I-8571, para 12.

[65] See in this context K Lenaerts, 'In the Union We Trust: Trust-Enhancing Principles of Community Law'
[2004] CML Rev 317, 339), who states that the Commission is obliged to undertake a diligent and impartial
examination of the complaints addressed to it and that fulfilment of this obligation should be amenable to
judicial review.

[66] See Ch 9, 'Procedural Infringements', para 9.31 et seq; Ch 11, 'Infringement Decisions and Penalties',
para 11.27.

[67] Council Reg 2988/74 concerning limitation periods in proceedings and the enforcement of sanctions
under the rules of the European Economic Community relating to transport and competition [1974] OJ
L319/1.

[68] See in this context Joined Cases T-22/02 and T-23/02 *Sumitomo Chemical v Commission* [2005] ECR
II-4065, para 129 et seq where the Court rejected the argument that limitation periods should also be applicable to merely declaratory prohibition decisions.

C. General Principles and ECHR Case Law

1.22 Case law is an important source of EU law. The sometimes imprecise, incomplete, or excessively general nature of the provisions of the TFEU and the fact that the instruments containing secondary legislation are often flawed, aided and abetted by political compromise and the linguistic and legal diversity of the EU, offers the EU Courts an opportunity to establish what the law is. In short, they fill the gaps where neither primary nor secondary law has provided an adequate solution to the problems caused by the development of the EU. In carrying out this quasi-legislative task, the EU Courts use very dynamic interpretative methods and resort extensively to general principles of law. For example, the ECJ has recognized that although the Commission is not a 'tribunal' within the meaning of Article 6 of the European Convention on Human Rights ('ECHR'),[69] the observance of fundamental rights forms part of the EU legal order.[70] Regulation 1/2003 specifically states that it respects the fundamental rights and observes the principles recognized, in particular, by the Charter of Fundamental Rights which is now part of the TFEU with all legally binding effects.[71] Regulation 1/2003, which spells out a number of guarantees on which undertakings may rely during the investigation stage,[72] must be interpreted and applied with respect to those rights and principles. The main provisions of the Charter that are relevant in the context of EU antitrust enforcement are contained in Article 7 (respect for private life, home, and communications); Article 41 (right to good administration, including *inter alia* the right to be heard and the right to have access to one's own case file); Article 47 (right to an effective remedy and to a fair trial); Article 48 (presumption of innocence and right of defence); Article 49 (principles of legality and proportionality of criminal offences and penalties); and Article 50 (right not to be tried or punished twice in criminal proceedings for the same criminal offence).[73]

---

[69] Convention for the Protection of Human Rights and Fundamental Freedoms (The European Human Rights Convention) (Rome, 4 November 1950; TS 71 (1053); Cmd 8969). R Wesseling and M Van der Woude, 'The Lawfulness and Acceptability of Enforcement of European Cartel Law' (2012) 35(4) World Competition 573.

[70] Joined Cases 209/78 to 215/78 and 218/78 *Van Landewyck v Commission* [1980] ECR 3125, para 81; Joined Cases 100/80 to 103/80 *Musique Diffusion Française and others v Commission* [1983] ECR 1825, para 7; Case T-11/89 *Shell v Commission* [1992] ECR II-757, para 39; Case C-299/95 *Kremzow v Austria* [1997] ECRI-2629, para 14; Case T-83/96 *Van der Wal* [1998] ECR II-545, para 46; Case T-112/98 *Mannesmannröhren-Werke v Commission* [2001] ECR II-729, para 60; Case T-9/99 *HFB Holding für Fernwärmetechnik Beteiligungsgesellschaft mbH & Co KG and others v Commission* [2002] ECR II-1487, para 377; Case C-94/00 *Roquette Frères* [2002] ECR I-9011 para 35; Opinion 2/94 [1996] ECR I-1759, para 33.

[71] The Charter of Fundamental Rights was initially solemnly proclaimed by the Presidents of the European Parliament, the Council, and the Commission at the Nice European Council on 7 December 2000, but this was merely a political commitment carrying no binding legal effect. Article 1(8) of the Treaty of Lisbon provides that Art 6(1) TEU is to be replaced by the following text: 'The Union recognises the rights, freedoms and principles set out in the Charter of Fundamental Rights of the European Union of 7 December 2000, as adapted at Strasbourg, on 12 December 2007, which shall have the same legal value as the Treaties.' See also in this respect WPJ Wils, 'EU Antitrust Enforcement Powers and Procedural Rights and Guarantees: The Interplay between EU Law, National Law, the Charter of Fundamental Rights of the EU and the European Convention on Human Rights' (2011) 34(2) World Competition 189. See also United Kingdom House of Lords, European Union Committee, 10th Report of Session 2007–08, *The Treaty of Lisbon: an impact assessment*, Volume I: Report, paras 5.37–5.103.

[72] Recital 37 of Reg 1/2003. Reg 1/2003 refers to the right not to incriminate oneself in Recital 23 or the control exercised by national courts regarding assistance during inspections (Arts 20 and 21).

[73] According to the explanation of Art 52(3) of the Charter of Fundamental Rights of the EU, the meaning and scope of rights that correspond to those guaranteed by the ECHR are to be determined not only by reference to the text of the Convention, but also, *inter alia*, by reference to the case law of the European Court of Human Rights (ECtHR). See on the process of accession of the EU to the ECHR: <http://www.coe.int/t/dghl/standardsetting/hrpolicy/Accession/default_en.asp>.

The case law of the EU Courts has also developed a series of general principles inspired by **1.23** the legal traditions of the different Member States,[74] which must be applied together with the Treaty provisions and secondary legislation. EU competition procedure takes all of these principles into account, which guide the conduct of authorities responsible for ensuring compliance with the competition rules.[75] It should be noted, however, that not every procedural irregularity will be sufficient to vitiate a decision. As a general principle of EU law, a person seeking the annulment of an administrative decision on the grounds of a procedural irregularity must be able to show at least the possibility that the outcome would have been different but for the irregularity complained of.[76]

At the same time, in recent years, fundamental rights invoked under the ECHR have steadily **1.24** grown in importance.[77] This has caused the EU Courts to pay increasing regard to the case law of the European Court of Human Rights ('ECtHR'). One of the recurring themes is how far the EU system for judicial review of decisions by the Commission imposing fines in competition cases is compatible with Article 6(1) of the ECHR. In a recent judgment, the ECtHR had the occasion to apply these principles to a case in which the Italian national competition authority had imposed a fine in an antitrust enforcement case.[78] The decision was confirmed on appeal. The Italian national competition authority is (like the Commission) an integrated authority that adopts decisions imposing fines, subject to a two-tier judicial control. While every system has its particularities, the institutional set-up in this case is thus not very dissimilar from the EU system. In this case, the ECtHR ruled that Article 6 ECHR was complied with in particular in view of the circumstance that the decisions of the administrative

---

[74] Joined Cases C-238/99, C-244/99, C-245/99, C-247/99, C-250/99 to C-252/99, and C-254/99 *Limburgse Vinyl Maatschappij (LVM) and others v Commission* [2002] ECR I-8375, para 217; see also WPJ Wils, 'Powers of Investigation and Procedural Rights and Guarantees in EU Antitrust Enforcement', First Lisbon Conference on Competition Law and Economics, Belém, 3–4 November 2005, paras 53–4; WPJ Wils, 'EU Antitrust Enforcement Powers and Procedural Rights and Guarantees: The Interplay between EU Law, National Law, the Charter of Fundamental Rights of the EU and the European Convention on Human Rights' (2011) 34(2) World Competition 189; See A Scordamaglia, 'Cartel Proof, Imputation and Sanctioning in European Competition Law: Reconciling Effective Enforcement and Adequate Protection of Procedural Guarantees' (2011) 7(1) Competition Law Review 5, 11 et seq.

[75] These principles will be considered below in greater detail, each in the context in which it has been dealt with in the case law. Thus, for example, proportionality will be considered in the context of fines; the rights of the defence in the context of observations from the parties, and so on.

[76] Case T-44/00 *Mannesmannröhren-Werke AG v Commission* [2004] ECR II-2223, para 55: 'the rights of the defence are infringed by virtue of a procedural irregularity only in so far as that irregularity had a definite impact on the possibilities for the undertakings implicated to defend themselves'. In Case T-62/98 *Volkswagen v Commission* [2000] ECJ II-2707, paras 279–83, the GC found that the Commission had infringed the principle of good administration as a result of its disclosure of the likely level of the fine prior to the decision, but considered that the decision's content would not have differed in the absence of this irregularity. K Lenaerts and J Maselis, 'Procedural Rights and Issues in the Enforcement of Articles 81 and 82 of the EC Treaty' [2001] Fordham International Law Journal 1615, 1637); A Scordamaglia, 'Cartel Proof, Imputation and Sanctioning in European Competition Law: Reconciling Effective Enforcement and Adequate Protection of Procedural Guarantees' (2011) 7(1) Competition Law Review 5, 12 et seq with more references. See also Ch 15, 'Steps Following the Adoption of a Formal Decision', para 15.69.

[77] M Bronckers and A Vallery, 'No Longer Presumed Guilty: The Impact of Fundamental Rights on Certain Dogmas of EU Competition Law' (2012) 34(4) World Competition 535. Kerse & Khan, *EC Antitrust Procedure* (6th edn, Sweet & Maxwell 2012) para 3-003.

[78] *A Menarini Diagnostics SRL v Italy*, App no 43509/08 (ECtHR, 27 September 2011), paras 64 and 65. See M Bronckers and A Vallery, 'Business as usual after Menarini?' [January–March 2012] Mlex Magazine 43, raising the question whether *post*-Menarini the marginal review undertaken by EU Courts in questions like market definition would amount to a full effective review; P Olivier, ' "Diagnostics" a Judgment Applying the Convention of Human Rights to the Field of Competition' [2012] Journal of Competition Law & Practice 163 notes that this judgment is unlikely to have satisfied the concerns of the critics of the current judicial review.

competition authority were subject to judicial review, in which it was assessed whether the competition authority had used its powers appropriately; and with respect to fines, the court could verify the suitability of the sanction and had the power to change the amount imposed.[79]

1.25 Based on a dataset of 207 competition judgments delivered by the GC between 1 September 2000 and 30 September 2010, it has been found that provisions of the ECHR have been cited by the GC in 23.8 per cent of cases, almost a quarter of its competition judgments.[80] Allegedly, the limited number of references obtained in relation to the Charter and the ECtHR case law (5.8 per cent and 2.3 per cent respectively) might have to do with the fact that the first lacked binding force until the adoption of the Lisbon Treaty in 2009. Regarding the latter, the GC and, more generally, the EU Courts have arguably sought to promote their own interpretation of fundamental rights.[81] Additionally, two other general principles of EU law (ie the principles of *legal certainty* and *legitimate expectations*) and of one general principle of EU competition law (the reference to *free and undistorted competition* that appeared under Article 3(1)(g) of the EC Treaty) can be spotted in the competition judgments of the GC. It has turned out that the GC discusses general principles of law in approximately one-fifth to one-third of the competition cases which it deals with. The relatively high number of cases referring to the principles of legal certainty and legitimate expectations would suggest that both the parties and the GC pay close attention to general principles of EU law, which generally protect the subjects of EU competition law. In any event, it appears these indicators show that the EU Courts constitute a forum where fundamental values are discussed.[82]

1.26 Without intending to be exhaustive, the paragraphs that follow describe some of the main principles. Where appropriate, references will be made to the case law of the ECHR.

1. The principle of proportionality

1.27 The principle of proportionality means that the acts of EU institutions should not be unnecessarily burdensome for those to whom they are addressed, and must be limited to what is strictly necessary to attain the objectives pursued.[83] The principle is of particular relevance in

---

[79] See OECD, Directorate for Financial and Enterprise Affairs/Competition Committee, OECD policy roundtable discussion 'Procedural fairness: competition authorities, courts and recent developments 2011, European Union', 192; C Bellamy, 'ECHR and Competition Law *post*-Menarini: An Overview of EU and National Case Law', e-Competitions, No 47946, available at <http://www.concurrences.com>. See also Case C-272/09 P *KME Germany and others v Commission* [2011] OJ C32; Case C-386/10 P *Chalkor AE Epexergasias Metallon v Commission* [2012] OJ C32. See also Opinion of AG Kokott of 12 January 2012 in Joined Cases C-628/10 P and C-14/11 P *Alliance One International Inc v Commission* [2012] OJ C295/6, whose para 95 states that 'intensity of review which the General Court should assume in that respect towards the Commission...concerns an issue which is time and again the subject of discussion and currently—not least in light of the Charter of Fundamental Rights—of increasing attention'. According to the case law of the ECHR, 'a judicial body with full jurisdiction is one which has the power to quash in all respects, on questions of fact and law, the contested decision adopted by the lower body. It must, inter alia, have jurisdiction to examine all questions of fact and law relevant to the dispute before it' (see *Menarini v Italy*, App no 43509/08 (ECtHR, 27 September 2011) § 59).

[80] See for more details, D Geradin and N Petit, 'Judicial Review in European Union Competition Law: A Quantitative and Qualitative Assessment', Tilburg Law and Economics Center (TILEC) Law and Economics Discussion Paper No 2011-008 and Tilburg Law School Legal Studies Research Paper No 01/2011 (26 Oct 2010), 29.

[81] See for more details on this survey, D Geradin and N Petit, 'Judicial Review in European Union Competition Law: A Quantitative and Qualitative Assessment' TILEC Law and Economics Discussion Paper No 2011-008 and Tilburg Law School Legal Studies Research Paper No 01/2011 (26 Oct 2010), 29.

[82] D Geradin and N Petit, 'Judicial Review in European Union Competition Law: A Quantitative and Qualitative Assessment' TILEC Law and Economics Discussion Paper No 2011-008 and Tilburg Law School Legal Studies Research Paper No 01/2011 (26 Oct 2010), 29.

[83] This principle is of particular relevance to the imposition of fines: defendants often claim that the amount of the fines imposed must be in proportion to the impact of the infringement. It is nevertheless for the Court to verify whether the amount of the fine imposed is in proportion to the duration and gravity of

the context of Commission investigations, where the coercive measures must be proportional to the subject matter of the investigation and must not constitute a disproportionate and intolerable interference.[84] In this respect, in *Roquette Frères*[85] the ECJ confirmed its previous decision in *Hoechst*[86] and held that the Commission must respect national law procedures when exercising its investigative powers, and at the same time national authorities must respect general principles of EC law, notably the principle of proportionality.[87] As regards the imposition of fines,[88] the amount of the fine must be proportionate in relation to the factors taken into account in the assessment of the gravity of the infringement.[89] However, fines do not have to be in direct proportion to the size of the market affected, that factor being just one amongst others. The fine imposed on an undertaking for an infringement of the competition rules must be proportionate to the infringement as a whole and, in particular, to the gravity of that infringement.[90] Regard must be had to a large number of factors, the nature and importance of which vary according to the type of infringement in question and the particular circumstances of the case.[91] While the Commission has a degree of discretion

the infringement: Opinion of AG Mischo in Case C-283/98 *Mo och DomsjöAB v Commission* [2000] ECR I-9855, para 125 et seq; Case T-62/98 *Volkswagen AG v Commission* [2000] ECR II-2707, paras 335–48; Case T-31/99 *ABB Asea Brown Boveri Ltd v Commission* [2002] ECR II-1881, paras 137–72; Joined Cases T-109/02, T-118/02, T-122/02, T-125/02, T-126/02, T-128/02, T-129/02, T-132/02, and T-136/02, *Bolloré SA et al v Commission* [2007] ECR II-947, para 468.

[84] Case C-331/88 *Fedesa and others* [1990] ECR I-4023, para 13; Joined Cases C-143/88 and C-92/89 *Zuckerfabrik Süderdith-marschen and Zuckerfabrik Soest* [1991] ECR I-415, para 73; Case C-233/94 *Germany v Parliament and Council* [1997] ECR I-2405, para 57; Case 233/94 *Germany v Parliament and Council* [1997] ECR I-2405, para 57 and Case C-200/96 *Metronome Musik* [1998] ECR I-1953, paras 21 and 26; Case C-94/00 *Roquette Frères* [2002] ECR I-9011, paras 53 and 73; Case C-180/00 *Netherlands v Commission* [2005] ECR I-6603; Case T-339/04, *France Télécom SA* [2007] ECR II-521, paras 117 and 118. See also the Opinion of AG Kokott in Case C-17/10 *Toshiba Corporation and Others* [2012] OJ C98/3, para 90: 'That principle [proportionality], to which the EU legislature expressly referred in the preamble to Regulation No 1/2003, has fundamental, not to say constitutional, significance within the Treaty system. It states that the content and form of Union action must not exceed what is necessary to achieve the objectives of the Treaties.'

[85] Case C-94/00 *Roquette Frères SA* [2002] ECR I-9011, para 27. During investigations, following *Roquette Frères*, Art 21(3) of Reg 1/2003 states that the national judicial authority shall ensure that the Commission decision is authentic and that the coercive measures envisaged are neither arbitrary nor excessive, having regard to the subject matter of the inspection. In this sense, the ECJ has held that review of whether the coercive measures envisaged are proportionate to the subject matter of the investigation involves establishing that such measures do not constitute, in relation to the aim pursued by the investigation in question, a disproportionate and intolerable interference.

[86] Cases 46/87 and 227/88 *Hoechst AG v Commission* [1989] ECR 2859, para 19.

[87] Case C-94/00 *Roquette Frères SA* [2002] ECR I-9011, paras 34 and 81: 'in order for the competent national court to be able to carry out the review of proportionality which it is required to undertake, the Commission must in principle inform that court of the essential features of the suspected infringement, so as to enable it to assess their seriousness, by indicating the market thought to be affected, the nature of the suspected restrictions of competition and the supposed degree of involvement of the undertaking concerned.'

[88] For more details see Ch 11, 'Infringement Decisions and Penalties', para 11.29.

[89] Joined Cases T-202/98, T-204/98, and T-207/98 *Tate & Lyle and others v Commission* [2001] ECR II-2035, para 106; Joined Cases T-236/01, T-239/01, T-244/01 to T-246/01, T-251/01, and T-252/01 *Tokai Carbon and Others v Commission* [2004] ECR II-1181, para 219; T-38/02 *Groupe Danone v EC Commission* [2005] II-4407, paras 50 and 51; Case T-18/03 *CD-Contact Data GmbH v EC Commission* [2009] ECR II-1021, para 105; Case T-161/05 *Hoechst GmbH v EC Commission* [2009] ECR II-3555, para 124. See also Case T-450/05 *Automobiles Peugeot SA and others v Commission* [2009] ECR II-2533, para 275, pointing out that '[the] assessment of the proportionate nature of a fine imposed with regard to the gravity and duration of an infringement, criteria formerly referred to…in Article 23(3) of Regulation No 1/2003, falls within the unlimited jurisdiction conferred on the Court of First Instance by Article 31 of that regulation.' For more details on the scope of review see Ch 11, 'Infringement Decisions and Penalties', para 11.40 with more references.

[90] Case T-229/94 *Deutsche Bahn v Commission* [1997] ECR II-1689, para 127; T-30/05 *William Prym GmbH & Co KG and Prym Consumer GmbH & Co KG v Commission* [2007] ECR II-107, para 224; Cases T-117/07 and T-121/07 *Areva et al v Commission* [2011] ECR II-633, para 350.

[91] Joined Cases 100/80 to 103/80 *Musique Diffusion Française and others v Commission* [1983] ECR 1825, para 120; Case T-50/00 *Dalmine SpA v Commission* [2004] ECR II-2395, para 259; Case T-66/01 *Imperial Chemical Industries Ltd v Commission* [2010] ECR II-2631, para 432; Case T-279/02 *Degussa v Commission*

when fixing the amount of each fine and is not obliged to apply a precise mathematical formula in this regard, it is nevertheless for the EU Courts to review whether the amount of the fine imposed is proportionate, given the duration of the infringement and the other factors capable of forming part of the assessment of its seriousness.[92]

2. The principle of observance of the right to a fair hearing[93]

1.28 The right to a fair hearing includes different aspects and notably comprises the threefold right of individuals:

- To be assisted by lawyers and enjoy confidentiality in respect of correspondence with them.[94] Article 6 ECHR grants the right of the accused to participate in an effective manner in a criminal or administrative-sanctions procedure. It includes not only the right to be physically present but also the right to be assisted by a lawyer.[95] The ECJ has recognized the role of the lawyer as collaborating in the administration of justice by the courts and as being required to provide, on a fully independent basis and without constraints, the legal assistance that the client needs.[96] In competition cases, lawyers may assist their clients in answering written requests for information.[97] They may also be present when an interview is carried out in accordance with Article 19 of Regulation 1/2003. Legal assistance during inspections pursuant to Article 20 of Regulation 1/2003 is not regulated either in Regulation 1/2003 or in Regulation 773/2004. It is, however, consistent Commission practice to allow undertakings to consult their lawyer and to ask them to be present, although the presence of a lawyer is not a legal condition for the validity of the inspection.

[2006] ECR II-897, para 272; Case T-446/05 *Amann & Söhne GmbH & Co KG and Cousin Filterie SAS v Commission* [2010] ECR II-1255, para 175; T-456/05 and T-457/05 *Gütermann AG and Zwicky & Co AG v Commission* [2010] ECR II-1443, para 264.

[92] Joined Cases T-202/98, T-204/98 and T-207/98 *Tate & Lyle and others v Commission* [2001] ECR II -2035, para 106; Case T-150/89 *Martinelli v Commission* [1995] ECR II-1 165, para 59; Case T-229/94 *Deutsche Bahn v Commission* [1997] ECR II-1689, para 127; Case T-352/94 *Mo och Domsjö v Commission* [1998] ECR II-1989, para 268, confirmed on appeal in Case C-283/98 P *Mo och Domsjö v Commission* [2000] ECR I-9855, para 45. Case C-359/01 P *British Sugar plc v Commission* [2004] ECR I-4933, paras 105–6. Regarding the case law of the ECtHR, see, *Schmautzer v Austria*, App no 15523/89 (ECtHR, 23 October 1995), para 36; *Valico SRL v Italy*, App no 70074/01 (ECtHR, 21 March 2006), 20 and case law cited; most recently, *A Menarini Diagnostics SRL v Italy*, App no 43509/08 (ECtHR, 27 September 2011), paras 58 and 59, where the ECtHR found, having regard to the criteria set out in its judgment in *Engel and Others v Netherlands, Engel et al v The Netherlands*, App nos 5100/71, 5101/71, 5102/71, 5354/72, 5370/72 (ECtHR, 8 June 1976), paras 82 and 83, that a fine of EUR 6 million imposed on an undertaking for anti-competitive practices was of a penal nature, so that Art 6(1) ECHR was applicable in the criminal respect (para 44).

[93] Joined Cases 100/80 to 103/80 *Musique Diffusion Française and others v Commission* [1983] ECR 1825, paras 10 and 14; Case T-54/03 *Lafarge SA v Commission* [2008] ECR II-120, para 37. See for more details on the observance of such principle during the *inter-partes* stage, Ch 10 'Procedures to Establish the Existence of an Infringement', para 10.18 et seq.

[94] Case T-99/04 *AC Treuhand v Commission* [2008] ECR II-1501, para 38; Case C-94/00 *Roquette Frères* [2002] ECR I-9011 para 46: 'without prejudice to the guarantees under domestic law governing the implementation of coercive measures, undertakings under investigation are protected by various Community guarantees, including, in particular, the right to legal representation and the privileged nature of correspondence between lawyer and client'. As regards the scope of the right, see in more detail Case C-550/07 P *Akzo Nobel Chemicals Ltd v Commission*, [2010] ECR I-8301, para 40 et seq.

[95] For example, Judgment of the ECtHR of 21 February 1984, *Öztürk v Germany, Application*, App no 8544/79 (EctHR, 21 February 1984); EU courts: Joined Cases 100/80 to 103/80 *Musique Diffusion Française and others v Commission* [1983] ECR 1825 para 8. Joined Cases T-305/94 to T-307/94 T-313/94 to T-316/94, T-318/94, T-325/94, T-328/94, T-329/94, and T-335/94 *Limburgse Vinyl Maatschappij and others v Commission* [1999] ECR II-931 ('*PVC II*'), para 120 et seq; Cases T-213/95 and T-18/96 *SCK and FNK v Commission* [1997] ECR II-1739, para 56; Case T-99/04 *AC Treuhand v Commission* [2008] ECR II-1501, para 38.

[96] Case 155/79 *AM &S Europe Limited v Commission* [1982] ECR 1575, paras 18 and 24.

[97] Article 18(4) of Reg 1/2003.

- To be allowed the same knowledge of the file used in the Commission's proceedings as the Commission itself, which presupposes that in a competition case the knowledge which the undertaking concerned has of the file used in the proceeding is the same as that of the Commission, including both the incriminating and potentially exculpatory documents (principle of 'equality of arms'). The Commission must give the undertaking concerned the opportunity to examine all the documents in the investigation file that may be relevant for its defence.[98] Access to the file is one of the procedural safeguards intended to protect the rights of the defence. These principles imply that all parties involved in a case are awarded the same knowledge in order to secure the observance of their defence rights.[99] The ECtHR has emphasized the need to respect the right to adversarial procedure, noting that this entails the parties' right to have knowledge of and comment on all evidence adduced or observations filed.[100] Recognizing these procedural safeguards, the ECJ has indicated that nonetheless the ECtHR has held that, just like the observance of the other procedural safeguards enshrined in Article 6(1) of the ECHR, compliance with the adversarial principle relates only to judicial proceedings before a 'tribunal' and that there is no general, abstract principle that the parties must in all instances have the opportunity to attend the interviews carried out or to receive copies of all the documents taken into account in the case of other persons.[101] The failure to communicate a document would constitute a breach of the rights of the defence only if the undertaking concerned shows, first, that the Commission relied on that document to support its objection concerning the existence of an infringement.[102] If there were other documentary evidence of which the parties were aware during the administrative procedure that specifically supported the Commission's findings, the fact that an incriminating document not communicated to the person concerned was inadmissible as evidence would not affect the validity of the objections upheld in the contested decision.[103] The principle of access to the file was established in the *Soda Ash* cases, which related to a concerted practice between Solvay and ICI and abuses of a dominant position by the two companies.[104]

---

[98] *Foucher v France*, App no 2209/93 (ECtHR, 18 March 1997), para 36.

[99] *Niederöst-Huber v Switzerland*, App no 18990/91 (ECtHR, 18 February 1997), para 24.

[100] *Brandstetter v Austria*, App nos 11170/84, 12876/87, 13468/87 (ECtHR, 28 August 1991),para 67.

[101] *Kerojärvi v Finland*, App no 17506/90 (ECtHR, 19 July 1995), para 42, and *Mantovanelli v France*, App no 21497/93 (ECtHR, 18 March 1997), para 33.

[102] Case 322/81 *Michelin v EC Commission* [1983] ECR 3461, paras 7 and 9; Case 107/82 *AEG v EC Commission* [1983] ECR 3151, paras 24–30.

[103] Joined Cases C-204/00 P, C-205/00 P, C-211/00 P, C-213/00 P, C-217/00 P, and C-219/00 P *Aalborg Portland and others v EC Commission* [2004] ECR I-123, para 70.

[104] In the course of the administrative proceedings the parties were unable to have access to the files related to one another: Case T-36/91 *Imperial Chemical Industries plc v Commission* [1995] ECR II-1847, paras 93 and 111. See also Case T-30/91 *Solvay SA v Commission* [1995] ECR II-1775, para 83 and 101 (these two cases related to the decisions under Art 101 TFEU). Case T-175/95 *BASF Lacke + Farben AG v Commission* [1999] ECR II-1581, para 46; Case T-23/99 *LRAF 1998A/S, formerly Løgstør Rør A/S v Commission* [2002] ECR II-1705, para 171: 'Having regard to the general principle of equality of arms, it is not acceptable for the Commission to be able to decide on its own whether or not to use documents against the undertakings, when the undertakings had no access to them and were therefore unable to decide whether or not to use them in their defence...the Commission is to deal, in its decisions, only with those objections in respect of which the undertakings have been afforded the opportunity of making known their views.' Case T-314/01 *Coöperatieve Verkoop- en Productievereniging van Aardappelmeel en Derivaten Avebe BA v Commission* [2006] ECR II-3085, para 66. Article 27(2) of Reg 1/2003 is based on the principle of equality of arms and provides that the parties involved shall be entitled to have access to the Commission's file subject to the classic exceptions relating to business secrets, other confidential information, and internal documents of the Commission. The arrangements to give access to all relevant files are contained in the Commission Notice on Access to the file [2005] OJ C325/7 which shall ensure compatibility with the requirements of the *Soda Ash* cases. As regards the Commission Notice of 13 December 2005 on the rules for access to the Commission file pursuant to Articles 81 and 82 EC Treaty [2005] OJ C252/7, see Ch 10, 'Procedures to Establish the Existence of an Infringement', para 10.38 et seq.

The GC ruled that in the case of illegal non-disclosure of exculpatory documents the only remedy is for the decision as a whole to be annulled, since it cannot be known what the result of the proceedings would have been, had such documents been disclosed to the companies.[105] The GC stated that the Commission had failed to respect the rights of the defence by not allowing the companies to have access to specific documents. In particular, the Commission had not prepared a list of all of the documents in the *Soda Ash* file because it considered this to be of no use in this case[106] and had not shown to ICI and Solvay certain allegedly confidential documents belonging to the other party.[107] Nor did the Commission provide the companies with a non-confidential summary of such documents because it considered that this was not possible in this case.[108] However, the GC took the view that by deleting their confidential parts, or by summarizing them, all documents, including both incriminating evidence and exculpatory evidence, could have been made available to the other party and it was not for the Commission to decide which documents were useful for the defence. In *Hercules*, the GC defined the limits of access to the file stating that 'the Commission has an obligation to make available to the companies involved in Article 101(1) proceedings all documents, whether in their favour or otherwise, which it has obtained during the course of the investigation, save where the business secrets of other undertakings, the internal documents of the Commission or other confidential information are involved'.[109] In *Cimenteries CBR,* the GC dismissed an application brought against the refusal of the Commission to disclose certain documents of the statement of objections, stating that, before the decision on the existence of an infringement, the Commission can still rectify procedural irregularities by granting access to the file but also emphasized that the infringement of a right of full access can lead to the annulment of the Commission's contested decision.[110] It would seem that access to the file is an integral part of the right to be heard and not a right in itself.[111] The right of access to the file is set out in Article 27(2) of Regulation 1/2003 and expanded

---

[105] Case T-30/91 *Solvay SA v Commission* [1995] ECR II-1775, paras 58, 97, and 98. The EU courts quashed the initial Commission decision, which was then readopted in 2000. Solvay lodged appeals against both of the decisions adopted in December 2000. The GC handed down separate judgments on 17 December 2009 (Cases T-57/01 (Art 102) and T-58/01 (Art 101)). On 25 October 2011, the ECJ ultimately annulled fines of EUR 23 million imposed by the Commission on Solvay for competition law infringements in the soda ash market. The Court ruled that Solvay's defence rights had been breached in the re-adoption procedure, since it could not have access to all of the documents in the file, some of which may have enabled the company to offer a 'different interpretation' of the facts of the case.

[106] See Case T-36/91 *ICI* [1995] ECR II-1847, paras 60, last indent, 61, 63, and 64. The Commission had actually joined all the documents that it considered could be shown to the Statement of Objections.

[107] See Case T-30/91 *Solvay SA v Commission* [1995] ECR II-1775, paras 8 and 90; Case T-36/91 *ICI v Commission* [1995] ECR II-1847, paras 8, 56, 61, and 100.

[108] According to the Commission, what the undertakings wanted to have access to was, precisely, the other party's business secrets. See Case T-36/91 *ICI v Commission* [1995] ECR II-1847, para 56.

[109] Case T-7/89 *Hercules v Commission* [1991] ECR II-1711, para 54; Joined Cases T-10/92 to T-12/92 and T-15/92 *Cimenteries CBR and Others v Commission* [1992] ECR II-2667, paras 39–41; Case T-57/01 *Solvay SA v Commission* [2009] ECR II-4621, para 453; Case C-407/08 P *Knauf Gips KG* [2010] ECR I-6371, para 22.

[110] Joined Cases T-10/92 to T-12/92 and T-15/92 *Cimenteries CBR, SA and others v Commission* [1992] ECR II-2667, paras 39–42, 47. See also Case T-7/89 *Hercules v Commission* [1991] ECR II-1711, para 38.

[111] Case C-51/92 P *Hercules Chemicals NV v Commission* [1999] ECR I-4235, para 75: 'access to the file in competition cases is intended in particular to enable the addressees of statements of objections to acquaint themselves with the evidence in the Commission's file so that on the basis of that evidence they can express their views effectively on the conclusions reached by the Commission in its statement of objections'. Joined Cases T-191/98, T-212/98 to T-214/98 *Atlantic Container Line and Others v Commission* [2003] ECR II-3275, para 334; Case T-161/05 *Hoechst GmbH v Commission* [2009] ECR II-3555, para 160.

upon in Articles 15 and 16 of Regulation 773/2004[112] and also included in the EU Charter of Fundamental Rights of the EU.[113]

• To be granted a hearing and make submissions before any public authority takes measures which might affect their interests; a person against whom the Commission has initiated administrative proceedings must have been afforded the opportunity, during those proceedings, to make known his or her views on the truth and relevance of the facts and circumstances alleged and on the documents used by the Commission to support its claim that there has been an infringement of EU law.[114] Observance of the right to be heard in all proceedings in which sanctions, in particular fines or penalty payments, may be imposed constitutes a fundamental principle of EU law which must be respected even if the proceedings in question are administrative proceedings.[115] The right to be heard is normally exercised in writing by way of reply containing observations on the accuracy of the facts and the validity of the arguments. The undertaking may also adduce evidence of its own in support of its defence. In this respect, in *Transocean Marine Paint Association v Commission*, the ECJ reiterated the general principle of EU law which requires that a person whose interests are appreciably affected by a decision taken by a public authority must be given the opportunity to make his point of view known.[116] This requirement also applies where the relevant regulation does not explicitly provide for this opportunity.[117]

For its part, the ECtHR has interpreted the right to a fair hearing before an independent and impartial tribunal in a liberal manner,[118] regardless of whether the matter is to be classified as civil or criminal. The provision is applicable to administrative procedures as well as to disciplinary procedures.[119] Article 6 ECHR is applied in a more or less strict fashion depending on **1.29**

---

[112] The Commission Notice of 13 December 2005 on the rules for access to the Commission file in cases pursuant to Arts 81 and 82 EC, Arts 53, 54, and 57 of the EEA Agreement, and Council Regulation (EC) 139/2004 provides the framework for the exercise of the right set out in these provisions [2005] OJ C325/7. The notice has replaced the 1997 notice on the internal rules of procedure for processing requests for access to the file.

[113] Title V, Art 41(2)(b). See also Ch 10, 'Procedures to Establish the Existence of an Infringement', para 10.38 et seq.

[114] Article 27(1) of Reg 1/2003 provides that, before taking its decision, the Commission is to give the undertakings 'the opportunity of being heard on the matters to which the Commission has taken objection'. This is reiterated in Art 11(2) of Reg 773/2004. See also Case 234/84 *Belgium v Commission* [1986] ECR 2263, para 27; opinion of AG Mischo in C-254/99 *ICI v Commission* [2002] ECR I-8375, para 133; Case T-54/03 *Lafarge SA v Commission*, para 68; Case T-24/07 *ThyssenKrupp Stainless AG v Commission* [2009] ECR II-2309, para 286.

[115] Case C-289/04 *Showa Denko* [2006] ECR 1-5859, para 68; Case T-170/06 *Alrosa Company Ltd v Commission* [2007] ECR II-2601, para 191.

[116] Case 17/74 *Transocean Marine Paint Association v Commission* [1974] ECR 1063, para 15: 'this rule requires that an undertaking be clearly informed, in good time, of the essence of conditions to which the Commission intends to subject an exemption [under Art 83(3) EC][103(3)] and it must have the opportunity to submit its observations to the Commission. This is especially so in the case of conditions which...impose considerable obligations having far-reaching effects.' See also Case T-79/00 *Rewe ZentralAG v OAMI* [2002] ECR II-705, para 14.

[117] See also Case T-214/06 *Imperial Chemical Industries Ltd v European Commission*, para 222; Case C-269/90 *Technische Universitat München v Hauptzollamt* [1991] ECR I-5469, paras 23–5. See also J Flattery, 'Balancing Efficiency and Justice in EU Competition Law: Elements of Procedural Fairness and their Impact on the Right to a Fair Hearing' (2010) 7(1) Competition Law Review 53 with more references to the case law.

[118] *Piersack v Belgium*, App no 8692/79 (ECtHR, 1 October 1982), paras 28–32; *Vilho Eskelinen & Ors Finland*, App. no 63235/00 (ECtHR, 19 April 2007); *Köksal and Durdu v Turkey*, App nos 27080/08 and 40982/08 (ECtHR, 15 June 2010).

[119] *Le Compte, Van Leuven and De Meyere*, App no 6878/75 and 7238/75 (ECtHR, 23 June 1981), paras 41–8; for example, concerning an administrative penalty imposed following a road traffic accident, see *Öztürk v Germany, Application*, App no 8544/79 (EctHR, 21 February 1984); concerning a penalty imposed for a customs offence, see *Salabiaku v France*, App no 10519/83 (ECtHR, 7 October 1988); concerning a penalty imposed by the French Financial Markets Board, see *Didier v France*, App no 58188/00 (EctHR, 27 August

whether the offence is of a criminal or non-criminal nature.[120] Although national law may not necessarily classify a matter as 'criminal', the ECtHR may do so, taking into account the nature of the offence and the severity of the penalty. Where a penalty is liable to be imposed on all persons infringing a rule and is imposed to deter and to punish infringements, and where those penalties are substantial, the matter would be classified as criminal.[121] The fact that Regulation 1/2003 states the fines being imposed 'shall not be of a criminal law nature' would not bind the ECtHR.[122] In *Societé Stenuit v France* the ECtHR considered a matter of French administrative law which concerned the imposition of a fine under French competition law for participation in a cartel as a criminal proceedings, notwithstanding the non-criminal charge of the penalty under French law.[123] The Union courts have accepted this interpretation and do not seem to contest the criminal nature of the Commission's decisions in which it imposes fines.[124]

3. The principle of presumption of innocence[125]

1.30 This principle means that any accused person is presumed innocent until proven guilty, therefore prohibiting any formal finding of responsibility for a person charged with an offence without that person having had the benefit of all guarantees inherent in the exercise of the rights of the defence.[126] The indictment or formal charge against any person is not evidence of guilt. The law does not require a person to prove his innocence or produce

---

2002); concerning a tax surcharge imposed in the context of a reassessment by the tax authorities, see *Jussila v Finland*, App no 73053/01 (ECtHR, 23 November 2006); and, concerning a reprimand given by the French Banking Commission (where it held that there were criminal charges of differing weight and that, for areas outside the 'hard core of criminal law', 'the criminal-head guarantees will not necessarily apply with their full stringency'), *Dubus SA v France* App no 5242/04 (ECtHR, 11 June 2009).

[120] M Ameye, 'The Interplay between Human Rights and Competition Law' [2004] ECLR 332, 333. Article 6(1) ECHR applies in civil matters as well as in the criminal sphere.

[121] *Bendemoun v France*, App no 12547/86 (ECtHR, 24 February 1994), para 47.

[122] Article 23(5) of Reg 1/2003. Kerse & Khan, *EC Antitrust Procedure* (6th edn, Sweet & Maxwell 2012) para 3-011, stating that this affirmation, although probably unsustainable from the perspective of the ECHR, would leave unresolved the precise extent to which procedural safeguards under Art 6 ECHR are applicable.

[123] The fine imposed was not large but the law allowed a fine of up to 5 per cent of turnover. The ECtHR held that the criminal nature of the case was 'revealed unambiguously' by the possibility of severe and deterrent maximum fines in the event of a breach. *Société Stenuit v France*, App no 11598/85 (ECtHR, 27 February 1992). It further observed that penalties were levied against undertakings that committed acts constituting 'infractions', and that the maximum fine that could be imposed (5 per cent of the undertaking's annual turnover) 'shows quite clearly that the penalty in question was intended to be deterrent' (paras 62–4). See, however, *OOO Neste St Petersburg v Russia*, App no 69042/01 (ECtHR, 3 June 2004), in which penalties under Russian competition law were not considered of being of criminal nature.

[124] C Bellamy and G Child, *EC Law of Competition* (6th edn, Oxford University Press 2008) para 13-030. See, however, Kerse & Khan, *EC Antitrust Procedure* (6th edn, Sweet & Maxwell 2012) para 3-011, n 24—with ample references—indicating that the Court's approach to the classification of competition proceedings as a civil or criminal matter has been inconsistent.

[125] See 'Soda Ash': Case T-30/91 *Solvay SA v Commission* [1995] ECR II-1775, paras 72 and 73 and Case T-36/91 *Imperial Chemical Industries plc v Commission* [1995] ECR II-1847, paras 82 and 83; Case C-199/92 *Hüls AG v Commission* [1999] ECR I-4287, para 150; Case T-62/98 *Volkswagen AG v E Commission* [2000] ECR II-2707, para 281: 'it should be borne in mind that the principle of the presumption of innocence applies to the procedures relating to infringements of the competition rules by undertakings that may result in the imposition of fines or periodic penalty payments…That presumption of innocence is clearly not respected by the Commission where, prior to formally imposing a penalty on the undertaking charged, it informs the press of the proposed finding which has been submitted to the Advisory Committee and the College of Commissioners for deliberation'. See also opinion of AG Mazák, Joined Cases C-322/07 P, C-327/07 P, and C-338/07 P *Papierfabrik August Köhler* [2007] ECR I-7191, para 132; Case C-413/08 P *Lafarge SA v Commission* [2010] ECR I-5361, para 92 (both with references to ECtHR case law); Case T-110/07 *Siemens AG v Commission* [2011] ECR II-477, para 45.

[126] Case T-474/04 *Pergan v Commission* [2007] ECR II-4225, paras 75–7; Case T-174/05 *Elf Aquitaine SA v Commission* [2009] ECR II-183, para 196.

any evidence at all. The prosecution has the burden of proving a person guilty beyond a reasonable doubt, and if it fails to do so the person is (so far as the law is concerned) not guilty.[127] The ECtHR states that Article 6(2) ECHR, which enshrines the presumption of innocence, governs criminal proceedings in their entirety, irrespective of the outcome of the prosecution. In its case law, the presumption of innocence is violated if, without the accused having previously been proved guilty according to law and, notably, without having had the opportunity of exercising his or her rights to a fair defence, a judicial decision concerning him or her reflects a guilty verdict.[128] Given the nature of the infringements in question and the nature and degree of severity of the ensuing penalties, the principle of the presumption of innocence applies to the procedures relating to infringements of the competition rules that may result in the imposition of fines or periodic penalty payments.[129] Under this principle, the Commission is required to produce sufficiently precise and consistent evidence to support the firm conviction that the alleged competition infringement has taken place.[130] However, it is important to emphasize that it is not necessary for every item of evidence produced by the Commission to satisfy those criteria in relation to every aspect of the infringement. It is sufficient if the body of evidence relied on by the institution, viewed as a whole, meets that requirement.[131] In this respect, this principle is closely connected with that of *in dubio pro reo* and with the duty to comply with the legally required standard to demonstrate the existence of the circumstances constituting an infringement.[132] The Court examines whether 'the

---

[127] *Minelli v Switzerland*, App no 8660/79 (ECtHR, 25 March), para 37.

[128] *Barberà, Messegué and Jabardo v Spain*, App no 10590/83 (ECtHR, 6 December 1988), para 91.

[129] Case C-199/92 P *Hüls v Commission* [1999] ECR I-4287, paras 149 and 150, where the Court observed that the presumption of innocence resulting in particular from Art 6(2) of the ECHR is one of the fundamental rights which, according to the Court's settled case law, reaffirmed in the preamble to the Single European Act and in Art 6(3) TEU, are protected in the EU legal order; Case C-235/92 P *Montecatini v Commission* [1999] ECR I-4539, paras 175 and 176 (see the judgments of the ECHR in *Öztürk v Germany, Application*, App no 8544/79 (EctHR, 21 February 1984) and in *Lutz v Germany*, App no 9912/82 (ECtHR, 25 August 1987)). Case T-110/07 *Siemens AG v Commission* [2011] ECR II-477, para 45.

[130] See, to that effect, Joined Cases 29/83 and 30/83 *CRAM and Rheinzink v Commission* [1984] ECR 1679, para 20; Joined Cases C-89/85, C-104/85, C-114/85, C-116/85, C-117/85, and C-125/85 to C-129/85 *A Ahlström Osakeyhtiö and others v Commission ('Woodpulp II')* [1993] ECR I-1307, para 157; Joined Cases T-68/89, T-77/89, and T-78/89 *SIV and others v Commission* [1992] ECR II-1403, paras 193–5, 198–202, 205–10, 220–32, 249, 250, and 322–8; and Case T-62/98 *Volkswagen v Commission* [2000] ECR II-2707, paras 43 and 72; Case T-377/06 *Comap SA v Commission* [2011] ECR II-1115, para 56; Case T-384/06 *IBP Ltd and International Building Products France SA v Commission* [2011] ECR II-1177, para 57.

[131] See, to that effect, Joined Cases T-305/94 to T-307/94, T-313/94 to T-316/94, T-318/94, T-325/94, T-328/94, T-329/94, and T-335/94 *Limburgse Vinyl Maatschaapij and others v Commission ('PVC II')* [1999] ECR II-931, paras 768–78, and in particular para 777, confirmed on the relevant point by the ECJ, on appeal, in its judgment in Joined Cases C-238/99 P, C-244/99 P, C-245/99 P, C-247/99 P, C-250/99 P to C-252/99 P, and C-254/99 P *LVM and others v Commission* [2002] ECR I-8375, paras 513–23; Joined Cases T-67/00, T-68/00, T-71/00, and T-78/00 *JFE Engineering v Commission* [2004] ECR II-2501, paras 179 and 180; Joined Cases T-109/02, T-118/02, T-122/02, T-125/02, T-126/02, T-128/02, T-129/02, T-132/02, and T-136/02 *Bolloré SA et al v Commission* [2007] ECR II-947, para 155; Case T-377/06 *Comap SA v Commission* [2011] ECR II-1115, para 57.

[132] The principle *of in dubio pro reo* is laid down in Art 48 of the Charter of Fundamental Rights and Art 6 ECHR. It is one of the fundamental principles which are protected by EU law. See in particular ECJ Case C-199/92 P *Hüls v Commission* [1999] ECR I-4287, para 149; see also Joined Cases T-5/00 and T-6/00 *Nederlandse Federatieve Vereniging voor de Groothandel op Elektrotechnisch Gebied and Technische Unie BV v Commission* [2003] ECR II-5761, para 210, rejecting that the Commission failed to demonstrate to a sufficient legal standard that its findings regarding the gentlemen's agreement were vitiated or contained material inaccuracies of such a kind as to render them invalid. It also rejected the allegation that certain documents adverse to the applicant were ambiguous and that the applicant should be granted the benefit of the doubt pursuant to the maxim *in dubio pro reo*.

Commission gathered sufficiently precise and consistent evidence to give grounds for a firm conviction that the alleged infringement took place'.[133] The Court is expected not to conclude that the Commission has established the existence of the infringement at issue to the requisite legal standard if it still entertains doubts on whether the evidence and other information relied on by the Commission are sufficient to establish the existence of the alleged infringement, in particular in proceedings for the annulment of a decision imposing a fine.[134]

4. The privilege against self-incrimination

1.31 The privilege against self-incrimination means that no one can be compelled to produce evidence against oneself. This includes the right of silence and the right not to answer questions. Although not expressly mentioned in Article 6 ECHR, the ECtHR has held that this privilege is part of the notion of the right to a fair procedure provided by Article 6 ECHR.[135] The ECtHR has not yet heard a case where a legal entity sought to invoke the right of silence. Its case law solely relates to situations where a natural person was questioned and refused to answer.[136] The first step in recognizing the privilege against self-incrimination was taken in *Funke*.[137] That case was based on a complaint by a French citizen against France. French custom officers had searched Mr Funke's home and requested him to produce statements concerning foreign bank accounts and financial information by customs authorities. Mr Funke was fined, pursuant to the French Customs Code, for refusing to provide the statements. The ECtHR considered that:

> the customs secured Mr Funke's conviction in order to obtain certain documents which they believed must exist, although they were not certain of the fact. Being unable or unwilling to procure them by some other means, they attempted to compel the applicant himself to provide the evidence of offences he had allegedly committed.

The ECtHR concluded that:

> [t]he special features of customs law…cannot justify such an infringement of the right of anyone 'charged with a criminal offence', within the autonomous meaning of this expression in Article 6 [ECHR], to remain silent and not contribute to incriminating himself.[138]

---

[133] Joined Cases T-185/96, T-189/96, and T-190/96 *Riviera Auto Service and others v Commission* [1999] ECR II-93, para 47; Case T-62/98 *Volkswagen v Commission* [2000] ECR II-2707, para 43; Joined Cases T-109/02, T-118/02, T-122/02, T-125/02, T-126/02, T-128/02, T-129/02, T-132/02, and T-136/02 *Bolloré SA et al v Commission* [2007] ECR II-947, para 257. The EU Courts seem to take the view that this is less stringent than the criminal law standard of 'beyond reasonable doubt'. In *Woodpulp II*, AG Darmon's interpretation to that effect of the concept of sufficiently precise and coherent evidence was not adopted by the Court: Opinion of AG Darmon in Joined Cases C-89/85, C-104/85, C-114/85, C116/85, C-117/85, and C-125/85 to C-129/85 *Ahlström Osakeyhtiö and others v Commission* ('Woodpulp II') [1993] ECR I-1307, para 195. Case T-53/03 *BPB plc v Commission* [2008] ECR-1333, para 64: 'It is apparent from that case-law that the Court must reject the applicant's assertion that the Commission must adduce proof "beyond reasonable doubt" of the existence of the infringement in cases where it imposes heavy fines.' See Ch 4, 'The Organization of EU Commission Proceedings', para 4.36 et seq.

[134] Joined Cases T-67/00, T-68/00, T-71/00, and T-78/00 *JFE Engineering Corp and others v Commission* [2004] ECR II-2501, para 177; Case T-56/02 *Bayerische Hypo- und Vereinsbank AG v Commission* [2004] ECR II-3495, paras 92–119, in which the Court found the evidence adduced by the Commission 'debatable' or 'not convincing'.

[135] *John Murray v United Kingdom*, App no 18731/91 (ECtHR, 8 February 1996), para 45. See for more details on the privilege against self-incrimination, Ch 7, 'Investigation of Cases (II): Formal Investigative Measures in General, Requests for Information, and Interviews', para 7.44 et seq.

[136] K Dekeyser and C Gauer, 'The New Enforcement System For Articles 81 and 82 and the Rights of Defence', ch 23 in BE Hawk (ed), *International Antitrust Law & Policy*, (Annual Proceedings of the Fordham Institute, 2005) 549, 562.

[137] *Funke v France*, App no 10828/84 (ECtHR, 25 February 1993). In *Orkem* the ECJ seemed to take the view that neither the wording of Art 6 ECHR nor the decisions of the ECtHR indicated that it upheld the right not to give evidence against oneself. Case 374/87 *Orkem v EC Commission* [1989] ECR 3283, para 30.

[138] *Funke v France*, App no 10828/84 (ECtHR, 25 February 1993), para 44.

This interpretation was further developed in the *John Murray* and *Saunders* judgments,[139] **1.32** although the latter seems to circumscribe the privilege more narrowly by excluding documents from the scope of Article 6 ECHR.[140] In *Saunders*, the ECtHR ruled that the right not to incriminate oneself 'cannot reasonably be confined to statements of admission of wrongdoing or to remarks that are directly incriminating'. On the other hand, the Court also stated that '[t]he right not to incriminate oneself is primarily concerned...with respecting the will of an accused person to remain silent'. Therefore:

> it does not extend to the use in criminal proceedings of material which may be obtained from the accused through the use of compulsory powers but which has an existence independent of the will of the suspect such as, inter alia, documents acquired pursuant to a warrant, breath, blood and urine samples and bodily tissue for the purpose of DNA testing.[141]

The ECtHR further noted that:

> [t]estimony obtained under compulsion which appears on its face to be of a non-incriminating nature—such as exculpatory remarks or mere information on questions of fact—may later be deployed in criminal proceedings in support of the prosecution case, for example to contradict or cast doubt upon other statements of the accused or evidence given by him during the trial or to otherwise undermine his credibility.[142]

In contrast to documents acquired pursuant to a warrant, the latter suggests a broad approach **1.33** to the nature of statements made by the accused which benefit from the privilege.[143] This interpretation went beyond the protection against actual admissions, but the GC seemed to take the view in *Mannesmannröhren-Werke*[144] that interpretations of certain rights in competition proceedings did not have to coincide exactly with those of the ECtHR when the latter deals with criminal procedures involving natural persons.[145] However, later the ECJ explained in *PVC II* in very explicit terms that it was ready to analyse the privilege against self-incrimination based on the ECtHR case law and even found that there had been considerable evolutions in the case law of the ECtHR since *Orkem* 'which the Community judicature must take into account when interpreting the fundamental rights'.[146] This stance contrasts with previous statements to the effect that the interpretations of fundamental rights by the Union courts did not have to coincide exactly with those of the ECtHR, and fits in with a more general trend of the Union courts of relying extensively on the case law of the ECtHR[147] and the express reference by the Charter of Fundamental Rights to the case law of the ECtHR.[148]

---

[139] *John Murray v United Kingdom*, App no 18731/91 (ECtHR, 8 February 1996), para 45; *Saunders v United Kingdom*, App no 19187/91 (ECtHR, 17 December 1996), para 71.

[140] C Bellamy and G Child, *EC Law of Competition* (6th edn, Oxford University Press 2008) para 13-058, suggesting that the *Saunders* case overruled the *Funke* case.

[141] *Saunders v United Kingdom*, App no 19187/91 (ECtHR, 17 December 1996), para 69.

[142] *Saunders v United Kingdom*, App no 19187/91 (ECtHR, 17 December 1996), para 71 (emphasis added). Joined Cases C-204/00 P, C-205/00 P, C-211/00 P, C-213/00 P, C-217/00 P, and C-219/00 P *Aalborg Portland and others v EC Commission* [2004] ECRI-123, para 64.

[143] Kerse & Khan, *EC Antitrust Procedure* (6th edn, Sweet & Maxwell 2012) para 3-035.

[144] Case T-112/98 *Mannesmannröhren-Werke v EC Commission* [2001] ECR II-729.

[145] B Vesterdorf, 'Legal Professional Privilege and the Privilege Against Self-Incrimination in EC Law: Recent Developments and Current Issues', ch 27 in BE Hawk (ed), *International Antitrust Law & Policy* (Annual Proceedings of the Fordham Institute 2004) 701, 713.

[146] Joined Cases C-238/99, C-244–245/99, C-247/99, C250–252/99, and C-254/99 *Limburgse Vinyl Maatschappij (LVM) and others v EC Commission* [2002] ECR I-8375, para 274.

[147] For example, the ECJ interpreted a directive mainly exclusively in light of the ECtHR case law on Art 8 ECHR (Joined Cases C-465/00, C-138/01, and C-139/01 *Österreichischer Rundfunk and others* [2003] ECR I-4989), para 73 et seq.

[148] See Recital 5 of the Charter of fundamental rights of the European Union [2010] OJ C83/391: '[t]his Charter reaffirms, with due regard for the powers and tasks of the Community and the Union and the

5. The principle that administrative measures must be lawful

1.34 The lawfulness of administrative measures comes into play as regards the obligation to state the reasons on which Union measures are based (Article 296 TFEU) so that the addressees are informed of the reasons for their adoption and the Court is able to undertake judicial review as to the legality of those decisions and to provide the party concerned with the necessary information so that it may establish whether they are well founded.[149] The extent of that obligation depends on the circumstances of each particular case, in particular the content of the measure in question, the nature of the reasons given, and the interest which the addressees of the measure, or other parties to whom it is of direct and individual concern, may have in obtaining explanations[150] but the Commission must disclose in a clear and unequivocal fashion its reasoning so that the persons concerned can know the reasons for the measure and defend their rights, and the EU courts can carry out their review.[151] In the context of the Commission's investigatory powers, the Commission is required to state the reasons for the decision ordering an investigation by specifying its subject matter and purpose. The EU Courts have held that this is a fundamental requirement, designed to enable the undertakings to assess the scope of their duty to cooperate, whilst at the same time safeguarding their defence rights.[152] Where the Commission finds in a decision that there has been an infringement of the competition rules and imposes fines on the undertakings participating in it, the Commission must, if it systematically took into account certain basic factors when setting the amount of the fines, set out those factors in the body of the decision in order to enable the addressees of the decision to verify that the level of the fine is correct.[153] It is not necessary for the reasoning to go into all of the relevant facts and points of law, since the question whether the statement of reasons meets the requirements of Article 296 TFEU must be assessed with regard not only to its wording but also to its context and to all of the legal rules governing the matter in question.[154] It is sufficient if the Commission sets out the facts and

---

principle of subsidiarity, the rights as they result, in particular, from … *the case-law of the* Court of Justice of the European Communities and of *the European Court of Human Rights*' (emphasis added). Article 6(3) of the TEU provides that: 'The Union recognises the rights, freedoms and principles set out in the Charter of Fundamental Rights of the European Union of 7 December 2000, as adapted at Strasbourg, on 12 December 2007, which shall have the same legal value as the Treaties.'

[149] Case C-350/88 *Delacre and Others v Commission* [1990] ECR I-395, para 15 and Case T-504/93 *Tiercé Ladbroke v Commission* [1997] ECR II-923, para 149. See eg Case T-44/90 *La Cinq v Commission* [1992] ECR II-1, para 42 and Case T-7/92 *Asia Motor France and others v Commission* [1993] ECR II-669, para 30. Accordingly, the Commission must explain its reasoning when it adopts a decision which goes appreciably further than its previous decisions (Case 73/74 *Papier Peints v Commission* [1975] ECR 1491, para 31).

[150] Joined Cases C-121/91 and C-122/91 *CT Control (Rotterdam) and JCT Benelux v Commission* [1993] ECR I-3873, para 31; Case C-56/93 *Belgium v Commission* [1996] ECR I-723, para 86; Joined Cases C-329/93, C-62/95, and C-63/95 *Germany and others v Commission* [1996] ECR I-5151, para 31; Case T-24/05 *Alliance One International and others v Commission* [2010] ECR II-5329, para 149; Cases T-117/07 and T-121/07 *Areva and others v Commission* [2011] ECR II-633, para 88.

[151] Case T-171/97 *Swedish Match Philippines v Council* [1999] ECR II-3241, para 82, and the case law cited there, and Joined Cases T-12/99 and T-63/99 *UK Coal v Commission* [2001] ECR II-2153, para 196. Case T-155/06 *Tomra Systems and others v Commission* [2010] OJ C288/31, para 227. In the case of a decision adopted pursuant to Art 102 TFEU, that principle requires that the contested decision mentions facts forming the basis of the legal grounds of the measure and the considerations which led to the adoption of the decision (see, to that effect, Case T-340/03 *France Télécom v Commission* [2007] ECR II-107, para 57, not appealed on that point).

[152] Case T-59/99 *Ventouris Group Enterprises SA* [2003] ECR II-5257, para 124; Case T-65/99 *Strintzis Lines Shipping SA* [2003] ECR II-5433, para 44; Case T-66/99 *Minoan Lines SA v Commission* [2003] ECR II-5515, paras 54 and 55.

[153] Case C-248/98 P *NV Koninklijke KNP BP v Commission* [2000] ECR I-9641, para 78; Case C-291/98 P *Sarrió SA v Commission* [2000] ECR I-9991, para 352.

[154] Case T-150/89 *GB Martinelli v Commission* [1995] ECR-II-1165 para 65; Case C-367/95 P *Commission v Sytraval and Brink's France* [1998] ECR I-1719, para 63 and the case law cited therein; Case

legal considerations which are of crucial importance to the decision.[155] Lack of reasoning in a decision amounts to an infringement of an essential procedural requirement.[156]

6. The principle of sound administration

The principle of sound administration encompasses a range of different aspects. It presupposes, **1.35** *inter alia*, that the Commission must act within a reasonable time in adopting decisions following administrative proceedings relating to competition policy[157] and that it must adopt the behaviour of an administrative authority exercising ordinary care, diligence, and good faith[158] in dealing with the information obtained. In particular, the Commission must examine carefully and impartially all relevant aspects of the individual case and the right of the person concerned to make his or her views known and to receive an adequately reasoned decision.[159] The principle is often invoked when the Commission fails to divulge, divulges partially, or fails to take into account certain evidence in the applicant's favour, makes a decision public before notifying it to the addressees,[160] takes excessive time to take a decision,[161] discloses matters under deliberation to the press,[162] or does not comply with its duty to carry out a thorough and impartial

---

T-122/04, *Outokumpu Oyj v Commission* [2009] ECR II-1135, para 49; Case T-378/06 *IMI plc v Commission* [pending publication] judgment of 24 March 2011 [2011] OJ C145/20, para 6.

[155] Case T-44/90 *La Cinq v Commission* [1992] ECR II-1, para 35 and Case T-7/92 *Asia Motor France and others v Commission* [1993] ECR II-669, para 31; Case T-211/05 *Italy v Commission* [2009] ECR II-2777, para 68 and the case law cited therein; Case T-427/08 *Confédération européenne des associations d'horlogers-réparateurs (CEAHR)* [2011] ECR II-5685, para 161.

[156] See Ch 15, 'Steps Following the Adoption of a Formal Decision', para 15.74.

[157] Joined Cases T-213/95 and T-1 8/96 *SCK and FNK v Commission* [1997] ECR II-1739, paras 55 and 56; Case T-66/01 *Imperial Chemical Industries Ltd v Commission* [2010] ECR II-2631, para 109. As regards the application of the competition rules, exceeding a reasonable time can constitute a ground for annulment only in the case of a decision finding infringements, provided that it has been established that the breach of that principle adversely affected the defence rights of the undertakings concerned. Joined Cases T-305/94 to T-307/94, T-313/94 to T-316/94, T-318/94, T-325/94, T-328/94, T-329/94, and T-335/94 *Limburgse Vinyl Maatschappij and Others v Commission* [1999] ECR II-931, para 122; Case T-62/99 *Sodima v Commission* [2001] ECR II-655, para 94; Case C-105/04 P *Nederlandse Federatieve Vereniging voor de Groothandel op Elktrotechnisch Gebied v Commission* [2006] ECR I-8725, paras 42–4.

[158] See Case T-44/90 *La Cinq v Commission* [1992] ECR II-1, para 86; Case C-269/90 *Technische Universität München* [1991] ECR I-5469, paras 14 and 26; Joined Cases T-528/93, T-542/93, T-543/93, and T-546/93 *Métropole Télévisionand Others v Commission* [1996] ECR II-649, para 93; Case C-367/95 P *Commission v Sytraval and Brink's France* [1998] ECR I-1719, para 62; see Case T-62/98 *Volkswagen AG v Commission* [2000] ECR II-2707, paras 269–70.

[159] Case T-44/90 *La Cinq v Commission* [1992] ECR II-1, para 86; Case C-269/90 *Technische Universität München* [1991] ECRI-5469, paras 14 and 26, where the ECJ held that this also applies where the Commission has great power of appraisal; and Joined Cases T-528/93, T-542/93, T-543/93, and T-546/93 *Métropole Télévision and others v Commission* [1996] ECR II-649, para 93, Case T-410/03 *Hoechst GmbH v Commission* [2008] ECR II-81, para 129; Case C-367/95 P *Commission v Sytraval and Brink's France* [1998] ECR I-1719, para 62. In the event of an action brought against an administrative decision, it must also be observed in the judicial proceedings before the EU Courts: Case C-185/95 P *Baustahlgewebe GmbH v Commission* [1998] ECR I-8417, para 21. K Lenaerts, 'In the Union We Trust: Trust-Enhancing Principles of Community Law' (2004) CML Rev 317, 337 suggested that it would be more appropriate to refer to the principles of sound administration, encompassing standards of (i) administrative care and diligence; (ii) administrative fairness; and (iii) legal certainty. See also Art 41(1) of the EU Charter on Human Rights, which recognizes every person's right 'to have his or her affairs handled impartially, fairly and within a reasonable time by the institutions and bodies of the Union'.

[160] Joined Cases 96-102, 104/82, 105/82, 108/82, and 110/82 *IAZ v Commission* [1983] ECR 3369, para 16.

[161] Joined Cases T-213/95 and T-18/96 *SCK and FNK v Commission* [1997] ECR II-1739, para 56 and Case T-127/98 *UPS Europe v Commission* [1999] ECR II-2633, para 37; Case T-213/00 *CMA CGM and others v Commission* [2003] ECR-913 II, para 317; Case C-105/04 P *Nederlandse Federatieve Vereniging voor de Groothandel op Elektrotechnisch Gebied v Commission* [2006] ECR I-8725, para 35; Case C-113/04 P *Technische Unie BV v Commission* [2006] ECR I-8831, para 40 et seq.

[162] Case T-62/98 *Volkswagen v Commission* [2000] ECR II-2707, para 281. Contrary to the situation which gave rise to the judgment in this case, in Case T-279/02 *Degussa AG v Commission* [2006] ECR II-897,

examination.[163] The ECHR establishes in Article 6(1) that every person has the right to have his or her affairs handled impartially, fairly, and within a reasonable time. The reasonableness of the length of proceedings is to be assessed in the light of the circumstances of the case and having regard to the criteria laid down in the Court's case law, in particular the complexity of the case[164] and the conduct of the applicant and of the relevant authorities. On the latter point, what is at stake for the applicant in the litigation has to be taken into account, but in any case, the applicant must not slow down the proceedings with a dilatory intention. The judicial authorities have to be prompt in rendering their decisions. The ECtHR has pointed out that the ECHR places a duty on the Member States to organize their legal systems so as to allow the courts to comply with the requirements of Article 6(1), including that of trial within a 'reasonable time'. On a number of occasions, the GC has had regard to the case law on delays under Article 6 ECHR in considering whether or not the Commission had taken a more than reasonable time to reach its decision.[165]

1.36 The EU Courts have stated that irregularities of this kind might lead to the annulment of the decision in question if it is shown that the content of that decision would have differed if that irregularity had not occurred.[166] For example, a failure to act within a reasonable time can constitute a ground for annulment only in the case of a decision finding infringements, where it has been proved that infringement of that principle has adversely affected the ability of the undertakings concerned to defend themselves. That apart, failure to comply with the principle that a decision must be adopted within a reasonable time cannot affect the validity of the administrative procedure under Regulation 1/2003.[167] In most cases the

---

para 409 et seq, it was not established that the Commission was behind the press disclosure of the content of the Decision. The information came from sources close to the Commission.

[163] In Case C-170/02 P *Schlüsselverlag JS Moser v Commission* [2003] ECR I-9889, para 29, the Commission stated that there was no obligation to take a position with respect to complaints lodged by competitors in the context of merger control proceedings. By contrast, the ECJ held that the Commission 'cannot refrain from taking account of complaints from undertakings which are not party to a concentration . . . likely to bring about an immediate change in the complainants' situation on the market or markets concerned' and 'that nothing justifies the Commission in avoiding its obligation to undertake, in the interests of sound administration, a thorough and impartial examination of the complaints which are made to it'. See also Case T-417/05 *Endesa, SA v Commission* [2006] ECR II-18, para 100.

[164] *Vallée v France*, App no 22121/93 (ECtHR, 26 April 1994), para 34.

[165] Joined Cases T-213/95 and T-1 8/96 *SCK and FNK v EC Commission* [1997] ECRII-1739, para 56; Joined Cases T-305/94 to T-307/94, T-313/94 to T-316/94, T-318/94, T-325/94, T-328/94, T-329/94, and T-335/94 *Limburgse Vinyl Maatschappij and others v EC Commission* [1999] ECR II-931, para 120 et seq; Case T-228/97 *Irish Sugar v Commission* [1999] ECR II-2969, para 276 et seq; and Joined Cases T-5/00 and T-6/00 *Nederlandse Federatieve Vereniging voor de Groothandel op Elektrotechnisch Gebied v EC Commission* [2003] ECR II-5761, para 73 et seq. In that connection, it must be observed, first, that in criminal matters the reasonable time referred to in Art 6(1) ECHR runs from the time at which a person is charged (see *Corigliano v Italy*, App no 8304/78 (ECtHR, 10 December 1982), para 34) and, secondly, that the fundamental rights guaranteed by the ECHR are protected as general principles of EU law. In a procedure relating to EU competition policy, of the kind at issue in this case, the persons concerned are not the subject of any formal accusation until they receive the statement of objections. Accordingly, the prolongation of this stage of the procedure alone is not in itself capable of adversely affecting the rights of the defence.

[166] Joined Cases 40/73 to 48/73, 50/73, 54/73 to 56/73, 111/73, 113/73, and 114/73 *Suiker Unie and others v Commission* [1975] ECR 1663, para 91; Case T-43/92 *Dunlop Slazenger v Commission* [1994] ECR II-441, para 29; Case T-62/98 *Volkswagen v Commission* [2000] ECR II-2707, para 283; Case T-279/02 *Degussa AG v Commission* [2006] ECR II-897, para 416.

[167] Case T-26/99 *Trabisco v Commission* [2001] ECR II-633, para 52, and Case T-62/99 *Sodima v Commission* [2001] ECR II-655, para 94; see also the Opinion of AG Mischo in Joined Cases C-238/99 P, C-244/99 P, C-245/99 P, C-247/99 P, C-250/99 P to C-252/99 P, and C-254/99 P *Limburgse Vinyl Maatschappij and others v Commission* [2002] ECR I-8375, in particular points 75–86 of the Opinion of AG Mischo in Case C-250/99; Case T-276/04 *Compagnie Maritime Belge SA v Commission* [2008] ECR II-1277, para 45.

infringement is not of sufficient magnitude to lead the Court to annul the decisions.[168] In *JFE*,[169] the Commission could not produce the relevant documentation relating to the EC–Japanese voluntary restraint agreement which was crucial to the determination of the duration of the infringement. Referring to the principle of sound administration, the GC found that the Commission's 'inexplicable inability' to produce evidence should not be to the detriment of the undertakings allegedly in breach, which, unlike the Commission, were not in a position to provide the missing evidence (in particular, on the duration of the infringement). Therefore, the GC limited the length of the infraction to the duration which the Commission had been able to prove.[170]

7. The principle that undertakings' business secrets must be protected

It is legitimate for an undertaking to request confidential treatment of its business secrets to **1.37** prevent substantial damage to its commercial interests.[171] According to a general principle which applies during the course of the administrative procedure, undertakings have a right to the protection of their business secrets.[172] However, the right must be balanced against safeguarding the rights of the defence. This cannot therefore justify the Commission's refusal to make disclosure to an undertaking, even in the form of non-confidential versions or by sending a list of documents gathered by the Commission of evidence in the case file which the undertaking might use in its defence. The Commission could protect these secrets by deleting the sensitive passages from the copies of the documents in accordance with DG COMP's general practice in this area, by either sending copies of these documents right away or by granting access to these documents with the business secrets deleted. In *Imperial Chemical Industries*, the Court reasoned that if during the administrative procedure the applicant had been able to rely on documents which might exculpate it, it might have been able to influence the assessment of the College of Commissioners, at least with regard to the conclusiveness of the evidence of its alleged passive and parallel conduct as regards the beginning and therefore the duration of the infringement.[173] Yet the possibility that a document

---

[168] In Case T-62/98 *Volkswagen v Commission* [2000] ECR II-2707, para 270, the GC held that 'the material nature of an infringement which has actually been proved at the end of an administrative procedure cannot be called in question by evidence of the Commission's premature display, during that procedure, of its belief as to the existence of that infringement'. The GC considered that the company failed to show that the Commission did in fact pre-judge the contested decision or lacked objectivity in its investigation (para 272). See also Case T-31/99 *ABB Asea Brown Boveri Ltd v Commission* [2002] ECR II-1881, paras 102–4, where the *'regrettable conduct'* on the part of a member of the team dealing, within the Commission, with a case involving an infringement of the EU competition rules, did not in itself vitiate the legality of the decision adopted in that case. Even if that official had infringed the principle of sound administration, the contested decision was not adopted by the official in question but by the College of Commissioners.

[169] Cases T-67/00, T-68/00, T-71/00, and T-78/00 *JFE Engineering Corp v Commission* [2004] ECR II-2501, paras 341–3. See also Case T-44/00 *Mannesmannröhren-Werke AG* [2004] ECR II-2223, para 262, referring to principle of proper administration.

[170] See also Case C-137/92 P *Commission v BASF and others* [1994] ECR I-2555, where the Commission was ordered to pay the costs of the court proceedings leading to the annulment of an initial decision due to its failure to authenticate it according to its own procedural rules.

[171] See Art 28 of Reg 1/2003, which obliges the Commission and NCAs to respect the principle of professional secrecy. As regards the unauthorized disclosure of confidential information to third parties, see Case 209/78 *FEDETAB* [1980] ECR 3125, paras 41–7.

[172] Case T-36/91 *ICI v Commission* [1995] ECR II-1847, para 98; Case C-36/92 P *SEP v Commission* [1994] ECR I-1911, para 36. The Court indicated in *ICI v Commission* that the Commission could either annex to the Statement of Objections all the documents which it wished to use to demonstrate the objections raised, including evidence which might 'clearly' be considered to be in favour of exculpating the undertaking concerned, or send that undertaking a list of relevant documents and grant it access 'to the file', ie allow it to inspect the documents at the Commission's premises.

[173] Case T-36/91 *ICI v Commission* [1995] ECR II-1847, para 108; Cases T-10/92, T-11/92, T-12/92, and T-15/92 *Cimenteries CBR and others v Commission* [1992] ECR II-2667, para 47.

which was not disclosed might have influenced the course of the proceedings and the content of the Commission's decision can be established only if a provisional examination of certain evidence shows that the undisclosed documents might, in the light of that evidence, have had a significance which ought not to have been disregarded.[174]

8. The right to respect for private and family life, home, and correspondence

1.38 Article 8 of the ECHR states that everyone has the right to respect for his private and family life, his home, and his correspondence. Even though the ECtHR has been willing to extend the right to respect for a home to business premises, it does not recognize Article 8 as an absolute right. Interferences are allowed as long as they are in accordance with the law, pursue a legitimate aim, and are necessary. These exceptions are to be interpreted narrowly,[175] and are easier to justify where business premises are involved than where a case concerns wholly domestic premises. In *Roquette Frères*, which concerned a request for a preliminary ruling requesting clarification on how should the *Hoechst* case on the inviolability of corporate domicile be interpreted, the ECJ examined how much regard it should have to the ECHR and the jurisprudence of the ECtHR.[176] In addition to laying down an entirely new standard for the division of functions between national courts and the Union courts in these matters,[177] the Court considered whether the applicable national rules for ordering entry upon premises and seizures are compatible with Union law, including, as the case may be, the rights established by the ECHR as general principles of law, observance of which is to be ensured by the ECJ.[178] The ECJ went on to state that to determine the scope of the protection against arbitrary or disproportionate intervention by public authorities in the sphere of the private activities of any person in relation to the protection of business premises, regard must be had to the case law of the ECtHR subsequent to the judgment in *Hoechst*. According to that case law, the ECJ concluded that, first, the protection of the home provided for in Article 8 ECHR may in certain circumstances be extended to cover business premises and, second, that the right of interference established by Article 8(2) ECHR might well be more far-reaching where professional or business activities or premises were involved than would otherwise be the case.[179]

---

[174] Joined Cases C-204/00 P, C-205/00 P, C-211/00 P, C-213/00 P, C-217/00 P, and C-219/00 P *Aalborg Portland and Others v Commission* [2004] ECR I-123, paras 74–6; Case T-24/07 *ThyssenKrupp Stainless AG v Commission* [2009] ECR II-2309, para 274.

[175] *Société Colas Est and others v France*, App no 37971/97 (ECtHR, 16 April 2002), in which the ECtHR ruled for the first time that in certain situations the rights guaranteed by Art 8 apply to a company's head office, branch office, or place of business. In this case, the investigators entered the applicant's premises without a prior judicial warrant and without a police officer with judicial investigation powers being present. The ECtHR ruled that the inspections were disproportionate to the legitimate purposes pursued. See also J Temple Lang and C Rizza, 'The Ste Colas Est and others v France case European Court of Human Rights Judgment of 16 April 2002' [2002] ECLR 413, who question the compatibility of the Commission inspections with the Colas judgment. See also K Dekeyser and C Gauer, 'The New Enforcement System for Arts 81 and 82 and the Rights of Defence', ch 23 in BE Hawk (ed), *International Antitrust Law & Policy* (Annual Proceedings of the Fordham Institute 2004) 549, 556.

[176] See Case C-94/00 *Roquette Frères* [2002] ECR I-9011, paras 22–9. In Joined Cases T-305/94, T-306/94, T-307/94, T-313/94 to T-316/94, T-318/94, T-325/94, T-328/94, T-329/94, and T-335/94 *Limburgse Vinyl Maatschappij NV (LVM) and others v EC Commission* [1999] ECR II-931, paras 419–20, the CFI rejected an invitation to qualify Hoechst in the light of *Niemietz v Germany*, App no 13710/88 (ECtHR, 16 December 1992). See C Bellamy and G Child, *EC Law of Competition* (6th edn, Oxford University Press 2008) para 13.046.

[177] See Ch 8 on 'Inspections', para 8.74 et seq.

[178] Case C-94/00 *Roquette Frères* [2002] ECR I-9011, para 26.

[179] Case C-94/00 *Roquette Frères* [2002] ECR I-9011, para 29, which expressly refers to the *Colas* judgment.

9. The principle of the protection of legitimate expectations

By virtue of this principle, the authorities should act in accordance with measures already **1.39** adopted by them and with their own prior conduct.[180] The concept of legitimate expectations presupposes that the person concerned entertains hopes based on specific assurances given to him or her by the EU administration.[181] Based on this principle, therefore, the authorities should act in accordance with measures already adopted by them and their own prior conduct.[182] The principle extends to any individual who is in a situation in which it is apparent that the EU administration has led him to entertain reasonable expectations by giving him '*precise* assurances'.[183] Nobody may plead infringement of this principle unless he or she has been given precise, unconditional, and consistent assurances, from authorized, reliable sources, by the administration.[184] Conversely, individuals cannot claim that the principle has been violated on the basis of beliefs deduced from informal contacts or vague or general statements made by the Commission officials or even the Commissioner.[185] Similarly, when lodging a complaint with

---

[180] Case T-465/93 *Murgia Messapica v Commission* [1994] ECR II-361, para 67 and Order in Case T-195/95 *Guérin Automobiles v Commission* [1996] ECR II-171, para 20. However, there is nothing to prevent the Commission from reconsidering its decisions or departing from its earlier interpretation of the competition rules. This principle must be seen, therefore, not as an obligation arising from *res judicata* but as one of consistency *rebus sic stantibus*. See Case 245/81 *Edeka* [1982] ECR 2745, para 27, Case 350/88 *Delacre and others v Commission* [1990] ECR I-395, para 33, and Case C-1/98 P *British Steel v Commission* [2000] ECR I-10349, para 52.

[181] Case T-465/93 *Murgia Messapica v Commission* [1994] ECR II-361, para 67 and Case T-195/95 *Guérin Automobiles v Commission* [1996] ECR II-171, para 20.

[182] See also Case T-1 15/94 *Opel Austria GmbH v Council* [1997] ECR II-39, para 93, where the GC declared that the principle of good faith is the corollary in public international law of the principle of protection of legitimate expectations which, according to the case law, forms part of EU law.

[183] Joined Cases T-485/93, T-491/93, T-494/93, and T-61/98 *Dreyfus and others v Commission* [2000] ECR II-3659, para 85; Case T-465/93 *Consorzio Gruppo di Azione Locale Murgia Messapica v Commission* [1994] ECR II-361, para 67; Case T-195/95 P *Guérin Automobiles v Commission* [1996] ECR II-679, para 14; Case T-266/97 *Vlaamse Televisie Maatschappij v Commission* [1999] ECR II-2329, para 71; Case T-65/98 *Van den Bergh Foods v Commission* [2003] ECR II-4653, para 192; Case T-191/98 *Atlantic Container Line and others v Commission* [2003] ECR II-3275, para 1565 et seq; Case T-220/00 *CheilJedang Corporation v Commission* [2003] ECR II-2473, para 40; Case T-73/04 *Carbone-Lorraine v Commission* [2008] ECR II-2661, para 146.

[184] Case T-29/05 *Deltafina SpA v Commission* [2010] ECR II-4077, para 427. In this case, the fact that, in a number of decisions preceding the organic peroxides decision, the Commission did not hold liable for infringement of Art 81(1) EC (current Art 101(1) TFEU) undertakings which contributed to the implementation of a cartel but were not active in the market affected by the infringement could not give rise to a legitimate expectation on the part of Deltafina that the Commission would refrain in future from pursuing and penalizing such undertakings. In Case T-13/03 *Nintendo Co Ltd, Nintendo of Europe GMBH v Commission* [2009] ECR II-975, para 202 et seq, the Commission's representative stated merely that the payment of compensation to third parties 'would be relevant in the calculation of any fine'. That statement cannot, in any case, be described as a precise and unconditional assurance that all compensation would be deducted from the final amount of the fine. In any event, in order to be able to give rise to a legitimate expectation, the assurances provided must emanate from authorized and reliable sources (see, to that effect, in the case of a statement by the Director-General competent for competition matters, Joined Cases T-236/01, T-239/01, T-244/01 to T-246/01, T-251/01, and T-252/01 *Tokai Carbon and Others v Commission* [2004] ECR II-1181, paras 152–3). In the light of the exclusive competence of the College of Commissioners to adopt a decision imposing a fine, a Commission official cannot have provided Nintendo, at an informal meeting with its representatives, with precise assurances from an authorized, reliable source that the compensation offered to the third parties in question would be deducted from the final amount of the fine.

[185] Cases T-190/95 and T-45/96 *Sodima v Commission* [1999] ECR II-3617, para 25; Case T-195/95 P *Guérin Automobiles v Commission* [1996] ECR II-679, para 20; Case T-213/95 and Case T-18/96 *SCK & FNK v Commission* [1997] ECR II-1739, para 83. See also in this respect, the possibility of pleading legitimate expectations obtained from NCAs in EU competition proceedings as a mitigating circumstance (Case T-203/01 *Michelin v Commission* [2003] ECR II-4071, para 305 et seq). For example, in Case T-30/05 *William Prym GmbH & Co KG and Prym Consumer GmbH* [2007] ECR II-107, para 67, the GC recalled the case law which held that a Director-General is not able to give specific assurances which will give rise to legitimate expectations in an area where his/her competence is limited to submitting proposals to the College

the Commission, the parties should know that they had no right to obtain a decision finding an infringement of the Treaty.[186] As regards fines, the Commission may not depart from the rules which it has imposed on itself. In particular, whenever the Commission adopts guidelines for the purpose of specifying, in accordance with the Treaty, the criteria which it proposes to apply in the exercise of its discretion, it limits its own discretion inasmuch as it must then follow those guidelines. Further, undertakings cannot have a legitimate expectation that an existing situation that is capable of being altered by the EU institutions in the exercise of their discretion will be maintained forever.[187] This is the case, for instance, when the Commission adopts preliminary positions that are capable of being modified.[188] The EU Courts have recognized that the Leniency Notice[189] may lead a company to entertain legitimate expectations, but this does not automatically justify a reduction in the amount of the fine.[190] In the field of competition law, the principle of legitimate expectations is often linked to the level of fines,[191] the reduction of fines under the Leniency Notice,[192] the weight given to mitigating circumstances,[193] and so on. In this respect, the CFI (now the GC) has stated that undertakings involved in administrative proceedings which

---

of Commissioners, who may accept or reject them. This principle would apply *a fortiori* to lower rank public officials.

[186] Case T-5/93 *Roger Tremblay and others v Commission* [1995] ECR II-185, para 79; Case T-24/90 *Automec v Commission* [1992] ECR II-2223, para 75.

[187] See Case 245/81 *Edeka v Germany* [1982] ECR 2745, para 27; Case C-350/88 *Delacre and others v Commission* [1990] ECR I-395, para 33; Case C-1/98 P *British Steel v Commission* [2000] ECR I-10349, para 52; and Case T-191/98 *Atlantic Container Line and others v Commission* [2003] ECR II-3275, para 1567; Case T-29/05 *Deltafina SpA v Commission* [pending publication] [2010] ECR II-4077, para 425 et seq, Deltafina had attempted to use the principle of legitimate expectations to obtain a symbolic fine of EUR 1,000, as this was the amount imposed on the undertakings which were not active in the market in the organic peroxides decision (as the Commission considered that it was taking a new approach in this area). The Court points to a number of elements which prove that Deltafina could not have legitimately expected that its penalty would also be symbolic.

[188] Case T-65/98 *Van den Bergh Foods v Commission* [2003] ECR II-4653, para 194, as regards a preliminary position of the Commission as published in a notice taking into account observations of interested third parties, on the basis of Art 19(3) of Reg 17.

[189] Commission Notice on the non-imposition or reduction of fines in cartel cases ([1996] OJ C207/4–6), first replaced by the Commission notice on immunity from fines and reduction of fines in cartel cases ([2002] OJ C45/3-5) and then by the 2006 Notice ([2006] OJ C298/11).

[190] Case T-48/00 *Corus UK v Commission* [2004] ECR II-2325, para 193, noting that it would not be sufficient for an undertaking to state in general terms that it does not contest the facts alleged, in accordance with that Leniency Notice, if, in the circumstances of the case, that statement is not of any help to the Commission at all. See also Case T-23/99 *LR AF 1998 v Commission* [2002] ECR II-1705, para 245; Joined Cases T-101/05 and T-111/05 *BASF AG* [2007] ECR II-4949, paras 89–92; Case C-510/06 P *Archer Daniels Midland Co* [2009] ECR I-1843, para 60.

[191] See Cases T-191/98 *Atlantic Container Line and others v Commission* [2003] ECR II-3275, para 1571; Case T-23/99 *LRAF 1998 v Commission* [2002] ECR II-1705, para 241; and Case T-220/00 *Cheil Jedang Corporation v Commission* [2003] ECR II-2473, para 35. In that case, Cheil, relying on previous cases and the 1996 Leniency Notice, exposed itself to a fine by cooperating with the Commission. The application of the 1998 Guidelines on setting fines to the case at hand resulted in a fine more than seven times greater than that calculated under the previous method. The GC stated that the effective application of the competition rules meant that the Commission could adjust the level of fines at any time to match the needs of EU competition policy. Consequently, the fact that, in the past, the Commission had imposed fines at a certain level for certain types of infringements does not preclude it from raising that level, subject to the limits indicated in former Reg 17 (now Reg 1/2003). In this respect, the Commission was neither bound to announce or to mention in the Statement of Objections the possibility that it would change its policy as regards the general level of fines. According to the Court, the only legitimate expectation which the applicant was entitled to entertain was one relating to the conditions under which a reduction would be allowed in recognition of its cooperation, not to the amount of the fine which would otherwise have been imposed upon it or to the calculation method that might be used to that end.

[192] Case T-48/00 *Corus UK v Commission* [2004] ECR II-2325, paras 192–200. Case T-26/02 *Daiichi Pharmaceutical v Commission* [2006] ECR II-713, para 147 and the case law cited therein.

[193] Cases T-347/94 *Mayr-Melnhof v Commission* [1998] ECR II-1751, para 368; Case T-23/99 *LRAF 1998 v Commission* [2002] ECR II-1705, para 244.

may lead to a fine cannot entertain legitimate expectations that the Commission will not exceed the level of fines previously applied[194] or apply the same considerations as in previous similar cases.[195] Moreover, the Commission is not bound to mention, in the Statement of Objections, the possibility of a change in its policy as regards the general level of fines, because that possibility is dependent on general competition policy considerations that have no direct relationship with the particular circumstances of the case at hand.[196]

10. The requirement of legal certainty

The requirement of legal certainty[197] is a corollary of the principle of legality and is a fundamen-   **1.40**
tal principle of EU law. This principle requires any legal measure adopted to be clear and precise in order to ensure that 'situations and legal relationships governed by Community law remain foreseeable'.[198] The Court has consistently held that 'the principle of legal certainty must be observed all the more strictly in the case of a measure liable to have financial consequences'.[199] The legal measure must be brought to the notice of the person concerned in such a way that he can ascertain exactly the time at which it comes into force and starts to have legal effect.[200] This principle, which is common to Member States and is enshrined in various international treaties (including the ECHR) must be observed with regard both to penal provisions and to specific administrative instruments imposing penalties or permitting their imposition.[201] It is therefore essential that the EU institutions observe the principle that they may not alter measures which they have adopted and which affect the legal and factual position of persons. Accordingly, those acts may only be amended in accordance with the rules on competence and procedure.[202] In certain instances, however, the Commission may exceptionally amend the fine post-decision

---

[194] Case T-23/99 *LRAF 1998 v Commission* [2002] ECR II-1705, para 243. See also Joined Cases C-189/02 P, C-205/02 P, C-206/02 P, C-207/02 P, C-208/02 P, C-213/02 P *Dansk Rørindustri A/S v Commission* [2005] ECR I-5425, para 169 et seq and Opinion of AG Antonio Tizzano of 8 July 2004, paras 134–55.

[195] Case T-23/99 *LRAF 1998 v Commission* [2002] ECR II-1705, para 244.

[196] Joined Cases 100/80 to 103/80 *Musique Diffusion Française and others v Commission* [1983] ECR 1825, para 22. Joined Cases T-109/02, T-118/02, T-122/02, T-125/02, T-126/02, T-128/02, T-129/02, T-132/02, and T-136/02 *Bolloré SA v Commission* [2007] ECR II-947, para 376: 'The proper application of the Community competition rules requires that the Commission be able at any time to adjust the level of fines to the needs of that [Community competition] policy.'

[197] Case C-234/89 *Stergios Delimitis v Henninger Bräu AG* [1991] ECR I-935, para 47: 'Account should here be taken of the risk of national courts taking decisions which conflict with those taken or envisaged by the Commission in the implementation of Arts [105(1)], [101(1)], and [106] [102], and also of Arts [105(3)] and [101(3)]. Such conflicting decisions would be contrary to the general principle of legal certainty and must, therefore, be avoided when national courts give decisions on agreements or practices which may subsequently be the subject of a decision by the Commission.'

[198] Case C-63/93 *Duff and others v Minister for Agriculture and Food and Attorney General* [1996] ECR I-569, para 20; Case T-73/95 *Oliveira v Commission* [1997] ECR II-381, para 29; Case T-57/01 *Solvay v Commission* [2009] ECR II-4621 para 106. See also recently Joined Cases T-22/02 and T-23/02 *Sunitomo Chemical v Commission* [2002] ECR II-4065, paras 80–91.

[199] See in particular Case C-248/04 *Koninklijke Coöperatie Cosun* [2006] ECR I-10211, para 79 and the case law cited; AG Bot in Case C-76/06 P *Britannia Alloys & Chemicals Ltd v Commission* [2007] ECR I-4405, para 12.

[200] K Lenaerts, 'In the Union We Trust: Trust-Enhancing Principles of Community Law' [2004] CML Rev 317, 340.

[201] Case T-446/05 *Amann & Söhne GmbH & Co KG and Cousin Filterie SAS v Commission* [2010] ECR II-1255, para 125.

[202] Joined Cases T-79/89, T-84/89, T-85/89, T-86/89, T-89/89, T-91/89, T-92/89, T-94/89, T-96/89, T-98/89, T-102/89, and T-104/89 *BASF and others v Commission* [1992] ECR II-315, para 35, and Joined Cases T-80/89, etc *BASF and others v Commission* [1995] ECR II-729, para 73. In *Opel Austria*, the EU Council adopted a regulation establishing an import duty on gearboxes in December 1993 when it knew with certainty that the EEA Agreement would enter into force on 1 January 1994. The GC found that the Council knowingly created a situation in which, with effect from January 1994, two contradictory rules of law would coexist, namely the contested regulation, which was directly applicable in the national legal systems and re-established a 4.9 per cent import duty on F-15 gearboxes produced by the applicant; and Art 10 of the EEA

in order to correct errors in the calculation, Companies can also invoke their inability to pay ('ITP') and request a reduction of the fine post-decision in view of their alleged critical financial situation. The applications can lead to reducing the amount of the fine to a level that the company is currently able to pay or, if necessary, to zero (no fine at all).[203]

II. The Authorities Empowered to Apply the Competition Rules

A. Antitrust Law and Decentralization[204]

1.41 When introducing Regulation 1/2003, the Commission took the view that ensuring the effective protection of the competition rules would require new forms of enforcing the rules which would maintain the Commission's traditional responsibility for defining competition policy and applying the rules in individual cases while involving national bodies more in this process.[205] As far as public enforcement is concerned, Regulation 1/2003 empowers NCAs to apply Articles 101 and 102 TFEU in their entirety and makes it compulsory to apply EU law whenever it is applicable, ie whenever the agreement or practice under review may affect trade between Member States.[206] Both the Commission and NCAs are responsible for enforcing the EU competition rules. NCAs apply their own procedural rules and are empowered to order the infringement to be brought to an end, take interim measures, accept commitments from the infringing parties, and impose fines or other penalties provided for in their national

Agreement, which had direct effect and prohibited customs duties on imports and any charges having equivalent effect. Consequently, the contested regulation could not be regarded as Community legislation which was certain and its operation could not be regarded as foreseeable by those subject to it. Thus, the Council also infringed the principle of legal certainty. See Case T-115/94 *Opel Austria GmbH v EC Commission* [1997] ECR II-39, para 125. The Court also held that another infringement of the same principle was the fact that the Council deliberately backdated the issue of the OJ in which the contested regulation was published. The issue was dated 31 December 1993. According to Art 2, the Regulation was to enter into force on the day of its publication in the OJ. However, according to written replies from the Publications Office to questions put by the Court, the OJ of 31 December 1993 was not made available to the public at the head office of the Publications Office in all the official languages of the Community until 11 January 1994.

[203] See Ch 15, 'Steps Following the Adoption of a Formal Decision'.

[204] The first edition of this book discussed these aspects under the heading of 'Antitrust Law and Subsidiarity'. Given that the notion of subsidiarity could arguably give rise to some confusion (Case C-91/95 *Tremblay and others v EC Commission* [1995] ECR I-5547, paras 22–5, Opinion of AG Jacobs), the term 'decentralization' is now widely used in this context and may better encapsulate the essence of the process, ie the application of EU competition law by the Member States. See A Schaub, *EC Competition System— Proposals for Reform* (Fordham Corporate Law Institute 1998), ch 1, who refers in the same context to *subsidiarity* and *proportionality*.

[205] Under Regulation 17, undertakings had to notify agreements to the Commission in order to benefit from the exception contained in Art 101(3) TFEU. The Commission had exclusive competence to apply this provision by way of formal exemption decisions, with NCAs and courts not being empowered to grant exemptions. The Commission's monopoly on the application of Art 101(3) and the system of prior notification and administrative authorization resulted in a significant backlog of notifications, the closure of 90 per cent of notifications informally, and a diversion of resources away from the investigation and prosecution of serious antitrust infringements.

[206] For more details on the effect on trade concept, Commission Notice—Guidelines on the effect on trade concept contained in Arts 81[101] and 82[102] of the Treaty [2004] OJ C101/81 paras 19 et seq. The Guidelines are designed to assist NCAs and national courts to decide whether an agreement or practice 'may affect trade between Member States' and is thus caught by Arts 101 and 102 TFEU. While for the most part the Guidelines contain a restatement of the EU Courts' case law, they also introduce a new rule (the non-appreciable affectation of trade rule or 'NAAT' rule) that attempts to link the absence of an effect on trade to specific market and revenue ceilings.

laws.[207] In its five-year review, the Commission has stated that the change from a system of notification and administrative authorization to one of direct application has been remarkably smooth in practice.[208] Overall, neither the decision-making practice of the Commission and NCAs nor the experience reported by the business and legal community would indicate major difficulties with the direct application of Article 101(3) TFEU.

One of the main features of the system set up by Regulation 1/2003 is the European Competition **1.42** Network (ECN). The ECN provides a platform for Member States' NCAs to constructively coordinate enforcement action, ensure consistency, and discuss policy issues of common interest.[209] However, the Commission retains an important role. In particular, it may start proceedings either on its own initiative or following complaints made directly to it. It can also deal with a case allocated to it in the ECN because it is best placed to act[210] and may provide a guidance letter at the request of the parties.[211] Finally, it has a key consultative role in NCA proceedings.[212]

Regulation 1/2003 has also served as a first step to open the way for the increased private **1.43** enforcement of Articles 101 and 102 TFEU, the importance of which has been expressly recognized by the ECJ.[213] The Commission has launched a further policy initiative in this area with a view to encouraging private damages claims.[214] Thus, the decentralization of the enforcement of EU competition law put in place by Regulation 1/2003 envisages not only a role for Member States' NCAs, but also for private litigation in national courts in this regard.[215]

Due to the decentralized implementation of Articles 101 and 102 TFEU, the Commission can **1.44** focus more on tackling the most serious antitrust infringements, resulting in it adopting more prohibitions and imposing more fines. In its first five-year review, the Commission stated that by adopting thirty-four decisions imposing fines in cartel cases since the entry into application of Regulation 1/2003 until 31 March 2009, compared with twenty-seven in the period from 1 January 2000 to 30 April 2004, it had not only maintained but also increased its focus on enforcement against cartels despite the heightened awareness of infringing undertakings of this fact and the ensuing increased difficulty of investigations. By contrast, during the entire decade

---

[207] Article 5 of Reg 1/2003.

[208] [COM(2009)206 final] Communication from the Commission to the European Parliament and Council, Report on the functioning of Regulation 1/2003 [COM(2009)206 final] 29 April 2009, para 11.

[209] See eg the activities listed in [COM(2011) 328 final] Commission Staff Working Paper accompanying the report from the Commission on Competition Policy 2010, para 393 et seq; see also ECN Briefs that periodically published and posted on the DG COMPS's website.

[210] This includes the possibility of clawing back a case from an NCA, for example to prevent conflicting decisions or because of the need for effective EU-wide enforcement. See Art 11(6) of Reg 1/2003. For more details, see Ch 3, 'The Role of National Competition Authorities', para 3.28 et seq.

[211] See Commission Notice on cooperation within the Network of Competition Authorities (2004/C 101/03).

[212] Recital 38 of Reg 1/2003. Commission Notice on informal guidance relating to novel questions concerning Arts 81[101] and 82[102] of the EC Treaty [TFEU] that arise in individual cases [2004] OJ C101/78.

[213] Case C-453/99 *Courage v Crehan* [2001] ECR I-6297, para 26–7, as confirmed by Joined Cases C-295/04 to C-298/04 *Manfredi* [2006] ECR I-6619, paras 60–1.

[214] See Commission White Paper on Damages Actions for Breach of the EC Antitrust Rules (COM (2008) 165, 2.4.2008) and Commission Green Paper on Consumer Collective Redress (COM (2008) 794 final, 27.11.2008). On 11 June 2013, the Commission published a proposal for a Directive on certain rules governing actions for damages under national law for infringements of competition law. The Directive is intended to ensure the effective enforcement of EU competition law by optimizing the interaction between public and private enforcement and ensuring that victims of competition law infringements can obtain full compensation. In particular, the proposed directive contains provisions relating to disclosure of evidence, including absolute protection of corporate leniency statements and settlement submissions. Commission Press Release IP/13/525 'Antitrust: Commission proposes legislation to facilitate damage claims by victims of antitrust violations' 13 June 2013. The text of the proposal for a Directive adopted by the Commission and all other relevant documents are available at <http://ec.europa.eu/competition/antitrust/actionsdamages/documents.html>.

[215] As regards the role of the national courts in private enforcement, see para 1.46 et seq and Ch 2, 'The Role of National Judicial Authorities', para 2.07 et seq.

from 1 January 1990 until 31 December 1999, the Commission only adopted eighteen decisions against cartels. Moreover, since 1 May 2004 the Commission has adopted twenty-seven decisions enforcing Articles 101 and 102 (final decisions on substance) not concerning cartels.[216] By comparison, between 1 January 2000 and 30 April 2004, only seventeen prohibition decisions were adopted.[217]

1.45 The decentralization process has inevitably had an impact on the EU Courts. Whereas the GC is in charge of direct actions against the Commission by private individuals relating to the implementation of the competition rules applicable to undertakings, the ECJ, besides its appellate jurisdiction, is involved in competition law issues mainly through preliminary rulings requested by national courts pursuant to Article 267 TFEU.[218]

B. The National Judicial Authorities

1. Role of the national courts

1.46 Regulation 1/2003 eliminated the Commission's monopoly on granting the exemption, and national judges can now rule on whether Article 101(3) TFEU is applicable. Article 6 states that national courts have the power to apply Articles 101 and 102 TFEU (in their entirety). The elimination of the monopoly on granting the exemption and the related abolition of the notification system aims to encourage private parties to bring more actions for damages before national courts. Moreover, Article 3 of Regulation 1/2003 provides that national courts shall apply EU competition law to anticompetitive behaviour which may affect trade between Member States where they apply national competition law to such behaviour.

1.47 Articles 101 and 102 may become relevant in proceedings before national courts in various ways and in different types of cases, for example where a party challenges the enforceability of contracts on the basis that their provisions are contrary to Article 101(1) and void under

---

[216] In 2010 the Commission adopted seven cartel decisions imposing fines totalling over EUR 3 billion on seventy undertakings (see Commission Staff Working Paper Accompanying the Report from the Commission on Competition Policy 2010 [COM(2011) 328 final], para 50); Commission Staff Working Paper, Accompanying the Report from the commission on Competition Policy 2011 [COM(2012) 253 final], 13 stating that it adopted four cartel decisions imposing fines totalling over EUR 614 million on 14 undertakings).

[217] [COM(2009)206 final] Communication from the Commission to the European Parliament and Council, Report on the functioning of Regulation 1/2003 [COM(2009)206 final] 29 April 2009, para 19.

[218] Given the significant financial interest of addressees of Commission cartel decisions in challenging these decisions, the allegedly perceived uncertainty about some procedural rights for companies and obligations for the Commission it is likely that appeals be lodged against almost all Commission decisions. Where an action for annulment is brought against a decision of the Commission finding an infringement of Arts 101 and 102 TFEU, the review of the EU Courts is two-fold. They must carry out the review of legality incumbent upon them on the basis of the evidence adduced by the applicant in support of the pleas in law put forward. In carrying out such a review, 'the Courts cannot use the Commission's margin of discretion—either as regards the choice of factors taken into account in the application of the criteria mentioned in the Guidelines or as regards the assessment of those factors—as a basis for dispensing with the conduct of an in-depth review of the law and of the facts'. The review of legality is supplemented by the unlimited jurisdiction under Art 31 of Reg No 1/2003, in accordance with Art 261 TFEU. That jurisdiction empowers the Courts, in addition to carrying out a mere review of the lawfulness of the penalty, to substitute their own appraisal for the Commission's and, consequently, to cancel, reduce, or increase the fine or penalty payment imposed (see Case C-272/09 P *KME Germany and Others v Commission* [2012] OJ C32/4, paras 102 and 103). Joined Cases T-25/95 etc *Cimenteries CBR and others v Commission* [2000] ECR II-491, para 719; Case T-65/98 *Van den Bergh Foods v Commission* [2003] ECR II-4653, para 60. See comment of R Wessling on Joined Cases C-238/99 P, C-244/99 P, C-245/99 P, C-247/99 P, C-250/99 P to C-252/99 P, and C-254/99 P *Limburgse Vinyl Maatschappij NV (LVM) and others v Commission* [2002] ECR I-8375, [2004] CMLR 1141–55. K Lenaerts and D Gerard, 'Decentralisation of EC Competition Law Enforcement: Judges in the Frontline' [2004] World Competition Law and Economics 313, 340.

Article 101(2) TFEU. National courts may also award damages for loss suffered as a result of the infringement of Article 101 and 102 TFEU. Thus, the antitrust prohibitions could then be used as a shield when they are invoked as a defence against a contractual claim for performance or for damages or conversely as a sword to obtain an injunction to restrain unlawful conduct and/or to obtain damages. Regulation 1/2003 allowed national courts to apply Article 101(3) TFEU themselves. While it is true that Regulation 1/2003 cannot be said to be a private remedies charter, there is agreement that it contains a number of provisions which may support private actions in national courts.[219] The direct applicability of Article 101(3) TFEU is supplemented by rules on the burden of proof of meeting the conditions of Article 101(3) TFEU on the party claiming its benefit and provisions empowering the Commission to make written submissions in cases pending in national courts. At the same time, national courts may continue to seek assistance from the Commission in a specific case. The Commission hopes that the new regime of cooperation embodied in Article 15 of Regulation 1/2003 will establish a more fertile climate for private actions.[220]

The case for increased private enforcement received a significant boost from the ECJ preliminary ruling in *Courage Ltd v Crehan*, where the Court decided that individuals must have the opportunity and the right to claim damages for losses caused by any kind of behaviour liable to restrict or distort competition. As the Court put it: **1.48**

> the full effectiveness of Article [101 TFEU] and, in particular, the practical effect of the prohibition laid down in Article [101(1)] would be put at risk if it were not open to any individual to claim damages for loss caused to him by a contract or by conduct liable to restrict or distort competition…the existence of such a right strengthens the working of the Community competition rules and discourages agreements or practices, which are frequently covert, which are liable to restrict or distort competition. From that point of view, actions for damages before the national courts can make a significant contribution to the maintenance of effective competition in the Community.[221]

Subsequently, in *Manfredi*, an Italian citizen and other individuals claimed damages from a number of Italian insurance companies that had been found by the Italian competition authority to have engaged in an unlawful exchange of information, with a view to maintaining higher insurance premiums. The ECJ expressly recognized the right of private litigants to claim compensation for loss suffered as a result of a breach of the competition rules. It also offered guidance on the definition of 'damages'. Its decision represents a further step in the development of the law following the *Courage* judgment, which had confirmed that, in certain circumstances, a party to a contract had the right to claim damages for infringement of Article 101 TFEU.[222] **1.49**

---

[219] CA Jones, 'Private Antitrust Enforcement in Europe: A Policy Analysis and Reality Check' [2004] World Competition 13, 14; L Ortiz Blanco and A Lamadrid de Pablo, 'EU Competition Law Enforcement, Elements for a Discussion on Effectiveness and Uniformity' in Annual Proceedings of the Fordham Competition Law Institute, International Antitrust and Policy [2011] Fordham 38th Conference on International Antitrust Law and Policy 45, 87 et seq.

[220] See Recital 7 of Reg 1/2003.

[221] Case C-453/99 *Courage Ltd v Bernard Crehan and Bernard Crehan v Courage Ltd and others* [2001] ECR I-6297, paras 26–7.

[222] Joined Cases C-295/04 to C-298/04 *Vincenzo Manfredi and Others v Lloyd Adriatico Assicurazioni SpA and Others* [2006] ECR I-6619, paras 60–3. 'Quantifying antitrust damages. Towards non-binding guidance for courts' Study prepared for the European Commission, Oxera, and a multi-jurisdictional team of lawyers led by Dr Assimakis Komninos. With economic assistance from Dr Walter Beckert, Professor Eric van Damme, Professor Mathias Dewatripont, Professor Julian Franks, Dr Adriaan ten Kate, and Professor Patrick Legros, December 2009: <http://ec.europa.eu/competition/antitrust/actionsdamages/quantification_study.pdf>.

2. Actions before national courts

1.50 As stated, Regulation 1/2003 envisages a complementary role for enforcement through litigation between private parties before the national courts. It eliminates the exemption system and the Commission's monopoly on the application of Article 101(3) TFEU and as a result national judges will be able to rule on whether this provision applies.

Request to the Court for a preliminary ruling

1.51 Decentralization brings with it the possibility of divergent decisions where Member States' national courts have jurisdiction to hear direct actions concerning Articles 101 and 102 TFEU or actions against decisions of the NCAs.[223] Where the law is unclear, the national court can request assistance from the Commission in specific cases.[224] Access to the EU Courts is solely through the preliminary ruling procedure under Article 267 TFEU, which provides that the ECJ has jurisdiction to give preliminary rulings on questions concerning, *inter alia*, the interpretation of the Treaty and the validity and interpretation of EU legislation. With regard to DG COMP's activities, this may be, for instance, a question on the interpretation of the powers of an NCA in applying EU antitrust law. A national court or tribunal[225] can make a request for a preliminary ruling where such a question is raised before it and the court considers that a decision is necessary to enable it to give judgment. A preliminary ruling from the ECJ on the legality of a Commission decision is the only way that a national court can bypass such a decision when applying EU competition law to the case before it. In other words, if a national court intends to take a decision that runs counter to that of the Commission, it must first refer the question to the ECJ for a preliminary ruling.[226]

Procedure for cooperation between national courts and the Commission

1.52 Regulation 1/2003 sets out the areas of cooperation between the Commission and national courts. In particular, Article 15 of Regulation 1/2003 deals, *inter alia*, with the transmission of information by the Commission and of the Commission's opinions, both at the request of a national court.[227] It

---

[223] L Sevón, 'The National Courts and the Uniform Application of EC Competition Rules, Preliminary Observations on Council Regulation 1/2003' in M Hoskins and W Robinson (eds), *A True European—Essays for Judge David Edward* (Hart Publishing 2003) 145, distinguishes four ways of diminishing the risk of diverging case law: (i) Application of Arts 101and 102 by national courts; (ii) national courts may ask the Commission to transmit to them information in its possession or its opinion on questions concerning the application of the EU competition rules (Art 15(1) of Reg 1/2003); (iii) Member States shall forward to the Commission a copy of any written judgment on the application of Arts 101 and 102 TFEU and the Commission may submit written observations to national courts; and (iv) the request for preliminary rulings.

[224] See Art 15 of Reg 1/2003.

[225] For the criteria used to determine which entities can be regarded as courts or tribunals within the meaning of Art 267 TFEU, see, eg Case C-516/99 *Schmid* [2002] ECR I-4573, para 34: 'The Court takes account of a number of factors, such as whether the body is established by law, whether it is permanent, whether its jurisdiction is compulsory, whether its procedure is inter pares, whether it applies rules of law and whether it is independent.' The ECJ declined jurisdiction in a reference for preliminary ruling from the Greek Competition Commission as to whether the latter was a court or tribunal within the meaning of Art 267 TFEU in Case C-53/03 *Syfait and others v Glaxo SmithKline* [2005] ECR I-4609, paras 30–7.

[226] Article 16 of Reg 1/2003 codifies the ECJ ruling in *Masterfoods* (Case C-344/98 [2000] ECR I-11369, para 60), which brought into sharp relief the problem of the parallel jurisdiction of national courts and the Commission, in particular where each of them reaches opposite conclusions in concurrent proceedings. Where the outcome of the dispute before the national court of appeal depends on the validity of a Commission decision that is being appealed before the EU courts, the obligation of sincere cooperation under Art 4(3) TFEU means that the national court of appeal should stay the proceedings pending the judgment by the EU Courts in the appeal proceedings against the Commission decision, unless a reference to the ECJ for a preliminary ruling is warranted. Thus, national courts are bound in a specific case by any previous Commission decision subject to any contrary ruling by the EU Courts, either on Art 263 TFEU appeal or following an Art 267 TFEU reference. See National Courts Cooperation Notice [2004] OJ C101/54, para 13. See Ch 2, 'The Role of National Judicial Authorities', para 2.27 et seq.

[227] For more detail, see E Gippini-Fournier, 'The Modernisation of European Competition Law: First Experiences with Regulation 1/2003—Institutional Report' in HF Koeck and MM Karollus (eds), The

also includes the possibility of the Commission submitting written observations on its own initiative and oral observations with the permission of the court. Observations may relate to the economic analysis of the case as well as legal issues. The Commission may request copies of all documents relevant to the case in order to prepare its observations.[228] While these observations are not legally binding on the national courts, they will certainly carry a great deal of weight. Under the former system, a mechanism for facilitating the cooperation between the Commission and national courts—as well as between the Commission and NCAs—already existed but was rarely applied.[229] While it is settled law that national courts cannot disregard the EU competition rules, it is also well established that the Commission is under a general duty to cooperate with national courts to ensure that EU law is applied and respected.[230] Article 15 of Regulation 1/2003 and its implementation under the National Courts Cooperation Notice has taken this further and is intended to serve as a practical tool for national judges who apply Articles 101 and 102 TFEU in accordance with Regulation 1/2003. The National Courts Cooperation Notice covers, among other things, the competence of national courts to apply the EU competition rules, procedural aspects of the application of the EU competition rules by national courts, parallel or consecutive application of the EU competition rules by the Commission and national courts, the Commission as *amicus curiae*, transmission of national courts' judgments to the Commission, and the role of national courts in the context of a Commission inspection. This is considered in more detail in Chapter 2.

The National Courts Cooperation Notice is aimed at those courts and tribunals of the EU **1.53** Member States which are entitled to refer a question for a preliminary ruling to the ECJ pursuant to Article 267 TFEU.[231] In addition, it includes the national courts designated as

Modernisation of European Competition Law—Initial Experiences with Regulation 1/2003, FIDE XXIII Congress Linz 2008—Congress Publications Vol 2 (Nomos 2008) 375, 463 et seq; see also Recommendations to national courts and tribunals in relation to the initiation of preliminary ruling proceedings [2012] OJ C338/1.

[228] See E Gippini-Fournier, 'The Modernisation of European Competition Law: First Experiences with Regulation 1/2003—Institutional Report' in HF Koeck and MM Karollus (eds), The Modernisation of European Competition Law—Initial Experiences with Regulation 1/2003, FIDE XXIII Congress Linz 2008—Congress Publications Vol 2 (Nomos 2008) 375, 463 et seq, who reports that in 2006 the Commission made use of this possibility for the first time by presenting written observations to the *Cour d'appel de Paris* (France) concerning the interpretation of the motor vehicle block exemption in a case involving quantitative selective distribution. In this case, the Commission did not receive the parties' pleadings. On 15 March 2007, the Commission sought to lodge observations as *amicus curiae* in a second case, pending before the *Gerechtshof Amsterdam* (The Netherlands). The case concerned the issue of tax deductibility of fines imposed by the Commission under national law.

[229] Notice on cooperation between national courts and the Commission in applying Arts 85 and 86 of the EEC Treaty [1993] OJ C39/6, now replaced by the National Courts Cooperation Notice, at para 43. Commission Notice on cooperation between national competition authorities and the Commission in handling cases falling within the scope of Arts 85 or 86 of the EEC Treaty [1997] OJ C313/3, now replaced by the ECN Cooperation Notice [2004] OJ C101/43, para 71.

[230] Case C-234/89 *Stergios Delimitis v Henninger Bräu AG* [1991] ECR I-935, para 53: 'It should be noted in this context that it is always open to a national court, within the limits of the applicable national procedural rules and subject to Art [339 TFEU], to seek information from the Commission on the state of any procedure which the Commission may have set in motion and as to the likelihood of its giving an official ruling on the agreement in issue pursuant to [Reg] 17. Under the same conditions, the national court may contact the Commission where the concrete application of [Art [101](1)] or of [Art [102]] raises particular difficulties, in order to obtain the economic and legal information which that institution can supply to it. Under Art [4.3 TFEU], the Commission is bound by a duty of sincere cooperation with the judicial authorities of the Member State, who are responsible for ensuring that Community law is applied and respected in the national legal system.'

[231] National Courts Cooperation Notice [2004] OJ C101/54 para 1; as indicated, the ECJ rejected a preliminary reference in Case C-53/03 *Synetairismos Farmakopoion Aitolias & Akarna-nias (Syfait) and others v GlaxoSmithKline plc and others* [2005] ECR I-4609, paras 30–7. The ECJ found that it has no jurisdiction to answer the questions referred by the Greek NCA (Epitropi Antagonismou) since that body is not a 'court or tribunal' within the meaning of Art 267 TFEU—the provision which allows national courts or tribunals to refer questions to the Court for a preliminary ruling—because it does not have certain of the features required for it to be classified as such, namely independence and the fact of being called upon to give judgment in

NCAs pursuant to Article 35(1) of Regulation 1/2003. The National Courts Cooperation Notice applies where national courts are called upon to apply Articles 101 and 102 TFEU in actions between private parties. To the extent that they act as public enforcers, they are subject to the Notice on cooperation within the network of competition authorities. National courts also play a role in Commission investigations, where national legislation requires a court to authorize national enforcement authorities to assist the Commission in its inspections at a company's premises. Further, pursuant to Article 21 of Regulation 1/2003, a prior authorization from a national court is needed for inspection of premises other than those of the undertakings themselves.[232]

C. National Authorities for Upholding Competition[233]

1. Substantive powers

1.54 The system under Regulation 17 was based on an administrative control of agreements in which the Commission bore almost sole responsibility for enforcing the competition rules. NCAs rarely dealt with infringements of Articles 101 and 102 TFEU. Under Regulation 1/2003, the NCAs have been assigned a much more significant role in the public enforcement of the EU competition rules. Regulation 1/2003 created a system of parallel competences in which the competition rules are enforced by a network of competition authorities as well as by the national courts. Provided trade between Member States is affected, Regulation 1/2003 allows NCAs to apply Articles 101 and 102 TFEU but leaves the Member State to determine which body will enforce the rules and which mechanism for investigating infringements and enforcing decisions will apply.[234] It is true that Regulation 1/2003 still provides that if the Commission decides to start proceedings for the adoption of a decision, this automatically ends the NCAs' jurisdiction to apply Articles 101 and 102 TFEU. Yet a central feature of Regulation 1/2003 is that NCAs have the power to apply Article 101 and 102 TFEU in individual cases. The Commission has

---

proceedings intended to lead to a decision of a judicial nature. On the definition of this notion, see E Gippini-Fournier, 'The Modernisation of European Competition Law: First Experiences with Regulation 1/2003—Institutional Report' in HF Koeck and MM Karollus (eds), The Modernisation of European Competition Law—Initial Experiences with Regulation 1/2003, FIDE XXIII Congress Linz 2008—Congress Publications Vol 2 (Nomos 2008) 375, (463–4) in HF Koeck and MM Karollus (eds), *The Modernisation of European Competition Law* (Nomos 2008).

[232] In this regard, Arts 20 and 21 of Reg 1/2003 and paras 38–41 of the National Courts Cooperation Notice have codified the case law in Case C-94/00 *Roquette Frères* [2002] ECR I-9011.

[233] E Gippini-Fournier, 'The Modernisation of European Competition Law: First Experiences with Regulation 1/2003—Institutional Report' in HF Koeck and MM Karollus (eds), The Modernisation of European Competition Law—Initial Experiences with Regulation 1/2003, FIDE XXIII Congress Linz 2008—Congress Publications Vol 2 (Nomos 2008) ; see also KJ Cseres, 'The Impact of Regulation 1/2003 in the New Member States' (2010) 6(2) Competition Law Review 145.

[234] Under Art 35 of Reg 1/2003, the designation of the bodies responsible for the application of the rules is left to the Member States. In practice, the nature of those bodies varies from country to country: a single administrative authority may be in charge of investigation, prosecution, and decision making (eg Bundeskartellamt in Germany), but more often a dual structure has been set up, whereby a section of the Ministry for Economic Affairs is responsible for investigating a particular conduct, whilst an independent administrative authority or court is endowed with the power to adopt decisions and impose sanctions (eg Austria, Finland, Ireland). Various Member States have chosen to give the body vested with the power to decide in competition matters the status of administrative or ordinary court. Hence, whether or not it was expressly provided for under national law, some of these specialist courts have considered that their jurisdiction entitled them to request preliminary rulings from the ECJ on the interpretation of EU competition provisions. See eg Spain and the preliminary ruling requested by the now extinct *Tribunal de Defensa de la Competencia* in Case C-67/91 *Asociación Española de Banca Privada (AEB)* [1992] ECR I-4785.

withdrawn the competence of NCAs by starting proceedings, in a limited number of cases, in very specific circumstances.[235]

One of the objectives of Regulation 1/2003 was to encourage the consistent application of EU competition rules by NCAs. NCAs must give priority to the enforcement of EU law over national competition laws. Thus, the Regulation provides that where NCAs apply national competition law to agreements, decisions by associations of undertakings, or concerted practices within the meaning of Article 101 TFEU which may affect trade between Member States, they shall apply Article 101 TFEU.[236] In addition, where they apply national competition law to any abuse prohibited by Article 102 TFEU, they shall apply Article 102 TFEU. Thus, Regulation 1/2003 had an impact on the powers of NCAs only to the extent that they apply EU law and to ensure a sufficiently uniform application throughout the EU. Whether national competition law leads to a stricter outcome than the position under EU competition law will depend upon whether Article 101 TFEU or Article 102 TFEU applies. In relation to conduct which may affect trade between Member States, Article 3(2) of Regulation 1/2003 permits the application of stricter national law than Article 102 TFEU to prohibit or sanction unilateral conduct. Regulation 1/2003 does not, however, lay down the procedures to be followed by NCAs in applying Articles 101 and 102 TFEU. Neither does Regulation 1/2003 harmonize powers of enforcement or procedures between Member States. Instead, it limits itself to setting out the type of decisions that NCAs can take, namely requiring that an infringement be brought to an end; ordering interim measures; accepting commitments; and imposing fines, periodic penalty payments, or any other penalty provided for in their national law.[237] The latter may also include imprisonment or criminal sanctions on natural persons.[238] NCAs are entitled to establish their own enforcement priorities, including the right to decide which agreements and conduct to investigate.

1.55

2. Cooperation between the Commission and NCAs and the European Network of Competition Authorities

Under the system of parallel competence, the Commission and the NCAs must apply the EU competition rules in close cooperation.[239] Together, the NCAs and the Commission form a network of European competition authorities (the ECN), which serves as a forum for discussion and cooperation in the application of Articles 101 and 102 TFEU.[240] Essentially, the ECN is an informal network whose aim is to ensure both an efficient division of labour and the consistent application of the EU competition rules. The ECN provides the framework for the sharing of work between the Commission and the NCAs, on the one hand, and between the NCAs, on the other, through mutual information about new cases, especially in order to ensure the efficient

1.56

---

[235] ECN Cooperation Notice [2004] OJ C101/43 para 54.

[236] National law may be applied if the agreement does not affect trade between Member States or because there is no agreement (unilateral conduct).

[237] Art 5 of Reg 1/2003. Under Art 29(2), NCAs are also empowered to withdraw the benefit of a block exemption regulation under certain conditions. Where, in any particular case, agreements, decisions by associations of undertakings, or concerted practices to which a block exemption applies have effects which are incompatible with Art (101)(3) TFEU in the territory of a Member State or in part thereof, which has all the characteristics of a distinct market, the NCA of that Member State may withdraw the benefit of the block exemption in question in respect of that territory.

[238] This could mean that NCAs could have stronger powers than the Commission under Regulation 1/2003. The Commission can only impose fines on undertakings for infringements of Art 101 or 102 TFEU, while Art 23(5) of Reg 1/2003 clarifies that fines 'shall not be of a criminal law nature'.

[239] Art 11(1) of Reg 1/2003. See for more details Ch 3, 'The Role of National Competition Authorities', para 3.11 et seq.

[240] Recital 15 of Reg 1/2003.

allocation of cases, and the possibility of exchanging information and giving assistance.[241] The fact that a case under Article 101 or 102 TFEU affecting trade between Member States can be dealt with by either the Commission or a single national authority or various national authorities acting in parallel has led to the increased enforcement of EU competition law. Although Regulation 1/2003 has spelled out the objective that each competition case should be handled by a single authority, the ECN does not, however, take any decisions on the division of work between the enforcers; it cannot compel its Member States to act in a certain way. Furthermore, neither the Commission nor the NCAs take 'referral' decisions, referring cases from one to another. The ECN Cooperation Notice sets out the case allocation principles.

D. The Commission

1. The Commission's monitoring powers

1.57 Article 17(1) TFEU entrusts the Commission with the task of ensuring that both the Treaty provisions and the measures adopted by the EU institutions for their implementation are observed. This obligation is reflected in the description of the Commission as 'the guardian of the Treaty'.[242] Its task includes the duty to investigate and punish individual infringements, but it also encompasses the duty to pursue a general policy designed to apply, in competition matters, the principles laid down by the Treaty and to guide the conduct of undertakings in the light of those principles.[243] While the decentralization of the enforcement of competition policy had been at the core of the modernization process, the Commission retained its major enforcement role.[244] By abolishing the notification system, the Commission was able to redefine its enforcement priorities and concentrate its resources on the most serious infringements.[245] The detection, prosecution, and punishment of serious violations have become the core task of all parts of the DG COMP, which is responsible for EU competition policy.[246] In parallel with the reforms of

---

[241] While it has been possible in the past to pass on information to the Commission (*British Sugar* [1999] OJ L76/1; *Nathan-Bricolux* [2001] OJ L54/1), Reg 1/2003 is a significant improvement in this respect.

[242] See Case C-431/92 *Commission v Germany* [1995] ECR I-2189, para 22.

[243] Case T-228/97 *Irish Sugar v Commission* [1999] ECR II-2969, para 245; Joined Cases T-202/98, T204/98, and T-207/98 *Tate & Lyle plc/British Sugar/Napier Brown & Co Ltd v Commission* [2001] ECR II-2035, para 100; Case T-31/99 *ABB Asea Brown Boveri v Commission* [2002] ECR II-1881, para 166. There has been some debate on the role of the Commission as an investigator, prosecutor, judge, and jury. While this combination of powers is a common feature of a number of administrative systems in Europe, the real issue should be whether the Commission's decisions are subject to effective checks and balances. See former President of the GC, Judge Bo Vesterdorf, 'Judicial Review and Competition Law—Reflections on the Role of the Community Courts in the EC system of Competition Law Enforcement', Speech at the International Forum on EC Competition Law, Brussels, 8 April 2005. See also the published and edited paper version of the speech in (2005) 1(2) Competition Policy International 6.

[244] See generally L Ortiz Blanco and A Lamadrid de Pablo, 'EU Competition Law Enforcement, Elements for a Discussion on Effectiveness and Uniformity' in Annual Proceedings of the Fordham Competition Law Institute, International Antitrust and Policy' [2011] Fordham 38th Conference on International Antitrust Law and Policy 45, 87 et seq.; Vice President of the European Commission responsible for Competition Policy, J Almunia, 'Cartels: The Priority in Competition Enforcement 15th International Conference on Competition: A Spotlight on Cartel Prosecution Berlin', SPEECH/11/268, 14 April 2011; Director-General at DG COMP A Italianer, 'Priorities for Competition Policy' St Gallen International Competition Law Forum, 20 May 2010; see also former Director-General at DG COMP P Lowe, 'Reflections on the Past Seven Years—"Competition Policy Challenges in Europe"' GCR 2009 Competition Law Review, Keynote address, 17 November 2009.

[245] WPJ Wils, 'Community Report' in D Cahill (ed), *The Modernization of EU Competition Law Enforcement in the EU: FIDE National Reports* (Cambridge University Press 2004) 661, 677. The notification-related work had consumed about half of the resources of the DG COMP not dealing with mergers or State aid.

[246] Competence over State aid is sometimes shared with other DGs concerned.

the legal instruments, in recent years DG COMP has changed its internal structures and processes to align these more closely with the requirements of a modern competition policy framework. There have been two major reorganizations of the DG COMP, supplemented in between by a number of other incremental changes. In 2003–2004, DG COMP for the first time created a matrix structure by integrating merger units with antitrust units in directorates dedicated to enforcement action in key sectors of the EU economy such as energy, telecommunications, transport, financial services, and information technology. The 2007 reorganization went one step further and integrated State aid units with antitrust and merger teams in five 'market and cases' directorates. It aimed to pool and increase market knowledge so that investigations would be more informed and effective. Its aim is to establish closer links between competition policy and other EU sectoral policies and to allow for more effective competition advocacy.[247] The leniency programme, unannounced visits (or on-the-spot investigations), and severe sanctions (ie high fines) are the three pillars of the Commission's deterrence policy.[248]

In addition to its primary task of prosecuting the most serious infringements, the Commission **1.58** should deal with those cases which raise concerns in more than three Member States or which raise new issues calling for the development of competition policy. While the Commission does not fulfil the function of a 'clearing house', it recognizes its role of a *primus inter pares* within the ECN with a view to ensuring the consistent application of competition law.[249] Member States must inform the Commission before or without delay after commencing the first formal investigative measures and at least thirty days before a decision is taken on the intended course of action.[250] While it is true that Regulation 1/2003 does not require NCAs to consult the Commission formally before a decision is taken (ie the NCA in question can take the envisaged decision once the thirty days' deadline has expired), the Commission can make written observations on the decision prior to its adoption and can thus influence the findings where it sees fit. In exceptional cases, particularly when the consistent application of EU competition law is at stake, it can also relieve NCAs of their competence to apply Articles 101 and 102 TFEU.[251]

The second tool enabling the Commission to maintain the consistent application of EU com- **1.59** petition law is intellectual leadership when it comes to formulating competition law policy. In this respect the Commission can make use of a number of instruments, such as taking up cases raising new issues or issues of particular interest.[252] Another possibility is the adoption and subsequent publication of a guidance letter, in which important points of law are clarified. As the EU Courts have made clear, the powers vested in the Commission, particularly those deriving earlier from Regulation 17 and now from Regulation 1/2003, are intended to enable it to carry out its duty under the EU Treaties of ensuring that the competition rules are applied in the internal market. The function of those rules, as is apparent from the fourth recital in the preamble to the Treaty, Article 3(g) and Articles 101 and 102 TFEU,

---

[247] Former Director-General of DG COMP P Lowe, 'The Design of Competition Policy Institutions for the 21st Century—The Experience of the European Commission and DG Competition' (2008) 3 Competition Policy Newsletter 1, 7.

[248] European Commission, DG COMP Management Plan 2013, 20 et seq.

[249] Former Director-General of DG COMP P Lowe, 'The Role of the Commission in the Modernisation of EC Competition Law', Speech at the UKAEL Conference on Modernisation of EC Competition Law: Uncertainties and Opportunities, 23 January 2004.

[250] Article 11(3) and (4) of Reg 1/2003.

[251] The tool can be found in Art 11 (6) of Reg 1/2003, which allows the Commission to initiate formal proceedings. However, before making use of this crude instrument, the Commission will discuss the matter with the NCA concerned.

[252] Article 10 of Reg 1/2003.

is to prevent competition from being distorted to the detriment of the public interest, individual undertakings, and consumers. The exercise of these powers given to the Commission must contribute to the maintenance of the system of competition intended by the Treaty with which undertakings have an absolute duty to comply.[253] Article 17(1) TFEU provides that, in order to ensure the proper functioning and development of the internal market, the Commission is to 'have its own power of decision' and 'exercise the powers conferred on it by the Council for the implementation of the rules laid down by the latter'. Articles 288 to 292 TFEU describe the principal features of decisions, which may be classified as true administrative measures for the implementation of primary and secondary EU law. In this respect, Regulation 1/2003 empowers the Commission to adopt decisions in order to ensure compliance with the EU competition rules contained in the Treaty. Thus, as stated, when dealing itself with an individual case, the Commission combines investigative, prosecutorial, and adjudicative functions.[254]

2. The internal procedure for the adoption of decisions

General principles relating to Commission decision making

1.60 A detailed account of the relevant rules relating to decision making within the Commission in general and DG COMP in particular is contained in the Antitrust Manual of Procedures ('Manproc') published in March 2012, in which the Commission explains in detail the empowerment, sub-delegation, and delegation procedures.[255]

1.61 The way in which the Commission operates and takes decisions is set forth in the following documents:

---

[253] Case 374/87 *Orkem v Commission* [1989] ECR 3283 para 19, which in turn cites Case 136/79 *National Panasonic v Commission* [1980] ECR 2033. See also Case C-94/00 *Roquette Frères* [2002] ECR I-9011, para 42; T-59/99 *Ventouris v Commission* [2003] ECR II-5257, para 120.

[254] As to whether this system is compatible with Art 6(1) ECHR, see WPJ Wils, 'Community Report' in D Cahill (ed), *The Modernization of EU Competition Law Enforcement in the EU: FIDE National Reports* (Cambridge University Press 2004), paras 174–7. The ECtHR has recently ruled that there was an adequate means for challenging the fines imposed by the Italian competition authority (under an institutional framework which is similar to that of the EU) in *A Menarini Diagnostics SRL v Italy*, App no 43509/08 (ECtHR, 27 September 2004). Arguments alleging breach of Art 6(1) of the ECHR are increasingly being used as a tool in appeals in competition cases, and questions are also being raised about the compatibility with the ECHR of the EU institutional and procedural framework, particularly given the increase in the level of antitrust fines imposed by the European Commission in recent years. See eg the discussion of AG Sharpston in the appeal by KME against the GC's judgment dismissing an appeal against the European Commission's decision on the copper industrial tubes cartel (Case C-272/09 P *KME Germany AG, KME France SAS and KME Italy SpA v European Commission* (pending publication) [2012] OJ C32/4, para 99 et seq). The Commission is of the view that the ECtHR in *Menarini* and the ECJ in its *Copper Industrial Tubes and Copper Plumbing Tubes* (C-386/10 P *Chalkor v Commission* [2012] OJ C32/9, para 54 and Case C-272/09 P *KME v Commission* [2012] OJ C32/4 and C-389/10 P *KME Germany and Others v Commission* [2012] OJ C32/10) confirmed that the institutional framework for the enforcement of competition law, by which an administrative organ such as the Commission takes decisions which are subject to full judicial review, ensures an adequate protection of the fundamental rights of the persons concerned by those decisions. See Commission Staff Working Paper Accompanying the Report from the Commission on Competition Policy 2011 [COM(2012) 253 final], 30 May 2012, 10.

[255] Antitrust Manual of Procedures Internal DG Competition working documents on procedures for the application of Articles 101 and 102 TFEU, March 2012. The text is available at <http://ec.europa.eu/competition/antitrust/information_en.html>. This section largely draws on information contained in the Manproc, also taking into account the fact that it refers in part to decisions and internal Commission documents which are not accessible from outside the Commission. See Kerse & Khan, *EC Antitrust Procedure* (6th edn, Sweet & Maxwell 2012) para 6-009, pointing out the distinction between the delegation of powers to adopt a decision and the delegation of signature. A task may be the responsibility of the College of Commissioners, or one Commissioner, but another may be able to sign any necessary measure alone, on behalf of the decision-maker.

- The Rules of Procedure of the Commission.[256] These describe the various procedures for adopting Commission acts, how those decisions are prepared and implemented, and how the departments supporting the Commission are to be organized.
- The Rules giving effect to the Rules of Procedure of the Commission.[257] These supplement the Rules of Procedure and spell out in detail how the latter are to be applied in practice.[258]

According to Article 17(6) TFEU and Article 1 of the Rules of Procedure, decision making in **1.62** the Commission is based on the principle of collegiality.[259] This results from the equality of the members of the Commission in decision taking, and means, in particular, that decisions should be discussed and adopted jointly, and also that all Commission members are politically responsible for all decisions adopted.[260] The delegation of decision-making powers to individual Commissioners or Directors-General is regarded by the Treaty and the Rules of Procedure as an exception rather than the rule and is therefore subject to limitations.[261] Commission decisions are either taken at the Commission's weekly meeting ('oral procedure'), by written procedure, by empowerment (which includes the possibility of sub-delegation), or by direct delegation.[262] Moreover, since empowerment/sub-delegations/delegations are exceptions to the general principle of collegiality, they must be construed narrowly (in principle, there is no 'implicit' empowerment or empowerment 'by analogy'). Before adopting a measure under the empowerment, sub-delegation, or delegation procedure the empowered Commissioner, Director-General,

---

[256] 24.2.2010 (C (2010)1200 final) (hereinafter the 'Rules of Procedure').

[257] Implementing Rules giving effect to the Rules of Procedure of the Commission (C (2010)1200 final) (hereinafter the 'Rules giving effect'), adopted on 24 February 2010. The Rules giving effect are not publicly accessible.

[258] Antitrust Manual of Procedures, Internal DG Competition working documents on procedures for the application of Articles 101 and 102 TFEU, March 2012, Module 1 'Decision-making procedure' para 2 indicates that explanations covering the rules contained in those two basic documents, as well as useful information on their application in practice are accessible via the Manual Operating Procedures on the Secretariat intranet site (only accessible for DG COMP officials).

[259] Article 250 TFEU provides that the Commission shall act by a majority of the number of members provided for in Art 245. A meeting of the Commission shall be valid only if the number of members laid down in its rules of procedure is present. Article 7 of the Rules of Procedure provides that the number of Members whose presence is necessary to constitute a quorum shall be equal to a majority of the number of Members specified in the Treaty (at present fourteen out of a total of twenty-seven). There is currently one Commissioner from each EU country.

[260] Case 5/85 *AKZO v Commission II* [1986] ECR 2585, para 30 et seq, and Case C-137/92 P *Commission v BASF and others (PVCII)* [1994] ECR I-2555, paras 62 and 63. K Lenaerts and J Maselis, 'Procedural Rights and Issues in the Enforcement of Articles 81 and 82 of the EC Treaty' [2001] Fordham International Law Journal 1615, 1646–7.

[261] Antitrust Manual of Procedures Internal DG Competition working documents on procedures for the application of Articles 101 and 102 TFEU, March 2012, Module 1 'Decision-making procedure' para 17. As indicated, Commission decisions delegating the adoption of certain kinds of decisions in proceedings for the application of EU competition law have not been published. In Case 5/85 *AKZO Chemie v Commission* II [1986] ECR 2585, paras 35–9, the Court upheld the principle of delegating the adoption of merely administrative decisions to individual members of the Commission, subject to review by the latter, but recommended that the decisions delegating such powers be published. Similarly, see Joined Cases 46/87 and 227/88 *Hoechst v Commission III* [1989] ECR 2859, paras 44–6.;Case T-275/94 *Carte Bleu v Commission II* [1995] ECR II-2169, paras 69–71, and the case law cited therein. Regarding public access to documents, see Reg (EC) 1049/2001 of the European Parliament and of the Council of 30 May 2001 regarding public access to European Parliament, Council, and Commission documents [2001] OJ L145/43 and Commission Decision of 5 December 2001 amending its rules of procedure [2001] OJ L345/94 by which Reg 1049/2003 is annexed to these rules of procedure. See also K Lenaerts, 'In the Union We Trust: Trust-Enhancing Principles of Community Law' (2004) CML Rev 317, 324, who notes that it is highly likely that in the future EU institutions will no longer be able to refer to an excessive administrative burden in order to decline a reasonable request for access to documents on the basis of Art 15 TFEU.

[262] Antitrust Manual of Procedures Internal DG Competition working documents on procedures for the application of Articles 101 and 102 TFEU, March 2012, Module 1 'Decision-making procedure' para 4.

or Head of Service must always determine whether, on the grounds of political sensitivity or because of its importance, the matter must be brought before the full College.[263]

1.63 **Oral and written procedure**   As a general rule, all decisions of principle involving a degree of political discretion or assessment must be adopted by the College by oral or written procedure. Formal Commission measures must be approved by a majority of its members, at present fourteen out of a total of twenty-seven.[264] Such decisions of principle cannot be delegated to individual Commissioners, let alone the Commission services.[265]

- The oral procedure (Articles 5 to 11 of the Rules of Procedure) mirrors the collegiate nature of Commission decision making, since it provides for an opportunity for discussion between Commissioners. Commission acts are adopted during the weekly meeting (normally on Wednesday) either without discussion (A point) or following discussion between Commissioners (B point).[266] If the Competition Commissioner considers, after having consulted the President of the Commission, that in view of their economic or political importance the measures in issue should be debated, the oral procedure is used.[267]
- The written procedure (Article 12 of the Rules of Procedure) aims to relieve the Commissioners of the need to debate matters in relation to which the adoption of decisions is not controversial and have been discussed between the head of Cabinets at preparatory meetings on the basis of the submitted documents for adoption, approved by the Legal Service and other departments directly involved during the inter-service consultation.[268] The written procedure is generally used for all measures which must be adopted directly by the College itself, but which do not require a debate in the College.[269] Prior approval of the Legal Service and agreement of the Directorates-General with a legitimate interest in the draft text are required before a written procedure can be started.[270]

1.64 Before draft measures are adopted by the College under the oral or written procedure, they must be submitted to an inter-service consultation of the 'departments with a legitimate interest in the draft text'.[271] The purpose of that consultation at services level is to prepare the decision of the College of Commissioners. Where one or more services disagree, the measure must be adopted under the oral procedure. Otherwise it can be adopted under the written procedure.

---

[263] Point 13/14-3.2 of the joint Rules giving effect to Arts 13 and 14 of the Rules of Procedure.

[264] See Annex to the Commission Decision of 24 February 2010 amending its Rules of Procedure (Art 8 of the Rules of Procedure of the Commission [2010] OJ L55/60).

[265] Antitrust Manual of Procedures Internal DG Competition working documents on procedures for the application of Articles 101 and 102 TFEU, March 2012, Module 1 'Decision-making procedure' para 3.

[266] Antitrust Manual of Procedures Internal DG Competition working documents on procedures for the application of Articles 101 and 102 TFEU, March 2012, Module 1 'Decision-making procedure' para 6.

[267] Antitrust Manual of Procedures Internal DG Competition working documents on procedures for the application of Articles 101 and 102 TFEU, March 2012, Module 1 'Decision-making procedure', para 19.

[268] Antitrust Manual of Procedures Internal DG Competition working documents on procedures for the application of Articles 101 and 102 TFEU, March 2012, Module 1 'Decision-making procedure', para 7. Under the written procedure, the draft decision is circulated amongst all the members of the Commission and is approved and becomes a final decision of the Commission if no member either opposes it before a specified date or requests discussion of the matter by the full Commission.

[269] Antitrust Manual of Procedures Internal DG Competition working documents on procedures for the application of Articles 101 and 102 TFEU, March 2012, Module 1 'Decision-making procedure', paras 20 and 21.

[270] Article 12(1) of the Rules of Procedure and Antitrust Manual of Procedures Internal DG Competition working documents on procedures for the application of Articles 102 and 102 TFEU, March 2012, Module 'Decision-making procedures', para 1 citing Article 12(1) of the Rules of Procedure and points 12-3.3 and 23.6 of the Rules giving effect.

[271] Article 23(3) of the Rules of Procedure.

It should be noted that an inter-service consultation must also take place before an indi- **1.65** vidual Commissioner or DG COMP adopts a draft measure also under the empowerment, sub-delegation, or delegation procedure. Where a so-called associated service issues a nega- tive opinion in the course of that inter-service consultation, the measure cannot any longer be adopted under the empowerment, sub-delegation, or delegation procedure, but must be submitted to the oral procedure.[272] The prior agreement of the Legal Service is always required; other interested services are generally only informed and invited to provide com- ments within a given deadline. In the context of the empowerment, sub-delegation, and delegation procedure, the inter-service consultation thus acts as a safeguard for the principle of collegiality.[273]

Measures of (pure) administration   A category of measures to be distinguished from the **1.66** decisions of principle are the so-called measures of management or administration ('*mesures de gestion ou d'administration*'). Such measures are viewed as merely preparatory to future action by the Commission and can be delegated by the College of Commissioners to indi- vidual Commissioners, who then adopt the measure under the so-called empowerment pro- cedure ('*procédure d'habilitation*').[274] Empowerments are either 'general' (a Commissioner is empowered to adopt a given category of acts) or 'ad hoc' (a Commissioner is empowered to adopt a specific act in a specific case).[275] These measures can also be sub-delegated, by an empowered Commissioner to a Director-General or Head of Service who then adopts the measures under the sub-delegation procedure[276] or exceptionally delegated directly by the College to Directors-General or Heads of Service (eg Competition Hearing Officers).[277] The measures of management include those:

- of an investigatory or preparatory nature only,[278] in view of a later final decision to be taken by the College; and/or
- that leave the Commission no or only a limited degree of appreciation or discretion; and/or
- that are routine matters, whose adoption by the College would entail a disproportionate demand on Commissioners' time.

Lastly, a third category of measures are the so-called measures of pure administration ('*mesures* **1.67** *de pure gestion*'). Measures of pure administration are routine measures of a technical nature and/or with no legal consequences and therefore not covered by the principle of collegiality,

---

[272] Rules giving effect to Art 21, point 6.
[273] Antitrust Manual of Procedures Internal DG Competition working documents on procedures for the application of Articles 101 and 102 TFEU, March 2012, Module 1 'Decision-making procedures', paras 13 and 14.
[274] Article 13(1) of the Rules of Procedure.
[275] Such ad hoc empowerments are systematically added when adopting commitment decisions based on Art 9 of Reg 1/2003 in order to facilitate the adoption of Commission decisions implementing commitments such as the setting or extending of deadlines, approval of a purchaser in case of divestiture, or nomination of a trustee/independent auditor, for which no general empowerment of the Competition Commissioner has yet been requested, due to the novelty of Art 9 decisions, when the general empowerment decision has been adopted in 2004. Antitrust Manual of Procedures Internal DG Competition working documents on procedures for the application of Articles 101 and 102 TFEU, March 2012, Module 1 'Decision-making procedures' paras 38–9.
[276] Article 13(3) of the Rules of Procedure.
[277] Direct delegation, Art 14 of the Rules of Procedure.
[278] Case 5/85 *AKZO Chemie v Commission* [1986] ECR 2585, para 38: 'A decision ordering an undertak- ing to submit to an investigation is a form of preparatory inquiry and as such must be regarded as a straight- forward measure of management.'

ie they neither constitute acts which are reserved for adoption by the College, nor acts of management and administration open to empowerment and sub-delegation.[279]

Decision-making procedure in antitrust cases

1.68 **Measures reserved to the College** All final decisions on substance (including interim measures) and/or decisions of principle involving a wide degree of discretion are reserved to the College. These acts cannot be delegated. According to the Manproc, such decisions are:

- all Commission decisions finding and ordering the termination of an infringement (Article 7 of Regulation 1/2003);
- all Commission decisions ordering and renewing interim measures (Article 8(1)(2) of Regulation 1/2003);
- all Commission decisions making commitments binding (Article 9(1) of Regulation 1/2003);
- all Commission decisions finding the inapplicability of Articles 101 or 102 TFUE (Article 10 of Regulation 1/2003);
- all Commission decisions imposing fines for breaches of procedural or substantive law (Article 23(1) and (2) of Regulation 1/2003), as well as all related Commission decisions finally granting immunity or reduction of fines or rejecting immunity and leniency applications;
- all Commission decisions on the final amount of a periodic penalty payment (Article 24(2) (sentence 1) of Regulation 1/2003);
- all Commission decisions to withdraw the benefit of a block exemption regulation (Article 29(1) of Regulation 1/2003).[280]

1.69 Additionally, the Manproc indicates that 'for the time being and until sufficient experience has been gained with the following measures, these measures are also reserved for adoption by the College':[281]

- the issuing of informal guidance letters (Commission Notice on informal guidance relating to novel questions read in conjunction with recital 38 of the preamble of Regulation 1/2003);
- the initiation of proceedings in the situation foreseen in Article 11(6) in combination with Article 11(4) of Regulation 1/2003;
- decisions to launch an inquiry into a particular sector of the economy or into a particular type of agreement across various sectors (Article 17(1) first sentence of Regulation 1/2003).

1.70 **Empowerment of the Competition Commissioner for the application of Regulation 1/2003** By various Commission decisions, the Competition Commissioner has been empowered to adopt a series of acts. When adopting acts by empowerment, reference must be made to the empowerment decision which specifically refers to the act to be adopted.[282] Set out in the paragraphs that follow are various decisions by which powers have been delegated to the Commissioner.[283]

---

[279] They can therefore be taken directly by the services of DG Competition according to the internal division of tasks without involvement of the Legal Service or other departments.

[280] Antitrust Manual of Procedures Internal DG Competition working documents on procedures for the application of Articles 101 and 102 TFEU, March 2012, Module 1 'Decision-making procedures' para 17.

[281] Antitrust Manual of Procedures Internal DG Competition working documents on procedures for the application of Articles 101 and 102 TFEU, March 2012, Module 1 'Decision-making procedures' para 18.

[282] Since May 2008, all documents are adopted via e-Greffe within the Commission.

[283] Before entry into force of Regulation 1/2003 and of the new empowerments, the Commission decision-making procedures in the antitrust field were governed by a complex set of empowerment and sub-delegation decisions from 1965, 1980, 1990, 1996, 2000, and 2002. Where those empowerment decisions concern measures to be taken under Reg 17, they are no longer applicable and only of historical relevance. Some of the older empowerment decisions concern however measures not directly based on Reg 17 and continue therefore to apply in parallel with the new empowerments.

In April 2004, the Commission adopted a decision with a comprehensive set of empower- **1.71**
ments.[284] The introductory explanatory memorandum of the empowerment decision provides
information about the rationale and functioning of the empowerments and the involvement
of other services.[285] Other empowerments listed in Article 1 of the decision concern measures
which have been created by the new enforcement system, such as the following:

- preliminary assessment (Article 9(1) of Regulation 1/2003) and decision to reopen proceedings
  after a commitment decision (Article 9(2) of Regulation 1/2003);
- opinions for national courts and refusal to supply confidential information (Article 15(1) of
  Regulation 1/2003);
- Commission decision ordering inspections of other premises (Article 21 of Regulation 1/2003).

Under Article 13(3) of the Rules of Procedure, a Commissioner can sub-delegate the powers **1.72**
granted to him to a Director-General and Head of Service unless this is expressly prohibited in the
empowerment decision. The empowerment decision of 28 April 2004 prohibits the sub-delegation
only as regards the determination and issue of a statement of objections. The latter is the only
empowerment which must be exercised in agreement with the President of the Commission.[286]

---

[284] Commission Decision PV (2004) 1655, SEC(2004) 520/2, as extended by PV(2006) 1763, SEC(2006)
1368 for the Competition Commissioner for the application of Regulation No 1/2003 and implementing
Commission Regulation No 773/2004, 28 April 2004 ('Empowerment Decision') cited by Antitrust Manual
of Procedures Internal DG Competition working documents on procedures for the application of Articles
101 and 102 TFEU, March 2012, Module 1 'Decision-making procedures', para 23.

[285] Cited by the Antitrust Manual of Procedures Internal DG Competition working documents on
procedures for the application of Articles 101 and 102 TFEU, March 2012, Module 1 'Decision-making
procedures', para 23. The Competition Commissioner has been empowered to adopt roughly twenty-one different measures for which the Competition Commissioner already held an empowerment under the former
Regulation 17. The Manproc lists the following (Antitrust Manual of Procedures Internal DG Competition
working documents on procedures for the application of Articles 101 and 102 TFEU, March 2012, Module
1 'Decision-making procedures', para 25):

- Rejection of complaint by Commission decision (Article 7(2) of Regulation 1/2003 and Article 7(2) of
  Regulation 773/2004; Article 13(1) second sentence, Article 13(2) of Regulation 1/2003, and Article 9
  of Regulation 773/2004; Article 29(1) of Regulation 1/2003);
- Commission decision requesting information from undertakings and associations of undertakings
  (Article 18(3) of Regulation 1/2003);
- Commission decision ordering inspections of undertakings and associations of undertakings (Article
  20(4) of Regulation 1/2003);
- determination and issuance of a statement of objections to undertakings or associations of undertakings and setting of a time limit for reply (Article 27(1) of Regulation 1/2003 and Article 10(1)(2) of
  Regulation 773/2004).

[286] According to the Explanatory Memorandum of the Empowerment Decision, cited in the Manproc, in
this case the President of the Commission intervenes in his capacity as guarantor both of the principle of collegiality and of the credibility of the Commission as an impartial and objective enforcer of the law. Antitrust
Manual of Procedures Internal DG Competition working documents on procedures for the application of
Articles 101 and 102 TFEU, March 2012, Module 1 'Decision-making procedures', para 31. A footnote
referred to at the end of paragraph 45 of the Explanatory Memorandum states that: 'in view of the specificities of transport and given the fact that an ongoing process of liberalisation and market opening is being
carried out, the Commission notes that it remains possible for the member of the Commission responsible
for Transport to request the President, in accordance with the Commission's rules of procedure, that the
Commission may examine any draft decision proposing a statement of objections in transport antitrust, if the
political sensitivity or importance of the case would justify such an examination'. Before adoption of the 2004
empowerment package DG TREN was the only DG whose prior approval was necessary in order to adopt a
statement of objections. The 2004 empowerment package abolished that special right and introduced instead
the footnote above. That footnote does not, however, add anything, since it merely reiterates the rights which
the Transport Commissioner has in any event under the general Rules of Procedure of the Commission. See
Antitrust Manual of Procedures Internal DG Competition working documents on procedures for the application of Articles 101 and 102 TFEU, March 2012, Module 1 'Decision-making procedures', paras 32 and 33.

1.73 By decision of 27 May 2004 the Commissioner for Competition has sub-delegated a number of the above powers to the Director-General of DG COMP. As a result of those sub-delegations, only the following measures listed in the empowerment decision of 28 April 2004 are actually directly adopted by the Competition Commissioner:

- initiation of proceedings (Article 2(1) of Regulation 773/2004 and Article 11(6) of Regulation 1/2003) except in the situation foreseen in Article 11(4) of Regulation 1/2003;[287]
- determination and issuance of a statement of objections to undertakings or associations of undertakings (Article 27(1) of Regulation 1/2003 and Article 10(1)(2) of Regulation 773/2004). This empowerment shall be exercised in agreement with the President of the Commission;[288]
- preliminary assessment in the procedure for the adoption of a decision-making commitment binding (Article 9(1) of Regulation 1/2003);
- publication of a summary of the case and request for comments on commitments (Article 27(4) of Regulation 1/2003);
- Commission decision to re-open proceedings after a decision making commitments binding (Article 9(2) of Regulation 1/2003);
- Commission decision imposing (provisional) periodic penalty payments for breach of substantive rules (if not yet imposed by a previous Commission decision ordering termination of these breaches, Article 24(1)(a)(b)(c) of Regulation 1/2003) or for breach of procedural rules (Article 24(1)(e) of Regulation 1/2003); the decision on periodic penalty payments in order to compel undertakings to supply complete and correct information requested by decision taken pursuant to Articles 17 or 18(3) of Regulation 1/2003 (Article 24(1)(d)) is sub-delegated to the Director-General;[289]
- rejection of complaint by Commission decision (Article 7(2) of Regulation 1/2003 and Article 7(2) of Regulation 773/2004; Article 13(1) second sentence and 13(2) of Regulation 1/2003 and Article 9 of Regulation 773/2004; Article 29(1) of Regulation 1/2003);
- Commission decision ordering inspections of other premises (Article 21(1) of Regulation 1/2003) except where the decision must be taken urgently and the Competition Commissioner cannot be reached in time; for the latter exceptional cases there is a sub-delegation to the Director-General;
- Commission decision requesting an NCA to undertake inspections (Art. 22(2) of Regulation 1/2003).

1.74 All of these empowerments must be exercised in accordance with the general rules relating to the empowerment procedure. In particular, before taking a decision, the Commissioner must determine whether the matter should be brought before the full Commission on grounds of political sensitivity or because of its importance. If there is any doubt, the President should be consulted. DG COMP's services must draw the Commissioner's attention to those circumstances which might convince the Commissioner to bring the matter before the full Commission.

---

[287] The initiation of proceedings in the situation foreseen in Art 11(4) of Reg 1/2003, ie after a competition authority of a Member State has informed the Commission that it will adopt a decision requiring that an infringement be brought to an end, accepting commitments or withdrawing the benefit of a block exemption situation, is for the time being reserved for adoption at the level of the College. According to the Manproc, practical experience will show whether it is necessary to maintain this exception. See Antitrust Manual of Procedures Internal DG Competition working documents on procedures for the application of Articles 101 and 102 TFEU, March 2012, Module 1 'Decision-making procedures', note 4.

[288] Antitrust Manual of Procedures Internal DG Competition working documents on procedures for the application of Articles 101 and 102 TFEU, March 2012, Module 1 'Decision-making procedures', para 28.

[289] Antitrust Manual of Procedures Internal DG Competition working documents on procedures for the application of Articles 102 and 102 TFEU, March 2012, Module 1 'Decision-making procedures', para 40.

As regards the empowerments relating to the Leniency Notices, it should be recalled that **1.75** there are three different Leniency Notices, adopted in 1996, 2002, and 2006 respectively, each with different empowerment decisions. By decision of 4 April 2007 (PV(2007)1783, SEC(2007)439), the Commission empowered the Competition Commissioner to adopt the following decisions in relation to the application of the most recent 2006 Leniency Notice:[290]

- to inform the companies that the evidence described which they propose to disclose at a later date is of such a nature and content that it would meet the conditions required to obtain conditional immunity from fines (point 19 of the Commission Notice);
- to reject an application for conditional immunity where the evidence that the undertaking proposes to disclose at a later date is not of such a nature and content that it meets the requirements for conditional immunity from fines to be granted, and to inform the undertaking accordingly in writing (point 19 of the Commission Notice);
- to grant conditional immunity from fines in writing to the undertakings which meet the conditions set out in the Notice (points 18 and 19 of the Commission Notice);
- to reject an application for conditional immunity from fines where it is found that the conditions laid down in the Notice have not been met, and to inform the undertaking accordingly in writing (point 20 of the Commission Notice);
- to inform in writing the undertakings which meet the relevant conditions of the Commission's intention to apply a reduction of a fine within a specified band (point 29 of the Commission Notice);
- to reject an application for reduction of fines where it is found that the conditions laid down in the Notice have not been met, and to inform the undertaking accordingly in writing (point 29 of the Commission Notice).[291]

With respect to empowerments relating to cooperation with the United States and Canada, the **1.76** Competition Commissioner is empowered to issue requests to the competition authorities of these countries in order to investigate anticompetitive practices under their national laws and to adopt decisions to investigate anticompetitive practices at the request of these authorities.[292]

Measures sub-delegated by the Competition Commissioner to the Director-General[293] As **1.77** mentioned by the decision of 27 May 2004,[294] the Competition Commissioner has sub-delegated to the Director-General the following powers which are granted to him in the empowerment decision of 28 April 2004:

- Decision imposing (provisional) periodic penalty payments on undertakings or associations of undertakings in order to compel them to supply complete and correct information requested by decision taken pursuant to Articles 17 or 18(3) of Regulation 1/2003

---

[290] With respect to empowerments relating to the 2002 Leniency Notice, see also Antitrust Manual of Procedures Internal DG Competition working documents on procedures for the application of Articles 101 and 102 TFEU, March 2012, Module 1 'Decision-making procedures', para 35.

[291] Antitrust Manual of Procedures Internal DG Competition working documents on procedures for the application of Articles 101 and 102 TFEU, March 2012, Module 1 'Decision-making procedures', para 36.

[292] See Article V of the Agreement with the United States of 1995, Article III of the second agreement with the United States of 1998, and Article V of the Agreement with Canada of 1999 (PV (2002) 1572, SEC(2002) 669). Antitrust Manual of Procedures Internal DG Competition working documents on procedures for the application of Articles 101 and 102 TFEU, March 2012, Module 1 'Decision-making procedures', para 37.

[293] Please note that the measures delegated by the Commission to the Hearing Officer will be treated in the context of the description of the tasks of the Hearing Officer. See Ch 10 'Procedures to Establish the Existence of an Infringement', para 10.14 et seq. See also Antitrust Manual of Procedures Internal DG Competition working documents on procedures for the application of Articles 101 and 102 TFEU, March 2012, Module 1 'Decision-making procedures', paras 44–5.

[294] PH/2004/769. The sub-delegation decision was signed on 27 May 2004 and entered into force on 3 June 2004.

(Article 24(1)(d) of Regulation 1/2003); the power to impose periodic penalty payments for breaches of substantive rules (Article 24(1)(a)(b)(c)) and under Article 24(1)(e) is not sub-delegated and remains therefore with the Competition Commissioner under the empowerment procedure.

- Closure of proceedings (Article 2(1) of Regulation 773/2004 and Article 11(6) of Regulation 1/2003).
- Announcement by the Commission to the complainant that it intends to reject the complaint (Article 7(2) of Regulation 1/2003 and Article 7(1) of Regulation 773/2004).
- Refusal by the Commission to send confidential information to national courts (Article 15(1) of Regulation 1/2003).
- Determination of the content of an opinion to be sent to a national court (Article 15(1) of Regulation 1/2003).
- Decision requesting information from undertakings and associations of undertakings (Article 18(3) of Regulation 1/2003).
- Decision ordering inspections of undertakings and associations of undertakings (Article 20(4) of Regulation 1/2003).
- Decision to order inspections of premises other than business premises (Article 21 of Regulation 1/2003) limited to those cases in which the decision must be taken urgently and the Competition Commissioner cannot be reached in time; accordingly, in normal circumstances the decision to inspect premises other than business premises must be taken by the Commissioner under the empowerment procedure.
- Written commitment by the Commission not to use information which an NCA obtained under a national leniency programme.[295]

1.78 Before taking a decision the Director-General must always determine whether, on the grounds of political sensitivity or because of its importance, the matter must be brought before the Competition Commissioner. Where the Director-General for Competition is prevented from exercising the sub-delegated powers, for example during holiday periods, Article 27 of the Rules of Procedure of the Commission applies according to strict rules of seniority.

1.79 **Measures of pure administration ('de pure gestion')** Measures of pure administration are not decisions, submitted to a formal adoption procedure; rather they are issued by the services of DG COMP according to the internal division of tasks without the involvement of the Legal Service or other departments. In practice, measures of pure administration are mostly routine measures of a technical nature and/or acts having no binding effect. While the Manproc indicates that it would be impossible to list all measures of pure administration, since every measure which is not reserved to the full Commission or for decision under empowerment falls within that category, the measures of pure administration adopted by case-handlers would include the following:

- Simple requests for information (Article 18(2) of Regulation 1/2003).
- Simple inspection based merely on written authorization by the Director-General (Article 20(2)).
- Access to file.
- Publication of the summary of the decision in the OJ (Article 30 of Regulation 1/2003).
- Extension of time limit for written reply to the statement of objections (Article 9 of the Hearing Officer Terms of Reference).

---

[295] Antitrust Manual of Procedures Internal DG Competition working documents on procedures for the application of Articles 101 and 102 TFEU, March 2012, Module 1 'Decision-making procedures', para 40.

- Convening and chairing the Advisory Committee (Article 14(3) of Regulation 1/2003).
- Determining the summary of the case and the preliminary draft decision to be sent to the Advisory Committee (Article 14(3) of Regulation 1/2003).
- Transmission to NCAs of the most important documents with a view to applying Articles 7 to 10 and 29(1) of Regulation 1/2003(Articles 11(2) first and second sentences of Regulation 1/2003).
- Transmitting information in the Commission's possession to national courts (Article 15(1) first alternative, of Regulation 1/2003).[296]

Involvement of other services

Inter-service consultation prior to the adoption of measures reserved to the College   Under **1.80** Article 23(4) of the Rules of Procedure, the Legal Service must always be consulted on all drafts or proposals for legal instruments and on all documents which may have legal implications. With respect to DG COMP, this means that the Legal Service must be consulted on every act prepared by it to be adopted by the College or under the empowerment or sub-delegation procedures.

Under Article 23(5) of the Rules of Procedure, the Secretary General must be consulted in **1.81** specific circumstances. The Secretary General must be consulted on all initiatives that (a) are of political importance; or (b) are part of the Commission's annual work programme; or (c) concern institutional issues; or (d) are subject to impact assessment or public consultations. In concrete terms, with regard to DG COMP's activities, the Secretary General will only be consulted in exceptional situations, for instance in relation to the preparation of legislative acts or policy statements (draft regulations, draft notices, etc).

Under Article 23(2) of the Rules of Procedure other Directorates-General with a legitimate **1.82** interest in an initiative shall also be formally consulted on the drafts of all decisions which will be adopted by the College, either under the oral or written procedure.[297]

Under Article 23(6) of the Rules of Procedure, DG Budget (DG BUDG) shall be con- **1.83** sulted on documents which may have implications for the budget and finances. Specifically, this means that the operative part of a prohibition decision with fines should be sent to DG BUDG.

DG COMP must allow the Legal Service and the Directorate-Generals consulted at least ten **1.84** working days to respond (fifteen working days if the main body of the text (minus annexes) is longer than twenty pages). Departments unable to reply within the time limit for reasons beyond their control can ask for an extension provided they do so before the deadline. Any such requests should remain exceptional and must be duly substantiated. If a department consulted does not respond within the time limit, in legal terms this is taken to signify tacit approval (Point 23-4 of the Rules giving effect). Where the Legal Service or another

---

[296] Antitrust Manual of Procedures Internal DG Competition working documents on procedures for the application of Articles 101 and 102 TFEU, March 2012, Module 1 'Decision-making procedures', paras 46–9.

[297] Antitrust Manual of Procedures Internal DG Competition working documents on procedures for the application of Articles 101 and 102 TFEU, March 2012, Module 1 'Decision-making procedures', para 53 indicates that, in practice, with regard to DG COMP's activities, Directorates-General with a legitimate interest are mostly DGs Enterprise and Industry (ENTR), Economic and Financial Affairs (ECFIN), Energy (ENER), Mobility and Transport (MOVE), Information Society and Media (INFSO), Education and Culture (EAC), Employment, Social Affairs and Inclusion (EMPL), Internal Market and Services (MARKT), Agriculture and Rural Development (AGRI), and Health and Consumers (SANCO). The list of DGs obviously depends on the subject matter of the act to be adopted.

consulted Directorate-General disagrees, the proposal cannot be adopted under the written procedure but must be submitted to the oral procedure.

1.85 **Involvement of other services prior to the adoption of measures under the empowerment and sub-delegation procedures** With regard to measures adopted under the empowerment procedure granted in the competition field, since the first empowerment decision in 1965, Commission services other than the Legal Service are only informed in advance of and not consulted about certain envisaged measures. For the exercise of all empowerments and sub-delegations, the prior approval of the Legal Service is always necessary.[298] A formal inter-service consultation of the Legal Service is therefore required.

1.86 The extent of the involvement of services other than the Legal Service depends on the type of acts to be adopted. Each decision that empowers the Commissioner for Competition to adopt certain acts specifies the involvement of services other than the Legal Service

1.87 Prior to the exercise of the most important empowerments and sub-delegations, DG COMP must 'inform' the Directorates-General 'primarily responsible for the products, services or policy areas in issue' and give them the opportunity to state their views. The exercise of those empowerments and sub-delegation, however, is not subject to their prior approval.[299]

1.88 The 'information' procedure grants other DGs beyond a 'right to know' a true 'right to be heard'. Where prior information is required, the following rules apply:

- DG COMP must send the draft measure in sufficient time prior to its adoption so as to give the other department an effective opportunity to state its views;
- except in duly justified circumstances of urgency, the other department will be given ten working days to state its views;
- DG COMP will take the greatest possible account of the opinion expressed by the other departments; and
- on request by one of the other departments, an inter-service meeting will be held in good time.

1.89 **Measures for which prior information of other services is obligatory** The measures for which the prior information of services other than the Legal Service is obligatory are as follows:

- The initiation of proceedings (Article 2(1) of Regulation 773/2004 and Article 11(6) of Regulation 1/2003) except in the situation foreseen in Article 11(4) of Regulation 1/2003. In the latter case the decision is taken at the College level after normal inter-service consultation.
- Determination and issuance of a statement of objections to undertakings or associations of undertakings (Article 27(1) of Regulation 1/2003 and Article 10(1)(2) of Regulation 773/2004).[300]

---

[298] Article 23(4), second paragraph, of the Rules of Procedure; Antitrust Manual of Procedures Internal DG Competition working documents on procedures for the application of Articles 102 and 102 TFEU, March 2012, Module 1 'Decision-making procedures', para 10, citing Article 23(4) second paragraph of the Rules of Procedure; point 13/14-3.3 of the Rules giving effect and empowerment decisions in the competition field.

[299] Most of the time there will only be one service 'primarily responsible' (ENTR, INFSO, MARKT, EAG, EMPL, ENER, ECFIN, or MOVE). Depending on the nature of the case, however, there may also be more than one other department involved. Footnote 14 of the explanatory memorandum states: 'Departments which have not been informed and which regard themselves as also primarily responsible for the products, services or policy areas in issue in a given case may be informed at all times upon making a reasoned request.'

[300] As explained earlier, the Competition Commissioner must exercise the empowerment for sending the statement of objections in agreement with the President of the Commission. Despite the involvement of the President at the College level, the Secretariat General (SG) does not have to be involved in the inter-service consultation. The SG is not a 'service responsible for the products, services or policy areas in issue'. Since the Competition Commissioner needs to obtain the agreement of the President prior to the adoption of the

- The preliminary assessment in the procedure for the adoption of a decision making commitments binding (Article 9(1) of Regulation 1/2003).
- Publication of a summary of the case and request for comments on commitments (Article 27(4) of Regulation 1/2003).
- Commission decision to reopen proceedings after a decision making commitments binding (Article 9(2) of Regulation 1/2003).
- Commission decision imposing (provisional) periodic penalty payments for breach of substantive rules (if not yet imposed by a previous Commission decision ordering termination of these breaches, Article 24(1)(a)(b)(c) of Regulation 1/2003, or for breach of procedural rules of Article 24(1)(d)(e) of Regulation 1/2003). The decision to impose periodic penalty payments on undertakings or associations of undertakings in order to compel them to supply complete and correct information requested by decision taken pursuant to Article 17 or 18(3) of Regulation 1/2003 (Article 24(1)(d) of Regulation 1/2003 is sub-delegated to the Director-General). This is is the only sub-delegated measure prior to the adoption of which services other than the Legal Service must be 'informed'.
- Rejection of complaint by Commission decision for insufficient grounds for acting by conducting a further investigation ('lack of EU interest').

Acts for which no provision of prior information to other services is required   For a **1.90** number of measures to be adopted by empowerment or sub-delegation, no provision of prior information to other services is foreseen (with the exception of the Legal Service, whose prior approval must always be sought). This is the case where (a) strict confidentiality is necessary, such as in the case of unannounced inspections ordered by decision or the handling of leniency applications;[301] or (b) the measure is one of technical case administration in respect of the conduct of the proceedings or in respect of the oral hearing, publication of Commission acts in the Official Journal or access to the file. The no information regime applies to the following measures:

- The closure of proceedings (Article 2(1) of Regulation 773/2004 and Article 11(6) of Regulation 1/2003).
- Announcement by the Commission to the complainant that it intends to reject his complaint (Article 7(2) of Regulation 1/2003 and Article 7(1) of Regulation 773/2004).
- Rejection of complaint by Commission decision (Article 7(2) of Regulation 1/2003 and Article 7(2) of Regulation 773/2004; Article 13(1) second sentence, Article 13(2) of Regulation 1/2003, and Article 9 of Regulation 773/2004; Article 29(1) of Regulation 1/2003), except for rejections of complaints for lack of EU interest, which are subject to the normal prior information regime and rejections of complaints on substantive grounds, for which a special involvement regime applies.
- Refusal by the Commission to transmit confidential information (Article 15(1) first alternative of Regulation 1/2003).[302]
- Commission decision requesting information from undertakings and associations of undertakings (Article 18(3) of Regulation 1/2003).
- Commission decision ordering inspections of undertakings and associations of undertakings (Article 20(4) of Regulation 1/2003).

---

statement of objections, the Commissioner must be fully informed about any possible disagreements during the inter-service consultation/information. Antitrust Manual of Procedures Internal DG Competition working documents on procedures for the application of Articles 101 and 102 TFEU, March 2012, Module 1 'Decision-making procedures', para 65.

[301] See Commission decision of 13.2.2002, PV(2002)1555 adopting document SEC(2002)119.
[302] National Courts Cooperation Notice [2004] OJ C101/54, paras 23–6.

- Commission decision to order inspections of other premises (Article 21(1) of Regulation 1/2003).
- Commission decision requesting an NCA to undertake an inspection (Article 22(2) of Regulation 1/2003).
- Written commitment by the Commission not to use certain information exchanged in the ECN for imposing sanctions on a leniency applicant or certain other persons (point 41(2) of the Commission Notice on cooperation within the network of competition authorities).
- The refusal by the Commission to allow the complainant to express his views at the oral hearing (Article 7(2) of Regulation 1/2003 and Article 6(2) of Regulation 773/2004).
- Refusal by the Commission to hear third parties (other than addressees of a statement of objections or complainants) for lack of sufficient interest (Article 27(3) of Regulation 1/2003 and Article 13(1) of Regulation 773/2004).
- Refusal by the Commission to invite third parties (other than addressees of a statement of objections or complainants) to develop their arguments at the oral hearing (Article 27(3) of Regulation 1/2003 and Article 13(2) of Regulation 773/2004).

1.91 The 'no information' regime also applies with regard to the application of the empowerment on the application of the 2002 and 2006 Leniency Notices. Decisions to grant (or not to grant) conditional immunity or acts informing applicants of the Commission's intent to grant a reduction of fines (or to reject it) can therefore be adopted without prior information of services other than the Legal Service (the prior approval of which remains necessary). Finally, all decision-making powers delegated to the Hearing Officer do not require prior information of any other service but the Legal Service, whose agreement is always required.

1.92 **Special case of rejections of complaints on substantive grounds**   Rejections of complaints on substantive grounds occurs where, after an assessment of the known facts, the Commission considers that the conduct complained of does not infringe Articles 101 or 102 TFEU. They are to be distinguished from rejections of complaints on other grounds, which include rejections of complaints for lack of sufficient EU interest, procedural reasons (eg under Article 13 of Regulation 1/2003), or lack of sufficient substantiation by the complainant of the allegations put forward.

1.93 For the exercise of the empowerment for rejections of complaints on substantive grounds, the empowerment decision exceptionally foresees the need to obtain the prior approval of both the Legal Service and the Commission departments responsible for the products, services, or policy areas in question. This leads to the following complicated involvement regime for rejections of complaints:

- For rejections of complaints on substantive grounds, the prior approval of the departments primarily responsible is necessary (exception to the normal prior information regime).
- For rejections of complaints for insufficient grounds for acting by conducting a further investigation ('lack of EU interest'), the departments primarily responsible must be informed (normal prior information regime).
- No services other than the Legal Service must be informed in advance as regards rejections of complaints on other grounds;
- For Article 7 letters (announcement by the Commission to the complainant that it intends to reject his complaint, Article 7(2) of Regulation 1/2003 and Article 7(1) of Regulation 773/2004) no services other than the Legal Service have to be informed in advance.

Consequences of a failure to observe the decision making formalities

Failure by the Commission to observe the decision-making formalities may constitute a breach **1.94** of an essential procedural requirement and may well render the decision void if an action is brought under Article 263 TFEU. In *PVC*, the full Commission had only agreed the supposed authentic text of a decision imposing fines in languages which were not the languages of certain of the undertakings to whom the decision was addressed (Italian and Dutch). The decision, with some modifications, was later adopted in these other languages by the Commissioner responsible for Competition. The GC held that the adoption of a decision was not a measure of management which could be delegated within the terms of the Commission's Rules of Procedure.[303] The case law suggests that certain matters cannot be delegated and must be dealt with by the Commissioners. This would concern decisions under Article 7 (termination of infringement), Article 8 (interim measures), Article 9 (acceptance of commitments), Article 10 (findings of inapplicability), and Articles 23 and 24 (fines and penalties).[304]

It should be noted that the applicant must produce evidence and specific facts to rebut **1.95** the presumption that EU acts are valid[305] before the Court will order the supply of the

---

[303] See Case C-137/92 P *Commission v BASF' AG and others* [1994] ECR I-2555, para 62 et seq. That judgment dealt with an appeal by the Commission against the GC's judgment in Joined Cases T-79/89, T-84 to 86/89, T-89/89, T-91 and 92/89, T-94/89, T-96/89, T-98/89, T-102/89, and T-104/89 *BASF AG and others v Commission* [1992] ECR II-315, in which the Court declared to be non-existent the Commission Decision of 21 December 1988 in the *PVC cartel* case [1989] OJ L74/1. The GC considered that there had been a breach of the principle of the inalterability of measures adopted by the Commission and that the member of the Commission responsible for competition matters lacked powers *ratione materiae* and *ratione temporis*. On appeal, the Court concluded that, although not sufficient for a decision of non-existence, one of the irregularities pointed out by the GC (specifically, failure to comply with Art 18 of the Commission's Rules of Procedure concerning *authentification* of its measures) constituted an essential procedural requirement under Art 263 TFEU, so that the *PVC* decision had to be annulled. The Court rejected the Commission's view that the Commissioners' decision-making process may be confined to expressing their will to act in a particular way, without having to take part in the drafting of the measure containing the decision or in giving it its final written form. According to the Court, the intellectual aspect and the formal aspect are wholly inseparable and the record of the measure in written form necessarily expresses the views of the authority adopting it. The *PVC II* judgment has been followed in Joined Cases T-80/89, T-81/89, T-87/89, T-88/89, T-90/89, T-93/89, T-95/89, T-97/89, T-99/89, T-100/89, T-101/89, T-103/89, T-105/89, T-107/89, and T-112/89 *BASF AG and others v Commission (LdPE)* [1995] ECR II-729, relating to the Commission Decision on the *LdPE* case [1989] OJ L74/21. The *LdPE* decision was adopted at the same time and contained more or less the same irregularities that led to the *PVC* decision being annulled. In particular, it was not adopted by the full Commission in all the languages in which it was binding. According to the GC, the Commission may delegate authority to one of its Members to adopt decisions only in those official languages in which the text is not authentic for the parties to the proceedings. See Case T-80/89, etc *BASF AG and others v Commission (LdPE)* [1995] ECR II-729, paras 96–102; Case C-287/95 and Case C-288/95 *Commission v Solvay* [2000] ECR I-2391, para 74, on the failure to authenticate decisions adopted by the College of Commissioners.

[304] Adoption of such decisions by other than the full Commission would infringe the principle of collegiate responsibility. See Joined Cases T-79/89, etc *BASF AG and others v Commission* [1992] ECR II-315, para 71. On the other hand, a decision by which the Commission requires default interest to be paid following a judgment of the GC upholding in part a decision imposing a fine subject to accrual of default interest must, in so far as it is a measure giving effect to the original decision setting the fine and the rate of interest, be regarded as no more than a management and administrative measure. This has been the view taken by the GC in Case T-275/94 *Groupement des Cartes Bancaires 'CB' v Commission* [1995] ECR II-2169, paras 70 and 71, in which the GC stated that 'measures which create rights and obligations for individuals amount to decisions which must be deliberated upon by the members of the Commission together' and 'measures which merely ratify those decisions constitute accessory measures of management which may be taken pursuant to a delegation of authority'. See also Kerse & Khan, *EC Antitrust Procedure* (6th edn, Sweet & Maxwell 2012) para 6-006, who note that the Commissioners need not have read the complete case file in order to adopt a valid decision. The Court would consider it sufficient that the Commissioners had received complete and detailed information regarding the essential points of the case and had access to the entire file. Cases 41/69, 44/69, and 45/69 *ACF Chemiefarma v Commission* [1970] ECR 661, paras 21–3.

[305] Case T-43/92 *Dunlop Slazenger International Ltd v Commission* [1994] ECR II-441, para 24.

relevant internal EU documents. In *British Airways v Virgin*, British Airways argued that the Commission had acted *ultra vires* by adopting the contested decision in July 1999, since the members of the Santer Commission, who had resigned on 16 March 1999 in order to avoid a motion of censure by the Parliament, only had the authority to deal with current business within the meaning of Article 234 TFEU (applied by analogy) until the appointment of the members of the new Commission. The GC disagreed and took the view that the Treaty would not prohibit Commissioners who had resigned from exercising their normal powers until their resignation took effect on the date of their actual replacement in September 1999. Until this time, they retained their full powers.[306]

1.96 The importance of the Commission's internal decision-making procedure for ensuring a system of checks and balances should not be underestimated. It is fair to say that where the Commission considers that it has jurisdiction to act, it has the power to investigate, prosecute and decide a case, which could make it vulnerable to some sort of '*prosecutorial bias*' against the undertakings being investigated.[307] However, draft decisions are scrutinized by a large number of people inside the Commission, including the Legal Service, the team of the Chief Economist,[308] and Peer Review Panels[309]—which are particularly important in merger

---

[306] Case T-219/99 *British Airways plc v Commission* [2003] ECR II-5917, paras 46–57.

[307] D Geradin and N Petit, 'Judicial Review in European Union Competition Law: A Quantitative and Qualitative Assessment' TILEC Law and Economics Discussion Paper No 2011-008/Tilburg Law School Legal Studies Research Paper No 01/2011, 26 October 2010 pointing out on page 19 that: 'checks and balances should be part of every legal regime that can lead to the adoption of decisions with adverse effects on individuals (or groups of individuals). In most antitrust regimes, such checks and balances are ensured through the separation of the investigative and decision-making functions as the decision-maker will control the quality of the evidence and the strength of the case that has been put together by the investigating body. Such a separation does not exist under Regulation 1/2003'. The fairness of the Commission's procedures for deciding competition cases has been discussed widely in the doctrine, eg I Forrester, 'Due Process in EC Competition C: A Distinguished Institution with Flawed Procedures' (2009) 34 EL Rev 817; W Wils, 'The Increased Level of EU Antitrust Fines, Judicial Review and the ECHR' (2010) 33 World Competition 5; F Castillo de la Torre, 'Evidence, Proof and Judicial Review in Cartel Cases' (2009) 32 World Competition 505; D Slater, S Thomas, and D Waelbroeck, 'Competition Law Proceedings before the European Commission and the Right to a Fair Trial: No Need for Reform?' Global Competition Law Centre Working Paper 04/08; 'Enforcement by the Commission: The Decisional and Enforcement Structure in Antitrust Cases and the Commission's Fining System', report presented at the Fifth Annual Conference of the Global Competition Law Centre, 11–12 June 2009.

[308] D Geradin and N Petit, 'Judicial Review in European Union Competition Law: A Quantitative and Qualitative Assessment' TILEC Law and Economics Discussion Paper No 2011-008/Tilburg Law School Legal Studies Research Paper No 01/2011, 26 October 2010, pointing out on page 19 that: 'the CET [Chief Economist Team], which is now composed of about twenty PhD economists, has also shown independence in that it has expressed, on a number of occasions, disagreement with the theories of harm developed by case teams. The (degree of) involvement of the CET, however, varies depending on the cases and the CET has no ability to block the issuance a statement of objections and eventual adoption of an infringement decision even if it disagrees with the theories of harm developed by the case team. In addition, as "intellectually" independent he may be, the Chief Economist is part of the DG Competition hierarchy and reports to the Director General'.

[309] D Geradin and N Petit, 'Judicial Review in European Union Competition Law: A Quantitative and Qualitative Assessment' TILEC Law and Economics Discussion Paper No 2011-008/Tilburg Law School Legal Studies Research Paper No 01/2011, 26 October 2010, indicating on page 19 that: 'These panels, which are composed of three officials of units that have not been involved in the investigation, play a useful role in that they provide a second opinion on whether the Commission should proceed with a given case... The setting up of these panels does not, however occur as a matter of course and, although it is the authors' understanding that panel members usually perform a good and thorough scrutiny of the case file, their independence is not guaranteed since these officials, as the Chief Economist, belong to DG Competition. In any event, their role is only advisory. Their opinion does not bind the DG Competition hierarchy.' See OECD Directorate For Financial and Enterprise Affairs Competition Committee, Procedural Fairness: Transparency Issues in Civil and Administrative Enforcement Proceedings 2010, 'European Union' 205, stating that the

proceedings and which reflect the Commission's efforts to increase the informal procedural safe-guards.[310] These internal checks and balances are complemented by external review, in the shape of judicial control by the EU Courts.[311]

3. Commission policy documents

Best Practices and Manual of Procedures

Best Practices   In an attempt to enhance the transparency and predictability of the Commission's   **1.97**
proceedings, in October 2011 the Commission published its Commission notice on best prac-tices for the conduct of proceedings concerning Articles 101 and 102 TFEU ('Best Practice guide-lines').[312] For the first time they provide guidance on how Article 101/102 proceedings take place before the Commission, and give parties and other stakeholders a clear picture of what to expect at each stage. The measures consist of the Commission's Notice on best practices in the conduct of anti-trust proceedings under Article 101 TFEU (prohibition of anti-competitive agreements) and Article 102 TFEU (prohibition of abuses of dominance), a new mandate for the Hearing Officer and, as indicated earlier, best practices for the submission of economic evidence ('Best Practices Package').

The following are the most relevant points of the Best Practice guidelines: **1.98**

- Relevant parameters for the calculation of fines will be outlined at the statement of objections stage.

Peer Review panels are set up in order to provide a 'fresh pair of eyes', checking the factual, legal, and eco-nomic basis of cases and procedural issues and coherence. The aim of the Peer Review Panel would be to have an open discussion on the line proposed by the case team. It can either identify areas where further work is necessary; identify objections that should be dropped; recommend that the case is not pursued further; or recommend that the case team continue with the case on an unchanged basis. The organization of the panel and the members of the Peer Review team are not made public and the peer review of a case does not involve in any way the parties subject to the proceedings or any third party.

[310] D Geradin and N Petit, 'Judicial Review in European Union Competition Law: A Quantitative and Qualitative Assessment' TILEC Law and Economics Discussion Paper No 2011-008/Tilburg Law School Legal Studies Research Paper No 01/2011, 26 October 2010, however take the view (pp 19/20) that the measures adopted by the Commission to improve its enforcement processes only provide a feeble not a com-prehensive system of 'checks and balances'. See in contrast former Director General of DG COMP, P Lowe 'Cartels, Fines, and Due Process' (2009) June(2) Online Magzine for Global Competition Policy Release 6, stating that a 'case has to pass several checkpoints both within and outside DG Competition before a deci-sion is adopted. These ensure that, of the Commission's cases, "only the strong survive".' J Temple Lang 'The Strengths and Weaknesses of the DG Competition Manual of Procedure' (2013) 1(1) Journal of Antitrust Enforcement 132, 152 observes a 'diffusion and vagueness of responsibility' in the Commission's procedure that is also owed to informally constituted panels with no clear rules. It would be difficult for people both inside and outside the Commission to identify the key decision-makers.

[311] Former President of the GC, Judge Bo Vesterdorf, 'Judicial Review and Competition Law—Reflections on the Role of the Community Courts in the EC System of Competition Law Enforcement', Speech at the International Forum on EC Competition Law, Studienvereinigung Kartellrecht, Brussels 8 April 2005. See also the edited paper version of the speech in [2005] 1(2.7) Competition Policy International; see also DG at DG COMP A Italiener, 'Best Practices for Antitrust Proceedings and the Submission of Economic Evidence and the Enhanced role of the Hearing Officer', OECD Competition Committee Meeting 18 October 2011, Paris, who takes the view that the system is sound and fair, anchored in the rule of law, respects the rights of parties, and has performed well over the years. There is therefore no need for radical reform. See, however, U Soltész, 'What (Not) to Expect From the Oral Hearing—Oral Hearings and the Best Practices Guidelines' (2010) March (1) The Competition Policy International Antitrust Journal. See also J Temple Lang 'The Strengths and Weaknesses of the DG Competition Manual of Procedure' (2013) 1(1) Journal of Antitrust Enforcement 132.

[312] On 6 January 2010 the European Commission published for consultation draft best practice guide-lines on the conduct of antitrust proceedings. It published the final version of its Notice on best practices for the conduct of proceedings concerning Articles 101 and 102 of the TFEU, 17 October 2011 [2011] OJ C308/6. MEMO/11/703 Competition: Best Practices to increase interaction with parties and enhanced role of hearing officer—frequently asked questions, 17 October 2011; IP/11/1201 Commission reforms antitrust procedures and expands role of Hearing Officer. 17 October 2011.

- State of play meetings will be held in cases concerning Article 101 TFEU (including cartel cases) and abuse of dominance.
- Access to 'key submissions', such as the non-confidential version of the complaint, and economic studies, will be granted prior to the statement of objections.
- The mandate and role of the Hearing Officer have been extended.
- The rejection of complaints will be published.
- The standard of analysis for economic evidence has been clarified.[313]

1.99 It is fair to say that the Best Practice guidelines offer no revolutionary changes. Their main value is that they provide an up-to-date, coherent, and transparent set of rules on which undertakings can rely in antitrust investigations, while introducing some new elements that could be beneficial for companies under investigation, complainants, and interested third parties if handled in the right way. Their real impact will depend largely on the Commission's future practice.[314]

1.100 **Antitrust Manual of Procedures**   Furthermore, on 30 March 2012, the Commission published its Antitrust Manual of Procedures, disclosing parts of its internal guidelines applicable to investigations on procedures for the application of Articles 101 and 102 TFEU ('Manproc'). The Manproc is another step in the Commission's efforts to shed light on how it conducts administrative procedures.[315] From the outset, the Commission has been keen to

---

[313] The Best Practices for the submission of economic evidence outlines the criteria that economic evidence must fulfil to be acceptable to the Commission, and explains the interaction between Chief Economist, case teams, and third parties providing such evidence. According to the Guidelines, any tested hypotheses need to be explicitly formulated and based on economic theory, and datasets need to undergo thorough inspection and quality control. Although it recognizes the limitations of imperfect data, the paper provides that these limitations should not preclude economic analysis, and statistical techniques should be used to improve the quality of the analysis in such cases. The chosen methodology should be substantiated by explicitly providing its pros and cons, and generally accepted methods are preferred. Any necessary documentation must be shared to allow for timely replication of the analysis. Results must be reported in the standard format found in academic papers, and a robustness analysis should always accompany any economic and econometric analysis. The parties should be careful to avoid presenting economic opinions misleadingly as statements of fact, and, given that parties often use data that they have not audited or verified themselves, the parties should carefully acknowledge the sources of information. Lastly, the paper provides that data provided in response to Data Requests need to be complete, correct, and timely.

[314] See also Director-General at DG COMP, A Italianer, 'Best Practices for Antitrust Proceedings and the Submission of Economic Evidence and the enhanced role of the Hearing Officer' OECD Competition Committee Meeting, 18 October 2011, Paris. Kerse & Khan, *EC Antitrust Procedure* (6th edn, Sweet & Maxwell 2012) paras 1-090–1-091, commenting on Commission efforts to improve transparency. See also J Temple Lang 'The Strengths and Weaknesses of the DG Competition Manual of Procedure' (2013) 1(1) Journal of Antitrust Enforcement 132 arguing that while the Best Practices would not deal with various 'unresolved and unsatisfactory' issues, they provide nevertheless some helpful comments.

[315] The publication is the result of a complaint by a lawyer who made a request under Regulation 1049/2001, asking the Commission to provide access to Manproc. The Commission initially refused this request, arguing that the manual was a working document which had been prepared for purely internal purposes. It argued that disclosure of its internal procedures would be highly detrimental to its investigation and decision-making processes. Finally, in October 2011, the European Ombudsman published its decision on the complaint that the Commission had failed to provide access to DG COMP's internal procedural manual (see Decision of the European Ombudsman closing his inquiry into complaint 297/2010/(ELB)GG against the European Commission of 26 September 2011, see also Mlex, 'EC to disclose "version" of antitrust handbook next month' 30 September 2012). The Ombudsman accepted that the Commission had been entitled to refuse access to certain parts of the internal manual on the grounds that disclosure would reveal its investigatory strategy and so undermine the purpose of investigations and its decision-making process. However, it provisionally concluded that the Commission should have at least made partial disclosure and its failure to do so amounted to maladministration. In response to the Ombudsman's recommendation for an amicable settlement, the Commission agreed to produce a publicly disclosable version of the internal manual. It stated that it intended to publish this at the same time, or soon after, the publication of the final version of the Best Practices document, which took place on 17 October 2011. According to press reports, however, the move to

stress that this is merely an internal document to help staff at DG COMP to investigate cases under Article 101 and 102 TFEU. The Guidance is not binding on DG COMP staff and most importantly has not been adopted by the Commission.[316]

The Commission explained that the Manproc would be an internal working tool intended to give practical guidance to DG COMP staff on how to conduct an investigation applying Articles 101 and 102 TFEU. It will not contain binding instructions for staff, and the procedures set out in it might have to be adapted to the circumstances of individual cases. It will be oriented towards the practical needs of case teams, but will not claim to provide complete or exhaustive practical guidance. As a practical working tool, it will evolve through updates made on a regular basis to reflect new experience gained in applying the competition rules of the Treaty, and the Regulations, notices, and other guidance. In the case of any discrepancy, these rules will take precedence over the Manproc. **1.101**

While the published modules therefore do not create or alter any rights or obligations arising under the EU competition rules, the Manproc is expected to be of great value for practitioners because it provides a valuable insight into internal Commission procedures. In particular, it clarifies issues not covered by specific competition guidance, such as the decision-making process within the Commission, the use of languages, the consultation obligations within the Commission and the recovery of penalties. The section on commitments decisions, in particular, provides additional guidance to that contained in the Best Practices as this is one procedural area where there is no separate Commission notice.[317] **1.102**

It is also worthy of note that the document published does not contain any information on the Commission's internal procedures relating to conducting inspections or in its prioritization of the cases to pursue (except in relation to not pursuing complaints due to a lack of EU **1.103**

---

publish a version of the internal manual does not spell the end of the dispute. Only weeks after the document was made available, the Commission faced new requests for access to versions of the Manproc. See Mlex, 'EC Faces Further Demands for Internal Antitrust Guidebook', 12 April 2012.

[316] The Commission makes clear in the prologue that 'the fact that the modules are in the public domain does not change their character as purely internal guidance to staff' and that 'the practical guidance given in the manual does not claim to be complete or exhaustive'. See also J Temple Lang 'The Strengths and Weaknesses of the DG Competition Manual of Procedure' (2013) 1(1) Journal of Antitrust Enforcement 132 who states that the Manual may give rise to legitimate expectations on the part of the companies indicating that the Manual may lead the GC to be more careful to ensure that the Commission treats companies in different cases equally.

[317] The Manproc contains 28 chapters and is 277 pages long. The Manproc includes the following modules: 1. Decision-making procedures—19 pages; 2. Relations with the Hearing Officers—5 pages; 3. Cooperation with National Competition Authorities (ECN)—14 pages; 4. Cooperation between the Commission and National Courts—8 pages; 5. Cooperation with Competition Authorities in Third Countries—7 pages; 6. Requests for information (Article 18 of Regulation 1/2003)—15 pages; 7. Sector inquiry (Article 17 of Regulation 1/2003) [*under construction*]; 8. Power to take statements (Article 19 of Regulation 1/2003)—6 pages; 9. Dealing with leniency applications—18 pages; 10. Opening of Procedures—6 pages; 11. Statement of Objections—15 pages; 12. Access to file and confidentiality—25 pages; 13. Right to be heard (written phase and hearing)—11 pages; 14. Advisory Committee on restrictive practices and dominant positions—5 pages; 15. Adoption of a prohibition decision (Article 7 of Regulation 1/2003)—5 pages; 16. Commitment decisions (Article 9 of Regulation 1/2003)—13 pages; 17. Interim measures (Article 8 of Regulation 1/2003)—5 pages; 18. Finding of inapplicability (Article 10 of Regulation 1/2003)—9 pages; 19. Remedies and fines (Article 23 of Regulation 1/2003) [*under construction*]; 20. Periodic penalty payment (Article 24 of Regulation 1/2003)—3 pages; 21. Handling of complaints—11 pages; 22. Informal guidance—7 pages; 23. Closure of proceedings—3 pages; 24. Administrative closure of the file—3 pages; 25. Follow-up of decisions—6 pages; 26. Court litigation—8 pages; 27. Use of languages—7 pages; 28. Publication of decisions—15 pages. See also J Temple Lang 'The Strengths and Weaknesses of the DG Competition Manual of Procedure' (2013) 1(1) Journal of Antitrust Enforcement 132 who regrets that the Manual says little about due process and policy.

interest).[318] This reflects the fact that the Ombudsman agreed with the Commission that it was entitled to refuse to disclose sensitive internal information and strategies, and guidance on investigations, which could undermine the successful conduct of future investigations.[319]

4. Function and terms of reference of the Hearing Officer

1.104 Further, as part of the package of measures aimed at improving interaction with parties in antitrust proceedings and reinforcing the mechanisms for safeguarding parties' procedural rights, the mandate of the Hearing Officer was also strengthened. The Hearing Officer has been in charge of guaranteeing the respect of the right to be heard in antitrust and merger proceedings since 1982. Nowadays, Hearing Officers are mainly responsible for ensuring that the effective exercise of procedural rights is respected. They have various functions and powers. First, they decide, on behalf of the Commission, on certain procedural issues.[320] Generally, parties, complainants, and interested third parties involved in the proceedings must first raise these issues with DG COMP. It is only in the event of disagreement that the issue may be referred to the Hearing Officers.[321] Second, Hearing Officers have the power to make recommendations in relation to certain procedural issues. Third, Hearing Officers can report on any procedural incidents in their interim and final reports.[322] They may also submit observations on any matter arising out of any proceedings to the Competition Commissioner at any point in time. Finally, they are responsible for the organization and conduct of oral hearings.[323]

1.105 The Hearing Officer's decisional powers were previously limited to the stages following the sending of the statement of objections. In order to reinforce overall protection of procedural fairness, the Commission has now extended this role. Under the revised mandate, parties now have a right to an independent review of their procedural claims during the entire procedure, since Hearing Officers have new functions throughout competition proceedings, including the investigation phase and in the context of commitments decisions. They also have a new role in intervening to ensure that the Commission informs an undertaking of its procedural status. The extensive role of Hearing Officers means that they may examine all major types of Commission proceedings.[324]

---

[318] The chapters on sector inquiries and remedies and fines have also yet to be published, as they are still under review.

[319] The European Ombudsman (see Art 228 TFEU) adds another mechanism for external administrative control to the review procedures. The Ombudsman receives complaints concerning instances of maladministration in the activities of all EU institutions, bodies, offices, or agencies etc. See N Diamandouros, 'Improving EU Competition Law Procedures by Applying Principles of Good Administration: The Role of the Ombudsman' (2010) 1(5) Journal of European Competition Law & Practice 379; A Scordamaglia-Tousis, 'The Role of the European Ombudsman in Competition Proceedings: A Second Guardian of Procedural Guarantees' (2010) 3(1) Journal of European Competition Law & Practice 29.

[320] See notably Arts 4(2c, d), 5(2), 6(2), 7(3), 8, and 9 of the Hearing Officer's Mandate.

[321] Article 3(7) of the Hearing Officer's Mandate.

[322] See Arts 14(1) and 16–17 of the Hearing Officer's Mandate. According to Art 14(2) of the Hearing Officer's Mandate, at the occasion of an administrative oral hearing, the Hearing Officer may also make observations on the substance of the case, such as on the further progress of the proceedings and the need for the formulation or the withdrawal of certain objections.

[323] Antitrust Manual of Procedures Internal DG Competition working documents on procedures for the application of Articles 101 and 102 TFEU, March 2012, Module 2, para 3.

[324] See the overview of WP Wils, 'The Role of the Hearing Officer in Competition Proceedings before the European Commission' (2012) 35(3) World Competition 431.

E. The EU Courts

1. The EU judicature

At present, the judicial function in the European Union is discharged by two courts: the Court of **1.106** Justice (ECJ) and the General Court (GC).[325] The GC is attached to the ECJ and its jurisdiction has gradually increased with successive Treaty amendments (ie Maastricht, Amsterdam, Nice, and Lisbon). The functions of the GC are identical to those of the ECJ—ie to review the legality of the acts of the EU institutions—but are limited in terms of the matters on which it may adjudicate.

At present, both the GC and the ECJ are composed of twenty-seven judges (ie one per **1.107** Member State).[326] The ECJ also includes eight Advocates General. Unlike judges, Advocates General do not decide cases; instead they provide the Court with their opinion of the case and the legal solution that should be applied in their view. Opinions of Advocates General are made public. The GC does not have permanent Advocates General, but may appoint one in a particularly complex case, although it has not done so for many years.

One of the GC's main areas of jurisdiction is judicial review actions brought by private persons **1.108** against EU institutions, including against Commission decisions in competition cases.[327] The GC reviews the Commission's findings, both as regards the facts and the law.[328] The GC is the principal forum for competition cases, ie challenges to Commission decisions applying Articles 101 and 102 TFEU, but remains subordinated to the ECJ. Its creation was also due to the need for judicial control which reviews comprehensively and rigorously the factually complex decisions that the Commission adopts in competition cases.[329] Appeals (on a point of law only) seeking to set aside decisions of the GC may be brought before the ECJ.[330] EU case law has clarified which of the Commission's acts can be challenged and who may lodge such challenges.

---

[325] Article 256 TFEU on the jurisdiction of the GC was added by Art 11 of the Single European Act [1987] OJ L169/1. See also Council Decision 88/591 [1988] OJ L319/1, which is the enabling provision for establishing the new court. The objective was to improve judicial protection of individual interests, particularly in cases requiring the examination of complex facts, while at the same time reducing the ECJ's workload.

[326] There is a plan to add eight further judges to the GC.

[327] The initial jurisdiction of the GC encompassed (i) staff cases; (ii) certain cases under the European Coal and Steel Community Treaty; (iii) actions against the Commission relating to the enforcement of the EU competition rules and damages claims (Art 340 TFEU) arising from an act or failure to act which is the subject of an action under any of the first three matters. In 1993, the GC's jurisdiction was extended to cover all direct actions brought by natural or legal persons.

[328] According to the Former President of the GC, Judge Bo Vesterdorf, acting as Advocate General in Case T-7/89 *Hercules SA v EC Commission* [1991] ECR II-867: 'the very creation of the Court of First Instance as a court of both first and last instance for the examination of facts in the cases brought before it is an invitation to undertake an intensive review in order to ascertain whether the evidence on which the Commission relies in adopting a contested decision is sound'. It is notable that the Courts therefore act as judicial review courts and not as courts of full appellate jurisdiction with the power to adopt decisions on the merits of the case themselves; see in this sense B Vesterdorf, 'The Court of Justice and Unlimited Jurisdiction: What Does it Mean in Practice?' (2009) June (2) Online Magazine for Global Competition Policy Release 1.

[329] Case C-185/95 P *Baustahlgewebe* [1998] ECR I-8417, para 41: 'the purpose of attaching the Court of First Instance to the Court of Justice and of introducing two levels of jurisdiction was, first, to improve the judicial protection of individual interests, in particular in proceedings necessitating close examination of complex facts, and, second, to maintain the quality and effectiveness of judicial review in the Community legal order'. A consolidated version of the Rules of Procedure of the GC is available at <http://curia.europa. eu/jcms/upload/docs/application/pdf/2008-09/txt7_2008-09-25_14-08-6_431.pdf> (last amendment 24 May 2011). A reform of those rules is currently under discussion (see also next note on revised ECJ Rules of Procedure).

[330] Articles 49–54 of the Statute of the Court of Justice, inserted by Art 7 of Council Decision 88/591 [1988] OJ L319/1. A consolidated version of the ECJ Statute is available at <http://curia.europa.eu/jcms/ upload/docs/application/pdf/2011-07/rp_cjue_en.pdf>. Note also that a new revised version of the Rules of

2. Main types of proceedings

Actions in general

1.109 Article 19 TFEU provides that 'the Court of Justice shall ensure observance of the law in the interpretation and application of the Treaty'. Its jurisdiction includes competence to deal with questions concerning the interpretation and application of Articles 101 and 102 TFEU by the judicial authorities of Member States. The courts have been extremely active, not only in the interpretation, but also in the creation of EU competition law by gradually extending the scope of judicial review in the field of competition law as regards both the acts that can be challenged and the persons who may lodge the challenge. As a general rule, all decisions producing legal effects that affect the interest of an applicant by bringing about a distinct change in his or her legal position may be subject to an action for annulment.[331] Additionally, by way of preliminary rulings in response to questions submitted by the national courts under Article 267 TFEU and by giving judgment in proceedings brought before it concerning Commission decisions, the Court has developed a substantial body of case law and EU precedents. As has been seen, these have allowed the development of legal principles to foster the free market and to attain the economic integration of Member States. In some cases, this goes far beyond what the Commission and the Council, because of timidity and lack of political will, respectively, could have proposed or accepted.

1.110 In statistical terms, both the nature and the volume of litigation before the EU Courts have changed radically in recent years, mainly because of the development of EU law in new areas and the increase in the number of Member States. The enlargement of the EU has also had a considerable effect on the internal structure of the courts, mainly because of the increase in the number of their members and in the number of languages that can be used in litigation.[332] Of particular complexity are competition cases, challenges by undertakings to Decisions made by the Commission allowing or refusing mergers, or concerning anti-competitive behaviour.[333] A strand of the discussions—focusing on changing the statutes of the court—has been put on hold for the time being, while stakeholders discuss more technical and procedural aspects of the dossier. The EU's GC has already scaled back its duty to prepare reports in advance of case hearings, in particular removing references to parties' rights to use the document as

---

Procedure of the European Court of Justice (ECJ) was published in the Official Journal ([2012] OJ L265/1) that apply from 1 November 2012. The new Rules reflect the fact that references for a preliminary ruling now constitute the primary category of cases brought before the ECJ (rather than direct actions). Therefore, the new Rules distinguish more clearly between the procedures for each type of action that can be brought before the ECJ, while drawing together common procedural provisions. The Rules have also been supplemented or clarified in light of experience. Certain procedures, such as review procedures, have been simplified. Further, in an endeavour to shorten time periods, the opportunities for the ECJ to rule by reasoned order have been extended and the rules relating to intervention have been simplified. See also ECJ Press Release No 122/12 of 3 October 2012 explaining the rationale for the new rules.

[331] Case T-87/96 *Assicurazioni Generali and Unicredito v Commission* [1999] ECR II-203, para 37; Joined Cases T-125/97 and T-127/97 *Coca-Cola v Commission* [2000] ECR II-1733, para 77.

[332] See Marc Jaeger, President of the GC, 'Is it time for reform? The Court of First Instance of the European Communities is celebrating its 20th anniversary' (*European Voice*, 23 September 2009) available at <http://europeanvoice.com>, where Marc Jaeger has pleaded for EU policy makers to provide the means to tackle a mounting backlog. He pointed out that the number of new cases brought each year before the GC rose from 238 in 1998 to 466 in 2003 and 629 in 2008, an increase of over 160 per cent in ten years. See also Commission Opinion of 30 September 2011 on the requests for the amendment of the Statute of the Court of Justice of the European Union, presented by the Court.

[333] A Scordamaglia, 'Cartel Proof, Imputation and Sanctioning in European Competition Law: Reconciling Effective Enforcement and Adequate Protection of Procedural Guarantees' (2011) 7(1) Competition Law Review 5, 43, pointing to a growing need of judicial review in antitrust matters. Today's extensive body of case law on cartels extends up to a total of 245 judgments, 99 by the ECJ, and 146 by the CFI/EGC (as of 25 Feb 2011).

a check on the judges' understanding of the pleas.[334] This change comes ahead of a broader reform effort that involves increasing the number of GC judges.[335]

Direct actions available to undertakings

Proceedings under Articles 267 and 258 TFEU fall to be instituted, respectively, by the **1.111** national courts and the Commission. Actions under the second paragraph of Article 340, in conjunction with Article 268, raise general questions of non-contractual liability which typically fall outside the sphere of competition law.[336] However, two types of direct action procedures are of particular interest with regard to competition cases. First, the GC has jurisdiction to review decisions of the Commission under Article 261 TFEU and may cancel, reduce, or increase the fine or penalty payment imposed. Secondly, it also has jurisdiction to review the legality of all decisions taken by the Commission under Article 263 TFEU. Proceedings may be brought by any natural or legal person to whom the decision is addressed.[337] Direct actions against Commission decisions or against the Commission's failure to act are brought under Article 265, third paragraph TFEU. As well as actions under these two provisions, proceedings may also be brought under Articles 278 and 279 TFEU. Notwithstanding the fact that the Court may order suspension of enforcement of a contested measure, actions brought before the Court do not have suspensive effect, pursuant to Article 278 TFEU.[338] Regulation 1/2003 expressly provides that particular acts of the Commission are to be in the form of decisions which makes them amenable to review under Article 263 TFEU.[339]

---

[334] Mlex, 'General Court pares back hearing documents' 8 July 2011. According to a change in the GC's 'practice directions to parties', the GC has already deleted references to the function of the hearing reports. It has removed a passage detailing that the hearing report 'provides an objective summary of the case'. Further, it has deleted the text that says that the report 'is meant to enable the parties to check that their pleas and arguments have been properly understood and to facilitate study of the documents before the Court by the other Members of the bench hearing the case.' See also Mlex, 'EU court-hearing transparency under scrutiny in reform debate' 25 January 2012. One of the proposals concerns the abolition of reports prepared by the Court outlining litigants' arguments in a dispute. In the past, these reports have served as a starting point for the debates during oral hearings, and provided insight into the proceedings for outside observers. The court's plan to abolish them has been questioned by certain Member States' governments, who fear that proceedings will be less transparent and that litigants will no longer have access to the summary of the case. For the court, the reports are costly due to the number of legal staff—judges, rapporteurs, and translators—required for the drafting. The court believes efficiency in proceedings should override any of the concerns voiced. Already, such reports have been reduced in size, offering less insight into the parties' arguments.

[335] Mlex, 'EU considers hiring more senior clerks to clear court caseload' 17 September 2012, reporting that EU governments are considering suggestions to hire more senior clerks, or 'référendaires', to assist judges at the GC and tackle a growing backlog of cases. National officials would still discuss plans to increase the number of judges at the court, but in view of Croatia's anticipated entry to the EU, there would be options for an extra 5, 8, 11, or 14 members to join the EU bench; Mlex, 'General Court judge pushes for specialised judges in EU competition cases' 11 March 2011, citing Nicholas Forwood, a leading judge at the GC in Luxembourg, has said the time may be ripe to consider a specialization of European judges in competition law, in particular on points of economics, to ensure the European Commission's decision are adequately reviewed. Mlex, 'Talks stall on increasing number of EU judges, again' 10 June 2013, indicating that European Union governments have again failed to find common ground on appointing new judges to the EU courts as they would become stretched by more and more litigation.

[336] See, however, Case 145/83 *Stanley Adams v Commission* [1985] ECR 3539, para 44, in which the Commission was found liable under Art 288 EC for the unauthorized disclosure of confidential information by Commission staff. The Commission might have the duty to take reasonable steps to avoid any disclosure (eg identity of an informant) that might cause a party harm.

[337] They may also be brought by any natural or legal person against a decision which, although addressed to another person, is of direct and individual concern to the applicant. Article 10 of Reg 1/2003 still entitles the Commission in exceptional cases 'where the Community public interest ... so requires' to find by decision that Art 101 TFEU is not applicable to a specific agreement or practice. One might imagine that competitors could be entitled to challenge such a decision before the GC on the basis of Art 263 TFEU, in the same way that they used to challenge the legality of authorization decisions of the Commission under the previous regime.

[338] A more detailed description of these applications is given in Ch 15, 'Steps Following the Adoption of a Formal Decision', para 15.31 et seq.

[339] Chapter III of Reg 1/2003.

1.112 The court with jurisdiction over proceedings of this kind is the GC. Thus, pursuant to Article 256 TFEU, the GC has jurisdiction to hear and determine at first instance actions or proceedings referred to in Articles 263, 265, 268, 270, and 272 TFEU.[340] Applications lodged at the same time as the main actions, such as applications for suspension of enforcement or for interim measures under Articles 278 and 279 TFEU, are also dealt with by the GC. The GC pays more attention to the factual issues underlying Commission decisions than the ECJ, which is mainly concerned with legal issues.[341] Historically, for reasons of 'institutional balance'[342] the EU courts have in fact declined to substitute their own analysis of complex economic data for that of the Commission and have tended to review the latter's decisions with a degree of self-restraint,[343] accepting that the Commission has some discretion when making complex and technical assessments. An act or decision will not be annulled on matters of substance unless the Commission has manifestly erred in its assessment. However, within the limits of the review to which it is entitled, the GC has increasingly conducted its review in a comprehensive manner as to whether the Commission provided adequate reasoning, based

---

[340] Note that according to Art 51 of the ECJ Statute, jurisdiction shall be reserved to the ECJ in certain actions referred to in Arts 263 and 265 TFEU when they are brought by a Member State.

[341] See recently Opinion of AG Bot in Case C-89/11 P *E.ON Energie AG v Commission*, delivered on 21 June 2012, ECJ judgment of 22 November 2012, para 26: '[i]t has consistently been held that...an appeal must be limited to points of law and may be based on grounds of lack of competence of the [GC], a breach of procedure before it and infringement of Union law by the [GC]. Therefore, the [GC] has in principle sole jurisdiction to find and appraise the facts, except in a case where the factual accuracy of its findings arises from evidence adduced before it. In that case, the Court of Justice has jurisdiction under Art. 256 TFEU solely to review the legal characterisation of those facts by the [GC], and the legal conclusions it has drawn from them'. Case C-62/01 P *Campogrande v Commission* [2002] ECR I-3793, para 24; Case C-24/05 P *Storck v OHIM* [2006] ECR I-5677, paras 34 and 35; and Case C-95/04 P *British Airways v Commission* [2007] ECR I-2331, para 137.

[342] Former President of the GC, Judge Bo Vesterdorf, 'Judicial Review and Competition Law—Reflections on the Role of the Community Courts in the EC system of Competition Law Enforcement', Speech at the International Forum on EC Competition Law, Brussels, 8 April 2005. See also the published and edited paper version of the speech in (2005) 1(2) Competition Policy International 3, noting that the Commission and courts should stick to their primary functions, competition policy and enforcement on the one hand and judicial review, on the other hand. More recently, see also the President of the GC, M Jaeger, 'The Standard of Review in Competition Cases Involving Complex Economic Assessments: Towards the Marginalisation of the Marginal Review' (2011) 2(4) Journal of European Competition Law Practice 295. Judge at the GC N Forewood, 'The Commission's "More Economic Approach"—Implications for the Role of the EU Courts, the Treatment of Economic Evidence and the Scope of Review' 255 in CD Ehlermann and M Marquis (eds), *European Competition Law Annual 2009* (Hart Publishing 2011). In this context see also Opinion of AG Tizzano in Case C-12/03 *Commission v Tetra Laval BV* [2005] ECR I-987, para 89: 'The rules on the division of powers between the Commission and the Community judicature, which are fundamental to the Community institutional system, do not, however, allow the judicature to go further, and particularly—as I have just said—to enter into the merits of the Commission's complex economic assessments or to substitute its own point of view for that of the institution.' However, for example in Case C-389/10 P *KME Germany and Others v Commission* [2012] OJ C32/10, para 129, the Court held that the EU Courts cannot use the Commission's margin of discretion as a basis for dispensing with the conduct of an in-depth review of the law and of the facts. This may well be interpreted as an invitation to restrict limited review to the bare minimum, or even to leave it aside.

[343] In its order in Joined Cases 142 and 156/84 R *BAT and Reynolds v Commission* [1986] ECR 1899, para 11, eg the ECJ stated 'examination by the Court of the Commission's internal file...would constitute an exceptional measure of inquiry'. From the beginning, the GC's practice has been different. See, *inter alia*, Case T-19/91 *Société d'Hygiène Dermatologique de Vichy v Commission* [1992] ECR II-415, para 7, where the Court requested that the Commission produce a copy of a study which was undertaken for the Commission; in particular Joined Cases T-79/89, T-84-86/89, T-91 and 92/89, T-94/89, T-98/89, and T-104/89 *BAS and others v Commission (PVC)* [1992] ECR II-315, para 25 et seq, in which the Commission submitted a series of documents to the Court for its review. Note that according to Art 51 of the ECJ Statute, jurisdiction shall be reserved to the ECJ with respect to certain actions referred to in Arts 263 and 265 TFEU, when they are brought by a Member State. See, for more details on the scope of review, Ch 15, 'Steps Following the Adoption of a Formal Decision', para 15.32 et seq.

on accurate and persuasive evidence.[344] The intensity of control varies depending on whether the GC reviews the correctness of the facts or the correct application of the law, both of which are subject to full control, and the correctness of the Commission's assessment of complex economic matters, where control is more restrained.[345]

Competition cases before the GC are complex, with lengthy pleadings and an enormous amount of evidence which require a significant effort on the part of the Court to ascertain all of the arguments at stake. Given this, it is hardly surprising that the normal GC procedure takes more than thirty months.[346] With a view to accelerating the review procedure, the EU Courts have adopted two types of fast-track procedure: **1.113**

(1) The *'expedited procedure'* enables the GC to expedite the hearing and determination of appeals.[347] In 2001, the GC's Rules of Procedure were amended to allow it to use a special accelerated or 'fast track' procedure. Under that procedure, particularly urgent cases may be dealt with immediately, whereas under the normal procedure they would have to wait until earlier cases had been heard. Given the Court's limited resources, that procedure can only be used in cases where there is a genuine and pressing need for the Court to come to a decision quickly. To date, this procedure has been particularly used for the

---

[344] Case T-342/99 *Airtours v Commission* [2002] ECR II-2585; Case T-310/01 *Schneider Electric SA v Commission* [2002] ECR II-4071, para 349; Case T-5/02 *Tetra Laval v Commission* [2002] ECR II-4381, confirmed on appeal in Joined Cases C-12/03 and C-13/03 P *Commission v Tetra Laval* [2005] ECR I-987. In both cases the GC engaged in an exhaustive review of the substantive and procedural issues and annulled the decision.

[345] See Joined Cases C-204/00 P, C-205/00 P, C-211/00 P, C-213/00 P, C-217/00 P, and C-219/00 P *Aalborg Portland and others v Commission* [2004] ECR I-123, para 279. See also Case C-389/10 P *KME Germany and Others v Commission* [2012] OJ C32/10, para 121, where the Court seemed to reject the notion of light judicial review even in cases of complex economic assessments, stating that: 'whilst, in areas giving rise to complex economic assessments, the Commission has a margin of discretion with regard to economic matters, that does not mean that the Courts of the European Union must refrain from reviewing the Commission's interpretation of information of an economic nature. Not only must those Courts establish, among other things, whether the evidence relied on is factually accurate, reliable and consistent but also whether that evidence contains all the information which must be taken into account in order to assess a complex situation and whether it is capable of substantiating the conclusions drawn from it.' See also the other two judgments rendered on the same day, Cases C-386/10 P *Chalkor v Commission* [2012] OJ C32/9, para 54 and Case C-272/09 P *KME v Commission* [2012] OJ C32/4, para 94. As regards the submission of economic evidence in court proceedings, see Mlex, 'Economics pleas should be presented early in antitrust appeals, EU judge says' 1 November 2011, citing EU Judge Nicholas Forwood that: '[e]ven if there may not be any formal restriction to advancing economic arguments for the first time at the Court of Justice, practically, one has to realise that something that has been advanced with enormous conviction throughout the entire process is likely to be more favourably looked at than the rabbit produced out of the hat in the last minute'. See also Mlex, ' "Spill-over" of economics in competition cases won't limit judicial review, Jaeger says' 29 August 2011, citing Marc Jaeger, President of the GC, who stated that the more widespread use of complex economics in EU competition investigations will not limit judges' powers to review such decisions. Rather, a 'marginal review' should only apply to aspects where the European Commission makes an 'economic-based choice of policy'. For more details, see N Forwood, 'The Commission's "More Economic Approach"—Implications for the Role of the EU Courts, the Treatment of Economic Evidence and the Scope of Judicial Review' in CD Ehlermann and M Marquis (eds), *European Competition Law Annual 2009* (Hart Publishing 2011) 255. See also M Jaeger, 'The Standard of Review in Competition Cases involving Complex Economic Assessments: Towards the Marginalisation of Marginal Review?' (2011) 2(4) Journal of European Competition Law & Practice 295.

[346] House of Lords, European Union Committee 14th Report of Session 2010–11, The Workload of the Court of Justice of the European Union, April 2011.

[347] Article 76a of the Rules of Procedure of the GC of the European Communities, last amendment [2011] OJ L162/18. The expedited procedure entered into force on 1 February 2001 but rarely applies in cartel cases. A request to use the expedited procedure was accepted in Case T-170/06 *Alrosa v Commission* [2007] ECR II-260, paras 27–30, which involved a Commission decision under Art 9 of Reg 1/2003 in relation to an alleged abuse of a dominant position.

review of merger decisions and helped reduce the average time required to between seven and nineteen months.[348]

(2) The President may decide to apply the accelerated procedure to a reference for a preliminary ruling where the circumstances referred to establish that a ruling on the question put to the Court is a matter of exceptional urgency.[349]

1.114 In practice, however, accelerated procedures have had little impact on the judicial review of antitrust cases.[350] Unlike merger cases, there seems to be less urgency in antitrust cases because the judicial actions involve past events, and where this could lead to serious and irreparable damage, a company may resort to the possibility of applying for interim relief. To streamline the procedure, one possibility would be to switch to a more US-style prosecutorial system, in which the GC could not only annul a decision, but could also take a final decision on the merits.[351] This would mean definitely abandoning what still remains of the concept of restricted jurisdiction, apart from the full jurisdiction that the GC enjoys to review fines.[352] However, such a reform would have a significant effect on how the GC reviews cases and may even require amendment of the rules contained in the TFEU.

---

[348] For example, Case T-310/01 *Schneider Electric v Commission* [2002] ECR II-4071, paras 61–70; Case T-5/02 *Tetra Laval v Commission* [2002] ECR II-4381, confirmed on appeal in Case C-12/03 P and C-13/03 P *Commission v Tetra Laval* [2005] ECR I-987; Case T-87/05 *Energias de Portugal SA v Commission* [2005] ECR II-3745, paras 39–43. See also N Levy, *European Merger Control Law: A Guide to the Merger Control Regulation* (Matthew Bender 2008), § 20.05 with more references.

[349] Article 104a of the Rules of Procedure, last amended on 24 May 2011 [2011] OJ L162/17.

[350] In Case T-313/02 *Meca Medina v Commission* [2004] ECR II-3291, the GC refused to grant use of the expedited procedure in an appeal against a rejection of a complaint filed under Arts 101 and 102 TFEU. In April 2011, a committee of the UK House of Lords warned that the EU and the GC may struggle to keep up with their workload if structural reform is delayed further. An increase in the number of both Advocates General at the ECJ and GC judges ranks among the preferred solutions, but not the creation of specialist courts. See Mlex, 'UK Lords warn of "crisis" if EU courts not reformed' 6 April 2011, and the transcript of the debate: HL Deb, 17 October 2011, vol 731 col 205.

[351] In the context of this debate, EU judge N Wahl has advocated a 'contradictory style' regime, where the GC would be the first to pass binding decisions on fines. A prosecutorial system could solve many of the concerns over the protection of companies' fundamental rights. Mlex, 'Antitrust enforcement debate should focus on EC's dual powers, says EU judge Wahl' 8 October 2010. See also, amongst others, D Slater, S Thomas, and D Waelbroeck, 'Competition Law Proceedings before the European Commission and the Right to a Fair Trial: No Need for Reform?' GCLC Working Paper 04/08, available at <http://www.gclc.coleurope.eu>; see also Mlex, 'ECtHR ruling confirms legality of present antitrust system, General Court judge says' 5 October 2011, citing N Forwood as saying that post-*Menarini*, moving towards a prosecutorial system would be 'even less likely in the light of this judgment.' So long as the court would be able to conduct a full review of the facts and law before it, a split system—where an agency imposes sanctions but these are subject to full review by an independent court—should comply with fundamental rights law.

[352] M Bronckers and A Vallery, 'Business as usual after Menarini?' (January–March 2012) Mlex Magazine 43, suggest that in competition law cases a distinction could be made between decisions imposing fines and other decisions where they grant the Commission 'more or less discretion' and 'review its findings with more or less intensity'. As regards the scope of effective judicial review, see Ch 15, 'Steps Following the Adoption of a Formal Decision', para 15.32 et seq.

2

THE ROLE OF NATIONAL JUDICIAL AUTHORITIES

Luis Ortiz Blanco and Konstantin Jörgens

A. Jurisdiction of National Courts

National courts' involvement with the EU competition rules occurs at three different lev- **2.01** els. First, a specific court can be designated by a Member State as its national competition authority, thereby becoming a specialized body.[1] Second, particular courts may be vested with the power to review on appeal the decisions of the national competition authority, whether of an administrative or judicial nature. Finally, national courts are those which, in the exercise of their general jurisdiction, may be called upon to apply Articles 101 and 102 of the Treaty on the Functioning of the European Union ('TFEU') in claims between private parties at first instance or on appeal. It is the latter function that this chapter concentrates on. Before Regulation 1/2003 entered into force, the Commission had handled the vast major- ity of all antitrust cases. Its decisions were subject to judicial review by the General Court ('GC') and the Court of Justice ('ECJ') under Article 263 TFEU. As indicated, Regulation 1/2003 decentralized the enforcement of the EU competition rules. More responsibility for the enforcement of the antitrust rules was not only given to national competition authori- ties ('NCAs') but also to national courts. Both have the power to apply Articles 101 and

---

[1] In this situation, while keeping its judicial nature, the court will be subject to all obligations related to its position within the European Competition Network ('ECN'). Commission Notice on cooperation within the Network of Competition Authorities [2004] OJ C101/43. See Ch 3, 'The Role of National Competition Authorities'.

102 TFEU in individual cases. Therefore, national courts have the power to apply the rules directly and, additionally, the jurisdiction to hear appeals against decisions of the NCAs.[2]

1. Jurisdiction of national courts under Regulation 44/2001

2.02 Whether the ordinary courts of the Member States[3] are competent to deal with a case is determined according to national, EU, and international rules. Of particular relevance for determining the jurisdiction of national courts at the EU level is Council Regulation 44/2001, which unifies the rules on conflict of jurisdiction in civil and commercial matters and aims to simplify the formalities with a view to rapid and simple recognition and enforcement of judgments reached in other Member States.[4] According to Regulation 44/2001, a dispute involving a tort or contractual liability claim can be brought before the territorially competent court in the Member State where the defending party is domiciled.[5] In addition, contractual liability proceedings may be brought before the competent court for the 'place of performance' of the obligation in question and tort proceedings in the court for the place where the harmful event occurred (special jurisdiction).[6] The place where the harmful event occurred can be either where the event giving rise to the damage took place or where the damage itself occurred (*forum delicti*, at the choice of the claimant).[7] This could create problems where it

---

[2] Note that the Commission Notice on the cooperation between the Commission and the courts of the EU Member States in the application of Articles 81 [101 TFEU] and 82 EC [102 TFEU] ('National Courts Cooperation Notice') [2004] OJ C101/54, para 7 extends the competence to apply EU competition law to acts adopted by EU institutions in accordance with the TFEU or in accordance with the measures adopted to implement the EC Treaty, provided that these acts have direct effect, ie national courts may have to enforce Commission decisions or Commission regulations applying Art 101(3) TFEU. When applying these EU competition rules, national courts act within the framework of Community law and are bound to observe general EU law principles.

[3] In the discussion that followed the publication of the White Paper on the modernisation of the rules implementing Articles 81 EC [101 TFEU] and 82 EC [102 TFEU] [1999] OJ C132/1, it was suggested that the application of EU competition rules be entrusted to specialized courts. Initially, this had been the view of the European Parliament that considered it necessary to ensure consistency and legal certainty. The EU's Economic and Social Committee ('ECOSOC') was of the same opinion—in fact, it went even further, suggesting a system of appeals to supranational courts—as were other commentators from the industry and the legal profession. However, only three Member States supported this proposal.

[4] Council Reg (EC) 44/2001 of 22 December 2000 on jurisdiction and the recognition and enforcement of judgments in civil and commercial matters [2001] OJ L12/1. As regards the necessary nexus, this will be established if (i) the defendant is domiciled in a Regulation State; (ii) a court of a Member State has exclusive jurisdiction pursuant to Art 22 (which point is expanded on later); or (iii) where, in accordance with Art 23, the defendant is a party to an agreement that provides that the courts of a Member State are to have exclusive jurisdiction to settle any dispute which has arisen in connection with a particular legal relationship (usually with the aid of a choice of forum/jurisdiction clause). On 20 November 2012, the European Parliament adopted a 'recast' Regulation 44/2001. The new Regulation (EU) 1215/2012 on jurisdiction and the recognition and enforcement of judgments in civil and commercial matters (recast) [2012] OJ L351/1 will not be applied by Member State courts until 10 January 2015. Among other things, it aims to strengthen jurisdiction agreements by requiring Member State courts to stay proceedings where there is an exclusive jurisdiction agreement in favour of another Member State's court and that court has also been seized of proceedings, thereby defusing so-called 'torpedo' actions.

[5] Article 2 of Reg 44/2001. See also EC Commission, Green Paper—Damages actions for breach of the EC antitrust rules (SEC(2005) 1732)/(COM/2005/0672 final), 19 December 2005, at point 2.8

[6] Article 5(1) and (3) of Reg 44/2001. In Case 21/76 *Bier v Mines de Potasse d'Alsace* [1976] ECR 1735, the ECJ has construed this as meaning either the place of the event causing the loss or the place where the loss occurred. Later cases, however, restricted this wide interpretation by stating that Art 5(3) cannot mean any place where the adverse consequences of an event which has already caused actual loss elsewhere are felt.

[7] For example, in the *Vitamin* cartel, jurisdiction was established at the domicile of a victim of the cartel in Germany in relation to an antitrust damages action against a cartel member seated in Switzerland. Regional Court (*Landgericht*) Dortmund, Case 13 O 55/02, Judgment of 1 April 2004, IPRax 2005, p 542—*Vitamins* case. This decision concerned the corresponding provision in the Lugano Convention (Art 5(3)). See in this respect, T Schreiber, 'Private Antitrust Litigation in the European Union', Speech at the ABA section of the International Law Fall Meeting 2010, Paris, 3 November 2010, p 5, available at <http://www.carteldamage-claims.com>, or International Lawyer (2010) Winter, 44(4), 1157.

is difficult to pinpoint geographically where the intangible economic loss arose. Given that the cartels prosecuted by the Commission are typically international cartels with effects in various Member States, claimants will have a strong incentive to select the most convenient forum for the success of their claims, which in turn may lead to forum shopping, where they bring actions for damages against transnational cartels involving multinational defendants.[8] Claimants may prefer to bring their cases before common law jurisdictions with wide-reaching discovery rules which include the production of documents adverse to a party's own case.[9] Civil law countries do not always have any automatic disclosure requirements. This problem also encompasses the claim for damages as a result of a contractual dispute. If the dispute arises out of the operations of a branch, agency, or other establishments of the defendant, the defendant may be sued where it is situated.[10]

Further, Regulation 44/2001 also establishes a specific jurisdiction for collective litigation which is also suitable for antitrust damages actions against two or more infringers with their headquarters in different Member States. Pursuant to Article 6(1), several co-defendants can be sued at the domicile or seat of one co-defendant, provided that the   **2.03**

> claims are so closely connected that it is expedient to hear and determine them together to avoid the risk of irreconcilable judgments resulting from separate proceedings.

---

[8] See, eg the case before the UK courts, *Provimi Ltd v Roche Products Ltd and others* [2003] EWHC 961 (Comm), which interpreted Reg 44/2001 on jurisdiction and domestic English procedural rules in a way that greatly facilitated damages actions in European courts. In *Provimi*, the court allowed consolidation of EU actions in English courts, even where neither the claimant nor the defendant was English and where the contract contained a jurisdiction clause in favour of the German courts. The proceedings arose out of an investigation into the vitamins and pigment markets by the Commission, which found that two companies, Roche and Aventis, among others, had participated in the operation of cartels contrary to Art 101 TFEU in relation to the sale of vitamins in the EU (the *Vitamins Cartel* case). The *Provimi* case has allowed damages claims against Roche and Aventis to proceed to trial. The importance of the case is that it clears potential jurisdictional hurdles for damages claims against cartel members and shows how an English court can assert jurisdiction over claims between entities from other Member States in respect of products purchased at inflated cartel prices across Europe. However, there are limits on the jurisdiction of the English courts. In the *SanDisk* case (*SanDisk Corpn v Koninklijke Philips Electronics NV and others* [2007] EWHC 332 (Ch)), a US importer and seller of unlicensed MP3 players in the EU, SanDisk, brought proceedings in the High Court against a number of non-UK domiciled defendants, alleging that the terms of the defendants' licences, together with conduct such as alleged harassment through the enforcement of certain patents, amounted to an abuse of a dominant position in the market for the licensing of patents essential to the production, sale, and import of MP3 players and memory cards. The court, however, refused to accept jurisdiction in circumstances where none of the defendants was a UK company, none of the alleged acts of harassment or negotiations for licences had taken place in the UK, and no immediate damage had been caused to the claimant in the UK as a result of these alleged abuses. In those circumstances, the court considered that courts in other EU jurisdictions (where there had been border detentions as a result of legal and administrative actions) were better placed to hear the claim. L Farrell and S Ince, 'Private Enforcement in the UK' [2008] European Antitrust Review 226, 229.

[9] The UK is increasingly seen as an 'attractive place in which to litigate antitrust disputes'. Its appeal is explained by the broad approach of its national courts in affirming their own jurisdiction in cases with international elements, their well-established reputation, and speed. Similarly, Germany has established itself as a popular forum for damages claims due to recent changes in its law erasing previous obstacles to such claims and the cost-effectiveness of its legal system. L Farrell and S Ince, 'Private Enforcement in the UK' [2008] European Antitrust Review 226, 229; J Álvaro and T Reher, 'Towards the Directive on Private Enforcement of EC Competition Law: Is the Time Ripe?' [2008] European Antitrust Review 2008 44, 44. See also Mlex 'German court considers ECJ referral on CDC's bleach-chemical damage claim' 4 November 2011, where it was reported that a Dortmund court (Germany) was contemplating seeking guidance from the ECJ on whether it would be competent to review a private action brought by Cartel Damage Claims (CDCs) against members of a bleach cartel. The case raises questions over where damages actions are brought, and against whom. The defendants are said to have questioned whether companies not based in Germany could sue or be sued before the Dortmund court, and whether CDCs bringing claims acquired from individual plaintiffs is legal—particularly if some of them are based outside Germany. The action brings together thousands of individual claims from more than a dozen jurisdictions.

[10] Article 5(5) of Reg 44/2001 (special jurisdiction).

Such a factual and legal connection is typically established in cases concerning the enforcement of antitrust damages claims: (i) such claims result from the same anticompetitive conduct (eg price fixing or allocation of markets); and (ii) the infringers are jointly and severally liable for the overall damage caused by their illicit activities. This provision therefore designates alternative, equally competent courts that have jurisdiction for the place where the infringers have their seat.[11]

2. Applicable law under Regulation 864/2007

2.04 The competent court to hear and to adjudicate the case will, as a general rule, apply the procedural rules of the Member State in question (*lex fori*). In addition, it has to determine which substantive law will apply to claims for damages resulting from the violation of EU antitrust law. In this respect, Regulation (EC) No 864/2007 on the law applicable to non-contractual obligations ('Rome II Regulation') is relevant.[12] The Rome II Regulation, which entered into force on 11 January 2009, harmonized the private international law rules of the Member States concerning tortious liability. In this respect, Article 6(3) contains a special rule on the law applicable to non-contractual obligations arising out of antitrust infringements, covering violations of both European and national competition law. According to Article 6(3)(a) of the Rome II Regulation, the law applicable to claims resulting from the violation of competition law 'shall be the law of the country where the market is, or is likely to be, affected'. However, pursuant to Article 6(3)(b) of the Rome II Regulation:

> in cases where the market is, or is likely to be, affected in more than one country,...the claimant may instead choose to base his or her claim on the law of the court seized, provided that the market in that Member State is amongst those directly and significantly affected by the restriction of competition.

Therefore, should the claimant so choose, one the substantive law of one Member State will govern the claims for damages brought in different Member States.[13]

3. Issues of potential concern

2.05 While it has not led to substantial problems in practice so far, the recognition of foreign judgments and decisions of competition authorities in proceedings pending before a national court is still an area of potential conflict. Regulation 44/2001 provides that judgments given in a Member State must be recognized in all others 'without any special procedure being required', except, *inter alia*, 'if such recognition is manifestly contrary to the public policy in the Member State in which recognition is sought'.[14] Problems

---

[11] T Schreiber, 'Private Antitrust Litigation in the European Union', Speech at the ABA section of the International Law Fall Meeting 2010, Paris, 3 November 2010, 5.

[12] [2007] OJ L199/40.

[13] T Schreiber, Private Antitrust Litigation in the European Union, Speech at the ABA section of the International Law Fall Meeting 2010, Paris, 3 November 2010, 5, 6, notes that in relation to antitrust infringements that took place prior to the entry into force of Art 6(3) Rome II Regulation, there are good arguments that, in particular in cases where the main infringement (eg the first meeting of a cartel) took place in one Member State, the substantive law of that Member State is applicable to all damages claims, even if the economic effect (also) occurred in other Member States. In particular, the principle of effectiveness established by the EU Courts and mirrored in Art 6(3)b of the Rome II Regulation would imply the application of one coherent set of procedural and substantive rules to damages claims based on an infringement of EU antitrust law. However, as pointed out by S Poillot-Peruzzetto and D Lawnicka in J Basedow, S Francq and L Idot (eds), *International Antitrust Litigation: Conflict of Laws and Coordination* (Hart Publishing 2012) 135–6, it is not entirely clear whether all claims for compensation originating in breach of competition rules should be considered as tort claims irrespective of the source of restriction. In principle, actions for antitrust damages could also be based on Regulation (EC) No 593/2008 of the European Parliament and of the Council of 17 June 2008 on the law applicable to contractual obligations ('Rome I Regulation') [2009] OJ L 177/6.

[14] Articles 33 and 34 of Reg 44/2001. As regards enforcement, under the current rules, a judgment in one Member State does not automatically take effect in another. It first has to be validated and declared

may arise in regard to the notion of recognition. A judgment is *res judicata* between the parties to the dispute; the principle *non bis in idem* therefore prevents the same issues between the same parties being brought before another competent court. However, recognition of a foreign court's decision that clearly violates EU competition law may well be refused if it entails a manifest infringement of the *ordre public* of the Member State where such recognition is sought.[15] Determining whether the foreign judgment violates the *ordre public* might also require a thorough analysis of the case by the competent court, which could partly invalidate the automatic recognition mechanism under Regulation 44/2001.[16]

A second concern relates to the possible existence of networks of identical contracts between, for instance, a supplier (party A) and different dealers (parties B, C, D, and E).[17] From a legal point of view, each contract entails a separate relationship that may be subject to a separate legal review. From an economic point of view, however, competition is affected by the network of agreements as a whole. If a national court reaches the conclusion that one of the contracts, eg a contract between A and B, or even the entire network of contracts, is contrary to Article 101 or even Article 102 TFEU, and annuls it, it remains to be determined what the effects of that judgment will be on the same or similar disputes between A and C, D, or E, since they do not involve exactly the same parties. In the absence of any specific provision dealing with that issue in Regulation 1/2003, one may conclude that the outcome of the judgment between A and B may only qualify as an indisputable fact in the other proceedings. It could be considered as strong evidential value and may even result in a reversal of the burden of proof. Where the Commission is not seized of the matter, multiple and burdensome cases may thus be necessary to dismantle the anticompetitive network of agreements.[18] It is also conceivable that additional problems may arise where the same facts are not before the national courts involved. Markets evolve, and the effects of an agreement

2.06

---

enforceable in a special intermediate step by a court in the Member State of enforcement—the so-called '*exequatur*' procedure. In complex cases, this procedure may cost significant amounts in lawyers' fees, translation, and court costs. It could also take several months in some countries to have a judgment recognized and enforced. This procedure is a pure formality in almost 95 per cent of cases. The Commission has proposed to abolish it and to make judgments of a court in one Member State in civil and commercial matters automatically enforceable throughout the EU. The execution of the judgment could still be stopped by a court, but only under exceptional circumstances (such as a violation of a right to a fair trial by the court which passed the foreign judgment). See Commission Press Release IP/10/1705 'European Commission to cut red tape in cross-border court cases for businesses and consumers', 14 December 2010. See however the remarks in note 16 below regarding the abolition of *exequatur* under the recast Regulation 1215/2012.

[15] The EU Courts have repeatedly emphasized the public order nature of Arts [101] and [102 TFEU], see Joined Cases C-430/93 and C-431/93 *Jeroen van Schijndel and Johannes Nicolaas Cornelis van Veen v Stichting Pensioenfonds voor Fysiotherapeuten* [1995] ECRI-4705, para 21; Case C-126/97 *Eco Swiss China Time Ltd v Benetton International NV* [1999] ECR I-3055, para 39. This may, however, be different at the Member State and national competition law level.

[16] As indicated, the European Commission has published plans to streamline the enforcement of judgments across borders, with the abolition of the *exequatur* procedure for all cases other than libel and collective redress. There are also provisions to remove channels for abusive litigation in arbitration proceedings and 'torpedo' cases. See Commission Press Release IP/10/1705 'European Commission to cut red tape in cross-border court cases for businesses and consumers', 14 December 2010. The new 'recast' Regulation (EU) 1215/2012—which will substitute Regulation 44/2001 as of 10 January 2015—will make EU Member State judgments immediately enforceable across the EU without the need for an intermediate registration process in the enforcing state (ie abolishing the so-called 'exequatur' procedure); however, recognition or enforcement will be refused on various grounds, including, among other things, if recognition is manifestly contrary to public policy in the enforcing State.

[17] Example used by K Lenaerts and D Gerard, 'Decentralisation of EC Competition Law Enforcement: Judges in the Frontline' [2004] World Competition Law and Economics 313, 327.

[18] K Lenaerts and D Gerard, 'Decentralisation of EC Competition Law Enforcement: Judges in the Frontline' [2004] World Competition Law and Economics 313, 328.

may vary over time. A third issue has to do with the authority before a national court of an administrative decision given by a foreign competition authority; such a decision would not be covered by the recognition afforded under the terms of Regulation 44/2001, which only addresses the recognition of judgments. The jurisdiction of an NCA is limited to the territory of the Member State to which it belongs, and it would be difficult for the European Court of Justice ('ECJ') to extend Article 16(1) of Regulation 1/2003 by analogy to cover these NCA decisions.[19]

4. Actions before national courts

2.07 The Commission has continuously stressed that the application of Articles 101 and 102 TFEU by national courts has many advantages for individuals.[20] In the first place, national courts may award compensation for loss suffered as a result of a restrictive practice or agreement, a possibility not open to the Commission.[21] Secondly, national courts may adopt interim or protective measures more rapidly than the Commission. Thirdly, a national court may be seized simultaneously of actions under national law and actions under Community law; the same cannot be said of the Commission. Fourthly, national courts may award costs against the unsuccessful party, including lawyers' fees, a course of action not available in an administrative procedure. Besides, it would seem that national courts are the logical forum for commercial litigation and are in a better position than the Commission to resolve conflicts between private interests. The parties and their lawyers are also more familiar with the procedure to be followed before national courts and benefit from the fact that the latter are near at hand. Finally, administrative authorities—or at least the EU authorities—are not generally obliged to deal with specific cases or to handle every request made to them, being able to choose those which they consider most important.[22] National courts, on the other hand, are obliged to deal with all matters brought before them.[23]

2.08 With a view to fostering private enforcement of competition law rules, the Commission published a White Paper on damages actions for breach of the EC antitrust rules on 2 April 2008.[24] Together with its White Paper, the Commission published a detailed Staff Working Paper,[25] which provides the legal background, as well as a so-called 'Impact Assessment

---

[19] In the United States, in situations where the government obtains a civil or a criminal judgment against a defendant to the effect that he or she has violated the antitrust laws, it appears that the decision of an NCA could be treated as prima facie evidence of a violation of EU competition law in any other court proceedings between the defendant in the administrative procedure and third parties.

[20] For example, Commissioner and Vice-President of the Commission J Almunia 'Common standards for group claims across the EU', Speech at University of Valladolid, Valladolid Law Faculty, 15 October 2010; former Commissioner Neelie Kroes, Opening address at conference, 'Competition and Consumers in the 21st century', Brussels, 21 October 2009.

[21] Application of these Articles by the courts would have the additional advantage of encouraging compliance with EU law on the part of undertakings, which, finding themselves directly threatened by such actions by individuals, would be more careful not to infringe the EU competition rules.

[22] See Notice on handling of complaints [2004] C101/65, para 8. See Ch 12, 'Rejection of Complaints', para 12.07.

[23] In this context, it should be noted that in the United States, the real deterrent factor for companies in conducting their business is not so much public actions by competition authorities and the possible resulting fines, but rather the fear of private claims for damages, which can force undertakings to pay out huge amounts of money to settle the disputes.

[24] White Paper on damages actions for breach of the EC antitrust rules, COM (2008) 165 final. See also Rainer Becker, Nicolas Bessot, and Eddy De Smijter, DG COMP, 'The White Paper on damages actions for breach of the EC antitrust rules' (2008) 2 Competition Policy Newsletter 4; Andre Bouquet, 'The Judicial Application of European Competition Law', Proceedings of the FIDE XXIV, Congress Madrid 2010, Vol 2, Institutional Report, 17, 38–44, with an overview of the key developments at EU level.

[25] Commission Staff Working Paper accompanying the White Paper on damages actions for breach of the EC antitrust rules, SEC (2008) 404, 2 April 2008.

Report',[26] which contains an economic analysis of different potential private enforcement scenarios. In addition, an extensive economic study on the welfare impact of more effective private damages actions and an economic assessment of the quantification of antitrust damages were published on the Commission's website. The Commission's activity suggests that the approach to actions for damages resulting from infringements of EU antitrust law is currently changing to the benefit of victims of such infringements.[27] In addition to activity at the European level, national legislators have made important legislative changes at the national level in order to facilitate the private enforcement of antitrust damages claims.[28] Yet mixed messages over the fate of EU plans for promoting collective redress have given a foretaste of some of the battles ahead if legislation for private damages is ultimately adopted.[29] In June 2013, the Commission adopted a proposal for a Directive on how citizens and companies can claim damages when they are victims of infringements of the EU antitrust rules, such as cartels and abuses of a dominant market position. The goal of this legislation will be to standardize national procedural rules covering aspects such as access to evidence, the protection of submissions of leniency applicants, the legal force of NCA decisions, and potentially how claimants can group together to bring collective actions.[30]

Articles 101 and 102 TFEU may arise in a variety of contexts before national courts. **2.09**
National courts may be called upon to apply such rules in administrative, civil, or criminal

---

[26] Commission Staff Working Document accompanying document to the White Paper on damages actions for breach of the EC antitrust rules, Impact Assessment, SEC (2008) 405, 2 April 2008.

[27] In 2011, the Commission began a consultation on whether any EU measures are needed to facilitate consumers who group together to bring lawsuits against companies. Its careful wording suggests that, while there is an acknowledged problem regarding the lack of successful claims, all policy options are on the table, and legislation is far from assured. Commission Press Release IP/11/132 'Commission seeks opinions on the future for collective actions in Europe' of 4 February 2011. See also Commission Staff Working Document, Towards a Coherent European Approach to Collective Redress, SEC (2011)173 final. See also Mlex 'EC Statement: EC recommends collective redress mechanism to ensure effective access to justice' 11 June 2013 where the Commission has set out a series of common, non-binding principles for collective redress mechanisms in the Member States so that citizens and companies can enforce the rights granted to them under EU law where these have been infringed. The Recommendation aims to ensure a coherent horizontal approach to collective redress in the European Union without harmonizing Member States' systems. IP/13/525 'Commission Press Release Antitrust: Commission proposes legislation to facilitate damage claims by victims of antitrust violations', 11 June 2013; Commission MEMO/13/531 'Frequently Asked Questions: Commission proposes legislation to facilitate damage claims by victims of antitrust violations', 11 June 2013; the documents of the 'Legislative Initiative on Antitrust Damages', including the Proposal for a Directive of the European Parliament and of the Council on certain rules governing actions for damages under national law for infringements of the competition law provisions of the Member States and of the European Union are available at <http://ec.europa.eu/competition/antitrust/actionsdamages/documents.html>.

[28] For example, in Germany, the Seventh amendment to the German Act against Restraints of Competition ('ARC') entered into force on 1 July 2005. An English version of the ARC is available at the website of the Federal Cartel Office at <http://www.bundeskartellamt.de/wEnglisch/index.php>. See also overview in S Martinez-Lage and R Allendesalazar, 'The Judicial Application of European Competition Law', Proceedings of the FIDE XXIV, Congress Madrid 2010, Vol 2, General Report, 1, (14–16) and the EC Member State Reports.

[29] See interested parties' replies to the Consultation on collective redress, available at <http://ec.europa.eu/competition/consultations/2011_collective_redress/index_en.html>.

[30] Mlex, Proposal for a Directive of the European Parliament and of the Council on certain rules governing actions for damages under national law for infringements of the competition law provisions of the Member States and of the EU, COM(2013) 404, 11 June 2013. According to the Proposal, national courts will have the power to order companies to disclose evidence when victims claim compensation; decisions of NCAs finding an infringement will automatically constitute proof before national courts of all Member States that the infringement occurred; rules on limitation periods, ie the period of time within which victims can bring an action for damages, will be clarified; the liability rules in cases where price increases due to an infringement are 'passed on' along the distribution or supply chain will be clarified, and rules to facilitate consensual settlements will be put in place so as to allow a faster and less costly resolution of disputes.

proceedings.[31] While the National Courts Cooperation Notice makes reference to Article 6 of Regulation 1/2003 as the principal source of the ability of the national courts to apply Articles 101 and 102 TFEU in those disputes, this power already flows from the direct effect of these rules.[32] Thus, the role of the national courts in relation to EU competition rules was somehow defined by the Treaty itself. Article 101(2) TFEU provides that any agreement which infringes Article 101(1) TFEU is automatically void. Given that it falls to national courts to enforce lawful agreements, the nullity—and, therefore, the inapplicability—of agreements is a matter primarily for the national courts, which are under an obligation to apply that sanction.[33] Consequently, the parties to a restrictive agreement which is caught by Article 101(1) TFEU cannot ask the court to ensure that the agreement is performed. Since that provision is concerned with a matter of public policy, national courts are under an obligation to declare of their own motion that restrictive agreements are void if they find them to be in breach of Article 101(1) TFEU.[34] Thus, it is not only that national courts with jurisdiction are entitled to apply Articles 101 and 102 TFEU, since in particular circumstances they can apply such rules of their own motion and even be obliged to do so. Under the terms of the ECJ ruling in *Van Schijndel*,[35] national courts are obliged to apply of their own motion binding EU rules where under national law they are obliged to apply of their own motion binding national rules. In the same vein, where national courts have discretion to apply binding national rules, the same discretion must exist in relation to the application of binding EU law. However, national courts are not required to apply such rules of their own motion when that would oblige them to depart from the situation of judicial passivity imposed on them by national law, by going beyond the dispute as defined by the parties and relying on facts or circumstances not raised by the parties.[36] Conversely, the parties to a restrictive agreement may contend that it is void if they wish to escape a mandatory injunction to perform a contractual obligation or an award against them for damages in an action for breach of the agreement in question.[37]

See also Communication from the Commission on quantifying harm in actions for damages based on breaches of Article 101 or 102 TFEU [2013] OJ C167/19 and Commission Staff Working Document— Practical Guide on Quantifying Harm, also available at <http://ec.europa.eu/competition/antitrust/actions-damages/documents.html>.

[31] Regulation 1/2003 does not apply to national laws which impose criminal sanctions on natural persons, except to the extent that such sanctions are the means of enforcing the competition rules that apply to undertakings; however, it gives no indication of the circumstances where Regulation 1/2003 would indeed apply to criminal proceedings. See Recital 8 of Reg 1/2003, last sentence.

[32] National Courts Cooperation Notice [2004] OJ C101/54, para 3 note 5. See Case 127/73 *BRT v Sabam* [1974] ECR 51, paras 15 and 16.

[33] In Case T-24/90 *Automec v Commission* [1992] ECR II-2223, para 93, the Court of First Instance ('CFI') [now the GC] stated that 'the Treaty presupposes that national law gives the national courts the power to safeguard the rights of undertakings which have been subjected to anti-competitive practices'.

[34] The Commission can decide not to proceed with a complaint on the grounds that there is a lack of sufficient EU interest. See Ch 12, 'Rejection of Complaints', para 12.15 et seq.

[35] Joined Cases C-430/93 and C-431/93 *Van Schijndel/Stichting Pensioenfonds voor Fysiotherapeuten* [1995] ECR I-4705, paras 20–2.

[36] In *Peterbroeck*, however, the ECJ held that there was an obligation to raise an issue of Community law of its own motion where the effect of the national procedure would be to preclude any national court from considering an issue of Community law. Case C-312/93 *Peterbroeck v Belgian State* [1995] ECR I-4599, para 21. See C Bellamy and G Child, *European Community Law of Competition* (6th edn, Oxford University Press 2008), para 14.058, note 165, referring to the Opinion of AG Jacobs who suggested in *Schijndel* that where an agreement was manifestly illegal under Art 81(1) EC [101 TFEU], the national court could and should raise the point of its own motion, since it would do the same under domestic law.

[37] Thus, for example, distributors who fail to comply with an exclusive dealing clause or licensees of a patent subject to territorial restrictions who do not wish to pay royalties for using the patented invention could plead—and have done so in similar cases—a breach of Art 101(1) TFEU in order to escape their contractual obligations.

The task of national courts, however, goes much further than merely applying the penalty **2.10** of nullity.[38] Even in its earliest case law, the ECJ made it clear that, since the prohibitions laid down by Articles 101(1) and 102 TFEU are inherently capable of producing direct effects between individuals, these provisions create rights in favour of the persons concerned which the national courts must uphold.[39] This means that, in addition to the penalty of nullity, which derives directly from the TFEU, the national courts are obliged to provide adequate legal remedies or rights of action to enable individuals and undertakings to take action against restrictive or abusive practices. Such remedies may take many forms: striking out certain clauses of agreements as void, or indeed the agreement as a whole if the clauses in question are not severable; injunctions or orders to take or refrain from particular action; the award of compensation for loss and damage suffered through infringements of Articles 101 and 102 TFEU; or the recovery of sums unduly paid. If necessary, such remedies may be accompanied by protective or interim measures. Undertakings and individuals are therefore entitled to use Articles 101 and 102 TFEU both as a 'shield' and as a 'sword'.[40]

The means employed to ensure that individuals have at their disposal adequate ways of **2.11** enforcing their rights under EU law vary from one Member State to another. It is a matter for national law, following any guidelines laid down by EU law, to say how EU law is to be applied. The relevant principle is that the exercise of all rights of action under EU law must be available in order to ensure the fulfilment of EU provisions having direct effect, under the same conditions as those which apply to ensure compliance with national law.[41] However, this may not be sufficient. The ECJ has held that if the national law of a Member State lacks adequate legal remedies to deal with an infringement of national law and such remedies are necessary to enable an individual to enforce EU provisions, the national legislature is obliged to create *ex novo* the requisite remedies for the exercise of such rights of action. Consequently, if it were not possible to prescribe protective or interim measures or if no action for damages were available on such grounds, the national legislature would have to create the remedies needed to safeguard the individual rights and claims of private persons under EU law.[42]

---

[38] E Gippini-Fournier, 'The Modernisation of European Competition Law: First Experiences with Regulation 1/2003—Institutional Report' in HF Koeck and MM Karollus (eds), The Modernisation of European Competition Law—Initial Experiences with Regulation 1/2003, FIDE XXIII Congress Linz 2008—Congress Publications Vol 2 (Nomos 2008) , 375, 476, cautions against invoking the frequency of litigated areas where Art 101(2) is invoked as a yardstick against which to measure the vitality or good health of the private enforcement system. Truly serious infringements of Art 101 would never give rise to attempts at enforcement through contractual litigation because their nullity would be a known fact.

[39] Case 127/73 *BRT v Sabam II* [1974] ECR 313, para 16. It is precisely 'because Art [101(1)] and Art [106] of the Treaty is directly applicable, [that] the Commission and the national court have in fact concurrent jurisdiction to apply' those provisions: Case T-24/90 *Automec v EC Commission II* [1992] ECR II-2223, para 60, citing *BRT* and *Lauder* (judgment in Case 37/79 *Marty v Estée Lauder* [1980] ECR 2481).

[40] The terms are repeatedly used in the literature: L Ritter and WD Braun, *European Competition Law: A Practitioner's Guide* (3rd edn, Kluwer Law 2004) 1170; see also E Gippini-Fournier, 'The Modernisation of European Competition Law: First Experiences with Regulation 1/2003—Institutional Report' in HF Koeck and MM Karollus (eds), The Modernisation of European Competition Law—Initial Experiences with Regulation 1/2003, FIDE XXIII Congress Linz 2008—Congress Publications Vol 2 (Nomos 2008) 375, 475.

[41] See, among others, Case 158/80 *REWE v Hauptzollamt Kiel* [1981] ECR 1805 and Case 199/82 *San Giorgio* [1983] ECR 3595, para 12. Similarly in Case 106/77 *Simmenthal (II)* [1978] ECR 629, the Court held that when giving effect to Community rights in national courts, the latter must, if necessary, refuse to apply any conflicting provision of national law. The implementation of rights through the conduit of national remedies cannot render the exercise of such rights overly difficult.

[42] See Case 158/80 *REWE v Hauptzollamt Kiel* [1981] ECR 1805, para 44, where the Court stated that while 'the Treaty has made it possible in a number of instances for private persons to bring a direct action, where appropriate, before the ECJ, it was not intended to create new remedies in the national courts to ensure the observance of Community law other than those already laid down by national law. On the other hand the system of legal protection established by the Treaty, as set out in Art 177 [267 TFEU] in particular, implies that it must be possible for every type of action provided for by national law to be available for the purpose

2.12 The case law of the EU Courts has also emphasized the importance of the enforcement of EU competition law by private parties. In *Courage v Crehan*, the ECJ held that damages can be claimed before national courts for breaches of Article 101 TFEU, and parties to agreements violating Article 101 TFEU cannot be barred from claiming damages against co-contractors before national courts.[43] The ECJ reaffirmed that it is for national law to provide procedural rules, including remedies, for breaches of EU law as long as the remedy must not be less favourable than that available for domestic claims and it must not render ineffective the right under EU law. National rules may prevent unjust enrichment to litigants and may consequently prevent a party from benefiting from its own unlawful conduct by refusing to award it damages. Yet damages may only be refused with respect to parties who bear 'significant responsibility' for the distortion of competition caused by the agreement.[44] The ruling reflects the view that damages actions before the national courts are considered to make a significant contribution to the maintenance of effective competition in the EU.[45]

2.13 In its judgment in the *Manfredi* case,[46] the ECJ again took the opportunity to confirm these principles, already generally established in earlier case law, to safeguard the rights of civil parties claiming damages caused as a result of infringements of EU competition law.[47] The ECJ also confirmed that, once an infringement of Article 101 TFEU has been committed, any individual should be able to rely on the invalidity of an agreement or practice prohibited under that Article.[48] The ECJ also stated that a finding of an infringement of the national competition rules did not exclude an action for breach of the EU rules. Where there is a causal relationship between the infringement and any harm suffered, an individual should be able to claim compensation for the damages caused. EU law does not, however, involve

of ensuring observance of Community provisions having direct effect, on the same conditions concerning the admissibility and procedure as would apply were it a question of ensuring observance of national law.'

[43] Case C-453/99 *Courage v Crehan* [2001] ECR I-6297, para 11, the ECJ overturned the principle of English law that a party to an illegal act may not benefit from its own wrongdoing and therefore may not recover damages from other parties to an illegal agreement. Note that the overwhelming majority of judgments received by the Commission under Art 15(2) of Reg 1/2003 and posted on the DG COMP website resulted from private enforcement actions, in most cases aimed at the annulment of an agreement on the ground of its incompatibility with the EU competition rules. The non-confidential versions of these judgments are listed in this database, in their original language, classified according to the Member State of origin. For each Member State, the judgments are listed in chronological order. See <http://ec.europa.eu/competition/court/overview_en.html>.

[44] Case C-453/99 *Courage v Crehan* [2001] ECR I-6297, para 32 et seq, where the ECJ identified two main factors to be taken into account: (i) the economic and legal context; and (ii) the respective bargaining power of the parties, in particular where the party seeking damages was in a 'markedly weaker position' than the other party so as to seriously call into question that party's freedom to negotiate the terms of the contract and capacity to avoid or reduce the losses suffered.

[45] WP Wils, 'The Relationship between Public Antitrust Enforcement and Private Actions for Damages' (2009) 32(1) World Competition 3.

[46] Joined Cases C-295/04 to C-298/04 *Manfredi* [2006] ECR I-6619. The case follows on from a finding of the Italian competition authority that an agreement between automotive insurers infringed the competition rules. As a result of an unlawful exchange of information, the premiums charged to consumers were inflated by an average of 20 per cent. Mr Manfredi and the other applicants, who alleged that they had been overcharged, brought actions against their respective insurers to recover damages. See E Gippini-Fournier, 'The Modernisation of European Competition Law: First Experiences with Regulation 1/2003—Institutional Report' in HF Koeck and MM Karollus (eds), The Modernisation of European Competition Law—Initial Experiences with Regulation 1/2003, FIDE XXIII Congress Linz 2008—Congress Publications Vol 2 (Nomos 2008) 375, 477.

[47] See also Eddy De Smijter and D O'Sullivan, 'The Manfredi Judgment of the ECJ and How it Relates to the Commission's Initiative on EC Antitrust Damages Actions' (2006) 3 (Autumn) Competition Policy Newsletter 23.

[48] Joined Cases C-295/04 to C-298/04 *Manfredi* [2006] ECR I-6619, paras 58 and 59.

itself with the precise manner in which this right to claim damages for EU competition law infringements is exercised. It is, therefore, a matter for national law to provide the procedural safeguards for the exercise of that right.[49] This includes guidance on the concept of 'causal relationship', a principle that may vary slightly, according to national legal systems.

Although it would not be a matter for EU law to specify which courts or tribunals have **2.14** jurisdiction to hear actions for damages based on an infringement of EU competition law or to interfere with the detailed procedural rules governing those actions, the provisions that apply should be no less favourable than those that govern claims for damages based on an infringement of national competition rules. Furthermore, in order for those procedural rules not to infringe EU law, they should be framed in such a way that they do not render the exercise of the right to seek compensation for damages resulting from a practice prohibited under Article 101 and 102 TFEU either practically impossible or excessively difficult. This also applies to the limitation period for claims. Thus, if a limitation period is short and not capable of suspension, it could be contrary to EU law if, in practice, it renders the exercise of the right to seek compensation for damages practically impossible or excessively difficult.

Proceedings before national courts may be as slow, complicated, and expensive (even where **2.15** the unsuccessful party is ordered to pay the successful party's costs) as those before the Commission. Furthermore, many national courts may experience difficulties in carrying out extremely complicated economic evaluations. Since proceedings before national courts are adversarial, the parties must produce evidence to support their claims. They cannot rely on evidence being obtained by the courts, as would be the case in inquisitorial proceedings. Additionally, NCAs arguably place great emphasis on protecting leniency programmes for cartel whistle-blowers, to the detriment of other possible effective mechanisms for deterring anticompetitive behaviour. Often, regulators find themselves torn between ensuring that there is a sufficient incentive for companies to disclose illegal behaviour, and providing potential victims with information confided to them to enable such victims to claim compensation. These considerations continue to carry considerable weight and may prompt parties to turn to administrative authorities rather than to courts, at either the EU or national level.[50]

It should be noted that national courts act in their capacity as ordinary jurisdictional bodies, ie not as competition authorities. Thus, they are not part of the European Competition **2.16** Network ('ECN') and are not bound to give up a case because the Commission has started proceedings at the same time. Such a situation could conflict with the necessary independence of the judiciary, and with the different tasks assigned to courts and public authorities in charge of competition enforcement. Accordingly, parallel procedures are thus possible between national courts and competition authorities, even if they are not desired or desirable. A breach of Articles 101 or 102 TFEU may be pleaded and the national court may apply the prohibition contained in Article 101 before or at the same time as the Commission or an NCA, as the case may be, is carrying out its own investigation.

---

[49] By confirming that such actions are subject to national procedural rules, which vary considerably between EU Member States, this also increases the likelihood that forum shopping may play an important role in private EC antitrust litigation in the future.

[50] White Paper on damages actions for breach of the EC antitrust rules COM(2008) 165 final, 2 April 2008, points 1.1 and 1.2.; Commission Staff Working Paper accompanying the White Paper on Damages actions for breach of the EC antitrust rules, SEC(2008) 404, 4 April 2008, Chapter 1, in particular point 2. See, however, the Commission's proposal for a Directive on antitrust damages actions for breaches of EU competition law, presented on 11 June 2013, which is aimed to facilitate private enforcement (note 27 above).

B. The Application of Articles 101 and 102 by National Courts

1. General principles

2.17 Consistent enforcement of EU competition rules throughout the Union does not only mean the uniform application of such rules in substantive terms but also an equally effective application independently of the national court which is called on to apply them. In this respect, different national procedures may indeed result in *de facto* different enforcement of EU competition rules, eg due to different rules on the standard of proof,[51] investigative powers, criminal versus civil enforcement, access to the file, interim measures, etc.[52] The main obstacles have been described and analysed in the Green Paper and the 2005 Staff Working Paper: the rules on access to evidence; the fault requirement; the definition of damages; the availability of the passing-on defence; the question of the legal standing of indirect purchasers; collective redress mechanisms; the costs of actions; the issues regarding limitation periods and applicable law. Furthermore, the two limbs of coherent application—uniformity and effectiveness—are interrelated. In fact, a system of procedural autonomy between different jurisdictions may well jeopardize uniform application, eg where a national court is unable to make a specific finding—eg the existence of a cartel due to the lack of the necessary investigative powers—while another national court (or the Commission) enjoying different procedural powers might indeed be able to make such a finding in the same case.

2.18 While Member States are mainly free to choose their procedural conditions for the enforcement of EU competition rules, national courts need to take note of certain EU rules that determine the relationship between the Commission and the national courts. Procedural autonomy is also circumscribed by general principles of EU law, including, *inter alia*, the following:

(a) the requirement that national law provide effective, proportionate, and dissuasive sanctions for breaches of EU law;

(b) the availability, under certain circumstances, of damages for breaches of EU law;

(c) the principles of effectiveness and equivalence which require, respectively, that national procedural rules should not make excessively difficult or practically impossible the enforcement of EU law (effectiveness) nor should they be less favourable than the rules applicable to the enforcement of equivalent national law (equivalence).[53]

---

[51] While Art 2 of Reg 1/2003 harmonizes rules on the burden of proof, Recital 5 makes clear that the Regulation does not affect national rules on standard of proof or the obligations of the national court to ascertain the relevant facts of the case, subject to compliance with the general principles of Community law. See for the UK: Case Number 1021/1/2003 *Allsports Limited /OFT*, registered 1 October 2003; Case Number 1022/1/1/03 *JJB Sports PLC v Office of Fair Trading*, registered 1 October 2003, available at <http://www.catribunal.org.uk>.

[52] The relevant differences refer broadly to national procedures which would apply to litigation based on Arts 101 and 102. These may include not only differences in procedural rules *stricto sensu* (ie rules on investigative powers) but also differences in substantive rules which are nevertheless capable of affecting the application of Arts 101 and 102 in national proceedings (eg rules on fault as a condition of liability, causation, etc). See eg Commission Staff Working Paper accompanying the White Paper on damages actions for breach of the EC antitrust rules, SEC(2008) 404, 4 April 2008, para 5: 'the traditional tort rules of the Member States, either of a legal or procedural nature, are often inadequate for actions for damages in the field of competition law, due to the specificities of actions in this field. In addition, the different approaches taken by the Member States ... can lead to differences in treatment and to less foreseeability for the victims as well as the defendants, i.e. to a high degree of legal uncertainty.'

[53] The clearest recent statement of these principles may be found in Joined Cases C-279/96, C-280/96, and C-281/96 *Ansaldo Energia and others/Amministrazione delle Finanze dello Stato and others* [1998] ECR I-5025, para 27, where the Court stated that: 'in the absence of Community legislation governing a matter,

The National Courts Cooperation Notice seems to rate effectiveness higher than equivalence, **2.19**
which is consistent with the case law of the EU courts Indeed, the ECJ has established that
effectiveness prevails over equivalence, ie even if national procedural rules ensure equal treatment of a claim based on EU law and a similar national cause of action, that might not be
enough if it does not ensure the effective application of EU law.[54] The ECJ established these
two principles as general limits on national procedural autonomy, but it has also increasingly
imposed specific restraints on national courts' autonomy, including the requirement that
national law provide for specific remedies, such as damages or effective sanctions.[55]

2. Application of EU and national competition rules by national courts

To avoid the risk of inconsistency in the parallel application of national and EU competition **2.20**
rules, Regulation 1/2003 states that where the national courts apply national competition
law to agreements, decisions by associations of undertakings, or concerted practices within
the meaning of Article 101(1) TFEU which may affect trade between Member States within
the meaning of that provision, they shall also apply Article 101 TFEU to such agreements,
decisions, or concerted practices. Where the competition authorities of the Member States
or national courts apply national competition law to any abuse prohibited by Article 102
TFEU, they shall also apply Article 102 TFEU.[56] Whilst Article 3(1) of Regulation 1/2003
requires the application of Articles 101 and 102 TFEU to cases capable of affecting trade
between Member States,[57] it does not impose an obligation to apply national law at the same
time to such cases. The parallel application of national rules is thus optional and depends on

---

it is for the domestic legal system of each Member State to designate the national courts and tribunals having
jurisdiction and to lay down the detailed procedural rules governing actions for safeguarding rights which
individuals derive from Community law. However, such rules must not be less favourable than those governing similar domestic actions (principle of equivalence) and they must not render virtually impossible or
excessively difficult the exercise of rights conferred by Community law (principle of effectiveness).' National
Courts Cooperation Notice [2004] OJ 101/54. See also Commission Working Paper accompanying the
White Paper on damages actions for breach of the EC antitrust rules, SEC(2008) 404, 4 April 2008, para
77 et seq.

[54] See, eg Case C-199/82 *Amministrazione delle Finanze dello Stato v SpA San Giorgio* [1983] ECR I-3595,
para 17. In the field of competition law, the ECJ ruling in C-126/97 *Eco Swiss* [1999] ECR I-3055 might be
read as an application of this rule of effectiveness taking precedence over equivalence, although the ECJ actually based its ruling on the very nature and purpose of Art [101 TFEU] as a 'fundamental provision which is
essential for the accomplishment of the tasks entrusted to the Community and, in particular, for the functioning of the internal market'. On the other hand, another interpretation of the Court's ruling in *Eco Swiss* might
be that the proper way to establish whether Dutch law was in fact ensuring equal treatment to claims based
on Art [101 TFEU] was not the corresponding provision of Dutch competition law. Instead, the comparison
should be between Dutch public policy provisions on the one hand and Community public policy provisions
on the other hand, the latter including Art [101 TFEU].
[55] In Case C-453/99 *Courage v Crehan* [2001] ECR I-6297, paras 26–7. As regards sanctions, see, for
instance, in the field of employment, Case C-271/91 *M Helen Marshall v Southampton and South-West
Hampshire Area Health Authority* [1993] ECR I-4367, paras 36–7.
[56] Article 3 of the earlier draft Reg 1/2003 provided for the exclusive application of EC competition law
where applicable. 'Relationship between Arts [101] and [102] and national competition laws. Where an agreement, a decision by an association of undertakings or a concerted practice within the meaning of Art [101]
of the Treaty or the abuse of a dominant position within the meaning of Art [102] may affect trade between
Member States, Community competition law shall apply to the exclusion of national competition laws.'
[57] See Commission Staff Working Paper accompanying the Communication from the Commission to
the European Parliament and Council, Report on the functioning of Regulation 1/2003 (COM(2009) 206
final), para 145 noting that in a cartel case covering the territory of Austria, the GC confirmed the case law
according to which horizontal cartels covering the whole of a Member State are normally capable of affecting trade between Member States, even where the members of the cartel had not taken specific measures
to exclude foreign competitors from the market. See Joined Cases T-259/02 to T-264/02 and T-271/02
Raiffeisen Zentralbank Österreich AG and others [2006] ECR II-5169, confirmed in Joined Cases C-125/07 P,
C-133/07 P, C-135/07 P, and C-137/07 P *Erste Group Bank a.O. v Commission* [2009] ECR I-8681,
paras 36–48.

the respective national system. Certain Member States, such as Italy and Luxembourg, have indeed opted for the exclusive application of EC competition law to cases falling within its scope. Most Member States have, however, chosen the possibility of relying on a double legal base, and parallel application of the EC and national rules has become a well-established practice.[58]

2.21 Regulation 1/2003 requires that parallel application of national law should not lead to a different outcome than that which would result from the application of Article 101 TFEU. Under Article 3(2) of Regulation 1/2003, agreements which are permitted under Article 101 TFEU cannot be prohibited under national law,[59] nor can agreements which are prohibited under Article 101 TFEU be permitted under national law.[60] In particular, this convergence obligation applies in respect of:

> agreements, decisions by associations of undertakings or concerted practices within the meaning of Article 101(1) TFEU which may affect trade between Member States within the meaning of that provision.

Thus, national courts will have to determine whether the agreement in question is capable of affecting trade between Member States.[61] They also have to establish whether the agreement in question is an 'agreement...within the meaning of Article [101(1) TFEU]'. Such requirement will have to be construed as not only referring exclusively to the need to establish whether the conduct in question constitutes an agreement, as opposed, for instance, to

---

[58] See Commission Staff Working Paper accompanying the Communication from the Commission to the European Parliament and Council Report on the functioning of Regulation 1/2003 [COM(2009)206 final], whose para 148 notes that cases in which NCAs applied the EU competition rules amounted to a significant share of their overall antitrust caseload. Roughly one-half of the enforcement decisions adopted by the Italian competition authority during the reporting period were based on EU law. The French competition authority applied EU competition law in nearly 40 per cent of the cases, while the figure for the Belgian, Danish, and Dutch authorities was around 30 per cent of all cases dealt with in the antitrust field. In Portugal and Greece this ratio was approximately 25 per cent, whereas Hungary and Slovenia were close to 20 per cent.

[59] Article 3(2) of Reg 1/2003. It would appear that national law may also not be applied where the agreement serves some other legitimate purpose. In its preliminary ruling in Case C-309/99 *Wouters* [2002] ECR I-1577, the ECJ ruled that although a regulation concerning partnerships between members of the Bar and members of other liberal professions may fall within the scope of Art 101 TFEU, it may not amount to an infringement of the prohibition on anticompetitive agreements because despite their inherently anticompetitive nature, the Bar rules may be considered as necessary for the proper practice of the legal profession, as organized in the Member State concerned.

[60] Case 14/68 *Walt Wilhelm* [1969] ECR 1. In this case, the Berliner Kammergericht sought guidance under Art [267 TFEU] on how far the German authorities could continue with national cartel proceedings when the same case was being investigated by the Commission. See the question of whether whether a national competition authority can prosecute below the *de minimis* threshold, Case C-226/11 *Expedia Inc v Autorité de la concurrence and Others* [2013] OJ C38/6.

[61] See Commission Notice—Guidelines on the effect on trade concept contained in Articles 81[101] and 82[102] of the Treaty [2004] OJ C101/81, para 6 and what follows. Commission Staff Working Paper accompanying the Communication from the Commission to the European Parliament and Council Report on the functioning of Regulation 1/2003 (COM(2009)206 final), para 150, stating that some Member States' national courts have in certain cases construed the criterion of effect on trade more narrowly than the national competition authority. In Germany, for instance, the Higher Regional Court of Düsseldorf rejected the NCA's analysis in two decisions due to the lack of sufficient evidence of foreclosure and any appreciable effect on trade (Judgments in Cases VI-Kart, 14/06(V) and VI-2 Kart 12/04 (V)). In Italy, where national rules are not applied in parallel with Arts 101 and 102 TFEU, the Italian Supreme Administrative Court overturned a decision of the competition authority criticizing, *inter alia*, the lack of rigorous and concrete examination of the condition of effect on trade (Italian Supreme Administrative Court, 2 October 2007, judgment no 5085/07). The French Court of Cassation, in turn, concluded in *Bausch and Lomb v Medint*, that the Court of Appeal's decision was not well founded, as it had failed to establish whether the agreement concerning exclusive dealing between Chauvin and BL was liable to affect trade appreciably between Member States (Cours de Cassation, 12 December 2006, *Bausch and Lomb v Medint*).

unilateral conduct,[62] or whether it is an agreement between 'undertakings'. It also requires national courts to establish whether the agreement in question comes within the scope of Article 101(1) TFEU because it appreciably restricts competition.[63] Should the national court find that the agreement in question does not appreciably restrict competition, it would not have to apply Article 101 TFEU. Thus, the obligation to apply Article 101 TFEU in parallel with national competition law would not extend to agreements that, while affecting cross-border trade, do not have an appreciable effect on competition.[64] In its five-year review in 2009, the Commission reported that it would appear that there is generally a high degree of awareness on the part of national competition authorities and courts of the obligation to apply Articles 101 and 102 TFEU. After 1 May 2004, national competition authorities switched en masse to applying the EU competition rules in cases where trade may be affected.[65]

In regard to Article 102 TFEU, the Commission takes the view that Article 3(2) of Regulation **2.22** 1/2003 does not require a similar convergence between national and EU law with respect to unilateral conduct. Unilateral behaviour capable of affecting trade between Member States can thus be prohibited by national law, even if it occurs below the level of dominance or is not considered abusive within the meaning of Article 102. The last sentence of Article 3(2) thus contains an exception to the idea of the level playing field and implies that undertakings doing cross-border business in the internal market may be subjected to a variety of standards as to their unilateral behaviour.[66] However, it adds that the principle of the primacy of EU law requires national courts to disapply those provisions of national law that contravene EU rules.[67] In this context, it is important to note that when a national court is unsure about whether or not national legislation is incompatible with EU law, it can refer the matter to

---

[62] See T-208/01 *Volkswagen AG v EC Commission* [2003] ECR II-5141 and Joined Cases C-2/01 P and C-3/01 P *Bundesverband der Arzneimittel-Importeure eVand EC Commission v Bayer AG* [2004] ECR I-23.

[63] This conclusion is supported by a systematic interpretation of the first and second sentences of Art 3(1), which refer to the parallel application of Arts 101 and 102 TFEU, respectively. In particular, the last sentence of Art 3(1), dealing with Art 102, requires national courts to apply EU competition law in parallel with national competition law to 'any abuse prohibited by Art 102'. Thus, if national courts are required to establish whether the conduct in question is 'prohibited' in Art 102 cases in order to establish whether they should apply this Article in parallel with their national competition law, it seems that a similar requirement would apply in Art 101 cases, ie national courts would not only have to establish that the agreement in question is an 'agreement' for the purposes of Art 101, but also that Art 101 applies to that specific agreement, because it appreciably restricts competition.

[64] See on this point C Fellenius-Omnell, C Landström, and J Coyet, 'Modernizing EC Competition Law—Will a System of Parallel Application of EC and National Competition Laws Ensure Convergence?' in BE Hawk (ed), *International Antitrust Law & Policy* (Fordham Corporate Law Institute 2002) ch 7, 111. The authors suggest that Art 3(1) might not apply to agreements which are *de minimis* under the Commission De Minimis Notice ([2001] OJ C368/13), although Art 3(2) of Reg 1/2003 would still apply, thus preventing national courts from prohibiting under national law agreements which can be considered as *de minimis* under EU competition law. However, one might wonder whether, in order to establish if an agreement is *de minimis*, ie it does not appreciably restrict competition, national courts should apply the thresholds in the Commission's De Minimis Notice or whether they would have some discretion.

[65] Commission Staff Working Paper accompanying the Communication from the Commission to the European Parliament and Council Report on the functioning of Regulation 1/2003 (COM(2009)206 final), para 148.

[66] Commission Staff Working Paper accompanying the Communication from the Commission to the European Parliament and Council Report on the functioning of Regulation 1/2003 (COM(2009)206 final), para 160.

[67] Case C-198/01 *Consorzio Industrie Fiammiferi (CIF) v Autorità Garante della Concorrenza e del Mercato* [2003] ECR I-8055, para 49. In this preliminary ruling, the ECJ was asked whether in the event of an agreement between undertakings which adversely affected EU trade and which was required or facilitated by national legislation, Art [101 TFEU] requires or permits the NCA to disapply national law and to penalize the anticompetitive conduct in question. The ECJ ruled that Arts 81[101] and 82[102] in conjunction with Art 10 EC [4.3 TFEU] required that any provision which breached Community law had to be disapplied.

the ECJ for clarification within the preliminary ruling procedure.[68] It should be noted that Article 3(2) of Regulation 1/2003 itself expressly provides that Member States may adopt and apply in their territory *stricter* national laws which prohibit or sanction unilateral conduct. As an example of stricter national rules concerning unilateral conduct, Recital 8 of Regulation 1/2003 expressly refers to national provisions which prohibit or impose sanctions on abusive behaviour toward economically dependent undertakings. Apart from rules which specifically concern abuses of economic dependence, some national provisions regulate behaviour labelled as 'abuse of superior bargaining power' or 'abuse of significant influence'.

2.23 The aim of these kinds of rules is essentially to regulate unequal bargaining power in distribution relationships, including where neither the supplier nor the distributor holds a dominant position in a specific market.[69] Thus, Member States are indeed entitled to prohibit under national law abusive conduct that would not be prohibited under Article 102 TFEU. However, their national law cannot permit abusive conduct which would be prohibited under Article 102 TFEU. Apart from the rules applicable to unilateral behaviour by firms that expressly extend to undertakings that do not have a dominant position in the market within the meaning of Article 102 TFEU, national laws may also contain different standards for assessing dominance as well as stricter national provisions governing the conduct of dominant undertakings.

2.24 The Commission has reminded national courts that they might also have to apply other EU acts having direct effect, such as Commission decisions or block exemption regulations. It does not, however, mention the last provision of Article 3(2) of Regulation 1/2003, providing that the national courts' duties under Article 3(1) and (2)—including the convergence duty—do not preclude the application of national law pursuing predominantly an objective different from that of Articles 101 and 102 TFEU, '[w]ithout prejudice to the general principles and other provisions of Community law'. Regulation 1/2003 indicates as an example of such laws national legislation which imposes sanctions on unfair trading practices, including both unilateral and bilateral acts.[70]

It follows from this judgment that an NCA is bound to disapply national law incompatible with EU law. The consequences of the declaration of inapplicability was that all national courts and administrative bodies involved in the application of the national legislation incompatible with EU law were obliged to disapply it and the undertakings concerned had to terminate conflicting conduct required by such national legislation.

[68] A Kaczorowska, 'The Power of a National Competition Authority to Disapply National Law Incompatible with EC Law—and its Practical Consequences' [2004] ECLR 591, 595, which also points out that when a national court establishes the incompatibility of national legislation with Community law, its judgment removes all doubts in this area and provides the parties with a high degree of certainty, given that judgments are known to have binding force.

[69] Commission Staff Working Paper accompanying the Communication from the Commission to the European Parliament and Council Report on the functioning of Regulation 1/2003 (COM(2009)206 final), paras 162 and 163–4. In 2004, the Member States with specific provisions concerning the abuse of economic dependence or superior bargaining power notably included France, Germany, Italy, Portugal, and Spain, while Ireland and Slovakia had measures with a more limited scope covering groceries and retail trade, respectively. In Spain, these provisions were removed from the Spanish Competition Act in 2007, but abuse of economic dependence remains an infringement of the Spanish Unfair Competition Act (*Ley de Competencia Desleal*), which essentially concerns unfair competition and trading practices, and the new Spanish Competition Act allows the competition authority to pursue such conduct where the distortion of fair competition affects the public interest. Hungary, in turn, introduced legislation to prohibit abuses of significant market power in 2006, and Latvia did the same in 2008 both entrusting the enforcement of these provisions to the competition authority. In Greece, the prohibition of the abuse of a relationship of economic dependence was reintroduced in 2005, after having been abolished in 2000. The French, German, Greek, and Portuguese legislation concerning the abuse of 'economic dependence' apply to various types of exclusionary conduct on both the demand and supply sides and normally require that there is no reasonable alternative source of supply or demand of the product or service in question.

[70] Recital 9 of Reg 1/2003.

Where the line is drawn appears to be particularly difficult in relation to legislation concern- **2.25**
ing stricter competition rules for unilateral conduct, on the one hand, and that covering
unfair trading practices, on the other, both of which currently fall outside the scope of the
convergence rule. If the objective of the national rules is to regulate contractual relationships
between undertakings by stipulating the terms and conditions that, for instance, suppliers
must offer to distributors (rather than their competitive behaviour in the market), the proper
classification appears to be that of laws concerning unfair trading practices. On the other
hand, national rules combating excessive market power or protecting smaller undertakings
in a market against their larger competitors appear more likely to be treated as competition
law provisions.[71]

3. Parallel or subsequent application of the EU competition rules

While the concurrent application of EU competition law (ie the application of such rules to **2.26**
the same case) by the Commission and the NCAs is excluded by Regulation 1/2003 in the
event that the Commission initiates proceedings,[72] this does not apply to a situation where
national courts and the Commission examine a case at the same time. The National Courts
Cooperation Notice sets out the principles governing such concurrent application of the EU
competition rules. The problem is particularly one of timing.[73] Where the Commission and
the national courts can both apply Article 101 and/or Article 102 TFEU, the Commission
Notice attempts to avoid the risk of any conflicting decision being adopted in the event that
either the national courts or the Commission come to a decision first.

- *If the national court comes to a decision first, it must avoid taking a decision that would conflict with the decision contemplated by the Commission.* The National Courts Cooperation
  Notice has outlined a number of avenues open to national courts to ensure the consistency
  of their rulings with Commission practice.[74] The national court may seek information
  from the Commission as to whether the Commission has started proceedings, the status
  of any such proceedings, and the likelihood of a decision being adopted. This possibility
  was already envisaged by the 1993 Notice on cooperation between national courts and the
  Commission in applying Articles 81 and 82 EC,[75] based on the ECJ ruling in *Delimitis*,
  although it was made dependent on the national procedural rules of the requesting court,[76]
  while now it is expressly provided for in Article 15 of Regulation 1/2003.[77] Moreover, the
  national court may decide to stay proceedings until the Commission has reached a decision. The National Courts Cooperation Notice restates the Court's case law in *Delimitis*

---

[71] Commission Staff Working Paper accompanying the Communication from the Commission to the
European Parliament and Council Report on the functioning of Regulation 1/2003 (COM(2009)206 final),
para 181.
[72] Under Art 11(6) of Reg 1/2003 the initiation of proceedings by the Commission relieves NCAs of their
competence to apply EC competition rules.
[73] There are also some national courts that have not shied away from taking positions that may not be
shared by the Commission. In theory, the Commission could adopt an individual position on the agreement
that is being examined by the national court and use Art 16 of Reg 1/2003 to challenge the consistency of
the national court ruling.
[74] National Courts Cooperation Notice [2004] OJ C101/54, para 12.
[75] [1993] OJ C39/6.
[76] See Commission Notice on cooperation with national courts [1993] OJ C39/6 ('1993 NC Notice'),
para 37; Case C-234/89 *Stergios Delimitis v Henninger Bräu AG* [1991] ECR I-935, para 53, where the Court
states that the possibility for national courts to seek information from the Commission is 'always open to a
national court, within the limits of the applicable national procedural rules'.
[77] A different issue is whether a national court may request information from the Commission in respect of
proceedings concerning purely domestic competition law. Case C-275/00 *European Community v First NV and
Franex NV* [2002] ECR I-10943, para 49 may be read as meaning that the ECJ did not limit the Commission's
duty to cooperate with the national court to cases where the national court was applying EC law.

and confirms the Commission's commitment to give priority to cases suspended in this way as was the case under the 1993 National Courts Notice.[78] Where the national court cannot reasonably have any doubt regarding the Commission's contemplated decision or where the Commission has already decided in a similar case, the national court may rule in the case before it 'without it being necessary' to ask the Commission for the information mentioned earlier or to await the Commission's decision. Strictly speaking, however, whether it is 'necessary' either to ask the Commission for procedural information or to stay the proceedings is left to the national court's discretion. Indeed, the national court might instead decide to make a reference for a preliminary ruling to the ECJ.[79]

• *If the Commission comes to a decision first, under Article 16 of Regulation 1/2003, the national court cannot take a decision running counter to the decision adopted by the Commission.*[80] Based on the ECJ judgments in *Foto-Frost*[81] and *Masterfoods*,[82] the Commission recalls that in view of the binding nature of Commission decisions, national courts cannot hold a Commission decision invalid and cannot take a decision that runs counter to that of the Commission.[83] Instead, it should refer the matter to the ECJ, which has exclusive jurisdiction over that matter. Where the Commission's decision is the subject of an application for annulment under Article 263 TFEU[84] and the dispute before the national courts depends on the validity of the Commission decision, the national court should stay proceedings or,

---

[78] See 1993 National Courts Cooperation Notice [1993] OJ C93/6, para 37.

[79] Note that the Commission mentioned in the White Paper on the modernisation of the rules implementing Arts 81[101] and 82[102] [1999] OJ C132/1, para 102, that it could still intervene and adopt a prohibition decision—subject only to the principle of *res judicata* that applies to the dispute between the parties themselves, which has been decided once and for all by the national court after a national court had delivered a positive judgment (eg, rejecting an action on the ground that a restrictive practice satisfied the test contained in Art 101(3) TFEU, when the latter is either no longer open to appeal or has been confirmed on appeal). The argument of the Commission is that *res judicata* is valid only between the parties and that, taking into account the different mission of the competition authorities (acting in the public interest), nothing precludes it from acting afterwards in order to ensure consistency in the application of Arts [101] and [102][TFEU]. Recently, the Commission seems to take the view that the ECJ should have the final word on this issue. K Lenaerts and D Gerard, 'Decentralisation of EC Competition Law Enforcement: Judges in the Frontline' [2004] World Competition Law and Economics 313, 326.

[80] This rule is not without exceptions. Thus, Recitals 13 and 22 of Reg 1/2003 indicate that it would not apply to commitments decisions under Art 9, National Courts Cooperation Notice [2004] OJ 101/54, para 13.

[81] Case 314/85 *Foto-Frost v Hauptzollamt Lübeck-Ost* [1987] ECR I-4199.

[82] Case C-344/98 *Masterfoods Ltd v HB Ice Cream Ltd* [2000] ECR I-11369.

[83] See E Gippini-Fournier, 'The Modernisation of European Competition Law: First Experiences with Regulation 1/2003—Institutional Report' in HF Koeck and MM Karollus (eds), The Modernisation of European Competition Law—Initial Experiences with Regulation 1/2003, FIDE XXIII Congress Linz 2008—Congress Publications Vol 2 (Nomos 2008) 375, 471 points out that *Masterfoods* and Art 16 do not state that national courts are 'bound' by Commission decisions, but rather that they cannot take decisions 'running counter' to them. In the author's view, a national court should not issue an order requiring behaviour which would constitute a breach of the commitments made binding by the Commission in an Art 9 decision. The deference due to Commission decisions would also be linked to the exclusive competence of the EU Courts to review their legality (p 472).

[84] It is often claimed that the GC applies a 'self-imposed limited control' over the legality of Commission decisions in competition cases. Despite the language of Art 263 TFEU, however, the 'manifest error of appraisal' standard for reviewing the application by the Commission of Art 101(3) TFEU has evolved considerably over time towards a full review standard and does not *a priori* preclude the GC from undertaking a full and exhaustive review of the facts of the case and of the Commission's legal and economic analysis in the application of the four conditions required to declare Art 101(1) TFEU inapplicable. K Lenaerts and D Gerard, 'Decentralisation of EC Competition Law Enforcement: Judges in the Frontline' [2004] World Competition Law and Economics 313, 326. Note that the GC was established particularly in order to improve the judicial protection of individual interests in respect of actions requiring the close examination of complex facts. As regards the EU Courts' judicial review standard, see Ch 15, 'Steps Following the Adoption of a Formal Decision' para 15.32 et seq.

where it considers it appropriate, submit its question to the ECJ for a preliminary ruling on the validity of the Commission's decision.[85] The obligation for national courts not to adopt a decision conflicting with a prior Commission decision could play a role not only in avoiding conflicting decisions, but also in resolving conflicts which have already arisen. In particular, if a national court's judgment found that Article 101 TFEU does not apply, the Commission might still prohibit the agreement in question with effect *erga omnes*. In such a case, if the national court's judgment were appealed against, the appeal court would be bound by the Commission's decision.[86]

Request to the ECJ for a preliminary ruling[87]

As indicated, decentralization brings with it the possibility of divergent decisions where national courts of the Member States have jurisdiction to hear direct actions under Articles 101 and 102 TFEU or actions against decisions of the NCAs. Where the law is unclear, the national courts can request assistance from the Commission in specific cases,[88] or else they can request a preliminary ruling from the ECJ pursuant to Article 267 TFEU.[89] In particular, national courts may require guidance where they apply Article 101(3) TFEU. Note that the EU Courts have often granted the Commission some discretion when applying Article 101(3) TFEU, in particular where this involves 'complex economic' assessments. However, the arguments that have been put forward to justify the type of restricted jurisdiction exercised by the EU Courts, eg 'institutional balance' between the Commission and the EU Courts, or the prime responsibility of the Commission for conducting competition policy,[90] are difficult to use in the context of the review conducted by the national court. A national first instance court may not limit itself to a review of legality, but needs to examine the merits of the case. It applies Article 101 in its entirety, including the prohibition in Article 101(1) and the exception to the prohibition in Article 101(3).[91] Thus, the judge must carry out this assessment, however complicated it may be. Given that the case law of the EU Courts

2.27

---

[85] See Art 16(1) of Reg 1/2003; Case C-344/98 *Masterfoods Ltd v HB Ice Cream Ltd* [2000] ECR I-11369, paras 52–9.

[86] See also Case T-65/98 *Van den Berg Foods v EC Commission* [2003] ECR II-4653, para 199, stating that the Commission is at any time entitled to adopt a decision under Arts 101 and 102 TFEU, even though this may conflict with an earlier national court decision.

[87] See Recommendations to national courts and tribunals in relation to the initiation of preliminary ruling proceedings [2012] OJ C338/1. These recommendations follow on from the adoption on 25 September 2012 in Luxembourg of the new Rules of Procedure of the Court of Justice ([2012] OJ L265/1). They replace the information note on references from national courts for a preliminary ruling ([2011] OJ C160/1) and reflect innovations introduced by those Rules. They affect both the principle of a reference for a preliminary ruling to the Court of Justice and the procedure for making such a reference.

[88] See Art 15 of Reg 1/2003.

[89] This is particularly relevant if there is the risk of national courts taking a decision which might conflict with those taken by the Commission in applying Arts 101 and 102 TFEU, Case C-234/89 *Delimitis v Henninger Brau AG* [1991] ECR I-935, para 54. If the national court doubts the legality of the Commission's decision and intends to take a decision that runs counter to that of the Commission, it must refer a question to the ECJ. See National Courts Cooperation Notice [2004] OJ C101/54, para 54. In view of the binding effect of the Commission decisions under Art 16(1) of Reg 1/2003, a preliminary ruling from the ECJ on the compatibility of a Commission decision with EU law is the only way for a national court to actually *bypass* such a decision in the application of EU competition law to the case before it.

[90] President of the CFI, Judge Bo Vesterdorf, 'Judicial Review and Competition Law—Reflections on the Role of the Community Courts in the EC System of Competition Law Enforcement', speech at the International Forum on EC Competition Law, Brussels, 8 April 2005, and the edited paper version of the speech in Competition Policy International [2005] 1(2), 6.

[91] The finding of an infringement is only one side of the equation. Before a finding of illegality can be made, the Art 101(3) TFEU analysis must be carried out and it must be concluded that on balance the agreement is anticompetitive. See L Kjolbye, 'The New Commission Guidelines on the Application of Article 81(3)[101(3)]: An Economic Approach to Article 81' [2004] ECLR 566, 566. See Ch 15, 'Steps Following the Adoption of a Formal Decision', para 15.42.

gives very little guidance on this point, a national court may consider requesting the ECJ for orientation on how it should conduct its assessment where it believes that the Commission Guidelines on the application of Article 101(3) TFEU do not give it sufficient guidance.[92]

2.28 Any court or tribunal of a Member State[93] may ask the ECJ to interpret a rule of EU law, whether contained in the Treaties or in acts of secondary law, if it considers that this is necessary for it to give judgment in a case before it. Courts against whose decisions there is no judicial remedy under national law must refer questions of interpretation arising before them to the ECJ, unless the latter court has already ruled on the point or the correct application of the rule of EU law is obvious.[94] It should be noted that questions referred for a preliminary ruling must concern the interpretation or validity of a provision of EU law only, since the ECJ does not have jurisdiction to interpret national law or assess its validity.[95] The decision by which a national court or tribunal refers a question to the ECJ for a preliminary ruling may be in any form allowed by national procedural law. The reference of a question or questions to the ECJ generally causes the national proceedings to be stayed until the Court gives its ruling, but the decision to stay proceedings is one which the national court alone must take in accordance with its own national law.[96] A national court or tribunal may refer a question to the ECJ for a preliminary ruling as soon as it finds that a ruling on the point or points of interpretation or validity is necessary to enable it to pass judgment. It must be stressed, however, that it is not for the ECJ to decide issues of fact or differences of opinion as to the interpretation or application of rules of national law.[97] It is therefore desirable that a decision to make a reference should not be taken until the national proceedings have reached a stage where the national court is able to define, if only hypothetically, the factual and legal context of the question.[98] Thus, it is solely for the national court before which the dispute has been brought, and which must assume responsibility for the subsequent judicial decision, to determine, in the light of the particular circumstances of the case, both the need for a preliminary ruling in order to enable it to deliver judgment and the relevance of the questions which it submits to the Court.[99] Consequently, where the questions submitted by the national court

---

[92] F Montag and S Cameron, 'Effective Enforcement: The Practitioner's View of Recent Experiences under Regulation 1/2003', International Bar Association ('IBA') conference, Antitrust Reform in Europe: A Year in Practice, Brussels, 1–11 March 2005, 3, see a need for guidance in particular with regard to Art 81(3) EC.

[93] C-246/05 *Armin Häupl v Lidl Stiftung & Co. KG* [2007] ECR I-4673, para 16: 'in order to determine whether the body making a reference is a court or tribunal for the purposes of Article 234 EC, which is a question governed by Community law alone, the Court takes account of a number of factors, such as whether the body is established by law, whether it is permanent, whether its jurisdiction is compulsory, whether its procedure is inter partes, whether it applies rules of law and whether it is independent.' Case C-54/96 *Dorsch Consult* [1997] ECR I-4961, para 23, and Case C-53/03 *Syfait and Others* [2005] ECR I-4609, para 29.

[94] Recommendations to national courts and tribunals in relation to the initiation of preliminary ruling proceedings [2012] OJ C338/1, paras 12 and 13.

[95] See C-7/97 *Oscar Bronner GmbH & Co KG* [1997] ECR I-7791, para 17, stating that Art 234 EC [267 TFEU] is based on 'a clear separation of functions between national courts and this court [and] does not allow this court to review the reasons for which a reference is made. Consequently, a request from a national court may be rejected only if it is quite obvious that the interpretation of Community law or review of the validity of a rule of Community law sought by that court bears no relation to the actual facts of the case or to the subject-matter of the main action.'

[96] Recommendations to national courts and tribunals in relation to the initiation of preliminary ruling proceedings [2012] OJ C338/1, para 17.

[97] Recommendations to national courts and tribunals in relation to the initiation of preliminary ruling proceedings [2012] OJ C338/1, paras 7 and 8.

[98] The administration of justice may well be best served by waiting until both sides have been heard in the national court before referring a question for a preliminary ruling. Recommendations to national courts and tribunals in relation to the initiation of preliminary ruling proceedings [2012] OJ C338/1, para 19.

[99] Case 314/01 *Seimens ARGE Telekom & Partner* [2004] ECR I-2549, para 34: 'it is for the national court or tribunal seised of the dispute, which alone has direct knowledge of the facts giving rise to the dispute and must assume responsibility for the subsequent judicial decision, to determine in the light of the particular

concern the interpretation of EU law, the ECJ is, in principle, bound to give a ruling. The ECJ may refuse to rule on a question referred for a preliminary ruling by a national court only where it is quite obvious that the interpretation of, or assessment of the validity of, a provision of EU law that is sought by the referring court bears no relation to the actual facts of the main action or its purpose, where the problem is hypothetical, or where the Court does not have before it the factual or legal material necessary to provide a useful answer to the questions submitted to it.[100]

On average, the ECJ takes two to two-and-a-half years to pass judgment in preliminary ruling cases.[101] This relatively time-consuming process is perceived as a major problem[102] which is likely to worsen if the expected greater number of requests for preliminary rulings materializes. Arguably, a second drawback is the limitation inherent in the preliminary ruling mechanism, in that the ECJ only answers abstract questions regarding the interpretation of the law, while leaving the application of the law to the referring court. The ECJ has to give its answers based on the facts described by the referring court and by the parties, and does not examine the evidence.[103] Besides, although the ECJ is not competent to decide whether the disputed facts, including those of an economic nature, are material, it can nevertheless qualify the facts reported in the referral request with regard to EU law, and it is entitled to

2.29

---

circumstances of the case both the need for a preliminary ruling in order to enable it to deliver judgment and the relevance of the questions which it submits to the Court'.

[100] Joined Cases C-480/00 to C-482/00, C-484/00, C-489/00 to C-491/00 and C-497/00 to C-499/00 *Azienda Agricola Ettore Ribaldi and others* [2004] ECR I-2943, para 72.

[101] Recommendations to national courts and tribunals in relation to the initiation of preliminary ruling proceedings [2012] OJ C338/1, para 38, stating that 'Article 105 of the Rules of Procedure provides that a reference for a preliminary ruling may be determined pursuant to an expedited procedure derogating from the provisions of those Rules, where the nature of the case requires that it be dealt with within a short time. Since that procedure imposes significant constraints on all those involved in it, and, in particular, on all the Member States called upon to lodge their observations, whether written or oral, within much shorter time-limits than would ordinarily apply, its application should be sought only in particular circumstances that warrant the Court giving its ruling quickly on the questions referred.' The urgent preliminary ruling procedure referred to in para 39 of the *Recommendations* and provided for in Art 107 of the Rules of Procedure only applies in the areas covered by Title V of Part Three of the TFEU, relating to the area of freedom, security, and justice, and imposes even greater constraints on those concerned, since it limits in particular the number of parties authorised to lodge written observations, and, in cases of extreme urgency, allows the written part of the procedure before the Court to be omitted altogether.

[102] This is in contrast to the time frame envisaged for the opinions provided by the Commission under Art 15 of Reg 1/2003. The Commission has stated its willingness to answer requests for an opinion within four months. See National Courts Cooperation Notice [2004] OJ C101/54, para 28. A Commission opinion, however, is a non-binding clarification of aspects of an 'economic, factual or legal nature', whereas a ECJ preliminary ruling is a binding interpretation of EU law as applicable to the facts of the case. The former is thus arguably much broader in terms of the scope of the request that may be formulated, although it can be challenged.

[103] Case C-198/01 *Consorzio Industrie Fiammiferi (CIF) v Autorità Garante della Concorrenza e del Mercato* [2003] ECR I-8055, para 62: 'for the purposes of the procedure set out in Art [267 TFEU], which is based on a clear separation of functions between the national courts and the Court of Justice, the latter, when ruling on the interpretation or validity of Community provisions, is empowered to do so only on the basis of the facts which the national court puts before it... It is not for the Court of Justice to apply Community law to the dispute before the national court... or to assess the facts in the main proceedings.' For example, the nature and geographical extent of the markets in issue or the possible justification for alleged abusive conduct are matters for the national court to decide. Case 311/84 *CBM v CLT and IPB* [1985] ECR 3261. See C Bellamy and G Child, *European Community Law of Competition* (6th edn, Oxford University Press 2008), para 14.089 et seq. There is no second-guessing of the facts before the ECJ. C Baudenbacher, 'Judicialization of European Competition Policy' in BE Hawk (ed), *International Antitrust Law and Policy* (Fordham Corporate Law Institute 2002) 353, 359, citing the President of the CFI, Judge Bo Vesterdorf: 'This is not precisely a very nice situation if we have to go into an intensive evaluation of Art 81 (3) [101 (3)] if we cannot really deal with the facts, if we have no influence on the facts.' Baudenbacher believes that a certain weakening of the protection of individual rights appears to be an inevitable consequence of decentralization.

determine whether or not a specific fact is relevant in order to determine whether infringements of Articles 101or 102(1) have taken place. Thus, although the rulings of the ECJ in competition cases appear short and abstract, they are still very much based on an evaluation of the facts[104] as presented by the referring judge and therefore constitute a valid source of guidance for national courts.[105]

2.30 So far, Regulation 1/2003 has not given rise to a large number of references.[106] The case of *T-Mobile Netherlands and Others* concerned the evidence which must be adduced before national courts to prove an infringement of Article 101 TFEU, in examining whether there is a causal connection between the concerted practice and the market conduct of the undertakings participating in the practice. The reference for a preliminary ruling was made to the ECJ, asking whether the evidence of a causal connection between a concerted practice and market conduct is to be adduced and appraised in accordance with the EU case law, or whether the national court can apply the rules of national law pertaining to the burden of proof in this respect. The ECJ stated that the EC presumption of a causal connection stems from the interpretation of Article 101(1) by the European Courts. It would consequently form an integral part of applicable Community law. The national court is therefore required—subject to proof to the contrary to be adduced by the undertakings concerned—to apply the presumption of a causal connection established in the Court's case law, according to which, provided the undertakings in question would remain active on that market, they are presumed to take account of the information exchanged with their competitors.[107]

C. Cooperation between National Courts and the Commission

2.31 Because Regulation 1/2003 assumes that Article 101(3) TFEU will have direct effect, cooperation between the Commission and Member States' courts has acquired more importance. Given the central role of national courts, the success of decentralized competition law enforcement depends to a large extent on the national courts' ability to apply the law accurately and

---

[104] K Lenaerts and D Gerard, 'Decentralisation of EC Competition Law Enforcement: Judges in the Frontline' [2004] World Competition Law and Economics 313, 339, referring to Joined Cases C-264/01, C-306/01, C-354/01, and C-355/01 *AOK Bundesverband et al* [2004] ECR I-2493, in which the ECJ thoroughly examined the question of whether groups of sickness funds, such as the fund associations, constitute undertakings or associations of undertakings within the meaning of Art 101 TFEU. Note that the Court's jurisdiction under Art 263 TFEU is more limited to the extent that it will review a Commission decision which has already formed a view on the ancillary nature or otherwise of a restriction. In so doing, the Court must take into account the Commission's powers, especially when they involve complex evaluations on economic matters. D Bailey, 'The Scope of Judicial Review under Article 81' [2004] CML Rev 1327, 1346.

[105] Former President of the GC, Judge Bo Vesterdorf, 'Judicial Review and Competition Law—Reflections on the Role of the Community Courts in the EC System of Competition Law Enforcement', speech at the International Forum on EC Competition Law, Brussels, 8 April 2005, asked whether, for reasons of coherency, it would not be better to empower the GC, as the main body handling competition cases, to deal with preliminary rulings in this area as could be done under Art [256(3)]. See also the edited paper version of the speech in Competition Policy International [2005] 1(2), 27.

[106] C-360/09 *Pfleiderer AG v Bundeskartelamt* [2011] OJ C232/5 (Arts 11 and 12 of Reg 1/2003); C-17/10 [2012] OJ C98/3 (Arts 3(1) and 11(6) of Reg 1/2003); Case C-375/09 *Prezes Urzędu Ochrony Konkurencji i Konsumentów v Tele2 Polska sp. z o.o* [2011] OJ C186/04 (Art 5 of Reg 1/2003); Case-439/08 *Vlaamse federatie van verenigingen van Brood- en Banketbakkers, Ijsbereiders en Chocoladebewerkers (VEBIC)* [2011] OJ C55/2 (Art 35 of Reg 1/2003); Case C-429/07 *Inspecteur van de Belastingdienst* [2009] ECR I-4833 (Art 15 of Reg 1/2003). For a more detailed list of preliminary references in relation to Arts 101 and 102 TFEU, see Bruno Gencarelli in A Frignani and S Bariatti (eds), *Disciplina della concorrenza nella UE* (Cedam 2013).

[107] In Case C-8/08, *T-Mobile Netherlands BV, KPN Mobile NV, Orange Nederland NV, Vodafone Libertel NV* [2009] ECR I-4529, paras 44–53.

consistently. This means that arrangements must be established for cooperation between the courts of the Member States and the Commission.[108] A network involving the national courts similar to the ECN would sit uneasily with the independence of the judiciary. Nevertheless, Regulation 1/2003 provides for a number of devices to promote consistency, building on the mutual duty of loyal cooperation laid down in Article 10 EC.

Article 15 of Regulation 1/2003 sets out the areas of cooperation between the Commission **2.32** and the national courts, referring to the transmission by the Commission both of information and its opinions at the request of a national court and the possibility of the Commission submitting written observations on its own initiative and oral observations with the permission of the court.[109] The National Courts Cooperation Notice has further implemented the means of cooperation, which will be considered in more detail in the paragraphs that follow.[110]

These possibilities of cooperation become particularly relevant where the principles governing **2.33** the concurrent application of EU competition law by national courts and the Commission under Article 16 of Regulation 1/2003 are not applicable since the Commission has not—or will not—take a decision on the same matter. Two of the cooperation mechanisms established by Regulation 1/2003 operate at the request of national courts—transmission of information (Article 15(1)) and request for the Commission's opinion (Article 15(1))—while the third— Commission's observations (Article 15(3))—is left to the Commission's own initiative. The Commission has indicated that assistance to the national courts is carried out in such a way as to respect the latter's independence and ensure the Commission's own neutrality, adding that it understands that its neutral role as defendant of the public interest requires that it should not hear the parties on the issue of its assistance to the national courts.[111]

While the Commission does not rule out making contact with the parties,[112] the general rule **2.34** of not hearing the parties has attracted some criticism. Critics have pointed to the usefulness of a hearing which would enhance the effectiveness of the Commission's intervention—by

---

[108] Article 4(3) TFEU, as interpreted by the ECJ, in Order C-2/88 *Zwartveld* [1990] ECR I-3365, obliges the Commission to cooperate with national courts in the application of Arts 101 and 102 TFEU. 'That principle [of sincere cooperation] not only requires the Member States to take all the measures necessary to guarantee the application and effectiveness of Community law, if necessary by instituting criminal proceedings but also imposes on Member States and the Community institutions mutual duties of sincere cooperation. This duty of sincere cooperation imposed on Community institutions is of particular importance *vis-à-vis* the judicial authorities of the Member States, who are responsible for ensuring that Community law is applied and respected in the national legal system.' See also O Weber in JL Schulte and C Just (eds), *Kartellrecht* (Carl Heymanns Verlag 2012) Article 15 of Reg 1/2003, para 1. The obligation to assist national courts only exists when the latter apply EU law. See Antitrust Manual of Procedures Internal DG Competition working documents on procedures for the application of Articles 101 and 102 TFEU, March 2012, Module 4 'Cooperation between the Commission and national courts', para 5.

[109] Article 15(1) and (3) of Reg 1/2003. Pursuant to Art 15(2), Member States must forward to the Commission a copy of any written judgments that deal with the application of Arts [101] and [102 TFEU]. Commission Report on Competition Policy (2005) 805 final para 114, noting that the Commission had received thirty-six judgments since May 2004 which were put on the DG COMP website to the extent that the transmitting authority did not classify them as confidential.

[110] As of 31 March 2009, the Commission has issued opinions on eighteen occasions to national courts in Belgium (five), Spain (nine), Lithuania (one), The Netherlands (one), and Sweden (two). See Commission Staff Working Paper accompanying the Communication from the Commission to the European Parliament and Council Report on the functioning of Regulation 1/2003 (COM(2009)206 final), para 277.

[111] National Courts Cooperation Notice [2004] OJ C101/54, para 22.

[112] At least with respect to national courts' requests for information, the Commission indicates that it may have to consult those affected by the transmission of information (National Courts Cooperation Notice [2004] OJ C101/54, para 22). Furthermore, the Commission indicates that it will inform the national court where it has been contacted by the parties (National Courts Cooperation Notice [2004] OJ C101/54, para 19).

allowing it to make a 'useful objective intervention'[113] and ensuring that the parties' defence rights are upheld.[114] In addition, the Commission's neutrality in this respect would neither be feasible nor desirable.[115] Overall, it seems that hearing the parties is in no way incompatible with the Commission's impartiality. The fact that the Commission obtains information from the parties does not mean that it is prevented from objectively assessing such information and then making an independent intervention before the national courts. In other words, hearing the parties does not mean that the Commission must share their views. The real reason for there being no hearing might well be in order to avoid further administrative burdens and delays, but this is not acceptable if the parties' defence rights are harmed as a result.

2.35 Since the Commission has indicated that it will inform the parties of any such contact whether it took place before or after the national courts' request for information, it might well be that the parties will seek to use this channel to make their position known to the Commission. In fact, while the Commission cannot take the initiative to hear the parties, it is unlikely to refuse to listen to them if they contact it. Thus, while allowing parties to make their views known to the Commission might enhance their defence rights, this could give rise to concerns if only one of the parties has made use of this possibility. In the same vein, it is somewhat unfortunate that the Commission did not maintain its commitment in the earlier 1993 Notice to 'ensure that its answer reaches all the parties to the proceedings'.[116] In essence, the Commission leaves it to the national courts to guarantee the parties' access to the information, opinions or observations submitted by it. When dealing with the Commission's opinion in accordance with national procedural rules, the Commission obliges national courts to respect the general principles of EU law, which in turn should be understood as requiring the national courts to give the parties access to any such opinion and permit them to submit observations.

2.36 Lastly, it should be noted, however, that the National Courts Cooperation Notice is aimed at those courts and tribunals of Member States which are entitled to refer a question for a preliminary ruling to the ECJ pursuant to Article 267 TFEU.[117] Accordingly, the Commission did not extend the scope of the National Courts Cooperation Notice to cover arbitration panels or arbitrators.[118] Although they are not entitled to ask the ECJ for a preliminary

---

[113] See National Courts Cooperation Notice [2004] OJ C101/54, paras 28–33, which refer to the Commission being able to submit 'useful' opinions and observations.

[114] This was one concern voiced in the comments submitted by interested parties on the draft Notice.

[115] See H Gilliams, 'Modernization: From Policy to Practice' (2003) 28 EL Rev 451, 461. According to the author, where the Commission has already taken or is going to take some form of action against the practice regarding which the national court seeks assistance, it seems difficult for such assistance to be impartial. The author suggests that a better way for national courts to obtain the factual or legal information they need would be for the parties to ask the Commission for a reasoned opinion, which could then be introduced into the proceedings as evidence. This solution would have the double advantage of allowing the Commission to hear the parties before issuing its opinion and making such an opinion available to the general public, thus in turn contributing to reducing the risk of inconsistent decisions.

[116] 1993 National Courts Cooperation Notice [1993] OJ C039/6, para 42.

[117] As indicated previously, a national court or tribunal may refer a question to the ECJ for a preliminary ruling as soon as it finds that a ruling on the point or points of interpretation or validity is necessary to enable it to pass judgment. The Notice applies where national courts are called upon to apply Arts 101 and 102 TFEU in claims between private parties. To the extent that they act as a public enforcer, they will be subject to the National Courts Cooperation Notice.

[118] Note also that the ECJ has made it clear that an arbitration tribunal constituted pursuant to an arbitration agreement which is an expression of party autonomy is not a court or tribunal of a Member State within the meaning of Art [267 TFEU]: in Case 102/81 *Nordsee v Reederei Mond* [1982] ECR 1095, the Court applied the test of whether the Member State had entrusted or left to the arbitration tribunal the duty of ensuring compliance with the State's obligations under Community law. The Court found that the arbitration tribunal was purely private in nature because its authority derived solely from party autonomy. Given that the arbitration tribunal is not a public authority, the duty of cooperation under Art [4.3 TFEU] cannot be applied to those tribunals. On the other hand, national courts have the duty to ensure the uniform and

ruling,[119] they are also bound to apply Articles 101 and 102 TFEU as public order provisions and their awards may be annulled for failure to do so.[120] Although practical considerations would have made it desirable to include arbitrators, the fact that the legal basis of the National Courts Cooperation Notice, ie Article 10 EC (which was repealed and partly replaced by Article 4(3) TFEU),[121] which enshrines the principle of mutual loyal and constant cooperation between the Commission and the Member States, does not include arbitration panels formed by private parties which may have played a role.[122] Although nothing prevents the Commission from providing assistance to arbitrators by means of any other informal procedure,[123] it is likely that the lack of any rules in this respect may make it more difficult to institutionalize a similar exchange between the Commission and arbitration panels.[124]

1. Transmission of information

The National Courts Cooperation Notice suggests that the Commission's duty of assistance **2.37** to the national courts mainly consists of its obligation to transmit information to national courts.[125] The Notice itself does not give any indication as to the form a request for information should take; it simply states that any request for assistance can be sent in writing or electronically to the addresses indicated therein. Parties may try to participate in the formulation

---

effective application of EU competition law and policy exercising jurisdiction in respect of any matters arising out of arbitration proceedings (the 'second look' doctrine). For more details, see Ch 29 'EU Competition Arbitration'.

[119] Case 102/81 *Nordsee v Reederei Mond* [1982] ECR 1095, para 13. M Dolmans and J Greisens, 'Arbitration and the Modernization of EC Antitrust Law: New Opportunities and New Responsibilities' (2003) 14(2) ICC International Court of Arbitration 37, 42.

[120] Case C-126/97 *Eco Swiss China Time v Benetton International* [1999] ECR I-3055, paras 37 and 41. Note that the ruling related to Art 81(1) EC [101(1) TFEU], although the reasoning maybe extended to Art 81(3) EC [101(3) TFEU].

[121] Article 10 read as follows: 'Member States shall take all appropriate measures, whether general or particular, to ensure fulfilment of the obligations arising out of this Treaty or resulting from action taken by the institutions of the Community. They shall facilitate the achievement of the Community's tasks—They shall abstain from any measure which could jeopardise the attainment of the objectives of this Treaty.' See also J Temple Lang, 'Developments, Issues and New Remedies—The Duties of National Authorities and Courts under Art 10 of the EC Treaty' [2004] Fordham International Law Journal 1904.

[122] At the very least, such cooperation might have been addressed in the Regulation, based on Art [103] (2)(e), which allegedly would cover the establishment of procedural rules for the application of Arts [101] and [102], not only by the Commission and national courts and NCAs, but by anybody called on to apply such provisions.

[123] Arbitration bodies could ask the Commission for an opinion or specific information pursuant to Art 15 of Reg 1/2003; see also M Dolmans and J Greisens, 'Arbitration and the Modernization of EC Antitrust Law: New Opportunities and New Responsibilities' (2003) 14(2) ICC International Court of Arbitration 37, 50 on the interaction between the Commission and arbitrator panels under Art 15 of Reg 1/2003. Nothing prevents an arbitrator from asking a 'supporting judge' to request on his behalf the information or opinion necessary to settle the matter. In addition, considering that the ECJ has held that Arts [101] and [102] were provisions of *ordre public*, a losing party to an arbitration award claiming an erroneous application of Art [101](3) TFEU, should in principle be allowed to obtain the *reformation* of the award by a judicial court. See also R Nazzini, 'International Arbitration and Public Enforcement of Competition Law' [2004] ECLR 153.

[124] The definition of the relevant market, the weighing of anticompetitive and positive effects of the agreements, and the quantification of damages are as difficult before an arbitration tribunal as they are before a court. A national court, however, may avail itself of some procedural devices in order to save time and expenses and avoid handing down a judgment that may conflict with a Commission decision. For example, it may stay the civil proceedings and await the outcome of the administrative investigation. See for more details on this point Ch 29 'EU Competition Arbitration', para 29.75 et seq.

[125] There is, however, some scepticism as to the willingness of national courts to actually make use of this possibility—which was hardly used under the 1993 Notice—both because they are not used to taking inquiry measures themselves and because they might feel that cooperation with an administrative authority might impinge on their independence. See H Gilliams, 'Modernization: From Policy to Practice' (2003) 28 EL Rev 451, 461.

of the request for information. Before a national court submits a request for information, it is expected that it will hear the parties.[126] Article 15 of Regulation 1/2003 refers to the possibility of asking the Commission for 'information in its possession'. The National Courts Cooperation Notice specifies that national courts may request that the Commission transfer to it 'documents in its possession' or 'information of a procedural nature', the latter including information on whether a case is pending before the Commission, whether the Commission has initiated a procedure or whether it has already taken a position, as well as whether a decision is likely to be taken. The ECJ case law also refers to 'legal and economic information',[127] possibly included in the category of 'documents' mentioned in Article 15. Thus, the type of information requested is not restricted to information of a general nature. In *Postbank*, the ECJ has already upheld the transmission to national courts of documents relating to the position or conduct of the parties, such as a Statement of Objections.[128]

2.38 The ruling in *Postbank* also seems to suggest that documents obtained by the Commission might also be produced in proceedings between parties other than the parties to the Commission's proceedings from which such documents originate.[129] The actual limits on the scope of a request for information are difficult to establish in abstract terms, but at least two general points seem quite clear. First, as already indicated, such requests for information should relate to information 'in possession' of the Commission,[130] which might also be a criterion to distinguish a mere request for information from a request for an opinion. Second, under no circumstances should the Commission's reply concern the merits of the case pending before the national court, in line with the Commission's position with respect to opinions and as a guarantee of the parties' defence rights. Whether or not the information supplied by the Commission will be publicly available will depend on the content of the document in question.[131]

---

[126] A similar provision is contained in the ECJ Guidelines on References under Art 234 EC [267 TFEU], in which the ECJ states that without prejudice to the national court's discretion as to when to make a reference, it is advisable first to hear the parties. Information Note on References by National Courts for Preliminary Rulings, para 7, available at the Community Courts' website.

[127] See Case C-234/89 *Delimitis v Henninger Bräu AG* [1991] ECR I-935, para 53; Joined Cases C-319/93, C-40/94, and C-224/94 *Hendrik Evert Dijkstra v Friesland (Frico Domo)* [1995] ECR I-4471, para 34.

[128] Case T-353/94 *Postbank NV v EC Commission* [1996] ECRII-921. The fact that in this case the Statement of Objections was in fact forwarded to the NC not directly by the Commission but by a third party, which had in turn received it from the Commission, does not seem to preclude a direct transmission of such a document from the Commission to the national courts, always subject to the procedural safeguards required by the Court. Thus, when relying on the information received by the Commission, the national courts have to protect the defence rights of the parties concerned. In Case C-360/09 *Pfleiderer AG v Bundeskartellamt* [2011] ECR I-5161 the ECJ concluded that it would be for the Member State courts to apply national law to determine the conditions under which third party access to documents and information provided as part of a leniency application should be allowed or refused. In Case C-536/11 *Bundeswettbewerbsbehörde v Donau Chemie AG and others*, judgment of the ECJ of 6 June 2013, the ECJ essentially followed the *Pfleiderer* ruling by holding that national courts are to decide case-by-case as regards the disclosure of leniency documents. Therefore EU law would preclude national legislation which prohibits third party access to the court files in public law competition proceedings without the parties' consent.

[129] In Case T-353/94 *Postbank NV v EC Commission* [1996] ECR II-921, the Commission claimed that the action brought by Postbank against disclosure of the Statement of Objections sent to it in national court proceedings was inadmissible due to Postbank's lack of interest, on the grounds that such a document had been produced in national proceedings to which Postbank was not a party. The Court ruled that this circumstance (production in proceedings to which Postbank was not a party) was irrelevant in order to establish Postbank's interest to bring an action, since Postbank had an interest in protecting its confidential and secret business information in the same way as in proceedings to which it was a party. Thus, the Court indirectly admitted the possibility of producing information concerning an undertaking in proceedings to which the latter was not a party.

[130] A Klees, *Europäisches Kartellverfahrenrecht* (Carl Heymans Verlag 2005) §8, para 52.

[131] Regulation 1049/2001 regarding public access to European Parliament, Council and Commission documents [2001] OJ L145/43. The Commission has also said that it may make its opinions and observations available on its website. National Courts Cooperation Notice [2004] OJ C101/54, para 20.

The information requested will be mainly documents, although information of a procedural **2.39** nature can also be requested (eg whether the Commission has initiated proceedings in a given case, or when a decision is likely to be taken). Only information already in the possession of the Commission can be asked for. Consequently, no investigation should be carried out to obtain (further) information with the sole purpose of transmitting that information to the national court. The request for information must also be specific. In cases where a general request is made (eg for the whole file in a given case), the national court should be asked whether it can specify more precisely the information which it seeks. Where possible, the information transmitted should be in the language of the request. There is no obligation, however, to translate information before transmission takes place.[132]

The National Courts Cooperation Notice restates the principles established in the case law of **2.40** the EU Courts regarding disclosure to national courts of information covered by professional secrecy, including both confidential information and business secrets.[133] The general principle established in the case law is that the combined reading of Article 10 [repealed and partly replaced by Article 4.3 TFEU] EC and Article 339 TFEU does not prevent the disclosure of such information to national courts, provided that this does not undermine the guarantees given to the undertakings concerned by EU provisions on professional secrecy. This safeguard has two aspects.[134] First, it requires the Commission to adopt all precautions to ensure that the right of the undertaking concerned to the protection of such information is not undermined, including, in particular, informing the latter of the documents or the transfer of documents covered by professional secrecy. Secondly, it requires national courts to guarantee protection of the confidentiality of such information. The principle that information covered by professional secrecy may be disclosed to national courts is, however, subject to at least two sets of exceptions.[135]

• *First, the Commission is entitled to refuse transmission of such information where national courts cannot ensure the protection of the confidential information.* The Commission indicates that it will not transmit such information to the national court if, after asking whether it can and will guarantee protection of such information, the national court cannot offer such a guarantee.[136] However, the Commission has not given any indication as to what

---

[132] Antitrust Manual of Procedures Internal DG Competition working documents on procedures for the application of Articles 101 and 102 TFEU, March 2012, Module 4 'Cooperation between the Commission and national courts', paras 7–10.

[133] National Courts Cooperation Notice [2004] OJ C101/54, para 23. The Commission may refuse in specific circumstances to transmit information for overriding reasons relating to the need to avoid interference with its functioning and independence, in particular by jeopardizing the accomplishment of the tasks entrusted to it (see para 26 of National Courts Cooperation Notice [2004] OJ C101/54).

[134] See Case T-353/94 *Postbank NV v EC Commission* [1996] ECR II-921, paras 69 and 90, where the Court indicates that 'there is a presumption that the national courts will guarantee the protection of confidential information'.

[135] See National Courts Cooperation Notice [2004] OJ C101/54, paras 25–6; see also Case T-353/94 *Postbank NV v EC Commission* [1996] ECR II-921, para 93, where the Court states that '[s]uch a refusal [to provide national courts with information covered by professional secrecy] is justified only where it is the only way of ensuring "protection of the rights of third parties", which in principle is a matter for the national courts, or "where the disclosure of that information would be capable of interfering with the functioning and independence of the Community", which, in contrast, is a matter exclusively for the Community institutions concerned.'

[136] In Case T-39/90 *NV Samenwerkende Elektriciteits-Produktiebedrijven v Commission* [1991] ECR II-1497, paras 27–30, the Court held that the Netherlands Ministry of Industry (which at the time also dealt with Community competition matters in the Netherlands) should, when deciding on the commercial strategy of a State undertaking controlled by that Ministry (Gasunie), could not be expected to ignore the information provided to it by the Commission concerning relations between one of the latter's clients (SEP) and a competing supplier (Statoil). Mere knowledge of the contract entered into between SEP and Statoil might be taken into account in deciding the commercial policy of Gasunie, since the Netherlands Ministry of Industry was not required to disregard information transmitted to it.

type of safeguard is required. In adversarial proceedings, a court will not be able to use information which is not in the file, ie which has not been disclosed to the parties. Thus, if the national court were required to maintain the confidentiality of the documents transmitted by the Commission by not disclosing them to the parties, either the court might be unable to give such a guarantee if national law requires that the parties have access to all information available to the court, or the transmission of information would be deprived of its purpose, in the sense that it would be pointless for the national courts to request and obtain information which it cannot use.[137]

• *The second set of exceptions refers to the need to safeguard the interests of the EU or to avoid interfering with its functioning and independence.*[138] In this respect, one should welcome the Commission's amendment of the original draft National Courts Cooperation Notice to introduce into the final version an express commitment not to transmit to national courts information voluntarily submitted by leniency applicants without the consent of the latter.[139] This was indeed one of the main concerns of the business and legal communities, reflected in several comments submitted in relation to the Commission's draft National Courts Cooperation Notice. It should be pointed out, however, that such a limited guarantee is by no means equivalent to the one provided by Article 12 of the Regulation in relation to the exchange of information between the Commission and the national courts, since it does not address the use that national courts are entitled to make of the information received from the Commission.[140]

2.41 Article 12 of Regulation 1/2003 states expressly that the information exchanged between the Commission and NCAs may be used in evidence, subject to the restrictions established in the same provision. Regulation 1/2003 does not contain a similar provision in relation to information transmitted to national courts, nor does the National Courts Cooperation Notice give any indications in this respect. However, in the light of the case law of the EU Courts, it seems that national courts are equally entitled to use the information received from the Commission as evidence. Indeed, even in a situation where national courts were not allowed to use the information received by the Commission as evidence (but only for the purposes of deciding whether or not to initiate national proceedings), the Court held, in *Postbank*, that the same limitation did not apply to national courts.[141] In the same case, the Court indicated some ways in which the national court could guarantee that the use of such information respected the parties' defence rights in the particular circumstances of the case (which was concerned with disclosure of a statement of objections), namely by taking account of the provisional nature of the opinion expressed by the Commission in a statement of objections and of the possibility of suspending proceedings pending the adoption of the final Commission decision. Since national courts can therefore use

---

[137] See also J Temple Lang, 'Developments, Issues and New Remedies—The Duties of National Authorities and Courts under Art 10 of the EC Treaty' [2004] Fordham International Law Journal 1904, 1922, who notes that when companies receive information from the Commission and when the Commission has advised them that they are not free to use it for any other purpose than the Commission's procedure, a national court should enjoin them from using it in any other way and if appropriate order compensation for the owners of the documents. This obligation would result from Art 10 EC.

[138] Antitrust Manual of Procedures Internal DG Competition working documents on procedures for the application of Articles 101 and 102 TFEU, March 2012, Module 4 'Cooperation between the Commission and national courts', para 11.

[139] National Courts Cooperation Notice [2004] OJ C101/54, para 26.

[140] A national court should always receive the information that is publicly available via requests based on Regulation (EC) No 1049/2001 regarding public access to European Parliament, Council and Commission documents (OJ 2001, L145/43). See also O Weber in JL Schulte and C Just (eds), *Kartellrecht* (Carl Heymanns Verlag 2012) Article 15 of Reg 1/2003, para 6, which includes more references.

[141] See Case T-353/94 *Postbank NV v EC Commission* [1996] ECR II-921, para 71. Also, in *Zwartveld*, the Court ruled that the Commission was required to authorize its officials to give evidence in national proceedings, namely by being examined as witnesses. See Case 2/88 *Imm J J Zwartveld and others* [1990] ECR I-3365.

the information received by the Commission as evidence, it might have been appropriate to remind them that they must do so in accordance with the general principles of EU law, which should include the parties' right to have access to such information.[142] As indicated, the National Courts Cooperation Notice does so in relation to opinions and observations without, however, expressly stating the general principles of EU law which it refers to. On the other hand, unlike with opinions and observations, the Notice does envisage the possibility of 'consulting those who are directly affected by the transmission of the information'.[143] The Commission states in its Notice that it will endeavour to provide the information within one month from the date on which the Commission receives the request. Where Directorate-General for Competition ('DG COMP') has to ask the national court for further clarification or where it has to consult those directly affected by the transmission (eg the undertakings that provided the information), the period starts to run from the moment that it receives that additional information.[144]

Requests for transmission of information

The Antitrust Manual of Procedures (known as 'Manproc') published by the Commission pro- **2.42** vides details of the procedure for handling transmission of information requests.[145] Requests arrive electronically (preferably via the dedicated functional mailbox COMP-AMICUS) or via traditional mail at the registry. If another official in DG COMP receives a request for information from a national court, this should be passed on immediately to the registry for registration.[146] If the information that is requested may be covered by professional secrecy, the competent unit will ask the national court whether it can and will guarantee protection of that information. In order to inform the national court about which parts of the transmitted information cannot be publicly disclosed (where the national court has given a confidentiality guarantee) or in order to make a non-confidential version of the requested information (where the national court has not given a confidentiality guarantee), the competent unit should examine which documents (or parts thereof) are covered by professional secrecy. It may be necessary to consult the legal or natural person or authority from whom the information originates to determine whether or not the information is (still) covered by professional secrecy at the moment of transmission or if they have other grounds to oppose disclosure. In the event of disagreement with the disclosure of the requested information (or the arrangements for the protection of its confidentiality), the procedure laid down in *Akzo* would apply.[147]

---

[142] On the one hand, the GC clearly assumed in *Postbank* that the national courts must indeed guarantee the protection of confidential information pursuant to the principle of effective judicial protection. On the other hand, the GC recognized that a refusal by the Commission to disclose remains the only way of ensuring the protection of the rights of third parties. The Commission has interpreted this as meaning that where national rules fail to make adequate provisions for the protection of confidential information, the Commission is not obliged under Art 10 EC to supply documents requested by national judges. M Dougan, *National Remedies Before the Court of Justice—Issues of Harmonization and Differentiation* (Hart Publishing 2004) 364–5.

[143] 1993 National Courts Notice [1993] OJ C39/6, para 22.

[144] Antitrust Manual of Procedures Internal DG Competition working documents on procedures for the application of Articles 101 and 102 TFEU, March 2012, Module 4 'Cooperation between the Commission and national courts', para 14, which states that in order to comply with the one month deadline, it is advisable that the sectoral unit *chef de file* contacts Unit A1 when the request arrives and not only before the transmission of the information.

[145] Antitrust Manual of Procedures Internal DG Competition working documents on procedures for the application of Articles 101 and 102 TFEU, March 2012, Module 4 'Cooperation between the Commission and national courts', paras 15–22.

[146] The registry assigns the request upon receipt to the competent sectoral unit as *chef de file* (with a copy to Unit A1 for its information) where the request concerns sector-specific information. Unit A1 is put in copy. A1 is *chef de file* for non-sector specific requests. If necessary, the competent unit will ask for a translation of the request for its information.

[147] Antitrust Manual of Procedures Internal DG Competition working documents on procedures for the application of Articles 101 and 102 TFEU, March 2012, Module 4 'Cooperation between the Commission

2.43 The *chef de file* unit consults Unit A1 on the draft letter. The unit that is *chef de file* should consult the Legal Service, eg where the transmission of the information could give rise to a significant legal issue. The Legal Service must have at least five working days to give its opinion. The letter accompanying the transmission of the requested information is signed by the Director of the competent unit. The letter should be drafted in the language of the request. A copy of this letter must be transmitted to A1 to enable accurate records to be kept. In the event of a refusal to transmit information requested by a national court, grounds must be given. Unit A1 and the Legal Service must be consulted on the refusal and given five working days to reply. The letter of refusal has to be signed by the Director-General.

2. Opinions

2.44 Article 15 of Regulation 1/2003 entitles national courts to request from the Commission an 'opinion on questions concerning the application of the Community competition rules'.[148] Apart from recalling that such an opinion is, of course, not binding on the national court and without prejudice to the possibility or obligation to make an Article [267] reference to the ECJ, the Commission Notice does not say much more about either the scope or the procedural aspects of such an opinion. The Notice merely indicates that the opinion may concern economic, factual, and legal matters, and not 'the merits of the case pending before the national court'.[149] It adds that for the purpose of providing a 'useful opinion', the Commission may request further information from the national court, but will not hear the parties, who will have to 'deal with the Commission's opinion in accordance with the relevant national procedural rules, which have to respect the general principles of Community law'.[150]

2.45 Thus, as a result of the Commission providing scant description of how the relevant provision in Article 15 is meant to work, a number of issues arise in relation to the scope of the Commission's opinion, as regards its relation to references under Article 267 TFEU, and its use in national proceedings. A first question is the difference in scope between a transmission of information and an opinion.[151] A second relates to the actual scope of an opinion. The dividing

---

and national courts', para 19. The *Akzo* procedure refers to a procedural rule established by the ECJ in Case 53/85 *Akzo v Commission* [1986] ECR 1965, which has also been inserted into the mandate of the Hearing Officer and which concerns the disclosure of confidential documents or business information by the Commission. This rule says that where the Commission intends to disclose information which the company providing it wants to be treated as a business secret or confidential, it shall inform that company in writing of its intentions and the reasons for it. Where the company concerned objects to the disclosure of this information, but the Commission finds that the information is not protected and may therefore be disclosed, that finding shall be stated in a reasoned decision. This decision has to be notified to the company concerned, which has to be given the opportunity to bring an action before the GC with a view to having the Commission's assessments reviewed. See also Antitrust Manual of Procedures Internal DG Competition working documents on procedures for the application of Articles 101 and 102 TFEU, March 2012, Module 12 'Access to file and Confidentiality', para 54.

[148] 'Q&A on Modernization with Kris Dekeyser' (April 2005) 8(3) Global Competition Review 11, 12, reports that during the first year of the application of Reg 1/2003 the Commission has received ten requests for an opinion. Commissioner Report on Competition Policy [2004] 805 final para 112 mentions nine requests, of which six came from Spanish courts, and all dealt with a similar type of distribution agreement in the energy sector. The Commission's replies to these six requests were largely based on its preliminary assessment in *Repsol CPP* [2004] OJ C258/7. The remaining three requests came from Belgian courts which are obliged to make a reference to the Brussels Court of Appeal for a preliminary ruling whenever they have doubts as to the application of competition rules. The Court of Appeal forwarded these requests to the Commission.

[149] National Courts Cooperation Notice [2004] OJ 101/54.

[150] National Courts Cooperation Notice [2004] OJ 101/54, para 30.

[151] Although it may not be necessary to distinguish between opinion and information for the purposes of Art 15 of Reg 1/2003 because Art 15 treats them on equal terms. A Klees, *Europäisches Kartellverfahrensrecht* (Carl Heymanns Verlag 2005) §8, para 52.

line between transmission of information and delivering an opinion, though not completely clear-cut, was somewhat clearer under the 1993 National Courts Notice. While referring generally to 'information' which national courts may request from the Commission, the 1993 Notice further specified the scope of the national courts' request, by indicating that '[f]irst, they may ask for information of a procedural nature', '[n]ext, national courts may consult the Commission on points of law', and '[l]astly, national courts can obtain information from the Commission regarding factual data: statistics, market studies and economic analysis'. Thus, it appears that under the 1993 Notice one could distinguish between three categories of requests: a request for information per se, relating to information of a procedural nature; a request for an opinion, relating to points of law; and a request for specific documents. Furthermore, the 1993 Notice defined in greater detail the scope of an opinion on points of law, clarifying that it would have as its object the Commission's customary practice in relation to the principle of EU law at issue and, in particular, questions such as the effect on interstate trade and the appreciable effect of a restriction of competition, as well as eligibility for an individual exemption.

Under the applicable Cooperation Notice, a request for information to the Commission may **2.46** relate both to 'documents in its possession' and 'information of a procedural nature', whilst an opinion may deal not only with points of law but also with 'economic, factual and legal matters' and, in particular, include both 'factual information' and 'economic or legal clarification'.[152] Moreover, while Article 15, when referring to requests for information, expressly states that such requests should relate to information 'in possession' of the Commission, there is no similar provision in relation to opinions. Thus, it seems that when replying to a request for information, the Commission will limit itself to 'transmitting' data it already has, while, with respect to an opinion, the Commission might possibly take into account additional data specifically obtained *ex novo* in relation to the national court's request. As to the actual scope of an opinion, as indicated, the Notice does not give much guidance. However, based on the ECJ's judgment in *Van der Wal*, it is possible to distinguish two types. First, the Commission may limit itself to expressing an opinion of a general nature independent of the data relating to the case pending before the national court, or secondly, provide a legal or economic analysis on the basis of the data supplied by the national court.[153] It seems that such a distinction could still apply under the current Commission Notice. However, the question remains open as to how far the Commission can go in opinions of the second kind, taking into account that such opinions should not in any event address the merits of the case pending before the national court.

In sum, it would have been helpful if the Commission had expanded more on the scope of an **2.47** opinion, perhaps simply by reproducing the relevant explanation in the 1993 Notice regarding opinions on legal matters. The scope of a Commission's opinion could also have been more clearly defined by distinguishing it from that of an Article 267 TFEU request for a preliminary ruling. By explaining, for example, in more detail the differences in scope between both procedures, the Commission could have helped the national court to decide when, in a particular case, it could be more helpful to ask the Commission rather than the Court or vice versa.[154] In this respect, an initial distinction between the two procedures is that, unlike

---

[152] Antitrust Manual of Procedures Internal DG Competition working documents on procedures for the application of Articles 101 and 102 TFEU, March 2012, Module 4, para 8, pointing out that only information already in the possession of the Commission can be asked for. Consequently, no investigation should be carried out to obtain (further) information with the sole purpose of transmitting that information to the national court.

[153] Joined Cases C-174/98 P and C-189/98 P *Van der Wal v EC Commission* [2000] ECR I-1, paras 24 and 25.

[154] The longer duration of an Art 267 TFEU procedure is one of the elements that the national courts could possibly take into account in deciding whether to ask for an opinion from the Commission instead of making a reference for a preliminary ruling.

an Article 267 TFEU reference, a request for an opinion may not only relate to points of law, but also to factual and economic matters. This broader scope of the Commission's opinion might possibly lead the national court to consider whether to ask the Commission rather than the Court where, for instance, its doubts concern factual and/or economic matters in addition to legal issues. Furthermore, even where the national court's question specifically relates to a point of law, there might be reasons for preferring a request to the Commission rather than going to the ECJ. In particular, while the Article 267 TFEU procedure relates to the interpretation of EU law provisions (in addition to the separate issue of their validity), it seems that the scope of a Commission opinion under Article 15 of the Regulation may well go further, subject to the limit of not considering the merits of the case. Indeed, under Article 15 such an opinion concerns the 'application' of EU competition law. Thus, the possibility that, under certain circumstances, it might be more helpful to ask the Commission rather than the Court cannot be excluded, although the Commission has indicated that where the request raises novel issues, the opinion may also suggest to the national court that it request a preliminary ruling from the ECJ.[155] For instance, an opinion on the 'customary practice of the Commission', ie the application of the law in question to similar situations, could on occasions be sufficient for the national court to be able to decide how to apply the law to the case before it, without the need to make a reference to the ECJ. On the other hand, it has been anticipated that national courts will prefer to rely on Article 267 TFEU and that the absence of a specific procedure for making a request to the Commission would further discourage them from using this latter procedure.[156]

2.48   Article 15 of Regulation 1/2003 does not give any indication of the procedure for requesting an opinion from the Commission. The Commission states in its Notice that it will endeavour to provide the opinion within four months from the date on which the Commission receives the request. If DG COMP has to ask the national court for further clarification, the period starts to run from the moment that the latter receives that additional information. The Commission's ManProc states that requests are processed in the same way as incoming requests for the transmission of information.[157]

2.49   As regards the procedure to be followed for a reply to a request for an opinion, the task of issuing an opinion of the Commission requested by a national court has been conferred by the College to the Competition Commissioner by empowerment, who has sub-delegated

---

[155] Antitrust Manual of Procedures Internal DG Competition working documents on procedures for the application of Articles 101 and 102 TFEU, March 2012, Module 4 'Cooperation between the Commission and national courts', para 26.

[156] See A Riley, 'EC Antitrust Modernisation: The Commission Does Very Nicely—Thank You! Part Two: Between the Idea and the Reality: Decentralisation under Regulation 1' [2003] ECLR 657, 666.

[157] Antitrust Manual of Procedures Internal DG Competition working documents on procedures for the application of Articles 101 and 102 TFEU, March 2012, Module 4 'Cooperation between the Commission and national courts', paras 30–3. Requests arrive electronically (preferably via the dedicated functional mailbox COMP-AMICUS) or via traditional mail at the registry. If someone else in DG COMP receives a request from a national court, it should be passed on immediately to the registry for registration. The registry assigns the request upon receipt to the competent sectoral unit as *chef de file* (with copy to Unit A1 for its information) where the request concerns sector-specific information. Unit A1 is put in copy. A1 is *chef de file* for non-sector specific requests. The sectoral unit will normally be considered to be *chef de file* whenever the request is closely related to and focused on specificities of the sector and/or closely linked to a case (being) dealt with by the sectoral unit (eg market definition). Where both non-sector-specific policy issues and sectorial issues are at stake, the *chef de file* should be decided on a case-by-case basis, taking into account the relative weight of the issues involved. In that case, the other unit (*non-chef de file*) will be closely involved in the drafting of the opinion. If necessary, the competent unit will ask for a translation of the request.

it to the Director-General of DG COMP.[158] The Commission's reply to the request of a national court is composed of a letter of transmission and an opinion, which is annexed to this letter. The letter of transmission is signed by the Director-General and the annex contains the text of the opinion itself. This means that the content of the letter of transmission is not part of the opinion. The letter of transmission should draw the court's attention to the fact that the Commission may publish its opinions on its webpage and intends to do so in the relevant case once a judgment has been rendered. The letter should also give the court the opportunity to present any objections to such publication. If a working language version of the opinion exists in a more commonly understood language than the authentic version (for instance, where the opinion has internally been processed in English or French), it may also be appropriate to publish this working language version. If so, this should also be mentioned in the letter to the court.[159]

In line with the ECJ guidelines on Article 267 TFEU references, the minimum information **2.50** to be included in a request for an opinion must include the factual and legal background, the reasons which prompted the request, and possibly a summary of the parties' arguments. In particular, the need to include a summary of the parties' arguments could be particularly important in the light of the Commission's position not to hear the parties before submitting its opinion. More generally, one might wonder whether the parties may play any role in formulating the request for an opinion. In this respect, the 1993 Notice seemed to envisage some indirect involvement of the parties.[160] The new Notice is silent on this point. It may be assumed that, as with other points, the Commission understands that national procedural rules should apply. Indeed, the Notice states that the Commission's opinion should be 'dealt with' in accordance with national procedural rules, subject to the general principles of EU law. This leads to the thorny issue of the use that a national court can make of the Commission's opinion. All the Notice says is that the Commission's opinion is not binding, before making reference to national procedural rules, which in turn have to respect the general principles of EU law. However, there is no indication as to how such an opinion may be used and, in particular, whether it may be used in evidence. In *Van der Wal*,[161] the ECJ equated the Commission's opinions (of the second kind, ie providing a legal or economic analysis on the basis of data supplied by the national court) with expert reports and ruled that they should be subject to national procedural rules applying to expert reports, including rules on disclosure. Thus, the Court first clarified the 'status' of the Commission's opinions and then the treatment which should be given to them. While that case was concerned with the conditions for disclosure of such opinions to third parties, it seems that the same principles would apply to disclosure of a Commission's opinion to the parties in the proceedings, ie

---

[158] Antitrust Manual of Procedures, Internal DG Competition working documents on procedures for the application of Articles 101 and 102 TFEU, March 2012, Module 4 'Cooperation between the Commission and national courts', paras 34.

[159] Antitrust Manual of Procedures, Internal DG Competition working documents on procedures for the application of Articles 101 and 102 TFEU, March 2012, Module 4 'Cooperation between the Commission and national courts', paras 35–6.

[160] The 1993 Notice provided that '[a]s amicus curiae, the Commission is obliged to respect legal neutrality and objectivity. Consequently, it will not accede to requests for information unless they come from a national court, either directly, or indirectly through parties which have been ordered by the court concerned to provide certain information. In the latter case, the Commission will ensure that its answer reaches all the parties to the proceedings' (para 42). Taking into account that a request for 'information' under the 1993 Notice could be construed as also covering a request for an opinion (see above), one might argue that such direct involvement of the parties would be possible in all of the three possible requests for 'information' envisaged therein, including requests for an opinion.

[161] Joined Cases C-174/98 P and C-189/98 P *van der Wal v EC Commission* [2000] ECR I-1, para 25.

such disclosure will depend on the relevant national procedural rules. However, as indicated in the Commission's Notice, such rules must comply with the general principles of EU law. It seems that such principles include the parties' right to be heard (and/or submit observations on the Commission's opinion), whatever use the national courts might make of the Commission's opinion.

3. Observations

2.51 A genuinely new feature of cooperation introduced by Regulation 1/2003 was the possibility afforded to the Commission (and NCAs) to submit observations to national courts on issues relating to the application of Articles 101 and 102 TFEU.[162] While the transmission of information and the opinions provided for in Article 15(1) of Regulation 1/2003 are cooperation instruments which can be used at the initiative of national courts, the observations pursuant to Article 15(3) are submitted by the Commission of its own motion, although it needs the permission of the national court if it wishes to submit them orally.

2.52 Different from the requests for information or for an opinion, observations to a national court are submitted on the initiative of the Commission. Oral submissions can only be submitted with the national court's permission.[163] The Commission's Notice adds that, while it is for the Member States to establish the relevant procedural framework, in its absence, the procedure for the submission of observations should be determined by the national courts dealing with the case, subject to the principles of EU law, including respecting the parties' fundamental rights (mentioned here expressly, unlike in paragraph 30 in relation to opinions). As with the other two instruments of cooperation, a number of issues arise in relation to the scope, the purpose of, and the procedure for the submission of observations. The Commission will only submit observations when the consistent application of Articles 101 or 102 TFEU so requires.[164] Thus, compared to the other two cooperation instruments, here the actual purpose of this instrument—to ensure the consistent application of EU competition law—emerges even more clearly. Indeed, the very text of Article 15(3) envisages the submission of observations '[w]here the coherent application of Article 101 or [102] of the Treaty so requires'.[165] Unlike the other two instruments of cooperation, Regulation 1/2003 touches on

---

[162] 'Q&A on Modernization with Kris Dekeyser' (April 2005) 8(3) Global Competition Review, reports that the Commission has not submitted *amicus curiae* briefs during the first year of application of Reg 1/2003 because it has not identified any problem of coherence in the application of Arts [101] and [102 TFEU] by national courts.

[163] See also Antitrust Manual of Procedures, Internal DG Competition working documents on procedures for the application of Articles 101 and 102 TFEU, March 2012, Module 4 'Cooperation between the Commission and national courts', paras 37 and 38.

[164] Case C-429/07 *Inspecteur van de Belastingdienst* [2009] ECR I-4833, para 30: 'Consequently, a literal interpretation of the first subparagraph of Article 15(3) of Regulation No 1/2003 leads to the conclusion that the option for the Commission, acting on its own initiative, to submit written observations to courts of the Member States is subject to the sole condition that the coherent application of Articles 81 EC or 82 EC so requires. That condition may be fulfilled even if the proceedings concerned do not pertain to issues relating to the application of Article 81 or Article 82 of the Treaty.' In this respect, the Notice states at para 32: 'The regulation specifies that the Commission will only submit observations when the coherent application of Articles [101] or [102] EC so requires. That being the purpose of its submission, the Commission will limit its observations to an economic and legal analysis of the facts underlying the case pending before the national court.'

[165] The scope of the Commission's intervention seems narrower than originally envisaged in the draft Regulation, which provided that the Commission would be entitled to submit written (and oral) observations '[f]or reasons of the Community public interest'. See Proposal for a Council Regulation on the implementation of the rules on competition laid down in Arts 81[101] and 82[102] of the Treaty and amending Regs (EEC) 1017/68, (EEC) 2988/74, (EEC) 4056/86, and (EEC) 3975/87 ('Reg implementing Arts 81 and 82 of the Treaty'), COM(2000) 582 final [2000] OJ C365E/284. On the other hand, the scope of the

some procedural aspects concerning the submission of observations. Because NCAs can also submit observations to national courts, submissions by the Commission are more likely to be appropriate before last instance courts in the Member States.

Both Regulation 1/2003 and the Cooperation Notice are silent on the actual use which **2.53** the national court is entitled to make of the Commission's observations. However, in relation to the national procedural rules governing the submission of observations, the Notice states that those rules should be compatible with the fundamental rights of the parties involved in the case. Although the Commission might have been more explicit, this seems to indicate that the parties should be allowed not only to have access to the Commission's observations, but also to submit their own observations thereon.[166] This is even more important if, as seems to be the case, the Commission's observations may in fact address the merits of the case. A problem may arise in connection with the considerable weight that the Commission's or NCAs' observations inevitably have for a national judge, with the risks that this entails for the protection of the defence rights of the parties to the national proceedings and of the principle of 'equality of arms'. Those observations should thus be communicated to the parties and aired before the court. In this respect, the procedural stage when such observations are submitted may also be important. In the absence of any indication in the Regulation or the Notice, it seems that the Commission has some discretion as to when exactly to submit its observations, subject to any national procedural law requirements, which, in turn, are likely to differ not only between Member States but also between different proceedings within the same Member State. It is advisable to coordinate the timing of the submission of the intended amicus curiae observations at least informally with the addressee court.[167] It is submitted that if the Commission intervenes too early, it might not have everything it requires to make a 'useful' intervention (without prejudice to the possibility of requesting any necessary documents from the national court), while if it intervenes too late, it may delay the proceedings precisely because of the need to ensure that the parties are given an opportunity to reply.

As regards the internal procedure for the preparation of submissions, the submissions made **2.54** pursuant to Article 15(3) require the approval of the College of Commissioners. The approval to lodge submissions is sought by a communication of the President of the Commission in agreement with the Member of the Commission with special responsibility for competition. The Legal Service is *chef de file* both for requesting the approval of the College and for the actual submission. It will draft the written observations and present the oral observations

---

Commission's intervention also seems narrower than that of the NCAs, since Art 15(3) of Reg 1/2003 does not provide for any limit on the latter's intervention.

[166] However, this is not the only possible interpretation of Art 15 and para 35 of the Notice. See H Gilliams, 'Modernization: From Policy to Practice' [2003] 28 EL Rev 451, 461, who doubts whether national courts are required to communicate the Commission's observations to the parties and claims that the Commission (and the NCAs) should have been allowed to intervene as parties instead, applying for leave to intervene in accordance with national law and not as 'interveners with special rights'.

[167] See also Antitrust Manual of Procedures Internal DG Competition working documents on procedures for the application of Articles 101 and 102 TFEU, March 2012, Module 4 'Cooperation between the Commission and national courts', para 41. The Manproc indicates at para 40 of Module 4 'Cooperation between the Commission and national courts' that DG COMP may have knowledge about individual cases from different sources, notably because (one of) the parties inform(s) DG COMP (this does not oblige the Commission to act, though). Requests (eg by parties) to submit observations to a national court will be registered and passed to Unit A1; or because DG COMP receives a copy of the judgment under appeal pursuant to Art 15(2) of Reg 1/2003. Unit A1 or the competent sectoral unit may proactively wish to find out whether one of the parties seeks relief with the last instance court. Unit A1 unit or the competent sectoral unit will not contact the parties to this end, but it will consider whether information can be sought with the registry of the last instance court and may liaise with the Legal Service in this respect.

(possibly in the presence of the appropriate DG COMP official). Depending on the nature of the issue at stake (eg horizontal issue or sector-specific issue), assistance on the substance will be given by Unit A1 or by the sectoral unit, after having consulted Unit A1. Procedural assistance (eg asking the national court to transmit or ensure the transmission of a copy of all documents that are necessary for the assessment of the case) will be given by Unit A1. If no assistance is asked for by the Legal Service, Unit A1 will ensure that DG COMP is duly consulted about the content of the observations.[168]

2.55 It is also to note that there may also be a conflict between the principle of direct effect and respect for Member States' procedural autonomy. Article 15(3) of Regulation 1/2003 grants the Commission a directly applicable right to submit observations to national courts on its own initiative, but the Cooperation Notice adds that in the absence of a specific and uniform procedural framework for such submission, Member States' procedural rules and practices determine the relevant procedural framework. National courts thus have to provide within their system for the possibility of the Commission intervening, while ensuring at the same time respect for the fundamental rights of the parties and the general principles of EU law, such as the principles of effectiveness and equivalence.[169] Under the principle of effectiveness, the submission of observations may not be excessively (ie disproportionately) difficult or practically impossible. The principle of equivalence would require that the submission of observations by the Commission might not be subject to a more restrictive procedure than any other similar submission provided by national law. As a result, it may be that the Commission will in fact be granted the status of a non-party intervener with sufficient interest to submit observations to the court in proceedings in which issues of EC competition law arise.[170]

2.56 For its part, the Commission has decided to submit amicus curiae observations on two occasions during the first five years of the application of Regulation 1/2003, where it considered that there was an imminent threat to the coherent application of the EU competition rules. In sum, the Commission's amicus curiae brief pursuant to Article 15(3) of Regulation 1/2003 is to intervene in cases that have important policy implications for the application of Articles 101 and 102 TFEU. Stakeholders have called on the Commission to have greater recourse to this instrument and further reflection is required as to how this practice may be developed in the future.[171] By the end of 2011, there were in total nine interventions.[172]

---

[168] DG COMP Policy Director (Director of COMP/A), following a suggestion made by Unit A1 and in cooperation with the competent sectoral unit, may propose that the Commission submit observations to the national court. Unit A1, in cooperation with the competent sectoral unit, will solicit the views of the Legal Service on whether it agrees with the proposal to submit written or oral observations. Unit A1, in cooperation with the competent sectoral unit, will liaise with the cabinet of the Member of the Commission with special responsibility for competition to ask for approval of such a submission. See also Commission Antitrust Manual of Procedures, Internal DG Competition working documents on procedures for the application of Articles 101 and 102 TFEU, March 2012, Module 4 'Cooperation between the Commission and national courts', paras 42–7.

[169] See, eg Case C-147/01 *Weber's Wines World et al* [2003] ECR I-11365, paras 38–45.

[170] K Lenaerts and D Gerard, 'Decentralisation of EC Competition Law Enforcement: Judges in the Frontline' [2004] World Competition Law and Economics 313, 334.

[171] Commission Staff Working Paper accompanying the Communication from the Commission to the European Parliament and Council, Report on the functioning of Regulation 1/2003 (COM(2009)206 final), para 291. A more recent case involves 'Observations of the European Commission pursuant to Article 15(3) of Regulation 1/2003—*National Grid Electricity Transmission plc v ABB and others*', November 2011, where the Commission published the observations that it made to the English High Court in relation to an application (in a cartel damages action) for disclosure of leniency documents.

[172] Commission Staff Working Paper Accompanying the Report from the Commission on Competition Policy 2011 (COM(2012) 253 final), 30 May 2012, 15. See also the list contained on DG COMP's website <http://ec.europa.eu/competition/court/antitrust_amicus_curiae.html>. In 2012 the Commission filed an

4. Transmission of judgments

Article 15(2) of Regulation 1/2003 requires Member States to forward to the Commission **2.57** a copy of any written judgment passed by national courts deciding on the application of Articles 81[101] or 82 EC [102 TFEU]. These judgments must be sent 'without delay after the full written judgment is notified to the parties'. The Commission publishes a database of the judgments it receives from the Member States pursuant to Article 15(2). This database, although welcomed as potentially being a valuable source of case practice, is criticized by several stakeholders on the grounds that it is far from complete.[173] Some stakeholders have provided suggestions for improving the functioning of Article 15(2). For example, it has been proposed that NCAs should be given the task of assembling the relevant judgments in their respective territories and transmitting them to the Commission, as is currently done in several Member States. It is further proposed that this could be combined with litigants being obliged to serve their initial pleadings on the Commission and/or the NCA concerned, so that the latter could be alerted to the litigation at an early stage.[174] Overall, options for ensuring a more efficient and effective way of providing access to national court judgments should be contemplated.

D. National Courts' Assistance to the Commission

Regulation 1/2003 not only concerns the Commission's assistance to national courts, but **2.58** also national courts' assistance to the Commission. Such assistance is dealt with in Part B of Section III of the Commission's Notice. Apart from the transmission of documents necessary for the submission of observations (Article 15(3)) and written copy of the judgments applying EU competition law (Article 15(2)), such assistance basically takes place in the context of the Commission's inspections.[175] The Commission Notice reproduces the provisions of Regulation 1/2003 on the national courts' intervention in the context of an inspection of the

---

amicus curiae brief before the Belgian Constitutional Court case (Ruling no 161/2012 *Tessenderlo Chemie v Belgische Staat*, 20 December 2012, available at <http://ec.europa.eu/competition/court/antitrust_amicus_curiae.html>) which concerned the question whether or not fines imposed by the Commission for breach of Art 101 TFEU can be wholly or partially deductible from taxes. In its amicus curiae brief, the Commission set out the view that an interpretation of the Belgian Income Tax Code that allowed such fines to be deducted (in whole or in part) from taxable income would not be compatible with EU law. In particular, tax deductibility of the fine would undermine the required deterrent character of such a fine and endanger the objectives of EU competition law.

[173] In the five-year review carried out by the Commission, numerous stakeholders have highlighted the fact that they are aware of national court judgments in which Arts [101] or [102 TFEU] have been applied that do not appear in the database. The database of judgments transmitted by the Member States is currently supplemented by a compilation of judgments handed down by national courts from 2006 onwards, which is prepared by most NCAs for their respective jurisdictions and is made available on the DG COMP website at <http://ec.europa.eu/competition/elojade/antitrust/nationalcourts/>. Parts 3 of the 2004 and 2005 Annual Reports on Competition Policy, available at: <http://ec.europa.eu/competition/annual_reports/> also contain sections on the application of the EU competition rules by national courts.

[174] For instance, this is the practice in the UK where any party whose statement of case raises or deals with an issue relating to the application of Arts 101 and 102 TFEU or the equivalent national provisions must serve a copy of the statement of the case on the Office of Fair Trading at the same time as it is served on the other parties to the claim. See Practice Direction—Competition Law—Claims Relating to the Application of Articles 81 [101] and 82 [102] of the EC Treaty and Chapters I and II of Part 1 of the Competition Act 1998, para 3. The same duty of notification is imposed on appellants. See Practice Direction 52—Appeals, para 21.10A.

[175] See Ch 8, 'Inspections', para 8.74 et seq.

undertakings' premises as well as in the context of an inspection of other premises, adding only that the national court shall provide its assistance in an appropriate timeframe as established by ECJ case law.[176] As provided for in Articles 20 and 21 of Regulation 1/2003, while in the first case judicial assistance will only be required, if national law so provides, where the undertaking concerned opposes the Commission's inspection (although it might indeed be requested on a precautionary basis), in the second case prior authorization from the national court is required by the Regulation itself.

2.59 In both cases, the national court is entitled to a limited control with regard to the authenticity and the proportionality of the Commission's decision, but cannot call into question its necessity or validity, the latter being a matter exclusively for the ECJ. Nor can the national court, for the purposes of carrying out such control, request information which is in the Commission's file. However, with respect to inspections of other premises, the scope of control is somewhat broader than with respect to inspections of the premises of the undertaking concerned. In particular, as regards inspections of other premises, in its assessment of the proportionality of the Commission's decision, the national court may have regard not only to the seriousness of the suspected infringement and the involvement of the undertaking concerned, but also to the importance of the particular evidence sought and the reasonable likelihood that the documents which the Commission is seeking are kept in the premises for which authorization is requested. Furthermore, it may request explanations on (all) those elements necessary to allow its control of proportionality (ie not only on the grounds for suspecting an infringement—which should in any event be expressly stated in the decision pursuant to Article 21(2)—and the nature of the involvement of the undertaking concerned).[177]

---

[176] See also M Dougan, *National Remedies Before the Court of Justice—Issues of Harmonization and Differentiation* (Hart Publishing 2004) 365–7. Case C-94/00 *Roquette Frères* [2002] ECR I-9011, para 92.

[177] Case C-94/00 *Roquette Frères* [2002] ECR I-9011, para 92.

3

THE ROLE OF NATIONAL COMPETITION AUTHORITIES

Luis Ortiz Blanco and Konstantin Jörgens

A. Introduction

Regulation 17 of 1962 provided for a system of administrative control of agreements where, **3.01** in practice, the Commission had almost sole responsibility for enforcing the EU competition rules and the national competition authorities ('NCAs') only rarely dealt with infringements of Articles 101 and 102 of the Treaty on the Functioning of the European Union ('TFEU'). Under Regulation 1/2003, it is not only the Commission but also the NCAs that are responsible for enforcing the EU competition rules, the latter having been assigned a much more significant role in this regard.[1] Regulation 1/2003 created a system of parallel competences in which the competition rules are enforced by a network of competition authorities as well as by the national courts. Provided trade between Member States is affected, Regulation 1/2003 allows NCAs to apply Articles 101 and 102 TFEU, but leaves the Member State free to determine which body will enforce the rules and which mechanism for investigating infringements and enforcing decisions will apply.[2] Article 11(6) of Regulation 1/2003 provides that if the Commission initiates

---

[1] See Commission Staff Working Paper accompanying the Communication from the Commission to the European Parliament and Council 'Report on the functioning of Regulation 1/2003' (COM(2009)206 final), 29 April 2009, para 182: 'After five years, it is apparent that the key challenge in this respect, to boost enforcement results while ensuring the consistent and coherent application of EC competition rules, has been largely achieved.' (available at <http://ec.europa.eu/competition/antitrust/legislation/regulations.html>). See E Gippini-Fournier, 'The Modernisation of European Competition Law: First Experiences with Regulation 1/2003—Institutional Report' in HF Koeck and MM Karollus (eds), The Modernisation of European Competition Law—Initial Experiences with Regulation 1/2003, FIDE XXIII Congress Linz 2008—Congress Publications Vol 2 (Nomos 2008) 375, [70–108]; L Ortiz Blanco and A Lamadrid de Pablo, 'EU Competition Law Enforcement: Elements for a Discussion on Effectiveness and Uniformity' ch 4 in [2011] 38th Annual Fordham Competition Law Institute Conference on International Antitrust Law and Policy, 45, 48–9.

[2] Under Art 35 of Reg 1/2003, the designation of the bodies responsible for the application of the rules is left to the Member States. See Commission Staff Working Paper accompanying the Communication from the Commission to the European Parliament and Council 'Report on the functioning of Regulation 1/2003'

proceedings for the adoption of a decision, the NCAs no longer have jurisdiction to apply Articles 101 and 102 TFEU. Yet a central feature of Regulation 1/2003 is that NCAs may apply Articles 101 and 102 TFEU in individual cases.[3]

3.02 One of the objectives of Regulation 1/2003 was to encourage the consistent application of the EU competition rules by NCAs.[4] As with national courts, Regulation 1/2003 provides that where NCAs apply national competition law to agreements, decisions by associations of undertakings, or concerted practices within the meaning of Article 101 TFEU which may affect trade between Member States, they shall apply Article 101 TFEU.[5] Similarly, where NCAs apply national competition law to any abuse prohibited by Article 102 TFEU, they shall apply Article 102 TFEU. The obligation to apply EU competition law is intended to ensure that the EU competition rules are applied to all cases within their scope. Compliance also entails that the cooperation mechanisms involving the Commission, NCAs, and national courts, as set forth in Articles 11 to 13 and 15 of Regulation 1/2003, are fully applicable in such cases and are not avoided by applying only national law.

3.03 However, Article 3 of Regulation 1/2003 does not provide for the exclusive application of EU law. While the obligation of NCAs (and national courts) to apply Articles 101 and 102 TFEU in all cases that may affect trade between Member States remains, national law may also be applied at the same time. Furthermore, NCAs retained the right to apply national rules that are stricter than Article 102 TFEU in cases of unilateral conduct.[6] The application of national competition law may not, however, lead to the prohibition of agreements, decisions by associations of undertakings, or concerted practices which may affect trade between

---

(COM(2009)206 final) 29 April 2009, paras 192–3, stating that most Member States have one administrative authority which investigates and decides cases. Indeed, several Member States' systems have switched from dual administrative authority systems to a single authority. In Spain, for example, the two former competition bodies were replaced by a single independent authority—the National Competition Commission ('NCC') by the Competition Act 15/2007. Estonia changed its dual system into one single authority. The French system has also been subject to significant changes in 2008/2009, in particular providing the new *Autorité de la Concurrence* with extended powers in antitrust and merger cases. Belgium and Luxembourg currently still opt for a traditional dual administrative system. In Ireland and Austria, investigations are carried out by the respective competition authorities, with the decision-making powers having been transferred to courts. In Malta, the Office of Fair Competition is part of the Ministry of Finance. In Greece, Ireland, and the UK, sectoral regulators are empowered to enforce the EU competition rules in specific sectors, eg telecommunications, postal services, and energy. In all Member States the decisions of NCAs are subject to judicial review.

[3] Notice on cooperation within the Network of Competition Authorities ('ECN Cooperation Notice') [2004] OJ C101/43, para 54.

[4] Communication from the European Commission to the European Parliament and the Council 'Report on the functioning of Regulation 1/2003' (SEC(2009)574), 29 April 2009, para 23. L Ortiz Blanco and A Lamadrid de Pablo, 'EU Competition Law Enforcement: Elements for a Discussion on Effectiveness and Uniformity' ch 4 in [2011] 38th Annual Fordham Competition Law Institute Conference on International Antitrust Law and Policy, 45, 91–101.

[5] See also Ch 2, 'The Role of National Judicial Authorities', para 2.17 et seq.

[6] As an example of stricter national rules concerning unilateral conduct, Recital 8 of Reg 1/2003 explicitly mentions national provisions which prohibit or impose sanctions on abusive behaviour toward economically dependent undertakings. Besides rules specifically concerning the abuse of economic dependence, some national provisions regulate behaviour labelled as 'abuse of superior bargaining power' or 'abuse of significant influence'. The aim of these kinds of rules is essentially to regulate unequal bargaining power in distribution relationships, including where neither the supplier nor the distributor holds a dominant position in a specific market. See also Commission Staff Working Paper accompanying the Communication from the Commission to the European Parliament and Council 'Report on the functioning of Regulation 1/2003' (COM(2009)206 final), 29 April 2009, para 162. Furthermore, Regulation 1/2003 does not apply to national laws which impose criminal sanctions on natural persons unless such sanctions are the means whereby competition rules applying to undertakings are enforced. See also O Weber in JL Schulte and C Just (eds), *Kartellrecht* (Carl Heymanns Verlag 2012) Art 3 of Reg 1/2003, para 13 et seq.

Member States[7] but which do not restrict competition within the meaning of Article 101(1) TFEU, or which fulfil the conditions of Article 101(3) TFEU or which are covered by a regulation for the application of Article 101(3) TFEU. If the prohibition in Article 101(1) TFEU does not apply because competition is not restricted or Article 101(3) TFEU applies,[8] it cannot be prohibited under national law.[9] The objective of Article 3(2) of Regulation 1/2003 is thus to eliminate differing results of the application of national and EU law in situations where Article 101 TFEU may apply.[10]

For a large number of NCAs, cases in which they apply the EU competition rules represent a **3.04** significant share of their overall antitrust caseload.[11] Whilst Article 3(1) of Regulation 1/2003 requires the application of Articles 101 or 102 TFEU to cases capable of affecting trade between Member States, it does not impose an obligation to apply national law in parallel to such cases. The parallel application of national rules is thus optional and depends on the respective national system.[12] The primary interest of parallel application is that it protects enforcement decisions by NCAs against legal challenges based on the question of whether there is an effect on trade. In other words, if the EU law base is not upheld, the case would still stand for the infringement of national competition law.[13] In any event, Article 3 of

---

[7] In Joined Cases T-259/02 to T-264/02 and T-271/02 *Raiffeisen Zentralbank Österreich AG and others* [2002] ECR II-5169, confirmed in Joined Cases C-125/07 P, C-133/07 P, C-135/07 P, and C-137/07 P *Erste Group Bank a.O. v Commission* [2009] ECR I-8681, the General Court ('GC') confirmed, in a cartel case covering the territory of Austria, the established case law according to which horizontal cartels covering the whole of a Member State are normally capable of affecting trade between Member States, even where the members of the cartel had not taken specific measures to exclude foreign competitors from the market.

[8] See also Case C-309/99 *Wouters* [2002] ECRI-1577, para 97 et seq. Article 101(1) TFEU may also not apply where the agreement serves a legitimate purpose. See Ch 2, 'The Role of National Judicial Authorities', para 2.21, n 59.

[9] The ECJ has held that NACs can apply Art 101(1) to an agreement between undertakings that may affect trade between Member States, but that does not reach the thresholds specified by the Commission in its de minimis notice, provided that the agreement constitutes an appreciable restriction of competition within the meaning of Art 101. The ruling concerned a reference from the French Supreme Court on whether national competition authorities can take enforcement action against companies found to be in breach of Art 101 of the TFEU, but where the parties remain below the market share thresholds in the European Commission's de minimis notice Case C-226/11 *Expedia v Autorité de la concurrence and Others* [2013] OJ C38/6.

[10] Commission Staff Working Paper accompanying the Communication from the Commission to the European Parliament and Council 'Report on the functioning of Regulation 1/2003' (COM(2009)206 final), 29 April 2009, para 142. In the view of the Commission, Art 3 could be characterized as 'one of the major successes of Regulation 1/2003'. Stakeholders from the legal and business communities have largely confirmed that Reg 1/2003 has positively contributed to the creation of a level playing field, along with the substantive convergence of national laws with the EU competition rules. On the other hand, the divergence of standards regarding unilateral conduct has been criticized by the business and legal communities. For more details on this debate regarding the state of substantive convergence, see also L Ortiz Blanco and A Lamadrid de Pablo, 'EU Competition Law Enforcement: Elements for a Discussion on Effectiveness and Uniformity', ch 4 in [2011] 38th Annual Fordham Competition Law Institute Conference on International Antitrust Law & Policy, 45, [94–7].

[11] For more details, see Commission Staff Working Paper accompanying the Communication from the Commission to the European Parliament and Council 'Report on the functioning of Regulation 1/2003' (COM(2009)206 final), 29 April 2009, para 148. For example, the Commission reported that roughly one-half of the enforcement decisions adopted by the Italian competition authority during the reporting period were based on EU law. The French competition authority applied EU competition law in nearly 40 per cent of all cases dealt with in the antitrust field, and the Belgian, Danish, and Dutch authorities in around 30 per cent. Portugal and Greece reached approximately 25 per cent, whereas Hungary and Slovenia were close to 20 per cent.

[12] Commission Staff Working Paper accompanying the Communication from the Commission to the European Parliament and Council 'Report on the functioning of Regulation 1/2003' (COM(2009)206 final), 29 April 2009, para 152.

[13] Commission Staff Working Paper accompanying the Communication from the Commission to the European Parliament and Council 'Report on the functioning of Regulation 1/2003' (COM(2009)206 final), 29 April 2009, para 153.

Regulation 1/2003 only deals with substantive law and does not concern the application of procedural rules.

3.05 The 'remarkable level of convergence' referred to by the Commission in its five-year review in 2009 should not, however, lead to an underestimation of the continuing divergences on important procedural issues that may influence the outcome of individual cases, eg fines, criminal sanctions, liability of undertakings or associations of undertakings, succession of undertakings, prescription periods, standard of proof, and the power to impose structural remedies. Moreover, as the Commission itself admits, the ability of NCAs to set priorities would be greatly divergent in so far as a large number of authorities are obliged to investigate and/or rule on complaints that they are seized with, while others are legally empowered to set priorities in one form or another.[14]

3.06 Regulation 1/2003 sets out the powers of NCAs by defining the types of decisions that can be taken. The NCAs are given the power to apply Articles 101 and 102 TFEU in individual cases. For this purpose, acting on their own initiative or on a complaint, they may require that an infringement be brought to an end, order interim measures, accept commitments, and impose fines, periodic penalty payments, or any other penalty provided for in their national law.[15] The latter may also include imprisonment or criminal sanctions for natural persons.[16] At the same time, NCAs remain entitled to establish their own enforcement priorities, including the right to decide which agreements and conduct to investigate. The Commission, however, retained its specific role of clarifying the law, and NCAs do not have the power to adopt non-infringement decisions similar to the ones which the Commission may adopt, acting on its own initiative and where the EU public interest relating to the application of Articles 101 and 102 TFEU so requires.[17]

---

[14] Commission Staff Working Paper accompanying the Communication from the Commission to the European Parliament and Council 'Report on the functioning of Regulation 1/2003' (COM(2009)206 final), 29 April 2009, para 203. See also at para 206, where the Commission noted that stakeholders in the context of the public consultation for this Report have called strongly for further harmonization of procedures within the ECN. They particularly emphasized different national rules on sanctions/fines for violations of the antitrust rules, leniency, settlements, commitments, complaints, rules governing the admissibility of evidence (eg Legal Professional Privilege ('LPP')) and procedural rules (eg limitations, deadlines, procedural fines etc). According to stakeholders, these differences in national rules may lead to discrepancies in the outcome of a case depending on the jurisdiction in which it is reviewed and could therefore harm the rights of undertakings. L Ortiz Blanco and A Lamadrid de Pablo, 'EU Competition Law Enforcement: Elements for a Discussion on Effectiveness and Uniformity' ch 4 in [2011] 38th Annual Fordham Competition Law Institute Conference on International Antitrust Law and Policy, 45, 92–3, pointing out that: '[P]rocedural rules have a crucial influence over the outcome of cases, and the solution to each case should not depend on the particular procedural arrangements adopted in each jurisdiction.'

[15] Article 5 of Reg 1/2003. Under Art 29(2) NCAs are also empowered to withdraw the benefit of a block exemption regulation under certain conditions. Thus, where in any particular case, agreements, decisions by associations of undertakings, or concerted practices to which a block exemption applies have effects which are incompatible with Art 101(3) TFEU in the territory of a Member State or part thereof, which has all the characteristics of a distinct market, the NCA of that Member State may withdraw the benefit of the block exemption in question in respect of that territory.

[16] This could mean that the NCAs have stronger powers than the Commission under Reg 1/2003. The Commission can only impose fines on undertakings for infringements of Art 101 or 102 TFEU, while Art 23(5) of Reg 1/2003 clarifies that fines 'shall not be of a criminal law nature'. The German Federal Cartel Office (*Bundeskartellamt*) can impose fines on individuals such as directors or officers. In the UK, infringements of competition law can result for individuals in director disqualification orders of up to fifteen years and imprisonment for up to five years in relation to certain specified cartel arrangements.

[17] Article 10 of Reg 1/2003. See in this regard WP Wils, 'Community Report. The Modernisation of EU Competition Law Enforcement' in the EU FIDE 2004 National Reports 661, paras 49–50. In any event, if the Commission does not take up the case, companies may contact the NCAs whose territory is affected by the agreement in question in order to obtain a decision that there is 'no ground for action on their part' (Art 6(3) of Reg 1/2003). Despite the fact that such a decision would only bind the issuing authority, it would

As regards the scope of the powers of NCAs to take decisions under Regulation 1/2003, the **3.07** Grand Chamber of the Court of Justice ('ECJ') confirmed that only the Commission could reach a decision that no infringement existed as regards the compatibility of an undertaking's practices with EU competition law.[18] According to the Court, the most that a NCA could do was to close its investigation and declare that, based on the information in its possession, the conditions in Articles 101 and/or 102 TFEU were not met and that there were no grounds for action.[19] The case followed a reference from a Polish court, which was faced with the task of deciding whether, having found that the telecommunications incumbent Telekommunikacja Polska had engaged in no restrictive practices under national law, the Polish NCA could also bring the procedure under Article 102 TFEU to an end on the basis that it 'was devoid of purpose'. Rival Tele2 Polska—now Netia—complained that the authority was not empowered to adopt a 'non-infringement' decision for Telekommunikacja Polska. Instead, it could only close its investigation.

In the same judgment, the Court observed that Article 5 of Regulation 1/2003 would **3.08** limit the type of decisions that NCAs could issue. By virtue of Article 5(1), NCAs can require that an infringement be brought to an end; order interim measures; accept commitments; and/or impose fines or periodic penalty payments. Under Article 5(2), where the conditions for prohibition are not met, NCAs 'may likewise decide that there are no grounds for action on their part.'[20] Explicitly finding that there had been no infringement would make it impossible for other authorities to conduct investigations and only the Commission was empowered to find that there had been no breach of the rules described. The Court also referred to the Commission's power to issue decisions (on an exceptional basis) of a declaratory nature to ensure the consistent application of EU competition law.[21] The Grand Chamber stated that empowering NCAs to take 'negative' decisions that there has been no breach of EU competition rules would risk undermining the uniform application of Articles 101 and 102 TFEU, since it might prevent the Commission

---

provide a high degree of legal certainty in that it would be unlikely that other authorities, including the Commission, would subsequently impose fines on a company. C Canenbley and M Rosenthal, 'Cooperation between Antitrust Authorities In-and Outside the EU: What does it mean for Multinational Corporations?—Part 1' [2005] ECLR 106, 107.

[18] Case C-375/09 *Prezes Urzędu Ochrony Konkurencji i Konsumentów v Tele2 Polska sp. z o.o* [2011] ECR I-3055. Kerse & Khan, *EC Antitrust Procedure* (6th edn, Sweet & Maxwell 2012) para 5-011, pointing out, as a matter of textual and contextual interpretation, that Art 5 does appear to prevent NCAs from adopting decisions that formally declare Art 102 inapplicable, or that there has been no breach of Art 102. In practical terms, the position might not be clear-cut describing situations where NCAs and national courts may go beyond those limits of Article 5. Judge JD Cooke, 'Application of EC Competition Rules by National Courts', International Bar Association ('IBA') conference, Antitrust Reform in Europe: A Year in Practice, Brussels, 9–11 March 2005, 6, also noted that NCAs would seem to be entitled to decisions that there are no grounds for action but not to decisions of inapplicability. However, Cooke believed this might give rise to some problems before national courts, particularly in those Member States where, under the arrangements for implementing Reg 1/2003, the investigating and prosecuting functions of an NCA have been separated from the decision-making function. Where a court has been designated under Art 35 of Reg 1/2003 to decide upon infringements, it is presumably arguable that a judgment of the court dismissing the NCA prosecution case against defendant undertakings has precisely the effect of a decision that no infringement has taken place. The judgment in Case C-375/09 *Prezes Urzędu Ochrony Konkurencji i Konsumentów v Tele2 Polska sp. z o.o* [2011] ECR I-3055 has not expanded on this latter problem.

[19] Case C-375/09 *Prezes Urzędu Ochrony Konkurencji i Konsumentów v Tele2 Polska sp. z o.o* [2011] ECR I-3055, para 37.

[20] Case C-375/09 *Prezes Urzędu Ochrony Konkurencji i Konsumentów v Tele2 Polska sp. z o.o* [2011] ECR I-3055, paras 37 and 22.

[21] Article 10 of Reg 1/2003 and Recital 14. Case C-375/09 *Prezes Urzędu Ochrony Konkurencji i Konsumentów v Tele2 Polska sp. z o.o* [2011] ECR I-3055, para 25.

from subsequently finding that the practice in question amounted to a breach of those provisions.[22]

3.09 As regards the question of whether NCAs may adopt declaratory decisions in relation to past infringements, the Commission has indicated that given that Article 5 does not contain a provision equivalent to the last paragraph of Article 7(1) of Regulation 1/2003, there remains a question mark about whether the lack of an express provision may prevent NCAs from taking a decision on the basis of Articles 101 and 102 TFEU in relation to past infringements where they do not intend to impose a fine.[23]

3.10 In any event, the Commission is able to relieve the NCAs of their competence to deal with cases in certain circumstances, and NCAs cannot take decisions which would run counter to an earlier decision by the Commission regarding the same agreement or practice.[24] These are the main differences between the position of the Commission and that of the NCAs.[25]

B. Cooperation between the Commission and the NCAs[26]

3.11 Under the system of parallel competence, the Commission and the NCAs must apply the EU competition rules in close cooperation.[27] Together, the NCAs and the Commission form a

---

[22] Case C-375/09 *Prezes Urzędu Ochrony Konkurencji i Konsumentów v Tele2 Polska sp. z o.o* [2011] ECR I-3055, para 24.

[23] Commission Staff Working Paper accompanying the Communication from the Commission to the European Parliament and Council 'Report on the functioning of Regulation 1/2003' (COM(2009)206 final), 29 April 2009, para 198. See E Gippini-Fournier, 'The Modernisation of European Competition Law: First Experiences with Regulation 1/2003—Institutional Report' in HF Koeck and MM Karollus (eds), The Modernisation of European Competition Law—Initial Experiences with Regulation 1/2003, FIDE XXIII Congress Linz 2008—Congress Publications Vol 2 (Nomos 2008) 375, 416. The author suggests that the NCA could take the view that Art 5 does not oblige them (but does not prevent them either) from taking declaratory decisions in relation to past infringements if they can show a legitimate interest in the sense of the case law of the EU Courts.

[24] Article 16(2) of Reg 1/2003. This does not mean that, once the Commission initiates proceedings, the NCAs are permanently and definitively relieved of their power to apply national competition law. Depending on how the Commission proceedings end, there may be scope for national competition law to be applied by NCAs later, which retain their power to apply both EU and national competition laws even if the Commission has itself already taken a decision, as long as they respect the primacy of EU rules. See Case C-17/10 *Toshiba Corporation e.a.* [2012] OJ C98/3, paras 85 and 86.

[25] P Lowe, 'The Role of the Commission in the Modernisation of EC Competition Law', [2004] Speech at UKAEL Conference on Modernization of EC Competition Law: Uncertainties and Opportunities, suggested at the time of the adoption of Regulation 1/2003 that the role of the Commission would be of a 'primus inter pares'. See also DG COMP official T Toft, 'Introduction to EU Competition Policy: Past, Present and Future', EU–China Conference on the Anti-Monopoly Law Dalian, Liaoning Province, 11 May 2009: '[DG COMP] remains the focal point for Article [101 and 102 TFEU] cases in the EU. For example, if a novel or unresolved issue arises, where it is in the [EU interest], or where a case has an effect on a large number of Member States, [DG COMP] will be well placed to deal with the case, provided that the agreement or practice has an effect on trade between Member States.'

[26] See the general overview in L Ortiz Blanco and A Lamadrid de Pablo, 'EU Competition Law Enforcement: Elements for a Discussion on Effectiveness and Uniformity', ch 4 in [2011] 38th Annual Fordham Competition Law Institute Conference on International Antitrust Law and Policy, 45, 97–101.

[27] Article 11(1) of Reg 1/2003. As described in more detail at para 3.15, the Commission has created in the Directorate-General for Competition ('DG COMP') an 'ECN unit' that gives guidance to case-handlers on all aspects of Reg 1/2003, the implementing Reg 773/20043 and related instruments, as regards the functioning of the Network. In parallel, the mission of the ECN unit comprises the coordination of Director-Generals' relations with Member States in the field of antitrust, in particular with regard to the application of the antitrust rules by NCAs. The ECN unit manages the ECN's general and horizontal activities. Antitrust Manual of Procedures Internal DG Competition working documents on procedures for the application of Articles 101 and 102 TFEU, March 2012, Module 3 'Cooperation with National Competition Authorities and exchange of information in ECN', paras 10 and 11.

network of European competition authorities (the 'European Competition Network' or 'ECN'), which serves as a forum for discussion and cooperation in the application of Articles 101 and 102 TFEU.[28]

Essentially, the aim of the ECN is to ensure both an efficient division of work and the consistent **3.12** application of the EU competition rules. The fact that a case under Article 101 or 102 TFEU affecting trade between Member States can be dealt with by either the Commission or a single NCA or various NCAs acting in parallel undoubtedly led to an increased enforcement of EU competition law. For example, in the period from 1 May 2004 until 31 March 2009, when the Commission published its five-year assessment on the functioning of Regulation 1/2003, more than 1,000 cases were said to have been pursued on the basis of the EU competition rules.[29] Within this time period, the Commission had been informed of more than 300 envisaged decisions submitted by NCAs pursuant to Article 11(4) of Regulation 1/2003. Compared to the situation prior to Regulation 1/2003, these figures clearly demonstrated a significant increase of enforcement activities in the EU since 2004.[30]

The trend continued in 2010, whereas from 2011–2012 the number of cases involving EU **3.13** competition rules went down. The Commission was informed under Article 11(3) of Regulation 1/2003 of 158 new case investigations launched by NCAs in 2010 (in 2012: 106). Amongst the new cases for the last full year (2012), 61 per cent concerned the application of Article 101 TFEU, 28 per cent concerned the application of Article 102 TFEU, and the remainder concerned the application of both. The figure for Article 101 cases notably includes the enforcement action of NCAs in the area of cartels. Large numbers of cases could be observed *inter alia* in the transport, energy, manufacturing, media, and telecommunications sectors.[31] In 2010, the Commission services reviewed a record 94 envisaged decisions under Article 11(4) of Regulation 1/2003, as well as advised on a number of informal requests and queries from NCAs, a figure which has remained fairly stable until 2012 (91).[32]

1. The European Competition Network (ECN)

Regulation 1/2003 did not establish strict rules for the allocation of cases between the **3.14** Commission and the NCAs. Instead, it only provided a series of instruments to allow a flexible and consensual allocation of cases within the ECN.[33] The Commission sought to give guidance through its Notice on cooperation within the network of competition

---

[28] Apart from the cooperation mechanism described at para 3.54 et seq, an important development is the creation of working groups and sectoral subgroups in the ECN which allow for case and policy-related exchanges between experts of certain sectors. See already K Dekeyser, 'Regulation 1/2003: First Experiences' IBC Conference, London, 27 and 28 April 2005, who pointed to the importance of sharing information and experience in this regard. Commission Report on Competition Policy SEC (2004) 805 final para 104. Annex to Report on Competition Policy 2006, Brussels, 25 June 2007, Doc SEC(2007) 860 (COM(2007) 358 Final), paras 149–55.

[29] Updated figures and information are regularly published on the ECN website which was set up in April 2006 in order to provide information to the legal and business community and to citizens. For further information, see <http://ec.europa.eu/competition/ecn/index_en.html>. L Ortiz Blanco and A Lamadrid de Pablo, 'EU Competition Law Enforcement: Elements for a Discussion on Effectiveness and Uniformity', ch 4 in [2011] 38th Annual Fordham Competition Law Institute Conference on International Antitrust Law and Policy, 45, [48–9].

[30] Commission Staff Working Paper accompanying the Communication from the Commission to the European Parliament and Council 'Report on the functioning of Regulation 1/2003' (COM(2009)206 final), para 184.

[31] Commission Staff Working Paper, Accompanying the Report from the Commission on Competition Policy 2010 (COM(2011) 328 final), para 397.

[32] Commission Staff Working Paper, Accompanying the Report from the Commission on Competition Policy 2010 (COM(2011) 328 final), para 399. See, for more statistical information, <http://ec.europa.eu/competition/ecn/index_en.html>.

[33] This is in sharp contrast to the allocation mechanism provided in the merger control rules, where the Commission and the Member States do not have concurrent jurisdiction so that a clear division of

authorities ('ECN Cooperation Notice').[34] Thus, one very important issue dealt with in the ECN Cooperation Notice concerns the principles governing the division of work between the members of the network. This is required to enable an undertaking to carry out its self-assessment because this must be based not only on the Commission's practice but also on the decision-making practice of NCAs and national courts. Regulation 1/2003 established a system of parallel competences, whereby both the Commission and NCAs are competent to apply Articles 101 and 102 TFEU. This approach was taken to ensure efficient work sharing for all cases, including complex ones, without burdening the system with a rigid division of competences.[35]

3.15 Within the Commission, a dedicated ECN unit gives guidance to case-handlers on all aspects of Regulation 1/2003, the Commission implementing Regulation 773/2004[36] and the related instruments, as regards the functioning of the Network. The starting point is that in the system established by Regulation 1/2003, every case handler becomes involved in contacts and cooperation with Member States' NCAs. The Commission is at pains to stress that regular contacts at all levels, mutual trust, and solidarity are necessary to ensure the successful operation of the ECN.[37] In parallel, the mission of the ECN unit comprises the coordination of the Director-Generals' relations with Member States in the field of antitrust, in particular with regard to the application of the antitrust rules by NCAs. The ECN Unit manages the ECN's general and horizontal activities. Apart from the networking on horizontal policy issues, its tasks involve coordination work with regard to case alloca-tion, the monitoring and scrutiny (in close cooperation with the competent sectoral unit) of draft decisions/statement of objections from NCAs, advising on Article 11(6) measures, the provision of informal assistance to NCAs (essentially, help desk function), and the provision of assistance to sectoral units in the Directorate-General for Competition ('DG COMP') on ECN-related issues. The ECN unit should also ensure consistency across sectors in rela-tions with the various Member States throughout the handling of DG COMP's own cases.

---

competence is established (Art 21 of Council Regulation (EC) No 139/2004 states that 'Subject to review by the Court of Justice, the Commission shall have sole jurisdiction to take the decisions provided for in this Regulation').

[34] [2004] OJ C101/43. The ECN Cooperation Notice is based to a significant extent on the Joint Statement of the Council and the Commission on the functioning of the network of competition authorities, entered in the Council Minutes at the time of the adoption of Reg 1/2003; Council Document 15435/02 ADD 1 of 10 December 2002. Given that the Joint Statement is a political declaration, whose details were to be set out in the ECN Cooperation Notice, the analysis may therefore be limited to principles spelled out in the Notice. In Case T-339/04 *France Télécom SA v Commission* [2007] ECR II-521, para 85, the GC held that this statement was political in nature and that it did not create legal rights or obligations. The applicant could not therefore rely on such a document with a view to procuring the annulment of an act of EU law that adversely affected it. The notice replaced the earlier 'Commission notice on cooperation between national competition authorities and the Commission in handling cases falling within the scope of Arts 81 and 82 of the EC Treaty' [1997] OJ C313/3.

[35] K Dekeyser, 'Regulation 1/2003: First Experiences', IBC Conference, London, 27 and 28 April 2005, noted that the system had been built on the assumption that parallel competences serve effective enforce-ment. In a system of exclusive competences the victims of infringements would depend on a single enforcer which sets different priorities. See also C Gauer, 'Due Process in the Face of Divergent National Procedures and Sanctions', IBA conference, Antitrust Reform in Europe: A Year in Practice, Brussels, 9–11 March 2005, 2–3. See also, Antitrust Manual of Procedures, Internal DG Competition working documents on procedures for the application of Articles 101 and 102 TFEU, March 2012, Module 3 'Cooperation with National Competition Authorities in EU and exchange of information in ECN', para 2.

[36] Commission Regulation (EC) No 773/2004 of 7 April 2004 relating to the conduct of proceedings by the Commission pursuant to Articles 81 and 82 of the EC Treaty, [2004] OJ L123/18.

[37] See also Antitrust Manual of Procedures, Internal DG Competition working documents on procedures for the application of Articles 101 and 102 TFEU, March 2012, Module 3 'Cooperation with National Competition Authorities in EU and exchange of information in ECN', para 1.

It informs and where necessary consults within DG COMP on issues of relevance that come up in these contacts with the ECN.[38]

In its five-year assessment in 2009, the Commission took the view that the cooperation in the **3.16** ECN had surpassed expectations and had given a more 'structural impetus' to the enforcement of the EU competition rules. The possibility of (re)allocating cases to another well-placed authority and the cooperation mechanisms provided by Regulation 1/2003 would have been used reasonably and largely successfully and have significantly enhanced the enforcement activities within the ECN.[39] Informal exchanges and cooperation in various multilateral fora would have contributed towards building a common competition culture.[40]

Principles of case allocation

The competence of the NCAs   In principle, cases under Articles 101 and/or 102 TFEU **3.17** will be dealt with by (i) a single NCA, with the assistance or not of NCAs of other Member States; (ii) several NCAs acting in parallel; or (iii) the Commission.[41] The ECN Cooperation Notice sets out the criteria applied to determine which NCA is the best placed to handle the case. An authority can be considered to be well placed to deal with a case if the following three cumulative conditions are met:

  (i) The agreement or practice has substantial direct actual or foreseeable effects on competition within its territory, is implemented within, or originates from its territory. This will often coincide with the centre of gravity of the case, ie the Member State(s) where competition is substantially affected by the infringement.
 (ii) The authority is able to effectively bring to an end the entire infringement, ie it can adopt a cease-and-desist order, the effect of which will be sufficient to bring an end to the infringement, and it can, where appropriate, sanction the infringement adequately.[42]
(iii) The authority can gather, possibly with the assistance of other authorities, the evidence required to prove the infringement.[43]

Conditions (ii) and (iii) are related to the investigation and enforcement capabilities of the **3.18** authority so selected. These criteria suggest that a material link between the infringement and the territory of a Member State must exist in order for that Member State's competition authority to be considered well placed. In most cases the NCAs of those Member States will be well placed where competition is substantially affected by an infringement, provided that the NCA in question is capable of effectively bringing the infringement to an end through

---

[38] Antitrust Manual of Procedures Internal DG Competition working documents on procedures for the application of Articles 101 and 102 TFEU, March 2012, Module 3 'Cooperation with National Competition Authorities in EU and exchange of information in ECN', paras 10–11.

[39] Commission Staff Working Paper accompanying the Communication from the Commission to the European Parliament and Council 'Report on the functioning of Regulation 1/2003' (COM(2009)206 final), para 183. For an evaluation of functioning of the ECN see M Kekelekis, 'The European Competition Network (ECN): It Does Actually Work Well' [2009] EIPAScope 35; and with regard to leniency K Dekeyser and M Jaspers, 'A New Era of ECN Cooperation: Achievements and Challenges with Special Focus on Work in the Leniency Field' (2007) 30 World Competition 3.

[40] Antitrust Manual of Procedures Internal DG Competition working documents on procedures for the application of Articles 101 and 102 TFEU, March 2012, Module 3 'Cooperation with National Competition Authorities in EU and exchange of information in ECN', paras 13–14, stating that DG COMP case-handlers have direct access to the informatics application and its ECN case forms ('fiches'): a new case fiche, an envisaged decision fiche, and a closed case fiche.

[41] ECN Cooperation Notice [2004] OJ C101/43, para 5.

[42] The question whether an infringement having effects in several Member States can be adequately sanctioned by one NCA is a question which remains unanswered taking into account that no NCA has imposed so far sanctions in respect of infringement carried on outside its territory. On this point, see Kerse & Khan, *EC Antitrust Procedure* (6th edn, Sweet & Maxwell 2012) para 2-011.

[43] ECN Cooperation Notice [2004] OJ C101/43, para 8.

either single or parallel action—together with another NCA—unless the Commission is better placed to act.[44] In most instances, the NCA that receives a complaint or starts an *ex officio* procedure will remain in charge of the case.

3.19   A competition authority which is well placed and willing to investigate and sanction an infringement informs the network of its intentions at an early stage of the investigation by inserting some basic information into the ECN database. The number of case investigations initiated by NCAs and communicated to the network is considerable, being estimated at well over 100 new cases every year.[45]

3.20   The ECN uses an informatics application for recording the most important steps (opening of case, envisaged decision, and closure) in enforcement cases dealt with by all ECN members, including the Commission.[46] In parallel to the information received electronically via the informatics application, the Commission will receive from the NCAs draft documents by secure electronic mail or by secure courier. The envisaged statement of objections/draft decision arrives via encrypted mail at the antitrust registry, which decrypts it and uploads it into an internal database; the registry also sends an alert immediately to the ECN unit of the Commission and the competent sectoral unit for follow-up. The registry provides the submitting NCA with an acknowledgement of receipt. This mechanism aims to allow the network members to rapidly detect multiple proceedings and should ensure efficient work sharing within the ECN.[47]

3.21   With respect to the Commission, DG COMP must monitor the fiches submitted to the informatics application, informing the Commission of any step taken in national procedures applying Articles 101 and 102 TFEU.[48] Each sectoral unit would need an ECN responsible person, who regularly checks new fiches and, if appropriate, immediately brings to the attention of the head of unit cases of potential relevance to the unit (both with a view to avoiding duplication of efforts and ensuring consistency).[49] Other authorities may signal their interest

---

[44]   ECN Cooperation Notice [2004] OJ C101/43, para 9.

[45]   See E Gippini-Fournier, 'The Modernisation of European Competition Law: First Experiences with Regulation 1/2003—Institutional Report' in HF Koeck and MM Karollus (eds), The Modernisation of European Competition Law—Initial Experiences with Regulation 1/2003, FIDE XXIII Congress Linz 2008—Congress Publications Vol 2 (Nomos 2008) 375, 434.

[46]   IT application developed and centrally administered by the Commission (Unit COMP-R3). See Antitrust Manual of Procedures Internal DG Competition working documents on procedures for the application of Articles 101 and 102 TFEU, March 2012, Module 3 'Cooperation with National Competition Authorities and exchange of information in ECN', para 4. The Module explains the rules regarding the filling in and the follow-up of the information in the informatics application, including the possible reallocation of cases and taking over by the Commission of a case dealt with by a NCA. It also describes the work sharing between the ECN Unit and the sectoral units as well as the mechanism for the confidential transmissions of documents and information by way of a secure e-mail system operated by the Authorised Disclosure Officer ('ADO', see para 3.65). This means that case-handlers are not to make such transmissions themselves.

[47]   Antitrust Manual of Procedures Internal DG Competition working documents on procedures for the application of Articles 101 and 102 TFEU, March 2012, Module 3 'Cooperation with National Competition Authorities in EU and exchange of information in ECN', paras 13 and 18.

[48]   See E Gippini-Fournier, 'The Modernisation of European Competition Law: First Experiences with Regulation 1/2003—Institutional Report' in HF Koeck and MM Karollus (eds), The Modernisation of European Competition Law—Initial Experiences with Regulation 1/2003, FIDE XXIII Congress Linz 2008—Congress Publications Vol 2 (Nomos 2008) 375, 433, points out that, in practice, this requires NCAs to determine at an early stage whether they intend to 'act' under Art 101 or Art 102 TFEU. This, in turn, means that not every new complaint or preliminary step in a possible *ex officio* case triggers a communication to the Commission. Where NCAs receive complaints which they do not intend to investigate (eg because they appear unmeritorious), they have usually not communicated information about them to the network.

[49]   Antitrust Manual of Procedures Internal DG Competition working documents on procedures for the application of Articles 101 and 102 TFEU, March 2012, Module 3 'Cooperation with National Competition Authorities in EU and exchange of information in ECN', para 14.

to also act in the case, either in parallel with the first authority (in the case of NCAs) or solely (in the case of the Commission). In the rare case that authorities disagree on the most suitable allocation of the case, bilateral discussions take place between the concerned authorities.[50]

The ECN Cooperation Notice provides some practical examples of when it could be consid- **3.22** ered that one or various authorities are well placed to deal with a case;[51] in particular, parallel action by two or three NCAs may be appropriate where an agreement or practice has substantial effects on competition in their respective territories and the action of only one NCA would not be sufficient to bring the infringement to an end or to issue adequate sanctions. Conversely, where the action of a single NCA is sufficient to bring the entire infringement to an end, this may be appropriate, although more than one NCA can be regarded as well placed. One example of this scenario is the case of a joint venture operating a maritime transport service between two Member States.[52] The prohibition of the joint venture by one of the two authorities is sufficient to bring an end to the agreement. The Commission emphasizes that each NCA retains full discretion in deciding whether or not to investigate a case.[53]

According to the Commission, the experience of the first five years of work sharing within **3.23** the ECN had clearly demonstrated and confirmed the good functioning of the flexible and pragmatic approach introduced by Regulation 1/2003 and the ECN Cooperation Notice. Discussions on case allocation arose in only a few cases and actual reallocation of cases took place in even fewer. In other words, cases mostly remain with the competition authority that started the investigation.[54] While case allocations attracted considerable attention at the time that the modernization package was adopted, it is true that most of the fears surrounding case allocation have not materialized.[55]

A certain number of complaints received by the Commission or an NCA or both have been **3.24** passed on within the network. Important examples are the *Deutsche Post* cases, where the Commission and the German competition authority were seized with similar complaints referring to Article 102 TFEU concerning the same practice of Deutsche Post AG with regard to discounts for pre-sorted mail. Deutsche Post's practice was based on a provision of the German postal legislation which was the subject of a Commission procedure under Article

---

[50] Commission Staff Working Paper accompanying the Communication from the Commission to the European Parliament and Council 'Report on the functioning of Regulation 1/2003' (COM(2009)206 final), para 209. L Ortiz Blanco and A Lamadrid de Pablo, 'EU Competition Law Enforcement: Elements for a Discussion on Effectiveness and Uniformity', ch 4 in [2011] 38th Annual Fordham Competition Law Institute Conference on International Antitrust Law and Policy, 45, 97–9.

[51] ECN Cooperation Notice [2004] OJ C101/45, paras 10–15.

[52] K Dekeyser and C Gauer, 'The New Enforcement System for Articles 81 and 82 and the Rights of Defence', ch 23 in BE Hawk (ed), *International Antitrust Law & Policy* [2004] Annual Proceedings of the Fordham Institute 549, 75, n 91.

[53] ECN Cooperation Notice [2004] OJ C101/43, para 5. See C Gauer, L Kjolbye, D Dalheimer, E de Smijter, D Schnichels, and M Laurila, 'Regulation 1/2003 and the Modernization Package fully applicable since 1 May 2004' (Summer 2004) 2 Competition Policy Newsletter 1, 3: 'From a practical point of view this means that ... the Finnish authority would not seize itself with an infringement that happens in Greece, as there are already no effects in the Finnish market, not to mention the difficulty of gathering the relevant information and bringing the infringement to an end. On the other hand, if an infringement concerned for instance a shipping line between Italy and Greece, the Greek as well as the Italian competition authority might be well placed to deal with the case, depending on the circumstances.'

[54] Commission Staff Working Paper accompanying the Communication from the Commission to the European Parliament and Council 'Report on the functioning of Regulation 1/2003' (COM(2009)206 final), 29 April 2009, para 214.

[55] See E Gippini-Fournier, 'The Modernisation of European Competition Law: First Experiences with Regulation 1/2003—Institutional Report' in HF Koeck and MM Karollus (eds), The Modernisation of European Competition Law—Initial Experiences with Regulation 1/2003, FIDE XXIII Congress Linz 2008—Congress Publications Vol 2 (Nomos 2008) 375, 435.

106 TFEU. In this case, the Commission, whose experts were preparing the Article 106 TFEU decision, considered that the most effective and efficient way forward would be the investigation of the complaint by the Bundeskartellamt. The complainant agreed to withdraw the complaint filed with the Commission.[56] The work sharing proved successful inasmuch as both proceedings have now been concluded by decisions. In the Commission's view, these cases provide a remarkable example of how the action of the Commission and that of a Member State competition authority can effectively complement each other in practice.[57]

3.25 One issue which would have given rise to certain discussions in the network relates to the situation where an NCA is seized by a complainant but is not particularly well placed to deal with the case, as this requires extensive investigations in other Member States. However, the Commission or another NCA does not consider the case to be a priority. According to the Commission, such a 'negative conflict of allocation' scenario would have occurred on very few occasions. It is in the first place linked to the aforementioned issue that some authorities in the network are bound to deal with cases, even where they are not an enforcement priority, whereas others are not. Still, the Commission takes the view that the issue might merit further observation in the practice of the network, with a view to determining whether the mechanisms for assistance should be enhanced in order to further improve the ability of NCAs to deal with cases requiring fact-finding in other Member States.[58]

3.26 **The competence of the Commission** As regards the competence of the Commission, the ECN Cooperation Notice establishes that the Commission is particularly well placed if one or several agreement(s) or practice(s), including networks of similar agreements or practices, have an effect on competition in more than three Member States (cross-border markets covering more than three Member States or several national markets). If more than three authorities have opened investigations, the Commission has indicated that this nevertheless does not mean that it should systematically open investigations in such cases. The decision whether or not to investigate must be decided on the merits of the case.[59] The Antitrust Manual of Procedures ('Manproc') explains that the ECN unit monitors the opening of cases within the network from a general allocation perspective. The ECN responsible person of each unit should regularly examine all newly opened cases relevant to that unit. This monitoring aims at detecting multiple procedures and identifying cases where allocation criteria would normally favour action by the Commission.[60]

3.27 Given the very short timeframe within which the Commission has to examine envisaged decisions and, if so required, react, the information from NCAs on their statements of objections/

---

[56] Commission Decision of 20 October 2004 on the German postal legislation relating to mail preparation services (COMP/38.745); BKA, Decision of 11 February 2005 (B 9-55/03); See also M Martinez Lopez and S Obst, 'The BdKEP Decision: The Application of Competition Law to the Partially Liberalised Postal Sector' (2005) 1 Competition Policy Newsletter 31.

[57] Commission Staff Working Paper accompanying the Communication from the Commission to the European Parliament and Council 'Report on the functioning of Regulation 1/2003' (COM(2009)206 final), 29 April 2009, para 217.

[58] Commission Staff Working Paper accompanying the Communication from the Commission to the European Parliament and Council 'Report on the functioning of Regulation 1/2003' (COM(2009)206 final), 29 April 2009, para 222.

[59] Antitrust Manual of Procedures Internal DG Competition working documents on procedures for the application of Articles 101 and 102 TFEU, March 2012, Module 4 'Cooperation with National Competition Authorities', para 16, pointing to ECN Cooperation Notice [2004] OJ C101/45, para 15.

[60] If a sectoral unit considers that the Commission should pursue a case first opened by an NCA, it should liaise with the ECN unit. For this type of reallocation from an NCA to the Commission, see section 5. The follow-up of new case fiches may also indicate the possibility of applying Art 13 of Reg 1/2003 allowing the Commission to suspend proceedings or reject a complaint. This procedure is explained in the Complaint handling module; Antitrust Manual of Procedures Internal DG Competition working documents on procedures for the application of Articles 101 and 102 TFEU, March 2012, Module 3 'Cooperation with National Competition Authorities in EU and exchange of information in ECN', paras 15 and 17.

draft decisions should be dealt with by the ECN Unit as 'chef de file', in close cooperation with the operational units, whose involvement will depend on the language and economic sector involved. The ECN unit as 'chef de file' should inform by note the competent sectoral unit of the arrival of a new envisaged decision from an NCA and indicate the name of the coordinator in the ECN unit responsible for the case.[61] The appraisal of the envisaged draft act is carried out both by the ECN unit (from a horizontal coordination perspective) and by the competent sectoral unit(s) (from a sectoral perspective). The first step is to assess whether the NCA has submitted sufficient information for a proper assessment. Where that is not the case, the sectoral unit informs the ECN unit, which will take the matter up with the NCA concerned and keep the sectoral unit informed.[62]

Article 11(6) of Regulation 1/2003 states that the initiation by the Commission of proceed- **3.28** ings shall relieve all NCAs of their competence to apply Articles 101 and 102 TFEU.[63] This provision can come into play in two main situations. First, once the Commission has started proceedings, NCAs cannot act on the same legal grounds against the same agreement(s) or practice(s) by the same undertaking(s) in the same relevant geographic and product market. Secondly, the Commission can also relieve the NCA of their competence to deal with a particular case.[64] During the initial allocation period (indicative time period of two months), the Commission can initiate proceedings which will have the effect stated in Article 11(6) of Regulation 1/2003 after having consulted the NCAs concerned. If a case raises very significant issues of coherent application, the timing must be observed closely. Thus, according to the Manproc, the fourteenth calendar day is the latest day for deciding within DG COMP on the possible initiation of proceedings under Article 11(6); this is the practical deadline by which DG COMP will have to send a note to the Commissioner requesting permission to launch this procedure.[65] After the two-month allocation stage, the Commission will in principle only apply Article 11(6) of Regulation 1/2003 and disable the NCAs if one of the following situations arises:

(i) Network members envisage conflicting decisions in the same case.
(ii) Network members envisage a decision which is obviously in conflict with consolidated case law; the standards defined in the judgments of the EU Courts and in previous Commission decisions and regulations should serve as a yardstick; with regard to the assessment of the facts (eg market definition), only a significant divergence will trigger an intervention by the Commission.

---

[61] Antitrust Manual of Procedures Internal DG Competition working documents on procedures for the application of Articles 101 and 102 TFEU, March 2012, Module 3 'Cooperation with National Competition Authorities in EU and exchange of information in ECN', para 19.

[62] Antitrust Manual of Procedures Internal DG Competition working documents on procedures for the application of Articles 101 and 102 TFEU, March 2012, Module 3 'Cooperation with National Competition Authorities in EU and exchange of information in EC', para 20.

[63] The proceedings for the adoption of a decision under Chapter III concern decisions finding an infringement and/or ordering its termination, decisions ordering interim measures, decisions making commitments binding, and decisions finding that Arts 101 or 102 TFEU are not applicable to an agreement or practice. The case law of the ECJ with regard to the similarly worded Art 9(3) of Reg 17 lays down that the initiation of a procedure requires an 'authoritative act of the Commission evidencing its intention of taking a decision'. See Case 48/72 *Brasserie de Haecht v Wilkin-Janssen* [1972] ECR 88, para 16.

[64] Article 11(6) of Reg 1/2003; ECN Cooperation Notice [2004] OJ C101/43, para 54. This possibility should be used as an exception to the rule according to which EU competition law is uniformly and consistently applied by different NCAs and national courts. See also Antitrust Manual of Procedures, Internal DG Competition working documents on procedures for the application of Articles 101 and 102 TFEU, March 2012, Opening of proceedings 3–7.

[65] Antitrust Manual of Procedures Internal DG Competition working documents on procedures for the application of Articles 101 and 102 TFEU, March 2012, Module 3 'Cooperation with National Competition Authorities in EU and exchange of information in ECN', para 21.

(iii) Network member(s) is (are) unduly drawing out proceedings in the case.
(iv) There is a need to adopt a Commission decision to develop EU competition policy in particular when a similar competition issue arises in several Member States or to ensure effective enforcement.
(v) The NCA(s) concerned do not object.[66]

3.29   The actual initiation of proceedings by the Commission with a view to 'correcting' the approach taken by an NCA in an envisaged decision should be reserved to the severest problems of coherent application where they arise in a case that presents sufficient EU interest for the Commission to conduct its own procedure in the matter.[67] In practice, Article 11(6) is rarely used.

3.30   One rare example in which Article 11(6) was used occurred when the Commission reopened formal proceedings to investigate an alleged refusal by several luxury watch manufacturers to supply spare parts to independent repairers, in breach of EU competition rules. The opening of proceedings followed a judgment of the GC which annulled the Commission's decision to reject a complaint lodged by the European Confederation of Watch & Clock Repairers' Associations ('CEAHR').[68] The decision to reopen the case deprived the Spanish competition authority of their competence to investigate similar conduct which largely involved the same parties. The legal base of this procedural step was Article 11(6) of Regulation 1/2003.[69] In the Commission's view, the still very limited use of Article 11(6) could be attributed to various factors, particularly the NCAs' commitment to coherent application, extensive horizontal exchanges in the ECN (including in dedicated sectoral subgroups), as well as informal exchanges between the Commission services and NCAs in the context of Article 11(4) submissions.[70]

3.31   In Case T-339/04 *France Télécom SA v Commission*, the applicant argued that the French Competition Council would have been the best-placed authority to act in the case and the Commission was not better placed.[71] Therefore, the inspection could not lead to the Competition Council being relieved of the case and it being reallocated to the Commission, and the inspection ordered was therefore not lawful. Secondly, direct intervention by the Commission would have been unjustified because the Competition Council possesses inspection powers and the Commission could have requested it to use them. Thirdly, even if the inspection were to be regarded as lawful, the Commission should have applied Article 22(2) of Regulation 1/2003 and thus associated the French Competition Council with the measures of inspection and delegated to it all the tasks that could be delegated.

---

[66] Antitrust Manual of Procedures Internal DG Competition working documents on procedures for the application of Articles 101 and 102 TFEU, March 2012, Module 3 'Cooperation with National Competition Authorities in EU and exchange of information in ECN', para 73.

[67] See Commission Staff Working Paper accompanying the Communication from the Commission to the European Parliament and Council 'Report on the functioning of Regulation 1/2003' (COM(2009)206 final), 29 April 2009, para 264.

[68] Case T-427/08 *CEAHR v Commission* [2011] ECR II-5865.

[69] The Spanish competition authority closed its investigation after the European Commission consulted with the authority and announced that it would reopen its investigation. The Spanish competition authority considered itself deprived of its competence, pointing to Article 44 of the Competition Act ('When the National Competition Commission is not competent to prosecute the conduct detected or denounced in application of [Regulation 1/2003]').

[70] See Commission Staff Working Paper accompanying the Communication from the Commission to the European Parliament and Council 'Report on the functioning of Regulation 1/2003' (COM(2009)206 final), 29 April 2009, para 264.

[71] Case T-339/04 *France Télécom v Commission* [2007] ECR II-521, para 71.

The Court stated that Regulation 1/2003 would not call into question the general power that **3.32** the Commission is acknowledged to enjoy under the case law.[72] The Commission effectively has very wide powers of investigation under Regulation 1/2003 and is, in any event, entitled to decide to initiate proceedings relating to an infringement, which entails removing the case from the Member States' competition authorities. The Commission would thus retain a leading role in the investigation of infringements. In addition, there would be no provision in the regulation establishing a rule allocating powers, such as that alleged by the applicant, whereby the Commission is not authorized to carry out an inspection if an NCA is already dealing with the same matter. On the contrary, Article 11(6) of Regulation 1/2003 provides, subject only to consultation with the NCA concerned, that the Commission retains the option of initiating proceedings for the adoption of a decision, even where an NCA is already acting in the matter.

The Commission will only intervene where: (i) more than three Member States are involved; **3.33** (ii) there are EU provisions which may be exclusively or more effectively applied by the Commission; or (iii) if the EU interest requires the adoption of a Commission decision to develop EU competition policy when a new competition issue arises or to ensure effective enforcement.[73] Issues of case allocation could arise in the grey area where it is difficult to localize the effects of the infringement or where a single NCA appears unable to investigate the case properly or to bring the infringement to an end.

Procedural issues

The Manproc sets out a detailed procedure for ensuring consistency on the basis of the envis- **3.34** aged decision fiche and draft envisaged act. For all cases that do not give rise to a recommendation to initiate proceedings, the examination proceeds during the thirty-day period in the way initially agreed between the ECN unit and the sectoral unit, taking account of the time constraints arising due, for example, to absences in both services, exceptional requests from NCAs for early reaction, the need to consult the Legal Service etc.

During the examination of the case, the ECN unit and the sectoral unit should cooperate **3.35** closely, including meetings of the case handlers. In general, the sectoral unit sends an email or note setting out its position to the ECN unit when it has completed its examination. During the process, DG COMP can ask for additional information or clarification from the NCA in question (but does not make observations at this stage). Such contacts with the NCA are made either by the ECN unit or by the sectoral unit, as agreed in the case at hand. Where appropriate, the ECN unit also calls on the policy unit in Directorate A for feedback where cases raise policy issues. When setting up a team for scrutinizing an envisaged decision, the ECN unit takes into account whether any linguistic help is required. In cases where neither the coordinator in the ECN unit nor the case handler in the sectoral unit speak the language in question, this is done by calling upon a colleague from within DG COMP who does speak the language (language correspondent), or, if this is not possible, by asking for DG Translation's help.[74]

The results of the examination of the case are summarized in a case note that is normally **3.36** prepared by the ECN unit, with input from the sectoral unit. The case note summarizes the contents of the envisaged decision, reflects the comments of the sectoral unit (if any), and sets out the proposed follow-up. The case note is addressed to the Legal Service for consultation

---

[72] Case C-344/98 *Masterfoods* [2000] ECR I-11369, paras 46 and 48.
[73] ECN Cooperation Notice [2004] OJ C101/43, para 15.
[74] Antitrust Manual of Procedures Internal DG Competition working documents on procedures for the application of Articles 101 and 102 TFEU, March 2012, Module 3 'Cooperation with National Competition Authorities in the EU and exchange of information in ECN', paras 22–4.

before any observation is communicated to the NCA. The consultation is carried out by the ECN unit. The Legal Service must react within three days for notes without comments and oral comments, five days if it is proposed that a written note be sent to the NCA. Only after the agreement of the Legal Service is received can observations on the substance of the case be addressed to the NCA.

3.37 The reaction to the NCA will depend on the issues raised by the envisaged decision. When a case does not call for comments, the ECN Unit informs the NCA informally that the matter has been closed. When minor observations are made, the ECN unit will set up a conference call with the NCA, to which the sectoral case handler is invited. The line to be taken is determined by the case note and the corresponding reaction of the Legal Service. In cases which call for more fundamental observations, DG COMP's views can be set out in writing in a letter to the NCA. Any observations are to remain internal to the Network and are not disclosed to the parties.[75]

3.38 The Commission has undertaken to inform the other Network members about the important procedural steps in its cases by means of submitting new case 'fiches', envisaged decision 'fiches' (at the stage when the draft decision is sent to the Advisory Committee via encrypted mail), and closed case fiches. Case teams are responsible for ensuring that these fiches are completed and submitted in the informatics application.[76]

3.39 When a case dealt with by a sectoral unit raises an important issue of cooperation with the NCAs, the ECN unit should be consulted so as to maintain consistency across sectors in the relationships with the various NCAs. This consistency check should exist throughout the handling of cases by DG COMP and encompasses, for example, legal issues with respect to assistance during inspections and other general questions concerning investigative powers, issues concerning information exchanges, and discussions in the context of an individual case, on important general/policy issues, or on matters relating to the Advisory Committee.[77]

3.40 It is important to note that neither Regulation 1/2003 nor the ECN Cooperation Notice confer jurisdiction over Articles 101 or 102 TFEU cases. Any competition authority wishing or which has requested to investigate a matter must have jurisdiction. Regulation 1/2003 does not express any direct or indirect preference for enforcement by the NCAs or—for that matter—by the Commission. While it has been argued that the ECN Cooperation Notice creates legitimate expectations, it is also true that it does not state that one single authority will be well placed to deal with a given case. It stresses that all authorities retain full discretion in deciding whether or not to investigate a case.[78] The case must fall within the scope of Articles 101 or 102 TFEU and there must be an effect on competition in the affected Member State's territory. If, for example, the Belgian or the Luxembourg competition authorities were not to have sufficient resources to deal with a case for which the relevant geographic market is the Benelux area, the case could be dealt with by the Dutch competition authority or by the Commission. Thus, the NCA has no wider powers than it already had under its national laws to impose fines or to order remedies. It could be argued that the limitations inherent in public law which prohibits a sovereign State from exercising its powers outside its territory have not been addressed by Regulation 1/2003.

---

[75] This has been given rise to some controversy in the past. See references in note 318 of the Commission Staff Working Paper accompanying the Communication from the Commission to the European Parliament and Council 'Report on the functioning of Regulation 1/2003' (COM(2009)206 final), 29 April 2009, para 267.

[76] Antitrust Manual of Procedures Internal DG Competition working documents on procedures for the application of Articles 101 and 102 TFEU, March 2012, Module 3 'Cooperation with National Competition Authorities in EU and exchange of information in ECN', para 34.

[77] Antitrust Manual of Procedures Internal DG Competition working documents on procedures for the application of Articles 101 and 102 TFEU, March 2012, Module 3 'Cooperation with National Competition Authorities in EU and exchange of information in ECN', para 35.

[78] ECN Cooperation Notice [2004] OJ C101/43, para 15.

Therefore, an NCA can only order the termination and sanction the effects of infringements on its own territory.[79] Their decisions do not have an EU-wide effect and may not normally be enforced outside their borders. It could also be concluded from a combined reading of Article 4(3) TFEU, which requires the Member States to make penalties effective, proportionate, and dissuasive,[80] and Regulation 1/2003 that when sanctioning an infringement in the territory of other Member States, NCAs take into account the effects of the infringement in the territory of the Member State.[81] For example, the Office of Fair Trading ('OFT') in the UK has declared that if a penalty or fine has been imposed by the Commission, or by a court or other body in another Member State in respect of an agreement or conduct, it will take that penalty or fine into account when setting the amount of a penalty in relation to that agreement or conduct.[82]

So far, it appears that the situations where cases have changed hands are rare in comparison with the overall number of cases treated by the Network members. In several cartel cases, notably those in which parallel leniency applications were received, the Commission and NCAs cooperated at an early stage. In the *Flat Glass* cartel case,[83] for example, the Commission started its investigation in 2005 on the basis of information provided by several NCAs[84] which had received complaints or leads from customers or other third parties who suspected that a cartel existed. In the *iTunes* case concerning online delivery of music, the Commission was approached by the UK OFT, which was handling a complaint from a consumer organization. The Commission agreed to take up the case, which concerned several Member States, **3.41**

---

[79] See E Paulis and C Gauer, 'La reforme de règles d'application des Articles 81[101] et 82[102 TFEU] du Traité' [2003] 11 Journal de tribunaux droit européen 35. An earlier example of this system of restricted enforcement was the sanctioning of infringements of Art 101 TFEU in the shrimp industry in the Netherlands, Germany, and Denmark by the Dutch NCA. This was the first time that the Dutch authorities imposed a fine for an infringement of the EU competition rules and in view of the restricted jurisdiction to impose fines for conduct affecting commerce other than in the Netherlands, it decided to limit the fines for the parties involved to the effect of their behaviour on the Dutch part of the market. See R Wesseling report, 'The Netherlands' in *The Modernization of EU Competition Law Enforcement in the EU*, FIDE 2004 National Reports 407, 416. R Smits, 'The European Competition Network' [2005] Legal Issues of Economic Integration 175, 185 takes the view that had this case arisen later and therefore been allocated under Reg 1/2003 to a single rather than three cooperating NCAs, the NCAs concerned would have had to agree on a mechanism under which the findings of one of them would be followed up by the others imposing fines on the undertakings involved for the effects of the infringement on their part of the market.

[80] Case 68/88 *Commission v Greece* [1989] ECR 2965, paras 23–4; Case C-354/99 *Commission v Ireland* [2001] ECR I-7657, para 46.

[81] WPJ Wils, 'Community Report' in *The Modernisation of EU Competition Law Enforcement*, FIDE 2004 National Reports 661, para 134; see also Case T-102/96 *Glencor/Lonrho* [1999] ECR II-753, para 90. See also OFT's Guidance as to the appropriate amount of a penalty, OFT423, September 2012, at 2.6: 'In cases concerning infringements of Art 101 and/or Art 102, the OFT may, in determining the starting point, take into account effects in another Member State of the agreement or conduct concerned. The OFT will take into account effects in another Member State through its assessment of relevant turnover; the OFT may consider turnover generated in another Member State if the relevant geographic market for the relevant product is wider than the United Kingdom and the express consent of the relevant Member State or NCA, as appropriate, is given in each particular case.'

[82] This is to ensure that where an anticompetitive agreement or conduct is subject to proceedings resulting in a penalty or fine in another Member State, an undertaking will not be penalized again in the UK for the same anticompetitive effect. See OFT's Guidance as to the appropriate amount of a penalty—'Understanding Competition Law' [2004], para 2.6. For more details on the problem of *ne bis in idem* or double jeopardy, see para 3.48.

[83] Commission Decision in Case COMP/39.165 *Flat Glass* of 28 November 2007. See Summary Decision in [2008] OJ C127/9. See Commission Press Release, 'Antitrust: Commission fines flat glass producers €486.9 million for price fixing cartel' IP/07/1781 of 28 November 2007.

[84] German, French, Swedish, and British competition authorities; the Bundeskartellamt ('BKartA') had already asked the complainant for information when reallocation took place. See Commission Staff Working Paper accompanying the Communication from the Commission to the European Parliament and Council 'Report on the functioning of Regulation 1/2003' (COM(2009)206 final), para 216 also cites the *Power Transformers* case where the German Bundeskartellamt dealt with a separate but related case.

and initiated proceedings in April 2007.[85] After Apple's announcement that it was equalizing its prices for music downloads from iTunes in Europe in January 2008,[86] the case was closed.[87]

Reallocation

3.42 Reallocation can occur between NCAs or from NCAs to the Commission. Among NCAs, reallocation would only be envisaged at the outset of a procedure where either the NCA seized of the case considered that it was not well placed to act, or where other NCAs, having been informed of the fact that an authority has started to act in a certain case, express an interest in dealing with it. In order to detect multiple procedures and to ensure that a well-placed NCA deals with cases, network members have to be informed at an early stage of the cases pending before the various competition authorities. Where reallocation issues arise, they should be resolved swiftly within a period of two months starting from the date of the first information sent to the network.[88] Once this initial two-month allocation period has elapsed, reallocation of a case should only occur where the facts known about the case change materially during the investigation.

3.43 In those cases where various NCAs regard themselves as well placed to act, they might actually do so in parallel in the same proceeding. The ECN Cooperation Notice provides that:

> where reallocation is found to be necessary…network members *will endeavour* to reallocate cases to a single well placed competition authority as often as possible,[89]

but it does not provide for a proceeding to resolve disputes on allocation within the ECN. It only establishes that the Advisory Committee could serve as a forum for discussion in important cases, but the Advisory Committee does not have a legal mandate to ultimately settle disputes in a binding manner.[90] While this is deliberately conceived to leave room for flexible and pragmatic solutions, it is clear that this rather informal method of dispute resolution presupposes that NCAs wish to cooperate and to solve disputes amicably in a significant number of cases involving agreements or practices that affect more than one Member State. In any event, if the members of the network were not to reach an agreement as to which one of them should deal with a case, or if an NCA happens to disregard the principles of allocation set out in the ECN Cooperation Notice, the Commission can initiate proceedings itself, thus relieving the NCA in question of its competence to deal with the case.[91]

3.44 The ECN Cooperation Notice states that in a system of parallel competences, case allocation is considered as a mere division of labour and therefore it does not confer a right on the

---

[85] See Commission Press Release, 'Competition: European Commission confirms sending a Statement of Objections against alleged territorial restrictions in on-line music sales to major record companies and Apple' IP/07/126 of 03 April 2007.

[86] See Commission Press Release, 'Antitrust: European Commission welcomes Apple's announcement to equalise prices for music downloads from iTunes in Europe' IP/08/22 of 09 January 2008. On 18 March 2008, the Commission decided to close antitrust proceedings in cases COMP/C-2/39154 PO/iTunes and COMP/C-2/39174 Which/iTunes, initiated by the decision of 30 March 2007.

[87] See Commission Staff Working Paper accompanying the Communication from the Commission to the European Parliament and Council, 'Report on the functioning of Regulation 1/2003' (COM(2009)206 final), 29 April 2009, para 218.

[88] Art 11 of Reg 1/2003. Antitrust Manual of Procedures Internal DG Competition working documents on procedures for the application of Articles 101 and 102 TFEU, March 2012, Module 3 'Cooperation with National Competition Authorities in EU and exchange of information in ECN', para 12.

[89] ECN Cooperation Notice [2004] OJ C101/43, para 7.

[90] ECN Cooperation Notice [2004] OJ C101/43, para 62. C Gauer, 'Due Process in the Face of Divergent National Procedures and Sanctions', IBA conference, Antitrust Reform in Europe: A Year in Practice, Brussels, 9–11 March 2005. See also, Antitrust Manual of Procedures Internal DG Competition working documents on procedures for the application of Articles 101 and 102 TFEU, March 2012, Module 14 'Advisory Committee on Restrictive Practices and Dominant Positions', para 3.

[91] Article 11(6) of Reg 1/2003.

parties to have their case be decided by a particular NCA.[92] Thus, the case allocation princi-ples do not create individual rights for the companies involved in, or affected by, an infringe-ment to have a case dealt with by a particular authority.[93] Accordingly, the ECN Cooperation Notice merely provides that if a case is reallocated within the network, the undertakings concerned and the complainant(s) are informed as soon as possible by the NCAs involved.[94]

3.45 In practice, reallocation of cases between NCAs has rarely occurred. In its five-year review, the Commission reported that it had been informed only of the three cases cited in paragraph 3.41. These reallocations were mainly due to the fact that the locations of the companies concerned by the investigations were situated in another Member State.[95] The cases mentioned generally illustrate how work-sharing in the Network takes place in practice. As is well known, Regulation 1/2003 does not provide for a 'transfer' of cases as such. 'Reallocation' involves one authority going ahead with the investigation of a case while another authority abstains from acting or closes its file either on the basis of its discretion (not) to act or on the basis of Article 13 of Regulation 1/2003.[96]

3.46 From the Commission's perspective, the steps to be followed to reallocate a registered DG COMP case to a Member State competition authority are as follows. The sectoral unit responsible for the case consults the ECN unit on the basis of a short description of the case

---

[92] This is also why the Commission has always considered that the allocation of cases is not a 'decision'. Case allocation is mainly a work-sharing exercise between authorities. 'Q&A on Modernization with Kris Dekeyser' (April 2005) 8(3) Global Competition Review 11, 12. Kerse & Khan, *EC Antitrust Procedure* (6th edn, Sweet & Maxwell 2012) para 2-009, indicates that even such allocation/reallocation 'decisions' by NCAs were susceptible to judicial review under relevant national laws, it would seem that they could only be success-fully challenged in the most extreme circumstances, such as where there was a misuse of powers.

[93] See Commission Staff Working Paper accompanying the Communication from the Commission to the European Parliament and Council 'Report on the functioning of Regulation 1/2003' (COM(2009)206 final), para 208. The Network Notice, para 31. As indicated at para 3.31 above, this question was raised in Cases T-339/04 and T-340/04 *France Télécom* [2007] ECR II-521, where the applicants argued that the Commission was not competent to act, since the case-allocation criteria of the ECN Notice and the prin-ciple of subsidiarity, legal certainty, and loyal cooperation required the investigation to remain with the French competition authority, a better placed authority. The Court confirmed that Reg 1/2003 does not establish a system of allocation of competences. It stated, *inter alia*, at para 83: 'it must first be noted that paragraph 4 states that consultations and exchanges within the network are matters between public enforcers and that, according to paragraph 31, the Notice does not create individual rights for the companies involved to have the case dealt with by a particular authority. The applicant's contention that under the Notice only the Competition Council could deal with the case is therefore unfounded.' See E Gippini-Fournier, 'The Modernisation of European Competition Law: First Experiences with Regulation 1/2003—Institutional Report' in HF Koeck and MM Karollus (eds), The Modernisation of European Competition Law—Initial Experiences with Regulation 1/2003, FIDE XXIII Congress Linz 2008—Congress Publications Vol 2 (Nomos 2008) 375, 435, pointing out that the regulation does not envisage any reallocation decision. The only rule affecting the relationship between proceedings before the Commission and proceedings conducted by other authorities is Art 11(6). Gippini also adds (at 438) that the orders of the GC in Case T-109/06 *Vodafone v Commission* and Case T-295/06 *BASE v Commission* would further support the view that the allocation of cases among authorities within the ECN is not a matter open to challenge.

[94] ECN Cooperation Notice [2004] OJ C101/43, para 34. It should be noted that Reg 1/2003 does not oblige ECN members to inform the undertakings concerned of information exchange taking place. D Reichelt, 'To What Extent does the Cooperation within the European Competition Network Protect the Rights of the Undertakings?' (2005) CML Rev 745, 754 indicates that given the almost automatic exchange of certain information at particular procedural stages, the undertaking will, however, be able to learn what information will be transmitted.

[95] See Commission Staff Working Paper accompanying the Communication from the Commission to the European Parliament and Council 'Report on the functioning of Regulation 1/2003' (COM(2009)206 final), 29 April 2009, para 220.

[96] See Commission Staff Working Paper accompanying the Communication from the Commission to the European Parliament and Council 'Report on the functioning of Regulation 1/2003' (COM(2009)206 final), 29 April 2009, para 221.

regarding the opportunity to reallocate the case. As a matter of principle, reallocation of a case to an NCA should only occur for cases which are considered worth investigating. If there is agreement on the reallocation, the sectoral unit informally contacts the NCA concerned, describes the case, and inquires whether the NCA would be interested in dealing with it. However, if the sectoral unit does not know whom to address in the NCA, the ECN unit can assist with the contact.[97]

3.47 If the NCA is willing to take up the case, the sectoral unit prepares a letter transmitting the information pursuant to Article 12 of Regulation 2003 with a copy of the file attached. The letter should:

- state the legal basis of the transmission (Article 12);
- ask for confirmation on the part of the NCA that it will investigate the case;
- as appropriate, draw the attention of the NCA to confidential information or other points requiring attention.[98]

Principle of ne bis in idem[99]

3.48 The prohibition against prosecution and punishment for the same cause of action (*ne bis in idem* principle) is expressed in Article 50 of the Charter of Fundamental Rights and Article 4(1) of Protocol No 7 to the European Convention on Human Rights ('ECHR').[100] Even before the entry into force of Regulation 1/2003, the parallel application of Article 101 and national competition laws to the same matter has been consistent with the division of responsibilities between the Commission and Member States.[101] Potential conflicts did not

---

[97] Antitrust Manual of Procedures Internal DG Competition working documents on procedures for the application of Articles 101 and 102 TFEU, March 2012, Module 3 'Cooperation with National Competition Authorities in EU and exchange of information in ECN', paras 43–5.

[98] Antitrust Manual of Procedures Internal DG Competition working documents on procedures for the application of Articles 101 and 102 TFEU, March 2012, Module 3 'Cooperation with National Competition Authorities in EU and exchange of information in ECN', para 46.

[99] Although the concept is broadly similar to the common law principle of 'double jeopardy', the latter also covers the requirement to set off the first penalty imposed for the same offence in a previous case. In EU law, this is known as the requirement of natural justice. K Dekeyser and C Gauer, 'The New Enforcement System for Articles 81 and 82 and the Rights of Defence', ch 23 in BE Hawk (ed), *International Antitrust Law & Policy* [2004] Annual Proceedings of the Fordham Institute 549, 576. E Paulis and C Gauer, 'Le règlement n° 1/2003 et le principe du *ne bis in idem*' (2005) 32(1) Revue des droit de la concurrence 1. J Schwarze and A Weitbrecht, *Grundzüge des Europäischen Kartellverfahrensrechts* (2004) §7, paras 24–31; C Canenbley and M Rosenthal, 'Cooperation between Antitrust Authorities In-and Outside the EU: What does it mean for Multinational Corporations?—Part 2' [2005] ECLR 179, 181–3. C Gauer, 'Due Process in the Face of Divergence National Procedures and Sanctions', IBA conference, Antitrust Reform in Europe: A Year in Practice, Brussels, 9–11 March 2005, 7–8; F Louis and G Accardo, 'Ne bis in idem Bis, Part Bis' [2011] World Competition 34, 97–112; M Petr, 'The Ne Bis In Idem Principle in Competition Law' (2008) 29(7) European Competition Law Review 392; WPJ Wils. 'The Principle of Ne Bis in Idem in EC Antitrust Enforcement: A Legal and Economic Analysis (2003) 2 World Competition, 131; G Di Fiderico, 'EU Competition Law and the Principle of *Ne Bis In Idem*' (2011) 17(2) European Public Law 241.

[100] See R Sauer and O Weber in JL Schulte and C Just (eds), *Kartellrecht* (Carl Heymanns Verlag 2012), Art 23 of Reg 1/2003, para 47 et seq; F Louis and G Accardo, 'Ne bis in idem Bis, Part Bis' (2011) 34 World Competition 97, 98–9.

[101] Case 14/68 *Walt Wilhelm v Bundeskartellamt* [1969] ECR 1, paras 3 and 11. The ECJ decided that the application of national law and EU competition law to the same infringement does not raise a *ne bis in idem* issue because the interests protected by the two sets of rules are different. However, it considered that natural justice requires the fine set by the NCA for the infringement of national law to be taken into account by the Commission before imposing a fine for the infringement of EU competition law. See also Case T-141/89 *Tréfileurope v Commission* [1995] ECR II-791, in which the Commission took into account a fine imposed by the French authority under French law, Joined Cases C-204/00 P, C-205/00 P, C-211/00 P, C-213/00 P, C-217/00 P, and C-219/00 *Aalborg Portland and others v Commission* [2004] ECR I-123, Opinion of AG Ruiz-Jarabo delivered on 11 February 2003 in Case C-217/00 *Buzzi Unicem v Commission* [2004] ECR I-123, para 160.

really arise under Regulation 17, perhaps also because NCAs have only recently strengthened their enforcement efforts, for example by introducing leniency programmes of their own. While it is true that Regulation 1/2003 sets out the objective that each case should be handled by a single authority, the ECN Cooperation Notice does not rule out the possibility of parallel action by several NCAs,[102] unless the Commission has taken up the case under the claw-back mechanism of Article 11(6) of Regulation 1/2003.[103] Actually, according to the Commission, parallel proceedings between network members are also very rare. The vast majority of NCAs do not act in parallel to other NCAs or to the Commission. In its five-year assessment in 2009, the Commission reported one single case of parallel action in relation to a single infringement in which the German and Belgian competition authorities received a leniency application relating to a European wide price-fixing cartel for the chemical product Benzyl-Buthyl-Phtalat. Both authorities investigated the case and imposed fines.[104] The Belgian authority which imposed the second fine contemplated at length the issue of *ne bis in idem* and found, *inter alia*, that it was able to impose a fine regarding the effects of the cartel in Belgian territory based on the turnover in Belgium in so far as the first fine had been imposed by the German authority in view of the effects arising in the German territory only. The case might prima facie have presented the EU Courts (pursuant to an Article 267 TFEU reference) with the opportunity of clarifying questions relating to the principle of *ne bis in idem* and in particular the definition of 'idem'. However, no appeal was lodged against neither decision.[105]

On several occasions, the EU Courts have had to rule on the application of the *ne bis in idem* **3.49** principle in competition cases.[106] They defined this principle as precluding an undertaking from being found liable or proceedings from being brought against it a second time on the grounds of anticompetitive conduct in respect of which it has already either been penalized

---

[102] Joint Statement of the Council and the Commission on the functioning of the network, available at DG COMP's website at <http://ec.europa.eu/competition/index_en.html>, at 16 and 18; ECN Cooperation Notice [2004] OJ C101/43, paras 12–13. See also Recital 18 of Reg 1/2003 stating that the objective should be that each case is handled by a single authority. E Paulis and C Gauer, 'Le règlement n° 1/2003 et le principe du *ne bis in idem*' [2005] Revue des droit de la Concurrence 32, paras 11–15.

[103] This does not mean, however, that once the Commission initiates proceedings, the NCAs are permanently and definitively relieved of their power to apply national competition law. Depending on how the Commission proceedings are concluded, there may be scope for national competition law to be applied later by NCAs. The power of NCAs is restored when the Commission's investigation is concluded. Under Art 16(2) of Regulation 1/2003, NCAs may still take action, even where the Commission has adopted a decision. Article 16 prohibits national courts and NCAs from adopting decisions which are contrary to Commission decisions. It does not prohibit them from taking action in relation to cases where the Commission has adopted a decision. NCAs therefore retain their power to apply both EU and national competition laws even if the Commission has itself already taken a decision, as long as they respect the precedence of EU rules. In a recent case, for example, the contested decision of the Czech competition authority dealt with the anticompetitive consequences of the cartel before the Czech Republic's accession to the EU. The combination of Arts 11(6) and 3(1) of Reg 1/2003 did not represent an obstacle to the application of national law prior to 1 May 2004. See the judgment of the ECJ in Case C-17/10 *Toshiba Corporation e.a* [2012] OJ C98/3. See also D Gerard, 'The ECJ Advocate General Kokott renders her opinion in the Czech gas insulated switchgear case holding that the principle ne bis in idem does not preclude NCAs from prosecuting the same cartel with respect to different territories or periods (Toshiba)', e-Competitions, No 38780, available at <http://www.concurrences.com>.

[104] See Commission Staff Working Paper accompanying the Communication from the Commission to the European Parliament and Council 'Report on the functioning of Regulation 1/2003' (COM(2009)206 final), 29 April 2009, para 223, citing decision of the German Bundeskartellamt in Case B 11-23/05; decision of Belgian Competition Council of 4 April 2008.

[105] See Commission Staff Working Paper accompanying the Communication from the Commission to the European Parliament and Council 'Report on the functioning of Regulation 1/2003' (COM(2009)206 final), 29 April 2009, para 223.

[106] E Paulis and C Gauer, 'Le règlement n° 1/2003 et le principe du *ne bis in idem*' [2005] Revue des droit de la Concurrence 32, paras 27–33.

or declared not liable by a previous decision which is no longer subject to an appeal.[107] In the recent case *Toshiba and others*, the Court summarized its case law and stated that the application of *ne bis in idem* is subject to the threefold condition of identity of the facts, unity of offender, and unity of the legal interest protected. Under that principle, the same person cannot be sanctioned more than once for a single unlawful course of conduct designed to protect the same legal asset.[108] The ECJ also found that this principle did not preclude penalties which a national competition authority imposes on participants in a cartel on account of the anticompetitive consequences of the cartel in the territory of the Member State prior to its accession to the EU. This is the case as long as any fines previously imposed did not relate to those same consequences. More specifically, the Commission's decision did not cover any anticompetitive consequences of the cartel in the Czech Republic prior to 1 May 2004 and the Czech court had imposed fines only in relation to that territory and that period. Accordingly, although the decisions were based on infringements brought about by the same international cartel, they were otherwise based on different facts. Consequently, the Czech competition authority did not infringe the principle of *ne bis in idem*.[109]

3.50 In its earlier judgment relating to the *PVC II* decision,[110] the ECJ examined the question of whether the fact that the Commission had already ruled on the facts central to the case in

---

[107] Joined Cases C-238/99 P, C-244/99 P, C-245/99 P, C-247/99 P, C-250/99 P to C-252/99 P, and C-254/99 P *Limburgse Vinyl Maatschappij and Others v Commission* [2002] ECR I-8375, paras 59, 62, and 96; Case T-224/00 *Archer Daniels Midland v Commission* [2003] ECR II-2597, paras 85–9; Case T-322/01 *Roquette Frères v Commission* [2006] ECR II-3137, paras 277–92; Case T-43/02 *Jungbunzlauer v Commission* [2006] ECR II-343, paras 285–300; Joined Cases T-217/03 and T-245/03 *FNCBV and Others v Commission* [2006] ECR II-4987, paras 340–5; and Case C-17/10 *Toshiba Corporation and Others* [2012] OJ C98/3, paras 93–103.

[108] Case C-17/10 *Toshiba Corporation e.a* [2012] OJ C98/3, paras 94 and 97. See also Joined Cases C-204/00 P, C-205/00 P, C-211/00 P, C-213/00 P, C-217/00 P, and C-219/00 P *Aalborg Portland and others v Commission (Cement; appeal)* [2004] ECR I-123, Case C-213/00 P *Italcementi v Commission* [2003] ECR I-123, para 338, and Opinion of AG Ruiz-Jarabo Colomer, paras 88–9. AG Colomer distanced himself from the ruling in *Walt Wilhelm*, arguing that both national and EU competition law pursued the same objective, ie the protection of competition within the EU. The ECJ did not need to rule on this point because there was no identity of facts in that case. E Paulis and C Gauer, 'Le règlement n° 1/2003 et le principe du *ne bis in idem*' [2005] Revue des droit de la Concurrence 32, paras 29–30, noting that under Reg 1/2003 the issue raised in *Walt Wilhelm* has lost much of its relevance given that the Commission and the NCAs apply the same set of rules, although the Court refers to this consideration when it comes to international cartels where it has held that an undertaking may be a defendant in two parallel sets of proceedings concerning the same infringement and thus incur a double penalty, one imposed by the competent authority of a third country concerned and the other an EU penalty, since concurrent sanctions are justified where the two sets of proceedings pursue different ends. Joined Cases T-236/01, T-239/01, T-244/01 to T-246/01, T-251/01, and T-252/01 *Tokai Carbon Co Ltd and others v Commission* (Case T-236/01 [2004] ECR II-1181, paras 130–4); T-224/00 *Archer Daniels Midland Company and Archer Daniels Midland Ingredients Ltd v Commission* [2003] ECR II-2597, paras 85–94.

[109] The ECJ declared that it did not matter that the decision of a competition authority related to a period prior to the accession of a Member State to the EU. The application of the principle in the context of EU law does not depend on the date on which the facts at issue occurred, but on the situation for which the proceedings for the imposition of a penalty were initiated. The ECJ found that the Czech referring court was already a Member State of the EU when the main proceedings were opened and that the authority was therefore required to comply with the *ne bis in idem* principle. However, the ECJ did note that the principle did not prohibit more than one competition authority or court from penalizing competition restrictions resulting from the same cartel in different territories or during different periods of time. Kerse & Khan, *EC Antitrust Procedure* (6th edn, Sweet & Maxwell 2012) para 7-254, submits that outside the specific circumstances of the Toshiba case, it would not be possible for a fine to be imposed by the Commission in respect of an infringement already dealt with by an NCA in the sense of having been pursued it to a definitive conclusions, referring to Joined Cases T-144/07, T-147/07, T-148/07, T-149/07, T-150/07, and T-154/07 *ThyssenKrupp Liften Ascenseurs v Commission* [2011] OJ 211/45, para 160. See also Ch 11 'Infringement Decisions and Penalties', para 11.84.

[110] Joined Cases C-238/99 P, C-244/99 P, C-245/99 P, C-247/99 P, C-250/99 P to C-252/99 P, and C-254/99 P *Limburgse Vinyl Maatschappij NV LVM and others v Commission* [2002] ECR I-8375, paras 59–62. The *PVC* proceedings should be seen against the background of the end of the *PVC I* procedure. In *PVC I*, the Commission investigated the behaviour of fourteen undertakings active in the PVC industry and

its *PVC I* decision and the subsequent annulment of that decision by the ECJ was compatible with the principle of *ne bis in idem*. In its judgment relating to the *PVC II* decision, the GC had concluded that the *ne bis in idem* principle applies in EU law proceedings. According to the ECJ, the application of that principle presupposes that a ruling has been given on the question of whether an offence has in fact been committed or that the legality of the assessment thereof has been reviewed. The principle therefore merely prohibits a fresh in-depth assessment of the alleged commission of an act which would result in the imposition of either a second penalty or a first penalty in the event that a liability not established by the first decision is established by the second. However, the principle does not preclude the resumption of proceedings in respect of the same anticompetitive conduct where the first decision was annulled for procedural reasons without any ruling having been given on the substance of the alleged facts.[111] The ECJ considers that in such circumstances the annulment cannot be regarded as an 'acquittal' within the meaning given to that expression in criminal law.[112] Since the decision of the Commission had been annulled for purely procedural reasons and the Court did not pronounce on the substance of the case, it did not therefore preclude the Commission from reaching another decision. If the decision had been annulled because a given conduct had been considered unproven by the Court, further proceedings could not have been brought by the Commission.[113]

The ECJ case law in this respect does not, however, appear to be entirely coherent. In *Toshiba*, **3.51** AG Kokott pointed out that for the purposes of disciplinary proceedings under civil service law, the Court would be guided only by the factual situation (whether the facts were 'different'). Indeed, in the context of the rules governing the area of freedom, security, and justice (Article 54 of the Convention implementing the Schengen Agreement of 14 June 1985 ('CISA'))[114] the

---

fined all of them for infringement of Art 101 TFEU. On appeal, the GC held the decision to be non-existent and dismissed the application as inadmissible. The Commission appealed to the ECJ, which set aside the GC judgment and found the decision to be existent, but annulled it on procedural grounds. The Commission thereafter adopted a new decision which was addressed to almost all addressees of the original decision and which imposed fines of the same amounts. The *PVC* decision was again appealed. The GC dismissed almost all of the applications.

[111] Joined Cases C-238/99 P, C-244/99 P, C-245/99 P, C-247/99 P, C-250/99 P to C-252/99 P, and C-254/99 P *LVM v Commission* [2002] ECR I-8375, paras 61–2. Kerse & Khan, *EC Antitrust Procedure* (6th edn, Sweet & Maxwell 2012) para 7-255.

[112] In such a case, the penalties imposed by the new decision are not added to those imposed by the annulled decision but replace them. Joined Cases C-238/99 P, C-244/99 P, C-245/99 P, C-247/99 P, C-250/99 P to C-252/99 P, and C-254/99 P *LVM v Commission* [2002] ECR I-8375, para 62.

[113] It could be argued that in this case the first decision would have been annulled due to a lack of evidence, then the administrative procedure leading up to the decision would have been considered a 'trial' and the annulment of the first decision would have been considered as an 'acquittal' within the meaning Art 4(1) of Protocol No 7 to the ECHR, as well as Art 50 of the Charter. See also K Dekeyser and C Gauer, 'The New Enforcement System for Articles 81 and 82 and the Rights of Defence', ch 23 in BE Hawk (ed), *International Antitrust Law & Policy* [2004] Annual Proceedings of the Fordham Institute 549, 579; WPJ Wils, 'The Principle of Ne Bis In Idem in EC Antitrust Enforcement: A Legal and Economic Analysis' [2004] World Competition—Law and Economics Review 131, 142. Wils takes the view that, eg in a case in which the main producers of some product for which the relevant geographic market is Europe had held a meeting where they decided a concerted price increase, if this violation of Art 101 TFEU happens to be handled first by the competition authority of a Member State, then the Commission or the NCAs of the second Member State cannot deal with the case even if the competition authority only takes into account the effects of the violation on its own national territory, and/or that the national law of that Member State only provides for low fines for violations of Art 101 TFEU. According to Wils, such a case constitutes a single violation of Art 101 TFEU, irrespective of any effect it may or may not have had in any part of the EU. The principle of *ne bis in idem* prohibits multiple prosecution or punishments for the same offence, not merely for the same effects of an offence.

[114] Joined Cases C-187/01 and C-385/01 *Criminal proceedings against Hüseyin Gözütok and Klaus Brügge* [2003] ECR I-1345, paras 25–34. See also *Sergey Zolotukhin v Russia* App no 14939/03 (ECtHR, 10 February 2009), para 84: 'The Court's inquiry should therefore focus on those facts which constitute a set of concrete factual circumstances involving the same defendant and inextricably linked together.' Case C-436/04 *Van Esbroeck* [2006] ECR I-2333, para 36: 'In those circumstances, the only relevant criterion

Court has expressly considered the criterion of unity of the legal interest protected to be irrelevant.[115] In such circumstances, it has consistently held that the only relevant criterion is identity of the material acts, understood as the existence of a set of concrete circumstances which are inextricably linked together.[116] AG Kokott found that to interpret and apply the *ne bis in idem* principle so differently depending on the area of law concerned is detrimental to the unity of the EU legal order and that therefore account should henceforth be taken only of the identity of the facts (which necessarily includes the unity of the offender). The ECJ did not seem to have followed this approach and did not see a need to align its case law on the principle of *ne bis in idem* in competition law proceedings with its case law on Article 54 of the CISA. Instead, in *Toshiba* the ECJ held that in competition law cases the application of the principle of *ne bis in idem* is subject to the threefold condition of identity of the facts, unity of offender, and unity of the legal interest protected, as established in *Aalborg Portland A/S*.[117]

3.52 Acquittal and convictions in the enforcement system The prohibition of double prosecution and punishment does not exclude the possibility of parallel proceedings being conducted by several members of the ECN at the same time against the same defendants, as long as none of these proceedings has already reached the stage of final acquittal or conviction. This means that at a preliminary stage, when it may not yet be clear which member of the network is best placed to deal with the case, several competition authorities may investigate the same agreement or practice. However, no later than the moment when the first proceeding is ended by a final acquittal or conviction, the other authorities have to discontinue their proceedings with regard to the same defendants.[118] The question is only which decisions constitute an acquittal or a conviction for the application of the principle of *ne bis in idem*.[119] All competition authorities can adopt cease

---

for the application of Article 54 of the CISA is identity of the material acts, understood in the sense of the existence of a set of concrete circumstances which are inextricably linked together.' See also Case C-467/04 *Gasparini and Others* [2006] ECR I-9199, para 54; Case C-150/05 *Van Straaten* [2006] ECR I-9327, paras 41, 47, and 48; Case C-367/05 *Kraaijenbrink* [2007] ECR I-6619, paras 26 and 28; Case C-261/09 *Mantello* [2011] OJ C13/13, para 39.

[115] Convention implementing the Schengen Agreement ('CISA') signed in Schengen on 19 June 1990 [2000] OJ 2000 L239/19.

[116] See Opinion of AG Kokott in Case C-17/10 *Toshiba Corporation et al* [2012] OJ C98/3.

[117] Joined Cases C-204/00 P, C-205/00 P, C-211/00 P, C-213/00 P, C-217/00 P, and C-219/00 P *Aalborg Portland and Others v Commission* [2004] ECR I-123, paras 338–40. Kerse & Khan, *EC Antitrust Procedure* (6th edn, Sweet & Maxwell 2012) para 7-255, notes that while the Court seems to have endorsed the view that the pursuit of a matter under respectively national law and EU law there would be 'no unity of the legal interest protected', Art 3(1) of Reg 1/2003 would mean that NCAs no longer have the option of pursuing a matter under national law alone, if the requisites for applying EU law are fulfilled. Therefore, the application by the NCAs of EU competition law to a matter would mean further action by the Commission would violate the *ne bis in idem* principle because EU law would already have been applied to the matter.

[118] The principle of *ne bis in idem* enshrined in Art 50 (Right not to be tried or punished twice in criminal proceedings for the same criminal offence) of the Charter of Fundamental Rights of the European Union [2010] C83/389, applies not only within the jurisdiction of one Member State but also between the jurisdictions of several Member States. It thus forms part of those principles and fundamental rights which should also govern the interpretation and application of Reg 1/2003; see Reg 1/2003, Recital 37. Multiple prosecutions can be largely avoided on the ground that, when imposing fines in cases allocated to them, NCAs not only have the power, but are also obliged to take account of the effects of the infringement within the EU. In such cases, the principle of double jeopardy would prevent a subsequent prosecution and fine for the same offence by another EU competition law authority. See WPJ Wils, 'The Principle of Ne Bis In Idem in EC Antitrust Enforcement: A Legal and Economic Analysis' (2003) 26(2) World Competition 134. However, it is questionable whether the EU's intention was to grant new and extensive extra-territorial powers to the NCAs. See N Levy and R O'Donoghue, 'The EU Leniency Programme Comes of Age' [2004] World Competition—Law and Economics Review 75, 95, n 84.

[119] Following a Greek initiative (Initiative of the Hellenic Republic with a view to adopting a Council Framework Decision concerning the application of the *ne bis in idem* principle [2003] OJ C100/24), a Green Paper on Conflicts of Jurisdiction and the Principle of ne bis in idem in Criminal Proceedings was developed, which requires that whoever has been prosecuted and finally judged in one Member State cannot be prosecuted

and desist orders, decisions imposing fines, decisions accepting commitments, decisions rejecting complaints, and termination proceedings. While a decision imposing a fine for an infringement in regard to a certain market would prevent another authority from taking a decision concerning the effects in the same market,[120] the other types of decisions could require a closer analysis. Decisions accepting commitments do not take a position either on the existence of an infringement prior to the commitments or on the absence of an infringement after the commitments.[121] In addition, Regulation 1/2003 allows NCAs and national courts to act against the infringement after a commitment decision.[122] In the same vein, decisions rejecting complaints may not be regarded as acquittals either.[123] They are not addressed to the undertaking subject to the proceeding and merely settle the relationship between the authority and the complainant. The Commission may always act against an infringement, even if one or several NCAs have rejected a complaint against that same infringement. Conversely, NCAs may act against an infringement even if the Commission rejected a complaint against that same infringement.[124] More complicated are decisions ordering that an infringement be brought to an end without imposing a fine. While they contain a finding of an infringement, they do not impose a sanction on the undertaking for past infringement and

---

for the same acts in another Member State if either acquitted or convicted and serving or having served the sentence, subject to some restrictions. The Green Paper contains in its definition of 'criminal offences' the following (Art 1): 'acts which constitute administrative offences or breaches of order that are punished by an administrative authority by a fine...provided that they fall within the jurisdiction of the administrative authority and the person concerned is able to bring the matter before a criminal court.' Where administrative proceedings leading to the imposition of a fine for competition law infringement would be covered by this definition, the decision, if it becomes law, may affect the decentralized system of competition law enforcement. R Smits, 'The European Competition Network' [2005] Legal Issues of Economic Integration 175, 187.

[120] This would also hold true for 'leniency' decisions: where the Commission granted immunity or reduced the fine in EU-wide cartel proceedings, an NCA would be prevented from taking action concerning the same conduct. This may be the consequence of a combined reading of the principle of *ne bis in idem* and Art 4(3) TFEU which obliges NCAs and the Commission to assist each other in fulfilment of the principle of 'sincere cooperation'. See para 3.20.

[121] Article 9 of Reg 1/2003. E Paulis and C Gauer, 'Le règlement n° 1/2003 et le principe du *ne bis in idem*' [2005] Revue des droit de la Concurrence 32, para 61.

[122] Recital 13 of Reg 1/2003. K Dekeyser and C Gauer, 'The New Enforcement System for Articles 81 and 82 and the Rights of Defence', ch 23 in BE Hawk (ed), *International Antitrust Law & Policy* [2004] Annual Proceedings of the Fordham Institute 549, 579; Hawk at 82 points out that the preliminary ruling in *Brügge/Gözütok* might be construed as meaning that a settlement with a public prosecutor would trigger the application of the *ne bis in idem* principle and that commitment decisions are a kind of settlement with the competition authorities (Joined Cases C-187/01 and C-385/01 *Gözütok and Klaus Brügge* [2003] ECR I-1345). However, these decisions would not constitute a sanction of the infringement and they do not exclude any further prosecution. In the same sense, see E Paulis and C Gauer, 'Le règlement n° 1/2003 et le principe du *ne bis in idem*' [2005] Revue des droit de la Concurrence 32, para 61. See also more recently E Gippini-Fournier, 'The Modernisation of European Competition Law: First Experiences with Regulation 1/2003—Institutional Report' in HF Koeck and MM Karollus (eds), *The Modernisation of European Competition Law—Initial Experiences with Regulation 1/2003, FIDE XXIII Congress Linz 2008—Congress Publications Vol 2 (Nomos 2008) 375, 401, stating that: '[N]either do Article 9 decisions constitute an "acquittal" on substantive grounds, or because the case was time-barred. Article 9 decisions, according to recital 13 of Regulation 1/2003, do not conclude "whether or not there has been or still is an infringement". They therefore appear much closer to a decision not to pursue proceedings and close the case "without any determination whatsoever as to the merits of the case", a category of decisions which, according to the case law, does not trigger the application of the *ne bis in idem* principle.'

[123] K Dekeyser and C Gauer, 'The New Enforcement System for Articles 81 and 82 and the Rights of Defence', ch 23 in BE Hawk (ed), *International Antitrust Law & Policy* [2004] Annual Proceedings of the Fordham Institute 549, 579, take the view that this applies to all types of rejection of complaints, be it for lack of EU interest or for lack of substantiation etc. E Paulis and C Gauer, 'Le règlement n° 1/2003 et le principe du *ne bis in idem*' [2005] Revue de Droits de la Concurrence 32, paras 62–4.

[124] Commission Notice on the handling of complaints by the Commission under Articles 81[101] and 82 EC [102 TFEU] ('Notice on Handling of Complaints'), para 79. E Paulis and C Gauer, 'Le règlement n° 1/2003 et le principe du *ne bis in idem*' [2005] Revue des droit de la Concurrence 32, para 64, indicates that the rejection of complaints would not require prior consultation between the Commission and the NCAs.

may be considered as an acquittal as far as the imposition of fines is concerned.[125] Similar reasoning may apply to declarations of inapplicability under Article 10 of Regulation 1/2003.[126]

3.53 **Sanctions imposed by third-country authorities** The EU Courts have also decided on the application of the principle in cases where a third country competition authority and the Commission adopt decisions relating to a worldwide cartel. As indicated, in these cases, they have always rejected the application of the *ne bis in idem* principle, arguing that the two laws clearly pursue different ends. The Courts also rejected the idea that natural justice would require that the sanction imposed on a worldwide cartel by third country authorities must be deducted from any Commission sanction.[127] There is the suggestion that the Commission should be bound, at least, by a 'general requirement of natural justice' flowing from the general principle of proportionality and requiring the Commission to consider the amount of a first sanction imposed in non-EU Member States by reducing the amount of the (second) sanction. The objective of avoiding over-punishment should also apply outside the EU.[128]

2. The ECN and the cooperation mechanism

3.54 In order to find out about possible parallel proceedings and to ensure consistency, Regulation 1/2003 sets out a number of obligations for NCAs to provide information in regard to the opening of cases and the decisions that they intend to adopt. Exchanges of information

---

[125] K Dekeyser and C Gauer, 'The New Enforcement System for Articles 81 and 82 and the Rights of Defence', ch 23 in BE Hawk (ed), *International Antitrust Law & Policy* [2004] Annual Proceedings of the Fordham Institute 549, 579. E Paulis and C Gauer, 'Le règlement n° 1/2003 et le principe du *ne bis in idem*' [2005] Revue des droit de la Concurrence 32, para 66, suggest that the application of *ne bis in idem* should also be extended to cases where the Commission announces its intention to impose a fine but abstains from taking this step in view of the arguments put forward by the undertaking in question.

[126] E Paulis and C Gauer, 'Le règlement n° 1/2003 et le principe du *ne bis in idem*' [2005] Revue des droit de la Concurrence 32, para 67.

[127] Case 7/72 *Boehringer v Commission* [1972] ECR 1281, paras 3–6; Case T-224/00 *Archer Daniels Midland and Archer Daniels Midlands Ingredients v Commission* [2003] ECR II-2597, para 103, stating that it 'has in no way been shown that the penalty imposed in the United States related to application of the cartel or its effects other than in the United States…It continued and stated that an extension to the EEA would have *clearly encroached on the territorial jurisdiction of the Commission*'. See also Case T-71/03 *Tokai Carbon v Commission* [2005] ECR II-10, para 116: 'In so far as SGL claims that that agreement entails the application of the principle of ne bis in idem in relations between the United States and the Community, the applicant's argument is based on an erroneous reading of that agreement. It is clear from Art I(2) (b) and Art III of that agreement that the legal interests protected by the Community authorities and the US authorities are not the same and that the purpose of the agreement is not the principle of ne bis in idem but solely to enable the authorities of one of the contracting parties to take advantage of the practical effects of a procedure initiated by the authorities of the other.' In this case, the GC considered that the penalties imposed in the US for SGL's participation in the graphite electrodes cartel concerned a distinct market and involved different members. Note that SGL filed an appeal against the decision. Case C-328/05 P *SGL Carbon AG v Commission* [2007] ECR I-3921; and Case T-322/01 *Roquette Frères SA v Commission* [2006] ECR II-3137, paras 280–1: 'However, an undertaking may properly be the subject of two parallel procedures for the same unlawful conduct in so far as those procedures pursue different ends and there is not identity between the provisions infringed. On the facts, it is held that the proceedings by the Commission and US authorities do not pursue the same objectives: "[w]hereas, in the former, it is a question of preserving undistorted competition on the territory of the European Union or in the EEA, the protection sought, in the latter, concerns the American market". There is therefore no unity of the legal interest protected. Case T-43/02 *Jungbunzlauer v Commission* [2006] ECR II-3435, paras 286–8.

[128] C Canenbley and M Rosenthal, 'Cooperation between Antitrust Authorities In-and Outside the EU: What does it mean for Multinational Corporations?—Part 2' [2005] ECLR 179, 183, noting that pursuant to Art 23 of Reg 1/2003, the Commission is entitled to set fines on the basis of the *total* (worldwide) turnover of undertakings found to be in violation of Arts 101 and 102 TFEU. The authors also ask whether the Commission in *Microsoft* could impose such far-reaching remedies after the US Consent Decree had already redressed the anticompetitive behaviour (Case COMP/37.792 *Microsoft*. See Commission Press Release IP/04/382 'Commission concludes on Microsoft investigation, imposes conduct remedies and a fine').

between the Commission and NCAs can occur through various channels.[129] Furthermore, Regulation 1/2003 provided for a suspension mechanism with respect to parallel proceedings, which could lead an NCA to suspend a proceeding or reject a complaint where another NCA is already investigating the same agreement, decision of an association, or practice.[130] Both provisions are described in more detail at paragraph 3.110. In order to guarantee the consistency of the system, Article 11 of Regulation 1/2003 provides that NCAs should inform other members of the network of the cases they are dealing with.[131]

Certain information and documents are sent to the competition authorities of the Member **3.55** State without the need for a prior request.[132] This rule applies to the 'most important documents the Commission has collected with a view to applying Articles 7 to 10 and 29(1) of Regulation 1/2003'.[133] The legal basis for the foregoing is Article 11(2) of Regulation 1/2003. The documents that should systematically be transmitted to the Member States are:[134]

(i) all admissible complaints upon their registration as cases, subject to any redaction needed to respect requests for anonymity;
(ii) formal fact-finding measures
   – requests for information by decision pursuant to Article 18(3) are sent for information purposes to the competition authority of the Member State in whose territory the undertaking is located and whose territory is affected (see Article 18(5)). If this undertaking has a parent company in another Member State, a copy can also be sent to the latter Member State;
   – inspections based on a simple mandate (Article 20(3)): in good time before the inspection, the Commission must give notice of the inspection to the NCA of the Member State in whose territory it is to be conducted;
   – inspections ordered by decision (Article 20(4)): Advance consultation of the Member State in whose territory the inspection is to be conducted; where the officials of the Member State in question did not assist the Commission, information after the inspection may also ordered;

---

[129] Under Art 10(1) of Reg 17, the Commission was required to provide to the NCAs copies of the most important documents lodged with the Commission for purposes of establishing an infringement of Arts 101 or 102 or when it issued a negative clearance or a decision applying Art 101(3).

[130] Article 13 of Reg 1/2003.

[131] Former Director-General of DG COMP, P Lowe found that '... [Reg 17] created a star-like scheme that involves in particular considerable flows of information from the Commission to the national competition authorities about Commission cases and the opportunity for the national enforcers to comment collectively—through the Advisory Committee. Regulation 1/2003 turns the beams of this star-like system into two-way streets as Member States' authorities will now also inform the Commission about their cases and consult the Commission on their draft decisions. The Regulation moreover provides for the involvement of the other national competition authorities in the overall context of close co-operation as provided for in Art 11(1) of the new Regulation. Thus, the ultimate structure of the network is no longer that of a star but that of a web.' P Lowe, 'Implications of the Recent Reforms in the Antitrust Enforcement in Europe For National Competition authorities, Address at the Italian Competition Consumer Day', Rome, 9 December 2003.

[132] The legal basis is Art 11(2) of Regulation 1/2003. This transmission is done, systematically and upon instruction of the case team or the responsible unit. Antitrust Manual of Procedures Internal DG Competition working documents on procedures for the application of Articles 101 and 102 TFEU, March 2012, Module 3 'Cooperation with National Competition Authorities', para 53.

[133] Article 11(2) of Reg 1/2003. Therefore, the term 'most important' may generally refer to documents which the Commission collected when applying the (first) investigative measures under Chapter V of Reg 1/2003, leaving aside the withdrawal of block exemptions. It may be assumed that the Commission has the exclusive power to determine the most important documents.

[134] Antitrust Manual of Procedures Internal DG Competition working documents on procedures for the application of Articles 101 and 102 TFEU, March 2012, Module 3 'Cooperation with National Competition Authorities', para 54.

– sector inquiry decisions (Article 17): draft decision sent for Advisory Committee consultation;

(iii) decisions imposing provisional periodic penalty payments: a copy is sent to all Member States;

(iv) preparatory acts:

– initiation of proceedings (Article 11(6)): information is sent to all Member States;
– statement of objections: a copy is sent to all Member States;
– preliminary assessment in Article 9 proceedings;
– invitation to hearings: sent to all Member States;
– Article 27(4) market test publication for the Official Journal: a copy of the draft to all Member States after approval of the Commissioner and before publication;
– the tape recordings on hearings are sent to the Member States on a case–by–case basis, but only if they make an express request;
– the final report of the Hearing Officer;[135]

(v) undertakings' replies to Statements of Objections and to Article 27(4) publications: copy to all Member States;

(vi) information about closure of a case where proceedings have been opened:

– rejections of complaints pursuant to Article 13 of Regulation 1/2003 or Article 7 of Regulation 773/2004, subject to any redaction needed to respect request for anonymity;
– decisions which must be published (in summary format) (Art. 30 Regulation 1/2004): first, the Secretariat General ('SG') sends the operative part by fax to all NCAs; then, the case team instruct the Antitrust Register to send the full text of the decision (ie including confidential information and indication of figures on fines) to all NCAs in the languages available via the encrypted mail promptly (within two weeks) after the adoption of the decision;
– every three months a list of all closed cases is drawn up for the Member States by the Antitrust Registry.

3.56 On the basis of Article 11(2) of Regulation 1/2003, second sentence, the NCAs are also entitled to receive, upon request, copies of other existing documents necessary for the assessment of the case.

3.57 NCAs shall inform the Commission when they start a proceeding under Article 101 or 102 TFEU. This information may be available to other NCAs. In practice, this will be done in each case by means of the completion of a standard form containing limited details of the case, such as the authority dealing with the case, the product, territories and parties concerned, the nature and suspected duration of the alleged infringement, and the origin of the case.[136]

3.58 No later than thirty days prior to the adoption of a decision, NCAs shall supply the Commission with a summary of the case and a copy of the draft decision or, in the absence thereof, any other document indicating the proposed course of action.[137] Within this time

---

[135] See Decision of the President of the European Commission on the function and terms of reference of the hearing officer in certain competition proceedings ([2011] OJ L275/29), Art 16.

[136] Article 11(3) of Reg 1/2003. The undertaking subject to investigative measures by an NCA can expect this minimum information to be transmitted to all other ECN members, also because the Commission has stated that it automatically forwards the information on first investigative measures. D Reichelt, 'To What Extent does the Cooperation within the European Competition Network Protect the Rights of the Undertakings?' (2005) CML Rev 745, 760. It is essential to point out that, as a rule, the information will be made available to all members of the network. This can be deduced from para 10 of the Joint Statement of the Council and the Commission on the functioning of the network.

[137] By the end of 2009, the Commission had been informed of more than 300 envisaged decisions by NCAs on the basis of Art 11(4). None of these cases resulted in the Commission initiating proceedings pursuant

period, the Commission has been informed of more than 300 envisaged decisions submitted by NCAs pursuant to Article 11(4) of Regulation 1/2003. Compared to the situation before Regulation 1/2003 came into force, these figures clearly demonstrate a significant increase in enforcement activities in the EU since 2004.[138]

The purpose of Article 11(4) is to enable the Commission and NCAs to ensure that Articles **3.59** 101 and 102 TFEU are applied in a consistent manner within the network. The Commission may make written observations on cases about which it is informed pursuant to Article 11(4) to the NCA in question.[139] This information obligation applies to all types of envisaged decision referred to in Article 11(4) since the entry into application of Regulation 1/2003. The NCAs must submit the text of the envisaged decision and a summary of the case.[140] Instead of a draft decision, NCAs can also submit any other document which indicates the proposed course of action, in particular a statement of objections or other documents foreseen by national laws.[141] DG COMP acknowledges receipt of information on envisaged decisions pursuant to Article 11(4), permitting undertakings to verify compliance with the obligations provided for by Article 11(4) in the proceedings of the NCA or, where they deem it appropriate, in appeal proceedings in the Member States.[142]

---

to Art 11(6) to relieve an NCA of its competence for reasons of coherent application. Communication from the Commission to the European Parliament and Council Report on the functioning of Regulation 1/2003 SEC (2009) 574, para 28. Commission Staff Working Paper accompanying the Communication from the Commission to the European Parliament and Council, 'Report on the functioning of Regulation 1/2003', COM(2009)206 final, 29 April 2009, para 187. If the Commission so requests, the obligation to provide the information can also extend to other documents 'which are necessary for the assessment of the case' (Art 11(4)).

[138] See Commission Staff Working Paper accompanying the Communication from the Commission to the European Parliament and Council 'Report on the functioning of Regulation 1/2003' (COM(2009)206 final), 29 April 2009, para 184.

[139] See Commission Staff Working Paper accompanying the Communication from the Commission to the European Parliament and Council 'Report on the functioning of Regulation 1/2003' (COM(2009)206 final), 29 April 2009, para 253.

[140] Antitrust Manual of Procedures Internal DG Competition working documents on procedures for the application of Articles 101 and 102 TFEU, March 2012, Module 3 'Cooperation with National Competition Authorities', para 18, stating that the deadline set by Art 11(4) starts to run from the receipt of both the 'envisaged decision fiche' in the informatics application and the text of the envisaged decision.

[141] Antitrust Manual of Procedures Internal DG Competition working documents on procedures for the application of Articles 101 and 102 TFEU, March 2012, Module 3 'Cooperation with National Competition Authorities', para 20. The examination of the draft envisaged act is done both by the ECN unit (from a horizontal coordination perspective) and by the competent sectoral unit(s) (from a sectoral perspective). The first step is to assess whether the NCA has submitted sufficient information for a proper assessment. Where this is not the case, the sectoral unit informs the ECN unit, which will take the matter up with the NCA concerned and keep the sectoral unit informed.

[142] See Commission Staff Working Paper accompanying the Communication from the Commission to the European Parliament and Council 'Report on the functioning of Regulation 1/2003' (COM(2009)206 final), 29 April 2009, paras 254–5. E Gippini-Fournier, 'The Modernisation of European Competition Law: First Experiences with Regulation 1/2003—Institutional Report' in HF Koeck and MM Karollus (eds), The Modernisation of European Competition Law—Initial Experiences with Regulation 1/2003, FIDE XXIII Congress Linz 2008—Congress Publications Vol 2 (Nomos 2008) 375, 444–5) on the 'duty' to resubmit information where the envisaged decision (or other document indicating the 'proposed course of action') undergoes significant changes before it is effectively adopted. The author argues that a duty to resubmit information (triggering a fresh count of the standstill period) would appear most compelling when the contemplated decision changes to a different type of decision also contemplated in Art 11(4), ie where, for example, an NCA has informed the Commission of its intention to adopt a decision accepting commitments and ultimately modifies its approach and intends to adopt a decision finding an infringement.

3.60 In recent years, DG COMP has developed the practice of submitting observations to NCAs in many cases,[143] mostly orally but sometimes in writing. These observations have been multi-faceted. The Commission reported that in most cases they had covered minor comments or had been related to particular aspects of the envisaged decisions in order to promote a uniform approach on such aspects (eg product market definition); coordination with on-going Commission cases; or case law of the EU Courts. These observations did not contain any new evidence of any other information that would be exculpatory or incriminating for the parties to the proceedings.[144] Until 2009, in about 10 per cent of the cases the observations of DG COMP were provided in writing.[145] In 2011, no fewer than eighty-eight cases were submitted by the Member States to the Commission for consultation, increasing the total number of cases brought since May 2004 to 555.[146]

3.61 This prior consultation duty applies to: (i) prohibition decisions; (ii) acceptance of commitments; and (iii) withdrawal of block exemptions; but not to (i) rejections of complaints; or (ii) decisions to take no action.[147] The obligation to consult may serve as a check on concerns that NCAs could feel particularly tempted to prohibit or punish the behaviour of a foreign undertaking. If such bias exists, the Commission could remove the case from the acting NCA. As far as the exchange of information with other NCAs is concerned, as Article 11(3) states, the information may be shared with other NCAs.[148]

3.62 Generally, an NCA planning to adopt a decision is not required to take the Commission's comments into account. In all cases, the way in which it responds to observations from DG COMP is ultimately the responsibility of the NCA in question. As a rule, observations are left with the NCA to consider unless the NCA itself suggests another way of proceeding. In exceptional cases, DG COMP may ask for a further follow-up, such as the communication of a revised draft,

---

[143] See Antitrust Manual of Procedures Internal DG Competition working documents on procedures for the application of Articles 101 and 102 TFEU, March 2012, Module 3 'Cooperation with National Competition Authorities', para 26, stating that the reaction to the NCA will depend on the issues raised by the envisaged decision. When a case does not call for comments, the ECN unit informs the NCA informally that the matter has been closed. When minor observations are made, the ECN unit will set up a conference call with the NCA, to which the sectoral case handler is invited. The line to be taken is determined by the case note and the corresponding reaction of the Legal Service. In cases which call for more fundamental observations, DG COMP's views can be set out in writing in a letter to the NCA. Any observations are to remain internal to the Network and are not disclosed to the parties.

[144] See Commission Staff Working Paper accompanying the Communication from the Commission to the European Parliament and Council 'Report on the functioning of Regulation 1/2003' (COM(2009)206 final), para 257.

[145] See Commission Staff Working Paper accompanying the Communication from the Commission to the European Parliament and Council 'Report on the functioning of Regulation 1/2003' (COM(2009)206 final), para 257, note 312.

[146] Commission Staff Working Paper accompanying the Report from the Commission on Competition Policy 2011 (COM(2012) 253 final), 30 May 2012, 15.

[147] When comparing the list of types of decisions in the first sentence of Art 11(4) with the list of decisions in Art 5 of Reg 1/2003, it appears that there is no obligation for NCAs to consult the Commission on decisions imposing fines or other penalties unless these decisions also include an order requiring the infringement to be brought to an end (which may not be the case in decisions regarding past infringements). However, the understanding within the ECN network is that consultation will take place on all decisions imposing fines or other penalties. In this sense, WPJ Wils, 'Regulation 1/2003: A Reminder of the Main Issues' in D Geradin (ed), *Modernisation and Enlargement: Two Main Challenges for EC Competition Law* (Hart Publishing 2004) 57, n 223.

[148] It could be argued that the transmission referred to in Art 11(4) is limited to NCAs *dealing with the case* because the transmission of this information no longer occurs for the purpose of case allocation; rather, it concerns the procedural stage before the adoption of a decision. D Reichelt, 'To What Extent does the Cooperation within the European Competition Network Protect the Rights of the Undertakings?' (2005) CML Rev 745, 758–9.

transmission of the decision as finalized etc,[149] and the only way for the Commission to intervene is by taking over the case, a rather drastic measure that might have a significant impact on the companies under investigation.

The Commission is also under a duty to advise or consult the authorities in the Member States when it intends to carry out investigations in their territory. The NCAs must assist the Commission during such investigations. The Commission may further request NCAs to undertake investigations in their own territory to obtain information for the Commission.[150] Member States are entitled to take part in hearings at which undertakings submit their observations. Finally, the authorities in the Member States may be called on to cooperate in the enforcement of decisions imposing fines, in accordance with the procedure contained in Article 299 TFEU. Regulation 1/2003 provides that one NCA may ask another NCA for assistance in order to collect information on its behalf. **3.63**

Exchange of information

The question of gathering information has become more important in recent years. A number of EU judgments[151] indicate that the amount of information that the Commission should gather from undertakings in order to prove the existence of an anticompetitive practice is critical to the validity of its assessment. The ECN Cooperation Notice suggests that the functioning of the system is based to a large extent on the exchange of information between the NCAs, and in some respect on the voluntary submission of information from undertakings to either the Commission or an NCA. Article 12 of Regulation 1/2003 states that the Commission and the NCAs shall have the power to provide one another with and use in evidence any matter of fact or law, including confidential information.[152] The information transferred would not only cover the information collected under Article 22 (inspections) but presumably also information received and acquired from any party (including a complainant) without any need for the NCA to exercise powers of inquiry.[153] This means that exchange of information not only takes place between an NCA and the Commission, but also between and amongst NCAs. While this is an enabling power in that there is no duty on an ECN member to transmit information to another member,[154] it is the variety **3.64**

---

[149] Antitrust Manual of Procedures Internal DG Competition working documents on procedures for the application of Articles 101 and 102 TFEU, March 2012, Module 3 'Cooperation with National Competition Authorities', para 27.

[150] Under Art 22(2) of Reg 1/2003, the Commission can ask an NCA to carry out an inspection on its behalf.

[151] See, eg Case T-56/02 *Bayerische Hypo- und Vereinsbank AG v Commission* [2004] ECR II-3495, para 119: 'All of the evidence just examined permits the conclusion that the Commission has not adduced to the requisite legal standard proof of the existence of the agreement which it claimed to exist, relating both to the fixing of the prices for currency exchange services of the euro-zone currencies and also to the ways of charging those prices.'

[152] Kerse & Khan, *EC Antitrust Procedure* (6th edn, 2012) para 5-012, indicate that the wording of Art 12 is designed to overcome any problems caused by restrictions on use and confidentiality, whether under EU or national law. However, there is no express obligation to transfer relevant information under Art 12. The only exception to this rule is Art 22, which provides that the exchange and use of any information collected by one NCA in carrying out an inspection on behalf of another must be carried out under Art 12(2). D Reichelt, 'To What Extent does the Cooperation within the European Competition Network Protect the Rights of the Undertakings?' (2005) CML Rev 745, 754, regarding the question whether Arts 11 and 12 of Reg 1/2003 provide for the obligation to exchange information or the possibility of a voluntary exchange, respectively.

[153] Kerse & Khan, *EC Antitrust Procedure* (6th edn, 2012) para 5-013, who also note that this should also include information pulled together from the domestic files of an NCA. The objective of Art 12 would be frustrated if an NCA were unable to transfer all of the information on its file following a reallocation decision within the Network.

[154] K Dekeyser and E De Smijter, 'The Exchange of Evidence Within the ECN' [2005] Legal Issues of Economic Integration 161 (particularly 164–5), point to the question of how the option of Art 12 relates to the duty of loyal cooperation under Art 4(3) TFEU. The combined reading of both provisions may lead to an obligation for ECN members to exchange information between them.

in the types of penalties which can be imposed by the different members of the network of NCAs that could raise concerns with regard to the exchange of evidence within the network. However, Regulation 1/2003 contains certain safeguards with respect to the use of confidential information exchanged within the network, which the ECN Cooperation Notice and subsequently the Manproc have expanded on.[155]

3.65 It should be noted that the Commission and all other ECN members have appointed Authorised Disclosure Officers ('ADOs') to ensure that confidential information is transmitted in an appropriate way.[156] In the Commission, the ADO holds the key to the secure email system, and therefore is the person who receives/sends messages from/to NCAs where the use of this system is necessary. For the Commission, the antitrust ADO is the Head of the Antitrust Registry. For the purposes of sending documents to the Advisory Committee, the Secretariat of the Advisory Committee can also use the secure mailing system. Likewise, for the purposes of hearings, the Hearing Officer's team can use this system.

3.66 The Manproc provides detailed guidance on the procedure to be followed where the Commission takes the view that it is impossible to transmit the requested information in its possession.[157] This would be the case in the following situations:

- A leniency applicant does not consent to the forwarding of (some of) his submissions and consent is needed. This follows from the ECN Cooperation Network Notice.[158]
- The information was received from an informant who provided market information, as compared to a formal complainant, and the informant does not consent to the forwarding of the information in question. This is essential to respect the trust of the informant and to create a framework where potential informants are not inhibited from providing such information.

3.67 Other situations where the case-handler concludes that such impossibility exists should be communicated to the ECN unit so that a common position may be arrived at. The transmission of the requested information can be authorized by the responsible head of unit. Except in cases where no confidentiality issue could arise, case teams should not send the requested documents themselves but instead provide the necessary information and documents to the ADO of DG COMP, who takes care of the transmission.[159]

---

[155] ECN Cooperation Notice [2004] OJ C101/45, para 26. Antitrust Manual of Procedures Internal DG Competition working documents on procedures for the application of Articles 101 and 102 TFEU, March 2012, Module 3 'Cooperation with National Competition Authorities in EU and exchange of information', para 47 et seq.

[156] Antitrust Manual of Procedures Internal DG Competition working documents on procedures for the application of Articles 101 and 102 TFEU, March 2012, Module 3 'Cooperation with National Competition Authorities', para 47, n 7. The ADO function is essentially linked to the cooperation mechanisms established by the antitrust modernization under Regulation 1/2003 and more particularly to the Art 12 exchange of information and the Arts 20–22 investigation cooperation. Therefore, while many network members have organized their formal communication channels so that the ADO is the central entry and exit point between them and the Commission and also between all network members, the only communications which must go through the ADO are those which, strictly speaking, relate to enforcement cooperation between network members. This means, for instance, that when the Commission informs or consults NCAs with a view to applying Arts 7, 8, 9, 10, and 29(1) of Reg 1/2003, the participation of the ADO in this sense is not called for. Whether or not the ADO intervenes in person, the confidentiality of documents sent out by the Commission must in any event be fully protected by the receiving authority, but the Commission cannot widen the agreed scope of intervention of the ADO. This is why ECN members have asked the Commission to indicate in the transmissions what the legal basis is, so that they can easily assess whether the ADO must intervene in person.

[157] Antitrust Manual of Procedures Internal DG Competition working documents on procedures for the application of Articles 101 and 102 TFEU, March 2012, Module 3 'Cooperation with National Competition Authorities in EU and exchange of information', para 61 et seq.

[158] ECN Cooperation Notice [2004] OJ C101/45, paras 40–1.

[159] Antitrust Manual of Procedures Internal DG Competition working documents on procedures for the application of Articles 101 and 102 TFEU, March 2012, Module 3 'Cooperation with National Competition

The note accompanying the requested information should indicate several factors, including **3.68** in which case the information was obtained (eg case x against party y), the subject matter[160] for which it was collected, and where, when, and how the information was obtained (eg inspection, formal information request, informant, or informal telephone conversation).[161]

The transmission should take place as soon as possible and no later than within one month **3.69** from the date of receipt of the request.[162]

When a Network member sends a communication to DG COMP, the ADO must ensure **3.70** that it reaches, decrypted, the appropriate persons within DG COMP without delay. When information should be sent to Network members, the case-handling unit is responsible for determining in each particular case if the nature of the information is so sensitive—business secrets or other confidential information, as well as internal communications—that it needs to be sent encrypted via the ADO.[163]

Information supplied under Article 12 is provided exclusively for the purpose of applying the **3.71** EU rules and may only be used 'in respect of the subject matter for which it was collected'.[164] Regulation 1/2003 does not go into further detail about what is meant by 'subject matter' but it may be reasonably construed as meaning more than simply that both the transmitting and receiving NCA are pursuing the same parties in relation to the same infringement. Thus, it could be aimed at ensuring that the functioning of the ECN will not jeopardize the procedural guarantees in relation to the use of evidence in Articles 20(3) and (4) and 28(1) of Regulation 1/2003.[165] This would mean that information collected in the context of an investigation of a suspected cartel in a given product market (eg steel) could not be used as evidence against a cartel involving all or a number of the same parties in another product market (eg aluminium).[166] Thus, this would amount to a restriction of the use of information. Where the NCA wishes to use the information in the context of its own proceedings, Regulation 1/2003 is based on the premise that the enforcement of EU rules prevails over the enforcement of domestic law. The information can be used where national competition law is applied in the same case and in parallel to EU competition law and does not lead

---

Authorities in EU and exchange of information', para 64 et seq. The Manproc provides more details on procedural aspects.

[160] E Gippini-Fournier, 'The Modernisation of European Competition Law: First Experiences with Regulation 1/2003—Institutional Report' in HF Koeck and MM Karollus (eds), The Modernisation of European Competition Law—Initial Experiences with Regulation 1/2003, FIDE XXIII Congress Linz 2008—Congress Publications Vol 2 (Nomos 2008) 375, 441, submits that 'subject matter' in Art 12(2) might be reasonably read in the same manner as in Art 20(3), and that the limitations on the 'subject matter' for which information exchanged between authorities may be used in evidence will depend on how narrowly or broadly the collecting authority has defined the scope of the investigatory measure, within the limits of what is permissible within its own legal system.

[161] Antitrust Manual of Procedures Internal DG Competition working documents on procedures for the application of Articles 101 and 102 TFEU, March 2012, Module 3 'Cooperation with National Competition Authorities', para 68.

[162] Antitrust Manual of Procedures Internal DG Competition working documents on procedures for the application of Articles 101 and 102 TFEU, March 2012, Module 3 'Cooperation with National Competition Authorities', para 47.

[163] Antitrust Manual of Procedures Internal DG Competition working documents on procedures for the application of Articles 101 and 102 TFEU, March 2012, Module 3 'Cooperation with National Competition Authorities', para 50.

[164] The purpose restriction may be contrasted with Arts 11, 13, and 22 of Reg 1/2003 which contain a broad variety of specific situations in which rights and obligations of the ECN members to exchange information exist. D Reichelt, 'To What Extent does the Cooperation within the European Competition Network Protect the Rights of the Undertakings?' (2005) CML Rev 745, 754.

[165] Kerse & Khan, *EC Antitrust Procedure* (6th edn, 2012) para 5-039. The Commission refers to the ECJ ruling in Case 85/87 *Dow Benelux v Commission* [1989] ECR 3137, para 20.

[166] Kerse & Khan, *EC Antitrust Procedure* (6th edn, 2012) para 5-039.

to a different outcome. Possibly, a different outcome would mean that national law would authorize conduct prohibited under EU law and prohibit under national law conduct that is authorized under EU law. Regulation 1/2003 does not specify what would happen if an NCA ceases to apply EU law because there is no effect on inter-State trade. While it seems that the application of national law may be excluded because it would not apply 'in the same case and in parallel', it is also true that the limitation on the use of information in Article 12(2) restricts the use of evidence in national proceedings.

3.72 There has been some debate about how the option of Article 12 of Regulation 1/2003 relates to the duty of loyal cooperation contained in Article 4(3) TFEU. The ECJ has ruled that Article 4(3) imposes on the European institutions and EU Member States mutual duties of sincere cooperation with a view to attaining the objectives of the EU, which may also include the duty of the Commission to transmit the information it holds to national courts.[167] Conversely, an NCA may be under a duty to provide the Commission or another NCA with the information that it holds. This interpretation would reflect the need that EU institutions and NCAs have to assist one another in the application of competition rules, and Article 12 of Regulation 1/2003 may thus turn into an obligation.[168] If this is true, the obligation would not be unlimited: based on the ECJ's case law, the Commission may refuse to transmit information for overriding reasons relating to the need to safeguard the interest of the EU or to avoid any interference with its functioning and independence, in particular by jeopardizing the accomplishment of the tasks entrusted to it.[169] The safeguards relating to, for example, the protection of confidential information and leniency applications may thus be read in this sense.[170] For example, where the Commission has granted immunity to an undertaking under its leniency programme, an NCA may have the duty not to impose full fines under national law using information disclosed to the Commission.[171]

3.73 The possibility of exchanging and using information gathered by another competition authority has proven to be one of the cornerstones of the modernization package, given that it greatly enhances the overall efficiency within the network and that it is a pre-condition for a flexible case-allocation system. Since the entry into force of Regulation 1/2003, information exchanges pursuant to Article 12 have taken place to and from the Commission and between the NCAs, notably in the following three scenarios:

(i) In the context of inspections, information exchanges may enable several authorities that have received different pieces of information to obtain a more complete picture of a suspected infringement. Such exchanges strengthen the individual ECN members' ability

---

[167] See, eg Case 2/88 *Imm JJ Zwartfeld and others* [1990] ECR I-3365, para 17: 'relations between the Member States and the Community institutions are governed, according to according to Article 5 of the EEC Treaty, by a principle of sincere cooperation'. See also Case C-275/00 *European Community v First NV and Franex NV* [2002] ECR I-10943, para 49, in relation to the duties of national courts. As regards the duty of not only national courts but also State bodies, including administrative authorities, to disapply national legislation which contravenes EU law, see also Case C-198/01 *Consorzio Industrie Fiammiferi (CIF) v Autorità Garante della Concorrenza e del Mercato* [2003] ECR I-8055. See also J Temple Lang, 'Developments, Issues and New Remedies—The Duties of National Authorities and Courts under Art 10 of the EC Treaty' [2004] Fordham International Law Journal 1904, 1928.

[168] K Dekeyser and E De Smijter, 'The Exchange of Evidence within the ECN' [2005] Legal Issues of Economic Integration 161, 164–5.

[169] Case C-2/88 *Zwartfeld* [1990] ECR I-3365, para 17; Case C-275/00 *European Community v First NV and Franex NV* [2002] ECR I-1043, para 4.

[170] See para 3.79 et seq.

[171] See also J Temple Lang, 'Developments, Issues and New Remedies—The Duties of National Authorities and Courts under Art 10 of the EC Treaty' [2004] Fordham International Law Journal 1904, 1929, who bases this duty on Art 104(3) TFEU. Otherwise, if an NCA were able to use the information disclosed to impose a full fine for violation of *national* competition law, this would defeat the purpose of the Leniency Notice.

to detect infringements. They occur normally at a very early stage of an investigation (prior to inspections) and are highly confidential.

(ii) In the context of Article 22 inspections, the information collected on behalf of the requesting authority is transferred on the basis of Article 12.

(iii) If a case is allocated between authorities or reallocated to another authority, the information is passed on pursuant to Article 12.

Cases where information was not only exchanged but also used in evidence are more limited, and most of them are still ongoing. The majority of these cases would have related to the Article 22 scenario (eg *Flat Glass*, *Sanitary fittings*[172]). In this context, it was reported by NCAs that some difficulties were encountered in using the documents collected by another NCA due to different legislation on confidentiality requirements. **3.74**

As regards the conditions provided for by Article 12(3) and the use of evidence in cases of sanctions on individuals, experience is very limited. According to the Commission, no network member would have reported any particular case where it had to carry out an analysis of the conditions of Article 12(3) in view of using information received from another network member, or where it abstained from requesting potentially relevant information, or where it was unable to use in evidence information relevant to a case for the imposition of custodial sanctions received from another network member.[173] **3.75**

In exceptional cases where a risk exists that the NCA of a Member State could not guarantee that commercially sensitive information is not used by another 'arm of the State' for purposes other than the enforcement of Articles 101 and 102 TFEU, the Commission would need to take the necessary safeguarding measures respecting the ruling of the Court in *SEP*.[174] If it wishes to transmit a document to the competent NCAs, notwithstanding the claim that in the particular circumstances of the case that document is of a confidential nature with respect to those authorities, the Commission will have to adopt a reasoned decision amenable to judicial review through an action for annulment. It is through an action for the annulment of such a decision that the undertaking may effectively enforce its right to protection of its business secrets. **3.76**

In those cases where the Commission has decided which information is to be treated confidentially—for example, with respect to requests for public access to documents under Regulation 1049/2001 or with respect to questions decided by the Hearing Officer in the application of the *Akzo* procedure (very exceptionally, in the application of the *SEP* case law mentioned in the previous paragraph)—the transmission should indicate which parts of the exchanged information are thus regarded as confidential. Where the parties have provided a non-confidential version of the information, it is also recommended including this version in the transmission pursuant to Article 12.[175] **3.77**

Professional secrecy

Article 28(1) of Regulation 1/2003 provides that information obtained pursuant to Articles 17 and 22 can only be used for the purpose for which it was acquired. Accordingly, such **3.78**

---

[172] Commission decision of 28 November 2007 in Case COMP/39165 *Flat glass*; Commission Decision of 23 June 2012 in Case COMP/39.092 *Bathroom fittings and fixtures*.
[173] See Commission Staff Working Paper accompanying the Communication from the Commission to the European Parliament and Council 'Report on the functioning of Regulation 1/2003' (COM(2009)206 final), paras 242–4.
[174] Case C-36/92 P *Samenwerkende Elektriciteits-Produktiebedrijven (SEP) NV v Commission* [1994] ECR I-1911.
[175] Antitrust Manual of Procedures Internal DG Competition working documents on procedures for the application of Articles 101 and 102 TFEU, March 2012, Module 3 'Cooperation with National Competition Authorities', para 60.

information is not available for use by NCAs under their own competition rules or other national laws.[176] In addition, Article 34(2) TFEU imposes an obligation not to disclose information covered by professional secrecy, which includes business secrets and other confidential information, based on the right of undertakings to protect their business secrets.[177] Nevertheless, this obligation is without prejudice to the exchange of information required to prove an infringement of Articles 101 and 102 TFEU. The term 'professional secrecy' is an EU law concept that aims to create a common minimum level of protection throughout the EU.[178] Because of the primacy of EU law, NCAs cannot rely on national law provisions as a reason for not sending the confidential information to other ECN members[179] but they need to have an effective procedure in place in order to ensure that information which circulates within the ECN remains within the ECN. The creation of the ECN was surrounded by concerns about safeguarding confidential information among a plurality of enforcers. However, pursuant to Article 28 of Regulation 1/2003, the Commission and the Member States' competition authorities shall not disclose any information which is covered by the principle of professional secrecy. Article 28 applies to all Network members and thus sets a common standard which needs to be protected throughout the EU. The standard of Article 28 is inherited from Article 20 of Regulation 17. In the context of the latter, its main significance for Member States' competition authorities related to the documents that they received from the Commission in view of the meeting of the Advisory Committee. This aspect remained unchanged. Under Article 11(2) of Regulation 1/2003, the Commission is still obliged to provide an NCA with copies of the most important documents that it has collected with a view to taking decisions pursuant to Articles 7 to 10 and 29. This means that Member States' competition authorities are well aware of, and are used to, protecting case-related confidential documents emanating from another authority. The standard of protection that has always been applied to Commission documents is now extended to documents received from other Member State competition authorities.[180]

3.79 Before transmitting confidential information, the Commission may have to consider carefully the implications of the possibility of 'information leaks' from the competition authorities.[181] In *SEP*, the ECJ acknowledged that the prohibition on disclosure does not

---

[176] Kerse & Khan, *EC Antitrust Procedure* (6th edn, 2012), indicate that the restriction of use offsets the broad power of enquiry under Arts 17 and 22 and is necessary to ensure the undertaking's defence rights were the Commission able to rely on evidence obtained during an investigation that was unrelated to the subject matter of the proceedings.

[177] Article 28 of Reg 1/2003. See Ch 9, 'Procedural Infringements: Fines and Periodic Penalties', para 9.24 et seq. Case C-36/92 P *Samenwerkende Elektriciteits-Produktiebedrijven (SEP) NV v Commission* [1994] ECR I-1911, para 36.

[178] ECN Cooperation Notice [2004] C101/43, para 28.

[179] In those cases where the transmitting ECN member has, before or after transmission, classified information as confidential on the basis of national legislation, such classification would not bind the receiving ECN member, although the latter may take this classification into account as much as possible. K Dekeyser and E De Smijter, 'The Exchange of Evidence Within the ECN' [2005] Legal Issues of Economic Integration 161, 68 and n 14.

[180] See Commission Staff Working Paper accompanying the Communication from the Commission to the European Parliament and Council 'Report on the functioning of Regulation 1/2003' (COM(2009)206 final), paras 265–6.

[181] See Case T-39/90 *NV Samenwerkende Elektriciteits-Produktiebedrijven v Commission* [1991] ECR II-1497, para 7: 'By letter of 6 March 1990, the Commission requested the applicant, pursuant to Article 11(1) of Regulation No 17—under which the Commission, in carrying out its duty to monitor compliance with Articles 85 and 86 of the Treaty, may obtain "all necessary information", particularly from undertakings and associations of undertakings—to send to it: (a) the original gas supply contract concluded between SEP and Statoil and the correspondence relating to that agreement; (b) the new contract between SEP and Gasunie and the documents relating to the negotiations preceding its conclusion; (c) information concerning the role played by the Netherlands State in the conclusion of the agreement between SEP and Gasunie and any correspondence between the Netherlands State and SEP relating to that agreement'; para 12: 'On 14 December 1990 the applicant brought an appeal before the Court of Justice against the above mentioned

guarantee that information contained in the documents sent to NCAs will not be taken into consideration by them or by their officials for other purposes.[182] However, this does not, of course, result in an automatic ban on the exchange of confidential information, where the relevant undertaking would have to invoke before the Commission the confidential nature of a document vis-à-vis the competent NCAs.[183] The general principle of the protection of business secrets, referred to earlier, may limit the Commission's obligation under Article 12(1) of Regulation 1/2003—together with Article 10 4(3)TFEU—to transmit the document to the competent national authorities. Whether the *SEP* issue—ie parties raising the confidentiality of the material supplied—continues to be of particular relevance under Regulation 1/2003 remains to be seen. There is nothing in Regulation 1/2003 or the accompanying notices which would limit the freedom to transfer information to be used as a basis for applying Articles 101 or 102 TFEU, or which would make it possible for a party to contest such a transfer.[184] Notwithstanding this, information gathered in a national procedure and under national law cannot be freely used in EU procedures or any other NCA processes. The Commission has been at pains to point out that the same strict standard already applied under the old enforcement system, where the Member States' competition authorities were fully informed about the cases dealt with by the Commission, including

---

interlocutory order of the President of the Court of First Instance (Case C-372/90 P). By a separate document lodged at the Registry of the Court of Justice on the same date, it also applied for an order suspending the operation of the decision of 2 August 1990 and/or for interim measures. In this connection, the applicant requested the Court of Justice in the alternative "to order the Commission not to provide the Member States with a copy of the Statoil contract...until the Court of First Instance has given judgment...on the application for annulment...against (the) Commission's decision of 2 August 1990 or, in the event that the Court of Justice gives its decision before the Court of First Instance, until the Court of Justice has delivered a final judgment in Case T-39/90 R on the appeal by SEP against the order of the President of the Court of First Instance" (Case C-372/90 P-R). Finally, on 23 January 1991 the applicant lodged as a precautionary measure a second appeal against that order of the President of the Court of First Instance, seeking in addition an order from the ECJ requiring the Commission to return to it the Statoil contract, which it had sent to that institution in the light of the latter's aforementioned decision of 26 November 1990 imposing a periodical penalty payment. The applicant requested the ECJ in the alternative to make an order restraining the Commission from communicating copies of the contract in question to the authorities of the Member States (Case C-22/91 P)'; and para 25: 'Commission is entitled to require the disclosure only of information which may enable it to investigate putative infringements which justify the conduct of the inquiry and are set out in the request for information.'

[182] On appeal, the ECJ disagreed with the GC and stated that the restriction imposed by Art 20(1) of Reg 17 (now Art 28 of Reg 1/2003) would ensure that the Dutch authorities and officials who had received confidential information from the Commission could not effectively be required to disregard the relevant information regarding a competitor if it fell to them to determine the commercial policy of a public enterprise under their supervision. Case C-36/92 P *Samenwerkende Elektriciteits-Produktiebedrijven (SEP) NV v Commission* [1994] ECR I-1911, para 30.

[183] Parties supplying information to the Commission should clearly indicate relevant sensitive material and that the 'SEP proviso' has been invoked.

[184] Kerse & Khan, *EC Antitrust Procedure* (6th edn, 2012) para 5-021, note that the *SEP* situation has lost some of its relevance in that many Member States have independent competition authorities. Further, Art 35 of Reg 1/2003 imposes the obligation to designate competition authorities that are capable of 'effectively' complying with the requirements under Reg 1/2003. D Reichelt, 'To What Extent does the Cooperation within the European Competition Network Protect the Rights of the Undertakings?' (2005) CML Rev 745, 771, takes the view that the 'SEP proviso' may still be good law but is only applicable in a particular set of circumstances. It seems that the disclosure of business secrets within the ECN only affects the right to protect business secrets if one or more ECN members act(s) as an *economic entity*. Then, an exchange of information can be objected to on confidentiality grounds where one of the NCAs has to be classified as a 'third party'. C Gauer, 'Due Process in the Face of Divergent National Procedures and Sanctions', IBA conference Antitrust Reform in Europe: A Year in Practice, Brussels, 9–11 March 2005, 12–13, believes that the SEP situation would no longer exist. Member States have set up competition authorities which are not linked to State-owned companies and the risk has therefore disappeared. She points out that there is no decision to transmit the information which the undertaking could challenge, but they may challenge the collection of the evidence.

business secrets and other confidential information. Similarly, the Commission had the power to obtain all types of information from the Member States. This system never created any substantial problems. Regulation 1/2003 introduces the additional possibility of exchanging information between NCAs. This information also comes within the common standard of professional secrecy.[185]

3.80 **Evidence** Regulation 1/2003 draws a distinction between the use of information against legal and natural persons. Recital 16 provides that when the information is used by the receiving authority to impose sanctions on undertakings, there should be no other limit to the use of the information than the obligation to use it for the purpose for which it was collected. This is justified by the fact that the sanctions imposed on undertakings are of the same type in all systems and consequently the defence rights enjoyed by undertakings can be considered as sufficiently equivalent.[186] Article 12(2) of Regulation 1/2003 states that the exchanged information can only be used in evidence for the purpose of applying Article 101 or 102 TFEU and limited to the subject matter for which it was collected by the transmitting authority. It adds that where national competition law is applied in the same case and in parallel to EU competition law and does not lead to a different outcome, the information exchanged may also be used for the application of national competition law.

3.81 This limitation on the application of EU law is consistent with the overall scope and purpose of Regulation 1/2003, which is limited to the application of Articles 101 and 102 TFEU. The reference to 'national competition laws' must be read in the light of Article 3 of Regulation 1/2003, which contemplates the cumulative application of EU and national competition laws in given cases. The expression 'in the same case and in parallel' contained in Article 12 should restrict the recipient authorities' powers to the cumulative application governed by Article 3(1). There is no scope for the use of the information exchanged in the application of 'stricter national laws which prohibit or sanction unilateral conduct' under the second paragraph of the same Article, nor to cases where competition authorities apply 'merger control laws' or 'provisions of national law that predominantly pursue an objective different from that pursued by Articles 81[101] and 82[102]' under Article 3(3) of Regulation 1/2003.[187] For any such situations, the recipient NCA will remain bound by the 'acute amnesia' rule in *Spanish Banks*.[188] On the other hand, it is not entirely clear whether evidence received from another NCA can be used as the basis for an infringement of a national provision equivalent to Article 101. This point seems still to be uncertain, even if

---

[185] In practice, the transmission of confidential information between authorities will take place through encrypted mail or other secure means of transmission. C Gauer, L Kjolbye, D Dalheimer, E de Smijter, D Schnichels, and M Laurila, 'Regulation 1/2003 and the Modernisation Package fully applicable since 1 May 2004' (Summer 2004) 2 Competition Policy Newsletter 4.

[186] See JS Venit and T Louko, 'The Commission's New Power to Question and its Implications on Human Rights', ch 26 in BE Hawk (ed), *International Antitrust Law & Policy*, Annual Proceedings of the Fordham Institute [2004] 675, 679.

[187] M Araujo, 'The Respect of Fundamental Rights within the European Network of Competition Authorities', ch 21 in BE Hawk (ed), *International Antitrust Law & Policy*, Annual Proceedings of the Fordham Institute [2004] 511, 527. See also Ch 9, 'Procedural Infringements: Fines and Periodic Penalties', para 9.28, regarding the issue of whether Art 12 is a legislative modification of the ECJ case law in *Spanish Banks* (see n 187). See also D Reichelt, 'To What Extent does the Cooperation within the European Competition Network Protect the Rights of the Undertakings?' (2005) CML Rev 745, 777–8.

[188] Case C-67/91 *Dirección General de Defensa de la Competencia v Asociación Española de Banca Privada* [1992] ECR I-4785, paras 35–9. In this case the ECJ was not persuaded that the absence from Art 20 of Reg 17 of references to other provisions under which the Commission obtained information necessarily meant that information obtained otherwise under the Regulation could be freely used by national authorities as evidence in their national law procedures. NCAs were not, however, required to suffer 'acute amnesia'. They can consider the information in deciding whether to initiate national proceedings. Kerse & Khan, *EC Antitrust Procedure* (6th edn, 2012) para 5-020, n 25.

the application of EU law is abandoned at the outset because there is no evidence of effect upon inter-State trade.

As far as the restriction on the subject matter is concerned, the parallel provision in **3.82** Regulation 17 was interpreted by the ECJ in *Dow Benelux* as prohibiting 'that information obtained during investigations' may eventually be 'used for purposes other than those indicated in the order or decision under which the investigation is carried out'.[189] It is not entirely clear what the role of the 'subject matter' is in this context. It could refer to the specific complaint, which was being investigated by the transmitting authority so that its use would be confined to the undertakings identified in that complaint. It could also imply that the receiving authority would be entitled to make use of it in the course of an investigation into different undertakings suspected of a different practice, but in respect of the same reference market.[190]

Sanctions   Article 12(3) of Regulation 1/2003 regulates the circumstances under which the **3.83** exchanged information can be used for imposing sanctions on individuals. Regulation 1/2003 distinguishes between custodial sanctions and other types of sanctions such as fines. The exchange of information for the purpose of applying Articles 101 and 102 TFEU is precluded unless both the laws of the transmitting and receiving authorities provide sanctions of a similar kind in respect of individuals. Whether sanctions or procedures are classified at national level as administrative or criminal is irrelevant.[191]

In the event that the two legal systems involved do not provide sanctions of a similar kind, the **3.84** exchange of information can only take place if the same level of protection of the individual rights is given in both countries. In this latter case, however, the information cannot be used by the receiving authority in order to impose custodial sanctions. This provision should ensure that to the extent that differences in procedural rights and guarantees result from differences in the kind of sanctions which can be imposed by the different members of the network, the exchange of information within the network cannot lead to any procedural right or guarantee being weakened or undermined.[192]

This system gives rise to various questions: when the members of the network assist each other **3.85** in collecting evidence, it may well occur that one member of the network, either of its own initiative or at the second NCA's request, collects, in accordance with the law governing the investigative powers of the first NCA, evidence[193] which the second NCA could not have

---

[189] Case 85/87 *Dow Benelux v Commission* [1989] ECR 3137, para 17.

[190] JD Cooke, 'General Report' in *The Modernization of EU Competition Law Enforcement in the EU*, FIDE 2004 National Reports 630, 655.

[191] See Commission Staff Working Paper accompanying the Communication from the Commission to the European Parliament and Council 'Report on the functioning of Regulation 1/2003' (COM(2009)206 final), para 241.

[192] For example, this would prevent the Commission from transmitting information to NCA in relation to the questioning of an individual because Art 12(3) of Reg 1/2003 states that the information can only be used against the individual if it has been collected by an authority which has similar sanctions for individuals. K Dekeyser, 'Session IV, Rights, Privileges and Ethics in Competition Cases', ch 28 in BE Hawk (ed), *International Antitrust Law & Policy*, [2004] Annual Proceedings of the Fordham Institute 731, 741. C Gauer, 'Due Process in the Face of Divergent National Procedures and Sanctions', IBA conference, Antitrust Reform in Europe: A Year in Practice, Brussels, 9–11 March 2005, 15, notes, for example, that the commercial manager of a company could be asked to mention the meetings with the competitors he attended on behalf of the undertaking and that information could be used to establish his own role in the infringement. The undertaking is under an obligation to answer, but the individual speaking on behalf of the undertaking does not run any personal risk: his or her statements cannot be used against him in any proceedings because if he or she had been the target of the investigation he or she would have had a right to remain silent. See also Ch 7, 'Formal Investigation Measures', para 7.49 et seq.

[193] D Reichelt, 'To What Extent does the Cooperation within the European Competition Network Protect the Rights of the Undertakings?' (2005) CML Rev 745, 752, raises the issue that it may not always

lawfully collected under its own law, and transfers this evidence to the second NCA so that it can use the evidence. In Ireland, for example, where Articles 101 and 102 TFEU have been made part of criminal law, a person interrogated in connection with a potentially criminal offence is entitled to be cautioned that any information given may be used in evidence against him. If the Dutch NCA obtained information from interviews in the course of investigating a suspected infringement by Dutch and Irish undertakings, the question which arises is whether that information could be used if transmitted to the Irish NCA for the purpose of prosecuting the Irish company if it had been obtained without any caution being given in the Netherlands.[194]

3.86 This issue was raised in the UK consultation on the new OFT competition law guidelines, during which concern was expressed about the possibility that the OFT could use in evidence documents which might have benefited from legal professional privilege if they had been collected by the OFT in the UK, but which do not benefit from legal professional privilege in the Member State where the documents were actually collected. The OFT stated that when it receives information from another competition authority, it is the law of the Member State of the transmitting authority that governs whether the information was lawfully collected, not the relevant provisions of UK law.[195] Whether this would also be the case where an NCA, being aware of the existence of in-house counsel documentation concerning a given conduct (potentially as a result of a failed request for information or investigation) and unable to request it under national law, invites another authority able under its national rules to request that same documentation and transmit it under Regulation 1/2003, is open to question. In this situation, irrespective of whether this may be allowed under EU law, national law may prevent the use of information so collected. Assuming that the receiving authority should not be able to use evidence so obtained, the next question may be whether evidence not complying with national standards may be accepted at all. Regulation 1/2003 does not seem to distinguish between information received under a lower standard and information required specifically from another authority in the knowledge of such lower standards.[196]

---

be obvious to the transmitting authority whether the information gathering was in compliance with all of the relevant provisions of domestic law. Only the transmitting authority can exercise effective control over the information which is posted on the ECN.

[194] JD Cooke, 'General Report' in *The Modernization of EU Competition Law Enforcement in the EU*, FIDE 2004 National Reports 630, 655. See also Kerse & Khan, *EC Antitrust Procedure* (6th edn, 2012) para 5-032 regarding open issues in this respect. K Dekeyser and E De Smijter, 'The Exchange of Evidence Within the ECN' [2005] Legal Issues of Economic Integration 161, note that due to the mutual recognition of a common minimum standard of fundamental rights, these differences should not prevent the receiving NCA from using information legally collected by the transmitting ECN.

[195] Response to the points raised during the consultation on the competition law guidelines, guidance and the OFT's Rules, 24 December 2004, at points 2.22–2.27. See also K Dekeyser and E De Smijter, 'The Exchange of Evidence Within the ECN' [2005] Legal Issues of Economic Integration 161, as regards the example of legal privilege attached to documents established by in-house lawyers.

[196] In order to overcome these difficulties, when discussing draft Reg 1/2003, Marc van der Woude proposed three principles that these exchanges should comply with, as well as the appropriate procedural mechanism for their enforcement. These principles are: (i) the right to the highest standard of confidentiality; (ii) the right to the most favourable conditions; and (iii) the right to a complete transfer. These rights would essentially require a cumulative application of the procedural rights of the transmitting and receiving authorities. M van der Woude, 'Exchange of Information within the European Competition Network: Scope and Limits', in CD Ehlermann and I Atanasiu (eds), *European Competition Law Annual 2002: Constructing the EU Network of Competition Authorities* (Hart Publishing 2003) 14–16. As Reg 1/2003 stands today, it seems difficult to affirm those principles on the basis of the Regulation alone. If these principles are to be complied with, it will probably be on the basis of national laws. In contrast, the ECN Cooperation Notice (para 27) suggests that Art 12 should override any national laws on the basis of the principle of primacy.

According to the Commission, no network member has reported any particular case **3.87** where it had to carry out an analysis of the conditions of Article 12(3) as regards using information received from another network member, where it abstained from requesting potentially relevant information, or where it was unable to use in evidence information relevant to a case for the imposition of custodial sanctions received from another network member.[197]

Article 12 of Regulation 1/2003 does, however, depart from the principle that evidence **3.88** should be collected lawfully in accordance with the rules and procedures in the transmitting State if it is to be used in evidence by NCAs and recognized in the courts of the receiving State. Accordingly, under Article 12(1) of Regulation 1/2003, the receiving NCA could use the evidence which was collected by the first NCA and transmitted to it, even if it could not itself lawfully have collected this evidence, or could not have used it if it had collected it itself.[198] If the Commission is the receiving authority and EU law grants the protection (eg privilege against self-incrimination) it could be argued that protection will not be lost in proceedings before the Commission merely because the privileged information was collected in circumstances where that protection did not apply.[199] However, additional problems may arise where the law of the receiving State provides greater protection than that of the transmitting State. The example indicated would suggest that it would probably matter how this information was obtained. Where the NCA has deliberately chosen to have the information collected where similar protection did not exist, this would mean a breach of fundamental rights or the general principles of EU law.[200] Where the NCA did not seek to circumvent the defence rights afforded under the law of the receiving State, the receiving NCA would be free to use the information except in the specific situation of the imposition of sanctions on natural persons. As indicated, the receiving Member State can only impose those sanctions if the law of the transmitting authority foresees sanctions of a similar kind and where an equivalent level of protection exits in both the transmitting and the receiving State.[201]

While the normal flow of information within the network is essential for the whole sys- **3.89** tem to work, it is arguable whether the safeguards will prove sufficient. For example, in the first place, it was not even clear whether the affected companies would be informed of the exchange of information within the network before disclosure. Without such knowledge, companies cannot take legal action to safeguard their rights in those cases where they might wish to object to the exchange of confidential information. The Manproc now states that if the information was provided to the Commission by a complainant, the latter may be informed of the transmission, after contacting the receiving authority to make sure that

---

[197] See Commission Staff Working Paper accompanying the Communication from the Commission to the European Parliament and Council 'Report on the functioning of Regulation 1/2003' (COM(2009)206 final), para 244.

[198] Art 12 of Reg 1/2003 takes precedence over any contrary law of a Member State. The question whether information was gathered in a legal manner by the transmitting authority is governed on the basis of the law applicable to this authority. It is to be noted that in the ECN Cooperation Notice, the Commission states that the 'question whether information was gathered in a legal manner by the transmitting authority is governed on the basis of the law applicable to this authority' [2004] OJ C101/43, para 27.

[199] Kerse & Khan, *EC Antitrust Procedure* (6th edn, 2012) para 5-033, submit, based on the ECJ ruling in Case C-60/92 *Otto BV v Postbank NV* [1993] ECR I-5683, that even where the right or protection is not one recognized by EU law, such right may need to be respected by the receiving NCA.

[200] Cf by analogy the Court's doctrine on circumvention of national laws by individuals. See Case 33/74 *Van Binsbergen v Bedrijfsvereniging Metaalnijverheid* [1974] ECR 1299, para 13; Case C-212/97 *Centros Ltd v Erhvervs- og Selskabsstyrelsen* [1999] ECR I-1459, para 24, regarding freedom to supply services. Kerse & Khan, *EC Antitrust Procedure* (6th edn, 2012) para 5-037, note that in this case the receiving authority would be prevented from using the information in 'evidence' but Art 11(4) of Reg 1/2003 might still apply.

[201] Article 12(3) of Reg 1/2003.

such a measure would not jeopardize its investigations. The undertaking complained of and other parties, as suppliers of information, may also be informed if the relevant head of unit considers it appropriate and after contacting the receiving authority to make sure that such a measure would not jeopardize its investigations.[202]

3.90 The possibility of exchanging and using information gathered by another competition authority has proven to be one of the cornerstones of the modernization package, given that it greatly enhances the overall efficiency within the network and that it is a pre-condition for a flexible case-allocation system. Since the entry into force of Regulation 1/2003, information exchanges pursuant to Article 12 have taken place to and from the Commission and between NCAs, notably in the following three scenarios:

- In the context of inspections, information exchanges may enable several authorities that have received different pieces of information to obtain a more complete picture of a suspected infringement. Such exchanges strengthen the individual ECN members' ability to detect infringements. They normally occur at a very early stage of an investigation (prior to inspections) and are highly confidential.
- In the context of Article 22 inspections, the information collected on behalf of the requesting authority is transferred on the basis of Article 12.
- If a case is allocated between authorities or reallocated to another authority, the information is passed on pursuant to Article 12.

3.91 In addition, the rules concerning the protection of confidential information undoubtedly differ among Member States. Therefore, one may ask from the outset whether the classification as 'confidential' of any document by one NCA could be overruled by another NCA that has obtained the document through the ECN. This could occur where a document is transmitted from an NCA with high standards regarding the confidentiality protection to another NCA whose national law is less strict in this regard. Yet it seems that Regulation 1/2003 contains a common minimum standard for the protection of confidential information in the form of Article 28(2). By replacing national guarantees for the protection of confidential information, this provision somehow aims to release ECN members from a duty that might exist under their domestic law to verify and ascertain the confidential nature of the information they have obtained and intend to send to another member.[203] Nevertheless, it is also true that this may not be sufficient to remove the reluctance of companies to provide NCAs with confidential information if they are unable to assess the extent to which the information will be distributed within the ECN.

3.92 In addition, differences in procedural rights and guarantees exist today between Member States, or between Member States and the EU, which do not arise from different types of sanctions. The mere fact that there are differences in the procedural rules of the Member States should not prevent the exchange for the purpose of applying the common rules on competition. Procedural rules of all Member States and at EU level comply with high standards of protection of the defence rights under the control of independent courts. They are thus mutually compatible and Regulation 1/2003 takes a clear stance that in the light of an implicit mutual recognition of standards of fundamental rights the remaining divergences should not stand in the way of closer cooperation between authorities in the internal market. Nevertheless, some concerns remain. As a matter of principle, parallel application of national

---

[202] Antitrust Manual of Procedures Internal DG Competition working documents on procedures for the application of Articles 101 and 102 TFEU, March 2012, Module 3 'Cooperation with National Competition Authorities in EU and exchange of information in ECN', para 70.

[203] K Dekeyser and E De Smijter, 'The Exchange of Evidence Within the ECN' [2005] Legal Issues of Economic Integration 161, 172.

law may not make possible the use of evidence where Regulation 1/2003 would not so permit. In this regard, it is clear that national rules could not provide for the use of evidence gathered in one procedure for a 'subject matter' different to that for which it was collected by the transmitting authority. However, it is more questionable whether national laws may limit the use of information in cases not contemplated by Regulation 1/2003.[204] In addition to the examples mentioned previously, there may be national rules limiting the use by the recipient authority of confidential information in the light of extensive rights of access to the file. National rules may also differ on the relative weight of evidence, attaching low probative value to certain documents or testimonies. This suggests that inevitably the national law of the recipient authority will influence the use of evidence received under Article 12 of Regulation 1/2003. It is also apparent that these national provisions may be based on considerations concerning the protection of fundamental rights, thus resulting in an additional layer of protection to that provided by Regulation 1/2003. Indeed, these mechanisms may never make redundant the possibility that the recipient authority may use evidence received under Article 12, but the extent of their influence is unclear in this regard.

Leniency programmes   The Commission and a number of NCAs have leniency programmes, **3.93** under which they offer, subject to varying conditions, full immunity or a significant reduction in the penalties which they would otherwise impose or seek to have imposed on participants in cartels in exchange for the freely volunteered disclosure of information on the cartel which satisfies specific criteria prior to, or during, the investigative stage of proceedings. The ECN Cooperation Notice also deals with the impact of the new decentralized system on the leniency process, namely regarding information exchanges.[205] The Commission considers that the leniency programme has helped detect cartel activity by competition authorities and that it has deterred companies from participating in unlawful cartels. In fact, the Commission has acknowledged several times that most of the major cartel cases which it has recently investigated were initiated as a result of a leniency application.

The coexistence of several leniency programs within the European Union has been addressed **3.94** following the entry into force of Regulation 1/2003. In the ECN Cooperation Notice, potential applicants were advised that they might have an interest in protecting their position in several jurisdictions.[206] Moreover, safeguards concerning the transmission of leniency-related information within the ECN were put in place.[207]

As from 2005, a dedicated ECN Leniency Working Group prepared further measures, con- **3.95** sidering that certain discrepancies may indeed have adverse effects on the effectiveness of the programmes and on the incentives of undertakings to disclose their cartel activities throughout the EU. To address these concerns, the heads of all ECN members endorsed the ECN Model Leniency Programme[208] (the 'Model Programme') on 29 September 2006, whose aim is to remove certain discrepancies between the policies of the ECN Members and to facilitate multiple filings within the EU.

---

[204] JS Venit, 'Private Practice in the Wake of the Commission's Modernization Program' [2005] Legal Issues of Economic Integration 147, 157, suggests that private counsel should work on the assumption that all information provided to one competition authority will be promptly shared with other competition authorities and that even if they cannot directly use this information, they will be aware of the issue and will know where to look for the necessary information.

[205] ECN Cooperation Notice [2004] OJ C101/43, paras 37–42; see also Ch 6, 'Leniency Policy'.

[206] See ECN Cooperation Notice [2004] OJ C101/43, para 38.

[207] ECN Cooperation Notice [2004] OJ C101/43, paras 40 and 41.

[208] Available at <http://ec.europa.eu/competition/ecn/model_leniency_en.pdf>. See also MEMO/06/356 'Competition: the European Competition Network launches a Model Leniency Programme—frequently asked questions', 29 September 2006.

3.96 The Model Programme was drafted as a coherent document setting out the essential procedural and substantive elements that ECN members believe every leniency programme should contain. It concerns only secret cartels, which are difficult to detect by other means.[209] Its purpose is to harmonize the key elements of leniency policies, including the conditions for immunity from fines and the exclusion of certain applicants from protection, the marker system, information required for immunity and markers, conditions for the reduction of fines, and the maximum percentage for the reduction of fines.[210] It foresees that coercers of the cartel are excluded from immunity.[211] The Model Programme also introduces a uniform summary application system that facilitates the procedure when an applicant wants to protect its position with one or more NCAs in addition to the Commission.[212]

3.97 The Model Programme opted for a summary application system for cases in which the Commission is 'particularly well placed' to deal with the case (ie cases concerning more than three Member States).[213] Where a full application has been made with the Commission, NCAs can agree temporarily to protect the applicant's position on the basis of the very limited information foreseen in the Model Programme. This information is broadly equivalent to that needed for a marker and can be given orally.[214] Should an NCA act on the case, it will grant the applicant a period of time to complete its application.

3.98 In this system, summary applications facilitate multiple filings and their processing by competition authorities where it is likely that the Commission will deal with the case. Undertakings that take part in cross-border cartels expose themselves to penalties in several jurisdictions. It is for the applicant to take the steps which it considers appropriate to protect its position with respect to possible proceedings by the relevant authorities.[215]

3.99 In order to limit any negative consequences for leniency programmes by risk of disclosure of leniency information and documents, the Model Leniency Programme allows for oral applications in all cases where this would appear to be justified and proportionate.[216] The Model Leniency Programme also foresees that no access will be granted to any records of any oral statements before the statement of objections has been issued. Moreover, under the Model Leniency Programme, the exchange of records of oral statements between authorities is limited to cases where the protections afforded to such records by the receiving authority are equivalent to those afforded by the transmitting authority.

---

[209] See paras 1–2 of the Explanatory Notes.
[210] See the Explanatory Notes. For instance, reductions of fines should not exceed 50 per cent of the fine in order to ensure that there is a significant difference between immunity and reductions, so that it will be significantly more attractive to apply for immunity than wait to be second in line.
[211] Paragraph 8 of the Model Programme provides that an undertaking which took steps to coerce another undertaking to participate in the cartel will not be eligible for immunity from fines. In general, the Model Programme does not prevent ECN members from adopting a more favourable approach. However, some ECN Members' programmes are not applicable to the sole ringleaders (see also n 4 of the Model Programme). See also ECN Model Leniency Programme: Report on the Assessment of the State of Convergence, para 65 of which states that, with regard to procedural issues, most programmes make it necessary to apply expressly for leniency and provide that immunity will be granted and rejected in writing. Twenty programmes provide for a marker system. Summary applications alongside a Commission application in cases where the latter is particularly well placed are available in twenty-three Member States; seventeen of them accept summary oral applications. Full leniency applications are accepted orally under nineteen leniency programmes. MEMO/09/456 Antitrust: European Competition Network publishes report on leniency convergence, 15 October 2009.
[212] See paras 22–5 of the Model Programme and para 14 of the Network Notice.
[213] See ECN Cooperation Notice [2004] OJ C101/43, para 14.
[214] See, in particular, para 48 of the Explanatory Notes.
[215] See ECN Cooperation Notice [2004] OJ C101/43, para 38.
[216] According to para 14 of the Network Notice, oral applications are always justified and proportionate in cases where the Commission is 'particularly well placed' to act.

The decentralized system has changed the situation for leniency applicants. Prior to the entry **3.100** into force of the new system, an undertaking could expect that its application for leniency would remain in the possession of the NCA to which it was submitted. With the new system, some information regarding leniency applications may flow between NCAs. Under the ECN, the application of the allocation principles may give rise to uncertainties. These conflicts arise where it is ultimately decided within the ECN that the authority to which the leniency application was addressed is not competent. For example, where a leniency applicant approaches the Commission in the belief that the latter is best placed to act, but it later transpires that an NCA, or a number of NCAs, assume jurisdiction under the case reallocation procedures, the applicant may be faced with the risk of fines by these NCAs unless it has made a further application to them. Therefore, companies must not rely on a 'one-stop shop' procedure in the EU, and this would include the situation where they apply to the Commission and another cartel member blows the whistle at the national level. The Commission has been at pains to point out that the allocation rules are not rules of jurisdiction and would not create legitimate expectations on which companies can rely.[217] Conversely, where a leniency applicant believes that a cartel is confined to one or two Member States and makes applications at the national level, but later it turns out that the Commission assumes exclusive jurisdiction on the grounds that the cartel affected more than three Member States, the applicant may face the risk of substantial fines at the EU level.[218]

The ECN Notice suggests that a leniency applicant should present its application before **3.101** all the NCAs which have jurisdiction to apply Article 101 TFEU in the territory affected by the infringement.[219] However, where those effects are difficult to determine, an applicant should presumably apply for leniency in all Member States.[220] In a Union comprising twenty-seven Member States, seeking leniency simultaneously in several Member States may be burdensome and complicated. The ECN Cooperation Network addresses two possible concerns. The first of these is that, as a result of the cooperation provisions contained in Article 11 of Regulation 1/2003, a leniency application to one authority within the ECN might trigger an investigation by another ECN member to which the applicant has not also applied for leniency. The second potential concern is that the information which a leniency applicant has volunteered to one authority within the ECN, together with any information which that authority may obtain as a consequence, might be transmitted to another ECN member under Article 12 of Regulation 1/2003 and used as evidence to impose sanctions on the applicant.

---

[217] C Canenbley and M Rosenthal, 'Cooperation between Antitrust Authorities In and Outside the EU: What does it mean for Multinational Corporations?—Part 1' [2005] ECLR 106, 110–11, suggesting that the whistleblower who submits leniency applications to the Commission should also ask the latter for formal confirmation that it will deal with the case. S Blake and D Schnichels, 'Leniency following Modernisation: Safeguarding Europe's Leniency Programmes' (2004) 2 Competition Newsletter 7, 10, indicate that the network notice may create legitimate expectations in so far as the Commission is concerned.

[218] N Levy and R O'Donoghue, 'The EU Leniency Programme Comes of Age' [2004] World Competition—Law and Economics Review 75, 95.

[219] ECN Cooperation Notice [2004] OJ C101/43, paras 37–42.

[220] The Commission seems to have taken note of the fact that the present system of multiple filings with all relevant authorities within the ECN costs time and money and that differences between programmes might dissuade potential applicants from applying. N Kroes, 'Taking Competition Seriously—Anti-Trust Reform in Europe', IBA conference, Antitrust Reform in Europe: A Year in Practice, Brussels, 9–11 March 2005. D Schroeder, 'Leniency—Issues from a Private Practitioner's Perspective' in "Antitrust Reform in Europe: A Year in Practice' (9–11 March 2005), Brussels, available at <http://www.ibanet.org/Conferences/05_confs_antitrust_reform_in__Eu_A_year_in_Practice_papers.aspx>, also notes that the Commission advises that filings should be made simultaneously, but applicants might have to ask themselves whether they can afford to wait until they would be ready in all relevant Member States.

3.102   Regarding the publicity that should be given to a leniency application within the ECN, under the ECN Cooperation Notice an authority receiving a leniency application should inform the Commission and the other members of the network in application of Article 11(3) of Regulation 1/2003.[221] It is not clear whether this information should include the name of the applicant.[222] Moreover, the Notice makes clear that this information cannot be used by the NCA to start an investigation *ex officio*, whether under the EU competition rules or their national competition law. Notwithstanding this, although an NCA is prevented from using the information obtained from a leniency application filed with a different NCA to open an investigation on its own behalf, Regulation 1/2003 also establishes that an NCA can open an investigation on the basis of information received from other sources.[223] On the other hand, transmission of the information obtained through a leniency application between NCAs pursuant to Article 12 of Regulation 1/2003 would need the prior consent of the applicant.[224] This consent requirement also applies to information that has been obtained as a result of investigative measures 'which could not have been carried out except as a result of the leniency application'. Nevertheless, there are some circumstances in which the consent of the applicant is not required for the transmission of information to another NCA pursuant to Article 12 of the Regulation, namely:[225]

- *When the same applicant has presented another leniency application regarding the same infringement before the receiving authority, provided that he is not allowed to withdraw the information provided.* Once a leniency applicant has made the decision to apply to more than one ECN member, it must accept that the authorities to which it has applied will no longer require its consent in order to exchange information between themselves. The one proviso to this is that at the time that the information is transmitted, it must not be

---

[221] ECN Cooperation Notice [2004] OJ C101/43, para 39. The timing of the disclosure of information pursuant to Art 11(3) has certain importance. The earlier the information is disclosed, the easier it is to examine whether the case raises issues of parallel proceedings or whether reallocation to a better-placed authority should occur. NCAs frequently communicate informally with the Commission about new cases, sometimes well before the formal submission of information pursuant to Art 11(3). E Gippini-Fournier, 'The Modernisation of European Competition Law: First Experiences with Regulation 1/2003—Institutional Report' in HF Koeck and MM Karollus (eds), The Modernisation of European Competition Law—Initial Experiences with Regulation 1/2003, FIDE XXIII Congress Linz 2008—Congress Publications Vol 2 (Nomos 2008) 375, 434.

[222] It could be argued that the competition authority which receives a leniency application is obliged to forward the minimum information contained in the standard form to the other ECN members without any consent being required. This would mean that the authority has to indicate whether it is a leniency case, whether the identity must not be disclosed, and who the applicant is. The consent requirement would then only apply to any further information. See D Reichelt, 'To What Extent does the Cooperation within the European Competition Network Protect the Rights of the Undertakings?' (2005) CML Rev 745, 752.

[223] ECN Cooperation Notice [2004] OJ C101/43, para 40.

[224] ECN Cooperation Notice, para 40. K Dekeyser and E De Smijter, 'The Exchange of Evidence Within the ECC' [2005] Legal Issues of Economic Integration 161, 166, note that although these principles guarantee the required adequate protection of the leniency applicant, they might have the effect that not only the leniency applicant but also other participants in the behaviour infringing the competition rules will escape from effective sanctioning. This is because the would-be transmitting ECN member cannot—or can only partially—sanction the infringement, but the information being exchanged may not be of much use since the leniency applicant is only expected to give its consent when he does not risk any sanction being imposed by the would-be receiving authority.

[225] ECN Cooperation Notice [2004] OJ C101/43, para 41. K Dekeyser and E De Smijter, 'The Exchange of Evidence Within the ECC' [2005] Legal Issues of Economic Integration 161,167, add one further situation where consent is not required: if the ECN member that received the leniency application asks an NCA to carry out inspections on its territory, the latter NCA may send the information obtained to the ECN member that initially asked for this assistance. Commission Report on Competition Policy SEC (2004) 805 final para 109, stating that in 2004 in at least two instances information was exchanged in leniency cases with the consent of the leniency applicant.

open to the applicant to withdraw its leniency application from the authority to which the information is to be transmitted.

- *When the receiving authority has presented a written commitment stating that it or another authority will not use the received information in order to impose sanctions either on the leniency applicant, any other legal or natural person which is covered by the favourable treatment related to the leniency application, or on any employee of any of the persons mentioned before.* The authority requesting transmission of the information must guarantee that not only the information transmitted to it, but also any other information that it may subsequently obtain will not be used either by it or by any other authority to which the information is subsequently transmitted to impose sanctions on any of the following: the leniency applicant; any other person covered by the transmitting authority's leniency programme (eg the subsidiaries of the applicant); or any employee or former employee of either of the former two. It follows from this that unless the receiving authority was already in possession of sufficient evidence to impose a sanction on the transmitting authority's leniency applicant, the guarantee will *de facto* confer on the latter immunity from any fine which the receiving authority might otherwise have imposed on it.

As regards leniency cases, if the leniency applicant has consented to the transmission (and **3.103** in cases where the consent of the leniency applicant is not necessary for the transmission of information), the case-handling unit will inform the leniency applicant of the transmission as soon as possible after this takes place, after contacting the receiving authority to make sure that such a measure would not jeopardize its investigations.

For the avoidance of doubt, the ECN Cooperation Notice also expressly states that where **3.104** information has been collected by an ECN member under Article 22(1) of Regulation 1/2003 on behalf of the ECN member to which the leniency application was made, such information may be transmitted to the latter authority, notwithstanding that the information might otherwise technically be covered by the restriction on the transmission of information obtained during or by means of an inspection or other fact-finding measure that could not have been carried out except as a result of the leniency application. However, it is not entirely clear whether leniency applicants are well protected against investigations from other authorities. The Commission has made clear that 'an application for leniency to a given authority is not to be considered as an application for leniency to any other authority'.[226] Given that not all Member States act on the basis of different rules, it is still doubtful that the safeguards foreseen by the Commission in the ECN Cooperation Notice will overcome the risks that companies would reasonably like to avoid before presenting a leniency application. Actual or potential leniency applicants are understandably sensitive about the subsequent disclosure of both the information which they have volunteered and that which the authority's investigation later uncovers and which, but for the leniency application, would not have come to light.

The ECN Cooperation Notice foresees that information exchanged within the network on **3.105** newly opened cases will not be used by other ECN members to start their own proceedings. The Commission also points out that NCAs have signed a statement in which they declare that they will abide by the principles set out in the Commission Notice.[227] The mutual information in the network is organized in such a way that only those authorities that have committed to these principles receive information on leniency cases. In order to obtain detailed

---

[226] ECN Cooperation Notice [2004] OJ C101/43, para 38.
[227] For the list of NCAs that have signed the statement, which includes in particular a reference to the principles 'relating to the protection of applicants claiming the benefit of a leniency programme, in any case in which [they are] acting or act and to which those principles apply', see <http://ec.europa.eu/competition/ecn/list_of_authorities.pdf>.

information contained in a leniency application, the receiving authority will have to sign a declaration that it will not use the information transmitted or any other information gathered thereafter to impose sanctions on the leniency applicant. In this regard, it should also be noted that the competition authorities that operate leniency programmes have a clear interest not to undermine the functioning of their programmes by circulating the leniency information without appropriate guarantees for their leniency applicant.

3.106 Whilst NCAs would not necessarily have applied EU competition law prior to 1 May 2004, cartel members, then as now, nevertheless risked being sanctioned by the NCAs whose territories were affected by the infringement, either under the EU competition rules or under national competition law. Another ECN member will not be precluded from investigating the case altogether. It will still be free to open an investigation if it receives sufficient information to enable it to do so from another source, such as a complainant, an informant, or another leniency applicant. Moreover, it is important to note that the risk to the leniency applicant of an authority independently receiving information and initiating an investigation on its own behalf does not arise as a consequence of Regulation 1/2003.

3.107 The Commission has pointed out that the means of cooperation and the subjects of discussion have been manifold and have developed over time. Currently, policy work is organized at four different levels: yearly meetings of the Directors-General of the Commission and NCAs, plenary meetings, horizontal working groups, and sector-specific subgroups. Discussions in the different forums have promoted a coherent approach and the consistent application of the EU competition rules. The Director-Generals' meeting is the forum for discussing major policy issues within the Network and constitutes the top level of the ECN framework. It takes place once a year and discussions have, for example, taken place on major topics such as the review of the Commission's policy on Article 102 TFEU, the ECN Leniency Model Programme, increases in food and energy prices, and the financial crisis. Another central forum is the 'ECN Plenary', where horizontal antitrust issues of common interest are discussed, eg the ability of NCAs to disapply State measures in their application of the EU competition rules in combination with Article 4(3) TFEU, following the judgment of the ECJ in *CIF*.[228]

3.108 Cases undertaken by NCAs on this basis are typically complex and a debate was held on the conditions that must be met for the disapplication of anticompetitive State measures. Such exchange of experience and know-how has proved extremely beneficial in terms of further developing a common competition culture within the Network. Under the 'umbrella' of the Plenary, there is a varying number of working groups that deal with horizontal questions of a legal, economic, or procedural nature situated at the interface between EU law and diverse national laws (eg operational issues, leniency, sanctions and *ne bis in idem*, information and communication, Article 102 TFEU, competition chief economists, vertical restraints, and horizontal agreements). In addition to the horizontal working groups, the ECN also encompasses fifteen subgroups that deal with particular sectors. The work in the ECN subgroups has also resulted in, or contributed to, some sectoral guidance on the application of Articles 101 and 102 TFEU, eg in the area of sport and waste management systems. Moreover, the pharmaceuticals subgroup has been closely associated with the inquiry into this sector.[229]

---

[228] Case C-198/01 *Consorzio Industrie Fiammiferi (CIF) and Autorità Garante della Concorrenza e del Mercato* [2003] ECR I-8055.

[229] See Commission Staff Working Paper accompanying the Communication from the Commission to the European Parliament and Council 'Report on the functioning of Regulation 1/2003' (COM(2009)206 final), 29 April 2009, para 248.

This constant dialogue between the network members on all levels in recent years has sig- **3.109**
nificantly contributed to a coherent approach and the consistent application of the EU competition rules. The permanent exchange of experiences and views, very often in an informal
manner, has established confidence and trust between network members, increased expertise,
and promoted convergence. It has led to the creation of a space that allows fruitful discussions in a spirit of close cooperation and with the ultimate objective of promoting a common
competition culture in Europe.[230]

3. Suspension or termination of proceedings (Article 13 of Council Regulation 1/2003)

Article 13 of Regulation 1/2003 provides that the NCAs and the Commission have the right **3.110**
to suspend a proceeding or reject a complaint if the same case is, or has been, dealt with by
another NCA.[231] The NCA should be asked to confirm that they are actively dealing/have
actively dealt with the case by way of a standard form. The NCA should also be asked when
the complainant can be informed (as there would be a possibility of an embargo, if a surprise
inspection is planned). If the Commission comes to the conclusion that it should not pursue
the case, it will first inform the complainant in a meeting or by phone that it has come to the
preliminary view that the case may be rejected.[232]

The ECN Cooperation Notice points out that the possibility of suspending or rejecting a **3.111**
complaint is an option open to the NCAs and the Commission, not a duty. In the event of a
disagreement over the allocation of a case with sufficient EU interest, under Article 11(6) of
Regulation 1/2003 the Commission may itself initiate proceedings which will automatically
relieve the NCAs of their competence to proceed with the case.

Where an authority terminates or suspends proceedings because another authority is dealing **3.112**
with the case, it may transfer—in accordance with Article 12 of the Council Regulation—
the information provided by the complainant to the authority which is to deal with the
case.[233] The possibility of suspending or terminating proceedings can also be applied to
part of a complaint or to part of the proceedings in a case. It may be that only part of a
complaint or of an ex-officio procedure overlaps with a case already dealt with or being dealt
with by another competition authority. In that case, the competition authority with which
the complaint is filed is entitled to reject part of the complaint on the basis of Article 13 and
to deal with the rest of the complaint in an appropriate manner. The same principle applies
to the termination of proceedings.[234] The provision reflects the principle that the allocation
of cases is meant to be flexible. There is no obligation to terminate or suspend proceedings
on the ground that another authority is investigating the case, and there is no indication
as to which authority is supposed to suspend or to terminate. In a system of parallel competences, each authority decides for itself whether or not it wishes to act against a given

---

[230] See Commission Staff Working Paper accompanying the Communication from the Commission to
the European Parliament and Council 'Report on the functioning of Regulation 1/2003' (COM(2009)206
final), 29 April 2009, paras 248–9.

[231] A rejection pursuant to Art 13 is not a referral decision, it merely closes the complaint procedure by
the Commission.

[232] Antitrust Manual of Procedures Internal DG Competition working documents on procedures for the
application of Articles 101 and 102 TFEU, March 2012, Module 21 'Handling of complaints', paras 36–8.

[233] It should be noted that Art 13(1) does not provide expressly for an exchange of information subsequent to the termination or suspension. However, for the purposes of effective enforcement, the information
gathered by the terminating or suspending authority could be transmitted to the other ECN member which
continues to deal with the case. See D Reichelt, 'To What Extent does the Cooperation within the European
Competition Network Protect the Rights of the Undertakings?' (2005) CML Rev 745, 752.

[234] ECN Cooperation Notice [2004] OJ C101/43, paras 23 and 24.

infringement.[235] If a complaint was rejected by an authority following an investigation of the substance of the case, another authority may not want to re-examine the case. On the other hand, if a complaint was rejected for other reasons (eg the authority was unable to collect the evidence necessary to prove the infringement), another authority may wish to carry out its own investigation and deal with the case. This flexibility is also reflected, for pending cases, in the choice open to each NCA as to whether it terminates or suspends its proceedings. An authority may be unwilling to terminate a case before the outcome of another authority's proceedings is clear.[236] As regards the extent of procedural rights of complainants in the context of rejections pursuant to Article 13 of Regulation 1/2003, it is argued that the Commission should at least indicate its intention to reject the complaint and allow for a reasonable period for any comments.[237]

4. The role and the functioning of the Advisory Committee on Restrictive Practices and Monopolies[238]

3.113 The Advisory Committee on Restrictive Practices and Monopolies ('Advisory Committee') has been described in the Commission's ECN Notice as being the forum where officials from the different NCAs meet to discuss specific cases and general issues of EU competition law. The Advisory Committee should be composed of representatives of the NCAs, each Member State having one representative. Yet for meetings in which general issues are being discussed, Member States should be able to appoint an additional representative.[239] The Advisory Committee is consulted prior to the Commission taking decisions on infringement findings,[240] interim measures,[241] commitments,[242] findings of inapplicability of Articles 101 or 102 TFEU,[243] fines,[244]

---

[235] K Dekeyser and C Gauer, 'The New Enforcement System for Articles 81 and 82 and the Rights of Defence', ch 23 in BE Hawk (ed), *International Antitrust Law & Policy* [2004] Annual Proceedings of the Fordham Institute 549. See E Gippini-Fournier, 'The Modernisation of European Competition Law: First Experiences with Regulation 1/2003—Institutional Report' in HF Koeck and MM Karollus (eds), The Modernisation of European Competition Law—Initial Experiences with Regulation 1/2003, FIDE XXIII Congress Linz 2008—Congress Publications Vol 2 (Nomos 2008) 375 in HF Koeck and MM Karollus (eds), (2008). The author argues that the rejection of a complaint on the grounds that an NCA is dealing with a case is a challengeable decision because in this case the Commission would exercise its discretion. In addition, it would not be always obvious that a 'case' is being dealt with or has been dealt with by another authority. Defining 'cases' would require an assessment that should be amenable to judicial review (p 394–5).

[236] D Geradin and N Petit, 'Judicial Remedies under EC Competition Law: Complex Issues Arising from the Modernization Process', ch 17 in *Annual Proceedings of the Fordham Corporate Law Institute* (Fordham University School of Law 2006) 393, note that in legal terms Art 263 does not allow decisions by NCAs to reallocate a case to be challenged, as only decisions taken by an EU institution fall within this Article. See also para 3.14.

[237] E Gippini-Fournier, 'The Modernisation of European Competition Law: First Experiences with Regulation 1/2003—Institutional Report' in HF Koeck and MM Karollus (eds), The Modernisation of European Competition Law—Initial Experiences with Regulation 1/2003, FIDE XXIII Congress Linz 2008—Congress Publications Vol 2 (Nomos 2008) 375, 395. An action for the annulment of a rejection of complaint pursuant to Art 13 was introduced before the GC in Case T-153/06 *European Association of Euro Pharmaceutical Companies (EAEPC) v Commission*. The case was later withdrawn ([2008] OJ C92/46).

[238] For more details, see Antitrust, Manual of Procedures, Internal DG Competition working documents on procedures for the application of Articles 101 and 102 TFEU March 2012, Module 14, 'Advisory Committee on Restrictive Practices and Dominant Positions', para 10.

[239] Recital 20 of Reg 1/2003. This is without prejudice to members of the Committee being assisted by other experts from the Member States.

[240] Article 7 in connection with Art 14(1) of Reg 1/2003.

[241] Article 8 in connection with Art 14(1) of Reg 1/2003.

[242] Article 9 in connection with Art 14(1) of Reg 1/2003.

[243] Article 10 in connection with Art 14(1) of Reg 1/2003.

[244] Articles 23 (Fines) and 24(2) of Reg 1/2003 which allows the Commission to fix the amount of the periodic penalty payment at a figure lower than that which would arise under the original decision in the event that the undertaking has satisfied the obligation which the periodic payment was intended to enforce.

or withdrawal of the benefit granted under any exemption Regulation. The requirement of consultation also applies to sector inquiries.[245] Furthermore, the Commission or any Member State can request that a specific case dealt with by an NCA be put on the agenda of the Advisory Committee. In either situation, the Commission will put the case on the agenda after having informed the NCA concerned.[246] However, this discussion will not lead to a formal opinion. The ECN Notice provides that the Advisory Committee can be used as a forum for the discussion of case allocation. On the other hand, the Advisory Committee will also be consulted by the Commission on draft regulations and the adoption of notices and guidelines.[247]

The consultation of an Advisory Committee can take place either by oral procedure in a **3.114** meeting convened by the Commission (Article 14(3) of Regulation 1/2003) or by written procedure (Article 14(4)), unless any Member State objects to the latter. The oral procedure takes the form of a meeting of the Advisory Committee. Where the written procedure has not been expressly decided upon, the oral procedure will be organized by default.[248]

Under the normal procedural rules, the consultation may take place at a meeting convened and **3.115** chaired by the Commission, held not earlier than fourteen days after the invitation to the meeting is sent by the Commission, together with a summary of the case, an indication of the most important documents, and a preliminary draft decision.[249]

The decisions are sent to each Member State in its own official language (or languages). **3.116** Accompanying those documents, the Commission gives an indication of the most important documents in the case file. In respect of interim decisions, the meeting may be held seven days after the dispatch of the operative part of a draft decision.[250] Where the Commission dispatches a notice convening the meeting which gives a shorter period of notice than those specified, it may take place on the proposed date, provided no Member State objects.

During the meeting, case teams will reply to any point raised by the members of the Advisory **3.117** Committee. The Commission, as Chair, should determine the general structure of, and format for, the discussion to take place in the meeting. If necessary, the case team may give some additional explanation. At the end of the meeting, the Advisory Committee adopts an opinion (generally in English), normally signed by the nominated NCA representatives present. The Secretariat of the Advisory Committee distributes a copy to the representatives of the Member States before the conclusion of the meeting. The case team ensures the translation of the opinion into the two other working languages and keeps the signed original.

Accordingly, the obligation to consult does not concern the decision to impose periodic payments. For individual cases in which fines are imposed, there will often be two Advisory Committees, one discussing the substance of the case, and the other discussing the amount of the fines to be imposed. Antitrust, Manual of Procedures, Internal DG Competition working documents on procedures for the application of Articles 101 and 102 TFEU, March 2012, Module 14 'Advisory Committee on Restrictive Practices and Dominant Positions', para 1.

[245] Article 17 of Reg 1/2003, second para; Art 14 of Reg 1/2003.

[246] Article 14(7) of Reg 1/2003.

[247] ECN Cooperation Notice [2004] OJ C101/43 para 66.

[248] Antitrust, Manual of Procedures, Internal DG Competition working documents on procedures for the application of Articles 101 and 102 TFEU, March 2012, Module 14 'Advisory Committee on Restrictive Practices and Dominant Positions', paras 11–12.

[249] Article 14(3) of Reg 1/2003. ECN Cooperation Notice [2004] C101/43, para 65. Antitrust, Manual of Procedures, Internal DG Competition working documents on procedures for the application of Articles 101 and 102 TFEU, March 2012, Module 14 'Advisory Committee on Restrictive Practices and Dominate Positions', para 13, indicates that a shorter period can be set in the absence of an objection by any Member State.

[250] ECN Cooperation Notice [2004] C101/43, para 60 states that for decisions adopting interim measures, the procedure will be swifter and lighter and that the Advisory Committee must be provided with a short explanatory note and the operative part of the decision.

3.118 The Advisory Committee must deliver a written opinion on the Commission's preliminary draft decision, even if some members are absent and are not represented. At the request of one or more members, grounds must be given for the positions stated in the opinion. Where the Advisory Committee delivers a written opinion, this will be appended to the draft decision. The Commission must fully heed the opinion of the Advisory Committee and inform the Committee of the manner in which its opinion has been taken into account.[251] If the Advisory Committee recommends publication of the opinion, the Commission will publish it, taking into account the legitimate interest of undertakings in the protection of their business secrets.[252] Where, in cases where fines are imposed, a second Advisory Committee meeting takes place, a second opinion may be published in the OJ.

3.119 Under the written procedure, the Commission determines a time limit of not less than fourteen days within which the Member States are to put forward their observations for circulation to all other Member States.[253] The Commission must decide whether or not to propose to NCAs a written procedure, taking into account the likely efficiency gains for both NCAs and the Commission, having regard to the nature of the case, the type of draft decision being considered, and the likely nature of the comments if a meeting were held. The launching of the consultation under a written procedure is done by a notice from the Commission to the Advisory Committee, within the deadline prescribed in Article 14(4) of Regulation 1/2003, and together with the documents set out in Article 14(3) of Regulation 1/2003. If any Advisory Committee member considers that a case where the Commission has proposed an oral procedure would be suitable for a written procedure, he/she may communicate his/her opinion to the Commission. The Commission can follow up this suggestion by sending a notice to all Advisory Committee members, proposing that the consultation should take place by way of a written procedure. Pursuant to Article 14(4) of Regulation 1/2003, the Commission may set shorter deadlines than those provided in Article 14(3) and (4). Members should endeavour to indicate to the Commission as early as possible if they object to the shorter deadline. In the event of an objection, the deadlines foreseen in Article 14(3) and (4) of Regulation 1/2003 would apply, counting from the dispatch of the documents.[254]

---

[251] Article 14(5) of Reg 1/2003; ECN Cooperation Notice [2004] C101/43, para 59.

[252] Article 14(6) of Reg 1/2003 and ECN Cooperation Notice [2004] C101/43, para 68. Although not binding, the opinions expressed by the Member States in the reports and at the Committee meetings are scrutinized carefully by Commission officials to ensure that decisions are of a high quality. See also Kerse & Khan, *EC Antitrust Procedure* (6th edn, 2012) para 5-097, who consider that making the Committee's opinion public is a significant change, although this does not include opinions of the Committee on cases referred to it by an NCA. Under Reg 17, any opinion of the Committee was not revealed to the undertakings concerned. In *Pioneer*, the Court rejected the view that Reg 17 should be construed as meaning that the Committee's opinion needed to be disclosed to the undertakings. Whatever the Court's opinion might be, the Commission would be required to base its decisions only on facts about which the undertaking have had the chance of making known their views. Cases 100 and 100/80 *Musique Diffusion Francaise v Commission* [1983] ECR 1823, paras 34–6.

[253] Article 14(4) of Reg 1/2003. ECN Cooperation Notice, para 67. In *RTE*, the GC held that the fourteen-day notice period under Reg 17 was a purely internal procedural rule, and failure to comply with it would not by itself render a subsequent decision by the Commission ineffective. Case T-69/89 *Radio Telefis Eireann v Commission* [1991] ECR II-485, para 27. See also Antitrust, Manual of Procedures, Internal DG Competition working documents on procedures for the application of Articles 101 and 102 TFEU, March 2012, Module 14 'Advisory Committee on Restrictive Practices and Dominant Positions', para 23. As regards decisions taken pursuant to Article 8, the time limit of fourteen days is replaced by one of seven days. Where shorter time limits for the written procedure are proposed, they will be applicable in the absence of an objection by any Member State.

[254] Antitrust, Manual of Procedures, Internal DG Competition working documents on procedures for the application of Articles 101 and 102 TFEU, March 2012, Module 14 'Advisory Committee on Restrictive Practices and Dominant Positions', paras 24–7.

In a consultation conducted under the written procedure, it would be sufficient to sub- **3.120**
mit to the Advisory Committee a simple list of key questions. Its members may make
any observations in writing.[255] If the nature of the requests for explanations is such that
an open-to-all discussion is warranted, the Commission may organize a conference call/
videoconference to deal with the questions and then restate the deadline for the written replies. Alternatively, if the complexity of the issues justifies it or any member so
requests, it may 'switch' to the oral procedure by organizing a meeting on the date specified in the original invitation. The consultation would then be concluded in this meeting
(in which written replies already made would not be binding upon the members of the
Committee).[256]

Outside the scope of Articles 101 and 102 TFEU and pecuniary penalties, liaison with the **3.121**
Committee takes place prior to the adoption of decisions to initiate inquiries into different
economic sectors under Article 17(2) of Regulation 1/2003. It should be noted that the
Advisory Committee is allowed to discuss general issues of competition law, but cannot issue
opinions on cases dealt with by NCAs.[257]

Undertakings have no right to participate in Advisory Committee meetings. One of the rep- **3.122**
resentatives acts as rapporteur, being appointed on a rotating basis from among the members
of the Advisory Committee. In order to keep the proceedings to the point, the rapporteur
informs the other representatives of the main issues involved and usually submits a number of
questions to be considered by them. Those questions, which usually refer to the applicability
of Articles 101 and 102 TFEU to the case in question and the appropriateness or otherwise
of imposing fines, not normally dealt with in a second Advisory Committee meeting, are
dealt with in turn by each country's representative in alphabetical order. The members of the
Advisory Committee may address questions to and seek clarifications from the Commission.
After discussion, each of the rapporteur's questions is answered succinctly by the representatives of the Member States. The report reflects the views of all of the delegations, first
the majority opinion and then the minority opinions.[258] However, no particular majority
is required for the adoption of the report and there is no provision for individual views.
Failure to consult the Advisory Committee may constitute an infringement of a procedural
requirement in the application of the competition rules and could vitiate the Commission's
decision.[259] However, it is not regarded, in itself, as undermining the fundamental rights of
undertakings or their defence rights.[260] The EU Courts are unlikely to quash a decision of

---

[255] Antitrust Manual of Procedures, Internal DG Competition working documents on procedures for the
application of Articles 101 and 102 TFEU, March 2012, Module 14 'Advisory Committee on Restrictive
Practices and Dominant Positions', paras 28–9. These observations, or at least a summary thereof, should
be provided in a commonly understood and accepted language for the convenience of other Committee
members.
[256] Antitrust, Manual of Procedures, Internal DG Competition working documents on procedures for
the application of Articles 101 and 102 TFEU, March 2012, Module 14 'Advisory Committee on Restrictive
Practices and Dominant Positions', para 30.
[257] Article 14(7) third para of Reg 1/2003.
[258] See eg in relation to merger control. Opinion of the Advisory Committee on concentrations given at
its 113th meeting on 20 March 2003 concerning a draft decision relating to Case COMP/M.2876 *Newscorp/
Telepiù* [2004] OJ C102/25.
[259] See Opinion of AG Gand in Case 41/69 *ACF Chemiefarma v Commission* [1970] ECR 661, paras
709–11.
[260] Case T-19/91 *Vichy v Commission* [1992] ECR II-415, para 38. Where not all available information is
disclosed to the members of the Advisory Committee, the legality of the Commission's decisions will only be
affected if it is shown that failure to forward that information to the Committee did not allow the Committee
to deliver its opinion in full knowledge of the affects, that is to say, without being misled in material respect
by inaccuracies or omissions. Joined Cases T-25/95, T-26/95 etc *Cimenteries CBR SA and others v Commission*

the Commission for procedural irregularity unless it is sufficiently substantial and would have a harmful effect on the legal and factual situation of the party alleging the procedural irregularity.[261]

3.123 As regards the question of whether an NCA is entitled, by virtue of those provisions of the Regulation, to participate, as a defendant or respondent, in judicial proceedings concerning one of its own decisions, the ECJ ruled that Article 35 of the Regulation must be interpreted as precluding national rules which do not allow an NCA to participate, as a defendant or respondent, in judicial proceedings brought against a decision that the authority itself has taken. It is for the NCA to gauge the extent to which their intervention is necessary and useful, having regard to the effective application of EU competition law. However, if the NCA consistently fails to enter an appearance in such judicial proceedings, the effectiveness of Articles 101 TFEU and 102 TFEU will be jeopardized. In the absence of EU rules, the Member States remain competent, in accordance with the principle of procedural autonomy, to designate the body or bodies of the NCA which may participate, as a defendant or respondent, in proceedings brought before a national court against a decision that the authority itself has taken, while at the same time ensuring that fundamental rights are observed and that EU competition law is fully effective. An NCA's obligation to ensure that Articles 101 TFEU and 102 TFEU are applied effectively therefore means that an NCA should be entitled to participate, as a defendant or respondent, in proceedings before a national court which challenge a decision that the authority itself has taken.[262]

C. Principles and Procedures for Cooperation with Third Countries

3.124 The Commission emphasizes that it enhances effective enforcement of competition rules through international cooperation with third country authorities. Such cooperation may

---

[2000] ECR II-491, para 742. See also K Lenaerts and I Maselis, 'Procedural Rights and Issues in the Enforcement of Articles 81 and 82 of the EC Treaty' [2001] Fordham International Law Journal 1615, 1646.

[261] Case T-290/94 *Kaysersberg SA v Commission* [1997] ECR II-2247, para 88. In *PVC II*, the ECJ held that there was no need to consult the Advisory Committee where a second decision adopted to correct an illegal measure in the original decision did not substantially amend the first decision. Cases C-238, 244, 245, 247, 252, and 254/99 *Limburgse Vinyl Maarschappij v Commission (PVC II)* [2002] ECR I-8375, para 118.

[262] Case C-439/08 *Vlaamse federatie van verenigingen van Brood- en Banketbakkers, Ijsbereiders en Chocoladebewerkers (VEBIC)* [2011] ECR I-12471. The question raised by the Belgium national court was whether an NCA is entitled under Arts 2, 15(3), and 35(1) of Regulation 1/2003 to participate in judicial proceedings concerning one of its own decisions. According to the ECJ, designated NCAs have to make sure that Arts 101 and 102 are applied effectively in the general interest. Although Art 35(1) leaves it to the domestic law of Member States to determine the detailed procedural rules for legal proceedings brought against decisions of NCAs, the rules must not jeopardize the attainment of the objective of Reg 1/2003 to ensure that Arts 101 and 102 are applied effectively by NCAs. If the NCA is not afforded rights as a party to proceedings and is prevented from defending a decision that it has adopted in the general interest, there is a risk that the court before which the proceedings have been brought will be wholly 'captive' to the pleas and arguments put forward by the undertaking bringing the proceedings. In competition law, which involves complex legal and economic assessments, the existence of such a risk is likely to compromise the exercise of the obligation on national competition authorities to ensure the effective application of Arts 101 and 102 TFEU. An NCA's obligation to ensure that Arts 101 and 102 are applied effectively requires that the authority should be entitled to participate as a defendant or respondent in proceedings before a national court that challenge a decision that the authority has taken. N Petit 'The Judgment of the European Court of Justice in VEBIC: Filling a Gap in Regulation 1/2003' (2011) 2(4) Journal of European Competition Law & Practice 340.

include sharing experiences, coordination of enforcement actions, and exchanging information to facilitate enforcement activities.[263] Cooperation with third country enforcement authorities is agreed by bi-lateral or multi-lateral agreements or is arranged through regular contacts. The EU has agreements concerning competition matters with a number of countries and regions.[264]

So-called dedicated cooperation agreements on competition policy were signed with the **3.125** United States, Canada, Japan, and Korea.[265] Under these agreements, competition authorities exchange non-confidential information and coordinate their enforcement activities. Furthermore, each party may ask the other to take enforcement action (positive comity); and each party must take account of the other's significant interests when enforcing the competition rules (traditional comity).

That said, Regulation 1/2003 does not specifically regulate the exchange of information with **3.126** third country enforcement authorities. Article 12 of the Regulation is applicable only to the exchange of information between the Commission and the Member States for the application of Article 101 and 102 TFEU. Under the agreements with the United States, Canada, and Japan, the Commission and each respective competition authority exchange information. However, the existing cooperation agreements expressly exclude the exchange of protected or confidential information.[266] This means in practice that no information obtained through the formal investigative tools can be shared with the other authority without the specific consent ('waivers') of the companies involved.[267]

While the possibility of exchanging evidence between competition authorities is an essen- **3.127** tial element of efficient cooperation in the enforcement of the competition rules in an increasingly international context, the conclusion of an international cooperation agreement which allows for the exchange of evidence with enforcers in selected third countries with a criminal enforcement system comes up against the obstacle contained in Article 12(3), last sentence of Regulation 1/2003, prohibiting the use inside the EU of information collected by one authority by the receiving authority to impose custodial sanctions, in so far as the law of the transmitting authority does not provide for sanctions of a similar kind for the infringement of Articles 101 or 102 TEFU. This raises the difficulty that it would be awkward for the EU to go further in terms of information exchange with third country enforcers than is currently the case for enforcers inside the Union. It may therefore

---

[263] Commission Staff Working Paper accompanying the Communication from the Commission to the European Parliament and Council 'Report on the functioning of Regulation 1/2003' (COM(2009)206 final), 29 April 2009, para 302 et seq.

[264] A list of countries and regions with which the European Union has signed a bilateral or multilateral agreement concerning competition matters is available at: <http://ec.europa.eu/competition/international/bilateral/>.

[265] 1991 EU/US Competition Cooperation Agreement [1995] OJ 95/47; Agreement between the European Communities and the Government of Canada regarding the application of their competition laws [1999] OJ L175/50; Agreement between the European Community and the Government of Japan concerning cooperation on anti-competitive activities [2003] OJ L183/12; Agreement between the European Community and the Government of the Republic of Korea concerning cooperation on anti-competitive activities [2009] OJ L202/35. See for more details: <http://ec.europa.eu/competition/international/legislation/agreements.html>.

[266] Commission Staff Working Paper accompanying the Communication from the Commission to the European Parliament and Council 'Report on the functioning of Regulation 1/2003' (COM(2009)206 final), 29 April 2009, para 306.

[267] Commission Staff Working Paper accompanying the Communication from the Commission to the European Parliament and Council 'Report on the functioning of Regulation 1/2003' (COM(2009)206 final), 29 April 2009, para 306, n 350, citing the Opinion of AG Mengozzi in Case C-511/06 P *Archer Daniels Midland Co v Commission* [2009] ECR-I 5843, para 105.

be appropriate to reflect upon the limitations placed on authorities using information they have received to impose custodial sanctions as per Article 12(3), last sentence of Regulation 1/2003, and to examine whether other options are available, while fully preserving the parties' defence rights.

Disclosure to third country public authorities

3.128 The Manproc establishes guidelines for the implementation of international agreements which need to be respected when assessing a case with an international dimension. These guidelines are as follows.[268]

3.129 **Notification to third countries** A case officer should determine whether a third country with which the EU has concluded an agreement has an interest in a case for which he/she is responsible. The case officer should consider whether, *inter alia*, any of the following criteria are met:

- Is the case officer aware of a similar enquiry taking place in the third country?
- Does the case involve anticompetitive activities (other than a merger or acquisition) carried out in a significant part of the third country's territory?
- Is one or more of the undertakings under investigation or party to the transaction, or a company controlling such undertaking(s), a company incorporated or organized under the laws of the third country?
- Does the case involve conduct believed to have been required, encouraged or approved by the third country?

3.130 During the course of the investigation, the case officer should consider the following:

- Will DG COMP request information from any undertaking operating in the territory of the third country?
- Will the enforcement activity involve remedies that would, in significant respects, require or prohibit conduct in the third country?

3.131 Where a case meets any of these criteria, the case officer should verify if notification to the third country is obligatory and should inform Unit A5/International Relations. The relevant desk officer in Unit A5 will be available to provide assistance and advice.

3.132 **Notification from third countries** When a notification is received from the authorities of a third country, Unit A5 shall forward it to the operational units concerned and to the Member States whose interests are affected.

3.133 **Cooperation and coordination** If a case officer wishes to contact the authorities of a third country (request for assistance, material, or clarification about a parallel investigation etc), Unit A5 can arrange the initial contact. Where an operational Directorate believes that there are important EU interests which would necessitate an intervention by DG COMP with the authorities of the third country, ie to take action, to modify a proposed action, or to desist from taking action, it should immediately consult with Unit A5 to determine the most appropriate course of action.

3.134 **Positive comity requests** Positive comity enables one party adversely affected by anticompetitive conduct carried out in the other's territory to request the other party's competition authority to take enforcement action. There are general 'positive comity' provisions in the

---

[268] Antitrust Manual of Procedures Internal DG Competition working documents on procedures for the application of Articles 101 and 102 TFEU, March 2012, Module 3 'Cooperation with National Competition Authorities in EU and exchange of information in ECN', paras 28–39.

Cooperation Agreements with the USA (Article V 2), Canada (Article V 2), Japan (Article 5.1), and Korea (Article 6), according to which either party can invite the other party to take, on the basis of the latter's legislation, appropriate measures regarding anticompetitive behaviour implemented on its territory and which affects the important interests of the requesting party.

With regard to the USA, a special Positive Comity Agreement has existed since 1998. The **3.135** Agreement clarifies both the mechanics of the positive comity cooperation instrument, and the circumstances in which it can be used. In principle, one party may request the other party to remedy anticompetitive behaviour which originates in its jurisdiction but affects the requesting party as well.

In practice, the positive comity provisions would not be used frequently, as companies (ie **3.136** complainants) prefer to address directly the competition authority they consider to be best suited to deal with the situation. If, however, a case of positive comity arises, the case handler should contact Unit A5 to determine the appropriate course of action.[269]

---

[269] Antitrust Manual of Procedures Internal DG Competition working documents on procedures for the application of Articles 101 and 102 TFEU, March 2012, Module 3 'Cooperation with National Competition Authorities in EU and exchange of information in ECN', paras 40–2.

4

THE ORGANIZATION OF EUROPEAN COMMISSION PROCEEDINGS

Luis Ortiz Blanco, Konstantin Jörgens, and Marisa Tierno Centella

A. Outline of the Main Types of Procedure

1. Informal guidance[1]

The system of enforcement set out in Regulation 1/2003 is based on the premise that under-   **4.01**
takings are best placed to take an informed decision on whether an agreement or concerted
practice is compatible with Article 101 or Article 102 of the Treaty on the Functioning of the
European Union ('TFEU'). Any kind of notification/clearance procedure would run counter
to the Commission's key objective of dedicating its resources to tackling major cartels and
other serious anticompetitive practices. However, from the outset the Commission acknowledged that there might be cases which could give rise to genuine uncertainty because they
present novel or unresolved questions for the undertakings involved.[2] In these situations, the

---

[1] See European Commission Antitrust Manual of Procedures, Internal DG Competition working docu-
ments on procedures for the application of Articles 101 and 102 TFEU, March 2012, Module 22 'Informal
Guidance', para 1 et seq; E Gippini-Fournier, 'The Modernisation of European Competition Law: First
Experiences with Regulation 1/2003—Institutional Report' in HF Koeck and MM Karollus (eds), The
Modernisation of European Competition Law—Initial Experiences with Regulation 1/2003, FIDE XXIII
Congress Linz 2008—Congress Publications Vol 2 (Nomos 2008) 375, 419–21.
[2] Commission Notice on informal guidance relating to novel questions concerning Arts 81 and 82 of the
EC Treaty that arise in individual cases (guidance letters) [2004] OJ C101/78, para 5.

Commission is generally ready to issue informal guidance to aid the consistent application of the competition rules in a decentralized system, as long as this is compatible with its enforcement priorities.[3]

4.02 The Commission points out that when companies seek informal guidance, it should be made clear that: (i) the Directorate-General for Competition ('DG COMP') does not object to an exchange of views about market developments and may provide general indications about its case practice and policy; (ii) no definitive views can be given on a particular agreement, decision, or practice; (iii) an informal discussion with DG COMP cannot be construed as the Commission giving any form of 'clearance'; and (iv) the fact of meeting DG COMP does not confer any rights or expectations.

4.03 Aware that an over-generous system of acceding to requests for assistance and informal guidance could jeopardize the essence of the modernized enforcement of the EU competition rules,[4] the Commission makes guidance letters conditional on three cumulative requirements being met because issuing a guidance letter should remain exceptional.[5] First, the question must be novel. The problems must be real and identifiable ones. The Commission does not consider hypothetical questions and does not issue guidance letters on agreements or practices that are no longer being implemented by the parties. Where the parties present a request on an agreement, the implementation must have reached a sufficiently advanced stage. Secondly, the guidance letter should be appropriate and useful having regard to the economic implications of the transaction. Finally, expending the resources of the Commission must be compatible with the enforcement priorities of the Commission. In particular, this would mean that no further fact-finding is required.[6] In the context of its five-year assessment of Regulation 1/2003, the Commission reported that it had received very few requests for 'informal guidance' as set out in the Notice on guidance letters and that:

> [n]one of these approaches came close to fulfilling the conditions for making such a request, which must be made about novel or unresolved questions that give rise to genuine uncertainty, as opposed to providing what would amount to individual comfort letters as existed prior to modernisation.[7]

4.04 A request for a guidance letter is without prejudice to the power of the Commission to open proceedings in accordance with Regulation 1/2003 with regard to the facts presented in the

---

[3] As indicated before, guidance letters are based exclusively on the Notice, as they are not expressly foreseen by Regulation 1/2003. They are nonetheless indirectly referred to in Recital 38 of Regulation 1/2003. See also R Sauer in JL Schulte and C Just (eds), *Kartellrecht* (Carl Heymanns Verlag 2012), Art 10 of the Reg 1/2003, para 20.

[4] See European Commission Antitrust Manual of Procedures, Internal DG Competition working documents on procedures for the application of Articles 101 and 102 TFEU, March 2012, Module 22 'Informal Guidance', para 7.

[5] See also European Commission Antitrust Manual of Procedures, Internal DG Competition working documents on procedures for the application of Articles 101 and 102 TFEU, March 2012, Module 22 'Informal Guidance', para 2.

[6] Informal Guidance Notice [2004] OJ C101/78, paras 8–10, also European Commission Antitrust Manual of Procedures, Internal DG Competition working documents on procedures for the application of Articles 101 and 102 TFEU, March 2012, Module 22 'Informal Guidance', para 11. See also earlier E Paulis and E De Smitjer, 'Enhanced Enforcement of the EC Competition Rules Since 1 May 2004 by the Commission and the NCAs', International Bar Association ('IBA') conference, Antitrust Reform in Europe: A Year in Practice, Brussels, 9–11 March 2005, 15, who point out the exceptional character of guidance letters.

[7] Commission Staff Working Paper accompanying the Communication from the Commission to the European Parliament and Council, Report on the functioning of Regulation 1/2003{COM(2009)206 final}, 29 April 2009, para 45.

request. Therefore, information provided by means of guidance requests submitted by undertakings can in principle also serve as a starting point for ex officio procedures under Articles 7, 9, and 10 of Regulation 1/2003, provided that the respective requirements for opening a case and the relevant priority setting criteria are fulfilled.[8] The Commission also rules out the possibility of introducing an annulment decision against guidance letters by making it clear that the latter are not Commission decisions.[9] These factors underline the limited attractiveness of guidance letters for undertakings.[10]

2. Infringement proceedings and settlements[11]

Infringement proceedings

Infringement of the EU competition rules laid down in Articles 101 and 102 TFEU exposes undertakings to the risk of infringement proceedings being initiated against them, with the possibility of severe fines. Where it appears to the Commission—as a result of complaints from individuals, information from the undertakings themselves, or from its own sources[12]—that an infringement may exist, it initiates a procedure. The Notice on Antitrust Best Practices also provides that the Commission will open proceedings under Article 11(6) of Regulation 1/2003 when the initial assessment leads to the conclusion that the case merits further investigation and where the scope of the investigation has been sufficiently defined.[13] In cartel cases, the opening of proceedings normally takes place simultaneously with the adoption of the Statement of

4.05

---

[8] European Commission Antitrust Manual of Procedures, Internal DG Competition working documents on procedures for the application of Articles 101 and 102 TFEU, March 2012, Module 22 'Informal Guidance', para 4. The Commission has pointed out that its practice is to impose more than symbolic fines only where it is established, either in horizontal instruments or in the case law and decision-making practice, that certain behaviour constitutes an infringement. See para 4 of the Commission Notice on guidance letters and para 36 of the Guidelines on the method of setting fines imposed pursuant to Article 23(2)(a) of Regulation No 1/2003 [2006] OJ C210/2. As a result, companies engaging in activities about which genuine legal uncertainty exists are not at risk of being fined. Commission Staff Working Paper accompanying the Communication from the Commission to the European Parliament and Council, Report on the functioning of Regulation 1/2003{COM(2009)206 final} note 48.

[9] Informal Guidance Notice [2004] OJ C101/78, para 25. European Commission Antitrust Manual of Procedures, Internal DG Competition working documents on procedures for the application of Articles 101 and 102 TFEU, March 2012, Module 22 'Informal Guidance', para 15: 'Guidance letters are not Commission decisions and do not bind Member States' competition authorities or courts that have the power to apply Articles 101 and 102 TFEU. However, it is open to Member States' competition authorities and courts to take account of guidance letters issued by the Commission as they see fit in the context of a case.'

[10] See E Gippini-Fournier, 'The Modernisation of European Competition Law: First Experiences with Regulation 1/2003—Institutional Report' in HF Koeck and MM Karollus (eds), The Modernisation of European Competition Law—Initial Experiences with Regulation 1/2003, FIDE XXIII Congress Linz 2008—Congress Publications Vol 2 (Nomos 2008) 375, 421, noting that it is understandable that the Commission has sought to take a restrictive approach with regard both to the possibility of examining requests for guidance letters and to the effects of such letters. However, as a result, there would be a risk of this instrument becoming irrelevant in practice. Kerse & Khan, *EC Antitrust Procedure* (6th edn, Sweet & Maxwell 2012) para 2-086.

[11] See in more detail Ch 10, 'Procedures to Establish the Existence of an Infringement', para 10.01 et seq.

[12] Information from citizens and undertakings is important in triggering investigations by the Commission. As pointed out in its Commission notice on best practices for the conduct of proceedings concerning Articles 101 and 102 TFEU [2011] OJ C308/6, the Commission therefore encourages citizens and undertakings to inform it about suspected infringements of the competition rules. This can be done either by lodging a formal complaint or by simply providing market information to the Commission. Anyone who is able to show a legitimate interest as a complainant, and who submits a complaint in compliance with form C (Art 5(1) of the Implementing Regulation) enjoys certain procedural rights. The details of the procedure to be followed are set out in the Implementing Regulation and in the notice on the handling of complaints. See Commission Notice on best practices for the conduct of proceedings concerning Articles 101 and 102 TFEU (text with EEA relevance) [2011] OJ C308/6, paras 10 and 11.

[13] See Commission Notice on best practices for the conduct of proceedings concerning Articles 101 and 102 TFEU (text with EEA relevance) [2011] OJ C308/6, para 17.

Objections, though it may take place earlier.[14] Also in other cases, if by conducting limited further investigations the appropriate scope of the case can be determined with more certainty, it may be advisable to do this before proposing to open proceedings.[15] The opening of proceedings does not prejudge in any way the existence of an infringement; it merely indicates that DG COMP will further pursue the case as matter of priority. This important distinction is made clear in the decision notified to the parties, as well as in all public communications concerning the opening of the case.[16]

4.06   In general terms, the procedure has two main successive stages.[17] In the first stage, the Commission investigates the facts: for this purpose it is entitled to send requests for information to undertakings and to carry out inspections at their premises. Following the fact-finding stage, once it has gathered sufficient evidence of an infringement, the Commission gives the undertakings an opportunity to submit observations regarding the facts and objections on the basis of which the Commission intends to take a decision against them. To that end, it sends them a Statement of Objections setting out the infringements of which they are accused and the Commission's intentions, which will simply be to declare the existence of an infringement and, if necessary, impose a fine on the undertakings involved.[18] The undertakings are informed that they may make such submissions in writing and, in some cases, orally. In order to enable undertakings to prepare their defence better, the Commission allows them access to the case file. They will then be able to reply to the objections in writing, and it is at this time that, if they wish, they must ask for an administrative hearing. At hearings, undertakings have an opportunity to make such oral submissions to the Commission as they consider relevant to their defence. After the hearing, the Commission prepares a draft decision which is submitted to the Advisory Committee for a non-binding report to be given. The Advisory Committee is made up of the national authorities of the Member States responsible for competition matters. Commission officials at DG COMP amend the draft as they consider necessary.[19] It then becomes the final draft and is presented as such to the full meeting of the Commission. The decision may then be adopted by the Commission, which notifies it to the undertakings and publishes it in the Official Journal ('OJ'). It may be challenged before the General Court ('GC').

4.07   The Commission may commence proceedings following a complaint, on a request or transfer from a national competition authority ('NCA') or by simply acting on its own initiative.

---

[14] See Commission notice on best practices for the conduct of proceedings concerning Articles 101 and 102 TFEU (text with EEA relevance) [2011] OJ C308/6, para 24.

[15] European Commission Antitrust Manual of Procedures, Internal DG Competition working documents on procedures for the application of Articles 101 and 102 TFEU, March 2012, Module 10 'Opening of proceedings', para 4.

[16] European Commission Antitrust Manual of Procedures, Internal DG Competition working documents on procedures for the application of Articles 101 and 102 TFEU, March 2012, Module 10 'Opening of proceedings', para 13.

[17] See, eg Joined Cases C-238/99, C-244–245/99, C-247/99, C250–252/99, and C-254/99 *Limburgse Vinyl Maatschappij and others v Commission* [2002] ECR I-8375, paras 181–3; Case T-241/97 *Stork Amsterdam v Commission* [2000] ECR II-309, para 51.

[18] See Commission notice on best practices for the conduct of proceedings concerning Articles 101 and 102 TFEU (text with EEA relevance) [2011] OJ C308/6, para 76, stating that the Statement of Objections sets out the preliminary position of the Commission on the alleged infringement of Arts 101 and/or 102 TFEU, after an in-depth investigation. Its purpose is to inform the parties concerned of the objections raised against them with a view to enabling them to exercise their rights of defence in writing and orally (at the hearing). It thus constitutes an essential procedural safeguard which ensures that the right to be heard is observed. The parties concerned will be provided with all the information they need to defend themselves effectively and to comment on the allegations made against them.

[19] For more details on the Advisory Committee,see European Commission Antitrust Manual of Procedures, Internal DG Competition working documents on procedures for the application of Articles 101 and 102 TFEU, March 2012, Module 14 'Advisory Committee'.

This mirrors the different ways by which information relating to a suspected infringement of the EU competition rules may be brought to the knowledge of the Commission. As regards complaints, there is a formal complaint procedure through which a third party may make known evidence of a possible violation of Article 101 or 102 TFEU in a complaint.[20] The Commission may also receive information from a variety of other sources, eg monitoring of public information or through its discussions with other antitrust authorities. Sector inquiries may be of a particular sector of the economy or a particular type of agreement across various sectors.[21]

Settlement procedure[22]

In 2008, the Commission introduced a new mechanism which allows the Commission to settle cartel cases by means of a simplified procedure.[23] The settlement procedure, which is another string to the Commission's bow in its fight against cartels, allows companies to recognize their participation in an anticompetitive agreement. The Settlement Notice sets out the framework for 'rewarding cooperation in the conduct of Commission proceedings commenced in view of the application of Article [101 TFEU] to cartel cases.'[24] In a nutshell, it provides for the granting of a 10 per cent fine reduction to any undertaking involved in a Commission cartel investigation that agrees to have its case treated under the settlement procedure rather than under the general procedure.

4.08

Cooperation within the Settlements Package is different from the voluntary production of evidence to initiate or advance the Commission's investigation, which is already covered by the Leniency Notice. Parties have neither the right nor the duty to settle, but in cases where companies are convinced that the Commission could prove their involvement in a cartel to the required legal standard, a settlement can be reached with the Commission on the scope and duration of the cartel, and on the individual liability of the companies involved. The process seems intended primarily to reward firms that do not contest the Commission's view of the facts and application of the law. However, the process does allow for an exchange of views, and the Commission acknowledges that parties will 'have the opportunity to influence the Commission's objections through argument',[25] regardless of how such discussions are labelled. To this end, parties will be informed about the likely objections and the evidence supporting those objections, and will be given the opportunity to state their views before formal

4.09

---

[20] Commission Notice on the handling of complaints by the Commission under Articles 101 and 102 of the TFEU ('Notice on Complaints') [2004] OJ C10 1/65, paras 53–81.

[21] A relatively recent example includes the competition inquiry into the pharmaceutical sector, which was launched in January 2008 with unannounced inspections in a number of pharmaceutical companies in Europe. The inquiry is a competition investigation based on Art 17 of Reg 1/2003 on the application of the EU competition rules (Arts 81 and 82). The Commission is committed to a more frequent use of sector inquiries in the future. See Ch 5, 'Opening of the File and Proceedings; Transparency', para 5.01 et seq.

[22] For more details see Ch 10, 'Procedures to Establish the Existence of an Infringement', para 10.107 et seq; see also U Soltesz, 'EU Cartel Settlements in Practice—The Future of EU Cartel Law Enforcement?' [2011] 32(5) ECLR 258; ML Tireno Centella, 'La procedure de transaction communautaire' (2008) 2 Concurrences 76; K Dekeyser and C Roques, 'The European Commission's Settlement Procedure in Cartel Cases' (Winter 2010) 55(4) The Antitrust Bulletin 819.

[23] The settlements package, which entered into force on 1 July 2008, consisted of a Commission Regulation (Commission Regulation (EC) No 622/2008 of 30 June 2008 amending Regulation (EC) No 773/2004, as regards the conduct of settlement procedures in cartel cases ([2008] OJ L171/3)), accompanied by a Commission Notice (Commission Notice on the conduct of settlement procedures in view of the adoption of Decisions pursuant to Article 7 and Article 23 of Council Regulation (EC) No 1/2003 in cartel cases ([2008] OJ C167/1)).

[24] Commission Notice on the conduct of settlement procedures in view of the adoption of Decisions pursuant to Article 7 and Article 23 of Council Regulation (EC) No 1/2003 in cartel cases [2008] OJ C167/01, para 1.

[25] Commission Q&A accompanying the legislative package, MEMO/08/458 'Antitrust: Commission introduces settlement procedure for cartels—frequently asked questions' of 30 June 2008.

objections are sent out. If the parties choose to introduce a settlement submission acknowledging the objections, the Commission's statement of objections would reflect the contents of the submission by the parties and therefore could be much shorter than a statement of objection issued without prior cooperation.[26] Since parties will have been heard in anticipation of the 'settlement' Statement of Objections, other procedural steps can be simplified so that, following confirmation by the parties, the Commission can proceed swiftly to adopt a final decision after consulting Member States in the Advisory Committee of representatives of all Member States.

4.10 A settlement only takes place when the Commission decision reflects the parties' settlement submissions. The Commission may only depart from the parties' settlement submissions by reverting to the standard procedure. In addition, if no settlement were explored or reached, the standard procedure would apply by default. In 2010, the Commission adopted its first two settlement decisions: a full settlement decision in *DRAMs*[27] and a hybrid settlement decision in *Animal Feed Phosphates*.[28] A third decision adopted using the settlement procedure was announced in April 2011, when the Commission imposed fines on companies engaging in price fixing of consumer detergents.[29] In October 2011, the Commission adopted a fourth decision using the settlement procedure by imposing fines on companies involved in the Cathode Ray Tube ('CRT') glass cartel.[30] In December, the Commission adopted its fifth settlement decision in the market for refrigeration compressors.[31] In each of the 2011 cases, all of the parties in the case used the settlement procedure and were granted an extra 10 per cent discount from their fines. European Commission officials have expressed their expectation that more settlements in cartel investigations would be in the pipeline.[32] To date, the last cartel settlement published was

---

[26] Commission Staff Working Document, Accompanying the Report from the Commission on Competition Policy 2008 {COM(2009)374 final}, paras 9 and 10.

[27] Case COMP/38511 *DRAMs*. See IP/10/586 and MEMO/10/201 of 19 May 2010. See also Commission Staff Working Document, Accompanying the Report from the Commission on Competition Policy 2010 {COM(2011) 328 final}, paras 53–5.

[28] Case COMP/38866 *Animal Feed Phosphates*. See IP/10/985 of 20 July 2010. The procedure is termed 'hybrid' when at least one of the companies investigated declines to settle and insists on continuing with the ordinary investigation, thus leaving its defence options open when appealing against the Commission's Decision to the GC.

[29] Commission Press Release IP/11/473 'Antitrust: Commission fines producers of washing powder €315.2 million in cartel settlement case', 13 April 2011. Joaquín Almunia Vice President of the European Commission responsible for Competition Policy Statement by Commissioner Almunia on the detergent powder cartel settlement Statement in Berlaymont press room, Brussels, 13 April 2011.

[30] Commission Press Release IP/11/1214 'Antitrust: Commission fines producers of CRT glass €128 million in fourth cartel settlement', 19 October 2011.

[31] Commission Press Release IP/11/1511 'Antitrust: Commission fines producers of refrigeration compressors €161 million in fifth cartel settlement', 7 December 2011.

[32] Mlex, 'More cartel settlements soon, EC's chief competition lawyer says' 7 April 2011, *ICF 18th St Gallen International Competition Law Forum*. T Christoforou praised the way that the new procedure was working, and said that the 10 per cent fine reduction on offer appeared to be enticing enough for companies. He admitted that while the fast-track procedure was introduced three years ago, to that date it had been slow to reap results, given that it had resulted in only two cases, *DRAMs* and the *Animal Feed Phosphates* case. Christoforou also highlighted the fact that while previous decisions took more than a year to be reached, the average time now needed 'should be slightly more than six months'. The settlement procedure did not involve 'negotiation' with the parties on the level of fines or the scope of the infringement. Moreover, Christoforou pointed out that there would still be room for the companies to respond and clarify their views on the allegations made, but this should not be taken for a 'negotiation process'. See also Speech 12/428, 8 July 2012, 'Joaquín Almunia Vice President of the European Commission responsible for Competition Policy Antitrust enforcement: Challenges old and new 19th International Competition Law Forum, St. Gallen 8 June 2012': 'the recent decisions confirmed the growing success of our settlement procedure. In 2011, we adopted three settlement decisions in cases concerning consumer detergents, refrigeration compressors, and Cathode Ray Tube glass. Clearly, the settlement system has become a well-established and effective tool that can considerably shorten our proceedings and generate benefits for everyone. Let me add, however, that

announced on 27 June 2012 and concerned producers of water management products used in heating, cooling, and sanitation systems.[33]

3. Interim measures[34]

Pursuant to Article 8 of Regulation 1/2003, in cases of urgency the Commission, acting on its **4.11** own initiative, is empowered to adopt interim measures where there is a risk of serious and irreparable harm to competition and there is prima facie evidence of an infringement.[35] It is further stipulated that interim measures may be adopted for no more than one year, with a possibility of renewal. The exceptional character of this power has led to the adoption of less than a dozen decisions ordering interim measures which were partly annulled by the EU Courts.

Regulation 1/2003 specifically stipulates that interim measures may be ordered by the **4.12** Commission 'acting on its own initiative'. In its earlier practice under Regulation 17, the Commission had accepted that a complainant could request the Commission to issue interim measures in the same way that a litigant would seek an injunction from a court.[36] Under Article 8 of Regulation 1/2003, the Commission considers that it acts in the public interest and not in the interest of individual operators.[37] It therefore takes the view that complainants do not have a right to ask for interim measures under Regulation 1/2003, and it is therefore not obliged to decide on any (informal) request for interim measures and, if necessary, to reject it by decision. However, the Commission's decision to adopt interim measures is

---

settlements are not suitable in all cases and neither of the decisions we have taken so far in 2012 has been a settlement.' D Vascott 'EU Cartel Settlements: Are they Working?' Global Competition Review, May 2013.

[33] Commission Press Release IP/12/704 'Antitrust: Commission fines producers of water management products €13 million in sixth cartel settlement', 27 June 2012.

[34] See Ch 14, 'Interim Measures', paras 14.01–14.15. R Sauer in JL Schulte and C Just (eds), *Kartellrecht* (Carl Heymanns Verlag 2012), Art 8 of Reg 1/2003, para 1 et seq.

[35] Regulation 17 did not directly address the issue of whether the Commission could adopt interim measures in relation to a suspected infringement of Arts 101 and 102. However, in its 1980 order in the *Camera Care* case, the ECJ held that Art 3(1) of that regulation conferred on the Commission the power to take interim measures. See Case C-792/79 *Camera Care v Commission* [1980] ECR 119, para 18; European Commission Antitrust Manual of Procedures, Internal DG Competition working documents on procedures for the application of Articles 101 and 102 TFEU, March 2012, Module 7 'Interim measures', para 1.

[36] Case 792/79 *Camera Care v Commission* [1980] ECR 119, para 20 et seq; Case T-23/90 *Peugeot v Commission* [1991] ECR II-653, para 19; Case T-44/90 *La Cinq v Commission* [1992] ECR II-1, paras 1, 13, and 27; J Schwarze and A Weitbrecht, *Grundzüge des Europäischen Kartellverfahrensrecht* (Nomos 2004) § 6, para 47; Kerse & Khan, *EC Antitrust Procedure* (6th edn, Sweet & Maxwell 2012) para 6-061. If the application is rejected, it is debatable whether at present the applicant could have the refusal reviewed by the EU Courts. J. Temple Lang 'The Strengths and Weaknesses of the DG Competition Manual of Procedure' (2013) 1(1) Journal of Antitrust Enforcement 132, 145 notes that the Commission's policy on interim measures would be 'unsatisfactory and excessively concerned with administrative convenience rather than effectiveness in safeguarding competition'. The Manual of Procedure's Module on interim measures would be the most inadequate part of the Manual because it does not say anything on, for example, the important question of balance of interests.

[37] Proposal for a Council Regulation on the implementation of the rules on competition laid down in Arts 81 and 82 (EC) and amending Regs (EEC) 1017/68, (EEC) 2988/74, (EEC) 4056/86, and (EEC) 3975/87 (Draft Regulation implementing Articles 81 and 82 EC [2000] OJ C365E/284), Explanatory Memorandum, Commission document COM(2000)582 of 27 September 2000 [1999] OJ C132/1, Art 8; Notice on Complaints [2004] OJ C101/65, para 80. Article 8 decisions may be similar to decisions under former Art 15(6) of Reg 17 relating to the withdrawal of immunity from fines, where the GC ruled that third-party complaints have no legitimate interests in having immunity withdrawn. Kerse & Khan, *EC Antitrust Procedure* (6th edn, Sweet & Maxwell 2012) para 6-062, express doubts as to whether the Court will accept that the adoption of interim measures will be removed from the scope of judicially reviewable acts. D Geradin and N Petit, 'Judicial Remedies under EC Competition Law: Complex Issues Arising from the Modernization Process' ch 17 in International Antitrust & Policy, 32nd Annual International Antitrust Law & Policy Conference [2006] Fordham Corporate Law Institute 393, note that the formulation of Art 8 of Reg 1/2003 would be open to criticism and difficult to reconcile with the case law of the EU Courts which have acknowledged under certain conditions a right to interim relief by economic operators. See Ch 14, 'Interim Measures', para 14.07 et seq.

subject to appeal to the EU Courts.[38] Companies could always have recourse to national courts, the very function of which is to protect the rights of individuals.[39] Article 8(1) codifies the requirement laid down in the *Camera Care* case that the Commission must first show a *prima facie* case.[40] In *Peugeot* and *La Cinq*, the GC condemned the Commission for applying an overly stringent test.[41] The requirement of certainty demanded of a final decision was not needed to satisfy the condition relating to the probable existence of an infringement in interim measures proceedings. Further, Regulation 1/2003 provides that interim measures should only be granted in cases of urgency due to the risk of serious and irreparable harm to competition. To qualify as 'urgent', the case must call for immediate action on the part of the Commission, in order to avoid either a 'serious and irreparable damage' to the party seeking the adoption of interim measures, or to avoid a situation that is intolerable for the public interest.[42] With regard to the harm justifying intervention, in *Camera Care* the Court of Justice ('ECJ') treated damage to other undertakings and jeopardizing competition policy as separate criteria for adopting interim measures.[43] Article 8(1) refers to 'damage to competition', which could encompass damage to undertakings and to competition policy. Potential damage to an individual undertaking is therefore only to be considered where it coincides with damage to competition, in which case the interests of an undertaking may be protected by implication.[44] The practice of the Commission shows that the average period required for granting interim measures may vary to a certain extent, being approximately three to eight months. This can be explained by the procedural requirements which need to be fulfilled before adopting a decision taking interim measures.[45]

---

[38] European Commission Antitrust Manual of Procedures, Internal DG Competition working documents on procedures for the application of Articles 101 and 102 TFEU, March 2012, Module 17 'Interim measures', para 6. See also the Commission Notice on the handling of complaints by the Commission under Articles 81 and 82 of the EC Treaty (2004/C 101/05), para 77.

[39] J Schwarze and A Weitbrecht, *Grundzüge des Europäischen Kartellverfahrensrecht* (Nomos 2004) § 6, paras 48–9, indicate that this does not need to entail a restriction of the legal protection, given the increased role of national courts and that the assessment of the notion of public interest will also embrace the interests of individual companies.

[40] Camera Care, which sold and repaired cameras, complained to the Commission that it would be denied supplies of Hasselblad cameras by Hasselblad and its distributors. It therefore requested the Commission to take interim measures to protect its position while the matter was being investigated, but the Commission refused the request on the grounds that it had no power to do so. On appeal, the Court held that the Commission had the power to take interim measures. Case 792/79 *Camera Care v Commission* [1980] ECR 119, paras 19–20.

[41] Case T-23/90 *Peugeot v Commission* [1991] ECR II-653, paras 59–61; Case T-44/90 *La Cinq v Commission* [1992] ECR II-1, paras 61 and 62. Essentially, in proceedings relating to the legality of a Commission decision concerning the adoption of interim measures, the requirement of a finding of a *prima facie* infringement cannot be placed on the same footing as the requirement of certainty that a final decision must satisfy. The Commission is wrong to identify the requirement of a 'prima facie infringement' with the requirement of a finding of a 'clear and flagrant infringement' at the stage of interim measures. The GC only required the probability of a *prima facie* infringement. See also European Commission Antitrust Manual of Procedures, Internal DG Competition working documents on procedures for the application of Articles 101 and 102 TFEU, March 2012, Module 17 'Interim measures', para 13.

[42] European Commission Antitrust Manual of Procedures, Internal DG Competition working documents on procedures for the application of Articles 101 and 102 TFEU, March 2012, Module 17 'Interim measures', paras 14 and 15.

[43] Case 792/79 *Camera Care v Commission* [1980] ECR 119, para 19.

[44] European Commission Antitrust Manual of Procedures, Internal DG Competition working documents on procedures for the application of Articles 101 and 102 TFEU, March 2012, Module 17 'Interim measures', para 9.

[45] European Commission Antitrust Manual of Procedures, Internal DG Competition working documents on procedures for the application of Articles 101 and 102 TFEU, March 2012, Module 17 'Interim measures', para 20.

4. Rejection of complaints and declarations of inapplicability

Rejection of complaints[46]

Proceedings commenced by a complaint may conclude with a decision declaring and penal-   **4.13**
izing an infringement of Articles 101 and 102 TFEU or else with the rejection of the complaint. While the Commission has the duty 'to examine carefully the facts and points of law
brought to its notice by the complainant in order to establish whether they disclose conduct
liable to distort competition in a given area',[47] the Commission is not obliged to carry out an
investigation of every complaint submitted with a view to establishing whether the infringement has been committed.[48] During the first stage, the Commission examines the complaint
and may collect further information in order to decide what action it will take.[49] In the second stage, the Commission may investigate the case further with a view to initiating proceedings pursuant to Article 7(1) of Regulation 1/2003. Where the Commission has investigated
a complaint and intends not to pursue it, it will first inform the complainant in a meeting
or by phone that it has come to the preliminary view that the complaint may be rejected.
Once informed, the complainant may decide to withdraw the complaint, leading to the file
being closed. If the complainant maintains the complaint, the Commission will inform him
by formal letter pursuant to Article 7(1) of Regulation 773/2004 of its preliminary conclusion that there are insufficient grounds for acting and set a time limit for the submission of
written observations.[50] Article 7 of Regulation 773/2004 states that 'where the Commission
considers that on the basis of the information in its possession there are insufficient grounds
for acting on a complaint... [it will] set a time-limit' within which the complainant must
submit his or her views.[51] 'Article 7 letters' are similar to 'Article 6 letters' under Regulation
99/63 and seek to safeguard the rights of the complainant.[52]

---

[46] Ch 12, 'Rejection of Complaints'.
[47] Case T-575/93 *Koelman v Commission* [1996] ECR II-1, para 39.
[48] Notice on Complaints [2004] OJ C101/65, para 53.
[49] If the intention is to investigate the case further, the complainant should be informed. A short letter
by the Head of Unit is sufficient. The complainant should also be informed of the initiation of proceedings, unless such information is inappropriate. In the spirit of encouraging an open exchange of views, the
Commission will, in cases based on formal complaints, provide the parties subject to the proceedings, at an
early stage (unless such is considered likely to prejudice the investigation) and at the latest shortly after the
opening of proceedings, with the opportunity of commenting on a non-confidential version of the complaint.
See Commission Notice on best practices for the conduct of proceedings concerning Articles 101 and 102
TFEU (text with EEA relevance) [2011] OJ C308/6, para 69. European Commission Antitrust Manual of
Procedures, Internal DG Competition working documents on procedures for the application of Articles 101
and 102 TFEU, March 2012, Module 21 'Handling of complaints', paras 11–12,; Notice on Complaints
[2004] OJ C101/65, para 55.
[50] European Commission Antitrust Manual of Procedures, Internal DG Competition working documents
on procedures for the application of Articles 101 and 102 TFEU, March 2012, Module 21 'Handling of
complaints', paras 57–8.
[51] The Article 7 letter is a formal Commission act adopted by the Director-General, by sub-delegation.
The Legal Service must be consulted and give its approval before the Art 7 letter is adopted by the
Director-General. It expressly refers to Art 7 of Reg 773/2004, indicates a time limit for written observations
(at least four weeks), and refers to the legal consequences if no reply is received within the deadline. For more
details, see European Commission Antitrust Manual of Procedures, Internal DG Competition working documents on procedures for the application of Articles 101 and 102 TFEU, March 2012, Module 21 'Handling
of complaints', para 61.
[52] The Commission notes that this procedure between the complainant and the companies that are subject to the investigation is not adversarial. Consequently, these rights would be less far-reaching than those
of the companies under investigation. Notice on Complaints [2004] OJ C101/65, para 59. K Lenaerts and
J Maselis, 'Procedural Rights and Issues in the Enforcement of Articles 81 and 82 of the EC Treaty' [2001]
Fordham International Law Journal 1615, 1648–9, noting that the rights of complainants would be limited
to the right to 'participate' in the administrative procedure.

4.14 It is important to note that an 'Article 7' letter does not imply that the Commission will not change its position in the future.[53] A complainant who, pursuant to Article 7(1) of the Implementing Regulation, has been informed of the Commission's intention to reject its complaint, may request access to the documents on which the Commission has based its provisional assessment.[54] Such access is normally provided by annexing to the letter a copy of the relevant documents.[55] If the complainant does not respond within the time limit set, the complaint is deemed to have been withdrawn pursuant to Article 7(3) of Regulation 773/2004.[56] In all other cases, in the third procedural phase, the Commission takes cognizance of the observations submitted by the complainant and either initiates a procedure against the company under investigation or adopts a definitive decision rejecting the complaint, stating that on the basis of the facts and information in its possession the complaint is unjustified or does not merit further action by the Commission.[57] Regulation 773/2004 makes it clear that the complainant is entitled to a decision from the Commission on the matter of its complaint.[58]

4.15 The rejection decision itself is a formal decision by the Commission which is adopted by the duly empowered Commissioner. It can be appealed against to the EU Courts. The rejection decision is limited to rejecting the complaint, it does not 'bless' the agreement or practice complained of. Rejection of a complaint by the Commission is without prejudice to NCAs or national courts acting regarding the same case.[59]

4.16 Complaints can be rejected on the basis that there are insufficient grounds for acting. In particular, there can be insufficient grounds for acting if conducting a further investigation into the alleged infringement would, in view of the public interest and the circumstances of the individual case, not constitute a sufficiently high degree of priority for the Commission (also known as 'lack of European Union interest' or 'Union interest'). The case law (in particular *Automec II*)[60] has

---

[53] Case C-125/78 *GEMA v Commission* [1979] ECR 3173, para 17: 'Such a communication implies the discontinuance of the proceedings without, however, preventing the Commission from reopening the file if it considers it advisable, in particular where, within the period allowed by the Commission for that purpose in accordance with the provisions of Article 7 the applicant puts forward fresh elements of law or of fact'. The Art 7 letter does not itself constitute a decision challengeable before the Court in an action for annulment under Art 263 TFEU. See Case T-186/94 *Guérin Automobiles v Commission* [1995] ECR II-1753, para 32, confirmed on appeal in Case C-282/95 *Guérin Automobiles v Commission* [1997] ECR I-1503, para 34. It constitutes, however, a definition of the position within the meaning of Art 265, second para TFEU and cannot, therefore, be challenged on the basis of that provision. However, if the Commission fails either to initiate a proceeding against the subject of the complaint or to adopt a definitive decision within a reasonable time, the complainant may rely on Art 265 TFEU in order to bring an action for failure to act.

[54] Article 8(1) of Reg 773/2004. Note that the Commission Notice on Access to the file [2005] OJ C325/7, para 31, provides that the complainant will be provided access to such documents on a single occasion, following the issuance of the letter informing the complainant of the Commission's intention to reject its complaint.

[55] Commission Notice on the handling of complaints by the Commission under Articles 81 and 82 of the EC Treaty [2004] OJ C101/65, para 69.

[56] This would mean that the Commission is not required to take a decision formally rejecting the complaint. On the other hand, this should prevent the complainant from reviving the complaint and the Commission from reassessing its position in the light of any further information provided by the complainant. Kerse & Khan, *EC Antitrust Procedure* (6th edn, Sweet & Maxwell 2012) para 2-055.

[57] This decision can be challenged before the Court. In the context of such an action the complainant may rely on any legal defects prior to the definitive decision. Case C-282/95 *Guérin Automobiles v Commission* [1995] ECR I-1503, para 38. If the Commission fails either to initiate proceedings against the undertaking complained of or to adopt a definitive decision within a reasonable time the complainant may rely on Art 265 TFEU in order to bring an action for failure to act.

[58] Article 7(2) of Reg 773/2004.

[59] European Commission Antitrust Manual of Procedures, Internal DG Competition working documents on procedures for the application of Articles 101 and 102 TFEU, March 2012, Module 21 'Handling of complaints', paras 69–70.

[60] Case T-24/90 *Automec v Commission* [1992] ECR II-2223, para 85. Automec was a distributor of BMW vehicles in Italy. On expiry of its dealership, Automec brought proceedings before the national

recognized that the Commission is entitled to give differing degrees of priority to the complaints that it receives, taking into account the duration and extent of the infringements complained of and their effect on the competition situation in the EU.[61] As regards the grounds for rejecting a complaint, from the outset the Commission has discretion regarding which cases it will pursue. There can also be insufficient grounds for acting if the complaint is not substantiated or if there is no evidence to establish the existence of an infringement.[62]

Until now, the task of the Commission to consider attentively all the matters of fact and of law **4.17** which the applicant brought to its attention appeared to be a mere formality. However, by virtue of its strict scrutiny in Case T-427/08 *CEAHR v Commission*,[63] there is the perception that the obligation placed on the Commission to consider attentively all the matters of facts and law which the applicant has brought to its attention—in order to assess the Union interest related to the case—has become a material one.[64] The Court has held that in order to assess the Union interest in further investigating a case, the Commission must take account of the circumstances of the case, in particular the matters of law and fact set out in the complaint made to it. Above all, it must weigh the significance of the alleged infringement as regards the functioning of the internal market against the probability of it being able to establish the existence of the infringement and the extent of the investigative measures necessary in order to fulfil, under the best possible conditions, its task of ensuring compliance with Articles 101 and 102 TFEU.[65]

While the Commission's Notice on complaints sums up the case law as to when the Commission **4.18** may be justified in refusing a complaint on grounds of insufficient Union interest, the EU Courts have made it clear that there is not an exhaustive list of factors to which the Commission can

courts to compel BMW to continue the contractual relationship and subsequently lodged a complaint. The Commission sent Automec a letter stating that it had no power to grant its application. Automec brought the matter before the GC seeking annulment of the letter and damages for the Commission's failure to commence proceedings against BMW (Case T-64/89 *Automec v Commission* [1990] ECR II-367). Automec and the Commission continued their correspondence. In 1990 the Commission rejected Automec's complaint, stating that there was not a sufficient Community interest to justify an investigation. Automec appealed to the GC, which gave rise to *Automec II*.

[61] European Commission Antitrust Manual of Procedures, Internal DG Competition working documents on procedures for the application of Articles 101 and 102 TFEU, March 2012, Module 21 'Handling of complaints', para 41. For more details on the requisites for the notion of lack of EU interest: R Sauer in JL Schulte and C Just (eds), *Kartellrecht* (Carl Heymanns Verlag 2012), Art 7 of the Reg 1/2003, para 26 et seq.

[62] European Commission Antitrust Manual of Procedures, Internal DG Competition working documents on procedures for the application of Articles 101 and 102 TFEU, March 2012, Module 21 'Handling of complaints', para 41.

[63] Case T-427/08 *Confédération européenne des associations d'horlogers-réparateurs (CEAHR) v Commission* [2011] ECR II-5865, paras 20–178. In this case, the CEAHR challenged the Commission decision rejecting its complaint against several Swiss manufacturers of luxury watches on the grounds of a lack of Community interest. The question of the definition of the relevant market—vital in this case, which involved an analysis of the after-market—raised complex economic assessments. The judgment reviewed extensively the Commission's statements in relation to market definition and eventually found a manifest error of assessment, which ultimately vitiated the Commission's reasoning as to their being an insufficient EU interest. The Court found that the Commission had failed in its duty to assess carefully all matters of fact in order to assess the lack of Community interest. See also President of the GC, Marc Jaeger, 'The Standard of Review in Competition Cases Involving Complex Economic Assessments: Towards the Marginalisation of the Marginal Review?' (2011) 2(4) Journal of European Competition Law & Practice 295, 302.

[64] P van Ginneken, 'The CEAHR Judgment: Limited Discretion to Reject Complaints' (2011) 2(4) Journal of European Competition Law & Practice 348. See also A Mikroulea, 'Rejection of Complaint, Lack of Community Interest, Obligation of Motivation: How Does that all Fit Together?' (2011) 2(3) Journal of European Competition Law & Practice 241.

[65] European Commission Antitrust Manual of Procedures, Internal DG Competition working documents on procedures for the application of Articles 101 and 102 TFEU, March 2012, Module 21 'Handling of complaints', para 43; see for case in which the Commission denied the Union interest relative to an alleged Art 102 TFEU infringement, Case T-119/09 *Protégé International v Commission* [2012] OJ C319/6.

or should have regard.[66] Having a wide degree of discretion, the Commission is nevertheless required to state reasons if it declines to pursue a complaint.[67] In addition, the Commission cannot exclude certain types of cases from the investigation.[68] Accordingly there is no short cut for the Commission: it cannot consider certain situations as being excluded in principle.[69] Given the ruling in *CEAHR v Commission*, in future cases the Commission will probably be inclined only to set aside a complaint for lack of EU interest after an exhaustive assessment of all of the facts submitted.[70]

Declarations of inapplicability[71]

4.19 Article 10 of Regulation 1/2003 enables the Commission acting on its own initiative to adopt a decision finding that Article 101 TFEU is not applicable to an agreement either because the conditions of Article 101(1) TFEU are not fulfilled or because those contained in Article 101(3) TFEU are satisfied. Article 10 further states that the Commission may also make the same finding with reference to Article 102 TFEU.[72] The Commission has pointed out that a declaratory decision finding inapplicability can be proposed in exceptional cases where a Commission decision is needed, on a specific issue, in order to avoid or solve a problem of coherence resulting from conflicting interpretations by national courts in different Member States or by members of the European Competition Network ('ECN'). Such circumstances can justify allocating the Commission's resources to the preparation of this type of 'positive' decision.[73]

4.20 While the Commission issued a detailed Notice on Informal Guidance, there is no similar communication on the declarations of inapplicability. There is no prescribed form.[74] This demonstrates that the Commission is determined not to allow Article 10 to be used as a backdoor route for notifications which could jeopardize the main objective of Regulation 1/2003.[75] Article 10 of Regulation 1/2003 shows its exceptional character by stating that such decisions may be taken where 'the Community interest so requires'.[76] The objective of

---

[66] Case C-119/97 *Ufex and others v Commission* [1999] ECR I-1341, para 79: 'the number of criteria of assessment the Commission may refer to should not be limited, nor conversely should it be required to have recourse exclusively to certain criteria'. See also Case C-450/98 *IECC v Commission* [2001] ECR I-3947, para 58.

[67] The Commission is under an obligation to state reasons if it declines to continue with the examination of a complaint and those reasons must be sufficiently precise and detailed to enable the Court effectively to review the Commission's use of its discretion to define priorities. Case C-119/97 *Ufex v Commission* [1999] ECR I-1341, paras 89–95; Case T-26/99 *Trabisco v Commission* [2001] ECR II-633, para 31; Case T-115/99 *SEP v Commission* [2001] ECR II-691, para 32.

[68] Case C-119/97 *Ufex v Commission* [1999] ECRI-1341, paras 90–2.

[69] Kerse & Khan, *EC Antitrust Procedure* (6th edn, Sweet & Maxwell 2012) para 2-058.

[70] The Union interest was, however, denied in Case T-119/09 *Protégé International v Commission* [2012] OJ C319/6 and the ruling does not mention *CEAHR v Commission*.

[71] Ch 13, 'Voluntary Adjustments, Commitments, Finding of Inapplicability, Informal Guidance'.

[72] Kerse & Khan, *EC Antitrust Procedure* (6th edn, Sweet & Maxwell 2012) para 2-087, take the view that this type of decision covers the old 'negative clearance' and 'exemption', although a declaration under Art 10 would appear 'to be something more than the former but less than the latter'. The declaration of inapplicability may contain a statement as to whether Art 101(3) TFEU is satisfied (unlike 'negative decisions'), but it would not apply for a fixed period of time (unlike exemptions).

[73] European Commission Antitrust Manual of Procedures, Internal DG Competition working documents on procedures for the application of Articles 101 and 102 TFEU, March 2012, Module 18 'Decision finding inapplicability (Article 10 decision)', para 1.

[74] It seems that a letter would suffice in order to apply for a declaratory decision. Kerse & Khan, *EC Antitrust Procedure* (6th edn, Sweet & Maxwell 2012) para 2-088, suggest that given the similarity between a decision under Art 10 of Reg 1/2003 and the former negative clearance or exemption under Reg 17, the Commission may demand the amount of information it would have required under Form A/B.

[75] See Draft Regulation Implementing Articles 81 and 82 EC [2000] OJ C365E/284, Explanatory Memorandum Art 10: 'Such a possibility would seriously undermine the principal aim of the reform, which is to focus the activities of all competition authorities on what is prohibited.'

[76] See also Reg 1/2003 of Recital 14, stating that 'in exceptional cases where the public interest of the Community so requires, it may also be expedient for the Commission to adopt a decision of a declaratory

competition policy is to benefit consumers and the economy as a whole, in the framework of the internal market. The notion of 'Community public interest' contained in Article 10 refers to the fundamental commitment of the EU to a system of undistorted competition as a common public goal.[77] For this reason, and given that the Commission is under no obligation to make inapplicability declarations at the request of the parties, the Commission will only issue inapplicability decisions where, for example, the Commission wishes to make quasi-legislative statements in regard to new types of agreements or practices.[78] The terms of application of Article 10 have been clearly defined so that its use is confined to 'exceptional cases'[79] to clarify the law and ensure its consistent application throughout the EU, namely: (i) to 'correct' the approach of an NCA; or (ii) to send a signal to the ECN about how to approach a certain case.[80] The Commission has not, to date, adopted any decisions under Article 10.

In contrast to NCAs, which can decide that there are no grounds for an action, the **4.21** Commission may state that Articles 101 and 102 TFEU are not applicable.[81] As regards findings under Article 101(3) TFEU, the scope of Article 10 decisions may be weaker compared to exemption decisions under former Regulation 17. Where those decisions granted exemption for a fixed period of time and could only be withdrawn in limited circumstances, a decision under Article 10 does not protect the agreement in question for a specified period of time and in principle the Commission would be free at any time to reopen the case. Where the Commission intends to adopt a decision of inapplicability, it shall publish a concise summary of the case and the main content of the proposed course of action. Interested parties may submit their observations within a time limit fixed by the Commission.[82] Pursuant to Article 14 of Regulation 1/2003, prior to taking a decision under Article 10, the Advisory Committee must be consulted.

---

nature'. See also European Commission Antitrust Manual of Procedures, Internal DG Competition working documents on procedures for the application of Articles 101 and 102 TFEU, March 2012, Module 18 'Decision finding inapplicability (Article 10 decision)', para 5 stating that Art 10 decisions are not intended to replace negative clearance or exemption decisions under the previous enforcement system. Neither can they be legally 'applied for' by undertakings, nor should they be envisaged as a reaction to such requests. It is important to note that under the legal exception system, undertakings have the primary responsibility to assess the compatibility of their agreements and practices with the EU competition rules.

[77] See Commission Staff Working Paper SEC(2001) 1828 'The notion of 'Community public interest' in Article 10' of 13.11.2001, 5, section II, para 11. This notion should be clearly distinguished from the (lack of) 'Community interest' concept developed in connection with the *Automec* case law and governing the rejection of complaints.

[78] See also R Sauer in JL Schulte and C Just (eds), *Kartellrecht* (Carl Heymanns Verlag 2012), Art 10 of Reg 1/2003, para 21; J Schwarze and A Weitbrecht, *Grundzüge des Europäischen Kartellverfahrensrecht* (Nomos 2004) § 6, para 100, indicate that this situation may occur where an NCA has prohibited a specific agreement or concerted practice (or where such prohibition is forthcoming), which the Commission considers as permitted. Once the Commission has issued a decision, this would bind national courts and NCAs alike—see Art 16 of Reg 1/2003—although it would be questionable whether this would always be in line with the exceptional character of Art 10 and whether it would not be preferable for the Commission to apply Art 11(6) of Reg 1/2003 in these cases. F Montag and S Cameron, 'Effective Enforcement: The Practitioner's View of Recent Experiences under Regulation 1/2003', IBA conference, Antitrust Reform in Europe: A Year in Practice, Brussels, 9–11 March 2005, 6, also note that the Commission is expected to use Art 10, *in extremis*, to make pronouncements to protect the consistent application of EU Law.

[79] Recital 14 of Reg 1/2003: 'In exceptional cases where the public interest of the Community so requires . . .'.

[80] Commission Staff Working Paper accompanying the Communication from the Commission to the European Parliament and Council, Report on the functioning of Regulation 1/2003{COM(2009)206 final}, para 113.

[81] Article 5 of Reg 1/2003.

[82] J Schwarze and A Weitbrecht, *Grundzüge des Europäischen Kartellverfahrensrecht* (Nomos 2004) § 6, paras 102–5, point out that Art 27(1)–(3) of Reg 1/2003 which expands on sub-paragraph (1) does not refer to Art 10. Although the wording of Art 27 might suggest that defence rights are limited to the right to submit

5. Commitments and informal settlements[83]

4.22 Article 9(1) of Regulation 1/2003 provides that where the Commission intends to adopt a decision requiring that an infringement be brought to an end and the undertakings concerned offer commitments to meet the competition concerns, the Commission may make those commitments binding on the undertakings. The advantages include quicker cases and the fact that the voluntary nature of commitments may facilitate implementation. The choice of an Article 9 proceeding is thus often guided by considerations of expediency, as the procedure normally results in savings of administrative and investigative resources that would be required in an Article 7 procedure, as well as considerations about the effectiveness of commitments proposed for solving market problems expeditiously.[84] Disadvantages include the need to ensure that commitments fully address the competition problems, the lower precedent value, and the more limited deterrent effect.[85]

4.23 A commitment decision is usually intended to bring an apparent ongoing infringement to an end and restore competition in the market. However, commitments can still be appropriate if the undertakings have discontinued their presumed anticompetitive practice prior to, or during, the investigation. A commitment decision does not contain an infringement decision but just describes the concerns found in the investigation and merely concludes that there are 'no longer grounds for action' by the Commission.[86]

---

observations on the summary published in the OJ (see Art 27(4) of Reg 1/2003), Schwarze and Weitbrecht take the view that the defence rights referred to in Art 27(1)–(3) should also apply to proceedings under Arts 9 and 10. They argue that third parties should also be granted the right to challenge the decision under Art 10 of Reg 1/2003 on the basis of Art 263 fourth paragraph EC where (i) they have been heard; (ii) they submitted their observations and where the decision impairs their rights and interests; or (iii) where the third party is directly and individually concerned by the decision. See in this regard, J Schwarze and A Weitbrecht, *Grundzüge des Europäischen Kartellverfahrensrecht* (Nomos 2004) § 6, para 120. D Geradin and N Petit, 'Judicial Remedies under EC Competition Law: Complex Issues Arising from the Modernization Process' ch 17 in International Antitrust & Policy, 32nd Annual International Antitrust Law & Policy Conference, [2006] Fordham Corporate Law Institute 393, also take the view that these decisions show features of challengeable acts, also because they are binding upon NCAs and national courts.

[83] Informal settlements are to be distinguished from cartel settlements which have been dealt with at para 4.08. Cases may be closed without a formal decision also where the Commission cannot rule out the existence of an infringement but a formal decision appears impossible or inappropriate. See E Gippini-Fournier, 'The Modernisation of European Competition Law: First Experiences with Regulation 1/2003—Institutional Report' in HF Koeck and MM Karollus (eds), The Modernisation of European Competition Law—Initial Experiences with Regulation 1/2003, FIDE XXIII Congress Linz 2008—Congress Publications Vol 2 (Nomos 2008) 375, 398–419. H Schweitzer, 'Commitment Decisions under Article 9 of Regulation 1/2003: The Developing EC Practice and Case Law' in C-D Ehlermann and M Marquis (eds), *European Competition Law Annual* (Hart Publishing 2008) 547; J Davies and Manish Das, 'Private Enforcement of Commission Commitment Decisions: A Steep Climb, Not A Gentle Stroll', ch 10 in International Antitrust Law & Policy [2005] Fordham Corporate Law 199; see also Ch 13, 'Commitments, Voluntary Adjustments, Conclusion of the Procedure without a Formal Decision'.

[84] Commission Staff Working Paper accompanying the communication from the Commission to the European Parliament and Council report on the functioning of Regulation 1/2003 {Com(2009)206 final}, 29 April 2009, para 99.

[85] European Commission Antitrust Manual of Procedures, Internal DG Competition working documents on procedures for the application of Articles 101 and 102 TFEU, March 2012, Module 16 'Commitment decisions', para 6 et seq.

[86] Reg 1/2003, Recital 13. E Gippini-Fournier, 'The Modernisation of European Competition Law: First Experiences with Regulation 1/2003—Institutional Report' in HF Koeck and MM Karollus (eds), The Modernisation of European Competition Law—Initial Experiences with Regulation 1/2003, FIDE XXIII Congress Linz 2008—Congress Publications Vol 2 (Nomos 2008) 375, 401, argues that Art 9 decisions appear much closer to a decision not to pursue proceedings and close the case without any determination whatsoever as to the merits of the case. This would not bar a subsequent investigation or prosecution of the same facts by an NCA or a court.

Moreover, commitments are offered by undertakings on a voluntary basis. Conversely, **4.24** through an Article 7 decision, the Commission can impose remedies which are necessary to bring the infringement to an end (and/or fines) on undertakings. The required level of detail of a commitment decision may be lower than in the case of a 'prohibition' decision or 'imposed' remedy decision. However, the Commission must have at its disposal sufficient facts to allow it to make an informed and sound assessment of the relevant competition concerns. The Commission has so far adopted an increasing number of decisions under Article 9, relating to a variety of matters about which competition concerns were expressed under both Articles 101 and 102 TFEU.[87]

Undertakings may contact the DG COMP at any time to explore the Commission's readiness **4.25** to pursue the case with the aim of reaching a commitment decision. While a commitment decision can only be adopted after the Commission has begun proceedings, Article 9 requires that the Commission expresses its competition concerns in a preliminary assessment vis-à-vis the undertaking(s) concerned. The preliminary assessment principally creates the opportunity for the Commission to make its competition concerns known to the parties at an earlier stage of the proceedings with a view to open commitment discussions. The preliminary assessment does not, therefore, need to have the level of detail required for a statement of objections.[88] Commitments are not appropriate where the Commission contemplates imposing a fine.[89] Prior to Regulation

---

[87] 2005: COMP/37.214 *Bundesliga* [2005] OJ L134/46; COMP/39.116 *Coca-Cola* [2005] OJ L253/21. 2006: COMP/38.381 *De Beers* [2006] OJ L205/24–25; COMP/38.173 *FAPL* [2006] OJ C7/18; COMP/38.348 *Repsol* [2006] OJ L176/104; COMP/38.681 *Cannes Agreement* [2006] OJ L296/27–28. 2007: COMP/39.140 *DaimlerChrysler* [2007] OJ L317/76–78; COMP/39.141 *Fiat* OJ L332/77–79; COMP/39.143 *Opel* [2007] OJ L330/44–47; COMP/39.142 *Toyota Motor Europe* [2007] OJ L329/52–55; COMP/37.966 *Distrigaz* [2007] OJ C9/8. 2008: COMP/39.388, COMP/39.389 *E.ON German electricity market* [2008] OJ C36/8. 2009: COMP/39.402 *RWE Gas Foreclosure* [2009] OJ C133/10; Case COMP/39.416 *Ship classification* [2010] OJ C2/5; Case COMP/39.530 *Microsoft (Tying)* [2010] OJ C36/7; Case COMP/39.316 *GDF* [2010] OJ C57/13; Case COMP/38.636 *RAMBUS* [2010] OJ C30/17. 2010: Case COMP/39.351 *Swedish Interconnectors* [2010] C142/28; Case COMP/39.386 *Long Term Electricity Contracts France* [2010] C 133/5; Case COMP/39.317 *E.ON Gas* [2010] OJ C278/9; Case COMP/39.596 *British Airways/American Airlines/Iberia* [2010] OJ C278/14; Case COMP/39.315 *ENI* [2010] OJ C352/8; Case COMP/39.386 *Long Term Electricity Contracts France* [2010] OJ C133/5; Case COMP/39.398 *VISA MIF* [2011] OJ C79/8. 2011: Case COMP/39.592 *Standard & Poor's* [2012] C31/8; Case COMP/39.692 *IBM Maintenance Services* [2012] OJ C18/6; Case COMP/39736 *Areva SA/Siemens AG* (Commission Press Release IP/12/618 'Antitrust: Commission makes legally binding commitments by Siemens and Areva concerning nuclear technology markets', 18 June 2012) [2012] OJ C280/08. Commission MEMO/12/983, 'Antitrust: Commission accepts legally binding commitments from Simon & Schuster, Harper Collins, Hachette, Holtzbrinck and Apple for sale of e-books', 13 December 2012; Commission Press Release IP/12/1433 'Antitrust: Commission renders legally binding commitments from Thomson Reuters', 20 December 2012; Commission Press Release IP/12/1434 'Antitrust: Commission renders legally binding commitments from Rio Tinto Alcan', 20 December 2012; see also overview in R Saur in JL Schulte and C Just (eds), *Kartellrecht* (Carl Heymanns Verlag 2012), Art 9 of Reg 1/2003, para 34.

[88] Commission staff working paper accompanying the communication from the Commission to the European Parliament and council Report on the functioning of Regulation 1/2003 {COM(2009)206 final}, para 100. E Gippini-Fournier, 'The Modernisation of European Competition Law: First Experiences with Regulation 1/2003—Institutional Report' in HF Koeck and MM Karollus (eds), The Modernisation of European Competition Law—Initial Experiences with Regulation 1/2003, FIDE XXIII Congress Linz 2008—Congress Publications Vol 2 (Nomos 2008) 375, 404, points out that the preliminary assessments issued by the Commission after 1 May 2005 have been relatively short documents of twenty pages reminiscent of the warning letters sent by DG COMP, with the significant difference being that preliminary assessments are adopted by the Commission by the same procedure used for statements of objections.

[89] Recital 13 of Reg 1/2003. J Temple Lang, 'Commitments under Regulation 1/2003: Legal Aspects of a new Kind of Competition Decision' [2003] ECLR 347, 347, suggests that there would be no reason why a commitment decision could not be adopted in a case in which the Commission intended to impose a fine when it sent the statement of objections, but later decided that a fine was not necessary or justified. See also Commission Memo/04/217 'Commitment decisions (Article 9 of Council Regulation 1/2003 providing for a modernised framework for antitrust scrutiny of company behavior)' of 17 September 2004, stating that

1/2003, commitments offered by the parties aimed at terminating the infringement of the EU competition rules,[90] whilst the Commission could require the undertaking to submit proposals with a view to bringing the infringement to an end,[91] the difference being that the Commission could not make those commitments binding on the undertakings.

4.26 The Commission has broad discretion in relation to the acceptance of commitments.[92] It has pointed out that the advantages and disadvantages of a commitment decision have to be weighed carefully in each individual case.[93] Commitments may be behavioural or structural, may be limited in time, and varied or withdrawn if the facts change. In contrast to merger control proceedings where the Commission prefers the imposition of structural remedies,[94] in antitrust cases they might primarily be behavioural, given that they aim to terminate possible infringements.[95] In deciding whether or not to accept commitments, the Commission can take into consideration, together with the facts of the case, any breach of a previous commitment given by the undertaking in question. A decision under Article 9 would not constitute proof that there has (or has not) been an infringement. Article 9(2) stipulates that the Commission is entitled to reopen the procedure only if the facts on the basis of which

---

commitment decisions would be excluded in hard-core cartel cases. E Gippini-Fournier, 'The Modernisation of European Competition Law: First Experiences with Regulation 1/2003—Institutional Report' in HF Koeck and MM Karollus (eds), The Modernisation of European Competition Law—Initial Experiences with Regulation 1/2003, FIDE XXIII Congress Linz 2008—Congress Publications Vol 2 (Nomos 2008) 375, 399, notes that the statement in Recital 13 should not be interpreted rigidly. If a fine were excluded there would be little incentive for the undertakings concerned to offer commitments.

[90] Joined Cases 89/85, 104/85, 114/85, 116/85, 117/85, and 125/85 to 129/85 *Ahlström Osakeyhtiö and others v Commission, 'Woodpulp II'* [1993] ECR I-1307, para 117. See also M Busse and A Leopold, 'Entscheidungen über Verpflichtungszusagen nach Article 9 VO (EG) Nr. 1/2003' [2004] Wirtschaft und Wettbewerb 146, 147; J Schwarze and A Weitbrecht, *Grundzüge des Europäischen Kartellverfahrensrecht* (Nomos 2004) § 6, para 69. J Temple Lang, 'Commitment Decisions and Settlements with Antitrust Authorities and Private Parties under European Antitrust Law' in International Antitrust Law & Policy [2005] 32nd Annual International Antitrust Law & Policy Conference Fordham Corporate Law Institute 265.

[91] Cases 6/73 and 7/73 *Istituto Chemioterapico Italiano and Commercial Solvents v Commission* [1974] ECR 223, para 45.

[92] From a policy point of view, the different precedent value of commitment decisions compared to final decisions under Art 7 may be an argument against the 'commitment path'. Commitment decisions do not actually find an infringement, and the factual and legal assessment may be shorter than in Art 7 decisions. The more limited risk of an appeal may also reduce the Commission's chances of having contentious legal issues clarified by the Court. If the Commission therefore wants to establish an important precedent, it may prefer an Art 7 decision. European Commission Antitrust Manual of Procedures, Internal DG Competition working documents on procedures for the application of Articles 101 and 102 TFEU, March 2012, Module 16 'Commitment decisions', para 11. See also R Sauer in JL Schulte and C Just (eds), *Kartellrecht* (Carl Heymanns Verlag 2012), Art 9 of Reg 1/2003, para 10.

[93] European Commission Antitrust Manual of Procedures, Internal DG Competition working documents on procedures for the application of Articles 101 and 102 TFEU, March 2012, Module 16 'Commitment decisions', paras 9–10.

[94] Commission notice on remedies acceptable under Council Regulation (EC) No 139/2004 and under Commission Regulation (EC) No 802/2004 [2008] OJ 267/1, para 15. The Standard Model for Divestiture Commitments, originally developed for merger remedies, can be an appropriate 'base text' for antitrust commitments. Even where no pure divestiture commitment (such as licences or other non-structural/behavioural remedies) is proposed, the model text may still constitute a useful starting point. However, certain amendments to the merger model text are necessary to take into account that antitrust commitments are based on Art 9 of Reg 1/2003. See European Commission Antitrust Manual of Procedures, Internal DG Competition working documents on procedures for the application of Articles 101 and 102 TFEU, March 2012, Module 16 'Commitment decisions', para 40.

[95] M Busse and A Leopold, 'Entscheidungen über Verpflichtungszusagen nach Article 9 VO (EG) Nr. 1/2003' [2004] Wirtschaft und Wettbewerb 146, 148. Note that pursuant to Recital 12 of Reg 1/2003, structural remedies should only be imposed either where there is no equally effective behavioural remedy or where any equally effective behavioural remedy would be more burdensome for the undertaking concerned than the structural changes.

the Commission accepted the commitments have materially changed, if the undertaking offering the commitments has supplied incorrect, incomplete, or misleading information, or if the undertaking breaches the commitments. In accordance with Articles 23(2)(c) and 24(1)(c) of Regulation 1/2003, fines or periodic penalties may therefore be imposed for breach of a commitment. Where the Commission has evidence of a negligent or intentional non-compliance with an interim or commitment decision, it may impose a fine to sanction the 'bad faith' conduct of a company, independently of whether this infringement involved a breach of Articles 101 or 102 TFEU.[96] Pursuant to Article 27(4) of Regulation 1/2003, where the acceptance of commitments is envisaged, a summary of the case and the main content of the offered commitments must be published, inviting comments by interested parties. In addition, the Commission publishes the full text of the commitments in their original language on the Internet, giving interested parties one month within which to make comments. If this so-called market test reveals any weaknesses in the proposed course of action, the Commission can renegotiate or abandon the commitment option and, if appropriate, revert to the prohibition scenario.[97]

In the Commission's view, the experience so far shows that commitment decisions have functioned well and have been an effective means of addressing the competition problems at issue in several cases. As commitment decisions result from the parties' initiative and willingness to offer commitments, the same parties tend to be more readily inclined to implement their own voluntary commitments. Commitment decisions are also less likely to be challenged before the EU Courts than prohibition decisions. Indeed, thus far few commitment decisions adopted by the Commission have been appealed to the GC by third parties directly affected by the decision.[98] Consequently, Article 9 decisions have helped to expedite market changes. Through the lower litigation burden and other procedural economies, Article 9 has therefore **4.27**

---

[96] See Ch 11, 'Infringement Decisions and Penalties', para 11.22.

[97] Commission staff working paper accompanying the communication from the commission to the European Parliament and Council Report on the functioning of Regulation 1/2003, para 104, reported that there would be the perception that the overall duration of the administrative proceedings in certain cases decided under Art 9 was relatively long and thus did not fully yield the efficiencies pursued by the Regulation. A number of of cases decided under Art 9 so far had been started under Reg 17 and thus entered the commitment route after May 2004 (ie *DFB, Distrigaz, De Beers, Coca-Cola, FA Premier League, Repsol, Cannes Extension Agreement*). Even though from a procedural perspective in cases in which a statement of objections has been issued, the requirement of the preliminary assessment is fulfilled, a market test under Art 27(4) is still necessary. In most of these cases, the difficulty in arriving at a satisfactory outcome on substance has led to relatively prolonged discussions with parties before it was possible for the Commission to accept commitments. The procedure has generally been shorter in cases which followed the entry into force of Reg 1/2003. The car cases took less than three years each, whereas the E.ON cases were concluded in a relatively short time of less than two years.

[98] *Alrosa v Commission* is the first ECJ judgment concerning a decision to make commitments binding under Art 9 of Regulation 1/2003. It makes it clear that the Commission's proportionality assessment when deciding whether to accept commitments is conducted on a different basis to the assessment of an infringement decision under Art 7. In Case T-170/06 *Alrosa v Commission* [2007] ECR II-260, the GC had annulled the Commission Decision 2006/520/EC of 22 February 2006, in which De Beers, the number one buyer and trader of diamonds worldwide, unilaterally committed to stop its business relationship with the number two producer. The GC upheld Alrosa's appeal against the commitments decision and concluded that the Commission had breached the principle of proportionality. The Court concluded that the requirement that De Beers and Alrosa end their supply arrangements by 2009 was manifestly disproportionate and that the Commission had failed in its duty to consider less onerous alternative solutions. Further, the Commission breached Alrosa's right to be heard in relation to the commitments offered by De Beers. On appeal by the Commission, the GC judgment was, however, set aside. The ECJ ruled that the GC erred in holding that it would be contrary to the system created by Regulation 1/2003 for a decision that would be regarded as disproportionate to the infringement that had been established under Article 7 to be adopted as a binding commitment under Article 9. The ECJ considered that undertakings which offered commitments on the basis of Article 9 consciously accepted that the concessions which they made may go beyond the measures that the

also contributed favourably to resource allocation within the DG COMP, freeing resources for the prosecution and punishment of the most serious infringements.[99]

Informal settlements

4.28 As indicated, unlike to cartel settlements, cases may also be closed without a formal decision where the Commission cannot rule out the existence of an infringement but a formal decision appears impossible or inappropriate. The EU administrative procedure provides undertakings with an opportunity to adjust their agreements, practices, or conduct so as to comply with competition law. In principle, it is open to undertakings to secure a favourable decision from the Commission regarding their case—either formally or informally—if they voluntarily agree to comply with the requirements of Articles 101 and 102 TFEU. In general, the Commission may resolve cases of any kind either formally or informally. Although it does not appear that Article 9 would prevent the Commission from settling a case by any means other than a formal decision, there is the suggestion that the Commission is not inclined to pursue informal settlements, given the possibility of imposing commitments under Article 9. Moreover, having recourse to informal settlements could undermine interested parties' rights of due process.[100] Although the Commission no longer gives reassurance that the conduct in question does not amount to an infringement, it may close the file after an informal settlement. Cases may also be closed without a formal decision where the Commission cannot rule out the existence of an infringement but a formal decision appears impossible or inappropriate. This may be the case where a complaint is withdrawn, where devoting resources to an investigation appears disproportionate at an advanced stage, or when the alleged infringement has ceased and there is no legitimate interest in adopting a formal decision under Article 7 or Article 9.[101]

4.29 While informal settlements necessarily imply less transparency and the number of old-style informal settlements may decrease significantly given the procedure laid down in Article 9, the Commission cannot be understood to have waived its right to reach an amicable informal settlement with the parties during the preliminary investigation stage.[102] While the Commission is expected to focus its resources on high-profile cases, it should not be automatically forced to adopt a commitment decision under Article 9 of Regulation 1/2003 where it is agreed with the parties that the latter will behave in a given manner in order to avoid infringing the EU competition rules, at least where a statement of objections has yet to be issued. Another example would be where the conduct in question has already definitively ceased; here, the Commission's intervention under Article 9 (where no fines are imposed and no finding of an infringement is made) does not serve any useful purpose, unless there is a real danger of the

Commission could impose on them if it were to adopt an infringement decision under Art 7. The closure of the infringement proceedings when commitments were made binding allowed the undertaking to avoid being found to have breached the competition rules and a possible fine. Further, the GC had put forward its own assessment of complex economic circumstances and substituted its own assessment for that of the Commission. It had, therefore, encroached on the Commission's discretion instead of reviewing the lawfulness of its assessment. The ECJ found that this error, in itself, justified setting aside the judgment.

[99] Commission Staff Working Paper accompanying the Communication from the Commission to the European parliament and council Report on the functioning of Regulation 1/2003 {COM(2009)206 final}, para 100.

[100] Kerse & Khan, *EC Antitrust Procedure* (6th edn, Sweet & Maxwell 2012) para 6-091.

[101] E Gippini-Fournier, 'The Modernisation of European Competition Law: First Experiences with Regulation 1/2003—Institutional Report' in HF Koeck and MM Karollus (eds), The Modernisation of European Competition Law—Initial Experiences with Regulation 1/2003, FIDE XXIII Congress Linz 2008—Congress Publications Vol 2 (Nomos 2008) 375, 422.

[102] L Ritter and WD Brown, *European Competition Law: A Practitioner's Guide* (3rd edn, Kluwer 2004) 1041, also note that prior to the modernization the vast majority of cases were closed without reaching the formal decision stage and point out that in the 1996–2001 period the number of formal decisions annually was limited to 21–68, whereas 300–500 cases were closed without any formal decision. XXXI Report on Competition Policy [2001] after para 243.

conduct in question being resumed, or perhaps if the effects of the infringement persist in the market and could be counteracted or mitigated by commitments which bind the undertaking concerned.[103] It would then be a commitment, but not one which is formally binding.[104]

B. Use of Languages and Calculation of Time Limits

Pursuant to Article 2 of Regulation No 1, documents which an undertaking sends to the **4.30** Commission may be drafted in any of the official languages of the EU selected by the sender.[105] The reply and subsequent correspondence will be drafted in the same language. Pursuant to Article 3 of Regulation No. 1, documents which the Commission sends to an undertaking based in the European Union will be drafted in the language of the Member State in which the undertaking is based.[106] This also applies to oral communications between officials of the EU institutions and individuals. As regards simple requests for information, it is standard practice to send the cover letter in the language of the addressee's location or in English (including a reference to Article 3 of Regulation No 1) and to attach the

---

[103] E Gippini-Fournier, 'The Modernisation of European Competition Law: First Experiences with Regulation 1/2003—Institutional Report' in HF Koeck and MM Karollus (eds), The Modernisation of European Competition Law—Initial Experiences with Regulation 1/2003, FIDE XXIII Congress Linz 2008—Congress Publications Vol 2 (Nomos 2008) 375, 422, identifying a number of examples in which the investigation was closed through an informal settlement. IP/08/22 'Antitrust: European Commission welcomes Apple's announcement to equalise prices for music downloads from iTunes in Europe', 9 January 2008; IP/06/139 'Competition: Commission closes investigation following changes to Philips CD-Recordable Disc Patent Licensing', 9 February 2006; IP/05/519 'Competition: Commission welcomes improved access to tickets for the 2006 World Cup', 2 May 2005; IP/04/1314 'Commission closes investigation into contracts of six Hollywood studios with European pay-TVs', 26 October 2004. See also more recently IP/12/873 'Antitrust: Commission closes investigation in P&I Clubs case', 1 August 2012; IP/12/210 'Antitrust: Commission closes investigation in pharmaceutical companies AstraZeneca and Nycomed', 1 March 2012;

[104] J Temple Lang, 'Commitments under Regulation 1/2003: Legal Aspects of a New Kind of Competition Decision' [2003] ECLR 347, 347.

[105] EEC Council Regulation No 1 determining the languages to be used by the European Economic Community (French edn: [1958] OJ 385; English special edn: Series I Volume 1952–1958 P 59–59). See also Art 5(3) of Reg 773/2004. Official languages of the EU include virtually all the official languages of the various EU Member States. Council Regulation No 1 lists the following twenty-three official languages (in alphabetical order): Bulgarian, Czech, Danish, Dutch, English, Estonian, Finnish, French, German, Greek, Hungarian, Irish, Italian, Latvian, Lithuanian, Maltese, Polish, Portuguese, Romanian, Slovak, Slovenian, Spanish, and Swedish. (Croatia became the 28th Member State of the EU on 1 July 2013). The Official Journal of the European Union exists in all of these languages. EU regulations and other documents of general application (Directives, for instance) are published in the official languages. There is, however, an exception for Irish (until 1 January 2012): before that date, only regulations adopted jointly by the European Parliament and Council (not relevant to DG COMP's activities) had to be published in Irish. For other types of acts, such as all acts prepared by DG COMP, the institutions of the EU were not bound to publish in Irish.

[106] This provision has been invoked against the Commission's practice of sending the records of hearings in infringement procedures in the languages in which the various participants express themselves, without a translation. See Case T-77/92 *Parker Pen v Commission* [1994] ECR II-549, paras 72–5. The GC dismissed that case because the undertaking had had an opportunity to follow the hearings in its own language through simultaneous interpretation and because the undertaking had not alleged 'substantial inaccuracies or omissions which [might] have adverse legal consequences such as to vitiate the administrative procedure as a result of the fact that there was no translation of the parts drawn up in German'. Article 3 of Reg 1 has also been invoked against the practice of sending the annexes of statements of objections in their original language to the undertakings. The GC has differentiated between the statement of objections as such, which must be considered a 'text' within the meaning of the Article and which must therefore be sent to addressees in their own language, and its annexes. Annexes coming from the Commission are viewed as exhibits on which the Commission relies as evidence. They must therefore be brought to the attention of the addressee in their original state. This is so that the latter can see how the Commission has interpreted the evidence on which not only the statement of objections but also the formal decision itself is based. Moreover, as the GC has pointed out, statements of objections generally quote the most important parts of the annexes in the language of the addressees. See Case T-148/89 *Trefilunion v Commission* [1995] ECR II-1063, paras 19–21. See also

questionnaire in English with a view to allowing a more expeditious treatment. The addressee is also informed—in the language of the addressee's location—of its right to obtain a translation of the cover letter and/or questionnaire into the language of country where it is located, as well as the right to reply in that language.[107]

4.31 In order to avoid delays due to translation, addressees may waive their right to receive the text in the language resulting from this rule and opt for another language, for example English. Duly authorized language waivers can be given for some specific documents and/or for the whole procedure. The Statement of Objections, Preliminary Assessment and decisions pursuant to Articles 7, 9, and 23(2) of Regulation 1/2003 are notified in the authentic language of the addressee unless it has signed the language waiver.[108] Where the Commission relies on documentary evidence in support, for example, of the statement of objections, the original version should be made available to the undertakings concerned.[109] The parties must be able to evaluate the interpretation that the Commission has adopted.[110]

4.32 With respect to the calculation of the time limits applied by the Commission in EU competition law procedures (which are generally fixed in terms of days, weeks, or months), Articles 2 and 3 of Regulation 1182/71, which apply to all Commission measures under the TFEU, lay down rules similar to those contained in the national laws of Member States.[111]

C. General Characteristics of Proceedings

1. The nature of the Commission and its proceedings

4.33 The Commission is an administrative authority which plays several different roles at the same time. Its functions are legislative, administrative, and, consequently, political. Not only does it enforce competition law, it also creates it, and, by so creating and applying it, develops competition policy. The ECJ has stated, with regard to the Commission's administrative function, that, in applying EU competition law, it is not to be regarded as a 'tribunal' within the meaning of Article 6 of the ECHR.[112] This Article provides that every person is entitled to have his or her case fairly tried by an independent and impartial tribunal.[113] The Commission is, on the contrary, an administrative body responsible for ensuring compliance with certain

K Lenaerts and J Maselis, 'Procedural Rights and Issues in the Enforcement of Articles 81 and 82 of the EC Treaty' [2001] Fordham International Law Journal 1615, 1651–2.

[107] See Commission notice on best practices for the conduct of proceedings concerning Articles 101 and 102 TFEU Text with EEA relevance [2011] OJ C308/6, para 28.

[108] See Commission notice on best practices for the conduct of proceedings concerning Articles 101 and 102 TFEU Text with EEA relevance [2011] OJ C308/6, paras 27 and 29.

[109] While the observance of defence rights therefore requires that addressees of the statement of objections should have access during the administrative procedure to all the incriminating documents in their original versions, the Commission, in communicating those annexes in their original language, does not infringe the right to be heard of the undertakings concerned. Case T-25/95 *Cimenteries CBR v Commission* [2000] ECRII-491, para 635.

[110] Case T-148/89 *Tréfilunion v Commission* [1995] ECR II-1063, para 21; Case T-338/94 *Finnboard v Commission* [1998] ECR II-1617, para 53; Case T-9/99 *HFB v Commission* [2002] ECR II-1487, para 327.

[111] See Council Reg (EEC, Euratom) 1182/71 determining the rules applicable to periods, dates, and time limits [1971] OJ L124/1 (English special edn: Series I Chapter 1971(II) P 0354).

[112] Convention for the Protection of Human Rights and Fundamental Freedoms (European Human Rights Convention, 'ECHR')) (Rome, 4 November 1950; TS 71 (1953); Cmnd 8969).

[113] Joined Cases 209–215/78 and 218/78 *Van Landewyck v Commission* [1980] ECR 3125, para 81; Joined Cases 100/80 and 103/80 *Musique Diffusion Française v Commission* [1983] ECR 1825, para 7; Case T-1 1/89 *Shell v Commission* [1992] ECR II-757, para 39. K Lenaerts and J Maselis, 'Procedural Rights and Issues in the Enforcement of Articles 81 and 82 of the EC Treaty' [2001] Fordham International Law Journal 1615, 1616–17.

rules in the public interest of the Union. Like any administrative authority, the Commission undertakes preliminary inquiries, hears submissions of the parties, and then adopts the appropriate decision, imposing fines if necessary.[114] As the Court has held in competition cases:

> [s]uch an investigation…does not constitute adversary proceedings between the companies concerned; it is a procedure commenced by the Commission, upon its own initiative or upon application [complaint], in fulfilment of its duty to ensure that the rules on competition are observed.[115]

The Commission should not be viewed as a neutral civil authority in proceedings *inter partes*, **4.34** adopting its decision in favour of what it considers to be the more legitimate of two opposing positions put to it. Instead, the Commission pursues an inquisitorial model of decision making and therefore carries out its own investigation. It does not just review and adjudicate on material provided to it by the parties. The Commission has the burden of proving the infringement and throughout the proceedings it 'strives to respect the rights of defendants, complainants and third parties'.[116] Its conduct of proceedings is governed by the principle *audi alteram partem* and by the aim of establishing the objective truth by means of an inquisitorial procedure. The Commission must allow all possible addressees of a decision and third parties with an interest in it to make submissions and be heard impartially. Thereafter, it adopts its decision on the basis of the evidence before it and the submissions made. The criticism levelled at the Commission that it is both a judge and a party to its own proceedings is thus no better founded than the objections made against administrative proceedings in general.[117] For its part, the Commission accepts that, as an administrative authority, it cannot provide the same procedural safeguards as a court.[118]

---

[114] Fines under Art 23 of Reg 1/2003 are administrative and not criminal in nature as is made clear by Art 15(4). In practice undertakings may, however, perceive little difference between Commission fines and criminal law fines. This is particularly so in the light of the evolution of European Court of Human Rights (ECtHR) case law. In *Societé Stenuit v France* [1992] 14 EHRR 509, the European Commission of Human Rights considered the imposition of fines under French competition law as criminal for the purposes of the European Convention. Article 24 does not contain a similar disclaimer regarding the criminal nature of periodic penalties.

[115] See Joined Cases 142/84 and 156/84 *BAT and Reynolds v Commission* [1987] ECR 4487, para 19 and Case T-65/96 *Kish Glass v Commission* [2000] ECR II-1885, para 33. On the basis of this feature of the procedure, the Court classified the different procedural situations of undertakings involved in the proceedings as either subjects of complaints, on the one hand, or as complainants, on the other.

[116] Director-General of DG COMP, A Italiaener, 'European Commission regarding due process in antitrust proceedings' Fordham Competition Law Institute Annual Conference on International Antitrust Law and Policy Session on 'Enforcers' perspectives on international antitrust', Thursday 23 September 2010, 7.

[117] See, eg Case T-11/89 *Shell v Commission* [1992] ECR II-757, para 31 et seq. Shell accused the Commission of bias, in that it was possible for the same officials to investigate the case and report on it to the Commission. In fact, as from 1985, DG COMP ceased to have a Directorate with special responsibility for carrying out inspections, and the rapporteurs themselves began to carry out inspection duties. The GC rejected that submission, considering that the procedural safeguards provided by EU law did not require the Commission to adopt a form of internal organization which prevented the same official from acting in the same case both as investigator and as rapporteur. See also, Judge B Vesterdorf, 'Judicial Review in EC Competition Law: Reflections on the Role of the Community Courts in the EC System of Competition Law Enforcement', (2005) 1(2) Competition Policy International 6, who notes that a concentration of investigative, prosecutorial, and decision-making powers in the hands of a single body is not an unusual feature of administrative systems. S Durande and K Williams, 'The Practical Impact of the Exercise of the Right to be Heard: A Special Focus on the Effect of Oral Hearings and the Role of the Hearing Officers' (Summer 2005) 2 EC Competition Newsletter 22, 24–5, who also point to the adversarial aspects in the Commission's procedure. For example, the Commission must give the defendant an opportunity to comment in writing on the objections and, together with the oral hearing, reinforce the quasi-adversarial nature of the stage of the procedure where the Commission is no longer the sole master and where the role of the Hearing Officer is to protect the requirements of due process. There are a number of persons, whether consultative—such as Member States or the Hearing Officer—or decisive—Commission services and the Commissioners in the College—that may take account of the result of the hearing.

[118] Director-General of DG COMP, A Italiaener, 'Safeguarding Due Process in Antitrust Proceedings' Fordham Competition Law Institute Annual Conference on International Antitrust Law and Policy Session

4.35 However, although the proceedings are administrative, in competition matters they include—as a result of the particular manner in which the Commission observes the principle that the parties must be heard—safeguards similar to those available in judicial proceedings.[119] The administrative nature of the proceedings is evident in the preparatory phase, in which evidence is gathered.[120] Its quasi-judicial character is evident at the stage when submissions are made and the parties are heard, and is reflected by the procedural safeguards accorded to undertakings.[121] This specific feature of the proceedings has prompted the Court to state that, with regard to infringements, Regulation 1/2003 lays down two successive but clearly separate procedures. First, a preparatory investigation procedure, the purpose of which is to enable the Commission to obtain the information necessary to check the actual existence and scope of a specific factual and legal situation, and which includes the possibility of requesting information and carrying out inspections of undertakings' premises. A second *inter partes* procedure, governed by Article 27(1) and (2) of Regulation 1/2003 and Regulation 773/2004, commences with the statement of objections that the Commission sends to the undertakings when it has sufficient evidence of an infringement. In this second procedure, the undertakings have an opportunity to submit written and oral observations on the objections made against them. The Commission may only take a decision on objections about which the undertakings have had an opportunity to make their views known.[122] The Court thus refers to two procedures in the application of the competition rules, the second of which is an 'administrative procedure inter partes' of a quasi-judicial nature (rather than a

on 'Enforcers' perspectives on international antitrust', Thursday 23 September 2010, 7. See also J Almunia, Vice President of the European Commission responsible for Competition policy 'Due process and competition enforcement' Speech 10/449, IBA, 14th Annual Competition Conference Florence, 17 September 2010, who indicated that '[i]f I chose one issue which in my view will require particular effort to be improved, it is the way hearings take place, who is allowed to intervene and participate, how every participant is allowed to contribute, and how the conclusions of the hearing officer will be integrated into our decision.' While he recognized that there was 'room for improvement in due process and efficiency', in the administrative system of antitrust enforcement in Europe, he believed that it had proved 'very effective' from a European perspective. The way the Commission conducts its investigations and then gives companies a chance to answer the charges has come under pressure recently, with lawyers arguing that defence rights are being disregarded and that antitrust cases are unanswerable.

[119] Director-General of DG COMP, A Italianer 'European Commission Regarding Due Process in Antitrust Proceedings' Fordham Competition Law Institute Annual Conference on International Antitrust Law and Policy Session on 'Enforcers' perspectives on international antitrust', Thursday 23 September 2010, 7, refers to the right to receive a reasoned Statement of Objections, the right to access the case file, and the right to an oral hearing. These checks and balances would have provided meaningful results. 'Between 2007 and 2009, 17 out of 21 cartel cases were amended after the parties exercised their rights of defence, and one case dropped. Similarly 6 out of 7 abuse of dominance cases were also modified. Many of these amendments were substantial. And these statistics don't even take account of the cases we drop at earlier stages of the investigation.' The former Director-General of DG COMP, P Lowe has also pointed out that the results of Statements of Objections and hearings, on historical record, do not lead immediately to prosecution, in 'Reflections on the past seven years—Competition policy challenges in Europe', Speech at GCR's Competition Law Review, Brussels, 17 November 2009.

[120] Regarding the means of investigation available to the Commission, see Ch 7, 'Formal Investigative Measures' and Ch 8, 'Inspections'.

[121] Director-General of DG COMP, A Italianer, 'European Commission Regarding Due Process in Antitrust Proceedings' Fordham Competition Law Institute Annual Conference on International Antitrust Law and Policy Session on 'Enforcers' perspectives on international antitrust', Thursday 23 September 2010, 4, indicating that the Commission's Antitrust Best Practices would be 'intended to do the same: they complement rights of defence with additional measures, in the interest of ensuring procedural fairness across sectors. They detail our proceedings, starting with how the Commission decides upon case priority and ending with the adoption of a decision.'

[122] See Case 374/87 *Orkem v Commission* [1989] ECR 3283, paras 19–25; Case 27/88 *Solvay v Commission* [1989] ECR 3355, paras 16–22; Joined Cases T-10/92 to T-12/92 and T-15/92 *Cimenteries CBR and others v Commission* [1992] ECR II-2667, para 45; and Joined Cases T-191/98, T-212/98 to T-214/98 *Atlantic Container Line and others v Commission* [2003] ECR II-3275, para 110.

'civil procedure inter partes', as explained previously). Accordingly, the term 'procedure' will be used here in general to cover both of the procedures described; in other words, the whole sequence of measures and steps taken by the Commission from the initiation of a procedure until the adoption of a decision, and even thereafter. It must nevertheless be pointed out that the proceedings in the strict sense, or the proceedings for the adoption of a decision, are only initiated by means of an express Commission measure. This coincides with the second *inter partes* procedure referred to by the Court in *Orkem*, which extends from the issue of a statement of objections to the adoption of a formal decision. For this phase, the term 'formal proceedings' or 'proceedings for the adoption of a decision' will be used.[123]

2. Burden of proof/standard of proof

The distribution of the burden of proof between the enforcing authority and the companies **4.36** had been clear since the very first judgments of the ECJ reviewing the Decisions adopted by the Commission under Regulation 17. The Commission bears the burden of proving the elements of the infringement alleged against the relevant companies in antitrust cases; conversely, any company willing to claim that the conditions mentioned in Article 101(3) TFEU apply needs to adduce evidence to support the claim. However, this clear allocation became an issue during the discussions leading to the adoption of Regulation 1/2003. Under the new regulation, both the prohibition and the exception need to be analysed and applied together, since Article 1(2) of Regulation 1/2003 establishes that practices satisfying the conditions of Article 101(3) TFEU are no longer prohibited, without any prior decision (exemption) to that effect being required.[124] It became clear during the discussions leading to the adoption of Regulation 1/2003 that a new provision needed to be inserted for the avoidance of any doubt that the traditional allocation of the burden of proof remained unchanged.[125] Therefore, Article 2 of Regulation 1/2003 ensures that the relevant authority does not automatically bear the burden of proving both the elements of the infringement and the efficiencies that could be attached to the practices under review. Recital 5 of Regulation 1/2003 explains that it is necessary to regulate the burden of proof under the relevant provisions of the Treaty to ensure that the party or authority alleging an infringement bears the burden of proving its existence, while the undertaking invoking the benefit of a defence has to demonstrate that the conditions thereof are met.

In the context of a given investigation, once the Commission meets the standard of proof (in **4.37** the terms explained at paragraph 4.39 et seq), it has satisfied its burden of proof. From that moment on, it is up to the defendant to put forward a rebuttal. In this regard, the ECJ has

---

[123] This distinction will also be made later, in relation to the initiation of proceedings per se. See Ch 5, 'Opening of the File', para 5.33 et seq.

[124] Also, competition authorities and national courts of the Member States first became competent to apply that provision, in addition to Arts 81(1) EC and 82 EC (now respectively Arts 101(1) TFEU and 102 TFEU), which were already directly applicable by virtue of the case law of the ECJ. This marked the end of the exemption system monopolized by the European Commission.

[125] This solution was suggested by the representatives of the Dutch government in the Council working groups. See the article by Anne Willem Kist and María Luisa Tierno Centella, 'Coherence and Efficiency in a Decentralised Enforcement of EC Competition Rules: Some Reflections on the White Paper on Modernisation' in C-D Ehlermann and I Atanasiu (eds), *European Competition Law Annual 2000: Volume 5, The Modernisation of EC Antitrust Policy* (Hart Publishing 2001). Pending the discussions on the Commission White Paper on Modernisation, the authors drew attention to the consequences of the original wording (lacking a provision regulating the burden of proof): 'We should be very careful because that would put the whole burden of proof on the authority. In order to prove the infringement, we would be required to demonstrate also that the conditions in Article 81(3) had not been met…If Article 81(3) has to be applied ex officio and bearing the burden of proof, the system may here find its Achilles heel…Such an allocation of the burden of proof is not inherent in a legal exemption system; it can be conveniently adjusted by adding the necessary wording…'.

ruled, for instance, that where the Commission has been able to establish that an undertaking had attended meetings with other competitors of a manifestly anticompetitive nature, it is for the defendant to provide another explanation for the tenor of those meetings.[126]

4.38 A Commission decision relating to a fine for breach of a seal affixed on a door during inspections at the premises of E.ON has given the opportunity for an interesting exchange of arguments on the burden and standard of proof and to the judgment of the ECJ on 22 November 2012 confirming on appeal the judgment of the GC upholding the Commission's fine. The ECJ declared that once 'the Commission had determined that there had been a breach of seal on the basis of a body of evidence, including the breach of seal report,... it was for E.ON Energie to adduce evidence challenging that finding' and that this does not unduly reverse the burden of proof nor sets aside the principle of the presumption of innocence. In such circumstances, it is not sufficient for the defendant to simply raise the possibility that a circumstance arose which might affect the probative value of evidence meeting the legal standard of proof. It is for the defendant to prove to the requisite legal standard, both the existence of the circumstance relied upon and that the latter calls in question the probative value of the evidence adduced by the Commission.[127]

Standard of proof

4.39 In order to satisfy this burden of proof, the Commission must meet a certain legal standard of proof, a threshold of convincing evidence capable of supporting a finding. It must adduce evidence capable of demonstrating the existence of the facts constituting an infringement, thereby defeating the presumption of innocence.[128] This means that the evidence relied upon should found the firm conviction of the veracity of a given fact or objection[129] and that the company held liable must have been able to exercise its defence rights during the administrative proceedings leading to the decision in question.

4.40 In annulment proceedings, the GC assesses whether the evidence and other information relied on by the Commission in its decision are sufficient to establish the existence of the alleged infringement.[130] The objective is to ensure that a reviewing court entertains no doubt, since any such doubt operates to the advantage of the companies (*in dubio, pro reo*),[131] the standard of proof is not satisfied and the undertaking is presumed to be innocent. The presumption of

---

[126] Case C-235/92 P *Montecatini v Commission* [1999] ECR I-4539, para 181; Case C-89/11 P *E.ON Energie AG v Commission*, judgment of 22 November 2012, not yet published, para 75.

[127] Case C-89/11 P, *E.ON Energie AG v Commission*, judgment of 22 November 2012, not yet published, paras 76–9.

[128] 'The presumption of innocence implies that every person accused is presumed to be innocent until its guilt has been established according to law' (Joined Cases T-22/02 and T-23/02 *Sumitomo Chemical and Sumika Fine Chemical v Commission* [2005] ECR II-4065, at para 106). See also MJ Mélicias, ' "Did They Do It?" The Interplay between the Standard of Proof and the Presumption of Innocence in EU Cartel Investigations' (2012) 35(3) World Competition 471.

[129] See, eg Case C-185/95 P *Baustahlgewebe v Commission* [1998] ECR I-8417, para 58, and Case C-49/92 P *Commission v Anic Partecipazioni* [1999] ECR I 4125, para 86; see Case T-112/07 *Hitachi Ltd, Hitachi Europe Ltd, Japan AE Power Systems Corp* [2011] OJ C252/30, para 57; Case T-348/08, *Aragonesas Industrias y Energía, SAU v Commission* [2011] ECR II-3871, para 90; Joined Cases T-44/02 OP, T-54/02 OP, T56/02 OP, T-60/02 OP, and T-61/02 OP *Dresdner Bank and Others v Commission* [2006] ECR II-3567, para 59, and the case law cited therein.

[130] Joined Cases T-305/94, T-306/94, T-307/94, T-313/94 to T-316/94, T-318/94, T-325/94, T-328/94, T-329/94, and T-335/94 *Limburgse Vinyl Maatschappij and Others v Commission* ('PVC II') [1999] ECR II-931, para 891; Case T-348/08, *Aragonesas Industrias y Energía, SAU v Commission* [2011] OJ C355/15, para 92.

[131] Case T-112/07 *Hitachi Ltd, Hitachi Europe Ltd, Japan AE Power Systems Corp* [2011] ECR II-3871, para 58; Case T-348/08, *Aragonesas Industrias y Energía SAU v Commission* [2011] OJ C355/15, para 93; Joined Cases T-44/02 OP, T-54/02 OP, T-56/02 OP, T-60/02 OP and T-61/02 OP, *Dresdner Bank and Others v Commission* [2006] ECR II-3567, para 60.

innocence is a fundamental right contained in Article 6(2) of the ECHR[132] and constitutes a general principle of EU law. It has been declared by the courts that, given the nature of the infringements in question and the nature and degree of gravity of the ensuing penalties, the principle of the presumption of innocence applies in particular to the procedures relating to infringements of the competition rules applicable to undertakings that may result in the imposition of fines or periodic penalty payments.[133]

In the field of competition law, the principle of unfettered evaluation of evidence prevails **4.41** and any means of proof can be used.[134] In order to meet the legal standard of proof, the Commission must rely on a cogent 'body of evidence', which, taken as a whole, should constitute unequivocal proof—ie precise and consistent proof which leads to the firm conviction that a fact has actually taken place.[135] It is sufficient if the body of evidence relied on by the institution meets that requirement. Hence, it is not necessary for each item of evidence to meet that threshold on its own in relation to every aspect of the infringement[136] unless that specific item constitutes the sole basis of establishing a given fact or objection. In such a case:

> there is no principle of Community law which precludes the Commission from relying on a single document . . . provided that its evidential value is undoubted and that the document by itself definitely attests to the existence of the infringement in question.[137]

What constitutes reliable evidence and amounts to precise, consistent, and convincing une- **4.42** quivocal proof will often depend on the specific nature and features of each case. In cases involving non-contentious and prospective assessments such as mergers, companies are likely to be cooperative and offer precise data as evidence, although there is an inherent uncertainty in forecasting the likely effects. Accordingly:

> [n]ot only must the Community Courts, inter alia, establish whether the evidence relied on is factually accurate, reliable and consistent but also whether that evidence contains all the information which must be taken into account in order to assess a complex situation and whether it is capable of substantiating the conclusions drawn from it.[138]

---

[132] See eg Case C-199/92 P *Hüls v Commission* [1999] ECR I-4287, paras 149–50, and Case C-235/92 P *Montecatini v Commission* [1999] ECR I-4539, paras 175–6.

[133] Joined Cases T-44/02 OP, T-54/02 OP, T-56/02 OP, T-60/02 OP and T-61/02 OP *Dresdner Bank and Others v Commission* [2006] ECR II-3567, para 61; Case T-112/07 *Hitachi Ltd, Hitachi Europe Ltd, Japan AE Power Systems Corp* [2011] ECR II-3871, para 59; Case T-348/08 *Aragonesas Industrias y Energía, SAU v Commission* [2011] OJ C355/15, para 94. In particular, regarding the application of those principles to *procedural* infringements, see Case C-89/11 P *E.ON Energie AG v European Commission*, judgment of the ECJ, 22 November 2012, not yet published, para 73.

[134] 'It is important to note that the activity of the ECJ and thus also that of the CFI is governed by the principle of the unfettered evaluation of evidence, unconstrained by the various rules laid down in the national legal systems. Apart from the exceptions laid down in the Communities' own legal order, it is only the reliability of the evidence before the Court which is decisive when it comes to evaluations' (Case T-7/89 *SA Hercules Chemicals v Commission* [1991] ECR II-954). See also Case T-50/00 *Dalmine v Commission* [2004] ECR II-2395, para 72; Case T-113/07 *Toshiba Corp v Commission* [2011] ECR II-3989, para 87 (appeal pending); Case T-112/07 *Hitachi Ltd, Hitachi Europe Ltd, Japan AE Power Systems Corp* [2011] ECR II-3871, para 64; Case T-348/08 *Aragonesas Industrias y Energía, SAU v Commission* [2011] OJ C355/15, para 98.

[135] L Ortiz Blanco, 'Standards of Proof and Personal Conviction in EU Antitrust and Merger Control Procedures' in CD Ehlermann and M Marquis (eds), *European Competition Law Annual 2009* (Hart Publishing 2011) 175.

[136] Joined Cases T-44/02 OP, T-54/02 OP, T-56/02 OP, T-60/02 OP, and T-61/02 OP *Dresdner Bank and Others v Commission* [2006] ECR II-3567, paras 62–3; Case T-112/07 *Hitachi Ltd, Hitachi Europe Ltd, Japan AE Power Systems Corp* [2011] ECR II-3871, para 60; Case T-348/08 *Aragonesas Industrias y Energía, SAU v European Commission* [2011] OJ C355/15, paras 95 and 96.

[137] Case T-25/95 *Cimenteries CBR v Commission* [2000] ECR II-491, para 1838.

[138] Case C-12/03, *Commission v Tetra Laval BV* [2005] ECR I-987, para 39.

The same applies in cases involving the investigation of past infringements (abuses of a dominant position[139] and anticompetitive agreements and concerted practices[140]). The next section will examine the complexities of the assessment of evidence during the investigation of cartel infringements.

Assessment of evidence in cartel cases[141]

4.43 The case law on the assessment of evidence is inevitably richer in cartel cases, since they are a source of numerous judgments due both to the number of cartel decisions and the multiple addressees entitled to challenge each decision.

4.44 Moreover, in cartel cases, the Commission relies typically on a set of coherent documentary evidence, corporate statements, and/or witness statements provided by the companies, and sometimes has to resort to inferences from indicia or market conduct. This is because it is difficult to gather straightforward documentary evidence of cartels, since cartels are widely known to be prohibited and cartel members deliberately conceal their existence and implementation. Commission records show that meetings or contacts may happen as a result of advantage being taken of other meetings or in the framework of other practices, and companies would typically take every measure to avoid leaving traces behind. Sometimes they have used highly sophisticated means of concealing their conduct. In the *Gas Insulated Switchgear* cartel, the parties not only used codes, but, over time, they encrypted their exchanges and used dedicated devices, such as mobile phones and faxes and anonymous email boxes, for cartel affairs. Occasionally, companies' premises are located outside of the EEA, which reduces the Commission's compulsory powers of investigation. These are some of the factors that make it particularly difficult to find and decode direct incriminating evidence of the existence of cartels. The introduction of leniency programmes into cartel enforcement attests to these difficulties.

4.45 In those circumstances, the Commission must indicate evidence capable of establishing up to the requisite legal standard the existence of the facts constituting an infringement and the basis on which this can be attributed to the relevant undertakings and the legal entities within. This means finding, interpreting, and assessing the evidence of the existence of a cartel, but also of its essential aspects and developments when they lead to legal consequences. It also involves assessing evidence to establish the continuity or repetition of the conduct at stake and the involvement of the different undertakings and legal entities, their awareness of the issues in which they are not directly involved, and the duration, scope, and circumstances around their conduct.[142] Any Commission official dealing with a cartel file is confronted on a daily basis with the need to disregard some allegations and even pieces of evidence when

---

[139] Case T-201/04 *Microsoft Corp v Commission* [2007] ECR II-3601, para 89: 'However, the Community Courts must not only establish whether the evidence put forward is factually accurate, reliable and consistent but must also determine whether that evidence contains all the relevant data that must be taken into consideration in appraising a complex situation and whether it is capable of substantiating the conclusions drawn from it (see, to that effect, concerning merger control, Case C-12/03 P *Commission v Tetra Laval* [2005] ECR I-987, para 39).'

[140] Joined Cases 29/83 and 30/83 *CRAM and Rheinzink v Commission* [1984] ECR 1679, para 20; Case T-62/98 *Volkswagen v Commission* [2000] ECR II-2707, paras 43 and 72.

[141] See also O Weber in JL Schulte and C Just (eds), *Kartellrecht* (Carl Heymanns Verlag 2012), Art 2 of Reg 1/2003, para 12 et seq.

[142] By way of example, the ECJ has recently considered that the company Coppens could not be held liable for all the components of an otherwise single and continuous infringement found in the international removals cartel, because it could not adduce evidence to prove that 'Coppens intended, through its participation in the agreement on cover quotes, to contribute to the common objectives pursued by all the other participants in the cartel and that it was aware of the agreement on commissions put into effect by them or that it could reasonably have foreseen that agreement and was prepared to take the risk'. See eg Case C-441/11 P, *Commission v Verhuizingen Coppens NV*, judgment of 6 December 2012, not yet published, paras 64–6.

they do not appear to be sufficiently convincing or duly corroborated to support one or other finding.

The EU Courts are well aware of this and have established the general rules on assessment of **4.46** evidence, introducing a number of nuances, delicate countervailing factors, and guarantees. The case law tends to render possible the investigation of cartel infringements, while ensuring that companies' liability does not go beyond their own involvement or responsibility.

As in any other competition case, the relevant facts and circumstances can be established **4.47** on the basis of a cogent body of evidence. This also makes possible a global assessment of incriminating and exculpating evidence. On the one hand, the reliability and contents of the different items of evidence have to be assessed to verify whether they support a firm conviction that cannot be undermined by the elements put forward by the defending parties. On the other hand, the same exercise has to be carried out in relation to the elements of proof with potentially mitigating or exculpatory value found during the investigation or which have been alleged by the defendants. Even if the conviction of the veracity of a fact or objection normally depends on the combined assessment of a body of evidence, this also requires an assessment of the relative reliability and content of each item of evidence which constitutes the whole. According to the ECJ, the sole criterion relevant in evaluating the probative value of the various items of evidence is its reliability.[143]

Guidance from the Leniency Notice

The Commission Notice on immunity from fines and reduction of fines in cartel cases[144] **4.48** ('Leniency Notice') provides interesting guidance to leniency candidates on the relative value of evidence from a Commission perspective. According to the Notice, companies willing to obtain a reduction of their fine must provide the Commission with evidence representing significant added value compared to the evidence already in the Commission's possession at the time they produce it. Point 25 of the Leniency Notice clarifies the concept of 'added value', which is to be understood as meaning 'added probative value':

> The concept of 'added value' refers to the extent to which the evidence provided strengthens, by its very nature and/or its level of detail, the Commission's ability to prove the alleged cartel.

While the assessment of the relevant level of detail offered by a piece of evidence is directly related to the facts of a case, the nature of a piece of evidence can be discussed in more abstract terms, based on the case law.

The Leniency Notice introduces the concept of 'compelling evidence' as self-standing evi- **4.49** dence capable of proving a point on its own, by contrast to other evidence, such as statements:

> Similarly, the degree of corroboration from other sources required for the evidence submitted to be relied upon against other undertakings involved in the case will have an impact on the value of that evidence, so that compelling evidence will be attributed a greater value than evidence such as statements which require corroboration if contested.

For a piece of isolated evidence to be compelling, it seems to be necessary for it to constitute unambiguous documentary evidence or an outright admission.

---

[143] See eg Case T-44/00 *Mannesmannröhren-Werke v Commission* [2004] ECR II-2223, para 84; Joined Cases T-67/00, T-68/00, T-71/00, and T-78/00 *JFE Engineering Corp and Others* [2004] ECR II-2501, para 273; Case T-50/00 *Dalmine v Commission* [2004] ECR II-2395, para 72; Case T-112/07 *Hitachi Ltd, Hitachi Europe Ltd, Japan AE Power Systems Corp* [2011] ECR II-3871, paras 69 and 79; Case T-348/08, *Aragonesas Industrias y Energía, SAU v European Commission* [2011] OJ C355/15, para 102.
[144] [2006] OJ C298/17–22.

4.50 Point 25 of the Leniency Notice compares the relative probative value of other pairs of possible characteristics that evidence may present and considers that, all other factors being equal, the fact that an item was written or recorded at the time of the infringement, increases its reliability as proof of the facts it supports:

> In this assessment, the Commission will generally consider written evidence originating from the period of time to which the facts pertain to have a greater value than evidence subsequently established.

Direct and indirect incriminating evidence are also addressed:

> Incriminating evidence directly relevant to the facts in question will generally be considered to have a greater value than that with only indirect relevance.

Reliability of documentary evidence

4.51 The Commission can certainly rely on documentary evidence establishing the existence of a cartel either directly or indirectly. According to the general rules on evidence, the reliability, and therefore the probative value of a document depends on its origin, the circumstances in which it was drawn up, the person to whom it is addressed, and its contents.[145] Particular importance is given to the circumstance that a document has been 'established in direct connection with the facts'[146] or by a direct witness of the facts.[147] In those cases, the Commission often refers to the document as 'contemporaneous evidence' and it is considered to carry great probative value (provided it is not ambiguous), because it is deemed to reflect the true situation at that time (*in tempore non suspecto*) without there being a connection with the subsequent investigation. We have seen that point 25 of the Leniency Notice follows the same line of reasoning.

Reliability of corporate statements and witness statements

4.52 The Commission can rely against an undertaking on that undertaking's own admissions.[148] In addition, no provision or general principle of EU law prohibits the Commission from relying, against an undertaking, on statements made by other undertakings accused of having participated in the cartel. If that were not the case, the burden of proving conduct contrary to Article 101 TFEU and Article 53 EEA, which is borne by the Commission, would be unsustainable and incompatible with the task of supervising the proper application of those provisions.[149] It has been ruled that 'statements which run counter to the interest of the declarant must in principle be regarded as particularly reliable evidence'.[150]

---

[145] See eg Joined Cases T25/95, T-26/95, T-30/95, T-31/95, T-32/95, T-34/95, T-35/95, T-36/95, T37/95, T-38/95, T-39/95, T-42/95, T-43/95, T-44/95, T-45/95, T-46/95, T48/95, T-50/95, T-51/95, T-52/95, T-53/95, T-54/95, T-55/95, T-56/95, T57/95, T-58/95, T-59/95, T-60/95, T-61/95, T-62/95, T-63/95, T-64/95, T65/95, T-68/95, T-69/95, T-70/95, T-71/95, T-87/95, T-88/95, T-103/95, and T-104/95 *Cimenteries CBR and Others v Commission* [2000] ECR II-491, paras 1053 and 1838; Case T-112/07 *Hitachi Ltd, Hitachi Europe Ltd, Japan AE Power Systems Corp* [2011] ECR II-3871, para 70; Case T-348/08 *Aragonesas Industrias y Energía, SAU v European Commission* [2011] ECR II-4091, para 103.

[146] Case T-157/94 *Ensidesa v Commission* [1999] ECR II-707, para 312; Joined Cases T-5/00 and T-6/00 *Nederlandse Federatieve Vereniging voor de Groothandel op Elektrotechnish Gebied et Technische Unie v Commission* [2003] ECR II-5761, para 181.

[147] Joined Cases T-67/00, T-68/00, T-71/00, and T-78/00 *JFE Engineering Corp and Others* [2004] ECR II-2501, para 207.

[148] Case T-133/07 *Mitsubishi Electric Corp v Commission* [2011] ECR II-4219, para 135; Case T-132/07 *Fuji Electric Co Ltd v Commission* [2011] OJ C252/31, paras 245 and 246.

[149] Joined Cases T-67/00, T-68/00, T-71/00, and T-78/00 *JFE Engineering Corp and Others* [2004] ECR II-2501, para 192; Case T-112/07 *Hitachi Ltd, Hitachi Europe Ltd, Japan AE Power Systems Corp* [2011] ECR II-3871, paras 59 and 67; Case T-348/08 *Aragonesas Industrias y Energía, SAU v Commission* [2011] OJ C355/15, para 100.

[150] Joined Cases T-67/00, T-68/00, T-71/00, and T-78/00 *JFE Engineering Corp and Others* [2004] ECR II-2501, paras 211–12: '211. In addition, the Commission correctly points out that statements which run

Here again, a corrective element has been introduced in favour of any undertaking accused in a **4.53** corporate statement by another undertaking: if the accusations are contested the Commission must adduce corroborating evidence. That said, the degree of corroboration required may be lower in view of the reliability of the statements at issue.[151] Corroborating evidence can be, but is not necessarily, documentary. Two independent corporate statements may corroborate each other. We seen that according to Point 25 of the Leniency Notice, corporate statements are generally not compelling evidence in the sense of self-standing evidence.

Corporate statements are typically, but not necessarily, those submitted by leniency appli- **4.54** cants. It has been ruled that even if some caution has to be applied as to the evidence provided by leniency applicants in case they tend to play down their own contribution and highlight that of the others, they are in principle reliable. The reason is that any attempt to mislead the Commission would jeopardize its chances of benefiting from leniency and inaccuracies, and distortions are likely to be detected and corrected because contested statements must be corroborated by other evidence.[152]

Witness statements of employees and former employees can be provided by the undertaking **4.55** or gathered otherwise. In *JFE Engineering*, the GC insisted that:

> answers given on behalf of an undertaking as such carry more weight than that of an employee of the undertaking, whatever his individual experience or opinion.[153]

In that case, the statements of a particular witness were attributed with particularly great probative value because:

 (i)　they were reliable;
 (ii)　they were made on behalf of an undertaking;
(iii)　they were made by a person under a professional obligation to act in the interests of that undertaking;
(iv)　they went against the interests of the person making the statements;
 (v)　they were made by a direct witness of the circumstances to which they relate; and
(vi)　they were provided in writing deliberately and after mature reflection.[154]

However, those statements do not constitute independent evidence capable of corroborating corporate statements if the witnesses have expressed themselves in front of the Commission

---

counter to the interests of the declarant must in principle be regarded as particularly reliable evidence. In this case, Mr Verluca's statements clearly ran counter to the interests of Vallourec, which he represented, given that the Commission had opened an investigation into that company. 212. In particular, it must be concluded that where a person who has been asked to comment on documents, as Mr Verluca was requested to do by Commission staff, admits that he committed an infringement and thus admitted the existence of facts going beyond those whose existence could be directly inferred from the documents in question, that fact implies, a priori, in the absence of special circumstances indicating otherwise, that that person had resolved to tell the truth.'

 [151] Joined Cases T-67/00, T-68/00, T-71/00, and T-78/00 *JFE Engineering Corp and Others* [2004] ECR II-2501, paras 219–20; Case T-112/07 *Hitachi Ltd, Hitachi Europe Ltd, Japan AE Power Systems Corp* [2011] ECR II-3871, para 68; Case T-348/08 *Aragonesas Industrias y Energía, SAU v Commission* [2011] OJ C355/15, para 101.
 [152] Case T-120/04 *Peróxidos Orgánicos v Commission* [2006] ECR II4441, para 70; Case T-112/07 *Hitachi Ltd, Hitachi Europe Ltd, Japan AE Power Systems Corp* [2011] ECR II-3871, paras 72–3; Case T-348/08 *Aragonesas Industrias y Energía, SAU v Commission* [2011] OJ C355/15, paras 105–6.
 [153] Joined Cases T-67/00, T-68/00, T-71/00, and T-78/00 *JFE Engineering Corp and Others* [2004] ECR II-2501, para 205.
 [154] Joined Cases T-67/00, T-68/00, T-71/00, and T-78/00 *JFE Engineering Corp and Others* [2004] ECR II-2501, paras 205–10; Case T-112/07 *Hitachi Ltd, Hitachi Europe Ltd, Japan AE Power Systems Corp* [2011] ECR II-3871, para 71; Case T-348/08 *Aragonesas Industrias y Energía, SAU v Commission* [2011] OJ C355/15, para 104.

upon the initiative of that same undertaking in the framework of its obligation to cooperate under the Leniency Notice, in the presence of the company's legal counsel. Having the same origin, those witness statements can supplement the corresponding corporate statements and add to their reliability, but cannot corroborate them, and they need to be corroborated by other evidence if contested by the party concerned by the information.[155]

Relying on fragmentary evidence together with inferences from market conduct

4.56 There may be situations where no documents or statements expressly attesting to contacts between cartel members are available. In the absence of another plausible explanation, the Commission can reconstitute some circumstances concerning a cartel relying on the fragmentary and sporadic evidence in the file supplemented by inferences from coincidences and circumstantial evidence, such as the undertakings' market conduct. However, conclusions inferred only from the companies' conduct in the market on the basis that the established facts cannot be explained other than by the existence of anticompetitive behaviour may be rebutted by simply proving the existence of circumstances which cast the facts in a different light and thus allow another plausible alternative explanation.[156] The same rule applies whenever the evidence in a case is insufficient to establish the existence of an infringement unequivocally and without any need for interpretation.[157]

4.57 The standard for rebuttal is low, since it does not seem necessary for a truthful alternative explanation to be put forward, but merely the casting of doubt. Any innocent company should easily meet the rebuttal standard by simply arguing the truth as a plausible alternative explanation.

4.58 The principle that it is sufficient for the applicants to prove circumstances which cast the facts established by the Commission in a different light and allow for an alternative explanation thereof is not applicable where the Commission's findings are based on evidence. Undertakings cannot resort to an alternative version of the facts in cases where the existence of an infringement is established unequivocally and without the need for interpretation, even if documentary evidence is lacking (a point that will be taken into account in the global assessment of the set of indicia), or the findings are inferred from other facts established on the basis of indirect or non-documentary evidence. The GC has already rejected the claim that any finding made on evidence or indicia different from non-documentary evidence was

---

[155] See Case T-112/07 *Hitachi and Others v Commission* [2011] ECR II-3871, para 129: 'It should be noted, at the outset, that the witness statements of the employees and of the former employee of ABB do not constitute evidence which is distinct and independent from ABB's statements, since the witnesses made them before the Commission on ABB's initiative and in the context of the latter's duty to cooperate under the Leniency Notice, while benefiting from the presence of ABB's outside counsel. Consequently, the witness statements concerned are not such as to corroborate ABB's statements for the purposes of the case law cited in paragraph 68 above. Rather, they are complementary to those and can explain them and express them in concrete form. Consequently, they must also be corroborated by other evidence.'

[156] See eg from the ECJ: Joined Cases 29/83 and 30/83 *CRAM and Rheinzink v Commission* [1984] ECR 1679, para 16; Joined Cases C-89/95, C-104/85, C-114/85, C-116/85, C-117/85, and C-125/85 to C-129/85 *Ahlström and Others v Commission* [1993] ECR I-1307, paras 126 and 127; Case C-89/11 P *E.ON Energie AG v Commission*, judgment of 22 November 2012, not yet published, para 74. See also eg from the GC: Joined Cases T-305/94 to T-307/94, T-313/94 to T-316/94, T-318/94, T-325/94, T-328/94, T-329/94, and T-335/94 *Limburgse Vinyl Maatschappij and Others v Commission ('PVC II')* [1999] ECR II-931, paras 725–7; Joined Cases T-67/00, T-68/00, T-71/00, and T-78/00 *JFE Engineering and Others v Commission* [2004] ECR II-2501, paras 186–7; Case T-112/07 *Hitachi Ltd, Hitachi Europe Ltd, Japan AE Power Systems Corp* [2011] ECR II-3871, paras 61–2; Case T-113/07 *Toshiba Corp v Commission* [2011] OJ C252/30, para 85; Case T-348/08 *Aragonesas Industrias y Energía, SAU v Commission* [2011] ECR II-3989, para 97.

[157] Case T-36/05 *Coats Holdings and Coats v Commission* [2007] ECR II-110, para 74; Case T-113/07 *Toshiba Corp v Commission* [2011] ECR II-3989, para 86.

subject to the rule that it could be contradicted by simply resorting to an alternative plausible explanation.[158]

Concept and reliability of indirect evidence

Point 25 of the Leniency Notice suggested back in 2006 that evidence could be considered as **4.59** direct or indirect depending on whether it was directly or indirectly relevant to the facts it was deemed to prove. There have been interesting developments in recent GC judgments regarding the concept and probative value of indirect evidence, demonstrating that it can be decisive in corroborating statements or complementing intermittent or sporadic documentary evidence. On the one hand, it appears from the judgments of 12 July 2011 (concerning the Japanese members of the Gas Insulated Switchgear (GIS) cartel), that the existence of an infringement can be inferred from some facts which are well established to the extent that they lead to that conclusion (those facts would qualify as indirect evidence of the infringement). On the other hand, it appears from the recent judgment in *Aragonesas* that indirect documentary evidence constitutes *prima facie* evidence ('*un commencement de preuve*', '*un début de preuve*', '*un principio de prueba*'), requiring some corroboration to establish a given fact.

Indirect evidence in the GIS cartel

The GC upheld the finding that the cartel between the two groups of Japanese and European **4.60** GIS producers affected the EU/EEA market. The Commission case against Japanese companies depended on whether it could prove that the Japanese producers had committed to refrain from competing in Europe.[159] Since the object of that commitment was to determine the conduct of the Japanese undertakings in relation to the EEA market, that understanding effectively amounted to reserving the EEA market for European producers and had an effect on trade between Member States.[160] The GC ruled that the commitment by the Japanese was established on the basis of 'a coherent body of incriminating evidence' encompassing both contemporaneous documents and (corporate and witness) statements. Although there was direct evidence on this point,[161] the novelty in this case is the detailed analysis of indirect evidence for an unwritten agreement.

Japanese and European companies constituted two separate groups and each of them was **4.61** entitled to a quota in the GIS projects which they managed to rig around the world. The Commission established that cartel members relied on an unwritten agreement composed of three elements: thus (i) the European producers undertook to refrain from competing for projects in Japan; (ii) the European producers undertook to notify the Japanese cartel members of the GIS projects which they obtained in Europe outside their 'home countries'[162] and to include the value of those projects in the joint worldwide quota of the European group;

---

[158] Case T-112/07 *Hitachi Ltd, Hitachi Europe Ltd, Japan AE Power Systems Corp* [2011] ECR II-3871, para 63; Case T-113/07 *Toshiba Corp v Commission* [2011] ECR II-3989, para 87.

[159] Case T-112/07 *Hitachi Ltd, Hitachi Europe Ltd, Japan AE Power Systems Corp v European Commission* [2011] ECR II-3871, para 76; Case T-113/07 *Toshiba Corp v European Commission* [2011] OJ C252/30, para 97; Case T-133/07 *Mitsubishi Electric Corp v European Commission* [2011] ECR II-4219, para 91.

[160] Case T-133/07 *Mitsubishi Electric Corp v European Commission* [2011] ECR II-4219, para 233.

[161] Documentary evidence of a proposal to review the scope of the European area reserved to the European companies (Case T-112/07 *Hitachi Ltd, Hitachi Europe Ltd, Japan AE Power Systems Corp v Commission* [2011] ECR II-3871, para 254), there was also an admission by Fuji (Case T-112/07 *Hitachi Ltd, Hitachi Europe Ltd, Japan AE Power Systems Corp v European Commission* [2011] ECR II-3871, para 172; Case T-132/07 *Fuji Electric Co Ltd v Commission* [2011] ECR II-4091, paras 245–6, and Case T-133/07 *Mitsubishi Electric Corp v European Commission* [2011] ECR II-4219, para 135), as well as statements describing a common understanding between European and Japanese producers which included this element (Case T-112/07, *Hitachi Ltd, Hitachi Europe Ltd, Japan AE Power Systems Corp v Commission* [2011] ECR II-3871, para 253).

[162] Japan was a home country left to the Japanese companies and there were also some 'home countries' within Europe (attributed to the incumbents). Projects in home countries were neither discussed by the cartel members nor counted in the worldwide quota attributed to the relevant group.

and (iii) the Japanese producers would refrain from competing for GIS projects in the vast majority of Europe, which was thereby reserved to the European group.[163] The Commission and the GC believed that the purpose of the notification and project loading mechanism was to offer compensation to the Japanese undertakings, viewed by the European undertakings as potential competitors in the EEA market.

4.62 Among the various components of the common understanding, the GC recalled that it was the alleged undertaking of the Japanese companies not to enter the EEA market which constituted the basis of the Commission's case against the applicants and which needed to be established to the requisite legal standard. It then declared that the other components of the common understanding, if proven, may also serve as indirect evidence from which the existence of the corresponding undertaking on the part of the Japanese firms may be inferred.[164] The perception that the Japanese could have competed in Europe if they had not undertaken to refrain from doing so explains why the European companies agreed to notify and load European projects into their worldwide quota to the detriment of obtaining a higher proportion of projects elsewhere in the world. Therefore, the notification and loading mechanism constituted indirect evidence of the Japanese firms' commitment not to contest the European market in exchange for that reward,[165] as well as 'a serious indicator' that Japanese companies were perceived as credible competitors in Europe outside the home countries and this justified their compensation.[166] The GC ruled that the direct evidence establishing the two remaining elements of the common understanding constituted indirect evidence[167] of the existence of the undertaking given by the Japanese firms (the third element which could be inferred therefrom). In this scenario, the defendants could not simply resort to an alternative version of the facts, because the Commission was not only relying on indicia and coincidences.[168] They must first prove that the conclusion does not flow from the premise.

Indirect evidence in the Aragonesas judgment

4.63 In the *Aragonesas* judgment,[169] the GC held that indirect documentary evidence constituted *prima facie* evidence, requiring some corroboration to establish the fact in question. In this case, the presumption of innocence prevailed over indirect evidence, even if it was contemporaneous to the infringement. The GC considered that single pieces of indirect evidence must be corroborated by other pieces of evidence in order for the necessary conviction to be established. The notes taken of direct discussions between their author and three other interlocutors containing references to previous contacts between Aragonesas and either of the

---

[163] Mitsubishi and Toshiba are the only companies who have appealed these findings to the ECJ. See Case C-489/11 P *Mitsubishi Electric Corp v Commission*, pending and Case C-498/11 P *Toshiba v Commission*, appeals pending.

[164] Case T-112/07 *Hitachi Ltd, Hitachi Europe Ltd, Japan AE Power Systems Corp v Commission* [2011] ECR II-3871, para 76; Case T-113/07 *Toshiba Corp v Commission* [2011] OJ C252/30, para 97; Case T-133/07 *Mitsubishi Electric Corp v European Commission* [2011] ECR II-4219, para 91.

[165] Case T-112/07 *Hitachi Ltd, Hitachi Europe Ltd, Japan AE Power Systems Corp v Commission* [2011] ECR II-3871, paras 230 and 255; Case T-113/07 *Toshiba Corp v Commission* [2011] OJ C252/30, paras 189 and 206; Case T-133/07 *Mitsubishi Electric Corp v European Commission* [2011] ECR II-4219, paras 175 and 214.

[166] Case T-112/07 *Hitachi Ltd, Hitachi Europe Ltd, Japan AE Power Systems Corp v Commission* [2011] ECR II-3871, para 226; Case T-113/07 *Toshiba Corp v Commission* [2011] OJ C252/30, para 186; Case T-133/07 *Mitsubishi Electric Corp v Commission* [2011] ECR II-4219, para 174.

[167] Specifically, two corporate statements and a witness statement directly proved that the Japanese accepted the regular notification by the Europeans of the projects obtained in most of the EEA (outside 'home countries') and the counting thereof in the European quota.

[168] Case T-132/07 *Fuji Electric Co Ltd v Commission* [2011] ECR II-4091, paras 247, 251, and 252; Case T-112/07 *Hitachi Ltd, Hitachi Europe Ltd, Japan AE Power Systems Corp v Commission* [2011] ECR II-3871, para 261.

[169] Case T-348/08 *Aragonesas Industrias y Energía, SAU v Commission* [2011] OJ C355/15.

interlocutors or a third party only amounted to indirect evidence against Aragonesas. Those notes would have constituted direct evidence (and had greater probative value) had they been obtained directly from Aragonesas or had their author reported on his/her own direct conversations with Aragonesas. In the Court's view, it was the multiplication of the number of intermediaries involved in reporting the facts that reduced the credibility of the item of evidence.[170]

3. Choice of priorities and role of complainants

While Regulation 1/2003 provides the basis for the Commission's enforcement procedure and gives it the power to investigate and take decisions requiring the termination of infringements, it has led to a change of focus in DG COMP's activities. As the Commission is an administrative authority which must act in the public interest, and since it is responsible not only for the application of the competition rules but also for the shaping of competition policy,[171] a fundamental task inherent in the exercise of the Commission's administrative activity by which it directs its policy is 'setting priorities within the limits laid down by the law'.[172] Under Regulation 1/2003, the Commission does not investigate all of the matters brought to its attention.[173] Nor does it observe the same degree of formality in every case it deals with, since that is not its function and, in any event, it does not have the material resources to do so. A fundamental criterion applied by the Commission in determining whether a case is sufficiently important, is the extent to which it involves an EU interest. That may be assessed, in the case of complaints, by reference, *inter alia*, to the impact of the alleged infringements on the functioning of the common market and the probability of establishing the infringement by a level of investigative activity commensurate to the importance of the case.[174] In other instances, the novelty of the problems raised and the economic significance of cases are taken into account.[175] DG COMP is mainly involved with cases that are liable to result in prohibition decisions and decisions imposing fines. Tackling cartels will remain a clear priority.[176]

4.64

---

[170] The conclusion that a lower credibility based on the number of intermediaries is able to turn contemporaneous evidence which is directly relevant to a given fact into indirect evidence may arguably not be straightforward. See María Luisa Tierno Centella, 'Indirect Evidence of a Cartel in the GIS Judgments Saga' Journal of European Competition Law and Practice, first published online 7 March 2012, available at <http://jeclap.oxfordjournals.org>: 'Without going into the merits of this reasoning, it is however not clear why this affects the direct or indirect nature of the references to Aragonesas, rather than just the credibility of their content.'

[171] Case T-24/90 *Automec v Commission* [1992] ECR II-2223, para 73, citing Case C-234/89 *Delimitis v Henninger Bräu* [1991] ECR I-935.

[172] See Case T-24/90 *Automec* [1992] ECR II-2223, para 77.

[173] Regarding the treatment of complaints, see Ch 12, Rejection of Complaints.

[174] See Case T-24/90 *Automec* [1992] ECR II-2223, para 86. But see also Case T-427/08 *Confédération européenne des associations d'horlogers-réparateurs (CEAHR) v Commission* [2011] ECR II-5865.

[175] For example, in connection with the an alleged abuse of a dominant position by the US chipset manufacturer, Qualcomm Incorporated (COMP/39247 *Texas Instruments/Qualcomm*), the Commission stated that the case had raised important issues about the pricing of technology after its adoption as part of an industry standard. It considered that its assessment in these cases might 'be complex, and that anti-trust enforcers have to be very careful about overturning commercial agreements'. Although the Commission has investigated whether royalties charged by Qualcomm since its technology became part of Europe's 3G standard could be unreasonably high, it has not reached any formal conclusions about whether Qualcomm has breached Art 102 TFEU. The complainants withdrew (or indicated their intention to withdraw) their complaints, and, in view of its priorities, the Commission decided not to invest further resources in its investigation. MEMO/09/516 'Antitrust: Commission closes formal proceedings against Qualcomm', 24 November 2009.

[176] Director-General of DG COMP, A Italianer, 'Recent developments regarding the Commission's cartel enforcement our strong anti-cartel enforcement activity', Studienvereinigung Kartellrecht Conference, Brussels, 14 March 2012, emphasizing that 2011 saw a steady flow of immunity applications, covering a range of European and global cartels in different industries. In 2010–2011, eleven investigations involving eighty-three corporations were concluded and the total fines imposed amounted to EUR 3.5 billion. See also

4.65 Citizens and undertakings are encouraged to inform the Commission about suspected infringements of the competition rules. There are two ways of doing this: market information; and a
complaint under Article 7(2) of Regulation 1/2003. Citizens and undertakings who wish to
inform the Commission about suspected infringements of Articles 101 or 102 are invited to
write to the Commission. This information can be the starting point for a Commission investigation, but it does not trigger the formal complaints procedure.

4.66 The Commission will endeavour to inform complainants of the action that it proposes to take on
a complaint within an indicative time frame of four months from the receipt of the complaint.[177]
This is, however, subject to the circumstances of the individual case and, in particular, depends
on whether DG COMP has received sufficient information from the complainant or third parties, notably in response to its requests for information, in order for it to decide whether or not
it intends to investigate the case further.

4.67 Formal complaints made on the basis of Article 7(2) of Regulation 1/2003 oblige the Commission
to react in specific ways. Articles 5 to 9 of Regulation No 773/2004 lay down specific rules
concerning the handling of such complaints. According to the Commission, complainants are
'closely associated with the proceedings'.[178] If they are able to show a legitimate interest and
provide comprehensive information, then they benefit from a range of procedural rights. The
Commission is under an obligation to 'examine carefully' the complaint, to decide on it within
a 'reasonable time' and to subsequently involve the complainant to an extent in the procedure
should it be opened (copy of non-confidential statement of objections, oral hearing, etc). If the
Commission does not pursue the case, the complainant is entitled to have its complaint rejected
by a reasoned decision which it can challenge before the EU Courts.

D. Commission Decisions

1. General characteristics of decisions

4.68 During the procedures described earlier in this chapter, or at their culmination, the
Commission adopts various types of decisions which, pursuant to the fourth paragraph of
Article 288 TFEU, are binding in all respects on their addressees. As is apparent from the
case law of the EU Courts on measures which may be challenged under Article 263 TFEU,
Commission decisions produce legal effects and are liable to have a considerable impact on
the legal situation of their addressees—and other interested parties—and thus affect their
interests.[179] The vast majority of Commission decisions in competition matters are addressed
to undertakings[180] and apply the EU competition rules in a specific manner to specific cases.

---

his speech entitled 'Zero tolerance for international cartels', ICN Cartel Workshop 2011, Bruges, 10–13
October.

[177] Notice on Complaints [2004] OJ C10 1/65, para 61.

[178] See also Commission notice on best practices for the conduct of proceedings concerning Articles 101
and 102 TFEU [2011] OJ C308/6, para 104.

[179] See, among others, Case 53/85 *AKZO v Commission* [1986] ECR 1965, para 16. A statement of objections cannot, therefore, be regarded as a decision against which proceedings may be brought: Case 60/81 *IBM
v Commission* [1981] ECR 2639, para 11. D Geradin and N Petit, 'Judicial Remedies under EC Competition
Law: Complex Issues Arising from the Modernization Process' ch 17 in International Antitrust & Policy,
32nd Annual International Antitrust Law & Policy Conference [2006] Fordham Corporate Law Institute,
393, suggest that the ruling in *IBM* permits an exception to the principle that the act must be of a definitive
nature where the acts fall within a phase which can be separated from the course of proceedings leading to the
definitive act. This point will be considered in greater detail in Ch 10, 'Procedures to Establish the Existence
of an Infringement'.

[180] However, a decision rejecting a complaint may be addressed to an individual. Regarding the main types
of decision, see para 4.70 et seq.

In that sense, its decisions may be regarded as equivalent to administrative measures under national law and constitute a means of administrative enforcement of EU law available to the Commission. All in all, decisions often have a value which goes beyond the mere determination of specific cases with which the Commission has to deal. The particular way in which the Commission—and more particularly DG COMP—works, dictated by the impossibility of dealing formally with all cases, makes it necessary to select those cases which will be brought to a formal conclusion and to some extent makes these decisions precedents for the future.[181] The Commission is under an obligation to state reasons if it declines to continue with the examination of a complaint, and those reasons must be sufficiently precise and detailed to enable the Court effectively to review the Commission's use of its discretion to define priorities. The GC verifies whether this condition has been complied with.[182]

The case law of the GC interprets the obligation to state reasons as a requirement that the **4.69** Commission state clearly and unequivocally the reasoning followed in adopting its decisions. The reasons must disclose the Commission's arguments to the addressees, thus enabling them to judge whether or not the decision is well founded and, ultimately, properly to defend their rights. The obligation to state reasons also exists so that the Court can carry out its task of judicial review.[183] The obligation to state reasons is highly important and must be fulfilled with particular care where a Commission decision goes significantly further than any previously adopted.[184] A contradiction in the statement of reasons on which a decision is based constitutes a breach of Article 296 TFEU. If the reasons are not stated adequately, or at all, the decision will be rendered void.[185] In particular, the Court has held that the statement of reasons must enable 'the persons concerned to ascertain the reasons for the measure and to enable the competent Community court to exercise its power of review. It is not necessary for the reasoning to go into all the relevant facts and points of law'. Whether a statement of reasons is adequate must be assessed 'with regard not only to its wording but also to its context and to all the legal rules governing the matter in question'.[186]

2. Types of decision

The Commission may take a final decision ordering the termination of the infringements of the **4.70** competition rules and may take procedural decisions during the course of its investigation. As indicated, it may also take interim measures in order to prevent irreparable damage before it can

---

[181] This does not mean that the Commission is unable to re-focus its policy regarding specific restrictive agreements and conduct, as has already been seen. The value as a precedent does not go as far as the common law concept of *stare decisis*.

[182] Case T-427/08 *Confédération européenne des associations d'horlogers-réparateurs (CEAHR) v Commission* [2011] ECR II-5865, para 28.

[183] For the interpretation of Art 296 TFEU in the context of competition law proceedings, see Joined Cases 142/84 and 156/84 *BAT and Reynolds v Commission* [1987] ECR 4487, para 72; Case T-76/89 *ITP v Commission* [1991] ECR II-575, paras 62–6; Case T-44/90 *La Cinq v Commission* [1992] ECR II-1, para 42; Case T-16/91 *Rendo v Commission* [1992] ECR II-2417, para 124; Case T-7/92 *Asia Motor France and others v Commission* [1993] ECR II-669, para 80; Case T-102/92 *Viho Europe BV v Commission* [1995] ECR II-17, paras 75–6; and Case T-114/92 *BEMIM v Commission* [1995] ECR II-147, para 41. The Commission is not required, however, to deal with all matters of fact and law which may have arisen in the course of the procedure. It is sufficient for the Commission to refer to it in general terms: Joined Cases 43/82 and 63/82 *VBVB and VBBB v Commission* [1984] ECR 19, para 22. Note that recent practice, however, has been to state at length the evidence relied on. See Case COMP/36.571/D *Austrian Banks* [2004] OJ L56/1.

[184] If the Commission's decision breaks new ground, it must give more extensive legal reasoning. See Case 73/74 *Papiers Peints v Commission* [1975] ECR 1491, para 31 and Joined Cases 142/84 and 156/84 *BAT and Reynolds v Commission* [1987] ECR 4487, para 71.

[185] Ex post reasoning, such as during proceedings before the Court, cannot salvage an inadequately reasoned decision. Joined Cases T-236/01, T-239/01, T-244/01 to T-246/01, T-251/01, and T-252/01 *Tokai Carbon v Commission* [2004] ECR II-1181, para 415.

[186] Case T-199/08 *Ziegler SA v Commission* [2011] ECR II-3507, para 87.

come to a final decision. In addition, it has two further powers under Regulation 1/2003: firstly, it may take a decision making commitments binding but without finding an infringement, and secondly it may reach a 'positive' decision finding that Article 101 or 102 TFEU is inapplicable.

4.71 Under Article 7(1) of Regulation 1/2003, a decision finding an infringement may therefore order undertakings to bring the infringement to an end to the extent that it has not been definitely terminated already. These are 'cease-and-desist' orders. The decision may also contain a 'like effects order' whereby the parties are prohibited from entering into similar arrangements.[187] Regulation 1/2003 expressly gives the Commission power to make orders by stating that it may impose 'any behavioural…remedies which are proportionate to the infringement committed and necessary to bring the infringement effectively to an end'. As regards infringements of Article 101 TFEU, however, the GC has ruled that the Commission does not have the power to order a party to enter into a contractual relationship where there are other ways of making the party end the infringement.[188]

3. Notification of decisions and information to the Member States

Notification

4.72 Pursuant to Article 297 TFEU, decisions 'shall be notified to those to whom they are addressed and shall take effect upon such notification.'[189] The Secretariat General ('SG') is in charge of the notification process, which will take place in two rounds. In the first stage, immediately after the decision has been adopted by the College, the SG notifies by fax[190] the operative part of the decision ('dispositif') to the parties (not to their external legal counsel, except if parties waived the notification rights to their empowered attorney); the SG also notifies the operative part of the decision to the NCAs. In the second stage, the SG notifies a certified copy of the decision to the parties,[191] as well as a copy of the final report of the Hearing Officer by express courier service.

4.73 The Court has made it clear that a decision is deemed to be duly notified when received by its addressee and the latter has an opportunity to take note of its content.[192] The Court takes an objective approach. If the document containing the notification has been presented to an undertaking, the latter cannot allege lack of notification merely because it refuses to admit that it has been notified. Irregularities affecting the method of notification do not constitute a defect affecting the legality or propriety of the notified measure in itself.[193]

---

[187] Case IV/31.553 *Welded Steel Mesh* [1989] OJ L260/1, paras 209 and 210.

[188] Case T-24/90 *Automec v Commission* [1992] ECR II-2223, paras 51–4.

[189] European Commission Antitrust Manual of Procedures, Internal DG COMP working documents on procedures for the application of Articles 101 and 102 TFEU, March 2012, Module 15 'Adoption of a Prohibition Decision', para 27.

[190] See Case T-46/92 *Scottish Football v Commission* [1994] ECR II-1039, para 4, which seems to indicate that notification of a decision by fax does not constitute formal notification. However, this could to ensure that undertakings are made aware of decisions before details appear in the press, which has occurred in the past. The Court has stated that, although regrettable, the fact that a decision is made public before it is notified to its addressee is not a formal defect such as to invalidate it (Joined Cases 96/82 to 102/82, 104/82, 105/82, 108/82, and 110/82 *IAZ v Commission* [1983] ECR 3369, para 16). See also Case T-43/92 *Dunlop v Commission* [1994] ECR-II 441, paras 27–9.

[191] If there is no serious indication of any irregularity, this copy is conclusive as to the content of a decision. See Joined Cases 97/87, 98/87, and 99/87 *Dow Chemical Ibérica and others v Commission* [1989] ECR 3165, para 59, and the GC judgments in Case T-43/92 *Dunlop Slazenger v Commission* [1994] ECR II-441, paras 24 and 25, Case T-34/92 *Fiatagri UK and New Holland Ford v Commission* [1994] ECR II-905, para 27, and Case T-35/92 *John Deere v Commission* [1994] ECR II-957, para 31.

[192] See Case 48/69 *ICI v Commission* [1972] ECR 619, paras 34–44, and Case 6/72 *Europemballage Corp and Continental Can Co v Commission* [1973] ECR 215, para 10, both cited in Case 374/87 *Orkem v Commission* [1989] ECR 3283, para 6.

[193] See Case 48/69 *ICI v Commission* [1972] ECR 619, paras 39–40, and Case 52/69 *Geigy AG v Commission* [1972] ECR 787, para 18, cited in Case T-43/92 *Dunlop Slazenger v Commission* [1994] ECR-II

The only exception to this concerns the notification of inspection decisions, which takes place **4.74** upon commencement of inspections by the officials responsible for performing them. The date of formal notification of the decision as a whole—which will generally be the date on which the addressees sign the postal form for acknowledgement of receipt[194]—marks the start of the time limit for commencing proceedings before the GC. Traditionally, decisions have been signed by the member of the Commission responsible for competition matters or by the senior DG COMP official (normally the Director-General) to whom the Commission and the relevant member of the Commission have delegated that authority.[195] The judgment in the *PVC* cartel has prompted the Commission to redouble its precautions regarding signature and completion of other formalities.[196] In any event, no provision requires the copy of the notified decision to be signed by the competent member of the Commission.[197]

441, para 25. It does not seem to matter whether the addressee is situated outside of the EU. See also Kerse & Khan, *EC Antitrust Procedure* (6th edn, Sweet & Maxwell 2012) para 6-026. K Lenaerts and J Maselis, 'Procedural Rights and Issues in the Enforcement of Articles 81 and 82 of the EC Treaty' [2001] Fordham International Law Journal 1615, 1648, noting that an irregularity in the notification may sometimes prevent the period within which an application must be lodged from starting to run.

[194] See Case T-12/90 *Bayer v Commission* [1991] ECR II-219 (in particular para 20), in which the GC held that postal receipt provides conclusive evidence of the date of notification and takes precedence over other acknowledgements of receipt which, although sent by the Commission to the parties, are of subsidiary status. The subsequent appeal against this decision was rejected by the Court: see Case C-195/91 *Bayer v Commission* [1994] ECR I-5619. At para 21, the Court confirmed that an undertaking is taken to have notice of a Commission decision from the time when the form containing the decision (sent by registered post) arrives at its registered office. The GC, however, has accepted that when it has been established that the information contained in the postal record of delivery is incorrect, it must be disregarded. See Joined Cases T-80/89, T-81/89, T-87/89, T-88/89, T-90/89, T-93/89, T-95/89, T-97/89, T-99/89, T-100/89, T-100/89, T-101/89, T-103/89, T-105/89, T-107/89, and T-112/89 *BASF and others v Commission* [1995] ECR II-729, paras 58–61.

[195] The Commission adopted a decision with a comprehensive set of empowerments (PV(2004) 1655, SEC(2004) 520/2) as extended by PV(2006) 1763, SEC(2006) 1368 for the Competition Commissioner for the application of Regulation No 1/2003 and implementing Commission Regulation No 773/2004. It must be borne in mind that under Art 13(3) of the Rules of Procedure, a Commissioner can sub-delegate the powers granted to him to a Director-General and Head of Service unless this is expressly prohibited in the empowerment decision. The empowerment decision of 28 April 2004 prohibits the sub-delegation only as regards the determination and issuance of a statement of objections. By decision of 27 May 2004, the Commissioner for Competition has therefore sub-delegated a number of the above powers to the Director-General of DG COMP. All final decisions on substance (including interim measures) and/or decisions of principle implying a wide margin of appreciation are reserved to the College. Those acts cannot be delegated. To these Commission acts belong: all Commission decisions finding and ordering the termination of an infringement (Art 7 of Reg 1/2003); all Commission decisions ordering and renewing interim measures (Art 8(1)(2) of Reg 1/2003); all Commission decisions making commitments binding (Art 9(1) of Reg 1/2003); all Commission decisions finding the inapplicability of Arts 101 or 102 TFEU; all Commission decisions imposing fines for breaches of procedural or substantive law (Art 23(1)(2) of Reg 1/2003); as well as all related Commission decisions finally granting immunity or reduction of fines or rejecting immunity and leniency applications (1996, 2002, and 2007 Leniency Notices); all Commission decisions on the final amount of a periodic penalty payment (Art 24(2) (sentence 1) of Reg 1/2003) and all Commission decisions to withdraw the benefit of a block exemption regulation (Art 29(1) of Reg 1/2003). See Antitrust Manual of Procedures, Internal DG Competition working documents on procedures for the application of Articles 101 and 102 TFEU, March 2012, Module 1 'Decision-making procedure', paras 11 and 17–18.

[196] In its judgment in Joined Cases T-79/89, T-84 to 86/89, T-89/89, T-91 and 92/89, T-94/89, T-96/89, T-98/89, T-102/89, and T-104/89 *BASF and others v Commission* [1992] ECR II-315, paras 76–83, the GC declared the Commission Decision in *PVC Cartel* [1988] OJ L/74/1 non-existent because of a number of formal defects. By its judgment in Case C-137/92 *Commission v BASF and others* [1994] ECR I-2555, paras 75–8, the Court set aside the GC judgment, taking the view that the formal defects in the Commission's Decision were such that it should be declared void rather than non-existent.

[197] Joined Cases 97/87, 98/87 and 99/87 *Dow Chemical Ibérica and others v Commission* [1989] ECR 3165, para 59. Cited in the GC judgment in Case T-43/92 *Dunlop Slazenger* [1994] ECR-II 441, para 25.

Information to Member States concerning adopted decisions

4.75 The Member States have decisions notified to them, in the same way as the direct address-ees of decisions, whenever the decision has been the subject of a report by the Advisory Committee. The operative part of the decision is communicated by fax and the full text is subsequently sent by post.

4. Publication of decisions and other measures

The Official Journal

4.76 Article 30 of Regulation 1/2003 requires the Commission to publish its decisions (find-ing and termination of infringement, interim measures, commitments, finding of inap-plicability, and penalties). Decisions in competition matters are published in the L series (legislation) of the OJ, Part II: 'measures whose publication is not a precondition for their applicability'. The obligation to publish in the OJ extends to the final report of the Hearing Officer,[198] as well as to the opinion of the Advisory Committee, if the Advisory Committee so recommends.[199] According to Article 27(4) of Regulation 1/2003, when the Commission intends to adopt a decision pursuant to Article 9 or 10 of Regulation 1/2003, it has to publish a summary of the case and the main content of the commitment or the proposed course of action (the Article 27(4) 'market test' notice). Addressees of decisions adopted under the above-mentioned articles have no specific right to prevent the publication by the Commission in the Official Journal and, where relevant, on the DG COMP's website, of information which, even though not confidential, includes more than the 'main content' essential for understanding the operative part of those decisions.[200]

4.77 Decisions other than those mentioned in the previous paragraph may also be published if the Commission considers them sufficiently important for the development of competition policy. For example, there may be publication of decisions to inspect, those rejecting com-plaints,[201] and others.[202] The published decisions often do not contain all of the information included in the decisions notified to the undertakings. In preparing the non-confidential version of the decision for publication, the Commission must balance its professional secrecy obligation and interest in protecting its investigations on the one hand with the aim of pro-viding maximum transparency on the other.

---

[198] Article 17(3) of the Decision of the President of the European Commission of 13 October 2011 on the function and terms of reference of the hearing officer in certain competition proceedings, OJ L275, 20.10.2011, p. 29 ('Hearing Officer Terms of Reference').

[199] Article 14(6) of Reg 1/2003. For decisions imposing fines, the opinion of the Advisory Committee consists of two parts (one on the substance and one on the fines). In line with Art 14 of Reg 1/2003, this section refers to both parts as the 'opinion of the Advisory Committee'.

[200] European Commission Antitrust Manual of Procedures Internal DG Competition working docu-ments on procedures for the application of Articles 101 and 102 TFEU, March 2012, Module 28, para 4. Citing Case T-198/03 *Bank Austria Creditanstalt v Commission* [2006] ECR II-1429, para 77: 'the interest of an undertaking which the Commission has fined for breach of competition law in the details of the offend-ing conduct of which it is accused not being disclosed to the public does not warrant any particular protec-tion, given the public interest in knowing as fully as possible the reasons behind any Commission action, the interest of the economic operators in knowing the sort of behaviour for which they are liable to be penalised and the interest of persons harmed by the infringement in being informed of the details thereof so that they may, where appropriate, assert their rights against the undertakings punished, and in view of the fined under-taking's ability to seek judicial review of such a decision.'

[201] Director-General of DG COMP, A Italianer, 'European Commission regarding due process in antitrust proceedings' Fordham Competition Law Institute Annual Conference on International Antitrust Law and Policy Session on 'Enforcers' perspectives on international antitrust', Thursday 23 September 2010, 8, indi-cating that the Commission will 'give publicity'.

[202] In the relevant sections, reference is made to certain decisions of this kind which have been published in the OJ.

The information that will be deleted refers to the following:[203]   **4.78**

- Confidential information, in particular business secrets.[204] Under Article 339 TFEU, the Commission and its staff are bound by the obligation of professional secrecy.[205] This obligation covers business secrets[206] and other confidential information, provided that it meets the criteria set out in the case law.
- Personal data.[207] The Commission must consider the requirements of Regulation EC No 45/2001.[208] Personal data must, in principle, be removed from documents before their publication.
- Information the publication of which may jeopardize Commission investigations.[209] The publication of certain types of information may jeopardize the Commission's ability to conduct its investigations, both in specific cases and in general. In particular, this can be the case as regards admissions provided by the parties under the Leniency Notice and voluntary admissions of the participation in an infringement made by parties during inspections, in replies to requests for information and during the oral hearing. Therefore, the Commission redacts certain information falling within this category in the public version of the decision.[210]

The Commission considers, however, that undertakings are not entitled to request confi-   **4.79** dentiality for information establishing or proving the existence or seriousness of an infringement.[211] It is up to the parties themselves to mark proposals for redaction of information such as quotes stemming from their own corporate statements or other information stemming from their corporate statements to the extent that they are traceable to them. The Commission,

---

[203] European Commission Antitrust Manual of Procedures Internal DG Competition working documents on procedures for the application of Articles 101 and 102 TFEU, March 2012, Module 28 'Publication of decisions', para 92 et seq.

[204] Pursuant to Art 30(2) of Reg 1/2003, the publication of the decision shall have regard to the legitimate interest of undertakings to protect their business secrets. The same applies to the final report of the Hearing Officer (Art 17(3) of the Hearing Officer Terms of Reference) and the opinion of the Advisory Committee (Art 14(6) of Reg 1/2003).

[205] Article 339 TFEU provides as follows: 'The members of the institutions of the Union, the members of committees, and the officials and other servants of the Union shall be required, even after their duties have ceased, not to disclose information of the kind covered by the obligation of professional secrecy, in particular information about undertakings, their business relations or their cost components.'

[206] Which are expressly mentioned in Art 30(2) of Reg 1/2003.

[207] Regulation (EC) No 45/2001 of the European Parliament and of the Council of 18 December 2000 on the protection of individuals with regard to the processing of personal data by the Community institutions and bodies and on the free movement of such data [2001] OJ L8/1–22.

[208] Regulation (EC) No 45/2001 of the European Parliament and of the Council of 18 December 2000 on the protection of individuals with regard to the processing of personal data by the Community institutions and bodies and on the free movement of such data [2001] OJ L8/1–22.

[209] Case T-198/03 *Bank Austria Creditanstalt v Commission* [2003] ECR II-4879, para 39, in which the GC identified an ambiguity in Art 9(3) of the Mandate of the Hearing Officer, questioning whether the Hearing Officer has to decide also whether or not parts of a Commission decision, being not part of the decision's 'main content', should be published under Art 21 of Reg 17 (Art 30 of Reg 1/2003).

[210] Commission Antitrust Manual of Procedures, Internal DG Competition working documents on procedures for the application of Articles 101 and 102 TFEU, March 2012, Module 28 'Publication of Decisions', para 105. See Ch 6, 'Investigation of Cases (I): Leniency Policy', para 3.43 et seq.

[211] Commission Antitrust Manual of Procedures, Internal DG Competition working documents on procedures for the application of Articles 101 and 102 TFEU, March 2012, Module 12 'Access to file and confidentiality', para 40. For an example, where the President of the GC ordered that the Commission refrain from publishing a decision with allegedly confidential information: T-345/12 *Akzo Nobel and others v Commission*, order of the GC of 16 November 2012; Case T-462/12, *Pilkington Group v Commission*, Order of the President of the GC of 11 March 2013, where the GC partially upheld and partially dismissed Pilkington Glass Ltd's application for interim relief in relation to its appeal against a Commission decision refusing its request for the confidential treatment of certain information relating to its participation in the car glass cartel.

however, ultimately decides whether the publication of certain information would jeopardize the Commission's investigation and whether other information than that marked by the parties should be redacted to avoid such adverse effects on the functioning of the Commission. As established by the GC in *Pergan*,[212] findings relating to an infringement by any third parties who may have participated in the infringement but who are not mentioned in the operative part of the decision must be removed from the published version of the decision. In general, the adopted version of the decision should avoid references to any such undertakings, in particular in the Commission's narratives. It is possible, however, that, for example, quoted documents, such as price tables found during inspections, contain names of undertakings that may have participated in the infringement but which are not mentioned in the operative part.[213]

4.80 There are no express legal requirements regarding the timing of the publication in the OJ.[214] Once all official language versions have been received, the case team sends the texts that need to be published (summary, final report of the Hearing Officer, opinion of the Advisory Committee) to the relevant functional mailbox, indicating the name and number of the case as well as the date of adoption of the decision. The Secretariat General transmits the documents to be published to the Publications Office in Luxembourg, which fixes the date of publication and communicates it to the Secretariat General of the Commission.[215] The Commission has a long-established practice of publishing its final antitrust decisions on the DG COMP's website in order to ensure transparency, predictability, and legal certainty, even though it is under no legal obligation to do so.[216] In addition, all of the documents published in the OJ are also available on the DG COMP website via a direct link.[217]

Press releases

4.81 The Commission always issues a press release when it adopts a formal decision under Articles 101 and 102 TFEU. Press releases (or Commission 'Memos') are not usually issued regarding measures or decisions of a procedural nature, unless the cases involved are already public knowledge and the Commission wishes to clarify some aspect of the situation.[218] The Commission may consider it appropriate to rely on a press release to clarify matters relating to its policy or to make

---

[212] Case T-474/04 *Pergan Hilfsstoffe für industrielle Prozesse v Commission* [2007] ECR II-4225, paras 71–81, stating, *inter alia*, that 'since the Commission's findings relating to an infringement committed by an undertaking are capable of infringing the principle of the presumption of innocence, those findings must, in principle, be regarded as confidential as regards the public, and therefore as being of the kind covered by the obligation of professional secrecy. This principle stems, inter alia, from the need to respect the reputation and dignity of the person concerned as that person has not been finally found guilty of an infringement.' (para 78)

[213] Commission Antitrust Manual of Procedures, Internal DG Competition working documents on procedures for the application of Articles 101 and 102 TFEU, March 2012, Module 28 'Publication of Decisions', paras 109–10.

[214] The publication of the summary of the decision in the OJ will be relevant to triggering the deadline for an appeal by third parties to the European Courts. Ch 15, 'Steps Following the Adoption of a Formal Decision. Judicial Review', para 15.03, n 10.

[215] Commission Antitrust Manual of Procedures, Internal DG Competition working documents on procedures for the application of Articles 101 and 102 TFEU, March 2012, Module 28 'Publication of Decisions', paras 83–5. The summary, the final report of the Hearing Officer, and the opinion of the Advisory Committee are published in the OJ in series C under the heading IV—Notices—Notices from European Union institutions, bodies and agencies.

[216] See Case T-198/03 *Bank Austria Creditanstalt v Commission* [2006] ECR II-1429, para 76: 'that provision [Art 21(2) of Reg 17] does not limit the Commission's power to publish the full text of its decisions, if, resources permitting, it considers it appropriate to do so'; and para 79: 'the aim of Article 21(2) of Regulation No 17 is not to limit the Commission's freedom to publish, of its own volition, a version of its decision that is fuller than the minimum necessary and also to include information whose publication is not required, in so far as the disclosure of that information is not inconsistent with the protection of professional secrecy.'

[217] The bibliographic link allows viewers to choose the desired format and language.

[218] See Commission Memo/12/78 'Antitrust: Commission confirms unannounced inspections in the electricity sector', 7 February 2012, in which the Commission confirmed that Commission officials undertook

undertakings or consumers aware of the more interesting points in their decisions where the case in question may be a source of useful information. Generally, there is no publication in respect of intermediate steps such as the statement of objections. Sometimes, if the issue involved is of sufficient importance, being novel or likely to affect other cases, the Commission may issue a press release concerning measures adopted by other institutions or national authorities and courts. These are fairly frequent in cases heard by the Court under Article 267 TFEU (preliminary rulings). Press releases may also be issued regarding GC cases.[219] Press releases can be obtained from the Commission Press Offices and may be consulted on the Commission's Rapid Database.[220]

Periodical publications

Undertakings and individuals can periodically familiarize themselves with the Commission's **4.82** activities in competition matters through a number of Commission publications. The *Bulletin of the European Union* provides a monthly insight into the activities of the Commission and the other EU institutions. It is published by the Secretariat-General of the Commission and appears ten times a year in all EU languages, providing information about the Commission activities, including competition policy.[221] As regards the latter, the annual report contains general information on the development of EU competition policy and comments on the relevant decisions of the Commission and the EU Courts. Finally, the Commission regularly prepares a number of information leaflets on competition policy[222] and issues a regular EC Competition Policy Newsletter in electronic format to keep undertakings and practitioners informed of the latest developments.[223]

Europe Direct, European Documentation Centres, and the Internet

In addition to the formal requirements contained in Regulation 1/2003 to publish notices **4.83** and decisions, the Commission has been constantly trying to improve the transparency of EU policy and its application in practice. For example, Europe Direct encompasses an extensive network of information centres and contact points set up by the EU for the public.[224] Official publications can be consulted at a large number of European Documentation Centres. The DG COMP Internet homepage contains material on all of the main areas of EU competition policy. Under each heading (antitrust, mergers, etc) the user can search an increasing number of sections containing a variety of documents, including press releases, EU legislation, and case law.

E. Confidentiality

1. Professional secrecy and business secrets

Undertakings dealing with the Commission will naturally wish to ensure that confidential **4.84** information given to the Commission is protected from disclosure. According to Article 339 TFEU, the members of the institutions, as well as officials and other servants of the EU, are

---

unannounced inspections at the premises of companies active in managing power exchanges in several Member States.

[219] For example, see MEMO/12/233 'Antitrust: Commission welcomes General Court judgments in Telefónica case', 29 March 2012. Note that both of the EU Courts publish their own press releases.
[220] <http://europa.eu/rapid/search.htm>.
[221] <http://europa.eu/archives/bulletin/en/welcome.htm>. The Bulletin is supplemented by the General Report on the activities of the EU which provides an overview of the activities of the previous year.
[222] Most of them can be downloaded from the DG COMP's website.
[223] The three yearly newsletters may be supplemented by special editions.
[224] <http://europa.eu/europedirect/index_en.htm>. Europe Direct can also be contacted by a single free-phone number (00 800 67 89 10 11) from anywhere in the EU.

obliged not to disclose 'information of the kind covered by the obligation of professional secrecy'. In order for information to be of the kind to fall within the scope of the professional secrecy obligation:

> it is necessary, first of all, that it be known only to a limited number of persons. It must then be information whose disclosure is liable to cause serious harm to the person who has provided it or to third parties. Finally, the interests liable to be harmed by disclosure must, objectively, be worthy of protection. The assessment as to the confidentiality of a piece of information thus requires the legitimate interests opposing disclosure of the information to be weighed against the public interest that the activities of the Community institutions take place as openly as possible.[225]

Confidentiality applies in particular[226] to 'information about undertakings, their business relations or their cost components' (Article 339 TFEU). This refers to information which, by reason of its content, in principle falls within the category of business secrets, as defined by the ECJ.[227] Business secrets relate to the activities of undertakings and concern information for which not only disclosure to the public but also mere transmission to a person other than the one who provided it may seriously harm the latter's interests.[228] In addition, confidential information other than business secrets is also protected.[229]

---

[225] Case T-198/03 *Bank Austria Creditanstalt v Commission* [2006] ECR II-1429, para 71. According to the judgment (paras 74–5): '[i]n so far as [such] provisions of secondary legislation prohibit the disclosure of information to the public or exclude public access to documents containing it, that information must be considered to be covered by the obligation of professional secrecy. Conversely, to the extent that the public has a right of access to documents containing certain information, that information cannot be considered to be of the kind covered by the obligation of professional secrecy.' Consequently, Art 28 of Reg 1/2003 'prohibits, besides the disclosure of business secrets, in particular the publication of information covered by the exceptions to the right of access to documents that are laid down in Article 4 of Regulation No 1049/2001 or information which is protected under other rules of secondary legislation, such as Regulation No 45/2001. Conversely, this provision is not a bar to publication of information with which the public has the right to be acquainted through the right of access to documents.' See also European Commission Antitrust Manual of Procedures, Internal DG Competition working documents on procedures for the application of Articles 101 and 102 TFEU, March 2012, Module 12 'Access to file and confidentiality', paras 38–9, pointing out that the GC had confirmed (Case T-198/03 *Bank Austria Creditanstalt v Commission* [2006] ECR II-1429, para 29) that the concept of professional secrecy is broader than that of business secrets and therefore documents protected by the principle of professional secrecy can be disclosed when granting access to the file for the purpose of defence rights, provided that they do not contain business secrets.

[226] In *Adams*, the ECJ clarified that the confidentiality requirement also applies to information supplied by natural persons, if that information is 'of the kind' that is confidential. That includes the statements of an informant where the information is supplied on a purely voluntary basis but accompanied by a request for confidentiality in order to protect the informant's anonymity. See Case 145/83 *Stanley Adams v Commission* [1985] ECR 3539, para 34. As regards the Commission's findings relating to an infringement committed by an undertaking see also Case T-474/04 *Pergan Hilfsstoffe für industrielle Prozesse v Commission* [2007] ECR II-4225, paras 65, 78, and 80.

[227] See Case T-353/94 *Postbank v Commission* [1996] ECR II-921, para 86.

[228] See Commission Notice on the rules for access to the Commission file in cases pursuant to Articles 81 and 82 of the EC Treaty, Articles 53, 54 and 57 of the EEA Agreement and Council Regulation (EC) No 139/2004, OJ C325/7, 22.12.2005, para 18.

[229] Case T-353/94 *Postbank v Commission* [1996] ECR II-921, para 86; Case T-62/98 *Volkswagen v Commission* [2000] ECR II-2707, para 279; Case T-474/04 *Pergan Hilfsstoffe für industrielle Prozesse v Commission* [2007] ECR II-4225, para 63. See also Commission Notice on the rules for access to the Commission file in cases pursuant to Articles 81 and 82 of the EC Treaty, Articles 53, 54, and 57 of the EEA Agreement and Council Regulation (EC) No 139/2004 [2005] OJ C325/7, para 19 et seq. See also European Commission Antitrust Manual of Procedures, Internal DG Competition working documents on procedures for the application of Articles 101 and 102 TFEU, March 2012, Module 12 'Access to file and confidentiality', para 29, describing business secrets as confidential information about an undertaking's business activity, the disclosure of which could cause serious harm to that undertaking. Examples of information that may qualify as business secrets include: technical and/or financial information relating to an undertaking's know-how, methods of assessing costs, production secrets and processes, supply sources, quantities

By way of example, the Commission has indicated in the Antitrust Manual of Procedures **4.85** (Manproc) that it does not normally accept the following type of information as business secrets and other confidential information:[230]

- Data from or about another company (such as price announcements, sales data etc other than that received pursuant to a contract with that company), unless confidentiality has been claimed (eg to prevent disclosure of the knowledge of this information).
- Information made known outside the company concerned (such as price targets, increases, dates of implementation and customer names, if made known to third parties).
- Facts relating to an application for immunity or a reduction of fines, where these facts aim at providing evidence of an alleged infringement, unless the disclosure of such facts could harm the Commission's leniency policy.
- Names and positions of employees or other persons involved in an infringement.[231]

The Commission also adds that business secrets and other confidential documents would **4.86** cease to be confidential if they are already known outside or have lost their commercial importance, for instance due to the passage of time (as a general rule, parties' turnover, sales, market-share data, and similar information which is more than five years old is no longer confidential).[232] Personal data has to be processed in accordance with Regulation 45/2001.[233] In the view of the Commission, correspondence relating to the granting of confidentiality (including cover emails etc) would be so closely interrelated to the issue of confidentiality that it need normally not be disclosed to the parties. The index should make clear that the document concerned constitutes 'correspondence on confidentiality claims', so that the parties can understand why the document is not accessible.[234]

Article 28 of Regulation 1/2003 applies the general concept of professional secrecy to the **4.87** enforcement of the competition rules. The protection provided for is twofold.[235] First, paragraph 2 of that provision prohibits the *disclosure of information* acquired as a result of the application of Regulation 1/2003 and of the kind covered by the obligation of professional

---

produced and sold, market shares, customer and distributor lists, marketing plans, cost and price structure and sales strategy.

[230] See also DG Competition informal guidance paper on confidentiality claims (16 March 2012), which sets out informal guidance for the recipients of a request for information on how to claim confidentiality for information in theory submission.

[231] European Commission Antitrust Manual of Procedures, Internal DG Competition working documents on procedures for the application of Articles 101 and 102 TFEU, March 2012, Module 12 'Access to file and confidentiality', para 31.

[232] Notice on Access to the file [2005] OJ C325/7, para 23.

[233] Regulation (EC) 45/2001 of the European Parliament and of the Council of 18 December 2000 on the protection of individuals with regard to the processing of personal data by the Community institutions and bodies and on the free movement of such data [2001] OJ L8/1.

[234] European Commission Antitrust Manual of Procedures, Internal DG Competition working documents on procedures for the application of Articles 101 and 102 TFEU, March 2012, Module 12 'Access to file and confidentiality', paras 32–4.

[235] See generally Case T-39/90 *Samenwerkende Elektriciteitsproduktiebedrijven (SEP) v Commission* [1991] ECR II-1497, para 55; Case C-67/91 *Dirección General de Defensa de la Competencia (DGDC) v Asociación Española de Banca Privada (AEB) and others* [1992] ECR I-4785, para 37. On appeal in the *SEP* case, the ECJ stressed the limits of such protection, while at the same time referring to the general right of undertakings to the protection of their business secrets as a basis of constraining the Commission's powers to transmit certain information even to the competent Member States authorities. See Case C-36/92 P *Samenverkende Elektriciteits-produktiebedrijven (SEP) v Commission II* [1994] ECR I-1911, para 27 et seq. European Commission Antitrust Manual of Procedures, Internal DG Competition working documents on procedures for the application of Articles 101 and 102 TFEU, March 2012, Module 12 'Access to file and confidentiality', para 30. As regards the question of whether the 'SEP-scenario' still applies, see Ch 3, 'The Role of National Competition Authorities', para 3.76 et seq.

secrecy.[236] Secondly, without prejudice to Articles 12 and 15 of Regulation 1/2003, Article 28(1) prohibits the *use of information* acquired as a result of the application of Articles 17 to 22 (measures of enquiry) for any purpose other than that for which it has been requested.[237] These two safeguards are of a complementary nature. They have to be respected by both the EU and national administrations, which means that the requirement of confidential treatment also concerns information transmitted to Member States as a result of cooperation between authorities as provided in Article 12 of Regulation 1/2003.[238] In addition, Article 28(2) of Regulation 1/2003 also applies to all representatives and experts of Member States attending meetings of the Advisory Committee pursuant to Article 14 of Regulation 1/2003.[239]

4.88 The general principle of the protection of business secrets is also reflected in other provisions.[240] For instance, Article 30(2) of Regulation 1/2003 provides that the publication of decisions 'shall have regard to the legitimate interest of undertakings in the protection of their business secrets.' Despite its seemingly more restrictive wording, this again also includes any information covered by the professional secrecy obligation.[241]

2. Use of the information

4.89 Article 28(1) of Regulation 1/2003 provides that '[w]ithout prejudice to Articles 12 and 15, information collected pursuant to Articles 17 to 22 shall be used only for the purpose for which it was acquired'.[242] Measures of inquiry, like requests for information, interviews, or inspections require the Commission, or the competent national authority acting at its request, to inform the addressee of the specific purpose of the investigation. Information[243] and documents obtained as a result of such investigative measures may be used only to determine whether or not Articles 101 and 102 TFEU have been infringed in the specific case at hand. Conversely, they must not be used either in other types of proceedings (eg, merger control, criminal, or customs cases) or in other proceedings (for different purposes) based on the same competition rules. However, Article 28(1) should not be construed as meaning:

> that the Commission is barred from initiating an inquiry in order to verify or supplement information which it happened to obtain during a previous investigation if that information

---

[236] This obligation gives effect to Art 339 TFEU, see Case C-67/91 *Dirección General de Defensa de la Competencia (DGDC) v Asociación Española de Banca Privada (AEB) and others* [1992] ECR I-4785, para 21.

[237] This also prevents the sharing of such information with other administrative departments that deal with matters unrelated to competition policy (eg departments at national level which are responsible for managing public undertakings). See Case T-39/90 *Samenwerkende Elektriciteitsproduktiebedrijven (SEP) v Commission* [1991] ECR II-1497, paras 55–6. For the use of information obtained during an inspection in a subsequent investigation against another undertaking, or against the same undertaking with regard to a different subject matter, see Case 85/87 *Dow Benelux v Commission* [1989] ECR 3137, paras 17–20; Joined Cases C-238/99 C-245/99, C-247/99, C-250/99, C-252/99, and C-254/99 *Limburgse Vinyl Maatschappij NV and others v Commission* [2002] ECR I-8375, paras 298–307.

[238] See Case T-39/90 *Samenwerkende Elektriciteitsproduktiebedrijven (SEP) v Commission* [1991] ECR II-1497, para 55, *in fine.*

[239] See also Commission Notice on best practices for the conduct of proceedings concerning Articles 101 and 102 TFEU [2011] OJ C308/6, para 144.

[240] See also Arts 14(6), 27(2), (4), and 30(2) of Reg 1/2003 as well as Arts 8, 14(6) and (8), 15(2) to (4), and 16 of Reg 773/2004.

[241] See Case T-198/03 *Bank Austria Creditanstalt v Commission* [2006] ECR II-1429, paras 76, 79, and 88; Case T-474/04 *Pergan Hilfsstoffe für industrielle Prozesse v Commission* [2007] ECR II-4225, para 64.

[242] The same should apply to other information obtained by the Commission during investigations with regard to individual cases, for instance information included in commitment offers pursuant to Art 9 of Reg 1/2003. See by analogy Case C-67/91 *Dirección General de Defensa de la Competencia (DGDC) v Asociación Española de Banca Privada (AEB) and others* [1992] ECR I-4785, para 48 et seq (concerning information transmitted in applications or notifications for individual clearance or exemption in the framework of Reg 17).

[243] Unlike Art 28(2) of Reg 1/2003, Art 28(1) is not limited to information of the kind covered by the professional secrecy obligation.

indicates the existence of conduct contrary to the competition rules in the Treaty. Such a bar would go beyond what is necessary to protect professional secrecy and the rights of the defence and would thus constitute an unjustified hindrance to the performance by the Commission of its task of ensuring compliance with the competition rules in the common market and to bring to light infringements of Articles [101] and [102] of the Treaty.[244]

Hence, the Commission is not prevented from requesting the same documents in connection with another procedure, or to initiate further inspections based on information obtained during a prior, lawful[245] investigation.[246]

The prohibition on the use of information is without prejudice to Articles 12 and 15 of Regulation 1/2003. Article 12 of Regulation 1/2003 allows the Commission and NCAs to 'provide one another with and use in evidence any matter of fact or of law, including confidential information'.[247] Several limitations apply, which can be summarized as follows:[248] **4.90**

(a) The information exchanged may be used only 'for the purpose of applying Articles [101] and [102] of the Treaty', although it may also be used to apply national competition law 'in the same case and in parallel' to EU rules where this 'does not lead to a different outcome'.

(b) Information exchanged shall only be used in respect of the subject matter for which it was collected.

(c) Information exchanged can only be used in evidence to impose sanctions on natural persons where (i) the law of the transmitting authority foresees sanctions of a similar kind in relation

---

[244] See Case 85/87 *Dow Benelux v Commission* [1989] ECR 3137, paras 19–20.

[245] The Commission has to explain the purpose of its investigation and may only request information, or carry out an inspection, which is 'necessary' (Arts 18(1), 20(1) of Reg 1/2003). Also, both requests for information and inspections require that the Commission acts on the basis of some initial suspicion based on verifiable facts. See, for instance, Case C-94/00 *Roquette Frères SA v Directeur général de la concurrence, de la consommation et de la répression des fraudes, and Commission* [2002] ECR I-9011, paras 54, 55, 61, and 99; Case T-339/04 *France Télécom v Commission* [2007] ECR II-521, paras 60 and 62; Case T-99/04 *AC-Treuhand v Commission* [2008] ECR II-1501, para 55. The requirement to indicate the presumed facts which the Commission seeks to investigate is to ensure that the latter does not carry out its investigation on a speculative basis, without having any concrete suspicion (a 'fishing expedition'). See Opinion of AG Kokott in Case C-109/10 P *Solvay SA v Commission* [2011] OJ C370/12, para 138.

[246] See Joined Cases T-305/94, T-306/94, T-307/94, T-313/94 to T-316/94, T-318/94, T-325/94, T-328/94, T-329/94, and T-335/94 *Limburgse Vinyl Maatschappij NV and others v EC Commission* [1999] ECR II-931, paras 472–7. See also Case C-67/91 *Direccion General de Defensa de la Competencia (DGDC) v Asociación Española de Banca Privada (AEB) and others* [1992] ECR I-4785, paras 39, 42, and 43 (no 'acute amnesia'); Case 112/98 *Mannesmannröhren-Werke v Commission* [2001] ECR II-729, paras 85–7.

[247] See also Commission Notice on cooperation within the Network of Competition Authorities [2004] OJ C101/43, paras 26–9 and 40–2. This new information exchange system has been somewhat criticized on the basis that the information handled by the Commission and NCAs will now be subject to both national and EU law, with different standards and guarantees. See Kerse & Khan, *EC Antitrust Procedure* (6th edn, Sweet & Maxwell 2012) para 5-032 (for example on legal professional privilege); M Araujo, 'The Respect of Fundamental Rights within the European Network of Competition Authorities' ch 21 in BE Hawk (ed), International Antitrust Law & Policy, Annual Proceedings of the Fordham Institute (2004) 511, 526–7 and n 61, regarding the compatibility of Art 12 with the ruling in Case C-67/91 *Direccion General de Defensa de la Competencia (DGDC) v Asociación Española de Banca Privada (AEB) and others* ('Spanish Banks') [1992] ECR I-4785. D Reichelt, 'To What Extent does the Cooperation within the European Competition Network Protect the Rights of the Undertakings?' (2005) CML Rev 745, 777–8.

[248] See also Recital 16 of Reg 1/2003 and Commission Notice on cooperation within the Network of Competition Authorities [2004] OJ C101/43, para 28. As regards corporate statements under the Leniency Notice, see Commission Notice on Immunity from fines and reduction of fines in cartel cases [2005] OJ C298/17, para 35. As regards settlement submissions see Commission Notice on the conduct of settlement procedures in view of the adoption of Decisions pursuant to Art 7 and Art 23 of Council Regulation (EC) No 1/2003 in cartel cases [2008] OJ C167/1, para 37. See Ch 3, 'The Role of the National Competition Authorities'.

to an infringement of Articles 101 or 102 TFEU; (ii) the information has been collected in a way which respects the same level of protection of the defence rights of natural persons as provided for under the national rules of the receiving authority. In the latter case, the receiving authority may not use the information exchanged to impose custodial sanctions.[249]

4.91 In addition, in proceedings for the application of Articles 101 and 102 TFEU, courts of the Member States may ask the Commission to transmit to them information in its possession (Article 15(1) of Regulation 1/2003).[250] This obligation, which seeks to protect the rights of litigants deriving from the direct effect of Articles 101 and 102 TFEU which the national courts must safeguard, is an expression of the principle of sincere cooperation (Article 4(3) TEU) which requires the Commission to provide active assistance to any national judicial authority dealing with the infringement of EU rules.[251]

4.92 In so far as documents from the Commission's administrative file are produced to the national court, there is a presumption that the latter will guarantee professional secrecy, and in particular protect business secrets.[252] At the same time, the Commission must take all necessary precautions to ensure that the right of the undertakings concerned with protection of that information is not undermined by or during the transmission of the documents to the national courts.[253] This

---

[249] According to the EU legislature, 'the rights of defence enjoyed by undertakings in the various systems can be considered as sufficiently equivalent' (Recital 16 of Reg 1/2003). However, it should be noticed that differences among ECN members still exist. For instance, Belgium and the UK deem as eligible for non-disclosure lawyer–client communications with in-house legal counsel, while other members exclude in-house lawyers' correspondence from the mentioned privilege either completely (Spain, France, Sweden, or the European Commission itself) or partially (as in the Netherlands, where legal privilege merely applies to correspondence between undertakings and lawyers admitted to the bar, in-house lawyers seldom being admitted to the bar). See M Araujo, 'The Respect of Fundamental Rights within the European Network of Competition Authorities' ch 21 in BE Hawk (ed), International Antitrust Law & Policy, Annual Proceedings of the Fordham Institute (2004) 511, 523; M van der Woude, 'Exchange of Information within the European Competition Network: Scope and Limits' in *European Competition Law Annual 2002: Constructing the EU Network of Competition Authorities* (2002) 13. K Dekeyser and E De Smijter, 'The Exchange of Evidence Within the ECN' [2005] Legal Issues of Economic Integration 161, 171, state that because of mutual recognition, such a difference in standards cannot prevent the receiving ECN member from using in evidence information exchanged to the extent that it was legally collected by the transmitting ECN member according to its home rules. At the time when the draft Reg 1/2003 was under discussion, M van der Woude suggested a number of principles that should be cumulatively respected in the course of information exchanges and indicated several procedural mechanisms for their enforcement. These principles would include: (i) the right to the highest standard of confidentiality; (ii) the right to the most favourable conditions; and (iii) the right to a complete transfer. While these principles may not exist under Reg 1/2003, national law could help to implement them.
[250] See Commission Notice on the co-operation between the Commission and the courts of the EU Member States in the application of Articles 81 and 82 EC [2004] OJ C101/54, paras 21–6. See also Commission Notice on the conduct of settlement procedures in view of the adoption of Decisions pursuant to Article 7 and Article 23 of Council Regulation (EC) No 1/2003 in cartel cases [2008] OJ C167/1, para 39. For information on the application of Art 15(1) of Reg 1/2003, see also DG COMP's website at <http://ec.europa.eu/competition/court/antitrust_requests.html>.
[251] Case T-353/94 *Postbank v Commission* [1996] ECRII-921, paras 64, 65, and 67.
[252] Case T-353/94 *Postbank v Commission* [1996] ECRII-921, paras 69 and 72. There may also be a duty under Art 4(3) TEU for national courts to prevent the misuse of documents obtained in competition cases. See J Temple Lang, 'Developments, Issues and New Remedies—The Duties of National Authorities and Courts under Article 10 of the EC Treaty' [2004] Fordham International Law Journal 1904, 1922. See Ch 2, 'The Role of National Judicial Authorities', para 2.40 et seq.
[253] In Case T-164/12 *Alstom v Commission* (pending), Alstom has appealed to the GC against the Commission's disclosure of certain documents to the High Court of England and Wales in connection with an action for damages against the cartel participants of the Gas Insulated Switchgear cartel It also applied for interim measures to prevent disclosure. The President of the GC concluded that the balance of interests lay in favour of granting interim measures to suspend transmission to the High Court of the confidential version of Alstom's reply to the Commission's statement of objections in the cartel case, pending the conclusion of the appeal, Case T-164/12 R *Alstom v Commission*, Order of the President of the GC of 29 November 2012.

may include, in particular, informing these undertakings of the documents to be transmitted and giving them the opportunity to state their views.[254] Also, before transmitting information covered by professional secrecy to a national court, the Commission will remind the court of its obligation under EU law to uphold the rights which Article 339 TFEU confers on natural and legal persons and it will ask the court whether it can and will guarantee protection of confidential information and business secrets. Only if the national court has offered such a guarantee will the Commission transmit the information requested, indicating those parts which are covered by professional secrecy and those which are not and can therefore be disclosed.[255] In exceptional cases, the Commission may even refuse transmission of information and/or documents to the national courts where this is the only way of ensuring protection of the rights of third parties or for overriding reasons relating to the need to safeguard the interests of the EU, for instance in order to avoid the accomplishment of the tasks entrusted to the Commission being jeopardized. This may, for instance, be relevant for leniency statements given the need to safeguard the incentives for undertakings to apply for leniency and admit participation in cartel infringements Accordingly, the Commission will not transmit to national courts information voluntarily submitted by a leniency applicant without the consent of that applicant.[256]

Article 339 TFEU and Article 28 of Regulation 1/2003 do not require the Commission to **4.93** prohibit third parties from producing, in national legal proceedings, documents received in the procedure before the Commission which contain confidential information and business secrets. These provisions, even if they prevent undertakings from transmitting such documents to third parties, allow their disclosure to the national courts.[257] However, as in the situation of a direct transmission from the Commission to the national court, the Commission has to take all necessary precautions to protect the interests of the undertakings from which the information and/or document originates as well as the interests of the Union (see paragraph 4.96 et seq).

3. Protection of information

While Article 28(2) of Regulation 1/2003 protects information covered by the obligation of pro- **4.94** fessional secrecy,[258] this is without prejudice to the exchange and use of information foreseen in Articles 11, 12, 14, 15, and 27. However, since the Commission and the Member States' authorities are equally covered by the obligations of Article 28(2), and since the national courts have to guarantee an adequate level of protection in the context of their duty of loyalty (Article 4(3) TEU),[259] these exceptions do not constitute actual limitations for professional secrecy. At the same time, a real restriction stems from the right of certain parties to be heard. Here, the interest in protecting the information and the interest in their disclosure has to be balanced.[260] As regards the addressees of the Statement of Objections, protection of their defence rights requires that they obtain access to those pieces of evidence on which the Commission intends to rely for

---

[254] Case T-353/94 *Postbank v Commission* [1996] ECR II-921, paras 90–1 and 94–5 (the so-called 'Akzo procedure').

[255] Commission Notice on the co-operation between the Commission and the courts of the EU Member States in the application of Articles 81 and 82 EC [2004] OJ C101/54, para 25.

[256] See Commission Notice on immunity from fines and reduction of fines in cartel cases [2005] OJ C298/17, paras 6, 40, and Commission Notice on the co-operation between the Commission and the courts of the EU Member States in the application of Articles 81 and 82 EC [2004] OJ C101/54, para 26 *in fine*.

[257] See Case T-353/94 *Postbank v Commission* [1996] ECR II-921, paras 66 and 89. While it is no longer true that Reg 1/2003 does not cover the cooperation between the Commission and national courts (cf Art 15 of Reg 1/2003), the reasoning in para 89 of the judgment remains valid.

[258] European Commission Antitrust Manual of Procedures, Internal DG COMP working documents on procedures for the application of Articles 101 and 102 TFEU, March 2012, Module 12 'Access to file and confidentiality', paras 38–9.

[259] See Case T-353/94 *Postbank v Commission* [1996] ECR II-921, paras 66–70.

[260] Case T-198/03 *Bank Austria Creditanstalt v Commission* [2006] ECR II-1429, para 71; Case T-474/04 *Pergan Hilfsstoffe für industrielle Prozesse v Commission* [2007] ECR II-4225, para 65.

its final decision. Consequently, the duty to protect confidential information does not prevent the Commission from disclosing and using information necessary to prove an infringement.[261]

4.95 The provisional qualification of a piece of information as confidential is not a bar to its disclosure if it is 'inculpatory' (necessary to prove an alleged infringement) or could be 'exculpatory' (necessary to exonerate a party).[262] In this case, the need to safeguard the parties' defence rights through the provision of the widest possible access to the Commission's file may outweigh the obligation to protect other parties' confidential information.[263]

4.96 It is for the Commission to assess whether the need to prove an infringement or the parties' defence rights may outweigh the protection of confidentiality, in any specific situation. In other words, for each individual document it has to assess whether the need to disclose is greater than the harm which might result from disclosure,[264] which may justify only granting access to non-confidential summaries or protecting the identity of informants.[265] The Commission should make this assessment as soon as possible. According to the Manproc, the following factors, even if potentially conflicting, may be taken into account:[266]

- The relevance of the information in determining whether or not an infringement has been committed, and its probative value.
- Whether the information is indispensable.
- The degree of sensitivity involved (to what extent would disclosure of the information harm the interests of the person or undertaking in question).
- The preliminary view of the seriousness of the alleged infringement.

4.97 The Commission points out that the public interest in proving a competition law infringement, the parties' interest in having exculpatory information in the file at their disposal for the preparation of their defence, and the information providers' interest in protecting the confidential information will have to be weighed up.[267] The latter interest depends on the damage that the disclosure could cause in the individual case. For example, if information is to be divulged to companies with significant market power, the danger of retaliation against the information providers needs to be taken into account.[268] Information provided by individuals who request confidentiality/anonymity should be treated with the utmost care.[269]

---

[261] Article 27(2), last sentence, of Reg 1/2003; Art 15(3) of Reg 773/2004.

[262] See Art 27(2) of Reg 1/2003; Art. 15(3) of Reg 773/2004, Notice on access to file, para 24.

[263] Case T-30/91 *Solvay v Commission* [1995] ECR II-1775, para 81: 'In the defended proceedings for which Regulation No 17 provides it cannot be for the Commission alone to decide which documents are of use for the defence. The Commission must give the advisers of the undertaking concerned the opportunity to examine documents which may be relevant so that their probative value for the defence can be assessed.'

[264] Recital 14 of Reg 773/2004. See also Commission Notice on the rules for access to the Commission file in cases pursuant to Articles 81 and 82 of the EC Treaty, Articles 53, 54 and 57 of the EEA Agreement and Council Regulation (EC) No 139/2004 [2005] OJ C325/7, para 14.

[265] See Case T-5/02 *Tetra Laval v Commission* [2002] ECR II-4381, paras 99–100; Case 145/83 *Stanley Adams v Commission* [1985] ECR 3539, para 34 et seq.

[266] European Commission Antitrust Manual of Procedures, Internal DG Competition working documents on procedures for the application of Articles 101 and 102 TFEU, March 2012, Module 12 'Access to file and confidentiality', paras 43–4.

[267] European Commission Antitrust Manual of Procedures, Internal DG Competition working documents on procedures for the application of Articles 101 and 102 TFEU, March 2012, Module 12 'Access to file and confidentiality', para 43.

[268] Case T-65/89 *BPB Industries and British Gypsum* [1993] ECR II-389; Case C-310/93 P *BPB Industries and British Gypsum* [1995] ECR I-865.

[269] Exceptionally, the Commission may even have to abstain from using inculpatory evidence which is not essential but whose disclosure could inflict disproportionate harm on the informant. See Case 107/82 *Allgemeine Elektrizitäts-Gesellschaft AEG-Telefunken AG v Commission* [1983] 3151, para 24.

The practical guidance given by the Manproc allows the Commission case team to choose to **4.98**
provide the information providers with a draft non-confidential version of their documents.
However, depending on the characteristics of the individual case, to reconcile conflicting interests it can prove useful to reveal the confidential information (only) partially or in an anonymous
manner.[270]

As set out in detail in the Manproc, the Commission considers that it is entitled to do the **4.99**
following:

- Use information against the addressee of the final decision in a non-confidential or anonymous manner. According to the case law,[271] the Commission would have the right to use in
  its final decision confidential information that has only been revealed in a non-confidential or
  anonymous manner.[272]
- Oblige the information providers to (partially) reveal information which is to be used in the
  final decision or which could be exculpatory. According to Regulations 1/2003 and 773/2004,
  the confidential nature of a document is not a bar to its disclosure in these cases. Pursuant to
  Article 27 (2) in fine of Regulation 1/2003, the Commission is not prevented from disclosing
  and using information necessary to prove an infringement (using the 'Akzo' procedure).

In the Commission's opinion, many disputes can be avoided if it is made clear to the parties **4.100**
that a confidentiality claim is accepted or refused with a view to establishing a Statement of
Objections and in no way precludes a later assessment of the confidentiality of the information in the public version of the decision that will be published online.

As regards third parties (Article 27(3) of Regulation 1/2003), their right to be heard is more **4.101**
limited than that of the parties concerned. Consequently, they will not have access to business
secrets, nor to other confidential information, at least generally.[273]

Requests for confidentiality are quite common in practice. Information will be classified as **4.102**
confidential where the information provider has substantiated its confidentiality claim and provided a non-confidential version that has been provisionally accepted by the Commission.[274]
Article 16 of Regulation 773/2004 provides for a procedure for the identification and protection of confidential information.[275] According to Article 16(1) of Regulation 773/04, the

---

[270] This should only be done if it is indeed impossible for the companies to which the information is disclosed to identify directly or indirectly the provider of the information. This will depend on the circumstances
of each case. European Commission Antitrust Manual of Procedures, Internal DG Competition working
documents on procedures for the application of Articles 101 and 102 TFEU, March 2012, Module 12 'Access
to file and confidentiality', para 44.

[271] Case T-44/00 *Mannesmann Röhrenwerke* [2004] ECR II-2223, para 84.

[272] The GC would have acknowledged that the Commission may make use of an element of evidence
even if it would not disclose the identity of the informant to the addressee of the Statement of Objections.
European Commission Antitrust Manual of Procedures, Internal DG Competition working documents on
procedures for the application of Articles 101 and 102 TFEU, March 2012, Module 12 'Access to file and
confidentiality', para 44.

[273] Articles 6(1), 8(1), 14(6), (8) of Reg 773/2004. See, however, Case 53/85 *AKZO Chemie v Commission*
[1986] ECR 1965, para 27; Case T-9/99 *HFB Holding für Fernwärmetechnik-Beteiligungsgesellschaft and
Others v Commission* [2002] ECR II-1487, para 364.

[274] European Commission Antitrust Manual of Procedures, Internal DG COMP working documents on
procedures for the application of Articles 101 and 102 TFEU, March 2012, Module 12 'Access to file and
confidentiality', para 35. See also para 46, which provides that after inspections and the unsolicited submission of information, the case team should clarify which documents can be returned on the basis that they are
not objectively linked to the investigation and request immediately the confidentiality status of the remaining
documents by sending a letter to the parties asking them for a non-confidential version of those documents,
to be enclosed, by copying them on a CD-ROM, if appropriate.

[275] See also the Commission Notice on the rules for access to the Commission file in cases pursuant to
Articles 81 and 82 of the EC Treaty, Articles 53, 54 and 57 of the EEA Agreement and Council Regulation

Commission will not communicate or make accessible confidential information or documents, and in particular business secrets. Therefore, any person who makes known his/her views, or subsequently submits further information to the Commission in the course of the same procedure, must clearly identify any material which is considered to be confidential, giving the reasons for this, and provide a separate non-confidential version by the date set by the Commission. This concerns parties or complainants who submit observations on the Statement of Objections (Articles 6(1), 10(2)), complainants who comment on a letter rejecting their complaint (Article 7(1)), or third parties who have been given the opportunity to make their views known (Article 13(1) and (3)).[276]

4.103 Instructions on how to submit claims for non-confidentiality are set out in the annex on business secrets and other confidential information, based on Article 16 of Regulation 773/2004 and paragraphs 39 to 43 of the Notice on access to the file, sent together with the Commission's request for information or request for non-confidential versions. The Manproc describes the procedure as follows:[277]

- The case-team may/will ask the provider of information to provide draft non-confidential versions of the documents in which the provider should first only highlight the information considered confidential or a business secret so that it remains legible.
- The information that the provider of information considers confidential can then be readily identified by the case team. The highlighted text together with the table of confidentiality claims, providing the reason for the confidentiality claim and, if necessary, a non-confidential summary of the confidential information, will form the basis of any discussions on the treatment of the content.
- At the latest, once the case team is preparing access to the file, it will assess the claims for confidential treatment and review the documents submitted accordingly.
- Once the claims for confidentiality are accepted, the case team asks for a final, blacked-out version of the document (including annexes) to be produced.
- In general, confidentiality cannot be claimed for the entire or whole sections of the document as it is normally possible to protect confidential information with limited redactions.
- The non-confidential document should keep the same format as the original version. Thus, if the provider of information claims confidentiality for only some parts of a document, the provider is requested to furnish an accessible non-confidential version of the entire document. In other words, if a five-page document has been submitted, the non-confidential version of that document must also contain five pages. Headings of the documents and/or the headings of the columns should not be redacted, nor columns or spaces in tables and/or pictures left empty.

4.104 Where information providers do not respond or fail to comply with the provisions setting out how to submit confidentiality claims (in particular with the obligation to properly justify the claim and submit a meaningful summary of the redacted information), the Commission may assume that the documents or statements concerned do not contain confidential information and that the undertaking has no objections to the disclosure thereof in their entirety. The standard confidentiality annex expressly reminds companies of these consequences (see

---

(EC) No 139/2004 [2005] OJ C325/7, and the Commission Notice on best practices for the conduct of proceedings concerning Articles 101 and 102 TFEU [2011] OJ C308/6, paras 41 and 94.

[276] There may be other parties from which, or circumstances in which, the Commission receives confidential information.

[277] European Commission Antitrust Manual of Procedures, Internal DG Competition working documents on procedures for the application of Articles 101 and 102 TFEU, March 2012, Module 12 'Access to file and confidentiality', para 47.

also Article 16(4) of Regulation 773/2004).[278] However, in view of Article 339 TFEU, the Commission may not rely on this provision of secondary law in order to disclose information which is obviously of a confidential nature.

Article 16 of Regulation 773/2004 does not contain any legal obligation to send a reminder **4.105** to an information provider if the request is not answered within the time limit. In particular, in cases where an information provider is represented by an external lawyer, it can be presumed that they are aware of the legal provisions and their consequences.[279]

As regards dealing with confidentiality claims, the Commission considers it preferable to set- **4.106** tle all claims for confidentiality before the notification of the Statement of Objections to the parties, in order to ensure complete access to the file.[280] In practice, the case team should try to solve unjustified confidentiality claims informally with the information provider.[281] The DG COMP informs the information provider in writing that:

- it will provisionally accept those claims which seem justified. In any event, the information provider should be reminded of the Commission's right to reconsider its initial evaluation at a later stage of the handling of the case;[282] or
- it does not agree with the confidentiality claim in whole or in part, provides reasons why it intends to disclose this information, and sets a time limit within which the information provider may inform the Commission in writing of its views.[283]

Where the Commission does not agree with the confidentiality claim from the outset or **4.107** where it takes the view that the provisional acceptance of the confidentiality claim should be reversed, and thus intends to disclose information, it will grant the person or undertaking in question an opportunity to express its views.[284] In such cases, DG COMP will inform the person or undertaking in writing of its intention to disclose information, unless a reasoned

---

[278] European Commission Antitrust Manual of Procedures, Internal DG COMP working documents on procedures for the application of Articles 101 and 102 TFEU, March 2012, Module 12 'Access to file and confidentiality', para 48.

[279] European Commission Antitrust Manual of Procedures, Internal DG Competition working documents on procedures for the application of Articles 101 and 102 TFEU, March 2012, Module 12 'Access to file and confidentiality', para 49.

[280] European Commission Antitrust Manual of Procedures, Internal DG Competition working documents on procedures for the application of Articles 101 and 102 TFEU, March 2012, Module 12 'Access to file and confidentiality', para 50. See also para 42 of the Notice on access to file: 'Where the Directorate General for Competition does not agree with the confidentiality claim from the outset or where it takes the view that the provisional acceptance of the confidentiality claim should be reversed, and thus intends to disclose information, it will grant the person or undertaking in question an opportunity to express its views. In such cases, the Directorate General for Competition will inform the person or undertaking in writing of its intention to disclose information, give its reasons and set a time-limit within which such person or undertaking may inform it in writing of its views. If, following submission of those views, a disagreement on the confidentiality claim persists, the matter will be dealt with by the Hearing Officer according to the applicable Commission terms of reference of the Hearing Officers.'

[281] European Commission Antitrust Manual of Procedures, Internal DG Competition working documents on procedures for the application of Articles 101 and 102 TFEU, March 2012, Module 12 'Access to file and confidentiality', para 52.

[282] One should keep in mind that the Notice on access to the file expressly foresees the possibility of provisionally accepting substantiated confidentiality claims accompanied by non-confidential versions, while reserving the possibility of reversing a provisional acceptance at a later stage (see para 42 of the Notice on access to the file).

[283] European Commission Antitrust Manual of Procedures, Internal DG Competition working documents on procedures for the application of Articles 101 and 102 TFEU, March 2012, Module 12 'Access to file and confidentiality', para 52.

[284] European Commission Antitrust Manual of Procedures, Internal DG Competition working documents on procedures for the application of Articles 101 and 102 TFEU, March 2012, Module 12 'Access to file and confidentiality', para 53.

request for confidentiality is lodged with the Hearing Officer within a given deadline. This letter is sent by a form requiring acknowledgement of receipt with a copy to the Hearing Officer.[285]

4.108 If the information provider maintains its position, the Hearing Officer will address the issue and, if necessary, apply the Akzo Procedure,[286] in accordance with Article 8 of the Hearing Officer Terms of Reference.[287]

- In practice, the Hearing Officer may send a 'pre Article 8' letter.
- If the company concerned still objects to the disclosure of this information, but the Commission finds that it should not be protected and may therefore be disclosed, that finding must be stated in a reasoned decision of the Hearing Officer (an Article 8 Decision).
- This decision is adopted by delegation procedure by the Hearing Officer and notified to the concerned company.
- The company concerned is thereby given the opportunity to bring an action before the GC with a view to having the Commission's assessment reviewed.
- The company concerned must inform the Hearing Officer within a given time limit from the day of notification of the Article 8 Decision whether they intend to lodge an appeal with the GC and to apply for interim measures.[288]

4.109 If the company concerned has lodged an appeal and applied for interim measures before that deadline, the Commission cannot disclose the relevant information until the Court has taken a decision on the request for interim relief. In order for the protection pursuant to Article 339 TFEU to be effective, the decision of the Hearing Officer may not be implemented prior to the court's ruling on the interim measure application.[289] Thus, undertakings will be able to prevent disclosure until the GC has had an opportunity to examine the merits of the Commission's intention to disclose the document or information at issue to third parties.

4.110 Under Article 8(2) of the Hearing Officer Terms of Reference, where the undertaking or person concerned objects to the disclosure of the information but it is found that the information is not protected and may therefore be disclosed, that finding shall be stated in a reasoned decision which is notified to the undertaking or person concerned. The decision must specify the date after which the information will be disclosed, which cannot be less than one week from the date of notification.[290] Partial access can be granted in a manner determined by the Hearing Officer, where appropriate.[291] If information providers misuse the procedure to delay the Commission's investigation, they should be reminded that the Commission may

---

[285] Commission Notice on the rules for access to the Commission file in cases pursuant to Articles 81 and 82 of the EC Treaty, Articles 53, 54 and 57 of the EEA Agreement and Council Regulation (EC) No 139/2004 [2005] OJ C325/7, para 42. This prior information by the services of DG COMP is in itself not a challengeable act. See Case T-90/96 *Automobiles Peugeot SA v Commission* [1997] ECR II-663, paras 33–7; Case T-213/01 R *Österreichische Postsparkasse AG v Commission* [2001] ECR I-3963, paras 46 and 49.

[286] As first set out by the ECJ in Case 53/85 *AKZO Chemie v Commission* [1986] ECR 1965.

[287] Decision of the President of the European Commission of 13 October 2011 on the function and terms of reference of the hearing officer in certain competition proceedings [2011] OJ L275, para 29.

[288] European Commission Antitrust Manual of Procedures, Internal DG Competition working documents on procedures for the application of Articles 101 and 102 TFEU, March 2012, Module 12 'Access to file and confidentiality', para 54.

[289] See Case 53/85 *AKZO Chemie v Commission* [1986] ECR 1965, para 29.

[290] As stated, the basic features of this procedure were essentially established in the *Akzo*, Case 53/85 *AKZO Chemie v Commission* [1986] ECR 1965. See also Case T-219/01 *Commerzbank AG v Commission* [2003] ECR II-2843, paras 69–70.

[291] See also Commission Notice on best practices for the conduct of proceedings concerning Articles 101 and 102 TFEU [2011] OJ C308/6, para 98.

consider this an event of non-cooperation and take it into account as an aggravating factor when setting a possible fine against the information providers.[292]

According to the Notice on Antitrust Best Practices,[293] further to the possibilities contem-   **4.111**
plated in the Notice on access to the file, there are two additional procedural practices that may be used for the purpose of alleviating the burden on the parties to redact their submissions in relation to confidential information. These procedural practices—the negotiated disclosure procedure and the rules governing access to confidential information in a data room—may be offered by DG COMP where it considers it to be useful, and are typically conducted in cases where there is only a limited number of undertakings. In the Manproc, the Commission stresses that both procedural practices can be beneficial not only for the party being granted access to the file, but also for the information providers, since they would not have to redact their confidential material.[294]

Under the negotiated disclosure procedure, in certain cases, especially those with a very   **4.112**
voluminous file or which raise serious concerns about the full disclosure of information to addressees of the Statement of Objections, DG COMP may accept that the parties agree voluntarily to use a negotiated disclosure procedure. The party entitled to access to the file agrees bilaterally with the information providers claiming confidentiality to receive all or some of the information they have provided to the Commission and is contained in the Commission's file, including confidential information (instead of only being given access to the redacted version of their submissions).

The party being granted access to the file limits access to the information to a restricted   **4.113**
circle of persons (to be decided on a case-by-case basis, if requested, under the supervision of DG COMP). To the extent that this type of access to the file would amount to a restriction of a party's right to have full access to the investigation file, it must waive its right to have access to the file vis-à-vis the Commission. Normally, the party would receive the information subject to the negotiated disclosure procedure directly from the information provider. However, if the information that is subject to such an agreement were, exceptionally, provided to the restricted circle of persons by the Commission, the information providers would have to waive their rights to confidentiality vis-à-vis the Commission.[295]

Exceptionally, the Commission may also grant access to the file through a 'data room' proce-   **4.114**
dure organized by DG COMP.[296] This procedure is typically used for the disclosure of quantitative data relevant for econometric analysis. The purpose of this procedure is to provide access under strict rules to sensitive data constituting business secrets from third parties in

---

[292] Commission Antitrust Manual of Procedures, Internal DG Competition working documents on procedures for the application of Articles 101 and 102 TFEU, March 2012, Module 12 'Access to file and confidentiality', para 56.

[293] Commission Notice on best practices for the conduct of proceedings concerning Articles 101 and 102 TFEU [2011] OJ C308/6, paras 96–7.

[294] European Commission Antitrust Manual of Procedures, Internal DG Competition working documents on procedures for the application of Articles 101 and 102 TFEU, March 2012, Module 12 'Access to file and confidentiality', para 106.

[295] Commission Notice on best practices for the conduct of proceedings concerning Articles 101 and 102 TFEU [2011] OJ C308/6, para 96. European Commission Antitrust Manual of Procedures, Internal DG Competition working documents on procedures for the application of Articles 101 and 102 TFEU, March 2012, Module 12 'Access to file and confidentiality', paras 107–10.

[296] Commission Notice on best practices for the conduct of proceedings concerning Articles 101 and 102 TFEU [2011] OJ C308/6, para 97. European Commission Antitrust Manual of Procedures, Internal DG Competition working documents on procedures for the application of Articles 101 and 102 TFEU, March 2012, Module 12 'Access to file and confidentiality', paras 111–19.

order to verify the Commission's methodology and conclusions drawn from the data, economic or otherwise, underlying the reasons behind the Statement of Objections, whilst still maintaining the necessary confidentiality.

4.115 Empirical analysis sometimes requires the Commission to review highly confidential data provided by different market participants that in principle includes both the methodologies applied by the Commission and the general structure and nature of the data itself. Depending on the type of data used, this can raise difficult confidentiality issues. In such a case, a 'data room' is organized that allows a restricted group of persons, ie the external legal counsel and/or the economic advisers of the addressee(s) of a Statement of Objections, to access, within DG COMP's premises, confidential information obtained from third parties during the course of the investigation so as to verify the Commission's analysis and to advise the parties as regards this confidential information whilst maintaining the necessary confidentiality. The advisers may make use of the information contained in the data room for the purpose of defending their client, but may not disclose any confidential information to their client. This has been applied several times to quantitative data, most often in relation to an econometric exercise. The Commission indicates that whether and in what form third parties need to be contacted before their data is used for a data room is very case-specific, ie it depends on the type of data-room procedure and the type of data involved. It is recommended that the appropriate arrangements be discussed beforehand with the Hearing Officer's team.

4.116 To the extent that this type of access to the file would amount to a restriction of a party's right to have full access to the investigation file, the procedural guarantees provided for in Article 8 of the Hearing Officer's Terms of Reference (the so-called 'Akzo procedure') apply. Equally, the Hearing Officer may decide pursuant to Article 8(4) of these Terms of Reference that the data-room procedure should be used in those limited cases where access to certain confidential information is indispensable for a party's defence rights and where the Hearing Officer considers that, on balance, the conflict between respect for confidentiality and defence rights is best solved in this way. The Hearing Officer will not take such a decision if he considers that the data room is not appropriate and that access to the information should be given in a different form (eg following the standard procedure through non-confidential versions).

4.117 The data-room rules need to be adjusted to the specific nature of each case. The advisers of the addressee(s) of a Statement of Objections are provided with access to several PC workstations in a 'data room' on the Commission's premises, equipped with the necessary software and, if relevant, the necessary data sets and a log of the regressions used to support the Commission's case. There is no network connection and no external communication is allowed. The advisers are permitted to remain in the room during normal working hours and, if justified, access should be provided for consecutive days (typically two to three days). The advisers are strictly prohibited from taking copies, notes, or summaries of the documents, and may remove from the data room only a final report, which is verified by the case team in order to ensure that it does not contain any confidential information. Each adviser signs a Confidentiality Agreement and is presented with a set of Conditions of Special Access to the Data Room before entering the data room.

4.118 The PCs or notebooks are provided by DG COMP's IT Service. The DG COMP's PCs/notebooks are not normally equipped with econometrics software, and installation on several machines takes some time. The IT Services will provide memory sticks to move data between PCs. Advisers must not use any of their own storage devices and wifi, Bluetooth, and similar connections must be disabled.

The advisers' final report is intended to enable them to verify the veracity and accuracy of the   **4.119**
Commission's analysis and the nature of the underlying data. However, it must not reveal any
business secrets. What constitutes a business secret must be assessed carefully in each case. In
short, the data-room procedure can be a useful tool reconciling confidentiality requirements
with considerations relating to the right to be heard in a pragmatic fashion, especially in those
cases where empirical analysis plays a key role.

5

OPENING OF THE FILE AND
OF PROCEEDINGS; TRANSPARENCY

Luis Ortiz Blanco and Konstantin Jörgens

A. Action Taken by the Commission before a File is Opened

1. Sources of information[1]

Instead of spending its time processing notifications of largely benign agreements, the objective of Regulation 1/2003 was to enable the Commission to use its limited resources to crack down on serious infringements, such as cartels. The widening of the Commission's investigatory powers was precisely aimed at enhancing methods of discovering cartel activity at all levels of enforcement.[2] However, in so doing it is dependent on receiving information from third parties, either informally or through formal complaints. In essence, cartels and other anticompetitive practices can come to light either directly, through whistle-blowers[3] and complaints by **5.01**

---

[1] See also R Sauer in JL Schulte and C Just (eds), *Kartellrecht* (Carl Heymanns Verlag 2012), Art 7 of the Reg 1/2003, para 5 et seq

[2] As regards the Commission's increased investigative powers, see Ch 7, 'Formal Investigative Measures' and Ch 8, 'Inspections'. See also Director-General at Directorate-General for Competition ('DG COMP'), A Italianer, 'Zero Tolerance for International Cartels', Speech at ICN Cartel Workshop 2011, Bruges, 10–13 October 2011, who pointed out that the investigative technique has significantly improved. Since 2006, the Commission has used forensic IT support in about seventy inspections, at 210 sites. The Commission now has in-house trained staff that can proficiently perform such searches. The inspectors, and those of the sister agencies of the European Competition Network ('ECN') are specifically trained. They would also be able to retrieve electronic data that has been hidden, whilst respecting the confidentiality that some of that data may have. The knowledge gained, as well as that of other agencies, is regularly shared in the ECN Forensic IT Working Group and in the ICN Cartel Working Group.

[3] See Observations of the European Commission pursuant to Article 15(3) of Regulation 1/2003 *National Grid Electricity Transmission plc v ABB* and others, November 2011 (available at <http://ec.europa.eu/competition/court/amicus_curiae_2011_national_grid_en.pdf>), in which the Commission published the observations that it made to the English High Court in relation to an application (in a cartel damages action) for disclosure of leniency documents. The Commission explains the importance of its leniency programme with respect to its ability to enforce EU competition law (para 20). The willingness of companies to provide

third parties, or indirectly, through other regulatory activities, such as sector inquiries or merger investigations. The Commission strongly encourages citizens and undertakings to inform public enforcers about suspected infringements of the competition rules as complainants.[4] Thus, to supplement formal complaint proceedings, the Commission also seeks to collect information which does not need to be submitted pursuant to the requirements for complaints under Regulation 1/2003 and Regulation 773/2004,[5] but which may nevertheless be relevant with a view to detecting competition law violations. For this purpose, the Commission created a special website to collect information from citizens and undertakings and their associations who wish to inform the Commission about suspected infringements of Articles 101 and 102 of the Treaty on the Functioning of the European Union ('TFEU').[6] Anyone who is able to show a legitimate interest as a complainant and who submits a complaint in compliance with Form C enjoys certain procedural rights.[7]

---

comprehensive and candid information would be crucial to the success of the leniency programme which is the most effective tool available to the Commission in detecting secret cartels.

[4] Commission Notice on the handling of complaints by the Commission under Articles 81 and 82 of the EC Treaty ('Notice on Handling of Complaints') [2004] OJ C101/65 sets out a detailed procedure for lodging a complaint with the Commission. See also former Commissioner for Competition Policy, M Monti, 'Proactive Competition Policy and the role of the Consumer', Speech at the European Competition Day, Dublin, 29 April 2004: 'it is of crucial importance that we have active consumers and consumer associations which provide the competition authorities with market information, given that it is consumers who are usually on the receiving end of anti-competitive practices. While a simple letter from one consumer is rarely enough, a series of complaints or a complaint submitted by a consumer association, where the conduct complained of is likely to affect the interests of its members, can normally provide the Commission with a basis to open an investigation'. Vice President of the European Commission responsible for Competition Policy, J Almunia, 'Competition—what's in it for consumers?', Speech at European Competition and Consumer Day, Poznan, 24 November 2011: 'Consumers and consumers' organisations can help us and national competition authorities carry out our work. I urge everyone, especially consumer organisations, to come forward with factual information that may help our investigations. We always welcome this sort of cooperation when it is accompanied by solid and well researched data. There have been cases of successful cooperation with consumers. For instance, the French mobile telephone operators case of 2005, where the French competition authority fined several companies for agreements that distorted competition in the market. The investigation into one of those agreements had been triggered by a complaint from the consumer association "UFC Que Choisir".' See Case C-119/97 *Ufex v Commission* [1999] ECR I-1341, para 74, Opinion of AG Ruiz-Jarabo Colomer in Case C-119/97 *Ufex v Commission* [1999] ECR I-1341, para 7: 'Undertakings which complain of anti-competitive practices perform an activating function or, so to speak, act as catalysts for measures by the Commission involving two orders of interests—the interests of the undertakings themselves in averting commercial damage as a result of the unlawful practices of their competitors, and the general interest that the competition rules should be observed, an interest which is safeguarded by Community law and must be protected by the Commission'. See also the website operated by the Commission: <http://ec.europa.eu/competition/consumers/index_en.html>.

[5] Article 7(2) of Reg 1/2003 and Art 5 (admissibility of complaints) of Reg 773/2004.

[6] There are two ways to inform about suspected infringements: Parties who feel directly affected by the potentially restrictive practice may lodge a formal complaint. The complaint form ('Form C') is available in the Annex to Regulation 773/2004. For more details, see para 5.19. Under Arts 5–9 of the Regulation, formal complaints have to fulfil certain requirements. Information contained in submissions that do not respect these requirements may nevertheless be taken into account as market information. See also Commission Notice on best practices for the conduct of proceedings concerning Articles 101 and 102 TFEU [2011] OJ C308/6, note 18. Market information can be reported by using the following email address: comp-market-information@ec.europa.eu or postal address: European Commission, Competition DG, B–1049 Brussels.

[7] Commission Notice on best practices for the conduct of proceedings concerning Articles 101 and 102 TFEU [2011] OJ C308/6, para 10. The details of the procedure to be followed are set out in Reg 773/2004 ([2004] OJ L123/18) and in the Notice on Handling of Complaints ([2004] OJ C101/65). Natural and legal persons, other than complainants, who show a sufficient interest to be heard and who are admitted to the proceedings by the Hearing Officer also enjoy certain procedural rights in accordance with Art 13 of Reg 773/2004. Conversely, where a complaint is taken up by the Commission only as an own-initiative matter because of the complainant's lack of legitimate interest, no procedural rights will flow to the complainant, see Kerse & Khan, *EC Antitrust Procedure* (6th edn, Sweet & Maxwell 2012) para 2-022.

Further, the Consumer Liaison Office of the Directorate-General for Competition ('DG COMP')   **5.02**
is responsible for receiving information and requests concerning competition problems faced by
end consumers and customers. A team of Consumer Liaison Correspondents responsible for
each economic sector will give advice to consumers within a month of any query. If DG COMP
is not the correct department it will transfer the information to other Directorates-General in
the Commission or to a national authority dealing with competition and consumer protection.[8]
Such information can be the starting point for an investigation by the Commission.[9]

The Commission also relies on the work of the specialist press or may receive information from   **5.03**
internal sources. It may also use information contained in a request for a guidance letter[10] or
information gathered in the context of a sector inquiry under Article 17 of Regulation 1/2003.[11]
Requests for information under Article 18 of Regulation 1/2003[12] and investigations under
Articles 19 (Power to take statements),[13] 20 (inspections), and 21 (inspections of other premises),[14] which have been carried out in the market for a given product, may reveal prohibited
practices in other markets which affect other products.

The Court of Justice ('ECJ') interpreted Article 20(1) of former Regulation 17, which pro-   **5.04**
vided—in the same sense as Article 28 of Regulation 1/2003—that 'information acquired as a
result of the application of Articles 11, 12, 13, and 14 shall be used only for the purpose of the
relevant request or investigation',[15] as not preventing the Commission from relying on information concerning markets or products not directly investigated initially, in order to commence
a new and separate investigation into them.[16] In such cases, the ECJ ruled that Article 28(1)

---

[8] The Consumer Liaison Office was established in December 2003 in order to ensure a permanent dialogue with European consumers. Its tasks include (i) acting as primary contact point for consumer organizations, but also for individual consumers, by establishing more regular and intensified contacts with consumer
organizations; (ii) alerting consumer groups to competition cases when their input might be useful, and advising them on the way they can provide input and express their views; (iii) maintaing contacts with national
competition authorities ('NCAs') regarding consumer protection matters; and (iv) intensifying contacts
between the competition and other Directorates-General, most notably the Health and Consumer Protection
Directorate-General.
[9] Notice on Handling of Complaints [2004] OJ C101/65, paras 3–4. In practice, complaints have
tended not to be the starting point for Commission cartel investigations, although they have been the norm
for NCAs in some Member States. Complaints rarely provide as much evidence as leniency applications, as
the innate secrecy of a cartel prevents third parties from possessing sufficient information. The Commission
will only open an investigation if there is a realistic chance of uncovering sufficient evidence to prove a cartel.
[10] The information remains with the Commission and can be used in subsequent procedures under Reg
1/2003. A request for a guidance letter is without prejudice to the power of the Commission to open proceedings in accordance with Reg 1/2003. Commission Notice on informal guidance relating to novel questions
concerning Articles 81 and 82 of the EC Treaty that arise in individual cases ('Notice on Informal Guidance')
[2004] OJ C101/78, paras 11 and 18.
[11] See para 5.09 et seq.
[12] See Ch 7, on 'Investigation of Cases (II): Formal Investigative Measures in General, Requests for
Information, and Interviews', para 7.24 et seq.
[13] See Ch 7, 'Investigation of Cases (II): Formal Investigative Measures in General, Requests for
Information, and Interviews', para 7.53 et seq.
[14] See Ch 8, 'Investigation of Cases (III): Inspections', para 8.28 et seq and 8.66 et seq.
[15] Articles 11, 12, 13, and 14 of former Reg 17 are equivalent to Arts 18, 17, 22, and 20, respectively, of
Reg 1/2003.
[16] See Case 85/87 *Dow Benelux v Commission* [1989] ECR 3137, para 19. To interpret that provision
otherwise would be tantamount to granting impunity for restrictive practices which come to the notice of
Commission officials accidentally or incidentally. In the Court's view, this would prevent the Commission
from effectively upholding the EU legal order. Indeed, if the fact that such information became known
informally prevented the initiation of proceedings and the imposition of penalties, undertakings themselves
would have an interest in letting information slip out regarding other possible restrictive practices on their
part affecting markets or products not directly under investigation, in order to obtain immunity from penalties in those other areas.

merely obliged the Commission to obtain the necessary information as part of a new procedure separate from the one in which evidence emerged of a different infringement.

5.05   Whilst it is true, therefore, that in EU law—except where there is a specific provision to the contrary—a particular fact may be proved by any *form of evidence* and determination of the probative value of an item of evidence is a matter for the EU Courts, not for legislation, it cannot be maintained that every *item of evidence* produced is usable and has to be evaluated as to its merits by the Commission or the EU judicature.[17] Indeed, according to the case law of the EU Courts, the Commission cannot use the following as evidence in proceedings:[18]

- Statements or documents acquired by the Commission in an earlier case under the same regulation.[19]
- Documents in respect of which the undertaking under investigation has not had an opportunity to exercise its right to be heard during the course of that investigation.[20]
- Communications between lawyers and clients of a legally protected confidential nature.[21]
- Statements made by executives of an undertaking in reply to questions put to them in the course of a preliminary examination of witnesses prior to the initiation of national civil proceedings, where the reply entails admission of an infringement of the competition rules.[22]
- Minutes of questioning from national criminal proceedings, where transmission thereof to the Commission has been declared unlawful by the competent national court.[23]

5.06   Information may also be received from other competition enforcement authorities. A central feature of the modernization of the competition rules is that the Commission and national

---

[17] This applies to both the Commission and NCAs.

[18] See overview given by AG Mengozzi, in Case C-511/06 P *Archer Daniels Midland Co v Commission* [2009] ECR I-5843, 406, para 114

[19] Case 85/87 *Dow Benelux v Commission* [1989] ECR 3137, paras 17–19. See Joined Cases C-238/99 P, C-244/99 P, C-245/99 P, C-247/99 P, C-250/99 P to C-252/99 P, and C-254/99 P *Limburgse Vinyl Maatschappij and Others v Commission ('PVC II')* [2002] ECR I-8375, paras 298–300 and 305.

[20] Case 107/82 *AEG-Telefunken v Commission* [1983] ECR 3151, according to which the Commission could not take account in the final decision, as not being mentioned in the statement of objections, either particular events (see paras 21 and 28) or particular documents (see paras 21 and 27).

[21] See Case 155/79 *AM & S v Commission* [1982] ECR 1575, paras 29–31; see also the more recent rulings in Joined Cases T-125/03 and T-253/03 *Akzo Nobel and Akcros v Commission* [2007] ECR II-3523; Case C-550/07 P *Akzo Nobel Chemicals Ltd and Akcros Chemicals Ltd v European Commission* [2010] ECR I-8301.

[22] See Case C-60/92 *Otto v Postbank* [1993] ECR I-5683, paras 16–20. The Court so held in answering a preliminary question as to whether a party to civil proceedings could shield itself by reliance on the judgment of the Court in Case 374/87 *Orkem v Commission* [1989] ECR 3283 and thereby decline to answer certain questions which might have caused it to admit an infringement of Arts 101 and 102 TFEU. The Court held that EU law did not allow an undertaking in such circumstances to refuse to answer. The quid pro quo for the disclosure to the Commission of such information was that the latter could not rely on it as proof or possible evidence of an infringement. It thus seems that the Commission will, although to a very limited extent, be obliged to suffer 'acute amnesia' (see Case C-67/91 *Dirección General de Defensa de la Competencia (DGDC) v Asociación Española de Banca Privada (AEB) and others* [1992] ECR I-4785, para 39), if anyone supplies it with information from civil proceedings in which a party has been compelled to admit an infringement of the competition rules. As a result, if EU infringement proceedings were initiated on the basis of the same facts, the Commission could be called on to indicate the evidence on which it relied in order to commence its investigations, if the *Otto* judgment were invoked against it.

[23] AG Mengozzi, Conclusions in Case C-511/06 P *Archer Daniels Midland Co v Commission* [2009] ECR I-5843, 406, para 115: 'To those examples of evidence which the Commission is not permitted to use, the judgment under appeal in the present case adds another: that of statements made in a proceeding other than the proceeding being conducted by the Commission itself, where the interested party was not given benefit of the procedural rights to which he was entitled in that context or those he would have enjoyed under Community law if those statements had been taken directly by the Commission.'

competition authorities ('NCAs') should form a network and work closely together in the application of Articles 101 and 102 TFEU. This network provides an infrastructure for the mutual exchange of information, including confidential information, and assistance, thereby expanding considerably the scope for each member of the network to enforce Articles 101 and 102 TFEU effectively.[24] In addition, the Commission is a member of the International Competition Network ('ICN')[25] and has agreements with a number of other antitrust authorities outside the EU under which information may be passed.

2. Sector inquiries[26]

The Commission constantly monitors the EU economy. Direct observation of the various industrial and commercial sectors enables it to detect and then investigate both abuses and agreements infringing competition law. Against these, the Commission will initiate a procedure on its own initiative with a view to imposing a penalty. Regulation 1/2003 enables the Commission to undertake inquiries into sectors of the economy where there is evidence to suggest that competition is being restricted or distorted in an economic sector of the internal market.[27] Sector inquiries are essentially an investigatory tool that allows the Commission to address directly those features of a market that restrict competition.[28]   **5.07**

Inquiries into sectors of the economy may serve to pave the way for individual procedures under Regulation 1/2003. Their main purpose remains, however, to discover possible and emerging restrictions and distortions of competition in a given sector, enabling the Commission better to apprehend the underlying economic situation and take the appropriate remedial action. Data collection undertaken in a sector inquiry covers the legal environment as well as business practices, contracts, technical elements, and financial conditions which help to define which competition law principles should apply to a given sector.[29] Where the Commission has focused its resources on investigating serious infringements, awareness of market dynamics and performance, sector particularities, and obstacles to competition have   **5.08**

---

[24] See Ch 2, 'The Roles of National Competition Authorities', para 3.11 et seq.

[25] <http://www.internationalcompetitionnetwork.org/>.

[26] See N Calvino and A Gee, 'Enquêtes sectorielles: Complément ou substitut de l'action des autorites de concurrence? Le point de vue de la Commission européene' (2010) 2 Concurrences, New Frontiers of Antitrust Conference, 15 February 2010, 9, who point out the increasing importance of this instrument; N Petit, 'Enquêtes sectorielles: Complement ou substitut de l'action des autorites de concurrence? Le "couteau suisse" du droit européen de la concurrence' (2010) 2 Concurrences, New Frontiers of Antitrust Conference, 15 February 2010, 17, which includes a chart showing the results of the sector inquires during the period 2001–2009 (at 27). The author advocates setting up best practices for conducting sector inquiries; I Forrester, 'Sector Inquiries: Complements or Substitutes for Antitrust Enforcement? A European paradox: Imposing maket reform "voluntarily"' (2010) 2 Concurrences, New Frontiers of Antitrust Conference, 15 February 2010, 29, who takes the view that sector inquiries are vehicles for gathering information, but not for launching prosecutions.

[27] See D Wood and N Baverez, 'Sector Inquiries under EU Competition Law' (2005) (Feb) Competition Law Insight 3.

[28] See also former Commissioner for Competition, N Kroes, 'Fact-based competition policy—the contribution of sector inquiries to better regulation, priority setting and detection', Speech 07/186 given at the 13th International Conference on Competition and the 14th European Competition Day, Munich, 26 March 2007, pointing to the perceived benefits of a sector inquiry including (i) the knowledge gained via an inquiry can be used to guide thinking in merger and state aid cases; (ii) sector inquiries can inform and guide proposals for legislation, embedding competition principles and sectoral knowledge into the Commission's wider policy work; (iii) inquiries highlighting problems with sectors in competition terms can help with identifying far-reaching and durable solutions to structural problems with markets; and (iv) sector inquiries can help to identify the right balance between competition policy and regulatory intervention, particularly important for newly liberalized or regulated sectors.

[29] A Crawford and P Adamopoulos, 'Using the Instrument of Sector-Wide Inquiries: Inquiry into Content for 3G Services' (2004) 2 Competition Newsletter 63, 64.

become increasingly important, in particular in emerging and technology-based markets.[30] In this regard, in the Commission's view, sector inquiries provide a particularly appropriate tool for investigating cross-border market concerns and examining sector-wide practices that do not normally fall within the scope of an individual case.[31] In assessing markets to be reviewed, DG COMP typically focuses on sectors where there are only a few players, where cartel activity is recurrent, or where abuses of market power are typical.[32] At one time, this instrument seemed to fall into disuse, or was even abandoned.[33] However, sector inquiries have made a reappearance as one of the key investigatory tools for DG COMP, given its increased focus on major infringements.[34] Such inquiries are aimed at allowing the Commission to analyse allegedly anticompetitive practices in a systematic and transparent manner, and to give NCAs the opportunity to launch their own parallel national investigations on the basis of the Commission's findings.

5.09   The opening of a sector inquiry presupposes, under Article 17(1) of Regulation 1/2003, the adoption of a decision to that effect by the Commission. Since it is not a purely routine decision—despite not being one whose publication is required pursuant to Article 30 of Regulation 1/2003—it must be adopted by the full Commission,[35] after the opinion of the Advisory Committee has been obtained.[36] The decision will define the economic sector

---

[30] See D Wood and N Baverez, 'Sector Inquiries under EU Competition Law' [2005] Competition Law Insight 3, 4; A Crawford and P Adamopoulos, 'Using the Instrument of Sector-Wide Inquiries: Inquiry into Content for 3G Services' (2004) 2 Competition Newsletter 63, 64 with respect to 3rd generation mobile telecommunications networks.

[31] The following sectors have been subject to sector inquiries: pharmaceuticals (see MEMO/09/321 'Antitrust: shortcomings in pharmaceutical sector require further action—frequently asked questions', 8 July 2009), financial services (MEMO/07/382 'Competition: final report of the sector inquiry into business insurance—frequently asked questions', 25 September 2007; MEMO07/40 'Competition: Final report on retail banking inquiry—frequently asked questions', 31 January 2007); energy (MEMO07/15 'Energy sector competition inquiry—final report—frequently asked questions and graphics', 10 January 2007). Earlier sector inquiries related to media (see 'Public presentation of the preliminary findings of the New Media (3G) Sector Inquiry', Brussels, 27 May 2005, available on DG COMP website); the local loop (Commission Press Release IP/02/348 'Slow progress in unbundling of the local loop: Commission publishes report on sector enquiry', 1 March 2002); leased lines (Commission Press Release IP/02/1852 'Price decreases of up to 40% lead Commission to close telecom leased line inquiry' of 12 November 2002); roaming (MEMO 01/262 'Statement on inquiry regarding mobile roaming', 11 July 2001).

[32] Vice President of the European Commission responsible for Competition, J Almunia, 'Competition v Regulation: where do the roles of sector specific and competition regulators begin and end?', Speech at the Centre on Regulation in Europe ('CERRE'), Brussels, 23 March 2010 indicating that the remedies in the Commission's antitrust cases address concrete competition concerns in individual investigations, but that 'the [energy] sector inquiry also helped the Commission to better identify shortcomings and loopholes in the regulatory framework in place and to develop adequate regulatory solutions.' Commission Communication 'A Pro Active Competition Policy for a Competitive Europe' (COM(2004)(204) 293 final); see also former Commissioner for Competition, N Kroes, 'Fact-based competition policy—the contribution of sector inquiries to better regulation, priority setting and detection', Speech 07/186 given at the 13th International Conference on Competition and the 14th European Competition Day, Munich, 26 March 2007, indicating that the Commission should focus on areas where there appear to be durable competition problems; the problems may be due to competition infringements, there are implications for better regulation and the sector is key for consumers and/or competitiveness.

[33] See earlier inquiries in the beer brewing sector Commission Decision 71/257/EEC in *Albra-Brasserie Espérance* [1971] OJ L161/2; *Union des Brasseries* [1971] OJ L161/6; *Maes* [1971] OJ L161/10.

[34] See D Wood and N Baverez, 'Sector Inquiries under EU Competition Law' [2005] Competition Law Insight 3, 5. Sector inquiries came into focus again in the telecommunications sector in 1999.

[35] The Commission has indicated that for the time being, until sufficient experience has been gained, this measure is one of those reserved for adoption by the College. Commission Antitrust Manual of Procedures, Internal DG Competition working documents on procedures for the application of Articles 101 and 102 TFEU, March 2012, Module 1 'Decision-making procedures', para 18.

[36] See Art 17(2) of Reg 1/2003. Commission Antitrust Manual of Procedures, Internal DG Competition working documents on procedures for the application of Articles 101 and 102 TFEU, March 2012, Module 14 'Advisory Committee on restrictive practices and dominant positions', para 2.

concerned and identify the undertakings required to provide information. Decisions under Article 17 of Regulation 1/2003 enable the Commission to exercise fully its investigative powers under Articles 18,[37] 19, 20,[38] and 22[39] of Regulation 1/2003 without having first opened an individual procedure in which specific investigative measures may be decided upon and without having to prove the need for such measures.[40] These powers are therefore exactly the same as those which the Commission may exercise when conducting an investigation into potential breaches of Articles 101 and 102 of the TFEU. However, unlike, for example, in a cartel investigation, the Commission does not have the power during a sector inquiry to inspect non-business premises, that is, the homes and other premises of directors, managers, and other company or trade association employees. In its requests for information and its inspections, the Commission need refer only to the decision to open an investigation enquiring into a particular economic sector in order to justify the specific investigative measure vis-à-vis the undertakings concerned. Thus, the Commission may ask undertakings to supply information necessary to carry out its inquiry. Undertakings concerned are obliged to answer the Commission's questionnaires and even to provide documents, if so required.[41]

In practice, the Commission initially seeks to engage in a dialogue with, and address questionnaires to, companies and trade associations in the sector under investigation. It will also contact Member State authorities, users of the products/services subject to the inquiry, and relevant consumer organizations. Following a review of the information gathered in this exercise, the Commission may send additional questionnaires seeking more detailed follow-up information. It may also conduct oral hearings. **5.10**

The Commission may subsequently publish a report on the results of its inquiry and invite comments from interested parties.[42] While it is under no obligation to publish its findings, in practice, in the inquiries conducted under Regulation 1/2003, it has published its preliminary findings, to give companies, trade associations, and third parties an opportunity to comment, as well as its final report and recommendations. The main advantage of sector inquiries for the Commission thus lies in the breadth of the powers available to it, which are not constrained by the requirement to prove the need for investigative measures that apply in individual cases. **5.11**

---

[37] Regarding requests for information, see Ch 7, 'Investigation of Cases (II): Formal Investigative Measures in General, Requests for Information and Interviews', para 7.36 et seq.

[38] Regarding inspections, see Ch 8, 'Investigation of Cases (III): Inspections', para 8.18 et seq.

[39] See Ch 8 , 'Investigation of Cases (III): Inspections', para 8.77 et seq.

[40] The exercise of the Commission's investigative powers is generally based on the existence of evidence showing the involvement of the undertakings investigated. See below Ch 7, 'Investigation of Cases (II): Formal Investigative Measures in General, Requests for Information and Interviews'.

[41] Article 23 allows the Commission to impose fines on undertakings and associations of undertakings which, in response to a request for information, either supply incorrect or misleading information or do not supply it at all. Such fines may reach 1 per cent of the total turnover in the preceding business year. Pursuant to Art 24, periodic penalties of up to 5 per cent of the average daily turnover of the firm may also be imposed.

[42] Article 17, third subparagraph. In the energy sector inquiry, the Commission also first published an issues paper setting out various initial findings, which it discussed with NCAs and electricity and gas regulators before publishing its preliminary findings for general consultation. Upon publication of its preliminary report in the retail banking sector inquiry, the Commission published a feedback form for both phases of its inquiry seeking views from market participants and authorities on its provisional findings. Copies of all final reports and recommendations have been published, usually in the form of a Communication from the Commission summarizing its main findings, and an accompanying staff working paper, which sets out its analysis, conclusions, and recommendations in more detail.

B. Complaints

1. Introduction

5.12   Under Article 7(2) of Regulation 1/2003, Member States and any natural or legal persons who claim a legitimate interest are entitled to apply to the Commission for a finding of an infringement of Articles 101 and 102 TFEU. Under Regulation 17, the EU Courts held that the fact of lodging a complaint under Article 3 of Regulation 17 did not confer upon the complainant the right to obtain from the Commission a decision within the meaning of Article 288 TFEU, regarding the existence or otherwise of an infringement of Article 101 or 102 TFEU, or both.[43] Rather, the Commission is entitled to give different degrees of priority and may decide on the order in which they are to be examined.[44] The current enforcement system requires potential complainants and their advisers to consider most carefully the appropriate authority to which a complaint should be addressed. The Commission is not the first and not necessarily the only authority which will receive complaints. Nor does it have the role of a case allocation agency.[45] For this reason, the complainant is therefore well advised to identify the competition authority or authorities best placed to handle the complaints, and also in order to reduce the risk of any delay caused by a possible reallocation. A complainant may consider the legal powers and procedural rules available to a given NCA in addition to its reputation for effectiveness.

5.13   Of particular importance for the complainant, however, are the rules which the Commission and the NCAs themselves apply with a view to determining which authority will deal with a complaint. Guidance for the work sharing between the Commission and the NCAs are laid down in the ECN Cooperation Notice,[46] which should help complainants to determine the authority most likely to be well placed to deal with their case. In principle, a case may be dealt with by one NCA, several NCAs acting in parallel, or the Commission. In essence, the Commission considers an NCA as being well placed to deal with a case if there is a *material link* between the infringement and the territory of the Member State to which the NCA in

---

[43]   Case 125/78 *GEMA v Commission* [1979] ECR 3173, para 17 and Case T-16/91 *Rendo v EC Commission* [1994] ECR II-2417, para 98; Case T-24/90 *Automec Srl v Commission (Automec II)* [1992] ECR II-2223, paras 75–6; and Case T-114/92 *BEMIM v Commission* [1995] ECR II-147, para 62.

[44]   See eg Case T-26/99 *Trabisco SA v Commission* [2001] ECR II-633, para 30, where the GC held that the Commission is not required to join the procedures for examining different complaints concerning the conduct of a particular undertaking, since the conduct of an investigation falls within the scope of its discretion. In particular, the fact that there are a number of complaints from operators belonging to different categories such as, in the context of this case, independent resellers, authorized intermediaries, and dealers, cannot preclude the dismissal of those complaints which appear, according to the evidence available to the Commission, to be unfounded or lack a Community interest. See also Case T-5/93 *Tremblay and others v Commission* [1995] ECR II-185, para 60. The position is different only if the complaint comes within the exclusive remit of the Commission, as in the case of withdrawal of an exemption granted under Reg 1/2003 Art 81(3) EC. Notice on Handling of Complaints [2004] OJ C101/65, para 41.

[45]   Former Director-General at DG COMP, P Lowe, 'The Role of the Commission in the Modernisation of EC Competition Law', Speech at the UKAEL Conference on Modernisation of EC Competition Law: Uncertainties and Opportunities, 23 January 2004: 'The Commission cannot and will not act as a clearing house between independent national authorities, but will leave it to the authorities to agree on the appropriate case allocation. The Commission will also not undermine the parallel application of European competition law—the very aim of the modernisation exercise. And it will finally not go against the political compromise reached in the Council as regards the number of countries that need to be concerned before the Commission is considered to be best placed to deal with a case. In the case allocation process the Commission is thus merely a primus inter pares'.

[46]   ECN Cooperation Notice [2004] OJ C101/43, paras 5–15; Notice on Handling of Complaints [2004] OJ C101/65, paras 19–25.

question belongs.[47] In most cases, the authorities of those Member States where competition is substantially affected by an infringement are expected to be well placed—either through single or parallel action—unless the Commission is better placed to act. A single NCA is usually well placed to deal with agreements or practices that substantially affect competition mainly within its territory. Parallel action by two or three NCAs may be appropriate where an agreement or practice has substantial effects on competition mainly in their respective territories and the action of only one NCA would not be sufficient to bring the entire infringement to an end and/or where the evidence is most likely to be found in more than one Member State. Conversely, the Commission is 'particularly well placed' if one or several agreement(s) or practice(s), including networks of similar agreements or practices, have effects on competition in more than three Member States (cross-border markets covering more than three Member States or several national markets). Moreover, the Commission considers that it is well placed to deal with a case if it is closely linked to other EU provisions which may be exclusively or more effectively applied by the Commission, if the (European) Union interest[48] requires the adoption of a Commission decision to develop EU competition policy when a new competition issue arises or to ensure effective enforcement.

Within the European Competition Network ('ECN'), information on cases that are being **5.14** investigated following a complaint will be made available to the other members of the network before or immediately after commencing the first formal investigative measure.[49] Where the same complaint has been lodged with several authorities or where a case has not been lodged with an authority that is well placed, the members of the network will endeavour to determine, within an indicative time period of two months, which authority or authorities should be in charge of the case. In conclusion, complainants themselves have an important role to play in reducing the potential need for reallocation of a case originating from their complaint when deciding on where to lodge their complaint. If a case is nonetheless reallocated within the network, the undertakings concerned and the complainant(s) are informed as soon as possible by the competition authorities involved.[50] The Commission may reject a complaint in accordance with Article 13 of Regulation 1/2003, on the grounds that an NCA is dealing with or has dealt with a given case. In rejecting any complaint, the Commission must, in accordance with Article 9 of Regulation 773/2004, inform the complainant without delay of the NCA concerned.

Apart from approaching public enforcers, a complainant may also envisage bringing mat- **5.15** ters before national courts. It may be easier to obtain interim relief in a national court or to receive damages for loss suffered as a result of the infringement.[51] In addition, it may be easier for the complainant to control the proceedings, for example, if it wishes it may simply withdraw a claim, whereas a public enforcer could investigate a case on its own motion. A complainant may be reluctant to take action before national courts because litigating the matter

---

[47] For more details, see Ch 3, 'The Role of National Competition Authorities', para 3.18 et seq.

[48] The Commission is entitled to refer to the Community interest (now Union interest) in order to determine the degree of priority to be applied to the complaints it receives and may reject a complaint on the grounds that there is insufficient EU interest to justify an investigation. In its Report on Competition Policy 2005, the Commission announced a set of criteria which it uses in order to decide whether or not there is sufficient Community interest to carry out an in-depth investigation. E Gippini-Fournier, 'The Modernisation of European Competition Law: First Experiences with Regulation 1/2003—Institutional Report' in HF Koeck and MM Karollus (eds), The Modernisation of European Competition Law—Initial Experiences with Regulation 1/2003, FIDE XXIII Congress Linz 2008—Congress Publications Vol 2 (Nomos 2008) 375, 396.

[49] ECN Cooperation Notice [2004] OJ C101/43, para 17.

[50] Notice on Handling of Complaints [2004] OJ C101/65, para 24.

[51] Article 8 of Reg 1/2003 provides that the Commission may adopt interim measures only on its own initiative.

may involve more costs. Further, the complainant may be faced with a myriad of different and often burdensome rules of civil procedure in Member States.[52] While the Commission is at pains to stress the complementary role of private and public enforcement, the decision of whether to have recourse to the Commission, an NCA, or a national court hinges on various factors which must be carefully weighed up in each individual case.

2. Informal or unofficial complaints

5.16 Complaints may be (i) formal or (ii) informal or unofficial. That said, those of an unofficial nature do not formally rank as complaints; the identity of the persons who make them is not disclosed, either because they are made anonymously or because the complainants ask the Commission to keep their identity secret. In the latter case, the Commission is careful at all times to maintain the anonymity of the complainant[53]—who in reality is merely an informant. This is in order to obviate problems of the kind which gave rise to the judgment of the ECJ in *Stanley Adams v Commission*, where it was held that where information is supplied on a voluntary basis and accompanied by a request for confidentiality in order to protect the informant's anonymity, the Commission is legally bound to comply with that condition.[54] Informal complaints may be made orally or in writing and do not constitute 'formal applications' or formal complaints, and for that reason those who make them do not enjoy the legal and procedural safeguards available to other complainants.[55] The Commission is under no obligation to investigate informal complaints and they are acted upon only if the person in charge of the relevant sectoral unit or another DG COMP senior official decides to do so. In such cases, the informal complaint will serve as the factual basis for the commencement of a procedure on the Commission's own initiative. The Commission takes care to ensure that the documents and submissions supporting informal complaints are not shown to the undertakings whose conduct is complained of, except where there is no risk whatever that the anonymity of the complainants might be breached—otherwise they could not be used.[56] Where it is impossible to show the documents to the undertakings concerned so that the latter can verify them, the Commission prefers to take a more adventurous approach and use its own investigative facilities to gather evidence of the infringement (and perhaps not

---

[52] Kerse & Khan, *EC Antitrust Procedure* (6th edn, Sweet & Maxwell 2012) para 2-019; see also the advantages of private action before national courts highlighted by the Notice on Handling of Complaints [2004] OJ C101/5, para 6.

[53] Notice on Handling of Complaints [2004] OJ C101/05, para 81.

[54] Case 145/83 *Stanley Adams v Commission* [1985] ECR 3539. Stanley Adams was an informant whose identity was disclosed by the Commission during the investigation of restrictive practices in the vitamins market (Commission Decision of 9 June 1976 [1976] OJ L223/27), with serious consequences. The informant, employed by the Swiss multinational Hoffmann-La Roche, was tried and imprisoned in Switzerland, where any person who divulges business secrets of his employer is liable to imprisonment. Judgment was given against the Commission in proceedings for non-contractual liability.

[55] See Ch 12, 'Rejection of Complaints'.

[56] In *Plasterboard*, the ECJ acknowledged the need to provide protection to customers of the firm being investigated. Case C-310/93 P *BPB Industries and British Gypsum v Commission* [1995] ECR I-865, para 26–7; see also Case T-9/99 *HFB v Commission* [2002] ECR II-1487, para 225 and Joined Cases T-191/98, T-212/98 to T-214/98 *Atlantic Container Line v Commission* [2003] ECR II-3275, para 393: 'the Commission may in any event refuse access to the correspondence with third parties by reason of its confidential nature, since an undertaking to which a statement of objections has been addressed, and which occupies a dominant position in the market, may adopt retaliatory measures against a competing undertaking, a supplier or a customer who has collaborated in the investigation carried out by the Commission'. However, there is no absolute guarantee of confidentiality. Article 15(3) of Reg 773/2004 states that 'nothing in this Regulation prevents the Commission from disclosing and using information necessary to prove an infringement of Article 81 or 82 EC'. Circumstances where the disclosure of the identity of the complainant would become indispensable to proving an infringement are likely to be rare, but nevertheless in some cases, eg infringements of Art 102 TFEU by a refusal to supply, the identity of the complainant is likely to be obvious to the addressee of such a decision. Kerse & Khan, *EC Antitrust Procedure* (6th edn, Sweet & Maxwell 2012) para 2-033.

find the documents or information sought) rather than jeopardize the interests of informal complainants.

3. Formal complaints

Complaints under Article 7 of Regulation 1/2003 are subject to the formalities laid down in Article 5 of Regulation 773/2004. Under Regulation 17, old Form C was the standard form for complaints,[57] but in practice no particular or special form was required, in sharp contrast with applications for negative clearance and notifications for exemption, which required Form A/B to be used. The only formal requirement was the disclosure of the identity of the complainant or that of its authorized representative. At present, any person having a legitimate interest—not only undertakings—is empowered to lodge complaints, and Article 5(1) of Regulation 773/2004 provides that they must contain the information required by Form C. Nevertheless, in the past, the Commission has rarely rejected a complaint because of formal defects. In practice, it was sufficient for complaints to be submitted in writing and signed by the complainant, who, as stated previously, may not request anonymity if he or she wishes to enjoy the procedural rights of a formal complainant. Formal complaints made under Article 7(2) of Regulation 1/2003 oblige the Commission to react in specific ways. Articles 5 to 9 of Regulation 773/2004 lay down specific rules concerning the handling of such complaints. In addition, a Commission Notice on the handling of complaints by the Commission under Articles 101 and 102 of the Treaty[58] (the 'Notice on Handling of Complaints') provides guidance on the subject. A formal complaint can only be made about an alleged infringement of Article 101 and/or 102 of the Treaty by undertakings.[59] In addition, the complainant must show a legitimate interest. Finally a complaint has to comply with Form C that is annexed to Regulation 773/2004.[60]

Legitimate interest

The following are considered, in principle, to have a legitimate interest:[61]

5.18

- Undertakings (themselves or through associations entitled to represent their interests[62]) can claim a legitimate interest where they are operating in the relevant product market or where the conduct complained of is liable to directly and adversely affect their interests.[63]

---

[57] Form C was annexed to the original version of Reg 27 ([1962] OJ 1118/62, [1959–62] OJ Spec Ed 132) and was updated by Reg 3666/93 ([1993] OJ L336/1) (English special edn 1959–1962, P 132).

[58] [2004] OJ C101/65.

[59] No formal complaint can be made under Reg 1/2003 about infringements by Member States. Sometimes a complaint also concerns a State measure caught by Art 106 TFEU or by Art 4(3) TEU. In such circumstances, the different aspects of the complaint will be handled separately.

[60] Article 5(2) of Reg 773/2004. Also explained in Notice on Handling of Complaints [2004] OJ C101/65, para 29. R Sauer in JL Schulte and C Just (eds), *Kartellrecht* (Carl Heymanns Verlag 2012), Art 7 of the Reg 1/2003, para 10 et seq.

[61] Cf also the explanations in the Notice on Handling of Complaints [2004] OJ C10 1/65, para 33 et seq. Antitrust Manual of Procedures, Internal DG Competition working documents on procedures for the application of Articles 101 and 102 TFEU, March 2012, Module 21 'Handling of complaints', paras 4–6.

[62] Joined Cases T-133/95 and T-204/95 *International Express Carriers Conference (IECC) v Commission* [1998] ECR II-3645, paras 79–83, as confirmed in Joined Cases T-213 and 214/01 *Österreichische Postsparkasse AG and Bank für Arbeit und Wirtschaft AG v Commission* [2006] ECR II-1601, para 112.

[63] Antitrust Manual of Procedures, Internal DG Competition working documents on procedures for the application of Articles 101 and 102 TFEU, March 2012, Module 21 'Handling of complaints', para 6, note 7, indicates that this would confirm the established practice of the Commission according to which a legitimate interest can, for instance, be claimed by the parties to the agreement or practice which is the subject of the complaint, by competitors whose *interests* have allegedly been damaged by the behaviour complained of or by undertakings excluded from a distribution system. Notice on Handling of Complaints [2004] OJ C101/65, para 36.

- Consumer associations can also lodge complaints with the Commission.[64]
- Individual consumers are considered to be in a position to show a legitimate interest when their economic interests have been harmed or are likely to be harmed as a result of the restriction of competition in question.[65]
- Local or regional public authorities may be able to show a legitimate interest in their capacity as buyers or users of goods or services affected by the conduct complained of.
- Member States are deemed to have a legitimate interest in all complaints they choose to lodge.

Form C

5.19   Complaints should be in one of the official EU languages and, in order to be admissible, must contain the information requested in Form C.[66] Correspondence to the Commission that does not comply with the formal requirements set out in Article 5 of Regulation 773/2004 does not constitute a complaint within the meaning of Article 7(2) of Regulation 1/2003 and will be considered as general information which may lead to an investigation of its own motion.[67] Form C requires complainants to submit comprehensive information in relation to their complaint and to use their best efforts to complete it as fully as possible. If the complainant believes any detail asked for to be unavailable, a reasoned explanation should be given. The Commission may waive the obligation to provide any particular information, including documents, where it considers that such information is not necessary for the examination of the case.[68] This may enable, where appropriate, a complaint to be tailored to the particular case so that the key information strictly needed for the Commission's preliminary examination is provided. Where a complainant is uncertain how to complete Form C or wishes further explanation, he or she may contact DG COMP to obtain guidance from Commission officials. Preliminary contacts can help to identify what DG COMP regards as necessary in a particular commercial or industry context. Such contacts may facilitate completion of the form and serve to speed matters up later in the procedure. Any material which the complainant considers to be confidential or contains business secrets should be clearly marked and the Commission's attention drawn to any restrictions on its use. It is common practice for parties to submit documents where each page is marked that it contains 'Business Secrets', but it may sometimes be worth indicating specifically the confidential items in a given document. Where Form C contains confidential information, it is necessary to attach a non-confidential version.[69] The reason for this is that the full complaint, subject to the exclusion of business secrets, will eventually be shown to the undertaking which is the subject of the complaint. The complainant should follow the style and order of the Form and make clear at the outset, using the headings given in Regulation 773/2004, that the document is a complaint on Form C. A complainant should expressly refer to Regulation 1/2003 and Form C in making its complaint in order to demonstrate clearly that reliance is also being placed on the provisions of the Regulation.[70]

---

[64] Case T-37/92 *Bureau Européen des Unions des Consommateurs (BEUC) v Commission* [1994] ECR II-285, para 36.

[65] Joined Cases T-213 and T-214/01 *Österreichische Postsparkasse et al v Commission* [2006] ECR II-1601, para 114.

[66] Form C is available at the DG COMP website at <http://ec.europa.eu/competition/index_en.html> and is also annexed to the Notice on Handling of Complaints [2004] OJ C101/65.

[67] Notice on Handling of Complaints [2004] OJ C101/65, para 32.

[68] Article 5(1) of Reg 773/2004; Notice on Handling of Complaints [2004] OJ C101/65, para 31, where the Commission states that this possibility can play a role in facilitating complaints by consumer associations which will not have access to the relevant information held by the undertakings concerned.

[69] Article 5(2) of Reg 773/2004.

[70] As the GC has indicated, the nature of a complaint may be determined by reference to its purpose and not only its form. Case T-117/96 *Intertronic F Cornelis GmbH v Commission* [1997] ECR II-141 (Summary Publication): 'Mere reference to [Art 7 of Reg 1/2003], without further observation, in a letter to the Commission cannot serve to give that letter the character of a complaint under that article when it is apparent that its purpose is to obtain a declaration that a Member State has failed to fulfil its obligations under the Treaty.'

Information regarding the parties Section I of Form C requires the identification of the **5.20** complainant. Where the complainant is an undertaking, information is required about any group to which it belongs. The complaint must also give the names and addresses of the undertaking or undertakings which are the subject of the complaint, as well as the nature and scope of their business activities. The relationship (eg competitor, customer) should also be given and could be further expanded in Section III, where the complainant has to demonstrate its legitimate interest.

Details of alleged infringement Section II requires a description of the arrangements or **5.21** behaviour in question. The details will largely depend on the circumstances of the particular case. The substance of the complaint should be set out as clearly as possible: copies of all relevant correspondence and other documents, if any, should be attached. A description of the relevant products or services should be given, particularly where they have a specialist or technical nature: where appropriate, photographs, diagrams, catalogues, price lists, etc may be supplied. Some indication should be given of the nature and structure of the relevant market and position of the undertakings concerned in it: any available statistical information and other published reports and materials may be referred to or copies or extracts supplied. Where the contents of agreements or practices in question are not, or are only partially, available in writing or documents are not available to the complainant, the fullest possible description should be given. Details should be given of provisions restricting—or perceived to restrict—parties in their freedom to take independent commercial decisions in relation to a variety of matters, such as prices, choice of markets, and sources of supply. Section II is also the place to give the names and addresses of any other relevant persons, eg those who may be able to corroborate any statements made by the complainant or who can provide other information or assistance in the matter. Although the Commission will not necessarily adopt the complainant's legal analysis and arguments, the latter should nevertheless indicate how Article 101 or 102 EC and/or Article 53 or 54 EEA is thought to apply in the circumstances. Where the complainant wants the Commission to investigate the alleged infringement under both Articles 101 and 102 TFEU, it should indicate this and substantiate its allegations with facts and data. The complainant may need to show how the agreements in question affect competition to an appreciable extent. Information must be given on how the agreement affects trade between Member States and/or European Free Trade Association ('EFTA') States.

Finding sought from the Commission This section of the complaint addresses two distinct **5.22** issues. First, the complainant should state exactly what 'finding or action' is being sought. As mentioned previously, where the infringement of a number of Treaty Articles is alleged, these must all be specified in the complaint and in calling on the Commission to act. The introduction of a specific invitation to the complainant to identify the relief sought might appear somewhat surprising, given that Article 8 of Regulation 1/2003 seems to deny complainants any standing to seek interim measures. Since the question is nevertheless raised on Form C, complainants should not hesitate to request interim measures, even if Article 8 does prove to constitute a barrier to obtaining relief against a refusal to order interim measures. Where specific relief is sought, the complainant should be careful to identify what the Commission can, and should, grant in the circumstances.[71] The complainant might usefully summarize any reasons for any claim that the case involves an issue of exceptional urgency. In addition, it should adduce evidence to show that he or she has a 'legitimate interest' within the meaning of Article 7(2) of Regulation 1/2003.

---

[71] In *Automec II*, the complainant unsuccessfully sought injunctive relief requiring supply of vehicles to it for resale. The GC held that although the Commission could have granted alternative forms of relief which might in fact have had the same result of resuming supply to the complainant, it was not the Commission's duty to redefine the complainant's application. Case T-24/90 *Automec II* [1992] ECR II-2223, paras 52–4. Kerse & Khan, *EC Antitrust Procedure* (6th edn, Sweet & Maxwell 2012) para 2-041.

5.23 **Proceedings before NCAs or national courts** Section IV is especially important in the context of the new enforcement regime. If a similar complaint (ie one concerning the same or a closely related subject matter) has been made to any other authority (eg the NCA of a Member State or the EFTA Surveillance Authority) or is the subject of proceedings in a national court, the current position of such complaint or action should be made known to the Commission. The authority or court must be identified and details given of submissions made. It may also be relevant to explain, where applicable, why no national remedies are available or why they would be inadequate. Finally under this section, the applicant is asked to say whether it intends to produce further supporting facts or arguments not yet available and, if so, to identify the relevant points.

5.24 **Other formal requirements** The complaint must be signed by the complainant, under a formal declaration that the information in the form has been given in good faith. Where a representative signs the complaint, written proof of his/her authority to act should be supplied. Without this, a notification signed by an officer of the company or companies concerned is not considered to be signed by a representative. The complaint must be submitted in three paper copies and, if possible, an electronic copy.

Initial assessment

5.25 The purpose of the initial assessment is to filter the admissible complaints in order to find those which seem most to merit further investigation by the Commission.[72] The Commission will endeavour to inform complainants of the action that it proposes to take on a complaint within an indicative time frame of four months from the receipt of the complaint.[73] According to the Antitrust Manual of Procedures ('Manproc'), this will, however, be subject to the circumstances of the individual case and, in particular, will depend whether DG COMP has received sufficient information from the complainant or third parties, notably in response to its requests for information, to enable it to decide whether to investigate the case further.[74]

5.26 The Commission can undertake preliminary investigations in order to assess whether the case should be a priority. For example, these could look for prima facie indications of the alleged infringement and try to determine a possible theory of harm.[75] The initial assessment should make it clear whether the complaint:

- is a potential case for further investigation by the Commission;
- should be re-allocated to an NCA; or
- contains insufficient grounds for acting.

5.27 If the intention is to investigate the case further, the complainant should be informed. A short letter by the Head of Unit is sufficient. The complainant should also be informed of the initiation of proceedings, unless it is inappropriate to provide this information.[76] In order to encourage an open exchange of views, in cases based on formal complaints the Commission will provide the parties subject to the proceedings at an early stage (unless such is considered likely to prejudice the investigation) and, at the latest, shortly after the

---

[72] Antitrust Manual of Procedures, Internal DG Competition working documents on procedures for the application of Articles 101 and 102 TFEU, March 2012, Module 21 'Handling of complaints', para 7.

[73] Notice on Handling of Complaints [2004] OJ C101/65, para 61.

[74] Antitrust Manual of Procedures, Internal DG Competition working documents on procedures for the application of Articles 101 and 102 TFEU, March 2012, Module 21 'Handling of complaints', para 8.

[75] Antitrust Manual of Procedures, Internal DG Competition working documents on procedures for the application of Articles 101 and 102 TFEU, March 2012, Module 21 'Handling of complaints', para 9.

[76] Antitrust Manual of Procedures, Internal DG Competition working documents on procedures for the application of Articles 101 and 102 TFEU, March 2012, Module 21 'Handling of complaints', para 11.

opening of proceedings, with the opportunity to comment on a non-confidential version of the complaint.[77]

According to Article 27 of Regulation 1/2003, before the Commission takes decisions under Articles 7, 8, 23, and 24(2), complainants should be associated closely with the proceedings.[78] The complainant can help the Commission in supplying evidence of the anticompetitive practice and thus in establishing the infringement. However, the formal complainant has less extensive procedural guarantees than the company subject to the investigation.[79] **5.28**

Where appropriate, documents such as replies to requests for information can be provided to the complainant in so far as business secrets are duly protected and the suppliers of the information have been informed.[80] A non-confidential version of the reply of the party subject to the investigation to the complaint may be provided to the complainant. However, this may not be the case where the complaint is rejected at an early stage without further in-depth investigation.[81] **5.29**

According to Article 6(1) of Regulation 773/2004, the Commission provides the complainant with a copy of the non-confidential version of the Statement of Objections and sets a time limit within which the complainant may make known its views in writing. A deadline of a maximum of one month is given for comments. The transmission is made for the sole purpose of the proceedings under Regulation 1/2003, without prejudice to the case law of the EU Courts.[82] **5.30**

Where appropriate, non-confidential versions of the replies to the Statement of Objections can be given to the complainant, provided that business secrets are not disclosed and that the suppliers of the information have been consulted.[83] **5.31**

In the same way, non-confidential versions of the complainants' comments may be sent to the undertaking(s) complained of.[84] Pursuant to Article 6 of Regulation 773/2004, the Commission may afford complainants with the opportunity of expressing their views at the oral hearing of the parties to which a Statement of Objections has been issued, if they so request in their written comments.[85] **5.32**

---

[77] Commission Notice on best practices for the conduct of proceedings concerning Articles 101 and 102 TFEU (text with EEA relevance) [2011] OJ C308/6, para 71; Antitrust Manual of Procedures, Internal DG Competition working documents on procedures for the application of Articles 101 and 102 TFEU, March 2012, Module 21 'Handling of complaints', para 12.

[78] Commission Notice on best practices for the conduct of proceedings concerning Articles 101 and 102 TFEU (text with EEA relevance) [2011] OJ C308/6, para 104.

[79] Antitrust Manual of Procedures, Internal DG Competition working documents on procedures for the application of Articles 101 and 102 TFEU, March 2012, Module 21 'Handling of complaints', para 13.

[80] Antitrust Manual of Procedures, Internal DG Competition working documents on procedures for the application of Articles 101 and 102 TFEU, March 2012, Module 21 'Handling of complaints', para 14.

[81] Commission Notice on best practices for the conduct of proceedings concerning Articles 101 and 102 TFEU (text with EEA relevance) [2011] OJ C308/6, para 71.

[82] See eg Case T-353/94 *Postbank* [1996] ECR II-921; Antitrust Manual of Procedures, Internal DG Competition working documents on procedures for the application of Articles 101 and 102 TFEU, March 2012, Module 21 'Handling of complaints', para 16.

[83] Antitrust Manual of Procedures, Internal DG Competition working documents on procedures for the application of Articles 101 and 102 TFEU, March 2012, Module 21 'Handling of complaints', para 17.

[84] Antitrust Manual of Procedures, Internal DG Competition working documents on procedures for the application of Articles 101 and 102 TFEU, March 2012, Module 21 'Handling of complaints', para 18.

[85] Antitrust Manual of Procedures, Internal DG Competition working documents on procedures for the application of Articles 101 and 102 TFEU, March 2012, Module 21 'Handling of complaints', para 19.

C. Initiating Proceedings

5.33 Proceedings conducted by the Commission in competition matters may be commenced by the Commission on its own initiative, or in response to a complaint. Article 2 of Regulation 773/2004 provides that the Commission may decide to initiate proceedings with a view to adopting a decision pursuant to Articles 7 to 10 of Regulation 1/2003.[86] There is no specified time or moment for the initiation of proceedings—this can occur at any stage in the investigation of a case. In particular, the initiation of proceedings is not necessary before the Commission can exercise its powers of investigation.[87] Pursuant to Article 2 of Regulation 773/2004, the Commission may decide to open proceedings with a view to adopting a decision pursuant to Chapter III (Article 7 to 10) of Regulation 1/2003 at any point in time, but no later than the date on which it issues a Statement of Objections,[88] a preliminary assessment as referred to in Article 9(1) of Regulation 1/2003 or a Notice pursuant to Article 27(4) of Regulation 1/2003 (for instance in an Article 10 procedure), whichever is the earlier.[89] It follows that proceedings cannot be opened if, at the material point in time, the Commission does not intend to adopt a decision.[90]

5.34 All cases, irrespective of their origin, are subject to an initial assessment phase. During this phase the Commission examines whether the case merits further investigation and, if so, provisionally defines its focus, in particular with regard to the parties, the markets, and the conduct to be investigated. During this phase, the Commission may make use of investigative measures such as requests for information in accordance with Article 18(2) of Regulation 1/2003. In practice, the system of initial assessment means that some cases will be discarded at a very early stage and do not qualify for further investigation. In this regard, the Commission is expected to focus its enforcement resources on cases where it appears likely that an infringement may be found, in particular on cases with the most significant impact on the functioning of competition in the internal market and risk of consumer harm, as well as on cases which are likely to contribute to defining EU competition policy and/or to ensuring the coherent application of Articles 101 and/or 102 TFEU.[91] Also in other cases, if by conducting limited further investigations the appropriate scope of the case can be determined with more certainty, it may be advisable to carry out such further investigation before proposing to open proceedings.[92]

---

[86] Finding and termination of infringement (Art 7), interim measures (Art 8), commitments (Art 9), and finding of inapplicability (Art 10). Under Art 2(4) of Reg 773/2004, proceedings do not have to be commenced in order to reject a complaint.

[87] Article 2(3) of Reg 1/2003.

[88] Commission Notice on best practices for the conduct of proceedings concerning Articles 101 and 102 TFEU (text with EEA relevance) [2011] OJ C308/6, para 24. In practice, proceedings will not be formally initiated until just before the statement of objections is served on the parties.

[89] Commission Antitrust Manual of Procedures, Internal DG Competition working documents on procedures for the application of Articles 101 and 102 TFEU, March 2012, Module 10 'Opening of proceedings', para 4.

[90] Antitrust Manual of Procedures, Commission Antitrust Manual of Procedures, Internal DG Competition working documents on procedures for the application of Articles 101 and 102 TFEU, March 2012, Module 10 'Opening of proceedings', para 5.

[91] Commission Notice on best practices for the conduct of proceedings concerning Articles 101 and 102 TFEU (text with EEA relevance) [2011] OJ C308/6, paras 12 and 13. During the first phase, the Commission will also consider the allocation of cases within the ECN.

[92] Antitrust Manual of Procedures, Internal DG Competition working documents on procedures for the application of Articles 101 and 102 TFEU, March 2012, Module 10 'Opening of proceedings', para 4.

When the first investigative measure is addressed to them (normally a request for informa- **5.35** tion[93] or an inspection), undertakings are informed of the fact that they are subject to a preliminary investigation and of its subject matter and purpose. In the context of requests for information, they will further be reminded that if the behaviour under investigation is confirmed to have taken place, this might constitute an infringement of Articles 101 and/or 102 TFEU. After having received a request for information or being subject to an inspection, parties may at any time ask the DG COMP about the status of the investigation, including before the opening of proceedings. If such an undertaking considers that it has not been properly informed by DG COMP of its procedural status, it may refer the matter to the Hearing Officer for resolution, after having raised the matter with the DG COMP.[94] If at any stage during the initial assessment phase, the Commission decides not to investigate the case further (and thus not to open proceedings), it will, of its own initiative, inform the party subject to the preliminary investigation of this fact.[95]

The Commission will open proceedings under Article 11(6) of Regulation 1/2003 when **5.36** the initial assessment leads to the conclusion that the case merits further investigation and where the scope of the investigation has been sufficiently defined.[96] The main consequence of the initiation of the formal proceedings by the Commission is laid down in Article 11(6) of Regulation 1/2003, which states that the initiation by the Commission of proceedings for the adoption of a decision under Chapter III[97] will relieve all NCAs of their competence to apply Articles 101 and 102 TFEU. Consequently, once the Commission has started proceedings, NCAs cannot act under the same legal basis against the same agreement(s) or practice(s) by the same undertaking(s) in the same relevant geographic and product market.[98]

Firstly, where the Commission is the first competition authority to initiate proceedings in **5.37** a case for the adoption of a decision, NCAs may no longer deal with the case. Article 11(6) provides that once the Commission has initiated proceedings, NCAs can no longer start their own procedure with a view to applying Articles 101 and 102 TFEU to the same agreement(s) or practice(s) by the same undertaking(s) in the same relevant geographic and product market.

Secondly, where one or more NCAs have informed the network pursuant to Article 11(3) that **5.38** they are acting in a given case, Article 11(6) requires the Commission to consult in writing the authority in question before the opening of proceedings.

---

[93] See Case T-99/04 *AC Treuhand* v *Commission* [2008] ECR II-1501, para 56.

[94] The Hearing Officer shall take a decision that the DG COMP will inform the undertaking or association of undertakings that made the request of their procedural status. This decision shall be communicated to the undertaking or association of undertakings that made the request. Article 4(2)(d) of the terms of reference of the Hearing Officer.

[95] Commission Notice on best practices for the conduct of proceedings concerning Articles 101 and 102 TFEU (text with EEA relevance) [2011] OJ C308/6, para 15.

[96] Commission Notice on best practices for the conduct of proceedings concerning Articles 101 and 102 TFEU (text with EEA relevance) [2011] OJ C308/6, para 17.

[97] Articles 7–10 of Reg 1/2003.

[98] Note that the application of Art 11(6) of the Regulation is limited and governed by Art 35(3) of Reg 1/2003, which states that the effects of Art 11(6) shall not extend to courts in so far as they act as review courts in respect of the types of decisions foreseen in Art 5 of Reg 1/2003. According to Art 35(4), where, for the adoption of certain decisions foreseen in Art 5, 'an authority in a Member State brings an action before a judicial authority that is separate and different from the prosecuting authority and provided that the terms of this paragraph are complied with, the effects of Article 11(6) shall be limited to the authority prosecuting the case which shall withdraw its claim before the judicial authority when the Commission opens proceedings and this withdrawal shall bring the national proceedings effectively to an end.'

5.39 Two situations may need to be distinguished here:

- if the opening is envisaged during the indicative case-allocation period, a simple bilateral consultation will suffice. The other authorities are given an opportunity to respond within two weeks;[99] and
- after the indicative case-allocation period.

5.40 In the second situation, after the allocation phase, the Commission will in principle only apply Article 11(6) if there is a risk of inconsistency or if network members are unduly delaying proceedings in a given case. In particular, the ECN Cooperation Notice acknowledges the possibility of the Commission using its power under Article 11(6) when:

(i) network members envisage conflicting decisions;

(ii) 'network members envisage a decision which is obviously in conflict with consolidated case law; the standards defined in the judgments of the Community courts and in previous decisions and regulations of the Commission should serve as a yardstick';[100]

(iii) network member(s) is (are) unduly drawing out proceedings in the case;

(iv) there is a need to adopt a Commission decision to develop Community competition policy in particular when a similar competition issue arises in several Member States or to ensure effective enforcement; or

(v) the NCA(s) concerned do not object.[101]

5.41 In addition to the provisions of Article 11(6) of Regulation 1/2003, paragraphs 54 to 56 of the ECN Cooperation Notice require the Commission to:

- consult formally the NCA(s) concerned, explaining in writing to them—and also to other network members—the reasons for the opening of proceedings; and
- announce its intention to open proceedings in due time, so that network members can request an Advisory Committee meeting.

The consultation must contain specific reasoning as to why the Commission finds that it is appropriate for it to open proceedings.[102]

5.42 In *IBM*, the ECJ held that the initiation of proceedings was merely a procedural measure adopted as a preparatory step prior to the decision, which represents its culmination.[103] By the same token, the initiation of proceedings under Regulation 1/2003 is not a challengeable act within the meaning of Article 267 TFEU. The initiation of proceedings is made

---

[99] In principle this case-allocation period is two months from the date when either the Commission or an NCA first informs the network of an investigation, but in case of a disagreement it is implicitly extended until a solution is found. An initiation decision is the ultimate way to end extended case-allocation discussions, but an agreement is by far a preferred solution to a unilateral de-seizure.

[100] WPJ Wils, 'Community Report' in *The Modernization of EU Competition Law Enforcement in the EU, FIDE 2004 National Reports* (Cambridge University Press 2004) 661, para 1.68.

[101] Commission Antitrust Manual of Procedures, Internal DG Competition working documents on procedures for the application of Articles 101 and 102 TFEU, March 2012, Module 10 'Opening of the proceedings', para 8.

[102] Commission Antitrust Manual of Procedures, Internal DG Competition working documents on procedures for the application of Articles 101 and 102 TFEU, March 2012, Module 10 'Opening of the proceedings', para 9, where it is pointed out that this can be done by explaining why one or more of the scenarios described in para 54 of the ECN Cooperation Notice is at stake. The consultation document is signed by the Director-General of DG COMP and copied to the other network members, and a period of two weeks is given for replies.

[103] Case 60/81 *IBM v Commission* [1981] ECR 2639, para 21; this also applies to the statement of objections, Joined Cases T-191/98, T-212/98 to T-214/98 *Atlantic Container Line and others v Commission* [2003] ECR I-3275, para 114.

with a view to adopting a definitive or final measure under Articles 7 to 10 of Regulation 1/2003. Accordingly it is only those measures which definitively determine the position of the Commission upon the conclusion of that procedure which are open to challenge and not intermediate measures whose purpose is to pave the way for the final decision, which would arguably also exclude decisions by the Commission under Article 11(6) of Regulation 1/2003 from the scope of challengeable acts.[104] Any legal defects therein may be relied upon in an action directed against the definitive act for which they represent a preparatory step.[105]

The Commission may also wish to reopen an investigation which it had previously closed. **5.43** To do so it must, however, set out the reasons for having changed its opinion. In *Storck Amsterdam*, the Commission informed the parties to an agreement by decision that it would not take any further action on the matter because of its limited economic importance at EU level. Later, the Commission changed its previous position on this point and the Court found that the reasons for that change of position were not explained by the Commission, nor could they be inferred from the context of the decision. In particular, the decision to re-examine the case was not based on the presence or awareness of new points of fact or law warranting re-examination of the matter. The GC annulled the decision to reopen the investigation due to the inadequacy of the statement of reasons, since the parties were not in a position to ascertain the reasons for the contested decision, which meant that the Commission took the view that the matter was of sufficient economic importance to warrant its staff conducting a thorough examination.[106] It is should be noted that the opening of proceedings does not limit the right of the Commission to extend (or reduce) the scope and/or the addressees of the investigation at a later point in time; eg the in-depth investigation or a reorientation of the case may imply taking up and investigating new aspects, or dropping some existing aspects of the case.[107] Where the investigation is extended, it is necessary to open proceedings in respect of additional infringements at the latest at the Statement of Objections or Preliminary Assessment stage.[108]

---

[104] Case 60/81 *IBM v Commission* [1981] ECR 2639, paras 9–10; Case T-95/99 *Satellim-ages TV5 SA v Commission* [2002] ECR II-1425, para 32. D Geradin and N Petit, 'Judicial Remedies under EC Competition Law: Complex Issues Arising from the Modernization Process' ch 17 in International Antitrust & Policy, 32nd Annual International Antitrust Law & Policy Conference [2006] Fordham Corporate Law Institute 393, acknowledge that the *IBM* case law, which excludes decisions to initiate a procedure from the scope of challengeable acts on the grounds that these acts are a preparatory step towards a final decision, could also be transposed to Art 11(6) decisions, maintains, however, that Commission decisions recalling cases from the national level deserve special treatment and may be considered as 'challengeable' within the meaning of Art 263 TFEU, also because—by way of analogy—the GC has held that the decision to refer a case under Art 9 of the Merger Control Regulation (Reg 139/2004) affects the legal situation of the parties to the concentration and could therefore be the subject of an action for annulment (Case T-1 19/02 *Royal Philips Electronics BV v Commission* [2003] ECR II-1433, para 281). See also Judge JD Cooke, 'Application of EC Competition Rules by National Courts', International Bar Association ('IBA') conference, Antitrust Reform in Europe: A Year in Practice, Brussels, 9–11 March 2005, 7, indicating that the parties may have invested considerable time and money in defending themselves, and are then faced with the prospect of having to start all over again in a different forum.
[105] Case 60/81 *IBM v Commission* [1981] ECR 2639, para 12; Case T-241/97 *Storck v Commission* [2000] ECR II-309, para 49; Case T-189/95 *SGA v Commission* [1999] ECR II-3587, para 26; Order of the President of the GC in Case T-213/01 *Österreichische Postparkasse v Commission* [2001] ECR II-3963, para 46; Case T-95/99 *Satellimages TV5 SA v Commission* [2002] ECR II-1425, para 32.
[106] Case T-241/97 *Storck Amsterdam BV v Commission* [2000] ECR II-309, paras 70–83.
[107] In deciding whether to include new elements, the trade-off between the scope and duration of the investigation must be taken into account.
[108] Antitrust Manual of Procedures, Internal DG Competition working documents on procedures for the application of Articles 101 and 102 TFEU, March 2012, Module 10 'Opening of the proceedings', para 20.

5.44 The decision to open proceedings identifies the parties and briefly describes the scope of the investigation. In particular, it sets out the behaviour constituting the alleged infringement of Articles 101 and/or 102 TFEU to be covered by the investigation and normally identifies the territory and sector(s) where that behaviour takes place. Pursuant to Article 2 of Regulation 773/2004, the Commission may make the opening of proceedings public. The Commission's policy is to publish the opening of proceedings on the DG COMP's website and issue a press release, unless such publication may harm the investigation.

5.45 The Manproc provides that the parties subject to the investigation should be informed orally or in writing of the opening of proceedings sufficiently ahead of the opening of proceedings being made public so as to enable them to prepare their own communication (in particular in relation to shareholders, the financial institutions, and the press).[109] After the notification of the decision to open proceedings, the case team will prepare a short information note for the ECN and instruct the Antitrust Registry to send the note to the NCAs, mentioning Article 11(6) of Regulation 1/2003 and the case number (but no case name in the subject line) and, if appropriate, to the EFTA Surveillance Authority ('ESA')[110] by mentioning Article 2 of Protocol 23 to the EEA Agreement.[111]

5.46 The publication of the press release and of the website notice should take place after the notification of the decision to open proceedings. The Manproc indicates that the case team has to await the acknowledgement of receipt of the notification (DHL slip signed by the addressee(s) of the decision). Only once this has been received should they inform the spokesperson to trigger the communication as well as launch the publication on the DG COMP website within one to two days, depending on whether or not the addressee was aware of the intention to open proceedings and could therefore prepare its own communication (in particular, as stated, in relation to shareholders, the financial institutions, and the press).[112]

5.47 The Manproc indicates that the decision to open proceedings is usually kept short. Since the decision as such is notified to the parties, it has to be drafted in the authentic language, ie the language of the addressee (the language of the jurisdiction where it is domiciled).[113]

---

[109] Commission Notice on best practices for the conduct of proceedings concerning Articles 101 and 102 TFEU (text with EEA relevance) [2011] OJ C308/6, paras 19–21. In *Dyestuffs*, it was argued that the Commission had violated the procedural rules then contained in Reg 17 by communicating to the parties its statement of objections at the same time as it announced the initiation of proceedings to determine whether any infringements had taken place. The ECJ rejected this argument, emphasizing that the statement of objections was the crucial document in this regard. See Case 57/69 *Azienda Colori Nazionali—ACNA SpA v Commission* [1972] ECR 933, paras 10–11: 'neither the provisions in force nor the general principles of law require notice of the decision to initiate the procedure to establish an infringement to be given prior to the notification of the objections adopted against the interested parties in the context of such proceedings...It is the notice of objections alone and not the decision to commence proceedings which is the measure stating the final attitude of the Commission concerning undertakings against which proceedings for infringement of the rules on competition have been commenced'. Kerse & Khan, *EC Antitrust Procedure* (6th edn, Sweet & Maxwell 2012) para 2-103.

[110] Antitrust Manual of Procedures, Internal DG Competition working documents on procedures for the application of Articles 101 and 102 TFEU, March 2012, Module 10 'Opening of the proceedings', para 18.

[111] Antitrust Manual of Procedures, Internal DG Competition working documents on procedures for the application of Articles 101 and 102 TFEU, March 2012, Module 10 'Opening of the proceedings', para 17. The EEA Agreement entered into force on 1 January 1994, available at <http://www.efta.int/eea/eea-agreement.aspx>.

[112] Commission Antitrust Manual of Procedures, Internal DG Competition working documents on procedures for the application of Articles 101 and 102 TFEU, March 2012, Module 10 'Opening of proceedings', para 18.

[113] Commission Antitrust Manual of Procedures, Internal DG Competition working documents on procedures for the application of Articles 101 and 102 TFEU, March 2012, Module 10 'Opening of proceedings', para 11; Module 27 'Use of languages in antitrust proceedings', para 8.

In essence, the decision states that it has been decided to open the proceedings pursuant to Article 11(6) of Regulation 1/2003 and Article 2 of Regulation 773/2004 in the case at stake, and that the NCAs are relieved of their competence to apply Articles 101 and 102 of the TFEU to the same case. The decision to open proceedings identifies the parties subject to the proceedings and briefly describes the scope of the investigation. In particular, it sets out the behaviour constituting the alleged infringement of Articles 101 and/or 102 TFEU to be covered by the investigation and normally identifies the territory and sector(s) where that behaviour takes place.[114] The opening of proceedings does not prejudge in any way the existence of an infringement. It merely indicates that the DG COMP will further pursue the case as a matter of priority. This important distinction is made clear in the decision notified to the parties, as well as in all public communications concerning the opening of the case.[115]

Regardless of whether there is a complaint or a procedure is commenced on the Commission's **5.48** own initiative, each case receives a Registry number and name when it is initiated. The number and name serve to identify the case in DG COMP files and appear in all subsequent correspondence as a reference both for the undertakings concerned and for the Commission itself. When the file thus opened relates to another procedure already at the investigative stage, the Registry still gives it its own number, even though the processing of the cases, and the final decision, may be the same for the original procedure and for subsequent procedures if combined with the first one. There are no formal rules for the joining of procedures. In general, a decision must relate to at least one infringement. In view of the fact that a procedure may relate to several infringements and several procedures may relate to a single infringement, a procedure may result in one decision or several, as the case may be. Given the possibility of joining procedures, a single decision may deal with several infringements and several procedures. The ECJ has confirmed the Commission's authority to deal with several infringement procedures in a single decision, provided that the decision enables each addressee to determine precisely what conduct has been attributed to it.[116]

As already indicated, the Commission may open a case on its own initiative (*ex officio*). It may **5.49** do so when certain facts have been brought to its attention, or further to information gathered in the context of sector enquiries, informal meetings with industry, market monitoring, or on the basis of information exchanged within the ECN or competition authorities of third countries. Cartel cases can also be initiated on the basis of an application for leniency by one of the cartel members.[117] This can happen without the need for any action by the persons concerned. However, the fact that an infringement is public and notorious does not impose a duty on the Commission to initiate a procedure under Articles 101(1) or 102 TFEU, at least in the absence of a formal complaint.[118]

---

[114] Commission Antitrust Manual of Procedures, Internal DG Competition working documents on procedures for the application of Articles 101 and 102 TFEU, March 2012, Module 10 'Opening of proceedings', para 12.

[115] Commission Antitrust Manual of Procedures, Internal DG Competition working documents on procedures for the application of Articles 101 and 102 TFEU, March 2012, Module 10 'Opening of proceedings', paras 11–13.

[116] See Joined Cases 48/73, 50/73, 54–56/73, 111/73, 113/73, and 114–73 *Suiker Unie and others v Commission* [1975] ECR 1663, para 111; and Joined Cases 209–15/78 and 218/78 *Van Landewyck v Commission (FEDETAB)* [1980] ECR 3125, para 77; Opinion of AG General Ruiz-Jarabo Colomer in Joined Cases C-204/00 P *Aalborg Portland v Commission* [2003] ECR I-123, para 86: 'That approach is legitimate and is based on the Commission's power to adopt a single decision covering several infringements.'

[117] Commission Notice on best practices for the conduct of proceedings concerning Articles 101 and 102 TFEU (text with EEA relevance) [2011] OJ C308/6, para 11.

[118] Case T-29/92 *Vereniging van Samenwerkende Prijsregelende Organisatie in de Bouwnijverheid (SPO) and others v Commission* [1995] ECR II-289, para 360.

5.50 The communication of the initiation of the proceedings to an undertaking may produce effects in relation to the interruption of the limitation period under Article 25 of Regulation 1/2003. This may be of relevance where the Commission has to demonstrate that it acted in a timely fashion. The risk of being time barred does not appear to be particularly significant, given that it is most likely that the Commission will have carried out one of the other acts which interrupts the running of time under Article 25(3) before it reaches the stage of deciding to initiate proceedings.[119] The Commissioner for Competition has been empowered by the College to adopt the decision to open proceedings, except in cases in which the Commission wishes to relieve an NCA of its competence following a consultation by the NCA on its envisaged decision pursuant to Article 11(6) of Regulation 1/2003.

D. Possible Outcomes of the Investigation Phase

5.51 Once the Commission has reached a preliminary view of the main issues raised by a case, the following different procedural paths may be envisaged:

- The Commission may decide to proceed towards the adoption of a Statement of Objections with a view to adopting a prohibition decision relating to all or some of the issues identified when proceedings are opened (see paragraph 5.30 et seq).
- The parties subject to the investigation may consider offering commitments which address the competition concerns arising from the investigation, or at least show their willingness to discuss such a possibility; in that case, the Commission may decide to engage in discussion with a view to a commitment decision.
- The Commission may decide that there are no grounds to continue the proceedings with regard to some or all of the parties and close the proceedings accordingly. If the case originated via a complaint, before closing it the Commission will give the complainant the possibility to express its views.[120]

5.52 When closing a case in relation to one or several parties in multi-party proceedings at an early stage after these have been formally opened, normally the Commission will not only notify the decision to those parties but also, in those cases where the opening thereof has been made public, note the closure on its website and/or issue a press release. The same applies in cases where proceedings have not been formally opened but the Commission has already made public its investigation (eg by having confirmed that inspections have taken place).[121]

E. Transparency

5.53 Throughout the procedure, the Commission has indicated that, on its own initiative or upon request, it endeavours to give parties subject to the proceedings ample opportunity for open and frank discussions—taking into account the stage of the investigation—and to make their points of view known.

---

[119] Kerse & Khan, *EC Antitrust Procedure* (6th edn, Sweet & Maxwell 2012) para 2-098.
[120] Commission Notice on best practices for the conduct of proceedings concerning Articles 101 and 102 TFEU (text with EEA relevance) [2011] OJ C308/6, para 75.
[121] Commission Notice on best practices for the conduct of proceedings concerning Articles 101 and 102 TFEU (text with EEA relevance) [2011] OJ C308/6, para 76.

1. State of Play meetings

In this respect, the Commission will offer 'State of Play' meetings at certain stages of the proce- **5.54**
dure. These meetings, which are completely voluntary in nature for the parties, aim to contribute
to the quality and efficiency of the decision-making process and to ensure transparency and
communication between the DG COMP and the parties, notably to inform them of the status
of the proceedings at key points. State of Play meetings will only be offered to the parties being
investigated and not to the complainant (except where the Commission has opened proceedings
pursuant to Article 11(6) of Regulation 1/2003 and intends to inform the complainant that it
will reject its complaint by formal letter under Article 7(1) of the Implementing Regulation) or
third parties. Where several parties are investigated, State of Play meetings will be offered to each
party separately.[122]

The Notice on Best Practices provides that DG COMP endeavours to give, on its own initia- **5.55**
tive or upon request, parties subject to the proceedings ample opportunity for open and frank
discussions and to make their points of view known throughout the procedure.[123] Thus, DG
COMP will offer a State of Play meeting (in principle, although not normally in cartel proceedings) shortly after the opening of proceedings informing the parties subject thereto of the issues
identified at this stage and of the anticipated scope of the investigation. This meeting provides
the parties with an opportunity to react initially to the issues identified and may also help the DG
COMP to decide the appropriate framework for its further investigation.[124]

This initial meeting may also be used to discuss with the parties any relevant language waivers **5.56**
that may be appropriate for the conduct of the investigation. DG COMP may at this stage
indicate a tentative timetable for the case which, if appropriate, will be updated following State
of Play meetings. State of Play meetings are normally conducted at the Commission's premises, but they may be held by telephone or videoconference. Senior DG COMP management
(Director-General or Deputy Director-General) will normally chair the meetings. However, in
cases involving multiple parties, the meeting may be chaired by the responsible head of unit.
The Legal Service and the Hearing Officer will be invited to the State of Play meetings and may
decide to participate.[125]

2. Triangular meetings

In addition to bilateral meetings between the DG COMP and each individual party (such as **5.57**
State of Play meetings), the Commission may exceptionally decide to invite the parties subject to

---

[122] Commission Notice on best practices for the conduct of proceedings concerning Articles 101 and 102
TFEU (text with EEA relevance) [2011] OJ C308/6, para 61. In cartel proceedings, one State of Play meeting
will be offered after the oral hearing (para 65).
[123] Commission Notice on best practices for the conduct of proceedings concerning Articles 101 and 102
TFEU (text with EEA relevance) [2011] OJ C308/6, para 60.
[124] See Commission Notice on best practices for the conduct of proceedings concerning Articles 101 and
102 TFEU (text with EEA relevance) [2011] OJ C308/6, para 63(1). Further State of Play meetings will be
offered at a sufficiently advanced stage in the investigation as well as after the parties' reply to the Statement of
Objections or after the Oral Hearing (see Commission Notice on best practices for the conduct of proceedings concerning Articles 101 and 102 TFEU (text with EEA relevance) [2011] OJ C308/6, paras 63(2) and
64). A meeting at an advanced stage of the investigation will give the parties the opportunity to understand
the Commission's preliminary views on the status of the case following the investigation, and on the competition concerns identified. The meeting can be used to clarify the issues and facts relevant to the outcome of the
case. At the final State of Play meeting (other than in commitment cases, where two further meetings will be
held), the parties will usually be informed of how the Commission intends to pursue the case.
[125] Commission Antitrust Manual of Procedures, Internal DG Competition working documents on procedures for the application of Articles 101 and 102 TFEU, March 2012, Module 10 'Opening of proceedings', para 26.

the proceedings, and possibly also the complainant and/or third parties, to a so-called 'triangular' meeting.[126] Such a meeting will be held if the DG COMP believes it to be in the interests of the investigation to hear all of the parties' views on, or to verify the accuracy of, factual issues in a single meeting. Such a meeting could be useful to the investigation, for example, where two or more opposing views or pieces of information have been put forward with respect to key data or evidence. Any triangular meeting would normally take place at the initiative of the Commission and on a voluntary basis. Triangular meetings are normally chaired by senior management at DG COMP (Director-General or Deputy Director-General). The Legal Service and the Hearing Officer will systematically be informed of and invited to triangular meetings.[127]

5.58   Where triangular meetings are held, this should be done as early as possible during the investigatory phase (after the opening of proceedings and before any issuing of the Statement of Objections) in order to help the Commission reach a conclusion on substantive issues before it decides whether to issue a Statement of Objections. However, the holding of such meetings after the issue of the Statement of Objections in appropriate cases is not excluded.[128] The Manproc provides that triangular meetings should be prepared on the basis of an agenda established by the DG COMP after consulting all parties that agree to attend. The preparation of the meeting may include a mutual exchange of non-confidential submissions between the attending parties sufficiently in advance of the meeting.[129]

3. Review of key submissions

5.59   In the spirit of encouraging an open exchange of views, in cases based on formal complaints the Commission will provide the parties subject to the proceedings with the opportunity of commenting on a non-confidential version of the complaint at an early stage (unless this is considered as likely to prejudice the investigation) and at the latest shortly after the opening of proceedings.[130] However, this may not be the case where the complaint is rejected at an early stage without any further in-depth investigation (eg based on 'insufficient grounds for acting by conducting a further investigation', also known as 'lack of European Union interest').[131] Early access to the complaint may allow the parties to provide useful information at an early stage of the procedure and facilitate the assessment of the case.[132]

5.60   In addition, shortly after the opening of the proceedings, the Commission's objective will be to provide the parties thereto with the opportunity to review non-confidential versions of other 'key submissions' which have already been submitted. This would include significant submissions of the complainant or interested third parties, but not, for example, replies to requests for information. The review of key submissions does not replace the formal access to the file procedure.

---

[126] See Commission Notice on best practices for the conduct of proceedings concerning Articles 101 and 102 TFEU (text with EEA relevance) [2011] OJ C308/6, paras 67–9.

[127] See Commission Notice on best practices for the conduct of proceedings concerning Articles 101 and 102 TFEU (text with EEA relevance) [2011] OJ C308/6, para 68.

[128] See Commission Notice on best practices for the conduct of proceedings concerning Articles 101 and 102 TFEU (text with EEA relevance) [2011] OJ C308/6, para 69.

[129] Commission Antitrust Manual of Procedures, Internal DG Competition working documents on procedures for the application of Articles 101 and 102 TFEU, March 2012, Module 10 'Opening of proceedings', para 30.

[130] A non-confidential version of the reply of the party subject to the investigation to the complaint may thereafter be provided to the complainant.

[131] Commission Notice on best practices for the conduct of proceedings concerning Articles 101 and 102 TFEU (text with EEA relevance) [2011] OJ C308/6, para 71.

[132] Commission Notice on best practices for the conduct of proceedings concerning Articles 101 and 102 TFEU (text with EEA relevance) [2011] OJ C308/6, para 72.

After this early stage, later submissions will only be shared with the parties if this is in the **5.61** interest of the investigation and would not risk unduly slowing down the investigative phase. The Commission will respect justified requests by the complainant or interested third parties for non-disclosure of their submissions prior to the issuing of a Statement of Objections where they have genuine concerns regarding confidentiality, including fears of retaliation and the protection of business secrets. The review of key submissions will not be offered in the context of cartel proceedings.[133]

---

[133] Commission Notice on best practices for the conduct of proceedings concerning Articles 101 and 102 TFEU (text with EEA relevance) [2011] OJ C308/6, para 73.

6

INVESTIGATION OF CASES (I): LENIENCY POLICY

Corneliu Hödlmayr, Luis Ortiz Blanco, and Konstantin Jörgens

A. Policy and Objectives

Nowadays, competition authorities around the world encourage companies to report their own **6.01** antitrust violations in exchange for 'amnesty' or 'leniency' from fines.[1] Simply put, leniency programmes offer companies incentives to 'blow the whistle' on cartels, making cartel participation riskier and creating a 'race to confess' in order to obtain full immunity. Such a policy is based on the recognition that while cartels rank among the most serious violations of competition rules, the collection of evidence to prosecute them is increasingly difficult. In earlier decisions, the Commission had already taken account of the existence or absence of cooperation on the part of undertakings.[2] Encouraged by the experiences of the operation of a leniency

---

[1] See overview in OECD, *Fighting Hardcore Cartels: Harm, Effective Sanctions, and Leniency Programmes* (2002), available on the OECD website at <http://www.oecd.org>. The OECD has identified an increasingly successful 'carrot-and-stick' approach—applying stiffer punishment for cartel operators and enhancing programmes aimed at rewarding cartel members who decide to defect and cooperate with the authorities. At the EU level, the first Member States that have adopted leniency programmes were Germany, France, Ireland, the Netherlands, and the United Kingdom. See also comprehensive overview of the worldwide leniency regimes in SJ Mobley and R Denton, *Global Leniency Manual 2010* (OUP 2010). Twenty-six authorities in EU Member States which operate a leniency programme: Austria, Belgium, Bulgaria, Cyprus, the Czech Republic, Denmark, Estonia, Finland, France, Germany, Greece, Hungary, Ireland, Italy, Latvia, Lithuania, Luxembourg, the Netherlands, Poland, Portugal, Romania, Slovakia, Slovenia, Spain, Sweden, and the United Kingdom. Malta does not dispose of any formal leniency regime, but the Maltese competition authority may accord leniency on the basis of discretion and upon request, see Mobley and Denton, *Global Leniency Manual 2010*, 298. See also DJ Arp and CRA Swaak, 'A Tempting Offer: Immunity from Fines for Cartel Conduct under the European Commission's New Leniency Notice' [2003] ECLR 9, 9. Croatia introduced a leniency policy with the Competition Act 2009 which became applicable as of 1 October 2010; see also Alexandr Svetlicinii, 'The Croatian Government adopts leniency guidelines under the new law on protection of competition', 11 November 2010, e-Competitions, No 33581, <www.concurrences.com>.

[2] Eg Decision 82/253 *National Panasonic* [1982] OJ L354/28.

programme by the US Department of Justice, in 1996 the Commission adopted the Notice on the non-imposition or reduction of fines in cartel cases (the '1996 Notice').[3] This first guidance was updated twice, taking account of the practical experience gathered since its first instatement in 1996. The 1996 Notice was replaced in February 2002 by the '2002 Notice'[4] that changed the earlier system, and was largely modelled on the US 'amnesty' programme. In December 2006 the leniency regime was again updated by the '2006 Notice'.[5]

6.02   Under the 1996 Notice, the first company to provide 'decisive evidence' of a cartel could gain between a 75 per cent reduction to full immunity from fines. Besides, where the Commission had already begun an investigation, a company providing 'decisive evidence' could obtain a reduction of 50 to 75 per cent. Finally, those companies not satisfying the latter conditions that nevertheless cooperated with the Commission could benefit from a reduction in fines from 10 to 50 per cent. By April 2007, the 1996 Notice has been applied in twenty-three cases and the 2002 Notice in eight.[6] By December 2010, the total amount of fine reductions granted on the basis of all leniency notices since the 2006 fining guidelines was of EUR 911 million respectively 18 per cent of the total fines imposed in these thirteen cartel decisions.[7]

6.03   The 1996 Notice was subject to criticism because it was considered as providing insufficient incentive for a whistle-blower to approach the Commission about a cartel unknown to it. Companies that 'confessed' were given little or no indication until the very end of the administrative process of the reduction in fines, if any, that they would receive in return for their cooperation.[8] Under the 1996 Notice, the decision on the granting of immunity would not be taken until the adoption of the final decision imposing fines, which could take place several years after the application. Further, the 'decisive evidence' criterion was unclear and necessarily subjective.[9] The requirement that a company should not have acted as a ringleader could easily disqualify a whistle-blower with the most abundant information about the cartel from the 'very substantial reduction or non-imposition'.

6.04   In response to the shortcomings of the 1996 Notice, the Commission adopted the 2002 Notice, mainly for two reasons. First, the leniency programme's effectiveness would be improved by increasing the transparency and certainty of the conditions on which any reduction of fines would be granted. The Commission considered it necessary to ensure greater coherence between the level of reduction of fines and the value of a company's contribution to establishing the infringement. Secondly, the 1996 Notice excluded from immunity those companies that had played 'a determining role in the illegal activity'.[10] Such a concept was considered as insufficiently precise and it was thought that it could deter companies from

---

[3] Commission Notice on the non-imposition or reduction of fines in cartel cases [1996] OJ C207/4.

[4] Commission Notice on immunity from fines and reduction of fines in cartel cases [2002] OJ C45/3.

[5] Commission Notice on immunity from fines and reduction of fines in cartel cases [2006] OJ C298/17.

[6] A Stephan, 'An Empirical Assessment of the European Leniency Notice' (Sept 2009) 5(3) Journal of Competition Law & Economics 537, 539.

[7] Cento Veljanovski, European Cartel Fines under the 2006 Penalty Guidelines, 10 December 2010, Case Associates, published by the Social Science research Network and available on its website at <http://www.ssrn.com>.

[8] M Jephcott, 'The European Commission's New Leniency Notice—Whistling the Right Tune' [2002] ECLR 378, 378; DJ Arp and CRA Swaak, 'A Tempting Offer: Immunity from Fines for Cartel Conduct under the European Commission's New Leniency Notice' [2003] ECLR 9, 11.

[9] F Arbault and F Peiró, 'The Commission's New Notice on Immunity and Reduction of Fines in Cartel Cases: Building on Success' (2002) June (2) Competition Policy Newsletter 15, 22. JM Joshua and PD Camesasca, 'Where Angels Fear to Tread: The Commission's "New" Leniency Policy Revisited' (2005) 1(5) European Antitrust Review 10, 10, taking the view that the 1996 Notice—in essence—called for the production of the 'smoking gun'.

[10] DJ Arp and CRA Swaak, 'A Tempting Offer: Immunity from Fines for Cartel Conduct under the European Commission's New Leniency Notice' [2003] ECLR 9, 13.

informing the Commission of their participation in illegal cartels. Like its US counterpart, the 2002 Notice continues to be an important case generator.[11]

On 8 December 2006, the 2006 Notice entered into force.[12] The new regime, *inter alia*, clari- **6.05** fies the handling of hypothetical leniency applications and formalizes the so-called 'marker system' by which applicants are given the possibility of protecting their position in the queue for a certain period of time without having to provide the full information necessary for immunity. Furthermore, the 2006 Notice introduced a compulsory corporate statement by which the applicant has to explain in detail its involvement in the cartel, its main characteristics, and its functioning. Finally, the standard necessary to qualify for immunity was slightly adjusted: while the 2002 Notice required evidence that may either enable the Commission in its view 'to carry out an investigation' or 'to find an infringement', the 2006 Notice attempts to address criticism of a too vague standard by replacing the first alternative with a requirement for evidence for the granting of immunity that, in the view of the Commission, will enable it 'to carry out a targeted inspection in connection with the alleged cartel'.

The leniency policy of the Commission aims to create a race between cartel members where the **6.06** last company to confess will face difficulties in avoiding the imposition of heavy fines, not only because this company will probably not benefit from the leniency notice, but also because by then the Commission will have acquired all the necessary information to build a strong case.[13]

The 1996 Notice applied to all requests for leniency filed with the Commission after its publica- **6.07** tion on 18 July 1996. The 2002 Notice started applying as of 14 February 2002 to all requests the Commission was made aware of after that date.[14] Finally, all points of the 2006 Notice except points 31 to 35 apply to cases where the Commission has not been contacted by any party to a cartel before 7 December 2006.[15] Points 31 to 35 of the 2006 Notice on the procedures applying to the submission of corporate statements and the access of third parties thereto apply to all pending immunity/leniency applications without any inter-temporal limitations.

As already partly detailed, the two updates since 1996 mainly introduced changes with regard **6.08** to the following questions:

(1) At what time does the window for requesting immunity close?
(2) What quality of evidence is needed for a successful leniency application?

---

[11] As a result of the 2002 Notice, there has been an increase in the number of cases; XXXIII Report on Competition Policy (2003), paras 29 and 30. This trend towards more cartel decisions continued up to 2010, when the Commission had taken a total of sixty-nine decisions per undertaking/association, and seems to have stayed at that high level in 2012 (with a total of twenty-nine decision until June 2012) despite a drop to only fourteen cartel decisions that were taken in 2011; Cartel Statistics available at <http://ec.europa. eu/competition/cartels/statistics/statistics.pdf> (Version of 27 June 2012). Out of all cartel investigations about 75 per cent are based on immunity applications; Report on Competition Policy (2009), para 100. B Van Barlingen and M Barennes, 'The European Commission's Leniency Notice in Practice' (2005) Autumn (3) Competition Policy Newsletter 6, 6, notes 6 and 7, point out that the most interesting aspect is not so much the high number of leniency applications under the 2002 Notice (compared to a total of eighty leniency applications under the 1996 Notice), than the fact that the large majority of leniency applications under the 1996 Notice were made only after the Commission had undertaken inspections and resulted in a reduction of fines. Under the 2002 Notice more than half of all the leniency applications have been made before any inspection took place. See also K Nordlander, 'Discovering Discovery—US Discovery of EC Leniency Statements' [2004] ECLR 646, 646–7.

[12] See para 37 of the 2006 Notice [2006] OJ C298/19.

[13] This aim of the leniency notices to trigger a race amongst cartel participants for the best cooperation with the Commission is also recognized by the Court: Case T-127/04 *KME v Commission* [2009] ECR II-1167, para 130.

[14] See point 28 of the 2002 Notice.

[15] See point 37 of the 2006 Notice [2006] OJ C298/19.

(3) Can the applicants continue to participate in the cartel without losing the benefits of its application?

(4) What entitlement to leniency do leading members of a cartel (ie ringleaders) have?

(5) When and how is the applicant deemed to have sufficiently cooperated to obtain immunity or leniency?

(6) Can the applicant make an anonymous and hypothetical immunity application to test its chances of obtaining immunity?

(7) Can the applicant reserve its place in the queue before it has completed the often burdensome evaluation of its cartel participation?

6.09 Given the rules of inter-temporal application, it can be virtually excluded that the 1996 and 2002 Notices would apply to any new leniency application.[16] However, the 2002 Notice is still the basis for many recent Commission cartel decisions. The following explanations will therefore relate to the 2006 Notice and will indicate when the case law and academic writing relate to the areas in which changes have occurred, and will explain whether the findings and statements made with regard to former versions of the Notice can be transferred to the present situation.

B. Procedures

6.10 According to the wording of the 2006 Notice, leniency or immunity is applied for and granted to undertakings in the competition law sense (ie single economic units which may consist of a multitude of natural or legal persons[17]). Given that prohibition decisions with fines and conditional immunity decisions (see paragraph 18 of the 2006 Notice) are addressed to legal persons,[18] it is important to determine which legal persons belong to the undertaking and thus are meant to be covered by a leniency application and which may ultimately benefit from immunity from fines or a reduction of fines. This is of particular relevance to groups of companies, in which case leniency applications may be made, for example, by either the subsidiary or a joint venture ('JV') that is involved in the infringement or their parent company or companies. Generally all undertakings belonging to a single economic unit at the time of the immunity or leniency application would be covered by an immunity or leniency decision.[19]

---

[16] The 2002 Notice would only apply to a newly introduced application if another member of the cartel had approached the Commission for Leniency before 8 December 2006. Given that usual cartel investigations do not take longer than five years, this is very unlikely to be the case.

[17] Settled case law of the EU courts since Case 170/83 *Hydrotherm v Compact* [1984] ECR 2999, para 11.

[18] WPJ Wils, 'Powers of Investigation and Procedural Rights and Guarantees in EU Antitrust Enforcement', First Lisbon Conference on Competition Law and Economics, Belém, 3–4 November 2005, note 31, states that as regards the choice of the person or persons to whom a violation is to be imputed, the general rule formulated by the EU Courts is that 'when…a violation is found to have been committed, it is necessary to identify the natural or legal person who was responsible for the operation of the undertaking at the time when the violation was committed, so that it can answer for it' (C-279/98 P *Cascades v EC Commission* [2000] ECR I-9709, para 78). If the undertaking found to have committed a violation were found to consist of an unincorporated business (eg several natural persons operating a single business), the Commission would necessarily have to address its fining decision to the natural persons operating the business. However, under Reg 17 and Reg 1/2003 up to now, this situation has not yet occurred. All fines have been imposed on companies or other legal persons. WPJ Wils refers to Decision of the Commission of 21 October 1998 (COMP IV/35.691/ E.4—*Pre-Insulated Pipes* [1999] OJ L24/1, paras 157–60, where the Commission appears to have made an effort to avoid imposing the fine on a natural person (Dr W Henss) who managed and controlled one of the undertakings concerned. See also Case T-9/99 *HFB v EC Commission* [2002] ECR II-1487, para 105.

[19] Case T-161/05 *Hoechst v Commission* [2009] ECR II-3555, paras 75–9.

Despite the Notice's clear wording, in certain cases it would appear that limiting an immu- **6.11** nity/leniency application to a single economic unit would run counter to its effective appli- cation. Such a situation could occur, for instance, where two parent companies of a JV or successive parents of a subsidiary (or JV) would apply for immunity. In most such cases, it is not clear at the time of the leniency application whether both JV parents can be seen as belonging to one single economic unit, since the Commission will not dispose of any proof of actual control at such an early stage of the investigation.[20] Nevertheless, denying immunity/ leniency to one of them while the other discloses the cartel in which both have participated may deter both companies from approaching the Commission and thus would run coun- ter to the aims of the Commission's leniency policy.[21] Therefore, there are good reasons to grant immunity or the same level of leniency to two undertakings on the basis of a single immunity or leniency application. Such a decision would have to be taken on a case-by-case basis and would depend to a large extent on whether the prospective fine of both undertak- ings is roughly equal, so that the benefit of the immunity/leniency application of only one undertaking would be offset by the payment of the fine through the other undertaking. This is typically the case in JV situations, where the JV parents had been equally involved in the cartel.[22] Conversely, in situations of successive parents, a former parent usually is not directly or by imputation responsible for the full period of the cartel and, moreover, does not neces- sarily internalize the risks of the fine payment with the succeeding parent. In such a situation the old parent on the one hand and the new parent and the directly involved subsidiary on the other have each a sufficiently strong isolated interest to apply separately for immunity/ leniency, so that no exception from the rule that only one undertaking can apply is justified. As a result, the facts of each individual case (ie contractual relationship between undertakings internalizing the fining risks, level of involvement in the cartel) should play a decisive role for the acceptance of joint applications.

1. Conditions for the granting of complete immunity

The 2006 Notice largely maintains the generous approach introduced by the 2002 Notice **6.12** and makes it easier than the 1996 Notice for companies to obtain full immunity[23] or a reduc- tion of the fine.[24] In particular, it offers two alternative thresholds. Complete immunity from fines may be obtained by the one undertaking that is the first to submit evidence which in the Commission's view may enable either:

(i) an on-the-spot investigation to be carried out, provided the Commission does not already have sufficient evidence to launch such an inspection (paragraphs 8(a) and 10); or
(ii) the establishment of an infringement of Article 101 TFEU with an alleged cartel that affects the Community, provided that the Commission does not already have sufficient evidence to reach such a finding (paragraphs 8(b) and 11).

---

[20] The daughter and both parents of a 50 per cent/50 per cent full function joint venture can be regarded as one undertaking and a single economic unit if the Commission shows that the two mother companies both exercise actual control over the subsidiary: see Judgment of 2 February 2012 in Case T-76/08 *Dupont v Commission*, paras 58–83, under appeal on this specific point in Case C-172/12.

[21] Groups and JVs tend to internalize the penalty risks associated with a cartel participation, and thus the sanctioning of one undertaking within the JV or group would in certain cases also be sufficient to take away the entire leniency benefit from the party that formally succeeds with its immunity/leniency application before the Commission.

[22] For instance in the Sodium Gluconate cartel both JV parents (Akzo and Avebe) were fined as partici- pants in the cartel and shared the starting amount for the calculation of the fine; for a description of the functioning of that JV see findings of the Court in Case T-314/01 *Avebe v Commission* [2006] ECR II-3085, paras 138–41.

[23] 2006 Notice [2006] OJ C298/19, paras 8–13.

[24] 2006 Notice [2006] OJ C298/19, paras 23–6.

6.13 In the first case the undertaking should provide the Commission with 'concrete and reliable' information in order to launch a 'dawn raid'. The quality of the information is assessed *ex ante* to the inspection, and therefore information found at the inspection cannot be used to counter the value of the information provided by the applicant prior to the inspection.[25] Immunity under paragraph 8(a) could even be obtained if inspections cannot be conducted because of all company premises being located outside the EU.[26] The standard for the quality of the information required for this alternative is high as regards the description of the cartel in terms of geography, product market, and duration, and also depends largely on the information that was already held by the Commission at the time of the immunity application: merely supporting an already existing Commission investigation will not be sufficient, since information is required that leads to the detection of a cartel of which the Commission was unaware.[27] Accordingly, the mere fact that an inspection was conducted by the Commission also on the basis of the information provided in the application is not on its own sufficient indication that the information provided justifies immunity status.[28] Based on the change of the wording in the 2006 Notice that the information must be sufficient to conduct a 'targeted' inspection, the requirements regarding the precision of the information on the cartel provided in the corporate statement will have to be even higher than they were already under the 2002 Notice. In contrast to the 2002 Notice, which only stated that 'sufficient evidence' for conducting an inspection must be provided, the 2006 Notice now stipulates in more detail categories and types of information that has to be provided in order to qualify for immunity. In particular the applicant now must provide a corporate statement that explains its involvement in the cartel and the main characteristics of the cartel (paragraph 9(a) of the 2006 Notice) together with all the actual, preferably contemporaneous, evidence available to it at the time of the application (paragraph 9(b) of the 2006 Notice).

6.14 In the second alternative of paragraph 8 of the 2006 Notice, immunity may be granted if the applicant adds sufficient information to the facts about the cartel already known to the Commission to enable it to conclude on an infringement of Article 101 TFEU equally accompanied by an obligatory corporate statement.[29] This requirement is more demanding than the first alternative in terms of the quality of the documentary evidence that has to be provided, because the evidence has to be very concrete and direct, which means that the applicant for immunity must volunteer clear information suggesting the existence of an infringement.[30] The undertaking will only be granted immunity if the Commission did not have, at the time of the submission, sufficient evidence to find an infringement of Article 101

---

[25] See footnote 1 of 2006 Notice [2006] OJ C298/19.

[26] While this could be seen as a circumvention of the higher standard for information under para 8(b), the Commission is granting immunity in such cases in order to encourage companies outside the EU to come forward with immunity and thus in order to preserve the efficiency of the Leniency Programme. Whether such cases will, however, in practice be investigated and brought to decision stage by the Commission remains to be seen.

[27] Judgment of 13 July 2007 in Case T-151/07 *Kone v Commission*, paras 111 and 113.

[28] In Judgment of 13 July 2007 in Case T-151/07 *Kone v Commission*, para 117f, the immunity applicants had provided the Commission with information that was in principle suitable for the preparation of a second inspection in the case. The Commission then also conducted an inspection partly basing itself on the information provided by the applicant. Nevertheless, at the time of the application the Commission had already gathered information on the *geographic and product coverage* of the cartel that was sufficient to carry out an inspection. Since the applicant could not prove that the information it had provided served the preparation of inspections regarding a different infringement than the one already known by the Commission (ie other products or geographic coverage), it could not benefit from immunity under para 8(a) of the 2006 Notice. With regard to the provision of information that leads to an increase in the duration of the infringement, see para 6.25 et seq on partial immunity.

[29] 2006 Notice [2006] OJ C298/19, para 11.

[30] See eg Commission Press Release IP/04/1313 'Commission fines Coats and Prym for a cartel in the needle market and other haberdashery products' of 26 October 2004, when fining Coats and Prym for a

TFEU in connection with the alleged cartel.[31] It is therefore in the interests of applicants to provide as much evidence as possible in a timely manner. This is even more important since the provision of inaccurate or incomplete evidence may be seen at a later stage as a lack of cooperation, leading to the loss of immunity and leniency.[32]

The Commission retains a wide margin of appreciation to determine whether the information **6.15** supplied by the applicant fulfils the conditions of paragraph 8 of the 2006 Notice.[33] In general immunity from fines can only be accorded in strictly exceptional situations.[34] The Commission may assess the quality of the information and statement provided in comparison with the information and statements provided by other immunity applicants, and could subsequently conclude on the basis of such comparative analysis that the applicant did not genuinely cooperate.[35] Thus, the level of cooperation needed for immunity will also very much depend on the specifics of each individual cartel: in cartels in which secrecy played a particularly important role and the Commission is unable to obtain any information via its investigative powers, a lower level of cooperation may suffice for immunity than in cartels where the Commission was already able to investigate most details of the cartel via its investigative instruments. The discretion has to be exercised by the Commission in the limits set by the 2006 Notice and is only subject to a limited EU Courts review of manifest errors of assessment of the quality of the information in the context of the concrete cartel investigation.[36] It is is incumbent on a party wishing to show that the information provided by another applicant was not good enough to prove that in the absence of such information the Commission would not have been able to prove the essential elements of the infringement and therefore to adopt a decision imposing fines.[37] Such proof of hypothetical decision making within the Commission will regularly

---

cartel in the needle market and other haberdashery products. Entaco benefited from full immunity of fines because it came forward and disclosed information which enabled the Commission to take this decision; see also Commission Press Release IP/05/61 'Antitrust: Commission imposes €216.91 million in fines on MCAA chemicals cartel' of 19 January 2005, in which Clariant received full immunity for being the first to provide evidence of the existence of the cartel to the Commission. B Van Barlingen and M Barennes, 'The European Commission's Leniency Notice in Practice' (2005) Autumn (3) Competition Policy Newsletter 6, 7, note 1, explain that the Commission policy is to use the lower of the two thresholds for conditional immunity whenever both options have been applied for because the legal position of the applicant would not be different under para 8(a) and para 8(b) of the 2002 Notice. The Commission would be able to grant conditional immunity more quickly than if it first had to make a definitive analysis of whether the evidence provided for is sufficient to establish an infringement of Art 101 TFEU. The General Court confirmed that the evidence for immunity under para 8b needs to be 'precise and consistent documentary evidence', thus in other words evidence will not suffice on which the Commission cannot directly base the finding of an infringement in its decision; Judgment of 13 June 2011 *Kone v Commission*, paras 94, 99, and 105.

[31] 2006 Notice [2006] OJ C298/19, para 11.

[32] Joined Cases C-189/02 P, C-202/02 P, C-205/02 P to C-208/02 P, and C-213/02 P *Dansk Rørindustri A/S v Commission* [2005] ECR I-5425, para 395 f.

[33] Joined Cases C-189/02 P, C-202/02 P, C-205/02 P to C-208/02 P, and C-213/02 P *Dansk Rørindustri A/S v Commission* [2005] ECR I-5425, para 394; Joined Cases C-125/07 P, C-133/07 P, C-135/07 P, and C-137/07 P *Erste Group Bank AG v Commission* [2009] ECR I-8681, para 248f; Case T-343/08, *Arkema France v Commission* [2011] ECR II-2287, paras 134 and 135.

[34] Judgment of 18 June 2013, C-681/11 *Schenker and others v Bundeswettbewerbsbehörde*, para 49.

[35] In Case C-328/05 P *SGL Carbon AG v Commission* 2007 [ECR] I-3921, para 88f, the Court indicates the discretion of such comparative analysis only with regard to the level of cooperation of the company and not with regard to the quality of the information provided. According to para 21 of the 2006 Notice, the Commission will only consider a single immunity application at a time and thus a comparative analysis is at least excluded for the first application submitted and will often not be the basis for any decision on conditional immunity. Thus, once the Commission has decided on a provisional basis on conditional immunity, it can withdraw the immunity granted only if it finds out about a lack of genuine cooperation on the basis of applications from other leniency applicants or through other sources or about the coercion of another undertaking in the sense of para 22 of the 2006 Notice.

[36] Case C-511/06 *Archer Daniels v Commission* [2009] ECR I-5843, para 152.

[37] Case T-343/08 *Arkema France v Commission* [2011] ECR II-2287, para 135.

be almost impossible to provide. However, when exercising its discretion the Commission must furthermore respect the principle of equal treatment.[38] If the information provided only repeats or even corroborates information provided by another applicant, the Commission will not normally grant immunity or even any leniency reduction.[39] Similarly, if none of the information provided is relevant for the setting of a fine under Regulation 1/2003, neither immunity nor leniency will be granted.[40] Leniency and immunity may also not be granted if the information provided was in principle useful but would have required that the Commission further investigate details that, although possibly known to the applicant, were not provided to the Commission.[41] Thus it is not sufficient to provide the Commission with information that is in principle useful; indeed, the applicant has to significantly ease the Commission's investigative tasks.[42] Conversely, if the inspection or subsequent information requests reveal that the information provided, albeit being detailed, was incomplete or inaccurate in a way that raises doubts as to the genuine cooperation of the applicant, this may lead to the total loss of immunity or leniency benefits;[43] while it is in theory not excluded that other applicants may move up into the position of the applicant that lost immunity or leniency, in practice this appears almost impossible, since the information provided by the applicant that lost immunity or leniency usually remains on the file and constitutes the benchmark for the assessment of the 'value' of subsequent applications.[44]

6.16 Given the wording of the 2006 Notice it is questionable, whether the Commission will grant immunity if the corporate statement does not exhaustively describe all the aspects of the cartel required under paragraph 9(a) but the evidence provided under paragraph 9(b) is already *prima facie* sufficient to conduct an inspection or to conclude on an infringement of

---

[38] Case T-29/05 *Deltafina SpA v Commission* [2010] ECR II-4077, para 399.
[39] Joined Cases T-456/05 and T-457/05 *Gütermann and Zwicky v Commission* [2010] ECR II-1443, para 222; Case T-38/02 *Groupe Danone v Commission* [2005] ECR II-4407, para 455; Case T-343/08, *Arkema France v Commission* [2011] ECR II-2287, para 137.
[40] Case T-224/00, *Archer Daniels (lysine) v Commission* [2003] ECR II-2597, para 297. Case T-448/05 *Oxley Threads v Commission* [2010] ECR II-69, para 125.
[41] Case T-343/08 *Arkema France v Commission* [2011] ECR II-2287, para 151.
[42] See analysis undertaken in Case T-343/08 *Arkema France v Commission* [2011] ECR II-2287, para 157.
[43] Joined Cases C-189/02 P, C-202/02 P, C-205/02 P to C-208/02 P, and C-213/02 P, *Dansk Rørindustri A/S v Commission* [2005] ECR I-5425, para 395f. Similarly, if the applicant goes beyond its obligation to reply to questions of the Commission but rather misleads the Commission by inaccurate or incomplete information, it may lose any leniency benefit: see Case T-101/05 *BASF and UCB v Commission* [2007] ECR II-4959, para 92.
[44] According to para 8 of the 2006 Notice [2006] OJ C298/19, the Commission will grant immunity only to the applicant that is *first* to submit information that enables the Commission *in its view* to carry out a targeted inspection (lit a) or to find an infringement in connection with the alleged cartel (lit b). It could be inferred from this wording that immunity is 'consumed' to the detriment of potential second candidates once the Commission has received the information mentioned, even if the first applicant is eventually not granted immunity because, for example, it does not comply with its duty of cooperation under para 12 of the 2006 Notice, or it emerges that he coerced another undertaking to participate in the cartel in the sense of para 22 of the 2006 Notice. In the authors' view there is no reason to per se exclude access to immunity for the second applicant in such a situation. In the contrary, the availability of immunity or higher reduction band for leniency may serve as a further incentive for the second applicant to cooperate better and provide even more information. However, the second applicant would only be able to receive immunity if the information '*enables*' the Commission to carry out a targeted inspection. As long as the information of the first applicant that in the Commission's view in the provisional immunity decision enabled it to conduct a targeted inspection is still on the file, it is hard to conceive a situation where the second applicant would be able to satisfy the conditions of para 8 of the 2006 Notice. A more likely possibility to do so could be given if the first applicant decides to withdraw its corporate statement from the Commission's file on the basis of para 20 of the 2006 Notice. With regard to leniency, the question in principle has to be answered in analogy to what is submitted on immunity: the assessment of significant added value in the sense of para 24 of the 2006 Notice has to be undertaken by the Commission at the point in time when the application of the second applicant was submitted. Since for a leniency application there is no option for the first applicant to withdraw the information from the Commission's file, the second applicant can in practice not be seen as having submitted significant added value regarding the investigation of the cartel as the first. Thus, moving up the rank for a leniency applicant seems in theory only possible if it provided information about a competition law infringement (ie other product or geographic coverage) other than the first applicant.

Article 101 TFEU.[45] The Commission does not appear to have formed a definitive view on this point. The wording of the 2006 Notice is not clear, since on the one hand it links the two requirements for information and evidence, ie paragraphs 9(a) and 9(b), with the conjunction '*and*' indicating a cumulative requirement, but on the other hand it requires under paragraph 9(a) only the provision of information '*insofar as known to the applicant*', which indicates some flexibility and also margin of appreciation for the Commission when assessing the completeness of the corporate statement. The obligatory requirement to provide a corporate statement is the major change introduced by the 2006 Notice. Despite not being clearly delineated in the motivations for the 2006 Notice, the requirement was aimed not only at procedurally clarifying the protection of corporate statements from private litigation discovery,[46] but also at ensuring that the Commission is always provided with a corporate statement and not just with huge amounts of documentary information where it is not immediately clear whether it contains the relevant quality for immunity/leniency. Therefore, in the interests of a swift and clear decision on immunity, the Commission is likely to see the existence of a full and complete corporate statement at the point at which the full application should have been provided as a condition *sine qua non* for the granting of immunity. Thus, written reassurance about the completeness of the corporate statement should be sought from the Commission as early as possible in the application process, and the statement should always clearly and comprehensively cover all points mentioned in paragraph 9(a) of the notice. Conversely, the provision of a corporate statement alone will also not suffice for receiving immunity. The statement also has to be accompanied by all documentation available at the time of the inspection in the sense of paragraph 9(b) of the 2006 Notice.

The receipt of immunity is excluded if the applicant has coerced another undertaking to participate in the cartel.[47] A coercer may, however, still qualify for leniency. This exemption has so far never been applied in practice. However, under the 2006 Guidelines for setting fines,[48] coercion is an aggravating circumstance that has been applied in practice several times.[49] Thus, immunity might be withdrawn on the basis of paragraph 22 of the Notice if the Commission comes to the conclusion in the fining section of the decision that the immunity applicant was acting as a coercer. Conversely, unlike in the 1996 Notice, no exclusion of immunity is foreseen for the instigator, albeit it is somewhat unclear where the distinctive line between coercer and instigator lies and whether in practice the two concepts might overlap. For coercion one would have to ask for some sort of pressure being exercised on another participant of the cartel, while for instigation it would appear to already be sufficient to have been the first undertaking that convinced other participants of its idea for the cartel. The 2006 Notice has now made the concept of coercion more precise by specifying in its paragraph 13 that the coercion must relate to forcing[50] another undertaking to either

6.17

---

[45] This situation will often occur when companies are trying to reserve the first place in the queue by sending all available information on the cartel to the Commission, but are not yet able to complete a corporate statement as required by para 9(a) of the 2006 Notice. The marker, if applicable, would not always help in such a situation, since the deadline set for the submission of the full corporate statement may be too short for the applicant to acquire the full information necessary to complete the corporate statement.

[46] See for instance the explanatory note for the consultation of the 2006 Notice available at <http://ec.europa.eu/competition/cartels/legislation/leniency_2006_en.pdf>.

[47] See 2006 Notice [2006] OJ C298/19, paras 13 and 22.

[48] Guidelines on the method of setting fines imposed pursuant to Article 23(2)(a) of Regulation No 1/2003 [2006] OJ C210/2.

[49] See Ch 11, Infringement Decisions and Penalties, at para 11.60(v) for examples of coercion as an aggravating circumstance.

[50] The German text uses the even term 'gezwungen', while the French, like the English text, is much wider, using the term 'contraindre'. A meaningful interpretation of the concept of coercion used here cannot mean to force another undertaking in the sense of *vis absoluta* (which would exclude the liability of the

join the cartel or to remain in it.[51] A mere attempt to force a participant is not sufficient;[52] it is required that the threats used by the coercer are actually the cause of the participation of another undertaking in a cartel. Therefore, it is difficult for an undertaking to claim that it has been actually coerced to participate in a cartel (and to thereby deprive the immunity applicant of receiving immunity and possibly improve its position in the leniency race), if it has not either shown somehow that it distanced itself from the cartel or has approached the Commission with a complaint describing its coercion prior to the immunity application.[53]

2. The procedure to obtain immunity

6.18 As we have seen, the procedures introduced by the 2002 Notice were intended to address the weaknesses of the 1996 Notice, in particular in regard to the uncertainty as to whether full immunity or only a leniency reduction will be granted.[54] The 2006 Notice has continued on this path by introducing a marker procedure.

6.19 Under the 2006 Notice an immunity applicant has three options for approaching the Commission for immunity:

(1) to provide a full immunity application to the Commission;[55] or
(2) to apply for a marker and only provide the full immunity application at the time set by the Commission in the marker;[56] or alternatively
(3) to introduce a so-called hypothetical application which omits the disclosure of the identity of the applicant until the Commission has verified the value of the available information on the product or service concerned by the alleged cartel, its geographic scope, and its estimated duration.[57]

6.20 Upon request, the Commission will provide an acknowledgement of receipt that confirms the date and time of the application.[58] The Commission will not consider other applications for immunity from fines before it has taken a position on the pending application of each specific undertaking in relation to the same suspected infringement.[59]

---

other undertaking under Arts 101 and 102), but rather must relate to *vis compulsiva*, which implies that the other undertaking took a wilful decision to participate in the cartel on the basis of threats or similar incentives imposed by the coercer (for instance the threat and application of physical violence to compel another undertaking to participate in a cartel, Decision in Case C 38.279 *French Beef* [2003] OJ L209/12, para 173).

[51] 2006 Notice [2006] OJ C298/19, para 22 does not make these specifications but would have to be interpreted in light of the clearer formulation in para 13 of the Notice.

[52] Judgment of 2 February 2012 in Case T-83/08 *Denka Chemicals and others v Commission*, paras 61 and 62.

[53] Judgment of 2 February 2012 in Case T-83/08 *Denka Chemicals and others v Commission*, paras 61 and 62. It is conceivable that the coerced undertaking can prove the coercion if it can provide the Commission with documentary evidence that shows threats of such a nature that it appears convincing that it has been actually coerced into participation in the cartel. Conversely, the fact that an undertaking has been put under pressure to participate in a cartel does not, no matter how great the pressure, relieve the undertaking concerned of its liability for the infringement committed, does not alter the gravity of the cartel, and cannot constitute an attenuating circumstance for the purpose of the setting of fines, since the undertaking concerned could have reported any pressure to the competent authorities and made a complaint to them (see to that effect, Joined Cases C-189/02 P, C-202/02 P, C-205/02 P to C-208/02 P, and C-213/02 P, *Dansk Rørindustri A/S v Commission* [2005] ECR I-5425, paras 369 and 370, and Case T-62/02 *Union Pigments v Commission* [2005] ECR II-5057, para 63).

[54] 2002 Notice [2002] OJ C45/3, paras 12–19.

[55] 2006 Notice [2006] OJ C298/19, paras 14, 16(a), and 18.

[56] 2006 Notice [2006] OJ C298/19, paras 14, 15, and 16(a).

[57] 2006 Notice [2006] OJ C298/19, paras 14, 16(b), and 19.

[58] 2006 Notice [2006] OJ C298/19, para 17.

[59] 2006 Notice [2006] OJ C298/19, para 21. It is not conceivable that several separate undertakings sign the same application and receive immunity together, since only one undertaking can effectively apply for leniency. See also the different suggestion by Philippe Billiet, 'How Lenient is the EC Leniency Policy? A Matter of Certainty and Predictability' [2009] 30(1) ECLR 20.

Once the Commission has received evidence that fulfils the various criteria, it grants the **6.21** company conditional immunity from fines in writing. Note that an undertaking which fails to meet the conditions set out in paragraph 8(a) and (b), as appropriate, may withdraw the evidence disclosed for the purposes of its immunity application or request the Commission to consider it under Section III of the 2006 Notice.[60] The return of the information does not, however, prevent the Commission from using its investigative powers to eventually uncover the potential cartel of which it has been made aware by the attempt of an unsuccessful immunity application. In that context the Commission may request the same or similar information that it has returned to the applicant by its investigative powers under Articles 18(2) and (3) of Regulation 1/2003.[61]

In order to enhance the chances of being the first, an immunity applicant in principle **6.22** now has the possibility, under the 2006 Notice, of obtaining a marker that allows it to preserve its place in the queue until it has been able to complete all the investigations and drafting necessary for a valid immunity application. The marker has to be requested from the Commission and is granted upon its discretion ('may'). The Commission decides whether a marker is granted and sets the deadline by which time the marker has to be perfected. The system was introduced to further enhance competition amongst immunity applicants for the first place in the queue in exceptional circumstances where an applicant has good reasons why an application cannot immediately be handed in, such as, for instance, recent changes in the company's management requiring further investigations for the completion of the required company statement.[62] Conversely the marker procedure is not meant to make it possible for parties to make use of a 'salami' tactic with regard to the information provided to the Commission in an attempt to provide a minimum possible of self-incriminating information for the receipt of immunity. Therefore, the request for a marker will regularly have to justify why the information cannot be immediately provided, and the Commission has to be reassured of the applicant's genuine cooperation. Equally, the timelines for the perfection of the marker will be very short and normally will not exceed one month.[63]

An undertaking may initially present this evidence in hypothetical terms,[64] in which case it **6.23** must present a descriptive list of the evidence it proposes to disclose at a later agreed date. If these conditions are not satisfied, the undertaking may withdraw the evidence disclosed. Withdrawal of the application may only be a viable option where an application has not gone beyond the hypothetical stage. While the Commission would be required to use its ordinary investigative powers to obtain the relevant information outside the framework of the immunity application, it may not be expected to adopt a position of 'acute amnesia' towards the

---

[60] 2006 Notice [2006] OJ C298/19, para 20.

[61] In that context note that EU law recognizes only a very limited right to not incriminate oneself in competition proceedings, Ch 7, 'Investigation of Cases (II): Formal Investigative Measures in General, Requests for Information and Interviews', para 7.43. The Commission will not, however, be able to use its knowledge of the returned information to prove under Arts 23 or 24 of Reg 1/2003 that the company would have provided inaccurate, incomplete, or misleading information in reply to a request pursuant to Art 18 of Reg 1/2003.

[62] See MEMO06/357, 'Competition: Commission proposes changes to the Leniency Notice—frequently asked questions', 29 September 2006.

[63] The Commission will strive to create the greatest possible competition amongst several applicants by not preventing the possibility of others receiving immunity through an over-long deadline for the perfection of the marker.

[64] Through this hypothetical offer companies are able to discuss anonymously with the Commission officials if they are in position to seek leniency without making admissions or revealing incriminating documents. See 'Hypothetical applications', para 6.19.

existence of the infringement that has been brought to its attention.[65] The fall-back option is to request the Commission to consider it to proceed to a reduction of the fine.[66] Once the administrative procedure is finished, the Commission will check the undertaking has met the cumulative conditions[67] and, if so, the Commission will grant the undertaking the immunity in the relevant decision.

6.24 If the company is represented by counsel, the application should include a power of attorney.

3. Partial or *de facto* immunity

6.25 The Court had already established for the 1996 Notice that:

> It is inherent in the logic of immunity from fines that only one of the cartel members can have the benefit, given that the effect being sought is to create a climate of uncertainty within cartels by encouraging their denunciation to the Commission. That uncertainty results precisely from the fact that the cartel participants know that only one of them can benefit from immunity from being fined by denouncing the other participants in the infringement, thereby exposing them to the risk that they face more severe fines.[68]

This logic has not changed with the 2002 Notice. However, since then a company other than the first may obtain what colloquially is called 'partial' or '*de facto* immunity' if it is the first to provide compelling evidence that has an influence on the gravity or duration of the infringement. According to paragraph 26 of the 2006 Notice, the applicant that is first to provide compelling evidence increasing the gravity or the duration of the infringement will be treated for the calculation of its fine as if that information was not in the Commission's possession. Evidence is compelling if it does not necessarily require corroboration. Unilateral statements which are not supported by precise and consistent documentary evidence of the infringement are not sufficient.[69] Also not sufficient is information that provides merely significant added value for the detection of the cartel as it is required for obtaining leniency but is not explicitly and directly related to the gravity and duration of the infringement which was previously unknown to the Commission.[70] Pursuant to paragraph 26 of the 2006 Notice, *de facto* immunity is granted for the period of time of the infringement that has been uncovered by a specific applicant or for an applicant that is the first to provide compelling evidence that would justify increasing the fine as an aggravating circumstance.

6.26 Unlike point 23 of the 2002 Notice, the 2006 Notice does not explicitly require that the facts submitted to the Commission for partial immunity need to be previously unknown to the Commission. The Commission had placed great importance on the wording of the 2002 Notice as excluding partial immunity if the evidence only critically reinforces the ability of

---

[65] The principles set out in Case C-67/91 *Dirección General de Defensa de la Competencia (DGDC) v Asociación Española de Banca Privada (AEB) and others ('Spanish Banks')* [1992] ECR I-4785, may prevent the Commission from using as direct evidence the information obtained earlier, but it may still be able to initiate its own inquiry aimed at also procuring the very same pieces of information that had previously been returned to the anonymized applicant from all players active in the respective industry.

[66] JM Joshua and PD Camesasca, 'Where Angels Fear to Tread: The Commission's 'New' Leniency Policy Revisited' (2005) 1(5) European Antitrust Review 10, 12, noting that in practice the Commission will not entertain any approach unless the applicant commits in advance to converting the application on the spot to one for a fine reduction rather than walk out.

[67] 2002 Notice [2002] OJ C45/3, para 11. B Van Barlingen and M Barennes, 'The European Commission's Leniency Notice in Practice' (2005) Autumn (3) Competition Policy Newsletter 6.

[68] Case T-127/04 *KME v Commission* [2009] ECR II-1167, para 130.

[69] Judgment of 15 June 2012 in Case C-494/11 P *Otis et al v Commission*, para 89; related still to the 2002 Notice.

[70] Judgment of 27 September 2012 in Case T-347/06 *Nynas v Commission*, para 32f.

the Commission to prove certain facts with regard to which it already had evidence on its file.[71] This had also been confirmed by the court.[72]

4. The conditions for the grant of a leniency fine reduction

In the context of leniency, several scenarios can arise:[73] **6.27**

First, it may be that the facts reported to the Commission are not covered by the material **6.28** scope of the Leniency Notice because they do not relate to cartel arrangements. In these cases, the Commission services address so-called 'non-eligibility letters' to the applicant, which are short standard letters indicating that—without prejudice to the compatibility of the reported arrangements with EC competition rules—those arrangements do not fall within the scope of the 2006 Notice and the applicant may withdraw the evidence disclosed.

Secondly, immunity applications may not meet the substantive conditions for conditional **6.29** immunity under paragraph 8(a) of the 2006 Notice. This means that carrying out an inspection would not be possible on the basis of the information provided. The Commission adopts a 'rejection decision' whereby it denies conditional immunity. In instances where the application for immunity cannot be granted, the undertakings usually opt for a reduction of fine rather than withdrawing the evidence. The application for a reduction of fine then remains on the record, but only becomes active if the Commission decides to investigate the matter further.

Thirdly, it may occur that *prima facie*, not all of the conditions of the 2006 Notice are met (eg **6.30** the effects of the infringement are geographically limited) and the case is not suitable for further investigation in accordance with the priorities that the Commission has established for its enforcement policy. It appears that the Commission will then send a so-called 'no action letter' stating that it does not intend to investigate the matter further without prejudice to the power to take a position on the application for immunity at a later stage. The decision on the initial immunity is somehow put on hold in case the applicant does not withdraw its application.[74]

Lastly, as indicated earlier, a loss of leniency may occur where the company does not cooper- **6.31** ate fully with the Commission throughout the procedure (eg the applicant does not terminate its involvement in the cartel or reveals that it may face liability for an antitrust infringement under the rules of the US Securities and Exchange Commission). Rather than withdrawing the conditional immunity it had granted, the Commission will decide in its prohibition decisions not to grant immunity.

All these four scenarios involve provisional measures not affecting the rights of the applicant **6.32** unless there is a final fining decision; therefore they could only be appealed before the Court in the context of an appeal against any final fining decision.[75]

---

[71] See Commission Decision of 12 November 2008 in Case COMP/39125 *Carglass*, para 725.

[72] Judgment of 27 September 2012 in Case T-347/06 *Nynas v Commission*, para 32f.

[73] See generally, B Van Barlingen and M Barennes, 'The European Commission's Leniency Notice in Practice' (2005) Autumn (3) Competition Policy Newsletter 6, 11, who refer to applications for immunity which concern the review of clauses in business contracts. Those may raise issues under Art 101 TFEU, but would certainly not reflect secret cartel arrangements. When asking for immunity for such agreements, the companies would attempt to create something similar to the previous but abolished notification system.

[74] See B Van Barlingen and M Barennes, 'The European Commission's Leniency Notice in Practice' (2005) Autumn (3) Competition Policy Newsletter 6, 11–13.

[75] According to settled case law, only measures which produce binding legal effects such as to affect the interests of an applicant by bringing about a distinct change in his legal position may be the subject of an action for annulment under Art 267 TFEU: Case T-125/03 *Akzo and others v Commission* [2007] ECR II-3523, para 45.

6.33   Companies that are unable to obtain full or partial immunity may still obtain a reduction of the fine according to a decreasing scale.[76] As its predecessor from 2002, the 2006 Notice requires those undertakings requesting a reduction to contribute with evidence of the suspected infringement that has 'significant added value' ('SAV') with respect to the evidence already in the Commission's possession.[77] Paragraph 25 of the 2006 Notice describes the concept of SAV by referring to the extent to which the evidence provided strengthens, by its very nature and/or its level of detail, the Commission's ability to prove the facts in question.[78] The Commission enjoys a broad margin of assessment, reviewable by the Courts only for manifest errors, when it is required to determine whether the evidence provided by an undertaking that has stated that it wishes to benefit from leniency represents SAV.[79]

6.34   For the assessment of the significance of evidence provided in a leniency application, paragraph 25 of the 2006 Notice sets out a hierarchy on the basis of which the Commission will assess its significance and value:

(i) Written contemporaneous evidence (ie notes from meetings, email exchanges, calendar entries) has a higher value than evidence subsequently established (ie interviews with employees, corporate statements).

(ii) Direct evidence of a cartel (ie evidence of an agreement contrary to Article 101 TFEU) has a higher value than indirect evidence (ie indicia that, seen together, make it appear plausible that an agreement contrary to Article 101 TFEU has been concluded).

(iii) The degree of corroboration from other sources required for the evidence submitted to be relied upon (ie typically corporate statements inculpating other participants in the cartel alone only exceptionally represent evidence of SAV since they require corroboration from other sources in order to constitute sufficient proof of a cartel involvement[80]).

6.35   Furthermore the question of what is evidence of SAV will depend on the knowledge of the Commission of the cartel, the application of the principle of equality with regard to the assessment of the application in comparison with the applications of other leniency applicants, and the specifics of the individual case.[81] Once the quality of the evidence (SAV) has been established,

---

[76] Since in many cases partial immunity may be more beneficial than leniency, it has to be carefully considered which of the two alternatives is chosen in order to achieve the maximum possible reduction of the fine.

[77] 2002 Notice [2002] OJ C45/3, para 21.

[78] B Van Barlingen and M Barennes, 'The European Commission's Leniency Notice in Practice' (2005) Autumn (3) Competition Policy Newsletter 6, 13, describe the situations where it is only through the second applicant that the Commission was able to find an infringement. Where the Commission has already granted immunity under para 8(a) of the 2006 Notice but is not yet able to prove the infringement, a leniency applicant that submits sufficient new evidence to allow the Commission to prove the infringement will be considered as having provided SAV. The same applies where a leniency applicant does not necessarily bring new evidence, but confirms existing evidence where such confirmation is needed to prove the infringement.

[79] Judgment of 15 June 2012 in Joined Cases T-141/07, T-142/07, T 145/07, and T-146/07 *Otis and others v Commission*, paras 263 and 265. With regard to the recognition of evidence as being of SAV please refer also to the explanations given on the quality of evidence required for immunity in paras 6.33–6.36.

[80] 'Statements by one undertaking accused of having participated in a cartel, the accuracy of which is contested by several other undertakings similarly accused, cannot be regarded as constituting adequate proof of an infringement committed by the latter unless it is supported by other evidence, although the degree of corroboration required may be lesser in view of the reliability of the statement at issue', Judgment of 25 October 2011 in Case T-348/08 *Aragonesas Industrias, SAU v Commission*, para 206.

[81] Judgment of 15 June 2012 in Joined Cases T-141/07, T-142/07, T 145/07, and T-146/07 *Otis and others v Commission*, paras 274–8. In that judgment the Court dealt with two leniency applications of Kone and Otis that were related to two different geographic markets. The Court concluded that the principle of equality could not be inferred in that case in that Kone obtained a higher reduction than Otis, since the prior knowledge of the Commission was not identical with regard to the two markets and Kone was earlier with

the level of reduction depends on the point in time when evidence has been provided. According to paragraph 26 of the 2006 Notice, three bands for the level of reduction of fines are available:

(i)   30 to 50 per cent for the first undertaking providing SAV;
(ii) 20 to 30 per cent for the second undertaking providing SAV; and
(iii) 0 to 20 per cent for any subsequent undertaking providing SAV.

Within the bands, the Commission also has a margin of discretion as to what level of leniency   **6.36**
it accords to each individual applicant.[82] The actual amount fixed depends in particular upon the point in time at which the undertakings started to cooperate, the quality of the evidence submitted, and the extent of cooperation throughout the proceedings.[83]

5. The procedure for obtaining a leniency fine reduction

Undertakings that wish to obtain a reduction in their fines must contact the Directorate-General   **6.37**
for Competition ('DG COMP') and submit the formal leniency application identifying the evidence of the cartel that they want to be considered for leniency.[84] As for immunity applications, the Commission only considers other applications for reduction once it has formed its opinion on the existing application regarding the same infringement.[85] Similar to applications for immunity, the Commission will initially take a conditional decision, the definitive one being reserved for the adoption of the final decision. Upon explicit request, the applying undertakings will receive an acknowledgement of receipt from DG COMP recording the date on which the relevant evidence was submitted.[86] When the Commission comes to the preliminary conclusion that the evidence qualifies as SAV and the negative conditions for the granting of immunity are met, it will inform the undertaking in writing no later than the day on which the statement of objections is notified.[87] As with applications for immunity, this preliminary conclusion is conditional. The same notification is also sent to undertakings of which the Commission rejects the applications. The letters assigning bands of reduction are only conditional decisions that do not assign rights to parties before the final fining decision is taken; thus, they are not individually challengeable before the EU Courts.[88] At the end of the administrative procedure the

---

its application related to the German market than Otis was with the submission of evidence related to the Belgian market.

[82] Judgment of 15 June 2012 in Joined Cases T-141/07, T-142/07, T 145/07, and T-146/07 *Otis and others v Commission*, para 264.

[83] The degree of cooperation can be influenced by factors such as the contestation of the facts after receipt of the statement of objections; see Case T-37/05 *World Wide Tobacco España, SA v Commission* [2011] ECR II-41, para 193ff, where, under the 1996 Notice, the Court has not seen the contestation of the effects of the alleged conduct as a contestation of the facts relevant for the infringement and has lowered the fine accordingly for another 10 per cent (from the 25 per cent granted by the Commission for cooperation to 35 per cent).

[84] 2006 Notice [2006] OJ C298/19, para 27. The wording of the 2006 Notice that, unlike for immunity applications, does not set out the requirement of a compulsory corporate statement, indicates lower requirements for a leniency application than for a corporate statement (ie it would appear that a leniency application does not need to contain a comprehensive description of the cartel but is rather satisfactory when it lists the evidence submitted; however, the more precisely the cartel is described, the more likely is a higher reduction within a band).

[85] 2006 Notice [2006] OJ C298/19, para 28.

[86] 2006 Notice [2006] OJ C298/19, para 28.

[87] 2006 Notice [2006] OJ C298/19, para 29. The notification of the statement of objections thus seem to mark the end of availability of leniency; yet where an undertaking reveals another dimension to a cartel which would result in issuing a further statement of objections, a fine reduction might still be available. Kerse & Khan, *EC Antitrust Procedure* (5th edn, 2005), para 7-060. B Van Barlingen and M Barennes, 'The European Commission's Leniency Notice in Practice' (2005) Autumn (3) Competition Policy Newsletter 6, 15, on procedural issues.

[88] See also Ch 15, 'Steps Following the Adoption of a Formal Decision. Judicial Review'.

Commission may adopt a fining decision where it will definitively evaluate the level of reduction of the fine.

6.38 The 2006 Notice is silent on the possibility of using the hypothetical application for a leniency in a similar way as it can be used for immunity application. *E contrario* one therefore has to conclude that hypothetical leniency applications are not acceptable. In practice, a hypothetical leniency application makes little sense, since leniency applications are usually preceded by an immunity application that has ultimately revealed the identity of the cartel participants.

6. Reasons for exclusion or loss of provisionally granted immunity or leniency

6.39 In addition, the 2006 Notice requires all undertakings to meet three further cumulative conditions in order to be granted immunity or leniency in the final Commission decision. The undertaking must:

(i) genuinely and fully cooperate with the Commission on a continuous basis, including but not limited to: providing all evidence that comes into its possession relating to the suspected infringement; remaining at the Commission's disposal to answer requests or to make available (former) employees for interviews; not destroying, falsifying, or concealing relevant information or evidence; not disclosing the fact of the application or its content before a statement of objections has been issued;[89]

(ii) end its involvement in the cartel no later than the time when it submits evidence except for what would be in the Commission's view reasonably necessary to preserve the integrity of the inspections;[90]

(iii) when contemplating making its application to the Commission, not have destroyed, falsified, or concealed evidence of the alleged cartel nor disclosed the fact or any of the content of its contemplated application, except to other competition authorities.[91]

6.40 The decision to apply for leniency also requires the cooperation of the applicant during the entire duration of the Commission's investigation and therefore usually excludes the applicant from making use of its privilege not to incriminate itself.[92] The lack of cooperation can lead to the loss of immunity or leniency, even if the applicant had initially provided sufficient information

---

[89] 2006 Notice [2006] OJ C298/19, para 121(a).

[90] 2006 Notice [2006] OJ C298/19, para 121(b). In *Italian Raw Tobacco*, *Deltafina* had been granted conditional immunity at the beginning of the procedure under the terms of the Leniency Notice, but the Commission decision withheld final immunity 'due to a serious breach by *Deltafina* of its co-operation obligations': having received conditional immunity, *Deltafina* revealed to its main competitors that it had applied for leniency with the Commission (Commission Decision of 20 October 2005, COMP/C.38.261, OJ L353/45 2006, paras 408–60). This occurred before the Commission could carry out surprise inspections, so that when these took place, most companies concerned were already aware of the existence of the Commission investigation. See Commission Press Release IP/05/1315 'Competition: Commission fines companies €56 million for cartel in Italian raw tobacco market', 20 October 2005.

[91] 2006 Notice [2006] OJ C298/19, para 12(c).

[92] See U Soltész, 'Der "Kronzeuge" im Labyrinth des ECN' [2005] Wirtschaft und Wettbewerb 616, 617, who criticizes the fact that undertakings may have less incentive to invoke their rights of defence because they can only obtain a reduction if they cooperate. Such criticism is, however, misplaced: a company that is or has to be fully aware of the self-incriminating nature of its cooperation under the leniency notice renounces in a tradeoff to the protection under the *nemo tenetur principle* in exchange for immunity or leniency. Since the cooperation triggering immunity is also possible and required after the receipt of the statement of objections, cooperation may necessarily imply the abandonment of certain defence possibilities against the Commission's objections. Denying the factual findings of the Commission in full usage of the rights of defence may be the worse alternative, if other cartelists confirm the same findings to the Commission: in such a situation the defence is very likely to be unsuccessful and the then more obvious lack of cooperation will in addition lead to a total loss of any leniency benefit. Giving companies the choice of avoiding such a situation is precisely the sense of the Commission's leniency policy (see Joined Cases C-189/02 P, C-202/02 P, C-205/02 P to C-208/02 P, and C-213/02 P *Dansk Rørindustri A/S v Commission* [2005] ECRI-5425, para 419).

to receive provisional immunity but later failed to genuinely cooperate.[93] Cooperation to avoid the loss of immunity may also be required from an applicant who does not know what the precise subject matter of the Commission's investigation is, since failure to submit any information to the Commission (even such information which is not related to the subject matter of the Commission's investigation) has to be seen as a lack of cooperation and leads to the loss of immunity and leniency benefits.[94] While immunity under the 2006 Notice in principle requires that the applicant ends its involvement in the cartel immediately, it also takes account of the fact that the surprise factor of inspections might be lost if the undertaking stops its activity in the cartel without good reason.[95] Thus, the Commission may, upon request, authorize a certain level of participation in the cartel, if it prevents the other participants from becoming suspicious of the possibility of an inspection. The 2006 Notice extended the duty of cooperation to the period in which an applicant is contemplating about an immunity or leniency application on the basis that it would not be in conformity with the idea of leniency if an applicant was attempting to conceal information related to the cartel before making an application.[96]

Some authors found it debatable under the 2002 Notice whether an immunity applicant that **6.41** has lost its provisionally granted immunity for not satisfying one of the criteria described earlier before the final decision regarding the cartel is adopted may still apply for leniency.[97] Given that the criteria under the 2006 Notice exclude equally the granting of immunity and of leniency, the granting of leniency will now regularly be excluded if immunity has been lost. Leniency may only be considered if immunity has been lost on the basis of coercion under paragraph 22 of the 2006 Notice.[98] Furthermore, a reduction of the fine equal to leniency may be granted under the fining guidelines as a reward for the undertaking's cooperation.[99]

7. Cooperation outside the 2006 Notice

According to paragraph 29 of the 2006 Fining Guidelines, the active cooperation of an **6.42** undertaking may also be taken into account for a reduction of the fine outside the scope of the 2006 Notice. Such a reduction would take place in the context of the calculation of the fine before the application of the 10 per cent cap and will regularly be lower than any reduction on the basis of the 2006 Notice.[100]

C. Protection from Access to Immunity/Leniency Materials versus Private Enforcement Action

Most major cartels operate on a global basis, and parallel or consecutive enforcement action **6.43** by administrative authorities in several jurisdictions is the norm. Cartel participants are in

---

[93] The level of cooperation required is described in examples set out in paras 12(a) and 24 of the 2006 Notice [2006] OJ C298/19.

[94] Case T-410/09 *Almamet v Commission*, paras 57–61.

[95] 2006 Notice [2006] OJ C298/19, paras 12(b) and 24.

[96] 2006 Notice [2006] OJ C298/19, paras 12(c) and 24. See also MEMO/06/356 'Commission proposes changes to the Leniency Notice—frequently asked questions', 29 September 2006.

[97] F Arbault and E Sakkers in J Faul and A Nikpay, *Faul and Nikpay, The EC Law of Competition* (2nd edn, 2007) para 8.149, n 438, in contradiction with the detailed reasoning in Commission Decision of 20 October 2005, COMP/C.38.281 *Deltafina* [2006] OJ L353/45, paras 461–84, denying such a possibility to maintain a failed immunity application as a leniency request. This debate has become moot under the 2006 Notice for other cases than coercion.

[98] See also section on coercion under para 6.17.

[99] Commission Decision of 20 October 2005, COMP/C.38.281 *Deltafina* [2006] OJ L353/45, paras 385–98.

[100] For further details see Ch 11, 'Infringement Decisions and Penalties', para 11.62 at (iv).

parallel also exposed to private enforcement action in various jurisdictions. If leniency materials fell into the hands of private enforcement plaintiffs, this could significantly increase the risk of high damages payments by a cartelist. Thus, cartelists usually expect reassurances from the competition authority that the leniency information will not be disclosed to third parties as a precondition for introducing an immunity/leniency application.

6.44 How far the risk of disclosure of leniency information to private plaintiffs is, indeed, a deterrent for immunity/leniency applicants to come forward is somewhat difficult to quantify and may vary from case to case for a number of reasons.

6.45 Private enforcement systems of the key competition enforcers in the US and the EU continue to diverge largely with regard to their effectiveness: while in the US, a company may be sentenced to pay (treble) damages which are comparable in size or even larger than the cartel fines in the EU, private enforcement action in the EU does not (yet) lead to such high payment risks.[101] This results in leniency/immunity applicants being mainly concerned by disclosure of leniency material in the course of US pre-trial discovery.[102] The increasing popularity of private enforcement in the EU may add to disclosure concerns in the future.

6.46 The national procedural rules on the basis of which plaintiffs may gain access to leniency materials are very different. For instance US discovery rules are extremely far reaching and may cover millions of internal corporate documents, including all of the documents supporting a leniency/immunity application and, if no safeguards are applied, even the immunity/leniency application itself with the implicit or explicit admission of guilt usually contained therein. Conversely, EU private litigation evidentiary rules usually do not contain such far-reaching investigative possibilities in the course of private enforcement actions, making it more attractive to plaintiffs in private enforcement actions against cartelists to seek access to the information contained in the Commission's file.

6.47 The conditions for access to the files of EU competition authorities by plaintiffs litigating against cartelists have not yet been fully clarified by the Union Courts. In particular, there is no final ruling on the balance between the interests of competition authorities to preserve the effectiveness of their investigation by not creating disincentives for leniency applicants to come forward, on the one hand, and the interest to establish an effective private enforcement mechanism in the

---

[101] The deterrent effect is proportionate to the likelihood of private enforcement proceedings being successful and to the amount of damages that can be incurred by the defendant in such proceedings. Furthermore, the level of the fine imposed by the competition authority is also relevant for the risk assessment. So far, such private liability that matches or even exceeds the fines of the Commission can be incurred only in the US, where treble damages settlements can reach much higher amounts than the EU's highest fines. For instance, in the *Microsoft* case the fine confirmed by the General Court ('GC') in Case T-201/04 *Microsoft v Commission* [2007] ECR II-3601 of EUR 497 million (at the time USD 610 million) was exceeded even by the settlement amount reached by RealNetworks (USD 761 million) with regard to conduct (the tying of the Windows media player with the Windows operating system) that justified only a fraction of the EU decision's fine. Conversely, EU private enforcement still does not appear to represent any significant financial risk for cartelists: the method normally applied for the calculation of the incurred damages (limited to only the cartel overcharge) in the EU has not led to the award of compensation that would exceed the EUR 1 million threshold (see for instance Karlsruhe Court of Appeals, Decision of 11 June 2010, Case 6 U 118/05, not even confirmed on appeal with regard to the non-applicability of the passing on defence, BGH, Decision of 28 June 2011, KZR 75/10). See in that regard also the Commission's current consultation on the calculation of damages available at <http://ec.europa.eu/competition/consultations/2011_actions_damages/index_en.html>.

[102] K Nordlander, 'Discovering Discovery—US Discovery of EC Leniency Statements' [2004] ECLR 646, 658, shows that these concerns should not be taken too seriously, in that any admission of guilt contained in a leniency statement despite all possible precautions can easily be used against a cartelist in US court proceedings when the Commission has based a fining decision against the cartelist on it, since the Commission's decision itself constitutes proof in private litigation and key executives can be interrogated about its veracity.

EU, where private plaintiffs would have sufficient access to all documents proving the competition law infringement, on the other. It would go beyond the ambit of this book to describe the file access rules in each individual jurisdiction; the remainder of this section is therefore limited to explaining the access rules to the leniency materials held by the EU Commission.[103]

One of the first safeguards by which the Commission attempted to shield immunity/leniency **6.48** applicants mainly from US pre-trial discovery was to introduce the possibility of oral applications.[104] This procedure has now been formalized and explained in detail in paragraphs 32 to 35 of its 2006 Leniency Notice. Such oral applications made to the Commission are supposed to avoid the existence of a document at the premises of the cartel participants that would be accessible via US discovery rules.[105] In the course of this procedure the applicant's oral corporate statement is usually recorded on tape by the Commission and transcribed.[106] Access to file after the statement of objections is granted to these transcripts and the tape recordings of the leniency statement at the Commission's premises in a so-called 'oral procedure' that is now explicitly described in paragraph 33 of the 2006 Notice.[107] The parties given access to the material are not allowed to make any copy of the leniency statement by mechanical or electronic means.[108] However, they usually make verbatim notes of the recordings in order to defend themselves effectively during the Commission's cartel proceedings. These notes will be fully discoverable in the US and national cartel proceedings unless they are protected by legal privilege.[109] Similar to

---

[103] For access to the file in general see Ch 10, 'Procedures to Establish the Existence of an Infringement'.

[104] The case law before the 2006 Notice [2006] OJ C298/19, had already indicated that transcripts of oral statements made before the Commission could serve as leniency applications: see Joined Cases T-236/01, T-239/01, T-244/01 to T-246/01, and T-252/01 *Tokai Carbon v EC Commission (Graphite Electrodes)* [2004] OJ C251/13, para 431. Such a procedure was first implemented in the Commission's Decision in Case COMP/36.604 *Citric Acid* [2001] L239/18. The 2002 Notice did not mention such procedure explicitly, but *de facto* excluded the use of oral applications by stating in para 33 that only written documents would be added to the Commission's file, making oral applications impossible, given that access to file needs to be granted to any document on which the Commission intends to rely in its statement of objection and final decision.

[105] The Courts of EU Member States are in principle able to request, on the basis of Art 15(1) of Reg 1/2003, a copy of all documents in the Commission's possession, including the transcripts of oral statements made by immunity/leniency applicants vis-à-vis the Commission. However, according to the case law of the EU Courts, the Commission's obligation to transmit such documents is limited if disclosure to the national court would be capable of interfering with the functioning and independence of the Union (see the Order of President of the Court of Justice of 6 December 1990 in Case C-2/88 *Zwartveld and Others* [1990] ECR 1-4405, paras 10 and 11; Case 145/83 *Adams v Commission* [1985] ECR 3539, paras 43–4; Case T-253/94 *Postbank v Commission* [1996] ECR II-921, para 93). This limitation is interpreted in point 26 of the Notice on the Co-Operation with National Courts ([2004] OJ C101/54–64) as excluding the transmission of leniency materials submitted voluntarily by an immunity/leniency applicant without its consent.

[106] 2006 Notice [2006] OJ C298/19, para 32.

[107] This procedure should not be confused with the special access to file procedures mentioned in Art 8, para 4 of the Hearing Officer's Mandate and in the Commission Notice on best practices on the conduct of proceedings concerning Articles 101 and 102 TFEU [2011] OJ C308/6, paras 95–8. Such special procedures are, for instance, the data room procedure, where access is given to economic data that by its nature is difficult to redact from confidential information. For a detailed description of all access procedures to the Commission's file please refer to Ch 10, 'Procedures to Establish the Existence of an Infringement', paras 10.45–10.46.

[108] 2006 Notice [2006] OJ C298/19, para 33.

[109] Since the parties outside counsel will usually take the notes at the Commission's premises, these notes will not be discoverable as long as the counsel does not exchange them with his client. Exchanges with the client's in-house counsel may be protected under national laws of the EU Member States and in the US, despite the lack of protection of in-house counsel correspondence at EU-level, see Ch 8, 'Investigation of Cases (III): Inspections', paras 8.44–8.50. A further important risk that the leniency statement becomes discoverable is during the appeal proceedings regarding the Commission's cartel decision before the GC. in these proceedings the Commission usually makes reference to the full leniency statement in its defence without providing them as an annex to its defence, and explains to the Court that these statements can be provided under Article 65 of the GC's rules of procedure. Under this provision the applicant will not be served with the

written statements, which form part of the Commission's file, oral applications may not be used by the parties being granted access to the file for any purpose other than administrative or legal proceedings for the application of EU competition rules at issue in the related administrative proceedings.[110]

6.49 The Commission's information obtained as a result of an immunity/leniency application may itself be subject to Court discovery or attempts of private plaintiffs in damages action to obtain information further substantiating their claims. The Commission is in principle in the possession of three types of leniency-related materials that would be subject to such access requests:

(i) the leniency/immunity statement itself or a transcript thereof usually containing the undertaking's implicit or explicit admission of guilt (ie of its participation in the cartel);

(ii) pre-existing supporting documents submitted voluntarily by the applicant together with that leniency/immunity application;[111]

(iii) pre-existing documents investigated by the Commission in an inspection or pursuant to an information request on the basis of the knowledge obtained through the leniency application.

So far, it appears that none of these documents have successfully been claimed from the Commission. However, not all possibilities are yet exhausted by which such documents could in theory be obtained, and recent case law of the EU courts may encourage further attempts to obtain leniency materials in the future.[112]

6.50 Plaintiffs in private enforcement action could obtain leniency/immunity-related documents or information from the Commission in two different ways.

6.51 First, it is conceivable that a Court called to decide on a private enforcement action against a cartel member addresses a discovery request or a request for documents directly to the Commission. If the Court is located in one of the EU Member States, then according to paragraph 26 of the Notice on Cooperation with National Courts,[113] all documents voluntarily provided by cartelists during a leniency/immunity application (ie all leniency materials except the ones obtained by the Commission through its own investigations) will not be disclosed to the Court without the agreement of the cartelist. If a US Court addresses the Commission with a request for the transcript of an immunity/leniency statement, then such request may be refused by the Commission on the basis of investigatory privilege on which competition authorities can normally rely under US law.[114] Furthermore, the Commission has succeeded in protecting such information on the

---

documents and the leniency statements are safe from discovery. However, if the Court requests the documents under Art 64 of the GC's rules of procedure, the leniency statement will be served upon the applicant, which creates the risk of discovery. See in that regard Case T-113/07 *Toshiba v Commission* [2011] ECR II-3989.

[110] 2006 Notice [2006] OJ C298/19, para 34.

[111] The term 'pre-existing' thereby refers to the existence of the documents prior to the commencement of the Commission's investigation. Such documents are drafted *in tempore non suspectu*, therefore have a high probative value, and are usually also subject to discovery proceedings at the cartelists' premises.

[112] On 11 June 2013 the Commission adopted a proposal for a directive on certain rules governing actions for damages under national law for infringements of European and national competition law (COM(2013) 404 final). The proposal attempts to introduce an absolute protection from disclosure of the leniency/immunity statements and a temporary protection for the duration of the Commission's investigation of pre-existing documents. Arguably, there is a tension between the absolute protection suggested by this proposal in its Article 6(1) and the case law of the EU Courts foreseeing a case-by-case balancing exercise between the rights of plaintiffs derived from Art 101 to be effective in private enforcement actions versus the specific and substantiated public interest to preserve the effectiveness of competition investigations. Since the case law is largely based on the interpretation of Treaty provisions and general principles of European law, there may be doubts whether a directive like this can prevail over the court rulings described in the following paragraphs.

[113] [2004] OJ C101/54–64.

[114] K Nordlander, 'Discovering Discovery—US Discovery of EC Leniency Statements' [2004] ECLR 646, 657, explaining on the basis of the *Vitamins* case that the oral procedure explained earlier would also help the

basis of the principle of international comity, arguing that disclosure 'would be highly detrimental to the sovereign interests and public policies of the EU, and would substantially undermine the Commission's ability to detect and punish unlawful cartel activity'.[115]

Secondly, according to Article 2(1) and (3) of Regulation 1049/2001 on transparency and **6.52** access to documents,[116] any natural or legal person residing or having its registered office in a Member State has a right of access to documents of the Commission, including all documents submitted during an immunity or leniency application. The Commission has so far successfully attempted to protect access to immunity/leniency documents based on Article 4(2) and (3) second indent of Regulation 1049/2001. The possibility of such protection has currently been challenged in numerous proceedings and is subject to scrutiny by the EU Courts. Article 4(2) of Regulation 1049/2001 allows for a refusal to grant access to a document where disclosure would undermine the protection of:

  (i)   commercial interests of a natural or legal person, including intellectual property;
 (ii)   court proceedings and legal advice; and
(iii)   for the purpose of inspections, investigations, and audits.

Article 4(3) allows refusal of access if disclosure of the document would seriously undermine **6.53** the institution's decision-making process. All these exceptions from the access right have to be interpreted strictly.[117] The most appropriate category of exemption appeared to be that of commercial interests, whereby these would be understood as the immunity/leniency applicants' interest not to be exposed to private enforcement actions. However, the General Court ('GC') has not seen this interest to be worthy of protection on the basis that:

> the interest of a company which took part in a cartel in avoiding such actions cannot be regarded as a commercial interest and, in any event, does not constitute an interest deserving of protection, having regard, in particular, to the fact that any individual has the right to claim damages for loss caused to him by conduct which is liable to restrict or distort competition.[118]

Thus, it appears that the immunity/leniency applicant can avoid disclosure of the docu- **6.54** ments under the first indent of Article 4(2) only if it had successfully claimed, vis-à-vis the Commission, confidentiality on the basis of the access to file and publication rules of Article 28 of Regulation 1/2003.[119] Thus, a leniency/immunity applicant can only protect

---

Commission with claiming investigatory privilege for the leniency materials on its file. However, Nordlander seems to depart from the assertion that if investigatory privilege were not granted to the Commission, it might be under an obligation to disclose the leniency statement in the US discovery proceedings. Such an obligation is, however, far from clear, since public authorities may refuse to comply with such an order (as many of the EU Member State authorities do with regard to discovery in treble damages cases). Another question would be whether the Commission would feel obliged under the principle of comity to comply with a discovery order, which seems rather doubtful given that the US judge ordering discovery has in the first place overridden the Commission's interest in protecting the efficiency of its investigation.

[115] See Mlex, 'New York judge sides with EC in protection of air-cargo cartel decision' 22 December 2011; the confidential air cargo decision in this case contained the usual references to the statements of leniency applicants. The Commission is supported by the Department of Justice ('DoJ') in its attempt to protect the efficiency of its leniency program, see Mlex, 'DOJ pledges support for protection of EC leniency documents in US courts' 22 November 2011.

[116] [2001] OJ L145/43.

[117] Judgment of 15 December 2011 in Case T-437/08 *CDC Hydrogene Peroxide v Commission*, para 63.

[118] Judgment of 15 December 2011 in Case T-437/08 *CDC Hydrogene Peroxide v Commission*, para 49.

[119] This can be deduced by analogy from Judgment of 28 June 2012 in Case C-139/07 P *Commission v Technische Glaswerke Ilmenau* [2010] ECR I-5885, paras 53 and 54, which brings in line the confidentiality protection under Reg 1049/2001 with the protection granted under the State aid rules, and Judgment of 28 June 2012 in Case C-404/10 P *Éditions Odile Jacob SAS v Commission*, para 117, which brings in line the confidentiality protection under Reg 1049/2001 with the protection awarded to parties in the field of mergers.

commercially sensitive information on the basis of Article 4(2) of Regulation 1049/2001, but not the admission to have participated in the cartel as such. A further means of avoiding disclosure under Regulation 1049/2001 based on the need to protect the efficiency of the Commission's leniency regime could be the exemption under the third indent of Article 4(2) of Regulation 1049/2001 ('for the purpose of inspections, investigations and audits'),[120] which would apply only for the period during which the Commission's investigation is still ongoing (ie until the adoption of the final decision in a cartel case),[121] or Article 4(3) of Regulation 1049/2001 (access 'would seriously undermine decision making process'), which has a particularly high threshold for the access refusal.[122] Such exemption would not apply to the non-confidential information the Commission has obtained through investigative measures that were made possible by the immunity/leniency application (ie information which has not been sent to it voluntarily by the immunity/leniency applicant).[123] With regard to the information that has been voluntarily submitted by the immunity/leniency applicant, the Commission has failed in its attempt to protect a list of the leniency documents on its file with the argument that the category of leniency materials on its file overall deserves absolute protection.[124] In that regard the latest case law of the Court of Justice ('ECJ') also indicates, that the interest of the Commission to preserve the effectiveness of its leniency regime is not absolute and needs to be explained in detail and balanced against the interests of the information seekers to use information for the pursuit of their damages claims.[125] This balancing exercise is difficult to perform and hard to predict at this stage for a number of reasons:

(i) The Commission's claim that the effectiveness of its investigation needs to be preserved is very abstract and ultimately can only be substantiated by the commercial interest of the immunity/leniency applicant to avoid discovery of its admission of having participated in a cartel in damages proceedings against him[126]

---

[120] The third indent of Art 4(2) of Reg 1049/2001 applies only to ongoing investigations until the Commission has taken a final decision in the case even if that decision is appealed in Court; Case T-437/08 Judgment of 15 December 2011 in *CDC Hydrogene Peroxide v Commission*, paras 60–2. So far the Commission has not relied on Art 4(3) of Reg 1049/2001, under which a longer lasting protection of leniency materials could, in principle, also be envisaged.

[121] See Case T-344/08 *EnBW Energie Baden-Württemberg AG v Commission*, not yet reported, paras 116–22.

[122] The threshold for an access rejection under Art 4(3) of Reg 1049/2001 is very high, since the EU Courts require a particularly severe risk for the decision-making process which is imminent and not purely hypothetical. Case T-403/05 *My Travel/Commission* [2008] ECR II-2027, para 54; Judgment of 28 June 2012 in Case T-237/05 *Éditions Odile Jacob SAS v Commission*, para 141 et seq.

[123] This can already be deduced from the fact that under para 26 of the Commission Notice on co-operation between the Commission and the courts of the EU Member States in the application of Articles 81 and 82 EC [2004] OJ C101/54, such documents can also be requested by a judge in national private enforcement proceedings.

[124] Judgment of 15 December 2011 in Case T-437/08 *CDC Hydrogene Peroxide v Commission*, paras 76–7.

[125] Judgment of 14 June 2011 in Case C-360/09 *Pfleiderer AG v Bundeskartellamt*, paras 30–1. See also Antonio Caruso, 'Leniency Programmes and Protection of Confidentiality: The Experience of the European Commission' (2010) 1(6) Journal of European Competition Law & Practice 453; Alfred Dittrich, 'Kronzeugenanträge und Rechtsschutz' (2012) 2 WuW 133; Caroline Cauffman, 'Access to Leniency-Related Documents after Pfleiderer' (2011) 34(4) World Competition 597; Gaetane Goddin, 'The Pleiderer Judgment on Transparency: The National Sequel of the Access to Document Saga' (2012) 3(1) Journal of European Competition Law & Practice 40; Ingrid Vanderborre, 'The Confidentiality of EU Commission Cartel Records in Civil Litigation: The Ball is in the EU Court' (2011) 32(3) European Competition Law Review 116.

[126] This has also been pointed out by the GC in Judgment of 15 December 2011 in Case T-437/08 *CDC Hydrogene Peroxide v Commission*, para 73. In the latest judgment on this matter the Court of Justice has been even more specific by explicitly stating that an undermining of the effectiveness of a leniency programme 'cannot justify a refusal to grant access' to leniency material as such; Judgment of 6 June 2013 in Case C-536/11 *Donau Chemie and others v Bundeswettwerbsbehörde*, para 46.

(ii) As outlined previously, such substantiation is very difficult to make in view of the complex procedural and substantive rules of the various private enforcement proceedings that can be undertaken against a cartelist.[127]

(iii) The EU Courts do not appear to accept the risk of private enforcement proceedings (at least in litigation before Courts of EU Member States) as a valid commercial interest that would suffice to substantiate the refusal of access to voluntarily submitted immunity/leniency material.[128]

(iv) The latest case law in the area of mergers indicates that the GC might have introduced the possibility for the Commission to refuse access under Article 4(2) of Regulation 1049/2001 to entire categories of documents (in the case in question, internal advice of the Legal Service and documents exchanged by the Commission with the merging parties) based on a general presumption of their confidentiality without analysing the actual sensitivity of every piece of information contained in the documents in question.[129]

Such refusal to grant access by category may substantially extend the protection of leniency **6.55** statements, since by its nature it implies that numerous pieces of information which on their own could not be protected after an individual balancing exercise would benefit from an *en bloc* protection by category. Nevertheless, the presumption by category would require a detailed reasoning of why leniency documents as a category are confidential, tailored to the specific case.[130] While an analogy to the merger case law would appear desirable in terms of a reduction of administrative burden on the Commission to justify the protection of leniency statements, there are very significant legal obstacles to it:

(i) Unlike information in merger proceedings, leniency statements are not protected by any legal act at the level of a Regulation (*in casu* Regulation 139/2004) but only by the non-legally binding paragraph 33 of the 2006 Notice).[131]

(ii) Confidentiality interests of parties in merger proceedings are entirely different from those of immunity/leniency applicants who have infringed competition law and such interests are not worthy of protection against parties seeking access to information directly related to the infringement for the pursuit of their legitimate private enforcement actions.

In view of these arguments, it currently appears unlikely that the EU Courts would broadly **6.56** accept a denial of access to immunity/leniency statements under Regulation 1049/2001. Moreover, a refusal by category can hardly be reconciled with the requirements of a case-by-case analysis imposed by the Court of Justice in its *Pfleiderer* and *Donau Chemie* judgments.[132] While the risk that leniency materials may have to be disclosed to private plaintiffs

---

[127] In the *Pfleiderer* case the national tribunal which made the reference to the ECJ ultimately decided not to grant access to the leniency statements made before the Bundeskartellamt. Decision of Amtsgericht Bonn of 18 January 2012, Az 51 Gs 53/09.

[128] Judgment of 15 December 2011 in Case T-437/08 *CDC Hydrogene Peroxide v Commission*, para 49; Judgment of 14 June 2011 in Case C-360/09 *Pfleiderer AG v Bundeskartellamt*, paras 28–30.

[129] Judgment of 28 June 2012 in Case C-477/10 *Agrofert Holding a.s. v Commission*, paras 59–64.

[130] Judgment of 28 June 2012 in Case C-477/10, *Agrofert Holding a.s. v Commission*, paras 63 and 79, which concludes that for internal Commission legal advice a presumption of confidentiality cannot apply.

[131] This is a fundamental difference from the *Agrofert* situation, since an act in the status of a Regulation (ie Reg 1049/2001) cannot be limited by an act in the status of non-binding guidelines like the 2006 Leniency Notice. See also the article by GC judge A Dittrich, 'Kronzeugenanträge und Rechtsschutz' (2012) 2 WuW 139, in relation to the sister case in the area of State aids, Case C-139/07 P *Technische Glaswerke Ilmenau* [2010] ECR I-5885. A protection of leniency materials at the level of a directive is currently proposed in Art 6(1) of the proposal for a directive on certain rules governing actions for damages under national law for infringements of the competition law provisions of the Member States and of the European Union; COM(2013) 404 final.

[132] Judgment of 6 June 2013 in Case C-536/11 *Donau Chemie and others v Bundeswettbewerbsbehörde*, paras 42–6; Judgment of 14 June 2011 in Case C-360/09 *Pfleiderer AG v Bundeskartellamt*, paras 25–7 and 31.

is not to be neglected, it also has to be assessed in the light of the access possibilities that private litigants have by other means (discovery, the non-confidential version of the decision etc). In view of these possibilities the risk under Regulation 1049/2001 might in many cases not be significant enough to be taken into account when applying for immunity or leniency.

6.57 In recent cases regarding decisions taken against *Akzo* and *Evonik Degussa*, the Commission started implementing a policy to publish increasingly detailed versions of its cartel decisions on the DG COMP's webpage. In this context, the Commission wishes to rely on information contained in leniency statements. This has been provisionally stopped in the two cases mentioned by the President of the GC, *inter alia*, with the argument that information provided in leniency applications might be protected from publication under Article 8 of the Convention for the Protection of Human Rights and Fundamental Freedoms (European Convention on Human Rights, 'ECHR').[133]

D. Multijurisdictional Applications

6.58 According to Articles 4 and 5 of Regulation 1/2003, the national competition authorities ('NCAs') have full parallel competence to investigate and sanction one and the same cartel.[134] Each national authority has its own leniency regime and therefore applications can only be introduced separately before each authority and have only effects with regard to a single authority's investigation. Thus, in case several national authorities are in charge in parallel, an immunity/leniency applicant has to introduce an application before each of them in order to preserve its place in the queue.

6.59 If the Commission takes up a cartel investigation, all other EU competition authorities are relieved of their competence to further investigate the same cartel.[135] In such cases an immunity/leniency application introduced before DG COMP suffices to preserve the applicant's ability to obtain immunity or leniency and the applicant in principle does not need to worry about further liability for the same cartel before one of the EU NCAs. However, in rare cases, the Commission, may within the framework of cooperation with other competition authorities (the European Competition Network, 'ECN'), possibly after a preliminary analysis of the case based on the leniency/immunity application, conclude that one or several national authorities may be better placed to deal with a cartel and refer the case to them.[136] In such a situation the leniency application introduced before the Commission does not have an

---

[133] Judgment of 16 November 2012 in Case T-341/12 R *Evonik Degussa v Commission*, para 26 et seq; Case T-345/12 R *Akzo Nobel NV et al v Commission*, para et seq 32.

[134] See also para 5 of the Commission Notice on the cooperation with the Network of Competition authorities [2004] OJ C101/43 and point 11 of the Joint Statement of the Council and the Commission on the functioning of the network, Council document 15435/02 ADD 1.

[135] See Art 11(6) of Reg 1/2003.

[136] According to para 8 of the Commission Notice on cooperation within the Network of Competition Authorities OJ [2004] C101/43, an authority can be considered to be well placed to deal with a case if three cumulative conditions are met: (1) The agreement or practice has substantial direct actual or foreseeable effects with its territory, is implemented within or originates from its territory; (2) The authority is able to effectively bring to an end the entire infringement, ie it can adopt a cease-and-desist order, the effect of which will be sufficient to bring an end to the infringement and it can, where appropriate, sanction the infringement adequately; (3) It can gather, possibly with the assistance of other authorities, the evidence required to prove the infringement.

effect under the leniency regime of the NCA. If another party had applied to the national authority prior to the referral by the Commission, it will benefit from a better place in the queue even if the applicant in the Commission proceedings had submitted its application to the Commission earlier. Thus, the referral renders the earlier application made to the Commission ineffective.

From the point of view of a leniency applicant, it might be prudent to apply to all competi- **6.60** tion authorities who might be likely to investigate the cartel in order to preserve its place in the queue in all circumstances.[137] Such a multijurisdictional application is now eased to a certain extent by the increasing convergence of national leniency regimes in the context of the Model Leniency Programme.[138] In the course of the harmonization through this leniency programme, many of the features of the EU leniency regime, such as markers, the possibility of oral applications, and confirmatory letters after the receipt of an application, have been introduced in the Member States' regimes.[139] The Model Leniency Programme also attempts to avoid multiple fully fledged applications by introducing an indefinite marker under Member States' leniency regimes (called 'summary application') for applicants that have already submitted a full leniency application to DG COMP. Such procedure is, however, only available in cases in which the alleged anticompetitive practices have effects in more than three Member States (so-called Type 1A cases as defined in paragraph 14 of the Network Notice).[140] All twenty-six Member States with a leniency system have introduced the possibility of such a summary application, albeit the requirements for the information that still needs to be provided together with such an application in order to conserve the place in the queue varies from Member State to Member State.[141]

Conversely, applying to several or even all EU authorities also entails the risk that the informa- **6.61** tion submitted to them is less secure from third party access for private enforcement purposes than if it had only been submitted to the Commission.[142] This risk has to be weighed against the risk of losing the first place in the queue before NCAs to which the Commission may delegate the case.

The risk assessment is additionally complicated by the fact that the Commission may exchange **6.62** information from leniency applicants with other competition authorities in the framework of the ECN and thereby still maintains full competence for its assessment. In such cases the applicants may face the risk that the authorities receiving the Commission's leniency information may use it to bring proceedings against them with regard to a different cartel than the one investigated and ultimately decided upon by the Commission.

The NCAs and the Commission have sought to address these concerns via a number of informa- **6.63** tion exchange rules in section 2.3.3 of the Commission's ECN Cooperation Notice,[143] which

---

[137] S Blake and D Schnichels, 'Leniency Modernization: Safeguarding Europe's Leniency Programmes' (2004) Summer (2) Competition Policy Newsletter 7, 11; U Soltész, 'Der "Kronzeuge" im Labyrinth des ECN' [2005] Wirtschaft und Wettbewerb 616, 619, criticizes the fact that this would require substantial efforts on the part of the undertaking and would defeat the purpose of efficient allocation of resources.

[138] Available at <http://ec.europa.eu/competition/ecn/model_leniency_en.pdf>. On 22 November 2012, the ECN published a further refinement of the existing convergence rules available at <http://ec.europa.eu/competition/ecn/documents.html>.

[139] For an overview see V Jukneviciute and J Capiau, 'The State of ECN Leniency Convergence' (2010) 1 Competition Policy Newsletter.

[140] Commission Notice on cooperation within the Network of Competition Authorities [2004] OJ C101/43.

[141] V Jukneviciute and J Capiau, 'The State of ECN Leniency Convergence' (2010) 1 Competition Policy Newsletter, point 3.4.

[142] With regard to the protection mechanisms against disclosure of leniency applications held by the Commission see paras 6.49–6.57.

[143] [2004] OJ C101/43–53.

makes the exchange of leniency information via Article 11(2), (3) and Article 12(1) of Regulation 1/2003 partly dependent on the consent of the leniency applicant. The mechanisms are aimed at ensuring that there is no disincentive to be lenient under the existing leniency programmes and create legitimate expectations vis-à-vis the Commission and the NCAs which have committed themselves to respecting the principles set out in the ECN Cooperation Notice.[144]

6.64 Article 11(2) of Regulation 1/2003 in its first sentence contains an explicit *obligation* of the Commission to exchange the most important documents with the Member States' Competition Authorities. However, the leniency application, its supporting documents, and the documents and statements gathered by the Commission through investigations triggered by the leniency application are not seen as such 'most important documents'.[145] It is only at the explicit request of a competition authority of a Member State that the Commission should provide such documents to the national competition authority to the extent that the document is necessary for the assessment of the cartel case investigated by the Commission (Article 11(2) second sentence of Regulation 1/2003). Such requests will be rare, though, since the procedural documents submitted by the Commission, like, for instance, the statement of objections, should suffice for understanding the content of any leniency document on which the Commission's objections is based. If, nevertheless, another competition authority requests leniency-related documents, the wording of Article 11(2) second sentence ('should') indicates no discretion of the Commission to refuse to provide the requested documents. However, according to paragraph 39 of the ECN Cooperation Notice 'such documents cannot be used by the national competition as the basis for starting an investigation on their own behalf whether under the competition rules of the Treaty or, in the case of NCAs, under their national competition law or other laws'.[146]

6.65 According to Article 12 of Regulation 1/2003 the Commission and competition authorities of the Member States have the power (not the obligation) to provide one another with the leniency/immunity statements, their supporting documents, and any documents investigated on the basis of the leniency/immunity application. This provision leaves it to the discretion of the Commission and of the competition authorities of the Member States which documents to exchange.[147] If the discretionary decision is taken to exchange any leniency/immunity material, paragraphs 40 and 41 of the ECN Cooperation Notice provide for further limitations to the exchange.[148] In line with the procedures set out in the Manual of

---

[144] K Dekeyser, 'Regulation 1/2003: First Experiences', IBC Conference, London, 27 and 28 April 2005, D Reichelt, 'To What Extent does the Cooperation within the European Competition Network Protect the Rights of the Undertakings?' (2005) CML Rev 745, 767–70.

[145] See European Commission Antitrust Manual of Procedures, Internal DG Competition working documents on procedures for the application of Articles 101 and 102 TFEU, March 2012, Module 3 'Cooperation with National Competition Authorities in EU and exchange of information in ECN', para 54.

[146] This usage limitation is in line with the case law of the EU courts with regard to the preceding Reg 17; Case C-67/91 *Dirección General de Defensa de la Competencia (DGDC) v Asociacion Española de Banca Privada (AEB) and others ('Spanish Banks')* [1992] ECR I-4785, para 42.

[147] It is partly submitted that, despite its clear wording, Art 12(1) should entail an obligation to exchange information when read in conjunction with the duty to cooperate under Art 4(3) TFEU. However, such an obligation will regularly not exist when the interests of the leniency applicants and of competition enforcement would be affected by its instatement; see J Faul and A Nikpay, *Faul and Nikpay, The EC Law of Competition* (2nd edn, 2007), para 2.165.

[148] Regulation 1/2003 has thereby changed the approach taken in Reg 17 and '*Spanish Banks*', Case C-67/91 *Dirección General de Defensa de la Competencia (DGDC) v Asociacion Española de Banca Privada (AEB) and others* [1992] ECR I-4785, para 42. While under that case law, NCAs were not entitled to use the information transmitted by the Commission to pursue competition cases under their own competition laws, Reg 1/2003 now in principle allows for the application of national competition law on the basis of the transmitted information (see Art 12(2) and (3) of Reg 1/2003). Now the ECN Cooperation Notice rather limits the transmission of the leniency-related information without the leniency applicant's consent.

Procedures,[149] the Commission will in general not provide the leniency application and its supporting documents (ie documents that have been transmitted to the Commission voluntarily) absent the explicit consent of the leniency applicant (paragraph 40 of the ECN Cooperation Notice).[150] If the consent is refused, all documents that the Commission would not have been able to investigate itself via inspections and information requests without the leniency/immunity application are also barred from transmission under Article 12(1) of Regulation 1/2003.[151] However, according to paragraph 41 of the Cooperation Notice, the consent of the leniency/immunity applicant is not necessary for the transmission in any of the following circumstances:

(i) If the receiving authority has also received a leniency application relating to the same infringement from the same applicant as the transmitting authority, provided that at the time the information is transmitted it is not open to the applicant to withdraw the information which it has submitted to that receiving authority.

(ii) If the receiving authority has provided a written commitment that neither the information transmitted to it nor any other information it may obtain following the date and time of transmission as noted by the transmitting authority, will be used by it or by any other authority to which the information is subsequently transmitted to impose sanctions:[152]

    (a) on the leniency applicant;

    (b) on any other legal or natural person covered by the favourable treatment offered by the transmitting authority as a result of the application made by the applicant under its leniency programme;

    (c) on any employee or former employee of any of the persons covered by (a) or (b).

A copy of the receiving authority's written commitment will be provided to the applicant.

6.66 In the case of information collected by a network member in the context of an inspection under Article 22(1) of Regulation 1/2003 on behalf of and for the account of the network member to whom the leniency application was made, such information may be transmitted to, and used by, the network member to whom the application was made. In the case of an international cartel, the applicant may decide to apply for leniency to antitrust authorities in other jurisdictions.[153] In these cases the applicant should provide a waiver to the Commission in order to discuss the case and share information, as well as allowing for simultaneous dawn raids in different parts of the world.

---

[149] European Commission Antitrust Manual of Procedures, Internal DG Competition working documents on procedures for the application of Articles 101 and 102 TFEU, March 2012, Module 3 'Cooperation with National Competition Authorities in EU and exchange of information in ECN', paras 61–9.

[150] Conversely, documents that have been uncovered by compulsion at inspections or through information requests on the basis of the leniency/immunity application may be exchanged with other competition authorities without the consent of the leniency/immunity applicant.

[151] See para 40 second sentence of the ECN Cooperation Notice.

[152] K Dekeyser, 'Q&A on Modernization with Kris Dekeyser' (April 2005) 8(3) Global Competition Review 11, 14, notes that this may lead to a situation where the company obtains immunity in a Member State that does not have a leniency programme.

[153] For example, USA, Australia, Canada, and Japan.

7

INVESTIGATION OF CASES (II): FORMAL INVESTIGATIVE MEASURES IN GENERAL, REQUESTS FOR INFORMATION, AND INTERVIEWS

Manuel Kellerbauer, Ralf Sauer, Corneliu Hödlmayr,
Luis Ortiz Blanco, and Konstantin Jörgens

A. Formal Investigative Measures in General[1]

1. Principles applicable in the initial investigative phase

The Commission is empowered to investigate possible infringements of Articles 101 and **7.01**
102 of the Treaty on the Functioning of the European Union ('TFEU') and, where appropriate, impose penalties on undertakings and associations of undertakings. To this end, it
performs the activities both of fact-finding and evaluation.[2] Often, the Commission needs to

---

[1] For an overview see Commission Notice on best practices for the conduct of proceedings concerning Articles 101 and 102 TFEU [2011] OJ C308/6, sections 2.5 and 2.6; European Commission Antitrust Manual of Procedures, Internal DG Competition working documents on procedures for the application of Articles 101 and 102 TFEU, March 2012, Module 6 'Requests for information' and Module 8 'Power to take statements'. See also European Commission, 'Dealing with the Commission—Notification, complaints, inspections and fact-finding powers under Articles [101] and [102] of the [TFEU]' (1997 edn) sections 3.1–5.7.

[2] The alleged role of the Commission as an investigator, prosecutor, and judge has been subject to criticism, but the case law of both the European Court of Human Rights ('ECtHR') and the EU Courts seems to confirm the legality of the system in so far as Commission decisions are subject to full judicial review in the sense

take investigatory steps to establish with certainty the existence of the suspected infringements. In that respect, its central role in the application of the principles laid down in Articles 101 and 102 TFEU has been maintained[3] and its powers of investigation granted under Regulation 17 have been further strengthened. As before, its two principal instruments are requests for information and on-site inspections. In addition, the Commission has been explicitly empowered to conduct interviews of natural or legal persons. As was the case under Regulation 17, the investigative powers set out in Regulation 1/2003 apply only to the Commission. Whenever national competition authorities ('NCAs') and national courts are required to apply Articles 101 and 102 TFEU, their powers of investigation and procedures are governed by national law.[4]

7.02 Chapter V of Regulation 1/2003 and the implementing Regulation 773/2004[5] lay down the conditions for the exercise by the Commission of its formal powers of investigation. Generally, its powers have increased in several respects, particularly as regards the collection of information and the imposition of fines in case of a violation of the undertaking's duties during an investigation.[6] By extending the Commission's investigative powers as compared to Regulation 17, it shall be better equipped to detect infringements of the competition rules, which has become increasingly difficult.[7] The exercise of the powers of investigation pursuant to Chapter V of Regulation 1/2003 is not limited by reference to the time of stage reached in a particular case, and thus can stretch from before initiating proceedings[8] until the period following the Statement of Objections and even the final decision.[9]

---

of Art 6 Convention for the Protection of Human Rights and Fundamental Freedoms (European Convention on Human Rights, 'ECHR'). See eg Case T-156/94 *Siderúrgica Aristrain Madrid v Commission* [1999] ECR II-645, para 2642; Judgment of 13 July 2011 in Case T-138/07 *Schindler v Commission*, paras 54 and 56; *A Menarini Diagnostics SRL v Italy* App no 43509/08 (ECtHR, 27 September 2011), paras 58 and 59. See also EFTA Court, Judgment of 18 April 2012 in Case E-15/10 *Posten Norge v EFTA Surveillance Authority*, para 91. For a more detailed discussion see Ch 4, 'The Organization of EU Commission Proceedings' and K Lenaerts, 'Due Process in Competition Cases', May 2013 1(5) *Neue Zeitschrift für Kartellrecht - NZKart.*

[3] See Ch 3, 'The Role of National Competition Authorities', para 3.05 et seq.

[4] Apart from obtaining assistance from Member States for the inspections it conducts itself, the Commission may also request NCAs to conduct inspections on its behalf pursuant to Art 22 of Reg 1/2003. The officials of the NCA responsible for conducting these inspections, as well as other persons authorized or appointed by them, shall exercise their powers in accordance with national law. According to WPJ Wils, 'Powers of Investigation and Procedural Rights and Guarantees in EU Antitrust Enforcement', First Lisbon Conference on Competition Law and Economics, Belém, 3–4 November 2005, para 26, it follows from the principles of effectiveness and equivalence that these powers must be effective, and at least equivalent to what the Member State would provide for in comparable situations of enforcement of its own national law.

[5] Commission Regulation (EC) 773/2004 relating to the conduct of proceedings by the Commission pursuant to Articles 81 and 82 of the EC Treaty [2004] OJ L123/18. Regulation 773/2004 was adopted pursuant to Art 33 of Reg 1/2003.

[6] K Dekeyser and C Gauer, 'The New Enforcement System for Articles 81 and 82 and the Rights of Defence' ch 23 in BE Hawk (ed), *International Antitrust Law and Policy* (Annual Proceedings of the Fordham Institute 2004) 545, 550. WPJ Wils, 'Powers of Investigation and Procedural Rights and Guarantees in EU Antitrust Enforcement', First Lisbon Conference on Competition Law and Economics, Belém, 3–4 November 2005, paras 32–3, has indicated that the powers of some NCAs appear to be more far-reaching than those of the Commission under Reg 1/2003. Article 5 of Reg 1/2003 allows NCAs to impose any other penalty provided for in their national law, which may include prison sanctions for directors or managers responsible for their companies' behaviour.

[7] See Recital 25 of Reg 1/2003.

[8] Article 2(3) of Reg 773/2004.

[9] For instance, the Commission may seek clarifications of issues discussed at the oral hearing (see eg *Glaxo Wellcome* [2001] OJ L302/1, para 7) or request turnover figures in order to be able to determine the fine (see eg Case T-213/00 *CMA CGM and Others v Commission* [2003] ECR II-913, para 482 et seq and 490). The Commission is also empowered to monitor the situation on the market following an infringement decision. According to the General Court ('GC'), '[t]he Commission cannot be deprived of its powers of investigation into facts subsequent to those penalized in a decision, even if such facts are identical to those on which that decision is based'. Case T-34/93 *Société Générale v Commission* [1995] ECR II-545, para 77.

Article 18 ('Requests for information'), Article 19 ('Power to take statements'), and Article 20 **7.03**
('The Commission's powers of inspection') of Regulation 1/2003 allow the Commission to
request such information and the production of documents, including during an inspection,
as is necessary to detect any agreement, decision, or concerted practice prohibited by Article
101 TFEU or any abuse of a dominant position prohibited by Article 102 TFEU.[10] The EU
Courts have repeatedly ruled that, as regards the need for information, the Commission
enjoys a considerable margin of appreciation. Even if the Commission already has indications, or indeed proof, of the existence of an infringement, it may legitimately take the view
that it is necessary to take further investigatory steps enabling it to better define the scope
of the infringement, to determine its duration, or to identify the circle of undertakings
involved.[11] In the same vein, the Courts have held that the Commission enjoys a margin of
discretion to set priorities when enforcing the competition rules.[12] At the same time, in using
its investigative powers under Regulation 1/2003, the Commission is required to observe the
general principles and fundamental rights prescribed by EU law.[13] Of particular relevance in
this regard are the principle of proportionality and the protection against arbitrary investigations.[14] However, and in particular as regards inspections, the rights of the undertaking have
to be balanced against the *effet utile* of the investigation.[15]

In its preliminary ruling in *Roquette Frères*, the Court of Justice ('ECJ') clarified this balance when **7.04**
it was asked to consider the scope of review to be undertaken by a national court on an application for assistance made under Article 14(6) of Regulation 17, the equivalent of Article 20(6) of
Regulation 1/2003.[16] Although the ruling concerned the judicial control of national enforcement
measures (search and seizure), the ECJ took the opportunity to spell out the general principles

---

[10] Articles 18 and 20 of Reg 1/2003 correspond to Arts 11 and 14 of Reg 17, respectively.

[11] Case C-94/00 *Roquette Frères v Directeur Général de la Concurrence, de la Consommation et de la Répression des Fraudes ('Roquette Frères')* [2002] ECR I-9011, para 78. In relation to additional requests for information see Judgment of 22 March 2012 in Joined Cases T-458/09 and T-171/10 *Slovak Telekom v Commission*, para 42 with further references. See also Case T-39/90 *Samenwerkende Elektriciteits-Produktiebedrijven (SEP) v Commission* [1991] ECR II-1497, para 30.

[12] Case T-24/90 *Automec Srl v Commission (Automec II)* [1992] ECR II-2223, paras 73–7 and 83; Case C-119/97 P *Ufex and Others v Commission* [1999] ECR I-1341, para 88. For instance, in Case T-219/99 *British Airways v Commission* [2003] ECR II-6917, paras 65, 66, and 70, the GC dismissed claims that the Commission had infringed the principle of non-discrimination by bringing an Art 102 TFEU case against British Airways but not against others.

[13] Opinion of AG Ruiz-Jarabo in Joined Cases C-204/00, C-205/00, C-211/00, C-213/00, C-217/00 and C-219/00 *Aalborg Portland and Others v Commission* [2004] ECR I-123, para 26: 'the Commission has wide powers of investigation and inquiry but, precisely because of that nature and because one and the same body is invested with the power to conduct investigations and the power to take decisions, the rights of defence of those subject to the procedure must be recognised without reservation and respected.' See also Case T-99/04 *AC-Treuhand v Commission* [2008] ECR II-1501, paras 50–6; Judgment of 27 September 2012 in Case T-357/06 *Koninklijke Wegenbouw Stevin v Commission*, para 227; European Commission, 'Dealing with the Commission—Notification, complaints, inspections and fact-finding powers under Articles [101] and [102] of the [TFEU]' (1997 edn) point 3.1.

[14] See Case C-94/00 *Roquette Frères* [2002] ECR I-9011, paras 27, 50, and 52; Judgment of 22 March 2012 in Joined Cases T-458/09 and T-171/10 *Slovak Telekom v Commission*, para 83.

[15] Judgment of 27 September 2012 in Case T-357/06 *Koninklijke Wegenbouw Stevin v Commission*, paras 230 and 231.

[16] When an inspection is ordered by decision of the Commission, it is current practice in certain Member States that the competent NCA requests, as a precautionary measure, judicial authorization by the national courts to overcome resistance in case the undertaking concerned refuses to submit to the investigation. In Case C-94/00 *Roquette Frères* [2002] ECR I-9011, the search warrant had been issued against Roquette Frères by a French regional court in the course of the Commission's investigation into the sodium gluconate cartel and had been challenged before the French Court of Appeals by its addressee. The Court of Appeals had subsequently asked the ECJ to clarify the scope of the review by national courts of the requests submitted to them pursuant to Art 14(6) of Reg 17.

which govern the exercise of the Commission's powers of investigation. Confirming its previous ruling in *Hoechst*, the Court held that the powers conferred on the Commission are designed to enable it to perform its task of ensuring that the competition rules are applied.[17] Without prejudice to the guarantees under national law governing the use of coercive measures, undertakings under investigation are protected by various guarantees under EU law, including, in particular, the right to legal representation and the privileged nature of correspondence between lawyer and client.[18] The ECJ also pointed out the fundamental importance of specifying the subject matter and purpose of an inspection (in line with Article 20(4) of Regulation 1/2003), as this allows the undertakings concerned to assess whether the proposed entry onto their premises is justified and to understand the scope of their duty to cooperate, whilst at the same time safeguarding their rights of defence.[19] Judicial review of the Commission's exercise of its investigative powers ensures that undertakings are protected against arbitrary measures and that such measures stay within the limits of what is necessary in order to perform the Commission's task of ensuring that the competition rules are applied.[20] Thus, when exercising its powers of investigation, the Commission must observe some principles in substance and others in form: substantively, the principles of necessity, appropriateness as regards the means deployed, proportionality, and observance of the rights of the defence;[21] and formally, the obligation to inform the undertakings concerned of the reasons justifying its action. However, this does not detract from the Commission's relatively wide discretion in carrying out its investigative duties.

2. The obligations of undertakings

7.05 During the investigation, undertakings are required to cooperate actively with the Commission.[22] This principle applies both to requests for information—the responses to which must not be evasive and should be a best-effort to address the Commission's questions[23]—and to inspections—in which the undertaking must assist the Commission in its search for documents rather than merely allowing the inspectors access to its premises. For instance, in *Fabbricca Pisana*, the Commission stated that the company has to do more than merely give the inspectors access

---

[17] Case C-94/00 *Roquette Frères* [2002] ECR I-9011, para 42; Joined Cases 46/87 and 227/88 *Hoechst v Commission* [1989] ECR 2859, para 25; Joined Cases C-204/00, C-205/00, C-211/00, C-213/00, C-217/00 and C-219/00 *Aalborg Portland and Others v Commission* [2004] ECR I-123, para 54.

[18] Case 155/79 *AM & S Europe v Commission* [1982] ECR 1575, paras 18–27, which stated that certain communications with external lawyers concerning legal advice were protected from Commission investigations whereas communications with in-house lawyers do not profit from such privilege protection. This has in the meantime been confirmed by the Grand Chamber of the Court of Justice as being continuous and established case law; Case C-550/07 P *Akzo v Commission* [2010] ECR I-8301, paras 40–50; Joined Cases 46/87 and 227/88 *Hoechst v Commission* [1989] ECR 2859, para 16; Judgment of 27 September 2012 in Case T-357/06 *Koninklijke Wegenbouw Stevin v Commission*, para 228 et seq. For more details see Ch 8, 'Investigation of Cases (III): Inspections'.

[19] Case C-94/00 *Roquette Frères* [2002] ECR I-9011, para 47; Joined Cases 46/87 and 227/88 *Hoechst v Commission* [1989] ECR 2859, para 29.

[20] Case C-94/00 *Roquette Frères* [2002] ECR I-9011, paras 42 and 50.

[21] Unlike Reg 17, Reg 1/2003 is more explicit and spells out a number of guarantees. See, eg, the right not to incriminate oneself in Recital 23 or the control exercised by national courts during inspections as provided in Arts 20(7), (8), and 21(3) of Reg 1/2003. K Dekeyser and C Gauer, 'The New Enforcement System for Articles 81 and 82 and the Rights of Defence' ch 23 in BE Hawk (ed), *International Antitrust Law and Policy* (Annual Proceedings of the Fordham Institute 2005) 549, 551.

[22] See Case T-46/92 *Scottish Football Association v Commission* [1994] ECR II-1039, para 31; Case T-34/93 *Société Générale v Commission* [1995] ECR II-545, para 72; Judgment of 27 September 2012 in Case T-357/06 *Koninklijke Wegenbouw Stevin v Commission*, para 236; Joined Cases C-204/00, C-205/00, C-211/00, C-213/00, C-217/00 and C-219/00 *Aalborg Portland and Others v Commission* [2004] ECR I-123, para 61.

[23] Cf European Commission, 'Dealing with the Commission—Notification, complaints, inspections and fact-finding powers under Articles [101] and [102] of the [TFEU]' (1997 edn) section 4.5: 'Firms must give an extensive response to the request which is sent to them; they must carefully interpret the questions posed in the light of the objectives pursued and the spirit and purpose of the investigation.'

to information they require: it should actually produce the specific documents required.[24] On this ground, the company's argument that the inspectors failed to examine the business records which were kept in its administration department was rejected, because the inspectors had not been told that the documents requested were, or might have been, kept in that department and there was otherwise no reason to suppose that documents of that nature might be found there.

The fact that in the undertaking's view the Commission has no grounds for action under **7.06** Articles 101 and/or 102 TFEU does not entitle it to resist a request.[25] In *CSM NV*, the Commission imposed a fine because CSM refused to hand over documents which it regarded as irrelevant for the investigation; providing these documents later did not mitigate the fine. The Commission took the view that it alone (under the control of the EU Courts) should decide what lies within the scope of the investigation. While the decision stated that inspectors are not entitled to examine business records if they are obviously not related to the subject matter of the investigation, companies cannot enforce this on their own initiative.[26] Generally, undertakings must make available to the Commission all information concerning the subject matter of the investigation.[27] At the same time, the EU Courts have also pointed out that defence rights must not be irremediably impaired during (preliminary) investigation procedures. Although Regulation 1/2003 (like Regulation 17) does not provide for an absolute right to silence in competition proceedings, it is necessary to reconcile the Commission's powers to investigate during the preliminary stage with the need to safeguard the undertakings' defence rights.[28] In this regard, the General Court ('GC') stated in *Mannesmannröhren-Werke* that the Commission is entitled to compel an undertaking to provide all necessary information concerning such facts as may be known to it and to disclose to the Commission, if necessary, such documents relating thereto as are in its possession,

---

[24] *Fabbrica Pisana* [1980] OJ L75/30, para 10: 'The argument that Fabbrica Pisana had satisfactorily fulfilled its obligations by generally putting all its files at the investigators' disposal must be rejected, since the obligation on undertakings to supply all documents required by Commission inspectors must be understood to mean not merely giving access to all files but actually producing the specific documents required.'

[25] See eg *Fire Insurance* [1982] OJ L80/36, paras 4 and 19; *Deutsche Castrol Vertriebsgesellschaft mbH* [1983] OJ L114/26, paras 4 and 5. Even if the undertaking were able to show that the Commission could not reasonably suspect an infringement, and would thus challenge the Arts 18(3) or 20(4) decision, it would still have to comply, given that an annulment action does not have a suspensory effect (Art 278 TFEU). The only way to avoid this outcome would be a request for interim measures which, however, is unlikely to succeed and—in the case of inspections—would typically come too late. See Joined Cases 46/87 and 227/88 *Hoechst v Commission* [1989] ECR 2859, paras 63 and 64. Cf also Order of the President of 29 July 2011 in Case T-293/11 R *Holcim v Commission* (on the lack of urgency).

[26] Case IV/33.791 *CSM NV* [1992] OJ L305/16, at section II.1.: '... The Commission does not call into question that in the first instance it is up to the company itself to assess its rights in the framework of a verification in the case of dispute. However, at issue is the question how an undertaking should assert its rights. The answer is that the undertaking cannot take matters into its own hands but must apply to the Court of First Instance of the European Communities, which alone is competent to supervise the Commission's conduct.'

[27] Case T-9/99 *HFB and Others v Commission* [2002] ECR II-1487, para 561. Note that the obligation to provide the relevant information also applies to governments and NCAs under the terms of Art 18(6) of Reg 1/2003 (former Art 11 of Reg 17). While the Commission has on rare occasions made use of that power (see eg *Cast iron and steel rolls* [1983] OJ L317/1, para 2, in which an information request was directed to the German *Bundeskartellamt*), the provision is of little practical relevance given the possibility of requesting information based on Art 12 of Reg 1/2003. See European Commission Antitrust Manual of Procedures, Internal DG Competition working documents on procedures for the application of Articles 101 and 102 TFEU, March 2012, Module 6 'Requests for information', para 86.

[28] Case 374/87 *Orkem v Commission* [1989] ECR 3283, paras 28–35; Case C-301/04 P *SGL Carbon v Commission* [2006] ECR I-5915, paras 40–4 and 48; Case T-112/98 *Mannesmannröhren-Werke v Commission* [2001] ECR II-729, paras 62–7; Case T-446/05 *Amann & Söhne and Cousin Filterie v Commission* [2010] ECR II-1255, paras 325–9. See also Recital 23 of Reg 1/2003. The privilege against self-incrimination will be further discussed at para 7.49 et seq.

even if the latter may be used to establish, against it or another undertaking, the existence of anticompetitive conduct.[29]

3. Persons concerned by investigatory measures

7.07 While the ultimate objective of all investigatory measures foreseen in Chapter V of Regulation 1/2003 is to determine whether an undertaking or association of undertakings has infringed the competition rules, and which factors might be relevant for any possible sanction, the addressees of such measures can vary. Both requests for information pursuant to Article 18(3), (4) and inspections pursuant to Article 20 of Regulation 1/2003 are directed at undertakings and associations thereof, even though these can be third parties not suspected of having committed the infringement themselves. Requests for information may also be addressed to the government or competition authority of a Member State (Article 18(6)). Where they are addressed to undertakings, their owners, representatives, or the persons authorized to represent them by law or by their constitution, as well as lawyers duly authorized to act on their behalf, may supply the information requested, pursuant to Article 18(4). Inspections may also be carried out at non-business premises (eg the private home of a director), and in this case an inspection decision pursuant to Article 21(1), (2) will be addressed (also) to the individual whose premises shall be inspected. Finally, pursuant to Article 19, the Commission may interview any natural or legal person who consents to be interviewed for the purpose of collecting information relating to the subject matter of an investigation; such an interview may (or may not) take place on the premises of an undertaking.[30] The most typical candidates for this type of interview are undertakings applying for immunity or leniency (acting through their company or legal representatives), members of their staff (eg those who participated in person during cartel contacts), or complainants (who may be natural or legal persons).[31]

7.08 As regards requests for information, a distinction must be drawn between the *addressee of the request*—who is responsible under Articles 23(1)(a), (b) and 24(1)(d) of Regulation 1/2003 that the information provided to the Commission is correct and not misleading, as well as complete and timely in the case of a request by formal decision—and the *natural persons who actually put together the information and transmit it* to the Commission. In this regard, Article 18(2), (3) of Regulation 1/2003 state that requests for information have to be addressed to 'undertakings and associations of undertakings', thereby using the same wording and concept as Articles 101 and 102 TFEU.[32] Consequently, the functional concept of the 'undertaking' defines the scope and availability of the information on the basis of which the completeness of the response will be assessed. The response will be considered complete if it includes all the

---

[29] Case T-112/98 *Mannesmannröhren-Werke v Commission* [2001] ECR II-729. The GC held that some of the questions asked by the Commission, namely the request for a description of the object of certain meetings and of decisions adopted during those meetings, went further than permitted under the earlier ruling in *Orkem*. These were not purely factual questions and effectively required Mannesmann to admit participation in a cartel (para 65). See PR Willis, 'You Have the Right to Remain Silent . . . Or Do You? The Privilege against Self-incrimination following *Mannesmannröhren-Werke* and other Recent Decisions' [2001] ECLR 313.

[30] This is different, however, from the power to put oral questions to a representative or member of staff of an undertaking during the course of an ongoing inspection (Art 20(2)(e) of Reg 1/2003). See European Commission Antitrust Manual of Procedures, Internal DG Competition working documents on procedures for the application of Articles 101 and 102 TFEU, March 2012, Module 8 'Power to take statements', para 3.

[31] For further examples see European Commission Antitrust Manual of Procedures, Internal DG Competition working documents on procedures for the application of Articles 101 and 102 TFEU, March 2012, Module 8 'Power to take statements', para 12.

[32] For the complex nature of the competition law concept of an undertaking that may encompass a multitude of legal persons see eg Richard Whish and David Bailey, *Competition Law* (Oxford University Press 2012) 84–91.

requested information that already exists or can be compiled without excessive effort based on existing data;[33] where necessary, this implies a duty to search for the information within the undertaking.[34]

Article 18(4) of Regulation 1/2003 deals with the natural persons who are in charge to put **7.09** together the information for the undertaking and to provide it to the Commission. While it limits the circle of potential representatives—owners, representatives, or lawyers—it does not prescribe who is to act on behalf of the undertaking. These individuals are neither addressees of the request for information nor subject to sanctions in case the information is incomplete, incorrect, or misleading (which may, however, be imposed on the undertaking).[35] They merely help the undertaking to comply with its obligations vis-à-vis the Commission and are only liable to the undertaking on the basis of their legal obligations towards it.

It is not only undertakings which are parties to agreements or are involved in anticompeti- **7.10** tive conduct that are subject to the Commission's investigative powers. Regulation 1/2003 empowers the Commission to request and obtain information from all 'undertakings and associations of undertakings'. For instance, whenever necessary, the Commission may request information from customers, suppliers, competitors, distributors, or any other undertakings that might be in possession of relevant information as regards a possible infringement of Articles 101 and/or 102 TFEU.[36]

4. Extraterritoriality and cooperation with other competition authorities

Undertakings in countries of the European Free Trade Association ('EFTA') which are **7.11** parties to the Agreement on the European Economic Area ('EEA') are also subject to the

---

[33] Cf Case COMP/M.1634 *Mitsubishi Heavy Industries* [2001] OJ L4/31. In Case T-34/93 *Société Générale v Commission* [1995] ECR II-545, para 73, the Court concluded that the respondent to an information request is under a 'duty of active cooperation', which means that it must be prepared to make *any* information relating to the object of the inquiry available to the Commission' (emphasis added). Whether this also entails an obligation to provide information (eg economic data) that may not be available in the format requested by the Commission is not yet entirely clear and subject to seven pending cases before the GC (Cases T-293/11 *Holcim v Commission*; T-296/11 *Valderrivas v Commission*; T-302/11 *HeidelbergCement v Commission*; T-292/11 *Cemex v Commission*; T-297/11 *Buzzi v Commission*; T-306/11 *Schwenk v Commission*; T-305/11 *Italmobiliare v Commission*). It should be noted that, in discussing the privilege against self-incrimination, the GC considered that the recipient of a request for information is entitled 'to confine himself to answering questions of a purely factual nature and to producing only the *pre-existing* documents and materials sought'. See Case T-112/98 *Mannesmannröhren-Werke v Commission* [2001] ECR II-729, paras 77 and 78.

[34] The undertaking might also be obliged to procure information from outside the undertaking if it can reasonably be expected that it has access to it (eg electronic access to a server located elsewhere) or can obtain the information from a third party without particular effort. For instance, in *San Michele*, the Directorate-General for Steel of the High Authority requested the undertakings to provide, or to ask their suppliers of electric energy to provide, the High Authority with invoices relating to the electric energy consumed during a certain period. On appeal, the ECJ considered that the request was not excessive and that, 'even if the applicants had destroyed or lost or had never kept the originals of the invoices at issue, they ought to have asked the electricity supply companies for copies of them upon being notified of the Decisions'. However, any difficulties in obtaining the documents from the energy suppliers had to be taken into account in fixing the time from which the periodic penalty payments imposed by the Commission applied. See Joined Cases 5 to 11 and 13 to 15/62 *Società Industriale Acciaierie San Michele and Others v High Authority of the European Coal and Steel Community* [1962] ECR 449; Joined Cases 2/63 to 10/63 *Società Industriale Acciaierie San Michele and Others v High Authority of the European Coal and Steel Community* [1963] ECR 327.

[35] This does not exclude that 'the undertaking' and the natural person owning it and putting together the information are one and the same, since the concept of undertaking may encompass natural persons. See eg Case C-309/99 *Wouters and Others v Algemene Raad van de Nederlandse Orde van Advocaten* [2002] ECR I-1577, para 49.

[36] See also European Commission Antitrust Manual of Procedures, Internal DG Competition working documents on procedures for the application of Articles 101 and 102 TFEU, March 2012, Module 9 'Requests for information', para 12.

Commission's investigative powers, albeit subject to certain conditions.[37] Particular issues arise with regard to undertakings that have no business establishment at all in any EU or EEA Member State, or where at least the requested information is held by an entity within the undertaking that is established outside the EU/EEA. While the Commission cannot address a decision pursuant to Article 18(3) of Regulation 1/2003 requesting information (directly) to undertakings outside the EU/EEA[38]—nor carry out an inspection abroad[39]— simple requests for information pursuant to Article 18(2) which do not entail an element of compulsion may be sent to a company abroad.[40] Where the undertaking has a subsidiary in the EU/EEA, the request may in parallel also be sent to that entity.[41] Identical rules apply to associations of undertakings which may be subject to all types of investigatory measures (including inspections) if located in the EU/EEA. Whether a trade association (also) represents non-EU undertakings is irrelevant, and the association may not refuse to submit to the investigation on that ground.[42] If the Commission carries out an investigation in a new EU

---

[37] See Art 8 of Protocol 23 to the EEA Agreement and European Commission Antitrust Manual of Procedures, Internal DG Competition working documents on procedures for the application of Articles 101 and 102 TFEU, March 2012, Module 9 'Requests for information', paras 17 and 18. Regarding the exercise of the investigative powers conferred by the competition provisions of the EEA Agreement, see Part V of this book.

[38] As regards the inadmissibility of taking binding measures outside the EU, see eg the Opinion of AG Mayras of 2 May 1979 in Case 48/69 *Imperial Chemical Industries v Commission* [1972] ECR 619 (695): 'These facts lead me to adopt the distinction made in international law by the Commission and by academic writers between "prescriptive jurisdiction" and "enforcement jurisdiction", or between *jurisdictio* and *imperium*. Whether it be criminal law or, as in the present cases, administrative proceedings that are involved, the courts or administrative authorities of a State—and, *mutatis mutandis*, of the Community—are certainly not justified under international law in taking coercive measures or indeed any measure of inquiry, investigation or supervision outside their territorial jurisdiction where execution would inevitably infringe the internal sovereignty of the State on the territory of which they claimed to act.' See also the Opinion of AG Darmon of 25 May 1988 in Joined Cases 89, 104, 114, 116, 117 and 125 to 129/85 *A Ahlström Osakeyhtiö and Others v Commission* [1988] ECR 5193, 5220. This does not exclude the possibility that a foreign state might grant the Commission jurisdiction to adopt a formal decision by way of an international agreement. In at least one case, the Commission addressed a formal decision requesting information both to a company situated outside the EU/EEA and its EU subsidiary, but gave as address for the parent company that of the subsidiary ('c/o Dalmine'). See Case T-596/97 *Dalmine v Commission* [1998] ECR II-2383, para 6. The application brought by the Argentinian parent company Siderca SAIC, by which it claimed, *inter alia*, a violation of international law, was later withdrawn. See Case T-8/98 *Siderca v Commission* [1998] OJ C72/24 (summ pub). In addition, the Commission considers that it may address a formal request for information to an EU subsidiary even if the objective is to obtain documents or data from the parent company abroad if both form part of one undertaking. In this scenario, the undertaking may be deemed to have a presence (and an address for notification) inside the EU, thus conferring jurisdiction onto the Commission. See Commission Decision of 15 February 2007 in Case COMP/39.309 *Thin Film Transistors Liquid Crystal Displays*. Also in this case, the application challenging the decision was later withdrawn. See Case T-140/07 *Chi Mei Optoelectronics Europe v Commission* [2007] OJ C155/28 (summ pub).

[39] European Commission, 'Dealing with the Commission—Notification, complaints, inspections and fact-finding powers under Articles [101] and [102] of the [TFEU]' (1997 edn) section 3.1.

[40] See eg Case IV/E-1/35.860 *Seamless Steel Tubes* [2003] OJ L140/1, para 4 and Art 6, where the Commission sent information requests, among others, to Sumitomo, Nippon Steel, Kawasaki Steel, and NKK, all of which were situated in Japan.

[41] See European Commission Antitrust Manual of Procedures, Internal DG Competition working documents on procedures for the application of Articles 101 and 102 TFEU, March 2012, Module 9 'Requests for information', para 19. According to para 20, the letter can be sent directly to the (association of) undertakings and does not need to be channelled through a delegation of the EU in the respective (non-EU) country. However, this may not always be an appropriate solution. For instance, in the past companies located in Switzerland have invoked Swiss legislation which expressly prohibits the use of public power by a foreign authority on Swiss territory; this may also apply to the notification of requests for information by the Commission in Switzerland. In such cases it might indeed be necessary to use diplomatic channels, for instance by transmitting the request via a Permanent Representative to the European Commission.

[42] Cases IV/32.448 and IV/32.450 *Ukwal* [1992] OJ L121/45.

Member State and discovers information relating to anticompetitive conduct prior to that State's accession to the EU, the Commission is entitled to take that information into account in so far as it is relevant for assessing whether an infringement affecting competition in the EU has been committed, even if, for the territory of that State, such an infringement could only be established as of the date of accession.[43]

Irrespective of the limited possibilities under Regulation 1/2003 for obtaining information from undertakings outside the EU jurisdiction, competition authorities have become increasingly aware that, since national systems of competition law are not always adequate to deal with cartels and anticompetitive practices that cross national boundaries, international cooperation between them may increase the chances of achieving a successful solution. The establishment of the International Competition Network ('ICN') bears testimony to these efforts. The ICN's work is complementary to that of the United Nations Conference on Trade and Development ('UNCTAD'), the Organisation for Economic Co-operation and Development ('OECD'),[44] and the World Trade Organization ('WTO'). As an informal, virtual network of competition authorities that seeks to facilitate cooperation between competition authorities and to promote procedural and substantive convergence of competition laws and administrative practice,[45] the ICN has no rule-making powers. **7.12**

International cooperation between competition authorities has also been advanced by the adoption of several bilateral agreements.[46] Most notably, US and EU antitrust enforcement authorities remain committed to cooperating in the detection and punishment of international cartel activities. Cooperation and convergence in cartel enforcement provide powerful incentives for cartel participants to avail themselves of effective leniency programmes and to report illegal activity in all jurisdictions where they might be exposed to risks of sanctions. Indeed, the most profound boost to cooperation in cartel enforcement resulted from collaboration between US and EU officials on the convergence of the respective amnesty programmes in both jurisdictions.[47] According to US antitrust officials, the Commission's revised programme 'has led to a surge in parallel amnesty applications to both the Commission and the Division'.[48] In turn, this has led to an increased level of cooperation between both antitrust authorities. **7.13**

---

[43] Cases 97–99/87 *Dow Chemical Ibérica v Commission* [1989] ECR 3165, paras 61–4; Judgment of 22 March 2012 in Joined Cases T-458/09 and T-171/10 *Slovak Telekom v Commission*, paras 45–62.

[44] As regards the OECD Competition Committee see <http://www.oecd.org/competition>. In October 2005, the committee published 'Best Practices for the formal exchange of information between competition authorities in hard core cartel investigations'.

[45] The ICN's website is a valuable source of material, including links to the sites of its member competition authorities. Established in October 2001, the ICN seeks to promote more efficient, effective antitrust enforcement worldwide by enhancing convergence and cooperation. Unlike the ECN, it is not a vehicle for exchanging detailed information on individual cases. One of its sections, the ICN Cartel Working Group, seeks to address the challenges of repressing cartels at national and international levels, with a view to reaching an international consensus on when to intervene in such cases. For more information in general see <http://www.internationalcompetitionnetwork.org>.

[46] See the list of bilateral agreements on the website of the Directorate-General for Competition ('DG COMP') at <http://ec.europa.eu/competition/international/bilateral/index.html> and at <http://ec.europa.eu/competition/international/legislation/legislation.html>. The annual Commission Report on Competition Policy provides an overview of the status of international agreements and cooperation.

[47] Based in part on shared insights and experiences in fighting the increasing 'internationalization' of cartel activity, the European Commission revised its leniency programme in 2002 and again in 2006 to provide more transparency for applicants and less discretion for enforcers in administering the programme. The Commission's revised leniency programme now substantially mirrors the corporate amnesty policy of the US Department of Justice. See BMB Newman and M Delgado Echevarría, 'Gaps and Bridges: Transatlantic Cooperation' [2005] European Antitrust Review 26.

[48] R Hewitt Pate, 'Antitrust in a Transatlantic Context—From the Cicada's Perspective', address at the Antitrust in a Transatlantic Context Conference, 7 June 2004, cited by BMB Newman and M Delgado Echevarría, 'Gaps and Bridges: Transatlantic Cooperation' [2005] European Antitrust Review 26, 29.

7.14 More specifically, the US Government and the EU have entered into two agreements regulating cooperation on antitrust matters in which their interests overlap. The first agreement, entered into in 1991, demonstrates the efforts being made to coordinate an international approach to competition policy ('1991 Agreement').[49] The Commission and the Antitrust Division of the US Department of Justice ('DoJ') will now notify each other whenever they become aware that their enforcement activities may affect important interests of the other party, exchange information,[50] consult each other upon request, and coordinate and cooperate in enforcement activities to the extent their respective laws allow.[51] In particular, one agency may be asked by its counterpart to take action in order to remedy anticompetitive behaviour in its jurisdiction if such conduct affects the territory of its counterpart.[52] The 1991 Agreement was complemented by a second agreement on the application of positive comity principles in the enforcement of competition laws in both jurisdictions ('1998 Agreement'[53]), which further develops the principle of positive comity laid down in Article V of the 1991 Agreement. Antitrust authorities of both jurisdictions may request their counterpart to investigate and, if warranted, to remedy anticompetitive activities in accordance with its own competition laws. The 1998 Agreement clarifies both the mechanism of positive comity and the circumstances in which this cooperation instrument can be employed. In particular, it describes the conditions under which the requesting party should normally suspend its own enforcement actions and make a referral.[54]

7.15 The timing of an investigation is increasingly being influenced by cooperation efforts between cartel agencies worldwide due to the growing number of cases with an international dimension. One example is the *Heat Stabilisers* case (Case COMP/38.589), where, in 2003, the Commission and the antitrust authorities in the US, Canada, and Japan closely coordinated their investigative actions and undertook near-simultaneous inspections and other investigative measures. Another example is the *Industrial Copper Tubes* case (Case C.38.240), decided

---

[49] The Agreement was approved on behalf of the (then) European Communities by Decision of the Council and Commission of 10 April 1995 concerning the conclusion of the Agreement between the European Communities and the Government of the United States of America regarding the application of their competition laws, Decision 95/145/EC, ECSC, [1995] OJ L95/45. The act whereby the Commission initially sought to conclude the agreement on its own was annulled by the Court in Case C-327/91 *France v Commission* [1994] ECR I-3641, after the French Government successfully challenged the legal basis on which the Commission had proceeded. The text of the Agreement is annexed to the Decision ([1995] OJ L95/47) and is accompanied by a letter with two interpretative statements, the first dealing with the type of information that may be exchanged under the Agreement, the second confirming that the respective authorities should protect any information received from the other party in confidence.

[50] According to Art III of the 1991 Agreement, officials from both competition authorities shall meet at least twice a year, unless otherwise agreed, to (a) exchange information on their current enforcement activities and priorities; (b) exchange information on economic sectors of common interest; (c) discuss policy changes which they are considering; and (d) discuss other matters of mutual interest relating to the application of competition laws. Also, each Party will provide the other Party with any significant information about anticompetitive activities that its competition authorities believe is relevant to, or may warrant, enforcement activity by the other Party's competition authorities. Finally, upon receiving a request from the other Party, and within the limits of Arts VIII and IX, a Party will provide any information within its possession that according to the other Party is relevant to an enforcement activity being considered or conducted by its competition authorities.

[51] See Arts II–IV, VII of the 1991 Agreement.

[52] See Art V of the 1991 Agreement. However, such a request does not limit the *discretion* of the other Party whether or not to initiate enforcement actions. It merely requires the other Party to *consider* such action.

[53] Agreement between the European Communities and the Government of the United States of America on the application of positive comity principles in the enforcement of their competition laws [1998] OJ L173/28. The first investigation to be initiated on the basis of positive comity was the *Sabre* case. See XXX Report on Competition Policy [2000], para 191.

[54] Article IV of the 1998 Agreement.

in December 2003, where much of the evidence on which the decision relied resulted from inspections that were coordinated with the US antitrust authorities. In the *Bulk Liquids Shipping* case (Case 38624), the Commission, in a joint effort with the EFTA Surveillance Authority ('ESA') and the Norwegian authorities, undertook inspections simultaneously with the DoJ.[55] Likewise, in the *Marine Hoses* case (Case 39406), the Commission conducted surprise inspections coordinated with several other jurisdictions, including the US.[56] In the *Power Exchanges* case, the Commission participated in inspections carried out by ESA.[57]

To the extent that it is permitted, information sharing between US and EU authorities hap- **7.16** pens routinely. However, despite the remarkable level of coordination that antitrust authorities from both jurisdictions have achieved in their cartel enforcement efforts, practical impedi- ments to cooperation remain. Antitrust agencies are more limited in their ability to share information in this area than in the merger control context, due primarily to applicable rules prohibiting the sharing of information obtained in the course of investigations. With respect to the ECN, Article 28 of Regulation 1/2003 prevents the Commission and also the NCAs from disclosing (confidential) information obtained from companies during the course of their investigations outside the EU.[58] For instance, in the absence of a 'second generation' cooperation agreement providing for the exchange of such information, the Commission cannot share information obtained from an employee with non-EU antitrust authorities who could use it to prosecute antitrust violations outside the EU.[59] Also, the US and the EU both maintain policies of not disclosing an amnesty applicant's identity, or any information obtained from the applicant, to foreign authorities without the applicant's consent. Policy convergence may eventually break down these barriers, but still has to be achieved in a num- ber of areas. Moreover, given the decentralization of EU competition law brought about by Regulation 1/2003, existing agreements between the US and each EU Member State will be of increasing importance, since the 1991 and 1998 Agreements between the EU and the US are not binding on national jurisdictions.[60]

5. Retroactivity of the Commission's investigative powers

In an action for the annulment of an inspection decision put into effect in Spain one year **7.17** after accession, it was pleaded that Spanish undertakings could not be subjected to an inves- tigation relating to conduct preceding accession, since at that time the undertakings in ques- tion were outside the Commission's jurisdiction. In other words, the argument was that the Commission's powers could not be exercised retroactively.[61] The ECJ held, first, that since the Act of Accession of Spain to the European Communities contained no derogation to Regulation 17, undertakings established in Spain could be the subject of Commission

---

[55] XXXIII Report on Competition Policy [2003], paras 32 and 684. For more recent examples see Commission Report on Competition Policy 2009, para 66.
[56] Commission Press Release IP/09/137 'Commission fines marine hose producers €131 million for market sharing and price-fixing cartel' of 28 January 2009.
[57] MEMO/12/78 'Antitrust: Commission confirms unannounced inspections in the electricity sector' of 7 February 2012.
[58] For the applicability of these safeguards also in the relationship to the US authorities see Art VIII and the interpretative statements accompanying the 1991 Agreement. See also C Canenbley and M Rosenthal, 'Cooperation between Antitrust Authorities In- and Outside the EU: What does it mean for Multinational Corporations?—Part 2' [2005] ECLR 178, 179.
[59] See JS Venit and T Louko, 'The Commission's New Power to Question and its Implications on Human Rights' ch 26 in BE Hawk (ed), *International Antitrust Law and Policy* (Annual Proceedings of the Fordham Institute 2005) 675, 682.
[60] BMB Newman and M Delgado Echevarría, 'Gaps and Bridges: Transatlantic Cooperation' [2005] European Antitrust Review 26, 28.
[61] See Joined Cases 97/87 to 99/87 *Dow Chemical Ibérica v Commission* [1989] ECR 3165, para 61.

investigations as from 1 January 1986. Secondly, it stressed that the subject matter of the investigation could only be limited by the scope of the EU competition rules. The Court concluded that, since there was no EU provision restricting the Commission's investigative powers to conduct occurring after accession, the applicants' argument had to be rejected.[62] The same applies to the Member States which have joined the EU in the last decade, given that no restrictions in relation to the Commission's powers were stipulated under Regulation 1/2003.[63]

7.18　More generally, the GC has stressed that the powers of investigation provided for in Article 18(1) of Regulation 1/2003 are subject only to the requirement that the information requested must be necessary, and that this is for the Commission to evaluate. Hence, if the Commission can reasonably assume that information relating to an earlier period during which the competition rules of the EU did not (yet) apply is necessary for the finding of a possible infringement of Articles 101 and/or 102 TFEU (from the point in time when they became applicable), it may request such information. If it were to ignore this information, the Commission would go against its duty to examine carefully and impartially all the relevant evidence in the case under investigation. Often, certain conduct can only (or at least better) be assessed in the light of earlier events, be it objectively (eg cost figures of an earlier period may be important in analysing a margin squeeze) or as regards the subjective intentions of market players (eg their aim to eliminate competitors).[64]

6. The choice of investigative measures

7.19　Subject to the principle of proportionality[65]—which includes the aspects of necessity and non-arbitrariness—the Commission has discretion to choose among the investigatory powers available to it and is not bound to any particular chronological order. Thus, an inspection may precede a request for information, and vice versa, the information obtained at the first stage, whatever it might be, being used to guide the investigation at the next stage. Early on, the ECJ has clarified that Articles 11 (requests for information) and 14 (inspections) of Regulation 17 provided for two entirely independent procedures.[66] The fact that an inspection has already taken place does not in any way limit the Commission's powers to issue a request for information, and it might even ask for the disclosure of documents which it was unable to copy during an inspection at an earlier stage.[67] Likewise, even if it already has indications, or indeed proof, of the existence of an infringement, the Commission may legitimately take the view that it is necessary to request further information to enable it to better define the scope of the infringement, to determine its duration, or to identify the circle of undertakings involved.[68] Where such information is not likely to be obtained by way of a request for information, the Commission may proceed to an(other) inspection.[69]

---

[62] Joined Cases 97/87 to 99/87 *Dow Chemical Ibérica v Commission* [1989] ECR 3165, paras 62–3. Like any other companies located outside the EEA, undertakings in a country seeking accession may have infringed Arts 101, 102 TFEU prior to its accession to the EU, for which reason it would seem logical for their earlier activities to be open to investigation and even liable to fines, if the limitation period has not expired.

[63] Unlike the State aid sector which has been subject to a number of transitional arrangements.

[64] Joined Cases T-458/09 and T-171/10 *Slovak Telekom v Commission*, paras 42 and 45 et seq.

[65] See Case T-339/04 *France Télécom v Commission* [2007] ECR II-573, para 118 (inspections); Judgment of 22 March 2012 in Joined Cases T-458/09 and T-171/10 *Slovak Telekom v Commission*, para 81 (requests for information).

[66] Case 136/79 *National Panasonic v Commission* [1980] ECR 2033, paras 9–15; Case 374/87 *Orkem v Commission* [1989] ECR 3283, para 14. See also Case T-266/03 *Groupement des cartes bancaires (CB) v Commission* [2007] ECR II-83, para 64.

[67] Case 374/87 *Orkem v Commission* [1989] ECR 3283, para 14.

[68] Case 374/87 *Orkem v Commission* [1989] ECR 3283, para 15.

[69] Case T-339/04 *France Télécom v Commission* [2007] ECR II-573, paras 119 and 122.

The ECJ has held that in respect of inspections, the Commission's choice between a simple **7.20** authorization and an inspection decision does not depend on matters such as the particular seriousness of the situation, or extreme urgency, but rather on the need for an appropriate inquiry, having regard to the special features of the case. In particular, the Court has concluded that, where an inspection shall enable the Commission to gather the information needed to assess whether the competition rules have been infringed, such a measure is not contrary to the principle of proportionality.[70] As regards requests for information, Regulation 1/2003 no longer foresees a two-stage procedure whereby the Commission first has to send a simple request.[71] Consequently, it does not infringe the principle of proportionality if the Commission proceeds straight to a request by decision pursuant to Article 18(3) of Regulation 1/2003.[72] This means that the Commission is in principle free to choose between both options and may adopt a (binding) decision whenever it considers that there is a risk (even a slight one) that otherwise the response might be delayed or incomplete.

7. Cooperation with Member States' authorities

As regards inspections, if these are carried out by NCAs under Article 22(2) of Regulation **7.21** 1/2003, there will be a close collaboration between the Commission and the respective national authority. If carried out by the Commission, it must consult the NCA before adopting an inspection decision (Article 20(4)), or at least inform the NCA of its intentions '[i]n good time before the inspection' in case of a simple authorization (Article 20(3)).[73] At the request of the Commission, NCA officials must actively assist the Commission inspectors during the investigation (Article 20(5)). Where an undertaking refuses to submit (fully) to an inspection, the Member State concerned must afford the Commission the necessary assistance to enable the inspections to take place: this may entail the involvement of the police or an equivalent enforcement authority (Article 20(6)). Depending on the applicable national law, such assistance may require prior judicial authorization (Article 20(7)), something which is always mandatory in case non-business premises are to be inspected (Article 21(3)). In this regard, Articles 20(8) and 21(3) reflect the ECJ's judgment in *Roquette Frères* on the role of the national judge.[74] Finally, where a suspected infringement has an EEA dimension, the authority carrying out the inspection—be it the Commission or the ESA—shall inform the other authority of that fact and, upon request, transmit the relevant results of the inspection.[75]

As regards requests for information, the Commission has the duty to forward a copy of the simple **7.22** request or of the decision to the NCA in whose jurisdiction the (association of) undertaking(s) is situated, as well as to the NCA of the Member State whose territory is affected (Article 18(5) of Regulation 1/2003). Similar rules apply in the EEA context in case the Commission or ESA address an undertaking outside their jurisdiction.[76] Upon receipt of the response from the undertaking, the Commission services will voluntarily provide the NCA with a copy thereof.[77] Finally,

---

[70] Case C-94/00 *Roquette Frères* [2002] ECR I-9011, para 77; Case 136/79 *National Panasonic v Commission* [1980] ECR 2033, paras 28–30.

[71] See Art 11(5) of Reg 17 of 1962.

[72] Judgment of 22 March 2012 in Joined Cases T-458/09 and T-171/10 *Slovak Telekom v Commission*, para 90.

[73] A change from Reg 17 is that the Commission no longer has to provide the identity of the authorized officials (see last sentence of Art 14(2) of Reg 17).

[74] Case C-94/00 *Roquette Frères* [2002] ECR I-9011. See Ch 8, 'Investigation of Cases (III): Inspections', para 8.62 et seq.

[75] See Art 8(5) of Protocol 23 to the EEA Agreement.

[76] See Art 8(1) of Protocol 23 to the EEA Agreement.

[77] European Commission Antitrust Manual of Procedures, Internal DG Competition working documents on procedures for the application of Articles 101 and 102 TFEU, March 2012, Module 6 'Requests for information', para 40.

Article 19(2) of Regulation 1/2003 foresees that, where the Commission intends to conduct an interview at the premises of an undertaking, it has to inform the NCA in whose jurisdiction the interview will take place.[78] The NCA can then request that its officials assist the officials and other accompanying persons authorized by the Commission to conduct the interview.

8. Consequences of non-compliance

7.23 Refusal to cooperate with or attempts to obstruct the Commission's investigation may be fined as a procedural infringement pursuant to Article 23(1) of Regulation 1/2003, and can lead to the imposition of periodic penalty payments pursuant to Article 24(1)(d) and (e). Moreover, in line with point 28 of the 2006 Fining Guidelines, refusal to cooperate with as well as the obstruction of the Commission in carrying out its investigation may constitute an aggravating circumstance leading to an increased fine for any antitrust violations found as a result of the investigation.[79]

B. Requests for Information

1. Introduction

7.24 Pursuant to Article 18 of Regulation 1/2003, the Commission may request undertakings or associations of undertakings to provide it with all information it deems necessary in order to carry out the duties assigned to it by Regulation 1/2003. Undertakings can be required to provide the Commission with all the information specified in the request, and can therefore be compelled to hand over existing documents or to provide answers to questions within the time limit fixed.[80] This power may be seen as a specific example of its general investigative powers set out in Article 337 TFEU. Written requests for information constitute the method most commonly used by the Commission in its investigations, and the number of such requests far exceeds the number of inspections. As stated previously, they may be made at any stage of the procedure, even before initiating proceedings against an undertaking,[81] until adoption of the decision, and even afterwards, for instance in order to verify compliance. The Commission has discretion to decide whether it is necessary to employ requests for information,[82] and it is not unusual for one and the same undertaking to receive several (follow-on) requests in the course of the same procedure. The term 'information' must be interpreted as also including specific documents, so that the Commission may request such business records[83] as it considers appropriate. Article 18 of Regulation 1/2003 empowers the Commission not only to request explanations, figures, or statistical tables, but also to ask for specific documents in the possession

---

[78] According to Commission practice, the NCA should normally be informed at least two weeks in advance. See European Commission Antitrust Manual of Procedures, Internal DG Competition working documents on procedures for the application of Articles 101 and 102 TFEU, March 2012, Module 8 'Power to take statements', para 11.

[79] For a detailed overview see Chapter 11, para 11.60 (iii).

[80] Article 18(6) of Reg 1/2003, like formerly Art 11 of Reg 17, also includes the possibility of obtaining information from the governments and competent authorities of the Member States. Under Reg 17, the vast majority of requests for information were sent to undertakings; Art 12 of Reg 1/2003 also provides for the possibility of exchanging information between the Commission and the NCAs, and amongst the NCAs themselves.

[81] Article 2(3) of Reg 773/2004.

[82] Case 27/88 *Solvay v EC Commission* [1989] ECR 3355, paras 12–13; Case 374/87 *Orkem v EC Commission* [1989] ECR 3283, paras 15–16; Joined Cases 46/87 and 227/88 *Hoechst AG v EC Commission* [1989] ECR 2859, para 25. As regards the Commission's discretion in shaping the enquiry, see Case T-141/94 *Thyssen Stahl v Commission* [1999] ECR II-347, para 110; Case T-9/99 *HFB and Others v Commission* [2002] ECR II-1487, para 384 and Case T-48/00 *Corus UK v Commission* [2004] ECR II-2325, para 212.

[83] See Ch 9, 'Procedural Infringements: Fines and Periodic Penalties', para 9.09 et seq regarding the term 'business records'.

of undertakings that may contain information needed for the purposes of the investigation. The information demanded need not be confined to the firm's own business, but may extend to questions about the background of the industry and the market as far as the requested information is available to, or can be estimated by, the addressee. Furthermore, the GC held that the Commission, in order to investigate a potential infringement of the EU competition rules that would fall within its jurisdiction, also has the power to require undertakings to provide information that stems from a period during which the competition rules of the EU did not apply.[84]

The Commission enjoys considerable discretion in determining what information is 'neces- **7.25** sary' for its inquiries and the EU Courts merely exercise a limited review in that regard. The GC held that, given the wording and purpose of Article 18(1) of Regulation 1/2003, the powers of investigation provided for in that provision are subject only to the requirement that the information requested be necessary, which it is *for the Commission* to evaluate, in order to assess the putative infringements justifying the undertaking of the investigation and to detect an infringement of Articles 101 and/or 102 TFEU.[85] The meaning of 'necessary information' was considered by the EU Courts in *SEP*,[86] and, more recently, in *Slovak Telecom*.[87] The GC stated that the term 'necessary information' must be interpreted by reference to the purposes for which the powers of investigation in question have been conferred upon the Commission. The requirement that there must exist a correlation between the request for information and the putative infringement will be satisfied if, at the respective stage in the proceedings, the request may legitimately be considered as having a connection with the putative infringement, in the sense that the Commission may *reasonably suppose* that the document would help it to determine whether the alleged infringement had taken place.[88] The Commission cannot be required, before having received the information requested, to be familiar with the content of the requested documents and their relative importance for the investigation.[89] The ECJ upheld this interpretation in *SEP*.[90] The Commission's margin of discretion in considering the information necessary for an investigation was also highlighted by the GC in *Corus*.[91] The GC also held that the Commission is under no obligation, during its investigation, to put the same questions to all the undertakings it suspects of participating in an infringement. Such an obligation would detract from the Commission's freedom of action in the conduct of its investigations in competition cases and would therefore undermine their effectiveness.[92]

It could be argued that the concept of 'necessary information' as explained earlier already encom- **7.26** passes the requirement that requests for information made by the Commission to an undertaking must comply with the principle of proportionality. The EU Courts have nevertheless highlighted specifically that the obligation imposed on an undertaking to supply information should not be

---

[84] See Judgment of 22 March 2012 in Joined Cases T-458/09 and T-171/10 *Slovak Telekom v Commission*, paras 45 and 72. The GC held that information and documents pre-dating the accession of the Slovak Republic to the EU and the period of infringement could prove necessary for the Commission to be able to undertake the tasks assigned to it by Reg 1/2003 in an impartial and fair manner.

[85] See Judgment of 22 March 2012 in Joined Cases T-458/09 and T-171/10 *Slovak Telekom v Commission*, para 45.

[86] Case T-39/90 *SEP v Commission* [1991] ECR II-1497.

[87] Judgment of 22 March 2012 in Joined Cases T-458/09 and T-171/10 *Slovak Telekom v Commission*, para 42 et seq.

[88] Case T-39/90 *SEP v Commission* [1991] ECR II-1497, para 29 et seq; Judgment of 22 March 2012 in Joined Cases T-458/09 and T-171/10 *Slovak Telekom v Commission*, para 42.

[89] See Judgment of 22 March 2012 in Joined Cases T-458/09 and T-171/10 *Slovak Telekom v Commission*, para 55.

[90] Case C-36/92 P *SEP v Commission* [1994] ECR I-1911.

[91] Case T-48/00 *Corus UK v Commission* [2004] ECR II-2325, para 212.

[92] Case T-48/00 *Corus UK v Commission* [2004] ECR II-2325, para 212.

a burden on that undertaking which is disproportionate to the needs of the inquiry.[93] However, so far undertakings have not succeeded in demonstrating this. In view of the Commission's broad discretion to decide whether particular items of information are necessary for the investigation,[94] it is not easy to show that the request is disproportionate, even in cases where the undertaking had to provide a broad range of information or invest significant resources in that regard. This does not mean that the Commission may embark on a 'fishing expedition' and that the EU Courts would not be prepared to hold, in an appropriate case, that it has exceeded its powers.[95] Also, irrespective of the Commission's exclusive power to shape its investigation, DG COMP is generally willing to discuss with the addressees the scope and the format of the request for information. This may be particularly useful in cases of requests concerning quantitative data.[96]

7.27 The power to request information has been strengthened in comparison with the situation under Regulation 17.[97] Article 11 of Regulation 17 laid down a two-step procedure for such requests which the Commission was bound to follow. In the first phase, the Commission had to send a simple request for information to the undertaking. Only if a complete reply had not been given by the undertaking within the prescribed time limit could the Commission proceed to the second phase and send a request for information by binding decision. Pecuniary penalties could only be imposed if the undertaking refused to reply a second time.[98] Under Regulation 1/2003, the Commission has the choice: information can be requested by simple letter ('simple request', Article 18(2)) or (directly) by decision (Article 18(3) of Regulation 1/2003). The principle of proportionality in principle does not require the Commission to first send a simple request before adopting a binding decision.[99] Nevertheless, typically the Commission will still start by issuing a simple request addressed to the undertaking, unless it has any reasons to believe that they will be uncooperative or if the Commission cannot run the risk of receiving belated answers in view of the particular urgency of the case. If the Commission issues a simple request, undertakings are not compelled to respond, and hence they incur no penalty if they decide not to provide the requested information, but they may then be deemed uncooperative by the Commission. Moreover, even in case of a simple request the provision of incorrect or misleading information may lead to the imposition of a fine of up to

---

[93] See Judgment of 22 March 2012 in Joined Cases T-458/09 and T-171/10 *Slovak Telekom v Commission*, para 81; Case C-36/92 P *SEP v Commission* [1994] ECR I-1911, paras 51–2; Joined Cases T-191/98, T-212/98 to T-214/98 *Atlantic Container Line and Others v Commission* [2003] ECR II-3275, paras 404 and 418. Likewise, the Commission Notice on best practices for the conduct of proceedings concerning Articles 101 and 102 TFEU [2011] OJ C308/6, para 33 n 31, acknowledges that in exercising its discretion as to the scope of requests for information, the Commission is bound by the principle of proportionality.

[94] See Judgment of 22 March 2012 in Joined Cases T-458/09 and T-171/10 *Slovak Telekom v Commission*, para 43; Case 155/79 *AM & S Europe v Commission* [1982] ECR 1575, para 17; Case C-94/00 *Roquette Frères* [2002] ECR I-9011, para 78; and Case T-340/04 *France Télécom v Commission* [2007] ECR II-573, para 148.

[95] See Case 155/79 *AM & S Europe v Commission* [1982] ECR 1575 paras 14–16; Case 374/87 *Orkem v Commission* [1989] ECR 3283, para 15. Currently seven cases are pending before the GC regarding the proportionality of information request decisions asking for very extensive pre-existing economic data for the purpose of proving a concerted practice in the cement industry: Cases T-306/11 *Schwenk v Commission*; T-305/11 *Italmobiliare v Commission*; T-302/11 *HeidelbergCement v Commission*; T-297/11 *Buzzi Unicem v Commission*; T-296/11 *Cementos Portland Valderrivas v Commission*; T-293/11 *Holcim v Commission*; T-292/11 *Cemex and others v Commission*.

[96] Commission Notice on best practices for the conduct of proceedings concerning Articles 101 and 102 TFEU [2011] OJ C308/6, para 34 with n 32.

[97] A Riley, 'EC Antitrust Modernisation: The Commission Does Very Nicely—Thank You! Part One: Regulation 1 and the Notification Burden' [2003] ECLR 604, 608.

[98] See Case 136/79 *National Panasonic v Commission* [1980] ECR 2033, para 10. This was repeatedly confirmed, eg in Case T-39/90 *Samenwerkende Elektriciteits-Produktiebedrijven (SEP) v Commission* [1991] ECR II-1497, para 26; in Case T-46/92 *The Scottish Football Association v Commission* [1994] ECR II-1039, para 30; and in Case T-34/93 *Société Générale v Commission* [1995] ECR II-545, para 38.

[99] See Judgment of 22 March 2012 in Joined Cases T-458/09 and T-171/10 *Slovak Telekom v Commission*, para 81; Case C-36/92 P *SEP v Commission* [1994] ECR I-1911, para 90.

1 per cent of the undertaking's turnover in the previous year, pursuant to Article 23(1)(a) of Regulation 1/2003.[100] If the Commission requests information by decision, undertakings are also compelled to provide information in a complete and timely manner, or otherwise will risk a fine at the indicated level, pursuant to Article 23(1)(b) of Regulation 1/2003.

Under Article 3 of Regulation 1/1958,[101] undertakings are entitled to receive requests for infor- **7.28** mation in the official EU language or languages[102] of the country in which they are situated. As far as complainants are concerned, requests for information must be in the language of their complaint (as long as is it one of the EU official languages) even if this is not the language of the Member State where they are located.[103] However, as a matter of practice, the Commission sometimes formulates its requests in English or another widely used language in order to be able to proceed more swiftly. The addressees are informed—in the language used at their location—of their right to obtain a translation of the cover letter and/or questionnaire, as well as the right to reply in that language.[104] If the undertakings accept this correspondence, the Commission will continue addressing them in its chosen language. The companies may either reply in English, the language in which the request is formulated, or in their own language. Conversely, at the request of an undertaking, the Commission may agree to send requests and other correspondence in an EU language other than that of the place where that undertaking is established.[105] Requests for information are usually sent by fax or email, if channels of communication with the addressee have already been established. The addressee will be asked to return the acknowledgement of receipt accompanying the request.[106] Such a request can also be made electronically through the eQuestionnaire application, which provides respondents with a secure and efficient web-based workspace to submit their replies to the Commission.[107] Registered mail or courier may also be sued, in particular if a large number of documents or handwritten documents are attached to the request. In this case, when setting the deadline for reply, account must be taken of the time necessary to deliver the letter.[108] The period within which a reply must be given starts to run from the day following the date of receipt. In order to avoid any argument as to whether a means of transmission such as fax provides conclusive

---

[100] Regarding the possibility of imposing fines in these situations, see Ch 9, 'Procedural Infringements: Fines and Periodic Penalty Payments' para 9.04 et seq.

[101] Council Reg 1 of 25 April 1958 determining the languages to be used by the EEC ([1952–58] OJ Spec Ed 59), last modified by Annex II, ch 22, para 1, of the Accession Act [2003] OJ L236/791. Article 3 of Reg 1/1958 provides: 'Documents which an institution of the Community sends to a Member State or to a person subject to the jurisdiction of a Member State shall be drafted in the language of such State.' Neither the EU Treaties nor Reg 1/2003 contain any express provisions determining the languages to be used by the Commission or by the NCAs.

[102] Regarding official languages, see Ch 4 'The Organization of EU Commission Proceedings', para 4.30 et seq.

[103] European Commission Antitrust Manual of Procedures, Internal DG Competition working documents on procedures for the application of Articles 101 and 102 TFEU, March 2012, Module 6 'Requests for information', para 21.

[104] European Commission Antitrust Manual of Procedures, Internal DG Competition working documents on procedures for the application of Articles 101 and 102 TFEU, March 2012, Module 6 'Requests for information', para 22.

[105] An example might be an undertaking with a US parent company whose branch in the EU is located in Germany. A US undertaking might prefer to receive correspondence in English and could make a request to the Commission to that effect; the Commission will, in general, agree.

[106] European Commission Antitrust Manual of Procedures, Internal DG Competition working documents on procedures for the application of Articles 101 and 102 TFEU, March 2012, Module 6 'Requests for information', para 35.

[107] European Commission Antitrust Manual of Procedures, Internal DG Competition working documents on procedures for the application of Articles 101 and 102 TFEU, March 2012, Module 6 'Requests for information', para 37.

[108] European Commission Antitrust Manual of Procedures, Internal DG Competition working documents on procedures for the application of Articles 101 and 102 TFEU, March 2012, Module 6 'Requests for information', para 36.

evidence that the request has been received, the Commission usually calculates its time limits by reference to the date on the acknowledgement of receipt returned by the postal authorities, even where it has sent the letter first by fax. Requests for information are always sent to undertakings as such, and not personally to their directors, managers, or representatives. Nor are they sent to lawyers acting for them, unless they have expressly been authorized to provide the information on behalf of their clients.[109]

7.29 As regards the type of information which the Commission may ask from an undertaking, the EU Courts have upheld the Commission's prerogatives as to the appropriateness and content of its requests for information in most cases—*inter alia* in its judgments in the *Orkem, Solvay*, and *SEP* cases.[110] The Commission is well advised to ensure that its questions are as precise as possible, in order to enable undertakings to reply to them clearly and completely. Despite the latitude which it enjoys in asking questions, the Commission is required to scrupulously observe undertakings' defence rights when formulating them. It may not frame its questions in such a manner that an undertaking cannot reply without admitting that it has infringed the competition rules or pursued objectives which in themselves would be regarded as constituting an infringement.[111] If an undertaking answers to questions that the Commission was not allowed to ask, the reply might have to be taken into account as voluntary cooperation in the context of the calculation of the fine.[112] It is incumbent upon the Commission to prove the infringement, and it may therefore not ask undertakings simply to admit guilt—if it does, the relevant question(s) in its request would not have to be answered and incorrect answers could not be sanctioned.[113] This does not apply to purely factual questions, as they are not capable of requiring the undertaking to admit the existence of an infringement of the competition rules. The same applies to requests to provide pre-existing documents which might prove the infringement, or factual explanations related to these documents. However, these questions must be framed in such a way that they do not solicit self-incriminatory replies.[114] According to the case law, questions like the following are not permitted:[115]

- Questions relating to the purpose of the action taken and the objectives pursued.
- A request for details of any method which allowed the attribution of sales targets or quotas to several undertakings.

---

[109] In contrast to Art 11 of Reg 17, note that Art 18(4) of Reg 1/2003 expressly refers to this possibility.

[110] Case 374/87 *Orkem v Commission* [1989] ECR 3283, paras 14–17; Case 27/88 *Solvay v Commission* [1989] ECR 3355, para 8, and Case T-39/90 *Samenverkende Elektriciteits-Produktiebedrijven (SEP) v Commission* [1991] ECR II-1497, paras 25–8.

[111] The fact that an undertaking is not entitled to base a refusal to reply on the grounds that the objective information or documents requested by the Commission could be used as evidence against it, is not unproblematic. By contrast to the situation under criminal law in the Member States, EU competition law guarantees no right to silence, and only a partial protection against self-incrimination. However, the right not to give evidence against oneself only relates to natural persons accused of a criminal offence, while lesser restrictions may apply in administrative proceedings against firms. Unlike eg in German antitrust law (see $$ 81 et seq of the German Act Against Restrictions of Competition (GWB) and $ 9 of the German Administrative Offences Act (OWiG)), only firms (not their individual executives or officials) are liable to penalties for antitrust infringements under EU law.

[112] Chapter 11, para 11.62 (iv).

[113] In its judgments in Case 374/87 *Orkem v Commission* [1989] ECR 3283 and Case 27/88 *Solvay v Commission* [1989] ECR 3355, the Court annulled certain questions put by the Commission to these two undertakings on the ground that they required them to admit an infringement of former Art 85 of the EC Treaty [now Art 101 TFEU]. In doing so, the Commission infringed their defence rights and disregarded the rules concerning the burden of proof (paras 41 and 37 respectively). Regarding the interpretation of the *Orkem* judgment and its inapplicability to civil proceedings on the basis of Arts 101 and 102 TFEU, see Case C-60/92 *Otto v Postbank* [1993] ECR I-5683, para 11 et seq.

[114] European Commission Antitrust Manual of Procedures, Internal DG Competition working documents on procedures for the application of Articles 101 and 102 TFEU, March 2012, Module 6 'Requests for information', para 45.

[115] For more details, see para 7.41 et seq.

- A request for details of any method facilitating the monitoring of compliance with any system of targets in terms of volume or quotas.

Generally, the Commission allows undertakings to supply unsolicited information or docu- **7.30**
ments which they consider to be important to the investigation of the case, and which they
may use in their defence at a later stage. Further, where the Commission has received a formal complaint, the sending of a request for information may be an opportunity to ask the
undertakings for their views on the action attributed to them by the complainant.[116] Such
information is not covered by the rules in Article 18 of Regulation 1/2003, which means
that the Commission cannot insist on receiving it, and therefore can only set indicative time
limits. Undertakings provide their views on complaints forwarded to them only if they wish
to do so.

2. Simple requests

Due to their non-binding nature, simple requests for information issued pursuant to **7.31**
Article 18(2) of Regulation 1/2003 are measures of pure administration, which do not
require the Commission's approval and can be undertaken by officials within DG COMP
without involvement of other Commission departments.[117] They usually incorporate two
distinct parts: first, an accompanying letter which contains the necessary formal and substantive clarifications to enable the undertakings to reply to the request; and secondly, as an annex
to the letter, a questionnaire specifying in detail the information and documents requested.
Both parts (not merely the questions contained in the questionnaire) comprise the request
for information pursuant to Article 18 of Regulation 1/2003. When the first investigative
measure is taken in respect of an undertaking, including by way of a request for information
under Article 18 of Regulation 1/2003, the Commission is required to inform the undertaking concerned, *inter alia*, of the subject matter and purpose of the on-going investigation.[118]
In *AC Treuhand*, the GC held that, with regard to requests for information, the reasoning
does not need to be as extensive as that required for decisions ordering an inspection, owing
to the more restrictive nature of the latter and their particularly intense impact on the legal
situation of the undertaking concerned. Nevertheless, that reasoning must still enable the
undertaking to understand the purpose and subject matter of the investigation, which means
that both the putative infringement and the fact that the undertaking may be faced with allegations in that regard must be specified, so that it can take the measures which it deems useful
to exonerate itself and, thus, prepare its defence at the *inter partes* stage of the administrative
procedure.[119] Concerning the suspected infringement of Articles 101 and/or 102 TFEU, the
Commission must specify it 'with reasonable precision'.[120] Moreover, the Commission has to
demonstrate that it could reasonably assume that the sought-for information might enable

---

[116] See Ch 5, 'Opening of the File and of Proceedings: Transparency', para 5.15 et seq.

[117] European Commission Antitrust Manual of Procedures, Internal DG Competition working documents
on procedures for the application of Articles 101 and 102 TFEU, March 2012, Module 1 'Decision-making
procedures', para 49.

[118] See Case T-99/04 *AC Treuhand v Commission* [2008] ECR II-1501, para 56. After having received a
request for information or being subject to an inspection, parties may at any time inquire with DG COMP
about the status of the investigation, even before the formal opening of proceedings. If an undertaking considers that it has not been properly informed by DG COMP of its procedural status, it may refer the matter to
the Hearing Officer for resolution, after having raised the matter with DG COMP. See Commission Notice
on best practices for the conduct of proceedings concerning Articles 101 and 102 TFEU [2011] OJ C308/6,
para 15.

[119] See Case T-99/04 *AC Treuhand v Commission* [2008] ECR II-1501, para 56.

[120] See Opinion of AG Jacobs in Case C-36/92 P *SEP v Commission* [1994] ECR I-1911, para 30;
endorsed by ECJ in Case C-36/92 P *SEP v Commission* [1994] ECR I-1932, para 21.

it to investigate the putative infringement which justifies the enquiry and is set out in the request for information.[121] While the Commission must thus clearly indicate the alleged facts which it intends to investigate by giving a concise indication of the putative infringement and the firm's suspected involvement, it is not obliged to disclose all the known facts.[122] Article 18 of Regulation 1/2003 has codified these requirements and states that in simple requests, the Commission is obliged to indicate:

- the legal basis of the request;
- the purpose of the request, ie a brief description of the type of activity investigated, allegedly constituting an infringement of the competition rules;[123]
- a specification of the requested information;
- the time limit within which the information has to be provided.[124]
- the penalties for providing incorrect information. The provision of incorrect or misleading information may lead to the imposition of a fine of up to 1 per cent of the undertaking's turnover in the previous year, pursuant to Article 23(1)(a) of Regulation 1/2003. The text of this provision is usually reproduced in the letter.

7.32 In addition, simple requests for information always contain a statement that both the questions and the replies are covered by professional secrecy under Article 28 of Regulation 1/2003.[125] Given that, at a later stage, the Commission may nevertheless be obliged to grant access to the addressees of a statement of objections,[126] or may consider it appropriate to disclose the replies to specified third parties (in particular the complainant), who may be customers or competitors of the undertaking responding to an information request, the Commission asks the respondents to clearly identify what parts they regard as business secrets that must not be disclosed to third parties or published. In accordance with Article 16(3) of Regulation 773/2004, the addressee must substantiate any such claims individually with regard to each item of information and provide a non-confidential version thereof. Such a non-confidential version should be provided in the same format as the confidential information, replacing deleted passages by summaries thereof. Unless otherwise agreed, a non-confidential version

---

[121] Judgment of 22 March 2012 in Joined Cases T-458/09 and T-171/10 *Slovak Telekom v Commission*, paras 42–3; Case T-34/93 *Société Générale v Commission* [1995] ECR-II 545, para 40.

[122] Joined Cases 46/87 and 227/88 *Hoechst AG v Commission* [1989] ECR 2859, paras 39–43; Case 136/79 *National Panasonic v Commission* [1980] ECR 2033, paras 24–7; Case 85/87 *Dow Benelux v Commission* [1989] ECR 3137, paras 6–11.

[123] As the Court has held: 'By disclosing its suspicion of the existence of agreements contrary to Article 85(1) of the Treaty [101(1) TFEU], the Commission merely complied with the obligations imposed on it by Article 11(3) to state the purpose of its request'—see Case 374/87 *Orkem v Commission* [1989] ECR 3283, para 11 and Case 27/88 *Solvay v Commission* [1989] ECR 3355, para 8.

[124] Article 18(2) of Reg 1/2003 does not specify the time limit for a reply, which may be expressed as a period (several days or weeks) or end date. DG COMP sets the time limit for answers at its own discretion, according to the complexity of the questions. In general, this time limit will be at least two weeks from the receipt of the request, but may be longer where this is considered necessary. When the scope of the request is limited, for example if it only covers a short clarification of information previously provided or information readily available to the addressee of the request, the time limit will normally be shorter (one week or less). See Commission Notice on best practices for the conduct of proceedings concerning Articles 101 and 102 TFEU [2011] OJ C308/6, para 38. Upon reasoned request (by letter or email), sufficiently in advance of the expiry of the time limit, the Commission may grant additional time. It may also agree with the addressee of the request that certain parts of the requested information that are of particular importance or easily available for the addressee will be supplied within a shorter time limit, whereas additional time will be granted for supplying the remaining information (para 39).

[125] European Commission Antitrust Manual of Procedures, Internal DG Competition working documents on procedures for the application of Articles 101 and 102 TFEU, March 2012, Module 6 'Requests for information', para 26.

[126] See Art 15 of Reg 773/2004.

should be provided at the same time as the original submission.[127] If undertakings fail to comply with these requirements, the Commission may assume that the documents or statements concerned do not contain confidential information, pursuant to Article 16(4) of Regulation 773/2004. In order to provide the undertakings with a point of contact if they have any doubts about the content of the request or the procedure to be followed in answering the questions, towards the end of the letter DG COMP usually indicates the name and telephone number of the officials in charge of investigating the case.[128] Where this is necessary to communicate properly, the officials concerned will seek the assistance of a colleague who speaks the language of the undertaking's representative.

The Commission may request information from undertakings not directly involved either in   **7.33**
the proceedings or in the infringement under investigation if they possess information needed for the investigation.[129] It may also approach any undertaking directly or indirectly affected by the suspected infringement. As always, the Commission must observe the generally applicable rules for such a request and in particular give reasons for its request, indicating its legal basis and purpose. The undertakings concerned will also be informed whether or not the procedure is directed against them (at that stage, at least).[130] However, in principle, the Commission is not required in the initial phase of the investigation to reveal the identity of the (other) undertakings allegedly involved in the putative infringement; neither does it have to contact each and every legal entity that ultimately may be held liable for such an infringement.[131] Information obtained under Article 18 of Regulation 1/2003 must not be used for purposes other than that for which it was requested and both the Commission and the competent authorities of the Member States are required to observe professional secrecy.[132] This requirement:

> is intended to protect, in addition to the professional secrecy... the undertakings' defence rights... which not only form part of the fundamental principles of Community law but are also enshrined in Article 6 of the ECHR. Those rights would be seriously endangered if the Commission were able to rely on evidence against undertakings which was obtained during an investigation but was not related to the subject-matter or purpose thereof.[133]

However, in so far as that information provides indications for further anticompetitive conduct, it may be taken into account to justify initiation of another (including a national) procedure.[134]

---

[127] European Commission Antitrust Manual of Procedures, Internal DG Competition working documents on procedures for the application of Articles 101 and 102 TFEU, March 2012, Module 6 'Requests for information', para 26; Commission Notice on best practices for the conduct of proceedings concerning Articles 101 and 102 TFEU [2011] OJ C308/6, para 41.

[128] European Commission Antitrust Manual of Procedures, Internal DG Competition working documents on procedures for the application of Articles 101 and 102 TFEU, March 2012, Module 6 'Requests for information', para 24.

[129] For instance, in Case AF/IV/372 *Fides* [1979] OJ L57/33, the Commission compelled a management company not active on the market concerned by the infringement to produce documentation regarding various undertakings for which it carried out services. The decision concerned an inspection, but the same principles apply as regards a request for information.

[130] If the addressees are themselves subject to the investigation (ie suspected of having participated in the putative infringement), they shall be informed of this fact as well as the subject matter and purpose of the investigation. See Commission Notice on best practices for the conduct of proceedings concerning Articles 101 and 102 TFEU [2011] OJ C308/6, para 15.

[131] See Judgment of 29 September 2011 in Case C-521/09 P *Elf Aquitaine v Commission*, paras 118–22.

[132] See Recital 16 and Art 28 of Reg 1/2003.

[133] Joined Cases C-238/99 P, C-244/99 P, C-245/99 P, C-247/99 P, C-250/99 P to C-252/99 P and C-254/99 P *Limburgse Vinyl Maatschappij and Others v Commission* [2002] ECR I-8375, paras 299 and 300.

[134] Case C-67/91 *Dirección General de Defensa de la Competencia v Asociación Española de Banca Privada* ('*Spanish Banks*') [1992] ECR I-4785, para 39: 'The Member States are not required to ignore the information disclosed to them and thereby undergo, to echo the expression used by the Commission and the national

7.34 As has been seen, simple requests for information may also be sent to undertakings/associations of undertakings outside the EEA.[135] In such cases, the Commission usually writes directly to the head of the foreign company. The letters can be sent directly to the undertakings and do not need to be channelled through delegations of the EU in the respective countries.[136] Where the undertaking has a subsidiary within the EEA, the request may be sent in addition to that subsidiary. If sent to the undertaking located outside the EEA, the Commission's internal manual of procedure foresees that the request will not contain the reference to potential fines that would normally be included.[137] As regards the EEA, Article 8(1) of Protocol 23 to the EEA Agreement empowers the Commission to send requests for information to undertakings in the territory of the EFTA (except Switzerland) under conditions very similar to those applicable to companies in the EU. Requests sent to undertakings and associations of undertakings in such EEA countries (ie Norway, Iceland, Liechtenstein) can be drafted in the same way as requests to companies located within the EU, including any reference to the possibility of imposing fines.[138] The EFTA Surveillance Authority (ESA) must receive a copy of such requests. This will be indicated on the stamp showing to whom copies of the request for information must be sent.[139] The Commission will also inform the authorities of certain non-EEA countries with whom it has concluded a formal agreement[140] (or at least found some kind of arrangement concerning the application of competition rules) that a request for information has been dispatched which might be relevant to the enforcement activities of the foreign competition authority.[141]

---

court, "acute amnesia". That information provides circumstantial evidence which may, if necessary, be taken into account to justify initiation of a national procedure'. Note that under Art 12 of the Reg 1/2003, the information exchanged may be used only for the purposes of applying Arts 101 and 102 TFEU, or national competition laws 'in the same case and in parallel' to EU rules. This expression should restrict the recipient authorities' powers to the cumulative application governed by Art 3(1) of the Regulation. There is no scope for the use of the information exchanged in the application of 'stricter national laws which prohibit or sanction unilateral conduct' under Art 3(2), or in cases where competition authorities apply 'merger control laws' or 'provisions of national law that predominantly pursue an objective different from that pursued by Arts 101 and 102 TFEU' under Art 3(3). M Araujo, 'The Respect of Fundamental Rights within the European Network of Competition Authorities' ch 21 in BE Hawk (ed), *International Antitrust Law and Policy* (Annual Proceedings of the Fordham Institute 2005) 511, 527.

[135] See 'Undertakings which may be investigated', para 7.11 et seq.

[136] European Commission Antitrust Manual of Procedures, Internal DG Competition working documents on procedures for the application of Articles 101 and 102 TFEU, March 2012, Module 6 'Requests for information', para 20. In accordance with OECD Council Recommendation Concerning Cooperation between Member Countries on Restrictive Practices Affecting International Trade, 27–28 July 1995 C(95)130/final, the government of the foreign company's country and those of other affected non-EU countries would be informed.

[137] European Commission Antitrust Manual of Procedures, Internal DG Competition working documents on procedures for the application of Articles 101 and 102 TFEU, March 2012, Module 6 'Requests for information', para 19. Presumably, the reason is that the Commission could not enforce its powers of investigation by way of a fine outside its jurisdiction. The Manproc also excludes a reference to periodic penalty payments, which in any event, however, are not foreseen for simple requests for information pursuant to Art 18(2) of Reg 1/2003.

[138] European Commission Antitrust Manual of Procedures, Internal DG Competition working documents on procedures for the application of Articles 101 and 102 TFEU, March 2012, Module 6 'Requests for information', para 17.

[139] European Commission Antitrust Manual of Procedures, Internal DG Competition working documents on procedures for the application of Articles 101 and 102 TFEU, March 2012, Module 6 'Requests for information', para 18.

[140] This might occur, eg, in relation to the US authorities under Art III of the 1991 Agreement, see para 7.14. This Article provides, *inter alia*, for the exchange of information between the Justice Department and the Commission, meetings at least twice a year, and the establishment of a mutual request procedure on enforcement activities.

[141] This would be the case with OECD countries. See, eg OECD Council Recommendation concerning Cooperation between Member Countries on Anticompetitive Practices affecting International Trade, 27 July 1995 C(95)130/final and Recommendation of the Council concerning Effective Action Against Hard Core

When undertakings do not reply to an initial request or reply incompletely or incorrectly, **7.35** the Commission may, on expiry of the time limit, send an administrative letter containing a formal reminder before requesting the information by binding decision. The Commission will typically refer the undertaking to its earlier communication and grant an additional period (which is shorter and ends on a specified date) for it to reply. Generally, when an undertaking requests an extension of the time limit for replying based on sound reasons, the Commission will accede to that request. Unlike for decisions pursuant to Article 18(3) of Regulation 1/2003, the undertaking cannot turn to the Hearing Officer to request an extension if the extra time has been refused by DG COMP.[142] However, it is important to note that the Commission cannot impose a penalty for a total or partial failure to reply (ie an incomplete answer) to a simple request for information. In both cases, the Commission has no alternative but to request the information not supplied, wholly or in part, by means of a binding decision. The question arises as to the consequences of such a lack of cooperation in terms of assessing the level of the fine to be potentially imposed on the undertakings in question in a final decision sanctioning a breach of competition law. In the absence of an obligation to reply to a simple request for information, it can be argued that only incorrect or misleading replies may be conducive to an increase of such fines.[143] Despite the lack of such an obligation, questions contained in a simple request for information should not invite self-incriminatory replies.[144]

3. Requests for information by means of a binding decision

Requests for information by means of a decision differ from simple requests in that the **7.36** addressee is compelled to respond. Accordingly, decisions pursuant to Article 18(3) of Regulation 1/2003 go beyond measures of pure administration and must be adopted by the Commissioner responsible for competition matters, who is empowered for that purpose by the Commission. By contrast, they do not need to be published or submitted to the Advisory Committee, even where they threaten a periodic penalty payment.[145] However, the national authorities in the Member State in whose territory the undertaking is located will always receive a copy of the decision. In case the Commission requests the information by decision, fines pursuant to Article 23(1)(b) of Regulation 1/2003 may be imposed either if the reply is incorrect, incomplete, or misleading, or if the information is not provided within the time limit set by the Commission, and the undertaking is at fault. The Article 18(3) decision can be combined with a decision setting the provisional amount of periodic penalty payments pursuant to Article 24(1)(d) of Regulation 1/2003 in case of non-compliance. In this case, the decision will specify the provisional level of the daily penalty payments (up to 5 per cent

---

Cartels 25 March 1998 C(98)35/final. The non-EU members of the OECD are Australia, Canada, the US, Iceland, Japan, New Zealand, Norway, Switzerland, Turkey, and South Korea.

[142] See Hearing Officer's Mandate, Arts 3(7) and 4(c).
[143] See, by analogy, Case T-384/06 *IBP et International Building Products France v Commission* [2011] ECR II-1177, para 109 et seq. On the other hand, early cooperation with the Commission that goes beyond a company's legal obligations can prompt the Commission to reduce the fine imposed for the participation in an infringement. For instance, this has been the case in the Commission's decision in the *Cartonboard* cartel, Case IV/31865 *Cartonboard* [1994] OJ L243/1; see Commission Press Release IP/94/642 'The Commission condemns a cartel of European Cartonboard Producers and imposes substantial fines' of 13 July 1994. See also Ch 9, 'Procedural Infringements: Fines and Periodic Penalty Payments', para 9.17 et seq.
[144] European Commission Antitrust Manual of Procedures, Internal DG Competition working documents on procedures for the application of Articles 101 and 102 TFEU, March 2012, Module 6 'Requests for information', para 28. As regards the scope of the privilege against self-incrimination see para 7.43 et seq; for the requirement that an element of compulsion exists for the privilege against self-incrimination to apply, see paras 7.47 and 7.48.
[145] See Ch 3, 'The Role of National Competition Authorities', para 3.45 et seq.

of the average daily turnover in the preceding business year). The final amount of the penalty will then be fixed in a second decision pursuant to Article 24(2) of Regulation 1/2003.[146]

7.37 Article 18(3) of Regulation 1/2003 lays down the essential elements of the statement of reasons for a decision requesting information. The Commission must state the legal basis and the purpose of the request, specify what information is required, and fix the time limit within which it is to be provided. As regards the purpose of the request, the Commission is not required to communicate to the addressee all the information at its disposal concerning presumed infringements or to make a precise legal analysis of those infringements, although it must clearly indicate the presumed facts which it intends to investigate.[147] In addition, the Commission must also indicate the penalties which may be imposed under Articles 23 and 24 should the undertaking in question fail to comply with the decision, and the right to have the decision reviewed by the ECJ according to Article 263 TFEU (typically combined with a warning that such appeal does not have suspensive effect unless expressly accorded by the GC, Article 278 TFEU). Finally, the addressee of an Article 18(3) decision will be reminded of the privilege against self-incrimination as defined by the case law of the EU Courts and that, if the behaviour under investigation is confirmed to have taken place, this might constitute an infringement of Articles 101 and/or 102 TFEU.[148] Where the addressee of an Article 18(3) decision considers that the time limit granted for the reply is too short and where it is unable to resolve its concerns through contacts with DG COMP, it may refer the matter to the Hearing Officer. Such a request should be made in due time before the expiry of the original time limit set. The Hearing Officer then decides on whether an extension of the time limit should be granted, taking account of the length and complexity of the request for information and the requirements of the investigation.[149]

C. The Reply

1. Persons obliged and authorized to supply information

7.38 According to Article 18(4) of Regulation 1/2003, the owners of the undertaking or its representatives and, in the case of legal persons, companies or firms or associations having no legal personality, the persons authorized to represent them by law or by their constitution, are to supply the information requested. The aim of this provision is to ensure that replies are made by persons with sufficient seniority to reply on the undertaking's behalf. This guarantees that the replies legally bind the undertakings and, as a practical matter, that those replying enjoy access to all sources of information within the undertaking under investigation. However, it is not necessary for the executives or directors of undertakings to sign replies to requests for information. It is sufficient for replies to be signed by someone who is entitled to act on behalf of the undertaking, if necessary giving proof to that effect.[150] Consequently, even where executives or directors are

---

[146] For the imposition of periodic penalty payments see also Ch 9, 'Procedural Infringements: Fines and Periodic Penalty Payments', para 9.18 et seq and Ch 11, 'Infringement Decisions and Penalties', para 11.87.

[147] See Judgment of 22 March 2012 in Joined Cases T-458/09 and T-171/10 *Slovak Telekom v Commission*, not yet published, para 77.

[148] See Commission Notice on best practices for the conduct of proceedings concerning Articles 101 and 102 TFEU [2011] OJ C308/6, para 36 and European Commission Antitrust Manual of Procedures, Internal DG Competition working documents on procedures for the application of Articles 101 and 102 TFEU, March 2012, Module 6 'Requests for information', para 52. As to the scope of the privilege against self-incrimination see para 7.43 et seq.

[149] See European Commission Antitrust Manual of Procedures, Internal DG Competition working documents on procedures for the application of Articles 101 and 102 TFEU, March 2012, Module 6 'Requests for information', para 55 and Art 4(2)(c) of the Hearing Officer's Mandate.

[150] When the reply is signed by a person whose level of responsibility in the undertaking is unknown, the Commission may make a written request for confirmation that the person concerned had authority to provide a reply.

unaware of the content of the replies, the latter will be binding on the undertaking if another authorized person within the undertaking has replied on its behalf.

Given that in practice the management of undertakings will often have an interest in entrust- **7.39** ing the drafting of replies to their legal advisors, Article 18(4) has provided for the possibility that duly authorized lawyers may supply the information for their client. This should apply to both (independent) law firms and the undertaking's own in-house lawyers where they act upon a clear authorization. Each time, the undertakings remain fully responsible if the information is incomplete, incorrect, or misleading. If no lawyer has been duly authorized, the request for information must be addressed directly to the undertaking or association of undertakings.[151] Conversely, if a duly authorized lawyer has been appointed (power of attorney in the file), a request for information can either be sent to the undertaking care of (c/o) its lawyer (alternatively, it might be addressed to the undertaking with a courtesy copy sent to the lawyer).

2. Content of the replies

It is not for undertakings to judge whether or not a request for information or documents **7.40** is justified or whether the period for which the information is requested is appropriate.[152] Neither may they choose between information which they consider useful for the investigation and information for which this is, in their view, not the case, or put into question the initial suspicion of an infringement. At this investigatory stage, undertakings should merely give their replies, since they will be entitled subsequently, in the observations phase, to put forward arguments on those points and on any other matters.[153] When replies are given to requests for information, it is important to bear in mind that the Commission may request the documents in which the requisite information is contained, whether they be agreements, balance-sheets, statistical tables or any other kind of document. Undertakings may not decline to supply them on the pretext that they are confidential,[154] because Article 28 of Regulation 1/2003 guarantees confidential treatment of the information obtained during investigations.[155] By contrast, undertakings can invoke their right to legal professional privilege ('LPP') as a justification not to transmit documents requested by the Commission.[156] When, in a reply to a request for information, undertakings submit manifestly irrelevant

---

[151] European Commission Antitrust Manual of Procedures, Internal DG Competition working documents on procedures for the application of Articles 101 and 102 TFEU, March 2012, Module 6 'Requests for information', paras 14 and 15.

[152] *Fédération Chaussure de France* [1982] OJ L319/12, para 8 (for a request for documents within the context of an inspection).

[153] In the case of a decision requesting information, undertakings could, however, endeavour not to reply by applying to the GC for interim measures under Arts 278 and 279 TFEU, with a view to having the Court suspend the operation of the Commission Decision. Such a request for interim measures would, however, be unlikely to succeed, as it would be difficult for the undertakings concerned to demonstrate the irreparable harm resulting from the obligation of a timely reply to a decision requesting information. Cf eg Order of the President of the GC of 29 July 2011 in Case T-302/11 R *HeidelbergCement v Commission*, para 15 et seq; Order of the President of the GC in Case T-296/11 R *Cementos Portland Valderrivas v Commission* [2011] ECR II-246, para 33.

[154] *Fédération Chaussure de France* [1982] OJ L319/12, para 8. Cf eg Order of the President of the GC of 29 July 2011 in Case T-302/11 R *HeidelbergCement v Commission*, para 28.

[155] Even where the production of documents is prohibited by national law and gives rise to penalties imposed by non-EU authorities (eg the Swiss legislation which gave rise to Case 145/83 *Stanley Adams v Commission* [1985] ECR 3539), it is unlikely that the Commission would refrain from this investigative measure. This is because limitations on the use of documents and the principle of professional secrecy guarantee to undertakings (except where there are errors, as in the *Adams* case) that the information supplied to the Commission will remain confidential. Where the supply of the information is accompanied by a request for confidentiality to protect anonymity, the Commission is bound to comply with such a condition. See Case 145/83 *Stanley Adams v Commission* [1985] ECR 3539, para 34.

[156] Chapter 8, para 8.52 et seq.

information (in particular documents which are clearly not related to the subject matter of the investigation), DG COMP may, in order not to unnecessarily burden the often voluminous administrative file, return such information to the addressee of the request as early as possible after having received the reply. A short notice reporting this fact will be put in the file.[157]

7.41 The Commission may sometimes request information or documents not in the possession of the undertakings or not immediately available to them or available in a form other than that requested by the Commission. If what is requested is absolutely unavailable to them and they have no way of obtaining it, their reply to the Commission must say so. If the information is not immediately available and the time limit allowed is insufficient for them to obtain it, undertakings must, before the expiry of the time limit, write to the Commission requesting an extension. If they have information similar to, but not exactly the same as, the information requested, the undertakings should make direct contact with the official in DG COMP responsible for the conduct of the case and ask him/her whether it would be possible to substitute the information available for that requested. This may facilitate the preparation of their reply and they may also receive more favourable treatment in the event of fines being imposed for substantive infringements if the Commission takes into account their cooperation in the investigation.[158]

7.42 It is advisable for undertakings to examine the Commission's requests for information in their entirety, and provide such information as may help to clarify the facts to which the investigation relates, even if such information is not directly requested from them by the Commission. The Commission, in turn, assesses and evaluates the replies from undertakings in their entirety.[159] It does not confine itself to the literal terms of the replies to the specific questions contained in the questionnaire forming part of the request for information. It also takes account of any information which goes further than the specific terms of the questions and any information given by undertakings on a voluntary basis, even though it may not relate directly to the headings in the questionnaire.[160] The provision of complete and detailed information on a voluntary basis may not only obviate recourse by the Commission to more coercive methods of investigation (for example, surprise inspections), but may also be taken into account by the Commission so as to reduce a possible fine for an infringement of Articles 101 and/or 102 TFEU.

7.43 Articles 23(1) and 24(1) of Regulation 1/2003 restore the deterrent effect of the Commission's system of procedural fines. This may well encourage the Commission to make greater use of its power to issue Article 18(3) decisions requiring information to be provided. Where it knows that certain information is available at the undertaking, an Article 18(3) decision backed up by significant fines for non-compliance may well save the Commission the time

---

[157] European Commission Antitrust Manual of Procedures, Internal DG Competition working documents on procedures for the application of Articles 101 and 102 TFEU, March 2012, Module 6 'Requests for information', para 10.

[158] For the calculation of fines and 'mitigating' circumstances, see Ch 11, 'Infringement Decisions and Penalties'.

[159] For the 'Commission's duty to examine carefully and impartially all the relevant aspects of the individual case...and to take its decision on the basis of all the information which might influence that decision', see Judgment of 22 March 2012 in Joined Cases T-458/09 and T-171/10 *Slovak Telekom v Commission*, para 45, 71.

[160] In practice, the questionnaires may contain an invitation to undertakings to provide any other unsolicited information they consider relevant. However, this information must not mislead the Commission (see Art 23(1)(a) of Reg 1/2003) in an attempt to divert it from its enquiry. The inclusion of information intended to set the Commission on a false trail may attract a fine. See, by analogy, Case T-384/06 *IBP and International Building Products France v Commission* [2011] ECR I-1177, para 109 et seq.

and resources of organizing an inspection under Article 20. It may also impose periodic penalty payments in order to enforce an obligation to submit information and/or documents.

3. The problem of self-incrimination[161]

According to the case law of the EU Courts,[162] during the preliminary investigation procedure **7.44**
EU law incorporates certain specific guarantees for the undertakings concerned which must be
observed by the Commission. However, as with Regulation 17, Regulation 1/2003 does not
grant an undertaking subject to investigation any express right to refuse to comply with a measure on the grounds that it might thereby provide evidence of its participation in an infringement of EU competition rules. Recital 37 of Regulation 1/2003 (which pre-dates the Lisbon
Treaty), contains a general statement that the regulation 'respects the fundamental rights and
observes the principles recognised in particular by the Charter of Fundamental Rights of the
European Union. Accordingly, this Regulation should be interpreted and applied with respect
to those rights and principles.' Additionally, Recital 23 codifies the principles developed in
Orkem and *Mannesmannröhren-Werke*, stating that an undertaking cannot be forced to admit
that it has committed an infringement. However, this right has to be contrasted with the obligation to cooperate actively, ie to answer factual questions and to provide documents, even if this
information could be used to establish the existence of an infringement. In order to ensure the
effectiveness of Article 18(3) of Regulation 1/2003, there is thus no absolute 'right to silence'.
Rather, the Commission is entitled to compel undertakings to provide all necessary information
concerning such facts as may be known to them and to disclose to the Commission, if necessary, such documents relating thereto as are in their possession, even if the latter may be used to
establish the existence of anticompetitive conduct.[163] The Commission considers that, in line
with the existing case law, two types of questions are fully compatible with the privilege against
self-incrimination (ie these types of questions are lawful):

(i) the provision of documentary evidence already in the possession of the undertaking
    may always be requested without infringing the privilege against self-incrimination—
    this applies regardless of whether or not the documents at issue contain incriminating
    evidence which may be used against the addressee of the request or against any other
    third party; and

(ii) questions seeking purely factual information are normally admissible and do not infringe
     the privilege against self-incrimination.[164]

In the absence of a 'right of silence' expressly enshrined in Regulation 17 and Regulation **7.45**
1/2003, the EU courts have gone a long way to considering to what extent general principles of law, including fundamental rights which must underlie the interpretation of EU law,

---

[161] See in relation to the problem in the context of Reg 1/2003, WPJ Wils, 'Self-Incrimination in EC
Antitrust Enforcement, A Legal and Economic Analysis' [1994] World Competition 567, 574; Judge B
Vesterdorf, 'Legal Professional Privilege and the Privilege against Self-incrimination in EC Law: Recent
Developments and Current Issues' ch 27 in BE Hawk (ed), *International Antitrust Law & Policy* (Annual
Proceedings of the Fordham Institute 2004) 701, 709–18.

[162] See Case 374/87 *Orkem v Commission* [1989] ECR 3283 and Case 27/88 *Solvay v Commission* [1989]
ECR 3355, paras 26 and 23–37, respectively.

[163] See Recital 23 of Reg 1/2003; Judgment of 22 March 2012 in Joined Cases T-458/09 and T-171/10
Slovak Telekom v Commission, para 41. See also, by analogy, in relation to the application of Reg 17, Case
374/87 *Orkem v Commission* [1989] ECR 3283, paras 34 and 35; Joined Cases C-204/00 P, C-205/00 P,
C-211/00 P, C-213/00 P, C-217/00 P and C-219/00 P *Aalborg Portland and Others v Commission* [2004]
ECR I-123, para 61; Case C-301/04 P *Commission v SGL Carbon* [2006] ECR I-5915, para 41; and Case
T-446/05 *Amann & Söhne and Cousin Filterie v Commission* [2010] ECR II-1255, para 327.

[164] See European Commission Antitrust Manual of Procedures, Internal DG Competition working documents on procedures for the application of Articles 101 and 102 TFEU, March 2012, Module 6 'Requests
for information', paras 76–8.

imply recognition of an undertaking's right not to provide information that might be used to incriminate it.[165] In *Orkem*, the undertaking challenging a request for information asserted that several questions asked by the Commission infringed 'the general principle that no one may be compelled to give evidence against himself'.[166] In response, the ECJ noted that, in general, the laws of the Member States afforded the right not to give evidence against oneself only to a *natural person* charged with an offence *in criminal proceedings.* By contrast, there was no principle common to the laws of the Member States which allowed *legal entities* to claim a right against self-incrimination in the context of alleged infringements *in the economic sphere.*[167] Further, the ECJ considered that, although Article 6 ECHR may be invoked by an undertaking subject to an investigation relating to competition law, neither the wording of that provision nor the decisions of the European Court of Human Rights ('ECtHR') indicated that it recognized the right not to give evidence against oneself.[168] Accordingly, the ECJ ruled that none of the legal bases relied upon by the applicant supported the right invoked.

7.46 Nevertheless, the ECJ considered that the Commission may not, by means of a decision requesting information, undermine the defence rights of the undertaking concerned.[169] It therefore examined whether certain limitations on the Commission's powers of investigation were 'implied by the need to safeguard the rights of the defence which the [ECJ] has held to be a fundamental principle of the Union legal order'.[170] In that regard, while holding that the Commission was entitled to compel an undertaking to provide all necessary information concerning such *facts* as may be known to it and to disclose to the Commission, if necessary, such *documents* relating thereto as are in its possession, even if the latter may be used to establish the existence of anticompetitive conduct, 'the Commission may not compel an undertaking to provide it with answers which might involve an admission on its part of the existence of an infringement which it is incumbent upon the Commission to prove'.[171] The scope of this principle was further delimited three years later in *Otto*, a case in which the ECJ ruled that the privilege against self-incrimination could not be claimed in the context of national civil proceedings before a court applying Articles [101] and/or [102 TFEU], on the grounds that civil proceedings cannot lead, directly or indirectly, to the imposition of a penalty by a public authority.[172] This was followed by

---

[165] See also Ch 4, 'The Organization of EU Commission Proceedings', para 4.36. K Dekeyser and C Gauer, 'The New Enforcement System for Articles 81 and 82 and the Rights of Defence' ch 23 in BE Hawk (ed), *International Antitrust Law & Policy* (Annual Proceedings of the Fordham Institute 2005) 549, 562, submit that the reasoning behind the right to silence in the ECtHR case law is to protect the accused against improper psychological or even physical pressure of the authorities and to avoid miscarriages of justice. This would not apply to undertakings.

[166] The applicant submitted that the principle was supported by three different legal bases: (i) the laws of the Member States; (ii) the ECHR; and (iii) the International Covenant on Civil and Political Rights of 19 December 1966 ('ICCPR'). The ECJ considered that the right not to give evidence against oneself or to confess guilt enshrined in Art 14(3)(g) of the ICCPR related only to persons accused of a criminal offence in court proceedings and thus had no bearing on investigations in the field of competition law. Case 374/87 *Orkem v Commission* [1989] ECR 3283, para 31 (see also opinion of AG Darmon, in the same case, para 127).

[167] Case 374/87 *Orkem v Commission* [1989] ECR 3283, para 29 (see also opinion of AG Darmon in the same case, paras 98–121).

[168] Case 374/87 *Orkem v Commission* [1989] ECR 3283, para 30.

[169] Case 374/87 *Orkem v Commission* [1989] ECR 3283, para 34.

[170] Case 374/87 *Orkem v Commission* [1989] ECR 3283, paras 32–3.

[171] Case 374/87 *Orkem v Commission* [1989] ECR 3283, para 35. See also Case T-34/93 *Société Générale v Commission* [1995] ECR II-545, para 75.

[172] Case C-60/92 *Otto v Postbank* [1993] ECR I-5683. In this case, Postbank contended in its defence that, in so far as the Dutch procedural rules compelled it to produce the information requested, they were incompatible with EU law. The question was to what extent the *Orkem* principles applied, by virtue of EU law, as part of the rights of the defence, in national civil proceedings. The ECJ stated at paras 15–17 that '[t]he guarantees necessary to ensure respect for the right of the defence of an individual in the course of an

the judgment in *Mannesmannröhren-Werke*, where the GC was again faced with an argument of self-incrimination in a competition case.[173] In this case, the applicant submitted, *inter alia*, that, based on the ECtHR ruling in *Funke*, the scope of the privilege against self-incrimination as laid down by the ECJ in *Orkem* had to be extended. The GC recalled that it had no jurisdiction to apply the ECHR when reviewing an investigation under competition law, because the ECHR as such is not part of EU law.[174] However, the court stressed that the EU Courts draw inspiration from the constitutional traditions common to the Member States and from the guidelines supplied by international treaties for the protection of human rights on which the Member States have collaborated and to which they are signatories; in this regard, it highlighted the special significance of the ECHR.[175] The GC considered that the privilege against self-incrimination was not absolute, because such a solution 'would go beyond what is necessary in order to preserve the rights of defence of undertakings, and would constitute an unjustified hindrance to the Commission's performance of its duty'.[176] As a result, it confirmed the ruling in *Orkem* that an undertaking in receipt of a request for information pursuant to a binding decision could be granted a right to silence 'only to the extent that it would be compelled to provide answers which might involve an admission on its part of the existence of an infringement which it is incumbent upon the Commission to prove'.[177]

In the *PVC II* appeal, the ECJ indicated that it was ready to assess the privilege against self-incrimination based on ECHR case law.[178] In the case before the GC,[179] the applicants had submitted that the Commission should not have used allegedly incriminating replies given by *any of the* final decision's addressees (ie not only their own answers) under *any* legal basis (ie be it Article [18(1)] or Article [18(3)] of Regulation [1/2003]).[180] The GC found that **7.47**

---

administrative procedure such as that at issue in the *Orkem* case are different from those which are necessary to safeguard the rights of the defence of a party involved in civil proceedings. Where, as in the main proceedings, a procedure is involved which concerns exclusively private relations between individuals and cannot lead directly or indirectly to the imposition of a penalty by a public authority, Community law does not require a party to be granted the right not to give answers which might entail admission of the existence of an infringement of the competition rules. That guarantee is essentially intended to protect an individual against measures of investigation ordered by public authorities to obtain his admission of the existence of conduct laying him open to administrative or criminal penalties. It follows that the limitation on the Commission's power of investigation under Regulation No 17 with regard to an undertaking's obligation to reply to questions, which the Court deduced from the principle of respect for the rights of the defence in the *Orkem* case, cannot be transposed to national civil proceedings involving the application of Articles 85 and 86 of the Treaty which exclusively concern private relations between individuals, since such proceedings cannot lead, directly or indirectly, to the imposition of a penalty by a public authority'.

[173] Case T-112/98 *Mannesmannröhren-Werke v Commission* [2001] ECR II-729.
[174] Case T-112/98 *Mannesmannröhren-Werke v Commission* [2001] ECR II-729, paras 59 and 75, citing Case T-347/94 *Mayr-Melnhof v Commission* [1998] ECR II-1751, para 311.
[175] Case T-112/98 *Mannesmannröhren-Werke v Commission* [2001] ECR II-729, para 60.
[176] Case T-112/98 *Mannesmannröhren-Werke v Commission* [2001] ECR II-729, para 66.
[177] Case T-112/98 *Mannesmannröhren-Werke v Commission* [2001] ECR II-729, para 67. Judge Vesterdorf has indicated that *Mannesmannröhren-Werke* could be interpreted as a signal to the effect that the EU Courts' interpretation of certain rights in competition proceedings did not have to coincide exactly with those of the ECtHR when the latter deals with criminal procedures involving natural persons, while noting that more recently the EU Courts have made an effort to make these interpretations converge. Judge B Vesterdorf, 'Legal Professional Privilege and the Privilege against Self-incrimination in EC Law: Recent Developments and Current Issues' ch 27 in BE Hawk (ed), *International Antitrust Law & Policy* (Annual Proceedings of the Fordham Institute 2005) 701, 713–14.
[178] Joined Cases C-238/99 P, C-244/99 P, C-245/99 P, C-247/99 P, C-250/99 P to C-252/99 P and C-254/99 P *Limburgse Vinyl Maatschappij and Others v Commission* ('PVC II') [2002] ECR I-8375.
[179] Joined Cases T-305/94 to T-307/94, T-313/94 to T-316/94, T-318/94, T-325/94, T-328/94, T-329/94 and T-335/94 *Limburgse Vinyl Maatschappij and Others v Commission* [1999] ECR II-931.
[180] LVM, DSM, and ICI contended that Art 6 ECHR, as interpreted by the ECtHR (relying on *Funke* and *Saunders*), laid down an absolute right to remain silent and in no way to contribute to one's own

the questions contained in the decisions requiring information and which were challenged by the applicants were identical to those annulled by the ECJ in *Orkem* and therefore unlawful.[181] Yet, the GC also indicated that the undertakings had either refused to answer those questions or denied the facts on which they were being questioned, which meant that the illegality of the questions could not affect the legality of the decision by which the Commission had fined them.[182] The Court added that simple requests for information do not contain any element of compulsion and that undertakings submitting a reply therefore cannot validly claim the privilege against self-incrimination.[183]

7.48 On appeal, the ECJ first noted that the GC had confirmed the main principles laid down in *Orkem*.[184] Having summarized these findings, the ECJ considered that there had been further developments in the case law of the ECtHR since *Orkem* 'which the Union judicature must take into account when interpreting the fundamental rights'.[185] However, the ECJ concluded that both the *Orkem* judgment and the recent case law of the ECtHR required, first, the exercise of coercion against the suspect in order to obtain information from him and, second, 'the existence of an actual interference with the right which they define', namely the right not to be compelled by the Commission to admit his participation in an infringement.[186] On this basis, the ECJ first considered that the GC had correctly drawn the appropriate distinction between (i) a simple request for information, which left the undertaking the possibility not to reply; and (ii) a decision requiring information, which additionally subjected an undertaking to a penalty in the event of a refusal to reply: only the latter exerts actual compulsion on the recipient undertaking.[187] Second, as regards requests pursuant to a binding decision, for which an element of compulsion exists,

---

incrimination. Joined Cases T-305/94 to T-307/94, T-313/94 to T-316/94, T-318/94, T-325/94, T-328/94, T-329/94 and T-335/94 *Limburgse Vinyl Maatschappij and Others v Commission* [1999] ECR II-931, paras 429 and 448.

[181] Joined Cases T-305/94 to T-307/94, T-313/94 to T-316/94, T-318/94, T-325/94, T-328/94, T-329/94 and T-335/94 *Limburgse Vinyl Maatschappij and Others v Commission* [1999] ECR II-931, para 451.

[182] Joined Cases T-305/94 to T-307/94, T-313/94 to T-316/94, T-318/94, T-325/94, T-328/94, T-329/94 and T-335/94 *Limburgse Vinyl Maatschappij and Others v Commission* [1999] ECR II-931, paras 452-3; Judge B Vesterdorf, 'Legal Professional Privilege and the Privilege against Self-incrimination in EC Law: Recent Developments and Current Issues' ch 27 in BE Hawk (ed), *International Antitrust Law & Policy* (Annual Proceedings of the Fordham Institute 2004) 701, 714.

[183] Joined Cases T-305/94 to T-307/94, T-313/94 to T-316/94, T-318/94, T-325/94, T-328/94, T-329/94 and T-335/94 *Limburgse Vinyl Maatschappij and Others v Commission* [1999] ECR II-931, paras 455-7. See also Joined Cases T-25/95, T-26/95, T-30/95 to T-39/95, T-42/95 to T-46/95, T-48/95, T-50/95 to T-65/95, T-68/95 to T-71/95, T-87/95, T-88/95, T-103/95 and T-104/95 *Cimenteries CBR SA and Others v Commission* [2000] ECR II-491, paras 731-6 where the GC pointed out that the parties are free to decide whether or not to reply to such a request for information. In addition, only the undertakings that have given the relevant answers have grounds, if at all, for claiming that, during the course of the administrative procedure, their right not to give evidence against themselves has been infringed. See also K Lenaerts and J Maselis, 'Procedural Rights and Issues in the Enforcement of Articles 81 and 82 of the EC Treaty' [2001] Fordham International Law Journal 1615, 1621. *Austrian Banks* [2004] OJ L56/1, para 485 et seq and para 544 et seq discusses extensively whether companies who give more than they have to in response to requests for information should receive cooperation credit for doing so. See also J Ratliff, 'Major Events and Policy Issues in EC Competition Law, 2003–2004 (Part 2)' [2005] ICCLR 109, 112–13.

[184] Joined Cases C-238/99 P, C-244/99 P, C-245/99 P, C-247/99 P, C-250/99 P to C-252/99 P, and C-254/99 P *Limburgse Vinyl Maatschappij and Others v Commission* ('PVC II') [2002] ECR I-8375, para 272, referring to the principles set out at paras 27, 28, and 32–35 of *Orkem*.

[185] Joined Cases C-238/99 P, C-244/99 P, C-245/99 P, C-247/99 P, C-250/99 P to C-252/99 P and C-254/99 P *Limburgse Vinyl Maatschappij and others v Commission* ('PVC II') [2002] ECR I-8375, para 274.

[186] Joined Cases C-238/99 P, C-244/99 P, C-245/99 P, C-247/99 P, C-250/99 P to C-252/99 P and C-254/99 P *Limburgse Vinyl Maatschappij and others v Commission* ('PVC II') [2002] ECR I-8375, paras 273 and 275.

[187] Joined Cases C-238/99 P, C-244/99 P, C-245/99 P, C-247/99 P, C-250/99 P to C-252/99 P and C-254/99 P *Limburgse Vinyl Maatschappij and others v Commission* ('PVC II') [2002] ECR I-8375, para 279.

the ECJ observed that the applicants did not indicate any aspects of those answers which were *in fact* used to incriminate them or the addressees of the requests.

The EU courts in *PVC II* broke new ground by expressly making the privilege against self-incrimination dependent on an element of compulsion or coercion.[188] Furthermore, the ECJ very clearly emphasized the relevance of the case law of the ECtHR for the purpose of interpreting fundamental rights, something which also follows from Article 52(3) of the Charter of Fundamental Rights given that the meaning and scope of rights under the Charter shall be the same as corresponding rights in the ECHR.[189] Later in *Tokai Carbon*,[190] the GC confirmed its previous finding in *Mannesmannröhren-Werke* that '[a] right to silence can be recognised only to the extent that the undertaking concerned would be compelled to provide answers which might involve an admission on its part of the existence of an infringement which it is incumbent upon the Commission to prove'.[191] The GC also reiterated its previous finding that the Commission 'is entitled to compel the undertakings to provide all necessary information concerning such facts as may be known to them and to disclose to the Commission, if necessary, such documents relating thereto as are in their possession, even if the latter may be used to establish the existence of anti-competitive conduct'.[192] Further, the GC considered that this power did not fall foul of either Article 6(1), (2) ECHR or the

7.49

---

[188] Joined Cases C-238/99 P, C-244/99 P, C-245/99 P, C-247/99 P, C-250/99 P to C-252/99 P, and C-254/99 P *Limburgse Vinyl Maatschappij and Others v Commission* [2002] ECR-I-8375, para 275 et seq. Voluntary statements given under Art 19 and statements given to the Commission under Art 20(2)(e) of Reg 1/2003 in case of an inspection by simple authorization are made free of state coercion. Thus, it would seem that no privilege against self-incrimination could be asserted by the undertaking concerned. This should be different in case of an inspection ordered pursuant to Art 20(4) of Reg 1/2003, where the undertaking has to provide a complete answer (see Art 23(1)(d), third indent). The individual respondent itself is not the object of the investigation, and the Commission has no powers to impose sanctions on members of staff or company representatives. The question arises whether the person could still claim privilege for himself when he is requested to make statements that would incriminate him under certain national laws. However, it seems doubtful that such a situation will often arise in practice: an admission by a person who is authorized to speak in the name of an undertaking to the effect that he personally participated in a breach of Arts 101 and/or 102 TFEU will, in most instances, incriminate the company itself (and therefore be covered by the latter's potential privilege).

[189] See Explanations relating to the Charter of Fundamental Rights [2007] OJ C303/17, Explanation on Article 52—Scope and interpretation of rights and principles. As Judge Vesterdorf noted, this contrasts with earlier statements to the effect that the interpretations of fundamental rights by the EU Courts did not have to coincide exactly with those of the ECtHR. B Vesterdorf, 'Legal Professional Privilege and the Privilege against Self-incrimination in EC Law: Recent Developments and Current Issues' ch 27 in BE Hawk (ed), *International Antitrust Law & Policy* (Annual Proceedings of the Fordham Institute 2004) 701, 716. See eg Opinion of AG Darmon in Case 374/87 *Orkem v Commission* [1989] ECR 3283, paras 139–40 ('the existence in Community law of fundamental rights drawn from the [ECHR] does not derive from the wholly straightforward application of that instrument as interpreted by the Strasbourg authorities...This Court may...adopt, with respect to provisions of the [ECHR], an interpretation which does not coincide exactly with that given by the Strasbourg authorities, in particular the [ECtHR]. It is not bound, in so far as it does not have systematically to take into account, as regards fundamental rights under Community law, the interpretation of the Convention given by the Strasbourg authorities.').

[190] Joined Cases T-236/01, T-239/01, T-244/01 to T-246/01, T-251/01 and T-252/01, *Tokai Carbon and Others v Commission* [2004] ECR II-1181. The question of the privilege against self-incrimination came up in the specific context of the assessment of the fine for which SGL sought a reduction due to its cooperation with the Commission (see paras 401–11). SGL argued that it had provided the Commission with information that it could have withheld (because it was covered by the privilege against self-incrimination) and that accordingly it should have benefited from an additional reduction of the fine imposed on it.

[191] Joined Cases T-236/01, T-239/01, T-244/01 to T-246/01, T-251/01 and T-252/01, *Tokai Carbon and Others v Commission* [2004] ECR II-1181, para 402, citing Case T-112/98 *Mannesmannröhren-Werke v Commission* [2001] ECR II-729, paras 66 and 67.

[192] Joined Cases T-236/01, T-239/01, T-244/01 to T-246/01, T-251/01 and T-252/01 *Tokai Carbon and Others v Commission* [2004] ECR II-1181, para 403, citing Case T-112/98 *Mannesmannröhren-Werke v Commission* [2001] ECR II-729, para 65.

ECHR case law, noting that in *PVC II* the Court had not reversed its previous case law in spite of the ECtHR's judgments in *Funke* and *Saunders*.[193]

7.50 While in *Tokai Carbon* the GC expressly restated the principles laid down in *Mannesmannröhren-Werke*, when applying these principles to the facts of the case the court seemed to take a broader view of the scope of the privilege against self-incrimination. The GC first considered that the privilege applied to requests to describe the purpose, content and conclusions of a number of meetings 'when it was clear that the Commission suspected that the object of the meetings was to restrict competition'. More controversially, the GC also considered that the privilege applied to certain types of pre-existing *documents* related to these meetings (eg preparatory documents, planning and discussion documents, working documents, (handwritten) notes and conclusions, protocols).[194] This judgment posed a serious problem: if the Commission would not be empowered to request the production of such documents, its enforcement powers would become dependent on either voluntary cooperation or the use of dawn raids. However, on appeal the ECJ set aside the GC's judgment. It specified that addressees of an Article 18(3) decision may lawfully be required to provide pre-existing documents, such as minutes of cartel meetings, even if those documents may incriminate the party providing them.[195] While it is evident that the rights of the defence should be respected, the undertaking concerned is still able, either during the administrative procedure or in the proceedings before the EU Courts, to contend that the documents produced have a different meaning from that ascribed to them by the Commission.[196] It follows that the provision of documentary evidence already in the possession of the undertaking may always be requested without infringing the privilege against self-incrimination. This applies regardless of whether or not the documents at issue contain incriminating evidence which may be used against the addressee of the request or against any other third party.[197]

7.51 The revised Mandate of the Hearing Officer provides for a role of the Hearing Officer in facilitating the resolution of claims that replies to a question for information would go against the

---

[193] Joined Cases T-236/01, T-239/01, T-244/01 to T-246/01, T-251/01 and T-252/01 *Tokai Carbon and Others v Commission* [2004] ECR II-1181, paras 404 and 405. The GC further considered that 'the mere fact of being obliged to answer purely factual questions put by the Commission and to comply with its requests for the production of documents already in existence cannot constitute a breach of the principle of respect for the rights of defence or impair the right to fair legal process, which offer, in the specific field of competition law, protection equivalent to that guaranteed by Article 6 [ECHR].' The GC explained this stance on the grounds that '[t]here is nothing to prevent the addressee of a request for information from showing, whether later during the administrative procedure or in proceedings before the Community Courts, when exercising his rights of defence, that the facts set out in his replies or the documents produced by him have a different meaning from that ascribed to them by the Commission' (citing Case T-112/98 *Mannesmannröhren-Werke v Commission* [2001] ECR II-729, paras 77 and 78).

[194] Joined Cases T-236/01, T-239/01, T-244/01 to T-246/01, T-251/01 and T-252/01 *Tokai Carbon and Others v Commission* [2004] ECR II-1181, para 408. K Dekeyser and C Gauer, 'The New Enforcement System for Articles 81 and 82 and the Rights of Defence' ch 23 in BE Hawk (ed), *International Antitrust Law & Policy* (Annual Proceedings of the Fordham Institute 2004) 549, 561 have stressed that the GC ruling suffered from an 'internal contradiction' which consists in denying the privilege against self incrimination for all pre-existing documents in its para 406 while apparently granting that privilege for a large amount of pre-existing documents in para 408 and later accepting the submission of such documents in reply to an information request as voluntary cooperation capable of justifying a reduction of the fine.

[195] Case C-301/04 P *Commission v SGL* [2006] ECR I-5915, paras 41, 44, and 48.

[196] Case C-301/04 P *Commission v SGL* [2006] ECR I-5915, para 49.

[197] See European Commission Antitrust Manual of Procedures, Internal DG Competition working documents on procedures for the application of Articles 101 and 102 TFEU, March 2012, Module 6 'Requests for information', para 77.

privilege against self-incrimination as determined by the case law of the EU Courts.[198] Where the addressee of an informal request for information pursuant to Article 18(2) of Regulation 1/2003 considers whether to refuse to reply to a question in order to not incriminate itself, it may refer the matter in due course to the Hearing Officer, after having raised the matter with DG COMP before the expiry of the original time limit set. In appropriate cases, and having regard to the need to avoid undue delay in proceedings, the Hearing Officer may make a reasoned recommendation as to whether the privilege against self-incrimination would apply in case of a decision pursuant to Article 18(3) of Regulation 1/2003 and inform the director responsible of the conclusions drawn. Although the recommendation is non-binding on the Commission, it is 'to be taken into account in case of any decision taken subsequently pursuant to Article 18(3) of Regulation 1/2003'.[199] The addressee of the request shall receive a copy of the reasoned recommendation.[200] While the addressee of an informal request for information could in any event not be fined if it fails to reply, and could not be compelled to reply by way of periodic penalty payments (cf Articles 23(1)(a), (b) and 24(1)(d) of Regulation 1/2003), this procedure allows discussions with the addressee on possibly self-incriminatory questions to be settled at an early stage, before issuing a binding decision pursuant to Article 18(3) of Regulation 1/2003.

4. Cooperation with the authorities of the Member States

7.52 The Commission is obliged to forward copies of all simple requests and requests by decision to the national competition authority (NCA) in the Member State in whose territory the undertaking or association of undertakings concerned has its seat, and the NCA whose territory is affected.[201] The President of the GC has clarified, however, that the obligation on the part of the Commission to transmit to the NCAs copies of the most important documents it has collected with a view to, *inter alia*, finding an infringement, does not require the Commission automatically to forward all replies received by it from undertakings.[202] Furthermore, the obligation to transmit the most important documents to the Member States must be interpreted in the light of the general principle that undertakings are entitled to protection of their business secrets.[203] The Commission services may provide NCAs with copies of replies to a request for information, but the provisions of Article 11(2) of Regulation 1/2003 are not regarded by DG COMP as containing any obligation in this respect. If the undertaking concerned has claimed confidentiality in respect of certain parts of its reply, the NCA should be reminded of the fact that the provision of information is

---

[198] See Recital 10 and Art 4(2)(b) of the Hearing Officer's Mandate. The reference to the case law of the ECJ makes clear that the Hearing Officer is not empowered to apply a concept of the privilege against self-incrimination that would be inspired by his personal views of procedural fairness. See also Commission Notice on best practices for the conduct of proceedings concerning Articles 101 and 102 TFEU [2011] OJ C308/6, para 36.

[199] Article 4(2)(b) of the Hearing Officer's Mandate.

[200] See Commission Notice on best practices for the conduct of proceedings concerning Articles 101 and 102 TFEU [2011] OJ C308/6, para 36 and Art 4(2)(b) of the Hearing Officer's Mandate.

[201] Article 18(5) of Reg 1/2003. As regards the competition authority of the Member State whose territory is affected, the Commission used to send a copy of the requests to the authorities of all the Member States which would be concerned, for one reason or another, with the case, although Reg 17 did not expressly provide for this requirement. Internally, the case team must indicate on the minute to which NCAs the request must be copied. See European Commission Antitrust Manual of Procedures, Internal DG Competition working documents on procedures for the application of Articles 101 and 102 TFEU, March 2012, Module 6 'Requests for Information', para 39.

[202] See Order of the President of the GC of 21 November 1990 in Case T-39/90 R *Samenwerkende Elektriciteits-Produktiebedrijven (SEP) v Commission* [1990] ECR II-649, para 28.

[203] A principle which Art 339 TFEU and various provisions of Reg 1/2003, such as Arts 28(2) and 30(2), embody.

governed by Articles 11 and 28 of Regulation 1/2003, and be informed about the undertaking's confidentiality claims. Alternatively, the case team and the NCA may agree that the latter receives the non-confidential version for the reply.[204] Similar rules apply in the EEA context where the Commission or ESA address an undertaking outside their jurisdiction.[205] Similarly, Article 19(2) of Regulation 1/2003 foresees that, where the Commission intends to conduct an interview at the premises of an undertaking, it has to inform the NCA in whose jurisdiction the interview shall take place.[206] The NCA can then request that its officials may assist the officials and other accompanying persons authorized by the Commission to conduct the interview.

D. Interviews and Oral Statements

7.53 Under Article 19 of Regulation 1/2003, the Commission is empowered to interview (ie take oral statements from) individuals and legal persons (through their company representatives) for the purpose of collecting information relevant to an investigation. This investigation tool was not available under Regulation 17 except in the context of inspections pursuant to Article 14(1)(c) of Regulation 17 (now Article 20(2)(e) of Regulation 1/2003).[207] The purpose of the introduction of Article 19 was to 'fill a gap in the Commission's powers by allowing for oral submissions to be recorded and used as evidence in proceedings'.[208] In other words, Article 19 was meant to facilitate the introduction of evidence in competition proceedings by granting the Commission the power of carrying out formal interviews where deemed appropriate. The possibility for the Commission to hold meetings with third parties without the formal recording and access to file requirements of Article 19 (which already existed prior to Regulation 1/2003) was not meant to be replaced by Article 19 but to coexist with it. Hence, Article 19 does not introduce a general obligation to carry out formal interviews for every meeting, phone call, or video conference organized by the Commission relating to an investigation. Whether the Commission, nevertheless, is under an obligation to conduct every oral contact (ie meetings, phone and video calls) with third parties pursuant to the procedural rules of Article 19 in connection with Article 3 of Regulation 773/2004 is currently subject to court scrutiny in the *Intel* case, where Intel has argued that its rights

---

[204] European Commission Antitrust Manual of Procedures, Internal DG Competition working documents on procedures for the application of Articles 101 and 102 TFEU, March 2012, Module 6 'Requests for information', para 40. As regards the protection of confidentiality in the transmission to Member States authorities, see Case T-39/90 *Samenwerkende Elektriciteits-Produktiebedrijven (SEP) v Commission* [1991] ECR II-1497, paras 53 and 55.

[205] See Art 8(1) of Protocol 23 to the EEA Agreement. See also European Commission Antitrust Manual of Procedures, Internal DG Competition working documents on procedures for the application of Articles 101 and 102 TFEU, March 2012, Module 6 'Requests for information', paras 18, 61, and 65.

[206] According to Commission practice, the NCA should normally be informed at least two weeks in advance. See European Commission Antitrust Manual of Procedures, Internal DG Competition working documents on procedures for the application of Articles 101 and 102 TFEU, March 2012, Module 8 'Power to take statements', para 11.

[207] Article 20(2)(e) provides for a fundamentally different interview by the Commission, since it is not conducted on a voluntary basis and the correctness of the answers given can be sanctioned on the basis of Art 24(1)(e) of Reg 1/2003. Already under Reg 17 undertakings could of course voluntarily provide oral information to the Commission, for instance as part of a leniency application. Cf eg *Zinc Phosphate* [2003] OJ L153/1, para 57. See also European Commission Antitrust Manual of Procedures, Internal DG Competition working documents on procedures for the application of Articles 101 and 102 TFEU, March 2012, Module 8 'Power to take statements', para 4: 'While Article 19 confirms previous Commission practice in leniency cases, it provides for the first time a possibility to conduct interviews and record statements in all other cases.'

[208] Explanatory memorandum for the Regulation implementing articles 81 and 82 of the Treaty of 27 September 2000, COM(2000)582 final.

of defence would be infringed if potentially exculpatory oral statements made vis-à-vis the Commission were not accurately recorded and made available to it via access to file.[209] The court's decision in this case has been preceded by a finding of the European Ombudsman that the principle of good administration would oblige the Commission to record every oral contact under the rules of Article 19 in order to avoid a bias by allowing the Commission to select the facts that it introduces into its file.[210] The Commission does not agree with this finding, which would fundamentally change the way it is interacting with parties, but absent the ruling of the court, it has adopted a provision in its Best Practices providing for certain recording requirements also for informal oral contacts with third parties not falling under Article 19.[211] In the meantime, the court has, in contradiction to the opinion of the European Ombudsman, confirmed that the Commission does not have to record meetings with parties and only needs to put records on its file in as far as they contain inculpatory information that it intends to use against parties.[212]

Unlike for other investigative tools, the Commission is not entitled to adopt a decision to compel a person to give a statement; the relevant individual or company must consent to the interview taking place. Article 19 is not restricted to officers or employees of undertakings suspected of infringements. Because of its voluntary nature, no penalties apply to a refusal to grant an interview, nor do penalties apply to the supply of incorrect information. This makes information gathered during such interviews somewhat less reliable than information gathered by information requests, where sanctions may apply if the answers submitted by the interviewee are incorrect, incomplete, or misleading.[213] Given the lack of such sanctions in order to secure complete and correct statements, it is submitted that the Commission should have discretion as to whether it takes an interview on the basis of Article 19 or not, taking into account such factors as the type of information sought or the involvement of the individual in the infringement under investigation. However, if a party wishes to submit information on the basis of Article 19, then the Commission must take such a statement subject to the needs and requirements of a proper conduct of the investigation.[214] **7.54**

---

[209] Case T-286/09 *Intel v Commission* (summary of the application in [2009] OJ C220/41). The oral hearing of the case took place in June 2012.

[210] Decision of the European Ombudsman of 14 July 2009 in Case 1935/2008/FOR available on the website of the European Ombudsman at <http://www.ombudsman.europa.eu/en/cases/home.faces>.

[211] See Commission Notice on best practices for the conduct of proceedings concerning Articles 101 and 102 TFEU [2011] OJ C308/6, paras 43 and 44, which provide that: 'When a meeting takes place at the request of the parties, complainants or third parties, they should as a general rule submit in advance a proposed agenda of topics to be discussed at the meeting, as well as a memorandum or a presentation which covers these issues in more detail. After meetings or phone calls on substantive issues, the parties, complainants or third parties may substantiate their statements or presentations in writing. Any written documentation prepared by the undertakings which attended a meeting that is communicated to DG COMP will be put on the file. A non-confidential version of such documentation, together with a brief note prepared by the Directorate-General for Competition, will be made accessible to the parties subject to the investigation during their access to the file, if the case is further pursued. Subject to any anonymity requests this note will mention the undertaking(s) attending the meeting (or participating in the phone call relating to substantive issues) and the timing and topic(s) covered by the meeting (or phone call). Such a brief note will also be prepared when the meeting takes place on the Commission's initiative (e.g. State of Play meetings).' These best practices do not apply in the context of leniency applications, where special rules are laid out in the leniency notice; see also Ch 6, 'Investigation of Cases (I): Leniency Policy'.

[212] Judgment of 14 March 2013 in Case T-587/08 *Fresh Del Monte Produce v Commission*, paras 724–6.

[213] While direct sanctions for incorrectness and incompleteness of Art 19 replies are not foreseen, a company is 'indirectly' sanctioned if it provides misleading evidence in the course of an Art 19 interview for the purpose of obtaining leniency. In such a situation, the evidence provided is seen as more reliable by the court in view of the potential loss or reduction of leniency if the information proves to be inaccurate at a later stage; see Judgment of 3 March 2011 in Case T-110/07 *Siemens AG v Commission*, paras 64–5 and 70.

[214] See Commission Notice on best practices for the conduct of proceedings concerning Articles 101 and 102 TFEU [2011] OJ C308/6 Module 8, para 49.

7.55 Oral statements under Article 19 may be provided to the Commission by employees (or former employees) of undertakings either in their private capacity[215] or on behalf of the undertaking.[216] Furthermore a lawyer acting on behalf of an undertaking can introduce information orally into the Commission's file via Article 19.[217] Interviewees making statements in their private capacity cannot be prohibited from doing so by their former employer.[218] At the same time, the Commission may be under a duty of confidentiality not to disclose the identity of an informant to the undertaking concerned and to protect the identity of the information in order to shield him or her from disadvantages deriving from the disclosure of the information pursuant to national law.[219]

7.56 The power to take statements is of great importance within the context of leniency proceedings, as it makes possible the introduction of evidence in the oral procedure that has become the norm under the Leniency Notice 2006.[220] Commission Regulation 773/2004 requires the Commission to state the legal basis and purpose of the interview and to recall its voluntary nature. The Commission shall also inform the person interviewed of its intention to make a record of the interview.[221] The interview may be conducted in any format, including by telephone or electronic means,[222] and concern any 'information relating to the subject-matter of an investigation'. Thus, it might have a potentially wider scope than explanations requested under Article 20(2)(e), which must concern facts or documents relating to the subject matter and purpose of an inspection. The interviewee may be accompanied by a lawyer during the interview.[223] While the Commission is allowed to record the interview in any form, it must first inform the interviewee of its intention to do so. A copy of the record must

---

[215] In which case the employer has no right to be informed or to participate in any way in the interview; European Commission Antitrust Manual of Procedures, Internal DG Competition working documents on procedures for the application of Articles 101 and 102 TFEU, March 2012, Module 8 'Power to take statements', para 15. Moreover, the interviewee has to be informed about his right to stay anonymous in any subsequent access to file proceedings; European Commission Antitrust Manual of Procedures, Internal DG Competition working documents on procedures for the application of Articles 101 and 102 TFEU, March 2012, Module 8 'Power to take statements', paras 20 and 31.

[216] European Commission Antitrust Manual of Procedures, Internal DG Competition working documents on procedures for the application of Articles 101 and 102 TFEU, March 2012, Module 8 'Power to take statements', para 12.

[217] European Commission Antitrust Manual of Procedures, Internal DG Competition working documents on procedures for the application of Articles 101 and 102 TFEU, March 2012, Module 8 'Power to take statements', para 12.

[218] European Commission Antitrust Manual of Procedures, Internal DG Competition working documents on procedures for the application of Articles 101 and 102 TFEU, March 2012, Module 8 'Power to take statements', para 14. This provision also clarifies that the motivation of an employee to make inculpatory statements about his employer will regularly be an aspect to be taken into account by the Commission when assessing the probative value of the statement.

[219] Cf Case 145/83 *Stanley George Adams v Commission* [1985] ECR 3539, para 34.

[220] At the same time, this may have an adverse effect on the probative value of the evidence, given the lack of sanctions for the provision of wrong or misleading information. JM Joshua, 'Oral Statements in EC Competition Proceedings: A Due Process Short-cut?' (2004) 26 Competition Law Insight 1, 5–6. However, it should not be overlooked that an undertaking making false (leniency) statements risks the loss of leniency benefits (see para 7.53), and possibly an increase of its fine based on aggravating circumstances. For the latter see, by analogy, Case T-384/06 *IBP and International Building Products France v Commission* [2011] ECR II-1177, paras 111, 113, and 114.

[221] Article 3(1) of Reg 773/2004.

[222] Article 3(2) of Reg 773/2004. The Commission may record the statements made by the persons interviewed in any form. A copy of any recording shall be made available to the person interviewed for approval. Where necessary, the Commission shall set a time limit within which the person interviewed may communicate to it any correction to be made to the statement; Art 3(3) of Reg 773/2004.

[223] See Commission Notice on best practices for the conduct of proceedings concerning Articles 101 and 102 TFEU [2011] OJ C308/6, para 48.

be made available to the interviewee for approval. Further, where necessary the Commission shall set a time limit within which the interviewee can correct his or her statement, although no sanctions follow from an incorrect statement.[224] Since the interview takes place on a voluntary basis (ie only with the consent of the interviewee, without any form of coercion or compulsion),[225] it seems clear that no privilege of self-incrimination could be asserted by the individual or legal entity concerned.[226] Where the interview is conducted at the premises of an undertaking, Article 19(2) gives the NCA of the territory in which the interview takes place the right to be present.[227]

---

[224] Article 3(3) of Reg 773/2004. See also European Commission Antitrust Manual of Procedures, Internal DG Competition working documents on procedures for the application of Articles 101 and 102 TFEU, March 2012, Module 8 'Power to take statements', para 27. During the consultations regarding the modernization package, various submissions were made asking that the recordings of statements be made available to the undertakings concerned in order to ensure the defence rights of the parties. See eg Responses to European Commission Consultation on the Modernization Package: submissions by Baker and McKenzie, 23 December 2003, point 7.1, and Cleary, Gottlieb, Steen, and Hamilton, 5 December 2003, point VIII.1.

[225] Cf European Commission Antitrust Manual of Procedures, Internal DG Competition working documents on procedures for the application of Articles 101 and 102 TFEU, March 2012, Module 8 'Power to take statements', para 13.

[226] Cf European Commission Antitrust Manual of Procedures, Internal DG Competition working documents on procedures for the application of Articles 101 and 102 TFEU, March 2012, Module 8 'Power to take statements', paras 7, 20, and 23. Judge Vesterdorf has argued that the protection of those persons is enhanced by the requirements stipulated in Art 3(1) of Reg 773/2004. See also Recital 3 of Reg 773/2004, including its reference to the guarantees enshrined in Art 12(3) of Reg 1/2003. It could be argued that the Commission shall also inform the individual that before (s)he answers the question, (s)he should be aware that the Commission has the right to transmit the information to other competition authorities and that it may also be accessed by third parties on the basis of rights of access to the Commission's file. See B Vesterdorf, 'Rights, Privileges and Ethics in Competition Cases Roundtable' in BE Hawk (ed), *International Antitrust Law & Policy* (Annual Proceedings of the Fordham Institute 2005) 731, 739.

[227] European Commission Antitrust Manual of Procedures, Internal DG Competition working documents on procedures for the application of Articles 101 and 102 TFEU, March 2012, Module 8 'Power to take statements', para 11.

8

INVESTIGATION OF CASES (III): INSPECTIONS

Ralf Sauer, Luis Ortiz Blanco, and Konstantin Jörgens

A. Overview

The power to request information or documents and the power to carry out inspections at **8.01** the premises of an undertaking to gather evidence directly often complement each other in antitrust investigations, and may be employed in the same case. However, while requests for information are valuable for obtaining company and/or market data,[1] for eliciting particulars of contractual arrangements, or even for seeking information on anticompetitive behaviour where the Commission can ask targeted questions based on some prior knowledge, only unannounced on-the-spot inspections ('dawn raids') have the surprise effect which may be of

---

[1] This may even include detailed market information (eg pricing, places of delivery) which could be used as (supplementary) evidence to prove anticompetitive behaviour like price coordination or market sharing. See Case COMP/39.520 *Cement and related products*, Commission Press Release IP/10/1696 'Commission opens antitrust proceedings against a number of cement manufacturers' of 10 December 2010.

crucial importance in order to detect the existence of hardcore cartels[2] or abuses of a dominant position by uncovering direct evidence located in business premises[3] or private homes.[4] The Commission takes the view that the carrying out of inspections is of value, not only as a means of uncovering unlawful conduct, but also in itself, as companies usually stop their illegal behaviour in a given business sector immediately after the Commission's intervention.[5]

8.02 Article 20(1) of Regulation 1/2003 grants the Commission powers to conduct 'all necessary inspections' of undertakings and associations of undertakings. This concerns investigations at the undertaking's premises, land, and means of transport (see Article 20(2)(a)). Although the powers of inspection pursuant to Regulation 1/2003 are very similar to those stipulated in Article 14 of Regulation 17, there are a number of significant extensions, including the power to carry out inspections on domestic property ('homes of directors, managers and other members of staff', see Article 21(1)). In addition, Regulation 1/2003 incorporates some of the case law on inspections developed under Regulation 17. According to Article 20(2), inspectors may examine the books and other records related to the business, 'irrespective of the medium on which they are stored'. This and the related power 'to take or obtain in any form copies of or extracts from' such records provides the Commission with a legal basis allowing it to search and copy electronic data.[6] Besides, of the five powers listed in Article 20(2), the power to seal any business premises or records did not appear in Regulation 17, and the power to ask for explanations on facts or documents arguably is wider than the power to ask for 'oral explanations on the spot' under Article 14(1) of Regulation 17/62. The Commission has been given the power to seal any business premises and books or records

---

[2] Cartel activities have been described as the 'supreme evil of antitrust' and the 'scourge of the economy'. See XXXIII Report on Competition Policy [2003], para 717. One of the stated objectives of the modernization package was to focus the Commission's enforcement activities on hard-core cartels by freeing resources that previously were spent on dealing with notifications. This also led to the creation of a dedicated Cartel Directorate in the Directorate-General for Competition ('DG COMP'). Overall, the fifteen years from 1996 to 2010 saw a significant increase in the number of cartel decisions (in total and by number of undertakings), which was accompanied by a considerable surge in the number of unannounced inspections. However, this was followed by a considerable decline in enforcement activity in 2011 (only four cartel decisions, down from seven cartel decisions in 2010) and 2012 (only three cartel decisions, plus readoption). See Cartel Statistics (last change: 5 December 2012). Between 1 May 2004 and the end of 2008, the Commission conducted twenty-nine inspections in cartel cases covering a large number of sites. See Commission Staff Working Paper accompanying the Report on the functioning of Regulation 1/2003, SEC(2009) 574 final, para 70; Commissioner N Kroes, 'Tackling cartels—a never ending task' SPEECH/09/454 of 8 October 2009. In 2009 alone, the Commission published press releases on a total of nine inspections. In 2008, the sector inquiry into the pharmaceuticals industry was launched through inspections. See Report on Competition Policy 2008, COM(2009) 374 final, para 96.

[3] Joined Cases 46/87 and 227/88 *Hoechst v Commission* [1989] ECR 2859, para 26: 'the right to enter any premises, land and means of transport of undertakings is of particular importance inasmuch as it is intended to permit the Commission to obtain evidence of infringements of the competition rules in the places in which such evidence is normally to be found, that is to say, on the business premises of undertakings.'

[4] The new power to inspect non-business premises (Art 21 of Reg 1/2003) was first used in the investigation of the *Marine Hoses* cartel in May 2007. See Commission Press Release IP/09/137 'Commission fines marine hoses producers € 131 million for market sharing and price-fixing cartel' of 28 January 2009. Since then, the Commission has inspected private homes at least two more times. See also Commission Staff Working Paper accompanying the Report on the functioning of Regulation 1/2003, SEC(2009) 574 final, paras 74 and 75.

[5] XXXIII Report on Competition Policy [2003], para 28.

[6] See Explanatory note to an authorisation to conduct an inspection in execution of a Commission decision under Article 20(4) of Council Regulation No 1/2003, para 9. This includes searching the IT environment, storage media, and hardware of the undertaking, for instance based on keywords or with the help of dedicated search software. Where appropriate, eg where access to selected data is not possible *in situ* or the data is too voluminous to finish the search, the Commission may take an integral copy of any digital storage medium (so-called forensic image) to be searched in the presence of company representatives at the Commission's premises. Explanatory note at paras 10 and 11.

for the period and to the extent necessary for the inspection. This power serves to ensure the effectiveness of inspections, in particular in cases where an inspection is carried out over the course of more than one day and the officials have to leave the premises of the company during the night before finishing their search. Although an informal seal procedure existed before, the recognition of a formal power to seal provides a secure basis for the procedure and has encouraged the Commission to affix seals regularly.[7] Pursuant to Article 23(1)(e) of Regulation 1/2003, breaching the seals affixed by Commission officials or other authorized persons may lead to a fine of up to 1 per cent of the annual turnover of the undertaking.[8] The Commission is also entitled to ask any representative or member of staff of the undertaking or association of undertakings for explanations on facts or documents relating to the subject matter and purpose of the inspection and to record the answers.[9] The former Article 14 of Regulation 17 was unclear as to the scope of the Commission's power to ask questions during inspections. The Court of Jusice ('ECJ') indicated in *National Panasonic*[10] that Commission officials conducting on-the-spot investigations were empowered to pose questions regarding the books and business records being examined. The new legal framework goes further by allowing inspectors to ask for explanations regarding either the *facts* or documents *related to the subject matter and purpose of the inspection*, and to record them. Further details, including the right of the undertaking or association of undertakings to rectify, amend, or supplement the explanations provided by a member of its staff, are set out in Regulation 773/2004.[11] Where the undertaking or association of undertakings fails in its duties, a sanction may be imposed pursuant to Article 23(1)(d) of Regulation 1/2003.[12]

Pursuant to Article 20(3) of Regulation 1/2003, the Commission may carry out an inspection at company premises simply upon the production of a 'written authorisation'. The inspectors may come without warning (although the Commission has to 'give notice' in good time before the inspection to the national competition authority ('NCA') of the Member State in whose territory the inspection is to be conducted) but are likely to give advance notice of their arrival. This is because, if they only have the Article 20(3) 'authorisation', an undertaking is under no legal obligation to submit to the inspection.[13] This form of inspection may, for instance, be **8.03**

---

[7] Commission Staff Working Paper accompanying the Report on the functioning of Regulation 1/2003, SEC(2009) 574 final, para 72: 'Seals have been regularly used during inspections since 2004. They are particularly useful when a considerable number of offices need to be inspected, numerous documents are found which cannot all be copied and registered in one day and when Forensic IT is used which often requires overnight scanning of IT files.'

[8] See on this Ch 9, 'Procedural Infringements: Fines and Periodic Penalty Payments'.

[9] Article 20(2)(e) of Reg 1/2003.

[10] Case 136/79 *National Panasonic v Commission* [1980] ECR 2033, para 15. See also Proposal for a Regulation implementing Articles 81 and 82 of the Treaty, COM(2000) 582 final, p. 25.

[11] See Recital 4 and Art 4 of Reg 773/2004.

[12] See on this Ch 9, 'Procedural Infringements: Fines and Periodic Penalty Payments'.

[13] However, as long as the undertaking voluntarily submits to the inspection, it may not obstruct the investigation. See European Commission, 'Dealing with the Commission—Notifications, complaints, inspections and fact-finding powers under Articles [101] and [102] of the [TFEU]' (1997 edn) point 5.2. For instance, if the required books are produced in an incomplete form, the undertaking may be liable to fines. Consequently, the standard form for the written authorization stipulates that the inspectors have been invested with the powers set out in Art 20(2) of Reg 1/2003 and draws attention (as required by Art 20(3)) to the penalties foreseen in Art 23 'in case the production of the required books or other records related to the business is incomplete or where the answers to questions asked under [Art 20(2)] are incorrect or misleading' (see Art 23(1)(c), (d)). See also K Lenaerts and J Maselis, 'Procedural Rights and Issues in the Enforcement of Articles 81 and 82 of the EC Treaty' [2001] Fordham International Law Journal 1615, 1622–3; A Klees, *Europäisches Kartellverfahrensrecht* (Carl Heymanns Verlag 2005) § 9, para 61. At the same time, since the inspection is voluntary, the undertaking may subsequently decide to terminate its cooperation. If this happens—and such a change of direction would have to be clearly communicated to the inspectors—the Commission will have to either leave the premises or produce an inspection decision. In addition, Art 20(3) and Art 23(1)(c) and (d) of

considered where the company management cooperates with the Commission but prefers an inspection in order to surprise staff members who otherwise might seek to hide incriminating material. Conversely, pursuant to Article 20(4) undertakings *must* submit to inspections ordered by decision of the Commission.[14] Article 20(4) requires the Commission to 'consult' the NCA of the Member State in whose territory the inspection is to take place before adopting an inspection decision.

8.04 In line with the ECJ ruling in *Roquette Frères*,[15] Article 20(8) clarifies the role of national courts in the context of Commission inspections. Where inspectors encounter opposition on the side of the undertaking, they may ask the Member State for the necessary assistance to overcome such opposition, which includes assistance of the police or of an equivalent enforcement authority (Article 20(6)). If under national law this assistance requires authorization from a national judge, the Member State authorities have to apply for such authorization. This may also be done as a precautionary measure, in case there are grounds for apprehending such opposition and/or attempts at concealing or destroying the evidence[16] (Article 20(7)). The national judge must limit its review to ensuring that the Commission's inspection decision is authentic and that the coercive measures requested by the Commission as assistance under Article 20(6) are neither arbitrary nor excessive.[17] It may ask for detailed explanations allowing it to assess the proportionality of the measures,[18] but is not entitled to question the necessity of the inspection as such or to request access to the information in the Commission's file. In so far as a judicial authorization is required under national law for the use of public force in case of opposition by an undertaking, this leads to a double judicial control: a control on the proportionality of the coercive measures exercised by the national judge, on the one hand, and a full control over the legality of the Commission's inspection decision exercised by the EU Courts, on the other hand.[19]

Reg 1/2003 appear to draw a distinction between the *incomplete production of records* (which can be sanctioned) and the *incomplete answer to questions* (which cannot). Hence, representatives and/or staff members of the undertaking may decide not to provide complete answers when asked for explanations during a simple inspection. However, without an express indication as to its incompleteness the answer might be considered misleading, thereby exposing the undertaking to the risk of being sanctioned pursuant to Art 23(1)(d), first indent. See also Ch 9, 'Procedural Infringements: Fines and Periodic Penalty Payments'.

[14] Where the undertaking does not submit to an inspection based on a written authorization, the Commission would have to resort to an inspection decision in order to trigger the legal obligation under Art 20(4) of Reg 1/2003. As regards the parallel situation under Reg 17, see eg *Vereinigung deutscher Freiformschmieden* [1978] OJ L10/32. Cf also Case 5/85 *AKZO Chemie v Commission* [1986] ECR 2585, para 38. Generally, the Commission may choose between the two types of measures. See Joined Cases 46/87 and 227/88 *Hoechst v Commission* [1989] ECR 2859, para 22.

[15] Case C-94/00 *Roquette Frères v Directeur Général de la Concurrence, de la Consommation et de la Répression des Fraudes* ('*Roquette Frères*') [2002] ECR I-9011. The judgment dates from 22 October 2002 and thus less than two months before the adoption of Reg 1/2003 on 16 December 2002.

[16] See Case C-94/00 *Roquette Frères* [2002] ECR I-9011, paras 74 and 75.

[17] See also Case C-94/00 *Roquette Frères* [2002] ECR I-9011, paras 52, 54, 71, and 76.

[18] In this assessment, the national judge may in particular take into account the grounds for suspecting an infringement, the seriousness of the suspected infringement. and the involvement of the undertaking concerned, as well as the importance of the evidence sought. See Art 20(8) of Reg 1/2003 and Case C-94/00 *Roquette Frères* [2002] ECR I-9011, paras 61 and 79–81. K Dekeyser and C Gauer, 'The New Enforcement System for Articles 81 and 82 and the Rights of Defence', ch 23 in BE Hawk (ed), *International Antitrust Law & Policy* (Annual Proceedings of the Fordham Institute 2005) 549, 554–8, have noted that the more intrusive the measures of constraint, the stricter is likely to be the proportionality test carried out by the national judge. J Schwarze and A Weitbrecht, *Grundzüge des europäischen Kartellverfahrensrechts* (2004) § 4, para 24, have criticized the fact that the national courts do not have access to the Commission file, but have to rely on *second-hand* explanations by the Commission which can decide on the nature and scope of the information provided. See also A Klees, *Europäisches Kartellverfahrensrecht* (Carl Heymanns Verlag 2005) § 6, paras 75–80.

[19] See Case C-94/00 *Roquette Frères* [2002] ECR I-9011, paras 39, 40, and 54–8, pointing out that there is 'no fundamental difference' between the review of the national judge and the review which the EU judicature may be called upon to ensure that the inspection decision itself is in no way arbitrary. See also

Notwithstanding some earlier pronouncements by the EU Courts on the compatibility of the **8.05** Commission's investigative powers with fundamental rights,[20] the question has been raised whether Commission inspections, even in the absence of opposition on the side of the undertaking, might always require a prior judicial authorization by which the proportionality of the inspection could be assessed in advance.[21] While it seems clear that such an authorization could only come from the EU courts[22]—and that the current legal framework (Treaty on the Functioning of the European Union ('TFEU'), Regulation 1/2003, but also the Statute of the ECJ and its Rules of Procedure) does not foresee such a possibility[23]—there are also good reasons to consider that this is not required by EU law, including the fundamental rights and general principles of law enshrined in the Charter of Fundamental Rights[24] and the ECHR.[25]

K Dekeyser and C Gauer, 'The New Enforcement System for Articles 81 and 82 and the Rights of Defence', ch 23 in BE Hawk (ed), *International Antitrust Law & Policy* (Annual Proceedings of the Fordham Institute 2005) 549, 555.

[20] See eg Case 136/79 *National Panasonic v Commission* [1980] ECR 2033, paras 17–20; Case 5/85 *AKZO Chemie v Commission* [1986] ECR 2585, para 27; Joined Cases 46/87 and 227/88 *Hoechst v Commission* [1989] ECR 2859, para 10 et seq; Case 85/87 *Dow Benelux v Commission* [1989] ECR 3137, para 22 et seq; Joined Cases T-305/94, T-306/94, T-307/94, T-313/94, T-314/94, T-315/94, T-316/94, T-318/94, T-325/94, T-328/94, T-329/94 and T-335/94 *Limburgse Vinyl Maatschappij and Others v Commission* [1999] ECR II-931, paras 417–22 (confirmed in Joined Cases C-238/99 P, C-244/99 P, C-245/99 P, C-247/99 P, C-250/99 P to C-252/99 P and C-254/99 P *Limburgse Vinyl Maatschappij and Others v Commission* [2002] ECR I-8375, paras 249–51); Case T-266/03 *Groupement des cartes bancaires (CB) v Commission* [2007] ECR II-83, paras 68–72; Case T-23/09 *CNOP and CCG v Commission* [2010] ECR II-5291, para 40. See also Case C-94/00 *Roquette Frères* [2002] ECR I-9011, paras 22–9, 52, where the ECJ referred to the *Colas Est* judgment of the European Court of Human Rights ('ECtHR') without putting in question the legality of the EU system with regard to Commission inspections. This was in line with AG Mischo's Joined Opinion of 21 February 1989 in Joined Cases 46/87 and 227/88 *Hoechst v Commission*, Case 85/87 *Dow Benelux v Commission*, and Joined Cases 97/87, 98/87 and 99/87 *Dow Chemical Ibérica and Others v Commission* ('Joined Opinion in Cases 46/87, 85/87, 97/87, 98/87, 99/87 and 227/88 *Hoechst and Others v Commission*') [1989] ECR 2859, paras 46 and 47. For a critical discussion of the compatibility of inspections under EU law with fundamental rights, see D Théophile and I Simic, 'Legal Challenges to Dawn Raid Inspections under the Principles of EU, French and ECHR law' (2012) 3 JECL 511.

[21] The question has been raised in Case T-274/10 *Suez Environnement Company and Lyonnaise des Eaux France v Commission* (withdrawn) and in Cases T-289/11, T-290/11, and T-521/11 *Deutsche Bahn and Others v Commission* (pending).

[22] See Arts 20(8) and 21(3) of Reg 1/2003 and Case C-94/00 *Roquette Frères* [2002] ECR I-9011, paras 39, 40, and 96, which indicate that it is not for the national courts to assess the necessity of an inspection. This is important also to ensure a uniform interpretation and application of the legal requirements for inspections and thereby the equal treatment of undertakings in the context of inspections. Cf Case C-550/07 P *Akzo Nobel and Others v Commission* [2010] ECR I-8301, para 115, and the Opinion of AG Kokott in the same matter, para 168; AG Mischo, Joined Opinion in Cases 46/87, 85/87, 97/87, 99/87 and 227/88 *Hoechst and Others v EC Commission* [1989] ECR 2859, para 52.

[23] See also AG Mischo, Joined Opinion in Cases 46/87, 85/87, 97/87, 98/87, 99/87 and 227/88 *Hoechst and Others v Commission* [1989] ECR 2859, para 153: 'The only solution which would not be open to criticism would obviously be to supplement the EEC Treaty itself.'

[24] Charter of Fundamental Rights of the European Union ('Charter') [2000] OJ C364/1. According to Art 6(1) of the Treaty on European Union ('TEU'), the rights enshrined in the Charter have the same legal value as the Treaties and pursuant to Art 37 of Reg 1/2003 the Regulation (including Art 20 thereof) must be interpreted with respect to those rights. Among others, Art 7 of the Charter guarantees everyone's 'right to respect for his or her private and family life, home and communications.'

[25] Convention for the Protection of Human Rights and Fundamental Freedoms (European Convention on Human Rights, 'ECHR'), Council of Europe Treaty Series No 5. According to Art 6(3) TEU, fundamental rights as guaranteed by the ECHR and as they result from the constitutional traditions common to the Member States shall constitute general principles of EU law. Moreover, Art 6(2) TEU foresees that the rights of the Charter shall be interpreted in accordance with the general provisions in Title VII of the Charter and with due regard to the explanations referred to in the Charter. Article 52(3) of the Charter stipulates that Charter rights which correspond to rights guaranteed by the ECHR shall have the same meaning and scope.

This includes the inviolability of the home guaranteed in Article 7 of the Charter (in line with Article 8 ECHR).[26] Compatibility with these rights depends on whether the legal regime as a whole provides sufficient protection against arbitrary or disproportionate intervention,[27] and the case law of the EU Courts confirms that this is indeed the case with respect to inspections.[28] Among others, inspection decisions must be based on reasonable grounds for suspicion[29] and include sufficient reasoning;[30] the measure of inquiry must relate to the ground for suspicion and the aim of the investigation;[31] it must be proportionate; and the powers of the inspectors under Article 20 of Regulation 1/2003 are limited (in particular they do not include any power of coercion).[32] Moreover, inspected undertakings enjoy various EU guarantees, including, in particular, the right to legal representation and the privileged nature of correspondence between lawyer and client.[33] In addition, the EU system provides for several layers of judicial protection, including the *ex post facto* review of the inspection decision[34] and certain individual

---

[26] As regards their applicability in case of inspections see Judgment of 12 December 2012 in Case T-410/09 *Almamet v Commission*, paras 22 and 23 with further references. According to the explanations provided by the Praesidium of the Convent [2007] OJ C303/17, the rights guaranteed in Art 7 of the Charter as well as the limitations which may legitimately be imposed correspond to those guaranteed by Art 8 of the ECHR which stipulates the following: '1. Everyone has the right to respect for his private and family life, his home and his correspondence. 2. There shall be no interference by a public authority with the exercise of this right except such as in accordance with the law and is necessary in a democratic society in the interests of national security, public safety or the economic well-being of the country, for the prevention of disorder or crime, for the protection of health or morals, or for the protection of the rights and freedoms of others.'

[27] *Varga v Romania* App no 73957/01 (ECtHR, 1 April 2008), para 70; *Mastepan v Russia*, App no 3708/03 (EctHR, 14 January 2010), paras 41 and 43. In keeping with the idea that an overall assessment is required, the ECtHR has indicated that deficiencies in the limitation of the scope of the search warrant (inspection decision) may be offset by sufficient procedural safeguards if these are 'capable of protecting the applicant against any abuse or arbitrariness'. See *Robathin v Austria* App no 30457/06 (ECtHR, 3 July 2012) para 47.

[28] Case C-94/00 *Roquette Frères* [2002] ECR I-9011, para 50. Likewise, the General Court ('GC') has emphasized that 'European Union law provides undertakings with a range of guarantees against arbitrary or disproportionate intervention by public authorities in the sphere of their private activities'. See Judgment of 12 December 2012 in Case T-410/09 *Almamet v Commission*, para 27.

[29] Case C-94/00 *Roquette Frères* [2002] ECR I-9011, paras 54 and 55; Judgment of 14 November 2012 in Case T-135/09 *Nexans v Commission*, paras 43 and 45.

[30] For an overview of the obligations to delimit the subject matter and purpose of the inspection see Judgment of 14 November 2012 in Case T-135/09 *Nexans v Commission*, para 38 et seq, with further references.

[31] See, with respect to requests for information, Judgment of 22 March 2012 in Joined Cases T-458/09 and T-171/10 *Slovak Telekom v Commission*, paras 42 and 43. It appears, though, that the GC grants the Commission considerable leeway in this assessment, since it has stressed that 'it is for the Commission to decide' whether a particular request is in fact necessary.

[32] See, *inter alia*, Joined Cases 46/87 and 227/88 *Hoechst v Commission* [1989] ECR 2859, paras 28–31 and 41; Case 85/87 *Dow Benelux v Commission* [1989] ECR 3137, paras 17 and 18; Case C-94/00 *Roquette Frères* [2002] ECR I-9011, paras 47, 48, 55, and 83; Case T-339/04 *France Télécom v Commission* [2007] ECR II-573, paras 56–60; Case T-266/03 *Groupement des cartes bancaires (CB) v Commission* [2007] ECR II-83, paras 35–7 and 72. The investigatory powers conferred on the Commission by Art 20(1) of Reg 1/2003 are limited to authorizing its officials to enter such premises as they choose and to have the documents they request and the contents of any piece of furniture which they indicate shown to them. See, for Reg 17/62, Joined Cases 46/87 and 227/88 *Hoechst v Commission* [1989] ECR 2859, para 31. The sealing of offices does not constitute a coercive measure, as it merely creates a financial risk in case of a breach and makes it possible to detect any potential access to a particular room or file cabinet. It is thus an auxiliary tool which protects the investigation without imposing excessive burdens on the inspectors.

[33] Case 155/79 *AM & S Europe v Commission* [1982] ECR 1575, paras 18–27; Joined Cases 46/87 and 227/88 *Hoechst v Commission* [1989] ECR 2859, para 16; Case 85/87 *Dow Benelux v Commission* [1989] ECR 3137, para 27; Joined Cases T-125/03 and T-253/03 *Akzo Nobel Chemicals and Akcros Chemicals v Commission* [2007] ECR II-3523 (confirmed in Case C-550/07 P *Akzo Nobel Chemicals and Akcros Chemicals v Commission* [2010] ECR I-8301).

[34] In case the decision in question is annulled, the Commission would be prevented from using, for the purposes of proceedings in respect of an infringement of the EU competition rules, any documents or evidence

measures,[35] plus the *ex-ante* review of coercive measures where this is required under national law.[36] In case the Commission has to rely on the assistance of national authorities, their conduct has to respect all procedural guarantees under national law.

This analysis is not put into doubt by the judgment of the European Court of Human Rights **8.06** ('ECtHR') in *Colas Est*,[37] which has to be read in its specific context. In particular, from the description of the facts and arguments by the parties in that case, it transpires that the ECtHR considered the conduct of the French authorities at issue as excessive (abuse of power) and the safeguards at national level to be insufficient.[38] It should also be noted that the judgment in *Colas Est* was rendered before the ECJ's judgment in *Roquette Frères* (which makes explicit reference to *Colas Est*), without there being any indication by the ECJ that it read the ECtHR judgment as putting into doubt the legality of the EU system for inspections. Other judgments by the ECtHR have confirmed that an *ex-post* judicial control may be sufficient to protect against arbitrary and/or disproportionate intrusions into private homes.[39]

As indicated earlier, the exercise of the power of inspection complements the power to request **8.07** information pursuant to Article 18 of Regulation 1/2003. However, it is not necessary to make a prior request for information, and undertakings do not have to refuse to provide such information before an inspection can be carried out. In practice, the Commission is entitled to exercise both powers independently, so that on some occasions inspections will follow requests for information (eg where the reply given by the undertaking is unsatisfactory) and in other cases the order will be reversed (eg where the Commission seeks clarifications concerning documents and information obtained during an inspection).[40] Depending on the circumstances, it may also be legitimate to have several rounds of inspections, in particular where prior investigative measures reveal information that invites further investigation or where the Commission refocuses its investigation.[41] In terms of the object of the investigation, Article 20 of Regulation 1/2003 does

---

which it has obtained in the course of that investigation, as otherwise the decision on the infringement might equally be annulled in so far as it was based on such evidence. See the Orders of 26 March 1987 in Case 46/87 R *Hoechst v Commission* [1987] ECR 1549, para 34, and of 28 October 1987 in Case 85/87 R *Dow Chemical Nederland v Commission* [1987] ECR 4367, para 17; Joined Cases T-305/94, T-306/94, T-307/94, T-313/94, T-314/94, T-315/94, T-316/94, T-318/94, T-325/94, T-328/94, T-329/94 and T-335/94 *Limburgse Vinyl Maatschappij and Others v Commission* [1999] ECR II-931, para 472.

[35] See eg Joined Cases T-125/03 and T-253/03 *Akzo and Akcros v Commission* [2007] ECR II-3523, para 45.

[36] Article 20(6), (7) of Reg 1/2003 and Case C-94/00 *Roquette Frères* [2002] ECR I-9011, paras 52, 76, and 80. Where the national judge considers this necessary, it may make a reference for a preliminary ruling to the ECJ. See Case T-339/04 *France Télécom v Commission* [2007] ECR II-573, para 51.

[37] *Colas Est and Others v France* ('*Colas Est*') App no 37971/97 (ECtHR, 16 April 2002).

[38] Cf *Colas Est*, paras 48 and 49. Several factors might have led to that conclusion: the inspection was based directly on an ordinance, without any inspection decision or warrant that could have been challenged; the Ordinance of 1945 was probably not in line with the French constitution and thus constituted a doubtful legal basis even under national law; for those reasons it was soon after the inspection replaced by a new law guaranteeing prior judicial review; the inspectors had wide powers which included coercive measures (seizure of documents); the inspection was large scale (fifty-six companies) and might have involved abusive conduct (seizure of a large number of documents, partly outside the scope of the inspection, and without a complete inventory to check which documents had been taken).

[39] See *Harju v Finland*, App no 56716/09 (ECtHR, 15 February 2011), paras 44–6, and *Heino v Finland*, App no 56720/09 (ECtHR, 15 February 2011), paras 45–7. See also *Mastepan v Russia*, App no 3708/03 (ECtHR, 14 January 2010), para 43; *Société Métallurgique Liotard Frères v France*, App no. 29598/08 (ECtHR, 5 May 2011), para 18. For an overview of the situation in the Member States at the time see AG Mischo, Joined Opinion in Cases 46/87, 85/87, 97/87, 98/87, 99/87 and 227/88 *Hoechst and Others v Commission* [1989] ECR 2859, para 49 et seq.

[40] See Case T-339/04 *France Télécom v Commission* [2007] ECR II-573, para 122; Case T-266/03 *Groupement des cartes bancaires (CB) v Commission* [2007] ECR II-83, paras 64 and 65.

[41] Cf Case C-94/00 *Roquette Frères* [2002] ECR I-9011, para 78. This may also become relevant in case of 'chance findings' during a first inspection which reveal other, additional types of anticompetitive conduct that

not define the types of undertakings which the Commission can target, with the result that it is entitled—as in the case of requests for information—to order inspections not only at the premises of undertakings allegedly implicated in an infringement, but with regard to any undertaking which might be in possession of information regarding the anticompetitive conduct under investigation.[42] In addition, the Commission has the power to search premises, land, or means of transport other than those of an undertaking or association of undertakings, where reasonable suspicion exists that records related to the business[43] and to the subject matter of an investigation into a serious violation of Articles 101 and 102 TFEU are kept there. Article 21(1) of Regulation 1/2003 describes these premises as including the homes of directors, managers, and other members of staff of the undertaking or association of undertakings concerned. This power can only be exercised by decision, and such decisions may only be taken after the Commission has consulted the NCA of the Member State in whose territory the inspection is to be conducted. Article 21(3) provides that the national judge must give prior authorization for the execution of the Commission's decision.

8.08 While written authorization pursuant to Article 20(3) of Regulation 1/2003 is considered a measure of pure administration which is taken by the Director-General of the Directorate-General for Competition ('DG COMP'),[44] decisions to order an inspection pursuant to Articles 20(4) and 21 of Regulation 1/2003 are in principle for the College of Commissioners to adopt, but the Commissioner with special responsibility for competition has been empowered to act in its stead. As regards business premises (Article 20(4)), this power is sub-delegated to the Director-General of DG COMP, whereas in the case of non-business premises (Article 21) the latter may act in sub-delegation only if the decision must be taken urgently and the Competition Commissioner cannot be reached in time.[45]

B. Types of Inspections

1. Alternatives

8.09 Article 20 of Regulation 1/2003 describes two types of inspections: inspections based on a written authorization ('simple inspection'), and inspections ordered by formal decision ('inspection by decision' or 'mandatory inspection'). These constitute alternatives and the Commission is entitled at its discretion to decide which type is most appropriate in each case.[46] Hence, it may decide to proceed immediately with an inspection by decision without

---

the Commission then seeks to investigate with a second round of inspections. See Case 85/87 *Dow Benelux v Commission* [1989] ECR 3137, paras 17–20; Joined Cases T-305/94, T-306/94, T-307/94, T-313/94, T-314/94, T-315/94, T-316/94, T-318/94, T-325/94, T-328/94, T-329/94 and T-335/94 *Limburgse Vinyl Maatschappij and Others v Commission* [1999] ECR II-931, paras 474 and 477.

[42] This possibility, however, has been used rarely. Typically, the Commission prefers to request information from third parties by letter. For a special case involving a company organizing and operating cartel agreements for other manufacturers, see *Fides* [1979] OJ L57/33.

[43] According to Case C-94/00 *Roquette Frères* [2002] ECR I-9011, para 45, 'the scope of the Commission's investigatory powers does not extend to cover, in particular, documents of a non-business nature, that is to say, documents not relating to the market activities of the undertaking'.

[44] European Commission Antitrust Manual of Procedures, Internal DG Competition working documents on procedures for the application of Articles 101 and 102 TFEU, March 2012, Module 1 'Decision-making procedures', paras 46 and 49.

[45] European Commission Antitrust Manual of Procedures, Internal DG Competition working documents on procedures for the application of Articles 101 and 102 TFEU, March 2012, Module 1 'Decision-making procedures', paras 25, 26, 28, and 40.

[46] See Case 136/79 *National Panasonic v Commission* [1980] ECR 2033, para 12: 'those two procedures do not necessarily overlap but constitute two alternative checks the choice of which depends upon the special features of each case.' See also Joined Cases 46/87 and 227/88 *Hoechst v Commission* [1989] ECR 2859,

having previously tried a simple inspection[47] or even made a request for information. Like Regulation 17 before, Regulation 1/2003 recognizes that the Commission may wish to carry out a surprise visit, whether it has previously encountered resistance on the part of the undertaking or not. In case of a simple inspection, the officials may either give advance notice of their arrival or come without warning (although they have to give notice 'in good time before the inspection' to the NCA of the Member State in whose territory the inspection is carried out). Given that only an inspection provides for a surprise element and allows the Commission (if necessary through the assistance of national authorities) to act independently of the undertaking's assistance, a prior request for information is not necessary, nor does the fact that the undertaking has previously responded to such a request render an inspection disproportionate.[48]

2. Simple inspections[49]

Reasonable grounds for suspecting an infringement

Even though a simple inspection pursuant to Article 20(3) of Regulation 1/2003 may only **8.10** be carried out with the consent of the undertaking concerned, the Commission must have reasonable grounds for suspecting an infringement. Given the limited interference with the business sphere of the undertaking of an agreed inspection, the requirements in this regard are likely to be low. They will always be fulfilled where the Commission acts on the basis of information from the undertaking's management itself indicating anticompetitive conduct.

Content of the authorization

Article 20(3) of Regulation 1/2003 provides that officials and other accompanying persons **8.11** mandated by the Commission for this purpose (inspectors) are to exercise their powers upon production of a written authorization[50] provided by the Director-General of DG COMP under sub-delegation.[51] The authorization to inspect, which will be drafted in the official language of the Member State where the undertaking is located,[52] must specify:

(i) the name or trading name of the undertaking or association of undertakings under investigation;

(ii) the subject matter and purpose of the inspection; and

---

para 22; European Commission, 'Dealing with the Commission—Notifications, complaints, inspections and fact-finding powers under Articles [101] and [102] of the [TFEU]' (1997 edn) points 5.1, 5.3: 'The Commission does not have to give reasons which specifically justify why an inspection has been ordered by decision rather than conducted on the basis of authorisation.' This parallels the situation with respect to (informal and formal) requests for information. See Judgment of 22 March 2012 in Joined Cases T-458/09 and T-171/10 *Slovak Telekom v Commission*, para 90.

[47] With respect to Reg 17, see Case 136/79 *National Panasonic v Commission* [1980] ECR 2033, para 11.

[48] Case T-266/03 *Groupement des cartes bancaires (CB) v Commission* [2007] ECR II-83, paras 62–72.

[49] See also the overview in para 8.01 et seq.

[50] See Explanatory note to an authorisation to conduct an inspection in execution of a Commission decision under Article 20(4) of Council Regulation No 1/2003, para 1: 'Written authorisations serve to name the officials and other accompanying persons authorised by the Commission to conduct the inspection. They prove their identity by means of their staff card.' For officials and persons authorized or appointed by the NCA, see para 5. Pursuant to former Art 14(2) of Reg 17, the Commission was explicitly required to indicate the identity of the authorized officials to the responsible NCA. Article 20(3) of Reg 1/2003 no longer contains this requirement.

[51] European Commission Antitrust Manual of Procedures, Internal DG Competition working documents on procedures for the application of Articles 101 and 102 TFEU, March 2012, Module 1 'Decision-making procedures', para 49.

[52] European Commission Antitrust Manual of Procedures, Internal DG Competition working documents on procedures for the application of Articles 101 and 102 TFEU, March 2012, Module 27 'Use of languages in antitrust proceedings', para 21.

(iii) the penalties provided for in Article 23 of Regulation 1/2003 in cases where the required books or other business records are produced in incomplete form or where the answers to questions asked under Article 20(2) are incorrect or misleading.

Name or trading name of the undertaking

8.12 As for decisions pursuant to Article 20(4), the written authorization to be produced to the undertaking at the start of the inspection will typically name the undertaking—often a parent company as well as all companies directly or indirectly controlled by it—and provide an address of the legal entity (or entities) which is (are) the immediate target of the inspection. At the same time, the authorization will clarify that any of the undertaking's premises may be inspected.[53] If their search for information makes this necessary, inspectors are thus not prevented from entering buildings, premises, or offices owned by the undertaking and located at a place other than that specifically indicated in the authorization.[54] The essential component, therefore, is the name of the undertaking[55] and not any address given in the authorization, which is foremost an additional element for the identification of the undertaking.

Officials authorized to carry out inspections

8.13 On-site inspections are carried out by Commission officials as well as by 'other accompanying persons' authorized for that purpose by the Commission.[56] Especially where it is necessary to carry out several inspections simultaneously at the premises of many undertakings located in different Member States, inspection teams may be quite large. This also has as a consequence that not all the inspectors will be familiar with the case file, or even the business sector at issue. In order to allow for a targeted inspection, the inspectors will normally be briefed beforehand about any available information on the presumed anticompetitive conduct, the goods or services at stake, the industry and market structure (competitors, clients, etc), details of the organizational structure of the undertaking(s) to be investigated, as well as the purpose of the inspection, and in particular the evidence to look for, *inter alia*, so that they can perform their duties efficiently. Regulation 1/2003 does not specify who can be appointed as 'other accompanying persons'. In addition to national experts or other persons working for DG COMP without the status of an official, this could also cover external help, for instance

---

[53] In line with Art 20(2)(a) of Reg 1/2003, which foresees that the Commission may 'enter any premises, land and means of transport' of the respective undertaking.

[54] In Case T-66/99 *Minoan Lines v Commission* [2003] ECR II-5515, para 58 et seq, the Commission conducted the investigation not at the premises of Minoan Lines (to whom the inspection decision was addressed) but at the premises of the European Trust Agency ('ETA'), a different legal entity. ETA had no parent/subsidiary relationship with Minoan but was merely Minoan's agent. The Court held that in carrying out its functions as agent and representative of Minoan, ETA had authority to present itself to the public at large and to the Commission during the investigation as Minoan. Also, Minoan had delegated the conduct of its business to ETA to the point that this agency housed in fact the real centre of Minoan's commercial activities and was therefore the place where the books and business records relating to the activities in question were held. Whilst ETA was legally a separate entity from Minoan, in its role as Minoan's representative and sole manager of those of Minoan's affairs which were the subject matter of the investigation, its identity merged with that of its principal. Consequently, it was under the same obligation to cooperate as Minoan. The Court found that the Commission acted diligently and amply fulfilled its duty to make as sure as possible, before the investigation began, that the premises which it targeted indeed belonged to the legal entity which it sought to investigate. See also Case T-59/99 *Ventouris Group Enterprises v Commission* [2003] ECR II-5257, para 111 et seq; Case T-65/99 *Strintzis Lines Shipping v Commission* [2003] ECR II-5433, para 48 et seq.

[55] The ECtHR has interpreted this requirement broadly by stating that it may not be relevant whether the inspection decision refers to the correct legal form of the company, as long as the identity of the respective entity or entities can be ascertained. See *Société Canal Plus and Others v France*, App no 29408/08 (ECtHR, 21 December 2010), paras 8 and 52.

[56] Article 20(2) of Reg 1/2003. Former Art 14 of Reg 17 did not mention 'other accompanying persons'.

from IT experts who can assist with gaining access to information stored electronically.[57] Unless specifically stated in the mandate, these 'other accompanying persons' are not limited in their powers vis-à-vis the other inspectors. For each business premise to be inspected, a 'team leader' will be appointed who functions as the contact person for company representatives and their lawyers during the inspection and takes any measures on-site,[58] where necessary, in close contact with the 'home base' of DG COMP in Brussels.

Subject matter and purpose of inspections

Article 20(3) defines the essential elements which have to be present in the written authorization, by stating that it must specify the subject matter and purpose of the inspection. **8.14** The subject matter of inspections encompasses the specific anticompetitive agreements and/ or concerted practices of the undertakings under investigation in relation to the supply of specified products or services in the EU.[59] The aim of the inspection will in all cases be to verify or determine the existence of an infringement of Articles 101 and/or 102 TFEU and to establish its legal and economic context[60] for the purpose of antitrust proceedings. The Commission's obligation to indicate the subject matter and purpose of the inspection in its authorization will be fulfilled if it describes, at least succinctly, the nature of the putative infringement which it seeks to uncover and thus what it is looking for. According to the ECJ, the requirement that the Commission informs the undertakings of the subject matter and purpose of the inspection constitutes a fundamental safeguard of the rights of the defence of undertakings under investigation.[61] Therefore, the obligation to state reasons cannot be limited by virtue of considerations relating to the effectiveness of the investigation. Although the Commission is not required to inform undertakings of all the evidence in its possession concerning the putative infringement,[62] or to make a precise legal analysis of that

---

[57] This reflects the reality that inspections are no longer just about going through drawers or paper files, but increasingly involve a high-tech search of computer systems for information.

[58] See eg Case T-141/08 *E.ON Energie v Commission* [2010] ECR II-5761, paras 4, 103, 138, and 254, according to which the head of the inspection team affixed the seals, instructed the company representatives about their importance as well as the potential consequences of a seal breach, and ultimately signed the respective minutes both for the sealing and the seal breach.

[59] An investigation under Reg 1/2003 can only be used to prosecute antitrust violations *in the EU* because its 'subject matter' may not cover non-EU territories. However, even if the Commission may only exercise its powers of inspection within the EU's jurisdiction and therefore at premises within this geographic area, this does not exclude that certain findings relate to conduct or perpetrators located outside the EU. See Joined Cases 89, 104, 114, 116, 117, and 125 to 129/85 *A Ahlström Osakeyhtiö and Others v Commission* [1988] 5193, para 11 et seq; Judgment of 14 November 2012 in Case T-135/09 *Nexans v Commission*, para 99. Likewise, an inspection may cover evidence from a period during which the competition rules of the EU were not (yet) applicable in a specific territory. See, for requests for information, Judgment of 22 March 2012 in Joined Cases T-458/09 and T-171/10 *Slovak Telekom v Commission*, para 45 et seq.

[60] See, with respect to requests for information, Judgment of 22 March 2012 in Joined Cases T-458/09 and T-171/10 *Slovak Telekom v Commission*, paras 48 and 51.

[61] Joined Cases 46/87 and 227/88 *Hoechst v Commission* [1989] ECR 2859, paras 29 and 41; Case T-66/99 *Minoan Lines v Commission* [2003] ECR II-5515, para 55: 'As the Court has held, that requirement is intended to protect the rights of defence of the undertakings concerned, which would be seriously compromised if the Commission could rely on evidence against undertakings which was obtained during an investigation but was not related to the subject matter or purpose thereof [referring to Case 85/87 *Dow Benelux v Commission* [1989] ECR 3137, para 18, and Case C-94/00 *Roquette Frères* [2002] ECR I-9011, para 48].'

[62] Some commentators have raised the question whether the undertaking under investigation should be given access to the information underlying the investigation already at the time of the inspection as this would strengthen its defence rights. See M Araujo, 'The Respect of Fundamental Rights within the European Network of Competition Authorities' ch 21 in BE Hawk (ed), *International Antitrust Law & Policy* (Annual Proceedings of the Fordham Institute 2004) 511, 514. However, the Commission has to protect its investigation against obstruction by the inspected undertaking and has a legitimate interest in keeping the incentive for leniency submissions which might be lost if the details of the information available to the Commission are known. Also, there is a clear need to protect certain sources, in particular the identity of complainants

infringement,[63] it shall nevertheless describe it 'as precisely as possible'.[64] So far, the EU Courts appear to have been rather lenient regarding the extent of the reasoning that the Commission must provide. According to case law, the Commission does not have to delimit precisely the relevant market, specify the exact legal nature of the putative infringements, or the period during which those infringements were committed.[65] In practice, the level of detail in this respect will very much depend on the quantity and quality of the information which prompted the Commission to open the file and order an inspection.[66] Often, the Commission will prefer not to delineate the putative infringement to be investigated too narrowly in order to avoid the need for a subsequent extension of the authorization, or a further inspection. This can create a conflict with the rights of defence of the undertakings concerned, given that their ability to determine the scope of their duty of cooperation, and to satisfy themselves that the evidence gathered is relevant to the subject matter of the inspection, depends on the clarity of the mandate.[67] In any event,

---

or whistle-blowers, which could be put at risk by providing more detailed information to the inspected undertaking(s). Therefore, it should be sufficient if the Commission describes the presumed infringement in some detail, thereby demonstrating that it possesses relevant information. In *France Télécom*, the GC stipulated the following requirements: 'In order to establish that the inspection is justified, the Commission is required to show, in a properly substantiated manner, in the decision ordering the inspection that it is in possession of information and evidence providing reasonable grounds for suspecting the infringement of which the undertaking subject to inspection is suspected'; Case T-339/04 *France Télécom v Commission* [2007] ECR II-573, paras 60 and 62. It should be noted, though, that for this the GC refers to passages of the *Roquette Frères* judgment which deal with the explanations provided by the Commission to the national judge, not with the content of the inspection decision. Cf Case C-94/00 *Roquette Frères* [2002] ECR I-9011, para 97.

[63] See eg Case T-23/09 *CNOP and CCG v Commission* [2010] ECR II-5291, paras 41 and 68; Case T-57/01 *Solvay v Commission* [2009] ECR II-4621, paras 219–26 and AG Kokott, Opinion of 14 April 2011 in Case C-109/10 P *Solvay v Commission*, paras 138–44 (no need to make a final assessment as to whether certain conduct constitutes an anticompetitive agreement between undertakings, a decision by an association of undertakings, or the abuse of a dominant position).

[64] Joined Cases 46/87 and 227/88 *Hoechst v Commission* [1989] ECR 2859, para 41; Case T-266/03 *Groupement des cartes bancaires (CB) v Commission* [2007] ECR II-83, paras 36 and 37. See also Case T-339/04 *France Télécom v Commission* [2007] ECR II-573, para 58 (Commission must 'state as precisely as possible the presumed facts which it intends to investigate, namely what it is looking for and the matters to which the investigation must relate').

[65] See Case 85/87 *Dow Benelux v Commission* [1989] ECR 3137, paras 7–10, and Cases 97–99/87 *Dow Chemical Ibérica v Commission* [1989] ECR 3165, paras 44–6; Case C-94/00 *Roquette Frères* [2002] ECR I-9011, para 82; Judgments of 14 November 2012 in Case T-135/09 *Nexans v Commission*, paras 54, 97, and in Case T-140/09 *Prysmian v Commission*, para 55 (as regards the timing). At the same time, the GC stipulated the following requirements in Case T-339/04 *France Télécom v Commission* [2007] ECR II-573, para 59: 'the Commission is also required to state in a decision ordering an inspection the essential features of the suspected infringement by indicating the market thought to be affected, the nature of the suspected restrictions of competition and the supposed degree of involvement of the undertaking concerned, the evidence sought and the matters to which the investigation must relate as well as the powers conferred on the Community investigators'. However, it should be noted that for this the GC referred to passages of the *Roquette Frères* judgment which do not deal with the content of the inspection decision but rather with the explanations provided by the Commission to the national judge where judicial authorization is required. Cf Case C-94/00 *Roquette Frères* [2002] ECR I-9011, para 97. In a subsequent case, the GC held that the Commission must 'identify the sectors covered by the alleged infringement with which the investigation is concerned with a degree of precision sufficient to enable the undertaking in question to limit its cooperation to its activities in the sectors in respect of which the Commission has reasonable grounds for suspecting an infringement of the competition rules...and to make it possible for the Court of the European Union to determine, if necessary, whether or not those grounds are sufficiently reasonable for those purposes.' This, however, does not exclude that the sector described covers several (competition law) markets. See Judgment of 14 November 2012 in Case T-135/09 *Nexans v Commission*, paras 45 and 57.

[66] Cf Case C-94/00 *Roquette Frères* [2002] ECR I-9011, para 78: 'Even if it already has evidence, or indeed proof, of the existence of an infringement, the Commission may legitimately take the view that it is necessary to order further investigations enabling it to better define the scope of the infringement, to determine its duration or to identify the circle of undertakings involved.'

[67] Case C-94/00 *Roquette Frères* [2002] ECR I-9011, para 48; Case T-339/04 *France Télécom v Commission* [2007] ECR II-573, para 57.

as long as the description of the putative infringement is sufficiently precise, the Commission is not required to identify in advance the type of evidence it seeks to gather during the inspection.[68]

Clear details of possible sanctions

Article 23(1)(c) of Regulation 1/2003 empowers the Commission to impose fines on undertak- **8.15** ings which, having submitted to a simple inspection with written authorization, produce the required books or other business records in incomplete form. In obvious parallel with simple requests for information, simple inspections are not compulsory, and undertakings must decide whether or not to submit to them. However, once they have allowed an inspection to commence, undertakings may not obstruct the investigative work of the inspectors. Thus, simple inspections, once agreed to voluntarily by the undertaking, in principle proceed in the same way as inspections undertaken pursuant to a formal decision[69] (with the difference that the undertaking may decide to terminate its cooperation). This also includes that the inspectors have the power to request explanations (and their recording) pursuant to Article 20(2)(e) of Regulation 1/2003.[70] The Commission may impose a fine based on Article 23(1)(d) where (i) the answers to such questions are incorrect or misleading, or (ii) the undertaking fails to rectify within a set time limit such incorrect or misleading answers.[71] Both of the above fining powers have to be spelt out in the written authorization.

Explanatory note

In order to inform undertakings of some of their rights and obligations, the Commission has **8.16** prepared an explanatory note setting out the powers of the inspectors and certain aspects of the procedure during a simple inspection.[72] In accordance with consistent administrative practice,

---

[68] Case C-94/00 *Roquette Frères* [2002] ECR I-9011, para 84; Case T-57/01 *Solvay v Commission* [2009] ECR II-4621, para 218; Judgment of 14 November 2012 in Case T-135/09 *Nexans v Commission*, para 62. Early on, the EU Courts took the view that the Commission cannot know (and thus describe) in advance which documents it expects to find. See Case 31/59 *Brescia v High Authority* [1960] ECR 153, paras 80 and 81: 'it is only the object in view which must serve as the criterion and not an a priori statement of the results expected which drawn up unilaterally and without knowledge of the facts, may change by reasons of the checks when they are carried out'.

[69] The fact that undertakings (have to) submit to simple inspections voluntarily does not mean that they will be less rigorous. As for inspections by decision, the Commission may rely on the active assistance of the national authorities pursuant to Art 20(5) of Reg 1/2003. Conversely, the use of coercive measures by national authorities pursuant to Art 20(6) presupposes that an inspection has been 'ordered', which refers only to Art 20(4) but not to Art 20(3) inspections.

[70] According to the Commission Notice on best practices for the conduct of proceedings concerning Articles 101 and 102 TFEU, [2011] OJ C308/6, n 39, this must be distinguished from the power to take statements pursuant to Art 19 of Reg 1/2003. See also European Commission Antitrust Manual of Procedures, Internal DG Competition working documents on procedures for the application of Articles 101 and 102 TFEU, March 2012, Module 8 'Power to take statements', para 3: 'Only with respect to oral questions asked during inspections employees of an undertaking (be it representatives who have the authority to speak on behalf of the undertaking or other members of staff) are obliged to answer to questions. Only with respect to these questions may the Commission under certain conditions impose fines'.

[71] See Explanatory note for an authorisation to conduct an inspection based on a Commission authorisation under Article 20(3) of Council Regulation No 1/2003, paras 7 and 8, which refers to the procedure in Art 4 of Reg 773/2004. At the same time, Reg 1/2003 appears to treat simple inspections in the same way as simple requests for information (Art 18(2)) in the sense that the undertaking is not required to provide a complete reply to questions asked during an inspection (unless an incomplete answer is in itself misleading). This makes some sense as otherwise the Commission could circumvent the requirement for a formal decision pursuant to Art 18(3) of Reg 1/2003 by asking questions during a simple inspection based solely on a written authorization. If the Commission realizes that it has received an incomplete answer, it will have to resort to a request for information by decision, pursuant to Art 18(3) (in which case an incomplete answer carries the risk of a fine pursuant to Art 23(1)(b)).

[72] Explanatory note for an authorisation to conduct an inspection based on a Commission authorisation under Article 20(3) of Council Regulation No 1/2003. The explanatory note (which is not available on the internet) is an informal document that does not affect the powers of the inspectors, but explains how the

the inspectors deliver a copy of the memorandum to the undertaking together with the written authorization. It explicitly informs the undertaking that it is not obliged to submit to the inspection and may accordingly refuse to submit to it.

Procedure and judicial review

8.17	In good time before the inspection, DG COMP must give notice of the inspection to the NCA of the Member State in whose territory it is to be conducted.[73] On the day of the inspection, the inspectors have to produce the written authorization and, upon request, will provide explanations on the subject matter and purpose of the proposed inspection, as well as on procedural matters (eg confidentiality)—even though in most cases this will not be necessary, as the undertaking has already been informed about the inspection in advance. In case the undertaking refuses the inspection, the inspectors will minute this refusal and hand a copy of the minute to a company representative upon request.[74] The written authorization to carry out an inspection pursuant to Article 20(3) of Regulation 1/2003 is not a challengeable act. However, its legality may be questioned in the context of a possible annulment action against a subsequent decision finding an infringement on substance if this is based on evidence obtained during the inspection.[75]

3. Inspections by decision[76]

Reasonable grounds for suspecting an infringement

8.18	In order to avoid an arbitrary interference with the business sphere of the undertaking concerned, the Commission must have reasonable grounds for suspecting an infringement of the competition rules in order to carry out any inspection.[77] If the undertaking challenges the inspection decision in this respect, the EU Courts must satisfy themselves that such grounds exist.[78] This does not require documentary evidence in the form of a 'smoking gun', but at least some credible information (eg from a complainant) concerning a possible infringement of the

---

inspection will proceed as regards certain important aspects, and describes some of the basic rights of the company being inspected. Among others, the explanatory note covers the request for oral explanations from representatives or members of staff, the examination of electronic information (including the blocking of email accounts, keyword and other electronic searches, or the taking of a forensic image of digital storage mediums) and the procedure for the sealing of business premises, rooms, cabinets, etc.

[73] See European Commission Antitrust Manual of Procedures, Internal DG Competition working documents on procedures for the application of Articles 101 and 102 TFEU, March 2012, Module 3 'Cooperation with National Competition Authorities in EU and exchange of information in ECN', at para 54(b).

[74] For these procedural steps see Explanatory note for an authorisation to conduct an inspection based on a Commission authorisation under Article 20(3) of Council Regulation No 1/2003, paras 1–3 and 6.

[75] Joined Cases T-305/94 to T-307/94, T-313/94 to T-316/94, T-318/94, T-325/94, T-328/94, T-329/94 and T-335/94 *Limburgse Vinyl Maatschappij and others v Commission* [1999] ECR II-931, para 412.

[76] See also the explanations with respect to simple inspections which apply *mutatis mutandis* also to mandatory inspections. This section deals mostly with those aspects in which mandatory inspections differ from simple inspections.

[77] Case C-94/00 *Roquette Frères* [2002] ECR I-9011, paras 54 and 55; Judgment of 14 November 2012 in Case T-135/09 *Nexans v Commission*, para 43. According to the ECtHR, 'the existence of reasonable suspicion is to be assessed at the time of issuing the search warrant', so that subsequent events (eg finding that the infringement or the participation of the undertaking therein cannot be established) do not render the inspection unlawful. See *Robathin v Austria* App no 30457/06 (ECtHR, 3 July 2012) para 46. Cf also Judgment of 22 March 2012 in Joined Cases T-458/09 and T-171/10 *Slovak Telekom v Commission*, para 85; Judgment of 12 December 2012 in Case T-410/09 *Almamet v Commission*, para 52. In order to allow the EU Courts to assess whether the Commission acted upon a reasonable suspicion, the latter has to sufficiently identify the sectors covered by the putative infringement with which the investigation is concerned. See Judgment of 14 November 2012 in Case T-135/09 *Nexans v Commission*, para 45.

[78] Judgment of 14 November 2012 in Case T-135/09 *Nexans v Commission*, para 43. In order to challenge the lack of a reasonable suspicion for adopting the inspection decision, the undertaking merely has to raise doubts in this regard (paras 69–72). If it turns out that the Commission had reasonable grounds of suspicion only for certain aspects of the investigation, this will lead to a partial annulment (at paras 91 and 93–4).

competition rules in the economic sector that shall be investigated. In line with the rather lenient requirements as regards the definition (in the decision) of the subject matter and purpose of the inspection,[79] such prior information does not have to be specific as to the temporal and geographic scope of the infringement.

Content of the decision

Article 20(4) of Regulation 1/2003 provides that '[u]ndertakings and associations of undertakings are required to submit to inspections ordered by decision of the Commission'. Unlike simple inspections, which undertakings may oppose without thereby committing any infringement, inspections pursuant to a decision are mandatory.[80] As stated earlier, the Commission has discretion in choosing between methods of investigation and types of inspections. In general, this choice will depend on the circumstances of the case, including the attitude previously displayed by the undertaking. For example, the Commission may consider a mandatory inspection where the undertaking refused to agree to a simple inspection in the past or, after it had agreed, obstructed an earlier inspection by providing records in incomplete form; where the Commission has sufficient indications to believe that the evidence or documents sought are at risk of being destroyed or removed elsewhere if some other investigation method is employed, or if it suspects the existence of particularly serious infringements (eg, cartels) for which it would be naïve to rely on the cooperation of the undertakings concerned at the stage of the inspection.[81] Generally, the choice of a mandatory inspection will be the norm rather than the exception. Before carrying out such an inspection, the Commission must first 'consult' the NCA with jurisdiction in the respective territory. However, this can be done informally, if necessary by phone.[82] **8.19**

The Commission is expected to take particular care in drafting binding inspection decisions and in stating the grounds on which they are based.[83] Besides subject matter and purpose,[84] the decision must indicate the (earliest) date on which the inspection is to begin and the penalties provided for in Article 23 (fine of up to 1 per cent of the total turnover of the undertaking in the preceding business year for any violation of its procedural duties) and Article 24 (penalty of up to 5 per cent of the average (total) daily turnover of the undertaking in the preceding business year per day of delay in fulfilling its duties). In addition, the Commission shall also refer to the right to have the decision reviewed by the EU Courts. **8.20**

---

[79] See para 8.14.

[80] Undertakings could, in theory, attempt to paralyse the course of an inspection by applying to the GC for interim measures under Arts 278 and 279 TFEU. However, according to Art 278 cl 1 TFEU the mere application for interim relief, like the main action, does not have suspensory effect and it is unrealistic to consider that it would be dealt with by the GC, even by way of an *ex parte* order, before the inspection has been completed. See also Kerse & Khan, *EC Antitrust Procedure* (6th edn, Sweet & Maxwell 2012) para 3-134, indicating that the balance of interests (weighing up the possibility of serious and irreparable damage to the undertaking and the risk of evidence disappearing) will likely be in favour of the Commission. However, the undertaking will be able to seek judicial redress before the GC *ex post* by lodging an action for annulment against the decision ordering an inspection, a right of which the addressee has to be informed in the decision itself pursuant to Art 20(4) of Reg 1/2003.

[81] However, even then the Commission might combine mandatory and simple inspections, with the latter targeted at the immunity applicant that can be assumed to cooperate during the investigation.

[82] Case 5/85 *AKZO Chemie v Commission* [1986] ECR 2585, para 24. See also European Commission Antitrust Manual of Procedures, Internal DG Competition working documents on procedures for the application of Articles 101 and 102 TFEU, March 2012, Module 3 'Cooperation with National Competition Authorities in EU and exchange of information in ECN', para 54(b).

[83] In *Roquette Frères*, the ECJ indicated that it suffices if the decision—the operative part and the recitals which motivate the decision—summarizes the main features of the infringement of Arts 101 and 102 TFEU (product, types of anticompetitive conduct and possibly their setting) and the undertaking's participation therein. See Case C-94/00 *Roquette Frères* [2002] ECR I-9011, paras 10, 11, and 87–9, and the earlier explanations with respect to simple inspections.

[84] See para 8.14.

Such judicial review is independent of any final decision on an infringement of Articles 101 and 102 TFEU which might be adopted at the conclusion of the investigation. The undertaking may apply for annulment under Article 263 TFEU, without such action, however, having any suspensory effect, as provided in Article 278 TFEU.[85] Where the undertaking has not sought its annulment, it will be prevented from pleading the illegality of the inspection decision in any subsequent action for annulment of the Commission decision finding a substantive infringement.[86] Conversely, since in the context of an action for the annulment of the inspection decision, an undertaking may not challenge the lawfulness of the way in which an inspection has been carried out,[87] the latter aspect may (only) be raised in an action against the final decision (on substance) adopted by the Commission.[88]

8.21 Not mentioned in Article 20(4) as an element of the inspection decision, probably because it is obvious, is the name or trading name of the undertaking to be investigated and the address of a legal entity (or entities) forming part of the undertaking. The (trading) name is important, since the Commission's powers relate to the undertaking as defined in the decision. Linked to this is the information concerning the address, which serves to identify the undertaking, rather than to limit the Commission's powers to the specific location.[89] Typically, the inspection

---

[85] Under EU law, the undertaking has to accept that measures adopted by the institutions are fully effective as long as they have not been declared invalid by the courts, and to recognize their enforceability unless the courts have decided to suspend the operation of the said measures. See Joined Cases 46/87 and 227/88 *Hoechst v Commission* [1989] ECR 2859, para 64. If the decision in question is annulled by the EU judicature, the Commission will be prevented from using, for the purposes of proceedings in respect of an infringement of the EU competition rules, any documents or evidence which it might have obtained in the course of that investigation. An infringement decision based on such evidence would be illegal and could itself be annulled by the EU judicature. See Case C-94/00 *Roquette Frères* [2002] ECR I-9011, para 49; Case T-59/99 *Ventouris v Commission* [2003] ECR II-5257, para 126. It is therefore not necessary, but also not admissible, in an annulment action against the inspection decision to ask the court to order the Commission to remove the evidence obtained during an illegal inspection from the file. See Case T-266/03 *Groupement des cartes bancaires (CB) v Commission* [2007] ECR II-83, para 78. However, as Art 266 TFEU requires the Commission 'to take the necessary measures to comply with the judgment', it has to return the evidence obtained in case the inspection decision is annulled (unless it is covered by a subsequent request for information by which the Commission has legitimately extended the scope of the investigation, see Judgment of 12 December 2012 in Case T-410/09 *Almamet v Commission*, para 50 et seq).

[86] Cf Joined Cases T-305/94 to T-307/94, T-313/94 to T-316/94, T-318/94, T-325/94, T-328/94, T-329/94 and T-335/94 *Limburgse Vinyl Maatschappij and others v Commission* [1999] ECR II-931, paras 396, 397, 406, and 408–10. This is different where the inspection decision was addressed to another undertaking (para 411). For a special case in which the undertaking contested the legality of the decision finding an infringement of Art 101 TFEU on the ground that the inspected entity was not the addressee of the inspection decision, which meant that the evidence would have been illegally obtained, see Case T-66/99 *Minoan Lines v Commission* [2003] ECR II-5515, para 41 et seq.

[87] See Case 85/87 *Dow Benelux v Commission* [1989] ECR 3137, para 49; Judgment of 14 November 2012 in Case T-135/09 *Nexans v Commission*, para 115 et seq. The latter case concerned an action for annulment concerning two acts, namely the taking by the inspectors of an integral copy of a computer hard drive and the request for certain explanations from a company employee. The GC considered that these acts constituted intermediate measures (merely) implementing the inspection decision and that any refusal to comply could only have been penalized based on a separate decision pursuant to Art 23(1) of Reg 1/2003 which could be challenged before the EU Courts. It indicated that the assessment might be different if the undertaking had claimed that specific documents were protected under EU law (eg legal professional privilege, 'LPP').

[88] Cf Joined Cases T-305/94 to T-307/94, T-313/94 to T-316/94, T-318/94, T-325/94, T-328/94, T-329/94 and T-335/94 *Limburgse Vinyl Maatschappij and others v Commission* [1999] ECR II-931, paras 396, 397, 405, and 413; Judgment of 14 November 2012 in Case T-135/09 *Nexans v Commission*, para 132 (indicating that a challenge could be brought against a separate decision imposing fines pursuant to Art 23(1) of Reg 1/2003). Likewise, the allegation that the inspection impinged upon the right of self-incrimination may also be raised in an appeal against the final decision. See Kerse & Khan, *EC Antitrust Procedure* (6th edn, Sweet & Maxwell 2012), para 3-136. See also K Lenaerts and J Maselis, 'Procedural Rights and Issues in the Enforcement of Articles 81 and 82 of the EC Treaty' [2001] Fordham International Law Journal 1615, 1624.

[89] See *Akzo Chemicals* [1994] OJ L294/31, para 16.

decision will be addressed to the company which, based on the information at hand, was directly involved in the putative infringement, and, where applicable, the parent company of the group (or at least an intermediate holding having sector responsibility), with a further reference to 'all companies directly or indirectly controlled by it'. The decision will also make clear that inspections may be carried out at all premises of any of these companies. Although the Commission is under no obligation to disclose the evidence in its possession, the ECJ held in its judgment in *Hoechst* that the Commission must clearly indicate in its decision the allegations it intends to substantiate through the inspection.[90] The date on which the inspection 'is to begin' must also be indicated in the decision, but is not necessarily the actual day of commencement but rather marks the earliest point in time at which the inspection may take place (and this is how it is often indicated in inspection decisions). Inspections may not begin on the first day indicated but one or more days later because of unforeseen delays. Commencement on a date later than indicated does not render the inspection unlawful, provided that it takes place within a reasonable period of time thereafter. No end date has to be given and in fact could be fixed as the duration of an inspection depends on various factors which cannot be foreseen from the outset (eg the scope of the investigation, including the volume of electronic data,[91] the size and number of the premises ultimately inspected, technical problems encountered on site, obstruction, etc). As regards penalties, the decision indicates the potential fines provided for in Article 23(1)(c) to (e) which may be imposed in the event of a refusal to submit to the inspection, the production of required books or other business records in incomplete form, the failure or refusal to provide a complete answer as well as incorrect or misleading answers in response to questions on the spot (Article 20(2)(e)), or the breach of a seal affixed in accordance with Article 20(2)(d).[92] It also details the periodic penalty payments which may be applied for a refusal to submit to the inspection.[93]

Irrespective of the requirements for a sufficient motivation of the inspection decision, the Commission may be under a duty, first formulated by the ECJ in *Roquette Frères* and then adopted into Articles 20(8) and 21(3) of Regulation 1/2003, to provide more detailed explanations to the national judge where his prior judicial authorization is required.[94] In this regard, the ECJ has explained that: **8.22**

> [w]hilst the matters which must feature in the investigation decision itself, particularly under Article 14(3) of Regulation No 17 [now Article 20(4) of Regulation 1/2003], correspond in part to the information which must be communicated to the competent national court so as to enable that court to carry out its review, that information may also emanate from other sources.[95]

---

[90] Joined Cases 46/87 and 227/88 *Hoechst v Commission* [1989] ECR 2859, para 41. See also the earlier explanations with respect to simple inspections on the requirement to set out the subject matter and purpose of the inspection (para 8.14).

[91] In fact, para 11 of the Explanatory note to an authorisation to conduct an inspection in execution of a Commission decision under Article 20(4) of Council Regulation No 1/2003 foresees the possibility of taking an integral copy of a digital storage medium (forensic image), for instance where access to selected data is not possible in situ. In this case a digital copy will be taken to the Commission's premises (Brussels) in a sealed envelope, where it will be searched in the presence of company representatives. This procedure can significantly prolong the inspection, which will only be considered complete once the search has been concluded and the undertaking has been handed a signed list of the copies taken from the forensic image.

[92] Article 23(1)(c) of Reg 1/2003.

[93] Article 24(1)(e) of Reg 1/2003.

[94] Case C-94/00 *Roquette Frères* [2002] ECR I-9011, paras 61, 81, and 99. According to Art 20(8) of Reg 1/2003, the Commission may be required to provide 'detailed explanations in particular on the grounds the Commission has for suspecting [an] infringement of Articles [101] and [102] of the Treaty, as well as on the seriousness of the suspected infringement and on the nature of the involvement of the undertaking concerned.'

[95] Case C-94/00 *Roquette Frères* [2002] ECR I-9011, para 97.

Hence, when seeking judicial authorization, the Commission (as well as the NCA) may rely on additional information not included in the inspection decision.

Procedure

8.23 As regards the adoption of inspection decisions, there is no requirement for the undertaking concerned to be allowed to submit observations, for a consultation of the Advisory Committee, or for the decision to be published.[96] Any decision is adopted, in the official language of the Member State where the undertaking is located,[97] by the Director-General of DG COMP in sub-delegation from the Member of the Commission with special responsibility for competition (who in turn has been empowered to act on behalf of the Commission).[98] Inspection decisions which impose periodic penalty payments are subject to the special rules governing such penalties.[99]

Other documents

8.24 Together with the inspection decision in the strict sense, the inspectors deliver to the undertaking both the authorization empowering them personally to carry out the inspection,[100] and an explanatory note setting out the rights and duties of the undertaking and certain powers of the inspectors.[101] At the time a certified copy of the decision is delivered, the inspectors draw up a minute of notification (to be signed by the undertaking).[102]

---

[96] Although inspection decisions are not published, the Commission services will typically confirm the carrying out of inspections by way of a press release if there are press inquiries or announcements by the inspected undertakings. See eg MEMO/04/20 'Spokesperson's statement on inspections at manufacturers of elevators and escalators' of 29 January 2004.

[97] European Commission Antitrust Manual of Procedures, Internal DG Competition working documents on procedures for the application of Articles 101 and 102 TFEU, March 2012, Module 27 'Use of languages in antitrust proceedings', para 21.

[98] See European Commission Antitrust Manual of Procedures, Internal DG Competition working documents on procedures for the application of Articles 101 and 102 TFEU, March 2012, Module 1 'Decision-making procedures', paras 25–8 and 40. The Court confirmed the legality of the empowerment in its judgments in Case 5/85 *AKZO v Commission* [1986] ECR 2585, paras 28–41, Joined Cases 46/87 and 227/88 *Hoechst v Commission* [1989] ECR 2859, paras 44–6, and Joined Cases 97–99/87 *Dow Chemical Ibérica v Commission* [1989] ECR 3165, para 57–9. According to the latter judgment (para 59), there is no provision which requires that the copy of the decision notified to the undertaking must be signed by the person exercising the delegated power. Instead, the decision may be duly certified as authentic by signature of the Secretary-General of the Commission.

[99] See Ch 9, 'Procedural Infringements: Fines and Periodic Penalty Payments'. It should be noted that the decision imposing (provisional) periodic penalty payments pursuant to Art 24(1)(e) of Reg 1/2003 must be directly adopted by the Competition Commissioner. See European Commission Antitrust Manual of Procedures, Internal DG Competition working documents on procedures for the application of Articles 101 and 102 TFEU, March 2012, Module 1 'Decision-making procedures', paras 28 and 40.

[100] The name of the authorized official must be correctly stated, together with the number of the staff card by which the inspectors prove their identity.

[101] Explanatory note to an authorisation to conduct an inspection in execution of a Commission decision under Article 20(4) of Council Regulation No 1/2003 (available at DG COMP's website at <http://ec.europa.eu/competition/antitrust/legislation/explanatory_note.pdf>). This note differs from the one used in simple inspections as regards aspects which only apply to mandatory inspections, but is otherwise identical. One important difference is that, in case of an inspection by formal decision, the inspectors 'cannot be required to enlarge upon the subject matter as set out in the decision or to justify in any way the taking of the decision.' Conversely, in case of a simple inspection 'the Commission officials shall, at the undertakings' request, provide explanations on the subject matter and purpose of the proposed inspection'. The difference should not be surprising, given that a written authorization (unlike an inspection decision) cannot be challenged in court and that in a simple inspection the inspectors can only act in agreement with the undertaking which first might have to be persuaded that the inspection is indeed justified.

[102] Explanatory note to an authorisation to conduct an inspection in execution of a Commission decision under Article 20(4) of Council Regulation No 1/2003, para 3. According to case law, '[a] decision is properly notified within the meaning of the Treaty, if it reaches the addressee and puts the latter in a position to take

4. Surprise inspections

For obvious reasons, Article 20 of Regulation 1/2003 does not require the Commission to **8.25**
give undertakings prior notice of inspections. Giving prior notice (Article 20(3)) or carrying
out a consultation (Article 20(4))[103] is required only with regard to the competent authorities of the Member State concerned. Whether to proceed by simple or mandatory inspection
is a matter for the Commission to decide, taking into account the circumstances of each
individual case.[104] Simple inspections are usually announced in advance, as the undertaking
may in any event refuse to submit to them. The responsible officials may in such cases speak
directly by phone with the executives representing the undertaking[105] to explain the purpose
of the inspection and to set a date for it to be carried out. Inspections pursuant to a binding
decision could in principle also be announced, but are typically surprise inspections without
prior notice. They are warranted in particular where the Commission believes that there is
a risk that documents will be destroyed if the company is alerted beforehand.[106] In the early
days, the Commission resorted very rarely to surprise inspections, often referred to as 'dawn
raids'.[107] The toughening of EU competition policy in the 1990s gave rise—in addition to
increased fines for infringements of Articles 101 and 102 TFEU[108]—to a refocusing of investigatory work, reflected in the increased use of unannounced inspections.

Today, the Commission resorts with more frequency to surprise inspections. If it were unable **8.26**
to do so, it would be deprived of a particularly effective method of uncovering incriminating
evidence, and its position in annulment actions brought by undertakings against infringement decisions would be considerably weakened. In this respect, the surge in the number of
unannounced inspections can also be explained by the top priority given by the Commission
to the fight against illegal cartel activity. In *National Panasonic*, the ECJ confirmed the legality of surprise inspections. According to the court, such inspections do not infringe the fundamental rights of the undertaking, including Article 8 ECHR (inviolability of the home).[109]
In its view, the exercise of the investigative powers vested in the Commission contributes to

---

cognizance of it'. See Case 6/72 *Europemballage Corporation and Continental Can v Commission* [1973] ECR
215, para 10.

[103] This can be done informally, for instance by telephone. See Case 5/85 *AKZO Chemie v Commission*
[1986] ECR 2585, para 24.

[104] Case 136/79 *National Panasonic v Commission* [1980] ECR 2033, para 29: 'The Commission's
choice between an investigation by straightforward authorisation and an investigation ordered by a decision
[depends]...on the need for an appropriate inquiry, having regard to the special features of the case.'

[105] In order to be able to initiate an inspection, it is sufficient that the company representatives submit to
it, not each and every employee. In fact, it is not atypical that the management of the undertaking does not
inform the employees beforehand, for instance when it suspects that some of them have been involved in a
cartel and might not cooperate voluntarily in the investigation.

[106] For an example, see *Graphite Electrodes* [2002] OJ L100/1, para 33: 'by the time the investigation
started, all the relevant files had been "reviewed" and incriminating documents destroyed or moved to a
safe location away from offices and private homes.' The Commission does not need to set out whether
and why it is concerned that an undertaking might conceal or destroy evidence. For other reasons why the
Commission might decide to undertake a mandatory inspection see European Commission, 'Dealing with
the Commission—Notifications, complaints, inspections and fact-finding powers under Articles [101] and
[102] of the [TFEU]' (1997 edn) point 5.3 (company has refused to submit to voluntary inspection; in the
past it has refused to cooperate voluntarily, for instance with regard to a request for information; it has previously made false statements or otherwise misled the Commission; the investigation involves a number of
different companies located in more than one Member State and it is important for the effectiveness of the
investigation for the Commission to be able to conduct simultaneous inspections at a number of premises).

[107] European Commission, 'Dealing with the Commission—Notifications, complaints, inspections and
fact-finding powers under Articles [101] and [102] of the [TFEU]' (1997 edn) points 5.1, 5.3.

[108] See Ch 11, 'Infringement Decisions and Penalties'.

[109] As regards the applicability of Art 8 ECHR and Art 7 of the Charter of Fundamental Rights of the
European Union, see paras 8.05 and 8.06.

the maintenance of the system of competition intended by the Treaty which undertakings are absolutely bound to comply with.[110]

8.27 Nor does an unannounced inspection as such[111] infringe the right to be heard. As the ECJ has pointed out, the immediate objective of a Commission inspection is not to terminate an infringement or to establish that a certain conduct is incompatible with Articles 101 or 102 TFEU. Its sole aim is to enable the Commission to gather the necessary information for checking the actual existence and scope of a potential infringement.[112] This also affects the extent of the motivation which must be provided in the inspection decision.[113] The need for the Commission to collect the necessary information in order to appraise whether an infringement of the Treaty rules on competition has been committed provides sufficient justification for surprise inspections as regards the proportionality principle.[114]

C. Representation of Undertakings during Inspections

1. Representatives and members of staff

8.28 Article 20 of Regulation 1/2003, unlike Article 18(4) in relation to requests for information, does not specify who is permitted to represent undertakings during inspections. However, Article 18(4) reflects the general principle that it is for the undertakings to designate the person or persons who will represent them in the investigation. This also implies a responsibility to swiftly come forward with a representative who may act on behalf of the undertaking during the inspection.[115] The Commission inspectors have neither the authority nor the means

---

[110] See Case 136/79 *National Panasonic v Commission* [1980] ECR 2033, para 20. See also Case 5/85 *AKZO Chemie v Commission* [1986] ECR 2585, para 27.

[111] However, this does not mean that the undertaking could not claim (the violation of) certain rights of defence, for instance the right to involve a lawyer or the right to LPP. See Joined Cases 46/87 and 227/88 *Hoechst v Commission* [1989] ECR 2859, paras 15 and 16. See also Case 85/87 *Dow Benelux v Commission* [1989] ECR 3137, para 18.

[112] Case 136/79 *National Panasonic v Commission* [1980] ECR 2033, para 21. See also Joined Cases 97/87, 98/87 and 99/87 *Dow Chemical Ibérica v Commission* [1989] ECR 1369, para 55 (with respect to the presumption of innocence).

[113] See Case T-23/09 *CNOP and CCG v Commission* [2010] ECR II-5291, paras 41 and 68. This parallels the situation as regards requests for information. Cf Opinion of AG Kokott of 14 April 2011 in Case C-109/10 P *Solvay v Commission*, para 144.

[114] Case 136/79 *National Panasonic v Commission* [1980] ECR 2033, para 30. The fact that the inspection decision has to be sufficiently motivated and that the inspectors only have limited powers (they cannot use force to compel the undertaking to submit to an inspection or provide access to specific documents) also plays a role here, as these elements provide safeguards against arbitrary or disproportionate intervention. See Joined Cases 46/87 and 227/88 *Hoechst v Commission* [1989] ECR 2859, paras 19, 29, 31, and 37, and the explanations at para 8.05.

[115] European Commission, 'Dealing with the Commission—Notification, complaints, inspections and fact-finding powers under Articles [101] and [102] of the [TFEU]' (1997 edn) point 5.6: 'the firm has the responsibility of designating competent representatives to deal with requests from the Commission's inspectors. Such persons must be well informed and able to provide the inspectors with the assistance they require.' In *Mewac* [1993] OJ L20/6, the Secretary-General as the sole representative of the association was absent at the time the inspection decision was notified. When the inspectors contacted him by phone, he claimed that in the absence of any lawyer who could represent him at the premises, he could not allow the inspectors access to any documents until his return the following day. The Commission considered this as a refusal to submit to the inspection by stating that 'there was no material reason why the Commission decision could not be implemented: had the Conference so wished, the Commission officials could have been joined either promptly by any legal representative or adviser designated by the Conference or, later in the day, by the Secretary-General himself or his Paris-based lawyer; in the latter case, the Conference could have allowed the Commission officials, with the help of the Conference staff present at the time, to begin an initial examination of documents relating to the subject-matter of the investigation, on the understanding that the Secretary-General or his representative could, as soon as they arrived, add any appropriate comments.'

to safely judge the competence or knowledge of the persons designated by the undertaking[116]—it does so at its own risk[117]—and their prime interest is to have a proper interlocutor during the inspection to whom any requests can be addressed. It is for the undertakings to ensure that their representatives on such occasions are competent and well informed, as this helps not only the inspectors but also (and perhaps even in particular) benefits their own interests. The undertakings may ask for their legal advisers to be present in order to exercise their rights of defence during the inspection, which, however, is not a prerequisite for the investigation to be lawful.[118]

2. Oral explanations and rectification

It should be noted that the officials and other accompanying persons authorized by the **8.29** Commission to conduct an inspection have the power to ask any representative or member of staff of the undertaking or association of undertakings for explanations on facts and documents relating to the subject matter and purpose of the inspection. The corresponding provision in Regulation 17 (Article 14(1)(c)) empowered the inspectors 'to ask for oral explanations on the spot' and there was a surprising lack of authority on what this meant. The generally accepted view was that it encompassed asking questions directly arising from the books and records being examined (eg explanations of specific terms or abbreviations), but did not allow for a general interrogation of officers or employees of the undertaking.[119] Also, Article 14 of Regulation 17 did not specify who should answer the oral questions put to the undertaking, but a failure by the undertaking to come forward with a suitable representative could be construed as a refusal to cooperate. These uncertainties have been remedied by Article 20(2)(e) of Regulation 1/2003, which has expanded the Commission's powers to ask questions.[120] The inspectors may now inquire with 'any representative or member of staff' for explanations on *facts* and documents relating to *the subject matter and purpose* of the inspection. The answers can be recorded.

Article 23(1)(d) provides that the Commission may fine undertakings up to 1 per cent of **8.30** their total turnover in the preceding business year if, in response to a question asked in accordance with Article 20(2)(e):

- they give an incorrect or misleading answer;
- they fail to rectify within a time limit set by the Commission an incorrect, incomplete, or misleading answer given by a member of staff; or
- they fail or refuse to provide a complete answer on facts relating to the subject matter and purpose of an inspection ordered by a decision adopted pursuant to Article 20(4).

---

[116] Cf *Fabbrica Pisana* [1980] OJ L75/30, para 10: 'it is not for the Commission's inspectors to assess or dispute the competence or extent of knowledge of the representatives of the undertakings they are investigating. The undertakings named in investigation authorisations are alone responsible for designating their representatives.'

[117] In *Fabbrica Pisana* [1980] OJ L75/30, the Commission explained that it is not permissible for an undertaking which has not produced certain documents requested by the inspectors to argue that its failure to do so was caused by the absence of its general manager and that the sales manager was unaware of the whereabouts of the documents concerned.

[118] Judgment of 27 September 2012 in Case T-357/06 *Koninklijke Wegenbouw Stevin v Commission*, para 232.

[119] See also European Commission, 'Dealing with the Commission—Notifications, complaints, inspections and fact-finding powers under Articles [101] and [102] of the [TFEU]' (1997 edn) point 5.6: 'the power should not be used to pressure the officials of a firm into making oral admissions which they would not make if they had the time for reflection afforded them by a written request under Article 11.'

[120] Proposal for a Council Regulation on the implementation of the rules on competition laid down in Articles 81 and 82 of the Treaty, COM(2000) 582 final, explanations on Art 20 of Reg 1/2003.

8.31 Unlike some national laws, Regulation 1/2003 grants no powers to impose fines on individuals, but only on the undertakings for which they act or which employ them. As regards members of staff who were not authorized to act on behalf of the undertaking, a fine may be imposed on the undertaking for failure or refusal to rectify any incomplete, incorrect, or misleading answers provided by the employee during the inspection. The Commission shall set a time limit within which the undertaking (or association of undertakings) may communicate to the Commission any rectification, amendment, or supplement to the explanations given by such member of staff.[121] It should be noted, though, that the failure (or refusal) to supply a *complete* answer cannot be sanctioned in case of simple inspections,[122] which logically entails that the same applies where the undertaking fails to rectify an incomplete answer. Hence, with regard to simple inspections, Article 23(1)(d), second indent, has a narrower scope of application than its wording appears to suggest.

8.32 The possibility of rectification is only granted with regard to members of staff 'not authorised by the undertaking or association of undertakings to provide explanations'. Undertakings might also wish, however, to rectify or supplement answers provided by staff 'authorised' to act on behalf of the undertaking or association. Whether the Commission will accept such rectification without imposing a fine will likely depend on the circumstances of the case, for instance on the functional authority of the employee who replied or whether there are any indications of bad faith on the part of the undertaking at the time the incorrect or misleading answer was provided.[123]

3. Assistance from a lawyer or legal adviser

8.33 The right to be assisted by a lawyer during inspections is stipulated neither in Regulation 1/2003 nor in the Implementing Regulation 773/2004. It is, however, consistent Commission practice to allow undertakings to consult their own legal advisers or independent lawyers. This results from the general principle that undertakings under investigation are protected by various EU guarantees, including, in particular, the right to legal representation.[124] However, that right does not imply any limitation on the investigative powers of the Commission. The EU Courts have clarified that an inspection carried out without awaiting the arrival of an undertaking's legal adviser is lawful, and that the undertaking commits a procedural infringement if it prevents the inspectors from entering on the ground that it is not represented by legal counsel.[125] At the same

---

[121] Article 4(3) of Reg 773/2004. Recital 4 of Reg 773/2004 clarifies that the original answer will remain in the Commission file as recorded during the inspection. This suggests that the original answer, albeit rectified, may be used by the Commission as evidence, at least in order to counter the revised version of facts submitted by the undertaking's (legal) representatives.

[122] See Art 20(3) and Art 23(1)(d), third indent, which shows that a sanction can only be imposed if the inspectors acted on the basis of a formal decision pursuant to Art 20(4) of Reg 1/2003. See also Ch 9, 'Procedural Infringements: Fines and Periodic Penalty Payments'. At the same time, Art 23(1)(d), second indent, allows for a sanction where incorrect or misleading answers from an unauthorized member of staff are not rectified on time, even in the case of simple inspections.

[123] Cf A Jones and B Sufrin, *EC Competition Law* (2nd edn, Oxford University Press 2004) 1071.

[124] Case C-94/00 *Roquette Frères* [2002] ECR I-9011, para 46, with further references. See also Case 155/79 *AM & S Europe Limited v Commission* [1982] ECR 1575, paras 18–27 (on LPP).

[125] Judgment of 27 September 2012 in Case T-357/06 *Koninklijke Wegenbouw Stevin v Commission*, paras 225–32 and 233. Cf also Case 136/79 *National Panasonic v Commission* [1980] ECR 2033, paras 6 and 21. According to A Jones and B Sufrin, *EC Competition Law* (2nd edn, Oxford University Press 2004) 1064, Commission officials arrived at Panasonic's offices in Slough at 10.00am. The directors asked if the inspection could be delayed to await the arrival of their solicitor, who was in Norwich. The officials waited until 10.45am and then proceeded with the inspection. The solicitor did not arrive until 1.45pm and the inspection finished at 5.30pm. The Court held that National Panasonic's fundamental rights had not been infringed during the investigation, although it did not expressly consider the legal adviser point. Note that refusing to submit to the inspection until a particular designated representative of the firm or a particular lawyer can be present may lead to the imposition of a fine pursuant to Art 23(1)(c) of Reg 1/2003.

time, there is some debate as to whether the added power of the Commission to address a member of staff for providing oral explanations presupposes that such persons be assisted by their own lawyer. Depending on national rules, they may be liable to sanctions for their personal involvement in anticompetitive practices.[126] However, for the purpose of the Commission investigation, the staff member is not the real subject of the inquiry as he or she is only questioned on behalf of the undertaking[127] and no incrimination of that individual may occur under EU competition law.[128] Hence, there does not appear to be a legal duty for the Commission to refrain from interviewing staff members in the absence of a lawyer,[129] even though it might be appropriate to give the employee an opportunity to consult a lawyer where there is a clear risk of self-incrimination and the employee has specifically requested this.

In procedural terms, the Commission has a policy of allowing firms a reasonable time to **8.34** secure the services of an in-house legal adviser or lawyer of their choice, although it will not permit undue delay.[130] During any waiting period the undertaking's management must ensure that business records remain as they were on the officials' arrival and the officials have to be allowed to enter and remain in the offices of their choice.[131] In other words, there must be no opportunity for the operation of the paper-shredder or the wiping of the hard-drive.

D. The Commission's Ordinary Powers during Inspections

The powers of the Commission during inspections are the same for simple inspections, pur- **8.35** suant to Article 20(3), and those based on a binding decision pursuant to Article 20(4) of

---

[126] While national sanctions may be envisaged, Art 12(3) of Reg 1/2003 limits the possibility that the information collected during a Commission investigation be used by a national authority to impose sanctions on natural persons, and in all cases excludes custodial sanctions on that basis. If an individual provides incriminating information in a Commission investigation, or refuses to answer, a Member State should not be permitted to use the statements or the fact of such silence in subsequent national criminal proceedings targeting that individual. See E Gippini-Fournier, 'Legal Professional Privilege in Competition Proceedings before the European Commission: Beyond the Cursory Glance' ch 24 in BE Hawk (ed), *International Antitrust Law & Policy* (Annual Proceedings of the Fordham Institute 2004) 587, 643.

[127] This is why the undertaking has the right to rectify, amend, or supplement statements made by unauthorized members of staff. See Art 4(3) of Reg 773/2004.

[128] The member of staff would not face any personal sanction, neither for incomplete, incorrect, or misleading answers, nor for the infringement as such. Article 23(1)(d) of Reg 1/2003 foresees that fines may only be imposed on the undertaking. K Dekeyser and C Gauer, 'The New Enforcement System for Articles 81 and 82 and the Rights of Defence' ch 23 in BE Hawk (ed), *International Antitrust Law & Policy* (Annual Proceedings of the Fordham Institute 2005) 549, 559–64. However, if during a mandatory inspection, the individual requested to provide oral explanations refuses to answer the question and the undertaking does not provide the information by other means, the latter may be held liable.

[129] This is different from interviews pursuant to Art 19 of Reg 1/2003. See European Commission Antitrust Manual of Procedures, Internal DG Competition working documents on procedures for the application of Articles 101 and 102 TFEU, March 2012, Module 8 'Power to take statements', para 15: 'The interviewee may decide to be accompanied by a person of his/her choice, e.g. a lawyer.' See also para 20, where it is recommended to draw the attention of the interviewee to the fact that he or she is entitled to be accompanied by a lawyer.

[130] European Commission, 'Dealing with the Commission—Notifications, complaints, inspections and fact-finding powers under Articles [101] and [102] of the [TFEU]' (1997 edn) point 5.5. See also the Explanatory note to an authorisation to conduct an inspection in execution of a Commission decision under Article 20(4) of Council Regulation No 1/2003, para 6, according to which any delay must be kept 'to the strict minimum'. The inspectors will allow the company to call its external lawyers to attend the inspection. However, they are not obliged to wait until the lawyers arrive, and in practice are unlikely to wait for more than a short time period before proceeding with the investigation. See Judgment of 27 September 2012 in Case T-357/06 *Koninklijke Wegenbouw Stevin v Commission*, para 232.

[131] Judgment of 27 September 2012 in Case T-357/06 *Koninklijke Wegenbouw Stevin v Commission*, para 232.

Regulation 1/2003. The main difference lies in the fact that undertakings may object to the former but not to the latter (and thus may be fined and forced to comply if they do not voluntarily submit to the inspection). However, if undertakings agree to submit to a simple inspection, the legal framework pursuant to Articles 20(3) and 23(1)(c), (d) of Regulation 1/2003 suggests that they are required to enable the inspectors to exercise all their powers and must present all documentation requested in complete form, as if the inspection would be carried out pursuant to a decision. As for simple requests for information, representatives of the undertaking and other members of staff are not obliged to provide *complete* answers when asked for explanations during a simple inspection, but this should be made transparent, as otherwise the undertaking faces the risk of being sanctioned pursuant to Article 23(1)(d), first or second indent, if such an answer is misleading (and if it is not rectified on time by the undertaking where the answer was provided by an unauthorized member of staff).

8.36 Pursuant to Article 20(2) of Regulation 1/2003 the Commission powers include the right to:

(i) enter any premises, land, and means of transport of undertakings and associations of undertakings;

(ii) examine the books and other records related to the business, irrespective of the medium on which they are stored;

(iii) take or obtain in any form copies of or extracts from such books or records;

(iv) seal any business premises and books or records for the period and to the extent necessary for the inspection;

(v) ask any representative or member of staff of the undertaking or association of undertakings for explanations on facts or documents relating to the subject matter and purpose of the inspection and to record the answers.

8.37 In the sections that follow, the five powers pursuant to Article 20(2) will be dealt with in turn, and the practical implications of each will be considered.

1. Access to premises, land, and means of transport of undertakings or associations of undertakings

8.38 Commission inspectors are entitled to unrestricted access[132] to all buildings, land, and vehicles of undertakings.[133] This includes, in particular, access to all offices which may contain documents and/or files relating to the investigation. Regulation 1/2003 does not speak exclusively of administrative premises or in any way restricts the access of the inspectors. It is up to them to select the premises, dwellings, land, or vehicles for their investigation. The Commission takes the view that its powers of inspection are not limited to premises owned or leased by the undertaking; what matters is where the business of the undertaking is carried out.[134]

---

[132] Undertakings may not prevent Commission officials from entering by claiming inviolability of their premises. See Cases 46/87 and 227/88 *Hoechst v Commission* [1989] ECR 2859, para 17 et seq and 26–7. The Court has recognized 'that the need for protection against arbitrary or disproportionate intervention by public authorities in the sphere of the private activities of any person, whether natural or legal, constitutes a general principle of Community law', but that the existence of the power of judicial review conferred on the EU courts and the detailed rules governing the exercise by the Commission of its investigatory powers help to protect undertakings against arbitrary measures and to keep such measures within the limits of what is necessary in order to prevent competition from being distorted to the detriment of the public interest, individual undertakings and consumers. See Case C-94/00 *Roquette Frères* [2002] ECR I-9011, paras 27 and 29 and 50; Case T-266/03 *Groupement des cartes bancaires (CB) v Commission* [2007] ECR II-83, paras 68–72; Case T-23/09 *CNOP and CCG v Commission* [2010] ECR II-5291, para 40.

[133] For the interpretation of the term 'undertaking' see Case T-23/09 *CNOP and CCG v Commission* [2010] ECR II-5291, para 67 et seq.

[134] See *Akzo Chemicals* [1994] OJ L294/31, para 19.

Also, the inspection may encompass business premises occupied by third parties which are authorized (for instance as an agent) to act in the undertaking's stead.[135] However, this power does not extend to premises of external lawyers or accountants used by the undertaking, even if such persons may well hold 'books or other business records' belonging to the undertaking being investigated.[136]

The extent of the Commission's powers was explained in *Hoechst*.[137] Inspectors are empow-   **8.39** ered to enter such premises as they choose and to have shown to them the contents of any piece of furniture (eg cupboard, drawer) they indicate, as well as any document they request. They are *not* empowered to obtain access to premises or furniture by force or to carry out searches without the undertaking's consent. If the undertaking does not submit to the investigation, Article 20(6) of Regulation 1/2003 comes into play and the Commission has to rely on the assistance of the Member State authorities.[138]

The Commission is also entitled to investigate businesses which themselves are not suspected   **8.40** of any infringement of the competition rules. It may wish to see documents in the possession of competitors, customers or suppliers, or of third party complainants. However, in such cases the Commission is unlikely to carry out an inspection but will rather request such information by simple letter (Article 18(2)) or formal decision (Article 18(3) of Regulation 1/2003); if an inspection is considered necessary at all, the Commission would be likely to warn the relevant business in advance (no surprise inspection). The power of entry under Regulation 17 did not extend to a director's private home. In practice, if documents were located outside the company's premises, the inspectors could only request the company to produce them. Under Regulation 1/2003, the Commission has been granted an express power to inspect non-business premises, including private homes of directors, managers, and other members of staff.[139]

2. Examination of books and other business records

Business records in general

The term 'business records' embraces all documentation, in writing or otherwise, related to the   **8.41** undertaking's business.[140] Records include correspondence, calendars, business and financial

---

[135] See Case T-66/99 *Minoan Lines v Commission* [2003] ECR II-5515, paras 69, 70, 77, and 80–90. However, '[i]t would be excessive and contrary to the provisions of Regulation No 4056/86 [the old maritime equivalent of Reg 1/2003] and fundamental principles of law to allow the Commission a general right of access, based on an investigation decision addressed to one legal entity, to inspect premises belonging to another legal entity simply on the pretext that the latter is closely connected with the addressee of the investigation decision or that the Commission believes it will find there documents belonging to the addressee of the decision' (para 83).

[136] See Kerse & Khan, *EC Antitrust Procedure* (6th edn, Sweet & Maxwell 2012) para 3-114. Unless a decision is adopted which allows the Commission to enter the premises of these outside *advisers*, it can only require the *undertaking* under investigation to produce any relevant documents (but communications with external *lawyers* might be protected by LPP). For the obligation of undertakings to, in turn, request certain documents from third parties, see Joined Cases 2/63 to 10/63 *Società Industriale Acciaierie San Michele and Others v High Authority of the European Coal and Steel Community* [1963] ECR 327, 343. Cf also, with regard to documents held by linked undertakings, § 59(1) of the German Act against Restraints of Competition (GWB)).

[137] Cases 46/87 and 227/88 *Hoechst v Commission* [1989] ECR 2859, paras 31, 32, and 37.

[138] Where a company refuses to submit to the inspection, the Commission may impose penalty payments or fines and can obtain appropriate assistance, such as a warrant, from a national judge at the request of the NCA. See eg s 62 of the UK Competition Act 1998.

[139] Article 21 of Reg 1/2003.

[140] See, for instance, *FNICF* [1982] OJ L319/12, paras 3 and 5: correspondence, internal memoranda, minutes, or records of meetings.

documents (eg invoices, balance sheets), but also microfilms, magnetic tapes, photographs, films, videocassettes, audio cassettes, CDs, DVDs, memory sticks, data saved on desktops, laptops, or servers (including Word programs, Excel sheets, email accounts), and so on. In other words, inspections extend to all possible physical materials for the recording of information, not only written documents.[141] The only requirement is that they should relate to the economic activity of the undertaking.[142] The ECJ has also stressed how important it is to preserve the effectiveness of investigations as a necessary tool for the Commission to carry out its role as guardian of the Treaty in competition matters, ruling that the right of access would serve no useful purpose if the Commission's officials could do no more than ask for documents or files which they could identify precisely in advance. Hence, the Commission is empowered to search for any conceivable item of information, irrespective of whether it is already known or can be fully identified in advance. Without such a power, it would be impossible for the Commission to obtain the information necessary to carry out the investigation.[143]

8.42 The business nature of a document cannot be determined until after the inspectors have at least superficially examined it. In principle, a document may be assumed to be a business record if it is found at the premises and in the files of an undertaking. However, if, after examination, a document proves in fact to be entirely private, the inspectors will not study it further or take copies. In the case of written documents, the investigation may cover both final documents which have been used by undertakings for formal purposes (eg correspondence) and unofficial or informal documents (internal memoranda and minutes of meetings, hand-written notes, drafts of documents not yet finalized, etc). Regulation 1/2003 does not limit the powers of inspectors regarding the type of document to be investigated. In view of the fact that many restrictive practices—or at least, some of the most seriously restrictive ones—are secret, it would be impractical to require the Commission to find a public or formal physical record of them which often does not exist. If it were otherwise, the Commission would be prevented from exercising its powers exactly against the most reprehensible conduct from the point of view of competition law.

8.43 During the inspection, the Commission may examine information stored in electronic data systems (computers or servers) and take digital or paper copies of such information.[144] The word 'examine' should be construed broadly so as to include the right of reasonable access and use of necessary facilities for the analysis of such records.[145] In searching the IT environment, storage media, and hardware, the inspectors may thus use the search tools built into the storage media themselves (eg a document search with Windows Search or a keyword search with the Find function in Word or Windows Explorer) and/or employ dedicated software or hardware brought from outside (eg software which allows the inspectors to recover data).[146]

---

[141] Article 20(2)(b) of Reg 1/2003 specifies that the Commission may examine business records 'irrespective of the medium on which they are stored'. Hence, this power to examine encompasses all forms of information technology.

[142] Case 155/79 *AM& S Europe v Commission* [1982] ECR 1575, para 16: 'Article 14(1) [now Article 20(2)(b)] in particular empowers the Commission to require production of business records, that is to say, documents concerning market activities of the undertaking, in particular as regards compliance with those rules.' According to the ECJ, 'the scope of the Commission's investigatory powers does not extend to cover, in particular, documents of a non-business nature, that is to say, documents not relating to the market activities of the undertaking'. Case C-94/00 *Roquette Frères* [2002] ECR I-9011, para 45.

[143] Cases 46/87 and 227/88 *Hoechst v Commission* [1989] ECR 2859, para 27; Case T-59/99 *Ventouris v Commission* [2003] ECR II-5257, para 122.

[144] See Explanatory note to an authorisation to conduct an inspection in execution of a Commission decision under Article 20(4) of Council Regulation No 1/2003, para 9.

[145] Kerse & Khan, *EC Antitrust Procedure* (6th edn, Sweet & Maxwell 2012), para 3-116.

[146] See Explanatory note to an authorisation to conduct an inspection in execution of a Commission decision under Article 20(4) of Council Regulation No 1/2003, para 10.

The Commission's explanatory note on mandatory inspections also foresees that inspectors may **8.44** take an integral copy[147] of a digital storage medium (forensic image), for example where access to specific data is not possible *in situ* with the tools available, where the selection of documents and data would take a considerable amount of time (thus prolonging the inspection for many days), or where the inspectors consider this necessary for the preservation of information that otherwise could be lost. In this case the digital copy (DVD, hard disc, etc) is put in a sealed envelope and a replica of that copy is handed to the undertaking. The undertaking will then be invited by the Commission to attend the opening of the sealed envelope and the examination of the digital copy at the Commission's premises in Brussels, where it will receive a copy of any paper copies made and a signed list of those copies.[148] This procedure raises a number of legal questions, which so far have not been decided by the EU Courts.[149]

The limitation of the inspection to the undertaking's 'premises' in Article 20(2)(a) of Regulation **8.45** 1/2003 does not necessarily mean that the records susceptible to inspection under Article 20(2)(b) have to be *located on* the premises if instead they are *accessible from* there. This may apply to information stored in a computer system: where undertakings use computers to access information stored on a server situated elsewhere, that information is likely to be considered as coming within the ambit of the inspection.[150] Failure to cooperate in this respect—on the pretext, for example, that no one capable of operating the electronic system is available on-site—could be regarded as incomplete production of the respective business records, liable to a penalty under Article 23(1)(c) of Regulation 1/2003.

---

[147] The GC has indicated that this constitutes the taking of copies from a business record within the meaning of Art 23(2)(c) of Reg 1/2003. See Judgment of 14 November 2012 in Case T-135/09 *Nexans v Commission*, paras 28, 119, 120, and 125.

[148] See Explanatory note to an authorisation to conduct an inspection in execution of a Commission decision under Article 20(4) of Council Regulation No 1/2003, paras 11 and 12.

[149] Taking a forensic image of an entire storage medium (eg the hard disc of a computer) reverses the normal sequence of first examining the records and then taking copies of those documents which are related to, and thus relevant for, the specific investigation. However, there is no indication that the powers provided in Art 20(2) of Reg 1/2003 would have to be exercised in a particular order (cf. eg Art 20(2)(d) and (e)) and the copying of an entire storage medium does not necessarily entail a greater risk of a 'fishing expedition', given the right for company representatives to be present during the examination at the Commission's premises. Nor can it be required that the steps foreseen in Art 20(2)(b) and (c) (examination, taking of copies) necessarily have to be carried out at the premises or land where the inspection took place (Art 20(2)(a)). Rather, what seems to matter is that the inspection decision has been duly notified to the undertaking and that the copy (of the hard disc) was taken at its premises, in the course of the investigation. It has also been questioned whether the examination of the forensic image at the Commission's premises in Brussels requires the Belgian NCA (as the competition authority of the Member State where the search takes place) to be informed (Art 20(3)) or consulted (Art 20(4)). However, such information/consultation has to take place *before* the inspection takes place, which means it should rather be the NCA in the Member State where the undertaking has its premises. In case the undertaking allows the taking of an integral copy but then objects to the examination of the forensic image in Brussels, any assistance pursuant to Art 20(6) of Reg 1/2003 could indeed only be provided by the Belgian NCA, but would not be necessary given the Commission's possession of the storage medium; besides, any opposition at this stage should be considered irrelevant where the undertaking did not oppose the taking of the forensic image at its premises. Overall, there appear to be sufficient safeguards in place given that the undertaking: (i) may oppose the taking of an integral copy at its premises (the Commission then has to rely on the national authorities to overcome such opposition, and these authorities have to respect national rules and guarantees of procedure); and (ii) may be present during the examination of the datafiles to protect its rights of defence. With these safeguards, the procedure can be justified, also with a view to the principle of proportionality, bearing in mind that the alternative would be an extended inspection at the business premises, which can be very disruptive.

[150] Cf also s 27(5)(e) of the UK Competition Act 1998, which includes the power for inspectors to request access to any 'information' held in a computer and which is accessible from the premises. This suggests that even information stored on a server outside the competition authority's jurisdiction could be obtained within the framework of an inspection at the company's premises, provided there is a link to the server.

8.46 The logical basis for these wide powers of examination is the fact that it is often impossible for the Commission to specify in advance the exact documents which might be of interest for the investigation.[151] Instead, the relevance of a particular document will often become apparent only during the inspection. For obvious reasons, the undertaking itself is not entitled to determine whether any document requested to be produced is relevant.[152] However, in addition to the documents or data requested and examined by the inspectors, the undertaking is entitled to draw attention to other documents, data or information if it considers this necessary for the purpose of protecting its legitimate interest in a complete and objective clarification of the matters raised, provided that the inspection is not thereby unduly delayed.[153]

Limits to the Commission's powers, chance findings

8.47 Despite the power of Commission inspectors to examine all business records, they are authorized to take away (by obtaining copies or extracts) only those that relate directly or indirectly to the subject matter and purpose of the inspection. Hence, while the general accessibility and unrestricted *examination* of business records is essential to establish in the first place whether specific records could be relevant for the investigation—which means that only those which are manifestly outside the scope of the inspection mandate cannot be looked at[154]—their removal and *subsequent use* in Commission procedures is more narrowly circumscribed. However, even the Commission's power to take away copies is not limited to those pieces of information that are directly related to the subject matter of the investigation. For instance, in order to arrive at a more informed judgment as to the existence of an alleged infringement, it may be necessary to obtain documents of a general nature relating to the business of the undertaking in the relevant economic sector, and in particular its business strategy.[155]

8.48 As indicated, the fact that the Commission must observe certain limits in *collecting* information from undertakings does not mean that those limits apply in the same way to what the inspectors

---

[151] See Cases 46/87 and 227/88 *Hoechst v Commission* [1989] ECR 2859, para 27. Occasionally, the Commission might know exactly what documents it is looking for, for instance when it has been contacted by a whistle-blower from inside the company or by an immunity applicant. Even in such cases, however, the Commission is not obliged to specify these documents in the inspection decision or authorization if it does not wish to do so, for instance to protect the identity of the informant or any further steps in the investigation.

[152] *FNICF* [1982] OJ L319/12, para 8; *CSM* [1992] OJ L305/16. See also AG Mischo, Joined Opinion in Cases 46/87, 85/87, 97/87, 98/87, 99/87 and 227/88 *Hoechst and Others v Commission* [1989] ECR 2875, paras 27, 28, 36, 174, and 186; Case 155/79 *AM & S Europe v Commission* [1982] ECR 1575, para 17: 'since the documents which the Commission may demand are, as Article 14(1) confirms, those whose disclosure it considers "necessary" in order that it may bring to light an infringement of the Treaty rules on competition, it is in principle for the Commission itself, and not the undertaking concerned or a third party, whether an expert or an arbitrator, to decide whether or not a document must be produced to it'. This parallels the case law on requests for information, see Judgment of 22 March 2012 in Joined Cases T-458/09 and T-171/10 *Slovak Telekom v Commission*, paras 42, 43, and 55.

[153] See Explanatory note to an authorisation to conduct an inspection in execution of a Commission decision under Article 20(4) of Council Regulation No 1/2003, para 14. With respect to requests for information see also Judgment of 22 March 2012 in Joined Cases T-458/09 and T-171/10 *Slovak Telekom v Commission*, paras 71 and 72: 'It is in particular as a result of the Commission's duty to examine carefully and impartially all the relevant aspects of the individual case that it is required to prepare a decision with the required level of diligence and to take its decision on the basis of all the information which might influence that decision.'

[154] In particular, it would be naïve to think that undertakings store incriminating evidence (eg print-outs of emails, notebooks, etc) in places where they can easily be found. Rather, it must be assumed that undertakings try to hide such evidence by placing it in unexpected locations, for instance in offices where such records would not normally be expected, in files which bear an innocent label, etc. Therefore, the Commission must be allowed to search broadly without this being considered a 'fishing expedition'.

[155] For the 'Commission's duty to examine carefully and impartially all the relevant evidence in the case under investigation', and the legitimate objective of describing the wider (factual and historical) context of the conduct at issue, see Judgment of 22 March 2012 in Joined Cases T-458/09 and T-171/10 *Slovak Telekom v Commission*, paras 45, 48, 51, and 71. For the relevance of examining the business strategy in abuse cases, see Judgment of 19 April 2012 in Case C-549/10 P *Tomra Systems and Others v Commission*, paras 17–20.

may *see* (access) and *examine*. In fact, without a power to search broadly for information related to the subject matter of the investigation, it would be impossible to determine which documents are relevant and which are not. Furthermore, undertakings could impede inspections if it were left to them to decide what inspectors might or might not be allowed to examine.[156] Given its broad powers of investigation and assessment, the Commission thus has a margin of appreciation as to the business records it examines, and the extent to which it does so. In principle, its inspectors will have access to *all* information (concerning the *whole* business) accessible at the premises, on the land, or in the means of transport of the undertaking.[157]

Nevertheless, the Commission has acknowledged that its inspectors are under 'an obligation not to examine business records, or to stop examining such records, if they are obviously or in the Commission officials' opinion not related to the subject matter of the investigation'.[158] This is important to avoid 'fishing expeditions'[159] and in the light of the fact that the Commission may initiate a new inquiry or extend its investigation (eg by way of an amended or additional inspection decision, or a subsequent request for information) 'in order to verify or supplement information which it happened to obtain during a previous investigation if that information indicates the existence of conduct contrary to the competition rules in the Treaty'.[160] The characterisation

8.49

---

[156] See Judgment of 27 September 2012 in Case T-357/06 *Koninklijke Wegenbouw Stevin v Commission*, para 238; Judgment of 14 November 2012 in Case T-135/09 *Nexans v Commission*, paras 62–4. See also AG Mischo, Joined Opinion in Cases 46/87, 85/87, 97/87, 98/87, 99/87 and 227/88 *Hoechst and Others v Commission* [1989] ECR 2875, paras 28 and 36: Inspectors 'must certainly be given every facility to ensure that no document of relevance escapes their scrutiny. In order to do so, they must have…the right to have the files and documents contained in any cabinet they designate submitted to them because otherwise how could they find any information as to the conduct of the undertaking which the latter has an interest in hiding and which it will ensure does not appear in its "classic" files?' With respect to requests for information see Judgment of 22 March 2012 in Joined Cases T-458/09 and T-171/10 *Slovak Telekom v Commission*, paras 42, 43, and 45.

[157] See Case T-57/01 *Solvay v Commission* [2009] ECR II-4621, para 218.

[158] *CSM* [1992] OJ L305/16. See also AG Mischo, Joined Opinion in Cases 46/87, 85/87, 97/87, 98/87, 99/87 and 227/88 *Hoechst and Others v Commission* [1989] ECR 2875, para 207.

[159] See AG Kokott, Opinion of 14 April 2011 in Case C-109/09 P *Solvay v Commission*, para 138.

[160] Case 85/87 *Dow Benelux v Commission* [1989] ECR 3165, paras 19 and 20; Judgment of 12 December 2012 in Case T-410/09 *Almamet v Commission*, para 30. See also AG Mischo, Joined Opinion in Cases 46/87, 85/87, 97/87, 98/87, 99/87 and 227/88 *Hoechst and Others v Commission* [1989] ECR 2875, para 206, and Case C-67/91 *Dirección General de Defensa de la Competencia v Asociación Española de Banca Privada and Others* [1992] ECR I-4785, para 39 (no 'acute amnesia'). While the Commission is thus allowed to use 'chance findings' in order to initiate a new inquiry, there is a question as to how it may deal with those findings in the course of the original inspection. Where the Commission realizes that it has chanced upon information for an infringement not covered by the initial inspection decision, it may not *take copies* before a new inspection decision has been notified to the undertaking. Whether it may nevertheless *single out* the documents at the premises of the undertaking without copying them, for instance by marking the documents with stickers or by putting them on the side, is a question currently debated in two pending court cases before the GC (see Case T-290/11 *Deutsche Bahn and Others v Commission* [2011] OJ C238/22; Case T-521/11 *Deutsche Bahn and Others v Commission* [2011] OJ C355/23). Where the Commission seizes the documents while under the legitimate impression that they related to the subject matter of the initial inspection, it cannot be criticized for a breach of the undertaking's procedural safeguards. It may then be sufficient if the Commission extends its investigation and makes a fresh request to the undertaking pursuant to Art 18 of Reg 1/2003 for the production of those documents, which in turn enables the undertaking to assert its rights of defence. If the undertaking, in its response, refers to the documents already seized, the Commission may simply keep them as part of the evidence collected within the ambit of the new (enlarged) investigation. See Judgment of 12 December 2012 in Case T-410/09 *Almamet v Commission*, paras 45–56 and 62–79. Without such further investigatory steps, the Commission is barred from using chance findings directly for proving an infringement. See Joined Cases T-305/94, T-306/94, T-307/94, T-313/94, T-314/94, T-315/94, T-316/94, T-318/94, T-325/94, T-328/94, T-329/94 and T-335/94 *Limburgse Vinyl Maatschappij and Others v Commission* [1999] ECR II-931, para 474 (confirmed in Joined Cases C-238/99 P, C-244/99 P, C-245/99 P, C-247/99 P, C-250/99 P to C-252/99 P and C-254/99 P *Limburgse Vinyl Maatschappij and Others v Commission* [2002] ECR I-8375, paras 302 and 305).

as a 'chance finding' may be rejected where the inspectors actively search for information beyond their mandate (eg through keywords) or intensively examine documents which clearly fall outside its scope.[161]

8.50 In practice, it often happens that the scope of the inspection is broadly defined because of the Commission's lack of specific knowledge of the business under investigation and/or the suspected infringement. In this case, attempts to avoid handing over certain documents or to prevent inspectors from taking copies could be seen as obstructive and lead to the company being sanctioned.[162] Undertakings may want to register their protest if they consider that the material collected by the inspectors falls outside the scope of the mandate by not being related to the subject matter and purpose of the inspection. Such a protest, however, is not a formal precondition for raising a plea as to the inadmissibility of certain pieces of evidence in an action for annulment against the decision on the merits.[163] If a finding of illegality is made by the General Court ('GC'), the Commission will then be barred from using the evidence which it has obtained unlawfully.[164] Undertakings may also request that copies which, in their view, have no bearing on the subject matter of the inspection be returned.[165]

8.51 The documents and data copied during an inspection will be covered by the provisions of Article 28 of Regulation 1/2003 concerning professional secrecy. If, at a later stage of the

---

[161] For the distinction between an (active) *search* for information possibly going beyond the subject matter and purpose of the inspection and the mere *examination* of business records even if it is not clear whether they relate to activities covered by the inspection decision, see Judgment of 14 November 2012 in Case T-135/09 *Nexans v Commission*, paras 63 and 64. This also entails that the Commission, once it has realized after examination of a business record that it does not relate to the activities covered by the inspection decision, refrains from using that document for the purpose of its investigation. Still, this leaves open the possibility of initiating a new investigation or enlarging the ambit of the ongoing investigation with a view to covering the possible additional infringement (see previous footnote).

[162] The Commission has stressed that undertakings may not substitute their own interpretation of the inspection decision for that of the Commission, since only the GC 'is competent to supervise the Commission's conduct'. See *CSM* [1992] OJ L305/16.

[163] Conversely, 'an undertaking cannot plead the illegality of the investigation procedures as a ground for annulment of the measure on the basis of which the Commission carried out that investigation'. See the references in the Order of the President in Joined Cases 125/03 R and T-253/03 *Akzo Nobel Chemicals and Akcros Chemicals v Commission* [2003] ECR II-4771, paras 68 and 69. This means that the legality of the inspection decision as such is not affected by any subsequent errors during the inspection, including excessive searches for documents.

[164] Case 85/87 *Dow Benelux v Commission* [1989] ECR 3165, para 18; Case C-94/00 *Roquette Frères* [2002] ECR I-9011, para 49. It should be noted that undertakings may only claim a violation of their rights of defence if the inspection was carried out at their own premises, related to documents that belonged to them or if they had at least a specific right to those documents. Otherwise, their rights of defence are sufficiently protected if, at the beginning of the administrative *inter partes* stage, the Commission provides access to the documents seized, thereby enabling them to take them into account when formulating their reply to the Statement of Objections. See Judgment of 12 December 2012 in Case T-410/09 *Almamet v Commission*, para 34. At the same time, 'any cartel participant may rely on the inadmissibility of evidence...obtained by the Commission in disregard of the procedure laid down for gathering it, such as the inspection procedure provided for in Article 20 of Regulation No 1/2003'. However, there is again a difference between the undertaking directly concerned and third parties: '[I]f the Commission has used the appropriate procedure laid down for gathering such evidence, any procedural irregularities may be invoked only by those directly concerned by them..., that is in the case of an inspection, in principle, by the person who submitted to the inspection. [Where] a party other than the party that submitted to an inspection...invokes an infringement, during that inspection, of safeguards designed to ensure respect for fundamental rights, the Court must confine itself to checking that the Commission did in fact use the procedure laid down to that effect, without going into the details of the conduct of that procedure unless the party in question invokes a procedural irregularity likely to concern it directly' (paras 40–2). Finally, 'if the holder of evidence obtained by the Commission decides, in full knowledge of his rights, not to object to its use by the Commission even though he could have done so, he clearly cannot take issue with the Commission for having used that evidence in its investigation' (para 43).

[165] See eg in *CSM* [1992] OJ L305/16.

procedure, it becomes necessary to grant other parties access to those documents or data, the undertaking will be asked to identify any business secrets or other confidential information contained therein, to justify those claims and to provide non-confidential copies or summaries for the purpose of granting access to the file.[166] Given this level of protection, undertakings may not rely on confidentiality arguments for refusing access to certain documents or data,[167] except for certain correspondence with lawyers as explained in the next section.

Correspondence with lawyers[168]

The general power of examination enjoyed by inspectors in Commission investigations[169] **8.52** is subject to the requirement to respect confidentiality in the correspondence between undertakings and their (external) lawyers. Although neither Regulation 17 nor Regulation 1/2003 contain a special provision dealing with lawyer-client communications, in *AM & S v Commission*[170] the ECJ held that Regulation 17 must be interpreted as providing protection for such correspondence and defined the conditions under which such protection is available, as well as the manner in which undertakings and the Commission must behave in such cases.

---

[166] See Explanatory note to an authorisation to conduct an inspection in execution of a Commission decision under Article 20(4) of Council Regulation No 1/2003, para 13. See also Art 27(2) of Reg 1/2003, Arts 15, 16 of Reg 773/2004 and the Commission Notice on the rules for access to the Commission file in cases pursuant to Articles 81 and 82 of the EC Treaty, Articles 53, 54 and 57 of the EEA Agreement and Council Regulation (EC) No 139/2004, [2005] OJ C325/7. If the Commission intends to disclose information for which confidential treatment has been claimed, the undertaking concerned shall be informed in writing of this intention and given the opportunity to comment. It may then refer the matter to the Hearing Officer. If the Hearing Officer finds that the information may be disclosed, such finding shall be stated in a reasoned decision to be notified to the undertaking. The decision shall specify the date after which the information may be disclosed, which shall not be less than one week from the date of notification in order to allow for an annulment action and a request for interim measures. See Decision of the President of the European Commission of 13 October 2011 on the function and terms of reference of the hearing officer in certain competition proceedings [2011] OJ L275/29, Art 8. See also Joined Cases T-213/01 and T-214/01 *Österreichische Postsparkasse v Commission* [2006] ECR II-1601, para 66.

[167] See, with respect to requests for information, Case C-36/92 *Samenwerkende Elektriciteits-Produktiebedrijven v Commission* [1994] ECR I-1911, paras 22–42; Case T-9/99 *HFB and Others v Commission* [2002] ECR II-1487, paras 561 and 562. See also Order of the President of 29 July 2011 in Case T-302/11 R *HeidelbergCement v Commission*, para 28.

[168] For an overview see Commission Notice on best practices for the conduct of proceedings concerning Articles 101 and 102 TFEU, [2011] OJ C308/6, point 2.7. See also E Gippini-Fournier, 'Legal Professional Privilege in Competition Proceedings before the European Commission: Beyond the Cursory Glance' ch 24 in BE Hawk (ed), *International Antitrust Law & Policy* (Annual Proceedings of the Fordham Institute 2004) 587, 621–6; J Temple Lang, 'The AM & S Judgment' ch 12 in M Hoskins and W Robinson (eds), *A True European—Essays for Judge David Edward* (Hart Publishing 2003) 153–60; J Joshua, 'Privilege in Multi-Jurisdictional Cartel Investigations: Are European Courts Missing the Point' (February 2004) Global Competition Review 39.

[169] The Courts have explicitly referred to a 'Community concept of LPP'. See Joined Cases T-125/03 and T-253/03 *Akzo Nobel Chemicals and Akcros Chemicals v Commission* [2007] ECR II-3523, para 176. Different rules may apply for investigations carried out at national level, ie by NCAs applying their national rules. See Case C-550/07 P *Akzo Nobel Chemicals and Akcros Chemicals v Commission* [2010] ECR I-8301, paras 102 and 104. However, where NCAs merely assist the Commission (cf Art 20(5), (6) of Reg 1/2003), the question of which business records may be examined is determined exclusively in accordance with EU law (including the LPP rules set out in this section). See Case C-550/07 P *Akzo Nobel Chemicals and Akcros Chemicals v Commission* [2010] ECR I-8301, para 119. The same should apply where NCAs undertake inspections at the Commission's request pursuant to Art 22(2) of Reg 1/2003.

[170] Case 155/79 *AM & S Europe v Commission* [1982] ECR 1575. The case originated in a dispute over the confidentiality of a series of documents found at the premises of AM & S during an inspection by written authorization into a cartel among zinc producers. The company claimed these were privileged written communications between lawyer and client and refused to show them to the Commission. The Commission then issued an inspection decision which specifically required AM & S to produce the documents. The parties agreed that the LPP issue needed to be resolved by the Union Courts and that the Commission would therefore not impose a sanction for obstruction.

The conditions for this so-called legal professional privilege ('LPP') have been further developed in subsequent judgments.[171]

8.53 Taking as a starting point the fact that correspondence between an undertaking and a lawyer may form part of the business records referred to in Article 14 of former Regulation 17 (now Article 20 of Regulation 1/2003), that the Commission is empowered to require production of the business records of undertakings and that it is in principle for the Commission—not the undertaking concerned or any third party—to decide whether or not a document should be produced to it, the Court nevertheless confirmed that certain business records, in particular correspondence between undertakings and lawyers, may be recognized as confidential. This right to confidentiality reflects the requirement, the importance of which is recognized in all the Member States, that every person must be entirely free to consult a lawyer whose profession entails the giving of independent legal advice to all those in need of it.[172] LPP therefore applies to written communications between lawyer and client that are made for the purpose of and in the interest of the client's right of defence and can be described as having a relationship with the subject matter of (competition) law proceedings. As the protection granted is solely to the benefit of the undertaking (the client), it may always choose to disclose the written communications with its lawyer where it considers that this is in its best interest.[173]

8.54 According to settled case law, the right to claim LPP is only recognized where the communication involves an independent lawyer, that is to say a lawyer not linked to the undertaking by an employment relationship.[174] Hence, LPP does not cover exchanges with in-house lawyers (inside a company or group).[175] As for external lawyers, they must be entitled (as an admitted member of the Bar[176]) to practise their profession in one of the EU Member States, regardless of the Member State in which the undertaking is located.[177] The same benefit is available to undertakings seeking advice from lawyers in European Free Trade Association ('EFTA') countries which are parties to the European Economic Area ('EEA') agreement.[178] Conversely, it appears that correspondence

---

[171] See Case T-30/89 *Hilti v Commission* [1991] ECR II-1439; Joined Cases T-125/03 and T-253/03 *Akzo Nobel Chemicals and Akcros Chemicals v Commission* [2007] ECR II-3523 (confirmed in Case C-550/07 P *Akzo Nobel Chemicals and Akcros Chemicals v Commission* [2010] ECR I-8301).

[172] Case 155/79 *AM & S Europe v Commission* [1982] ECR 1675, para 18. The Court considered that the protection of confidentiality between lawyer and client is an essential corollary to the rights of defence, observance of which is a fundamental principle of EU law now enshrined in Art 48(2) of the EU Charter of Fundamental Rights. See Case 155/79 *AM & S Europe v Commission* [1982] ECR 1675, para 23; Case C-550/07 P *Akzo Nobel Chemicals and Akcros Chemicals v Commission* [2010] ECR I-8301, para 92.

[173] Case 155/79 *AM & S Europe v Commission* [1982] ECR 1675, para 28.

[174] Case 155/79 *AM & S Europe v Commission* [1982] ECR 1675, paras 21 and 24. The Commission rejected Audi's LPP claim regarding documents emanating from the internal legal department in *Volkswagen* [1998] OJ L124/60, paras 198–9.

[175] Case C-550/07 P *Akzo Nobel Chemicals and Akcros Chemicals v Commission* [2010] ECR I-8301, para 44. The Court clarified (para 45) that 'the concept of the independence of lawyers is determined not only positively, that is by reference to professional ethical obligations, but also negatively, by the absence of an employment relationship'. In the Court's view, given its economic dependence and the fact that it will not be able to ignore the commercial strategies of the client, an in-house lawyer is less able to deal effectively with any conflicts between those strategies and his professional obligations, and will therefore not be able to ensure a degree of independence comparable to that of an external lawyer (paras 45–9 and 57). Thus, 'when an undertaking seeks advice from its in-house lawyer, it is not dealing with an independent third party, but with one of its employees, notwithstanding any professional obligations resulting from enrolment at a Bar or Law Society' (para 94).

[176] The French text speaks of '*les avocats inscrits au barreau*'.

[177] Case 155/79 *AM & S Europe v Commission* [1982] ECR 1675, para 25.

[178] Individuals and undertakings have the right to be represented, before the GC and ECJ as well as before the EFTA Court, by lawyers entitled to practise either before the EU or EFTA national courts. Whether the proceedings are conducted by the European Commission or the EFTA Surveillance Authority ('ESA'), correspondence with lawyers from EFTA/EEA States is protected under LPP rules. See J Temple Lang 'The AM

between an undertaking and its non-EU lawyers does not fall under the LPP rules.[179] Moreover, LPP does not extend to other professional advisers such as patent attorneys, accountants, etc.[180]

In terms of timing, the protection of confidentiality in administrative proceedings before **8.55** the Commission extends to all correspondence exchanged after the initiation of proceedings which may lead to a decision on the application of Articles 101 or 102 TFEU (and possibly the imposition of a sanction), but also to earlier communications which are clearly related to the subject matter of that procedure.[181] Since the formal initiation of proceedings in the sense of Article 2(1) of Regulation 773/2004[182] usually takes place *after* a preliminary investigation (including inspections)[183]—and in cartel cases will typically coincide with the Statement of Objections[184]—it makes sense that LPP applies already to earlier communications and indeed once the file for a particular (at least broadly defined) investigation has been opened.[185] Such correspondence may include, for example, letters exchanged between undertaking and lawyer concerning a complaint or related to an investigative step (eg a request for information).[186] If the content of such communications has been reproduced or reported in documents inside the undertaking (internal notes), those notes must also be regarded as being protected by LPP.[187]

& S Judgment' ch 12 in M Hoskins and W Robinson, *A True European—Essays for Judge David Edward* (Hart Publishing 2003) 157.

[179] For a critical view on this point, see J Joshua, 'Privilege in Multi-Jurisdictional Cartel Investigations: Are European Courts Missing the Point' (February 2004) Global Competition Review 39, 40; J Temple Lang, 'The AM & S Judgment' ch 12 in M Hoskins and W Robinson (eds), *A True European—Essays for Judge David Edward* (Hart Publishing 2003) 153–60. Indeed, there appears to be no good reason why correspondence with lawyers practising elsewhere (eg from the American Bar) should not be protected, as long as their professional and ethical obligations ensure a comparable level of independence from the client.

[180] Commission Notice on best practices for the conduct of proceedings concerning Articles 101 and 102 TFEU [2011] OJ C308/6, n 43.

[181] Case 155/79 *AM & S Europe v Commission* [1982] ECR 1675, para 23. However, for a legal communication exchanged before the start of the investigation or the initiation of proceedings to be privileged, it should be required that it has been made in anticipation of such proceedings, ie as a preparatory step in the undertaking's defence. Cf Order of the President of 30 October 2003 in Joined Cases T-125/03 R and T-253/03 *Akzo Nobel Chemicals and Akcros Chemicals v Commission* [2003] ECR II-4771, para 113 (documents that relate to 'facts which are prima facie capable of justifying consultation of a lawyer and of being connected either with the investigation currently being carried out by the Commission or with other investigations which the applicants were reasonably able to fear or anticipate and in view whereof they intended to draw up a strategy and prepare in advance, if necessary, the exercise of their rights of defence').

[182] Article 2(1) of Reg 773/2004 foresees that the Commission may decide to initiate proceedings with a view to adopting a decision pursuant to Chapter III of Reg 1/2003 at any point in time, but not later than the date on which it issues a Preliminary Assessment as referred to in Art 9(1) of Reg 1/2003 or a Statement of Objections or the date on which a notice pursuant to Art 27(4) of Reg 1/2003 is published, whichever is the earlier. According to the ECJ, the initiation of proceedings presupposes an 'authoritative act of the Commission, evidencing its intention to take a decision'. See Case 48/72 *Brasserie de Haecht v Wilkin-Janssen* [1973] ECR 77, para 16.

[183] According to Art 2(3) of Reg 773/2004, the Commission may exercise its powers of investigation pursuant to Chapter V of Reg 1/2003 before (formally) initiating proceedings.

[184] See Commission Notice on best practices for the conduct of proceedings concerning Articles 101 and 102 TFEU [2011] OJ C308/6, para 24.

[185] Cf Kerse & Khan, *EC Antitrust Procedure* (6th edn, Sweet & Maxwell 2012) para 3-045, noting that there should be no discouragement from taking legal advice at the earliest opportunity.

[186] According to the Best Practices, '[w]hen the first investigative measure is addressed to them (normally a request for information or an inspection), addressees are informed of the fact that they are subject to a preliminary investigation and about the subject matter and purpose of such investigation'. See Commission Notice on best practices for the conduct of proceedings concerning Articles 101 and 102 TFEU [2011] OJ C308/6, para 15.

[187] Case T-30/89 *Hilti v Commission* [1991] ECR II-1439, paras 16–18.

8.56 Generally, whether or not a document is privileged will depend on the parties to the communication and the purpose for which the document came into existence. The current rules can be summarized as follows:

- *Legal advice of a general nature.* Since the communication must have been made for the purposes and in the interest of the client's rights of defence,[188] general legal advice unrelatead to the particular investigation will not be privileged (but equally will not be relevant to the inspection).
- *Communications inside the company with an in-house lawyer.* These communications are not privileged under EU law.[189] Thus LPP does not apply to (i) written advice given by the in-house lawyer to the company; or (ii) a written request from the company to its in-house lawyer for legal advice. This applies even if the request would subsequently be passed on to an external lawyer.[190]
- *Communications between the company and an external lawyer.* Correspondence between a company and an external lawyer will be protected by LPP as long as (i) it is made for the purposes and in the interest of the client's defence rights; and (ii) the external lawyer is qualified to practise in an EEA country.[191] If these conditions are satisfied, protection extends to all written communications exchanged after the Commission has started an investigation which may lead to a decision under Articles 101 or 102 TFEU (including the imposition of a fine). In addition, it covers earlier written communications clearly related to the same subject matter (see paragraph 8.55). There is no requirement that the communication was actually sent to the lawyer, but it suffices that it was prepared with that purpose (for instance a draft letter).[192] LPP protection also applies if the company (client) acts through an in-house lawyer, for instance if he is the first recipient of the communication from the external lawyer and the document is passed on without any changes. In this context, the question arises whether under the principles established in *Hilti*, the privilege will no longer apply if the communication is amended by the in-house lawyer or any other person within the company. While certain (limited) amendments will not entail the loss of LPP protection, it is difficult to define operative criteria. In any event, legal advice which is circulated and discussed widely within the company may well lose its privileged status.
- *Internal reports on the advice received from external lawyers, prepared by an in-house lawyer or other employee.* Internal notes which merely report the text or content of communications from an external lawyer that would have been protected under LPP if received in writing from the external lawyer will themselves be privileged.[193] However, not all aspects of such an internal note are likely to be covered. For example, a report which includes an

---

[188] Case 155/79 *AM & S Europe v Commission* [1982] ECR 1675, para 21. See also Order of the President of 30 October 2003 in Joined Cases T-125/03 R and T-253/03 *Akzo Nobel Chemicals and Akcros Chemicals v Commission* [2003] ECR II-4771, para 113.

[189] For a critique see J Temple Lang, 'The AM & S Judgment' ch 12 in M Hoskins and W Robinson (eds), *A True European—Essays for Judge David Edward* (Hart Publishing 2003) 155, who has submitted that this runs counter to the policy of Reg 1/2003 to emphasize the self-assessment as regards compliance with EU competition law, because it discourages consultation of employed lawyers.

[190] See Joined Cases T-125/03 and T-253/03 *Akzo Nobel Chemicals and Akcros Chemicals v Commission* [2007] ECR II-3523, para 123: 'the mere fact that a document has been discussed with a lawyer is not sufficient to give it such protection.'

[191] See para 8.54 as regards the question whether such a limitation as to the personal scope of LPP is justified.

[192] Joined Cases T-125/03 and T-253/03 *Akzo Nobel Chemicals and Akcros Chemicals v Commission* [2007] ECR II-3523, para 118.

[193] Order in Case T-30/89 *Hilti v Commission* [1990] ECR II-163, para 18: 'Thus the principle of the protection of written communications between lawyer and client must, in view of its purpose, be regarded as extending also to the internal notes which are confined to reporting the text or the content of those communications'.

expression of opinion or amendments made by the in-house lawyer or other employee will not be privileged, at least in so far as those amendments are considerable and/or if the expression of that opinion or those amendments is clearly separable.[194]

- *Preparatory documents within the company drawn up exclusively for the purpose of seeking legal advice from an external lawyer.* It may be necessary, in certain circumstances, for the client (company) to prepare certain documents as a means of gathering information which will be useful to the external lawyer for an understanding of the context, nature, and scope of the facts for which his assistance is sought. Such preparatory documents, even if they were not exchanged with the lawyer, may still be covered by LPP if they were drawn up exclusively for the purpose of seeking legal advice in the exercise of the rights of defence.[195] In principle, this could also cover requests for information from the in-house lawyer to the company for the purpose of instructing an external lawyer, and responses to such requests. However, the possibility of treating a preparatory document as covered by LPP must be construed restrictively, and the mere fact that a document has been discussed with an external lawyer is not sufficient to grant it protection under LPP.[196] It is for the undertaking relying on LPP protection to prove that the documents in question were drawn up with the sole aim of seeking legal advice; this should be unambiguously clear from the content of the documents themselves or the context in which those documents were prepared and/or found.[197]
- *Communications related to advice from professional advisers other than an external lawyer.* Requests from the company to the in-house lawyer to obtain advice from professional advisers other than an external lawyer and requests from the in-house lawyer or other employee to such professional advisers for information or advice will not be privileged under EU law. The same applies to communications from the professional advisers themselves.
- *File notes.* File notes prepared by an in-house lawyer or other employee will not be privileged. The only possible exception is where the note records advice received from external legal advisers, and no significant comment or modification has been added. As indicated earlier, this might raise difficult questions as to how to delineate privileged from non-privileged content.

It is for the undertaking claiming the protection of LPP with regard to a given document **8.57** to provide the Commission with appropriate justification and relevant material to substantiate its claim, without disclosing the contents of such document. In order to do so,

---

[194] See for instance *Opel* [2001] OJ L59/1, n 18. Opel Nederland BV claimed that an internal document which included *inter alia* guidance on how dealers verify whether sales are compatible with the dealer contract should be protected by legal privilege, as it was based on advice from an independent legal adviser. The Commission rejected this argument as the document in question was not confined to reporting the text or the content of such advice.

[195] Joined Cases T-125/03 and T-253/03 *Akzo Nobel Chemicals and Akcros Chemicals v Commission* [2007] ECR II-3523, paras 122 and 123. See also Order of the President of 30 October 2003 in Joined Cases T-125/03 R and T-253/03 *Akzo Nobel Chemicals and Akcros Chemicals v Commission* [2003] ECR II-4771, paras 102–4.

[196] Joined Cases T-125/03 and T-253/03 *Akzo Nobel Chemicals and Akcros Chemicals v Commission* [2007] ECR II-3523, paras 123 and 124. However, a more lenient interpretation might be given in interim measures cases where the President only has to establish a prima facie infringement of LPP rules. See Order of the President of 30 October 2003 in Joined Cases T-125/03 R and T-253/03 *Akzo Nobel Chemicals and Akcros Chemicals v Commission* [2003] ECR II-4771, para 109–14.

[197] Joined Cases T-125/03 and T-253/03 *Akzo Nobel Chemicals and Akcros Chemicals v Commission* [2007] ECR II-3523, para 124. The fact that a document was drawn up under a competition law compliance program is not sufficient in itself for that document to benefit from protection under LPP. In particular, the fact that an outside lawyer has put together and/or coordinated a compliance program cannot automatically confer LPP protection on all the documents drawn up under that program or in relation with it (para 127). See also Order of the President of 30 October 2003 in Joined Cases T-125/03 R and T-253/03 *Akzo Nobel Chemicals and Akcros Chemicals v Commission* [2003] ECR II-4771, para 107.

the undertaking concerned may, in particular, inform the Commission of the author of the document and for whom it was intended, explain the respective duties and responsibilities of author and likely recipient, and refer to the objective and the context in which the document was drawn up. Also, the undertaking may mention the circumstances in which the document was filed, disclose certain passages thereof (for example, the letterhead of the external lawyer), or produce any related documents.[198] The inspectors may ask for additional explanations and evidence, unless they consider the information provided as sufficient to accept the LPP claim. Where the undertaking has (i) not substantiated its claim that the document is covered by LPP; (ii) has only invoked reasons that, according to the case law, cannot justify such protection; or (iii) bases itself on factual assertions that are manifestly wrong, the Commission considers that it may immediately read the content of the document and take a copy of it.[199] Otherwise, the inspectors are prohibited from examining the document until the Commission has given the undertaking the opportunity to refer the matter to the EU Courts.[200] Before adopting a challengeable act rejecting the LPP claim, the inspectors will, however, seek to confirm the accuracy of the reasons invoked by the undertaking by taking a cursory look at the general layout, heading, title, or other superficial features of the document. While this might often solve the issue, in certain cases there would be a risk that, even with a cursory look at the document, and in spite of the superficial nature of their examination, the inspectors would gain access to information covered by LPP.[201] The undertaking may then refuse to allow the inspectors even a cursory look, provided that it gives appropriate reasons to justify why such a cursory look would necessarily reveal the content of the document.[202] In such a situation, or when the inspectors, following a cursory look in agreement with the undertaking, cannot rule out that the document might

---

[198] See Joined Cases T-125/03 and T-253/03 *Akzo Nobel Chemicals and Akcros Chemicals v Commission* [2007] ECR II-3523, para 80.

[199] See Commission Notice on best practices for the conduct of proceedings concerning Articles 101 and 102 TFEU, [2011] OJ C308/6, paras 54 and 57. This is likely based on the ruling in Joined Cases T-125/03 and T-253/03 *Akzo Nobel Chemicals and Akcros Chemicals v Commission* [2007] ECR II-3523, paras 80 and 85, where the GC appears to distinguish between situations where the undertaking produces 'no relevant material of such a kind as to prove that [the document] is actually protected by LPP', and situations where the Commission 'is not satisfied with the material and explanations provided...for the purposes of proving that the document concerned is covered by LPP'. Paragraph 80 could thus be read as an indication that, in the first scenario, inspectors are allowed to immediately read the document. It should be noted, though, that in para 86 et seq the GC explains in detail why it considers that the Commission must not be allowed to read the content of a document for which LPP has been claimed 'until it has given the undertaking concerned the opportunity to refer the matter to the [EU Courts]' (para 88). Moreover, in para 89 the GC rejects the Commission's argument that undertakings may abuse the LPP procedure 'by making requests, merely as a delaying tactics, for protection under LPP which are clearly unfounded, or by opposing, without objective justification, any cursory look', as the Commission would have the means to discourage and penalize such conduct. Hence, it cannot be excluded that the GC is opposed to the immediate reading of any document for which LPP has been claimed, even if the justification is 'clearly unfounded'. See, however, Order of the President of 30 October 2003 in Joined Cases T-125/03 R and T-253/03 *Akzo Nobel Chemicals and Akcros Chemicals v Commission* [2003] ECR II-4771, paras 133 and 134. In any event, where the Commission seizes the document of which LPP is claimed and places it in the investigation file rather than a sealed envelope, and without first taking a formal decision rejecting the LPP claim, that physical act necessarily entails a 'tacit decision' to reject LPP which is open to challenge by an annulment action. See Joined Cases T-125/03 and T-253/03 *Akzo Nobel Chemicals and Akcros Chemicals v Commission* [2007] ECR II-3523, para 49. If this is followed by a more formal rejection decision, that (second) decision may also be challenged (para 53).

[200] Joined Cases T-125/03 and T-253/03 *Akzo Nobel Chemicals and Akcros Chemicals v Commission* [2007] ECR II-3523, para 88. See also Case 155/79 *AM & S Europe v Commission* [1982] ECR 1675, paras 31 and 32.

[201] Joined Cases T-125/03 and T-253/03 *Akzo Nobel Chemicals and Akcros Chemicals v Commission* [2007] ECR II-3523, para 81. That may be the case, in particular, if the confidentiality of the document in question is not clear from external indications and thus could only be established following a closer examination of the text.

[202] Joined Cases T-125/03 and T-253/03 *Akzo Nobel Chemicals and Akcros Chemicals v Commission* [2007] ECR II-3523, para 82.

be privileged (even if they consider that LPP protection has not been sufficiently established), they will place a copy of the contested document in a sealed envelope and take it to the Commission's premises, with a view to a subsequent resolution of the dispute.[203] In this case, the inspectors will draw up a minute[204] which states that the Commission inspectors agreed to place a copy of the disputed document in a sealed envelope 'not [to] be opened until (i) such time as the Commission has received written agreement of the undertaking to do so; or (ii) the date indicated in the Commission's written position following [a specified] procedure'. This procedure entails the setting of a time limit of two weeks for the undertaking to submit written arguments in support of its LPP claim. If the Commission is satisfied with the arguments submitted it will return the envelope (unopened) to the undertaking. If not, it will formulate a written position indicating the date on which it intends to open the envelope and place the document on the file.

If, possibly following further submissions from the undertaking, DG COMP continues to **8.58** disagree with the undertaking as to the privileged nature of the document, the undertaking may refer the matter to the Hearing Officer in order for him to examine the LPP claim and in particular the document concerned (as well as related documents that the Hearing Officer considers necessary for his review). After examination of the issue, and without revealing the potentially privileged content of the document, the Hearing Officer shall communicate his preliminary view to the responsible Director in DG COMP and the undertaking concerned. In addition, he may suggest 'appropriate steps to promote a mutually acceptable resolution' of the conflict.[205] If no such resolution is reached, the Hearing Officer may formulate a reasoned recommendation[206] to the competent member of the Commission (again, without revealing the potentially privileged content of the document) of which the undertaking claiming LPP shall receive a copy. Whatever the outcome, the Commission is not bound by this recommendation. It may either grant LPP or adopt a decision rejecting the LPP claim.[207] Even if it takes the latter course of action, it will not open the sealed envelope and read the contents of the document before the undertaking had the opportunity to apply for interim relief (which also presupposes an annulment action) and until the EU Courts have decided on such an application for interim measures.[208] If the EU Courts annul the rejection decision in the main action, the Commission is then prevented from using the privileged documents for the

---

[203] Joined Cases T-125/03 and T-253/03 *Akzo Nobel Chemicals and Akcros Chemicals v Commission* [2007] ECR II-3523, para 83.

[204] This is an official form used by DG COMP and entitled 'Minute of the inspection concerning documents containing alleged legally privileged information.' It will be signed by a Commission inspector and (ideally) a representative of the undertaking.

[205] See Decision of the President of the European Commission of 13 October 2011 on the function and terms of reference of the hearing officer in certain competition proceedings [2011] OJ L275/29 ('Terms of Reference'), Art 4(2)(a). According to DG COMP's Manual of Procedure, the Hearing Officer will discuss his preliminary assessment with the undertaking and DG Competition. See European Commission Antitrust Manual of Procedures, Internal DG Competition working documents on procedures for the application of Articles 101 and 102 TFEU, March 2012, Module 2 'Relations with the Hearing Officers', para 13.

[206] According to Recital 11 of the Terms of Reference, the Hearing Officer's recommendation shall refer to 'the applicable case-law of the Court of Justice'. Hence, undertakings should not expect that the Hearing Officer would recommend protection under a concept of LPP which goes beyond the limits of established jurisprudence.

[207] The decision whereby the Commission rejects an LPP request produces binding legal effects for the undertaking concerned and therefore constitutes a challengeable act. See Joined Cases T-125/03 and T-253/03 *Akzo Nobel Chemicals and Akcros Chemicals v Commission* [2007] ECR II-3523, paras 45–8. As regards the restitution of the documents placed in the sealed envelope, see Order of the President of 27 September 2004 in Case C-7/04 P(R) *Akzo Nobel Chemicals and Akcros Chemicals v Commission* [2004] ECR I-8739, para 46.

[208] Commission Notice on best practices for the conduct of proceedings concerning Articles 101 and 102 TFEU, [2011] OJ C308/6, para 57 with n 48. It should be noted that in the *Akzo/Akcros* case, the

purpose of finding an infringement, and would be required to remove them from its file by returning them to the undertaking.[209] Conversely, where the undertaking made LPP claims that were clearly unfounded in order to delay the inspection, or opposed any cursory look without objective justification, the Commission might impose fines pursuant to Article 23(1)(c) of Regulation 1/2003, or take such conduct into account as an aggravating circumstance in any decision imposing a fine for an infringement of Articles 101 and/or 102 TFEU.[210]

3. Taking of copies and extracts of records in any form

8.59   The main aim of inspections is to obtain documents concerning the possible restrictions of competition described in the authorization or decision to inspect. Since the Commission is not empowered to seize and retain original documents, it copies them in most cases (extracts are rarely taken). As stated earlier, the information contained in the copied documents must be directly or indirectly related to the subject matter and purpose of the inspection, the criteria by which the scope of the inspection is defined.[211] Practical arrangements for the identification and copying of documents will vary from one investigation to another. While in principle the company might undertake the copying on their behalf, inspectors will typically take charge of copying arrangements themselves.[212] As most businesses now work and communicate primarily in electronic form, access to computer and email systems forms an increasingly important part of an inspection. In particular, the inspectors may search the IT environment and electronic storage media (for instance through a keyword search), recover data through specialized software or hardware, and then take paper or digital copies of the information.[213] Special questions arise where the inspectors make 'chance findings' that are not related to the subject matter of the on-going inspection but might be used as information to support an additional investigation or a broadening of the mandate.[214]

Commission voluntarily stated that it would not allow third parties to have access to documents for which LPP claims had been made until judgment in the main action was given by the GC. See Joined Cases T-125/03 and T-253/03 *Akzo Nobel Chemicals and Akcros Chemicals v Commission* [2007] ECR II-3523, paras 19 and 24. The effect of this has been that the investigation was significantly delayed, resulting in prescription for certain undertakings and a voluntary reduction of the fine for delay in the administrative procedure for others. See Commission Decision of 11 November 2009 in Case COMP/38.589 *Heat Stabilisers*, summ pub [2010] OJ C307/9.

[209] See Order of the President of 27 September 2004 in Case C-7/04 P(R) *Akzo Nobel Chemicals and Akcros Chemicals v Commission* [2004] ECR I-8739, paras 37–9.

[210] Commission Notice on best practices for the conduct of proceedings concerning Articles 101 and 102 TFEU, [2011] OJ C308/6, para 58, with reference to Joined Cases T-125/03 and T-253/03 *Akzo Nobel Chemicals and Akcros Chemicals v Commission* [2007] ECR II-3523, para 89.

[211] Where these requirements are fulfilled, the mere fact that inspectors copy a large number of documents in itself does not render the inspection unlawful. See Joined Cases T-305/94, T-306/94, T-307/94, T-313/94, T-314/94, T-315/94, T-316/94, T-318/94, T-325/94, T-328/94, T-329/94 and T-335/94 *Limburgse Vinyl Maatschappij and Others v Commission* [1999] ECR II-931, para 425.

[212] The undertaking has no obligation to make photocopying facilities available to the inspectors, although this will avoid extending the length of the inspection. See, in relation to Reg 17, European Commission, 'Dealing with the Commission—Notification, complaints, inspections and fact-finding powers under Articles [101] and [102] of the [TFEU]', at point 5.6. Where the photocopying is done with equipment available on site, the Commission shall, at the request of the undertaking, reimburse the cost. See Explanatory note to an authorisation to conduct an inspection in execution of a Commission decision under Article 20(4) of Council Regulation No 1/2003, para 12.

[213] See paras 8.02, 8.21, and 8.43–8.45 with accompanying footnotes. With respect to the special procedure for taking an integral copy of a digital storage medium ('forensic image'), see para 8.43 and the Commission's Explanatory note to an authorisation to conduct an inspection in execution of a Commission decision under Article 20(4) of Council Regulation No 1/2003, para 11.

[214] See para 8.49 and accompanying footnotes.

According to the explanatory note handed to the undertaking at the beginning of the **8.60** inspection, it will receive a copy of all the documents and data copied by the inspectors and may request a signed list of the copies and extracts taken during the inspection.[215] Nevertheless, the company might want to ensure that it maintains its own inventory. Also, a note should be kept of the names and location of the files from which copies were taken. Where inspectors take copies of records which in the view of the undertaking are not related to the subject matter of the investigation, it may ask the Commission to return those copies,[216] although the Commission is unlikely to do so unless they are clearly unrelated (and hence have been copied by mistake).[217] The documents and data copied during an inspection will be covered by the provisions of Article 28 of Regulation 1/2003 concerning professional secrecy. If, at a later stage of the procedure, it becomes necessary to grant other parties access to those documents and/or data, the undertaking will be asked to identify any business secrets or other confidential information contained in the documents or data, to justify those claims, and to provide non-confidential copies for the purpose of granting access to the file.[218]

4. Sealing of business premises, books, or records for the period and to the extent necessary for the inspection

Given that the detection of infringements is growing ever more difficult, and that inspec-   **8.61** tions are one of the most important instruments in securing the evidence for anticompetitive conduct, Regulation 1/2003 enlarges the powers of the Commission during investigations (see Recital 25 of Regulation 1/2003).[219] One of the new powers is the power to seal any business premises and books or records for the period and to the extent necessary for the inspection.[220] Affixing seals allows the Commission to secure documents or data stored on site (eg in certain rooms, cupboards,[221] hard drives,[222] etc) if it is not possible for the inspectors to examine or copy them immediately, and if otherwise there would be a risk that third parties (eg company staff) could use the delay to destroy, conceal, or tamper with the evidence.[223] This applies in particular to paper searches when documents have been

---

[215] Explanatory note to an authorisation to conduct an inspection in execution of a Commission decision under Article 20(4) of Council Regulation No 1/2003, para 12.

[216] *CSM* [1992] OJ L305/16.

[217] See Commission Notice on the rules for access to the Commission file in cases pursuant to Articles 81 and 82 of the EC Treaty, Articles 53, 54 and 57 of the EEA Agreement and Council Regulation (EC) No 139/2004, [2005] OJ C325/7, para 9 (documents shall be returned if, following a more detailed examination, they 'prove' to be unrelated to the subject matter of the investigation).

[218] Explanatory note to an authorisation to conduct an inspection in execution of a Commission decision under Article 20(4) of Council Regulation No 1/2003, para 13.

[219] Beforehand, the Commission had to rely on the powers of NCAs to seal cupboards or offices. See Speech by Director-General of DG COMP, Philip Lowe, 'What's the Future for Cartel Enforcement', Understanding Global Cartel Enforcement, Brussels, 11 February 2003, available at <http://ec.europa.eu/competition/speeches/text/sp2003_044_en.pdf>.

[220] Recital 25 of Reg 1/2003 foresees that seals should normally not be affixed for more than seventy-two hours, but already the wording makes clear that this is no absolute requirement.

[221] See Proposal for a Council Regulation implementing Articles 81 and 82 of the Treaty, COM(2000) 582 final, point II.C.1.c.

[222] Cf Explanatory note to an authorisation to conduct an inspection in execution of a Commission decision under Article 20(4) of Council Regulation No 1/2003, para 11: 'If the selection of the relevant documents for the investigation is not finished during the inspection, the digital copy (DVD, Hard Disk, ...) of the data still to be searched is put in an envelope which will be sealed in situ and carried off by the officials ... The undertaking will then be invited by the Commission to attend the opening of the sealed envelope and the selection process in the Commission's premises.'

[223] See Commission Staff Working Paper accompanying the Report on the functioning of Regulation 1/2003, SEC(2009) 574 final, para 72. As regards the necessity to affix seals, see Commission decision of 30 January 2008 in Case COMP/39.326 *E.ON Energie AG*, paras 71–3 and 99.

selected for further examination or copying, but the volume is too large to carry out that work within one day. In this case, the inspectors will typically store those documents in a designated room which will then be sealed overnight. Both the sealing of the door (and, where appropriate, window(s)) and the removal of the seal(s) will be documented in a minute to be signed by the inspectors and a company representative. At the time of removal, the inspectors will also record any changes in the appearance of the seals that could indicate a possible breach.[224] While the room or other storage medium is sealed, the undertaking is expected to ensure that the seal(s) as well as the immediate environment of the place where they have been affixed remain untouched.[225] This entails, in particular, that the undertaking locks the door and prevents any (inadvertent) interference with the seal,[226] for instance by putting up a warning sign, placing a physical object in front of the door, or even guarding the door through security personnel. If the seal is broken[227] upon return of the inspectors and the undertaking cannot show that this was due to *force majeure*, it is likely to be fined pursuant to Article 23(1)(e) of Regulation 1/2003.[228]

5. Request for oral explanations on facts or documents relating to the subject matter and purpose of the inspection

8.62 For the better performance of their tasks during an inspection and to obtain additional relevant information, inspectors often ask for oral explanations from the representatives[229] or staff members of the undertaking concerned. The primary aim of seeking oral explanations is to facilitate the conduct of inspections, in particular through a better understanding of the company structure and organization, business activities, etc, as well as the content and meaning of certain information discovered during the investigation (for instance, specific abbreviations used in company documents which may constitute useful evidence). Pursuant to Article 20(2)(e) of Regulation 1/2003, the inspectors may ask any representative or member of staff of the undertaking for explanations on facts or documents relating to the subject matter and purpose of the

---

[224] Explanatory note to an authorisation to conduct an inspection in execution of a Commission decision under Article 20(4) of Council Regulation No 1/2003, para 15. It appears that in more recent inspections Commission officials also take photos both at the time the seal is affixed and upon their return when the seal is removed, and attach those to the respective minutes. See Commission Decision of 24 May 2011 in Case COMP/39.796 *Suez Environnement breach of seal*, paras 23, 27, 58, and 63.

[225] Explanatory note to an authorisation to conduct an inspection in execution of a Commission decision under Article 20(4) of Council Regulation No 1/2003, para 15. In the Commission's view, Art 23(1)(e) of Regulation 1/2003 implies that the undertaking has to take all necessary measures in order to prevent any manipulation of the affixed seals. This responsibility is also recalled in the minute drawn up at the time the seal is affixed. See Commission Decision of 24 May 2011 in Case COMP/39.796 *Suez Environnement breach of seal*, paras 21 and 71; Case T-141/08 *E.ON Energie v Commission* [2010] ECR II-5761, paras 216 and 260 (confirmed on appeal in Case C-89/11 *E.ON Energie v Commission*).

[226] See Commission Decision of 24 May 2011 in Case COMP/39.796 *Suez Environnement breach of seal*, paras 73 and 74.

[227] The way the seals currently in use indicate a seal breach is explained in Case T-141/08 *E.ON Energie v Commission* [2010] ECR II-5761, paras 137, 218, and 256; Commission Decision of 30 January 2008 in Case COMP/39.326 *E.ON Energie AG*, paras 6, 7, 74 et seq, 100; Commission Decision of 24 May 2011 in Case COMP/39.796 *Suez Environnement breach of seal*, paras 18, 19, 61, and 69.

[228] See Commission Decision of 30 January 2008 in Case COMP/39.326 *E.ON Energie AG*, paras 74 et seq and 101–3. See also Ch 9, 'Procedural Infringements: Fines and Periodic Penalty Payments'.

[229] E Gippini Fournier has argued that (only) the persons authorized to provide explanations on behalf of the undertaking should be deemed 'representatives', for whom rectification or amendment is excluded, whereas all employees without such authority are 'members of staff' whose explanations may be rectified, amended, or supplemented. E Gippini-Fournier, 'The Modernisation of European Competition Law: First Experiences with Regulation 1/2003—Institutional Report' in HF Koeck and MM Karollus (eds), The Modernisation of European Competition Law—Initial Experiences with Regulation 1/2003, FIDE XXIII Congress Linz 2008—Congress Publications Vol 2 (Nomos 2008) 60.

inspection. The undertaking has a duty to cooperate actively[230] and it should therefore ensure that the best-placed employees of sufficient seniority and knowledge of operations are available to deal with the inspectors' enquiries.[231] Generally, it is advisable to identify one member of staff to act as a central point of contact for all queries. If the undertaking fails or refuses to provide a complete answer, if the answer is incorrect or misleading, or (in case an unauthorized member of staff gave the answer) the undertaking fails to rectify within a time limit set by the Commission an incorrect, incomplete, or misleading answer, a fine may be imposed pursuant to Article 23(1)(d) of Regulation 1/2003.[232] In order to make such rectification possible, oral explanations provided during an inspection may be recorded (in any form), and a copy of any recording will be made available to the undertaking after the inspection.[233] The undertaking may then communicate to the Commission any rectification, amendment, or supplement within a time limit set by the Commission.[234] The power under Article 20(2)(e) should be distinguished from that pursuant to Article 19.[235]

Under Regulation 17, the ECJ considered that inspectors had the power to ask specific questions related to the examination of books and business records.[236] Such questions could concern practical matters such as the location, organization, and layout of offices or files. In addition, they could relate to the contents of documents or files, for example questions on the job description and broad responsibilities of certain individuals involved in the communication, or requests for an explanation of internal reporting structures. At the same time, no clear guidance existed as to whether inspectors could ask questions related to the ongoing investigation as such and its subject matter. This left some uncertainty about the Commission's powers under Regulation 17 to request information, and whether inspectors could also address individuals other than those identified by the undertaking.[237] Article 20(2)(e) of Regulation 1/2003 clarifies these powers to some extent. In doing so, it 'supplement[s]' (recital 25) them by allowing inspectors to ask for **8.63**

---

[230] In *Orkem* the ECJ stressed that undertakings have an obligation to cooperate actively during an investigation. This obligation implies that they 'must make available to the Commission all information relating to the subject matter of the investigation'; Case 374/87 *Orkem v Commission* [1989] ECR 3283, para 27. Likewise, the GC has referred to a duty of active cooperation. See Case T-34/93 *Société Générale v Commission* [1995] ECR II-545, para 72; Judgment of 22 March 2012 in Joined Cases T-458/09 and T-171/10 *Slovak Telekom v Commission*, para 44.

[231] See, in relation to Reg 17, European Commission, 'Dealing with the Commission—Notification, complaints, inspections and fact-finding powers under Articles [101] and [102] of the [TFEU]', point 5.6.

[232] However, incomplete answers and their non-rectification can only be sanctioned in case of an inspection by formal decision. See paras 8.03, 8.15, 8.31, and 8.32 with accompanying footnotes.

[233] Article 4(1) and (2) of Reg 773/2004.

[234] Article 4(3) of Reg 773/2004. The rectification, amendment, or supplement shall be added to the original explanations as recorded; these explanations will remain in the Commission file. See Recital 4 of Reg 773/2004.

[235] For the latter see European Commission Antitrust Manual of Procedures, Internal DG Competition working documents on procedures for the application of Articles 101 and 102 TFEU, March 2012, Module 8 'Power to take statements'.

[236] Case 136/79 *National Panasonic v Commission* [1980] ECR 2033, para 15; Case T-9/97 *Elf Atochem v Commission* [1997] ECR II-919, para 23. See also E Gippini-Fournier, 'The Modernisation of European Competition Law: First Experiences with Regulation 1/2003—Institutional Report' in HF Koeck and MM Karollus (eds), The Modernisation of European Competition Law—Initial Experiences with Regulation 1/2003, FIDE XXIII Congress Linz 2008—Congress Publications Vol 2 (Nomos 2008) 59: 'Under Regulation 17, "oral explanations" were viewed as a simple extension of the power to inspect documents and records, and therefore questions would cover only matters strictly related to the records themselves ("who wrote this?" "who has access to this computer?" "whose signature is this?" "where are the records relating to travel expenses of sales managers last year?" "what are these figures?", and so on).'

[237] See, in relation to Reg 17, European Commission, 'Dealing with the Commission—Notification, complaints, inspections and fact-finding powers under Articles [101] and [102] of the [TFEU]', at point 5.6: 'The extent of the inspectors' powers to request on-the-spot oral explanations has never been fully clarified by the Court of Justice or the Court of First Instance.'

explanations on any facts or documents relevant to the inspection, and to put these questions to any member of staff or representative of the undertaking, even employees other than those identified by the company as being best-placed to answer. This creates a certain risk that the power could be used to conduct general interrogations outside of Articles 18, 19 of Regulation 1/2003,[238] which is only somewhat mitigated by the possibility for the undertaking to rectify oral observations by unauthorized members of staff. As it is, the wording of Article 20(2)(e) is quite broad and thus leaves room for disagreement. In line with the Commission's own assessment under Regulation 17,[239] it has been suggested that any question asked pursuant to Article 20(2)(e) should be such that it can be reasonably answered in the circumstances of the inspection. Indeed, fining the undertaking for incorrect answers made on the spot to questions which require reflection and internal investigation will not always be justified, but the outcome will depend on the specific circumstances of each case.[240]

8.64 As indicated, the Commission may record the explanations it receives in any form and then needs to provide a copy of the record to the company. The recorded explanations (only) of unauthorized members of staff are then subject to rectification or amendment. Recital 4 of Regulation 773/2004 nevertheless specifies that the answer given by the staff member shall remain in the Commission file as recorded during the inspection. One probably has to interpret this as meaning that the original reply, albeit rectified, may still be used as evidence. This could become relevant where the Commission concludes that the revised answer, rather than the original reply, is incorrect and/or misleading. The original reply might then be used as evidence in a (procedural) infringement case against the undertaking,[241] as well as to corroborate the evidence by other parties in the case on substance (eg cartel decision).[242]

8.65 In the case of an inspection based on a decision, any refusal by the undertaking (ie its representatives and/or members of staff) to provide explanations may be regarded by the Commission as an infringement of its procedural duty of active cooperation and might give rise to fines and periodic penalty payments.[243] In a simple inspection, such a refusal might lead to a suspension of the inspection. However, any question that would lead to self-incrimination in violation of the *nemo tenetur* principle is inadmissible; as the undertaking has a right not to respond to such questions, the Commission may not sanction a refusal to reply. If it receives a response nevertheless, that

---

[238] A Jones and B Sufrin, *EC Competition Law* (2nd edn, Oxford University Press 2004) 1070. See also Kerse & Khan, *EC Antitrust Procedure* (6th edn, Sweet & Maxwell 2012) para 3-128; A Klees, *Europäisches Kartellverfahrensrecht* (Carl Heymanns Verlag 2005) § 9, paras 101–5.

[239] See European Commission, 'Dealing with the Commission—Notification, complaints, inspections and fact-finding powers under Articles [101] and [102] of the [TFEU]', point 5.6: 'The inspectors are certainly entitled to demand oral explanations where these arise directly out of the documents produced (or not produced), and they may ask for more extensive explanations. However, this power must be read in the light of Article 11 and the safeguards it contains for firms requested to provide information. In particular, the power should not be used to pressure the officials of a firm into making oral admissions which they would not make if they had the time for reflection afforded them by a written request under Article 11.'

[240] Kerse & Khan, *EC Antitrust Procedure* (6th edn, Sweet & Maxwell 2012) para 3-129. It should be noted that Recital 4 and Art 4 of Reg 1/2003 foresee the possibility of a rectification only in case the answer had originally been given by an *unauthorized staff member*. Conversely, where *company representatives* or *authorized staff members* provide incorrect answers, the Commission may in principle directly impose a fine pursuant to Art 23(1)(d), first indent, of Reg 1/2003.

[241] This could lead to the imposition of a fine pursuant to Art 23(1)(d), first indent, of Reg 1/2003, where the Commission would consider the rectification as the (final) incorrect answer of the undertaking.

[242] See Kerse & Khan, *EC Antitrust Procedure* (6th edn, Sweet & Maxwell 2012) para 3-131.

[243] It should be noted that Art 23(1)(d) of Reg 1/2003 relates to the failure or refusal to provide a complete answer by the undertaking. Hence, where an employee refuses to answer a question (for instance out of fear that the information could be used against him to establish his criminal liability in a national jurisdiction), the undertaking might be able to avoid the imposition of fines by providing a satisfactory reply through another member of staff or company representative.

information cannot be used to prove the infringement unless the answer has been provided by a representative or duly authorized staff member in full knowledge that the undertaking was not obliged to respond. However, these restrictions only apply to questions which would (directly) lead the undertaking to admit its involvement in the infringement. Purely factual questions (for instance, as to the participation of staff members in specific meetings, or the existence and location of certain documents) have to be answered, even if the reply can be used by the Commission to prove anticompetitive conduct.[244] Where for any reason it is not possible for the undertaking to give an immediate answer, the inspectors may agree to receive the requested explanations subsequently in writing, in the same way that, if certain documents requested are not available, they may accept an offer by the undertaking to send them to the Commission after completion of the inspection. This does not affect the Commission's powers to request such explanations (or documents) subsequently under Article 18 of Regulation 1/2003. Conversely, the Commission has no power to *compel* representatives or members of staff of undertakings to respond to its questions during an inspection. This may be different for some national competition laws which include powers of enforcement exercisable not only against undertakings but also against their representatives, and also provide for criminal or administrative penalties for executives guilty of not cooperating in the investigation.[245]

E. The Commission's Power to Inspect other Premises

One of the most remarkable extensions to the Commission's investigative powers is its right **8.66** to conduct inspections of non-business premises, including private homes of directors, managers, and other staff members. The use of this new power is restricted to the search for books or other records relevant to prove a 'serious violation' of Articles 101 and/or 102 TFEU and requires a decision by the Competition Commissioner.[246] It has been introduced in particular because the Commission's experience showed that there are cases where business records are kept in the homes of directors or other persons working for an undertaking, and the Commission seeks to ensure that its efforts to crack down on hard-core cartels will not be frustrated by this practice.[247] The Commission's original proposal for Regulation

---

[244] See Recital 23 of Reg 1/2003 and the jurisprudence concerning requests for information, eg Case 374/87 *Orkem v Commission* [1989] 3283, para 34 et seq; Case C-301/04 P *Commission v SGL Carbon* [2006] ECR I-5915, para 43 et seq; Case T-112/98 *Mannesmannröhren-Werke v Commission* [2001] ECR II-729, para 65 et seq; Joined Cases T-236/01, T-239/01, T-244/01 to T-246/01, T-251/01 and T-252/01 *Tokai Carbon and Others v Commission* [2004] ECR II-1181, para 402 et seq; Case T-446/05 *Amann & Söhne and Cousin Filterie v Commission* [2010] ECR II-1255, para 325 et seq. See also European Commission Antitrust Manual of Procedures, Internal DG Competition working documents on procedures for the application of Articles 101 and 102 TFEU, March 2012, Module 6 'Requests for information (Article 18 of Regulation 1/2003)', paras 74–8, and Ch 7, 'Investigation of Cases (II): Formal Investigative Measures in General, Requests for Information and Interviews'.

[245] See JD Cooke, 'General Report' in D Cahill (ed), *The Modernisation of EU Competition Law Enforcement in the European Union: FIDE National Reports* (Cambridge University Press, 2004) 630, 645–6.

[246] See European Commission Antitrust Manual of Procedures, Internal DG Competition working documents on procedures for the application of Articles 101 and 102 TFEU, March 2012, Module 1 'Decision-making procedures', paras 23 and 26–8.

[247] See Recital 26 of Reg 1/2003 and the Proposal for a Council Regulation implementing Articles 81 and 82 of the Treaty, COM(2000) 582 final, explanations to Art 20: 'This extension is based on experience gained in recent cases where it appeared that company employees kept relevant documents in their private homes. Evidence was found suggesting that incriminatory documents were deliberately stored in private homes. Under the existing rules, this enables companies effectively to undermine inspections by the Commission. In order to ensure that the effectiveness of inspections against secret infringements is maintained, it is therefore necessary to extend the powers of the Commission inspectors to search private homes of companies' personnel where professional documents are likely to be kept.' For an example, see *SAS/Maersk Air* [2001]

1/2003 foresaw an extension of its powers of inspection under Article 20 to include private homes, with a requirement to seek a judicial warrant.[248] The fact that Regulation 1/2003 now devotes a separate provision to the inspection of other premises indicates both the importance of this new power and the awareness that it must be strictly circumscribed.[249] So far, the Commission has used that power only in a limited number of cases.[250]

8.67 Article 21 specifies that:

> [i]f a reasonable suspicion exists that books or other records related to the business and to the subject matter of the inspection, which may be relevant to prove a serious violation of Article [101] or Article [102] [TFEU], are being kept in any other premises, land and means of transport, including the homes of directors, managers and other members of staff of the undertakings and associations of undertakings concerned, the Commission can by decision order an inspection to be conducted in such other premises, land and means of transport.

The reference to 'other premises' distinguishes this power from Article 20(2)(a) which permits inspections at the premises of undertakings. While Regulation 1/2003 only makes express reference to the homes of directors, managers, and other members of staff, this may also include the private premises of members of the supervisory board or the owner(s) of the undertaking.[251]

8.68 Given that the search at private premises goes to the core of Article 7 of the Charter,[252] there must be at least a 'reasonable likelihood'[253] that business records relating to the subject matter of the inspection and relevant to prove an infringement are kept there, and the inspection decision must contain specific motivation on this point.[254] Likewise, the Commission must have in its file information and evidence providing reasonable grounds for supporting the suspicion of a serious violation of Articles 101 and/or 102 TFEU.[255] Regulation 1/2003 provides no guidance as to what is meant by a 'serious' infringement in this regard.[256] However,

---

OJ L265/15, para 89, reporting on a meeting note which recorded a Maersk representative as saying that 'all material on price agreements, market-sharing agreements and the like had to be destroyed before going home today. Anything that might be needed had to be taken home.'

[248] Proposal for a Council Regulation implementing Articles 81 and 82 of the Treaty, OM(2000) 582 final, Art 20: '2. The officials authorized by the Commission to conduct an inspection are empowered: . . . (b) to enter any other premises, including the homes of directors, managers and other members of staff of the undertakings and associations of undertakings concerned, in so far as it may be suspected that business records are being kept there; . . . 7. Where the officials authorised by the Commission wish to exercise the power provided for by paragraph 2(b), authorisation from the judicial authority must be obtained beforehand.'

[249] Kerse & Khan, *EC Antitrust Procedure* (6th edn, Sweet & Maxwell 2012) para 3-139–3-140.

[250] See para 8.01 with accompanying footnote.

[251] Cf Proposal for a Council Regulation implementing Articles 81 and 82 of the Treaty, COM(2000) 582 final, Art 20(2)(b). Indeed, the German language version of Art 21(1) of Reg 1/2003 not only refers to members of the Board of Directors (captured by the term 'directors' in the English language version), but also to members of the Supervisory Board ('Aufsichtsorgan').

[252] As the ECJ explained in *Roquette Frères* with regard to ECtHR jurisprudence, 'the right of interference established by Article 8(2) of the ECHR might well be more far-reaching where professional or business activities or premises were involved than would otherwise be the case'. See Case C-94/00 *Roquette Frères* [2002] ECR I-9011, para 29. This suggests that the requirements for interfering with private homes are particularly stringent. See also *Buck v Germany* App no 41604/98 (ECtHR, 28 April 2005), para 51, according to which 'it must be clearly established that the proportionality principle has been adhered to' in order for a home search to be justified under the ECHR.

[253] See Art 21(3) of Reg 1/2003.

[254] Article 21(2) of Reg 1/2003. Given that the interference with fundamental rights is particularly intense for decisions pursuant to Art 21 of Reg 1/2003, the requirement as to their motivation is particularly high.

[255] Case C-94/00 *Roquette Frères* [2002] ECR I-9011, para 61; Case T-339/04 *France Télécom v Commission* [2007] ECR II-521, paras 60 and 62.

[256] It has been suggested that determining the seriousness of the infringement requires an overall assessment taking into account all relevant factors (nature of the infringement, level of fault, concerned market, potential

it seems clear that the investigation of cartels, which will be the typical application of Article 21, should sufficiently justify the inspection of private premises. While Article 21(3) refers to the seriousness of the suspected infringement (including the involvement of the undertaking concerned), the degree of likelihood that business records relating to the subject matter of the inspection might be kept at the premises, and the importance of the evidence sought as factors in determining the *proportionality of any coercive measures* that may be envisaged, these are also important when determining the *necessity of the inspection* as such.[257]

As for the powers of the inspectors, they are more limited: the Commission has the right to   **8.69** examine business records (irrespective of the storage medium) and take copies thereof, but is not empowered to conduct interviews or to seal cupboards, rooms, or premises.[258] It is also worth noting that neither Article 21 nor Articles 23 or 24 refer to any Commission power to impose fines and/or penalty payments in relation to inspections under Article 21. The likely reason is that the undertaking cannot be held liable for obstructive behaviour on the side of the individual whose private premises are searched.[259] This also speaks against any increase in the fine on account of aggravating circumstances (obstruction) in case the undertaking is subsequently held liable for a substantive infringement of the competition rules.

Where the Commission intends to inspect non-corporate premises pursuant to Article 21   **8.70** of Regulation 1/2003, it will often make sense to address the inspection decision to both the individual occupying the premises[260] and the undertaking concerned (based on Article 20(4)).[261] The first decision, however, cannot be executed without prior authorization from the competent judicial authority of the Member State concerned (Article 20(3) of Regulation 1/2003).[262] The national judge will ensure that the Commission decision is authentic—and,

---

damage to competition, etc). See O Weber in JL Schulte and C Just (eds), *Kartellrecht* (Carl Heymanns Verlag 2012), Art 21 of Reg 1/2003, para 7. Some inspiration could be drawn from the 1998 Fining Guidelines which, for the purpose of setting fines, distinguished between 'minor', 'serious', and 'very serious' infringements and provided examples for each category. See Guidelines on the method of setting fines imposed pursuant to Article 15 (2) of Regulation No 17 and Article 65 (5) of the ECSC Treaty, [1998] OJ C9/3.

[257] Cf Case C-94/00 *Roquette Frères* [2002] ECR I-9011, para 55.

[258] Article 21(4) of Reg 1/2003. This deviates from what was originally foreseen in the Commission's legislative proposal which did not distinguish between inspections at company or private premises as regards the powers of the inspectors. See also K Dekeyser and C Gauer, 'The New Enforcement System for Articles 81 and 82 and the Rights of Defence' ch 23 in BE Hawk (ed), *International Antitrust Law & Policy* (Annual Proceedings of the Fordham Institute International Antitrust Law and Policy 2005) 545, 557.

[259] Kerse & Khan, *EC Antitrust Procedure* (6th edn, Sweet and Maxwell 2012), para 3-144.

[260] Where private dwellings are concerned, there are good arguments to consider that the individual residing, occupying or using the premises (usually having *de jure* control of access as an owner or lessee) should be named as addressee. See E Gippini-Fournier, 'The Modernisation of European Competition Law: First Experiences with Regulation 1/2003—Institutional Report' in HF Koeck and MM Karollus (eds), The Modernisation of European Competition Law—Initial Experiences with Regulation 1/2003, FIDE XXIII Congress Linz 2008—Congress Publications Vol 2 (Nomos 2008) 64. If other persons have special rights to control the premises (eg the owner of an appartment that is rented out to a staff member of the undertaking), the inspection decision empowers the Commission to interfere with these rights. However, those other persons might have a right to challenge the decision as the inspection is of direct and individual concern to them.

[261] This is particularly important where office space and private rooms cannot easily be distinguished (for instance in a small family business), or where it is suspected that managers regularly transfer business documents between their office and private home. In case the Commission adopts parallel decisions pursuant to Arts 20 and 21 of Reg 1/2003, each of them has to fulfill the applicable legal requirements and may be challenged separately. See also E Gippini-Fournier, 'The Modernisation of European Competition Law: First Experiences with Regulation 1/2003—Institutional Report' in HF Koeck and MM Karollus (eds), The Modernisation of European Competition Law—Initial Experiences with Regulation 1/2003, FIDE XXIII Congress Linz 2008—Congress Publications Vol 2 (Nomos 2008) 63.

[262] In practice, the NCA will cooperate and transmit the inspection decision to the judicial authority on behalf of the Commission. However, the Commission should also be allowed to file or join the application,

where this is requested as a precautionary measure, that the coercive measures envisaged[263] are neither arbitrary nor excessive[264]—but must not call into question the necessity of the inspection as such, which is for the EU Courts alone to review (in case of an annulment action against the inspection decision). Article 21(3) states that the national judge shall assess the proportionality of the interference with the undertaking's rights with due regard to the seriousness of the infringement, the involvement of the undertaking concerned, the importance of the evidence sought, and the reasonable likelihood that such evidence will be located on the premises. This is akin to the requirements under Article 20(8),[265] even though it can be expected that the level of scrutiny is likely to be higher in case an inspection at a private home is at issue. In order to carry out its task, the national judge may ask the Commission, directly or through the NCA, for detailed explanations concerning these elements; it cannot demand, however, that it be provided with documents in the Commission's file.[266]

F. Cooperation between the Commission and the NCAs

1. Involvement of the NCAs

Prior notice or consultation

8.71 In the case of simple inspections by authorization, Article 20(3) requires the Commission 'in good time before the investigation... [to] give notice of the inspection to the competition authority of the Member State in whose territory it is to be conducted'. In the case of inspections pursuant to a binding decision, Articles 20(4) and 21(2) provide that 'the Commission shall take such decisions after consulting the competition authority of the Member State in whose territory the inspection is to be conducted.' In general, the Commission strives to provide the NCAs with at least two weeks' notice. However, there are no formal rules requiring it to observe that time limit or to involve the NCA in any particular form. Thus, depending on the circumstances of the case (eg a particular concern that information might leak to the undertaking concerned) the Commission may choose to contact the NCA informally by telephone and on short notice,[267] as long as this provides the NCA with sufficient time to be

---

and to be present at any hearing before the judge. See E Gippini-Fournier, 'The Modernisation of European Competition Law: First Experiences with Regulation 1/2003—Institutional Report' in HF Koeck and MM Karollus (eds), The Modernisation of European Competition Law—Initial Experiences with Regulation 1/2003, FIDE XXIII Congress Linz 2008—Congress Publications Vol 2 (Nomos 2008) 63.

[263] Cf Case C-94/00 *Roquette Frères* [2002] ECR I-9011, para 58.

[264] E Gippini Fournier has argued that judicial authorization pursuant to Art 21(3) would at the same time also fulfill the function of an authorization for assistance by the national authorities, also because Art 21(4) does not make any reference to the authorization pursuant to Art 20(7). See E Gippini-Fournier, 'The Modernisation of European Competition Law: First Experiences with Regulation 1/2003—Institutional Report' in HF Koeck and MM Karollus (eds), The Modernisation of European Competition Law—Initial Experiences with Regulation 1/2003, FIDE XXIII Congress Linz 2008—Congress Publications Vol 2 (Nomos 2008) 63, n 186.

[265] See also Case C-94/00 *Roquette Frères* [2002] ECR I-9011, paras 52, 54, and 79–80. According to the ECJ, judicial review by the national court of any coercive measures envisaged involves establishing that such measures (i) 'are appropriate to ensure that the investigation can be carried out' and (ii) 'do not constitute, in relation to the aim pursued by the investigation in question, a disproportionate and intolerable interference' (paras 71 and 72).

[266] See Case C-94/00 *Roquette Frères* [2002] ECR I-9011, paras 61–2, 91–3, and 97–8.

[267] The ECJ has stated that it is of little importance if the consultation took place informally or by telephone, without any record of it being made. Since the purpose of Art 14(2) of Reg 17 [now Art 20(3) of Reg 1/2003] is to enable the Commission to carry out surprise inspections at the premises of undertakings suspected of infringements of the Union competition rules, the Commission must be in a position to take a decision without being bound by formal conditions which would delay its adoption. See Case 5/85 *AKSO Chemie v Commission* [1986] ECR 2585, para 24.

present during the inspection and prepare the necessary steps, including, where appropriate, any application for judicial authorization as a precautionary measure.[268] However, in case of an inspection decision the 'consultation' is normally more formal than the notice given for a simple inspection (which depends on the voluntary cooperation of the undertaking and excludes any kind of enforcement action). Generally, a two-way consultation process also benefits the Commission, as the NCA might possess additional information on the undertaking and/or market environment, which helps to better prepare the investigation.

Assistance and inspection work by national officials alongside Commission inspectors

While there is no general duty for the NCAs to be present—and absences do indeed occur **8.72** at times, at least during part of the inspection—Article 20(5) of Regulation 1/2003 foresees that NCA officials (or those authorized or appointed by it) 'shall, at the request of that authority or of the Commission, actively assist' the Commission inspectors. In case of assistance they enjoy the same powers as the Commission inspectors pursuant to Article 20(2). Hence, they do not act as arbiter or neutral observer, but rather help the Commission inspectors to locate, read, and copy or take extracts from business records. In addition, where the Commission inspectors find that an undertaking opposes an inspection ordered by decision, the Member State concerned shall afford them the necessary assistance by way of coercion, requesting where appropriate the help of the police or an equivalent enforcement authority (Article 20(6)).

Inspections facilitated by measures of constraint

As indicated, the role of the Member States becomes particularly important if the undertakings **8.73** do not submit to the inspection, obstruct its course, or otherwise fail to cooperate. The duty to submit to a decision ordering an inspection is a continuing one, which means that the undertaking not only has to allow the inspection to begin but must also cooperate (actively) thereafter. However, the Commission's officials lack the power to enforce these duties, other than by imposing penalty payments, which make for an inadequate tool in the context of (surprise) inspections. The Commission therefore must rely on the NCAs, and possibly the assistance of national enforcement authorities, to overcome opposition[269] on the side of the undertaking. While these authorities have the investigative powers conferred upon the Commission under Article 20(2) of Regulation 1/2003, and act within the scope of the inspection as defined by EU law,[270] their enforcement powers derive from national law. In carrying out their tasks, they must follow the procedures laid down in national law and observe the procedural safeguards foreseen in this respect.[271] Article 20(6) of Regulation 1/2003 provides that, where the officials

---

[268] See Art 20(7) of Reg 1/2003. This will be particularly relevant where the Commission itself requests the assistance of the NCA as a precautionary measure in order to overcome any potential opposition on the part of the undertaking, including attempts at concealing or disposing of evidence. See Joined Cases 46/87 and 227/88 *Hoechst v Commission* [1989] ECR 2859, para 32; Case C-94/00 *Roquette Frères* [2002] ECR I-9011, paras 73 and 74. Where such assistance by the NCA presupposes prior judicial authorization, it is for the Commission to provide the competent national court with the explanations needed by that court to satisfy itself that otherwise the investigation would be jeopardized.

[269] As regards reliance on the national authorities as a precautionary measure, see Case C-94/00 *Roquette Frères* [2002] ECR I-9011, paras 73–5.

[270] Articles 20(5) and 21(4) of Reg 1/2003. See also Art 20(7) ('according to national rules') and Case C-94/00 *Roquette Frères* [2002] ECR I-9011, paras 35–6 and 44–6; Case C-550/07 P *Akzo Nobel Chemicals and Akcros Chemicals v Commission* [2010] ECR I-8301, para 119.

[271] Joined Cases 46/87 and 227/88 *Hoechst v Commission* [1989] ECR 2859, para 32–4; Case C-94/00 *Roquette Frères* [2002] ECR I-9011, para 34. Once the national authorities take enforcement measures—where appropriate, based on an authorization from a national judge—failure by the undertaking and its staff to comply may lead to sanctions under national law. See European Commission, 'Dealing with the Commission: Notification, complaints, inspections and fact-finding powers under Articles [101] and [102] of the [TFEU]' (1997 edn), point 5.4.1.

and other accompanying persons authorized by the Commission find that an undertaking opposes an inspection ordered pursuant to this Article, the Member State concerned shall afford them the necessary assistance, requesting where appropriate the assistance of the police or an equivalent enforcement authority, so as to enable the Commission inspectors to conduct their inspection.[272] If such assistance requires authorization from a judicial authority under national law (ie because national rules require that a court controls coercive measures such as forcible entry and/or the seizure of documents), this must be applied for.[273] The powers and duties of review of the national court in this context, which were not specifically addressed in Regulation 17, are now expressly regulated in Articles 20(8) and 21(3) of Regulation 1/2003, in line with the ECJ's judgment in *Roquette Frères*,[274] which was rendered only two months before the adoption of the new regulation.

8.74 In *Roquette Frères*, the ECJ held that, in ruling on the request for a search warrant, the national court could not review the need for the Commission's investigation. In order to ensure the uniform interpretation and application of EU law, control over the legality of an EU act may only be exercised by the EU Courts.[275] However, it stated that the national court may examine whether the coercive measures envisaged to overcome opposition by the undertaking would be arbitrary or disproportionate (excessive) relative to the subject matter of the investigation.[276] While the national judge may not demand that it be provided with the information and evidence in the Commission's file—as this could threaten the anonymity of informants and possibly slow down the Commission's investigation, especially where simultaneous inspections are carried out in several Member States—it may ask for detailed explanations.[277] As regards the proportionality of the coercive measures to the subject matter of the investigation, it must be established that such measures are appropriate to ensure that the investigation can be carried out and that they 'do not constitute, in relation to the aim pursued by the investigation in question, a disproportionate and intolerable interference'.[278] This requires informing the national court about the:

> essential features of the suspected infringement, so as to enable it to assess their seriousness, by indicating the market thought to be affected, the nature of the suspected

---

[272] If a Member State would fail to provide the necessary assistance in this regard, the Commission could bring an action against that Member State before the ECJ under Art 258 TFEU. See W Wils 'Powers of investigation and procedural rights and guarantees in EU antitrust enforcement', First Lisbon Conference on Competition Law and Economics, November 2005, para 23 and n 28.

[273] Article 20(7) of Reg 1/2003. Such judicial authorization is always required for inspections of private homes pursuant to Art 21(3) of Reg 1/2003.

[274] Case C-94/00 *Roquette Frères* [2002] ECR I-9011, para 39 et seq.

[275] Case C-94/00 *Roquette Frères* [2002] ECR I-9011, paras 39 and 51. It has been suggested that the system of double control (review by the national judge of the proportionality between the coercive measures applied for and the seriousness of the suspected infringement, review by the EU Courts of the legality of the EU act) is confusing for applicants who do not always clearly understand which ground they may invoke before which court. In addition, where the Commission conducts inspections simultaneously in various Member States, it may become necessary to seek numerous court warrants before various national courts. For these and other reasons, AG Mischo has argued in favour of a unified system of prior control in the hands of the EU Courts, which, however, would be likely to require a change of the Treaties. AG Mischo, Joined Opinion in Cases 46/87, 85/87, 97/87, 98/87, 99/87 and 227/88 *Hoechst and Others v Commission* [1989] ECR 2859, para 146 et seq.

[276] Case C-94/00 *Roquette Frères* [2002] ECR I-9011, paras 36, 40, and 52.

[277] Case C-94/00 *Roquette Frères* [2002] ECR I-9011, paras 54–66. Although the Commission had not indicated the nature of the evidence on which its suspicions were based (eg a complaint, testimony, or documents exchanged between the participants in the suspected cartel), the ECJ considered it sufficient that the Commission provided a detailed account of the available information concerning the specific subject matter of the suspected cartel such as to enable the competent national court to establish a firm basis for its conclusion that the Commission does indeed possess such evidence (para 70).

[278] Case C-94/00 *Roquette Frères* [2002] ECR I9011, paras 71 and 76. In case assistance by the national authorities is requested as a precautionary measure in order to overcome potential opposition, it is ultimately

restrictions of competition and the supposed degree of involvement of the undertaking concerned.[279]

The Commission also has to indicate as precisely as possible the evidence sought and the matters to which the investigation relates. However, this can be done in a general way without reference to specific documents or files the Commission is looking for, given that it is entitled to search for items not already known or identified in advance.[280]

The competent national court might refuse to grant the coercive measures applied for where **8.75** the suspected impairment of competition is so minimal, the extent of the likely involvement of the undertaking concerned so limited, or the evidence sought so peripheral, that the intervention in the business sphere of a legal person which a search using law enforcement authorities entails would appear manifestly excessive in the light of the objectives pursued by the investigation. Similar considerations will determine the review of a request for prior authorization as regards inspections of private homes (Article 21(3) of Regulation 1/2003), even though the judge is likely to require a higher level of justification. In either case, a national court cannot simply dismiss an application for coercive measures where it considers the information provided by the Commission to be insufficient. Before doing so, it must as rapidly as possible inform the Commission, or the national authority which has brought the latter's request before it, of the difficulties encountered, where necessary by requesting any additional information required to conduct its review. In turn, the Commission is obliged to transmit, with a minimum of delay, such additional information, which might even be provided orally.[281] The national court may delay a final ruling on the coercive measures until it obtains the requested clarifications.[282]

It should be noted that the fact of having finally gained access to the premises of undertakings **8.76** by force does not prevent the Commission from imposing a fine where the inspection has been impeded. In fact, the Commission does not hesitate to impose penalties for such procedural infringements.[283] Alternatively—and this might have an even greater impact financially—a refusal by the undertaking to cooperate with the Commission may be taken into account as an aggravating circumstance in the calculation of the fine which may be imposed for the infringement on substance (eg the cartel fine).[284]

2. Inspections carried out pursuant to Article 22 of Regulation 1/2003 and Article 8 of Protocol 23 to the EEA Agreement

Article 22 of Regulation 1/2003 is modeled on Article 13 of Regulation 17, but has been **8.77** adapted to the new European Competition Network ('ECN') system; it complements

---

for the Commission to provide the competent national court with the explanations needed by that court to satisfy itself that, otherwise, 'it would be impossible, or very difficult, to establish the facts amounting to the infringement'. Hence, there must be grounds for apprehending opposition to the investigation and/or attempts at concealing or disposing of evidence in the event that an investigation ordered by decision is notified to the undertaking concerned (paras 74 and 75).

[279] Case C-94/00 *Roquette Frères* [2002] ECR I-9011, para 81. See also Arts 20(8) and 21(3) of Reg 1/2003.

[280] Case C-94/00 *Roquette Frères* [2002] ECR I-9011, paras 83 and 84.

[281] See Case C-94/00 *Roquette Frères* [2002] ECR I-9011, para 98.

[282] Case C-94/00 *Roquette Frères* [2002] ECR I-9011, paras 90–4.

[283] See eg the Decision in *MEWAC* [1993] OJ L20/6 applying the procedural rules of the Reg concerning maritime transport.

[284] See point 28, second indent, of the Guidelines on the method of setting fines imposed pursuant to Article 23(2)(a) of Regulation No 1/2003 [2006] OJ C210/2.

Articles 11 to 14 of Regulation 1/2003. The provision regulates two types of action: first, the competence[285] of an NCA to carry out any fact-finding measures (including inspections)[286] on behalf of the NCA of another Member State (Article 22(1)); and second, the legal obligation for an NCA to carry out an inspection of business premises[287] on its territory at the request[288] of the Commission (Article 22(2)).[289] Such cooperation is necessary in order to allow effective cooperation within the European network of competition authorities.[290] It enables the Commission to save (limited) resources, and the NCAs to effectively deal with cases even if some of the evidence is located in another Member State. In fact, without such mechanisms, a real decentralization of the application of EU competition rules might not work. Each time, the NCA carrying out the inspection applies its own national law and the investigative powers granted therein.[291] Upon request by the Commission itself, or the NCA in whose territory the inspection is to be conducted, officials and/or other accompanying persons authorized by the Commission may assist the NCA officials, in which case their actions will be based on national law. Any exchange and use of the information collected will be governed by Article 12.[292]

8.78 As far as judicial control is concerned, competences are split: while the request for assistance and any finding of an infringement based on the evidence collected fall under the legal regime of the requesting authority (Member State, EU), the collection of the evidence (and thus the way the investigation is conducted) must follow the procedural rules of the Member State where the investigation takes place; this also determines the judicial body competent to review the respective measures.[293] Where the NCA charged with the investigation violates applicable procedural safeguards, the information collected may not be used as evidence. In addition safeguards provided for in Article 12(2) and (3) of Regulation 1/2003 apply.

8.79 Assistance will also be provided between the European Commission and the EFTA Surveillance Authority ('ESA'). Hence, where a suspected infringement extends across the

---

[285] Article 22(1) of Reg 1/2003 confers a competence, not an obligation. However, the NCA which has been requested to assist in fact-finding measures must exercise its discretion in a spirit of sincere cooperation (Art 4(3) TEU). In case the request is rejected, the requesting NCA may consult the Commission pursuant to Art 11(5) of Reg 1/2003.

[286] According to the Commission, assistance has mainly been requested and provided in the context of inspections, witness interviews, and requests for information. See Commission Staff Working Paper accompanying the Report on the functioning of Regulation 1/2003, SEC(2009) 574 final, para 246.

[287] As the reference in Art 22(2) of Reg 1/2003 to Art 20 indicates, the provision does not apply to inspections of non-business premises within the meaning of Art 21.

[288] The request to the NCA based on Arts 20(4) and 22(2) is likely to be in the form of a decision addressed to the Member State. The Commissioner with special responsibility for competition has been empowered to make such a request on behalf of the College (SEC(2006) 1368).

[289] The Commission has used this instrument in the context of the *Flat glass* investigation in France and Germany in February 2005. See Commission MEMO/05/63 'Anti-trust: Commission investigation in the flat and car glass sector' of 24 February 2005 and Commission Decision of 28 November 2007 in Case COMP/39.165 *Flat Glass*, para 61. It is particularly useful in investigations where a large number of sites need to be inspected simultaneously and the Commission lacks the necessary resources. See Commission Staff Working Paper accompanying the Report on the functioning of Regulation 1/2003, SEC(2009) 574 final, para 80.

[290] Recital 28 of Reg 1/2003.

[291] See Commission Notice on cooperation within the Network of Competition Authorities [2004] OJ C101/43, paras 29 and 30. The assisting authority may use all investigative tools at its disposal, independently of the fact that they may differ from the investigative tools at the disposal of the requesting authority. See Commission Staff Working Paper accompanying the Report on the functioning of Regulation 1/2003, SEC(2009) 574 final, para 79.

[292] See also Commission Notice on cooperation within the Network of Competition Authorities [2004] OJ C101/43, paras 26–9.

[293] See O Weber in JL Schulte and C Just (eds), *Kartellrecht* (Carl Heymanns Verlag 2012), Art 22 of Reg 1/2003, paras 5 and 7.

EEA, the 'competent surveillance authority'[294] may request the other authority to carry out inspections within its territory (European EU, EFTA States), in accordance with its internal rules.[295] The requesting authority is entitled to be represented and take an active part in such inspections. Immediately after the inspection, it will receive all information obtained.[296]

G. The Conduct of Inspections

1. Arrival of inspectors

Although Regulation 1/2003 does not stipulate that inspections may only be carried out **8.80** during office hours, the Commission must conduct itself in a way that is proportionate and not arbitrary. Hence, the Commission inspectors, accompanied if appropriate by national officials assisting them, always arrive at the premises of the undertaking during office hours. The first thing they do is to inform the staff members who receive them that they are EU officials and ask to speak with those in charge. The inspectors will also allow the company to contact its external lawyers to attend the inspection.[297] However, the inspectors are not obliged to wait until the lawyers arrive and in practice will accept only a short delay before starting with the inspection. In order to ensure that no evidence is destroyed or tampered with in the meantime, they will enter the premises and occupy the relevant offices of their choice without delay.[298] While waiting for the arrival of external lawyers, legal advice may be obtained by telephone.

The company should ensure that, with the consent of the inspectors, a senior member of the **8.81** legal department (if there is one on site) or an appropriately senior company representative is immediately alerted to the arrival of the inspectors. In addition, in order to ensure that the investigation is appropriately managed and supervised, the company is well advised to establish a team of employees headed by a senior company representative who will take overall responsibility. With the consent of the inspectors, other relevant staff (eg the IT department) should be informed that an investigation is underway, of their duty of active cooperation during the inspection, and the potential consequences of obstructive behaviour. The company may want to set aside a meeting room as a place where files can be examined and any necessary discussions with inspectors can be held.

2. Designated representatives

The inspectors may not know in advance the identity of those individuals they will encounter **8.82** on the day of the inspection, unless they have informed the undertaking of the inspection

---

[294] Article 56 of the EEA Agreement.

[295] For instance, where the ESA acts upon request of the Commission, it will itself adopt an inspection decision based on the EFTA Agreement and implementing rules. Pursuant to Art 8(2) of Protocol 23 to the EEA Agreement, the ESA would be obliged to follow such a request, which will likely be in the form of a Commission decision based on Arts 20(4) of Reg 1/2003, Art 8 of Protocol 23 to the EEA Agreement. See also Art 5(1) of Reg 2894/94.

[296] Article 8(3) of Protocol 23 to the EEA Agreement. See also European Commission Antitrust Manual of Procedures, Internal DG Competition working documents on procedures for the application of Articles 101 and 102 TFEU, March 2012, Module 5 'International relations: cooperation with competition authorities in third countries', para 23.

[297] If available, external lawyers with training on how to deal with inspections should supervise the investigatory steps taken by the inspectors and note down any irregularities.

[298] See Explanatory note to an authorisation to conduct an inspection in execution of a Commission decision under Article 20(4) of Council Regulation No 1/2003, para 6. This approach has been confirmed by the GC, see Judgment of 27 September 2012 in Case T-357/06 *Koninklijke Wegenbouw Stevin v Commission*, para 232.

beforehand (simple inspection) and thus already had prior contacts with the relevant company representatives. Hence, in the case of surprise inspections, the inspectors' first task will be to discover, without delay, who is to represent the undertaking during the inspection. In practice, the team leader for the inspection will typically ask for the company organization chart and to be received by a higher-ranking company representative (eg directors, commercial managers, or heads of the relevant departments). However, it is for the undertaking, not the Commission, to designate its representatives. At the same time, the inspectors are empowered to ask questions and request clarifications from any members of staff who, by reason of their office, seem well placed to provide such information (Article 20(2)(e) of Regulation 1/2003).

3. Identification and documentation

8.83 Once the undertaking has decided who is to represent it, the officials proceed to identify themselves, EU officials by means of their 'staff cards', which show their photographs, and national officials by means of an equivalent identity document (according to their national rules). The inspectors then hand to the undertaking's representatives the documentation necessary for the exercise of their powers of inspection and inform the undertaking of its rights (as well as certain of its duties). Thus, respectively, they will hand over:

(1) In simple inspections:
  (a) the written authorization to inspect;[299]
  (b) the explanatory memorandum concerning inspections pursuant to Article 20(3) of Regulation 1/2003.
(2) In inspections pursuant to a binding decision:
  (a) an authenticated copy of the inspection decision;
  (b) the written authorization to inspect (mandate for the individual inspectors);
  (c) the explanatory memorandum concerning inspections pursuant to Article 20(4) of Regulation 1/2003.

8.84 When the copy of the decision is handed over to a representative of the undertaking, the inspectors draw up a formal minute of notification. The fact of signing the record does not imply that the undertaking accepts the legality of the decision and/or agrees to submit to the inspection. Rather, it is a simple acknowledgement of receipt.[300]

4. Clarifications and legal representation

8.85 The inspectors then ask the representatives of the undertaking to read the explanatory note and, if so requested, they explain particular aspects of the inspection.[301] Where the inspection

---

[299] This mandate also serves to name the officials and other accompanying persons authorized to conduct the inspection. If the identity of any inspector does not coincide with the particulars given in the authorization, the undertaking may request that the person concerned refrains from taking part in the inspection.

[300] Explanatory note to an authorisation to conduct an inspection in execution of a Commission decision under Article 20(4) of Council Regulation No 1/2003, para 3.

[301] In particular, further instructions as to the handling of electronic data might be provided. See eg Commission Decision of 28 March 2012 in Case COMP/39.793 *EPH and others*, para 40: 'As electronic files are much easier and quicker to destroy during the inspection than paper files, the Commission inspectors routinely take steps at the beginning of inspections to ensure that they will have access to complete files as foreseen by Regulation (EC) No 1/2003. In particular they identify the e-mail accounts of the key persons in the undertaking for the business subject to the inspection and they ask the IT department to change the password required to connect to those e-mail accounts to a password which is only known to the Commission inspectors. This procedure ensures an exclusive access for the Commission inspectors until they have completed their review of the e-mails... The Commission inspectors unblock the accounts as quickly as possible and at the latest when they leave the premises on the last day of the inspection. The Commission may and does review not only e-mails that have been received or sent before the inspection but also e-mails that are

constitutes the first investigative measure against the undertaking, it shall be informed that it is subject to a preliminary investigation and of its procedural status in this respect (typically that of an undertaking concerned).[302] In simple inspections, the EU officials may also provide explanations regarding both the subject matter and purpose of the inspection, as well as matters of procedure[303] (including questions of confidentiality and the use of documents, the right to involve a lawyer, the voluntary nature of the inspection and, notwithstanding such voluntary nature, the obligation not to obstruct the inspection once the undertaking has decided to submit to it[304]). In the case of inspections pursuant to a decision, there is no need for the inspectors to explain the subject matter and purpose of the inspection, or the reasons for which the decision to inspect was taken. The decision itself should deal with all those points in some detail, and the inspectors are instructed not to 'enlarge upon the subject matter as set out in the decision or to justify in any way the taking of the decision'.[305] However, they may clarify points of procedure (for example the confidential treatment and limited use of the information obtained), indicate the consequences of a refusal to submit to the inspection or any obstruction, and indicate the right of the undertaking to be assisted by a lawyer or legal adviser.[306] The explanations given must not be understood as replacing the written authorization or inspection decision, nor the accompanying explanatory note. The time spent on such explanations will be as short as possible, so as not to delay the start of the inspection to an extent that could neutralize the surprise effect.

In the case of a surprise inspection, if the undertaking has no internal legal advisers at hand, the **8.86** inspectors may nevertheless refuse to put the inspection on hold until a lawyer arrives. However, they might wait at least for a short period of time.[307] In this case, the inspectors will likely require that the undertaking guarantees, first, that no business records will be interfered with during the delay and, second, that they will not be prevented from entering the premises and occupy the offices they may choose.[308] If an advance notice has been given of a (simple) inspection, inspectors will not await the arrival of the undertaking's lawyer. Nor will the start of the inspection normally be delayed if undertakings have their own legal advisers but wish to be assisted by independent lawyers.

---

received during the course of the inspection and thus become part of the body of documentation subject to the inspection.' The Commission considered that instructions to the head of the IT department were sufficient, as that person would then be responsible for disseminating the information promptly to the rest of the IT staff (including the helpdesk) (para 73). See also Explanatory note for an authorisation to conduct an inspection based on a Commission authorisation under Article 20(3) of Council Regulation No 1/2003, para 9.

[302] Commission Notice on best practices for the conduct of proceedings concerning Articles 101 and 102 TFEU, [2011] OJ C308/6, para 15. If the undertaking considers that it has not been properly informed by DG COMP of its procedural status, it may refer the matter to the Hearing Officer for resolution, after having raised the issue with DG COMP. If the complaint is upheld, the Hearing Officer will take a decision that DG COMP shall inform the undertaking of its procedural status. See Decision of the President of the European Commission of 13 October 2011 on the function and terms of reference of the hearing officer in certain competition proceedings [2011] OJ L275/29, Art 4(2)(d).

[303] See Explanatory note for an authorisation to conduct an inspection based on a Commission authorisation under Article 20(3) of Council Regulation No 1/2003, para 2.

[304] See European Commission, 'Dealing with the Commission—Notifications, complaints, inspections and fact-finding powers under Articles [101] and [102] of the [TFEU]' (1997 edn) point 5.2.

[305] Explanatory note to an authorisation to conduct an inspection in execution of a Commission decision under Article 20(4) of Council Regulation No 1/2003, para 2.

[306] See Case C-94/00 *Roquette Frères* [2002] ECR I-9011, para 46.

[307] See para 8.80.

[308] Explanatory note to an authorisation to conduct an inspection in execution of a Commission decision under Article 20(4) of Council Regulation No 1/2003, para 6; European Commission, 'Dealing with the Commission—Notifications, complaints, inspections and fact-finding powers under Articles [101] and [102] of the [TFEU]' (1997 edn) point 5.5.

5. Submission to inspections

8.87 After the written authorization to conduct a (simple) inspection has been produced, and possibly further explanations, the undertaking has to decide whether or not to agree to such an inspection. The Commission will not accept a partial or conditional submission to an inspection. Although this point has not been dealt with in the case law so far, the Commission's view seems to be that if the undertaking agrees to the commencement of a simple inspection—and has not expressly revoked that agreement later on—it must fully submit to it, as in the case of an inspection pursuant to a decision.[309] Thus, any obstruction of the investigation by the undertaking might give rise to a fine pursuant to Article 23(1)(c) to (e) of Regulation 1/2003.[310] In the event of an upfront opposition to a simple inspection, the Commission officials shall minute this refusal, 'no particular form being required'. The undertaking shall receive a copy of the minute, if it so wishes, following which the inspectors leave the premises. The Commission will then be forced (if it wants to continue the investigation) to adopt a decision ordering an inspection. Experience shows that the Commission can act very quickly in such cases. Therefore, undertakings should not hope to gain much time by opposing a simple inspection.[311] However, the Commission clearly runs the risk that incriminating evidence may no longer be found at the premises of the undertaking when inspections are subsequently carried out pursuant to a decision. This is the reason why in most cases simple inspections will only be carried out in cooperation with the undertaking, or at least its top management.[312]

6. Enforcement

8.88 EU officials are not entitled to enter the premises of an undertaking by force, or to enforce their powers of inspection. If undertakings oppose an inspection, the Commission merely documents the opposition but then has to rely on NCAs or other national authorities to assist the inspectors by taking coercive measures, in accordance with Article 20(6) of Regulation 1/2003. Opposition must not be interpreted as being confined to an outright refusal to allow inspectors to enter an undertaking's premises or to examine business records. It includes any attempt by the undertaking (ie its staff or representatives) to hamper the inspectors' work once an inspection has commenced. The form of any assistance by Member States authorities is determined by national law and is confined by the procedural safeguards provided therein, including the potential need to obtain authorization from a national court. However, as indicated earlier, the national judge is not empowered in such cases to substitute its own view

---

[309] See European Commission, 'Dealing with the Commission—Notifications, complaints, inspections and fact-finding powers under Articles [101] and [102] of the [TFEU]' (1997 edn) point 5.2, and the Explanatory note for an authorisation to conduct an inspection based on a Commission authorisation under Article 20(3) of Council Regulation No 1/2003, para 9, which states that while email accounts are blocked 'the undertaking must not interfere in any way with these blocked accounts.' Likewise, para 15 stipulates that the undertaking 'has to ensure that seals that have been affixed as well as the immediate environment of the place where they have been affixed . . . remain untouched until the seals are removed by the Commission's representative.' However, Arts 20(3), 23(1)(d) of Reg 1/2003 suggest that the undertaking cannot be sanctioned for providing incomplete replies, unless doing so would be tantamount to a misleading and/or incorrect answer.

[310] See eg *FNICF* [1982] OJ L319/12.

[311] See European Commission, 'Dealing with the Commission—Notifications, complaints, inspections and fact-finding powers under Articles [101] and [102] of the [TFEU]' (1997 edn) point 5.2.

[312] Problems can arise in case of immunity applications where only the top management of the undertaking cooperates, or where the application also extends to joint venture companies which the applicant owns together with another parent company that is not part of the application. Here, it might be a sensible course of action to inspect the joint venture company, or even the applicant company itself, but if this is done by way of a simple inspection there is a certain risk that company employees will not cooperate, or that the other parent company will instruct the joint venture company not to cooperate during the investigation. For this reason, the Commission might act upon a written authorization, but already prepare an inspection decision to be notified in case problems arise.

of the necessity of the inspection for that of the Commission, the latter's assessment being subject only to legality review by the EU Courts.[313] This means that the judge may only verify the authenticity of the inspection decision, ensure that the coercive measures envisaged are not arbitrary or disproportionate in relation to the subject matter of the inspection, and guarantee that the provisions of national law are observed during the inspection.

In some Member States, the NCA always applies for a court order allowing the search of premises in case of opposition,[314] thereby avoiding any discussion as to the general need for such an authorization as a matter of fundamental rights.[315] Where necessary, assistance in executing the court order will be provided by national law-enforcement authorities. If such a search warrant has not been applied for as a precautionary measure, and the undertaking refuses access to the building, the Commission officials might request the national authorities to seal the offices, cupboards, etc where documents relating to the subject matter of the inspection may be located while waiting for the court order, if this can be done without such an order or where the undertaking agrees. While national authorities might be empowered to actively search for business records, depending on their national law, the Commission is only entitled to request that certain documents be produced by the undertaking.[316] **8.89**

7. Investigative steps

Once the undertaking has consented to a simple inspection or has complied with an inspection decision, both types of inspection follow the same pattern. The inspectors usually request details of the layout of the premises and the location of offices or cupboards/files where business records related to the investigation might be found. Once they have arrived at the relevant offices, they might ask the undertaking to produce specific documents which the undertaking then must make available. In this case, staff members have to open the cupboards and filing cabinets and hand the documents to the inspectors who, except by way of the assistance of national authorities, may not themselves remove them from their location[317]—unless the undertaking prefers that they do so and voluntarily grants its permission for that purpose, which is typically the case. Similarly, in contrast with certain national authorities, the Commission is not empowered to retain original documents, and therefore inspectors merely take copies. Finally, the inspectors may ask any representative or member of staff for explanations on facts or documents relating to the subject matter and purpose of the inspection and record the answers. **8.90**

Article 20 of Regulation 1/2003 requires the active participation of undertakings, and the latter do not fulfil their obligation to produce in complete form the documents requested by the Commission unless those documents are actually delivered to the inspectors.[318] This **8.91**

---

[313] Case C-94/00 *Roquette Frères* [2002] ECR I-9011, paras 39 and 51.

[314] As regards the requirements for such a precautionary measure, see Case C-94/00 *Roquette Frères* [2002] ECR I-9011, paras 73–5.

[315] On this point, see paras 8.05 and 8.06.

[316] Joined Cases 46/87 and 227/88 *Hoechst v Commission* [1989] ECR 2859, paras 30–2 and 37. See also AG Mischo, Joined Opinion in Cases 46/87, 85/87, 97/87, 98/87, 99/87 and 227/88 *Hoechst and Others v Commission* [1989] ECR 2859, paras 28–42.

[317] See Case 85/87 *Dow Benelux v Commission* [1989] ECR 3137, para 42.

[318] This also applies to the undertaking's obligation to make available email accounts for search by the inspectors. As the Commission noted in a case in which the undertaking deviated incoming emails from the inbox of certain key staff to a central server: 'Commission inspectors must have access to all e-mails in the account, including e-mails entering the account during the entire inspection until such point as the inspection ends...Exclusive access during the entire inspection means that the settings of the account must not be changed by the undertaking without prior notification to and agreement by the Commission inspectors...The duty of active cooperation does not merely mean passively allowing access to all files but also indicating where the relevant information can be found and actually producing specific documents as requested.'

implies that it is the undertaking which must locate them and remove them from their filing cabinets, whereas it is generally not sufficient to simply make the premises, archives, and all documents available to the inspectors. Any 'go slow' attitude on the part of the representatives and staff of the undertaking may be penalized as being tantamount to a breach of the obligation to actively cooperate and provide complete information.[319] In short, this means that the representatives of the undertakings must accompany the inspectors throughout the inspection or at least be available at all times.

8.92 Where undertakings decline to produce specific documents, the inspectors will record that refusal. The Commission may then penalize the undertaking for failure to produce the business records in complete form.[320] Apart from any such penalty, the inspectors may request the assistance of the national authorities in the form of coercive measures to secure the production of particular documents.[321] Where the undertaking claims LPP for certain documents, it must provide explanations for such a claim; depending on the arguments raised, the inspectors will either put the documents in a sealed envelope for future determination of the matter, or examine them directly if the LPP claim appears manifestly unfounded or is just a delaying tactic.[322] Furthermore, the undertaking may draw the attention of inspectors to particular documents, data, or information relating to the subject matter of the inspection which are favourable to it and have not been examined by the inspectors, provided that the inspection is not thereby unduly delayed.[323] These documents will be placed with the others, if the undertaking so wishes, and will be examined as part of the overall assessment of the case.

8. Inventory of copies or extracts taken

8.93 Inspectors are also entitled to take photocopies of any business records related to the investigation. Practical arrangements for the copying of documents will vary from one inspection to another. Typically, the inspectors will take charge of copying arrangements, but it is not excluded that the company might be asked to undertake the copying on their behalf.[324] On completion of the inspection, the undertaking will receive a copy of all the documents and data copied by the inspectors and may request a list (inventory) of the copies and extracts taken.[325] The list will be signed by both an inspector and a company representative.

9. The completion and other records

8.94 Once the inspection is completed, the inspectors will typically draw up a record of the results of the inspection. This record is treated as an internal Commission document and will

---

By changing the settings for the email account, 'the companies de facto reduced the scope of access to the e-mail account; they therefore de facto refused to submit fully to the inspection.' See Commission Decision of 28 March 2012 in Case COMP/39.793 *EPH and others*, paras 58–61.

[319] See eg *Fabbrica Pisana* [1980] OJ L75/30.

[320] See Ch 9, 'Procedural Infringements: Fines and Periodic Penalty Payments'.

[321] The Commission could also choose to impose periodic penalty payments if subsequently the documents are not submitted. See eg *CSM* [1992] OJ L305/16.

[322] See para 8.52 et seq.

[323] See Explanatory note to an authorisation to conduct an inspection in execution of a Commission decision under Article 20(4) of Council Regulation No 1/2003, para 14.

[324] Where the undertaking makes available photocopies of documents at the request of the Commission, it may ask that the cost of the photocopies be reimbursed. See Explanatory note to an authorisation to conduct an inspection in execution of a Commission decision under Article 20(4) of Council Regulation No 1/2003, para 12.

[325] Explanatory note to an authorisation to conduct an inspection in execution of a Commission decision under Article 20(4) of Council Regulation No 1/2003, para 12.

therefore not be shared with the undertaking.[326] However, the undertaking will obtain copies of the minutes reporting specific events that occurred during the inspection.

10. Duration and timing of inspections

The period from the arrival of the inspectors at the undertaking's premises until their depar-   **8.95**
ture can vary significantly, but will typically range between one and three days.[327] The Commission endeavours to keep them as short as possible in order not to disrupt the normal business operations of the undertaking. It is required to carry out its inspections at times when the premises and buildings of the undertakings are normally open. During the inspection, inspectors may ask the undertaking to provide them with a place (a room, cupboard, or filing cabinet) which can be sealed overnight in order to protect the integrity of documents or other records which have not yet been examined, copied, and/or listed in the inventory. Where the inspectors encounter problems with analysing electronic storage media, or where this would take a long time, the Commission may decide to copy the content onto a DVD to be searched at its premises in Brussels. In this case, the DVD will be put in a sealed envelope and the undertaking will be invited to be present when the envelope is opened and to attend the search. It will also receive a copy of the DVD and a duplicate of any paper copies taken from electronic data.

---

[326] See European Commission, 'Dealing with the Commission—Notifications, complaints, inspections and fact-finding powers under Articles [101] and [102] of the [TFEU]' (1997 edn) point 5.6.

[327] As regards private homes, E Gippini-Fournier has argued that the absence of any power to affix seals may constitute an indication that such inspections should not extend beyond one day, in order to limit the degree of invasion of privacy involved. See E Gippini-Fournier, 'The Modernisation of European Competition Law: First Experiences with Regulation 1/2003—Institutional Report' in HF Koeck and MM Karollus (eds), *The Modernisation of European Competition Law—Initial Experiences with Regulation 1/2003*, FIDE XXIII Congress Linz 2008—Congress Publications Vol 2 (Nomos 2008) 61, 62.

9

PROCEDURAL INFRINGEMENTS: FINES AND PERIODIC PENALTY PAYMENTS

Ralf Sauer, Luis Ortiz Blanco, and Konstantin Jörgens

A. Introduction

Undertakings which fail to fulfil their procedural obligations during an investigation may be **9.01** held responsible and fined. European Union competition law provides for two types of pecuniary penalties, which, however, have 'shared characteristics and objectives':[1] first, fines which sanction past unlawful behaviour but are considered as non-criminal by the EU legislator;[2] and second, periodic penalty payments, which accumulate daily for each day the undertaking fails to comply with its obligations; the final amount is typically calculated once compliance is achieved, by multiplying the daily amount with the number of days of delay. The objective of fines is twofold: they are designed (i) to penalize infringements (the punitive aspect); and (ii) to ensure that undertakings in general (the exemplary or dissuasive aspect) and specifically the infringing undertaking (the coercive aspect) refrain(s) from hampering Commission investigations. As for periodic penalty payments, their central objective is to induce undertakings by way of a financial incentive[3] to take, or refrain from taking, certain action. In both cases, the Commission seeks to ensure the effectiveness of the investigatory process, and in particular to avoid that decisions on substance are taken on the basis of incomplete, incorrect or misleading information. However, while Article 23(1) requires that the infringement be committed 'intentionally or negligently', periodic penalties may be imposed irrespective of fault.

---

[1] See Judgment of 27 June 2012 in Case T-167/08 *Microsoft v Commission*, para 94. The General Court ('GC') explained that 'a fine and a periodic penalty payment both relate to the conduct of an undertaking as revealed in the past and both of them require a deterrent effect in order to prevent repetition or continuation of the infringement.'

[2] See Art 23(5) of Reg 1/2003. However, this does not exclude that they may be considered as 'criminal charge' within the autonomous meaning of the Convention for the Protection of Human Rights and Fundamental Freedoms (European Convention on Human Rights, 'ECHR'). See Ch 11, 'Infringement Decisions and Penalties', para 11.11.

[3] Depending on the level of the amounts imposed, these 'incentives' will also have an element of coercion.

9.02 Article 23(1) of Regulation 1/2003 largely follows Article 15(1) of Regulation 17, but it partly enlarges the Commission's powers and significantly increases the level of fines that may be imposed. Whereas fines under Article 15(1) of Regulation 17 were limited to a range of between ECU 100 and 5,000, under Article 23(1) of Regulation 1/2003 the Commission may by decision impose on undertakings[4] fines of up to 1 per cent of total turnover in the preceding business year. This modification, like the increase in the scale of periodic penalty payments under Article 24, was triggered by the consideration that the previous amounts did not have any deterrent effect.[5] In this respect, one also has to bear in mind the potential level of the fines for any substantive infringement, given that the obstruction of the investigation will often be aimed at preventing the Commission from making such a finding.[6] However, there can be an infringement under Article 23(1) even if there is no proven infringement of Articles 101 or 102 TFEU. Moreover, third parties not suspected of having infringed the competition rules are also required to submit to Commission inspections and inquiries and can therefore be liable to a fine or periodic penalty payment if they do not cooperate with the Commission. Whether or not to proceed with these sanctions is a matter of discretion for the Commission.

B. Fines[7]

9.03 Article 23(1) of Regulation 1/2003 allows the Commission to sanction procedural infringements relating to its powers of investigation pursuant to Articles 17, 18, and 20. Given that interviews pursuant to Article 19 are voluntary, the refusal to answer, as well as any incomplete answer, cannot be fined. Nor does Article 23(1) foresee any sanction in case of incorrect or misleading answers during such an interview.[8] As for inspections at non-business premises (Article 21), inspectors only have limited powers (see Article 21(4) which only refers to the powers pursuant to Article 20(2)(a), (b) and (c)). Moreover, obstruction by directors, managers etc at their private

---

[4] The term 'undertaking' should be interpreted uniformly across Reg 1/2003, given that it stems from primary law (Arts 101, 102 TFEU; see also Art 103(2)(a) TFEU which provides the basis for Arts 23, 24 of Reg 1/2003). This has been confirmed both by the Commission (see Commission Decision of 24 May 2011 in Case COMP/39.795 *Suez Environnement breach of seal*, paras 88, 89, and 91) and the GC (see Judgment of 26 October 2010 in Case T-23/09 *CNOP and CCG v Commission*, para 67). Consequently, the rules for delineating the boundaries of the undertaking, including those for the relationship between parent company and subsidiary, should equally apply in the context of procedural violations. See R Sauer in JL Schulte and C Just (eds), *Kartellrecht* (Carl Heymanns Verlag 2012), Art 23 of Reg 1/2003, paras 69–71, and P Kienapfel, 'Geldbuße im Siegelbruch-Fall bestätigt', in: 2 Österreichische Zeitschrift für Kartellrecht (2011) 67. Hence, it should only be relevant whether the parent company exercised control over the subsidiary's *commercial policy*, rather than the *specific conduct constituting the infringement*. This is in line with the interpretation of the concept of undertaking in the context of Art 23(2) when obstruction is considered an aggravating circumstance leading to an increase of the fine. See eg Commission Decision of 20 November 2007 in Case COMP/38.432 *Professional Videotapes*, paras 8–10, 45, 219–27, and 263. Of course, the Commission may always decide to address the decision only to the subsidiary. See eg Commission Decision of 30 January 2008 in Case COMP/39.326 *E.ON Breach of Seal*.

[5] See Proposal for a Regulation implementing Articles 81 and 82 of the Treaty ('Draft Regulation') COM(2000) 582 final—CNS 2000/0243, Explanatory Memorandum, Art 22. See also Recital 29 of Reg 1/2003: 'appropriate levels of fine should also be laid down for infringements of the procedural rules'. According to the Explanatory Memorandum, the idea was to align the procedural fines under the EC Treaty [now Treaty on the Functioning of the European Union ('TFEU')] with those under the ECSC Treaty (Art 47).

[6] Cf Case T-141/08 *E.ON Energie v Commission* [2010] ECR II-5761, para 288.

[7] For a critical account of the Commission's practice of fining procedural infringements see G-K de Bronett, 'Die Rechtmäßigkeit der neueren Geldbußenpraxis der EU-Kommission wegen Verstoß gegen Verfahrenspflichten nach Art. 23 Abs. 1 Verordnung Nr. 1/2003' (2012) 12 Wirtschaft und Wettbewerb 1163.

[8] See European Commission Antitrust Manual of Procedures, Internal DG Competition working documents on procedures for the application of Articles 101 and 102 TFEU, March 2012, Module 8 'Power to take statements', para 3.

homes cannot normally be imputed to the undertaking, which explains why Article 23(1) does not foresee any sanction in this regard.[9]

1. In relation to requests for information

Under Article 23(1) of Regulation 1/2003, the Commission may by decision impose on undertakings and associations of undertakings fines not exceeding 1 per cent of the total turnover in the preceding business year where, intentionally or negligently: **9.04**

(i) they supply incorrect or misleading information in response to a request made pursuant to Article 17 or Article 18(2);
(ii) in response to a request made by decision adopted pursuant to Article 17 or Article 18(3) they supply incorrect, incomplete, or misleading information or do not supply information within the required time limit.

Article 23(1)(a) and (b) of Regulation 1/2003 is similar to the wording of Article 15(1)(b) of Regulation 17, but extends the scope to cover not only information that is 'incorrect' but also 'incomplete or misleading'. It should be noted, though, that under Regulation 17, the Commission considered that incorrect information had been supplied when the information was so incomplete that the reply as a whole would be likely to be misleading.[10] To some extent, therefore, this extension simply codifies a former practice. Undertakings have no duty to reply to simple requests for information pursuant to Article 18(2) of Regulation 1/2003, which also means that in principle they cannot be sanctioned for submitting information late or in incomplete form. However, if they do reply (voluntarily or because the request is made by decision pursuant to Article 18(3) of Regulation 1/2003), undertakings must answer correctly all of the Commission's questions.[11] This may depend on the context in which the information has been requested[12] and will be assessed by comparing it with facts or figures clearly established by other means. Moreover, firms are under an obligation to carefully interpret the questions in the light of the objective pursued and the spirit and purpose of the investigation.[13] Information is misleading if it gives a distorted view of reality, ie if it 'would tend to suggest to a normal or reasonable reader that the situation is other than it is.'[14] Aside from using ambiguous language, this includes the failure to disclose pertinent information without highlighting this to the Commission, and can even occur where the undertaking's response goes beyond the question asked.[15] Finally, where a request is **9.05**

---

[9] It would seem that the same applies when it comes to the question whether obstruction in the context of interviews or inspections at private homes could be taken into account as aggravating circumstances for a fine under Art 23(2) of Reg 1/2003 (substantive infringement). However, incorrect or misleading replies by employees that have been offered as witnesses by an immunity or leniency applicant might be considered as a violation of the duty to cooperate under the Leniency Notice, depending on the circumstances. See European Commission Antitrust Manual of Procedures, Internal DG Competition working documents on procedures for the application of Articles 101 and 102 TFEU, March 2012, Module 8 'Power to take statements', para 4.
[10] *Telos* [1982] OJ L58/19, para 21: 'Any statement is incorrect which gives a distorted picture of the true facts asked for, and which departs significantly from reality on major points.' See also *Theal-Watts* [1977] OJ L39/19 Art 4.
[11] Case T-9/99 *HFB and Others v Commission* [2002] ECR II-1487, para 561.
[12] See eg *Comptoir d'importation* [1982] OJ L27/31. See also Case 28/77 *Tepea v Commission* [1978] ECR 1391, paras 69–72, where the Court took the view that the notification form clearly drew Theal's attention to its duty to inform the Commission of the agreement and its content, and to state whether it involved market sharing.
[13] European Commission, 'Dealing with the Commission—Notification, complaints, inspections and fact-finding powers under Articles [101] and [102] of the [TFEU]' (1997 edn) point 4.5.
[14] See, in the merger context, *Tetra Laval/Sidel* [2005] OJ L98/27, paras 60, 89, and 94.
[15] See Judgment of 24 March 2011 in Case T-384/06 *IBP and International Building Products France v Commission*, paras 111 and 114.

made by way of a decision pursuant to Article 18(3) of Regulation 1/2003, undertakings may be fined when they do not submit the information within the imposed time limit, or submit incomplete information. This also covers the refusal to submit any response. In its assessment of the level of any fine, the Commission takes into account the importance of the requested information and thus the consequences that an incorrect or belated response may have for the investigation (eg length of the obstruction; risk of adopting an erroneous decision based on misleading information), as well as the degree of fault (eg whether the procedural violation was intentional, or if it could have been avoided given the undertaking's easy access to legal advice).[16]

9.06 In the past, the Commission has not shied away from imposing the maximum fines amount (ECU 5,000) in case of obstruction, although it was ready to consider specific circumstances. For instance, in *Peugeot*,[17] the Commission took into account that the infringement had been committed partly intentionally and partly negligently and imposed a slightly reduced fine (ECU 4,000). The persons who drafted the replies to the Commission's requests for information were not fully acquainted with the facts. Nevertheless the Commission found that the company did not exercise sufficient supervision within the group to prevent false statements being made. Similarly, in *Anheuser-Busch/Scottish & Newcastle*,[18] the Commission accepted that there was no intention to provide incorrect information and that the parties had voluntarily corrected their response after a relatively short time period. Overall, the Commission has fined undertakings for supplying incorrect information in reply to Article 11(3) requests for information under Regulation 17 on around half a dozen occasions, with most decisions dating back to the 1980s.[19] However, the relatively small number of cases should not be taken as a sign that the Commission may be reluctant to use the equivalent power granted by Regulation 1/2003. On the contrary, the Commission has shown a determination to penalize companies found to have frustrated competition law investigations by whatever means. While the range of fines available in the past might have been inadequate to make this a useful tool, that is no longer true for Regulation 1/2003. Still, so far the Commission appears to have initiated only one proceeding for a procedural infringement in relation to a request for information under Regulation 1/2003.[20] At the same time, there are some examples of similar proceedings under the corresponding provision of Regulation 139/2004 (the EC Merger Regulation).[21]

---

[16] See *Telos* [1982] OJ L58/19, paras 27–9; *National Panasonic* [1982] OJ L113/18, para 22; *Peugeot* [1986] OJ L295/19, para 50; *Anheuser-Busch/Scottish Newcastle* [2000] OJ L49/37, paras 72, 77, and 82. For a maritime transport case under Reg 4056/86 see *Secrétama* [1991] OJ L35/23, para 15; for an example in the merger context see *Mitsubishi Heavy Industries* [2001] OJ L4/31, paras 14–16 and 18. In *Deutsche Post/trans-o-flex* the Commission considered that causality was not a requirement for imposing a fine. See *Deutsche Post/trans-o-flex* [2001] OJ L97/1, para 111.

[17] *Peugeot* [1986] OJ L295/19.

[18] *Anheuser-Busch/Scottish Newcastle* [2000] OJ L49/37.

[19] See M Van der Woude and C Jones, *EC Competition Law Handbook* (Sweet & Maxwell 2004) 197, which includes a comprehensive list of cases in which fines were imposed for infringement of procedural rules.

[20] See Commission Press Release IP/10/1009 'Commission sends Statement of Objections to Servier for providing misleading and incorrect information', of 26 July 2010. The request (in form of a questionnaire) had been made within the context of the pharmaceutical sector inquiry. In its Statement of Objections, the Commission concluded provisionally that Servier had provided incorrect and misleading information.

[21] See eg *Sanofi/Synthélabo* [2000] OJ L95/34; *Mitsubishi Heavy Industries* [2001] OJ L4/31; *Deutsche Post/trans-o-flex* [2001] OJ L97/1; *BP/Erdölchemie* [2004] OJ L91/40; *KLM/Martinair III* [2005] OJ L50/10; *Tetra Laval/Sidel* [2005] OJ L98/27. In view of the importance of a full disclosure of relevant information in merger cases, the EC Merger Regulation, in force since 1 May 2004, has increased the maximum penalty for each infringement from EUR 50,000 to a maximum of 1 per cent of total turnover.

2. In relation to inspections

According to Article 23(1)(c) of Regulation 1/2003, fines may be imposed on undertakings where: **9.07**

> they produce the required books or other records related to the business in incomplete form during inspections under Article 20 or refuse to submit to inspections ordered by a decision adopted pursuant to Article 20(4).

On the face of it, this appears to relate to two separate types of infringements ('or'), which would mean that the incomplete production of books or other records would not amount to a refusal to submit to an investigation. However, in *Orkem* the European Court of Justice ('ECJ') already confirmed that undertakings have an obligation to cooperate *actively* during an investigation,[22] despite the wording of Regulation 17 (and Regulation 1/2003[23]) that undertakings shall '*submit*' to investigations ordered by Commission decision. This means cooperation in all aspects of the inspection, which includes an obligation to indicate where the relevant information can be found and to produce specific documents as requested:

> the obligation on undertakings to supply all documents required by Commission inspectors must be understood to mean not merely giving access to all files but actually producing the specific documents required.[24]

Consequently, an undertaking's refusal to hand over a document during an inspection in principle fulfils the conditions of both alternatives stipulated in Article 23(1)(c) of Regulation 1/2003 as it demonstrates that the undertaking is not (actively) cooperating. In fact, in *CSM*, the undertaking's refusal to let certain documents be copied which it considered as not relevant was treated as a refusal to submit to the investigation.[25] Still, the category of producing business records in incomplete form retains an independent meaning where the Commission conducts an inspection on the basis of a written authorization (Article 20(3) of Regulation 1/2003). Here, the undertaking is not obliged to submit to the inspection, but has to produce the documents in complete form if it does so voluntarily.[26] The provision is applicable to inspections carried out by Commission officials (inspections under Article 20(3) and (4)) as well as those carried out by the competition authorities of the Member States on behalf of the Commission (Article 22 in conjunction with Article 20(3) and (4)).

Failure to submit to an inspection, including opposition

This may include the outright refusal as well as any delay to let the inspectors enter the **9.08**
premises,[27] but also any partial refusal (eg when the undertaking does not allow access to

---

[22] Case 374/87 *Orkem v Commission* [1989] ECR 3283, para 27: 'Regulation No 17 does not give an undertaking under investigation any right to evade the investigation on the ground that the results thereof might provide evidence of an infringement by it of the competition rules. On the contrary, it imposes on the undertaking an obligation to cooperate actively.' See also Case T-34/93 *Société Générale v Commission* [1995] ECR II-545, para 72 ('duty of active cooperation').

[23] Article 20(4) of Reg 1/2003 only speaks of the duty of undertakings to submit to the inspection. And Art 20(2) only mentions the Commission's competences, for instance to examine business records, not the corresponding duties of the undertaking. However, both Arts 20(3) and 23(1)(c) clearly presuppose the duty of the undertaking to 'produce' those books and records.

[24] *Fabbrica Pisana* [1980] OJ L75/30, para 10.

[25] *CSM* [1992] OJ L305/16. The undertaking's obligation to cooperate in the investigation is not limited to supplying those documents it considers relevant. See also *FNICF* [1982] OJ L319/12, in which FNICF refused to produce minutes of the meetings of its Federal Council, alleging that the documents were confidential and related to questions which had no bearing on the subject matter of the investigation.

[26] See eg *Fabbrica Pisana* [1980] OJ L75/30.

[27] Judgment of 27 September 2012 in Case T-357/06 *Koninklijke Wegenbouw Stevin v Commission*, para 233. See also *Ukwal* [1992] OJ L121/45; *Mewac* [1993] OJ L20/6.

certain offices or pieces of furniture (desk, drawer, etc)).[28] Disguised opposition, that is to say any subterfuge intended to delay and hamper the inspection, on various pretexts, may also be sanctioned, for example if the inspectors are made to wait at the entrance for more than a short time.[29] The Commission has stressed that it is not for the undertaking concerned to decide on the timing of the investigation.[30] Asking for a postponement until a particular designated representative of the firm or a particular lawyer can be present may also constitute a refusal to submit.[31] Likewise, any impediment to the Commission's exercise of its powers under Article 20(2) of Regulation 1/2003 falls into this category, for example where the undertaking refuses to let the inspectors take copies of documents or seal offices.[32] In the age of electronic communications, this also applies to IT access[33] (computers, servers) and the tampering with email accounts (for instance, the failure to block an email account or the diversion of in-coming emails).[34] The fact that the Commission may have succeeded in enforcing its decision with the assistance of national authorities does not prevent it from imposing a fine for opposition on the part of the undertaking. However, where the inspectors act merely on a written authorization, the refusal to submit to the inspection cannot be sanctioned. Rather, the Commission would first have to adopt a formal decision.

---

[28] Judgment of 27 September 2012 in Case T-357/06 *Koninklijke Wegenbouw Stevin v Commission*, paras 235–9; *Akzo Chemicals* [1994] OJ L294/31 (incorrect information on the existence of a manager's office and refusal to let the inspectors access a particular room).

[29] Usually, and as long as it is guaranteed that this does not put at risk the inspection, the Commission accepts a short delay during which the undertaking may seek legal assistance. See Explanatory note to an authorisation to conduct an inspection in execution of a Commission decision under Article 20(4) of Council Regulation No 1/2003, para 6: 'The undertaking may consult a legal adviser during the inspection . . . However, the presence of a lawyer is not a legal condition for the validity of the inspection. The [inspectors] can enter the premises, notify the decision ordering the inspection and occupy the offices of their choice without waiting for the undertaking to consult its lawyer. [They] will accept only a short delay pending consultation of the lawyer before starting [the inspection]. Any such delay must be kept to the strict minimum.' See also *Ukwal* [1992] OJ L121/45, para 4. In *MEWAC*, the Commission considered that the association had held up matters for what was manifestly an unreasonably long period (until the next day), *Mewac* [1993] OJ L20/06, para 7. In this case, the national authorities sealed the premises until the inspection could begin the following day.

[30] *Mewac* [1993] OJ L20/06, para 7; *Ukwal* [1992] OJ L1 21/45, para 9.

[31] European Commission, 'Dealing with the Commission—Notification, complaints, inspections and fact-finding powers under Articles [101] and [102] of the [TFEU]' (1997 edn) point 4.5.

[32] The Commission has stressed that the duty to submit to the inspection is a continuing one, and that therefore a company may not at any point in time obstruct the Commission's investigation. See European Commission, 'Dealing with the Commission—Notification, complaints, inspections and fact-finding powers under Articles [101] and [102] of the [TFEU]' (1997 edn) point 5.3.

[33] According to Art 20(2)(b) and (c) of Reg 1/2003 the inspectors are empowered to examine and take copies of the books and other records related to the business, 'irrespective of the medium on which they are stored'. Moreover, in the Commission's view the right to uninhibited and exclusive access implies, as far as electronic documents are concerned, that passwords which may be used to secure certain files, folders, or email accounts have to be provided to the inspectors who may block access to them by resetting the password.

[34] See Commission Press Release IP/10/627 'Commission opens proceedings against Czech J&T Group for obstruction during inspection' of 28 May 2010; Commission Press Release IP/10/1748 'Commission sends Statement of Objections to Czech energy companies Energetický a průmyslový holding and J&T Investment Advisors for obstruction during inspection' of 20 December 2010; Commission Press Release IP/12/319 'Commission fines Czech energy companies Energetický a průmyslový holding and EP Investment Advisors €2.5 million for obstruction during inspection' of 28 March 2012. In the Commission's provisional assessment, the IT department charged by J&T (now EPH) with assisting the inspectors unblocked an email account (ie allowed access to the account holder) which the inspectors had requested to be blocked during the inspection; evidence showed that the account holder accessed his account. Also, the Commission considered that the undertaking had given an instruction to divert all newly arriving emails for certain key accounts to the main server, which prevented the inspectors from having complete access to those accounts, thereby limiting the scope of the inspection. The latter could also have been qualified as the production of business-related records in incomplete form. The Commission's decision has been challenged in Case T-272/12 (OJ C250/17).

Production of business records in incomplete form

Article 23(1)(c) of Regulation 1/2003 is identical on substance to its predecessor Article **9.09** 15(1)(c) of Regulation 17, and earlier practice therefore remains directly relevant. The obstruction may be attributable to the objective fact that the documentation produced is not complete, but also to the conduct of the undertaking during an inspection. As stated earlier, the obligation to provide the requested information calls for active cooperation on the part of undertakings and a 'go slow' attitude or unwillingness to assist in the localization of specific files might be regarded by the Commission as equivalent to the production of incomplete documentation. For example, during its first investigation of the glass market in Italy, the Commission fined two undertakings producing documents in incomplete form. In *Fabbrica Sciarra*, the Commission's inspectors asked specific questions about the relation of the company with Fides and requested the company to produce all correspondence with Fides or other glass manufacturers. Considering that the requests were so precise that *Fabbrica Sciarra* could have been left in no reasonable doubt as to the exact nature of the documents sought, the Commission considered their incomplete production as intentional.[35] A similar reasoning led to the imposition of a fine on *Fabbrica Pisana*.[36] In *FNICF*[37] and *CSM*,[38] the Commission considered that it was not up to the association to decide whether a particular document was relevant or fell within the ambit of the inspection, and that even a temporary refusal would justify a fine. And in *Sanofi-Aventis*, the Commission initiated proceedings because of the company's refusal to let inspectors examine and copy relevant documents until the French authorities produced a national search warrant.[39] Moreover, in one case the Commission indicated that it could consider the failure to open encrypted emails as also falling into this category.[40]

The power to fine the incomplete production of records also applies with respect to sim- **9.10** ple inspections based on a written authorization (see Articles 20(3), 23(1)(c) of Regulation 1/2003). It must be remembered that once a simple inspection has been agreed to and has commenced, it follows mostly the same course as an inspection based on a formal decision. Hence, undertakings may not refuse to produce a document or information on the pretext that, if they are entitled to refuse to submit to the inspection as such, they may choose the lesser option of refusing to hand over a document. They may in principle withdraw their agreement to submit to the inspection and this cannot be fined, but such a withdrawal has to be clearly communicated to the inspectors in order to allow the Commission to adopt a formal inspection decision; it would impede the deterrent effect of the power to fine the incomplete production of records if such conduct could instead be construed as an implicit (partial) refusal to submit to the inspection.

---

[35] *Fabbrica Sciarra* [1980] OJ L75/35.
[36] *Fabbrica Pisana* [1980] OJ L75/30.
[37] *FNICF* [1982] OJ L319/12, para 8.
[38] *CSM* [1992] OJ L305/16.
[39] Commission MEMO/08/357 'Commission opens formal proceedings against sanofi-aventis for possible procedural infringement' of 2 June 2008. The case was closed without decision.
[40] Commission Press Release IP/10/1748 'Commission sends Statement of Objections to Czech energy companies Energetický a průmyslový holding and J&T Investment Advisors for obstruction during inspection' of 20 December 2010; Commission Press Release IP/12/319 'Commission fines Czech energy companies Energetický a průmyslový holding and EP Investment Advisors €2.5 million for obstruction during inspection' of 28 March 2012. Emails fall into the broad category of 'records' within the meaning of Arts 20(2)(b) and 23(1)(c) of Reg 1/2003, as the latter is not limited to a particular storage medium. Given the duty to cooperate actively, the inspectors must be granted access to all (business-related) emails. Where emails are encrypted, this entails that the undertaking opens the email or provides the inspectors with the password.

Incorrect, incomplete, or misleading answers

9.11 Pursuant to Article 23(1)(d) of Regulation 1/2003, fines may be imposed on undertakings where, in response to a question asked in accordance with Article 20(2)(e):

> (i) they give an incorrect or misleading answer;
>
> (ii) they fail to rectify within a time limit set by the Commission an incorrect, incomplete, or misleading answer given by a member of staff; or
>
> (iii) they fail or refuse to provide a complete answer on facts relating to the subject matter and purpose of an inspection ordered by a decision adopted pursuant to Article 20(4).

9.12 This new provision supplements Article 23(1)(b) and should resolve the lingering uncertainty under Regulation 17 as to whether the ambit of its Article 15(1)(c) was wide enough to deal with cases where an undertaking either refused to provide oral explanations or gave a false explanation. In *Akzo Chemicals*, the Commission imposed the maximum fine where the surprise effect of its unannounced inspection was frustrated by the undertaking giving incorrect information as to whether it had offices at a certain location and by denying access to the office of one of its directors.[41] Whilst the latter clearly fell under Article 15(1)(c) of Regulation 17, it was arguable whether that provision also provided a legal basis to penalize the false explanations. By virtue of Article 23(1)(d), this question is now settled. Incorrect and misleading answers by persons who are authorized to provide explanations on behalf of the undertaking (eg directors, board members) may always be sanctioned (see first indent). Where other members of staff give incorrect and/or misleading answers during an inspection, this may lead to a sanction if the undertaking does not rectify the information within a time limit set by the Commission pursuant to Article 4(3) of Regulation No 773/2004[42] (see second indent). As regards incomplete answers, Article 23(1)(d) foresees the possibility of a sanction only in case of inspections ordered by formal decision (see third indent); this is also apparent from the wording of Article 20(3), according to which the written authorization shall only refer to the penalties provided for in Article 23 'where the answers to questions asked under [Article 20(2)] are incorrect or misleading'. Against this background, Article 23(1)(d), second indent, should be interpreted narrowly: since Regulation 1/2003 appears to impose a duty to *provide complete* answers only in case of mandatory inspections, the failure to *rectify* an *incomplete* answer can also only be relevant in this context.[43] However, depending on the circumstances, providing an incomplete answer without revealing this to the inspectors can be misleading and thus lead to a fine pursuant to Article 23(1)(d), first indent, even in the case of an inspection by written authorization.

Breach of seal

9.13 Fines may also be imposed on undertakings where, intentionally or negligently, seals affixed in accordance with Article 20(2)(d) by officials or other accompanying persons authorised by the Commission have been broken. The sealing of furniture (eg filing cabinets), rooms, or data carriers (eg hard drive) is a new competence which the Commission acquired only with the

---

[41] *Akzo Chemicals* [1994] OJ L294/31.

[42] Commission Regulation (EC) No 773/2004 of 7 April 2004 relating to the conduct of proceedings by the Commission pursuant to Articles 81 and 82 of the EC Treaty [2004] OJ L123/18. See also Recital 4 of Reg 773/2004.

[43] It should also be noted that Art 4(3) of Reg 773/2004 allows for a rectification only where the original answer was provided by an unauthorized member of staff. If a fine for a failure to rectify an incomplete answer could be imposed pursuant to Art 23(1)(d), second indent, also in the case of simple inspections, the liability risk for the undertaking would therefore be higher when the answer is provided by an unauthorized staff member than when it comes from a company representative, given that for the latter Art 23(1)(d), third indent, foresees a power to impose a fine only in case of inspections based on a formal decision.

adoption of Regulation 1/2003.[44] It becomes relevant where the inspectors have to adjourn the inspection with regard to certain locations or objects, in particular where the inspection cannot be finished within one day. In the latter scenario, the Commission typically stores the folders or documents which have not yet been examined in one or more rooms and then seals them overnight.[45] Simply locking the door in such a situation would not provide sufficient assurance that the room will not be entered, because the inspectors can never be certain they have received all the keys.[46] Once the seal has been affixed, it is the responsibility of the undertaking to ensure that no breach occurs, for instance by placing a security guard in front of the door or by obstructing access to it; at the very least, it is advisable to inform all staff that rooms have been sealed and to mark the locations where seals have been affixed (eg by putting a clearly visible warning sign up on the door).[47] The power to fine pursuant to Article 23(1)(e) of Regulation 1/2003 does not require the proof that the sealed door has been opened or that documents stored in the sealed room were altered or taken out: 'Not the opening of a door, but the breaking of the seal is the object of the fines provision.'[48] Consequently, any change in the appearance of the seal which, by its design, indicates a seal breach, is sufficient to trigger liability.[49] What matters is the (abstract) risk that, despite sealing, the undertaking may have obtained access to the sealed room or object.[50]

So far, the Commission has found a breach of seal in two cases. In *E.ON Energie*,[51] it imposed a fine of EUR 38 million on E.ON Energie AG, a subsidiary of E.ON AG (but did not also sanction the parent company). In relative terms, this fine constituted 0.14 per cent of E.ON Energie's total turnover.[52] The company did not cooperate during the administrative procedure but instead had tried to argue that the appearance of the VOID signs[53] across the **9.14**

---

[44] See Recital 25 of Reg 1/2003.

[45] Commission Decision of 30 January 2008 in Case COMP/39.326 *E.ON Energie*, para 99: 'The purpose of the sealing is to prevent (the possibility of) evidence being lost during the inspection. Sealing is thus a guarantee of the effectiveness of the Commission's investigatory activities during the course of inspections. It is intended to ensure that objects or rooms remain intact and to prevent the opening of the sealed object or room by unauthorised persons, or to make evident that such opening has occurred. The sealing of rooms is also intended to ensure that the relevant rooms do not have to be placed under permanent guard (e.g. overnight).'

[46] See Commission Decision of 30 January 2008 in Case COMP/39.326 *E.ON Energie*, paras 72 and 98.

[47] See Case T-141/08 *E.ON Energie v Commission* [2010] ECR II-5761, paras 216 and 260. See also Commission Decision of 24 May 2011 in Case COMP/39.796 *Suez Environnement breach of seal*, paras 73 and 74, where the Commission considered the conduct of Lyonnaise des Eaux as at least negligent because it had not taken all the necessary measures to ensure the integrity of the seal, in particular by locking the door and placing a physical obstacle before it.

[48] Commission Decision of 30 January 2008 in Case COMP/39.326 *E.ON Energie*, paras 98 and 100. In para 111 the Commission also stressed that it would not constitute an attenuating factor if it could not be demonstrated that the door to the sealed room had actually been opened or that documents had been removed. See also Case T-141/08 *E.ON Energie v Commission* [2010] ECR II-5761, paras 85, 256, and 291 (confirmed on appeal in Judgment of 22 November 2012 in Case C-89/11 P *E.ON Energie v Commission*, paras 128 and 129).

[49] With the seals currently used by the Commission, this merely presupposes the showing of VOID signs on the seal's surface. It is not necessary that the seal has been damaged (eg by cutting or buckling) or completely removed.

[50] Commission Decision of 30 January 2008 in Case COMP/39.326 *E.ON Energie*, para 100.

[51] Commission Decision of 30 January 2008 in Case COMP/39.326 *E.ON Energie*. See also Commission Press Release IP/08/108 'Commission imposes €38 million fine on E.ON for breach of a seal during an inspection' of 30 January 2008; MEMO/08/61 'Commission imposes fine on E.ON for the breach of a seal during inspection—frequently asked questions' of 30 January 2008.

[52] The Commission stressed, however, that one of the reasons why it had not opted for a higher fine was that this case constituted the first one in which the Commission sanctioned a breach of seal. See MEMO/08/61 'Commission imposes fine on E.ON for the breach of a seal during inspection—frequently asked questions' of 30 January 2008.

[53] The Commission's seals are adhesives made of a very strong plastic film. If they are removed from the surface, they do not tear but show irreversible 'VOID' signs across the seal. Moreover, when the seal is

seal—which is the typical mechanism to show that the seal had been detached from the surface—might have been caused by a slippage of the seal rather than a breach. Among the various
explanations provided were insufficient adhesion (due to the age of the seal,[54] prior damage when
removing the seal from its liner, or surface conditions), the use of an aggressive cleaning product
with respect to the seal by the cleaning lady, and vibrations in the wall panels caused by the frequent opening and closing of another office door close by. In order to assess these arguments, the
Commission carried out a thorough investigation, including the use of outside experts to test the
seals in various conditions. It concluded that none of the alleged factors could explain the state of
the seal on the morning when the inspectors returned. Likewise, E.ON's arguments were rejected
by the EU Courts when the decision was challenged.[55]

9.15   In *Suez Environnement*,[56] the situation was different. After the breach had been detected by
the inspectors at the premises of Lyonnaise des Eaux ('LDE'), the company and its parent,
Suez Environnement, immediately started an internal investigation to establish what had
happened. They then admitted an inadvertent breach by a company employee[57] and cooperated fully during the administrative procedure (eg by allowing the Commission to interview
the employee who had breached the seal). This was taken into account by the Commission
when determining the level of the fine, which was set at EUR 8 million (0.065 per cent
of total turnover). Suez Environnement was held jointly and severally liable for the fine,
together with its subsidiary LDE, on the basis that the infringement could also be imputed
to it. This finding rested on a number of factual elements showing that both before and after
the affixing of the seal, Suez Environnement had been directly involved in the inspection
conducted at the premises of LDE (eg its lawyers had been present at the premises during
the inspection and it had taken a leading role in the internal investigation following the
breach).[58] Moreover, the Commission considered that the rules for determining the relevant
undertaking as the subject of the competition rules should be identical for both substantive and
procedural infringements and pointed to the 'economic, organisational and legal links' between

---

removed and re-affixed, some glue will often become visible next to the seal since it is very difficult to re-affix
the seal at exactly the same place as before. For a description of the functioning of the seals currently in use
see C Gauer, K Bansard, and F Christ, 'The Suez Environnement seal case—EUR 8 million fine for breaching
a Commission seal during an inspection' (2011) 3 Competition Policy Newsletter 8.

[54] The seal had been produced in December 2002 and was used during an inspection in May 2006. The
technical bulletin published by the producer indicated a so-called 'shelf life' of two years. However, it turned
out that this indication had nothing to do with the seal being over-aged. More importantly, perhaps, the
producer had indicated that, even if the adhesive strength of the seal would diminish over time, this could
only result in a 'false negative' (no appearance of VOID signs despite a breach of seal), but not a 'false positive'
(appearance of VOID signs without a breach of seal). Nevertheless, in order to avoid any further discussion of
that sort, the Commission subsequently replaced the batch of seals at issue with new ones.

[55] Case T-141/08 *E.ON Energie v Commission* [2010] ECR II-5761 (confirmed on appeal in the Judgment
of 22 November 2012 in Case C-89/11 P *E.ON Energie v Commission*).

[56] Commission Decision of 24 May 2011 in Case COMP/39.796 *Suez Environnement breach of seal*. See
also Commission Press Release IP/11/632 'Commission fines Suez Environnement and Lyonnaise des Eaux
€8 million for the breach of a seal during an inspection' of 24 May 2011, and C Gauer, K Bansard, and F
Christ, 'The Suez Environnement seal case—EUR 8 million fine for breaching a Commission seal during an
inspection' (2011) 3 Competition Policy Newsletter 8.

[57] The employee had been instructed by his superior to fetch a document. When he found the door of
the relevant office to be closed, he tried his luck next door, which was the one that had been sealed. He realized that something was wrong when he felt resistance (from the seal) while opening the door, and therefore
immediately closed it again. The room had not been locked by the company, but it had placed a large warning
sign on the door which the employee had overlooked. Video footage of the elevators in the building, which
showed the employee arriving on the floor and soon after leaving again, suggested that indeed there would
not have been much time for him to enter and search the room.

[58] Commission Decision of 24 May 2011 in Case COMP/39.796 *Suez Environnement breach of seal*,
paras 101–4.

LDE and Suez Environnement, namely the 100 per cent ownership and the strategic role of Suez Environnement as head of the group.[59]

General considerations

It should be noted that there are also numerous cases where the Commission has not established **9.16** a procedural violation as a separate infringement pursuant to Article 23(1) of Regulation 1/2003, but rather considered it as an aggravating circumstance[60] in the determination of the fine for a substantive infringement (eg a cartel).[61] In absolute terms, this has led to increases of the fine between EUR 2 million and EUR 20 million (or up to 3 per cent of total turnover).[62] Imposing both a fine for a procedural infringement and an increase of the fine for a substantive infringement would most certainly violate the principle of *ne bis in idem*.[63] Where the Commission is not sure whether the investigation will lead to a finding of a substantive infringement, or where it considers it important to react quickly (and with particular publicity) to a procedural violation, it is likely to be inclined to impose an (autonomous) fine pursuant to Article 23(1) of Regulation 1/2003.[64]

When determining the level of the fine for a procedural infringement, the Commission has to **9.17** consider its gravity and duration (Article 23(3) of Regulation 1/2003), but also respect the proportionality principle[65] and the principle of equal treatment. In its practice, the Commission takes particular account of the nature of the infringement and its (potential) consequences for the investigation in question.[66] Obstructions during an inspection will certainly be among the most serious violations and hence justify significant fines.[67] Other factors that may be relevant,

---

[59] Commission Decision of 24 May 2011 in Case COMP/39.796 *Suez Environnement breach of seal*, paras 88–9 and 91. In n 56 the decision makes reference to Case T-141/08 *E.ON Energie v Commission* [2010] ECR II-5761, para 258, where, in the context of a procedural infringement, the GC applied the normal rules for imputing the behaviour of employees to the undertaking (hence suggesting that the interpretation of the notion of undertaking in both substantive and procedural infringements should be identical).

[60] See para 28 of the 2006 Fining Guidelines ('refusal to cooperate with or obstruction of the Commission in carrying out its investigations').

[61] See Ch 11, 'Infringement Decisions and Penalties', para 11.60 (iii).

[62] In one case (COMP/38.121 *Fittings*) the increase would have been 12 per cent of total turnover but the fine was capped pursuant to Art 23(2) of Reg 1/2003. The GC has stressed that an increase of the fine for the aggravating circumstance of obstruction may go beyond the limit foreseen in Art 23(1) of Reg 1/2003 (1 per cent). See Judgment of 24 March 2011 in Case T-384/06 *IBP and International Building Products France v Commission*, paras 109 and 110.

[63] Cf Judgment of 27 September 2012 in Case T-343/06 *Shell Petroleum and Others v Commission*, para 118. While the GC has taken the view that Art 23(1) and Art 23(2) 'relate to different infringements', it nevertheless considered that 'if conduct is classified under one of those heads, it cannot at the same time be classified under the other'. See Judgment of 24 March 2011 in Case T-384/06 *IBP and International Building Products France v Commission*, paras 109 and 110.

[64] C Gauer, K Bansard, and F Christ, 'The Suez Environnement seal case—EUR 8 million fine for breaching a Commission seal during an inspection' (2011) 3 Competition Policy Newsletter 8, 9–11.

[65] Case T-141/08 *E.ON Energie v Commission* [2010] ECR II-5761, paras 286–7 and 294. See also AG Bot, Opinion of 21 June 2012 in Case C-89/11 P *E.ON Energie AG v Commission*, para 123 et seq.

[66] Commission Decision of 30 January 2008 in Case COMP/39.326 *E.ON Energie*, paras 107 and 108.

[67] See eg Commission Decision of 30 January 2008 in Case COMP/39.326 *E.ON Energie*, para 105: 'Quite apart from this specific case, breaches of seals must in principle be regarded as a serious infringement' (confirmed in Case T-141/08 *E.ON Energie v Commission* [2010] ECR II-5761, paras 288 and 294). See also Commission Press Release IP/08/108 'Commission imposes €38 million fine on E.ON for breach of a seal during an inspection' of 30 January 2008: 'The Commission cannot and will not tolerate attempts by companies to undermine the Commission's fight against cartels and other anti-competitive practices by threatening the integrity and effectiveness of our investigations. Companies know very well that high fines are at stake in competition cases, and some may consider illegal measures to obstruct an inquiry and so avoid a fine. This decision sends a clear message to all companies that it does not pay off to obstruct the Commission's investigations.' The importance of inspections and the need to ensure the full effectiveness of the power to inspect, in particular as regards the search of electronic files, has been reiterated in Commission Decision of 28 March 2012 in Case COMP/39.793 *EPH and others*, paras 85–7.

depending on the circumstances of the case, are the duration of the infringement[68] (eg the time until a correct and/or complete answer to a request for information has been provided) and/or the degree of fault.[69] Finally, from the fact that the statutory limit of the fine relates to the overall turnover, hence a relative value, it follows that the aspect of deterrence may also play a role.[70] Sufficient deterrence must be ensured in particular with respect to those undertakings that are suspected of substantive infringements. For them, it must not pay off to obstruct the investigation in order to avoid a high fine.[71] The gravity of the procedural violation might be mitigated if the undertaking's failure to fulfil its duties was negligent and it rectifies the error on its own initiative; if it cooperates fully with the Commission once the error has been discovered; and/or if it openly acknowledges the procedural infringement.[72] No fining guidelines exist. Hence, the Commission is not bound by any particular methodology and may carry out an overall assessment of gravity.[73]

C. Periodic Penalty Payments

9.18 Article 24 of Regulation 1/2003 empowers the Commission to impose periodic penalty payments not exceeding 5 per cent of the average daily[74] (total) turnover of the undertaking or association of undertakings in the preceding business year per day of non-compliance with

---

[68] See eg Commission Decision of 28 March 2012 in Case COMP/39.793 *EPH and others*, para 90: 'The longer an e-mail account is unblocked or e-mails are diverted, the higher the risk that e-mails are tampered with.' See also Judgment of 12 December 2012 in Case T-332/09 *Electrabel v Commission*, para 267.

[69] Case T-322/01 *Roquette Frères v Commission* [2006] ECR II-3137, para 315; Commission Decision of 30 January 2008 in Case COMP/39.326 *E.ON Energie*, para 110. See also AG Bot, Opinion of 21 June 2012 in Case C-89/11 P *E.ON Energie AG v Commission*, para 130, and C Gauer, K Bansard, and F Christ, 'The Suez Environnement seal case—EUR 8 million fine for breaching a Commission seal during an inspection' (2011) 3 Competition Policy Newsletter 8, 9. The GC has stressed the Commission's margin of appreciation when deciding whether to take into account negligence as a mitigating factor, while considering that the type of fault does not necessarily affect the degree of gravity of the infringement. See Judgment of 12 December 2012 in Case T-332/09 *Electrabel v Commission*, paras 237, 239, and 272. As the intentional character of procedural infringements may often be difficult to establish, it may be justified *not* to take (presumed) negligence into account as a mitigating circumstance (para 273). See also, for a failure to comply with a commitment decision, Commission Decision of 6 March 2013 in Case AT.39530 *Microsoft (Tying)*, paras 49–53 and 69.

[70] Case T-141/08 *E.ON Energie v Commission* [2010] ECR II-5761, para 288. See also AG Bot, Opinion of 21 June 2012 in Case C-89/11 P *E.ON Energie AG v Commission*, para 129: 'Finally, it is by taking into consideration the appellant's size and global resources that it is possible to ensure that the fine has a sufficient deterrent effect through the impact on the appellant, and to ensure that the sanction is not negligible in the light, particularly, of its financial capacity.'

[71] Case T-141/08 *E.ON Energie v Commission* [2010] ECR II-5761, para 288 (confirmed on appeal in Judgment of 22 November 2012 in Case C-89/11 P *E.ON Energie v Commission*, para 132); Commission Decision of 28 March 2012 in Case COMP/39.793 *EPH and others*, para 83. Consequently, the gravity and duration of the potential substantive infringement may also be relevant. See also Commission Decision of 30 January 2008 in Case COMP/39.326 *E.ON Energie AG*, paras 105 and 107; AG Bot, Opinion of 21 June 2012 in Case C-89/11 P *E.ON Energie AG v Commission*, paras 123 and 128.

[72] *Anheuser-Busch/Scottish Newcastle* [2000] OJ L49/37, paras 80, 81; Commission Decision of 24 May 2011 in Case COMP/39.796 *Suez environnement breach of seal* (IP/11/632: 'The Commission however took into account the immediate and constructive cooperation of Suez Environnement and LDE, which provided more information than was its obligation, when setting the fine'); Commission Decision of 6 March 2013 in Case AT.39530 *Microsoft (Tying)*, paras 66 and 70–1. As regards non-contestation see *BP/Erdölchemie* [2004] OJ L91/40, para 54. In Commission Decision of 28 March 2012 in Case COMP/39.793 *EPH and others*, para 102, the Commission took into account the cooperation of the parties, but considered that it had not occurred spontaneously and that the parties generally sought to put in doubt the existence of any procedural violation.

[73] Case T-141/08 *E.ON Energie v Commission* [2010] ECR II-5761, para 284. Cf also Judgment of 12 December 2012 in Case T-332/09 *Electrabel v Commission*, paras 227, 228, and 292.

[74] Given that the number of working days differs between EU Member States, this must be read as a reference to calendar days.

procedural rules or substantive decisions. As regards procedural rules, periodic penalty payments may be imposed for any delay in supplying complete and/or correct information requested by decision pursuant to Article 17 or 18(3) of Regulation 1/2003, or for each day of failing to submit to an inspection ordered by decision pursuant to Article 20(4). Regulation 1/2003 foresees a two-stage procedure whereby a first decision is taken to set the (provisional) amount of the daily periodic penalty payment and the starting date for the calculation (Article 24(1)) and a second decision fixes the final amount (Article 24(2)).[75] While Article 24(1) decisions may be adopted by the Competition Commissioner (empowerment) or, for decisions taken to enforce compliance with a formal request for information, by the Director-General of the Directorate-General for Competition ('DG COMP') (sub-delegation), the final Article 24(2) decision is reserved for the College of Commissioners, which will normally adopt it in written procedure.[76]

Periodic penalty payments provide the Commission with an instrument to exert pressure on the **9.19** undertaking, by creating a strong financial incentive to behave in a certain way. This is important given the Commission's lack of actual enforcement powers (cf Article 20(6) of Regulation 1/2003 for inspections). Since periodic penalty payments are not punitive, their imposition does not require fault on the side of the undertaking. As regards procedural obligations, periodic penalty payments play a supporting role in the investigation. The Commission resorts to them mainly to ensure that obstacles to its investigative work, when encountered, are removed, or where there are grounds for doubting that undertakings cooperate. Periodic penalty payments may follow,[77] but will often already accompany decisions requesting information.[78] In the first case, the Commission will adopt a further, separate decision imposing the periodic penalty payment.[79] In the second case, the decision in question will stipulate both the procedural obligations

---

[75] Joined Cases 46/87 and 227/88 *Hoechst v Commission* [1989] ECR 2859, para 55. According to Art 24(1) of Reg 1/2003, the Commission may 'impose' periodic penalty payments. However, despite this wording, this refers to the announcement of an intention to impose penalty payments (up to a certain amount) from a specified date in the future if by that date the addressee has not complied with its obligations. The actual amount of any penalty payment may only be 'fixed' (in the wording of Art 24(2) of Reg 1/2003) once it is clear that the undertaking has failed to comply. Unlike a decision pursuant to Art 24(2) of Reg 1/2003 the preliminary act announcing the intention to impose periodic penalty payments pursuant to Art 24(1) is not preceded by a statement of objections, access to file or an administrative hearing (see Art 27(1) of Reg 1/2003).

[76] European Commission Antitrust Manual of Procedures, Internal DG Competition working documents on procedures for the application of Articles 101 and 102 TFEU, March 2012, Module 20 'Periodic penalty payments', paras 5 and 16.

[77] For a recent example see the Commission decisions addressed to several companies in the cement case (COMP/39.520 *Cement and related products*). The Art 24(1) decision had been preceded by a formal request for information pursuant to Art 18(3) of Reg 1/2003. While all the companies replied to this request, some accompanied their reply by a general caveat that the time limit had been too short to validate the data and ensure completeness, and that therefore such data could not be used to draw reliable conclusions with respect to the companies' market behaviour. Both the Art 18(3) decision (Cases T-292/11, T-293/11, T-296/11, T-297/11, T-305/11 and T-306/11) and the Art 24(1) decision (Case T-49/12 *Lafarge v Commission*, later withdrawn) have been challenged in court.

[78] See eg *JCB* [2002] OJ L69/1; *Mercedes-Benz* [2002] OJ L257/1. See also Commission Decision of 19 December 2007 in Cases COMP/34.579 *Mastercard*, COMP/36.518 *EuropeCommerce*, and COMP/38.580 *Commercial Cards* ([2009] OJ C264/8 (summ pub)). For a recent example see Commission Decision of 14 June 2011 in Case COMP/39.736 *Siemens/Areva*. Despite the different wording of Arts 18(3) and 20(4), this should also apply in case of an inspection decision, even though it will usually not make much sense to resort to periodic penalty payments in this context given the loss of the surprise effect if the investigation is delayed. Hence, the Commission will rather have to rely on the deterrent effect of fines pursuant to Art 23(1) of Reg 1/2003.

[79] The imposition of a periodic penalty payment may not have retroactive effect in such cases since its objective is to ensure that the undertaking changes its conduct in the future (compliance). Moreover, the fixing of any periodic penalty payments (pursuant to Art 24(2) of Reg 1/2003) presupposes that such payments have first been imposed, which in turn requires that an Art 24(1) decision has been notified beforehand. Therefore, the delay for calculating periodic penalty payments cannot start before the day of notification of the Art 24(1) decision.

(eg to reply within a given deadline) and a periodic penalty payment to be imposed in the event the undertaking does not comply.[80] Provided it observes the principle of proportionality, there is nothing to prevent the Commission from deciding to request information (or to undertake an inspection) and at the same time imposing periodic penalty payments in the event of a failure to reply (or opposition).[81] The particular character of periodic penalty payments as an instrument of coercion (rather than punishment of past behaviour) makes them independent from, yet capable of accompanying, the imposition of fines.[82] Thus, for example, an incomplete reply to a formal request for information may give rise not only to a fine but also to the imposition of a periodic penalty payment in case the undertaking does not rectify its failure to comply within a given time limit.

9.20 If the undertaking (or association of undertakings) fails to comply with its procedural obligations by the prescribed deadline, and following a decision pursuant to Article 24(1) of Regulation 1/2003 threatening periodic penalty payments up to a certain amount, the Commission may fix their definitive amount by decision pursuant to Article 24(2). For this to happen, it is not necessary that the undertaking has complied in the meantime,[83] even though the Commission may take such compliance into account when setting the daily penalty level.[84] While it may go up to the limit which follows from multiplying the maximum *per diem* amount announced in the Article 24(1) decision with the length (number of days) of the delay, the Commission may also fix the payment 'at a figure lower than that which would arise under the original decision' (see Article 24(2) of Regulation 1/2003). Unlike the announcement of the intention to impose periodic penalty payments pursuant to Article 24(1),[85] the fixing of the definitive amount pursuant to Article 24(2) of Regulation 1/2003 is a challengeable act.[86]

---

[80] In its Antitrust Manual of Procedure, the Commission has stated that its 'usual practice is to combine an Article 24(1) decision with the decision that the periodic penalty payments are intended to enforce'. See European Commission Antitrust Manual of Procedures, Internal DG Competition working documents on procedures for the application of Articles 101 and 102 TFEU, March 2012, Module 20 'Periodic penalty payments', para 7.

[81] For instance, in Case COMP/39.523 *Slovak Telekom* the Commission imposed periodic penalty payments (Art 24(1)) as part of two formal requests for information pursuant to Art 18(3) of Reg 1/2003. It noted that Slovak Telekom had previously refused to provide certain information and documents following a simple request for information pursuant to Art 18(2) of Reg 1/2003, and that there was thus a risk of further delays. The legality of both decisions has been confirmed in the Judgment of 22 March 2012 in Joined Cases T-458/09 and T-171/10 *Slovak Telekom v Commission*.

[82] For an example of a case where the Commission imposed both a fine and periodic penalty payments in case of a substantive infringement see *JCB* [2002] OJ L69/1. Given their different object (past/future behavior), this should be admissible notwithstanding the Court's finding that 'a fine and a periodic penalty payment both relate to the conduct of an undertaking as revealed in the past and both of them require a deterrent effect in order to prevent repetition or continuation of the infringement.' See Judgment of 27 June 2012 in Case T-167/08 *Microsoft v Commission*, para 93.

[83] In *Microsoft*, the Commission was faced with continued obstruction on the side of the undertaking which for almost two years did not comply with its obligations under Commission Decision of 24 March 2004 in Case COMP/37.792 *Microsoft*. Following an earlier Art 24(1) decision on 10 November 2005, by which it had imposed periodic penalty payments of EUR 2 million per day, on 12 July 2006 the Commission fixed the definitive amount of the penalty payments for the period 16 December 2005 to 20 June 2006 (Art 24(2)). In the same decision it also imposed new periodic penalty payments at an increased amount of EUR 3 million per day as of 31 July 2006 (Art 24(1)). See Commission Decision of 12 July 2006 in Case COMP/37.792 *Microsoft*.

[84] See *Baccarat* [1991] OJ L97/16, para 10.

[85] Joined Cases 46/87 and 227/88 *Hoechst v Commission* [1989] ECR 2859, para 55; Order of 24 June 1998 in Case T-596/97 *Dalmine v Commission* [1998] ECR II-2383, paras 30–2 and 36. However, as a necessary step in the procedure, its legality can be challenged in an application for annulment against the subsequent decision fixing the definitive amount of the periodic penalty payment.

[86] Order of 24 June 1998 in Case T-596/97 *Dalmine v Commission* [1998] ECR II-2383, para 32.

No guidelines exist for determining the level of periodic penalty payments. The Commission **9.21** has to take into account all relevant facts and in particular balance the need to ensure compliance by creating sufficient incentives with the economic situation and financial strength of the undertaking.[87] As regards substantive obligations, the potential benefits for the undertaking from non-compliance may also be considered.[88] Other relevant factors include the consequences of the failure to comply for the market (restriction of competition)[89] or for the Commission's investigation;[90] the delay in complying;[91] or the undertaking's fault in non-compliance. Conversely, doubts on the side of the undertaking as to the legality of the decision imposing procedural or substantive obligations will generally not be considered relevant.[92] Given the difficulties in ruling out that the undertaking is merely dragging its feet, any claim that it *attempted* to live up to its obligations, albeit unsuccessfully, is unlikely to be accepted either.[93] While the 10 per cent cap foreseen for fines in Article 23(2) of Regulation 1/2003 does not apply, the Commission has to respect the proportionality principle and thus must ensure that the definitive payment is not excessive given the financial means of the undertaking.[94] When reviewing the decision pursuant to Article 24(2) of Regulation 1/2003, the EU Courts may modulate the definitive amount of the penalty payment in their unlimited jurisdiction (Article 31 of Regulation 1/2003).[95]

---

[87] See Judgment of 27 June 2012 in Case T-167/08 *Microsoft v Commission*, paras 220 and 207–8, where the GC referred to Microsoft's size in terms of turnover, the delay in complying with its obligations, the benefit this entailed for its position on the market, the need for deterrence and the fact that it finally complied. See also *IMA-Statut* [1980] OJ L318/1 and, for the relevance of the size and economic power of the undertaking in the determination of fines, Joined Cases 100/80 to 103/80 *Musique diffusion française v Commission* [1983] ECR 1825, para 120; Case T-48/98 *Acerinox v Commission* [2001] ECR II-3859, paras 89 and 90.

[88] Commission Decision of 10 November 2005 in Case COMP/37.792 *Microsoft*, para 202 (Art 24(1) of Reg 1/2003); Commission Decision of 12 July 2006 in Case COMP/37.792 *Microsoft*, para 242 (Art 24(2) of Reg 1/2003); Commission Decision of 27 February 2008 in Case COMP/37.792 *Microsoft*, paras 293 and 294 (Art 24(2) of Reg 1/2003) (confirmed in the Judgment of 27 June 2012 in Case T-167/08 *Microsoft v Commission*, para 220).

[89] See Judgment of 27 June 2012 in Case T-167/08 *Microsoft v Commission*, para 220.

[90] See eg *Hasselblad* [1982] OJ L161/18; Commission Decision of 10 November 2005 in Case COMP/37.792 *Microsoft*, paras 197 and 198 (Art 24(1) of Reg 1/2003); Commission Decision of 12 July 2006 in Case COMP/37.792 *Microsoft*, paras 242 and 247 (Arts 24(1), (2) of Reg 1/2003).

[91] See Commission Decision of 12 July 2006 in Case COMP/37.792 *Microsoft*, paras 247 and 248 (Art 24(2) of Reg 1/2003); Commission Decision of 27 February 2008 in Case COMP/37.792 *Microsoft*, paras 291 and 292 (Art 24(2) of Reg 1/2003). The GC considered that this also includes time periods where the Commission assesses whether the undertaking's conduct constitutes compliance, and that the existence of an arbitration mechanism did not counter-balance the fact of non-compliance. See Judgment of 27 June 2012 in Case T-167/08 *Microsoft v Commission*, paras 115–17, 219, and 221.

[92] Joined Cases 46/87 and 227/88 *Hoechst v Commission* [1989] ECR 2859, paras 62–5. If the undertaking entertains doubts, it has to challenge the decision imposing such obligations.

[93] See Commission Decision of 27 February 2008 in Case COMP/37.792 *Microsoft*, para 295 (Art 24(2) of Reg 1/2003). However, in para 296 the Commission nevertheless took into account that at some point Microsoft had taken measures to limit the negative effects on the market of its failure to comply.

[94] In should be noted that, depending on the percentage level chosen by the Commission, penalty payments could exceed 10 per cent of the undertaking's turnover if the delay in complying is longer than two years (see Art 24(1)), and that the 10 per cent turnover limit in Art 23(2) has been stipulated by the legislator in order to ensure that the sanction imposed is 'not excessive and disproportionate'. See Joined Cases C-189/02 P, C-202/02 P, C-205/02 P to C-208/02 P and C-213/02 P *Dansk Rørindustri and Others v Commission* [2005] ECR I-5425, para 281.

[95] See Judgment of 27 June 2012 in Case T-167/08 *Microsoft v Commission*, para 217, where the GC stressed that the exercise of its unlimited jurisdiction 'may justify the production and taking into account of additional information which is not as such required, by virtue of the duty to state reasons under Article 253 EC, to be set out in the decision'.

1. In relation to requests for information

9.22 Pursuant to Article 24(1)(d) of Regulation 1/2003, the Commission may impose periodic penalty payments on undertakings or associations of undertakings in order to compel them 'to supply complete and correct information which it has requested by decision taken pursuant to Article 17 or Article 18(3)'. Periodic penalty payments may therefore be imposed, not only when no or only partial answers are provided within the given time limit,[96] but also when the answers are incorrect in the sense that the information provided is not what was asked for or the answers are vague or unclear. Under Regulation 17, in most cases the Commission did not adopt a decision when requesting information, which was already then the prerequisite for imposing periodic penalty payments.[97] Undertakings generally cooperated with the Commission at the stage of ordinary requests, which meant that in nearly all cases it was unnecessary to adopt a formal request for information or impose periodic penalty payments. Moreover, pursuant to Article 11(5) of Regulation 17, a formal decision requesting information could only be adopted where the undertaking had failed to supply the information previously asked for by ordinary request within the time limit fixed by the Commission, or where previously it had supplied incomplete information. This subsidiarity principle no longer applies: pursuant to Article 18(3) of Regulation 1/2003, the Commission may now *directly* proceed to a decision requiring the disclosure of information.[98] Still, so far the Commission has only rarely made use of this power in antitrust cases.[99]

2. In relation to inspections

9.23 Article 24(1)(d) of Regulation 1/2003 also empowers the Commission to impose (daily) periodic penalty payments in order to compel undertakings 'to submit to an inspection which it has ordered by decision taken pursuant to Article 20(4)'. Normally, the Commission makes no provision in its inspection decisions for the imposition of periodic penalty payments in the event of opposition on the part of the undertaking. The obvious reason is that the success of any inspection (pursuant to Article 20(4)) crucially depends on its surprise effect, and that any delay in carrying out the inspection creates the risk that important documents might disappear. In fact, undertakings might be willing to accept penalty payments (eg for not granting access to their premises) in an attempt to destroy or tamper with incriminating evidence on site if this might help them to avoid high fines for any substantive infringement. Consequently, in case of opposition, the Commission will rather rely on the national authorities to enforce submission to an inspection (see Article 20(6) of Regulation 1/2003), and in addition impose fines pursuant to Article 23(1)(c) to (e) of Regulation 1/2003. Conversely, it is unlikely that periodic penalty payments and enforcement measures could be applied in parallel, since the success of the latter would typically preclude the former.[100]

---

[96] Where the addressee of a decision requesting information pursuant to Art 18(3) of Reg 1/2003 considers that the time limit imposed for its reply is too short, it may refer the matter to the hearing officer. See Art 4(2)(c) of the Decision of the President of the European Commission of 13 October 2011 on the function and terms of reference of the hearing officer in certain competition proceedings [2011] OJ L275/29.

[97] Art 16(1)(c) of Reg 17.

[98] See Judgment of 22 March 2012 in Joined Cases T-458/09 and T-171/10 *Slovak Telekom v Commission*, para 90. Generally, Art 18(3) of Reg 1/2003 stipulates the same formalities which also apply for a simple request pursuant to Art 18(2) of Reg 1/2003, with the additional requirement that the Commission shall 'indicate or impose the penalties provided for in Art 24'.

[99] One prominent exception is the *Cement* case, where the Commission adopted a formal decision after previous attempts to obtain complete and coherent information from the undertakings concerned had failed (see Commission Decision of 30 March 2011 in Case COMP/39.520 *Cement and related products*). Almost all addressees have challenged the Art 18(3) decision in court (Cases T-292/11, T-293/11, T-296/11, T-297/11, T-305/11, and T-306/11).

[100] See, however, Joined Cases 46/87 and 227/88 *Hoechst v Commission* [1989] ECR 2859, paras 3–5.

D. Procedure

1. General

Procedural infringements on the part of undertakings may lead to autonomous penalty pro- **9.24** ceedings, ancillary to the main procedure on substance. For instance, where undertakings refuse to allow inspectors to enter their premises or to have full access to the undertaking's books or other records, the Commission would be empowered to impose a fine in respect of such action,[101] but also periodic penalty payments if, for any reason, enforcement measures prove unsuccessful.[102] This could lead to three Commission procedures:

(i)   a procedure pursuant to Article 24(1)(e) of Regulation 1/2003, intended to compel the undertaking to submit to the inspection;
(ii) a procedure for an infringement of Article 20(4), pursuant to Article 23(1)(c) of Regulation 1/2003, with a view to the imposition of fines for opposition to an inspection;
(iii) a main procedure for an infringement of Articles 101(1) and/or 102 TFEU.

Each procedure would follow its own independent course—although in parallel—until the **9.25** possible adoption of three final decisions. All three procedures would typically be dealt with by the same officials within DG COMP. However, a decision concerning procedural violations (eg obstruction) does not presuppose that the undertaking is also the subject of investigations concerning an infringement on substance (ie Articles 101, 102 TFEU). Rather, in so far as the Commission has reasonable suspicions of anticompetitive conduct, all undertakings (including third parties[103]) are required to submit to the investigation, even if it later turns out that no substantive infringement can be established. All, therefore, are liable to a pecuniary penalty if they do not cooperate with the Commission.

2. Procedure for the imposition of periodic penalty payments

Article 27(1) of Regulation 1/2003 provides that before adopting the decisions provided for, **9.26** *inter alia*, in Articles 23 and 24(2), the Commission will give undertakings and associations of undertakings an opportunity to submit their observations on the objections or charges made by the Commission against them.[104] In addition, pursuant to Article 14(1) of Regulation 1/2003, the Advisory Committee on Restrictive Practices and Dominant Positions is also consulted.[105]

As indicated earlier, the imposition of a periodic penalty payment comprises two phases.[106] **9.27** In the first phase—either as part of the investigatory measure (Article 18(3), 20(4)) or by an independent decision—the Commission determines the (maximum) amount of the periodic penalty payment per day of delay. In this first phase, the Commission is not required to send a statement of objections, or to allow undertakings to submit observations, be it in

---

[101] Alternatively, the Commission may treat the obstructive behaviour as an aggravating circumstance in any substantive fine pursuant to Art 23(2) of Reg 1/2003. See point 28, second indent, of the 2006 Fining Guidelines.
[102] Cf Joined Cases 46/87 and 227/88 *Hoechst v Commission* [1989] ECR 2859, paras 3–8.
[103] For instance, undertakings which—without having been parties to an anticompetitive agreement or concerted practice—are in possession of information which they refuse to disclose to the Commission.
[104] See also Arts 10–12, 14 of Reg 773/2004.
[105] See Ch 3, 'The Role of National Competition Authorities'.
[106] Joined Cases 46/87 and 227/88 *Hoechst v Commission* [1989] ECR 2859, para 55. For an overview of the procedure see European Commission Antitrust Manual of Procedures, Internal DG Competition working documents on procedures for the application of Articles 101 and 102 TFEU, March 2012, Module 20 'Periodic penalty payments', para 4 et seq.

writing or orally.[107] Nor is it necessary for the Commission to submit a draft decision to the Advisory Committee. If the undertaking complies with its obligations, it will face no adverse consequences. If it fails to do so within the fixed time limit, the responsible Director-General in DG COMP will send the undertaking a brief letter reminding it of the financial consequences of non-compliance,[108] namely that, for each day that passes, the penalty will increase.

9.28 When the undertaking finally complies (after the time limit), or if the Commission considers that a (first) penalty should be fixed despite continued non-compliance, the second phase commences. In this phase the Commission determines by (independent) decision the definitive amount of the periodic penalty payment. Pursuant to Article 24(2) of Regulation 1/2003:

> where the undertakings or associations of undertakings have satisfied the obligation which it was the purpose of the periodic penalty payment to enforce, the Commission may fix the total amount of the periodic penalty payment at a lower figure than that which would arise under the original decision.

It has discretion in this regard, but may consider a reduction:

> if the undertaking has taken some steps towards compliance or if, having heard the undertaking concerned, the Commission is persuaded that a lower amount than that set in the Article 24(1) decision was appropriate for any reason.[109]

9.29 The second decision fixing the amount of the penalty payment can only be adopted after a Statement of Objections has been sent and the undertaking had the opportunity to submit observations.[110] Given that the objections raised in an Article 24 proceeding normally do not require an in-depth analysis by the undertaking concerned, the Commission will in general consider it appropriate to set the time limit for observations at four weeks.[111] In addition, the Advisory Committee will be consulted and the Commission will have to 'take the utmost account' of the opinion it delivers (Article 14(5) of Regulation 1/2003).[112] These procedural steps shall put both the undertaking concerned and the Advisory Committee:

> in a proper position to express their views on all the matters on the basis of which the Commission has imposed the periodic penalty payment and fixed the definitive amount thereof.[113]

9.30 By virtue of Article 30(1) of Regulation 1/2003, the decisions pursuant to Articles 23 and 24 have to be published.

---

[107] See Art 27(1) of Reg 1/2003 in conjunction with Arts 10–13 of Reg 773/2004, which is in conformity with earlier case law (Joined Cases 46/87 and 227/88 *Hoechst v EC Commission* [1989] ECR 2859, paras 55 and 56). This also means that no access to the file is granted. See Art 15(1) of Reg 773/2004.

[108] European Commission Antitrust Manual of Procedures, Internal DG Competition working documents on procedures for the application of Articles 101 and 102 TFEU, March 2012, Module 20 'Periodic penalty payments', para 9.

[109] European Commission Antitrust Manual of Procedures, Internal DG Competition working documents on procedures for the application of Articles 101 and 102 TFEU, March 2012, Module 20 'Periodic penalty payments', para 11.

[110] Even if the Statement of Objections is adopted before the procedural infringement has ended, the subsequent period (up until the decision pursuant to Art 24(2)) may still be counted for calculating the penalty payment if the Commission has indicated in the Statement of Objections that the infringement has not yet ended, and only takes into consideration such facts on which the undertaking had the opportunity to comment. See Judgment of 27 June 2012 in Case T-167/08 *Microsoft v Commission*, para 186.

[111] European Commission Antitrust Manual of Procedures, Internal DG Competition working documents on procedures for the application of Articles 101 and 102 TFEU, March 2012, Module 20 'Periodic penalty payments', para 14. See also Arts 10(2), 17(1), (2) of Reg 773/2004.

[112] See Case T-596/97 *Dalmine v Commission* [1998] II-2383, para 32.

[113] Joined Cases 46/87 and 227/88 *Hoechst v EC Commission* [1989] ECR 2859, para 56.

E. Limitation Period[114]

Since the adoption of Regulation 2988/74,[115] the Commission's power to impose penal- **9.31**
ties for infringements of EU competition law is subject to a statute of limitation.[116] In this
regard, Regulation 1/2003 has taken over the rules contained in Regulation 2988/74 with
some minor changes in order to adapt the enforcement system to the new decentralized
application of the competition rules.[117] Pursuant to Article 25(1) of Regulation 1/2003, the
limitation period for the imposition of fines or periodic penalty payments for procedural
infringements is three years. Time begins to run on the day on which the infringement is
committed. However, in the case of continuing infringements, the starting date is the day
on which the infringement ceases[118] (Art 25(2) of Regulation 1/2003). As regards periodic
penalty payments, this will be the day when the undertaking fulfils its procedural or substantive obligations.

According to Article 25(3) of Regulation 1/2003, any action taken by the Commission for **9.32**
the purpose of the investigation or proceedings in respect of an infringement shall interrupt the limitation period for the imposition of fines or periodic penalty payments.[119]
The limitation period is interrupted with effect from the date on which the action is notified to the undertaking, which comprises notification to a subsidiary with which the parent company forms one economic entity.[120] Among[121] the actions which interrupt the
running of the limitation period are written requests for information,[122] the initiation of

---

[114] See also Ch 11, 'Infringement Decisions and Penalties', para 11.27 et seq.
[115] Council Reg 2988/74 concerning limitation periods in proceedings and the enforcement of sanctions
under the rules of the European Economic Community relating to transport and competition [1974] OJ
L319/1, as amended.
[116] On the *ratio legis* see Joined Cases T-22/02 and T-23/02 *Sumitomo v Commission* [2005] ECR II-4065,
paras 80 and 82, and the opinion of AG Bot of 26 October 2010 in Case C-352/09 P *ThyssenKrupp Nirosta v
Commission*, para 188. Normally, the prescription issue will be less relevant for cases of procedural violations.
However, there are scenarios where this could become an issue, for instance if the Commission originally
intended to sanction the procedural violation as an aggravating circumstance in the substantive case (eg cartel
decision), but later on abandons that route and reverts back to an autonomous infringement case pursuant
to Art 23(1) of Reg 1/2003.
[117] Pursuant to Art 37 of Reg 1/2003, Reg 2988/74 has been amended so that it does not apply to measures taken under Reg 1/2003.
[118] See eg Case C-235/92 P *Montecatini v Commission* [1999] ECR I-4539, paras 195 and 196.
According to settled case law, 'if there is no evidence directly establishing the duration of an infringement,
the Commission should adduce at least evidence of facts sufficiently proximate in time for it to be reasonable
to accept that that infringement continued uninterruptedly between two specific dates'. See Case T-61/99
Adriatica di Navigazione v Commission [2003] ECR II-5349, para 125. This question cannot be answered
in the abstract, but has to be assessed according to the mode of operation of the individual infringement.
See eg Case T-18/05 *IMI et al v Commission* [2010] ECR II-1769, paras 89 and 96. In case of procedural
infringements, it should normally not be too difficult to establish their duration. Often they will be punctual
events, or otherwise the beginning and end date will be marked by events that can easily be established (eg the
deadline set for a reply in a request for information; the date when the reply is finally submitted).
[119] The same applies for actions taken by the competition authority of a Member State (national competition authority, 'NCA'), but it is difficult to imagine that this could play a role in case of procedural
infringements.
[120] See Case T-405/06 *Arcelor Mittal Luxembourg and Others v Commission* [2009] ECR II-789, para 146.
[121] This is a non-exhaustive list, see Joined Cases C-238/99 P, C-244/99 P, C-245/99 P, C-247/99 P,
C-250/99 P to C-252/99 P and C-254/99 P *Limburgse Vinyl Maatschappij and Others v Commission* [2002]
ECR I-8375, para 141. However, the GC has stressed the need for a restrictive interpretation in this regard. See
Case T-213/00 *CMA CGM v Commission* [2003] II-913, para 484; Case T-405/06 *ArcelorMittal Luxembourg
and Others v Commission* [2009] ECR II-789, para 154.
[122] Pursuant to Art 18(2) or (3) of Reg 1/2003. For instance, a request to the undertaking asking it to explain
the measures it had undertaken to prevent a breach of seal. Any interruption presupposes that the request for

proceedings,[123] and/or the notification of the Statement of Objections.[124] With respect to periodic penalty payments, the announcement of the intention to impose such payments (Article 24(1) of Regulation 1/2003) interrupts the limitation period for a decision fixing the definitive amount pursuant to Article 24(2) of Regulation 1/2003.

9.33 For prescription purposes, time starts running afresh after each interruption. Irrespective of such interruption, the powers pursuant to Articles 23(1) and 24(1) of Regulation 1/2003 will be prescribed (for procedural infringements) after six years if the Commission fails to impose a fine or other penalty.[125] This maximum time limit will be extended by the time during which the limitation period was suspended, ie for as long as the decision of the Commission is the subject of proceedings before the GC or ECJ.[126] Unlike an interruption of the limitation period, suspension only has *inter partes* effects and this applies even to companies which are part of the same undertaking.[127] In case the limitation period has elapsed, the Commission is barred from imposing fines or periodic penalty payments, but not prevented from finding a procedural infringement[128] if it can show a legitimate interest in doing so.[129]

9.34 Article 26(1) of Regulation 1/2003 specifies a limitation period of five years in respect of the Commission's power to enforce any decision imposing a fine and/or periodic penalty payment under Articles 23 and 24 of Regulation 1/2003. Time starts to run on the day on which the decision becomes final. The limitation period for the enforcement of penalties is interrupted (i) by notification of a decision varying the original amount of the fine or periodic penalty payment or refusing an application for variation; and (ii) by any action of the Commission or of a Member State, acting at the request of the Commission, designed to enforce payment of the fine or periodic penalty payment. Any interruption has only *inter partes* effects. The limitation period for the enforcement of penalties is suspended for as long as (i) time to pay is allowed; and (ii) enforcement of payment is suspended pursuant to a decision of the EU Courts. There is no case law on these provisions, but in practice the far-reaching possibilities for interruption render it unlikely that prescription will prevent the Commission from recovering a fine.

---

information was actually necessary. See Case T-213/00 *CMA CGM v Commission* [2003] II-913, para 488 in which the General Court held that the interruption of the limitation period has to be interpreted restrictively and the Commission cannot make a request for information for the sole purpose of prolonging that time period. However, unless there are indications that the Commission abused its investigatory powers, necessity can *prima facie* be assumed. See Case T-276/03 *Compagnie maritime belge v Commission* [2008] ECR II-1277, para 32.

[123] See Art 2(1), (2) of Reg 773/2004.

[124] See Art 10(1) of Reg 773/2004.

[125] Article 25(5) of Reg 1/2003: 'the limitation period shall expire at the latest on the day on which a period equal to twice the limitation period has elapsed without the Commission having imposed a fine or a periodic penalty payment'.

[126] Article 25(6) of Reg 1/2003. For the *ratio legis* see Joined Cases C-238/99 P, C-244/99 P, C-245/99 P, C-247/99 P, C-250/99 P to C-252/99 P and C-254/99 P *Limburgse Vinyl Maatschappij and Others v Commission* [2002] ECR I-8375, paras 144 and 151. The suspension effect is independent of the outcome of the case and in fact becomes most relevant when a decision is annulled (for a procedural error) and the Commission proceeds to a re-adoption (paras 67 and 153).

[127] Case T-405/06 *Arcelor Mittal Luxembourg and Others v Commission* [2009] ECR II-789, paras 151–8 (confirmed on appeal by Judgment of 29 March 2011 in Joined Cases C-201/09 P and C-216/09 P *ArcelorMittal Luxembourg v Commission* and *Commission v ArcelorMittal Luxembourg and Others*, paras 143–7).

[128] If one assumes that the power to find an infringement (of procedural rules) is inherent in the power to impose fines or periodic penalty payments pursuant to Arts 23(1), 24(1) of Reg 1/2003. Cf Case 7/82 *GVL v Commission* [1983] ECR 483, para 23.

[129] Case 7/82 *GVL v Commission* [1983] ECR 483, para 24; Joined Cases T-22/02 and T-23/02 *Sumitomo Chemical v Commission* [2005] ECR II-4065, paras 63 and 130 et seq.

10

PROCEDURES TO ESTABLISH THE EXISTENCE OF AN INFRINGEMENT

Manuel Kellerbauer, Luis Ortiz Blanco, Konstantin Jörgens, and Marisa Tierno Centella

I. Introduction

A. The Steps of the Procedure and its Formal Initiation

The administrative procedure under Regulation 1/2003, which takes place before the **10.01** Commission, is divided into two distinct and successive stages, namely a preliminary investigation stage and an *inter partes* stage. The preliminary investigation stage covers the period up until the notification of the statement of objections. It is intended to enable the Commission, with the help of the powers of investigation provided for in Regulation 1/2003, to gather all the relevant information tending to prove or disprove the existence of an infringement of the competition rules and to adopt an initial position on the course of the procedure and how it is to proceed. By contrast, the *inter partes* stage, which covers the period from the notification of the statement of objections to the adoption of the final decision, must enable the Commission to reach a final decision on the potential infringement concerned.[1] The *inter partes* stage involves frequent contacts with the companies subject to investigation and this is also with a view to ensuring that they have ample opportunity to comment on all elements of fact and of law which the Commission may take into account when adopting the final decision.

10.02 The initiation of proceedings by the Commission is a formal act by which the Commission indicates its intention to adopt a decision under Chapter III of Regulation 1/2003.[2] The Commission will open proceedings under Article 11(6) of Regulation 1/2003, where the initial assessment of the evidence acquired leads to the conclusion that the case merits further investigation and where the scope of the investigation has been sufficiently defined.[3] Proceedings are opened 'with a view to adopting a decision'[4] under Articles 7 to 10 of Regulation 1/2003. It follows that proceedings cannot be opened if, at the material point in time, the Commission does not intend to adopt a decision. Given the legal consequences attached to the opening of proceedings, the Commission's view must be underpinned by a certain number of objective factors. According to the Commission's Manual of Procedures, there must be reasonable indications of a likely infringement for proceedings to be opened.[5] In order to be in a position to conduct this initial assessment, the Commission can already exercise its powers of investigation.[6] The initiation of proceedings is not a requirement for the Commission to reject a complaint pursuant to Article 7 of Regulation 773/2004.[7] The opening of the 'procedure' in the strict sense usually occurs after the preliminary investigation stage of the case, but not later than the date when the Commission:

(i) issues a statement of objections (Article 27(1) of Regulation 1/2003), or
(ii) issues a preliminary assessment (Article 9(1) of Regulation 1/2003), or
(iii) issues a notice pursuant to Article 27(4) of Regulation 1/2003 summarizing the case and the main content of the commitments or the proposed course of action, whichever date is the earlier.[8]

---

[1] See Case T-348/08 *Aragonesas Industrias y Energía v Commission* [2011] OJ C355/15, para 109, and, by analogy, C-254/99 P *Limburgse Vinyl Maatschappij and Others v Commission* [2002] ECR I-8375, para 38.

[2] Case 48/72 *Brasseries de Haecht v Wilkin-Janssen* [1973] ECR 77, para 16, with regard to Reg 17/1962.

[3] See Commission Notice on best practices for the conduct of proceedings concerning Articles 101 and 102 TFEU [2011] OJ C308/6, para 17. If by conducting limited further investigations the appropriate scope of the case can be determined with more certainty, it may be advisable to carry out such further investigation before opening proceedings.

[4] See Art 2 of Reg 773/2004.

[5] See European Commission Antitrust Manual of Procedures, Internal DG Competition working documents on procedures for the application of Articles 101 and 102 TFEU, March 2012, Module 10 'Opening of proceedings', para 5.

[6] Article 2(3) of Reg 773/2004.

[7] Article 2(4) of Reg 773/2004.

[8] See Art 2(1) of Reg 773/2004, which refers to the catalogue of formal decisions adopted by the Commission under Chapter III of Reg 1/2003 (Art 7—finding and termination of infringement, Art 8—interim measures, Art 9—commitment decisions, and Art 10—finding of inapplicability). The notice mentioned in Art 27(4) of Reg 1/2003 refers to Arts 9 and 10 of Reg 1/2003. See also Commission Notice on best practices for the conduct of proceedings concerning Articles 101 and 102 TFEU [2011] OJ C308/6, n 27.

The formal initiation of the procedure for the adoption of a decision itself takes the form of **10.03** a *sui generis* Commission decision. Decisions to initiate the procedure do not prejudge in any way the existence of an infringement and merely indicate that the Commission will further pursue the case. Therefore, they cannot be challenged under Article 263 of the Treaty on the Functioning of the European Union ('TFEU'). The EU Courts have defined them as 'procedural measures adopted preparatory to the decision which represents their culmination'.[9] As the Commission may decide to initiate proceedings at any point in time, it may well decide to do so prior to the statement of objections, quite independently.[10] However, in cartel cases, the opening of proceedings normally takes place simultaneously with the adoption of the statement of objections, though it may take place earlier.[11] The main legal effect of formal initiation of proceedings is that the Commission becomes the sole *administrative* authority competent to apply Articles 101 and 102 TFEU to the matter in question thereby relieving national competition authorities ('NCAs') of their jurisdiction to apply these provisions.[12] Furthermore, initiating proceedings signals the Commission's commitment to allocating resources to the case and to endeavouring to deal with the case in a timely manner.[13] The opening of proceedings does not limit the right of the Commission to extend (or reduce) the scope and/or the addressees of the investigation at a later point in time; eg the in-depth investigation or a reorientation of the case may imply taking up and investigating new aspects, or dropping some existing aspects of the case. Where the investigation is extended, it is necessary to open proceedings in respect of additional infringements at the latest at the stage of the statement of objections or, prior to decisions pursuant to Article 9 of Regulation 1/2003, the Preliminary Assessment.[14]

The decision opening proceedings should be kept short. Since the decision as such is notified to **10.04** the parties, it has to be drafted in the authentic language. In essence the decision states that it has been decided to open the proceedings pursuant to Article 11(6) of Regulation 1/2003 and Article 2 of Regulation 773/2004 in the case at stake, and that the NCAs are relieved of their competence to apply Articles 101 and 102 TFEU to the same case. The decision to open proceedings identifies the parties subject to the proceedings and briefly describes the scope of the investigation. In particular, it sets out the behaviour constituting the alleged infringement of Articles 101 and/or 102 TFEU to be covered by the investigation and normally identifies the territory and sector(s) where that behaviour takes place. It is also emphasized that the opening of proceedings does not

---

[9] See Case 60/81 *IBM v Commission* [1981] ECR 2639, para 21; Case T-241/97 *Stork Amsterdam v Commission* [2000] ECR II-309, para 49. The initiation of proceedings remains a preparatory step and is made 'with a view to adopting' a definitive or final measure under Arts 7–10 of Reg 1/2003. See also on this discussion on whether (re-) allocation decisions within the ECN are challengeable, Ch 3, 'The Role of the National Competition Authorities', para 3.14 et seq.

[10] The Commission may in its discretion choose the time for formal initiation of the procedure, which usually follows—but may precede specific investigative measures. See Case 107/82 *AEG v Commission* [1983] ECR 3151, paras 19–20.

[11] See Commission Notice on best practices for the conduct of proceedings concerning Articles 101 and 102 TFEU [2011] OJ C308/6, para 24.

[12] Article 11(6) of Reg 1/2003. This relates to the application of competition law by NCAs, in administrative proceedings, in order to bring to an end conduct contrary to Arts 101 and 102 TFEU. It does not concern the application of competition provisions by national courts or judges in civil proceedings with a view, *inter alia*, to the annulment of agreements or the award of damages. National courts may continue to apply the EU competition law in that way, even after exclusive competence has become vested in the Commission.

[13] See Commission Notice on best practices for the conduct of proceedings concerning Articles 101 and 102 TFEU [2011] OJ C308/6, para 18.

[14] European Commission Antitrust Manual of Procedures, Internal DG Competition working documents on procedures for the application of Articles 101 and 102 TFEU, March 2012, Module 10 'Opening of proceedings', para 20.

prejudge in any way the existence of an infringement.[15] The parties subject to the investigation are usually informed of the opening of proceedings when they receive the statement of objections or the notice pursuant to Article 27(4) of Regulation 1/2003 summarizing the case and the main content of the commitments or the proposed course of action. Where the procedure is initiated before that stage, the undertakings are informed by letter. If the decision to open proceedings is made public, the parties subject to the procedure are informed sufficiently in advance so as to enable them to prepare their own communication (in particular in relation to shareholders, the financial institutions, and the press).[16] Complainants and other natural or legal persons with a 'sufficient interest' may also be informed by the Commission of the initiation of the proceedings.[17]

10.05 The Member States are informed of the initiation of a procedure immediately after it has been decided upon, so as to make it clear to them that the Commission now has jurisdiction under Article 11(6) of Regulation 1/2003. The letter by which the Member States are informed stipulates that the Commission has decided to initiate a procedure and that it intends adopting a decision of the kind provided for in Articles 7, 8, 9, or 10 of Regulation 1/2003. If an NCA has already been informed that they are acting on a given case, Article 11(6) of Regulation 1/2003 requires that the Commission consults in writing with the authority in question before initiating proceedings. In this regard two situations need to be distinguished. If the opening is envisaged during the indicative case-allocation period,[18] a simple bilateral consultation will suffice. The other authorities are given an opportunity to react within two weeks. If the opening is envisaged after the indicative case-allocation period, paragraphs 54 to 56 of the Commission's Network Notice[19] require that the Commission formally consults the authority or authorities concerned, explaining the reasons for the opening in writing to the NCA(s) concerned and also to other network members, and announces the intention to open proceedings in due time, so that network members have the opportunity to ask for an Advisory Committee meeting. The consultation must contain a specific reason as to why the Commission finds that it is appropriate for it to open proceedings. This can be done by explaining why one or more of the scenarios described in paragraph 54 of the Network Notice is at stake.[20]

---

[15] European Commission Antitrust Manual of Procedures, Internal DG Competition working documents on procedures for the application of Articles 101 and 102 TFEU, March 2012, Module 10 'Opening of proceedings', paras 11 and 12.

[16] Article 2(2) of Reg 773/2004. See also Commission Notice on best practices for the conduct of proceedings concerning Articles 101 and 102 TFEU [2011] OJ C308/6, para 21 and European Commission Antitrust Manual of Procedures, Internal DG Competition working documents on procedures for the application of Articles 101 and 102 TFEU, March 2012, Module 10 'Opening of proceedings', para 18.

[17] According to Art 27(1) of Reg 1/2003, complainants shall be closely associated with the proceedings.

[18] According to the European Commission Antitrust Manual of Procedures, Internal DG Competition working documents on procedures for the application of Articles 101 and 102 TFEU, March 2012, Module 10 'Opening of proceedings', note 8, this case-allocation period is in principle two months from the date when either the Commission or an NCA first informed the network of an investigation, but in case of a disagreement it is implicitly extended until a solution is found. An initiation decision is the ultimate way to end extended case-allocation discussions, but an agreement is by far a preferred solution to a unilateral de-seizure.

[19] Commission Notice on cooperation within the Network of Competition Authorities [2004] OJ C101/3.

[20] Paragraph 54 of the Commission Notice on cooperation within the Network of Competition Authorities [2004] OJ C101/3 holds that: 'After the allocation phase, the Commission will in principle only apply Article 11(6) of [Regulation 1/2003] if one of the following situations arises: (a) Network members envisage conflicting decisions in the same case; (b) Network members envisage a decision which is obviously in conflict with consolidated case law; the standards defined in the judgments of the Community courts and in previous decisions and regulations of the Commission should serve as a yardstick; concerning the assessment of the facts (e.g. market definition), only a significant divergence will trigger an intervention of the Commission; (c) Network member(s) is (are) unduly drawing out proceedings in the case; (d) There is a need to adopt a Commission decision to develop Community competition policy in particular when a similar competition issue arises in several Member States or to ensure effective enforcement; (e) The NCA(s) concerned do not object.' See for more details, Ch 3, 'The Role of National Competition Authorities', para 3.26 et seq.

Shortly after the opening of proceedings, the Directorate-General for Competition ('DG **10.06** COMP') will inform the parties subject to the investigation of the issues identified at this stage and of the anticipated scope of the investigation. This first 'State of Play meeting' provides the parties with an opportunity to react initially to the issues identified and may also serve to assist the DG COMP in deciding on the appropriate framework for its further investigation.[21] This State of Play meeting may also be used to discuss any relevant language waivers that may be appropriate for the conduct of the investigation. The DG COMP will normally indicate a tentative timetable for the case.[22] Such tentative timetable will, if appropriate, be updated at later State of Play meetings at a sufficiently advanced stage in the investigation. State of Play meetings are normally chaired by the senior management of DG COMP (Director-General or Deputy Director-General) and conducted at the Commission's premises.[23]

In cases based on formal complaints, the Commission will usually also provide the parties **10.07** subject to the proceedings at an early stage, and at the latest shortly after the opening of proceedings, with the opportunity of commenting on a non-confidential version of the complaint.[24] However, this will not be the case where the complaint is rejected at an early stage without further in-depth investigation, or where disclosing the complaint is considered likely to prejudice the investigation.[25] Shortly after the opening of proceedings, the Commission will also endeavour to provide the parties subject to the proceedings with the opportunity to review non-confidential versions of other so-called 'key submissions' already submitted to the Commission. This includes significant submissions of the complainant or interested third parties, but not, for example, replies to requests for information.[26] However, it is important to note that no early access to key submission is granted in cartel cases.[27]

Once the Commission has reached a preliminary view of the main issues raised by a case, the **10.08** following procedural paths may be envisaged:[28]

• The Commission may decide to proceed towards the adoption of a statement of objections with a view to adopting a prohibition decision relating to all or some of the issues identified at the opening of proceedings.

---

[21] See Commission Notice on best practices for the conduct of proceedings concerning Articles 101 and 102 TFEU [2011] OJ C308/6, para 63.

[22] See Commission Notice on best practices for the conduct of proceedings concerning Articles 101 and 102 TFEU [2011] OJ C308/6, para 63.

[23] See Commission Notice on best practices for the conduct of proceedings concerning Articles 101 and 102 TFEU [2011] OJ C308/6, para 62. However, in cases involving multiple parties, the meeting may be chaired by the responsible head of unit. It can also be held by telephone or videoconference where appropriate.

[24] See Commission Notice on best practices for the conduct of proceedings concerning Articles 101 and 102 TFEU [2011] OJ C308/6, para 71.

[25] See Commission Notice on best practices for the conduct of proceedings concerning Articles 101 and 102 TFEU [2011] OJ C308/6, para 71.

[26] See Commission Notice on best practices for the conduct of proceedings concerning Articles 101 and 102 TFEU [2011] OJ C308/6, para 73. The Commission points out that it will respect justified requests by the complainant or interested third parties for non-disclosure of their submissions prior to the issuing of a statement of objections where they have genuine concerns regarding confidentiality, including fears of retaliation and the protection of business secrets.

[27] The Commission defines cartels in its notice on immunity from fines and reduction of fines in cartel cases ([2006] OJ C298/17) as 'agreements and/or concerted practices between two or more competitors aimed at coordinating their competitive behaviour on the market and/or influencing the relevant parameters of competition through practices such as the fixing of purchase or selling prices or other trading conditions, the allocation of production or sales quotas, the sharing of markets including bid-rigging, restrictions of imports or exports and/or anticompetitive actions against other competitors'.

[28] See Commission Notice on best practices for the conduct of proceedings concerning Articles 101 and 102 TFEU [2011] OJ C308/6, para 75.

- The parties subject to the investigation may consider offering commitments which address the competition concerns arising from the investigation, or at least show their willingness to discuss such a possibility; in that case, the Commission may decide to engage in discussions with a view to a commitment decision (see Chapter 13, 'Commitments, Voluntary Adjustments, Conclusion of the Procedure without a Formal Decision', para 13.08).
- The Commission may decide that there are no grounds to continue the proceedings with regard to all or some of the parties and close the proceedings accordingly. If the case originated via a complaint, the Commission shall, before closing the case, give the complainant the possibility to express its views (Chapter 12 'Rejection of Complaints', para 12.20 et seq).

B. Overview of the Procedural Guarantees

10.09 The initiation of a procedure potentially leading to the establishment of an infringement requires the Commission to put into place and observe a set of procedural guarantees aimed at protecting the parties' rights of defence. Notwithstanding the Commission's lack of a judicial role, the conduct of its administrative procedures establishing the existence of an infringement must respect certain guarantees that constitute general principles of EU law.[29] As the EU Courts have repeatedly made clear, fundamental rights—defence rights included—form part of the EU legal order and are to be respected by EU institutions according to Member States' common constitutional traditions and the Convention for the Protection of Human Rights and Fundamental Freedoms (European Convention on Human Rights, 'ECHR').[30] These rights must also be respected in the absence of an express provision recognizing them in the procedural rules or where the existing provisions do not in themselves take account of them.[31]

10.10 Regulation 1/2003 specifically states in its Recital 37 that it respects fundamental rights and follows the principles enshrined in the EU Charter of Fundamental Rights.[32] Furthermore, both Regulation 1/2003 (Article 27) and Regulation 773/2004 (Article 11) provide that the Commission must respect undertakings' defence rights by requiring it to base its decisions only on elements of fact and law on which the parties concerned have been able to comment. The EU Courts have recognized that the rights of the defence include, among others, the right to be heard, the right of access to the file, the right against self-incrimination, the right to be assisted by a lawyer, legal professional privilege, and the principle of good administration.[33] The principle

---

[29] See recently, Joined Cases C-204/00 P, C-205/00 P, C-211/00 P, C-213/00 P, C-217/00 P, and C-219/00 P *Aalborg Portland and Others v Commission* [2004] ECR I-123, para 64; Case T-99/04 *AC-Treuhand v Commission* [2008] ECR II-1501, para 46; Case C-109/10 P *Solvay v Commission* OJ C370/12, para 52.

[30] See, eg Case C-299/95 *Kremzow* [1997] ECR I-2629, para 14; Case T-1 12/98 *Mannesmannröhren-Werke v Commission* [2001] ECR II-729, para 60. Joined Cases T-67/00, T-68/00, T-71/00, and T-78/00 *JFE Engineering Corp and others v Commission* [2004] OJ C239/1, para 178. According to the case law, fundamental rights are protected in the EU legal order, as reaffirmed in the preamble to the Single European Act, by Art 6 TEU and by Art 47 of the Charter of Fundamental Rights of the European Union; see, eg Case T-348/08 *Aragonesas Industrias y Energía v Commission* [2011] OJ C355/15, para 94. See Ch 1, 'The Institutional Framework' para 1.22 et seq.

[31] See Joined Cases 234/84 and 40/85 *Belgium v Commission* [1986] ECR 2263, para 27; Case C-301/87 *France v Commission* [1990] ECR I-307, para 29; Case C-32/95 P *Commission v Lisrestal [1996]* ECR I-5373, para 21; Case C-1 35/92 *Fiskano v Commission* [1994] ECR I-2885, para 39; Case T-251/00, *Lagardère and Canal+ v Commission* [2002] II-4825, para 94.

[32] [2007] OJ C303/1. This obligation now also results from Art 6(1) TEU.

[33] See, eg the former President of the General Court ('GC'), Judge Bo Vesterdorf, 'Judicial Review and Competition Law—Reflections on the Role of the Community Courts in the EC System of Competition Law Enforcement', Speech at the International Forum on EC Competition Law, Brussels, 8 April 2005, noting that important due process rights include the requirement for the Commission to address its objections in writing, the right of the parties to respond in writing or orally to those objections, and the right to have access to the Commission's file. See also a published and edited paper version of this speech in (2005) 1(2) Competition Policy International 7. See also Ch 1, 'The Institutional Framework', para 1.27 et seq.

of good administration first and foremost entails the obligation for the Commission to examine carefully and impartially all the relevant elements of the case.[34] Secondly, as an element of the right to good administration, the Commission is obliged to act within a reasonable time in conducting administrative proceedings relating to competition policy.[35]

As regards the right to be heard enjoyed by undertakings prior to the adoption of decisions as **10.11** provided for in Articles 7, 8, 23, and 24(2) of Regulation 1/2003, EU competition law generally distinguishes between the right to be heard of undertakings under investigation (the so-called 'parties'[36] or 'undertakings concerned'),[37] on the one hand, and the right to be heard of complainants and other third parties showing a sufficient interest on the other.[38] The parties are notified by a statement of objections and granted access to file,[39] on the basis of which they are given the opportunity to comment in writing[40] and at a formal oral hearing.[41] Interested third parties are informed of the nature and subject matter of the proceedings.[42] However, in principle, they do not enjoy a right to access to file or a right to have an oral hearing organized upon their request.[43]

Only the parties can exercise their right to be heard during the Commission proceedings as **10.12** a right of defence. Its purpose is to allow the company under investigation to make known its views on the truth and relevance of the legal arguments and the facts alleged and on the documents used by the Commission to support its claim that there has been an infringement of the Treaty.

The right to be heard of the undertakings under investigation comprises the following: **10.13**

- The right to obtain a precise and complete statement of objections; in particular, the statement of objections must supply the undertaking with all the information necessary to enable it properly to defend itself before the Commission adopts a final decision.[44]
- The opportunity for the party to submit its observations on the documents and information on which the Commission bases its objections and arguments to reach a decision. The undertaking concerned must be afforded the opportunity to put forward its view as

---

[34] Case T-44/90 *La Cinq v Commission* [1992] ECR II-1, para 86; Case T-410/03 *Hoechst v Commission* [2008] ECR II-881, para 129; Judgment of 22 March 2012 in Joined Cases T-458/09 and T-171/10 *Slovak Telekom v Commission*, para 68.

[35] Case C-282/95 P *Guérin automobiles v Commission* [1997] ECR I-1503, paras 36 and 37; Joined Cases C-238/99 P, C-244/99 P, C-245/99 P, C-247/99 P, C-250/99 P to C-252/99 P, and C-254/99 P *LVM v Commission* [2002] ECR I-8375, paras 167–71; Case T-67/01 *JCB Service v Commission* [2004] ECR II-49, para 36. This right is also enshrined in Art 41(1) of the Charter of Fundamental Rights of the European Union.

[36] Article 27(1) of Reg 1/2003, second sentence.

[37] See Arts 7(1) and 9(1).

[38] Article 27(1) 3rd sentence and Art 27(3) of Reg 1/2003.

[39] Article 27(2) of Reg 1/2003, Art 15 of Reg 773/2004.

[40] Article 27(1) of Reg 1/2003, Art 10, 11(1) of Reg 773/2004.

[41] Article 12 of Reg 773/2004.

[42] See Art 13(1) of Reg 773/2004. Pursuant to Art 6 of Reg 773/2004, complainants are in addition entitled to receive a non-confidential copy of the statement of objections. Usually, this copy is also transmitted to interested third parties, although they do not enjoy a right in this respect; see Case T-213/01 *Österreichische Postsparkasse v Commission* [2006] ECR II-1601, para 107.

[43] If the Commission refuses to follow up on a complaint, the complainant enjoys a right to access to file pursuant to Art 8(1) of Reg 773/2004, which, however, is limited to the documents on the basis of which the Commission intends to reject the complaint. Furthermore, pursuant to Art 6(2), 13(2) of Reg 773/2004, complainants and other interested third parties can be admitted to an oral hearing which was requested by the parties.

[44] Case 45/69 *Boehringer Mannheim v Commission* [1970] ECR 769, para 9; Case 52/69 *Geigy v Commission* [1972] ECR 787, para 11; Case 27/76 *United Brands v Commission* [1978] ECR 207, paras 274 and 277; Joined Cases C-89/85, C-104/85, C-114/85, C-116/85, C-117/85, and C-125/85 to C-129/85 *Ahlström Osakeyhtiö and others v Commission* ('*Woodpulp II*') [1993] ECR I-1307, para 42.

to the truth and relevance of the facts and circumstances alleged and objections raised by the Commission.[45] In this context, the parties are also entitled to express their views in a formal oral hearing organized and chaired by the Hearing Officer.[46]

• The right to be generally allowed the same case knowledge used by the Commission in the proceedings, which implies access to the Commission's file on the same terms as the latter. This is also referred to as the principle of equality of arms, which means that, when adopting a decision, it is generally impossible for the Commission to take into account information not disclosed to the undertaking concerned on the grounds that it is covered by the principle of confidentiality.[47] According to settled case law the Commission has an obligation to make available to the parties all documents, whether in their favour or otherwise, which it has obtained during the course of the investigation, save where the business secrets of other undertakings, the internal documents of the Commission or other confidential information are involved.[48] It appears from the case law that 'access to the file' is an integral part of the right to be heard and not a right in itself because it would be intended to enable the addressees to acquaint themselves with the evidence in the Commission's file so that on the basis of such evidence they can express their views effectively on the conclusions reached by the Commission.[49] The right of access to the file is set out in Article 27(2) of Regulation 1/2003 and explained in more detail in Regulation 773/2004. The practicalities of access to the file, as well as detailed indications on the type of documents that will be accessible and confidentiality issues, are covered in a Commission notice on access to file.[50]

• It is worth noting that the EU Courts have ruled that the breach of an undertaking's right to be heard in general and breach of the right to access to the Commission's administrative file in particular does not warrant annulment of a decision, unless the ability of that undertaking to defend itself has been affected.[51] Where access to the file, and particularly to exculpatory documents, is not granted during the administrative proceedings, the undertaking concerned has to show, not that if it had had access to the non-disclosed documents, the Commission decision would have been different in content, but only that those documents could have been useful for its defence.[52] In such a case the infringement is not remedied by the mere fact that access was made possible during the judicial proceedings.[53]

---

[45] Case T-228/97 *Irish Sugar v Commission* [1999] ECR II-2969, para 35.

[46] Article 12 of Reg 773/2004.

[47] However, in order to strike the right balance between the right to confidentiality and the right to be heard, the Commission can rely on inculpatory information that has been disclosed only in a restrictive manner, eg by redacting the author or provider of the document or by disclosing the document only to representatives of the company entitled to access to file that have signed a confidentiality declaration. For more details, see para 10.57.

[48] eg Joined Cases C-238/99 P, C-244/99 P, C-245/99 P, C-247/99 P, C-250/99 P to C-252/99 P, and C-254/99 P *Limburgse Vinyl Maatschappij and Others v Commission* [2002] ECR I-8375, para 315; Joined Cases C-204/00 P, C-205/00 P, C-211/00 P, C-213/00 P, C-217/00 P, and C-219/00 P *Aalborg Portland and Others v Commission* [2004] ECR I-123, para 68; Case C-109/10 P *Solvay v Commission* [2011] OJ C370/12, para 54.

[49] eg Case T-7/89 *SA Hercules Chemicals NV v Commission* [1991] ECR II-1711, paras 51–3; Joined Cases T-10/92 to T-12/92, T-14/92, and T-15/92 *Cimenteries CBR SA v Commission* [1992] ECR II-2667, para 38.

[50] Commission Notice on the rules for access to the Commission file in cases pursuant to Articles 81 and 82 of the EC Treaty, Arts 53, 54, and 57 of the EEA Agreement, and Council Regulation (EC) No 139/2004 [2005] OJ C325/7–15. See also para 10.38 et seq.

[51] eg Joined Cases T-25/95, T-26/95, T-30/95 to T-39/95, T-42/95 to T-46/95, T-48/95, T-50/95 to T-65/95, T-68/95 to T-71/95, T-87/95, T-88/95, T-103/95, and T-104/95 *Cimenteries CBR SA and others v Commission* [2000] ECR II-491, paras 240–1.

[52] Case C-199/99 P *Corus UK v Commission* [2003] ECR I-11177, para 128; Case C-109/10 P *Solvay v Commission* [2011] OJ C370/12, para 57.

[53] Joined Cases C-238/99 P, C-244/99 P, C-245/99 P, C-247/99 P, C-250/99 P to C-252/99 P, and C-254/99 P *Limburgse Vinyl Maatschappij and Others v Commission* [2002] ECR I-8375, para 318.

C. The Role of the Hearing Officer in Ensuring the Respect of Procedural Guarantees

The Hearing Officer plays an important role in ensuring the respect of companies' proce- **10.14** dural rights.[54] In particular, companies can turn to the Hearing Officer in charge of their competition proceeding when they consider that they should be granted further access to the Commission's file[55] or that they were not granted sufficient time to make known their views on the Commission's objections.[56] In order to further strengthen the role of Hearing Officers in competition proceedings, in 2011 the Commission attributed them with the function of safeguarding the effective exercise of companies' procedural rights in the context of the Commission's powers of investigation under Chapter V of Regulation 1/2003 and with specific functions during this investigative phase in relation to claims for legal professional privilege, the privilege against self-incrimination, deadlines for replying to decisions request- ing information pursuant to Article 18(3) of Regulation No 1/2003, as well as with regard to the parties' right to be informed of their procedural status.[57] The Hearing Officers also draw up reports to the competent member of the Commission and the public on the hearing of the parties and the respect for the effective exercise of procedural rights.[58] For a detailed description of the role of the Hearing Officer in competition proceedings, reference is made to Chapter 1 ('The Institutional Framework'), paragraph 1.100.

The following decisional powers of the Hearing Officer are of particular importance to the **10.15** procedural rights of parties and third parties:

- Deciding, after consultation with the Director responsible for investigating the case, on applications from third parties to be heard in writing in a competition procedure. The third party must submit an application together with a written statement explaining his or her interest in the outcome of the procedure.[59]
- Deciding, after consultation with the Director responsible for investigating the case, whether complainants and interested third parties are to be heard orally.[60] Parties to whom the Commission has addressed a statement of objections are always entitled to an oral hearing.[61]
- Deciding on applications for extensions of time limits from parties that consider that the time limit given to them for commenting on the statement of objections is too short, or from complainants or interested third persons that consider that the time limit to make their views known in writing is insufficient.[62]

---

[54] The post of the Hearing Officer was first established in 1982 in order to enhance impartiality and objectivity in competition proceedings before the Commission. Over the years, the significance of the post has increased leading, *inter alia*, to enhanced terms of reference in 1994, 2001, and 2011. The Commission usually appoints two Hearing Officers. Currently, Michael Albers and Wouter Wils are in office. For each competition proceeding before the Commission, one of them is in charge.

[55] See Art 7 of the Decision of the President of the European Commission of 13 October 2011 on the function and terms of reference of the hearing officer in certain competition proceedings [2011] OJ L275/29 (the 'Hearing Officer's Mandate').

[56] See Art 9 of the Hearing Officer's Mandate.

[57] See Recital 10 to the preamble of the Hearing Officer's Mandate. See also Arts 4 and 9 of the Hearing Officer's Mandate.

[58] See Arts 14 and 16 of the Hearing Officer's Mandate.

[59] Article 5 of the Hearing Officer's Mandate.

[60] Article 6(2) of the Hearing Officer's Mandate.

[61] Article 6(1) of the Hearing Officer's Mandate.

[62] Article 9 of the Hearing Officer's Mandate.

- Deciding, in response to a reasoned application, whether the parties to whom a statement of objections has been addressed are entitled to have access to additional documents which the undertaking has reason to believe that the Commission has in its possession and that are necessary for the proper exercise of the right to be heard.[63] In the same vein, complainants and interested third parties may make a reasoned request to the Hearing Officer for further access to information in certain circumstances, although both are not entitled to access to file.[64]

10.16 In order to safeguard the effective exercise of procedural rights which arise in the context of the exercise of the Commission's powers of investigation under Chapter V of Regulation 1/2003, in 2011 the Hearing Officer has been granted the following additional powers:[65]

- The Hearing Officer may be asked to issue non-binding recommendations to the Competition Commissioner with regard to claims that a document required by the Commission is covered by legal professional privilege.
- The Hearing Officer may be asked to issue non-binding recommendations to the director responsible for the investigation where the addressee of a request for information pursuant to Article 18(2) of Regulation No 1/2003 refuses to reply to a question invoking the privilege against self-incrimination.
- The Hearing Officer may be asked to extend the time limit for a decision requesting information pursuant to Article 18(3) of Regulation No 1/2003.
- The Hearing Officer ensures upon request that undertakings are duly informed of their procedural status, in particular whether they are subject to an investigation and, if so, the subject matter and purpose of that investigation.

10.17 Finally—and this is of the utmost importance—the Hearing Officer decides on what allegedly confidential information obtained from undertakings may be disclosed to other undertakings or persons upon their request or be published pursuant to the relevant provisions of Regulation 1/2003, for which purpose he will follow a procedure equivalent to that described by the Court in its judgment in *Akzo I*.[66] It is important to note, however, that the Hearing Officer does not deal with requests for access to documents and ensuing questions of confidentiality under Regulation No 1049/2001.

---

[63] Article 7(1) of the Hearing Officer's Mandate.

[64] Article 7(2) of the Hearing Officer's Mandate. In particular, complainants that have been informed of the Commission's intention to reject their complaint can request access to further documents on which the Commission intends to base its rejection decision (Art 8(1) of Reg 773/2004), and complainants and interested third parties can request to be informed in more detail about the Commission's case before exercising their right to comment in writing (Arts 6(1) and 13(1) of Reg 773/2004).

[65] Article 4(2) of the Hearing Officer's Mandate.

[66] See Art 8 of the Hearing Officer's Mandate. Such a procedure—'*Akzo Procedure*'—was set out by the Court in Case 53/85 *Akzo Chemie v Commission ('Akzo I')* [1986] ECR 1965, para 29. Firstly, the undertaking must be given an opportunity to state its views. Then, the Commission is required to adopt a decision in that connection containing an adequate statement of the reasons on which it is based and which must be notified to the undertaking concerned. Taking into account the serious damage which could result from improper disclosure of confidential information, the Commission must, before implementing its decision, give the undertaking or person concerned an opportunity to bring an action before the Court within one week, with a view to having the assessments made reviewed by it and to preventing disclosure of the documents in question. Only requests for interim relief will prompt the Hearing Officer to delay the disclosure.

II. The *Inter Partes* Stage: Rights of Defence and the Formal Adoption of Decisions

The general principle of observance of the rights of the defence, which the Court has held **10.18** to be a fundamental principle of the EU legal order,[67] requires the Commission and all EU institutions, in all circumstances, to allow persons to make observations and be heard before the EU institutions adopt any measures which might adversely affect them, despite the fact that proceedings are of an administrative nature.[68] Similarly, they may not irreversibly compromise the future exercise of such rights during the conduct of the administrative procedure.[69] With respect to procedures establishing the existence of an infringement, Article 27(2) of Regulation 1/2003 expressly provides that the rights of defence of the parties concerned will be fully respected in the proceedings. For such purposes, when the Commission intends to adopt a decision against the interests of undertakings, it will draw up a statement of objections on which the undertakings will be given the opportunity of being heard in writing and, upon request, orally. Also, the addressees of a statement of objections will be granted access to all documents in the file, with the exception of confidential information of other undertakings and internal documents of the Commission.[70] Those steps together constitute part of the *inter partes* stage of procedures establishing the existence of an infringement, after which, following the report from the Advisory Committee and the report from the Hearing Officer, the Commission will adopt its final decision or close the proceedings. In most cases, nearly one year will have elapsed between the end of the investigation and the adoption of the final decision.

A. The Statement of Objections

1. Introduction

According to settled case law, in all proceedings in which sanctions, especially fines or penalty **10.19** payments, may be imposed, observance of the rights of the defence is a fundamental principle of EU law which must be complied with.[71] It requires that the undertakings concerned be afforded the opportunity, from the stage of the administrative procedure, to make known

---

[67] See Case 322/81 *Nederlandsche Banden Industrie NV Michelin v Commission* [1983] ECR 3461, para 7; Joined Cases C-204/00 P, C-205/00 P, C-211/00 P, C-213/00 P, C-217/00 P, and C-219/00 P *Aalborg Portland and Others* v *Commission* [2004] ECR I-123, para 64; Case C-109/10 P *Solvay v Commission* [2011] OJ C370/12, para 52.

[68] See Case C-109/10 P *Solvay v Commission* [2011] OJ C370/12, para 53; Case C-328/05 P *SGL Carbon v Commission* [2007] ECR I-3921, para 70; Cases 100–103/80 *Musique Diffusion Française v Commission (Pioneer)* [1983] ECR 1825, para 10; Case 85/76 *Hoffmann-La Roche v Commission* [1979] ECR 461 para 9; Joined Cases T-305/94, T-306/94, T-307/94, T-313/94 to T-316/94, T-318/94, T-325/94, T-328/94, T-329/94, and T-335/94 *Limburgse Vinyl Maatschappij and others v Commission* [1999] ECR II-931, para 246; Case T-308/94 *Cascades v Commission* [1998] ECR II-925, para 39; Case T-348/94 *Enso Española v Commission* [1998] ECR II-1875, para 80. See also Joined Cases T-5/00 and T-6/00 *Nederlandse Federatieve Vereniging voor de Groothandel op Elektrotechnisch Gebied and Technische Unie BV v Commission* [2003] ECR II-4121, para 32.

[69] See, eg Joined Cases 46/87 and 227/88 *Hoechst v Commission III* [1989] ECR 2859, para 15; Joined Cases C-204/00 P, C-205/00 P, C-211/00 P, C-213/00, P, C-217/00 P, and C-219/00 P *Aarlborg et al v Commission* [2004] ECR II-123, para 63.

[70] In accordance with Art 27(1) of Reg 1/2003, Arts 10 and 11 of Reg 773/2004 and the Notice on Access to File, para 10. See also, Case C-109/10 P *Solvay v Commission* [2011] OJ C370/12, para 54; Joined Cases T-236/01, T-239/01, T-244/01 to T-246/01, T-251/01, and T-252/01 *Tokai Carbon Co Ltd and others v Commission* [2004] ECR II-1181, para 38.

[71] Case C-308/04 P *SGL Carbon v Commission* [2006] ECR I-5977, para 94, and Joined Cases C-125/07 P, C-133/07 P, C-135/07 P, and C-137/07 P *Erste Group Bank and Others v Commission* [2009] ECR I-8681, para 270.

their views on the truth and relevance of the facts, objections, and circumstances put forward by the Commission.[72] In particular in the following proceedings enumerated in Article 27(1) of Regulation 1/2003, the issuing of a statement of objections is legally required:

- In procedures in which the Commission, acting on a complaint or on its own initiative, might find pursuant to Article 7(1) of Regulation 1/2003 that there is an infringement of Article 101 or Article 102 of the Treaty.
- In procedures for the adoption of interim measures based on Article 8 of Regulation 1/2003.[73]
- Whenever, for any reason, the Commission intends imposing fines or periodic penalty payments under Articles 23 and 24(2) of Regulation 1/2003.

10.20 The statement of objections serves to inform undertakings of the Commission's objections against them with a view to enabling them to exercise their right to be heard.[74] It grants them an opportunity to reply to the Commission setting out all the facts known to them that are relevant to their defence against the objections raised: whether the facts are correctly stated; whether the legal reasoning relied on against them by the Commission is well founded; and whether the Commission's conclusions fit the facts and the legal provisions relied on by it.[75] The addressees of a statement of objections have the right to have their observations taken into account by the Commission—that is to say, the right to expect that their cases will not be prejudged. Finally they have the right not to have any finding made against them in the final decision otherwise than in respect of the objections on which they have had a chance to give their views.[76]

10.21 Where a statement of objections is issued, the parties will also be offered a State of Play meeting after their reply to the statement of objections or after the oral hearing, should one be held: at this meeting the parties will normally be informed of the Commission's preliminary view on how it intends to pursue the case further.[77] The sending of the statement of objections may be an occasion for undertakings to modify their agreements and practices and bring them in line with EU competition law. Yet, the statement of objections does not in itself place undertakings under an obligation to modify or reconsider their commercial practices.[78] The provisions applicable to the statement of objections clearly indicate that it is provisional. The Commission highlights in its Best Practices that the statement of objections

---

[72] Case 85/76 *Hoffmann-La Roche* [1979] ECR 461, para 11, and Case T-314/01 *Avebe v Commission* [2006] ECR II-3085, para 49; Case C-511/06 *Archer Daniels Midland v Commission* [2009] ECR I-5843, para 85; Case T-83/08 *Denki Kagaku Kogyo Kabushiki Kaisha, Denka Chemicals v Commission* [2012] OJ C80/16 para 82.

[73] See Ch 14, 'Interim Measures', para 14.12.

[74] See Joined Cases 142–156/84 *BAT and Reynolds Industries v Commission* [1987] ECR 4487, para 14 et seq; Case C-511/06 *Archer Daniels Midland v Commission* [2009] ECR I-5843, para 85 et seq; Case T-445/07 *Berning & Söhne v Commission* [2012] OJ C243/12, para 47 et seq.

[75] The statement of objections must clearly set out the facts on which the Commission relies, and the legal inferences to be drawn from them. See Case C-62/86 *Akzo v Commission III* [1991] ECR I-3359, para 29; and Joined Cases T-5/00 and T-6/00 *Nederlandse Federatieve Vereniging voor de Groothandel op Elektrotechnisch Gebied and Technische Unie BV v Commission* [2003] ECR II-5761, para 33; Case C-407/04 P *Dalmine v Commission* [2007] ECR I-829, para 44; Case T-445/07 *Berning & Söhne v Commission* [2012] OJ C243/12, para 47 et seq.

[76] See Art 11(2) Reg 773/2004. See also Joined Cases C-238/99 P, C-244/99 P, C-245/99 P, C-247/99 P, C-250/99 P to C-252/99 P, and C-254/99 P *Limburgse Vinyl Maatschappij (LVM) and others v Commission* [2002] ECR I-8375, para 103; Joined Cases T-236/01, etc *Tokai Carbon Co Ltd and others v Commission* [2004] ECR II-1181, para 47; Case T-445/07 *Berning & Söhne v Commission* [2012] OJ C243/12, para 48.

[77] Commission Notice on best practices for the conduct of proceedings concerning Articles 101 and 102 TFEU [2011] OJ C308/6, para 64.

[78] Case 60/81 *IBM v Commission* [1981] ECR 2639, para 19.

only sets out its preliminary position on the alleged infringement of Articles 101 and/or 102 TFEU, albeit after an in-depth investigation.[79] Because it is a procedural and preparatory document, the Commission is not prevented from withdrawing the statement of objections, either in whole or part, or from dropping or amending specific objections.[80] For the same reason, the statement of objections is not a decision or other act which may be challenged before the Court under Article 263 TFEU.[81] The adoption of a statement of objections may well lead to the closing of the case without the adoption of a prohibition decision or a commitment decision.[82]

If the Commission bases its decisions on objections on which the parties concerned have not **10.22** been able to comment, the decision will be void.[83] For that reason, the Commission must set out in the statement of objections exhaustively—but not necessarily at great length[84]—each and every instance of conduct and each and every legal argument on which it proposes to rely for its decision. Similarly, the Commission is obliged to mention all documents that it intends to use as evidence in the final decision, together with the inferences which the Commission intends to draw from them.[85] That is why it is only after an in-depth investigation—which may last several months or several years—that the Commission decides to take this measure. The final decision adopted by the Commission does not necessarily have to be a copy of the statement of objections.[86] The rights of the defence are not breached by an inconsistency between the statement of objections and the final decision unless a criticism contained in the latter had not been set out in the former sufficiently clearly to enable the addressees to defend themselves.[87] In the same vein, a document brought to the attention of the addressee of a statement of objections may be used by the Commission in support of an objection in the final decision if the addressee could reasonably deduce from the statement

---

[79] Commission Notice on best practices for the conduct of proceedings concerning Articles 101 and 102 TFEU [2011] OJ C308/6, para 82.
[80] Final Report of the Hearing Officer in *GVG/FS* [2004] OJ C12/2 and in *Brasseries Kronenbourg Brasseries Heineken* [2005] OJ C175/4; see also Case C-125/07 P *Erste Group Bank and others v Commission* [2009] OJ C282/3, para 310 et seq. Case T-445/07 *Berning & Söhne v Commission* [2012] OJ C243/12, para 50.
[81] Case 60/81 *IBM v Commission* [1981] ECR 2639, para 21. Case T-10/92 *Cimenteries CBR v Commission* [1992] ECR II-2667, para 47.
[82] Commission Notice on best practices for the conduct of proceedings concerning Articles 101 and 102 TFEU [2011] OJ C308/6, para 77.
[83] See the Joined Cases C-89/85, C-104/85, C-114/85, C-116/85, C-117/85, and C-125/85 to C-129/85 *Ahlström Osakeyhtiö and others v Commission* [1993] ECR I-1307, paras 40–54 and 148–54, in which the Court partially annulled the decision which the Commission had adopted on the merits. The portion annulled concerned certain conduct objected to and the participation of certain undertakings therein, about which the objections were not sufficiently clear or were silent. As a result, the undertakings were not able to defend themselves properly in the administrative procedure. See also Case T-213/00 *CMA CGM and others v Commission* [2003] ECR II-913, para 109.
[84] The length of the statement of objections is very variable and depends on the complexity and novelty of the matter. The statement of objections fulfils its function by being clear and informing the undertakings of the essential facts and arguments relied on against them, albeit succinctly. See Case 27/76 *United Brands v Commission* [1978] ECR 207, para 274. See also, Case T-50/00 *Dalmire SpA v Commission* [2004] OJ C239/13, para 145; Case T-213/00 *CMA CGM v Commission* [2003] ECR II-347, para 109; and Case T-5/00 R *Nederlandse Federatieve Vereniging voor de Groothandel op Elektrotechnisch Gebied and Technische Unie BV v Commission* [2003] ECR II-5761, para 33; Case T-410/03 *Hoechst v Commission* [2008] ECR II-881, para 416.
[85] See Case T-446/05 *Amann & Söhne and Cousin Filterie v Commission* [2010] ECR II-1255, para 314; Case 107/82 *AEG-Telefunken v Commission* [1983] ECR 3151, para 27; Case C-62/86 *AKZO v Commission* [1991] ECR I-3359, para 21; Case T-11/89 *Shell v Commission* [1992] ECR II-757, para 55.
[86] See Case T-48/00 *Corus UK Ltd v Commission* [2004] OJ C239/12, paras 100–1; Case T-228/97 *Irish Sugar* [1999] ECR II-2969, para 35.
[87] See Joined Cases T-67/00, T-68/00, T-71/00, and T-78/00 *JFE Engineering Corp and others v Commission* [2004] ECR II-2501, para 429.

of objections and the contents of the document the conclusions which the Commission intended to draw from it.[88]

10.23 The Commission must take into account the factors emerging from the whole of the administrative procedure, in order either to abandon such objections as have been shown to be unfounded or to amend and supplement its arguments, both in fact and in law, in support of the objections which it maintains. In this context, the statement of objections does not prevent the Commission from altering its standpoint in favour of the undertakings concerned.[89] Partial withdrawal of objections is quite frequent, although it is rare for objections to be completely withdrawn.[90] Furthermore, arguments put forward by undertakings during the administrative procedure can be taken into account provided that consideration of the argument in the final decision does not alter the nature of the complaints against them.[91] If certain objections were not included in the statement of objections—because the events occurred, or came to the notice of the Commission, after the statement of objections was sent—the Commission needs to send a supplementary statement of objections and again grant the addressees the opportunity to state their views in writing and orally.[92] For example a supplementary statement of objections would be issued if the new evidence allows the Commission to extend the duration of the infringement, the geographic scope, or the nature or scope of the infringement.[93] If the Commission wishes to adduce further evidence in support of existing objections, it suffices to submit a so-called 'letter of facts'.[94] Issuing a letter of facts does not entitle the addressees to request a (second) oral hearing.[95]

2. Layout and general scheme of the statement of objections

10.24 The Commission's practice is to produce statements of objections comprising three parts. With the statement of objections in the strict sense an accompanying letter is sent, containing a number of statements—most of which are of a mandatory nature—together with any

---

[88] Case T-446/05 *Amann & Söhne and Cousin Filterie v Commission* [2010] ECR II-1255, para 315; Case T-11/89 *Shell v Commission* [1992] ECR II-757, para 62.

[89] Case C-125/07 P *Erste Group Bank and others v Commission* [2009] ECR I-8681, para 310. See also Joined Cases T-10/92, T-1 1/92, T-12/92, and T-15/92 *Cimenteries CBR SA v Commission* [1992] ECR II-2667, para 47 'until a final decision has been adopted, the Commission may, in view, in particular, of the written and oral observations of the parties, abandon some or even all of the objections initially made against them.'

[90] A Commission case in which the objections were withdrawn in their entirety was *BAT and Reynolds v Phillip Morris*. See Joined Cases 142 and 156/84 *BAT and Reynolds v Commission* [1987] ECR 4487, paras 26 and 27. Regarding the need to take account of the action taken when withdrawing or amending objections, see also Case 60/81 *IBM v Commission* [1981] ECR 2639, paras 18 and 21, and Joined Cases 100 to 103/80 *Musique Diffusion Française v Commission (Pioneer)* [1983] ECR 1825, paras 13–14. In the ruling on the 'Cement Cartel', Joined Cases C-204/00 P, C-205/00 P, C-211/00 P, C-213/00 P, C-217/00 P, and C-219/00 P *Aarlborg et al v Commission* [2004] ECR II-123, para 192, the ECJ found that an interested party is not entitled to be informed by the Commission if the latter drops certain objections (in the that case, in relation to certain conduct on the Italian market). The ECJ reiterated that it would be only necessary to inform a would-be addressee of such a decision if there would be a material alteration in the evidence relied on in a decision or if new evidence would be taken into account.

[91] See Case T-86/95, *Compagnie générale maritime and Others v Commission* [2002] ECR II-1011, para 447; Case T-228/97 *Irish Sugar v Commission* [1999] ECR II-2969, paras 34 and 36.

[92] See Case T-67/01 *JCB Service v Commission* [2004] ECR II-49, para 52.

[93] Commission Notice on best practices for the conduct of proceedings concerning Articles 101 and 102 TFEU [2011] OJ C308/6, note 70.

[94] See Case T-340/03 *France Telecom v Commission* [2007] ECR II-107, para 34 et seq; Case T-110/07 *Siemens AG v Commission* [2011] ECR II-477, paras 87–9.

[95] See Art 12 of Reg 773/2004, according to which only the addressees of a statement of objections and not the addressees of a letter of facts are entitled to an oral hearing. Furthermore, it can be argued that company's right to be heard can be exercised in writing where the objections remain the same and the Commission merely intends to take account of additional elements of fact.

annexes referred to in the statement of objections or the letter. Although under no legal obligation in this respect, in order to increase transparency, the Commission has announced that it will also endeavour to include in the statement of objections any matters relevant to any subsequent calculation of fines, including the relevant sales figures to be taken into account and the year(s) that will be considered for the value of such sales.[96] However, such information may also be provided to the parties separately after the statement of objections. Personal data, that is any information relating to an identified or identifiable natural person (eg names of company representatives) should for reasons of personal data protection only be mentioned in the statement of objections if this is necessary to support the objections against the undertaking concerned or to allow parties to properly exercise their rights of defence.[97]

The statement of objections strictly speaking

In general terms, the structure of the statement of objections is very similar to that of a Commission decision applying Articles 101(1) and 102 TFEU, which in turn are similar—formally, and only in part—to a judicial decision. The content of decisions will be examined in detail in due course, but in the statement of objections there are two distinct parts: the descriptive part (the facts), and the legal conclusions drawn from the evidence (the legal grounds) regarding the infringement. They are accompanied by certain statements from the Commission concerning its conclusions and intentions, for example to prohibit an agreement or practice, impose a fine, etc. The statement of objections is therefore, in appearance, a decision in embryo. **10.25**

The letter accompanying the statement of objections—time limit for a reply

Together with the statement of objections, strictly speaking, the Commission sends a letter which is also of great importance. It should indicate clearly: **10.26**

(i) The nature of the letter, the statement of objections and the annexes thereto. In other words, it is made clear that the communication constitutes a statement of objections issued pursuant to Article 27 of Regulation /2003 in respect of a potential infringement of the EU competition provisions.

(ii) The commencement of the procedure (unless the commencement of the procedure was communicated to the addressee already at an earlier stage).

(iii) The time limit within which observations may be submitted in response to the statement of objections. In setting the time limit for the reply to the statement of objections, the Commission will take into account both the time required for the preparation of the submission and the urgency of the case.[98] The period allowed might not be less than four weeks, pursuant to Article 17(2) of Regulation 773/2004. In practice, depending on the size and complexity of the file (eg the number of infringements, the alleged duration of the infringement(s), the size and number of documents, and/or the size and complexity of expert studies), the time of year (Christmas, Easter, or summer holidays), whether the addressee of the statement of objection making the request has had prior access to information (eg key submissions), and/or any other objective obstacles which may be faced by the addressee of the statement of objections making the request in providing its observations,

---

[96] Commission Notice on best practices for the conduct of proceedings concerning Articles 101 and 102 TFEU [2011] OJ C308/6, para 85.

[97] See European Commission Antitrust Manual of Procedures, Internal DG Competition working documents on procedures for the application of Articles 101 and 102 TFEU, March 2012, Module 11 'Drafting of Statement of Objections', para 12.

[98] Commission Notice on best practices for the conduct of proceedings concerning Articles 101 and 102 TFEU [2011] OJ C308/6, para 100, referring to Case T-44/00 *Mannesmannröhren-Werke AG v Commission* [2004] ECR II-2223, para 65.

the Commission normally sets a period of two months.[99] However, for proceedings initiated with a view to adopting interim measures pursuant to Article 8 of Regulation 1/2003, the time limit may be shortened to one week. An addressee of a statement of objections may, within the original time limit, seek an extension of the time limit to reply by means of a reasoned request to the DG COMP at least ten working days before the expiry of the original time limit.[100] If such a request is not granted or the addressee of the statement of objections disagrees with the length of the extension granted, it may refer the matter to the Hearing Officer for review before the expiry of the original time limit.[101]

(iv) The fact that, in response to the statement of objections, undertakings are entitled to make any submissions and raise any matters relevant to their defence. To substantiate facts, the undertakings may, if they wish, append documents of any kind. The Commission requests that in such cases the undertakings clearly identify—preferably in a separate annex—the documents which contain business secrets or other confidential information.

(v) The modalities for submission of the reply are set out in Article 10(3) of Regulation 773/2004,[102] which contains the following provisions:

> The parties may, in their written submissions, set out all facts known to them which are relevant to their defence against the objections raised by the Commission. They shall attach any relevant documents as proof of the facts set out. They shall provide a paper original as well as an electronic copy or, where they do not provide an electronic copy, 28 paper copies of their submission and of the documents attached to it. They may also propose that the Commission hear persons who may corroborate the facts set out in their submission.

(vi) That the undertakings may orally expound their views at an administrative hearing which, if requested, would be arranged by the Commission. Undertakings may, when lodging written observations, ask to give oral arguments at an administrative hearing, under Article 12 of Regulation 773/2004. They may also request, pursuant to Article 13 of Regulation 773/2004, that other persons (witnesses or experts) be heard and be allowed to appear and participate in the administrative hearing, in order to make oral observations confirming the facts on which they rely in their defence. The request for an oral hearing is to be lodged with the Hearing Officer.[103] The Commission services will usually indicate that an oral hearing, if requested by the parties, would be likely to take place about a month following their reply to the statement of objections.[104]

(vii) That if undertakings want to have access to the file, they have to make a written request within five working days after receipt of the statement of objections, in order to collect the CD-ROM/DVD at DG COMP premises or receive the CD-ROM/DVD by registered letter with receipt of delivery and/or to have access to corporate statements in case of leniency cases.[105]

---

[99] Commission Notice on best practices for the conduct of proceedings concerning Articles 101 and 102 TFEU [2011] OJ C308/6, para 100, referring to Case T-44/00 *Mannesmannröhren-Werke AG v Commission* [2004] ECR II-2223, para 100.

[100] Commission Notice on best practices for the conduct of proceedings concerning Articles 101 and 102 TFEU [2011] OJ C308/6, para 101.

[101] Hearing Officer's Mandate, Art 9(1).

[102] See European Commission Antitrust Manual of Procedures, Internal DG Competition working documents on procedures for the application of Articles 101 and 102 TFEU, March 2012, Module 11 'Drafting of Statement of Objections', para 57.

[103] See Art 6(1) of the Hearing Officer's Mandate.

[104] See European Commission Antitrust Manual of Procedures, Internal DG Competition working documents on procedures for the application of Articles 101 and 102 TFEU, March 2012, Module 13 'Right to be heard', para 13.

[105] See European Commission Antitrust Manual of Procedures, Internal DG Competition working documents on procedures for the application of Articles 101 and 102 TFEU, March 2012, Module 10 'Opening of proceedings', para 59.

(viii) That the deadline to reply to the statement of objections starts running when the parties have received the most important documents from the Commission file.[106] Deadlines start to run as from the day after the receipt of these documents (Article 3 of Council Regulation No 1182/71 of 3 June 1971 determining the rules applicable to periods, dates, and time limits[107]).

(ix) That the Hearing Officer is at the undertakings' disposal for any query in relation to their procedural rights. Usually, the Hearing Officer in charge of the proceeding is indicated to the undertakings subject to the investigation at the latest when the statement of objections is issued.

(x) That pursuant to Article 15(4) of Regulation 773/2004, documents obtained through access to the file shall only be used for the purposes of judicial or administrative proceedings for the application of Articles 101 and 102 of the Treaty.

The annexes to the statement of objections

Together with the accompanying letter and the statement of objections itself, and with a view to **10.27** expediting the procedure as much as possible, the Commission encloses a list of annexes. Those annexes are documents that usually do not emanate from the Commission and must be regarded as supporting documentation on which the Commission relies and must therefore be brought to the attention of the addressee in their original language, so that the addressee can apprise himself of the interpretation of them which the Commission has adopted and on which it has based its statement of objections.[108] However, the Commission will not annex all other documents which the parties may be entitled to inspect under the access to the file procedure. For the purpose of access to the file, the Commission provides a CD-ROM containing a list of all the documents of the file, giving both the number of each document, the nature of it,[109] and its content when it is not confidential. This includes the documentary evidence on which it relied in drawing up the statement of objections, and even evidence which is already well known to the undertakings.[110]

3. Formal conditions

The statement of objections, as already described, must be formally sent to the undertakings **10.28** so that they are able to exercise their defence rights.[111] Article 10(1) of Regulation 773/2004

---

[106] Case T-44/00 *Mannesmannröhren-Werke v Commission* [2004] ECR II-2223, para 65. The most important documents usually comprise the access to file CD/DVD and potential corporate statements made under the leniency programme.

[107] [1971] OJ L124/1.

[108] See Case T-148/89 *Tréfilunion SA v Commission* [1995] ECR II-1063, para 21. For a detailed description of the summary list of documents annexed to a statement of objections, see Case T-65/89 *BPB v Commission* [1993] ECR II-389, para 31; Joined Cases T-305/94, T-306/94, T-307/94, T-313/94 to T-316/94, T-318/94, T-325/94, T-328/94, T-329/94, and T-335/94 *Limburgse Vinyl Maatschappij (LVM) and others v Commission* [1999] ECR II-931, paras 337–8. T-338/94 *Finnboard v Commission* [1998] ECR II-1617, para 53; T-9/99 *HFB v Commission* [2002] ECR II-1487, para 327.

[109] In general terms, the Commission classifies them as accessible (A), non-accessible (NA), 'internal', 'EC premises' (for all corporate statements and immunity/leniency related decisions or correspondence only accessible at DG COMP premises) or by default, before determining the right classification, as 'undefined'. See European Commission Antitrust Manual of Procedures, Internal DG Competition working documents on procedures for the application of Articles 101 and 102 TFEU, March 2012, Module 12 'Access to file and confidentiality', para 59.

[110] See Case 107/82 *AEG v Commission* [1983] ECR 3151, para 26, where the ECJ pointed out that it is not the documents themselves that are important but the conclusions drawn from them by the Commission. The Court held that if documents were not mentioned in the statement of objections, AEG could reasonably conclude that they were not important for the case.

[111] If the statement of objections is sent to the undertakings only for their information and without a time limit for a response, the defence rights are infringed, since the possibility cannot be excluded that the result of the procedure would have been different if the undertakings had had an opportunity to give their views on the statement. See Joined Cases T-39 and T-40/92 *Carte Bleu v Commission* [1994] ECR II-49, para 46

provides that the statement of objections must be notified to each of the undertakings and/ or associations of undertakings concerned. It is addressed and notified individually to each party by the Secretariat General together with the cover letter explaining the rights of the addressees.[112] The Secretariat General sends the statement of objections only to the undertakings, not to their lawyers. However, if regarded as useful, a courtesy copy to the lawyers can be sent by the Head of Unit responsible.[113] In view of its importance, the statement objections must unequivocally identify the legal persons upon whom a fine is likely to be imposed and be addressed to the latter.[114] In the case of associations of undertakings, however, in order to comply with the principle of observing the defence rights, statements of objections do not have to be sent to an association's members; at least if it appears from their internal rules that the members are liable for the debts of the association.[115] However, in certain cases the Commission may not be entitled to separate the evidence regarding several related infringements in the statement of objections—with the result that separate decisions are adopted—if by so doing it prevents the undertakings from examining relevant documents for their defence which may have been placed in other files, thus infringing the undertakings' defence rights.[116]

10.29 Statements of objections do not have to be limited to dealing with a single infringement— they may refer to several, although these must be connected. It is normal for them to be addressed to several undertakings at the same time and for them to relate to different undertakings and to varying extents. The Commission may also bring together in one statement of objections facts which have been the subject of separate complaints. It is not required to draw up a separate statement of objections for each complaint and it is entitled to join related cases without any formal requirement to adopt a reasoned decision for that purpose.[117]

10.30 Pursuant to Article 3 of Regulation 1/58,[118] statements of objections are sent in the EU language of the country where the addressee undertakings are situated. The Commission may agree to send statements of objections in another EU language, if undertakings so argue or

---

et seq, in particular paras 58 and 60. In this case, the Commission had sent a supplementary statement of objections, solely for information, to one of the undertakings involved, which had in fact had the first statement notified to it formally.

[112] In Cases T-24/93, T-26/93 and T-28/93 *Compagnie Maritime Belge Transports v Commission* [1996] ECR II-1201, para 35 the GC adopted the view that a party cannot complain if the statement of objections does not properly name it where it is otherwise clear that it is the intended addressee and has the opportunity to exercise its defence rights. However, on appeal, the ECJ disagreed and annulled the fines for the appellants. It ruled that 'It is clear that a statement of objections which merely identifies as the perpetrator of an infringement a collective entity, such as Cewal, does not make the companies forming that entity sufficiently aware that fines will be imposed on them individually if the infringement is made out. Contrary to what the [GC] held, the fact that Cewal does not have legal personality is not relevant in this regard...Similarly, a statement of objections in those terms is not sufficient to warn the companies concerned that the amount of the fines imposed will be fixed in accordance with an assessment of the participation of each company in the conduct constituting the alleged infringement.' Joined Cases C-395/96 P and C-396/96 P *Compagnie Maritime Belge Transports SA v Commission* [1996] ECR I-1365, paras 144–5.

[113] See European Commission Antitrust Manual of Procedures, Internal DG Competition working documents on procedures for the application of Articles 101 and 102 TFEU, March 2012, Module 10 'Opening of proceedings', para 30.

[114] Joined Cases C-65/02 P and C-73/02 P *ThyssenKrupp v Commission* [2005] ECR I-6773, para 92; Case C-176/99 P *ARBED v Commission* [2003] ECR I-10687, para 21.

[115] In Joined Cases T-39/92 and T-40/92 *Carte Bleu v Commission* [1994] ECR II-49, the GC considered that it was lawful, by implication, for the Commission to send the statement of objections to two associations and not to its members (paras 22 and 25) and held that the Commission had not infringed the principle of the individual nature of penalties by imposing on the association a fine exceeding ECU 1 million (para 139).

[116] See Case T-36/91 *Imperial Chemical Industries plc (ICI) v Commission* [1995] ECR II-1847, para 94; and Case T-30/91 *Solvay SA v Commission* [1995] ECR II-1775, para 84.

[117] See Joined Cases 209/78 and 218/78 *Van Landewyck v Commission (FEDETAB)* [1980] ECR 3125, paras 29 and 32.

[118] [1958] OJ 17/385.

request.[119] It often happens that undertakings having their registered offices and/or head-quarters outside the EU/EEA, also have subsidiaries or branches in the territory of the EU/EEA. In such cases the statement of objections can be notified to the undertaking concerned at the address ('c/o') of a subsidiary in the EU/EEA representing the business activities if the registered office and/or headquarters outside the EU/EEA has agreed to it. If an undertaking has no establishment in the EU/EEA, the letter communicating the statement of objections must be sent directly to the registered office or headquarters located outside the EU/EEA.[120]

4. Substantive conditions—evidential documents

The Commission must establish clearly and exhaustively in the statement of objections the **10.31** accusations—administrative, not criminal[121]—made against the undertakings suspected of infringing EU competition law. Regardless of whether they have knowledge of facts and documents mentioned in the statement of objections, the undertakings must be informed of all the conduct and documents on which the Commission intends to rely for its decision. As stated, pursuant to Article 27(1) of Regulation 1/2003, the final decision may be based only on the objections and the documents in respect of which the undertakings have had an opportunity to give their views or version of events. EU competition procedure is essentially a written procedure and where necessary the Commission cites the documents which lead it to think that there has been an infringement of the Treaty provisions. Nevertheless, as has already been stated, what is important in the statement of objections is not the documents themselves but the conclusion arrived at by the Commission on the basis of them.[122] As regards documents, if the Commission failed to identify those that would be used in the decision, together with the inferences which the Commission intends to draw from them, it would prevent the latter from giving their views on their evidential value and infringe the rights of the defence, with the result that such documents could not be regarded as valid evidence against them.[123] The Commission must therefore take care to indicate in its statement of objections the evidential documents on which it relies. As regards annexed documents which have not been referred to in the statement, they may be used in the final decision only to the extent to which the addressees could reasonably have drawn from the statement of objections the same conclusions as the Commission drew from those documents.[124] The

---

[119] Regarding EU languages, see Ch 4, 'The Organization of EU Commission Proceedings', para 4.30 et seq.

[120] See European Commission Antitrust Manual of Procedures, Internal DG Competition working documents on procedures for the application of Articles 101 and 102 TFEU, March 2012, Module 10 'Opening of proceedings', para 35.

[121] See Art 23(5) of Reg 1/2003.

[122] See Case 107/82 *AEG v Commission* [1983] ECR 3151, paras 24–8, in particular para 27. See also C-62/86 *Akzo v Commission III* [1991] ECR I-3359, para 21, and the polypropylene cartel cases, *inter alia*, Case T-9/89 *Hüls v Commission* [1992] ECR II-499, para 38; Case T-11/89 *Shell v Commission* [1992] ECR II-757, para 55; Case T-446/05 *Amann & Söhne and Cousin Filterie v Commission* [2010] ECR II-1255, para 314.

[123] See Case T-148/89 *Tréfilunion SA v Commission* [1995] ECR II-1063, para 25. Here the GC stated that: '[t]he Court finds that the documents mentioned by the applicant were not disclosed to it when the statement of objections was sent. It follows that the applicant was entitled to consider that they were not important to the case. It follows that they cannot be regarded as admissible evidence as far as it is concerned', referring to Case C-62/86 *Akzo v Commission III* [1991] ECR I-3359, para 21, and Case T-8/89 *DSMNV v Commission* [1991] ECR II-1833, para 37.

[124] See Case T-446/05 *Amann & Söhne and Cousin Filterie v Commission* [2010] ECR II-1255, para 315; Joined Cases T-191/98 and T-212/98 to T-214/98 *Atlantic Container Line v Commission* [2003] ECR II-3275, paras 162, 171, 173, and 263; Case T-9/89 *Hüls v Commission* [1992] ECR II-499, para 39; Case T-11/89 *Shell v Commission* [1992] ECR II-757, para 56; and Case T-15/89 *Chemie Linz v Commission* [1992] ECR II-1275, para 37. See also Case T-4/89 *BASF v Commission* [1991] ECR II-1523 at paras 36 and 37.

Commission may, even after sending the statement of objections, issue a so-called letter of facts in order to forward evidential documents to undertakings so that they may make their observations on them.[125] As in the case of facts and evidential documents, undertakings must be given an opportunity to contest the legal conclusions concerning the alleged infringements adopted by the Commission, and its assessments as to their gravity, whether they were committed deliberately, and their duration.[126] The importance of the latter requirement lies in the fact that such circumstances will serve as the basis for calculating the fines in those cases where the statement of objections indicates that they will be imposed.

5. Publicity of the statement of objections

10.32 In order to enhance the transparency of the proceedings, the Commission generally publishes a press release setting out the key issues in the statement of objections shortly after it is received by its addressees.[127] This press release, which is usually published on the website of DG COMP, should explicitly state that the statement of objections does not predetermine the final outcome of the proceedings, once the parties have been heard. For the sake of promoting the implementation of competition policy, the Commission can also refer to the issue of a statement of objections in a particular case in its annual report on competition policy. The obligation of professional secrecy imposed on the Commission by Article 28 of Regulation 1/2003 does not prevent it from making a public announcement as to the issue of a statement of objections, provided the Commission does not divulge business secrets or other confidential information. There is no principle or rule whatsoever preventing the Commission from releasing 'information relating to particular undertakings' involved in procedures being conducted by it. The Commission must take care, in any event, that there is no confusion on the part of readers of a press notice between a statement of objections and a final decision finding an infringement, and that the notice is not made public before the statement of objections reaches its addressees.

6. Cases where a financial penalty is envisaged

10.33 If the Commission plans to impose a fine or fix the amount of a periodic penalty payment, the statement of objections must clearly indicate that the Commission will consider whether it is appropriate to impose fines on the undertakings concerned and point out the main factual and legal criteria capable of giving rise to a fine, such as the gravity and the duration of the alleged infringement and whether that infringement was committed intentionally or negligently.[128] The statement of objections must also clearly indicate whether the Commission intends to impose other remedies (structural or behavioural), should the objections be upheld, referring to the evidence and facts supporting such measures.[129] As regards the actual level of the envisaged fines, it is settled case law that to give indications of the level of the contemplated fines, when the undertakings have not been in a position to put forward their observations on the objections held against them, would be tantamount to anticipating

---

[125] See Case T-340/03 *France Telecom v Commission* [2007] ECR II-107, para 34 et seq; Case T-110/07 *Siemens AG v Commission* [2011] ECR II-477, paras 87–9; Joined Cases T-236/01, T-239/01, T-244/01 to T-246/01, T-251/01, and T-252/01 *Tokai Carbon Co Ltd and others v Commission* [2004] ECR II-1181, para 45.

[126] Commission Notice on best practices for the conduct of proceedings concerning Articles 101 and 102 TFEU [2011] OJ C308/6, para 84.

[127] Commission Notice on best practices for the conduct of proceedings concerning Articles 101 and 102 TFEU [2011] OJ C308/6, para 91.

[128] Case C-125/07 *Erste Group Bank and Others v Commission* [2009] ECR I-8681, para 181; Joined Cases C-189/02 P, C-202/02 P, C-205/02 P to C-208/02 P, and C-213/02 P *Dansk Rørindustri and Others v Commission* [2005] ECR I-5425, para 428.

[129] Commission Notice on best practices for the conduct of proceedings concerning Articles 101 and 102 TFEU [2011] OJ C308/6, para 83.

inappropriately the Commission's decision.[130] Nevertheless, although under no legal obligation in this respect, the Commission announced that it would endeavour to include in the statement of objections further matters relevant to any subsequent calculation of fines, including the relevant sales figures to be taken into account and the year(s) that will be considered for the value of such sales.[131]

If the fines are for procedural infringements in connection with requests for information[132] **10.34** or inspections,[133] the Commission is also obliged to inform the undertakings of its objections. The period allowed for written observations is usually between fifteen days and one month. If the Commission envisages imposing periodic penalty payments, the statement of objections is sent before the adoption pursuant to Article 24(2) Regulation 1/2003 of the decision as an enforceable measure, but after the adoption pursuant to Article 24(1) Regulation 1/2003 of the decision in which the periodic penalty payment is announced for the case of non-compliance.[134] The procedure for the imposition of fines for the infringement of procedural rules is different from the main procedure. It follows its own course separately from the latter, the result of which has no bearing on any finding of procedural infringements committed by the undertakings involved in the procedure. Where, after a first phase of resistance or opposition to the Commission's action, the undertakings modify their agreements or practices in order to make them conform with EU requirements or reach an amicable settlement with the Commission under Article 9 of Regulation 1/2003, those facts do not release the undertakings from their liability for infringing the provisions of Regulation 1/2003 relating to the Commission's powers of investigation (for example, by giving incorrect information or opposing an inspection). The Commission's consistent practice shows that even in cases with a 'happy ending', infringements which offend against the Commission's investigative powers do not go unpunished.

7. New objections and new evidence

Despite the Commission's scrupulous care not to omit any important aspect of the case from **10.35** the statement of objections, it may happen that new matters come to light on which the undertakings have not had an opportunity to express their views. This may be as a result of a fresh complaint or from the observations of the undertakings accused of restrictive practices at this stage of the procedure, or information obtained by the Commission in the exercise of its investigative powers. In such circumstances, the Commission may be required to send a supplementary statement of objections and to give the parties the necessary time to submit their views on the new material. Three situations may arise. Firstly, the new facts and the legal conclusions to be drawn from them may differ substantially from those previously described and detailed by the Commission in the statement of objections so that, even if the undertakings are the same, the new information may not be sufficiently related to the Commission's actual proceedings. In such cases, the Commission may choose to initiate a new substantive procedure to establish the existence of an infringement or else may deal with both infringements in the same decision. The second situation which may arise is that, despite the emergence of new information in the case

---

[130] Case C-125/07 *Erste Group Bank and Others v Commission* [2009] ECR I-8681, para 182; Joined Cases C-189/02 P, C-202/02 P, C-205/02 P to C-208/02 P, and C-213/02 P *Dansk Rørindustri and Others v Commission* [2005] ECR I-5425, para 434.

[131] Commission Notice on best practices for the conduct of proceedings concerning Articles 101 and 102 TFEU [2011] OJ C308/6, para 85.

[132] Article 23(1)(a) and (b) of Reg 1/2003.

[133] Article 23(1)(c), (d), and (e) of Reg 1/2003. See Ch 9, 'Procedural Infringements: Fines and Periodic Penalty Payments'.

[134] Regarding the procedure for the imposition of periodic penalty payments, see Ch 9, 'Procedural Infringements: Fines and Periodic Penalty Payments'.

which might give rise to new objections, the legal conclusions about the incriminated agreements, practices, or conduct is basically the same—there are no new infringements but there are new objections in respect of the same infringements. The same proceedings will continue, and there will be only one substantive decision, which will set out both the original (in whole or in part) and the new objections and will refer to the infringements indicated originally. The third situation that may arise is that the Commission has obtained new evidence corroborating the objections previously notified to the undertakings. There will be no new objections, but there will be factual information over and above that already known to the undertakings.

10.36   In the first two situations, additional objections are issued and/or the intrinsic nature of the infringement with which an undertaking is charged is modified. Hence the Commission should send an additional statement of objections to the undertakings concerned. Before doing so, a State of Play meeting will normally be offered to the parties.[135] The rules on setting the time limit for the reply to a statement of objections apply (see Chapter 9, 'Procedural Infringements: Fines and Periodic Penalty Payments', paragraphs 9.24 et seq), although a shorter time limit will typically be set in this context.[136] In the third, the Commission will choose to communicate to the undertakings involved the new information in support of the existing objections, in a 'letter of facts' allowing the parties to submit observations on the new evidence within a specified time limit.[137] This information does not alter the conclusions drawn earlier in the statement of objections that was sent earlier.[138]

10.37   The procedural rights which are triggered by the sending of the statement of objections apply *mutatis mutandis* where a supplementary statement of objections is issued, including the right of the parties to request an oral hearing.[139] Access to all evidence gathered between the initial statement of objections and the supplementary statement of objections will also have to be provided. If a letter of facts is issued, access will in general be granted to evidence gathered after the statement of objections up to the date of the said letter of facts. However, in cases where the Commission only intends to rely upon specific evidence that concerns one or a limited number of parties and/or isolated issues (in particular those regarding the determination of the amount of the fine or issues of parental liability), access will be provided only to the parties directly concerned and to the evidence relating to the issue(s) in question.[140] A letter of facts will not give rise to an(other) oral hearing. The letter will not reproduce the objections—they having been notified previously—nor will new reasoning be called for (still less a repetition of that already set out). The Court has generally accepted this practice.[141]

---

[135] Commission Notice on best practices for the conduct of proceedings concerning Articles 101 and 102 TFEU [2011] OJ C308/6, para 110.

[136] Commission Notice on best practices for the conduct of proceedings concerning Articles 101 and 102 TFEU [2011] OJ C308/6, para 110.

[137] Commission Notice on best practices for the conduct of proceedings concerning Articles 101 and 102 TFEU [2011] OJ C308/6, para 111. The Best Practices highlight that when the Commission merely communicates to a party a non-confidential version (or specific excerpts thereof) of the other parties' written replies to the Statement of Objections and gives it the opportunity to submit its comments, this does not constitute a letter of facts.

[138] A straightforward example may be that the Commission has gathered further evidence for meetings that the parties to a cartel allegedly held. This would not affect, as such, the finding on the duration of the infringement contained in the statement of objections and would thus not raise new objections.

[139] Commission Notice on best practices for the conduct of proceedings concerning Articles 101 and 102 TFEU [2011] OJ C308/6, para 112.

[140] Commission Notice on best practices for the conduct of proceedings concerning Articles 101 and 102 TFEU [2011] OJ C308/6, para 112.

[141] See Case T-340/03 *France Telecom v Commission* [2007] ECR II-107, para 34 et seq; Case T-110/07 *Siemens AG v Commission* [2011] ECR II-477, paras 87–9.

B. The Granting of Access to the File

1. Introduction

Once informed of the objections, the undertakings involved have an opportunity to submit **10.38** observations. To enable them to do so in full knowledge of the facts, undertakings are allowed, when receiving the statement of objections, to obtain access to the Commission's investigation file. Access to the Commission's file is one of the procedural guarantees intended to apply the principle of equality of arms and to protect the rights of the defence.[142] This is a procedural requirement deriving from case law[143] with which the Commission has complied with good grace[144] and which has now a legal basis in Article 27(1) and (2) of Regulation 1/2003. While it is true that initially the Commission imposed on itself certain rules and patterns of action as regards granting access to the file, as the Court of Justice ('ECJ') recognized, it now forms part of the EU Charter of Fundamental Rights,[145] which is not dependent upon a self-imposed obligation by the Commission. Article 15(1) of Regulation 773/2004 provides that the Commission shall grant access to the file to the parties to whom it has addressed a statement of objections. Pursuant to Article 15(2) of Regulation 773/2004, the right of access to the file shall not extend to business secrets, other confidential information, and internal documents of the Commission or of the competition authorities of the Member States.[146] The provision is in line with settled case law, according to which internal documents of the Commission and confidential information are in principle inaccessible.[147] Article 16(2) of Regulation 773/2004 obliges parties and third parties to indicate the material they consider as confidential in their submission and the obligation to explain the reasons and to provide a non-confidential version. The practicalities of access to the file, as well as detailed indications on the type of documents that will be accessible and confidentiality issues, are covered by a Commission Notice on access to file.[148] It should be borne in mind that access to the file is not a special procedure distinct from the procedure to establish the existence of an infringement, but a procedural stage in contentious competition cases.

---

[142] See, most recently, Case C-109/10 P *Solvay v Commission* [2011] OJ C370/12, para 53; Case T-83/08 *Denki Kagaku Kogyo Kabushiki Kaisha, Denka Chemicals v Commission* [2012] OJ C80/16, para 83.

[143] See the Joined Cases 56/64 and 58/64 *Consten & Grundig v Commission* [1966] ECR 299, para 5, and Case 85/76 *Hoffmann-La Roche v Commission* [1979] ECR 461, para 11.

[144] Joined Cases T-10/92, T-11/92, T-12/92, and T-15/92 *Cimenteries CBR v Commission* [1992] ECR II-1571, para 38; Case T-7/89 *SA Hercules Chemicals NV v Commission* [1991] ECR II-1711, para 53, established that the Commission may not depart from the rules imposed by it on itself, in that specific case those concerning access to the file. To the same effect, see also the judgments of the GC in all the polypropylene cartel cases—eg Case T-9/89 *Hüls v EC Commission* [1992] ECR II-499, para 42 et seq.

[145] See Art 41(2)(b) of the Charter of Fundamental Rights of the European Union. In fact, the ECJ has already referred to the EU Charter in various cases, which is now enshrined in Art 6(1) TEU (see, eg Case C-109/10 P *Solvay v Commission* [2011] OJ C370/12, para 53; Joined Cases C-204/00 P, C-205/00 P, C-211/00 P, C-213/00 P, C-217/00 P, and C-219/00 P *Aalborg et al v EC Commission* [2004] ECR II-123, para 94). The principle has also been already recognized by the case law of the European Court of Human Rights ('ECtHR') when interpreting Art 6(1) of the Convention for the Protection of Human Rights and Fundamental Freedoms (European Convention of Human Rights, 'ECHR'), to which refers Art 6(2) of the EU Treaty. See Ch 1, 'The Institutional Framework', para 1.28 et seq.

[146] As the case law had already recognized: Case T-7/89 *SA Hercules Chemicals NV v Commission* [1991] ECR II-1711, para 54.

[147] Joined Cases C-238/99 P, C-244/99 P, C-245/99 P, C-247/99 P, C-250/99 P to C-252/99 P, and C-254/99 P *Limburgse Vinyl Maatschappij and Others v Commission* [2002] ECR I-8375, para 315, and Joined Cases C-204/00 P, C-205/00 P, C-211/00 P, C-213/00 P, C-217/00 P, and C-219/00 P *Aalborg Portland and Others v Commission* [2004] ECR I-123, para 68.

[148] The Notice was adopted on 13 December 2005, see Commission Press Release IP/05/1581 'Competition: Commission improves rules for access to the file in merger and antitrust procedures' of 13 December 2005. See also Commission Notice of 13 December 2005 on the rules for access to the Commission file pursuant to Articles 81 and 82 EC Treaty [2005] OJ C252/7, para 1.

10.39 The term 'access to the file' is used here exclusively to mean access granted to those parties to whom the Commission has addressed a statement of objections.[149] The GC has stated that complainants do not have the same rights as the parties under investigation.[150] Consequently, complainants cannot claim a right of access to the file as established for the parties.[151] The term 'file' refers to the Commission's investigation file in a proceeding, which consists of all documents, which have been obtained, produced, and/or assembled by DG COMP, during the investigation.[152] In this context, the term 'document' is used for all forms of information support, irrespective of the storage medium.[153] The investigation file also comprises documents that the Commission does not intend to rely on as inculpatory evidence and that are in the Commission's opinion useless for the defence of the addressees of the statement of objections. It cannot be for the Commission alone to decide which documents are of use for the defence of undertakings in proceedings involving infringement of the competition rules. In particular, having regard to the general principle of equality of arms, it is not acceptable for the Commission to be able to decide on its own whether or not to use them against the parties, when the latter had no access to them and were therefore unable likewise to decide whether or not it would use them in their defence[154] Even internal documents of the Commission and confidential information form part of the investigation file, although they are in principle inaccessible. This implies, in particular, that the Hearing Officers have access to these documents and can be called upon to review their classification as confidential or internal.[155] In specific circumstances the file may even include documents that are physically contained in folders relating to other infringements. In the case of documents that are confidential but possibly aid the defence, the Commission may be obliged to provide non-confidential summaries.

2. Limits on access to the file

10.40 By virtue of its obligation to respect defence rights, the Commission must grant undertakings allegedly implicated in an infringement access to the evidence and documents on which it relies for its objections, as set out in the statement of objections or the annexes to it,[156] and on which it may finally base its decision, so that they can submit their observations on them.[157] However, in view of the exceptions from access to the file that apply to confidential

---

[149] Commission Notice on the rules for access to the Commission file pursuant to Articles 81 and 82 EC [2005] OJ C325/7, para 3.

[150] See Case T-17/93 *Matra-Hachette SA v EC Commission* [1994] ECR II-595, para 34. The Court ruled that the rights of third parties, as laid down by Art 19 of Reg 17 (now replaced by Art 27 of Reg 1/2003), were limited to the right to participate in the administrative procedure.

[151] Commission Notice on the rules for access to the Commission file pursuant to Articles 81 and 82 EC [2005] OJ C325/7, paras 3 and 7. The situation of complainants is different in that they are not entitled to access to file *stricto sensu*. Rather, where the Commission intends to reject their complaint, they are entitled to be provided with a non-confidential version of those documents on which the Commission would base the rejection of complaint; see Art 8 of Regulation 773/2004. Other interested third parties are not entitled to have access to documents to the investigation file under EU competition law.

[152] See Commission Notice on the rules for access to the Commission file pursuant to Articles 81 and 82 EC [2005] OJ C325/7, para 8.

[153] This covers also any electronic data storage device as may be or become available; see Commission Notice on the rules for access to the Commission file pursuant to Articles 81 and 82 EC [2005] OJ C325/7, para 8, n 6.

[154] Case T-30/91 *Solvay v Commission* [1995] ECR II-1775, para 83; Case T-314/01, *Avebe v Commission* [2006] ECR II-3085, para 66.

[155] See Arts 3(3) and 7(1) of the Hearing Officer's Mandate.

[156] See Case 322/82 *Michelin v EC Commission* [1983] ECR 3461, para 7.

[157] As already explained, documents not shown to the undertakings will not be available as evidence against them in the Commission's final decision.

and internal documents, in practice, not all the documents contained in the file are shown to the undertakings.[158]

First, documents in the file regularly do not stem from the addressee of the statement of **10.41** objections only, but from its suppliers, clients, competitors, or employees, and disclosing the information or the identity of the information provider can cause significant harm.[159] However, since access to confidential information can be useful or even necessary for the exercise of the rights of defence, the latter need to be balanced against the right to confidentiality resulting from Article 339 TFEU and Article 28 of Regulation 1/2003.[160] Hence, the Commission needs to verify for each individual document whether the need for access constitutes an overriding interest which justifies the risk of harm caused by its disclosure.[161] Often, granting access to a non-confidential version of the document in question constitutes the best compromise between the conflicting interests. Problems unrelated to confidentiality may arise where two undertakings are the subject of the same complaint. In such cases, access to the file must not enable the undertakings—which in many cases will be competitors, in theory at least—to exchange information that in any other circumstances would in itself be contrary to the competition rules.

The Court has on numerous occasions ruled on the scope of 'business secrets', and other **10.42** information covered by the obligation of professional secrecy, the latter being also referred to as 'other confidential information'.

According to settled case law, three conditions need to be fulfilled for a piece of information **10.43** to be *confidential*:[162]

  (i)   it must be known to a limited number of persons only;
 (ii)   it must be information whose disclosure is liable to cause serious harm to the person
        who has provided it or to third parties; and
(iii)   the interests liable to be harmed by disclosure must, objectively, be worthy of protection.

---

[158] See Art 27(2) of Reg 1/2003, Arts 15(2) and 16(1) of Reg 773/2004. Those exceptions are confirmed in settled case law. See Case T-7/89 *SA Hercules Chemicals NV v EC Commission* [1991] ECR II-1711, para 54; Joined Cases C-204/00 P, C-205/00 P, C-211/00 P, C-213/00 P, C-217/00 P, and C-219/00 P *Aalborg Portland and Others v Commission* [2004] ECR I-123, para 68; Case C-109/10 P *Solvay v Commission* [2011] OJ C370/12, para 54. Whilst it is not for the Commission alone to decide which documents in the file may be useful for the purposes of the defence (see Case T-30/91 *Solvay v Commission* [1995] ECR II-1775, paras 81–6, and Case T-36/91 *ICI v Commission* [1995] ECR II-1847, paras 91–6), the Commission is nevertheless allowed to preclude evidence which has no relation to the allegation of fact and of law in the statement of objections. Joined Cases C-204/00 P etc, *P Aalborg Portland v Commission* [2004] ECR I-123, para 126.

[159] It should be borne in mind that when complaints contain business secrets, described as such by the complainant, the Commission may not disclose any copy until it has deleted all confidential information from them—if the complainant did not place the confidential documents and information in special annexes. Article 16(2) of Reg 773/2004 establishes that any party which makes known its views shall clearly identify any material which it considers to be confidential, giving reasons, and provide a separate non-confidential version by the date set by the Commission for making its views known. If it does not do so by the set date, the Commission may assume that the submission does not contain such materials.

[160] See Case T-30/91 *Solvay v Commission* [1995] ECR II-1775, para 88; Case T-36/91 *ICI v Commission* [1995] ECR II-1847, para 98; Case T-25/95 *Cimenteries CBR v Commission* [2000] ECR II-495, para 147.

[161] See Recital 14 of Reg 773/2004; Notice on access to file, para 14. See also Case T-198/03 *Bank Austria Creditanstalt v Commission* [2006] ECR II-1429, para 71; Case T-474/04 *Pergan v Commission* [2007] ECR II-4225, para 63 et seq; Case T-36/91 *ICI v Commission* [1995] ECR II-1847, para 98.

[162] Case T-198/03 *Bank Austria Creditanstalt v Commission* [2006] ECR II-1429, para 71; Case T-474/04 *Pergan v Commission* [2007] ECR II-4225, para 65.

The assessment as to the confidentiality of a piece of information thus requires the legitimate interests opposing disclosure of the information to be weighed against the private or public interest requiring its divulgation.[163]

10.44 The concept of other confidential information comprises details that might make it possible to identify a complainant where the latter could suffer serious harm by calling into question his anonymity. It also includes military secrets.[164]

10.45 The term 'business secret' designates a category of confidential information that is afforded very special protection.[165] In order to qualify as a business secret, information must be known to a limited number of persons only.[166] In addition, the concept of business secrets only concerns information of which not only disclosure to the public but also mere transmission to a person other than the one who provided the information may seriously harm the latter's interests.[167] In general, information supplied by an undertaking, which contains strategic information as to its business activities, must be regarded as constituting business secrets.[168] The Commission's Notice on Access to the File also puts forward some examples of business secrets in order to provide guidance.[169]

10.46 Second, internal Commission documents are inaccessible. If the Commission chooses to make notes of meetings with any persons or undertakings, such documents constitute the Commission's own interpretation of what transpired at the meeting (unless the person or undertaking has agreed the minutes).[170] Nevertheless, the Commission renders accessible brief notes outlining the contents of meetings with parties and third parties, subject to legitimate requests for confidentiality.[171] A particular case of internal documents is the Commission

---

[163] See Case T-198/03 *Bank Austria Creditanstalt v Commission* [2006] ECR II-1429, para 71. The judgment concerned the publication of a Commission decision adopted pursuant to Art 7 of Reg 1/2003. Therefore, the legitimate interests opposing disclosure of the information had to be weighed against the public interest that the activities of the EU institutions take place as openly as possible.

[164] Commission Notice on the rules for access to the Commission file pursuant to Articles 81 and 82 EC [2005] OJ C325/7, para 20.

[165] According to the Court's *Akzo I* ruling, complainants must not be granted access to business secrets which the Commission has obtained in the course of its investigation; Case 53/85 *Akzo Chemie v Commission* [1986] ECR 1965, para 28. A similar statement has not been made with regard to other confidential information that does not constitute a business secret.

[166] Case T-474/04 *Pergan v Commission* [2007] ECR II-4225, para 65.

[167] T-353/94 *Postbank v Commission* [1996] ECR II-9 para 87; Case T-198/03 *Bank Austria Creditanstalt v Commission* [2006] ECR II-1429, para 30.

[168] In different judgments, the Community Courts and the Commission have given examples of types of information constituting business secrets. See in particular Case T-9/89 *Hüls v Commission* [1992] ECR II-499, paras 127 and 294; Case C-7/95 P *John Deere* [1998] ECR I-3111, para 89; T-353/94 *Postbank v Commission* [1996] ECR II-9, para 86; or Case T-9/99 *HBF Holding v Commission* [2002] ECR II-1487, para 367 and *Polypropylene* [1986] OJ L230/1, regarding sales volumes, selling prices, deliveries, profitability thresholds, stock levels, cost components, or the commercial strategy.

[169] Commission Notice on the rules for access to the Commission file pursuant to Articles 81 and 82 EC [2005] OJ C325/7, para 18: 'Examples of information that may qualify as business secrets include: technical and/or financial information relating to an undertaking's knowhow, methods of assessing costs, production secrets and processes, supply sources, quantities produced and sold, market shares, customer and distributor lists, marketing plans, cost and price structure and sales strategy.' The Notice on Access to the File also sets out the criteria according to which the Commission will accede to requests for confidential treatment (paras 21–5).

[170] Commission Notice on the rules for access to the Commission file pursuant to Articles 81 and 82 EC, para 13. Studies commissioned as part of the investigation will be disclosed, para 11; see qualification in para 14. In *Sorbates*, the Hearing Officers considered the notes of telephone conversations between the parties and Commission officials are internal documents of the Commission and thus, in principle, non-accessible. Final Report of the Hearing Officer in Case COMP/37.370 *Sorbates* [2003] OJ C173/5.

[171] Commission Notice on best practices for the conduct of proceedings concerning Articles 101 and 102 TFEU [2011] OJ C308/6, para 44.

correspondence between it and the authorities of the Member States. The Notice on Access to the File establishes as examples of internal documents four different types of Commission's correspondence with other public authorities:[172]

- Correspondence between the Commission and the competition authorities of the Member States (NCAs), or between the latter, referring to Article 27(2) of Regulation 1/2003 and Article 15(2) of Regulation 773/2004.
- Correspondence between the Commission and other public authorities of the Member States.[173]
- Correspondence between the Commission, the EFTA Surveillance Authority, and public authorities of EFTA States.
- Correspondence between the Commission and public authorities of non-member countries, including their competition authorities, in particular where the Union and a third country have concluded an agreement governing the confidentiality of the information exchanged.

However, the Notice states that in certain exceptional circumstances access is granted to documents originating from Member States, or the EFTA Surveillance Authority of EFTA States, after deletion of any business secrets or other confidential information.[174]

The Commission seeks to ensure that documents of which disclosure might have serious **10.47** consequences for the information providers are not shown to people who might guess their origin and the identity of the Commission's informant.[175] That is not a purely hypothetical concern.[176] An important action to establish non-contractual liability[177] in which judgment was given against the Commission arose from just such a case of carelessness on the part of the Commission.[178]

The limits on access to information are even stricter for complainants before formal rejection **10.48** of their complaint and for complainants and other third parties involved in infringement procedures against other undertakings. This is due to the fact that such persons do not enjoy a

---

[172] Commission Notice on the rules for access to the Commission file pursuant to Articles 81 and 82 EC [2005] OJ C325/7, para 15. This is not an exhaustive enumeration, but merely examples.

[173] See Joined Cases T-134/94, T-136/94, T-1 37/94, T-138/94, T-141/94, T-145/94, T-1 47/94, T-148/94, T-151/94, T-156/94, and T-157/94 *NMH Stahlwerke and others v Commission* [1997] ECR II-2293, para 36, and Case T-65/89 *BPB Industries and British Gypsum v Commission* [1993] ECR II-389, para 33 (correspondence with Member States).

[174] See Commission Notice on the rules for access to the Commission file pursuant to Articles 81 and 82 EC [2005] OJ C325/7, para 16.

[175] As regards the correspondence and other documents provided by third-party undertakings during the Commission's investigations, the Court has stated that it is clear that third parties that submit such documents and consider that reprisals might be taken against them as a result can do so only if they know that account will be taken of their request for confidentiality. See Commission Notice on the rules for access to the Commission file pursuant to Articles 81 and 82 EC [2005] OJ C325/7, para 19. Case C-310/93 P *BPB Industries Plc and British Gypsum Ltd v Commission II* [1995] ECR I-865, paras 29–35. In practice the Commission is extremely cautious about disclosing third-party documents in all the circumstances, even if it has not received a formal request for confidentiality.

[176] The EU Courts have pronounced upon this question both in cases of alleged abuse of a dominant position (Art 82 EC): Case T-65/89 *BPB Industries and British Gypsum v Commission* [1993] ECR II-389, para 33; and Case C-310/93P *BPB Industries and British Gypsum v Commission* [1995] ECR I-865, para 26; and in merger cases: Case T-221/95 *Endemol v Commission* [1999] ECR II-1299, para 69, and Case T-5/02 *Tetra Laval v Commission* [2002] ECR II-4381, para 98 et seq.

[177] See the second para of Art 340 TFEU.

[178] See Case 145/83 *Stanley Adams v Commission* [1985] ECR 3539, para 44. Hoffmann-La Roche had been able to identify Adams as the informant as a result of carelessness by the Commission, and although he had left the company he was arrested for economic espionage in Switzerland. Whilst he was held in solitary confinement by the Swiss authorities, his wife committed suicide.

right to access to file *stricto sensu*, which would result from the right to defend themselves, but merely a right to give their informed views on agreements or restrictive conduct in which they have a sufficient interest, provided for by Article 27(3) of Regulation 1/2003 and by Articles 6(1) and 13 of Regulation 773/2004. Therefore, only complainants are granted access to a limited number of documents in the Commission's file, to the extent that the Commission intends to base its decision to reject a complaint on these documents.[179] In view of the special protection granted to business secrets,[180] pieces of information pertaining to this category of confidential information must never be disclosed to complainants and third parties.[181]

3. Access to the file and confidential documents

10.49 The application of the rules mentioned in the previous paragraphs might lead to disagreements between the participants in the procedure and the Commission as to whether access to certain documents may be granted. The most common source of disagreement is the view taken by some undertakings that they are entitled to see documents which information providers consider to be confidential or the Commission considers to be internal. In such cases, the undertakings must first make a reasoned request to the Commission service in charge of the investigation.[182] They must call on it to reconsider the list of disclosable documents and to send them a larger number of documents, or a specific document.[183] If the disagreement persists, the Hearing Officer can be called upon to decide on whether further documents need to be rendered accessible to respect parties' right to access to file.[184]

10.50 Where an information provider has raised no objection to its disclosure to other participants in the procedure, the Commission can nevertheless consider that it should not be shown to the other parties in order to ensure that no restriction of competition comes into being between the parties. If the Commission considers that the information in question may have an adverse impact on competition between the undertakings, it is not only empowered but also obliged to ensure that no such veiled exchange of information between undertakings occurs.

10.51 Where an information provider refuses to allow disclosure of documents which the Commission regards as essential for the parties' proper exercise of defence rights—in particular because the documents prove the existence of an infringement of the competition rules—the Commission is in principle under an obligation to render the document accessible. Even where the Commission must observe its obligation to maintain professional secrecy, laid

---

[179] Article 8(1) of Reg 773/2004.

[180] Case T-198/03, *Bank Austria Creditanstalt v Commission* [2006] ECR II-1429, para 29 et seq; Case 53/85 *Akzo v Commission I* [1986] ECR 1965, para 28. The distinction between business secrets and other confidential information is less clear in Case T-474/04 *Pergan v Commission* [2007] ECR II-4225, para 65.

[181] See Case 53/85 *Akzo v Commission I* [1986] ECR 1965, para 27; Case T-9/99 *HFB Holding für Fernwärmetechnik Beteiligungsgesellschaft mbH & Co KG (HFB) and others v Commission* [2002] ECR II-1487, para 364.

[182] According to the Commission Notice on best practices for the conduct of proceedings concerning Articles 101 and 102 TFEU [2011] OJ C308/6, para 93, granting access to the Commission file is primarily the responsibility of DG COMP. Hence, requests for further access to file are first to be addressed to the services within DG COMP that are in charge of the investigation. The same follows from Art 7(1) in conjunction with Art 3(7) of the Hearing Officer's Mandate.

[183] The GC ruled that the Commission is obliged to provide a company with a list and summaries of the documents on the file only where the company submits a request to this effect. Joined Cases T-236/01, T-239/01, T-244/01 to T-246/01, T-251/01, and T-252/01 *Tokai Carbon Co Ltd and others v Commission* [2004] ECR II-1181, para 39; Joined Cases T-25/95, T-26/95, T-30/95 to T-39/95, T-42/95 to T-46/95, T-48/95, T-50/95 to T-65/95, T-68/95 to T-71/95, T-87/95, T-88/95, T-103/95, and T-104/95 *Cimenteries CBR SA and others v Commission* [2000] ECR II-491, para 383.

[184] See Art 7(1) of the Hearing Officer's Mandate.

down in Article 28 of Regulation 1/2003, that obligation must be interpreted without prejudice to the right of the parties to be heard in accordance with Article 27.[185] The Commission is thus obliged to disclose the essential parts of the file to the participants in the procedure so that they are in a position to give their views. If the Commission did not show certain evidence to the undertakings to which the procedure relates, it must be disregarded for the purposes of its decision.[186] Therefore, if a document to be relied upon by the Commission in its final decision contains confidential information, the Commission will at least render accessible a non-confidential version or grant access to the document in the context of a negotiated disclosure to a restricted circle of persons or via a data room procedure.[187]

However, as noted earlier, not every failure to disclose documents will lead to an outright **10.52** annulment of the Commission's decision, as this will rest on the content, weight, and significance of the non-disclosed documents and the objections raised by the Commission in the particular case. In this line, the distinction between incriminatory and exculpatory documents established by the Court[188] shows that non-disclosure of certain documents may not have any influence on defence rights. Thus, for instance, if an inculpatory document has not been disclosed, the undertaking concerned cannot allege a breach of its rights of defence when there are other documents disclosed on which the Commission has equally relied upon to prove an infringement.[189] Where access to potentially exculpatory documents is not granted during the administrative proceedings, the undertaking concerned has to show, not that if it had had access to the non-disclosed documents the Commission decision would have been different in content, but only that those documents could have been useful for its defence.[190] In such a case the infringement is not remedied by the mere fact that access was made possible during the judicial proceedings.[191] In *Solvay*, whole sub-files had disappeared during the administrative proceedings, and the Commission was not able to submit these documents even during the judicial proceedings. The ECJ held that in such circumstances it cannot be ruled out that the documents could have contained essential documents relating to the procedure before the Commission, which may have been relevant to Solvay's defence, and annulled the Commission Decision for infringement of the rights of defence.[192]

The EU Courts have highlighted that business secrets of undertakings involved in com- **10.53** petition proceedings deserve utmost protection.[193] However, the protection of confidential

---

[185] See Case 85/76 *Hoffmann-La Roche v Commission* [1979] ECR 461, para 13.

[186] Case 107/82 *AEG v Commission* [1983] ECR 3151, paras 22–5; Case T-83/08 *Denki Kagaku Kogyo Kabushiki Kaisha, Denka Chemicals v Commission* [2012] OJ C80/16, para 84.

[187] See paras 10.57 and 10.58.

[188] Joined Cases T-25/95, T-26/95, T-30/95 to T-39/95, T-42/95 to T-46/95, T-48/95, T-50/95 to T-65/95, T-68/95 to T-71/95, T-87/95, T-88/95, T-103/95, and T-104/95 *Cimenteries CBR SA and others v Commission* [2000] ECR II-491, paras 248 and 284. See also Commission Notice on the rules for access to the Commission file pursuant to Articles 81 and 82 EC [2005] OJ C325/7, para 24.

[189] Case T-83/08 *Denki Kagaku Kogyo Kabushiki Kaisha, Denka Chemicals v Commission* [2012] OJ C80/16, para 84. In the 'Cement Cartel', certain applicants succeeded in demonstrating that documents which had not been disclosed to them shed a different light on the documentary evidence used by the Commission to prove their participation in the cartel. The GC was of the view that there was a chance that the outcome could have been different if they had been given access to these documents. The Court therefore annulled the decision as regards those applicants (eg Joined Cases T-25/95 etc *Cimenteries CBR SA and others v Commission* [2000] ECR II-491, paras 2205–12, 2224, 2225, 2284–90 etc).

[190] Case C-199/99 P *Corus UK v Commission* [2003] ECR I-11177, para 128; Case C-109/10 P *Solvay v Commission* [2011] OJ C370/12, para 57.

[191] Joined Cases C-238/99 P, C-244/99 P, C-245/99 P, C-247/99 P, C-250/99 P to C-252/99 P, and C-254/99 P *Limburgse Vinyl Maatschappij and Others v Commission* [2002] ECR I-8375, para 318.

[192] Case C-109/10 P *Solvay v Commission* [2011] OJ C370/12, para 63 et seq.

[193] See Case 53/85 *Akzo v Commission I* [1986] ECR 1965, para 28. This interpretation appears to be confirmed both by Joined Cases T-10–12 and T-15/92 *Cimenteries and others v Commission III* [1992] ECR

information is not absolute. The protection of business secrets and other confidential information must be balanced with other interests, such as the rights of the defence or the requirement of effective legal protection.[194] This begs the question as to how the Commission addresses a conflict between the principle of the protection of business secrets, on one hand, and the principle of upholding defence rights on the other.[195] In practice, the conflict described does not arise with regard to (allegedly) exculpatory information. If the Commission believes that a confidential document shows that all or part of the preliminary conclusions set out in the statement of objections are flawed, it will withdraw or modify the objections when adopting its final decision, thereby depriving the document of its exculpatory nature. By contrast, if only the addressee of the statement of objections takes the view that the confidential document is exculpatory, whilst the Commission has checked the document and is convinced that it does not stand against its case, the Commission would, on balance, not grant access to information providers' business secrets. The situation is different for confidential inculpatory documents that the Commission intends to rely on in its final decision.[196] Generally speaking, Article 27(2) of Regulation 1/2003 authorizes the Commission to use such documents even if they contain business secrets: 'Nothing in this paragraph shall prevent the Commission from disclosing and using information necessary to prove an infringement'. However, in such cases, the Commission would first endeavour to take due account of confidentiality by rendering accessible a non-confidential version of the document in question or by applying a negotiated disclosure procedure or a data room procedure.[197] If that proved impossible, the Commission would weigh up the respective and opposing interests, after allowing both the information provider and the company requesting access to file to make observations. A fair balance would then need to be established between safeguarding defence rights and the right to protection of business secrets.[198] In *Belgian Architects Associations*, the danger of retaliation led the Hearing Officer to refuse access to a document in the file which would have allowed the parties to identify the informant.[199]

10.54 Finally, a reference should be made to the specific cases in which the parties to an antitrust procedure before the Commission have been capable of exchanging information and documents among themselves or have agreed on the form in which confidential information on the Commission's file was to be made accessible. In *Intel*, the company subject to investigation agreed bilaterally with each of the information providers to receive the entirety or a distinct part of their information located on the Commission's file in unredacted form (that

---

II-2667 and by Case C-36/92 P *Samenverkende Elektriciteits-produktiebedrijven (SEP) v Commission II* [1994] ECRI-1911, para 28 et seq. The legitimate interest in the protection of confidential information submitted in the context of a competition proceeding also needs to be respected when access to documents is requested under Reg 1049/2001; see case C-404/10 *Commission v Editions Odile Jacob* [2012] OJ C258/3, para 115 et seq.

[194] See Case C-450/06 *Varec* [2008] ECR I-581, paras 49–52. See also Case 53/85 *AKZO Chemie and AKZO Chemie UK v Commission* [1986] ECR 1965, paras 28–9 and Judgment of 29 March 2012 in Case C-1/11 *Interseroh Scrap and Metals Trading*, paras 44–5.

[195] No such conflict exists where the Commission does not accept an information provider's claim that its document(s) contain(s) business secrets. In such case the Hearing Officer would adopt a decision pursuant to Art 8 of the Hearing Officer's Mandate and apply the so-called *Akzo procedure* (Case 53/85 [1986] ECR 1965) so that the Commission would ultimately be authorized to render the document accessible.

[196] By contrast, if a piece of confidential inculpatory evidence could easily be replaced by a non-confidential piece of evidence with the same probative value, the Commission could simply decide to have recourse to the latter.

[197] See paras 10.57 and 10.58.

[198] See Case T-36/91 *ICI v Commission* [1995] ECR II-1847, para 98.

[199] Final report of the hearing officer in Case COMP/38.549 *Architects' Association* [2005] OJ C3/4. The anonymity of a person who supplies information must be respected if that person so requests and may otherwise be open to reprisals (Case 143/83 *Stanley Adams v Commission* [1985] ECR 3539, para 34).

is, including confidential information) in exchange for limiting the access to this information to a restricted circle of persons (its outside counsels and economic advisers and, in some
cases, certain in-house counsels).[200] In *Soda Ash*, some documents had in fact been exchanged
between the parties. However, this possibility of 'self-help between the parties',[201] which may
lend itself also to problems under Article 101(1) TFEU,[202] may not relieve the Commission
from fully complying with its obligations regarding access to the file. The fact that the parties could have access to certain documents by means of cooperation and exchanges with
other parties to the proceedings cannot be an argument for lessening the Commission's duty
to ensure that the parties' defence rights are respected.[203] It cannot be expected in all circumstances that such an exchange will take place, particularly when the parties involved are
competitors.

4. Forms of access to the file

In antitrust proceedings, access to the file will be granted upon request and, normally, on **10.55**
a single occasion, following the notification of the Commission's objections to the parties. However, a party will be granted access to documents received after notification of the
objections at later stages of the administrative procedure, prior to the adoption of a formal
decision, where such documents may constitute new evidence pertaining to the allegations
against that party in the Commission's statement of objections. Similarly, the issuance of a
supplementary statement of objections triggers a new round of access to file.

As a general rule, disclosure is now effected by means of sending one or more CD-ROMs upon **10.56**
request by the addressee of the statement of objections (in the case of undertakings implicated
in an infringement). However, the possibility cannot be excluded that, where it is advisable
to do so in the circumstances of the case, the Commission might resort to the procedure of
convening the undertakings and their lawyers to a meeting at the offices of DG COMP to
familiarize themselves with the administrative file. In order to protect the effectiveness of the
Commission's leniency policy, corporate statements made by applicants in accordance with
the Commission Notice on immunity from fines and reduction of fines in cartel cases are rendered accessible only at the Commission premises.[204] The Hearing Officer's Mandate and the
Commission's Best Practices also provide for special procedures for facilitating the exchange of
confidential information between parties to the proceedings, which deviate from the rule of giving unrestricted access by means of CD-ROMs. Two additional procedures may be used for the
purpose of alleviating the burden of drawing up non-confidential versions of submissions: the
negotiated disclosure to a restricted circle of persons, and the data room procedure.[205]

---

[200] See Commission Decision of 13 May 2009, D(2009) 3726 in Case COMP/C-3/37.990 *Intel*, para 29.
[201] Kerse & Khan, *EC Antitrust Procedure* (6th edn, Sweet & Maxwell 2012) para 4-092.
[202] As stated, in certain cases such an exchange of information may even constitute an infringement of
the competition rules.
[203] Case T-23/99 *LR AF 1998 v Commission* [2002] ECR II-1705, para 184: 'by suggesting that the
undertakings concerned facilitate access to the documents by exchanging documents among themselves, and
at the same time itself ensuring the right of access to the entire investigation file, the Commission had due
regard to the requirements laid down in the case-law of the Court of First Instance, namely that an exchange
of documents between the undertakings cannot in any event eliminate the Commission's own duty to ensure
that during the investigation of an infringement of competition law the rights of defence of the undertakings
concerned are respected.' See also Case T-30/91 *Solvay v Commission* [1995] ECR II-1775, paras 85–6, and
Case T-36/91 *ICI v Commission* [1995] ECR II-1847, paras 95–6.
[204] See Commission Notice on Immunity from fines and reduction of fines in cartel cases [2006] OJ
C298/11, para 7. Corporate statements may take the form of written documents signed by or on behalf of
the undertaking or be made orally.
[205] See Art 8(4) of the Hearing Officer's Mandate and Commission Notice on best practices for the conduct of proceedings concerning Articles 101 and 102 TFEU [2011] OJ C308/6, paras 95–8.

10.57   First, DG COMP may accept in certain cases, especially those with a very voluminous file, that the parties agree voluntarily to use a negotiated disclosure procedure. Under this procedure, the party entitled to access to file agrees bilaterally with the information providers claiming confidentiality to receive all or some of the information which the latter has provided to the Commission, including confidential information. The party being granted access to file limits access to the information to a restricted circle of persons, normally the external legal advisers and/or economic advisers of the company concerned. To the extent that such negotiated access to the file would amount to restricting a party's right to have access to the investigation file, that party must waive its right to access to the file vis-à-vis the Commission. Normally, the party would receive the information subject to the negotiated disclosure procedure directly from the information provider. However, if the information that is subject to such an agreement would, exceptionally, be provided to the restricted circle of persons by the Commission, the information providers must waive their rights to confidentiality vis-à-vis the Commission.

10.58   Second, DG COMP may organize a so-called data room procedure. This procedure is typically used for the disclosure of quantitative data relevant for econometric analysis. Under this procedure, part of the file, including confidential information, is gathered in a room, at the Commission's premises (the data room). Access to the data room is granted to a restricted group of persons, ie the external legal counsel and/or the economic advisers of the party (collectively known as the 'advisers'), under the supervision of a Commission official. The advisers may make use of the information contained in the data room for the purpose of drawing up their client's comments on the statement of objections, but may not disclose any confidential information to their client. The data room is equipped with several PC workstations and the necessary software (and, if relevant, the necessary data sets and a log of the regressions used to support the Commission's case). There is no network connection and no external communication is allowed. The advisers are permitted to remain in the data room during normal working hours and, if justified, access may be provided for several days. The advisers are strictly prohibited from taking copies, notes, or summaries of the documents, and may only remove a final report from the data room, which is to be verified by the case team in order to ensure that it does not contain any confidential information. Each adviser will sign a confidentiality agreement and will be presented with the conditions of special access to the data room before entering. The Hearing Officer will usually decide that the data room procedure shall be used where access to certain confidential information is indispensible for a party's rights of defence and where the Hearing Officer considers that, on balance, the conflict between respect for confidentiality and the rights of defence is best solved in this way.

5. Access to documents pursuant to Regulation 1049/2001

10.59   The right of access to the file in antitrust and merger proceedings is distinct from the general right of access to documents provided for in Regulation 1049/2001 of the European Parliament and of the Council regarding public access to European Parliament, Council and Commission documents.[206] The latter is subject to different criteria and pursues a different purpose. Public access to Commission documents follows from Article 1(2) TEU,[207] Article 15(3) TFEU, Article 42 of the Charter of Fundamental Rights of the European Union, and Article 2(1) of Regulation 1049/2001. Contrary to the right to access to file granted under competition law, Article 2(1) of the Transparency Regulation grants '[a]ny citizen of the

---

[206]   [2001] OJ L145/43.
[207]   In its first recital, Regulation 1049/2001 recalls that Art 1(2) TEU enshrines the concept of openness, stating that the Treaty marks a new stage in the process of creating an ever closer union among the peoples of Europe, in which decisions are taken as openly as possible and as closely as possible to the citizen.

Union, and any natural or legal person residing or having its registered office in a Member State...a right of access to documents of the [EU] institutions'.[208] Applicants seeking access to documents in the investigation file of a competition proceeding pursuant to Regulation 1049/2001 do not require a specific role in the competition proceedings and do not need to await the issuance of a statement of objections. Therefore, the question arises whether the right to public access can be invoked in competition proceedings to circumvent the restrictions on access to file provided for under competition law or whether the exceptions from public access to documents set out in Article 4 of Regulation 1049/2001[209] need to be interpreted in the light of EU competition law.

With regard to access to documents contained in the file in merger proceedings, the ECJ held in **10.60** *Edition Odile Jacobs* and *Agrofert* that for the purposes of interpreting Regulation 1049/2001 it is necessary to take account of the specific rules on access to file resulting from EU merger control law, because generalized access on the basis of Regulation 1049/2001 would undermine the limitations on access to file introduced by that legislation.[210] In principle, both protection of the objectives of investigation activities and that of commercial interests of the companies involved in merger procedures require that documents in the investigation file are presumed to be generally inaccessible under Regulation 1049/2001.[211] Therefore, it is for an applicant to show that a document requested pursuant to Regulation 1049/2001 is not covered by that presumption or that there is a higher public interest justifying the disclosure of the document concerned by virtue of Article 4(2) of Regulation 1049/2001. It can be expected that the ECJ will apply the same principles when deciding on requests for public access to documents resulting from an antitrust investigation.[212] Therefore, in conclusion, access to documents under Regulation 1049/2001 does not present an alternative to the right to access to file under competition law. However, where a competition proceeding is definitively closed, Regulation 1049/2001 can be invoked to obtain access to documents that may prove useful for the preparation of a private follow-on action.[213]

C. The Reply to the Statement of Objections

1. Introduction

Pursuant to Article 27(1) of Regulation 1/2003, the Commission is required to give the under- **10.61** takings and associations of undertakings investigated the opportunity of making known their

---

[208] Article 2(2) of Reg 1049/2001 enables the institutions to grant access to documents to any natural or legal person not residing or not having its registered office in a Member State. The Commission has made use of this possibility in its detailed rules for the application of Reg 1049/2001; see annex to Commission decision of 5 December 2001 [2001] OJ L345/94.

[209] Article 4 of Reg 1049/2001 contains a list of exceptions of which Art 4(1) lit. b) (protection of privacy and the integrity of the individual), (2) first indent (protection of commercial interests), (2) second indent (protection of legal advice), (2) third indent (protection of the purpose of inspections and investigations), and (3) (protection of the decision-making process with regard to documents drawn up for internal use) are of particular importance for public access to documents contained in the investigation file of a competition procedure.

[210] See Case C-404/10 P *Commission v Éditions Odile Jacob* [2012] OJ C258/3, para 121 et seq and Case C-447/10 P *Commission v Agrofert Holding* [2012] OJ C258/4, para 61 et seq.

[211] For Commission internal documents, this presumption of inaccessibility applies only until the merger decision is no longer subject to judicial review; Case C-404/10 *Commission v Editions Odile Jacob* [2012] OJ C258/3, para 127 et seq.

[212] Articles 17 and 18(3) of Reg 139/2004 as well as Art 17 of Reg 802/2004, which restrict the use of information gathered in the context of merger control proceedings by limiting access to certain parties and specific purposes find their equivalent in Art 27(2) of Reg 1/2003, as well as Art 15 of Reg 773/2004.

[213] See para 10.59.

views on the objections against them. This is a fundamental right of the parties to be heard. Undertakings are entitled in their written comments to set out 'all facts relevant...to their defence'.[214] This means that in principle the company can include in its defence such factual, legal, and economic arguments and material as it considers necessary. Where it is necessary to rectify any factual information supplied previously to the Commission, the correction should be explained in detail.[215]

10.62 Issuing a statement of objections does not form part of the Commission's powers of investigation.[216] There is no legal obligation to reply to the Commission's statement of objections. Neither does the failure to comment on the elements of facts and law set out in the statement of objections prevent the addressees from contesting these elements when they challenge the Commission's final decision before the Court. The GC held that where a party does not expressly acknowledge the facts during the administrative proceedings, the Commission must prove the facts, and the undertaking is free to put forward, in the procedure before the Court, any plea in its defence which it deems appropriate.[217] The ECJ confirmed that there is no requirement under EU law that the addressee of the statement of objections must challenge its various matters of fact or law during the administrative procedure, if it is not to be barred from doing so later at the stage of judicial proceedings.[218] The case is different where the undertaking expressly, clearly, and specifically acknowledges the facts: where it expressly admits during the administrative procedure the substantive truth of the facts which the Commission alleges against it in the statement of objections, those facts must thereafter be regarded as established and the undertaking stopped in principle from disputing them during the court proceedings.[219]

10.63 The principle of good administration requires that addressees of a statement of objections must be given a reasonable time to comment, bearing in mind both the time required for preparation of comments and the urgency of the case, for example, where there is a competitor or customer who may be suffering immediate loss as a result of the alleged breach of Articles 101 and 102 TFEU. The EU Courts have held, in a number of cases involving voluminous documentation, that a two-month period was sufficient for submission of observations on the statement of objections.[220] The minimum time limit allowed is four weeks, except where interim measures are being proposed when it may be reduced to one week.[221] The Hearing Officer can extend the time limit where the parties make a reasoned request before the expiry of the original time limit.[222] After hearing the director responsible, the Hearing Officer will decide on whether an extension of the time limit is necessary to allow the addressee of a statement of objections to exercise its right to be heard effectively, while

---

[214] Article 10(3) of Reg 773/2004.

[215] Case T-334/94 *Sarrio SA v Commission* [1998] II-1439, paras 380–1.

[216] Consequently, the statement of objections is anchored in Art 27(1) of Reg 1/2003, rather than in any of the articles pertaining to Chapter V ('Powers of Investigation') of Regulation 1/2003.

[217] Joined Cases T-236/01, T-239/01, T-244/01 to T-246/01, T-251/01, and T-252/01 *Tokai Carbon and others v Commission* [2004] ECR II-1181, para 108; Case C-297/98 P *SCA Holding v Commission* [2000] ECR I-10101, para 37.

[218] Case C-407/08 P *Knauf Gips v Commission* [2010] ECR I-6375, para 89.

[219] Case C-407/08 P *Knauf Gips v Commission* [2010] ECR I-6375, para 89; Case T-330/01 *Akzo v Commission* [2006] ECR II-3389, para 85 et seq; Joined Cases T-236/01, T-239/01, T-244/01 to T-246/01, T-251/01, and T-252/01 *Tokai Carbon and others v Commission* [2004] ECR II-1181, para 108.

[220] Case 27/76 *United Brands v Commission* [1978] ECR 207, paras 272 and 273; Joined Cases 40/73 to 48/73, 50/73, 54/73 to 56/73, 111/73, 113/73, and 114/73 *Suiker Unie and others v Commission* [1975] ECR 1663, paras 94–9; see also Case T-9/99 *HFB v Commission* [2002] ECR II-1487, para 344 (fourteen weeks).

[221] Article 17(2) in conjunction with Art 10(2) of Reg 773/2004.

[222] Article 9(1) of the Hearing Officer's Mandate. The applicant must first address the director in charge of the investigation with a timely request for an extension of the time limit.

also having regard to the need to avoid undue delay in proceedings. In doing so, the Hearing Officer will in particular take into account the following elements:

(i) the size and complexity of the file;
(ii) whether the addressee of the statement of objections making the request has had prior access to information;
(iii) any other objective obstacles which may be faced by the addressee of the statement of objections making the request in providing its observations.[223]

Article 27(3) of Regulation 1/2003 makes provision for the participation of other persons **10.64** after the issuance of the statement of objections. First, according to Article 27(3), first sentence and third sentence, where the Commission or the competent authorities of the Member States consider it necessary, any natural or legal persons may be invited to express their views. Second, according to Article 27(3), second sentence, applications to be heard from third parties should be granted where they show a sufficient interest. The addressee for such applications is the Hearing Officer, to whom applicants must explain their interest in the outcome of the procedure. The Hearing Officer then decides on behalf of the Commission after consulting the director responsible.[224] Complainants are generally entitled to make their views known in writing on the statement of objections without applying to the Hearing Officer.[225]

Observations by the addressee of the statement of objections are submitted in writing and **10.65** orally. As stated earlier, EU competition procedures are principally written procedures and written observations are made in nearly all cases. However, under Article 12 of Regulation 773/2004 the Commission must also give the parties to whom it has addressed a statement of objections the opportunity to develop their arguments at an oral hearing, if they so request in their written submissions. In effect, pursuant to the same provision, the first precondition for a hearing is a request to that effect from the addressees of the statement of objections, who must ensure that their wish to be heard *viva voce* is put forward in their written observations on the statement of objections. For them to be entitled to be heard orally, it is essential for the undertakings to reply in writing to the objections within the time limit laid down by the Commission.[226] Third parties and complainants are not entitled to have an oral hearing organized. However, the Hearing Officer can admit them upon request to an oral hearing that is organized for the addressees of the statement of objections.[227]

Apart from the *right of* the parties and interested third parties to be heard orally (the latter **10.66** only in certain cases), the Commission has the *power* to allow any other person—not merely the undertakings involved, the complainants, or third parties that show sufficient interest and that have made a request to that effect—the opportunity to express their views at the oral hearing of the parties to whom a statement of objections has been addressed (Article 13(3) of Regulation 773/2004 in conjunction with the first sentence of Article 27(3) of Regulation 1/2003). In such cases, it is not necessary for such persons to submit written observations before the oral hearing. The Commission exercises this power only when a hearing has already been arranged at the request of the interested parties.

---

[223] For the purposes of assessing point (a), Art 9(1) of the Hearing Officer's Mandate indicates that the number of infringements, the alleged duration of the infringement(s), the size and number of documents, and the size and complexity of expert studies may be taken into consideration.

[224] Article 5 of the Hearing Officer's Mandate. See also Art 13(1) of Reg 773/2004.

[225] Article 6(1) of Reg 773/2004.

[226] See Joined Cases 209/78 and 218/78 *Van Landewyck v Commission (FEDETAB)* [1980] ECR 3125, para 24. See also Commission Decision of 13 May 2009, D(2009) 3726 in Case COMP/C-3/37.990 *Intel*, paras 24–6.

[227] Article 6(2) of the Hearing Officer's Mandate.

2. Written observations

10.67 In summary, the following parties are entitled to submit written observations following the issuance of the statement of objections:

    (i) The addressees of the statement of objections (the 'parties') and complainants.

    (ii) Third parties that have demonstrated a sufficient interest in the outcome of the procedure in an application lodged with the Hearing Officer.

    (iii) Other persons allowed to submit written observations because the Commission, either on its own initiative or upon the request of the competition authority of a Member State, considers it necessary in the interest of the investigation.

10.68 The Hearing Officer may reject applications by third parties to submit observations, on the grounds that they lack a sufficient interest. However, the Hearing Officer must inform them in advance of its reasons for rejecting their observations and allow them to make comments in this regard. If the third party makes known its views as to why it has an interest in the outcome of the procedure within the time limit set, and its submission still does not lead to the conclusion that it has a sufficient interest, this finding will be stated in a reasoned decision notified to the applicant.[228]

10.69 The written comments submitted by the parties and third parties within the period allowed by the Commission become part of the file and serve as a reference for the parties in the subsequent stages of the administrative procedure and, if appropriate, for proceedings before the GC after the administrative phase is completed. The parties' observations are also notified to the competition authorities in the Member States and the relevant Commission departments. The Hearing Officer and the Legal Service also receive a copy of these observations.

10.70 According to the Best Practices Notice,[229] where required by the rights of defence,[230] or where it may in the Commission's view help to further clarify factual and legal issues relevant for the case, the Commission may give parties a copy of the non-confidential version (or specific parts thereof) of other parties' written replies to the statement of objections. This would normally be done prior to the oral hearing, so as to allow parties to comment on them at the oral hearing. The Commission may also decide to do so in appropriate cases with respect to complainants and admitted third parties. If access to other parties' replies is granted because it is required for the rights of the defence, parties are also entitled to have sufficient additional time to comment on these replies.[231] The parties' replies to the statement of objections and observations made by other persons in accordance with Article 13 of Regulation 773/2004 constitute information which does not form part of the investigation file to which access to file is granted. In principle, the Commission terminates the investigation when the statement of objections is issued. Accordingly, information received after this point does not form part of the investigation file. Otherwise, the proceedings could be delayed significantly by requests to comment on new documents submitted belatedly and subsequent requests to submit further remarks on such comments.[232]

---

[228] Article 5(3) of the Hearing Officer's Mandate.

[229] Commission Notice on best practices for the conduct of proceedings concerning Articles 101 and 102 TFEU [2011] OJ C308/6.

[230] See Joined Cases T-191/98 and T-212/98 to T-214/98 *Atlantic Container Line and Others v Commission* [2003] ECR II- 3275; Case T-54/03 *Lafarge v Commission* [2008] ECR II-120, paras 69–73; Case T-52/03 *Knauf v Commission* [2008] ECR II-115, paras 41–7 and 67–79; Case C-407/08 P *Knauf v Commission* [2010] ECR I-6375, paras 23–8.

[231] See European Commission Antitrust Manual of Procedures, Internal DG Competition working documents on procedures for the application of Articles 101 and 102 TFEU, March 2012, Module 13 'Right to be heard', para 25.

[232] See European Commission Antitrust Manual of Procedures, Internal DG Competition working documents on procedures for the application of Articles 101 and 102 TFEU, March 2012, Module 13 'Right to be heard', para 26.

3. The oral hearing[233]

As regards the oral hearing: **10.71**

(i)   The Hearing Officer is required to arrange for an oral hearing to be held if the under-taking to which the statement of objections has been addressed requests an oral hearing (Article 12 of Regulation 773/2004, Article 6(1) of the Hearing Officer's Mandate).[234]

(ii) The Hearing Officer may invite complainants and interest third parties to an oral hearing when they apply and show a sufficient interest in giving their views orally, over and above their interest in submitting written observations (Article 13(2) of Regulation 773/2004, Article 6(2), first sentence of the Hearing Officer's Mandate). Whilst oral hearings will not be organized solely upon the request of complainants and interested third parties,[235] the Hearing Officer will usually not be overly strict when it comes to admitting complainants and interested third parties to an oral hearing organized upon the parties' request. However, the participation of complainants and interested third parties can depend on the interest which the Commission has in their contribution or its probative value.[236]

(iii) The right to make oral observations is usually conditional upon previous submission of written observations, without which the Hearing Officer will often decline to hear oral submissions from the person concerned.

(iv) The Commission may in any case invite any person to make oral observations, without it being necessary in such cases for written observations to be submitted beforehand (Article 13(3) of Regulation 773/2004). The Hearing Officer may also invite representatives from competition authorities from third countries to attend the oral hearing as observers in accordance with agreements concluded between the EU and third countries (Article 6(2), second sentence of the Hearing Officer's Mandate). Normally in such cases the Hearing Officer will ask the parties if they do not object to the admission of observers.[237]

The procedure for hearings is governed by Regulation 773/2004, in particular, Articles 12 to   **10.72**
14, and the Hearing Officer's Mandate, in particular Articles 10 to 13. The hearing always takes place after the end of the period set for a reply to the statement of objections and before

---

[233] The oral hearing in Competition Proceedings before the European Commission is explained in detail by W Wils, who is currently one of the two Hearing Officers, in 'The Oral Hearing in Competition Proceedings before the European Commission', (2012) 35(3) World Competition, 397–430.

[234] S Durande and K Williams, 'The Practical Impact of the Exercise of the Right to be Heard: A Special Focus on the Effect of Oral Hearings and the Role of the Hearing Officers' (2005) Summer (2) EC Competition Newsletter 22, 23, note that defendants are sometimes reluctant to make use of their right to express their views at an oral hearing. They often fear that oral hearings would give third parties an opportunity to present their views and that, secondly, given that the Commission is unlikely to change its opinion, they would be unlikely to reverse the orientation of the case. Accordingly, the general perception would be that the value of those hearings is at best limited. However, Durande and Williams (Hearing Officers at the time when the article was written) take the view that oral hearings would provide defendants with the widest possible audience they can reach in the Commission's proceedings. More importantly, the strength of the Commission's case would be tested and the really significant issues could be more easily identified than in the written comments. It would not be too bold to argue that oral hearings circumscribe the genuine object of the debate. Experience would show that in a number of instances the orientations of cases have been altered quite dramatically subsequent to the explanations given in oral hearings, even leading the Commission to drop entirely its objections, ie to abandon the case.

[235] See European Commission Antitrust Manual of Procedures, Internal DG Competition working documents on procedures for the application of Articles 101 and 102 TFEU, March 2012, Module 13 'Right to be heard', para 32.

[236] The Commission enjoys a 'reasonable margin of discretion' in deciding which persons are to be heard, according to the relevance of their participation in the investigation of the case. See Joined Cases 43/82 and 63/82 *VBVB and VBBB v Commission* [1984] ECR 1984, para 18.

[237] See European Commission Antitrust Manual of Procedures, Internal DG Competition working documents on procedures for the application of Articles 101 and 102 TFEU, March 2012, Module 13 'Right to be heard', para 38.

a meeting of the Advisory Committee on Restrictive Practices and Dominant Positions is convened.[238]

Preparation for the hearing

10.73 Whenever it is foreseeable that the parties will ask for and be granted a hearing, the Commission will, at the outset, indicate in the statement of objections an approximate date for it to be held. The cover letter sent with the statement of objections usually indicates that an oral hearing, if requested by the parties, would be likely to take place about a month following their reply to the statement of objections.[239] The final date, determined by the Hearing Officer after consulting the director responsible,[240] will be notified later, but always allowing sufficient time to make due preparations for the hearing. However, the Commission is not obliged to observe a minimum period between the date of the summons and that of the hearing, by contrast with the position regarding convening of the Advisory Committee.[241] Undertakings may request that the date for the hearing be postponed, but the Hearing Officer is rather less compliant in such cases than where a similar request is made regarding the period for replying to the statement of objections.[242] The physical arrangements for the hearing are so complex that there is little room for a flexible approach, and only in rare cases will the Commission agree to a deferment. For that reason, if, having received the statement of objections, undertakings foresee some difficulty in attending the hearing on the dates provisionally suggested, or on dates on which it is foreseeable that hearings might be held, it is advisable for them to inform the Hearing Officer and suggest a time convenient to them before the dates are fixed definitively. The Hearing Officer will endeavour as far as possible to strike a balance between the interests of the undertakings and the need to ensure the proper conduct of the procedure.

10.74 As stated earlier, the Commission does not query the interest of the undertakings allegedly implicated in the infringement in the organization of an oral hearing, even where it has no intention of imposing a fine on them. As regards other interested parties not directly implicated in the alleged infringement, the Hearing Officer usually does not query the interest of the complainants in participating in an oral hearing (Article 27(1) of Regulation 1/2003 read in conjunction with Article 6(2) of Regulation 773/2004). The same applies to third parties that have shown their sufficient interest in the outcome of the procedure and that might contribute new information or arguments to the procedure. According to Article 13(3) of Regulation 773/2004, the Commission can also allow any other person to express their views, thus allowing the possibility of summoning persons capable of providing useful and relevant information even in the absence of a 'sufficient interest'.

10.75 In practice, when the undertakings wish to have evidence given by experts or witnesses—whose status in this administrative procedure is hybrid and is not precisely the same as in civil proceedings in the Member States—they should mention it in their written reply to the statement of objections. The undertakings may annex to their submissions such opinions or reports as they consider appropriate, send them to the Commission after lodging their reply

---

[238] Regarding this Committee, see Ch 3 'The Role of the National Competition Authorities', para 3.113 et seq.
[239] See European Commission Antitrust Manual of Procedures, Internal DG Competition working documents on procedures for the application of Articles 101 and 102 TFEU, March 2012, Module 13 'Right to be heard', para 13.
[240] See Art 12(1) of the Hearing Officer's Mandate.
[241] See Art 14(3) of Reg 1/2003.
[242] According to Art 12(1) of the Hearing Officer's Mandate it is for the Hearing Officer to decide on requests to postpone the Oral Hearing.

but before the hearing, or hand them to the Commission at the start of the hearing. When information of this kind from experts or special witnesses is to be given orally—regardless of whether or not it has been submitted in writing earlier or at the same time—it is preferable to give the Hearing Officer advance notice of that fact. The Hearing Officer may then ask for a summary of the draft of the contribution to be made by such persons, if one has not previously been received from the undertakings (which will enable him/her to consider whether or not their participation is relevant), and define the limits of that contribution in the context of the hearing. The preparatory meetings mentioned at paragraphs 10.80 et seq are used for this purpose.[243] The Hearing Officer does not usually object to the participation of such persons in hearings, and in the rare cases in which it limits the duration of the statements or determines their subject-matter, its intention is principally to concentrate discussions within a limited time frame; hearings do not usually last more than two or three days, and a large number of people may take part in them in order to speak or ask questions.[244] That said, the Commission has no alternative in most cases but to accede to the parties' wishes. The hearings are held at the request of the parties and it is the parties which have to make the observations in the first place. Other contributions to hearings, both from the complainants and other interested third parties, are less important. The Commission services will usually content themselves with a very limited time frame, since the oral hearing does not have the purpose of allowing the Commission to defend its case.[245]

As regards the category of persons whose involvement is considered useful or necessary by the Commission in accordance with Article 13(3) of Regulation 773/2004, it may also include other experts or witnesses whose participation is desired by the Commission. The summonses to hearings are sent by the Commission to the persons named by the undertakings for that purpose. They may contain certain information from the Hearing Officer concerning the central issues and the matters about which the Commission would like to hear in more detail from the undertakings. The competition authorities of the Member States are invited to attend the hearing, pursuant to Article 14(3) of Regulation 773/2004. Officials and civil servants of other authorities of the Member States may also be invited to the hearing.[246] The summonses sent to undertakings are, strictly speaking, nothing more than invitations. **10.76**

The Commission cannot compel the undertakings or specific officers of them to attend, nor may it impose any penalty for non-attendance. Nor is the Commission granted powers to oblige witnesses or experts to attend an oral hearing. According to Article 14(4) and (5) of Regulation 773/2004: **10.77**

> [p]ersons invited to attend shall either appear in person or be represented by legal representatives or by representatives authorized by their constitution as appropriate. Undertakings and associations of undertakings may also be represented by a duly authorized agent appointed from among their permanent staff. Persons heard by the Commission may be assisted by their lawyers or other qualified persons admitted by the Hearing Officer.

This provision must be interpreted primarily as meaning that it allows the undertakings involved to be represented at the hearings both by their management or by persons whose **10.78**

---

[243] See Art 11 of the Mandate of the Hearing Officer.

[244] In addition to the undertakings, complainants, and interested third parties, the Commission services and representatives of the Member States can raise questions at the oral hearing.

[245] The brevity of the Commission's presentations at an oral hearing might sometimes give the incorrect impression that the Commission's case is weak and that the Commission is not in a position to address the parties' counterarguments. For the Commission, this is the 'price to pay' for the very purpose of the oral hearing, which is to allow the parties to exercise their right to be heard to the fullest extent possible.

[246] Article 6(2) second sentence of the Hearing Officer's Mandate.

offices normally enable them to represent the undertakings in all kinds of proceedings, and by members of their staff who have been appointed and empowered by the undertakings specifically in order to participate in this stage of the procedure. The 'duly authorized agent' must therefore have sufficient powers to speak on behalf of the undertaking or undertakings represented by him at hearings. The requirement that the persons representing the undertakings which are to present observations are to be members of their permanent staff is intended to make the hearings more fruitful as regards the information or clarifications which may be given to the Commission during them. The advantage of having representatives directly involved in the management of the undertakings lies in the fact that they may have more detailed or far-reaching knowledge than the lawyers or other legal advisers, of technical details or economic or commercial information about the products and services concerned and their markets.

10.79   Secondly, Article 14(5) of Regulation 773/2004 provides for the participation of lawyers, or 'other qualified persons', who may assist those who are to be heard. The Hearing Officer interprets this rule very flexibly. Thus, lawyers of non-member countries may generally take part in hearings, even where there is no reciprocal arrangement and the countries of origin of those lawyers do not allow EU lawyers to take part in similar proceedings. The lawyers or legal advisers should not in such cases be regarded as representatives of the undertakings, except for the purpose of defending them in legal proceedings. If the undertakings were represented solely by independent lawyers, that would—quite apart from matters relating to rights of the defence—to some extent frustrate the Commission's expectations regarding hearings, at which the Commission has an opportunity of putting questions to the representatives of the undertakings, and would render the procedure less helpful to it. The phrase 'other qualified persons' also seems to leave the door open for non-lawyers to defend the interests of participants in hearings.[247]

10.80   It is the prerogative of the Hearing Officer in certain cases to request the attendance of undertakings to a meeting prior to the hearing in order to focus the debate on the aspects of the case which in its view call for most attention.[248] Such meetings are attended both by the undertakings and by the officials of DG COMP who are directly conducting the case. They also provide an opportunity to make preparations as to how exactly the hearing is to be conducted. Thus, for example, arrangements may be made regarding the order in which the participants are to be heard in those cases where several wish to put their views forward (for example, several undertakings involved in the procedure and several complainants and third parties); the arrangements for the participation of persons involved in the defence of the undertakings (usually witnesses and experts) in accordance with Article 10(3) of Regulation 773/2004; the maximum time allowed for speaking according to the time available, and so on.

10.81   At the preparatory meeting or in a different context, the Hearing Officer may indicate to the persons invited to the hearing the focal areas for debate. In this respect, the facts and issues that the addressees of the statement of objections want to raise will be decisive.[249] Since it can be advantageous for the attendees at an oral hearing to know in advance what will be stated by the other participants, the Hearing Officer may also ask for prior notification of the essential contents of the intended statements.[250] This can also help parties to exercise their defence rights. The Hearing Officer may also, after consulting the director responsible,

---

[247] This could give rise to an unusual problem of professional encroachment if it were intended that such persons should act mainly in order to provide legal defence.
[248] Article 11(2) of the Hearing Officer's Mandate.
[249] Article 11(1) of the Hearing Officer's Mandate.
[250] Article 11(3) of the Hearing Officer's Mandate.

supply in advance to the parties invited to the hearing a list of the questions on which he/she wishes them to make known their views.[251] If third parties' contributions contain new facts or conclusions that the Commission might want to take into account in its final decision against the addressees, it will be obliged to give the parties an opportunity to express their views on these elements either at the oral hearing itself or at a later stage by means of a supplementary statement of objections or a letter of facts. The parties are more likely to be in a position to express their views at the oral hearing itself if they have been given the opportunity to prepare for such third party contributions.

The conduct of the hearing

The main steps at the oral hearing are the following:[252]   **10.82**

- The Hearing Officer opens the hearing and invites DG Competition to summarize the facts and principal arguments of the Commission (usual time allocated around 20 minutes).
- The party(ies) and third parties are given the opportunity to be heard.
- The Hearing Officer decides whether new documents should be admitted during the hearing.
- The Hearing Officer allows the parties, complainants and third parties, the Commission services and the representatives of the Member States to ask questions during the hearing to all attendees. If, exceptionally, a party cannot answer a question at the hearing, the Hearing Officer may allow such party to give an answer in writing within a set time limit.
- Where appropriate, in view of the need to ensure the right to be heard, the Hearing Officer may, after consulting the Director responsible, afford the parties concerned, other involved parties, complainants or interested third persons the opportunity of submitting further written comments after the oral hearing and fix a date by which such submissions may be made.
- Before closing the oral hearing the Hearing Officer invites the parties to make final remarks.
- During the hearing, the case team/secretary should take all necessary precautions in order to avoid any inadvertent disclosure of information covered by professional secrecy.

Administrative hearings are not public.[253] Only persons duly summoned to attend may do   **10.83** so. Article 14 of Regulation 773/2004, Articles 10 to 13 of the Hearing Officer's Mandate, and paragraphs 106 to 108 of the Commission's Best Practices, lay down rules for the manner in which oral hearings are to be conducted. In addition, the Commission's consistent administrative practice has led to the emergence of a general pattern that, with slight variations, is followed by the EU administration in all cases. In view of the limited time available, and having regard to the number of participants, the Hearing Officer will grant each a period in which to present oral observations.[254] The speaking time is always flexible, the intention being that no participant should not be heard as a result of insufficient time. The speaking time varies according to the nature of the participants. In most cases, the presentation of oral observations by the undertakings involved in the procedure—the period granted to them is usually the longest—does not take longer than three hours. The GC has pointed out that:

> the mere fact that the Commission imposes a programme for the hearings does not of itself constitute an infringement of the rights of the defence. There can be such an infringement

---

[251] See European Commission Antitrust Manual of Procedures, Internal DG Competition working documents on procedures for the application of Articles 101 and 102 TFEU, March 2012, Module 13 'Right to be heard', para 43.

[252] See European Commission Antitrust Manual of Procedures, Internal DG Competition working documents on procedures for the application of Articles 101 and 102 TFEU, March 2012, Module 13 'Right to be heard', paras 57–63.

[253] Article 14(6) Reg 773/2004.

[254] See Chapter 6 of the Hearing Officer's Mandate. In principle, according to Art 12(2) of the Hearing Officer's Mandate, the Hearing Officer can even decide 'which persons should be heard on behalf of a party'.

only where the applicants concerned prove that the organisation of the hearings prevented them from attending the hearings relating to objections raised against them or from putting forward orally their arguments against such objections.[255]

Participants in the oral hearing may request to be heard in an EU official language other than the language of proceedings. In that case, interpretation will be provided during the oral hearing, as long as sufficient advance notice of this requirement is given to the Hearing Officer.[256]

10.84 The Hearing Officer opens the session and calls on the investigating official or the head of the unit dealing with the case to speak. One of the latter briefly sets out the facts and states the alleged infringement. The summary thus given is useful because it allows the undertakings to focus discussion on the points which most concern, or are of most interest to, the Commission. Furthermore, the Commission's account may give the undertakings a first inkling of how their written arguments (reply to the statement of objections) have been received by the Commission. The undertakings involved then present their observations. These do not necessarily have to be limited to what has already been touched on in writing, but may cover new points not previously raised. Since there is little point in repeating aloud arguments already set out in the reply to the statement of objections, the Commission has made it clear that the advantage of a hearing lies in the opportunity thereby given to undertakings to clarify anything not properly dealt with in their written submissions and to lay down the main lines of their defence. This is the appropriate time for the persons who are able to confirm the facts set out in the reply to the statement of objections (the already-mentioned *sui generis* witnesses or experts) to speak. If its contribution has been properly prepared, the Commission will already have available at the start of the meeting a sufficient number of copies of the report, opinion, or evidence[257] that will be appended to the file.[258] This does not mean that such documents cannot be produced at the hearing. In this way, the oral observations can concentrate on the most important specific details, or on the general outlines of the document—merely repetitive reading thus being avoided. Any members of the management of the undertaking who wish to do so may also make their observations at this stage. Those who take part in the administrative hearing do not do so under oath. Nor are they even formally called upon to state the truth. As regards the experts, witnesses, and other persons involved in defending the undertakings, their statements must be regarded as reflecting the best of their knowledge and belief. Their reliability and objectivity—despite the fact that they are brought in by the undertakings involved—will be appraised by the Commission. The undertakings usually give the Commission information as to the standing and professional competence of their experts and witnesses. The statements made by undertakings at the hearing are not covered by the same obligations as those imposed by Articles 18 and 20 of Regulation 1/2003 (requests for information and inspections) as regards the truth of the information given to the Commission, and undertakings cannot be fined if for any reason they give incorrect information or particulars that do not reflect the true position. Neither Article 23(1) of Regulation 1/2003—relative to fines—nor Regulation 773/2004 provide for such a possibility.

---

[255] Joined Cases T-25/95 etc *Cimenteries CBR and Others v Commission* [2000] ECR II-508, para 663; see also para 674 of the same judgment as to the length of the speaking time.
[256] Commission Notice on best practices for the conduct of proceedings concerning Articles 101 and 102 TFEU [2011] OJ C308/6, para 31. Usually, translation from and into the two usual working languages of the Commission, namely English and French, does not pose a problem.
[257] Numerous persons may be involved in hearings and will each require a copy.
[258] The appropriate stage in the procedure for this may be the reply to the statement of objections, or between the end of the period allowed for a reply and the date of the hearings.

By contrast with the investigation phase, in which the undertakings are obliged to give true **10.85** and accurate information to the Commission, in the knowledge that if they do so they might incriminate themselves,[259] the hearing is a phase of the procedure in which the rights of the defence prevail over all other considerations. This does not mean that the Commission has no interest in whether the information given at this stage reflects the true situation. Although it may subsequently check such information, the position is that in order to ensure that the rights of the defence are fully safeguarded, the Commission simply has no powers, in this phase of the procedure, to impose penalties of the kind described above.[260] As regards written reports and evidence, they and any other documents should be forwarded to the Commission with the minimum delay, if possible well before the hearings—although they can in fact be produced at the hearing.[261] If they contain business secrets, the Commission must be informed. It is important to note that the Hearing Officer—who will give a decision on the matter—may be asked that, in order to safeguard the business secrets of the undertakings making oral statements, certain undertakings should leave the room for a short time so that the speakers will not be heard by the other undertakings present at the hearing.[262] Since the complainants—who are usually customers or competitors—often take part in the hearings, this situation can arise frequently.

The complainants may be heard after the undertakings involved. Practice varies regarding **10.86** the order in which they take part. In most cases, complainants speak after the undertakings involved. In each case, the order depends largely on what has been previously agreed between the undertakings and the Hearing Officer. After the undertakings have spoken, the Commission may ask questions if it wishes to do so. It is under no obligation to ask questions and the fact of not putting questions to the undertakings cannot be regarded as an indication that it has prejudged the case. When it decides to ask questions, the Commission must confine itself to those facts or arguments, put forward in the statement of objections or the comments thereon that call for clarification. It is important to note that, for the Commission, this step in the procedure is not investigative; the facts on which it seeks to rely must already have been set out in the statement of objections, and any request for clarification must be specifically directed towards those facts. The hearing cannot be treated by the Commission as a means of obtaining particulars and information that could be satisfactorily obtained by the exercise of its investigative powers under Articles 18 and 20 of Regulation 1/2003.

It is also important to note that the hearing cannot operate as a substitute for a statement of **10.87** objections. If the Commission advances new allegations of infringements or new essential facts, different from those contained in the statement of objections, it has to issue a supplementary statement of objections (which would then entail the right to a new oral hearing) or at least a letter of facts.[263] Nevertheless, the Commission's statements at the oral hearing can

---

[259] Regarding the problem of self-incrimination, or the right to remain silent, in relation to the Commission's investigative powers, see Ch 7, 'Investigation of Cases (II): Formal Investigative Measures in General, Requests for Information, and Interviews', para 7.39 et seq.

[260] See Ch 9 'Procedural Infringements: Fines and Periodic Penalty Payments', para 9.01 et seq.

[261] The Hearing Officer may in any event 'ask for prior written notification of the essential contents of the intended statement of persons whom the undertakings concerned have proposed for hearing' (Art 11(3) of the Mandate of the Hearing Officer).

[262] Article 14(6) of Reg 773/2004, Art 13 of the Hearing Officer's Mandate.

[263] Article 12(2) of the Hearing Officer's Mandate states that new documents may be admitted during the Hearing with the Hearing Officer's consent. The admission of those documents would seem appropriate where they may shed light on some points of law or fact on which the Commission has not reached a clear understanding. S Durande and K Williams, 'The Practical Impact of the Exercise of the Right to be Heard: A Special Focus on the Effect of Oral Hearings and the Role of the Hearing Officers' (2005) Summer (2) EC Competition Newsletter 22, 25. In any event, the rights of defence require that parties are given sufficient opportunity to make their views known on such new documents.

put the parties in a position reasonably to infer the conclusions that the Commission intends to draw from a piece of evidence, which can exclude a breach of the right to be heard.[264] Similarly, if the undertakings agree to discuss facts and arguments not contained in the statement of objections—and which do not materially differ from those raised in the statement of objections[265]—and have an opportunity to give their views on them at the hearing and produce evidence relating to them, they cannot later contend that the decision is vitiated because it does not correspond precisely to the statement of objections.[266] Just as the undertakings involved are not under a specific obligation to tell the truth and are not liable to fines in the event that the particulars or information they give in their oral observations are incomplete, misleading, or false, the Commission has no procedural means of making the undertakings answer its questions or of making them give true and complete answers if they do not wish to do so. In practice, the undertakings only very rarely refuse to answer the Commission's questions, and only then in cases where it is not possible to give replies—not even approximate replies—on the spot. In such cases, the undertakings may reply in writing after the hearing to the Commission's questions that were left unanswered. The details regarding the time limit for such replies can be settled at the end of the hearing between the Hearing Officer and the undertakings. The written replies are likewise not covered by Article 18 and do not allow the Commission to fine undertakings when the information provided is incorrect. Quite apart from this possibility, the Commission is in all cases entitled, after the hearing, formally to call for more precise details and information to supplement the statements made by the participants at this stage.[267]

10.88 It is then the turn of the NCAs of the Member States, who, like the Commission, may put questions to the undertakings in the person of their lawyers, those supporting them, or their executives. In view of the fact that the NCAs will have an opportunity to question the Commission at meetings of the Advisory Committee, it is better for them to defer putting questions to the Commission until then. Finally, before the hearing ends, the undertakings have a further opportunity to speak, briefly. The undertakings involved may thereby respond to the comments made by the complainants. It is the appropriate point in the procedure for them to request measures which they consider appropriate; for example, that the infringement procedure be suspended or that fines should not be imposed or should be reduced, and so forth. The Hearing Officer, who will have chaired the proceedings throughout, intervening when necessary, then closes the hearing.

Record of the hearings

10.89 Article 14(8) of Regulation 773/2004 provides as follows:

> The statements made by each person heard shall be recorded. Upon request, the recording of the hearing shall be made available to the persons who attended the hearing. Regard shall also be had to the legitimate interest of the parties in the protection of their business secrets and other confidential information.

---

[264] See, by analogy, Joined Cases T-191/98 and T-212/98 to T-214/98 *Atlantic Container Line v Commission* [2003] ECR II-3275, paras 162, 171, 173 and 263.

[265] As regards the question of fresh evidence and the requirement to issue a new statement of objections, para 10.35 et seq.

[266] See Cases 100–103/80 *Musique Diffusion (Pioneer) v Commission* [1983] ECR 1825, paras 18–19.

[267] The Commission can always issue formal information requests under Art 18 of Reg 1/2003. The Commission powers are not limited by reference to time or the stage reached in the case, so that they can be used after completion of the investigation, during the observations phase, between the latter phase and the adoption of a decision, and even afterwards. See Ch 7, 'Investigation of Cases (II): Formal Investigative Measures in General, Requests for Information, and Interviews', para 7.03 and the possibility of the Commission sanctioning the supply of incorrect or misleading information Ch 9, 'Procedural Infringements: Fines and Periodic Penalty Payments', para 9.03 et seq.

Thus, while the recording sets out a record of the entire proceedings, regard must be had to the legitimate interest of the parties in the protection of their business secrets and other confidential information. It is no longer the Commission's practice to prepare written minutes and to submit them to the parties for their approval in order to enable them to check what they said at the hearing to ensure that they contained a true record of the substance of what they had said. After the hearing, the Hearing Officer sends a copy of the audio recording to the Antitrust Registry, who encodes it in the case management application. Parties who attended the hearing and have requested the audio recording may collect it at the Hearing Office. Parties who did not attend the hearing do not have a right to obtain a copy of the recording.[268]

The Hearing Officer's interim report

Article 14(1) of the Hearing Officer's Mandate provides that the Hearing Officer shall submit **10.90** an interim report to the Competition Commissioner on the conclusions to be drawn from the oral hearing with regard to the respect for the effective exercise of procedural rights. In addition to, and separately from, this interim report, the Hearing Officer may also make observations on the further progress and impartiality of the proceedings.[269]

Such observations may concern, among other things: **10.91**

(i) whether due account is taken of all the relevant facts;
(ii) the need for further information;
   – the withdrawal of certain objections;
   – the formulation of further objections; or
   – suggestions for further investigative measures pursuant to Chapter V of Regulation 1/2003 (eg, request for information, interview of natural or legal persons).[270]

The Hearing Officer sends his draft interim report and observations to the case team for **10.92** information and comments on the facts before sending it to the Competition Commissioner, after having seen the case team's report on the hearing.[271] It follows that an oral hearing can also prompt the Hearing Officer to submit comments on the substance of the case, in particular if the parties' observations at the hearing reveal insufficiencies in the Commission's case. It needs to be emphasized that, contrary to the final report, the Hearing Officer's interim observations are only for internal use by the Commission, and are not communicated to any of the parties to the proceedings.[272]

4. Participation of the complainants and of other third parties

Status of complainants

Procedures for the application of EU competition law conducted by the European **10.93** Commission are administrative procedures which are commenced on the initiative of the Commission.[273] This is due to the fact that the EU competition rules form part of EU public

---

[268] See European Commission Antitrust Manual of Procedures, Internal DG Competition working documents on procedures for the application of Articles 101 and 102 TFEU, March 2012, Module 13 'Right to be heard', para 55.

[269] Article 14(2) of the Hearing Officer's Mandate.

[270] See European Commission Antitrust Manual of Procedures, Internal DG Competition working documents on procedures for the application of Articles 101 and 102 TFEU, March 2012, Module 13 'Right to be heard', para 59.

[271] See European Commission Antitrust Manual of Procedures, Internal DG Competition working documents on procedures for the application of Articles 101 and 102 TFEU, March 2012, Module 13 'Right to be heard', para 60.

[272] See Case T-191/06 *FMC Foret v Commission* [2011] ECR II-2959, para 143.

[273] For more detailed treatment of this point, see Ch 5, 'Opening of the File', para 5.08 et seq.

policy, and their implementation by administrative authorities is not a matter where private initiative should prevail. In that respect, private individuals are above all, as far as the Commission is concerned, informants and not always parties to procedures in the strict sense, even when they may in fact have prompted the Commission to take action. Regardless of the starting point of procedures, it is always the Commission that decides how and when the various stages of the procedure are to take place once the EU machinery has been put into action. The limitations on the Commission's discretionary powers on procedural issues derive solely from the procedural regulations themselves and do not result from requests from those involved, except of course to the extent to which they reflect the procedural rules.

10.94 From the procedural point of view, this has an important practical consequence: the only necessary parties to infringement procedures are the undertakings implicated in the agreements, practices, or abuses contrary to Articles 101 and 102 of the Treaty. Other 'parties' rank as such only in the sense that they 'take part', and although complainants 'shall be associated closely with the proceedings',[274] even their participation is to a certain extent a matter for the Commission's discretion. This applies even more to other, so-called 'interested third parties' that demonstrate a legitimate interest in having their *written* views on the nature and subject matter of the procedure considered (Article 27(3) of Regulation 1/2003 in conjunction with Article 13(1) of Regulation 773/2004). Hence, the following remarks on the participation of the complainants applies all the more to interested third parties and to other third parties that are called on by the Commission to express their views (Article 13(3) of Regulation 773/2004).

10.95 The Commission's interest in the participation of the complainants in competition procedures lies in the fact that, through their first-hand knowledge of the market and of the infringements which constitute the factual basis of the procedure—the most usual complainants are customers or competitors of the undertakings involved—they provide enormous help to the Commission in proving infringements of Articles 101 and 102 TFEU. The Commission is also obliged to examine the matters of fact and law which the complainants have brought to its notice and to allow them to defend their legitimate interests during the administrative procedure.[275] However, despite their considerable usefulness, complainants do not enjoy the same rights and procedural safeguards as the undertakings implicated in an infringement.[276]

10.96 The *Österreichische Postsparkasse* judgment clarified the requirements that a person needs to meet in order to qualify as a 'complainant' in antitrust proceedings.[277] First, the GC confirmed that applicants qualify as complainants if they justify their 'legitimate interest' by demonstrating that the alleged infringement might harm their economic interests. The Commission is obliged to establish whether persons claiming to be complainants might indeed be harmed in their economic interests.[278] By contrast, it is not for the Commission to examine whether the person pursues motives other than the termination of the infringement.[279] In the case at hand, the banks' claim that the complainant pursued political interests rather than its

---

[274] Article 27(1) of Reg 1/2003.

[275] See Case 298/83 *CICCE v Commission* [1985] ECR 1105, cited in Joined Cases 142/84 and 156/84 *BAT and Reynolds Industries v Commission* [1987] ECR 4487, para 20.

[276] See Joined Cases 209/78 and 218/78 *Van Landewyck v Commission ('FEDETAB')* [1980] ECR 3125, para 18, and Joined Cases 142/84 and 156/84 *BAT and Reynolds Industries v Commission* [1987] ECR 4487, paras 19–20.

[277] Joined Cases T-213 and 214/01 *Österreichische Postsparkasse v Commission* [2006] ECR II-1601. See in this respect M Kellerbauer and L Repa, 'The Court of First Instance Upholds Two Decisions of the Hearing Officer Clarifying Important Procedural Questions in Antitrust Investigations' (2007) 28(5) ECLR 297.

[278] Joined Cases T-213 and 214/01 *Österreichische Postsparkasse v Commission* [2006] ECR II-1601, paras 124–9.

[279] Joined Cases T-213 and 214/01 *Österreichische Postsparkasse v Commission* [2006] ECR II-1601, para 118.

interests as a consumer was therefore deemed to be irrelevant. Second, the fact that the Commission has already initiated the antitrust investigation the complaint refers to, either on its own ('ex officio') or due to another complaint, is not a bar to the applicant's qualification as a complainant.[280] Irrespective of whether the complainants submit substantial new evidence, they can always 'jump on the bandwagon' of a pending Commission investigation, even at a late stage.[281] Any person claiming the status of 'complainant' but not justifying their legitimate interest can still be entitled to be heard as an interested third party, provided that they demonstrate a sufficient interest in the outcome of the proceedings and are granted the status of 'interested third party' by the Hearing Officer.[282]

Participation of complainants

Traditionally, the role of the complainant in infringement procedures has primarily been that of an informant.[283] However, in view of the added value that a more active role of the complainant entailed in the proceedings, the Commission considered it advisable to allow complainants to participate actively in the procedure following the filing of the initial complaint, so that they could give their views, in writing or orally, on the statement of objections and even on the defence put forward by the undertakings implicated in the infringements. **10.97**

Modernization rules (both Regulation 1/2003 and Regulation 773/2004) have enshrined such a *de facto* position of complainants by conferring them a specific status in the proceedings.[284] Thus, first, according to Article 27(1) of Regulation 1/2003, 'complainants shall be associated closely with the proceedings'. Secondly, Regulation 773/2004, while establishing a clear distinction between complainants and other third parties, does not require complainants to prove a 'sufficient interest' after having shown a 'legitimate interest' in lodging a complaint—as required by Article 5(1). It is obvious, therefore, that the special position that complainants were previously afforded in the Commission's practice has now been legally recognized. Regarding the rights of the complainant, where the Commission considers that there are insufficient grounds for acting on the complaint, it will inform the complainant of its reasons setting a time limit for the complainant to make known its views in writing.[285] If the Commission raises objections relating to a matter in respect of which a complaint has been lodged, it will provide the complainant with a copy of the non-confidential version of the statement of objections and will set a time limit within which the complainant may make known its views in writing.[286] The GC has confirmed that complainants may ask for a non-confidential version of the statement of objections even after an oral hearing has taken place and up until the very moment the Advisory Committee **10.98**

---

[280] Joined Cases T-213 and 214/01 *Österreichische Postsparkasse v Commission* [2006] ECR II-1601, para 92.

[281] See European Commission Antitrust Manual of Procedures, Internal DG Competition working documents on procedures for the application of Articles 101 and 102 TFEU, March 2012, Module 13 'Right to be heard', para 5.

[282] See European Commission Antitrust Manual of Procedures, Internal DG Competition working documents on procedures for the application of Articles 101 and 102 TFEU, March 2012, Module 13 'Right to be heard', para 6.

[283] In the words of AG Lenz, '[T]he complainant is limited to a role which corresponds to the position, under criminal procedure, of a person who reports a matter to the authorities'. Opinion in *Akzo I* Case 53/85 *Akzo v Commission* I [1986] ECR 1965.

[284] It must be pointed out, however, that Reg 2842/1998—repealed by Reg 773/2004—already foresaw the recognition of the specific status of complainants.

[285] Article 7(1) of Reg 773/2004. In this respect, the complainant is also granted a limited right to access to file, albeit only to the documents on which the Commission intends to base its decision to reject the complaint. See Art 8 of Reg 773/2004.

[286] Article 6(1) of Reg 773/2004. The complainant may raise issues about the extent of the deletions in the non-confidential version of the statement of objections sent to it, and may refer the matter for decision to the Hearing Officer in case of disagreement with the case team pursuant to Art 7(2)(c) of the Hearing Officer's Mandate.

convenes to decide on the draft decision imposing fines.[287] However, in cases where the cartel settlement procedure applies, complainants do not receive a non-confidential version of the statement of objections, but are merely informed in writing of the nature and subject matter of the procedure.[288] Furthermore, the presence of complainants during the oral hearing requires their admission by the Hearing Officer.[289]

10.99 During the investigation phase, the Commission may in addition inform complainants both of the content of the requests for information sent to the undertakings involved in the alleged infringement of the competition provisions of which they complain, and of the answers given by the undertakings to such requests and to the complaints themselves if copies were forwarded to the undertakings. Three comments are called for in this respect. The first is that the Commission has a discretion as to whether or not the complainants should receive those documents.[290] In many cases the Commission waits until the hearing before asking for the opinion of the complainants on the information given and the defence put forward by the undertakings against which the complaints are directed. The second is that while respecting the safeguards contained in Article 28(1) and (2) of Regulation 1/2003, the Commission may make non-confidential information available to the complainant or to other third parties.[291] Finally, while Article 15(1) of Regulation 773/2004 establishes that access to the file is to be granted only to the addressees of the statement of objections, it might be argued that the Commission may rely on Article 15(3) to make certain pieces of information in the investigation file available to the complainant, provided it relates to the subject matter for which it was acquired and is not covered by the obligation of professional secrecy and confidentiality. However, complainants have no right to examine the documents in the Commission's investigation file.[292]

10.100 In order to safeguard the rights of the defence, the observations expressed by the complainants and other third parties concerning the statement of objections will generally be communicated to the undertaking directly involved in the alleged infringement, subject to their legitimate interest in confidentiality.[293] The forwarding of a copy may be sufficient in those cases where the statements from such persons do not contain new matters of fact to be taken into account in the final decision, or else contain new facts for which it is clear which

---

[287] Joined Cases T-213 and 214/01 *Österreichische Postsparkasse v Commission* [2006] ECR II-1601, para 149.

[288] Article 6(1) of Reg 773/2004.

[289] Article 6(2) of Reg 773/2004, Art 6(2) Hearing Officer's Mandate. The Hearing Officer decides after consulting with the Director responsible.

[290] According to the Commission Notice on best practices for the conduct of proceedings concerning Articles 101 and 102 TFEU [2011] OJ C308/6, n 51, a non-confidential version of the reply of the party subject to the investigation to the complaint *may* be provided to the complainant.

[291] Complainants and other third parties cannot claim a right of access to the file as established for parties; Commission Notice on the rules for access to the Commission file pursuant to Articles 81 and 82 EC [2005] OJ C325/7, para 30. In any event, according to the Court's *Akzo I* ruling, they must not be granted access to business secrets which the Commission has obtained in the course of its investigation; Case 53/85 *Akzo Chemie v Commission* [1986] ECR 1965, para 28; see also Case T-5/97 *Industrie des poudres sphériques SA v Commission* [2000] ECR II-3755, para 229.

[292] It is only where the Commission intends to reject a complaint that the complainant is granted, pursuant to Article 8 of Reg 773/2004, access to a non-confidential version of the documents on which the Commission intends to base its decision to reject the complaint.

[293] According to the Commission Notice on best practices for the conduct of proceedings concerning Articles 101 and 102 TFEU [2011] OJ C308/6, para 73, the Commission intends to provide the parties subject to the proceedings shortly after the opening of proceedings with the opportunity to review non-confidential versions of other 'key submissions' already submitted to the Commission. This would include significant submissions of the complainant or interested third parties, but not, for example, replies to requests for information. After this point, the Commission will share other such submissions with the parties only if this is in the interest of the investigation and would not risk unduly slowing down the investigative phase.

existing conclusions contained in the statement of objections are corroborated. Where the Commission intends to use such observations to raise new objections, it becomes necessary to send a supplementary statement of objections. Where new facts are used in support of existing objections and the conclusions to be drawn from these facts might not be clear to the parties, the Commission will observe the rights of the defence by allowing the undertakings concerned to submit observations in response to a letter of facts.

Complainants and interested third parties can be interested in commenting in turn on **10.101** the comments that parties had on their observations. However, this should not lead to a procedure which is comparable to one of replies and rejoinders of the kind typical of civil proceedings.[294] The Commission's intention is to scrupulously observe undertakings' defence rights and ensure that the right to a fair hearing is upheld, and it does not, in principle, consider it appropriate to allow an exchange of mutual accusations between undertakings. Therefore, complainants and interested third parties are generally afforded only one opportunity to comment on the submissions made by the addressees of a statement of objections.[295]

Other third parties

As explained earlier, third parties must apply to be heard by showing a 'sufficient interest' in **10.102** the outcome of the procedure to the Hearing Officer (Article 13(1) of Regulation 773/2004, Article 5 of the Hearing Officer's Mandate). It may therefore be affirmed that third parties are not accorded a status similar to that of complainants,[296] let alone to that of the parties to whom the Commission has addressed a statement of objections. Any third party applying to be heard directly to the case team should be told to address its application, including a statement explaining the applicant's interest in the outcome of the procedure, to the Hearing Officer.[297] Once their application is granted by the Hearing Officer, pursuant to Article 13(1) of Regulation 773/2004, third parties shall be informed in writing of the 'nature and subject matter of the procedure'. Therefore, the Commission is not legally required to send a non-confidential version of the statement of objections to interested third parties, but only to inform them of a summary of the facts and of the legal assessment set forth in the statement of objections.[298] This is to be seen as an additional sign of the secondary or less important status of third parties in terms of possibilities to be heard. However, in practice, the Commission usually sends a non-confidential version of the statement of objections not only to complainants, but also to interested third parties[299] and the GC confirmed the lawfulness

---

[294] The Community administrative procedure in competition matters is not a civil adversarial procedure. See also the judgment in Joined Cases 142/84 and 156/84 *BAT and Reynolds Industries v Commission* [1987] ECR 4487, para 19. Nevertheless, the Court itself has described the procedure following a statement of objections as contentious proceedings. See Joined Cases 46/87 and 227/88 *Hoechst v Commission III* [1989] ECR 2859, para 16; Case 27/88 *Solvay v Commission* [1989] ECR 3355, paras 17 and 21–2; and Case 374/87 *Orkem v Commission* [1989] ECR 3283, paras 20, 24, and 25. In those cases, the Court makes it clear that the opposing parties are the undertakings involved and the Commission, and that there is no adversarial litigation between complainants and undertakings, in the civil procedural sense.

[295] See also para 10.70.

[296] As stated, complainants are supposed to have a sufficient interest once they have shown a legitimate interest to be entitled to lodge a complaint.

[297] See European Commission Antitrust Manual of Procedures, Internal DG Competition working documents on procedures for the application of Articles 101 and 102 TFEU, March 2012, Module 13 'Right to be heard', para 10.

[298] See European Commission Antitrust Manual of Procedures, Internal DG Competition working documents on procedures for the application of Articles 101 and 102 TFEU, March 2012, Module 11 'Drafting of Statement of Objections', para 38.

[299] See Final reports of the Hearing Officer in *UEFA Champions League* [2003] OJ C269/22 and *Deutsche Telekom AG* [2003] OJ C288/2.

of this practice.[300] Third parties may complain to the case team about the appropriateness of the information they received for the purposes of making known their views, and refer the matter for decision to the Hearing Officer in case of disagreement with the case team.[301]

10.103 While it is not completely clear what 'sufficient interest' within the meaning of Article 13(1) of Regulation 773/2004 means[302]—and no ruling of the EU Courts has yet been given on the matter—it must be pointed out that in any event the Commission has a wide margin of discretion as to the persons to be heard, apart from the parties to the proceedings and complainants, since Article 13(3) of Regulation 773/2004 recognizes the power of the Commission to hear 'any other person' to express its views in writing and to attend the oral hearing. Once a third party is capable of showing a sufficient interest and is informed of the nature and subject matter of the procedure, Article 13(1) provides that the Commission shall set a time limit in order to allow such third party to make observations in writing. Finally, and regarding the possibility of attending the oral hearing and developing arguments, third parties must make such a request in their written comments, the Hearing Officer having the last word on the matter (Article 13(2) of Regulation 733/2004 and Article 6(2) of the Hearing Officer's Mandate).

Triangular meetings

10.104 Bilateral State of Play meetings are usually only offered to the parties being investigated and not to the complainant nor to third parties.[303] However, the Commission may exceptionally decide to invite the parties subject to the proceedings, the complainant and/or interested third parties, to a so-called 'triangular' meeting. Such a meeting will be organized if DG COMP believes it to be in the interests of the investigation to hear the views on, or to verify the accuracy of, factual issues of all participants to the proceedings in a single meeting.[304] This can particularly be the case where two or more opposing views or pieces of information have been put forward as to key data or evidence. Triangular meetings normally take place at the initiative of the Commission and on a voluntary basis. They are usually chaired by senior management of DG COMP (Director-General or Deputy Director-General), who will also establish an agenda after consulting all parties that agree to attend the meeting. Triangulars meeting are not meant to replace the formal oral hearing chaired by the Hearing Officer.[305] Where triangular meetings are held, the Commission intends to hold them as early as possible during the investigatory phase (ie after the opening of proceedings and before any issuing of statement of objections) in order to help the Commission reach a conclusion on substantive issues before the Commission decides whether to issue a statement of objections. However, the holding of such meetings after the issue of the statement of objections in appropriate cases is not excluded, either.[306] Triangular meetings should be prepared

---

[300] Joined Cases T-213 and 214/01 *Österreichische Postsparkasse v Commission* [2006] ECR II-1601, para 107.

[301] Article 7(2) of the Hearing Officer's Mandate.

[302] Article 5(1) of the Hearing Officer's Mandate specifies that a third party's 'sufficient interest' must relate to the third party's interest in the outcome of the procedure.

[303] An exception is made where the Commission has opened proceedings pursuant to Article 11(6) of Regulation 1/2003 and intends to inform the complainant that it will reject its complaint by formal letter under Article 7(1) Regulation 773/2004. Commission Notice on best practices for the conduct of proceedings concerning Articles 101 and 102 TFEU [2011] OJ C308/6, para 61.

[304] Commission Notice on best practices for the conduct of proceedings concerning Articles 101 and 102 TFEU [2011] OJ C308/6, paras 67–9.

[305] Commission Notice on best practices for the conduct of proceedings concerning Articles 101 and 102 TFEU [2011] OJ C308/6, para 68.

[306] Commission Notice on best practices for the conduct of proceedings concerning Articles 101 and 102 TFEU [2011] OJ C308/6, para 69.

on the basis of an agenda established by DG COMP after consulting all parties that agree to attend the meeting. The preparation of the meeting may include a mutual exchange of non-confidential submissions between the attending parties sufficiently in advance of the meeting.[307]

D. The Remaining Stages of the Procedure until the Adoption of a Decision

Where a statement of objections is issued, the parties will also be offered a State of Play meeting after their reply to the statement of objections or after the oral hearing, should one be held. At this meeting the parties will normally be informed of the Commission's preliminary view on how it intends to pursue the case further.[308] In the context of cartel proceedings one State of Play meeting will be offered after the oral hearing.[309] The Commission emphasizes that State of Play meetings do not in any way preclude discussions between the parties, complainants, or third parties and the DG COMP on substance or on timing issues at any point throughout the procedure as appropriate.[310]   **10.105**

The further procedural stages, following the observations under Article 27(1) of Regulation   **10.106**
1/2003, have been considered in general terms in Chapter 1, dealing with the manner in which the Commission adopts decisions in competition matters.[311] In short, once the observations phase is completed, DG COMP prepares, in all cases with the approval of the Legal Service and, in some cases, with the involvement of other departments concerned,[312] a draft decision which is referred to the Advisory Committee, made up of the representatives of NCAs, for its opinion.[313] DG COMP, taking into account that opinion, then prepares a final draft, which is again approved by its Legal Service. The full Commission then approves the draft, with or without amendments, notifies its decision to the undertakings, and publishes it in the Official Journal together with the Final Report of the Hearing Officer.[314] The final report considers (Article 16(1) of the Hearing Officer's Mandate) whether participants in antitrust proceedings have been able to effectively exercise their procedural rights and whether the draft decision deals only with objections in respect of which the parties have been afforded the opportunity of making known their views. It is submitted to the Competition Commissioner, the Director-General for Competition and the Director responsible for the investigation, and is communicated to the competent authorities of the Member States and, in accordance with the provisions on cooperation laid down in Protocol 23 of the EEA Agreement, to the EFTA Surveillance Authority (Article 16(2) of the Hearing Officer's Mandate). The final report is notified to the parties and published together with the

---

[307] See European Commission Antitrust Manual of Procedures, Internal DG Competition working documents on procedures for the application of Articles 101 and 102 TFEU, March 2012, Module 10 'Opening of proceedings', para 30.

[308] Commission Notice on best practices for the conduct of proceedings concerning Articles 101 and 102 TFEU [2011] OJ C308/6, para 64.

[309] Commission Notice on best practices for the conduct of proceedings concerning Articles 101 and 102 TFEU [2011] OJ C308/6, para 65.

[310] Commission Notice on best practices for the conduct of proceedings concerning Articles 101 and 102 TFEU [2011] OJ C308/6, para 66.

[311] See Ch 4, 'The Organization of European Commission Proceedings', para 4.05 et seq.

[312] Only the report of the Legal Service is required in cases dealt with under Reg 1/2003, but the Commission may obtain the opinion of other Directorates-General in individual cases.

[313] See Ch 3, 'The Organization of European Commission Proceedings', para 3.113 et seq.

[314] Article 16(3) of the Hearing Officer's Mandate.

final decision.[315] Member States must have the draft final report when discussing the draft decision at the Advisory Committee. The report may be modified by the Hearing Officer in the light of any amendments to the draft decision up to the time the Commission adopts the decision.[316]

III. Settlement Procedures[317]

A. Origin and Context

1. Legislative history

10.107 On 30 June 2008, after a public consultation,[318] the European Commission adopted the legislative package introducing the settlement procedure, providing for a new and stream-lined infringement procedure under EU law.[319] The so-called 'settlements package' consists of 'Commission Regulation (EC) No 622/2008 of 30 June 2008 amending Regulation (EC) No 773/2004, as regards the conduct of settlement procedures in cartel cases'[320] and 'Commission Notice on the conduct of settlement procedures in view of the adoption of Decisions pursuant to Article 7 and Article 23 of Council Regulation (EC) No 1/2003 in cartel cases'[321] ('Settlements Notice').

10.108 The settlements package was introduced into the existing institutional and legal framework by adjustments only at the level of implementing legislation avoiding other longer and more burdensome procedures. It did not involve any amendment of Council Regulation 1/2003, but merely of Commission Regulation 773/2004, which itself is adopted on the basis of Article 33 of Regulation 1/2003. This course of action allowed the Commission to introduce the settlement procedure in a much faster way, albeit at the price of being restricted to the confines of Regulation 1/2003.[322] Although the introduction of a specific settlement procedure, different from the infringement procedure governed by Regulation 1/2003, would have allowed the Commission to move beyond these limitations, the introduction of an optional simplification of the current well-known procedure maintains coherence and avoids confusion.

---

[315] See European Commission Antitrust Manual of Procedures, Internal DG Competition working documents on procedures for the application of Articles 101 and 102 TFEU March 2012, Module 13 'Right to be heard', paras 62 and 63.

[316] See European Commission Antitrust Manual of Procedures, Internal DG Competition working documents on procedures for the application of Articles 101 and 102 TFEU, March 2012, Module 13 'Right to be heard', paras 65 and 66.

[317] The first version of this section was drafted by Clio Zois and Michal Bobek, and then revised by Marisa Tierno Centella.

[318] See Commission Press Release IP/07/1608 'Antitrust: Commission calls for comments on a draft legislative package to introduce settlement procedure for cartels' of 26 October 2007.

[319] See Commission Press Release IP/08/1056 'Antitrust: Commission introduces settlement procedure for cartels' of 30 June 2008.

[320] [2008] OJ L171/3.

[321] [2008] OJ C167/1–6.

[322] See L Ortiz Blanco, A Givaja Sanz, and A Lamadrid De Pablo, 'Fine Arts in Brussels: Punishment and Settlement of Cartel Cases under EC Competition Law' in: *Antitrust between EC law and national law — Antitrust fra diritto nazionale e diritto comunitario* 22–23 May/Maggio 2008 Tome 6 (Bruylant 2009), 155.

2. EU legal framework

Under EU law, a settlement (decision) is a formal infringement decision reserved to cartel **10.109** cases, which is adopted pursuant to Articles 7 and 23 of Regulation 1/2003 at the end of a simplified procedure. Its core feature is the express acceptance of liability for an infringement of Article 101 TFEU by the undertakings involved, for which they are granted a fine reduction.

EU settlements, following a rationale of their own, are designed to fit into the existing **10.110** European institutional framework. According to the European Commission, they are neither driven by an intention to emulate other settlement procedures, nor do they respond to the need to cope with a hypothetical backlog of the Commission.[323]

Settlements and leniency

The cooperation covered by the Settlements Notice is different from the voluntary produc- **10.111** tion of evidence to trigger or advance the Commission's investigation, which is covered by the Leniency Notice.

The Leniency Notice rewards companies involved in cartels that decide to disclose the exist- **10.112** ence of a cartel and provide evidence to prove an infringement.[324] It encourages self-reporting whilst ensuring that companies are better off by cooperating with the Commission. The first to self-report receives a 100 per cent fine reduction, while subsequent leniency applicants can obtain lower reductions when producing evidence that is of significant added value.

Unlike leniency, the settlement procedure is not used as an investigative tool but rather **10.113** as a 'case closure mechanism'[325] to reward specific contributions to procedural efficiency. Therefore, by the time settlement discussions take place, the possibility of applying for leniency lapses, as the main investigation has already taken place and consequently the Commission has no further interest in rewarding companies for the information provided under the leniency programme.[326]

Furthermore, from the undertaking's point of view, the incentive to 'race for immunity' and **10.114** self-report beforehand would be reduced if the undertakings were allowed to do so even during the settlement discussions, upon hearing the Commission's allegations and seeing the evidence.

Contrary to the leniency programme, in the settlement procedure each party to the proceed- **10.115** ings contributes in an equivalent way to allow for procedural efficiencies to be obtained. Whether procedural efficiencies can be obtained depends not only on one company, but on the overall behaviour of all parties. It is therefore the Commission who will assess whether the settlement procedure in a given cartel case is likely to result in a settlement and is therefore worthwhile pursuing. If it is not, the Commission will opt for the ordinary procedure.

As the leniency programme and the settlement procedure follow different objectives, **10.116** they must always be regarded as two separate but complementary tools.[327] Since leniency

---

[323] K Mehta, ML Tierno Centella, 'EU Settlement Procedure: Public Enforcement Policy Perspective' in C-D Ehlermann and M Marquis (eds), *European Competition Law Annual 2008: Antitrust Settlements under EC Competition Law* (Hart Publishing 2009) 391, Section II.1.

[324] Commission Notice on immunity from fines and reduction of fines in cartel cases [2006] OJ C298/17, paras 4 and 5. See Ch 6 'Investigation of Cases (I): Leniency Policy'.

[325] J Joshua, K Hugmark, and I Daems, 'What's the Deal? Navigating the European Commission's 2008 Settlement Notice' [2009] The European Antitrust Review 23.

[326] Commission Notice on the conduct of settlement procedures in view of the adoption of Decisions pursuant to Article 7 and Article 23 of Council Regulation (EC) No 1/2003 in cartel cases [2008] OJ C167/1, para 13.

[327] See Commission Notice on the conduct of settlement procedures in view of the adoption of Decisions pursuant to Article 7 and Article 23 of Council Regulation (EC) No 1/2003 in cartel cases [2008] OJ C167/1, para 33.

applications require active cooperation with the Commission, it is likely that the settlement procedure will be particularly successful with cases involving several leniency applicants willing to take the next step in that cooperation.

Settlements and commitments

10.117   Another instrument that needs to be distinguished from settlements pursuant to the settlements package is that of commitments. Commitment decisions are adopted pursuant to Article 9 of Council Regulation 1/2003 and involve only a preliminary assessment raising concrete competition concerns. They do not formally establish an infringement, nor do they impose a fine. In cases where the Commission suspects the existence of illegal behaviour, the commitment decision imposes on companies the commitments offered by the latter to meet the Commission's concerns.[328] Commitments are published in the Official Journal to allow interested third parties to submit comments.[329]

10.118   Commitment decisions simply conclude that 'there are no longer grounds for action by the Commission'[330] and are therefore not suitable for cases where the Commission intends to impose a fine,[331] as is expected for all cartel cases against which the Commission decides to act.[332]

10.119   On the other hand, settlement decisions are adopted pursuant to Articles 7 and 23 of Regulation 1/2003. They establish the existence of an infringement, require its termination and impose a fine.

10.120   Both the commitment and the settlement procedure require cooperation of the parties, but apart from that should be seen as separate proceedings with different objectives that are used for different kinds of infringements.

B. Policy Objectives: Rewards and Advantages

1. Policy objectives

10.121   The settlement procedure has been introduced to allow the Commission to handle more cartel cases in a faster and more efficient way with the same resources. This should help to deliver effective and timely punishment, while increasing overall deterrence.[333]

10.122   The main efficiencies to be achieved with the settlement procedure are two-fold. First, a successful settlement allows the Commission to draft shorter statements of objections and shorter final decisions, because of parties' acknowledgement of liability in their settlement submissions and because substantive contestation in Court is not expected. Furthermore, substantial administrative economies can be achieved as many procedural steps, such as the screening for confidentiality, the processing of substantive replies to adversarial statements

---

[328] See Recital 13 and Art 9 of Reg 1/2003; see MEMO/08/458 'Antitrust: Commission introduces settlement procedure for cartels—frequently asked questions' of 30 June 2008; see Guidelines of 1 September 2006, on the method of setting fines imposed pursuant to Art 23(2)(a) of Reg 1/2003 [2006] OJ C210/2, para 28.

[329] See Art 27(4) of Reg 1/2003.

[330] See Art 9 of Reg 1/2003.

[331] Recital 13 of Reg 1/2003.

[332] See K Mehta and ML Tierno Centella, 'EU Settlement Procedure: Public Enforcement Policy Perspective' in C-D Ehlermann and M Marquis (eds), *European Competition Law Annual 2008: Antitrust Settlements under EC Competition Law* (Hart Publishing 2009) 391, Section II.4. Especially in the case of cartels, it is crucial to set a fine at a deterrent level.

[333] Commission Notice on the conduct of settlement procedures in view of the adoption of Decisions pursuant to Article 7 and Article 23 of Council Regulation (EC) No 1/2003 in cartel cases [2008] OJ C167/1, para 1.

of objections, access to the full file, translations, and the holding of an oral hearing, are of a more limited nature or have become redundant under the settlement procedure.[334]

However, not every cartel case will be open to settlement. The Commission has a broad degree of discretion to determine which cases are suitable in this regard and undertakings are not ultimately obliged to enter into settlement discussions or to settle.[335] **10.123**

The Settlements Notice makes it clear that settlements can only be reached in cartel cases pending before the Commission as of 2 July 2008. Cartels are deliberate and hard-core infringements of Article 101 TFEU and such cases are particularly suitable for settlement because litigation focuses on the probative value of the evidence in the file to establish the existence, extent, and duration of the infringement, the attribution of liability within groups of companies, procedural issues, and the level of the fine (and thus there tends to be little discussion on the more debatable issues of intent, market definition or anticompetitive effects). **10.124**

2. Rewards and advantages

Cooperation with and submission to the settlement procedure is rewarded by a 10 per cent reduction of the fine,[336] which is the first straightforward incentive for companies to settle.[337] The second reward is that the 'increase for deterrence [...] used in their regard will not exceed a multiplication by two.'[338] 'While often overlooked, this second benefit is potentially of much greater significance [especially] for large companies.'[339] **10.125**

As to the fine reduction's underlying rationale, it is important that the settlement procedure should not undermine the crucial importance of deterrence, nor should it diminish the incentive for cartel members to 'blow the whistle'. 'If the settlement of cases were to lead to much lower penalties there is a danger that these two important features of the current system could be harmed.'[340] An amount of 10 per cent leaves enough room between the reduction under the Settlements Notice and the smallest range of reduction of up to 20 per cent under the Leniency Notice.[341] **10.126**

Apart from the reduction of the fine, the settlement procedure gives parties a unique opportunity to be informed of the likely objections and of the evidence which the Commission already has against them at a very early stage and to put forward their arguments in reply.[342] They can also discover the likely range of fines quite some time before the adoption of the final decision.[343] **10.127**

---

[334] See K Mehta and ML Tierno Centella, 'EU Settlement Procedure: Public Enforcement Policy Perspective' in C-D Ehlermann and M Marquis (eds), *European Competition Law Annual 2008: Antitrust Settlements under EC Competition Law* (Hart Publishing 2009) 391, Section II.2.

[335] Commission Notice on the conduct of settlement procedures in view of the adoption of Decisions pursuant to Article 7 and Article 23 of Council Regulation (EC) No 1/2003 in cartel cases [2008] OJ C167/1, para 5.

[336] Commission Notice on the conduct of settlement procedures in view of the adoption of Decisions pursuant to Article 7 and Article 23 of Council Regulation (EC) No 1/2003 in cartel cases [2008] OJ C167/1, para 32.

[337] Because all parties involved in the settlement procedure have to contribute to the same extent for the procedure to be successful, any distinctions in the particular reductions of the fine would have to be considered discriminatory. Therefore, all settling companies receive the same percentage reduction.

[338] Commission Notice on the conduct of settlement procedures in view of the adoption of Decisions pursuant to Article 7 and Article 23 of Council Regulation (EC) No 1/2003 in cartel cases [2008] OJ C167/1, para 32.

[339] DW Hull and MJ Clancy, 'The European Commission's New Settlement Procedure for Cartel Cases: A Defense Counsel's Perspective' in C Gheur and N Petit (eds), *Alternative Enforcement Techniques in EC Competition Law* (Bruylant 2009) 107, 112.

[340] R Whish, Competition Law (6th edn, Oxford University Press 2009) 259.

[341] Leniency Notice, para 26.

[342] See Recital 2 of Reg 622/2008.

[343] Commission Notice on the conduct of settlement procedures in view of the adoption of Decisions pursuant to Article 7 and Article 23 of Council Regulation (EC) No 1/2003 in cartel cases [2008] OJ C167/1, para 16.

Further benefits for the companies lie in putting the procedure behind them more quickly and thus reducing the damage to their reputation due to adverse publicity. This also reduces their legal costs and frees up managerial resources. In addition, the undertakings obtain a unique opportunity to have an impact on the wording which the Commission will use in public statements and possibly reduce the ability for private claimants to pursue follow-on cases, creating further incentives for them to settle.

3. Initiation of proceedings

10.128 Like the ordinary infringement procedure, the settlement procedure commences with an investigation by the Commission pursuant to Article 2(3) of the amended Regulation 773/2004 and Chapter V of Regulation 1/2003.[344] Any undertaking becoming aware of the existence of such an investigation may already indicate at this stage to the Commission its interest in exploring settlements.[345]

10.129 Once the Commission has investigated and qualified the facts of a certain case,[346] it will examine whether the case is suitable for settlement. Paragraph 5 of the Settlements Notice states that the Commission retains a broad degree of discretion in this regard.[347] In assessing whether a particular case is suitable for settlement, the Commission may take the following factors into account:[348]

- the probability of reaching a common understanding regarding the scope of the potential objections within a reasonable timeframe with the parties involved in view of:
  a. the number of parties;
  b. foreseeable conflicting positions on the attribution of liability;
  c. the extent to which the facts are contested;
- the prospect of achieving procedural efficiencies, *inter alia* in view of access to non-confidential documents of the file; and
- the possibility of setting a precedent. This factor may sometimes favour having recourse to the ordinary procedure, to the extent that parties could be less inclined to accept that a case be treated in a novel manner if they consider that they stand a chance of putting forward an alternative defence.

10.130 Paragraph 5 does not set out a definitive list of the factors that the Commission may take into account in considering whether a case is suitable for settlement. By way of example, in international cartels prosecuted by other agencies worldwide, it would be sensible for the Commission to take into account whether all parties have already settled the case in

---

[344] As a consequence, the Commission's investigative tools are identical under the settlement procedure and the ordinary infringement procedure.

[345] MEMO/08/458 'Antitrust: Commission introduces settlement procedure for cartels – frequently asked questions' of 30 June 2008, 3.

[346] K Mehta and ML Tierno Centella, 'EU Settlement Procedure: Public Enforcement Policy Perspective' in C-D Ehlermann and M Marquis (eds), *European Competition Law Annual 2008: Antitrust Settlements under EC Competition Law* (Hart Publishing 2009) 391, Section IV.3.1.

[347] It is to be noted here that the Commission retains a broad degree of discretion throughout the entire settlement procedure as it may further decide whether or not to engage in settlement discussions and as it may at any time until the adoption of the final decision decide to discontinue the settlement attempts and revert back to the ordinary procedure (see, to this end, paras 5 and 29 Settlements Notice). The extent to which the Commission 'has the whip hand' is not uncontroversial. See JD Cook, 'Negotiated Settlements under EC Competition Law: A Judicial Perspective' in *European Competition Law Annual 2008: Antitrust settlements under EC Competition Law* (Hart Publishing 2009) 262, and more generally the responses to the public consultation published at <http://ec.europa.eu/competition/cartels/legislation/cartels_settlements/index.html>.

[348] Commission Notice on the conduct of settlement procedures in view of the adoption of Decisions pursuant to Article 7 and Article 23 of Council Regulation (EC) No 1/2003 in cartel cases [2008] OJ C167/1, para 5. On the other hand, parties having participated in settlement discussions may also decide to discontinue settlement attempts until they make the choice to introduce a settlement submission, turning back to the ordinary procedure (see para 10.132).

jurisdictions applying criminal sanctions to individuals, since the timing of the Commission settlement proceedings could be compromised if the parties do not feel comfortable about admitting to their infringement in a settlement submission before having settled the case elsewhere. Following paragraph 6 of the Settlements Notice, when the Commission considers a case to be suitable for settlement, it will explore all parties' interests in settling. Thus, at this stage the Commission will typically entertain informal contacts with the parties' lawyers to assess whether settlement discussions are viable.[349] Often, lawyers signal to the Commission their interest in participating in eventual settlement discussions once they see that the investigation is advancing with regard to their clients.

Once the prospects of a successful settlement are good, the Commission will initiate proceedings **10.131** pursuant to Article 10a of the amended Regulation 773/2004 and Article 11(6) of Regulation 1/2003.[350] This entails that, as in the ordinary infringement procedure, once the decision to initiate proceedings is taken, the Commission becomes the only competition authority competent to apply Article 101 TFEU.[351] Whenever the Commission initiates proceedings against two or more parties within the same undertaking, these parties are required to appoint a joint representative to act on their behalf during the subsequent settlement discussions.[352]

The initiation of proceedings formally identifies the parties to the proceedings and thereby **10.132** opens the window for settlement discussions and settlement submissions, which closes with the adoption of the statement of objections. With its decision to initiate proceedings, the Commission will set a time limit of no less than two weeks within which parties must confirm in writing their interest in engaging in settlement discussions.[353] This written declaration neither amounts to an admission by the parties that they have participated in an infringement or are liable for it,[354] nor creates a duty for the parties concerned to settle.[355] In addition, pursuant to paragraph 13 of the Settlements Notice, the time limit referred to previously also constitutes the deadline for undertakings to make leniency applications under the Leniency Notice; in other words, 'the window for leniency applications closes before the window for settlement discussions opens'.[356]

---

[349] D Gabathuler, 'The Emerging Practice of EU Cartel Settlement' [2011] Mlex Magazine 2011 47.

[350] Pursuant to para 9 of the Settlements Notice, the Commission has to take the decision to initiate proceedings 'no later than the date on which it either issues a statement of objections or requests the parties to express in writing their interest to engage in settlement discussions, whichever is the earlier'. Note that if the Commission decides to pursue the settlement procedure, the latter date, namely the request to the parties to express their interest in settling, will constitute the deadline for taking the decision to initiate proceedings, since, as will be seen below, in the settlement procedure the issuing of a statement of objections takes place only towards the end of the procedure.

[351] Article 11(6) of Reg 1/2003 and Commission Notice on the conduct of settlement procedures in view of the adoption of Decisions pursuant to Article 7 and Article 23 of Council Regulation (EC) No 1/2003 in cartel cases [2008] OJ C167/1, para 10.

[352] Article 10(a)(1) of the amended Reg 733/2004 and Commission Notice on the conduct of settlement procedures in view of the adoption of Decisions pursuant to Article 7 and Article 23 of Council Regulation (EC) No 1/2003 in cartel cases [2008] OJ C167/1, para 12.

[353] Articles 10(a)(1) and 17(3) of the amended Reg 733/2004 and Commission Notice on the conduct of settlement procedures in view of the adoption of Decisions pursuant to Article 7 and Article 23 of Council Regulation (EC) No 1/2003 in cartel cases [2008] OJ C167/1, para 11.

[354] Commission Notice on the conduct of settlement procedures in view of the adoption of Decisions pursuant to Article 7 and Article 23 of Council Regulation (EC) No 1/2003 in cartel cases [2008] OJ C167/1, para 11.

[355] ML Tierno Centella, 'The New Settlement Procedure in Selected Cartel Cases', (2008) 3 Competition Policy Newsletter 30, 32. See also Commission Notice on the conduct of settlement procedures in view of the adoption of Decisions pursuant to Article 7 and Article 23 of Council Regulation (EC) No 1/2003 in cartel cases [2008] OJ C167/1, para 11.

[356] S Holmes and P Girardet, 'Settling Cartel Cases: Recent Developments in Europe' [2011] International Comparative Legal Guide to: Cartels and Leniency 2.

C. Settlement Discussions

1. Nature and conduct of discussions

10.133   Settlement discussions occur on a bilateral basis[357] between the Commission's DG COMP and the undertaking(s) wishing to settle[358] and aim at allowing both the Commission and the parties to assess whether settling is beneficial to them[359] and thereafter to exchange arguments—and eventually reach common ground—on potential objections, liability and the range of fines.[360] Such discussions are pursued on a strictly confidential basis.[361] Parties 'may not disclose to any third party in any jurisdiction the contents of the discussions or of the documents which they have had access to in view of settlement',[362] unless authorized beforehand by the Commission.[363] Participation in settlement discussions does not imply any admission of illegal conduct or duty to settle for the parties concerned.

10.134   Settlement discussions are generally structured around a minimum of three formal meetings with each undertaking, although there may be a larger number, including also technical meetings or calls. These meetings are grouped in rounds, which is why it is more appropriate to speak about three rounds of meetings. However, there may be more meetings of a technical nature, including phone conferences, between the settling parties and the Commission's services,[364] which are largely contemporaneous for all of them. During the first meeting or round of meetings, the Commission will present the parties with an oral presentation of the case, stating the preliminary views of the case team on how a future statement of objections[365] would look, thereby outlining the key objections of its case and referring to some essential evidence supporting them. In preparation of the second round of meetings, the parties will have access to all of the evidence in support of the objections, including that which is used to the benefit of the companies.[366] Parties will be given the opportunity to respond to the case as initially outlined by the Commission between meeting rounds or at the second round of meetings, when the Commission will present its views on the arguments raised by the parties.

---

[357] For the Commission, the reasoning behind the bilateral nature of settlement discussions is 'to focus efficiently on the concerns of the relevant undertaking in a relatively short sequence of meetings, without having to get into comparative exercises.' See ML Tierno Centella, 'The New Settlement Procedure in Selected Cartel Cases' (2008) 3 Competition Policy Newsletter, 32.

[358] Commission Notice on the conduct of settlement procedures in view of the adoption of Decisions pursuant to Article 7 and Article 23 of Council Regulation (EC) No 1/2003 in cartel cases [2008] OJ C167/1, para 14.

[359] K Mehta and ML Tierno Centella, 'Settlement Procedure in EU Cartel Cases' [2008] June Competition Law International 13.

[360] Section III of final 'Overview' section of the Commission Notice on the conduct of settlement procedures in view of the adoption of Decisions pursuant to Article 7 and Article 23 of Council Regulation (EC) No 1/2003 in cartel cases [2008] OJ C167/1.

[361] Article 10a(2) of the amended Reg 773/2004.

[362] Commission Notice on the conduct of settlement procedures in view of the adoption of Decisions pursuant to Article 7 and Article 23 of Council Regulation (EC) No 1/2003 in cartel cases [2008] OJ C167/1, para 7.

[363] Furthermore, pursuant to para 7 of the Settlements Notice [2008] OJ C167/1, any breach of this confidentiality requirement may lead the Commission to disregard an undertaking's request to follow the settlement procedure and may also constitute an aggravating circumstance within the meaning of point 28 of the Guidelines on fines.

[364] C Cook and M Piergiovanni, 'Implications of Settling an EU Cartel Investigation for a Prospective Civil Damages Defendant: Bad or Good?' (2011) 4(2) Global Competition Litigation Review 62.

[365] See L Ortiz Blanco, A Givaja Sanz, and A Lamadrid De Pablo, 'Fine Arts in Brussels: Punishment and Settlement of Cartel Cases under EC Competition Law', in: *Antitrust between EC law and national law—Antitrust fra diritto nazionale e diritto comunitario*-22–23 May/Maggio 2008–Tome 6, (2009, Bruylant), 155.

[366] Commission Notice on the conduct of settlement procedures in view of the adoption of Decisions pursuant to Article 7 and Article 23 of Council Regulation (EC) No 1/2003 in cartel cases [2008] OJ C167/1, para 15 and Art 10a(2) of the amended Reg 773/2004.

During the third round of settlement meetings, the Commission will disclose the final parameters of its case and the fine range it envisages imposing on the parties composing the undertaking concerned.[367] The Commission does not disclose the fines imposed on other parties, except for the obvious inference that any successful immunity applicant will not pay a fine.

The Commission retains a broad degree of discretion in determining the appropriateness **10.135** and speed of the settlement discussions.[368] This means that the Commission does not only determine the sequence and order of the settlement discussions but also the timing of the disclosure of information to the parties, including the evidence in the Commission file used to establish the envisaged objections and the potential fine.[369] However, parties are guaranteed that they may not be asked to make any settlement submission without having had the opportunity to have access to all of the evidence to be used in the statement of objections and decision settling the case.

The Commission has been keen to stress that settlement discussions do not imply negotia **10.136** tions[370] and are thus dissimilar to the American plea-bargaining system.[371] However, in its Frequently Asked Questions Press Release, the Commission equally admits that 'parties will also be heard effectively on the framework of the settlement procedure and parties will therefore have the opportunity to influence the Commission's objections through argument',[372] thereby possibly even persuading the Commission to modify its initial stance.[373] How in practice 'negotiations' differ from 'influencing through argument' is nevertheless debatable and it seems that the line between these two concepts, if it exists, is wafer-thin.[374] The Commission refuses, using the term 'negotiations' to stress that it engages in technical discussions and exchanges of views on matters of fact and law, such as the value of the evidence and

---

[367] C Cook and M Piergiovanni, 'Implications of Settling an EU Cartel Investigation for a Prospective Civil Damages Defendant: Bad or Good?' (2011) 4(2) Global Competition Litigation Review 62.

[368] Commission Notice on the conduct of settlement procedures in view of the adoption of Decisions pursuant to Article 7 and Article 23 of Council Regulation (EC) No 1/2003 in cartel cases [2008] OJ C167/1, para 15. See also Art 10a(2) of the amended Reg 773/2004.

[369] Commission Notice on the conduct of settlement procedures in view of the adoption of Decisions pursuant to Article 7 and Article 23 of Council Regulation (EC) No 1/2003 in cartel cases [2008] OJ C167/1, para 15. As to the 'potential fine', n 1 to para 15 of the Settlements Notice specifies that this reference 'affords the Commission services the possibility to inform the parties concerned by settlement discussions of an estimate of their potential fine in view of the guidance contained in the Guidelines on fines, the provisions of this Notice and the Leniency Notice, where applicable'.

[370] Commission Notice on the conduct of settlement procedures in view of the adoption of Decisions pursuant to Article 7 and Article 23 of Council Regulation (EC) No 1/2003 in cartel cases [2008] OJ C167/1, para 2; European Commission, MEMO/08/458 'Antitrust: Commission introduces settlement procedure for cartels – frequently asked questions' of 30 June 2008, 1; K Mehta and ML Tierno Centella, 'EU Settlement Procedure: Public Enforcement Perspective' [2008] European Competition Law Annual 391.

[371] A Stephan, 'The Direct Settlement of EC Cartel Cases' (2009) 58 International Comparative Law Quarterly 627; A O'Brien, 'Cartel Settlements in the US and EU: Similarities, Differences & Remaining Questions' [2008] European Competition Law Annual 182–3.

[372] See Commission Press Release IP/07/1608 'Antitrust: Commission calls for comments on a draft legislative package to introduce settlement procedure for cartels' of 26 October 2007 and European Commission MEMO/07/433 'Antitrust: Commission calls for comments on a draft legislative package to introduce settlement procedure for cartels—frequently asked questions' of 26 October 2007. See also European Commission MEMO/08/458 'Antitrust: Commission introduces settlement procedure for cartels – frequently asked questions' of 30 June 2008, 1.

[373] K Mehta and ML Tierno Centella, 'EU Settlement Procedure: Public Enforcement Perspective' [2008] European Competition Law Annual, Section IV.3.4.

[374] See further L Ortiz Blanco, A Givaja Sanz, and A Lamadrid De Pablo, 'Fine Arts in Brussels: Punishment and Settlement of Cartel Cases under EC Competition Law', in: *Antitrust between EC law and national law— Antitrust fra diritto nazionale e diritto comunitario* 22–23 May/Maggio 2008 Tome 6, (Bruylant 2009), 155, where the analogy is drawn with Magritte's famous 'ceci n'est pas une pipe' painting. See also M Schinkel, 'Bargaining in the Shadow of the European Settlement Procedure for Cartels' Amsterdam Centre for Law & Economics Working Paper No 2010-17, 25.

the basis for its allegations, so that the parties can present their defence, but the Commission should not be expected to engage in any bargaining to accommodate the fine or the facts to the wishes of the party. Compared to the ordinary procedure, the contact between the Commission and the parties is closer and a change of mind is already possible at the stage of preparation of the statement of objections, influencing the content of the latter itself.

10.137 Settlement discussions are conducted on the basis of a settlement submission template in order to facilitate agreement on the wording of the subsequent settlement submission.[375] When a common understanding can be reached between the parties 'regarding the scope of the potential objections and the estimate of the range of likely fines to be imposed by the Commission'[376] and the Commission takes the preliminary view that procedural efficiencies are likely to be achieved in view of the progress made overall during the procedure, the Commission may grant a final (extendable) time limit of at least fifteen working days for the introduction of parties' settlement submissions.[377] Should no agreement be reached or should the parties concerned fail to introduce a settlement submission, the procedure will revert back to the ordinary infringement procedure.[378]

2. Parties' procedural rights: access to the file and hearing

10.138 The settling parties cannot be asked to formally acknowledge their guilt or accept a potential range of fines in subsequent settlement submissions unless they have been given the possibility during the settlement discussions of exercising effectively their procedural rights. For this purpose, the settlement procedure offers parties the opportunity to have access to the file and to be heard, albeit to a more limited extent than in the ordinary infringement procedure.

10.139 With regard to the right to information, the settlement procedure allows for early[379] but limited access to the file. The Commission will disclose information 'in a timely manner as settlement discussions progress'[380] and will provide the parties with information concerning 'the essential elements taken into consideration so far, such as the facts alleged, the classification of those facts, the gravity and duration of the alleged cartel, the attribution of liability, an estimation of the range of likely fines, as well as the evidence used to establish the potential objections'.[381]

10.140 Furthermore, parties will be provided with a list of all accessible documents in the case file and, upon their request, the Commission may grant access to non-confidential versions of any specified accessible document listed therein, 'in so far as this is justified for the purpose

---

[375] K Mehta and ML Tierno Centella, 'Settlement Procedure in EU Cartel Cases' (2008) June Competition Law International 14.

[376] Commission Notice on the conduct of settlement procedures in view of the adoption of Decisions pursuant to Article 7 and Article 23 of Council Regulation (EC) No 1/2003 in cartel cases [2008] OJ C167/1, para 17.

[377] Articles 10a(2) and 17(3) of the amended Reg 773/2004.

[378] Commission Notice on the conduct of settlement procedures in view of the adoption of Decisions pursuant to Article 7 and Article 23 of Council Regulation (EC) No 1/2003 in cartel cases [2008] OJ C167/1, paras 5 and 19. See also S Holmes and P Girardet, 'Settling Cartel Cases: Recent Developments in Europe' [2011] International Comparative Legal Guide to: Cartels and Leniency 3.

[379] Namely before any statement of objections is sent to the parties concerned. See Van Bael and Bellis, *Competition Law of the European Community* (5th edn, Kluwer Law International 2010) 1182.

[380] Commission Notice on the conduct of settlement procedures in view of the adoption of Decisions pursuant to Article 7 and Article 23 of Council Regulation (EC) No 1/2003 in cartel cases [2008] OJ C167/1, para 15.

[381] Commission Notice on the conduct of settlement procedures in view of the adoption of Decisions pursuant to Article 7 and Article 23 of Council Regulation (EC) No 1/2003 in cartel cases [2008] OJ C167/1, para 16 in conjunction with Arts 10a(2) and 15(1a) of Reg 773/2004. This makes the access to the file under the settlement procedure more limited than under the ordinary infringement procedure, where parties are granted access to all of the non-confidential documents making up the Commission's file.

of enabling the party to ascertain its position regarding a time period or any other aspect of the cartel'[382] and where this disclosure 'does not jeopardize the overall efficiency sought with the settlement procedure'.[383] The previously mentioned access to information generally takes place after the first settlement meeting[384] and is only available *before* the Commission sets a time limit for the introduction of the settlement submissions, unless the subsequently issued statement of objections does not reflect the contents of parties' settlement submissions.[385]

With regard to the right to be heard, during the settlement discussions the parties will be **10.141** allowed to assert their views on the Commission's objections and on the evidence supporting these.[386] If the parties manage to convince the Commission, some of the initial objections may be dropped or modified thereby potentially altering the fine range.[387] Furthermore, pursuant to paragraph 18 of the Settlements Notice, parties may at any time during the settlement procedure call upon the Hearing Officer for issues that might arise in relation to due process.

Some commentators have taken the view that in the EU settlement procedure, the right to be **10.142** heard is 'formally [as opposed to legally] affected'.[388] This is because, on the one hand, parties are (legally) heard during the settlement discussions and through their settlement submissions.[389] On the other hand, when parties introduce their settlement submissions, they must declare that they have already been individually heard to their satisfaction and, therefore, that they will not ask to participate in a collective hearing if the subsequent statement of objections reflects the contents of their settlement submissions.[390] Should a party consider that it has not been heard to its satisfaction, this would of course mean that it is not ready to settle on terms agreeable to the Commission. In that scenario, the ordinary procedure would apply instead. In any event, the right to participate in a collective oral hearing is not always exercised by the parties, even in the ordinary procedure. It is submitted that in the settlement

---

[382] Commission Notice on the conduct of settlement procedures in view of the adoption of Decisions pursuant to Article 7 and Article 23 of Council Regulation (EC) No 1/2003 in cartel cases [2008] OJ C167/1, para 16. This could for instance be the case when a party engaged in settlement discussions genuinely lacks information about its own past behaviour or about a certain aspect of the alleged cartel. See ML Tierno Centella, 'The New Settlement Procedure in Selected Cartel Cases' (2008) 3 Competition Policy Newsletter 33.

[383] MEMO/08/458 'Antitrust: Commission introduces settlement procedure for cartels—frequently asked questions' of 30 June 2008, 4. With regard to these files, the undertakings' lawyers will be permitted to take notes but not to copy documents. This review will be limited in time. See I Daems, K Hugmark, and J Joshua, 'Cartels and Leniency' [2011] The European Antitrust Review 3.

[384] C Cook and M Piergiovanni, 'Implications of Settling an EU Cartel Investigation for a Prospective Civil Damages Defendant: Bad or Good?' (2011) 4(2) Global Competition Litigation Review 62.

[385] Articles 10a(2) and 15(1a) Reg 733/2004 and Commission Notice on the conduct of settlement procedures in view of the adoption of Decisions pursuant to Article 7 and Article 23 of Council Regulation (EC) No 1/2003 in cartel cases [2008] OJ C167/1, para 27. It is here that another difference between the settlement procedure and the ordinary infringement procedure can be found, as the right to access to the file (and, as will be seen below, the right to be heard) are only available before the issuing of a formal statement of objections, whilst under the ordinary infringement procedure, these procedural rights can be exercised after parties have received a statement of objections.

[386] Commission Notice on the conduct of settlement procedures in view of the adoption of Decisions pursuant to Article 7 and Article 23 of Council Regulation (EC) No 1/2003 in cartel cases [2008] OJ C167/1, para 16.

[387] K Mehta and ML Tierno Centella, 'Settlement Procedure in EU Cartel Cases' (2008) June Competition Law International 13. See also the discussion on the prohibition of 'negotiation' at para 10.136.

[388] Eg, Van Bael and Bellis, *Competition Law of the European Community* (5th edn, Kluwer Law International 2010) 1183.

[389] Recital 2 of Reg 622/2008 and Commission Notice on the conduct of settlement procedures in view of the adoption of Decisions pursuant to Article 7 and Article 23 of Council Regulation (EC) No 1/2003 in cartel cases [2008] OJ C167/1, para 25.

[390] Article 12(2) of Reg 733/2004 and Commission Notice on the conduct of settlement procedures in view of the adoption of Decisions pursuant to Article 7 and Article 23 of Council Regulation (EC) No 1/2003 in cartel cases [2008] OJ C167/1, para 28.

procedure, a hearing after having issued a statement of objections reflecting a party's settlement submission would be an unnecessary, redundant formality, deprived of any purpose.

3. Settlement submission

10.143 Upon the successful completion of the settlement discussions, the parties must make a formal request to settle in the form of a settlement submission.[391] Pursuant to Article 10a(2) of the amended Regulation 733/2004 and paragraph 20 of the Settlements Notice, settlement submissions, which can in principle be made both orally and in writing,[392] must contain the following five features:

(i) an acknowledgement in clear and unequivocal terms of the parties' liability for the infringement, which is summarily described as regards its object, its possible implementation, the main facts, their legal definition, including the party's role and the duration of their participation in the infringement in accordance with the results of the settlement discussions;

(ii) an indication of the maximum amount of the fine which the parties foresee being imposed by the Commission and which the parties would accept under a settlement procedure;

(iii) the parties' confirmation that they have been sufficiently informed of the objections which the Commission envisages raising against them and that they have been given sufficient opportunity to make their views known to the Commission;

(iv) the parties' confirmation that, in view of the above, they do not envisage requesting access to the file or requesting being heard again in an oral hearing, unless the Commission does not reflect their settlement submissions in the statement of objections and the decision;

(v) the parties' agreement to receive the statement of objections and the final decision pursuant to Articles 7 and 23 of Regulation 1/2003 in an agreed official language of the European Union.[393]

10.144 Given the parties' recognition of their participation and liability for the infringement and their choice of putting an end to the exercise of two of their formal procedural rights (having further access to the file and participating in an oral hearing), settlement submissions can be seen as the core element of the settlement procedure.[394]

10.145 Under paragraph 21 of the Settlements Notice, the acknowledgments and confirmations provided by the parties in view of settlement constitute the expression of their commitment to cooperate in the expeditious handling of the case following the settlement procedure.[395] However, it is important to stress that those acknowledgments and confirmations are conditional upon the Commission meeting their settlement submission, including the anticipated maximum amount of the fine, in the subsequent statement of objections and in the final decision.[396] If either the statement of objections or final decision goes beyond what has been acknowledged and

---

[391] Commission Notice on the conduct of settlement procedures in view of the adoption of Decisions pursuant to Article 7 and Article 23 of Council Regulation (EC) No 1/2003 in cartel cases [2008] OJ C167/1, para 20.

[392] Commission Notice on the conduct of settlement procedures in view of the adoption of Decisions pursuant to Article 7 and Article 23 of Council Regulation (EC) No 1/2003 in cartel cases [2008] OJ C167/1, para 38.

[393] Article 10a(2) Reg 773/2003 and Commission Notice on the conduct of settlement procedures in view of the adoption of Decisions pursuant to Article 7 and Article 23 of Council Regulation (EC) No 1/2003 in cartel cases [2008] OJ C167/1, para 20.

[394] Van Bael and Bellis, *Competition Law of the European Community* (5th edn, Kluwer Law International 2010), 1176–7.

[395] Commission Notice on the conduct of settlement procedures in view of the adoption of Decisions pursuant to Article 7 and Article 23 of Council Regulation (EC) No 1/2003 in cartel cases [2008] OJ C167/1, para 21.

[396] Commission Notice on the conduct of settlement procedures in view of the adoption of Decisions pursuant to Article 7 and Article 23 of Council Regulation (EC) No 1/2003 in cartel cases [2008] OJ C167/1, para 21.

agreed upon in the settlement submission, 'the party concerned is no longer bound by its submission, and the acknowledgments provided cannot be used in evidence against any of the parties to the proceedings'.[397] In other words, unless the Commission's subsequent statement of objections and final decision do not reflect the settlement submissions, the latter cannot be withdrawn unilaterally.[398]

4. Statement of objections and reply

Pursuant to Article 10(1) of the amended Regulation 773/2004, the issuing of a statement of objections is mandatory for the Commission before adopting any final decision, including a settlement decision.[399] However, statements of objections drawn up in the framework of the settlement procedure differ from those drawn up in the ordinary infringement procedure in two main respects. **10.146**

First of all, statements of objections drawn up in the settlement procedure are much shorter than those issued in the ordinary infringement procedure, as the Settlements Notice specifies that they are meant to contain the information necessary to enable the parties to corroborate that they reflect their settlement submissions and provide a clear view of what the subsequent settlement decision will look like.[400] **10.147**

Secondly, statements of objections are issued at a much later stage in the settlement procedure than in the ordinary infringement procedure, where statements of objections are issued at the beginning of the procedure, at the latest with the decision to initiate formal proceedings.[401] This last paragraph need not necessarily be disadvantageous for parties involved. On the one hand, in the settlement procedure, parties will formally receive the allegations and evidence against them at a later stage than is 'ordinarily' the case. However, as noted earlier, at the start of the settlement discussions, the Commission will in practice be relying on the Commission services' view of the case, which some have called a 'mini-oral Statement of Objections',[402] outlining the main evidence in its file as well as the envisaged objections and **10.148**

---

[397] K Mehta and ML Tierno Centella, 'EU Settlement Procedure: Public Enforcement Policy Perspective' in C-D Ehlermann and M Marquis (eds), *European Competition Law Annual 2008: Antitrust Settlements under EC Competition Law* (Hart Publishing 2009) 391, Section IV.3.5. See also paras 27 and 29 of the Settlements Notice.

[398] Commission Notice on the conduct of settlement procedures in view of the adoption of Decisions pursuant to Article 7 and Article 23 of Council Regulation (EC) No 1/2003 in cartel cases [2008] OJ C167/1, para 22. This para further clarifies that a statement of objections is deemed to have endorsed the settlement submissions if it reflects their contents on the issues mentioned in para 20(a) of the Settlements Notice relating to the various aspects of parties' liability for the infringement. Additionally, for a final decision to be deemed to have reflected the settlement submissions, it should also impose a fine which does not exceed the maximum amount indicated therein.

[399] See also Commission Notice on the conduct of settlement procedures in view of the adoption of Decisions pursuant to Article 7 and Article 23 of Council Regulation (EC) No 1/2003 in cartel cases [2008] OJ C167/1, para 23.

[400] Commission Notice on the conduct of settlement procedures in view of the adoption of Decisions pursuant to Article 7 and Article 23 of Council Regulation (EC) No 1/2003 in cartel cases [2008] OJ C167/1, para 23, n 1. Thus, 'a settlement Statement of Objections and decision include a concise and "high level" description of the infringing conduct, with few (or no) references to specific meetings, their participants, the details of the discussions that took place, and/or of the agreements that were reached. These documents also typically do not include the names of specific customers and include fewer references to documents in the Commission's case file than ordinary Statement of Objections and decisions.' See C Cook and M Piergiovanni, 'Implications of settling an EU cartel investigation for a prospective civil damages defendant: bad or good?' (2011) 4(2) Global Competition Litigation Review 65–6.

[401] Article 2(1) of Reg 773/2004.

[402] See L Ortiz Blanco, A Givaja Sanz, and A Lamadrid De Pablo, 'Fine Arts in Brussels: Punishment and Settlement of Cartel Cases under EC Competition Law', in: *Antitrust between EC law and national law—Antitrust fra diritto nazionale e diritto comunitario* 22–23 May/Maggio 2008 Tome 6, (Bruylant 2009), 155: 'each of the settlement candidates will be orally informed of the essential elements taken into consideration so far in order to enable them to *"assert their views of the potential objections against them"* as well as to

the potential fine.[403] Furthermore, as specified in paragraph 25 of the Settlements Notice, by introducing a formal settlement request in the form of a settlement submission prior to the notification of the statement of objections, the parties concerned enable the Commission to effectively take their views into account already when drafting the statement of objections,[404] rather than only before the consultation of the Advisory Committee or before the adoption of the final decision.[405]

10.149 Hence, if the parties' settlement submissions mirror the agreement reached during the settlement discussions, the Commission should normally issue a short, streamlined statement of objections which will reflect their content.[406] In this case, within a time limit of at least two weeks the parties should reply 'by simply confirming (in unequivocal terms) that the Statement of Objections corresponds to the contents of their settlement submissions and that they therefore remain committed to follow the settlement procedure'.[407] Should a party fail to reply within the stipulated time period, the Commission will note the party's breach of commitment and may disregard its request to follow the settlement procedure.[408]

10.150 However, the Commission preserves the right to issue a statement of objections which does not reflect the parties' settlement submission.[409] In this case, the parties would revert to the ordinary infringement procedure, the involved undertakings would be able to present their full defence anew, and they would no longer be bound by their settlement submissions which could not be used in evidence against them.[410]

5. Commission decision

10.151 Upon the parties' positive replies to the statement of objections, the Commission may, after consulting the Advisory Committee,[411] proceed immediately to the adoption of a final, streamlined, and short settlement decision[412] pursuant to Articles 7 and/or 23 of Regulation 1/2003.[413] This decision will be accompanied by a report from the Hearing Officer, as occurs in the ordinary infringement procedure.

---

allow them to decide whether or not to pursue a settlement procedure. In practice this means that at this stage the Commission services would be relying on a *"mini-oral Statement of Objections"*.'

[403] Commission Notice on the conduct of settlement procedures in view of the adoption of Decisions pursuant to Article 7 and Article 23 of Council Regulation (EC) No 1/2003 in cartel cases [2008] OJ C167/1, para 15.

[404] See also Recital 2 of Reg 622/2008.

[405] This being required by Art 11(1) of Reg 773/2004 and Art 27(1) of Reg 1/2003.

[406] K Mehta and ML Tierno Centella, 'Settlement Procedure in EU Cartel Cases' (2008) June Competition Law International 15.

[407] Commission Notice on the conduct of settlement procedures in view of the adoption of Decisions pursuant to Article 7 and Article 23 of Council Regulation (EC) No 1/2003 in cartel cases [2008] OJ C167/1, para 26 and Art 10(3) of Reg 773/2004.

[408] Commission Notice on the conduct of settlement procedures in view of the adoption of Decisions pursuant to Article 7 and Article 23 of Council Regulation (EC) No 1/2003 in cartel cases [2008] OJ C167/1, para 26.

[409] Commission Notice on the conduct of settlement procedures in view of the adoption of Decisions pursuant to Article 7 and Article 23 of Council Regulation (EC) No 1/2003 in cartel cases [2008] OJ C167/1, para 27.

[410] Commission Notice on the conduct of settlement procedures in view of the adoption of Decisions pursuant to Article 7 and Article 23 of Council Regulation (EC) No 1/2003 in cartel cases [2008] OJ C167/1, para 27, in conjunction with Arts 10(2), 12(1) and 15(1) of Reg 773/2004.

[411] Article 10a(3) of Reg 773/2004 in conjunction with para 28 Commission Notice on the conduct of settlement procedures in view of the adoption of Decisions pursuant to Article 7 and Article 23 of Council Regulation (EC) No 1/2003 in cartel cases [2008] OJ C167/1 and Art 14 of Reg 1/2003.

[412] Van Bael and Bellis, *Competition Law of the European Community* (5th edn, Kluwer Law International 2010), 1178–9.

[413] Paragraph 28 of the Settlements Notice specifies that this implies that no oral hearing or access to the file may be requested by those parties once their settlement submissions have been reflected by the statement of objections, in line with Arts 12(2) and 15(1a) of Reg 773/2004.

However, the Commission preserves the right to depart from its statement of objections **10.152** in its final decision, either in view of the opinion provided by the Advisory Committee or because of other appropriate considerations bearing in mind the Commission's ultimate decision-making autonomy.[414] Should the Commission choose to go down this path,[415] the parties would revert to the ordinary infringement procedure. Pursuant to paragraph 29 of the Settlements Notice, this means that the Commission must inform the parties of its decision and serve on them a new statement of objections. Parties can exercise their full rights of defence anew and the acknowledgments made by them in their settlement submissions would be deemed to have been withdrawn and cannot be used in evidence against them.

Upon successful completion of the settlement procedure, parties receive a 10 per cent fine **10.153** reduction applied to the normal fine resulting from the Commission's Fining Guidelines.[416] Furthermore, any specific increase for deterrence will be limited to multiplication by two, double the original fine. All parties settling a case with the Commission will be given the same percentage reduction.[417] Where applicable, this 10 per cent reduction will be cumulative with the fine reduction under the Commission's leniency programme.[418]

Any final settlement decision is subject to judicial review under Article 263 TFEU. Moreover, **10.154** the ECJ has unlimited jurisdiction to review decisions on fines adopted pursuant to Article 23 of Regulation 1/2003.[419] However, the usefulness of such review is critically questioned in view of the parties' recognition of the infringement and of their liability and acceptance of the reduced fine.[420]

D. Confidentiality Issues in Settlement Cases

1. Confidentiality issues

Information relating to settlements is protected in a similar way as information under the **10.155** Leniency Notice, where the leniency applicant is protected from discovery in civil actions for damages. Settlements are conducted behind closed doors and will result in a more streamlined decision, possibly not giving as much detail on the internal workings of a cartel as a fully fledged

[414] Commission Notice on the conduct of settlement procedures in view of the adoption of Decisions pursuant to Article 7 and Article 23 of Council Regulation (EC) No 1/2003 in cartel cases [2008] OJ C167/1, para 29. For instance, the Commission is deemed to have departed from its statement of objections if it imposes a fine in its final decision which exceeds the maximum amount indicated by the parties in their settlement submissions. See Van Bael and Bellis, *Competition Law of the European Community* (5th edn, Kluwer Law International 2010), 1178.
[415] Even though the Commission itself acknowledges that 'this should occur only exceptionally if the usefulness of the settlement instrument is to be preserved.' See European Commission, MEMO/08/458 'Anti trust: Commission introduces settlement procedure for cartels—frequently asked questions' of 30 June 2008.
[416] Commission Notice on the conduct of settlement procedures in view of the adoption of Decisions pursuant to Article 7 and Article 23 of Council Regulation (EC) No 1/2003 in cartel cases [2008] OJ C167/1, para 32. See Guidelines on the method of setting fines imposed pursuant to Article 23(2)(a) of Regulation 1/2003, [2006] OJ C210/2.
[417] K Mehta and ML Tierno Centella, 'Settlement Procedure in EU Cartel Xases' (2008) June Competition Law International 15.
[418] Commission Notice on the conduct of settlement procedures in view of the adoption of Decisions pursuant to Article 7 and Article 23 of Council Regulation (EC) No 1/2003 in cartel cases [2008] OJ C167/1, para 33.
[419] Commission Notice on the conduct of settlement procedures in view of the adoption of Decisions pursuant to Article 7 and Article 23 of Council Regulation (EC) No 1/2003 in cartel cases [2008] OJ C167/1, para 41.
[420] D Waelbroeck, 'Le développement en droit européen de la concurrence des solutions négociées (engagements, non-contestations des faits et transactions): que va-t-il rester aux juges?' [2008] GCLC Working Paper 1/08 23–4; W Wils: 'The Use of Settlements in Public Antitrust Enforcement' in *European Competition Law Annual* (2008) 42. Van Bael and Bellis, *Competition Law of the European Community* (5th edn, Kluwer Law International 2010), 1180–1. S-P Brankin, 'All Settled: Where are the European Commission's Proposals

decision would. Access to settlement submissions is also very restricted.[421] It must be noted that the confidentiality concerning documents and written or recorded statements in the context of the Settlements Notice is retained even after the settlement decision has been taken.[422]

10.156 From a prospective settling party's perspective, it has been argued that having only limited access to the Commission's file during the settlement procedure may deprive the company involved of the ability to access potentially exculpatory documents from other cartel participants that could be present in the undisclosed part of the Commission's file.[423] However, the Commission states otherwise, indicating that documents that are obviously exculpatory will be provided to the parties, and used by the Commission. The parties are usually aware of what they have done and will try to submit arguments and documents that benefit their case. In any event, if they are not convinced, they are not obliged to settle.

10.157 Commissioner Almunia has often declared that the Commission is determined to protect both leniency and settlement submissions. It remains to be seen whether the Commission will be able to continue to resist disclosure in the context of discovery. In the corresponding context of the leniency programme, a number of decisions adopted by the Commission in which it refused to disclose documents that had been provided to it by leniency applicants, were appealed to the GC. Thus, in *CDC Hydrogen Peroxide v Commission*,[424] the GC annulled the Commission decision to disclose certain documents on the ground that disclosure of the statement of contents undermined both the protection of the purpose of the investigation activities and the protection of the undertaking's commercial interests which took part in the cartel, as well as undermining the Commission's decision-making process. The GC did not rule that the documents at issue were not capable, in principle, of falling within the claimed exceptions, but only that the Commission had failed to conduct a sufficient examination of the individual documents and to explain how the exceptions applied to each of those documents. This could be an indication that the GC places quite a high burden on the Commission in dealing with requests for disclosure of information in relation to competition cases. The Commission cannot simply refuse requests due to the general nature of the document, but must assess each document to see if it falls within the exceptions provided in Article 4 of Regulation 1049/2000 in full or in part. In *ENBW Energie*

Post Consultation?' [2008] Competition Law Journal 170. See however *contra*: C Cook and M Piergiovanni, 'Implications of settling an EU cartel investigation for a prospective civil damages defendant: bad or good?' (2011) 4(2) Global Competition Litigation Review 65.

[421] Pursuant to para 35 of the Settlements Notice, 'access to settlement submissions is only granted to those addressees of a Statement of Objections who have not requested settlement, provided that they commit ... not to make any copy by mechanical or electronic means of any information in the settlement submissions to which access is being granted and to ensure that the information to be obtained from the settlement submission will solely be used for the purposes of judicial or administrative proceedings for the application of the Union competition rules at issue in the related proceedings. Other parties such as complainants will not be granted access to settlement submissions.' See further, para 39 of the Commission Notice on the conduct of settlement procedures in view of the adoption of Decisions pursuant to Article 7 and Article 23 of Council Regulation (EC) No 1/2003 in cartel cases [2008] OJ C167/1.

[422] See Commission Notice on the conduct of settlement procedures in view of the adoption of Decisions pursuant to Article 7 and Article 23 of Council Regulation (EC) No 1/2003 in cartel cases [2008] OJ C167/1, para 40; see A Caruso, 'Leniency Programmes and Protection of Confidentiality: The Experience of the European Commission' (2010) 1(6) Journal of European Competition Law & Practice 453, 466.

[423] M Siragusa and E Guerri, 'Antitrust Settlements under EC Competition Law: The Point of View of the Defendants' in C-D Ehlermann and M Marquis (eds), *European Competition Law Annual 2008: Antitrust Settlements under EC Competition Law* (Hart Publishing 2009) 251, 196.

[424] See Case T-437/08 *CDC Hydrogen Peroxide v Commission* [2012] OJ C32/18; Case T-380/08 *Kingdom of Netherlands v Commission* (pending); Case T-344/08 *EnBW Energie Baden-Württemberg v Commission* [2012] OJ C194/18. See also G Olsen and M Jephcott, 'Sharing the Benefits of Procedural Economy: The European Commission's Settlement Procedure' (2010) 25(1) Antitrust 76, 79.

Baden Würtemberg v Commission,[425] the GC applied similar reasoning and found that the Commission should have undertaken a concrete, individual examination of the documents covered by the request.

2. Private litigation

The confidentiality of certain documents provided to the Commission by the settling parties, especially the settlement submission, may not have such a substantial impact on private litigation as might appear at first sight. This is because the Commission decision constitutes sufficient evidence of a company's participation in, and liability for, a cartel. In any event, even if the settlement submission were to be discoverable, its content would probably match that of the statement of objections and the final decision very closely. Therefore, the only benefit of such discovery for private claimants would be to obtain the contents of the likely decision a few months before it is adopted.[426]   **10.158**

Only in jurisdictions in which the claimant also bears the burden of proving the defendant's fault could the discovery of the settlement submission theoretically worsen the settling party's position.[427]   **10.159**

Since settlement decisions will not necessarily be very detailed, there is a risk that this would prevent private plaintiffs from alleviating their burden of proof with respect to an infringement,[428] thus increasing their cost and thereby reducing the likelihood of private actions.[429] According to some commentators, this is likely to be one of the most convincing arguments for cartel members who are considering submitting to the settlement procedure.[430] Others have demonstrated, based on the US model, that the level of detail disclosed does not have a particular effect on the likelihood of private actions.[431] The application of the settlement procedure should lead to more decisions and more cartels being uncovered. This could have a positive effect on private enforcement, because with more cases uncovered, despite the lesser degree of detail, victims could bring a follow-on action in more cases.[432] The time factor will probably be equally important to   **10.160**

---

[425] Case T-344/08 EnBW *Energie Baden-Württemberg v Commission* [2012] OJ C194/18; see also Case T-380/08 *Kingdom of Netherlands v Commission*, appeal pending. See also G Olsen and M Jephcott, 'Sharing the Benefits of Procedural Economy: The European Commission's Settlement Procedure' (2010) 25(1) Antitrust 76, 79. See also: Case T-345/12 *Akzo Nobel and others v Commission*, Order of the GC of 16 November 2012 and more recently, Case T-462/12, *Pilkington Group v Commission*, Order of the President of the GC of 11 March 2013, where the GC partially upheld and partially dismissed Pilkington Glass Ltd's application for interim relief in relation to its appeal against a Commission Decision refusing its request for the confidential treatment of certain information relating to its participation in the car glass cartel. Case T-465/12 *AGC Glass Europe and Others v Commission*, pending.

[426] See C Cook and M Piergiovanni, 'Implications of Settling an EU Cartel Investigation for a Prospective Civil Damages Defendant: Bad or Good?' (2011) 4(2) Global Competition Litigation Review 62.

[427] V van Vormizeele, 'The Fault Requirement in European Private Antitrust Litigation and Compliance Programmes as Exculpating or Mitigating Factor' (2010) 3(1) Global Competition Litigation Review, 44.

[428] See J Burrichter, DJ Zimmer, 'Reflections on the Implementation of a "Plea Bargaining"/"Direct Settlement" System In EC Competition Law' in C-D Ehlermann and I Atanasiu (eds), *European Competition Law Annual 2006: Enforcement of Prohibition of Cartels* (Hart Publishing 2007) 611, Section 3.3.

[429] See L Coppi and RJ Levinson, 'The Interaction between Settlements and Private Litigation—An Economic Perspective' in C-D Ehlermann and M Marquis (eds), *European Competition Law Annual 2008: Antitrust Settlements under EC Competition Law* (Hart Publishing 2009) 687, 692.

[430] MP Schinkel, 'Bargaining in the Shadow of the European Settlement Procedure for Cartels' (2010) Amsterdam Center for Law & Economics Working Paper No 2010-17, 10.

[431] See L Coppi and RJ Levinson, 'The Interaction between Settlements and Private Litigation—An Economic Perspective' in C-D Ehlermann and M Marquis (eds), *European Competition Law Annual 2008: Antitrust Settlements under EC Competition Law* (Hart Publishing 2009) 687, 693.

[432] See K Dekeyser, R Becker, and D Calisti, 'Impact of Public Enforcement on Antitrust Damages Actions: Some Likely Effects of Settlements and Commitments on Private Actions for Damages' in C-D Ehlermann and M Marquis (eds), *European Competition Law Annual 2008: Antitrust Settlements under EC Competition Law,* (Hart Publishing 2009) 677, Section II.2.b.

infringers, as a faster streamlined decision that is unlikely to be appealed will become final much earlier and will expose them to private actions for damages much sooner.[433]

10.161 As the bringing of private actions for damages is not (yet) very common in Europe, the effects of settlements in this regard remain to be seen.

E. First Cases Decided

10.162 At the time of writing, six settlement decisions have been issued by the Commission, the first one having been delivered two years after the introduction of the settlement procedure. The first five cases which ended with a settlement are: *DRAM*,[434] adopted on 19 May 2010; *Animal Feed Phosphates*,[435] adopted on 20 July 2010; *Consumer Detergents*,[436] adopted on 13 April 2011; *CRT Glass*,[437] adopted on 19 October 2011; *Refrigerator Compressors*, adopted on 7 December 2011;[438] and *Water Management Products*,[439] adopted on 27 June 2012. Settlements currently account for more than 30 per cent of the total amount of cartel fines imposed under the mandate of Vice President Almunia so far. According to the Competition Commissioner, 'this share of the total fines and the shorter duration of settlement cases is concrete proof of quick results in cartel enforcement and effective impact on the market'.

DRAM

10.163 The first settlement decision can be viewed as a milestone in the Commission's anti-cartel enforcement.[440] The case concerned a cartel involving ten producers of memory chips (DRAMs) used in computers and servers, and was triggered by a successful immunity application by one of the parties, which revealed the existence of the cartel to the Commission in 2002, ending with a decision in May 2010. The settlement process was concluded in slightly over a year, with only three months between the statement of objections and the decision being adopted. Companies that are first to reveal cartels to the Commission enjoy immunity from fines under the Commission's 2002 Leniency Notice, but the Commission also took account of the cooperation of five other companies under the Leniency Notice and granted a fine reduction to these as well.

10.164 The settlement discussions in this case took place as from March 2009, after the companies indicated that they were prepared to engage in such discussions. In December 2009, they all made formal settlement submissions. A statement of objections reflecting the parties'

---

[433] K Dekeyser, R Becker, and D Calisti, 'Impact of Public Enforcement on Antitrust Damages Actions: Some Likely Effects of Settlements and Commitments on Private Actions for Damages' in C-D Ehlermann and M Marquis (eds), *European Competition Law Annual 2008: Antitrust Settlements under EC Competition Law* (Hart Publishing 2009), Section II.3.b.

[434] European Commission Press Release IP/10/586 'Antitrust: Commission fines DRAM producers €331 million for price cartel; reaches first settlement in a cartel case' of 19 May 2010.

[435] European Commission Press Release IP/10/985 'Antitrust: European Commission fines animal feed phosphates producers €175 647 000 for price-fixing and market-sharing in first 'hybrid' cartel settlement case' of 20 July 2010.

[436] European Commission Press Release IP/11/473 'Antitrust: Commission fines producers of washing powder €315.2 million in cartel settlement case' of 13 April 2011.

[437] European Commission Press Release IP/11/1214 'Antitrust: Commission fines producers of CRT glass €128 million in fourth cartel settlement' of 19 December 2011.

[438] European Commission Press Release IP/11/1511 'Antitrust: Commission fines producers of refrigeration compressors €161 million in fifth cartel settlement' of 07 December 2011.

[439] European Commission Press Release IP/12/704 'Antitrust: Commission fines producers of water management products €13 million in sixth cartel settlement' of 27 June 2012.

[440] European Commission Press Release IP/10/586 'Antitrust: Commission fines DRAM producers €331 million for price cartel; reaches first settlement in a cartel case' of 19 May 2010.

submissions was notified to them on 8 February 2010 and the parties all confirmed that its content reflected their submissions and they wished to continue with the settlement procedure. The Advisory Committee on Restrictive Practices and Dominant Positions issued a favourable opinion on 7 May 2010 and finally the Commission adopted the Decision on 19 May 2010.[441]

The DRAM case was rather lengthy and suggests that dealing with the procedure was a learning **10.165** process for the Commission and practitioners alike.[442] The novelty of the procedure explains why the first settlement took so long, although the steps of the settlement procedure had been tested before in the *Animal Feed Phosphates* case, which took longer only because one of the companies opted out of the settlement. As the Commission gains experience and standard practices build up, it is to be expected that future cases will proceed more smoothly and quickly.[443]

Animal Feed Phosphates

First hybrid settlement

The second settlement decision concerned producers of animal feed phosphates. This case, **10.166** although the second decision issued under the settlement procedure, was a 'first' in that it was a hybrid settlement, where not all parties to the cartel opted for the settlement procedure. Moreover, this was the first case which went through all of the settlement phases (the first case in which all settlement discussion rounds took place, in which the settlement fines were disclosed and the settlement submissions were introduced and agreed upon). However, since one of the participating undertakings, Timab Industries SA and Compagnie Financière et de Participation Roullier, a French company (hereafter CFPR/Timab), discontinued the settlement procedure after having been invited to introduce the settlement submission on the terms agreed in principle with the Commission, this case was overtaken by the DRAMs decision, because the Commission had to wait until the end of the ordinary procedure with respect to the company opting out before adopting the final decisions in this case. The Commission chose to adopt two decisions: 'a streamlined settlement decision for those undertakings which [had] agreed to settle and admitted their participation in the cartel and, on the other hand, a standard decision for one company which decided not to settle and for which the ordinary procedure was followed'.[444] Both decisions were adopted on 20 July 2010. Had the settlement decision preceded the ordinary decision, this would have prevented the Commission from taking into account the arguments of the non-settling undertaking regarding a time when they could have an influence on the overall case and on the fine parameters common to all parties. In the Commission's view, it was sensible not to decide all of those elements in advance in a settlement decision for all other parties to the same cartel, because this could have been seen as pre-empting Timab's arguments with the consequent factual or formal impact on the latter's rights of defence.

The parties were notified of the decision to initiate settlement proceedings by letter dated 19 January **10.167** 2009. Following settlement discussions, all parties introduced their settlement submissions, with

---

[441] Summary of Commission Decision of 19 May 2010 relating to a proceeding under Article 101 of TFEU and Article 53 of the EEA Agreement (Case COMP/38.511 *DRAMs* [2011] OJ C170, 15–17).

[442] See K van Hove and R Burton, 'Direct Settlement: The European Commission's Decision in the Recent DRAM Case Sheds Light on How the Cartel Settlement Procedure is Working in Practice' (2010) 6 Competition Law Insight 8; G Olsen and M Jephcott, 'Sharing the Benefits of Procedural Economy: The European Commission's Settlement Procedure' (2010) 25(1) Antitrust 76, 79.

[443] Joaquín Almunia in SPEECH/10/247 of 19 May 2010 'Joaquín Almunia Vice-President of the European Commission responsible for Competition policy First cartel decision under settlement procedure—Introductory remarks Press conference—Berlaymont press room Brussels, 19 May 2010' stated 'As the procedure will start to be applied to new cases it is expected to speed up investigations significantly', adding that future settlement cases will take no more than six months, in some cases less.

[444] European Commission Press Release IP/10/985 'Antitrust: European Commission fines animal feed phosphates producers €175 647 000 for price-fixing and market-sharing in first "hybrid" cartel settlement case', 20 July 2010.

the exception of CFPR/Timab, who discontinued the settlement procedure. On 23 November 2009, the Commission adopted a bundle of six statements of objections addressed to all of the parties. With the exception of CFPR/Timab, all of the parties replied by confirming that the statements of objections corresponded to the contents of their settlement submissions and that they therefore remained committed to following the settlement procedure.[445]

Fallback onto the ordinary procedure

10.168   After having been granted full access to the file by way of a DVD and, at the Commission's premises, to corporate statements as well as a non-confidential version of the other parties' settlement submissions, CFPR/Timab then replied in writing to the statement of objections on 2 February 2010 and participated in an oral hearing held on 24 February 2010. In addition, it was, upon request, subsequently granted additional access to the settling parties' acknowledgments of the statement of objections at the Commission's premises.[446] Even though the settling parties had renounced their right to request an oral hearing in the settlement submission, 'the Hearing Officer responsible for the case at the time decided, as a matter of transparency and fairness, to invite them to the hearing'.[447]

10.169   The settlement process took just under eighteen months, with a period of eight months between the issuing of the statement of objections and the adoption of a decision. This is due to the fact that CFPR/Timab decided to pull out of the settlement procedure at a rather advanced stage of the discussions, once all settlement discussions had taken place and after having been invited to introduce their settlement submission and also because further procedural steps had been requested by the new legal advisers.

Loss of efficiencies and appeal by CFPR/Timab

10.170   Due to the withdrawal of CFPR/Timab from the settlement procedure, many of the envisaged procedural savings were lost. By falling back onto the more cumbersome ordinary procedure for just one party, the Commission had to issue a full statement of objections, allow further access to the file, and hold an oral hearing. Yet all of these extra procedural steps had to be taken only in relation to one company. Procedural efficiencies had been achieved vis-à-vis the settling parties and the only point which needed to be further argued with CFPR/Timab concerned the scope of its infringement.

10.171   Because regular settlement decisions are unlikely to be appealed, a hybrid settlement decision reduces procedural efficiencies further, as the non-settling party is more likely to appeal the decision. On the other hand, the credibility of the arguments of the non-settling party is likely to be compromised as regards the common cartel features that have been expressly described and acknowledged by all other cartelists.

10.172   CFPR/Timab appealed against the Commission decision by bringing an action before the GC on 1 October 2010,[448] seeking the annulment of the Commission decision or alternatively the annulment of Article 1 of the decision and a substantial reduction of the fine. CFPR/Timab put forward eight pleas in support of its action.

10.173   In its appeal, CFPR/Timab argued that it had been penalized for withdrawing from the settlement proceedings and that this was the reason that the Commission had substantially lowered the amount of the fine reduction under the Leniency Notice. However, the Commission

---

[445] Summary of Commission Decisions of 20 July 2010 relating to a proceeding under Article 101 TFEU and Article 53 of the EEA Agreement (Case COMP/38.866 *Animal feed phosphates*) [2011] OJ C111/15–18, 19–21.
[446] Final report of the Hearing Officer, Case COMP/38.866 *Animal feed phosphates* [2011] OJ C111/14, 13–14.
[447] Final report of the Hearing Officer, Case COMP/38.866 *Animal feed phosphates* [2011] OJ C111/14.
[448] Action brought on 1 October 2010 Case T-456/10 *Timab Industries and CFPR v Commission* [2010] OJ C346/46.

explained that a lower leniency reduction had been decided on because of the companies' contestation of the Commission's interpretation of their own leniency submissions as being self-incriminating regarding a long period for which they were the only evidence against CFPR/Timab. As a result, under the new scenario only a much shorter infringement by CFPR/Timab could be taken into account, which could be established on the basis of other evidence in the file and, more generally, the case against the other companies could be built to a large extent on the basis of evidence obtained from other sources. Therefore, the Commission argued that the added value of CFPR/Timab's leniency submissions was considerably reduced compared to the length of the violation considered during the settlement discussions. In addition, there was the paradox that the calculation of the so-called 'entry fee' on the basis of an average year of the shorter duration had as a mathematical consequence a higher 'entry fee' than the one originally calculated for an average year of the longer duration. This is due to the fact that CFPR/Timab's relevant turnover was much higher than the last years of the infringement (which were retained) than during the first period (which was dropped upon CFPR/Timab's new arguments of defence). Apart from the pleas concerning the penalization by misapplication of the Leniency Notice, allegedly because of the withdrawal from settlement discussions, CFPR/Timab alleged inadequate and contradictory grounds and also the infringement of its defence rights. It must be noted, however, that as far as CFPR/Timab is concerned, an ordinary procedure took place. At the time of writing, the case is still pending before the GC. This will be the first case in which an EU court has had the chance to scrutinize the settlement procedure (albeit indirectly), to reveal some of the internal processes at work and evaluate the settlement procedure from a legal perspective. Whether the Court will take this opportunity remains to be seen and is highly anticipated, as is how far it will go.

This case shows that the Commission is in principle willing to use the settlement procedure even in cases where not all parties are willing to settle, essentially so as to prevent parties from acquiring a veto right over each other's settlement chances. However, the extent to which the Commission will accept hybrid settlements where more than one party refuses to settle and procedural efficiencies are evidently lower remains to be seen.[449] **10.174**

Consumer Detergents

The third cartel settlement, announced on 13 April 2010, concerned a cartel in the household laundry powder detergents market which operated in eight EU countries for over three years from 2002 to 2005. The settlement discussions started in June 2010, after the companies indicated that they were prepared to engage in such discussions. Subsequently, in January 2011, they all introduced formal settlement submissions. After acknowledging their respective liability in the settlement submissions filed in January 2011, a statement of objections was notified to them in February 2011. A streamlined decision was adopted as little as two months later.[450] **10.175**

This case was triggered by an immunity application submitted on 13 May 2008 by one of the parties, who was the first to inform the Commission about the existence of the cartel. After the Commission carried out inspections, the other two companies involved also applied for leniency. In a case where all parties are leniency applicants, and thus willing to fully cooperate with the Commission, the efficiencies of the settlement procedure can be exploited to the full. **10.176**

---

[449] F Distefano, 'Cartel Risks in the Chemicals Sector—Lessons to Draw from Recent Cases and Areas to Watch' [2011] The European Antitrust Review 84.

[450] Summary of Commission Decision of 13 April 2011 relating to a proceeding under Article 101 TFEU and Article 53 of the EEA Agreement (Case COMP/39.579 *Consumer detergents*) [2011] OJ C193/14–16.

CRT Glass

10.177   The fourth cartel settlement, announced on 19 October 2011, concerned four producers of cathode ray tube ('CRT') glass used in televisions and computer screens which operated in the European Economic Area ('EEA') for over five years from 1999 to 2004.[451] The investigation was triggered by initial information pointing to a possible cartel in this market. Shortly after, the Commission received a request for immunity from one of the companies which led to inspections taking place. The fine on three of the companies included a 10 per cent reduction for acknowledging their participation in the cartel, thereby helping the Commission to conclude the case more rapidly. Besides, some of these companies were also granted another reduction for cooperation under or outside the Leniency Notice. The fourth company was granted full immunity under the Commission's 2006 Leniency Notice for being the first to give information about the cartel.

Refrigeration Compressors

10.178   Announced on 7 December 2011, this cartel settlement concerned producers of household and commercial refrigeration compressors used in fridges, freezers, vending machines, and ice-cream coolers.[452] The companies concerned operated a cartel that covered the whole EEA from April 2004 until October 2007. The fine included a reduction of 10 per cent for the companies' acknowledgement of their participation in the cartel and their liability in respect of such participation. Three of the companies also received a further reduction for cooperation under the Leniency Notice, while another one received a further reduction for its cooperation outside the Leniency Notice. On the other hand, Tecumseh was not fined at all as it benefited from immunity under the 2006 Leniency Notice for revealing the existence of the cartel to the Commission. This case is interesting, since it contained a factor which had not appeared previously: the inability to pay. Thus, one of the undertakings invoked its inability to pay the fine under point 35 of the 2006 Guidelines; as a result of this assessment, the Commission granted a fine reduction.

Water Management Products

10.179   The last cartel settlement published until now was announced on 27 June 2012 and concerned producers of water management products used in heating, cooling, and sanitation systems.[453] The three companies that behaved in an anticompetitive way initially operated in the German market from June 2006 until May 2008, and in thirteen other Member States, for a limited period of three months. The Commission reduced the fines imposed by 10 per cent as the companies concerned acknowledged their participation in the cartel and liability in this respect, agreeing to reach a settlement with the Commission. Moreover, one of the companies was not fined as it benefited from immunity under the Commission's 2006 Leniency Notice for revealing the existence of the cartel to the Commission.

---

[451] Summary of Commission Decision of 19 October 2011 relating to a proceeding under Article 101 of the Treaty and Article 53 of the EEA Agreement (Case COMP/39.605 *CRT Glass*) [2012] OJ C48/18; see also IP/11/1214 'Antitrust: Commission fines producers of CRT glass €128 million in fourth cartel settlement', 19 October 2011.

[452] IP/11/1511, Antitrust: Commission fines producers of refrigeration compressors €161 million in fifth cartel settlement', 7 December 2012. Summary of Commission Decision of 7 December 2011 relating to a proceeding under Article 101 TFEU and Article 53 of the EEA Agreement (Case COMP/39.600 *Refrigeration compressors*) [2012] OJ C122/6.

[453] Commission Press Release IP/12/704 'Antitrust: Commission fines producers of water management products €13 million in sixth cartel settlement', 27 June 2012.

11

INFRINGEMENT DECISIONS AND PENALTIES

Ralf Sauer

I. General Content of Infringement Decisions

A. Layout

There is no specific requirement for the Commission as to the way in which it structures com-   **11.01** petition decisions, but they must meet the requirements contained in Article 296 of the Treaty on the Functioning of the European Union ('TFEU'). The basic layout of decisions applying Articles 101 and 102 TFEU consists of (1) a title; (2) a preamble referencing the legal basis; (3) recitals that contain a summary of the various procedural steps, an account of the facts, a legal assessment of those facts, as well as, where applicable, an explanation of the level of any sanctions (fines, penalty payments); and (4) the Articles of the decision, known as the operative part or simply the 'decision'. The operative part sets out the finding of an infringement and its duration for specific addressees (legal entities), the remedies required by the Commission (including a cease and desist order), the amounts of any sanctions with arrangements for their payment, and an indication that the decision shall be enforceable pursuant to Article 299 TFEU.[1] It should be borne in mind that the Commission may withdraw its objections against

---

[1] Note that *infringement* decisions make no reference to the right of undertakings to contest the decision before the General Court ('GC')—within a period of two months from the day following the date of notification, under the fourth paragraph of Art 263 TFEU. That formal requirement applies only to procedural decisions adopted under the Commission's investigative powers pursuant to Arts 18(3) (decisions to request information), 20(4) and 21(2) (inspection decisions) of Reg 1/2003.

undertakings wholly or in part, and amend, correct, or supplement them in the light of the replies by the undertakings concerned to the statement of objections. Decisions are not, therefore, a copy of the statement of objections.[2] It should also be remembered that although decisions must specify the evidence on which the Commission's findings are based, they do not have to enumerate exhaustively every available item of evidence.[3] As regards the reasoning on which its decisions are based, it is true that, under Articles 296(2) TFEU, 41(2)(c) of the Charter of Fundamental Rights, the Commission is required to give a statement of the reasons for its decisions, indicating the matters of fact and of law on which it relied in adopting them.[4] However, the Commission cannot be required to discuss each and every one of the points of fact and law submitted by each of the parties involved in the course of the administrative procedure.[5]

11.02   The present chapter will focus on infringement decisions as such, with particular attention paid to the operative part. This also includes declaratory decisions, enforcement decisions (ie orders), as well as fines and periodic penalty payments imposed on undertakings for infringements of the substantive provisions of Articles 101 and 102 TFEU.

B. Declarations and Orders

11.03   Commission decisions in competition matters contain both declaratory and enforcement elements in the operative part. In the following, the first are referred to as declaratory decisions, the second, which are strictly speaking 'orders', as enforcement decisions.[6]

1. Declaratory decisions

11.04   Infringement decisions always contain a finding to the effect that the agreements or conduct to which the procedure relate(s) constitute(s) an infringement of Article 101(1), Article 102

---

[2] eg Case T-191/98 *Atlantic Container Line and Others v Commission* [2003] ECR-II 3275, para 191. Case T-48/00 *Corus UK v Commission* [2004] ECR II-2325, para 101: 'the assessment appearing in a statement of objections is often more succinct than that contained in the final decision as adopted, since it only represents the Commission's provisional view. Divergences of wording between a statement of objections and a final decision, deriving from the difference between the respective purposes of those two documents, are not, in principle, capable of infringing the rights of the defence.' For more details on the required degree of similarity of the statement of objections and the final decision, see Ch 10, 'Procedures to Establish the Existence of an Infringement'.

[3] See Case T-2/89 *Petrofina v Commission* [1991] ECR II-1087, para 39; Case T-43/92 *Dunlop v Commission* [1994] ECR II-441, para 34.

[4] According to settled case law, the operative part of a decision has to be interpreted in the light of the statement of reasons. See Joined Cases T-80/89, T-81/89, T-87/89, T-88/89, T-90/89, T-93/89, T-95/89, T-97/89, T-99/89, T-100/89, T-101/89, T-103/89, T-105/89, T-107/89 and T-112/89 *BASF and Others v Commission* [1995] ECR II-729, para 76; Judgment of 30 November 2011 in Case T-208/06 *Quinn Barlo and Others v Commission*, para 131. See, however, Case T-301/04 *Clearstream v European Commission* [2009] ECR II-3155, para 210. This is of particular importance where, for example, in *Vitamins* [2003] OJ L6/1, the Articles of the decision simply refer to the undertakings having infringed Art 81 EC [now Art 101 TFEU] by participating in agreements affecting the EU. As far as the operative part is concerned, the EU Courts do not seem to require more than an identification of the identity of the undertakings concerned and the duration of the infringement. See *Seamless Steel Tubes* [2003] OJ L140/1, Art 2, upheld in this respect by Case T-48/00 *Corus UK v Commission* [2004] ECR II-2325, para 87.

[5] Case T-8/89 *DSM v Commission* [1991] ECR II-1833, para 257; Case T-2/93 *Air France v Commission* [1994] ECR II-323, para 92; Case T-198/98 *Micro Leader Business v Commission* [1999] ECR II-3989, para 40; Case C-521/09 P *Elf Aquitaine v Commission*, para 150: 'It is not necessary for the reasoning to go into all the relevant facts and points of law, since the question whether the statement of reasons meets the requirements of Article 253 EC must be assessed with regard not only to its wording but also to its context and to all the legal rules governing the matter in question.' See also Case C-367/95 P *Commission v Sytraval and Brink's France* [1998] ECR I-1719, para 64: 'The Commission is not required, however, to define its position on matters which are manifestly irrelevant or insignificant or plainly of secondary importance.'

[6] The term used in French is '*injonction*'.

TFEU, or both (eg abuse of a collective dominant position deriving from an agreement or restrictive practice).[7] Although Article 7(1) of Regulation 1/2003 merely states that the Commission may by 'decision require the undertakings or associations of undertakings concerned to bring such infringement to an end', the EU Courts have always taken the view that a cease and desist order implies the power to find an infringement, also on the grounds that the Commission has a legitimate interest in clarifying its position in law and in preventing any future infringement of the same or a similar kind.[8] Where undertakings have brought the infringement to an end before the initiation[9] or during the course of the proceedings, the Commission may confine itself to declaring that the conduct to which the procedure relates constituted an infringement of the EU competition rules. However, according to Article 7(1) of Regulation 1/2003,[10] this requires that the Commission can demonstrate a legitimate interest in doing so.[11] The Commission has adopted declaratory decisions of this kind on several occasions where there was a palpable risk that anticompetitive behaviour would be resumed, thus calling for a definitive clarification of the legal situation.[12] Beyond this, the General Court ('GC') has stressed the need for a case-by-case demonstration of any legitimate interest.[13] It is therefore not sufficient to point, in the abstract, to a category of cases in which such an interest may arise. Moreover, it has been argued[14] that such an interest must always be related to considerations of special deterrence (eg a tangible risk of recidivism,[15] the interest to present the anticompetitive behaviour of an undertaking in its entirety[16]). Conversely, mere considerations of general deterrence (eg the interest to promote

---

[7] See also Cases C-395/96 P and 396/96 P *Compagnie Maritime Belge Transports v Commission* [2000] ECR I-1365, stating that because a practice is exempted under Art 81(3) EC [now Art 101(3) TFEU], this does not mean that the same practice may not be challenged under Art 82 EC [now Art 102 TFEU].

[8] See Case 7/82 *GVL v Commission* [1983] ECR 483, paras 16–28.

[9] This applies even where the Commission's competence to impose a sanction is prescribed. See Joined Cases T-22/02 and T-23/02 *Sumitomo Chemical v Commission* [2005] ECR II-4065, paras 61–3, 109, and 131.

[10] See also Recital 11 of Reg 1/2003.

[11] For the need to demonstrate such an interest at least during the court procedure in case of an annulment action directed against the fines part of the challenged decision (eg by invoking prescription of the power to sanction) see Judgment of 16 November 2011 in Case T-68/06 *Stempher and Koninklijke Verpakkingsindustrie Stempher v Commission*, para 44.

[12] Case 7/82 *GVL v Commission* [1983] ECR 483, para 27. See also Commission Decision of 26 October 2004 in Case COMP/38.662 *GDF/ENEL*, para 162; Commission Decision of 14 September 2005 in Case COMP/38.337 *PO/Garne*, paras 408–17. This applies all the more so in cases where the conduct at issue is itself in disregard of a prior cease-and-desist order. See Commission Decision of 3 May 2006 in Case COMP/38.620 *Hydrogen peroxide (and perborate)*, para 369.

[13] Joined Cases T-22/02 and T-23/02 *Sumitomo Chemical v Commission* [2005] ECR II-4065, paras 137–8. See, however, for the legitimate interest in finding an infringement without imposing penalties, Opinion of AG Kokott of 28 February 2013 in Case C-681/11 *Schenker and Co AG and Others*, para 114. While the Advocate-General did not specifically address the question of whether an isolated finding of an infringement can be justified once it has been terminated, and possibly after the power to fine has been prescribed, her arguments at least indicate that general and specific deterrence (recidivism) as well as the support for civil damage claims constitute important considerations for competition law enforcement.

[14] See E Gippini-Fournier, 'The Modernisation of European Competition Law: First Experiences with Regulation 1/2003—Institutional Report' in HF Koeck and MM Karollus (eds), The Modernisation of European Competition Law—Initial Experiences with Regulation 1/2003, FIDE XXIII Congress Linz 2008—Congress Publications Vol 2 (Nomos 2008), 19.

[15] However, the mere objective of discouraging any repeat infringement in the future is not sufficient to demonstrate a legitimate interest. See Joined Cases T-22/02 and T-23/02 *Sumitomo Chemical v Commission* [2005] ECR II-4065, paras 137–8.

[16] See Commission Decision of 1 October 2008 in Case COMP/39.181 *Candle Waxes*, para 617; Commission Decision of 11 November 2009 in Case COMP/38.589 *Heat Stabilisers*, para 437. See also Commission Decision of 23 June 2010 in Case COMP/39.092 *Bathroom Fittings*, para 1179.

lawful competitive behaviour[17]) or the goal to prepare claims for damages[18] may not suffice. However, it should be noted that, according to the explanatory memorandum accompanying the draft of Regulation 1/2003, the mere clarification, in the public interest, of new legal questions could justify the adoption of purely declaratory decisions.[19]

2. Enforcement decisions: remedies

11.05 This category includes both orders to bring infringements to an end and orders to carry out specific acts, as well as the obligations which the Commission may attach to such orders. Sometimes, it may be decided to impose a periodic penalty payment in order to ensure the fulfillment of such obligations.[20]

Order to bring infringement to an end

11.06 Article 7(1) of Regulation 1/2003 establishes that where the Commission, acting on a complaint or on its own initiative, finds an infringement of Article 101 or of Article 102 TFEU, it may by decision require the said infringement to be brought to an end.[21] The Commission adopts such 'cease and desist' orders where the undertakings have not cooperated with the Commission by cancelling their restrictive agreements or desisting from their unlawful conduct prior to the decision, or where it is not sure that the undertakings have in fact terminated the infringement to which the procedure relates.[22] Cease and desist orders are, in principle, proportionate, even if the undertaking offered commitments pursuant to Article 9 of Regulation 1/2003 (as the Commission is not obliged to adopt a commitment decision).[23] The same applies to a 'like effects order', whereby the parties are prohibited from entering into similar arrangements which may have the same effect or object as the conduct which has been found to be anticompetitive.[24] Such an order does not depend on the specific situation

---

[17] See Joined Cases T-22/02 and T-23/02 *Sumitomo Chemical v Commission* [2005] ECR II-4065, paras 137–8. During the court procedure, the Commission had explicitly referred to the contestation of an infringement by the undertaking concerned as a factor justifying a declaratory decision.

[18] See, however, Joined Cases C-295/04 to C-298/04 *Manfredi* [2006] ECR I-6619, para 91, according to which 'actions for damages before the national courts can make a significant contribution to the maintenance of effective competition in the Community'. In this respect, victims of competition law infringements may want to rely on the Commission's findings based on its comprehensive powers of investigation, in particular as regards cross-border infringements. Regarding actions for damages as well as other actions in which EU competition law is applied directly by national courts, see Ch 2, 'The Role of National Judicial Authorities'.

[19] Draft Reg implementing Arts 81 and 82 of the Treaty, COM (2000) 582 final [2000] OJ C365 E/284, Explanatory Memorandum, 20. See also the Commission's past practice, eg Cases IV/33.378 and IV/33.384 *Distribution of Package Tours 1990 World Cup*, para 126; Cases IV/31.550, IV/31.898 *Zera/Montedison* and *Hinkens/Staehler*, paras 131–2.

[20] Regarding the procedure for the imposition of periodic penalty payments, see also Ch 9, 'Procedural Infringements: Fines and Periodic Penalty Payments'.

[21] This is the most straightforward type of decision. See Joined Cases 6/73 and 7/73 *Istituto Chimioterapico Italiano and Commercial Solvents v Commission* [1974] ECR 223, para 45; Judgment of 14 March 2013 in Case T-587/08 *Fresh Del Monte v Commission*, para 291. See also *Frankfurt Airport* [1998] OJ L72/30, para 1; *Irish Sugar plc* [1997] OJ L258/1, para 3.

[22] See *Industrial and medical gases* [2003] OJ L84/1, para 2; *Food Flavour Enhancers* [2004] OJ L75/1, para 2; *Opel* [2001] OJ L59/1, para 2.

[23] Judgment of 29 November 2012 in Case T-491/07 *Groupement des cartes bancaires (CB) v Commission*, paras 429 and 430.

[24] Case T-311/94 *BPB de Eendracht NV v Commission* [1998] ECR II-1129, para 275; Joined Cases T-305/94, T-306/94, T-307/94, T-313/94 to T-316/94, T-318/94, T-325/94, T-328/94, T-329/94 and T-335/94 *Limburgse Vinyl Maatschappij and Others v Commission* [1999] ECR II-931, paras 1252–7; Case T-410/08 R *GEMA v Commission* [2008] ECR II-268, para 66. See also Commission Decision of 29 March 2006 in Case COMP/38.113 *Prokent-Tomra*. As regards the proportionality of such measures, see Judgment of 29 November 2012 in Case T-491/07 *Groupement des cartes bancaires (CB) v Commission*, paras 439 and 440. However, in *Langnese-Iglo* (Cases T-7/93 and T-9/93 *Langnese-Iglo & Schöller Lebensmittel v Commission* [1995] ECR II-1533, paras 205–9, upheld by the ECJ in Case C-279/95P *Langnese Iglo v Commission* [1998]

of the undertaking concerned, for instance on whether it has terminated the infringement in the meantime or even retreated from the business area at issue.[25] When imposing these measures, the Commission must respect the principle of legal security, which requires that at least the grounds of the decision are sufficiently clear as to the type of conduct that is prohibited.[26]

Orders to take specific action[27]

In addition, Article 7(1) of Regulation 1/2003 empowers the Commission to impose on undertakings that have infringed Articles 101 and/or 102 TFEU all remedies necessary to bring the infringement to an end,[28] including (i) behavioural, or (ii) structural remedies. As regards behavioural remedies, the Court of Justice ('ECJ') had already interpreted Article 3 of Regulation 17 (the equivalent provision to Article 7(1) of Regulation 1/2003) as enabling the Commission not only to require an end to certain conduct contrary to the Treaty (cease and desist orders), but also to order undertakings to carry out certain actions if it finds that the undertaking's failure to act has been unlawful.[29] However, it is not for the Commission to impose on the parties its own choice from among the various potential courses of action which are in accordance with the Treaty.[30] More generally, any order requiring an undertaking

11.07

ECR I-5609, para 74), the ECJ held that the Commission was not entitled to forbid undertakings from entering into exclusive purchasing agreements *in the future*, given that the anticompetitive nature of such conduct, and whether it might satisfy Art 101(3) TFEU, depended on the factual context in which it might occur. See also Case T-34/92 *Fiatagri UK and New Holland Ford v Commission* [1994] ECR II-905, para 39 on the declaratory nature of an order to refrain from entering into any information exchange system having an object identical or similar to an anticompetitive agreement. For the general wording of a 'like effects order' see European Commission Antitrust Manual of Procedures, Internal DG Competition working documents on procedures for the application of Articles 101 and 102 TFEU, March 2012, Module 25 'Follow-up of decisions', n 5.

[25] Judgment of 28 April 2010 in Joined Cases T-456/05 and T-457/05 *Gütermann und Zwicky v Commission*, paras 65–6; Case T-410/03 *Hoechst v Commission* [2004] ECR II-4451, paras 199–200.

[26] Judgment of 29 November 2012 in Case T-491/07 *Groupement des cartes bancaires (CB) v Commission*, paras 443–9.

[27] J Schwarze and A Weitbrecht, *Grundzüge des Europäischen Kartellverfahrensrechts* (Nomos 2004) § 6, para 21, have proposed the following categories: (i) reporting obligations; (ii) obligations to modify the undertaking's pricing policy; (iii) obligations to modify the terms and conditions of sale; (iv) obligations to grant access to infrastructure, licences; (v) obligations to supply; and (vi) obligations to divest or sell shareholdings or businesses. See also A Klees, *Europäisches Kartellverfahrensrecht* (Carl Heymanns Verlag 2005) § 6, para 70 et seq.

[28] Judgment of 29 November 2012 in Case T-491/07 *Groupement des cartes bancaires (CB) v Commission*, paras 437 and 438.

[29] Joined Cases C-241/91 P and C-242/91 P *Radio Telefis Eireann and Independent Television Publications Ltd (ITP) v Commission* [1995] ECR I-743, para 90, citing Joined Cases 6/73 and 7/73 *Istituto Chimioterapico Italiano and Commercial Solvents Corp v Commission* [1974] ECR 223, para 45 (in which the dominant undertaking was ordered to supply a certain amount of raw material to the complainant which involved the parties entering into contractual relations); Case T-228/97 *Irish Sugar v Commission* [1999] ECR II-2969, para 298. See also Commission Decision of 24 March 2004 in Case COMP/37.792 *Microsoft*, in which the Commission ordered Microsoft to offer versions of Windows without Windows Media Player incorporated and to make available certain interoperability information; see Commission Press Release IP/04/382 'Commission concludes Microsoft investigation, imposes conduct remedies and a fine', of 24 March 2004. For an order based on Art 106(3) TFEU see Commission Decision of 4 August 2009 in Case COMP/38.700 *Greek Lignite* and Commission Press Release IP/09/1226 'Commission accepts commitments by Greece to ensure fair access to Greek lignite deposits', of 6 August 2009.

[30] See Case T-24/90 *Automec v Commission* [1992] ECR II-2223, para 52. The GC held that infringements arising out of the application of an illegal distribution system could also be eliminated by the abolition or amendment of the distribution system instead of imposing the obligation to allow the use of certain trademarks. Thus, the Commission could not order the party to enter into a contractual relationship, as this would constitute a disproportionate restriction of the freedom of contract. See also Case T-7/93 *Langnese-Iglo v Commission* [1995] ECR II-1533, paras 205–9; Judgment of 27 June 2012 in Case T-167/08 *Microsoft v Commission*, para 95; Case T-425/08 R *KODA v Commission* [2008] ECR-II 303, paras 43 and 46.

to take or refrain from certain actions, with a view to bringing the infringement to an end, must not exceed what is appropriate and necessary to attain the objectives pursued (cf Article 7(1) of Regulation 1/2003).[31] In practice, the Commission does not hesitate to use 'injunctions' where this is considered necessary to remedy the consequences of an abuse of a dominant position,[32] although it appears to take a more cautious stance with regard to agreements and restrictive practices caught by Article 101(1) TFEU.[33] Where an infringement can be remedied in several alternative ways, the Commission may also request the undertaking concerned to come forward with its own proposals.[34]

11.08 As regards the implementation of structural remedies, Regulation 17 did not specifically provide for such a possibility. Yet Article 7(1) of Regulation 1/2003 expressly empowers the Commission to impose on undertakings structural remedies:

> provided that there is no equally effective behavioural remedy or that any equally effective behavioural remedy would be more burdensome for the undertaking concerned than the structural remedy.[35]

This may become relevant, for instance, with regard to cooperation agreements and abuses of a dominant position, if a divestiture of certain assets appears necessary.[36] Under the EU Courts' case law, the Commission's discretion in this area remains restricted by the principle of proportionality, which implies that:

> [t]he burdens imposed on undertakings in order to bring an infringement of competition law to an end must not exceed what is appropriate and necessary to attain the objective sought, namely re-establishment of compliance with the rules infringed.[37]

---

[31] Joined Cases C-241/91 P and C-242/91 P *Radio Telefis Eireann and Independent Television Publications Ltd (ITP) v Commission* [1995] ECR I-743, para 93; Case T-410/03 *Hoechst v Commission* [2004] ECR II-881, para 198; Case T-201/04 *Microsoft v Commission* [2007] ECR II-3601, paras 1276–7. See also Case T-9/93 *Schöller Lebensmittel v Commission* [1995] ECR II-1611, paras 159–61.

[32] Where an undertaking abuses its dominant position by, for example, a refusal to supply, it may be difficult to contemplate any other remedy than an order to supply. See, eg, Joined Cases 6/73 and 7/73 *Istituto Chimioterapico Italiano and Commercial Solvents v Commission* [1974] ECR 223, para 45. Many subsequent Art 102 cases on refusal to supply and essential facilities have involved ordering a dominant undertaking to supply or share facilities. For instance, in *Magill TV Guide* the Court upheld the Commission's decision ordering compulsory licensing of the applicant's television programme listings. See Joined Cases C-241/91 P and C-242/91 P *Radio Telefis Eireann and Independent Television Publications Ltd (ITP) v Commission* [1991] ECR I-743. See also Commission Decision of 24 March 2004 in Case COMP/37.792 *Microsoft*, para 998 et seq.

[33] See eg *Astra* [1993] OJ L20/23, para 3, which provided that customer contracts should be renegotiated and readjusted. *Volkswagen* [1998] OJ L124/60, para 203: 'In order to bring the infringements established in this case to an end, taking into account the fact that they still persist today...the Italian authorised dealers must be informed that the warnings, instructions and penalties have been declared invalid. Furthermore, the contracts with the Italian dealers must be amended with respect to the bonus and margin schemes. All authorised dealers within the Community must be told that cross-deliveries within the Community are allowed and not to be penalised in any way.' See, however, Case T-395/94 *Atlantic Container Line v Commission* [2002] ECR II-875, paras 410–16, in which the obligation imposed by the Commission to inform customers that they were entitled, if they so wished, to renegotiate the terms of those contracts or to terminate them was considered as unnecessary.

[34] Joined Cases 6/73 and 7/73 *Istituto Chimioterapico Italiano and Commercial Solvents Corp v Commission* [1974] ECR 223, para 45; Case T-201/04 *Microsoft v Commission* [2007] II-3601, para 1255. See also Commission Decision of 5 March 2008 in Case COMP/38.700 *Greek Lignite*, paras 248, 251, and Art 2.

[35] A Klees, *Europäisches Kartellverfahrensrecht* (Carl Heymanns Verlag, 2005) § 6, paras 80 and 81, suggests that it would be more adequate to require that structural remedies should only be taken if behavioural remedies are not '*sufficiently* effective'.

[36] Draft Reg implementing Arts 81 and 82 of the Treaty, COM (2000) 582 final [2000] OJ C365 E/284, Explanatory Memorandum, Art 7.

[37] See Case T-7/93 *Langnese-Iglo v Commission* [1995] ECR II-1533, para 209; Case T-9/93 *Schöller v Commission* [1995] ECR II-1611, para 163; Joined Cases C-241/91 P and C-242/91 P *Radio Telefis Eireann*

An order to divest assets will only stand the proportionality test in exceptional circumstances.[38] In particular:

> [c]hanges to the structure of an undertaking as it existed before the infringement was committed would only be proportionate where there is a substantial risk of a lasting or repeated infringement that derives from the very structure of the undertaking (Recital 12 of Regulation 1/2003).

Less burdensome might be a decision pursuant to Article 9, where the undertaking concerned can exert a stronger influence on the design of the structural remedy. So far, the Commission has not made use of its competence to order structural remedies based on Article 7(1) of Regulation 1/2003.[39]

Additional obligations

Sometimes, the Commission requires undertakings to grant access to certain information or **11.09** infrastructure.[40] Together with this, it may impose obligations which enable it to ascertain whether or not the undertakings are changing their conduct to comply with their (positive or negative) duties.[41] Often, such obligations consist in providing the Commission or third parties with specific information.[42] For example, in *JCB*[43] the Commission required the parties to inform dealers of the changes in their agreements and in particular their right to carry out passive sales to end-users and other authorized distributors. Limits apply where the decision attempts to regulate the legal relationship between the undertaking concerned and other private parties, given that the consequences in civil law attaching to an infringement of Articles 101 and 102 TFEU, such as the obligation to make good the damage caused to a third party or a possible obligation to enter into a contract, are generally to be determined under national law.[44]

---

and Independent Television Publications v Commission [1995] ECR I-743, para 93 (confirming Case T-76/89 *ITP v Commission* [1991] ECR II-575, para 80). See also Case T-151/01 R *Duales System Deutschland v Commission* [2001] ECR II-3295, para 169.

[38] See eg *Continental Can* [1972] OJ L7/25; *Warner-Lambert/Gillette and Others* and *BIC/Gillette and Others* [1993] OJ L116/21. Today, these operations might fall under merger control rules, but the investigations were initiated before the entry into force of the former EC Merger Control Reg 4069/89. J Schwarze and A Weitbrecht, *Grundzüge des Europäischen Kartellverfahrensrechts* (Nomos, 2004) § 6, para 41.

[39] Commission Staff Working Paper, SEC(2009)574 final, para 92. However, the Commission has accepted structural remedies as part of commitments under Art 9 of Regulation 1/2003. See eg *German Electricity Wholesale Market* [2009] OJ C36/8; *RWE Gas Foreclosure* [2009] OJ C133/10.

[40] *Magill TV Guide/ITP, BBC and RTE* [1989] OJ L78/43 (confirmed in T-69/89 *Radio Telefís Eireann v Commission* [1991] ECR II-485 and Joined Cases C-241/91 P and C-242/91 P *Radio Telefís Eireann and Independent Television Publications v Commission* [1991] ECR I-743), imposing the requirement to supply competitors and third parties, upon request and on a non-discriminatory basis, with advance weekly programme listings and to permit reproduction of those listings.

[41] In *Microsoft* the Commission provided for a Monitoring Trustee to ensure Microsoft's interface disclosures were complete and accurate. See Commission Decision of 24 March 2004 in Case COMP/37.792 *Microsoft*. This obligation was quashed by the GC on the grounds that the Monitoring Trustee did not merely assist the Commission, but was rather intended to assume its competences, and that the Commission was not authorized to delegate such powers. See Case T-201/04 *Microsoft v Commission* [2007] II-3601, paras 1251–72.

[42] See eg to that effect *ECS/Akzo* [1985] OJ L374/1 Arts 4 and 5; *Tetra Pak* [1992] OJ L72/1 Art 4 (confirmed in Case T-83/91 *Tetra Pak v Commission* [1994] ECR-II 755 and Case C-333/94 P *Tetra Pak v Commission* [1996] ECR I-5951); Commission Decision of 19 December 2007 in Cases COMP/34.579 *MasterCard*, COMP/36.518 *EuroCommerce* and COMP/38.580 *Commercial Cards* Arts 4 and 5. See also *VBBB/VBVB* [1982] OJ L54/36, para 4. For the general wording of such obligations, see European Commission Antitrust Manual of Procedures, Internal DG Competition working documents on procedures for the application of Articles 101 and 102 TFEU, March 2012, Module 25 'Follow-up of decisions', para 26.

[43] *JCB* [2002] OJ L69/1 Art 3. See also *Mercedes* [2002] OJ L257/1. As for prohibitions imposed on the undertaking, such additional obligations may not exceed what is appropriate and necessary in order to attain the objectives sought, namely to restore compliance with the infringed rules. See eg Case T-310/94 *Gruber + Weber GmbH & Co KG v Commission* [1998] ECR II-1043, para 178.

[44] Case T-395/94 *Atlantic Container Line and Others v Commission* [2002] ECR II-875, para 414.

Decision to impose a periodic penalty payment

11.10 Sometimes, particularly where the Commission fears open opposition or reluctance on the part of undertakings to fulfill their obligations, it also imposes periodic penalty payments as a means of coercion in order to prevent a refusal to comply or delay in complying.[45] Such a measure may be combined with the original decision,[46] or adopted separately later. The penalty payment must not exceed 5 per cent of the average daily turnover in the preceding business year per day. The outcome is then in the hands of the undertaking, which can avoid the imposition of any penalty by complying with the Commission's orders within the prescribed deadline.[47] Given their different objectives, penalty payments may be imposed in addition to fines pursuant to Article 23 of Regulation 1/2003.[48] Their level depends on a number of factors, such as the delay in complying, the benefits which that delay might have entailed for the undertaking, its size (turnover), and the need for deterrence.[49]

II. Penalties

A. Introduction

11.11 The following sections will deal only with the pecuniary penalties that the Commission may impose for infringements of Articles 101 and 102 TFEU—based on Article 23(2)(a) of Regulation 1/2003—to the exclusion of pecuniary penalties for infringements of decisions adopted pursuant to Article 8 (interim measures[50]), Article 9 (commitments[51]), and for infringements of procedural rules (in relation to Articles 17 to 22 of Regulation 1/2003 concerning requests for information, the power to take statements and inspections).[52] Fines

---

[45] Article 24(1)(a) of Reg 1/2003. See Commission Decision of 10 November 2005 imposing a periodic penalty payment on Microsoft Corporation (Case COMP/37.792 *Microsoft*). Microsoft was ordered to comply with the conditions of an earlier Commission decision, failing which a periodic penalty payment of EUR 2 million per day, calculated from that date, would be imposed. As Microsoft had not (fully) complied with its obligations, the Commission in a subsequent decision of 12 July 2006 ([2008] OJ C138/10; Press Release IP/06/979 'Commission imposes penalty payment of €280.5 million on Microsoft for continued non-compliance with March 2004 Decision', of 12 July 2006) increased that amount to EUR 3 million per day. See also paras 11.26 and 11.88–11.91 of this chapter and Commission Decision of 19 December 2007 in Cases COMP/34.579 *MasterCard*, COMP/36.518 *EuroCommerce*, and COMP/38.580 *Commercial Cards* Art 7. Unlike Reg 17, Art 24(1)(b) and (c) of Reg 1/2003 provides that periodic penalty payments may also be imposed to compel undertakings to comply with interim measures (Art 8) and commitment decisions (Art 9), respectively. In the past, the Commission has used the threat of periodic penalty payments to achieve compliance with interim measures, see eg *Ford Werke* [1982] OJ L256/20.

[46] See eg *ECS/Akzo* [1985] OJ L374/1 Art 6 in which the Commission imposed a periodic penalty payment of ECU 1,000 per day of delay in fulfilling each of the obligations which it had imposed on AKZO in Arts 4 and 5. See also *Irish Sugar* [1997] OJ L258/1 Art 5; *Volkswagen* [1998] OJ L124/60 Art 5.

[47] At the same time, where the Commission considers that the undertaking concerned has not (fully) complied with its obligations, this can lead to significant penalties. See eg Commission Decision of 12 July 2006 in Case COMP/37.792 *Microsoft* (EUR 280.5 million); Commission Decision of 27 February 2008 in Case COMP/37.792 *Microsoft* (EUR 899 million). The ultimate penalty imposed can be lower than originally indicated in the decision pursuant to Art 24(1) of Reg 1/2003.

[48] See *JCB* [2002] OJ L69/1 Arts 4, 6; *Mercedes-Benz* [2002] OJ L 257/1 Arts 3, 5.

[49] See Judgment of 27 June 2012 in Case T-167/08 *Microsoft v Commission*, para 220.

[50] See Ch 14, 'Interim Measures'.

[51] See Ch 13, 'Commitments, Voluntary Adjustments, Conclusion of the Procedure without a Formal Decision'. For a decision imposing fines for a breach of commitments see Commission Decision of 6 March 2013 in Case AT.39530 *Microsoft (Tying)*.

[52] See Ch 9, 'Procedural Infringements: Fines and Periodic Penalty Payments'.

for substantial infringements represent the central tool in the enforcement of EU competition law. Their increased level in recent years shows the Commission's determination to tackle abuses of dominant positions and in particular cartel activity.[53] However, similar trends can be seen with regard to other types of infringements.[54]

According to case law, the Commission may impose a single fine for multiple infringements. **11.12** While this is rather exceptional, it may be appropriate where the infringements form part of a coherent overall strategy, or are concerned with the same type of conduct on different markets, and the undertakings involved are largely the same.[55]

1. Nature of sanctions

The pecuniary penalties imposed by the Commission in competition matters, like other **11.13** measures adopted by the Commission under Regulation 1/2003, are imposed on undertakings.[56] EU competition law—by contrast with that of the US and a small number of EU Member States[57]—does not allow criminal or administrative proceedings to be initiated against

[53] See Cartel Statistics (8 March 2013), point 1.5 'Ten highest cartel fines per case (since 1969)—period 2007–2012' (available at the website of the Directorate-General for Competition ('DG COMP')); Commission Vice President and Commissioner for Competition, J Almunia, 'Cartels: the priority in competition enforcement', Speech/11/268, 15th International Conference on Competition, Berlin, 14 April 2011; MEMO/09/496 'Commission acting against cartels—Questions and answers' of 11 November 2009. See also Commissioner for Competition N Kroes, 'Delivering on the crackdown: recent developments in the European Commission's campaign against cartels', 10th Annual Competition Conference at the EUI, Fiesole, on 13 October 2006.

[54] See eg the increase in the fines level for procedural infringements between Commission Decision of 30 January 2008 in Case COMP/39.326 *E.ON Breach of Seal* (0.14 per cent of total turnover) and Commission Decision of 28 March 2012 in Case COMP/39.793 *EPH and Others* (0.25 per cent of total turnover). For an earlier observation in this direction see D Geradin and D Henry, 'The EC Fining Policy for Violation of Competition Law: An Empirical Review of the Commission Decisional Practice and the Community Courts' Judgments' [2005] European Competition Law Journal 401.

[55] See Judgment of 28 April 2010 in Case T-446/05 *Amann & Söhne v Commission*, paras 154–6, with further references.

[56] Article 23(1) and (2) of Reg 1/2003. In competition law, the concept of undertaking is an economic and functional rather than a legal one, namely that of an economic unit participating in commercial dealings, regardless of its legal structure and status. See Opinion of AG Kokott of 23 April 2009 in Case C-97/08 P *Akzo Nobel and Others v Commission*, para 36 et seq.; Case C-97/08 P *Akzo Nobel and Others v Commission* [2009] ECR I-8237, para 54. Certain natural persons may be regarded as undertakings, eg inventors, artists, independent entrepreneurs, etc where they commercially exploit the product of their talent. If the undertaking found to have committed a violation consisted of an 'unincorporated' business, the Commission would have to address its fining decision to the natural persons operating the business.

[57] In the US, the Antitrust Criminal Penalty Enhancement and Reform Act 2004 raised the statutory maximum fine for corporations to USD 100 million (from USD 10 million) and for individuals to USD 1 million (from USD 350,000). In addition, the Act increased the maximum prison term to ten years per violation (from three years). For the justification and practice of applying criminal sanctions in the US, see GJ Werden, SD Hammond, and BA Barnett, 'Deterrence and Detection of Cartels: Using all the Tools and Sanctions' (1 March 2012). As regards the EU, JD Cook, 'General Report' in 'The Modernization of EU Competition Law Enforcement in the EU' [2004] FIDE 2004 National Reports (Cambridge University Press) 635, has reported that criminal sanctions continue to play a relatively limited role in the enforcement of competition law rules. Ireland appears to be the only one of the old Member States which has provided criminal sanctions in the form of both fines and imprisonment for an infringement of Arts 101 and 102 TFEU as well as the corresponding rules of national law. In Denmark, criminal fines for the infringement of competition rules can be imposed by the criminal courts, but sanctions in the form of prison sentence are not provided for. Also, in two Member States (Austria and France), criminal sanctions for competition infringements which had existed under earlier laws have been removed. In all Member States, of course, it is recognized that some conduct may at the same time infringe the competition rules and constitute a criminal offence under the Penal Code, for example the manipulation of auctions or collusive tendering (eg Germany). The UK Enterprise Act 2002 establishes a 'cartel offence' punishable by imprisonment of up to five years and/or an unlimited fine. The conduct covered includes 'bid-rigging' as well as a number of activities similar to those described in sub-paras (a)–(e) of Art 101(1) TFEU. In addition, an infringement of

natural persons, such as chief executives, employees of undertakings, or any other persons directly responsible for conduct contrary to Articles 101 and 102 TFEU. In EU law, competition law penalties are considered as not having a criminal-law nature; instead, both the sanctions[58] and antitrust proceedings before the European Commission[59] are seen as administrative. However, this does not rule out that sanctions for competition law infringements are considered 'criminal' within the autonomous meaning of the European Convention for the Protection of Human Rights and Fundamental Freedoms (European Convention on Human Rights, 'ECHR')[60] and the Charter of Fundamental Rights.[61] While the EU courts[62] have so far not taken a definitive position in this regard, the jurisprudence of the European Court of Human Rights ('ECtHR') firmly points in that direction.[63] At the same time, it appears that competition law sanctions are

---

Arts 101 and 102 TFEU and the corresponding provisions of the national rules can lead to the disqualification of the directors of corporate undertakings by the court.

[58] According to Art 23(5) of Reg 1/2003, decisions imposing fines 'shall not be of a criminal nature'. See Case T-83/91 *Tetra Pak v Commission* [1994] ECR II-755, para 235; Case T-220/00 *Cheil Jedang v Commission* [2003] ECR II-2473, para 44; Case T-276/04 *Compagnie maritime belge v Commission* [2008] ECR II-1277, para 66; Judgment of 16 June 2011 in Case T-191/06 *FMC Foret v Commission*, para 138. Such qualification was important given that, as a general rule, 'neither criminal law nor the rules of criminal procedure fall within the Community's competence'. See Case C-176/03 *Commission v Council* [2005] ECR I-7879, para 47. The qualification may be relevant when it comes to the status of antitrust fines under national law, eg whether they are tax deductible in some Member States. However, the case law of the EU Courts has clarified that fines must not be tax deductible as otherwise they would be partly paid by the taxpayer. See Case T-10/89 *Hoechst v Commission* [1992] ECR-II 629, para 369; Case C-429/07 *Inspecteur van de Belastingdienst v X BV* [2009] ECR I-4833, para 39. J Temple Lang, 'Developments, Issues and New Remedies—The Duties of National Authorities and Courts under Art 10 of the EC Treaty' [2004] Fordham International Law Journal 1904, 1910, has argued that it would be contrary to Art 10 EC (now Art 4(3) TEU) for a Member State to reduce the effect of a Commission fine by allowing it to be deducted for tax purposes, or otherwise to reduce the costs of the infringement. For a recent ruling by the Belgian Constitutional Court confirming that EU cartel fines are not tax-deductible, see Judgment No 161/2012 of 20 December 2012.

[59] See Case 45/69 *Boehringer Mannheim v Commission* [1970] ECR 769, para 23; Joined Cases C-204/00 P, C-205/00 P, C-211/00 P, C-213/00 P, C-217/00 P and C-219/00 P *Aalborg Portland and Others v Commission* [2004] ECR I-123, para 200. See, however, Opinion of AG Bot of 26 October 2010 in Joined Cases C-201/09 P and C-216/09 P *ArcelorMittal Luxembourg v Commission* and *Commission v ArcelorMittal Luxembourg and Others*, para 41; Opinion of AG Kokott of 14 April 2011 in Case C-109/10 P *Solvay v Commission*, paras 255 and 329.

[60] See Arts 6, 7 and Protocol No 7. According to Art 6(3) of the Treaty on European Union ('TEU'), '[f]undamental rights, as guaranteed by the European Convention for the Protection of Human Rights and Fundamental Freedoms and as they result from the constitutional traditions common to the Member States, shall constitute general principles of the Union's law'.

[61] See Arts 49, 50. According to Art 6(1) TEU, the rights, freedoms, and principles set out in the Charter 'shall have the same legal value as the Treaties'. They 'shall be interpreted in accordance with the general provisions in Title VII of the Charter governing its interpretation and application and with due regard to the explanations referred to in the Charter, that set out the sources of those provisions.' Article 52(3) of the Charter stipulates that: 'In so far as this Charter contains rights which correspond to rights guaranteed by the Convention for the Protection of Human Rights and Fundamental Freedoms, the meaning and scope of those rights shall be the same as those laid down by the said Convention. This provision shall not prevent Union law providing more extensive protection.' Cf Judgment of 26 February 2013 in Case C-617/10 *Åklagaren v Hans Åkerberg Fransson*, para 20.

[62] See Case C-45/08 *Spector Photo Group and Van Raemdonck* [2009] ECR I-12073, para 42, with reference to Case C-199/92 P *Hüls v Commission* [1999] ECR I-4287, paras 149–50; Case T-279/02 *Degussa v Commission* [2006] ECR II-897, paras 71 and 115; Case T-99/04 *AC-Treuhand v Commission* [2008] ECR II-1501, para 24 with further references. See also Opinion of AG Bot of 26 October 2010 in Joined Cases C-201/09 P and C-216/09 P *ArcelorMittal Luxembourg v Commission* and *Commission v ArcelorMittal Luxembourg and Others*, para 42; Opinion of AG Sharpston of 10 February 2011 in Case C-272/09 P *KME Germany v Commission*, paras 63 and 64.

[63] The standard test relies on the so-called 'Engel criteria', namely the legal qualification of the applicable norm within the respective legal order, the nature of the infringement as well as the nature and severity of the sanction. See *Engel and Others v The Netherlands* App nos 5100–5102/71 (ECtHR, 8 June 1976), para 82; *Jussila v Finland* App no 73053/01 (ECtHR, 23 November 2006), paras 29–32. Hence, while the legal

not considered as part of the 'hard core' criminal law for which the criminal law principles of the ECHR would apply with their full stringency.[64]

2. The object of sanctions: undertakings, successors, and accessories

The concept of the undertaking and parental liability[65]

In the case of a group of companies, the Commission's starting point is that the competition rules are aimed at 'economic units, each of which consists of a unitary organisation of personal, tangible and intangible elements which pursues a specific economic aim on a long-term basis'.[66] Given that infringements are committed by undertakings as economic units while enforcement decisions can only be addressed to legal persons, the Commission in each case has to determine the 'boundaries' of the undertaking and thus the legal person(s) to whom an infringement by the undertaking is to be attributed.[67] According to settled case law, the fact that a subsidiary has separate legal personality is not sufficient to exclude the possibility that it constitutes one undertaking with the parent company, especially where the subsidiary does not independently decide its own conduct on the market, but carries out, in all material respects, the instructions given to it by the parent company, having regard in particular to the economic and legal links between them.[68] This requires that the parent company (i) was able to exercise decisive influence

11.14

---

qualification as 'non-criminal' in Art 23(5) of Reg 1/2003 serves as a starting point, it is rather of secondary importance. See *Öztürk v Germany* App no 8544/79 (ECtHR, 23 October 1984), para 52. For competition law infringements see *Menarini Diagnostics v Italy* App no 43509/08 (ECtHR, 27 September 2011), paras 39–44. See also Opinion of AG Bot of 26 October 2010 in Joined Cases C-201/09 P and C-216/09 P *ArcelorMittal Luxembourg v Commission* and *Commission v ArcelorMittal Luxembourg and Others*, para 42. Following the judgment in *Menarini*, the EFTA Court has confirmed that the antitrust proceedings carried out by the EFTA Surveillance Authority 'fall, as a matter of principle, within the criminal sphere for the purposes of Article 6 ECHR' and that, having regard to the nature and severity of the applicable sanctions (EUR 12.89 million in the case at hand) as well as the stigma attached to being held accountable for an abuse of a dominant position, the criminal charge could not be considered as being of minor weight. See Judgment of 18 April 2012 in Case E-15/10 *Posten Norge v EFTA Surveillance Authority*, paras 88 and 90.

[64] See *Jussila v Finland* App no 73053/01 (ECtHR, 23 November 2006), para 43; *Hüseyin Turan v Turkey* App no 11529/02 (ECtHR, 4 March 2008), para 32; *Menarini Diagnostics v Italy* App no 43509/08 (ECtHR, 27 September 2011), paras 59 and 62 ('Par ailleurs, la Cour rappelle que la nature d'une procédure administrative peut différer, sous plusieurs aspects, de la nature d'une procédure pénale au sens strict du terme. Si ces différences ne sauraient exonérer les Etats contractants de leur obligation de respecter toutes les garanties offertes par le volet pénal de l'article 6, elles peuvent néanmoins influencer les modalités de leur application'). See also Case T-99/04 *AC-Treuhand v Commission* [2008] ECR II-1501, para 113; Judgment of 13 July 2011 in Case T-138/07 *Schindler v Commission*, para 52; Opinion of AG Kokott of 14 April 2011 in Case C-109/10 P *Solvay v Commission*, para 256, and Opinion of 18 April 2013 in Case C-501/11 P *Schindler Holding and Others v Commission*, paras 25, 34–5 and 151. But see EFTA Court, Judgment of 18 April 2012 in Case E-15/10 *Posten Norge v EFTA Surveillance Authority*, paras 89 and 90. For an analysis of the compatibility of EU antitrust procedures and sanctions with ECHR law, see W Wils, 'The Increased Level of EU Antitrust Fines, Judicial Review, and the European Convention on Human Rights' (March 2010) 33(1) World Competition; Coutrelis, 'Amendes, procedures *antitrust* et CEDH: l'harmonie plutôt que la confrontation' (2011) 29 Revue Lamy de la Concurrence 108.

[65] For an overview of the EU Courts' case law on parental liability, see J Kokott and D Dittert, 'Die Verantwortlichkeit von Muttergesellschaften für Kartellvergehen ihrer Tochtergesellschaften im Lichte der Rechtsprechung der Unionsgerichte', 2012 Wirtschaft und Wettbewerb 670–83. For an analysis of the compatibility of the case law on parental liability with corporate law principles and its basis in the EU Treaties, see Opinion of AG Kokott of 18 April 2013 in Case C-501/11 P *Schindler Holding and Others v Commission*, paras 65–67, 74–77 and 84.

[66] Case T-11/89 *Shell v Commission* [1992] ECR II-757, para 311. See also Case T-352/94 *Mo och Domsjö v Commission* [1998] ECR II-1989, para 87; Judgment of 25 October 2011 in Case T-349/08 *Uralita v Commission*, para 35.

[67] Judgment of 25 October 2011 in Case T-349/08 *Uralita v Commission*, para 36.

[68] Case 6/72 *Europemballage and Continental Can v Commission* [1973] ECR 215, para 15; Case C-294/98 P *Metsä-Serla and Others v Commission* [2000] ECR I-10065, para 27; Case 97/08 P *Akzo Nobel and Others v Commission* [2009] ECR I-8237, paras 58–9. At the same time, the fact that the subsidiary is

on the subsidiary's commercial policy; and (ii) has effectively exercised this power.[69] Commercial policy in this context will be interpreted broadly as relating to strategic orientations and overall business objectives, rather than the operational business.[70] Consequently, it is not necessary for the parent company to have exercised decisive influence specifically as regards the business sector where the infringement occurred.[71] Also, rather than steering the subsidiary's daily conduct by way of instructions, it will often be sufficient for the parent company to rely on an *ex-post* control, with intervention when problems arise.[72] Where the parent company forms part of the infringing undertaking because it exercises control, it is deemed to have committed the infringement itself (personal responsibility).[73] This justifies the joint and several liability of both parent and subsidiary.[74] Given that the parent company is liable as one of the principals of an economic unit together with the subsidiary, it is not necessary that it carries out an economic business itself.[75]

---

not acting autonomously does not relieve it of responsibility (Joined Cases T-236/01, T-239/01, T-244/01 to T-246/01, T-251/01 and T-252/01 *Tokai Carbon and Others v Commission* [2004] ECR II-1181, para 279) and the Commission has discretion in choosing which company (subsidiary or parent) to hold liable. See Case T-299/08 *Elf Aquitaine v Commission* [2011] ECR II-2149, para 60; Judgment of 25 October 2011 in Case T-349/08 *Uralita v Commission*, para 60.

[69] Case 107/82 *AEG-Telefunken v Commission* [1983] ECR 3151, para 50; Case 97/08 P *Akzo Nobel and Others v Commission* [2009] ECR I-8237, para 60. Most cases have so far concerned the attribution of liability to a parent company for an infringement in which one of its subsidiaries was directly implicated. However, a strict parent–subsidiary relationship is not a necessary condition. This has been confirmed by judgments like the one in Case T-43/02 *Jungbunzlauer v Commission* [2006] ECR II-3435, paras 125–30, which concerned the management of the group by a subsidiary which thereby exercised decisive influence over a sister company.

[70] See Judgments of 12 October 2011 in Case T-41/05 *Alliance One International v Commission*, para 162 and in Case T-38/05 *Agroexpansión v Commission*, para 172; Judgment of 2 February 2012 in Case T-77/08 *The Dow Chemical Company v Commission*, paras 93 and 107; Judgment of 29 June 2012 in Case T-360/09 *E.ON Ruhrgas and E.ON AG v Commission*, para 280; Order of 15 June 2012 in Case C-494/11 P *Otis Luxembourg and Others v Commission*, para 42; Judgment of 12 December 2012 in Case T-392/09 *1. garantovaná v Commission*, paras 48 and 49; Judgment of 8 May 2013 in Case C-508/11 P *Eni v Commission*, para 64. Ultimately, what matters is the unity of the conduct on the market. See Judgment of 25 October 2011 in Case T-349/08 *Uralita v Commission*, para 37.

[71] Judgment of 12 October 2011 in Case T-38/05 *Agroexpansión v Commission*, paras 164 and 167; Judgment of 16 November 2011 in Case T-72/06 *Groupe Gascogne v Commission*, para 81; Judgment of 8 May 2013 in Case C-508/11 P *Eni v Commission*, paras 64–5; Judgment of 17 May 2013 in Case T-146/09 *Parker v Commission*, para 181.

[72] See Judgment of 16 November 2011 in Case T-72/06 *Groupe Gascogne v Commission*, paras 76–8 and 82–9. Moreover, the GC considers that 'as a result of the parent company's power of supervision, the parent company has a responsibility to ensure that its subsidiary complies with the competition rules. An undertaking which has the possibility of exercising decisive influence over the business strategy of its subsidiary may therefore be presumed, in the absence of proof to the contrary, to have the possibility of establishing a policy aimed at compliance with competition law and to take all necessary and appropriate measures to supervise the subsidiary's commercial management. Mere failure to do so by the shareholder with a power of supervision over such matters cannot in any event be accepted as a ground on which he can decline his liability. Accordingly, since any gains resulting from illegal activities accrue to the shareholders, it is only fair that that those who have the power of supervision should assume liability for the illegal business activities of their subsidiaries.' Judgment of 2 February 2012 in Case T-77/08 *The Dow Chemical Company v Commission*, para 101.

[73] Judgment of 27 June 2012 in Case T-372/10 *Bolloré v Commission*, paras 51, 52, and 193. See also Judgment of 29 September 2011 in Case C-521/09 P *Elf Aquitaine v Commission*, para 87. While in EU law the personal responsibility attaches to the undertaking as a whole (of which the parent company forms one part), this derogation from the principles of company law is justified by the need to ensure an effective and deterrent competition poliy. See Judgment of 13 December 2012 in Case T-103/08 *Versalis and ENI v Commission*, para 77.

[74] Judgment of 27 September 2012 in Case T-360/06 *Heijmans v Commission*, para 50. See also Opinion of AG Kokott of 29 November 2012 in Case C-440/11 P *Commission v Stichting Administratiekontoor Portielje*, para 32. On the concept of joint and several liability of the undertaking in EU law see A Böhlke, 'Die gesamtschuldnerische Verantwortlichkeit im EU-Wettbewerbsrecht', EuZW 20/2011, 781–4.

[75] Opinion of AG Kokott of 29 November 2012 in Case C-440/11 P *Commission v Stichting Administratiekontoor Portielje*, paras 36 and 55. See, however, the divergent view of the GC in the judgment under appeal (Judgment of 16 June 2011 in Joined Cases T-208/08 and T-209/08 *Gosselin Group and Stichting Administratiekantoor Portielje v Commission*).

The Commission bears the burden of proof for the exercise of decisive influence by the parent **11.15** company over the subsidiary, and may for this rely on a bundle of indicia relating to the legal, organizational, and economic links between them.[76] However, in case a subsidiary is wholly or nearly wholly[77] owned, there is a rebuttable presumption (the '*Stora* presumption') that the second condition is fulfilled.[78] In order to avoid liability, the parent company must rebut the presumption, which means that it has to adduce sufficient evidence to show that its subsidiary in fact acted fully[79] autonomously on the market.[80] This question cannot be assessed solely on the basis of the relevant company law, but must take account also of economic reality, which includes informal ways to exercise control.[81] Any rebuttal will typically be difficult, as it requires a negative fact to be proven, ie that the parent company did not actually exercise control.[82] However,

---

[76] Judgment of 27 September 2012 in Case T-347/06 *Nynäs Petroleum and Nynas Belgium v Commission*, para 55.

[77] In its Decision of 19 January 2005 in Case COMP/E-1/.37.773 *MCAA*, paras 257–8, the Commission relied on the presumption of decisive influence in a case where Elf Aquitaine held 98 per cent of the shares in its subsidiary Atofina. This has been confirmed, in principle, by the EU Courts. See Case T-174/05 *Elf Aquitaine v Commission* [2009] ECR II-183, paras 120, 125 and 156–7 (on this point confirmed in Case C-521/09 P *Elf Aquitaine v Commission*, para 63, but annulled for other reasons). See also Judgment of 7 June 2011 in Case T-206/06 *Elf Aquitaine and Total v Commission*, para 56 (shareholding of 96.48 per cent).

[78] Case C-286/98 *Stora Kopparbergs v Commission* [2000] ECR I-9925, paras 26–9; Case 97/08 P *Akzo Nobel and Others v Commission* [2009] ECR I-8237, para 60. As to the *raison d'être* of the (rebuttable) presumption and its compatibility with human rights principles see also Judgment of 13 July 2011 in Joined Cases T-141/07, T-142/07, T-145/07, and T-146/07 *Otis and Others v Commission*, paras 71–7; Judgment of 27 June 2012 in Case T-372/10 *Bolloré v Commission*, paras 31–50; and Judgment of 29 September 2011 in Case C-521/09 P *Elf Aquitaine v Commission*, paras 59–60 and 62. In the past, some doubt prevailed as to whether the Commission could simply rely on the 100 per cent ownership by the parent company to shift the burden of proof, or whether it needed to present additional indicia supporting the presumption. See, eg, Case T-325/01 *DaimlerChrysler v Commission* [2005] ECR II-3319, para 219; Joined Cases T-109/02, T-118/02, T-122/02, T-125/02, T-126/02, T-128/02, T-129/02, T-132/02 and T-136/02 *Bolloré v Commission* [2007] ECR II-947, para 132. However, the ECJ has made clear that while the Commission may adduce such further indicia, it is not required to do so. Case 97/08 P *Akzo Nobel and Others v Commission* [2009] ECR I-8237, paras 61–2; Judgment of 29 September 2011 in Case C-521/09 P *Elf Aquitaine v Commission*, paras 80 and 96; Judgment of 7 June 2011 in Case T-206/06 *Elf Aquitaine and Total v Commission*, paras 48 and 51–2. See also Opinion of AG Kokott of 23 April 2009 in Case 97/08 P *Akzo Nobel and Others v Commission*, paras 49–76. For the question whether the reliance, only for some parent companies, on additional indicia may violate the principle of non-discrimination see Judgment of 29 September 2011 in Case C-521/09 P *Elf Aquitaine v Commission*, para 97; Joined Cases C-628/10 P and C-14/11 P *Alliance One International and Standard Commercial Tobacco v Commission* and *Commission v Alliance International and Others*, paras 49–53 and 59.

[79] Cf Order of 15 June 2012 in Case C-493/11 P *United Technologies v Commission*, para 38.

[80] Case 97/08 P *Akzo Nobel and Others v Commission* [2009] ECR I-8237, para 61. The parent is not barred from presenting new rebuttal evidence in court. See Judgment of 16 November 2011 in Case T-54/06 *Kendrion v Commission*, para 71; Judgment of 27 September 2012 in Case T-360/06 *Heijmans v Commission*, para 63. At the same time, the Commission may present additional clarifications in order to complement an already sufficient motivation. See Judgment of 27 September 2012 in Case T-348/06 *Total Nederland v Commission*, para 113. In case the parent sells the subsidiary, it has to ensure that it preserves the necessary information for rebuttal, eg by agreeing on a right of access to the transferred archives. See Judgment of 27 June 2012 in Case T-372/10 *Bolloré v Commission*, paras 137 and 152. For constellations which could in principle constitute a successful rebuttal see the Opinion of AG Kokott in Case C-97/08 P *Akzo Nobel and Others v Commission* at n 67, referenced in the Judgment of 12 December 2012 in Case T-392/09 *1. garantovaná v Commission*, para 52. According to AG Wahl, the case law does not clarify whether decisive influence can be exercised passively, thus begging the question whether 'abstention from exercising decisive influence … can be the basis for rebuttal of the presumption'. See N Wahl, 'Parent Company Liability—A Question of Facts or Presumption?', 19th St Gallen International Competition Law Forum, 7 and 8 June 2012.

[81] Opinion of AG Kokott of 29 November 2012 in Case C-440/11 P *Commission v Stichting Administratiekontoor Portielje*, paras 71–4. Hence, it may not be sufficient to present evidence of only the formal management structure (eg voting rights, reporting lines). Rather, rebuttal evidence might also have to cover the everyday commercial dealings within the group (see paras 77 and 90).

[82] In *Souris-Topps*, the Commission stated that 'successful rebuttal must rather be based on precise explanations on how the relationship between the parent and its subsidiaries is governed', and not 'on general

this does not amount to a *probatio diabolica* and is in fact normal in cases where a presumption applies.[83] Where parent and/or subsidiary submit arguments and evidence to demonstrate the autonomy of the subsidiary, the Commission has to analyse and take a position on them in the decision; insufficient motivation in this regard can lead to the annulment of the decision.[84] Moreover, the rejection of arguments advanced in order to rebut the presumption is subject to judicial control for manifest errors of assessment.[85]

11.16 The presumption also applies in cases where the ultimate parent is linked to the subsidiary via intermediate holding companies, as long as it holds (nearly) 100 per cent of the shares in the subsidiary.[86] As for the case of joint ventures, the *Stora* presumption does not strictly apply, given that the Commission first has to demonstrate the existence of a 'joint management power' by the respective parent companies before the exercise of decisive influence can be presumed.[87] This will ususally entail a case-by-case analysis of the legal, organizational, and economic links between these parent companies and the joint venture. However, once joint

---

assertions'. See Commission Decision of 26 May 2004 in Case COMP/37.980 *Souris-Topps*, para 165. This is in line with settled case law, according to which 'it is for the parent company to put before the Court any evidence relating to the economic and legal organisational links between its subsidiary and itself which in its view are apt to demonstrate that they do not constitute a single economic entity'. See Case T-112/05 *Akzo Nobel and Others v Commission* [2007] ECR II-5049, para 65; Opinion of AG Kokott of 18 April 2013 in Case C-501/11 P *Schindler Holding and Others v Commission*, paras 104–5. Morover, the EU Courts have stressed that mere assertions are insufficient and that actual proof of autonomy is required. See eg Case T-174/05 *Elf Aquitaine v Commission* [2009] ECR II-183, paras 157–8, 162–5, 167, and 169; Judgment of 29 September 2011 in Case C-521/09 P *Elf Aquitaine v Commission*, paras 60–1; Order of 13 September 2012 in Case C-495/11 P *Total and Elf Aquitaine v Commission*, paras 56 and 57 (not just plausible alternative). At the same time, however, the GC has stated 'qu'il n'est pas exigé des parties concernées qu'elles rapportent une preuve directe et irréfutable de l'autonomie de comportement de la filiale sur le marché, mais uniquement qu'elles produisent des éléments de preuve susceptibles de démontrer cette autonomie'. Case T-174/05 *Elf Aquitaine v Commission* [2009] ECR II-183, para 173.

[83] See Judgment of 29 September 2011 in Case C-521/09 P *Elf Aquitaine v Commission*, paras 65–6 and 70; Judgment of 27 September 2012 in Case T-343/06 *Shell Petroleum and Others v Commission*, para 54. See also Opinion of AG Kokott of 29 November 2012 in Case C-440/11 P *Commission v Stichting Administratiekontoor Portielje*, para 53.

[84] Case T-185/06 *L'Air liquide v Commission* [2011] ECR II-2809, para 60 et seq; Case T-196/06 *Edison v Commission*, para 56 et seq; Case C-521/09 P *Elf Aquitaine v Commission*, para 144 et seq. Cf also Judgment of 13 December 2012 in Case C-654/11 P *Transcatab v Commission*, para 36. However, 'the Commission is not obliged to adopt a position on all the arguments relied on by the parties concerned but it is sufficient if it sets out the facts and the legal considerations having decisive importance in the context of the decision. In particular, the Commission is not required to define its position on matters which were manifestly irrelevant or insignificant or plainly of secondary importance'. Case T-185/06 *L'Air liquide v Commission*, para 64. See also Order of 7 February 2012 in Case C-421/11 P *Total and Elf Aquitaine v Commission*, para 43 et seq; Order of 13 September 2012 in Case C-495/11 P *Total and Elf Aquitaine v Commission*, paras 46–53.

[85] Case C-90/09 P *General Química and Others v Commission* [2011] ECR I-1, para 78. The ECJ has indicated that it is for the GC alone to appreciate rebuttal arguments, with only limited grounds for appeal. See Judgment of 3 May 2012 in Case C-298/11 P *Legris Industries v Commission*, para 53.

[86] Case C-90/09 P *General Química and Others v Commission* [2011] ECR I-1, para 90; Judgment of 12 October 2011 in Case T-38/05 *Agroexpansión v Commission*, para 108; Judgment of 6 March 2012 in Case T-65/06 *FL Smidth & Co v Commission*, paras 22–4.

[87] See Case T-314/01 *Avebe v Commission* [2006] ECR II-3085, para 135 et seq and 138. While it has occasionally been argued that *Avebe* does not constitute a valid precedent as the joint venture in that case had no legal personality, the GC dismissed this objection in its Judgment of 2 February 2012 in Case T-77/08 *The Dow Chemical Company v Commission*, para 94. For further cases dealing with joint venture situations see Judgment of 27 October 2010 in Case T-24/05 *Alliance One International and Others v Commission*, para 163 et seq (confirmed in Joined Cases C-628/10 P and C-14/11 P *Alliance One International and Standard Commercial Tobacco v Commission* and *Commission v Alliance International and Others*, paras 101 and 103); Judgment of 13 July 2011 in Joined Cases T-141/07, T-142/07, T-145/07, and T-146/07 *Otis and Others v Commission*, paras 91 et seq, 106 et seq.; Judgment of 14 March 2013 in Case T-587/08 *Fresh Del Monte v Commission*, para 60 et seq.

management power has been established, for instance by reference to the voting rights on the relevant boards, that may be sufficient to show the exercise of decisive influence.[88]

Special problems may arise where there is no legal person at the head of a group of companies. For instance, in *Aristrain* the Commission based its decision solely on the fact of common ownership by certain family members when imputing to *Siderúrgica Aristrain Madrid* the conduct of its sister company *José Maria Aristrain*. The ECJ stated that: **11.17**

> the simple fact that the share capital of two separate commercial companies is held by the same person or the same family is insufficient, in itself, to establish that those two companies are an economic unit with the result that, under Community competition law, the actions of one company can be attributed to the other and that one can be held liable to pay a fine for the other.[89]

Where there is no legal person at the head of a group of companies, as the person responsible for coordinating the group's activities, the Commission may nevertheless hold the various group companies jointly and severally liable for the acts of the group if there are factors which show that they constitute one economic unit. This may be the case, for instance, where a natural person with key functions in the various group companies represents them in the cartel as a group.[90] The same applies to companies which are family-owned and where there are close economic links or dependencies and/or one company represents the rest of the group on the market.[91]

Where several group companies are all controlled by one parent company, the existence of one undertaking is not in question, which in principle would allow the Commission to hold each entity liable for the infringement committed by the undertaking as a whole. Nevertheless, the Commission may hold only one company liable for the conduct of other group companies where this is justified by the particular circumstances of the case, for instance where it has supervisory or coordinating functions.[92] The joint and several liability together with other group companies can also be relevant for the amount of the fine in so far as it is influenced by the size of the undertaking (eg deterrence multiplier, 10 per cent turnover cap).[93] **11.18**

---

[88] See Order of 15 June 2012 in Case C-494/11 P *Otis Luxembourg and Others v Commission*, paras 43 and 49; Judgment of 27 September 2012 in Case T-343/06 *Shell Petroleum and Others v Commission*, paras 45, 46, and 51.

[89] Case C-196/99 P *Siderúrgica Aristrain Madrid v Commission* [2003] ECR I-11005, paras 96–9. See C Steinle 'Kartellgeldbußen gegen Konzernunternehmen nach dem Aristrain Urteil des EuGH' [2004] Europäisches Wirtschafts- und Steuerrecht (EWS) 118. A Montesa and A Givaja 'When Parents Pay for their Children's Wrongs: Attribution of Liability for EC Antitrust Infringements in Parent-Subsidiary Scenarios' [2006] World Competition 555, 570, have argued that the only material difference between *Aristrain* and *Stora* lies in the fact that the head of the group of undertakings was a natural person in the former case and a legal person in the latter case.

[90] See eg Case T-9/99 *HFB and Others v Commission* [2002] ECR-II 1487, paras 54–67 (confirmed on appeal in Joined Cases C-189/02 P, C-202/02 P, C-205/02 P to C-208/02 P and C-213/02 P *Dansk Rørindustri and Others v Commission* [2005] ECR I-5425, paras 116–20), where the conclusion that an economic unit existed was reached on the basis of a series of documents which established that a natural person controlled the various companies concerned, held key functions in the managing bodies of those companies, and also represented them, as a group, at meetings where the cartel was arranged.

[91] See Case T-52/03 *Knauf Gips v Commission* [2008] ECR II-115, para 337 et seq (annulled on appeal in Case C-407/08 P *Knauf Gips v Commission* [2010] ECR I-6375, para 63 et seq, which nevertheless confirmed the decision).

[92] See eg Case T-11/89 *Shell v Commission* [1992] ECR II-757, paras 308–15; Case T-43/02 *Jungbunzlauer v Commission* [2006] ECR II-3435, paras 122–30 (see also paras 131–3 for the applicant's economic succession to the liability incurred by another group company which formerly coordinated the group activities in the relevant business sector).

[93] Case T-37/05 *World Wide Tobacco España v Commission* [2011] ECR II-41, para 124; Joined Cases T-71/03, T-74/03, T-87/03 and T-91/03 *Tokai Carbon and Others v Commission* [2005] ECR II-10, para 390; Case T-52/03 *Knauf Gips v Commission* [2008] ECR II-115, para 353.

Legal and economic succession

11.19 A change in the legal form and name of an undertaking as such does not exonerate it from liabil-ity for anticompetitive behaviour.[94] By the same token, where an economic operator transfers its business activities to another undertaking, the transferor undertaking continuing in existence remains liable for any past infringement.[95] This also applies where the infringing business is carried out through a subsidiary, the shares of which are sold to another parent. In both cases, liability is split between the former operator (including the former parent) and the new operator (including the new parent) according to the periods in which each of them controlled the busi-ness.[96] In the event that the business has been *merged* with that of another undertaking, with the result that the original undertaking has ceased to exist, the responsibility may lie with the merged entity in line with the principle of legal continuity.[97] Conversely, if the business is *transferred*, the question is whether there is an economic and functional continuity between the original undertaking and its successor.[98] Where, between the commission of the infringement and the time the undertaking in question must answer for it, the person responsible for the operation of that undertaking has *ceased to exist* in law, it is necessary

> to find the combination of physical and human elements which contributed to the commis-sion of the infringement and then to identify the person who has become responsible for their operation,

so as to avoid the situation whereby, because of the disappearance of the person responsible for its operation when the infringement was committed, the undertaking may fail to answer for it.[99] Furthermore, even where the infringing company continues to exist as an economic operator, the

---

[94] Joined Cases 29/83 and 30/83 *CRAM and Rheinzink v Commission* [1984] ECR 1679, para 9; Case C-297/98 P *SCA Holding v Commission* [2000] ECR I-10101, para 29; Case C-280/06 *ETI and Others* [2007] ECR I-10893, paras 42 and 43. See also Joined Cases T-117/07 and T-121/07 *Areva and Others v Commission* [2011] ECR II-633, para 59; *Welded Steel Mesh* [1989] OJ L260/1, para 195.

[95] Case C-49/92 P *Commission v Anic* [1999] ECR I-4125, para 145; Case T-327/94 *SCA Holding v Commission* [1998] ECR II-1373, para 63; Case T-195/06 *Solvay Solexis v Commission* [2011] ECR II-178 (summ pub), para 310. When the infringing entity is still in existence, it must be held liable for the infringe-ment, irrespective of the nature of its current activities in the market: see *Welded Steel Mesh* [1989] OJ L260/1, para 194; *Amino Acids* [2001] OJ L152/24, para 444.

[96] See Joined Cases T-122/07 to T-124/07 *Siemens AG Österreich and Others v Commission*, paras 139 and 141–4. In particular, the new parent is not liable for the past conduct of its newly acquired subsidiary. See Case 279/98 P *Cascades v Commission* [2000] ECR I-9693, paras 78 and 79; Case T-9/99 *HFB and Others v Commission* [2002] ECR II-1487, paras 103 and 104; *Cartonboard* [1994] OJ L243/1, para 145. This applies even where the acquirer is aware that the subsidiary participated in an infringement prior to the acquisition. See Case C-286/98 P *Stora Kopparbergs Bergslags v Commission* [2000] ECR I-9925, paras 37–9. As regards the determination of the basic amount of the fine in case of a change of parents see Judgment of 6 March 2012 in Case T-64/06 *FLS Plast v Commission*, paras 100, 101, and 186.

[97] Judgment of 9 September 2011 in Case T-25/06 *Alliance One v Commission*, paras 219 and 220; Judgment of 25 October 2011 in Case T-349/08 *Uralita v Commission*, paras 65–8. See *Food Flavour Enhancers* [2004] OJ L75/1, para 192: 'Miwon Corporation Limited's full merger with Sewon Co. Ltd to form Daesang Corporation means that responsibility passes to the new entity. There is an obvious continuity between Miwon and the new entity into which it has been subsumed. Miwon ceased to exist in law and its legal personality as well as all its assets and staff were transferred to Daesang Corporation.'

[98] Joined Cases 40–48/73, 50/73, 54–56/73, 111/73, 113/73 and 114/73 *Coöperative Vereniging 'Suiker Unie' v Commission* [1975] ECR 1663, paras 75–88; Case C-49/92 P *Anic Partecipazioni v Commission* [1991] ECR I-4125, para 145; Opinion of AG Mischo of 18 May 2000 in Case C-297/98 *SCA Holding v Commission* [2000] ECR I-10101, para 16; Opinion of AG Kokott of 3 July 2007 in Case C-280/06 *ETI and Others*, para 75 et seq. See also *Welded Steel Mesh* [1989] OJ L260/1, para 194.

[99] Case T-6/89 *Enichem Anic v Commission* [1991] ECR II-1623, paras 236–8; Joined Cases T-305/94 to T-307/94, T-313/94 to T-316/94, T-318/94, T-325/94, T-328/94, T-329/94 and T-335/94 *Limburgse Vinyl Maatschappij and Others v Commission* [1999] ECR II-931, para 953. If the original undertaking does no longer carry out economic activities this may be treated the same way as cases where the legal person ceases to exist. See Case C-280/06 *ETI and Others* [2007] ECR I-10893, para 40; Case T-134/94 *NMH Stahlwerke v Commission* [1999] ECR II-239, paras 137–8.

Commission may hold another company liable to which the relevant business was sold as part of a *group restructuring*, as long as both are part of one economic unit (undertaking) or at least are tied to each other by structural links (group companies).[100] Finally, liability may also be transferred where such restructurings are carried out in bad faith, after the Commission or national competition authority ('NCA') has initiated investigations, with the intention to *circumvent* liability for past infringements.[101] Conversely, the mere contractual arrangement to indemnify the seller from liability (eg in a sale and purchase agreement) does not lead to a transfer of responsibility under the competition rules.[102] Where a decision seeks to attribute liability for an infringement to the purchaser or other successor of an undertaking alleged to have committed the infringement, the Commission must clearly identify the identity of the legal entity which is the legal successor and demonstrate the continuance by that entity of the business activity in question.[103]

The liability of accessories

The Commission decision in *Organic Peroxyde* sets out the Commission's views on the liability **11.20** of consultancy companies[104] which provided services to a price-fixing and market-sharing cartel agreement but did not manufacture and/or sell the products. The Commission found that AC-Treuhand, a Swiss-based consultancy company, played an important role in the organization and implementation of the infringement, and therefore imposed a sanction. Among other

---

[100] Joined Cases C-204/00 P, C-205/00 P, C-211/00 P, C-213/00 P, C-217/00 P, and C-219/00 P *Aalborg Portland and Others v Commission* [2004] ECR I-123, paras 344 and 359 (50 per cent participation); Case C-280/06 *ETI and Others* [2007] ECR I-10893, paras 41–51; Case T-405/06 *ArcelorMittal Luxembourg and Others v Commission* [2009] ECR II-789, para 109; Case T-194/06 *SNIA v Commission* [2011] ECR II-3119, paras 64–6. See also Joined Cases T-305/94, T-306/94, T-307/94, T-313/94 to T-316/94, T-318/94, T-325/94, T-328/94, T-329/94 and T-335/94 *Limburgse Vinyl Maatschappij and Others v Commission* [1999] ECR II-931, paras 943 and 956–8. For the succession into the liability of a company that coordinated the business activities of a group see also Case T-43/02 *Jungbunzlauer v Commission* [2006] ECR II-3435, para 131. In a recent judgment, the GC rejected economic succession in a case where the subsidiary to which the business was transferred had been created with a view to (immediately) selling its shares to an independent third party. See Judgment of 17 May 2013 in Case T-146/09 *Parker v Commission*, paras 83–121.

[101] See Case C-280/06 *ETI and Others* [2007] ECR I-10893, para 41 (and the Opinion of AG Kokott in this case, paras 74, 79, and 82); Case C-49/92 P *Anic Partecipazioni v Commission* [1991] ECR I-4125, para 146; Case T-9/99 *HFB and Others v Commission* [2002] ECR II-1487, para 107; Judgment of 17 May 2013 in Case T-146/09 *Parker v Commission*, paras 95 and 96. An even more far-reaching view has been presented by AG Bot in Opinion of 26 October 2010 in Joined Cases C-201/09 P and C-216/09 P *ArcelorMittal Luxembourg v Commission* and *Commission v ArcelorMittal Luxembourg and Others*, para 233: 'As I have stated, ProfilARBED continues to be a wholly-owned subsidiary of ARBED. In addition, industrial activities whose market value is the consequence, at least in part, of the anti-competitive agreements in which ARBED and TradeARBED participated were transferred to it. Consequently, I think that ProfilARBED could not be unaware of the partially fraudulent origin of the assets which it inherited, since it was set up by ARBED shortly after the infringement had been committed, as a wholly-owned subsidiary. In those circumstances, I am of the opinion that its situation can be assimilated to that of a "receiver" in domestic criminal law. To my mind, only that analysis would justify the Commission, in application of the rules normally and traditionally applicable in relation to criminal penalties, being entitled, in Article 2 of the contested decision, to involve ProfilARBED in the payment of the fine and, if necessary, if it commits further infringements, to regard it as a repeat offender.'

[102] Case T-161/05 *Hoechst v Commission* [2009] ECR II-3555, para 65. This may be different where the Commission explicitly agrees with such a transfer of liability, depending on the specific circumstances of the case. See Joined Cases T-45/98 and T-47/98 *Krupp Thyssen Stainless v Commission* [2001] ECR II-3757, paras 59–62 (confirmed on appeal in Joined Cases C-65/02 P and C-73/02 P *ThyssenKrupp v Commission* [2005] ECR I-6773, paras 81–2, 86, and 93); Case T-24/07 *ThyssenKrupp Stainless v Commission* [2009] ECR II-2309, paras 139–40 and 144 (confirmed on appeal in Case C-352/09 P *ThyssenKrupp Nirosta v Commission*, para 153; in his Opinion in that case, AG Bot had disagreed with such an outcome, see, paras 161–73).

[103] See Kerse & Khan, *EC Antitrust Procedure* (6th edn, Sweet & Maxwell 2012), para 7-015. Where imputation of liability is disputed, the Commission decision should contain a more detailed account of the grounds for holding the successor entity liable for the infringement.

[104] This may include lawyers where they support anticompetitive practices by way of legal opinions tailored to their client's interests, see Opinion of AG Kokott of 28 February 2013 in Case C-681/11 *Schenker and Co AG and Others*, para 73.

things, it had a key role in determining the methods of implementing the cartel by carrying out auditing of the cartel members. The relatively modest fine of EUR 1,000 was attributable to the fact that the imposition of a sanction on a third party in these circumstances was 'to a certain extent a novelty'.[105] This approach was confirmed by the GC which held that:

> the objective condition for the attribution of various anti-competitive acts constituting the cartel as a whole to the undertaking concerned is satisfied where that undertaking has contributed to its implementation, even in a subsidiary, accessory or passive role, for example by tacitly approving the cartel and by failing to report it to the administrative authorities,

and that

> those principles apply mutatis mutandis to the participation of an undertaking whose economic activity and professional expertise mean that it cannot but be aware of the anti-competitive nature of the conduct at issue and enable it to make a significant contribution to the committing of the infringement. In those circumstances, the applicant's argument that a consultancy firm cannot be regarded as a co-perpetrator of an infringement—because it does not carry out an economic activity on the relevant market affected by the restriction of competition and because its contribution to the cartel is merely subordinate—cannot be upheld.[106]

In a subsequent case, again involving AC-Treuhand, the Commission imposed fines for two separate infringements, in each case up to the maximum amount determined by the 10 per cent turnover cap (EUR 174,000).[107]

3. The purpose of penalties

11.21 In imposing fines and periodic penalty payments, the Commission's central objective is to ensure that the prohibited conduct does not recur.[108] Hence, the essential purpose of penalties is to deter and persuade. In the specific case of fines, the EU Courts have recognized their twofold character, in that they punish past acts and have a deterrent effect for the future.[109] This applies not only to the undertakings involved in the infringement, but also to other economic operators that might be tempted to engage in the same type of conduct.[110]

---

[105] Commission Decision of 10 December 2003 in Case COMP/37.857 *Organic peroxyde*, para 454.

[106] Case T-99/04 *AC-Treuhand v Commission* [2008] ECR II-1501, paras 133 and 136. See also Case T-36/05 *Coats Holdings and Coats v Commission* [2007] ECR II-110, paras 109–22; Case T-29/05 *Deltafina v Commission* [2010] ECR II-4077, paras 53–64; Judgment of 29 November 2012 in Case T-491/07 *Groupement des cartes bancaires (CB) v Commission*, para 83.

[107] Commission Decision of 11 November 2009 in Case COMP/38.589 *Heat Stabilisers* ([2010] OJ C307/09). The decision has been appealed in Case T-27/10 *AC-Treuhand v Commission* ([2010] C100/45).

[108] Case 45/69 *Boehringer Mannheim v Commission* [1970] ECR 769, para 53; Case T-18/97 *Atlantic Container Line and Others v Commission* [2002] ECR II-1125, para 50; Case T-15/02 *BASF v Commission* [2003] ECR II-213, para 218, with further references.

[109] Recital 4 of the 2006 Guidelines (specific and general deterrence); Case 49/69 *BASF v Commission* [1972] ECR 713, para 38; Joined Cases 100–103/80 *Musique Diffusion Française v Commission* [1983] ECR 1825, para 106; Case C-289/04 P *Showa Denko v Commission* [2006] ECR I-5859, para 16. See also Joined Cases T-202/98, T-204/98 and T-207/98 *Tate & Lyle and Others v Commission* [2001] ECR II-2035, paras 133–5; Case T-203/01 *Michelin v Commission* [2003] ECR-II 4071, para 293. The Commission has repeatedly emphasized the importance of 'credible deterrence' for potential offenders. See eg XXXIII Report on Competition Policy [2003], paras 722 and 725. The need to ensure sufficient deterrence, where it does not lead the Commission to raise the general fines level as a policy choice, requires 'that the amount of the fine be adjusted in order to take account of the desired impact on the undertaking on which it is imposed, so that the fine is not rendered negligible, or on the other hand excessive, notably by reference to the financial capacity of the undertaking in question, in accordance with the requirements resulting from, first, the need to ensure that the fine is effective and, second, respect for the principle of proportionality'. See Judgment of 12 December 2012 in Case T-352/09 *Nováčke chemické závody v Commission*, para 46.

[110] For the same reason, there is still a need for deterrence even if a parent company has subsequently sold the infringing business. See Judgment of 16 November 2011 in Case T-54/06 *Kendrion v Commission*,

Consequently, deterrence is a relevant factor at all stages of the fines calculation.[111] It is of particular relevance where the infringement involves large undertakings. Not only are they presumed to have the legal and economic knowledge that will enable them to recognize more easily the anticompetitive character of their conduct, they can also 'spread the risks connected with the commission of the infringement over a broad financial base'.[112] The 2006 Fining Guidelines therefore foresee the possibility of applying a so-called 'deterrence multiplier' to the fine of undertakings which have a particularly large turnover beyond the cartelized turnover.[113] The Commission may also impose fines where the infringement has already come to an end[114] and is not precluded from imposing a fine by the fact that no fine was imposed in other (similar) cases in the past.[115] Periodic penalty payments, for their part, are mainly coercive. They are intended to either prevent specific conduct contrary to the competition provisions or to compel undertakings to comply with Commission decisions seeking to enforce those provisions, or to investigate possible infringements.

4. Intentional or negligent infringement

Article 23(2) of Regulation 1/2003 states that the infringement must have been committed 'intentionally or negligently'. This requirement applies independently of the question of gravity of the infringement. Indeed, Article 23 deals with two distinct issues: first, it sets out that the infringement must be intentional or negligent in order that a fine may be imposed. Second, the provision governs the determination of the fine, which depends on the gravity and duration of the infringement.[116] Gravity, in turn, has to be determined by reference to numerous factors, such as the particular circumstances of the case, its context, and the dissuasive effect of fines.[117] When ascertaining the gravity of an infringement, the Commission is generally not required to distinguish between the two alternative types of fault. Infringements committed negligently are not, from the point of view of competition, less serious than those committed intentionally.[118] It should be noted, though, that paragraph 29 of the 2006 Fining Guidelines foresees the possibility of reducing the fine on account of mitigating circumstances

11.22

---

paras 174–6; Judgment of 6 March 2012 in Case T-64/06 *FLS Plast v Commission*, paras 146–7; Order of 7 February 2012 in Case C-421/11 P *Total and Elf Aquitaine v Commission*, paras 80 and 82.

[111] Judgment of 6 March 2012 in Case T-53/06 *UPM-Kymmene v Commission*, para 136. Often, the Commission explicitly justifies the imposition of a high fine by the need to exclude, through its deterrent effect, any repetition of the behaviour in question. See eg *Opel* [2001] OJ L59/1, para 194.

[112] Case T-38/02 *Groupe Danone v Commission* [2005] ECR II-4407, paras 175 and 359; Judgment of 6 March 2012 in Case T-53/06 *UPM-Kymmene v Commission*, paras 77 and 78; *Methylglucamine* [2004] OJ L38/18, para 239.

[113] The EU Courts have confirmed that such an approach is justified. See Judgment of 6 March 2012 in Case T-53/06 *UPM-Kymmene v Commission*, para 81.

[114] Joined Cases 41/69, 44/69 and 51–57/69 *ACF Chemiefarma v Commission* [1970] ECR 661, paras 170–5.

[115] Case 32/78 *BMW Belgium v Commission* [1979] ECR 2435, paras 52 and 53. Generally, according to settled case law, the Commission's decision-making practice does not in itself serve as a legal framework for assessing fines in competition matters. Case T-241/01 *Scandinavian Airlines System v Commission* [2005] ECR II-2917, para 87; Case T-73/04 *Le Carbone Lorraine v Commission* [2008] ECR II-2661, para 92.

[116] Case C-137/95 P *Vereniging van Samenwerkende Prijsregelende Organisaties in de Bouwnijverheid (SPO) and Others v Commission* [1996] ECR I-1611, para 53.

[117] Joined Cases 100–103/80 *Musique Diffusion Française v Commission* [1983] ECR 1825, para 129; Case C-219/95 P *Ferriere Nord v Commission* [1997] ECR I-4411, para 33; Joined Cases C-189/02 P, C-202/02 P, C-205/02 P to C-208/02 P and C-213/02 P *Dansk Rørindustri and Others v Commission* [2005] ECR I-5425, para 241. As regards some of the possible criteria for assessing the gravity of infringements of Art 102 TFEU, see also Case T-66/01 *Imperial Chemical Industries v Commission* [2010] ECR II-2631, para 372.

[118] Case C-137/95 P *SPO and Others v Commission* [1996] ECR I-1611, paras 55–7; Judgment of 12 December 2012 in Case T-332/09 *Electrabel v Commission*, paras 237–9. For a procedural violation (breach of seal) see Case T-141/08 *E.ON Energie v Commission* [2010] ECR II-5761, para 289.

'where the undertaking provides evidence that the infringement has been committed as a result of negligence'.[119]

11.23 While the reference to an 'intentional' or 'negligent' infringement relates to culpability on the part of the undertakings concerned, it is clear that an undertaking acts through human agency, and any intentions or negligence are in effect those of its directors and employees. In EU law, the undertaking is responsible for the conduct of its directors and employees as long as the natural person at issue was *generally* authorized to act on behalf of the undertaking and *generally* did not exceed the powers conferred on him/her (eg, as a sales person),[120] leaving aside any general instructions not to infringe competition rules.[121] In *Volkswagen*, the ECJ held that it was not necessary for the Commission to identify the persons whose conduct was indicative of the intentional or negligent nature of the infringement.[122] Neither does it have to investigate the subjective knowledge or objectives of such persons, but may rely on an 'objective assessment of the facts'.[123]

11.24 An intentional infringement requires at least the deliberate commission of an act which aims to achieve anticompetitive ends, or which is committed in the knowledge that anticompetitive effects would ensue. This requires an intention to restrict competition, but not an objective to infringe the competition rules.[124] Hence, 'it is not necessary for an undertaking to have been aware that it was infringing those rules; it is sufficient that it could not have been unaware that

---

[119] In this respect, AG Bot has considered that negligence constitutes a mitigating factor that needs to be taken into account as a matter of proportionality. See Opinion of 21 June 2012 in Case C-89/11 P *E.ON Energie v Commission*, para 130.

[120] Joined Cases 100–103/80 *Musique Diffusion Française v Commission* [1983] ECR 1825, paras 97–8; Case T-9/99 *HFB and Others v Commission* [2002] ECR II-1487, para 275; Case T-141/08 *E.ON Energie AG v Commission* [2010] ECR II-5761, para 258; Judgment of 6 March 2012 in Case T-64/06 *FLS Plast v Commission*, para 69. It is not necessary for there to have been action by, or even knowledge on the part of, the partners or principal managers of the undertaking concerned. Joined Cases 100–103/80 *Musique Diffusion Française v Commission* [1983] ECR 1825, para 97; Judgment of 7 February 2013 in Case C-68/12 *Protimonopolný úrad Slovenskej republiky v Slovenská sporitel'na*, paras 25, 26, and 28; Judgment of 14 March 2013 in Case T-588/08 *Dole Food and Dole Germany v Commission*, paras 581–2; Opinion of AG Kokott of 18 April 2013 in Case C-501/11 P *Schindler Holding and Others v Commission*, paras 129–32. At the same time, the mere fact than an employee of a company participating in a cartel is seconded to another company does not in itself imply that the latter automatically becomes responsible for any infringement. Judgment of 13 July 2011 in Case T-42/07 *The Dow Chemical Company and Others v Commission*, para 93.

[121] While undertakings should have effective compliance programmes to prevent infractions of the competition rules, such programmes neither prevent their liability in case of an infringement nor constitute a mitigating circumstance for the determination of the fine. Joined Cases C-189/02 P, C-202/02 P, C-205/02 P to C-208/02 P and C-213/02 P *Dansk Rørindustri and Others v Commission* [2005] ECR I-5425, para 373; Case T-66/01 *Imperial Chemical Industries v Commission* [2010] ECR II-2631, para 420. See Vice President and Commissioner for Competition Policy Almunia 'Cartels: the priority in competition enforcement', 15th International Conference on Competition, Berlin, 14 April 2011 (SPEECH/11/268); European Commission, 'Compliance matters: What companies can do better to respect EU competition rules' (November 2011).

[122] Case C-338/00 *Volkswagen v Commission* [2003] ECR I-9189, paras 94–8.

[123] See, in this respect, *Nederlandse Federatieve Vereniging voor de Groothandel op Elektrotechnisch Gebied and Technische Unie (FEG and TU)* [2000] OJ L39/1, paras 131–5, confirmed in Joined Cases T-5/00 and T-6/00 *Nederlandse Federatieve Vereniging voor de Groothandel op Elektrotechnisch Gebied v Commission* [2003] ECR II-5761, in particular, paras 396–7.

[124] Joined Cases 100–103/80 *Musique Diffusion Française v Commission* [1983] ECR 1825, paras 111–12; Case T-66/92 *Herlitz v Commission* [1994] ECR II-531, paras 45–6; Case T-52/02 *Société nouvelle des couleurs zinciques SA (SNCZ) v Commission* [2005] ECR II-5005, para 83; Joined Cases T-259/02 to T-264/02 and T-271/02 *Raiffeisen Zentralbank and Others v Commission* [2006] ECR II-5169, paras 205–6 (the latter also as regards the effect on trade criterion). As regards infringements of Art 102 TFEU, undertakings act intentionally if they are aware of the factual elements justifying both the finding of the existence of a dominant position and the assessment of the conduct as an abuse of that position. See Case 322/81 *Michelin v Commission* [1983] ECR 3461, para 107; Judgment of 29 March 2012 in Case T-336/07 *Telefónica and Telefónica de España v Commission*, paras 320–6.

its conduct was aimed at restricting competition'.[125] Given their extended legal and economic resources as well as organizational infrastructures, lack of awareness will be particularly hard to argue for large undertakings.[126] Also, given the long-standing practice of sanctioning hardcore cartels, such as price-fixing agreements, these will almost certainly be considered as a deliberate infringement.[127]

Negligence implies that the undertaking concerned did not act intentionally, but could rea-   **11.25**
sonably foresee that its conduct would infringe the competition rules.[128] In case of organizational failures leading to procedural infringements, the question will be whether the undertaking
has violated a particular duty to act of which it should have been aware.[129] Hence, negligence
does not constitute a kind of fall-back position in case intention cannot be proven, but requires
an analysis of the specific circumstances in each individual case. Even where the Commission
assumes negligence, it may set a lower fine where the conduct concerned an area of activity where
uncertainty as to the proper type of behaviour prevailed.[130] Also, in exceptional circumstances
the fact that undertakings acted under pressure may lead the Commission to impose no fine at
all.[131] However, given that undertakings can usually evade pressure by informing the competent

---

[125] Judgment of 5 October 2011 in Case T-11/06 *Romana Tabacchi v Commission*, para 227; Judgment of 18 June 2013 in Case C-681/11 *Schenker and Others*, paras 37–8. See also *British Sugar* [1999] OJ L76/1, para 191. Undertakings from new Member States cannot invoke lack of knowledge of EU law to escape a sanction in case of competition law infringements. See eg *Austrian Banks* [2004] OJ L56/1, paras 494–501.
[126] See eg *Methyglucamine* [2004] OJ L38/18, para 239 (on the issue of deterrence); Commission Decision of 6 March 2013 in Case AT.39530 *Microsoft (Tying)*, paras 49 and 50.
[127] See eg *PO v Interbrew and Alken Maes* [2003] OJ L200/58, para 296; *Methylglucamine* [2004] OJ L38/18, para 224; Commission Decision of 15 December 2008 in Case COMP/39.188 *Bananas*, para 314; Commission Decision of 8 December 2010 in Case COMP/39.309 *Liquid Crystal Displays*, para 433. As regards infringements of Art 102 TFEU see eg *Michelin* [2002] OJ L143/1, para 352; Case T-229/94 *Deutsche Bahn v Commission* [1997] ECR II-1689, para 128.
[128] Case 27/76 *United Brands v Commission* [1978] ECR 207, paras 299–301; Opinion of AG Mayras of 29 October 1975 in Case C-26/75 *General Motors v Commission* [1975] ECR 1367 (stating that 'the concept of negligence must be applied where the author of the infringement, although acting without any intention to perform an unlawful act, has not foreseen the consequences of his action in circumstances where a person who is normally informed and sufficiently attentive could not have failed to foresee them'). For a discussion of negligence in the case of an avoidable error of law based on incorrect legal advice, see Opinion of AG Kokott of 28 February 2013 in Case C-681/11 *Schenker and Others*, para 47 et seq (not followed by the ECJ in its Judgment of 18 June 2013, see para 43).
[129] See eg Case T-141/08 *E.ON Energie v Commission* [2010] ECR II-5761, paras 254 and 260; Commission Decision of 28 March 2012 in Case COMP/39.793 *EPH and Others*, paras 72 and 73.
[130] For instance, following up a complaint filed by the UK Post Office, the Commission decided that Deutsche Post AG had abused its dominant position in the German letter market by intercepting, surcharg-ing and delaying incoming international mail which it erroneously classified as domestic mail. However, owing to the legal uncertainty that prevailed at the time of the infringement, the fine was set at the token figure of EUR 1,000. See *Deutsche Post/British Post Office* [2001] OJ L331/40, paras 192–3: 'An infringement of the competition rules like the present one should normally be penalised by fines varying in accordance with the gravity and duration of the infringement. However, in certain cases the Commission may impose a symbolic fine...DPAG has behaved in a manner which—at least partially—is in accordance with the case law of German courts. Despite the fact that the Commission considers that DPAG's behaviour in some respects goes beyond what can be determined with certainty from German case law, it must be concluded that the said case law resulted in a situation where the legal situation was unclear. Moreover, at the time when the majority of the interceptions, surcharging and delays in the present case took place, no Community case law existed that concerned the specific context of cross-border letter mail services'.
[131] See eg *Opel* [2001] OJ L59/1, para 174: 'The Dutch Opel dealers, as participants together with Opel Nederland BV through agreements to prevent or limit exports, are victims of the restrictive policy decided by their contracting party, to which they had to agree under pressure. The dealers did not participate actively. The Commission is therefore of the opinion that no fine should be imposed on them.' In the *French Beef* case, the pressure exerted on certain undertakings and associations did not lead to an exemption from any fine, or a symbolic fine, but to a reduction on the basis of mitigating circumstances. See *French Beef* [2003] OJ L209/12, paras 121, and 176–7.

competition authorities, the Commission is generally not required to grant a reduction on that ground.[132]

5. Compatibility of fines and periodic penalty payments

11.26 Although at first sight it looks as if Article 23 of Regulation 1/2003 (fines) seeks to punish past infringements, while Article 24 of Regulation 1/2003 (periodic penalties) deals with continuing and future infringements, it must not be forgotten that deterrence is one of the central objectives of fines, which are therefore aimed also at changing future behaviour. Consequently, it has been argued that by imposing both fines and sanctions at the same time, the Commission is penalizing the same conduct twice.[133] However, while the *objectives* might be partly aligned, the *object* of both types of sanctions is different: even if the decision imposing fines might also include a cease and desist order in order to prevent the continuing violation of the competition rules, the fine must necessarily be determined on the basis solely of *past behaviour*, the gravity and duration of which has to be established in accordance with Article 23(3) of Regulation 1/2003; conversely, periodic penalty payments are there to compel a change of conduct (ie, future behaviour) and are 'calculated from the date appointed by the decision' (Article 24(1) of Regulation 1/2003) in case the undertaking fails to follow suit. Hence, similar to Regulation 17, Regulation 1/2003 does not limit the Commission's recourse to either penalty, or exclude the imposition of both at the same time.[134]

6. Limitation periods[135]

11.27 The Commission's power to impose penalties[136] for infringements of EU competition law is subject to a statute of limitation.[137] The relevant provisions of Regulation 1/2003 fix two types of limitation periods: those relating to the Commission's powers to impose fines and penalties (Article 25); and those relating to the enforcement of such sanctions (Article 26). Within its scope of application, Regulation 1/2003 has taken over the rules contained in Regulation 2988/74,[138] with some minor changes in order to adapt the enforcement system

---

[132] See Joined Cases C-189/02 P, C-202/02 P, C-205/02 P to C-208/02 P, and C-213/02 P *Dansk Rørindustri and Others v Commission* [2005] ECR I-5425, paras 369–70; Case T-38/02 *Groupe Danone v Commission* [2005] ECR II-4407, paras 167–8; Case T-195/06 *Solvay Solexis v Commission* [2011] ECR II-178, paras 251–2.

[133] See Kerse & Khan, *EC Antitrust Procedure* (6th edn, Sweet & Maxwell 2012) para 7-263. In the authors' view, subjecting the same conduct (eg a refusal to submit to an inspection) to two different sanctions would lead to a conflict with Art 50 of the EU Charter of Fundamental Rights and general principles of law.

[134] For an example of a case where both fines and periodic penalty payments have been imposed see *JCB* [2002] OJ L69/1 Arts 4 and 6. See, however, Judgment of 27 June 2012 in Case T-167/08 *Microsoft v Commission*, para 94.

[135] See also Ch 9, 'Procedural Infringements: Fines and Periodic Penalty Payments', paras 9.31–9.34.

[136] In *Sumitomo Chemical*, the GC reaffirmed that the five-year limitation period pursuant to Art 25(1)(b) of Reg 1/2003 only applies to the Commission's power to impose a fine, not to its power to make a finding of an infringement of Arts 101 and 102 TFEU. See Joined Cases T-22/02 and T-23/02 *Sumitomo Chemical v Commission* [2005] ECR II-4065, para 61. Neither does it apply to the finding of recidivism as a prerequisite for increasing the fine based on aggravating circumstances. See Case T-38/02 *Groupe Danone v Commission* [2005] ECR II-4407, para 360 (confirmed on appeal in Case C-3/06 *Groupe Danone v Commission* [2007] ECR I-1331, para 38).

[137] On the *ratio legis* see Joined Cases T-22/02 and T-23/02 *Sumitomo v Commission* [2005] ECR II-4065, paras 80 and 82, and the Opinion of AG Bot of 26 October 2010 in Case C-352/09 P *ThyssenKrupp Nirosta v Commission*, para 188.

[138] Council Reg 2988/74 concerning limitation periods in proceedings and the enforcement of sanctions under the rules of the European Economic Community relating to transport and competition [1974] OJ L319/1. As is recounted in Art 37 of Reg 1/2003, Reg 2988/74 has been amended and does not apply to measures taken under Reg 1/2003. It continues to apply in the transport sector as well as with regard to merger control procedures.

to the new decentralized application of competition rules. Pursuant to Article 25(1) of Regulation 1/2003, the imposition of penalties will be prescribed after a period of five years for substantive infringements, whereas a period of three years applies to procedural violations. The Commission is not prevented from taking any action after these periods have elapsed, but is merely prohibited from imposing fines. Thus, where the Commission can show a legitimate interest, it may still adopt a decision declaring that an infringement has taken place (Article 7(1) of Regulation 1/2003),[139] which may have consequences for the finding of liability before a national court.

Time begins to run on the day on which the infringement has been committed. However, in the **11.28** case of continuing or repeated infringements, the limitation period starts with the day on which the infringement ceases.[140] The Commission principally bears the burden of proof for the duration of anticompetitive practices, but may rely on an overall assessment of various coincidences and indicia in this regard. Hence, the fact that no evidence exists in relation to certain specific periods does not preclude the infringement from being regarded as established for a longer overall period, if such a finding is supported by objective and consistent indicia.[141] However:

> if there is no evidence directly establishing the duration of an infringement, the Commission should adduce at least evidence of facts sufficiently proximate in time for it to be reasonable to accept that that infringement continued uninterruptedly between two specific dates.[142]

Whether a series of acts together constitutes a *continuous* infringement depends on a case-by-case analysis, taking into account the objectives pursued, as well as a number of other factors, such as the geographic scope of the activities, the identity of the parties, or the organizational structure of their contacts.[143] This also includes the period separating two manifestations of infringing conduct; however, the question of whether that period is long enough to constitute an interruption of the infringement needs to be assessed in the context of the functioning of the cartel in question.[144] Over time, anticompetitive conduct will typically evolve and

---

[139] See also Case 7/82 *GVL v Commission* [1983] ECR 483, para 23; Judgment of 29 June 2012 in Case T-370/09 *GDF Suez v Commission*, para 272. With respect to the requirements for a declaratory decision, see above para 11.04.

[140] For a case in which the GC, based on the view that insufficient evidence had been presented of the existence of a continuous infringement between two dates (1977, 1985) on which anticompetitive conduct occurred, applied the prescription rules to the first infringement period, see Case T-43/92 *Dunlop v Commission* [1994] ECR II-441, para 84. The judgment seems misconceived given that the court considered that prescription affected the finding of an infringement. Conversely, where the Commission can demonstrate continuity of behaviour, even a longer interruption does not prevent it from imposing a fine taking into account also the earlier period of the infringement. See Case T-18/05 *IMI and Others v Commission* [2010] ECR II-1769, para 89, 96–7; Case T-382/06 *Tomkins v Commission* [2011] ECR II-1157, paras 48–53.

[141] Judgment of 6 December 2012 in Case C-441/11 P *Commission v Verhuizingen Coppens*, paras 71, 72, and 75.

[142] Case T-120/04 *Péroxidos Orgánicos v Commission* [2006] ECR II-4441, paras 51–2; Case T-61/99 *Adriatica di Navigazione v Commission* [2003] ECR II-5349, para 125. See also Joined Cases C-204/00 P, C-205/00 P, C-211/00 P, C-213/00 P, C-217/00 P and C-219/00 P *Aalborg Portland and Others v Commission* [2004] ECR I-123, para 260: 'In the context of an overall agreement extending over several years, a gap of several months between the manifestations of the agreement is immaterial. The fact that the various actions form part of an 'overall plan' owing to their identical object, on the other hand, is decisive.' This can include considerable gaps, see eg Judgment of 27 June 2012 in Case T-439/07 *Coats Holdings v Commission*, paras 149–54; Judgment of 2 February 2012 in Case T-83/08 *Denki Kagaku Kogyo and Denka Chemicals*, para 224.

[143] It is for the Commission to demonstrate both an objective and subjective link between two sets of anticompetitive conduct. See eg Case T-110/07 *Siemens AG v Commission* [2011] ECR II-477, paras 241–52. See also Case T-377/06 *Comap v Commission* [2011] ECR II-1115, paras 85–8; Case T-385/06 *Aalberts Industries v Commission* [2011] ECR II-1223, paras 86–8, 105 and 110. The subjective intention of the various undertakings will be taken into account only in the context of assessing their individual participation. See Case T-110/07 *Siemens AG v Commission* [2011] ECR II-477, para 246.

[144] Judgment of 30 November 2011 in Case T-208/06 *Quinn Barlo v Commission*, para 159.

adapt to changing circumstances, but this does not necessarily affect the finding of a continuous infringement.[145] In case of interruptions, the Commission may nevertheless assume a 'repeated' infringement where it can establish an objective and subjective link between the earlier and later actions.[146]

11.29   As regards the running of time, any action taken by the Commission or by the competition authority of a Member State (NCA)[147] for the purpose of the investigation or proceedings in respect of an infringement will interrupt the limitation period for the imposition of fines or periodic penalty payments in relation to both procedural and substantive infringements (Article 25(3) of Regulation 1/2003). These actions shall include in particular[148] the following:

  (i) written requests for information by the Commission[149] or an NCA;
  (ii) written authorizations to conduct inspections issued to its officials by the Commission[150] or an NCA;
  (iii) the initiation of proceedings by the Commission[151] or an NCA;
  (iv) notification of the statement of objections of the Commission[152] or an NCA.

In *FETTSCA*, the GC made it clear that the interruption of the five-year limitation period is an exception to the rule and must be interpreted narrowly.[153] Moreover, written requests for information must be for the purpose of the preliminary investigation or proceedings in respect of an infringement, and they must be necessary in the sense that they can legitimately be regarded as having a connection with the putative infringement. Information requests aimed at artificially prolonging the limitation period cannot be considered as necessary in this regard.[154] The limitation period is interrupted as of the date on which the action is

---

[145] See eg Case T-377/06 *Comap v Commission* [2011] ECR II-1115, paras 85–8.

[146] See Case T-18/05 *IMI v Commission* [2010] ECR II-1769, para 97; Judgments of 17 May 2013 in Joined Cases T-147/09 and T-148/09 *Trelleborg v Commission*, paras 72–94; and in Case T-154/09 *Manuli v Commission*, paras 199–201. See also Case T-110/07 *Siemens AG v Commission* [2011] ECR II-477, para 237 et seq.

[147] This is irrespective of any request for action from the Commission.

[148] This is a non-exhaustive list, see Joined Cases C-238/99 P, C-244/99 P, C-245/99 P, C-247/99 P, C-250/99 P to C-252/99 P and C-254/99 P *Limburgse Vinyl Maatschappij and Others v Commission* [2002] ECR I-8375, para 141. For the interruption by a decision imposing fines or periodic penalty payments see Case T-276/04 *Compagnie maritime belge v Commission* [2008] ECR II-1277, para 33. The issue of whether a decision granting conditional immunity under the 2002 Leniency Notice may constitute an action interrupting the limitation period is litigated in Case T-250/12 *Uralita v Commission* ([2012] OJ C243/26). With regard to periodic penalty payments, the announcement of the intention to impose such payments (Art 24(1) of Reg 1/2003) interrupts the limitation period for a decision fixing the definitive amount pursuant to Art 24(2) of Reg 1/2003.

[149] Pursuant to Art 18(2) or (3) of Reg 1/2003. See eg Case T-120/04 *Peróxidos Orgánicos v Commission* [2006] ECR II-4441, paras 46–7. This may also apply to a request for information seeking turnover figures with a view to checking the applicability of the 10 per cent turnover cap. See Case T-213/00 *CMA CGM and Others v Commission* [2003] ECR II-913, para 490.

[150] See Case T-405/06 *ArcelorMittal Luxembourg and Others v Commission* [2009] ECR II-789, para 147 (notification of inspection decision).

[151] See Art 2(1), (2) of Reg 773/2004. The Commission may exercise its powers of investigation pursuant to Chapter V of Regulation (EC) No 1/2003 before initiating proceedings (Art 2(3) of Reg 773/2004), which will typically lead to an earlier interruption.

[152] See Art 10(1) of Reg 773/2004 and Case T-405/06 *ArcelorMittal Luxembourg and Others v Commission* [2009] ECR II-789, para 147.

[153] Case T-213/00 *CMA CGM and Others v Commission* [2003] ECR II-913, para 484. See also Case T-405/06 *ArcelorMittal Luxembourg and Others v Commission* [2009] ECR II-789, para 154.

[154] See Case T-213/00 *CMA CGM and Others v Commission* [2003] ECR II-913, paras 486–8. However, under normal circumstances it can be presumed that information requests sent out by the Commission are necessary for the investigation. See Case T-276/04 *Compagnie maritime belge v Commission* [2008] ECR II-1277, para 32: 'It must be considered prima facie that the requests for information in question were necessary for the preliminary investigation or the proceedings.'

notified to at least one undertaking or association of undertakings which has participated in the infringement (Article 25(4) of Regulation 1/2003: effect *erga omnes*).[155]

For limitation purposes, time starts to run again after each interruption has ended.[156] Moreover, **11.30** the time bar will take effect in any event after six years (for procedural infringements) or ten years (for substantive infringements) if the Commission fails to impose a fine or other penalty.[157] This time limit will be extended by the period during which prescription was suspended as a result of proceedings before the GC and/or ECJ[158] following an action against a Commission decision.[159] Unlike for measures which interrupt the limitation period, the suspension during a court procedure only has *inter partes* effects.[160] The suspensory effect is independent of the outcome of the legal proceedings.[161] Hence, where a final decision is annulled for a procedural error, the Commission may re-start the administrative proceeding with a view to re-adoption.[162]

---

[155] See Judgment of 27 June 2012 in Case T-372/10 *Bolloré v Commission*, paras 199 and 203. This applies even in cases where another undertaking was not yet the object of investigatory measures (eg the Commission was unaware of its participation in the infringement; it did not yet know that another company formed part of the same undertaking). See Case T-276/04 *Compagnie maritime belge v Commission* [2008] ECR II-1277, para 31; Case T-405/06 *ArcelorMittal Luxembourg and Others v Commission* [2009] ECR II-789, paras 143 and 145.

[156] Article 25(5) of Reg 1/2003.

[157] Article 25(5) of Reg 1/2003: 'the limitation period shall expire at the latest on the day on which a period equal to twice the limitation period has elapsed without the Commission having imposed a fine or a periodic penalty payment.'

[158] In the past, the EU Courts did not have to decide whether the limitation period is also suspended during the period *between* a judgment by the GC and the filing of an appeal against that judgment before the ECJ. See, eg, Joined Cases C-238/99 P, C-244/99 P, C-245/99 P, C-247/99 P, C-250/99 P, C-251/99 P, C-252/99 P and C-254/99 P *Limburgse Vinyl Maatschappij and Others v Commission* [2002] ECR I-8375, paras 147 and 157; Case T-276/04 *Compagnie maritime belge v Commission* [2008] ECR II-1277, para 34; Case T-405/06 *ArcelorMittal Luxembourg and Others v Commission* [2009] ECR II-789, para 148; Case T-57/01 *Solvay v Commission* [2009] II-4621, para 98. However, in a recent case the GC explicitly included that interval into the suspension period. See Judgment of 27 June 2012 in Case T-372/10 *Bolloré v Commission*, paras 213 and 216.

[159] Article 25(6) of Reg 1/2003. See eg *PVC* [1994] OJ L239/14, paras 56–8. That decision followed the annulment of the first *PVC* Decision by the ECJ, after the GC had declared it non-existent. See also Joined Cases T-305/94, T-306/94, T-307/94, T-313/94 to T-316/94, T-318/94, T-325/94, T-328/94, T-329/94 and T-335/94 *Limburgse Vinyl Maatschappij and Others v Commission* [1999] ECR II-931, para 1098 (confirmed on appeal in Joined Cases C-238/99 P, C-244/99 P, C-245/99 P, C-247/99 P, C-250/99 P, C-251/99 P, C-252/99 P and C-254/99 P *Limburgse Vinyl Maatschappij (LMV) and Others v Commission* [2002] ECR I-8375, paras 144 and 151). The suspension effect is independent of the outcome of the case and in fact becomes most relevant were a decision is annulled (for a procedural error) and the Commission proceeds to a re-adoption. See Joined Cases C-238/99 P, C-244/99 P, C-245/99 P, C-247/99 P, C-250/99 P, C-251/99 P, C-252/99 P and C-254/99 P *Limburgse Vinyl Maatschappij (LMV) and Others v Commission* [2002] ECR I-8375, paras 67 and 153.

[160] Case T-405/06 *ArcelorMittal Luxembourg and Others v Commission* [2009] ECR II-789, paras 151–8 (confirmed on appeal in Joined Cases C-201/09 P and C-216/09 P *ArcelorMittal Luxembourg v Commission* and *Commission v ArcelorMittal Luxembourg and Others* [2011] ECR I-2239, paras 143–7). This applies even to legal entities which are part of the same undertaking but did not participate in the court proceedings. See Case T-405/06 *ArcelorMittal Luxembourg and Others v Commission* [2009] ECR II-789, paras 157–8.

[161] Joined Cases T-305/94, T-306/94, T-307/94, T-313/94 to T-316/94, T-318/94, T-325/94, T-328/94, T-329/94 and T-335/94 *Limburgse Vinyl Maatschappij and Others v Commission* [1999] ECR II-931, para 1100 (confirmed on appeal in Joined Cases C-238/99 P, C-244/99 P, C-245/99 P, C-247/99 P, C-250/99 P, C-251/99 P, C-252/99 P and C-254/99 P *Limburgse Vinyl Maatschappij and Others v Commission* [2002] ECR I-8375, paras 67 and 153). The opposing view by AG Bot, Opinion of 26 October 2010 in Case C-352/09 P *ThyssenKrupp Nirosta v Commission*, paras 183 and 198–206, has not been followed.

[162] See Joined Cases T-305/94, T-306/94, T-307/94, T-313/94 to T-316/94, T-318/94, T-325/94, T-328/94, T-329/94 and T-335/94 *Limburgse Vinyl Maatschappij and Others v Commission* [1999] ECR II-931, para 1098.

11.31 Similar principles apply to the limitation period for the enforcement of sanctions pursuant to Article 26 of Regulation 1/2003.[163] However, there are differences as regards:

(i) the beginning and length of the limitation period (always five years, starting from the date the decision becomes final);

(ii) the interruption of the limitation period, both for the types of measures having such effect (eg, modification of the fines amount by court judgment, enforcement actions) and their effects (only *inter partes*);

(iii) the suspension of the limitation period (granting of payment facilities, suspension of enforcement through the EU courts); and

(iv) the lack of an absolute time bar.

11.32 In *Ferriere Nord*, the undertaking claimed that the Commission's power to bring legal proceedings to enforce its decision of August 1989 was time-barred and therefore unlawful because they were initiated after the limitation period contained in Regulation 2988/74 had expired. In 2004, the Commission had requested that Ferriere Nord pay the fine it owed in accordance with the original decision which was upheld by the GC in 1995 and by the ECJ in 1997. The Commission stated that once the payment was made, it would waive a bank guarantee that had been issued by Banco di Roma to the Commission in respect of the payment due from Ferriere Nord. The Court concluded that the Commission's requests (by letter and telefax) were acts of an administrative nature, rather than actions in a contractual dispute based on the bank guarantee, as claimed by the Commission. Thus, the demand for payment and the notice regarding the execution of the guarantee constituted enforcement of the original decision. Based on this, the Court agreed with Ferriere Nord that the Commission's power to enforce the penalty set out in its original decision expired in September 2002, given that the limitation period first began to run on the date of notification of the ECJ's judgment in 1997, which was only interrupted once when the Commission rejected Ferriere Nord's request that the penalty figure be reduced.[164]

7. Procedure

11.33 Throughout the procedure, the Commission must respect the fundamental rights developed by the case law of the EU Courts and enshrined in the Charter of Fundamental Rights.[165] In this regard, the Commission's Notice on Best Practices set out in more detail the procedural steps undertaken in a typical antitrust investigation.[166] In particular, fines and periodic penalty payments for breach of decisions under Article 8 (interim measures) and Article 9

---

[163] Article 26 of Regulation 1/2003 specifies a limitation period of five years in respect of the Commission's power to enforce any decision imposing a fine and/or periodic penalty payment pursuant to Arts 23 and 24 of Reg 1/2003. Time begins to run on the day on which the decision becomes final. The limitation period is interrupted (i) by the notification of a decision varying the original amount of the fine or periodic penalty payment or refusing an application for variation; and (ii) by any action of the Commission or of a Member State, acting at the request of the Commission, designed to enforce payment of the fine or periodic penalty payment. Unlike for the limitation period pursuant to Art 25(3), any interruption only has *inter partes* effects. The limitation period for the enforcement of penalties is suspended for so long as (i) time to pay is allowed; and (ii) enforcement of payment is suspended pursuant to a decision of the EU Courts. There is no case law on these provisions, but in practice the far-reaching possibilities of interrupting actions will make it unlikely that limitation periods will prevent the Commission from recovering a fine.

[164] Case T-153/04 *Ferriere Nord v Commission* [2006] ECR II-3889.

[165] Recital 37 of Reg 1/2003. For the judicial control by the EU Courts see Case T-43/02 *Jungbunzlauer v Commission* [2006] ECR II-3435, paras 74 and 78; Case T-99/04 *AC-Treuhand v Commission* [2008] ECR II-1501, para 45. See also Ch 1, 'The Institutional Framework', paras 1.21, 1.23–1.37, and Ch 10, 'Procedures to Establish the Existence of an Infringement'.

[166] Commission Notice on best practices for the conduct of proceedings concerning Articles 101 and 102 TFEU [2011] OJ C308/6.

(commitments) of Regulation 1/2003, those for substantive infringements (of Articles 101 and 102 TFEU), and those for procedural infringements (of Articles 18 to 22 of Regulation 1/2003) must be preceded by a statement of objections (Article 27(1) of Regulation 1/2003, Articles 10 to 12 of Regulation 773/2004).[167] In order to comply with the rights of defence, the Commission is required to include in the statement of objections addressed to an under-taking on which it intends to impose a penalty for infringement of competition rules, the essential factors taken into consideration against that undertaking, such as the facts alleged, the classification of those facts, and the evidence on which the Commission relies, so that the undertaking may submit its arguments effectively during the administrative procedure brought against it.[168] Given its importance, the statement of objections must specify une-quivocally the legal person on whom fines may be imposed and be addressed to that entity.[169]

The fines are dealt with in a specific section of the statement of objections. The Commission has pledged that it will indicate the: **11.34**

> essential facts and matters of law which may result in the imposition of a fine, such as the duration and gravity of the infringement and that the infringement was committed inten-tionally or by negligence. The Statement of Objections will also mention in a sufficiently precise manner that certain facts may give rise to aggravating circumstances and, to the extent possible, to attenuating circumstances.

Moreover, in order to increase transparency and avoid unnecessary litigation related to the level of the fine, the Commission:

> will endeavour to include in the Statement of Objections (using information available) fur-ther matters relevant to any subsequent calculation of fines, including the relevant sales figures to be taken into account and the year(s) that will be considered for the value of such sales.[170]

---

[167] See Commission Notice on best practices for the conduct of proceedings concerning Articles 101 and 102 TFEU [2011] OJ C308/6, paras 81–91 and 109–12; European Commission Antitrust Manual of Procedures, Internal DG Competition working documents on procedures for the application of Articles 101 and 102 TFEU, March 2012, Module 11 'Drafting of Statement of Objections'. As regards the right to be heard see also Commission Notice on best practices, paras 78–80 and 92–108.

[168] Joined Cases C-322/07 P, C-327/09 P and C-338/07 P *Papierfabrik August Koehler and Others v Commission* [2009] ECR I-7191, paras 34–9; Joined Cases C-189/02 P, C-202/02 P, C-205/02 P to C-208/02 P and C-213/02 P *Dansk Rørindustri and Others v Commission* [2005] ECR I-5425, para 428.

[169] Case C-176/99 *Arbed and Others v Commission* [2003] ECR I-10687, paras 19–24. The ECJ held that although the applicant was aware of the statement of objections addressed to its subsidiary TradeARBED and of the procedure which had been initiated against that subsidiary, it could not be concluded from that fact that the appellant's rights of defence were not infringed. Ambiguity as to the legal entity to which the fines would be imposed, and which could have been dispelled only by properly addressing a fresh statement of objections to the appellant, persisted up to the end of the administrative procedure. See also Joined Cases C-395/96 P and C-396/96 P *Compagnie Maritime Belge Transports and Others v Commission* [2000] ECR I-1365, para 144: 'It is clear that a statement of objections which merely identifies as the perpetrator of an infringement a collective entity, such as Cewal, does not make the companies forming that entity sufficiently aware that fines will be imposed on them individually if the infringement is made out. Contrary to what the Court of First Instance held, the fact that Cewal does not have legal personality is not relevant in this regard.' In addition see Joined Cases T-45/98 and T-47/98 *Krupp Thyssen Stainless v Commission* [2001] ECR II-3757, paras 57–68 (confirmed on appeal in Joined Cases C-65/02 P and C-73/02 P *ThyssenKrupp v Commission* [2005] ECR I-6773, paras 80–8 and 92–6); Joined Cases C-322/07 P, C-327/09 P and C-338/07 P *Papierfabrik August Koehler and Others v Commission* [2009] ECR I-7191, paras 37–9; European Commission Antitrust Manual of Procedures, Internal DG Competition working documents on procedures for the application of Articles 101 and 102 TFEU, March 2012, Module 11 'Drafting of Statement of Objections', paras 31–2.

[170] Commission notice on best practices for the conduct of proceedings concerning Articles 101 and 102 TFEU [2011] OJ C308/6, paras 84–5. See also European Commission Antitrust Manual of Procedures, Internal DG Competition working documents on procedures for the application of Articles 101 and 102 TFEU, March 2012, Module 11 'Drafting of Statement of Objections', paras 15 and 17, with further reference to case law.

Finally, the Commission will also inform the addressees that 'in exceptional cases, it may, upon request, take account of the undertaking's inability to pay…according to point 35 of the Guidelines on setting fines'.[171]

11.35 In their observations on the statement of objections and during the administrative hearing, the undertakings may give their views not only on the infringements of which the Commission accuses them, but also on the seriousness and estimated duration of the infringements, matters which the Commission will take into account in determining the amount of the fine. In practice, there is no procedure for the imposition of fines for substantive infringements that is separate from the procedure for the establishment of the infringement as such. However, there will be a separate procedure for the infringement of interim measures[172] and for commitment decisions,[173] as well as with regard to fines for procedural infringements. The procedure for the imposition of periodic penalty payments has certain particular features, as already indicated.[174]

B. Fines

1. Quantitative limits: the 10 per cent cap

11.36 Pursuant to Article 23(2) of Regulation 1/2003, the Commission may by decision impose fines on undertakings or associations of undertakings which shall not exceed 10 per cent of their respective total turnover in the preceding business year. This sum does not constitute a maximum fine, to be imposed only in respect of the most serious infringements, but a 'capping ceiling', the only possible consequence of which is that the amount of the fine calculated on the basis of the criteria of gravity and duration will be reduced to the maximum permitted level.[175] Given that

---

Information on the reference year and the value of sales may also be provided to the parties after the statement of objections. As regards the legal requirements for drafting the statement of objections in relation to fines, see Judgment of 12 December 2012 in Case T-392/09 *1. garantovaná v Commission*, paras 68, 69, 73, 78, and 79.

[171] Commission notice on best practices for the conduct of proceedings concerning Articles 101 and 102 TFEU [2011] OJ C308/6, para 87.

[172] See European Commission Antitrust Manual of Procedures, Internal DG Competition working documents on procedures for the application of Articles 101 and 102 TFEU, March 2012, Module 17 'Interim Measures (Article 8 of Reg. 1/2003)'.

[173] See Commission notice on best practices for the conduct of proceedings concerning Articles 101 and 102 TFEU [2011] OJ C308/6, paras 115–33; European Commission Antitrust Manual of Procedures, Internal DG Competition working documents on procedures for the application of Articles 101 and 102 TFEU, March 2012, Module 16 'Commitment decisions (Article 9 of Reg. 1/2003)'. Unless the commitment route is taken only at a late stage, a commitment decision is preceded by a so-called preliminary assessment, not a statement of objections. See Art 9(1) of Reg 1/2003.

[174] Periodic penalty payments may be imposed by adopting an Art 24(1) decision on a stand-alone basis or by including the provisions relating to their imposition in the decision that the periodic penalty payments are intended to enforce (eg an Art 18(3) decision). The usual practice is to follow the second option. See European Commission Antitrust Manual of Procedures, Internal DG Competition working documents on procedures for the application of Articles 101 and 102 TFEU, March 2012, Module 20 'Periodic penalty payment', paras 7–8.

[175] Judgment of 12 December 2012 in Case T-352/09 *Novácke chemické závody v Commission*, paras 161 and 163. See also Joined Cases T-236/01, T-239/01, T-244/01 to T-246/01, T-251/01 and T-252/01 *Tokai Carbon and Others v Commission* [2004] ECR II-1181, para 368; Case T-52/03 *Knauf Gips v Commission* [2008] ECR II-115, paras 452–4; Judgment of 5 October 2011 in Case T-11/06 *Romana Tabacchi v Commission*, para 257; F Castillo de la Torre 'The 2006 Guidelines on Fines: Reflections on the Commission's Practice' (2010) 33 World Competition 396, 397. The opposite view is taken by the civil courts in Germany, see Oberlandesgericht Düsseldorf, Judgment of 29 June 2009 (VI-2a Kart 2-6/08 OWi), and Bundesgerichtshof, Order of 26 February 2013 (KRB 20/12). The latter has ruled that, in order to avoid a conflict with the principle of legal certainty in criminal matters, the national provision corresponding to Art 23(2) of Reg 1/2003 must be interpreted as the upper limit of a fines band, to be reached only for the most

this cap relates to the relevant undertaking as described in the Commission decision, the attribution of responsibility to a parent company will generally increase the ceiling of any potential fine.[176] This requires a finding in the decision that several entities constitute one undertaking, but not necessarily that each of them is also held liable as an addressee.[177] In case of hierarchical groups, the Commission may rely on the consolidated turnover of the (top) parent company to which the decision is addressed, without having to demonstrate that all companies whose turnover is consolidated form part of the undertaking.[178] Where the economic unit between a parent and its subsidiary has broken up prior to the Commission's decision, the 10 per cent cap will be calculated separately for each legal entity, based on its own turnover.[179] Conversely, where during the infringement period a company acquires control over another entity directly participating in the cartel (and remains in control until adoption of the Commission's decision), the overall turnover will be relevant even if the infringement did not continue for an extended period following the acquisition.[180] Finally, if the Commission finds that two sets of anticompetitive activities constitute separate infringements, this may also have the effect that the 10 per cent cap will apply separately to the fine imposed for each individual infringement.[181]

As regards the interpretation of the notion of 'turnover', the EU Courts have confirmed that **11.37** this refers to the *total, worldwide turnover* of the undertaking in question, not its volume of sales in the EU or its turnover in respect of the products in the market where the infringements of Articles 101 and 102 TFEU occurred.[182] As will be seen, the latter figure will be

---

serious infringements. Only within such a band could the criteria of gravity and duration be considered as sufficient guidance from the legislator; conversely, fining guidelines could not substitute for the required legislative framework. See, however, Opinion of AG Kokott of 18 April 2013 in Case C-501/11 P *Schindler Holding and Others v Commission*, paras 148–57, with further references to case law.

[176] For a special scenario see *Industrial and Medical Gases* [2003] OJ L84/1, in particular nn 20 and 282. The Commission fined seven companies in a Dutch industrial gases price-fixing cartel between 1993 and 1997, which included AGA Gas BV. Following the liquidation of AGA Gas BV after the infringement period, AGA AB accepted liability for the acts of its subsidiary and became the addressee of the decision. As AGA AB was held liable for its former subsidiary, AGA Gas BV, the fine was reduced to 10 per cent of the last turnover of AGA Gas BV.

[177] See Case T-52/03 *Knauf Gips v Commission* [2008] ECR II-115, para 337 et seq, 339 (confirmed on appeal in Case C-407/08 P *Knauf Gips v Commission* [2010] ECR I-6375).

[178] See Case T-26/06 *Trioplast Wittenheim v Commission* [2010] ECR II-188 (summ pub), para 115; Case T-384/06 *IBP v Commission* [2011] ECR II-1177, para 101; Judgment of 9 September 2011 in Case T-25/06 *Alliance One v Commission*, para 210; Judgment of 16 November 2011 in Case T-72/06 *Groupe Gascogne v Commission*, paras 110–12.

[179] Judgment of 16 November 2011 in Case T-54/06 *Kendrion v Commission*, para 92.

[180] See Case T-26/06 *Trioplast Wittenheim v Commission* [2010] ECR II-188 (summ pub), para 114; Joined Cases T-122/07 to T-124/07 *Siemens AG Österreich and Others v Commission* [2011] ECR II-793, para 189. See also Judgment of 12 October 2011 in Case T-38/05 *Agroexpansión v Commission*, paras 194 and 195; Judgment of 16 November 2011 in Case T-79/06 *Sachsa Verpackung v Commission*, para 108; Judgment of 27 June 2012 in Case T-448/07 *YKK Corp and Others v Commission*, paras 190–5. However, in one case the Commission appears to have applied the cap pro rata according to the periods during which the parent company exercised decisive influence. See Commission Decision of 4 April 2011 in Case COMP/38.344 *Prestressing Steel* (Commission Press Release IP/11/403). AG Sharpston has argued that the Commission is legally obliged to proceed in this way. See Opinion of 30 May 2013 in Case C-40/12 P *Gascogne Sack Deutschland v Commission*, paras 81–9.

[181] Judgment of 27 June 2012 in Case T-439/07 *Coats Holding v Commission*, para 146.

[182] See eg Joined Cases 100–103/80 *Musique Diffusion Française v Commission* [1983] ECR 1825, para 119; Joined Cases T-67/00, T-68/00, T-71/00 and T-78/00 *JFE Engineering and Others v Commission* [2004] ECR II-2501, para 533; Case T-112/05 *Akzo Nobel v Commission* [2007] ECR II-5049, para 90. For a confirmation that the 10 per cent figure refers to worldwide turnover, see Case C-279/87 *Tipp-Ex v Commission* [1990] ECR I-261, para 39; Judgment of 12 December 2012 in Case T-410/09 *Almamet v Commission*, para 225. Input costs which the undertaking has to bear in order to obtain the products or services which it provides to customers are not deducted. See Judgment of 12 December 2012 in Case T-410/09 *Almamet v Commission*, para 225.

used to determine the basic amount of the fine. The Commission must, in principle, take into account the turnover achieved by the undertaking concerned in the *last full business year before the date of adoption* of the decision imposing the fine. However, where the turnover in that period does not represent a full year of normal economic activity over a period of twelve months, and thus does not provide any useful indication as to the actual economic situation of the undertaking concerned, or where the Commission does not have at its disposal the turnover for the last business year preceding the date of adoption of the decision,[183] it has to rely on the turnover achieved in an earlier year.[184] The lack of audited turnover figures does not constitute a further exception, unless the undertaking provides sound and consistent evidence showing that the non-audited figures are unreliable.[185]

11.38 Following the Commission's practice, the 10 per cent limit only applies to the final amount of the fine, after considering any aggravating and/or mitigating factors and before applying any reduction granted under the Commission Notice on immunity from fines and reduction of fines in cartel cases ('Leniency Notice'),[186] the Commission Notice on the conduct of settlement procedures ('Settlements Notice'),[187] or based on an assessment of the undertaking's inability to pay.[188] The Court has clarified that Article 23(2) of Regulation 1/2003 does not prohibit the Commission from using an intermediate amount in its calculations higher than 10 per cent of the turnover of the affected undertaking, provided that the ultimate fine imposed does not

---

[183] This may for instance be the case where the annual accounts of the undertaking have not yet been drawn up, have not been disclosed to the Commission, or have only been produced for a period shorter than twelve months. The Commission must then rely on an earlier complete year for which annual accounts have been drawn up. See Judgment of 12 December 2012 in Case T-410/09 *Almamet v Commission*, para 215. However, the undertaking cannot simply avoid the normal application of Art 23(2) of Reg 1/2003 by failing to produce annual accounts for the business year preceding the date of adoption of the decision, without providing credible reasons why it could not do so. Otherwise, the undertaking could try to reduce its fine by only producing the annual accounts of an earlier year with lower turnover figures.

[184] See Case T-33/02 *Britannia Alloys & Chemicals v Commission* [2005] ECR II-4973, para 37 et seq (confirmed in Case 76/06 P *Britannia Alloy & Chemicals v Commission* [2007] ECR I-4405, para 25 et seq); Judgments of 12 December 2012 in Case T-392/09 *1. garantovaná v Commission*, paras 86–88, 105, and 106; and in Case T-410/09 *Almamet v Commission*, para 215. See also Commission Decision of 22 July 2009 in Case COMP/39.396 *Calcium Carbide*, para 334. Conversely, 'as long as an undertaking has in fact achieved a turnover during a complete year in which economic activities, albeit on a reduced scale, have been carried on, the Commission must take the undertaking as it stands when setting the upper limit provided for in Article 15(2) of Regulation No 17', even if the turnover has been negatively influenced by exceptional circumstances (eg, sector crisis, plant accident). See Case T-33/02 *Britannia Alloys & Chemicals v Commission* [2005] ECR II-4973, para 49; Judgment of 28 April 2010 in Joined Cases T-465/05 and T-457/05 *Gütermann & Zwicky v Commission*, para 97; Judgment of 12 December 2012 in Case T-410/09 *Almamet v Commission*, para 216. According to the GC, the reference in the case law to a 'full year of normal economic activity' is intended to ensure that 'a year in which the undertaking concerned was in the process of winding down its business, although economic activity had not yet entirely come to an end, is precluded from being taken into account, as, more generally, is a year in which the market conduct of the undertaking concerned did not correspond to that of an undertaking carrying on an economic activity on the usual terms. On the other hand, the mere fact that turnover or the profits generated in a particular year are significantly lower, or higher, than in previous years does not mean that the year in question does not constitute a full year of normal economic activity.' See Judgment of 12 December 2012 in Case T-410/09 *Almamet v Commission*, para 253.

[185] Judgment of 12 December 2012 in Case T-410/09 *Almamet v Commission*, paras 250–2.

[186] Commission Notice on immunity from fines and reduction of fines in cartel cases [2006] OJ C298/17. The application of the Leniency Notice after the 10 per cent cap is justified by the need to ensure its effectiveness. See Case T-52/02 *Société nouvelle des couleurs zinciques (SNCZ) v Commission* [2005] ECR II-2005, para 41.

[187] Commission Notice on the conduct of settlement procedures in view of the adoption of Decisions pursuant to Article 7 and Article 23 of Council Regulation (EC) No 1/2003 in cartel cases [2008] OJ C167/1.

[188] Paragraph 35 of the 2006 Guidelines. See also Note of Vice President and Competition Commissioner Almunia and Budget Commissioner Lewandowski, 'Inability to pay under paragraph 35 of the 2006 Guidelines and payment conditions pre- and post-decision finding an infringement and imposing fines' Sec(2010)737.

exceed this maximum limit. In this respect, the fact that, due to the capping, certain factors (eg duration, mitigating circumstances) will not influence the final amount of the fine is a simple consequence of this statutory provision.[189] The mere fact that mono-product companies (ie companies which achieve most of their overall turnover with the cartelized product) will often receive a higher fine *in relative terms* than more diversified groups[190] should not matter either, given that they will also benefit the most from the cartel activity and that *in absolute terms* their fine will be much lower than what would be justified based on the gravity and duration of their cartel participation.[191] There is, however, an on-going debate as to whether the Commission (or at least the Court under its unlimited jurisdiction) should re-establish the differences in the relative weight of each undertaking's participation in the infringement when calculating the fine in case the fine of several undertakings is capped.[192]

With respect to the imposition of fines on associations of undertakings, their own turnover will be an appropriate measure for the cap if the association is itself active in the market, has its own sales, and if the infringement relates to this activity. However, where this is not the case and the infringement is rather related to the activities of its members, Article 23(2) of Regulation 1/2003 provides that an association can be fined an amount of **11.39**

---

[189] See Joined Cases C-189/02 P, C-202/02 P, C-205/02 P to C-208/02 P and C-213/02 P *Dansk Rørindustri and Others v Commission* [2005] ECR I-5425, paras 278 and 279; Judgment of 12 July 2011 in Case C-181/11 P *Compañía española de tabaco en rama (Cetarsa) v Commission*, paras 80–7; Case T-52/02 *Société nouvelle des couleurs zinciques (SNCZ) v Commission* [2005] ECR II-2005, paras 38–40; Case T-73/04 *Le Carbone Lorraine v Commission* [2008] ECR II-2661, para 123.

[190] Cf Judgment of 16 November 2011 in Joined Cases T-55/06 and T-66/06 *RKW and JM Gesellschaft für industrielle Beteiligungen v Commission*, para 24. The Court stressed, however, that even this was justified by the application of the statutory cap in Art 23(2) of Reg 1/2003.

[191] Judgment of 12 July 2011 in Case C-181/11 P *Compañía española de tabaco en rama (Cetarsa) v Commission*, paras 84 and 87. In Case T-64/02 *Dr Hans Heubach v Commission* [2005] ECR II-5173, para 39, the GC indicated that the 1998 Guidelines would enable the Commission to take into consideration, where circumstances so require, the particular circumstances of SMEs compared to undertakings with a higher turnover in the relevant market and higher overall turnover. At the same time, other judgments have stressed that there is no requirement to ensure that the ratio between the fine imposed on SMEs and their overall turnover does not exceed the ratio for larger undertakings. See Case T-21/99 *Dansk Rørindustri v Commission* [2002] ECR II-1681, para 203; Case T-52/03 *Knauf Gips v Commission* [2008] ECR II-115, para 423; Judgment of 16 November 2011 in Case T-54/06 *Kendrion v Commission*, para 149; Judgment of 12 December 2012 in Case T-352/09 *Novácke chemické závody v Commission*, paras 158 and 160. Neither does the characterization as an SME constitute a mitigating circumstance. See Joined Cases C-189/02 P, C-202/02 P, C-205/02 P to C-208/02 P and C-213/02 P *Dansk Rørindustri and Others v Commission* [2005] ECR I-5425, para 366; Case T-379/06 *Kaimer v Commission* [2011] ECR II-64, para 101; Judgment of 5 October 2011 in Case T-11/06 *Romana Tabacchi v Commission*, paras 228 and 260. Nevertheless, in one recent case the Commission reduced the fine based, among others, on the mono-product character of the undertakings involved. See Commission Decision of 28 March 2012 in Case COMP/39.452 *Mountings for windows and window-doors*. In this regard, the GC has indicated that the concentration of the product portfolio may constitute a legitimate factor when determining the amount of the fine. See Judgment of 12 December 2012 in Case T-352/09 *Novácke chemické závody v Commission*, para 138 et seq.

[192] For instance, AG Tizzano has stated that with higher fines, a calculation method which has the effect that in many cases the fining amounts exceed the 10 per cent limit, and where therefore the final amount of the fine is determined solely by that cap, may violate the proportionality, equity, and transparency principles. This could particularly hit small-and medium-sized undertakings, making it questionable whether the results would comply with the principles of reasonableness and fairness. See Opinion of 8 July 2004 in Joined Cases C-189/02 P, C-202/02 P, C-205/02 P to C-208/02 P and C-213/02 P *Dansk Rørindustri and Others v Commission* [2005] ECR I-5425, paras 129–33. However, the ECJ did not follow the Advocate-General in that case. For the 2006 Guidelines, the Advocate-General's Opinion has been taken up by the GC in an *obiter dictum* in Case T-211/08 *Putters International v Commission* [2011] ECR II-3729, para 75. The court hinted that there might be cases where it would have to rectify this situation based on its power of unlimited jurisdiction, thereby indicating that it might not consider this as a question of legality, but of fairness. Conversely, in its Judgment of 16 November 2011 in Case T-54/06 *Kendrion v Commission*, para 107, the GC rejected a discrimination argument based on the application of the 10 per cent cap.

up to 10 per cent of the joint turnover of those members active on the market affected by the infringement.[193] Given that such an amount is likely to exceed the financial means of the association, Regulation 1/2003 provides for new solutions in cases where it is unable to pay the fine.[194] According to Article 23(4), in the event of insolvency, the association is obliged to call for contributions from its members to cover the amount of the fine. If such contributions have not been made to the association within the time limit fixed by the Commission, it may seek to recover the fine directly from any of the undertakings whose representatives were members of the decision-making bodies of the association.[195] Moreover, if such payments are not sufficient to ensure full payment of the fine, the Commission may require payment of the balance by any of the members of the association that were active on the market where the infringement occurred, after giving them an opportunity to be heard.[196] In each scenario, the members have the possibility of exculpating themselves based on the grounds set out in Article 23(4) of Regulation 1/2003. Moreover, the respective liability of each member is limited to 10 per cent of its overall turnover in the preceding business year (Article 23(5) of Regulation 1/2003).

11.40 According to the ECJ, the quantitative limits determined by Regulation 1/2003 for fines with respect to infringements of Articles 101 and 102 TFEU seek to ensure that the sanction is not disproportionate to the size and hence financial capacity of the undertaking.[197] However,

---

[193] See also paras 14 and 33 of the 2006 Guidelines. To some extent this codifies earlier case law with regard to Reg 17. See eg Joined Cases T-213/95 and T-18/96 *SCK and FNK v Commission* [1997] ECR II-1739, para 252; Case T-9/99 *HFB and Others v Commission* [2002] ECR II-1487, para 529; Joined Cases T-217/03 and T-245/03 *FNCBV and Others v Commission* [2006] ECR II-4987, paras 318–25 (confirmed on appeal in Case C-101/07 P *Coop de France bétail et viande and Others v Commission* [2008] ECR I-10193, para 98); Case C-298/98 P *Metsä-Serla Sales v Commission* [2000] ECR I-10157, para 66.

[194] See Art 23(4) of Reg 1/2003. Article 15 of Reg 17 did not provide for such a mechanism, despite the fact that the 1998 Guidelines foresaw the possibility of imposing an overall fine on the association 'calculated according to the [normal principles] but equivalent to the total of individual fines which might have been imposed on each of the members of the association'. This could make the collection of the fine impossible. See the Commission's White Paper on Modernization [1999] OJ C132/1, paras 127–8 referring to Joined Cases T-213/95 and T-18/96 *SCK and FNK v Commission* [1997] ECR I-1739 where the problem arose. So far, the Commission has indicated the potential need for making use of the new mechanism only in one case. See Commission Decision of 8 December 2010 in Case COMP/39.510 *LABCO/ONP* (Commission Press Release IP/10/1683).

[195] The Commission has discretion in choosing the members that it wants to hold liable. However, it 'should have regard to the relative size of the undertakings belonging to the association and in particular to the situation of small and medium-sized enterprises' (Recital 30 of Reg 1/2003). The same applies where the Commission, in a further step, seeks recovery of the fine from other members active on the affected market.

[196] The Commission is not obliged to send a statement of objections to the member undertakings of an association where it intends to impose a fine *on the association*, even if that fine is calculated with a view to the members' combined turnover. See Joined Cases T-39/92 and T-40/92 *Groupement des Cartes Bancaires (CB) and Europay International v Commission* [1992] ECR II-49, paras 22, 25, and 139; Joined Cases T-217/03 and T-245/03 *FNCBV and Others v Commission* [2006] ECR II-4987, para 343. However, where the Commission seeks recovery of the fine *from members of the association*, their rights of defence would seem to require that not only can they put in question their liability under Art 23(4), but also the finding of an infringement against the association which forms its basis. Hence, for reasons of economy of procedure, they should be given the opportunity to make observations at the stage when the statement of objections has been sent to the association. This could be achieved by informing them of the procedure and the sending of the statement of objections through a notice in the Official Journal ('OJ'), which would allow interested members to request to be heard based on Art 27(3) of Reg 1/2003, Art 13 of Reg 773/2004. See the Commission's White Paper on Modernization [1999] OJ C132/1, para 128.

[197] Joined Cases 100–103/80 *Musique Diffusion Française v Commission* [1983] ECR 1825, para 119; Joined Cases C-189/02 P, C-202/02 P, C-205/02 P to C-208/02 P and C-213/02 P *Dansk Rørindustri and Others v Commission* [2005] ECR I-5425, para 281; Joined Cases T-67/00, T-68/00, T-71/00 and T-78/00 *JFE Engineering and Others v Commission* [2004] ECR II-2501, para 533; Joined Cases T-236/01, T-239/01, T-244/01 to T-246/01, T-251/01 and T-252/01 *Tokai Carbon v Commission* [2004] ECR II-1181, paras 200 and 368.

the Commission must bear in mind that, in specific cases, even within the limits laid down by Regulation 1/2003, the fines it seeks to impose may be disproportionate, and therefore it should moderate their amount.[198]

2. Calculation: the Commission's Fining Guidelines[199]

Aside from laying down certain maximum figures or caps, Regulation 1/2003 states that in fixing **11.41** the amount of the fine the Commission shall have regard to both the duration and gravity of the infringement (Article 23(3)).[200] Until 1998, the Commission's normal practice had been to determine the amount of fines in relation to the turnover with the products concerned.[201] However, the GC voiced some mild criticism regarding the level of motivation in the Commission's decisions on the grounds that the addressees should be able to assess the correctness of the (level of the) fine and whether there had been any discrimination.[202] Thus, in order to ensure the transparency of its decision-making process, the Commission in 1998 adopted its first fining guidelines ('1998 Guidelines').[203] At the same time, the system set out by the Commission in the 1998 Guidelines also seemed to provide a response to the criticism that the Commission should not have unfettered discretion in relation to the level of fines.[204] Yet, the 1998 Guidelines neither indicated the fines level, nor did they refer to a specific overall amount. Far from surrendering

---

[198] Case T-30/05 *Prym v Commission* [2007] ECR II-107, para 226; Judgment of 12 December 2012 in Case T-410/09 *Almamet v Commission*, para 228. See also, by analogy, Judgment of 5 October 2011 in Case T-11/06 *Romana Tabacchi v Commission*, paras 279–85, in which the GC adjusted the amount of the fine in its unlimited jurisdiction with regard to, among others, the particular financial situation of the undertaking concerned.

[199] For a general appraisal of the objective and consequences of adopting fining guidelines see Judgment of 5 October 2011 in Case T-11/06 *Romana Tabacchi v Commission*, paras 71–3. For their conformity with the principle of legal certainty (foreseeability) see Judgment of 2 February 2012 in Case T-83/08 *Denki Kagaku Kogyo and Denka Chemicals v Commission*, paras 114 and 117–26. The Fining Guidelines only apply for sanctions set pursuant to Art 23(2)(a) of Reg 1/2003. They do not provide a general method for the determination of fines in the field of competition law. See Judgment of 12 December 2012 in Case T-332/09 *Electrabel v Commission*, paras 227 and 228.

[200] As regards the compatibility of this provision with the principle of legal certainty (nulla poena sine lege certa), see Judgment of 12 December 2012 in Case T-400/09 *Ecka Granulate and non ferrum Metallpulver v Commission*, paras 24–34, with further references.

[201] See eg Case T-347/94 *Mayr-Melnhof Kartongesellschaft v Commission* [1998] ECR II-1751, para 276; Joined Cases C-189/02 P, C-202/02 P, C-205/02 P to C-208/02 P and C-213/02 P *Dansk Rørindustri and Others v Commission* [2005] ECR I-5425, para 260. See also Commission Press Release IP/94/1108 of 30 November 1994 on the *Cement* case: 'The basic levels of the fines imposed on the undertakings and associations of undertakings were set in accordance with usual practice, applying the provisions laid down under community law. Fines can in theory amount to 10% of a company's total turnover, but calculation is normally based on the Community turnover in the product concerned. The level of fines takes account of the seriousness of the infringement (market sharing and exchanges of information), its duration (since 1983), the involvement of the undertakings or associations of undertakings in each of the practices, and market conditions.'

[202] See Case T-347/94 *Mayr-Melnhof Kartongesellschaft v Commission* [1998] ECR II-1751, paras 280 and 282, referring to Case T-148/89 *Tréfilunion v Commission* [1995] ECR II-1063, para 142.

[203] Guidelines on the method of setting fines imposed pursuant to Article 15(2) of Regulation 17 and Article 65(5) of the ECSC Treaty [1998] OJ C9/03. The 1998 Guidelines were later also applied to fines imposed under Reg 1/2003. For an overview of the methodology applied under the 1998 Guidelines see Case T-23/99 *LR AF 1998 v Commission* [2002] ECR II-1705, para 224 et seq.

[204] See R Whish, *Competition Law* (5th edn, LexisNexis Butterworths 2003) 268; A Jones and B Sufrin, *EC Competition Law* (2nd edn, Oxford University Press 2004) 1127. However, the Court has always acknowledged that the Commission has a margin of discretion when fixing the amount of the fine and is not obliged to apply a precise mathematical formula for that purpose. Case T-150/89 *Martinelli v Commission* [1995] ECR II-1165, para 59; Case T-352/94 *Mo och Domsjö v Commission* [1998] ECR II-1989, para 268, confirmed on appeal in Case C-283/98 P *Mo och Domsjö v Commission* [2000] ECR I-9855, in particular, para 47.

the Commission's discretion[205] they established a 'tariff' or 'flat-rate' approach[206] to calculate the amount of fines from a basic amount determined in accordance with the gravity and duration of the infringement. In its ruling on the appeal against the judgment of the General Court in the *Pre-insulated pipes* cartel, the Court of Justice confirmed for the first time the legality of the 1998 Guidelines and in particular the application of the method of calculating the amount of the fines while underlining the wide discretion of the Commission in the field of competition policy.[207] It took the view that the Commission remained within the legal framework laid down by Article 15(2) of Regulation 17 [now Article 23(2) of Regulation 1/2003] and did not exceed the discretion conferred on it by the legislature.[208]

11.42 In June 2006, the Commission adopted new fining guidlines ('2006 Guidelines').[209] While further developing its methodology, the Commission also increased the likely level of fines in individual cases, which it may do as a matter of principle,[210] in particular as regards cartels affecting large markets or which are of longer duration. The new policy applies to all cases, including pending cases, for which a statement of objections has been issued after 1 September 2006, the date on which the 2006 Guidelines were published in the Official Journal. Adherence to the methodology in the 2006 Guidelines does not relieve the Commission of its obligation to ensure that the fines imposed in a particular case accord with the principles of proportionality and equal treatment.[211] Furthermore, in paragraph 37 of the 2006 Guidelines, the Commission has reserved the right to depart from the methodology or from the limits specified in those guidelines where this is justified by the particularities of a case

---

[205] The 1998 Guidelines contained a large number of variables, in particular as regards the determination of the starting amount of the fine for which the guidelines merely provided an open-ended bracket ('above ECU 20 million') when it came to 'very serious infringements' like cartels. Hence, many matters continued to fall within the Commission's discretion, which made it difficult, if not impossible, for undertakings to compute the fine that they might have to face. See JM Joshua and PD Camesasca, 'EC Fining Policy against Cartels after the Lysine Ruling: The Subtle Secrets of X' [2004] The European Antitrust Review, Global Competition Review 5, 6–7.

[206] See Joined Cases C-189/02 P, C-202/02 P, C-205/02 P to C-208/02 P and C-213/02 P *Dansk Rørindustri and Others v Commission* [2005] ECR I-5425, para 225; Case T-64/02 *Dr Hans Heubach v Commission* [2005] ECR II-5137, para 44.

[207] Joined Cases C-189/02 P, C-202/02 P, C-205/02 P to C-208/02 P and C-213/02 P *Dansk Rørindustri and Others v Commission* [2005] ECR I-5425, para 169 et seq.

[208] Joined Cases C-189/02 P, C-202/02 P, C-205/02 P to C-208/02 P and C-213/02 P *Dansk Rørindustri and Others v Commission* [2005] ECR I-5425, para 252. The Commission welcomed the judgment as confirmation of the method of calculating fines it had been using in its decisions since 1998. See I Breit, 'The "Pre-insulated Pipes" Judgment: The European Court of Justice Confirms the Legality of the Commission's Guidelines on Fines' (2005) 3 EC Competition Policy Newsletter 78; P Lowe, 'Enforcement Antitrust Roundtable' 32rd Annual Conference Fordham Corporate Law Institute, in International Antitrust Law & Policy 43, 45.

[209] Guidelines on the method of setting fines imposed pursuant to Article 23(2)(a) of Regulation No 1/2003 [2006] OJ C210/2. The Commission has stressed that the 2006 Guidelines present the general methodology for the setting of fines without prejudicing the possibility of departing from this methodology where the particularities of a given case or the need to achieve deterrence may so require. See para 37 of the 2006 Guidelines.

[210] The Commission may at any time adjust the level of fines to ensure the effective implementation of EU competition policy. See Joined Cases 100–103/80 *Musique Diffusion Française v Commission* [1983] ECR 1825, para 109. In raising the level of the fines, the Commission may take into account that, despite the sanctions imposed in the past, the number of infringements is still high. See Case T-9/99 *HFB and Others v Commission* [2002] ECR II-1487, para 457. The EU Courts have taken the view that undertakings involved in an administrative procedure in which fines may be imposed cannot acquire a legitimate expectation that the Commission will not exceed the level of fines previously imposed or will use a particular method of calculating fines. See Joined Cases C-189/02 P, C-202/02 P, C-205/02 P to C-208/02 P and C-213/02 P *Dansk Rørindustri v Commission* [2005] ECR I-5425, paras 228–30; Case T-59/02 *Archer Daniels Midland v Commission* [2006] ECR II-3627, paras 47 and 49.

[211] Judgment of 12 December 2012 in Case T-352/09 *Novácke chemické závody v Commission*, para 48.

or the need to achieve sufficient deterrence.[212] Such deviation must, however, be in conformity with the principle of equal treatment.[213]

The determination of the basic amount

The determination of the basic amount remains the core element of the Commission's fining **11.43** policy. It determines to a great extent the final amount, at least where the fine is not 'capped' at the 10 per cent limit of the undertaking's overall turnover. Under the 2006 Guidelines, the starting point for the fine is a percentage of the value of sales related to the infringement for each undertaking, depending on the degree of gravity of the infringement, and multiplied by the number of years of its participation therein (so-called 'variable amount'). For hard-core infringements (horizontal price-fixing, market-sharing, and output-limitation agreements) the variable amount is then further increased by an additional amount (sometimes in appropriately called the 'entry fee'[214]) which effectively adds the portion of another year of turnover. This has as its objective 'to deter companies from even entering into illegal practices'.[215] The imposition of an additional amount is optional for other types of infringements.[216]

Value of sales

By using a clearer reference to each undertaking's 'value of sales' to which the infringement **11.44** directly or indirectly relates, the 2006 Guidelines intend to reflect the economic importance of the infringement as a whole, as well as the relative weight of each undertaking participating therein.[217] In general, the scope of the relevant products or services will be determined by the undertakings and the objectives they pursue with the infringement; it is not necessary to demonstrate actual effects.[218] Indirect sales may also be covered, for instance where parties reach a price agreement on a given product and it can be shown that this price then serves as a basis for the price of lower or higher quality products.[219] The value of sales of goods and services will be

---

[212] The legality of such a deviation has been confirmed by the GC, see Judgment of 12 December 2012 in Case T-410/09 *Almamet v Commission*, para 233. According to the GC, 'the undertaking concerned may challenge the Commission's decision not to grant it a reduction of the fine under point 37 of the Guidelines, or may claim that any reduction that it may have been granted is insufficient, in the light of the wording of that provision of the Guidelines and general principles of law including, in particular, the principle of proportionality' (para 245).

[213] Judgment of 12 December 2012 in Case T-352/09 *Nováčke chemické závody v Commission*, para 135.

[214] See Commission Press Release IP/06/857 'Commission revises Guidelines for setting fines in antitrust cases' of 28 June 2006.

[215] 2006 Guidelines, para 7.

[216] 2006 Guidelines, para 25.

[217] 2006 Guidelines, para 6. See also Hubert de Broca, 'The Commission Revises its Guidelines for Setting Fines in Antitrust Cases' (2006) Autumn (3) Competition Policy Newsletter 1, 1.

[218] Case T-211/08 *Putters International v Commission* [2011] ECR II-3729, paras 58–62; Joined Cases T-204/08 and T-212/08 *Team Relocations v Commission* [2011] ECR II-3569, paras 63–7. See also Judgment of 29 June 2012 in Case T-370/09 *GDF Suez v Commission*, para 423. According to the GC, the market share of each undertaking provides an adequate indication of its responsibility for the infringement, even in the absence of any effects. See Judgment of 9 September 2011 in Case T-12/06 *Deltafina v Commission*, para 273. Also, it is settled case law that the intentional aspect is most relevant for the fines determination, whereas the actual impact is not a decisive factor. See eg Judgment of 5 June 2012 in Case T-214/06 *Imperial Chemical Industries v Commission*, para 112, with further references. However, the GC has stressed that, to be able to rely on sales invoiced in the EEA, the Commission must assess whether it is the best criterion for ascertaining the effects of the cartel. See Judgment of 17 May 2013 in Case T-146/09 *Parker v Commission*, paras 209–11.

[219] See n 1 of the 2006 Guidelines. See also Judgment of 14 March 2013 in Case T-588/08 *Dole Food and Dole Germany v Commission*, para 638 et seq; Hubert de Broca, 'The Commission Revises its Guidelines for Setting Fines in Antitrust Cases' (2006) Autumn (3) Competition Policy Newsletter 1, 2–3. This may also justify the inclusion of 'internal sales' within a vertically integrated group where it can be established on the basis of objective indicia that the downstream market has been affected. See Case C-248/98 P *Koninklijke KNP v Commission* [2000] ECR I-9641, paras 61–2; Case T-304/94 *Europa Carton v Commission* [1998] ECR II-869, paras 121–30; Case T-16/99 *Lögstör Rör v Commission* [2002] ECR II-1633, paras 358–61;

determined before VAT and other taxes directly related to the sales,[220] and the Commission is not required to deduct costs (eg production costs).[221] Although the relevant turnover of each undertaking is in principle determined by the extent of the infringement for which it can be held liable (which includes the actions of other participants of which the undertaking was aware or at least should have been aware), the Commission may already at this stage take into account a more limited individual participation.[222] In case the ultimate parent company of a group is held liable, the relevant sales of all group companies may be used to determine the basic amount.[223]

11.45   Where the geographic scope of an infringement extends beyond the European Economic Area ('EEA'), the Commission may assess the total value of the sales of goods or services to which the infringement relates, determine the share of sales of each undertaking to the infringement on that market, and apply this share to the aggregate sales within the EEA of each of the undertakings concerned.[224]

11.46   In terms of timing, the Commission will normally take into account the relevant sales made by the undertakings during the last full year of their participation in the infringement.[225] Where sales during the last year are clearly not representative (eg the geographic scope of the

---

Case T-26/02 *Daiichi v Commission* [2006] ECR II-713, paras 61 and 63; Case T-452/05 *Belgian Sewing Thread v Commission* [2010] ECR II-1373, para 82. See also Commission Decision of 3 December 2003 in Case COMP/38.359 *Electrical and mechanical carbon and graphite products*, para 292; Commission Decision of 8 December 2010 in Case COMP/39.309 *Liquid Crystal Displays*, para 382. However, the Commission is not obliged to take such internal sales into account where it has established anticompetitive conduct only in respect of sales to independent customers, without any finding that vertically integrated groups drew an additional competitive advantage. See Judgment of 27 September 2012 in Case T-82/02 *Guardian Industries and Guardian Europe v Commission*, paras 104–6 (appeal pending, Case C-580/12 P).

[220] 2006 Guidelines, para 17. See Judgment of 18 June 2013 in Case T-406/08 *ICF v Commission*, paras 175 and 176. In case of sales in foreign currency, the exchange rate at the time of the infringement (sales moment) will apply. See Commission Decision of 19 June 2013 in Case AT.39226 *Lundbeck*, para 1372.

[221] See Case T-122/04 *Outokumpu v Commission* [2009] ECR II-1135, para 82; Case T-11/05 *Wieland-Werke v Commission* [2010] ECR II-86, para 161; Judgment of 8 December 2011 in Case C-272/09 P *KME Germany and Others v Commission*, para 53; Judgment of 18 June 2013 in Case T-406/08 *ICF v Commission*, para 176.

[222] This can, for instance, relate to the geographic scope of the infringement (see eg Commission Decision of 23 June 2010 in Case COMP/39.092 *Bathroom Fittings*, paras 1199 and 1208; see also Case T-28/99 *Sigma Tecnologie v Commission* [2002] ECR II-1845, paras 81, 82, 93, and 94), or the products covered (see eg Commission Decision of 23 June 2010 in Case COMP/39.092 *Bathroom Fittings*, paras 1199 and 1208; see also Case T-18/05 *IMI and Others v Commission* [2010] ECR II-1769, para 156 et seq and 162–4). For the need to take such differences into consideration in assessing gravity, see Judgment of 6 December 2012 in Case C-441/11 P *Commission v Verhuizingen Coppens*, para 74.

[223] See Judgment of 14 March 2013 in Case T-588/08 *Dole Food and Dole Germany v Commission*, paras 619 and 622. This is in line with the case law on the groupings under the 1998 Guidelines (see eg Joined Cases T-259/02 to T-264/02 and T-271/02 *Raiffeisen Zentralbank Österreich and Others v Commission* [2006] ECR II-5169, paras 360 and 374 et seq; Joined Cases C-125/07 P, C-133/07 P, C-135/07 P and C-137/07 P *Erste Group Bank and Others v Commission* [2009] ECR I-8681, paras 172–9). For the parallel question of determining the overall turnover of the undertaking for the 10 per cent cap, see para 11.36.

[224] 2006 Guidelines, para 18. See also Commission Decision of 7 October 2009 in Case COMP/39.129 *Power Transformers*, paras 231–6; Commission Decision of 28 January 2009 in Case COMP/39.406 *Marine Hoses*, paras 429–2; Commission Decision of 25 June 2008 in Case COMP/39.180 *Aluminium Fluoride*, paras 230–1. For an overview see F Castillo de la Torre 'The 2006 Guidelines on Fines: Reflections on the Commission's Practice' [2010] World Competition 33, 372–3. Determining the geographic scope of the infringement requires no market definition, and only the sales of cartel participants count. See Judgments of 18 June 2013 in Case T-404/08 *Fluorsid and Minmet v Commission*, para 158, and in Case *ICF v Commission*, paras 183–7.

[225] 2006 Guidelines, para 13. See Judgment of 2 February 2012 in Case T-83/08 *Denki Kagaku Kogyo and Denka Chemicals v Commission*, paras 134–6. For the appropriateness of using the last business year as reference year for the groupings under the 1998 Guidelines see Case C-196/99 P *Aristrain v Commission* [2003] ECR I-11005, para 128; Case T-175/05 *Akzo Nobel v Commission* [2009] ECR II-184, para 143; Judgment of 3 March 2011 in Joined Cases T-122/07–T-124/07 *Siemens AG Österreich and Others v Commission*, paras 124–7 and 241.

infringement significantly changed during the lifetime of the infringement), then alternative periods may be used,[226] for instance a different reference year[227] or a multi-annual reference period.[228] Also, the Commission has to ensure as much as possible that the undertaking's respective sales are comparable, which normally requires using a unified reference period.[229] This can justify departing from the last year of the infringement and instead using an earlier year during which all addressees were still involved in the infringement.[230] As for the individual undertaking, it:

> cannot compel the Commission to rely, in its case, upon a period different from that used for the other undertakings, unless it proves that, for reasons peculiar to it, its turnover in the latter period does not reflect its true size and economic power or the scale of the infringement which it committed.[231]

This could become relevant where the undertaking sold all or a substantial part of its relevant business in relative proximity to the end of the infringement period, or, conversely, acquired the business of one of its competitors.

Gravity factor (percentage value)

Only a fraction of the value of sales (per year) will be taken for the determination of the basic **11.47** amount. The percentage applied in each case will be based on the gravity of the infringement and, as a general rule, can go up to 30 per cent.[232] In cases of hard-core infringements the actual percentage will generally be set 'at the higher end of the scale'[233] (ie 15 per cent and higher). Unless the Commission stays close to that lower threshold, it has to explain its choice of percentage or risks the case being annulled for lack of motivation.[234]

---

[226] Hubert de Broca, 'The Commission Revises its Guidelines for Setting Fines in Antitrust Cases' (2006) 3 Competition Policy Newsletter 1 & 3. See also Case T-319/94 *Fiskeby Board v Commission* [1998] II-1331, paras 42–6; Case T-175/05 *Akzo Nobel v Commission* [2009] ECR II-184, paras 142 and 144–5; Case T-40/06 *Trioplast Industrier v Commission* [2010] ECR II-4893, paras 91–3 and 94–7; Case T-192/06 *Caffaro v Commission* [2011] ECR II-3063, paras 87–90; Judgment of 5 October 2011 in Case T-11/06 *Romana Tabacchi v Commission*, paras 177, 183–5 and 190. Normal growth of business leading to higher sales in later years of the cartel will usually not trigger a different reference period. See Judgment of 13 July 2011 in Case T-42/07 *The Dow Chemical Company v Commission*, paras 133–5. This may be different in exceptional circumstances, see Commission Decision of 28 January 2009 in Case COMP/39.406 *Marine Hoses*, para 422 (general instability of sales); Commission Decision of 22 June 2011 in Case COMP/39.525 *Telekomunikacja Polska*, para 896 (significant increase of sales in a developing market).

[227] See eg Commission Decision of 7 October 2009 in Case COMP/39.129 *Power Transformers*, paras 227–8.

[228] See eg Commission Decision of 1 October 2008 in Case COMP/39.181 *Candle Waxes*, para 634; Commission Decision of 28 November 2009 in Case COMP/39.401 *E.ON/GDF*, paras 352–6. See also Commission Decision of 28 November 2007 in Case COMP/39.165 *Flat Glass*, para 486 n 415; Commisson Decision of 9 November 2010 in Case COMP/39.258 *Air Freight*, para 1173.

[229] Joined Cases 100–103/80 *Musique Diffusion Française v Commission* [1983] ECR 1825, para 122; Case C-196/99 P *Aristrain v Commission* [2003] ECR I-11005, para 129; Case T-327/94 *SCA Holding v Commission* [1998] ECR II-1373, para 185; Case T-175/05 *Akzo Nobel v Commission* [2009] ECR II-184, paras 142–3; Judgment of 12 July 2011 in Case T-133/07 *Mitsubishi v Commission*, paras 268 and 276–8.

[230] Judgment of 16 November 2011 in Case T-76/06 *Plasticos Españoles (ASPLA) v Commission*, paras 112 and 113.

[231] Judgment of 6 March 2012 in Case T-53/06 *UPM-Kymmene v Commission*, para 88.

[232] 2006 Guidelines, paras 21 and 22. So far, the lowest percentage applied has been 5 per cent (Commission Decision of 13 May 2009 in Case COMP/37.990 *Intel*, paras 1778 et seq and 1786), the highest percentage 25 per cent (Commission Decision of 28 January 2009 in Case COMP/39.406 *Marine Hoses*, paras 437 et seq, 445, and 450). In cartel cases, the percentages are typically 15 per cent or higher, whereas abuse cases might lead to lower percentages (see eg Commission Decision of 22 June 2011 in Case COMP/39.525 *Telekomunikacja Polska*, para 908: 10 per cent).

[233] 2006 Guidelines, para 23.

[234] Case T-199/08 *Ziegler v Commission* [2011] ECR II-3507, paras 92–3 and 140–2. The same applies to the determination of the percentage for the additional amount (paras 25 and 22 of the 2006 Guidelines).

11.48 In deciding what percentage of the value of sales should be used, the Commission will consider the gravity of the infringement (paragraphs 19 and 22 of the 2006 Guidelines) (taking into account any partial immunity[235]). While this determination will be inspired by similar principles as under the 1998 Guidelines, the formal distinction between minor,[236] serious,[237] and very serious[238] infringements, as previously employed, has been abandoned. The relatively broad range of percentage values in paragraph 21 of the 2006 Guidelines (from 0 to 30 per cent) reflects the wide discretion the Commission enjoys in assessing gravity. However, the guidelines state that for determining whether the proportion of the value of the sales to be considered in a given case should be at the lower or higher end of the scale, the Commission will have regard to a number of factors, such as (i) the nature of the infringement; (ii) the combined market share of all the undertakings concerned; (iii) the geographic scope of the infringement; and (iv) whether or not the infringement has been implemented.[239]

11.49 Where a single infringement combines several types of conduct, relating to different products, it may be appropriate to determine separate percentages for the sales with each product.[240] Moreover, although the basic amount in principle relates to the infringement as a whole, not the individual participation of each undertaking,[241] the application of different percentage values

---

[235] See para 26 of the 2006 Leniency Notice. For further details see Ch 6, 'Investigation of Cases (I): Leniency Policy'.

[236] Under the 1998 Guidelines restrictions of a vertical nature with a limited market impact were deemed minor infringements. The only time the Commission has qualified an infringement as minor was in *Nathan Bricolux* [2000] OJ L54/01, para 131, indicating that although the infringement could be considered as serious, the restrictions in question were not implemented systematically in French-speaking Belgium and France. In *Deutsche Telekom AG* [2003] OJ L263/9, para 207, the Commission found that Deutsche Telekom (DT) had charged its competitors and end-users unfair monthly and one-off charges for access to the local network which it considered a serious infringement, although this became a minor infringement when DT reduced the margin squeeze.

[237] This category included horizontal or vertical restrictions with a wider market impact. Also, abuses of a dominant position such as a refusal to supply, price discrimination, exclusion, or loyalty discounts applied by dominant firms in order to shut competitors out of the market, etc could fall into this category. See eg *Michelin* [2002] OJ L143/1 (confirmed in Case T-203/01 *Michelin v Commission* [2003] ECR II-4071); *Virgin/British Airways* [2000] OJ L30/1 (confirmed in T-219/99 *British Airways v Commission* [2003] ECR II-5917). See also *Deutsche Post AG* [2001] OJ L125/27. In *Greek Ferries* [1999] OJ L109/24, the Commission asserted that the relevant market of ferry transport in question was small compared to the cross-Baltic and cross-Channel markets and therefore qualified the price-fixing agreement as a 'serious' infringement. *FETTCSA* [2000] OJ L268/1 also concerned a price-fixing agreement which was classified as a serious infringement on account of the fact that there was no evidence of the effects of the infringement on the level of prices even though horizontal price agreements were normally regarded as very serious infringements.

[238] This category was generally represented by horizontal restrictions including price cartels and market-sharing quotas, which jeopardize the functioning of the single market, and clear-cut abuses of a dominant position by undertakings holding a virtual monopoly. See eg *Carbonless Paper* [2004] OJ L115/1, para 378 (price fixing/market sharing); *Nintendo* [2003] OJ L255/33, para 374 (market partitioning); *Methionine* [2003] OJ L255/1, para 273 (market sharing/price fixing). In *Volkswagen* [1998] OJ L124/60 (partially annulled in Case T-62/98 *Volkswagen v Commission* [2000] ECR II-2707), the Commission stated that the steps taken by VW to prevent its Italian dealers from supplying the German and Austrian markets were contrary to the Common Market and therefore the infringement was qualified as 'very serious'. See also D Geradin and D Henry, 'The EC Fining Policy for Violation of Competition Law: An Empirical Review of the Commission Decisional Practice and the Community Courts' Judgments' [2005] European Competition Law Journal 401, 434–5.

[239] 2006 Guidelines, para 22.

[240] See Commission Decision of 1 October 2008 in Case COMP/39.181 *Candle Waxes*, paras 293–4, 297, 610–11, 630, 653, 656–7, and 660–1 (paraffin, slack wax); Commission Decision of 22 July 2009 in Case COMP/39.396 *Calcium carbide*, paras 174, 177, 280, 287–8, and 303–4.

[241] Judgment of 25 October 2011 in Case T-348/08 *Aragonesas Industrias y Energía v Commission*, paras 265–7 and 273; Judgment of 12 December 2012 in Case T-352/09 *Novácke chemické závody v Commission*, para 58.

might still be necessary in order to reflect deviations in the scope of participation as regards clearly defined aspects of the cartel.[242]

The EU Courts have consistently stated that in assessing the gravity of an infringement, 'regard **11.50** must be had to a large number of factors, the nature and importance of which vary according to the type of infringement in question'; these include:

> the particular circumstances of the case, its context and the dissuasive element of fines…, no binding or exhaustive list of the criteria which must be applied has been drawn up.[243]

Moreover,

> it is important not to confer on one or other of those factors an importance which is disproportionate in relation to other factors. In this context, the principle of proportionality requires the Commission to set the fine proportionately to the factors taken into account for the purposes of assessing the gravity of the infringement and also to apply those factors in a way which is consistent and objectively justified.[244]

According to the case law, the *nature of the infringement* plays a primary role in classifying **11.51** infringements as more or less serious, whereas the impact on competition is not a relevant criterion.[245] As indicated, horizontal price fixing, market sharing, and output limitation agreements will be heavily fined as a matter of policy, since they are, by their nature, the most harmful restrictions of competition;[246] the proportion of the value of sales taken into account in these cases will generally be set at 15 per cent or more,[247] irrespective of the number of Member States to which the infringement relates.[248] Higher percentage values may be used

---

[242] See Joined Cases T-208/08 and T-209/08 *Gosselin Group and Stichting Administratiekantoor Portielje v Commission* [2011] ECR II-3639, paras 143–5; Judgment of 16 November 2011 in Case T-79/06 *Sachsa Verpackung v Commission*, paras 136–8; Judgment of 30 November 2011 in Case T-208/06 *Quinn Barlo and Others v Commission*, paras 197–200; Judgment of 5 June 2012 in Case T-214/06 *Imperial Chemical Industries v Commission*, para 43. See also F Castillo de la Torre, 'The 2006 Guidelines on Fines: Reflections on the Commission's Practice' (2010) 33 World Competition 377. For variations in the intensity of the infringement see Case T-18/05 *IMI and Others v Commission* [2010] ECR II-1769, paras 159–66; Joined Cases T-208/08 and T-209/08 *Gosselin Group and Stichting Administratiekantoor Portielje v Commission* [2011] ECR II-3639, paras 143–5, 184; Joined Cases T-204/08 and T-212/08 *Team Relocations v Commission* [2011] ECR II-3569, para 128; Case T-211/08 *Putters International v Commission* [2011] ECR II-3729, para 83. For differences in the geographic scope of the respective infringements see Case T-28/99 *Sigma v Commission* [2002] ECR II-1845, paras 81–2 and 93–4. Alternatively, the more limited participation may be reflected in the value of sales, see para 11.44.

[243] See Joined Cases 100–103/80 *Musique Diffussion Francaise and Others v Commission* [1983] ECR 1825, paras 120, 129; Case C-219/95 *Ferriere Nord v Commission* [1996] ECR I-4411, para 33; Case C-137/95 *SPO and Others v Commission* [1995] ECR I-1611, para 54; Case T-9/99 *HFB and Others v Commission* [2002] ECR II-1487, para 443. See also Judgment of 28 April 2010 in Case T-446/05 *Amann & Söhne v Commission*, para 272 for the 1998 Guidelines. Various apects of a single infringement may be considered together. See Case T-73/04 *Le Carbone Lorraine v Commission* [2008] ECR II-2661, paras 47–9.

[244] Case T-446/05 *Amann & Söhne v Commission* [2010] ECR II-1255, para 171.

[245] See eg Case C-194/99 P *Thyssen Stahl v Commission* [2003] ECR I-10821, para 118; Case T-241/01 *Scandinavian Airlines System v Commission* [2005] ECR II-2917, paras 84 and 130; Joined Cases T-259/02 to T-264/02 and T-271/02 *Raiffeisen Zentralbank Österreich v Commission* [2006] ECR II-5169, paras 240 and 241 (confirmed in Joined Cases C-125/07 P, C-133/07 P, C-135/07 P, and C-137/07 P *Erste Group Bank and Others v Commission* [2009] ECR I-8681, para 103); Judgment of 13 July 2011 in Joined Cases T-141/07, T-142/07, T-145/07, and T-146/07 *Otis and Others v Commission*, paras 158–60; Judgment of 9 September 2011 in Case T-12/06 *Deltafina v Commission*, para 268; Judgment of 29 June 2012 in Case T-370/09 *GDF Suez v Commission*, para 423; Judgment of 8 May 2013 in Case C-508/11 P *Eni v Commission*, paras 96–8.

[246] See Judgment of 27 September 2012 in Case T-353/06 *Vermeer Infrastructuur v Commission*, para 115.

[247] Cf Joined Cases T-208/08 and T-209/08 *Gosselin Group and Stichting Administratiekantoor Portielje v Commission* [2011] ECR II-3639, paras 131 and 132.

[248] For example, in *Bathroom Fittings* the undertakings Artweger (Austria) and Rubinetteria Teorema (Italy) were found to have infringed the competition rules only in one Member State, but nevertheless a percentage value of 15 per cent was applied to their value of sales. See Commission Decision of 23 June 2010 in

where there are several types of anticompetitive behaviour (eg, market sharing, price collusion).[249] The Commission may also take into account that the undertakings have taken extensive precautions to avoid detection (secrecy).[250]

11.52 Already in the past, the *combined market share* of all cartel participants was considered as an indicator for the potential effects of an infringement.[251] In the Commission's practice under the 2006 Guidelines so far, it may slighly vary the percentage value depending on the level of the combined market share; however, it appears that a higher percentage applies only as of a certain threshold (around 70 to 80 per cent).[252]

11.53 The Commission will also take into account the *geographic scope of the infringement*, which can lead to an increase of the percentage value to be applied if the infringement covers (nearly) the entire EEA.[253] Conversely, the fact that an infringement might be limited to only one Member State will generally not lead to a reduced percentage value.[254] Whether the infringement also relates to countries outside the EU is generally irrelevant,[255] but may affect the value of sales (see paragraph 18 of the 2006 Guidelines).

11.54 Unlike the 1998 Guidelines, according to which the actual effects of the infringement on the market would be taken into account for gravity if they could be measured,[256] the 2006 Guidelines

---

Case COMP/39.092 *Bathroom Fittings and Fixtures*, para 1220. Cf also Commission Decision of 11 March 2008 in Case COMP/38.543 *International Removal Services*, paras 542–3 (Belgium).

[249] Commission Decision of 11 March 2008 in Case COMP/38.543 *International Removal Services*, paras 541–3; Commission Decision of 1 October 2008 in Case COMP/39.181 *Candle Waxes*, para 653.

[250] Judgment of 27 September 2012 in Case T-362/06 *Ballast Nedem Infra v Commission*, para 106. The GC has described the secret nature of a cartel as a 'factor liable to exacerbate its gravity'. See Joined Cases T-259/02 to T-264/02 and T-271/02 *Raiffeisen Zentralbank Österreich and Others v Commission* [2006] ECR II-5169, para 252.

[251] Case T-127/04 *KME Germany v Commission* [2009] ECR II-1167, paras 69 and 70; Case T-43/02 *Jungbunzlauer v Commission* [2006] ECR II-3435, para 159. See also Case T-279/02 *Degussa v Commission* [2006] ECR II-897, para 232.

[252] Castillo de la Torre 'The 2006 Guidelines on Fines: Reflections on the Commission's Practice' (2010) 33 World Competition 380, nn 108, 109.

[253] For the relevance of the scope of the affected geographic market in determining the gravity of the infringement see Judgment of 19 December 2012 in Case C-452/11 P *Heineken Nederland v Commission*, para 111; Judgment of 13 July 2011 in Case T-151/07 *Kone and Others v Commission*, para 52 (considering as relevant the larger size of the German market when compared to the other geographic markets affected by the *Elevators and Escalators* cartel). In order to establish the geographic scope of the infringement, it is sufficient for the Commission to assess the greater or lesser extent of the market(s) concerned, without being required to define them precisely, and without demonstrating any effects. See Judgment of 27 September 2012 in Case T-82/08 *Guardian Industries and Guardian Europe v Commission*, para 90.

[254] Cf the case law concerning the 1998 Guidelines, eg Case T-241/01 *Scandinavia Airlines System v Commission* [2005] ECR II-2917, paras 87–9; Joined Cases T-259/02 to T-264/02 and T-271/02 *Raiffeisen Zentralbank Österreich v Commission* [2006] ECR II-5169, paras 311–13; Case T-29/05 *Deltafina v Commission* [2010] ECR II-4077, paras 238–41; Case T-240/07 *Heineken v Commission* [2011] ECR II-3355, paras 337–8, 341; Judgment of 9 September 2011 in Case T-12/06 *Deltafina v Commission*, paras 248 and 251; Judgment of 29 March 2012 in Case T-336/07 *Telefónica and Telefónica de España v Commission*, para 413.

[255] See Joined Cases T-236/01, T-239/01, T-244/01 to T-246/01, T-251/01 and T-252/01 *Tokai Carbon and Others v Commission* [2004] ECR II-1181, para 200 (lack of jurisdiction). See also Commission Decision of 9 November 2010 in Case COMP/39.258 *Air Freight*, para 1186.

[256] While the Commission sometimes seemed to accept that infringements might have only a limited impact (eg *Greek Ferries* [1999] OJ L109/24, paras 148 and 149), usually it was reluctant to rely on actual impact where this was difficult to establish. Instead, it looked at the object of the agreement or concerted practices which was to restrict competition and how vigorously the parties pursued (implemented) them, rather than actual effects. This was prudent given that the EU Courts will carefully check the evidence for actual impact where the Commission refers to it as an element in determining the level of the fine. See eg Case T-30/05 *Prym v Commission* [2007] ECR II-107, paras 108–11 (confirmed on appeal in Case C-534/07 P *Prym v Commission* [2009] ECR I-7415, in particular, para 82). Notwithstanding these requirements, the Commission in some cases could point to actual proof of effects. For instance, in *SAS/Maersk Air* [2001]

only consider relevant 'whether or not the infringement has been implemented'. This element had been considered relevant by the courts[257] in the past, as it provides at least an indication of the potential effects of the infringement on competition.[258] In its practice, the Commission examines in each individual case the degree of *implementation*, but in most cases has decided against an increase of the percentage value despite certain indications for implementing measures.[259] Conversely, limited implementation will typically not lead to a reduced percentage value.[260] Even though the Commission does not have to show actual effects, it is still conceivable that it might increase the fine where such a demonstration[261] is possible. According to paragraph 31 of the 2006 Guidelines, the Commission may even take into account actual gains 'improperly made as a result of the infringement where it is possible to estimate that amount'.[262]

Duration factor

The percentage of the relevant turnover determined by gravity will be multiplied by the num- **11.55** ber of years of the undertaking's participation in the infringement[263] (taking into account any partial immunity[264]). This approach, which ensures that each year of participation will be fully reflected in the level of the fine,[265] constitutes a notable change from the 1998

OJ L265/15, para 92, the Commission could establish that the parties withdrew from or reduced their frequencies on certain routes. See also *Amino Acids* [2001] OJ L152/24, para 261 et seq (referring to the cartel participants' own assessment as shown by statements made *in tempore non suspectu*).

[257] See eg Case T-69/04 *Schunk and Schunk Kohlenstoff-Technik v Commission* [2008] ECR II-2567, paras 167 and 168. See also Judgment of 9 September 2011 in Case T-12/06 *Deltafina v Commission*, paras 277–9.

[258] Case T-322/01 *Roquette Frères v Commission* [2006] ECR II-3137, para 77; Case T-168/05 *Arkema v Commission* [2009] ECR II-180, para 165. See also Joined Cases C-125/07 P, C-133/07 P, C-135/07 P and C-137/07 P *Erste Group Bank and Others v Commission* [2009] ECR I-8681, para 117.

[259] See eg Commission Decision of 12 November 2008 in Case COMP/39.125 *Car Glass*, para 673; Commission Decision of 15 October 2008 in Case COMP/39.188 *Bananas*, paras 459 and 460. However, the Commission increased the percentage value in its Decision of 5 December 2007 in Case COMP/38.620 *Chloroprene Rubber*, paras 526 and 535.

[260] Commission Decision of 20 November 2007 in Case COMP/38.432 *Professional videotapes*, para 214.

[261] According to the GC, 'actual impact of a cartel on the market must be regarded as sufficiently demonstrated if the Commission is able to provide specific and credible evidence indicating with reasonable probability that the cartel had an impact on the market'. Case T-127/04 *KME Germany v Commission* [2009] ECR II-1167, para 68. See also Case C-534/07 P *Prym v Commission* [2009] ECR I-7415, para 82. It does not have to 'quantify that impact or provide any assessment in figures in this respect'. Case T-59/02 *Archer Daniels Midland v Commission* [2006] ECR II-3627, para 160; Case T-54/03 *Lafarge v Commission* [2008] ECR II-120, paras 583 and 584. In case of complex economic assessments, judicial review is limited to checking for manifest errors. See Judgment of 29 March 2012 in Case T-336/07 *Telefónica and Telefónica de España v Commission*, para 409. Solely relevant are the effects of the infringement as a whole, not whether the specific actions of individual cartel participants have an impact on competition. See Case C-49/92 P *Anic Partezipazioni v Commission* [1999] ECR I-4125, para 152; Judgment of 16 November 2011 in Case T-79/06 *Sachsa Verpackung v Commission*, para 120; Judgment of 30 November 2011 in Case T-208/06 *Quinn Barlo and Others v Commission*, para 185. Neither is it necessary, in general, to assess each affected market or each affected product separately. See Case T-73/04 *Le Carbone Lorraine v Commission* [2008] ECR II-2661, paras 46, 80, and 97.

[262] At the same time, the Commission is not obliged to consider whether an undertaking has *failed* to derive any benefit from the infringement. See Case T-213/00 *CMA CGM and Others v Commission (FETTCSA)* [2003] ECR II-913, para 340; Case T-30/05 *Prym v Commission* [2007] ECR II-107, paras 190 and 191. In one case, the GC appears to have considered that actual effects would henceforth *only* be relevant under point 31 of the 2006 Guidelines. See Judgment of 14 March 2013 in Case T-587/08 *Fresh Del Monte v Commission*, paras, 772 and 774.

[263] 2006 Guidelines, para 24.

[264] See para 26 of the 2006 Leniency Notice. For further details see Ch 6, 'Investigation of Cases (I): Leniency Policy'.

[265] The underlying idea is that, for deterrence reasons, the fine should reflect a certain portion of the annual turnover with the products or services concerned, taking into account average price mark-ups as a consequence of the infringement, as well as the likelihood of detection by the competition authorities.

Guidelines, where each year of involvement in the cartel merely led to an increase of 10 per cent of the basic amount of the fine.[266] It should not be overlooked, though, that the methodology has been modified *as a whole*: the *percentage of the value of sales* which forms the basis for the calculation under the 2006 Guidelines is not identical to the *starting amount* under the 1998 Guidelines and can be (much) smaller than the minimum threshold of EUR 20 million foreseen therein.[267] Hence, the new methodology will likely result in (significantly) higher fines for long-lasting infringements, whereas it may produce less severe outcomes (vis-à-vis the 1998 Guidelines) in situations where the market size is relatively small and the infringement of a relatively short duration. In calculating the factor for duration, the 2006 Guidelines allow for a rounding-up: periods less than six months shall be counted as half a year,[268] periods longer than six months (but shorter than one year) as a full year.[269] However, the Commission is equally justified in deviating from this methodology in its discretion by applying finer differentations (eg by month). In fact, in more recent decisions the Commission has increasingly made use of that possibility.[270]

11.56 The Commission is not required to establish a direct relation between the length of the infringement (duration) and an increased damage to competition.[271] Nor does it have to modulate the factor for duration where the intensity of the infringement varies over time,[272] or with respect to the weight of the individual participation of each undertaking,[273] as long as the percentage applied to the value of sales adequately reflects the gravity of the infringement as a whole. However, where the infringement consists of clearly separable types of conduct (eg relating to different products) it may be appropriate to apply separate multipliers for duration, even if an objective link and common objective between the various actions can be

---

[266] However, the EU Courts appear to accept that, within the Commission's discretion, the applicable guidelines may clarify the impact of the duration factor (Art 23(3) of Reg 1/2003) in the fines calculation. See Judgment of 8 December 2011 in Case C-386/10 P *Chalkor AE Epexergasias Metallon v Commission*, paras 71 and 77; Judgment of 27 June 2012 in Case T-439/07 *Coats Holdings v Commission*, para 187.

[267] Assuming a percentage value of at least 15 per cent for hard-core infringements, as applied to the value of sales, the individual turnover in the last year of the infringement with the products or services concerned has to be at least EUR 134 million in order for the amount determined on that basis to exceed EUR 20 million.

[268] This applies even to infringements of a very short duration, see eg Commission Decision of 25 June 2008 in Case COMP/39.180 *Aluminium fluoride*, para 241 (50 per cent for a duration of five months) (confirmed in the Judgment of 18 June 2013 in Case T-406/08 *ICF v Commission*, para 206).

[269] This is generally permissible, see Case T-220/00 *Cheil Jedang v Commission* [2003] ECR II II-2473, paras 128–37; Case T-299/08 *Elf Aquitaine v Commission* [2011] ECR II-2149, para 314; Judgment of 2 February 2012 in Case T-77/08 *The Dow Chemical Company v Commission*, paras 142–3 and 148–9. Generally, there is no requirement to fix the amount of the fine at a level that is strictly proportionate to the duration of an undertaking's participation in the infringement. See Judgment of 27 September 2012 in Case T-362/06 *Ballast Nedam Infra v Commission*, para 142.

[270] See eg Commission Decision of 11 November 2009 in Case COMP/38.589 *Heat Stabilisers*, paras 671 and 712–13; Commission Decision of 23 June 2010 in Case COMP/39.092 *Bathroom Fittings and Fixtures*, para 1223; Commission Decision of 9 November 2010 in Case COMP/39.258 *Air Freight*, para 1189. See also Commission Decision of 22 June 2011 in Case COMP/39.525 *Telekomunikacja Polska*, paras 910–11.

[271] Judgment of 8 December 2011 in Case C-272/09 P *KME Germany and Others v Commission*, paras 64, 65, and 67–9. Generally, the factor for duration is independent of the actual effects of the infringement or its implementation. Case T-213/00 *CMA CGM and Others v Commission* [2003] ECR II-913, para 280; Judgment of 27 June 2012 in Case T-439/07 *Coats Holdings v Commission*, paras 187 and 189.

[272] Judgment of 8 December 2011 in Case C-272/09 P *KME Germany and Others v Commission*, para 66; Case T-30/05 *Prym v Commission* [2007] ECR II-107, para 196; Case T-52/03 *Knauf Gips v Commission* [2008] ECR II-115, para 438; Case T-13/03 *Nintendo v Commission* [2009] ECR II-975; Case T-377/06 *Comap v Commission* [2011] ECR II-1115, para 113; Judgment of 29 March 2012 in Case T-336/07 *Telefónica and Telefónica de España v Commission*, para 450; Judgment of 27 June 2012 in Case T-439/07 *Coats Holdings v Commission*, para 187.

[273] Case T-50/03 *Gyproc Belgium v Commission* [2008] ECR II-114, paras 107 and 108; Case T-12/03 *Itochu v Commission* [2009] ECR II-909, paras 120 and 121.

established.[274] The same applies where individual companies forming one undertaking have participated in the infringement during different time periods.[275]

In principle, the basic amount for each undertaking will be tailored to its individual cir- **11.57** cumstances, subject to two exceptions.[276] First, the Commission may set an identical basic amount for two undertakings, even though they only have similar, but not identical, turnover figures. This can be justified since, where the relevant sales of two or more undertakings are similar, the difference between their likely weight in the infringement and the respective impact of their behaviour on the market is probably not such that different fines are necessary. Secondly, rounded figures will be used for the basic amount.[277]

Additional amount

An important innovation introduced by the 2006 Guidelines is the additional amount **11.58** (sometimes inappropriately called the 'entry fee').[278] This is an extra amount ranging from 15 to 25 per cent of the undertaking's relevant turnover.[279] It applies 'irrespective of duration', ie also for one-off or very short infringements, with a view to deterring undertakings from even trying out anticompetitive behaviour by threatening a substantial fine.[280] Hence, it applies once, whatever the duration of the infringement, and, contrary to the variable amount of the fine, is not multiplied by the number of years of participation in the infringement. Imposing an additional amount is generally foreseen for hard-core infringements,[281] whereas it is optional otherwise.[282] The percentage value will be determined on the basis of the same factors as have been considered for the variable amount. Consequently, and despite the different bands established in paragraphs 21 and 25 of the 2006 Guidelines, the percentage values for the variable and additional amount are normally identical.[283] Where a subsidiary that participates in an infringement is transferred to a different undertaking during the

---

[274] See eg Commission Decision of 1 October 2008 in Case COMP/39.181 *Candle Waxes*, paras 610 and 611. See also Castillo de la Torre 'The 2006 Guidelines on Fines: Reflections on the Commission's Practice' (2010) 33 World Competition 385, nn 133, 134.

[275] Commission Decision of 11 November 2009 in Case COMP/38.589 *Heat Stabilisers*, para 713. Where this is the case, the limitation periods count separately for parent and subsidiary. Cf Judgment of 27 June 2012 in Case T-372/10 *Bolloré v Commission*, para 194.

[276] 2006 Guidelines, para 26.

[277] See Hubert de Broca, 'The Commission Revises its Guidelines for Setting Fines in Antitrust Cases' (2006) Competition Policy Newsletter' 1 & 4.

[278] The GC has already endorsed this element of the fine, see Case T-299/08 *Elf Aquitaine v Commission* [2011] ECR II-2149, para 289; Joined Cases T-204/08 and T-212/08 *Team Relocations v Commission* [2011] ECR II-3569, paras 117 and 118; Judgment of 13 December 2012 in Case T-103/08 *Versalis and ENI v Commission*, para 248. See also AG Kokott, Opinion of 24 May 2012 in Case C-441/11 P *Commission v Verhuizingen Coppens*, para 66 with n 48.

[279] 2006 Guidelines, para 25.

[280] In so far as the objective of the additional amount is general deterrence, it plays a role separately from the variable amount, the aggravating circumstance of recidivism and any deterrence multiplier based on the overall size of the undertaking. See Judgment of 13 December 2012 in Case T-103/08 *Versalis and ENI v Commission*, paras 247 and 316.

[281] This includes not just horizontal agreements, but also concerted practices and decisions by associations of undertakings. See Judgment of 14 March 2013 in Case T-587/08 *Fresh Del Monte v Commission*, paras 781 and 782.

[282] Possible examples for the latter scenario might be where the anticompetitive character of the conduct was rather obvious (eg consistent line of previous decisions) or where the infringement, despite its very short duration, produced or was likely to produce significant effects (eg serious abuses of a dominant position or restrictions of, parallel trade). However, no additional amount was imposed in either *Intel* (Commission Decision of 13 May 2009 in Case COMP/37.990) or *Telekomunikacja Polska* (Commission Decision of 22 June 2011 in Case COMP/39.525).

[283] The Commission applied different percentage values only in the first three decisions adopted under the 2006 Guidelines (COMP/38.432 *Professional Videotapes*; COMP/39.165 *Flat glass*; COMP/38.629 *Chloroprene Rubber*).

infringement period, *both parents* (old and new) will *each* receive an additional amount, whereas the *subsidiary* remains liable for a *single* additional amount only.[284]

11.59 In comparison with the 1998 Guidelines, the calculation of the fine under the 2006 Guidelines will generally be better tailored to the individual circumstances of each participant in the infringement. At the same time, there is no uniform answer to the question as to whether the outcome will be better or worse for each individual undertaking, as this will depend on the value of sales at stake and the duration of its participation in the infringement (for the 2006 Guidelines), but also the other characteristics of the infringement, for instance the type of infringement or the size of the overall market affected (both in geographic and volume terms) (for the 1998 Guidelines). Two examples may help to demonstrate the divergent results to which the application of the 2006 Guidelines may lead. Suppose that the Commission finds that an undertaking with a turnover of EUR 300 million in the relevant product market is involved in a cartel. In an average case, the variable amount could then be around EUR 51 million (ie 17 per cent[285] of EUR 300 million). If the cartel lasted for six years, that amount is multiplied by six, increasing it to EUR 306 million. In addition, the Commission will impose an additional amount of (again) EUR 51 million (basically, the portion of another year of turnover). Overall, and leaving aside any adjustments for aggravating or mitigating circumstances, the basic amount would therefore add up to EUR 356 million, which is likely to be higher than the fine imposed on the undertaking under the 1998 Guidelines.[286] At the same time, an undertaking with a turnover of EUR 20 million in the relevant product market would receive a variable amount of around EUR 10.2 million for a cartel of three years and an additional amount of EUR 3.4 million, thus leading to a basic amount of EUR 13.5 million. This would be below the minimum threshold of EUR 20 million foreseen in the 1998 Guidelines for a hard-core infringement.

Adjustments to the basic amount

11.60 The basic amount of the fine may be increased or reduced if any aggravating or mitigating circumstances apply.[287] The relevant factors in this respect deal with the specific role performed by each undertaking and/or the individual gravity of its participation in the infringement, as well as its conduct during the course of the investigation.[288] The 2006 Guidelines provide an illustrative

---

[284] Commission Decision of 22 July 2009 in Case COMP/39.396 *Calcium carbide*, paras 307 and 308.

[285] This corresponds to the average percentage value applied in the twenty-four cartel cases that have been adopted in the first five years of the application of the 2006 Guidelines.

[286] In fact, in only two cases under the 1998 Guidelines (*Vitamins*: Hoffmann-La Roche with EUR 462 million; *Gas-insulated switchgear*: Siemens with EUR 396 million) did the fines for an individual undertaking exceed that amount. See Cartel Statistics (8 March 2013), para 1.6. 'Ten highest cartel fines per undertaking (since 1969)'.

[287] 2006 Guidelines, para 27. In case several factors apply, such as aggravating and mitigating circumstances, each modulation will (again) be carried out with regard to the full basic amount. See Case T-38/02 *Groupe Danone v Commission* [2005] ECR II-4407, para 521: 'the percentages corresponding to increases or reductions applied to reflect aggravating or attenuating circumstances must be applied to the basic amount of the fine set by reference to the gravity and duration of the infringement, and not to the figure resulting from any initial increase or reduction to reflect an aggravating or attenuating circumstance.' See also Case T-224/00 *Archer Daniels Midland v Commission* [2003] ECR II-2597, para 378.

[288] It should be noted, though, that already some of the factors that are relevant for determining the *basic amount* relate not to the infringement as such but to *elements specific to each undertaking*. This applies in particular to the value of sales and the factor for duration. In addition, depending on the circumstances it might be justified to differentiate the percentage value(s) to be applied to the relevant turnover in accordance with the scope of participation of the respective undertaking in the infringement (eg as regards the geographic scope, see Commission Decision of 28 March 2012 in Case COMP/39.452 *Mountings for windows and window-doors*, para 480).

but not exhaustive list of adjustment factors.[289] The list of aggravating and mitigating circumstances is similar to the one under the 1998 Guidelines, with certain differences, for instance as regards recidivism (earlier decisions of NCAs under Articles 101 and 102 TFEU also count)[290] and substantially limited participation (which replaces the former 'passive role' and requires competitive conduct on the market). According to paragraph 27 of the 2006 Guidelines, the Commission will make 'an overall assessment which takes account of all the relevant circumstances'.[291] Cases are inevitably fact-specific and reflect how the Commission exercises its discretion in this overall assessment, both as regards the application of adjustment factors and the specific level of any increase or reduction.[292]

Aggravating circumstances

The 2006 Guidelines set out five specific forms of aggravating circumstances in paragraph 28.[293] **11.61**
The term 'such as' underlines that this is not a closed list and thus, as under the previous regime, arguably leaves scope for the development of new categories:

(i) *Continuation of the infringement after intervention by the Commission.* One of the aggravating factors that has been applied on several occasions is continuing the infringement following intervention by the Commission.[294] While the 2006 Guidelines explicitly refer to a prior 'finding' of an infringement, an aggravating circumstance might also apply where the undertaking had at least received an explicit warning from the Commission or an NCA.[295] It will then be necessary to assess whether it continued the infringement knowing that it was subject to a Commission inquiry.[296] In *Graphite Electrodes*,[297] the Commission increased the amount of the fine for a number of undertakings because they continued their participation in the infringement after the Commission had initiated its investigation (inspections; requests for information). In *French Beef*,[298] the undertakings 'continued

---

[289] This is already clear from the wording of the 2006 Guidelines ('such as'). See also Joined Cases T-236/01, T-239/01, T-244/01 to T-246/01, T-251/01 and T-252/01 *Tokai Carbon and Others v Commission* [2004] ECR II-1181, para 314; Judgment of 25 October 2011 in Case T-348/08 *Aragonesas v Commission*, para 281.

[290] The severe punishment of repeat offenders was one of the main objectives of the 2006 reform. See European Commission, MEMO/06/256 'Competition: revised Commission Guidelines for setting fines in antitrust cases—frequently asked questions' of 28 June 2006.

[291] See the references in the sub-section on mitigating circumstances, at para 11.63. The Commission is generally not bound by its assessment in previous decisions. See Case T-30/05 *Prym v Commission* [2007] ECR II-107, para 205.

[292] See Judgment of 12 October 2011 in Case T-38/05 *Agroexpansión v Commission*, para 227; Judgment of 29 March 2012 in Case T-336/07 *Telefónica and Telefónica de España v Commission*, para 455.

[293] Regarding the 1998 Guidelines, see also D Geradin and D Henry, 'The EC Fining Policy for Violation of Competition Law: An Empirical Review of the Commission Decisional Practice and the Community Courts' Judgments' [2005] European Competition Law Journal 401, 443–8.

[294] The increase of the fine in these cases has been confirmed by the EU Courts in the past. See Case T-31/99 *Asea Brown Boveri v Commission* [2002] ECR II-1881, paras 211–14; Joined Cases T-236/01, T-239/01, T-244/01 to T-246/01, T-251/01 and T-252/01 *Tokai Carbon v Commission* [2004] ECR II-1181, paras 292–5 and 310; Case T-13/03 *Nintendo v Commission* [2009] ECR II-975, paras 142 and 144–5; Case T-384/06 *IBP and International Building Products France v Commission* [2011] ECR II-1177, para 105.

[295] For example *Pre-Insulated Pipes* [1999] OJ L24/1, para 108 et seq and 171; Joined Cases T-217/03 and T-245/03 *FNCBV and Others v Commission* [2006] ECR II-4987, para 271. But see also Case T-141/94 *Thyssen Stahl v Commission* [1999] ECR II-347, paras 619–24 (not where the undertaking was merely the addressee of an inspection decision and the statement of objections concerning another infringement).

[296] See Case T-28/99 *Sigma Tecnologie v Commission* [2002] ECR II-1845, paras 102–7. The Court partly annulled the decision because no inspections had been carried out at the premises of the applicant and it could not be demonstrated that it knew of the on-going investigation.

[297] *Graphite Electrodes* [2002] OJ L100/1, paras 160 and 164 (SGL); 187 and 192 (UCAR); 209 and 210 (Tokai, SEC, Nippon).

[298] *French Beef* [2003] OJ L209/12, para 174 (confirmed in this respect in Joined Cases T-217/03 and T-245/03 *FNCBV and Others v Commission* [2006] ECR II-4987, para 271).

their agreement in secret, in another form…even though they had received a letter of formal notice from the Commission, and had given an assurance that the written agreement…would not be extended'. In *Fittings*, Aalberts, Delta, Comap, and Advanced Fluid Connections (IBP) had their fines increased by 60 per cent because they continued their illegal arrangements after the Commission's initial inspections.[299]

(ii)   *Repeated infringement of a similar type by the same undertaking(s) after a prior finding of an infringement by the Commission or an NCA.* According to the 2006 Guidelines, the basic amount of the undertaking's fine may be increased by up to 100 per cent for each prior infringement.[300] This shows that the Commission considers repeat offences as a very serious aggravating circumstance deserving a significant increase in the fine, and that 'multi-recidivists' should be hit particularly hard. However, in its practice so far the Commission has not made full use of that 100 per cent band, but instead applied only an increase of 50 per cent for a *single* prior infringement.[301] Higher increases applied in cases of *several* prior infringements.[302] No increase has yet been based on a prior infringement decision by an NCA, given that the Commission considers that a finding of recidivism in this respect will only be warranted where the subsequent infringement continued (for some time at least) following the publication of the 2006 Guidelines.[303] The meaning of a *'similar' infringement* is broad: it suffices if the undertaking violated the same legal norm[304] (or the parallel provision in the ECSC Treaty[305]) in the past. Conversely, the particular circumstances of the prior infringement,[306] including the economic sector[307] or geographic market affected,[308] are not relevant. The *mere finding of an infringement*

---

[299] Commission Decision of 20 September 2006 in Case COMP/38.121 *Fittings*, paras 779–83 and 785 (confirmed, for example, in Case T-284/06 *IBP and International Building Products France v Commission* [2011] ECR II-1177, para 105; for different reasons, the decision against Aalberts was annulled as a whole in Case T-385/06 *Aalberts Industries and Others v Commission* [2011] ECR II-1223).

[300] Although this increase also serves the objective of deterrence, it plays a role different from the increase for deterrence which may be imposed on larger undertakings (so-called multiplier). See Judgment of 6 March 2012 in Case T-53/06 *UPM-Kymmene v Commission*, paras 134–7.

[301] eg Commission Decision of 23 January 2008 in Case COMP/38.628 *Nitrile Butadiene Rubber*, para 182; Commission Decision of 7 October 2009 in Case COMP/39.129 *Power Transformers*, paras 254–6. This level has been confirmed by the EU Courts, see Joined Cases T-101/05 and T-111/05 *BASF and UCB v Commission* [2007] ECR II-4949, para 69. Generally, the courts have emphasized that recidivism is a factor which justifies a 'significant' increase in the basic amount of the fine. Case T-203/01 *Michelin v Commission* [2003] ECR II-4071, para 293; Case T-38/02 *Groupe Danone v Commission* [2005] ECR II-4407, para 348 (confirmed on appeal in Case C-3/06 *Groupe Danone v Commission* [2007] ECR I-1331, para 47).

[302] An increase of 60 per cent was applied for two prior infringements (eg Commission Decision of 12 November 2008 in Case COMP/39.125 *Car Glass*, paras 695 and 696), 90 per cent for three prior infringements (Commission Decision of 11 November 2009 in Case COMP/38.589 *Heat Stabilisers*, para 718; Judgment of 17 May 2011 in Case T-343/08 *Arkema v Commission*, paras 103, 104, and 204), and 100 per cent for four prior infringements (Commission Decision of 22 July 2009 in Case COMP/39.396 *Calcium carbide*, para 310 n 631).

[303] However, it appears that the Commission indicated the possibility of increasing the fine on this basis in the statement of objections issued in Case COMP/39.633 *Shrimps* (Commission Press Release IP/12/782). There, the previous finding of an infringement by the Dutch NCA dated from before the publication of the 2006 Guidelines.

[304] Joined Cases T-101/05 and T-111/05 *BASF and UCB v Commission* [2007] ECR II-4949, para 64. No recidivism will be assumed, however, if the prior infringement concerned a violation of Art 101 TFEU, whereas subsequently the undertaking infringed Art 102 TFEU. See Case T-57/01 *Solvay v Commission* [2009] ECR II-4621, para 510.

[305] Case T-122/04 *Outokumpu v Commission* [2009] ECR II-1135, paras 55–7.

[306] See Case T-122/04 *Outokumpu v Commission* [2009] ECR II-1135, paras 58 and 64.

[307] Case T-161/05 *Hoechst v Commission* [2009] ECR II-3555, para 147 (concerning Commission Decision of 19 January 2005 in Case COMP/37.773 *MCAA*, paras 311 and 312: 'There is no requirement that the business, products and personnel should be consistent between decisions'). See also Judgment of 6 March 2012 in Case T-53/06 *UPM-Kymmene v Commission*, para 133; Commission Decision of 22 July 2009 in Case COMP/39.396 *Calcium carbide*, paras 309 and 310, n 631.

[308] Case T-203/01 *Michelin v Commission* [2003] ECR II-4071, para 288 (different national markets).

(without imposing a sanction) suffices,[309] even if legal proceedings against such a finding have been initiated.[310] The Commission has to demonstrate and sufficiently reason the *identity of the undertaking* that committed the past and present infringement(s).[311] In this respect, in some cases the GC appears to require that an increase of the fine for recidivism is justified only for those legal entities which had already been the addressees of an earlier decision finding an infringement.[312] However, other judgments accept that the Commission may find recidivism where one group company commits an infringement of the same type as that for which another was previously sanctioned, as long as it can show that the same undertaking continued to exist.[313] For this, it may be sufficient that the former perpetrator was a wholly-owned subsidiary of a parent company that forms part of an undertaking with the later perpetrator.[314] In establishing a repeat offence, the Commission is not bound by any limitation period. However, it has to take the length of *time that has elapsed* between the infringements in question into consideration as an indication that may confirm, or speak against, the undertaking's propensity to disregard the

---

[309] Case T-38/02 *Groupe Danone v Commission* [2005] ECR II-4407, para 363 (confirmed on appeal in Case C-3/06 P *Groupe Danone v Commission* [2007] ECR I-1331, para 41).

[310] Case T-410/03 *Hoechst v Commission* [2008] ECR II-881, para 466; Case T-43/03 *Lafarge v Commission* [2008] ECR II-120, paras 734–7 (confirmed on appeal in Case C-413/08 P *Lafarge v Commission* [2010] ECR I-5361, paras 81–6). However, the ECJ made clear that, if the prior decision forming the basis for recidivism is subsequently annulled, 'the Commission is required, under Article 233 EC [now: Article 266 TFEU], to take the measures necessary to comply with the judgment of the Court, by amending, as appropriate, the later decision in so far as it includes an increase of the fine for repeated infringement'. See Case C-413/08 P *Lafarge v Commission*, para 88.

[311] Judgment of 12 July 2011 in Case T-59/07 *Polimeri Europa v Commission*, paras 298–303; Judgment of 8 May 2013 in Case C-508/11 P *Eni v Commission*, para 129. In addition, in *PO/Interbrew Alken Maes* [2003] OJ L200/1, para 314, the Commission took into account that the same person occupied the post of chairman and chief executive during the period in which the past and subsequent infringements were committed, and that two directors also worked in the company's business divisions concerned by these infringements.

[312] Judgment of 13 July 2011 in Joined Cases T-144/07, T-147/07, T-148/07, T-149/07, T-150/07, and T-154/07 *ThyssenKrupp Liften Ascenseurs and Others v Commission*, paras 314–15, 318–19, and 322. While the Commission cross-appealed the judgment on this point, the ECJ never ruled on the cross-appeal because ThyssenKrupp subsequently withdrew its appeal. See also Judgment of 13 December 2012 in Case T-103/08 *Versalis and ENI v Commission*, paras 272–4, and the *obiter dictum* in Case T-206/06 *Total and Elf Aquitaine v Commission* [2011] ECR II-163, para 213.

[313] Judgment of 27 September 2012 in Case T-343/06 *Shell Petroleum and Others v Commission*, para 248 et seq; Judgment of 6 March 2012 in Case T-53/06 *UPM-Kymmene v Commission*, para 129. See also Case T-161/05 *Hoechst v Commission* [2009] ECR II-3555, para 147; Commission Decision of 22 July 2009 in Case COMP/39.396 *Calcium carbide*, para 311. More expansively, in an earlier judgment the GC considered it sufficient that the addressee of the later decision had been linked to the addressee of the prior decision through a parent company which held the entire share capital in both legal entities (but where the Commission had not established the existence of one undertaking in the first decision). See Case T-203/01 *Michelin v Commission* [2003] ECR II-4071, para 290. It is this view which was rejected in the Judgment of 13 July 2011 in Joined Cases T-144/07, T-147/07, T-148/07, T-149/07, T-150/07 and T-154/07 *ThyssenKrupp Liften Ascenseurs and Others v Commission*, para 314 et seq; and in the Judgment of 13 December 2012 in Case T-103/08 *Versalis and ENI v Commission*, para 272–4, and 281.

[314] Judgment of 27 September 2012 in Case T-343/06 *Shell Petroleum and Others v Commission*, para 263. Where the Commission indicates in the statement of objections that the same undertaking had already been held liable for a similar infringement in the past, the addressee has the opportunity to contest this finding, thereby safeguarding its rights of defence (para 275). While this was the view of the Sixth Chamber, in a subsequent judgment the Seventh Chamber of the GC held that the entity for which recidivism shall be established must have had the opportunity, *during the administrative procedure leading up to the decision finding the previous infringement*, to contest that it exercised decisive influence on the legal entity directly participating in that infringement. See Judgment of 13 December 2012 in Case T-103/08 *Versalis and ENI v Commission*, para 274. At the same time, however, the GC considered that it was sufficient for increasing the fine for both parent and subsidiary on grounds of recidivism if a repeat offence could at least be established vis-à-vis the subsidiary (paras 276–80 and 367).

competition rules.[315] The relevant time period in this regard is that between the finding of the prior infringement and the beginning of the new infringement. Where the time periods of the earlier and later infringement overlap, the Commission may increase the fine imposed for the second infringement if it continues to run for some (material) time after the finding of the first infringement.[316] The finding of an earlier infringement may be considered for recidivism even if it has already been taken into account as an aggravating circumstance in other cases.[317] Finally, the *absence* of any previous infringement is a normal circumstance which the Commission does not have to take into account as a mitigating factor.[318]

(iii) *Refusal to cooperate or obstruction of the Commission's investigation.* The Commission may also take into account the (obstructive) conduct of the undertaking during the administrative procedure, in particular the investigation stage.[319] An obstruction of the investigation may take different forms, for example a warning to other cartel members of a forthcoming inspection,[320] the prevention of an inspection (eg by not letting the inspectors enter the premises or a particular office),[321] the destruction of documents during an inspection,[322] or disclosure to the co-conspirators of statements submitted to the Commission in response to a request for information.[323] Also, clearly unfounded requests for protection

---

[315] Case C-3/06 P *Groupe Danone v Commission* [2007] ECR I-1331, paras 38 and 39; Case C-413/08 P *Lafarge v Commission* [2010] ECR I-5361, paras 70 and 72. At least a period of (only) ten years will not prevent the Commission from establishing recidivism. Case T-38/02 *Groupe Danone v Commission* [2005] ECR II-4407, paras 354 and 355 (confirmed on appeal in Case C-3/06 P *Groupe Danone v Commission* [2007] ECR I-1331, para 40). If the period is longer, it may also be relevant whether there have been intermediary findings of an infringement which provide for a closer temporal link. See Judgment of 17 May 2011 in Case T-343/08 *Arkema v Commission*, paras 69–73. In some cases, the Commission has relied on prior findings of an infringement which dated back more than twenty years. See eg Commission Decision of 29 September 2004 in Case COMP/37.750 *Brasseries Kronenbourg, Brasseries Heineken*, para 93; Commission Decision of 9 December 2004 in Case COMP/37.533 *Choline Chloride*, para 208 (confirmed in Joined Cases T-101/05 and T-111/05 *BASF and UCB v Commission* [2007] ECR II-4949, paras 18 and 67–72); Commission Decision of 19 January 2005 in Case COMP/37.773 *MCAA*, para 309 (confirmed in Case T-161/05 *Hoechst v Commission* [2009] ECR II-3555, paras 141 and 142). In a more recent judgment, the GC considered that a time lapse of fifteen years does not confirm a tendency to infringe the competition rules. See Judgment of 27 September 2012 in Case T-82/08 *Guardian Industries and Guardian Europe v Commission*, para 123.

[316] Commission Decision of 22 July 2009 in Case COMP/39.396 *Calcium carbide*, para 309, n 631; Commission Decision of 9 November 2010 in Case COMP/39.258 *Air Freight*, para 1220. See Case T-161/05 *Hoechst v Commission* [2009] ECR II-3555, paras 10, 21, and 142; Case T-54/03 *Lafarge v Commission* [2008] ECR II-120, paras 738 and 739. If this is the case, the basic amount as a whole will be increased and not just a part corresponding to the period following the finding of the earlier infringement. Case T-53/03 *BPB v Commission* [2008] ECR II-1333, paras 369 and 391–2. However, no increase may be justified where most parts of the subsequent infringement preceded the finding of the earlier infringement. See Case T-141/94 *Thyssen Stahl v Commission* [1999] ECR II-347, paras 617 and 618.

[317] Case T-217/06 *Arkema v Commission* [2011] ECR II-2593, paras 297–300; Judgment of 14 July 2011 in Case T-189/06 *Arkema v Commission*, paras 126–30 and 132–4. See also Commission Decision of 19 January 2005 in Case COMP/37.773 *MCAA*, para 313 (confirmed in Case T-161/05 *Hoechst v Commission* [2009] ECR II-3555, para 150).

[318] Case T-8/89 *DSM v Commission* [1991] ECR II-1833, para 317.

[319] Judgment of 27 September 2012 in Case T-357/06 *Koninklijke Wegenbouw Stevin v Commission*, para 249.

[320] Joined Cases T-236/01, T-239/01, T-244/01 to T-246/01, T-251/01 and T-252/01 *Tokai Carbon and Others v Commission* [2004] ECR II-1181, paras 310, 312–13, and 315 (confirmed on appeal in Case C-308/04 P *SGL Carbon v Commission* [2006] ECR I-5977, paras 64–72).

[321] Commission Decision of 13 September 2006 in Case COMP/38.456 *Bitumen Netherlands*, paras 340 and 341 (confirmed in Case T-357/06 *Koninklijke Wegenbouw Stevin v Commission*, paras 233 and 239).

[322] Commission Decision of 30 November 2005 in Case COMP/38.354 *Industrial bags*, paras 790–5; Commission Decision of 20 November 2007 in Case COMP/38.432 *Professional Videotapes*, paras 219–27.

[323] Case T-66/99 *Minoan Lines v Commission* [2003] ECR II-5515, para 338. Likewise, the attempt to coordinate the responses to a request for information may constitute obstruction. See *Bayo-n-ox* [1990] OJ L21/71, paras 32 and 69.

under 'legal professional privilege' ('LPP')—merely as a delaying tactic—may lead to an increase of the fine.[324] Conversely, the mere assertion of one's rights of defence (for example by rejecting the tentative findings in the statement of objections) cannot constitute an aggravating circumstance.[325] Nevertheless, where the undertaking of its own motion makes factual assertions, or submits evidence (eg witness statements), it has to ensure their accuracy.[326] In the Commission's view, a simple attempt to obstruct, irrespective of any actual effects, may justify an increase of the fine.[327] Depending on the circumstances, this might also apply in the case of negligent conduct. In some cases, the Commission has significantly increased the basic amount under this heading.[328] Alternatively, the refusal to submit to an inspection and other types of obstructive behaviour (eg incorrect replies to a request for information) can lead to the finding of a separate, procedural infringement pursuant to Article 23(1) of Regulation 1/2003 and the imposition of a fine on that ground.[329] This may be particularly warranted if there are doubts as to whether the investigation will ever proceed to the finding of an infringement on substance. However, once the Commission has imposed a procedural fine, the principle of *ne bis in idem* would likely rule out a subsequent increase, for the same conduct, of the substantive fine.[330]

(iv) *Role as ring leader or instigator of the infringement.* The role as *instigator* concerns the initiation or expansion of a cartel,[331] in particular where the undertaking has persuaded or encouraged others to establish the cartel, or to join in it.[332] This entails that it must have taken the initiative, 'for example by suggesting to the other[s] an opportunity for collusion or by attempting to persuade [them] to do so'.[333] Conversely, the role as *ring leader* concerns

---

[324] Joined Cases T-125/03 and T-252/03 *Akzo Nobel Chemicals and Akcros Chemicals v Commission* [2007] ECR II-3523, para 89.

[325] Case T-9/99 *HFB and Others v Commission* [2002] ECR II-1487, para 478 (confirmed on appeal in Joined Cases C-189/02 P, C-202/02 P, C-205/02 P to C-208/02 P and C-213/02 P *Dansk Rørindustri and Others v Commission* [2005] ECR I-5425, paras 352 and 353).

[326] Case T-384/06 *IBP and International Building Products France v Commission* [2011] ECR II-1177, paras 111 and 114.

[327] Commission Decision of 30 November 2005 in Case COMP/38.354 *Industrial bags*, para 794; Commission Decision of 20 November 2007 in Case COMP/38.432 *Professional Videotapes*, para 221. See also Section B.2 of the 1998 Guidelines.

[328] In *Greek Ferries* [1999] OJ L109/24, paras 160 and 161, Minoan attempted to obstruct the investigation by suggesting to its co-conspirators a slight differentiation in prices in order to disguise the collusion; this led to an increase of the basic amount by 10 per cent (see Case T-66/99 *Minoan Lines v Commission* [2003] ECR II-5515, paras 335–8). In *Pre-Insulated Pipes* [1999] OJ L24/1, paras 157–60 and 179, Henss/Isoplus attempted to mislead the Commission about the group's corporate structure; the Commission increased the fine for this and another aggravating circumstance by 30 per cent (see Case T-9/99 *HFB and Others v Commission* [2002] ECR II-1487, paras 555–65). In *Graphite Electrodes* [2002] OJ L100/1, para 160, the Commission applied an increase of 25 per cent to the fine of SGL for having warned other members of the cartel of the forthcoming Commission investigations (see Joined Cases T-236/01, T-239/01, T-244/01 to T-246/01, T-251/01 and T-252/01 *Tokai Carbon v Commission* [2004] ECR II-1181, paras 310 and 312–17).

[329] On the relationship between such a procedural infringement and the increase of a fine for a substantive infringement (eg a violation of Art 101 TFEU) on account of an aggravating circumstance see Case T-384/06 *IBP and International Building Products France v Commission* [2011] ECR II-1177, paras 108–10; Judgment of 27 September 2012 in Case T-357/06 *Koninklijke Wegenbouw Stevin v Commission*, paras 245 and 251.

[330] Cf Judgment of 27 September 2012 in Case T-343/06 *Shell Petroleum and Others v Commission*, para 118.

[331] See Case T-110/07 *Siemens AG v Commission* [2011] ECR II-477, para 348.

[332] Judgment of 27 September 2012 in Case T-343/06 *Shell Petroleum and Others v Commission*, paras 155 and 156. See eg *Pre-Insulated Pipes* [1999] OJ L24/1, paras 121 and 171; *Greek Ferries* [1999] OJ L109/24, para 159. By contrast, it is not sufficient merely to have been a founding member of the cartel.

[333] Case T-15/02 *BASF v Commission* [2003] ECR II-213, paras 316 and 321; Joined Cases T-117/07 and T-121/07 *Areva and Others v Commission* [2011] ECR II-633, para 290. For examples see Joined Cases T-109/02, T-118/02, T-122/02, T-125/02 and T-126/02, T-128/02 and T-129/02, T-132/02 and T-136/02 *Bolloré and Others v Commission* [2007] ECR II-947, para 586. The mere fact that an undertaking belongs to the founding members of a cartel is not sufficient. Case T-15/02 *BASF v Commission* [2003] ECR II-213, para 456.

the actual functioning of the cartel, for example its organization and implementation.[334] It does not imply that the undertaking exerted pressure or even dictated the behaviour of other cartel members (which may nevertheless constitute an aggravating circumstance); neither does the Commission have to demonstrate the undertaking's particular market power.[335] Rather, it is 'sufficient that the undertaking was a significant driving force for the cartel, which may be inferred in particular from the fact that it took upon itself responsibility for developing and suggesting the conduct to be adopted by the members of the cartel, even if it was not necessarily in a position to impose it upon them.'[336] This will require an overall assessment of all relevant circumstances, including for example the market position of the undertaking and/or the functioning of the cartel.[337] The Commission may assume a leading role where the undertaking has taken special iniatives in the cartel,[338] or where it made particular efforts in ensuring its stability and success.[339] The latter may include a coordinating role in the cartel (eg cartel secretariat) or an otherwise central role for its functioning (eg substantial tasks with regard to the organization of meetings or the information flow; chairmanship; representation of several other cartel members; mediation of conflicts; allocation of market shares; negotiation and monitoring of agreements).[340] Also, the fact that an undertaking has determined the strategic orientation of the cartel may be important.[341] However, the Commission is not required to demonstrate that the infringement would have been less serious without the leadership role of the undertaking.[342] There might be more than one instigator or ring leader in a cartel.[343] Where the cartel has two

---

[334] For an overview see Case T-110/07 *Siemens AG v Commission* [2011] ECR II-477, paras 333–69; Joined Cases T-117/07 and T-121/07 *Areva and Others v Commission* [2011] ECR II-633, paras 280–93 and 300; Judgment of 27 September 2012 in Case T-343/06 *Shell Petroleum and Others v Commission*, paras 198–202. For examples see Case T-15/02 *BASF v Commission* [2003] ECR II-213, paras 374 and 404; Case T-59/02 *Archer Daniels Midland v Commission* [2006] ECR II-3627, paras 305 and 306; Case T-29/05 *Deltafina v Commission* [2010] ECR II-4077, para 335. For price initiatives see Case T-15/02 *BASF v Commission* [2003] ECR II-213, paras 348 and 427.

[335] Joined Cases T-117/07 and T-121/07 *Areva and Others v Commission* [2011] ECR II-633, paras 284 and 290–1. Neither is it relevant whether the undertaking accepted its role as leader voluntarily or whether its room for manoeuvre was limited (para 292).

[336] Case T-15/02 *BASF v Commission* [2003] ECR II-213, para 374; Case T-110/07 *Siemens AG v Commission* [2011] ECR II-477, paras 337 and 342; Joined Cases T-117/07 and T-121/07 *Areva and Others v Commission* [2011] ECR II-633, paras 287, 291, and 293 (pre-eminent position in terms of the duration, intensity, and significance of the functions carried out in the cartel organization).

[337] Case T-15/02 *BASF v Commission* [2003] ECR II-213, paras 299 and 300; Judgment of 27 September 2012 in Case T-357/06 *Koninklijke Wegenbouw Stevin v Commission*, para 299.

[338] Case T-66/99 *Minoan Lines v Commission* [2003] ECR II-5515, para 332 (expansion of the cartel); Case T-15/02 *BASF v Commission* [2003] ECR II-213, para 404 (proposals as to the functioning of the cartel and the scope of the agreements).

[339] Joined Cases T-117/07 and T-121/07 *Areva and Others v Commission* [2011] ECR II-633, para 283. In one case, the GC considered it a strong element of proof that the undertaking had regularly made available its premises for cartel meetings. See Judgment of 27 September 2012 in Case T-357/06 *Koninklijke Wegenbouw Stevin v Commission*, paras 295 and 296.

[340] Case T-29/05 *Deltafina v Commission* [2010] ECR II-4077, para 335; Case T-110/07 *Siemens AG v Commission* [2011] ECR II-477, paras 337 and 338; Joined Cases T-117/07 and T-121/07 *Areva and Others v Commission* [2011] ECR II-633, para 287. See also Commission Decision of 20 October 2004 in Case COMP/38.238 *Raw Tobacco Spain*, paras 365 and 435; Commission Decision of 3 October 2007 in Case COMP/38.710 *Bitumen Spain*, para 535.

[341] Case T-224/00 *Archer Daniels Midland v Commission* [2003] ECR II-2597, para 247; Joined Cases T-236/01, T-239/01, T-244/01 to T-246/01, T-251/01 and T-252/01 *Tokai Carbon v Commission* [2004] ECR II-1181, paras 303 and 304 (planning, establishment, implementation).

[342] Case T-13/03 *Nintendo v Commission* [2009] ECR II-975, para 130.

[343] Case T-110/07 *Siemens AG v Commission* [2011] ECR II-477, paras 344 and 345; Case T-59/02 *Archer Daniels Midland v Commission* [2006] ECR II-3627, para 276. See also Commission Decision of 28 January 2009 in Case COMP/39.406 *Marine Hoses*, para 457 et seq, 463. However, the fact that (nearly) all cartel members participated actively may also indicate a 'joint initiative cartel' where no one is considered as a leader. See Commission Decision of 19 January 2005 in Case COMP/37.773 *MCAA*, paras 304–7.

or more consecutive leaders, the duration of their respective leadership term must be considered when determining the relative level of increase in their fines.[344] Given the special responsibility for the infringement following from the role of instigator or leader,[345] and for reasons of deterrence, this aggravating circumstance may justify a significant increase in the fine.[346]

(v)   *Coercive and/or retaliatory measures against other undertakings with a view to enforcing practices which constitute an infringement.* As for the case of an instigator or ring leader of an antitrust infringement, the Commission will also pay particular attention to any coercive and/or retaliatory measures[347] against other undertakings with a view to enforcing[348] the practices constituting the infringement. In both cases, the mere threat may be sufficient if it has an impact on the conduct of the affected undertaking.[349] In the past, the Commission has increased the fine for such measures on various occasions. For example, in *Pre-insulated Pipes*,[350] ABB's fine was increased by 50 per cent for a series of aggravating circumstances, among others its role as instigator and ring leader, the fact that it put pressure on other undertakings to persuade them to enter the cartel, and its 'systematic orchestration of retaliatory measures against Powerpipe, aimed at its elimination from the market'.[351] In *French Beef*, the Commission increased the fine of the farmers' associations by 30 per cent for the fact that they 'used violence in order to compel the slaughterers' federations to accept the agreement of 24 October

---

[344]   Joined Cases T-117/07 and T-121/07 *Areva and Others v Commission* [2011] ECR II-633, paras 300 and 307.

[345]   See eg Case T-352/94 *Mo och Domsjo v Commission* [1998] ECR II-1989, para 371 (confirmed on appeal in Case C-283/98 P *Mo och Domsjö v Commission* [2000] ECR I-9855, para 45); Joined Cases T-236/01, T-239/01, T-244/01 to T-246/01, T-251/01 and T-252/01 *Tokai Carbon v Commission* [2004] ECR II-1181, para 301.

[346]   Case T-110/07 *Siemens AG v Commission* [2011] ECR II-477, paras 367 and 368; Joined Cases T-117/07 and T-121/07 *Areva and Others v Commission* [2011] ECR II-633, para 319. See also Commission Decision of 1 October 2008 in Case COMP/39.181 *Candle Waxes*, para 681 et seq and 686. So far the maximum increase has been 50 per cent. See eg *Graphite Electrodes* [2002] OJ L100/1, paras 160–4 and 187–92 (confirmed in Joined Cases T-236/01, T-239/01, T-244/01 to T-246/01, T-251/01 and T-252/01 *Tokai Carbon v Commission* [2004] ECR II-1181, paras 291 and 303–10); *Vitamins* [2003] OJ L6/1, paras 712–18 (Hoffmann-La Roche and BASF were found to be joint leaders, but BASF received a milder increase of 30 per cent as the Commission found Roche to be the prime mover); *Nintendo* [2003] OJ L255/33, paras 228–38 and 406 (confirmed in Case T-13/03 *Nintendo and Nintendo of Europe v Commission* [2009] ECR II-975, paras 125 et seq and 215); *Carbonless Paper* [2004] OJ L115/1, paras 418–24 (confirmed in Joined Cases T-109/02, T-118/02, T-122/02, T-125/02, T-126/02, T-128/02, T-129/02, T-132/02 and T-136/02 *Bolloré and Others v Commission* [2007] ECR II-947, paras 559 et seq and 581–90, with an analysis of Commission decisional practice); Commission Decision of 24 January 2007 in Case COMP/38.899 *Gas insulated switchgear*, paras 511–14 (confirmed for Siemens in Case T-110/07 *Siemens AG v Commission* [2011] ECR II-477, paras 363–8).

[347]   Retaliatory measures in principle constitute an aggravating circumstance separate from that of being a ring leader. See Joined Cases T-109/02, T-118/02, T-122/02, T-125/02, T-126/02, T-128/02, T-129/02, T-132/02, and T-136/02 *Bolloré and Others v Commission* [2007] ECR II-947, para 587. However, the Commission may take them into account in an overall assessment. See Case T-31/99 *Asea Brown Boveri v Commission* [2002] ECR II-1881, para 205 et seq.

[348]   The same may apply where an undertaking (successfully) forces another cartel member to extend the scope of anticompetitive cooperation. See Case T-38/03 *Groupe Danone v Commission* [2005] ECR II-4407, paras 280 and 281. In *PO/Interbrew and Alken-Maes* [2003] OJ L200/1, para 315, the Commission held that Danone's threat to destroy Interbrew on the French market if a significant amount of beer was not transferred to Alken-Maes led to an extension of the cartel to market-sharing. However, the Court considered that the causal link was not sufficiently proven. See Case T-38/02 *Groupe Danone v Commission* [2005] ECR II-4407, paras 283–311.

[349]   Case T-38/03 *Groupe Danone v Commission* [2005] ECR II-4407, paras 281 and 283.

[350]   *Pre-Insulated Pipes* [1999] OJ L24/1, para 171.

[351]   See Case T-31/99 *Asea Brown Boveri v Commission* [2002] ECR II-1881, paras 205–10 (confirmed on appeal in Joined Cases C-189/02 P, C-202/02 P, C-205/02 P–C-208/02 P, and C-213/02 P *Dansk Rørindustri and Others v Commission* [2005] ECR I-5425).

2001. They also used physical force to set up mechanisms to verify that the agreement was being applied, such as the illegal "inspections" to establish the place of origin of meat.'[352] In *Volkswagen*,[353] VW's fine was increased by 20 per cent because it not only put direct pressure on dealers to enforce price discipline, but also used them as informers by calling on them to report on breaches of price discipline by others. In *JCB*,[354] the Commission decided to increase the basic amount of the fine imposed on JCB by twice the amount of the sanction which JCB had imposed on a distributor for not complying with the agreement.

11.62   Unlike in the 1998 Guidelines, the need to increase the penalty in order to exceed the amount of gains improperly made as a result of the infringement (when it is objectively possible to estimate the amount) is no longer listed among the aggravating circumstances, but under a separate sub-heading within the section on further adjustments to the basic amount (specific increase for deterrence).[355] In order to safeguard the undertakings' rights of defence, it is sufficient that the Commission announces in the statement of objections that it will take the individual role of each undertaking into account and that the amount of the fine will reflect any aggravating circumstances.[356]

Mitigating circumstances

11.63   The 2006 Guidelines also mention five specific forms of mitigating circumstances which are partly similar to, partly different from the 1998 Guidelines. A new mitigating factor—where an undertaking proves that its involvement was substantially limited and that it actually adopted competitive conduct in the market—replaces two separate mitigating factors under the 1998 Guidelines ('exclusively passive role', 'non-implementation in practice of the offending agreements'). While it appears to have been the Commission's objective to raise the bar for claiming a mitigating circumstance in this regard when compared to the 1998 Guidelines,[357] the GC has sent conflicting messages as to whether 'passive role' still survives as an (unnamed) mitigating circumstance.[358] Generally, the

---

[352] *French Beef* [2003] OJ L209/12, para 173.

[353] *Volkswagen* [2001] OJ L262/14, para 121. The Commission found that circulars and individual letters were not just intended to restrict the freedom of dealers to set their prices, but warnings were given and legal action (or even termination of contract) was threatened unless dealers demonstrated greater price discipline.

[354] *JCB* [2002] OJ L69/1, paras 255 and 256.

[355] 2006 Guidelines, para 31.

[356] Judgment of 27 September 2012 in Case T-357/06 *Koninklijke Wegenbouw Stevin v Commission*, para 217.

[357] See Commission Decision of 8 December 2010 in Case COMP/39.309 *Liquid Crystal Displays*, para 439, according to which 'the mere fact that an undertaking takes a passive role should not be rewarded by a reduction in the applicable fine. Even if an undertaking only adopts a passive or 'follow-my-leader' approach, it still participates in the cartel. This means that, on the one hand, it derives its own commercial benefits from its participation in the cartel and, on the other hand, it encourages the other cartelists to participate and to implement the arrangements. Therefore, a passive or 'follow-my-leader' role does not constitute a mitigating circumstance'.

[358] See, on the one hand, Judgment of 25 October 2011 in Case T-348/08 *Aragonesas v Commission*, paras 281 and 284 et seq, Judgment of 12 December 2012 in Case T-352/09 *Novácke chemické závody v Commission*, paras 92–4, Judgment of 14 March 2013 in Case T-587/08 *Fresh Del Monte v Commission*, paras 800–1, and, on the other hand, Judgment of 2 February 2012 in Case T-83/08 *Denki Kagaku Kogyo and Denka Chemicals v Commission*, para 253. In any event, a lower fine may (have to) be imposed where the undertaking has not participated in all aspects of the infringement. See Case C-49/92 P *Anic Partecipazioni v Commission* [1999] ECR I-4125, para 90; Joined Cases T-204/08 and T-212/08 *Team Relocations v Commission* [2011] ECR II-3569, paras 127–8. For example, this may be the case where it has not participated in all aspects ('branches') of the collusion. See eg Joined Cases T-109/02, T-118/02, T-122/02, T-125/02, T-126/02, T-128/02, T-129/02, T-132/02 and T-136/02 *Bolloré and Others v Commission* [2007] ECR II-947, para 429; Commission Decision of 3 October 2007 in Case COMP/38.710 *Bitumen Spain*,

wording of paragraph 29 of the 2006 Guidelines ('such as') leaves room for the development of further categories of mitigating circumstances.[359] In each case, the Commission must make an overall assessment of all relevant facts[360] and it has discretion both as regards this assessment and the level of any possible reduction of the fine.[361] While it has to examine the existence of mitigating circumstances of its own motion,[362] undertakings wishing to invoke the benefit of mitigating circumstances should nevertheless ensure that they draw the Commission's attention to the merits of their case as early as possible during the course of the investigation. However, even where undertakings fail to make their case during the administrative procedure, the GC might still consider such facts within its unlimited jurisdiction.[363] The 2006 Guidelines set out the following categories of mitigating circumstances:

(i)   *Proven termination of the infringement as soon as the Commission intervened.* Although the Commission has already on several occassions granted a reduction where the undertaking ceased participation in the infringement following its intervention,[364] the courts have made clear that the requirements for doing so will be interpreted restrictively.[365] Therefore, no reduction of the fine will apply where the termination of the infringement was actually not triggered by the Commission's intervention (eg because the undertaking had already decided to cease its participation).[366] Neither will a reduction be

---

para 567; Commission Decision of 9 November 2010 in Case COMP/39.258 *Air Freight*, para 1234. See also paras 11.44 and 11.49.

[359] See eg Judgment of 14 March 2013 in Case T-587/08 *Fresh Del Monte v Commission*, paras 800–1 ('passive role') and 824–5 ('reasonable doubt').

[360] See Case T-50/00 *Dalmine v Commission* [2004] ECR II-2395, paras 325–6; Joined Cases T-109/02, T-118/02, T-122/02, T-125/02, T-126/02, T-128/02, T-129/02, T-132/02 and T-136/02 *Bolloré and Others v Commission* [2007] ECR II-947, para 602; Case T-25/05 *KME Germany v Commission* [2010] ECR II-91, paras 125–6; Case T-37/05 *World Wide Tobacco España v Commission* [2011] ECR II-41, para 152; Judgment of 30 November 2011 in Case T-208/06 *Quinn Barlo and Others v Commission*, para 245; Judgment of 2 February 2012 in Case T-83/03 *Denki Kagaku Kogyo and Denka Chemicals v Commission*, para 240. The Commission is generally not bound by its previous decisions, see Case T-30/05 *Prym v Commission* [2007] ECR II-107, para 205.

[361] See Case T-191/06 *FMC Foret v Commission* [2011] ECR II-2959, para 333; Case T-461/07 *Visa Europe v Commission* [2011] ECR II-1729, para 303; Case T-50/00 *Dalmine v Commission* [2004] ECR II-2395, para 326. In this assessment, the Commission may take into account that the fine imposed is not deprived of its deterrent effect. See Judgment of 2 February 2012 in Case T-83/03 *Denki Kagaku Kogyo and Denka Chemicals v Commission*, para 237.

[362] Case T-191/06 *FMC Foret v Commission* [2011] ECR II-2959, para 330.

[363] Case T-73/04 *Le Carbone Lorraine v Commission* [2008] ECR II-2661, paras 186 et seq and 194 (however, even though the applicant had not specifically asked the Commission to consider a mitigating circumstance, it had at least informed the Commission of the relevant facts). See also Judgment of 16 November 2011 in Case T-79/06 *Sachsa Verpackung v Commission*, para 211: 'La circonstance que la requérante n'a pas invoqué son rôle passif au sein de l'entente au stade de la procédure administrative diminue ainsi quelque peu le crédit que le Tribunal serait susceptible d'attacher à cette allégation dans le cadre de l'exercice de sa compétence de pleine juridiction'. As regards the burden of demonstrating the existence of a mitigating circumstance, see Joined Cases T-259/02 to T-264/02 and T-271/02 *Raiffeisen Zentralbank and Others v Commission* [2006] ECR II-5169, para 485; Joined Cases T-109/02, T-118/02, T-122/02, T-125/02, T-126/02, T-128/02, T-129/02, T-132/02 and T-136/02 *Bolloré and Others v Commission* [2007] ECR II-947, paras 601–2.

[364] eg *FETTCSA* [2000] OJ L268/1, para 188; *Nathan-Bricolux* [2001] OJ L54/1, para 134.

[365] Case T-329/01 *Archer Daniels Midland v Commission* [2006] ECR II-3255, paras 278–80 (confirmed on appeal in Case C-510/06 P *Archer Daniels Midland v Commission* [2009] ECR I-1843, paras 144–8).

[366] Case C-407/04 P *Dalmine v Commission* [2007] ECR I-829, para 158; Case T-44/00 *Mannesmannröhren-Werke v Commission* [2004] ECR II-2223, paras 280–2. Where the undertaking terminated its participation prior to the intervention by the Commission, this is sufficiently taken into account through the (lower) factor for duration. See eg *Vitamins* [2003] OJ L6/1, paras 707 and 730–2.

granted where the anticompetitive character of the behaviour was manifest.[367] Hence, 'this will not apply to secret agreements or practices (in particular cartels)'.[368]

(ii) *Proven negligence in the commission of the infringement.* Infringements committed as a result of negligence were already considered favourably under the 1998 Guidelines.[369] While the EU courts have held that infringements committed by negligence are not less serious than intentional infringements, at least as regards their effects on competition,[370] the type of fault is nevertheless one of the factors that in principle[371] will be taken into account when determining the undertaking's personal responsibility. Consequently, where there are indications of negligent conduct, and in particular where the undertaking has claimed negligence by providing relevant information in this regard, the burden should be on the Commission to prove intention.[372] In case of doubt it has to assume negligence. Conduct may be negligent if the undertaking has reasonable doubts as to the anticompetitive object or effect of its actions (eg because the behaviour is not manifestly anticompetitive and no decisional practice exists),[373] or if it is not aware of all aspects of the cartel (but could have reasonably foreseen them, so that it can still be held responsible for the cartel as a whole).[374] The establishment of a compliance programme is no longer considered as a mitigating circumstance, as

---

[367] eg *Austrian Banks* [2004] OJ L56/1, para 529 (confirmed in Joined Cases T-259/02 to T-264/02 and T-271/02 *Raiffeisen Zentralbank Österreich and Others v Commission* [2006] ECR II-5169, paras 497–9 and 503 et seq). See also Case T-329/01 *Archer Daniels Midland v Commission* [2006] ECR II-3255, para 282 (confirmed on appeal in Case C-510/06 P *Archer Daniels Midland v Commission* [2009] ECR I-1843, paras 149–50); Case T-53/03 *BPB v Commission* [2008] ECR II-1333, paras 439–40; Judgment of 5 October 2011 in Case T-39/06 *Transcatab v Commission*, para 284. This may be different where an undertaking had reasonable doubts as to the illegality of its conduct. See Joined Cases T-259/02 to T-264/02 and T-271/02 *Raiffeisen Zentralbank and Others v Commission* [2006] ECR II-5169, para 499; Case T-54/03 *Lafarge v Commission* [2008] ECR II-120, para 782.

[368] 2006 Guidelines, para 29. The underlying idea is that otherwise undertakings could always enter into secret anticompetitive arrangements, knowing that they would in any event get the benefit of a mitigating circumstance if they stop their conduct once it has been discovered. Hubert de Broca, 'The Commission Revises its Guidelines for Setting Fines in Antitrust Cases' (2006) Competition Policy Newsletter 1 & 5. See also Case T-199/08 *Ziegler v Commission* [2011] ECR II-3507, paras 151–2; Case T-211/08 *Putters v Commission* [2011] ECR II-3729, para 82; Judgment of 5 October 2011 in Case T-39/06 *Transcatab v Commission*, para 284.

[369] However, in practice the types of conduct which are fined by the Commission rarely appear to be 'infringements by negligence', so that this mitigating circumstance plays a rather marginal role. Hubert de Broca, 'The Commission Revises its Guidelines for Setting Fines in Antitrust Cases' (2006) Competition Policy Newsletter 1 & 5.

[370] See Judgment of 12 December 2012 in Case T-332/09 *Electrabel v Commission*, paras 237–9.

[371] See Judgment of 12 December 2012 in Case T-332/09 *Electrabel v Commission*, paras 272–4, according to which the Commission has a certain margin of appreciation as regards the taking into account of negligence as a mitigating circumstance. Cf also Commission Decision of 6 March 2013 in Case AT.39530 *Microsoft (Tying)*, para 69.

[372] However, in certain types of cases the Commission may presume an anticompetitive objective (eg where an undertaking participates in cartel meetings without distancing itself). See Case C-510/06 P *Archer Daniels Midland v Commission* [2009] ECR I-1843, para 119.

[373] Cf Commission Decision of 2 June 2004 in Case COMP/38.096 *Clearstream*, para 344. For Art 102 TFEU see also Commission Decision of 4 July 2007 in Case COMP/38.784 *Wanadoo España v Telefónica*, paras 720–30 and 764–6. For a discussion of negligence in the case of an avoidable error of law based on incorrect legal advice or statements made by an NCA or national court, see Opinion of AG Kokott of 28 February 2013 in Case C-681/11 *Schenker and Co AG and Others*, paras 47 et seq and 82 et seq.

[374] Commission Decision of 15 October 2008 in Case COMP/39.188 *Bananas*, paras 252 et seq and 476. The undertaking can be held liable for the infringement as a whole where it intended to contribute by its own conduct to the common objectives pursued by all the participants and was aware of the actual conduct planned or put into effect by other undertakings in pursuit of those same objectives, or could reasonably have foreseen it, and was prepared to take the risk. See Case C-49/92 P *Commission v Anic Partecipazioni* [1999] ECR I-4125, para 87.

the question of a reduction in the fine only arises where the programme has *failed* to prevent anticompetitive conduct.[375] Neither can the parent company of a group of companies free itself of responsibility (or claim mere negligence) with the argument that it has done everything it could to avoid competition law infringements, given that Article 23(2) of Regulation 1/2003 relates not to each individual legal entity within the group but to the undertaking as a whole.

(iii) *Substantially limited role in the infringement and competitive conduct.* This factor replaces two mitigating circumstances in the 1998 Guidelines, namely the undertaking's exclusively passive or 'follow-my-leader' role in the infringement[376] and its non-implementation of the offending agreements or practices. It should be distinguished from a *limited participation in the infringement* in the sense that the undertaking did not participate in certain aspects of the cartel (eg certain countries, certain types of behaviour) which may be taken into account as an unnamed mitigating circumstance[377] or within the determination of the basic amount by adapting the gravity factor applied to the value of sales of the individual undertaking.[378] The third indent of paragraph 29 of the 2006 Guidelines stipulates two cumulative conditions, even though it appears that in some decisions the Commission has relied only, or mainly, on merely one of them.[379] These conditions have to be interpreted strictly.[380] The Commission will assume a '*substantially limited involvement*' where the undertaking acted in the 'periphery' of the cartel,

---

[375] Joined Cases C-189/02 P, C-202/02 P, C-205/02 P to C-208/02 P and C-213/02 P *Dansk Rørindustri and Others v Commission* [2005] ECR I-5425, para 373; Case T-66/01 *Imperial Chemical Industries v Commission* [2010] ECR II-2631, para 420. In *British Sugar* [1999] OJ L76/1, para 208, the fact that the undertaking violated its own compliance programme (which had been assessed as a mitigating factor in a previous case) was considered an aggravating circumstance.

[376] As to the question whether the mitigating circumstance still applies as such under the 2006 Guidelines, see para 11.63.

[377] See eg *Pre-Insulated Pipes* [1999] OJ L24/1, para 182 (reduction of the fine for Ke-Kelit for 'minor role' and because its participation was limited to Austria) (confirmed in Case T-17/99 *KE KELIT v Commission* [2002] ECR II-1647).

[378] See Joined Cases T-204/08 and T-212/08 *Team Relocations and Others v Commission* [2011] ECR II-3569, para 127; more restrictive is the judgment in Case T-21/05 *Chalkor v Commission* [2010] ECR II-1895, para 85 (assessment within the gravity of the infringement). This may occur, for example, where the undertaking did not know the entire scope of the cartel (Commission Decision of 15 October 2008 in Case COMP/39.188 *Bananas*, para 476); did not participate in all aspects of the cartel, or in some aspects only to a limited extent (Commission Decision of 20 October 2010 in Case COMP/38.281 *Raw Tobacco Italy*, para 380; Commission Decision of 3 October 2007 in Case COMP/38.710 *Bitumen Spain*, para 567; Commission Decision of 1 October 2008 in Case COMP/39.181 *Candle Waxes*, paras 653 and 660–1; Commission Decision of 9 November 2010 in Case COMP/39.258 *Air Freight*, para 1234; Joined Cases T-109/02, T-118/02, T-122/02, T-125/02, T-126/02, T-128/02, T-129/02, T-132/02 and T-136/02 *Bolloré and Others v Commission* [2007] ECR II-947, paras 417 et seq and 429; Joined Cases T-208/08 and T-209/08 *Gosselin v Commission* [2011] ECR II-3639, paras 143–5 and 183); did not participate with regard to all products covered by the cartel (Commission Decision of 31 May 2006 in Case COMP/38.645 *Methacrylates*, para 335; Commission Decision of 23 June 2010 in Case COMP/39.092 *Bathroom Fittings and Fixtures*, paras 1199 and 1208; Case T 18/05 *IMI and Others v Commission* [2010] ECR II-1769, paras 156 et seq and 162–4); or where its participation was more limited in geographic terms (Case T-28/99 *Sigma Tecnologie v Commission* [2002] ECR II-1845, paras 81–2 and 93–4; Commission Decision of 30 November 2005 in Case COMP/38.354 *Industrial bags*, para 776; Commission Decision of 23 June 2010 in Case COMP/39.092 *Bathroom Fittings and Fixtures*, paras 1199 and 1208; Commission Decision of 30 June 2010 in Case COMP/38.344 *Prestressing Steel*).

[379] See Commission Decision of 19 May 2010 in Case COMP/38.511 *DRAMs*, para 110; Commission Decision of 9 November 2010 in Case COMP/39.258 *Air Freight*, para 1234 (both limited participation); Commission Decision of 19 May 2010 in Case COMP/38.511 *DRAMs*, para 109 (competitive conduct on the market). See also Commission Decision of 30 June 2010 in Case COMP/38.344 *Prestressing Steel*, paras 1022 and 1023.

[380] Cf Judgment of 8 December 2011 in Case C-389/10 P *KME Germany and Others v Commission*, paras 95 and 96.

ie only participated at the margins.[381] In line with case law on the 'exclusively passive role' of a cartel member, the mere fact that an undertaking has been passive during certain periods, or with regard to individual agreements, will not be sufficient.[382] Nor can the undertaking invoke the more active role of others.[383] The further aspect of demonstrating *competitive conduct on the market* is at least similar to the former mitigating circumstance of 'non-implementation in practice of the offending agreements' in its interpretation by the EU Courts.[384] The mere fact that an undertaking occasionally or even often does not follow the anticompetitive arrangements (eg by charging lower prices than agreed) is not decisive, as it 'may simply be trying to exploit the cartel for its own benefit [cheating]'.[385] Rather, a reduction of the fine presupposes that the undertaking showed a truly independent and pro-competitive conduct on the market which is capable of countering the (likely) anticompetitive effects of the infringement.[386] At least, the undertaking must demonstrate 'that it clearly and substantially breached the obligations relating to the implementation of

---

[381] Commission Decision of 19 May 2010 in Case COMP/38.511 *DRAMs*, para 110; Commission Decision of 9 November 2010 in Case COMP/39.258 *Air Freight*, para 1234.

[382] Case T-73/04 *Le Carbone Lorraine v Commission* [2008] ECR II-2661, paras 179–80; Case T-168/05 *Arkema v Commission* [2009] ECR II-180, para 153; Case T-26/06 *Trioplast Wittenheim v Commission* [2010] ECR II-4893, para 103; Judgment of 16 November 2011 in Joined Cases T-55/06 and T-66/06 *RKW and JM Gesellschaft für industrielle Beteiligungen*, para 89. Neither has a 'passive role' been assumed where the undertaking organized or prepared cartel meetings. Case T-43/02 *Jungbunzlauer v Commission* [2006] ECR II-3435, para 257; Joined Cases T-456/05 and T-457/05 *Gütermann & Zwicky v Commission* [2010] ECR II-1443, paras 190–4; Judgment of 5 October 2011 in Case T-11/06 *Romana Tabacchi v Commission*, para 223.

[383] Cf Judgment of 16 November 2011 in Joined Cases T-55/06 and T-66/06 *RKW and JM Gesellschaft für industrielle Beteiligungen*, para 83; Judgment of 6 March 2012 in Case T-65/06 *FLSmidth & Co. v Commission*, para 59. The fact that an undertaking has been the participant which attended the cartel meetings least regularly or limited itself to receiving information passed on unilaterally by competitors, without expressing any reservations or objections, does not suffice to establish a passive role. Judgment of 27 September 2012 in Case T-82/08 *Guardian Industries and Guardian Europe v Commission*, para 111.

[384] Judgment of 12 December 2012 in Case T-400/09 *Ecka Granulate and non ferrum Metallpulver v Commission*, paras 85–6. For earlier case law see Case T-26/02 *Daiichi v Commission* [2006] ECR II-713, para 113; Judgment of 12 July 2011 in Case T-59/07 *Polimeri Europa v Commission*, paras 306–9.

[385] Case T-50/00 *Dalmine v Commission* [2004] ECR II-2395, para 291; Joined Cases T-71/03, T-74/03, T-87/03 and T-91/03 *Tokai Carbon v Commission* [2005] ECR II-10, paras 74 and 297; Judgment of 12 December 2012 in Case T-400/09 *Ecka Granulate and non ferrum Metallpulver v Commission*, paras 87–9. See also Judgment of 15 September 2011 in Case T-216/06 *Lucite v Commission*, paras 130 et seq, 134, 137–8, 141, 166–7, and 171; Commission Decision of 8 December 2010 in Case COMP/39.309 *LCD*, para 438; *Food flavour enhancers* [2004] OJ L75/1, para 270; *Austrian Banks* [2004] OJ L56/1, para 530: 'nor is it a mitigating circumstance that during the period in question there were repeated instances of lack of discipline or indeed price wars. Like many other cartels, the Lombard cartel went through good times and less good times, and had to endure crises on occasion. Some banks did repeatedly attempt to gain market share by undercutting or exceeding the agreed rates for short periods. But such conduct is typical of many cartels, and cannot be considered a mitigating circumstance. All the participants, including the occasional "price breakers", profited to the same extent from the action decided jointly, and from the information they regularly exchanged on the future conduct on the market of their competitors. Even those banks that on occasion took commercial decisions that departed from the agreements were exploiting the cartel to their advantage.'

[386] Judgment of 29 June 2012 in Case T-370/09 *GDF Suez v Commission*, para 443; Judgment of 27 September 2012 in Case T-348/06 *Total Nederland v Commission*, paras 81 and 83. See also Case T-220/00 *Cheil Jedang v Commission* [2003] ECR II-2473, para 196; Case T-73/04 *Le Carbone Lorraine* [2008] ECR II-2661, para 208; Case T-33/05 *Cetarsa v Commission* [2011] ECR II-12, para 216; Commission Decision of 19 May 2010 in Case COMP/38.511 *DRAMs*, para 109. For price collusion see Case T-224/00 *Archer Daniels Midland v Commission* [2003] ECR II-2597, paras 269–73; Case T-26/02 *Daiichi v Commission* [2006] ECR II-713, paras 109 and 117 et seq; Joined Cases T-109/02, T-118/02, T-122/02, T-125/02, T-126/02, T-128/02, T-129/02, T-132/02 and T-136/02 *Bolloré and Others v Commission* [2007] ECR II-947, paras 631 and 633. The fact that the cartel as a whole was not fully effective during certain periods is not relevant. See Judgment of 30 November 2011 in Case T-208/06 *Quinn Barlo and Others v Commission*, para 244.

the cartel to the point of disrupting its very operation'.[387] This presupposes that the under-taking 'did not give the appearance of adhering to the agreement and thereby incite other undertakings to implement the cartel in question'.[388] The burden of proof for showing the existence of this mitigating circumstance is on the undertaking.[389]

(iv) *Effective cooperation with the Commission outside the scope of the Leniency Notice*[390] *and beyond a legal obligation to do so.* Unlike the reduction for cooperation under the Leniency Notice, this reduction will normally apply *before* the 10 per cent turnover limit[391] and will typically be more limited given that the undertaking does not have to respect the Leniency Notice's strict cooperation requirements.[392] For the same reason, in order to preserve the practical effect of the Leniency Notice, a reduction under this heading will be granted only in exceptional circumstances.[393] This may be the case where the undertaking provides self-incriminating evidence without being able to profit from partial immunity,[394] or where it informs the Commission of the lack of cooperation of another cartel member that has applied for leniency.[395] At the same time, cooperation

---

[387] Commission Decision of 8 December 2010 in Case COMP/39.309 *Liquid Crystal Displays*, para 438; Commission Decision of 28 March 2012 in Case COMP/39.452 *Mountings for Windows and Window-Doors*, para 494 (each time with reference to Case T-26/02 *Daiichi v Commission* [2006] ECR II-713, para 113). See also Commission Decision of 27 November 2002 in Case COMP/37.152 *Plasterboard*, paras 574 and 575; Commission Decision of 20 October 2005 in Case COMP/38.281 *Raw Tobacco Italy*, para 380; Judgment of 25 October 2011 in Case T-348/08 *Aragonesas v Commission*, para 298.

[388] Judgment of 29 June 2012 in Case T-370/09 *GDF Suez v Commission*, para 439; Case T-44/00 *Mannesmannröhren-Werke v Commission* [2004] ECR II-2223, paras 277–8. The non-participation in certain anticompetitive activities (Case T-195/06 *Solvay Solexis v Commission* [2011] ECR II-178, paras 269–72) or occasional conflicts among cartel participants will generally not suffice (see Case T-62/02 *Union Pigments v Commission* [2005] ECR II-5057, para 131). The same applies where the undertaking sends conflicting messages, Joined Cases T-259/02 to T-264/02 and T-271/02 *Raiffeisen Zentralbank Österreich and Others v Commission* [2006] ECR II-5169, para 494.

[389] Judgment of 29 June 2012 in Case T-370/09 *GDF Suez v Commission*, para 443; Judgment of 16 November 2011 in Joined Cases T-55/06 and T-66/06 *RKW and JM Gesellschaft für industrielle Beteiligungen*, para 83 (for passivity). See also Judgment of 30 November 2011 in Case T-208/06 *Quinn Barlo and Others v Commission*, paras 238 and 239.

[390] Currently: Commission Notice on immunity from fines and reduction of fines in cartel cases [2006] OJ C 298/17.

[391] Case T-381/06 *FRA.BO v Commission* [2011] ECR II-66, paras 50 et seq, 57, and 61.

[392] Judgment of 5 October 2011 in Case T-39/06 *Transcatab v Commission*, para 329; Judgment of 5 June 2012 in Case T-214/06 *Imperial Chemical Industries v Commission*, para 258. See also Commission Decision of 28 March 2012 in Case COMP/39.452 *Mountings for Windows and Window-Doors*, paras 513–14. There, the Commission granted a 5 per cent reduction before the 10 per cent cap for cooperation outside leniency that was self-incriminating and brought significant added value.

[393] Case T-44/00 *Mannesmannröhren-Werke v Commission* [2004] ECR II-2223, para 308; Case T-343/08 *Arkema v Commission* [2011] ECR II-2287, paras 169–70; Judgment of 5 October 2011 in Case T-39/06 *Transcatab v Commission*, paras 328–34; Judgment of 13 December 2012 in Case T-103/08 *Versalis and ENI v Commission*, para 336. The last two judgments even suggest that this mitigating circumstance would only apply with regard to infringements which do not fall within the scope of the Leniency Notice, and thus not to cartels. See also Opinion of AG Kokott of 18 April 2013 in Case C-501/11 P *Schindler Holding and Others v Commission*, para 197; Commission Decision of 25 June 2008 in Case COMP/39.180 *Aluminium fluoride*, paras 249–50; Commission Decision of 7 October 2009 in Case COMP/39.129 *Power Transformers*, paras 267 and 273; Commission Decision of 30 June 2010 in Case COMP/38.344 *Prestressing Steel*, para 1008; Commission Decision of 8 December 2010 in Case COMP/39.309 *LCD*, para 440.

[394] Commission Decision of 30 June 2010 in Case COMP/38.344 *Prestressing Steel*, paras 1010–11. See also Commission Decision of 10 December 2003 in Case COMP/37.857 *Organic Peroxides*, paras 493–6; Commission Decision of 19 January 2005 in Case COMP/37.773 *MCAA*, para 318.

[395] Case T-224/00 *Archer Daniels Midland v Commission* [2003] ECR II-2597, paras 304–7. For further exceptions see Commission Decision of 7 October 2009 in Case COMP/39.129 *Power Transformers*, paras 270–2 and 307 et seq; Commission Decision of 20 October 2005 in Case COMP/38.281 *Raw Tobacco Italy*, paras 385–98 and 441 et seq.

which by its nature could fall under the Leniency Notice[396] will generally not constitute a mitigating circumstance[397] since the objective is not to provide a reduction for failed leniency applications. Even where the circumstances might speak in favour of a reduction, it will be required that the cooperation has a close link to the investigation[398] and that the Commission's task has effectively been made easier.[399] In more recent cases, the GC has suggested a standard of 'objective usefulness', namely that the Commission relied in its final decision on evidence 'which an undertaking has submitted to it in the context of its cooperation, [and] without which the Commission would not have been in a position to penalise the infringement concerned in whole or in part.'[400] The mere cooperation during an inspection or the mere reply to a request for information (without going beyond the addressee's legal obligations) does not justify a reduction.[401] The same applies where the undertaking merely chooses not to defend itself against the allegations in the statement of objections by remaining silent. In case of an explicit *non-contestation*, the question whether or not to reduce the fine will again depend on the 'objective use' of such a statement.[402] It is for the undertaking to put forward arguments establishing that its non-contestation has

---

[396] This only applies to cartel cases, whereas, for example, infringements within a vertical relationship are not covered. Cf Case T-13/03 *Nintendo v Commission* [2009] ECR II-975, para 157 et seq; Judgment of 13 December 2012 in Case T-103/08 *Versalis and ENI v Commission*, para 336. For the infringement of a commitment decision, see Commission Decision of 6 March 2013 in Case AT.39530 *Microsoft (Tying)*, para 66.

[397] Case T-186/06 *Solvay v Commission* [2011] ECR II-2839, paras 314 and 315; Case T-195/06 *Solvay Solexis v Commission* [2011] ECR II-178, paras 283–6; Judgment of 14 July 2011 in Case T-189/06 *Arkema v Commission*, paras 178–81; Judgment of 27 September 2012 in Case T-347/06 *Nynäs Petroleum v Commission*, paras 114–16; Judgment of 14 March 2013 in Case T-587/08 *Fresh Del Monte v Commission*, paras 857 and 864 (for non-contestation). See also Commission Decision of 20 October 2005 in Case COMP/38.281 *Raw Tobacco Italy*, paras 386–7.

[398] Case T-448/05 *Oxley Threads v Commission* [2010] ECR II-69, paras 126 and 129.

[399] Case T-15/02 *BASF v Commission* [2006] ECR II-213, para 588; Commission Decision of 30 October 2010 in Cases COMP/35.587, 35.706, 35.321 *PO/Video Games, PO/Nintendo Distribution and Omega/Nintendo*, paras 454, 456, and 459 (confirmed in Case T-13/03 *Nintendo v Commission* [2009] ECR II-975, para 160). See also Commission Decision of 7 October 2009 in Case COMP/39.129 *Power Transformers*, paras 1007 and 1009.

[400] Case T-343/08 *Arkema v Commission* [2011] ECR II-2287, para 170; Judgment of 16 November 2011 in Case T-79/06 *Sachsa Verpackung v Commission*, para 225; Judgment of 12 December 2012 in Case T-352/09 *Novácke chemické závody v Commission*, paras 115 and 119. See also Judgment of 5 June 2012 in Case T-214/06 *Imperial Chemical Industries v Commission*, para 266, and *Nathan-Bricolux* [2001] OJ L54/01, para 130. In another judgment, the GC held that the Commission may reserve the application of this mitigating circumstance to the undertaking 'which is the first to provide it with information enabling it to expand its investigation and to undertake the necessary measures in order to establish a more serious infringement or an infringement of greater duration'. See Judgment of 30 November 2011 in Case T-208/06 *Quinn Barlo and Others v Commission*, para 272. While the benchmark established in the former judgments is similar to that of partial immunity, the standard developed in this last judgment seems to mix elements from partial and point 8(a) immunity.

[401] Commission Decision of 22 July 2009 in Case COMP/39.396 *Calcium carbide*, para 322. However, it may be justified to grant a reduction where an undertaking's response to a request for information goes beyond its legal obligations (even though it could apply for leniency in this regard, see Commission Decision of 8 December 2010 in Case COMP/39.309 *LCD*, para 471).

[402] Case T-343/08 *Arkema v Commission* [2011] ECR II-2287, paras 189 and 190; Judgment of 5 June 2012 in Case T-214/06 *Imperial Chemical Industries v Commission*, para 265. For a less restrictive interpretation see Case T-199/08 *Ziegler v Commission* [2011] ECR II-3507, para 160. In the Commission's view, generally no reduction will apply. See eg Commission Decision of 13 September 2006 in Case COMP/38.456 *Bitumen Netherlands*, para 370; Commission Decision of 20 November 2007 in Case COMP/38.432 *Professional Videotapes*, para 239; Commission Decision of 11 March 2008 in Case COMP/38.543 *International removal services*, para 595; Commission Decision of 22 July 2009 in Case COMP/39.396 *Calcium carbide*, para 323; Commission Decision of 30 June 2010 in Case COMP/38.344 *Prestressing Steel*, para 1009. This is an admissible deviation from previous Commission practice; see Judgment of 12 December 2012 in Case T-400/09 *Ecka Granulate and non ferrum Metallpulver v Commission*, paras 58–62. See also Judgment of 16 June 2011 in Case T-211/08 *Putters International v Commission*, para 85. For an exceptional case see Judgment of 13 July 2011 in Joined Cases T-144/07, T-147/07, T-148/07, T-149/07, T-150/07 and T-154/07 *ThyssenKrupp Liften*

facilitated the Commission's task, and the latter enjoys a broad discretion in assessing that question.[403] If the non-contestation is ambiguous,[404] or where the Commission already possessed sufficient elements in order to establish the facts in question, its tasks will be unlikely to have been facilitated.[405] Depending on the circumstances, a reduction might be more justified in case of an *explicit acknowledgment* of the infringement.[406]

(v) *Authorization or encouragement by public authorities or by legislation (without prejudice to any action that may be taken against the Member State).* Under the 1998 Guidelines, the 'existence of reasonable doubt on the part of the undertaking as to whether the restrictive conduct does indeed constitute an infringement' constituted a mitigating circumstance.[407] Beyond this, the Commission in some situations took into account the effects of the (national) legislative or administrative context.[408] For example, in *Welded Steel Mesh*,[409] it considered the fact that the German cartel office had authorized the formation of a structural crisis cartel in Germany as a mitigating factor for producers outside Germany, as it provided a motive for them to protect themselves. Among other cases, the legal context and its effects on the undertaking (doubts) also led to a reduction of the fine in: *Building and Construction Industry in the Netherlands*,[410]

Ascenseurs v Commission, paras 429 and 431–2. In this context, it should be noted that any non-contestation during the administrative procedure is not binding at the court stage. See Joined Cases T-236/01, T-239/01, T-244/01 to T-246/01, T-251/01 and T-252/01 *Tokai Carbon v Commission* [2004] ECR II-1181, para 108. If the undertaking (for the first time) contests the Commission's findings before the court, the Commission will have to prove them by other means. Case C-297/98 P *SCA Holding v Commission* [2000] ECR I-10101, para 37; Case T-69/04 *Schunk and Schunk Kohlenstoff-Technik v Commission* [2008] ECR II-2567, para 84. Still, it should be noted that at least in one case the GC appears to have taken the view that a clear and unequivocal non-contestation would *generally* facilitate the Commission's task. See Case T-161/05 *Hoechst v Commission* [2009] ECR II-3555, para 97.

[403] Cf Judgment of 6 March 2012 in Case T-65/06 *FL Smidth & Co v Commission*, para 97.

[404] Judgment of 16 November 2011 in Joined Cases T-55/06 and T-66/06 *RKW and JM Gesellschaft für industrielle Beteiligungen v Commission*, paras 102–5.

[405] Judgment of 27 June 2012 in Case T-372/10 *Bolloré v Commission*, para 258; Judgment of 12 December 2012 in Case T-400/09 *Ecka Granulate and non ferrum Metallpulver v Commission*, paras 65–6. Neither will a cooperation that merely reduces the burden of the Commission's administrative tasks to a limited extent, without allowing it to find and terminate the infringement, justify a reduction (para 67).

[406] For the legal (evidentiary) value of such an acknowledgment see Case C-297/98 P *SCA Holding v Commission* [2000] ECR I-10101, para 37; Case C-407/08 P *Knauf Gips v Commission* [2010] ECR I-6375, para 90; Joined Cases T-71/03, T-74/03, T-87/03 and T-91/03 *Tokai Carbon v Commission* [2005] ECR II-10, para 324; Case T-375/06 *Viega v Commission* [2011] ECR II-60, para 40; Judgment of 25 October 2011 in Case T-348/08 *Aragonesas v Commission*, paras 217–18 and 227; Judgment of 12 December 2012 in Case T-332/09 *Electrabel v Commission*, para 35. As for the difference between an explicit acknowledgment of the infringement and a mere non-contestation, see Joined Cases C-65/02 P and C-73/02 P *ThyssenKrupp v Commission* [2005] ECR I-6773, para 58.

[407] See Case T-66/99 *Minoan Lines v Commission* [2003] ECR II-5515, paras 347 and 353; Joined Cases T-191/98, T-212/98 to T-214/98 *Atlantic Container v Commission* [2003] ECR II-3275, paras 1611 et seq and 1633; Case T-461/07 *Visa Europe and Visa International Service v Commission* [2011] ECR II-1729, paras 248 and 250–52. But see, for example, Joined Cases T-49/02 to T-51/02 *Brasserie nationale v Commission* [2005] II-3033, paras 191–3.

[408] This presupposes that the legislative and/or administrative context leaves some room for undertakings to decide independently their action on the market. If anticompetitive conduct is *required* of undertakings by national legislation, or if the latter creates a legal framework which itself *eliminates* any possibility of competitive activity on their part, Arts 101, 102 TFEU do not apply. In such a situation, the restriction on competition is not attributable to the autonomous conduct of the undertaking. See eg Joined Cases C-359/95 P and C-379/95 P *Commission and France v Ladbroke Racing* [1997] ECR I-6265, para 33; Case T-513/93 *Consiglio Nazionale degli Spedizionieri Doganali v Commission* [2000] ECR II-1807, paras 58–9.

[409] *Welded Steel Mesh* [1989] OJ L260/1, para 206.

[410] *Building and Construction Industry in the Netherlands* [1992] OJ L92/1, para 141 (national legislation may have created a certain ambiguity as to the compatibility of the collusion with EU competition rules).

Greek Ferries,[411] *Luxembourg Brewers,*[412] *Deutsche Telekom,*[413] *French Beef,*[414] and *Spanish Raw Tobacco.*[415] In other cases, the national government's knowledge of the infringements did not represent a valid defence, for example in *Zinc Producers Group.*[416] As for the 2006 Guidelines, both the national and the EU legal framework can be taken into account.[417] For instance, in *Bananas,*[418] the Commission granted a reduction of the fine, *inter alia*, because the affected business was regulated by sector-specific legislation which influenced the competition parameters on the market. Likewise, in *Air Freight,*[419] the Commission has considered the 'general regulatory environment' as a mitigating factor, since it could be viewed as encouraging price coordination. Moreover, depending on the specific circumstances of each case, the actions by national authorities[420] or the Commission may constitute a mitigating factor. However, the mere inaction of authorities, despite their knowledge of anticompetitive behaviour, is not akin to an authorization or encouragement on their side.[421] No reduction of the fine is explicitly foreseen for cases where the undertaking harbours a 'reasonable doubt' as to the legality of its conduct. Nevertheless, such doubts may exclude intention (and therefore lead to a lower fine because of negligence) or constitute an unnamed mitigating circumstance.[422] At the

---

[411] *Greek Ferries* [1999] OJ L109/24, para 163 (usual practice of fixing domestic fares through consultation of all domestic operators and the involvement of the ministry in the price fixing for domestic routes may have created doubt as to whether price fixing consultation for international routes constituted an infringement).

[412] *Luxembourg Brewers* [2002] OJ L253/21, para 100 (Luxembourg case law might have created doubts as to the legality of certain restrictions).

[413] *Deutsche Telekom* [2003] OJ L263/9, para 212 (national, sector-specific regulation of charges).

[414] *French Beef* [2003] OJ L209/12, para 176 (strong intervention by ministry in favour of conclusion of the agreement, putting pressure on slaughterers).

[415] Commission Decision of 20 October 2004 in Case COMP/38.238 *Spanish Raw Tobacco*, paras 427–8 and 437 (encouragement by the ministry to go ahead with joint negotiation of agreements, thereby engendering a considerable degree of uncertainty as to the legality of the undertakings' conduct).

[416] *Zinc Producer Group* [1984] OJ L220/27, para 74 (however, this is only discussed in the context of the application of [then] Art 81 EC, not the fine).

[417] See Case C-198/01 *CIF v Commission* [2003] ECR I-8033, paras 56–7; Case T-271/03 *Deutsche Telekom v Commission* [2008] ECR II-477, paras 311–13 (confirmed on appeal in Case C-280/08 P *Deutsche Telekom v Commission* [2010] ECR I-9555, para 278).

[418] Commission Decision of 15 October 2008 in Case COMP/39.188 *Bananas*, paras 456 and 467.

[419] Commission Decision of 9 November 2010 in Case COMP/39.258 *Air Freight*, para 1241. See Commission Press Release IP/10/1487 'Commission fines 11 air cargo carriers €799 million in price fixing cartel' of 9 November 2010.

[420] Case T-271/03 *Deutsche Telekom v Commission* [2008] ECR II-477, paras 311–13; Joined Cases T-259/02 to T-264/02 and T-271/02 *Raiffeisen Zentralbank and Others v Commission* [2006] ECR II-5169, para 505.

[421] Case T-199/08 *Ziegler v Commission* [2011] ECR II-3507, para 157.

[422] Judgment of 14 March 2013 in Case T-587/08 *Fresh Del Monte v Commission*, para 825. In the past, the Commission sometimes imposed a lower fine—or no fine at all—where its decision was the first to deal with an infringement in a particular sector. See eg *London European/Sabena* [1988] OJ L317/47, para 40; *Eurocheque: Helsinki Agreement* [1992] OJ L95/50, para 90; *GVG/FS* [2004] OJ L11/17, para 164 ('novelty of the case'). In *Akzo*, the ECJ reduced the fine, among other reasons, because of its view that 'abuses of this kind come within the field of law in which the rules of competition have never been determined precisely'. Case 62/86 *Akzo v Commission* [1996] ECR I-3359, para 163. Likewise, the Commission considered in *Deutsche Post* that, because of German case law, the legal situation was unclear and that 'no Community case law existed that concerned the specific context of cross-border letter mail services'. Hence, it imposed a token fine of EUR 1,000. *Deutsche Post AG-Interception of Cross-Border Mail* [2001] OJ L331/40, para 193. In *Deutsche Telekom*, 'the fact that a weighted method applied in this decision to determine the margin squeeze ha[d] not previously been the subject of a formal Commission decision' was one reason to consider the infringement only as 'serious', *Deutsche Telekom* [2003] OJ L263/9, para 206. But see Case T-83/91 *Tetra Pak v Commission* [1994] ECR II-755, para 239, where the GC concluded that, 'even if in some respects defining the relevant product markets and the scope of Article 86 may have been a matter of some complexity, that factor cannot in this case lead to a reduction in the amount of the fine because of the manifest nature and the particular gravity of the restrictions on competition resulting from the abuses in question. The applicant's allegations... relating to the allegedly unprecedented nature of certain legal assessments in the Decision cannot therefore be accepted.'

same time, reasonable doubts should be treated as a necessary requirement to acknowledge as a mitigating circumstance the authorization or encouragement by authorities. In this respect, the resources available to the undertaking to obtain accurate legal information have to be considered.[423]

(vi) *Other mitigating circumstances.* Given that the 2006 Guidelines do not provide an exhaustive list of mitigating circumstances, the Commission may also take into account other factors, depending on the factual elements present in each case. Aside from the (exclusively) 'passive role' or 'follow-my-leader' role discussed earlier,[424] a reduction has been granted in a number of cases, for example where the undertaking acted on instructions[425] or under pressure,[426] constituted a destabilizing element which helped to limit the impact of the cartel on the market,[427] participated in only one aspect of the overall cartel,[428] had compensated victims of the cartel,[429] or because of the excessive length of the investigative procedure.[430] At the same time, the EU Courts have on many occasions

---

This was confirmed on appeal in Case C-233/94 *Tetra Pak v Commission* [1996] ECR I-5951, paras 46–9. See also Case T-37/05 *World Wide Tobacco España v Commission* [2011] ECR II-41, para 160; Case T-321/05 *AstraZeneca v Commission* [2010] ECR II-2805, para 901; Judgment of 12 December 2012 in Case T-332/09 *Electrabel v Commission*, paras 251–5; *French-West African Shipowners Committees* [1992] OJ L134/1, para 74(a), (g). In a recent case the Commission considered that the 2006 Guidelines no longer foresee a reduction in case of reasonable doubts: Decision of 19 June 2013 in Case AT.39226 *Lundbeck*, paras 1343 and 1377.

[423] Joined Cases T-259/02 to T-264/02 and T-271/02 *Raiffeisen Zentralbank and Others v Commission* [2006] ECR II-5169, paras 503–5; Judgment of 5 October 2011 in Case T-39/06 *Transcatab v Commission*, para 298. See also Judgment of 29 March 2012 in Case T-336/07 *Telefónica and Telefónica de España v Commission*, para 458, according to which the authorization or toleration of an infringement by national authorities may not be taken into account for negligence if the undertakings concerned had the necessary ressources to obtain precise and correct legal advice.

[424] See para 11.63.

[425] Commission Decision of 17 December 2002 in Case COMP/37.667 *Specialty graphite*, paras 515–16 (distributor).

[426] *French Beef* [2003] OJ L209/12, para 177 (physical coercion). However, in most cases the Commission has rejected the existence of a mitigating circumstance as the undertakings which are pressed by others to participate in an infringement normally have the possibility to turn to the authorities or national courts. See eg *French-West African Shipowners' Committees* OJ [1992] L134/1, para 74(e); *Amino Acids* [2001] OJ L152/24, paras 387 and 391; *Citric Acid* [2002] OJ L239/18, paras 274, 277 and 283; *Carbonless Paper* [2004] OJ L115/1, paras 425 and 427. See also Joined Cases C-189/02 P, C-202/02 P, C-205/02 P to C-208/02 P and C-213/02 P *Dansk Rørindustri and Others v Commission* [2005] ECR I-5425, paras 369–70; Case T-38/02 *Groupe Danone v Commission* [2005] ECR II-4407, paras 163–4; Case T-33/05 *Cetarsa v Commission* [2011] ECR II-12, para 217; Case T-195/06 *Solvay Solexis v Commission* [2011] ECR II-178, paras 251–2; Judgment of 5 October 2011 in Case T-11/06 *Romana Tabacchi v Commission*, paras 212 and 213; Judgment of 2 February 2012 in Case T-83/08 *Denki Kagaku Kogyo and Denka Chemicals v Commission*, para 62.

[427] Commission Decision of 27 November 2002 in Case COMP/37.152 *Plasterboard*, paras 574–5 and 589.

[428] Judgment of 14 March 2013 in Case T-587/08 *Fresh Del Monte v Commission*, paras 814–17. For alternative methods of taking this aspect into account in determing the fine see paras 11.44 and 11.49.

[429] Commission Decision of 30 October 2010 in Cases COMP/35.587, 35.706, 35.321 *PO/Video Games, PO/Nintendo Distribution and Omega/Nintendo*, paras 440–1.

[430] Commission Decision of 11 November 2009 in Case COMP/38.589 *Heat Stabilisers*, paras 722–3 and 771. In *Commercial Solvents*, the ECJ reduced the fine on account of duration, arguing that the infringement could have been significantly shorter had the Commission intervened more quickly following a complaint. Joined Cases 6/73 and 7/73 *Istituto Chimioterapico Italiano and Commercial Solvents v Commission* [1974] ECR 223, paras 51–2. A similar claim was rejected, however, in Joined Cases 32/78, 36/78 to 82/78 *BMW Belgium v Commission* [1979] ECR 2435, para 45. In *NFVGE and TU*, the GC accepted the Commission's approach to grant a reduction of EUR 100,000 for the excessive length of the procedure. See Joined Cases T-5/00 and T-6/00 *NFVGE and Technische Unie v Commission* [2003] ECR II-5761, paras 436–8. Conversely, in *Bavaria* it considered that a reduction of the fine by EUR 100,000 for the excessive length of the administrative procedure was insufficient, given the level of the basic amount (EUR 22.94 million), and therefore granted a reduction of 5 per cent under its unlimited jurisdiction. See Case T-235/07 *Bavaria v Commission* [2011] ECR II-3229, paras 341 and 343 (confirmed on appeal in the Judgment of 19 December 2012 in Case C-445/11 P *Bavaria v Commission*, para 80). See also Case T-235/07 *Heineken v Commission* [2011] ECR II-3355, paras 429–34; Judgment of 5 June 2012 in Case T-214/06 *Imperial Chemical Industries v Commission*, para 290

rejected claims for a reduction of the fine based on alleged mitigating circumstances. Such factors include: the lack of secrecy of the anticompetitive conduct;[431] the (economic) dependency of an undertaking;[432] the lack of mechanisms for enforcement and/or control in the implementation of the cartel;[433] the fact that an undertaking did not actively participate in the cartel[434] or had good intentions;[435] the fact that no high-ranking representatives of the undertaking participated in, or even knew of, the infringement;[436] the lack of any benefit drawn from the infringement,[437] or even that an undertaking suffered economic disadvantages;[438] the SME character of the undertaking;[439] the fact that the undertaking committed its first infringement;[440] the fact that the cartel did not concern all sectors in which an undertaking is active;[441] the voluntary waiver of an administrative hearing;[442] the existence/introduction of a compliance programme[443] or the initiation of disciplinary

---

et seq; AG Kokott, Opinion of 8 December 2005 in Case C-113/04 P *Technische Unie v Commission*, paras 139–41, and Opinion of 14 April 2011 in Case C-109/10 P *Solvay v Commission*, paras 331, 351–2 and 355. Where the length of the proceedings had a negative effect on the exercise of the undertaking's rights of defence, it may even lead to the annulment of the finding of an infringement. Case C-113/04 P *Technische Unie v Commission* [2006] ECR I-8831, paras 132–6; Case T-410/03 *Hoechst v Commission* [2008] ECR II-881, paras 227–8; Case T-57/01 *Solvay v Commission* [2009] ECR II-4621 (annulled for other reasons in the Judgment of 25 October 2011 in Case C-109/10 P *Solvay v Commission*). See also Case T-235/07 *Bavaria v Commission* [2011] ECR II-3229, paras 325–36. However, the undertaking bears the burden of proof in this regard and hence must demonstrate that its difficulties are actually a direct consequence of the length of the procedure and not of own negligence. Cf Judgment of 27 June 2012 in Case T-372/10 *Bolloré v Commission*, paras 128, 137, 152, 182, and 183. As regards the possible impact of the length of judicial proceedings on the fine see AG Sharpston, Opinion of 30 May 2013 in Case C-58/12 P *Groupe Gascogne v Commission*, para 72 et seq.

[431] Case T-66/01 *ICI v Commission* [2010] ECR II-2631, para 447. See also Joined Cases T-259/02 to T-264/02 and T-271/02 *Raiffeisen Zentralbank Österreich and Others v Commission* [2006] ECR II-5169, para 252: 'although the secret nature of a cartel is a factor liable to exacerbate its gravity, it is not an indispensable condition for an infringement to be classified as "very serious"'.

[432] Case T-192/06 *Caffaro v Commission* [2011] ECR II-3063, paras 41 and 43. See also Judgment of 16 November 2011 in Case T-51/06 *Fardem Packaging v Commission*, para 100.

[433] Case T-38/02 *Groupe Danone v Commission* [2005] ECR II-4407, para 393.

[434] Joined Cases T-204/08 and T-212/08 *Team Relocations v Commission* [2011] ECR II-3569, para 124. See also the further explanations above on the mitigating circumstance of 'substantially limited participation'.

[435] Judgment of 16 November 2011 in Case T-51/06 *Fardem Packaging v Commission*, paras 95 and 110.

[436] Judgment of 15 September 2011 in Case T-216/06 *Lucite v Commission*, paras 95–105.

[437] Case T-64/02 *Dr Hans Heubach v Commission* [2005] ECR II-5137, paras 184–6; Joined Cases T-109/02, T-118/02, T-122/02, T-125/02, T-126/02, T-128/02, T-129/02, T-132/02 and T-136/02 *Bolloré and Others v Commission* [2007] ECR II-947, paras 671–3; Judgment of 16 November 2011 in Case T-76/06 *Plasticos Españoles (ASPLA) v Commission*, para 128.

[438] Case T-192/06 *Caffaro v Commission* [2011] ECR II-3063, para 60–2. See also Judgment of 12 July 2011 in Case T-112/07 *Hitachi v Commission*, para 327; *Zinc Phosphate* [2003] OJ L153/1, para 330.

[439] See Joined Cases C-189/02 P, C-202/02 P, C-205/02 P to C-208/02 P and C-213/02 P *Dansk Rørindustri and Others v Commission* [2005] ECR I-5425, para 366; Case T-52/02 *SNCZ v Commission* [2005] ECR II-5005, para 84; Case T-446/05 *Amann & Söhne v Commission* [2010] ECR II-1255, paras 198–200; Case T-379/06 *Kaimer v Commission* [2011] ECR II-64, para 101; Judgment of 5 October 2011 in Case T-11/06 *Romana Tabacchi v Commission*, paras 226, 228, and 260.

[440] Case T-329/01 *Archer Daniels Midland v Commission* [2006] ECR II-3255, para 300; Judgment of 30 November 2011 in Case T-208/06 *Quinn Barlo and Others v Commission*, paras 255 and 264; Judgment of 12 December 2012 in Case T-400/09 *Ecka Granulate and non ferrum Metallpulver v Commission*, para 71. Likewise, 'the Commission is not required to moderate fines when taking action for the first time in a particular sector'. See Judgment of 5 October 2011 in Case T-39/06 *Transcatab v Commission*, para 343. This is particularly so if the undertaking must have been aware of the anticompetitive nature of its conduct and should have expected it to be incompatible with the competition rules. Cf Judgment of 6 December 2012 in Case C-457/10 P *AstraZeneca v Commission*, para 164.

[441] Judgment of 12 December 2012 in Case T-400/09 *Ecka Granulate and non ferrum Metallpulver v Commission*, para 70.

[442] Case T-18/03 *CD-Contact Data v Commission* [2009] ECR II-1021, para 125.

[443] Joined Cases C-189/02 P, C-202/02 P, C-205/02 P to C-208/02 P and C-213/02 P *Dansk Rørindustri and Others v Commission* [2005] ECR I-5425, para 373; Case T-352/94 *Mo och Domsjö v Commission* [1998]

actions against 'rogue employees';[444] the payment of compensation to affected customers[445] or other measures to remedy the infringement;[446] the imposition of sanctions for other infringements in the recent past[447] or in jurisdictions outside the EU.[448] Finally, according to settled case law, the Commission is not required to take into account the *poor (economic or financial) state of the business sector* in question since, as a general rule, cartels come into being when a sector encounters problems.[449] The same applies to the *poor financial situation of the undertaking* concerned, given that recognition of an obligation to reduce the fine would be tantamount to giving an unjustified competitive advantage to undertakings least well adapted to market conditions.[450] However, even if, therefore, the 'inability to pay' of an undertaking does not constitute a mitigating circumstance, the Commission will take this factor into account pursuant to paragraph 35 of the 2006 Guidelines.[451]

Deterrence multiplier

Pursuant to paragraph 30 of the 2006 Guidelines, the Commission will pay particular attention to the need to ensure that fines have sufficient deterrent effect.[452] This may **11.64**

ECR II-1989, para 417; Case T-66/01 *ICI v Commission* [2010] ECR II-2631, para 420; Judgment of 30 November 2011 in Case T-208/06 *Quinn Barlo and Others v Commission*, paras 256 and 257. See also *Zinc Phosphate* [2003] OJ L153/1, paras 331–2; Commission Decision of 1 October 2008 in Case COMP/39.181 *Candle Waxes*, para 698; Commission Decision of 6 March 2013 in Case AT.39530 *Microsoft (Tying)*, para 73. The Commission's position has been summarized in a Manual 'Compliance matters: What companies can do better to respect EU competition rules' (November 2011) (available at DG COMP webpage).

[444] Case T-28/99 *Sigma Tecnologie v Commission* [2002] ECR II-1845, para 127; Joined Cases T-101/05 and T-111/05 *BASF and UCB v Commission* [2007] ECR II-4949, para 129; Judgment of 12 December 2012 in Case T-400/09 *Ecka Granulate and non ferrum Metallpulver v Commission*, paras 79 and 80. See also Case T-241/01 *Scandinavian Airlines System v Commission* [2005] ECR II-2597, paras 222–9; Commission Decision of 9 December 2004 in Case COMP/37.533 *Choline Chloride*, para 217.

[445] Case T-59/02 *Archer Daniels Midland v Commission* [2006] ECR II-3627, paras 349–55.

[446] Cf Commission Decision of 6 March 2013 in Case AT.39530 *Microsoft (Tying)*, para 71.

[447] Case T-206/06 *Total and Elf Aquitaine v Commission* [2011] ECR II-163, paras 297–8. However, the particular circumstances of the individual case might justify taking this factor into account (para 299).

[448] Joined Cases T-71/03, T-74/03, T-87/03 and T-91/03 *Tokai Carbon v Commission* [2005] ECR II-10, paras 334–7.

[449] Judgment of 8 December 2011 in Case C-389/10 P *KME Germany and Others v Commission*, para 97; Joined Cases T-236/01, T-239/01, T-244/01 to T-246/01, T-251/01 and T-252/01 *Tokai Carbon and Others v Commission* [2004] ECR II-1181, para 345; Judgment of 5 October 2011 in Case T-39/06 *Transcatab v Commission*, paras 352–3. While the Commission in the past did occasionally take into account the financial state of the sector (for example *Alloy surcharge* [1998] OJ L100/55, paras 83–4; see also Case T-38/02 *Groupe Danone v Commission* [2005] ECR II-4407, para 414, referring to an 'exceptional structural or economic situation capable of being taken into account in determining the amount of the fine'), the more recent Commission practice shows a rather negative attitude towards a reduction on that basis (Commission Decision of 9 December 2004 in Case COMP/37.533 *Choline Chloride*, para 216; see Castillo de la Torre, 'The 2006 Guidelines on Fines: Reflections on the Commission's Practice' (2010) 33 World Competition, n 207 with accompanying text). In any event, the Commission has a margin of discretion when assessing the relevant facts in this regard. Joined Cases T-109/02, T-118/02, T-122/02, T-125/02, T-126/02, T-128/02, T-129/02, T-132/02, and T-136/02 *Bolloré and Others v Commission* [2007] ECR II-947, para 664.

[450] Judgment of 8 December 2011 in Case C-389/10 P *KME Germany and Others v Commission*, paras 103–4 with further references, Case T-319/94 *Fiskeby Board v Commission* [1998] ECR II-1331, paras 75–6; Case T-38/02 *Groupe Danone v Commission* [2005] ECR II-4407, para 413; Judgment of 16 November 2011 in Case T-54/06 *Kendrion v Commission*, paras 162–3. See also Commission Decision of 9 December 2004 in Case COMP/37.533 *Choline Chloride*, para 215. Even if the imposition of the fine would lead to the insolvency or even liquidation of the undertaking, this is not as such prohibited by EU law. Joined Cases T-236/01, T-239/01, T-244/01 to T-246/01, T-251/01 and T-252/01 *Tokai Carbon v Commission* [2004] ECR II-1181, para 372; Case T-64/02 *Dr Hans Heubach v Commission* [2005] ECR II-5137, para 163; Judgment of 12 December 2012 in Case T-392/09 *1. garantovaná v Commission*, paras 119, 131, and 132. See, however, Judgment of 5 October 2011 in Case T-11/06 *Romana Tabacchi v Commission*, para 258, 279–84.

[451] Cf Case T-213/00 *CMA CGM and Others v Commission* [2003] ECR II-913, paras 351–2.

[452] According to the ECJ, in assessing the gravity of an infringement, the Commission 'must ensure that its action has the necessary deterrent effect, especially as regards those types of infringement which

require that the amount of the fine is adjusted in order to take account of the desired impact on the undertaking on which it is imposed, so that the fine is not rendered negligible or excessive, notably by reference to the financial capacity of the undertaking in question.[453] To this end, the Commission has the power (but not the obligation)[454] to increase the fine to be imposed on (multi-product[455]) undertakings which have a particularly large overall turnover beyond the sales of goods or services to which the infringement relates.[456] In the Commission's view such an increase is justified where an undertaking as a whole has very significant financial resources, and thus is more easily able to pay any sanction,[457] but where its fine might be comparatively small because its sales in the market affected by the cartel are limited.[458] This rationale, which was already applied under the 1998 Guidelines,[459] remains valid under the 2006 Guidelines given that the basic amount is heavily influenced by the sales to which the infringement relates, while ignoring the overall size and economic strength of the undertaking.[460] Under the 1998 Guidelines, the question whether to apply a multiplier was part of the assessment of gravity. Under the 2006 Guidelines, it will occur at a later stage of the determination of the fines, as part of the 'adjustment factors'. This is in line with the overall logic of the guidelines as Section 1 concerns the assessment of the infringement, while Section 2 deals with factors that are specific to each undertaking. Since the application of the multiplier relates to the size of the individual undertaking, it has been considered more appropriate to assess it in Section 2 of the Guidelines rather than in Section 1.[461] The consequence is a difference

---

are particularly harmful to the attainment of the objectives of the Community.' Joined Cases 100–103/80 *Musique Diffusion Française v Commission* [1983] ECR 1825, para 106. Deterrence is an objective of the fine that is to be taken into account throughout the calculation of the fine. See Judgment of 6 March 2012 in Case T-53/06 *UPM-Kymmene v Conmission*, para 136; Judgment of 13 December 2012 in Case T-103/08 *Versalis and ENI v Commission*, paras 315–6 (distinguishing the deterrence multiplier from the additional amount and any increase for recidivism). See also para 4 of the 2006 Guidelines according to which both the need for 'special deterrence' (with regard to the undertaking concerned) and 'general deterrence' (with regard to other undertakings) (as regards the latter, see Case T-224/00 *Archer Daniels Midland v Commission* [2003] ECR II-2597, para 110; Case T-12/03 *Itochu v Commission* [2009] ECR II-909, paras 93–4) must be ensured. See Case C-413/08 P *Lafarge v Commission* [2010] ECR I-5361, para 102; Judgment of 5 October 2011 in Case T-39/06 *Transcatab v Commission*, para 221; Judgment of 16 November 2011 in Case T-54/06 *Kendrion v Commission*, para 175. For the difference in rationale from the additional amount see Case T-299/08 *Elf Aquitaine v Commission* [2011] ECR II-2149, para 289; Judgment of 13 December 2012 in Case T-103/08 *Versalis and ENI v Commission*, para 318.

[453] Judgment of 5 October 2011 in Case T-39/06 *Transcatab v Commission*, para 217.
[454] Judgment of 12 December 2012 in Case T-352/09 *Novácke chemické závody v Commission*, paras 62–4.
[455] The fact that an undertaking is a multi-product enterprise, or operates on the international level, may be an indication of special economic power. See Case T-38/02 *Groupe Danone v Commission* [2005] ECR II-4407, paras 172, 175, and 359; Judgment of 5 October 2011 in Case T-39/06 *Transcatab v Commission*, paras 217 and 223; Judgment of 13 December 2012 in Case T-103/08 *Versalis and ENI v Commission*, para 316.
[456] For an overview see T-217/06 *Arkema v Commission* [2011] ECR II-2593, paras 211–14. As regards the justification see Judgment of 6 March 2012 in Case T-53/06 *UPM-Kymmene v Conmission*, para 81.
[457] See Case T-15/02 *BASF v Commission* [2006] ECR II-497, paras 234–5. Large undertakings are 'in a position to spread the risks connected with commission of the infringement over a broad financial base'. See Judgment of 6 March 2012 in Case T-53/06 *UPM-Kymmene v Conmission*, para 78.
[458] See eg Case T-48/98 *Acerinox v Commission* [2001] ECR II-3859, paras 88–9.
[459] One of the first cases was *Pre-Insulated Pipes* [1999] OJ L24/1, paras 168–9, where ABB's starting amount was increased by 250 per cent. See also *Graphite Electrodes* [2002] OJ L100/1, paras 152–4; *Vitamins* [2003] OJ L6/1, paras 697–9; *Citric Acid* [2002] OJ L239/18, paras 240–6; *Carbonless Paper* [2004] OJ L115/1, paras 410–12.
[460] According to settled case law, the overall turnover of the undertaking 'gives an indication, albeit approximate and imperfect, of the size of the undertaking and of its economic power'. Case T-23/99 *LR AF 1998 v Commission* [2002] ECR II-1705, para 280; Case T-213/00 *CMA CGM and Others v Commission* [2003] ECR II-913, para 399.
[461] Hubert de Broca, 'The Commission Revises its Guidelines for Setting Fines in Antitrust Cases' (2006) Competition Policy Newsletter 1 & 5.

in the fines calculation with regard to past practice, since aggravating or mitigating circumstances lead to adjustments of the basic amount which, under the 1998 Guidelines, already included the deterrence factor, whereas it does not under the 2006 Guidelines. The potential application of a deterrence multiplier does not have to be explicitly announced in the statement of objections.[462] For the decision, the Commission may simply refer to the factors mentioned in paragraph 30 of the 2006 Guidelines, without having to set out the methodology applied in the case at hand.[463] While the 1998 Guidelines also indicated that account might be taken of:

> [the] fact that large undertakings usually have legal and economic knowledge and infrastructures which enable them more easily to recognize that their conduct constitutes an infringement and be aware of the consequences stemming from it under competition law,[464]

this is no longer mentioned in the 2006 Guidelines. Arguably, these elements are more closely linked to the relative gravity of the individual infringement than to any deterrence objective. Where appropriate, they might be considered separately as an aggravating circumstance.[465]

The starting point for the assessment is the overall (worldwide) turnover of the undertaking for which the infringement has been established,[466] in the last business year before the adoption of the decision.[467] In addition, the Commission may compare the situation of other cartel participants. Generally, the determination of the deterrence multiplier is not based on a mathematical formula and does not have to be (directly) proportionate to the overall turnover.[468] Nevertheless, the Commission has to respect general principles of law, in particular **11.65**

---

[462] Case T-13/03 *Nintendo v Commission* [2009] ECR II-975, para 87.

[463] Case T-15/02 *BASF v Commission* [2006] II-497, paras 208–15; Case T-240/07 *Heineken v Commission* [2011] ECR II-3355, paras 374–5; Case T-186/06 *Solvay v Commission* [2011] ECR II-2839, paras 294–6.

[464] Section 1.A of the 1998 Guidelines. See Case T-38/02 *Groupe Danone v Commission* [2005] ECR II-4407, paras 175 and 359.

[465] Consequently, the relevant reference year in this respect should be the last year of the infringement rather than the last business year before the adoption of the decision (as is the case for the deterrence multiplier). See Case T-279/02 *Degussa v Commission* [2006] ECR II-897, paras 289–90; Case T-410/03 *Hoechst v Commission* [2008] ECR II-881, para 382; Case T-386/06 *Pegler v Commission* [2011] ECR II-1267, paras 125 and 129.

[466] Case C-289/04 P *Showa Denko v Commission* [2006] ECR I-5859, paras 16 and 17; Case T-37/05 *World Wide Tobacco España v Commission* [2011] ECR III-41, paras 124 and 128 (consolidated turnover of the top holding company). The assessment has to take into account any changes in the size of the undertaking, including any acquisitions or divestitures. See Case T-386/06 *Pegler v Commission* [2011] ECR II-1267, para 133; Judgment of 9 September 2011 in Case T-25/06 *Alliance One v Commission*, paras 257–8; Judgment of 12 October 2011 in Case T-38/05 *Agroexpansión v Commission*, para 194. See also Commission Decision of 11 June 2008 in Case COMP/38.695 *Sodium Chlorate*, paras 524–5, 548, and 552. Conversely, it is not relevant whether the undertaking is still active in the specific market where the infringement occurred. See Order of 7 February 2012 in Case C-421/11 P *Total and Elf Aquitaine v Commission*, paras 80 and 82; Judgment of 6 March 2012 in Case T-64/06 *FLS Plast v Commission*, para 147. Nor does the worldwide size of the undertaking have to be balanced against other factors like its position on the market or role in the cartel. Judgment of 6 March 2012 in Case T-53/06 *UPM-Kymmene v Commission*, para 79. Taking into account the turnover of the group as a whole does not violate the principle of personal responsibility. See Judgment of 27 September 2012 in Case T-348/06 *Total Nederland v Commission*, para 106.

[467] Case T-279/02 *Degussa v Commission* [2006] ECR II-897, paras 278 and 285–6; Judgment of 12 October 2011 in Case T-41/05 *Alliance One International v Commission*, paras 210 and 211; Judgment of 27 June 2012 in Case T-448/07 *YKK Corp and Others v Commission*, para 204.

[468] Joined Cases T-109/02, T-118/02, T-122/02, T-125/02, T-126/02, T-128/02, T-129/02, T-132/02 and T-136/02 *Bolloré and Others v Commission* [2007] ECR II-947, para 532; Case T-175/05 *Akzo Nobel v Commission* [2009] ECR II-184, paras 152 and 155; Judgment of 5 June 2012 in Case T-214/06 *Imperial Chemical Industries v Commission*, para 174; Judgment of 13 June 2013 in Case C-511/11 P *Versalis v Commission*, para 105. Cf also Judgment of 2 February 2012 in Case T-77/08 *The Dow Chemical Company v Commission*, para 156.

those of equal treatment[469] and proportionality.[470] This entails that the respective steps between the multipliers fixed for the various undertakings must be objectively justified.[471] Moreover, the need to ensure proportionality between the overall fine and the (relative) gravity of the individual infringement[472] sets an absolute upper limit. This may have the consequence that no multiplier is justified, even for a multi-product undertaking. At the same time, the imposition of a deterrence multiplier does not depend on whether the undertaking is likely to commit further infringements in the future.[473] Nor is the Commission required to take into account that the undertaking has cooperated during the investigation, has introduced a compliance programme, or has received additional sanctions for other infringements.[474]

11.66 The deterrence multipliers applied under the 2006 Guidelines generally appear to be (much) lower than those typically imposed under the 1998 Guidelines. So far, the highest multiplier was set at 100 per cent (factor 2)[475] while in the past factors of 2.5 or higher were not uncommon. Moreover, the turnover threshold as of which a multiplier is at all considered appropriate appears to have increased. In settlement cases the multiplier may never exceed factor 2.[476]

Improper gains

11.67 The Commission will also take into account the need to increase the fine in order to exceed the amount of gains improperly made as a result of the infringement where it is possible to estimate such gains.[477] Before the adoption of the 1998 Guidelines, the Commission at times took into account the benefits for the infringing undertakings in its assessment of gravity.[478] Under the 2006 Guidelines, this factor will only become relevant if it is clear that the calculation based on other factors produces a fine that does not capture the benefit derived by the undertakings from the infringement. This presupposes that the benefit can be assessed properly. As this is exceedingly difficult to show, so far the Commission has never made use of that option.

---

[469] Case T-279/02 *Degussa v Commission* [2006] ECR II-897, paras 335 and 338; Judgment of 13 December 2012 in Case T-103/08 *Versalis and ENI v Commission*, paras 323–5.

[470] Case T-54/03 *Lafarge v Commission* [2008] ECR II-120, para 670; Case T-116/04 *Wieland-Werke v Commission* [2009] ECR II-1087, para 95. For the judicial control of that principle see also Case T-110/07 *Siemens AG v Commission* [2011] ECR II-477, para 323.

[471] Case T-279/02 *Degussa v Commission* [2006] ECR II-897, para 329 et seq. However, strict proportionality is not required. See Case T-330/01 *Akzo Nobel v Commission* [2006] ECR II-3389, para 126.

[472] Case T-116/04 *Wieland-Werke v Commission* [2009] ECR II-1087, para 192.

[473] Joined Cases T-259/02 to T-264/02 and T-271/02 *Raiffeisen Zentralbank and Others v Commission* [2006] ECR II-5169, para 383; Case T-13/03 *Nintendo v Commission* [2009] ECR II-975, paras 72–4.

[474] Joined Cases T-101/05 and T-111/05 *BASF and UCB v Commission* [2007] ECR II-4949, paras 52–3; Case T-168/05 *Arkema v Commission* [2009] ECR II-180, paras 182–3; Case T-13/03 *Nintendo v Commission* [2009] ECR II-975, para 74; Case T-446/05 *Amann & Söhne v Commission* [2010] ECR II-1255, paras 159–60; Case T-217/06 *Arkema v Commission* [2011] ECR II-2593, paras 228–31 and 235–6; Judgment of 13 July 2011 in Joined Cases T-141/07, T-142/07, T-145/07, and T-146/07 *General Technic-Otis and Others v Commission*, paras 245 and 247–8. However, the cumulation of sanctions in case of several infringements may become relevant with regard to the proportionality principle, as well as the undertaking's ability to pay.

[475] Commission Decision of 1 October 2008 in Case COMP/39.181 *Candle Waxes*, para 713 (ExxonMobil, Shell).

[476] Commission Notice on the conduct of settlement procedures in view of the adoption of Decisions pursuant to Article 7 and Article 23 of Council Regulation (EC) No 1/2003 in cartel cases [2008] OJ C167/1, para 33.

[477] Joined Cases C-189/02 P, C-202/02 P, C-205/02 P to C-208/02 P and C-213/02 P *Dansk Rørindustri and Others v Commission* [2005] ECR I-5425, paras 292 and 294; Case T-213/00 *CMA CGM and Others v Commission* [2003] ECR II-913, paras 342–6; Case T-15/02 *BASF v Commission* [2006] ECR II-497, para 227.

[478] In *Gosme/Martell*, the Commission took into account the extent to which one party may have derived more benefits than another, setting different levels of fines for parties involved in the same infringement. See *Gosme/Martell-DMP* [1991] OJ L185/23, paras 42–3. The Commission stated that Martell was the primary beneficiary with regard to the collusion and imposed on it a much higher fine than on DMP, the other undertaking involved.

Application of the 10 per cent cap and possible further adjustments: settlements and leniency

The individual adjustments (aggravating and mitigating circumstances, where relevant, and **11.68** specific increase for deterrence) modify the basic amount of the fine. Once these calculations have been made, the Commission has to ensure that the overall amount does not exceed 10 per cent of the worldwide turnover of the undertaking, ie the maximum allowed pursuant to Article 23(2) of Regulation 1/2003.[479] If this is the case, the overall amount will be reduced to this threshold[480] (for details see paragraphs 11.36 to 11.40). However, in one recent case[481] the Commission has indicated that, in exceptional circumstances, it may take into account that for cartels involving mostly (small) mono-product companies, the differences in their liability (relative gravity, duration) might be lost due to the fact that the fines for most or even all of them would be capped.[482] As a consequence, the Commission in this case used its discretion to further adjust the fine by applying downward multipliers of varying levels.[483] This adjustment was formally based on paragraph 37 of the 2006 Guidelines, which foresees the possibility of departing from the general methodolgy set out in the guidelines.

Further adjustments will be made in case the undertaking cooperates under the Leniency **11.69** Notice[484] or participates in a settlement of the case under the Settlement Notice.[485] Under the terms of the Leniency Notice, the first undertaking to submit information and evidence which, in the Commission's view, will enable it to (i) carry out a targeted inspection in connection with an alleged cartel (point 8(a)), or (ii) find an infringement of Article 101 TFEU in connection with the alleged cartel (point 8(b)) may receive *full immunity* from fines. Undertakings that do not meet these conditions, but provide the Commission with evidence of the alleged infringement which represents significant added value with respect to the evidence already in the Commission's possession may receive a *reduction* of their fines (points 23 to 26). The level of such reduction depends on the order in which the applicants fulfilled this condition, as they will be grouped in certain bands (first undertaking: 30 to 50 per cent reduction; second undertaking: 20 to 30 per cent; subsequent undertakings: up to 20 per cent);

---

[479] 2006 Guidelines, para 32. For associations of undertakings see para 33.

[480] According to settled case law, intermediate amounts in the determination of the fine may exceed the 10 per cent turnover threshold, even if this means that certain factors will not have any effect on the final amount of the fine. See Joined Cases C-189/02 P, C-202/02 P, C-205/02 P to C-208/02 P and C-213/02 P *Dansk Rørindustri and Others v Commission* [2005] ECR I-5425, paras 278–9; Case T-31/99 *ABB Asea Brown Boveri v Commission* [2002] ECR II-1881, para 184; Case T-73/04 *Le Carbone Lorraine v Commission* [2008] ECR II-2661, para 123. This applies even in cases where already the basic amount exceeds the threshold. See Case T-52/03 *SNCZ v Commission* [2005] ECR II-5005, paras 39 and 40. For a more detailed overview see paras 11.36–11.40.

[481] Commission Decision of 28 March 2012 in Case COMP/39.452 *Mountings for Windows and Window-doors*, paras 517–23.

[482] This concern had previously been raised by the GC in Case T-211/08 *Putters v Commission* [2011] ECR II-3729, para 75. Cf also the Opinion of AG Tizzano in Joined Cases C-189/02 P, C-202/02 P, C-205/02 P to C-208/02 P and C-213/02 P *Dansk Rørindustri and Others v Commission* [2005] ECR I-5425, paras 129–33, which, however, was not followed by the ECJ. Leaving aside the *obiter dictum* in *Putters*, the EU Courts have consistently rejected the idea that the capping of fines pursuant to Art 23(2) of Reg 1/2003 could entail the violation of the principles of equality and/or proportionality. See paras 11.36–11.40.

[483] The level of the reduction varied between 45 per cent and 87 per cent depending on the mono-product ratio of the individual undertakings, the relative gravity of their participation in the infringement, and the need to achieve sufficient deterrence. The decision has nevertheless been challenged by several addressees (Cases T-248/12, T-252/12, T-256/12, T-257/12, and T-259/12), *inter alia* claiming insufficient motivation and discriminatory treatment.

[484] Commission Notice on immunity from fines and reduction of fines in cartel cases [2006] OJ C298/17 ('Leniency Notice'). For further details see Ch 6, 'Investigation of Cases (I): Leniency Policy'.

[485] Commission Notice on the conduct of settlement procedures in view of the adoption of Decisions pursuant to Article 7 and Article 23 of Council Regulation (EC) No 1/2003 in cartel cases [2008] OJ C167/1. For further details see Ch 10, 'Infringement Procedures'.

within these bands, the reduction level is determined by the added value as well as the timing of the cooperation (point 26). If the conditions for a settlement are fulfilled, the Commission will *reduce by 10 per cent* the amount of the fine to be imposed after the cap has been applied. Also, for such an undertaking, any specific increase for deterrence (multiplier) will not exceed factor 2.[486] If the settlement involves a leniency applicant, the reduction of the fine granted on that account will be added to the leniency reward.[487]

Inability to pay ('ITP')[488]

11.70 In exceptional cases, the Commission may, upon request, take account of the undertaking's inability to pay in a specific social and economic context in order to reduce the fine otherwise imposed under the guidelines, or to grant special payment facilities.[489] However, it will not base any reduction granted for this reason on the mere finding of an adverse or loss-making financial situation, but rather require objective evidence that imposition of the fine would irretrievably jeopardize the economic viability of the undertaking concerned and cause its assets to lose all their value.[490] The burden of proof for demonstrating this rests on the undertaking,[491] and the conditions should be interpreted narrowly, given that a reduction of the fine for inability to pay risks granting a competitive advantage to undertakings that are the least well adapted to market conditions.[492] In analysing ITP, the Commission has a margin of assessment which the courts will only control for manifest errors.[493] As for the timing, what matters in principle is the undertaking's financial situation (immediately) prior to the Commission decision; however, in

---

[486] Commission Notice on the conduct of settlement procedures in view of the adoption of Decisions pursuant to Article 7 and Article 23 of Council Regulation (EC) No 1/2003 in cartel cases [2008] OJ C167/1, para 32.

[487] Commission Notice on the conduct of settlement procedures in view of the adoption of Decisions pursuant to Article 7 and Article 23 of Council Regulation (EC) No 1/2003 in cartel cases [2008] OJ C167/1, para 33.

[488] See para 35 of the 2006 Guidelines and the Note of Vice President and Competition Commissioner Almunia and Budget Commissioner Lewandowski 'Inability to pay under paragraph 35 of the 2006 Guidelines and payment conditions pre- and post-decision finding an infringement and imposing fines', SEC(2010) 737 ('ITP Note'). For an instructive overview see F Castillo de la Torre 'The 2006 Guidelines on Fines: Reflections on the Commission's Practice' (2010) 33 World Competition 397; P Kienapfel and G Wils, 'Inability to Pay—First Cases and Practical Experiences' [2010] Competition Policy Newsletter 3, 3–7.

[489] According to the ITP Note, para 13, the possibility of granting deferred and unsecured payments by instalments will only be considered in exceptional circumstances as an alternative to fine reductions. See also European Commission Antitrust Manual of Procedures, Internal DG Competition working documents on procedures for the application of Articles 101 and 102 TFEU, March 2012, Module 25 'Follow-up of decisions', paras 9 and 10, distinguishing between payment facilities granted by the Accounting Officer pursuant to Art 85 of the Implementing Rules [now: Art 89 of the Rules of Application of the Financial Regulation] and by College decision based on para 35 of the 2006 Guidelines.

[490] 2006 Guidelines, para 35.

[491] Judgment of 16 November 2011 in Case T-54/06 *Kendrion v Commission*, para 163; Judgment of 12 December 2012 in Case T-400/09 *Ecka Granulate and non ferrum Metallpulver v Commission*, para 112; Judgment of 12 December 2012 in Case T-352/09 *Nováčke chemické závody v Commission*, para 201. Where the undertaking fails to provide evidence as regards all conditions pursuant to para 35, the Commission may summarily reject the request. See Judgment of 12 December 2012 in Case T-400/09 *Ecka Granulate and non ferrum Metallpulver v Commission*, paras 115–16 (no lack of motivation).

[492] H de Broca, 'The Commission Revises its Guidelines for Setting Fines in Antitrust Cases' (2006) 3 Competition Policy Newsletter 1 & 6, with reference to Case C-308/04 P *SGL Carbon v Commission* [2006] ECR I-5977, para 105. See also the ITP Note, para 4: 'taking into account the distressed financial situation of a company can carry the inherent risk of favouring those companies that are inefficient, badly managed or over-leveraged at the expense of well managed and financially prudent companies. It may also encourage strategic behaviour (moral hazard), in particular financial engineering or corporate restructuring, aimed at avoiding the payment of the fine...A generous treatment of such ITP requests may also diminish the deterrent effect of the Commission's fines.'

[493] See Joined Cases T-109/02, T-118/02, T-122/02, T-125/02 and T-126/02, T-128/02 and T-129/02, T-132/02 and T-136/02 *Bolloré and Others v Commission* [2007] ECR II-947, para 664.

exceptional cases the Commission will also enter into a post-decision ITP analysis, which may lead to a reduction or even a waiver of the fine.[494] Any ITP reduction will be applied after the 10 per cent cap pursuant to Article 23(2) of Regulation 1/2003. By spring 2013 such a reduction had been granted to a total of thirteen undertakings in seven different cartel decisions.[495] Reductions on this basis have ranged from 25 per cent to 75 per cent. The Commission has expressed its aim to settle around half of its cartel investigations in 2013.[496]

According to settled case law, the Commission is not required, when determining the amount **11.71** of the fine, to take into account the poor financial situation of an undertaking concerned.[497] Furthermore, the fact that a measure taken by an EU authority leads to the insolvency or liquidation of a given undertaking is not as such prohibited by EU law.[498] Consequently, any reduction for inability to pay requires fulfillment of the specific requirements set out in paragraph 35 of the 2006 Guidelines.[499] These conditions have been further explained in an information note of 2010 by the Commissioners with special responsibility for Competition and Budget.[500]

---

[494] This requires a College decision, see ITP Note, para 19. For an example of a post-decision ITP reduction, see Commission Decision of 31 March 2011 amending Decision C(2007) 4257 final of 19 September 2007 in Case COMP/39.168 *PO/Hard Haberdashery: Fasteners* [2011] OJ C210/26. The full text (in French) is available at <http://ec.europa.eu/competition/antitrust/cases/dec_docs/39168/39168_1108_5.pdf>. For a (partial) waiver of the recovery of fines pursuant to Art 80 of the Financial Regulation ([2012] OJ L298/1) and Art 91 of the Rules of Application ([2012] OJ L362/1) see European Commission Antitrust Manual of Procedures, Internal DG Competition working documents on procedures for the application of Articles 101 and 102 TFEU, March 2012, Module 25 'Follow-up of decisions', paras 14–24.

[495] *Heat Stabilisers* (COMP/38.589, Decision of 11 November 2009), *Bathroom Fittings* (COMP/39.093, Decision of 23 June 2010), *Prestressing Steel* (COMP/38.344, Decision of 30 June 2010), *Animal Feed* (COMP/38.866, Decision of 20 July 2010) (settlement case), *Refrigeration Compressors* (COMP/39.600, Decision of 7 December 2011) (settlement case), *Mountings for Windows and Window-doors* (COMP/39.452, Decision of 28 March 2012) and *TV and Computer Monitor Tubes* (COMP/39.437, Decision of 5 Decision 2012). In an additional two cases (Interdean in *International Removal Services* (COMP/38.543, Decision of 24 July 2009); Almamet in *Calcium Carbide* (COMP/39.396, Decision of 22 July 2009)) the Commission applied a *sui generis* reduction based on para 37 of the 2006 Guidelines taking into account the particular financial situation of the respective undertaking.

[496] Statement by Vice President and Competition Commission Almunia at a conference of the College of Europe, 14 January 2013 (as reported by Mlex).

[497] Joined Cases C-189/02 P, C-202/02 P, C-205/02 P to C-208/02 P and C-213/02 P *Dansk Rørindustri and Others v Commission* [2005] ECR I-5425, para 327; Case C-328/05 *SGL Carbon v Commission* [2007] ECR I-3921, para 100; Case T-213/00 *CMA CGM and Others v Commission* [2003] ECR II-913, para 351; Case T-38/02 *Groupe Danone v Commission* [2005] ECR II-4407, para 413. This case law is not put in question by para 35 of the 2006 Guidelines, which, however, lead to a self-limitation by the Commission. See Judgment of 16 November 2011 in Case T-54/06 *Kendrion v Commission*, paras 162 and 163.

[498] Judgments of 12 December 2012 in Case T-400/09 *Ecka Granulate and non ferrum Metallpulver v Commission*, para 50 with further references, and in Case T-392/09 *1. garantovaná v Commission*, paras 119, 131, and 132. According to the GC, only the loss of all personal, tangible and intangible assests represented by the undertaking may justify taking into account the risk of insolvency or of the dissolution of the undertaking as a consequence of the fine. See Case T-400/09 *Ecka Granulate and non-ferrum Metallpulver v Commission*, paras 51 and 96.

[499] At the same time, para 35 guarantees that the Commission's decision does not violate the proportionality principle. Given that the Commission must not act arbitrarily, it will usually have to grant an ITP reduction where the conditions of para 35 are fulfilled. See Judgments of 12 December 2012 in Case T-400/09 *Ecka Granulate and non ferrum Metallpulver v Commission*, paras 48 and 100; and in Case T-352/09 *Novácke chemické závody v Commission*, paras 185–90 and 238.

[500] Note of Vice President and Competition Commissioner Almunia and Budget Commissioner Lewandowski 'Inability to pay under paragraph 35 of the 2006 Fining Guidelines and payment conditions pre- and post-decision finding an infringement and imposing fines', SEC(2010) 737 ('ITP Note'). The ITP Note, paras 14–16, also highlights the right of undertakings to choose between provisional payment and provision of a bank guarantee in case of an annulment action against the Commission decision. On this see also Art 90 of the Rules of Application of the Financial Regulation ([2012] OJ L362/1) and the European Commission Antitrust Manual of Procedures, Internal DG Competition working documents on procedures for the application of Articles 101 and 102 TFEU, March 2012, Module 25 'Follow-up of decisions', paras 6 and 7.

Procedurally, this presupposes a specific ITP request[501] by the undertaking that explains its financial situation and provides detailed and up-to-date financial information to support its request.[502] Usually, the Directorate-General for Competition ('DG COMP') will be in contact with the undertaking in order to collect additional information and/or clarify the information obtained, which will allow it to bring further relevant data to the attention of the Commission.[503] In order to ensure that companies are systematically made aware of the possibility of invoking ITP, an explicit reference to paragraph 35 of the 2006 Guidelines shall be included in every statement of objections in antitrust cases where fines are likely to be imposed, or in the requests for information that are sent out closer to the adoption date of the decision in order to collect the parties' latest turnover figures.[504]

11.72 As for the substance, the most important part of the ITP test is whether the fine imposed by the Commission will 'irretrievably jeopardise the economic viability of the undertaking and cause its assets to lose all their value'. According to the ITP Note, the Commission assesses the financial situation of the undertaking on the basis of a number of indicators for profitability, capitalization, solvency, and liquidity (derived from recognized bankruptcy prediction models, including the so-called *Altman Z-score* test).[505] Using not only historical data but also projections,[506] in particular regarding cash flows, it assesses whether and how the fine would cause these financial indicators to deteriorate.[507] In this context, the Commission will also consider the undertaking's relations with outside financial partners (access to credit, including undrawn credit facilities)[508] and with

---

[501] See Case T-199/08 *Ziegler v Commission* [2011] ECR II-3507, para 165; Joined Cases T-204/08 and T-212/08 *Team Relocations v Commission* [2011] ECR II-3569, paras 172 and 176; Judgment of 16 November 2011 in Case T-54/06 *Kendrion v Commission*, paras 137 and 165.

[502] See Commission Notice on best practices for the conduct of proceedings concerning Articles 101 and 102 TFEU [2011] OJ C308/6, para 89: 'The assessment of the financial situation is carried out for all undertakings that have made an inability to pay request close to the adoption of the decision and on the basis of up-to-date information, irrespective of when the request was submitted.' For the undertaking's duties in this regard, see Case T-64/02 *Dr Hans Heubach v Commission* [2005] ECR II-5137, paras 164–5.

[503] Commission Notice on best practices for the conduct of proceedings concerning Articles 101 and 102 TFEU [2011] OJ C308/6, para 88.

[504] ITP Note, para 6. See also Commission Notice on best practices for the conduct of proceedings concerning Articles 101 and 102 TFEU [2011] OJ C308/6, para 87.

[505] In this regard, the Commission 'gives more emphasis to solvency and liquidity relative to capitalisation and profitability'. See ITP Note, para 7. In several decisions, the Commission explained that it takes into account information like the balance sheet, the income statement, the statement of changes in equity and the cash-flow statement, usually of the last five financial years, as well as projections. The time horizon for such projections into the future is likely to vary according to the special circumstances of each individual case. While the ITP Note mentions cash flow projections 'for the current year and two future years' (para 7), in other cases a more extended time period into the future has been assessed. See eg Commission Decision of 28 March 2012 in Case COMP/39.452 *Mountings for Windows and Window-doors*, para 547, where a five-year period was taken into account. The Commission has explained that it focuses on the presence and the immediate future; its analysis is dynamic, taking into account the consistency over time of the submitted projections. It also considers possible restructuring plans and their implementation.

[506] According to the Commission Notice on best practices for the conduct of proceedings concerning Articles 101 and 102 TFEU [2011] OJ C308/6 (para 88), when assessing an ITP request, 'the Commission looks in particular at the financial statements for recent years and forecasts for the current and coming years'.

[507] See ITP Note, para 7. Thus, if there is sufficiently clear evidence that a company is in immediate danger of bankruptcy, the Commission will try to assess whether it is likely that such bankruptcy would indeed be caused by the fine. For the causality link see Case T-62/02 *Union Pigments v Commission* [2005] ECR II-5057, para 178. Cf also, for interim measures, Order of the President of 29 July 2011 in Case T-292/11 R *Cemex and Others v Commission*, para 24.

[508] In this regard, the Order of the President of 13 April 2011 in Case T-393/10 R *Westfälische Drahtindustrie* appears to have eased the burden on undertakings to show that they cannot obtain credit support from financial institutions, at least in the context of interim measures. The President of the GC rejected the Commission's arguments on the inherent alignment of interests between banks, shareholders and companies in arguing the impossibility of receiving/granting support, and in particular allowed the undertaking to rely on refusal letters from banks where the latter have been sufficiently informed about the undertaking's

shareholders.[509] Aside from controlling shareholders, this also includes such natural persons[510] or (group) companies, the (business) interests of which are aligned with the company requesting ITP.[511] The necessary causal link may be missing where the undertaking's existence is irrevocably threatened, even without the fine,[512] or where the fine imposed is very small when compared to the overall turnover and assets of the undertaking, so that it cannot be expected that the fine will have a decisive influence on its financial situation.[513] Moreover, the causal link might be interrupted where the undertaking causes its inability to pay on purpose,[514] or where this is the direct consequence of a lack of diligence in deploying its financial resources.[515]

While paragraph 35 of the 2006 Guidelines further presupposes that the undertaking's assets **11.73** lose 'all their value', it has become apparent that a literal interpretation would lead to an almost systematic rejection of all ITP claims, since even in a bankruptcy situation, individual assets will normally retain at least a certain operational and resale value. The Commission therefore considers that this condition is already fulfilled if the fine 'would not only be likely to lead to the bankruptcy of an undertaking as such, but also that it would cause its productive assets to lose 'significantly' their value'.[516] This might be the case if the bankruptcy would lead to the

---

financial situation (as reflected in the respective rejection letters). The requirements in this regard for the interim measures procedure have been further clarified in the Order of the President of the ECJ of 20 April 2012 in Case C-507/11 P(R) *Indústria de Fapricela v Commission*, para 36 et seq. Where the banks refuse support despite the existence of a larger group (with potentially larger financial resources), the undertaking has to provide the judge with detailed and certified documentation showing that the banks knew the financial situation of its shareholders. See Order of the President of the ECJ of 20 April 2012 in Case C-507/11 P(R) *Indústria de Fapricela v Commission*, paras 35, 67, and 68.

[509] Commission Notice on best practices for the conduct of proceedings concerning Articles 101 and 102 TFEU [2011] OJ C308/6, para 88. As regards the possibility to receive financial support from shareholders see Commission Decision of 9 November 2010 in Case COMP/39.258 *Air Freight*, para 1379 n 1566 with references to the case law in the context of interim measures (Order of the President of 14 December 1999 in Case C-335/99 P(R) *HFB Holding für Fernwärmtechnik Beteiligungsgesellschaft and Others v Commission* [1999] ECR I-8705; Order of the President of 23 March 2001 in Case C-7/01 P(R) *Nederlandse Federatieve Vereniging voor de Groothandel op Elektrotechnisch Gebied v Commission* [2001] ECR I-2559; Order of the President of 7 May 2010 in Case T-410/09 R *Almamet v Commission* [2010] ECR II-80).

[510] Order of the President of 30 June 2009 in Case T-550/08 R *Tudapetrol Mineralölerzeugnisse Nils Hansen v Commission*, para 45.

[511] See Order of the President of 30 April 2010 in Case C-113/09 P(R) *Ziegler v Commission* [2010] ECR I-50, paras 44–8. This may also comprise minority shareholders. See Order of the President of 16 December 2010 in Case C-373/10 P(R) *Almamet v Commission*, paras 22–3 and 27; Order of the President of 24 January 2011 in Case T-370/10 R *Rubinetterie Teorema v Commission*, paras 37 et seq and 41; Order of 13 April 2011 in Case T-393/10 R *Westfälische Drahtindustrie and Others v Commission*, para 37 et seq.

[512] See Commission Decision of 30 June 2010 in Case COMP/38.344 *Prestressing Steel*, paras 1178–9.

[513] See Commission Decision of 9 November 2010 in Case COMP/39.258 *Air Freight*, paras 1387, 1390, 1394, and 1398. See, however, Case T-199/08 *Ziegler v Commission* [2011] ECR II-3507, para 167.

[514] Cf Judgment of 12 December 2012 in Case T-392/09 *1. garantovaná v Commission*, paras 144 and 146.

[515] However, according to the President of the GC in interim measures, the causal link remains intact where, even after the statement of objections, the undertaking reduces its funds as a consequence of normal business (investment) decisions or intra-group transfers which have the objective to prevent the insolvency of other group companies. See Order of the President of 2 March 2011 in Case T-392/09 R *1.garantovaná v Commission*, para 87; Order of 13 April 2011 in Case T-393/10 R *Westfälische Drahtindustrie and Others v Commission*, para 51. At the same time, the failure to make sufficient provisions may, depending on the facts of the case, constitute a lack of diligence. See Order of the President of 13 April 2011 in Case T-413/10 R *Socitrel v Commission*, para 53.

[516] The GC has stressed that the mere risk that the fine might lead to bankruptcy is not sufficient as regards the application of para 35 of the 2006 Guidelines. According to the court, 'while bankruptcy adversely affects the financial interests of the owners or investors concerned, it does not necessarily mean that the undertaking in question will disappear. That undertaking may continue to exist as such, either—in the case of the recapitalisation of the company declared bankrupt—as a legal person operating that undertaking, or—in the case of the acquisition by another entity of all its assets and thus of the undertaking—as an entity carrying out an economic activity. Such an acquisition of the assets may take the form either of a voluntary purchase

disappearance of the undertaking as a going concern (because of dismantling and/or closure), its jobs being lost and the assets (property, buildings, machinery etc) being sold separately at substantially discounted prices.[517] This requires a prospective, case-by-case analysis, for which the Commission is not bound by (but might take into account) national insolvency rules.

11.74 According to paragraph 35 of the 2006 Guidelines, the Commission will assess the undertaking's inability to pay (and thus its likely disappearance from the market) against the social and economic context in which it operates, in order to see whether this context is in any way 'special'. In practice, this condition is interpreted rather broadly. The specific economic context can be argued in times of general economic crisis (often leading to a slump in demand)[518] or if the specific sector concerned by the decision is going through a cyclical crisis[519] (eg suffering from overcapacity or falling prices), but it may also be considered whether companies have difficulties in obtaining access to capital or credit as a result of the prevailing economic conditions (credit crunch).[520] A specific social context may be present in cases of high and/or mounting unemployment (at a regional or wider level), where the bankruptcy of the undertaking might (significantly) contribute to a further increase.[521] The burden of demonstrating such effects is again on the undertaking, which must show not only the (high) likelihood of such effects, but also the causal link with the fine to be imposed.[522]

11.75 If the Commission intends to reject an ITP application, it has to sufficiently justify its conclusion by providing at least a brief summary of the evidence and findings substantiating the outcome.[523] Even where the conditions of paragraph 35 of the 2006 Guidelines are not fulfilled,

---

or of a forced sale of the assets of the bankrupt company with its continued operation.' See Judgment of 12 December 2012 in Case T-352/09 *Novácke chemické závody v Commission*, paras 189, 220, and 228.

[517] ITP Note, para 9; Press Release IP/10/790 'Commission fines 17 bathroom equipment manufacturers €622 million in price fixing cartel' of 23 June 2010. Conversely, there would be no significant asset loss if the undertaking will likely be acquired and its business continued as a going concern (ie without job losses etc.) by another company in insolvency proceedings. This standard has been by and large confirmed by the GC, see eg Judgments of 12 December 2012 in Case T-400/09 *Ecka Granulate and non ferrum Metallpulver v Commission*, paras 96–8 and 115; in Case T-352/09 *Novácke chemické závody v Commission*, paras 190 and 191; and in Case T-410/09 *Almamet v Commission*, paras 265–9. In Commission Decision of 20 July 2010 in Case COMP/38.866 *Animal Feeds*, para 231, the Commission explained that the undertaking has to demonstrate that no viable alternatives exist which would allow the undertaking to be restructured, within a reasonably short period of time, such that the undertaking is maintained as a going concern (possibly as part of insolvency proceedings); where this is not the case, the Commission will assume a sufficiently high risk that the undertaking will go into forced liquidation and that this would lead to a significant loss of asset value.

[518] See Commission Decision of 11 November 2009 in Case COMP/38.589 *Heat Stabilisers*, para 779 et seq; Commission Decision of 23 June 2010 in Case COMP/39.092 *Bathroom Fittings*, para 1320 et seq; Commission Decision of 30 June 2010 in Case COMP/38.344 *Prestressing Steel*; Commission Decision of 28 March 2012 in Case COMP/39.452 *Mountings for Windows and Window-doors*.

[519] See Joined Cases T-217/03 and T-245/03 *FNCBV and Others v Commission* [2006] ECR II-4987, para 356.

[520] ITP Note, para 8. Effects on economic sectors up- or downstream may also figure in the overall assessment. See Joined Cases T-236/01, T-239/01, T-244/01 to T-246/01, T-251/01 and T-252/01 *Tokai Carbon and Others v Commission* [2004] ECR II-1181, para 371; Judgment of 12 December 2012 in Case T-400/09 *Ecka Granulate and non ferrum Metallpulver v Commission*, para 99.

[521] ITP Note, para 8. See also Case C-308/04 P *SGL Carbon v Commission* [2006] ECR I-5977, para 106; Case T-25/05 *KME Germany and Others v Commission* [2010] ECR II-91, paras 166 and 170.

[522] Case T-62/02 *Union Pigments v Commission* [2005] ECR II-5075, para 176; Case T-25/05 *KME Germany and Others v Commission* [2010] ECR II-91, para 170.

[523] Judgment of 12 December 2012 in Case T-352/09 *Novácke chemické závody v Commission*, para 207. However, if the applicant fails to explain (and prove) how the imposition of the fine would jeopardize its economic viability as an undertaking and would cause its assets to lose all their value, the Commission may confine itself to a finding that the requirements of para 35 have not been satisfied (paras 209 and 210). Even if the Commission's decision is vitiated by an inadequate statement of reasons, the EU Courts may nevertheless conclude, in the exercise of their unlimited jurisdiction and based on additional information produced

however, the Commission may still accept a lower fine based on the particular (economic) circumstances which the undertaking faces, based on paragraph 37 of the 2006 Guidelines.[524] Alternatively, a payment plan could be imposed, but this constitutes the exception. Moreover, post-decision, the accounting officer generally requires a bank guarantee covering the outstanding amount (at any point in time) in such a scenario. This requirement may exceptionally be waived when the undertaking 'is willing and able to make the payment in the additional time period but is not able to lodge such guarantee and is in a distressed situation'.[525]

3. Final amount and judicial review

The Commission is not required: **11.76**

> to ensure, where fines are imposed on a number of undertakings involved in the same infringement, that the final amounts of the fines resulting from its calculations for the undertakings concerned reflect any distinction between them in terms of their overall turnover or their turnover in the relevant product market.[526]

This also applies to small and medium companies as:

> the Commission is under no obligation to reduce the fines where the undertakings concerned are SMEs. There is no reason to treat SMEs differently from other undertakings.[527]

The Commission's policy on fines

After the adoption of Regulation 17, whereby it was empowered to sanction undertakings   **11.77** which had infringed the EC competition rules, the Commission for many years showed a very restrained attitude regarding fines[528]—so much so that between 1962 and 1969 no fines at all were imposed—and when finally, in 1969, the first undertaking was penalized in *Quinine*,[529] the sanction was of an almost token amount. The turning point in the Commission's policy on fines was marked by its 1980 decision in *Pioneer*,[530] where the Commission went so far as

---

only at the litigation stage, that the fine imposed is appropriate (paras 212 and 214). See also Judgment of 14 March 2013 in Case T-588/08 *Dole Food and Dole Germany v Commission*, para 668, according to which the reasons in the decision have to be read in conjunction with the wording in para 35 of the 2006 Guidelines.

[524] See eg Commission Decision of 11 March 2008 in Case COMP/38.543 *International Movers*, paras 634 et seq, 652 and 654. See also Commission Decision of 22 July 2009 in Case COMP/39.396 *Calcium Carbide*, paras 371 and 372, nn 684 and 685; Judgments of 12 December 2012 in Case T-352/09 *Novácke chemické závody v Commission*, para 139 et seq; and in Case T-410/09 *Almamet v Commission*, paras 233, 271, and 274. For the necessity to deviate from its own guidelines based on the particular circumstances of an individual case see Judgment of 12 December 2012 in Case T-400/09 *Ecka Granulate and non ferrum Metallpulver v Commission*, paras 42–6. The resulting difference in treatment of several participants in an infringement must be compatible with the principle of equal treatment. See Judgment of 12 December 2012 in Case T-352/09 *Novácke chemické závody v Commission*, para 135.

[525] See Art 89 of the Rules of Application of the Financial Regulation ([2012] OJ L362/1); ITP Note, paras 13 and 17–19. For the replacement of the obligation to pay the fine by a payment plan, as an interim solution, see Order of the President of 13 April 2011 in Case T-393/10 R *Westfälische Drahtindustrie and Others v Commission*. See also Order of the President of 13 July 2006 in Case T-11/06 R *Romana Tabacchi v Commission* [2006] ECR II-2491.

[526] Case T-23/99 *LR AF 1998 v Commission* [2002] ECR II-1705, para 278; Judgment of 5 October 2011 in Case T-11/06 *Romana Tabacchi v Commission*, para 259.

[527] Judgment of 5 October 2011 in Case T-11/06 *Romana Tabacchi v Commission*, para 260. See also Judgment of 16 November 2011 in Case T-54/06 *Kendrion v Commission*, para 149.

[528] See D Geradin and D Henry, 'The EC Fining Policy for Violation of Competition Law: An Empirical Review of the Commission Decisional Practice and the Community Courts' Judgments' [2005] European Competition Law Journal 401, 404–8.

[529] *Quinine* [1969] OJ L192/5. The highest fine for an undertaking was ECU 210,000 and it may safely be assumed, considering the gravity and duration of the infringement in this case, that the fines would have been much higher if the case were to be considered now.

[530] *Pioneer Hi-Fi Equipment* [1980] OJ L60/21.

to impose fines of up to 4 per cent of the total turnover for certain of the infringing undertakings.[531] In the ensuing court case, the Commission justified this by stating that:

> [a]fter 20 years of Community competition policy an appreciable increase in the level of fines is necessary...at least for types of infringement which have long been well defined and are known to those concerned, such as prohibitions on exports and imports...Heavier fines are particularly necessary where, as in the present case, the principal aim of the infringement is to maintain a higher level of prices for consumers.

It also stressed that:

> many undertakings carry on conduct which they know to be contrary to Community law because the profit which they derive from their unlawful conduct exceeds the fines imposed hitherto. Conduct of that kind can only be deterred by fines which are heavier than in the past.[532]

In its judgment, the ECJ, although reducing the amount of the fines, gave clear support for the Commission's new policy of attempting to discourage anticompetitive conduct on the part of undertakings by fines of an exemplary nature. The Court stated that it was indeed appropriate to raise the level of fines in order to increase their deterrent effect.[533] As a result of that judgment, the Commission made it known in its *Thirteenth Report on Competition Policy* (1983) that in the future it would continue to impose high fines in order to create the dissuasive effect which so far had not been achieved.[534] From the mid-1980s onwards, the size of fines increased considerably. In 1991, a fine of ECU 75 million was imposed on Tetra Pak[535] for abuse of a dominant position. This amounted to almost 2.5 per cent of its overall turnover. Forty-one participants were sanctioned in the *Cement* cartel with a total fine of ECU 248 million in 1994.[536]

11.78 The 1998 Guidelines introduced a new method for setting fines: the starting amount was determined in absolute terms according to the intrinsic gravity of the infringement, while

---

[531] Pioneer Electronic Europe NV received the highest fine of ECU 4.35 million (in court, this was reduced to ECU 2 million). In their applications to the ECJ, the companies argued that the Commission had taken advantage of their case 'to introduce a new policy intended to increase the general level of fines for certain infringements of Community law'. See Joined Cases 100–103/80 *Musique Diffusion Française v Commission* [1983] ECR 1825, para 101. In response, the Commission acknowledged 'that the present cases are the first in which it has imposed a level of fines considerably higher than in the past. Before the adoption of the contested decision it had not imposed fines exceeding 2% of the total turnover of the undertaking, even for serious infringements. In these cases the fines range from 2 to 4% of turnover' (para 103).

[532] As reported in Joined Cases 100–103/80 *Musique Diffusion Française v Commission* [1983] ECR 1825, para 104.

[533] Joined Cases 100–103/80 *Musique Diffusion Française v Commission* [1983] ECR 1825, para 106. In para 108, the Court confirmed that it was 'open to the Commission to have regard to the fact that practices of this nature, although they were established as being unlawful at the outset of Community competition policy, are still relatively frequent on account of the profit that certain of the undertakings concerned are able to derive from them and, consequently, it was open to the Commission to consider that it was appropriate to raise the level of fines so as to reinforce their deterrent effect.'

[534] XIII Report on Competition Policy [1983], paras 56–8. The Commission concluded that '[a]fter about 20 years' experience of enforcing the competition rules, during which time it had imposed relatively light fines, the Commission found that fines of this size were not proving adequate to deter companies from continuing to commit even quite clear-cut infringements'. As for the purpose of fines, those were twofold: 'to impose a pecuniary sanction on undertakings for the infringement and prevent a repetition of the offence, and to make the prohibition in the Treaty more effective'.

[535] *Tetra Pak II* [1992] OJ L72/1 (confirmed in Case T-83/91 *Tetra Pak International v Commission* [1994] ECR II-755).

[536] *Cement* [1994] OJ L343/1. Some of these fines were reduced on appeal, in particular because the Commission had not proven the full length of the infringement: Joined Cases T-25/95, T-26/95, T-30/95 to T-39/95, T-42/95 to T-46/95, T-48/95, T-50/95 to T-65/95, T-68/95 to T-71/95, T-87/95, T-88/95, T-103/95 and T-104/95 *Cimenteries CBR and Others v Commission* [2000] ECR II-491.

duration was generally taken into account by an increase of 10 per cent per year. One year later, the Commission imposed a fine of ECU 272.98 million on the parties to the Trans-Atlantic Conference Agreement ('TACA'),[537] a group of shipping companies providing scheduled container transport for freight between ports in northern Europe and the US. In 2001 the Commission sanctioned fifty-six companies with fines totalling EUR 1,836 million, nearly half of which were imposed in the *Vitamins*[538] cartel case. Hoffmann-La Roche, one of the undertakings involved in this case, was fined EUR 462 million because of its participation in a price-fixing cartel for eight different vitamins, considered to be eight separate infringements. One year later, the largest fine for a vertical agreement, totalling EUR 167.9 million, was imposed on eight undertakings in *Nintendo*.[539] In the same year, one single undertaking, the French company Lafarge, was fined EUR 249.6 million.[540] Taken together, in the four years from 2000 to 2003, the Commission adopted twenty-six cartel decisions with fines totalling EUR 3,330 million, compared with eight decisions (EUR 552 million) in the 1996 to 1999 period, and eleven decisions (EUR 393 million) from 1992 to 1995.[541] In early 2004, the Commission in its *Microsoft* decision[542] imposed what was at the time the largest fine ever on an individual undertaking, with a total amount of EUR 497.2 million relating to a proceeding under Article 102 TFEU. Fines imposed for cartel cases rose from a total of EUR 3,463 million in the period 2000 to 2004 to a total of EUR 9,648 million in the period 2005 to 2009,[543] however with significant variations in individual years.[544] The Commission fined six undertakings a total of EUR 519 million in 2006 for participating in a cartel to fix prices and share customers for certain types of synthetic rubber.[545] In 2007 it imposed fines of EUR 486.9 million on four

---

[537] [1999] OJ L95/01.

[538] *Vitamins* [2003] OJ L6/01. The overall fine imposed on the eight undertakings amounted to EUR 855 million. This compared to an overall size of the product market concerned in the EEA of EUR 800 million in 1998 (para 15), with the various infringements ranging in duration from three to ten years (para 2). By far the largest fines were imposed on Hoffmann-La Roche (EUR 462 million) and BASF (EUR 296.16 million), which, however, were also by far the largest players on the market (para 10). In court, BASF's overall fine was reduced to EUR 236.85 million (Case T-15/02 *BASF v Commission* [2006] ECR II-497).

[539] *Nintendo* [2003] OJ L255/33. By far the largest individual fine of EUR 149.13 million was imposed on Nintendo Corporation Ltd/Nintendo of Europe GmbH (in court, this fine was reduced to EUR 119.24 million, see Case T-13/03 *Nintendo v Commission* [2009] ECR II-975).

[540] *Plasterboards* [2005] OJ L166/8 (summ pub). The overall fine imposed amounted to 478.3 million euros for a cartel of six years, which compared to an overall size of the product market concerned of EUR 1,210 million in each of 1997 and 1998 (para 8). The fine for Lafarge was upheld in Case T-54/03 *Lafarge v Commission* [2008] ECR II-120 (confirmed on appeal in Case C-413/08 P *Lafarge v Commission* [2010] ECR I-5361).

[541] M Bloom, 'The Great Reformer: Mario Monti's Legacy in Art 81 and Cartel Policy' [2005] Competition Policy International 55, 69.

[542] Commission Decision of 24 March 2004 in Case COMP/37.792 *Microsoft* (the fine was upheld in Case T-201/04 *Microsoft v Commission* [2007] ECR II-3601). It should be noted that at the time of the decision Microsoft had approximately EUR 50 billion in cash reserves. Consequently, the fine imposed by the Commission amounted to no more than 1 per cent of its worldwide turnover.

[543] DG COMP, Cartel Statistics (version of 27 June 2012). At the same time, it should be noted that the number of decisions (per undertaking/assocation) also increased significantly, from 157 in 2000–2004 to 203 in 2005–2009.

[544] For instance, in 2009 (six cartel cases) the overall amount of the fines imposed was EUR 1,541 million, compared to EUR 3,313 million in 2007 (eight cartel cases). In 2010, the overall fines again reached EUR 2,869 million (seven cartel cases).

[545] Commission Decision of 29 November 2006 in Case COMP/38.638 *Butadiene Rubber and Emulsion Styrene Butadiene Rubber*. This compared to an overall size of the market with the products concerned of around EUR 482 million in 2001, in a cartel that lasted more than six years (paras 2, 55, and 60). The highest individual fine of EUR 272.3 million was imposed on ENI (reduced to EUR 181.5 million in the Judgment of 13 July 2011 in Case T-39/07 *ENI v Commission*).

undertakings participating in the *Flat Glass* cartel,[546] EUR 748.7 million on thirteen undertakings participating in the *Gas Insulated Switchgear* (GIS) cartel,[547] and EUR 992.3 million on five undertakings participating in four separate cartel infringements in the markets for the installation and maintenance of *Elevators and Escalators* in Germany and the Benelux countries.[548] Large fines were also imposed in 2008, with a total of EUR 676 million in the *Candle Waxes* cartel[549] and EUR 1383.9 million in the *Car Glass* cartel[550] (where Saint-Gobain alone received a fine of EUR 896 million). This continued in 2009 where a fine of EUR 1,106 million was imposed on E.ON and GdF for a market-sharing agreement regarding the MEGAL gas pipeline.[551] In the same year, *Intel* received a fine of EUR 1,060 million for abusing its dominant position.[552] The following year (2010) saw an all-time high in cartel enforcement activity, with the Commission addressing cartel decisions to sixty-nine undertakings at an overall fines amount of EUR 2,869 million. This included a total fine of EUR 799 million for the participation of eleven undertakings in the *Air Freight* cartel,[553] of EUR 649 million for the participation of six

---

[546] Commission Decision of 28 November 2007 in Case COMP/39.165 *Flat Glass*. This compared to an overall size of the market with the products concerned of EUR 1,700 million in 2004, in a cartel that lasted about one year (paras 41 and 457). The highest individual fine of EUR 148 million was imposed on Guardian, the only undertaking to have challenged the decision (rejected in the Judgment of 27 September 2012 in Case T-82/08 *Guardian Industries and Guardian Europe v Commission*; the appeal in Case C-580/12 P is currently pending).

[547] Commission Decision of 24 January 2007 in Case COMP/38.899 *Gas Insulated Switchgear*. This compared to an overall size of the market with the products concerned of EUR 320 million in 2003, in a cartel that lasted more than sixteen years (paras 3 and 4). The highest individual fine of EUR 396.6 million was imposed on Siemens AG (upheld in Case T-110/07 *Siemens AG v Commission* [2011] ECR II-477; the appeal in Case C-239/11 P *Siemens AG v Commission* is currently pending).

[548] Commission Decision of 21 February 2007 in Case COMP/38.823 *PO/Elevators and Escalators*. This compared to an overall size of the market with the products concerned of around EUR 1,123 million in 2003, in four infringements that lasted between four and eight years (paras 71 and 610). The highest overall fine of EUR 479.7 million was imposed on various companies of the ThyssenKrupp group. While the decision was upheld for the rest, the fine on ThyssenKrupp was reduced to EUR 319.78 million because the GC considered that the aggravating circumstance of recidivism did not apply (Judgment of 13 July 2011 in Joined Cases T-144/07, T-147/07, T-148/07, T-149/07, T-150/07, and T-154/07 *ThyssenKrupp Liften Ascenseurs and Others v Commission*). All undertakings appealed to the ECJ, but the appeals of the ThyssenKrupp companies were later withdrawn following a cross-appeal by the Commission on the point of recidivism.

[549] Commission Decision of 1 October 2008 in Case COMP/39.181 *Candle Waxes*. This compared to an overall size of the market with the products concerned of EUR 485 million in 2004, in a cartel that lasted over twelve years (paras 71 and 610). The highest individual fine of EUR 318.2 million was imposed on Sasol (challenged in Case T-541/08 *Sasol and Others v Commission*).

[550] Commission Decision of 12 November 2008 in Case COMP/39.125 *Car Glass*. This compared to an overall size of the market with the products concerned of [2000–2500] EUR million in 2002, in a cartel that lasted five years (paras 4 and 5). Saint Gobain's fine has been challenged in Case T-56/09 *Saint-Gobain France and Others v Commission*.

[551] Commission Decision of 8 July 2009 in Case COMP/39.401 *E.ON/GDF*. The fine, which was calculated on the basis of the 2006 Guidelines, would normally have been much higher for E.ON but was 'capped' on the basis of the fine imposed on GDF, because the Commission considered that, as equal partners in the market-sharing agreement, both undertakings should receive the same fine. The percentage value applied to the relevant sales was 15 per cent (paras 365 and 375), the duration for the German and French market varied between five and seven years, and no aggravating or mitigating circumstances were present. Both undertakings challenged the decision in court (Case T-360/09 *E.ON Ruhrgas and E.ON v Commission*; Case T-370/09 *GDF Suez v Commission*). In its judgments of 29 June 2012 the GC considered that the Commission had not sufficiently established the finding of an infringement on the German market from 1980 until April 1998 (which had not been taken into account for the fine) and on the French market from August 2004 until September 2005 (which formed part of the fines calculation). On that basis, and in its unlimited jurisdiction, the GC reduced the fine for each undertaking from EUR 553 million to EUR 320 million.

[552] Commission Decision of 13 May 2009 in Case COMP/37.990 *Intel*. In this case, the Commission applied the lowest percentage value to the relevant sales so far (5 per cent). The decision has been challenged in Case T-286/09 *Intel v Commission*.

[553] Commission Press Release IP/10/1487 'Commission fines 11 air cargo carriers €799 million in price fixing cartel' of 9 November 2010. The cartel lasted for over six years. All carriers received a reduction of

undertakings in the *LCD* cartel,[554] and of EUR 622 million for the participation of seventeen undertakings in the *Bathroom Fittings* cartel.[555] Since then, however, the pace seems to have slowed down. In 2011, the Commission only adopted four cartel decisions against fourteen undertakings, with fines totalling EUR 614 million. Three decisions concerned settlement cases, and the only non-settlement case (*Exotic Fruit*[556]) led to a fine of merely EUR 8.9 million. While the first half of 2012 saw three cartel decisions (and one re-adoption) against twenty-nine undertakings, fines were again rather low.[557] Only one further decision was adopted in the second half of 2012, but it imposed fines totalling EUR 1.470 million.[558] No cartel decision was taken in the first half of 2013, but the Commission fined anticompetitive agreements in two cases: EUR 79 million in *Telefónica/Portugal Telecom* (IP/13/39) and EUR 146 million in *Lundbeck* (IP/13/563). In addition, *Microsoft* was fined EUR 561 million for non-compliance with a commitment decision (IP/13/196). Since the introduction of the new settlement procedure in summer 2008, the Commission has also adopted six settlement decisions with fines between EUR 13 million and EUR 331 million.[559]

Even though the Commission has stressed that the elements set out in the 2006 Guidelines **11.79** 'should not be regarded as the basis for an automatic and arithmetical calculation method',[560]

---

15 per cent on account of the general regulatory environment in the sector which could be seen as encouraging price coordination. The highest individual fine of EUR 310.1 million was imposed on Air France/KLM, who have challenged the decision in Case T-62/11 *Air France-KLM v Commission* [2011] OJ C95/8.

[554] *Liquid Crystal Displays (LCD)* [2001] OJ L295/8. See also Commission Press Release IP/10/1685 'Commission fines six LCD panel producers €648 million for price fixing cartel' of 8 December 2010. The cartel lasted for over four years. The highest individual fine of EUR 300 million was imposed on Chimei InnoLux Corporation, which has challenged the decision in Case T-91/11 *Chimei InnoLux v Commission* [2011] OJ C113/18.

[555] Commission Press Release IP/10/790 'Commission fines 17 bathroom equipment manufacturers €622 million in price fixing cartel' of 23 June 2010. The cartel lasted for twelve years and concerned six Member States. The highest individual fine of EUR 326 million was imposed on Ideal Standard.

[556] Commission Press Release IP/11/1186 'Commission imposes €8.9 million fine in banana cartel' of 12 October 2011. The cartel only comprised two undertakings, Chiquita (which received immunity) and Pacific Fruit, lasted less than a year, and only affected customers in Greece, Italy, and Portugal with a market volume of about EUR 525 million. The decision followed an earlier finding in 2008 of a cartel in the bananas sector covering Germany and seven other Northern European countries (IP/08/1509).

[557] Leaving aside the readoption decision in the *GIS* case (IP/12/705), the fines imposed were EUR 86 million in the *Mountings* case (COMP/39.452), EUR 169 million in the *Freight forwarding* case (COMP/39.462), and EUR 13 million in the *Water management products* case (COMP/39.611). The outcome in the *Mountings* case could have been higher, but the Commission used its discretion to exceptionally reduce the fines in light of the special circumstances of the case (most of the addressees were mono-product companies and their fine would have been capped at 10 per cent of their total turnover). The size of the affected market was estimated to be at least EUR 1 billion and the cartel lasted for more than seven years. See Commission Press Release IP/12/313 'Commission fines nine producers of window mountings €86 million for price fixing cartel' of 28 March 2012.

[558] Commission Decision of 5 December 2012 in Case COMP/39.437 *TV and Computer Monitor Tubes* (Press Release IP/12/1317). The decision involved seven undertakings and concerned two cartels concerning colour picture tubes used for televisions and colour display tubes used in computer monitors, which lasted for almost ten years. The highest fine of EUR 391.9 million was imposed on Philips and LG Electronics, jointly and severally.

[559] Commission Decision of 19 May 2010 in Case COMP/38.511 *DRAM* ([2011] OJ C180/15; IP/10/586); Commission Decision of 20 July 2010 in Case COMP/38.866 *Animal Feed Phosphates* ([2011] OJ C180/15; IP/10/985); Commission Decision of 13 April 2011 in Case COMP/39.579 *Consumer Detergents* ([2011] OJ C193/14; IP/11/473); Commission Decision of 19 October 2011 in Case COMP/39.605 *CRT glass bulbs* (IP/11/1214); Commission Decision of 7 December 2012 in Case COMP/39.600 *Refrigeration compressors* ([2012] OJ C122/6; IP/11/1511); Commission Decision of 27 June 2012 in Case COMP/39.611 *Water management products* (IP/12/704). Case COMP/38.866 was 'hybrid' in the sense that one cartel participant (Timab) ultimately decided not to settle. It has challenged the (regular) decision taken against it in Case T-456/10 *Timab Industries and CFPR v Commission* [2010] OJ C346/46.

[560] 2006 Guidelines, para 6.

it is clear that the determination of fines has become significantly more transparent and predictable. While the Commission still has to decide on the gravity (percentage) value to be applied to the relevant sales and possible adjustment factors, the fine is to a large extent determined by product turnover and duration. Hence, although the *introduction* of the 2006 Guidelines marked a significant change, any increase in fine levels *since then* primarily has to do with the features of the individual infringement in question (eg the size of the affected market(s); duration; aggravating circumstances), rather than a policy choice to impose ever higher sanctions. In this regard, the determination of DG COMP to focus its enforcement policy on particularly damaging anticompetitive behaviour also plays a role.[561] Another key element has been the adoption of the Leniency Notice and the actual implementation of the leniency programme since then.[562] A further increase in anti-cartel enforcement shall be achieved once the settlement procedure has gained full momentum. At the same time, cartel decisions like *Vitamins* or *Elevators and Escalators* and abuse decisions like *Microsoft* demonstrate that high fines could also result from the 1998 Guidelines, depending on the particular circumstances of each individual case. While the starting amounts under the 1998 Guidelines were typically higher, in relative terms, for smaller markets, the 2006 Guidelines lead to results which are more proportionate to the size of the affected market and the weight of each infringing undertaking on that market. As for the 1998 Guidelines,[563] the EU Courts appear to have accepted the fines method applied under the 2006 Guidelines.

Judicial review of the fine

11.80 In the event of a challenge in court, the GC and the ECJ are empowered to exercise judicial control over the amount of the fine, having regard to the circumstances of the case. In this regard they enjoy a two-fold competence. First, they carry out a legality review which, *inter alia*, covers conformity with the Commission's fining guidelines,[564] as well as general principles of law, like the principles of proportionality[565] and equal treatment.[566] In the absence of any further guidance by the legislature, the EU courts will normally accept that the guidelines clarify the application of the relevant fining factors in Article 23(3) of Regulation 1/2003 (gravity and duration).[567]

---

[561] A dedicated cartel unit central to the overall process of enhancing the Commission's efficiency in its fight against cartels was created in 1998, thus concentrating the existing know-how in investigating cartels. In 2002, a further increase of resources was achieved by the creation of a second cartel unit. M Bloom, 'The Great Reformer: Mario Monti's Legacy in Article 81 and the Cartel Policy' [2005] Competition Policy International 55, 71–3; JM Joshua and PD Comesasca, 'EC Fining Policy against Cartels after the Lysine Ruling: The Subtle Secrets of X' [2004] The European Antitrust Review, Global Competition Review 5. Since June 2005, an entire directorate (Directorate G, currently comprising six cartel units) in DG COMP has the exclusive task of detecting and combating cartels. See Commission MEMO 05/454/2005 'Competition: Commission action against cartels—Questions and answers' of 30 November 2005. One of the cartel units deals specifically with settlement cases.

[562] See Ch 6, 'Investigation of Cases (I): Leniency policy'.

[563] Joined Cases C-189/02 P, C-202/02 P, C-205/02 P to C-208/02 P and C-213/02 P *Dansk Rørindustri and Others v Commission* [2005] ECR I-5425, paras 240–96, in particular, paras 252 and 253. In fact, the ECJ found that the method applied under the 1998 Guidelines 'seems to correspond better with the principles laid down by Regulation No 17 as interpreted by the ECJ, notably in its judgment in *Musique Diffusion française and Others v Commission*, than what is alleged to be the Commission's earlier practice, referred to by the applicants, in which the relevant turnover played a predominant and relatively mechanical role' (para 260).

[564] See Case T-127/04 KME *Germany v Commission* [2009] ECR II-1167, para 34: 'It is therefore for the Court to verify, when reviewing the legality of the fines imposed by the contested decision, whether the Commission exercised its discretion in accordance with the method set out in the Guidelines and, should it be found to have departed from that method, to verify whether that departure is justified and supported by sufficient legal reasoning.'

[565] See Judgment of 22 November 2012 in Case C-89/11 P *E.ON Energie v Commission*, para 126.

[566] For the different ways to restore the balance in case of unequal treatment see Judgment of 12 December 2012 in Case T-352/09 *Nováčke chemické závody v Commission*, paras 55 and 56.

[567] Cf Judgment of 8 December 2011 in Case C-386/10 P *Chalkor AE Epexergasias Metallon v Commission*, para 71 (for the duration factor). See also paras 75–7: 'The large number of factors to be taken into account

Although the courts have sometimes suggested that, where the applicable rules leave room for discretion, judicial review will be limited to manifest errors of assessment,[568] often this is more rhetoric than reality.[569] Typically, the courts will review the Commission's analysis in detail where the applicant has advanced specific arguments and not just general complaints. Indeed, while they 'cannot use the Commission's margin of discretion—either as regards the choice of factors taken into account in the application of the criteria mentioned in the Guidelines or as regards the assessment of those factors—as a basis for dispensing with the conduct of an in-depth review of the law and of the facts',[570] they do not have to carry out a full review of their own motion.[571] In the context of the review of legality, the assessment is based solely on the elements of fact and law existing at the time when the measure was adopted, and in particular the information available to the Commission at that time.[572] In terms of the outcome, where a plea is only directed at a specific part of the Commission's decision, it will only lead to a partial annulment, provided the annulled part can be severed from the remainder and the undertaking had been put in a position to defend itself, during the administrative procedure, against its liability for the remaining part.[573]

The review of legality provided for under Article 263 TFEU is supplemented by the unlimited jurisdiction in respect of the amount of the fine, provided for under Article 31 of Regulation 1/2003 (which in turn is based on Article 261 TFEU).[574] In exercising that jurisdiction, the court is: **11.81**

---

necessarily gives the Commission a variety of options in its assessment of those factors, their weighting and their evaluation so as adequately to punish the infringement. However, the Commission remains subject to certain obligations.'

[568] See eg Judgment of 16 November 2011 in Joined Cases T-55/06 and T-66/06 *RKW and JM Gesellschaft für industrielle Beteiligungen v Commission*, para 205. For the assessment of the quality of cooperation during the investigation, also in comparison to other leniency applicants, see Case C-328/05 P *SGL Carbon v Commission* [2007] ECR I-3921, para 88; Joined Cases T-71/03, T-74/03, T-87/03 and T-91/03 *Tokai Carbon and Others v Commission* [2005] ECR II-10, para 362; Case T-343/08 *Arkema v Commission* [2011] ECR II-2287, paras 81 and 134–6. See also Opinion of AG Kokott of 18 April 2013 in Case C-501/11 P *Schindler Holding and Others v Commission*, para 190.

[569] Cf Judgment of 8 December 2011 in Case C-386/10 P *Chalkor AE Epexergasias Metallon v Commission*, paras 47 and 82.

[570] Judgment of 6 November 2012 in Case C-199/11 *Europese Gemeenschap v Otis and Others*, para 61.

[571] Judgment of 8 December 2011 in Case C-386/10 P *Chalkor AE Epexergasias Metallon v Commission*, paras 62, 66, and 70. See also Judgment of 8 December 2011 in Case C-389/10 P *KME Germany and Others v Commission*, para 63: 'in an action on a decision relating to a competition matter, it is for the applicant to formulate his pleas in law and not for the General Court to review of its own motion the weighting of the factors taken into account by the Commission in order to determine the amount of the fine.' However, the Commission has to explain the weighting and assessment of those factors in the decision, and the EU Courts must check the motivation in this regard on their own motion. See Judgment of 6 November 2012 in Case C-199/11 *Europese Gemeenschap v Otis and Others*, para 60. Moreover, in the case of a parent-subsidiary relationship, where both companies are liable as part of one undertaking, the EU Courts may rely on the outcome of the annulment action by the respective other company in a separate case as long as both have brought a plea with the 'same object'. See Judgment of 22 January 2013 in Case C-286/11 P *Commission v Tomkins*, paras 43, 49, and 56.

[572] Judgment of 27 September 2012 in Case T-343/06 *Shell Petroleum and Others v Commission*, para 104: 'No one, therefore, can rely before the Court of the European Union on matters of fact which, since they were not put forward in the course of the administrative procedure, could not be taken into acccount at the time of adoption of that measure'.

[573] See Judgment of 6 December 2012 in Case C-441/11 P *Commission v Verhuizingen Coppens*, paras 36–8, 46, and 51. The requirement of severability is not satisfied where the partial annulment of a measure would cause the substance of that measure to be altered. This must be determined objectively and not with a view to the political intentions of the authority which adopted the measure at issue (para 38).

[574] See Case C-297/98 P *SCA Holding v Commission* [2000] ECR I-10101, paras 53–5; Case T-48/02 *Bouwerij Haacht v Commission* [2005] ECR II-5259, para 44; Joined Cases T-259/02–T-264/02 and T-271/02 *Raiffeisen Zentralbank and Others v Commission* [2006] ECR II-5169, para 391. According to

empowered, in addition to carrying out a mere review of the lawfulness of the penalty, to substitute its own appraisal for the Commission's and, consequently, to cancel, reduce or increase the fine or penalty payment imposed.[575]

Hence, it may also consider questions of expediency, appropriateness, and fairness.[576] Independent of any legal error by the Commission,[577] and without annulling its decision, the courts may vary the sanction[578]—which will often be a reduction[579] but can also involve an increase of the fine (no *reformatio in peius*).[580] It is not entirely clear, though, whether the exercise of this power merely requires that the question of the amount of the fine in general is before the court,[581] or whether the court can only act upon specific pleas.[582] Given that the procedure before the EU courts is adversarial in nature, and that the right to effective judicial review (Article 47 of the Charter of Fundamental Rights) does not require an *ex officio* review, the latter seems to be more in line with standard procedural rules. On appeal, the ECJ restricts

the GC: 'Article 261 TFEU (formerly Article 229 EC) does not constitute an autonomous legal remedy; its sole effect is to enlarge the extent of the powers the Courts of the Union have in the context of the action referred to in Article 263 TFEU (formerly Article 230 EC).' Judgment of 12 July 2011 in Case T-132/07 *Fuji v Commission*, para 207. See also Case T-69/04 *Schunk and Schunk Kohlenstoff-Technik v Commission* [2008] ECR II-2567, para 246.

[575] Case C-3/06 P *Groupe Danone v Commission* [2007] ECR I-1331, para 61.
[576] AG Kokott, Opinion of 8 December 2005 in Case C-113/04 P *Technische Unie v Commission*, para 132.
[577] See Case C-3/06 P *Groupe Danone v Commission* [2007] ECR I-1331, para 61; Case T-343/08 *Arkema v Commission* [2011] ECR II-2287, para 203 et seq. In the past, this was less clear. See the ECJ's Annual Report 2006, at 124.
[578] Case C-534/07 P *Prym and Prym Consumer v Commission* [2009] ECR I-7415, para 86.
[579] Joined Cases T-217/03 and T-245/03 *FNCBV v Commission* [2006] ECR II-4987, paras 355 et seq and 361.
[580] See eg Joined Cases T-101/05 and T-111/05 *BASF and UCB v Commission* [2007] ECR II-4949, paras 24 and 212–23. This includes the possibility that the court may not maintain a reduction granted by the Commission. See Judgment of 12 December 2012 in Case T-410/09 *Almamet v Commission*, para 275. The Commission itself may request the Court to exercise its unlimited jurisdiction, for example where the applicant had received a reduction of the fine for non-contestation but then contests certain facts before the court. See Case T-69/04 *Schunk and Schunk Kohlenstoff-Technik v Commission* [2008] ECR II-2567, paras 244 and 247; Joined Cases T-67/00, T-68/00, T-71/00 and T-78/00 *JFE Engineering and Others v Commission* [2004] ECR II-2501, para 575. An increase of the fine by the court will always require that the undertaking had the opportunity to exercise its rights of defence by making known its views. See Joined Cases T-67/00, T-68/00, T-71/00 and T-78/00 *JFE Engineering and Others v Commission* [2004] ECR II-2501, para 578. See also Case C-3/06 P *Groupe Danone v Commission* [2007] ECR I-1331, para 70 et seq; Joined Cases T-101/05 and T-111/05 *BASF and UCB v Commission* [2007] ECR II-4949, para 212. This allows the undertaking to withdraw its application in order to avoid a higher fine.
[581] Cf Case C-3/06 P *Groupe Danone v Commission* [2007] ECR I-1331, para 62. See also Opinion of AG Bot of 21 June 2012 in Case C-89/11 P *E.ON Energie v Commission*, para 115. In this direction also Opinion of AG Mengozzi of 19 July 2012 in Case C-286/11 P *Commission v Tomkins*, para 37 et seq, according to which the GC may take into account its own findings in a parallel case (against the subsidiary) when making use of its unlimited jurisdiction in the case brought by the parent company. However, this opinion was not followed by the ECJ in its judgment of 22 January 2013 in that case.
[582] Judgment of 8 December 2011 in Case C-386/10 P *Chalkor AE Epexergasias Metallon v Commission*, paras 64–6 and 70: 'With the exception of pleas involving matters of public policy which the Courts are required to raise of their own motion, such as the failure to state reasons for a contested decision, it is for the applicant to raise pleas in law against that decision and to adduce evidence in support of those pleas...What the applicant is required to do in the context of a legal challenge is to identify the impugned elements of the contested decision, to formulate grounds of challenge in that regard and to adduce evidence—direct or circumstantial—to demonstrate that its objections are well founded.' The same view has been taken by the EFTA Court in Case E-15/10 *Posten Norge v EFTA Surveillance Authority*, para 268. See also Judgment of 27 June 2012 in Case T-372/10 *Bolloré v Commission*, para 220; Judgment of 29 June 2012 in Case T-360/09 *E.ON Ruhrgas and E.ON AG v Commission*, paras 295–8; Judgment of 12 December 2012 in Case T-332/09 *Electrabel v Commission*, para 222, and Judgment of 14 March 2013 in Case C-276/11 P *Viega v Commission*, paras 57 and 59.

its review to legal errors. Hence, it will not, on grounds of fairness, substitute its own assessment for that of the GC exercising its unlimited jurisdiction to rule on the amount of the fine.[583] At the same time, it has unlimited jurisdiction to determine the fine when it sets aside the judgment of the GC.[584]

In exercising its unlimited jurisdiction, the court is not bound by the fining methodology applied in the decision (eg the 2006 Guidelines or the Leniency Notice)[585] and generally should form its own view of an appropriate fines level.[586] At the same time, like the Commission, it has to respect general principles of law, both of a procedural (eg rights of defence) and of a substantive nature (eg 10 per cent turnover limit).[587] This applies in particular to the principle of equal treatment, which is why the judges should provide a justification if it chooses to deviate from the fines method applied to the other addressees in the contested decision.[588] It is thus not surprising that the EU Courts usually correct errors in the fines calculation in line with the method applied by the Commission, at least where there are other undertakings which also received a fine.[589] In fact, as the President of the GC has stressed, 'the choice to follow an existing calculation method, such as the Commission's fining guidelines, is also the expression of its unlimited jurisdiction'.[590] The assessment may justify the

11.82

---

[583] Judgment of 6 December 2012 in Case C-457/10 P *AstraZeneca v Commission*, para 162. However, the question of whether the fine is disproportionate is a legal question that may be raised on appeal. See Judgment of 22 November 2012 in Case C-89/11 P *E.ON Energie v Commission*, para 126.

[584] Judgment of 6 December 2012 in Case C-441/11 P *Commission v Verhuizingen Coppens*, para 79.

[585] Joined Cases T-101/05 and T-111/05 *BASF and UCB v Commission* [2007] ECR II-4949, paras 17, 213, and 219; Judgment of 5 October 2011 in Case T-11/06 *Romana Tabacchi v Commission*, para 266; Judgment of 29 June 2012 in Case T-370/09 *GDF Suez v Commission*, para 462; Judgment of 30 May 2013 in Case C-70/12 P *Quinn Barlo v Commission*, para 53.

[586] Judgment of 17 May 2013 in Joined Cases T-147/09 and T-148/09 *Trelleborg v Commission*, para 114. On the need for an appraisal which is 'sufficiently independent of that of the Commission' see Opinion of AG Bot of 21 June 2012 in Case C-89/11 P *E.ON Energie v Commission*, paras 116 et seq and 119. However, the fact that the EU Courts have unlimited jurisdiction does not mean that they must always fix the fine themselves, especially where the applicant merely advances general pleas without explaining why the fine might be disproportionate etc. See M Jaeger, 'Standard of Review in Competition Cases: Can the General Court Increase Coherence in the European Union Judicial System?' in T Baumé, E Oude Elferink, P Phoa, and D Thiaville (eds), *Today's Multilayered Legal Order: Current Issues and Perspectives, Liber Amicorum in Honour of Arjen WH. Meij* (Paris Legal Publishers 2011) 136: 'Too often I read comments that judges do not exercise their competences fully, as granted pursuant to Article 261 TFEU and Article 31 of Regulation 1/2003—the reason is, most of the time, much simpler: they are not convinced by the arguments put forward by the applicants! And thus, they do not need to go beyond what is necessary to render justice. Full jurisdiction is not a synonym of judicial activism. It should never be forgotten that the General Court, even in the exercise of its unlimited jurisdiction, is constrained by the principle of party disposition and the inherent limits of the notion of public order grounds that can be raised on the General Court's own motion.'

[587] Opinion of AG Maduro of 16 November 2006 in Case C-3/06 P *Groupe Danone v Commission*, para 53; Judgment of 12 July 2011 in Case T-132/07 *Fuji v Commission*, para 209. See also Case C-3/06 P *Groupe Danone v Commission* [2007] ECR I-1331, paras 68–70 (as regards the rights of defence).

[588] Case C-291/98 P *Sarrió v Commission* [2000] ECR I-9991, paras 97 and 98; Case C-338/00 *Volkswagen v Commission* [2003] ECR I-9189, para 146; Case T-213/00 *CMA CGM and Others v Commission* [2003] ECR I-913, para 462; Case T-217/06 *Arkema France v Commission* [2011] ECR II-2593, para 342; Judgment of 27 September 2012 in Case T-362/06 *Ballast Nedam Infra v Commission*, para 143.

[589] Judgment of 6 December 2012 in Case C-441/11 P *Commission v Verhuizingen Coppens*, para 80. See eg Case C-3/06 P *Groupe Danone v Commission* [2007] ECR I-1331, para 82; Case T-161/05 *Hoechst v Commission* [2009] ECR II-3555, paras 100–101 and 196–198; Case T-37/05 *World Wide Tobacco España v Commission* [2011] ECR II-41, para 198; Case T-461/07 *Visa Europe v Commission* [2011] ECR II-1729, para 291.

[590] M Jaeger, 'Standard of Review in Competition Cases: Can the General Court Increase Coherence in the European Union Judicial System?' in T Baumé, E Oude Elferink, P Phoa, and D Thiaville (eds), *Today's Multilayered Legal Order: Current Issues and Perspectives, Liber Amicorum in Honour of Arjen WH. Meij* (Paris Legal Publishers 2011) 130. See also 122: 'If, as sometimes criticised, the General Court does not very often exercise its unlimited jurisidiction to depart from the Commission's methodology to set fines, one must counterbalance this observation with the necessity of legal certainty. Indeed, the intervention of the General Court

production and taking into account of additional information which the duty to state reasons did not require to be set out in the Commission decision.[591] Also, the court may take into account mitigating circumstances, even if the applicant had not made such a request during the administrative procedure.[592]

11.83 The legality review provided for in Article 263 TFEU, supplemented by the unlimited jurisdiction in respect of the amount of the fine, provided for in Article 31 of Regulation 1/2003, meets the requirements of the principle of effective judicial protection in Article 47 of the Charter of Fundamental Rights.[593]

4. Ne bis in idem

11.84 Undertakings involved in international cartels that also extend to non-Member States cannot request a reduction of their fine by arguing that they were already sanctioned in another jurisdiction. The GC held that the principle of *ne bis in idem*, according to which a person who has already been tried may not again be prosecuted or fined for the same conduct, does not apply where the different proceedings are brought by the Commission and the authorities of a non-Member State, as they do not protect the same legal interest.[594] Neither do considerations of fairness require that the Commission, when fixing the amount of a fine, takes into account previous fines imposed by authorities or courts of a non-EU Member State.[595] The situation is different within the European Union where Article 50 of the Charter of Fundamental Rights explicitly stipulates the applicability of the *ne bis in idem* principle.[596] Its application is subject

---

would be counterproductive if each time it had to review a decision it would substitute its own assessment to determine a new amount of the fine. The existence of Guidelines, claimed in essence to increase transparency, allows the parties concerned to know the rules of the game ... Unlimited jurisdiction with regard to the fine has to be used wisely and carefully not to create legal uncertainty either for the administration or for companies.'

[591] Case T-220/00 *Cheil Jedang v Commission* [2003] ECR-II-2473, para 215, with further references; Case T-15/02 *BASF v Commission* [2006] ECR II-497, paras 303, 354, 394, 534, and 542; Judgment of 27 September 2012 in Case T-343/06 *Shell Petroleum and Others v Commission*, para 176. See also Joined Cases T-101/05 and T-111/05 *BASF and UCB v Commission* [2007] ECR II-4949, paras 70–2, as regards an increase of the fine on account of recidivism for an earlier finding of an infringement not mentioned in the challenged decision. However, where, during the administrative procedure, the undertaking failed to submit, even negligently, decisive evidence for the setting of the amount of the fine and then relies on such evidence only at the court stage, the EU Courts may take this failure into account when re-setting the fine (by applying a certain increase). See Judgment of 27 September 2012 in Case T-343/06 *Shell Petroleum and Others v Commission*, paras 118–9.

[592] See Case T-73/04 *Le Carbone Lorraine v Commission* [2008] ECR II-2661, paras 186 et seq, 187, and 194–5. However, the court has indicated that this might require that at least the relevant facts were known to the Commission before it adopted the decision. See Case T-322/01 *Roquette Frères v Commission* [2006] ECR II-3137, para 327.

[593] Judgment of 6 November 2012 in Case C-199/11 *Europese Gemeenschap v Otis and Others*, paras 63 and 64. See also *Menarini Diagnostics v Italy* App no 43509/08 (ECtHR, 27 September 2011), paras 58–67; EFTA Court, Judgment of 18 April 2012 in Case E-15/10 *Posten Norge v EFTA Surveillance Authority*, paras 91 and 100.

[594] See eg Case T-223/00 *Kyowa Hakko Kogyo and Others v Commission* [2003] ECR II-2553, paras 102 and 103. See also Case C-397/03 P *Archer Daniels Midland v Commission* [2006] ECR I-4429, para 69; Case C-289/04 P *Showa Denko v Commission* [2006] ECR I-5859, para 55; Joined Cases T-236/01, T-239/01, T-244/01 to T-246/01, T-251/01 and T-252/01 *Tokai Carbon and Others v Commission* [2004] ECR II-1181, para 135; Case T-43/02 *Jungbunzlauer v Commission* [2006] ECR II-3435, para 387.

[595] Case C-289/04 P *Showa Denko v Commission* [2006] ECR I-5859, paras 57–8 and 60–1; Case C-328/05 P *SGL Carbon v Commission* [2007] ECR I-3921, paras 31–4. See also Case T-69/04 *Schunk and Schunk Kohlenstoff-Technik v Commission* [2008] ECR II-2567, para 210.

[596] See Joined Cases C-204/00 P, C-205/00 P, C-211/00 P, C-213/00 P, C-217/00 P and C-219/00 P *Aalborg Portland and Others v Commission* [2004] I-123, paras 338–40; Case C-289/04 P *Showa Denko v Commission* [2006] ECR I-5859, para 54; Judgment of 13 July 2011 in Joined Cases T-144/07, T-147/07,

to the threefold condition of identity of the facts,[597] unity of the offender,[598] and unity of the legal interest protected.[599] The burden of proof for the fulfilment of these conditions is on the undertaking which invokes the *ne bis in idem* principle.[600] With regard to the identity of facts, the ECJ has clarified that:

> [w]hether undertakings have adopted conduct having as its object or effect the prevention, restriction or distortion of competition cannot be assessed in the abstract, but must be examined with reference to the territory, within the Union or outside it, in which the conduct in question had such an object or effect, and to the period during which the conduct in question had such an object or effect.[601]

This allows for parallel proceedings and sanctions even within the EU, as long as the geographic and/or temporal scope of each case is different. In so far as authorities within the European Competition Network ('ECN') close their case with a view to the parallel competence of another authority, this does not constitute a final disposal of the case,[602] which could bar further investigation.[603] The same applies to conditional immunity decisions which guarantee a certain procedural status but where the granting of immunity still depends on the fulfillment of certain conditions (in particular the continued cooperation of the undertaking).[604]

5. The payment of fines and interim measures

Infringement decisions contain a number of provisions in their operative part regarding the payment of fines.[605] In the first place, the decision determines the amount of the fine in euros and the interest for late payment,[606] plus the details of the Commission bank account into

11.85

T-148/07, T-149/07, T-150/07, and T-154/07 *ThyssenKrupp Liften Ascenseurs and Others v Commission*, para 162. See also Case T-223/00 *Kyowa Hakko Kogyo and Others v Commission* [2003] ECR II-2553, para 103.

[597] See Case T-11/05 *Wieland-Werke and Others v Commission* [2010] ECR II-86, para 82 et seq.

[598] As regards associations of undertakings, see Joined Cases T-217/03 and T-245/03 *FNCBV and FNSEA v Commission* [2006] ECR II-4987, paras 343–4.

[599] Joined Cases C-204/00 P, C-205/00 P, C-211/00 P, C-213/00 P, C-217/00 P and C-219/00 P *Aalborg Portland and Others v Commission* [2004] I-123, para 338; Case T-24/07 *ThyssenKrupp Stainless v Commission* [2009] ECR II-2309, para 179. Advocate-General Kokott has suggested that the three-pronged test (identity of facts, persons, and legal interest) in competition cases should be replaced by the standard applied in Strasbourg case law, which only looks to the identity of facts. See Opinion of 8 September 2011 in Case C-17/10 *Toshiba Corporation and Others*, para 114 et seq, with reference to the judgment in *Zolotukhin v Russia* App no 14939/03 (ECtHR (Grand Chamber), 10 February 2009). However, in its judgment of 14 February 2012 in that case, the ECJ maintained its traditional view (para 97).

[600] Case 7/72 *Boehringer Mannheim v Commission* [1972] ECR 1281, para 5; Case T-322/01 *Roquette Frères v Commission* [2006] ECR II-3137, para 289.

[601] Judgment of 14 February 2012 in Case C-17/10 *Toshiba Corporation and Others*, para 99.

[602] Cf Case C-469/03 *Miraglia* [2005] ECR I-2009, para 34.

[603] For Art 54 of the Convention implementing the Schengen Agreement see Joined Cases C-187/01 and C-385/01 *Gözütok and Brügge* [2003] ECR I-1345, para 26 et seq; Case C-467/04 *Gasparini* [2006] ECR I-9199, paras 34–7.

[604] Judgment of 9 September 2011 in Case T-12/06 *Deltafina v Commission*, para 114–118; Judgment of 13 July 2011 in Joined Cases T-144/07, T-147/07, T-148/07, T-149/07, T-150/07 and T-154/07 *ThyssenKrupp Liften Ascenseurs and Others v Commission*, para 167.

[605] See also European Commission Antitrust Manual of Procedures, Internal DG Competition working documents on procedures for the application of Articles 101 and 102 TFEU, March 2012, Module 25 'Follow-up of decisions', para 2.

[606] Art 78(4) of the Financial Regulation ([2012] OJ L298/1) together with Art 83 of the Rules of Application ([2012] OJ L362/1). See also Case T-275/94 *Groupement des Cartes Bancaires (CB) v Commission* [1995] ECR II-2169, para 47: 'The power conferred on the Commission covers the power to determine the date on which the fine is payable and that on which default interest begins to accrue, the power to set the rate of such interest and to determine the detailed arrangements for implementing its decision by requiring, where appropriate, the provision of a bank guarantee covering the principal amount of the fine imposed plus interest.' The legality of interest being charged by the Commission in the event of delay in paying a fine had already been confirmed by the ECJ in Case 107/82 *AEG v Commission* [1983] ECR 3151, paras 141–3.

which the undertakings must (provisionally) pay the fine. The rate will be that applied by the European Central Bank to its main refinancing operations, plus 3.5 per cent.[607] Secondly, decisions set a time limit for payment, usually three months. Payment must be made before the end of that period (cf Articles 278, 299 TFEU) in order to avoid forced recovery. However, where the undertaking has challenged the decision in court it may choose[608] to either make a provisional payment or furnish a bank guarantee[609] covering the principal amount of the fine and interest on it[610] until judgment. Proceedings before the EU Courts do not have suspensive effect.[611] If the undertaking is unable to provide a bank guarantee (or to make a provisional payment), it must request suspension of the decision or interim measures pursuant to Articles 278, 279 TFEU, Articles 104 et seq of the Rules of Procedure of the GC in order to avoid a forced recovery of the fine. The costs incurred in providing a bank guarantee are not recoverable, even where the undertaking wins its case.[612] Exceptionally, where the conditions of Article 89 of the Rules of Application of the Financial Regulation are met, the addressee of the decision may be granted additional time for payment by the Accounting Officer of the Commission. Payment facilities may also take the form of payments by instalment, ie the company agrees to pay a certain sum at

---

[607] See Art 83(2)(b) of the Rules of Application ([2012] OJ L362/1) and Case T-68/04 *SGL Carbon v Commission* [2008] ECR I-2511, para 144. According to the EU Courts, the Commission is entitled 'to adopt a higher rate than that charged by the European Monetary Cooperation Fund in the event of late payment and in any event, as far as proceedings are concerned, to discourage manifestly unfounded actions brought with the sole object of delaying payment of the fine'. Case T-142/89 *Boël v Commission* [1995] ECR II-867, para 138; Case T-23/99 *LRAF 1998 v Commission* [2002] ECR II-1705, paras 397–8. The GC also implicitly confirmed the legality of the Commission's practice of applying a higher interest rate for (unjustified) late payment when compared to undertakings that bring an action before the Court. See Case T-275/94 *Groupement des Cartes Bancaires (CB) v Commission* [1995] ECR II-2169, para 83; Case T-142/89 *Boël v Commission* [1995] ECR II-867, para 139.

[608] Art 90(1) of the Rules of Application ([2012] OJ L362/1). See also European Commission Antitrust Manual of Procedures, Internal DG Competition working documents on procedures for the application of Articles 101 and 102 TFEU, March 2012, Module 25 'Follow-up of decisions', para 6: 'The addressee is informed of that possibility in the cover letter of notification of the decision imposing a fine sent by the Secretariat-General.'

[609] The Commission is not required to accept other types of securities, eg a mortgage. See Joined Cases T-236/01, T-239/01, T-244/01 to T-246/01, T-251/01 and T-252/01 *Tokai Carbon and Others v Commission* [2004] ECR II-1181, para 479. If the company opts for a bank guarantee (which complies with certain minimum requirements and is accepted by the Accounting Officer), the payment of the fine (and default interest as the case may be) will be deferred until the judgment; depending on the outcome of the court case, the guarantee will be enforced or released. See Art 90(3), (4) of the Rules of Application ([2012] OJ L362/1) and the European Commission Antitrust Manual of Procedures, Internal DG Competition working documents on procedures for the application of Articles 101 and 102 TFEU, March 2012, Module 25 'Follow-up of decisions', paras 6 and 7.

[610] See Art 90(1) of the Rules of Application ([2012] OJ L362/1). The applicable interest rate is the ECB rate plus 1.5 per cent. See also Case T-275/94 *Groupement des Cartes Bancaires (CB) v Commission* [1995] ECR II-2169, paras 53 and 54; European Commission Antitrust Manual of Procedures, Internal DG Competition working documents on procedures for the application of Articles 101 and 102 TFEU, March 2012, Module 25 'Follow-up of decisions', n 3.

[611] Pursuant to Art 297(2) TFEU, decisions finding an infringement and imposing fines take effect upon notification and shall be enforceable (Art 299(1) TFEU). Actions brought before the EU Courts do not have suspensory effect (Art 278 TFEU).

[612] See Case 183/83-DEPE *Krupp Stahl v Commission* [1987] ECR 4611, para 10; Case T-77/92 *Parker Pen v Commission* [1994] ECR II-549, para 101. The GC stated that the costs incurred by the applicants in guaranteeing payment of a fine are not recoverable costs under the Rules of Procedure, since they cannot be regarded as costs incurred 'for the purpose of the proceedings'. In *Holcim*, the GC dismissed Holcim's request for reimbursement of its costs for providing a bank guarantee instead of paying the fine. The Court held that the illegality of the Commission decision fining Holcim for its participation in a cartel in the cement sector (which was earlier annulled by the GC) did not to trigger liability, among others because the voluntary decision to provide a bank guarantee meant that the latter was not a direct consequence of such illegality: Case T-28/03 *Holcim (Deutschland) v Commission* [2005] ECR II-1357 (confirmed on appeal in Case C-282/05 P *Holcim (Deutschland) v Commission* [2007] ECR I-2941).

regular points in time.[613] This presupposes that the undertaking provides a bank guarantee, which, however, may exceptionally be waived if the undertaking is not able to lodge such guarantee and is in a distressed situation.[614] Alternatively, the College may grant a partial reduction, or even the full cancellation of the fine; for this the undertaking will have to claim and demonstrate 'inability to pay' in the sense of paragraph 35 of the 2006 Guidelines.[615] Finally, there is also the possibility of a waiver of the recovery of fines, again only under (highly) exceptional circumstances.[616]

If the undertakings do not pay before the expiry of the period for voluntary payment of the **11.86** fine, or challenge the decision in court and do not make a provisional payment/provide a bank guarantee, the Commission is entitled to start execution to secure payment, even while court proceedings are pending.[617] However, in line with its administrative practice, where undertakings request interim measures, the Commission will not enforce its decision pursuant to Article 299 TFEU until the President of the GC has decided on the application. Exceptionally the President has suspended the execution of decisions imposing fines without lodging a bank guarantee when the undertaking faces serious difficulties in obtaining the guarantee, or if its cost would cause serious and irreparable damage.[618] In rendering such a decision, the President has a wide margin of discretion.[619] The requirements are strict. First, with regard to the merits of the

---

[613] European Commission Antitrust Manual of Procedures, Internal DG Competition working documents on procedures for the application of Articles 101 and 102 TFEU, March 2012, Module 25 'Follow-up of decisions', para 9.

[614] Article 89 of the Rules of Application ([2012] OJ L362/1). See also Note of Vice-President and Competition Commissioner Almunia and Budget Commissioner Lewandowski, 'Inability to pay under paragraph 35 of the 2006 Guidelines and payment conditions pre- and post-decision finding an infringement and imposing fines' Sec(2010)737, para 11: 'The second option would be not to reduce the amount of the fine but to grant deferred payment by instalments, unsecured by a bank guarantee for the amount that the company is currently unable to pay (this amount would then be paid in yearly instalments over a certain time period, normally not exceeding 3 to 5 years).' However, paras 12 and 13 stress that a fine reduction is the preferred option in cases of 'inability to pay', whereas deferred and unsecured payments will only be granted in exceptional circumstances; the same applies to a possible combination of the two options. In exceptional circumstances, it may also be possible for the undertaking to receive a deferred payment plan without bank guarantee after the decision has become definitive, in case no guarantee has been provided by that time. See ITP-Note, para 18(c).

[615] European Commission Antitrust Manual of Procedures, Internal DG Competition working documents on procedures for the application of Articles 101 and 102 TFEU, March 2012, Module 25 'Follow-up of decisions', para 10. The rejection of a post-decision request invoking inability to pay is done by administrative letter signed by the Director-General of DG COMP. So far, there is no clarification from the EU Courts as to whether such a letter would constitute a challengeable act.

[616] Article 91 of the Rules of Application ([2012] OJ L362/1). For an overview see European Commission Antitrust Manual of Procedures, Internal DG Competition working documents on procedures for the application of Articles 101 and 102 TFEU, March 2012, Module 25 'Follow-up of decisions', paras 14–24.

[617] For the procedure in this regard see European Commission Antitrust Manual of Procedures, Internal DG Competition working documents on procedures for the application of Articles 101 and 102 TFEU, March 2012, Module 25 'Follow-up of decisions', paras 11–13.

[618] For example, in *Cartonboard* the undertaking Cascades was ordered to guarantee 30 per cent of the fine immediately and the remainder within six months, while its appeal was pending. Case T-308/94 R *Cascades v Commission* [1995] ECR II-265. In *Prestressing Steel*, the President allowed the undertaking to pay in instalments, without any bank guarantee, pending its application in the main case. Order of 13 April 2011 in Case T-393/10 R *Westfälische Drahtindustrie and Others v Commission*. See also Case T-11/06 R *Romana Tabacchi v Commission* [2006] ECR II-2491; Order of 2 March 2011 in Case T-392/09 R *1. garantovaná v Commission*. Exceptionally, the undertaking may also request a waiver of the obligation to provide a bank guarantee from the Accounting Officer, either under the conditions of Article 89 of the Rules of Application ([2012] OJ L362/1), or based on a College decision if within three months of the notification of the decision it makes a request showing that the requirements under para 35 of the 2006 Guidelines are fulfilled. See Note of Vice President and Competition Commissioner Almunia and Budget Commissioner Lewandowski, 'Inability to pay under paragraph 35 of the 2006 Guidelines and payment conditions pre- and post-decision finding an infringement and imposing fines' Sec(2010)737, para 18(a). See also, para 18(b) for the possibility of a so-called 'post-decision ITP request'.

[619] Case T-9/99 *HFB and Others v Commission* [1999] ECR II-2429, para 25; Order of 2 March 2011 in Case T-392/09 R *1. garantovaná v Commission*, para 22.

main action, it must be clear that at least some pleas put forward are *prima facie* relevant and not entirely unfounded (*fumus boni iuris*).[620] Second, there must be a sufficient likelihood that the fulfillment of the obligation to provide a bank guarantee would lead to serious and irreparable harm (urgency).[621] It is for the applicant to present objective and reliable evidence in order to demonstrate that it cannot wait for the outcome of the main proceedings without suffering such harm. Finally, a suspension requires that the balance of interests at stake is in favour of granting that measure.[622] Urgency will only be assumed in exceptional circumstances,[623] in particular where it is objectively impossible for the undertaking to provide the bank guarantee, or where the requirement to provide a bank guarantee would jeopardize the undertaking's very existence.[624] In order to prove a risk for survival, the undertaking has to come forward with detailed and precise information, as well as documentary evidence, regarding its financial situation.[625] Depending on the circumstances of the case, in particular the financial situation of the undertaking, this may include letters from the banks rejecting the provision of a financial guarantee.[626] However, in order to assess its ability to provide the guarantee in question, account should also be taken of the group of undertakings to which it belongs directly or indirectly, as this can influence the possibility of providing the security which the banks will typically require.[627] This may even include

---

[620] Case T-395/94 R *Atlantic Container Line and Others v Commission* [1995] ECR II-595, para 49 (confirmed on appeal in Case C-149/95 P(R) *Commission v Atlantic Container Line and Others* [1995] ECR I-2165, paras 26 and 27). See also Case T-9/99 *HFB and Others v Commission* [1999] ECR II-2429, paras 26 and 27.

[621] Case T-9/99 *HFB and Others v Commission* [1999] ECR II-2429, paras 28 and 29; Case T-550/08 R *Tudapetrol v Commission* [2009] ECR II-92, para 19.

[622] Case T-104/95 *Tsimenta Chakidos v Commission* [1995] ECR II-2235, para 19; Case C-445/00 R *Austria v Council* [2001] ECR I-1461, para 73. See eg Case T-245/03 R *FNSEA and Others v Commission* [2004] ECR II-271, in particular, paras 119–30, where the President suspended the obligation on certain agricultural syndicates to provide a bank guarantee under very strict conditions based on a balance of interests. In this assessment, the fact that the applicant has raised particularly serious doubts as to the legality of the decision may be taken into account. See Case T-295/94 R *Buchmann v Commission* [1994] ECR II-1265, para 27.

[623] Case C-364/99 P(R) *DSR Senator Lines v Commission* [1999] ECR I-8733, para 48; Case T-9/99 *HFB and Others v Commission* [1999] ECR II-2429, para 17.

[624] Case C-361/00 P(R) *Cho Yang Shipping v Commission* [2000] ECR I-11657, para 88; Case T-199/08 R *Ziegler v Commission* [2009] ECR II-2, paras 44 and 45; Case T-30/10 R *Reagens v Commission* [2010] ECR II-83, para 43. See also Case T-9/99 R *HFB and Others v Commission* [1999] ECR II-2429, paras 34 and 38, stating that the mere risk that the parties concerned might be obliged to request the opening of insolvency proceedings as a consequence of the obligation to provide a bank guarantee does not as such demonstrate serious and irreversible damage; rather, evidence must be provided that liquidation is foreseeable with a sufficient degree of probability. See also Case T-295/94 R *Buchmann v Commission* [1994] ECR II-1265, para 23. It remains to be seen whether this case law still applies following the introduction of Art 89 of the Rules of Application ([2012] OJ L362/1) (which merely refers to a 'distressed situation').

[625] Case T-30/10 R *Reagens v Commission* [2010] ECR II-83, para 45.

[626] See eg T-9/99 R *HFB and Others v Commission* [1999] ECR II-2429, para 37; Case T-370/10 R *Rubinetterie Teorema v Commission* [2011] ECR II-9, para 36; Case T-392/09 R *1. garantovaná v Commission* [2011] ECR II-33, paras 63 and 64; Case T-393/10 R *Westfälische Drahtindustrie and Others v Commission* [2011] ECR II-1697, paras 29–35. In this regard, the Order of the President of 13 April 2011 in Case T-393/10 R *Westfälische Drahtindustrie* appears to have eased the burden on undertakings to show that they cannot obtain credit support from financial institutions, at least in the context of interim measures. The President of the GC rejected the Commission's arguments on the inherent alignment of interests between banks, shareholders, and companies in arguing the impossibility of receiving/granting support, and in particular allowed the undertaking to rely on refusal letters from banks in so far as the latter appeared to be sufficiently informed about the undertaking's financial situation (where this was reflected in the respective rejection letters). The requirements in this regard for the interim measures procedure have been further clarified in the Order of the President of the ECJ of 20 April 2012 in Case C-507/11 P(R) *Indústria de Fapricela v Commission*, para 36 et seq.

[627] Case T-301/94 R *Laakmann Karton v Commission* [1994] ECR II-1279, para 26; Case T-295/94 R *Buchmann v Commission* [1994] ECR II-1265, para 26; Case C-364/99 P(R) *DSR Senator Lines v Commission* [1999] ECR I-8733, para 49 et seq; Case T-199/08 R *Ziegler v Commission* [2009] ECR II-9, para 50 et seq (confirmed in Case C-113/09 P(R) *Ziegler v Commission* [2010] ECR I-50, para 44). Likewise, where the damage to an association of undertakings is at issue, the financial situation of its members must be taken into account where the objective interests of the association are not autonomous in relation to those of the

natural persons[628] and minority shareholders.[629] The President will not only look at the financial capacity of these companies or persons, but also assess whether their economic interests are aligned with those of the applicant.[630] The simple unilateral refusal of assistance by the principal shareholder does not, as such, preclude the financial situation of the group as a whole from being taken into account.[631]

As a general rule, the decision determines the amount of the fine payable by each undertaking for **11.87** its participation in the infringement covered by the procedure. Where the undertaking consists of several companies which are the addressees of the decision, the Commission has to determine the extent to which they are jointly and severally liable.[632] Moreover, in two judgments of March 2011, the GC concluded that the Commission also needs to determine the distribution of liability between those co-debtors.[633] The Commission has appealed these judgments, arguing that they disregard the fact that the object of the EU competition rules (including Article 23 of Regulation 1/2003) is the undertaking, not the legal entities of which it is composed. In the case of an association of undertakings, the Commission may also declare the joint and several liability of the association with its members.[634] Fine amounts form part of the EU's budgetary revenue as soon as the decision imposing them has become definitive; they reduce the contribution of the respective Member State to the EU budget.[635]

C. Periodic Penalty Payments

In accordance with Article 24(1) of Regulation 1/2003, the Commission may, by decision, **11.88** impose on undertakings periodic penalty payments not exceeding 5 per cent of the average daily

---

undertakings belonging to it (see Case C-268/96 P(R) *SCK and FNK v Commission* [1996] ECR I-4971, paras 35–8). The undertaking has to submit information for the group or otherwise risk that its application for interim measures is rejected. See Case T-385/10 R *ArcelorMittal Wire France v Commission* [2010] ECR II-262, para 53. It is not sufficient for the undertaking to claim that its banks (which have refused support) knew the financial situation of the company's shareholders. See Order of the President of the ECJ of 20 April 2012 in Case C-507/11 P(R) *Indústria de Fapricela v Commission*, paras 35, 67, and 68.

[628] Case T-550/08 R *Tudapetrol v Commission* [2009] ECR II-92, para 45.

[629] Case T-410/09 R *Almamet v Commission* [2010] ECR II-80, para 57 (confirmed in Case C-373/10 P(R) *Almamet v Commission* [2010] ECR I-171, para 17 et seq); Case T-393/10 R *Westfälische Drahtindustrie and Others v Commission* [2011] ECR II-1697, para 38.

[630] This is unlikely to be the case where a minority shareholder belongs to another group of companies which competes with the applicant: Case T-393/10 R *Westfälische Drahtindustrie and Others v Commission* [2011] ECR II-1697, para 40.

[631] Case C-364/99 P(R) *DSR Senator Lines v Commission* [1999] ECR I-8733, para 54. See also Case T-385/10 R *ArcelorMittal Wire France v Commission* [2010] ECR II-262, para 40.

[632] See Joined Cases T-122/07 to T-124/07 *Siemens Österreich and VA Tech Transmission & Distribution v Commission* [2011] ECR II-793, paras 149–54. For the relationship between parent company and subsidiary see Case T-405/06 *ArcelorMittal Luxembourg and Others v Commission* [2009] ECR II-789, paras 115–17. On the concept of joint and several liability of the undertaking in EU law, see A Böhlke, 'Die gesamtschuldnerische Verantwortlichkeit im EU-Wettbewerbsrecht', EuZW 20/2011, 781–4.

[633] Joined Cases T-122/07 to T-124/07 *Siemens Österreich and VA Tech Transmission & Distribution v Commission* [2011] ECR II-793, paras 122, 153, and 156–7 (appealed in Case C-231/11 P *Commission v Siemens Österreich and Others*), and in Joined Cases T-117/07 and T-121/07 *Areva and Others v Commission* [2011] ECR II-633, para 214. See also Judgment of 16 November 2011 in Case T-54/06 *Kendrion v Commission*, para 96.

[634] See eg Joined Cases T-339/94, T-340/94, T-341/94 and T-342/94 *Metsä-Serla and Others v Commission* [1998] ECR II-1727, para 41 et seq. However, it should be noted that in the Court's view 'Finnboard in practice formed an economic unit with each of its cartonboard-producing member companies' (para 58). See also the ECJ's assessment on appeal in Case C-294/98 P *Metsä-Serla and Others v Commission* [2000] ECR I-10065, paras 27 and 36.

[635] Article 83 of the Financial Regulation ([2012] OJ L298/1). See Case T-171/99 *Corus v Commission* [2001] ECR II-2967, para 30; MEMO/06/256 'Competition: revised Commission Guidelines for setting

turnover in the preceding business year[636] per day. Unlike for fines, in order to impose periodic penalty payments the Commission does not have to show that the undertaking acted intentionally or negligently. There are two stages in the imposition of periodic penalty payments, at each of which the Commission adopts a decision: (i) the initial decision announcing that it will impose such payments in case the addressee does not comply with specific duties within a certain time frame, and setting a maximum amount of such payments for each day of delay;[637] and (ii) the decision on the final amount of the payment, which may be below the sum which would follow from the initial decision in view of the actual delay (see Article 24(2) of Regulation 1/2003[638]). While the initial decision is merely a preparatory act which is not directly challengeable,[639] the decision on the final amount constitutes an enforceable title pursuant to Article 299 TFEU against which the addressee may bring an annullment action.

11.89 The first stage of the procedure may coincide both with decisions intended to ensure compliance with procedural rules (periodic penalty payments in the event of delay in supplying the information requested by decision,[640] or for each day of non-compliance in the case of inspections) and with substantive decisions (periodic penalty payments imposed in order to compel undertakings to comply with (i) a decision ordering to put an end to an infringement of Article 101 or 102 TFEU; (ii) a decision ordering interim measures pursuant to Article 8 of Regulation 1/2003; or (iii) a commitment made binding by a decision pursuant to Article 9 of Regulation 1/2003). However, the Commission may also, in the case of both procedural and substantive infringements, initiate proceedings for the imposition of periodic penalty payments separately from, and at a later stage than, the decisions with which they are associated. Where obligations are attached to an infringement decision, the Commission may impose periodic penalty payments for each obligation of which it seeks to ensure fulfilment, as long as it complies with the principle of proportionality. The second stage of the procedure (imposition of the final penalty) starts with the issuing of a statement of objections. This does not presuppose that the infringement has already ended, as long as the Commission clearly identifies in the statement of objections the conduct complained of, and in the final decision only takes into consideration facts on which the undertaking had the opportunity to comment.[641]

11.90 No guidelines exist for determining the level of the penalty payment.[642] However, it seems obvious that it needs to be fixed at an amount which provides sufficient financial incentives

---

fines in antitrust cases—frequently asked questions' of 26 June 2006, stating that the amount of the fines will be paid into the EU Budget. The fines therefore help to finance the EU and reduce the tax burden on individuals.

[636] This requires dividing the overall turnover of the undertaking during the last business year by the number of calender days (not: working days) in that year.

[637] In most cases the Commission sets a fixed percentage of turnover (or absolute amount) for each day of delay. However, in one case the Commission threatened penalty payments of 'up to 5%'. See Commission Decision of 14 June 2011 in Case COMP/39.736 *Siemens/Areva*.

[638] The wording of Art 24 of Reg 1/2003 is somewhat misleading: the Commission may impose a lower amount than originally foreseen even where the undertaking's failure to comply continues. For a case where the undertaking had in the meantime complied, see Commission Decision of 15 March 1991 in Case IV/33.300 *Baccarat*, paras 10 and 11.

[639] Joined Cases 46/87 and 22/88 *Hoechst v Commission* [1989] ECR 2859, para 55; Case T-596/97 *Dalmine v Commission* [1998] ECR II-2383, paras 30–2 and 36. However, as the first decision constitutes a necessary step to be taken prior to the second decision fixing the final amount of the penalty, the review of the legality of the first decision may be part of the assessment of the second decision when that decision is challenged.

[640] Article 18(3) of Reg 1/2003: 'Where the Commission requires undertakings and associations of undertakings to supply information by decision, it shall... indicate or impose the penalties provided for in Article 24.' Informal requests for information pursuant to Art 18(2) of Reg 1/2003 are not compulsory and therefore cannot be enforced by way of penalty payments.

[641] Judgment of 27 June 2012 in Case T-167/08 *Microsoft v Commission*, para 186.

[642] However, the GC has provided some guidance in its judgment in Microsoft. See Judgment of 27 June 2012 in Case T-167/08 *Microsoft v Commission*, para 220.

for the addressee to comply. Hence, the Commission will consider the economic situation and financial strength of the undertaking.[643] Where it shall be compelled to comply with substantive requirements, it may also be relevant to consider what benefits the undertaking might draw from not fulfilling its duties.[644] Furthermore, the importance of the failure to comply (eg the consequences for competition on the market and/or for customers; the consequences for the success of the investigation) will be taken into account.[645] Other elements can also play a role, for instance the particular length of non-compliance,[646] or any other factors showing intent or gross negligence.[647] In the *Microsoft* case, the Commission did not consider as relevant the company's claim that it had (unsuccessfully) attempted to comply with the decision.[648] Under Regulation 17, due to the low amounts involved and the very nature of periodic penalty payments—which are almost always imposed in cases where undertakings obstruct the Commission procedures—the amount was frequently the maximum daily figure.[649]

Microsoft is the first case under Regulation 1/2003 in which the Commission has imposed a penalty payment under Article 24(1)(a). Aside from sanctioning Microsoft's past abusive behaviour, in its March 2004 decision[650] the Commission also ordered Microsoft to produce complete and accurate documentation containing specifications on its products, so that the servers developed by Microsoft's competitors could eventually interoperate freely with the Windows environment. This technical documentation was to be provided within 120 days. Subsequently, in November 2005, the Commission set a new deadline (15 December 2005) combined with penalty payments of EUR 2 million per day in case of non-compliance.[651] In July 2006 it then fixed the definitive amount of the penalty payment for the period 16 December 2005 until 20 June 2006 at EUR 280.5 million. At the same time, that decision increased the penalty payments to EUR 3 million per day.[652] Finally, on 27 February 2008 the Commission fixed a further definitive amount of the penalty payment for the period 21 June 2006 to 21 October 2007 at EUR 899 million.[653]

11.91

---

[643] See eg *IMA Rules* [1980] OJ L318/1. See also Joined Cases 100–103/80 *Musique Diffusion Française v Commission* [1983] ECR 1825, para 120; Case T-48/98 *Acerinox v Commission* [2001] ECR II-3859, paras 89 and 90 (for the relevance of the size and economic strength of the undertaking in the determination of fines).

[644] See eg Commission Decision of 10 November 2005 in Case COMP/37.792 *Microsoft*, para 202; Commission Decision of 12 July 2006 in Case COMP/37.792 *Microsoft*, para 242; Commission Decision of 27 February 2008 in Case COMP/37.792 *Microsoft*, paras 293 and 294.

[645] See eg *Hasselblad* [1982] OJ L161/18; Commission Decision of 10 November 2005 in Case COMP/37.792 *Microsoft*, paras 197 and 198; Commission Decision of 12 July 2006 in Case COMP/37.792 *Microsoft*, paras 242 and 247.

[646] Commission Decision of 12 July 2006 in Case COMP/37.792 *Microsoft*, paras 247 and 248; Commission Decision of 27 February 2008 in Case COMP/37.792 *Microsoft*, paras 291–2.

[647] Generally, the mere existence of doubts as to the legality of the decision does not justify non-compliance as the undertaking may seek judicial review (which does not have suspensory effect). See Joined Cases 46/87 and 22/88 *Hoechst v Commission* [1989] ECR 2859, paras 62–5.

[648] Commission Decision of 27 February 2008 in Case COMP/37.792 *Microsoft*, para 295. However, the Commission nevertheless took into account that, from a certain moment onwards, Microsoft had taken measures (reduction of fees) which limited the effects of the infringing behaviour (para 296).

[649] See *Commercial Solvents* [1972] OJ L299/51 (Art 4); *ECS/Akzo* [1985] OJ L374/1 (Art 6) (ECU 1,000).

[650] Commission Decision of 24 March 2004 in Case COMP/37.792 *Microsoft* (largely confirmed in Case T-201/04 *Microsoft v Commission* [2007] ECR II-3601).

[651] Commission Decision of 10 November 2005 in Case COMP/37.792 *Microsoft*.

[652] Commission Decision of 12 July 2006 in Case COMP/37.792 *Microsoft*. In technical terms, the original decision of 27 February 2008 was amended as concerns the level of the periodic penalty payments.

[653] Commission Decision of 27 February 2008 in Case COMP/37.792 *Microsoft* (largely confirmed by the Judgment of 27 June 2012 in Case T-167/08 *Microsoft v Commission*).

12

REJECTION OF COMPLAINTS

Manuel Kellerbauer, Luis Ortiz Blanco, and Konstantin Jörgens

A. Introduction

Procedures can be commenced by a formal complaint.[1] It is also possible that the Commission **12.01** initiates a procedure *ex officio* with regard to conduct that is the subject of a complaint at a later stage.[2] In both cases, the procedure may conclude as requested by the complainants with a decision finding an infringement of Articles 101 and 102 of the Treaty on the Functioning of the European Union ('TFEU'), or else with a rejection of the complaint.[3] In some cases, a procedure to establish the existence of an infringement following a complaint may give rise to a decision rendering commitments binding pursuant to Article 9 of Regulation 1/2003, a finding of inapplicability decision pursuant to Article 10 Regulation 1/2003, or possibly an informal settlement[4] between the undertakings complained of and the Commission, as

---

[1] For the difference between unofficial or informal and official or formal complaints, see Ch 5, 'Opening of the File and of Proceedings: Transparency', para 5.42. The term complainants is used only for formal complainants, since proceedings initiated in response to an unofficial or informal complaint are, for administrative purposes, deemed to be procedures commenced on the Commission's own initiative in which the complainants do not play a role or do not have the rights of a formal complainant.

[2] See Joined Cases T-213/01 and T-214/01 *Österreichische Postsparkasse v Commission* [2006] ECR II-1601, para 91 et seq; Joined Cases T-259/02 to T-264/02, T-271/02 *Raiffeisen Zentralbank v Commission* [2006] ECR II-5169, para 96. The General Court ('GC') held that for the purposes of recognition of status as a complainant it is not required that the complaint in question forms the basis for the Commission opening an infringement proceeding.

[3] The Commission must define its position regarding all the alleged infringements that the complainants have referred to it. The Commission may determine which legal basis for a complaint is best suited for resolving a competition matter, but if a complainant relies both on Arts 101 and 102 TFEU, the Commission cannot be regarded as having satisfied its demands when it acts on the basis of only one of those provisions. See Case T-74/92 *Ladbroke Racing (Deutschland) GmbH v Commission* [1995] ECR II-115, paras 60–1, replying to the arguments of the Commission in paras 50–1. See also Case T-548/93 *Ladbroke Racing Limited v Commission* [1995] ECR II-2565, paras 50–1.

[4] By contrast, settlements pursuant to Art 10a of Reg 773/2004 will usually result in a Commission decision establishing and penalizing the infringement complained of.

a result of which the complainant may be discontented if the result does not, or does not fully, respond to his concerns.[5] In these cases, a rejection of the complaint is also necessary where the complainant continues to pursue his complaint.[6] The procedure for the rejection of complaint should then be done in parallel with the Article 9 or Article 10 of the decision procedure.[7]

12.02 Upon receipt of a complaint the Commission can choose one of the following options:

(i) to initiate proceedings for examining the existence of a breach of Article 101(1) and/or Article 102 TFEU; or

(ii) to dismiss the complaint after having sent the complainant a letter under Article 7(1) of Regulation 773/2004[8] with or without a formal decision,[9] either on the ground of lack of EU interest[10] or for other reasons.

Initiating proceedings does not prevent the Commission from changing its mind at a later stage and from rejecting the complaint after the proceedings have commenced.

B. The Treatment of Complaints

12.03 The Commission is required to

examine carefully the factual and legal particulars brought to its notice by the complainant in order to decide whether they disclose conduct of such a kind as to distort competition in the [Internal] Market and affect trade between Member States.[11]

The Commission is required to consider attentively all the matters of fact and of law which the complainant brings to its attention.[12] Nevertheless, the Commission is not obliged to investigate all the complaints it receives.[13] The General Court ('GC') considers that 'setting priorities within the limits prescribed by the law' is 'an inherent feature of administrative activity',[14] so that the Commission may give priority to certain complaints, which will indeed be investigated, and reject others without having taken any specific investigative measures. This results from the task assigned to the Commission of ensuring application of Articles 101 and 102 TFEU and

---

[5] Whilst the commitments rendered binding in a decision pursuant to Art 9 of Reg 1/2003 can respond to the complainant's expectations, the complainant might as well hope for a decision finding an infringement of Arts 101 and/or 102 TFEU in order to facilitate private litigation.

[6] See para 12.20.

[7] European Commission Antitrust Manual of Procedures, Internal DG Competition working documents on procedures for the application of Articles 101 and 102 TFEU, March 2012, Module 21 'Handling of complaint', para 65.

[8] This is the equivalent of former Art 6 of Reg 99/63 and of Reg 2842/98 (repealed).

[9] See para 12.23.

[10] See para 12.15 et seq.

[11] See Case T-24/90 *Automec v Commission II* [1992] ECR II-2223, para 79; Joined Cases T-189/95, T-39/96, and T-123/96 *Service pour le groupement d'acquisitions (SGA) v Commission* [1999] ECR II-3587, para 53; Case T-575/93 *Koelman v Commission* [1996] ECR II-1, para 39, confirmed on appeal by Case C-59/96 P *Koelman v Commission* [1997] ECR I-4809; Case T-432/05 *EMC Development v* Commission [2010] ECR II-1629, para 59.

[12] Case 210/81 *Schmidt v Commission* [1983] ECR 3045, para 19; Case 298/83 *CICCE v Commission* [1985] ECR 1105, para 18; Joined Cases 142/84 and 156/84 *British American Tobacco and Reynolds Industries v Commission* [1987] ECR 4487, para 20; Case C-119/97 *Union française de l'express (Ufex) and others v Commission* [1999] ECR I-1341, para 86; and Case C-449/98 *International Express Carriers Conference (IECC) v Commission* [2001] ECR I-3875, para 45.

[13] Case T-24/90 *Automec v Commission II* [1992] ECR II-2223, para 76 et seq.

[14] See Case T-24/90 *Automec v Commission II* [1992] ECR II-2223, para 77; Case C-119/97 P *Ufex and others v Commission* [1999] ECR I-1341, para 88; Case T-219/99 *British Airways v Commission* [2003] ECR II-5917, para 68.

its responsibility for defining and implementing effectively the orientation of EU competition policy.[15] Regulations 1/2003 and 773/2004 do not contain express provisions relating to the action to be taken concerning the substance of a complaint, and any obligations on the part of the Commission to carry out an investigation. The EU Courts held that the Commission is under no obligation to initiate procedures to establish possible infringements of EU law and that the rights conferred on complainants by those regulations do not include the right to obtain a final decision as to the existence or non-existence of the alleged infringement.[16] Also the notice on the handling of complaints highlights that the Commission has limited resources and must therefore set priorities, in accordance with the principles set out at paragraphs 41 to 45 thereof.[17]

Whilst the Commission may not reject a complaint without undertaking a detailed exami- **12.04**
nation of its contents, it is not obliged to initiate proceedings[18] and to investigate the case by, for example, making requests for information and carrying out inspections. Moreover, to reject a complaint on the ground that the conduct complained of does not infringe the EU competition rules or does not fall within their scope of application, the Commission is not obliged to take into account circumstances that have not been brought to its attention by the complainant and that it could only have uncovered by the investigation of the case.[19] However, once the Commission has decided to investigate a case, it must do so carefully, seriously, and diligently so as to enable it to appraise, in full knowledge of the circumstances, the matters of fact and of law which the complainants have referred to it for consideration.[20]

The Commission is required, where appropriate, to inform the complainants of the reasons **12.05**
why it considers that the information gathered by it does not justify upholding the complaint and to allow them a period within which to submit any observations in writing, in accord-ance with Article 7(1) of Regulation 773/2004. The notice on the handling of complaints establishes that the statement of reasons must disclose in a clear and unequivocal fashion the reasoning followed by the Commission in such a way as to enable the complainant to ascertain the reasons for the decision and to enable the competent EU Court to exercise its power of review. However, the Commission is not obliged to adopt a position on all the argu-ments relied on by the complainant in support of its complaint. It only needs to set out the facts and legal considerations, which are of decisive importance in the context of the decision.[21] The Commission is obliged to carry out an investigation or take a final decision on the existence of the alleged infringement only if the complaint is within its jurisdiction.[22]

---

[15] Case T-77/95 *RV Union française de l'express (Ufex) and others v Commission* [2000] ECR II-2167, para 39.

[16] Order of the Court in Case C-367/10 P *EMC Development AB* [2011] ECR I-46, para 73; Case C-119/97 P *Ufex and Others v Commission* [1999] ECR I-1341, para 87; Case C-449/98 P *IECC v Commission* [2001] ECR I-3875, para 35; Case T-432/05 *EMC Development v Commission* [2010] ECR II-1629, para 57.

[17] Commission Notice on the handling of complaints [2004] OJ C101/65.

[18] Article 2(4) of Reg 773/2004.

[19] See Commission Notice on the handling of complaints [2004] OJ C101/65, para 47.

[20] In the absence of the requisite care, integrity, and diligence, a rejection decision following an investiga-tion carried out incorrectly would be annulled. See Case T-7/92 *Asia Motor France v Commission II* [1993] ECR II-669. See in the same sense Case T-319/99 *Federación Nacional de Empresas de Instrumentación Científica, Médica, Técnica y Dental (FENIN) v Commission* [2003] ECR II-357, para 43: 'the Commission is not required, when considering a complaint, to examine facts which have not been brought to its notice by the complainant before rejecting a complaint on the ground that the practices complained of do not infringe [EU] competition rules or do not fall within the scope of the [EU] competition rules…An applicant bringing an action against a decision of the Commission rejecting its complaint in a competition matter can-not, therefore, criticise the Commission for failing to take account of facts which it has not brought to the Commission's attention and which the Commission could only have discovered by investigation.'

[21] Commission Notice on the handling of complaints [2004] OJ C101/65, para 75.

[22] Regarding the Commission's obligations deriving from its exclusive powers, see Case T-24/90 *Automec v Commission II* [1992] ECR II-2223, para 75.

12.06   Having followed the rejection procedure, the complainant is entitled to obtain a formal decision from the Commission on its complaint.[23] However, the Commission is not required to
adopt a decision compelling undertakings to bring an infringement to an end, once it has been
found to exist, since Article 7 of Regulation 1/2003 indicates that the Commission *may* adopt
such a decision.[24] Sometimes part of a complaint triggers a Commission investigation, while
the remainder is not followed up on, for example for lack of EU interest. If the 'remainder' is
a separate alleged infringement, it will in principle be treated as a complaint in its own right
and may hence need to be rejected separately. Before such a 'partial rejection', the Commission
will usually contact the complainant and verify whether the complainant is willing partially to
withdraw the complaint.[25]

C. Reasons for Rejecting Complaints

12.07   The main reasons for which the Commission may reject a complaint after the prescribed detailed
examination of its content are: (i) lack of a legitimate interest on the part of the complainant for
lodging a complaint;[26] (ii) lack of substantiation provided by the complainant as to the existence
of the alleged infringement; (iii) lack of evidence found during the investigation for the existence
of an infringement; (iv) lack of any connection with Articles 101 and 102 TFEU; (v) the applicability of an individual[27] or block exemption; (vi) the fact that a national competition authority
('NCA') is dealing or has already dealt with the same case; and—most importantly—(vii) the
lack of any EU interest in the matter complained of.[28] Another obvious reason for rejecting a
complaint after a preliminary examination, which will not be considered in detail here, is the fact
that the complainant has again raised the same issue without adducing fresh evidence, after its
first complaint was definitively rejected.[29]

---

[23] See Commission Notice on the handling of complaints [2004] OJ C101/65, para 28. Case C-282/95 P
Guérin Automobiles v Commission [1997] ECR I-1503, para 36; Case T-77/95 RV *Union française de l'express
(Ufex) and others v Commission* [2000] ECR II-2167, para 37: 'complainants are entitled to have the fate of
their complaint settled by a decision of the Commission against which an action may be brought'; T-127/98
UPS Europe SA v Commission [1999] ECR II-2633, para 36: 'when a complainant has submitted his observations on the notification under [Art 7 of Reg 773/2004], the Commission is required either to initiate a
procedure against the person who is the subject of the complaint or to adopt a definitive decision rejecting
the complaint, which may be the subject of an action for annulment before the [EU Courts]'; Case C-282/95
P *Guérin Automobiles v Commission* [1997] ECR I-1503, para 36.
[24] Case C-449/98 *International Express Carriers Conference (IECC) v Commission* [2001] ECR I-3875,
para 35 in which the Court of Justice ('ECJ') states that Art 3 of Reg 17 [now Art 7 of Reg 1/2003] does not
give a person making an application under that Article the right to insist that the Commission take a final
decision as to the existence or non-existence of the alleged infringement and does not oblige the Commission
to continue the proceedings, whatever the circumstances, right up to the stage of a final decision.
[25] European Commission Antitrust Manual of Procedures, Internal DG Competition working documents
on procedures for the application of Articles 101 and 102 TFEU, March 2012, Module 21 'Handling of
complaint', para 55.
[26] See also Commission Notice on the handling of complaints [2004] OJ C101/65 paras 33–40.
[27] Decisions adopted pursuant to Art 81(3) EC (now Article 101(3) TFEU) remain valid until they expire.
See Art 43(1) of Reg 1/2003.
[28] See also Commission Notice on the handling of complaints [2004] OJ C101/65 paras 41–5.
[29] Commission Notice on the handling of complaints [2004] OJ C101/65 para 79. Opinion of AG Alber
in Joined Cases C-172/01 P, C-175/01 P, C-176/01 P, and C-180/01 P *International Power plc, British Coal
Corporation, PowerGen (UK) plc and Commission v National Association of Licensed Opencast Operators* [2003]
ECR I-11421 para 99: 'If the complainant then lodges a fresh complaint which does not contain any significant new facts, the Commission is not obliged to re-examine the matter. Its rejection of the complaint on that
ground is merely confirmation of the earlier decision and cannot be challenged.'

1. Lack of a legitimate interest to lodge a complaint[30]

Pursuant to Article 5 of Regulation 773/2004, natural and legal persons shall show a 'legiti-   **12.08**
mate interest' in order to be entitled to lodge a complaint for the purposes of Article 7 of
Regulation 1/2003.[31] Where a natural person or legal entity lodging a complaint is unable to
demonstrate a legitimate interest, the Commission is entitled not to pursue the complaint.[32]
The complainant must set out in its written complaint the reasons justifying its legitimate
interest,[33] complying with Form C that is annexed to Regulation 773/2004. It is not sufficient to make a general allegation that the person concerned considers itself adversely affected
by the alleged infringement. The Commission is obliged to investigate the complainant's
legitimate interest[34] and may ascertain whether this condition is met at any stage of the
investigation.[35] It should not be concluded, however, that a decision finding an infringement under Article 7(1) of Regulation 1/2003 would be unfounded if the procedure had
been initiated in response to a complaint from a person lacking a legitimate interest within
the meaning of Article 7(2), since the Commission, under Article 7(1), is entitled to commence infringement proceedings on its own initiative, without any outside intervention.[36]
It could use information obtained from a complainant without a legitimate interest in order
to initiate or advance proceedings. If a complainant does not have a legitimate interest, it
would nevertheless be regarded as an informant or, possibly, an informal complainant with
limited procedural rights. The Court has drawn attention to the relationship between Article
7(2) of Regulation 1/2003 and Article 263 TFEU, taking the view that a complainant may,
under the fourth paragraph of Article 263 TFEU, bring an action for the annulment of an
individual exemption decision in favour of agreements complained of by him.[37]

Neither Regulation 1/2003 nor Regulation 773/2004 define the concept of 'legitimate inter-   **12.09**
est' referred to in Article 7(2) of Regulation 1/2003 (formerly Article 3(2)(b) of Regulation
17). The Commission has interpreted it as requiring that the complainant must be adversely
affected by the alleged infringement, since otherwise its legitimate interests would not be

---

[30] As will be seen later, in the EU competition law context, the terms 'interest' and 'legitimate interest'
are *sui generis* and may have little in common with similar expressions used in any of the national laws of the
Member States.

[31] According to the European Commission Antitrust Manual of Procedures, Internal DG Competition
working documents on procedures for the application of Articles 101 and 102 TFEU, March 2012, Module
13 'Right to be heard', para 4, there are two conditions for a person to qualify as a complainant in antitrust
proceedings. First, such person must file a formal complaint pursuant to Art 5(1) of Reg 773/2004. Second,
the person must have a legitimate interest.

[32] Commission Notice on the handling of complaints [2004] OJ C101/65 para 40.

[33] Article 7 (2) of Reg 1/2003, Art 5 (1) of Reg 773/2004. See also Commission Notice on the handling
of complaints [2004] OJ C101/65 para 40.

[34] See Joined Cases T-213/01 and T-214/01 *Österreichische Postsparkasse AG v Commission* [2006] ECR
II-1601, paras 124 and 134–6.

[35] Joined Cases T-133/95 and T-204/95 *International Express Carriers Conference (IECC) v Commission*
[1998] ECR II-3645 para 79.

[36] See Joined Cases 32/78 and 36/78 to 82/78 *BMW Belgium v Commission* [1979] ECR 2435, para 18.

[37] See Case 26/76 *Metro v Commission I* [1977] ECR 1875, para 13. In Case 75/84 *Metro v Commission
II* [1986] ECR 3021, paras 20–3, the Court went even further and established a link between the fourth para
of Art 263 TFEU (then the second para of Art 173 EC) and Art 19(3) of Reg 17 (see now Art 27(4) of Reg
1/2003), placing on the same footing the 'interested third parties' referred to in the latter provision and the
'natural or legal persons who claim a legitimate interest' referred to in Art 3(2)(b) of Reg 17 (now Art 7(2)
of Reg 1/2003). In the Court's opinion, proof that Metro was a person 'directly and individually' concerned
by a decision by which the Commission renewed an individual exemption for SABA derived from the fact
that Metro had submitted observations after the publication prescribed by Art 19(3) of Reg 17. The Court
stated that: '[t]he Commission recognized that Metro had a legitimate interest in submitting its observations
in accordance with Article 19(3) of Regulation 17', thereby assimilating 'interested third parties' to 'natural
or legal persons who claim a legitimate interest'.

affected. Only Member States are deemed to have legitimate interest for all complaints they choose to lodge.[38] According to the Commission's Notice on the handling of complaints[39] and the Antitrust Manual of Procedure,[40] the following are considered, in principle, to have a legitimate interest:

- undertakings can claim a legitimate interest where they are operating in the relevant product market or where the conduct complained of is liable to directly and adversely affect their interests;[41]
- An association entitled to represent the interests of its members can claim a legitimate interest, provided that the conduct complained of is liable to adversely affect the members' interests;[42]
- consumer associations can lodge complaints with the Commission;[43]
- individual consumers are considered to be in a position to show a legitimate interest when their economic interests have been harmed or are likely to be harmed as a result of the restriction of competition in question;[44]
- local or regional public authorities may be able to show a legitimate interest in their capacity as buyers or users of goods or services affected by the conduct complained of.

2. Lack of substantiation

12.10 There may be cases where a natural or legal person shows a sufficient 'legitimate interest' in order to be entitled to lodge a complaint, whilst providing wholly insufficient evidence in support of the claim that EU competition law has been infringed. An admissible complaint may be rejected for lack of substantiation, when it fails to submit even a minimum of *prima facie* evidence necessary to substantiate one or several conditions for an infringement of Articles 101 or 102 TFEU.[45] In such cases, there is no need for the Directorate-General for Competition

---

[38] Article 7(2) of Reg 1/2003; Commission Notice on the handling of complaints [2004] OJ C101/65, para 33.

[39] Commission Notice on the handling of complaints [2004] OJ C101/65, paras 34–40.

[40] European Commission Antitrust Manual of Procedures, Internal DG Competition working documents on procedures for the application of Articles 101 and 102 TFEU, March 2012 Module 21 'Handling of complaint', para 6.

[41] This confirms the established practice of the Commission according to which a legitimate interest can, for instance, be claimed by the parties to the agreement or practice which is the subject of the complaint, by competitors whose *interests* have allegedly been damaged by the behaviour complained of or by undertakings excluded from a distribution system. Cf Commission Notice on the handling of complaints [2004] OJ C101/65 para 36.

[42] Case T-114/92 *Bureau Européen des Médias et de l'Industrie Musicale (BEMIM) v Commission* [1995] ECR II-147, para 28. Associations of undertakings were also the complainants in the cases underlying the judgments in Case 298/83 *Comité des industries cinématographiques des Communautés européennes (CICCE) v Commission* [1985] ECR 1105 and Case T-319/99 *Federación Nacional de Empresas de Instrumentación Científica, Médica, Técnica y Dental (FENIN) v Commission* [2003] ECR II-357; see also Joined Cases T-213 and 214/01 *Österreichische Postsparkasse v Commission* [2006] ECR II-1601 (*Austrian Banks*), para 112.

[43] Case T-37/92 *Bureau Européen des Unions des Consommateurs (BEUC) v Commission* [1994] ECR II-285, para 36. However, according to Recital 11 of Regulation 773/2004, consumer associations that apply to be heard as a third party should generally be regarded as having a sufficient interest only 'where the proceedings concern products or services used by the end-consumer or products or services that constitute a direct inputs into such products or services'. The rationale for this requirement also applies to the 'legitimate interest' that consumer associations need to show in order to lodge a complaint.

[44] See Joined Cases T-213/01 and T-214/01 *Österreichische Postsparkasse AG v Commission* [2006] ECR II-1601, paras 114–17 and 131. The question was raised in a procedure before the GC regarding the legitimate interest of a political party whose members were likely to be affected in the *Austrian Banks* case. The Commission has also accepted as complainant an individual consumer in *Greek Ferries* [1999] OJ L109/24 para 1.

[45] Case 298/83 *Comité des industries cinématographiques des Communautés européennes (CICCE) v Commission* [1985] ECR 1105, para 21–4 et seq; Case T-198/98 *Micro Leader Business v Commission* [1999] ECR II-3989, para 32 et seq.

('DG COMP') to inform associated or concerned Directorate-Generals within the Commission. The so-called 'Article 7 letter' (pre-rejection letter) and a later rejection decision will be carefully worded and point out why the complaint fails to provide a minimum of indications of a competition law infringement.[46]

3. Unfounded complaints

Even where a complainant provides sufficient evidence for the Commission to initiate an investi-   **12.11**
gation, the complaint may be rejected as unfounded where, during the investigation, insufficient evidence has been obtained to substantiate it. Where an infringement has not been proved, there is no alternative but to reject the complaint (rejection on factual grounds).[47] Similarly, a complaint may be rejected where, after sufficient evidence has been obtained, the conduct is found not to be contrary to Articles 101 and 102 TFEU.[48] In the absence of an infringement, the complaint must be rejected (rejection on legal grounds).

4. Complaints having no connection with Articles 101 and 102 TFEU

Sometimes DG COMP receives complaints from individuals which relate to conduct uncon-   **12.12**
nected with Articles 101 and 102 TFEU. Thus, complaints may be made concerning particular situations which are not the responsibility of the undertakings,[49] or one undertaking may complain about another on the ground that the latter is taking action which is more properly described as unfair competition[50] and is in principle a matter for the competent national courts or authorities, rather than the Commission.[51] Alternatively, an undertaking may incorrectly approach DG COMP to raise a matter which should be dealt with by other departments of the Commission, using different legal instruments from those used by DG COMP. In this case DG COMP will on its own initiative refer the matter to the Secretariat General of the Commission for allocation, or else directly to the competent department of the Commission, informing the

---

[46] See European Commission Antitrust Manual of Procedures, Internal DG Competition working documents on procedures for the application of Articles 101 and 102 TFEU, March 2012, Module 21 'Handling of complaint', para 55.

[47] European Commission Antitrust Manual of Procedures, Internal DG Competition working documents on procedures for the application of Articles 101 and 102 TFEU, March 2012, Module 21 'Handling of complaint', para 41.

[48] For example in Case COMP/A36.568 *Scandlines v Port of Helsingborg* and Case COMP/A36.570 *Sundbusserne v Port of Helsingborg*, Commission Decision of 23 July 2004, the Commission came to the conclusion that the available evidence was insufficient to demonstrate to the requisite legal standard that the prices at issue were excessive. These two parallel complaints related to alleged abuses within the meaning of Art 82 EC [now Art 102 TFEU] involving excessive port fees.

[49] Such as, eg, national regulations on prices, entry into the market, etc in particular sectors. For a rejection of a complaint based on the existence of national restrictive rules, see *Ijsselcentrale and others* [1991] OJ L28/32, and Case T-16/91 *Rendo v Commission I* [1992] ECR II-2417, para 42 et seq. It should be borne in mind, however, that EU law does not allow national rules that reinforce pre-existing restrictive agreements between undertakings, even though such agreements may appear in principle to pursue laudable aims, such as combating unfair competition. In that connection, *inter alia*, see Case 311/85 *Vlaamse Reisbureaus (VVR) v Sociale Dienst* [1987] ECR 3801.

[50] Regarding 'unfair competition', it is interesting to observe that sometimes agreements between undertakings designed to eliminate such competition may simply be disguised cartels—as in the case of the agreements between Flemish travel agents, which gave rise to *Vlaamse Reisbureaus (VVR) v Sociale Dienst*, cited in n 49. Allegedly unfair competition on the part of two German agencies also gave rise to the judgment in Case 66/86 *Ahmed Saeed and another v ZBW* [1989] ECR 803.

[51] An example might be misleading advertising or any other typical act of unfair competition. The fact that EU competition law does not in principle deal with such issues does not mean that, in particular circumstances, certain unfair conduct cannot be dealt with under Arts 101 and 102 TFEU. For instance, reference can be made to Case T-321/05, *AstraZeneca v Commission* [2010] ECR II-2805, para 377, where the GC held that representations made to public authorities with a view to unlawfully obtaining exclusive rights can constitute an abuse within the meaning of Art 102 TFEU.

complainants that it has done so.[52] More generally, there may be complaints concerning matters clearly outside the scope of the EU antitrust provisions, which strictly speaking cannot be regarded as complaints within the meaning of Article 7(2) of Regulation 1/2003.[53] Since the Commission has no power to act upon this type of complaint, the communication to the complainant informing it of the steps taken on the complaint does not constitute a decision which may be subject to an action before the GC. If a matter brought before the Commission falls outside the terms of reference of the EU competition authorities, in that it does not fulfil the requirements of Articles 101 and 102 TFEU (in particular as regards effects on trade between Member States), the Commission may raise the issue within the European Competition Network ('ECN')[54] and advise the complainants to invoke national competition law and to approach the relevant authorities for its application.

5. Exempt agreements

12.13 The Commission may also receive a complaint concerning an agreement or a practice which has been authorized individually under Regulation 17 or under a block exemption regulation. Unless the complainants refer to conduct not covered by the exempting decision or regulation, or request withdrawal of the exemption on substantive grounds (breach of the decision or of Article 101(3) TFEU[55]), the Commission will also reject complaints in such cases. For the Commission to withdraw the benefit of the block exemption pursuant to Article 29 of Regulation 1/2003, it must find that upon individual assessment an agreement to which the exemption regulation applies has certain effects which are incompatible with Article 101(3) TFEU.

6. National competition authority dealing with the same case

12.14 If an NCA is dealing or has already dealt with the same case, the Commission will inform the complainant accordingly in order to allow him/her to withdraw the complaint.[56] The notion of 'same case' essentially implies: infringement of the same nature, same product market, same geographic market, at least one of the same undertakings, same period of time.[57] If the complainant nevertheless decides to maintain the complaint, the Commission may reject it by decision pursuant to Article 13 of Regulation No 1/2003 in conjunction with Article 9 of Regulation 773/2004. The rejection identifies the agreements or practice complained of, states that the same case is or has been dealt with by the NCA, and, to the extent necessary, specifies why the cases are identical. It also specifies the NCA's proceedings by reference to the national case number(s), dates of measures taken, national rejection decision or equivalent identifiers.[58] A rejection pursuant to Article 13 is not a referral decision;[59] it merely closes the

---

[52] See European Commission Antitrust Manual of Procedures, Internal DG Competition working documents on procedures for the application of Articles 101 and 102 TFEU, March 2012, Module 21 'Handling of complaint', para 5.

[53] Not even when they have been submitted on the legal basis of the EU competition provisions concerning state aid. See the order of the GC in Case T-36/92 *SFEI v Commission I* [1992] ECR II-2479.

[54] See Ch 3, 'The Role of National Competition Authorities', para 3.11 et seq.

[55] Regarding the procedure for withdrawal of a block exemption on an individual basis, see Ch 14, 'Interim Measures', para 14.23 et seq.

[56] Commission Notice on best practices for the conduct of proceedings concerning Articles 101 and 102 TFEU [2011] OJ C308/6, para 138.

[57] Commission notice on best practices for the conduct of proceedings concerning Articles 101 and 102 TFEU [2011] OJ C308/6, para 138, n 83.

[58] See European Commission Antitrust Manual of Procedures, Internal DG Competition working documents on procedures for the application of Articles 101 and 102 TFEU, March 2012, Module 21 'Handling of complaint', para 38.

[59] In the field of antitrust, the Commission and the NCAs have parallel competences to deal with cases under Arts 101 and 102 of the Treaty (as long as the Commission does not formally initiate proceedings). 'Re-allocation'

complaint procedure by the Commission. The NCA will usually be asked to confirm that they are actively dealing/have actively dealt with the case by way of a standard form. The forms do not need to be translated. The NCA should also be asked when the complainant can be informed (possibility of an embargo, if a surprise inspection is planned).[60] By contrast, if a national court is dealing or has already dealt with the same case, the Commission may reject the complaint based on lack of EU interest.

7. Lack of EU interest

The concept of EU interest or, more properly, lack of EU interest, as such, does not appear **12.15** in the TFEU, nor could it be inferred from any provision of Regulation 1/2003. Having previously been used more or less sporadically by the Commission, it was incorporated into legal jargon at the time of the *Automec II* judgment, in which the existence of a sufficient EU interest was seen only as a criterion for the attribution, by the Commission, of varying degrees of priority when investigating a complaint.[61] The concept relates exclusively to the Commission's obligations regarding the investigation of conduct complained of. As regards the authority to adopt or not adopt a decision, the GC takes the view that the Commission is under no obligation to rule on the existence or otherwise of an infringement in every case.[62]

The Notice on the handling of complaints establishes that: **12.16**

> the Commission is entitled to give different degrees of priority to complaints made to it and may refer to the Union interest presented by a case as a criterion of priority. The Commission may reject a complaint when it considers that the case does not display a sufficient Union interest to justify further examination.[63]

This is in line with settled case law.[64] In this respect, the Commission differs from a civil court, which must uphold the subjective rights of private individuals in their reciprocal relations.[65] As to the point in time when the Commission can invoke the lack of EU interest to reject a complaint, in *BEMIM*, the GC made it clear that the Commission might take a decision to shelve a complaint for lack of a sufficient EU interest not only before commencing an investigation of the case, but also after taking investigative measures, if that course seems appropriate to it at that stage of the proceedings.[66]

---

in the ECN implies that one authority goes ahead with a case while another abstains from acting or closes its file. There is no need to 'transfer' the case or, a fortiori, to 'transfer' the competence to deal with the case.

[60] See European Commission Antitrust Manual of Procedures, Internal DG Competition working documents on procedures for the application of Articles 101 and 102 TFEU, March 2012, Module 21 'Handling of complaint', para 37.

[61] Opinion of AG Ruiz-Jarabo Colomer in Joined Cases in C-449/98 P and C-450/98 P *International Express Carriers Conference (IECC) v Commission* [2001] ECR I-3875, para 57: 'It is no more than an abbreviated formula, a shortcut, to describe, succinctly, the discretion—neither unfettered nor arbitrary, since it is subject to judicial review—which the Treaties confer on the Commission for its examination of a complaint alleging the existence of anti-competitive practices. The substance of that concept varies very considerably, to the same extent as the widely differing circumstances which surround cases involving infringements of the competition rules.'

[62] See Case T-24/90 *Automec v Commission II* [1992] ECR II-2223, para 84 et seq.

[63] Commission Notice on the handling of complaints [2004] OJ C101/65, para 28. Similarly European Commission Antitrust Manual of Procedures, Internal DG Competition working documents on procedures for the application of Articles 101 and 102 TFEU, March 2012, Module 21 'Handling of complaint', para 42.

[64] The Court said the Commission 'is entitled to give differing degrees of priority to the complaints brought before it'. Case C-119/97 *Union française de l'express (Ufex) and others v Commission* [1999] ECR I-1341, paras 88 and 89, and Case C-449/98 P *International Express Carriers Conference (IECC) v Commission* [2001] ECR I-3875, para 3.

[65] See Case T-24/90 *Automec v Commission II* [1992] ECR II-2223, para 85.

[66] See Case T-114/92 *Bureau Européen des Médias et de l'Industrie Musicale (BEMIM) v Commission* [1995] ECR II-147, para 81 and Case C-449/98 P *International Express Carriers Conference (IECC) v Commission* [2001] ECR

12.17 The GC considers, however, that the Commission may not confine itself to referring abstractly to the lack of EU interest, but must specifically indicate the factual and legal considerations which prompted it to conclude that there was no EU interest, in accordance with Article 296 TFEU. In order to assess the EU interest in further investigation of a case, the Commission must take account of the specific circumstances of the case and, in particular, weigh the significance of the alleged infringement as regards the functioning of the internal market against the probability of establishing the existence of the infringement and the extent of the investigative measures necessary.[67] The Commission may not exclude *a priori* and in general certain situations from its task as enforcer of the competition rules. Furthermore, a rejection for lack of EU interest must be based on a consistent set of reasons.[68] In order to satisfy its duty to state reasons, it is sufficient if the Commission sets out the facts and the legal considerations that have decisive importance in the context of the decision.[69] The GC's recent scrutiny in Case T-427/08 *CEAHR*[70] illustrates the obligation placed on the Commission to consider a complaint attentively and to provide sufficient reasons for its rejection.[71] The Court held that the Commission's view that the conduct complained of concerned only one market or a segment of a market of limited size, with the result that its economic importance was limited, was vitiated by a lack of reasoning and an infringement of the duty to consider attentively all the matters of fact and of law which the complainant brought to its attention.[72]

12.18 If the Commission decides not to pursue a complaint on the ground of lack of a EU interest, it must first adopt a formal decision against which an action may be brought.[73] The purpose of the potentially ensuing Court review is to ascertain whether or not the contested decision is based on materially incorrect facts, or is vitiated by an error of law, a manifest error of appraisal, or misuse of powers. By contrast, the review by the EU Courts of the

---

I-3875, para 37: 'The existence of that discretion does not depend on the more or less advanced stage of the investigation of a case. However, that element forms part of the circumstances of the case which the Commission is required to take into consideration when exercising its discretion.'

[67] See Case T-24/90 *Automec v Commission II* [1992] ECR II-2223, para 86; Case T-5/93 *Roger Tremblay and others v Commission* [1995] ECR II-185, para 62; and Case T-62/99 *Sodima v Commission* [2001] ECR II-655, para 46; Joined Cases T-189/95, T-39/96, and T-123/96 *SGA v Commission* [1999] ECR II-3587, para 52; Joined Cases T-185/96, T-189/96, and T-190/96 *Riviera Auto Service and others v Commission* [1999] ECR II-93, para 46.

[68] European Commission Antitrust Manual of Procedures, Internal DG Competition working documents on procedures for the application of Articles 101 and 102 TFEU, March 2012, Module 21 'Handling of complaint', para 45.

[69] Case T-211/05 *Italy v Commission* [2009] ECR II-2777, para 68.

[70] Case T-427/08 *Confédération européenne des associations d'horlogers-réparateurs (CEAHR) v Commission* [2010] ECR II-5865. In this case, the CEAHR challenged the Commission decision rejecting its complaint against several Swiss manufacturers of luxury watches on the grounds of a lack of EU interest. The question of the definition of the relevant market—vital in this case, which involved an analysis of the after-market—raised complex economic assessments. The judgment reviewed extensively the Commission's statements in relation to market definition and eventually found a manifest error of assessment, which ultimately vitiated the Commission's reasoning as to their being an insufficient EU interest. The Court found that the Commission had failed in its duty to assess carefully all matters of fact in order to assess the lack of EU interest. See also President of the GC, Marc Jaeger, 'The Standard of Review in Competition Cases Involving Complex Economic Assessments: Towards the Marginalisation of the Marginal Review?' (2011) 2(4) Journal of European Competition Law & Practice 295, 302.

[71] See A Mikroulea, 'Rejection of Complaint, Lack of Community Interest, Obligation of Motivation: How Does that all Fit Together?' (2011) 2(3) Journal of European Competition Law & Practice 241.

[72] Case T-427/08 *Confédération européenne des associations d'horlogers-réparateurs (CEAHR) v Commission* [2010] ECR II-5865, paras 33, 49, and 164.

[73] See Case T-37/92 *BEUC and others v Commission* [1994] ECR II-285, para 47. The *BEUC* judgment was confirmed in Case T-114/92 *Bureau Européen des Médias et de l'Indus-trie Musicale (BEMIM) v Commission* [1995] ECR II-147; Order of the Court of 31 March 2011 in Case C-367/10 P *EMC Development v Commission*, para 75.

Commission's exercise of the discretion conferred on it for dealing with complaints must not lead them to substitute their assessment of the EU interest for that of the Commission, but focuses on whether the contested decision is based on materially incorrect facts, or is vitiated by an error of law, manifest error of appraisal, or misuse of powers.[74] In that regard, the Court must, *inter alia*, examine whether it is clear from the decision that the Commission weighed the significance of the impact which the alleged infringement may have on the functioning of the internal market, the probability of its being able to establish the existence of the infringement, and the extent of the investigative measures required. A manifest error of assessment is not sufficient to warrant annulment of the contested decision if, in the particular circumstances of the case, it could not have had a decisive effect on the outcome.[75] In *CEAHR*, the Court held that in the light of several manifest errors of assessment and insufficient reasoning it had to be concluded that the illegalities were such as to affect the Commission's assessment of the existence of sufficient EU interest. Therefore, the decision by which the Commission had rejected the complaint was annulled.[76]

The Commission has provided some guidance for assessing the EU interest of a case in its **12.19** Notice on the handling of complaints.[77] The criteria highlighted by the Commission are based on the case law of the EU Courts. When deciding whether there is a sufficient degree of EU interest for acting, the Commission will in particular look at the following criteria:

- The fact that the complainant can bring an action to assert its rights before national courts, where the effects of the infringements alleged in a complaint are essentially confined to the territory of one Member State[78] and where proceedings have been brought before the courts and competent administrative authorities of that Member State by the complainant against the body complained of.[79] The Commission's power to reject a complaint on these grounds is nevertheless conditional on the availability of appropriate remedies at national level.[80]

---

[74] Case T-115/99 *SEP v Commission* [2001] ECR II-691, para 34, and Case T-193/02 *Piau v Commission* [2005] ECR II-209, para 81.

[75] Case T-60/05 *Ufex and Others v Commission* [2007] ECR II-3397, para 77; Case T-126/99 *Graphischer Maschinenbau v Commission* [2002] ECR II-2427, paras 48 and 49.

[76] See Case T-427/08 *Confédération européenne des associations d'horlogers-réparateurs (CEAHR) v Commission* [2010] ECR II-5865, in particular paras 177 and 178.

[77] Commission Notice on the handling of complaints [2004] OJ C101/65 para 44. See European Commission Antitrust Manual of Procedures, Internal DG Competition working documents on procedures for the application of Articles 101 and 102 TFEU, March 2012, Module 21 'Handling of complaint', para 47 et seq.

[78] By contrast, the fact that the market affected by the conduct complained of is of EU dimension does not in itself suffice to justify an EU interest. In Case T-60/05 *UFEX v Commission* [2007] II-3397, para 158, the GC rejected the complainant's argument based on the EU dimension of the market concerned holding that: '[i]n so far as there is concurrent competence on the part of the Commission and the national competition authorities, the [EU] dimension of a market is not such as to oblige the Commission to conclude that an infringement was of a certain seriousness or that there was a [EU] interest in a given case.'

[79] Case T-24/90 *Automec v Commission II* [1992] ECR II-2223, para 88 et seq; Case T-5/93 *Roger Tremblay and others v Commission* [1995] ECR II-185, para 65 et seq; Case T-575/93 *Casper Koelman v Commission* [1996] ECR II-1, paras 75–80.

[80] See most recently, Case T-427/08 *Confédération européenne des associations d'horlogers-réparateurs (CEAHR) v Commission* [2010] ECR II-5865, para 173; Case T-458/04 *Au lys de France v Commission* [2007] ECR II-71, para 83. According to the GC in Case T-5/93 *Roger Tremblay and others v Syndicat des Exploitants de Lieux de Loisirs (SELL)* [1995] ECR II-185, para 68: 'the rights of a complainant could not be regarded as sufficiently protected before the national court if that court were not reasonably able, in view of the complexity of the case, to gather the factual information necessary in order to determine whether the practices criticized in the complaint constituted an infringement of [Art 101] or [Art 102] of the Treaty or of both', citing the judgment in Case T-24/90 *Automec v Commission* [1992] ECR II-2223, paras 89–96.

- The impact on trade between Member States and the duration and the extent of the infringements complained of.[81]
- The significance of the alleged infringement as regards the functioning of the Internal Market, the probability of establishing the existence of the infringement, and the scope of the investigation.[82]
- The more or less advanced stage of the investigation of a case.[83]
- The fact that the practices in question have ceased.[84] However, the EU Courts held that 'the Commission...cannot rely solely on the fact that practices alleged to be contrary to the Treaty have ceased, without having ascertained that anti-competitive effects no longer continue and, if appropriate, that the seriousness of the alleged interferences with competition or the persistence of their consequences has not been such as to give the complaint a [EU] interest'.[85]
- The acceptance by the undertakings concerned to change their conduct in such a way that it can consider that there is no longer a sufficient interest warranting intervention.[86] In particular, where commitments have been made binding by a Commission decision pursuant to Article 9 Regulation 1/2003 or where the undertaking complained of has changed its behaviour for other reasons, provided that neither significant persisting anticompetitive effects nor the seriousness of the alleged infringement constitute sufficient grounds for conducting a further investigation in spite of the cessation of modification.[87]

D. Rejection Procedure[88]

1. First stage: informal contacts

12.20 The rejection of complaints may involve three stages. There is an initial assessment which serves the purpose of screening the admissible complaints for those which seem most to merit

---

[81] Case C-119/97 P *Union Française de l'Express (Ufex) and others v Commission* [1999] ECR I-1341, paras 92–3. Order of the GC of 19 March 2012 in Case T-273/09 *Associazione 'Giúlemanidallajuve' v Commission*, para 50 et seq.

[82] Case T-24/90 *Automec v Commission* [1992] ECR II-2223, para 86.

[83] Case C-449/98 P *International Express Carriers Conference (IECC) v Commission* [2001] ECR I-3875, para 37.

[84] Case T-77/95 *Syndicat Français de l'Express International and others v Commission* [1997] ECR II-1, para 57; see also GC judgment following the referral of the case back to the GC, Case T-77/95 *Ufex v Commission* [2000] ECR II-2167, para 43 et seq, in which the GC concluded that the Commission did not assess the seriousness and duration of the infringements complained of and whether their effects were continuing: 'By considering, finally, that it was not obliged to investigate past infringements if the sole purpose or effect of such an investigation was to serve the individual interests of the parties, the Commission misunderstood its task in the field of competition, which was not indeed to apply itself to establishing the conditions for compensation for the pecuniary loss said to have been suffered by one or more undertakings, but to ensure, following the complaint brought by an organisation representing almost all the French private operators active in the market in question, a state of undistorted competition'. See also the rejection Decision in *UFEX* (COMP/38.663) which notes that the practices complained of—which had not in any event been duly established—were brought to an end more than ten years ago and that, since then, no lasting anticompetitive effects attributable to them had been apparent in the relevant market, cited in Commission Report on Competition Policy [2004], SEC (2005) 805 final, para 102.

[85] See Case C-119/97 P *Union Française de l'Express (Ufex) and others v Commission* [1999] ECR I-1341, para 95. See also Case T-60/05 *UFEX v Commission* [2007] II-3397, para 65.

[86] Case T-110/95 *International Express Carriers (IECC) v Commission and others* [1998] ECR II-3605, para 57, upheld by Case C-449/98 P *International Express Carriers (IECC) v Commission and others* [2001] ECR I-3875, paras 44–7. See Ch 13 'Commitments, Voluntary Adjustments, Conclusion of the Procedure without a Formal Decision', para 13.01 et seq.

[87] European Commission Antitrust Manual of Procedures, Internal DG Competition working documents on procedures for the application of Articles 101 and 102 TFEU, March 2012, Module 21 'Handling of complaint', para 52.

[88] The procedure for the rejection of complaints has been described by the GC in Case T-64/89 *Automec v Commission I* [1990] ECR II-367, paras 45–7, and developed in the XX Report on Competition Policy

being further investigated by the Commission.[89] The Commission will endeavour to inform complainants of the action that it proposes to take on a complaint within an indicative time frame of four months from the receipt of the complaint.[90] In those cases where it is appropriate to reject a complaint, the Commission first contacts the complainants and informally explains the reasons why it is not possible to follow up on their complaint or ascertain the existence of an infringement of the EU competition rules. It will usually be the head of the competent administrative unit of DG COMP who informs the complainants of the provisional and informal conclusions reached by the department responsible for dealing with the complaint, either in a meeting or over the phone.[91] Where the complaints are not adequately supported, the Commission official will ask the complainant for additional factual information or legal considerations which might enable the Commission to conclude that there has been an infringement or which can help establish the EU interest in following up on the complaint. This is an informal step in the procedure prior to formal rejection of the complaint; it does not constitute a decision and as such does not bind the Commission. Contacts of this kind are purely preliminary and are without prejudice to the rights of the complainants, and therefore they are not actionable.[92] The Commission uses them to allow complainants to put forward new information and arguments, without which it would be impossible to ascertain an infringement. In practice, if, after a considerable lapse of time, the complainants have not supplied any new information or arguments and they have not expressly asked for a more detailed explanation of the Commission's reasoning, the latter will close the file.

2. Second stage: Article 7(1) letter

In cases where the complainants express interest in receiving a more detailed explanation, the **12.21** Commission sends a formal letter before rejecting the complaint, as provided for in Article 7(1) of Regulation 773/2004. The obligation to deliver this type of letter is one of the most important procedural guarantees for complainants in order to safeguard their right to be heard.[93] The so-called 'Article 7 letter' sets out the Commission's provisional position on the complaint, subject to the observations that the complainant may submit in reply to the letter.

[1990], paras 163–5. It is also set out in the Commission Notice on best practices for the conduct of proceedings concerning Articles 101 and 102 TFEU [2011] OJ C308/6, paras 137–41, and in European Commission Antitrust Manual of Procedures, Internal DG Competition working documents on procedures for the application of Articles 101 and 102 TFEU, March 2012, Module 21 'Handling of complaint', para 57 et seq, although the Manproc refers to two steps instead of three because the initial contacts before issuing the Art 7(1) letter are not considered a 'step' as such.

[89] See European Commission Antitrust Manual of Procedures, Internal DG Competition working documents on procedures for the application of Articles 101 and 102 TFEU, March 2012, Module 21 'Handling of complaint', para 7.

[90] Commission Notice on the handling of complaints [2004] OJ C101/65, para 61.

[91] Commission notice on best practices for the conduct of proceedings concerning Articles 101 and 102 TFEU [2011] OJ C308/6, para 139. European Commission Antitrust Manual of Procedures, Internal DG Competition working documents on procedures for the application of Articles 101 and 102 TFEU, March 2012, Module 21 'Handling of complaint', para 57, seems to reject implicitly that the Commission will inform the complainant by letter at this stage.

[92] Case T-64/89 *Automec v Commission I* [1990] ECR II-367, para 45.

[93] The disappearance of the restriction of competition which was the subject matter of the complaint 'could not entitle the Commission to dispense with the requirement of defining its position on the applicant's complaint, in conformity with the procedural guarantees provided for in Article [7] of Regulation [1/2003] and Article [7] of Regulation [773/2004]'. Case T-74/92 *Ladbroke Racing (Deutschland) GmbH v Commission* [1995] ECR II-115, para 67. Case C-282/95 P *Guérin Automobiles v Commission* [1997] ECR I-1503, para 35: 'The purpose of that intermediate phase in the administrative procedure before the Commission is, in fact, to safeguard the rights of the complainant, to whom an unfavourable decision should not be addressed without first giving him the opportunity to submit observations on the grounds upon which the Commission intends to rely.' See also Order of the Court in Case C-367/10 P *EMC Development v Commission* [2011] ECR I-46, para 76.

As the GC has stated, the purpose of these Article 7 letters is to enable a complainant to be informed of the reasons which have led the Commission to conclude that there are insufficient grounds for granting the complainant's application.[94] Whilst these so-called 'Article 7 letters' are normally complex and lengthy, briefer and less detailed 'Article 7 letters' may be considered to satisfy all the formal requirements in that provision.[95] National courts are not bound by the Commission's appraisals contained in such letters regarding the applicability or otherwise of Articles 101 and 102 TFEU.[96] Their content corresponds to that of a statement of objections in an infringement procedure (in a way, they are statements of objections, but in reverse), and, like statements of objections, they are not measures against which proceedings may be brought.[97] By contrast, a statement of objections serves to define the Commission's position when the Commission intends to act against the alleged infringements and usually renders an Article 7 letter superfluous.[98] If, in the course of its examination of the complaint, the Commission has opened proceedings pursuant to Article 11(6) of Regulation 1/2003 a 'State of Play' meeting will be offered to the complainant prior to sending such a letter.[99]

12.22 Article 7 letters contain a factual part and a legal part, which are both generally very detailed. The Article 7 letter is a formal Commission act adopted by the Director-General, by subdelegation, after consultation with the Legal Service.[100] Formally, the letters contain an express reference to Article 7(1) of Regulation 773/2004, an invitation to the complainants to submit their observations on the letter in writing, generally within a period of at least four weeks,[101] and, as an annex, the documents from the file to which they are entitled to have access pursuant to Article 8(1) of Regulation 773/2004.[102] The time limit will start to run from the date when access to the main documents on which the Commission's preliminary assessment was made has been granted.[103] The complainant can request an extension of this time period with the Hearing Officer, provided an extension was unsuccessfully requested with DG COMP before the expiry of the original time limit.[104] When responding to an 'Article 7 letter', the complainant has also

---

[94] Case 125/78 *GEMA v Commission II* [1979] ECR 3173, para 17.

[95] See Case T-186/94 *Guérin Automobiles v Commission* [1995] ECR II-1753, paras 8 (which contains the text of a short Art 7 letter), 28, and 29.

[96] See Case T-114/92 *Bureau Européen des Médias et de l'Industrie Musicale (BEMIM) v Commission* [1995] ECR II-147, para 65 and Case T-575/93 *Casper Koelman v Commission* [1996] ECR II-1, paras 41–3.

[97] See Case T-64/89 *Automec v Commission I* [1990] ECR II-367, para 46 and Case T-28/90 *Asia Motor France v Commission I* [1992] ECR II-2285, para 42. Both judgments cite Case 125/78 *GEMA v Commission II* [1979] ECR 3173. See also Case T-17/93 *Matra v Commission* [1994] ECR II-595, para 35, which cites *Automec I*. See further T-186/94 *Guérin Automobiles v Commission* [1995] ECR II-1753, para 34 (confirmed by Case C-282/95 P *Guérin Automobiles v Commission* [1997] ECR I-1503); Case T-37/92 *Bureau Européen des Unions des Consommateurs (BEUC) and others v Commission* [1994] ECR II-285, paras 27 and 30 and Case T-241/97 *Stork Amsterdam BV v Commission* [2000] ECR II-309, para 52.

[98] The Commission will not send an 'Article 7 letter' if it does not have the intention to reject a complaint, and is actually pursuing the procedure for investigating the alleged breaches of the competition rules. See Case T-74/92 *Ladbroke Racing (Deutschland) GmbH v Commission* [1995] ECR II-115, para 44.

[99] Commission notice on best practices for the conduct of proceedings concerning Articles 101 and 102 TFEU [2011] OJ C308/6, para 139.

[100] See European Commission Antitrust Manual of Procedures, Internal DG Competition working documents on procedures for the application of Articles 101 and 102 TFEU, March 2012, Module 21 'Handling of complaint', para 61.

[101] See Art 17(2) of Reg 773/2004.

[102] Access is usually only granted to the non-confidential version of the documents on which the Commission bases its provisional assessment. The Commission Notice on the handling of complaints [2004] OJ C101/65, para 69, provides that access is normally provided by annexing to the letter a copy of the relevant documents.

[103] Commission notice on best practices for the conduct of proceedings concerning Articles 101 and 102 TFEU [2011] OJ C308/6, para 139.

[104] Decision of the President of the European Commission of 13 October 2011 on the function and terms of reference of the hearing officer in certain competition proceedings [2011] OJ L275/29, Art 9(2);

the right to turn to the Hearing Officer to request further access to documents on which the Commission has based its provisional assessment but which have not been provided.[105] If the complainant does not respond to the statement submitted by the Commission in the 'Article 7 letter', the complaint is deemed to have been withdrawn and the rejection procedure will end.[106] In this case, the complainant will be informed accordingly about the administrative closure of the case. As will be apparent, the Article 7 procedure presents similarities with the procedure considered in connection with the statement of objections. In these cases, however, no formal administrative hearing will be held, and access to the file is only granted to the documents on which the Commission bases its provisional assessment of the complaint.

3. Third stage: Article 7(2) decision

If a complainant has submitted written observations responding to the 'Article 7 letter' and insisted on obtaining a formal decision, the third stage will start and the Commission will continue to examine the complaint on the basis of the additional observations provided by the complainant. If the Commission decides definitely to reject the complaint, a rejection decision on the basis of Article 7(2) of Regulation 773/2004 will be adopted and signed, by virtue of a delegation of powers from the Commission, by the member of the Commission responsible for competition. It will not require to be reported on by the Advisory Committee, nor will it necessarily be published in the Official Journal—although a non-confidential version is usually made available on the DG COMP website. As regards the content and the effects of such decisions, the EU Courts have stated that they have the following features: they bring the investigation to an end, they contain an assessment of the agreements or practices in question, and they prevent the complainants from requiring a reopening of the investigation, unless they put forward new evidence.[107] By contrast, if the complainant's submissions in response to the Commission's Article 7 letter lead to a different assessment of the complaint, the Commission will continue its investigation.[108]

12.23

Whilst the Commission must give adequate reasons for its decision rejecting a complaint, it suffices to set out the decisive facts and legal considerations.[109] The Commission is not obliged to adopt a position on all the arguments raised, but only needs to set out the considerations which are decisive for the rejection of the complaint. If the Commission has adopted a decision pursuant to Article 10 or Article 9, that decision can be referred to in the rejection and serve as reasoning.[110] However, the reasons stated must be sufficiently precise

12.24

Commission Notice on best practices for the conduct of proceedings concerning Articles 101 and 102 TFEU [2011] OJ C308/6, para 139.

[105] Decision of the President of the European Commission of 13 October 2011 on the function and terms of reference of the hearing officer in certain competition proceedings [2011] OJ L275/29, Art 7(2) lit.b). According to Art 3(7), as for deadline extension, the request requires that the issue of insufficient access has first been raised with the DG COMP.

[106] Article 7(3) of Reg 773/2004.

[107] See Joined Cases 142/84 and 156/84 *BAT and Reynolds v Commission* [1987] ECR 4487, para 12; Case T-64/89 *Automec v Commission I* [1990] ECR II-367, para 57; Case T-116/89 *Prodifarma v Commission* [1990] ECR II-843, para 70; Case T-16/91 *Rendo and others v Commission* [1992] ECR II-2417, para 49; and Order of the GC in T-36/92 *SFEI v Commission I* [1992] ECR II-2479, para 29. All these GC decisions cite Joined Cases 142/84 and 156/84 *BAT and Reynolds v Commission* [1987] ECR 4487. See also Case 210/81 *Demo-Studio Schmidt v Commission* [1983] ECR 3045 and Case 298/83 *CICCE v Commission* [1985] ECR 1105.

[108] Commission Notice on best practices for the conduct of proceedings concerning Articles 101 and 102 TFEU [2011] OJ C308/6, para 141.

[109] Case T-387/94 *Asia Motor France SA v Commission* [1996] ECR II-961, para 104; Case T-111/96 *ITT Promedia v Commission* [1998] ECR II-2937, para 79.

[110] See European Commission Antitrust Manual of Procedures, Internal DG Competition working documents on procedures for the application of Articles 101 and 102 TFEU, March 2012, Module 21 'Handling of complaint', para 73.

and detailed to enable the GC effectively to review the Commission's use of its discretion to define priorities.[111] Complainants are entitled to have the fate of their complaint settled by a decision of the Commission against which an action may be brought.[112] The complainants will have a period of two months after notification of the decision to commence proceedings before the GC in accordance with Article 263 TFEU. Upon appeal, the Court assesses whether the rejection decision contains an appropriate examination of the factual and legal particulars submitted for the Commission's appraisal in the context of the administrative procedure.[113] In that regard, the EU Courts have established that the judicial review of Commission measures involving appraisal of complex economic matters is limited to verifying whether the relevant rules on procedure and on the statement of reasons have been complied with, whether the facts have been accurately stated, and whether there has been any manifest error of assessment or a misuse of powers.[114]

---

[111] Case C-119/97 P *Ufex and others v Commission* [1999] ECR I-1341, paras 90 and 91.

[112] Interestingly, it was the Commission itself which proposed this solution (see Case T-186/94 *Guérin Automobiles v Commission* [1995] ECR II-1753, para 16). Relying on the Opinion of Judge Edward acting as Advocate-General ('AG') in *Automec II*, Case T-24/90 *Automec v Commission II* [1992] ECR II-2223, paras 22 and 23, and citing Case 377/87 *Parliament v Council* [1988] ECR 4017, paras 7 and 10, and Case 302/87 *Parliament v Council* [1988] ECR 5615, para 16, the GC considered 'Article 6 letters [now Article 7 letters]' as acts which are the prerequisite for the next step in a procedure which culminates in a legal act which is itself open to an action for annulment under the conditions laid down in Art 230 EC. Referring to the previous case law—in particular, Case 125/78 *GEMA v Commission* [1979] ECR 3173, para 17; Case T-24/90 *Automec v Commission II* [1992] ECR II-2223, paras 75 and 76; and Case T-16/91 *Rendo and Others v Commission* [1992] ECR II-2417, para 98—and citing the judgments in Case 222/84 *Johnston v Chief Constable of the Royal Ulster Constabulary* [1986] ECR 1651, para 18, and Case C-249/88 *Commission v Belgium* [1991] ECR I-1275, para 25, the GC stated that there is nothing in the approach taken in these judgments to prevent a complainant from obtaining 'a Commission decision on its complaint capable of forming the subject-matter of an action for annulment, in accordance with the general principle that there is a right of access to judicial review'. Accordingly, the GC concluded that there is an obligation for the Commission to adopt such a rejection decision, or risk an action for failure to act under Art 265 TFEU.

[113] Case T-432/05 *EMC Development v Commission* [2010] ECR II-1629, para 60.

[114] Case T-432/05 *EMC Development v Commission* [2010] ECR II-1629, para 60; Case T-24/90 *Automec v Commission II* [1992] ECR II-2223, para 80; Case T-198/98 *Micro Leader v Commission* [1999] ECR II-3989, para 27.

13

VOLUNTARY ADJUSTMENTS, COMMITMENTS, FINDING OF INAPPLICABILITY, INFORMAL GUIDANCE

Luis Ortiz Blanco, Konstantin Jörgens, and Manuel Kellerbauer

I. Voluntary Adjustments

A. The Administrative Procedure as an Opportunity for Adjustment

Under Regulation 17, undertakings could reach an amicable agreement with the Commission **13.01** from the very beginning of the case if they agreed to bring their activities into line with EU competition law.[1] The Annual Reports of the Commission showed that a high number of cases were indeed resolved by way of a settlement.[2] In some cases, the terms of the settlement were published in the Annual Report or even in the Official Journal of the European Union ('OJ'), which was indicative of the Commission's flexible and quite pragmatic approach in this regard. Where the companies made enough concessions to satisfy the Commission and where the Commission considered nothing would be gained by pursuing formal proceedings further, an informal settlement often appeared as the most expedient way to terminate the matter.[3]

13.02 Regulation 1/2003 does not prevent the Commission from settling cases by way of informal arrangements.[4] While Article 9 of Regulation 1/2003 empowers the Commission to adopt decisions accepting commitments offered by undertakings in the course of proceedings,[5] the Commission continues to end cases by informal settlements if, all things considered, it deems that this is the best way to settle a matter. The Commission's power under Article 9 of Regulation 1/2003 to terminate its proceedings by binding companies to the commitments they offer thus does not create an obligation to this effect.[6] Nor is the Commission obliged to adopt any other formal decision provided by Regulation 1/2003.

13.03 Examples of such informal settlements are situations where it is agreed with the parties that the latter will behave in a given manner in order to avoid infringing the EU competition rules, at least where a statement of objections has yet to be issued[7] or where the conduct in question has

---

[1] Under Reg 17, the administrative procedure already specifically gave undertakings an opportunity to explain their conduct and adjust their agreements to the requirements of Community law. See Joined Cases 142/84 and 156/84 *BAT and Reynolds v Commission* [1987] ECR 448, para 23.

[2] Some of these cases also related to notified agreements which enjoyed immunity from fines, and where, therefore, a formal decision would have served little purpose. For example, see European Commission, Report on the Application of Competition Rules in conjunction with XXXIII Report on Competition Policy [2003] 203 et seq. See also 'Dealing with the Commission—Notification, complaints, inspections and fact-finding powers under Articles [101] and [102] of the [TFEU]' (edn 1997), para 8.3: 'In numerical terms, the informal settlements the Commission makes are of much greater significance than formal decisions.' L Ritter and WD Brown, *European Competition Law: A Practitioner's Guide* (3rd edn, Kluwer Law International 2004) 1041, also note that the vast majority of cases were closed without reaching the stage of formal decision.

[3] A Jones and B Sufrin, *EC Competition Law* (4th edn, Oxford University Press 2010) 1130.

[4] Commission Report on Competition Policy [2004], SEC (2005) 805 final 57, stating that out of 391 cases closed in 2004, 363 were solved informally (called 'Informal Procedure') and only 28 of them by formal decision.

[5] Kerse & Khan, *EC Antitrust Procedure* (6th edn, Sweet & Maxwell 2012) para 6-091, argue that although Art 9 of Reg 1/2003 would not prevent the Commission from settling a matter other than by formal commitments imposed on the parties, it would be surprising if the Commission were to continue to use informal settlements rather than commitment decisions. The provision would confer procedural rights on third parties and recourse to an informal settlement could be open to criticism as circumventing third parties' procedural rights.

[6] J Temple Lang, 'Commitment Decisions and Settlements with Antitrust Authorities and Private Parties under European Antitrust Law', ch 13 in *32nd Annual International Antitrust Law & Policy Conference Fordham Corporate Law Institute* (Juris Publishing 2005) 265–74 et seq, 8 elaborates on the reasons why the Commission may consider imposing commitment decisions. Commitment decisions are unlikely to be used when the Commission seeks to establish a clear precedent. See para 13.08 et seq.

[7] However, the Commission may also settle after the statement of objections. In connection with the investigation in relation to alleged agreements between Apple and a number of record companies restricting music sales (via iTunes online stores), statement of objections to major record companies and Apple, alleging that agreements between the record companies and Apple restricted music sales via iTunes online stores by imposing territorial restrictions and so infringed Art 101. After Apple announced its decision to equalize prices for downloads of songs from its iTunes online store in Europe thereby ending the different treatment of UK consumers and the Commission's further investigation showed that country-specific aspects of copyright laws, and not the agreements between Apple and the major record companies determine how the iTunes store is organized in Europe, the Commission therefore decided to close the file on its investigation. Commission Press Release IP/08/22 'Antitrust: European Commission welcomes Apple's announcement to equalize prices for music downloads from iTunes in Europe', 9 January 2008.

already definitively ceased.[8] In the latter case, the Commission's intervention under Article 9 (where no fines are imposed and no finding of an infringement is made) does not serve any useful purpose, unless there is a real danger of the conduct in question being resumed, or perhaps if the effects of the infringement persist in the market and could be counteracted or mitigated by commitments which bind the undertaking concerned.[9] It would then be a commitment, but not one which is formally binding.[10] It may also happen that regulatory changes obviate the need to continue the investigation.[11] It should be noted that the Commission may also pass a file to a better placed national competition authority ('NCA'): such reallocation of the file to an NCA in accordance with the European Competition Network ('ECN') Network Notice should not be considered a settlement, as it is for that NCA to decide on the future course of action in the case.[12]

Therefore, it is no surprise that informal settlements have not disappeared entirely: there are **13.04** fewer cases solved this way, but there will also be fewer cases the Commission will investigate, due to its focus on serious infringements of competition rules and the fact that the work will be shared with other 'well-placed' ECN members having enforcement powers parallel to those of the Commission. As regards the application of Article 9 of Regulation 1/2003, the Commission may prefer to adopt a commitment decision where it has followed through the procedure up to a point, for example where it has taken investigation measures, or where it has sent a statement of objections, whereas it may be more open to the possibility of 'informal settlements' at an earlier stage.

---

[8] In connection with the joint venture of the iron producers Rio Tinto and BHP Billiton, the Commission found that the joint venture could have a negative effect on competition on the worldwide market for seaborne iron ore and so could amount to a breach of Art 101. Shortly afterwards, the companies confirmed to the Commission that they had abandoned the plan. Midday Express/10/1206 'Commission closes investigation into proposed JV between BHP Billiton and Rio Tinto' 6 December 2010.

[9] E Gippini-Fournier, 'The Modernisation of European Competition Law: First Experiences with Regulation 1/2003—Institutional Report' in HF Koeck and MM Karollus (eds), The Modernisation of European Competition Law—Initial Experiences with Regulation 1/2003, FIDE XXIII Congress Linz 2008—Congress Publications Vol 2 (Nomos 2008) 375, 422, identifying a number of examples in which the investigation was closed through an informal settlement. Commission Press Release IP/08/22, 'Antitrust: European Commission welcomes Apple's announcement to equalise prices for music downloads from iTunes in Europe' of 9 January 2008; Commission Press Release IP/06/139, 'Competition: Commission closes investigation following changes to Philips CD-Recordable Disc Patent Licensing' of 9 February 2006; Commission Press Release IP/05/519 'Competition: Commission welcomes improved access to tickets for the 2006 World Cup' of 2 May 2005; Commission Press Release IP/04/1314 ' Commission closes investigation into contracts of six Hollywood studios with European pay-TVs' of 26 October 2004. See also, more recently, Commission Press Release IP/12/873 'Antitrust: Commission closes investigation in P&I Clubs case' of 1 August 2012; Commission Press Release IP/12/210 'Antitrust: Commission closes investigation in pharmaceutical companies AstraZeneca and Nycomed' of 1 March 2012; see Commission Press Release IP/09/5 15 'Antitrust: Commission welcomes IPCom's public FRAND declaration' and MEMO/09/143 of 1 April 2009. The Commission also 'welcome[d] the public declaration by German IP licensing company IPCom, following discussions with the Commission, that it is ready to take over Bosch's previous commitment to grant irrevocable licences on fair, reasonable and non-discriminatory (FRAND) terms to patents held by IPCom which are essential for various standards set by the European Telecommunications Standard Institute (ETSI) and Universal Mobile Telecommunications System (UMTS)' rather than adopting an Art 9 decision in this regard. See Commission Press Release MEMO/09/549 of 10 December 2009.

[10] J Temple Lang, 'Commitments under Regulation 1/2003: Legal Aspects of a new Kind of Competition Decision' [2003] 24 European Competition Law Review 347, 347.

[11] Commission Press Release IP/07/1113 'Antitrust: Commission closes proceedings against past roaming tariffs in the UK and Germany' of 18 July 2007, where the Commission has decided to close these cases following the entry into force of a European Regulation on 30 June 2007, which addresses the issue of high roaming charges.

[12] See Ch 3, 'The Role of National Competition Authorities', para 3.12 et seq.

13.05   The Commission usually informs undertakings of the investigations it has commenced concerning them at the earliest stage of the inquiries and, in particular, always sends the undertakings a copy of the formal complaints received against them, usually before, but certainly no later than, the sending of the statement of objections.[13] Moreover, the Commission is open to all kinds of direct contact, which enable undertakings to gain better knowledge both of the procedures and of the substantive rules of competition law.[14] This means that in many cases the undertakings themselves, aware of the Commission's critical view of particular agreements, conduct, or practices, change their own behaviour appropriately, thus avoiding the initiation of an infringement procedure or the adoption of a formal decision against them.[15] Voluntary adjustments would thus appear possible at any time, and the undertaking is itself responsible for assessing whether they suffice to comply with Articles 101 and 102 of the Treaty on the Functioning of the European Union ('TFEU'). In principle, the Commission does not formally approve any such voluntary adjustments.

13.06   There are various moments when a voluntary adjustment may be possible, from the moment the file is opened and even before, and coming to an end immediately before the formal decision declaring the infringement. Thus, formalities such as the transmission of the complaint to the undertakings to which they relate (where this is done separately), a request for information or an inspection, a statement of objections,[16] or even the administrative hearings may prompt the undertakings to reflect and facilitate the adjustment of their agreements, practices and conduct in order to comply with EU law. A unilateral declaration made in the course of proceedings that the agreements criticized in the statement of objections will cease to be applied wholly or in part may, in practice, be insufficient to avoid continuation of the infringement procedure and, in appropriate cases, the imposition of fines.[17] It may also be that from time to time the Commission considers it convenient to hold a 'State of Play' meeting with the parties.[18] However, at the same time, the Commission will avoid issuing

---

[13] See Ch 10, 'Procedures to Establish the Existence of an Infringement', para 10.03.

[14] After the initiation of proceedings, so-called 'State of Play' meetings allow for regular exchanges between the companies subject to investigation and the Commission. See Commission Notice on best practices for the conduct of proceedings concerning Articles 101 and 102 TFEU [2011] OJ C308/6, para 60 et seq.

[15] In its investigation into the rough diamond market, on the basis of increased transparency in De Beers' distribution arrangements, known as Supplier of Choice ('SOC'), the Commission requested De Beers to improve the transparency and the checks and balances of the SOC selection process. In response, De Beers significantly revised the Ombudsman's mandate, which led the Commission to close the investigation. Commission Press Release IP/07/122 'Competition: Commission closes investigation in rough diamonds sector following improvements to De Beers' distribution system' of 31 January 2007. See also Commission Press Release IP/10/1175 'Antitrust: Statement on Apple's iPhone policy changes' of 25 September 2010.

[16] Nevertheless, the statement of objections has the purpose of allowing the addressee to exercise its right to be heard. It does not in itself impose an obligation on undertakings to modify or reconsider their commercial practices. See Case 60/81 *IBM v Commission* [1981] ECR 2639, para 21. When the Commission sends a statement of objections concerning agreements or practices which require modification for the legal exception in Art 101(3) TFEU to be applied, the Commission may, but is not obliged to, give guidance to the undertakings as to possible alternative solutions, in other words regarding the specific changes to be made. See Joined Cases 43/82 and 63/82 *VBVB and VBBB v Commission* [1984] ECR 19, para 19.

[17] The scope of a procedure is not automatically changed just because the undertakings unilaterally announce in the course of the procedure that they will cease in part to apply the agreements covered by the statement of objections, particularly if that intention has not been notified to the Commission or verified in practice. See Case T-66/89 *The Publishers' Association v Commission* [1992] ECR II-1995, para 53, citing Cases 142/84 and 156/84 *BAT and Reynolds v Commission* [1987] ECR 4487, para 22. The judgment of the Court of First Instance ('CFI') was quashed in Case C-360/92 P *The Publishers Association v Commission II* [1995] ECR I-23, but the dicta cited remain valid.

[18] See Commission Notice on best practices for the conduct of proceedings concerning Articles 101 and 102 TFEU [2011] OJ C308/6, para 60 et seq.

any communication which could be compared to the instruments formerly used under Regulation 17 (exemption, negative clearance, or comfort letter). Thus, the Commission takes care that these informal contacts will not lead to a notification procedure through the back door. Nothing should be construed as altering the principle that companies should perform their self-assessment under EU competition rules.[19] Undertakings are generally considered as being well placed to assess the legality of their actions in such a way as to enable them to take an informed decision on whether to go ahead with an agreement or practice in whatever form, all the more so since the Commission's past decisional practice provides them with guidance.

B. Procedure after Voluntary Adjustment

Once they comply with the competition rules, the undertakings' agreements, conduct, and **13.07** practices may be dealt with by the Commission either formally or informally. One example might be a case where, despite termination of the infringement, the Commission considered it necessary to adopt a formal decision covering the period before the undertakings brought their behaviour into line with the EU rules.[20] It would then have to send a statement of objections and go through the entire infringement procedure, if it had not already done so. The Commission's reasons for adopting such a stringent approach are various. It may doubt that the agreement, practice, or conduct objected to will actually be abandoned by the undertakings. Or else the complainants may have asked the Commission for a formal decision to enable them to seek damages with confidence before a national court.[21] The Commission may also wish to set a precedent[22] or penalize particularly serious infringements (for example in cases of abuse of a dominant position).[23] Informal abandonment of the procedure after voluntary adjustments

---

[19] Recital 38 of Reg 1/2003 states that where cases give rise to genuine uncertainty because they present novel or unresolved questions for the companies, they may wish to seek guidance from the Commission. According to JS Venit, 'Private Practice in the Wake of the Commission's Modernization Program' [2005] Legal Issues of Economic Integration 147, 148–9, the significance of this 'loss' needs to be qualified: under the old system, where an agreement was highly questionable, it would have been seldom notified, and if it was, it brought with it the risk of forceful Commission intervention. Besides, the need for self-assessment would hardly be new; in the past responsible firms would also have been unlikely to negotiate an agreement or enter into it without having first concluded that it would fall outside the scope of Art 101(1) TFEU or, if caught by the prohibition, could prove exemptable under Art 101(3) TFEU. What is genuinely new is the increasing sophistication of this assessment considering the economically oriented approach of the regulator and courts.

[20] Note that under Art 7 of Reg 1/2003 in conjunction with Recital 11, the Commission is empowered to adopt a decision finding an infringement not only when it orders the termination of an infringement or imposes a fine, but also where the infringement has already come to an end and no fine is imposed. The power of the Commission to adopt an infringement decision in such circumstances is limited to cases where it has a legitimate interest to do so. This may be the case where there is a danger that the addressee might re-offend, or where the case raises new issues, the clarification of which is in the public interest.

[21] There appears to be a clear public interest in establishing an infringement by a Commission decision in the light of *Courage and Crehan* (Case C-453/99 [2001] ECR I-6297) and the policy objective inherent in Reg 1/2003 of using national courts to enforce EC competition rules. Kerse & Khan, *EC Antitrust Procedure* (6th edn, Sweet & Maxwell 2012) para 6-019.

[22] Thus, eg in *London European Airways v SABENA* [1988] OJ L317/47, the Commission imposed a token fine on Sabena for an abuse of a dominant position which had already ceased, in so far as the Belgian airline gave certain undertakings regarding its future conduct in the Belgian computer flight reservation market. See also *PO Video Games v PO Nintendo Distribution/Omega-Nintendo* [2003] OJ L255/33, para 371: 'However, the Commission has wide discretionary powers when determining the amount of fines to be imposed, including the power not to impose a fine at all or merely a symbolic fine'.

[23] See *Tetra Pak II* [1992] OJ L72/1. As is clear from Annex 7 to the decision, Tetra Pak's undertakings did not enable it to avoid the imposition of a fine of EUR 75 million.

will be due either to the fact that the case has low priority or is of little relevance to competition policy, or to the impossibility of dealing with the case formally by means of a favourable decision. An example would be a procedure commenced on the basis of a complaint or on the Commission's own initiative, in the course of which the undertakings change their agreements to the satisfaction of the Commission.[24]

II. Commitments

A. The Purpose and Main Aspects of Commitment Decisions

13.08 For a long time, the Commission has accepted commitments to settle antitrust proceedings on an informal basis. A number of cases have been resolved through informal commitments, called 'undertakings', offered by the undertaking concerned and considered by the Commission as acceptable.[25] The Court of Justice ('ECJ') even considered that providing the undertakings concerned with an opportunity to bring the practices complained of into line with the competition rules of the Treaty could be a requirement of good administration.[26] Nevertheless, it was not until Regulation 1/2003 that this practice was given an express legal basis and clear legal consequences. Article 9 of Regulation 1/2003 empowers the Commission to adopt decisions accepting commitments offered by undertakings in the course of proceedings in which the Commission intends to adopt a decision that orders termination of a potential infringement.[27] Such commitments must constitute an appropriate remedy to the competition concerns identified by the Commission during the proceedings and are rendered binding upon the undertaking to which the so-called 'Article 9 decision' or

---

[24] Commission Press Release IP/10/1175 'Antitrust: Statement on Apple's iPhone policy changes' of 25 September 2010, where the Commission investigated, among others, Apple's 'country of purchase' rule, where repairs services were only available in the country where the iPhone was purchased. The Commission was concerned that this made it difficult for consumers who had purchased an iPhone in another EU/EEA country to exercise their warranty rights in their home country. In response to this, Apple announced that it would no longer be enforcing the 'country of purchase' rule within the EU/EEA. It appointed independent authorized service providers to offer cross-border iPhone warranty services in those Member States where Apple does not currently directly take charge of repairs. It also removed the restrictions previously introduced on the development tools used to create iPhone apps. Conversely, in the investigation of the aftermarket for IBM mainframe computer ('Mainframes') maintenance, IBM informed the Commission that it had taken steps to modify the conditions under which it made the relevant inputs available to third party maintainers ('TPMs') of IBM Mainframes. However, because of their unilateral character, IBM's declarations were not enforceable by TPMs. For this reason, the Commission considered that IBM's unilateral declarations did not obviate the need for formal commitments pursuant to Art 9: Case COMP/39.692 *IBM Maintenance Services* [2012] OJ C18/6. F Domanico and M Angeli, 'An Analysis of the IBM Commitment Decision concerning the Aftermarket for IBM Mainframe Maintenance' (2012) 1 Competition Policy Newsletter.

[25] A review of the Commission's informal practice prior to Reg 1/2003 shows that the informal decisions where undertakings or commitments were given most frequently concerned high technology industries where the implementation of undertakings by the parties was a rapid and effective form of resolving the specific problems of constantly changing markets for which there was no solution under Reg 17: *IBM* [1985] OJ L118/24; Case COMP/30.566 *United International Pictures BV (UIP)*; Commission Press Release IP/99/681 'Commission renews UIP authorisation for five years' of 14 September 1999; *Irish Distillers Group* (XVIII Competition Report [1988]); *Coca-Cola* (XIX Competition Report [1989]); *Microsoft I* (XXIV Competition Report [1994]); *Digital* (XXVII Report on Competition Policy [1997]). See also, with more references to the case law until 2005, J Temple Lang, 'Commitment Decisions and Settlements with Antitrust Authorities and Private Parties under European Antitrust Law', *32nd Annual International Antitrust Law & Policy Conference Fordham Corporate Law Institute* (Juris Publishing 2005) 265–324.

[26] Case 96/82 *IAZ v Commission* [1983] ECR 3369, para 15.

[27] Article 9 of Reg 1/2003 should be read together with Recital 13. By virtue of Art 5 of Reg 1/2003, NCAs will also be entitled to adopt commitment decisions.

'commitment decision' is addressed. A commitment decision is usually intended to bring an apparent on-going infringement to an end and restore competition in the market. However, commitments can still be appropriate if the undertakings have discontinued their presumed anticompetitive practice prior to, or during, the investigation. This is to ensure that the undertakings will also continue to abide by the EU competition rules in the future, which in itself would constitute a legitimate interest for taking a formal Article 9 decision.[28]

Under Article 9 of Regulation 1/2003, the Commission 'may' but is never obliged to terminate **13.09** its proceedings by adopting a commitment decision.[29] This also applies if the Commission previously adopted a decision pursuant to Article 9 of Regulation 1/2003 in a similar case.[30] The Commission can consider such a decision if and when (i) the companies under investigation are willing to offer commitments which remove the Commission's initial competition concerns as expressed in a preliminary assessment; (ii) the case is not one where 'the Commission intends to impose a fine';[31] (iii) efficiency reasons justify that the Commission limits itself to making the commitments binding, and does not issue a formal prohibition decision.[32] In the event of multi-party infringements, this instrument may also be used vis-à-vis one undertaking, whereas the Commission may at the same time continue its infringement procedure against the others that do not offer sufficient commitments.[33] To date, under Regulation 1/2003 there has been a steadily increasing number of cases, in which Article 9 has been applied.[34] The fact that the Commission resorts to this instrument in a rising number of

---

[28] European Commission Antitrust Manual of Procedures, Internal DG Competition working documents on procedures for the application of Articles 101 and 102 TFEU, March 2012, Module 16 'Commitment decision (Article 9 of Reg. 1/2003)', para 15.

[29] The absence of an obligation to adopt a commitment decision also follows from the wording in Recital 13 of Reg 1/2003, which refers to the Commission's *ability* to adopt decisions which make commitments binding if certain requirements are met.

[30] European Commission Antitrust Manual of Procedures, Internal DG Competition working documents on procedures for the application of Articles 101 and 102 TFEU, March 2012, Module 16 'Commitment decision (Article 9 of Reg. 1/2003)', para 16.

[31] See Recital 13, 3rd sentence of Reg 1/2003. In the light of the preparatory work for Reg 1/2003, this statement merely seems to indicate that where the Commission decides to accept commitments, it cannot impose a fine. See Council of the European Union, Report of the Competition Working Party of 8 November 2002 (2000/0243(CNS)) ('the possibility for the Commission to adopt commitment decisions has been limited to cases in which it does not intend to impose a fine. This is however logical given that the regulation does not provide for a possibility to settle on the payment of an amount of money'). The Commission has excluded the adoption of Art 9 decisions in hardcore cartel cases (see Commission MEMO/04/217 'Commitment decisions (Article 9 of Council Regulation 1/2003 providing for a modernised framework for antitrust scrutiny of company behaviour' of 17 September 2004), but has made use of the new legal instrument in cases of rather serious infringements; see for instance, Decision of 18 March 2009, COMP 39402, *RWE gas foreclosure.*

[32] Commission MEMO/04/217 'Commitment decisions (Art 9 of Council Reg 1/2003 providing for a modernised framework for antitrust scrutiny of company behaviour)' of 17 September 2004.

[33] There can be no conflict with the principle of equal treatment where the Commission communicates its competitive concerns to all undertakings concerned, thus giving them the opportunity of submitting a proposal for commitments.

[34] Since 2004, the following decisions pursuant to Art 9 have been adopted (with Summary Decision in the OJ): Decision of 19 January 2005 COMP 37214 *DFB* [2005] OJ L134/46; Decision of 22 June 2005 COMP 39116 *Coca-Cola* [2005] OJ L134/46; Decision of 11 October 2007 COMP 37966 *Distrigaz* [2008] OJ C9/8; Decision of 22 March 2006 COMP 38173 *The Football Association Premier League Limited* [2008] OJ C7/18; Decision of 12 April 2006 COMP 38348 *REPSOL C.P.P. SA* [2006] OJ L176/104; Decision of 22 February 2006 COMP 38381 *De Beers* [2006] OJ C L205/24; Decision of 9 December 2009 COMP 38636 *Rambus* [2010] OJ C30/17; Decision of 4 October 2006 COMP 38681 *Cannes Agreement* [2007] OJ L296/27; Decision of 3 December 2009 [2007] OJ L296/27; Decision of 3 December 2009 COMP 39316 *GDF foreclosure* [2010] OJ C57/13; Decision of 26 November 2008 COMP 39388 *German electricity wholesale market* [2009] OJ C36/8; Decision of 26 November 2008 COMP 39389 *German electricity balancing market* [2009] OJ C36/8; Decision of 18 March 2009 COMP 39402 *RWE gas foreclosure* [2009] OJ C133/10; Decision of 14 October 2009 COMP 39416 *Ship Classification* [2010] OJ C2/5; Decision of 16

cases is already indicative of a certain popularity of commitment decisions. In some of these cases, the Commission has raised concerns as regards practices that could infringe Article 101 TFEU, particularly as regards vertical agreements (eg *German Bundesliga*,[35] *Repsol CPP SA*, *Premier League*).[36] Other cases involve Article 102 (eg *Coca Cola, Rambus, Microsoft, IBM Maintenance Service*) or both Articles 101 and 102 TFEU (eg *Alrosa-De Beers*). Further, some of the cases were originally petitions for individual authorization which the Commission, with the coming into force of Regulation 1/2003, turned into commitment decisions (eg *German Bundesliga, Repsol CPP SA, Premier League, Austrian Airlines/SAS*). At present, it seems safe to assume, therefore, that the new legal instrument is and will be applied across the board to all types of potential infringements of Articles 101 and 102 TFEU, with exception being made for hardcore infringements and other breaches of an obvious nature.[37]

13.10   One of the unique features of commitment decisions—which fundamentally differentiates them from finding and termination of infringement decisions, or inapplicability decisions— is the scope of the assessment that the Commission carries out. Article 9 provides that commitment decisions will only state that there are no longer reasons for the Commission to intervene. Recital 13, 2nd sentence of Regulation 1/2003 provides that such decisions will not declare whether or not an infringement of EU competition rules has occurred or whether it continues to exist. Therefore, the Commission is not obliged to carry out an exhaustive assessment of the matter, and can instead choose to decide that the commitments offered are sufficient to remove its concerns about the case in question. As a consequence, the companies under investigation avoid prohibition decisions based on Article 7 of Regulation 1/2003 that can harm their reputation and that can be used against them as proof of competition law infringements before national courts.[38] For the Commission, commitment decisions can save resources, allow for a speedier solution of competition cases in fast moving markets, and hence achieve more efficient changes in the competitive landscape than the adversarial disposal of a case pursuant to Article 7 of Regulation 1/2003.[39] Furthermore, the consensual nature of commitment decisions significantly reduces the risk of litigation before the EU

December 2009 COMP 39530 *Microsoft (Tying)* [2013] OJ C120/15; Decision of 17 March 2010 COMP 39386 *Long term electricity contracts in France* [2010] OJ C133/5; Decision of 14 April 2010 COMP 39351 *Swedish Interconnectors* [2010] OJ C142/28; Decision of 4 May 2010 COMP 39317 *E.On gas foreclosure* [2010] OJ C278/9; Decision of 14 July 2010 COMP 39.596 *BA/AA/IB* [2010] OJ C278/14; Decision of 29 September 2010 COMP 39315 *ENI* [2010] OJ C352/8; Decision of 08 December 2010 COMP 39398 *VISA MIF* [2011] OJ C79/8; Decision of 13 December 2011 COMP 39692 *IBM Maintenance Service* [2012] OJ C18/6; Decision of 18 June 2012 COMP 39736 *Siemens/Areva* [2012] OJ C280/8; Decision of 12 December 2012 COMP 39847 *E-books* [2013] C73/17.

[35] *German Bundesliga* (Art 27(4) notice in [2004] OJ C229/13 and summary in [2005] OJ L134/46), was the first case in which the Commission has applied Art 9. This procedure resulted from the request of the German Football Federation (DFB) for a negative clearance decision, or alternatively an individual exemption under Art 81(3) EC [now Article 101(3) TFEU], for the centralized marketing of the TV and radio broadcasting rights. See also T Körber, 'Die erstmalige Anwendung der Verpflichtungszusage gemäss Art 9 VO 1/2003' [2005] Wettbewerb in Recht und Praxis 463.

[36] By contrast, the *VISA MIF* Decision related to agreements of a horizontal nature.

[37] For a more detailed description of all Art 9 decisions adopted up to January 2010 see S Rab, D Monnoyeur, and A Sukhtankar, 'Commitments in EU Competition Cases Article 9 of Regulation 1/2003, Its Application and the Challenges Ahead' (2010) 1(3) Journal of European Competition Law & Practice 171.

[38] See also Art 16. However, according to Recital 13, commitment decisions are without prejudice to the powers of competition authorities and courts of the Member States to find an infringement and decide upon the case. Nevertheless, the entire lack of binding effect on national courts is controversially discussed in academia; see, in this respect, H Schweitzer, 'Commitment Decisions under Art. 9 of Regulation 1/2003' (2008) 22 EUI Working Papers Law 24.

[39] In addition to the traditional, fully adversarial procedure, the Commission has recently introduced a specific procedure which allows the Commission to settle cartel cases. Parties can choose to acknowledge their involvement in a cartel and their liability for it. In return, the Commission can reduce the fine imposed by

Courts.[40] Nevertheless, allowing the NCAs to examine cases which have already been decided by the Commission could present a problem, since this could seriously undermine the legal certainty provided by the decision, which would in turn dissuade companies from using this mechanism. However, so far, there was no intervention on the part of NCAs which would have resulted in contradictions with one of the Commission's Article 9 decisions.

B. The Procedure

1. The initiation of commitment discussions and the first State of Play meeting

Since commitments may be withdrawn until the adoption of the commitment decision, and given that a market test may show that the commitments are not appropriate, there is always a risk that antitrust investigations are significantly delayed by unsuccessful commitment discussions. From the Commission's perspective, it is therefore crucial to hold commitment discussions with the parties (which are also called 'undertakings concerned'),[41] before engaging in an Article 9 procedure in order to ascertain their willingness to settle and verify whether the commitments appear sufficiently likely to resolve the identified competition problems.[42] Undertakings may contact the Directorate-General for Competition ('DG COMP') at any point in time to explore its readiness to enter into commitment discussions. DG COMP encourages undertakings to signal at the earliest possible stage their interest in discussing commitments.[43] A State of Play meeting will be offered to parties which signal an interest in discussing commitments.[44] In practice, the description of the case as given in this State of Play meeting is the main basis for the undertakings concerned to decide whether to submit commitments or not.[45] Therefore, the summary of the competition concerns presented at the State of Play meeting is of great importance. Even if the Commission's competition concerns are only presented orally to the parties, the Commission's presentation should be well-structured and allow them to understand exactly the theory of harm and the underlying factual evidence. The parties will also be given the opportunity to ask questions regarding the competition concern in

13.11

---

10 per cent. This 'settlement' has to be distinguished from Art 9 decisions, as it results in a decision pursuant to Art 7 establishing an infringement and imposing fines under Article 23. See Commission Regulation (EC) No 622/2008 of 30 June 2008 amending Regulation (EC) No 773/2004, as regards the conduct of settlement procedures in cartel cases [2008] OJ L171/3 and Commission Notice on the conduct of settlement procedures in view of the adoption of Decisions pursuant to Article 7 and Article 23 of Council Regulation (EC) No 1/2003 in cartel cases, [2008] OJ C167/1. See in this respect Ch 11, 'Infringement Decisions and Penalties', para 11.11.

[40] To date, commitment decisions remain unchallenged by the addressees. Only in three cases have applications against Art 9 decisions been lodged by third parties: apart from the Commission Decision in *Alrosa*, which will be discussed in more detail later, the Commission Decision of 12 April 2006 COMP 38348 *REPSOL C.P.P. SA*, and the Decision of 9 December 2009 COMP 38636 *Rambus* were challenged by third parties. The applications against the *Repsol* Decision were dismissed by the GC as inadmissible, having been brought out of time; see Orders of the GC in Cases T-45/08 *Transportes Evaristo Molina, SA v Commission* [2008] ECR II-265 and T-274/06 *Estaser El Mareny, SL v Commission* [2008] ECR II-143. The applications against the *Rambus* Decision are still pending (Cases T-148/10 and T-149/10).

[41] See Arts 7(1) and 9(1) of Reg 1/2003.

[42] European Commission Antitrust Manual of Procedures, Internal DG Competition working documents on procedures for the application of Articles 101 and 102 TFEU, March 2012, Module 16 'Commitment decision (Article 9 of Reg. 1/2003)', para 10.

[43] European Commission Antitrust Manual of Procedures, Internal DG Competition working documents on procedures for the application of Articles 101 and 102 TFEU, March 2012, Module 16 'Commitment decision (Article 9 of Reg. 1/2003)', para 19.

[44] Commission Notice on best practices for the conduct of proceedings concerning Articles 101 and 102 TFEU [2011] OJ C308/6, para 121.

[45] Undertakings concerned will usually only receive a written 'preliminary assessment' after they have stated their initial readiness to offer commitments.

order to be able to report the Commission's concerns clearly to their internal decision-making bodies. The Commission will also indicate to the undertaking the timeframe within which the discussions on potential commitments should be concluded.[46] The Commission services should clarify that the State of Play meeting is without prejudice to the decision of the Commissioner for Competition on whether to proceed along the commitment decision track. Therefore, during the ensuing discussions on potential commitments, no final position can be taken on their appropriateness.[47] Should the parties, after being confronted with the Commission's concerns in the State of Play meeting, decide to offer commitments, they should outline the main elements of the—at this stage informal—commitment proposal. This may, in practice, happen by submitting a 'term sheet' describing the main elements of the commitments, but sometimes already with a first draft of a commitment text.[48] If the Commission services are convinced that the commitments informally proposed by the undertaking may address the competition concerns and that the undertaking is seriously interested in submitting adequate formal commitments, they will propose to the Commissioner to draft a preliminary assessment.

2. The preliminary assessment

13.12 Article 9 states that undertakings will be able to offer commitments 'to meet the concerns expressed to them by the Commission in its preliminary assessment'. A preliminary assessment is not identical to a statement of objections,[49] although the Commission can adopt an Article 9 decision also on the basis of commitments offered in response to a statement of objections and has already done so in a few cases (eg *Premier League, Santiago Agreement, Rambus*).[50] The preliminary assessment is usually shorter than a statement of objections in that it merely summarizes the main facts of the case and identifies the competition concerns that would warrant a decision requiring that the infringement is brought to an end.[51] In previous decisions, the lengths of preliminary assessments varied from around ten to seventy pages,[52] which is about one-tenth of the length of a statement of objections. Preparing a statement of objections entails a great deal of work by the Commission and, in a proceeding

---

[46] European Commission Antitrust Manual of Procedures, Internal DG Competition working documents on procedures for the application of Articles 101 and 102 TFEU, March 2012, Module 16 'Commitment decision (Article 9 of Reg. 1/2003)', para 20.

[47] European Commission Antitrust Manual of Procedures, Internal DG Competition working documents on procedures for the application of Articles 101 and 102 TFEU, March 2012, Module 16 'Commitment decision (Article 9 of Reg. 1/2003)', para 21.

[48] European Commission Antitrust Manual of Procedures, Internal DG Competition working documents on procedures for the application of Articles 101 and 102 TFEU, March 2012, Module 16 'Commitment decision (Article 9 of Reg. 1/2003)', para 22.

[49] Article 2(1) of Reg 773/2004 distinguishes between a preliminary assessment as referred to in Art 9(1) of Reg 1/2003 and a statement of objections that companies receive prior to decisions enumerated in Art 27(1) of Reg 1/2003. In its decisional practice, the Commission also distinguishes between statements of objections and preliminary assessments in its decisions and sometimes issues statement of objections also in commitment procedures. See, for instance, Decision of 19 January 2005 COMP 37214 *Joint selling of the media rights to the German Bundesliga*, para 17 et seq; Decision of 16 December 2009 COMP 39530 *Microsoft (Tying)*, [2013] OJ C120/15, para 6.

[50] If a statement of objections has already been sent to the parties, commitments may nevertheless still be accepted, in appropriate cases. In these circumstances, a statement of objections fulfils the requirements of a preliminary assessment, as it contains a summary of the main facts, as well as an assessment of the competition concerns identified. See Commission Notice on best practices for the conduct of proceedings concerning Articles 101 and 102 TFEU [2011] OJ C308/6, para 121. According to Art 2 of Reg 773/2004, the issuance of a preliminary assessment or a statement of objections also obliges the Commission to initiate proceedings.

[51] See Commission Notice on best practices for the conduct of proceedings concerning Articles 101 and 102 TFEU [2011] OJ C308/6, para 121.

[52] European Commission Antitrust Manual of Procedures, Internal DG Competition working documents on procedures for the application of Articles 101 and 102 TFEU, March 2012, Module 16 'Commitment decision (Article 9 of Reg. 1/2003)', para 26.

leading to a decision adopted pursuant to Article 9 of Regulation 1/2003, it may not be necessary for undertakings to be aware of the Commission's concerns in great detail. The preliminary assessment is not published and not made available to third parties.[53] It is supposed to serve as a basis for the parties to formulate appropriate commitments addressing the competition concerns expressed by the Commission, or to better define previously discussed commitments.[54] Preliminary assessments are notified in the authentic language of the addressee, unless the latter has signed a language waiver.[55] The Commissioner needs to give his/her approval to adopt the preliminary assessment and to engage in formal commitment discussions with the parties. If proceedings have not been initiated before, the adoption of the preliminary assessment will be combined with the initiation of the proceedings.

C. The Commitments

1. The formal requirements for the timely submission of commitment proposals

After receiving the preliminary assessment, the parties will normally have one month to **13.13** formally submit their commitments. If they have received a statement of objections and subsequently decide to submit commitments, the time limit to reply to the statement of objections will generally not be extended.[56] The commitments proposed will only be accepted if they are unambiguous and self-executing, ie their implementation must not be dependent on the will of a third party which is not bound by the commitments. Although there is no specific standard text for antitrust commitments, the Standard Model for Divestiture Commitments,[57] originally developed for merger remedies, can be an appropriate reference for antitrust commitments. Even where no pure divestiture commitment (such as licences or other non-structural/behavioural remedies) is proposed, the model text may still constitute a useful starting point. However, certain amendments to the merger model text are necessary to take into account that antitrust commitments are based on Article 9 of Regulation 1/2003. Examples of previous antitrust commitments may provide useful guidance on which formulation may be appropriate in the individual case. Proposals for changes to the model put forward by the parties should, however, be carefully verified and only accepted if appropriate in the individual case.[58] When commitments cannot be implemented without the agreement of third parties (eg where a third party that would not be a suitable buyer under the commitments holds a pre-emption right), the undertaking should submit evidence of the third party's agreement. If need be, a trustee can be appointed to assist the Commission in monitoring the implementation of proposed commitments.[59]

---

[53] European Commission Antitrust Manual of Procedures, Internal DG Competition working documents on procedures for the application of Articles 101 and 102 TFEU, March 2012, Module 16 'Commitment decision (Article 9 of Reg. 1/2003)', para 36.

[54] See Commission Notice on best practices for the conduct of proceedings concerning Articles 101 and 102 TFEU [2011] OJ C308/6, para 122.

[55] See Commission Notice on best practices for the conduct of proceedings concerning Arts 101 and 102 TFEU [2011] OJ C308/6, para 29.

[56] Commission Notice on best practices for the conduct of proceedings concerning Articles 101 and 102 TFEU [2011] OJ C308/6, para 126.

[57] Accessible at <http://ec.europa.eu/competition/mergers/legislation/divestiture.html>.

[58] European Commission Antitrust Manual of Procedures, Internal DG Competition working documents on procedures for the application of Articles 101 and 102 TFEU, March 2012, Module 16 'Commitment decision (Article 9 of Reg. 1/2003)', para 40.

[59] Commission Notice on best practices for the conduct of proceedings concerning Articles 101 and 102 TFEU [2011] OJ C308/6, para 128.

2. The types of commitments to be accepted

13.14 The Commission has a wide discretion in relation to the type of commitments to be accepted.[60] Commitments can be behavioural (eg a supply obligation) or structural (eg divestiture of a part of a company).[61] As opposed to merger control proceedings, they might be primarily behavioural given that this will in most cases suffice to terminate potential (behavioural) infringements.[62] The Commission requires 'that commitments should provide that a lasting improvement of the market structure is achieved within a foreseeable timeframe'.[63] To date, a number of commitment decisions have been published (eg *Bundesliga, Repsol, Coca-Cola,* and *De Beers-Alrosa, Austrian Airlines/SAS, Microsoft Tying, VISA MIF*). Of these, it can be concluded that, in general, the Commission will look favourably on those commitments that aim to ensure that there is no foreclosure of the market, for instance:

(i) by offering the product in question to the greatest number of possible purchasers (*Bundesliga* and *De Beers-Alrosa*);

(ii) by opening as far as possible distribution networks so that suppliers can have access to these and thus distribute their products (*Repsol*);

(iii) by ending practices such as tying or discounts for bulk purchase that oblige clients to buy only that company's products (*Coca-Cola*);

(iv) by offering contracts through transparent procedures (*Bundesliga*);

(v) by including a 'choice screen' into the dominant company's operating system, enabling users to choose in an informed and unbiased manner which web browser(s) they wanted to install in addition to, or instead of, the dominant company's web browser (*Microsoft tying*);

(vi) by surrendering take-off and landing slots to enable competition on affected air routes (*Austrian Airlines/SAS*); and

(vii) by reducing the product scope and duration of a non-compete obligation in the market for nuclear technologies (*Siemens/Areva*).

However, the commitment not to charge royalties during a certain period or to commit to a maximum royalty rate with regard to certain standard essential patents, rendered binding in *Rambus*, demonstrated that Article 9 Decisions have also been used with regard to potential exploitative abuses of a dominant position.

3. The proportionality of commitments

13.15 Article 9 of Regulation 1/2003 stipulates that the commitments must meet the concerns expressed by the Commission.[64] By contrast, the wording of the provision does not allow for

---

[60] The Commission has described commitment decisions as 'a formal settlement solicited by a company under investigation and agreed by the Commission where its enforcement priorities justify this choice'. Commission MEMO/04/217 'Commitment decisions (Art 9 of Council Reg 1/2003 providing for a modernised framework for antitrust scrutiny of company behaviour)' of 17 September 2004.

[61] Commission Notice on best practices for the conduct of proceedings concerning Articles 101 and 102 TFEU [2011] OJ C308/6, para 127. The boundaries between both commitment types are not always entirely clear. See eg Commission Notice on remedies acceptable under the Council Regulation (EC) No 139/2004 and under Commission Regulation (EC) No 802/2004, [2008] OJ C267/1–27, para 22 et seq.

[62] However, the Commission has accepted structural rather than, or in addition to, behavioural commitments in a number of Art 9 decisions. See, in particular, Decision of 14 July 2010 COMP 39.596 *BA/AA/IB* [2010] OJ C278/14 and Decision of 29 September 2010 COMP 39315 *ENI* [2010] OJ C352/8.

[63] European Commission Antitrust Manual of Procedures, Internal DG Competition working documents on procedures for the application of Articles 101 and 102 TFEU, March 2012, Module 16 'Commitment decision (Article 9 of Reg. 1/2003)', para 51.

[64] According to settled case law (see eg Case C-119/97 *Ufex* [1999] ECR I-1341, para 88 et seq; Case T-24/90 *Automec* [1992] ECR II-2223, para 77 et seq), the Commission is entitled to apply different degrees

conclusions as to whether the Commission may render commitments binding which 'overshoot the mark' in that they go beyond what is objectively required to ensure the respect of competition law. Contrary to Article 7, Article 9 makes no reference to the principle of proportionality.[65] This begs the question whether the Commission can render binding 'disproportionate' commitments, the contents of which could not have lawfully been imposed on the addressees in a decision pursuant to Article 7 of Regulation 1/2003. The response has been given in the ECJ's ruling in *Alrosa*.[66] The Court emphasized the different aims of decisions pursuant to Articles 7 and 9 of Regulation 1/2003: in contrast to Article 7, which aims at establishing and terminating an infringement, Article 9 is intended to provide for a more rapid solution to the competition problems identified by enabling the companies concerned fully to participate in the procedure.[67] In view of the consensual nature of commitment proceedings, the Commission's task is confined to examining, and possibly accepting, the commitments offered by the undertakings concerned.[68] Accordingly, the measures which can be imposed in the context of proceedings pursuant to Article 7 of Regulation 1/2003 cannot serve as a reference for the purpose of assessing the proportionality of commitments accepted under Article 9 of Regulation 1/2003.[69] Rather, the proportionality of Article 9 decisions merely requires that the commitments in question address the concerns the Commission expressed, and that the companies concerned have not offered less onerous commitments that also address those concerns adequately.[70] By contrast, the Commission is not obliged itself to seek out less onerous or more moderate solutions than the commitments proposed.[71] In the light of this case law, the responsibility for avoiding disproportionate commitment decisions lies in the first place with the undertakings concerned.[72] In this context, it should be recalled that both sides, Commission and parties, can revoke at any time the willingness to cooperate required for commitment procedures.[73]

---

of priority in dealing with the cases submitted to it and to refrain from pursuing cases that do not raise sufficient EU interest to justify its investigations. Therefore, it can be argued that the Commission is not prevented from closing a procedure on the basis of commitments which do not fully eliminate a (potential) breach of competition law.

[65] The principle of proportionality requires that the measures adopted by EU institutions must not exceed what is appropriate and necessary for attaining the objective pursued, which implies that the disadvantages caused must not be disproportionate to the aims pursued and that when there is a choice between several appropriate measures, recourse must be had to the least onerous. See Case 331/88 *The Queen/Ministry of Agriculture, Fisheries and Food, ex parte FEDESA and others* [1990] ECR I-4023; Case C-180/00 *Netherlands v Commission* [2005] ECR I-6603, para 103; and Case C-174/05 *Zuid-Hollandse Milieufederatie and Natuur en Milieu* [2006] ECR I-2443, para 28.

[66] For a detailed discussion of the ECJ's ruling in *Alrosa* see M Kellerbauer, 'Playground instead of Playpen: The Court of Justice of the European Union's Alrosa Judgment on Article 9 of Regulation 1/2003' (2011) 32(1) European Competition Law Review 1; F Wagner-von Papp, 'Best and Even Better Practices in Commitment Procedures after Alrosa: The Dangers of Abandoning the "Struggle for Competition Law"' (2012) 49(3) Common Market Law Review 934; S Rab, D Monnoyeur, and A Sukhtankar, 'Commitments in EU Competition Cases Article 9 of Regulation 1/2003, its Application and the Challenges Ahead' (2010) 1(3) Journal of European Competition Law & Practice 182.

[67] Case C-441/07 *Commission v Alrosa* [2010] ECR I-5949, paras 35 and 46.

[68] Case C-441/07 *Commission v Alrosa* [2010] ECR I-5949, para 40.

[69] Case C-441/07 *Commission v Alrosa* [2010] ECR I-5949, para 47 et seq. In view of the advantages of Art 9 decisions for the undertakings concerned, the ECJ finds it acceptable that concessions they make may go beyond what the Commission could itself impose on them in a decision adopted under Art 7.

[70] Case C-441/07 *Commission v Alrosa* [2010] ECR I-5949, paras 35 and 41.

[71] Case C-441/07 *Commission v Alrosa* [2010] ECR I-5949, paras 40, 41, and 61.

[72] See in this respect M Kellerbauer, 'Playground instead of Playpen: The Court of Justice of the European Union's Alrosa Judgment on Article 9 of Regulation 1/2003' (2011) 32(1) European Competition Law Review 1.

[73] This is also highlighted in para 125 of the Commission Notice on best practices for the conduct of proceedings concerning Articles 101 and 102 TFEU [2011] OJ C308/6.

4. The duration of commitments

13.16 Under Article 9 of Regulation 1/2003, commitment decisions 'may be adopted for a specific period', thereby leaving open whether commitments can be rendered binding for an indefinite period. The General Court ('GC') in *Alrosa* held in this respect:

> As regards the period in which the decision making commitments binding may remain in force, it should be noted that while Article 9(1) of Regulation No 1/2003 provides that such a decision may be adopted for a specified period, it does not, however, require this. The definitive wording of Article 9 of Regulation No 1/2003 falls to be distinguished in that regard, as the Commission rightly points out, from the wording which had been used at the stage of the Commission proposal for a Council Regulation on the implementation of the rules on competition laid down in Articles 81 [EC] and 82 [EC] (COM(2000) 582 final), which provided that such a decision was 'to be adopted for a specified period'. There is, accordingly, no reason of principle which prohibits the Commission from making commitments for an indefinite period binding.[74]

As the GC's ruling was quashed by the ECJ for reasons other than the consideration set out earlier, it seems plausible that the GC will continue to hold in the future that the Commission is not prohibited from making commitments binding for an indefinite period. The principle of proportionality does not stand against this finding, Article 9(2)(a) of Regulation 1/2003 enables the Commission to reopen proceedings where an overly lengthy commitment is no longer adequate in the light of the material change in any of the facts on which the decision was based.[75] This ensures that disproportionately lengthy commitments can be avoided.

13.17 Generally, however, commitment decisions will be adopted for a specific time period only. This time period will depend on when the Commission expects the factual situation to change, and such change will either make the commitments unnecessary, or mean that they must be updated. From this it can be deduced that time periods will usually be shorter when the undertakings making the commitments in question are operating in markets undergoing rapid change.[76] In most of the decisions taken to date, commitments have been imposed for a period between four and five-and-a-half years.[77] Review clauses, including clauses extending deadlines of the commitments, should normally be limited to exceptional circumstances, as provided in the model text for divestiture commitments. Circumstances which are likely or at least possible to occur during the time of the implementation of the commitment should normally be

---

[74] Case T-170/06, *Alrosa v Commission* [2007] ECR II-260, para 91.

[75] For an example of such a review clause see Annex 'commitments' of Decision of 22 February 2006, Case COMP/B-2/38.381 *De Beers*, published in summary in [2006] OJ L205/24: 'Pursuant to Article 9.2(a) of Regulation No 1/2003, De Beers may request the Commission to reopen the proceedings with a view to modifying the present Commitments where there has been a material change in any of the facts on which the Commitment Decision is based.'

[76] This will be particularly important in high technology and starting industries.

[77] In *Bundesliga* the commitments were made binding taking effect on 9 January 2005 until June 2009. See Commission Press Release IP/05/62 'Competition: German Football League commitments to liberalise joint selling of Bundesliga media rights made legally binding by Commission decision' of 19 January 2005. See also summary of the commitment decision in [2005] OJ L134/46. In *Coca-Cola*, the commitment has been binding until December 2010. Commission Press Release IP/05/775 'Competition: Commission makes commitments from Coca-Cola legally binding, increasing consumer choice' of 22 June 2005; see also summary of the commitment decision in [2005] OJ L253/21. In *VISA (MIF)*, the commitments were rendered binding on Visa for four years following notification of the Decision: Commission Press Release IP/10/1684 'Antitrust: Commission makes Visa Europe's commitments to cut interbank fees for debit cards legally binding' of 8 December 2010. In *IBM Maintenance Service*, the commitments were rendered binding on IBM for five years following notification of the Decision. See summary of the Commitment Decision of 13 December 2011 in Case COMP/39.692 *IBM Maintenance Services* in [2012] OJ C18/6.

addressed in the commitments themselves and not be left to the review clause. It is worth noting that, in an antitrust case, a review clause as foreseen in the model text would be in addition and without prejudice to the possibility of Article 9(2)(a) of Regulation 1/2003 according to which the addressee can request a re-opening of the proceedings where a material change in the facts has occurred.[78]

5. The market test of the commitments

Pursuant to Article 27(4) of Regulation No 1/2003, the Commission conducts a market test of **13.18** the commitments before making them binding by decision. The Commission will do so only if it considers that the commitments offered *prima facie* address the competition concerns identi- fied.[79] The Commission publishes in the OJ a notice which contains a concise summary of the case and the main content of the commitments, whilst respecting the obligations of professional secrecy. Failure to comply with this requirement set out in Article 27(4) of Regulation 1/2003 can be a ground for annulment via the procedure contained in Article 263 TFEU. In addition, the Commission usually publishes on DG COMP's website the full text of the commitments in the authentic language.[80] In order to enhance the transparency of the process, the Commission also publishes a press release setting out the key issues of the case and the proposed commit- ments. The Commission will at this stage also inform the complainant and interested third par- ties about the market test and invite the complainant to submit comments. The publication of the Article 27(4) Notice opens up a phase of market testing of the commitments offered which will last at least one month.[81]

After receipt of the replies to the market test, the parties will be informed of the substance **13.19** of the replies at a State of Play meeting.[82] Where the results of the market test and, poten- tially other information at the Commission's disposal, indicate that the competition concerns identified in the preliminary assessment or statement of objections have not been addressed, or that the commitments need to be amended in order to become effective, the Commission will inform the undertakings concerned accordingly. The obligation to carry out a market test should not be misunderstood as requiring the approval of the market for the commit- ments. The market test is not an opinion poll which determines the fate of the remedies. The Commission can take a commitment decision, even in cases in which participants in the mar- ket test requested to reject the commitment offer. However, the market test often provides the Commission with useful indications on how the commitments could be improved.[83] If the Commission identifies shortcomings in the commitment proposal and the under- takings concerned are willing to address them, they should submit an amended version of

---

[78] European Commission Antitrust Manual of Procedures, Internal DG Competition working documents on procedures for the application of Articles 101 and 102 TFEU, March 2012, Module 16 'Commitment decision (Article 9 of Reg. 1/2003)', para 52.

[79] See Commission Notice on best practices for the conduct of proceedings concerning Articles 101 and 102 TFEU [2011] OJ C308/6, para 129; European Commission Antitrust Manual of Procedures, Internal DG Competition working documents on procedures for the application of Articles 101 and 102 TFEU, March 2012, Module 16 'Commitment decision (Article 9 of Reg. 1/2003)', para 55.

[80] See Commission Notice on best practices for the conduct of proceedings concerning Articles 101 and 102 TFEU [2011] OJ C308/6, para 129.

[81] European Commission Antitrust Manual of Procedures, Internal DG Competition working documents on procedures for the application of Articles 101 and 102 TFEU, March 2012, Module 16 'Commitment decision (Article 9 of Reg. 1/2003)', para 63.

[82] See Commission Notice on best practices for the conduct of proceedings concerning Articles 101 and 102 TFEU [2011] OJ C308/6, para 132.

[83] European Commission Antitrust Manual of Procedures, Internal DG Competition working documents on procedures for the application of Articles 101 and 102 TFEU, March 2012, Module 16 'Commitment decision (Article 9 of Reg. 1/2003)', para 66.

the commitments. A new market test is only required if the commitments are substantially revised.[84] If the undertakings are unwilling to submit an amended version of the commitments, where this is required by the Commission's assessment of the result of the market test, the Commission can revert to the traditional procedure which can result in a decision pursuant to Article 7 of Regulation 1/2003.

6. Publicity of the decision-making process

13.20   The publication pursuant to Article 27(4) of Regulation needs to be distinguished from the publication of the final decision pursuant to Article 30 of Regulation 1/2003, which occurs after the commitments are accepted by the Commission, taking into account the legitimate interest in confidentiality of the companies concerned. The commitment decision to be published under Article 30 of Regulation 1/2003 should state the material facts of the case and the prima facie evidence of the suspected infringement, and incorporate the accepted commitments.[85]

D. The Procedural Rights

1. The distinction between parties and third parties

13.21   As regards the procedural rights enjoyed by undertakings in antitrust proceedings, Regulation 1/2003 generally distinguishes between parties[86] or undertakings concerned,[87] on the one hand, and complainants and other third parties showing a sufficient interest on the other.[88] The ECJ's ruling following the Commission's Article 9 decision in *Alrosa-De Beers* shed light on this distinction. In the case in question, the Commission granted the procedural rights of an undertaking concerned only to De Beers, although both Alrosa and De Beers had originally been subject to the Commission's investigation and been involved in commitment discussions. The Commission treated Alrosa as a third party because only De Beers had eventually offered commitments deemed sufficient by the Commission, which led to an Article 9 decision addressed to De Beers. However, De Beers' unilateral commitment also restricted *de facto* the possibility of Alrosa continuing its long-lasting bilateral trading relationship with De Beers. Therefore, Alrosa claimed that in the procedure that had resulted in the Article 9 Decision addressed to De Beers, the Commission should have granted the procedural rights of an undertaking concerned to both De Beers and Alrosa.[89]

13.22   Whilst the GC granted Alrosa's application, upon appeal, the ECJ confirmed that the Commission had not been obliged to grant Alrosa the procedural rights of an undertaking concerned. The ECJ observed that the Commission had initiated a second, separate proceeding under Article 102 TFEU which concerned De Beers's conduct and in which a second statement of objections had been notified to De Beers only.[90] It followed that Alrosa could have had the status of

---

[84]   See Commission Notice on best practices for the conduct of proceedings concerning Articles 101 and 102 TFEU [2011] OJ C308/6, para 133; European Commission Antitrust Manual of Procedures, Internal DG Competition working documents on procedures for the application of Articles 101 and 102 TFEU, March 2012, Module 16 'Commitment decision (Article 9 of Reg. 1/2003)', para 67.

[85]   Proposal for a Council Regulation implementing Arts 81 and 82 of the Treaty, COM (2000) 582 final-CNS 2000/0243 Explanatory Memorandum Art 8.

[86]   Article 27(1) 1st and 2nd sentence of Reg 1/2003.

[87]   See Arts 7(1) and 9(1) of Reg 1/2003.

[88]   Article 27(1) 3rd sentence and Art 27(3) of Reg 1/2003.

[89]   Alrosa also invoked other reasons and in particular the fact that the two sets of proceedings, one initiated against Alrosa and De Beers under Art 101 TFEU, and the other against De Beers under Art 102 TFEU, were so closely connected that they had at all times been treated *de facto* as being a single set of proceedings.

[90]   Case C-441/07 *Commission v Alrosa* [2010] ECR I-5949, para 88.

undertaking concerned only in the context of the proceedings brought under Article 101 TFEU, which concerned both Alrosa and De Beers, but in which no decision had been taken.[91] With regard to the proceedings conducted exclusively against de Beers, Alrosa merely enjoyed the less extensive rights of an interested third party, which the Commission had fully granted the company.[92] As a result of the ECJ's *Alrosa* judgment, the Commission also has a margin of discretion to conduct separate Article 9 proceedings against two undertakings if the commitments proposed by one of them are aimed at terminating contractual relations between the two. There are limits to this discretion: the Commission misuses its power if it makes a single factual situation the subject of two separate sets of proceedings without an objective reason. In such cases both companies must be accorded the right of an undertaking concerned in both proceedings.[93] In *Alrosa*, the ECJ considered that it was objectively justified for the Commission to conduct two separate sets of administrative proceedings with regard to the agreement between Alrosa and De Beers in view of the different material legal bases applied. With regard to the proceedings under Article 102 TFEU, only De Beers, as the presumed dominant undertaking, could have been the addressee of the statement of objections and the Commission's final decision.[94]

2. The procedural rights granted to parties ('undertakings concerned')

Prior to a decision establishing an infringement pursuant to Article 7 of Regulation 1/2003, the **13.23** parties are notified of a statement of objections and granted access to file[95] on the basis of which they are given the opportunity to comment in writing[96] and at a formal oral hearing.[97] According to Regulations 1/2003 and 773/2004, these rights do not seem to be granted to the same extent in proceedings leading to the adoption of a commitment decision. Pursuant to Article 9, undertakings concerned only need to be sent a preliminary assessment in which the Commission expresses its 'concerns' about their potentially anticompetitive practice.[98] As explained previously, this preliminary assessment is not identical to a statement of objections, the issuance of which usually triggers the right to access to the file[99] and the right to a formal oral hearing.[100] Furthermore, there is no indication in Regulations 1/2003, Regulation 773/2004, or case law as to the necessary contents of a preliminary assessment. However, since the rights of defence must be respected in proceedings liable to culminate in a measure adversely affecting a person also in the absence of an express provision recognizing them in the procedural rules or where the existing provisions do not in themselves take account of them,[101] the Commission is also obliged to ensure the respect of the right to be heard in commitment proceedings.[102] It follows that the

---

[91] Case C-441/07 *Commission v Alrosa* [2010] ECR I-5949, para 88.

[92] Case C-441/07 *Commission v Alrosa* [2010] ECR I-5949, para 91 et seq.

[93] Case C-441/07 *Commission v Alrosa* [2010] ECR I-5949, para 88 et seq.

[94] Case C-441/07 *Commission v Alrosa* [2010] ECR I-5949, para 89.

[95] Article 27(2) of Reg 1/2003, Art 15 of Regulation 773/2004.

[96] Article 27(1) of Reg 1/2003, Arts 10, 11(1) of Reg 773/2004.

[97] Article 12 of Reg 773/2004.

[98] It was also explained earlier that an Art 9 decision can also be adopted on the basis of commitments proposed subsequent to a statement of objections. In the latter case, the rights of parties, complainants, and interested third parties are more closely aligned to those applying in infringement procedures.

[99] See Art 27(2) of Reg 1/2003, Art 15(1) of Reg 773/2004, which seem to indicate that only the addressee of a statement of objections is entitled to access to the file.

[100] According to Art 12 of Reg 773/2004, the opportunity to express their arguments at an oral hearing is reserved to the 'parties whom [the Commission] has addressed a statement of objections'.

[101] See Joined Cases 234/84 and 40/85 *Belgium v Commission* [1986] ECR 2263, para 27; Case C-301/87 *France v Commission* [1990] ECR I-307, para 29; Case C-32/95 P *Commission v Lisrestal* [1996] ECR I-5373, para 21; Case C-1 35/92 *Fiskano v Commission* [1994] ECR I-2885, para 39; Case T-251/00 *Lagardère and Canal+ v Commission* [2002] ECR II-4825, para 94.

[102] Despite the consensual nature of commitments proceedings, non-compliance with commitments rendered binding pursuant to Art 9 can entail severe sanctions according to Arts 23(2)(c) and 24(1)(c) of Reg 1/2003. See for example IP/13/196 'Antitrust: Commission fines Microsoft for non-compliance with browser choice commitments', 6 March 2013.

Commission must issue a preliminary assessment that allows the addressee adequately to assess whether the essential facts are correctly stated and whether the provisional legal reasoning relied on is well founded.[103] Furthermore, upon request, the Commission must grant access to the file.[104] Whilst parties will usually waive their right to access to the file where the Commission is likely to accept the commitments they are willing to propose, the Commission should not exert any pressure in this respect.

3. The procedural rights granted to complainants and other third parties

13.24 Whilst complainants are entitled, pursuant to Article 6(1) of Regulation 773/2004, to receive a non-confidential version of the statement of objections, no such right is enshrined in Regulation 773/2004 with regard to commitment procedures in which a preliminary assessment is issued. Similarly, Article 27(3) of Regulation 1/2003, which obliges the Commission to hear third parties that show a sufficient interest, only seems to apply to the decisions enumerated in Article 27(1).[105] With regard to commitment decisions, it can be argued that Article 27(4) of Regulation 1/2003, which stipulates that third parties are heard on the basis of the publication of a concise summary of the case and the main content of the commitments, constitutes *lex specialis*. If the case is based on a complaint, this market test will be sent to the complainant. The Commission can also send the publication in the OJ directly to other interested third parties known to be potentially concerned by the outcome of the case (eg third parties admitted to the procedure, consumer associations etc) and explicitly ask for their comments.[106] In the market test, the Commission then generally invites interested third parties to submit their observations within a fixed time limit which may not be less than one month.[107] Triangular meetings with the parties and the complainant and/or admitted third parties can be organized at the Commission's discretion.[108] These steps are supposed to ensure full involvement of those undertakings most concerned.[109] However, the publication pursuant to Article 27(4) of Regulation 1/2003 can be insufficient in cases where a decision on commitments constitutes an individual measure which adversely affects specific third parties. In such cases, the right to a fair hearing, which is a general principle of EU law, can require that such third parties be heard more extensively upon request.[110] In cases of a formal

---

[103] However, the case law requirements applying to a statement of objections would not be adequate for a preliminary assessment, since the latter is not supposed to put the addressee in a position to state its views on the Commission's preliminary view that a breach of EU competition law has occurred.

[104] Case T-170/06 *Alrosa v Commission* [2007] ECR II-260, para 197. Although the GC's ruling was quashed on different grounds by the ECJ, the GC is likely to maintain its reasoning on this point, which was based on Recital 37 of and Art 27(2) of Reg 1/2003, Recital 10 of Reg 773/2004 and Case C-32/95 P *Commission v Lisrestal* [1996] ECR I-5373, para 21; Joined Cases T-191/98 and others *Atlantic Container Line v Commission* [2003] ECR II-3275, para 334; and Case T-38/02 *Groupe Danone v Commission* [2005] ECR II-4407, para 33.

[105] Although the wording of Art 13(1) of Reg 773/2004 is not explicit in this respect, it would seem that the right of interested third parties to be informed of the nature and subject matter of the procedure depends on the issuance of a statement of objections.

[106] See Commission Notice on best practices for the conduct of proceedings concerning Arts 101 and 102 TFEU [2011] OJ C308/6, para 131.

[107] European Commission Antitrust Manual of Procedures, Internal DG Competition working documents on procedures for the application of Articles 101 and 102 TFEU, March 2012, Module 16 'Commitment decision (Article 9 of Reg. 1/2003)', para 63.

[108] See Commission Notice on best practices for the conduct of proceedings concerning Arts 101 and 102 TFEU [2011] OJ C308/6, para 129.

[109] European Commission Antitrust Manual of Procedures, Internal DG Competition working documents on procedures for the application of Articles 101 and 102 TFEU, March 2012, Module 16 'Commitment decision (Article 9 of Reg. 1/2003)', para 61.

[110] See Opinion of AG Kokott in Case C-441/07 *Commission v Alrosa* [2010] ECR I-5949, para 191.

complaint, where the Commission has obtained commitments that it considers adequate, a letter pursuant to Article 7(1) of Regulation 773/2004 has to be issued well before the adoption of the Article 9 decision, informing the complainant of the Commission's preliminary conclusion that, were the commitments accepted, there would no longer be grounds for the Commission to pursue the case.[111]

E. The Reopening of Proceedings. The Consequences of Non-Compliance

Article 9(2) of Regulation 1/2003 sets out three situations where the Commission may, either following a request or of its own initiative, reopen proceedings. Article 9(2)(a) provides that, where the facts with respect to an essential element of the decision have materially changed, the Commission can decide to reopen proceedings. This means that the Commission must give sufficient detail in the commitment decision of the most relevant facts, so that it can evaluate whether at any given moment such facts have changed. In turn, a change in circumstances may also lead the Commission to reassess whether the commitments are still necessary.[112] Whilst the Commission generally has discretion to refuse to reopen,[113] it can be argued that there is an obligation to that effect where the commitments appear manifestly excessive in the light of the changed circumstances.[114] According to Article 9(2)(b) of Regulation 1/2003, the Commission can reopen proceedings where the undertakings concerned do not comply with their commitments.[115] The same applies pursuant to Article 9(2)(c) of Regulation 1/2003, where the decision was based on 'incomplete, incorrect or misleading information provided by the parties'. Undertakings that do not comply with commitments made binding by a decision pursuant to Article 9 of Regulation 1/2003, or that have omitted information or furnished incorrect information in response to a decision pursuant to Article 18(3) of Regulation 1/2003, may also have penalty payments imposed on them with the aim of changing their conduct.[116] To date, Article 9(2) of Regulation 1/2003 has not been used to reopen proceedings. **13.25**

Article 23(2)(c) of Regulation 1/2003 enables the Commission to impose fines on undertakings where they fail to comply with a commitment made binding by a decision pursuant to Article 9. In this case, the Commission may impose a fine of up to 10 per cent of the undertaking's total turnover in the preceding business year.[117] However, it is not clear which specific criteria the Commission will apply when it imposes fines for non-compliance with commitment **13.26**

---

[111] European Commission Antitrust Manual of Procedures, Internal DG Competition working documents on procedures for the application of Articles 101 and 102 TFEU, March 2012, Module 16 'Commitment decision (Article 9 of Reg. 1/2003)', para 68.

[112] Some of the Commission's Art 9 Decisions explicitly refer to the Commission's willingness to reopen proceedings and to re-examine the remedy imposed if certain facts change. See eg Commission Decision of 11 October 2007, Case COMP/37.966 *Distrigaz*, para 36 et seq.

[113] Case T-170/06 *Alrosa v Commission* [2007] ECR II-260, para 155. As the GC's ruling was quashed by the ECJ on other grounds, it seems plausible that the GC will continue to hold in the future that the Commission has discretion to refuse to reopen Art 9 proceedings.

[114] See also Commission MEMO/04/217 'Commitment decisions (Art 9 of Council Reg 1/2003 providing for a modernised framework for antitrust scrutiny of company behaviour)' of 17 September 2004.

[115] The first case in which the Commission investigated whether the addressee of an Art 9 decision failed to comply with its commitments is the *Microsoft (tying)* case. See IP/13/196 'Antitrust: Commission fines Microsoft for non-compliance with browser choice commitments', 6 March 2013.

[116] Article 24(1)(c) and (d) of Reg 1/2003.

[117] Already in its early press releases on commitment decisions, the Commission emphasized that it would have the power to impose a fine amounting to 10 per cent of the companies' total worldwide turnover if

decisions. Although the Commission's 2006 'Guidelines on the method of setting fines'[118] do not apply to these types of fines, the Commission is likely to have recourse to some of the criteria set out therein. In particular, mitigating circumstances, such as the immediate termination of the infringement upon the Commission's intervention or the mere negligence rather than intent on the part of the infringing company, might be taken into account.[119]

13.27 While the Commission has reserved the right to impose the same type of fines of up to 10 per cent of the company's total turnover to two different types of infringement, on the one hand the infringement of Article 9 of Regulation 1/2003, and on the other hand the substantive infringement of Article 101 and/or Article 102 TFEU, the issue arises whether the Commission would impose in both cases the maximum amount of up to 10 per cent of the company's total turnover, as the wording of Article 23(2) of Regulation 1/2003 may suggest. It could be argued that, where the Commission has evidence of a negligent or intentional non-compliance with a commitment decision, the Commission may impose a fine to sanction the 'bad faith' conduct of the company, independently of whether this non-compliance involved a breach of Articles 101 or 102 TFEU.[120] Yet, the fact that the Commission does not need to show that there has been an infringement of Articles 101 and 102 TFEU where it fines a company for non-compliance with an Article 9 Decision, may lead to the assumption that in these cases the Commission will not exhaust the maximum limit of 10 per cent of the company's turnover, which could be as high as the fine the Commission would impose to sanction an actual infringement which has been proven. It might be justified—although the wording of Article 23(2) suggests otherwise—to put *a priori* a limit of 1 per cent of the company's turnover when the Commission sanctions the non-compliance with a commitment decision. This is the maximum amount under Article 23(1) of Regulation 1/2003 with which to sanction procedural infringements and may thus also be used as guidance where an infringement of Articles 101 and 102 TFEU has not been proven. Where the Commission wishes to impose a higher fine, it should reopen the procedure and prove that the breach of the commitments amounted at the same time to an infringement of Articles 101 and 102 TFEU.[121]

13.28 Faced with a breach of commitments, the Commission could generally adopt two decisions sanctioning the undertaking concerned. First, it could impose a fine pursuant to Article 23(2)(c) of Regulation 1/2003 for breach of the commitments. Second, it could reopen the procedure and impose another fine pursuant to Article 23(2)(a) for the infringement of Articles 101 and/or 102 TFEU. However, if the Commission decides to impose a double

---

the latter breached their commitments. See eg *Coca-Cola* (Commission Press Release IP/05/775 'Competition: Commission makes commitments from Coca-Cola legally binding, increasing consumer choice' of 22 June 2005).

[118] Guidelines on the method of setting fines imposed pursuant to Article 23(2)(a) of Regulation No 1/2003 [2006] OJ C210/2. Note that the same questions arise in respect to the breach of interim decisions under Art 8 of Reg 1/2003. As regards the application of Art 23(2)(b), see Ch 14, 'Interim Measures', para 14.19.

[119] See Guidelines on the method of setting fines imposed pursuant to Article 23(2)(a) of Regulation No 1/2003 [2006] OJ C210/2, para 29.

[120] As indicated, it is already sufficient that the Commission has identified concerns during a preliminary assessment. M Busse and A Leopold, 'Entscheidungen über Verpflichtungszusagen nach Art 9 VO (EG) Nr. 1/2003' [2005] Wirtschaft und Wettbewerb 146, 152; A Klees, 'Europäisches Kartellverfahrensrecht' [2005] Wirtschaft und Wettbewerb § 10, para 44, proposes that minor forms of non-compliance, to be judged by their gravity and duration, may not be sanctioned if this appears disproportionate.

[121] A Klees, 'Europäisches Kartellverfahrensrecht' [2005] Wirtschaft und Wettbewerb § 10, para 43, who also indicates that a fine of up to 10 per cent of the company's turnover applies typically to hardcore cartels for which commitment decisions do not provide an appropriate remedy (see Recital 13 of Reg 1/2003).

sanction, the general principle of proportionality would require the Commission to take the prior fine under Article 23(2)(c) into account when setting the amount of the fine in relation to the substantive infringement. Ultimately, it is reasonable to assume that the amount of the double fine should not exceed 10 per cent of the turnover of the companies concerned. Where the Commission reopens the proceedings, two types of decisions need to be distinguished: (i) the decision to reopen the proceedings as such; and (ii) where relevant, the decision on the infringement or the lifting of the commitments. Given that only measures that definitively determine the Commission's position upon the conclusion of the procedure are open to challenge, and not intermediate measures whose purpose is to prepare for the final decision,[122] only the second decision would be subject to judicial review. This decision constitutes a measure the legal effects of which are binding on, and capable of affecting the interests of, the undertaking in question by bringing about a distinct change in its legal position.

F. Review of Commitment Decisions

1. The scope of judicial review

Regulation 1/2003 does not provide any specific mechanism for the review of commitment decisions. Nevertheless, as with any other decision, nothing prevents a commitment decision from being challenged under Article 263 TFEU by any company to which it is of direct and individual concern.[123] However, given the nature of these decisions, where the Commission has a great degree of discretion, it might be difficult to appeal successfully.[124] When reviewing an Article 9 decision, the Court is confined to establishing manifest errors of assessment by examining whether the Commission's conclusion is obviously unfounded, having regard to the facts established by it.[125] It has been argued that an analogy can be drawn with judicial review in mergers, where a merging party will succeed only where it has been able to show that it has been arbitrarily forced by the Commission to propose the remedies rendered binding.[126] Addressees of an Article 9 decision are unlikely to prevail with the assertion that the Commission forced it to accept the undertakings, given that Article 9 is based on the premise that companies need to offer the commitments[127] and given that the addressees are granted the possibility to:

13.29

---

[122] Case 60/81 *IBM v Commission* [1981] ECR 2639, para 9; Joined Cases C-68/94 and C-30/95 *France and others v Commission* [1998] ECR I-1375, para 62; Case T-241/97 *Storck Amsterdam BV v Commission* [2000] ECR II-309, para 49. J Temple Lang, 'Commitment Decisions and Settlements with Antitrust Authorities and Private Parties under European Antitrust Law', *32nd Annual International Antitrust Law & Policy Conference Fordham Corporate Law Institute* (Juris Publishing 2005) 265–74 et seq, noting that the terms of a commitment can be altered only through a second formal commitment decision.

[123] This could also include third parties that may assert that the commitment decisions are not apt to eliminate the risk of an infringement of Arts 101 or 102 TFEU.

[124] As regards the Commission's discretion with regard to the commitments to be rendered binding see para 13.11.

[125] See Case C-441/07 *Commission v Alrosa* [2010] ECR I-5949, paras 42 and 63.

[126] H Schweitzer, 'Commitment Decisions under Art. 9 Regulation 1/2003: The Developing EC Case Law' (2008) 22 EUI Workings Papers Law refers to the GC's ruling in *Cementbouw* (Case T-282/02, confirmed in Case C-202/06), para 319, where it was held 'that it has not been established that the notifying parties were arbitrarily forced by the Commission to propose the corrective measure consisting in the dissolution of CVK within a period of [confidential] from the adoption of the contested decision. Nor is it apparent from the documents in the case-file that the parties were arbitrarily forced to propose the other corrective measures in their final commitments designed to restore effective competition.'

[127] M Busse and A Leopold, 'Entscheidungen über Verpflichtungszusagen nach Art 9 VO (EG) Nr. 1/2003' [2005] Wirtschaft und Wettbewerb 146, 153. AG Kokott held that the necessity of the commitments may be presumed as a matter of course vis-à-vis the company that has offered commitments voluntarily. See her opinion in Case C-441/07 *Commission v Alrosa* [2010] ECR I-5949, paras 50 and 60.

call upon the hearing officer at any stage in the procedure pursuant to [Article 9 Regulation 1/2003], in order to ensure the effective exercise of their procedural rights.[128]

In view of the Commission's discretion as to whether to make use of an Article 9 procedure,[129] an undertaking that had its commitment proposal rejected will also find it difficult to use this fact as the basis of an appeal against any final infringement decision.

13.30 The ECJ observed that when carrying out the assessment of the proportionality of commitments proposed, the Commission must also take into consideration the interests of third parties.[130] However, if these third parties offer alternative commitments that in their view amount to less onerous solutions to the competitive problems identified, the Commission has wide discretion to reject them and to accept the commitments originally proposed by the undertakings concerned.[131] Therefore, there is more chance of an appeal being successful if it is based on formal grounds, for example, if the Commission has not given third parties concerned the opportunity of making submissions on the proposed commitments, thereby breaching Article 27(4) of Regulation 1/2003. However, in such cases, it would need to be established that the breach of procedural rules could have had an impact on the outcome of the proceedings, ie on the contents of the commitments rendered binding.[132] The company on which the commitment has been made binding may challenge a Commission refusal to lift a commitment that the company considers no longer appropriate.

2. Other safeguards

13.31 The wording of Regulation 1/2003 does not place any limit on the Commission's powers to negotiate commitments.[133] Based on the ECJ's understanding that commitment decisions are not unilateral instruments for finding and terminating infringements of competition law, but rather a flexible mechanism speedily to resolve competition problems in cooperation with the undertakings concerned, the Commission has wide discretion when deciding on

---

[128] See Art 15(1) of the Hearing Officer's Mandate. By contrast, it can safely be assumed that the addressee of an Art 9 decision is entitled to challenge the decision before the Court. See, by analogy Case T-282/02 *Cementbouw v Commission* [2006] ECR II-319, in which the notifying party that offered commitments in a merger proceeding was entitled to challenge the Commission decision pursuant to Art 8(2) of Reg 139/2004.

[129] According to the very wording of Art 9 of Reg 1/2003, the Commission 'may' by decision make commitments binding where they meet the competitive concerns expressed. Similarly, Recital 13 of Reg 1/2003 grants the Commission the possibility of adopting commitment decisions rather than creating an obligation in this respect once sufficient commitments are proposed. Paragraph 115 of the Commission Notice on best practices for the conduct of proceedings concerning Articles 101 and 102 TFEU [2011] OJ C308/6, recalls that '[i]t is at the discretion of the Commission whether or not to accept commitments'. Therefore, companies cannot claim legitimate expectations that their breach of competition law could not be established in a decision pursuant to Art 7 of Reg 1/2003 if they offer sufficient commitments.

[130] See Case C-441/07 *Commission v Alrosa* [2010] ECR I-5949, para 41.

[131] See Case C-441/07 *Commission v Alrosa* [2010] ECR I-5949, para 93 et seq. The ECJ rejected the third party's claim that it could have proposed new joint commitments with the addressee of the Art 9 decision if the Commission had granted it further opportunities to be heard.

[132] See, by way of analogy, the case law on breaches of the right to be heard in infringement proceedings, eg Joined Cases T-25/95, T-26/95, T-30/95 to T-39/95, T-42/95 to T-46/95, T-48/95, T-50/95 to T-65/95, T-68/95 to T-71/95, T-87/95, T-88/95, T-103/95, and T-104/95 *Cimenteries CBR SA and others v Commission* [2000] ECR II-491, paras 240–1; Case C-199/99 P *Corus UK v Commission* [2003] ECR I-11177, para 128; Judgment of 25 October 2011 in Case C-109/10 P *Solvay v Commission*, para 57.

[133] It is interesting to note that in the US, proceedings in which consent decrees are adopted are regulated in greater detail. Compared to commitment decisions, consent decrees are a mechanism in which the competition authority enjoys considerable discretion. See M Furse, 'The Decision to Commit: Some pointers from the US' [2004] European Competition Law Review 5, 10; in regard to Australia, see S Eibl, 'Commitment Decisions: An Australian Perspective' [2005] European Competition Law Review 328, 332–7.

the proportionality of commitments.[134] Consequently, the responsibility for avoiding disproportionate commitment decisions lies in the first place with the companies concerned. It is for them to refuse commitments that go beyond what is required to solve the competitive concerns raised and to offer alternative, less onerous remedies. Nevertheless, concern has been expressed about the possibility of the Commission abusing its position, as it might be tempted to encourage undertakings to offer commitments which produce results that it would find hard to impose through the usual enforcement procedure, and which might not be judicially tested.[135] The revised Mandate of the Hearing Officer might help alleviate such concerns. Parties to Article 9 proceedings may call upon the Hearing Officer at any time in relation to the effective exercise of their procedural rights.[136] Wils, currently one of the two Hearing Officers at the Commission, wrote in an earlier publication that the risk that, faced with the alternative of long and costly infringement proceedings, undertakings may be prepared to offer commitments that go beyond what is proportional and necessary to enforce Articles 101 and 102 TFEU, could be reduced to some extent by ensuring that the undertakings' consent is an informed consent and by giving the undertakings the right of access to the Commission's file.[137]

G. Effects of Commitment Decisions[138]

From the scope of commitment decisions, it is clear that the effects of such decisions will differ, according to whether they are effective with respect to: (i) the undertakings concerned; (ii) national courts; or (iii) NCAs. With regard to the legal effects of commitment decisions vis-à-vis the Commission, reference is made to Section F in this chapter, where it is explained under which conditions the Commission is entitled to reopen proceedings.[139]   **13.32**

1. Effects on the undertakings concerned

Article 9 and Recital 13 of Regulation 1/2003 provide that through the adoption of a commitment decision, the Commission converts such commitments into obligations for the undertakings concerned. Consequently, the company to whom the decision is addressed must respect the commitments that the Commission rendered binding,[140] and if it fails to do so, the Commission will be able to impose fines and periodic penalty payments.[141] The possibility of substantial fines may give undertakings even more reason to consider the implications of the commitments. However, under Regulation 17, the Commission gave undertakings the possibility of terminating a commitment if there are 'relevant, material or   **13.33**

---

[134] See M Kellerbauer, 'Playground instead of Playpen: The CJEU's Alrosa Judgment on Article 9 of Regulation 1/2003' (2011) 32(1) European Competition Law Review 1.

[135] See, most recently, F Wagner-von Papp, 'Best and Even Better Practices in Commitment Procedures after Alrosa: The Dangers of Abandoning the Struggle for Competition Law' (2012) 49(3) Common Market Law Review 929.

[136] See Commission Notice on best practices for the conduct of proceedings concerning Articles 101 and 102 TFEU [2011] OJ C308/6, para 124, and Art 15(1) of the Hearing Officer's Mandate.

[137] W Wils, 'Settlements of EU Antitrust Investigations: Commitment Decisions under Article 9 of Regulation No 1/2003' [2006] World Competition 352.

[138] The effects of commitment decisions are discussed in detail in W Wils, *Efficiency and Justice in European Antitrust Enforcement* (Hart Publishing 2008), paras 122–50.

[139] If none of these conditions are met, commitment decisions provide legal certainty for undertakings that the Commission will not review the case and impose any fine.

[140] Commission MEMO/04/217 'Commitment decisions (Art 9 of Council Reg 1/2003 providing for a modernised framework for antitrust scrutiny of company behaviour)' of 17 September 2004, as regards the scope of the effects of a commitment decision.

[141] Articles 23(2)(c) and 24(1)(c) of Reg 1/2003.

objective circumstances that justify such a termination'.[142] There is no reason why this practice should not be maintained under Regulation 1/2003 as long as the possibility of termination is expressly provided for in the commitment decision.[143]

2. Effects on national courts

13.34 Recital 13 states that the commitment decisions are without prejudice to the powers of the courts of the Member States to make a finding of infringement of Articles 101 or 102 TFEU and decide upon the case. It is clear from this that national courts can reassess matters which have already been the subject of a Commission decision and decide whether or not there has been a breach of Articles 101 and 102 TFEU or whether such a breach still exists. The possibility of national courts judging a case that has already been decided by the Commission is logical, since the former have the task of defending a different legal interest from that which is protected by the Commission; the Commission is entrusted with defending the public interest, whereas the national courts protect private interests; in other words, they will hear cases concerning the possible harm caused to third parties and, where appropriate, will award damages. Since the national courts are the only ones which can award damages for breach of Articles 101 and 102 TFEU,[144] it is essential that their powers in this regard are not limited. Further, as noted before, it should not be forgotten that commitment decisions do not decide whether or not there is or has been a breach of Articles 101 and/or 102 TFEU. This has two consequences. The first is that commitment decisions cannot protect undertakings which were parties to agreements or carried out practices capable of being contrary to Article 101 and/or Article 102 from private third party actions. The second is that a customer or a competitor possibly seeking private enforcement in national courts still needs to prove the illegality of the former behaviour to obtain compensation for damages.[145]

13.35 The question arises whether third parties can invoke the commitments rendered binding by the Commission before national courts in order to seek injunctions or claim damages where these commitments are breached. The Commission's initial proposal for what has become Regulation 1/2003 stated in Recital 12 that the Commission should be able to adopt decisions making commitments binding 'so that the commitments can be relied upon by third parties before national courts'.[146] By contrast, Regulation 1/2003 in its current form is silent on the subject. In its Notice on cooperation with national courts, the Commission considers that national courts are competent to apply acts adopted by EU institutions in accordance with the EU Treaty and could be asked to enforce Commission decisions taken pursuant to Article 9 of Regulation 1/2003.[147] However, it appears doubtful whether such private enforcement is required or even appropriate to ensure the effective application of EU law.

---

[142] See, eg *La Poste v Swift GUF* [1997] OJ L335/3, para 3(3).

[143] M Busse and A Leopold, 'Entscheidungen über Verpflichtungszusagen nach Art 9 VO (EG) Nr. 1/2003' [2004] Wirtschaft und Wettbewerb 146, 153.

[144] See Recital 7 and Art 6 of Reg 1/2003.

[145] Commission MEMO/04/217 'Commitment decisions (Art 9 of Council Reg 1/2003 providing for a modernised framework for antitrust scrutiny of company behaviour)' of 17 September 2004. Therefore, in order to seek private enforcement, a commitment decision is substantially less valuable for the claimant than a Commission decision finding that an infringement has been committed, which leaves a claimant only with the task of proving causation and quantum of damage. J Temple Lang, 'Commitments under Reg 1/2003: Legal Aspects of a New Kind of Competition Decision' [2003] European Competition Law Review 347, 350.

[146] COM(2000)582 final of 27 September 2000.

[147] Commission Notice on the co-operation between the Commission and the courts of the EU Member States in the application of Articles 81 and 82 EC, [2004] OJ C101/54, para 7 and n 15.

As noted earlier, there is no such necessity with regard to Articles 101 and 102 TFEU, since Article 9 Decisions leave open whether these Treaty provisions have been infringed. With regard to the Article 9 Decision, the Commission itself seems to be best placed to investigate and act upon potential breaches of commitments it rendered binding.[148] The fact that the Council did not follow the Commission's initial proposal to refer to the possibility of private enforcement in Regulation 1/2003 also indicates that the legislator took the view that the possibilities of enforcement by the Commission itself, through fines, periodic penalty payments, and reopening of proceedings, would appear sufficiently effective to ensure compliance with commitment decisions.[149]

3. Effects on national competition authorities

The possibility of NCAs adopting a potentially diverging decision on the basis of the same facts as the Commission is the aspect that has engendered most controversial discussions.[150] The conclusions that can be reached from a reading of Recitals 13 and 22 are as clear as they are surprising. NCAs may decide whether or not there has been a breach of Articles 101 and 102 TFEU or whether this still exists, and therefore impose a fine. In addition, it is specifically stated that the decisions of the Commission where commitments are imposed do not affect the powers of the courts and competition authorities of the Member States to apply Articles 101 and 102 TFEU.[151] Although the principles stated earlier are unambiguous, the decision-making practice is still at an early stage, and these rules—which to some extent clash with the general principles laid down in Regulation 1/2003—have proved very controversial. This has led to various theories concerning the scope and legal effect of commitment decisions vis-à-vis NCAs. It has been suggested that the Commission, through a commitment decision, decides that the EU interest—within the meaning laid down in *Automec II*[152]—makes it advisable to end the proceedings and, therefore, will not carry out any assessment as to whether or not there has been an infringement. This approach would fit in perfectly with the provisions that regulate commitment decisions, which limit their scope to 'finding' that there are no longer grounds for action by the Commission.[153] It has also been argued that an Article 9 decision reflects the implicit finding that the Commission has assessed the factual situation and has concluded that the agreement or practice as modified by the commitments is in line with EU competition law.[154]

13.36

---

[148] J Davies and M Das, 'Private Enforcement of Commission Commitment Decisions: A Steep Climb not a Gentle Stroll' in BE Hawk (ed), *Annual Proceedings of the Fordham Corporate Law Institute* (Juris 2005) 214.

[149] See W Wils, *Efficiency and Justice in European Antitrust Enforcement* (Hart Publishing 2008), paras 139–40.

[150] See F Wagner-von Papp, 'Best and Even Better Practices in Commitment Procedures after Alrosa: The Dangers of Abandoning the Struggle for Competition Law' (2012) 49(3) Common Market Law Review 951; S Rab, D Monnoyeur, and A Sukhtankar, 'Commitments in EU Competition Cases Article 9 of Regulation 1/2003, its Application and the Challenges Ahead' (2010) 1(3) Journal of European Competition Law & Practice 184; M Marquis, 'Introduction: Cartel Settlements and Commitment Decisions' in C-D Ehlermann and M Marquis (eds), *European Competition Law Annual 2008: Antitrust Settlements under EC Competition Law* (Hart Publishing 2010) 29; H Schweitzer, 'Commitment Decisions under Art. 9 of Regulation 1/2003: The Developing EC Practice and Case Law' (2008) 22 EUI Working Paper Law 25.

[151] Recital 22 of Reg 1/2003.

[152] Case T-24/90 *Automec Srl v Commission* [1992] ECR II-2223. J Temple Lang, 'Commitments under Regulation 1/2003: Legal Aspects of a New Kind of Competition Decision' [2003] European Competition Law Review 347, 348–9.

[153] Recital 13 of Reg 1/2003.

[154] See F Montag and S Cameron, 'Effective Enforcement: The Practitioner's View of Recent Experiences under Regulation 1/2003', International Bar Association ('IBA') conference 'Antitrust Reform in Europe: A Year in Practice', 9–11 March 2005, Brussels, 14, noting that NCAs are unlikely to pursue behaviour which has been subject of a negotiated settlement between a company and the Commission unless there are important national peculiarities which have not been taken into account by the Commission's investigation.

This theory, which would restrict NCAs' freedom to take a decision about a given matter, gains credence taking into account the following:

(i) the task of both the Commission and NCAs is to protect the public interest;
(ii) certain provisions of Regulation 1/2003; and
(iii) the Commission's declarations concerning Article 9.

13.37 As noted, both the NCAs and the Commission must act in the public interest. It therefore follows that if, on the basis of the agreed commitments, the Commission has already decided that the public interest is safeguarded, there is no reason for the NCA to reach a different decision. The possibility that a Commission decision may be reviewed by an NCA contradicts (i) Article 13(2) of the Regulation 1/2003, as regards the principles that govern the way cases are to be allocated between the Commission and NCAs;[155] (ii) Article 11(6) of Regulation 1/2003;[156] and (iii) Article 16(2), which concerns the uniform application of Community competition law.[157] These three provisions clearly show that if the Commission has reached a decision concerning a case, the NCAs must either reject the claim brought against the agreement in question or reach the same decision as the Commission. Under no circumstances can it contradict the Commission's decision.[158] Although it is true that Recital 22 provides a derogation to these principles (especially as regards the rule on conflicting decisions contained in Article 16) for commitment decisions, it will be interesting to see how this plays out in practice. In fact, the first cracks have already appeared following the publication of the Commission's memorandum, in which the Commission made the application by national courts and NCAs of Articles 101 and 102 TFEU subject to the condition that 'the uniform application (of Articles 101 and 102 TFEU) throughout the EU is not jeopardised'.[159] This statement, which is not to be found in either Article 9 or Recital 13, introduces the first limitation on the free rein that Recital 22 appears to give NCAs when applying Articles 101 and 102 TFEU. Further, by imposing this limit, the Commission has circumscribed the power of NCAs, and it is possible that it will continue to interpret and, arguably, narrow down the extent of this unprecedented freedom, which flies in the face of the general principles governing relations between the NCAs and the Commission. Nevertheless, a communication like the Commission Memorandum has limited legal effect, whereas Article 9 and Recitals 13 and 22 clearly provide for the possibility of revision by the NCAs. Thus, the Commission or ultimately the ECJ may clarify this issue, which will largely define the degree of legal certainty that undertakings can obtain from such decisions and the extent to which undertakings will use this mechanism. However, it also needs to be emphasized that the issue has so far proved to be of little practical relevance. To date, NCAs have avoided establishing breaches

---

[155] 'Where a competition authority of a Member State or the Commission has received a complaint against an agreement, decision of association or practice which has already been dealt with by another competition authority, it may reject it.'

[156] '[T]he initiation by the Commission of proceedings for the adoption of a decision under Chapter III shall relieve the competition authorities of the Member States to apply Arts [101 and 102 TFEU].'

[157] 'When competition authorities of the member states rule on agreements, decisions or practices under [Arts 101 and 102 TFEU] which are already the subject of Commission decisions, they cannot take decisions which would run counter to the decision adopted by the Commission.'

[158] M Sousa Ferro, 'Committing to Commitment—Unanswered Questions on Article 9 Decisions' [2005] European Competition Law Review 451, 455–6, indicates that Art 10 EC [now Art 4(3) TEU] imposes on NCAs a duty to closely cooperate with the Commission in applying Union competition law. This may also give additional support to the view that companies who accept commitments will be protected from further investigation into the same practices; it could be argued that this obligation also extends to national courts with the result that they are prevented from saying that a commitment decision gave rise to a presumption that the conduct in question had been illegal under EU law in the past.

[159] See Commission MEMO/04/217 'Commitment decisions (Art 9 of Council Regulation 1/2003 providing for a modernized framework for antitrust scrutiny of company behaviour)' of 17 September 2004.

of Articles 101 and 102 TFEU with regard to conduct on the basis of which the Commission adopted decisions pursuant to Article 9 of Regulation 1/2003.

III. Finding of Inapplicability

A. Policy Objective

Article 10 of Regulation 1/2003 regulates decisions where the Commission finds that Articles **13.38** 101 and/or 102 TFEU do not apply. It provides that where the EU public interest relating to the application of Articles 101 and 102 so requires, the Commission, acting on its own initiative, may by decision find that Article 101 TFEU is not applicable to an agreement, a decision by an association of undertakings, or a concerted practice, either because the conditions of Article 101(1) TFEU are not fulfilled or because the conditions of Article 101(3) TFEU are satisfied. A similar finding may be made with respect to Article 102 TFEU. The Antitrust Manual of Procedures ('Manproc') adds that such a declaratory decision finding inapplicability can be proposed in exceptional cases where a Commission decision is needed, on a specific issue, in order to avoid or solve a problem of coherence resulting from divergent interpretations by national courts in different Member States or by members of the ECN. Such circumstances could justify allocating the Commission's resources to the preparation of this type of 'positive' decision.[160]

In this sense, Recital 14 of Regulation 1/2003 indicates the Commission's intention that only **13.39** in exceptional cases where the public interest of the EU so requires, could it be expedient for the Commission to adopt a decision finding that the prohibition in Article 101 or Article 102 TFEU does not apply.[161] This could help clarify the law and ensure its consistent application throughout the EU. Together with Article 11(6) of Regulation 1/2003, under which the Commission may relieve NCAs of their competence to deal with the same case, and the rule laid down in Article 16(2) of the Regulation, according to which NCAs cannot take decisions which would run counter to an earlier decision by the Commission concerning the same agreement or practice, the possibility of adopting inapplicability decisions differentiates the position of the Commission from that of the NCAs.[162]

---

[160] Antitrust Manual of Procedures, Internal DG Competition working documents on procedures for the application of Articles 101 and 102 TFEU, March 2012, Module 18 'Decision finding inapplicability (Article 10 Decision)', para 1.

[161] Note that the Explanatory Memorandum of the draft Reg 1/2003 stated that inapplicability decisions 'can be adopted only at the Commission's own initiative and in the Community public interest. These conditions ensure that decisions making a finding of inapplicability cannot be obtained on demand by companies. Such a possibility would seriously undermine the principal aim of the reform, which is to focus the activities of all competition authorities on what is prohibited. In the decentralised system the Commission, as the guardian of the Treaty and the centrally placed authority, has a special role to play in setting competition policy and in ensuring that Articles 81 and 82 are applied consistently throughout the single market. To that end it is necessary to empower the Commission to adopt positive decisions if the Community public interest so requires. This power allows the Commission to adopt a decision making a finding of inapplicability, in particular in respect of new types of agreements or practices or issues that have not been settled in the existing case-law and administrative practice.' Draft Regulation implementing Articles 81 and 82 of the Treaty COM (2000) 582 final [2000] OJ C365E/284, Explanatory Memorandum Art 10.

[162] WPJ Wils, 'Community Report' in D Cahill (ed), *The Modernization of EU Competition Law Enforcement in the EU* FIDE National Reports (Cambridge University Press 2004) 661, para 50. See E Gippini-Fournier, 'The Modernisation of European Competition Law: First Experiences with Regulation 1/2003—Institutional Report' in HF Koeck and MM Karollus (eds), The Modernisation of European Competition Law—Initial Experiences with Regulation 1/2003, FIDE XXIII Congress Linz 2008—Congress Publications Vol 2

B. Legal Nature

13.40 The legal nature of inapplicability decisions is open to debate.[163] In the first place, it is not easy to differentiate them for a decision to reject a complaint; and secondly they are both declaratory and binding in nature. As regards the difference with the rejection of complaints, the Commission Notice on the handling of complaints under Articles 101 and 102 TFEU ('Notice on Complaints') states that the decision to reject a complaint does not involve a definitive declaration regarding the existence or not of a breach of Articles 101 and 102, even where the Commission has evaluated the facts on the basis of these Articles.[164] This differentiates these acts from the findings of inapplicability. The assessments carried out by the Commission in a decision rejecting a complaint cannot prevent the national judge or competition authority from applying Articles 101 and 102 TFEU to the agreements and practices in issue, which again differs from the situation pertaining to decisions under Article 10. The Commission's assessments in a decision rejecting a complaint are factual matters that the national courts or NCAs may take into account when examining whether the agreements or practices in question comply with Articles 101 and 102. In addition, the Notice on Complaints clarifies that:

> [w]here the Commission rejects a complaint in a case that also gives rise to a decision pursuant to Article 10 of Regulation 1/2003 (Finding of inapplicability of Articles 101 or 102) or Article 9 of Regulation 1/2003 (Commitments), the decision rejecting a complaint may refer to that other decision adopted on the basis of the provisions mentioned.

From this it seems clear that Article 10 declarations and acts where complaints are rejected are two different ways of ending proceedings. The Commission can choose between a simple rejection, or alternatively it can adopt an Article 10 decision. If it opts for this second course of action, its decision will bind national courts and NCAs. By contrast, the national authorities cannot adopt Article 10 decisions, although obviously in a decision closing the file, they could find that there are no grounds for it to act. This statement will have no binding effect on other public enforcers or national courts.[165]

13.41 Further, a decision under Article 10 is by nature declaratory but binding for the NCAs and courts of the Member States.[166] Certain authors doubted that they would be binding.[167] Others limited themselves to highlighting their declaratory nature without drawing any

---

(Nomos 2008), available at <http://papers.ssrn.com/sol3/papers.cfm?abstract_id=1139776>, 470–1, pointing out that *Masterfoods* and Art 16 do not state that national courts are 'bound' by Commission decisions, but they cannot take decisions 'running counter' to them.

[163] Kerse & Khan, *EC Antitrust Procedure* (6th edn, Sweet & Maxwell 2012) para 2-089, take the view that the new decision covers the old 'negative clearance' and 'exemption' decisions, though declarations under Art 10 appear to be something more than the former but less than the latter.

[164] Commission Notice on the handling of complaints by the Commission under Articles 81 and 82 of the EC Treaty [2004] OJ C101/65, para 79.

[165] C Gauer, D Dalheimer, L Kjolbye, and E De Smitjer 'Reg 1/2003: A Modernized Application of EC Competition Rules' (2003) 1 Competition Policy Newsletter 3, 5–6. WPJ Wils, 'Community Report' in D Cahill (ed), *The Modernization of EU Competition Law Enforcement in the EU FIDE National Reports* (Cambridge University Press 2004) 661, para 49. It remains to be seen whether in practice, NCAs will not also adopt decisions which are quite similar to decisions under Art 10. See in this respect, Kerse & Khan, *EC Antitrust Procedure* (6th edn, Sweet & Maxwell 2012) para 5-004 and Ch 3, 'The Role of the National Competition Authorities', para 3.03.

[166] Article 16(1) and (2) of Reg 1/2003.

[167] M Siragusa, 'A Critical Review of the White Paper on the Reform of the EC Competition Law Enforcement Rules,' ch 15 in BE Hawk (ed), *International Antitrust and Policy* (Iuris Publishing 1999) 273, 282.

conclusions as to whether or not they were binding.[168] In this regard, during the process to approve the Regulation, the Commission made it clear that inapplicability decisions were declaratory in nature in the sense that they do not 'create' rights, unlike the former exemption decisions under Article 101(3) EC. For this reason, their 'declaratory' nature, defined in such terms, is compatible with their binding nature with respect to national courts and NCAs.

This is reflected in the justifications of the Commission contained in the proposed **13.42** Regulation.[169] Decisions under Article 10 of Regulation 1/2003 thus differ significantly from the exemption decisions adopted under Article 101(3) TFEU, which create rights with effect *erga omnes* for the duration of the decision, regardless of any material change in the facts.[170] Non-infringement decisions will have the effects of EU acts. Article 16 has created a general obligation for NCAs and national courts to make every effort to avoid decisions conflicting with decisions adopted by the Commission. A finding of inapplicability by the Commission pursuant to Article 10 can therefore make an important contribution to the uniform application of EU competition law.[171] These decisions would have the effects laid down in Article 16, ie national courts and NCAs may not adopt decisions that would run counter to a decision of the Commission. Accordingly, such decisions would thus not be intended as a replacement for the exemption decisions of the old system or to function as an instrument to 'bless' individual agreements in the absence of any issue of coherent application or policy. In short the declaratory nature of inapplicability decisions does not prevent them from having binding effect for national courts and NCAs (under Article 16 of Regulation 1/2003). They would be similar to qualified guidance letters, although unlike the latter, they would have binding effect.

C. The Application of Article 10 of Regulation 1/2003 in Practice

The Commission has not, to date, adopted any decisions under Article 10. This is also **13.43** explained by the intention of the Commission to only use Article 10 decisions as a means of steering the way in which EU competition law is applied to (i) new situations; or (ii) cases where EU competition law has been applied inconsistently by national courts or competition authorities.[172] It could also use them to put a brake on what it sees as an excessively rigorous application of EU competition law by national courts or NCAs, for example where an NCA has prohibited an agreement or practice which the Commission deemed to be lawful. Thus, the application of Article 10 should be confined to 'exceptional cases'[173] to clarify the law

---

[168] For more details on the debate, see R Sauer in JL Schulte and C Just (eds), *Kartellrecht* (Carl Heymanns Verlag 2012), Art 10 of Reg 1/2003, para 17; A Riley, 'EC Antitrust Modernisation: The Commission does very nicely—Thank you! Part One: Regulation 1 and the Notification Burden' [2003] European Competition Law Review 604, 608, stating that the provision should be of a declaratory nature and would not be intended to provide a back door notification procedure. H Gilliams, 'Modernization: From Policy to Practice' [2003] European Law Review 451, 461, put emphasis on the aspect that the Commission has reserved the power to adopt decisions 'acting on its own initiative', ie not pursuant to a notification or complaint, for certain landmark cases.

[169] Draft Reg implementing Arts 81 and 82 EC, COM (2000)582 final [2000] OJ C365E/284, Explanatory Memorandum.

[170] Unlike an exemption decision under Reg 17, which granted exemption for a fixed period of time (often as long as ten years) and could be withdrawn in limited circumstances, a decision under Art 10 does not protect the agreement in question for a specified time.

[171] C Gauer, D Dalheimer, L Kjolbye, and E De Smitjer 'Reg 1/2003: A Modernized Application of EC Competition Rules' (2003) 1 Competition Policy Newsletter 3, 5–6.

[172] Antitrust Manual of Procedures, Internal DG Competition working documents on procedures for the application of Articles 101 and 102 TFEU, March 2012, Module 18 'Decision finding inapplicability (Article 10 Decision)', para 1.

[173] Recital 14 of Reg 1/2003 states: 'In exceptional cases where the public interest of the Community so requires...'

and ensure its consistent application throughout the Community, namely: (i) to 'correct' the approach of an NCA; or (ii) to send a signal to the ECN about how to approach a certain case.[174] Given that such an *ex ante* means of ensuring consistency has largely been overtaken by the extensive efforts of the ECN in promoting the coherent application of the EU antitrust rules, the Commission has had no reasons to proceed under Article 10 to date.[175]

1. EU public interest justifying intervention[176]

13.44 According to its terms, Article 10 can be applied where 'the Community [EU] public interest relating to the application of Articles 81 and 82 of the Treaty [ie Articles 101 and 102 TFEU]' so requires. Article 10 decisions are not intended to replace negative clearance or exemption decisions under the previous enforcement system. Neither can they be legally 'applied for' by undertakings, nor should they be envisaged as a reaction to such requests. It is important to note that under the legal exception system, undertakings have the primary responsibility to assess the compatibility of their agreements and practices with the EU competition rules. Thus, the risk of having to defend their case before a national court is in principle the same for all undertakings. Therefore, the existence of that responsibility/risk in itself cannot be invoked as a valid reason for assuming a problem of consistent application of EU competition law possibly giving rise to the adoption of an Article 10 decision.[177]

13.45 The Manproc points out that the notion of 'Community public interest' in Article 10 refers to the fundamental commitment of the EU to a system of undistorted competition as a common public goal.[178] The notion of 'EU public interest' is strictly linked to the implementation of Articles 101 and 102 TFEU. It would follow that other public policy considerations (eg industrial interests) cannot be invoked to establish that there is 'EU public interest' within the meaning of Article 10.[179]

13.46 The term 'public' included in the notion of 'EU public interest' has been introduced to underline the public policy dimension and discretionary nature of the Commission's intervention

---

[174] Commission Staff Working Paper accompanying the Communication from the Commission to the European Parliament and Council, Report on the functioning of Regulation 1/2003 {COM(2009)206 final}, 29 April 2009, para 113 indicated that it is therefore opposed to demands by stakeholders that greater legal certainty would be guaranteed if the Commission were to adopt decisions under Art 10 of Reg 1/2003.

[175] Commission Staff Working Paper accompanying the Communication from the Commission to the European Parliament and Council, Report on the functioning of Regulation 1/2003 {COM(2009)206 final}, 29 April 2009, para 114 emphasizes that the extent to which the ECN would have proven to be a successful forum to discuss general policy issues was not anticipated at the time of the adoption of Reg 1/2003. Horizontal working groups and sector-specific subgroups have been set up where the case-handlers of the different authorities have been extremely proactive in exchanging views and learning from each others' experiences with particular issues or with particular sectors.

[176] See R Sauer in JL Schulte and C Just (eds), *Kartellrecht* (Carl Heymanns Verlag 2012), Art 10 of Reg 1/2003, para 5 et seq.

[177] Antitrust Manual of Procedures, Internal DG Competition working documents on procedures for the application of Articles 101 and 102 TFEU, March 2012, Module 18 'Decision finding inapplicability (Article 10 Decision)', para 5; see also earlier C Gauer, D Dalheimer, L Kjolbye, and E De Smitjer 'Regulation 1/2003: A Modernized Application of EC Competition Rules' (2003) 1 Competition Policy Newsletter 3, 5–6.

[178] See Commission Staff Working Paper SEC(2001) 1828 'The notion of "Community public interest" in Article 10' of 13 November 2001, 5, section II, para 11. This notion should be clearly distinguished from the (lack of) 'EU interest' concept developed in connection with the *Automec* case law and governing the rejection of complaints.

[179] Antitrust Manual of Procedures, Internal DG Competition working documents on procedures for the application of Articles 101 and 102 TFEU, March 2012, Module 18 'Decision finding inapplicability (Article 10 Decision)', para 4. 'It follows that other public policy considerations (eg industrial interests) cannot be invoked to establish that there is "EU public interest" in the sense of Article 10.'

on the basis of Article 10 and, conversely, the implicit judgment that individual interests of companies are not sufficient to activate the Commission decision-making process in this context. This is further confirmed by the fact that Article 10 specifies that the Commission acts 'on its own initiative' rather than on application (further stressing the Commission's discretion).

The term 'Community' (ie, European Union) constitutes the second important facet of the **13.47** notion 'EU public interest'. It underlines the fact that Commission decisions pursuant to Article 10 are designed to serve exclusively the common public goal of undistorted competition within the internal market and, accordingly, the development of EU competition policy to safeguard that public goal.

In accordance with the EU dimension of the notion of 'EU public interest' and given the **13.48** exceptional nature of Article 10 decisions in a legal exception system, the problem of inconsistent application of the law (see Recital 14) needs to have a substantial impact on the functioning of competition within the internal market. Inconsistent application of the competition rules, in particular if sustained over a long period of time, may lead to discrimination between economic operators and unequal opportunities to compete. The market process itself, which the competition rules are designed to protect, may be substantially impeded.

The risk of divergence in the application of the competition rules, entailing a substantial **13.49** impediment to competition within the internal market may, exceptionally, also arise in the context of novel and unresolved questions, in so far as they trigger parallel proceedings before NCAs and courts, so that clarification by way of an Article 10 decision may be appropriate. However, recourse to an Article 10 decision in such a situation should normally only be had if other means of preventing the risk of divergence, such as an *amicus curiae* intervention of the Commission in proceedings before national courts, is unlikely to be sufficient. On the other hand, minor divergences in the interpretation of the rules, with only a minimal impact on the functioning of competition within the internal market, should not give rise to the adoption of Article 10 decisions.

Where the request for an Article 10 decision is rejected, a simple letter will usually suffice as **13.50** reply, indicating that the Commission does not issue Article 10 decisions upon request.[180]

2. Procedural aspects[181]

The Commission is the only body with the power to take inapplicability decisions. The only **13.51** guidance on the procedure to be followed is contained in the Manproc. As regards NCAs, Article 5 *in fine* states that they can only decide that 'there are no grounds for action on their part' because the information at their disposal does not show that the conditions for a prohibition exist, but it does not give them the power to end a procedure with an Article 10 decision.[182]

---

[180] Antitrust Manual of Procedures, Internal DG Competition working documents on procedures for the application of Articles 101 and 102 TFEU, March 2012, Module 18 'Decision finding inapplicability (Article 10 Decision)', para 6.

[181] See R Sauer in JL Schulte and C Just (eds), *Kartellrecht* (Carl Heymanns Verlag 2012), Art. 10 of Reg 1/2003, paras 10–12.

[182] In Case C-375/09 *Tele2 Polska sp* [2011] ECR I-3055, the Court observed that Art 5 of Reg 1/2003 limits the type of decisions NCAs can issue. By virtue of Art 5(1), NCAs can require that an infringement be brought to an end; order interim measures; accept commitments; and/or impose fines or periodic penalty payments. By virtue of Art 5(2), where the conditions for prohibition are not met, the NCAs 'may likewise decide that there are no grounds for action on their part'. On 3 May 2011, the Grand Chamber of the ECJ ruled on two preliminary references submitted by the Polish Supreme Court. The judgment clarifies the

- The Commission commences the Article 10 procedure on its own initiative, which means that the case will normally be opened '*ex officio*'. However, although in principle, no request is necessary, it is not excluded either (from a party or an NCA).[183]
- DG COMP provides early information indicating that an Article 10 decision is being considered in a specific case and stating the reasons for such consideration.
- Then, an investigation and internal consultation on priority assessment takes place.
- Finally, it comes to the initiation of formal proceedings as laid down by Article 11(6) Regulation 1/2003 and Article 2 of Regulation 773/2004. Pursuant to Article 2 of Regulation 773/2004, the initiation of the proceeding cannot be done later than the date on which the Article 27(4) Notice is published. If the initiation of proceedings is a reaction to an envisaged decision communicated by an NCA to the Commission pursuant to Article 11(4), the proceedings need to be opened without delay. It is only after this initiation of proceedings that all other competition authorities are relieved, in accordance with said Article 11(6) and Articles 35(3) and 35(4), of their competence to apply Articles 101 and 102 TFEU to the same case.

13.52 It is also only after this that, pursuant to Article 16 of Regulation 1/2003, all national courts must avoid giving decisions which would conflict with a decision contemplated by the Commission in proceedings it has initiated. The initiation of the proceedings is immediately notified to the undertakings concerned. Pursuant to Article 2(2) of Regulation 773/2004, the initiation of proceedings is to be communicated to the parties concerned prior to its being made public in the appropriate way. The competition authorities of the Member States are to be informed of the initiation. If the case has EEA relevance, the EFTA Surveillance Authority ('ESA') should be informed of the initiation of the proceedings.

13.53 Where there is an intention to adopt an Article 10 decision, pursuant to Article 27(4) of Regulation 1/2003, the Commission must publish a concise summary of the case and the main content of the proposed course of action.[184] Interested third parties may submit their observations within a time limit which is fixed in the publication. That time limit may not be less than one month. The decision to publish a summary of the case pursuant to Article 27(4) is taken by the Commissioner responsible for competition by empowerment. The Article 27(4) Notice is not a decision which can be the subject matter of an action for annulment (Article 263 TFEU).[185]

---

division of powers between the European Commission and national competition authorities ('NCAs') as laid down in the 'Modernisation Regulation' (Reg 1/2003). It does so by stressing that, even if the Regulation obliges NCAs to apply the European competition rules (Arts 101 and 102 TFEU) side by side with national competition rules, only the European Commission is empowered to make a finding that there has been no breach of the former rules. For the sake of ensuring a consistent application of EU competition rules, the NCAs can only decide that there are no grounds for action on their part.

[183] Antitrust Manual of Procedure, Internal DG Competition working documents on procedures for the application of Articles 101 and 102 TFEU, March 2012, Module 18 'Decision finding inapplicability (Article 10 Decision)', paras 6 and 7.

[184] The main points to mention in an Art 27(4) Notice are: (i) a summary of the facts; (ii) the parties; (iii) the relevant market; (iv) the agreement/practice; (v) the proposed course of action; (vi) invitation for third party observations, including an explicit request for a non-confidential version of those observations; (vii) deadline for observations: the deadline will usually be, and should not be less than, one month. Business secrets must not be included. Internal DG Competition working documents on procedures for the application of Articles 101 and 102 TFEU, March 2012, Module 18 'Decision finding inapplicability (Article 10 Decision)', para 19.

[185] For the reasoning, see Case T-74/92 *Ladbroke* [1995] ECR II-115, para 72, concerning notices published pursuant to Art 19(3) of Reg 17.

A copy of the draft Article 27(4) Notice is sent to the parties, asking them to identify busi- **13.54**
ness secrets (pursuant to Article 16 of Regulation 773/2004), and to rectify any material
errors of fact. The parties are not consulted on the wording of or assessment in the Article
27(4) Notice. In the event of disagreement between the Commission and the parties as to
whether the text of the Article 27(4) Notice contains business secrets, the Hearing Officer is
competent to decide. The Article 27(4) Notice is to be submitted for translation into all EU
languages. Before publication, the text of the Article 27(4) Notice is sent to the parties and,
at the same time, parties are informed of the formal initiation of proceedings.[186]

The Member States' competition authorities must be informed of the initiation of proceedings. **13.55**
In addition, the initiation of proceedings will be made public on DG COMP's website. Parties
are to be informed prior to publication pursuant to Article 2(2) of Regulation 773/2004.[187]

Observations can be received from companies, private citizens, or Member States. For each **13.56**
submission received, an acknowledgment of receipt will be sent. The case team should examine the observations received, and determine whether any of the third party observations call
into question the overall orientation of the case.[188]

- A copy of the draft Article 10 Decision has to be sent to the Hearing Officer in all cases in
  which a draft decision is being submitted to the Advisory Committee, because the Hearing
  Officer has to prepare a final report.
- The Advisory Committee must be consulted pursuant to Article 14 of Regulation 1/2003.
  Consultation may also take place by written procedure (see Article 14(4) of Regulation
  1/2003), but in any case any Member State so requests, the Commission has to convene a
  meeting.[189]
- A Commission decision should be notified to addressees and copies transmitted to com-
  petition authorities of the Member States. It should be noted that in the case of Article 10
  Decisions, the internal procedure to follow for adoption by the Commission could in principle be the written procedure. The decision has to be notified to the addressees, and a copy
  should be transmitted to the competition authorities of the Member States and ESA.[190]
- At the end, a publication in accordance with Article 30 of Regulation 1/2003 is made.
  Decisions finding inapplicability of Articles 101 and 102 have to be published as provided
  for in Article 30 of Regulation 1/2003. The publication must state the names of the parties and the main content of the decision. It must have regard to the legitimate interest of
  undertakings in the protection of their business secrets. In addition, the legal basis of the
  decision should be indicated.[191]

---

[186] Antitrust Manual of Procedure, Internal DG Competition working documents on procedures for the
application of Articles 101 and 102 TFEU, March 2012, Module 18 'Decision finding inapplicability (Article
10 Decision)', para 24.
[187] Antitrust Manual of Procedure, Internal DG Competition working documents on procedures for the
application of Articles 101 and 102 TFEU, March 2012, Module 18 'Decision finding inapplicability (Article
10 Decision)', paras 25–6.
[188] Antitrust Manual of Procedure, Internal DG Competition working documents on procedures for the
application of Articles 101 and 102 TFEU, March 2012, Module 18 'Decision finding inapplicability (Article
10 Decision)', paras 27–9.
[189] Antitrust Manual of Procedure, Internal DG Competition working documents on procedures for the
application of Articles 101 and 102 TFEU, March 2012, Module 18 'Decision finding inapplicability (Article
10 Decision)', paras 41 and 42.
[190] Antitrust Manual of Procedures, Internal DG Competition working documents on procedures for the
application of Articles 101 and 102 TFEU, March 2012, Module 18 'Decision finding inapplicability (Article
10 Decision)', paras 43 and 44.
[191] Antitrust Manual of Procedures, Internal DG Competition working documents on procedures for the
application of Articles 101 and 102 TFEU, March 2012, Module 18 'Decision finding inapplicability (Article
10 Decision)', para 45.

3. Effects of Article 10 Decisions

13.57   Although an Article 10 Decision is declaratory in nature (as a corollary of the legal exception system), it is nonetheless capable of producing the legal effects laid down in Article 16 of Regulation 1/2003. As a result of the ECJ's judgment in *Masterfoods*[192] and of the latter's codification in Article 16 of Regulation 1/2003, Commission decisions have EU-wide legally binding effect. This binding effect is equally extended to decisions based on Article 10. In concrete terms, when national courts rule on agreements or practices which are the subject of a Commission decision, they cannot take decisions running counter to that decision, unless they first refer to the ECJ for a preliminary ruling on the validity of that decision. They must also avoid decisions which would conflict with a decision contemplated by the Commission.[193]

13.58   The Article 10 Decision is of a declaratory nature, and based on the circumstances known to the Commission at the moment of its adoption and explained in some detail in the decision. The Commission indicates that if the circumstances change to an extent that materially affects the findings set out in the decision, it does not need to be revoked, but simply may no longer be invoked by the parties to their benefit, and will no longer block national proceedings within the meaning of Article 16 of Regulation 1/2003.[194]

4. Content of an Article 10 Decision

13.59   The Article 10 Decision states that Article 101 TFEU is not applicable to an agreement, a decision by an association of undertakings, or a concerted practice, either because the conditions of Article 101(1) are not fulfilled, or because the conditions of Article 101(3) are satisfied. In practice, this means that an agreement or a particular clause is not void under Article 101(2). It can also state that the conditions of Article 102 TFEU are not fulfilled and that an agreement, a particular clause, or a practice does not constitute an abuse of a dominant position.[195]

13.60   The decision is addressed to the undertaking(s) and/or associations of undertakings whose practices or agreements are examined and to which Articles 101 or 102 are found to be inapplicable. In cases of distribution agreements with one supplier and numerous distributors, the decision can be addressed to the supplier only.[196]

5. Challenge before EU Courts

13.61   As regards whether a decision under Article 10 could be challenged under Article 263, fourth paragraph TFEU, there is the suggestion that a decision under Article 10 can be challenged before the EU Courts. The beneficiary of a declaration under Article 10 will have no interest in contesting

---

[192] C-344/98 *Masterfoods* [2000] ECR I-11369, para 51 et seq.

[193] Antitrust Manual of Procedures, Internal DG Competition working documents on procedures for the application of Articles 101 and 102 TFEU, March 2012, Module 18 'Decision finding inapplicability (Article 10 Decision)', para 31.

[194] Antitrust Manual of Procedures, Internal DG Competition working documents on procedures for the application of Articles 101 and 102 TFEU, March 2012, Module 18 'Decision finding inapplicability (Article 10 Decision)', para 32. See also Kerse & Khan, *EC Antitrust Procedure* (6th edn, Sweet & Maxwell 2012) para 2-089, stating that if the terms of the agreement have been altered, a national court might reasonably hold that it was faced with case which did not fall within the scope of the Art 10 decision and that to reach a different conclusion would not be to take an inconsistent decision.

[195] Antitrust Manual of Procedures, Internal DG Competition working documents on procedures for the application of Articles 101 and 102 TFEU, March 2012, Module 18 'Decision finding inapplicability (Article 10 Decision)', paras 32–3.

[196] Antitrust Manual of Procedures, Internal DG Competition working documents on procedures for the application of Articles 101 and 102 TFEU, March 2012, Module 18 'Decision finding inapplicability (Article 10 Decision)', para 35.

the decision, but a competitor may do so provided the declaration is of direct and individual concern to it.[197] This may be the case in two situations: first, where the competitor participated in the proceedings and was heard as an affected third party, although this might need to go beyond the mere submission of observations under Article 27(4) of Regulation 1/2003; and secondly, where the competitor did not participate in the administrative procedure and claims rights that might be available to it before the Court. In this latter case, the competitor must show that it is individually affected in accordance with the general rules established by the ECJ.[198]

IV. Informal Guidance

Together with the declarations of inapplicability, guidance letters are an exception to the system of self-assessment and provide orientation on which undertakings can rely to some extent. As indicated, Regulation 1/2003 placed a burden of complete self-reliance upon companies and their legal advisors to determine whether their arrangements satisfy the criteria for exception. Undertakings can rely on the existing Commission decision-making practice, EU Court case law, and the Commission's guidance, including block exemptions and Commission Notices. One of the main concerns of businesses when this reform was announced had been that there would be reduced legal certainty, in particular because agreements and commercial arrangements would no longer be able to be notified to the Commission and receive either a positive exemption decision, or an informal 'comfort letter'. The Commission has taken this concern into account and has recognized that there may be cases where assistance is effectively needed. These novel questions require a greater legal certainty than the explanations of the existing rules can provide. The Commission adopted a Notice on Informal Guidance relating to unresolved questions concerning Articles 81 [101] and 82 [102] EC [TFEU],[199] which offers undertakings the possibility of requesting from the Commission an assessment regarding the compatibility of their conduct with the EU Competition rules. **13.62**

The Manproc stresses that requests by individual undertakings for guidance should be clearly distinguished from suggestions by interested undertakings to the Commission to adopt a decision within the meaning of Article 10 of Regulation 1/2003.[200] Both Article 10 decisions and guidance letters are to be adopted very exceptionally, but Article 10 decisions are taken on the Commission's own initiative and exclusively in the EU public interest relating **13.63**

---

[197] See Art 267(4) TFEU. See R Sauer in JL Schulte and C Just (eds), *Kartellrecht* (Carl Heymanns Verlag 2012), Art 10 of Reg 1/2003, para 14.

[198] See R Sauer in JL Schulte and C Just (eds), *Kartellrecht* (Carl Heymanns Verlag 2012), Art 10 of Reg 1/2003, para 15; see also in respect to the possibility of third parties challenging a decision under Art 10: J Schwarze and A Weitbrecht, *Grundzüge des europäischen Kartellverfahrensrechts* (Nomos 2004) § 6, paras 108 21, referring to the ECJ case law in C-263/02P *Jégo-Quéré* [2004] ECR I-3425, para 44 et seq. The ECJ reiterated that a natural or legal person is to be regarded as individually concerned by an EU measure of general application that concerns him or her directly if the measure in question affects his or her legal position, in a manner which is both definite and immediate. A person would be affected by reason of certain attributes peculiar to them, or by reason of a factual situation which differentiates them from all other persons and distinguishes them individually in the same way as an addressee. Internal DG Competition working documents on procedures for the application of Articles 101 and 102 TFEU, March 2012, Module 18 'Decision finding inapplicability (Article 10 Decision)', para 36 indicates that the publication of the decision in full text should ensure that the other parties' rights are sufficiently protected and that they have the necessary information to seek judicial review if they deem it necessary.

[199] Commission Notice on informal guidance relating to novel questions concerning Articles 81 and 82 of the EC Treaty that arise in individual cases (guidance letters) 'Notice on Informal Guidance' [2004] OJ C101/78.

[200] AntitrustAntitrust Manual of Procedures, Internal DG Competition working documents on procedures for the application of Articles 101 and 102 TFEU, March 2012, Module 22 'Informal Guidance', para 3.

to the application of Articles 101 and 102 TFEU. As stated, the latter notion refers to the need for the Commission to act in order to solve a problem of coherent application or to set policy,[201] whereas guidance letters are designed in the first place to serve the interest of the individual undertakings in obtaining guidance that should assist them for the assessment of their actions where a novel question exists. In order not to blur the distinction between both situations, guidance letters should not refer to the concept of EU public interest relating to the application of Articles 101 and 102 TFEU or otherwise use terminology from the Article 10 Regulation 1/2003 context.[202] These are therefore discussed in the same context.

A. Guidance Letters

13.64 As stated in Recital 3 of Regulation 1/2003, one of the primary objectives of this Regulation is to allow the Commission to concentrate its resources on curbing the most serious infringements. For this reason, the possibility of requesting informal guidance should not lead to some kind of notification/clearance procedure, which would interfere with the Commission's main task of ensuring effective enforcement of the competition rules. Such guidance is issued at the Commission's discretion and subject to its other enforcement priorities. Providing guidance to individual companies is not the principal business of the Commission under Regulation 1/2003, which is to ensure effective enforcement of EU competition law. Indeed, a main principle introduced by Regulation 1/2003 is that, as a rule, undertakings have to self-assess their compliance with EU competition law. Therefore, the criteria for the issuing of a guidance letter, set out in the Notice, must be carefully respected. Issuing a guidance letter should remain exceptional.[203] Regulation 1/2003 does not make express provision for guidance letters, but limits itself to stating that where cases give rise to genuine uncertainty because they present novel or unresolved questions, individual undertakings may wish to seek informal guidance from the Commission.[204]

13.65 DG COMP receives numerous informal solicitations for guidance; for example, that undertakings send information about and/or the text of their agreements and solicit a reaction from DG COMP, ask for a meeting to discuss an agreement or practice, and/or ask for specific information or clarification on a competition law issue (in writing or orally).[205] Moreover, undertakings may seek informal contacts with a view to discussing the possibility of obtaining a guidance letter. They will want to describe the case and the issue for which they would envisage a request. DG COMP is at pains to stress that it does not object to an exchange of views about market developments and may provide general indications about its case practice and policy. However, no definitive views can be given on a particular agreement, decision, or practice. Moreover, an informal discussion with DG COMP should not be construed as the Commission giving any form of 'clearance'. The fact that a meeting is held with DG COMP does not confer any rights or expectations.[206]

---

[201] Cf Recital 14 of Reg 1/2003.
[202] Antitrust Manual of Procedures, Internal DG Competition working documents on procedures for the application of Articles 101 and 102 TFEU, March 2012, Module 22 'Informal Guidance', para 3.
[203] Antitrust Manual of Procedures, Internal DG Competition working documents on procedures for the application of Articles 101 and 102 TFEU, March 2012, Module 22 'Informal Guidance', para 3.
[204] Recital 38 of Reg 1/2003.
[205] Antitrust Manual of Procedures, Internal DG Competition working documents on procedures for the application of Articles 101 and 102 TFEU, March 2012, Module 22 'Informal Guidance', para 5.
[206] Antitrust Manual of Procedures, Internal DG Competition working documents on procedures for the application of Articles 101 and 102 TFEU, March 2012, Module 22 'Informal Guidance', paras 6–7.

1. The three cumulative conditions

13.66 The Commission may only consider issuing a guidance letter if the nature of the question being considered is not hypothetical and where the transaction has reached a sufficiently advanced stage. Conversely, it will not consider the issue if the agreement or practice is no longer implemented. In addition, the Notice on Informal Guidance stipulates that three positive cumulative conditions must be fulfilled.[207]

- Firstly, the assessment of conduct with regard to Articles 101 and/or 102 TFEU should pose a question for which the existing EU legal framework does not provide any answer or clarification. This means that the question raised is so original that no case of the EU Courts can be found on the point, nor is there any general guidance, precedent in decision-making practice, or previous guidance letters.[208]
- Secondly, after a preliminary evaluation of the characteristics and background of the case, the Commission will decide whether or not the issuance of a guidance letter will help find the adequate answer to the question raised. The Commission will have to appraise the usefulness of a guidance letter considering:
  - the economic importance from the point of view of the consumer of the goods or services concerned by the agreement or practice;
  - the extent to which the agreement corresponds or is liable to correspond to a more widespread economic usage in the market place;
  - the size of investments regarding the transaction taking into account the size of the companies concerned and the extent to which the transaction affects a structural operation, such as the creation of a non-full function joint venture.[209]
- Finally, it is possible to issue a guidance letter on the basis of the information provided, ie no further fact-finding is required.[210] However, the Commission is free to use any other public or private source available and may ask the applicant(s) to provide supplementary information.[211] If one condition fails, the request should be rejected. In its five-year assessment in 2009, the Commission has indicated that none of the approaches for informal guidance came close to fulfilling the conditions for making such a request.[212]

13.67 Furthermore, the Commission will not consider a request for a guidance letter in any of the following circumstances:[213]

- The questions raised in the request are identical or similar to issues raised in a case pending before EU Courts.

---

[207] Notice on Informal Guidance [2004] OJ C101/78, para 8(a)-(c); see also Internal DG Competition working documents on procedures for the application of Articles 101 and 102 TFEU, March 2012, Module 22 'Informal Guidance', para 11.

[208] Notice on Informal Guidance [2004] OJ C10 1/78, para 8(a).

[209] Notice on Informal Guidance [2004] OJ C101/78, para 8(b).

[210] Notice on Informal Guidance [2004] OJ C101/78, para 8(c). Internal DG Competition working documents on procedures for the application of Articles 101 and 102 TFEU, March 2012, Module 22 'Informal Guidance', paras 20–1. The Commission will in principle evaluate the request on the basis of the information provided by the undertakings. It follows that a request which does not set out the facts in a conclusive manner should be rejected. The Commission may use additional information at its disposal from public sources, former proceedings or any other source and may ask the applicant(s) to provide supplementary information.

[211] Notice on Informal Guidance [2004] OJ C101/78, para 15.

[212] Commission Staff Working Paper accompanying the Communication from the Commission to the European Parliament and Council, Report on the functioning of Regulation 1/2003 {COM(2009)206 final}, 29 April 2009, para 45.

[213] Antitrust Manual of Procedures, Internal DG Competition working documents on procedures for the application of Articles 101 and 102 TFEU, March 2012, Module 22 'Informal Guidance', para 11.

- The agreement or practice to which the request refers is subject to proceedings pending with the Commission, a Member State court, or a Member State competition authority.
- The Commission will not consider hypothetical questions and will not issue guidance letters on agreements or practices that are no longer being implemented by the parties. Undertakings may, however, present a request for a guidance letter to the Commission in relation to questions raised by an agreement or practice that they envisage, ie before the implementation of that agreement or practice. In this case the transaction must have reached a sufficiently advanced stage for a request to be considered.[214]

2. Procedure

13.68 Either one undertaking or a group of them can present a request for guidance in order to clarify the questions raised by an agreement or practice into which they have entered that could fall within the scope of Articles 101 and/or 102 TFEU. There is no specific request form to fill out, but the requests should be accompanied by a memorandum which contains the relevant information. The memorandum must be addressed to DG COMP, and include the following items:[215]

- the identity of all undertakings concerned as well as a single address for contacts with the Commission;
- the specific questions on which guidance is sought;
- full and exhaustive information on all points relevant for an informed evaluation of the questions raised, including pertinent documentation;
- detailed reasoning, explaining why the request presents a novel question;
- all other information that permits an evaluation of the request in the light of the aspects explained in the Notice, including in particular a declaration that the agreement or practice to which the request refers is not subject to proceedings pending before a Member State court or competition authority;
- where the request contains elements that are considered business secrets, a clear identification of these elements;
- any other information or documentation relevant to the individual case.[216]

13.69 When the Commission receives a request for a guidance letter, it will first consider whether or not it is appropriate to process it. A first reply should be sent by the unit dealing with the request to the applicant(s) within fifteen working days following receipt.[217] The Manproc states that two answers would be possible at this stage:

- A letter directly rejecting the request: this will allow immediate rejection of requests which obviously (i) do not fulfil the criteria; or (ii) are not considered as a priority. The letter rejecting the request will not refer to the substance but only to the fact that the Commission does not consider it as a priority. It should also state that the Commission is not precluded from subsequently examining that same agreement or practice in a procedure under Regulation 1/2003.
- A holding reply, if the request seems to fulfil the criteria detailed previously and merits being further analysed. The letter will indicate that the Commission services are currently

---

[214] Antitrust Manual of Procedures, Internal DG Competition working documents on procedures for the application of Articles 101 and 102 TFEU, March 2012, Module 22 'Informal Guidance', para 11.

[215] Notice on Informal Guidance [2004] OJ C101/78, para 14.

[216] Antitrust Manual of Procedures, Internal DG Competition working documents on procedures for the application of Articles 101 and 102 TFEU, March 2012, Module 22 'Informal Guidance', para 9.

[217] Antitrust Manual of Procedures, Internal DG Competition working documents on procedures for the application of Articles 101 and 102 TFEU, March 2012, Module 22 'Informal Guidance', para 16.

analysing the request and that the final evaluation (issuance of a guidance letter or refusal) will follow.[218]

In order to make this first assessment of the request, the unit should: **13.70**

- make a first assessment of the request against the conditions set out in the Notice: as indicated, if one condition fails, the request shall be rejected;
- check the facts set out by the undertakings: the Commission will in principle evaluate the request on the basis of the information provided by the undertakings. It follows that a request that does not set out the facts in a conclusive manner should be rejected. The Commission may use additional information at its disposal from public sources, former proceedings or any other source and may ask the applicant(s) to provide supplementary information;[219]
- make an initial assessment of whether it is appropriate to prepare a Guidance letter in the light of DG COMP's enforcement priorities: the unit in charge of the request should also make an initial assessment of whether the issuing of a guidance letter is appropriate in the light of the enforcement priorities. For this purpose, the priority-setting principles can be applied correspondingly. A request that is not considered as a priority in the light of the enforcement policy should be rejected.[220]

The Commission can share all of this information with the NCAs through the ECN,[221] which **13.71** will allow it to receive information from the ECN as well as to discuss the substance of the request with the NCAs before issuing a guidance letter. Where the Commission ultimately decides not to issue a guidance letter, it will inform the applicant accordingly. The Notice on Informal Guidance contains no rules on time periods in this respect. Given the wide discretion of the Commission to issue guidance letters, one may not expect that the Commission will need to explain in great detail the reasons for its refusal to consider the request. The applicants may withdraw their request for guidance at any point in time. Nevertheless, in any case all of the supplied information will remain with the Commission, which can initiate proceedings in accordance with Regulation 1/2003 with regard to the facts stated in the request.

If it is decided to issue a guidance letter, it might be necessary to collect supplementary infor- **13.72** mation, including by informal enquiries, while respecting the normal rules on professional secrecy with regard to the information supplied by the applicant(s).

According to the Notice on Informal Guidance, a guidance letter sets out:[222] **13.73**

- a summary description of the facts on which it is based;
- the principal legal reasoning underlying the Commission's understanding of novel questions relating to Articles 101 and/or 102 TFEU raised by the request. According to the Notice on Informal Guidance, a guidance letter may be limited to part of the questions raised in the request. It may also include additional aspects to those set out in the request.[223]

---

[218] Antitrust Manual of Procedures, Internal DG Competition working documents on procedures for the application of Articles 101 and 102 TFEU, March 2012, Module 22 'Informal Guidance', para 16.
[219] Antitrust Manual of Procedures, Internal DG Competition working documents on procedures for the application of Articles 101 and 102 TFEU, March 2012, Module 22 'Informal Guidance', paras 17 and 20–1.
[220] Antitrust Manual of Procedures, Internal DG Competition working documents on procedures for the application of Articles 101 and 102 TFEU, March 2012, Module 22 'Informal Guidance', paras 17 and 22–3.
[221] Notice on Informal Guidance [2004] OJ C101/78, para 16.
[222] Notice on Informal Guidance [2004] OJ C101/78, paras 19–21.
[223] Notice on Informal Guidance [2004] OJ C101/78, para 17.

13.74 The Notice on Informal Guidance provides that where no guidance letter is issued, the Commission should inform the applicant(s) accordingly. In practice, this will normally be done by a letter signed by the competent Director.[224]

3. Effects of a guidance letter

13.75 The Commission stresses that guidance letters are in the first place intended to help undertakings carry out, by themselves, an informed assessment of their agreements and practices.[225] A guidance letter cannot prejudge the assessment of the same question by the EU Courts. Where an agreement or practice has formed the factual basis for a guidance letter, the Commission is not precluded from subsequently examining that same agreement or practice in a procedure under Regulation 1/2003, in particular following a complaint.[226] In that case, the Commission will take the previous guidance letter into account,[227] subject in particular to changes in the underlying facts, to any new aspects raised by a complaint, to developments in the case law of the EU Courts, or wider changes in the Commission's policy.[228]

4. Publication of the Informal Guidance

13.76 According to the Notice on Informal Guidance, the guidance letter will be posted on the Commission's website, having regard to the legitimate interest of undertakings in the protection of their business secrets. Before issuing a guidance letter, the Commission will agree with the applicants on a public version. It follows that the service in charge of the preparation should ask the undertakings at an early stage for a definitive position on whether their request contains business secrets or other confidential information that they would not wish to see used in the published guidance letter. The case-handling unit should explore with the undertaking the possibilities of protecting the information for which confidentiality is claimed, while making public meaningful guidance. If the contacts with the undertakings on this matter lead to the conclusion that useful guidance could only be issued (and made public) if certain information is revealed that the undertakings do not wish to see disclosed, the request for a guidance letter should be rejected.

13.77 Before the draft guidance letter is submitted for adoption, the Competition Commissioner should be asked to give his/her approval. The guidance letter is adopted by the College (normally by written procedure), following an inter-service consultation. Once adopted, the guidance letter is sent by the Secretariat General to the applicant(s).[229]

---

[224] Notice on Informal Guidance [2004] OJ C101/78, para 17.

[225] Antitrust Manual of Procedures, Internal DG Competition working documents on procedures for the application of Articles 101 and 102 TFEU, March 2012, Module 22 'Informal Guidance', para 12.

[226] Notice on Informal Guidance [2004] OJ C101/78, para 24. Kerse & Khan, *EC Antitrust Procedure* (6th edn, Sweet & Maxwell 2012) para 2-086, note that the very limited interest to date in seeking informal guidance may be a reflection of the fact that a guidance letter would be of limited utility being not a formal Commission decision.

[227] Notice on Informal Guidance [2004] OJ C101/78, para 24. This may lead to the paradoxical situation of an undertaking being fined by an NCA or a national court for having followed the guidance received by the Commission, although this is unlikely to occur where the undertaking can allege that it followed in good faith the Commission's guidance. As a result, guidance letters may lead to disputes until the EU Courts decide the matter.

[228] Notice on Informal Guidance [2004] OJ C101/78, para 25, indicating that guidance letters are not Commission decisions and do not bind Member States' competition authorities or courts that have the power to apply Arts 101 and 102 TFEU. However, it is open to Member States' competition authorities and courts to take account of guidance letters issued by the Commission as they see fit in the context of a case. Antitrust Manual of Procedures, Internal DG Competition working documents on procedures for the application of Articles 101 and 102 TFEU, March 2012, Module 22 'Informal Guidance', paras 14–15.

[229] Antitrust Manual of Procedures, Internal DG Competition working documents on procedures for the application of Articles 101 and 102 TFEU, March 2012, Module 22 'Informal Guidance', para 30.

According to the Notice on Informal Guidance, the Guidance letter will be posted on the **13.78** Commission's website, subject to the legitimate interest of undertakings in the protection of their business secrets.[230] Before issuing a guidance letter, the Commission will agree with the applicant(s) on a public version. DG COMP will consequently send a letter to the applicant(s) to ask them to provide a non-confidential version of the guidance letter in order to publish it on the DG COMP website. It should be indicated on the website that the publication is for information purposes only and should not be considered as an official publication.[231]

---

[230] Notice on Informal Guidance [2004] OJ C101/78 para 21.
[231] Antitrust Manual of Procedures, Internal DG Competition working documents on procedures for the application of Articles 101 and 102 TFEU, March 2012, Module 22 'Informal Guidance', para 12. Notice on Informal Guidance [2004] OJ C101/78, para 33.

14

OTHER SPECIAL PROCEDURES

Ralf Sauer, Luis Ortiz Blanco, and Konstantin Jörgens

I. Interim Measures

A. Origin and Legal Basis[1]

Article 8 of Regulation 1/2003[2] empowers the Commission, '[i]n cases of urgency due to the **14.01** risk of serious and irreparable damage to competition...acting on its own initiative', to take a decision ordering interim measures 'on the basis of a prima facie finding of infringement'. Such decisions apply for a specified period of time but may be renewed in so far as this is necessary and appropriate.[3] Former Regulation 17 did not expressly grant the Commission such a power. However, in *Camera Care*,[4] the Court of Justice ('ECJ') ruled that in certain circumstances the Commission was entitled to adopt interim measures under Article 3 of Regulation 17. This provision—which more generally referred to cease-and-desist orders—was interpreted

---

[1] For an overview see European Commission Antitrust Manual of Procedures, Internal DG Competition working documents on procedures for the application of Articles 101 and 102 TFEU, March 2012, Module 17 'Interim measures'. See also R Sauer in JL Schulte and C Just (eds), *Kartellrecht* (Carl Heymanns Verlag 2012), Art 8 of Reg 1/2003. The 'interim measures' referred to in this chapter should not be confused with those granted under Art 279 TFEU.

[2] In addition, the Commission has been expressly granted the power to order interim measures by specific regulation, such as Reg 3975/87 as regards the application of the competition rules to the air transport sector and Reg 659/1999 as regards state aids. See European Commission Antitrust Manual of Procedures, Internal DG Competition working documents on procedures for the application of Articles 101 and 102 TFEU, March 2012, Module 17 'Interim Measures', para 4.

[3] Article 8(2) of Reg 1/2003.

[4] Case 792/79 R *Camera Care v Commission* [1980] ECR 119. That case arose when a complainant applied for interim measures, which the Commission refused on the grounds that Reg 17 did not empower it to adopt them. However, the ECJ took the opposite view at paras 17–19: 'As regards the right to take decisions conferred upon the Commission by Article 3(1) [of Reg 17], it is essential that it should be exercised in the most efficacious manner best suited to the circumstances of each given situation. To this end the possibility cannot be excluded that the exercise of the right to take decisions conferred upon the Commission should comprise successive stages

by the Court as empowering the Commission to adopt interim measures if these could be considered as indispensable for the effective exercise of its functions. In practice, the Commission has made rather limited use of this power since *Camera Care*,[5] although it has extended the concept to include not only prohibitory orders but also positive (prescriptive) measures.[6] The Commission did not make any use of Article 8 of Regulation 1/2003 since the power to adopt interim measures was explicitly prescribed in law in 2004.[7]

14.02 In terms of the basic requirements for interim measures, Article 8 of Regulation 1/2003 largely reflects the conditions developed in the case law of the Union courts starting with *Camera Care*.

---

so that a decision finding that there is an infringement may be preceded by any preliminary measures which may appear necessary at any given moment. From this point of view the Commission must also be able…to take protective measures to the extent to which they might appear indispensable in order to avoid the exercise of the power to make decisions given by Article 3 from becoming ineffectual or even illusory because of the action of certain undertakings. The powers which the Commission holds under Article 3(1) of [Reg 17] therefore include the power to take interim measures which are indispensable for the effective exercise of its functions and, in particular, for ensuring the effectiveness of any decisions requiring undertakings to bring to an end infringements which it has found to exist. However, the Commission could not take such measures without having regard to the legitimate interests of the undertaking concerned by them. For this reason it is essential that interim measures be taken only in cases proved to be urgent in order to avoid a situation likely to cause serious and irreparable damage to the party seeking their adoption, or which is intolerable for the public interest. A further requirement is that these measures be of a temporary and conservatory nature and restricted to what is required in the given situation. When adopting them the Commission is bound to maintain the essential safeguards guaranteed to the parties concerned by [Reg 17], in particular by Article 19 [concerning the right to be heard]. Finally, the decisions must be made in such a form that an action may be brought upon them before the Court of Justice by any party who considers he has been injured.' See also Joined Cases 228/82 and 229/82 *Ford v Commission* [1984] ECR 1129, paras 18 and 19; Case T-23/90 *Peugeot v Commission* [1991] ECR II-653, paras 19–22 and 61–3; Case T-44/90 *La Cinq v Commission* [1992] ECR II-1, paras 27–30, 61, 62, and 79–81. See also Order of the President in Case T-184/01 R *IMS Health v Commission* [2001] ECR II-3193, paras 53–5, 92, 120, and 141.

[5] See eg *Ford Werke—Interim Measures* [1982] OJ L256/20 (annulled by the ECJ in Joined Cases 228/82 and 229/82 *Ford v Commission* [1984] ECR 1129); *ECS/AKZO—Interim Measures* [1983] OJ L252/13; *BBI/Boosey and Hawkes—Interim Measures* [1987] OJ L286/36; *Eco System/Peugeot—Interim Measures* (Case IV/33.157; Commission Press Release IP/90/233 of 27 March 1990); *Mars/Langnese and Schoeller—Interim Measures* (Case IV/34.072; Commission Press Release IP/92/222 of 25 March 1992) (partially suspended in Joined Cases T-24/92 R and T-28/92 R *Langnese-Iglo and Schöller v Commission* [1992] ECR II-1839). See also Case IV/34.174 *B&I/Sealink* (Press Release IP/92/478 of 11 June 1992; unofficially published in [1992] 5 CMLR 255), in which the decision was adopted on the basis of Art 10 of Reg 4056/86, the equivalent for maritime purposes of Art 3 of Reg 17. On other occasions, the Commission terminated the procedure before adopting a formal decision, either because the undertakings ceased their activities in breach of the EU competition rules (eg *IGR Stereo Television I*, XI Commission Report on Competition Policy (1981), para 94; *Amicon/Fortia*, XI Commission Report on Competition Policy (1981), para 112) or because an amicable settlement was reached with the undertaking concerned in the form of commitments given by them (eg *Eurofix-Bauco/Hilti* [1988] OJ L65/19, para 29; *Napier Brown/British Sugar* [1988] OJ L284/41, para 9; *MTV Europe RMC Records (UK) Ltd* [1995] 1 CMLR 437, para 13). In *Sea Containers v Stena Sealink—Interim Measures* [1994] OJ L15/8, the Commission by decision rejected an application for interim measures.

[6] See eg *Ford Werke AG—Interim Measures* [1982] OJ L256/20, para 26 ('measures necessary for ensuring the effectiveness of any decision…[may] comprise both an order to perform some act and to desist from some act'). See also *NDC Health/IMS Health—Interim Measures* [2002] OJ L59/18, where the Commission imposed a requirement on IMS Health to grant a licence, upon request and on a non-discriminatory basis, to competitors for the use of its '1860 brick structure' in order to collect and sell regional pharmaceutical sales data formatted according to this structure. In giving an *ex-parte* order suspending the decision until final decision in the proceedings for interim judicial relief, the President of the General Court ('GC') expressed doubts over whether such measures were still within the scope of the Commission's powers in interim proceedings. See Case T-184/01 R *IMS Health v Commission* [2001] ECR II-2349, para 25. Both the President of the GC and the ECJ upheld this suspension in the interim measures case brought by IMS Health. Subsequently, the Commission withdrew its decision on the ground that IMS's competitors no longer needed a licence to compete with IMS. See Orders of the President in Case T-184/01 R *IMS Health v Commission* [2001] ECR II-3193; Case C-481/01 P(R) *NDC Health v IMS Health and Commission* [2002] ECR I-3401.

[7] See, for the period until April 2009, the Commission staff working paper accompanying the Communication from the Commission to the European Parliament and Council—Report on the functioning of Regulation 1/2003, SEC(2009) 574 final.

The main difference to the situation under Regulation 17 is that interim measures will now be ordered by the Commission (College[8]) 'on its own initiative' and hence in the exercise of its discretion. The Commission should only intervene where there is a risk of serious and irreparable harm to *competition*,[9] while individual operators (competitors, customers) may seek to have their individual interests protected before national courts.[10] Relying on the complementary role of private action vis-à-vis public enforcement, the Commission has been at pains to reiterate in its notices that national courts are better placed to grant interim relief at the request of third parties, and that Article 8 of Regulation 1/2003 shall be construed as meaning that interim measures cannot be applied for by complainants pursuant to Article 7(2) of Regulation 1/2003.[11] Hence, the Commission is no longer obliged to decide on any (informal) request for interim measures, or to reject it by decision.[12] It is unlikely that the Commission will change its practice in this regard; hence, it reserves the adoption of interim measures to exceptional circumstances where the public interest so requires.[13] This does not mean, however, that the Commission would ignore information brought to its attention by economic operators on possible infringements of the competition rules which might require urgent action.[14]

B. Conditions for Granting Interim Measures

Article 8 of Regulation 1/2003 describes the conditions that must be satisfied in order for the Commission to adopt interim measures.[15] Such measures presuppose: **14.03**

- a *prima facie* case establishing an infringement; and
- an urgent need for protective measures because of the risk of serious and irreparable harm to competition.[16]

---

[8] As a decision on substance which can have considerable consequences, interim measures are reserved to the College (no empowerment of the Competition Commissioner). See European Commission Antitrust Manual of Procedures, Internal DG Competition working documents on procedures for the application of Articles 101 and 102 TFEU, March 2012, Module 1 'Decision-making procedures', para 17.

[9] See Recital 9 of Reg 1/2003, according to which Articles 101 and 102 TFEU have as their objective the protection of 'competition on the market'.

[10] See Draft Reg implementing Arts 81 and 82 of the Treaty COM (2000) 582 final—CNS 2000/243 Explanatory Memorandum, Art 8. In a decentralized enforcement system, national competition authorities (NCAs) may equally take interim measures, which may also be adopted at the request of complainants. See Art 5 of Reg 1/2003 and the Commission Notice on the handling of complaints by the Commission under Articles 81 and 82 of the EC Treaty [2004] OJ C101/65, n 70. See also AG Mazák, Opinion of 7 December 2010 in Case C-375/09 *Prezes Urzedu Ochrony Konkurencji i Konsumentów c v Tele2 Polska* [2011] ECR I-3055, para 58.

[11] Commission Notice on the handling of complaints by the Commission under Articles 81 and 82 of the EC Treaty [2004] OJ C101/65, paras 16 and 80. See also Commission Notice on the co-operation between the Commission and the courts of the EU Member States in the application of Articles 81 and 82 EC [2004] OJ C101/54, paras 14 and 21, stating that it is incumbent on the national courts to assess whether it might be necessary to order interim measures to safeguard the interests of the parties.

[12] See European Commission Antitrust Manual of Procedures, Internal DG Competition working documents on procedures for the application of Articles 101 and 102 TFEU, March 2012, Module 17 'Interim Measures', para 6.

[13] J Schwarze and A Weitbrecht, *Grundzüge des Europäischen Kartellverfahrensrechts* (Nomos 2004) § 6, paras 48–50; see para 14.03 et seq.

[14] See European Commission Antitrust Manual of Procedures, Internal DG Competition working documents on procedures for the application of Articles 101 and 102 TFEU, March 2012, Module 17 'Interim Measures', para 6: 'Complainants or third parties who can demonstrate sufficient interest to be heard may encourage the Commission to adopt such measures. However, under [Art 8 of Reg 1/2003], the Commission acts *ex officio*.'

[15] See also European Commission Antitrust Manual of Procedures, Internal DG Competition working documents on procedures for the application of Articles 101 and 102 TFEU, March 2012, Module 17 'Interim Measures', paras 8–19.

[16] See also Case T-184/01 *IMS Health Inc v Commission* [2001] ECR II-3193, para 52.

14.04 In *Akzo* and other decisions, the Commission had considered that urgency constituted an independent third condition for the grant of interim measures,[17] but in *La Cinq*, the General Court ('GC') clarified that it rather forms part of the second condition to which it is inextricably linked.[18] Hence, if a risk of serious and irreparable harm exists, urgency is simultaneously established.[19] Since the conditions for ordering interim measures are cumulative, failure to fulfill one of them will prevent the Commission from exercising its power to adopt interim measures.[20]

14.05 In addition, any measures that the Commission takes must be of a temporary and conservatory nature (Article 8(2) or Regulation 1/2003)[21], and restricted to what is necessary in the situation at hand.[22] The Commission also has to balance the public interest in adopting interim measures with the legitimate interests of the undertaking which is the object of such measures,[23] and maintain the essential procedural safeguards guaranteed to it.[24] Finally, interim measures 'must come within the framework of the final decision',[25] ie they must not go beyond the scope of the Commission's powers pursuant to Article 7 of Regulation 1/2003 to bring an infringement to an end.[26]

1. *Prima facie* case of an infringement

14.06 In *Peugeot* and *La Cinq*, the GC stressed that—contrary to the interpretation adopted by the Commission which, in *La Cinq*, had assumed the need for finding a 'clear and flagrant' infringement—the case law of the EU Courts only presupposed a *prima facie* case that certain behaviour violates the competition rules.[27] The GC observed that the Commission's

---

[17] *ECS/AKZO—Interim Measures* [1983] OJ L252/13, para 23. See also *BBI/Boosey and Hawkes—Interim Measures* [1987] OJ L286/36, para 14.

[18] See Case T-44/90 *La Cinq v Commission* [1992] ECR II-1, paras 25 and 29. In its earlier judgment in Case T-23/90 *Peugeot v Commission* [1991] ECR II-653, paras 65 and 77, the GC had not clearly rejected the applicants' contention that urgency was a separate condition to be fulfilled.

[19] Case T-184/01 R *IMS Health Inc v Commission* [2001] ECR II-3193, para 54: 'It follows, since if a risk of serious and irreparable harm exists urgency is inevitably simultaneously established, that the three conditions enumerated by the Commission in the contested decision fall correctly to be characterised as constituting effectively two conditions.'

[20] See Case T-44/90 *La Cinq v Commission* [1992] ECR II-1, para 30; Case T-184/01 R *IMS Health Inc v Commission* [2001] ECR II-3193, para 55.

[21] See *ECS/AKZO—Interim Measures* [1983] OJ L252/13, para 36: 'The measures to be adopted must be of a temporary nature, designed to restore the status quo...'

[22] Case 792/79 R *Camera Care v Commission* [1980] ECR 119, para 19. See also European Commission Antitrust Manual of Procedures, Internal DG Competition working documents on procedures for the application of Articles 101 and 102 TFEU, March 2012, Module 17 'Interim Measures', n 11: 'The measures must be kept within the limits and not exceed what is strictly necessary to remedy a situation. The measures must aim at safeguarding...the public interest. The measures must be temporary or interim and can only be valid until a decision is adopted on the substance or until a higher instance annuls them.'

[23] See *ECS/AKZO—Interim Measures* [1983] OJ L252/13, paras 24 and 36; *BBI/Boosey and Hawkes—Interim Measures* [1987] OJ L286/36, para 14; *Sea Containers/Stena Sealink—Interim Measures* [1994] OJ L15/8, para 56; *NDC Health/IMS Health—Interim Measures* [2001] OJ L59/18, paras 42 and 199 (balance of interests). See also Case 792/79 R *Camera Care v Commission* [1980] ECR 119, para 19; Case T-23/90 *Peugeot v Commission* [1991] ECR II-653, paras 73–6.

[24] Case 792/79 R *Camera Care v Commission* [1980] ECR 119, para 19.

[25] Joined Cases 228 and 229/82 R *Ford v Commission* [1982] ECR I-3091, para 19; Case T-23/90 *Peugeot v Commission* [1991] ECR II-653, paras 20 and 54–7.

[26] Cf *Sea Containers/Stena Sealink—Interim Measures* [1994] OJ L15/8, para 56; *NDC Health/IMS Health—Interim Measures* [2001] OJ L59/18, para 42. This includes both behavioural and structural remedies, although it may be doubtful whether the latter could be applied as a temporal measure. It is not a requirement that in its final decision the Commission could impose a penalty in respect of the conduct at issue. See Case T-184/01 R *IMS Health Inc v Commission* [2001] ECR II-3193, para 92.

[27] Case T-44/90 *La Cinq v Commission* [1992] ECR II-1, paras 32 and 62.

interpretation would be tantamount to requiring, for the adoption of interim measures, a degree of certainty as to the existence of an infringement which would be sufficient for the adoption of a final decision in the case at hand, thereby rendering interim measures unnecessary and pointless.[28] Therefore, the Commission only needs to show the appearance or probability of an infringement,[29] which presupposes a less detailed analysis both as regards the underlying facts and the legal arguments.[30]

2. Urgency due to the risk of serious and irreparable harm to competition

In its *Camera Care* judgment, the ECJ had stressed the importance 'that interim measures be **14.07** taken only in cases proved to be urgent in order to avoid a situation likely to cause serious and irreparable damage to the party seeking their adoption, or which is intolerable for the public interest'.[31] Article 8(1) of Regulation 1/2003 is more limited in this respect, as it only refers to the risk[32] of serious and irreparable damage to competition. Due to the shift to a legal framework in which complainants are no longer able to apply for interim measures solely on the basis of the damage inflicted on them, the focus now is to avoid a situation which causes 'intolerable damage to the public interest'. Potential damage to an individual undertaking will only be considered where it coincides with damage to competition.[33] Consequently, and

---

[28] Case T-44/90 *La Cinq v Commission* [1992] ECR II-1, para 61.

[29] See European Commission Antitrust Manual of Procedures, Internal DG Competition working documents on procedures for the application of Articles 101 and 102 TFEU, March 2012, Module 17 'Interim Measures', para 13. The exact standards applied in case law and Commission practice vary. See eg Case T-44/90 *La Cinq v Commission* [1992] ECR II-1, paras 32, 59, 62, and 66 ('probable existence of an infringement'); Case T-23/90 *Peugeot v Commission* [1991] ECR II-653, paras 21 and 63 (finding that certain conduct 'at first sight' exceeds the limits of the EU competition rules, 'thus giving rise to serious doubts as to its compatibility with those provisions'); Order of the President of 26 October 2001 in Case T-184/01 R *IMS Health v Commission* [2001] ECR II-3139, para 68 (suggesting that the Commission 'is not obliged to establish, as a matter of probability, the existence of a prima facie violation of the Community competition rules before adopting a decision imposing interim measures'). In *Ford Werke AG—Interim Measure* [1982] OJ L256/20, para 25, the Commission referred to the 'distinct likelihood of infringement' as the applicable standard, although in para 49 it also considered that it had to show that the infringement is 'highly probable'.

[30] See Case T-184/01 R *IMS Health Inc v Commission* [2001] ECR II-3193, para 68, according to which the Commission's decision 'is inherently not based on a full and final appreciation of the facts and law in question'. This corresponds to the earlier finding in Case T-23/90 *Peugeot v Commission* [1991] ECR II-653, para 61 that, 'in proceedings relating to the legality of a Commission decision imposing provisional measures, the requirement of a finding of a prima facie infringement cannot be placed on the same footing as the requirement of certainty that a final decision must satisfy'. In its practice, the Commission has considered it sufficient to provide legal and factual elements showing a reasonably strong *prima facie* case. See *BBI/Boosey and Hawkes—Interim Measures* [1987] OJ L286/36, para 15; *NDC Health/IMS Health—Interim Measures* [2001] OJ L59/18, para 43.

[31] Case 792/79 R *Camera Care v Commission* [1980] ECR 119, para 19. See also Case T-44/90 *La Cinq v Commission* [1992] ECR II-1, para 28; Case T-184/01 R *IMS Health Inc v Commission* [2001] ECR II-3193, para 53. In *Camera Care*, the concept of public interest related to the preservation of EU competition policy objectives, as well as the interest of Member States and their citizens.

[32] In the past, this has sometimes been interpreted as the 'likelihood' of serious and irreparable damage. See eg *ECS/AKZO—Interim Measures* [1983] OJ L252/13; *BBI/Boosey and Hawkes—Interim Measures* [1987] OJ L286/36, para 23; *NDC Health/IMS Health—Interim Measures* [2002] OJ L59/18, paras 40 and 41. In *La Cinq*, the Court equated cases of proven urgency with a 'situation likely to cause serious and irreparable damage'; see Case T-44/90 *La Cinq v Commission* [1992] ECR II-1, paras 28 and 32.

[33] European Commission Antitrust Manual of Procedures, Internal DG Competition working documents on procedures for the application of Articles 101 and 102 TFEU, March 2012, Module 17 'Interim Measures', para 9. See eg *BBI/Boosey and Hawkes—Interim Measures* [1987] OJ L286/36, para 22: 'An eventual finding in the main decision that B&H had abused its dominant position under Art [102 TFEU] would be illusory if meanwhile BBI and the other undertakings had been put out of business. If the applicants go into liquidation, B&H will be confirmed as effectively the only producer of instruments suitable for brass bands in the Community.' In *IMS Health*, the Commission considered that without interim measures it would not be possible to compete on the market and that IMS Health would 'revert to being the sole provider of regional sales data in Germany.' This would be likely to lead to a 'complete foreclosure of the relevant

given its discretion in deciding whether it is necessary to take interim measures,[34] it seems unlikely that the Commission would intervene where an identifiable victim could seek relief before national courts or NCAs.

14.08 So far there is little guidance as to when the Commission might assume a 'risk of serious and irreparable damage to competition'. This will always require a case-by-case analysis,[35] taking into account the 'inherently exceptional nature of the power to adopt interim measures'[36] based on a *prima facie* finding of an infringement. The notion of 'serious' damage implies a certain degree of magnitude (quantitative criterion) and/or severity (qualitative criterion) that justifies the taking of such exceptional measures.[37] While in the past the Commission has sometimes used its powers to issue interim measures in cases involving a suspected infringement in only one Member State,[38] the principles of case allocation amongst the members of the European Competition Network ('ECN') and the emphasis on the particular competence of national courts in resolving bilateral disputes suggest that it will be rather reluctant to do so in the future.[39]

14.09 The ECJ has stated that damage is deemed to be 'irreparable' if it can no longer be remedied by a subsequent decision during the *Commission's* administrative procedure.[40] Therefore, 'irreparable' damage may even be assumed in a scenario where it could potentially be repaired by *court judgment*, be it on a national or the EU level.[41] Interim measures must be indispensable in order to avoid the exercise of the powers pursuant to Article 7 of Regulation 1/2003 from becoming ineffectual or even illusory because of the (continuing) actions of the undertaking concerned.[42] This requirement concerns both the urgent need for (any) action and the extent of such measures, as they must be 'restricted to what is necessary to uphold the effective exercise of the Commission's right of decision'.[43] It also means that interim measures must be of a temporary and conservatory nature.[44]

14.10 Damage is likely to be regarded as 'irreparable' if it leads to market developments that will be very difficult to reverse.[45] Conversely, financial loss is not regarded as irreparable unless

---

market.' *NDC Health/IMS Health—Interim Measures* [2002] OJ L59/18, paras 190, 195, and 196. At the same time, the ECJ has emphasized that the interests of competing undertakings 'cannot be separated from the maintenance of an effective competition structure'. See Case C-481/01 P(R) *NDC Health v Commission and IMS Health* [2002] ECR I-3401, para 84.

[34] Case T-184/01 R *IMS Health Inc v Commission* [2001] ECR II-3193, para 120. See also Case T-44/90 *La Cinq v Commission* [1992] ECR II-1, para 27.

[35] See European Commission Antitrust Manual of Procedures, Internal DG Competition working documents on procedures for the application of Articles 101 and 102 TFEU, March 2012, Module 17 'Interim Measures', para 16.

[36] Case T-184/01 R *IMS Health Inc v Commission* [2001] ECR II-3193, para 144.

[37] Kerse & Khan, *EC Antitrust Procedure* (6th edn, Sweet & Maxwell 2012) para 6-068. See eg *Ford Werke AG—Interim Measures* [1982] OJ L256/20, paras 42 and 43, where the Court referred to the 'interests of countless individual consumers and of numerous dealers' and a distribution system which 'puts the whole system of competition in the Community into jeopardy in an unacceptable fashion and cannot be counterbalanced'.

[38] See eg *NDC Health/IMS Health—Interim Measures* [2002] OJ L59/18 (Germany).

[39] Kerse & Khan, *EC Antitrust Procedure* (6th edn, Sweet & Maxwell 2012) para 6-067.

[40] Case 792/79 R *Camera Care v Commission* [1980] ECR 119, para 14.

[41] Case T-44/90 *La Cinq v Commission* [1992] ECR II-1, para 80.

[42] Case 792/79 R *Camera Care v Commission* [1980] ECR 119, para 18. For examples see European Commission Antitrust Manual of Procedures, Internal DG Competition working documents on procedures for the application of Articles 101 and 102 TFEU, March 2012, Module 17 'Interim Measures', paras 18 and 19.

[43] Case T-23/96 *Peugeot v Commission* [1990] ECR II-195, para 22.

[44] Case 792/79 R *Camera Care v Commission* [1980] ECR 119, para 19; *Ford Werke AG—Interim Measures* [1982] OJ L256/20, para 47.

[45] Case T-184/01 R *IMS Health Inc v Commission* [2001] ECR II-3193, paras 121, 128, and 129. See European Commission Antitrust Manual of Procedures, Internal DG Competition working documents on

the survival of the undertaking concerned is threatened and this could seriously damage competition.

C. Procedure for Rejection or Adoption

As indicated, the main difference between the former practice under Regulation 17 and Article **14.11** 8 of Regulation 1/2003 is that the Commission may order interim measures 'acting on its own initiative'. Under the previous regime, it was accepted that complainants could request the Commission to issue interim measures based on its powers under Article 3 of Regulation 17. The wording of Article 8 of Regulation 1/2003 (also when compared to Article 7[46]) and the Explanatory Memorandum accompanying the legislative proposal[47] reflect the determination to remove the complainant's right to apply for interim relief.[48] Consequently, inaction on the side of the Commission to adopt interim measures should fall outside the scope of Article 265 of the Treaty on the Functioning of the European Union ('TFEU'), and any letter[49] informing a complainant that the Commission will not adopt interim measures should no longer be considered a challengeable act (unlike the rejection of a complaint pursuant to Article 7(2) of Regulation 773/2004).[50] While this may somewhat contradict the ruling in *Camera Care*, where the Court considered that the power to adopt interim measures was inherent to the responsibilities of a public enforcer entrusted with the task of receiving complaints and protecting third parties against damage to their interests,[51] it is plain that Regulation 1/2003 foresees a more limited mandate. In fact, the power to adopt interim measures no longer emanates from the Commission's powers contained in Article 7 of Regulation 1/2003 (formerly, Article 3 of Regulation 17), but by now has its own (expressly confined) basis in Article 8 of Regulation 1/2003. There may be some doubts as to whether this shift will ultimately survive the test of the EU Courts in view of the earlier case law,[52] but for the time being the adoption of interim measures constitutes

---

procedures for the application of Articles 101 and 102 TFEU, March 2012, Module 17 'Interim Measures', para 17.

[46] Article 7 of Reg 1/2003 specifically foresees that the Commission may act upon the complaint of a third party, which, however, must show a legitimate interest in the matter. Conversely, according to Art 8 of Reg 1/2003, the Commission explicitly acts only on its own initiative. See Commission Notice on the handling of complaints by the Commission under Articles 81 and 82 of the EC Treaty [2004] OJ C101/65, para 80.

[47] Draft Reg implementing Arts 81 and 82 of the Treaty COM (2000) 582 final—CNS 2000/243 Explanatory Memorandum, Art 8.

[48] This is also the view expressed in European Commission Antitrust Manual of Procedures, Internal DG Competition working documents on procedures for the application of Articles 101 and 102 TFEU, March 2012, Module 17 'Interim Measures', para 6, according to which the Commission acts *ex officio* and 'complainants do not have a right to ask for interim measures'.

[49] See European Commission Antitrust Manual of Procedures, Internal DG Competition working documents on procedures for the application of Articles 101 and 102 TFEU, March 2012, Module 17 'Interim Measures', para 6: 'the Commission is therefore no longer obliged to decide on any (informal) request for interim measures and, if necessary, to reject it by decision'.

[50] Cf Case C-141/02 P *Commission v T-Mobile Austria (max-mobil)* [2005] ECR I-1283, paras 69 and 70, for the Commission's powers pursuant to Art 106(3) TFEU. See also the Order in Case T-18/97 *Atlantic Container Line and Others v Commission* [1998] ECR II-589, para 15, on the withdrawal of immunity from fines pursuant to Art 15(6) of Reg 17/62, where the GC drew a distinction between measures (directly) protecting the interests of third parties (which could be challenged) and those which are taken on the basis of considerations of expediency and the general interest (which could not be challenged).

[51] Case 792/79 R *Camera Care v Commission* [1980] ECR 119, paras 14, 15, and 20.

[52] For instance, Kerse & Khan, *EC Antitrust Procedure* (6th edn, Sweet & Maxwell 2012) para 6-062, have submitted that although Art 8 of Reg 1/2003 seems to preclude the review of a refusal to adopt interim measures by providing that these are taken by the Commission acting on its own initiative, this may not prevent judicial review of inaction on the part of the Commission in the face of requests from complainants. However, a case for failure to act could at most be successful if the Commission did not react *at all* to the request (not even by a letter rejecting the request). Even then, it cannot be overlooked that the current legal

the culmination of a special procedure, which is distinct from the one foreseen in Article 7 of Regulation 1/2003 in which third party complainants retain their full rights.[53] Complainants may nevertheless suggest the adoption of interim measures, and the Commission may come to the conclusion that the information provided warrants doing so.[54] Indeed, the official form provided for complaints (Form C) allows third parties to indicate which measures or action they want the Commission to take and that may include interim measures.[55]

14.12 Where the Commission proceeds to issue interim measures, it is required to observe the basic procedural safeguards provided for by Regulation 1/2003 (in particular Article 27(1)) and Regulation 773/2004.[56] This also includes a duty to examine carefully and impartially all the relevant aspects of the individual case.[57] As a necessary step in the preliminary investigation, the Commission must formally open proceedings[58] indicating a potential conflict of the undertaking's conduct with the competition rules. The interim measures procedure will typically be commenced together with the main (ordinary) procedure. Before the Commission can adopt interim measures, it has to inform the undertaking of its *prima facie* objections and the factors demonstrating urgency, in order to allow the addressee to exercise its rights of defence by submitting observations.[59] The statement of objections will also indicate the measures the Commission intends to adopt in case the undertaking does not cease its conduct. Access to the file is granted by including the documents which may be disclosed to the undertaking as an annex to the statement of objections, in electronic format or otherwise. If appropriate, it may be accompanied by a copy of the complaint and the request for interim measures, from which confidential information has been duly deleted.

14.13 According to Article 17(2) of Regulation 773/2004, the period for responding to the statement of objections is at least four weeks. However, Article 17(2) also provides that the time limit for proceedings initiated with a view to adopting interim measures pursuant to Article 8 of Regulation 1/2003 may be shortened to one week. The date of the administrative hearing may in principle be fixed shortly after the end of the period for submitting observations, if the undertaking requests a hearing in its written submission, but the timing is determined

---

framework (Arts 7 and 8 of Reg 1/2003; Arts 5 and 7 of Reg 773/2004) draws a clear distinction between the main case (finding of an infringement) and an interim measures case (provisional measures in case of a *prima facie* infringement). Not only does the Commission act 'on its own initiative' when considering interim measures, it also protects solely the public interest. In the absence of any statutory endorsement of a right to protection by interim measures, or even to have the Commission decide on such a request, the Commission could only be obliged to act (in a particular way) if such a duty would follow from fundamental rights of the complainant. However, given the case law on the rejection of complainants for 'lack of Community interest', it seems rather doubtful whether the EU Courts would endorse a fundamental right to protection against anticompetitive behaviour in the market.

[53] This is the description used by the GC for Art 15(6) decisions under Reg 17 in Case T-18/97 *Atlantic Container Line and Others v Commission* [1998] ECR II-589, para 16.

[54] See European Commission Antitrust Manual of Procedures, Internal DG Competition working documents on procedures for the application of Articles 101 and 102 TFEU, March 2012, Module 17 'Interim Measures', para 6. See also A Klees, *Europäisches Kartellverfahrensrecht* (Carl Heymanns Verlag 2005) § 6, para 99.

[55] See Section III 6 of Form C, Annex to the Commission Notice on the handling of complaints by the Commission under Articles 81 and 82 of the EC Treaty [2004] OJ C101/65.

[56] See Case 792/79 R *Camera Care v Commission* [1980] ECR 119, para 19. The Commission notice on best practices for the conduct of proceedings concerning Articles 101 and 102 TFEU ([2011] OJ C308/6) does not cover interim measures, see para 1 n 5.

[57] Case T-44/90 *La Cinq v Commission* [1992] ECR II-1, para 86.

[58] Article 2(1) of Reg 773/2004. See European Commission Antitrust Manual of Procedures, Internal DG Competition working documents on procedures for the application of Articles 101 and 102 TFEU, March 2012, Module 17 'Interim Measures', para 22.

[59] Article 27(1) of Reg 1/2003; Art 10 of Reg 773/2004.

by the Hearing Officer.[60] As in ordinary procedures, third parties who show a sufficient interest and ask to be heard may comment in writing and/or be admitted to take part in the hearing.[61] After this phase, the Commission draws up a draft decision and consults the Advisory Committee.[62] Given the urgency, Article 14(3) and (4) of Regulation 1/2003 allows the Commission to set shorter deadlines for this consultation.[63] The decision on interim measures is then adopted by the full Commission (no empowerment).[64] Pursuant to Article 30 of Regulation 1/2003 it is among those for which a summary publication is required. It can be expected that the Commission will publish a full version on the webpage of the Directorate-General for Competition ('DG COMP') if only a summary is published in the Official Journal ('OJ'). The heavy procedure, which makes a swift response to an urgent problem rather difficult, probably explains why the Commission has not yet made use of its powers under Article 8 of Regulation 1/2003.

D. Content of the Decision

1. General features

Interim measures have to be adopted in such a way that the affected undertaking (addressee) **14.14** may challenge them before the GC.[65] The acts foreseen in Article 8 of Regulation 1/2003 constitute decisions within the meaning of Article 288 TFEU and, as regards their general layout, do not differ from decisions in the main proceedings (but might be more concise). Pursuant to Article 296 TFEU, the decision must be duly motivated, failing which it will be void, and takes effect as from notification (Article 297 TFEU). By contrast to Article 7 decisions, which the Commission adopts after a full investigation, interim measures do not aim to definitively establish an infringement but limit themselves to demonstrating the existence of a *prima facie* infringement and urgency. Given the need to achieve quick results, it will often make sense to simultaneously impose periodic penalty payments in case the addressee fails to comply with the interim order, pursuant to Article 24(1)(b) of Regulation 1/2003.

2. Limitations

The operative part of the decision will contain the specific measures adopted by the **14.15** Commission. Where necessary, it may include a provision that no conduct to the same effect as the one against which the decision is directed must be adopted, in order to prevent any

---

[60] See Art 12 of Reg 773/2004 and Art 12(1) of the Decision of the President of the European Commission of 13 October 2011 on the function and terms of reference of the hearing officer in certain competition proceedings [2011] OJ L275/29.

[61] Article 13 of Reg 773/2004.

[62] Article 14(1) of Reg 1/2003. With respect to the situation under Reg 17, see Case T-19/91 *Vichy v Commission* [1992] ECR II 415, para 37.

[63] See also Commission Notice on cooperation within the Network of Competition Authorities [2004] C101/43, para 60, according to which the Advisory Committee is consulted following a swifter and lighter procedure, on the basis of a short explanatory note and the operative part of the decision.

[64] See European Commission Antitrust Manual of Procedures, Internal DG Competition working documents on procedures for the application of Articles 101 and 102 TFEU, March 2012, Module 1 'Decision-making procedures', para 17.

[65] See Case 792/79 R *Camera Care v Commission* [1980] ECR 119, para 19. Given that Art 8(1) of Reg 1/2003 explicitly refers to action by the Commission 'on its own initiative' (unlike for Art 7(1) of Reg 1/2003 which in addition foresees action 'on a complaint'), an application for failure to act pursuant to Art 265 TFEU would be likely to be inadmissible because such failure does not constitute an infringement of the applicable rules. See para 14.11.

circumvention.[66] Moreover, in order to monitor observance of the interim measures, reporting obligations can be imposed.[67]

14.16 As regards their nature, it can be stated in general that, first, the measures must be limited in time and scope and, secondly, that they must fall within the scope of the subject matter of the main procedure. Concerning the limitations in time, Article 8(2) of Regulation 1/2003 states that '[a] decision under paragraph 1 shall apply for a specified period of time and may be renewed in so far this is necessary and appropriate'.[68] The measures must be interim, ie temporary, and will only be valid until a decision in the main proceedings is adopted or they are annulled by the GC, whichever occurs earlier.[69] Furthermore, they must stay within the limits of what is indispensable (ie strictly necessary) to remedy a particular competition problem, which means that they will be purely protective and conservatory.[70] Nevertheless, the Commission is not confined to only imposing negative measures to desist from certain action, but may also include a positive order to perform some act.[71] As already indicated, under Regulation 1/2003 the measures imposed must safeguard the public interest in open competition (and not individual interests) by restoring the *status quo ante*,[72] but possibly also by forcing a change in the market.[73] Finally, the Commission must have regard to the legitimate interests of the undertaking to which the interim measures are addressed[74] and balance them against the likely harm to competition.[75] This also implies that, from the range of measures available to remedy a given situation, it must choose those which are the least burdensome, thereby ensuring proportionality.[76] In making this choice, however, it enjoys a margin of assessment (discretion).

---

[66] See eg *Ford Werke AG—Interim Measures* [1982] OJ L256/20, para 48 and Art 1.

[67] See eg *BBI/Boosey and Hawkes—Interim Measures* [1987] OJ L286/36, para 25 and Arts 2(2), 3.

[68] This deviates from the original Commission proposal, which had foreseen that decisions on interim measures 'shall apply for a maximum of one year but shall be renewable'. See Proposal for a Council Regulation on the implementation of the rules on competition laid down in Articles 81 and 82 of the Treaty and amending Regulations (EEC) 1017/68, (EEC) 2988/74, (EEC) 4056/86 and (EEC) 3975/87, COM(2000) 582 final.

[69] Cf *ECS/AKZO—Interim Measures* [1983] OJ L252/13, para 37, where the Commission, however, announced its intention to alter the decision in the meantime if circumstances so required. In *Ford*, the decision on the merits (*Ford Werke AG* [1983] OJ L327/31) explicitly revoked the interim measures decision (*Ford Werke AG—Interim Measures* [1982] OJ L256/20), despite the fact that the latter already stipulated that it would only apply 'until adoption of the Decision concluding the proceeding'.

[70] Case 792/79 R *Camera Care v Commission* [1980] ECR 119, paras 18 and 19. Regarding the principle of proportionality, see Case T-76/89 *ITP v Commission* [1991] ECR II-575, para 80, citing Case 181/84 *The Queen, ex parte E.D. & F. Man (Sugar) Ltd v Intervention Board for Agricultural Produce (IBAP)* [1985] ECR 2889, para 20.

[71] See para 14.01.

[72] *Ford Werke AG—Interim Measures* [1982] OJ L256/20, paras 44 and 45; *ECS/AKZO—Interim Measures* [1983] OJ L252/13, para 36; *BBI/Boosey and Hawkes—Interim Measures* [1987] OJ L286/36, para 24. See also Case T-184/01 R *IMS Health v Commission* [2001] ECR II-2349, para 25.

[73] See eg *Sea Containers v Stena Sealink—Interim Measures* [1994] OJ L15/8, paras 57, 67, and 79 (measures to enable a new competitor to enter a market in the face of a refusal to supply). In *NDC Health/IMS Health—Interim Measures* [2002] OJ L59/18, the Commission sought to impose an obligation to provide a licence to IMS's brick structure. This was, however, viewed critically by the President of the GC in its Order in Case T-184/01 R, *IMS Health v Commission* [2001] ECR II-2349, para 25, where it noted that the interim measures decision did not just preserve the *status quo ante*, but rather appeared to legitimize conduct (through a forced licence) that was previously illegal. In the President's view, the applicant 'ha[d] made out a not unconvincing case that the interim measures adopted by the Commission in the contested decision exceed the scope of the Commission's powers to adopt interim measures on the basis of the *Camera Care* case-law.'

[74] Case 792/79 R *Camera Care v Commission* [1980] ECR 119, para 19; *NDC Health/IMS Health—Interim Measures* [2002] OJ L59/18, para 42.

[75] *ECS/AKZO—Interim Measures* [1983] OJ L252/13, para 24; *NDC Health/IMS Health—Interim Measures* [2002] OJ L59/18, paras 199, 217 and Art 1.

[76] Cf Commission Press Release IP/92/478 'Commission orders interim measures against Sealink' of 11 June 1992, where the Commission emphasized that its interim measures would be 'limited to the minimum

In *Ford*, the Commission's interim measures were annulled because, since the main proceed- **14.17**
ings were concerned with the dealer agreement between Ford and its concessionaires, the measures ordered by the Commission—which related to a refusal to supply—did not fall within the
framework of a possible decision on the merits.[77] By contrast with the position in *Ford*, in *Peugeot*
(which was concerned with a Commission decision on a circular sent by Peugeot to its concessionaires to the effect that they should not supply new vehicles to the company Ecosystem), the
GC held that both the interim measures procedure and the main procedure were concerned
with the same issues (namely, the legality of the circular under Article 81(1) EC) and that there
was no reason for the decision to be annulled on that ground.[78] From both judgments it may
be concluded that the interim measures will (only then) not be acceptable where they concern a
different subject matter and (thus) exceed the scope of the main procedure.[79]

While the interim measures must be indispensable to avoid the exercise of the Commission's **14.18**
power to adopt prohibition decisions pursuant to Article 7 of Regulation 1/2003 from becoming ineffectual or even illusory because of the action of certain undertakings, the Commission
must also avoid imposing measures on the basis of a *prima facie* finding of an infringement
which definitively determine the conduct of these undertakings. In other words, these measures
must not prejudice the merits of the case, which should only be dealt with in the final decision.
Therefore, they must be not only temporary but also provisional.[80]

E. Imposition of Financial Penalties

The Commission may impose pecuniary penalties in order to compel undertakings to com- **14.19**
ply with the measures adopted. Article 23(2)(b) of Regulation 1/2003 expressly empowers the
Commission to impose fines on undertakings where they contravene a decision ordering interim
measures under Article 8.[81] Perhaps more importantly, the Commission may supplement the

---

necessary to achieve' their objective. This may also require that any measure imposed is limited in time to
what is strictly necessary. Cf *BBI/Boosey and Hawkes—Interim Measures* [1987] OJ L286/36, para 24. In its
interim order in *Ford*, the President of the Court considered that the detrimental effects of the Commission
decision ordering interim measures 'exceed those of a conservatory measure and in the meantime cause damage considerably in excess of the inevitable but short-lived disadvantages arising from such a measure'. See
Joined Cases 228 and 229/82 R *Ford v Commission* [1982] ECR I-3091, para 14.

[77] Joined Cases 228 and 229/82 R *Ford v Commission* [1982] ECR I-3091, paras 19–22.
[78] See Case T-23/90 *Peugeot v Commission* [1991] ECR II-653, paras 54–7.
[79] See Case T-23/90 *Peugeot v Commission* [1991] ECR II-653, para 57.
[80] Case T-23/90 *Peugeot v Commission* [1991] ECR II-653, paras 19–20 and 22. See also Joined Cases
T-24/92 R and T-28/92 R *Langnese-Iglo and Schöller v Commission* [1992] ECR II-1839, para 29, where the
President of the GC noted that '[i]mmediate implementation of the contested decision is liable seriously to
undermine the distribution systems set up by the applicants, thereby creating a development in the relevant
market which there are serious reasons for believing would be very difficult, if not impossible, to reverse at
a later stage'. In balancing the interests of the parties the President therefore imposed a temporary solution
(limited, as it had to be in an interim judicial procedure, until the time the GC would definitively decide in
the main case on the Commission's interim measures decision).
[81] Given that interim measures presuppose at least a *prima facie* finding of an infringement of Art 101
and/or Art 102 TFEU, the question arises—similar to the discussion relating to the imposition of fines for
a breach of a commitment decision under Art 9—whether the 10 per cent cap for the fine foreseen in Art
23(2) of Reg 1/2003 would apply only once for any infringement of the interim measures decision *and*
any subsequent decision establishing an infringement of Arts 101, 102 TFEU, or whether each fine would
have its own, separate cap. While both constitute separate infringements—one against the decision ordering
certain (interim) measures, the other against the EU competition rules—it would still seem appropriate that
the Commission takes into account a previous fine for the infringement of an interim measures decision
when deciding on the fine in the main case. This would also avoid exceeding the 10 per cent cap through the
accumulation of two fines. See also A Klees, *Europäisches Kartellverfahrensrecht* (Carl Heymanns Verlag 2005)
§ 10, paras 35–8, who suggests that the Commission will refrain from imposing a fine under Art 23(2)(b)

interim measures decision with the imposition of periodic penalty payments (or impose them later by separate act) in order to ensure compliance with the measures ordered (Article 24(1) (b) of Regulation 1/2003).[82] In setting the level of such periodic penalty payments within the statutory limits of 5 per cent of the average daily turnover in the preceding business year per day of non-compliance, the Commission may take into account the 'risk of serious and irreparable damage to competition' which justifies the adoption of interim measures in the first place.

F. Judicial Review

14.20 Early on the ECJ stressed the need for an appropriate judicial recourse[83] for the addressee of an interim measures decision, including interim relief.[84] Special issues arise in the latter type of proceedings (which always presuppose an application for annulment against the interim measures decision, ie a main case). In accordance with Article 104(2) of the Rules of Procedure of the GC, the President of the Court must ascertain whether the undertaking can demonstrate a *prima facie* illegality of the Commission's interim measures decision and an urgent need for relief to avoid serious and irreparable damage. Even where those conditions are fulfilled, it will in addition be necessary to balance the interests at stake, bearing in mind that the Commission's decision is itself an interim and provisional measure adopted in the course of a preliminary investigation.[85] In cases of particular urgency for the applicant, the President may also suspend the operation of the interim measures decision by an *ex-parte* order based on Article 105(2) of the Rules of Procedure until the order terminating the proceedings for interim relief is rendered.[86]

14.21 The Court has clarified that, even where an application for interim relief is directed against an (urgent) interim measures decision, the applicant is not required to demonstrate a particularly strong or serious *prima facie* case of illegality, or that the Commission's appraisal as to urgency is manifestly flawed.[87] Rather, both elements, as well as the Commission's assessment of the balance of interests in the interim measures decision, form part of the President's standard judicial control of the decision's *prima facie* legality. What the applicant needs to

---

in the first place when it subsequently considers imposing a fine for the substantial infringement. In setting the fine, the Commission might then take into account the breach of the interim measures decision as an aggravating factor under the Guidelines on the method of setting fines ([2006] OJ C210/2).

[82] Not surprisingly for decisions based on urgency, the Commission has often imposed periodic penalty payments. See, eg, *Ford Werke—Interim Measures* [1982] OJ L256/20, para 49 and Art 2; *ECS/AKZO—Interim Measures* [1983] OJ L252/13, para 38 and Art 6; *NDC Health/IMS Health—Interim Measures* [2002] OJ L59/18, para 220 and Art 3.

[83] For the standard of review, see Case T-44/90 *La Cinq v Commission* [1992] ECR II-1, paras 84 and 85.

[84] Case 792/79 R *Camera Care v Commission* [1980] ECR 119, para 20.

[85] Joined Cases 228 and 229/82 R *Ford v Commission* [1982] ECR I-3091, para 11; Case T-23/90 R *Peugeot v Commission* [1990] ECR II-195, para 24.

[86] For an example, see Order of the President of 10 August 2001 in Case T-184/01 R *IMS Health v Commission* [2001] ECR II-2349. In this order imposing 'provisional interim measures', the President examined whether the applicant had made out a 'provisional prima facie case' that the Commission acted in breach of the law and pointed to the potentially serious (non-) economic consequences for the applicant of the Commission's interim measures decision. This was balanced against the opposing interests by considering that the suspension would not cause irreparable harm either to the Commission's interest or that of competitors. See also Order of the President of 26 October 2001 in Case T-184/01 R *IMS Health v Commission* [2001] ECR II-3139, para 32.

[87] However, the strength or weakness of the pleas relied upon to show a *prima facie* case may be taken into consideration by the judge in his assessment of urgency and, if appropriate, of the balance of interests. See Order of the President of 11 April 2002 in Case C-481/01 P(R) *NDC Health v Commission and IMS Health* [2002] ECR I-3401, para 63.

show is the existence of a 'serious dispute' or at least 'reasonable doubts' regarding the correctness of the Commission's assessment with regard to one or more of the conditions for adopting an interim measures decision.[88] With respect to urgency, it must prove that there is a need for interim relief in order to avoid serious and irreparable damage. Particularly where this depends on a number of factors, it is sufficient for the harm to be foreseeable with a sufficient degree of probability. However, given that the Commission decision is itself an interim measure adopted in the course of a preliminary investigation, the judge will consider:

> whether or not there is a serious risk that the detrimental effects of the contested [interim measures] decision would, if it were put into operation immediately, exceed those of a conservatory measure and, in the meantime, cause damage considerably in excess of the inevitable but short-lived disadvantages arising from such an interim decision.[89]

Finally, the judge must balance the interests relied upon by the Commission to justify its interim measures decision against those invoked by the applicant in favour of the interim relief sought.[90] This analysis may also include the strength or weakness of the pleas relied upon to show a *prima facie* case.[91] Where risks of serious and irreparable damage exist on both sides, the President might seek a temporary solution balancing those interests until such time as the Court decides on the merits of the interim measures decision (in the main annulment action).[92] Generally, the judge has a wide discretion when ordering interim relief.[93]   **14.22**

II. Withdrawal of the Benefit of a Block Exemption[94]

The Commission may revoke a block exemption[95] in individual cases, without the need to modify the Regulation under which that exemption was granted. The procedure for this is laid down in Article 29(1) of Regulation 1/2003 which empowers the Commission, acting on its own initiative or on a complaint, to withdraw the benefit of an exemption Regulation   **14.23**

---

[88] Order of the President of 26 October 2001 in Case T-184/01 R *IMS Health v Commission* [2001] ECR II-3139, paras 60–73 and 93; confirmed in the Order of the President of the Court of Justice of 11 April 2002 in Case C-481/01 P(R) *NDC Health v Commission and IMS Health* [2002] ECR I-3401, para 59.

[89] Order of the President of 26 October 2001 in Case T-184/01 R *IMS Health v Commission* [2001] ECR II-3139, paras 116, 117, and 132; Order of the President of 21 May 1990 in Case T-23/90 R *Peugeot v Commission* [1990] ECR II-195, para 24. In the latter case, the President noted that the mere imposition of penalty payments could not be regarded as an argument establishing urgency as it was in the hands of the applicant to avoid such harm by complying with the interim measures decision.

[90] Order of the President of 26 October 2001 in Case T-184/01 R *IMS Health v Commission* [2001] ECR II-3139, paras 133 and 141. According to the President, the judge hearing the case will take account both of the Commission's analysis of the urgency that justified the adoption of the interim measures decision and the reasons why it balanced the interests involved in favour of adopting such measures (para 73).

[91] Order of the President of 26 October 2001 in Case T-184/01 R *IMS Health v Commission* [2001] ECR II-3139, para 144; confirmed in the Order of the President of the Court of Justice of 11 April 2002 in Case C-481/01 P(R) *NDC Health v Commission and IMS Health* [2002] ECR I-3401, para 63.

[92] See Joined Cases T-24/92 R and T-28/92 R *Langnese-Iglo and Schöller v Commission* [1992] ECR II-1839, paras 28–30.

[93] Order of the President of the Court of Justice of 11 April 2002 in Case C-481/01 P(R) *NDC Health v Commission and IMS Health* [2002] ECR I-3401, para 63.

[94] Since it has no longer any practical relevance, the revocation or amendment of an individual exemption adopted under Regulation 17 is no longer treated here (for more details, see *EC Competition Procedure* (2nd edn), paras 14.20–14.25).

[95] On the concept of Block Exemption Regulations see Guidelines on the application of Art 81(3) of the Treaty [2004] OJ C101/97, para 35. A list of such regulations can be found on DG COMP's website at: <http://ec.europa.eu/competition/antitrust/legislation/legislation.html>.

when it finds that in any particular case an agreement, decision, or concerted practice to which the exemption Regulation applies has certain effects which are incompatible with Article 101(3) TFEU.[96] Additionally, when such practices to which a Commission block exemption applies have effects which are incompatible with Article 101(3) TFEU in the territory of a given Member State, or in a part thereof, and which has all the characteristics of a distinct geographic market, the NCA of that Member State may also withdraw the benefit of the Regulation in question in respect of that territory.[97]

A. Withdrawal of a Block Exemption by the Commission

14.24 At the EU level, the procedure may be commenced on the Commission's own initiative or in response to a complaint from natural or legal persons claiming a legitimate interest. Since the withdrawal of a block exemption on an individual basis is one of its exclusive prerogatives,[98] the Commission may be obliged to adopt a formal decision withdrawing the exemption or rejecting the complaint.[99] As a result of the withdrawal, the previously exempt[100] agreement or conduct is prohibited in that specific case by virtue of Article 101(1) TFEU since it no longer enjoys the benefit of Article 101(3). The Commission may then initiate a procedure of the kind usual in cases of infringement (in particular Article 7 of Regulation 1/2003). Indeed, the withdrawal procedure will be an accessory to the infringement procedure and the final decision will combine several measures (withdrawal of the block exemption, finding of the infringement, cease-and-desist/appropriate measures order).[101] According to Article 14(1) of Regulation 1/2003 the Advisory Committee shall be consulted prior to the taking of any decision under Article 29(1).[102] The decision to withdraw eliminates any legitimate expectations which the infringing undertaking may have had as to the legality of its actions, and thus from that point on exposes it to potential fines.[103]

---

[96] Guidelines on the application of Art 81(3) of the Treaty [2004] OJ C101/97, para 36. This is a measure reserved to the College of Commissioners that cannot be delegated. See Ch 1, 'Institutional Framework', para 1.68. Antitrust Manual of Procedures Internal, DG Competition working documents on procedures for the application of Articles 101 and 102 TFEU, March 2012, Module 1 'Decision-making procedures', para 17.

[97] Given the limited scope of such a decision, the courts of other Member States are not bound by it, which may entail problems where the jurisdiction for an agreement, which was the object of the national withdrawal procedure, lies with the courts of another Member State.

[98] As regards the possibility for Member States of withdrawing the benefit of a block exemption under Art 29(2) of Reg 1/2003, see Ch 3 'The Role of NCAs', para 3.06, n 15.

[99] See Case T-24/90 *Automec v Commission II* [1992] ECR II-2223, para 75.

[100] Art 29 of Reg 1/2003 likely has to be interpreted as an exception to Art 1(1) of Reg 1/2003, according to which 'Agreements, decisions and concerted practices caught by Article 81(1) of the Treaty which do not satisfy the conditions of Article 81(3) of the Treaty shall be prohibited, no prior decision to that effect being required'. See also paras 2 and 37 of Guidelines on the application of Art 81(3) of the Treaty [2004] OJ C101/97.

[101] See eg *Langnese-Iglo* [1993] OJ L183/19 (partially annulled in Case T-7/93 *Langnese-Iglo v Commission* [1995] ECR II-1533, as confirmed in Case C-279/95 P *Langnese-Iglo v Commission* [1998] ECR I-5609). Given the (overall) negative effect of such a decision on the position of the undertaking concerned, it will have to be heard beforehand, including on the withdrawal of the Block Exemption Regulation. Cf. Art 27(1) of Reg 1/2003 and Case C-32/95 P *Commission v Lisrestal and Others* [1996] ECR I-5373, para 21. See also Kerse & Khan, *EC Antitrust Procedure* (6th edn, Sweet & Maxwell 2012) para 6-081.

[102] For more details, see Antitrust, Manual of Procedures, Internal DG Competition working documents on procedures for the application of Articles 101 and 102 TFEU, March 2012, Module 14, 'Advisory Committee on Restrictive Practices and Dominant Positions', para 1.

[103] Since any challenge against such a withdrawal decision has no suspensory effect (Art 278 TFEU), there is no reason to consider that the withdrawn Block Exemption Regulation could continue to shield the undertaking until the decision has become definitive.

There have been only a couple of cases so far: In *Langnese-Iglo*, the Commission withdrew a **14.25** block exemption on an individual basis in respect of certain exclusive dealing agreements covered by Regulation 1984/93, without at the same time granting an individual exemption.[104] The Commission also threatened to withdraw a block exemption enjoyed by the Peugeot vehicle distribution network.[105]

B. Withdrawal of a Block Exemption by a NCA

Article 29(2) of Regulation 1/2003 gives the NCAs—but not national courts—the power to **14.26** withdraw the benefit of block exemptions for their own territory, provided that it constitutes a distinct relevant geographic market.[106] Before Regulation 1/2003 came into force, NCAs had such a power only in respect of vertical agreements.[107] To ensure consistency in the application of block exemption regulations, which are Union acts, Regulation 1/2003 provides for prior consultation with the Commission in respect of national decisions withdrawing the benefit of a block exemption.[108] The NCA must demonstrate that the agreement infringes Article 101(1) TFEU and that it does not satisfy the conditions laid down in Article 101(3) TFEU before it can withdraw the block exemption. In practice, NCAs are expected to use this power only rarely. They will also have to observe the standard procedural safeguards, ie they will give written notice to the parties to that agreement and give them the opportunity to make representations. As regards national courts, they have no power to withdraw the benefit of block exemption regulations. Moreover, when applying block exemption regulations, they may not modify their scope by extending their sphere of application to include agreements not covered by the block exemption regulation in question.[109]

---

[104] *Langnese-Iglo* [1993] OJ L183/19.
[105] *Ecosystem/Peugeot* [1992] OJ L66/1. The block exemption in that case was the one granted by Commission Reg (EEC) 123/85 on the distribution of motor vehicles [1985] OJ L15/16.
[106] Guidelines on the application of Art 81(3) of the Treaty [2004] OJ C101/97, para 36.
[107] See Art 1(4) of Council Reg (EC) 1215/1999 ([1999] OJ L48/1) amending Reg 19/65/EEC on the application of Art 81(3) EC to certain categories of agreements and concerted practices.
[108] Art 11(4) of Reg 1/2003.
[109] Guidelines on the application of Art 81(3) of the Treaty [2004] OJ C101/97, para 37.

15

STEPS FOLLOWING THE ADOPTION OF A FORMAL DECISION. JUDICIAL REVIEW

Luis Ortiz Blanco and Konstantin Jörgens

I. Monitoring of Formal Decisions

The Commission's activity does not cease with the adoption of formal decisions in matters referred to it for examination. In all such cases, the Commission monitors developments in order to ensure that the requirements of its decisions are complied with. In the case of infringement decisions—with the exception of purely declaratory decisions without pecuniary penalties—the Commission collects the fines and checks that its notices and orders, and the undertakings' obligations under its decision, are complied with. **15.01**

A. Infringement Decisions

1. Collection of fines and periodic penalty payments

The General Court ('GC') has made it clear that the Commission has: **15.02**

> the power to determine the date on which the fine is payable and that on which default interest begins to accrue, the power to set the rate of such interest and to determine the detailed

arrangements for implementing its decision by requiring, where appropriate, the provision of a bank guarantee covering the principal amount of the fine imposed plus interest.[1]

The GC considers that if the Commission had no such power, the advantage which undertakings might be able to derive from late payment of fines would weaken the effect of penalties imposed by the Commission. In the Court's view, the charging of default interest on fines is not only justified by the need to ensure that the enforcement of EU competition rules is not rendered ineffective by practices applied unilaterally by undertakings which delay paying fines imposed on them, but also to ensure that such undertakings do not enjoy an advantage over those which pay their fines within the stipulated period.[2]

15.03 An undertaking that challenges a Commission decision imposing a fine can choose between different options: (i) pay the fine together with any default interest, if applicable, (ii) apply for payment facilities, and (iii) invoke the inability to pay the fine or apply for a reduction. Proceedings before the EU Courts do not have suspensive effect.[3] In order to avoid enforcement proceedings to obtain payment of the fine, undertakings can make provisional payment[4] or provide a bank guarantee as security for payment (iv).[5] The payment of the fine (and default interest, as applicable)[6] will then be deferred until judgment.[7] The addressee of a decision can also (v) apply for suspension of the fining decision or interim measures pursuant to Articles 278 and 279 of the Treaty on the Functioning of the European Union ('TFEU') and Articles 104 et seq of the Rules of Procedure of the GC without providing a bank guarantee.[8] Such a request, however, will only be granted by the courts if it is established that their adoption is *prima facie* justified in fact and in law that their adoption is necessary to avoid serious and irreparable damage and that the balance of interests

---

[1] Case T-257/94 *Groupement des Cartes Bancaires 'CB' v Commission* [1995] ECR II-2169, para 47; Joined Cases T-236/01, T-239/01, T-244/01 to T-246/01, T-251/01, and T-252/01 *Tokai Carbon and others v Commission ('Graphite Electrodes')* [2004] ECR II-1181, para 475.

[2] Joined Cases T-236/01, T-239/01, T-244/01 to T-246/01, T-251/01, and T-252/01 *Tokai Carbon and others v Commission* [2004] ECR II-1181, para 475; see also Case T-52/03 *Knauf Gips KG v Commission* [2008] ECR II-115, para 495: 'In the absence of such a power [requiring, where appropriate, a bank guarantee covering the principal amount and interest on the fines imposed], the fact that undertakings would be likely to make late payment would weaken the sanctions imposed by the Commission as part of its task of ensuring the implementation of competition rules. Thus, the application of default interest to fines is justified to prevent the *effet utile* of the Treaty from being undermined by companies delaying the payment of their fines and to exclude that certain undertakings may be advantaged over those who paid their fines when they were due', indicating that the Commission is authorized to take as a point of reference, a higher level than the rate proposed to an average borrower, applicable in the market, to the extent necessary to discourage delaying behaviour.

[3] Pursuant to Art 297, second paragraph TFEU decisions finding an infringement and imposing fines take effect upon notification and shall be enforceable (Art 299(1) TFEU). Actions brought before the EU Courts do not have suspensive effect (Art 278 TFEU).

[4] See Kerse & Khan, *EC Antitrust Procedure* (6th edn, Sweet & Maxwell 2012) para 7-284. Provisional payment means that the funds are not released into the funds available under the budget but are deposited in a bank pending the outcome of the proceedings.

[5] Where there is an appeal against the decision imposing a fine and the applicant is ready to provide a bank guarantee, it is not necessary to apply for interim measures to suspend the obligation to pay the fine.

[6] Commission Antitrust Manual of Procedures, Internal DG Competition working documents on procedures for the application of Articles 101 and 102 TFEU, March 2012, Module 25 'Follow-up decisions', para 7, n 3, indicating that the default interest in case of a bank guarantee is lower than the default interest applicable to a company that simply does not pay (rate applied by the European Central Bank ('ECB') to its principal refinancing operations in force on the first calendar day of the month in which the decision is adopted plus 1.5 per cent in the case of a bank guarantee, instead of 3.5 per cent in other cases) (see Art 86 of the Implementing Rules).

[7] Depending on the outcome of the court case, the guarantee will be enforced or released. Commission Antitrust Manual of Procedures, Internal DG Competition working documents on procedures for the application of Articles 101 and 102 TFEU, March 2012, Module 25 'Follow-up decisions', para 7.

[8] An applicant can only ask for interim measures in parallel to its main action. For instance, with regard to the antitrust activities of the Directorate-General for Competition ('DG COMP'), an applicant can bring an action for annulment of a prohibition decision imposing a fine on it (main proceedings) and, in parallel,

favours such an order.[9] In very limited circumstances, the Commission repeals or modifies a fine which has become final.[10]

Voluntary payment

Chapter 11 explains the content and structure of infringement decisions, and fines and peri-   **15.04**
odic penalty payments imposed by the Commission, and how the Commission describes in minute detail in its decisions the way in which such pecuniary penalties are to be paid.[11] The Commission not only fixes a sum in euros,[12] but also indicates the bank account into which payment is to be made. A judgment of the EU Courts annulling a Commission decision, or resetting the fine at a lower level, has retroactive effect, and the Commission is obliged to reimburse the fine already paid with interest.[13]

---

ask the Court to suspend payment of the fine while the main proceedings are pending. Commission Antitrust Manual of Procedures, Internal DG Competition working documents on procedures for the application of Articles 101 and 102 TFEU, March 2012, Module 26 'Court Litigation', para 13.

[9] See the detailed overview given by F Castillo de la Torre, 'Interim Measures in Community Courts: Recent Trends' (2007) 44 Common Market Law Review 273; Commission Antitrust Manual of Procedures, Internal DG Competition working documents on procedures for the application of Articles 101 and 102 TFEU, March 2012, Module 25 'Follow-up decisions', para 8.

[10] The deadline for actions of annulment is fixed at two months (Art 267 TFEU). Within that period, the addresses of the measure, as well as other persons to whom it is of direct and individual concern, may apply to the GC for review. Consistently, the Court has rejected invitations by persons who would have been entitled to bring an action under Art 267 TFEU to review the legality of measure after expiry of the deadline, even if it later turns out to be illegal. F Neumayr and H Kühnert, 'The Repeal of Decisions by the European Commission Based on Considerations of Fact or Law' (2011) 3(1) Journal of European Competition Law & Practice 4, 6, point out that under general EU rules, however, EU institutions will be required to reconsider a decision, which has become definitive, if the request to do so is based on substantial new facts. In competition cases, the Court of Justice ('ECJ') has indicated in an *obiter dictum* in *Lafarge* that the Commission may impose a higher fine for recidivism even if the decision has not yet become final. Where the first decision is annulled, the Court indicated that the Commission will have to reconsider the second decision ('In such a case, the Commission is required, under Article 233 EC, to take the measures necessary to comply with the judgment of the Court, by amending, as appropriate, the later decision in so far as it includes an increase of the fine for repeated infringement'; see Case C-413/08 P *Lafarge v Commission* [2010] ECR I-5361, para 88). See also for the application of the deadline to actions by the parent company/subsidiary, judgment of the GC of 18 June 2013, Case T-404/08 *Fluorsid and Minmet v Commission*, Judgment of 18 June 2013, paras 47– 64 where the Court concluded that the parent company's Minmet appeal was out-of-time and therefore inadmissible in so far as this appeal was directed at the decision addressed to it. It would be irrelevant that the action was brought jointly by Fluorsid and Minmet, as an economic unit, against the contested decision, without any distinction between the individual decisions addressed to them respectively. This action could not have the consequence that Minmet benefits from the same time-limit for bringing proceedings as Fluorsid.

[11] See Ch 11, 'Infringement Decisions and Penalties', para 11.85. As regards the tax-deductability of fines see C-429/07 *Inspecteur van de Belastingdienst v X BV* [2009] ECR I-4833, para 39, where the ECJ stated that it might compromise the coherent application of Arts 101 and 102 TFEU. In particular, according to the Court, the effectiveness of the Commission's fining decision might be significantly reduced if the company concerned were allowed to deduct fully or in part the amount of that fine from the amount of its taxable profits, since such a possibility would have the effect of offsetting the burden of that fine with a reduction of the tax burden. See Kerse & Khan, *EC Antitrust Procedure* (6th edn, Sweet & Maxwell 2012) para 7-287.

[12] Since 1 January 1999, fines have been stated in euros. In looking at past cases and decisions, the units of account and ECUs in which the fines and penalties were expressed can be taken as the equivalent to the sum in euros. See Art 2(1) of Council Reg 1103/97 on certain provisions relating to the introduction of the euro [1997] OJ L162/1, under which every reference in a legal instrument to the ECU, as referred to in Art 118 EC and as defined in Council Reg (EC) 3320/94 of 22 December 1994 on the consolidation of the existing Community legislation on the definition of the ECU following the entry into force of the Treaty on European Union [1994] OJ L350/27, is to be replaced by a reference to the euro at a rate of one euro to one ECU.

[13] Case T-171/99 *Corus UK v Commission* [2001] ECR II-2967. See WPJ Wils, 'The Increased Level of EU Antitrust Fines, Judicial Review and the ECHR' (2010) 33(1) World Competition 5, 21, indicating that the fact that, if the company chooses to provide a bank guarantee instead of immediately paying the fine, it will

Application for payment facilities

15.05 Where undertakings apply for payment facilities, the Commission may, in exceptional cases, grant them. Such facilities basically consist of the deferred or staged payment of one or more instalments of the fine (against payment of interest) or in the scheduling of the periodic penalty payment.[14] The Antitrust Manual of Procedures ('Manproc') indicates that such facilities will only be granted if, among other things, the provision of a bank guarantee covering the outstanding debt in terms of both the principal sum and interest is provided.[15]

Inability to pay/requests for reduction

15.06 After the adoption of the fining decision,[16] companies can also invoke their inability to pay ('ITP') and request a reduction of the fine post-decision in view of their alleged critical financial situation. An ITP analysis should be carried out, similar to those performed where such a request is made before the decision is taken, in order to assess the company's financial situation.[17] The basic principles under which the Commission may take into account a company's inability to pay are those set forth in paragraph 35 of the 2006 Fining Guidelines, which are

---

not receive reimbursement of the bank guarantee charges, is not problematic, because the company always has the option of paying the fine, and thus being guaranteed interest upon reimbursement in case of annulment or reduction thereof; see Case T-28/03, *Holcim (Deutschland) v Commission* [2005] ECR II-1357, confirmed on appeal in Case C-282/05 P, *Holcim (Deutschland) v Commission* [2007] ECR I-2941. For more details, see also Ch 11 'Infringement Decisions and Penalties' para 11.85 et seq.

[14] Order of the President of the GC in Case T-393/10 *Westfälische Drahtindustrie and Others v Commission* [2011] ECR II-1697, para 69, where the obligation to provide a bank guarantee was suspended on condition that the applicant would pay the Commission a certain sum upfront, the rest being paid in monthly instalments of EUR 300,000 until further notice, but not beyond delivery of judgment in the main proceedings. Case T-11/06 R *Romana Tabacchi SpA v Commission* [2006] ECR II-2491, para 146, where a staged payment was combined with a bank guarantee covering partly the amount of the fine. Joined Cases T-213/95 and T-18/96 R *Kraanverhuurbedrijf v Commission* [1996] ECR II-407, para 31; Case T-141/94 *Thyssen Stahl AG v Commission* [1999] ECR II-347, para 683, pointing out that '[i]t must also be pointed out that the possibility offered to the undertakings concerned to pay their fines in the form of five annual instalments subject, until their due date, to the basic EMCF rate, in conjunction with the possibility of obtaining a suspension of recovery measures in the event of an action being brought, represents an advantage vis-à-vis the formula traditionally used by the Commission where an action has been brought before the Community Judicature'. E Barbier de la Serre and C Winckler, 'A Landmark Year for the Law on Fines imposed in EU Competition Proceedings' (2012) 3(4) Journal of European Competition Law & Practice 351, note that the President of the GC in Case T-393/10 *Westfälische Drahtindustrie and Others v Commission* [2011] ECR II-1697 seemed quite irritated that the Commission itself had decided to reduce the fine on another company participating in the cartel after he himself had dismissed the application for interim relief (paras 10, 52, and 66 of the judgment). See Ch 11, 'Infringement Decisions and Penalties', para 11.86, n 618.

[15] Commission Antitrust Manual of Procedures, Internal DG Competition working documents on procedures for the application of Articles 101 and 102 TFEU, March 2012, Module 25 'Follow-up decisions', para 9.

[16] As regards the possibility of invoking inability to pay before the adoption of the decision, see Ch 11, 'Infringement Decisions and Penalties', para 11.70.

[17] In June 2011, the European Commissioners J Almunia (Competition) and J Lewandowski (Budget) circulated an information note on the inability to pay under para 35 of the 2006 Fining Guidelines and payment conditions pre- and post-decision finding an infringement and imposing fines ('the Information Note'). See J Almunia and J Lewandowski, 'Information Note—Inability to pay under paragraph 35 of the 2006 Fining Guidelines and payment conditions pre- and post-decision finding an infringement and imposing fines', Document SEC(2010) 737/2 12 June 2010. Almost at the same time, DG COMP officials supplemented this communication with further observations on the handling of ITP requests. See also P Kienapfel and G Wils, 'Inability to Pay—First Cases and Practical Experiences' (2010) 3 Competition Policy Newsletter. J Imgrund, 'The "Inability to pay" Doctrine in European Competition Law' (2012) 33(12) European Competition Law Review 560.

also of relevance for ITP applications prior to the adoption of the decision.[18] The number of companies doing this has risen significantly in recent years.[19]

The applications can lead to reducing the amount of the fine to a level that the company is cur- **15.07** rently able to pay or, if necessary, to zero (no fine at all).[20] Financial relief should only be granted if the criteria for the assessment of ITP claims under paragraph 35 of the 2006 Guidelines are fulfilled, in particular when it can be demonstrated with a sufficient degree of probability that it is the Commission's fine (covered by a security) that is likely to cause the company's bankruptcy.[21] A reduction granted on the grounds that an undertaking is unable to pay would be based solely on objective evidence that the fine would irretrievably jeopardize the economic viability of the undertaking concerned and cause its assets to lose their value.[22]

The determination of the competent authority within the Commission to waive recovery of a **15.08** fine depends on the amount to be waived (this amount includes the fine and the default interest). The Directorate-General for Competition ('DG COMP') is responsible for the waiver decision since the Director-General of DG COMP is by delegation the Authorising Officer ('ordonna- teur') of the fine in the Commission's financial procedure. However, in practice waivers of the

---

[18] Paragraph 35 reads: 'In exceptional cases, the Commission may, upon request, take account of the undertaking's inability to pay in a specific social and economic context. It will not base any reduction granted for this reason in the fine on the mere finding of an adverse or loss-making financial situation. A reduction could be granted solely on the basis of objective evidence that imposition of the fine as provided for in these Guidelines would irretrievably jeopardise the economic viability of the undertaking concerned and cause its assets to lose all their value.' See eg Case COMP/39.600 *Refrigeration compressors* [2012] OJ C122/6, para 20, stating that one of the undertakings in this case 'invoked inability to pay' under para 35 of the 2006 Guidelines on the method of setting the fines. The Commission reviewed this application, carefully ana- lysed the available financial data, and granted a reduction of the fine. In *International Removal Services*, the Commission reduced the fine on Interdean by 70 per cent (Commission Press Release IP/08/415 'Antitrust: Commission fines providers of international removal services in Belgium over €32.7 million for complex cartel', 11 March 2008. The decision also states that five other undertakings raised arguments relating to their inability to pay the fines which the Commission rejected). In March 2011, the Commission reduced a fine imposed on William Prym by more than half for its involvement in a haberdashery cartel (2007), after the fas- teners maker pleaded ITP. Thus, Prym's fine was reduced by EUR 25 million to EUR 15.5 million, from the initial penalty of EUR 40.5 million levied four years previously (COMP/39.168 *William Prym*, Commission Decision of 31 March 2011). Commission Antitrust Manual of Procedures, Internal DG Competition work- ing documents on procedures for the application of Articles 101 and 102 TFEU, March 2012, Module 25 'Follow-up decisions', para 10, stating that the rejection of a post-decision plea of inability to pay is done by administrative letter signed by the Director-General of DG COMP.

[19] According to a Global Competition Review ('GCR') survey of cartel fines based on publicly avail- able documents, available at <http://www.globalcompetitionreview.com>, the Commission has accepted only thirteen poverty pleas since 2005—all of which came after 2009, most likely as a result of the global financial crisis. See also 'CRT cartelist obtains record inability-to-pay fine cut—The European Commission has granted its largest ever inability-to-pay fine reduction, cutting Technicolor's fine in the cathode ray tubes (CRT) cartel decision by €219 million, *GCR* has learned', available at <http://www.globalcompetitionre- view.com>. Commission Press Release IP/12/313 'Antitrust: Commission fines nine producers of window mountings €86 million for price fixing cartel' of 28 March 2012, where the Commission granted to one company a 45 per cent reduction of the fine. See also MLEx 'Cap on window-mounting cartel fines prompts college debate on antitrust sanctions', 25 April 2012, pointing to the minutes of the 1996th meeting of the Commission on 28 March 2012, where the Commission discussed the impact of the decision, and, more widely, the need for an internal policy debate on antitrust fines.

[20] This is to distinguish from the situation where the Commission may exceptionally amend the fine post-decision in order to correct errors in the calculation. See para 15.15.

[21] See also Commission Antitrust Manual of Procedures, Internal DG Competition working documents on procedures for the application of Articles 101 and 102 TFEU, March 2012, Module 25 'Follow-up deci- sions', paras 15–20, citing Art 73 of the Financial Regulation and Arts 87 et seq of the Implementing Rules that govern the waiver of the recovery of fines.

[22] See J Almunia and J Lewandowski, 'Information Note—Inability to pay under paragraph 35 of the 2006 Fining Guidelines and payment conditions pre- and post-decision finding an infringement and impos- ing fines', Document SEC(2010) 737/2 12 June 2010, para 4.

recovery of antitrust fines are most often granted by the College, as the waiving of recovery of an established amount receivable may not be delegated where the amount to be waived exceeds a certain threshold.[23] The Manproc provides more details of the preparation of the decision to waive the recovery of the fine.[24]

Suspension of payment obligation with and without a bank guarantee

15.09   Companies that appeal against the fine imposed on them must either pay the fine provisionally, as indicated earlier, or provide a bank guarantee covering the full amount, in accordance with Article 85a of the implementing rules for the Financial Regulation.[25] Similarly, they may request, post-decision, exemption from the obligation to provide security pending the appeal before the Court, and the full or partial release from security already provided.

15.10   Under the current rules, the Commission admits that it is not entirely clear whether companies which have sufficient liquidity to provisionally pay the fine have the right to provide a bank guarantee as security, or whether they may only provide a bank guarantee if they can demonstrate to the Accounting Officer that they have insufficient liquidity.[26] The Commission points out that bank guarantees involve a higher financial risk (depending on the standing of the issuing bank). In addition, the management of fine guarantees and their safekeeping impose an administrative burden on the Commission that does not exist in the case of provisional payments. In practice, however, the Commission considers that the undertakings concerned have the right to choose between providing valid bank guarantees or making a provisional payment until the conclusion of the appeal, because in either case the payment of the fine will be secured.[27]

15.11   Generally, the EU Courts consider the possibility of requiring the provision of a financial guarantee to be a general and reasonable way for the Commission to act,[28] and that the party seeking interim relief can be exempted only in exceptional circumstances from the obligation to provide a bank guarantee as a condition for the Commission not immediately recovering a fine imposed

---

[23] EUR 1 million or more, or EUR 100,000 or more, where this represents 25 per cent or more of the established amount receivable (Art 87(4) of the Implementing Rules). Commission Antitrust Manual of Procedures, Internal DG Competition working documents on procedures for the application of Articles 101 and 102 TFEU, March 2012, Module 25 'Follow-up decisions', paras 18–20.

[24] Commission Antitrust Manual of Procedures, Internal DG Competition working documents on procedures for the application of Articles 101 and 102 TFEU, March 2012, Module 25 'Follow-up decisions', paras 21–4.

[25] Article 85a of the implementing rules for the Financial Regulation reads as follows: 'Where an action is brought before a Community court against a Commission decision imposing a fine, periodic penalty payment or other penalty under the EC Treaty or Euratom Treaty and until such time as all legal remedies have been exhausted, the accounting officer shall provisionally collect the amounts concerned from the debtor or request him to provide a financial guarantee.' See also J Almunia and J Lewandowski, 'Information Note—Inability to pay under paragraph 35 of the 2006 Fining Guidelines and payment conditions pre- and post-decision finding an infringement and imposing fines', Document SEC(2010)737/2, 12 June 2010, para 14 et seq.

[26] J Almunia and J Lewandosky, 'Information Note—Inability to pay under paragraph 35 of the 2006 Fining Guidelines and payment conditions pre- and post-decision finding an infringement and imposing fines', Document SEC(2010) 737/2 12 June 2010, para 15.

[27] As the choice of option can have financial consequences for the companies concerned, the Commission deems it necessary to amend the implementing rules for Financial Regulation in order to clarify that, in such situations, the undertakings concerned may choose between providing valid bank guarantees (ie fulfilling the relevant criteria which will be established and, for transparency reasons, made public by the Accounting Officer) or making a provisional payment, because in either case the payment of the fine will be secured. See J Almunia and J Lewandosky, 'Information Note—Inability to pay under paragraph 35 of the 2006 Fining Guidelines and payment conditions pre- and post-decision finding an infringement and imposing fines', Document SEC(2010) 737/2 12 June 2010, para 15.

[28] Case 384/06 R *IBP v Commission* [2007] ECR II-30, para 57; Case T-79/03 R *IRO v Commission* [2003] ECR II-3027, para 25.

by it.[29] A request for dispensation from the obligation to provide a bank guarantee, where that guarantee is the condition imposed in return for staying enforcement of a Commission fine for infringement of the competition rules, cannot be granted unless the provision of a guarantee would threaten the very existence of the undertaking or where the grounds upon which the decisions in the main application imposing the fine are challenged cast serious doubt on the legality of the decision.[30] The EU Courts seem to take a rigorous approach to evidence intended to show an undertaking's poor financial situation, which requires the undertaking concerned to produce actual proof of its inability to obtain a bank guarantee, ie adducing its rejected application to the bank.[31] The mere risk that the undertaking concerned might be obliged to commence winding-up proceedings as a consequence of the obligation to provide a bank guarantee may not necessarily constitute serious and irreversible damage, which has to be assessed on a case-by-case basis.[32]

The existence of such exceptional circumstances may, in principle, be regarded as established **15.12** where the party seeking dispensation from the obligation to provide the requisite bank guarantee adduces evidence that it is objectively impossible for it to provide the guarantee in question,[33] or that doing so would imperil its existence.[34] In this connection, not only does

---

[29] Orders in Case 107/82 R *AEG-Telefunken v Commission* [1982] ECR 1549, para 6; Case C-361/00 P(R) *Cho Yang Shipping v Commission* [2000] ECR I-11657, para 88; Case C-7/01 P(R) *FEG v Commission* [2001] ECR I-2559, para 44; and in Case T-30/10 *Reagens v Commission* [2010] ECR II-83, para 42.

[30] '*Cartonboard*' cases: Case T-295/94 R *Buchmann v Commission* [1994] ECR II-1265, paras 22, 24, and 27; Case T-301/94 R *Laakmann Karton GmbH v Commission* [1994] ECR II-1279, para 22 et seq; and Case T-308/94 R *Cascades SA v Commission* [1995] ECR II-265, para 43 et seq. See also *TACA* cases: eg Case T-191/98 R II *Cho Yang Shipping v Commission* [2000] ECR II-2551, para 42 et seq, confirmed on appeal in Case C-361/00 *Cho Yang Shipping Co Ltd v Commission* [2000] ECR I-11657, paras 88–93.

[31] Joined Cases T-236/01, T-239/01, T-244/01 to T-246/01, T-251/01, and T-252/01 *Tokai Carbon and others v Commission* ('*Graphite Electrodes*') [2004] ECR II-1181, para 480. See Case T-414/10 R, *Companhia Previdente—Sociedade de Controle de Participações Financeiras SA v Commission* [2011] ECR II-173, where the applicant claimed that it was unable to provide a bank guarantee as financial institutions had drastically reduced its lines of credit and that the banks were also unwilling to provide a guarantee. However, the President of the GC also found that Companhia Previdente had failed to provide any proof that it had attempted to obtain a bank guarantee. A reduction of credit lines or the refusal of a loan did not imply that a bank would refuse to give a bank guarantee, ie Companhia Previdente's claim that its financial situation did not permit it to pay the Commission's fine did not prove that it was unable to obtain a bank guarantee. It had also not provided the required specific and precise particulars (supported by documentary evidence) that refusal of interim measures would result in its liquidation. In short, it had not established a 'true and global' picture of its financial situation such that the Court could examine whether the provision of a bank guarantee would jeopardize its existence.

[32] Order of the President of the GC in Case T-9/99 R *HFB Holding v Commission* [1999] ECR II-2429, para 28; on appeal Order of the President of the Court in Case C-335/99 P (R) *HFB Holding v Commission* [1999] ECR I-8705, para 55 et seq.

[33] Case T-79/03 R *IRO v Commission* [2003] ECR II-3027, para 26 and the case law cited therein.

[34] See eg Order of the President of the GC in Case T-352/09 R *Nováčke chemické závody, as v Commission* [2009] ECR II-208, para 52 (the appeal was rejected in the main proceedings Case T-352/09 *Nováčke chemické závody, as v Commission* [2013] OJ C32/15; Order of the President of the GC in Case T-30/10R *Reagens SpA v Commission* [2010] ECR II-83, paras 42–3. The Commission has also signalled that the possibility cannot be totally excluded in pending or forthcoming cases that a company will claim inability to pay immediately after the adoption of that decision and claim that it is unable to provide security to the Accounting Officer. In order to address this type of situation, it is proposed to amend the implementing rules of the Financial Regulation to the effect that the companies can make a well-documented request to the Accounting Officer for an exemption from the obligation to provide security in combination with a deferred payment plan (which will incur late payment interest). Financial relief can only be envisaged after an ITP analysis evidencing the distressed situation of the company, unless such an analysis has been performed recently. The request for such financial relief is examined by the Accounting Officer in collaboration with DG COMP. J Almunia and J Lewandowski, 'Information Note—Inability to pay under paragraph 35 of the 2006 Fining Guidelines and payment conditions pre- and post-decision finding an infringement and imposing fines', Document SEC(2010)737/2, 12 June 2010, para 18.

the applicant have to provide documents concerning its individual financial status, but also 'unequivocal and sufficiently complete information on the banks' letters of refusal upon which it relies in order to prove that it was objectively impossible for it to provide the requisite bank guarantee.'[35]

15.13 When assessing the ability of undertakings to give a bank guarantee, the EU Courts also look at the group of undertakings to which the applicant belongs and, in particular, the resources available to that group as a whole, on the basis that the objective interests of the undertaking concerned are not independent of those of the individuals or legal entities with a controlling interest in it. Consequently, the serious and irreparable nature of the damage alleged must be assessed at the level of the group comprising those individuals or legal entities. In particular, given that the interests at stake overlap, the undertaking's interest in its own survival cannot be viewed in isolation from the interest of those controlling it in prolonging its existence indefinitely. In this regard, a simple unilateral refusal of assistance by the principal shareholder cannot be enough to preclude the financial situation of the group as a whole from being taken into account.[36] Where the applicant is not the subsidiary of a parent company and it does not belong to a larger group or a network or have a major shareholder whose resources should be taken into account, this may lead to the conclusion that the financial situation of the company is such that it is objectively impossible for it to provide a bank guarantee.[37]

---

[35] In Case T-392/09 *1. garantovaná as v Commission* [2011] ECR II-33, para 53, the Court considered that Garantovaná had provided sufficiently specific and precise information, supported by detailed and current documents, and had provided a faithful overall picture of its financial situation. Additionally, Garantovaná provided copies of five letters from various banks refusing its application for a bank guarantee. Despite certain objections from the Commission, the GC concluded that the applications for a bank guarantee had to be regarded as serious. Therefore, the refusal of the banks to provide Garantovaná with a bank guarantee served to establish that it was objectively impossible for Garantovaná to provide such a guarantee. Ultimately, the suspension of the requirement to provide a bank guarantee was made subject to a series of conditions requiring the company to provide a EUR 2.1 million payment and to undertake not to turn the subsidiary into an 'empty shell'. The appeal in the main proceedings was ultimately rejected, Case T-392/09 *1. garantovaná as v Commission* [2013] OJ C32/16. The GC rejected an application for interim measures of two other alleged cartel members (calcium carbide and magnesium based reagents): Case T-352/09 *Novácke chemické závody (NCHZ) v Commission* [2009] ECR II-208, holding in particular that since NCHZ had already started national insolvency proceedings, the interim measures would serve no purpose, as that harm had already occurred and could not be avoided by the grant of the interim relief sought. Case T-410/09 *Almamet v Commission* [2010] ECR II-80, confirmed in Case C-373/10 P(R) *Almamet v Commission* [2010] ECR I-171.

[36] Order of the President in Case T-352/09 R *Novácke chemické závody, as v Commission* [2009] ECR II-208, para 53; Case C-364/99 P (R) *DSR-Senator Lines GmbH v Commission* [1999] ECR I-8733, paras 53–4. Accordingly, the extent of the loss cannot flow from the unilateral intent of the majority shareholder of the undertaking seeking suspension.

[37] Case T-392/09 *1. garantovaná as v Commission* [2011] ECR II-33, para 66 et seq. As regards the assessment of the financial resources, the EU Courts typically consider whether (i) the applicant is a subsidiary of a parent company (Case T-352/09 R *Novácke chemické závody v Commission* [2009] ECR II-208, paras 53–5), (ii) whether the applicant has a majority shareholder (orders in Case C-364/99 P(R) *DSR-Senator Lines v Commission* [1999] ECR I-8733, paras 10 and 49 et seq; in Case T-11/06 R *Romana Tabacchi v Commission* [2006] ECR II-2491, para 111 et seq; and in the Orders in Case T-410/09 *Almamet v Commission* [2010] ECR II-80, paras 47, 48, and 57). In Case T-352/08 R *Pannon Hőerőmű v Commission* [2009] ECR II-9, paras 47–8, where the Court stated that the interests of certain minority shareholders also might no less justify their financial resources being taken into account in the analysis of that party's situation and, most particularly, in the assessment of whether a bank guarantee may be provided. See also in relation to 'network', Case C-113/09 P(R) *Ziegler v Commission* [2010] ECR I-50, para 48. See also in this regard E Barbier de la Serre and C Winckler 'A Landmark Year for the Law on Fines imposed in EU Competition Proceedings' (2012) 3(4) Journal of European Competition Law & Practice 351, 367.

Except in cases where security or a bank guarantee are given, undertakings are required to **15.14** make payment in accordance with the instructions set out by the Commission in the operative part of the infringement decision. Even then, deferment is subject to the conditions laid down by the Commission.[38] Failure to pay voluntarily within the prescribed time limits— whether imposed in the decision itself or in connection with the payment facilities or judgments—triggers the enforcement machinery.[39]

Repeal or modification of the fining decision

In two relatively recent cases, the Commission has reconsidered fines imposed by way of **15.15** repeal. It repealed the fines imposed on Ciba/BASF and Elementis in the *Heat Stabilizer* case two years after the adoption of the original decision.[40] In the *Pre-stressing Steel* case, the Commission's decision has been subject to two modifications.[41] Commentators are of the

---

[38] The Commission has indicated that it might grant deferred payment by instalments, unsecured by a bank guarantee, for the amount that the company is currently unable to pay (this amount would then be paid in yearly instalments over a certain time period, normally not exceeding three to five years). However, only in exceptional circumstances should the possibility of granting deferred and unsecured payments by instalments, specified with corresponding deferred due dates in the fine decision, be considered as an alternative to fine reductions. J Almunia and J Lewandowski, 'Information Note—Inability to pay under paragraph 35 of the 2006 Fining Guidelines and payment conditions pre- and post-decision finding an infringement and imposing fines', Document SEC(2010) 737/2, 12 June 2010, paras 11 and 13.

[39] Order of the President of the GC of 12 March 2012 in Case T-42/11 *Universal Corp v Commission*, where Universal brought an action before the GC seeking annulment of the decision contained in the Commission's letters addressed to Universal stating that as a consequence of the withdrawal of Universal's appeal, the Italian raw tobacco cartel decision had become legally binding with regard to Universal and that it had to pay the fine. The GC concluded that the contested letters had no autonomous legal effect capable of bringing about a distinct change in Universal's legal position. The letters were merely a request for the payment of the fine, together with default interest, which was imposed in the cartel decision. The withdrawal of the appeal had rendered definitive Universal's obligation to pay the sum ordered in the decision. In so far as the letters merely required such payment, they did not produce any legal effects. They merely constituted acts preparatory to pure enforcement, which are not open to challenge.

[40] Commission Press Release IP/11/820 'Antitrust: Commission repeals Heat Stabilisers cartel decision for Ciba/BASF and Elementis after EU Court judgment', 4 July 2011, where the Commission announced that it had repealed a decision of 11 November 2009 finding a cartel in the market for heat stabilizers in so far as it concerns the companies Ciba/BASF and Elementis. The judgment in an unrelated case (Joined Cases C-201/09 and C-216/09 *ArcelorMittal Luxembourg v Commission and Commission / ArcelorMittal Luxembourg and Others* [2011] ECR I-2239) would have clarified the legal rules as to limitation periods for the imposition of fines by the Commission under Arts 101 and 102 TFEU. As a result of that clarification, it was clear that the Commission decision of 2009 was incorrect in that the limitation period on these two companies had expired. As a result of that decision, Ciba/BASF and Elementis would have to pay no fine for their participation in the heat stabilizers cartel. The 2009 decision remains valid for the nine other undertakings which took part in the cartel.

[41] By decision of 4 April 2011, the Commission amended the fines for ArcelorMittal and OriMartin/ Siderurgica Latina Martin. By decision of 30 September 2010, the Commission had already corrected errors in the calculation of the fines of ArcelorMittal, Emesa/Galycas/ArcelorMittal (España), WDI/Pampus, and Rautaruukki/Ovako. See Commission Press Release IP/10/1297 'Antitrust: Commission fines prestressing steel producers €458 million for two decades long price-fixing and market-sharing cartel' and Commission Press Release IP/11/403 'CORRECTED[1] Antitrust: Commission fines prestressing steel producers €269 million for two-decades long price-fixing and market-sharing cartel' of 4 April 2011. J Imgrund, 'The "Inability to pay" Doctrine in European Competition Law' (2012) 33(12) European Competition Law Review 560, 564, points out that '[a]llegedly, the reduction was made because the subsidiaries involved in the cartel itself were unable to pay the fine and the parent company was *not willing* to do so'. See also Commissioner for Competition J Almunia, 'Recent developments and future priorities in EU competition policy', SPEECH/11/243, 8 April 2011, indicating that 'the parent companies were liable for only a small proportion of the infringement and therefore of the fine, while the subsidiaries were solely liable for a much greater portion of the fine. In other words, the liability gap was very wide and the normal application of our rules resulted in excessive and non-recoverable fines for the subsidiaries—several times their turnover, in fact. This is why we have greatly reduced the fines we had imposed earlier; a reduction that I consider necessary on grounds of proportionality and effectiveness.' In Midday Express/13/0306 'Antitrust: Commission

view that these cases are unlikely to be indicative of a paradigm shift within the Commission to the effect that the Commission would now feel obliged to reconsider illegal decisions after they have been adopted, but rather a pragmatic solution chosen by the Commission in exceptional circumstances.[42] Undertakings are of course free to bring to the attention of the Commission illegalities that are contained in an already final decision; with the exception of very limited circumstances only, the Commission appears free to act or not to act upon such a request.

Enforcement procedure

15.16 The collection of fines is not administered directly by DG COMP but by the Commission's Directorate-General for Budget ('DG BUDGE').[43] DG COMP, however, retains the right to grant an extension of the time limit for voluntary payment. In such circumstances, it informs the relevant Commission departments, which must take account of the new time limit granted. Failure to pay within the time limit (usually three months from the date of notification to the undertaking) has two main consequences. First, most decisions provide that interest must be directly paid at 3.5 per cent above the rate charged by the European Central Bank ('ECB') on the first working day of each month. The GC has upheld the right to charge default interest, stating that:

> if the Commission did not have the power to charge default interest on fines, undertakings which delayed paying their fines would enjoy an advantage over those which paid their fines within the period laid down.[44]

Second, DG Budget will write to the undertakings in question requiring payment ('formal notice').[45] In the absence of a satisfactory response to its letter—and the only satisfactory response is payment, no deferment having been granted—DG Budget forwards the file to the Commission's Legal Service, which enforces the decision by approaching the competent national authorities or courts.[46] The usual practice is for the Legal Service to entrust enforcement proceedings to independent lawyers practising in the country in question. The Legal Service does not become directly involved, as such, in proceedings of this kind. DG COMP is merely informed of non-payment within the time limit, the forwarding of the demand for payment, and the stage reached in the enforcement proceedings—if any—commenced before a national authority or court.

---

reduces fines of Saint-Gobain and Pilkington for their participation in car glass cartel', 6 March 2013, the Commission announced that it had reduced the fines imposed on Saint-Gobain and Pilkington for their participation in the car glass cartel. The corrections became necessary because of two errors in computing the fines when it had included some of the sales of these two companies in the sales figure used as a basis to set their respective fines.

[42] F Neumayr and H Kühnert, 'The Repeal of Decisions by the European Commission Based on Considerations of Fact or Law' (2011) 3(1) Journal of European Competition Law & Practice 4, 9 and 10; see also J Imgrund, 'The "Inability to Pay" Doctrine in European Competition Law' (2012) 33(12) ECLR 560, 564.

[43] The functions of 'Financial Control'—which in the past were attributed to former DG XX (Financial Control) that also participated in the collection of fines (see 1st edn of this book, ch 12.(A)1.(b))—have now been decentralized to and within the Commission's various Directorate-Generals. The monies provided by the fines form part of the revenues of the EU and are included in the general budget. Kerse & Khan, *EU Antitrust Procedure* (Sweet & Maxwell 2012) para 7-280.

[44] Case T-275/94 *Groupement des Cartes Bancaires v Commission* [1995] ECR II-2169, paras 48–9. Case T-23/99 *LR af 1998 v Commission* [2002] ECR II-1705, para 395.

[45] Commission Antitrust Manual of Procedures, Internal DG Competition working documents on procedures for the application of Articles 101 and 102 TFEU, March 2012, Module 25 'Follow-up decisions', para 12.

[46] Commission Antitrust Manual of Procedures, Internal DG Competition working documents on procedures for the application of Articles 101 and 102 TFEU, March 2012, Module 25 'Follow-up decisions', para 13.

The implementing provisions in such cases are Article 299 TFEU and the rules adopted by **15.17** the Member States to give effect to it. In general, with regard to procedures under Article 299, although the EU authorities (in particular the Commission) may impose pecuniary penalties, the enforcement of such penalties is a matter solely for the Member States, which are required to grant the EU authorities direct access to national civil proceedings for enforcement under a simplified procedure, without the need for any *exequatur*. Article 299 in fact provides that Commission decisions are enforceable measures. Enforcement is governed by the rules of civil procedure in force in the Member State where the addressees of the decisions are located. The only precondition for ordinary enforcement is verification by national authorities designated for that purpose that the decision is genuine. On completion of that formality, the Commission may proceed to enforcement in accordance with national law by bringing the matter directly before the competent authority. The national authority empowered to verify the authenticity of the document varies from Member State to Member State. In practice, the Commission would ask the Permanent Representation to the EU of the country concerned to verify the authenticity of the decision. It would take the necessary steps in the country concerned and return the decision to the Commission in a form fully enforceable under domestic law. The application for enforcement of the Commission's independent lawyers entrusted with the collection of the sums due would be processed by the ordinary civil court, which would be required to treat the decision as if it were a final judgment of a civil court.[47] It will be recalled that the European Union has legal personality (Article 47 of the TEU) and may be a party to legal proceedings in order to uphold its rights under the same conditions as an individual. Finally, enforcement may be suspended only by a decision of the ECJ. However, the courts of the country concerned have jurisdiction to hear complaints that enforcement is being carried out in an irregular manner.[48]

In some cases, the Commission gives up the pursuit of outstanding fines where, for example, **15.18** the company concerned has become insolvent.[49]

2. Monitoring of compliance with 'injunctions'

Pursuant to Article 7(1) of Regulation 1/2003, the Commission may include whatever is **15.19** necessary to bring to an end the infringements of the competition rules which have been ascertained. The Commission is empowered not only to require the cessation of specific conduct (earlier referred to as 'negative injunctions', which literally reflect the content of that provision), but also to require certain conduct by undertakings (earlier referred to as 'positive

---

[47] In the UK, the European Communities ('Enforcement of Community Judgments') Order enables the Commission's decisions imposing fines to be registered in the High Court and be given the same treatment as if they had been issued by the High Court itself. The European Communities (Enforcement of Community Judgments) Order 1972, SI 1972/1590, as amended by SI 1998/1259 and by SI 2003/3204. Kerse & Khan, *EC Antitrust Procedure* (6th edn, Sweet & Maxwell 2012) para 7-289.

[48] In *Pioneer* [1980] OJ L60/21 and Joined Cases 100–103/80 *Musique Diffusion Française v Commission* [1983] ECR 1825, one of the undertakings, the German company C Melchers & Co, which was fined ECU 400,000, applied to the European Commission of Human Rights for a finding against the Federal Republic of Germany on the ground that its Ministry of Justice had issued an order under Art 256 EC at the request of the European Commission of the European Communities. Melcher claimed that its fundamental rights had not been observed during the Community procedure. See the decision of the European Commission of Human Rights of 9 February 1990 on the admissibility of Application No 13258/87 of *C Melchers & Co v Germany*, DR 64, 138.

[49] See Mlex, 'EC writes off EUR18.9 mln in fines due to insolvent firms', 12 June 2012. In 2010, the European Commission wrote off EUR 4.8 million in fines, unable to recover the money from insolvent firms. Those failing to pay were a Dutch technical association and two Greek ferry lines. The Commission managed to seize assets, but eventually gave up the pursuit of the fines (see Mlex, 'EC writes off EUR 4.8 mln in fines as firms go insolvent', 4 July 2011). The 2009 Competition Report saw orders totalling EUR 14 million issued.

injunctions' or orders to take—as opposed to refrain from—action, in respect of which the Commission's powers have been upheld by the Court).[50]

15.20 In its decision, the Commission may confine itself to prohibiting or requiring a particular conduct, without further details being given. If no time limit is set for compliance and no express penalty is imposed for non-compliance, the position is deemed to be that the orders contained in the Commission decisions must be complied with immediately[51] and that the requirements or orders will be enforced—to put it bluntly—by the imposition of periodic penalty payments in the event of delay.[52] The Commission has no other means of requiring undertakings to comply with its decisions. In other cases, the decision itself may provide for the manner in which the operative part of the decision, as regards cessation of the infringement, is to be monitored. The Commission may attach obligations to its decisions which facilitate monitoring. Thus, for example, an undertaking in a dominant position may be required to inform the Commission periodically of its prices, to allow it to verify that the infringement—for example, a discriminatory or 'predatory' pricing policy destroying competition—has in fact been brought to an end,[53] or to notify to the Commission those contracts in which prohibited clauses were found in the course of the procedure, so that the Commission can determine whether those clauses are no longer being applied. In such cases, the Commission may provide for periodic penalty payments in the infringement decision itself, which will be applied if the undertakings do not fulfil the obligation.[54]

15.21 To date, the Commission itself has always tried to monitor compliance with its antitrust decisions.[55] Unlike its practice in the merger control area, where it has developed Best Practice Guidelines for Divestiture Commitments and Trustee Mandate,[56] the Commission does not use a similar set of rules for monitoring commitments imposed in proceedings under Articles 101 and 102 TFEU. One reason may be that most of Commission's decisions in this field have involved mere reporting duties or less complex remedies than in the field of mergers. Not only because Article 7 of Regulation 1/2003 expressly provides for the Commission's power to impose any remedy, whether behavioural or structural, which is necessary to bring the infringement effectively to an end, but also because proceedings may become increasingly complex, Regulation 1/2003 calls for a more sophisticated monitoring mechanism in the future and perhaps also some guidelines from the Commission.[57]

---

[50] See Ch 11, 'Infringement Decisions and Penalties', para 11.02 et seq.

[51] Commission Antitrust Manual of Procedures, Internal DG Competition working documents on procedures for the application of Articles 101 and 102 TFEU, March 2012, Module 25 'Follow-up decisions', para 26.

[52] The Commission may, however, where immediate cessation is not possible for objective reasons, grant a limited period—as short as possible—to undertakings in order to bring the infringement to an end.

[53] See Art 5 of Commission Decision in *ECS v Akzo II* [1985] OJ L374/1; see also Case T-128/98 *Aérports de Paris v Commission* [2000] ECR II-3929, paras 82–3, regarding the obligation to apply a non-discriminatory scheme of commercial fees at the airport of Paris.

[54] Article 6 of Commission Decision in *ECS v Akzo II* [1985] OJ L374/1; see also eg Art 5 of *Mercedes* [2002] OJ L257/1.

[55] Article 7 of Commission Decision in *DSD* [2001] OJ L166/1: 'DSD shall inform the Commission, within three months of notification of this Decision, of the fulfilment of the commitments under Arts 3 to 6'. See also Commission Antitrust Manual of Procedures, Internal DG Competition working documents on procedures for the application of Articles 101 and 102 TFEU, March 2012, Module 25 'Follow-up decisions', paras 25–9.

[56] Commission Press Release IP/03/614 'Commission publishes best practice guidelines for divestiture commitments in merger cases', 2 May 2003. Explanatory Note on the Commission's Model Texts for Divestiture Commitments and the Trustee Mandate under the EU Merger Control Reg and the Standard Models available at DG COMP's website. See Part II, Chs 16 and 17.

[57] The Commission seems to have recognized this; 'Q&A on modernization with Kris Dekeyser' (April 2005) 8(3) Global Competition Review 11.

At the internal level, the Manproc has indicated that the monitoring of cease and desist **15.22** orders may be based on tools provided for in the decision itself, such as a reporting obligation.[58] The follow-up actions (such as a decision on periodic penalty payments) do not require the adoption of a decision to open proceedings, neither do they require a decision to close proceedings once monitoring is no longer deemed necessary. The Commissioner can, however, issue a public statement to take note that the addressees of the prohibition decision have adjusted their behaviour to the cease and desist orders. Instead of pursuing an undertaking for violation of a cease and desist order, the Commission may equally decide to open a new investigation (with a decision to open proceedings) in the case of infringements that were continued or repeated despite a prohibition decision including a cease and desist order. The starting date of such a new infringement would be the date of the previous Commission decision or a subsequent date from which the recommencing of the infringement can be proven. In such a case, the legal entities within the undertaking that continued or repeated the same infringement may also be liable for the aggravating circumstance of recidivism.[59]

Microsoft illustrates a complex case in which the Commission took action against Microsoft's **15.23** alleged non-compliance with its infringement decision.[60] Further to the 2004 decision finding that Microsoft had abused its dominant position in the market for client PC operating systems by refusing to supply interoperability information between Windows software and non-Microsoft work group server operating systems,[61] Microsoft was also required to notify the Commission of measures that it proposed to take to implement the interoperability remedy. The decision gave the Commission the power to appoint a monitoring trustee to monitor Microsoft's compliance with the decision and to provide the Commission with impartial advice. Microsoft appealed this decision to the GC and sought interim relief to suspend the operative parts of the decision. The interim measures application was rejected by the President of the GC in December 2004.[62] The remedies imposed in the Commission's decision became effective after interim measures were not granted. Microsoft made available an unbundled version of Windows, but discussions continued with the Commission about the scope of the interoperability remedy. In December 2005, the Commission declared that it had issued a statement of objections to Microsoft, alleging its breach of the interoperability remedy by virtue of its failure to comply with its obligation to supply complete and accurate interoperability information.[63] In July 2006, the Commission announced that it had decided to impose penalty payments totalling EUR 280.5 million on Microsoft (EUR 1.5 million per day for the period 16 December 2005 to 20 June 2006) in relation to Microsoft's failure to provide interoperability information that was accurate and complete.[64] In March 2007, the Commission announced that it had sent Microsoft a further statement of obligations alleging

---

[58] See also Commission Antitrust Manual of Procedures, Internal DG Competition working documents on procedures for the application of Articles 101 and 102 TFEU, March 2012, Module 25 'Follow-up decisions', paras 27–9. For example, a dominant company having abused its position through an illegal pricing policy may have to regularly report its prices to the Commission over a number of years.

[59] Commission Antitrust Manual of Procedures, Internal DG Competition working documents on procedures for the application of Articles 101 and 102 TFEU, March 2012, Module 25 'Follow-up decisions', para 29.

[60] See also Ch 11, 'Infringement Decisions and Penalties', para 11.91.

[61] See Case COMP/C-3/37.792 *Microsoft* [2007] OJ L32/23.

[62] See Order of the President of the GC in Case T-201/04 R *Microsoft v Commission* [2004] ECR II-4463.

[63] Commission Press Release IP/05/1695 'Competition: Commission warns Microsoft of daily penalty for failure to comply with 2004 decision' of 22 December 2005; MEMO/05/499 'Competition: Statement of Objections to Microsoft for non-compliance with March 2004 decision—frequently asked questions' of 22 December 2005.

[64] Commission Press Release IP/06/979 'Competition: Commission imposes penalty payment of €280.5 million on Microsoft for continued non-compliance with March 2004 Decision' of 12 July 2007. MEMO/06/277 'Competition: Commission Decision of 12 July 2006 to impose penalty payments on Microsoft—frequently asked questions' of 12 July 2006.

that it had not complied with the obligation to provide interoperability information on reasonable and non-discriminatory terms.[65] The Commission considered that the interoperability information provided by Microsoft contained no significant innovation and, therefore, the prices charged by Microsoft for it were unreasonable. In October 2007, the Commission announced that Microsoft had agreed to take the steps that the Commission considered to be necessary for it to comply fully with the remedial interoperability obligations.[66] On this basis, the Commission considered that the interoperability information being provided by Microsoft in accordance with the interoperability remedy was 'substantially complete'. However, the Commission stated that it would still issue a decision in relation to the past non-compliance highlighted in the March 2007 statement of objections. In February 2008, the Commission announced that it had imposed a penalty payment of EUR 899 million on Microsoft for non-compliance with its obligation in the 2004 decision to provide the interoperability information on reasonable terms. The 2008 penalty payment decision was adopted under Article 24(2) of Regulation 1/2003 and found that prior to 22 October 2007 Microsoft had charged unreasonable prices for access to interoperability documentation for work group servers and therefore did not comply with its obligations under the 2004 Microsoft Decision.[67] Further to Microsoft's appeal, the GC essentially upheld the Commission's main findings that Microsoft's pricing of interoperability information did not comply with the 2004 Microsoft Decision, whilst reducing the penalty payment marginally from EUR 899 million to EUR 860 million.

15.24 The Commission considered that the judgment confirmed its ability to impose significant periodic penalty payments in the event of non-compliance of remedial action required by its decisions, stating that it 'vindicates the enforcement action that the Commission took to ensure Microsoft's compliance with its obligations'.[68] The judgment would show that 'the imposition of such penalty payments remains an important tool at the Commission's disposal'. To date, Microsoft has been the only company to receive a periodic penalty payment under Article 24 of Regulation 1/2003.

II. Closing of the Proceedings and Closing or Shelving of the File

15.25 Files may be closed either because the matter has been disposed of formally by means of a decision or because the matter at issue is regarded by the Commission as no longer of importance at any stage of the procedure.[69] Thus, it is possible that such a proceeding will

---

[65] Commission Press Release IP/07/269 'Competition: Commission warns Microsoft of further penalties over unreasonable pricing as interoperability information lacks significant innovation' of 1 March 2007. MEMO/07/90 'Competition: Statement of Objections to Microsoft for non-compliance with March 2004 decision—frequently asked questions', 1 March 2007.

[66] Commission Press Release IP/07/1567 'Antitrust: Commission ensures compliance with 2004 Decision against Microsoft', 22 October 2007. MEMO/07/420 'Antitrust: Commission ensures Microsoft's compliance with the 2004 Decision—frequently asked questions', 22 October 2007.

[67] Case COMP/C-3/37.792 *Microsoft* [2009] OJ C166/20: Commission Press Release IP/08/318 'Antitrust: Commission imposes €899 million penalty on Microsoft for non-compliance with March 2004 Decision' of 27 February 2008; MEMO/08/125 'Antitrust: Commission Decision of 27 February 2008 to impose penalty payments on Microsoft—frequently asked questions', 27 February 2008. See for an example of non-compliance with a commitment decision: IP/13/196 'Antitrust: Commission fines Microsoft for non-compliance with browser choice commitments', 6 March 2013; see also Ch 13 'Voluntary Adjustments, Commitments, Finding of Inapplicability, Informal Guidance', para 13.25.

[68] See Case T-167/08 *Microsoft v Commission* [2012] OJ C243/13.

[69] As regards the possibility of re-allocating the file to an NCA, see Ch 3, 'The Role of National Competition Authorities', para 3.17 et seq.

end with the adoption of, for instance, a prohibition decision, a commitment decision, and/
or a decision to reject a complaint. Conversely, it may be that in the end no such decision is
adopted, for instance if it appears that there is not sufficient evidence to find an infringement
or if a complaint has been withdrawn.[70] For example, the Commission may take the decision
to shelve a complaint for lack of a sufficient EU interest, not only before commencing an
investigation of the case, but also after taking investigative measures, if that course of action
seems appropriate to it at that stage of the procedure.[71] It may also be that a prohibition
decision is adopted against some of the parties, but that the case needs to be closed against
others, for instance because of the lack of evidence of their involvement in the infringement
(partial closure).

A distinction has to be made between the closure of the proceedings and the closure of the   **15.26**
file. The closure of proceedings mirrors the decision of opening of proceedings in a given
case, under Article 11(6) of Regulation 1/2003 and Article 2(1) of Regulation 773/2004.
This is done by the adoption of a decision by the Director-General of DG COMP on the
basis of powers that have been sub-delegated to him.[72] In such situations, the proceedings
that have been opened[73] have to be closed (in full or in part) by a formal Commission decision (sub-delegated to the Director-General of DG COMP), since proceedings were also
initiated by Commission decision (taken by the Competition Commissioner under delegated
powers). The Manproc indicates that this closure decision will be brief, giving no details
as to the substance, but will simply state the fact of closure.[74] If the file to be closed has
been initiated under Article 11(6) of Regulation 1/2003, the Commission is also expected
to inform the Member States of the end of its investigation in the same way as it previously

---

[70] Commission Antitrust Manual of Procedures, Internal DG Competition working documents on procedures for the application of Articles 101 and 102 TFEU, March 2012, Module 23 'Closure of proceedings',
paras 3–4.
[71] See Opinion of AG Ruiz-Jarabo Colomer in Joined Cases C-449/98 P and C-450/98 P *International
Express Carriers Conference (IECC) v Commission* [2001] ECR I-3875, paras 54–6, who stated, alluding to
the GC case law, that '[t]o conclude otherwise would be tantamount to placing the Commission under an
obligation, once it had taken investigative measures following the submission of an application under Article
3(2) of Regulation No 17, to adopt a decision as to whether or not either Article [101] or Article [102] of the
[TFEU], or both, had been infringed, which would be contrary not only to the very wording of Article 3(1) of
Regulation No 17, according to which the Commission may adopt a decision concerning the existence of the
alleged infringement, but would also conflict with the settled case-law...according to which a complainant
has no right to obtain from the Commission a decision within the meaning of Article [288] of the [TFEU].'
See Joined Cases T-133/95 and T-204/95 *International Express Carriers Conference (IECC) v Commission*
[1998] ECR II-3645, paras 146–7.
[72] Commission Antitrust Manual of Procedures, Internal DG Competition working documents on procedures for the application of Articles 101 and 102 TFEU, March 2012, Module 23 'Closure of proceedings',
para 1. See Ch 1, Institutional Framework', para 1.77.
[73] In cases where no proceedings have been opened, such as in many complaint cases, it is obviously not
necessary to close proceedings.
[74] See Commission Antitrust Manual of Procedures, Internal DG Competition working documents on
procedures for the application of Articles 101 and 102 TFEU, March 2012, Module 23 'Closure of proceedings', paras 5 and 6–12. The Legal Service should be consulted on the proposal to close the case on the basis
of the draft decision. In cases of partial closure, the consultation may be done at the same time as the consultation on the rest of the case. In other words, if proceedings are to be closed against one company, while a prohibition decision is proposed against others, the consultation on the proposal to close and on the preliminary
draft prohibition decision may be done simultaneously. The power to adopt the decision to close proceedings
(in full or in part) has been sub-delegated to DG COMP, by decision of the Commissioner of 27 May 2004
(see in this regard Ch 1, 'Institutional Framework', para 1.73). Once the decision to close proceedings has
been adopted, the decision has to be notified to the parties in the authentic language. Member States are
informed of the decision to close proceedings. When closing proceedings in relation to one or several parties
at an early stage after proceedings have been formally opened and this has been made public, the Commission
will normally note the closure on its website (by a short standard text) and, if appropriate, issue a press release.

announced its intention to apply Article 11(6). National competition authorities ('NCAs') should then no longer be barred from applying Articles 101 and 102 TFEU to the same case. It may be recalled that in those cases where, pursuant to Article 9 of Regulation 1/2003, the Commission has opted for a decision by virtue of which commitments are made binding upon the undertaking(s) concerned, the proceedings are not definitely closed. Proceedings may be reopened in the following circumstances:

(i)   a material change in the facts on which the decision was based takes place;

(ii) undertakings fail to comply with their commitments; or

(iii) the decision is proven to have been based on incomplete, incorrect, or misleading information provided by the parties.[75]

15.27 Conversely, the closure of the file is a purely administrative step (which implies that the case, which bears a case management application number, does not remain endlessly 'open' in this database).[76] The Manproc provides that in order to close the file, the relevant Head of Unit signs and sends a 'note de classement' to the Registry, with an indication of the 'closure motive' and 'closure type'. This must be done even if it is expected that there may be an appeal against the decision adopted by the Commission (prohibition decision, commitment decision, rejection of complaint, etc). The Head of Unit should ensure that the case file is properly managed and that the file is complete at the time of the administrative closure. A case is complete once all relevant documents in the case are uploaded into the case management application, which represents the master file for the case.[77] Whenever there has been a formal initiation of proceedings or a submission of a formal complaint, parties and/or complainants will be informed of the outcome of the case (for example, by receiving a prohibition decision, a commitment decision, a decision to reject the complaint, a closure of proceedings decision etc). The Manproc therefore indicates that there is no need to inform them in addition of the administrative closure of the file[78] (see relevant chapters on decision types on the information and publication process).

15.28 However, where this has not been the case, the companies being investigated, particularly if involved earlier in the proceedings, should be informed by informal letter of the administrative closure of the case (eg when a company has been informed of investigations about it due to a complaint, which finally has been withdrawn or rejected or when finally solely an association

---

[75] For more details on commitment decisions, see Ch 13, 'Commitments, Voluntary Adjustments, Conclusion of the Procedure without a Formal Decision', para 13.06 et seq.

[76] See Commission Antitrust Manual of Procedures, Internal DG Competition working documents on procedures for the application of Articles 101 and 102 TFEU, March 2012, Module 23 'Closure of proceedings', para 1. Once a case has been attributed a number by the Antitrust Registry of DG COMP (and therefore loaded into the case management application), the case is 'ongoing' as long as it has not been closed. Therefore, whatever the ground for concluding the case (prohibition decision, commitment decision, rejection of complaint, withdrawal of the complaint, DG COMP decides not to investigate the case further, decision to close proceedings, etc), the case needs to be administratively closed in the case management system.

[77] Commission Antitrust Manual of Procedures, Internal DG Competition working documents on procedures for the application of Articles 101 and 102 TFEU, March 2012 Module 24 'Administrative closure of the file', paras 4–7. This is mainly done during the case life for all incoming and outgoing documents, no matter the format and the sender. Clearly non-related documents and duplicates are taken out. The file must then be archived. For cases numbered 39268 or more, the Registry holds the file via the case management application (the paper file no longer constitutes the original file). The case team will inform the Registry whether the closure is definitive or whether an appeal or needs of monitoring are likely.

[78] Commission Antitrust Manual of Procedures, Internal DG Competition working documents on procedures for the application of Articles 101 and 102 TFEU, March 2012 Module 24 'Administrative closure of the file', paras 8–10.

remains the addressee of the decision, but not the members of that association subject to the investigation).[79] Where inspections or other investigative measures involving companies have taken place and been confirmed on the DG COMP website and/or through a press release, but not led to a final decision, the closure of these investigations and case should normally be made public via the same means.[80]

All files disposed of are closed, unless: **15.29**

(i) the formal decision contains obligations or undertakings whose fulfilment must be moni-
    tored by the Commission, in which case the *rapporteur* or monitoring trustee responsible
    will follow developments during the period prescribed or necessary to verify fulfilment of
    the requirements imposed by the Commission. For example, this situation may arise in
    infringement decisions[81] or where commitments are imposed;[82]
(ii) the formal decision bringing the procedure to an end is challenged before the EU
    Courts, in which case the file will be forwarded to the Legal Service and to the Court
    itself.[83]

The ECJ considered that a letter sent in the course of an administrative procedure in which   **15.30**
the Commission stated that it was ending the investigation without offering the parties the
opportunity to submit their observations was a definitive act, and as such could be challenged. Indeed in *SFEI*, the Court stated:

> a letter closing the file may be analysed as a preliminary or preparatory statement only if the
> Commission has clearly indicated that its conclusion is valid only subject to submission by
> the parties of supplementary observations.[84]

Later, the ECJ further explained that letters definitely '[c]losing the file may be the subject
of an action, since they have the content and effect of a decision, inasmuch as they close
the investigation, contain an assessment of the agreements in question and prevent the
applicants from requiring the reopening of the investigation unless they put forward new
evidence'.[85]

---

[79] Commission Antitrust Manual of Procedures, Internal DG Competition working documents on procedures for the application of Articles 101 and 102 TFEU, March 2012 Modules 15–18 and 28.

[80] See Commission Notice on best practices on the conduct of proceedings in Articles 101 and 102 TFEU
[2011] OJ C308/6, para 76.

[81] An example might be an obligation to inform the Commission annually, over a specified period, of
the conditions under which a product is sold (Art 6 of Commission Decision in *ECS v Akzo II* [1985] OJ
L374/1).

[82] Thus, eg if need be on a daily basis, the *rapporteur* responsible for the case verifies the fulfilment of the
undertakings' commitments under Art 9 of Reg 1/2003.

[83] Before the creation of the GC, the ECJ generally only asked for complaints or notifications, the statement of objections and the reply from the undertakings, the minutes of administrative hearings, the opinion
of the Advisory Committee, and the decision itself, although it had access, if it so wished, to the entire file.
The Court itself expressed the view in its Order in Joined Cases 142/84 and 156/84 *BAT and Reynolds v
Commission* [1986] ECR 1899, para 11, that the examination of the Commission's file was an exceptional
measure of inquiry which could be contemplated if there was any suspicion of misuse of powers on the part
of the Commission. The GC seemingly has departed from the earlier practice and examines the administrative file in detail.

[84] This did not apply in Case C-39/93 P *Syndicat Français de l'Express international (SFEI) v Commission*
[1994] ECR I-2681, para 30; Opinion of AG Saggio in Case C-265/97 P *Coöperatieve Vereniging De Verenigde
Bloemenveilingen Aalsmeer BV (VBA) v Commission* [2000] ECR I-2061, para 34.

[85] See Case T-241/97 *Stork Amsterdam BV v Commission* [2000] ECR II-309, para 53; Case 210/81
Demo-Studio Schmidt v Commission [1983] ECR 3045, paras 14–15; Case 298/83 *CICCE v Commission*

III. Court Proceedings Concerning the Application of EU Competition Law

15.31 Commission decisions in antitrust cases are subject to judicial review by the EU Courts. The GC, created in 1989, was initially only competent to hear actions in competition (and staff) cases but its jurisdiction was subsequently enlarged to cover all direct actions brought by private parties. The ECJ deals only with appeals from the GC and questions referred to it by a national court. All other antitrust litigation is under the jurisdiction of the GC. Judgments of the GC can be appealed to the ECJ as of right.[86] The Manproc provides an overview of the EU Court system, including the basic elements of EU court procedures.[87]

A. Application for Annulment

1. Jurisdiction of the EU Courts

Overview

15.32 In most antitrust cases, addressees of fines seek above all the annulment of the Commission decision in regard to the penalties imposed or at least a reduction thereof.[88] The 'rigour of the judicial review' carried out by the GC is twofold.[89] The GC may be asked to undertake an exhaustive review of both the Commission's substantive findings of fact and its legal appraisal of those facts and to assess whether the evidence and other information relied on by the Commission in its decision are sufficient to establish the existence of the alleged infringement.[90] The provisions

---

[1985] ECR 1105, para 18, and Joined Cases 142/84 and 156/84 *BAT and Reynolds v Commission* [1987] ECR 4487, para 12.

[86] Commission Antitrust Manual of Procedures, Internal DG Competition working documents on procedures for the application of Articles 101 and 102 TFEU, March 2012, Module 26 'Court Litigation', para 31, indicates that, for all Court cases, the Legal Service represents the Commission. It is therefore the responsibility of the Legal Service to draft the various written pleadings in a case and to notify them to the Court, to present the oral arguments of the Commission at the hearing, or to reply to the questions of the Courts. The relevant Director-General assists the Legal Service in carrying out this responsibility.

[87] Commission Antitrust Manual of Procedures, Internal DG Competition working documents on procedures for the application of Articles 101 and 102 TFEU, March 2012, Module 26 'Court Litigation'.

[88] The Commission can also request that the GC increases the fine: Case T-69/04 *Schunk* [2008] ECR-II, paras 244 and 247. See R Sauer in JL Schulte and C Just (eds), *Kartellrecht* (Carl Heymanns Verlag 2012), Art 31 of the Reg 1/2003, para 5. Sometimes the principal interest of the undertaking may be to challenge the remedies imposed and not the fine. After having filed an appeal against the Commission's decision with the GC, Microsoft also lodged an application for suspension of the Commission decision obliging Microsoft to offer an unbundled version of Windows and to make available to its competitors certain technical interface information necessary to allow non-Microsoft work group servers to achieve full interoperability with Windows PCs. This application for interim relief was rejected in the Order of the President of the GC. See Case T-201/04 *Microsoft v Commission* [2004] ECR II-4463. See also main proceedings T-201/04 *Microsoft v Commission* [2007] ECR II-3601. The fine was already paid in full to the Commission on 29 June 2004.

[89] See Opinion of AG Bot of 21 June 2012 in Judgment of 22 November 2012 in Case C-89/11 P *E.ON Energie v Commission*, paras 104–11, 115, and 118–22, stating that '[t]he rigour of the judicial review carried out by the GC is therefore an essential condition for the actual procedure characterised, on the one hand, by the criminal nature of the procedure and the fines referred to in Article 23 of [Regulation 1/2003] and, on the other hand, by a concentration of powers in the hands of the Commission, to be compatible with the requirements of Article 6 ECHR and Article 47 of the Charter'. As regards the two-fold judicial review, see WPJ Wils, 'The Increased Level of EU Antitrust Fines, Judicial Review and the ECHR' (2010) 33(1) World Competition 5, 23. With regard to procedural infringements, see also F Christ y C. Gauer, 'Les infractions procédurales en droit européen de la concurrence' (2012) 4 Concurrences, no 49312, 29.

[90] Case T-18/03 *CD-Contact Data v Commission* [2009] ECR II-1021, para 50, stating that 'where the Court is faced with an application for the annulment of a decision applying Article [101 TFEU], it

applicable to requests for annulment are Articles 263, 264 and 266 TFEU. In actions under Article 263 TFEU, the GC exercises supervisory jurisdiction to the extent that it has to satisfy itself that the Commission's findings of fact and legal conclusions drawn from those facts are correct. In general terms, it is not concerned with the merits of a decision, but rather whether the Commission's findings regarding the facts and its legal assessment satisfy the requisite legal standard.[91]

In addition, under Article 261 TFEU in conjunction with Article 31 of Regulation 1/2003, the Court also has unlimited jurisdiction in respect of fines and penalties.[92] This enables the GC and the ECJ to adjudicate on the amount of the pecuniary penalties imposed by the Commission in

15.33

---

undertakes a comprehensive review generally of the question whether or not the conditions for the application of Article [101 TFEU] are met'. See Joined Cases T-25/95, T-26/95, T-30/95 to T-39/95, T-42/95 to T-46/95, T-48/95, T-50/95 to T-65/95, T-68/95 to T-71/95, T-87/95, T-88/95, T-103/95, and T-104/95 *Cimenteries CBR SA and others v Commission* [2000] ECR II-491, para 719; Joined Cases T-67/00, T-68/00, T-71/00, and T-78/00 *JFE Engineering Corp and others v Commission* [2004] ECR II-2501, para 175. In the case of a decision adopted pursuant to Art 102 TFEU, the contested decision must mention facts forming the basis of the legal grounds of the measure and the considerations which led to the adoption of the decision (see, to that effect, Case T-340/03 *France Télécom v Commission* [2007] ECR II-107, para 57). It should be noted that the legality of the contested measure must be assessed on the basis of the elements of fact and of law existing at the time when the measure was adopted, and in particular on the basis of the information available to the Commission when it was adopted; see recently Case T-343/06 *Shell Petroleum NV et al v Commission* [2012] OJ C 355/14 (appeal pending, Case C-585/12 P *Shell Petroleum and Others v Commission*), para 104.

[91] See D Bailey, 'Scope of Judicial Review under Article 81 EC' (2004) Common Market Law Review 1327, 1331. Joined Cases C-2/01 P and C-3/01 P *Bundesverband der Arzneimittel-Importeure eV (BAI) and Commission v Bayer* [2004] ECR I-23, para 62; Joined Cases T-67/00, T-68/00, T-71/00, and T-78/00 *JFE Engineering Corp v Commission* [2004] ECR II-2501, para 175: 'Thus, the role of a Court hearing an application for annulment brought against a Commission decision finding the existence of an infringement of the competition rules and imposing fines on the addressees consists in assessing whether the evidence and other information relied on by the Commission in its decision are sufficient to establish the existence of the alleged infringement'. See also Case T-360/09 *E.ON Ruhrgas v Commission* [2012] OJ C243/15, para 172 (see also A Wiesbrock 'E.ON/GDF: Revisiting the Standard of Judicial Review for Fines in Competition Cases', (2013) 4(1) Journal of European Competition Law & Practice 58–60); Case T-348/08, *Aragonesas Industrias y Energía v Commission* [2011] OJ 355/15, para 92; see also B Vesterdorf, 'The CFI: Judicial Review or Judicial Control', St Gallen International Cartel Forum 2006, 'Neueste Entwicklungen im europäischen und internationalen Kartellrecht' 21 at 29: 'Control of primary facts by the CFI is intensive and...there is no margin for discretion on the part of the Commission. This is inherent in the nature of a control of the accuracy of facts. Either a fact is correct or it is not.' H Legal, 'Standards of Proof and Standards of Judicial Review in EU Competition Law' ch 5 in *Annual Proceedings of the Fordham Corporate Law Institute* (Juris Publishing 2006) 107 at 109–10. Both are cited by J Ratliff 'Judicial Review in EC Competition Cases before the European Courts:—Avoiding *double renvoi*' in C-D Ehlermann and M Marquis (eds), *European Competition Law Annual 2009: The Evaluation of Evidence and its Judicial Review in Competition Cases* (Hart Publishing 2010), 453: 'The [GC] observed that a court cannot conclude that the Commission has proved the existence of the infringement at issue to the requisite legal standard if it still entertains doubts on that point, in particular in proceedings for the annulment of a decision imposing a fine, this being in accordance with the principle of the presumption of innocence resulting in particular from Article 6(2) of the European Convention on Human Rights and Fundamental Freedoms.'

[92] Case T-59/02 *Archer Daniels Midland v Commission* [2006] ECR II-3627, para 443: 'It is apparent from the case-law that the fact that the examination of the pleas challenging the lawfulness of a Commission decision imposing a fine for infringement of the competition rules of the European Union has revealed an illegality does not dispense the Court from examining whether, in the light of the consequences of that illegality and in exercising its unlimited jurisdiction, it is required to amend the contested decision.' See also Opinion of AG J Kokott in Case C-11/04 *Technische Unie BV v Commission* [2006] ECR I-8831, para 132: 'it must be borne in mind that its unlimited jurisdiction to review fines is not subject to the same criteria as the annulment of the contested decision, for instance. In particular, its unlimited jurisdiction to review fines is not merely a review as to the legality of the Commission's decision. In exercising that jurisdiction, it may also consider questions of expediency, appropriateness, and fairness. Consideration must be given particularly to procedural defects such as a breach of the principle that action must be taken within a reasonable period, for example, which...constitute an infringement of a fundamental right even if they have not affected the content of the Commission's decision and therefore do not lead to its annulment.' See also R Sauer in JL Schulte

its infringement decisions. More than a simple review of legality, which merely permits dismissal of the action for annulment or annulment of the contested measure, the unlimited jurisdiction conferred on the GC by Article 31 of Regulation No 1/2003 in accordance with Article 261 TFEU authorizes it to vary the contested measure, even without annulling it, by taking into account all of the factual circumstances. It may, for example, amend the amount of the fine.[93] Thus, the Court also examines in each particular case whether the amount of the fine imposed by the Commission is reasonable and determines the appropriateness of the fine.[94] That assessment may justify the production and taking into account additional information which is not as such required, by virtue of the duty to state reasons under Article 296 TFEU, to be set out in the decision.[95]

15.34 On appeal, the ECJ's task is limited to examining whether, in exercising its power of review, the GC made an error of law.[96] Under Article 256 TFEU, second paragraph and Article 51, first paragraph of the Statute of the ECJ, an appeal must be limited to points of law and must lie on grounds of lack of competence of the GC, a breach of procedure before it which adversely affects the interests of the applicant or an infringement of EU law by the GC.

15.35 As regards the compatibility of the EU's judicial system with the requirements of the Convention for the Protection of Human Rights and Fundamental Freedoms (European Convention on Human Rights, 'ECHR'), the EU Courts have pointed out that the review provided for by the Treaties would involve a review by the Courts of both the law and the facts,

---

and C Just (eds), *Kartellrecht* (Carl Heymanns Verlag 2012), Art 31 of the Reg 1/2003, paras 2–3, with more references. WPJ Wils, 'The Increased Level of EU Antitrust Fines, Judicial Review and the ECHR' (2010) 33(1) World Competition 5, 23.

[93] Case C-534/07 *Consumer Prym v Commission* [2009] ECR I-7415, para 86; Case T-343/08 *Arkema* [2011] ECR II-2287, para 203; R Sauer in JL Schulte and C Just (eds), *Kartellrecht* (Carl Heymanns Verlag 2012), Art 31 of the Reg 1/2003, para 4.

[94] Case T-317/94 *Moritz J Weig v Commission* [1998] ECR II-1235, para 194: 'It follows that, when it finds in a decision that there has been an infringement of the competition rules and imposes fines on the undertakings participating in it, the Commission must, if it systematically took into account certain basic factors in order to fix the amount of fines, set out those factors in the body of the decision in order to enable the addressees of the decision to verify that the level of the fine is correct and to assess whether there has been any discrimination.' The statement of reasons must enable 'the persons concerned to ascertain the reasons for the measure and to enable the competent Community court to exercise its power of review. It is not necessary for the reasoning to go into all the relevant facts and points of law'. Whether a statement of reasons is adequate must be assessed 'with regard not only to its wording but also to its context and to all the legal rules governing the matter in question' (see Case T-199/08 *Ziegler SA v Commission* [2011] ECR II-3507, para 87).

[95] See Case C-248/98 *KNP BT v Commission* [2000] ECR I-9641, para 40. See also Case T-132/07 *Fuji Electric v Commission* [2011] ECR II-4091, para 209; Joined Cases T-236/01, T-239/01, T-244/01 to T-246/01, T-251/01, and T-252/01 *Tokai Carbon and Others v Commission* [2004] ECR II-1181, para 165, and case law cited, and Joined Cases T-71/03, T-74/03, T-87/03, and T-91/03 *Tokai Carbon and Others v Commission* [2005] ECR II-10, paras 59, 164, and 190. See also Case T-322/01 *Roquette Frères v Commission* [2006] ECR II-3137, para 327: 'However, having regard to the principle of legal certainty, that possibility must, in principle, be limited to taking into account information pre-dating the contested decision and which the Commission could have known at the time when it adopted that decision. A different approach would lead the Court to assume the role of the administration in assessing a question which the latter has not yet been required to examine, which would amount to encroaching on its powers and, more generally, to infringing the system of division of powers and the institutional balance between the judiciary and the administration.'

[96] The ECJ thus has no jurisdiction to find the facts or, as a rule, to examine the evidence which the GC accepted in support of those facts. Provided that the evidence has been properly obtained and the general principles of law and the rules of procedure in relation to the burden of proof and the taking of evidence have been observed, it is for the GC alone to assess the value which should be attached to the evidence produced to it. See, *inter alia*, order of the Court in Case C-19/95 P *San Marco Impex Italiana v Commission* [1996] ECR I-4435, para 40; Case C-53/92 P *Hilti v Commission* [1994] ECR I-667, para 42; and Joined Cases C-189/02 P, C-202/02 P, C-205/02 P to C-208/02 P, and C-213/02 P *Dansk Rørindustri and Others v Commission* [2005] ECR I-5425, para 177. However, in Case C-110/10 P, *Solvay v Commission* [2011] OJ C370/13,

meaning that they have the power to assess the evidence, to annul the contested decision, and to alter the amount of a fine.[97] Accordingly, the review of legality provided for under Article 263 TFEU, supplemented by the unlimited jurisdiction in respect of the amount of the fine provided for under Article 31 of Regulation 1/2003,[98] would not be contrary to the requirements of the principle of effective judicial protection enshrined in Article 6 of the ECHR and Article 47 of the Charter of Fundamental Rights.[99] Leaving aside the often expressed general critique of the whole EU competition law enforcement system and the role of the GC within that system, an applicant is always required to identify in each single case the specific failures in a judgment and it is on this basis that the EU Courts will undertake their

---

para 46, the ECJ stated that: 'Solvay is not criticising the findings of fact made at first instance, but the rules applied by the General Court as regards the standard of proof relating to the usefulness of the documents, some of which have been mislaid. The question of whether the [GC] applied the correct legal standard when determining the usefulness of those documents for Solvay's defence is a question of law, which is amenable to review by the Court of Justice on appeal.' See Case C-367/10 P *EMC Development AB v Commission* [2011] ECR I-46, para 108: 'The [GC] has exclusive jurisdiction to find the facts, except in a case where the substantive inaccuracy of its findings is apparent from the documents submitted to it, and to evaluate the evidence adduced. The establishment of those facts and the evaluation of that evidence do not, save where the clear sense of the evidence has been distorted, constitute a point of law which is subject as such to review by [ECJ] on appeal.' See also Joined Cases C-403/04 P and C-405/04 P *Sumitomo Metal Industries and Nippon Steel v Commission* [2007] ECR I-729, para 40, and Case C-413/06 P *Bertelsmann and Sony Corporation of America v Impala* [2008] ECR I-4951, para 117.

[97] On the compatibility with Art 47 of the Charter which implements in EU law the protection afforded by Art 6(1) of the ECHR, see also Case C-272/09 P *KME Germany and Others v Commission* [2012] OJ C32/4, para 91 et seq; C-386/10 P *Chalkor v Commission* [2012] OJ 32/9, para 45 et seq. Vice-President of ECJ, K Lenaerts 'Due Process in Competition Cases' (2013) 1(5) *Neue Zeitschrift für Kartellrecht—NZKart*, stating that the system of judicial review of Commission decisions affords all the safeguards required by Art 47. See also MEMO/11/888 'Antitrust: Commission welcomes European Court of Justice judgments in copper tubes cartels' of 8 December 2011, in which the Commission welcomed the ECJ's rulings stating that they confirm 'what the Commission has always defended, which is that the European Courts provide a thorough and effective review of our decisions in the competition policy area, including as regards the amount of the fines imposed, in accordance with the companies' fundamental right to an effective judicial protection.' See also I Nikolic, 'Full Judical Review of Antitrust Cases after KME: A New Formula of Review (2012) 33(12) ECLR 583, 587, who takes the view that the KME case would show that the ECJ is gradually intensifying its standard of review. Such an approach would be perfectly in conformity with the requirements of Art 6(1) ECHR.

[98] On appeal, the question arises whether the GC has in fact adequately exercised that jurisdiction. Whatever the extent of its jurisdiction, proceedings before the GC are adversarial in nature.

[99] See also, recently, Opinion of AG Kokott of 18 April 2013 in Case C-501/11 *Schindler Holding Ltd, Schindler Management AG, Schindler SA, Schindler Sarl, Schindler Liften BV, Schindler Deutschland Holding GmbH*, paras 25–30; WPJ Wils, 'The Increased Level of EU Antitrust Fines, Judicial Review and the ECHR' (2010) 33(1) World Competition 5, 18–20, adds that the ECtHR case law would not require several layers of full judicial review. It only requires that the addressee of an administrative decision imposing a criminal penalty on him can bring this decision before 'a judicial body' that has full jurisdiction, including the power to quash in all respects, on questions of fact and law, the challenged decision. The fact that, in the EU system, only the GC has jurisdiction over both questions of fact and law, whereas any further appeal to the ECJ is limited to points of law only, would thus not be problematic. See also the Opinion of AG Bot prior to the Judgment of 22 November 2012 in Case C-89/11 P *E.ON Energie v Commission*, stating that according to the case law, compliance with Art 6 of the ECHR 'does not preclude the Commission from having the function of carrying out the investigation, conducting the proceedings and adopting the decision on infringements of competition law, provided that the decision which is delivered is open to subsequent review by a judicial body that has unlimited jurisdiction'. (See *Schmautzer v Austria* App no 15523/89 (ECtHR, 23 October 1995), para 36; *Valico SRL v Italy* App no 70074/01 (ECtHR, 21 March 2006) , and the case law cited relating to the subsequent control by a judicial body that has full jurisdiction, and *A Menarini Diagnostics SRL v Italy* App no 43509/08 (ECtHR, 27 September 2011), paras 58–9, and case law cited.) In paras 104–7, AG Bot goes on to say that the 'judicial body must be able to examine all questions of fact and law relating to the dispute before it and must not be confined to examining a manifest error of assessment. Consequently, first, the judicial body must be able to ascertain whether, in relation to the particular circumstances of the case, the administrative authority made appropriate use of its powers. Secondly, the judicial body must be able to examine the merits and the *proportionality* of the choices of that authority and to verify its assessments of a

review.[100] According to the GC, nothing in Article 6 ECHR or the case law of the European Court of Human Rights ('ECtHR') would require the 'independent and impartial tribunal' to investigate, of its own motion, matters which are not raised before it. While the case law would require certain matters of public policy (essentially concerned with procedural guarantees) to be raised in that way, in other regards, the GC's exercise of its unlimited jurisdiction in relation to the penalties must be measured against the content of the allegations on which it has been asked to adjudicate.[101] In any appeal, the applicant has to identify those parts of the contested decision, to formulate grounds of challenge in that regard, and to adduce evidence—direct or circumstantial—to demonstrate that its objections are well founded.[102] The GC is then free in its absolute discretion to assess the value to be given to all the facts and evidence which have been submitted to it or which it has itself adduced.[103] There is no provision that prevents an applicant from submitting evidence offered in support before the Court, although it did not submit such evidence during the administrative procedure. None the less, the Court is required to take account of that circumstance when assessing the probative value of that evidence offered in support.[104]

15.36 In the ECJ's view, where the GC does not review the whole of a contested decision of the Court's own motion, this would not contravene the principle of effective judicial protection. Compliance with that principle would not require the GC—that would be obliged to respond to the pleas in law raised and to carry out a review of both the law and the facts—to undertake of its own motion a new and comprehensive investigation of the file.[105]

Scope of review

15.37 The ECJ has stated that the GC has exclusive jurisdiction:

> first, to establish the facts except where the substantive inaccuracy of its [Commission] findings is apparent from the documents submitted to it and, second, to assess those facts.[106]

As regards the review of fines, pursuant to Article 261 TFEU:

---

technical nature. Thirdly, the review of a penalty, according to the [ECtHR], means that the judicial body ascertains and determines in a *detailed* way whether the penalty is appropriate for the infringement, taking account of the relevant factors, including the *proportionality* of the penalty itself, and, as the case may be, replaces it.' The rigour of the judicial review would be an essential condition for the EU judicial review to be compatible with the requirements of Art 6 ECHR and Art 47 of the Charter. In Case C-272/09 P *KME v Commission*, Report for the Hearing, the Commission noted that in *Engel and Others v Netherlands, Engel et al v The Netherlands* App nos 5100/71, 5101/71, 5102/71, 5354/72, 5370/72 (ECtHR, 8 June 1976), paras 81 and 82, the ECtHR held that in order for a charge to be considered criminal in nature the following three criteria should be assessed: (i) the classification of the offence under domestic law; (ii) the nature of the offence; and (iii) the nature and severity of the penalty. The ECtHR would have also held in *Jussila v Finland* that there are criminal charges of differing weight and that, for areas outside the 'hard core of criminal law', 'the criminal-head guarantees will not necessarily apply with their full stringency' (*Jussila v Finland* App no 73053/01 (EctHR, 23 November 2006)). That would be the case for competition law fines, which Art 23(5) of Reg 1/2003 describes as non-criminal, even if they were nonetheless viewed as 'criminal charges' for the purposes of Art 6(1) ECHR. See in the same vein, Vice-President of ECJ, K Lenaerts 'Due Process in Competition Cases' (2013) 1(5) *Neue Zeitschrift für Kartellrecht—NZKart*.

[100] Opinion of AG Sharpston in Case C-272/09 P *KME Germany and Others v Commission* [2012] OJ C32/4, para 81.

[101] Opinion of AG Sharpston in Case C-272/09 P *KME Germany and Others v Commission* [2012] OJ C32/4, para 74.

[102] Case C-386/10 P *Chalkor v Commission* [2012] OJ 32/9, para 65.

[103] Order in Case C-360/02 P *Ripa di Meana v Parliament* [2004] ECR I-10339, para 28.

[104] Case T-343/06 *Shell Petroleum NV et al v Commission* [2012] OJ C355/14 (appeal pending, Case C-585/12 P *Shell Petroleum and Others v Commission*), para 160.

[105] C-386/10 P *Chalkor v Commission* [2012] OJ 32/9, para 66; Case C-272/09 P *KME Germany and Others v Commission* [2012] OJ C32/10, para 105.

[106] See Case C-7/95 P *John Deere v Commission* [1998] ECR I-3111, para 21; See Opinion of AG Mazák in Case C-328/05 P *SGL Carbon AG v Commission* [2007] ECR I-3921, para 46. Case C-425/07 P *AEPI v*

[r]egulations made by the Council pursuant to the provisions of this Treaty may give the Court of Justice unlimited jurisdiction in regard to the penalties provided for in such regulations.

In the context of competition proceedings, Article 31 of Regulation 1/2003 thus widens the scope of review and specifies that:

[t]he Court of Justice shall have unlimited jurisdiction to review decisions whereby the Commission has fixed a fine or periodic penalty payment; it may cancel, reduce or increase the fine or periodic penalty payment imposed' by the Commission.[107]

Also, sometimes because of a variation in wording in the case law of the EU Courts, which may reflect the difficulties of reconciling a clear strong control of all elements on which the Commission based its appraisal with the recognition of a certain discretion on the part of the Commission,[108] the question how the Courts exercise their review arguably continues to give rise to different interpretations.[109]

Review of lawfulness

As regards the lawfulness of the Commission's decision, the review undertaken by the GC under **15.38** Article 263 TFEU usually does not involve reassessing the facts of a case afresh.[110] While the GC

Commission, para 31: 'the Commission is responsible for defining and implementing Community competition policy and for that purpose has a discretion as to how it deals with complaints lodged with it'.

[107] Note that the Court is only entitled to 'cancel', 'reduce', or 'increase' the fine imposed by the Commission; it cannot impose a fine where none was imposed by the Commission in the first place. As regards the interpretation of Art 261 TFEU, see Case T-275/94 *Carte Bleu v Commission II* [1995] ECR II-2169, paras 57–65, in which the GC concludes that the fines it sets are not legally different from those imposed by the Commission. See also Case C-272/09 P *KME Germany and Others v Commission* [2012] OJ C32/10, para 103, stating that the '[unlimited] jurisdiction empowers the Courts, in addition to carrying out a mere review of the lawfulness of the penalty, to substitute their own appraisal for the Commission's and, consequently, to cancel, reduce or increase the fine or penalty payment imposed'. See also Joined Cases C-238/99 P, C-244/99 P, C-245/99 P, C-247/99 P, C-250/99 P to C-252/99 P, and C-254/99 P *Limburgse Vinyl Maatschappij and Others v Commission* [2002] ECR I-8375, para 692.

[108] See President of the GC M Jaeger, 'The Standard of Review in Competition Cases involving Complex Economic Assessments: Towards the Marginalization of the Marginal Review?' (2011) 22(4) Journal of European Competition Law & Practice 295, 304–5; see also in this context Mlex, 'Lawyers should differentiate cartel annulment and penalty-reduction pleas, says top EU court aide', 18 March 2011, citing Arnaud Bohler, GC President M Jaeger's head of cabinet, as saying that lawyers would be well advised to refine their arguments in an appeal, so that they would address requests for reductions in fines separately from challenges to the validity of decisions. Companies challenging cartel decisions would tend to ask the court for two things: first, to annul the decision, and as an alternative they request that the court use its 'unlimited jurisdiction' to evaluate and reduce the level of the fine. However, companies may be better off in developing arguments on fine reductions, because they can draw the court's attention to specific issues with the way the fines were calculated.

[109] President of the GC M Jaeger, 'The Standard of Review in Competition Cases involving Complex Economic Assessments: Towards the Marginalization of the Marginal Review?' (2011) 22(4) Journal of European Competition Law & Practice 295; Kerse & Khan, *EC Antitrust Procedure* (6th edn, Sweet & Maxwell 2012) para 8-088; D Salter, S Thomas, and D Waelbroeck, 'Competition Law Proceedings before the European Commission and the Right to a Fair Trial: No Need for Reform?' [2009] European Competition Journal 97; D Bailey, 'Scope of Judicial Review under Article 81 EC' [2004] Common Market Law Review 1337, who distinguishes between discretion (which tends to restrict the scope of judicial review by allowing the Commission to choose the criteria by which a decision is reached) and power of appraisal in regard to Art 101 TFEU, which is subject to comprehensive judicial review but which may be limited in cases involving complex economic assessment. See eg Case T-112/99 *Métropole Television v Commission* [2001] ECR II-2459, para 114. See also Case C-272/09 P *KME v Commission* [2012] OJ C32/4, para 109, stating that the GC had repeatedly referred to the 'discretion', the 'substantial margin of discretion', or the 'wide discretion' of the Commission; yet such references did not prevent the GC from carrying out the full and unrestricted review, in law and in fact, required of it. As regards the unlimited jurisdiction relating to the imposition of fine, Opinion of AG Bot in Judgment of the ECJ of 22 November 2012 in Case C-89/11 P *E.ON Energie v Commission*, para 110, who states that the GC therefore carry out its own appraisal.

[110] See Case T-342/00 *Petrolessence v Commission* [2003] ECR II-1161 para 103: 'it must be observed that the applicants have not established that the Commission's appraisal of those points is clearly mistaken

---

has demonstrated its willingness to resolve issues of economic importance and its commitment to a 'comprehensive judicial review' which will cause the Court to review a decision to the maximum extent possible,[111] the possibilities for challenging the Commission's appraisal are often limited to the party's defence rights and general principles (for example proportionality and equal treatment) because of the discretion that it enjoys.[112]

15.39   The EU Courts have always allowed the Commission considerable discretion and confined themselves to verifying that the limits of such discretion had not been exceeded and that an error of law has not occurred. In various judgments,[113] the EU Courts have justified the latitude available to the Commission by referring to the complex nature of the economic assessments which it must undertake in competition matters. In *Alrosa*, however, the ECJ found that the GC expressed its own differing assessment of the capability of the joint commitments to eliminate the competition problems identified by the Commission, before concluding that alternative solutions existed that were less onerous for the undertakings. By so doing, it stated that the GC had put forward its own assessment of complex economic circumstances and thus substituted its own analysis for that of the Commission. It therefore encroached on the discretion enjoyed by the Commission, rather than reviewing the lawfulness of its assessment.[114] In cases where the legal assessment is not straightforward and is related to economic analysis, the Courts normally confine the scope of their review. Where, for example, the object of an agreement is

---

and it must be concluded that the applicants' present arguments consist in inviting the [GC] to substitute a different appraisal of their candidacy for that of the Commission'. See also former President of the GC Judge B Vesterdorf, 'Judicial Review and Competition Law—Reflections on the Role of the Community Courts in the EC System of Competition Law Enforcement', Speech at the International Forum on EC Competition Law, Brussels, 8 April 2005, who takes the view that the case law (eg Case T-44/02 *German Banks v Commission* [2004] OJ C314/13 (not published in ECR), Case T-67/01 *JCB Service v Commission* [2004] ECR II-49, and Case T-208/01 *Volkswagen v Commission* [2003] ECR II-5141) shows that the GC does not shy away from examining closely and without restraint whether the Commission had got the core facts right. See also the published and edited paper version of Vesterdorf's speech in (2005) 1(2) Competition Policy International 15.

[111] See D Bailey, 'Scope of Judicial Review under Article 81 EC' [2004] Common Market Law Review 1327, 1332; Opinion of AG Cosmas in Case C-83/98 P *France v Ladbroke Racing and Commission* [2000] ECR I-3271, para 15; Opinion of Judge Vesterdorf acting as AG in Case T-7/89 *Hercules v Commission* [1992] II-1711, noting that the review is 'governed by the principle of the unfettered evaluation of evidence, unrestrained by the various rules laid down in national legal systems'. See also cases related to state aid: Case T-198/01 *Technische Glaswerke Ilmenau v Commission* [2004] ECR II-2717, para 79, indicating that comprehensive judicial review and discretion of the Commission go hand in hand: 'Where the Commission adopts a measure involving such an appraisal [private operator in market economy], it enjoys a wide discretion and, even though judicial review is in principle a comprehensive review of whether a measure falls within the scope of Article 87(1) EC, review of that measure is limited to establishing whether there has been compliance with the rules governing procedure and the statement of reasons, whether any error in law has been made, whether the facts on which the contested finding was based have been accurately stated and whether there has been any manifest error of assessment or a misuse of powers. In particular, the Court is not entitled to substitute its own economic assessment for that of the author of the decision.'

[112]   R Sauer in JL Schulte and C Just (eds), *Kartellrecht* (Carl Heymanns Verlag 2012), Art 31 of the Reg 1/2003, para 2, n 12, with references to the case law.

[113]   Case T-321/05 *AstraZeneca v Commission* [2010] ECR II-2805, para 33 (appeal pending, Case C-457/10 P *AstraZeneca v Commission*); Case C-194/99 P *Thyssen Stahl v Commission* [2003] ECR I-10821, para 78; Case T-17/93 *Matra Hachette SA v Commission* [1994] ECR II-595, para 104; and Case 42/84 *Remia and others v Commission* [1985] ECR 2545, para 34. A fundamental judgment with regard to the margin of assessment enjoyed by the Commission in competition proceedings was given in Case 42/84 *Remia v Commission* [1985] ECR 2545, para 34; see also Joined Cases 142/84 and 156/84 *British American Tobacco and Reynolds Industries v Commission* [1987] ECR 4487, para 62; and Joined Cases C-204/00 P, C-205/00 P, C-211/00 P, C-213/00 P, C-217/00 P, and C-219/00 P *Aalborg Portland and Others v Commission* [2004] ECR I-123, para 279.

[114]   Case C-441/07 P *Commission v Alrosa* [2010] ECR I-5949, paras 66–8. That error of the GC in itself would have justified setting aside the judgment under appeal.

not to restrict competition, it must be considered whether it has an anticompetitive effect. The effect of an agreement must be appraised in the legal and economic context in which it operates. In *Van den Bergh Foods*, the GC acknowledged that this might require the exercise of judgment as to the existence and extent of market foreclosure.[115] In such cases, accordingly, judicial review of Commission measures involving an appraisal of complex economic matters will be limited to verifying whether the relevant rules on procedure and on the statement of reasons have been complied with, whether the facts have been accurately stated, and whether there has been any manifest error of assessment or a misuse of powers.[116] Those guarantees include, in particular, the duty of the competent institution to examine carefully and impartially all of the relevant aspects of the individual case[117] and the parties' defence rights.[118]

A decision will be overturned if the Commission has manifestly erred in its judgment, which is to be decided on the basis of the persuasive evidence in each case; this involves the GC verifying objectively and materially the accuracy of certain facts and the correctness of the conclusions drawn. The review is more limited where the Commission enjoys some discretion.[119] **15.40**

---

[115] Case T-65/98 *Van den Bergh Foods Ltd v Commission* [1998] ECR II-2641, para 80. See also F Castillo de la Torre, 'Evidence, Proof and Judicial Review in Cartel Cases' (2009) 32(4) World Competition 505, 554, who proposes that the standard to be applied for assessing if the Commission has been right in its findings on impact is that of 'reasonable probability'. In Case T-25/05 *KME Germany et al v Commission* [2010] ECR II-91, para 85, the GC rejected the argument that, if the Commission relied on the concrete impact of the cartel in determining the amount of the fine, it was under a duty scientifically to demonstrate the existence of a tangible economic effect on the market and a link of cause and effect between the impact and the infringement, confirmed in Case C-389/10 P *KME Germany et al v Commission* [2010] OJ C32/10. See also Case T-59/02 *Archer Daniels Midland v Commission* [2006] ECR II-3627, paras 159–61; Case T-43/02 *Jungbunzlauer v Commission* [2006] ECR II-3435, paras 153–5; Case T-329/01 *Archer Daniels Midland v Commission* [2006] ECR II-3255, paras 176–8; Case T-322/01 *Roquette Frères v Commission* [2006] ECR II-3137, paras 73–5, indicating that the actual impact of a cartel on the market must be regarded as sufficiently demonstrated if the Commission is able to provide specific and credible evidence indicating with reasonable probability that the cartel had an impact on the market.

[116] Case T-65/98 *Van den Bergh Foods Ltd v Commission* [1998] ECR II-2641, paras 80 and 135. Interestingly, in this case, the GC has used similar language to describe the review under Art 101(1) and (3) EC—which may be indicative of similar standards—and states that the review carried out by the Court of the complex economic assessments undertaken by the Commission in the exercise of the discretion conferred on it by Art 101(3) TFEU in relation to each of the four conditions laid down therein, must be limited to ascertaining whether the procedural rules have been complied with, whether proper reasons have been provided, whether the facts have been accurately stated, and whether there has been any manifest error of appraisal or misuse of powers. See also Case T-432/05 *EMC Development AB v Commission* [2010] ECR II-1629, para 60; Case T-271/03 *Deutsche Telekom v Commission* [2008] ECR II-477, para 185; Case T-204/03 *HaladjianFrères v Commission* [2006] ECR II-3779, para 30 and the case law cited.

[117] Case T-154/98 *Asia Motor France SA, Jean-Michel Cesbron, Monin Automobiles SA and Europe Auto Service SA v Commission* [2000] ECR II-3453, para 54; Case C-269/90 *Technische Universität München* [1991] ECR I-5469, para 14; Case T-31/99 *ABB Asea Brown Boveri v Commission* [2002] ECR II-1881, para 99; Case T-343/08 *Arkema France v Commission* [2011] ECR II-2287, para 111; Case T-410/03 *Hoechst v Commission* [2008] ECR II-881. This obligation arises under the principle of sound administration; Case T-410/03 *Hoechst v Commission* [2008] ECR II-881, para 129; Case T-214/06, *Imperial Chemical Industries Ltd v Commission* [2012] OJ C209//, para 222.

[118] D Geradin and N Petit, 'Judicial Review in European Union Competition Law: A Quantitative and Qualitative Assessment', Tilburg Law and Economics Center (TILEC) Law and Economics Discussion Paper No 2011-008/Tilburg Law School Legal Studies Research Paper No 01/2011, 26 October 2010, available at <http://ssrn.com/abstract=1698342>, indicating on page 23 that many judgments of the GC dissect in the most minute details Commission decisions, and the Commission's inadequate treatment of the facts has led to the annulment of a significant number of Commission decisions both in the field of anticompetitive agreements and mergers. The authors point to the merger cases in Cases *Airtours v Commission* [2002] ECR II-2585; *Tetra Laval v Commission* [2002] ECR II-4519; and *Schneider v Commission* [2002] ECR II-4519. The GC took issue with the lack of cogent evidence supporting the assertions made by the Commission.

[119] See examples given by R Sauer in JL Schulte and C Just (eds), *Kartellrecht* (Carl Heymanns Verlag 2012), Art 31 of Reg 1/2003, para 3: Case T-235/07 *Bavaria v Commission* (determining the amount of a fine under Regulation No 1/2003) [2011] ECR II-3329, para 266; Case T-127/04 *KME Germany v Commission*

15.41 It is incumbent on the Commission to adduce evidence capable of demonstrating to the requisite legal standard the existence of circumstances constituting an infringement and it must produce sufficiently precise and consistent evidence to establish the existence of the infringement.[120] However, it is not necessary to satisfy these criteria for every item of evidence produced by the Commission in relation to every aspect of the infringement. It is sufficient if the body of evidence relied on by the institution, viewed as a whole, meets that requirement.[121] In *Sodium Chlorate*, the Court found that most of the evidence adduced by the Commission in its decision was unreliable and excessively sporadic and fragmented. Taken as a whole, the evidence adduced was not sufficiently precise and conclusive and did not found a firm conviction that Aragonesas had participated in the infringement throughout the period in question.[122] The Court only accepted that the Commission has sufficiently proven (on the basis of an acknowledgement by Aragonesas and statements and notes of the other participants) its participation in one cartel meeting. By referring to the general set up of the cartel, however, the Court found that the evidence of that single cartel meeting was sufficient to conclude that it had participated during the rest of that year (eleven months). Despite this finding, the Court annulled the fine in its entirety against Aragonesas.[123]

15.42 With respect to Article 101(3) TFEU, the review in the past seemed to be less intense.[124] The direct applicability of Article 101(3) TFEU would arguably require the GC to take a similar approach as with Article 101(1) TFEU. The GC may review the probative value of the evidence

---

[2009] ECR II-1167, para 141 (assessment of cooperation by the undertaking); and also Case T-240/07 *Heineken Nederland and Heineken v Commission* [2011] ECR II-3355, para 309; see also F Castillo de la Torre, 'Evidence, Proof and Judicial Review in Cartel Cases' (2009) 32(4) World Competition 505, 553, stating that the Commission may, in principle, choose which turnover to take in terms of territory and products in order to determine the fine, without being obliged to adhere precisely to the worldwide total turnover or turnover in the relevant product market, provided 'the choice made by the Commission is not vitiated by a manifest error of assessment'. The author points to Case T-52/02 *SNCZ v Commission* [2005] ECR II-5005, para 62 and Case T-241/01 *Scandinavian Airlines System v Commission* [2005] ECR II-2917, para 165. He adds that if the Commission makes certain claims as regards, for example, the product turnover of one undertaking, or asserts that prices were higher than they would have been, it may need to provide some evidence, but admits that no clear standards have been defined in general on these issues, and in particular on how much evidence needs to be provided and the sort of review the Commission's findings may undergo.

[120] Case T-214/06 *Imperial Chemical Industries Ltd v Commission* [2012] OJ C209/7, para 53 with more references. See in respect to Art 102 TFEU: Case T-321/05 *AstraZeneca v Commission* [2010] ECR II-2805, paras 474–7.

[121] Joined Cases T-67/00, T-68/00, T-71/00, and T-78/00 *JFE Engineering and Others v Commission* [2004] ECR II-2501, para 180, and the case law cited therein.

[122] Case T-348/08 *Aragonesas v Commission* [2011] OJ C355/15 paras 224–48.

[123] Case T-348/08 *Aragonesas v Commission* [2011] OJ C355/15, paras 90–249, especially paras 178–249; Kerse & Khan, *EC Antitrust Procedure* (6th edn, Sweet & Maxwell 2012) para 8-131.

[124] See C-D Ehlermann and I Atanasiu, 'The Modernization of EC Antitrust Law: Consequences for the Future Role and Functions of the EC Courts' [2002] European Competition Law Review 72, 74. According to these authors, the EU Courts have exercised a self-imposed limited control over Commission decisions under Art 101(3) TFEU. Reference is made to Case T-29/92 *Vereniging van Samenwerkende Prijsrege-lende Organisaties in de Bouwnijverheid and others v Commission* [1995] ECR II-289, para 288 (upheld on appeal in Case C-137/95 P *Vereniging van Samenwerkende Prijsregelende Organisaties in de Bouwnijverheid and others v Commission* [1996] ECR I-1611). The GC made the classic point that the review under Art 101(3) TFEU 'must be limited to ascertaining whether the procedural rules have been complied with, whether proper reasons have been provided, whether the facts have been accurately stated and whether there has been any manifest error of appraisal or misuse of powers.' See also Case T-65/98 *Van den Bergh Foods Ltd v Commission* [2003] ECR II-4653, para 135, and D Bailey, 'Scope of Judicial Review under Article 81 EC' [2004] Common Market Law Review 1327, 1347, pointing to the relatively few Art 101(3) TFEU decisions of the Commission which have been overturned: Case 17/74 *Transocean Marine Paint Association v Commission* [1974] ECR 1063 (procedural error); Case T-79/95 R *SNCF and BRB v Commission* [1996] ECR II-1491; and Joined Cases T-374/94, T-375/94, T-384/94, and T-388/94 *European Night Services v Commission* [1998] ECR II-3141, paras 180–9, the GC considered the Commission was wrong to conclude that the agreement was restrictive of competition within the meaning of Art 101(1). See also Joined Cases

taken into consideration by the Commission, in particular whether the efficiency gains flow-ing from an agreement outweigh its anticompetitive nature.[125] Similar to the assessment under Article 101(1) TFEU, what is fact and what comes within an assessment of facts is not always easy to decide. Where an issue involves a complex assessment which may lead two reasonable persons to disagree on the conclusions to be drawn, this may already fall outside the ambit of pure facts and could amount to an assessment of the facts. In any event, this does not relieve the Commission from the obligation to provide adequate reasons for its decision which the EU Courts consider as material to exercising their power of judicial review. Whether this opens the way to a 'normal' standard of judicial review in the context of Article 101(3) TFEU remains to be seen.[126] While the GC remains bound by its duty to control the legality of the Commission's decision, the EU Courts are unlikely to 'replace' the Commission's assessment of the four condi-tions of Article 101(3) but the Court will review the facts of the case and the interpretation of those facts by the Commission with due regard to economic theory.[127]

In *Tetra Laval*, a merger case, the ECJ summarized the scope of judicial review in competition cases as follows: **15.43**

> Whilst the Court recognises that the Commission has a margin of discretion with regard to economic matters, that does not mean that the [EU] Courts must refrain from reviewing the Commission's interpretation of information of an economic nature. Not only must the [EU] Courts, inter alia, establish whether the evidence relied on is factually accurate, reliable and consistent but also whether that evidence contains all the information which must be taken into account in order to assess a complex situation and whether it is capable of substantiating the conclusions drawn from it.[128]

T-185/00, T-216/00, T-299/00, and T-300/00 *Métropole télévision SA (M6) and others v Commission* [2002] ECR II-3805, in which the Court disagreed with the Commission's conclusion that the fourth condition of Art 101(3) (that the exempted agreement should not enable the undertakings concerned eliminate condition) was satisfied because non-members of the European Broadcasting Union ('EBU') have sufficient access to live TV rights that EBU members do not use.

[125] See Case T-65/98 *Van den Bergh Foods Ltd v Commission* [2003] ECR II-4653, para 74 (confirmed in Case C-552/03 P *Unilever Bestfoods (Former Van den Bergh Foods) v Commission* [2006] ECR I-9091): 'It is only within the specific framework of that provision that the pro and anti-competitive aspects of a restric-tion may be weighed'. See also the assessment in Joined Cases C-501/06 P, C-513/06 P, C-515/06 P, and C-519/06 P *GlaxoSmithKline Services Unlimited v Commission* [2009] ECR I-9291, para 79 et seq; Case 161/84 *Pronuptia* [1986] ECR 353, para 24; Case T-17/93 *Matra Hachette v Commission* [1994] ECR II-595, para 48; and Joined Cases T-374/94, T-375/94, T-384/94 and T-388/94 *European Night Services v Commission* [1998] ECR II-3141, para 136.

[126] In some decisions, the GC seems to consider that under both Art 101(1) and (3) TFEU, the judicial appraisal of complex matters is limited to examining whether procedural rules have been complied with, whether the Commission has accurately stated the reasons, and whether there has been any manifest error of assessment or misuse of powers. See Case T-65/98 *Van den Bergh Foods Ltd v Commission* [2003] ECR II-4653, paras 80 and 135.

[127] K Lenaerts and D Gerard, 'Decentralisation of EC Competition Law Enforcement: Judges in the Frontline' (2004) 27(3) World Competition 313, 327, n 128. See L Parret, 'Judicial Protection after Modernization of Competition Law' [2005] Legal Issues of Economic Integration 339, 363–4; see also Case T-168/01 *GlaxoSmithKline Services Unlimited v Commission* [2006] ECR II-2969, para 233 et seq where the GC held that the Commission had failed to conduct an adequate examination of GSK's notification for exemption of its sales conditions under Art 101(3). The GC concluded that the Commission's decision rejecting the application for exemption (on the basis that the first condition of Art 101(3) was not satisfied) is vitiated by a failure to conduct a proper examination. The Commission failed to take account of all the factual arguments and evidence submitted by Glaxo, it failed to refute certain substantiated arguments, and it failed to substantiate its own conclusions to the requisite legal standard. For the scope of the GC's review see also Judgment of 29 November 2012 in Case T-491/07 *CB v Commission*, para 278.

[128] Cases C-12/03 *Commission v Tetra Laval* [2005] ECR I-987, para 39. President of the GC M Jaeger, 'The Standard of Review in Competition Cases involving Complex Economic Assessments: Towards the Marginalization of the Marginal Review?' (2011) 22(4) Journal of European Competition Law & Practice

There is the suggestion that this clearly means that, while the EU Courts are ready to offer some leeway to the Commission, they will not authorize it to be careless in its assessments falling under the notion of complex economic appraisals.[129] This degree of judicial scrutiny implies that the GC would need to check whether other factors not mentioned by the Commission, or mentioned but to which the Commission did not pay proper attention, should be considered or whether other obvious elements should be taken into account.[130]

Unlimited jurisdiction

15.44 The unlimited jurisdiction conferred on the GC by Article 31 of Regulation 1/2003 in accordance with Article 261 TFEU authorizes the Court to vary the contested measure, even without annulling it, by taking into account all the factual circumstances, so as to amend the amount of the fine.[131] In exercising that jurisdiction, it may also consider questions of expediency, appropriateness, and fairness.[132] Yet, the unlimited jurisdiction does not amount to a review of the

---

295, 300–2, considers para 39 as the 'forgotten paragraph' in the sense that, while recognizing that the Commission has a certain discretion, the Courts would show 'an assured willingness to exercise a deep review' of the Commission's analysis. See also Case T-210/01 *General Electric v Commission* [2005] ECR II-5575. In this case, the same view, in even stronger terms, was also expressed by AG Tizzano, who claimed that: 'the fact that the Commission enjoys broad discretion in assessing whether or not a concentration is compatible with the common market does certainly not mean that it does not have in any case to base its conviction on solid elements gathered in the course of a thorough and painstaking investigation or that it is not required to give a full statement of reasons for its decision, disclosing the various passages of logical argument supporting the decision.' Opinion of AG Tizzano in Case C-12/03 P *Commission v Tetra Laval BV* [2005] ECR I-987, para 87; Case C-413/06 P *Bertelsmann and Sony Corporation of America v Impala* [2008] ECR I-4951, para 145; see for antitrust cases: C-386/10 P *Chalkor v Commission* [2012] OJ 32/9, para 54; Case C-272/09 P *KME Germany and Others v Commission* [2012] OJ 32/10, para 121; and state aid: Case C-525/04 P *Spain v Lenzing* [2007] ECR I-9947, paras 56 and 57. H Legal 'Standards of Proof and Standards of Judicial Review' ch 5 in BE Hawk (ed), *International Antitrust Law & Policy, 32nd Annual International Antitrust Law & Policy Conference Fordham Corporate Law Institute* (Juris Publishing 2006) 107–42, notes that this reasoning applies not only to merger cases but to all decisions involving interpretation of information of economic nature. He suggests that the Court's review aims to assess whether the material evidence is irrelevant, unreliable or otherwise insufficient to prove the point the Commission is trying to make. T Reeves and N Dodoo, 'Standards of Proof of Judicial Review in EC Merger Law' ch 6 in BE Hawk (ed), *International Antitrust Law & Policy, 32nd Annual International Antitrust Law & Policy Conference Fordham Corporate Law Institute* (Juris Publishing 2006) 117–42, note in the same context that in antitrust cases which often span several years with intensive fact-finding there might be less room for speculation than in a merger investigation which is by its very nature forward-looking.

[129] D Geradin and N Petit, 'Judicial Review in European Union Competition Law: A Quantitative and Qualitative Assessment', Tilburg Law and Economics Center (TILEC) Law and Economics Discussion Paper No 2011-008/Tilburg Law School Legal Studies Research Paper No 01/2011, 26 October 2010, 24.

[130] Case C-272/09 P *KME Germany and Others v Commission* [2012] OJ 32/4, para 102: 'In carrying out such a review, the Courts cannot use the Commission's margin of discretion—either as regards the choice of factors taken into account in the application of the criteria mentioned in the Guidelines or as regards the assessment of those factors—as a basis for dispensing with the conduct of an in-depth review of the law and of the facts.' Case C-386/10 P *Chalkor v Commission* [2012] OJ 32/9, para 62. Former President of the GC Judge Bo Vesterdorf 'Judicial Review and Competition Law—Reflections on the Role of the Community Courts in the EC system of Competition Law Enforcement', Speech at the International Forum on EC Competition Law, Brussels, 8 April 2005, argues that this may be considered as a 'slight tightening of the manifest error test.' See also the published and edited paper version of the speech in (2005) 1(2) Competition Policy International 16.

[131] Case C-534/07 P *Prym and Prym Consumer v Commission* [2009] ECR I-7415, para 86, and the case law cited; Case C-3/06 *Group Danone v Commission* [2007] ECR I-1331, para 62; Case T-252/03 *FNICGV v Commission* [2004] ECR II-3795, para 25 'an action in which the Community judicature is asked to exercise its unlimited jurisdiction with respect to a decision imposing a penalty necessarily comprises or includes a request for the annulment', cited by Kerse & Khan, *EC Antitrust Procedure* (6th edn, Sweet & Maxwell 2012) para 8-066.

[132] See Opinion of AG Kokott in C-113/04 P *Technische Unie BV v Commission* [2006] ECR I-8831, para 132.

Court's own motion. In *Group Danone*, the Court held that the EU Courts would be empowered to exercise unlimited jurisdiction where the question of the amount of the fine is before it and that the jurisdiction may be exercised to reduce that amount as well as to increase it.[133] In recent judgments, the Courts have emphasized that proceedings before the EU Courts are *inter partes*, which would imply that with the exception of pleas involving matters of public policy which the Courts are required to raise of their own motion, such as the failure to state reasons for a contested decision, it is for the applicant to raise pleas in law against the decision and to adduce evidence in support of those pleas.[134] More specifically, as regards the imposition of the fine, it is for the applicant to formulate his pleas in law and not for the GC to review of its own motion the weighting of the factors taken into account by the Commission in order to determine the amount of the fine.[135]

The Court may allow new pleas and arguments only on the twofold condition that those pleas **15.45** and arguments are effective for the purposes of that jurisdiction, and that they are not based on grounds of illegality different from those raised in the application.[136] Where a document was not expressly cited either by the Commission in the contested decision or in the statement of objections, but which none the less formed part of the Commission's administrative file, to which the applicants had access after notification of the objections, it could be taken into account by the Court in the exercise of its unlimited jurisdiction.[137]

Although the GC has full jurisdiction as a matter of law in determining the appropriate level of **15.46** fine and in verifying whether the amount of the fine imposed is in proportion to the duration and gravity of the infringement,[138] the GC has been at pains not to usurp a role which the Treaty has conferred on the Commission.[139] In this respect, the EU Courts have been mindful that fines are an instrument of competition policy and the level of fines may need to be adjusted to ensure

---

[133] Case C-3/06 *Group Danone v Commission* [2007] ECR I-1331, para 62.
[134] Case C-386/10 P *Chalkor v Commission* [2012] OJ C32/9, para 64; Case C-272/09 P *KME Germany and Others v Commission* [2012] OJ 32/10, para 131; see Case T-360/09 *E.ON Ruhrgas v Commission* [2012] OJ C243/15, para 298; Kerse & Khan, *EC Antitrust Procedure* (6th edn, Sweet & Maxwell 2012) para 8-070; as regards the issue of whether the GC is empowered to adjudicate on the amount of the fine without a request of the applicant, see also R Sauer in JL Schulte and C Just (eds), *Kartellrecht* (Carl Heymanns Verlag 2012), Art 31 of the Reg 1/2003, para 3.
[135] Case C-272/09 P *KME Germany and Others v Commission* [2012] OJ C32/10, para 63. See also Case T-372/10 *Bolloré v Commission* [2012] OJ C235/13, para 220.
[136] Case T-344/06 *Total v Commission* [2012] OJ C355/14, para 98 and Case T-343/06 *Shell Petroleum NV et al v Commission* [2012] OJ C355/14 (appeal pending, Case C-585/12 P *Shell Petroleum and Others v Commission*), para 272, referring both to Case C-104/97 P *Atlanta v European Community* [1999] ECR I-6983, paras 27–9.
[137] Case T-343/06 *Shell Petroleum NV et al v Commission* [2012] OJ C355/14 ((appeal pending, Case C-585/12 P *Shell Petroleum and Others v Commission*), para 176 (as regards the role in relation to the cartel) and 220 (as regards the appropriateness of the fine); Case C-297/98 P *SCA Holding v Commission* [2000] ECR I-10101, para 55; and Joined Cases T-236/01, T-239/01, T-244/01 to T-246/01, T-251/01, and T-252/01 *Tokai Carbon and Others v Commission* [2004] ECR II-1181 ('*Tokai I*'), para 165; and, for an application of this in relation to the role of leader, Case T-15/02 *BASF v Commission* [2006] ECR II-4971, para 354. In the Order of the President of the ECJ of 15 June 2012 in Case C-494/11 P *Otis Luxembourg and Others v Commission*, paras 35 and 46, the applicant alleged that the GC exceeded its competence in relying on evidence that was not referred to either in the contested decision or in the Commission's file. The ECJ stated the GC is entitled to examine and use evidence which is submitted to it by the parties and did not therefore exceed its competence in taking into account in the grounds of its judgment GTO's articles of association and the minutes of the board meetings which were submitted to the GC as an annex to a response to a series of questions raised by the GC by way of measures of organization of procedure.
[138] Case T-229/94 *Deutsche Bahn v Commission* [1997] ECR II-1689, para 127.
[139] Case T-150/89 *Martinelli v Commission* [1995] ECR II-1165, para 59, stating that the Commission has a margin of discretion and cannot be considered obliged to apply a precise mathematical formula when imposing a fine. See also Opinion of AG Geelhood in Case C-308/04 P *SGL Carbon AG v Commission* [2006] ECR I-5977, paras 16–19: 'the Court stated in its much-quoted judgment in *Musique Diffusion*

compliance with EU competition law.[140] In more recent judgments, it has stressed that the GC is called upon to make its own *independent* assessment.[141]

15.47 Where the Commission has not proved all of its case or where there has been some defect in reasoning in the Commission's decision which is not sufficient to justify complete annulment, the Court is ready to reduce fines.[142] The essential procedural requirement to state reasons is satisfied where the Commission indicates in its decision the factors which enabled it to determine

---

française...that the Commission's task certainly includes the duty to investigate and punish individual infringements, but also the duty to pursue a general policy designed to apply, in competition matters, the principles laid down by the Treaty and to guide the conduct of undertakings in the light of those principles...Furthermore, in assessing the gravity of an infringement for the purpose of fixing the amount of the fine, the Commission must take into consideration not only the particular circumstances of the case but also the context in which the infringement occurs and must ensure that its action has the necessary deterrent effect, especially as regards those types of infringement which are particularly harmful to the attainment of the objectives of the Community...Thus, the Court indicated in that judgment that the underlying rationale for the imposition of fines is to ensure the implementation of Community competition policy...It became clear, from that and from subsequent judgments, that numerous factors must be taken into account; that the Commission is not required to apply a precise mathematical formula...'. Case C-308/04 P *SGL Carbon AG v Commission* [2006] ECR I-5977, paras 46 and 47: 'the Commission enjoys a wide discretion as regards the method used for calculating fines and that it can, in this respect, take account of numerous factors, whilst complying with the ceiling on turnover laid down in [Regulation 17]...The [ECJ] has also stated that the calculation method set out in the Guidelines contains various flexible elements, enabling the Commission to exercise its discretion...as interpreted by the [ECJ].' Joined Cases C-189/02 P, C-202/02 P, C-205/02 P to C-208/02 P, and C-213/02 P *Dansk Rørindustri and Others v Commission* [2005] ECR I-5425, paras 240–3, and the case law cited; see also Case T-82/08 *Guardian Industries Corp et al v Commission* [2012] OJ C355/19, para 115 et seq.

[140] Case C-549/10 P *Tomra v Commission* [2012] OJ C165/6, para 105; 'the fact that the Commission has, in the past, imposed fines set at a specific level for certain categories of infringements cannot prevent it from setting fines at a higher level, if raising of penalties is deemed necessary in order to ensure the implementation of European Union competition policy, that policy continuing to be defined solely by Council Regulation [1/2003].' Case T-311/94 *BPB de Eendracht NV, formerly Kartonfabriek de Eendracht NV v Commission* [1998] ECR II-1129, para 303. D Geradin and N Petit, 'Judicial Review in European Union Competition Law: A Quantitative and Qualitative Assessment', Tilburg Law and Economics Center (TILEC) Law and Economics Discussion Paper No 2011-008/Tilburg Law School Legal Studies Research Paper No 01/2011, 26 October 2010, 12. See also B Vesterdorf 'The Court of Justice and Unlimited Jurisdiction: What Does it Mean in Practice?' (2009) June (2) Global Competition Policy (Online), Release 3, indicating that 'the exercise of the unlimited jurisdiction is, in practice, the very rare exception. This might, at least at first glance, seem somewhat at odds with Article 31, but follows in reality from the longstanding and firm case law of the [ECJ] according to which—quite correctly—it is for the Commission to decide which competition policy it finds appropriate at any given moment and in the circumstances of the market situation. Competition policy clearly also covers fining policy.'

[141] Case T-11/06 *Romana Tabacchi Srl v Commission* [2011] OJ C340/15, para 266: 'the fixing of a fine by the Court is not an arithmetically precise exercise. Furthermore, the Court is not bound by the Commission's calculations or by its Guidelines when it adjudicates in the exercise of its unlimited jurisdiction...but must make its own appraisal, taking account of all the circumstances of the case.' Judgment of GC of 17 May 2013 in Joined Cases T-147/09 and T-148/09, *Trelleborg Industrie SAS v Commission*, para 114. Case C-386/10 P *Chalkor v Commission* [2012] OJ C32/9, para 69, states that the GC is not bound by the Guidelines and is itself under a duty to verify whether the fine is proportionate in relation to the gravity of the unlawful conduct. See also Opinion of AG Bot of 21 June 2012 in Judgment of 22 November 2012 in Case C-89/11 P *E.ON Energie v Commission*, para 110, who states that '[t]he [GC] must therefore carry out *its own appraisal* and may therefore use a different calculation method even if it is less favourable for the undertaking concerned'.

[142] See Case T-311/94 *BPB de Eendracht NV, formerly Kartonfabriek de Eendracht NV v Commission* [1998] ECR II-1129, para 341 et seq: 'applicant's participation in the meetings of the JMC is proven only in regard to two of the 17 meetings of that body held during the period in which it is proved that the applicant committed an infringement of Art [101(1)]...As it is apparent...the applicant's participation in the meetings of that body was significantly more sporadic than that of the other undertakings regarded as 'ordinary members' of the cartel...Having regard to those factors, the applicant should have been regarded as having played a less significant role in the alleged cartel than that of the other undertakings considered to be "ordinary members" of it...Taking those factors into account, the Court, exercising its unlimited jurisdiction, will reduce the amount of the fine.'; Case 86/82 *Hasselblad (GB) Limited v Commission* [1984] ECR 883, para 57;

the gravity of the infringement and its duration. If those factors are not sufficiently stated, the decision is vitiated by failure to state adequate reasons.[143]

Where the Commission uses the calculation method that it has imposed on itself in the 2006 **15.48** Guidelines, it may not depart from those rules unless this is compatible with the principle of equality.[144] In this regard, a self-imposed limitation of that discretion arises inasmuch as it must then follow those guidelines.[145] The role of the GC is therefore to:

Case T-59/99 *Ventouris v Commission* [2003] ECR II-5257, paras 215–22; Case T-360/09 *E.ON Ruhrgas v Commission* [2012] OJ C243/15, paras 295–305, in particular para 300, where it states that the 'unlimited jurisdiction conferred on the Court…empowers the Court not only to carry out a simple review of the lawfulness of the penalty—which allows the Court only to dismiss the action for annulment or to annul the contested measure—but also to substitute its own appraisal for the Commission's and, consequently, to vary the contested measure—even without annulling it—in light of all the factual circumstances, by amending the fine imposed where the question of the amount of the fine is before it.' The GC confirmed the main points of the decision but found that the Commission committed an error as regards the duration of the infringement on each of the markets. See also Case C-3/06 P *Groupe Danone v Commission* [2007] ECR I-1331, paras 61 and 62, and Case C-534/07 P *Prym and Prym Consumer v Commission* [2009] ECR I-7415, para 86, and the case law cited therein.

[143] Case C-248/98 P *KNP BT v Commission* [2000] ECR I-9641, paras 42 and 45–6: 'Admittedly, the Commission cannot, by a mechanical recourse to arithmetical formulae alone, divest itself of its own power of assessment. However, it may in its decision give reasons going beyond the requirements, in particular by indicating the figures which, especially in regard to the desired deterrent effect, influenced the exercise of its discretion when setting the fines imposed on a number of undertakings which participated, in different degrees, in the infringement… It may indeed be desirable for the Commission to make use of that possibility in order to enable undertakings to acquire a detailed knowledge of the method of calculating the fine imposed on them. More generally, such a course of action may serve to render the administrative act more transparent and facilitate the exercise by the Court of First Instance of its unlimited jurisdiction, which enables it to review not only the legality of the contested decision but also the appropriateness of the fine imposed. However,…the availability of that possibility is not such as to alter the scope of the requirements resulting from the duty to state reasons.'

[144] Joined Cases C-189/02 P, C-202/02 P, C-205/02 P to C-208/02 P, and C-213/02 P *Dansk Rørindustri and Others v Commission* [2005] ECR I-5425, paras 209 and 210; Case C-520/09 P *Arkema v Commission*, paras 88 and 92: 'Guidelines merely constitute rules of practice from which the administration may not depart in an individual case without giving reasons that are compatible with the principle of equal treatment…The General Court thus in no way ruled out the possibility that the Commission, in compliance with European Union law and giving adequate reasons for so doing, may, where appropriate, use another methodology for calculating fines in the area of European Union competition law.' Case C-510/06 P *Archer Daniels Midland Co v Commission* [2009] ECR I-1843, para 60: 'The guidelines lay down rules of conduct from which the Commission cannot depart without being found to be in breach of general principles of law such as equal treatment and protection of legitimate expectations. They also provide legal certainty for the undertakings concerned.' See Case C-534/07 P *Prym and Prym Consumer v Commission* [2009] ECR I-7415, para 98: 'concerning the Commission's practice in previous decisions, suffice it to note that this does not serve as a legal framework for setting fines in competition matters, since the Commission enjoys a wide discretion in that area and, when exercising that discretion, is not bound by its past assessments.'

[145] See in respect to the 1998 Fining Guidelines: Case T-220/00 *Cheil Jedang v Commission* [2003] ECR II-2473, para 77 and the case law cited; and Case T-448/05 *Oxley Threads Ltd v* Commission [2010] ECR II-69, para 62. The 2006 fining guidelines were considered for the first time by the GC in the appeals by the alleged members of the *Sodium Chlorate* cartel (Case T-299/08 *Elf Aquitaine v Commission* [2011] ECR II-2149; Case T-343/08 *Arkema France v Commission* [2011] ECR II-2287; Case T-348/08 *Aragonesas v Commission* [2011] OJ C355/15; Case T-349/08 *Uralita SA v Commission* [2011] OJ C355/15) and by the alleged members of the *International Removal Services* cartel (Case T-199/08 *Ziegler SA v Commission* [2011] ECR II-3507; Joined Cases T-204/08 and T-212/08 *Team Relocations NV, Amertranseuro International Holdings Ltd and Others v Commission* [2011] OJ C226/24; Joined Cases T-208/08 and T-209/08 *Gosselin Group NV and Stichting Administratiekantoor Portielje v Commission* [2011] ECR II-3639 (appealed in Case C-440/11 P *Commission v Stichting Administratiekantoor Portielje and Gosselin Group NV*; see in this respect, Conclusions of AG Kokott of 29 November 2012): Cases T-210/08 *Verhuizingen Coppens NV v Commission* [2011] ECR II-3713—annulled in Judgment of 6 December 2012 in Case C-441/11 *Commission v Verhuizingen Coppens NV*—and Case T-211/08 *Putters International NV v Commission* [2011] ECR II-3729). The Court upheld the new methodology of the 2006 Fines Guidelines, confirming that the Commission has to be able to adapt the level of its fines to the needs of its enforcement policy at any time.

verify whether the Commission exercised its discretion in accordance with the method set out in the guidelines... to the extent to which it establishes any departure therefrom, to verify whether that departure is legally justified and supported by a statement of reasons to the requisite legal standard.[146]

15.49 While in exercising its jurisdiction the Court would not be bound by the Commission's Guidelines on the imposition of fines,[147] the Court has nevertheless followed the suggested approach of the Guidelines.[148] In the event that the applicant could successfully demonstrate that the Commission did not comply with the methodology set out in the Guidelines, this does not necessarily result in a reduction of fine which might have been the outcome where the Court had applied the Guidelines.[149] The Court is entitled to conduct its own assessment which may justify the production and taking into account of additional information,[150] but in most cases this does not lead to a significant reduction of a fine.[151] In most cases, the result of this form of exercise of its jurisdiction has been either full annulment or annulment of the fine as set by the Commission, replaced with a fine set by the GC. However, in fixing the new fine,

---

[146] Joined Cases T-259/02 to T-264/02 and T-271/02, *Raiffeisen Zentralbank Österreich AG et al v Commission* [2006] ECR II-5169, para 226; see also Case T-445/07 *Berning & Söhne* [2012] OJ C243/12, para 205, stating that the review is limited to obvious errors where the Commission has discretion.

[147] See, eg Case C-338/00 P *Volkswagen AG v Commission* [2003] ECR I-9189, para 147; Case 322/81 *Michelin v Commission* [1983] ECR 3461, para 111; Case T-148/94 *Preussag Stahl v Commission* [1999] ECR II-613, para 728; Case T-360/09 *E.ON Ruhrgas v Commission* [2012] OJ C243/15, para 301, stating that 'it should be observed that the Court is not bound by the Commission's calculations or by its Guidelines when it adjudicates in the exercise of its unlimited jurisdiction... but must make its own appraisal, taking account of all the circumstances of the case'; and Case T-370/09 *GDF Suez SA v Commission* [2012] OJ C243/16, para 461. Opinion of AG Mengozzi in Case C-511/06 P *Archer Daniels Midland v Commission* [2009] ECR I-5843, para 175, Opinion of AG Jacobs in Case C-167/04 P *JCB Service v Commission* [2006] ECR I-8935, para 141, and Judgment of the Court of First Instance of 12 December 2007 in Joined Cases T-101/05 and T-111/05 *BASF and UCB v Commission* [2007] ECR II-4949, para 213. See judgments of the ECJ of 30 May 2013 in Case C-70/12 P *Quinn Barlo Ltd v Commission*, para 53 stating that the Commission 'must observe the principle of the protection of legitimate expectations when it applies its self-imposed guidelines, that principle cannot bind the Courts of the Union in the same way, in so far as they do not propose to apply a specific method of setting fines in the exercise of their unlimited jurisdiction, but consider case by case the situations before them, taking account of all the matters of fact and of law relating to those situations.'

[148] Case T-220/00 *Cheil Jedang v Commission* [2003] ECR II-2473, paras 48–60, in which the GC sets out the methodology used by the Commission under the 1998 Guidelines; see also B Vesterdorf 'The Court of Justice and Unlimited Jurisdiction: What Does it Mean in Practice?' (2009) June (2) Global Competition Policy (Online), Release 3; Kerse & Khan, *EC Antitrust Procedure* (6th edn, Sweet & Maxwell 2012) paras 8-073–8-075, on the influence of the Commission's Fining Guidelines.

[149] A Scordamaglia, 'Cartel Proof, Imputation and Sanctioning in European Competition Law: Reconciling Effective Enforcement and Adequate Protection of Procedural Guarantees' (2011) 7(1) Competition Law Review 5, 43, indicates that fines are appealed in approximately 90 per cent of the Commission decisions, approximately 60 per cent of which are successful, with an average fine reduction of 19 per cent pointing to a study by C Veljanovski, 'European Cartel Prosecutions and Fines, 1998–2007—A Statistical Analysis' (2007), n 239 available at <http://papers.ssrn.com>.

[150] Case C-297/98 P *SCA Holding v Commission* [2000] ECR I-10101, paras 53–5. Where the Court recalculates the fine, it has to respect the principle of equality and the exercise of the unlimited jurisdiction shall not give rise to discrimination between the undertakings (Case T-362/06 *Ballast Nedam Infra v Commission* [2012] OJ C355/19, para 143).

[151] See the rulings in the synthetic rubber cartel: Case T-45/07 *Trade-Stomil v Commission* [2011] ECR II-4629, paras 48–68; Case T-44/07 *Kaucuk* [2011] ECR II-4601, paras 48–68. The Court annulled the fines for the two undertakings *Trade-Stomil1* and *Kaucuk/Unipetrol*, which participated in the cartel for respectively three months and three years. Although the Court recognized that there are elements in the file that have a certain probative value, it considered that in view of the lack of sufficiently specific proof and some contradictions in the evidence used in establishing their participation in the particularly important/core cartel meeting, there was a doubt as to the companies' participation which should be to their benefit. The evidence regarding the other meetings in which Kaucuk participated did not convince the Court either. See also the rulings in *Copper Fittings* cartel: Case T-385/06 *Aalberts Industries and Others v Commission* [2011] ECR II-1223, paras 47–69 and 83–119. The Court annulled the decision for *Aalberts* in its entirety and

the GC, in nearly all cases, simply applies the guidelines. Thus, instead of sending the case back to the Commission to allow it to recalculate the fine (which it would need to do if it lacked full jurisdiction), the GC applies its unlimited jurisdiction and recalculates the fine on the basis of the corrected facts (eg duration), but it does so still in application of the guidelines rather than applying its own methodology.[152]

In *Archer Daniels Midland*, the GC found that the Commission did not take account of **15.50** the turnover of each undertaking from sales in the market concerned by the infringement, namely the lysine market in the European Economic Area ('EEA'), but concluded that this failure to adhere to the Guidelines did not lead to a breach of the principle of proportionality in setting the fine.[153] In the same case, however, the GC found that the Commission did not apply the reductions granted on account of mitigating circumstances in the same way to all the undertakings concerned. It stated that the percentage increases or reductions adopted on account of aggravating or mitigating circumstances must be applied to the basic amount of the fine, determined by reference to the gravity and duration of the infringement, and not to the amount of an increase previously applied in respect of the duration of the infringement or to the figure resulting from the first increase or reduction adopted to reflect an aggravating or a mitigating circumstance. That method of calculating the fines should ensure equal treatment between the various undertakings participating in one and the same cartel.[154] In *Volkswagen*, the Court reduced the fine imposed on Volkswagen to EUR 90 million, in particular because it found that the infringement had lasted for only three years (from 1993 to 1996). However, the reduction granted was less than it could have been using the method set out in the 1998

---

partially for its subsidiaries, *Simplex* and *Aquatis*, because their participation in the cartel for the nine-month (post-inspection) period had not been established to the requisite legal standard. The Court found that, whereas *Aquatis* did indeed participate in one of the three aspects of the infringement (meeting of the professional organization, the other two being participation in anticompetitive bilateral contacts and contacts during a trade fair), this was not sufficient to conclude that it participated in the infringement, unless it was established that it knew or should have known that this behaviour was part of an overall plan made up of different parts that had a common purpose. As regards *Simplex*, the Court considered that its participation had not been proven to the requisite legal standard, highlighting in particular that a statement made in connection with a leniency application is not sufficient evidence in itself if the accuracy of that statement has been contested. The Commission appealed the ruling. Opinion of AG Mengozzi in Judgment of 28 February 2013 in Case C-287/11 P *Commission v Aalberts Industries NV*.

152 See also B Vesterdorf 'The Court of Justice and Unlimited Jurisdiction: What Does it Mean in Practice?' (2009) June (2) Online Magazine for Global Competition Policy Release 4. Vesterdorf indicates that quite often the Court may have found that the infringement in question had not been proven by the Commission to have lasted as long as postulated in the Commission decision. In such a case, the consequence would normally simply be that the fine is reduced to correspond to the period for which there was sufficient proof. If the decision and the fine were based on an alleged infringement period of five years, but the GC only found proof for four years, the fine will be reduced by one fifth. The same method is applied by the GC if it only finds proof of collusion concerning price fixing but not, as alleged in the Decision, of any clear effect of the price fixing on market prices. If the Decision, basing itself not only on object but also on effect, had increased the fine using the alleged effect as an aggravating circumstance, the GC can normally be expected to eliminate that increase in deciding the new fine. The same will be done if, for instance, the turnover for the product in question is found to be smaller than indicated in the Decision as an element for the calculation of the fine. A new fine will be calculated based on the smaller turnover. See, for an example in which the GC applied a further 10 per cent reduction for cooperation under the Leniency Notice: Case T-37/05 *World Wide Tobacco España, SA v Commission* [2012] ECR II-41, para 198, confirmed on appeal Case C-240/11 P *World Wide Tobacco España, SA v Commission*, [2012] OJ 303/4; Case T-452/05 *BST v Commission* [2010] ECR II-1373, paras 136–53. Where the GC granted BST, for its cooperation, a 10 per cent reduction in its fine, in addition to the 20 per cent reduction already granted.

153 Case T-224/00 *Archer Daniels Midland Company v Commission* [2003] ECR II-2597, paras 197–206.

154 See the Lysine cartel cases: Case T-220/00 *Cheil Jedang v Commission* [2003] ECR II-2473, para 229; see also Case T-224/00 *Archer Daniels Midland v Commission* [2003] ECR II-2597, para 378; Case T-230/00 *Daesang Corporation and Sewon Europe GmbH v Commission* [2003] ECR II-2733, para 152. In Case T-33/05 *Cetarsa v Commission* [2011] ECR II-12 (summary publication) the GC found that the Commission had not

Guidelines.[155] Thus, the reduction of the fine did not necessarily have to be proportionate to the reduction in the infringement period (which the Commission had taken into account) or correspond to the method of calculation which it had used. The ruling in *Dalmine* is an example of where the GC effectively reduced the fine using the Commission method to take account of the fact that the duration of the infringement found was erroneously fixed at four years instead of five.[156] Where the Court reviews the imposition of fines on several undertakings, it needs to give reasons if it departs from the methodology applied by the Commission in regard to any of the undertakings concerned.[157] These cases show that an applicant may be in a better position if it is able to obtain a reduction of a fine where it can be demonstrated that the infringement has not occurred to the extent alleged by the Commission (eg, with regard to duration where the Court often shortens the length of participation in the infringements for several companies). In most cases it happened because the Court did not accept the evidence used by the Commission to establish the starting date of the infringement as being up to the requisite legal standard.[158] Conversely, it may be more difficult to have the fine reduced on grounds that the infringement did not have the gravity alleged by the Commission.[159] The way of correcting the fines is a formal

---

sufficiently taken into account Cetarsa's cooperation in fine mitigation, making a manifest error of assessment when concluding that Cetarsa had contested certain facts in the statement of objections.

[155] Case T-62/98 *Volkswagen v Commission* [2000] ECR II-2707, para 347; confirmed by the ECJ in Case C-338/00 P *Volkswagen v Commission* [2003] ECR I-9189, para 146, where the Court pointed out that the exercise of unlimited jurisdiction should not result in discrimination between undertakings and that, if the GC intended, in the case of one of those undertakings, to depart specifically from the method of calculation followed by the Commission, which it had not called into question, it should have given reasons for doing so in the judgment under appeal. See also Case C-310/93 P *BPB Industries Plc and British Gypsum Ltd v Commission* [1995] ECR I-865, para 34.

[156] See the Seamless Steal Tube cartel cases: Case T-50/00 *Dalmine v Commission* [2004] ECR II-2395, paras 347–9; Case T-44/00 *Mannesmann v Commission* [2004] ECR II-2223, paras 314–16; Case T-48/00 *Corus UK Ltd, formerly British Steel plc v Commission* [2004] ECR II-2325, paras 219–21; Joined Cases T-67/00, T-68/00, T-71/00, and T-78/00 *JFE Engineering Corp and others v Commission* [2004] ECR II-2501, paras 588–90.

[157] Case C-291/98 P *Sarrió v Commission* [2000] ECR I-9991, para 98.

[158] Case T-44/00 *Mannesmannröhren-Werke AG v Commission* [2004] ECR II-2223, paras 259–70, in which the GC concluded that the correct duration of the infringement found was four years. The fine imposed on Mannesmann had therefore to be reduced accordingly. See the rulings in the *Plastic industrial bags* cartel: in November 2011, the GC reduced the fine imposed on Low & Bonar from EUR 12.24 million to EUR 9.18 million on the basis that the Commission had erred in finding that, prior to its attendance at an EU trade association meeting in November 1997, it had known, or ought to have known, that by participating in earlier national association meetings, it was joining a wider EU cartel. Therefore, it had not participated in a single and continuous infringement before November 1997. The GC also annulled the EUR 2.37 million fine imposed on Stempher on the basis that the Commission had not produced sufficiently precise and convincing evidence to establish Stempher's participation in the infringements after 20 June 1997, being the date five years before the Commission's first investigative steps. Therefore, the five-year limitation period in Art 25 of Reg 1/2003 applied and the Commission was precluded from fining Stempher. Case T-59/06 *Low & Bonar and Bonar Technical Fabrics v Commission* [2012] OJ C6/10; Case T-68/06 *Stempher and Koninklijke Verpakkingsindustrie Stempher v Commission* [2012] OJ C6/10. See also the fine reductions in Case T-53/06 *UPM-Kymmene Oyj v Commission* [2012] OJ C118/21 and Case T-64/06 *FLS Plast A/S v Commission* [2012] OJ C118/21. The Court, however, rejected all the arguments advanced by the other undertakings and decided, as a consequence, to uphold the fines imposed on them.

[159] Case T-59/99 *Ventouris v Commission* [2003] ECR II-5257, para 219, punished in like manner the undertakings which participated in two infringements and those which participated in only one of them, in disregard of the principle of proportionality. However, for reasons of equity and proportionality, the Court held that it is important that the companies whose involvement is limited to a single cartel are punished less severely than the companies which participated in all of the agreements at issue. The Commission cannot punish with the same degree of severity the companies which the Decision charges with two infringements and those which, like the applicant, are charged with only one. In Joined Cases T-67/00, T-68/00, T-71/00, and T-78/00 *JFE Engineering Corp and others v Commission* [2004] ECR II-2501, paras 566–88, the Court found that the Commission had violated the principle of equal treatment by omitting to take account of the European producers' second infringement (the contracts relating to the UK market) in determining the amount of the fine. Recognizing that the appropriate way of restoring a fair balance between the addressees of

exercise of the unlimited jurisdiction but, in reality, simply consists of adjusting the fine relative to errors found in the calculation or in the basis for the calculation made by the Commission. According to the former President of the GC Vesterdorf, it does not imply any independent and specific appraisal of the seriousness or lack thereof of the conduct to be sanctioned; neither the ECJ nor the GC has been easily convinced of arguments based on fines alleged to be excessive because of the very high levels at which fines are now increasingly often being set.[160]

Where the Commission asks the Court to exercise its unlimited discretion under Article 261 **15.51** TEFU and increase the fine imposed on an undertaking, the Court seems generally less inclined to accede to such requests.[161] In this regard, increase often means the withdrawal of a reduction which the Commission granted to an undertaking for not contesting the facts during the administrative procedure. One issue which arises in this context is whether an undertaking which received a reduction under the Leniency Notice during the administrative procedure may be estopped from contesting before the Courts the fact that it did not dispute or acknowledge it before the Commission, or whether this should open the way to a removal of the reduction.[162] In *Stora Kopparbergs Bergslags (Cartonboard)*, the GC held that the risk that an undertaking which has been granted a reduction in its fine in recognition of its cooperation will subsequently seek annulment of the decision finding the infringement of the competition rules and imposing a penalty on the undertaking responsible for the infringement, and will succeed before the EU Courts on appeal, is a normal consequence of the exercise of the remedies.[163] However, the mere fact that an undertaking has been successful before the EU Courts should not justify a fresh review of the size of the reduction granted to it.[164]

The issue of whether an undertaking can go back on its cooperation under the Leniency Notice **15.52** and claim before the Court that it had not participated in an infringement came before the Court again in *Tokai Carbon*. In this case, the Commission requested the GC to increase by 10 per cent the fine imposed on Nippon, which challenged the findings in respect of the duration of its infringement after having obtained a reduction of the same amount under the Leniency Notice. During the administrative procedure, Nippon had not disputed the facts on which the Commission based its allegations in the statement of objections, but it did not expressly accept them either. Referring to its earlier ruling in *SCA Holding*,[165] the Court held that where the undertaking does not expressly accept the facts, the Commission must prove the facts and the

---

its decision would have been to increase the amount of the fine imposed on each of the European producers, it finally decided for procedural reasons to reduce the amount decided on by the Commission in respect of the gravity of the infringement. Thus, in view of the fact that the Commission had not pleaded in its arguments that the amount of the fine should be revised upwards in this case, the Court held that the most suitable way of remedying the unequal treatment as between the European and Japanese producers was to reduce the amount of the fine imposed on each of the Japanese producers by 10 per cent.

[160] B Vesterdorf 'The Court of Justice and Unlimited Jurisdiction: What Does it Mean in Practice?' (2009) June (2) Global Competition Policy (Online), Release 5.

[161] For a case where the fine was increased, see Joined Cases T-101/05 and T-111/05 *BASF and UCB v Commission* [2007] ECR II-49449, para 24, 212–23: see also Case T-216/06 *Lucite v Commission* [2011] OJ C311/32, para 174 and Case T-41/05 *Alliance One International, Inc v Commission* [2011] OJ C347/26, paras 189 and 197, where the Commission request to increase the fine was rejected. E Barbier de la Serre and C Winckler, 'A Landmark Year for the Law on Fines imposed in EU Competition Proceedings' (2012) 3(4) Journal of European Competition Law & Practice 351, 368–9; Kerse & Khan, *EC Antitrust Procedure* (6th edn, Sweet & Maxwell 2012) para 8-079.

[162] See R Sauer in JL Schulte and C Just (eds), *Kartellrecht* (Carl Heymanns Verlag 2012), Art 31 of Reg 1/2003, para 5, with more references.

[163] Case T-354/94 *Stora Kopparbergs Bergslags v Commission* [2002] ECR II-843, para 67.

[164] Case T-61/99 *Adriatica di Navigazione v Commission* [2003] ECR II-5349, para 209 (confirmed in Case C-111/04 P *Adriatica di Navigazione v Commission* [2006] ECR I-22) referring to Case T-354/94 *Stora Kopparbergs Bergslags v Commission* [2002] ECR II-843, para 85.

[165] Case C-297/98 P *SCA Holding v Commission* [2000] ECR I-10101, para 37.

undertaking would be free to put forward any plea in its defence which it deems adequate.[166] Since Nippon did not 'expressly', 'clearly', and 'specifically' acknowledge its participation in the cartel during the procedure before the Commission, it was not prevented from contesting the evidence put forward by the Commission.[167] However, the Court stated that the Commission could take the view on the basis of the facts presented during the administrative procedure that Nippon participated in the cartel, irrespective of Nippon challenging certain facts. The GC partially allowed the request of the Commission to withdraw the reduction of the fine initially granted by the Commission to Nippon and increased Nippon's fine by 2 per cent. According to the Court, the Commission could establish that Nippon participated in the cartel during the relevant period and, secondly, Nippon's challenge made it necessary for the Commission to draft a defence dealing specifically with Nippon's challenge of facts which it considered that Nippon would no longer question.[168] The Court did not see a conflict with its earlier ruling in *Stora Kopparbergs Bergslags* because this latter case did not deal with the issue of fine reduction. Thus, the GC reiterated its right to increase the amount of the fine imposed on an undertaking which, after having had the benefit of a reduction in its fine in return for not having disputed the substantive truth of the facts established previously by the Commission, calls into question the accuracy of those facts for the first time before the GC.[169] On the other hand, in *Schunk*, the GC did not see any grounds to cancel the fine because Schunk had earlier expressly acknowledged certain facts and would now be barred from putting forward pleas disputing those facts in proceedings before the Court.[170] In the same ruling the Court held that the Commission was constrained

---

[166] Joined Cases T-236/01, T-239/01, T-244/01 to T-246/01, T-251/01, and T-252/01 *Tokai Carbon v Commission (Graphite Electrodes)* [2004] ECR II-1181, para 108.

[167] Joined Cases T-236/01, T-239/01, T-244/01 to T-246/01, T-251/01, and T-252/01 *Tokai Carbon v Commission (Graphite Electrodes)* [2004] ECR II-1181, para 109: 'Nippon's participation in the cartel between May 1992 and March 1993 was inferred by the Commission not from a clear and precise statement made by Nippon, referring expressly to that period, but from a range of evidence such as its conduct towards the Commission during the administrative procedure and its rather general no-contest statements. In those circumstances, Nippon cannot be prevented from pleading before the Court that that range of evidence was misinterpreted as proving its participation during the abovementioned period.'

[168] Joined Cases T-236/01, T-239/01, T-244/01 to T-246/01, T-251/01, and T-252/01 *Tokai Carbon v Commission (Graphite Electrodes)* [2004] ECR II-1181, para 112.

[169] Joined Cases T-236/01, T-239/01, T-244/01 to T-246/01, T-251/01, and T-252/01 *Tokai Carbon v Commission (Graphite Electrodes)* [2004] ECR II-1181, para 113: 'It should be pointed out, in that regard, that the judgment [in *Stora Kopparbergs Bergslags*] against which the appeal had been brought, had not adjudicated on the appropriateness or otherwise of the reduction of the fine granted to the undertaking in return for its cooperation and that the judgment of the [GC in *Stora Kopparbergs Bergslags*] which set aside in part the judgment of the [GC], had likewise not dealt with the problem of the reduction of the fine. Having regard to that particular procedural situation, the fact that the [GC] refused ... to embark upon a fresh review of the size of the reduction granted to the applicant in that case must not be interpreted as meaning that the [GC] cannot in any circumstances, in the exercise of its unlimited jurisdiction, increase the amount of the fine imposed on an undertaking which, after having had the benefit of a reduction in its fine in return for not having disputed the substantive truth of the facts established by the Commission during the administrative procedure, calls in question the veracity of those facts for the first time before the [GC].' In Case T-241/01 *SAS v Commission* [2005] ECR II-2917, paras 238–43, the Court found that the arguments of the applicant in this action could not therefore be regarded as a withdrawal of its acquiescence capable of justifying withdrawal of the 10 per cent reduction in its fine which was granted by the Commission. It would have only questioned whether the market sharing agreement had an impact.

[170] Case T-69/04 *Schunk v Commission* [2008] ECR II-2567, paras 251–9, see also paras 80, 81, and 84–5, stating that 'where the undertaking involved does not expressly acknowledge the facts, the Commission will have to prove those facts and the undertaking is free to put forward, at the appropriate time and in particular in the procedure before the Court, any plea in its defence which it deems appropriate. However, it follows that this cannot be the case where the undertaking at issue acknowledges the facts ... That case-law does not seek to restrict the bringing of actions by an undertaking sanctioned by the Commission, but to clarify the scope of the challenge which may be brought before the Court, in order to prevent the determination of the facts at the origin of the infringement concerned from being shifted from the Commission to the Court'.

to draw up a defence dealing with a challenge to facts, which it was entitled to consider that the applicant would no longer call into question, which would not be such as to justify, in the light of the two exclusive criteria for determining the amount of the fine, an increase of that fine.[171]

In its appeal in *Tomkins*, the Commission alleged that the GC had infringed the rule prohib- **15.53** iting a court from ruling *ultra petita* (the Court may not award more than the applicant actually requested) where it granted the parent company Tomkins the benefit of the partial fine reduction in reaction to the subsidiary.[172] The GC previously found that the Commission had erred in relation to the duration of the participation of Tomkins' subsidiary (Pegler) in the cartel and adjusted the fine. Since Tomkin was not held liable for the cartel on account of its direct participation in the cartel's activities, but held liable for the infringement only as parent company by virtue of Pegler's participation in the cartel, the GC took the view that Tomkins' liability could not exceed that of Pegler and that Tomkins had the benefit of the partial annulment of the Commission decision in relation to Pegler. Rejecting the argument of the Commission that a case lodged by one entity within a group does not affect the legal position of other entities within the same undertaking, the ECJ noted that in a situation in which the liability of the parent company is wholly derived from that of its subsidiary, and in which both of those companies have brought actions seeking, *inter alia*, that the GC reduce the fine by reason of a reduction in the duration of the infringement committed by the subsidiary, the notion of the 'same object' would not require that the scope of the applications of those companies, and the arguments on which they relied to contest the duration of the infringement, should be identical. Therefore, the ECJ ruled that the GC had been entitled, without ruling *ultra petita*, to take account of the outcome of the action brought by Pegler and to annul the contested decision.[173]

See R Sauer in JL Schulte and C Just (eds), *Kartellrecht* (Carl Heymanns Verlag 2012), Art 31 of Reg 1/2003, para 5, n 40, who raises the question of whether this view will still prevail after the ruling in Case C-407/08 P *Knauf Gips v Commission* [2010] ECR I-6375, paras 80 et seq and 90 ('there is no requirement under the law of the European Union that the addressee of the statement of objections must challenge its various matters of fact or law during the administrative procedure, if it is not to be barred from doing so later at the stage of judicial proceedings...Although an undertaking's express or implicit acknowledgement of matters of fact or of law during the administrative procedure before the Commission may constitute additional evidence when determining whether an action is well founded, it cannot restrict the actual exercise of a natural or legal person's right to bring proceedings before the General Court under the fourth paragraph of Article 263 TFEU.'); see also Case T-343/06 *Shell Petroleum NV et al v Commission* [2012] OJ C 355/14, para 116 (appeal pending, Case C-585/12 P *Shell Petroleum and Others v Commission*), where the Court added, however, that in the exercise of its unlimited jurisdiction, the Court might take account, where relevant, of an undertaking's lack of cooperation and consequently increase the fine imposed on it for infringement of Arts 101 or 102 TFEU, on condition that that undertaking has not been punished in respect of that same conduct by a specific fine based on the provisions of Art 23(1) of Reg No 1/2003.

[171] Case T-69/04 *Schunk v Commission* [2008] ECR II-2567, para 262, adding the expenses incurred by the Commission as a result of the proceedings before the Court would not be a criterion for determining the amount of the fine and must only be taken into account when applying the provisions of the Rules of Procedure relating to costs.

[172] Case C-286/11 P *Commission v Tomkins plc* [2013] OJ C/1/4.

[173] Case C-286/11 P *Commission v Tomkins plc* [2013] OJ C71/4, paras 32–50. The ECJ distinguished the situation in this case from that in other cases in which the *ultra petita* principle has been applied (paras 47 and 48). See in Case C-310/97 P *Commission v AssiDomän Kraft Products and Others* [1999] ECR I-5363, where AssiDomän Kraft Products AB and six other Swedish companies had not brought an action against the Commission's decision, which was annulled in part following an action brought by other undertakings; Joined Cases C-201/09 P and C-216/09 P *ArcelorMittal Luxembourg v Commission* and *Commission v ArcelorMittal Luxembourg and Others* [2011] ECR I-2239, the ECJ found that the case concerned a different legal issue that related to the suspension of the limitation period for the enforcement of penalties. While that case concerned three companies belonging to the same group the Commission's initial decision was directed exclusively against one of those companies, and that decision had been annulled by the GC with regard to that company alone. Therefore, no effect with regard to the other two companies could be inferred from that annulment.

15.54   As regards the ECJ, in the context of an appeal its role is twofold: first, to examine the extent to which the GC took into consideration, in a legally correct manner, all the essential factors to assess, for example, the infringement; and, second, to consider whether the GC responded to a sufficient legal standard to all the arguments raised by the appellant with a view to having the fine cancelled or reduced.[174] In *Volkswagen*, the ECJ stressed that when ruling on questions of law in the context of an appeal, it would not substitute, on grounds of fairness, its own assessment for that of the GC exercising its unlimited jurisdiction to rule on the amount of fines imposed on undertakings for infringements of EU law. At the appeal stage, therefore, the Court would not examine whether the amount of the fine fixed by GC, in the exercise of its unlimited jurisdiction, is proportionate in relation to the gravity and duration of the infringement as established by the GC on completion of its appraisal of the facts.[175] An appeal is inadmissible where it simply repeats or reproduces verbatim the pleas in law and arguments already put forward before the GC, including those which were based on facts expressly rejected by that Court. According to the ECJ, such an appeal would amount in reality to no more than a request for re-examination of the application submitted to the GC.[176] By contrast, where an appellant challenges the interpretation or the application of EU law by the GC, the points of law examined at first instance could be discussed again in the course of an appeal.[177]

2. Measures against which actions may be brought: *locus standi*

Actionable measures

15.55   Article 263 TFEU provides that '[t]he Court of Justice shall review the legality of acts of the...Commission other than recommendations or opinions'. The ECJ has made clear that '[a]s far as individuals are concerned, such measures must be in the nature of decisions and capable of affecting the applicant's interests by bringing about a significant change in his

---

[174] Cases C-322/07 P, C-327/07 P, and C-338/07 P *Papierfabrik August Koehler AG, Bolloré SA, Distribuidora Vizcaína de Papeles SL v Commission* [2009] ECR I-7191, para 125; see also Joined Cases C-204/00 P, C-205/00 P, C-211/00 P, C-213/00 P, C-217/00 P, and C-219/00 P *Aalborg Portland A/S and others v Commission* [2004] ECR I-123, para 47. See also Opinion of AG Geelhoed in Case C-407/04 P *Dalmine SpA v Commission* [2007] ECR I-829, para 296, stating that the ECJ would have only 'reason to substitute its own view for that of the [GC] only if there has been a manifest error of assessment of the facts or a manifest error of law'. R Sauer in JL Schulte and C Just (eds), *Kartellrecht* (Carl Heymanns Verlag 2012), Art 31 of the Reg 1/2003, para 7; see also Kerse & Khan, *EC Antitrust Procedure* (6th edn, Sweet & Maxwell 2012) para 8-055.Under Art 61 of the Statute of the Court of Justice, the ECJ must quash the GC's decision if an appeal is well founded. The ECJ may then give final judgment on the matter where it has sufficient information or refer the case back to the GC for judgment. In this respect, see Judgment of 6 December 2012 in Case C-441/11 P *Commission v Verhuizingen Coppens*, where the ECJ revised the fine.
[175] Case C-338/00 P *Volkswagen v Commission* [2003] ECR I-9189, para 151. See also Judgment of 22 November 2012 in Case C-89/11 P *E.ON Energie AG v Commission*, para 112, stating at para 126 that 'only inasmuch as the Court of Justice considers that the level of the penalty is not merely inappropriate, but also excessive to the point of being disproportionate, would it have to find that the General Court erred in law, due to the inappropriateness of the amount of a fine.'
[176] Judgment of 22 November 2012 in Case C-89/11 P *E.ON Energie AG v Commission*, para 112; see also Order of the ECJ of 13 December 2012 in Case C-593/11 P *Alliance One International Inc v Commission*, para 35: 'Therefore, inasmuch as, firstly, by the arguments thus relied on, AOI is in fact seeking a fresh assessment of the facts and, secondly, has in no way explained how the GC distorted the evidence, those arguments must be rejected as inadmissible'; Order of the ECJ of 13 December 2012 in Case C-654/11 P *Transcatab SpA v Commission*, para 39. See also Judgment of 14 March 2013 in Case C-276/11 P *Viega v Commission GmbH & Co KG*, para 28 et seq, stating that the ECJ cannot review the GC's factual assessments in the absence of evidence that the GC distorted the evidence.
[177] Judgment of 22 November 2012 in Case C-89/11 P *E.ON Energie AG v Commission*, para 113; see also Opinion of AG Sharpston of 30 May 2013 in Case C-58/12 P *Groupe Gascogne v Commission*, para 98 et seq where the AG took the view that for example an applicant is not precluded from raising the failure to adjudicate the case in reasonable time for the first time on appeal before the ECJ because the overall length of the proceedings would only be known when the GC renders its ruling.

legal position'.[178] The Court has adopted a broad interpretation of the nature of Commission measures against which actions may be brought, which is not confined to final formal decisions, but extends to certain decisions cloaked in administrative letters,[179] 'certain regulations',[180] and even 'other acts'.[181]

Regulation 1/2003 requires the Commission to adopt a formal decision in a number of circumstances, in particular where a fine is being imposed, but does not expressly provide for a similar requirement in all situations that may arise, although the Commission's act may affect the legal position of the parties to whom it is addressed. Thus, there may be measures that the Commission may take which may be decisions, though neither Regulation 1/2003 nor Regulation 773/2004 expressly refers to them. The important question in deciding whether a measure constitutes an actionable decision under Article 263 TFEU is not the form, but rather whether the content or substance of the measure itself is of direct and individual concern to an individual.[182] According to the Courts, the two main criteria for a measure to constitute a decision capable of being challenged under Article 263 TFEU are: (i) that it must constitute the Commission's final position—an aspect which is particularly important in the case of measures or decisions which go through various stages—and; (ii) that it produces binding legal effects capable of affecting the interests of the parties and clearly altering their legal position.[183] The particular form in which acts and decisions are adopted is, in principle, immaterial as regards the possibility of their being challenged by an action for annulment.[184] In accordance with those two criteria, various forms of administrative letters have been regarded as decisions capable of being subject to judicial review, for example administrative letters originally

15.56

---

[178] Case 60/81 *IBM v Commission* [1981] ECR 2639, para 9.

[179] However, it is not sufficient for a letter to have been sent by an EU institution to its addressee in response to a request from the latter for such a letter to be classifiable as a decision within the meaning of Art 263. See Case C-25/92 *Miethke v Parliament* [1993] ECR I-473, and Case T-83/92 *Zunis Holdings and others v Commission* [1993] ECR II-1169, para 30. More recently, Order of 12 March 2012 in Case T-42/11 *Universal Corp v Commission*, where the GC concluded that the Commission's letters requesting payment of the fine (and default interest) did not contain any decision which may be the subject of an action for annulment as they did not produce legal effects which changed Universal's legal position. Therefore, the action was inadmissible.

[180] See, eg outside the context of competition rules, Case 101/76 *Koninklijke Scholten Honig NV v Council and Commission* [1977] ECR 797, concerning an action for the annulment of an article of an agricultural Regulation. By virtue of Art 241 it would be possible for an undertaking to challenge an act which affects it individually if it is understood to have been adopted on the basis of an unlawful provision of a regulation.

[181] As stated in Case 60/81 *IBM v Commission* [1981] ECR 2639, para 9, and, even more explicitly, outside the sphere of competition rules, in its judgment in Case 22/70 *Commission v Council (ERTA)* [1971] ECR 263, paras 39–42, in which the delimitation of the external powers of each of those institutions was in issue.

[182] See Case T-37/92 *BEUC and another v Commission* [1994] ECR II-285, para 38. In its defence, the Commission had contended that the letter at issue could not constitute a decision because it had been signed by a Director-General of DG COMP. The GC held that the argument was not relevant to the examination of the admissibility of the action against that letter. I Parret, 'Judicial Protection after Modernization of Competition Law' [2005] Legal Issues of Economic Integration 339, 357, takes the view that the decisive criterion should be whether the decisions of the Commission contains an assessment of the factual and legal position of a party in such a way that this has consequences not only for the parties but possibly for third parties' rights.

[183] See Case 60/81 *IBM v Commission* [1981] ECR 2639; Case T-64/89 *Automec Srl v Commission I* [1990] ECR II-367, para 42; Joined Cases T-10/92 to T-12/92 and T-15/92 *Cimenteries v Commission III* [1992] ECR II-2667, para 28; and Case T-2/92 *Rendo v Commission* [1994] ECR II-2417, para 40. See also Case T-83/92 *Zunis Holdings v Commission* [1993] ECR II-1169, para 30; Case T-186/94 *Guérin Automobiles v Commission* [1995] ECR II-1753, para 39; Case T-241/97 *Stork Amsterdam BV v Commission* [2000] ECR II-309, para 49; and Joined Cases C-68/94 and C-30/95 *France and others v Commission* [1998] ECR I-1375, para 62.

[184] Case T-241/97 *Stork Amsterdam BV v Commission* [2000] ECR II-309, para 49; Case T-64/89 *Automec Srl v Commission I* [1990] ECR II-367, para 42; Case 60/81 *IBM v Commission* [1981] ECR 2639, para 9.

sent by the Commission under former Article 15(6) of Regulation 17—so-called 'provisional decisions';[185] a letter in which a Commission official declined to adopt interim measures because, in his view, the Commission had no powers to do so;[186] letters sent by the Commission announcing closure of the file or the rejection of complaints.[187]

15.57 The Court also held that an undertaking imposed in conjunction with a Commission decision is a measure that may be challenged under Article 263. The Commission had contended that the commitment in question constituted a unilateral act on the part of the undertakings which could not therefore be the subject of an action. The Court rejected the Commission's view outright and declared that the obligations resulting from the undertaking were to be assimilated to orders requiring infringements to be brought to an end of the kind provided for in Article 3 of Regulation 17 (Article 7 of Regulation 1/2003). Pursuing that particular course of conduct, the undertakings had, for personal reasons, agreed to acquiesce in a decision which the Commission could have adopted unilaterally.[188] The list is by no means exhaustive and the EU Courts may add to it if they consider it appropriate without the need to act according to a restrictive interpretation. With regard to the rejection of complaints, the Commission's decision will usually take the form of a letter signed by a senior official. The ECJ considers those rejections as 'decisions' for the purpose of Article 263: they have the content and effect of a decision, inasmuch as they end the investigation, contain an assessment of the agreements in question, and prevent the applicants from requiring the reopening of the investigation unless they put forward new evidence.[189]

---

[185] See Joined Cases 8–11/66 *Cimenteries v Commission I* [1967] ECR 75. See Ch 11.I.A of the first edn of this book.

[186] See Case 792/79R *Camera Care v Commission* [1980] ECR 119. Note that Art 8 of Reg 1/2003 now gives the Commission the express power to taken interim measures, but the extent to which refusals to take interim measures can be subject to judicial review remains to be seen, given that such measures are taken by the Commission 'acting on its own initiative'. See Ch 14, 'Interim Measures', para 14.09.

[187] See Case T-64/89 *Automec Srl v Commission I* [1990] ECR II-367, paras 52–8 and Case 142/84 *BAT and Reynolds v Commission* [1986] ECR 1899, para 2. The GC also treated as constituting an actionable decision statements made by the Commission spokesman concerning a concentration between air transport undertakings. See Case T-3/93 *Air France v Commission I* [1994] ECR II-121, para 44 et seq. The GC cites Joined Cases 316/82 and 40/83 *Kohler v Court of Auditors* [1984] ECR 641, in which an action brought against a purely oral decision was considered admissible. See also, for a case under state aid rules: Case C-521/06 P *Athinaïki Teckniki v Commission* [2008] ECR I-5829, where the ECJ held that a letter in which the Commission informed the complainant that it was closing the file because, on the basis of information available, there were no grounds to justify an investigation, was in fact a statement by the Commission that the review initiated had not enabled it to establish the existence of state aid within the meaning of Art 107 TFEU. In so doing it had implicitly refused to initiate the formal investigation procedure provided for in Art 108(2) TFEU. The informal nature of the decision and the fact that it left it open for the complainant to provide more information did not change its nature as a reviewable act. The ECJ therefore referred the matter back to the GC. The Commission then purported to withdraw the letter and reopen its examination of the complaint, leading the GC to dismiss the appeal, asserting that since the contested act (ie the letter) had been withdrawn, the appeal was devoid of purpose (Order of the GC of 29 June 2009 in Case T-94/05 *Athinaïki Tekniki v Commission*). In Case C-362/09 P *Athinaïki Tekniki v Commission* [2010] ECR I-13275, the ECJ annulled the GC's order stating that if the Commission were entitled to withdraw its act in those circumstances, it could perpetuate a state of inaction during the preliminary examination stage and avoid any judicial review. See V Rose in *Bellamy & Child European Competition Law of Competition, Second Cumulative Supplement* (Oxford University Press 2012) para 13.220.

[188] See Joined Cases C-89/85, C-104/85, C-114/85, C-116/85, C-117/85, and C-125/85 to C-129/85 *Ahlström, Osakeyhtiö and others v Commission* ('Woodpulp II') [1993] ECR I-1307, paras 180–2, citing the judgment in Joined Cases 6/73 and 7/73 *Istituto Chimioterapico Italiano and Commercial Solvents Corporation v Commission* [1974] ECR 223. In a different sense for Art 9 of Regulation 1/2003 decisions, see Case C-441/07 P *Commission v Alrosa* [2010] ECR I-5949 and Case T-170/06 *Alrosa v Commission* [2007] ECR II-2601(annulled) that seem to state the opposite.

[189] Case 210/81 *Demo-Studio Schmidt v Commission* [1983] ECR 3045, paras 14–15; Case 298/83 *CICCE v Commission* [1985] ECR 1105, para 18, and Joined Cases 142/84 and 156/84 *BAT and Reynolds v Commission* [1987] ECR 4487, para 12.

By virtue of these two criteria, none of the following have been regarded as decisions for the **15.58** purposes of Article 263 TFEU: the formal commencement of the procedure and the forward-ing of a statement of objections;[190] a refusal by the Commission to disclose certain documents contained in its files;[191] letters from the Commission asking complainants for submissions;[192] certain administrative letters sent by the member of the Commission responsible for compe-tition and DG COMP's staff during the investigation of a case, suggesting amendments to a notified agreement;[193] the Report of the Hearing Officer;[194] and the Commission's copying of the hard files of computers and requests for explanations from a certain individual during an inspection because these measures merely implement the decision under which the inspec-tion was ordered.[195]

In cases of acts or decisions drawn up in a procedure involving several stages, like the one **15.59** for rejecting a complaint, and particularly at the end of an internal procedure, it is generally only those measures which definitively determine the position of the institution upon the conclusion of that procedure which are open to challenge. and not intermediate measures whose purpose is to prepare for the final decision.[196] As explained,[197] during the first stage, following the lodging of the complaint, the Commission collects the information it needs to enable it to decide how to deal with the complaint. That stage may include an informal exchange of views between the Commission and the complainant, with a view to clarify-ing the factual and legal issues with which the complaint is concerned and to allowing the complainant an opportunity to expand on its allegations in the light of any initial reaction from Commission officials. These preliminary observations cannot be regarded as a measure which is open to challenge.[198] In the same vein, the existence of an internal Commission report which was used as a basis for discussion in an effort to reach a settlement with the parties involved does not confer on a provisional statement of the Commission[199] the nature

---

[190] See Case 60/81 *IBM v Commission* [1981] ECR 2639, para 21. Regarding the nature of the measure formally initiating the procedure and the nature of the statement of objections, see above, Ch 10, 'Procedures to Establish the Existence of an Infringement', para 10.01 et seq.

[191] See Joined Cases T-10/92, T-11/92, T-12/92, and T-15/92 *Cimenteries CBR SA v Commission* [1992] ECR II-2667, paras 42–8 and 53. It should be noted that the Hearing Officers will decide disputes between the parties, the information providers, and DG COMP over access to information contained in the Commission's file in accordance with the notice on access to file, the applicable regulations, and the principles laid down in the relevant case law. See Commission Notice on best practices for the conduct of proceedings concerning Articles 101 and 102 TFEU [2011] OJ C308/6, para 93.

[192] Case C-282/95 P *Guérin Automobiles v Commission* [1997] ECR I-1503, para 33 et seq.

[193] See Case T-113/89 *Nefarma v Commission* [1990] ECR II-797, paras 66–81 and Case T-116/89 *Prodifarma v Commission* [1990] ECR II-843, paras 75–87.

[194] Case T-52/03 *Knauf Gips KG v Commission* [2008] ECR II-115, para 125 and 126.

[195] Judgment of 14 November 2012 in Case T-135/09 *Nexans France SAS and Nexans SA v Commission*, paras 115–34. Judgment of 14 November 2012 in Case T-140/09 *Prysmian and Prysmian Cavi e Sistemi Energia v Commission*, paras 93–110 (in relation to the copying of the hard files of computers).

[196] However, D Geradin and N Petit, 'Judicial Remedies under EC Competition Law: Complex Issues Arising from the Modernization Process' ch 17 in BE Hawk (ed), *Annual Proceedings of the Fordham Corporate Law Institute* (Fordham University School of Law 2006) 393, 399, point out that in accordance with the *IBM* case law, acts must not always be of definitive nature for them to be challenged if they fall within a phase that can be separated from the course of the proceedings leading to the definitive act. See L Parret, 'Judicial Protection after Modernization of Competition Law' [2005] Legal Issues of Economic Integration 339, 359–61, who also argues that inter-ECN decisions should not be excluded *a priori* from judicial review; Kerse & Khan, *EC Antitrust Procedure* (6th edn, Sweet & Maxwell 2012) para 8-103.

[197] See Ch 5, 'Opening of the File and Proceedings, Transparency', para 5.12 et seq and Ch 12, 'Rejection of Complaints', para 12.03 et seq.

[198] Case T-64/89 *Automec v Commission I* [1990] ECR II-367, paras 45–6.

[199] Case T-95/99 *Satellimages TV 5 SA v Commission* [2002] ECR II-1425, paras 12–13: 'the Director in charge of the matter sent the applicant the letter...and stress[ed] that the...comments are provisional and based on the information available to [the] department at present. They do not constitute a final position of the European Commission and are subject to any further comments you or your client may wish to make.'

of a final position adopted by the Commission in relation to the complaint lodged by the applicant. The Commission is required to make a fresh analysis of the competition conditions, which will not necessarily be based on the same considerations as those underlying its previous internal report.[200] During the second stage, the Commission may indicate, in a notification to the complainant, the reasons why it does not propose to pursue the complaint, in which case it must offer the complainant the opportunity to submit any comments it may have within a time limit which it fixes for that purpose. In the third stage of the procedure, the Commission takes into consideration the observations submitted by the complainant and adopts a formal decision.

15.60 Letters setting out the Commission's views as to whether a document is protected by business secrecy and sent prior to a decision of the Hearing Officer on the matter are not actionable measures because they do not affect the undertaking's position immediately and irreversibly.[201] The refusal to give access to the Commission's file is not a reviewable act because it is a preparatory measure forming part of a preliminary administrative procedure. The Court takes the view that the Commission could rectify any procedural irregularities by subsequently granting access to the file. As a result, it could afford the undertakings concerned another opportunity to consult the file and to express their views.[202]

15.61 In *Intel Corp v Commission*, Intel challenged a decision by the Commissioner for refusing to procure, particularly from the complainant in the case, certain documentary evidence that Intel claimed to be directly relevant to the allegations made by the Commission in the statement of objections. It also contested a decision by the Hearing Officer, rejecting a submission by Intel that it cannot respond properly to the statement of objections without being provided with certain documents. The President of the GC rejected the application, stating that the decision of the Hearing Officer and the Commissioner's decision would be intermediate procedural measures taken in the context of the proceedings for the purpose of preparing the Commission's file. The Commission's proceedings may, ultimately, lead to the adoption of a decision establishing an infringement. In this respect, only measures whose legal effects are binding on the applicant would be capable of affecting its interests by bringing about a distinct change in his legal position. Only measures that definitively determine the position of the Commission on the conclusion of its procedure are open to challenge. Intermediate measures whose purpose is to prepare for the final decision cannot be challenged. Only measures that immediately and irreversibly affect the legal situation of the undertaking concerned would be of such a nature as to justify an action for annulment before the completion of the administrative procedure.[203]

---

[200] Case T-95/99 *Satellimages TV 5 SA v Commission* [2002] ECR II-1425, paras 34–41.

[201] Case T-90/96 *Automobiles Peugeot SA v Commission* [1997] ECR II-663. The letter merely stated that the Commission did not share the undertaking's point of view regarding the information which the latter maintained was protected by business secrecy, and that the Commission was prepared to communicate to the complainants more information than the applicant wished, and to allow the applicant time in which to submit its comments to the Hearing Officer.

[202] Case T-216/01 R *Reisebank AG v Commission* [2001] ECR II-3481, paras 46–8, referring to Cases T-10/92 to T-12/92 and T-14–15/92 *Cimenteries CBR SA v Commission* [1992] ECR II-2667, para 42.

[203] Intel had argued that the case law relating to the Commission's failure to grant access to documents on its file (which sets out that only definitive measures may be the subject of an action for annulment) did not apply in this case. The GC rejected this argument. Although Intel was not requesting access to documents on the Commission's file in this case, its objective was to compel the Commission to make available documents that Intel believed might affect the Commission's final decision. Whether the documents were in the file, but not accessible, or not in the file because the Commission had not included them, was immaterial to the finding that the decisions contested by Intel were merely preparatory measures. Any negative effects of the decisions would only be felt if there was a final infringement decision. Case T-457/08 R *Intel v Commission* [2009] ECR II-12, para 45 et seq. See also Opinion of AG Jacobs in Case C-123/03 P *Commission v Greencore* [2004] ECR I-11647, para 18, referring to Joined Cases T-83/99, T-84/99, and T-85/99 *Ripa di Meana v*

A decision under Article 24(1) of Regulation 1/2003 imposing a periodic penalty payment **15.62** does not produce binding legal effects and does not therefore constitute a challengeable measure. That decision constitutes only a procedural step before the Commission adopts, where appropriate, a decision definitively fixing the total amount of the periodic penalty payment which thus becomes enforceable.[204] By abolishing the notification system, Regulation 1/2003 has removed from controversy the legal status of acts whose judicial reviewability was discussed under Regulation 17, such as comfort letters.[205] Whether decisions may be subject to review will often depend on national law. For example, the lawfulness of the transmission to the Commission by a national prosecutor or the authorities competent in competition matters of information obtained in application of national criminal law, and its subsequent use by the Commission, are in principle questions covered by the national law governing the conduct of investigations by those NCAs, and also, in the case of court proceedings, by the jurisdiction of the national courts. In an action brought under Article 263 TFEU, the EU Courts would have no jurisdiction to rule on the lawfulness, as a matter of national law, of a measure adopted by a national authority.[206] A possible, albeit non-exhaustive, list of actionable measures may be as follows:[207]

- decisions ordering the cessation of an infringement under Article 7 of Regulation 1/2003;
- decisions adopting interim measures under Article 8 of Regulation 1/2003 (although it appears that this does not apply to the refusal to take interim measures);[208]
- decisions adopting commitments under Article 9 of Regulation 1/2003;
- finding of inapplicability under Article 10 of Regulation 1/2003;
- decisions rejecting a complaint under Article 7 of Regulation 773/2004; and
- refusal to accept the confidential nature of information supplied to the Commission.

These decisions are notified to the addressee. The date of notification or publication of the decision constitutes the starting point from which the two-month period laid down in Article 263, sixth paragraph, TFEU for the initiation of annulment proceedings begins to run.

Locus standi

Actions of this kind may be brought not only by Member States, the Council, the **15.63** Commission, and other Institutions, but also by natural or legal persons to whom the contested decision is addressed, and persons who, although not directly addressed, are directly

---

Commission [2000] ECR II-3493, para 33. See also Opinion of AG Jacobs in Case C-123/03 P *Commission v Greencore* [2004] ECR I-11647, para 18, referring to Joined Cases T-83/99, T-84/99, and T-85/99 *Ripa di Meana v Commission* [2000] ECR II-3493, para 33.

[204] Case T-596/97 *Dalmine v Commission* [1998] ECR II-2383, with reference to decisions issued under Art 16(1) of Reg 17: 'Consequently, in a decision adopted on the basis of Arts 11(5) and 16(1) of Reg No 17, a provision such as Art 2 of the contested decision is only preliminary in nature, serving as a warning for the undertaking concerned.'

[205] This question was dealt with by the Court in its judgments in the 'Perfume' cases. See specifically Joined Cases 253/78 and 1–3/79 *Procureur de la République v Guérlain* [1980] ECR 2327, paras 11–13 and Case 99/79 *Lancôme v Etos* [1980] ECR 2511, para 18.

[206] Case T-50/00 *Dalmine v Commission* [2004] ECR II-2395, para 86, referring 'by analogy' to Case C-97/91 *Oleificio Borelli v Commission* [1992] ECR I-6313, para 9 and Case T-22/97 *Kesko v Commission* [1999] ECR II-3775, para 83. See Ch 3, 'The Role of National Competition Authorities', para 3.14 et seq.

[207] D Geradin and N Petit, ch 17 'Judicial Remedies under EC Competition Law: Complex Issues Arising from the Modernization Process', in BE Hawk (ed), *Annual Proceedings of the Fordham Corporate Law Institute* (Juris Publishing 2006) 393, 401, argue that eg Commission decisions under Art 11(6) to recall cases from NCAs should also be challengeable on the ground that they constitute the end of a special procedure.

[208] See Ch 14, 'Interim Measures', para 14.11. As explained, the Commission may want the refusal to take interim measures to fall outside the category of reviewable acts.

and individually concerned by a decision addressed to another person (fourth paragraph of Article 263 TFEU).[209] As regards non-addressees of a decision, they may not claim that a decision affects them individually unless it does so by reason of certain attributes which are peculiar to them, or by reason of circumstances in which they differentiated from all other persons, with the result that it distinguishes them individually, just as in the case of the person addressed.[210] The mere fact that a measure may exercise an influence on the competitive relationships existing in the market in question is not sufficient to allow any trader in any competitive relationship whatsoever with the addressee of the measure to be regarded as directly and individually concerned by the measure.[211] The Court first allowed legal standing to a non-addressee in *Metro I* in respect of a party who had complained under Article 3(2)(b) of Regulation 17—the equivalent of Article 7(2) of Regulation 1/2003—and who objected to the granting of an exemption.[212] A complainant who is entitled to bring a complaint under Article 7(2) of Regulation 1/2003 and Article 5 of Regulation 773/2004 may sue under Article 263 TFEU. However, the GC has ruled that the fact that the applicants (in the procedure before the GC) have been identified in the contested decision as complainants is not sufficient for them to be considered as individually concerned by those parts of the contested decision which do not deal with the issues raised in their complaint.[213] In *Metro II*, the Court widened the complainant category to cover a party who had not formally complained, but who had taken part in the Commission's proceedings and had been recognized by the Commission as having a legitimate interest.[214] Conversely, the question arises as to whether

---

[209] In *Jégo-Quéré*, the GC undertook a review of the existing case law regarding the possibility of private parties challenging EU measures of a general nature and proposed a new criterion for analysing 'individual concern': Case T-177/01 *Commission v Jégo Quéré & Cie SA* [2002] ECR II-2365. The reasoning was mainly based on the principle of effective judicial review contained in the ECHR. On appeal, Case C-263/02 P *Commission v Jégo Quéré & Cie SA* [2004] ECR I-3425, the ECJ, however, refused to depart from the settled case law to allow more actions by private parties to be brought under Art 263 TFEU. The Court seemed to indicate that a more flexible interpretation of 'individual concern' in cases where there was no effective judicial review for parties went further than the text of the former EC Treaty allowed. Now, following the implementation of the Lisbon Treaty, the regulation adopted by the Commission challenged in *Jégo-Quéré* would most probably be considered a regulatory act and therefore the applicant would be granted standing under Art 263(4) TFEU, while an applicant must *still* be directly and individually concerned if it wishes to challenge measures adopted through the ordinary or special legislative procedure. By contrast, any other measure of general application that does not entail implementing measures (eg a Commission Regulation) can now be challenged by applicants that can demonstrate that they are directly concerned. The applicant no longer has to satisfy the Plaumann formula (Case 25/62 *Plaumann v Commission* [1963] ECR 95, at 107).

[210] See Case C-25/62 *Plaumann v Commission* [1963] ECR 199, cited in the GC judgment in Case T-2/93 *Air France v Commission II* [1994] ECR II-323, para 42. See also Case T-32/93 *Ladbroke v Commission* [1994] ECR II-1015, paras 41 and 42; Joined Cases T-447/93, T-448/93, and T-449/93 *AITEC and others v Commission* [1995] ECR II-1971, para 34; Case C-321/95 P *Stichting Greenpeace Council v Commission* [1998] ECR I-1651, and Case C-50/00 P *Unión de Pequeños Agricultores v Council* [2002] ECR I-6677.

[211] Despite the dictum in *Plaumann* to the effect that the provisions concerning individual entitlement to bring an action should not be interpreted restrictively (para 106); see also Case T-113/89 *Nefarma v Commission* [1990] ECR II-797, para 98, citing *Plaumann*.

[212] The EU Courts have held that complainants should be able, if their request is not complied with either wholly or in part, to institute proceedings in order to protect their legitimate interests. See Case 26/76 *Metro v Commission I* [1977] ECR 1875, para 13; Case 210/81 *Demo-Studio Schmidt v Commission* [1983] ECR 3045, para 14; Case T-37/92 *BEUC and NCC v Commission* [1994] ECR II-285, para 36; and Case T-114/92 *BEMIM v Commission* [1995] ECR II-147. On complainants and competitiors/customers, see Kerse & Khan, *EC Antitrust Procedure* (6th edn, Sweet & Maxwell 2012) paras 8-020–8-023.

[213] See Case T-16/91 *Rendo v Commission I* [1994] ECR II-2417, para 74. *Rendo* (para 72) relied on the case law of the Court whereby undertakings which have been identified in the act that they mean to contest or involved in preparatory inquiries may be directly and individually concerned by the said act. Joined Cases 239/82 and 275/82 *Allied Corporation v Commission* [1984] ECR 1005, para 12.

[214] The applicant in both *Metro* cases was a retailer who was excluded by the provisions of SABA's exempted selective distribution system from distributing SABA products. See Case 75/84 *Metro v Commission II* [1986]

the fact of having made adverse comments on Commission publications prior to the adoption of positive decisions, is an essential precondition for the EU Courts to treat third parties purporting to contest a decision of this kind as being directly and individually concerned. On one occasion, the Commission appears to have taken that approach, in connection with the monitoring of concentrations between undertakings.[215] In either case, however, it might be thought that, in analysing the interest of third parties in bringing proceedings, regard should be had rather to the applicant's circumstances as a whole, without including or excluding anything absolutely. If that were the case, and if the Court took that view, a person who had commented on a publication might be regarded as not being directly and individually concerned by a positive decision, and a person who had not made such comments might be regarded as qualified to bring an action for the annulment of a decision which he or she had not opposed previously.

In *Métropole Television*, Antena 3, a TV service provider, was refused admission to the **15.64** European Broadcasting Union ('EBU') as an active member before the Commission adopted a decision exempting EBU's rules. Antena 3 brought an action to have the decision annulled. The Commission argued that it was not individually and directly concerned and had not submitted observations. The GC, however, held that taking part in the administrative proceedings was not a prerequisite for being accorded legal standing, and its application to join the EBU distinguished Antena 3 in the same way as if it were an addressee of the decision.[216] Thus, it seems that where an applicant was actually denied access to the market, this party is likely to be accorded legal standing.

In *Kruidvat*, the Commission denied legal standing to a retailer who wished to challenge the **15.65** Article 101 TFEU exemption of Givenchy's selective distribution system. It had not taken part in the Commission's proceedings, complained to the Commission, or applied to become a member of Givenchy's network, nor did it seek to be one. The Commission declared that to grant Kruidvat legal standing would be to allow a practically limitless number of actions from unforeseeable sources to be brought. The GC agreed and stated that individual concern could not be established on the basis that the legality of the decision might affect indirectly related national proceedings.[217] As regards the addressees of a decision, the GC has held that even they must prove a 'vested and continuing' interest in the annulment of the contested measure. In the absence of such an interest, an action by an addressee of a decision may also be regarded as inadmissible.[218] However, in the case of a decision requesting information (and, by extension,

---

ECR 3021, para 20. See also Case 191/83 *FEDIOL v Commission* [1983] ECR 2913, para 28 et seq; Case 169/84 *COFAZ v Commission* [1986] ECR 391 and Case 43/85 *ANCIDES v Commission* [1987] ECR 3131, para 8. See also Case T-96/92R *Grandes Sources v Commission (Perrier)* [1992] ECR II-2579, paras 32–3, citing some of these judgments.

[215] Case T-3/93 *Air France v Commission II* [1994] ECR II-121, para 34.

[216] Joined Cases T-528/93, T-542/93, T-543/93, and T-546/93 *Métropole Télévision v Commission* [1996] ECR II-649, para 67. Nevertheless, L Parret, 'Judicial Protection after Modernization of Competition Law' [2005] Legal Issues of Economic Integration 339, 355, takes the view that it would seem advisable for interested parties to make sure that they have clearly manifested their interest at an early stage of a Commission investigation to have a stronger judicial case in terms of admissibility.

[217] Case T-87/92 *Kruidvat v Commission* [1996] ECR II-1931, paras 69–77.

[218] See Case T-138/89 *Nederlandse Bankiersvereniging and Nederlandse Vereniging van Banken v Commission (Dutch Banks)* [1992] ECR II-2181, paras 33–4. The Court considered that there was no vested (or 'present') interest in the annulment of the legal grounds of the Commission's negative clearance decision, since: (i) the banks' interest related to a future and uncertain legal situation (the possible action of the Netherlands' authorities, if they disagreed with the Commission and considered that the Dutch Banks' agreements were liable to affect intra-EU trade); and (ii) if the circumstances changed, so that intra-EU trade was affected, the applicant banks would have an opportunity to challenge a new Commission decision, if and when one was adopted.

ordering an inspection), by definition addressees always have a substantiated and real interest in obtaining its annulment.[219]

15.66 The ECJ has denied the possibility that customers of cartel members who may wish to bring follow-on damages actions can, on that ground alone, be party to appeal proceedings before the EU Courts. In this connection, the ECJ emphasized that it would not be the purpose of annulment actions brought to challenge Commission cartel decisions to facilitate the bringing of civil actions in national courts.[220]

3. Pleas in law

15.67 Article 263 TFEU provides for four pleas in law on which actions under it may be based, although they appear to be subsumed into the third one, the infringement of the Treaty or any rule of law relating to its application. Given the large degree of overlap, the EU Courts usually do not specify under which heading the reasons for an annulment fall. The fourth ground, misuse of powers, means that the EU institution has used its powers other than for the purpose for which they were conferred.

Lack of competence

15.68 The concept of lack of competence covers different situations, notably the lack of competence of the particular institution or official to adopt the challenged act. In such cases, parties allege that the power to take decisions was unlawfully delegated.[221] The delegation to the Commissioner for Competition of the power to take decisions ordering 'dawn raid' inspections under Regulation 17 was unsuccessfully challenged in *Akzo*.[222] Yet a challenge on both accounts (ie competence and infringement of an essential procedural requirement) of the infringement decision adopted by a single Commissioner succeeded in the *PVC* cartel case. The ECJ had, however, recognized a distinction between a delegation of powers and a delegation of signature, and acknowledged that the delegation of authority to sign is the normal means by which the Commission exercises its powers.[223] The plea of lack of competence has also been relied on in relation to allegedly extra-territorial action by the Commission, directed against non-EU undertakings or relating to

---

[219] See Case T-46/92 *Scottish Football Association v Commission* [1994] ECR II-1039, paras 13–14.

[220] See also Orders of the ECJ of 8 June 2012 in Case C-589/11 P(I) *Schenker v Air France and Commission*; Case C-590/11 P(I) *Schenker v Air France-KLM and Commission*; Case C-596/11 P(I) *Schenker v KLM and Commission*; Case C-598/11 P(I) *Schenker v Cathay Pacific Airways and Commission*; Case C-600/11 P(I) *Schenker v Lan Airlines and Others*; and Case C-602/11 P(I) *Schenker v Deutsche Lufthansa and Others*, where the ECJ held that the mere fact that an undertaking might possibly be affected by high prices caused by an alleged cartel does not distinguish it sufficiently from the other economic operators in the relevant sector which are also affected by the anticompetitive practices of the members of a cartel. The fact that an undertaking is a customer of the undertakings participating in a cartel is not sufficient, in itself, to establish the right to intervene in appeals challenging the legality of the decision establishing and punishing the alleged cartel. ECJ held that the GC had been previously correct to find that the purpose of actions seeking the annulment of a Commission cartel decision is not to make possible or facilitate the bringing of civil actions in a national court, such as claims for damages. Their purpose is to review the legality of the Commission's infringement decision and the fine imposed. See also Kerse & Khan, *EC Antitrust Procedure* (6th edn, Sweet & Maxwell 2012) paras 8-028–8-029.

[221] See, eg in Joined Cases 46/87 and 227/88 *Hoechst v Commission III* [1989] ECR 2859, in particular paras 44 and 47; see Case T-201/04 *Microsoft v Commission* [2007] ECR II-3601, para 1264 et seq, cited by Kerse & Khan, *EC Antitrust Procedure* (6th edn, Sweet & Maxwell 2012) para 8-138, where the GC denied that the Commission would have the authority to delegate to a private individual the enforcement powers conferred on it (ie, the right to appoint an independent monitoring trustee).

[222] Case 5/85 *Akzo Chemie BV v Commission* [1986] ECR 2585.

[223] 'Dutch Books' Joined Cases 43/82 and 63/82 *Vereniging ter Bevordering van het Vlaamse Boekwezen, VBVB, and Vereniging ter Bevordering van de Belangen des Boekhandels, VBBB v Commission* [1984] ECR 19, para 14.

agreements or action theoretically put into effect outside the EU frontiers.[224] The ECJ rejected the plea that the Commission had no jurisdiction to apply EU competition law in *Woodpulp*.[225] The case involved the anticompetitive conduct of forty-one producers and two trade associations having their registered offices outside the EU. The ECJ based the EU jurisdiction to apply its competition rules to such conduct on the territoriality principle in public law. The issue of lack of competence is a matter of public interest and should therefore be raised by the Court of its own motion.[226]

Infringement of an essential procedural requirement

Not every procedural irregularity will be sufficient to vitiate a Commission decision. The **15.69** ECJ has classified the Commission's procedure in competition cases as administrative and non-judicial. As a general principle of EU law, a person seeking the annulment of an administrative decision on the grounds of irregularity must be able to show at least a possibility that the outcome would have been different *but for the irregularity complained of*.[227] The Court has treated as infringements of essential procedural requirements, *inter alia*:

• the failure to hear the views of the undertakings concerned regarding the conditions and obligations which the Commission intended to attach to the renewal of an individual exemption;[228]
• the failure to give an adequate statement of the reasons for Commission decisions, in breach of Article 296 TFEU.[229] For example, in an early judgment in *Cimenteries* the Court took the view that a letter from a senior Commission official (in DG COMP) which presupposed an 'evaluation of facts and law' constituted a disguised decision.[230] The fact that the letter did not sufficiently state the reasons on which it was based for the purposes of Article 296 constituted grounds for the annulment of the decision. As regards third-party applicants, the fact that they are not addressees of the contested decision does not prevent them from alleging infringement of Article 296, since such interest as third parties directly and individually affected by a decision may have in receiving explanations must also be taken into account in evaluating the scope of the Commission's obligation to state the reasons for its decision;[231]
• the failure to communicate a document constitutes a breach of the rights of the defence only if the undertaking concerned shows, first, that the Commission relied on that document to support its objection concerning the existence of an infringement[232] and, second, that the

---

[224] eg in Case 57/69 *Azienda Colori Nazionali–ACNA SpA v Commission* [1972] ECR 933; Case 6/72 *Europemballage and Continental Can v Commission* [1973] ECR 215; and Joined Cases 6/73 and 7/73 *Istituto Chimioterapico Italiano and Commercial Solvents Corporation v Commission* [1974] ECR 223, among others.
[225] See Joined Cases 89/85, 104/85, 114/85, 116/85, 117/85, and 125–129/85 *A Ahlström Osakeyhtio and Others v Commission (Woodpulp-I)* [1988] ECR I-5193, paras 11–23.
[226] Joined Cases T-79/89, T-84/89, T-85/89, T-86/89, T-89/89, T-91/89, T-92/89, T-94/89, T-96/89, T-98/89, T-102/89, and T-104/89 *BASF and others v Commission* [1992] ECR II-315, para 31; on a 'more novel instance' of plea of lack of competence, see Kerse & Khan, *EC Antitrust Procedure* (6th edn, Sweet & Maxwell 2012) para 8-137, citing Joined Cases T-117/07 and T-121/07 *Areva and Others v Commission* [2011] II-633, where the applicant claimed that the Commission unlawfully delegated to a national court or arbitration panel the power to determine the extent of each undertaking's liability to pay the fine.
[227] See eg Case 30/78 *Distillers v Commission* [1980] ECR 2229, para 26.
[228] See Case 17/74 *Transocean Marine Paint Association v Commission* [1974] ECR 1063.
[229] Case T-241/97 *Storck Amsterdam v Commission* [2000] ECR II-309, para 82. Case T-196/06 *Edison SpA v Commission* [2011] OJ C226/22, para 56 et seq.
[230] Joined Cases 8–11/66 *Cimenteries v Commission I* [1967] ECR 93, para 92.
[231] See Case T-16/91 *Rendo v Commission* [1994] ECR II-2417, para 122, citing Case 41/83 *Italy v Commission* [1985] ECR 873 and Case 294/81 *Control Data v Commission* [1983] ECR 911.
[232] Case 322/81 *Michelin v Commission* [1983] ECR 3461, paras 7 and 9.

objection could be proved only by reference to that document.[233] The Courts have made a distinction between incriminating documents and exculpatory documents.[234] In the case of an incriminating document, it is for the undertaking concerned to show that the result at which the Commission arrived would have been different if that document had been disallowed. By contrast, where an exculpatory document has not been communicated, the undertaking concerned must only establish that its non-disclosure was able to influence, to its disadvantage, the course of the proceedings and the content of the Commission's decision;[235]

- the lack of sufficient evidence of the infringement;[236] and
- defects in the internal procedure for the adoption of the decision, such as the irregular authentication of the decision.[237]

15.70 Infringements of essential procedural requirements may be brought to the attention of the EU Courts by the parties involved in Commission proceedings, but may also be examined by the Courts of their own motion.[238] Where the Courts find that there has been an infringement of the defence rights of undertakings on account, in particular, of inconsistency between the statement of objections and the decision, it is very quick to protect the rights of undertakings and take a firm line with the Commission, by annulling the decision or that part of the decision relating to the facts or objections on which the parties have been unable to submit their observations. However, the Courts have not been excessively rigorous when interpreting the formal conditions

---

[233] Case 107/82 *AEG-Telefunken v Commission* [1983] ECR 3151, paras 24–30; Joined Cases C-204/00 P, C-205/00 P, C-211/00 P, C-213/00 P, C-217/00 P, and C-219/00 P *Aalborg Portland and Others v Commission* [2004] ECR I-123, para 71; Case T-30/91 *Solvay v Commission* [1995] ECR II-1775, para 58.

[234] See Case T-343/06 *Shell Petroleum NV et al v Commission* [2012] OJ C355/14, para 86 et seq (appeal pending, Case C-585/12 P *Shell Petroleum and Others v Commission*).

[235] To that effect, see Cases C-204/00 P, C-205/00 P, C-211/00 P, C-213/00 P, C-217/00 P, and C-219/00 P *Aalborg Portland and Others v Commission* [2004] ECR I-123, paras 73 and 74.

[236] Case T-56/02 *Bayerische Hypo- und Vereinsbank AG v Commission* [2004] OJ C314/14, para 119: 'All of the evidence just examined permits the conclusion that the Commission has not adduced to the requisite legal standard proof of the existence of the agreement which it claimed to exist, relating both to the fixing of the prices for currency exchange services of the euro-zone currencies and also to the ways of charging those prices. It follows that the pleas alleging that those findings of fact are incorrect and that the inculpatory evidence is not probative must be declared founded.' On the facts, the Court found for the applicant and annulled the decision. This occurred by way of a judgment in default; owing to a fax error, the Commission had not submitted its defence in time. Without taking into account the Commission defence, the Court assessed the applicant's arguments against those in the Commission's decision, but without the Commission defence, and concluded that the Commission's decision was not founded on sufficiently cogent evidence. For more references on this standard, see: Case T-110/07 *Siemens AG v Commission* [2011] ECR II-477, para 43 et seq; Joined Cases T-44/02 OP, T-54/02 OP, T-56/02 OP, T-60/02 OP, and T-61/02 OP *Dresdner Bank and Others v Commission* [2006] ECR II-3567, para 60: 'any doubt in the mind of the Court must operate to the advantage of the undertaking to which the decision finding an infringement was addressed. The Court cannot therefore conclude that the Commission has established the infringement at issue to the requisite legal standard if it still entertains any doubts on that point, in particular in proceedings for annulment of a decision imposing a fine.'

[237] When the Commission adopts an infringement decision, therefore, the Commissioner responsible for competition lays the draft before the whole College at one of its meetings and the measure is adopted by the College. The ECJ confirmed that the failure of the College to adopt an authenticated version of the decision was one reason for the annulment of the *PVC* decision in Case C-137/92 P *Commission v BASF AG and others* [1994] ECR I-2555.

[238] See eg on the obligation to state reasons Case T-31/91 *Solvay SA v Commission (Soda Ash—Art 81: Germany)* [1995] ECR II-1821, para 37 and Case T-32/91 *Solvay SA v Commission (Soda Ash—Art 82)* [1995] ECR II-1825, para 43. Case T-241/97 *Storck Amsterdam v Commission* [2000] ECR II-309, para 74: 'The obligation to state the reasons for a measure with sufficient precision, enshrined in Art [253 TFEU], is one of the fundamental principles of Community law which the Court has to ensure are observed, if necessary by considering of its own motion a plea of failure to fulfil that obligation.' Case C-265/97 *VBA v Florimex and others* [2000] ECR I-2061, para 93.

relating to Commission procedures and decisions, and in general have taken the view that formal defects are not a basis for annulling the decision, except where the parties' defence rights are undermined or where, had there been no irregularities, a different result might have been arrived at in the administrative procedure.[239]

In *Papierfabrik Köhler v Commission*, however, procedural grounds gave rise to annulment. In this case, the Commission's statement of objections made it clear that it intended to hold Bolloré liable for the infringement on account of its responsibility, as the parent company owning all the shares in Copigraph at the time of the infringement, for Copigraph's participation in the cartel. The GC correctly recognized that Bolloré's defence rights had been infringed, as the statement of objections did not make it aware of the fact that the Commission also intended to find it liable on the basis of its direct and personal involvement in the cartel. However, the GC held that this error could only result in the annulment of the Commission's decision if the allegations could not be substantiated from other evidence. It went on to decide that the Commission had been correct to hold Bolloré liable for the participation of its subsidiary in the cartel and that, therefore, the Commission's error did not have a decisive effect on the operative part of the decision, which was sufficiently based in law. On appeal, however, the ECJ found that the GC had erred in law in failing to draw any legal conclusion from its finding that Bolloré's defence rights had not been observed. Bolloré's first ground of appeal was therefore declared to be well founded.[240] **15.71**

In *PVC*, certain irregularities of competence and form prompted the GC not to annul a decision but to go so far as to declare it non-existent.[241] The GC found differences in both the statement of reasons and the operative part of the decision between the version adopted by the College of Commissioners at its relevant meeting and the version notified to the parties concerned. On appeal, the ECJ considered that the absence of an authenticated original was not of such obvious gravity that the decision must be treated as legally non-existent, but **15.72**

---

[239] See Case 30/78 *Distillers v Commission* [1980] ECR 2229, para 26. See also the Opinion of AG Warner in that case (2267). For AG Warner, EU law is distinct from French administrative law in that, under the French system, procedural defects in all cases render subsequent administrative decisions invalid. In EU law, those who attack the validity of an administrative decision are not entitled to rely on a procedural irregularity preceding the adoption of that decision unless they can demonstrate at least the possibility that, in the absence of that irregularity, the decision would have been different. This rule has been applied by the GC in both staff cases and in competition cases. Amongst the latter, AG Warner cited the cases on the *Quinine* cartel: Case 41/69 *ACF v Commission* [1970] ECR 661, paras 47–53; Case 44/69 *Buchler v Commission* [1970] ECR 733, paras 15, 35, and 36; and Case 45/69 *Boehringer Mannheim v Commission* [1970] ECR 769, paras 15, 39, and 40.

[240] Cases C-322/07 P, C-327/07 P, and C-338/07 P *Papierfabrik August Koehler AG, Bolloré SA, Distribuidora Vizcaína de Papeles SL v Commission* [2009] ECR I-7191, paras 40–5. See also Case T-410/03 *Hoechst GmbH v Commission* [2008] ECR II-881, paras 420–38, where the GC found that the statement of objections did contain the elements of fact on which the Commission ultimately relied in finding Hoechst to be a leader of the cartel. However, these elements were not linked together coherently or characterized in a particular way, and therefore the GC concluded that the statement did not specify the facts sufficiently precisely to enable Hoechst to defend itself properly. The lack of precision in the statement of objections meant that Hoechst's response only focused on certain issues (leadership of joint meetings, rather than leadership of the cartel as such). Hoechst was not able to adopt an effective defence to all of the points subsequently relied on in the Commission's decision. The Commission's decision was therefore amended in so far as it established the aggravating circumstance of Hoechst being a leader of the cartel.

[241] Case C-200/92 P *Imperial Chemical Industries plc (ICI) v Commission* [1999] ECR I-4399, paras 70–1: 'acts tainted by an irregularity whose gravity is so obvious that it cannot be tolerated by the Community legal order must be treated as having no legal effect, even provisional, that is to say they must be regarded as legally non-existent. The purpose of this exception is to maintain a balance between two fundamental, but sometimes conflicting, requirements with which a legal order must comply, namely stability of legal relations and respect for legality…From the gravity of the consequences attaching to a finding that an act of a Community institution is non-existent it is self-evident that, for reasons of legal certainty, such a finding is reserved for quite extreme situations.'

would nonetheless constitute an infringement of an essential procedural requirement and hence a ground for annulment under Article 263 TFEU.[242] As the GC has said:

> it is essential that the Community institutions observe the principle that they may not alter measures which they have adopted and which affect the legal and factual situations of persons, so that they amend those acts only in accordance with its rule on competence and procedure.[243]

---

[242] In Case C-137/92 P *Commission v BASF AG and others* [1994] ECR I-2555, the Court upheld as part of EU law the theory of the non-existence of administrative acts which prevails in various EU countries—led by France—but confined declarations of non-existence to extreme cases. The Court heard an appeal brought by the Commission against the GC judgment in Joined Cases T-79/89, T-84/89 to T-86/89, T-89/89, T-91, and 92/89, T-94/89, T-96/89, T-98/89, T-102/89, and T-104/89 *BASF AG and others v Commission* ('PVC') [1992] ECR II-315, in which the GC declared non-existent the Commission Decision concerning the PVC cartel [1989] OJ L74/1. The grounds for that finding were, *inter alia*, the lack of an original decision validly signed and duly authenticated discrepancies between the decision adopted and the version notified to the parties and published in the Official Journal ('OJ') (which indicated, in the GC's opinion, a breach of the principle of the inalterability of Commission measures) and certain differences between the language versions. The Court considered that the irregularities concerning powers and form highlighted by the GC, which related to the procedure for the adoption of the Commission decision, were not clearly serious enough for the decision to be declared non-existent, and set aside the GC judgment. However, the Court did not refer the case back to the GC but, giving judgment on the substantive issues, also annulled the Commission decision. It concluded that one of the irregularities referred to by the GC (specifically, the failure to comply with Art 12 of the Commission's Rules of Procedure regarding the authentication of its measures) constituted an infringement of an essential procedural requirement of the kind referred to in Art 263 of the Treaty, for which reason the *PVC* decision should also be annulled. Once the Court ruled that its first *PVC* decision, albeit existent, was to be annulled, the Commission adopted a new *PVC* decision rectifying its past internal procedural errors. See [1994] OJ L239/14, which was again subject to an appeal. Joined Cases T-305/94 to T-307/94, T-313/94 to T-316/94, T-318/94, T-325/94, T-328/94, T-329/94, and T-335/94 *Limburgse Vinyl Maatschaapij (LVM) and others v Commission* ('PVC II') [1999] ECR II-931, on appeal partly annulled in Joined Cases C-238/99 P, C-244/99 P, C-245/99 P, C-247/99 P, C-250/99 P to C-252/99 P, and C-254/99 P *LVM and others v Commission* [2002] ECR I-8375. The undertakings claimed that this would breach the principle of double jeopardy, or *non bis in idem*, and that the Commission had denied them the right to be heard by not sending a new statement of objections and holding hearings. The ECJ held that *non bis in idem* did not apply when the annulment was only on procedural grounds and that, given that the Court had not found any defects in the preliminary stages, there was no need to repeat those stages (para 54 et seq).

[243] Case T-229/94 *Deutsche Bahn AG v Commission* [1997] ECR II-1689, para 113 and Joined Cases T-79/89, T-84/89 to T-86/89, T-89/89, T-91/89, T-92/89, T-94/89, T-96/89, T-98/89, T-102/89, and T-104/89 *BASF and others v Commission* [1992] ECR II-315, para 35. The GC has followed the *PVC II* judgment in Joined Cases T-80/89, T-81/89, T-87/89, T-88/89, T-90/89, T-93/89, T-95/89, T-97/89, T-99/89, T-100/89, T-101/89, T-103/89, T-105/89, T-107/89, and T-112/89 *BASF AG and others v Commission* (LdPE) [1995] ECR II-729 (see especially para 73), relating to the Commission decision concerning *LdPE* [1989] OJ L74/21. The irregularities that made the *LdPE* decision be annulled were very similar to those of the *PVC* decision, which was adopted by the Commission at the same time. The *PVC II* judgment has also been followed by the GC in its *Soda Ash* judgments. In three of them, Case T-31/91 *Solvay SA v Commission (Soda Ash—Art 81: Germany)* [2000] ECR II-1821, Case T-37/91 *Imperial Chemical Industries plc (ICI) v Commission (Soda Ash—Art 82)* [1995] ECR II-1901, and Case T-32/91 *Solvay SA v Commission (Soda Ash—Art 82)* [2000] ECR I-2391, the Commission's decisions were quashed for lack of appropriate authentication. The annulment was upheld by the ECJ in C-287/95 P and C-288/95 P *Commission v Solvay* [2000] ECR I-2391. In the other two, Case T-36/91 *Imperial Chemical Industries plc (ICI) v Commission (Soda Ash—Art 81: UK-Continent)* and Case T-30/91 *Solvay SA v Commission (Soda Ash—Art 81: UK-Continent)*, the GC clearly suggested that it would have quashed the Commission's decisions for the same reasons, were it not because it found other grounds for annulment. See, in particular, Case T-36/91 *Imperial Chemical Industries plc (ICI) v Commission (Soda Ash—Art 81: UK-Continent)* [1995] ECR II-1847, paras 21 and 26, and Case T-30/91 *Solvay SA v Commission (Soda Ash—Art 81: UK-Continent)* [1995] ECR II-1775, paras 20 and 25. On the basis that the GC held the *PVC* decision to be non-existent for the reasons indicated, undertakings have claimed on various occasions in actions for annulment that irregularity of the internal procedure for the adoption of decisions constituted a breach of an essential procedural requirement, but so far without success. See Case T-43/92 *Dunlop v Commission* [1994] ECR II-441, paras 22–6, and Case T-77/92 *Parker Pen v Commission* [1994] ECR II-549, paras 22–3; Case T-34/92 *Fiatagri UK and another v Commission* [1994] ECR II-905, paras 25–7; and Case T-35/92 *John Deere v Commission* [1994] ECR II-957, paras 28–31. See

However, the Court has also stated that a measure which has been notified and published must be presumed to be valid. Accordingly, it would thus be for a person who seeks to allege the lack of formal validity or the non-existence of a measure to provide the Court with grounds enabling it to look behind the apparent validity of the measure which has been formally notified and published. Thus, the applicants should put forward any evidence to suggest that the measure notified and published has not been approved or adopted by the members of the Commission acting as a college. In particular, the applicant would have to adduce evidence that the principle of the inalterability of the adopted measure—leaving aside minor corrections of spelling and grammar—was infringed by a change to the text of the decision after the meeting of the College of Commissioners at which it was adopted.[244]

Where an EU institution is required to consult another prior to the adoption of an act, failure **15.73** to comply with this requirement may be challenged by means of an application for annulment.[245] Thus, the failure to consult the Advisory Committee would most likely represent an infringement of an essential procedural requirement.[246]

As regards the lack of reasoning, the extent of the obligation to state reasons depends on the **15.74** nature of the measure in question and the context in which it was adopted. The statement of reasons must disclose in a clear and unequivocal fashion the reasoning of the institution, in such a way as to give the persons concerned sufficient information to enable them to ascertain whether the decision is well founded or whether it is vitiated by a defect which may permit its legality to be contested, and to enable the EU Courts to review the legality of the measure.[247] It is not necessary for the reasoning to go into all of the relevant facts and points of law, since the requirements of Article 296 TFEU must be assessed with regard not only to its wording but also its context and all of the legal rules governing the matter in question.[248]

In many cases, the applicants invoke the excessive duration of the administrative proceedings, **15.75** which is not in itself such as to impair the undertaking's defence rights. For the purposes of applying the principle of good administration which involves a reasonable length of time to decide, the EU Courts distinguish between the investigative phase prior to the statement of objections and the remainder of the administrative procedure.[249] In a procedure relating

---

Case T-29/92 *Vereniging van Samenwerkende Prijsregelende Organisatie in de Bou-wnijverhe (SPO) and others v Commission* [1995] ECR II-289, in which the GC called on the Commission to produce the decision authenticated at the time of its adoption in the language in which it was binding. The GC had detected some evidence that the principles set down in *PVC II* might not have been respected—the undertakings had been consecutively notified of two different versions of the decision—but finally agreed that the text adopted by the Commission was the second one notified to the undertakings and that there was no irregularity that made the Commission's decision non-existent or void. See also Case T-106/89 REV *Norsk Hydro v Commission* [1994] ECR II-419, in which, relying on *PVC II*, and in view of the fact that the Commission *PVC* decision was not non-existent but had merely been annulled, the GC dismissed the application for revision brought by *Norsk Hydro*, an undertaking involved in the *PVC* cartel which did not contest the decision within the prescribed period and therefore had to pay the fine which the Commission had imposed on it.

[244] Case C-200/92 P *Imperial Chemical Industries plc (ICI) v Commission* [1999] ECR I-4399, paras 66–8.

[245] See Case C-21/94 *Parliament v Commission* [1995] ECR I-1827.

[246] *Quinine* cartel, see Case 41/69 *ACF Chemiefarma v Commission* [1970] ECR 661, cited by AG Warner in Case 30/78 *Distillers v Commission* [1980] ECR 2229. The AG also considered that the failure of the Advisory Committee itself to observe procedural requirements might be sufficient to vitiate the Commission's decision.

[247] Joined Cases T-213/95 and T-18/96 *Stichting Certificatie Kraanverhuurbedrijf (SCK) and Federatie van Nederlandse Kraanbedrijven (FNK) v Commission* [1997] ECR II-1739, para 226; T-241/97 *Storck Amsterdam v Commission* [2000] ECR II-309, para 73; Case C-278/95 P *Siemens v Commission* [1997] ECR I-2507, para 17; Case T-150/89 *Martinelli v Commission* [1995] ECR II-1165, para 65.

[248] Case C-367/95 P *Commission v Sytraval and Brink's France* [1998] ECR I-1719, para 63.

[249] AG Mischo in paras 40–53 of his Opinion in Case C-250/99 P *Limburgse Vinyl Maatschappij and others v Commission*, followed by the judgment [2002] ECR I-8375, para 178 et seq; as regards the length

to EU competition law, the persons concerned are not the subjects of any formal accusation until they receive the statement of objections.[250] Accordingly, the prolongation of this stage of the procedure alone is not in itself capable of adversely affecting defence rights.[251] In addition, in *FETTSCA*, the GC acknowledged that whilst the unreasonable length of the procedure, particularly where it infringes the parties' defence rights, justifies the annulment of a decision establishing an infringement of the competition rules, the same does not apply where the amount of the fines imposed by that decision is in dispute. The Commission's power to impose fines is governed by the rules on limitation periods, which cover in detail the periods within which the Commission may, without undermining the fundamental requirement of legal certainty, impose fines on undertakings which are the subject matter of procedures under the EU competition rules. Thus, the Commission could not put off a decision on fines indefinitely without incurring the risk of the limitation period expiring. In the light of those rules, there is no room for consideration of the Commission's duty to exercise its power to impose fines within a reasonable period.[252] The reasonableness of a period is to be appraised in the light of the circumstances specific to each case and, in particular, the importance of the case for the person concerned, its complexity, and the conduct of the applicant and of the competent authorities. The Court has held in that regard that that list of criteria is not exhaustive and that the assessment of the reasonableness of a period does not require a systematic examination of the circumstances of the case in the light of each of them, where the duration of the proceedings appears justified in the light of one of them. Thus, the complexity of the case may be deemed to justify a duration which is *prima facie* too long.[253]

15.76 However, in *Dutch Beer*, the GC found that the length of the administrative procedure infringed the principle that proceedings must be completed within a reasonable period. Accepting that over seven years constituted an unreasonable length of the administrative procedure in the present case, the Commission had reduced the fine on each undertaking by EUR 100,000. The Court criticized the missing link between the level of the fine imposed and the reduction granted by the Commission, considering that the flat-rate reduction given by the Commission did not take account of the amount of the fines, and was therefore not capable of adequately rectifying the violation resulting from the excessive duration of the procedure. It considered that, in order to give the companies just satisfaction for the excessive duration of the procedure, the reduction should be increased to 5 per cent of the fine. The main conclusion to be drawn from the Court's statement is therefore that fine reductions for

---

of the EU Courts procedure, see Opinion of AG Sharpston of 30 May 2013 in Case C-58/12 P *Groupe Gascogne v Commission*, Case C-40/12 P *Gascogne Sack Deutschland v Commission* and C-50/12 P *Kendrion v Commission* where the applicants claimed that the GC did not deal with their cases within a reasonable time. Agreeing that the applicants would be entitled to have their cases treated with reasonable dispatch, AG Sharpston recommended that the ECJ make it clear that it is open to the applicants to bring a separate action for damages for the excessive delay.

[250] However, when the first investigative measure is addressed to them (normally a request for information or an inspection), addressees are informed of the fact that they are subject to a preliminary investigation and about the subject matter and purpose of such investigation. See Commission Notice on best practices for the conduct of proceedings concerning Articles 101 and 102 TFEU [2011] OJ C308/6, para 15.

[251] Joined Cases T-5/00 and T-6/00 *Nederlandse Federatieve Vereniging voor de Groothandel op Elektrotechnisch Gebied and Technische Unie BV v Commission* [2003] ECR II-5761, paras 78–9.

[252] Case T-213/00 *CMA CGM and others v Commission ('FETTSCA')* [2003] ECR II-913, paras 321–4 with regard to Reg 2988/74, which is now replaced by the limitation periods of Arts 25 and 26 of Reg 1/2003. See also Case 48/69 *ICI v Commission* [1972] ECR 619, paras 46–9; Case 52/69 *Geigy v Commission* [1972] ECR 787, paras 20–2, and Joined Cases C-74/00 P and C-75/00 P *Falck v Commission* [2002] ECR I-7869, paras 139–41.

[253] Cases C-322/07 P, C-327/07 P, and C-338/07 P *Papierfabrik August Koehler AG, Bolloré SA, Distribuidora Vizcaína de Papeles SL v Commission* [2009] ECR I-7191, paras 144–6.

an excessively long procedure should be calculated as a percentage of the amount of the fine imposed.[254]

Infringement of the Treaty or of any provision of secondary law

This plea is put forward principally in connection with the Commission's interpretation of the competition rules and of general principles of EU law in its decisions. Viewed broadly, this plea could encompass the other three grounds on which proceedings may be brought. The GC will annul a decision where the Commission has misinterpreted the law or failed to abide by general principles of law, such as proportionality, non-discrimination, legitimate expectations, and the presumption of innocence or legal certainty. However, this would go beyond misinterpreting or misapplying the law. It would also cover a court finding that the Commission had committed 'a manifest error of appraisal' and that the evidence relied on by the Commission did not support the finding. The clearest cases of infringement of the Treaty rules may arise where the Commission has interpreted as restrictive or abusive a clearly defined course of action of which there is sufficient evidence and the Court interprets it as not being restrictive or abusive, which means that the Commission has incorrectly applied Articles 101 and 102 TFEU.[255]   **15.77**

Misuse of powers

EU law does not diverge significantly from the administrative law of Member States regarding the concept of misuse of powers. A decision is vitiated by misuse of powers only if it appears, on the basis of objective, relevant, and consistent factors, to have been taken for the purpose of achieving ends other than those stated or of evading a procedure specifically prescribed by the Treaty for dealing with the circumstances of the case.[256] This ground has not so far been successfully relied upon before the GC in competition cases and the case law shows the exceptional character of this concept.[257] For example, in *European Beams Producers*, one applicant alleged that the Commission had abused its powers by holding negotiations with the steel industry with a view to bringing about a thorough restructuring of the industry, negotiations which it broke off just a day before DG COMP imposed a penalty on various steel operators in the sector for competition law infringement. Neither the co-existence of parallel negotiations between the Commission and the industry on restructuring the European steel industry, dating back to the 1980s, or even the 1970s, nor the 'coincidence' between the failure of those negotiations and the adoption of the infringement decision, constituted per se evidence of abuse of powers. The ECJ dismissed the claim that   **15.78**

---

[254] Case T-240/07 *Heineken Nederland and Heineken v Commission* [2011] ECR II-3355, paras 425–36.

[255] Thus, eg in its judgment on the *Sugar* cartel in Joined Cases 40–48, 50, 54–56, 111, 113, and 114/73 *Suiker Unie and others v Commission* [1975] ECR 1663, the Court considered that certain conduct regarded as improper by the Commission did not constitute an abuse of a dominant position within the meaning of Art 102 TFEU, and therefore partially annulled the decision and reduced the fines which had been imposed on some of the members of the cartel for that reason. See in particular paras 492 and 493 of the judgment. Another example is 'Adalat', Cases C-2/01 P and C-3/01 P *Bundesverband der Arzneimittel–Importeure and Commission v Bayer* [2004] ECR I-23, which confirmed Case T-41/96 *Bayer v Commission* [2000] ECR II-3383. The GC had found that the Commission had not proved that there was an agreement within the meaning of Art 101(1) TFEU between Bayer and its Spanish and French wholesalers to limit parallel exports of Adalat to the UK.

[256] Case T-110/95 *IECC v Commission* [1998] ECR II-3605, para 188, with more references. Case T-299/08 *Elf Aquitaine SA v Commission* [2011] ECR II-2149, para 262.

[257] For examples of cases in which that ground was relied on yet rejected by the GC, see Case T-24/90 *Automec v Commission II* [1992] ECR II-2223, paras 102–8; Case T-5/93 *Roger Tremblay v Commission* [1995] ECR II-185, paras 85–93; see Case C-84/94 *United Kingdom v Council* [1996] ECR I-5755, para 69; and Case T-77/95 *SFEI and others v Commission* [1997] ECR II-1, para 116.

the administrative procedure was used for the purpose of forcing the steel industry to restructure itself or to penalize its lack of cooperation in that regard.[258]

4. Annulment of the contested measure

Partial nullity

15.79 The first paragraph of Article 264 TFEU provides that '[i]f the action is well founded, the Court of Justice shall declare the act concerned to be void'. However, the ECJ has consistently held that the nullity of measures of the other EU institutions may be partial, contrary to what might be thought if that provision were interpreted literally. Partial nullity of a measure will depend on whether the void part of the contested decision can be severed from the whole.[259] If the partial annulment of the contested act would have the effect of altering its substance, the result reached will be precisely as envisaged in Article 264: total nullity of the decision.[260] There is a relatively large number of examples in which Commission decisions in competition matters have been declared partially void.[261] If the Court opts for annulment, the Commission may restart the investigation at the point where the error occurred.[262] Partial annulment must

---

[258] Case C-196/99 P *Siderúrgica Aristrain Madrid SL v Commission* [2003] ECR I-11005, paras 526–32.

[259] Case C-244/03 *France v Parliament and Council* [2005] ECR I-4021, para 12; Case C-540/03 *Parliament v Council* [2006] ECR I-5769, para 27; Case C-295/07 P *Commission v Département du Loiret* [2008] ECR I-9363, para 105; and Case C-505/09 P *Commission v Estonia* [2012] OJ C151/2, para 11; Kerse & Khan, *EC Antitrust Procedure* (6th edn, Sweet & Maxwell 2012) para 8-155.

Regarding the question when the GC will annul an antitrust decision by the European Commission in its entirety and when must it be satisfied with a partial annulment, see Opinion of AG Kokott of 24 May 2012 in Case C-441/11 P *Commission v Verhuizingen Coppens NV*, who points out that 'the principle of procedural economy suggests that EU legal acts should be annulled only partially in cases of doubt, because it is then possible to avoid any repetition of the administrative procedure and possible fresh judicial proceedings or at least to restrict their subject-matter. In addition, in antitrust cases in particular, a repetition of the administrative procedure could, depending on the circumstances, be contrary to the *ne bis in idem* principle... Furthermore, only partial annulment of Commission decisions is more consistent with the fundamental requirement of an effective enforcement of the EU competition rules... than their complete annulment' (para 27). The judgment of 6 December 2012 in Case C-441/11 P *Commission v Verhuizingen Coppens*, ultimately set the GC judgment aside. The only circumstances in which the GC would have been justified, under Art 264 TFEU, in annulling the contested decision in its entirety in respect of Coppens would have been if the partial annulment of that decision would have altered the substance of the decision. However, the ECJ found that the GC had made an error in law by annulling the Commission decision in its entirety because it had not called in question Coppens' participation in the agreement on cover quotes or the anticompetitive nature of that agreement.

[260] AG Kokott of 24 May 2012 in Judgment of 6 December 2012 in Case C-441/11 P *Commission v Verhuizingen Coppens NV*, para 28 in note 20 with more references.

[261] Case C-295/07 P *Commission v Département du Loiret* [2008] ECR I-9363, paras 103–10. Decisions of this kind may eg lead to fine reductions imposed by the Commission.

[262] See eg Commission Decision of 30 April 2004 in *Compagnie Maritime Belge* (COMP/32.448 and 32/450), adopted after the ECJ annulled fines imposed in the original decision ([1993] OJ L34/20) in Joined Cases C-395/1996 P and C-396/1996 P *Compagnie Maritime Belge Transports SA v Commission* [2000] ECR I-1365. See also Case T-276/04 *Compagnie Maritime Belge v Commission* [2008] ECR II-1277, where the GC held that those parts of a Commission decision which are not annulled on appeal 'definitely form part of the Commission legal structure and produce their legal effects'. In that case, the annulment of a fine for purely procedural reasons did not in any way affect the legality of the finding of the infringement. The Commission could therefore rely on the parts of the decision that were not annulled for the purposes of adopting a later decision imposing a fine on the applicant for the abuses established in that earlier decision. See V Rose in *Bellamy & Child European Competition Law of Competition, Second Cumulative Supplement* (Oxford University Press 2012) para 13.238. See also Commission Press Release IP/10/788 'Antitrust: C ommission re-adopts fine on Bolloré for participation in carbonless paper cartel' of 23 June 2010, where the ECJ partially annulled the Commission decision on the grounds that Bolloré's rights of defence were infringed because it could not have foreseen from the wording of the original statement of objections that the Commission intended to hold it liable not only as a parent company of the cartel participant Copigraph, but also on account of its own involvement in the cartel. After sending a new statement of objections on 15 December 2009, which addressed both the parental liability and the direct involvement of Bolloré, the Commission has re-adopted the decision correcting the procedural error, which led to the annulment of the

respect the principle according to which the Court cannot remake a decision; while it may remove elements from the decision which may entail that the Court rewrites the decision to a certain extent, it abstains from adding new findings.[263] Typically, the Court might find that an infringement was only proved to exist for a shorter period of time than found by the decision. At the appeal level, the ECJ may also decide, for reasons of economy of procedure, to set aside the judgment of the GC or to vary it solely in relation to determining the amount of the fine.[264]

The Commission's obligations: claims for compensation

The annulment of a Commission decision takes effect *ex tunc* and thus has the effect of retroactively eliminating the annulled measure from the legal system.[265] The first paragraph of Article 266 TFEU provides that '[t]he institution whose act has been declared void…shall be required to take the necessary measures to comply with the judgment of the Court'. The defendant is thus required to take the necessary measures to reverse the effects of the illegalities as found in the judgment of annulment. In the case of an act that has already been executed, this may take the form of restoring the applicant to the position he was in prior to that act.[266] However, it is not for the Court to issue directions to the Commission or to substitute itself for it.[267] This is particularly the case in the context of judicial review, where the administration concerned is under a duty to take the necessary steps to comply with the judgment of the Court, which applies to both actions for annulment and actions for failure to act.[268] Accordingly, in judicial review proceedings under Article 263 TFEU, the Court may not order the Commission to adopt specific measures to replace the contested measure.[269] From a procedural point of view, it may be more effective if ending the litigation were achieved by allowing the GC to take a final decision on the merits, especially in those cases where it is not clear to the Commission which measures it should take.[270]

15.80

2001 decision. As during the re-adoption procedure, Bolloré no longer contested the participation of its former subsidiary Copigraph in the early stage of the cartel, the reduction for cooperation under the 1996 Leniency Notice was increased from 20 per cent to 25 per cent. The fine of Bolloré was therefore reduced from EUR 22.68 million to EUR 21.26 million.

[263] Joined Cases T-68/89, T-77/89, and T-78/89 *Societa Italiano Vetro SpA v Commission* [1992] ECR II-1403, para 319.

[264] Joined Cases C-120/06 P and C-121/06 P *FIAMM and Others v Council and Commission* [2008] ECR I-6513, paras 206–8, referring to Case C-185/95 P *Baustahlgewebe v Commission* [1998] ECR I-8417, paras 47, 48, and 101; see also Opinion of AG J Kokott in Case C-109/10 P *Solvay v Commission* [2011] OJ C370/12 and Case C-110/10 P *Solvay v Commission* [2011] OJ C370/13; Case T-214/06, *Imperial Chemical Industries Ltd v Commission* [2012] OJ C209/7, paras 278–91; Judgment of 6 December 2012 in Case C-441/11 P *Commission v Verhuizingen Coppens*

[265] See Joined Cases 97/86, 99/86, 193/86, and 215/86 *Asteris and others v Commission* [1988] ECR 2181, para 30; Joined Cases T-481/93 and T-484/93 *Exporteurs in Levende Varkens and others v Commission* [1995] ECR II-2941, para 46; Opinion of AG Léger in Case C-127/94 *The Queen v Ministry of Agriculture, Fisheries and Food, ex p H & R Ecroyd Holdings Ltd and John Rupert Ecroyd* [1996] ECR I-2731, para 74.

[266] Case 22/70 *Commission v Council* [1971] ECR 263, para 60; Case 92/78 *Simmenthal v Commission* [1979] ECR 777, para 32; Case 21/86 *Samara v Commission* [1987] ECR 795, para 7; Joined Cases T-480/93 and T-483/93 *Antillean Rice Mills and others v Commission* [1995] ECR II-2305, paras 59 and 60.

[267] See Joined Cases T-374/94, T 375/94, T-384/94, and T-388/94 *European Night Services and others v Commission* [1998] ECR II-3141, in which the GC refused to annul conditions which the Commission had attached to Art 101(3) exemption and leave the applicants with an unconditional decision. Instead, it annulled the decision completely.

[268] Case T-74/92 *Ladbroke Racing (Deutschland) GmbH v Commission* [1995] ECR II-115, para 75. Annulling judgments thus require the Commission to amend or apply its decisions in the manner indicated by the Court. One of the clearest cases is the judgment in Case 17/74 *Transocean Marine Paint Association* [1974] ECR 1063, already referred to frequently, which gave rise to the Commission decision in *Transocean III* [1975] OJ L286/24 (after the Commission had amended its Decision *Transocean II* [1974] OJ L19/18) and completed the procedural steps, the absence of which had given rise to the proceedings.

[269] See Joined Cases 142/84 and 156/84 *BAT and Reynolds v Commission* [1987] ECR 4487; Case T-191/98 *Atlantic Container Line v Commission* [2003] ECR II-3275, para 1643.

[270] President of the GC Judge Bo Vesterdorf 'Judicial Review and Competition Law—Reflections on the Role of the Community Courts in the EC system of Competition Law Enforcement', Speech at the

15.81 In *Corus*, the ECJ held that with regard to a judgment annulling or reducing the fine imposed on an undertaking for infringement of the EU competition rules, it is the Commission's obligation to repay all or part of the fine paid by the undertaking in question, in so far as that payment must be described as a sum unduly paid following the annulment ruling.[271] The ECJ considers that the payment of default interest on the amount overpaid would seem to be an essential component of the Commission's obligation to restore the applicant to his original position following an annulment judgment, or a judgment exercising the Court's unlimited jurisdiction, since complete reimbursement of an unduly paid fine cannot ignore certain factors, such as the lapse of time, which may in fact reduce its value and during which the applicant did not have the use of the sums it had unduly paid. A failure to reimburse interest could result in the unjust enrichment of the EU, which would be contrary to the general principles of EU law. It follows that the Commission is required to reimburse not only the principal amount of the unduly paid fine, but also the amount of any enrichment or benefit it has obtained as a result of such payment.

15.82 In *Greencore*, the applicant also requested the Commission to pay interest on the amount of the overpaid fine after the GC reduced the fine on Irish Sugar for breach of Article 102 TFEU. The Commission, however, transferred the principal amount due without interest. Following the ECJ ruling in *Corus*, the applicant repeated its request. In a letter to Greencore, the Commission indicated that payment of the principal sum without interest was tantamount to a refusal to pay any interest, of which Greencore sought annulment before the Court. In the action before the GC, the Commission raised an objection of inadmissibility on the basis that the letter merely provided information and did not change Greencore's legal position, arguing that the applicant should have brought an appeal when the Commission paid the principal amount. The GC dismissed the Commission's objection of inadmissibility,[272] and its ruling was confirmed by the ECJ, which stated that the Commission's silence could not be placed on the same footing as an implied refusal.[273] The letter therefore contained a refusal to pay interest and did not merely repeat an earlier refusal.[274]

15.83 The second paragraph of Article 266 TFEU also provides that the obligation to adopt a new measure complying with the judgment of the Court must not affect any obligation deriving from the second paragraph of Article 340 TFEU. This means that the subsequent adjustment of the contested measure so that it meets the requirements of EU law does not release the EU institutions from any non-contractual liability which they may have incurred as a result of the adoption of the measure in its original form.

15.84 If a Commission decision is annulled for formal defects, the Commission will not be required to terminate the proceedings and could rectify the errors and adopt a new decision in due

---

International Forum on EC Competition Law, Brussels, 8 April 2005. See also the published and edited paper version of the Vesterdorf's speech in (2005) 1(2) Competition Policy International 21.

[271] Case T-171/99 *Corus UK Ltd v Commission* [2001] ECR II-2967, paras 54–5; see also Case T-48/00 *Corus UK v Commission* [2004] ECR II-2325, para 223; Case T-53/03 *BPB plc v Commission* [2008] ECR II-13333, para 487.

[272] Order of the GC of 7 January 2003 in Case T-135/02 *Greencore Group v Commission*, not published, but referred to in Case T-135/02 *Greencore Group v Commission* [2005] ECR II-31, para 22.

[273] Case C-123/03 P *Commission v Greencore* [2004] ECR I-11647, para 45.

[274] It added that Greencore's failure to bring an action under Art 265 TFEU for failure to act to oblige the Commission to pay interest had no bearing on the question of the admissibility of its action. Case C-123/03 P *Commission v Greencore Group* [2004] ECR I-11647, para 46. See Case T-135/02 *Greencore Group v Commission* [2005] ECR II-31, in which the Court annulled the decision by which the Commission refused to grant Greencore the right to claim payment of default interest.

form, based on the same facts.[275] The reopening of the file in order to rectify errors and adopt a second decision in the same matter is also possible in the case of an infringement of defence rights.[276] Apart from that, it is increasingly common for undertakings to claim damages from the Commission where its decisions are annulled.[277] The GC has held that even if a decision were annulled, the Commission would not incur liability unless it had committed a sufficiently serious breach of a superior rule of law for the protection of the individual, or had manifestly and gravely disregarded the limits imposed on its powers.[278] Thus, the mere reversal of a decision is usually insufficient to establish fault. Fault has been found by the EU Courts in cases of 'inexcusable mistakes' and 'grave neglect of the duties of supervision and obvious lack of care'.[279] In *Holcim*, the Court dismissed a request for reimbursement of its costs providing a bank guarantee instead of paying the fine. The Court held that the illegality of a Commission decision fining Holcim for its participation in a cartel in the cement sector (which was earlier annulled by the GC) does not necessarily constitute a sufficient breach to trigger liability, also taking into account that the case was extremely complex and required intensive legal and factual analysis.[280] In *My Travel*, which related to the merger control area, the GC held that it could not be ruled out in principle that manifest and grave defects underlying the Commission's economic analysis of a merger could constitute breaches that are sufficiently serious to give rise to non-contractual liability on the part of the Commission. However, the complexity of merger control situations and the margin of discretion available to the Commission would have also to be taken into account. The GC concluded that the Commission did not commit a sufficiently serious infringement of a rule of law in either its assessment. Therefore, no non-contractual liability arose in this case.[281]

---

[275] See, eg Joined Cases T-305/94 to T-307/94, T-313/94 to T-316/94, T-318/94, T-325/94, T-328/94, T-329/94, and T-335/94 *Limburgse Vinyl Maatschaappij NV and others v Commission* [1999] ECR II-931, paras 151, 257, and 266. See *PVC II* [1994] OJ L239/14. The Commission relied on Art 3 of Reg 2988/74.

[276] See eg Case T-37/91 *Imperial Chemical Industries plc (ICI) v Commission (Soda Ash—Art 82)* [1995] ECR II-1901, para 72; Commission decision of 30 April 2004 in *Compagnie Maritime Belge* (COMP/32.448 and 32/450), adopted after the ECJ annulled fines imposed in the original decision ([1993] OJ L34/20) in Joined Cases C-395/96 P and C-396/96 P *Compagnie Maritime Belge Transports SA v Commission* [2000] ECR I-1365.

[277] For example, Case T-452/05 *Belgian Sewing Thread (BST) NV v Commission* [2010] ECR II-1373; Case 183/83 *Krupp v Commission* [1988] ECR 4611; and Case T-43/92 *Dunlop v Commission* [1994] ECR II-441, para 180 et seq (expenses incurred in providing security for payment of the fine); Case T-77/92 *Parker Pen v Commission* [1994] ECR II-549, paras 99–101 (claim for reimbursement of the expenses of providing the bank guarantee); Case T-387/94 *Asia Motor France SA v Commission* [1996] ECR II-961, paras 106–11. In the past, these claims often failed because the applicant could not prove the unlawfulness of the alleged conduct of the institution concerned, actual damage, and the existence of a causal link between that conduct and the damage pleaded.

[278] Case T-120/89 *Stahlwerke Peine-Salzgitter v Commission* [1991] ECR II-279, para 74, cited in its defence by the Commission in Case T-34/93 *Société Générale v Commission* [1995] ECR II-545, note on judgment in [1995] OJ C87/10, para 81. See also Case C-63/89 *Assurances du Crédit v Council and Commission* [1991] ECR I-1799, para 28, relied on in Case T-34/93 *Société Général* [1995] ECR II-545, para 82. In Joined Cases T-80/89, T-81/89, T-83/89, T-87/89, T-88/89, T-90/89, T-93/89, T-95/89, T-97/89, T-99/89, T-100/89, T-101/89, T-103/89, T-105/89, T-107/89, and T-112/89 *BASF and others v Commission (LdPE)* [1995] ECR II-729, paras 127–8, the GC dismissed the claim for damages of one of the undertakings because it was not supported by any argument or by any evaluation of the alleged damage so as to enable the GC to adjudicate on it.

[279] Case T-171/99 *Corus UK Ltd v Commission* [2001] ECR I-2967, para 45, citing the case law in regard to Art 34 of the ECSC Treaty, which is similar to Art 266 TFEU.

[280] Case T-28/03 *Holcim v Commission* [2005] ECR II-1357; confirmed on appeal in Case-282/05 *Holcim v Commission* [2007] ECR I-2941. See also Case T-113/04 *Atlantic Container Line and Others v Commission* [2007] ECR II-171.

[281] It appears that the GC placed considerable weight on the complexity of the analysis relating to collective dominance in finding that the Commission's errors of assessment were not sufficiently serious breaches: Case T-212/03 *MyTravel v Commission* [2008] ECR II-1967. In another case relating to the merger control area, the action was successful: Case T-351/03 *Schneider Electric v Commission* [2007] ECR II-2237, where the GC found that the Commission's breach of Schneider's rights of defence during its assessment of the merger amounted to a sufficiently serious breach of Community law to give a right to damages under Art 340 TFEU.

5. Enforceability

15.85 Article 280 TFEU provides that '[t]he judgments of the Court of Justice shall be enforceable under the conditions laid down in Article 299'. Article 299 TFEU gives detailed provision for the enforcement of financial obligations in accordance with the rules of civil procedure in the relevant EU Member State.[282] Such enforcement shall be governed by the rules of civil procedure of the state where it is carried out.

B. Proceedings for Failure to Act

15.86 Article 265 TFEU enables action to be taken against the Commission's failure to act.[283] The Court's approach in dealing with actions of this kind in competition matters is laid out in the judgment in *Lord Bethell v Commission*[284] and *GEMA II*.[285]

1. Actionable omissions

Nature of the action not taken

15.87 Article 265 TFEU provides that natural or legal persons may bring an action for failure to act where the EU institutions have failed to address to that person 'any act other than a recommendation or opinion'. The measures typically likely to be adopted by the EU institutions are mentioned in Article 288 TFEU. Once recommendations and opinions are eliminated, as expressly required by Article 265, and regulations and directives are also ruled out because they are of general application, the only measures whose non-adoption can be the subject of proceedings by individuals are decisions. However, in administrative proceedings before the Commission relating to the competition rules, there may be acts that fall short of formal decisions yet that can be subject to an action by individuals for failure to act, namely letters sent pursuant to Article 7 of Regulation 773/2004.[286]

However, the ruling was later overturned in Case C-440/07 P *Commission v Schneider Electric SA* [2009] ECR I-6413, concluded that the GC did not make an error in the legal characterization of the facts in finding there to be a sufficiently serious breach, but that it erred in finding that the Commission is liable for two-thirds of the losses incurred by Schneider due to the need to accept a lower sale price for Legrand in order to defer transfer until after proceedings before the GC were concluded. The ECJ founds that Schneider's losses in this regard did not arise directly, immediately, and exclusively from the Commission's unlawful act and, further, that Schneider had broken any causal link. A rare example of a successful claim for damages in the competition law context is Case T-88/09 *Idromacchnie Srl, Alessandro Capuzzo and Roberto Capuzzo v Commission* [2011] OJ C370/23, where the GC ordered the Commission to pay damages to Idromacchine Srl, a third party in state aid proceedings, for publication of its name and detrimental information relating to it in the OJ. The GC considered that certain information on Idromacchine about its contractual performance was confidential information according to Art 339 TFEU. It held that the publication of this information was detrimental to Idromacchine and had caused serious harm to Idromacchine's interests being worthy of protection

[282] Note that when the ECJ decides that an EU act does not comply with the treaties or when it interprets EU law, this decision has binding force and is applicable in all courts of the Member States. Thus, national courts are bound by the interpretation of the Court. This is also the case for public authorities.

[283] As has been seen, Art 266 TFEU refers both to actions for annulment and actions for failure to act.

[284] See Case 246/81 *Lord Bethell v Commission* [1982] ECR 2277.

[285] See Case 125/78 *GEMA v Commission II* [1979] ECR 3173. See also the judgment in Case 8/71 *Deutsche Kompanistenverband v Commission* [1971] ECR 705.

[286] See Case T-28/90 *Asia Motor France v Commission* [1992] ECR II-2285, para 42, referring to Case T-64/89 *Automec v Commission* [1990] ECR II-367 and Case 125/78 *GEMA v Commission* [1979] ECR 3173, para 21, stating that communications by which the Commission rules provisionally, under the conditions set out in Art 6 of Reg 99/63 (now Art 7 of Reg 1/2003), on a complaint referred to it under Art 3 of Reg 17 (now Art 7 of Reg 1/2003) are not in the nature of decisions capable of having adverse effects and are not therefore open to challenge by means of an action for annulment under Art 263 TFEU.

The failure to act must involve 'an infringement of the Treaty'. This requirement has been **15.88** interpreted as allowing proceedings not only where the Treaty has been infringed, but also where secondary EU law—which therefore includes Regulation 1/2003—has been infringed. Moreover, according to the Court, the term infringement implies that the Commission must be under a specific obligation to take action in the circumstances concerned.[287] Since the Commission can decide not to continue the proceedings whatever the circumstances, it is not under such an obligation vis-à-vis complainants under Article 7(1) of Regulation 1/2003 (former Article 3 of Regulation 17), in so far as complainants may not require the Commission to adopt a formal infringement decision in cases which they have brought to its attention.[288] Nevertheless, complainants may require the Commission to take action in two successive stages in proceedings for the rejection of their complaints. Firstly, under Article 7 of Regulation 773/2004—as under Article 6 of Regulation 99/63—complainants have traditionally been entitled to be informed of the lack of any grounds for their complaint to be acted upon, and therefore they are entitled to receive an explanation from the Commission. Secondly, although in the past complainants did not seem to be clearly entitled to require a formal rejection decision, the case law of the GC has established that having submitted comments in response to an [Article 7] letter, the complainant is entitled to obtain a definitive decision from the Commission on its complaint[289] and this element might have been picked up by Article 7(2) of Regulation 773/2004. Accordingly, although the Commission is not obliged to adopt an infringement decision, it shall not refuse to adopt formal decisions rejecting complaints provided the complainant so requests. If no answer is received within two months, the complainant can bring an action for failure to act.[290] In *Ryanair/Commission*, the Commission rejected the complaint that the Commission had failed to act in relation to its complaint about an abuse of dominance by Munich Airport. It stated that Ryanair's complaint could not be classified as a complaint brought in accordance with the requirements of Regulation 1/2003 or Regulation 773/2004. Therefore, when the Commission was formally called upon to define its position, it was not under a duty to act and cannot be criticized for failing to act.[291]

The need for applicants to be direct addressees

The third paragraph of Article 265 TFEU provides that any natural or legal person may **15.89** bring an action on the ground that 'an institution of the Community has failed to address to that person any act other than a recommendation or an opinion'. Initially, the applicant had to be a person to whom the legal measure which the Commission should have adopted without fail might potentially have been addressed.[292] That requirement was not fulfilled, for example, in the case of *Lord Bethell v Commission*,[293] in which Lord Bethell complained that the Commission had not adopted measures under Article 101 TFEU against infringements of the EU competition provisions committed by airlines. However, a decision under Article 101 TFEU would have been addressed to the airlines, not Lord Bethell. Nevertheless, the Court later changed the direction of its case law when it held that '[t]he possibility for individuals to assert their rights should not depend upon whether the institution concerned

---

[287] See Case 48/65 *Lutticke v Commission* [1966] ECR 27, in particular paras 24–5 and the Opinion of AG Gand in the same case.

[288] See Case 125/78 *GEMA v Commission II* [1979] ECR 3173, para 18.

[289] See Case T-186/94 *Guérin Automobiles v Commission* [1995] ECR II-1753, paras 23 and 34.

[290] Case T-28/90 *Asia Motor France v Commission* [1992] ECR II-2285, para 28.

[291] Case T-423/07 *Ryanair v Commission* [2011] ECR II-2397, para 40.

[292] See Case 246/81 *Lord Bethell v Commission* [1982] ECR 2277. See also Case C-371/89 *Emrich v Commission* [1990] ECR I-1555, paras 5–6; Case C-72/90 *Asia Motor France v Commission* [1990] ECR I-2181, paras 10–12; and Case T-3/90 *Prodifarma v Commission* [1991] ECR II-1, para 35, all of which are cited in Case T-471/93 *Ladbroke v Commission* [1995] ECR II-2537, para 40.

[293] See Case 246/81 *Lord Bethell v Commission* [1982] ECR 2277.

has acted or failed to act',[294] a statement that made it possible for undertakings to bring an action against a failure to act, provided that the omitted act is regarded as being of 'direct and individual concern' to them (in the sense previously explained), even in those cases where the addressee of the act would have been another party. For analogous reasons, complainants in proceedings for the application of the competition rules may not bring actions under Article 265 TFEU where the Commission takes a measure having the contrary or a different effect from that sought by them, since the Commission is not obliged to adopt a decision on the terms sought by the complainants—Article 7(1) of Regulation 1/2003 allows this, but does not compel it to do so, as has been seen. The only remedy available to a complainant in such circumstances is therefore an action for annulment under Article 263.

2. Preconditions

15.90 The second paragraph of Article 265 lays down as a precondition for proceedings of this kind the fact that the EU institution against which an action for failure to act has been brought before the EU Courts[295] has been called upon by the applicant to act. This must follow a reasonable period of time that will depend on the matter concerned[296] and clearly on the act required that it must indicate the intention of the party to start proceedings if a failure to act finally occurs. Only upon the expiry of two months after the EU institution has been called on to act without it having defined its position may an action be brought within a further period of two months. 'Defining their position' means that the EU institutions must adopt a formal measure—in this case, a decision on the issue raised, but not necessarily the decision sought by the applicant—or a clear and express view concerning that measure. This means, for example, a provisional communication under Article 7 of Regulation 773/2004 to the effect that with the information in its possession there are no grounds to conclude that the agreement complained of infringes Article 101 or 102 TFEU, the complainant being informed in both cases that it is inappropriate to adopt an infringement decision, and being allowed to submit observations.[297] Conversely, if the intention is to take up the complaint and start proceedings against the subject of the complaint, the Manproc indicates that, provided the investigation is completed, a letter informing the complainant of the initiation of proceedings against the subject of the complaint, with a copy of the position taken (ie a non-confidential version of the statement of objections) would be an act ending the failure to act.[298] If the complainant is ready to allow some additional delay, or if it can be justified that the investigation is still ongoing, a letter explaining the steps taken by the Commission and showing that the Commission has not been inactive might be sufficient to convince the complainant not to go to Court.[299] If the complainant continues correspondence with

---

[294] Case C-68/95 *T Port GmbH & Co KG v Bundesanstalt fur Landwirtschaft und Ernahrung* [1996] ECR I-6065, para 59.

[295] In proceedings for failure to act in competition matters, the EU institution will be the Commission and the judicial authority the GC.

[296] Case T-127/98 *UPS Europe v Commission* [1999] ECR II-2633, para 38.

[297] See Case C-282/95 P *Guérin Automobiles v Commission* [1997] ECR I-1503, para 31.

[298] Commission Antitrust Manual of Procedures, Internal DG Competition working documents on procedures for the application of Articles 101 and 102 TFEU, March 2012, Module 26 'Court Litigation', para 44.

[299] Commission Antitrust Manual of Procedures, Internal DG Competition working documents on procedures for the application of Articles 101 and 102 TFEU, March 2012, Module 26 'Court Litigation', para 44, n 8, states that, legally speaking, such a letter would not put an end to the failure to act (see Case T-95/96, *Gestevisión Telecinco v Commission* [1998] ECR II-3407, para 88: 'A letter from an institution called upon to act under Article 175 of the Treaty stating that the questions raised are being examined does not in fact amount to the defining of a position such as to release it from its duty to act'). But such a letter can be enough to convince the complainant that the Commission has been (and is still) actively dealing with the case, so that he does not need to go to Court (Case 13/83 *Parliament v Council* [1985] ECR 1513, para 25).

the Commission after the formal request for the Commission to act, then the Commission is entitled to regard the formal request to act as having been withdrawn. The Commission should then write to the complainant informing it of this.[300]

The fact that the Commission informs the person seeking the measure that it is consider- **15.91** ing the question is not sufficient to prevent that person from bringing an action for failure to act. If the Commission were to define its position in the manner described after the two-month time limit, and the person seeking the measure had already commenced proceedings within the further period of two months, the GC could halt the proceedings and order the Commission to pay the applicant's costs.[301]

3. Consequences of the action

Where an action for failure to act in competition matters is upheld by the GC, the **15.92** Commission will be found to be at fault and will be obliged to adopt the measures necessary to comply with the judgment (first paragraph of Article 266 TFEU). Since judgments in actions for failure to act are basically declaratory, the GC will merely state that the failure to act is contrary to the Treaty. It will not take any steps to rectify the omission or even require the Commission to adopt specific measures, although the measures which it considers appropriate may be inferred from the terms of the judgment. As in the case of actions for annulment, the fulfilment of the obligations stemming from judgments given in proceedings for the failure of EU institutions to act does not exclude non-contractual liability resulting from omissions declared by the GC to be contrary to the Treaty (second paragraph of Article 266). The judgments of the GC in actions for failure to act are also 'enforceable under the conditions laid down in Article 299' (Article 280 TFEU).

C. Applications to the Courts for Interim or Protective Measures

Where an applicant challenges a Commission decision under Article 261 or 263, the appli- **15.93** cation does not automatically stay the operation and the effect of the decision in question. Pursuant to Article 278 TFEU, actions brought before the EU Courts shall not have suspensive effect. However, Article 278 also gives the EU Courts the possibility of suspending the application of the contested act, where the circumstances so require. In addition, Article 279 TFEU provides that the EU Courts may prescribe any necessary interim measures in any cases which it hears. The nature of the measures which may be adopted by the EU Courts under either provision is basically the same; accordingly, they are both described here in general terms as interim measures.[302] In any event, in practice it is very common for actions to be brought jointly on the basis of both provisions. Applications of this kind are always related and subordinate to a main action—either under Article 263 TFEU (annulment) or Article 265 TFEU (failure to act)—and may be submitted only after or at the same time as the main action is brought.[303] In any event—and this is very important—submission must

---

[300] Commission Antitrust Manual of Procedures, Internal DG Competition working documents on procedures for the application of Articles 101 and 102 TFEU, March 2012, Module 26 'Court Litigation', para 45.

[301] See, eg Case 75/69 *Ernest Hake & Co v Commission* [1970] ECR 535, and Case T-186/94 *Guérin Automobiles v Commission* [1995] ECR II-1753.

[302] See F Castillo de la Torre, 'Interim Measures in Community Courts: Recent Trends' (2007) 44 Common Market Law Review 273,

[303] If the main action is manifestly inadmissible, the application for interim relief must also fail: see, eg Case C-117/91 R *Jean-Marc Bosnan v Commission* [1991] ECR I-3353, para 7.

be by means of a separate document, in which reasons must be set out justifying the urgent need for interim measures.

15.94 Applications for suspension of the operation of the contested measure under Article 263 TFEU may be brought concerning procedural decisions based on Article 18 and Article 20 of Regulation 1/2003 (ie requests for information and inspections) and substantive decisions, principally under Article 7 of Regulation 1/2003 (ie infringement of Articles 101 and 102 TFEU). In the past, undertakings have requested (and sometimes secured) both suspension of the implementation of Commission decisions imposing fines,[304] prescribing certain conduct or prohibiting other conduct,[305] the suspension of inspection decisions,[306] and the suspension of decisions requesting information under Article 18 of Regulation 1/2003[307] (although in such cases no undertaking has so far been successful). A request for an injunction against a third party not to make use in any way of the information contained in the statement of objections forwarded to it was ruled to be inadmissible.[308] By the same token,

---

[304] The EU Courts take a very strict approach to this issue, which has made it extremely difficult to be granted a suspension without a bank guarantee. The applicant seeking interim relief can be exempted only in exceptional circumstances from the obligation to provide a bank guarantee as a condition for the Commission's not immediately recovering a fine imposed by it. See eg Case T-398/10 R *Fapricela—Indústria de Trefilaria, SA v Commission* [2011] OJ C282/20, confirmed in Order of the President of the ECJ in Case C-507/11 P(R) *Fapricela—Indústria de Trefilaria, SA v Commission*; Case T-30/10 R *Reagens SpA v Commission* [2010] ECR II-83; Case T-410/09 *Almamet v Commission* [2010] ECR II-80; Cases T-104/95 R *Tsimenta Chalkidos v Commission* [1995] ECR II-2235 or T-18/96R *SCK & NCK v Commission* [1996] ECR II-407; see also Case T-191/98 R II *Cho Yang Shipping v Commission* [2000] ECR II-2551 and on appeal Case C-361/00 P(R) *Cho Yang Shipping v Commission* [2000] ECR I-11657. See also para 15.04 et seq.

[305] See, eg Case T-398/08 *Stowarzyszenie Autorów ZAiKS v Commission* [2008] ECR II-266; Case T-401/08 *Säveltäjäin Tekijänoikeustoimisto Teosto v Commission* [2008] ECR II-267; Case T-410/08 *GEMA v Commission* [2008] ECR II-268; Case T-411/08 *Artisjus Magyar Szerzői Jogvédő Iroda Egyesület v Commission* [2008] ECR II-270; Case T-422/08 *Sacem v Commission* [2008] ECR II-27; Case 27/76 R *United Brands v Commission* [1976] ECR 425, where the Court suspended part of the Commission's decision requiring United Brands to refrain from charging discriminatory and unfair selling prices for bananas; Cases 76–77/89 and 91/89 R *Radio Telefis Eireann v Commission (Magill)* [1989] ECR 1141, in which the Court suspended part of the Commission's decision which would have required the broadcasters to grant a compulsory licence of their programme schedules, admitting that the case raised delicate questions concerning the scope of Art 102; Case C-56/89 R *Publishers' Association v Commission* [1989] ECR I-1693, in which the Court suspended part of the Commission's decision requiring substantial amendments to the agreements in question.

[306] Eg *Hoechst* unsuccessfully sought suspension of a Commission inspection decision adopted in 1988. Case 46/87 R *Hoechst AG v Commission* [1987] ECR 1549. See also Case 85/87 R *Dow Chemical v Commission* [1987] ECR 4367. Nevertheless, the Court's approach seems to have changed. In an Order issued recently in *Akzo Nobel*, the President of the GC pointed out this tendency when assuring that, except in 'very special circumstances', defence rights prevail over 'considerations of administrative efficiency and of resource allocation'. Order of the President of the GC in Cases T-125/03 R and T-253/03 R *Akzo Nobel Chemicals v Commission* [2003] ECR II-4771, para 186, annulled in Case C-7/04 P(R) *Commission v Akzo Nobel* [2004] ECR I-8739.

[307] Orders of the GC of 29 July 2011 in Case T-292/11R *Cemex and others v Commission*; Case T-302/11 *Heidelberg Cement v Commission*; Case T-293/11 *Holcim (Deutschland) and Holcim v Commission*; Order of the President of the GC of 29 July 2011 in Case T-296/11 R *Cementos Portland Valderrivas, SA v Commission*, where the Court dismissed requests by four cement companies for interim measures to suspend an information request.

[308] Case T-12/07R *Polimeri Europa SpA v Commission* [2007] ECR II-38. The Commission argued that Polimeri's application was inadmissible, as it amounted to a request for the imposition of an injunction on a third party, which the Commission has no power to do, and also because such an order would not in fact change Polimeri's current position as the third party in this case, Manufacture Française des Pneumatiques Michelin (MFPM) is already bound by confidentiality undertakings agreed as a condition to it receiving a copy of the statement of objections. The GC President agreed that PE's application was inadmissible and, therefore, rejected the request. The President noted that the Commission has neither the power under either Reg 1/2003 or Reg 773/2004 to impose an order (whether general, as in this case, or specific) on third parties to proceedings or to draw up and, if necessary, impose sanctions on a third party to such administrative proceedings.

the GC rejected Intel's request for interim measures on the basis that the main action (i.e, the request for an extension of time in which to reply to the statement of objections) brought by Intel was manifestly inadmissible. It would not be for the EU judicature to issue directions to the Commission where the Court decides that the Commission's original decision cannot stand.[309]

Article 104(2) of the GC Rules of Procedure spells out the requirements for undertakings **15.95** that seek to apply for the suspension of an act or decision or any other interim relief, stating that '[a]n application [to suspend the operation of the measure or for any other interim measure] shall state the subject-matter of the proceedings, the circumstances giving rise to urgency and the pleas of fact and law establishing a prima facie case for the interim measures applied for.'[310] The President of the GC may grant the application even before the observations of the opposite party have been submitted.[311] This decision may be varied or cancelled even without any application being made by any party. The suspension may be partial and in practice is usually limited to certain parts of the contested decision, which in all other respects remains directly enforceable. The primary aim of interim measures in general is to guarantee the full effectiveness of the final future decision, in order to ensure that there is no lacuna in the legal protection provided by the EU Courts.[312]

An application under Article 279 TFEU to suspend the operation of a measure adopted by **15.96** an institution is admissible only if the applicant is challenging that measure in proceedings before the Court. In addition, an application for the adoption of any other interim measure referred to in Article 279 TFEU is admissible only if it is made by a party to a case before the GC and relates to that case. In order for a decision to be suspended, the applicants must state the circumstances giving rise to urgency and the pleas of fact and law establishing a *prima facie* case for the interim measures sought. The measures sought must be necessary in order to avoid serious and irreparable damage to the applicant's interests arising before a decision is reached in the main action and provisional in the sense that they must not prejudice that decision or neutralize in advance its effects.[313] Those conditions are cumulative, so that an application for interim measures must be dismissed if any one of them is not complied with.[314] It is for the party seeking suspension of the operation of an act to prove that it cannot wait for the outcome of the main proceedings without suffering damage of the type specified.[315] In the context of the overall examination, the GC must exercise the broad discretion which it enjoys when determining the manner in which those various conditions

---

[309] Case T-457/08 R *Intel Corp v Commission* [2009] ECR II-12, para 49, referring to Case T-126/99 *Graphischer Maschinenbau v Commission* [2002] ECR II-2427, para 17 and the case law therein cited.

[310] GC Rules of Procedure, as amended, last amendment [2011] OJ L162/18. See also the similar provision, Art 83(1) of the ECJ Rules of Procedure, as amended, last amendment [2011] OJ L162/17. Both sets of rules are available at <http://curia.eu.int>.

[311] Article 105(2) of the GC Rules of Procedure. See Case T-184/01 R *IMS Health v Commission* [2001] ECR II-3193.

[312] Case C-7/04 *Commission v Akzo Nobel* [2004] ECR I-8739, para 36.

[313] Case T-352/09 R *Novácke chemické závody, as v Commission* [2009] ECR II-208, para 13; Case T-184/01 R *IMS Health v Commission* [2002] ECR-II 3193, para 47; Case T-65/98 R *Van den Berg-Foods Ltd v Commission* [1998] ECR II-4653; Orders in Joined Cases 76/89 R, 77/89 R, and 91/89 R *RTE and others v Commission* [1989] ECR 1141, para 12; Case C-149/95 P(R) *Commission v Atlantic Container Line and others* [1995] ECR I-2165, para 22 and Case C-268/96 P(R) *SCK and FNK v Commission* [1996] ECR I-4971, para 30.

[314] Order of the President of the ECJ in Case C-7/04 P(R) *Commission v Akzo Nobel* [2004] ECR I-8739, para 28.

[315] Order of the President of the GC in Joined Cases T-38/99 R to T-42/99 R, T-45/99 R, and T-48/99 R *Sociedade Agrícola dos Arinhos and others v Commission* [1999] ECR II-2567, para 42.

are to be examined in the light of the specific circumstances of each case.[316] Article 107(1) of the GC Rules of Procedure states that '[t]he decision on the application shall take the form of a reasoned order'.[317] It has, however, been held that a judge dealing with an application for interim relief cannot be required to reply expressly to all of the points of fact and law raised in the course of the interim proceedings. In particular, it is sufficient that the reasons given by the judge dealing with the application at first instance validly justify his order in the light of the circumstances of the case and enable the ECJ to exercise its powers of review.[318]

15.97 The GC evaluates whether the arguments put forward by the applicant cannot be dismissed at that stage of the procedure without a more detailed examination.[319] In particular, where the applicant seeks interim relief against an interim decision, the applicant is not required to demonstrate a particularly strong or serious stateable case against the validity of what constitutes a *prima facie* evaluation by the Commission of the existence of an infringement of EU competition law.[320] The urgency of an application for interim relief must be assessed in the light of the need for an interlocutory order to avoid serious and irreparable damage to the party seeking the relief.[321] It is sufficient for the harm to be foreseeable with the appropriate degree of probability, particularly where it depends on the occurrence of a number of factors.[322]

15.98 The GC has generally ruled that pure financial loss cannot, save in exceptional circumstances, be regarded as irreparable, or even as being reparable only with difficulty, if it can ultimately

---

[316] Order in Case C-149/95 P(R) *Commission v Atlantic Container Line and Others* [1995] ECR I-2165, para 23; Case T-201/04 R *Microsoft v Commission* [2005] ECR II-3601, para 72; Order of the President of the GC in Case C-459/06 P(R) *Vischim v Commission* [2007] ECR I-53, para 25; Kerse & Khan, *EC Antitrust Procedure* (6th edn, Sweet & Maxwell 2012) para 8-183.

[317] As amended, last amendment [2011] OJ L162/18; see also Art 162(1) of the ECJ Rules of Procedure, as amended, last amendment [2012] OJ L265/1 available at <http://curia.eu.int>.

[318] Order of the President of the Court of Justice in Case C-159/98 P(R) *Netherlands Antilles v Council* [1998] ECR I-4147, para 70.

[319] Case T-395/94 R *Atlantic Container Line and others v Commission* [1995] ECR II-595, para 26; Case T-184/01 *IMS Health Inc v Commission* [2001] ECR II-3193, paras 59 and 60; Case T-41/96 R *Bayer AG v Commission* [1996] ECR II-381, para 42; Order of the President of the GC in Case T-201/04 R *Microsoft v Commission* [2005] ECR II-3601, paras 204–25, stating that arguments which Microsoft put forward concerning the issues raised in the main case could not be regarded as *prima facie* unfounded in the interim relief proceedings. Conversely, where the applicants cannot establish urgency, the President of the GC did not examine whether the other cumulative conditions for ordering the suspension had been satisfied, in particular whether the existence of a *prima facie* case had been established, see eg Case C-32/09 P (R) *Artisjus v Commission* [2010] ECR I-107, para 10.

[320] Case T-184/01 *IMS Health Inc v Commission* [2001] ECR II-3193, para 66; see also Order of the President of the GC of 13 April 2011 in Case T-393/10 *Westfälische Drahtindustrie and Others v Commission* [2011] ECR II-1697, para 60, stating that the possibility of the Court reducing the fine on the basis of its unlimited jurisdiction may in itself be sufficient to assert a *prima facie* case. E Barbier de la Serre and C Winckler, 'A Landmark Year for the Law on Fines imposed in EU Competition Proceedings' (2012) 3(4) Journal of European Competition Law & Practice 351, 367, note that in light of the power of the Court to exercise its unlimited jurisdiction as soon as 'the question of the amount of the fine is before it' (Case C-3/06 *Danone v Commission* [2007] ECR I-1331, para 62), this requisite of a *prime facie* case will be easily fulfilled in case of decisions imposing fines.

[321] Orders in Case T-352/09 R *Novácke chemické závody, as v Commission* [2009] ECR II-208, para 36 et seq; Case C-268/96 P(R) *Stichting Certificatie Kraanverhuurbedrijf (SCK) and Federa-tie van Nederlandse Kraanverhuurbedrijven (FNK) v Commission* [1996] ECR I-4971, para 30; Case C-329/99 P(R) *Pfizer Animal Health v Council* [1999] ECR I-8343, para 94; and Case C-471/00 P(R) *Commission v Cambridge Healthcare Supplies* [2001] ECR I-2865, para 107.

[322] Case C-335/99 P(R) *HFB and others v Commission* [1999] ECR I-8705, para 67; Case T-237/99 R *BP Nederland and others v Commission* [2000] ECR II-3849, para 49; Case T-201/04 R *Microsoft v Commission* [2005] ECR II-4463, para 241.

be the subject of financial compensation.[323] Interim relief is generally not granted in respect of financial loss unless the applicant is in a position to adduce evidence that would justify a *prima facie* finding that, failing the relief sought, the losses alleged would be such as to threaten its survival in the relevant market.[324]

However, in *IMS Health*, the GC stated that the case law on the interpretation of the notion **15.99** of damage is mainly based on the 'premise that damage of a financial nature that is not eliminated by the implementation of the judgment in the main proceedings constitutes an economic loss which may be made good by the means of redress provided for in the Treaty, in particular Articles [268 TFEU] and [340 TFEU]'.[325] It did state, however, that the prospects of an adequate redress would be difficult to ascertain where the applicant is basically limited to seeking redress before national courts. Having regard to the broad discretion enjoyed by the Commission in deciding whether it is appropriate to adopt interim decisions, it would seem unlikely that the applicant could succeed in any action for damages brought against the Commission on the grounds that the latter had manifestly and gravely disregarded the limits placed on its discretion.[326] While these factors as such did not threaten the survival of IMS Health in the market, the President of the GC concluded that there would be a real and tangible risk that execution of the Commission decision could, before judgment in the main action, cause serious and irreparable harm to IMS Health because it might trigger market developments that would be very difficult, if not impossible, to reverse later,[327] and it imposed significant restrictions on the freedom to define its business policy.[328]

Similarly, in *Adalat*, the President of the GC took the view that the immediate implementa- **15.100** tion of the prohibition imposed by the Commission to refuse supplies to wholesalers in order to prevent an increase in parallel exports might deprive Bayer of its independence in defining its business policy. The risk of serious damage would stem from price disparities in Member States over which Bayer had no control, which might cause Bayer to lower prices in those countries to which wholesalers might export the drug.[329]

In *Van den Bergh Foods*, the Commission adopted a decision in which an exclusivity require- **15.101** ment applicable to freezer cabinets and contained in distribution agreements was held to constitute an infringement of the EU competition rules. When assessing the degree of urgency resulting from the application to suspend the immediate revocation of the exclusivity

---

[323] Case T-392/09 *1. garantovaná v Commission* [2011] ECR II-33, para 38; Case C-213/91 *Abertal SAT Ltda and others v Commission* [1991] ECR I-5109, para 24; Case T-230/97 R *Comafrica and Dole v Commission* [1997] ECR II-1589, para 32; Case T-137/00 *Cambridge Healthcare Supplies Ltd v Commission* [2002] ECR II-4945, para 113; Case T-339/00 R *Bactria v Commission* [2002] ECR II-2287, para 94.

[324] Case T-181/02 R *Neue Erba Lautex v Commission* [2002] ECR II-5081, para 84; Case T-385/10 R *ArcelorMittal Wire France and Others v Commission* [2010] ECR II-262, para 37, where the ECJ considered that the applicant had failed to show that the constitution of bank guarantees would imperil their existence, the fact of the parent company's refusal to provide financial support being irrelevant. The letters from banks rejecting applicants for guarantees, produced by the applicants in evidence, were couched in very general terms and did not consider the global financial situation of the ArcelorMittal group.

[325] Case T-184/01 *IMS Health Inc v Commission* [2001] ECR II-3193, para 119, referring to the Orders in Case T-230/97 R *Comafrica and Dole v Commission* [1997] ECR II-1589, para 38 and in Case T-169/00 R *Esedra v Commission* [2000] ECR II-2951, para 47.

[326] Case T-184/01 *IMS Health Inc v Commission* [2001] ECR II-3193, paras 119–20; see also Case C-352/98 P *Bergaderm and Goupil v Commission* [2000] ECR I-5291, paras 41–4; Joined Cases T-198/95, T-171/96, T-230/97, T-174/98, and T-225/99 *Comafrica and Dole v Commission* [1997] ECR II-1589, para 134.

[327] See also Cases C-76/89, C-77/89, and C-91/89 R *Radio Telefis Eireann v Commission* [1989] ECR I-1141.

[328] Case T-184/01 *IMS Health Inc v Commission* [2001] ECR II-3193, paras 128–32.

[329] Case T-41/96 R *Bayer v Commission* ('*Adalat*') [1996] ECR II-381, paras 53–6.

requirement provided for in the Commission decision, the GC considered that this could have immediate serious and irreparable effects: competitors would make every effort to sell their products through outlets which had previously been less readily accessible. In addition, it was necessary to take into account the seasonal nature of sales of the products in question, which are purchased largely during the summer months.[330] In such a situation, if the decision in question were annulled, the financial losses would have been extremely difficult to quantify for the purposes of making reparation, in the light of unpredictable variations in the sales of such products. Moreover, there were serious grounds for believing that the market developments which immediate execution of the decision was likely to cause would be very difficult, if not impossible, to reverse if the application in the main action were subsequently successful.[331] The President of the GC therefore ordered the suspension of the Commission decision.

15.102 Previously, in *Atlantic Container Lines*, the Court found that the immediate effect of the Commission decision would have been to prevent the applicants from pursuing a practice which had been widespread in Europe since the early 1970s, ie the joint fixing of rates by shipping lines in respect of the inland portions of through-intermodal transport services in the maritime sector. The President of the GC agreed that the interruption of that practice might entail a risk for the operation of the transport market, since the applicants could put forward credible evidence that if they were unable to jointly fix rates for that type of transport, a general collapse of maritime transport rates would be likely to ensue.[332]

15.103 More recently, the President of the GC rejected applications by five collective rights associations for interim measures to suspend operative parts of the European Commission's decision that contracts and concerted practices between collecting society EEA members of the International Confederation of Societies of Authors and Composers ('CISAC') infringed Article 101 TFEU, rejecting a claim that implementation of the decision would reduce the income of the collecting societies dramatically, so potentially endangering their existence. The Commission only challenged the lawfulness of the concerted practice as regards exploitation by internet, satellite, and cable, which represented only a small fraction of the collecting societies' total income. The applicants had not, however, produced any evidence to demonstrate the seriousness of the alleged financial damage. In any event, damage of a financial nature will not, other than in exceptional circumstances, be regarded as irrevocable, since it can normally be the subject of later financial compensation.[333]

15.104 Ultimately, the Court's assessment hinges on striking a balance between the harm to the applicant from non-suspension—foreseeable with a sufficient degree of probability—with any harm which will be suffered by other parties if the suspension is granted.[334] In *IMS Health*, the President of the GC did not agree with the Commission decision which had

---

[330] Case T-65/98 *Van den Bergh Foods Ltd v Commission* [1998] ECR II-2641, paras 62 and 63.
[331] Case T-65/98 *Van den Bergh Foods Ltd v Commission* [1998] ECR II-2641, paras 65–7.
[332] Case T-395/94 R *Atlantic Container Line AB and others v Commission* [1995] ECR II-595, paras 51–7.
[333] Case T-398/08 *Stowarzyszenie Autorów ZAiKS v Commission* [2008] ECR II-266; Case T-401/08 *Säveltäjäin Tekijänoikeustoimisto Teosto v Commission* [2008] ECR II-267; Case T-410/08 *GEMA v Commission* [2008] ECR II-268; Case T-411/08 *Artisjus Magyar Szerzői Jogvédő Iroda Egyesület v Commission* [2008] ECR II-270; Case T-422/08 *Sacem v Commission* [2008] ECR II-271.
[334] Case C-445/00 R *Austria v Council* [2001] ECR I-1461, para 73; Case T-308/94 R *Cascades v Commission* [1995] ECR II-265. See also in relation to the suspension of fining decisions: Order of the President of the GC of 13 April 2011 in Case T-393/10 *Westfälische Drahtindustrie and Others v Commission* [2011] ECR II-1697, para 69 et seq; Order of the President of 31 August 2010 in Case T-299/10 R *Babcock Noell v European joint undertaking for ITER and the Development of Fusion Energy* [2010] OJ C301/31, para 64, 'the balance of interests requires the judge hearing the application to determine whether or not the interest of the applicant in obtaining the interim measures sought outweighs the interest in the immediate application

seemed to equate the interests of IMS' competitors with the interests of competition, thereby ignoring the primary purpose of Article 101 TFEU, namely to prevent the distortion of competition, and especially to safeguard the interests of consumers, rather than to protect the position of particular competitors.[335] In *Adalat*, the President of the GC weighed up the risk of major and irrevocable losses of profit faced by Bayer against the interests of wholesalers in Spain and France in increasing the volume of their exports to the UK, and concluded that the risk of damage to which Bayer would be exposed was disproportionate.[336] In *Van den Bergh Foods*, the GC not only weighed up the risk of damage to the applicant, but also noted a reduction in legal certainty as a result of a contradiction between the views of the Commission and those of the national courts in their application of EU competition law, which had earlier ruled that Van den Bergh's distribution system did not infringe Articles 101 and 102 TFEU.[337] As regards the fining decisions, the GC has typically to examine whether the interest of the applicants in suspension of the operation of the contested decision weighs more heavily than the interest in immediate implementation of that decision. In *Westfälische Drahtindustrie*, the GC acknowledged that the financial interests of the EU are of fundamental importance.[338] However, given that the applicants would be unable to pay the fine, it was unlikely that the Commission would receive the amount of the fines if it were to seek to enforce them. Additionally, the Commission's claim would not have any priority in the event of the bankruptcy of the applicants. Therefore, the GC found that the financial interests of the Commission would not be better protected if immediate compulsory enforcement were commenced, than it would be if the applicants were enabled to continue their business and pay their fines out of the proceeds.[339] There have also been interim decisions with regard to the publication of allegedly conmfidential information. For example, in *Alstom v Commission*, the President of the GC ordred the suspension of of the Commission's decision to transmit certain documents to the High Court of England and Wales to be used in a proceedings involving an action for damages against the cartel participants. The documents concerned material that was submitted by Alstom (or its predecessors) to the Commission during the course of the *Gas insulated switchgear* cartel investigation.[340] Weighing up the

---

of the contested act by examining, more specifically, whether the possible annulment of the act by the Court giving judgment in the main action would allow the situation brought about by its immediate implementation to be reversed and, conversely, whether suspension of operation of that act would be liable to prevent its full effect in the event of the main application being dismissed.'

[335] Case T-184/01 *IMS Health Inc v Commission* [2001] II-3193, para 145.

[336] Case T-41/96 R *Bayer v Commission* [1996] ECR II-381, paras 59–60.

[337] Case T-65/98 *Van den Bergh Foods Ltd v Commission* [1998] ECR II-2641, paras 70–4. The President took the view that the fact that Van den Bergh's competitors on the market found it difficult to distribute their products as a result of alleged structural barriers could not take precedence over the risks thus identified.

[338] Case T-393/10 *Westfälische Drahtindustrie and Others v Commission* [2011] ECR II-1697, para 65; Case 56/89 R *Publishers Association v Commission* [1989] ECR 1693, para 35; in Case T-245/03 R *FNSEA and Others v Commission* [2004] ECR II-271, para 119; and in Case T-11/06 R *Romana Tabacchi v Commission* [2006] ECR II-2491, para 135, indicates that this involves more generally weighing the applicant's interest in avoiding—in the event that it is unable to arrange a bank guarantee—immediate recovery of the fine against, on the other hand, the EU's financial interest in being able to recover that sum and, more generally, against the public interest in preserving the effectiveness of the competition rules and the deterrent effect of fines imposed by the Commission.

[339] Order of the President of the GC of 13 April 2011 in Case T-393/10 *Westfälische Drahtindustrie and Others v Commission* [2011] ECR II-1697, paras 65–70.

[340] Order of the President of the GC in Case T-164/12 R *Alstom v Commission*, 29 November 2012. The issue was whether the Commission, acceding to the High Court's request could involve an infringement of the obligation of professional secrecy protected in Art 339 TFEU. The President concluded that the appeal raised complex questions of law relating to the application of Art 339 TFEU. There would, therefore, be a *prima facie* case. The President ordered that the Commission's decision be suspended in so far as that decision concerns the transmission to the High Court of the confidential version of Alstom's reply to the statement of

different interests, the President of the GC decided that the suspension of of the contested decision would not preclude the Commission from adopting a new decision permitting the transmission of the non-confidential version of the documents at issue while awaiting the GC's ruling on the action for annulment in the main proceedings.[341] In *Microsoft*, however, the GC found that Microsoft had not adduced evidence that disclosure of the information previously kept secret would cause serious and irreparable damage. Following a factual examination of the actual consequences of disclosure as alleged by Microsoft, the President concluded that the required disclosure of information previously kept secret did not necessarily entail serious and irreparable damage and that, in the light of the circumstances of the case, such damage had not been demonstrated. Microsoft could not prove any of the following four points, namely that:

(i)   use by its competitors of the information disclosed would lead to its 'dilution';
(ii) the fact that the competing products would remain in the distribution channel after the decision had been annulled would constitute serious and irreparable damage;
(iii) it would be required to make a fundamental change in its business policy; or
(iv) the decision would cause an irreversible development on the market.[342]

---

objections. See also Order of the President of the GC of 11 March 2013 in Case T-462/12 *Pilkington Group v Commission*, where the GC made an order partially upholding and partially dismissing Pilkington Glass Ltd's application for interim relief in relation to its appeal against a decision of the Commission that refused its request for the confidential treatment of certain information relating to its participation in the car glass cartel. The Court found that Pilkington's application for interim measures must be upheld in so far as it would seek to prevent publication by the Commission of information relating to (i) customer names, product names or descriptions of products as well as any other information which might identify individual customers; and (ii) the number of parts supplied by Pilkington, the share of the business of a particular car manufacturer, pricing calculations or price changes etc.

[341] See Order of the President of the GC of 16 November 2012 in Case T-345/12 *Akzo Nobel and Others v Commission*, where the GC granted requests for interim relief in appeals challenging the Commission's refusal to grant confidential treatment for information in the decision on the bleaching chemicals cartel. The Commission intended to publish an extended non-confidential version of the cartel decision. The President of the GC concluded that the balance of interests lies in favour of granting interim measures to prevent publication of the contested information pending the conclusion of the appeal. For a more general view of the issues involved, see also Savvas S Papasavvas, 'Confidentiality Issues in Competition Law: The Impact of Confidentiality Issues on Proceedings before the CFI' in Heikki Kanninen, Nina Korjus, and Allan Rosas (eds), *EU Competition Law in Context: Essays in Honour of Virpi Tiili* (Hart Publishing 2009).

[342] Case T-201/04 R *Microsoft v Commission* [2004] ECR II-4463, para 266 et seq.

PART II

CONTROL OF CONCENTRATIONS
(REGULATION (EC) 139/2004)

16

GENERAL ISSUES: SCOPE OF CONTROL

Marcos Araujo Boyd and Nicolas von Lingen

A. Introduction

Council Regulation (EC) 139/2004 on the control of concentrations between undertak- **16.01**
ings[1] (hereinafter the 'Merger Control Regulation') sets out a common merger control in the
twenty-eight Member States of the EU. The Merger Control Regulation, which replaced former
Regulation (EEC) 4064/89,[2] is based on the necessity of ensuring that corporate transactions
do not distort competition between undertakings, while ensuring a level playing field between
undertakings operating in the different Member States.[3] It is based on the mandatory notification of corporate transactions above certain objective thresholds which define 'European Union
dimension'[4] and the application of common clearance criteria under the exclusive control of the
Commission.

---

[1] Council Reg (EC) No 139/2004 of 20 January 2004 on the control of concentrations between undertakings [2004] OJ L24/1.
[2] Council Reg (EC) No 4064/89 of 21 December 1989 on the control of concentrations between undertakings [1989] OJ L395/1 amended by Council Reg (EC) 1310/97 of 30 June 1997 [1997] OJ L180/1.
[3] Recitals 2–5 of the Merger Control Regulation. The Directorate-General for Competition ('DG
COMP') has published FAQs (Frequently Asked Questions) on its webpage explaining various aspects of the
Merger Control Regulation in brief notes.
[4] Consistent with the terminology of the Lisbon Treaty and the practice of the European Commission
after its entry into force, we use here the expressions 'Union dimension' or 'EU dimension' in reference to

16.02 The Merger Control Regulation is built upon the experience gained under former Regulation 4064/89. The Merger Control Regulation introduced a number of procedural improvements. Of particular significance are the changes with regard to the referral mechanisms of concentration cases, which seek to ensure that each case is dealt with by the competition authority that is best placed to do so, limiting as far as possible parallel notifications before multiple competition agencies. Further, in line with the reform of the rules approved in the context of Regulation 1/2003 for the application of Articles 101 and 102 of the Treaty on the Functioning of the European Union ('TFEU'), the Merger Control Regulation also widened the Commission's investigative powers.[5]

16.03 In parallel to the Merger Control Regulation, Article 57 of the Agreement on the European Economic Area ('EEA Agreement') also provides for a merger control regime which covers the geographic ambit of the EEA.[6] Under the EEA Agreement, if a concentration meets the turnover thresholds of the Merger Control Regulation, the Commission has sole competence to decide on the concentration. Concentrations with an 'EFTA [European Free Trade Association] dimension' as defined in Article 57 of the EEA Agreement and not having EU dimension are dealt with by the EFTA Surveillance Authority ('ESA').[7] However, to date no such concentrations have been notified to the EFTA Surveillance Authority. Where the Commission handles cases as a consequence of its competence under the EEA Agreement, ESA and the competition authorities of the EFTA States are involved in the proceedings.[8]

B. Basic Principles of Procedure under the Merger Control Regulation

1. Prior notification of concentrations

16.04 A fundamental principle of the system designed by the Merger Control Regulation is that undertakings must notify concentrations prior to their implementation and once an agreement has been reached, a public bid has been announced, or a controlling interest has been acquired.[9] Implementation of a concentration with no prior authorization may lead to severe

---

the minimum turnover requirements for European jurisdiction of mergers. Note, however, that Art 1 of the Merger Control Regulation still employs the expression 'Community dimension'.

[5] See Recital 38 of the Merger Control Regulation. This alignment is clear from a simple comparison of the powers contained in Arts 11–15 of the Merger Control Regulation and Arts 18–24 of Reg 1/2003. Both systems recognize the power of the Commission to send requests for information, carry out inspections on the premises of undertakings, examine books, and other materials stored on any medium whatever, take copies, seal premises, interview and request explanations, as well as record answers, impose fines and periodic penalty payments. However, unlike Art 21 of Reg 1/2003, the Merger Control Regulation says nothing about carrying out inspections at other premises, such as the homes of the directors, managers, and other members of staff of the undertakings concerned.

[6] The EEA, established under the Treaty of Porto of 2 May 1992, comprises the current EU countries plus Iceland, Liechtenstein, and Norway.

[7] See Annex XIV (Competition) to the EEA Agreement and Protocols 21 (on the implementation of competition rules applicable to undertakings) and 24 (on cooperation in the field of control of concentrations) to the EEA Agreement.

[8] See Protocol 24 (on cooperation in the field of control of concentrations) to the EEA Agreement.

[9] Article 4(1) of the Merger Control Regulation and Recital 34. Note that reference to the need to notify the operation within one week of reaching an agreement as contemplated in Reg 4064/89 has been removed, as well as the need for a binding agreement before notification is possible. It is now also possible to notify on the basis that the parties merely intend in good faith to enter into an agreement (Art 4(1) second sub-paragraph). Recital 34 of the Regulation requires that in such a case the parties must show the Commission that any such plan is sufficiently concrete, 'for example on the basis of an agreement in principle, a memorandum of agreement or a letter of intent signed by all undertakings concerned'. See Ch 17, 'Procedures', para 17.19.

sanctions.[10] In the initial years following the adoption of former Regulation 4064/89, the Commission was lenient with companies that did not notify or notified late, in particular when the operations concerned were complicated, it was not clear whether or not notification was necessary, and where there was no evidence that the companies concerned deliberately intended to breach the Regulation.[11] In 1998, a fine was imposed for the first time on a company for non-notification of a concentration in a case where deciding whether or not notification was necessary did not involve a complicated assessment of the relevant facts.[12] One year later, on 10 February 1999 the Commission imposed fines for failing to notify and for putting into effect three concentrations in breach of Arts 4 and 7(1) of Reg (EEC) 4064/89.[13] As can be seen from the *Electrabel/Compagnie nationale du Rhône* case from 2009, the current fining policy is more severe, at least with respect to early implementation of concentrations. In this case, the Commission imposed a fine of EUR 20 million for failure to suspend a concentration for a period of at least three years and seven months after having acquired *de facto* control, and this despite the fact that the transaction was later cleared unconditionally in phase one.[14] In practice, it is worth contacting the Commission, and, if appropriate, notifying an operation, even if the parties disagree about the need for this.[15]

---

[10] Under Art 14(2)(a) Merger Control Regulation, the fine could reach up to 10 per cent of the aggregate turnover of the undertakings concerned. See eg Case T-102/96 *Gencor v Commission* [1999] ECR II-753, para 76 and the General Court ('GC') judgment of 12 December 2012 in Case T-332/09 *Electrabel v Commission*, paras 234, 241, and 246–7.

[11] Case IV/M.157 *Air France/Sabena* [1992] OJ C272/5, para 21; Case IV/M.166 *Torras/Sarrió* [1992] OJ C58/20, para 3, in which the Commission abstained from imposing a fine in the light of the problems experienced by the parties when calculating turnover; COMP/JV.55 *Hutchison/RCPM/ECT* [2003] OJ C223/1, para 6, Commission Press Release IP/00/1199 'Commission prepares to take action against Hutchison and the Port of Rotterdam for failure to notify the acquisition of ECT as a merger' of 26 October 2000, in which the parties had notified the transaction in accordance with Reg 17 as a cooperation agreement. The Commission declared in the statement of objections that it was a concentration and threatened to impose a fine for breach of the duty to notify under former Reg 4064/89. Finally, the parties duly notified the concentration which was approved by the Commission. Distinguished from Case COMP/M.4994 *Electrabel/ Compagnie nationale du Rhône* [2009] in Case T-332/09 *Electrabel v Commission*, para 259.

[12] Commission Decision of 18 February 1998, imposing fines for failing to notify and for putting into effect a concentration in breach of Arts 4(1) and 7(1) of Council Reg (EEC) 4064/89 (Case IV/M.920 *Samsung/AST*) [1999] OJ L225/12, para 29.

[13] Case IV/M.969 *AP Møller* [1999] OJ L183/29, para 12. The size of the fines imposed on the Danish company AP Møller for failure to notify and for executing three concentrations without prior approval amounted to EUR 219,000.

[14] Commission Decision of 10 June 2009 imposing a fine of EUR 20 million on Electrabel, an electricity producer and retailer belonging to the Suez Group (now GDF Suez) for acquiring control of Compagnie Nationale du Rhône (CNR), another electricity producer, without having received prior approval under Reg 4064/89 (Case COMP/M.4994 *Electrabel/Compagnie Nationale du Rhône* [2009] OJ C279). Competition Commissioner Neelie Kroes said: 'It is essential for effective merger control that companies respect scrupulously the requirement to notify concentrations of a European dimension to the Commission before they are implemented. Implementing a transaction which has not received the clearance foreseen in EU law constitutes a serious breach of the Merger Regulation. Today's decision sends a clear signal that the Commission will not tolerate breaches of this fundamental rule of the EU merger control system.' Commission Press Release IP/09/895 'Mergers: Commission fines Electrabel 20 million euros for acquiring control of Compagnie Nationale du Rhône without prior Commission approval' of 10 June 2009. The finding of an infringement and the fine were upheld by the GC in its judgment of 12 December 2012 in Case T-332/09 *Electrabel v Commission*.

[15] Recital 11 of Commission Reg (EC) No 802/2004 dated 7 April 2004, applying the Merger Control Regulation [2004] OJ L133/1, amended by Commission Regulation (EC) No 1033/2008 of 20 October 2008 OJ L279/3 (hereinafter the 'Implementing Regulation') provides that the Commission must give the notifying parties the opportunity to discuss the proposed concentration in an informal and strictly confidential manner prior to notification. Regulation 802/2004 replaces Commission Reg (EC) 447/98 on the notifications, time limits, and hearings provided for in Reg 4064/89 [1998] OJ L61/1.

In this way, the parties may defend their position within the context of the Merger Control Regulation and avoid the risk of being fined.[16]

2. Mandatory suspension

16.05 Article 7(1) of the Merger Control Regulation requires that the implementation of a concentration that comes within the scope of the Merger Control Regulation is suspended until a definitive decision is adopted or the transaction is deemed to have been approved under Article 10(6) of the Regulation.[17] The exceptions to this principle are discussed later.

16.06 The Merger Control Regulation does not elaborate on what may constitute 'gun jumping', as the breach of the obligation to suspend implementation is known. However, in light of the purpose of this requirement, the acquisition of the capacity to influence the activities of the target undertaking is unlikely to be permitted.[18] The Commission has investigated some cases where parties seemed to have implemented a merger before approval had been obtained, and has intervened firmly in defence of this obligation.[19] It is arguable whether national courts may also have the power to intervene in order to ensure compliance with the prohibition to implement a merger.[20]

16.07 There are three important exceptions to the prohibition on implementation:

(i) with respect to public bids and operations concerning a series of transactions 'in securities admitted to trading on a market such as a stock exchange';

(ii) when the Commission grants a derogation from the suspension obligation in accordance with Article 7(3) of the Merger Control Regulation; and

(iii) concentrations referred by Member States, that may have been implemented provided that, in accordance with Article 22(4) of the Merger Control Regulation, the Commission has not informed the undertakings concerned that a request has been

---

[16] See the GC Judgment of 12 December 2012 in Case T-332/09 *Electrabel v Commission*, paras 253 and 255.

[17] Article 10(6) Merger Control Regulation provides that '[w]here the Commission has not taken a decision in accordance with Article 6(1)(b), (c) or Article 8 (1), (2), or (3) within the time limits set in paragraph 1 and 3 respectively, the concentration shall be deemed to have been declared compatible with the common market, without prejudice to Article 9.' In practice, this is rather unlikely to occur, as the Commission aims to adopt a formal decision pursuant to Article 6 or 8 Merger Control Regulation for each concentration notified to it.

[18] For a brief elaboration on this point see Case T-3/93 *Air France v Commission* [1994] ECR II-121, para 80. See also the GC Judgment of 12 December 2012 in Case T-332/09 *Electrabel v Commission*, para 246, last sentence.

[19] In addition to the cases mentioned in the previous section, the following may be noted: in Case IV/M.993 *Bertelsman/Kirch/Premiere* [1998] OJ L53/1, the Commission issued an order requiring the undertakings to stop marketing TV decoders before issuing its decision; in Case COMP/M.4730 *Yara/Kemira GrowHow* [2007] OJ C200/7, the Commission took the view that an infringement of the stand-still obligation in Article 7(1) and of the notification requirement in Article 4(1) could not be excluded; and in Case COMP/M.4734 *Ineos/Kerling* [2008] OJ C219/18 both the European Commission and the UK Office of Fair Trading are reported to have conducted unannounced inspections at two PVC producers to verify whether the parties had started implementing the transaction before the Commission's decision (N Tait, 'PVC companies raided over rules', Financial Times, 14 December 2007; F Depoortere and S Lelart, 'The Standstill Obligation in the ECMR' (2010) 33(1) World Competition 104). However, the Commission did not issue an Article 14 decision in any of these cases (D Lumdsen, 'EC closes "early implementation" probe as Ineos' Kerling purchase cleared', Mlex, 30 January 2008). In Case COMP/M.6106 *Caterpillar/MWM* [2011], inspections pursuant to Art 13(4) of the Merger Control Regulation took place at the premises of Caterpillar in the UK and of MWM in Germany following indications that the notified concentration had been implemented (para 14).

[20] As regards the civil consequences of implementation without authorization, see L Ritter, WD Braun, and F Rawlinson, *European Competition Law: A Practitioner's Guide* (Kluwer Law International 2004) 674, where the authors argue that the prohibition on implementing an operation without authorization would have direct effect in national law and could therefore give rise to claims for damages.

made. In this case, the obligation to suspend only applies if the concentration has not been implemented by the date on which the Commission informs the undertakings concerned that a referral request has been filed by one or more Member States.

Public bids and other transactions involving securities

The obligation to suspend the implementation of a concentration subject to the Merger Control **16.08** Regulation does not prevent the carrying out of a public bid or a series of transactions in securities admitted to trading on a market, such as a stock exchange, provided that the concentration arising therefrom is notified without delay to the Commission. In those cases, however, the acquirer may not exercise the voting rights attached to the securities in question, or may do so only to maintain the full value of its investments based on a derogation granted by the Commission.[21] These safeguards on the exercise of voting rights guarantee the objective pursued by the prohibition on implementation, preventing the acquirer from exercising its voting rights to determine the competitive strategy of the undertaking acquired before the Commission has cleared the transaction. If, after the examination procedure, the Commission considers that the notified operation must be prohibited, the securities acquired to implement the concentration have to be disposed of. Thus, the acquirer bears the risk of having the transaction prohibited.[22]

Derogations: lifting the suspension

The Commission may grant derogations from the obligation to suspend the implementation **16.09** of the operation, including the obligation to refrain from using voting rights mentioned in the preceeding paragraph.[23] This decision may refer to certain parts of the deal or territories in light of the requirements of each case.[24] There are pricipally two factors which the Commission must take into account when examining a reasoned request for a derogation:

(i) the potential damage or negative effect of the suspension for one or more undertakings concerned or for a third party;
(ii) the extent of the threat to competition caused by the concentration, arising from the need to prevent the operation from having adverse effects on the market.

A derogation may be subject to conditions and obligations aimed at guaranteeing effective **16.10** competition.[25] The breach of the conditions or obligations may result in the imposition of fines of up to 10 per cent of the total turnover of the undertaking concerned,[26] or periodic

---

[21] Article 7(2) of the Merger Control Regulation. The eventual decision to grant a derogation to enable the use of voting rights would be based on Art 7(3) of the Merger Control Regulation.

[22] Case T-411/07 *Aer Lingus Group v Commission* [2010] ECR II-3691, para 82 and Case C-440/07 P *Commission v Schneider Electric* [2009] ECR I-6413, para 204.

[23] Article 7(3) of the Merger Control Regulation.

[24] See eg Case COMP/M.4151 *ORICA/DYNO* [2006], para 3. More recently, in Case COMP/M.5969 *SC Johnson/Sara Lee* [2011], just before the Phase II investigation was initiated, SC Johnson applied to the Commission for a partial derogation under Art 7(3), asking to be allowed to execute the transaction only in countries and territories outside the EEA, claiming both that the suspension of the transaction would have negative effects on the Russian and Malaysian parts of the Sara Lee insecticide business and that the duration of the suspension would be disproportionate. Apart from concluding that SC Johnson had not shown that the suspension obligation could pose a real threat to the target business, the Commission indicated that: '[i]t is an inherent feature of the EU merger review system that the standstill obligation affects the whole concentration... and not only the part of that transaction that concerns the EEA markets. This is in conformity with the basis on which the Commission can claim jurisdiction under international law (Case T-102/96, *Gencor v Commission* [1999] ECR II-753), and other major jurisdictions with similar systems apply it in a comparable way' (para 40).

[25] For example, in Case IV/M.1305 *Eurostar* [1999] OJ C256/3, para 5, the derogation was linked to the condition that British Airways would not be involved in the preparation and approval of Eurostar's budget and business plan.

[26] Article 14(2)(d) of the Merger Control Regulation.

penalty payments of a maximum of 5 per cent of the average daily aggregate turnover of the undertakings concerned for each working day of delay, from the day laid down in the decision.[27]

16.11 The Merger Control Regulation does not lay down any special procedure for these decisions; quite the contrary, the request can be made and the derogation granted at any time, even before the notification itself has been filed.[28] Article 12 of the Implementing Regulation sets some more specific rules for cases in which adverse effects for any parties (the undertakings concerned and third parties) are anticipated.

16.12 In practice, the Commission is careful to ensure that the granting of the derogation is the exception rather than the rule. It therefore carries out an in-depth analysis to establish whether the circumstances really justify a derogation of the suspensive effect.[29] The following examples illustrate the practice of the Commission.

(i) *Urgent interim measures to ensure the success of the operation.* In *BT/Airtel*, the Commission granted a derogation to enable the parties to take certain measures to ensure the success of the operation.[30] Even as regards operations that consist in a simple restructuring, it is not sufficient to show that the operation does not damage competition. The parties must show the extent to which their situation is different from that of any other party that has acquired a new business and wishes to exercise control over that business as soon as possible.[31]

(ii) *Need to ensure no negative effect on competition.* The Commission has shown itself prepared to grant a derogation provided that the impact on competition has been examined first, and it has been concluded that there are no competition problems. For example, in *Philips/Lucent*[32] and *Matra Marconi*,[33] the Commission had already examined the relevant product and geographic market for satellites in two earlier decisions involving the same parties.[34]

---

[27] Article 15(1)(d) of the Merger Control Regulation.

[28] Article 7(3) *in fine* of the Merger Control Regulation. For example, see Case IV/M.573 *ING/Barings* [1995] OJ C114/6, para 7; Case IV/M.1365 *FCC/Vivendi* [1999] OJ C120/20, paras 1 and 2; Case COMP/M.3209 *WPP/Cordiant* [2003] OJ C212/9, para 6; Case COMP/M.5170 *Eon/Endesa Europa/Viesgo* [2010] OJ C237/1; Case COMP/M.5171 *Enel/Acciona/Endesa* [2010] OJ C170/5; Case COMP/M.5760 *Lotte Group/Artenius UK* [2010] OJ C90/2.

[29] In 2012, the Commission granted one derogation out of 283 notifications; in 2011, three derogations out of 309 notifications; in 2010, one derogation out of 274 notifications; in 2009, five derogations out of 259 notifications. Note, however, that the Commission does not state the number of petitions. These statistics can be found on DG COMP's webpage.

[30] Case COMP/JV.3 *BT/Airtel* [1998] OJ C181/2, para 6. The interim measures included the reduction in the number of Advisory Committee members, determining the special duties of the Managing Director and the creation of a committee to investigate technical areas in accordance with the agreement between the parties.

[31] Case COMP/M.1865 *France Telecom/Global One* [2000] OJ C43/3, para 7. The operation did not give rise to any competition law problems. However, the Commission rejected France Telecom's request to take certain preliminary decisions such as the appointment of executives, considering that France Telecom had not demonstrated the relevance and the negative impact involved in waiting for a period of three or four weeks to restructure Global One.

[32] Case IV/M.1358 *Philips/Lucent Technologies* [1999] OJ C39/13, para 7.

[33] Case IV/M.497 *Matra Marconi Space/Satcoms* [1994] OJ C307/3, paras 1 and 9.

[34] See also the decision of 28 April 2010 in Case COMP/M.5170 *Eon/Endesa Europa/Viesgo* [2010] OJ C237/1, para 17, where the Commission considered that it had already assessed and authorized the acquisition of control over Endesa Europa, Viesgo, and the additional Endesa assets by Eon in its decision of 6 August 2007, and it considered the changes to the transaction perimeter unlikely to have any impact on the competitive assessment carried out in its earlier decision.

(iii) *Fulfillment of prior commitments.* The purpose of the Mobil/JV operation (dissolution) was the cessation of Mobil's participation in a joint venture, which was the fulfillment of a commitment made by the parties in *Exxon/Mobil.*[35]

(iv) *Threat of serious damage for the parties and third parties.* In *Kelt/American Express*, the Commission granted the derogation because it was 'convinced of the need to swiftly effect the restructuring operation in order to prevent serious damage to one or more undertakings concerned by the concentration'.[36] Similarly, in *ING/Barings*, the derogation was granted because of the need to carry out the operation rapidly, so that Barings and third parties did not suffer serious harm while Barings Holding was subject to insolvency proceedings.[37] In *WPP/Cordiant*, the derogation was granted due to the situation of financial distress of the target company.[38] In *Lotte Group/Artenius UK*, the derogation was meant to allow production to restart at the target company placed under administration and to limit the costs of administration proceedings.[39] In *Sun Capital/SCS Group*, the Commission allowed Sun Capital to take all actions strictly necessary to restore the viability of the target company as a going concern (appointing a board representative, providing funding, and communicating and negotiating with suppliers and creditors). However, the management of the target had to continue to be responsible for its day-to-day operation, Sun Capital could not exercise any shareholder rights for other purposes, and an independent monitor had to be appointed.[40] In *Santander/Bradford & Bingley Assets*, the Commission accepted that B&B was in serious financial distress, and there was a real likelihood that, if the acquisition did not take place rapidly, B&B would cease to be a viable business. This would have an impact not only on B&B, but also on the stability of the financial markets. Therefore, the Commission granted the derogation to allow Santander to take all actions that were reasonably necessary to restore the viability of the target business and to contribute to ensuring financial stability.[41]

(v) *The need to fulfil legal requirements.* The Commission can grant a derogation if it considers this to be necessary to enable the parties, for example, to comply with the time periods stated in licences to build a telecommunications network.[42] In *Shell España/Cepsa/SIS JV*, the request for derogation was based on the fact that SIS had been awarded a concession to provide services at three Spanish airports. The concession imposed a number of preliminary measures, which according to Spanish law had to be implemented by SIS by specified dates. The parties argued that these preliminary steps could be viewed as implementation of the concentration. Therefore, the Commission granted a derogation which only related to certain administrative measures to enable SIS to enter into the concession contracts.[43]

---

[35] See Case IV/M.1822 *Mobil/JV Dissolution* [2000] OJ C112/6, para 2; see also Case IV/M.1419 *Groupe Cofinoga/BNP* [1999] OJ C80/7, para 2 (where it appears that there was little or no overlap between the parties' activities).

[36] Case IV/M.116 *Kelt/American Express* [1991] OJ C223/38, para 7.

[37] Case IV/M.573 *ING/Barings* [1995] OJ C114/6, para 7. See also Case IV/M.3148 *Siemens/Alstom Gas and Steam Turbines* [2003] OJ C207/25, para 7.

[38] Case COMP/M.3209 *WPP/Cordiant* [2003] OJ C212/9, para 6. See also Case COMP/M.5590 *3i Group/H.I.G. Capital/Volnay B.V.* [2009] OJ C199/5.

[39] Case COMP/M.5760 *Lotte Group/Artenius UK* [2010] OJ C90/2, paras 12–17.

[40] Case COMP/M.5267 *Sun Capital/SCS Group* [2008] OJ C240/1.

[41] Case COMP/M.5363 *Santander/Bradford & Bingley Assets* [2008] OJ C7/4. See also decision of 17 December 2012 in Case COMP/M.6812 *SFPI/Dexia*.

[42] Case IV/JV.2 *ENEL/FT/DT* [1998] OJ C178/15, para 8: 'derogation was granted in order to facilitate Wind's meeting the deadlines and obligations imposed by the licences granted in the fixed line sector and in order to enable Wind to start building its networks.' See Case IV/M.538 *Omnitel* [1995] OJ C96/3, para 6: 'This was necessary for OPI to be in a position to meet the deadlines established by the licence and to operate in competition with Telecom Italia, which has already built its GSM network and has a significant presence in the market for analogue mobile telephony in Italy.'

[43] Case COMP/M.3275 *Shell España/Cepsa/SIS JV* [2004] OJ C250/5.

(vi) *The need to comply with certain conditions of a bid.* In *Cinven Limited/Angel Street Holdings*, the Commission granted a derogation in order to facilitate a bid for a purchase of assets the sale of which had to be completed unconditionally on a given date. In the absence of the derogation, the parties would have been effectively excluded from the auction.[44] In *Cerberus/Torex*, due to the need to complete the sale of Torex quickly, potential bidders (such as Cerberus) who could not sign and complete simultaneously, due to the need to wait for merger clearance, would effectively be excluded from the procedure. The Commission granted the derogation solely in so far as it allowed Cerberus to take all actions that were reasonably necessary to restore the viability of Torex.[45]

(vii) *Derogations also possible in phase two.* In some exceptional cases, the Commission has granted derogations despite initiating a formal review procedure in light of the effects that the suspension may produce.[46]

Article 22(4) of the Merger Control Regulation

16.13 The principle of suspension of concentrations subject to the Merger Control Regulation applies in a special manner in respect of cases referred by national competition authorities. As explained in further detail later,[47] Article 22 of the Merger Control Regulation, also known as the 'Dutch clause', provides for the possibility of referral by national authorities to the Commission of concentrations that do not have an EU dimension that affect trade between Member States and threaten to affect competition in a significant way in the Member State or States making the request to the Commission. Cases referred by Member States under this mechanism may, in so far as permitted under national law, already have been implemented. That has already happened several times, for instance where there was no merger control regime or an ex-post merger control regime at national level.[48]

16.14 Article 22(4) provides for a limited application of the principle of suspension to these transactions. The obligation laid down in Article 7 to suspend the implementation will operate as long as the concentration has not been put in effect by the date when the Commission notifies the undertakings concerned that a request for referral has been made. If the concentration has already been implemented at that date, the Article 7 prohibition will not apply. If the transaction is finally prohibited, divestiture under Article 8(4) of the Regulation may be ordered.

3. Exclusive jurisdiction (the 'one-stop shop' principle)

16.15 Unlike the system of shared competences introduced by Regulation 1/2003 with respect to prohibited practices, concentrations which meet the thresholds that define EU dimension

---

[44] Case IV/M.2777 *Cinven Limited/Angel Street Holdings* [2002] OJ C147/20, para 2. See also Case IV/M.1365 *FCC/Vivendi* [1999] OJ C120/20, para 2.

[45] Case COMP/M.4763 *Cerberus/Torex* [2008] OJ C185/5.

[46] See Case IV/M.190 *Nestlé/Perrier* [1992] OJ L356/1, and Case IV/M.477 *Mercedes-Benz/Kässbohrer* [1995] OJ L211/1. Some derogations were granted under Art 7(4) in the original (and stricter) wording of former Reg 4064/89 ('to prevent serious damage to one or more undertakings concerned by a concentration or to a third party') whereas the wording of the Merger Control Regulation, which was the wording introduced into the former Reg 4064/89 following Reg 1310/97, appears to allow the Commission greater leeway ('the Commission shall take into account inter alia the effects of the suspension on one or more undertakings concerned by a concentration or on a third party and the threat to competition posed by the concentration'). The Commission is also reported to having granted a derogation subject to conditions after the opening of the Phase II investigation in Case COMP/M.4956 *STX/Aker Yards* [2008] OJ C147/14 (see 'Exemptions for crisis buy-outs possible, even during Phase II merger investigations', Mlex Comment, 21 October 2009 and n 50 of the Art 8(1) decision).

[47] See Section D of this chapter.

[48] Case IV/M.553 *Veronica/Endemol* [1995] OJ L134/32; Case IV/M.784 *Kesko/Tuko* [1996] OJ L110/53; Case IV/M.890 *Blokker/Toys 'R' Us* [1997] OJ C316/1; Case COMP/M.5020 *Lesaffre/GBI UK* [2008] OJ C308/7.

are examined under the Merger Control Regulation alone.[49] This is known as the 'one-stop shop' principle.[50] Conversely, the Commission has no jurisdiction with respect to concentrations that lack an EU dimension. In this case, the Member States remain free to apply their national competition laws.[51] This is consistent with the overall policy goal of establishing uniform conditions and guaranteeing the same notification requirements, procedure, and legal rules for all concentrations with significant cross-border effects through a single, centralized system of control.

The 'one-stop shop' principle is without prejudice to the participation of national authorities **16.16** in enforcement at EU level, which may also result in additional or parallel proceedings, and referrals to national authorities, which is discussed later.

The 'one-stop shop' principle finds an exception that results in parallel enforcement proceed- **16.17** ings where Member States need to act to protect certain legitimate interests other than those protected by the Merger Control Regulation. Besides this limitation of purpose, the intervention must be compatible with the provisions of EU law.[52] The Regulation expressly mentions certain of these legitimate interests: public security,[53] plurality of media,[54] and prudential rules, such as those applying in the insurance sector.[55] The Commission considers that these interests expressly listed should be subject to uniform interpretation, guided, where possible, by EU law in the field.[56]

Any other public interest must be notified by the Member State in question to the Commission, **16.18** who must recognize it, having first tested its compatibility with general principles (including

---

[49] The Merger Control Regulation is based on the principle of a clear division of powers between national and EU supervisory authorities. See Case C-170/02 P *Schlüsselverlag JS Moser and Others v Commission* [2003] ECR I-9889, para 32; Case C-42/01 *Portugal v Commission* [2004] ECR I-6079, para 50; Case C-202/06 P *Cementbouw Handel & Industrie v Commission* [2007] ECR I-12129, paras 35–8.

[50] Recital 8 of the Merger Control Regulation provides that '[s]uch concentrations should, as a general rule, be reviewed exclusively at EU level, in application of a *one-stop shop* system and in compliance with the principle of subsidiarity. Concentrations not covered by this Regulation come, in principle, within the jurisdiction of the Member States'.

[51] Case T-411/07 *Aer Lingus Group v Commission* [2010] ECR II-3691, para 91.

[52] Article 21(4) of the Merger Control Regulation. See Case C-196/07 *Commission v Spain* [2008] ECR I-41, para 37; Case T-65/08 R *Spain v Commission* [2008] ECR II-69, paras 22–40; Case T-200/09 *Abertis Infraestructuras v Commission* [2010] ECR II-85.

[53] See Recital 19 of the Merger Control Regulation. The scope of public security as a public interest that naturally involves questions concerning national defence must be understood without prejudice to the provisions of Art 346 TFEU, which is discussed later. However, the concept of public security also includes maintaining the supplies of those products or services that are considered to be vitally important in order to protect the health of the population. Case IV/M.336 *IBM France/CGI* [1993] OJ C151/5 regarding measures concerning two subsidiaries of CGI which previously worked for the French Ministry of Defence.

[54] Case IV/M.423 *Newspaper Publishing* [1994] OJ C 85/6, paras 22–3: in the UK, mergers that concern newspapers are subject to specific rules that involve reviewing specific aspects of the media industry (concerning the way news is presented or freedom of expression). As regards the annex to former Reg 4064/89 and in particular as regards the proportionality principle, in its authorization decision, the Commission imposed on the British authorities to be informed about any condition which they considered appropriate to attach to the concentration. In Case M.5932 *NewsCorp/BSkyB* [2010] OJ C37/5, the Commission cleared the transaction under Art 6(1)(b) of the Merger Control Regulation, but specified that its decision was without prejudice to the Media Plurality Review conducted by the relevant UK Authorities (para 310). See also the Commission Press Release IP/10/1767 'Mergers: Commission clears News Corp's proposed acquisition of BSkyB under EU merger rules': 'The UK remains free to decide whether or not to take appropriate measures to protect its legitimate interest in media plurality (as permitted under Article 21 of the EU Merger Regulation)'.

[55] Case IV/M.759 *Sun Alliance/Royal Insurance* [1996] OJ C225/12, paras 16–17: the Commission accepted that the UK was entitled to apply legislation concerning the authorization and supervision of insurance companies operating in the UK.

[56] Case IV/M.2491 *Sampo/Storebrand* [2001] OJ C290/3, para 39.

the principles of necessity, effectiveness, and proportionality) and other provisions of EU law. A case where the Commission also recognized interests that went outside these categories is *Lyonnaise des Eaux/Northumbrian Water*,[57] where the Commission accepted that the UK would take certain measures for the protection of consumer interests. It is noted that the legitimate interest exception is interpreted strictly, the Commission being careful to prevent concentrations with an EU dimension from being blocked by Member States for reasons other than those laid down in the Merger Control Regulation.[58]

16.19 The exclusivity of the European Commission's jurisdiction on mergers with an EU dimension has been enforced by the Commission in respect of actions by Member States seeking to block concentrations that had already been approved by the Commission for various reasons. The *BSCH/Champalimaud* case was the first time that the Commission formally used its powers under Article 21 of Regulation 4064/89 in order to prevent a Member State—*in casu*, Portugal—from blocking a concentration with EU dimension. The transaction in question had been notified on 30 June 1999 and authorized by the Commission on 3 August 1999.[59] During the approval procedure, the Portuguese government had already issued two decisions against the transaction, which forced the Commission to adopt an initial decision ordering the suspension of these national measures on 20 July 1999[60] even before the Commission had given its formal approval. On 20 October 1999, the Commission adopted a decision declaring that the Portuguese government's actions did not protect any legitimate interest admissible under Article 21(4) of Regulation 4064/89 and were an attempt to protect national strategic interests in a way that contravened that provision.[61] On 3 November 1999, it was made public that the Commission would bring an action before the Court of Justice ('ECJ') under Article 226 EC (now Article 258 TFEU) against the Portuguese Republic for failure to suspend the measures in issue. Finally, Portugal withdrew the measures and the Commission did not bring any action.[62]

16.20 The Commission followed a similar approach when the Portuguese government blocked the purchase by Secil Companhia Geral de Cal e Cimentos SA and Holderbank of the Portuguese company Cimpor Cimentos de Portugal SGPS.[63] In contrast with the *BSCH/Champalimaud* case, however, there was never a decision of the Commission on the transaction, given that the operation was abandoned by the parties in view of the opposition from

---

[57] Case IV/M.567 *Lyonnaise des Eaux/Northumbrian Water* [1995] OJ C 11/3, para 8.

[58] See in that regard the Commission's Art 21(3) Decision of 27 January 1999 in Case IV/M.1346 *EDF/London Electricity* [1999] OJ C92/10: the British authorities argued that the UK had a public interest in maintaining the legal system in the electricity sector and proposed changes to London Electricity's licence. However, the Commission concluded that it was not necessary to recognize a legitimate interest, since the changes proposed to the said licence amounted to the application of provisions of national law. Further, the changes did not refer to the concentration in itself, but rather to the management of the merged entities after the concentration, in order to guarantee that the regulatory body was capable of carrying out its tasks. XXIXth Report on Competition Policy [1999] 66–7.

[59] Case IV/M.1616 *BSCH/Champalimaud* [1999] OJ C306/37.

[60] Commission Decision of 20 July 1999, available on DG COMP's webpage.

[61] Commission Decision of 20 October 1999 available on DG COMP's webpage.

[62] Portugal, however, may have succeeded in making the transaction collapse. See for additional information on this interesting case Commission Press Releases IP/99/610 'Commission approves the acquisition of joint control by BSCH (Spain) over the Champalimaud group (Portugal)'; IP/99/669 'Commission opens infringement procedure against Portugal for not respecting its suspension decision in the BSCH/Champalimaud case'; IP/99/749 'Commission moves on with infringement procedure against Portugal for ignoring its suspension decision in the BSCH/Champalimaud case'; IP/99/774 'EU competition law: Commission overrules Portuguese measures against BSCH/Champalimaud operation'; IP/00/296 'Financial services: Commission closes infringement cases against Portugal concerning BSCH/Champalimaud'.

[63] COMP/M.2054 *Secil/Holderbank/Cimpor* [2000] OJ C198/5, withdrawn.

the Portuguese government. The Commission in any event did adopt a decision under Article 21 of Regulation 4064/89, which was challenged by the Portuguese government before the ECJ. In its judgment of 22 June 2004, the Court confirmed the validity of the Commission decision,[64] endorsing its interpretation of the 'one-stop shop' principle.

Article 21 was again used when the Spanish energy regulator decided to submit the planned **16.21** acquisition of Endesa by Enel and Acciona, which had been cleared by the European Commission,[65] to a number of conditions, which the Commission declared incompatible with the rules on the free movement of capital, the freedom of establishment, and the free movement of goods, and required their withdrawal.[66]

A special case of national interest is national security. Under Article 346 TFEU, Member **16.22** States may:

> take such measures as it considers necessary for the protection of the essential interests of its security which are connected with the production of or trade in arms, munitions and war material; such measures shall not adversely affect the conditions of competition in the internal market regarding products which are not intended for specifically military purposes.

Some Member States have relied on this provision vis-à-vis concentrations in the defence industry, instructing the notifying parties not to notify certain aspects of the concentration for national security reasons. For its part, the Commission has laid down certain conditions to enable the exemption to be invoked.[67]

---

[64] Case C-42/01 *Portuguese Republic v Commission* [2004] ECR I-6079.

[65] Case COMP/M.4685 *Enel/Acciona/Endesa* [2007] OJ C212/2.

[66] In particular, the incompatible conditions concerned: (i) the obligation to maintain Endesa as an independent company, including its brand, and its decision-making centre in Spain; (ii) a limitation in Endesa's debt service ratio; (iii) a limitation with respect to Endesa's dividends distribution policy; (iv) the obligation for certain of Endesa's generation assets to purchase certain amounts of national coal; and (v) the obligation to keep the assets of the insular and non-mainland electricity systems within the Endesa Group. These conditions were imposed by the National Energy Commission ('CNE') in its decision of 4 July 2007 and partially modified by the Minister of Industry on 19 October 2007. Case T-65/08 R *Spain v Commission* [2008] ECR II-69, paras 23–7: 'it is not for the Member State to assess whether national measures addressed to parties to a concentration declared compatible are aimed at protecting public safety, but for the Commission'. These conditions are broadly comparable to a number of conditions imposed in Case COMP/M.4197 *E.ON/ Endesa* [2006].

[67] Case IV/M.1438 *British Aerospace/GEC Marconi* [1999] OJ C241/8, para 2: 'The United Kingdom, relying upon Article 296(1)(b) of the EC Treaty [now Article 346(1)(b) TFEU], has instructed BAe not to notify the military aspects of this operation. The notification therefore relates only to the nonmilitary aspects of the transaction'; para 8 '[t]he Commission has considered the applicability of Article 296(1)(b) of the EC Treaty in the present case. In this context it has noted, on the basis of the information provided by the government of the United Kingdom, that the part of the concentration which has not been notified only relates to the production of or trade in arms, munitions and war material which are mentioned in the list referred to in Article 296(2) EC; the measures taken by the United Kingdom are necessary for the protection of the essential interests of its security; the measures taken will have no spillover effects on the non-military products of BAe and MES.' Paragraph 9 continues '[t]herefore, the Commission is satisfied that the measures taken by the United Kingdom fall within the scope of Article 296(1)b of the EC Treaty'. See also Case IV/1797 *Saab/ Celsius* [2000] OJ C46/25, para 2. In Case IV/M.1258 *GEC Marconi/Alenia* [1998] OJ C306/12, para 15, the Commission declared that 'the merger will have no significant impact on suppliers and sub-contractors of the undertakings concerned and on Ministries of Defence of other Member States'. In Case COMP/M.4160 *ThyssenKrupp/EADS/Atlas* [2006] OJ C177/35, the German government had, according to Art 296 of the EC Treaty (now Art 346 TFEU), instructed the Parties to notify the naval part of the transaction only in so far as no military secrets were concerned. 'The scope of the submitted notification, however, allowed the Commission to carry out a complete investigation of the markets affected by the transaction' (para 9). See also Judgment of 7 June 2012 in Case C-615/10 *Insinööritoimisto InsTiimi Oy*, paras 35–40, with respect to public contracts in the field of defence.

C. Competent Authorities in the Merger Control Area

1. The Directorate-General for Competition of the European Commission

16.23   As explained earlier in this book, the European Commission is divided into a series of Directorates-General or 'DGs', including the Competition DG (also known as 'DG COMP'). Below the Commissioner in charge of Competition Policy stands the Director-General of DG COMP and three Deputy Directors-General, one of whom has special responsibilities for mergers. DG COMP is further divided into nine Directorates, with five sectoral directorates organized into three main areas (antitrust, State aid, and concentrations), each constituting units with various teams of instructors. Until May 2004 there was a Directorate known as the Merger Task Force ('MTF') within the Competition DG, but it no longer exists.[68]

16.24   With the exception of Directorate A, which focuses on general competition policy and strategy, Directorates and the respective units of the Commission analyse the impact of the concentrations that have been notified in each of their sectors. The five sectoral Directorates with units that focus on the control of concentrations are: B (energy and environment); C (information, communication, and media); D (financial services); E (basic industries, manufacturing, and agriculture); and F (transport, post, and other services). Each possesses a unit which deals exclusively with concentrations. In addition, Directorate A (policy and strategy) comprises a unit which provides case support to the sectoral merger units and deals with the policy of mergers.

16.25   The role and capacity of analysis in the Commission's decision making has been reinforced by the ad hoc creation of groups of experts to evaluate, afresh, the conclusions of the case team ('peer review').[69] Civil servants with recognized experience in the field of concentrations conduct these evaluations. Their conclusions on given cases are then compared with those of the case team. This method of internal review is part of the organizational reform of DG COMP, in particular as regards the second-phase review. The revision of the functioning of the Commission has also led to the appointment of a Chief Economist who reports directly to the Director-General of DG COMP. The Chief Economist provides independent guidance on methodological issues of economics and econometrics in the application of EU competition rules, and contributes to individual competition cases (in particular those involving complex economic issues and quantitative analysis), to the development of general policy instruments, as well as assisting with cases pending before the EU Courts. The Chief Economist also acts as a focus for economic debate within DG COMP, in liaison with other Commission services and in association with the academic world. Members of his team organize training sessions on economic issues and give advice on studies of a general economic nature, as well as on market monitoring.

16.26   To all of this must be added the formalization of best practices in the conduct of merger proceedings,[70] which have been instrumental in providing a clearer procedural framework in the conduct of the procedure. Finally, other Commission services will be associated

---

[68] See Commission Press Release IP/03/603 'Commission reorganises its Competition Department in advance of Enlargement' of 30 April 2003. The updated organization chart of DG COMP is available on line on DG COMP's webpage.

[69] Commission Press Release IP/04/70 'EU gives itself new merger control rules for 21st century' of 20 January 2004. Peer review panels will usually be set up where a statement of objections has been addressed to the parties.

[70] DG Competition Best Practices on the conduct of merger proceedings of 20 January 2004, available at DG COMP's website.

throughout the process. This is the case for the Legal Service, which is formally consulted on each decision to be adopted by or on behalf of the Commission, or of DG Enterprise. Other Directorate-Generals are associated if the merger is within their sector of expertise (eg DG Mobility and Transport for mergers in the transport sector).

2. National competition authorities

The Merger Control Regulation provides for a framework of close cooperation between the **16.27** Commission and national competition authorities ('NCAs'). This is channelled through two distinct possibilities: one is the active participation of NCAs in the procedures run by the Commission, and is discussed here; the other takes place through case referral mechanisms, discussed in Section D of this chapter.

The Merger Control Regulation requires the Commission to deal with cases 'in close and **16.28** constant liaison with the competent authorities of the Member States'.[71] The importance of a close relationship is obvious given that there are many cases where a given Member State has a given interest and therefore maintains close contact with the Commission. The involvement of Member States enables them to be kept informed and make their views known. This is made possible through various procedural mechanisms.

In furtherance of this principle, the Commission is required to send to NCAs a copy of the **16.29** notifications within three working days, together with the most important documents that have been sent to it or that it has issued with respect to the notification.[72] In addition, when the Commission sends an undertaking a request for information adopted pursuant to Article 11(3), it will immediately send a copy of such a decision to the NCAs of the Member State where the headquarters of the undertaking or group of undertakings is located, and to the competent authority of the Member State whose territory is affected.[73] Further, the Commission will notify the NCAs of the said Member State in question that it has decided to carry out an inspection.[74] At the behest of the Commission, the NCAs of the Member States will proceed to carry out such verifications[75] or they may cooperate with the Commission's agents.[76] The NCAs are free to express their views at any time of the procedure, in particular as regards commitments that have been proposed to resolve competition issues.

Before adopting decisions at the end of the second phase or imposing sanctions under Articles **16.30** 14 or 15, the Commission must consult with the Advisory Committee on concentrations.[77] The Advisory Committee is made up of one or two representatives of the NCAs of each Member State, at least one of which must be an expert in restrictive practices and dominant positions.[78] The Merger Control Regulation reinforces the role of the Advisory Committee, whose influence

---

[71] Recital 13 and Art 19(2) of the Merger Control Regulation. Recital 14 alludes to the creation of a network of competition authorities, as well as to the principles of single authority, subsidiarity and the one-stop shop. As Recital 14 states, 'the Commission and the competent authorities of the Member States should form together a network of public authorities, applying their respective competences in close cooperation, using efficient arrangements for information-sharing and consultation, with a view to ensuring that a case is dealt with by the most appropriate authority, in the light of the principle of subsidiarity and with a view to ensuring that multiple notifications of a given concentration are avoided to the greatest extent possible.'

[72] Article 19(1) of the Merger Control Regulation. A third party may not rely on the failure to communicate a revised draft of the commitments to the NCAs to challenge the legality of an approval decision (Judgment of 7 June 2013 in Case T-405/08 *Spar Österreichische Warenhandels v Commission*, para 265).

[73] Article 11(5) of the Merger Control Regulation.

[74] Article 13(3)–(6) of the Merger Control Regulation.

[75] Article 12(1) of the Merger Control Regulation.

[76] Article 12(2) of the Merger Control Regulation.

[77] Article 19(3) of the Merger Control Regulation. See Ch 17, 'Procedures', para 17.82 et seq.

[78] Article 19(4) of the Merger Control Regulation.

should not be underestimated, in particular as regards those matters that involve markets with a national scope.[79]

16.31 In parallel to these cooperation schemes, NCAs cooperate when examining mergers that are not subject to EU merger control but require clearance in several Member States under flexible mechanisms, as they do for the enforcement of EU and national competition laws. On 9 November 2011, the Commission made public a set of Best Practices on Cooperation between EU National Competition Authorities in Merger Review, aimed at fostering and facilitating information sharing between national competition authorities in these situations.[80]

D. Referral of Concentrations

1. Basic principles

16.32 The system for the attribution of jurisdiction under the Merger Control Regulation is based on three basic principles: the one-stop shop, legal certainty, and subsidiarity.[81] These principles require a clear division of powers between the national and EU supervisory authorities, which is articulated through objective thresholds that define EU dimension.[82] While the system appoints a specific authority to examine a given matter, it provides by way of exception that a case may be transmitted to a different authority. These cases are hereafter denominated 'referrals'.

16.33 For reasons of legal certainty, referrals are limited to those cases where the principle of subsidiarity makes it advisable that another authority which is better placed to investigate is entrusted with the case. This may result in either the Commission or NCAs obtaining jurisdiction over a concentration in circumstances other than those initially resulting from the thresholds contained in Article 1 of the Merger Control Regulation.

16.34 Referrals may take place in both directions, ie from an NCA in favour of the Commission or vice versa, and at two different points of time in the procedure, ie either before a notification has been made, thereby avoiding a double filing, or after a notification has been filed. These four alternatives are examined in turn.[83]

---

[79] Pursuant to Art 19(7) of the Merger Control Regulation, 'the Commission shall communicate the opinion of the Advisory Committee, together with the decision, to the addressees of the decision. It shall make the opinion public together with the decision, having regard to the legitimate interest of undertakings in the protection of their business secrets.' In Case M.3796 *Omya/J.M. Huber PCC* [2006] OJ L72/24, some Member States expressed doubts concerning the effects of the transaction and the reliability of the econometric study, which led the Commission to verify the data provided by the notifying party and later to issue a statement of objections, although the Commission had initially submitted a draft clearance decision to the Advisory Committee (see Case T-145/06 *Omya v Commission* [2009] ECR II-145, paras 4, 59, 71–3, and 91).

[80] Available on DG COMP's webpage.

[81] Commission Notice on Case Referral in respect of concentrations [2005] OJ C56/2, (hereinafter the 'Case Referral Notice') also refers to a network of NCAs (paras 53–4), underlining the importance of cooperation and dialogue between the Commission and the NCAs in the case of concentrations that are the object of the referral system contained in the Reg.

[82] Case C-202/06 P *Cementbouw Handel & Industrie v Commission* [2007] ECR I-12129, para 35, referring to Case C-170/02 P *Schlüsselverlag JS Moser and Others v Commission* [2003] ECR I-9889, para 32, and Case C-42/01 *Portugal v Commission* [2004] ECR I-6079, para 50.

[83] The Commission made an assessment of the functioning of the referral mechanisms five years after the adoption of the Merger Control Regulations following a public consultation. See Communication from the Commission: Report from the Commission to the Council on the operation of Regulation (EC) No 139/2004 of 18 June 2009 COM(2009) 281 final and the accompanying Staff Working Paper of 30 June 2009 SEC(2009) 808 final/2. On 20 June 2013, the Commission also launched a public consultation to seek stakeholders' views on ways to streamline the referral system to avoid delays and improve its effectiveness. The paper discusses in particular (i) whether merging parties may notify a case that otherwise would be examined by three or more NCAs directly to the Commission without the prior step of the Form RS; and (ii) for cases referred to

2. Referral in favour of NCAs prior to notification of the operation (Article 4(4) of the Merger Control Regulation)

Article 4(4) of the Merger Control Regulation permits parties to a concentration with a **16.35** EU dimension to request that the examination of the operation is referred by the European Commission in favour of one or more Member States. Such a request must be based on the fact that the operation may significantly affect competition in a distinct market in the Member State in question.[84] This requirement aims to limit referrals to cases that cause competition problems, since otherwise there is no reason to make an exception to the general rules. Although the parties are not required to show a negative effect on competition, they must point to factors that normally suggest the existence of potential problems, such as, for example, the existence of affected markets.[85] In addition, the parties have to certify that the scope of the geographic market where the potential competition problem exists is national (or smaller).

This request is made by way of Form 'RS' (Reasoned Submission). Form RS is contained in **16.36** Annex III of the Implementing Regulation. Although the Commission will accept Form RS in any official EU language, the Case Referral Notice recommends that the undertakings file it in a language that will be understood by all of those to whom it is addressed to make it easier for the NCAs in question to deal with the request. The information that the parties include in the form has to be correct and complete. In the event of incorrect information, the Commission could impose fines in accordance with Article 14(1)(a) of the Merger Control Regulation.[86] The Commission could also request additional information. In an effort to prevent any problem concerning the possibility that the information is incomplete, prior contacts with the Commission and the NCAs are encouraged. The Commission undertakes to offer help in this regard.[87]

Once the request has been received, the Commission will transmit it to the 'affected' Member **16.37** States, that is, those to whom the case would be referred in the event that the request is authorized. The Commission has pledged in the Case Referral Notice to 'endeavour to transmit' the reasoned requests—by email, fax, or surface mail—within a period of one working day of being received. Confidential information is sent by protected means of communication, eg secure email.[88] The Member State(s) in question must agree or disagree within a maximum period of fifteen working days from receipt of the request. If a Member State is silent within this period, it is deemed to accept the referral. But in the event any, even just one affected Member State, states its disagreement, the referral will not take place. Even if there is agreement—express or implied—from all Member States affected, the Commission retains discretion in referring the matter to Member States.

The Commission will adopt its decision to proceed or not with the referral within a period **16.38** of twenty-five working days from its receipt of Form RS. The decision to refer will depend on whether the Commission considers that the NCA is the most appropriate authority to carry out the investigation, bearing in mind the effects of the operation; for example, it would

---

the Commission by one or several NCAs under Art 22 of the Merger Control Regulation, whether the review could cover the whole of the EEA and not just the territory of the Member State requesting the referral. See Commission Staff Working Document, 'Towards more effective EU merger control' and Commission Press release IP/13/584 of 20 June 2013.

[84] See Case Referral Notice, para 17.

[85] Section III of Form CO (Annex I of Reg 802/2004) defines markets affected as those where the joint market share of the parties to the concentration is over 15 per cent or where one or more of the parties are engaged in business activities in a product market, which is upstream or downstream of a product market in which any other party to the concentration is engaged, and any of their individual or combined market shares at either level is 25 per cent or more.

[86] Case Referral Notice, para 60.

[87] Case Referral Notice, para 64.

[88] Case Referral Notice, para 56.

normally make the referral if the effects of the proposed concentration were confined to a single Member State and national or infranational markets that did not constitute a substantial part of the internal market.[89] The Commission may also have regard to additional factors, especially the NCA's particular expertise in the sector.[90] Unless an expressly negative decision is adopted, it is presumed that the Commission has decided to refer. The Commission will inform the Member States and the undertakings concerned of its decision.[91]

16.39 Any referral may be in whole or in part.[92] If the Commission decides to refer part of the operation to the relevant NCA, the latter must begin to examine the part that has been referred in accordance with its national competition law without delay.[93] The Merger Control Regulation will be applied to the part of the operation not referred to the NCA. Total referral frees the parties of the obligation to notify the Commission in accordance with Article 1 of the Merger Control Regulation. The relevant national competition rules must be applied in accordance with the provisions of Article 9(6)–(9) of the Merger Control Regulation. These provisions require that the relevant NCA(s) decide(s) on the case in question without undue delay. It must, in turn, inform the undertakings concerned of its preliminary analysis and what it intends to do within a period of forty-five working days from the referral.

3. Referral in favour of the Commission prior to notification of the operation (Article 4(5) of the Merger Control Regulation)

16.40 Under Article 4(5) of the Merger Control Regulation, the parties to a concentration without EU dimension—and therefore, not capable of being notified to the Commission—may request that the Commission examine the operation under the Merger Control Regulation. This possibility is reserved for cases where the operation is capable of being analysed by virtue of the national competition rules of at least three Member States.[94] The request has to be made before a notification has been filed with the competent NCAs.[95]

16.41 As with Article 4(4), the referral request has to be made on Form RS. The Commission will transfer the request to all Member States within one working day. The affected Member States, that is those competent to examine the concentration under national rules, must be clearly identified in Form RS,[96] and they may oppose the referral request within fifteen working days from receipt of the request. If any of the affected Member States opposes the referral,

---

[89] These are the same factors that are taken into account in cases of referral of a notified concentration following a notification under Article 9 of the Merger Control Regulation, as discussed at para 16.50.

[90] See eg the reference to the OFT's extensive experience in assessing the impact of rail franchising and the previous referrals by the Commission in Case COMP/M.4797 *Govia/West Midlands Passenger Rail Franchise* [2007] or the fact that the NCA was undertaking a study into the aggregates market Case COMP/M.6153 *Anglo American/Lafarge/JV* [2011], para 37.

[91] As stated, the decision whether or not to refer will be made within a period of twenty-five working days from receipt of the Commission's request.

[92] Unlike Art 4(5) of the Merger Control Regulation, Art 4(4), para 3 of the Regulation allows a partial referral of the operation to one or more Member States, with the Commission retaining the rest of the case. However, neither the Commission nor the Member States can modify the scope of the request for total or partial referral.

[93] As required by Art 9(6) of the Merger Control Regulation, to which Art 4(4) refers.

[94] The Case Referral Notice confirms that it is not necessary for national law to require the operation to be notified; the fact that an operation comes within the jurisdiction of a Member State in accordance with its national competition law is sufficient (para 71).

[95] The referral mechanism under Art 4(5) can only be used if no national notification has yet been filed. See Case Referral Notice, para 69.

[96] If any Member State does not agree with being identified as 'competent' to examine the operation referred to in Form RS, it may inform the Commission of this within fifteen working days following receipt of the request (Case Referral Notice, para 75). If, due to incorrect information in Form RS, a Member State subsequently takes the view that, in contrast to the parties' submissions, it is competent to review the concentration, it could request that the Commission make a post-notification referral under Art 9 (Case Referral Notice, para 77).

it will not take place.[97] The Commission will inform without delay all Member States and the undertakings concerned of any disagreement of this nature, with the result that the parties will need to fulfil the applicable national rules regarding notifications. If, however, none of the affected Member States disagrees, the Commission will gain jurisdiction over the matter and the parties will notify the operation under the Merger Control Regulation. Unlike referrals under Article 4(4), partial referral is not possible; the whole operation has to be referred.

In analysing the chances of the referral request being accepted, the parties must consider **16.42** whether, in addition to the notification requirements that the operation must satisfy under each system of national law, the Commission will be the most appropriate authority to investigate the matter. This will be so when the effects of the concentration are not limited to the territory of a single Member State, or the case involves geographical markets which go beyond the national scope. Another important factor is the powers of investigation required in the case at hand. The Commission will also be seen as the most appropriate authority to assess operations that create competition problems in national geographic markets or even those that are smaller, but which overlap with those of other Member States.[98]

4. Post-notification referral of the operation in favour of NCAs (Article 9 of the Merger Control Regulation)

The Merger Control Regulation also contemplates referrals following a notification. In fact, this **16.43** was the only possibility in the original Regulation 4064/89, and assumes a decision following an initial examination by Member States. It is noted that, in contrast with the pre-notification referrals regulated by Article 4(4) and (5) of the Regulation, post-notification referral requests are made at the initiative of either Member States or the European Commission, and not of the parties. This section will discuss post-notification referrals to NCAs.

Under Article 9 of the Merger Control Regulation, at the request of one or more Member **16.44** States, whether of its own motion or upon the invitation of the Commission,[99] the Commission may refer to the authorities of the requesting Member State(s) a duly notified concentration with an EU dimension. In the event the referral takes place, the operation will be assessed in accordance with that Member State's national competition law.[100]

---

[97] This would not prevent the Member States from later making a post-notification referral to the Commission under Art 22 of the Merger Control Regulation.

[98] Case Referral Notice, para 20. See also Principles on the application, by National Competition Authorities within the ECA, of Articles 4(5) and 22 of the EC Merger Regulation (2005), paras 8 and 9, published by the network of European Competition Authorities ('ECA') available at <http://ec.europa.eu/competition/ecn/eca_referral_principles_en.pdf>.

[99] In its Green Paper on the review of Regulation 4064/89, the Commission suggested that '[i]n line with the objective of facilitating the referral of cases which, due to a lack of significant cross-border effects, would be most appropriately assessed at national level, it would be reasonable to provide the Commission with the possibility to refer such cases on its own initiative' (para 80).

[100] The GC confirmed in Case T-119/02 *Royal Philips Electronics NV v Commission* [2003] ECR II-1433, para 371, and Joined Cases T-346/02 and T-347/02 *Cableuropa and others v Commission* [2003] ECR II-451, para 217, that the NCAs are completely free to apply their national law and to achieve a completely independent result from that of the European Commission. In the *Royal Philips Electronics* case, the GC specifically stated that: 'However, provided they comply with those obligations [referring to Art 9 of Reg 4064/89 and Art 10 EC] the French competition authorities are free to rule on the substance of the concentration referred to them on the basis of a proper examination conducted in accordance with national competition law.' In the *Cableuropa* case, the GC explained in para 217: 'Consequently, as matters currently stand, the Court of First Instance cannot but find that, in the event of a partial referral to the national authorities, the risk that their decision will be inconsistent, or even irreconcilable, with the decision adopted by the Commission is inherent in the referral system established by Article 9 of Regulation No 4064/89' (see also in the *Royal Philips Electronics* case, para 381).

16.45   Article 9 was included in former Regulation 4064/89 at the request of, among others, Germany. It is frequently referred to as 'the German clause', and reflects a certain reluctance of Member States to abandon completely their competences and sovereignty, and therefore an interest to examine certain cases notwithstanding the European Commission's exclusive jurisdiction to examine all concentrations with a EU dimension.

16.46   For an operation to be totally or partially referred to a national competition authority, two elements are required. First, the operation must be likely to have significant effects on competition in a given market. Second, the market in question must come within the requesting Member State and have all the characteristics of a distinct market.

16.47   Article 9(2)(a) and (b) of the Merger Control Regulation differentiate two scenarios:

(i)   When a concentration threatens to affect competition significantly in a market within a Member State that *constitutes a substantial part of the internal market*, the said Member State may request to examine these effects if it can be demonstrated in accordance with Article 9(2)(a), following a preliminary examination, that:
   (a)   there is a real risk that the operation will have a significant negative effect on competition, and
   (b)   the geographic market or markets in which the competition will be affected have a national or infra-national dimension.

   In this case, the Commission retains a certain degree of discretion to decide whether or not it will refer the operation. If the Commission takes the view that Member States cannot safeguard or restore effective competition in the market concerned, it will not refer the case.[101]

(ii)   When a concentration threatens to affect a market within a Member State that *does not constitute a substantial part of the internal market*, in accordance with Article 9(2)(b) the Commission is under an obligation to refer the operation.[102] 'Distinct market' means an area that constitutes a separate geographic market within a Member State.[103] The concept of 'a substantial part of the internal market' is not clearly defined. The Commission has considered that markets which in principle could appear to be local have amounted to a substantial part of the internal market, in particular in circumstances where an interaction existed between certain local markets which produced regional or national effects.[104]

---

[101]   See Case T-119/02 *Royal Philips Electronics NV v Commission* [2003] ECR II-1433, paras 342–3; and Joined Cases T-346/02 and T-347/02 *Cableuropa and others v Commission* [2003] ECR II-451, para 175.

[102]   Note that the Art 9(2)(b) mechanism was introduced in 1997 in order to facilitate referral requests.

[103]   In Case IV/M.165 *Alcatel/AEG Kabel* [1992] OJ C6/23, paras 9 and 10, the Commission considered that there was no distinct German market for telecommunications cables and that although there was a German market for electrical cables, the concentration did not threaten to create or reinforce a dominant position in that market. The Case Referral Notice (n 22) states that when defining the geographic market, one has to take into account the typical factors that arise in national (or smaller) markets, such as significant transport costs, demand that is supplied in places close to its centres of activity, significant change in prices and market shares in different countries or the existence of legal barriers or other factors delimiting markets.

[104]   Case IV/M.890 *Blokker/Toys 'R' Us* [1998] OJ L316/1, para 38: retail sale is local in nature but it could have wider effects: '[a]lthough the catchment area of a retail outlet, which can be based on the distance the consumer is willing to travel to reach it, is of a local or regional scale, the catchment area does not necessarily determine the geographic market. In a situation where several retail chains operate networks of stores on a national scale, the important parameters of competition are determined on a national scale'. Case IV/M.784 *Kesko/Tuko* [1997] OJ L110/53, paras 21–3. The ECJ has also confirmed that geographically limited monopolies within a Member State which taken together covered the whole territory thereof, could make up a substantial part of the internal market when assessing a restriction on competition in that territory. Case C-323/93 *La Crespelle* [1994] ECR I-5889. However, in several recent cases also involving supermarkets, the Commission has adopted decisions on the basis of Art 9(2)(b) Merger Control Regulation (see Case COMP/M.4522 *Carrefour/Ahold Polska* [2007] OJ C39/29, para 36, Case COMP/M.5790 *Lidl/*

Being an exception to the general rule, these two scenarios should be interpreted restrictively **16.48** and therefore referrals to national authorities of concentrations with an EU dimension are limited to exceptional cases.[105]

The Commission's decision-making practice shows that concentrations have been referred to **16.49** NCAs on relatively few occasions, although in recent years more requests have been received and the Commission has been more ready to make referrals. Between 1990 and 1996, only six cases were referred to NCAs; fifty-nine were referred between 1997 and 2004, of which approximately half came within the period 2001/2004; and between 2005 and 2012, twenty-six cases have been referred to NCAs.[106] One reason for this increase in referrals is the increase in cooperation experience between the NCAs and the Commission, principally via the Advisory Committee; this has created a greater degree of trust between the different NCAs and their improved ability to carry out the analysis of these operations. This development must also be seen in the context of the Commission's policy of the increasingly decentralized application of EU competition law, which has made it more flexible when deciding whether or not to refer a case.[107] This tendency reflects a greater acceptance of the principle of subsidiarity and greater trust in the capacity of Member States to apply the competition rules rigorously.[108]

The practice of the Commission on this matter may be summarized as follows: **16.50**

(i) When it was a local market, the Commission was always more prepared to make the referral.[109]
(ii) When the geographic market affected was national or constituted a significant part of the internal market, the Commission indicated that the referral should only take place in exceptional circumstances. However, after a few years of operation the Commission seemed more willing to refer cases.[110]

Plus Romania/Plus Bulgaria [2010] OJ C123/15, paras 26–7). See also Case COMP/M.3669 *Blackstone (TBG CareCo)/NHP* [2005] OJ C312/4, paras 34–5, regarding care homes in three local UK authorities.

[105] Case T-119/02 *Royal Philips Electronics v Commission* [2003] ECR II-1433, para 354.

[106] European Commission figures as of end of December 2012, online at <http://ec.europa.eu/competition/mergers/statistics.pdf>.

[107] A Schaub, 'Developments of Competition Law and Policy—European and National Perspective', Conference of the Hellenic Competition Commission, 19 April 2002, available on DG COMP's webpage. The increase in the number of EU Member States with their own merger control regimes is also a factor that explains this tendency. See also the Report from the Commission to the Council on the operation of Regulation No 139/2004, 18 June 2009 as well as the Commission staff working paper accompanying the report (both available online).

[108] Article 5 TEU requires intervention to take place at the most adequate level to enable the objectives to be achieved in a sufficient manner. According to the Commission Report to the European Council on adapting Community legislation to the principle of subsidiarity (COM(93)545 final, of 24 November 1993), actions will take place at the most appropriate jurisdictional level, taking into account the objectives to be achieved and the means available to the Union and Member States. Green Paper on the review of Reg 4064/89 COM(2001)745 final, of 11 December 2001, para 16. As mentioned earlier, the Merger Control Regulation—and on numerous occasions the Case Referral Notice—stresses the importance of the principle of subsidiarity.

[109] See, *inter alia*, Case IV/M.1684 *Carrefour/Promodès* [2000] OJ C164/5, paras 3 and 19 (partial referral), Case IV/M.3373 *Accor/Colony/Barrière* [2004] OJ C196/8; Case COMP/M.3275 *Shell/Cepsa* [2004] OJ C250/5; Case COMP/M.3669 *Blackstone/NHP* [2005] OJ C312/4; Case COMP/M.5112 *Rewe/PLUS Discount* [2008] OJ C126/43; Case COMP/M.5677 *Schuitema/Super de Boer Assets* [2010] OJ C303/32.

[110] Case COMP/M.2662 *Danish Crown/Steff-Houlberg* [2002] OJ C114/22 and Case COMP/M.2044 *Interbrew/Bass* [2000] OJ C293/11, para 38, where the Commission 'concluded that the relevant geographic markets for the supply [of beer] to both the "on-trade" and the "off-trade" are no wider than the UK and therefore the UK presents all the characteristics of a distinct market, thereby satisfying the geographic criteria for referral to the competent UK authorities under Article 9(2)(a).'

(iii) The Commission also assessed the presence or otherwise of foreign companies that competed with national companies, for example in the case of military products. In *Krauss-Maffei/Wegmann*,[111] the Commission decided to refer to the German NCA the part of the operation concerning military armoured vehicles.

(iv) When the geographic market went beyond the limits of a Member State, the Commission often rejected the referral request. In *Alcatel/AEG Kabel*,[112] the Commission concluded that there was no distinct German market for telecommunications cables, and although there was a distinct German market for electrical cables, the notified operation did not threaten to create or reinforce a dominant position in that market.

(v) The fact that the NCAs have investigated or are investigating operations that affect the same companies and/or raise the same competition concerns in the same markets makes a referral appropriate in order to enable matters to be dealt with in a uniform way by the competent authority.[113]

(vi) In addition to the local dimension of markets, the Commission will refer the operation if there are significant competition problems. As regards whether the market in question constitutes a substantial part of the internal market, the Commission will leave this point open if the result of its analysis, in the light of the markets and the competition problems, is that the conditions for referral under Article 9 are fulfilled in any event, by applying either letter (a) or letter (b) of Article 9(2).[114]

Partial referrals

16.51 As under Article 4(4) of the Merger Control Regulation, Article 9 contemplates the possibility of a partial referral of the case. This enables the Commission to refer to an NCA the part of the transaction related to given markets and retain jurisdiction over other aspects of the concentration[115] or to refer the case to two authorities, each for their own markets.[116] In the event that an NCA is investigating another concentration in the same market or in a related market, or has previously done so, the Commission will consider referring a concentration to this NCA.[117] Similarly, when a concentration involves two concurrent offers concerning the same undertaking, one of which is already being investigated by the requesting authority, the

---

[111] Case IV/M.1153 *Krauss-Maffei/Wegmann* [1998] OJ C217/8, para 2.

[112] Case IV/M.165 *Alcatel/AEG Kabel* [1991] OJ C6/23, paras 9–10.

[113] Case COMP/M.3271 *Kabel Deutschland/Ish* [2004] OJ C111/6. See Commission Press Release IP/04/717 'Commission refers probe of KDG's acquisition of the North Rhine Westphalian broadband cable network to the German Federal Cartel Office'. Case COMP/M.3674 *Iesy Repositor/ISH* [2004] OJ C321/9. Case COMP/M.6525 *SESA/DISA/SAE/JV* [2012] OJ C135/22, paras 99–101. However, where the Commission has developed significant expertise, it may decide to examine the concentration itself (see the decision pursuant to Art 9(3) in Case COMP/M.5549 *EDF/Segebel* [2009] OJ C57/9, para 262).

[114] Case COMP/M.3275 *Shell España/CEPSA/SIS JV* [2004] OJ C250/5; Case COMP M.5637 *Motor Oil (Hellas) Corinth Refineries/Shell Overseas Holdings* [2010] OJ C46/5, para 98; Case COMP/M.5996 *Thomas Cook/Travel business of Co-operative Group/Travel business of Midlands Co-operative Society* [2011] OJ C309/12, para 99.

[115] See eg Case IV/M.1684 *Carrefour/Promodès* [2000] OJ C164/5; Case COMP/M.2533 *BP/E.ON* [2002] OJ L276/31, para 9; Case COMP/M.2389 *Shell v Dea* [2003] OJ L15/35, para 13; Case COMP/M.5200 *Strabag/Kirchner* [2008] OJ C281/3; COMP/M.5814 *CVC/Univar Europe/Eurochem* [2010] OJ C289/3; Case COMP/M.6321 *Buitenfood/AD Van Geloven Holding/JV* [2012] OJ C63/5. See also a situation where both the Commission and the NCA had relevant experience Case COMP/M.5996 *Thomas Cook/Travel business of Co-operative Group/Travel business of Midlands Co-operative Society* [2011] OJ C309/12, paras 88–90.

[116] Case COMP/M.5881 *ProSiebenSat.1/RTL interactive/JV* [2010] OJ C219/19 which was referred to Germany and to Austria.

[117] Commission Press Release IP/01/1247 of 6 September 2001 in Case COMP/M.2533 *BP/E.ON* [2001] OJ L276/31; Commission Press Release IP/01/1222 of 24 August 2001 in Case COMP/M.2389

Commission will refer the case given the administrative advantages of the second offer being examined by the same authority.[118]

Referral request

Within a period of fifteen working days, which begin to run after receipt of the copy of Form CO, Member States having an interest in seeking referral of a case must notify the Commission of their request.[119] This means that, in a relatively short period of time, Member States have to carry out an analysis that, in certain cases, may be complicated. As well as the problem posed by this short period of time, a post-notification referral request generally creates difficulties for the parties. During the period of time available for this assessment, Member States may only carry out the necessary investigation and take adequate measures for the application of Article 9(2) (and Article 4(4)).[120]   **16.52**

Effects on the time periods for deciding on the substance of the operation

The referral request automatically involves an extension of time in the first phase of ten working days, so that the period increases from twenty-five to thirty-five working days. Therefore, when a Member State files a referral request, the Commission will inform the notifying parties and extend the period within which the Commission can examine a notification. The fact that the period for the request is fifteen working days and that this does not start to run until receipt of Form CO by the NCAs means that, in certain cases,[121] the end of that period almost coincides with the end of the period corresponding to the first phase of the procedure before the Commission.   **16.53**

Referral decision

The Commission generally reaches a referral decision within a period of thirty-five working days from the day after receipt of the notification. When the Commission has set second phase proceedings in motion, it will take a decision on referral within sixty-five working days from the date of notification. When the Commission fails to take a referral decision within the period of sixty-five days despite the request of the Member State in question having been repeated, or has not taken the preparatory steps in order to adopt a decision under Article 8 to maintain or restore effective competition, it will be deemed to have adopted a decision referring the matter to the said Member State.[122] When the Commission considers that the conditions for a referral are not fulfilled, it will adopt a decision to that effect addressed to the Member State in question.[123] As has already been mentioned, there is a substantial difference in the discretion enjoyed by the Commission to make a referral depending on whether the case concerns an effect on competition in a market that   **16.54**

Shell/Dea OJ L15/35; Case COMP/M.5741 *CDC/Veolia Environnement/Transdev/Veolia Transport* [2010] OJ C266/2; Case COMP/M.5803 *Eurovia/Tarmac* [2010] OJ 286/3.

[118] Commission Press Release IP/96/254 of 22 March 1996 in Case IV/M.716 *GEHE/Lloyds* [1996]. The investigation of a national authority in relation to an offer in concurrent proceedings is considered a legitimate matter to be taken into account in a referral request.

[119] Article 9(2) of the Merger Control Regulation and Case Referral Notice, para 40.

[120] Article 21(3) of the Merger Control Regulation. The Commission nevertheless has the opportunity to conduct a market investigation before deciding on the Art 9 referral (see eg Case COMP/M.5996 *Thomas Cook/Travel business of Co-operative Group/Travel business of Midlands Co-operative Society* [2011] OJ C309/12).

[121] For instance where holidays do not coincide for the European Commission and the NCAs, which may delay the filing of the copy of Form CO or the referral request of the relevant NCA.

[122] Article 9(5) of the Merger Control Regulation.

[123] Article 9(3) of the Merger Control Regulation. DG COMP reports only six refusals to refer pursuant to Art 9(3) up to the end of 2012 (see statistics available on DG COMP's website). See Ch 18, 'Judicial Review of Commission Decisions Regarding Concentrations', para 18.15.

constitutes a substantial part of the internal market (Article 9(2)(a)) or not (Article 9(2)
(b)). In the former case, if the Commission considers that 'a concentration threatens to
affect significantly competition' in a distinct market, it will either deal with the case itself in
accordance with the Merger Control Regulation, or it will refer the operation—wholly or
in part—to the NCA(s). If the Commission considers that there is no distinct market or no
such threat exists, it will adopt a decision addressed to the Member State in question and
deal with the matter itself. In the latter case, if the Commission considers that the operation
affects competition in a distinct market that does not constitute a significant part of the
internal market, the Commission will proceed to refer the whole matter or that part which
is related to the distinct market.[124]

16.55 When the Commission refers a concentration to an NCA, that authority may only apply
national competition rules and can only take the measures that are strictly necessary to preserve or re-establish effective competition in the market in question.[125] Although the NCA
has some discretion as to how it will fulfil this obligation, it must comply with the principle
of proportionality which is now contained in Article 9(8) of the Merger Control Regulation.
National courts can review the use by Member States of this discretionary power.[126]

16.56 In accordance with Article 9(6) of the Merger Control Regulation, the NCA in question
must inform the undertakings concerned of the results of its preliminary analysis and, where
appropriate, the steps it intends to take, within a maximum period of forty-five working
days from the referral by the Commission or receipt of a complete notification by the NCA.

---

[124] Article 9(3)(b) of the Merger Control Regulation, last para.

[125] Article 9(8) of the Merger Control Regulation. See the decision pursuant to Art 9(3) in Case
COMP/M.5549 *EDF/Segebel* [2009] OJ C57/9, where the Commission also justified its decision not to refer
the case to the Belgian NCA by the fact that the transaction would have to be cleared automatically under
Belgian national law, ie without the Belgian authorities being in a position to require any remedies, including
those that were secured by the Commission under its Art 6(2) decision (para 263).

[126] There are at least four cases where the Commission referred the matter to NCAs and then the latter's final decisions were appealed before national courts. Case COMP/M.2044 *Interbrew/Bass* [2000] OJ
C293/11 concerned an operation that was referred to the UK in 2000. Once the British competition authorities had carried out an in-depth investigation, the Secretary of State for Trade and Industry reached a decision
requiring the complete divestments of the brewing activity of Bass, which effectively meant that the deal was
prohibited. Interbrew sought judicial review of this decision alleging that it was neither reasonable nor proportional, and was based on an abuse of due process. The High Court found against Interbrew as regards their
first (and main) allegation but agreed that the procedures of the British competition authorities were unfair
since Interbrew had not had a fair chance to resolve the fundamental problems relevant to assessing an alternative and less onerous solution. The second case concerned the supply of electricity in Case COMP/M.2216
Enel/FT/Wind/Infostrada [2001] OJ C39/9, which was referred to the Italian competition authorities. After
a detailed investigation, the Italian authorities approved the proposed merger, imposing on ENEL various
conditions. ENEL and CODACONS, the Italian consumer protection association, both appealed against the
decision and, in a judgment on both appeals, the competent Italian regional administrative tribunal (TAR,
'Tribunale Amministrativo Regionale') concluded that ENEL did not have a dominant position in the electricity supply market and also annulled the decision of the Italian competition authority regarding the conditions imposed. The third case was in Case COMP/M.2845 *Sogecable/Canalsatélite Digital/Vía Digital* [2002]
OJ C166/9, involving a concentration operation that was referred to the Spanish authorities under Art 9(2) of
Reg 4064/89. The Spanish cabinet approved the operation subject to various conditions in its Resolution of
29 November 2002 (BOE 14 January 2003, No 12, 1707), and various competitors brought judicial review
proceedings before the Spanish Supreme Court challenging these conditions. All the appeals were rejected by
the Supreme Court in its resolutions of 7 November 2005, 29 November 2005, and 3 October 2006. The
fourth case was Case COMP/M.2621 *SEB/Moulinex* [2003] OJ L138/18, involving a transaction that was
partially referred to the French authorities with respect to small electrical household appliances. That part
of the concentration was authorized by the Minister of Economics on 5 July 2002 on the basis of the failing
company defence. The decision was then annulled by the Conseil d'Etat on 6 February 2004. A challenge
against the second approval decision of the Minister of Economics of 16 August 2004 was rejected by the
Conseil d'Etat on 13 February 2006.

This provision involves a preliminary decision within the said period of forty-five working days from the referral of the operation, or, where appropriate, from the subsequent notification of the operation to the NCA. The wording of Article 9(6) of the former Regulation 4064/89 offered the NCA a time period of four months for 'the announcement of the findings of the examination', a longer period than the European Commission would have had to decide the matter if it had been entrusted with the examination. The new wording of Article 9(6) appears to reduce the period, although it should be noted that the Merger Control Regulation only requires the NCA to inform the undertakings concerned of the result of its preliminary analysis, rather than reach a final decision on whether or not to authorize an operation. As a result, the Green Paper's more ambitious idea of introducing a maximum period within which the NCAs must adopt a final decision has not seen the light of day.[127]

Article 9(6) of the Merger Control Regulation does, however, oblige NCAs to reach a decision according to their national law 'without undue delay'. This reference could be interpreted as meaning that the final decision on the concentration must be taken within the periods laid down in national law without any additional time being given on the grounds that it is a referral from the Commission. **16.57**

5. Post-notification referrals to the European Commission (Article 22 of the Merger Control Regulation)

Originally, the possibility of a referral to the European Commission was conceived of for the benefit of those Member States which lacked the necessary instruments to investigate mergers at a national level. The idea was to allow Member States to request the Commission to act in their stead and assess the effects of concentrations that did not reach the thresholds of former Regulation 4064/89. At the time of the adoption of former Regulation 4064/89, this was known as the Dutch clause, since it was introduced at the request of the Netherlands, which lacked its own system for the control of concentrations. In its original wording, Article 22 had a very limited scope.[128] **16.58**

The amendments that came into force in 1998 aimed to give the provision a new function by allowing two or more Member States to make joint referrals to the Commission when they considered that the latter was best placed to evaluate an operation. The declared intention was to consolidate both the application of EU competition law to cross-border cases and the **16.59**

---

[127] In the Green Paper on the review of Reg 4064/89 the Commission stated that: 'referred cases should arguably be treated on an equal footing to all cases subject to a merger control procedure within the specific reviewing authority. Nevertheless, there may be some merit in seeking to harmonise the timeframe in which the final decision is taken. A possibility would be to clarify the current rule in Article 9(6) so that a decision of a definitive nature comparable to an Article 8 decision under the Merger Regulation would have to be adopted within the same timeframe as would have applied for the Commission. Another more far-reaching possibility would be to provide, in the Merger Regulation, that any national authority dealing with a case that has been referred to it should do so under the procedure indicated in the Merger Regulation' (para 82).

[128] Up to the end of 2012, only seven concentrations have been referred to the Commission by a single Member State (as opposed to joint referral) under Art 22: Case IV/M.278 *British Airways/Dan Air* [1993] OJ C68/5 (air transport market), in which the first-phase investigation period started to run from the date of the submission of additional information by the Belgian authorities because the Commission considered itself unable to investigate the merger on the basis of previously submitted information; Case IV/M.553 *RTL/Verónica/Endemol* [1996] OJ L134/32 (Dutch TV market); Case IV/M.784 *Kesko/Tuko* [1997] OJ L110/53 (retail market in daily consumer goods in Finland); Case IV/M.890 *Blokker/Toys 'R' Us* [1998] OJ L316/1 (retail toy market in the Netherlands); and, after 1998, Case COMP/M.4465 *Thrane & Thrane/Nera* [2007] OJ C94/19 (mobile satellite maritime communication in the UK); Case COMP/M.4709 *Apax Partners/Telenor Satellite Services* [2007] OJ C230/1 (two-way telecommunication services in the UK); Case COMP/M.5020 *Lessafre/GBI UK* [2008] OJ C308/7 (manufacture and supply of yeast in the UK).

single authority principle, and to resolve the problem of multiple filings.[129] In 2002, for the first time two joint requests were filed by various Member States asking for the Commission to intervene in their stead.[130]

16.60 The new wording of Article 22 of the Merger Control Regulation has not affected its main features. Article 22(1) allows one or more Member States[131] to request the Commission to carry out the analysis of an operation that lacks an EU dimension if two cumulative requirements (that also existed under former Regulation 4064/89) are fulfilled:

- it affects trade between Member States (that is, it can have an appreciable influence on trade flows between Member States);[132] and
- it threatens to affect in a significant manner competition in the Member State(s) requesting referral. This requirement involves showing that there is a real risk of the operation having a significant negative effect on competition.

16.61 The Case Referral Notice defines two categories of cases most appropriate for referral.

- Cases which give rise to serious competition concerns in one or more markets which are wider than national, or where some of the potentially affected markets are wider than national, and where the main economic impact of the concentration is connected to such markets.
- Cases which give rise to serious competition concerns in a series of national or narrower than national markets located in a number of Member States, in circumstances where coherent treatment of the case (regarding possible remedies, investigative efforts) is considered desirable, and where the main economic impact of the concentration is connected to such markets.[133]

16.62 The question has been raised whether a Member State without jurisdiction to examine a merger may make or join a referral request. While Article 22(1) and (2) of the Merger Control Regulation would not seem to rule it out, Recital 5 of the Regulation states that '[o]ther Member States which are also competent to review the concentration should be able to join the request'. In its practice, the Commission has accepted referrals from Member States

---

[129] In the Green Paper on the review of Reg 4064/89, para 84, the Commission points out that this amendment was to some extent seen as complementary to the simultaneous introduction of the thresholds of Art 1(3), which in principle was aimed at resolving the same problems.

[130] Up to the end of 2012, there were sixteen joint referrals of various Member States to the Commission. In the case of the acquisition of Unison Industries by a subsidiary of General Electric, this was originally notified to various Member States (the UK, Germany, France, Italy, Spain, Austria, and Greece). These Member States decided to make a request to the Commission under Art 22 of Reg 4064/89. See Commission Press Release IP/02/578 of 17 April 2002, where the Commission recognized that '[t]his was only the second joint referral of a merger to the Commission by Member States in the almost eleven years that the Merger Regulation has been in place. The first such case was the *Promotech/Sulzer Textil* merger, on which the Commission started an in-depth investigation this week'. In Case COMP/M.2738 *GEES/Unison Industries* [2002], the requests by Member States contained *prima facie* indicators to suggest that the concentration would create or consolidate a dominant position which would enable the merged entity to obstruct significantly competition in the territory of the Member States concerned, as well as the cross-border trade concerned. See Commission Press Release IP/02/1140 of 24 July 2002, regarding Case COMP/M.2698 *Promotech/Sulzer Textil* [2002].

[131] Article 22 also allows the Commission to invite one or more Member States to present a referral request if the requirements for referral are fulfilled. See Case COMP/M.6796 *Aegean/Olympic II* [2013] OJ C70/12.

[132] On this point, the Case Referral Notice refers to the Guidelines on the effect on trade concept contained in Arts 81 and 82 of the EC Treaty [2004] OJ C101/81.

[133] In Case COMP/M.3986 *Gas Natural/Endesa* [2005], the Commission rejected the referral requests of Italy and Portugal. In Case COMP/M.4124 *Coca-Cola Hellenic Bottling Company/Lanitis Bros* [2006], the Commission considered that the concentration did not appear to belong to either category (paras 21–2). In at least two recent cases, the markets at stake had a national dimension; see Case COMP/M.5828 *Procter & Gamble/Sara Lee Air care* [2010] OJ C259/5; Case COMP/M.5969 *SCJ/Sara Lee* [2010] OJ C4/2.

which did not have jurisdiction, but that were joining Member States which had jurisdiction of an operation.[134]

16.63 Paragraph 2 of Article 22(1) of the Merger Control Regulation reduces the one-month period for filing the request contained in former Regulation 4064/89 to fifteen working days from 'the date on which the concentration was notified, or if no notification is required, otherwise made known to the Member State concerned'.[135] Once it has received the request, the Commission will notify all the Member States and undertakings concerned. Any Member State may join in the request within fifteen working days of receipt of the initial request (even if the operation has been notified in various Member States[136]). During this period, national time limits for assessing the concentration are suspended until the Commission adopts a decision on jurisdiction. This suspension will end with respect to any Member State from the moment that such State informs the Commission and the undertakings concerned that it does not wish to join the request.[137] After this period of fifteen working days, the Commission has ten working days to decide and duly inform all Member States and the undertakings concerned of its decision. If it does not expressly state its position within this time, it is deemed to have decided to examine the concentration in accordance with the request.

16.64 With regard to the effects of the referral decision, if the Commission accepts its competence to analyse the impact of the operation, the national control proceedings end and the Commission can require the parties to file a notification using Form CO. With respect to the scope of the investigation, the Commission will not assess the effects of the concentration in the territory of those Member States that have not joined the request, unless such an examination is necessary to evaluate the effects of the concentration within the territory of the requesting Member States (eg, if the geographic market extends beyond the territory of the requesting Member State(s)).[138] Once the operation has been referred to the Commission, the Member State cannot control the direction and scope of the Commission's investigation. The Commission can examine all of the relevant aspects of the concentration, independently of the scope of the request, with the exception previously mentioned that, in principle, it will

---

[134] See eg Case COMP/M.3796 *Omya/J.M. Huber PCC* [2005] OJ L72/24; Case COMP/M.4980 *ABF/GBI Business* [2007] OJ C145/12; Case COMP/M.5828 *Procter & Gamble/Sara Lee Air care* [2010] OJ C259/5; Case COMP/M.5969 *SCJ/Sara Lee Air Care* [2010] OJ C4/2; Case COMP/M.6191 *Birla/Columbian Chemicals* [2011] OJ C212/18.

[135] The Case Referral Notice clarifies that notification of a Member State must be interpreted here as meaning the notification of sufficient information to carry out a preliminary analysis in order to determine whether the criteria for requesting a referral under Art 22 are fulfilled (para 50).

[136] The Case Referral Notice encourages the parties to notify the operation simultaneously in all Member States so that all of the NCAs involved have the necessary information about the operation and can join in the request on a properly informed basis (para 50). When the parties to a concentration inform a NCA that the concentration is subject to review by another NCA, the information procedure as described in the ECA Procedures Guide will be put into effect and all NCAs within the ECA network should be informed of the concentration (see ECA principles on the application, by National Competition Authorities within the ECA, of Arts 4(5) and 22 of the Merger Regulation (2005), para 20).

[137] It is observed that, in contrast with pre-notification filings under Art 4(5) of the Merger Control Regulation, some Member States may retain the case and that would not prevent the Commission from accepting a referral. In Case COMP/M.5828 *Procter & Gamble/Sara Lee* [2010] OJ C259/5, the initial request was made by the German authorities, which were joined by six other Member States. However, four Member States competent to review the transaction did not request a referral.

[138] Case Referral Notice, para 50 and n 46. See eg Case COMP/M.5675 *Syngenta/Monsanto Sunflower Seed Business* [2010] OJ C182/1, where, besides the Spanish and Hungarian markets for the sale of sunflower seeds (for which it had received a referral request from these two Member States), the Commission also analysed the up-stream market for the trading of sunflower varieties. The Commission could not, however, deal with an important market downstream (France), given that the French authorities had not requested a referral pursuant to Art 22.

limit itself to examining the impact of the concentration in the territory or territories of the Member State(s) that made the referral request.

16.65 Unlike referrals under Article 9 of the Merger Control Regulation, Article 22 of the Merger Control Regulation does not permit partial referrals and therefore the Commission's investigations must be made in relation to the whole operation rather than just specific aspects of it, such as a particular product market. In practice, Article 22 results in an identical procedure to that applicable to concentrations with an EU dimension. In *Endemol Entertainment Holding*, the parties considered that the Commission's investigation should be limited to the market for TV advertising, since the Dutch government had only asked the Commission to examine whether the operation would create or reinforce a dominant position that would significantly obstruct effective competition in the Dutch TV advertising market. Since the Dutch government considered that there were no competition problems in other markets, in the opinion of the parties any investigation of other markets would go beyond the request made by the Dutch authorities.[139] However, the GC held that Article 22 grants no power to the Member State either to control the Commission's conduct of the investigation once it has referred the concentration in question to it, or to define the scope of the Commission's investigation. In that particular case, the GC found that the Dutch government had not sought in its request to restrict the Commission's examination of the concentration.[140]

16.66 Member States having referred the case lose the power to apply their national law to the concentration. In the event that the transaction is being examined by several NCAs, the Commission will decide on the operation on behalf of those Member States that have filed the referral request with respect to their territory, while those Member States that have not requested referral will continue to apply their national law. In the procedure, the Commission will apply the provisions of the Merger Control Regulation only, including any of the substantive decisions contemplated, *inter alia*, in Articles 6 and 8 thereof.[141]

E. Scope of the Merger Control Regulation: Concentrations with an EU Dimension

16.67 The Merger Control Regulation applies solely to concentrations (as defined in its Article 3) that have the minimum dimension defined in Article 1(2) and (3).

1. 'Concentration' as defined in Article 3 of the Merger Control Regulation

16.68 A concentration within the meaning of Article 3 of the Merger Control Regulation occurs when a single undertaking or two or more undertakings together permanently acquire control of another undertaking, or where previously independent undertakings merge. The concept of control under the Merger Control Regulation, which may be different from that applied in specific areas of legislation,[142] may be defined as the capacity of exercising a decisive influence on an undertaking, in particular where the undertaking with that power is able to impose choices on the other in relation to its strategic decisions.[143] Decisive influence, which has to

---

[139] Case T-221/95 *Endemol Entertainment Holding v Commission* [1999] ECR II-1229, para 37.
[140] Case T-221/95 *Endemol Entertainment Holding v Commission* [1999] ECR II-1229, paras 42–7.
[141] Case Referral Notice, n 45.
[142] Commission Consolidated Jurisdictional Notice under Council Regulation (EC) No 139/2004 on the control of concentrations between undertakings [1998] OJ C95/1 (hereinafter the 'Jurisdictional Notice'), para 23.
[143] Case T-411/07 *Aer Lingus Group v Commission* [2010] ECR II-3691, para 63.

be effective,[144] is obtained through rights, contracts, or other means, can refer to a part or the whole of the undertaking in question, or over a whole group of undertakings. The criterion of permanence serves to exclude transactions with no structural impact.[145]

The Regulation distinguishes three forms of concentrations: merger of undertakings, acquisition **16.69** of sole control, and acquisition of joint control over full-function undertakings. These three situations are examined in this section. The Commission has launched a reflection[146] to determine whether minority shareholdings that do not confer control[147] would create a gap in the enforcement and whether it would need to be closed.[148] In June 2013, the Commission launched a public consultation to elicit views of stakeholders as to whether the Merger Control Regulation should be amended to allow the Commission to also look at non-controlling minority shareholdings. The Commission presented a number of options to explore how these minority shareholdings could be controlled, without creating an undue burden for undertakings.[149]

Merger of two formerly independent entities

A concentration arises when two or more previously independent undertakings or parts of **16.70** undertakings merge. As explained in the Jurisdictional Notice, this may occur not only in the event of a legal merger, but also where the combining of the activities of previously independent undertakings results in the creation of a 'single economic unit', such as where two or more undertakings, while retaining their individual legal personalities or trade names,[150] establish contractually a common economic management. If this leads to a *de facto* amalgamation of the undertakings concerned into a genuine common economic unit, the operation is considered to be a merger. A prerequisite for the determination of a common economic unit is the existence of a permanent, single economic management. Other relevant factors may include internal profit and loss compensation as between the various undertakings within the group, and their joint liability externally. The *de facto* amalgamation may be reinforced by cross shareholdings between the undertakings forming the economic unit.

Acquisition of sole control

Another type of concentration arises where an undertaking acquires control over another **16.71** entity through rights, contracts, or other means and can thus determine the latter's commercial strategy. Article 3(1) of the Merger Control Regulation describes this as follows:

---

[144] Case T-282/02 *Cementbouw Handel & Industrie v Commission* [2006] ECR II-319, para 41.

[145] See Recital 20 Merger Control Regulation.

[146] See Commissioner Almunia, 'Merger Regulation in the EU after 20 years' SPEECH/11/166, 10 March 2011, and 'Higher Duty for Competition Enforcers', 15 June 2012. In November 2011, DG COMP announced its intention to conduct a study on the economic importance of minority shareholdings in the EU's economy and the need for the Commission to have the power to review the purchase of minority shareholdings.

[147] As defined in the Commission's call for tender for a 'Study on the importance of minority shareholdings in the EU' available at <http://ec.europa.eu/competition/calls/2011_016_tender_specifications_en.pdf>, minority shareholdings may involve a one-way direct stake in a company or may be reciprocal, where two companies hold shares in one another (or indeed amongst many competitors). Minority shareholdings may also arise through a third firm and thus be indirect.

[148] Two large Member States (Germany and the UK) currently have systems allowing for the control of minority shareholdings beyond certain thresholds.

[149] Should the scope of the Merger Control Regulation eventually be extended to cover non-controlling minority shareholdings, the Commission identified two options. One is to propose a selective system in which the Commission identifies the cases that may raise specific problems; the other would be a mandatory notification system of the kind in use today for mergers involving the acquisition of control. See Staff Working Document 'Towards more effective EU merger Control' and its two annexes, and Commission Press release IP/13/584 of 20 June 2013. See also 'Merger review: Past evolution and future prospects', SPEECH/12/773, 2 November 2012.

[150] See eg Case COMP/M.5747 *Iberia/British Airways* [2010] OJ C241/1, para 5.

(b) the acquisition, by one or more persons already controlling at least one undertaking,[151] or by one or more undertakings, whether by purchase of securities or assets, by contract or by any other means, of direct or indirect control of the whole or parts of one or more other undertakings.

16.72 The acquired entity may be a pre-existing undertaking or a part thereof. In the latter case, for there to be a concentration, the acquired entity needs to qualify as a separate 'undertaking' as opposed to a mere asset. The principal criterion in that regard is that the acquisition should affect a business with a market presence, to which a turnover can be clearly attributed.[152]

16.73 By way of exception, a concentration does not arise—and thus there is no obligation to notify—with respect to financial or credit entities or insurance companies whose normal activities include transactions and dealings in securities on their own account or on behalf of others which they have acquired solely in order to resell them. This is subject to the caveat that the acquirers do not exercise the voting rights in respect of the shares they hold, or they only exercise those rights to prepare the resale of the undertaking or its assets provided that the said resale occurs within a year of the date of purchase.[153] Similarly, under Article 3(5)(b), a concentration will not exist either if 'control is acquired by an office-holder according to the law of a Member States relating to liquidation, winding up, insolvency, cessation of payments, compositions or analogous proceedings'. Finally, Article 3(5)(c) provides that there is no concentration when the acquiring party is a financial holding company referred to in the Fourth Council Directive 78/660/EEC, provided that the voting rights in respect of the holding are only used to maintain the full value of the investment. The rationale for these exceptions is related with the absence of permanence of the situation of control.

16.74 Sole control may have a legal or a *de facto* basis. The elements that must be taken into account in the acquisition of sole control are as follows:

- The stake acquired: 50 per cent and one share of the share capital normally gives legal control. Ownership of 50 per cent of the shares normally means the ability to block, if not impose, most corporate decisions, leading to 'negative control'.[154]
- The percentage of voting rights that can be exercised in the shareholders' Annual General Meeting ('AGM'); the ability to exercise more than half of the voting rights normally confers legal control.
- The number of directors appointed on the Board of Directors of the acquired entity: the power to appoint more than half of the directors normally confers legal control, since, with the support of such directors, resolutions can be approved and therefore the competitive strategy of the acquired entity can be determined.

16.75 These aspects are often directly related, so that when an undertaking acquires most of the share capital in another company it normally also acquires most of the voting rights, and has the right to appoint more than half of the directors. Although this is the rule, in practice there are exceptions. The first aspect, then, which must be analysed is the proportion of share capital acquired, bearing in mind that normally a stake of more than 50 per cent of

---

[151] Note that the acquisition of sole control by an investor not controlling other undertakings would not be a concentration, as the Merger Control Regulation is not aimed at controlling property but amalgamations between independent companies.

[152] Jurisdictional Notice, para 24.

[153] Article 3(5)(a) of the Merger Control Regulation and paras 110–17 of the Jurisdictional Notice. See also Case T-279/04 *Editions Odile Jacob v Commission* [2010] ECR II-185. The Regulation provides for the possibility of the Commission extending the one-year period if the acquiring entities so request, provided that they can show that it was not 'reasonably possible' to make the disposal within the said period.

[154] Jurisdictional Notice, para 58.

the capital often confers control in the absence of other factors. It is, however, possible for minority shareholdings (below 50 per cent) to confer legal control if such shares have specific rights attached to them. These inherent rights may consist in preferential shares that give most of the voting rights or that allow the minority shareholder to determine exclusively the competitive strategy of the company in question. Among such rights, the power to appoint more than half of the members of the Board of Directors or the supervisory Board is seen as being very important.[155]

A minority shareholder may also exercise *de facto* sole control. An example may be a minority **16.76** shareholder without a majority of voting rights but having the ability to appoint the majority of directors.[156] If the other shares are widely dispersed, it is unlikely that all of the small shareholders will attend or be represented at the shareholders' AGM. If the average attendance at previous AGMs is observed, it may be that only half of the voting shares are represented. In such a situation, it is possible that with a stake of less than 50 per cent and using the same percentage of votes in the AGM, a company may be able to obtain approval of its resolutions. This would amount to an acquisition of control.[157] To determine whether control exists, a forecast or prediction will have to be made in each case, in which the extent of dispersion of shares as well as attendance at AGMs in the previous three years will be analysed, before deciding whether or not a given minority shareholder is capable of systematically obtaining the approval of its resolutions.[158] In addition, a situation of economic dependence may, in certain exceptional situations, result in the *de facto* acquisition of control when there are very substantial long-term supply agreements or credits granted by suppliers or clients, together with structural links that allow the latter to exercise a decisive influence over the acquired

---

[155] Jurisdictional Notice, para 57.

[156] Judgment of 12 December 2012 in Case T-332/09 *Electrabel v Commission*, paras 94–8. See also Case COMP/M.3330 RTL/M6 [2004] OJ C95/35 and Commission decision of 18 February 1998 imposing a fine for failure to notify and early implementation in Case IV/M.920 *Samsung/AST* [1998] OJ L225/12, where Samsung had appointed half of the members of the board despite the contractual limitation for participation in the capital of AST set at 49.9 per cent.

[157] Jurisdictional Notice, para 59. In Case IV/M.25 *Arjomari/Wiggins Teape* [1990], the Commission found that Arjomari had sole control with a minority stake of 39 per cent of WTA bearing in mind that none of WTA's remaining 107,000 shareholders owned more than 4 per cent of the company and only three shareholders had stakes of more than 3 per cent. See also Case COMP/M.4956 *STX/Aker Yards* [2008] OJ C147/14, where the Commission considered that given the shareholding structure of Aker Yards and the exercise of voting rights in Aker Yards at its last three shareholders' meetings, its shareholding of 39.2 per cent was highly likely to allow STX to acquire effective *de facto* control of Aker Yards (para 6); See also Case COMP/M.5250 *Porsche/Volkswagen* [2008] OJ C222/22, paras 7–13 and Case COMP/M.5508 *SoFFin/Hypo Real Estate* [2009]OJ C147/8, para 4. By contrast, in Case T-411/07 *Aer Lingus Group v Commission* [2010] ECR II-3691, para 67, Aer Lingus stated that Ryanair's 29.3 per cent shareholding gave it 'substantial opportunities to seek to interfere with the management and commercial strategy of Aer Lingus', but it agreed that this shareholding would not confer control within the meaning of Art 3 of the Merger Control Regulation.

[158] See Jurisdictional Notice, para 59. An example of such forecasting arose in Case IV/M.343 *Société Générale de Belgique/Générale de Banque* [1993] OJ C225/2, where Société Général de Belgique (SGB) increased its stake in Générale de Banque (GB) from 21 per cent to 26 per cent. The Commission considered that the 21 per cent stake which SGB had held was not enough to give it control, since although the other shareholders were quite dispersed, Groupe AG held almost 15 per cent of GB's share capital. The prediction of SGB's vote, taking into account attendance at the last three AGMs, gave it more than 40 per cent of the votes, but the Commission concluded that this did not amount to control. However, with the additional 5 per cent, giving it a total stake of 26 per cent, SGB was predicted to have almost 56 per cent of the votes in the AGM, and, therefore, the purchase of this additional stake was considered to be a *de facto* acquisition of control. A similar forecasting was undertaken by the Commission in Case COMP/M.4994 *Electrabel/Compagnie nationale du Rhône* [2009] OJ C279/9, paras 40–77. The Commission considered that as of 23 December 2003, Electrabel was assured of having a *de facto* majority at the general meeting of CNR shareholders based on the shareholding structure, at the presence at previous general meetings and the existence of a shareholder agreement between Electrabel and the second largest shareholder of CNR. This decision was upheld by the GC in their judgment of 12 December 2012 in Case T-332/09 *Electrabel v Commission*, paras 48–81, which relied also on the

entity.[159] An indicia of control can be the fact that the minority shareholder is the only industrial shareholder or has a central role in the operational control of the other undertaking.[160]

16.77 An option to purchase or convert shares will give the acquirer sole control if the purchase is made
through legally binding agreements.[161] If the exercise of the option in question is only probable,
its existence will be treated as merely another factor to be taken into account in assessing the
existence of control.[162] If the operation creates joint control for an initial period of time or on
start up, but legally binding agreements provide that this will subsequently become sole control,
the acquisition will be treated as one of sole control.[163]

Acquisition of joint control over full-function joint ventures

Joint control

16.78 When more than one independent entity jointly acquire control over another previously independent entity in the sense referred to earlier, a joint venture emerges.[164] The most common
transactions resulting in joint control are:

- two or more independent entities create an entity that they will jointly control;
- one or more undertakings takes a controlling stake in the share capital of another company controlled until that moment exclusively by a single undertaking which retains joint
  control;
- a *de facto* merger or combination of some of the activities of previously independent undertakings which, without amounting to a legal merger, results in the creation of a single
  economic entity under the joint management of the former entities.[165]

---

principles laid down in the Commission Notice on the concept of concentration under Council Regulation
(EEC) No 4064/89 on the control of concentrations between undertakings ([1998] C66/02, hereafter the
'Notice on the concept of concentration', now integrated in the Jurisdictional Notice).

[159] Case IV/M.258 *CCIE/GTE* [1992] OJ C265/.
[160] Case COMP/M.4994 *Electrabel/Compagnie nationale du Rhône* [2009] OJ C279/9, paras 128–37 confirmed
by the GC in their judgment of 12 December 2012 in Case T-332/09 *Electrabel v Commission*, paras 138–50.
[161] Case IV/M.259 *British Airways/TAT* [1992] OJ C326/16 and Case T-2/93 *Air France v Commission*
[1994] ECR II-323. In this case, the Commission concluded that BA had acquired joint rather than sole
control, despite acquiring 49 per cent of TATEA and an option to purchase the remaining 51 per cent of the
shares held by TAT, on the grounds that it was not definite that the option to purchase would be exercised.
The Commission Decision was appealed to the GC by Air France, one of BA's competitors. In its judgment,
the GC confirmed the Commission's assessment, holding that the exercise by BA of its option to purchase was
a hypothetical factor, and when the Decision was adopted it had not been proved that BA had the intention
to exercise it (para 71).
[162] Case COMP/M.4994 *Electrabel/Compagnie nationale du Rhône* [2009] OJ C279/9, paras 159–64,
confirmed by the GC in Case T-332/09 *Electrabel v Commission* [2012] ECR II-0000, paras 166–75.
[163] See para 34 of the Jurisdictional Notice and the reference to Case IV/M.425 *British Telecom/Banco
Santander* [1994] OJ C134/4, para 21. In this case the Commission concluded that since Banco Santander
could exercise a decisive influence over the joint venture BTSA only within the first three years of BTSA's
existence and that the investment was long term, the three-year period was insufficient to create a permanent
change in the structure of the undertakings concerned. Accordingly, Banco Santander did not acquire joint
control over BTSA and British Telecom had sole control.
[164] Jurisdictional Notice, para 91.
[165] Jurisdictional Notice, para 10. See Case JV.19 *Alitalia/KLM* [2000] OJ C96/5, Commission Press
Release IP/99/628 'Commission clears the alliance between Alitalia (Italy) and KLM (Netherlands) subject to
conditions'. In this case, despite the fact that the parties did not merge or create a joint venture as a separate
legal entity, the Commission examined the operation in accordance with former Reg 4064/89. Both undertakings continued to operate activities outside of the alliance as well as independent decision-making bodies.
However, the Commission considered that the parties had, through contractual means, achieved such a high
level of integration that the operation amounted to a full-function joint venture. This was the first time the
Commission established that there was a contractual joint venture or '*de facto* integration of the undertakings
concerned'. See Enrico Maria Armani, DG COMP-D–2, 'Alitalia-KLM: A new trend in assessing airline alliances?' (October 1999) 3 EC Competition Policy Newsletter 19.

Joint control exists when the parent companies must reach an agreement on most decisions   **16.79**
from a commercial point of view which affect the undertaking controlled. Unlike exclusive
power, which gives a shareholder the power to determine the strategic decisions of an undertaking, joint control is typified by the possibility of a deadlock situation, derived from the
power held by the parent companies of the joint venture to reject the strategic decisions proposed by one or other of the parties.[166] Joint control may therefore be defined in this negative
way as the power to block actions that determine the competitive strategy of an undertaking.[167] Joint control results naturally when the parent companies hold the same number of
shares, or the same amount of voting rights needed to approve resolutions at the shareholders'
AGM of the joint venture. There may also be a formal agreement between the parent companies concerning the number of representatives that each may appoint to the administrative
or decision-making bodies, or deciding who has a casting vote. In order for joint control to
exist, this agreement must provide that both parent companies have the right to appoint the
same number of directors and that none of them has the right to exercise a casting vote. If this
is not the case, it may be that one of the parent companies holds sole control.

Despite the fact that two or more parent companies in a joint venture may not be equally   **16.80**
represented in the decision-making bodies of the company, joint control may still exist in
the event of veto rights. In these cases, the mere possibility or power that the right may
be exercised is sufficient.[168] Veto rights that confer control must go beyond the rights that
protect the financial interests of minority shareholders. The latter category of rights protects
the shareholder with respect to decisions that create a risk for the very essence of the joint
venture, such as, *inter alia*, significant changes in the Articles, increases or reductions in the
share capital, the sale or liquidation of the undertaking, etc.[169] Veto rights must refer to questions such as the budget, the business plan, major investments, or the appointment of senior
executives. To obtain control it is not necessary to have veto rights over each and every one
of these aspects; sometimes, a veto right over only one may give control. Priority is given to
veto rights over the appointment of senior management, the budget, or the business plan,
which, in general, give control. In other cases, the acquisition of control will depend on both
the nature and number of veto rights, which will be assessed as a whole.[170] Even if there are
no veto rights, it is also possible for two or more undertakings that are minority shareholders
to exercise joint control. This would be the case if the minority shareholders jointly possessed
and exercised most voting rights. This situation may arise when there is a legally binding
agreement in this regard between the minority shareholders, if they create a holding company
to which they transfer their rights, or if there is *de facto* concerted action between them. As
regards this last point, the Commission may consider that *de facto* concerted action could
exceptionally be carried out if the minority shareholders held significant interests in common,
which would create a disincentive to adopt conflicting agreements within the joint venture.[171]
Examples of facts suggesting the existence of common interest would be the prior existence of
links between such shareholders or the acquisition of shares through concerted action.

---

[166] See Case T-282/02 *Cementbouw Handel & Industrie v Commission* [2006] ECR II-319, paras 42 in
general and 67 on the facts of the case.
[167] Jurisdictional Notice, para 62.
[168] See, to that effect, the judgment of 12 December 2012 in Case T-332/09 *Electrabel v Commission*, para
189, referring to Art 3(1) and (3) of Reg 4064/89 and para 9 of the Commission Notice on the concept of
concentration (now Jurisdictional Notice, para 16).
[169] Case IV/M.62 *Eridania/ISI* [1991] OJ C204/12. The Commission considered that the rights of certain
shareholders to oppose the ISI being taken over by another company, to closure, to changes to its share capital
or to the transfer of its headquarters did not confer control since they did not amount to veto rights but rather
the rights to protect the interests of minority shareholders.
[170] Jurisdictional Notice, para 73.
[171] Case COMP/JV.55 *Hutchison/RCPM/ECT* [2003] OJ L 223/1, para 15.

16.81 Joint control will also exist where there are various minority shareholders that make an essential contribution to the functioning of the joint venture, for example in terms of technology, know-how, or important supply agreements. The reason that such contributions can give control is that the only way the undertaking can be viable is if the contributors to such activities agree on the most important strategic decisions.[172] If one of the parent companies makes an essential contribution in this regard, while another parent company's role is limited, even to the point of playing no part in the day-to-day running of the company, the latter may still exercise joint control with the former, but only if there exists a real possibility of challenging or opposing the decisions adopted by the other parent company.

16.82 A casting vote in favour of a director appointed by a given undertaking normally confers sole control to that undertaking. However, there may not be sole control if the right can only be exercised after a series of arbitration procedures and attempts at reconciliation have been exhausted or its scope is very limited.[173]

16.83 It must be stressed that in order for there to be an acquisition of joint control, the undertakings that have the possibility of exercising control have to be the same with respect to all decisions that confer control. In other words, joint control will not exist in situations where, taking into account the majorities required for the approval of strategic agreements, it is possible that different combinations or coalitions of shareholders may approve specific agreements in certain circumstances, without there being a fixed majority (known as shifting alliances).

16.84 It is not unusual for the parties to allege that a situation of shifting alliances exists and, therefore, there is no acquisition of control and the underlying operation does not constitute a concentration. In such cases, the Commission will take into account whether it is more reasonable for the shareholders in question to act by exercising joint control in a permanent fashion instead of looking for occasional alliances with other minority shareholders.[174] The Commission will analyse whether the possible convergence of commercial interests or incentives of the different shareholders means that they always vote in the same way, rather than there being a situation of shifting alliances.[175]

16.85 **Full function**   Besides joint control, Article 3(4) of the Merger Control Regulation requires for a concentration to exist that the joint venture carries out 'on a lasting basis all of the functions of an autonomous economic entity', or all of the functions that are carried out by undertakings operating in the same activities. The Jurisdictional Notice[176] provides that for this to take place, the joint venture will require management dedicated to the day-to-day

---

[172] Jurisdictional Notice, para 77.

[173] Case IV/M.425 *British Telecom/Banco Santander* [1994] OJ C134/4, para 7, which suggested that the existence of a casting vote in favour of the Chairman appointed by BT did not in itself give the latter sole control because it only applied for a limited period of time and to a limited number of questions (three years and not with respect to certain strategic questions). The Commission concluded that BT had sole control for different reasons.

[174] Case IV/M.1157 *Skanska/Scancem* [1999] OJ L183/1, where the parties alleged that there was no joint control because they were in a situation of variable alliances. The factors that the Commission took into account when reaching the decision that Skanska and Aker exercised joint control over Scancem prior to the operation were, *inter alia*, that the prior acquisition of Scancem had taken place through the concerted action of both undertakings and that these had entered into a detailed shareholders' agreement which included an agreement with respect to the *Scancem* agreement.

[175] Case IV/M.1027 *Deutsche Telekom/BetaResearch* [1999] OJ L53/31, para 78, with respect to the commitments offered by the parties to avoid competition problems. See also the arguments that led the Commission to conclude that there was joint control in Case COMP/JV.55 *Hutchison/RCPM/ECT* [2003] OJ L223/1, para 15.

[176] Jurisdictional Notice, para 94.

running of the company, and have access to financial and human resources and assets (both tangible and intangible) in such a way that it carries out a business activity in a lasting manner. The specific functions that a joint venture must carry out will depend on the particular market, but generally it must be active in all of the typical functions such as production, distribution, and sales, thus enjoy access to the market. If the joint venture only carries out one of these functions, for example, it is only engaged in R&D, or it only manufactures products or distributes those made by its parent companies, it will be considered as an undertaking carrying out activities ancillary to those of its parent companies,[177] and this would not amount to notifiable concentrations within the Merger Control Regulation. These non-'full functional' entities may, however, be subject to Articles 101 and 102 TFEU.

In assessing whether a joint venture has full functionality, it is necessary to consider the presence of the parent companies in upstream or downstream markets vis-à-vis the market where the joint venture is present. In particular, the level of sales made by the joint venture to the parent companies or vice versa will have to be assessed to see whether it is a high proportion of total production. It may be concluded, for example, that the joint venture lacks full function because its activity is ancillary to the parent companies, since it supplies them almost exclusively and therefore depends on them. Nevertheless, if the joint venture has an initial start-up period during which time the parent companies acquire a substantial amount of its production, this will not prevent it being concluded that there is a full-function joint venture. This start-up period should normally not exceed three years.[178] If the substantial sales of the joint venture to the parent companies is not of final but rather of secondary products that are seen as being less important for the joint venture, such sales will not be considered to indicate a lack of full functionality.[179] **16.86**

Another relevant criterion in this assessment is whether or not the sales from the joint venture to the parent companies are carried out in normal market conditions; if, on the contrary, those sales are on more favourable terms (including prices) this suggests that the joint venture lacks full-functionality. If the joint venture acquires a large part of its supplies from one or more parent companies, whether or not it is full-function will depend on the added value which the joint venture contributes to the products or the services supplied by the parent company.[180] If the amount of this added value is low, the joint venture may be nothing more than a sales agency for the parent companies. **16.87**

---

[177] The Notice specifies at para 95 that the fact that a joint venture uses the distribution or sales networks of one or more of the parent companies does not necessarily mean that it lacks full functionality, provided that the parent companies act exclusively as agents of the JV. In Case IV/M.102 *TNT/Canada Post* [1991] OJ C322/19, paras 13–14, the Commission found that there was a full-function joint venture because it carried out all of the operational and administrative functions despite the fact that some operations could be contracted out to the post offices of its parent companies. The Commission considered that such access did not mean that the joint venture lacked full function since this was a normal market practice and, in addition, access to the post office outlets would take place on an agency basis. In this respect commercial risks attached to the JV operations would be its responsibility.

[178] Jurisdictional Notice, para 97.

[179] Case IV/M.550 *Union Carbide/Enichem* [1995] OJ C123/3. The Commission found that the products which the joint venture sold to its parent company, Enichem, were of little importance to the former: 'Enichem will also enter into long-term agreements to buy from Polimeri Europa all the ethylene by-products . . . currently produced by the two ethylene steam crackers that will be contributed to the venture. These purchases of ethylene by-products do not call into question the autonomy of the joint venture, because these by-products are of minor interest for the joint venture' (para 16).

[180] In Case IV/M.550 *Union Carbide/Enichem* [1995] OJ C123/3, there were also supply agreements from the parent company Enichem to the joint venture Polimeri Europa. The Commission found that '[t]hese supply agreements do not call into question the functioning of the joint venture as an autonomous economic entity. Given the significant added value between the raw material, ethylene, and the product manufactured, PE, Polimeri Europa cannot be considered as a commercial agency of Enichem.' (para 15).

16.88　A joint distribution organization may also assume the character of a full-function joint venture if, at the level of that organization, the products or services it distributes acquire significant added value, or if it functions as a genuine player on the market by obtaining supplies, to an appreciable extent, from other suppliers which compete with its own member undertakings.[181]

Duration

16.89　In line with the Merger Control Regulation's focus on structural changes on the market, the joint venture must be intended to operate on a lasting basis. Where the agreement between the two parents specifies a period for the duration of the joint venture, this period must be sufficiently long to bring about a lasting change in the structure of the undertakings concerned.[182] However, the joint venture will not be considered to operate on a lasting basis where it is established for a short finite duration, for instance to construct a specific project without being involved in the operation once the construction is completed.[183] This may also be the case where there are outstanding decisions of third parties that are of an essential core importance for starting the joint venture's business activity.[184] As soon as such a decision is taken in favour of the joint venture, a concentration arises.[185]

16.90　Changes in the activities of the joint venture may also result in a concentration. This may be the case where the parents decide to enlarge the scope of the activities of the joint venture in the course of its existence. The parents may need to notify the enlargement if it leads to the acquisition of the whole or part of an undertaking from the parents that would, on its own, qualify as a concentration under paragraph 24 of the Jurisdictional Notice.[186] A concentration may also occur through the transfer by the parent companies of significant additional assets, contracts, know-how, or other rights where these assets and rights allow the joint venture to extend its activities into other product or geographic markets.[187] Finally, the change in the activity of an existing non-full-function joint venture may give rise to a concentration if it leads to the creation of a full-function joint venture.[188]

The difference between concentrative and cooperative joint ventures

16.91　The original wording of Article 3(2) of former Regulation 4064/89 excluded from the scope of the Regulation those joint ventures that were called 'cooperative',[189] defined as those which had as their object or effect the coordination of the competitive behaviour of undertakings that would remain independent. In accordance with this system, only concentrative joint ventures had to be notified to the European Commission under former Regulation 4064/89, while cooperative joint ventures were subject to the competitive analysis under Article 81(1) and (3) EC (at present, Article 101(1) and (3) TFEU) and could be notified to the Commission or be investigated in accordance with

---

[181]　Case T-282/02 *Cementbouw Handel & Industrie v Commission* [2006] ECR II-319, para 276.

[182]　In this context, the Commission has considered that a minimum period of eight years was sufficient but not a period of three years. Jurisdictional Notice, para 103.

[183]　Jurisdictional Notice, para 104.

[184]　This applies only to decisions that go beyond mere formalities and the award of which is typically uncertain Jurisdictional Notice, para 105.

[185]　Regarding the award of passenger rail franchises, see Case COMP/M.4806 *DSB/First/Oresundstag* [2007] OJ C314/23, para 6.

[186]　Jurisdictional Notice, para 106. See regarding the extension of the activities of the joint venture in Case COMP/M.4806 following the award of an additional passenger rail franchise Case COMP/M.5753 *DSB/ First/DSBFirst Väst* [2010] OJ C340/1.

[187]　Jurisdictional Notice, para 107.

[188]　Jurisdictional Notice, para 109.

[189]　See Commission Notice on the difference between cooperative and concentrative joint ventures of 31 December 1994 [1994] OJ C385/1 which substituted the Commission Notice on the same matter of 25 July 1990 [1990] OJ C20/10.

the rules contained in Regulation 17.[190] Following the amendment in 1997 to former Regulation 4064/89,[191] both types of joint ventures came within the scope of the Regulation, provided they had full functionality. Nevertheless, the distinction between the two types of joint venture continues to be relevant, since concentrative joint ventures must be assessed according to whether they entail a significant impediment to effective competition, in particular, because they create or reinforce a dominant position, under Article 2(3) of the Merger Control Regulation, while the criteria contained in Article 101(1) and (3) TFEU will be applied to cooperative joint ventures.

In accordance with Article 2(4) and (5) of the Merger Control Regulation, the Commission **16.92** must assess whether the creation of the joint venture has as its object or effect the coordination of the competitive behaviour of the parent undertakings that remain independent. In order to carry out this assessment, the Commission must determine whether:

(i)   the parent companies retain a significant level of activity on the same market;
(ii) the creation of the joint venture directly causes coordination; and
(iii) the coordination would allow the elimination of competition 'in respect of a substantial part of the products or services in question'.

If it is concluded that the joint venture has coordination as its object or effect, the Commission will apply Article 101 TFEU.

The practice of the Commission shows that, in the first place, the markets where coordination **16.93** could take place must be identified. This means those markets where at least two parent companies retain activities to a significant degree in the same geographic market, whether the same market of the joint venture, or in an upstream, downstream, or neighbouring market. Sometimes in its assessment the Commission considers the position of the parent companies in the same market to see whether their presence is significant.[192] The next step is to see whether the creation of the joint venture will mean that the parent companies acquire certain incentives to coordinate their competitive behaviour, thus giving rise to an appreciable restriction of competition.[193] Here, the Commission assesses whether coordination provides the parent companies with sufficient market power to eliminate competition in a substantial part of those markets where coordination could occur. The Commission must also take into account whether the restriction of competition would have an effect on intra-EU trade.[194]

The factors that the Commission must take into account when carrying out the competi- **16.94** tive analysis are, *inter alia*, the joint market share of the parent companies,[195] the market

---

[190] Council Regulation (EEC) 17 of 1962: First Regulation implementing Arts 85 and 86 of the Treaty [1962] OJ 13/204.

[191] Regulation 1310/97 ([1997] OJ L180/1) introduced in former Reg 4064/89 a new para 4 into Art 2, which provided an examination of coordination under Art 81 of the EC Treaty (now 101 TFEU) within the Reg 4064/89 with respect to undertakings in cooperative joint ventures. Following this amendment, the Notice on the concept of full function joint venture was adopted ([1998] OJ C66/1). This 1998 Notice stated that it was the Commission's intention to adopt guidelines concerning the application of the said Art 2(4) that have yet to be adopted. The Notice provided that until such guidelines are adopted, the interested parties should refer to the principles laid down in paras 17–20 of the 1994 Notice on the difference between concentrative and cooperative joint ventures. Note also that the 2004 Guidelines on Horizontal Mergers do not apply to cooperative situations (see n 6 of those Guidelines).

[192] Case IV/JV.15 *BT/AT&T* [1999] OJ C390/21, para 170; Case IV/JV.17 *Mannesmann/Bell Atlantic/Opi* [1999] OJ C11/4, para 20; Case IV/M.2676 *Sampo/Varma Sampo/If Holding/JV* [2002] OJ C145/8, paras 34 and 37; Case IV/M.2744 *Rwe Gas/Lattice International/JV* [2002] OJ C205/9, para 34; Case IV/M.2840 *Danapak/Teich/JV* [2002] OJ C226/20, para 26; Case IV/M.2851 *Intracom/Siemens/Sti* [2003] OJ C49/3, para 41; Case IV/M.2982 *Lazard/Intesabci/JV* [2003] OJ C118/24, para 28.

[193] Case IV/M.2075 *Newhouse/Jupiter/Scudder/M&G/JV* [2000] OJ C322/12, para 19.

[194] Case IV/JV.15 *BT/AT&T* [1999] OJ C390/21, paras 176 and 191.

[195] An analysis of the Commission's practice reveals that if the joint market share of parent companies in markets where coordination could occur is less than 40 per cent, this usually means that there are no

structure,[196] asymmetry in the size of the parent companies,[197] the existence of barriers to entry,[198] the buying power of clients,[199] the nature of the product (whether homogeneous or heterogeneous[200]), the price of the intermediate product which the joint venture manufactures in relation to the price of the final product,[201] whether each parent company will have access to the confidential information of the other parent company or companies,[202] the geographic scope of the activities of the parent companies,[203] the limited importance of the activities of the joint venture for the parent companies,[204] or the importance of innovation in the market in question.[205]

2. EU dimension

16.95 Only those concentrations with an EU dimension[206] within the meaning of Article 1 of the Merger Control Regulation must be notified to the European Commission.[207] Where a

coordination problems. See Case IV/M.2211 *Universal Studio Networks/De Facto 829 (Ntl)/Studio Channel Limited* [2000] OJ C363/31, para 38; Case IV/M.2299 *BP Chemicals/Solvay/Hdpe JV* [2001] OJ C327/19, para 30; Case IV/M.2493 *Norske Skog/Abitibi/Papco* [2001] OJ C90/4, para 8; Case IV/M.2676 *Sampo/ Varma Sampo/If Holding/JV* [2002] OJ C145/8; Case IV/M.2874 *Starcore Llc* [2002] OJ C248/27, para 16; Case IV/M.2851 *Intracom/Siemens/Sti* [2003] OJ C49/3, paras 41 and 42; Case IV/M.3141 *Cementbouw/ Enci/JV* [2003] OJ C260/11, para 21. If the parent companies possess high market shares, it is very likely that the Commission will consider that the parent companies have an incentive to avoid competition and it is more likely that the restriction will be considered as being appreciable: *Elf Texaco/Antifreeze JV* [1998] OJ C16/8, paras 16–17; Case IV/JV.15 *BT/AT&T* [1999] OJ C390/21, para 175; Case IV/JV.42 *Asahi Glass/ Mitsubishi/F2 Chemicals* [2000] OJ C96/5, paras 21 and 23.

[196] The presence of strong competitors in markets where coordination is possible suggests a lack of incentive to coordinate. Case IV/M.2744 *Rwe Gas/Lattice International/JV* [2002] OJ C205/9, para 34, Case IV/M.2851 *Intracom/Siemens/Sti* [2003] OJ C49/3, para 43, Case IV/M.2676 *Sampo/Varma Sampo/ If Holding/JV* [2002] OJ C145/8, para 37, Case IV/JV.42 *Asahi Glass/Mitsubishi/F2 Chemicals* [2000] OJ C96/5, para 22.

[197] Case IV/M.2851 *Intracom/Siemens/Sti* [2003] OJ C49/3, para 44.

[198] Case IV/JV.14 *Panagora/Dg Bank* [1998] OJ C68/10, para 32.

[199] Case IV/M.2851 *Intracom/Siemens/Sti* [2003] OJ C49/3, para 43; Case IV/JV.42 *Asahi Glass/ Mitsubishi/F2 Chemicals* [2000] OJ C96/5, para 22.

[200] Case IV/M.2874 *Starcore Llc* [2002] OJ C248/27, para 16.

[201] If the price of the intermediate product is relatively low as compared with the total cost of the final product, the Commission may consider that the parties cannot use those prices as a means of coordinating the prices of the final product in which the parent companies are active. Case IV/JV.6 *Ericsson/Nokia/Psion* [1998] OJ C219/7, para 31.

[202] If this is so, it would help possible coordination. See Case IV/M.3101 *Accor/Hilton/Six Continents/JV* [2003] OJ C140/11, para 2. Case IV/M.2075 *Newhouse/Jupiter/Scudder/M&G/JV* [2000] OJ C322/12, para 21. The Commission may take into account the existence of 'Chinese walls' (see Case COMP/M.3099 *Areva/ Urenco/ETC JV* [2004] OJ L61/11, para 238-242 and Case COMP/M.4170 *LSG Lufthansa Service Holding/ Gate Gourmet Switzerland* [2006] OJ C11/2, paras 51–3).

[203] If a parent company is only present in one Member State whereas the other parent company is present throughout the EU, it is probable that the Commission will consider that it makes no sense for the parent companies to coordinate their behaviour. Case IV/M.2851 *Intracom/Siemens/Sti* [2003] OJ C49/3, para 44.

[204] Case IV/M.2851 *Intracom/Siemens/Sti* [2003] OJ C49/3, para 44, where the Commission considered the reduced size of the joint venture, which amounted to 0–10 per cent of the sales of the parent company Siemens in the EEA. See also Case IV/M.3101 *Accor/Hilton/Six Continents* [2003] OJ C140/11, para 28 and Case IV/M.2493 *Norske Skog/Abitibi/Papco* [2002] OJ C90/4, para 10. Case IV/JV.7 *Telia/Sonera/Lithuanian Telecommunications* [1998] OJ C178/16, para 31. Case M.4170 *LSG Lufthansa Service Holding/Gate Gourmet Switzerland* [2006] OJ C11/2, para 55.

[205] Case IV/M.2874 *Starcore Llc* [2002] OJ C248/27, para 16, Case IV/M.2851 *Intracom/Siemens/Sti* [2003] OJ C49/3, para 43.

[206] As noted earlier, Art 1 of the Merger Control Regulation uses the expression 'Community dimension', which is no longer in use by the Commission nor retained in this publication.

[207] Case T-282/02 *Cementbouw Handel & Industrie v Commission* [2006] ECR II-319, paras 114–15: 'the Commission is to become involved only where the proposed concentration—or the concentration already carried out—attains a certain economic size and geographic scope'. See also Case T-3/93 *Air France v Commission* [1994] ECR II-121, para 102.

concentration has an EU dimension, the Commission has exclusive competence to examine it. It does not, however, follow automatically that the Commission has exclusive competence to determine whether a concentration has an EU dimension. On the contrary, it is incumbent first of all on the undertakings concerned to make the initial assessment of a concentration's dimension and to determine as a result which authorities should be notified of the planned concentration. When a concentration is notified not to the Commission but to the authorities of one or more Member States, it is for those authorities, in particular in the light of the obligation of loyal cooperation contained in Article 4 TFEU, and in the light of Article 21 of the Regulation, to verify that the concentration referred to them does not have an EU dimension. It nevertheless remains possible in such situations for the Commission to decide that, contrary to the opinion of the authorities of the Member States, the concentration does have an EU dimension and falls within its exclusive competence.[208]

Thresholds in Article 1 of the Merger Control Regulation

Article 1(2) and (3) of the Merger Control Regulation contain the criteria used to determine **16.96** whether a concentration has an EU dimension. Each paragraph states a series of thresholds, based on the turnovers of the parties in different geographic areas. The foundation of the system of thresholds established by Article 1 of the Regulation is to provide a simple and effective method for determining the competent authority[209] in order to ensure legal certainty.[210]

The turnover must refer to the participants in the operation that are considered to be 'under- **16.97** takings concerned', a concept which is further described in the Commission's Jurisdictional Notice.[211] In summary, a distinction is drawn between undertakings concerned in the cases of mergers, acquisitions of sole control, and acquisitions of joint control as follows:

• As regards a merger between companies, the undertakings concerned will be those that merge, including their subsidiaries. Their parent companies will only be concerned if retaining control; if that is the case, the merger would be examined as an acquisition of control (in case the merged entity ends up individually controlled) or as the creation of a joint venture (in case there ends up being more than one parent company) and not a merger.
• As regards an acquisition, the undertakings concerned will be the acquiring and the acquired or target company. In the case of the purchaser, the turnover of the purchasing company includes the whole of its business group. The turnover established in Article 1 is therefore the global figure of the acquiring undertaking plus the whole of its business group. As regards the acquired entity, only the turnover of the acquired entity and eventually its subsidiaries (if transferred in the same operation) is relevant. If the purchase refers to part of an undertaking, with respect to the vendor, only the part transferred which is the object of the transaction will be taken into account.
• If the operation in question involves the acquisition of joint control over a joint venture, the undertakings concerned will be the parent companies and their respective business groups. If the joint venture already existed, then the joint venture itself would also be considered to be an undertaking concerned. In the same way, in the change from joint to sole control, the undertakings concerned will be the acquiring shareholder company which gains sole control and the joint venture. To avoid double counting, the turnover of the acquiring shareholder has to be calculated without the turnover of the joint venture.[212]

---

[208] Case T-417/05 *Endesa v Commission* [2006] ECR II-2533, paras 98–9.
[209] Case T-417/05 *Endesa v Commission* [2006] ECR II-2533, para 180.
[210] Case C-202/06 P *Cementbouw Handel & Industrie v Commission* [2007] ECR I-12129, para 38.
[211] Jurisdictional Notice, paras 129–53.
[212] Jurisdictional Notice, paras 158 and 188.

16.98 When the case involves a joint venture where there are changes in shareholdings, a concentration will exist when there is a change in either the identity or the quality of control. A change of identity takes place where a new shareholder, either by replacement or added to the pre-existing parent companies, acquires control. In that case, that new shareholder becomes an undertaking concerned. A change of quality takes place where a former jointly controlling undertaking turns into sole controlling entity or vice versa. However, where the acquiring party is a joint venture, it will be an undertaking concerned itself if it has the necessary financial and other resources to carry on a lasting business activity. However, if the joint venture is merely a vehicle of the parent companies in order to carry out the acquisition, its parent companies will be undertakings concerned.[213]

16.99 Article 5(2) of the Merger Control Regulation contains a special rule for the calculation of turnover in the event of operations between the same parties in a period of two years. These are considered as a concentration carried out on the date of the last such operation. Thus, if an operation between two parties—for example, the purchase of an entity—does not have to be notified, but then in the next two years another purchase takes place between the same parties, the turnovers of the entities acquired in the two transactions must be added together in order to assess whether the operation needs to be notified.[214] The examination will concern all the transactions that have taken place in the two-year period. This combination is made, irrespective of whether the initial transaction had been already notified.[215]

16.100 If certain undertakings jointly purchase a target undertaking in order to partition the assets immediately, despite the fact that there is a single operation, then each of the acquiring undertakings will be considered to be an undertaking concerned, as will the part of the target company that each has acquired as if there had been a series of independent operations.[216]

16.101 **Thresholds in Article 1(2) of the Merger Control Regulation** Article 1(2) Merger Control Regulation looks at both the worldwide and EU-wide turnover of the undertakings concerned. The worldwide threshold captures transactions having a certain global dimension, while the EU threshold seeks to determine whether the concentration involves a minimal level of activity in the EU. These criteria are cumulative and require that:

(i) the combined aggregate worldwide turnover of all the undertakings concerned is more than EUR 5,000 million; and
(ii) The aggregate EU-wide turnover of each of at least two of the undertakings concerned is more than EUR 250 million.

16.102 At the same time, in order for EU dimension to exist, a negative criterion known as the 'two-thirds rule' has to be fulfilled. Under this rule, in case all the undertakings concerned obtain more than two-thirds of their aggregate EU turnover in the same Member State, the concentration is seen as having an essentially national impact and therefore it will not be of EU dimension.[217]

---

[213] Jurisdictional Notice, paras 145 et seq.
[214] Jurisdictional Notice, paras 136 and 137. See also Case T-282/02 *Cementbouw Handel & Industrie v Commission* [2006] ECR II-319, paras 116–20.
[215] Jurisdictional Notice, para 137. This requirement to refile an initial transaction, especially if already cleared by the Commission, is arguably inconsistent with the underlying idea that this mechanism of accumulation is aimed at preventing circumvention of the obligation to file a notification. Cf Jurisdictional Notice, para 49.
[216] See eg Case COMP/M.5754 *Alstom Holdings/Areva T & D Transmission activities* [2010] OJ C122/1, paras 4–5 and Case COMP/M.5755 *Schneider Electric/Areva T&D* [2010] OJ C158/4, para 4.
[217] See eg Case T-417/05 *Endesa v Commission* [2006] ECR II-2533.

Thresholds in Article 1(3) of the Merger Control Regulation Article 1(3), introduced in **16.103** the 1997 reform with the aim of capturing smaller deals, reduces the turnover figure established in the worldwide and EU thresholds to EUR 2,500 and EUR 100 million respectively, and introduces and combines two thresholds with a national scope. These provide that at least two of the undertakings concerned must have at least a certain level of activity in at least three Member States. Thus, for an operation to be notifiable, in addition to fulfilling the reduced worldwide and EU thresholds, the following conditions must be met:

(i) the turnover of all of the undertakings concerned must be more than EUR 100 million in each of at least three Member States; and

(ii) the total turnover achieved individually by at least two of the undertakings concerned in at least three of the relevant Member States in (i)—ie those Member States where turnover is above EUR 100 million—is more than EUR 25 million.

Again, in order to have an EU dimension with this second threshold, the 'two-thirds rule' must not apply, ie, if more than two-thirds of the EU turnover of all undertakings concerned is obtained in the same EU country, there is no EU dimension.

Calculating the level of turnover

General rules Once the undertakings concerned have been identified, in order to evalu- **16.104** ate whether or not a concentration has an EU dimension it is necessary to calculate their turnover and see whether the thresholds established in Article 1 of the Merger Control Regulation are reached. This matter is regulated in Articles 1 and 5 of the Merger Control Regulation and developed further in the Jurisdictional Notice.[218] Article 1 of the Merger Control Regulation provides for the thresholds that give an operation an EU dimension. Article 5 provides for the manner in which the calculation has to be made in light of the companies' accounts.

The turnover must refer to the preceding financial year. If the information for the preced- **16.105** ing year is not available, the figures from the year immediately before that will be used. The Commission considers that the most reliable and exact information will come from company accounts that have been audited in accordance with accounting rules applicable to the undertaking in question, except that its attention is drawn to specific problems.[219] In line with the principle of assessing the undertaking's situation with the greatest possible rigour, the audited turnover must be adjusted if, prior to the concentration, purchases or sales of businesses have taken place. That said, the amount will not be adjusted to reflect purely temporary factors, such as a fall in orders. The turnover must include the sales figures not only of the specific acquiring entity or participant in the operation, but also all sales made by its business group.[220] This aspect should not be confused with the fact that Article 5 excludes from the calculation of turnover sales between undertakings of the same business group, in order to avoid double accounting. The sales to be taken into account for this calculation are therefore limited to sales to third parties.

---

[218] Jurisdictional Notice, para 157 et seq.

[219] Jurisdictional Notice, paras 169–71. Case T-417/05 *Endesa v Commission* [2006] ECR II-2533, para 115; it is nevertheless for the complainant to adduce information as to why such reliance is not warranted (*Endesa v Commission*, para 118).

[220] For a detailed calculation of the turnover under Art 5(4) of the Merger Control Regulation, see Case COMP/M.6447 *IAG/BMI* [2012], paras 7–30, where the Commission had to assess the links as provided for in Art 5(4) of the Merger Control Regulation existing between IAG, BA, and Iberia to establish the EU dimension of the acquisition of BMI by either IAG or BA (appeal pending on that point in Case T-344/12 *Virgin Atlantic Airways v Commission* [2012] OJ C161/2).

16.106 Article 5(2) excludes the turnover of the seller, not regarded as an 'undertaking concerned'.[221] The target undertaking, or part thereof, will be considered to be an undertaking concerned, regardless of whether it has legal personality, and therefore the turnover which it generates must be taken into account, without including that of undertakings that are connected through a relationship of control that are neither the target company nor retain control over it.

16.107 As already stated,[222] under Article 5(2) paragraph 2, when two or more operations between the same persons—natural or legal—are carried out in a staggered manner within a period of two years, they will be considered as a single concentration carried out on the date of the last operation, and therefore the turnover of the acquired entity must include that of the earlier operation or operations.[223] The purpose of this provision is to prevent concentrations from being fragmented into different parts to avoid having to notify, since no individual operation reaches the thresholds contained in Article 1 of the Merger Control Regulation.[224] This provision may be read as permitting undertakings not to notify fragmented operations until the moment when they carry out the last in the series of operations, although this is unclear and therefore, in case the earlier transactions meet the relevant thresholds, a discussion with the Commission seems necessary.

16.108 The amount of aid granted by State bodies must be included in the turnover if the undertaking is the beneficiary and the aid is directly linked to the sale of products and the provision of services by the undertaking. The aid is therefore an income of the undertaking from the sale of products or provision of services in addition to the price paid by the consumer.[225]

16.109 In the event that the undertakings concerned are the parent companies of a joint venture, the sales of the latter to its parent companies will not be included to avoid double counting. The sales of the joint venture to third parties, however, will be imputed in equal shares to the parent companies.[226] With regard to the calculation of the turnover of State-owned companies or holding companies, the fundamental principle is to identify the undertakings that constitute an independent economic entity equipped with autonomous decision-making power. Having identified this group and included its turnover, that of other State-owned groups must not be included.[227]

---

[221] Case T-282/02 *Cementbouw Handel & Industrie v Commission* [2006] ECR II-319, para 116, referring to Case T-3/93 *Air France v Commission* [1994] ECR II-121, para 103.

[222] See para 16.99.

[223] Jurisdictional Notice, para 137. See also Case COMP/M.5461 *Société Lyonnaise des Eaux/Sociétés de distribution d'eau et d'assainissement* I [2009] and II (Case M.5812) [2010] OJ C201/1.

[224] Case T-282/02 *Cementbouw Handel & Industrie v Commission* [2006] ECR II-319, paras 116–20.

[225] Case IV/M.156 *Cereol/Continentale Italiana* [1991] OJ C7/7. In this case, the Commission excluded EU aid from the calculation of turnover because the aid was not intended to support the sale of products manufactured by one of the undertakings involved in the merger, but the producers of the raw materials (grain) used by the undertaking, which specialized in the crushing of grain.

[226] Note that the percentage of the share capital held by each parent company in the joint venture is not important; the only relevant factor is that they have the rights or powers listed in Art 5(4)(b) of the Merger Control Regulation, which may differ with the criteria to establish control under Art 3 of the Regulation (Jurisdictional Notice, para 184). For example, if there are two parent companies, they will each be attributed with 50 per cent of the joint venture's sales, even if one has a 60 per cent stake and the other a 40 per cent stake; in the same way, if there were three parent companies, each would be attributed with 33.3 per cent of the sales. This method of imputing sales is also applicable to joint ventures between an undertaking concerned and third parties. See Art 5(5)(b) of the Merger Control Regulation and Jurisdictional Notice, paras 186 and 187.

[227] Recital 22 of the Merger Control Regulation. In Case COMP/M.5508 *SoFFin/Hypo Real Estate* [2009] OJ C147/8, paras 6–25, the Commission followed a two-step approach for determining whether or not the acquisition by the German Federal State via SoFFin of control of HRE was notifiable under the Merger Control Regulation. First, it established whether HRE would, post-transaction, make up an economic unit that retains an independent power of decision. Then, if this was not clearly the case, the Commission sought to establish

In order to apply the thresholds contained in Article 1, it is necessary to apportion the turnover for different geographic areas, in particular, in the EU and in each Member State where the undertaking concerned has activities. With respect to the geographic distribution of the turnover, this will be determined by the location of the client at the time of the transaction. Thus, Article 5 refers to the place where the sale takes place or where the service was provided. This is taken as the place where the client is located, since frequently it will coincide with the place where the transaction was carried out and where the undertaking has competed. The place where the goods or service are consumed will not be taken into account.[228]   **16.110**

Credit institutions   Article 5(3)(a) of the Merger Control Regulation sets forth special provisions for calculating the turnover of credit and other financial entities. The turnover will be substituted for the total obtained by adding together a series of income items (interest and other similar income, income from securities, commissions, net profits on financial operations, and other operating income) less VAT and other taxes that are directly related to these items. Paragraph 207 of the Jurisdictional Notice refers to the definitions contained in the First and Second Banking Directives, thus confirming that the term 'credit institution' means an undertaking whose activity consists in receiving deposits or other repayable funds from the public granting credits for its own account. 'Financial entity' means any undertaking other than a credit entity whose main activity consists in acquiring holdings or in exercising one or more of the activities listed in points 2 to 12 in the Annex to the Second Banking Directive.[229] The territorial attribution of each amount of income will be on the basis of the location of the branch or division of the corresponding entity.   **16.111**

Insurance companies   Article 5(3)(b) provides that with respect to insurance companies, turnover is to be substituted by the value of gross premiums written,[230] which will comprise all amounts received and receivable in respect of insurance contracts, including outgoing reinsurance premiums and parafiscal contributions applied to the total volume of such premiums. Such income will be attributed to the territory of the Member State where the client paying the premium resides. If an insurance company acquires an investment stake in another company without acquiring control, the sales of the latter company will not be taken into account when calculating turnover.   **16.112**

---

which was the ultimate acquiring entity (SoFFin or an entity ultimately controlling SoFFin, if SoFFin itself could not be considered as having an independent power of decision) and which other undertakings controlled by this ultimate acquiring entity needed to be considered for the purpose of calculating relevant turnover. See also Case COMP/M.5861 *Republic of Austria/Hypo Group Alpe Adria* [2010] OJ C236/1, para 9; or Case COMP/M.5549 *EDF/Segebel* [2009] OJ C57/9, where the Commission took into account the concept of economic unit with an independent power of decision when analysing the competition effects of a concentration involving entities (EDF and GDF) controlled by the French State (paras 89–99). For an analysis of enterprises owned or controlled by the Chinese State, see Case COMP/M.6113 *DSM/Sinochem/JV* [2011] OJ C177/1, paras 7–16; Case COMP/M.6141 *China National Agrochemical Corporation/Koor Industries/Makhteshim Agan Industries* [2011] OJ C309/1, paras 5–7.

[228] Jurisdictional Notice, paras 195–203.

[229] Paragraph 208 of the Jurisdictional Notice on the calculation of turnover explains that the term 'financial entity' covers both holding companies and those undertakings whose regular main activity is one of those contained in the list annexed to the Directive: lending, financial leasing, money transmission services, issuing and managing instruments of payment, giving guarantees, trading on own account or on account of clients in money market instruments, foreign exchange, financial futures and options, exchange and interest rate instruments, and transferable securities, participation in share issues, advice to undertakings on capital structure, industrial strategy etc, money broking, and others. As regards holding companies, paras 217–20 of the Jurisdictional Notice contain a specific method of calculating turnover.

[230] All premiums received, including outgoing reinsurance premiums, ie all amounts paid or payable by the undertaking concerned to obtain reinsurance cover. Both premiums paid for new insurance contracts entered into in the accounting year in question and those relating to contracts from previous years but which are still in force are counted.

17

PROCEDURES

Marcos Araujo Boyd and Nicolas von Lingen

A. Notification

The clearance procedure under the Merger Control Regulation commences with the formal **17.01** filing of complete documentation with the European Commission. This section discusses the main elements of that process.

1. The notifying parties and their representatives

The burden of filing rests with the party taking control of an undertaking. Hence, concentra- **17.02** tions that consist in the acquisition of sole control must be notified by the party acquiring control. When the concentration is the result of an acquisition of joint control, the notification is made jointly by the parties involved in the merger or acquisition of joint control.[1] In the event of a merger, again, the notification is made jointly by the parties to the merger.

---

[1] Article 4(2) of the Council Regulation (EC) No 139/2004 of 20 January 2004 on the control of concentrations between undertakings [2004] OJ L24/1 (hereinafter 'Merger Control Regulation').

When the case concerns a public bid to acquire the shares of an undertaking, it is the bidder that must notify.[2]

17.03   In certain situations, concentrations resulting from acquisitions of joint control in a joint venture may need to be notified jointly by parties to a transaction and others which are not, since all will participate in the joint control following the concentration. A clear example is that of the replacement of one parent company in an already jointly controlled entity. Irrespective of the fact that another parent company (or companies) may not have intervened in the deal in any manner, they are required to participate in the filing process as jointly controlling entity or entities.

17.04   Notification is normally made by legal representatives of the undertakings concerned, but there is no strict obligation to do so. Under the Implementing Regulation, these persons must provide written proof of authority.[3] Joint notifications must be filed through a representative appointed jointly by the parties empowered to transfer and receive documents on behalf of all notifying parties.[4] Despite a joint notification, the Commission may address separate requests for information to each party.

2. The notification form

Standard notification: the ordinary form or Form CO

17.05   The rules concerning notification are contained in the Implementing Regulation. The notification is made using Form CO, which is contained in Annex I of the Implementing Regulation. In the event of joint notification, a single form is used.[5] The form contains a series of questions about different aspects of the proposed concentration, which will be used to carry out the Commission's subsequent in-depth analysis. The parties must fill in Form CO in full and also provide all of the required documentation, unless the Commission considers that certain data or documents are not necessary to evaluate the concentration, in which case it may dispense with the need for them to be filed.[6]

17.06   The notification must be made in one of the official languages of the EU, which will then be the language to be used in the proceedings for the notifying parties. If notifications are made in accordance with Article 12 of Protocol 24 of the Agreement on the European Economic Area ('EEA Agreement') in an official language of an EFTA (European Free Trade Association) State, the notification must be accompanied simultaneously with a translation into an official EU language.[7] Supporting documents must be submitted in their original language, provided it is one of the official EU languages. If not, they will be translated into the language used in the proceedings.[8] Supporting documents must be originals or copies of originals, in which case the notifying party will confirm that they are authentic and complete.[9] One signed original on paper, five paper copies of the entire form, and thirty-three copies of the notification in CD- or DVD-ROM format must be filed with the Commission.[10]

---

[2] Annex I of the Commission Regulation (EC) No 1033/2008 of 20 October 2008 OJ L279/3 (hereinafter 'Implementing Regulation' (section 1.2). In March 2013, the Commission launched a public consultation on a proposal to amend the Implementing Regulation in order to update and streamline the notification process (Commission Press release IP/13/288 of 27 March 2013).

[3] Article 2(2) of the Implementing Regulation.

[4] Article 2(3) of the Implementing Regulation.

[5] Article 3(1) of the Implementing Regulation.

[6] Article 4(2) of the Implementing Regulation.

[7] Article 3(5) of the Implementing Regulation.

[8] Article 3(4) of the Implementing Regulation.

[9] Article 3(3) of the Implementing Regulation.

[10] Communication pursuant to Article 3(2) of Commission Regulation (EC) No 802/2004 implementing Council Regulation (EC) No 139/2004 on the control of concentrations between undertakings (2006/C 251/02), as informally corrected following the accession of Bulgaria and Romania to the EU in January 2007 and of Croatia on 1 July 2013.

Form CO requires the filing of detailed information, and to complete it properly generally **17.07** takes a considerable time (from two weeks to several months) and involves the joint effort of lawyers and notifying parties, as well as economists in many cases. The following categories of information must be initially supplied:

(i) Business and financial information concerning the notifying parties,[11] including personal and economic links between undertakings and previous acquisitions.[12]

(ii) Detailed information concerning the nature of the transaction, particularly where a joint venture is concerned, since determining whether or not the Merger Control Regulation applies may not always be straightforward.[13]

(iii) Supporting documents, copies of the final or most recent versions of all documents bringing about the concentration, copies of the most recent annual reports, and accounts of all the parties to the concentration. Further, copies of all analyses, reports, studies, and surveys prepared by or for any member or members of the board of directors or the supervisory board or the shareholders' meeting, for the purposes of assessing or analysing the concentration with respect to market share, competition conditions, actual or potential competitors, the rationale for the operation, the potential for sales growth or the expansion into other product or geographic markets, and the general market conditions.[14]

(iv) A description of the relevant markets, both product and geographic, which will determine the scope of the assessment of the concentration.[15]

(v) With respect to each of the product markets affected (defined as those where the parties have a joint share of 15 per cent where there is a horizontal overlap, or 25 per cent if a vertical relationship exists[16]) and for each of the last three financial years, extensive information on sales (volume and amount).[17]

(vi) General conditions of the affected markets, the structure of supply and demand of the affected markets, market access, information on research and development, cooperation agreements, and the lists of the parties' main independent suppliers, clients, and competitors.[18]

(vii) Cooperative effects of a joint venture, particularly if its creation may give rise to coordination between independent undertakings that restricts competition in the sense of Article 2(4) of the Merger Control Regulation.[19]

(viii) The worldwide context of the proposed concentration, and the effects that this may have on the interests of intermediate and final consumers and on technical and economic development.[20]

Form CO is more a report than just a form. It gives the parties the chance to make submissions **17.08** regarding the relevant market, the competitive context of the notified operation, and the effects of that operation. In preparing the form, the parties must take into account the fact that the Commission generally considers the approach it has taken in previous cases, particularly with respect to the definition of markets.[21] However, the Commission is not bound by its previous decisions and may modify its approach to a particular market when it feels this to be necessary. In addition, given that the Commission tries to confirm the situation stated in the form by

---

[11] Sections 2, 3, and 4 of Form CO.
[12] Section 4.2.3 of Form CO.
[13] Sections 1 and 3 of Form CO.
[14] Section 5 of Form CO.
[15] Section 6 of Form CO.
[16] Section 6 of Form CO.
[17] Section 7 of Form CO.
[18] Section 8 of Form CO.
[19] Section 10 of Form CO.
[20] Section 9 of Form CO.
[21] Case T-210/01 *General Electric v Commission* [2005] ECR II-5575, paras 118–20 and Case T-282/06 *Sun Chemical Group and others v Commission* [2007] ECR II-2149, para 88 and case law cited therein.

contacting the main operators in the industry in question, it is crucial that any relevant available evidence (for instance of an economic nature) be provided to back up the observations contained in the form, in particular, with regard to the definition of the relevant market(s). All internal documentation should be thoroughly revised to assess whether these contain incorrect and/or damaging observations and if these need any additional explanation, as these documents may be required under section 5(4) of Form CO or later requested by way of a request for information.

17.09 Notifications must in principle contain all the information, including the documents, requested in Form CO.[22] This information must be correct and complete.[23] The parties may request the Commission to accept the notification despite not having provided some information requested in the form, if that information is either partially or totally unavailable.[24] Further, the Commission may be requested to accept that the notification is complete and, therefore, valid despite a party not having made available the information required in the form if it is considered that some of the information required, whether in its full or abbreviated version, is not necessary for the Commission's analysis.[25] In general, the Commission is prepared to alleviate the notifying parties' obligation to complete certain parts of the form, in particular in cases where there is no significant overlapping or where the market shares are marginal.[26]

Simplified notification: the short form

17.10 A short-form notification also exists.[27] This can be used for filing those concentrations that *prima facie* do not pose any significant competition concerns, and which are generally authorized. A notification made under the short form usually leads to an abbreviated or simplified procedure.[28]

17.11 The short form may be used when:[29]

  (i) two or more undertakings acquire joint control of a joint venture provided that the latter does not operate nor is expected to operate within the European Economic Area ('EEA'), or when such activities are 'negligible'. Here, 'negligible' means that:

---

[22] Article 4(1) of the Implementing Regulation.

[23] Section 1.3 of Form CO.

[24] Implementing Regulation Annex I Form CO, s 1(3)(f): 'The Commission will consider such a request, provided that you give reasons for the unavailability of that information, and provide your best estimates for missing data together with the sources for the estimates.'

[25] Implementing Regulation, Annex I Form CO, s 1(3)(g): 'You may request in writing that the Commission accept that the notification is complete notwithstanding the failure to provide information required by this Form, if you consider that any particular information required, in the full or short form version, may not be necessary for the Commission's examination of the case.'

[26] See Directorate-General for Competition ('DG COMP') Best Practices on the conduct of EC merger control proceedings (20 January 2004, hereinafter 'Best Practice Guidelines on merger control proceedings', available online at <http://ec.europa.eu/competition/mergers/legislation/proceedings.pdf>), paras 6 and 19 and Art 3(2) of the Implementing Regulation.

[27] See Art 3(1) of the Implementing Regulation. The form is contained in Annex II of the Implementing Regulation.

[28] Commission Notice on a simplified procedure for treatment of certain concentrations under Council Reg (EC) 139/2004 [2005] OJ C56/32 (hereinafter the 'Simplified Procedure Notice'), which substitutes the previous Notice of 2000. Commissioner Almunia announced in November 2012 that his intention to make notifications easier and to streamline the system to focus on the more problematic cases which require complex analyses. He has indicated that: 'In practice this simplification exercise can be done within the current system. Once we have worked out the concrete proposals we will consult the stakeholders before adopting the final package, which can be introduced in a relatively short time in the course of next year.' ('Merger review: Past evolution and future prospects', SPEECH/12/773, 2 November 2012). On 27 March 2013, the Commission proposed a revised Simplified Procedure Notice which would expand the scope of this procedure (see Commission Press Release IP/13/288 of 27 March 2013). The proposed rules would raise the market share threshold for treatment under the simplified procedure for mergers between firms competing in the same market from 15% to 20% and from 25% to 30% for mergers between firms active in upstream and downstream markets, as well as where the market share increase is small even where the combined market share is above 20%.

[29] See point 5 of the Simplified Procedure Notice and s 1.1 of Annex II of the Implementing Regulation.

(a) the turnover of the joint venture or the turnover of the activities contributed (by the parent companies) is less than EUR 100 million within the EEA territory; and

(b) the total value of the assets transferred to the joint venture is less than EUR 100 million within the EEA territory;

(ii) two or more undertakings merge, or one or more undertakings acquires sole or joint control of another undertaking, provided that none of the parties to the concentration carries out business activities in the same product and geographic market or in a product market that is upstream or downstream from a product market in which any other party to the concentration operates;

(iii) two or more undertakings merge, or one or more undertakings acquire sole or joint control of another undertaking and:

(a) two or more of the parties to the concentration exercise business activities in the same product and geographic market (horizontal relationships), provided that their combined market share is less than 15 per cent (under the Commission's proposal for a revised Simplified Procedure Notice, this threshold would be set at 20 per cent); or

(b) one or more parties to the concentration carries out business activities in a product market which is upstream or downstream from a product market in which any other party to the concentration operates (vertical relationships) provided that none of their individual or combined market shares reaches 25 per cent (under the Commission's proposal for a revised Simplified Procedure Notice, this threshold would be set at 30 per cent);

(iv) a party to a concentration is to acquire sole control of an undertaking over which it already has joint control. This procedure is not appropriate for cases where the parties request an express assessment of the restrictions directly related to and necessary for the implementation.

The short form limits considerably the information that must be provided in sections 7 and 10 of the form and therefore the efforts that the notifying parties must make. In particular, they only have to submit market share data for the last year instead of the last three years,[30] and it is not necessary to offer all the detailed market information that is required in section 8 of the standard form. Notification on the short form, as with those cases notified on the normal form but which do not give rise to competition problems, will normally end in an abbreviated decision, which will be adopted within twenty-five working days of the date of notification. **17.12**

Despite having initiated the simplified procedure, the Commission may[31] conduct a full investigation leading to a standard decision. The Commission will also adopt a normal decision if a Member State expresses 'substantiated [competition] concerns' about the concentration within a period of fifteen working days from the date of receipt of the copy of the notification, or if a third party does the same within the time period laid down for such observations.[32] **17.13**

---

[30] The Simplified Procedure Notice requires market shares for relevant markets, both product and geographic, as well as all the plausible definitions of alternative relevant markets, both product and geographic, in which two or more parties develop business activities (regardless of their market share), or at least carry on activities in a market that is upstream or downstream from a market in which any other party to the concentration operates and in which its individual or combined market shares exceed 25 per cent.

[31] For example, in situations which may increase the parties' market power by combining technological, financial, or other resources even if the parties do not operate in the same market; in concentrations where any of the parties holds individually a market share of at least 25 per cent in any product market in which there is no horizontal or vertical relationship between the parties but it is a neighbouring market to another in which another party operates; in new or little developed markets where it is not possible to determine exactly what the market shares of the parties are; or in markets with high barriers to entry, a high degree of concentration, or other known competition problems (Simplified Procedure Notice, para 8). The Notice excludes from the procedure cases where it is difficult to define the relevant markets or determine the market shares of the parties, as well as concentrations that involve new legal aspects of a general interest (para 6).

[32] Paragraph 12 of the Simplified Procedure Notice. The Commission may also adopt a normal decision where it decides to take a different position from that put forward by the parties in their notification

17.14 The Simplified Procedure Notice disallows the simplified procedure when a Member State requests the referral of a concentration under Article 9 or where the Commission accepts a referral pursuant to Article 22 of the Merger Control Regulation. Short-form notification is, however, possible, despite the fact that the Commission had considered a referral on the basis of the parties' request under Article 4(4) or when a concentration is referred to it under Article 4(5) of the Merger Control Regulation. The decision taken by the Commission in these cases is also normally an abbreviated decision. Abbreviated decisions are limited to identifying the parties and the general features of the business, but they do not analyse the definition of the markets or the position of the parties in detail. These decisions also specify the basis for the approval by referring to paragraphs 5(a), (b), (c), and/or (d) of the Simplified Procedure Notice.[33]

3. Treatment of sensitive or confidential information

17.15 The Commission must respect undertakings' legitimate interest in protecting their business secrets and other confidential information.[34] This information will not be divulged nor will access be given to it if it contains the business secrets of any person or undertaking, in particular the notifying parties, other interested parties, and third parties, as well as no other confidential information which the Commission does not consider necessary to divulge for the purpose of the proceedings.[35] This covers any internal document of the Member States.[36]

17.16 In order to ensure the protection of confidential information, any person (notifying, interested, or third party[37]) who makes its point of view known through an invitation to submit observations on the text of a provisional decision to waive the obligation to suspend implementation of the concentration[38] or a statement of objections,[39] or in the oral hearing,[40] or a request for information,[41] should indicate clearly which elements it considers confidential and why. In addition, it will have to provide a separate non-confidential version of the document within the period laid down by the Commission.[42] The Commission may require the notifying parties and the undertakings that have filed documents in the proceeding to identify—and justify—the documents or parts thereof which they consider contain business secrets or other confidential information which belongs to them, and to identify as well the undertakings with respect to which the documents in question must be considered confidential.[43] This applies to confidential information

---

(see Case COMP/M.4920 *Haniel/Metro/Ruthebeck* [2008] OJ C10/1, where the Commission considered that the transaction led to the acquisition of sole control and not joint control as submitted by the parties (paras 5–11)).

[33] While ultimately declared inadmissible, it is of interest to note the first known action for annulment against a decision following the simplified procedure. See Case T-315/10 *Groupe Partouche v Commission* [2012] OJ C80/18.

[34] Article 339 TFEU: 'The members of the institutions of the Union, the members of committees, and the officials and other servants of the Union shall be required, even after their duties have ceased, not to disclose information of the kind covered by the obligation of professional secrecy, in particular information about undertakings, their business relations or their cost components.'

[35] Article 18 of the Implementing Regulation.

[36] Article 17 of the Implementing Regulation.

[37] Article 11 of the Implementing Regulation refers to the parties with the right to be heard and distinguishes between notifying parties, other involved parties (such as the seller or the target company), and third parties (clients, suppliers, and competitors, provided that a sufficient interest is justified). Under Art 11, all will have the right to be heard in the proceedings.

[38] Article 12 of the Implementing Regulation.

[39] Article 13 of the Implementing Regulation.

[40] Article 14 of the Implementing Regulation.

[41] Article 11 of the Merger Control Regulation.

[42] Article 18(2) of the Implementing Regulation.

[43] Article 18(3) of the Implementing Regulation.

contained in the statement of objections or in a decision.[44] If persons, undertakings, or associations of undertakings fail to comply with Article 18(2) or (3), the Commission may assume that the documents or statements concerned do not contain confidential information.[45] Whenever the Commission receives a request for access to the file, it must carry out a specific assessment in relation to each document.[46] It is considered that the interests of those parties would be prejudiced if the information provided to the Commission were published or divulged in any other form. Whenever the Commission is provided with information, it is recommended that any confidential information be sent separately, clearly marking each page 'Business secret'. It is also necessary to state why the information should not be divulged or made public.[47] When the case involves a merger or a joint acquisition, or when notification has been made by more than one of the parties, the documents protected by business secrets could be sent in a separate envelope, stating on the notification form that it is a confidential annex.

B. Key Procedural Deadlines

One of the most important procedural features of the Merger Control Regulation is the strict **17.17** adherence to mandatory deadlines.[48] This adherence is reinforced by the 'positive silence' mechanism provided in Article 10(6) of the Merger Control Regulation, which equates the effects of the Commission not having taken a decision at the end of either the first phase or the second phase within the applicable deadlines with an unconditional clearance.[49]

The 'positive silence' mechanism constitutes an exception to the general scheme of the Regulation, **17.18** based on the duty of the Commission to rule expressly and in a motivated manner on the concentrations which are notified to it. On the other hand, the legitimate need for legal certainty in exceptional situations, on which that mechanism is based, cannot go so far as to exclude decisions relating to concentrations in whole or in part from review by the EU Courts.[50]

1. Notification deadlines

There are no formal deadlines to file a notification. Article 4(1) of former Regulation 4064/89 **17.19** gave the parties one week within which to notify concentrations with an EU dimension to

---

[44] As clarified in 2008 by the introduction of Art 18(4) of the Implementing Regulation.

[45] Article 18(3), second para of the Implementing Regulation.

[46] The GC has established that the Commission cannot reject access to the whole file without having carried out a specific assessment and an individual examination of each document requested in order to determine whether access (even partial) is possible. The GC did add, however, that an individual examination may not be necessary in cases where it is obvious that access must be rejected or granted (Case T-2/03 *Verein für Konsumenteninformation v Commission* [2005] ECR II-1121, para 75).

[47] Where a third party submits confidential information vis-à-vis the notifying parties, it is in its interest to submit a non-confidential version, as otherwise the Commission would not be entitled to rely on it for the purposes of the decision (Case C-413/06 P *Bertelsmann and Sony Corporation of America v Commission* [2008] ECR I-4951, paras 101–2). See also Case T-210/01 *General Electric v Commission* [2005] ECR II-5575, paras 654 and 663.

[48] Case C-202/06 P *Cementbouw Handel & Industrie v Commission* [2007] ECR I-12129, para 39: The need for speed characterizes the general scheme of the Merger Control Regulation and requires the Commission to comply with strict time limits for the adoption of the final decision; Case T-417/05 *Endesa v Commission* [2006] ECR II-2533, para 66: 'In the case of time-limits which produce legal effects, any ground for suspension should be expressly provided for. In that regard, it is appropriate to note the importance of ensuring control of mergers within deadlines compatible with both the requirements of sound administration and the requirements of the business world (Case C-170/02 P *Schlüsselverlag J.S. Moser and Others v Commission* [2003] ECR I-9889, para 34).'

[49] The Commission will, however, normally adopt a formal decision.

[50] Case C-413/06 P *Bertelsmann and Sony Corporation of America v Commission* [2008] ECR I-4951, paras 48–9 and 171–5.

the Commission, a deadline that was in practice systematically exceeded.[51] This deadline was eliminated in 2004, and Article 4(1) of the Merger Control Regulation just requires that concentrations must be notified to the Commission prior to their implementation and following the conclusion of the agreement in question, the announcement of the public bid, or the acquisition of a controlling interest. While undertakings normally have an interest to notify as soon as possible, in practice it is not unusual that complicated cases, which require long pre-notification contacts, are filed several weeks or even months after the date on which the parties have entered into the agreement that gave rise to notification.

17.20 In contrast with the original version of Article 4.1, it is possible to notify in the absence of definitive agreements when the undertakings involved can show the Commission that their intention in good faith is to enter into an agreement, or when they have publicly announced their intention to make a bid, provided that the agreement or bid in question gives rise to a concentration of a EU dimension.[52]

2. Time periods in the first phase

17.21 The first phase should normally be cleared in twenty-five working days from the working day following effective notification. This period can be extended by ten working days if a Member State makes a referral request[53] or if the parties put forward commitments.[54] In the latter case, the commitments must be filed within a maximum period of twenty working days following receipt of notification.[55]

3. Time periods in the second phase

17.22 The maximum duration of the second phase is, in principle, ninety working days from the date on which it is formally initiated. This period may be extended by fifteen working days (giving a total of 105 working days) if the parties concerned propose commitments at least fifty-five days after the start of the second phase.[56] Commitments must be proposed within sixty-five working days from the date that second-phase proceedings are initiated.[57] However, if the period for adopting a decision is extended, the sixty-five working day period for filing commitments will automatically be extended by the same number of working days. The period for adopting a second-phase decision will exceptionally be suspended if, due to circumstances for which one of the undertakings involved in the concentration is responsible, the Commission has been forced to request information by decision in accordance with Article 11(3) or to order an inspection by decision pursuant to Article 13 of the Merger Control Regulation.[58]

---

[51] Case T-279/04 *Éditions Odile Jacob v Commission* [2010] ECR II-185, para 201. The fact that a concentration was not notified within the limit set by Art 4(1) of Reg 4064/89 could be sanctioned by fines, not by the prohibition of the concentration. See also Judgment of 6 November 2012 in Case C-551/10 P *Éditions Odile Jacob v Commission*, para 37.

[52] Recital 34 of the Merger Control Regulation clarifies that undertakings will comply with Art 4(1) if they can show that their plan for the proposed concentration is 'sufficiently concrete, for example on the basis of an agreement in principle, a memorandum of understanding, or a letter of intent signed by all undertakings concerned'.

[53] Article 9(2) of the Merger Control Regulation.

[54] Article 10(1) of the Merger Control Regulation. In cases characterized by a particular urgency, the Commission has adopted a decision within twenty-five working days, even where the concentration raises competition concerns and required a remedy (see Case COMP/M.5384 *BNP Paribas/Fortis* [2008] OJ C7/4 and Commission Press Release IP/08/1882 'Mergers: Commission clears acquisition of Fortis' Belgian and Luxembourg assets by BNP Paribas subject to divestment of BNP's Belgian consumer credit subsidiary').

[55] Article 19(1) of the Implementing Regulation.

[56] Article 10(3) of the Merger Control Regulation.

[57] Article 19(2) of the Implementing Regulation.

[58] Article 10(4) of the Merger Control Regulation which, according to Art 23 of the Merger Control Regulation, should be read in conjunction with Art 9(1) of the Implementing Regulation enumerating the

4. 'Stop the clock' provisions

The Merger Control Regulation has introduced limited flexibility in the deadlines in second-phase **17.23** procedures. Within the first fifteen working days of the initiation of a procedure under Article 6(1)(c) of the Regulation, the parties may request an extension. Alternatively, at any subsequent moment (provided the parties agree) the Commission may grant an extension of its own initiative. Any extension or extensions cannot exceed a maximum of twenty working days.[59]

C. Pre-Notification and First Phase

1. Pre-notification and waivers

Before an actual filing is made, informal contacts with the Commission usually take place. **17.24** This practice was, in the early days of the Regulation, rather informal. Currently, however, pre-notification meetings between the parties and the Commission are described in detail in the 'Best Practice Guidelines' issued by the Commission[60] and, while not mandatory, are formally regarded as a most important aspect of notification procedures under the Merger Control Regulation,[61] recognized by the Court of Justice ('ECJ') as an example of the principle of good administration.[62]

Pre-notification is based on the mutual interest of both the parties and the Commission. On the **17.25** one hand, it allows the Commission's services to find out about an operation in advance, which enables them to examine the case before notification actually takes place and the various time periods apply. Further, the notifying parties will obtain an initial idea of the Commission's view of the matter and can avoid the risk that the notification is declared incomplete.[63]

---

situations in which the time limits may be suspended. See also Case T-290/94 *Kaysersberg v Commission* [1997] ECR II-2137, paras 144 and 145. In *Schneider*, the GC clarified that the time limit is automatically suspended from the date on which it is found that the necessary information has not been provided until the date on which it is provided (Case T-310/01 *Schneider Electric v Commission* [2002] ECR II-4, para 106).

[59] Article 10(3) of the Merger Control Regulation, second para.

[60] Best Practice Guidelines on merger control proceedings: 'DG Competition finds it useful to have pre-notifying contacts with notifying parties even in seemingly non-problematic cases...Pre-notification contacts should preferably be initiated at least two weeks before the expected date of notification. The extent and format of these pre-notification contacts will depend on the complexity of the individual cases in question. In more complex cases a more extended pre-notification period may be appropriate and in the interests of the notifying parties. In all cases it is advisable to make contact with DG Competition as soon as possible as this will facilitate planning of the case. Pre-notification contacts should be launched with a submission that allows the selection of an appropriate DG Competition case team. This memorandum should provide a brief background to the transaction, a brief description of the relevant sector(s) and market(s) involved and the likely impact of the transaction on competition in general terms...In straightforward cases, the parties may choose to submit a draft Form CO as a basis for further discussions with DG Competition...Any submission sent to DG Competition should be provided sufficiently ahead of meetings or other contacts in order to allow for well prepared and fruitful discussions. In this regard, preparatory briefing memoranda/draft Form COs sent in preparation of meetings should be filed in good time before the meeting (at least three working days) unless agreed otherwise with the case team...DG Competition would normally require five working days to review the draft before being asked to comment, at a meeting or on the telephone, on the adequacy of the draft.' Paras 5, 10, 11, 14, and 15.

[61] See Recital 11 of the Implementing Regulation: 'The Commission should give the notifying parties and other parties involved in the proposed concentration, if they so request, an opportunity before notification to discuss the intended concentration informally and in strict confidence.'

[62] Case T-3/93 *Air France v Commission* [1994] ECR II-121, para 67. See also Best Practice Guidelines on merger control proceedings, paras 6 and 7.

[63] Best Practice Guidelines on merger control proceedings para 20 and Art 5(4) of the Implementing Regulation.

17.26 Before initiating these informal contacts with the Commission, parties should request the allocation of a case team to a merger which is to be notified and/or in relation to which pre-notification
discussions are to be held with the Commission. There is a standard case allocation request form
available on the website of the Directorate-General for Competition ('DG COMP'),[64] which
requires certain basic information relating to the transaction (parties, turnover, main products,
and markets), as well as reference to any prior discussions with DG COMP, identification of
confidentiality issues, indication of proposed case language, and expected dates of first draft and
notification.

17.27 The length of pre-notification discussion depends on the complexity of the case and other factors such as timing, availability of information, and prior experience of the Commission in the
same or closely related markets. While in some cases it involves the submission of several drafts
of the Form CO and replies to requests for information,[65] pre-notification contacts are advised,
even in cases perceived as straightforward, such as those handled under the Simplified Procedure
Notice.[66] Among the issues discussed, the following are particularly relevant:

(i) *The obligation to notify the operation under the Merger Control Regulation*: it is not
uncommon for the parties to consult the Commission on aspects, *inter alia*, related
to the acquisition of control,[67] the identification of affected undertakings, and the
turnover thresholds contained in Article 1 of the Merger Control Regulation.[68] If the
Commission considers that it does not have jurisdiction to deal with the case, it may
issue a letter confirming this.[69]

(ii) *Procedural matters* such as the possibility of requesting a derogation under Article 7(3)
of the Merger Control Regulation of the obligation to suspend implementation of
the concentration or jurisdictional aspects, such as whether it is appropriate to notify
national competition authorities ('NCAs') or use the prior referral mechanism.

(iii) *Waivers related to the information required*: Form CO requires the parties to supply
from the outset a significant amount of information. In many cases, a waiver can
be requested with respect to certain sections or aspects of Form CO.[70] The waiver
must be requested by the parties in a reasoned manner, justifying that the information
in question is not necessary for the Commission's assessment of the concentration.
Experience has shown that pre-notification meetings are extremely valuable, both for
the notifying party or parties and the Commission, in order to determine the precise
volume of information required in a notification; in addition, in the vast majority of

---

[64] Available at <http://ec.europa.eu/competition/mergers/case_allocation_request.rtf>.

[65] See eg Case COMP/M.5529 *Oracle/Sun* [2010] OJ C91/7, and the discussion on the definition of the
market for database products (paras 7 and 8).

[66] Simplified Procedure Notice, para 15.

[67] Judgment of 12 December 2012 in Case T-332/09 *Electrabel v Commission*, paras 253 and 255.

[68] Case T-417/05 *Endesa v Commission* [2006] ECR II-2533. In this case, Endesa requested the
Commission to give a ruling on whether it was competent to examine the concentration, since Endesa
considered that the Gas Natural/Endesa concentration, which had been previously notified to the Spanish
competition authority, had EU dimension within the meaning of Article 1 of the Regulation. According
to Endesa, this meant that the concentration should be notified to the Commission under Article 4 of the
Regulation and also that the Spanish competition authority had no power to give a ruling on that concentration. Note also that the GC indicated that there is no similarity between the situation of a Member
State which submits a request for referral under Art 22 and a situation in which an undertaking requests
the Commission to adopt a position on its competence, and there can be no obligation to suspend by mere
analogy (para 85).

[69] See also the letter sent following Aer Lingus' request to the Commission to apply Art 8 of the Merger
Control Regulation with respect to the 25.17 per cent shareholding held by Ryanair in Aer Lingus following
the decision declaring the acquisition incompatible with the common market (Case T-411/07 *Aer Lingus v
Commission* [2010] ECR II-3691, paras 24–30).

[70] Article 4(2) of the Implementing Regulation.

cases, they allow a significant reduction in the amount of information that must be filed.[71]

(iv) *Whether the concentration qualifies for short-form notification* if it does not cause any competition problems: as the Simplified Procedure Notice states, even with respect to cases where there may be complications even though they appear to be straightforward, it is worth resolving these problems in the pre-notification phase, contacting the Commission two weeks before the date of notification.[72]

(v) *A preliminary examination of competition law questions*: in these meetings potential difficulties related to the transaction can be identified in the light of the Commission's practice and previous experience in relevant markets. This may include reaching an agreement on the correct definition of markets, the methodology used to calculate market shares, possible markets affected, potential competition problems, and possible solutions. To increase the usefulness of these conversations, it is recommended that as much information as possible is provided. In practice, the Commission's services will request a memorandum which explains the most important features of the concentration, which will then form the basis of discussions in pre-notification meetings. These contacts can therefore highlight potential problems which can be resolved without entering into a more detailed analysis. In fact, without contacts in the pre-notification phase, it may be difficult to determine the need and the scope of the possible commitments to be made in the first phase of the investigation.

(vi) *Contacts between the Commission and other NCAs*: The European Commission encourages early discussions with potentially affected NCAs[73] in the EU and in other jurisdictions[74] at an early stage.

2. The first phase

Proceedings under the Merger Control Regulation have two phases, often just called phase 1 and phase 2. This two-stage technique, imported from the US Hart–Scott–Rodino Act of 1976,[75] reserves a more in-depth analysis for more complicated cases, thus enabling those matters less liable to damage competition to be dealt with speedily.

17.28

---

[71] Annex I of the Implementing Regulation states: 'It is recognised that the information requested in this Form is substantial. However, experience has shown that, depending on the specific characteristics of the case, not all information is always necessary for an adequate examination of the proposed concentration. Accordingly, if you consider that any particular information requested by this Form may not be necessary for the Commission's examination of the case, you are encouraged to ask the Commission to dispense with the obligation to provide certain information ("waiver").' Section 1.3.(g) of the Annex provides that: 'You may request in writing that the Commission accept that the notification is complete notwithstanding the failure to provide information required by this Form, if you consider that any particular information required, in the full or short form version, may not be necessary for the Commission's examination of the case.— The Commission will consider such a request, provided that you give adequate reasons why that information is not relevant and necessary to its inquiry into the notified operation. You should explain this during your pre-notification contacts with the Commission and, submit a written request for a waiver, asking the Commission to dispense with the obligation to provide that information, pursuant to Article 4(2) of the Implementing Regulation.'

[72] Simplified Procedure Notice, para 15.

[73] Principles on the application, by NCAs within the European Competition Authorities Association ('ECA'), of Arts 4(5) and 22 of the EC Merger Regulation (January 2002) available at <http://ec.europa.eu/competition/ecn/eca_referral_principles_en.pdf>.

[74] See, for instance, the 'Best Practices on Cooperation in Merger Investigations' (October 2011) prepared by the US–EU Merger Working Group between the Commission and the US authorities available at <http://ec.europa.eu/competition/mergers/legislation/best_practices_2011_en.pdf>.

[75] Hart–Scott–Rodino Antitrust Improvements Act of 1976 (Public Law 94-435).

17.29 The first phase is limited to determining whether there are serious doubts about the operation that justify initiating the second phase (Article 6 of the Merger Control Regulation). This involves an analysis of the markets affected. At the same time, other tasks are carried out, such as verifying that the notification is complete, that the Commission has jurisdiction, contacting NCAs and competitors, and, where appropriate, drafting and signing the decision. Within the first phase the following main stages can be identified:

Filing and completeness of the notification

17.30 First phase proceedings start with the filing of Form CO, usually following pre-notification contacts. This involves the delivery of one original, five paper copies, and thirty-three copies of the notification in CD- or DVD-ROM format to DG COMP.[76] The supporting documents must be originals or certified copies. It is convenient for the contact details required by Form CO (for clients, suppliers, and competitors) to be submitted to the Commission in an electronic version.[77] Notifications start to have effect on the date that they are received by the Commission.[78] The Commission will send to the notifying parties or their representatives an acknowledgement of receipt without delay.[79]

17.31 If the information contained in the notification, including the documents, is incomplete in relation to an essential point, the Commission will inform the notifying parties or their representatives in writing without delay and will fix an adequate period so that it can be completed. In these cases, a notification will have effect from the date on which the Commission receives the complete information.[80] There is no specific deadline for a declaration of incompleteness, and, in fact, it may be issued almost at the end of the procedure where, for instance, new relevant markets which had not been reported in the notification come to light.[81]

17.32 All essential amendments to the information contained in the notification which the notifying parties are or should be aware of must be notified to the Commission without delay. If such a modification could have a significant effect on the assessment of the operation, the Commission could consider that the notification takes effect from the date of receipt of the information concerning the essential change. The Commission will inform the parties or the representatives of this in writing and without delay.[82]

---

[76] Communication pursuant to Article 3(2) of Commission Regulation (EC) No 802/2004 implementing Council Regulation (EC) No 139/2004 on the control of concentrations between undertakings (2006/C 251/02), as informally corrected following the accession of Bulgaria and Romania to the EU in January 2007 and of Croatia on 1 July 2013.

[77] Best Practice Guidelines on the conduct of EC merger control proceedings, para 21.

[78] Article 5(1) of the Implementing Regulation. See also Annex I Introduction, s 1.3. 'a) In accordance with Article 10(1) of the EC Merger Regulation and Article 5(2) and (4) of the Implementing Regulation, the time-limits of the EC Merger Regulation linked to the notification will not begin to run until all the information that has to be supplied with the notification has been received by the Commission. This requirement is to ensure that the Commission is able to assess the notified concentration within the strict time-limits provided by the EC Merger Regulation.'

[79] Article 4(3) of the Implementing Regulation.

[80] Article 5(2) of the Implementing Regulation.

[81] See eg Case COMP/M.5253 *Sanofi-Aventis/Zentiva* [2009] OJ C66/24, paras 1–2: notification on 5 September 2008; declaration of incomplete notification on 2 October 2008; declaration of completeness on 5 December 2008; Case COMP/M.5454 *DSV/Versterhavet/DFDS* [2009] OJ C150/17: notification on 30 January 2009, declaration of incompleteness on 20 February 2002, declaration of completeness on 20 April 2009, Art 6(1)(c) decision on 12 June 2009, withdrawal of notification on 16 June 2009; and Case COMP/M.6059 *Norbert Dentressangle/Laxey Logistics* [2011] OJ C122, paras 1–2: notification of 3 January 2011, declaration of incomplete notification of 28 January 2011, declaration of completeness of 14 February 2011.

[82] Article 5(3) of the Implementing Regulation. See Case COMP/M.5096 *RCA/MAV Cargo* [2008] OJ C29/4, paras 10–11.

There are many reasons why a notification can be declared incomplete. However, three main **17.33** categories can be clearly identified.[83]

(i) Breach of certain formal requirements, for example failure to include all of the parties concerned.
(ii) The information requested in the notification is insufficient, for example, with respect to markets that are affected by the merger and the shares of the parties and competitors in those markets, or the Form CO lacks the necessary clarity to enable an adequate assessment of competition to be carried out. This latter aspect can be particularly important in the relatively frequent cases where the supporting documentation is voluminous and the possible markets affected both numerous and complicated.
(iii) Cases where the Commission's investigation reveals the existence of potentially affected markets that have not been mentioned by the notifying parties, and about which more information is needed, information that cannot be provided or assessed within the remaining time available.

In the first few years of the application of former Regulation 4064/89, the number of noti- **17.34** fications declared to be incomplete was relatively few. By the end of the 1990s, a significant increase in such declarations took place, partly because of the growing number of notifications and the pressure on the Commission's resources. However, following the adoption of the first Guidelines in 1998, this trend was reversed, and fewer declarations of incomplete notifications have been issued. The increase in pre-notification contacts between undertakings and the Commission in recent years, encouraged in the Guidelines, has been highlighted as one of the main reasons for this positive change.[84]

Appointment of case team

After receipt of the notification, the unit entrusted with the matter[85] will appoint a 'case **17.35** team', unless this had already been done in the pre-notification phase. The case team is normally made up of at least three people, an attempt being made to choose both lawyers and economists that are capable of working in the case language; experience in the relevant market(s) is also an important factor. A case manager will normally be designated and serve as a day-to-day interlocutor for the parties.

Market analysis: the 'market test'

One of the first initiatives of the case team is to carry out a global analysis of competition **17.36** conditions. Normally, the notification form is a useful starting point that the Commission completes with its own means of investigation.

After over twenty years controlling concentrations and after adopting more than 5,000 **17.37** decisions, the Commission has amassed a vast array of information on various markets. In addition, the Commission addresses requests for information to interested parties (competitors, customers, suppliers, business associations) to obtain their (preliminary) observations.[86]

---

[83] XXVIII [1998] Report on Competition Policy SEC/1999/0743 final, para 173.
[84] The immediate effect of the Guidelines was to reduce the proportion of notifications declared incomplete from 10–11 per cent in 1997–1999 to 6 per cent in 2000 and 2001. Green Paper, 'The Review of Regulation 4064/89' COM(2001)745 final 11 December 2001, para 199. From December 2004 to December 2012, the Commission has issued only seventeen declarations of incompleteness.
[85] At present there are five specialist units in the analysis of concentrations that are focused on different areas of activity (Units B-3, C-5, D-4, E-4, and F-4). One unit also forms part of the Directorate for general policy and strategic support, A-2, and is concerned with preparing general policy regarding concentrations and providing case support. See Ch 16, 'General Issues: Scope of Control', para 16.23.
[86] Best Practice Guidelines on merger control proceedings, para 27.

The replies of these undertakings are frequently decisive; if there is no opposition to the proposed concentration, it is unlikely that the Commission will continue with its assessment.
Conversely, if significant opposition is noted, and especially if it is felt that this may result in
a complaint or proceedings before the EU Courts, the first phase is likely to be more complicated for the notifying party.

17.38   Contact with interested third parties is possible as a result of the publicity given to the notification and the ensuing investigation. This occurs through the publication of a short notice
in the Official Journal of the European Union ('OJ'), noting the names of the undertakings
concerned, their country of origin, the nature of the concentration, and the economic sectors affected, as well as the date of receipt of the notification.[87] In addition, the Commission
enters into direct contact with possible interested parties, whose contact details must be supplied in the form, and are subject to the express warning that possible mistakes in addresses
and phone numbers may result in the notification being declared incomplete.[88] Third parties
wishing to exercise their right to be heard should make their request following notification
of the merger.[89]

Meetings—State of Play meetings, meetings with competitors, and triangular meetings

17.39   The Best Practice Guidelines refer to the need to give all the interested parties in the proceedings the opportunity to maintain free and frank channels of communication through various
types of meetings in order to make known to the Commission their points of view. Three
different types of meetings can be distinguished.

17.40   First, there are the 'State of Play' meetings between the Commission and the notifying parties
that can take place at crucial moments throughout the proceedings with respect to notifications that create competition problems, or at least potential problems. Thus, these meetings
take place during the second phase, or possibly in the first phase in relation to cases where,
if the parties do not put forward a clear solution to the problem, the second phase will be
initiated. These meetings may take place at the Commission, or alternatively by telephone or
video conference, and the agenda to be followed must be prepared well in advance. Although
there are five crucial moments when these meetings can be held, the parties can communicate
to the Commission important aspects at any time, such as a commitments proposal or written submissions on any other question already discussed in one such meeting.

17.41   The Best Practice Guidelines contemplate five different occasions during the proceedings
when a bilateral meeting between the parties and the Commission may take place:

(i)   In the first phase before the end of the three-week period from notification if there are
serious doubts about the compatibility of the operation with the internal market within
the meaning of Article 6(1)(c) of the Merger Control Regulation. The objective of this
meeting is for the parties to be aware of the Commission's concerns and for them to
have the opportunity to propose an acceptable solution in order for the operation to be
authorized without the second phase starting.

---

[87] Article 4(3) of the Merger Control Regulation and Art 5(5) of the Implementing Regulation. Since this
publication ensures that information on the notification of a concentration is made available to everyone,
third parties cannot claim to be unaware of the existence of a notification (Judgment of 12 October 2011 in
Case T-224/10 *Association Belge des Consommateurs Test-Achats v Commission*, paras 57 and 62).
[88] Best Practice Guidelines on merger control proceedings, para 20.
[89] See Judgment of 12 October 2011 in Case T-224/10 *Association Belge des Consommateurs Test-Achats v
Commission*, para 56. In that case, a consumer association had written to the Commission two months prior
to the notification of the merger, but had failed to submit or even confirm its observations following the
notification.

(ii) In the second phase, in the two-week period after a decision under Article 6(1)(c) has been adopted. In this meeting, the parties should provide the Commission with a written explanation of their position with respect to the competition concerns set out in the Article 6(1)(c) decision in advance of the meeting. The Commission will indicate to the parties whether or not they have properly understood its reasoning, and they could also discuss what should be the scope of the investigation, the definition of markets, and competition problems. They could also discuss the need to extend the second-phase time limit by up to twenty days.[90]

(iii) Before issuing a statement of objections once the second-phase investigation has started, in order to give the parties the opportunity to understand the Commission's preliminary point of view.

(iv) After the statement of objections and the hearing. This meeting gives the parties a clear idea of the Commission's position after the latter has had the opportunity to consider their reply to the statement of objections and their position in the hearing. It can also be used to discuss the scope and the timing for proposing remedies.

(v) Before the meeting of the Advisory Committee, in order to discuss with the Commission the proposed commitments, improvements made to these proposals, and, where appropriate, the results of the market test of such commitments.

A second type of bilateral meetings are those which take place between the Commission and third parties, and which show sufficient interest in the proceedings, such as customers, suppliers, competitors, members of managing bodies of undertakings concerned, or representatives of such undertakings. These mainly participate in the 'market test' through their answers to the request(s) for information sent by the Commission, but they may also be invited by the Commission to attend meetings. In appropriate cases, the Commission may offer these third parties a copy of (parts of) the statement of objections to allow them to make submissions about its content. Third parties may call the Commission's attention to a possible competition concern, or give a point of view that does not coincide with that presented to the Commission by the parties, but they must provide the Commission with proof of their submissions (examples, documents, any proof of the facts) as soon as possible.   **17.42**

Finally, triangular meetings between the Commission, the notifying parties, and other third parties are voluntary meetings that may take place if the Commission considers that, in the interest of the investigation, it could hear the opinion of all of them in a single forum. These occur in cases where there are different points of view as regards the key market information or the effects of the concentration on competition. These meetings do not replace the oral hearing. Both this type of meeting and the bilateral meetings between the Commission and third parties must take place as soon as possible to allow the Commission to reach the most detailed conclusions it can as regards the nature of the relevant market, and to clarify substantive aspects.[91] Triangular meetings will normally be preceded by an exchange of information filed by the notifying parties and third parties in sufficient time before the meeting, and will be chaired by a senior member of DG COMP.   **17.43**

First phase decisions

After the internal consultation process in the Commission, a draft decision that ends the first phase will be presented to the Commissioner for Competition or his or her substitute, authorized to take internal decisions on behalf of the College of Commissioners. One of three decisions is possible: a declaration of lack of competence (Article 6(1)(a) of the Merger   **17.44**

---

[90] Article 10(3) of the Merger Control Regulation, second para.
[91] Best Practice Guidelines on merger control proceedings, para 39.

Control Regulation); a definitive authorization declaring the concentration compatible with the internal market with or without commitments (Article 6(1)(b) of the Regulation); or a declaration that there are serious doubts about the compatibility of the concentration with the internal market, which initiates the second phase (Article 6(1)(c) of the Regulation).

17.45 **Article 6(1)(a) decision** The Commission will declare that the Merger Control Regulation is inapplicable when it reaches the conclusion that the notified operation is not a 'concentration' as defined in Article 3 of the Merger Control Regulation or that it does not have a EU dimension. The last such decision was adopted in 2002.[92]

17.46 **Article 6(1)(b) decision** When the Commission establishes that the notified concentration comes within the scope of the Merger Control Regulation, but does not raise serious doubts about its compatibility with the internal market, the Commission will decide not to oppose it and will declare it compatible with the internal market. The Commission may also take the initial view that the operation raises serious doubts, but that the changes that the undertakings have made to the concentration enable it to declare its compatibility with the internal market under Article 6(1)(b).

17.47 The General Court ('GC') has concluded that although the Commission has no discretion as regards initiating the second phase when it has serious doubts about the compatibility of a concentration with the internal market, it does enjoy a degree of discretion in the investigation and the examination of the circumstances of each specific case to determine whether these raise serious doubts or when commitments have been proposed or continue to be proposed, whether they remove the serious doubts.[93] It must be recalled that the Commission is required to examine the effects on competition in the markets in which there is a risk of damage to competition, even when a concentration may have such an effect in markets in which there is no overlap between the activities of the parties to a merger.[94] From 2000 to the end of 2012, about 99 per cent of final concentration decisions came within this category, and about 5 per cent of these were made subject to commitments.[95]

17.48 **Article 6(1)(c) decision** When the Commission finds that the notified concentration comes within the scope of the Merger Control Regulation and there are serious doubts about its compatibility with the internal market, it 'shall decide to initiate proceedings' or, as commonly

---

[92] Under Reg 4064/89, forty-eight decisions of this type were adopted from 1990 to 1998. From 1999 to 2002, however, only four such decisions were adopted, and none since the adoption of the new Merger Control Regulation. See Statistics at DG COMP website <http://ec.europa.eu/competition/mergers/statistics.pdf>. Although not necessarily in the form of Art 6(1)(a) decisions, but with similar legal effects, the Commission responds frequently to requests by interested parties to confirm whether a given transaction falls within the scope of the Merger Control Regulation. In Case C-170/02 P *Schlüsselverlag JS Moser GmbH et al v Commission* [2003] ECR I-9889, paras 26–30, the Court noted that the Commission has a legal duty to respond to these requests.

[93] Case T-119/02 *Royal Philips Electronics NV v Commission* [2003] ECR II-1433, para 77. Thus, even when the concept of serious doubts has an objective nature, the investigation of the existence of such doubts necessarily obliges the Commission to carry out complex economic appraisals, specifically the question of whether the commitments proposed by the parties to the concentration are sufficient to deal with such doubts. Where the Commission has approved a concentration without initiating the second phase in the light of the commitments given, it must have found that such commitments provided a direct and satisfactory answer to the concerns raised, unless there is a manifest error in its appraisal.

[94] Case T-177/04 *easyJet v Commission* [2006] ECR II-1913, para 63. Although its analysis of the effect on competition may be oriented, in part, towards the concerns raised by the third parties consulted during the administrative procedure, the Commission is bound, even in the absence of any express request by such third parties, but where there are serious indications to that effect, to assess the competition problems created by the merger on all the markets which may be affected by it (para 64).

[95] The statistics are available at DG COMP's website <http://ec.europa.eu/competition/mergers/statistics.pdf>.

described, will initiate second-phase proceedings. Article 6(1)(c) decisions involve a preliminary examination of the operation, justifying the opinion of the Commission that the operation is capable of being prohibited. However, an Article 6(1)(c) decision does not fix the definitive position of the Commission and hence is not open for legal challenge before EU Courts.[96] In 2010, 2011, and 2012, the number of decisions of this type that were adopted were four, eight, and nine respectively. This number is often roughly the same as the number of final decisions adopted at the end of the second phase, although some proposed concentrations are withdrawn by the parties during the second phase in order to avoid the bad publicity or precedent that a prohibition decision would entail.[97]

Publication of decisions

Once the decision has been signed by the Commissioner, it will be sent by the General **17.49** Secretariat of the Commission to the undertakings concerned, through the person appointed in the notification as legal representative for the receipt of all notices. The Commission is under a duty to inform both the undertakings concerned and the NCAs of its decision without delay.[98]

Article 20 of the Merger Control Regulation requires the Commission to publish decisions **17.50** ending the second phase.[99] However, there is no requirement to publish decisions ending the first phase, which only have to be notified to the parties to the concentration and the Member States.[100] In practice, the Commission publishes those decisions where concentrations are authorized at the end of the second phase in the OJ, and prepares a brief summary of its decisions in the form of a press release. As regards first-phase decisions approving concentrations, the Commission makes them available to the public on its website, publishes a short notice in the OJ,[101] and in some cases (notably decisions with commitments and cases having attracted public attention or raising new issues) also prepares a press release available upon adoption.[102]

Revocation or amendment of a first-phase decision

The Commission can only revoke or amend a first-phase decision in the following situations: **17.51**

(i) When the decision is based on incorrect information for which one of the undertakings is responsible or which has been obtained by fraudulent means.[103]

---

[96] Case C-188/06 P *Schneider Electric v Commission* [2007] ECR I-35, paras 34–5. Case T-279/04 *Éditions Odile Jacob v Commission* [2010] ECR II-185, para 89.

[97] On withdrawal of notifications, see para 17.52 et seq.

[98] Article 6(5) of the Merger Control Regulation.

[99] Decisions adopted under Art 8(1)–(6) of the Merger Control Regulation. As regards the obligation to publish these decisions, see Art 20(1) of the Merger Control Regulation. The obligation to publish decisions does not extend to provisional decisions pursuant to Art 7(3) (derogation from the suspension obligation) and Art 8(5) (interim measures to restore effective competition) of the Merger Control Regulation. The Commission nevertheless publishes a notice in the OJ when a case is withdrawn in the second phase (see eg Case COMP/M.5969 *SCJ/Sara Lee insecticides' business* [2011] OJ C168/18).

[100] Article 6(5) of the Merger Control Regulation.

[101] On the importance of publication for the start of the period for challenges to be brought by third parties see para 17.94 and the reference to Case T-48/04 *Qualcomm v Commission* [2009] ECR II-2029, paras 48 and 58.

[102] <http://ec.europa.eu/competition/mergers/cases/>.

[103] Article 6(3)(a) for the first phase and Art 8(6)(a) for the second phase. For a practical example, see Commission Decision in Case IV/M.1397 *Sanofi/Synthélabo* [1999] OJ C23/4, para 2: in this case, the Commission revoked its previous authorization when, following complaints made by third parties which led the Commission to question the compatibility of the operation, it was shown that the parties had not supplied the information required concerning a sector where their subsidiaries were active. Specifically, the breach committed by both Sanofi and Synthélabo consisted in the omission of information and in the notification of manifestly incorrect data with regard to the relevant markets. This led the Commission to impose

(ii) When the undertakings concerned have breached an obligation attached to the deci-sion.[104] In this case, the Commission could reach a new decision without being subject to the normal first-phase time periods.[105]

(iii) When it is concluded that the decision is illegal after its adoption. This extraordinary possibility of revision is open only within a reasonable period of time and must take into account the legitimate expectations of the beneficiary of the decision, which may have trusted its legality.[106]

Withdrawal of the notification: the right to a new notification

17.52 The notifying parties are free to withdraw their notification at any moment.[107] When the par-ties completely abandon the proposed concentration, the Commission loses its competence to examine it.[108] In the past, notifications have been withdrawn before the end of the first phase, amended to resolve the problems identified by the Commission and then notified again in order to avoid second-phase proceedings.[109]

17.53 In cases where notifications are withdrawn, the Commission's practice had been to issue a press release,[110] but without taking a formal decision. However, in June 2000, the Commission adopted a negative decision in *MCI WorldCom/Sprint*[111] one day after the par-ties had informed them of their intention to withdraw the notification, and that they no

---

˙ a maximum fine on each of the undertakings for the inexact nature of the information given: Commission Decision of 28 July 1999 imposing fines for having supplied incorrect information in a notification submit-ted pursuant to Art 4 of Council Reg 4064/89, Case IV/M.1543 *Sanofi/Synthélabo* [1999] OJ C95/34. In Case COMP/M.5047 *Rewe/Adeg* [2008] OJ C159/9, the Commission amended its decision almost two years after the initial Art 6(1)(b) decision to encompass two supermarkets the parties had failed to notify to the Commission (Decision of 29 April 2011, OJ C159/4).

[104] The Merger Control Regulation and the Acceptable Remedies Notice differentiate between con-ditions and obligations, aimed at guaranteeing that the undertakings concerned fulfill the obligations entered into with the Commission. The carrying out of each measure that leads to a structural change on the market is a condition; eg the transfer of an activity. The means to achieve this result are, in general, obligations imposed on the parties; eg the appointment of an administrator with the irrevocable power to sell that activity. If the parties breach an obligation, the Commission may revoke the decision of compat-ibility, and also impose periodic penalty payments. If the parties breach a condition, the compatibility decision will no longer be valid and, therefore, the Commission can take any measure to re-establish or maintain effective competition conditions, including divestments. See Section E of this chapter on commitments.

[105] Article 6(4) of the Merger Control Regulation.

[106] Case T-251/00 *Lagardère SCA and Canal+ SA v Commission* [2002] ECR II-4825, paras 139–41.

[107] DG Competition Information note on Art 6(1)c 2nd sentence of Reg 139/2004 (abandonment of concentrations), available at DG COMP's website.

[108] Case C-202/06 P *Cementbouw Handel & Industrie v Commission* [2007] ECR I-12129, para 40. However, the position is otherwise where the parties do no more than propose partial amendments to the draft (para 41). See also Case T-48/03 *Schneider Electric v Commission* [2006] ECR II-111, paras 96–100: after Schneider had transferred Legrand to the Wendel/KKR consortium, the notified transaction could not but be regarded as abandoned, and the procedure for the control of that transaction, which was resumed by the Commission after the annulment judgments of 22 October 2002, became devoid of purpose (upheld on appeal in Case C-188/06 P *Schneider Electric v Commission* [2007] ECR I-35, paras 78–83).

[109] eg Case IV/M.398 *Procter & Gamble/VP Schickedanz (I)* (withdrawn) and Case IV/M.430 *Procter & Gamble/VP Schickedanz (II)* [1994] OJ L354/32; Case IV/M.493 *Tractebel/Distrigaz (II)* [1994]; Case IV/M.422 *Unilever France/Ortiz Miko (II)* [1994].

[110] See, eg Commission Press Release IP/99/421 'KLM has withdrawn the notification of its planned merger with MARTINAIR' of 24 June 1999 in Case IV/M.1328 *KLM/Martinair*; Commission Press Release IP/00/258 'Alcan abandons its plans to acquire Pechiney to avoid the prospect of a decision by the European Commission to block the merger' of 14 March 2000 in Case IV/M.1715 *Alcan/Pechiney*.

[111] Case COMP/M.1741 *MCI WorldCom/Sprint* (2000) [2003] OJ L300/1.

longer intended to implement the proposed concentration in the way that it had been filed. The Commission took this decision on the basis that the undertakings involved had not formally abandoned the proposed concentration, since they had not withdrawn the merger agreement. On appeal, the GC annulled the Commission's decision, on the understanding that the distinction between the 'mere withdrawal of the notification' that the parties had entered into and the 'withdrawal of the merger agreement' which, according to the Commission, should have taken place, was excessively formalistic.[112] According to the GC, the Commission could not adopt a prohibition decision once the parties had notified by fax (signed by the lawyers) their intention to withdraw the notification and that they did not intend to implement the proposed concentration in the manner filed in the notification. The Court further held that in adopting its decision, the Commission had departed from its standard administrative practice, which was clearly known to the public through the various previous cases in which the Commission had closed the file without adopting any decision at all on the day that the parties had communicated their decision to withdraw the notification. In November 2005, the Commission published a Notice on withdrawal of notifications, setting out detailed requirements on the documentation that the Commission considers necessary for a formal withdrawal.[113]

D. Second Phase

1. Initiating proceedings: Article 6(1)(c) proceedings and fixing the timetable

Article 6(1)(c) of the Merger Control Regulation provides that 'where the Commission finds that **17.54** the concentration notified falls within the scope of this Regulation and raises serious doubts as to its compatibility with the internal market, it shall decide to initiate proceedings'. These decisions, which bring an end to the first phase and initiate the second, normally contain a lengthy statement of the Commission's doubts. In addition, the Commission often publishes a brief note referring to its decisions in a press release, as well as a notice in the OJ.[114]

While an Article 6(1)(c) decision is a formal decision within the meaning of Article 297 TFEU, **17.55** the EU Courts have confirmed that the Commission decision to start the second phase is an intermediate act in the proceedings, and it may therefore not be the object of an action for annulment before the EU Courts.[115]

Once this decision has been adopted, the Commission will invite the notifying parties to discuss **17.56** the timetable, with a view to making the investigation more effective, reducing the burden on

---

[112] Case T-310/00 *MCI v Commission* [2004] ECR II-3253, paras 83, 107, and 108.
[113] DG Competition Information note on Art 6(1)c 2nd sentence of Reg 139/2004 (abandonment of concentrations), available at DG COMP's website.
[114] In this notice, the Commission does not specify the serious doubts identified at the end of the first phase, but invites interested third parties to submit their observations on the proposed concentration to the Commission no later than fifteen days following the publication of the notice. By contrast, the Commission's press release usually outlines the main competition concerns identified by the Commission during the initial phase. The text of the Art 6(1)(c) decision is not made public.
[115] In the *Schneider Electric* case, both the GC and the ECJ clarified that Art 6(1)(c) decisions initiating second-phase proceedings are acts of a preparatory nature within the meaning of the *IBM* doctrine (Case 60/81 *IBM v EC Commission* [1981] ECR 2639, para 19) and therefore not open for review (Case T-48/03 *Schneider Electric v Commission* [2006] ECR II-111, paras 79–84, upheld on appeal in Case C-188/06 P *Schneider Electric v Commission* [2007] ECR I-35, para 70). See also Case T-279/04 *Éditions Odile Jacob v Commission* [2010] ECR II-185, paras 89–92. This point is further discussed in Ch 18, 'Judicial Review of Commission Decisions Regarding Concentrations'.

the notifying parties and third parties, and increasing transparency in the procedure.[116] While this aspect is often discussed in the pre-notification phase, in cases where the level of contacts or information supplied in that phase is limited, the agenda will be fixed when the second phase starts.

2. The statement of objections and the parties' observations

17.57   The issuance of a statement of objections is not a necessary prerequisite of a second-phase decision. Following the adoption of the Article 6(1)(c) decision, the Commission's in-depth investigation may lead it to conclude that the concentration does not lead to a significant impediment to effective competition[117] or that commitments offered by the parties allow the alleviation of the serious doubts identified in the decision opening the second phase.[118]

17.58   In the event the doubts of the Commission on the compatibility of the concentration with the internal market have not been resolved at the end of the in-depth investigation, the Commission is required to send to the parties a statement of objections so that they know exactly what issues they must deal with in their defence.[119]

17.59   The statement of objections is a procedural and preparatory document[120] whose objective is to merely set out, with sufficient clarity and precision, all of the grounds on which the Commission intends to base its final decision, and it may not contain the final analysis of the Commission.[121] The Commission is also not required, over and above the obligation to set out its objections in a statement of objections and to supplement that statement if it should then decide to adopt new objections, to indicate, after service of the statement of objections and before adoption of the final decision, its current thinking as to the possible means of resolving the problems it has identified.[122] Despite its preparatory nature, the Commission can only base its decisions on objections on which the interested parties have had the opportunity to make submissions.

---

[116] Best Practice Guidelines on merger control proceedings, para 25.

[117] This will lead to the adoption of an Art 8(1) decision (see for instance Case COMP/M.6214 *Seagate Technology/the HDD Business of Samsung Electronics* [2011] OJ C154/8; Case COMP/M.6314 *Telefonica UK/ Vodafone UK/Everything Everywhere/JV* [2012] OJ C66/5).

[118] According to Art 10(2) of the Merger Control Regulation, decisions pursuant to Art 8(2) of the Merger Control Regulation shall be taken as soon as it appears that any serious doubts referred to in Art 6(1) (c) of the Merger Control Regulation have been removed, particularly as a result of modifications made by the undertakings concerned (see Case COMP/M.5440 *Lufthansa/Austrian Airlines* [2009], para 10).

[119] Article 13(2) of the Implementing Regulation. Case C-413/06 P *Bertelsmann and Sony Corporation of America v Commission* [2008] ECR I-4951, paras 61 and 62: 'The right to a fair hearing, which is a fundamental principle of Community law and forms, in particular, part of the rights of the defence, requires that the undertaking concerned must have been afforded the opportunity, during the administrative procedure, to make known its views on the truth and relevance of the facts and circumstances alleged and on the documents used by the Commission to support its claim that there has been an infringement of the EC Treaty...that principle is laid down in the second sentence of Article 18(3) and, in more detail, in Article 13(2) of the Implementing Regulation.'

[120] It is therefore inherent in the nature of the statement of objections that it is provisional and subject to amendments to be made by the Commission in its further assessment on the basis of the observations submitted to it by the parties and subsequent findings of fact. Thus, the statement of objections does not prevent the Commission from altering its standpoint in favour of the undertakings concerned, and it is not obliged to explain any differences with respect to its provisional assessments set out in the statement of objections (Case C-413/06 P *Bertelsmann and Sony Corporation of America v Commission* [2008] ECR I-4951, paras 61–6).

[121] Case C-440/07 P *Commission v Schneider Electric* [2009] ECR I-6413, paras 130–2. See also Case T-145/06 *Omya v Commission* [2009] ECR II-145, para 46: 'the statement of objections records only the Commission's assessments which led it to identify potential competition problems and thus omits, in principle, the markets on which no risk was identified. Accordingly, its subject-matter is considerably more limited than that of the examination carried out at an earlier stage by the Commission.'

[122] Case T-209/01 *Honeywell v Commission* [2005] ECR II-5527, para 99 and the case law cited therein.

Neither the Merger Control Regulation nor the Implementing Regulation lay down any time **17.60** period for the adoption and sending to the parties of the statement of objections.

In the statement of objections, the Commission will fix the period within which the notify- **17.61** ing parties—or other interested parties—must file their observations concerning the issues, and it will not be obliged to deal with the submissions received after this period has ended.[123] In practice, the parties generally have two weeks within which to reply, which is often a very tight timeframe for the undertakings and their lawyers.[124]

The parties to whom the Commission has addressed the statement of objections may make **17.62** known in writing their viewpoint about the Commission's position. In their written observations and at the oral hearing following receipt of the statement of objections, the parties have the right to submit all material which they consider capable of refuting the Commission's objections and of leading it to approve their proposed concentration.[125] In order that they can reply effectively to the objections raised, the undertakings must be allowed to comment on the documents on which the Commission based its statement of objections.

3. Access to the file by the notifying parties

The notifying parties have the right of access to the Commission's file once the statement of **17.63** objections has been adopted[126] in order to examine evidence in the Commission's files so that they are in a position effectively to express their views on the conclusions reached by it in its statement of objections on the basis of that evidence.[127] This right extends to documentation received after the statement of objections has been adopted and until consultations take place with the Advisory Committee.[128] The right of access to the file may need to be adapted with the necessity for speed which characterizes the general scheme of the regulation,[129] and is justified by the need to guarantee the undertakings' rights to a fair defence against the allegations contained in the statement of objections.[130] The EU Courts have confirmed that the Commission may refuse

---

[123] Article 13(2) of the Implementing Regulation.

[124] A frequent problem is that the period for replying to the statement of objections coincides with the end of the period for filing commitments (now sixty-five working days from the start of the second phase). This creates problems for the parties, given the importance of preparing with sufficient time the observations on the statement of objections in the context of an administrative authorization proceeding. Further, the Commission may have little time to study the reply to the statement of objections before having to deal with commitments.

[125] Case C-413/06 P *Bertelsmann and Sony Corporation of America v Commission* [2008] ECR I-4951, para 89: 'Having regard to the requirements of the rights of the defence, the arguments of the notifying parties submitted in reply to the statement of objections cannot be subject to more demanding standards as to their probative value and their cogency than those imposed in relation to the arguments of competitors, customers and other third parties questioned by the Commission in the course of the administrative procedure or in the light of information provided by the notifying undertakings at a previous stage of the Commission's investigation.'

[126] Article 18(3) of the Merger Control Regulation; Art 13(3) of the Implementing Regulation. Best Practice Guidelines on merger control proceedings, para 42 et seq; and Commission Notice on the rules for access to the Commission file in case pursuant to Articles 81 and 82 of the EC Treaty, Articles 53, 54, and 57 of the EEA Agreement and Council Regulation (EC) No 139/2004 [2005] OJ C325/7, para 26 et seq.

[127] Case T-210/01 *General Electric v Commission* [2005] ECR II-5575, para 629; Case T-351/03 *Schneider Electric v Commission* [2007] ECR II-2237, para 241.

[128] Case T-210/01 *General Electric v Commission* [2005] ECR II-5575, para 684: the Commission is under no obligation to grant access to new material on the file late in the proceedings, nor to grant access to the file before the statement of objections (paras 692–6). See also Case T-351/03 *Schneider Electric v Commission* [2007] ECR II-2237, paras 240–1.

[129] Case T-210/01 *General Electric v Commission* [2005] ECR II-5575, para 631.

[130] Article 18(3) of the Merger Control Regulation and Art 13(3) of the Implementing Regulation: 'The Commission shall base its decisions only on objections on which the parties have been able to submit their observations. The rights of the defence shall be fully respected in the proceedings. Access to the file shall be

access, especially if no such request is made,[131] or provide a limited access[132] to certain types of documents, including the business secrets of other undertakings, the Commission's internal documents,[133] and other confidential information.[134] Otherwise, the right of access to the file does not extend to correspondence between the Commission and the competent authorities of the Member States,[135] nor does it give it the right to be informed that other persons have had access to certain information on that file.[136] In practice, after the issuance of the statement of objections, the Commission will usually grant access to documents in the file on a rolling basis.

17.64 A particular problem in this regard is access to observations made by third parties within the course of proceedings, whether of a formal or informal nature (telephone conversations, emails, meetings etc).[137] There is no consistent approach on this point, although it seems that the right to a fair defence should mean that the notifying parties have access to such observations, at the very least to a non-confidential version thereof.[138]

17.65 Once they have consulted the file, the parties will draft their observations. One original and thirty-five copies of these must be sent to the Commission, addressed to DG COMP, as well as one electronic version. The Commission will then send copies to the different NCAs.

open at least to the parties directly involved, subject to the legitimate interest of undertakings in the protection of their business secrets.' See also the Commission Notice on the rules for access to the Commission file in case pursuant to Articles 81 and 82 of the EC Treaty, Articles 53, 54, and 57 of the EEA Agreement and Council Regulation (EC) No 139/2004 [2005] OJ C325/7.

[131] Case T-417/05 *Endesa v Commission* [2006] ECR II-2533, para 75; Case T-351/03 *Schneider Electric v Commission* [2007] ECR II-2237, para 216.
[132] Case T-210/01 *General Electric v Commission* [2005] ECR II-5575, paras 653–5: 'Since the airlines had specifically asked for their identity not to be disclosed and for confidentiality, it must be held that the Commission was entitled to accord the parties to the merger disclosure in the form of a summary. Limited disclosure of that type is a balanced response, endorsed by the case-law, which allows, so far as is possible, the opposing interests of the parties to the merger, on the one hand, and the Commission and the complainants, on the other, to be reconciled.'
[133] Case T-210/01 *General Electric v Commission* [2005] ECR II-5575, para 671: the Commission is under no duty to disclose expert advice not relied upon. See also Case T-417/05 *Endesa v Commission* [2006] ECR II-2533, para 76.
[134] For an analysis of the right of access to the file enjoyed by undertakings involved in proceedings involving the application of Arts 101 and 102 TFEU, see Ch 10, 'Procedures to Establish the Existence of an Infringement'. The GC has considered that the same principles are applicable in concentration cases examined under the Merger Control Regulation. See Case T-290/94 *Kaysersberg v Commission* [1997] ECR II-2137, para 113; Case T-221/95 *Endemol Entertainment Holding BV v Commission* [1999] ECR II-1299, particularly para 68: 'The Court considers that the same principles are applicable to access to the files in concentration cases examined under Regulation No 4064/89, even though their application may reasonably be adapted to the need for speed, which characterises the general scheme of that regulation'; and para 66: 'the case-law also makes it clear that access to certain documents may be refused, in particular in the case of documents or parts thereof containing other undertakings' business secrets, internal Commission documents, information enabling complainants to be identified where they wish to remain anonymous and information disclosed to the Commission subject to an obligation of confidentiality.' Accordingly, 'the fact that the applicant had access only to non-confidential summaries of the replies to the questionnaires sent to the independent producers does not amount to an infringement of its rights of defence'; and Case T-210/01 *General Electric v Commission* [2005] ECR II-5575, para 631: 'the rights of the defence are not to be applied with a standard of protection which is different or more extensive in merger control cases than in proceedings involving infringements of Community competition law.'
[135] Article 17(3) of the Implementing Regulation. See Case T-417/05 *Endesa v Commission* [2006] ECR II-2533, para 76 (referring to Case T-65/89 *BPB Industries and British Gypsum v Commission* [1993] ECR II-389, para 33).
[136] Case T-417/05 *Endesa v Commission* [2006] ECR II-2533, para 74.
[137] See Case T-221/95 *Endemol v Commission* [1999] ECR II-1299, paras 83–91. In practice, the Commission will normally prepare agreed minutes of such meetings or telephone conversations, a non-confidential copy of which will be made available to the parties.
[138] Case C-413/06 P *Bertelsmann and Sony Corporation of America v Commission* [2008] ECR I-4951, paras 100–2.

4. Access to the file under Regulation 1049/2001[139]

Given the fact that the Merger Control Regulation does not provide for a right of access to documents in the Commission's files for purposes different to those of the specific procedure, and in no event in favour of third parties, a number of claimants interested in having access to the Commission's files beyond the constraints of the Merger Control Regulation have taken recourse to Regulation 1049/2001,[140] which provides for a general right of access to documents of the institutions of the EU. Of particular interest for the merger control area are the *Sweden/MyTravel*, *Odile Jacob*, and *Agrofert* access cases which are briefly discussed in the paragraphs that follow.

17.66

The first of these cases originates in the prohibition by the European Commission of the merger between Airtours and First Choice, which was subsequently annulled by the GC upon an appeal by Airtours (now MyTravel).[141] Following the annulment of that decision, MyTravel filed a claim for the damages allegedly caused by the prohibition.[142] In support of that claim it sought access to the Commission's files in the merger case. Against the refusal by the Commission, MyTravel filed another appeal before the GC.[143]

17.67

MyTravel's request in that latter case was partially accepted by the GC, which declared that the Commission should have performed an individual examination of each document to which it intended to refuse access. However, the GC sided with the Commission in disallowing access to its internal documents, including legal opinions from its services. That latter point was appealed by the Kingdom of Sweden before the ECJ.

17.68

In its judgment,[144] which was limited to the issue of the access to internal documents of the Commission, the ECJ dismissed the arguments of the Commission, which had argued that under Article 4(2) third indent of Regulation 1049/2001, it should be able to refuse to release internal documents which could affect its legal strategy. The Court particularly noted that the merger decision to which that material referred had already become final, and the Commission had not taken steps to re-examine that case, all of which reduced the risk that access may interfere with actions that the Commission may adopt. Therefore, it decided against a 'blanket approach' and imposed on the Commission a duty to carry out an individual examination of each document and to provide specific reasons for refusal of access.[145]

17.69

The issue of whether a specific examination of each document for which access had been requested is required (and the arguably opposite method based on general standards or presumptions that would apply to categories or groups of documents) would be qualified in the *Odile Jacob* access case. Similarly to the *MyTravel* case, the case was linked to other claims, in this case two appeals filed by Odile Jacob, one seeking the annulment of the decision conditionally approving the concentration between its competitor Lagardère and VUP,[146] and

17.70

---

[139] On this matter see Ingrid Vandenborre, 'The Confidentiality of EU Commission Cartel Records in Civil Litigation: The Ball is in the EU Court' (2011) 32(3) European Competition Law Review 116 and Rolf Hempel, 'Access to DG Competition's Files: An Analysis of Recent EU Court Case Law' (2012) 33(4) European Competition Law Review 195.

[140] Regulation (EC) No 1049/2001 of the European Parliament and of the Council of 30 May 2001 regarding public access to European Parliament, Council and Commission documents [2001] OJ L145/43.

[141] Case T-342/99 *Airtours Plc v Commission* [2002] ECR II-2585.

[142] Case T-212/03 *MyTravel Group Plc v Commission* [2008] ECR II-1967. That claim would ultimately be dismissed.

[143] Case T-403/05 *MyTravel Group Plc v Commission* [2008] ECR II-2027.

[144] Case C-506/08 P *Sweden v MyTravel and Commission* [2011] ECR I-6237.

[145] Case C-506/08 P *Sweden v MyTravel and Commission* [2011] ECR I-6237, paras 81, 89, 98, and 102.

[146] Case T-279/04 *Éditions Odile Jacob/Commission* [2010] ECR II-185, upheld on appeal, Judgment of 6 November 2012 in Case C-551/10 P *Editions Odile Jacob v Commission*.

another against the approval of Wendel Investissement SA as a suitable purchaser of certain assets to be divested by Lagardère.[147]

17.71 In the initial judgment, the GC ruled in favour of the applicant, noting that the Commission had failed to perform a concrete examination of the grounds for refusal of each specific document. However, the GC upheld the refusal by the Commission of access to one opinion of its Legal Service which the Commission had based on the exception for the protection of legal advice, given that Odile Jacob was challenging the decision in question. The Commission appealed that judgment with respect to the former issue and Odile Jacob later cross-appealed with respect to the latter issue.

17.72 On appeal by the Commission, the ECJ corrected the GC's approach and confirmed the validity of the decision from the Commission to refuse access.[148] Relying on the *Technische Glaswerke Ilmenau* case,[149] the Court noted that the original judgment had not had sufficient regard to the Merger Control Regulation[150] and the need to ensure a consistent application between that Regulation and Regulation 1049/2001.[151] In particular, the ECJ held that in light of the characteristics of merger control procedures, which oblige companies to surrender sensitive commercial information, a general presumption that access to the documentation would be liable to damage their commercial interests could be accepted,[152] and that failure to do so would jeopardize the proper functioning of the Merger Control Regulation and the specific guarantees provided for in Articles 17 and 18(3) of the Merger Control Regulation and Article 17 of the Implementing Regulation. As concerns the cross-appeal by *Odile Jacob*, the Court differentiated this case from the *Sweden/MyTravel* case. In particular, the ECJ observed that the requested documentation was linked to a decision of the Commission which was not definitive, as it had been appealed by Odile Jacob, unlike in the earlier case.[153]

17.73 *Agrofert*, the last case of relevance in the use of Regulation 1049/2001 in the merger control field, was decided on the same day as the *Odile Jacob* access case.[154] Again, it concerns a request for access in support of other claims, in this case a request by Agrofert for access to the Commission's merger control files in the *PKN Orlen/Unipetrol* merger case[155] in support of actions for damages by it and minority shareholders of Unipetrol. The Commission refused access, arguing that the claim had been formulated in a very wide manner (all documents on file, including those at the pre-notification phase). On appeal, however, the GC sided with the applicant essentially on the basis that, even if the exceptions to access of Regulation 1049/2001 were applicable, the Commission had failed in providing an individual assessment of each document.[156] On appeal, the ECJ drew a distinction between access to documents exchanged between the Commission and third parties and internal documents of the Commission. With regard to the former, it took a similar position to that of the *Odile Jacob* judgment of the same date[157] and consequently annulled the judgment of the GC on the basis of the admissibility of

---

[147] Case T-452/04 *Éditions Odile Jacob v Commission* [2010] ECR II-4713, upheld on appeal, Judgment of 6 November 2012 in Joined Cases C-553/10 P and C-554/10 P *Commission and Lagardère v Éditions Odile Jacob*.
[148] Judgment of 28 June 2012 in Case C-404/10 P *Commission v Éditions Odile Jacob*.
[149] Case C-139/07 P *Commission v Technische Glaswerke Ilmenau GmbH* [2011] ECR I-5885.
[150] Judgment of 28 June 2012 in Case C-404/10 P *Commission v Éditions Odile Jacob*, para 108 et seq.
[151] Judgment of 28 June 2012 in Case C-404/10 P *Commission v Éditions Odile Jacob*, para 110.
[152] Judgment of 28 June 2012 in Case C-404/10 P *Commission v Éditions Odile Jacob*, paras 118–25.
[153] Judgment of 28 June 2012 in Case C-404/10 P *Commission v Éditions Odile Jacob*, paras 128–34 and 138.
[154] Judgment of 28 June 2012 in Case C-477/10 P *Commission v Agrofert*.
[155] Case COMP/M.3543 *PKN Orlen/Unipetrol* [2005] OJ C129/2.
[156] Case T-111/07 *Agrofert v Commission* [2010] ECR II-128.
[157] Both judgments were adopted by the same Chamber of the ECJ (albeit with partly different compositions) and the part of the *Agrofert* judgment that deals with these documents closely follows the reasoning of

a general presumption that the system of the Merger Control Regulation may be impaired by access. However, in respect of the request for access to internal documents, the Court found the request more similar to *Sweden/MyTravel* than to *Odile Jacob*, since the decision to which the procedure referred was final and Agrofert was not challenging the validity of any decision. On that basis, the ECJ confirmed the GC's decision that the Commission should have provided an individual assessment on each document requested.

From these cases, it can be concluded that Regulation 1049/2001 can be used in order to gain **17.74** access to documents on file in merger control cases. While the Commission may rely on general presumptions of damage to refuse access to documents exchanged with third parties, a detailed assessment of specific documents may still be necessary.[158] An individual assessment will in any event be necessary to justify a refusal to grant access to internal documents of the Commission to parties not challenging the validity of decisions.

5. The right to be heard: the formal hearing

In their written submissions on the statement of objections, the notifying parties have **17.75** the right to request an oral hearing in order to present their arguments more fully.[159] The parties to whom the Commission has addressed its objections may also propose that the Commission hears those persons who can corroborate the truth of the facts on which the defence is based.[160]

Normally, the hearing takes place after the parties have filed their written observations in **17.76** reply to the statement of objections. The Commission must give the persons, undertakings, and associations of undertakings involved the right to be heard with regard to the objections raised against them at all stages of the proceedings prior to consultations with the Advisory Committee.[161] Other interested parties and third parties admitted may also, upon request, participate in the hearing and intervene on that occasion. The hearing normally takes one day, although in very complicated cases two or more days may be necessary, and it will be organized and presided over by the Hearing Officer in a totally neutral manner.[162]

The Commission is normally represented at the oral hearing by a team of civil servants that **17.77** usually includes the Deputy Director-General for mergers, the Director, the Head of Unit,

---

Odile Jacob. See Judgment of 28 June 2012 in Case C-404/10 P *Commission v Éditions Odile Jacob*, para 109 et seq and Case T-111/07 *Agrofert v Commission* [2010] ECR II-128, para 51 et seq.

[158] Judgment of 28 June 2012 in Case C-404/10 P *Commission v Éditions Odile Jacob*, para 126 and Case T-111/07 *Agrofert v Commission* [2010] ECR II-128, para 68.

[159] Article 14(1) of the Implementing Regulation. See also Article 6(1) of the Decision of the President of the European Commission of 13 October 2011 on the function and terms of reference of the hearing officer in certain competition proceedings [2011] OJ L275/29 ('Terms of Reference of the Hearing Officer').

[160] Article 13(3) of the Implementing Regulation.

[161] Article 13(1) of the Implementing Regulation in conjunction with Art 18(1) of the Merger Control Regulation. Note that Art 18 of the Merger Control Regulation provides that those with a right to be heard can exercise it 'at every stage of the procedure up to the consultation of the Advisory Committee'.

[162] Article 15(1) of the Implementing Regulation and Art 10(2) of the Terms of Reference of the Hearing Officer. In accordance with Art 14 of these Terms of Reference, the Hearing Officer will file his interim report directly to the competent Commissioner on the hearing and the conclusions he or she draws with regard to the respect for the exercise of procedural rights, which generally covers the questions of procedural guarantees, divulging documents, and access to the file, the time limits for replies to the statement of objections and what happened in the hearing, as well as possible oral observations regarding the future developments of the case (eg withdrawal of certain objections). His final report (which will be notified to Member States, attached to the draft final decision and published with the final decision in the OJ), will also consider whether the draft decision covers more than just the objections with respect to which the parties have had the opportunity to express their positions, and, where appropriate, the objective nature of any investigation with regard to the impact of commitments from the perspective of competition (Art 16 of the Terms of Reference). See Ch 10, 'Procedures to Establish the Existence of an Infringement'.

and the 'case team' that has carried out most of the investigation (including the peer review panel, composed of EU civil servants with lengthy experience in concentration cases)[163] and other civil servants of other Directorates-General, as well as the Legal Service and a member of the Cabinet of the Commissioner for competition.

17.78 Those invited to attend can either appear in person or with a legal or other representative, as allowed by their constitution. Undertakings or business associations may be represented by a duly authorized agent. Those whom the Commission hears may be assisted by lawyers or other duly 'qualified and duly authorized persons admitted by the Hearing Officer'.[164]

17.79 In addition, representatives of the NCAs of Member States may also attend.[165] The importance of a Member State's opinion, particularly with a view to the next procedural stage (the intervention of the Advisory Committee on concentrations), is clearly recognized by the parties, which often enter into bilateral contacts with the NCAs about the case.

17.80 Although each person should normally be heard in the presence of all other persons attending the oral hearing, the Hearing Officer may decide to hear persons separately in a closed session to protect business secrets or other confidential information.[166] No disclosure of or access to business secrets or other confidential information will be allowed which the Commission does not consider necessary to divulge for the purposes of the case at hand, or to the internal documents of either the Commission or the NCAs.[167] A record will be kept of the statements made by all those giving evidence at the hearing, and on request the record will be made available to all those attending.[168]

17.81 Apart from the notifying parties, the Commission may, in other phases of the proceedings, offer the notifying parties and any other interested party (for example, the seller and the target company) the chance to express their opinions orally.[169] The Merger Control Regulation and the Implementing Regulation provide for the possibility of hearing third parties that are defined as those natural or legal persons, including clients, suppliers, and competitors, provided that they can show a sufficient interest.[170]

17.82 The parties the Commission proposes to fine also have the same rights to an oral hearing.[171]

---

[163] Note that the setting up of these review panels in the second phase is not yet reflected in any rule. See Ch 16, 'General Issues: Scope of Control', para 16.25.

[164] Article 15(4) and (5) of the Implementing Regulation.

[165] Article 15(3) of the Implementing Regulation.

[166] Article 13 of the Terms of Reference of the Hearing Officer.

[167] Articles 15(8), 17, and 18 of the Implementing Regulation.

[168] Article 15(8) of the Implementing Regulation. At present, the record is in the form of a CD-ROM. See Ch 10, 'Procedures to Establish the Existence of an Infringement'.

[169] Articles 11 and 14 of the Implementing Regulation.

[170] Article 18 of the Merger Control Regulation and Arts 11 and 16 of the Implementing Regulation which particularly refers to members of the administrative or management bodies of the undertakings concerned, employees' representatives, and consumers' associations. In Case C-170/02 P *Schlüsselverlag JS Moser and others v Commission* [2003] ECR I-9889, the ECJ has confirmed that it is the Commission's duty to hear third parties, in this case competitors, with respect to their complaints concerning the breach of the obligation to notify to the Commission all operations with an EU dimension. With respect to Art 18 of the Merger Control Regulation, the ECJ stated that: 'the Commission cannot refrain from taking account of complaints from undertakings which are not party to a concentration capable of having a EU dimension. Indeed, the implementation of such a transaction for the benefit of undertakings in competition with the complainants is likely to bring about an immediate change in the complainants' situation on the market or markets concerned' (para 27). See also Case T-96/92 *CCE de la Société Générale des Grandes Sources and Others v Commission* [1995] II-1213, paras 55–7 and Case T-151/05 *NVV and Others v Commission* [2009] ECR II-1219, paras 200–15, and in particular paras 200–3.

[171] Article 11(d) of the Implementing Regulation.

6. Consultation with the Member States: the Advisory Committee

Throughout the procedure from the time of the notification, the Commission handles the **17.83** case in close and constant contact with the NCAs of Member States, as is required by Article 19(2) of the Merger Control Regulation.[172]

In the first phase, the Commission will send to the NCAs within three days a copy of the noti- **17.84** fication and the most important documents (including commitments) that have been lodged with or issued by the Commission in application of the Merger Control Regulation. Member States have the right to make observations with respect to the proceedings.[173] However, the Commission is not obliged to consult Member States before adopting a first-phase decision.

Throughout the second phase, the function of the Member States is much more formalized **17.85** within the Advisory Committee. This body is composed of representatives of the Member States' NCAs.[174] These representatives are normally specialists in their respective authorities dealing with concentrations with national dimensions, which allows a comparative debate to take place about the competition issues at stake in any given case. The Merger Control Regulation requires each Member State to appoint one or more representatives, and at least one of these must be a specialist in restrictive practices and dominant positions.

The Commission is obliged to consult the Advisory Committee before adopting one of the **17.86** decisions referred to in Article 8(1)–(6) of the Merger Control Regulation, that is, the decisions bringing an end to second-phase proceedings (authorizing—whether or not subject to conditions—or prohibiting the concentration), as well as the decisions on revocation, interim measures, or orders to dissolve the concentration, and those that impose sanctions under Articles 14 and 15 of the Merger Control Regulation.

Meetings of the Advisory Committee are called and chaired by a representative of the **17.87** Commission (normally by the Director or a Head of Unit in charge of coordination within DG COMP) and take place in Brussels. In accordance with Article 19 of the Merger Control Regulation, the meeting cannot take place before ten working days have passed from the date when the meeting was called, although in exceptional circumstances the Commission may reduce this period in order to prevent one or more undertakings affected by the operation from being seriously prejudiced. In practice, this ten-day period cannot always be respected for two main reasons. First, in the second phase the Commission is under extreme time pressure in cases where the parties offer last-minute commitments to resolve the competition problem in issue and try to avoid a prohibition. Secondly, minimal logistical needs related to the convening of the meeting (presentation of an explanatory note on the points to discuss, translations, etc) must be ensured. EU Courts have held that a failure to observe the notice period when calling a meeting of the Advisory Committee, even in the event that there are no exceptional circumstances related to the risk of a serious prejudice, is not in itself enough to make the final Commission decision illegal. A breach of this type can only make the final decision illegal when it is sufficiently substantial and it has a harmful effect on the legal and factual situation of the party alleging a procedural irregularity.[175]

---

[172] See Ch 16, 'General Issues: Scope of Control', para 16.27.
[173] Article 19(2) of the Merger Control Regulation.
[174] Articles 19(4) and 23(2) of the Merger Control Regulation.
[175] In its Judgment of 7 June 2013, Case T-405/08 *Spar Österreichische Warenhandels v Commission*, the GC held that a third party may not rely on the absence of communication of the revised draft of commitment offered by the parties since Article 19(1) of the Merger Control Regulation was not addressed to it (para 265). See also Case T-290/94 *Kaysersberg SA v Commission* [1997] ECR II-2137, para 88.

17.88 In meetings called to discuss a draft decision under Article 8 of the Merger Control Regulation, the representative of one of the Member States will act as *rapporteur* and will inform the representatives from the other Member States about the matter. After a debate about the content of the Commission's draft, the Committee will issue an opinion either in favour or against the draft decision as a whole or with regard to certain aspects of it (for example, disagreement about the case coming within the legal definition of a concentration, EU dimension, or on the market definition, about the Commission's finding of a significant impediment to effective competition or the creation or reinforcement of a dominant position in a given market affected by the concentration, and agreement with regard to the analysis in other markets). The meeting may lead the Commission to undertake further investigations and ultimately to change its views.[176] The Advisory Committee may give its opinion even when some of its members are not present or represented in the meeting. The Advisory Committee's meetings take place behind closed doors, and neither the parties nor any third parties may attend.

17.89 The Merger Control Regulation provides that a written opinion will be delivered and will be annexed to the draft decision. The Advisory Committee's opinions are not binding on the Commission,[177] which is only required to take 'the utmost account' of the Advisory Committee's opinion as well as the latter's report explaining the manner in which it has reached its opinion.[178] That report is made public together with the decision, taking into account the legitimate interest of undertakings in protecting their commercial secrets.[179]

7. Decisions at the end of the second phase: publication

Article 8(1) and (2) decisions

17.90 When the Commission finds that a notified concentration does not significantly impede effective competition in the internal market, either as notified (Article 8(1) of the Merger Control Regulation) or following the changes that the undertakings concerned may have made to it (Article 8(2) of the Regulation), it must take a decision declaring that the concentration is compatible with the internal market. The Commission may attach conditions to its decisions and agree to specific commitments aimed at guaranteeing that the undertakings comply with the obligations that they have entered into with the Commission in order to make the concentration compatible with the internal market. As already noted, second-phase decisions do not reach 4 per cent of the total number of notified operations. Out of this figure, nearly all of them are approval decisions.

Article 8(3) decisions

17.91 By contrast, if the Commission concludes that a proposed concentration will 'significantly impede effective competition in the internal market or in a substantial part of it', it must adopt a decision declaring that the concentration is incompatible with the internal market.[180]

---

[176] See Case COMP/M.3796 *Omya/J.M. Huber* [2006] OJ L72/24, where some Member States expressed doubts concerning the reliability of the econometric study (Case T-145/06 *Omya v Commission* [2009] ECR II-145, para 59), prompting the Commission to verify the accuracy of the data submitted by the parties and used in an econometric study (*Omya v Commission*, para 73). Whereas the Commission had at first submitted to the Advisory Committee a draft clearance decision, it later sent a statement of objections and adopted a clearance decision with commitments (decision of 19 July 2006 pursuant to Art 8(2) Merger Control Regulation, paras 4 and 9).

[177] Articles 19(3) and 23(2)(c) of the Merger Control Regulation.

[178] Articles 19(6) and 23(2)(c) of the Merger Control Regulation.

[179] Article 19(7) of the Merger Control Regulation.

[180] Up to the end of June 2013, there have been only twenty-four prohibitions, and only five since 2002, three in the airline sector (Case COMP/M.4439 *Ryanair/Aer Lingus* [2007] OJ C 47/9, Case COMP/M.5830 *Olympic/Aegean* [2011] OJ C195/11, and Case COMP/M.6663 *Ryanair/Aer Lingus III* [2013]), one in the financial services sector (Case COMP/M.6166 *Deutsche Börse/NYSE Euronext* [2012] OJ C234/2) and one in the small package delivery services sector (Case COMP/M.6570 *UPS/TNT Express* [2013]).

The parties run the risk of being fined if they implement an operation that has been declared incompatible with the internal market in a decision adopted under Article 8(3).[181]

Article 8(4) decisions

If a concentration which has been declared incompatible with the internal market has been implemented,[182] the Commission is empowered to force the undertakings concerned to put it to an end, in particular through the dissolution of the merger or the disposal of all the shares or assets acquired, so as to restore the situation prevailing prior to the implementation of the concentration. Alternatively, the Commission may order any other appropriate measure to achieve restoration of the *status quo ante*. If the prohibition decision is subsequently annulled, the divestiture is also annulled.[183]

17.92

Article 8(5) decisions

The Commission may take interim measures to restore or maintain effective competition when a concentration is implemented in breach of the obligation to suspend until a decision over the compatibility of the operation with the internal market is adopted.[184] Further, such measures could be taken when a concentration has been implemented in breach of one of the conditions attached to a first-phase decision.

17.93

Publication

The Commission will publish in the OJ the decisions adopted in accordance with Article 8, as well as those imposing sanctions under Articles 14 and 15, together with the report of the Advisory Committee.[185] The published decision will mention the undertakings concerned and all the relevant elements of the case, but not the undertakings' business secrets. To this end, it is a common practice of the Commission to make available to the undertakings concerned the draft decision to enable them to request that those aspects which they consider to be business secrets be treated as confidential (such as market share, prices, clients, suppliers, etc).[186]

17.94

Publication in the OJ will start the time limit for third parties to bring actions for annulment against the decision.[187] This holds true even if a third party had previous knowledge

17.95

---

[181] Article 14(2)(c) of the Merger Control Regulation.

[182] Implementation of a concentration may be either the result of a breach of Art 7 of the Merger Control Regulation or a case in which there was no obligation to suspend implementation. See Ch 16, 'General Issues: Scope of Control', para 16.05, esp para 16.07, for a discussion on these exceptions. Significant examples of Art 8(4) decisions are Case IV/M.784 *Kesko/Tusko* [1997] OJ L174/47 and the Decision of 30 January 2002 in Case COMP/M.2416 *Tetra Laval/Sidel* [2002] OJ L43/13. This latter decision would remain ineffective as a result of the annulment by the GC (and later confirmation by the ECJ) of the Commission decision prohibiting the concentration. In Case T-411/07 *Aer Lingus v Commission* [2010] ECR II-369, the GC stated that since Ryanair's shareholding in Aer Lingus did not confer on Ryanair the power to 'control' Aer Lingus, it could not be assimilated to a concentration which 'has already been implemented', even if the operation by which that shareholding was acquired had been declared incompatible with the common market. Thus, a measure pursuant to Art 8(4) of the Merger Control Regulation could not be adopted (paras 64–66 and 78). The reasoning regarding Art 8(4) of the Merger Control Regulation applies *mutatis mutandis* to Art 8(5) of the Merger Control Regulation (para 88).

[183] Case T-77/02 *Schneider Electric v Commission* [2002] ECR II-4201, paras 39–46; Case T-80/02 *Tetra Laval v Commission* [2002] ECR II-4825, paras 36–43.

[184] It is only the Merger Control Regulation that explicitly provided for such a possibility to take appropriate interim measures. This remains in any event at the discretion of the Commission (Judgment of 12 December 2012 in Case T-332/09 *Electrabel v Commission*, para 194).

[185] Article 20 of the Merger Control Regulation.

[186] For instructions on market share ranges in non-confidential versions of decisions see <http://ec.europa.eu/competition/mergers/legislation/market_share_ranges.pdf>.

[187] Article 263 TFEU.

of the decision (eg for having received a non-confidential version of the decision from DG COMP).[188]

Revocation or amendment of Article 8 decisions

17.96 Article 8(6) of the Merger Control Regulation provides for the revocation by the Commission of its decisions where (i) the declaration of compatibility with the internal market is the result of incorrect or fraudulent information; or (ii) where an obligation included in the decision is not complied with. These provisions are similar to those provided for in respect of decisions at the end of the first phase under Article 6(3) of the Merger Control Regulation.[189] It is submitted that the Commission is also able to amend its decisions for reasons of legality under the doctrine established by the GC in *Lagardère/Canal+*.[190] The Commission cannot revoke a decision declaring a concentration compatible with the internal market on the sole ground that it has been completed before having been notified.[191]

E. Remedies

1. Introduction

17.97 Notifying parties may propose solutions aimed at eliminating any competition problem and thus obtain authorization.[192] Normally, this involves reducing the market share of the parties to the concentration or facilitating entry of competitors.[193] Despite the fact that the decisions where commitments are offered are less than 5 per cent of all notifications received annually by the Commission, this is an area where the Commission has published a significant number of documents that provide assistance to the notifying parties.

17.98 The original wording of former Regulation 4064/89 only covered the Commission's power to negotiate, where appropriate, the acceptance of commitments from the parties to a concentration in the second phase.

17.99 Following the 1997 amendments, the acceptance of commitments in the first phase was expressly included in the Regulation.[194] The Commission noted that:

> [t]he formalization of phase I undertakings has proved of interest and benefit to merging parties and the Commission alike. It enables the delay and consequent uncertainty over the outcome of a notified transaction to be reduced, and avoids the need to deploy some of the

---

[188] Case T-48/04 *Qualcomm v Commission* [2009] ECR II-2029, paras 48 and 58. Compare with Opinion of AG Kokott in Case C-413/06 P *Bertelsmann and Sony Corporation of America v Commission* [2008] ECR I-4951, para 82.

[189] See para 17.51.

[190] Case T-251/00 *Lagardère SCA and Canal+ SA v Commission* [2002] ECR II-4825.

[191] Case T-279/04 *Éditions Odile Jacob v Commission* [2010] ECR II-185, paras 156 and 160.

[192] The Commission has the power to accept only such commitments as are capable of rendering the notified transaction compatible with the internal market. Case T-48/04 *Qualcomm v Commission* [2009] ECR II-2029, para 89, citing Case T-102/96 *Gencor v Commission* [1999] ECR II-753, para 318, and Case T-282/02 *Cementbouw Handel & Industrie v Commission* [2006] ECR II-319, para 294; see also, to that effect, Case T-87/05 *EDP v Commission* [2005] ECR II-3745, para 63.

[193] See Case COMP/M.5655 *SNCF/LCR/Eurostar* [2010] OJ C272/2, para 64.

[194] Recital 8 of Reg 1310/97 amending Reg 4064/89 [1997] OJ L180/1, provided that the Commission has the power to declare a concentration to be compatible with the internal market in the second phase, once the parties have presented commitments 'that are proportional to and would entirely eliminate the competition problem'. Recital 8 also states that 'it is also appropriate to accept commitments in the first phase of the procedure when the competition problem is readily identifiable and can easily be remedied' and that 'transparency and effective consultation of Member States and interested third parties should be ensured in both phases of the procedure'.

substantial extra resources (at the Commission as well as by the parties) required for a full phase II investigation and decision. Experience with the new power shows clearly that the revised system is able to deal both quickly—in a matter of weeks, rather than several months—and efficaciously with mergers where a potential dominant position may be created.[195]

Recitals 30 and 31 of the Merger Control Regulation require that commitments must be proportional to the competition problem in question and completely eliminate it. In accordance with Article 6(2) of the Merger Control Regulation, the Commission may declare a concentration to be compatible with the internal market when it can show that, once modified, it does not give rise to serious doubts about competition.[196] Article 8(2) of the Merger Control Regulation uses the same terms in relation to concentrations that are subject to second-phase proceedings.[197] **17.100**

In the first phase, the notifying parties can offer commitments within a maximum period of twenty working days from the date of receipt of notification.[198] The period for filing commitments in the second phase is sixty-five working days from the day on which proceedings were initiated. Where the parties submit commitments within less than fifty-five working days after the initiation of proceedings, the Commission has to take a final decision within not more than ninety working days of the date of initiation of proceedings. If the parties submit commitments on working day fifty-five or later, the period for the Commission to take a final decision is increased to 105 working days.[199] The regulations on concentrations impose no obligation on the Commission to accept commitments submitted after the deadline.[200] However, the Commission has agreed to examine modified commitments, including those submitted after the deadline, in specific circumstances.[201] During the second phase and before the Commission issues a statement of objections, the parties may nevertheless offer commitments that remove the serious doubts referred to in Article 6(1)(c) of the Merger Control Regulation. Where this occurs, and in accordance with Article 10(2) of the Merger Control Regulation, the Commission will then have to take a decision pursuant to Article 8(2) of the Merger Control Regulation without delay.[202] **17.101**

---

[195] XXVIII Report on Competition Policy [1998], para 142, insert 6.

[196] Judgment of 7 June 2013 in Case T-405/08 *Spar Österreichische Warenhandels v Commission*, para 47.

[197] As the GC has explained, commitments offered in the first phase enable, at the initial stage, the avoidance of the initiation of an in-depth investigation, or, thereafter, the prevention of a decision declaring that the concentration is incompatible with the internal market (Case T-212/03 *MyTravel v Commission* [2008] ECR II-1967, para 117). Commitments offered specifically for the purposes of obtaining a decision under Article 6(2) of the Merger Control Regulation are no longer valid where the Commission decides to open a second phase investigation (see Judgment of 1 September 2011 in Case T-132/10 *Communauté de Communes de Lacq v Commission*, paras 23–6).

[198] Article 19(1) of the Implementing Regulation. One of the widest commitments negotiated in first-phase proceedings was the subject matter of the Commission Decision of 9 August 1999 in Case IV/M.1378 *Hoechst/Rhône-Poulenc*. See XXIX Report on Competition Policy [1999], paras 182–3: the commitments included the divestiture of the chemical divisions of Rhodia and Celanese, as well as the veterinary division of Hoechst, HR Vet. In addition, commitments were given in response to the competition problems in various pharmaceutical and agrochemical markets that the Commission identified during its investigation. The commitments offered in Case COMP/M.2978 *Lagardère/Natixis/VUP* [2004] OJ L125/54 consisted in assets representing around 60 per cent of the acquired business (See Commission Press Release IP/04/15 of 7 January 2004).

[199] Article 10(3) of the Merger Control Regulation.

[200] Case T-87/05 *EDP v Commission* [2005] ECR II-3745, para 161; See also Case T-342/07 *Ryanair Holdings plc v Commission* [2010] ECR II-3457, para 455 and case law cited therein.

[201] Case T-87/05 *EDP v Commission* [2005] ECR II-3745, paras 161–6. See also Case T-212/03 *MyTravel Group plc v Commission* [2008] ECR II-1967, paras 124–7.

[202] Acceptable Remedies Notice, para 18. See Case COMP/M.5440 *Lufthansa/Austrian Airlines* [2009] OJ C16/11, para 10.

17.102 The time periods are short, and it is difficult for both the parties and the Commission to determine precisely the most appropriate type of commitments to propose. What the parties may consider to be the most acceptable proposal for the Commission after negotiations have taken place may be insufficient in light of the Commission's definition of the market or technical difficulties identified by the Commission once it has examined in detail the specific solutions proposed by the parties.[203] In cases where the parties suspect that the transaction may cause competition problems, they should contact the Commission as soon as possible, but especially before formal notification takes place. Further, a new feature of the Merger Control Regulation makes it important for the parties to evaluate whether they will need to request an extension of time within fifteen working days from the commencement of second-phase proceedings. Any such extension cannot exceed twenty days, during which time the 'clock stops' with respect to the time periods of general authorization.[204]

2. Notices adopted by the Commission in the field of remedies

17.103 In December 2000, the Commission adopted a first notice on remedies acceptable to resolve competition problems that arise in concentrations[205] aimed at giving guidance about amendments to concentrations, including commitments, based on the Commission's experience. The importance of this matter for the Commission was shown again in the creation in 2001 of an 'enforcement unit', whose task was to develop a consistent policy of assessment, acceptance, and implementation of the commitments.[206] Subsequently, the Commission adopted its 'Best Practice Guidelines for Divestiture Commitments', which contain model texts for divestiture commitments and the trustee's mandate, which will be examined later.[207] In October 2005, the Commission published a study evaluating the experience gathered so far in merger cases.[208]

17.104 Following the results of this study, in 2008 the Commission adopted a new Remedies Notice ('Acceptable Remedies Notice').[209] This new notice stands in contrast to the earlier notice in various aspects. Remedies are no longer declared insufficient for some operations, as former paragraph 14 of the older notice indicated. The text is much more detailed than its predecessor and discusses at length various manners in which the effects of a concentration may be corrected.

---

[203] Case T-210/01 *General Electric v Commission* [2005] ECR II-5575, para 52: '[t]he Commission is not responsible for technical or commercial gaps in the commitments in question (which led it to conclude that they were insufficient to permit it to approve the merger at issue); nor, more specifically, can those gaps be attributed to any unwillingness on its part to accept that other commitments, of a behavioural nature, might be effective. It was for the parties to the merger to put forward commitments which were comprehensive and effective from all points of view.' Case T-87/05 *EDP v Commission* [2005] ECR II-3745, para 105: 'The Commission had no obligation, even if it had been able to do so in the discussions with the parties, to establish a particular method of monitoring, notably one delegated to the competent national authorities. It was for the parties, on the contrary, to propose commitments that were full and effective from all aspects, especially if those behavioural commitments had intrinsic weaknesses as regards their binding nature that justified ex-post monitoring.'

[204] Article 10(3) of the Merger Control Regulation.

[205] Commission Notice on remedies acceptable under Council Reg (EEC) 4064/89 and Reg (EC) 447/98 [2001] OJ C68/3.

[206] See M Monti, 'The Commission notice on merger remedies—one year after', SPEECH/02/10, 18 January 2002, CERNA Paris, available at DG COMP's website.

[207] Best Practice Guidelines: The Commission's Model Texts for Divestiture Commitments and the Trustee Mandate under the EC Merger Regulation (hereafter, 'Best Practice Guidelines for Divestiture Commitments'), available at DG COMP's website.

[208] This *ex-post* analysis of ninety-six remedies included in merger decisions adopted in 1996–2000 is available at DG COMP's website.

[209] Commission Notice on remedies acceptable under Council Regulation (EC) No 139/2004 and under Commission Regulation (EC) No 802/2004 [2008] OJ C267/1.

3. Types of remedies

Remedies are often classified as either 'structural' (that is, those that modify the market struc-   **17.105**
ture through the sale or transfer of assets or undertakings) or 'behavioural'. Both structural and
behavioural remedies must be assessed on a case-by-case basis.[210] Structural remedies have traditionally been considered more apt to eliminate competition problems. This may no longer
be so, however. Among structural remedies, the most typical one is the divestiture or sale of
a subsidiary company.[211] The subject matter of the transfer may be a combination of tangible
and intangible assets; this may be a pre-existing undertaking or group of undertakings, or an economic activity that does not constitute an undertaking. The transfer of a viable business is seen as
the best means of restoring effective competition. A viable business is defined as an existing activity
that could be operated on a lasting basis independently of the parties to a notification as regards,
for example, the supply of consumables, or the purchase of products that it manufactures, or the
services that it provides (except during a start-up period). The objective is to create, through the
divestiture, an entity that will be a stable competitor in the market in question. Structural commitments will be capable of rendering the notified transaction compatible with the internal market
only if the Commission is able to conclude, with certainty, that it will be possible to implement
them and that the new commercial structures resulting from them will be sufficiently workable
and lasting to ensure that the creation or strengthening of a dominant position, or the impairment
of effective competition, which the commitments are intended to prevent, will not be likely to
materialize in the relatively near future.[212] If there is uncertainty that a number of potential acquirers are available, and the Commission cannot conclude with the requisite degree of certainty that
the business will be effectively divested to a suitable purchaser, the parties may have to undertake
that they will not complete the notified operation before having entered into a binding agreement
with a purchaser for the divested business, approved by the Commission ('up-front buyer' solution).[213] In cases where the identity of the purchaser is crucial for the effectiveness of the proposed
remedy, the parties may also identify and enter into a legally binding agreement with a buyer of
the business to be divested during the Commission procedure ('fix-it-first' solution).[214]

As regards commitments other than divestiture, the Acceptable Remedies Notice refers to   **17.106**
the elimination of structural links with a competitor in a market affected by the operation.
This may involve the sale of a stake that gives joint control in a joint venture or of a minority holding if it is felt that such a holding creates disincentives to compete.[215] Although the

---

[210] Case T-102/86 *Gencor v Commission* [1999] ECR II-753, para 40; Case T-5/02 *Tetra Laval v
Commission* [2002] ECR II-4381, para 161, confirmed in Case C-12/03 P *Commission v Tetra Laval* [2005]
ECR I-987, para 85; Case T-87/05 *EDP v Commission* [2005] ECR II-3475, para 100; Case T-177/04 *easyJet
v Commission* [2006] ECR II-1913, para 182.

[211] In Case T-102/86 *Gencor v Commission* [1999] ECR II-753, para 316, the GC laid down that structural commitments, such as the sale of a subsidiary, are preferable to behavioural commitments, in that they
eliminate the root of the competition problem and, in addition, they do not need supervision in the medium
or long term. In *Gencor*, the GC held that the commitments which consisted in mere promises to behave in
a certain way, such as the promise not to abuse a dominant position created by the concentration, would not
in itself be considered enough to make the operation compatible with the internal market. In the context
of the application of Arts 101 and 102 under Reg 1/2003, for the first time express mention is made of the
possibility of the Commission imposing any proportionate and necessary structural or behavioural remedies
in order to bring to an end a breach of these provisions (Art 7(1)). See para 11.04 et seq.

[212] See for instance Case T-210/01 *General Electric v Commission* [2005] ECR II-5575, para 555 and Case
T-342/07 *Ryanair Holdings plc v Commission* [2010] ECR II-3457, paras 453 and 496.

[213] Acceptable Remedies Notice, paras 53–5. See Case COMP/M.6203 *Western Digital Ireland/Viviti
Technologies* [2011] OJ C165/3, Commission Press Release IP/11/1395 of 23 November 2011, together with
Case COMP/M. 6531 *Toshiba/HDD Assets of Western Digital* [2012] OJ C96/3.

[214] Acceptable Remedies Notice, paras 56–7. See Case COMP/M.4187 *Metso/Aker Kvaerner* [2006] OJ
C6/11, para 148 and Commission Press Release IP/06/1762 of 12 December 2006.

[215] Acceptable Remedies Notice, paras 58–60.

divestiture of such stakes is the preferable solution, the Commission may exceptionally accept the waiving of rights linked to minority stakes in a competitor where it can be excluded, given the specific circumstances of the case, that the financial gains derived from a minority shareholding in a competitor would in themselves raise competition concerns.[216]

17.107 There are other acceptable solutions apart from the permanent transfer of businesses, such as facilitating market entry through giving access to consumables, or to the distribution network, or to certain infrastructures that are necessary to compete. This will include remedies such as terminating exclusivity agreements or guaranteeing that competitors have access to key technologies (including patents, know-how, and other intellectual property rights).[217]

17.108 The parties can offer a package of solutions combining a number of different remedies,[218] but the onus is on the parties to propose remedies that satisfy the Commission.[219]

4. Formal requirements for the filing of remedies

17.109 The filing of remedies was, in the first years of the Regulation, free from formal rules, as the Merger Control Regulation did not provide specific rules. However, bearing in mind the short time limits involved, in 2004 the Commission published guidelines and model texts concerning divestiture commitments, and the mandate of the trustee of the undertaking to be divested in order to assist undertakings when drawing up their proposed remedies and the said mandate.[220] More recently, in 2008, the Implementing Regulation was amended to include, among other elements, a specific form for submitting remedies. Form RM, contained in new Annex IV of the Implementing Regulation, complements the model texts that have been mentioned.

17.110 Under Form RM and the Model Texts, the proposed commitments must contain the following elements:

- In the case of a divestiture, a clear definition and description of its object including the links between the business to be divested and other undertakings controlled by the notifying parties (shared assets, personnel, systems, or customers, and supply, production, distribution, service, or other contracts) and all the elements of the activity being transferred: tangible assets (production plants, real property, distribution premises, sales offices, and others), intangible assets (IP, brands), personnel and key personnel, supply or sales agreements, client lists, technical assistance, financial data, etc.
- A description of the responsibilities of the parties vis-à-vis the Commission, the trustee and the business to be transferred, such as the commitment of the parties to preserve the full economic viability of the business until divestiture actually takes place, provide all of the assistance required by the trustee, or the parties' commitments not to take on employees that are part of the business to be divested.
- The possibility that the proposed purchaser can carry out a due diligence inspection of a company (process of examining the financial underpinnings of a company).

---

[216] See Case COMP/M.3653 *Siemens/VA Tech* [2005], para 327 et seq and *RCA/MAV Cargo* [2008] OJ L353/19, paras 94–7, 102–4, and 110 et seq.
[217] Acceptable Remedies Notice, paras 61–70.
[218] For mergers in the airline sector, a commitment to offer slots at an airport may not be sufficient and may have to be accompanied by other measures (Acceptable Remedies Notice, para 63 and n 4). See Case COMP/M.5335 *Lufthansa/SN Airholding (Brussels Airlines)* [2009] OJ C295/11, paras 443 and 458.
[219] Acceptable Remedies Notice, para 6.
[220] Available on DG COMP's website.

- The obligation of the parties to appoint an independent trustee,[221] the requirements that the latter must fulfill, the procedure for selection, the period within which it is to be elected, its duties and obligations, and remuneration. Both the actual trustee and the mandate must be approved by the Commission.[222]
- The criteria for the approval of the purchaser by the Commission (*inter alia*, being independent of the parties, or ensuring that the purchase will not create any competition concerns). If the purchase amounted to a concentration with an EU dimension, the new operation must be notified in accordance with the Merger Control Regulation in the usual way.

In broad terms, the commitments presented to the Commission in the first phase have to be **17.111** sufficient to remove the serious doubts concerning the compatibility of the operation with the internal market,[223] because there is no detailed investigation (this only occurs in the second phase) and the period within which the decision must be adopted is very short.[224] Accordingly, remedies are acceptable where there are readily identifiable concerns.[225] These commitments must fulfil the following requirements:

(i) they must be presented within the prescribed time limit;
(ii) they will specify the commitment entered into by the parties in sufficient detail to allow a complete evaluation;
(iii) they will explain how the commitments offered resolve the competition problems that have been defined by the Commission.

Following Articles 20 and 20(1a) of the Implementing Regulation, one original and ten **17.112** copies of the proposed commitments and of the information and documents prescribed by the Form RM must be sent to the Commission, together with an electronic version. Commitments must be signed by an authorized officer or a legal representative of the undertakings concerned.[226] The Commission will then send copies to the NCAs without delay. When presenting these commitments, the parties will give reasons why any information should be treated as confidential and they will supply a non-confidential version of the commitments for market testing.

The Commission will evaluate the parties' proposals in light of these requirements, in consul- **17.113** tation with the NCAs and, if it considers it appropriate, with third parties, as well as through

---

[221] The Model Texts distinguish between the administrator or 'Hold Separate Manager', who is responsible for running the business (and maintaining its viability until divestiture as per the commitment) and a trustee of the divestiture (who supervises the implementation of the commitments and periodically informs the Commission of any incident). Both functions can be carried out by the same person. On the independence of the trustee: Case T-452/04 *Éditions Odile Jacob v Commission* [2010] ECR II-4713, paras 83–119, upheld on appeal in Joined Cases C-553/10 P *Commission v Éditions Odile Jacob* and C-554/10 P *Lagardère v Éditions Odile Jacob* [2012], paras 48–53. See also the appeal against the second buyer approval decision of 13 May 2011 in Case COMP/M.2978 *Lagardère/Natexis/VUP* (Case T-471/11 *Éditions Odile Jacob v Commission* [2011] OJ C305/9 and Order of 24 November 2011 in Case T-471/11 R *Éditions Odile Jacob v Commission*).
[222] It is necessary to file the trustee's mandate with the Commission. The mandate will state the appointment and approval of the trustee, clarify the relation between the Commission, the trustee, and the parties, and set out the duties of the trustee, in order that it fulfills the obligations to implement the commitments. The commitments establish the main points that the mandate must cover. The guidelines establish that the mandate is the basis of a triangular relationship between the Commission, the trustee, and the parties. Despite the fact that the mandate puts the trustee in a contractual relationship with the parties, the latter cannot give instructions to the trustee (para 9).
[223] Case T-177/04 *easyJet v Commission* [2006] ECR II-1931, para 129 and case law cited.
[224] Acceptable Remedies Notice, para 18.
[225] Acceptable Remedies Notice, para 83.
[226] Case T-342/07 *Ryanair Holdings plc v Commission* [2010] ECR II-3457, paras 501–5.

a market test.[227] When the Commission's assessment confirms that the proposed remedies remove the grounds for serious doubts, it will declare that the concentration is compatible, and duly inform the parties of this.

17.114 Given that the object of the remedies proposed in the first phase is to obtain a direct solution to a clearly determinable competition problem, only limited modifications to the proposed commitments can be accepted.[228] These modifications, presented immediately after the results of the consultations, will include clarifications, refinements, and other improvements that guarantee that the commitments are 'workable and effective'.[229] If the parties have not removed the serious doubts, the Commission will issue an Article 6(1)(c) decision and start second-phase proceedings.

17.115 The requirements and procedure are similar in relation to commitments proposed in the second phase, apart from the time periods (sixty-five working days from the day on which proceedings were initiated[230]) and that the proposed commitments must tackle all of the competition concerns. The Commission is prepared to discuss the appropriateness of the commitments at any stage of the proceedings. However, at the more advanced stages of the procedure, the final offer of commitments must not only be binding on the party offering them, but also be sufficient in itself to allow the Commission to assess it without again having to seek the opinions of third parties on its content.[231]

5. Implementation of divestiture commitments

17.116 Designing commitments and assessing their viability is an exercise that is not free of difficulties, particularly because, by their nature, commitments can only be put into practice once the Commission has approved the proposed concentration. The Commission will assess the future impact of the commitments, and must also establish mechanisms that guarantee that the parties effectively implement them. The Commission will attach to its decision a series of conditions and obligations aimed at guaranteeing the implementation of the commitments. After this, the Commission must ensure that:

- the parties are doing everything necessary to implement correctly the commitments agreed with the Commission, including, as the case may be, ensuring that the divestiture takes place within the agreed time period. The Commission carries out this supervisory task on the basis of the reports supplied to it by the trustee;
- the business to be divested is kept independent of the activities retained by the parties and is managed as a distinct and saleable business by the hold separate manager, under the supervision of the monitoring trustee.[232] Since the Commission cannot participate in the day-to-day running of the business, this task is entrusted to the monitoring trustee,[233] who is chosen and paid by the parties and approved by the Commission, as is the monitoring trustee's mandate;

---

[227] It is arguable whether the Commission should have an obligation to market test any commitments offered, even if these commitments are clearly incapable of removing the serious doubts identified.

[228] See also Case T-87/05 *EDP v Commission* [2005] ECR II-3745, para 105, where the GC confirmed that the Commission does not have the right to modify the commitments. See also Case T-282/02 *Cementbouw Handel & Industrie v Commission* [2006] ECR II-319, para 311.

[229] Acceptable Remedies Notice, para 83 et seq.

[230] Acceptable Remedies Notice, para 88.

[231] Case T-342/07 *Ryanair Holdings plc v Commission* [2010] ECR II-3457, para 503.

[232] Acceptable Remedies Notice, para 112. Best Practice on Divestiture Commitments, para 21. The Hold Separate Manager is appointed by the parties and normally the manager of the business to be divested.

[233] The Acceptable Remedies Notice provides that the monitoring trustee is the general supervisor of the implementation of the commitments. He can normally propose or even impose measures to guarantee the fulfillment of the commitments as well as the presentation of periodical reports. He also oversees the parties' efforts to find an acceptable purchaser within the period established in the commitments; if they fail in this regard, the trustee will receive an irrevocable mandate to sell off the business within a specific time period at any price, subject to the Commission's prior approval. See also Article 20a of the Implementing Regulation.

- the viable business will be transferred to an appropriate purchaser within a specific period of time. The Commission will have to approve the potential purchaser and the purchase agreement, confirming that it is in line with the contents of the commitments offered. The purchaser must be an existing or potential competitor, and not have any connection whatsoever with the parties.

17.117 The trustee has special responsibility for vetting possible purchasers and must propose adequate purchasers to the Commission in accordance with the commitments given. Within the first period, when it is the parties' sole responsibility to find the right purchaser and they commit themselves to divesting the business (normally within a period of six months[234]), the business may be divested for the price which the parties consider to be appropriate. The parties are free to add of their own accord other assets to the deal in order to make a more attractive package. However, if at the end of this period they have not found an adequate purchaser, the trustee is empowered to carry out the divestiture at any price within what is known as the Extended Divestiture Period, which normally lasts for three months.[235]

6. Modifications of the commitments

17.118 As the Commission explains in its Acceptable Remedies Notice, commitments will usually include a review clause, and this irrespective of the type of remedy.[236] Under this review clause, the parties may request from the Commission the right to modify one or several aspects of the commitments upon request and where they can show good cause.

17.119 One of the more frequent requests is for the extension of deadlines, for instance to divest part of a business. In such cases, the extension will be granted only if the reasons for which the parties were not able to meet the deadline cannot be attributed to them and if the divestiture is likely to occur within a short time-frame.[237] Otherwise, the divestiture trustee will be considered better placed to fulfill the commitment, where necessary by way of a 'fire-sale'. Requests for waivers or modifications or substitutions of commitments will be accepted only in exceptional circumstances and will normally not apply to divestiture commitments.[238] This can be explained by the fact that the Commission considers it very unlikely that changes of market circumstances will have occurred in such a short time-frame.[239]

17.120 The Acceptable Remedies Notice indicates that a waiver, modification, or substitution of commitments may be more relevant for non-divestiture commitments, such as access commitments with a longer duration. Conditions remain a substantiated request from the parties and the demonstration that exceptional circumstances exist.[240] For that purpose, the parties

---

[234] The exact period may nevertheless be kept confidential towards third parties to ensure that in the first divestiture phase, the notifying parties can obtain the best possible price for the business to be sold.

[235] Best Practice Guidelines on Divestiture Commitments, para 15.

[236] Acceptable Remedies Notice, para 71. The Commission adds, however, that the review clause is of particular relevance for access remedies.

[237] Acceptable Remedies Notice, para 72.

[238] In Case COMP/M.5549 *EDF/Segebel* OJ C57/9, relying on significant and permanent changes in the conditions on the electricity market in Belgium since the adoption of the conditional clearance decision, EDF requested the Commission to grant it a postponement by two-and-a-half years of the deadline to comply with its commitment to either invest in a project or divest that project (see Order of the President of the GC of 11 October 2012 in Case T-389/12 R *EDF v Commission*, paras 3–4 (on appeal, Order of the Vice-President of the ECJ of 7 March 2013 in Case C-551/12 P(R) *EDF v Commission*). The Commission refused EDF's request for postponement, but granted an additional period of three-and-a-half months. This decision was challenged before the GC, and EDF asked that the case be decided under the expedited procedure, but that request was rejected (Case T-389/12 *EDF v Commission*).

[239] Acceptable Remedies Notice, para 73.

[240] Acceptable Remedies Notice, para 74.

could demonstrate that the market circumstances have changed significantly and on a permanent basis, and this normally several years after the adoption of the decision. The parties could also show that in light of the experience gained in the application of the commitments, the objectives pursued in the decision would be better served by modified commitments. Before taking a final position, the Commission will take into account the views of third parties[241] and the impact the modification may have on the position of third parties.[242]

17.121 In specific situations, the Commission has suggested that parties include a clause in the commitments allowing the Commission to trigger a limited modification to the commitments.[243] This may be appropriate where, at the time of the adoption of the decision, the Commission cannot foresee how the commitments would be implemented.

17.122 Procedurally, the Commission will usually adopt a formal decision for any waiver, modification, or substitution of commitments. However, the Acceptable Remedies Notice foresees that the Commission may simply take note of satisfactory amendments of the remedy by the parties, where such amendments improve the effectiveness of the remedy and result in legally binding obligations of the parties.[244] The Notice also clarifies that modifications of commitments are not foreseen to heal retroactively any breach of the commitments committed before the time of the modification. This means that the Commission remains free, where it deems appropriate, to pursue the parties for a breach under Articles 14 and/or 15 of the Merger Control Regulation.

7. Consequences of breach of the commitments

17.123 The Commission must ensure that the commitments offered by the parties are honoured and that they have the effect of making the operation compatible with the internal market. Commitments take the form of conditions and obligations which must be met by the undertakings.[245]

17.124 The consequences of a failure to comply by the undertakings concerned differ depending on whether the decision to authorize the operation is taken in the first or second phase and whether the infringement relates to conditions (eg the divestiture of an activity) or obligations arising from the decision (eg the appointment of a trustee).

Decisions adopted in the first phase

17.125 In the case of non-compliance with a condition, the Commission may:

- take appropriate provisional measures for the re-establishment or maintenance of effective competition conditions;[246] and/or

---

[241] In Case COMP/M.2876 *Newscorp/Telepiu* OJ C110/73, several third parties challenged the decision modifying the commitments and by which the Commission had authorized SKY to participate in the forthcoming tendering procedure for digital terrestrial television capacity (see Case T-501/10 *TI Media Broadcasting and TI Media v Commission* [2010] OJ C346/53 (rejected as partially devoid of purpose and partially inadmissible by order of 21 September 2012); Case T-504/10 *Prima TV v Commission* [2010] OJ C346/55 (later withdrawn, see Order of removal of 10 July 2012); and Case T-506/10 *RTI and Elettronica Industriale v Commission* [2010] OJ C346/56 (also withdrawn, see Order of removal of 10 July 2012), where the applicants claimed, *inter alia*, that the market circumstances on the basis of which the commitments were accepted in 2003 had neither changed significantly nor on a permanent basis when the Commission modified the commitments; as well as the fact that the Commission disregarded the serious concerns expressed during the market investigation preceding the adoption of the decision modifying the commitments).
[242] Case T-119/02 *Royal Philips Electronics v Commission* [2003] ECR II-1433, para 184.
[243] Acceptable Remedies Notice, para 75 and the reference to Case COMP/M.3868 *DONG/Elsam/Energi E2* [2006] OJ L133/24, para 24 of the Annex.
[244] Acceptable Remedies Notice, para 76.
[245] See the Merger Control Regulation, Recital 31. For a distinction between conditions and obligations, see paras 19–20 of the Acceptable Remedies Notice.
[246] Article 8(5)(b) of the Merger Control Regulation.

- adopt a decision (which may be to approve or prohibit the operation) but this shall not be subject to the time limit laid down in Article 10(1) of the Merger Control Regulation;[247] and/or
- decide to impose a fine of up to 10 per cent of the total turnover of the undertaking concerned.[248]

In the case of non-compliance with an obligation, the Commission may: **17.126**

- revoke the decision to authorize the operation;[249] and
- if revocation takes place, adopt a decision in the first phase—of approval or prohibition—subsequent to a new examination of the operation but this shall not be subject to the time limit laid down in Article 10(1) of the Merger Control Regulation for first phase decisions;[250] and/or
- by means of a decision, impose a fine of up to 10 per cent of the total turnover of the undertaking concerned; and/or
- impose a periodic penalty payment of up to 5 per cent of the average daily aggregate turnover of the undertakings for each working day of delay starting from the date laid down in the decision, in order that they comply with the obligation imposed in the first-phase authorization decision.[251]

Decisions adopted in the second phase

In the case of non-compliance with a condition, the Commission may: **17.127**

- demand, by means of a decision, that the concentration be dissolved, ie that the undertakings dissolve the concentration in such a manner that, by means of divestiture of acquired assets, the situation prior to the implementation of the concentration is re-established, or demand any other appropriate measure to guarantee the re-establishment of the prior situation;[252] and/or
- take appropriate provisional measures for the re-establishment or maintenance of effective competition conditions;[253] and
- adopt a decision (be it to approve or prohibit the operation) but without being subject to the time limit laid down in Article 10(3) of the Merger Control Regulation for the second phase;[254] and/or
- by means of a decision, impose a fine of up to 10 per cent of the total turnover of the undertaking concerned.

In the case of failure to comply with an obligation, the Commission may: **17.128**

- revoke the decision to authorize the operation;[255] and
- if revocation takes place, adopt a decision in the second phase but without being subject to the time limit laid down in Article 10(3); and/or
- by means of a decision, impose a fine of up to 10 per cent of the total turnover of the undertaking concerned and/or

---

[247] Article 8(7)(a)(i) of the Merger Control Regulation.
[248] Article 14(2)(d) of the Merger Control Regulation.
[249] Article 6(3) of the Merger Control Regulation.
[250] Article 6(4) of the Merger Control Regulation.
[251] Article 15(1)(c) of the Merger Control Regulation.
[252] Article 8(4)(b) of the Merger Control Regulation. This provision refers to the case that the compatibility of the concentration under Art 2(3) and (4) of the Merger Control Regulation depends on the fulfilment of the conditions attached to its authorization.
[253] Article 8(5)(b) of the Merger Control Regulation.
[254] Article 8(7) of the Merger Control Regulation.
[255] Article 8(6) of the Merger Control Regulation.

- impose a periodic penalty payment of up to 5 per cent of the average daily aggregate turnover of the undertakings for each working day of delay starting from the date laid down in the decision, in order that they comply with the obligation imposed in the second phase authorization decision.[256]

17.129 If a concentration is implemented and a condition has not been complied with (whether attached to a first- or second-phase decision), it is not necessary for the Commission to adopt a decision revoking the one which authorized the operation. It is considered that, having failed to comply with the condition, the situation which gave rise to the concentration being declared compatible with the internal market does not materialize. The concentration is therefore deemed to be 'non-notified' and implemented without authorization. Furthermore, Recital 31 of the Merger Control Regulation provides that if the Commission has concluded that, given the failure to comply with the condition in question, the concentration would be incompatible with the internal market, the Commission may order the dissolution of the concentration on the grounds of non-compliance. The Merger Control Regulation reserves the right to order the dissolution of the concentration to second-phase decisions, which, unlike the first phase, would probably be the only procedure where the Commission would have sufficient time to reach such a conclusion.

17.130 If a decision is revoked for reasons of non-compliance with an obligation, the Commission may subsequently adopt a new decision, but this shall not be subject to the usual time limits governing the first and second phases. The absence of time limits—something which is generally detrimental to the undertakings—would be justifiable, on the one hand, by the complexity of the relevant operation (shown by the fact that the undertakings have had to offer commitments) and also by a certain lack of trust on the Commission's part with respect to undertakings which have failed to comply with commitments that they themselves have given.

17.131 In the case of non-compliance with obligations, a combination of fines and periodic penalty payments can be imposed, and, at the same time, the undertakings can be ordered to adjust their behaviour so that they fulfill the commitment. The capacity to impose periodic penalty payments to obtain (belated) compliance following non-implementation is only possible with respect to the non-compliance of obligations. The imposition of periodic penalty payments implies that the decision approving the operation is not revoked, since the Commission is primarily interested in compliance with the commitments given.

17.132 Provisional measures for the re-establishment or maintenance of effective competition conditions are only possible in the case of non-compliance with conditions. In these cases, while revocation is not required, it may be necessary for reasons of legal certainty to adopt a decision whereby appropriate measures are taken for the re-establishment of effective competition.[257]

F. Investigative and Sanctioning Powers of the Commission

17.133 The Merger Control Regulation grants a number of prerogatives to the Commission for the purposes of carrying out investigations during the proceedings. These powers of investigation include the power to request information and the power to inspect the premises of undertakings. The Commission's investigative powers exist in both the first and second phases.

---

[256] Article 15(1)(c) of the Merger Control Regulation.
[257] Green Paper on the review of Reg 4064/89, para 223.

In general, the provisions in relation to investigative powers in the Merger Control Regulation **17.134** are similar to those in Regulation 1/2003 for the application of Articles 101 and 102 TFEU. These provisions are primarily related to requests for information and inspections carried out by the Commission. The remit of this part is limited to highlighting those matters that relate to concentrations, while Chapters 7 and 8 of this book offer a more detailed analysis of the relevant issues.

1. Requests for information

Article 11 of the Merger Control Regulation gives the Commission the right to request infor- **17.135** mation, in a broad sense of the word, from undertakings. This covers individuals, undertakings, or groups of undertakings, whether acquiring or acquirer, as well as other undertakings and business groups.[258] The Commission may exercise the powers conferred on it by Article 11 only to the extent that it considers that it is not in possession of all the information necessary to enable it to decide on the compatibility of the concentration concerned with the internal market.[259] The assessment of the necessity of the requested information must be made at the time the request is made and not whether it is actually needed in the subsequent procedure.[260] Similarly to requests under Regulation 1/2003, the request may be either a 'simple request for information' or a 'decision'. Unlike Regulation 1/2003, however, the Commission is not obliged to furnish the respective NCAs with a copy of all simple requests (Article 11(2)) and decisions (Article 11(3)) of this nature, unless there is a specific request from the NCA in question.[261]

Former Regulation 4064/89 had established a two-phase procedure whereby decisions to **17.136** request information could only be adopted if the undertakings failed to furnish requested information within the period stipulated in a simple request.[262] However, like Regulation 1/2003, the new Merger Control Regulation, from the very outset and at the discretion of the Commission, enables the adoption of a decision to request information without there being any prior need for a simple request.[263] Article 11(7) of the Merger Control Regulation has also incorporated the possibility for the Commission to obtain information by means of interviews with any natural or legal person that agrees to be interviewed for the purposes of obtaining information for the investigation, in parallel with Article 19 of Regulation 1/2003.

---

[258] When the Commission requires information from other market participants, it places particular importance on information furnished by clients and competitors with respect to the relevant market, the transaction under investigation and, where applicable, remedies offered.

[259] Case T-145/06 *Omya v Commission* [2009] ECR II-145, paras 28–34: 'In that connection, it must be recalled that, for the purposes of adopting a decision on a concentration, the Commission must examine, pursuant to Article 2 of Regulation No 139/2004, the effects of the concentration concerned on all the markets for which there is a risk that effective competition would be significantly impeded in the common market or in a substantial part of it.'

[260] Case T-145/06 *Omya v Commission* [2009] ECR II-145, para 30: 'that need is dependent on many factors and cannot therefore be determined with certainty at the time the request for information is made.'

[261] Article 11(5) of the Merger Control Regulation.

[262] Article 11(5) of Reg 4064/89 stated that 'where a person, undertaking or an association of undertakings does not provide the information requested within the period fixed by the Commission or provides incomplete information, the Commission shall by decision require the information to be provided'. That was in line with the procedural tools existing at the time for Arts 81 and 82 EC infringements under Art 11 of Reg 17 of 1962.

[263] This is the literal interpretation of the new rule. Although it can be inferred from reading Art 9(1) of the Implementing Regulation that decisions will be adopted if information is not furnished within the time limit established in a simple request, there is nothing to prevent the adoption of a decision even if non-compliance with a previously issued simple request has not occurred.

17.137 When sending a simple request for information the Commission shall state the legal basis and the purpose of the request, specify what information is required, and fix the time limit within which the information is to be provided,[264] as well as the penalties provided for in Article 14 for supplying incorrect or misleading information.[265] The Commission cannot be required to verify immediately and in detail the accuracy of all the information conveyed, since it is the parties that are best placed to ensure the information communicated is reliable.[266] Simple requests for information do not normally suspend calculation of the tight deadlines provided for in the Merger Control Regulation for the adoption of final decisions under the Regulation, including decisions on whether to refer concentration cases to the NCAs. By exception, however, Article 9 of the Implementing Regulation contemplates a suspension of these deadlines under the following circumstances:

- information sought by the Commission by means of a simple request to one of the notifying parties or another interested party[267] which has not been furnished within the period stipulated by the Commission or said information is incomplete; or
- information sought by the Commission by means of a simple request to a third party[268] that has not been furnished within the period stipulated by the Commission or said information is incomplete for reasons that can be attributed to one of the notifying parties or any other interested party.[269]

17.138 In the event of a suspension of time limits, this suspension operates between the elapsing of the period stipulated in the simple request for information or the decision and receipt of the correct and complete information.[270]

17.139 As concerns information requested through a formal decision, Article 9(2) of the Implementing Regulation provides that the time limits for final decisions, including referral decisions, will be suspended when the Commission, for reasons attributable to one of the undertakings participating in the concentration, has to take a decision to request information without proceeding first by way of a simple request.

2. Inspections

17.140 In general terms, the powers of the Commission concerning investigations are similar to those under Regulation 1/2003.[271] There is a marked exception, however: the Commission

---

[264] Case T-417/05 *Endesa v Commission* [2006] ECR II-2533, para 257. In this case, the GC validated a deadline of twenty-four hours set to reply to a request for information sent fifty days after the start of the proceedings, stating that the applicant did not ask for any extension of the deadline and was able to answer within the time limit set.

[265] See para 17.143.

[266] Case T-145/06 *Omya v Commission* [2009] ECR II-145, para 120.

[267] Article 9(1)(a) which refers to the interested parties of Art 11(2) of the Merger Control Regulation. The reference in this provision to 'other involved parties' would appear to encompass parties to the concentration other than the notifying parties, such as the seller or the undertaking which is the object of the concentration.

[268] Article 9(1)(b) which refers to 'third parties' in the sense of Art 11(c) of the Implementing Regulation, ie parties with the right to be heard in the proceedings apart from notifying parties and other interested parties such as clients, suppliers, and competitors, provided they show a sufficient interest.

[269] Article 9(1) of the Implementing Regulation.

[270] Article 9(3)(a) of the Implementing Regulation. Article 10(4) of the Merger Control Regulation provides for an exceptional indefinite suspension of time limits if, for circumstances that can be attributed to one of the undertakings participating in the concentration, the Commission is obliged to request information by means of a decision under Art 11 or order an inspection by means of a decision adopted under Art 13 of the Merger Control Regulation.

[271] See Ch 8, 'Investigation of Cases (III): Inspections'.

may not carry out inspections in the private residences of directors and persons related to the undertakings, unlike what is contemplated in Article 21 of Regulation 1/2003.[272]

Commission officials may verify books and other professional documents, irrespective of the **17.141** medium in which they may be stored; make or demand copies of books and professional documents in any format whatsoever; request any representative or member of staff to provide verbal explanations;[273] have access to any premises, land, or means of transport pertaining to the undertaking; and seal off[274] all premises and books belonging to the undertaking for the period necessary and to the degree necessary for the investigation to be carried out. The Commission may carry out an inspection through the use of a written authorization or by means of a decision. The two forms are alternatives, and the Commission has the discretion to choose what it considers to be the most appropriate method for a given case. The Commission can also request the competent authorities of the Member States to undertake inspections which it considers necessary; these officials shall conduct the inspections in accordance with their national law and may, upon the Commission's request, be assisted by Commission officials.[275]

Again, the time limits set out in the Merger Control Regulation to decide on the substance of **17.142** the matter or as regards referral cases under Article 9(4) may be affected by reasons attributable to the notifying parties or another interested party. In particular this is the case where any of these has refused to be the subject of a verification deemed necessary by the Commission, or has refused to cooperate with the Commission in accordance with the relevant provisions.[276] The period of suspension will span the period between the date of the failed attempt to carry out the verification and the date when the inspection, ordered by means of a decision, is deemed to have concluded.[277]

While requests for information are not infrequent in first and second phases, up to the pre- **17.143** sent date, inspections have only been used in exceptional cases under the Merger Control Regulation.[278]

3. Infringements and sanctions

Articles 14 and 15 of the Merger Control Regulation lay down two types of administrative **17.144** sanctions of a financial nature. The first—set out in Article 14—sanctions infringements that

---

[272] Former Competition Commissioner, Mario Monti, stated that certain powers were more necessary and appropriate for the discovery of cartels than for the enforcement of the Merger Control Regulation: 'For that reason, I remain unconvinced of the need and therefore, will not propose, that the Commission will be given the power to conduct home searches under the Merger Control Regulation'; Mario Monti, 'Roadmap for the reform project Conference on Reform of European Merger Control', Speech/02/252, 4 June 2002, British Chamber of Commerce review of the Merger Control Regulation, available on DGCOMP's website.

[273] Article 13(2)(e) of the Merger Control Regulation establishes that explanations must be limited to facts or documents related to the objective and purpose of the inspection.

[274] Recital (39) of the Merger Control Regulation limits the use of seals to exceptional circumstances and for the time that is strictly necessary for the inspection, which should normally not exceed forty-eight hours (contrast with the seventy-two hours referred to in Recital 25 of Reg 1/2003).

[275] Article 12 of the Merger Control Regulation.

[276] Article 9(1)(c) of the Implementing Regulation.

[277] Article 9(3)(b) of the Implementing Regulation.

[278] Article 10(4) of the Merger Control Regulation. See Case COMP/M.4734 *INEOS/Kerling* [2008] OJ C219/18, where the Commission suspected a possible early implementation of the concentration in breach of Art 7 of the Merger Control Regulation. The Commission did not find any evidence of the alleged violation (see (2008) 1 Competition Policy Newsletter 64). See also Case COMP/M.6106 *Caterpillar/MWM* [2011] OJ C60/5, where the Commission conducted investigations as it had suspicions that the notifying parties had (a) provided misleading information to the Commission in response to requests for information by the Commission, pursuant to Article 11 of Merger Control Regulation; (b) provided misleading information to the Commission in the notification; and (c) implemented the notified concentration before it had been cleared by the Commission in contravention of Art 7(1) of the Merger Control Regulation (para 14).

have already taken place, such as failure to notify prior to implementation, early implementation, implementation of a concentration that has been declared incompatible with the internal market, failure to comply with obligations and conditions imposed by the Commission, and conduct obstructing the investigation of the Commission. In these cases, a fixed fine is imposed. Article 15, in turn, allows periodic penalties aimed at forcing the undertakings to comply with obligations, such as responding to a request for information, agreeing to and cooperating with an inspection, and complying with the obligations imposed on the concentration. The periodic penalties vary according to the number of days undertakings take to comply.

17.145 The potentially most severe sanctions, reflecting the greater seriousness of the infringement,[279] are those laid down in Article 14(2) and can be as high as 10 per cent of the total turnover of the undertaking concerned.[280] This provision seems to have been drawn up along the lines of Article 23(2) of Regulation 1/2003. In setting the exact amounts of the fines, the Commission should take into account the nature, gravity, and duration of the infringement.[281]

17.146 Sanctions can be classified into three principal groups:

(i) procedural infringements, which are related to the investigation;
(ii) substantive infringements, which concern an improper implementation of the concentration; and
(iii) periodic penalty payments.

Sanctions for procedural infringements

17.147 The notifying parties must make known to the Commission, in a full and honest manner, the relevant facts and circumstances[282] for the adoption of a decision on the notified concentration.[283] The Commission places considerable importance on its duty to defend this essential principle in the exercise of its mission to monitor concentration operations with an EU dimension.[284] Failure to comply with this obligation, whether intentional

---

[279] See the GC Judgment of 12 December 2012 in Case T-332/09 *Electrabel v Commission*, paras 234–5, 246, and 280.

[280] This provision refers for the interpretation of the concept of 'undertaking concerned' to Art 5 of the Merger Control Regulation which, in conjunction with Art 3(1), should be understood to refer to the parties who merge or the acquirer or acquirers in their totality—the entire group of enterprises where relevant—and the acquired party—be it a group of undertakings, an undertaking or part of an undertaking—in the concentration (the GC Judgment of 12 December 2012 in Case T-332/09 *Electrabel v Commission*, paras 226 and 282). The concept of group refers to undertakings controlled as defined in Art 3 of the Merger Control Regulation; see Ch 16, 'General Issues: Scope of Control', para 16.97.

[281] Article 14(3) of the Merger Control Regulation. There is no Notice similar to the Guidelines on the method of setting fines imposed pursuant to Art 23(2)(a) of Reg 1/2003 [2006] OJ C210/2 (see the GC Judgment of 12 December 2012 in Case T-332/09 *Electrabel v Commission*, paras 227–8, 265, 272, and 299). See also for fines imposed for procedural infringements pursuant to Art 23(1)(e) of Reg 1/2003, for which the Commission has not adopted guidelines on fines either: for breach of seals during inspections (Case COMP/39.326 *E.On* [2008], confirmed by the GC in Case T-141/08 *E.On Energie v Commission* [2010] ECR II-5761, para 284, and on appeal by the ECJ in Case C-89/11 P *E.ON Energie v Commission* [2012]; Case COMP/39.796 *Suez* [2011]) and refusal to submit to an inspection (Case COMP/39.793 *EPH and others* [2012] on appeal Case T-272/12 *Energetický a průmyslový and EP Investment Advisors v Commission*). In its Art 14 decision in Case COMP/M.4994 *Electrabel/CNR*, the Commission explained that it had taken into account not only the nature, gravity, and duration of the infringement, but also any aggravating or mitigating circumstances (para 184).

[282] The Merger Control Regulation does not provide for a *de minimis* exception to its application, and therefore the fact that the turnover in a given market is not very significant cannot justify the exclusion of these activities from the notification form.

[283] Recital 5 and Art 4(1) of the Implementing Regulation.

[284] As stated in the Commission's Green Paper on the review of Reg 4064/89, Document COM (2001) 745/6 final, 11 December 2001, paras 197–202. See also with respect to the failure to notify and early implementation Commission Press Release IP/98/66 'Mergers: Commission fines Electrabel 20 million euros for

or negligent, will generate serious consequences. On the one hand, Article 14(1) of the Merger Control Regulation envisages a fine of up to 1 per cent of the total turnover of the relevant undertaking.[285] This fine will also apply if the parties furnish incorrect or misleading information[286] in response to a request for information, whether required through a simple request or by means of decision; in the latter case, the sanction will also be applicable if the information is incomplete or is not furnished within the period stipulated. Third parties to which the Commission has addressed a request for information may be sanctioned under these provisions as well.[287] On the other hand, Article 8(6)

---

acquiring control of Compagnie Nationale du Rhône without prior Commission approval' of 18 February 1998, in Case IV/M.920 *Samsung/AST* [1998] OJ L225/12; Commission Press Release IP/99/100 of 10 February 1999, in Case IV/M.969 *AP Møller* [1999]; and Commission Press Release IP/09/895 of 10 June 2009, in Case COMP/M.4994 *Electrabel/CNR* [2009] OJ L183/29, noting that Electrabel had the necessary knowledge and experience of the Merger Control Regulation to be aware of the rules. See also the GC Judgment of 12 December 2012 in Case T-332/09 *Electrabel v Commission*, paras 234 and 244–7.

[285] Article 14(1) of the Merger Control Regulation. Paragraph 225 of the Green Paper on the review of Reg 4064/89 referred to reviewing the calculation of fines as follows: 'It would be appropriate...to switch to a percentage-based calculation of fines for procedural rules (up to 1% of annual turnover). Moreover, it would be appropriate to add the violation of failing to comply with an obligation imposed by decision pursuant to Article 6(2) of the Merger Control Regulation to the list in Article 14(2)(a)...It would be appropriate...to switch to a percentage-based calculation of periodic penalty payments (up to 5% of average daily turnover). Again, it would be appropriate to add the violation of failing to comply with an obligation imposed by decision pursuant to Article 6(2) of the Merger Regulation to the list in Article 15(2)(a).'

[286] In December 1999, the Commission imposed a fine of EUR 50,000 on Deutsche Post for its notification in February 1999 of the proposed acquisition of a high-speed delivery service, trans-o-flex GmbH. Although Deutsche Post withdrew the notification in the second phase, the Commission held that Deutsche Post had deliberately given incorrect information in its notification and had subsequently failed to divulge information regarding a previous transaction (Case IV/M.1447 *Deutsche Post/trans-o-flex* OJ C38/6). Also in December 1999, the Commission imposed a fine on KLM (EUR 40,000), because KLM had furnished incorrect, incomplete, and misleading information. The Commission concluded that the conduct of KLM had been negligent, at the very least (Case IV/M.1608 *KLM/Martinair (III)* [1999] OJ L50/10). In announcing the decisions in both cases, former Competition Commissioner Mario Monti pointed out that an essential condition for the purposes of the application of competition rules was that the companies provided exact and complete information: '[t]hese decisions underline the Commission's determination to ensure that firms comply fully with their legal obligations. Firms which fail to do so—whether deliberately or through a failure to take proper care—should not expect to escape sanction in future.' Commission Press Release IP/99/985 'Commission fines Deutsche Post, KLM, Anheuser-Busch and Scottish & Newcastle for supplying incorrect or misleading information in competition procedures' of 14 December 1999. In Case COMP/M.1397 *Sanofi/Synthélabo* [2000] OJ C23/4, the Commission decided to impose a fine on the grounds of incorrect information furnished by the notifying parties. Following allegations made by third parties, the Commission reviewed the information provided by the notifying parties and revoked its initial authorization because it was based on incorrect information and manifestly incorrect statements. The Commission imposed the maximum fine at the time of EUR 50,000 and emphasized that the parties could not have ignored the monopolies enjoyed by each of them. Furthermore, the Commission considered that the fact that the initial notification had been declared incomplete should have drawn the attention of the parties and their representatives to the shortcomings in their preparatory work. Actually, the parties were given an additional period of eight days to check that their notification complied with the requirements of the Regulation. See also the decision adopted by the Commission on 7 July 2004 [2005] OJ L98/27 imposing a fine of EUR 90,000 against *Tetra Laval* for supplying misleading and incorrect information in the context of the *Tetra Laval/Sidel* notification (Case COMP/M.3255 *Tetra Laval/Sidel* [2004]). It is interesting to note that the Commission became aware of this failure in the context of the appeal brought by *Tetra Laval* against the Commission decision prohibiting that merger.

[287] The Commission fined Mitsubishi for providing incomplete information in response to a request for information under Art 11 of Reg 4064/89 with respect to the concentration in Case IV/M.1471 *Ahlstrom/Kvaerner* OJ C80/7, withdrawn. The Commission noted that it had been forced to estimate the market size for boilers and that the information was important in ensuring correct decisions. This is the first case of an undertaking being fined, with the exception of a notifying party, in merger control proceedings. Commission Press Release IP/00/764 'Commission fines Mitsubishi for failing to supply information on Kvaerner/Ahlström joint venture' of 12 July 2000.

(a) of the Regulation gives the Commission the power to revoke a decision which is based on incorrect information.[288]

17.148 The fines apply to the following cases, which represent obstacles to a Commission investigation:

- if the undertaking in question presents incomplete information in the context of an inspection;
- if it refuses to be made subject to an inspection required by decision;
- if it refuses to answer an oral question or answers it in an incomplete, incorrect or misleading manner;[289] or
- if it breaks the seals placed on the premises of the undertaking by agents of the Commission or their assistants.

Sanctions for substantive infringements

17.149 As mentioned, Article 14(2) of the Merger Control Regulation gives the Commission the power to impose fines of up to 10 per cent of the total turnover of the relevant undertaking. Infringements which may give rise to this sanction are the following, whether committed intentionally or negligently:[290]

- omission of the duty to notify prior to implementation;[291] or
- omission of the duty not to implement a concentration prior to notification and approval; or
- implementation of a concentration declared to be incompatible with the internal market; or
- failure to comply with measures imposed by the Commission in order to guarantee the dissolution of the concentration under the terms of Article 8(4) or appropriate provisional measures for the re-establishment or maintenance of effective competition conditions under the terms of Article 8(5); or
- failure to comply with conditions or obligations imposed on the undertakings with a view to making the concentration compatible with the internal market.[292]

17.150 When the Commission foresees the adoption of a decision under the terms of Article 14 or 15 of the Merger Control Regulation, before consulting the Advisory Committee on matters of concentration operations, it shall hear the undertakings on which it proposes to impose a fine or

---

[288] Case C-413/06 P *Bertelsmann and Sony Corporation of America v Commission* [2008] ECR I-4951, para 93.

[289] Article 14(1)(e), second para of the Merger Control Regulation provides that the person who has given incorrect or misleading information in response to requests for oral explanations can rectify the situation within the time period prescribed by the Commission for the purposes of avoiding a sanction.

[290] The GC Judgment of 12 December 2012 in Case T-332/09 *Electrabel v Commission*, para 237. The attempt to dissimulate the infringement could, however, possibly constitute an aggravating circumstance (para 277).

[291] Commission Decision of 5 October 1992 in Case IV/M.920 *Samsung/AST* [1999] OJ L225/12 para 29. The imposition of a fine included a (heavier) fine for the implementation of the operation without the authorization of the Commission. As mitigating factors, the Commission considered that omitting to notify did not have an impact on competition and that Samsung made its omission known to the Commission and cooperated during the proceeding. Commission decision of 10 February 1999 in Case IV/M.969 *AP Møller* OJ L183/29, para 12, where the Commission highlighted the importance of Arts 4(1) and 7(1) for the effectiveness of the Regulation. In spite of the imposition of modest fines the *Samsung/AST* and *AP Møller* decisions are not insignificant, since they indicate the determination of the Commission to use, when appropriate, the sanctioning powers it has under the Merger Control Regulation. Ten years later, still under Reg 4064/89, the Commission demonstrated its resolve by imposing a fine of EUR 20 million in Case COMP/M.4994 *Electrabel/CNR* [2009] OJ C126/3, despite the fact that the transaction was ultimately cleared unconditionally in the first phase. The GC upheld the decision and the fine, confirming that it constituted a serious infringement, which lasted a long duration (over three years) and that Electrabel had the necessary resources and experience with merger control law. The GC also rejected comparisons with the previous Commission decisions imposing modest fines on Samsung an AP *Møller*.

[292] As stated, the Acceptable Remedies Notice refers to the difference between conditions and obligations (paras 19–20).

a periodic penalty payment and will offer them the opportunity to verbally present their arguments in a formal hearing, if the undertakings have requested this in their written observations.[293]

Periodic penalty payments

Periodic penalty payments are aimed at obliging the undertakings to take certain action, **17.151** whether this be furnishing information or complying with an obligation. Their amount increases as time passes and the undertaking fails to take the action that has been required of it, and they end when compliance takes place. Article 15 of the Merger Control Regulation lays down that the Commission may impose periodic penalty payments of up to 5 per cent of the aggregate average turnover of the relevant undertakings or groups of undertakings concerned within the meaning of Article 5 for each working day of delay starting from the date stipulated in the decision, in order to oblige them to:

- supply in complete and correct form the information requested by Commission decision; or
- agree to an inspection ordered by Commission decision; or
- comply with an obligation imposed via decision or comply with measures ordered by a Commission decision adopted under Articles 8(4) (breach of the obligation not to implement unauthorized concentrations, or breach of the conditions for authorization) or 8(5) (interim measures).

Limitation periods

Unlike Regulation 1/2003 at Article 25, the Merger Control Regulation does not contain spe- **17.152** cific provisions regarding limitation periods for the imposition of penalties. The Commission has taken the view that Council Regulation (EEC) No 2988/74 of 26 November 1974 concerning limitation periods in proceedings and the enforcement of sanctions under the rules of the European Economic Community relating to transport and competition would apply to merger proceedings.[294] Article 1 of Regulation 2988/74 provides that the limitation period in proceedings is (i) three years in the case of infringements of provisions concerning applications or notifications of undertakings or associations of undertakings, requests for information, or the carrying out of investigations; and (ii) five years in the case of all other infringements.[295] Article 2 of that same Regulation 2988/74 provides that any action taken by the Commission for the purpose of the preliminary investigation or proceedings in respect of an infringement interrupts the limitation period in proceedings.[296]

Judicial review

The undertaking(s) fined may appeal to the GC by challenging the legality of the Commission's **17.153** decision by means of an action for annulment under Article 263 TFEU. The EU Courts also have unlimited jurisdiction under Article 262 TFEU to review both fines and periodic penalty payments, which means that they can annul, reduce, or increase them.[297]

---

[293] Articles 13(4) and 14(3) of the Implementing Regulation.

[294] OJ [1974] L319/1. See Commission Decision of 10 June 2009 in Case COMP/M.4994 *Electrabel/ CNR* OJ C126/3, paras 178 and 180.

[295] In the Judgment of 12 December 2012 in Case T-332/09 *Electrabel v Commission*, the GC held that the first category of infringements concerns those having a formal or procedural character and that the early implementation of a concentration is an infringement that does not enter into that category, as it is likely to produce substantial modifications of the competitive conditions (para 206, as well as paras 207–9). The GC further confirmed that the infringement of the obligation to suspend continues until the authorization of the concentration by the Commission or, where appropriate, an earlier date depending on the circumstances (para 212).

[296] See the GC Judgment of 12 December 2012 in Case T-332/09 *Electrabel v Commission*, para 214.

[297] Recital (43) and Art 16 of the Merger Control Regulation. See also the GC Judgment of 12 December 2012 in Case T-332/09 *Electrabel v Commission*, paras 221–2.

18

JUDICIAL REVIEW OF COMMISSION DECISIONS REGARDING CONCENTRATIONS

Marcos Araujo Boyd and Nicolas von Lingen

A. Introduction

The Courts of the EU have exclusive jurisdiction to control the legality of the decisions **18.01** adopted by the Commission in the field of concentrations.[1] Over the years, judicial review of these decisions has touched many aspects of the Commission's practice, raising questions as to where the balance of discretion of the Commission and intensity of the review should lie.[2] Independently of this debate, the important body of case law on the Merger Control Regulation must be hailed as a driving force that has been instrumental in the review and

---

[1] Articles 263 and 262 of the Treaty on the Functioning of the European Union ('TFEU') with respect to fines and periodic penalty payments. Under Arts 268 and 340(2) TFEU, the ECJ may also hear actions for damages arising from claims for non-contractual liability and in that context decide on the legality of decisions adopted under the Merger Control Regulation. Indirect legal review of these acts may also be available under Art 267 TFEU. Finally, the ECJ is competent to decide on actions for failure to act under Art 265 TFEU.

[2] In the *TetraLaval/Sidel* case, the Commission went as far as to appeal to the ECJ with the confessed intention of limiting the judicial review capacity of the General Court ('GC'). Commission Press Release IP/02/1952 'Commission appeals CFI ruling on Tetra Laval/Sidel to the European Court of Justice' of 20 December 2002. The appeal would ultimately be dismissed by the ECJ, Case C-12/03 P *Commission v Tetra*

improvement of the working methods of the Commission and has played a major instigating role in the reform process that the Directorate-General for Competition ('DG COMP') and the Merger Control Regulation[3] itself have undergone.

18.02 This chapter discusses some of the principles that can be extracted from the case law of the EU Courts regarding judicial review. The emphasis is placed on revision on matters of procedure, in line with the purpose of this publication.

B. Reviewable Acts

18.03 Articles 263 TFEU and 21(2) of the Merger Control Regulation provide for the direct review by the EU Courts of decisions adopted by the Commission under the Regulation. That principle is reiterated in respect of decisions imposing fines or periodic penalty payments by Article 16 of the Merger Control Regulation, where the courts enjoy unlimited jurisdiction pursuant to Article 262 TFEU. Other acts adopted by the Commission under the Merger Control Regulation may also be challenged before the EU Courts as discussed further in this chapter.

1. Form of the act not relevant

18.04 Article 263 TFEU provides that private persons may initiate actions for annulment as regards decisions addressed to the applicant or against a decision which, although in the form of a regulation or a decision addressed to another person, is of direct and individual concern to the former. According to the case law, the acts whose legal effects affect the interests of the applicants by bringing about a distinct change in their legal position may be challenged.[4] In principle, therefore, the form of such acts or decisions is irrelevant to the question of whether they can be reviewed under Article 263 TFEU.

18.05 *Dan Air*[5] is a good example of the judicial review of an informal decision of the Commission in the field of merger control. In this case, the General Court ('GC') accepted as admissible an annulment action brought by Air France against an oral statement made by the Competition Commissioner's spokesman, stating that the acquisition of Dan Air by British Airways was not notifiable under the Merger Control Regulation. The Court considered that the announcement had the same legal effects[6] as a formal decision, since it was not material that the decision took the unusual form of a verbal communication to the public at large.[7]

Laval [2005] ECR I-987. By contrast, in the *Sony/BMG* case, the ECJ quashed the judgment of the GC which had annulled the Commission's clearance decision and (re)stated some important principles concerning judicial review of merger decisions. See Case C-413/06 P *Bertelsmann and Sony Corporation of America v Commission* [2008] ECR I-4951.

   [3] Council Reg (EC) No 139/2004 of 20 January 2004 on the control of concentrations between undertakings [2004] OJ L24/1 (hereinafter 'Merger Control Regulation').

   [4] See Case 60/81 *IBM v Commission* [1981] ECR I-2639, para 9; Joined Cases C-68/94 and C-30/95 *France and others v Commission* [1998] ECR I-1375, para 62; Case T-87/96 *Assicurazioni Generali and Unicredito v Commission* [1999] ECR II-203, para 37; Joined Cases T-125/97 and T-127/97 *Coca-Cola Company v Commission* [2000] ECR II-1733, para 77 and Case T-57/07 *E.ON Ruhrgas and E.ON Földgáz Trade v Commission* [2009] ECR II-132, para 30.

   [5] Case T-3/93 *Air France v Commission* [1994] ECR II-121.

   [6] Case T-3/93 *Air France v Commission* [1994] ECR II-121, para 45.

   [7] A similar situation occurred in *Sogecable-Cablevisión*. Again, the challenged acts of the Commission were contained in certain letters and public declarations. Their content, however, was the exact opposite of that in *Dan Air*, since in the letters, the Commission affirmed its jurisdiction under former Reg 4064/89 regarding a concentration that had been notified to the Spanish competition authorities. In disagreement with the

However, in the *E.ON Ruhrgas and E.ON Földgáz Trade* case, a written expression of opinion by the European Commission was not regarded as capable of producing legal effects.[8]

2. Article 6 decisions

Article 6 of the Merger Control Regulation lists the different types of decisions that may be **18.06** adopted at the end of the first phase of the procedure. These are:

  (i) declarations that the Merger Control Regulation does not apply to a given transaction under Article 6(1)(a);
  (ii) clearance decisions at the end of the first phase under Article 6(1)(b), adopted either under the general or the simplified procedure;[9] and
  (iii) decisions to initiate second-phase proceedings under Article 6(1)(c).

There is no question that Article 6(1)(b) decisions are open to review, since these are final clearance decisions.[10] Whether or not the other two types of decision can be reviewed requires a closer look.

Article 6(1)(a) decisions are definitive acts of the Commission whose effect is the termination **18.07** of merger control procedures that open the door for potential action by the Commission or Member States under other competition rules. As already noted, in the *Dan Air* case, Air France challenged an informal declaration with a similar content (ie that the Commission was not competent to examine a transaction under the Merger Control Regulation). Subsequently, *Generali/Unicredito*[11] gave the GC an occasion to respond to that same question, albeit this time with respect to a formal Article 6(1)(a) decision. Not surprisingly, the Court affirmed that these decisions can be reviewed by the Courts. The Commission has, however, not adopted such a formal decision since 2002.[12]

The *Austrian Newspapers* case gave both EU Courts an occasion to review yet another case **18.08** involving letters from the Commission rejecting jurisdiction over a case.[13] On this occasion,

---

Commission over the issue of EU dimension, the parties appealed against the letters and declarations. The case was later withdrawn, but in the interim measures case, an order was rendered (Case T-52/96 R *Sogecable v Commission* [1994] ECR II-797). By contrast, in *Ryanair/Aer Lingus*, the Commission considered that it did not have the power to give a binding interpretation of Art 21 of the Merger Control Regulation regarding Ryanair's 25.17 per cent shareholding in Aer Lingus, as this provision was addressed to Member States, and that it was not in a position to act in response to Aer Lingus's request for an interpretation. While the admissibility of Aer Lingus's action for annulment against that response by the Commission was not contested, the application was dismissed. Case T-411/07 *Aer Lingus Group v Commission* [2010] ECR II-3691, paras 29 and 89–91.

  [8] Case T-57/07 *E.ON Ruhrgas and E.ON Földgáz Trade v Commission* [2009] ECR II-132, para 31, and case law quoted therein. In this case, the GC rejected as inadmissible a challenge against letters from DG COMP interpreting commitments provided by parties to a concentration. The GC held that neither the content nor the context in which they were adopted demonstrated that these letters were acts producing binding legal effects. The Commission would need to adopt a further decision to modify the parties' obligations flowing from the clearance decision.

  [9] Order in Case T-315/10 *Groupe Partouche v Commission* [2012] OJ C80/18 was the first case in which an Art 6(1)(b) decision adopted following the simplified procedure was challenged before the EU Courts. However, the GC did not have to decide on the substance of the case, given that the application was held inadmissible for failure to comply with Art 44(1)(c) of the GC's Rules of Procedure.

  [10] In Case T-151/06 *NVV and Others v Commission* [2009] ECR II-1219, the GC clarified that the correct legal basis for a challenge of a clearance decision in Phase I is Art 6 of the Merger Control Regulation and not Art 8 of the Merger Control Regulation (paras 65–8).

  [11] Case T-87/96 *Assicurazioni Generali SpA and Unicredito SpA v Commission* [1999] ECR II-203.

  [12] Case COMP/M.3003 *Electrabel/Energia Italiana/Interpower* [2002] OJ C25/2.

  [13] Case T-3/02 *Schlüsselverlag JS Moser GmbH et al v Commission* [2002] ECR II-1473. On appeal, Case C-170/02 P [2003] ECR I-9889. See also Case T-417/05 *Endesa v Commission* [2006] ECR II-2533.

the proposed concentration had been notified to and authorized by the relevant national competition authorities ('NCAs'), but the applicant argued that it had a Community dimension and filed a complaint to that effect. The Commission disagreed. Instead of challenging that decision, the applicants requested the Commission to act under Article 232 EC (now 265 TFEU) and subsequently brought an action for failure to act.

18.09 The GC rejected the application as inadmissible. Applying *Dan Air*, it held that the Commission had indeed acted through a decision, which the applicants could have challenged under Article 230 EC (now 263 TFEU). Interestingly, the Court of Justice ('ECJ') took a slightly different view on appeal. In its judgment, it avoided examining whether the letters in issue amounted to 'decisions', and instead found against the applicants on the basis of the lateness of their request to the Commission.[14]

18.10 In contrast, Article 6(1)(c) decisions, which result in the opening of the second phase of the examination of mergers, are not open to challenge before the Courts. This was decided in the *Schneider Electric* case both by the GC and the ECJ, which declared that these are acts of a preparatory nature within the meaning of the *IBM* doctrine[15] and therefore not open for review.[16] The GC held that it is simply a preparatory step whose sole aim is to undertake enquiries intended to identify the matters which will allow the Commission to rule, by means of a final decision at the end of that procedure, on the compatibility of the transaction with the internal market. While it involves extending the suspension of the transaction and the notifying party's obligation to cooperate with the Commission, these consequences derive directly from the Merger Control Regulation and are the ordinary effects of any procedural step; they do not therefore affect the party's legal position.[17]

3. Decisions imposing sanctions under the Merger Control Regulation

18.11 Article 16 of the Merger Control Regulation expressly provides that Commission decisions imposing sanctions on undertakings are open for review by the EU Courts. In Case T-29/00 *Deutsche Post AG v Commission*, the notifying party lodged an action for the annulment of the Commission Decision in Case IV/M.1610 *Deutsche Post/trans-o-flex*, imposing a fine for the supply of incorrect and misleading information under Article 14 of Regulation 4064/89, but the case was later withdrawn.[18]

18.12 Some years later, in 2009, Electrabel challenged the Commission decision to impose a fine for the implementation of the acquisition of CNR in violation of Article 7(1) of Regulation 4064/89 before the GC, who confirmed the validity of the Commission's decision.[19] The decision of the GC was appealed to the ECJ.[20]

---

[14] The ECJ also took the opportunity to firmly reject the Commission's argument that it was under no duty to take a position on requests by complainants to decide the applicability of the Merger Control Regulation to given cases. See paras 26–30. In the immediate aftermath of the prohibition decision in the *Ryanair/Aer Lingus* case, Aer Lingus requested the Commission to initiate proceedings under Art 8(4) and (5) of the Merger Control Regulation to order Ryanair to divest its shareholding of 25.17 per cent in Aer Lingus. The Commission's reply that it did not have the powers to do so was—unsuccessfully—challenged in an action for annulment under Art 263 TFEU (Case T-411/07 *Aer Lingus Group v Commission* [2010] ECR II-3691).

[15] See Case 60/81 *IBM v Commission* [1981] ECR 2639, paras 10–12.

[16] Case T-48/03 *Schneider Electric v Commission* [2006] ECR II-111, paras 79–84, upheld on appeal in Case C-188/06 P *Schneider Electric v Commission* [2007] ECR I-35, paras 34–5 and 67–73. See also Case T-279/04 *Éditions Odile Jacob v Commission* [2010] ECR II-185, paras 89–92.

[17] Case T-48/03 *Schneider Electric v Commission* [2006] ECR II-111, para 81, and on appeal Case C-188/06 P *Schneider Electric v Commission* [2007] ECR I-35, para 34.

[18] [2000] OJ C135/14 and [2001] OJ C161/26.

[19] Judgment of 12 December 2012 in Case T-332/09 *Electrabel v Commission*.

[20] Case C-84/13 P *Electrabel v Commission* [2013] OJ C32/15.

4. Referral decisions

Article 9 of the Merger Control Regulation, which deals with referral decisions, only **18.13** expressly provides for judicial review by the EU Courts upon application by Member States.[21] However, in *Philips Electronics*,[22] the GC rejected the objection of inadmissibility put forward by the Commission and declared that the act produced legal effects on the applicant's legal situation, since it had the effect of excluding the application of the Merger Control Regulation to the part of the concentration which had been referred and made that part of the concentration subject to exclusive review by the NCAs under their national competition law. As a result, the partial referral altered the criteria for the assessment of the lawfulness of the concentration, as well as the procedure and possible sanctions applicable to it. The applicant would therefore be deprived of the opportunity to have the Commission review the lawfulness of the concentration from the point of view of the Merger Control Regulation.[23]

This principle was later confirmed by the GC in the context of a full referral to a national **18.14** authority in *Cableuropa*.[24] This time the Court developed the argument further, stressing that the review of a concentration under the laws of a Member State cannot be considered, as regards its scope and effects, to be comparable with that carried out by the Commission under the Merger Control Regulation. Therefore, contrary to what the Commission had argued, referral decisions were capable of producing legally binding effects. The outcome of the transactions considered in both *Philips Electronics* and *Cableuropa* would later show that the referral of a merger might have a crucial impact on the chances of securing approval.

More recently, the refusal of the Commission to refer a case was challenged directly by a **18.15** NCA.[25] In the *Crédit Agricole/Cassa di Risparmio della Spezia/Agenzie Intesa Sanpaolo* case, the Italian competition authority contested, *inter alia*, the market definition retained by the Commission, arguing that a provincial banking services market existed and that this market did not form a substantive part of the internal market, and that the Commission therefore violated Article 9(2)(b) of the Merger Control Regulation.[26] The refusal to refer a case was also the subject of the *Association Belge des Consommateurs Test-Achats*[27] case, in which a consumer association was seeking the annulment of the Commission's conditional clearance decision in the *EDF/Segebel* case,[28] declaring the proposed concentration compatible with the internal market, and of the decision of the same day rejecting the request made by the Belgian authorities to refer the case in part to them.[29]

---

[21] Article 9(9) of the Merger Control Regulation.

[22] Case T-119/02 *Royal Philips Electronics v Commission* [2003] ECR II-1433, para 280.

[23] Case T-119/02 *Royal Philips Electronics v Commission* [2003] ECR II-1433, para 282. See also, by analogy, Case T-87/96 *Assicurazioni Generali and Unicredito v Commission* [1999] ECR II-203, paras 37–44.

[24] Joined Cases T-346/02 and T-347/02 *Cableuropa and others v Commission* [2003] ECR II-4251.

[25] Case T-45/11 *Italy v Commission* [2011] OJ C80/30, concerning Case COMP/M.5960 *Crédit Agricole/ Cassa di Risparmio della Spezia/Agenzie Intesa Sanpaolo* [2010] OJ C96/4. Later withdrawn (Order of 27 May 2013).

[26] See Ch 16, 'General Issues: Scope of Control', para 16.54.

[27] Judgment of 12 October 2011 in Case T-224/10 *Association Belge des Consommateurs Test-Achats v Commission*, paras 74–85.

[28] Case COMP/M.5549 *EDF/Segebel* [2009] OJ C59/7.

[29] Order of 20 January 2012 in Case T-315/10 *Groupe Partouche v Commission* [2012] OJ C80/18, a competitor of the notifying parties was challenging the refusal of the Commission to refer the concentration to the French competition authority, which had not even requested said referral under Art 9 of the Merger Control Regulation (paras 23 and 34).

5. Article 8 decisions

18.16 Clearance (whether conditional[30] or unconditional[31]) and prohibition[32] decisions under Article 8 of the Merger Control Regulation are reviewable acts and as such have been challenged on various occasions by the notifying parties. The discussion has, however, emerged concerning appeals brought by persons other than addressees of the decisions of the Commission. That is a *locus standi* issue and is therefore discussed in Section C of this chapter.

18.17 There may, however, be aspects within a decision that may not be capable of producing legal effects; the question would therefore arise as to whether those elements may be challenged. This is what happened in *Coca-Cola*,[33] where the GC did not allow *Coca-Cola* to challenge a finding of dominance in a decision unconditionally clearing the company's acquisition of its UK bottler. The Court held that none of the contested findings had any influence on the conclusions reached by the Commission in the operative part of the decision. As regards the concern that the contested findings might prejudice Coca-Cola in future cases, it held that any such findings did not constitute a legally binding precedent, either for the Commission or for national authorities and courts.

18.18 Acts amending final decisions by the Commission should be open to challenge in the same manner as the original decision. That was the situation in *Lagardère-Canal Plus*.[34] In this case the Commission argued that the amendment did not produce legal effects and therefore the challenge should not be admitted. The Commission relied particularly on the fact that the operative part of the decision had not been amended. The GC, however, affirmed that the measure in question, affecting the treatment of ancillary restrictions, would produce significant effects in the legal sphere of the applicant.

18.19 A divestiture decision pursuant to Article 8(4) of the Merger Control Regulation may also be challenged by the company to whom it is addressed. This may normally be the case where the notifying party also seeks to have a prohibition decision annulled. In this case, the illegality of the prohibition decision leads to the illegality of the divestiture decision and therefore to the latter's annulment.[35] A refusal to adopt an act under Article 8(4) or 8(5) of the Merger Control Regulation has also been challenged, with no success to date.[36]

---

[30] See Case T-282/02 *Cementbouw Handel & Industrie v Commission* [2006] ECR II-319. See also Case T-275/06 *Omya v Commission* ([2006] OJ C294/59), later withdrawn (see Order of the GC of 4 November 2008 [2008] OJ C80/18); Case T-60/12 *Western Digital and Western Digital Ireland v Commission* [2012] OJ C98/26, later withdrawn (see Order of the GC of 20 September 2012, OJ 355/38).

[31] See eg Case T-464/04 *Impala v Commission* [2006] ECR II-2289; Case T-292/10 *Monty Program v Commission* [2010] OJ C260/15, concerning an application for the annulment of the Commission's decision of 28 August 2009 in Case COMP/M.5529 *Oracle/Sun Microsystems*.

[32] See Case T-342/99 *Airtours v Commission* [2002] ECR II-2585; Case T-310/01 *Schneider Electric SA v Commission* [2002] ECR II-4071; Case T-5/02 *Tetra Laval v Commission* [2002] ECR II-4381; and Case T-310/00 *MCI v Commission* ECR II-3253; Case T-87/05 *EDP v Commission* [2005] ECR II-3745; Case T-209/01 *Honeywell v Commission* [2005] ECR II-5527; Case T-210/01 *General Electric v Commission* [2005] ECR II-5575; Case T-342/07 *Ryanair Holdings v Commission* [2010] ECR II-3457; Case T-202/11 *Aeroporia Aigaiou Aeroporiki and Marfin Investment Group Symmetochon v Commission* ([2011] OJ C160/25); Case T-175/12 *Deutsche Börse v Commission* ([2012] OJ C174/25); Case T-194/13 *United Parcel Service v Commission*; Case T-260/13 *Ryanair Holdings v Commission*.

[33] See Joined Cases T-125/97 and T-127/97 *Coca-Cola Company v Commission* [2000] ECR II-1733. See also Order of 21 September 2012 in Case T-501/10 *TI Media Broadcasting and TI Media v Commission*, para 56 et seq.

[34] Case T-251/00 *Lagardère and Canal+ v Commission* [2002] ECR II-4825, para 110.

[35] This is precisely what occurred in Case T-77/02 *Schneider Electric v Commission* [2002] ECR II-4201, paras 39–46; and in Case T-80/02 *Tetra Laval v Commission* [2002] ECR II-4825, paras 36–43.

[36] See Case T-411/07 R *Aer Lingus v Commission* [2008] ECR II-411 and Case T-411/07 *Aer Lingus Group v Commission* [2010] ECR II-3691, regarding minority shareholding not conferring control, and Case

6. Acts adopted in the implementation of merger clearance decisions

Conditional clearance decisions frequently require the Commission to take various initiatives **18.20** after the decision itself. There is a great variety of such initiatives, especially with regard to the management of the divestiture process. Some of these actions may give rise to reviewable acts.[37]

One example of such reviewable acts is found in *Petrolessence*,[38] concerning the implemen- **18.21** tation of certain conditions for the approval of the *TotalFina/Elf* concentration.[39] In that case, the compatibility of a concentration with the internal market was conditional upon the execution of commitments consisting in divesting assets to third parties, provided that such third parties had the ability to compete effectively on the relevant market.[40] Through a subsequent decision addressed to TotalFina Elf, the Commission indicated that the transfer of service stations to Petrolessence and Société de Gestion de Restauration Routière did not allow the continuation and development of effective competition, and therefore did not meet the conditions contained in the commitments. The said undertakings brought an action for annulment against that decision addressed to TotalFina Elf before the GC. In marked contrast to the doubts expressed by the Commission, the GC stated that 'it follows that the contested decision constitutes a refusal by the Commission to approve the applicants' candidacy, thus bringing about a significant change in their legal position'.[41] The GC also emphasized the definitive nature of the decision, since the rejection of the claimants as proposed acquirers did not require the Commission to take any further act and would automatically take effect if TotalFina Elf did not submit any observations,[42] as well as the fact that the claimants were excluded from the subsequent commercial negotiations that TotalFina Elf held at the time.[43]

Similarly, in the context of the *Lagardère/Natexis/VUP* case, a competitor successfully chal- **18.22** lenged before the GC the Commission's decision approving Wendel as a purchaser of the assets which formed part of the divestiture commitment. The GC held that the divestiture trustee was not independent from Editis (the assets to be divested), and that since the trustee's report had exercised a decisive influence on the Commission's assessment, the absence of independence vitiated the legality of the buyer approval decision.[44] This judgment was appealed by the Commission and by Lagardère, as the seller of the divested assets. While the Advocate-General ('AG') had suggested that the ECJ quash the judgment and reject the application at first instance, the ECJ upheld the GC's judgment. The ECJ held that, given that the GC correctly found that the trustee was not independent of the parties (as required under the commitments), it was under no obligation to examine whether that trustee actually acted in a way which was evidence of that lack of independence.[45] The second decision

---

T-279/04 *Editions Odile Jacob v Commission* [2010] ECR II-185, paras 191–5, regarding portage under Art 3(5)(a) of Reg 4064/89 (Art 3(5)(a) of the Merger Control Regulation) (and on appeal in Judgment of 6 November 2012 in Case C-551/10 P *Éditions Odile Jacob v Commission*, paras 33–42).

[37] The GC held, however, that a letter of the Commission's services providing their own provisional and non-binding interpretation of the commitments does not constitute a challengeable act: Case T-57/07 *E.ON Ruhrgas and E.ON Földgáz Trade v Commission* [2009] ECR II-132.

[38] Case T-342/00 *Petrolessence and SG2R v Commission* [2003] ECR II-1161.

[39] Case COMP/M.1628 *TotalFina/Elf* [2000] OJ L143/1.

[40] The case involved divesting seventy service stations owned by Elf, Total, and Fina located along French motorways.

[41] Case T-342/00 *Petrolessence and SG2R v Commission* [2003] ECR II-1161, para 38.

[42] Case T-342/00 *Petrolessence and SG2R v Commission* [2003] ECR II-1161, para 39.

[43] Case T-342/00 *Petrolessence and SG2R v Commission* [2003] ECR II-1161, para 41.

[44] Case T-452/04 *Odile Jacob v Commission* [2010] ECR II-4713, paras 83–119.

[45] Judgment of 6 November 2012 in Joined Cases C-553/10 P and C-554/10 P *Commission and Lagardère v Éditions Odile Jacob*, paras 37–53.

approving Wendel as a buyer of Editis adopted by the Commission following the annulment of the first decision was also appealed by Odile Jacob.[46]

18.23 The Commission's decision to accept a modification to the commitments submitted in the context of the *Newscorp/Telepiù* merger gave rise to three separate actions for annulment by third parties.[47] Two years later, in the *EDF/Segebel* case, EDF challenged the Commission's decision to refuse to grant it a postponement of the deadline to fulfill some of its commitments.[48] Even more recently, Aer Lingus appealed the Commission's decision evaluating bids for take-off and landing slots at Heathrow Airport that IAG was required to divest under the commitments in the *IAG/BMI* case,[49] and ranking the bid submitted by Virgin above the bid submitted by Aer Lingus for the London to Edinburgh route.[50]

7. Article 21 decisions

18.24 Decisions adopted by the Commission pursuant to Article 21(4) of the Merger Control Regulation may be challenged by the Member States to which they are addressed.[51] However, the decision by the Commission to close proceedings opened pursuant to Article 21(4) of the Merger Control Regulation against a Member State is not a challengeable act under Article 263 TFEU by third parties, including parties to the transaction affected by the measures taken.[52] The same holds true for the decision by the Commission not to bring infringement proceedings under Article 258 TFEU despite having addressed an Article 21(4) decision.[53]

8. Investigatory measures (Article 11 and Article 13 decisions)

18.25 Although not expressly mentioned in the Merger Control Regulation, other procedural decisions relating to investigatory measures such as formal requests for information under Article 11 of the Merger Control Regulation and decisions ordering investigations under Article 13 should also be challengeable along similar lines to the equivalent procedural decisions under Regulation 1/2003, which are discussed elsewhere in the book. For instance, in *Omya*, the notifying party challenged a request for information adopted pursuant to Article 11(3) of the Merger Control Regulation, in which the Commission had asked the parties to submit complete and correct information and had suspended the Phase II review of the merger until receipt of that information.[54]

---

[46] Case T-471/11 *Éditions Odile Jacob v Commission* [2011] OJ C305/9.

[47] Case T-501/10 *TI Media Broadcasting and TI Media v Commission* [2010] OJ C346/53, rejected by Order of 21 September 2012, OJ C355/26; Case T-504/10 *Prima TV v Commission* [2010] OJ C346/55, later withdrawn, see Order of 10 July 2012, OJ C273/23; Case T-506/10 *RTI and Elettronica Industriale v Commission* [2010] OJ C346/56, case closed on 10 July 2012, OJ C273/23.

[48] Case T-389/12 *Electricité de France v Commission* [2012] OJ C331/29.

[49] Case COMP/M.6447 *IAG/BMI* [2012] OJ C161/2.

[50] Case T-101/13 *Aer Lingus v Commission* [2013] OJ C101/31.

[51] Case C-42/01 *Portugal v Commission* [2004] ECR I-6079; Case T-65/08 R *Spain v Commission* [2008] ECR II-69.

[52] Case T-58/09 *Schemaventoto v Commission* [2010] ECR II-3863. A similar plea of inadmissibility was also raised in Case T-200/09 *Abertis Infraestructuras v Commission* [2010] ECR II-85, paras 33 and 65, but the GC dismissed the application for annulment as already inadmissible on the ground that it had been lodged out of time, ie nine months after Abertis had acquired knowledge of the Commission's decision to close proceedings.

[53] See, to that effect, Case T-443/03 *Retecal and Others v Commission* [2005] ECR II-1803, paras 41 and 43.

[54] Case T-145/06 *Omya v Commission* [2009] ECR II-145.

C. *Locus Standi*

Article 263 TFEU differentiates between two categories of applicants. First, there are 'privileged' **18.26**
applicants, namely Member States, the Commission, the Council, the European Parliament, as
well as, for the purpose of protecting their prerogatives, the Court of Auditors, the European
Central Bank, and the Committee of the Regions. These institutions may bring an annulment
action without having to show any special interest. With the exception of Article 21 cases,[55]
claims for judicial review concerning the control of concentrations are normally brought by
non-privileged plaintiffs. There are, however, some cases where Member States have intervened
in respect of other Merger Control Regulation decisions.[56]

As regards non-privileged applicants, Article 263 TFEU provides that any individual or under- **18.27**
taking can bring an action for judicial review against a decision which is addressed to them,
and also against decisions which, although in the form of a regulation or a decision addressed
to another person, affect them directly and individually. Besides direct and individual effect,
non-privileged applicants will also have to show an interest in bringing the proceedings.

1. The notifying party

In general, the party notifying a concentration will be the person, or one of the persons, to which **18.28**
the decision is addressed. Under Article 263, fourth paragraph TFEU, the addressees of a decision have *locus standi* to initiate an annulment action in the EU Courts. In these cases, the direct
and individual interest is obvious and there is therefore no need for it to be established.

The notifying party may, however, not be the addressee of the various acts capable of being **18.29**
reviewed, such as referral decisions. In such cases, its position will be the same as that of a
third party.

2. Competitors having actively participated in the procedure

Third parties in the sense of those that are not addressees of decisions may, in certain circum- **18.30**
stances, bring actions for the review of such decisions. The current criterion is based on the
rule laid down in *Plaumann*,[57] where the ECJ imposed on the claimants a very high standard,
based on the definition of 'individual concern'.[58]

---

[55] See para 18.24.

[56] Case C-68/94 *France and Société commerciale des potasses et de l'azote v Commission* [1998] ECR I-1375;
Case C-42/01 *Portugal v Commission* [2004] ECR I-6079. In addition to these instances of direct action,
Member States have occasionally intervened in support of undertakings, eg, in Case T-177/04 *easyJet v
Commission* [2006] ECR II-1913 (France); Case T-48/04 *Qualcomm v Commission* [2009] ECR II-2029
(Germany); and Case T-162/10 *Niki Luftfahrt v Commission* [2010] (Austria asked to intervene in addition
to the acquirer and the seller).

[57] Case 25/62 *Plaumann v Commission* [1963] ECR 95, para 107, confirmed in Case C-50/00 P *Unión de
Pequeños Agricultores v Council* [2002] ECR I-6677, para 36. See also Judgment of 12 October 2011 in Case
T-224/10 *Association Test Achats*, paras 32–7 and 65–7, in relation to the Charter and the right to effective
judicial protection.

[58] Establishing that an undertaking is 'individually concerned': 'if that decision affects them by reason of
certain attributes which are peculiar to them or by reason of the circumstances in which they are differentiated from all other persons and by virtue of these factors distinguishes them individually just as in the case
of the person addressed'. This standard has been seen as a barrier preventing EU citizens from having access
to justice, and various Advocates-General and the GC have tried to lower it. See eg Opinion of AG Jacobs in
Unión de Pequeños Agricultores (UPA), establishing a more straightforward test granting *locus standi* to third
parties whose interests are substantially prejudiced by the decision, but the ECJ has not accepted these invitations to change course (Case C-50/00 P *Unión de Pequeños Agricultores v Council* [2002] ECR I-6677; Case
C-263/02 P *Commission v Jego Quéré* [2004] ECR I-3425).

18.31 The standard of individual concern in merger cases is applied in a more flexible manner than in other areas. In particular, Courts usually give significant weight to the participation of the applicant in the procedure leading to the decision,[59] in particular once the formal investigation procedure is on-going following receipt of the notification by the Commission.[60] Depending on the circumstances of each case, third parties may be directly and individually concerned by a decision on the Commission's competence,[61] by a decision on the compatibility of a merger with the internal market and the commitments eventually imposed,[62] or with a decision by the Commission to refer a concentration under Article 9 of the Merger Control Regulation.[63]

18.32 Besides participation in the procedure, the Courts have given weight to the general principle that any competitor will be affected by the decision in question. Thus, in *TAT*,[64] the GC found that an individual concern of Air France existed not only because of that company's participation in the procedure through the submission of observations throughout (submissions which had been taken into account by the Commission), but also because Air France was BA's main competitor in the two markets identified in the concentration[65] and it had been obliged to divest in full its stake in TAT four months prior to the notification.

18.33 These principles were developed by the GC in *Babyliss*,[66] a case where doubts as to whether the claimant was even a competitor were raised. In this case, the Court began by recalling that mere participation in the administrative procedure is in itself not sufficient to show that the decision is of individual concern to the applicant. After examining the case law in competition matters, including the more specific area of the control of concentrations, the Court concluded that participation in the administrative procedure is a factor regularly taken into account when establishing, in conjunction with other specific circumstances, the *locus*

---

[59] The importance of participating in the procedure was made clear in the first sentence of Case T-3/93 *Air France v Commission* [1994] ECR II-121, where the possibility of acting in the proceedings in the event that the Commission had already initiated them was stated by the GC as one of the elements on which it would base a finding that an applicant had *locus standi*. See the references to the third party taking an 'active part in the administrative procedure' in Case T-177/04 *easyJet v Commission* [2006] ECR II-1913, paras 35 and 36, and Case T-151/06 *NVV and Others v Commission* [2009] ECR II-1219, para 44.

[60] See Judgment of 12 October 2011 in Case T-224/10 *Association Belge des Consommateurs Test-Achats v Commission*. In that case, a consumer association had sent comments to the Commission prior to the formal notification, but not when the Commission had elicited the views of third parties through publication of the notified concentration in the Official Journal of the European Union ('OJ').

[61] Case T-3/93 *Air France v Commission* [1994] ECR II-121, paras 79–82.

[62] Joined Cases C-68/94 and C-30/95 *France and Others v Commission* (*Kali and Salz*) [1998] ECR I-1375, paras 38–59.

[63] See eg Case T-119/02 *Royal Philips Electronics v Commission* [2003] ECR II-1433. By contrast, a third party is not entitled to challenge a decision by the Commission not to refer a concentration following a request by a Member State (Judgment of 12 October 2011 in Case T-224/10 *Association Belge des Consommateurs Test-Achats v Commission*, paras 74–85).

[64] Case T-2/93 *Air France v Commission* [1994] ECR II-323, paras 44–7.

[65] In the same sense, Case T-3/93 *Air France v Commission* [1994] ECR II-121, paras 80 and 81. Case T-119/02 *Royal Philips Electronics v Commission* [2003] ECR II-1433, para 292. 'The parties agree that the applicant is one of the principal current competitors of the parties to the concentration on the relevant markets. In recital 32 of the Approval Decision, the applicant is thus mentioned as one of the operators which, like SEB, Moulinex, Bosch, Braun and De'Longhi, offer a wide range of products in the small electrical household appliances sector and have a pan-European presence.' Case T-177/04 *easyJet v Commission* [2006] ECR II-1913, para 37: the applicant was one of Air France's main competitors in France on various—but not all—direct routes and one of KLM's main competitors on other direct routes. Moreover, the GC noted that easyJet competed on one of the markets on which both parties to the merger operate.

[66] In Case T-114/02 *BaByliss v Commission* [2003] ECR II-1279, the GC examined whether the Commission's decision to clear the concentration between *SEB* and *Moulinex* was open to challenge by *Babyliss*, a third party that had taken part in the Commission's procedure.

standi of the applicant.[67] As regards the applicant's status as a competitor, the GC stated that although the applicant's market presence was limited to only one of the markets in which SEB was active at the date of adoption of the contested decision, Babyliss should be regarded as at least a potential competitor.[68] That was judged sufficient to grant *locus standi*.

This definition was further broadened in *ARD v Commission*.[69] In this case, the GC consid- **18.34** ered that the fact that the applicant was not a competitor or even a potential competitor of KirchPayTV on the pay-TV market did not necessarily mean that it was not individually concerned by the decision. The GC considered that an action brought by an operator present only in the neighbouring upstream or downstream markets may be admissible under certain circumstances. The GC based its decision on five main arguments:

(i) the existence of some level of competition between free television and pay-TV;
(ii) the future convergence between free television and pay-TV due to digitalization;
(iii) the effect of the merger on digital interactive television services;
(iv) the applicant's participation in the FUN project;[70] and
(v) the acquisition of broadcasting rights.[71]

3. Customers

The standing of customers of the merging parties to bring an action against a clearance **18.35** decision was accepted in *Verband der freihen Rohrwerke* in respect of its purchaser (and competitor) Ferndorf[72] and later in *Sun Chemical*.[73] In this latter case, the Commission did not discuss the admissibility of the appeal brought by Sun Chemical, a customer that had actively participated in the procedure, but of the other two applicants, Siegwerk and Flint. The Commission particularly argued that their participation in the administrative procedure had been limited to submitting a reply to the Commission's customer questionnaire, that their replies were terse and general, and that they had failed to explain how they could be differentiated from other customers of the merging parties. In its judgment, the GC held that for reasons of economy of procedure, there was no need to consider the inadmissibility claim, since they had filed one single application together with Sun Chemical's whose admissibility was not disputed.[74] In any event, this case serves as a reminder of the importance of active participation in the procedure for these purposes.

---

[67] Case T-114/02 *BaByliss v Commission* [2003] ECR II-1279, para 95, with references to Case T-169/84 *Cofaz and others v Commission* [1986] ECR II-391, paras 24–5; Joined Cases C-68/94 and C-30/95 *France v Commission* [1998] ECR I-1375, para 54, and Case T-2/93 *Air France v Commission* [1994] ECR II-121, para 44. See also Case T-177/04 *easyJet v Commission* [2006] ECR II-1913, para 35.

[68] Case T-114/02 *BaByliss v Commission* [2003] ECR II-1279, para 99: 'in so far as it is entering the European market for small electrical household appliances and that the oligopolistic market is characterized by substantial barriers to entry arising from strong brand loyalty and by the difficulty of access to retail trading'.

[69] Case T-158/00 *ARD v Commission* [2003] ECR II-3825. In this case ARD, a company providing free-to-air TV services in Germany, appealed the Commission's decision to clear a concentration between Kirch Pay TV and BSkyB involving the markets for pay TV, digital interactive services, and the acquisition of broadcasting rights.

[70] 'Free Universe Network' is a platform set up to enable a second digital platform in Germany. See para 89 et seq of the judgment.

[71] Case T-158/00 *ARD v Commission* [2003] ECR II-3825, para 79.

[72] Case T-374/00 *Verband der freihen Rohrwerke and Others v Commission* [2003] ECR II-2275, para 51.

[73] Case T-282/06 *Sun Chemical Group and Others v Commission* [2007] ECR II-2149, para 49 and the case law cited. See also Case T-151/06 *NVV and Others v Commission* [2009] ECR II-1219, para 45. In para 48, the GC explained that the action brought jointly by NVV, Mr Schep, and NBHV did not contain pleas in law or arguments which relate exclusively to only one of those parties.

[74] The GC has consistently held that where one and the same action brought by a number of applicants is admissible with regard to one of those applicants, there is no need to consider whether the other applicants

18.36   By contrast, in *Wirtschaftskammer Kärnten* an action brought by a regional organization in charge of defending the interests of economic actors in competition matters was held inadmissible. The GC noted that the organization had not participated in the administrative procedure and found that neither itself nor its members were individually concerned by the clearance decision other than in their objective and abstract quality as consumers of electricity.[75] Similarly, the action for annulment against the *EDF/Segebel* conditional clearance decision brought by a Belgian consumer association was dismissed due to lack of active participation in the proceedings.[76]

4. Shareholders

18.37   The admissibility of appeals brought by shareholders against decisions deserves a special mention. In *Zunis Holding*,[77] three minority shareholders of Generali, each of which had a shareholding of less than 0.5 per cent, contested the Commission's decision that Mediobanca's increased shareholding in Generali was not sufficient to confer control over Generali. The GC held that the decision was not in itself sufficient to affect the substance or the extent of the rights of the shareholders, and that it did not affect the applicants individually, by virtue of any special attributes which differentiated them from other minority shareholders. Nevertheless, the Court left open the question of whether shareholders with larger stakes may be able to establish a direct and individual concern.[78]

5. Trade unions

18.38   Article 18(4) of the Merger Control Regulation grants to recognized representatives of the employees of an undertaking the right to be heard by the Commission upon application. That right, however, does not confer automatic *locus standi* under Article 263 TFEU to appeal against a Commission decision.

18.39   In *Nestlé/Perrier*,[79] it was ruled *in casu* that express and specific reference to the employee representatives among third persons showing a sufficient interest to submit their observations to the Commission was enough to differentiate them from all other persons, whether or not they have made use of their rights during the administrative procedure. The GC held, however, that they were not directly concerned, because any redundancies or changes in social benefits that could possibly arise following the merger were not an inevitable or direct consequence of the Commission's decision.

18.40   Trade unions may nevertheless be admitted as interveners, provided they can establish an interest in the result of the case.[80] This was the case in the *Schneider/Legrand* case, where both the European works council of the Legrand group and the works council of SA Legrand

---

are entitled to bring proceedings (see eg Case T-374/00 *Verband der freien Rohrwerke and Others v Commission* [2003] II-2275, para 57).

[75] Case T-350/03 *Wirtschaftskammer Kärnten and best connect Ampere Strompool v Commission* [2006] ECR II-68, paras 24–33.

[76] On this point, the Court relied on the fact that the applicant had requested to be heard before the notification had been filed and failed to approach the Commission thereafter. See Judgment of 12 October 2011 in Case T-224/10 *Association Belge des Consommateurs Test-Achats v Commission*.

[77] Case T-83/92 *Zunis Holding, Finan and Massinvest v Commission* [1993] ECR II-116, paras 34–7. See also on appeal Case C-480/93 P [1996] ECR I-1, although decided on other grounds.

[78] M Siragusa, 'Judicial Review of Competition Decisions under EC Law' 1–9 (2), available at <http://www.competition-commission.org.uk>.

[79] Case T-96/92 *Comité Central d'Entreprise de la Société Générale des Grandes Sources and others v Commission* [1995] ECR II-1213.

[80] See Art 40 of the Statute of the ECJ.

were granted leave to intervene in support of the Commission regarding the prohibition and divestiture decision adopted pursuant to Article 8(4) of Regulation 4064/89.[81]

6. Interest in bringing proceedings

Having demonstrated that the act is a challengeable act and that it is directly and individu- **18.41** ally concerned, a natural or legal person bringing an action for annulment will have to show that it has an interest in the proceedings. In accordance with settled case law, an action for annulment brought by a person other than a privileged applicant is admissible only in so far as that person has an interest in the annulment of the contested measure. In order for such an interest to be present, the annulment of the measure must of itself be capable of having legal consequences or, in other words, the action must be liable, if successful, to procure an advantage for the party that has brought it.[82] In this context, the situation of different types of potential applicants must be distinguished.

The EU Courts have consistently held that an undertaking has an interest in the annul- **18.42** ment of a prohibition decision addressed to it. This is the case even if the basis for the transaction has disappeared,[83] or where the applicant has complied with a prohibition decision[84] or has abandoned the concentration.[85] Notifying parties also have an interest in challenging conditions to which an authorization has been made subject, again irre- spective of the fact that the conditions may have been complied with at the time of the appeal.[86]

Competitors of the parties to the concentration also have an interest in challenging a deci- **18.43** sion authorizing a concentration that may affect their commercial situation.[87] However, in *Socratec*, the GC decided that there was no need to act on the application by a competitor who, less than a year after lodging its action for annulment of a decision had been declared in liquidation. The Court observed that under the applicable law, a company in liquidation no longer exercised any commercial activity and hence that it could no longer be considered a competitor of the parties.[88]

---

[81] Respectively Case T-310/01 *Schneider Electric v Commission* [2002] ECR II-4071 and Case T-77/02 *Schneider Electric v Commission* [2002] ECR II-4201, para 34.
[82] See eg Case T-310/00 *MCI v Commission* [2004] ECR II-3253, para 44 and the case law cited.
[83] Case T-102/96 *Gencor v Commission* [1999] ECR II-753, paras 40–5. In that case, the contested deci- sion would have constituted an obstacle to the exercise of Gencor rights of pre-emption.
[84] Case T-22/97 *Kesko v Commission* [1999] ECR II-3775, paras 55–65.
[85] Case T-310/00 *MCI v Commission* [2004] ECR II-3253, paras 44–57. In that case, the parties had announced to the Commission that they were withdrawing their notification and that they no longer wished to implement the proposed merger one day before the Commission adopted a prohibition decision.
[86] In *Kali & Salz*, third party interveners before the Court argued that since commitments which the applicants, here the merging parties, were subject to as a result of the conditions imposed by the decision had already been complied with, they no longer had any interest in the annulment by the Court of conditions which had thus become obsolete. The ECJ rejected that argument by holding that even if it proved impossible for the institution whose act had been declared void to fulfill the obligation to take the necessary measures to comply with the Court's judgment, the application for annulment would still constitute an interest at least as the basis for a possible action for damages. See Joined Cases C-68/94 and C-30/95 *France and Others v Commission* ('Kali & Salz') [1998] ECR I-1375, paras 70–5. See also Case T-269/03 *Socratec v Commission* [2009] ECR II-88, para 37.
[87] Case T-177/04 *easyJet v Commission* [2006] ECR II-1913, paras 40–1. The GC took into account the fact that the decision authorized, subject to certain conditions, a concentration between two of easyJet's competitors.
[88] Case T-269/03 *Socratec v Commission* [2009] ECR II-88, paras 40–1. See also paras 42–8 of the judg- ment responding to Socratec's alleged interest in bringing actions for damages against the notifying parties and the Commission.

18.44 In *Lebard*, a former manager of the merging parties sought the annulment of the Commission letter rejecting his request to revoke the *Rhodia/Donau Chemie/Albright & Wilson* decision[89] and refusing to reopen the file regarding the *Hoechst/Rhône Poulenc* decision,[90] arguing that these decisions were likely to affect his reputation as a businessman. While the GC recalled that the benefit for an applicant included the material interests as well as the moral interests and the future prospects of the person, it declared the heads of claims inadmissible, since the annulment of these decisions would not reinforce its reputation as a businessman.[91]

D. Actions for Damages

18.45 Under Articles 268 and 340(2) TFEU, the ECJ is competent to hear actions for damages arising from claims for non-contractual liability against the EU institutions. Settled case law of the EU Courts makes clear that compensation is due where EU institutions have committed a sufficiently serious breach of a rule of law intended to confer rights on individuals, and that there is direct causation between that breach and the harm suffered by the applicant. To date, three such cases have been decided in the merger control field. Both the first two concern situations where the Commission prohibited a transaction under the Merger Control Regulation and the prohibition had subsequently been annulled by the EU Courts.

18.46 In *My Travel*,[92] filed following the annulment of the *Airtours/First Choice* prohibition decision, the GC held that the Commission had not committed a sufficiently serious breach of a rule of law intended to confer rights on individuals as regards the analysis of (i) the concentration in the light of the criteria relating to collective dominance, and (ii) the commitments. However, in *Schneider/Legrand*,[93] the GC ordered the EU (then, the European Community ('EC')) to make good two-thirds of the loss claimed by Schneider as a result of the reduction in the transfer price of Legrand, which Schneider conceded to the transferee in exchange for the postponement of the effective date of sale until 10 December 2002. In addition, the Commission was ordered to reimburse Schneider for the loss represented by the costs incurred by Schneider as a result of its participation in the resumed merger control procedure which followed delivery of the judgments of the GC regarding the prohibition decision. On appeal lodged by the Commission, the ECJ held that there was no sufficiently direct link between the breach committed by the Commission and the reduction in the transfer price of Legrand and set aside that part of the judgment. However, the ECJ upheld the Community's liability for the costs of the resumed merger control procedure.[94] After some disagreement between the parties, the ECJ set the amount of the damages at EUR 50,000.[95]

18.47 A third action for damages was lodged by municipalities following the closure of a production site of the acquired company located on their territory. The action was dismissed as the GC found no fault with the Commission's refusal to force the parties to operate the production site for a duration of five years following completion.[96]

---

89 Case IV/M.1517 *Rhodia/Donau Chemie/Albright & Wilson* [1999] OJ C248/10.
90 Case IV.1378 *Hoechst/Rhône-Poulenc* [1999] OJ C42/22.
91 Case T-89/06 *Lebard v Commission* [2009] ECR II-201, paras 35–41.
92 Case T-212/03 *MyTravel Group plc v Commission* [2008] ECR II-1967.
93 Case T-351/03 *Schneider Electric SA v Commission* [2007] ECR II-2237.
94 Case C-440/07 P *Commission v Schneider Electric* [2009] ECR I-6413, paras 212–17.
95 Order of 9 June 2010 in Case C-440/07 P *Commission v Schneider Electric* [2010] ECR I-73, para 49.
96 Order of 1 September 2011 in Case T-132/10 *Communauté de communes de Lacq v Commission* [2011] OJ C319/21. The notifying party had offered a commitment to that effect in the first phase, but that commitment had been deemed insufficient and the concentration had eventually been cleared without remedies following an in-depth investigation.

E. Time-Period to Bring an Action

1. Action for annulment

Pursuant to Article 263, fifth paragraph, TFEU, actions for annulment against decisions of **18.48** the Commission must be brought within two months. While for addressees of such decisions (eg notifying parties) the time-period starts from notification of the decision, the question for non-addressees (eg competitors) was less straightforward. In *Qualcomm*, the Commission had argued that the action was out of time since the applicant, a competitor of the parties, had lodged its action nine months after receiving a non-confidential version of the clearance decision. The GC held, however, that the period for instituting proceedings must be calculated by reference to the first of the cases set out in the fifth paragraph of Article 230 EC (now Article 263 TFEU), namely from the time of publication in the Official Journal of the European Union ('OJ').[97] To extend the circle of 'addressees' would diminish the obligation provided for by Article 20(1) of the Merger Control Regulation to publish a notice of the decision in the OJ and confer on the Commission a discretion for the purpose of identifying those third parties/non-addressees who may bring an action from notification of a decision and not from its publication.[98]

Where an act is not published or not notified, the case law has determined that it is for **18.49** a party that has knowledge of a decision concerning it to request the whole text thereof within a reasonable period but, subject thereto, the period for bringing an action can begin to run only from the moment when the third party concerned acquires precise knowledge of the content of the decision in question and of the reasons on which it is based in such a way as to enable it to exercise its right of action.[99] In Case T-200/09, Abertis lodged an action for annulment of the decision of the Commission to close the procedure pursuant to Article 21(4) Merger Control Regulation concerning the Abertis/Autostrade case.[100] The GC declared the action out of time, considering that the applicant had already been informed by a letter some eight months beforehand that the Commission had decided to close the proceedings against Italy and that it had failed to ask the Commission for a copy of the full text of the letter addressed to the Italian authorities within a reasonable period.[101]

2. Action for failure to act

Under Article 265 TFEU, an action for failure to act shall be admissible only if the institu- **18.50** tion concerned has first been called upon to act. If, within two months of being so called upon, the institution concerned has not defined its position, the action may be brought within a further period of two months. In the *Austrian Newspapers* case, an eighteen-month period was judged unreasonable. The ECJ also noted that at the time the applicants made a complaint to the Commission, nearly four months had elapsed since the national authorities' decision approving completion of the transaction.[102]

---

[97] Case T-48/04 *Qualcomm v Commission* [2009] ECR II-2029, para 48.
[98] Case T-48/04 *Qualcomm v Commission* [2009] ECR II-2029, para 49. The GC also held that this could also entail a breach of the principle of equal treatment and explained that it was not always possible for the Commission to identify at the outset all the persons (eg actual or potential competitors) who may bring an action as from notification of a decision (para 49).
[99] See eg Case 236/86 *Dillinger Hüttenwerke v Commission* [1988] ECR 3761, para 14.
[100] Case COMP/M.4249 *Abertis/Autostrade* [2006] OJ C268/7.
[101] Case T-200/09 *Abertis Infraestructuras v Commission* [2010] ECR II-85, para 63.
[102] Case C-170/02 P *Schlüsselverlag JS Moser and Others v Commission* [2003] ECR I-9889, paras 36–8.

F. Scope of Revision and Discretion of the Commission

18.51   The margin of appreciation of the European Commission in merger cases does not only depend on the 'test' contained in the Merger Control Regulation. Arguably of greater importance is the standard of review, ie the intensity with which the Courts review the merits of the decisions adopted by the Commission under the Merger Control Regulation.[103] With respect to the standard of review of decisions imposing sanctions under Articles 14 or 15 of the Merger Control Regulation, the EU Courts have been specifically entrusted with unlimited jurisdiction within the meaning of Article 262 TFEU.[104] In the context of the review of a Commission decision imposing a fine for the implementation of a concentration in breach of the stand-still obligation under Article 7(1) of Regulation 4064/89, the GC relied on the case law regarding the imposition of fines for infringements of competition law, and held that the Commission's obligation is to produce sufficiently precise and coherent evidence to establish that the alleged infringement took place and that any doubt in the mind of the court must operate to the advantage of the addressees of the decision.[105] The GC also recalled that in the exercise of their unlimited jurisdiction under Article 16 of Regulation 4064/89 (unchanged in Regulation 139/2004), the EU Courts may, in addition to carrying out a mere review of the lawfulness of the penalty, substitute their own appraisal for the Commission's and, consequently, cancel, reduce or increase the fine or periodic penalty payment imposed. The GC pointed out, however, that this did not amount to a review of the Court's own motion, but that applicants had to raise pleas in law against the decision and adduce evidence in support of those pleas.[106]

18.52   For other decisions, the standard of review in merger control cases has also been built on the criteria for the review of the Commission's actions in other areas of competition law over the years, where EU Courts have developed a doctrine of marginal review aimed at avoiding replacing their own judgment with that of the Commission on policy decisions regarding complex economic matters. Early pronouncements in this line can be traced back to *Consten & Grundig*,[107] in which it was declared with regard to the granting of individual exemptions under Article 101(3) TFEU that judicial review should constrain itself 'to an examination of the relevance of facts and of the legal consequences arising therefrom'. That principle would be extended to the Commission's assessment under Article 101(1) TFEU in *Remia*,[108] where the Court acknowledged the Commission's margin of appreciation in competition matters declaring that 'the Court must therefore limit its review…to verifying whether the relevant procedural rules have been complied with, whether the statement of reasons is adequate, whether the facts have been accurately stated and whether there has been any manifest error of appraisal or misuse of power'.

---

[103] On this matter see generally M Jaeger, 'The Standard of Review in Competition Cases Involving Complex Economic Assessments: Towards the Marginalisation of the Marginal Review?' (2011) 2(4) Journal of Competition Law & Practice 295.

[104] Article 16 of the Merger Control Regulation.

[105] Judgment of 12 December 2012 in Case T-332/09 *Electrabel v Commission*, paras 31 and 106. The GC further observed that the Commission's analysis of the circumstances in which a concentration was put into effect is amenable to a full review by the Court and that the Commission did not enjoy any discretion in that regard (para 42).

[106] Judgment of 12 December 2012 in Case T-332/09 *Electrabel v Commission*, paras 221–2.

[107] Joined Cases 56 and 58/64 *Consten & Grundig v Commission* [1966] ECR 299.

[108] Case 42/84 *Remia v Commission* [1985] ECR 2545, p 34. The quote may be found in many competition cases after *Remia*; see eg Joined Cases 142/84 and 156/84 *BAT and Reynolds v Commission* [1987] ECR 4487, para 62 and Case C-7/95 P *Deere v Commission* [1988] ECR I-3111, para 76.

That approach would be directly transposed to merger cases. In *Kali & Salz*,[109] the ECJ acknowl- **18.53**
edged that the Commission should enjoy a 'discretionary margin implicit in the provisions
of an economic nature which form part of the rules on concentrations'. However, when the
GC annulled the merger prohibitions decided by the Commission in *Airtours*,[110] *Schneider*,[111]
and most importantly in *Tetra Laval*,[112] after conducting a particularly extensive review of the
Commission's analysis, the question arose as to whether the Court was abiding by that 'marginal
review' doctrine outlined earlier, or whether the examination was so intrusive as to risk that the
Courts would replace the Commission's assessment by their own.[113]

In the appeal judgment in *Tetra Laval*, the ECJ supported the approach adopted by the GC, **18.54**
declaring that:

> [w]hilst the Court recognises that the Commission has a margin of discretion with regard to
> economic matters, that does not mean that the Community Courts must refrain from review-
> ing the Commission's interpretation of information of an economic nature. Not only must the
> Community Courts, *inter alia*, establish whether the evidence relied on is factually accurate,
> reliable and consistent but also whether that evidence contains all the information which must
> be taken into account in order to assess a complex situation and whether it is capable of substan-
> tiating the conclusions drawn from it.[114]

It may therefore be concluded that the EU Courts recognize a 'certain degree of discretion' **18.55**
in favour of the Commission when carrying out complex economic assessments. That 'degree
of discretion' may vary according to the novelty and controversial or contested nature of the
economic theories upon which it bases its assessment.[115] In particular, a prohibition of a
concentration that potentially could have a conglomerate effect on a neighbouring market[116]
involves cause–effect relations that are not clearly perceptible, and that are uncertain and difficult to determine. In such cases, the Courts might be expected to invite the Commission

---

[109] Joined Cases C-68/94 and C-30/95 *France and Others v Commission ('Kali & Salz')* [1998] ECR
I-1375, paras 223 and 224.

[110] Case T-342/99 *Airtours v Commission* [2002] ECR II-2585.

[111] Case T-310/01 *Schneider Electric v Commission* [2002] ECR II-4071.

[112] Case T-5/02 *Tetra Laval v Commission* [2002] ECR II-4381.

[113] Actually, the Commission challenged the *Tetra Laval* GC judgment before the ECJ and issued a public statement affirming that it needed to do so in order to defend its prerogatives, as the GC had replaced
the 'manifest error of assessment' standard by one of 'convincing evidence'. Commission Press Release
IP/02/1952 'Commission appeals CFI ruling on Tetra Laval/Sidel to the European Court of Justice' of 20
December 2002.

[114] Case C-12/03 P *Commission v Tetra Laval* [2005] ECR I-987, para 39. That approach has since been
applied in other cases, such as Case T-201/05 *General Electric v Commission* [2005] ECR II-5575, paras
60–76, Case T-151/05 *NVV v Commission* [2009] ECR II-1291, para 54 and Case T-342/07 *Ryanair v
Commission* [2010] ECR II-3457, para 30.

[115] In this sense, see B Vesterdorf, 'Certain Reflections on Recent Judgments Reviewing Commission
Merger Control Decision' in M Hoskins and W Robinson (eds), *A True European, Essays for Judge David
Edward* (Hart Publishing 2003) 117, 142, 'when new theories advanced by the Commission in the context
of the exercise of its merger control function are contested before the Community judicature, it is, in my
view, the duty and responsibility of the CFI, so as to ensure effective judicial review, closely to scrutinize
the convincing nature of the evidence relied upon in the contested decision in support of such theories'.
Also B Vesterdorf, 'Standard of Proof in Merger Cases: Reflections in the Light of Recent Case Law of the
Community Courts' (2005) 1 European Competition Journal 3, 17–25.

[116] Case C-12/03 P *Commission v Tetra Laval* [2005] ECR I-987, para 44: 'The analysis of a
conglomerate-type' concentration is a prospective analysis in which, first, the consideration of a lengthy
period of time in the future and, secondly, the leveraging necessary to give rise to a significant impediment to
effective competition mean that the chains of cause and effect are dimly discernible, uncertain and difficult
to establish. That being so, the quality of the evidence produced by the Commission in order to establish
that it is necessary to adopt a decision declaring the concentration incompatible with the common market is
particularly important, since that evidence must support the Commission's conclusion that, if such a decision
were not adopted, the economic development envisaged by it would be plausible.'

to produce 'convincing evidence' as to how and why it is considered that competition will be significantly impeded.

18.56 That scrutiny does not, however, empower the EU Courts to alter the rules on the burden of proof and require either the Commission or the notifying parties to provide evidence against any conceivable theory of harm that may have emerged along the merger control procedure. That is the logic that made the ECJ correct the approach that the GC had adopted in its judgment of 13 July 2006, in which it had annulled a decision granting approval for Sony and Bertelsmann to merge their music units.[117] While agreeing that the actions by the GC consisting of 'an in-depth examination of the evidence underlying the contested decision' were consistent with its obligations under *Kali & Salz* and *Tetra Laval*,[118] the ECJ annulled the judgment, noting that the GC had required from the Commission:

> particularly demanding requirements as regard the probative character of the evidence and arguments put forward by the notifying parties in reply to the statement of objections and, secondly, in finding that the lack of additional market investigations after communication of the statement of objections and the adoption by the Commission of the appellants' arguments in defence amounted to an unlawful delegation to the parties to the concentration.[119]

18.57 By way of conclusion on the standard of review by the EU Courts in merger cases, three usual misconceptions can be avoided. First, the 'deferential' language which acknowledges a margin of discretion in favour of the Commission does not mean that it is an area free from review, but the recognition of a separation of powers provided for in the treaties. Secondly, 'marginal review' should not be confused with 'light review', as the review itself will be intense on questions of facts and on the analysis of the soundness of economic theories. Thirdly, complex economic assessments should not be mistaken for the complexity of calculations or data, for which there is no 'deference': any point of fact, including an economic argument, is open for review by the EU Courts.[120]

G. Interim Measures

18.58 Interim measures are very important in appeal procedures in general. This is even more so in merger control cases, where action often has to be taken immediately. Article 279 TFEU provides that '[t]he Court of Justice of the European Union may in any cases before it prescribe any necessary interim measures'. This provision does not establish what kind of interim measures might be granted, nor does it specify what conditions are required for them to be granted. The possibility of suspending the application of a contested decision is hinted at in Article 278 TFEU, which provides that '[t]he Court may, however, if it considers that circumstances so require, order that application of the contested act be suspended'. There is no list of possible interim measures that may be sought, so the parties might apply not only

---

[117] Case T-464 *Impala v Commission* [2006] ECR II-2289.
[118] Case C-413/06 P *Bertelsmann and Sony Corporation of America v Commission* [2008] ECR I-4951, para 146.
[119] Case C-413/06 P *Bertelsmann and Sony Corporation of America v Commission* [2008] ECR I-4951, para 95.
[120] See M Jaeger, 'The Standard of Review in Competition Cases Involving Complex Economic Assessments: Towards the Marginalisation of the Marginal Review?' (2011) 2(4) Journal of Competition Law & Practice 295.

for the suspension of the effects of a Commission's decision, but also for 'any other interim measure', according to the wording of Article 60 of the Statute of the Court of Justice.[121]

Article 39 of the Statute of the Court of Justice provides that the President of the Court **18.59** may, by way of summary procedure, adjudicate upon applications to suspend execution, as provided for in Article 278 of the TFEU, or to prescribe interim measures in pursuance of Article 279 of the TFEU, or to suspend enforcement in accordance with the fourth paragraph of Article 299 of the TFEU.

A successful application for interim measures requires a number of elements. First, the main **18.60** action should be validly lodged. Second, there has to be a sound *prima facie* case (*fumus boni iuris*). The applicant has to specify the circumstances of law and fact upon which the plea of urgency is based. Furthermore, it has to be proven that there is a serious risk of causing serious and irreparable harm to the applicant (*periculum in mora*). The measures applied for have to be necessary in order to avoid this serious damage, which has to be directly linked with the implementation of the contested decision. Ultimately, the decision requires a balancing of two conflicting interests: a public interest in ensuring an immediate application of the Commission decision, and the private interests of affected companies, including the beneficiary of the decision. In practice, the request is often limited to the specific mandates included in the decision that caused the irreparable harm.

The *Nestlé/Perrier* cases,[122] initiated by workers representatives, gave the President of the GC **18.61** the occasion to decide on interim measures in connection with disposals of businesses. The two orders strictly interpreted the requirements for the granting of interim measures in cases where the interests of persons not party to the procedure may be affected. Citing *Simmenthal v Commission*,[123] it was recalled that in these situations, interim measures could only be granted if there was a risk of the requesting parties disappearing. That was not found to be the case in *Nestlé/Perrier*. In addition, the President of the GC took the view that the allegedly irreparable effect that the transfer may have had on the level of employment had not been sufficiently established and the requests were dismissed.

Some months later, limited interim protection was granted to the applicant in *Kali & Salz*.[124] **18.62** In its decision, the Commission had, *inter alia*, imposed on the notifying parties a condition that they withdraw from a marketing joint venture (entered into with a competitor), which was active in third countries. The other shareholder in the joint venture, SCPA, and its parent company EMC asked the President of the Court to suspend that part of the decision pending judicial review. The request was granted, given the irreparable harm that the dissolution of the joint venture would cause to SCPA, an undertaking which was not a party to the procedure. It was also observed that the joint venture had existed for many years, and there was no good reason to dismantle it prior to the judicial review of the decision.

The application for interim relief in *Union Carbide*,[125] decided later in 1994, failed. The **18.63** applicant had a joint venture with Shell, and opposed the conditional clearance granted by the Commission in *Shell/Montecatini*.[126] The applicant claimed, *inter alia*, that certain

---

121 Protocol (No 3) on the Statute of the Court of Justice of the European Union annexed to the Treaty on the European Union, to the Treaty on the Functioning of the European Union and to the Treaty establishing the European Atomic Energy Community, as last amended [2010] OJ L83/210.

122 Case T-96/92 R *Comité Central d'Entreprise de la Société des Grandes Sources v Commission* [1992] ECR II-2579 and Case T-12/93 R *Comité Central d'Entreprise de la SA Vittel et Comité d'Etablissement de Pierval v Commission* [1993] ECR II-785.

123 Case 92/78 R *Simmenthal v Commission* [1978] ECR 1129.

124 Case T-88/94 R *SCPA and EMC v Commission* [1994] ECR II-401.

125 Case T-322/94 R *Union Carbide v Commission* [1994] ECR II-1159.

126 Case IV/M.269 *Shell/Montecatini* [1996] OJ L332/48.

commitments offered by Shell would damage the business of the existing UCC/Shell joint venture. The President of the GC dismissed these claims, considering that the causal link between the damage and the commitments had not been sufficiently well established.

18.64   A particular type of interim measure was requested in *Sogecable*,[127] where the measure sought was aimed at preventing the Commission from adopting any act within a merger control procedure. In the applicant's view, the case lacked a Community (now Union) dimension, and for this reason had been notified to the Spanish competition authorities. However, the Commission took the view that the case did have a Community dimension, and had therefore initiated proceedings under the Merger Control Regulation. The President of the GC rejected the request for interim measures, noting that the judge should not be empowered to grant such an open-ended measure that would prevent the Commission from adopting any conceivable measure, without prejudice to the review of the potentially actionable measures that the Commission may actually adopt within the said procedure.

18.65   Another example of interim measures in special circumstances is found in *Petrolessence*,[128] which concerned the rejection by the Commission of the applicants as potential purchasers of a business that had to be divested following *TotalFina/Elf*.[129] Again, based on the particularly strict test to be followed where the request may affect third parties not party to the procedure, the President of the GC rejected the request.[130]

18.66   The battle for the control of Endesa equally gave rise to specific requests for interim measures. In a first case,[131] Endesa applied for suspension of the decision whereby the Commission had informed Endesa that the proposed acquisition by Gas Natural did not have a Community dimension. Endesa put forward three types of harm which the company and its shareholders would suffer. The President of the GC only examined the condition relating to urgency, and concluded that Endesa had not demonstrated that it would suffer grave and irreparable damage in the absence of the relief sought. He recalled on two occasions that the harm possibly suffered by Endesa's shareholders could only be taken into account in the balance of interests but not in the assessment of urgency.[132]

18.67   In the second case,[133] Spain applied for annulment of the decision in which the Commission found that the adoption by the Spanish authorities of several measures constituted an infringement of paragraphs 2 and 4 of Article 21 of the Merger Control Regulation and sought the suspension of the application of the decision.[134] The President of the GC considered that the analysis of two of the conditions imposed on Enel and Acciona raised complex issues requiring the assessment of numerous factual and economic elements, and therefore that a *prima facie* case could not be ruled out.[135] Nevertheless, the request for interim measures was

---

[127] Case T-52/96 R *Sogecable v Commission* [1996] ECR II-797.

[128] Case T-342/00 R *Petrolessence and SG2R v Commission* [2001] ECR II-67.

[129] Case COMP/M.1628 *TotalFina/Elf* [2001] OJ L143/1.

[130] See also in *Aer Lingus*, where the President of the GC noted that the applicant would have to demonstrate a particularly strong *prima facie* case and the existence of very serious and irreparable harm before he could order Ryanair to divest its shares in Aer Lingus, in view of the fact that the measures would have a serious impact on the rights and interests of Ryanair as a shareholder of Aer Lingus (Case T-411/07 R *Aer Lingus v Commission* [2008] ECR II-411, para 135).

[131] Case T-417/05 R *Endesa v Commission* [2006] ECR II-18.

[132] Case T-417/05 R *Endesa v Commission* [2006] ECR II-18, paras 37 and 64.

[133] Case T-65/08 R *Spain v Commission* [2008] ECR II-69.

[134] It should be noted that, following the lodging of the request for interim measures, the Commission committed itself not to undertake new steps in the framework of the infringement procedure until the President of the GC had rendered its order (see Case T-65/08 R *Spain v Commission* [2008] ECR II-69, para 15).

[135] Case T-65/08 R *Spain v Commission* [2008] ECR II-69, para 62.

rejected again on the basis that Spain had not established urgency and that the balance of interest weighed against granting the relief sought.

In *EDF/Segebel*, EDF sought the annulment of the Commission's decision to reject its request **18.68** for a postponement of the deadline to implement one of the commitments by two-and-a-half years, and in essence requested the President of the GC to postpone the date by which EDF had to implement the commitment, pending a decision in the main case. In rejecting this request, the President considered that the alleged harm was of a purely financial nature and that EDF had not provided any information on the size and turnover of its undertaking, which would have allowed the establishment of an accurate overall picture of its financial situation and of that of the EDF group.[136] On appeal, and having heard the parties in writing and orally, the Vice-President of the ECJ quashed the decision at first instance, holding that the reasoning was vitiated by an error of law concerning the concept of serious harm. Although the size of the undertaking may have an influence on the assessment of the seriousness of the financial harm alleged, it could not be excluded that financial harm which was objectively significant and which allegedly resulted from the obligation to make a final commercial choice of some magnitude within a disadvantageous time-scale, could be considered as 'serious'.[137] The Vice-President of the ECJ then gave final judgment and rejected the application for interim measures, holding that the Commission's refusal to extend the time limit could not be considered as the decisive cause of the alleged harm. The Vice-President concluded that EDF had not established that it was likely to sustain serious or irreparable harm in the absence of the granting of the interim measures sought.[138]

Finally, it is worth mentioning that interim measures were requested in *Schnei-der/Legrand*[139] **18.69** and *Tetra Laval/Sidel*.[140] However, these applications were withdrawn after the Commission agreed to postpone enforcement of its decisions to divest shareholdings pursuant to Article 8(4) of the Merger Control Regulation until the end of the judicial review. This suggests that the Commission may take a flexible approach as regards enforcement in the context of appeals brought under the expedited procedure.

H. Procedure before European Courts

The judicial review of Commission decisions under the Merger Control Regulation is gov- **18.70** erned, besides the provisions of the Treaty and of the Statute of the Court of Justice, by the Rules of Procedure of the EU Courts. These cases are usually heard by the GC and, on appeal, by the ECJ. The main features of these procedures are summarized in the following paragraphs.

1. Ordinary procedure

The ordinary procedure, which is conducted in the language chosen by the applicant,[141] usually **18.71** consists of a written and an oral phase.[142]

---

[136] Order of 11 October 2012 in Case T-389/12 R *EDF v Commission* [2012] OJ C366/35, paras 3–4 and 19–21. Relying on publicly available figures, the President also compared the alleged harm to that of the considerable financial power of the EDF group (para 26).

[137] Order of 7 March 2013 in Case C-551/12 P(R) *EDF v Commission*, paras 32–3.

[138] Order of 7 March 2013 in Case C-551/12 P(R) *EDF v Commission*, paras 39–63.

[139] Case T-77/02 R *Schneider Electric v Commission* [2002] OJ C118/29.

[140] Case T-80/02 R *Tetra Laval v Commission* [2002] OJ C156/27.

[141] It should be noted that if the application for annulment is lodged in one language, an accompanying request for interim relief must be lodged in that same language of procedure (see Case T-417/05 R *Endesa v Commission* [2006] ECR II-18, para 13).

[142] If the courts consider themselves sufficiently informed by the pleadings of the parties and/or where the application is manifestly inadmissible, they may decide without hearing the parties orally.

18.72 The written phase begins with the filing of the application, which is composed of a pleading, together with all of the annexes mentioned therein, and the supporting documents.[143] The defendant must file a defence within two months of notification of the application, although this period may be extended if grounds are given. The supporting documents could be supplemented by way of further pleadings (a reply from the applicant and a rejoinder from the defendant), unless the Court considers this to be unnecessary.[144] During the proceedings, new documents cannot be adduced, unless new factual or legal reasons have come to light during the proceedings. Evidence can be proposed by both parties in the application or defence, and the Court can order the procedural steps or the production of evidence which it considers necessary. Once the evidential stage or any measures of procedural organization have taken place, the President will fix a date for opening the oral phase.

18.73 The oral submissions are made in a public hearing and simultaneously translated, where necessary. The Court may put questions to the agents, advisers, or lawyers. The oral phase will normally be declared to have ended once the hearing is finished. Finally, the judges will deliberate the matter and deliver the judgment in public.

18.74 The large number of procedural steps, together with the backlog of cases in the GC, are ill-suited for the review of concentrations. The effectiveness and speed of the notification procedure before the Commission, necessary in all concentration operations, is in marked contrast to the slowness of the procedure before the EU Courts, which has regularly frustrated the aspirations of the parties to concentrations. The system had become so slow and ineffective that the GC would often pass judgment in judicial review cases when it was no longer feasible to carry out the transaction that was the subject matter of the appeal. Ultimately, the severe criticism of this situation led to the introduction of the expedited or 'fast-track' procedure.

2. The expedited or 'fast-track' procedure

18.75 The expedited or 'fast-track' procedure in the GC was introduced in February 2001.[145] This procedure has significantly changed the position of the judicial review of Commission merger control decisions where fast-evolving markets mean that time is of the essence.

18.76 When introducing the fast-track procedure, the GC took into account the need to offer a rapid reply in actions for the judicial review of concentrations. Undertakings have clearly seen the benefits of this new procedure in concentration cases; in the first two years, eleven of the fourteen requests to use the fast-track procedure related to Commission decisions in the field of the control of concentrations.[146] However, the actions for annulment against three recent prohibition decisions challenged by the notifying parties themselves have not been accompanied by requests for an expedited procedure.[147]

---

[143] The application must contain the items listed in Art 44 of the Procedural Regulation of the GC. For instance, the application must spell out with sufficient clarity the elements of fact and law relied on (for an action for annulment against a clearance decision declared inadmissible for failure to comply with this provision see Order of 20 January 2012 in Case T-315/10 *Groupe Partouche v Commission*) [2012] OJ C80/18.

[144] Article 47(1) of the Rules of Procedure of the GC.

[145] Article 76a of the Rules of Procedure of the GC.

[146] B Vesterdorf, 'Certain Reflections on Recent Judgments Reviewing Commission Merger Control Decision' in M Hoskins and W Robinson (eds), *A True European, Essays for Judge David Edward* (Hart Publishing 2003) 117, 118.

[147] Case T-202/11 *Aeroporia Aigaiou Aeroporiki and Marfin Investment Group Symmetochon v Commission* [2011] OJ C160/25; Case T-175/12 *Deutsche Börse v Commisssion* [2012] OJ C174/25; Case T-260/13 *Ryanair Holdings v Commission*.

To date, eleven[148] cases have been reviewed under the fast-track procedure, and almost **18.77** all cases have taken less than one year from the lodging of the application at the GC.[149] *Schneider* and *Tetra Laval* were resolved within ten months of the time that the action began, and seven months from the moment that the applicability of the fast-track procedure was accepted. In *Babyliss* and *Philips*, judgment was given one year after the appeal started and nine months after the fast-track procedure commenced.[150] Judgment was delivered in a record time of seven months from the lodging of the action for annulment in *EDP*,[151] and nine months in *Endesa*.[152] In fact, it seems that the fast-track procedure may not take much longer than the time required for the Commission investigations that go into an in-depth investigation.[153]

Access to the fast track is not automatic. A series of requirements must be fulfilled, since **18.78** only those cases that are particularly urgent and which have special circumstances will be allowed to proceed in this way. The request must be filed by either of the parties and made on a separate document at the same time as the application or defence is filed, depending on who is making the request. The President of the Chamber to which the case has been assigned will hear the parties and decide whether or not a case qualifies for the fast track.[154] The GC has also held in the context of merger control that an expedited procedure, in which there is no second round of written submissions, presupposes that the applicant's arguments are clearly and definitively established at the outset of the application.[155] The GC also clarified that the applicant cannot reserve the option to put forward further pleas or arguments at a later date.[156]

It appears that, in general, cases concerning the judicial review of the Commission's decisions **18.79** on concentrations are likely to fulfill the requirements needed to qualify for the fast-track

---

[148] Case T-310/01 *Schneider Electric v Commission* [2002] ECR II-4071; Case T-77/02 *Schneider Electric v Commission* [2002] ECR II-4201; Case T-5/02 *Tetra Laval v Commission* [2002] ECR II-4381; Case T-80/02 *Tetra Laval v Commission* [2002] ECR II-4519; Case T-114/02 *BaByliss v Commission* [2003] ECR II-1279; Case T-119/02 *Royal Philips NV v Commission* [2003] ECR II-1433; Joined Cases T-346/02 and T-347/02 *Cableuropa and Others v Commission* [2003] ECR II-4251; Case T-87/05 *EDP v Commission* [2005] ECR II-3745; Case T-464/04 *Impala v Commission* [2006] ECR II-2289; Case T-417/05 *Endesa v Commission* [2006] ECR II-2533; and Case T-282/06 *Sun Chemical v Commission* [2007] ECR II-2149.

[149] One notable exception is the first *Impala* case before the GC, which took one year and eight months, in no small part due to the applicant's behaviour throughout the procedure (see Case T-464/04 *Impala v Commission* [2006] ECR II-2289, paras 546–51).

[150] B Vesterdorf, 'Certain Reflections on Recent Judgments Reviewing Commission Merger Control Decision' in M Hoskins and W Robinson (eds), *A True European, Essays for Judge David Edward* (Hart Publishing 2003) 117, 118.

[151] Case T-87/05 *EDP v Commission* [2005] ECR II-3745.

[152] In *Endesa*, this was all the more important because, following the Commission's decision that the merger between Gas Natural and Endesa lacked Community dimension, the concentration had been authorized by the Spanish Council of Ministers subject to conditions and soon thereafter suspended by the Commercial Court of Madrid (Case T-417/05 *Endesa v Commission* [2006] ECR II-2533).

[153] For instance, in *Schneider/Legrand* the Commission investigation lasted eight months and the procedure before the GC took slightly over ten months. In *EDP* the Commission investigation lasted five months and the procedure before the GC took seven months.

[154] Article 76a of the Rules of Procedure of the GC.

[155] Case T-87/05 *EDP v Commission* [2005] ECR II-3745, para 183. The GC held that, by implication, the limitation may not be circumscribed by systematic reference to voluminous and/or complex reports. See also Case T-417/05 *Endesa v Commission* [2006] ECR II-2533, para 247.

[156] Case T-417/05 *Endesa v Commission* [2006] ECR II-2533, para 251. See also Case T-119/02 *Royal Philips Electronics v Commission* [2003] ECR II-1433, para 205, where the GC considered that pleas raised for the first time by an intervener at the hearing could compromise the Commission's right to state its views properly.

procedure, since, in many cases, particular urgency will exist. However, there will be cases where, due to the peculiar circumstances of the appeal, for example where the application is based on a large number of grounds or is especially complicated, the fast-track procedure will not be appropriate.[157]

18.80   Although it could be thought that the speed of this procedure would mean that judgments would be shorter and less detailed, those fast-track judgments given to date are of the same quality as ordinary procedure judgments, both with respect to the grounds given and the detail of the examination and explanation of the Court's findings.[158] The fast track has been lauded by both academics and practitioners, but above all by undertakings; the latter have particularly welcomed this new system, which has enabled the GC to review decisions with a real sense of urgency, thus providing a convincing response to the criticism of the Commission's current role of investigator, prosecutor, and decision-maker.[159]

18.81   The benefit of the expedited procedure has been rejected in a number of instances.[160] This was the case in *Omya*, where the applicant was challenging an Article 11(3) Merger Control Regulation decision requesting information and stopping the clock in Phase II.[161] By the time the appeal was lodged, the Commission had already received the requested information, restarted the clock, and issued a statement of objections. This may have led the GC to consider that the expedited procedure would make little difference on the review of the merger. In the context of the appeal by Impala against the second clearance decision in the *Sony/BMG* case, the GC rejected the request for expedited proceedings five days after the ECJ had quashed the judgment of the GC having annulled the first *Sony/BMG* clearance decision.[162] A similar request was also rejected in Case T-411/07 *Aer Lingus*.[163] In that case, the applicant had also made an application for interim measures asking for the suspension of the Commission's decision rejecting Aer Lingus's request to order Ryanair to divest the shares it still held in its competitor Aer Lingus following the prohibition decision. However, the fact

---

[157] For example, in Case T-103/02 *Ineos Phenol* [2002] OJ C156/33, the GC refused the fast-track procedure because the issues were too complicated. The same happened in Case T-79/12 *Cisco Systems and Messagenet v Commission* [2012] OJ C109/31, but there was only one round of pleadings and the hearing took place only 15 months after the lodging of the application. In Case T-310/01 *Schneider Electric* [2002] ECR II-4071, the GC first refused the expedited procedure given the volume of the application and of the annexes submitted. However, after an informal meeting with the parties, the Court decided to grant the request when Schneider accepted to adhere to the abridged version of its application submitted after the meeting. In *EDP* (Case T-87/05), after an informal meeting at the GC, the applicant lodged its application in an abbreviated form. By contrast, in the first *Impala* case (Case T-464/04), the GC granted the expedited procedure, but noted disapprovingly in the judgment that the volume of the application and the number of pleas in law and arguments greatly exceed the recommended norms (para 547).

[158] In this sense, see J Temple Lang, 'Two Important Merger Regulation Judgments: The Implications of Schneider-Legrand and Tetra Laval-Sidel' (2003) 28 EL Rev 259, 259.

[159] B Vesterdorf, 'Certain Reflections on Recent Judgments Reviewing Commission Merger Control Decision' in M Hoskins and W Robinson (eds), *A True European, Essays for Judge David Edward* (Hart Publishing 2003) 117, 118.

[160] Of the cases which have reached judgment to date, the expedited procedure was refused in Case T-145/06 *Omya v Commission* [2009] ECR II-145, para 12 and in Case T-411/07 *Aer Lingus v Commission* [2010] ECR II-3691, para 35. In Case T-3/02 *Schlüsselverlag JS Moser and Others v Commission* [2002] ECR II-1473, the GC held that, since the action for failure to act was manifestly inadmissible, there was no need to give a decision on the application for the proceedings to be expedited.

[161] Case T-145/06 *Omya v Commission* [2009] ECR II-145, para 12.

[162] See Order of the GC of 30 September 2009 in Case T-229/08 *Impala v Commission* [2009] OJ C282/48, paras 11–13.

[163] Case T-411/07 *Aer Lingus v Commission* [2010] ECR II-3691, para 35.

that an interim measures procedure is pending does not necessarily lead to the rejection of the fast-track procedure.[164]

In cases for which no expedited procedure is requested or granted, the procedure before the **18.82** GC may be lengthy, even where the review of some decisions would appear to be urgent. For instance, the buyer approval decision in the *Lagardère/Natixis/VUP* case was annulled six years after its adoption, whereas the buyer had already resold the divested assets.[165] In three other recent cases, the procedure lasted over four years.[166] This will often occur in cases brought by third parties, such as competitors. The length of the procedure may depend on several factors, such as the complexity of the case, the volume of the application, the number of interveners, the need to resolve confidentiality concerns, or even the changes occurring in the composition of the chambers of the GC.

I. Appeals to the European Court of Justice

GC judgments that terminate proceedings, as well as those that partially resolve a substantive **18.83** issue or decide a procedural issue concerning a plea of lack of competence or inadmissibility,[167] or decide on a request for interim measures, may be appealed against to the ECJ within two months from the date of notification of the challenged judgment.[168] Any appeal to the ECJ must be limited to questions of law and must be based on one or more of the following grounds:

  (i) lack of competence of the GC;
 (ii) breach of procedure before it which adversely affects the interests of the appellant; and
(iii) infringement of EU law by the GC.[169]

This division of labour between the GC and the ECJ in the review of concentration decisions has been summarized by the ECJ in the *Sony/BMG* case.[170]

---

[164] In Case T-417/05 *Endesa v Commission* [2006] ECR II-2533, the expedited procedure was granted before the decision on interim measures was rendered and maintained, even after the President of the GC rejected the request for interim relief in Case T-417/05 R *Endesa v Commission* [2006] ECR II-18.

[165] Case T-452/04 *Éditions Odile Jacob v Commission* [2010] ECR II-4713.

[166] Case T-151/05 *NVV and Others v Commission* [2009] ECR II-1219; Case T-48/04 *Qualcomm v Commission* [2009] ECR II-2029; Case T-279/04 *Éditions Odile Jacob v Commission* [2010] ECR II-185; Judgment of 7 June 2013 in Case T-405/08 *SPAR Österreichische Warenhandel v Commission*.

[167] See Case C-188/06 P *Schneider Electric v Commission* [2007] ECR I-35, upholding the order in Case T-48/03 *Schneider Electric v Commission* [2006] ECR II-111.

[168] Article 56 of the Statute of the ECJ.

[169] Article 58 of the Statute of the ECJ.

[170] Case C-413/06 P *Bertelsmann and Sony Corporation of America v Commission* [2008] ECR I-4951, para 29: 'The Court of First Instance accordingly has exclusive jurisdiction, first, to find the facts, except where the substantive inaccuracy of its findings is apparent from the documents submitted to it and, second, to assess those facts. When the Court of First Instance has found or assessed the facts, the Court of Justice has jurisdiction under Article 225 EC to review the legal characterisation of those facts by the Court of First Instance and the legal conclusions it has drawn from them. The Court of Justice thus has no jurisdiction to establish the facts or, in principle, to examine the evidence which the Court of First Instance accepted in support of those facts. Provided that the evidence has been properly obtained and the general principles of law and the rules of procedure in relation to the burden of proof and the taking of evidence have been observed, it is for the Court of First Instance alone to assess the value which should be attached to the evidence produced to it. Save where the clear sense of the evidence has been distorted, that appraisal does not therefore constitute a point of law which is subject as such to review by the Court of Justice.' See also Opinion of AG Tizzano, delivered 25 May 2004 in Case C-12/03 P *Commission v Tetra Laval BV*, para 60.

18.84   Appeal proceedings may be started by filing a written appeal with the Registrar of the ECJ[171] by any parties whose submissions have been totally or partially dismissed by the GC. Interveners other than Member States and institutions may bring an appeal only where the decision of the GC directly affects them.[172] The procedure before the ECJ concerning an appeal against a GC ruling will usually consist of a written part and an oral part. After hearing the Advocate-General and the parties, the ECJ may dispense with the oral procedure.[173] The purpose of the appeal must be the total or partial annulment of the operative part of the judgment at first instance; the appeal cannot modify the subject matter of the case brought before the GC. Where the ECJ quashes the judgment at first instance in total or in part, it may decide on the matter definitively if there are no other pleas to which the GC did not reply and it has all the elements to decide upon that matter.

18.85   In the first few cases where an appeal took place,[174] the ECJ confirmed the GC's rulings. However, on some significant occasions the Grand Chamber of the ECJ has disagreed with the lower court. In *Sony/BMG*, the ECJ quashed the judgment of the GC and referred the case back to the GC, since only two of the five pleas relied on by Impala had been examined.[175] In the action for damages in *Schneider/Legrand*, the ECJ set aside the judgment of the GC in part and gave final judgment on Schneider's application for damages.[176] The ECJ also corrected the GC's approach in the *Odile Jacob* and *Agrofert* cases on access to documents.[177] Finally, in *EDF* the Vice-President of the ECJ quashed the decision of the President of the GC due to an error concerning the concept of serious harm, but eventually also rejected the request for interim measures in relation to the Commission's decision to refuse to grant EDF a postponement of the deadline to fulfil some of its commitments.[178]

J. Consequences of Judicial Review

18.86   The general rule concerning the consequences of Court decisions is set out in the Treaty itself. Under Article 266 TFEU, '(t)he institution whose act has been declared void or whose failure to act has been declared contrary to the Treaties shall be required to take the necessary

---

[171] Article 56 Statute of the ECJ.

[172] For examples of appeals brought by interveners, see Case C-413/06 P *Bertelsmann and Sony Corporation of America v Commission* [2008] ECR I-4951 (the purchaser and the seller) and Case C-554/10 P *Lagardère v Editions Odile Jacob* [2011] OJ C46/5 (the notifying party, with the purchaser of the assets under the commitments as intervener).

[173] Article 59 Statute of the ECJ.

[174] Case C-480/93 *Zunis Holding and others v* Commission [1996] ECR I-1 and Case C-170/02 P *Schlüsselverlag JS Moser GmbH et al v Commission* [2003] ECR I-9889. These appeals are limited to the question of admissibility (see also Case C-188/06 P *Schneider Electric v Commission* [2007] ECR I-35). For full appeals before the Court see Case C-12/03 P *Commission v Tetra Laval* [2005] ECR I-987 and Case C-202/06 P *Cementbouw Handel & Industrie v Commission* [2007] ECR I-12129.

[175] Case C-413/06 P *Bertelsmann and Sony Corporation of America v Commission* [2008] ECR I- 4951, para 190.

[176] Case C-440/07 P *Commission v Schneider Electric* [2009] ECR I-6413. The GC's judgment was set aside in so far as it had ordered the European Community to make good two-thirds of the loss claimed by Schneider as a result of the reduction in the transfer price of Legrand (para 208). The ECJ ordered the Community to make good the loss represented by the expenses incurred by Schneider as a result of its participation in the resumed merger control following the judgments annulling the prohibition decision (paras 212–17).

[177] Judgments of 28 June 2012 in Cases C-404/10 P *Commission v Odile Jacob* and C-477 P *Commission v Agrofert*. See Ch 17, 'Procedures'.

[178] Order of 7 March 2013 in Case C-551/12 P(R) *Electricité de France v Commission*.

measures to comply with the judgment of the Court of Justice of the European Union'. The necessary measures may, depending on the judgment, require the adoption of a new decision in accordance with the Merger Control Regulation. This may, for instance, raise the issue of whether the original notification needs to be updated and re-filed.

Originally, Regulation 4064/89 regulated the effects of Court decisions on mergers rather **18.87** cryptically. Article 10(5) stated that the periods laid down in the Regulation would start to run as from the date of the Court's judgment. The Regulation did not specify how these terms should be calculated, nor whether the analysis should be carried out, having regard to the circumstances prevailing at the time of the original notification or the later date where the decision was to be adopted.

In *Kali & Salz*,[179] the first case where the EU Courts reviewed the substance of a decision **18.88** adopted under the Merger Control Regulation, the Commission was confronted with the need to adopt the measures necessary to comply with the ECJ's judgment. In order to make a new examination, the Commission requested additional information from the parties in order to update the information on file.[180] Only following the receipt of this information, more than two months after the Court's judgment, did the Commission consider that the term had started to run. As to whether the analysis should be carried out having regard to current market conditions or those prevailing at the time of the initial case, the Commission seemingly adopted a mixed interpretation. As regards determining its competence over the concentration, it relied on data provided in the original notification to ascertain that the transaction had an EU dimension; however, concerning the competitive assessment, the Commission relied on the then-current situation, since any decision made on the basis of five-year-old data risked identifying competitive concerns that no longer existed. By way of exception, the possible availability of a 'failing firm defence' had to rely on the previous situation, since at the time of the re-examination the failing company no longer existed.[181]

A similar approach would be followed in *Tetra Laval/Sidel* following the annulment of **18.89** the first prohibition decision by the GC.[182] As the decision adopted by the Commission in the second procedure explains,[183] the Commission relied on Article 4(2) of the then implementing Regulation 447/98 and declared the notification incomplete in a material respect. Only following receipt of that information did the time limits start running again. The Commission finally cleared the transaction with conditions, noting, however, that its decision may depend on the outcome of the appeal that had been made before the ECJ.[184]

The precedents noted here have shaped the drafting of Article 10(5) of the Merger Control **18.90** Regulation, which now explains that, following a judgment that affects any decision subject to the time limits provided for in said Article 10,[185] a new examination will be made. The notifying parties will be required to either file a new notification or complete the notification

[179] Joined Cases C-68/94 and C-30/95 *France and others v Commission ('Kali & Salz')* [1998] ECR I-1375.
[180] See Case IV/M.308 *Kali und Salz/MDK/Treuhand* [1998] OJ C275/3, para 3.
[181] On this point, see N Hacker, 'The Kali und Salz case—the re-examination of a merger after an annulment by the Court' (1998) 3 (October) Competition Policy Newsletter 40.
[182] Case T-5/02 *Tetra Laval v Commission* [2002] ECR II-4381.
[183] Case COMP/M.2416 *Tetra Laval/Sidel* [2004] OJ L43/13.
[184] Case COMP/M.2416 *Tetra Laval/Sidel* [2004] OJ L43/13, para 3. In its Judgment of 18 March 2005, the Court dismissed the appeal made by the Commission. See Case C-12/03 P *Commission v Tetra Laval* [2005] ECR I-987.
[185] Or the time limits contained in Arts 6(4) and 8(7).

originally filed in the event that market changes have taken place, or certify otherwise that no such changes have occurred. The time periods laid down in the Merger Control Regulation will start to run once the new notification, supplemented notification, or certification, as the case may be, has been delivered to the Commission.

18.91　As regards the scope of the examination that the Commission would initiate, Article 10(5) paragraph 2 provides that, '[t]he concentration shall be reexamined in the light of current market conditions', which must be understood as meaning those existing at the time a new decision is adopted. That again is consistent with the Commission's practice in *Kali & Salz* and *Tetra Laval/Sidel*; actually, both cases resulted in a clearance of the transactions that in the initial assessment had been declared incompatible with the internal market. In both cases, the new circumstances were instrumental for the new assessment.[186]

18.92　In *Sony/BMG*, the first decision of compatibility was annulled by the GC on 13 July 2006.[187] Since the triggering event had occurred before the entry into force of Regulation 139/2004, Regulation 4064/89 was applied, including the pre-SIEC (significantly impede effective competition) dominance test, and the assessment only related to the countries which were Contracting Parties to the EEA Agreement at that time.[188] The concentration was, however, assessed under the market conditions existing at the time of the new filing. The Commission again declared the concentration compatible on 3 October 2007 without issuing a statement of objections or accepting commitments. This second decision was again challenged by *Impala*.[189] Following the ECJ's judgment on 10 July 2008, by which it quashed the GC's judgment in Case T-464/04 and referred the case back to the GC, on 11 September 2008 the GC ordered proceedings in Case T-229/08 to be stayed in accordance with Article 77(c) of the Rules of Procedure of the GC, until Impala lodged its statement of written observations concerning the steps to be taken, as regards the first action for annulment in Case T-464/04, in response to the judgment of the ECJ. By order of 30 June 2009, the GC held that there was no longer any need to adjudicate on the action against the first decision (Case T-464/04), since Impala's action had become devoid of purpose following the Commission's decision of 15 September 2008 declaring the acquisition by Sony of Bertelsmann's 50 per cent holding in the capital of Sony BMG to be compatible with the internal market.[190] Finally, upon request of all the parties, the GC declared by Order of 30 September 2009 that the action against the second clearance decision (Case T-229/08) had also become devoid of purpose and that it was no longer necessary to adjudicate following the third clearance decision.[191]

---

[186]　By contrast, the review of the *Schneider/Legrand* case following the annulment by the GC of the initial prohibition decision (Case T-310/01) resulted in second stage proceedings being opened. The ECJ confirmed that in its judgment in Case T-310/01, the GC had not given instructions to the Commission as to the stage at which it should restart its examination procedure and considered that by deciding to restart at the beginning of the second phase, the Commission had taken all necessary precautions to avoid a possible violation of Schneider's rights of defence (Case C-188/06 P *Schneider Electric v Commission* [2007] ECR I-35, paras 47 and 48). The notification was later withdrawn and a claim for damages filed with the GC (Case T-351/03 *Schneider Electric v Commission* [2007] ECR II-2237, on appeal Case C-440/07 P *Commission v Schneider Electric* [2009] ECR I-6413, and Order of the ECJ of 9 June 2010 [2010] ECR I-73).

[187]　Case T-464/04 *Impala v Commission* [2006] ECR II-2289.

[188]　Case COMP/M.3333 *Sony/BMG* [2008] OJ C94/19.

[189]　Case T-229/08 *Independent Music Publishers and Labels Association v Commission* [2003] OJ C197/33.

[190]　Case M.5272 *Sony/Sony BMG* [2008] OJ C259/5.

[191]　This third decision of 15 September 2008 in Case M.5272 concerned a different transaction from the two previous clearance decisions.

In the *Lagardère/Natixis/VUP* case, following the annulment by the GC of the decision   **18.93**
approving the purchase of Editis by Wendel,[192] the Commission adopted a new decision
approving the same buyer.[193]

---

[192] Case T-452/04 *Éditions Odile Jacob v Commission* [2010] ECR II-4713 and on appeal Judgment of 6
November 2012 in Joined Cases C-553/10 P and C-554/10 P *Commission v Éditions Odile Jacob*.

[193] The decision of the Commission was again challenged by Éditions Odile Jacob. In this particular case,
in the interim the buyer of the assets had resold them (Case T-471/11 *Éditions Odile Jacob v Commission*
[2011] OJ C305/9). The President of the GC rejected Éditions Odile Jacob's request for interim measure
(Order of 24 November 2011 in Case T-471/11 R *Éditions Odile Jacob v Commission* [2012] OJ C25/52).

PART III

PUBLIC UNDERTAKINGS AND EXCLUSIVE OR SPECIAL RIGHTS (ARTICLE 106(3) TFEU)

19

PROCEDURE ON STATE MEASURES—DECISIONS UNDER ARTICLE 106(3) TFEU[1]

José Luis Buendía Sierra

A. Introduction

This chapter will concentrate on the procedure for the application of rules regarding public **19.01** undertakings and special and exclusive rights in EU law, a question which is much more complicated and of greater scope than may first appear. In fact, Article 106(3) of the Treaty on the Functioning of the European Union ('TFEU') provides a special procedure intended not only to *bring an end to* infringements of Article 106(1) TFEU committed by Member States, but also to adopt general measures designed to *define* the scope of the obligations under Article 106(1) and/or to *prevent* future infringements of those obligations.[2] Thus, Article 106(3) grants to the Commission, on the one hand, the power to adopt *decisions* declaring that Member States have infringed the obligations under Article 106(1) and obliging the Member State to put an end to the infringement. Decisions adopted under the legal basis provided by Article 106(3) have also been issued by the Commission for taking note of remedies proposed by a Member State following up an Article 106(3) decision and making such commitments binding within a certain time frame.[3] This procedure constitutes

---

[1] The author of this chapter wishes to thank Jose Manuel Panero Rivas for his assistance in the drafting of certain sections.

[2] See JL Buendía Sierra, (Oxford University Press 1999) ch 10; F Blum and A Logue, (Wiley 1998) ch 3; C Hocepied, 'Les directives Article 90, paragraphe 3. Une espèce juridique en voie de disparition?' [1994] RAE ii 49; A Pappalardo, '(1991) 1 ECLR 29; M Kerf, 'The Policy of the Commission of EEC Toward National Monopolies. An Analysis of the Measures Adopted on the Basis of Article 90(3) of the EEC Treaty' (1993) 17(1) World Competition 73; LM Pais Antunes, 'L'Article 86 du Traité CEE—Obligations des Etats Membres et pouvoirs de la Commission' [1991] RTDE ii 187; F Melin-Soucramanien, '(1994) 382 RMCUE 601.

[3] Commission Decision (EC) of 4 August 2009, relating to a proceeding under Art [106(3) TFEU] establishing the specific measures to correct the anti-competitive effects of the infringement identified in the Commission Decision of 5 March 2008 on the granting or maintaining in force by the Hellenic Republic of rights in favour of Public Power Corporation SA for the extraction of lignite adopted in Case COMP/B-1/38.700 [2009] OJ C243/5 (summary publication)

an exception to the general procedure contained in Article 258 TFEU, in which it is up to the Court of Justice ('ECJ') to declare that the Treaty has been infringed, but it is not a revolutionary idea. Indeed, the Commission has similar powers as regards the anticompetitive behaviour of undertakings (Articles 101 and 102 TFEU) and State aid (Articles 107 and 108 TFEU). This suggests a system giving the Commission similar powers to react quickly against all restrictions of competition, irrespective of their public or private origin. Article 106(3) also provides the Commission with the power to adopt obligatory directives aimed at Member States, designed to define the scope of the rules under Article 106(1) and (2) and/or prevent future infractions of these rules. These two aspects of Article 106(3) raise some difficult questions of interpretation and delimitation with respect to other procedures provided for in the Treaty.

B. Procedures for the Application of the European Union Rules

19.02 The legal system of the EU consists of a set of rules which are addressed to Member States and/ or individuals.

1. Procedure regarding the behaviour of undertakings

19.03 Articles 101 and 102 TFEU are rules addressed to undertakings. These rules may be applied either by the national courts, by the competent national authorities, or by the European Commission. Naturally, in the exercise of these functions, the Commission is subject to the jurisdictional control of the General Court ('GC') and the ECJ. The application procedures of these provisions are currently contained in the so-called 'Modernisation' Regulation 1/2003 which is the object of other chapters of this book.[4]

2. Procedures regarding State measures

19.04 The normal procedure for the general application of the rules of the Treaty addressed to Member States is proceedings for failure to fulfil an obligation provided for in Article 258 TFEU. Apart from this general procedure, the Treaty has provided certain special procedures for the application of specific provisions. Thus, Article 108 provides a special procedure for the application of Article 107, which is a rule regarding State aid. In the same way, Article 106(3) provides a special procedure for the application of Article 106(1), a rule which concerns, *inter alia*, exclusive rights. Much of this chapter will be dedicated to this last mentioned procedure.

Application by the national courts and preliminary rulings (Article 267 TFEU)

19.05 It should be remembered that, apart from those procedures reserved to the institutions of the EU, individuals may bring an action before the *national* courts for the application of EU rules which have *direct effect*. The ECJ has recognized the direct effect of practically all of the rules regarding matters of exclusive rights, such as Articles 34, 35, 36, 37(1), 37(2), 49, 56, or 106(1). This means that the national courts are competent to judge the compatibility of exclusive rights with these provisions. Within this context, under Article 267 of the TFEU, national courts have the possibility (or the obligation if the national court's decision cannot be appealed) of referring a matter to the ECJ for a *preliminary ruling* on the interpretation of the provisions mentioned earlier.[5] The importance of Article 267 must not be underestimated. It is true that in the context of a preliminary ruling, the ECJ is in theory limited to offering an interpretation of the Treaty

---

[4] Regulation 1/2003 on the implementation of the rules on competition laid down in Arts 81 and 82 of the Treaty [2003] OJ L1/1.

[5] For a detailed study of the procedure for preliminary rulings under Art 267, see R Bray (ed), *Procedural Law of the European Union* (2nd edn, Sweet & Maxwell 2006) 36–85, 174–203, and 608–16; G Isaac, *Droit communautaire général* (4th edn, Masson 1994) 291–309. M Waelbroeck and D Waelbroeck, 'La Cour de Justice' in Various, *Commentaire Megret, Le Droit de la CEE*, Vol 10 (2nd edn, Editions de l'Université de Bruxelles 1993) 197.

provisions. It is not competent to judge on the legality or illegality of the State measure in question, since this is within the national courts' competence. In practice, however, the dividing line between 'interpret' the rules and 'apply' the rules is fairly unclear. The 'interpretation' of a rule makes no sense if it is not in reference to some facts.[6] Frequently, the interpretation given by the ECJ to a national court makes it absolutely clear as regards the legality or illegality of the national measure. In such cases the decision of the ECJ therefore determines beforehand the resolution of the proceedings.[7] However, there are many cases in which the ECJ prefers to limit itself to giving a general interpretation, with dubious usefulness for the national courts for resolving and settling proceedings.[8] In any case, it should be borne in mind that most of the judgments regarding Articles 37 and, above all, Article 106 have been given within the framework of preliminary rulings. The considerable changes experienced in the way that these provisions have been interpreted have almost always been as a result of individuals bringing legal proceedings before the national courts which have been referred for preliminary rulings. For this reason, it would be a serious mistake to perceive Article 267 as being of secondary importance in the application of EU rules concerning public undertakings and special and exclusive rights.

Proceedings for failure to fulfil an obligation (Article 258 TFEU)

Irrespective of the possible actions open to individuals, Article 17.1 of the Treaty on European Union ('TEU') entrusts to the Commission the task of acting as the guardian of the EU, thereby ensuring the application of the Treaties. The Commission's main instrument for carrying out this task is to bring an enforcement action for a Member State's failure to fulfil a Treaty obligation under Article 258: **19.06**

> If the Commission considers that a Member State has failed to fulfil an obligation under the Treaties, it shall deliver a reasoned opinion on the matter after giving the State concerned the opportunity to submit its observations.
>
> If the State does not comply with the opinion within the period laid down by the Commission, the latter may bring the matter before the Court of Justice of the European Union.

A detailed examination of Article 258 goes beyond the limits of this book,[9] but the principal features will be highlighted so that the originality of the special procedure of Article 106(3) of the TFEU can be appreciated. Following actions brought by individuals or by any other means, the Commission may conclude that a Member State is in breach of certain of its obligations under EU law. If it does so conclude, Article 258 confers upon it the power to bring proceedings before the ECJ for a declaration that the Member State is in breach of the obligation in question. Prior to bringing proceedings before the court, Article 258 provides for an obligatory informal or pre-contentious stage.[10] This initial stage of the procedure officially **19.07**

---

[6] M Waelbroeck and D Waelbroeck, 'La Cour de Justice' in Various, *Commentaire Megret, Le Droit de la CEE*, Vol 10 (2nd edn, Editions de l'Université de Bruxelles 1993) 197, 243.

[7] G Isaac, *Droit communautaire général* (4th edn, Masson 1994) 295.

[8] M Waelbroeck and D Waelbroeck, 'La Cour de Justice' in Various, *Commentaire Megret, Le Droit de la CEE*, Vol 10 (2nd edn, Editions de l'Université de Bruxelles 1993) 197, 243, n 266.

[9] For a detailed study of Art 258, see R Bray (ed), *Procedural Law of the European Union* (2nd edn, Sweet & Maxwell 2006) 128–74, JV Louis, 'Le rôle de la Commission dans la procédure en manquement selon la jurisprudence de la Cour de justice' in Various, *Du droit international au droit de l'intégration—Liber Amicorum Pierre Pescatore* (Nomos Verlagsgesellschaft 1987) 387–409; M Waelbroeck and D Waelbroeck, 'Article 169' in Various, *Commentaire Megret, Le Droit de la CEE*, Vol 10 (2nd edn, Editions de l'Université de Bruxelles 1993) 57–78.

[10] A relatively recent development on this area is the EU Pilot Programme designed to correct infringements of EU Law by Member States at a stage even earlier than the classic pre-contentious procedure. See Communication from the Commission, 'A Europe of results—applying community law' of 5 September 2007, COM(2007) 502 final, as well as Report from the Commission, 'EU Pilot evaluation report' of 3 March 2010 COM(2010) 70 final. For a detailed description of the pre-contentious stage, see R Bray (ed), *Procedural Law of the European Union* (2nd edn, Sweet & Maxwell 2006) 149–55, A Mattera, Le marché unique européen. Ses règles, son fonctionnement (Jupiter 1988) 569–93.

begins with the Commission sending a *letter of formal notice* to the Member State in which all the State measures that are considered to be incompatible with the Treaties are identified. The Commission sets out the arguments in support of its opinion, and the Member State is invited to submit its observations. If a satisfactory solution is not found, the Commission will proceed to issue a *reasoned opinion* in which the Member State is required to take action to end the infringement, normally within a specified time limit. Most of the cases are settled during this first conciliation stage. However, when the matter is not resolved and the Member State does not agree or comply with the requirements of the reasoned opinion, the Commission has the possibility of bringing proceedings for the failure to fulfil an obligation before the Court. This is the beginning of the formal or contentious stage. It must be emphasized that Article 258 provides the Commission with wide discretionary powers. The Commission is not obliged to commence proceedings or to follow them up once they have been started. It may therefore decide to begin or to continue proceedings not only for legal but also for tactical reasons. The Commission may, for example, favour using negotiations in order to eliminate a certain type of breach. From this it follows that individuals cannot bring a direct action under Article 263 for the annulment of a Commission decision not to institute infringement proceedings, nor may they bring an action under Article 265 against the inactivity of the Commission.[11] The purpose of Article 258 is not, then, to protect the rights that EU rules give to individuals. This protection has to be primarily sought before the national courts.

Proceedings for failure to fulfil an obligation of the ECSC Treaty

19.08 From an institutional point of view, Article 258 TFEU establishes a system whereby disagreements between the Commission and Member States concerning the scope of the latter's obligations are determined by the ECJ. This is not the only possible approach. In fact, proceedings for the infringement of the current Treaties are based on a very different rationale from proceedings for infringement of the old ECSC (European Coal and Steel Community) Treaty.[12] Proceedings under this latter treaty gave a much greater role to the Commission, as can be clearly seen from Article 88 of the ECSC Treaty:

> If the Commission considers that a State has failed to fulfil an obligation under this Treaty, it shall record this failure in a reasoned decision after giving the State concerned the opportunity to submit its comments. It shall set the State a time limit for the fulfilment of its obligation.
>
> The State may institute proceedings before the Court within two months of notification of the decision...

19.09 From an institutional point of view, the Commission's position in relation to Member States under the ECSC Treaty was much stronger than under the EU Treaty and the TFEU. In the procedure under Article 88 of the ECSC Treaty, the Commission established the existence of a breach and adopted a decision which required the Member State to bring the breach to an end. If the Member State did not agree with this decision, it had no other remedy but to bring an action against this decision before the Court within two months. By contrast, under Article 258 EC, the 'reasoned opinion' of the Commission is not binding upon the Member

---

[11] Case T-84/94 *German Accountants* [1995] ECR II-101, paras 21–6, upheld on appeal; Case C-107/95 P *Bundesverband der Bilanzbuchhalter eV v Commission (German Accountants (appeal))* [1997] ECR I-947, paras 17–19.
[12] The ECSC Treaty expired on 23 July 2002. Since then the coal and steel sectors were first included in the 'Community pillar' and thus subject to the EC Treaty and are currently subject, after the dismantling of the pillars' structure, to the TEU and the TFEU.

State and thus the Commission has no choice but to request the ECJ for a declaration of incompatibility.[13]

Special procedures of the TFEU

Nevertheless, it should not be forgotten that, although Article 258 contains the general procedure for rectifying infringements of Treaties' provisions, there are certain procedures applicable to specific TFEU rules which are closer to the approach taken under Article 88 of the ECSC Treaty than to Article 258. This is the case of the procedure laid down in Article 108(2) TFEU regarding State aids, and of the procedure under Article 106(3), which is applicable, amongst other matters, to exclusive rights. **19.10**

Special procedure regarding State aids (Article 108(2) EC)   The special procedure for State aids contained in Article 108(2) EC is an exception to the normal procedure under Article 258.[14] By virtue of Article 108(2), the Commission may order a Member State to suspend and to recover aid that is incompatible with the internal market. If the Member State does not agree with this decision, it must appeal under Article 263, requesting the Court to annul the decision within two months. If the Member State does not act within this given time limit, the legality of the decision may not be questioned. If the Member State does not comply with or enforce the decision within the time limit stated by the Commission, Article 108(2), paragraph 2 authorizes the Commission to bring the matter directly before the Court for a declaration that the Member State has not fulfilled its obligations. This special procedure of Article 108(2) is, therefore, fairly different from the general procedure under Article 258 of the TFEU and quite similar to the procedure under Article 88 of the ECSC Treaty. **19.11**

Special procedure relating to exclusive rights and other State measures concerning public or privileged undertakings (Article 106(3) TFEU)   As will now be explained in detail, Article 106(3) TFEU also provides a special procedure for the application of the remaining provisions of Article 106: **19.12**

> The Commission shall ensure the application of the provisions of this Article and shall, where necessary, address appropriate directives or decisions to Member States.

Thus, the procedure under Article 106(3) may be applicable when it is a question of ensuring that an exclusive right or any other State measure regarding public or privileged undertakings complies with Article 106(1) and (2).[15] Like the procedures under Article 88 of the old ECSC Treaty and Article 108(2) of the TFEU (and unlike the procedure under Article 258 of the TFEU), Article 106(3) allows the Commission itself to establish, through a binding decision, the non-compliance by a Member State with its obligations. If a Member State disagrees with the Commission's decision, it must bring an action before the Court requesting the annulment of the decision within two months. (It should be remembered that, under the general procedure of Article 258, the Commission's reasoned opinion is not binding upon the Member State and the onus is upon the Commission to bring an action before the

---

[13] On the procedure of Art 88 of the ECSC Treaty, see G Isaac, *Droit communautaire général* (4th edn, Masson 1994) 282–3; M Waelbroeck and D Waelbroeck, 'Article 169' in Various, *Commentaire Megret, Le Droit de la CEE*, Vol 10 (2nd edn, Editions de l'Université de Bruxelles1993) 58–9.

[14] For a description and examination of the procedure of Art 108, see Part IV of this book, and M Dony, *Commentaire Megret: Contrôle des aides d'Etat*, book 3, Vol 2 (3rd edn, Editions de l'Université de Bruxelles 2007); L Hancher, T Ottervanger, and PJ Slot, *EC State Aids* (3rd edn, Sweet & Maxwell 2006).

[15] Article 106(2) is applicable both to State measures and to the behaviour of undertakings. The application of Art 106(2) to justify the behaviour of undertakings which is contrary to Arts 101 and 102 may be carried out under Reg 1/2003. The application of Art 106(2) to justify State aid may be carried out in the context of an Art 108 procedure. In these cases, the Commission applies Art 106(2) without using the procedure under Art 106(3).

ECJ to seek a declaration of incompatibility). Article 106(3) thus provides a procedure for adopting *individual decisions* in order to end the specific breaches by Member States of their obligations. Although this procedure is different from the one provided for in Article 258, it is very similar to other procedures under EU law, and contains nothing strange or revolutionary. A detailed examination of this matter is dealt with in the next section of this chapter. What is much more original and controversial is the other facet of Article 106(3): the power conferred upon the Commission to adopt directives. This matter and its limits will be dealt with in Chapter 20.

C. Decisions under Article 106(3) TFEU

1. General points

19.13 The Commission has adopted twenty individual decisions based on Article 106(3) of the Treaty:

- Commission Decision (EEC) 85/276 [1985] OJ L152/25 regarding the insurance in Greece of public goods and of loans granted by Greek public banks;
- Commission Decision (EEC) 87/359 [1987] OJ L194/28 regarding the tariff reductions in air and shipping transport reserved exclusively to Spanish residents in the Canary and Balearic islands;
- Commission Decision (EEC) 90/16 [1990] OJ L10/47 regarding the provision in the Netherlands of courier postal services;
- Commission Decision (EEC) 90/456 [1990] OJ L233/19 regarding the provision in Spain of international courier postal services;
- Commission Decision (CE) 94/119 [1994] OJ L55/52 regarding the refusal of access to the installations of the port of Rødby (Denmark);
- Commission Decision (EC) 95/364 [1995] OJ L216/8 regarding the discount system in the landing tariffs in the national airport of Brussels;
- Commission Decision (EC) 95/489 [1995] OJ L280/49 regarding the conditions imposed upon the second operator of radio-telephonic GSM services in Italy;
- Commission Decision (EC) 97/181 [1997] OJ L76/19 regarding the conditions imposed upon the second operator of radio-telephonic services GSM in Spain;
- Commission Decision (EC) 97/606 [1997] OJ L244/18 on the exclusive right to broadcast television advertising in Flanders;
- Commission Decision (EC) 97/744 [1997] OJ L301/17 on the provisions of Italian ports legislation relating to employment;
- Commission Decision (EC) 97/745 [1997] OJ L301/27 regarding the tariffs for piloting in the Port of Genoa;
- Commission Decision (EC) 99/199 [1999] OJ L69/31 Portuguese airports;
- Commission Decision (EC) 2000/521 [2000] OJ L208/36 Spanish airports;
- Commission Decision (EC) 2001/176 [2001] OJ L63/59 in relation to the provision of certain new postal services with a guaranteed day- or time-certain delivery in Italy;
- Commission Decision (EC) 2002/344 [2002] OJ L120/19 on the lack of exhaustive and independent scrutiny of the scales of charges and technical conditions applied by La Poste to mail preparation firms for access to its reserved services;
- Commission Decision of 20 October 2004 K(2004)4001/3 (not published in the OJ) on the German postal legislation relating to mail preparation services in particular the access of self-provision intermediaries and consolidators to the public postal network and related tariffs;

- Commission Decision (EC) of 10 May 2007 (not published in the OJ) on the special rights granted by the French Republic to La Banque Postale, Caisses d'Epargne and Crédit Mutuel for the distribution of the *livret A* and *livret bleu*;
- Commission Decision (EC) of 5 March 2008 [2008] OJ C93/3 (summary publication) on the maintaining in force by the Hellenic Republic of rights in favour of Public Power Corporation SA for the extraction of lignite;[16]
- Commission Decision (EC) of 7 October 2008 [2008] OJ C322/10 (summary publication) on the Slovakian postal legislation relating to hybrid mail services;
- Commission Decision (EC) of 4 August 2009 [2009] OJ C243/5 (summary publication) establishing the specific measures to correct the anti-competitive effects of the infringement identified in the Commission Decision of 5 March 2008 on the granting of maintaining into force by the Hellenic Republic of rights in favour of Public Power Corporation SA for the extraction of lignite.[17]

These twenty decisions only constitute the tip of the iceberg.[18] Most of the cases dealt with by the Commission based on Article 106 are settled without the need to resort to a formal decision. The most significant cases are recorded in the annual reports on competition policy. Another decision which should be added to the decisions of the Commission mentioned here concerns the gaming machines sector, which was adopted by EFTA Surveillance Authority (ESA) on the basis of Article 59(3) of the European Economic Area Treaty, which is a rule similar to Article 106(3) of the TFEU.[19]

Application to the grant or maintenance of exclusive rights

The procedure under Article 106(3) only applies to State measures that infringe Article **19.14** 106(1). Accordingly, State measures relating to public undertakings or undertakings holding exclusive or special rights come within its scope. Thus, for instance, the grant or maintenance of an exclusive right which is incompatible with Article 106(1), together with another provision of the Treaty, can always be subject to the procedure under Article 106(3). In principle, the procedure under Article 106(3) does not allow the Commission to adopt decisions which are directly addressed to public undertakings or to undertakings holding exclusive or special rights.[20] To the extent that the autonomous behaviour of these undertakings infringes Articles 101 and 102, it must be dealt with under the Regulation 1/2003 procedure. This is clearly shown from the position taken by the ECJ in the context of Article 106(3) directives, a position which is also applicable to the individual decisions adopted on that legal basis:[21]

> [I]t should be noted that Article 90 [now Article 106] of the Treaty confers powers on the Commission only in relation to State measures . . . and that anticompetitive conduct engaged in by undertakings on their own initiative can be called in question only by individual decisions adopted under Articles 85 and 86 of the Treaty [now Articles 101 and 102].

---

[16] The Decision has been annulled by the GC by its Judgment of 20 September 2012 in Case T-169/08 *Dimosia Epicheirisi Ilektrismou AE (DEI) v Commission*.

[17] The Decision has been annulled by the GC by its Judgment of 20 September 2012 in Case T-421/09 *Dimosia Epicheirisi Ilektrismou AE (DEI) v Commission*.

[18] C Hocepied, 'Les directives articles 90, paragraphe 3. Une espèce juridique en voie de disparition?' [1994] RAE ii 52.

[19] Decision 336/94/COL of the EFTA Surveillance Authority of 30 December 1994, on exclusive rights regarding gaming machines in Finland.

[20] A Bercovitz, 'Normas sobre la competencia del Tratado de la AELC' in E Garcia de Enterria, JD Gonzalez Campos, and S Muñoz Machado (ed), *Tratado de Derecho comunitario*, Vol II (Civitas 1986) 437.

[21] Case C-202/88 *French Republic v Commission (Telecommunications Terminal Equipment)* [1991] ECR I-1272, paras 24 and 55. See also Joined Cases C-271/90, C-281/90, and C-289/90 *Spain, Belgium and Italy v Commission (Telecommunications Services)* [1992] ECR I-5866, para 24.

19.15 Nevertheless, there will be cases where, by virtue of Article 106(1), the veil will be lifted and certain behaviour of these undertakings will be attributed to the Member State. In these cases, at least, use of the Article 106(3) procedure will be fully justified.[22] Generally, the dividing line between the conduct of undertakings and State measures is rather blurred, which is an argument in favour of greater flexibility when delimiting the respective areas of Article 106(3) and Regulation 1/2003. Certain behaviour of public or private undertakings is likely to come within both areas when it is the result of 'incitement' by the authorities. In such cases the Commission should be able to proceed under either Article 106(3) or Regulation 1/2003.[23] This possibility seems to be accepted implicitly in the case law. Thus, the Court has only excluded from the scope of Article 106(3) anticompetitive behaviour which the undertakings have adopted 'on their own initiative'. It has also suggested that the behaviour of undertakings resulting from them being 'obliged or incited' by the State to behave in that way would come within the scope of Article 106(3).[24] In short, it is a question of proving the autonomous or non-autonomous character of the decisions of undertakings. Notwithstanding how clear the rule could theoretically be, this has proven to be a tricky question which can be highly controversial, depending on the facts at stake. An interesting analogy can be traced between this issue and the position adopted by the ECJ in the famous *Stardust* judgment regarding State aid rules. In this judgment the ECJ relied on a set of indicators 'arising from the circumstances of the case and the context in which that measure was taken' for determining the imputability to the State of the undertaking's behaviour that might be of interest for the purposes of proving whether or not the decisions of undertakings may be attributable to the State.[25]

Justification for a special procedure

19.16 The justification for the existence of the special procedure under Article 106(3) is controversial. The reason that is generally put forward is the existence of particularly close relations between Member States and public or privileged undertakings in addition to the difficulty of detecting the influence that those Member States may exercise over such undertakings.[26] However, this reasoning can only be used to justify the adoption of preventive measures through directives under Article 106(3). It cannot be used to justify the adoption of decisions under Article 106(3), the scope of which is limited to declaring the existence of an infringement and ordering that it be brought to an end, and which includes the possibility for the Commission to approve the measures proposed by the State in order to restore a situation compatible with EU law.[27] Indeed, the probability that Article 106(1) is infringed and that such infringements are detected is the same, irrespective of whether they are prevented by using Article 258 or Article 106(3) of the TFEU. It is submitted that the reason why the Treaty provided a procedure for adopting decisions under Article 106(3) is probably connected with the need to ensure that there is consistency in the removal of distortions in

---

[22] See the reference to the *Transmediterránea* case in XVIII Report on Competition Policy (1988), para 309.

[23] This position was suggested by J Temple Lang, 'Community Antitrust Law and Government Measures relating to Public and Privileged Entreprises: Article 90 EEC Treaty' [1984] FCLI 550, 564–5.

[24] Case C-202/88 *Telecommunications Terminal Equipment* [1991] ECR I-1272, paras 55–6; Joined Cases C-271/90, C-281/90, and C-289/90 *Telecommunications Services* [1992] ECR I-5866, paras 24–5.

[25] Case C-482/99 *France v Commission* [2002] ECR I-4397, paras 51–2 and 55–6.

[26] A Pappalardo, 'State Measures and Public Undertakings: Article 90 of the EEC Treaty Revisited' [1991] European Competition Law Review i 35; M Kerf, 'The Policy of the Commission of the EEC Toward National Monopolies. An Analysis of the Measures Adopted on the Basis of Article 90.3 of the EEC Treaty' (1993) 17(1) World Competition 77.

[27] See Commission Decision (EC) of 4 August 2009 [2009] OJ C243/5 (summary publication) establishing the specific measures to correct the anti-competitive effects of the infringement identified in the Commission Decision of 5 March 2008 on the granting or maintaining into force by the Hellenic Republic of rights in favour of Public Power Corporation SA for the extraction of lignite.

competition, whether such distortions are caused by the private or public sector.[28] Thus, the powers of rapid intervention that the Treaty gives to the Commission with respect to the behaviour of undertakings (Articles 101 and 102) are echoed in the field of State measures, whether they are State aids (Articles 107 and 108), special or exclusive rights, or other restrictive measures (Article 106(3)). Thus, in any event, the Commission itself has the power to find that an illegal restriction of the competition rules has occurred and the power to order that the restriction TREU in question is ended (including the possibility of approving the commitments submitted by the parties[29]) without having to bring proceedings before the ECJ. It is the responsibility of the party to whom the decision is addressed, whether an undertaking or a Member State, to appeal against the decision to the ECJ. As the ECJ has pointed out, the Treaty tries to grant to the Commission adequate and appropriate instruments to guarantee that the competition rules are respected both by undertakings and by Member States.[30]

Procedural sources

The procedure of Article 106(3) is not regulated in detail by the Treaty nor by secondary EU legislation. There is no supplementary text that specifies Article 106(3) procedure in greater detail. As a result, analogies with other procedures acquire great importance, the obvious ones being the antitrust procedure,[31] the State aids procedure,[32] or the Article 258 procedure.[33] However, these analogies have to be handled with care, and due account must be taken of the differences between these rules and Article 106.   **19.17**

Competent authority

The only authority competent to adopt decisions based on Article 106(3) is the European Commission. It does not make any difference that Article 106(1) is of direct effect.[34] The national courts and the ECJ may of course apply these substantive provisions and find that a national measure is contrary to Article 106, but may not adopt decisions under Article 106(3), as this power is expressly reserved to the European Commission.   **19.18**

The discretionary nature of the decision to initiate infringement proceedings

Article 17(1) TEU entrusts the Commission with the task of ensuring the application of the Treaties, and Article 106(3) TFEU entrusts it with a similar task as regards Article 106(1), but even if the Commission always has the ability to act (*ex officio* or following a complaint), it is not automatically obliged to initiate infringement proceedings whenever a breach of Article 106(1) comes to light. The infringement procedure is only one of the instruments that the Commission has at its disposal to carry out its function as the 'guardian of the Treaties'.   **19.19**

---

[28] This is the position advocated by H Papaconstantinou, *Free Trade and Competition in the EEC. Law, Policy and Practice* (Routledge 1988) 102–4, as well as by F Blum and A Logue, *State Monopolies under EC Law* (Wiley 1998).

[29] This possibility is provided as regards application of Arts 101 and 102 by Art 9 of Reg 1/2003, and as regards State aid, a similar effect is achieved by virtue of the possibility provided to Member States of modifying the notified measures or submitting commitments according to Art 7(3) and (4) of Council Regulation (EC) No 659/1999 of 22 March 1999 laying down detailed rules for the application of Art 93 of the EC Treaty [1999] OJ L207/37.

[30] Joined Cases C-48/90 and C-66/90 *Netherlands and Koninklijke PTT Nederland NV and PTT Post BV v Commission (PTT)* [1992] ECR I-635, para 30.

[31] Rejected by the GC in Case T-32/93 *Ladbroke I* [1994] ECR II-1015, para 38.

[32] Case C-18/88 *RTT* [1991] ECR I-5941, para 31; Opinion of AG La Pergola, Case C-107/95 P *Expert Accountants* [1996] ECR I-957, paras 14–21.

[33] Opinion of AG Van Gerven, Case C-18/88 *RTT* [1991] ECR I-5941, para 8; and C Hocepied, 'The Maxmobil Judgment: The Court of Justice Clarifies the Role of Complainants in Article 86 Procedures' (2005) 2 Competition Policy Newsletter 53.

[34] Case 66/86 *Ahmed Saeed Flugreisen and Silver Line Reisebüro GmbH v Zentrale zur Bekämpfung Unlauteren Wettbewerbs eV (Ahmed Saeed)* [1989] ECR 852, para 53.

Other more flexible instruments, such as recommendations or legislative proposals, may in certain cases effectively contribute towards ensuring that this function is carried out. The text of Article 106(3) only provides for the adoption of decisions or directives 'where necessary'. In this sense, the ECJ has held that the Commission enjoys a wide margin of discretion when deciding whether to initiate proceedings against a Member State for breach of Article 106(1) of the Treaty.[35] A 2002 judgment of the GC—then the Court of First Instance ('CFI')—in the *max.mobil* case put into jeopardy this well-established line of authority.[36] In this judgment, the GC seemed to narrow the margin of discretion of the Commission by making it clear that the Commission was obliged to examine complaints based on Article 106 TFEU in a diligent and objective way as a consequence of the general principle of good administration. This implied on the one hand that, after an analysis of the complaint, the Commission should at least give grounds explaining why it considered that there is (or there is not) an infringement and whether it considered it necessary to intervene. On the other hand, judicial review on these two points (and in particular on the opportunity to intervene) would in any case be minimal and limited to manifest errors.[37] However on appeal,[38] the ECJ overruled the GC on the grounds that, contrary to the position in cases involving Articles 101 and 102 TFEU, the Commission's refusal to act under Article 106 is not susceptible of judicial review under Article 263 TFEU, especially because that particular act could not be regarded as producing legal effects. This confirms that the Commission enjoys a wide margin of discretion when deciding whether to initiate proceedings against a Member State for breach of Article 106(1) of the TFEU.[39] As will be explained later, this discretion greatly limits the possibility of individuals who are complaining of such infringements successfully appealing against the Commission's decision. Such a distinctive feature of Article 106 cases is, perhaps, a consequence of a conception of Article 106(3) procedures as much closer to Article 258 procedures than to procedures based on Articles 101, 102, or State aid cases. It is doubtful whether this view can be shared, and perhaps the large margin of discretion given by the ECJ to the European Commission should be reconsidered.[40]

Optional nature of the procedure under Article 106(3)

19.20 It must be determined whether the Commission can choose between various infringement procedures when it decides in a particular case to act against an infringement of Article 106(1). Thus, while it is clear that the Commission *can* always use the special procedure under Article 106(3) in order to end infringements of Article 106(1), it is less clear whether the Commission *must* use the special procedure or not. In other words, if the Commission decides to intervene to end an infringement of Article 106(1), is it obliged to use the special procedure under Article 106(3) or may it opt for the general procedure under Article 258?

---

[35] Case C-163/99 *Portuguese Airports* [2001] ECR I-2613, para 20; Case T-266/97 *VTM* [1999] ECR II-2329, para 75; Case T-111/96 *ITT Promedia* [1998] ECR II-2937, para 97; Case T-575/93 *Koelman* [1996] ECR II-1, paras 70–3, confirmed by Case C-59/96 P *Koelman (appeal)* [1997] ECR I-4809, paras 57–8; Case T-32/93 *Ladbroke I* [1994] ECR II-1031, paras 37–8; Case T-548/93 *Ladbroke II* [1995] ECR II-2584, para 45; Case T-84/94 *Expert Accountants* [1995] ECR II-101, para 31 upheld by the ECJ on appeal, Case C-107/95 P *Expert Accountants (appeal)* [1997] ECR I-965, para 27.

[36] Case T-54/99 *max.mobil* [2002] ECR II-313.

[37] Case T-54/99 *max.mobil* [2002] ECR II-313, paras 56–9.

[38] Case C-141/02 P *max.mobil (appeal)* [2005] ECR I-1283, paras 68–73.

[39] On this case, see C Hocepied, 'The Maxmobil Judgment: The Court of Justice Clarifies the Role of Complainants in Article 86 Procedures' (2005) 2 Competition Policy Newsletter 53. See also Order of the General Court in Case T 568/10 *Vivendi v Commission* [2012] OJ C49/22 (summary publication).

[40] See para 19.25 et seq. See also JL Buendía Sierra 'Enforcement of Article 106(1)' presented in the 2013 EU Competition Law and Policy Proceedings of the European University Institute, Florence (July 2013), publication forthcoming.

Although this question has not been expressly dealt with by the ECJ, it is submitted that the Commission has the discretionary power to opt for either of the procedures.[41] This is also suggested in the text of Article 106(3), which provides for the adoption of decisions only 'where necessary'. A clear parallel can be drawn with the situation affecting State aids, where the Court has held that bringing proceedings under Article 108 does not prevent proceedings being brought under Article 258.[42] In conclusion, the possibility of using the Article 258 procedure always remains open, although the nature of Article 106(3) should normally make it the more probable choice.

Commencing proceedings ex officio

The Commission may at any time commence proceedings of its own motion under Article 106(3).[43] It is sufficient for the Commission to have obtained information regarding a possible infringement of Article 106(1) by a Member State and for it to consider that it is necessary to act. The information may have been obtained from any source; from the press, from questionnaires carried out by civil servants, from sector studies, from parliamentary questions, and so on. **19.21**

2. The processing of complaints and 'own initiative' proceedings

Commencing proceedings on the basis of a complaint

In many cases the Commission acts following complaints submitted by individuals or undertakings. These complaints constitute a very important source of information for the Commission, enabling it, for example, to go beyond the legal texts and to understand how the law is applied in practice by national authorities. The complaints are examined during the processing stage, following which the Commission decides whether or not to commence infringement proceedings by sending the letter of formal notice to the Member State. The processing stage of complaints (or where files are opened on the Commission's own initiative) should not be confused with the infringement procedure. **19.22**

The processing of complaints

Contrary to what happens with antitrust cases,[44] there are no particular formalities for the submission of a complaint for the breach of Article 106(1). It is sufficient to send a letter which clearly identifies the complainant, fully describes the facts or measures of a Member State which are alleged to have breached Article 106(1), and requests the Commission to act. It is advisable, although not essential, to attach to the complaint the legal grounds for stating that a breach of Article 106(1) has been committed. There is no particular application form which must be used. The complaint has to be submitted before the Commission. **19.23**

---

[41] Case T-266/97 *VTM* [1999] ECR II-2329, para 75. This question has hardly been dealt with by academics. In favour of the optional nature of Art 106(3) was H Papaconstantinou, *Free Trade and Competition in the EEC. Law, Policy and Practice* (Routledge 1988) 113; J Flynn and E Turnbull, 'Joined Cases C-48/90 and C-66/90, (the "Dutch Couriers" case)' (1993) 30 CML Rev 402; and C Hocepied, 'Les directives Article 90, paragraphe 3. Une espèce juridique en voie de disparition?' [1994] RAE ii 55. However, this author highlights the advantages of Art 106(3) and considers that the Commission should opt, whenever possible, for this procedure.

[42] M Waelbroeck and D Waelbroeck, 'Article 169' in Various, *Commentaire Megret, Le Droit de la CEE*, Vol 10 (2nd edn, Editions de l'Université de Bruxelles 1993) 61.

[43] For example, Cases C-157/94–C-160/94 *Gas and Electricity Monopolies* [1997] ECR I-5699, 5789, 5815, and 5851.

[44] The rules contained in Commission Notice on the handling of complaints by the Commission under Articles [101 and 102 TFEU] [2004] OJ C101/65 do not apply to complaints based on complaints that ask the Commission to take action against a Member State pursuant to Art 106(3) in conjunction with Arts 101 or 102 of the Treaty. See para 6 of the Notice.

It may be sent to the postal address of the Commission,[45] to its General Secretary, to the Directorate-General which is in principle competent, or to the offices of the Commission in the Member States. The complaints are registered at a central registry which is part of the Secretariat-General of the Commission. There they are attributed to the competent Directorate-General or Directorates-General for processing. Normally the complaints based on Article 106 are processed by the Directorate-General for Competition ('DG COMP'). However, very often the complaints are simultaneously directed against the behaviour of undertakings (Articles 101 and 102), against State aids (Articles 107 and 108), and/or against other State measures (Article 106). For that reason, many of these complaints are only initially registered at the special registries for State aids and antitrust, although subsequently those aspects concerning Article 106 are separated from other aspects of the complaint and registered at the central registry.

19.24 The Commission notifies the complainant by letter of the registration of his or her complaint. Further, the complainant is informed that a copy of the complaint will be sent to the relevant Member State in order that it may submit its observations. If the complainant does not wish the Member State to be aware that he or she has brought the complaint, he or she has to clearly state this in the actual complaint. In such cases the Commission may, if it considers it appropriate, use the information thus obtained to act on its own motion. The complaint is examined by the Commission, which proceeds, if necessary, to request additional reports from the complainant. Normally, a copy of the complaint is transferred to the Member State in question to allow it to submit its observations.[46] The Commission may also request additional information from the Member State as well as from the undertakings concerned in order to clarify the situation. In such a case, the principle of 'sincere co-operation' established in Article 4(3) TEU obliges the Member State to cooperate with the Commission, by providing it with the information that it has in its possession. If the Member State does not cooperate, this may give rise to a breach of this principle by the Member State, which may result in proceedings under Article 258, such proceedings being separate from the main proceedings. More doubtful is how the Commission should behave as regards the undertakings concerned and what its obligations are regarding them. As mentioned, it is not unusual for the Commission, when receiving a complaint on these grounds, to make a request of information from the undertaking concerned.[47] Should the Commission be concerned with an autonomous violation of Articles 101 or 102 TFEU, it is clear that the Commission is empowered to perform such request under Article 18 of Regulation 1/2003. However, it is more doubtful what legal basis the Commission may have for performing such a request for information when the infringement at stake is attributable to the State and not to the undertakings. Similar considerations can be made as regards the practice of submitting a copy of the complainant and/or the letter of formal notice to the undertakings. Even if this is a step in the direction of increasing the transparency of EU institutions decision-making, it is doubtful whether the Commission has a legal basis for doing so. This practice seems to undermine the Commission traditional position of Article 106(3) procedures as procedures exclusively between the Commission and the concerned Member State. In any event, once the information requested has been received, the Commission decides whether to commence infringement proceedings against the Member State, having analysed the facts and the law. If it decides to proceed,

---

[45] European Commission, Rue de la Loi, 200, B-1049 Brussels.

[46] Sometimes a copy of the complaint is also sent to the undertaking concerned (see para 26 of Commission Decision of 20 October 2004 K(2004)4001/3 (not published in the Official Journal, 'OJ')) on the German postal legislation relating to mail preparation services, in particular the access of self-provision intermediaries and consolidators to the public postal network and related tariffs.

[47] See, *inter alia*, para 118 of Commission Decision (EC) of 5 March 2008 on the maintaining in force by the Hellenic Republic of rights in favour of Public Power Corporation SA for the extraction of lignite [2008] OJ C93/3 (summary publication).

it sends the Member State a letter of formal notice.[48] This decision is discretionary. Even in the case of a formal complaint, the complainant cannot force the Commission to commence proceedings.[49] The Commission informs each complainant of the steps taken against the Member State and the possible decision to commence proceedings.

Processing 'own initiative' cases

The Commission may also, of its own initiative, investigate facts which seem to it capable of constituting an infringement of the Treaty. The processing of these claims is similar to that for complaints. At the end of the processing stage, the Commission has to decide whether to proceed by beginning infringement proceedings or whether the case should be closed. **19.25**

Dismissal of complaints or inactivity of the Commission

The Commission may, in principle, dismiss a complaint based on Article 106 for legal or opportunity reasons. If the complaint is dismissed for legal reasons, the Commission informs the complainant by letter of the reasons why it considers that there has not been a breach of EU law. If the complaint is dismissed because this is considered opportune, the Commission limits itself to informing the complainant that the complaint does not have sufficient interest to justify the Commission's intervention and recommends that the complainant seek redress in a national court. The GC considered in *max.mobil* that the Commission may react to a complaint based on Article 106 by adopting a decision refusing to take action and that an action for annulment by the complainant against such a decision may be admissible. On appeal, however, the ECJ rejected this approach in its 2005 judgment. According to this judgment, such letters cannot be regarded as producing legal effects and cannot be subject to an action for annulment.[50] Of course, persons and undertakings wishing to complain about an alleged infringement of Article 106(1) still have the right to invoke the direct effect of this provision before national courts. This right is totally independent from the possibility of filing a complaint with the Commission and—legally speaking—it is not affected by the outcome of such complaint. The possibilities for complainants to react to an implicit or explicit refusal by the Commission are much more limited. Traditionally it was considered that complainants did not have *locus standi* either to bring an Article 263 annulment action against the Commission's refusal to initiate proceedings[51] or to bring an Article 265 action against the Commission's failure to act following a complaint based on Article 106.[52] According to the ECJ, such actions could only be introduced in 'exceptional situations'.[53] **19.26**

In *max.mobil*, the GC tried to interpret these 'exceptional situations' very widely, declaring that a complainant could attack the Commission's refusal to act or its lack of action if the **19.27**

---

[48] This letter of formal notice can also be sent to the undertaking concerned (see para 1 of Commission Decision (EC) of 10 May 2007 (not published in the OJ) on the special rights granted by the French Republic to La Banque Postale, Caisses d'Epargne, and Crédit Mutuel for the distribution of the *livret A* and *livret bleu*).

[49] This, at least, is the position adopted by the GC in Case T-32/93 *Ladbroke I* [1994] ECR II 1031, paras 37 and 38, and Case T-548/93 *Ladbroke II* [1995] ECR II-2584, para 45, as well as in Case T-84/94 *German Accountants* [1995] ECR II-101, para 31. Similarly, although less emphatically, the ECJ, in Case C-107/95 P *German Accountants (appeal)* [1997] ECR I-965, para 27, did not completely exclude the possibility that, in exceptional circumstances, the Commission may be obliged to act under Art 106(3). See paras 19.26–19.30 for a detailed discussion of this point.

[50] Case C-141/02 P *max.mobil (appeal)* [2005] ECR I-1283, para 70. See Order of the GC in Case T 568/10 *Vivendi v Commission* [2012] OJ C49/22 (summary publication).

[51] Case T-84/94 *Expert Accountants* [1995] ECR II-101, para 31, confirmed by Case C-107/95 P *Expert Accountants (appeal)* [1996] ECR I-957, para 27.

[52] Case T-32/93 *Ladbroke I* [1994] ECR II-1015, paras 34–6.

[53] Case C-141/02 P *max.mobil (appeal)* [2002] ECR I-1283. See also Opinion of AG Poiares Maduro of 21 October 2004.

complaint refers not to measures in general but to specific measures favouring a competitor.[54] This distinction was, however, hardly relevant to cases under Article 106(1). Indeed, one of the necessary conditions for this provision to apply is precisely that the measure at stake is not general but specific to public or privileged undertakings, and therefore the 'specificity' criteria will—by definition—be automatically fulfilled in all Article 106(1) cases. On appeal in the *max.mobil* case,[55] the ECJ reversed the GC ruling on the basis that the Commission's refusal to act under Article 106 cannot be the subject of judicial review proceedings under Article 258 TFEU. This reversal unfortunately confirms that the Commission enjoys a wide margin of discretion when deciding whether to initiate proceedings against a Member State for breach of Article 106(1) of the Treaty.[56]

19.28 The fact that the complainant cannot bring actions against the Commission's decision not to act or against its inactivity under Article 106(3) derives from the analogical application of the doctrine applicable to the procedure under Article 258. In fact, this analogy seems to dominate the conception that the Commission, the GC, and the ECJ have of the procedure under Article 106(3). However, other more flexible possibilities might have been conceived of, such as the application by analogy of the remedies applicable in the field of State aids[57] or under Regulation 1/2003, procedures from which the Commission itself sometimes 'borrows' tools for Article 106(3) procedures. The question was raised for the first time in 1989 in *Ladbroke*. In this case the undertaking, Ladbroke, submitted a complaint before the Commission, based, *inter alia*, on former Article 90 (now Article 106), against the organization of the betting system for horse racing in France. In 1992, Ladbroke demanded that the Commission adopt a final and definitive decision concerning the complaint. The mandatory time limit of two months had elapsed without the Commission having taken any decision, therefore Ladbroke started proceedings for the Commission's failure to act in the GC. Ladbroke argued that an analogy should be drawn between Article 106(3) and the rights of

---

[54] Case T-17/96 *TF 1* [1999] ECR II-1757, paras 52–7; Case T-54/99 *max.mobil* [2002] ECR II-313, paras 64–72.

[55] Case C-141/02 P *max.mobil (appeal)* [2005] ECR I-1283, paras 68–73.

[56] See Case C-141/02 P *max.mobil (appeal)* [2005] ECR I-1283, paras 68–73; Order of the GC in Case T 568/10 *Vivendi v Commission* [2012] OJ C49/22 (summary publication); Case T-84/94 *German Accountants* [1995] ECR II-101, para 31, and the more qualified judgment of the ECJ in Case C-107/95 P *German Accountants (appeal)* [1997] ECR I-965, para 27. Against this position, see the Opinion of AG La Pergola in the same case, paras 14–22. See para 462 for a detailed discussion of this point. For a detailed study of annulment proceedings see R Bray (ed), *Procedural Law of the European Union* (2nd edn, Sweet & Maxwell 2006) 203–325; M Waelbroeck and D Waelbroeck, 'Article 173' in Various, *Commentaire Megret, Le Droit de la CEE*, Vol 10 (2nd edn, Editions de l'Université de Bruxelles 1993) 97–170. In the same way, in the event that the Commission does not make a decision regarding the complaint, the complainant has no grounds for bringing proceedings for failure to act under Art 265 of the Treaty. See Case T-32/93 *Ladbroke I* [1994] ECR II-1030, paras 34–46. The exceptional circumstances that according to the ECJ in *German Accountants (appeal)* would allow annulment proceedings to be brought should, logically, open the door to possible proceedings for failure to act. For a detailed study of proceedings for failure to act see Bray, *Procedural Law of the European Union*, 329–41; Waelbroeck and Waelbroeck, 'La Cour de Justice', in Various, *Commentaire Megret, Le Droit de la CEE*, Vol 10 (2nd edn, Editions de l'Université de Bruxelles 1993) 177.

[57] Opinion of AG Poiares Maduro, Case C-141/02P *max.mobil (appeal)* [2005] ECR I-1283. At the time of writing, the Commission has launched the EU State aid modernization ('SAM') initiative. According to the Commission proposals, the procedural regulation on State aid might be modified in order to allow the Commission to focus on cases that are more relevant for the internal market. At this stage it is unclear if this would crystallize in a *de facto* right of the Commission to refuse to take action in certain cases. We do not find this an appropriate idea, given the design of State aid control contained in the TFEU that, for good reasons, entrusts the Commission exclusively with the task of assessing the compatibility of State aid measures. See Communication from the Commission of 8 May 2012, to the European Parliament, the Council, the European Economic and Social Committee and the Committee of the Regions, EU State Aid Modernisation (SAM) COM (2012) 209 final.

complainants that are recognized in the antitrust field.[58] The Commission did not accept this analogy and submitted that the closest analogy to Article 106(3) was Article 258, and that therefore the complainants did not have any such rights. Accordingly, the Commission requested that the proceedings be declared inadmissible. In *Ladbroke I*, the GC fully supported the Commission's position and confirmed the wide discretionary margin that the Commission enjoys. It rejected the analogy with antitrust procedures, held that Ladbroke was not a party that was directly and individually interested and affected, and declared that the proceedings were inadmissible.[59]

This approach, whereby the rights of the complainant are excluded under Article 106(3), **19.29** was followed to the letter by the GC in *German Accountants*.[60] In this case, proceedings were brought by a German accountancy association against the Commission, who had rejected a complaint submitted by the German association. The complaint, based in particular on Article 106, had required the Commission to act against Germany because of legislation that reserved the exercise of tax consultancy services to certain professions, which did not include the complainant association. The President of the GC declared the proceedings for annulment to be inadmissible. The complainant association appealed to the ECJ. In his Opinion, Advocate-General ('AG') La Pergola rejected the analogy between the procedures under Articles 106(3) and 258. Instead, the AG, on the basis of the case law regarding State aids, argued for the right of individuals to appeal against Commission decisions for failure to act on the basis of Article 106(3).[61] According to the AG, however wide the Commission's discretion, this does not exclude the possibility of jurisdictional control.[62] On this basis, the AG recommended that the ECJ quash the judgment of the GC.

In *German Accountants*, the ECJ did not follow this recommendation and upheld the judg- **19.30** ment of the GC. However, it distanced itself from the restrictive conception of third party rights that the GC had favoured, by making the following exception:[63]

> The possibility cannot be ruled out that exceptional situations might exist where an individual or, possibly, an association constituted for the defence of the collective interests of a class of individuals has standing to bring proceedings against a refusal by the Commission to adopt a decision pursuant to its supervisory functions under Article 90(1) and (3) [now Article 106(1) and (3)].

Having left open this possibility for when some as yet undefined 'exceptional situations' arise, the ECJ returned to the well-known argument of the 'wide discretion'[64] of the Commission and it added another more original argument:[65]

> Moreover, an individual may not, by means of an action against the Commission's refusal to take a decision against a Member State under Article 90(1) and (3) [now Article 106(1) and (3)], indirectly compel that Member State to adopt legislation of general application.

The clear impression which this judgment gives is that the ECJ is against comparing com- **19.31** plainants under Article 106(3) with complainants in State aid procedures. The reason for this

---

[58] Case T-32/93 *Ladbroke I* [1994] ECR II-1222, para 7.
[59] Case T-32/93 *Ladbroke I* [1994] ECR II-1030, paras 34–46.
[60] Case T-84/94 *German Accountants* [1995] ECR II-101, paras 27–32.
[61] Opinion of AG La Pergola in Case C-107/95 P *German Accountants (appeal)* [1997] ECR I-953, paras 14–22.
[62] Opinion of AG La Pergola in Case C-107/95 P *German Accountants (appeal)* [1997] ECR I-954, para 18.
[63] Case C-107/95 P *German Accountants (appeal)* [1997] ECR I-964, para 25.
[64] Case C-107/95 P *German Accountants (appeal)* [1997] ECR I-965, para 27.
[65] Case C-107/95 P *German Accountants (appeal)* [1997] ECR I-965, para 28.

is probably because of the different consequences that arise from the different procedures for the Member State involved. While, with respect to aid, the most that the Member State normally risks is being required to refund the aid granted, as regards Article 106 the result would, in many cases, entail substantial legislative change in areas which are particularly politically sensitive. Recognizing the right of individuals to appeal against the inactivity of the Commission is the same as obliging it to act almost automatically. Such an automatic obligation is, to a certain extent, logical in cases of specific intervention, such as aid. However, it is more risky with respect to such delicate matters as exclusive rights, where sensitive issues of a legal, political, and economic nature come into play. While this is broadly true and it must be recognized that the argument has its merits, it should nevertheless be noted that State aid may also involve very sensitive political and economic questions and that, sometimes, the aid cannot be removed without structural changes leading to further consequences in sensitive areas. This is particularly true in the case of aid schemes under the form of fiscal aid, which can be as politically and economically sensitive as exclusive rights. Indeed, the removal of a fiscal measure considered by the Commission as a State aid almost automatically means the change of national tax legislation (and perhaps the recovery of past aid in the form of lower taxes applied), something *a priori* comparable to the substantial legislative changes in politically sensitive areas that normally follow an Article 106(3) decision. Therefore, we do not find this a valid reason per se for limiting the rights of complainants in Article 106(3) procedures as regards their rights in State aid procedures.

19.32 In *max.mobil*, the GC tried to extend the possibilities of complainants to appeal against a refusal by the Commission to act under Article 106.[66] The judgment seemed to reduce the Commission's margin of discretion by making it clear that the Commission was obliged to examine complaints based on Article 106 TFEU in a diligent and objective way. This implied, on the one hand, that the Commission should at least give its reasons for considering that there is (or there is not) an infringement and whether it is considered necessary to intervene. On the other hand judicial review regarding these two issues (particularly with respect to the need to intervene) would in any case be minimal and limited to manifest errors.[67] On appeal in *max.mobil*,[68] the ECJ reversed the GC judgment, and confirmed the traditional interpretation that the Commission enjoys a wide margin of discretion when deciding whether to initiate proceedings against a Member State for breach of Article 106(1) of the Treaty. Therefore, the current position is that individuals cannot in principle appeal against the Commission's refusal to take action under Article 106(3) as regards State measures. After this reversal, the GC has attached to the superior court the doctrine as shown in *UFEX*, where it considered that:

> [I]t follows from the wording of Article 86(3) of the Treaty [now 106(3)] and from the scheme of that article as a whole that the Commission is not obliged to bring proceedings within the terms of those provisions, as individuals cannot require the Commission to take a position in a specific sense. A decision by the Commission to refuse to act on a complaint requesting it to take action is not such as to constitute a measure that is capable of being the subject of an action for annulment.[69]

19.33 As mentioned previously,[70] sometimes there is only a thin line between behaviour of undertakings contrary to Articles 101 and 102 and State measures contrary to Article 106(1)

---

[66] Case T-54/99 *max.mobil* [2002] ECR II-313.
[67] Case T-54/99 *max.mobil* [2002] ECR II-313, paras 56–9.
[68] Case C-141/02 P *max.mobil (appeal)* [2005] ECR I-1283, paras 68–73.
[69] Case T-60/05 *Union française d'express (UFEX) and Others v Commission* [2007] ECR II-3397, para 189. See Order of the GC in Case T 568/10 *Vivendi v Commission* [2012] OJ C49/22 (summary publication).
[70] See para 19.15.

applied in combination with these Articles. Thus, it is common for complainants to explore both grounds simultaneously. However, the rule mentioned earlier also applies in these cases. It was clearly stated by the GC in *UFEX* where it held that:

> Nor ... may the fact that the complainants combined a complaint directed against a Member State with a complaint against an undertaking confer on them entitlement to challenge the part of the decision concerning the complaint directed against the Member State. Since the Commission is not obliged to initiate an action under Article 86 EC [now 106 TFEU], plainly individuals cannot require it to act in such a way by combining a complaint directed against a Member State with a complaint against an undertaking.[71]

More intriguing would be the situation for a hypothetical complaint referring to State aid **19.34** linked with national provisions contrary to Article 106 in connection with internal market rules. In this case, and following its previous case law in *Matra*,[72] the ECJ has recently held in *British Aggregates* that:

> It [is] ... settled case-law that, although the procedure provided for in Articles [107 TFEU] and [108 TFEU] leaves a margin of discretion to the Commission for assessing the compatibility of an aid scheme with the requirements of the [internal] market, it is clear from the general scheme of the [TFEU] that that procedure must never produce a result which is contrary to the specific provisions of the [TFEU].[73]

On this basis the Court concluded that:

> Accordingly, State aid, certain conditions of which contravene other provisions of the EC Treaty, cannot be declared by the Commission to be compatible with the common market[74]

Arguably, following this case law, a complaint on a State aid measure at its turn contravening **19.35** Article 106 in connection with internal market rules, should oblige the Commission—at least if the Commission assess the aid as compatible—to define its position not only on the assessment of the aid, but also on Article 106 grounds.[75] If, on the contrary, the complaint is limited to the ground of a violation by the Member State of Article 106 in connection with other articles—*inter alia*, internal market rules—the Commission may dismiss the complaint according to the *max.mobil* case law with a large margin of discretion and without being subject to judicial review. A comparison of both situations points to a lack of coherence in the system.

3. Infringement proceedings

Commencement of infringement proceedings

Normally infringement proceedings are commenced by the Commission sending a letter of **19.36** formal notice to the Member State. In certain cases, however, the letter could be preceded by the adoption of interim measures.

---

[71] Case T-60/05 *Union française d'express (UFEX) and Others v Commission* [2007] ECR II-3397, para 193.
[72] Case C-225/91 *Matra v Commission* [1993] ECR I-3203, para 41.
[73] Case T-359/04 *British Aggregates Association and Others v Commission* [2010] ECR II-4227, para 91.
[74] Case T-359/04 *British Aggregates Association and Others v Commission* [2010] ECR II-4227, para 92.
[75] Furthermore—and even if perhaps this is not the place to deal with the topic—this possible incoherence is not exclusive to Art 106 cases, as it also arises when comparing the situation of a complainant on a national measure contrary to the fundamental freedoms—where the Commission also has a large margin of discretion for deciding whether or not to initiate a procedure against the Member State—and a complainant on a State aid measure that in its turn contravenes those freedoms. The reason for this is the design of State aid control contained in the TFEU, that exclusively entrusts the Commission with the assessment of the compatibility of measures qualifying as State aid under Article 107 TFEU.

Interim measures

19.37 It is submitted that, by analogy with the approach of the ECJ in the field of antitrust cases,[76] the Commission may, when necessary, order specific measures which enable it to fulfil effectively the task that it is entrusted with under Article 106(3).[77] Thus, while Article 106(3) does not expressly say anything about interim measures, by taking this approach, it is possible for the Commission to adopt such measures under this provision. In any event, interim measures can only be adopted where an emergency situation exists and where, if they were not adopted, this would seriously and irreparably prejudice the concerned party or the general interest. The Commission may only order provisional measures after having heard the observations of the Member State,[78] and the objective of the measures thus adopted can only be to maintain the existing situation until the main proceedings are resolved.

The letter of formal notice

19.38 Article 106(3) is silent with respect to the letter of notice. However, in *PTT*, the ECJ held that the rights of defence of a Member State require the Commission to inform it in an exact and complete manner, before adopting the decision, of the charges against it and of the legal reasoning upon which the charges are based. This is necessary in order to give the Member State the opportunity to submit its observations.[79] This information is normally given in the form of a letter of formal notice sent by the Commission to the government of the Member State in question. In *PTT*, the Court examined two actions for annulment under Article 263 brought by the Dutch government and the public undertaking PTT Nederland NV against a decision adopted in 1989 by the Commission under Article 106(3) concerning courier mail services in the Netherlands.[80] In its decision, the Commission considered that the grant of exclusive rights by the State to the public undertaking PTT Nederland NV for the activities of courier mail services constituted a breach of the Treaty. The ECJ found that there was a case to answer in both actions: the action brought by the government of the Netherlands in its capacity as addressee of the decision, and the action brought by the beneficiary undertaking, as a directly interested party in the proceedings.

19.39 The ECJ annulled the decision of the Commission, holding that neither the Member State's right to a fair defence nor the beneficiary undertaking's right to be heard had been respected during the proceedings. The right to a fair defence of the Member State includes in particular the right to 'receive an exact and complete statement of the objections which the Commission intends to raise against it'.[81] This implies that the letter of formal notice must contain the following information: a statement of the State measure that is the object of the proceedings; the Treaty provisions which are considered to be breached by the Member State; and the reasons why the Commission considers that an infringement has occurred. The letter of formal notice sets a time limit within which the Member State must inform the Commission of the measures adopted in order to correct the position or notify the Commission of the reasons why the Member State disagrees with the Commission's position. The letter concludes by stating that the Commission may adopt a decision under Article 106(3) of the Treaty.[82] The object of the proceedings is set out in the letter of formal notice in such a way that any subsequent decision cannot be based on legal grounds that have not been stated in the letter. In addition, the

---

[76] Case 792/79 R *Camera Care Ltd v EC Commission* [1980] ECR 119.

[77] This is implied in the Opinion of AG Reischl in Joined Cases C-188–190/80 *Transparency Directive* [1982] ECR I-2587.

[78] Joined Cases C-48/90 and C-66/90 *PTT* [1992] ECR I-639, para 44.

[79] Joined Cases C-48/90 and C-66/90 *PTT* [1992] ECR I-639, para 45.

[80] Commission Decision (EEC) 90/16 *Courier Postal Services—The Netherlands* [1990] OJ L10/50.

[81] Joined Cases C-48/90 and C-66/90 *PTT* [1992] ECR I-639, para 45.

[82] Normally in the letter of formal notice, the Commission states whether it intends to proceed under Art 106(3) or Art 258. However, it is submitted that there is nothing to prevent the letter leaving both options open.

Commission cannot require measures that are not referred to in the letter to be modified. If the Commission considers that it is necessary to modify the object of the proceedings, it must offer the Member State an opportunity to submit its own observations, normally by sending an additional letter of formal notice. In general, the Commission does not publicize the fact that it has sent a letter of formal notice to a Member State: only the Member State is notified. Nevertheless, in certain cases the Commission may decide to give some publicity to its actions.

The rights of the Member State, the beneficiary undertaking, and the complainant

In *PTT*, the ECJ held that, although the procedure under Article 106(3) is only directed **19.40** against the Member State, which is the only party that enjoys the right to a fair defence,[83] the undertaking that benefits from the State measure in question has a right to be heard under the infringement procedure.[84] This means that there is a right to be informed of the Commission's position and a right to make comments to the Commission. However, the undertaking does not have a right to know the comments made by the Member State nor a right to obtain a copy of the complaint.[85] The impossibility for the beneficiary undertaking to have access to the Commission's file is similar to the traditional rule applying in State aid cases. However, recent developments in State aid case law merit some reflection in this regard. First, the ECJ case law has shown a more nuanced approach to the status of the beneficiary undertakings. Specifically, it has recognized in the *Ferriere Nord* case that parties concerned in State aid procedures, although they are not parties to the procedures and cannot rely on the rights of defence for that procedure, have the right to be associated with it in an adequate manner, taking into account the circumstances of the case at issue.[86] However, the very specific context of the case does not allow the extraction of further consequences from the rather vague statement of the Court. Secondly, the question on whether beneficiary undertakings could have access to the Commission's file in State aid cases has recently been subject to analysis by the GC and the ECJ. It is worth recalling in this regard the possible conflict between a radical denial of such access—arguably motivated in the risk that such disclosure poses to the protection of the objectives of the investigation activities—and the general right of access to documents of the EU's institutions established in Article 15(3) TFEU, Article 2(1) of Regulation 1049/2001,[87] and Article 42 of the Charter of Fundamental Rights of the European Union. In December 2006, the GC issued a judgment in the *Technische Glaswerke Ilmenau* case in which, in an approximation to the rules applicable under Regulation 1/2003, it stated that the Commission could only refuse beneficiary undertakings having access to documents in the Commission file after having performed an individual assessment, document by document, of:

> whether access to the document would specifically and actually undermine the protected interest and, secondly, in the circumstances referred to in Article 4(2) and (3) of Regulation No 1049/2001, whether there was no overriding public interest in disclosure. In addition, the risk of a protected interest being undermined must be reasonably foreseeable and not purely hypothetical.[88]

However, on appeal, the ECJ quashed the GC judgment and stated that:

---

[83] Joined Cases C-48/90 and C-66/90 *PTT* [1992] ECR I-640, para 49. See also Case T-226/97 *VTM* [1999] ECR II-2329, paras 32–7.

[84] Joined Cases C-48/90 and C-66/90 *PTT* [1992] ECR I-640, para 49.

[85] Case T-226/97 *VTM* [1999] ECR II-2329, para 37.

[86] Case C-49/05 P *Ferriere Nord SpA v Commission* [2008] ECR I-68, para 69.

[87] Regulation (EC) No 1049/2001 of the European Parliament and of the Council of 30 May 2001 regarding public access to European Parliament, Council and Commission documents [2001] OJ L145/43.

[88] Case T-237/02, *Technische Glaswerke Ilmenau GmbH v Commission* [2006] ECR II-5131, para 77.

[I]nterested parties other than the Member state concerned in the procedures for reviewing State aid do not have the right to consult the documents in the Commission's administrative file…[D]isclosure of documents in the administrative file in principle undermines protection of the objectives of investigation activities.[89]

19.41 Thus, the Commission can rely on such a general principle for denying access to documents in the Commission State aid file. However, the Court left open the possibility for the party to demonstrate that the specific documents for which access is requested is not protected by such principle as, in the words of the Court:

> that general presumption does not exclude the right of those interested parties to demonstrate that a given document disclosure of which has been requested is not covered by that presumption, or that there is a higher public interest justifying the disclosure of the document concerned by virtue of Article 4(2) of Regulation 1049/2001.[90]

It seems doubtful whether these parties could demonstrate that a document of which, by definition, the applicant does not have a precise knowledge is not covered by the presumption.[91] Given the similarities between State aid procedures and Article 106(3) procedures, it is probable that a similar rule could apply in procedures under Article 106(3). It will be interesting to see if any State aid beneficiary will be able to set aside the presumption and actually have access to the documents requested, and whether the circumstances of such a hypothetical case can be replicated in an Article 106(3) procedure.

19.42 As regards the complainant, as explained earlier, the case law offers limited rights, since he or she is considered as a third party without any direct and individual rights, and therefore is not legally able to bring proceedings for failure to act or for annulment.[92] Accordingly, the complainant has no right to participate in the proceedings, although the Commission may, if it considers it appropriate, notify the complainant of the nature of the response to the letter of formal notice and ask for the complainant's opinion, as well as any additional information. However, this level of participation does not make the complainant a party directly and individually concerned for the purpose of Articles 263 and 265.[93] In the event that the complainant or any other third party provides their opinion, the Commission would have to notify the Member State concerned before a decision is adopted.[94]

---

[89] Case C-139/07 *Commission v Technische Glaswerke Ilmenau* [2010] ECR I-5885, para 61.

[90] Case C-139/07 *Commission v Technische Glaswerke Ilmenau* [2010] ECR I-5885, para 62.

[91] For a subsequent case in which the GC applied the ECJ doctrine and refused access to the documents in the file, see Joined Cases T-494/08–T-500/08 and T-509/08 *Ryanair Ltd v Commission* [2010] ECR II-5723. See also Joined Cases T-109/05 and T-444/05 *Navigazione Libera del Golfo Srl (NLG) v Commission*, not yet reported, in which, even if reiterating the ECJ doctrine in *Commission v Technische Glaswerke Ilmenau*, the GC required the Commission to perform an individual examination of requests of information in the Commission file. In this case, the exception put forward by the Commission did not relate to 'undermining the objectives of investigation activities' but that the data requested (the costs taken into consideration for the evaluating the compensation of certain public services under EU State aid rules) might constitute commercial secrets.

[92] Case C-141/02 P *max.mobil (appeal)* [2005] ECR I-1283, para 70; Case T-32/93 *Ladbroke I* [1994] ECR II-1032, paras 40–2.

[93] Case C-141/02 P *max.mobil (appeal)* [2005] ECR I-1283, paras 70–3; Case T-32/93 *Ladbroke I* [1994] ECR II-1033, para 43.

[94] The fact that the Commission did not inform the Member State of the observations submitted by the courier undertakings was one of the reasons which led the Court to annul the decision in *PTT* (Joined Cases C-48/90 and C-66/90 *PTT* [1992] ECR I-639, para 46).

The termination of proceedings without a final decision being given

Decisions which have been formally adopted by the Commission on the basis of Article **19.43** 106(3) are rare, but those finally adopted only constitute perhaps the tip of the iceberg.[95] Arguably, in some cases, infringement proceedings end without a formal decision being adopted, either because the Member State accepts the Commission's requirements, or because the Commission modifies its position in light of the Member State's observations. If the case is sufficiently important, the settlement reached is given a degree of publicity.[96] However, the Commission is not bound under Article 106 to adopt a formal decision stating that this provision has not been infringed, and arguably most of the complaints on Article 106 finish at this dead end. So, contrary to what happens with regard to State aid cases, there are normally no 'positive' Article 106 decisions.[97] As the *Vivendi* case makes clear, a mere letter to the complainant rejecting its complaint does not have legal effect and therefore cannot prevent the Commission from taking action under Article 106(3) TFEU at a later stage.[98] Therefore, such a letter does not imply a 'positive' Article 106 decision. Given that the Commission seems not to adopt a proactive approach in these cases, a change in the lenient position of the ECJ in *max.mobil*, becoming closer to State aid procedures, would perhaps provide Article 106 with a necessary *élan vital*.[99]

4. The formal decision and its effects

Formal decisions under Article 106(3)

If the matter is not settled following the letter of formal notice, the Commission may proceed **19.44** to adopt a formal decision under Article 106(3). The Commission retains a wide margin of discretion to decide whether or not to adopt such a decision, and to date it has adopted twenty decisions of this kind.[100] Decisions adopted by the Commission under Article 106(3) are normal 'decisions', as provided by Article 288 of the TFEU.[101] By virtue of Article 296 TFEU, decisions 'shall state the reasons on which they are based'. The recitals describe the legal reasoning which led the Commission to the conclusion that the State measure in question breached Article 106(1) in conjunction with one or more Articles of the Treaty. The decision declares that the State measure is incompatible with the provisions referred to, and states the measures that the Member State must adopt in order to comply with its obligations under EU law.[102] In addition, the Member State is given a specific time limit within which it must notify the Commission that it has adopted the necessary measures. Thus, decisions adopted under Article 106(3) enable the Commission not only to declare that the Member

---

[95] C Hocepied, 'Les directives articles 90, paragraphe 3. Une espèce juridique en voie de disparition?' [1994] RAE ii 52.

[96] Through press releases, the Reports on Competition Policy, and the Commission's periodic publications.

[97] A possible *sui generis* exception to this is Commission Decision (EC) of 4 August 2009, relating to a proceeding under Article [106(3) TFEU] establishing the specific measures to correct the anti-competitive effects of the infringement identified in the Commission Decision of 5 March 2008 on the granting or maintaining in force by the Hellenic Republic of rights in favour of Public Power Corporation SA for the extraction of lignite adopted in case COMP/B-1/38.700 [2009] OJ C243/5 (summary publication). By this decision the Commission took the view that the measures proposed by Greece in order to correct the infringement of Art 106 were necessary and proportional in removing the effects of the infringement (see para 50 of the decision).

[98] Order of the GC in Case T 568/10 *Vivendi v Commission* [2012] OJ C49/22 (summary publication).

[99] See JL Buendía Sierra, 'Exclusive or Special Rights under Article 106: An Overview of EU and National Case Law' 20 March 2012, n 44436 e-competitions. See also JL Buendía Sierra 'Enforcement of Article 106(1)' presented in the 2013 EU Competition Law and Policy Proceedings of the European University Institute, Florence (July 2013), publication forthcoming.

[100] See para 19.13.

[101] For an analysis of the concept of 'decision' in the EC Treaty, see R Greaves, 'The Nature and Binding Effect of Decisions under Article 189 EC' [1996] ELR 3.

[102] Joined Cases C-48/90 and C-66/90 *PTT* [1992] ECR I-635, para 28; Case C-107/95 P *German Accountants (appeal)* [1997] ECR I-964, para 23.

State has committed a breach, but also to specify the particular measures that it must adopt to remedy the situation. This means that although the breach may, in principle, be eliminated in different ways, the Commission can require the Member State to proceed in the way that the Commission prefers.[103] Beside this, in a relatively recent case, and following a previous decision under Article 106(3) in which the existence of a State measure contrary to the Treaty was declared, the Commission has adopted a decision under Article 106(3) whose content—arguably inspired by antitrust procedures—consists of taking note of the remedies proposed by the Member State in question and making them binding within a certain time-frame.[104] According to Article 297(2) of the TFEU, the decision is notified to the Member State in question and takes effect from the date of its notification. Normally, decisions adopted under Article 106(3) are subsequently published in the OJ. However, there is an increasing—and regrettable—tendency in recent years to publish just the summary of decisions adopted under this legal basis, or even not to publish them at all in the Official Journal.[105]

The obligatory nature of Article 106(3) decisions

19.45 Decisions adopted under Article 106(3) are normal decisions, as provided for in Article 288 of the Treaty, and are therefore obligatory for the Member State to whom they are addressed.[106] Despite the wording of Article 106(3), there were some authors who initially doubted that Article 106(3) 'decisions' were truly binding decisions within the meaning of Article 288, and who maintained that they were in fact more similar to recommendations.[107] Such authors viewed Article 106(3) as being a derogation from the normal procedure under Article 258. According to them, the Commission cannot itself declare the existence of a breach by a Member State, nor is the Member State obliged to comply with a decision that is addressed to it by the Commission under Article 106(3). Such effects may only be obtained from a judgment of the ECJ in which the Court declares, in proceedings brought under Article 258, that the Member State had breached the Treaty. The fact that Article 106(3), unlike Article 108(2), does not expressly exclude Article 226 supports this argument.

19.46 This interpretation was defended by the Greek government in *Greek Insurance*,[108] a case that perfectly illustrates this issue. In 1985, the Commission adopted a decision based on Article 106(3) in which Greece was stated to have breached its obligations under Article 106(1) in conjunction with Articles 49 TFEU (former Article 52 EC), 53 EC (now derogated), 4(3) TEU (former Article 5 EC), and former Article 3 of the EC Treaty, by adopting legislation which obliged State banks to recommend to their clients that they obtain insurance from

---

[103] Joined Cases C-48/90 and C-66/90 *PTT* [1992] ECR I-635, para 28; Case C-107/95 P *German Accountants (appeal)* [1997] ECR I-964.

[104] Commission Decision (EC) of 4 August 2009 [2009] OJ C243/5 (summary publication) establishing the specific measures to correct the anti-competitive effects of the infringement identified in the Commission Decision of 5 March 2008 on the granting of maintaining into force by the Hellenic Republic of rights in favour of Public Power Corporation SA for the extraction of lignite.

[105] This is the case for Commission Decision of 20 October 2004, K(2004)4001/3 on the German postal legislation relating to mail preparation services, in particular the access of self-provision intermediaries and consolidators to the public postal network and related tariffs or Commission Decision of 10 May 2007 (not published in the OJ) on the special rights granted by the French Republic to La Banque Postale, Caisses d'Epargne and Crédit Mutuel for the distribution of the *livret A* and *livret bleu*. However, most of the decisions are available at DG COMP's website or can be requested from the Commission.

[106] Case C-136/99 *Portuguese Airports* [2001] ECR I-2613, paras 19–20; Case C-226/87 *Commission v Greece (Greek Insurance)* [1988] ECR I-3623, para 12.

[107] A Pappalardo, 'Régime de l'Article 90 du Traité CEE: les aspects juridiques' in Various, *L'entreprise publique et la concurrence. Les articles 90 et 37 du Traité CEE et leurs relations avec la concurrence* (Semaine de Bruges, 1968, De Temple, Bruges, 1969) 81; G Marenco, 'Public Sector and Community Law' [1983] 20 CML Rev 522.

[108] Case 226/87 *Greek Insurance* [1988] ECR 3611–3625.

State insurers.[109] The Commission decision ordering Greece to stop the breach was ignored by the Greek authorities, which neither complied with the decision nor appealed against it within the given time limits. The Commission therefore brought infringement proceedings under Article 258 against Greece, based not on the breach of Article 106(1) together with Articles 3, 5, 52, and 53 of the EC Treaty (currently Articles 49 TFEU and 4(3) of the EU Treaty) but on Greece's failure to respect the Commission's decision. These proceedings led to the judgment of the ECJ in *Greek Insurance*. In this judgment, the Court confirmed that the Greek Republic was obliged to execute the decision of the Commission unless the ECJ suspended or annulled it.[110] Given that the Greek republic had not appealed within the time limit of two months, nor had it applied for the suspension of the measure,[111] the decision had automatically become final. This meant that once the time limit had elapsed, the Greek government could no longer bring proceedings before the ECJ challenging the legality of the decision: it was obliged to comply with it.[112] The exception of illegality may only be adduced when the decision is so seriously defective that it could be classified as non-existent.[113] Such a very exceptional possibility has been subsequently mentioned by the ECJ case law, although—to our knowledge on this issue—it has never been applied.[114] The *Greek Insurance* and *Portuguese Airports* judgments confirmed that decisions under Article 106(3) bind the Member States to which they are addressed.[115] The obligatory nature also affects the judicial organs of the Member State.[116] To the extent that the decision imposes clear and unconditional obligations upon the Member State, the decision will probably have direct effect and may be invoked by individuals before the national courts once the deadline has expired without the measures being implemented.[117] For example, an undertaking that wishes to operate an activity which is subject to an exclusive right may base its case on a decision declaring an exclusive right to be contrary to the Treaty. As will be explained later, the decision could also serve as the basis for a claim for damages against the Member State under the rule in *Francovich*.[118]

Proceedings for annulment against a formal decision under Article 106(3)

The Member State to whom the decision is addressed has two months from the date of notification of the decision to bring proceedings for annulment before the ECJ under Article 263 of the Treaty.[119] Article 278 provides that the proceedings do not, in principle, have suspensory 　**19.47**

---

[109] Commission Decision (CEE) 85/276 concerning the insurance in Greece of public property and loans granted by Greek State-owned banks [1985] OJ L152/25.

[110] Case 226/87 *Greek Insurance* [1988] ECR 3623, para 12.

[111] Case T-23/01 R *Poste Italiane* [2001] ECR II-1479.

[112] Case 226/87 *Greek Insurance* [1988] ECR 3623–3624, paras 13–14.

[113] Case 226/87 *Greek Insurance* [1988] ECR 3624, para 16.

[114] See, *inter alia*, Case C74/91 *Commission v Germany* [1992] ECR I-5437, para 11; Case C404/97 *Commission v Portugal* [2000] ECR I-4897, para 35; Case C-404/00 *Commission v Spain* [2003] ECR I-6695, para 41; Case C-189/09 *Commission v Austria* [2010] ECR I-99, para 16.

[115] Case C-163/99 *Portuguese Airports* [2001] ECR I-2613, paras 19–20.

[116] R Greaves, 'The Nature and Binding Effect of Decisions under Article 189 EC' [1996] ELR xxi 13.

[117] LM Pais Antunes, 'L'Article 90 du Traité CEE—Obligations des Etats Membres et pouvoirs de la Commission' [1991] RTDE ii 205–6; C Hocepied, 'Les directives Article 90, paragraphe 3. Une espèce juridique en voie de disparition?' [1994] RAE ii 55. The direct effect of decisions in general was recognized by the Court in Case 9/70 *Franz Grad v Finanzamt Traunstein (Grad)* [1970] ECR 838 para 5; Case 249/85 *Albako Margarinefabrik Maria von der Linde GmbH & Co KG v Bundesanstalt für landwirtschaftliche Marktordnung—'Berlin butter' (Albako)* [1987] ECR 2345, para 17. See also G Isaac, *Droit communautaire général* (4th edn, Masson 1994) 129, 172–3; R Greaves, 'The Nature and Binding Effect of Decisions under Article 189 EC' [1996] ELR xxi 13–14.

[118] Joined Cases C-6/90 and C-9/90 *Francovich* [1991] ECR I-5357, paras 36–7.

[119] An action of this type was what gave rise to the *RTT* judgment (Case C-18/88 *Régie des télégraphes et des téléphones v GB-Inno-BM SA (RTT)* [1991] ECR I-5941). For a detailed study of actions for annulment see R Bray (ed), *Procedural Law of the European Union* (2nd edn, Sweet & Maxwell 2006) 203–325;

effect, but the Member State may request the Court to adopt an interim suspension.[120] The suspension would only be granted if the usual conditions for interim measures (*prima facie* good case, urgency and balance of public and private interest) are fulfilled. As regards the beneficiary undertaking of the State measure challenged, although the decision is not addressed to it, it is directly and individually affected by the decision. Therefore it has the right to bring an action for annulment under Article 263 of the Treaty.[121] In addition, other third parties that can show a direct and individual interest in the decision might be able to bring proceedings.[122] If, after the time limit of two months has expired, proceedings for annulment have not been brought, or having been brought, the proceedings have been dismissed by the ECJ, the decision becomes final and its legality cannot be further questioned, unless—as already stated—it is so seriously defective that it should be declared non-existent.[123]

Proceedings in the event of non-compliance with the decision by the Member State

19.48 Once the time limit stated in the decision has elapsed, and assuming that the Court has not suspended its execution under Article 278, if the decision has not been enforced by the Member State to whom it is addressed, the Commission may bring proceedings under Article 258, asking the Court to make a declaration that the Member State has failed to comply with the decision.[124] Whereas under Article 108(2), paragraph 2, concerning State aid cases, the Commission can bring an action directly to the ECJ without having to go through the pre-contentious stage as laid down in Article 258, Article 106(3) does not allow this 'fast-track' procedure. The Commission must send a letter of formal notice and subsequently a reasoned opinion to the Member State before it can commence proceedings under Article 258. It is important to emphasize that if proceedings are brought under Article 258 this does not mean a re-examination of the merits of the case. The ECJ will limit itself to examining whether the State has complied with the decision, without questioning its legality, unless—once again—it contains defects which are so serious that the decision is held to be non-existent.[125] If a Member State persists in refusing to comply with the decision after having been found by the ECJ to have failed to fulfil its obligations, Article 260(2) TFEU allows the Commission to initiate proceedings which can result in the ECJ imposing fines upon the Member State in question.

Liability of Member States for failure to fulfil their obligations under EU law

19.49 Apart from the actions of the Commission and the Court, following *Francovich*, individuals and undertakings that have suffered loss as a result of a Member State's failure to fulfil its obligations under Article 106 can sue the Member State in question for damages.[126]

G Isaac, *Droit communautaire général* (4th edn, Masson 1994) 245–57; M Waelbroeck and D Waelbroeck, 'Article 173' in Various, *Commentaire Megret, Le Droit de la CEE*, Vol 10 (2nd edn, Editions de l'Université de Bruxelles 1993) 97–170.

[120] See, eg Case T-53/01 R *Poste Italiane* [2001] ECR II-1479.

[121] This is clear from Joined Cases C-48 and 66/90 *PTT* [1992] ECR I-640, para 50, and from the Opinion of AG van Gerven in the same case (ECR I-593, para 5). See also Case C-107/95 P *German Accountants (appeal)* [1997] ECR I-947, para 24 'individuals may, in some circumstances, be entitled to bring an action for annulment'.

[122] The language of the Court appears deliberately loose in Case C-107/95 P *German Accountants (appeal)* [1997] ECR I-947, para 24.

[123] Case C-226/87 *Greek Insurance* [1988] ECR I-3623, paras 12–16.

[124] Case C-226/87 *Greek Insurance* [1988] ECR I-3623, paras 11–17; Joined Cases C-48/90 and C-66/90 *PTT* [1992] ECR I-637, para 36. The main features of Art 258 were examined in the previous section.

[125] Case C-226/87 *Greek Insurance* [1988] ECR I-3623, paras 13–16.

[126] Joined Cases C-6/90 and C-9/90 *Andrea Francovich and Danila Bonifaci and others v Italy (Francovich)* [1991] ECR I-5337, paras 36–7.

20

DIRECTIVES UNDER ARTICLE 106(3)[1]

José Luis Buendía Sierra

A. Functions of Directive under Article 106(3) TFEU

In order to fulfil the task of guardian that Article 106(3) of the Treaty on the Functioning of **20.01** the European Union ('TFEU') entrusts to the Commission, this institution has the power to address, 'where necessary', not only decisions but also directives to Member States. This power to adopt directives which Article 106(3) grants to the Commission gives rise to sensitive problems of a legal and, particularly, of a political nature. A full understanding of paragraphs 1 and 2 of Article 106 requires taking into consideration the institutional dimension implicit in Article 106(3). Thus, the interpretation given to the substantive rules contained in Article 106(1) and (2) becomes more important given the Commission's power to adopt directives under paragraph 3. In the same way, the significance, in terms of the institutional structure of the EU, of the rule-making power enjoyed by the Commission under Article 106(3) is largely due to the politically sensitive nature of the rules applied.

The relationship between the substantive and procedural rules in the field of exclusive rights **20.02** is particularly close. This particular closeness arises from certain fundamental differences in the nature of the EU legal system as compared with national legal systems. Thus, unlike most national constitutional rules regarding State intervention in the economy, which establish a programme of general goals to be attained (but which are nevertheless legally unenforceable), the Treaty rules directly impose legal obligations on Member States that they are obliged to respect and that—under certain conditions— individuals can invoke before the courts.[2] The primary function of Article 106(1) and (2) TFEU is not, therefore, to provide the legislator of the EU with a programme of general goals, but to impose obligations upon Member States. In turn, within their respective areas of competence, the Court of Justice ('ECJ'), the national

---

[1] The author of this chapter wishes to thank Jose Manuel Panero Rivas for his assistance on the drafting of certain sections.
[2] A Alonso Ureba, 'El marco constitucional económico español y la adhesión a las Comunidades europeas' in E Garcia de Enterria, JD Gonzalez Campos, and S Muñoz Machado (eds), Vol I (Civitas 1986) 253.

courts, and the Commission have to ensure that these obligations are observed. Some of the implications of this system are not always fully taken on board by everyone. In the legal system of the EU, unlike in other legal systems, the abolition of exclusive rights is not a question left to the free discretion of the legislator of the moment. Rather, it is a fundamental choice largely put into effect by the signatory States to the Treaty of Rome,[3] accepted by the new Member States, and ratified each time that the Treaties have been revised.[4] It is important not to lose sight of this point, since this characteristic of EU law in general and Article 106 in particular blurs the dividing line between what is 'creating law' and what is 'applying the law in force'.[5]

20.03 In addition, in the words of Advocate-General ('AG') Reischl: 'Montesquieu's principle is only partially put into effect in the European Union and it is not possible simply to identify the Commission with the executive and the Council with the legislature.'[6] In the legal system of the EU, the three classic functions cannot be perfectly identified with the institutions that exist.[7] Legislative power is currently shared by the Council and by the European Parliament, with the important qualification that the Commission has a quasi-monopoly over legislative initiative.[8] Executive power in the past tended to be identified with the Commission,[9] but

---

[3] This was explained by Baron Snoy et D'Oppuers, member of the Belgian delegation, during the *travaux préparatoires* for the Treaty, in an interesting article, 'La notion de l'intérêt de la Communauté à l'article 90 du Traité de Rome sur le marché Commun—rapport international' in *Concorrenza tra settore pubblico e privato nella CEE*, Colloquio di Bruxelles della 'Ligue Internationale contre la concurrence déloyale' 5–6 March [1963] RDI anno XII 252.

[4] An interesting—but already anecdotal—remark in this regard should be made on the text of the failed Constitutional Treaty, whose Article III-166(3), the equivalent to the current Article 106(3) TFEU, established that:

> The Commission shall ensure the application of this Article and shall, where necessary, adopt appropriate *European regulations* or decisions [emphasis added].

> This could be interpreted as an attempt to devaluate Article 106(3) directives. Indeed, it is worth recalling that under the Constitutional Treaty (see Article I-33) the equivalent to current directives were 'European Framework laws' and the equivalent to current Regulations 'European laws'. The term 'European Regulation' mentioned by the failed Article III-166(3) was reserved for [A]ct[s] of general application *for the implementation of legislative acts* and of certain provisions of the Constitution. It may either be binding in its entirety and directly applicable in all Member States, or be binding, as to the result to be achieved, upon each Member State to which it is addressed, but shall leave to the national authorities the choice of form and methods. (See Article I-33 of the Constitutional Treaty.)

However, this devaluation did not finally take place, as, when the content of the Constitutional Treaty was 'recycled' into the Treaty of Lisbon, the wording of Article 106(3) remained identical to the one of the former Article 86(3) EC, and the powers of the Commission to issue Directives under Article 106(3) remained unchanged.

[5] In fields such as EU law, where the legal instruments available do not match traditional legal methods, the words of Hans Kelsen make complete sense: 'Is interpretation an act of applying knowledge or is it instead an act of free will? There is no essential difference between, on the one hand, the preparation of a court judgment or an administrative act carried out in accordance with a statute and, on the other hand, the drafting of a statute in accordance with the Constitution...There is however a qualitative difference between these two cases, as the freedom of the legislator is, from a substantive point of view, greater than that of a judge. Nevertheless, a judge is also called on to create legal rules and enjoys a degree of freedom in his activity, since the creation of an individual rule [the judgment] is an act of will to the extent that it consists in completing the framework provided by one or more general rules.' *Théorie pure du droit*, Author's translation of French translation by H Thévenaz (Edn de la Baconnière 1988) 153.

[6] Opinion of AG Reischl in Cases 188–190/80 *Transparency Directive* [1982] ECR 2585.

[7] Neither do classifications other than that of Montesquieu fit, such as the distinction between functions of coordination, of policy-making, of administration, and of control, proposed by N Emiliou, (1993) 18(4) ELR 309. See also JP Jacqué, (6th edn, Dalloz 2010) 208–29, who considers that 'the institutional structure of the [EU] is based on a pragmatic approach that resists any comparison'.

[8] See JP Jacqué, *Droit institutionnel de l'Union européenne* (6th edn, Dalloz 2010) 365–9.

[9] See Art 211 EC, or Art 17 TEU.

two facts must be borne in mind: first, the Lisbon Treaty makes explicit that, in principle, the power of execution corresponds to the Member States *ex* Article 291(1) TFEU; and second, the power of Member States when making use of the 'comitology'.[10] The debate about the 'democratic deficit' adds another complicated dimension to the question of directives under Article 106(3) TFEU. The lack of sufficient democratic legitimacy is a structural problem that affects the EU as a whole. However, traditionally, the Commission, the 'technocratic' institution par excellence, has been considered in the past to be less 'democratic' than both the Council of Ministers, which represents the 'democratically elected' governments of Member States, and the European Parliament, which is elected by citizens through direct universal suffrage.[11] This then provides a brief outline of the political-institutional situation which provides the backdrop to any consideration of the two main schools of thought as regards the application of Article 106. On the one hand, there is the Commission's interpretation of the Treaty, repeatedly confirmed by the Court. This view sees the abolition of exclusive rights, at least in theory, as an obligation derived from the Treaty. As such it has an 'automatic' quality, and is therefore largely beyond the reach of the discretionary power of Member States and/or even the EU legislator. The second approach is based on an invocation of the principles of the separation of powers and of democratic legitimacy to resist this 'automatic' quality.

Two political debates are thus confused in the discussions over Article 106: the debate on **20.04** the limits of State intervention in the economy (free competition versus—State owned and/or State protected—monopoly) and the debate on the principle of 'subsidiarity' (intervention of the institutions of the EU versus intervention of national institutions). It is necessary to stress that these are two different, although related, debates. While it is true that most supporters of large-scale State intervention in the economy perceive this intervention as a national competence and invoke in support of their position the 'subsidiarity' argument, it would be quite feasible (and perhaps in some cases more effective) to carry out intervention at the level of the EU. It is also clear that some of the most fervent supporters of liberalization at any price are somewhat hostile to the idea of accepting any competence of the EU that affects 'national sovereignty'. The myth of the Commission's 'unbridled liberalism' therefore co-exists with the myth of the 'omnipresent intervention' of the Brussels bureaucrats, while the logical incompatibility between the two propositions goes largely unnoticed. In such a context, it would be impossible to try to present a 'politically neutral' interpretation of Article 106 TFEU.[12] The interpretation expressed here is neither politically neutral, nor is it the only interpretation legally possible. It is, however, submitted that it is a logical interpretation. Bearing these comments in mind, the law relating to directives under Article 106(3) TFEU will now be examined.

---

[10] See Reg (EU) 182/2011 of the Parliament and the Council of 16 February laying down the rules and general principles concerning mechanisms for control by Member States of the Commission's exercise of implementing powers [2011] OJ L 55/13.

[11] The innovation of the investiture of the Commission by the European Parliament (and the possibility of this latter organ bringing down the Commission through a vote of no confidence) brings a new dimension to the debate, by providing the Commission with an added dose of democratic legitimacy. This is—at least symbolically—reinforced by the fact that, under the Lisbon Treaty, it is the Parliament (Article 17(7) TEU) that *elects* the Commission's President (under the proposal of the qualified majority of the members of the Council), as well as by the fact that, when proposing the President of the Commission, the Council should '[take] account of the elections to the European Parliament' (see Declaration 11, Annex to the Treaty of Lisbon on Article 9 D(6) and (7) of the Treaty on European Union ('TEU')).

[12] C Hocepied, 'Les directives Article 90, paragraphe 3. Une espèce juridique en voie de disparition?' [1994] ii RAE 53.

B. Directives Adopted on the Basis of Article 106(3) TFEU

20.05 The Commission has made use of the power that Article 106(3) confers upon it to adopt directives on fourteen occasions. These fourteen directives can be divided into two groups. In the first group is the Transparency Directive,[13] originally adopted in 1980 and subsequently modified in 1985, 1993, 2000, and 2005.[14] In the second group are the directives relating to telecommunications. Thus, in 1988 the Commission adopted the Terminals Directive,[15] in 1990 the Services Directive,[16] in 1994 the Satellites Directive[17] that amends the two former directives, and from 1994 onwards, the Cable Directive (1995),[18] the Mobile Communications Directive (1996),[19] the Full Competition Directive (1996),[20] and a directive requiring that cable television networks and telecommunication networks owned by a single operator are separate legal entities (1999).[21] The last four directives modified the Services Directive. In 2002, the Commission consolidated all these instruments in a single text, Commission Directive (EC) 2002/77 on competition in the markets for electronic communications networks and services,[22] which, together with the Terminal Equipment Directive (formally derogated by its codification by Directive (EC) 2008/63[23]), are those currently in force.

1. Preventive function of directives under Article 106(3) TFEU

20.06 Article 106(3) states:

> The Commission shall ensure the application of the provisions of this Article and shall, where necessary, address appropriate directives or decisions to Member States.

---

[13] Commission Directive (EEC) 80/723 on the transparency of financial relations between Member States and public undertakings [1980] OJ L195/35 ('Transparency Directive').

[14] Commission Directive (EEC) 80/723 concerning the transparency of financial relations between Member States and their public undertakings [1980] OJ L195/35. This Directive has been modified by the following directives:

- Commission Directive (EEC) 85/413 [1985] OJ L229/20;
- Commission Directive (EEC) 93/84 [1993] OJ L254/16;
- Commission Directive (EC) 2000/52 [2000] OJ L193/75;
- Commission Directive (EC) 2005/81 [2005] OJ L312/47.

A consolidated version of the Transparency Directive can be found at: <http://eur-lex.europa.eu/LexUriServ/LexUriServ.do?uri=CONSLEG:1980L0723:20051219:EN:PDF>.

[15] Commission Directive (EEC) 88/301 on competition in the markets in telecommunications terminals equipment [1988] OJ L131/73 ('Terminals Directive').

[16] Commission Directive (EEC) 90/388 on competition in the markets for telecommunications services [1990] OJ L192/10 ('Services Directive').

[17] Commission Directive (EC) 94/46 amending Directive (EEC) 88/301 and Directive (EEC) 90/388 in particular with regard to satellite communications [1994] OJ L268/15 ('Satellites Directive').

[18] Commission Directive (EC) 95/51 amending Commission Directive (EEC) 90/388 with regard to the abolition of the restrictions on the use of cable television networks for the provision of already liberalized telecommunications services [1995] OJ L256/49 ('Cable Directive').

[19] Commission Directive (EC) 96/2 amending Directive (EEC) 90/388 with regard to mobile and personal communications [1996] OJ L20/59, ('Mobile Communications Directive').

[20] Commission Directive (EC) 96/19 amending Directive (EEC) 90/388 with regard to the implementation of full competition in telecommunications markets [1996] OJ L74/13 ('Full Competition Directive').

[21] Commission Directive (EC) 99/64 [1999] OJ L175/39 amending Directive 90/388/EEC in order to ensure that telecommunications networks and cable TV networks owned by a single operator are separate legal entities.

[22] Commission Directive (EC) 2002/77 on competition in the markets for electronic communications networks and services [2002] OJ L249/21.

[23] Commission Directive (EC) 2008/63 on competition in the markets in telecommunications terminal equipment (codified version) [2008] OJ L162/20.

This provision therefore entrusts the Commission with the task of ensuring that Member States fulfil their obligations under Article 106. In order to achieve this aim, Article 106(3) gives the Commission the possibility of using two legal instruments: decisions and directives. The role of Article 106(3) decisions as instruments designed to eliminate infringements has been examined in Chapter 19. The next step is therefore to examine the function or functions that Article 106(3) reserves to directives. Logically, the functions of the directives of Article 106(3) are going to be defined in light of the role of the guardian of the Treaties, which this provision gives to the Commission. Article 106(3) TFEU does not refer to 'regulations'. However, the Commission may also adopt decisions under Article 106(3) that are addressed not to one individual Member State but to all Member States.[24] The nature of such 'horizontal' decisions would be very similar to that of directives, both having binding effects on Member States. The main difference would be that decisions automatically have a 'direct effect', while directives only have such an effect in certain circumstances. The references made in this chapter to 'directives' may be understood to also apply to such kind of 'horizontal decisions'.

The two possible functions of directives under Article 106(3) TFEU are the creation of additional **20.07** but accessory obligations, and the 'specifying' of the obligations under the Treaty. The former function means that directives under Article 106(3) may impose upon Member States certain additional obligations to the extent that these are intended to facilitate the Commission's task of ensuring Article 106(1) is respected. The other possible function of the Article 106(3) directives is that of specifying the obligations under the Treaty. These two dimensions mean that the Commission enjoys a certain degree of rule-making power, although, as will be seen, this is subject to strict limits.[25] The aim of the two recognized functions of the directives under Article 106(3) is to *prevent* future infringements. Tackling infringements which have been committed is not a function of these directives.[26] As explained previously, within the scope of Article 106(3) this latter function corresponds to individual decisions. The prevention of infringements through Article 106(3) directives is done in two ways: first, by creating the necessary mechanisms to enable the Commission to detect infringements in the event that they occur; and secondly, by specifying the meaning and scope of the obligations that already exist under Article 106(1) and/or the exception under Article 106(2) TFEU so that legal certainty is increased and the risk of unintentional infringements is reduced. The first aspect was dealt with in the Transparency Directive; the second in the different directives regarding the liberalization of the telecommunications sector.

The Transparency Directive and the creation of additional accessory obligations through directives under Article 106(3)

Today it seems paradoxical to state that it was initially the Parliament which persistently **20.08** asked the Commission to adopt directives under Article 106(3) designed to eliminate distortions in competition between public and private undertakings. In its annual reports on

---

[24] Paradigmatic cases in this regard are Commission Decision of 20 December 2011 on the application of Art 106(2) of the Treaty on the Functioning of the European Union to State aid in the form of public service compensation granted to certain undertakings entrusted with the operation of services of general economic interest [2012] OJ 7/3, as well as the preceding Commission Decision of 28 November 2005 on the application of Article 86(2) of the EC Treaty to State aid in the form of public service compensation granted to certain undertakings entrusted with the operation of services of general economic interest [2005] OJ L312/67. The decision deals with public service compensation (ie aid granted by Member States to compensate undertakings in charge of services of general economic interest for the additional costs resulting from these missions). This instrument specifies that certain awards of compensation (those below a certain threshold and fulfilling certain conditions) are considered compatible with Art 106(2) and are exempted from the obligation to notify under Art 108 TFEU.

[25] M Kerf, 'The Policy of the Commission of the EEC Toward National Monopolies. An Analysis of the Measures Adopted on the Basis of Article 90(3) of the EEC Treaty' (1993) 17(1) World Competition 106.

[26] Case C-202/88 *Terminal equipment for telecommunications* [1991] ECR I-1223, para 17.

competition policy in the 1970s, the Commission announced that it was studying different directives under Article 106(3). Thus, in 1972, the Commission said it was considering:[27]

> the possibility of demanding (by appropriate directives or decisions under Article 90(3) [now Article 106(3)]) that the Member States, in certain fields where the risk of such behaviour is apparent, should take the necessary steps to stop the undertakings referred to in Article 90(1) [now Article 106(1)] from excluding all or some of the products or services of the other Member States when placing their contracts.

This aborted directive under former Article 90(3) EC [now 106(3) TFEU] provided a precedent for the subsequent Council directives concerning public procurement.

20.09 In 1975, it recommended an even more ambitious plan:[28]

> [A] directive based on Article 90(3) of the EEC Treaty [now Article 106(3)TFEU] with the three-fold aim of clarifying for Member States their responsibilities under Article 90 [now Article 106 TFEU] introducing rules which will put the Commission in a better position to check on compliance with the Treaty by Member States operating through public undertakings and by the undertakings themselves, and finally making the financial links between governments and public undertakings more transparent.

20.10 In 1976 the Commission clearly expressed the idea that directives under Article 106(3) could be merely preventive in nature and added:[29]

> This means that the Commission can have procedures and approaches initiated which are not necessarily linked to specific departures from the Treaty but which will serve generally to prevent them happening.

20.11 By 1977, the ambitious initial plans had been reduced to a draft directive under Article 106(3), which only concerned the transparency of financial relations between Member States and public undertakings. Despite Article 106(3) providing it with the power to adopt such a directive itself, the Commission commenced prior consultations with the Member States, the European Parliament, and the Economic and Social Committee. These consultations lasted for several years and finally led to the adoption of the Transparency Directive by the Commission in 1980.[30]

20.12 In its original version, the Transparency Directive[31] obliged Member States to guarantee the transparency of financial relations between public authorities and public undertakings so that the different types of financial transfers made from public authorities to public undertakings or from some public undertakings to others could be clearly followed. Amongst these transactions are compensation for operating losses, capital contributions, grants, loans on favourable terms, and so on. In particular, Member States were required to ensure the necessary transparency of these transactions and to keep records at the disposal of the Commission for a five-year period. In order for the directive to be applied, a definition of the term 'public undertaking' was given, based on the dominant influence of public authorities. In its original version, the directive did not apply to public undertakings which were active in a series of important sectors: water, energy, postal services, telecommunications, transport, banks, and

---

[27] III Report on Competition Policy (1972), para 129.
[28] V Report on Competition Policy (1975), para 159.
[29] VI Report on Competition Policy (1975), para 275.
[30] VII Report on Competition Policy (1975), para 271; VIII Report (1978), para 253; IX Report (1979), paras 207–8; X Report (1980), paras 235–9.
[31] Commission Directive (EEC) 80/723 on the transparency of financial relations between Member States and public undertakings [1980] OJ L195/35.

a good number of different services.[32] Following subsequent modifications, the Transparency Directive currently obliges Member States to guarantee not only the transparency of financial relations between public authorities and public undertakings, but also the transparency of the costs and revenues that are imputable to the different activities performed by the undertakings. A further development, introduced by Directive 2000/52 and modified by Directive 2005/81, consists of the obligation to maintain separate accounts for those undertakings enjoying special or exclusive rights or entrusted with the operation of services of general economic interest and that carry on other activities.

It is important to stress that the Transparency Directive did not itself prohibit any of the **20.13** transactions mentioned earlier from being carried out. The legality of these transactions had to be examined only in light of Articles 107 and 108 TFEU, the rules concerning State aids. The only thing that the directive did was to create an additional but related obligation for Members States: the obligation to ensure transparent accounting systems and to make information regarding its financial relations available to the Commission. It is a necessary obligation to enable the Commission to fulfil its task of guardian of the TFEU as regards State aids granted to public undertakings.[33] The modest objectives pursued by the directive did not prevent several Member States from bringing proceedings for annulment. These States were probably concerned by the institutional implications of the adoption of a directive by the Commission.

In the *Transparency Directive* case,[34] the ECJ, following the opinion of AG Reischl, confirmed **20.14** the validity of the directive and hence the power of the Commission to adopt directives of a preventive nature.[35] The Court first dealt with the arguments according to which the Commission had breached the division of powers provided for in the Treaty, and legislative powers were exclusively reserved to the Council. The Court pointed out that in EU law there was no general principle enshrining such a division of power[36] and that according to Article 249(1) EC (current Article 288 TFEU) both the Commission and the Council could adopt directives within the conditions laid down in the Treaty. Accordingly, it was a question of having regard to what the provisions of the different Articles stated. Since Article 106(3) expressly established that directives could be adopted by the Commission, it had to be concluded that the Commission was competent in principle to adopt them.[37] According to the Court, the fact that the rules of the directive could have been adopted by the Council on the basis of Article 109 TFEU in no way prevented the use of Article 106(3). The two provisions have different areas of application and different conditions as regards execution. Article 109 allows the Council to adopt all the regulations that are considered useful for the application of Articles 107 and 108 in general. On the other hand, under Article 106(3) the Commission's powers are limited to adopting measures which are necessary for it to fulfil

---

[32] These 'excluded sectors' were mostly subject to the directive as amended by Directive 85/413.

[33] See para 116 of Opinion of AG Geelhoed in Case C-295/05 *Tragsa* [2007] ECR I-2999, where he states: 'The risks which arise, in the light of the prohibition of State aid, from the absence of transparent financial or accounting relations between the State or other public authorities, on the one hand, and public undertakings and companies, on the other, have in the past led the Commission to introduce rules on the basis of Article 86(3) EC [currently Article 106.3 TFEU].'

[34] Joined Cases 188–190/80 *France, Italy, and the United Kingdom v Commission (Transparency Directive)* [1982] ECR 2545.

[35] The expression appears in the Opinion of AG Reischl in Joined Cases 188–190/80 *Transparency Directive* [1982] ECR 2545.

[36] It is worth adding that former Art 96(2) was not the only Treaty provision which authorized the Commission to adopt directives. See, eg former Arts 33(7) and 97 of the EC Treaty before they were derogated by the Treaty of Amsterdam, see [1992] OJ C-224/1.

[37] Joined Cases 188–190/80 *Transparency Directive* [1982] ECR 2545, paras 4–7.

effectively its role of guardian of Article 106 which this particular provision imposes on it as regards public and private undertakings. The competence of the Commission is limited to a specific area and is subject to very precise conditions, but it is not a residual competence, since it may exercise it even in areas in which the Council can act. In short, the Court admitted that there may be a certain amount of overlapping between directives adopted by the Commission under Article 106(3) and those adopted by the Council on other legal bases.[38]

20.15 The Court recognized that the obligations established by the directives were necessary in order for the Commission to fulfil effectively its task of controlling State aids granted to public undertakings. By virtue of Article 106(3), the Commission had the power of appraisal to specify what information was necessary for this purpose as regards State aids. The Court held that the Member States contesting the directive had not proved that it had exceeded or abused its authority by requesting unnecessary information. Further, the Court held that the directive did not breach the principal of equal treatment of public and private undertakings, since the situations of the two groups of undertakings as regards relations with public authorities were not comparable. In summary, the Transparency Directive confirmed that the Commission has its own power to adopt directives under Article 106(3) and that it can use this power, in a preventive way, to create related obligations that are necessary to enable it to carry out its task of guardian of the Treaties. However, it remained to be clarified whether the Commission's power to adopt directives under Article 106(3) allowed it to 'specify' the obligations derived under the Treaty and/or to declare that specific infringements exist.[39]

The Terminals Directive and the specification of Treaty obligations through directives under Article 106(3) TFEU

20.16 Subsequent judgments made clear that Article 106(3) directives may also be used to 'specify' the meaning and extent of the obligations that already exist under Article 106(1) TFEU.[40] The first example of this approach was the Terminals Directive, adopted by the Commission in 1988 on the basis of Article 106.[41] Unlike the Transparency Directive, this directive was not limited to creating related obligations aimed at facilitating the supervisory tasks of the Commission. Instead, its objective was to 'specify' the obligations that Article 106(1) imposed upon Member States as regards telecommunication terminals. However, these 'specifications' of the Commission were not simply a non-binding interpretation of Treaty provisions, but were directly imposed upon Member States as new obligations. Thus, the Commission considered that the exclusive rights for the import, marketing, connection, bringing into service, and maintenance of telecommunication terminals were incompatible with Article 106(1) in conjunction with those EC Treaty Articles equivalent to current Articles 34, 35, 56, and 102 TFEU. Accordingly, the directive ordered Member States to abolish such rights. France brought an action for annulment of this directive, based, *inter alia*, on arguments regarding the alleged lack of competence of the Commission.

---

[38] Joined Cases 188–190/80 *Transparency Directive* [1982] ECR 2545, paras 8–14.

[39] LM Pais Antunes, 'L'Article 86 du Traité CEE—Obligations des Etats Membres et pouvoirs de la Commission' [1991] RTDE ii 203, argued that if the Commission could create instrumental obligations necessary for its guardian role, *a fortiori* it should be able to create rules that were limited to specifying obligations that already existed in the Treaty. Similar reasoning is employed by A Deringer, 'Equal Treatment of Public and Private Enterprises. General Report' in Various, *Equal Treatment of Public and Private Enterprises*, Vol 2, (FIDE 1978) 1.33, para 92.

[40] Case C-163/99 *Portuguese Airports* [2001] ECR I-2613, paras 26 and 28.

[41] Commission Directive (EEC) 88/301 on competition in the markets in telecommunications terminals equipment [1988] OJ L131/73.

In his Opinion, AG Tesauro considered that to 'define the obligations incumbent on the **20.17** Member States' was a task that went beyond the limits of Article 106(3) and was therefore reserved to the Council.[42] The preventive function of Article 106(3) directives can only justify related obligations of the type contained in the Transparency Directive, designed to make possible the supervisory tasks of the Commission. However, it did not authorize, under the pretext of preventing future infringements, the detailed regulation of the sector through the creation of substantive obligations for the Member States.[43] According to AG Tesauro:[44]

> Certainly, the preventive effect will be achieved on a satisfactory and permanent basis by abolishing the legal situation which is liable to give rise to infringements of the Treaty, but whether doing so is a merely preventive action is very doubtful...[T]he Commission, unlike the Council, is not empowered to adopt all *appropriate* measures for the application of Article 90(1) [now Article 106(1)]...but only such measures as are *necessary* for the more effective performance of the duty of supervision. (emphasis added)

AG Tesauro therefore rejected the argument that Article 106 conferred upon the Commission the power to adopt directives designed to 'specify' the obligations derived from Article 106(1) TFEU.

In his Opinion, AG Tesauro also examined another possible justification of the directive; that **20.18** it was an example of the 'repressive' function underlying Article 106(3). According to this idea, the directive was simply a 'bundle' of decisions under Article 106(3). The Commission may, through a decision under Article 106(3), declare that a Member State has breached Article 106(1) and may order and impose upon it certain measures to bring the infringement to an end. In the same way, it can achieve the same end as regards all Member States through adopting a directive under Article 106(3). AG Tesauro rejected the idea that a directive could be used to declare the existence of specific breaches, and added that the general reasoning employed by the Commission may not serve as the basis for establishing specific infringements of the Treaty rules.[45] The ECJ, in its landmark judgment *Telecommunications Terminals*,[46] also rejected the argument that a directive under Article 106(3) can be used as a repressive instrument (to declare the existence of specific infringements and to require their elimination). Nevertheless, it gave a wide interpretation to the preventive function of directives under Article 106(3) and recognized that they could be used to specify the obligations that are derived from the Treaty. In the words of the Court:[47]

> Article 90(3) [now Article 106(3)] of the Treaty empowers the Commission to specify in general terms the obligations arising under Article 90(1) [now Article 106(1)] by adopting directives. The Commission exercises that power where, without taking into consideration the particular situation existing in the various Member States, it defines in concrete terms the obligations imposed on them under the Treaty. In view of its very nature, such a power cannot be used to make a finding that a Member State has failed to fulfil a particular obligation under the Treaty.

---

[42] Opinion of AG Tesauro in Case C-202/88 *Telecommunications Terminal Equipment* [1991] ECR I-1255, para 48. Similar reasoning appeared in Joined Cases C-271/90, C-281/90, and C-289/90 *Telecommunications Services* [1992] ECR I-5866, paras 24–6.

[43] Opinion of AG Tesauro in Case C-202/88 *Telecommunications Terminal Equipment* [1991] ECR I-1258, para 54.

[44] Opinion of AG Tesauro in Case C-202/88 *Telecommunications Terminal Equipment* [1991] ECR I-1256, paras 49 and 51.

[45] Opinion of AG Tesauro in Case C-202/88 *Telecommunications Terminal Equipment* [1991] ECR I-1250–1253, paras 32–40.

[46] Case C-202/88 *Telecommunications Terminal Equipment* [1991] ECR I-1264.

[47] Case C-202/88 *Telecommunications Terminal Equipment* [1991] ECR I-1264, para 17.

The Court repeated the rule established in the *Transparency Directive* case that the adoption by the Commission of a directive based on Article 106(3) was compatible with the existence of the legislative powers of the Council, such as those derived from Articles 103 and 114 TFEU.[48]

20.19 The judgment in *Telecommunications Terminal Equipment* was fully confirmed by the ECJ in *Telecommunications Services*.[49] In this case, various Member States brought annulment proceedings against the Telecommunications Services Directive, adopted in 1990 by the Commission on the basis of Article 106(3), which required the abolition of certain exclusive rights in the supply of telecommunications services.[50]

20.20 The Court confirmed once again that the scope of Article 106(3) directives was not limited to 'preventive' measures, stating:

> The Commission's power is not, therefore, limited to mere surveillance to ensure the application of the existing Community rules.

Instead, it also had the power 'to lay down general rules specifying the obligations arising from the Treaty which are binding on the Member States'.[51] The Court, following the Opinion of AG Jacobs,[52] rejected the submissions of the Belgium government that the Commission's recognized power of 'specification' should be limited to areas where the scope of Member States' obligations had been previously specified through Council directives. The judgment pointed out, quite logically, that such an interpretation would have deprived Article 106(3) of its *effet utile*.[53] What would be the sense of the power of 'specification' only being applied to situations which have been previously specified? The main use of Article 106(3) is precisely to specify the meaning of general rules whose specific scope is somewhat uncertain.

20.21 The 'specification' function of Article 106(3) is of course not restricted to 'obligations' imposed on Member States. It may also be used to 'specify' the meaning and extent of the exception foreseen in Article 106(2) TFEU for services of general economic interest.[54] This arises from the wording of Article 106(3), which expressly refers to 'the application of the provisions of this Article', thus clearly including the application of Article 106(2) TFEU. In this respect, on 28 November 2005 the Commission adopted a horizontal decision under Article 106(3) to deal with public service compensation (ie aid granted by Member States to compensate undertakings in charge of services of general economic interest for the additional costs resulting from these missions). This instrument specified that certain amounts of compensation (those below a certain threshold and fulfilling certain conditions) were considered compatible with Article 106(2) and were exempted from the obligation to notify under Article 108 TFEU.[55]

---

[48] Case C-202/88 *Telecommunications Terminal Equipment* [1991] ECR I-1265, paras 23–6.

[49] Joined Cases C-271/90, C-281/90, and C-289/90 *Telecommunications Services* [1992] ECR I-5833.

[50] Commission Directive (EEC) 90/388 on competition in the markets for telecommunications services [1990] OJ L192/10.

[51] Joined Cases C-271/90, C-281/90 and C-289/90 *Telecommunications Services* [1992] ECR I-5863, para 12.

[52] Opinion of AG Jacobs in Joined Cases C-271/90, C-281/90 and C-289/90 *Telecommunications Services* [1992] ECR I-5853, paras 39–41.

[53] Joined Cases C-271/90, C-281/90, and C-289/90 *Telecommunications Services* [1992] ECR I-5865, para 21.

[54] For an example, see Commission Directive (EEC) 90/388 [1990] OJ L192/10, on competition in the markets for telecommunications services, paras 18–20.

[55] Commission Decision of 28 November 2005 on the application of Article 86(2) of the EC Treaty to State aid in the form of public service compensation granted to certain undertakings entrusted with the operation of services of general economic interest [2005] OJ L312/67.

This decision has recently been replaced by a new horizontal Commission Decision of 20 December 2011, also issued under the legal basis provided by Article 106(3), which, although slightly amended, serves the same goal.[56]

2. The rules concerning directives under Article 106(3) TFEU

The approach laid down by the ECJ in the three cases mentioned previously, concerning the **20.22** Transparency, Terminals, and Services Directives, provided the basis for the rules concerning directives under Article 106(3) TFEU. In the following paragraphs these rules will be carefully analysed, with an examination not only of these three judgments, but also of other subsequent judgments and the practice of the Commission.

Preparation of Article 106(3) directives

The Commission has sole competence for adopting directives under Article 106(3). The **20.23** Treaty does not require the participation of any other institution in the preparation process. In practice, however, the Commission normally consults the other institutions, in particular the European Parliament, Member States, and even undertakings and interested individuals. The normal procedure for the preparation of Article 106(3) directives was explained by the Commission in its XXV Report on Competition Policy.[57] The initiative for preparing an Article 106(3) directive belongs to the Commission, which enjoys total discretion in deciding on the necessity for and the timing of the initiative.[58] Naturally, the European Parliament, Member States, associations, undertakings, and individuals are free to request the Commission to adopt a directive under Article 106(3) if they consider it necessary. However, it is the Commission alone who decides whether it will take action and whether such action must take the form of an Article 106(3) directive. It must not be forgotten that apart from this instrument, the Commission possesses various alternatives, such as adopting individual decisions under Article 106(3), bringing proceedings under Article 258, recommendations, proposing harmonization directives, and so on.

The Commission normally has recourse to Article 106(3) directives to deal with two princi- **20.24** pal situations: first, situations where the Commission cannot properly carry out its controlling function (as occurred with the control of State aids to public undertakings before the Transparency Directive); and second, when it considers them a suitable tool for addressing specific problems concerning a sector. The decision to boost liberalization in a given sector often underlies the use of directives under Article 106(3). In cases where the reason for the directive is based on the liberalization of a sector, before preparing the draft proposal the Commission often proceeds to carry out a previous consultation process about the general direction of this liberalization process or about certain aspects of it. This consultation can take the form of a Green Paper or of a Consultation Document, which is discussed with the interested parties

---

[56] Commission Decision of 20 December 2011 on the application of Article 106(2) of the Treaty on the Functioning of the European Union to State aid in the form of public service compensation granted to certain undertakings entrusted with the operation of services of general economic interest [2012] OJ 7/3. For a comparison with the precedent legal framework for the assessment of SGEI compensation under EU State aid rules, see JL Buendía Sierra and M Muñoz de Juan 'Some Legal Reflections on the Almunia Package' in Proceedings of the Conference 'The Reform of State Aid Rules on Services of general Economic Interest From the 2005 Monti-Kroes Package to the 2011 Almunia Reform', 2012, Lexxion, Berlin. As well as JL Buendía Sierra and JM Panero Rivas, 'The Almunia Package: State Aid and Services of General Economic Interest' in E Szyszczak and JW van de Gronden (eds), (T.M.C Asser Press 2013).
[57] XXV Report on Competition Policy (1995) COM (96) 126 final, para 100.
[58] In light of the judgments of both Courts in *Ladbroke* and *German Accountants*, the opinion of C Hocepied, 'Les directives articles 90, paragraphe 3. Une espèce juridique en voie de disparition?' [1994] ii RAE 60, that the Commission is obliged to act under Art 90(3) and could be sued if it did not act, no longer appears sustainable. See Ch 19, 'Procedure on State Measures—Decisions under Article 106(3) TFEU'.

(undertakings in the sector concerned, representatives of consumers associations, etc), with experts in the sector, with Member States, and/or with the other EU institutions.

20.25 The next step is for the Commission to prepare a draft directive, taking into particular account the results of the consultation process. The text is then adopted 'at first reading' by the Commission as a 'draft directive under Article 106(3)' and is sent for observations to the European Parliament, the Economic and Social Committee, the Committee of the Regions, and the Member States. The text is also published in the Official Journal of the European Union ('OJ') as a draft directive in order to give interested parties the opportunity to formulate any observations they may have about it. The Commission has committed itself to consider attentively the comments received (particularly those of the European Parliament, the Economic and Social Committee, the Committee of the Regions, and the Member States) before finally adopting the directive. In any event, it is clear that the opinions received by the Commission do not legally bind it. Despite that, the importance of this consultation process is considerable from a political point of view. Although the Commission has its own rule-making powers under Article 106(3), it will still attempt to reach the greatest degree of consensus possible on its proposals before adopting them. The adoption of a directive under Article 106(3) against the will of the majority of Member States and against the opinion of Parliament is a most unlikely scenario.

Adoption of the directive

20.26 In any event, the adoption of directives based on Article 106(3) TFEU belongs exclusively to the Commission. The ECJ has laid down the precise limits of the Commission's rule-making power under this provision, and accordingly it is possible to state what those limits are in some detail.

Limits on the rule-making power of the Commission

20.27 As is clear from the case law mentioned earlier, Article 106(3) does not provide the Commission with a general legal basis to adopt legislation. In fact, the situation is quite the reverse, since Article 106(3) confers on the Commission specific competence to adopt rules which specify Member States' obligations under Article 106(1) and (2). The limited nature of the Commission's competence gives rise to a series of consequences. The obligations which can be 'specified' by means of an Article 106(3) directive are solely those obligations that for Member States derive from Article 106(1) and (2) TFEU. Of course, given the character of Article 106(1) as a 'reference rule', this process of specifying Member States' obligations may also relate to other Treaty provisions, to the extent that they apply in conjunction with Article 106(1). It should be recalled that in order for Article 106(1) to apply, the State measures in question must concern public undertakings or undertakings which enjoy special or exclusive rights—although these concepts are wide. More specifically, the grant or maintenance of exclusive rights is a State measure which comes within the scope of Article 106(1). For this reason it is perfectly possible for the objective of a directive under Article 106(3) to be the abolition of exclusive rights. Other State measures which are not specifically related either to public undertakings or to special or exclusive rights cannot in principle be the object of a directive under Article 106(3).

Article 106(3) directives and the behaviour of undertakings

20.28 Article 106(3) only confers powers on the Commission as regards State measures. This means that the behaviour of an undertaking cannot, in principle, be the object of an Article 106(3) directive if such behaviour was due to the undertaking acting of its own free will. In the Terminals Directive and the Services Directive, the Commission obliged Member States, in addition to eliminating certain exclusive rights, to ensure that traditional telecommunications operators allowed clients to rescind their contracts concerning goods or services affected by the liberalization process whose duration was greater than one year. Clearly, the objective was to prevent the existence of long-term contractual obligations between these operators and their clients from turning the elimination of exclusive rights into a pointless exercise. Nevertheless, the ECJ annulled this part of both directives on the following basis:[59]

> [I]t should be noted that Article 90 [now Article 106] of the Treaty confers powers on the Commission only in relation to State measures…and that anticompetitive conduct engaged in by undertakings *on their own initiative* can be called in question only by individual decisions adopted under Articles 85 and 86 [now Articles 101 and 102] of the Treaty.

It does not appear, either from the provisions of the directive or from the preamble thereto, that the holders of special or exclusive rights were *compelled or encouraged by State regulations* to conclude long-term contracts.

> Article [106] cannot therefore be regarded as an appropriate basis for dealing with the obstacles to competition which are purportedly created by the long-term contracts referred to in the directive.

Nevertheless, it would be an error to interpret these judgments in a simplistic manner and con- **20.29** clude that directives under Article 106(3) can never be aimed at the behaviour of undertakings. In the public sector, the boundaries between the behaviour of undertakings and State measures are blurred, and Article 106 was included in the Treaty precisely in order to tackle this type of problem. A careful reading of these judgments reveals that the behaviour of public or privileged undertakings only escapes from the scope of Article 106(1) to the extent that it has been decided by the undertaking acting on its own initiative. The Court has recognized that the behaviour of public or privileged undertakings which are obliged or incited by a State rule to behave in that way can be the object of directives under Article 106(3). The same reasoning should be applied with respect to behaviour which is the result of the State obliging or inciting the undertaking to behave in a given way, not through a rule, but through less obvious but equally effective measures. This last category clearly causes evidential problems. How can it be proved that the apparently independent behaviour of an undertaking is in reality the result of the influence of public powers? The answer is 'with extreme difficulty'. Nevertheless, it is necessary to remember that one of the legal effects of Article 106(1) is to attribute to the State certain behaviour apparently carried out by public or privileged undertakings.[60] Accordingly there are no good reasons for excluding on principle these situations from the scope of directives under Article 106(3) TFEU.[61]

Article 106(3) authorizes the Commission to specify the scope of the obligations derived **20.30** from Article 106(1) and the exception contained in Article 106(2). The Commission will therefore jointly examine both sections in the light of the circumstances of the sector in question. The directive does not have to limit itself to prohibiting exclusive rights; it can also conclude that an exclusive right or another measure is justified, even in a transitional manner, on

---

[59] Case C-202/88 *Telecommunications Terminal Equipment* [1991] ECR I-1272, paras 55–7.

[60] An interesting analogy can be traced between this issue and the position adopted by the ECJ in the famous *Stardust* judgment regarding State aid rules. In this judgment, the ECJ relied on a set of indicators 'arising from the circumstances of the case and the context in which that measure was taken' for determining the imputability to the State of the undertaking's behaviour that might be of interest for the purposes of proving whether or not the decisions of undertakings may be attributable to the State. See Case C-482/99 *France v Commission* [2002] ECR I-4397, paras 51–2 and 55–6.

[61] Prior to the judgment in *Telecommunications Terminal Equipment*, academics took a more flexible approach to this question; see A Deringer, 'Equal Treatment of Public and Private Enterprises. General Report' in Various, *Equal Treatment of Public and Private Enterprises*, Vol 2 (FIDE 1978) 1.33 1.32–1.33, paras 92–3.

the basis of Article 106(2).[62] Directives under Article 106(3) can be employed to specify the scope of the exception contained in Article 106(2). Since this exception is applicable to both State measures and the behaviour of undertakings, an Article 106(3) directive could probably be used to specify the application of Article 106(2) to the behaviour of undertakings.

Clear and obscure acts

20.31 The power under Article 106(3) to specify Treaty obligations is not limited to those provisions whose interpretation is particularly difficult.[63] It is even less correct to say that the power is limited only to those provisions whose interpretation is unproblematic.[64] Article 106(3) allows the meaning of general rules whose specific scope is uncertain to be clarified, and also to remind Member States that they must fulfil the obligations contained in the Treaty, the interpretation of which is not in doubt.

How specific can directives under Article 106(3) be?

20.32 The function of specifying the obligations under the Treaty includes that of indicating to Member States what specific measures have to be adopted in order to comply with those obligations. However, there are obligations in the Treaty that, because of their general character, can be fulfilled by Member States in various ways, at least in the absence of directives under Article 106(3). The question that arises is whether directives under Article 106(3) can reduce this room for manoeuvre which, in principle, Member States enjoy, and impose on them a particular way of fulfilling Treaty obligations. The question of how specific directives can be in laying down obligations does not only arise in the field of Article 106(3): rather, it affects all directives. It must not be forgotten that, according to paragraph 3 of Article 288:

> A directive shall be binding, as to the result to be achieved, upon each Member State to which it is addressed, but shall leave to the national authorities the choice of form and methods.

Although the decision as to the form that national acts of transposition take without doubt corresponds to Member States, the boundary between 'the result to be achieved' and 'the methods' to achieve it is not easy to draw. The choice of methods used will depend heavily on the end pursued by the directive. The more specific the end of the directive, the less freedom Member States will have in their choice of means. In practice, the trend is for directives to be increasingly precise, thus reducing the room for manoeuvre of the Member States.[65]

20.33 In the context of Article 106(3), the question of how specific directives can be was raised by the Belgian government in its action against the Services Directive. In this action, the Belgian government criticized the Commission for having drastically reduced Member States' room

---

[62] For an example, see Commission Directive (EEC) 90/388 [1990] OJ L192/10, on competition in the markets for telecommunications services, paras 18–20. See also Commission Decision of 28 November 2005 on the application of Article 86(2) of the EC Treaty to State aid in the form of public service compensation granted to certain undertakings entrusted with the operation of services of general economic interest [2005] OJ L312/67.

[63] LM Pais Antunes, 'L'Article 90 du Traité CEE—Obligations des Etats Membres et pouvoirs de la Commission' [1991] ii RTDE 208; on the other hand, G Marenco, 'Public Sector and Community Law' [1983] xx CMLRev 522, was in favour of confining the use of Art 86(3) to situations whose compatibility with the Treaty was doubtful.

[64] Joined Cases C-271/90, C-281/90, and C-289/90 *Telecommunications Services* [1992] ECR I-5865, para 21.

[65] JV Louis, 'Les actes des institutions' in Various, *Commentaire Megret, Le Droit de la CEE*, Vol 10 (2nd edn, Editions de l'Université de Bruxelles 1993) 500–1; G Isaac, *Droit communautaire général* (4th edn, Masson 1994) 127–8; JP Jacqué, *Droit institutionnel de l'Union européenne* (6th edn, Dalloz 2010) 520–1.

for manoeuvre under the Treaty to fulfil their obligations in various ways.[66] According to the Belgian government, the Commission lacked, as regards Article 106(3) directives, the right to impose on Member States a particular means of fulfilling its obligations.[67] The Court rejected this argument, pointing out that, contrary to what was alleged by the Belgian government, the directive concerned had not specified in an exhaustive manner the methods open to Member States to fulfil their obligations.[68] This reasoning appeared to suggest that the Commission therefore does not have complete freedom to choose the methods Member States had to use. Some authors have even suggested that the Commission would exceed its powers if it were to impose on Member States the use of certain methods to fulfil their obligations in cases where the Treaty permitted them to choose freely the method they preferred in order to achieve the desired result.[69] Nevertheless, when the Commission has specified a method, it has in fact been more guilty of being excessively prudent than excessively zealous, to the extent that many of the provisions contained in the directives are dangerously ambiguous and could jeopardize the effectiveness of the liberalization process. It is submitted that more detailed rules should be adopted in the future.[70]

It is also submitted that the function of specifying the obligations contained in the Treaty can **20.34** include that of selecting from among the methods in principle available to Member States those that the Commission considers most appropriate. This principle has already been recognized by the case law as regards Article 106(3) individual decisions.[71] It should also apply as regards directives. The limits of this particular power of 'specification' are, on the one hand, respect for the principle of proportionality and, on the other hand, the inherent legal flexibility of directives.[72] Within these limits, an Article 106(3) directive can reduce the degree of freedom which Member States have and oblige them to use specific methods to comply with the Treaty. This appears to be clear from the *Taillandier, Lagauche,* and *Decoster* judgments, all given on 27 October 1993.[73] These cases concerned Article 6 of the Terminals Directive, which established an obligation on Member States to attribute the functions of the regulation of the telecommunications sector to a public entity, 'independent' from the public or private undertakings in that sector. The situations examined in the three cases were almost identical: criminal proceedings against people who had marketed non-approved terminals, thus breaching the Belgian (*Lagauche*) and French (*Taillandier* and *Decoster*) legislation. In the three cases, the submissions of the interested parties made it clear that the legislative provisions in question were incompatible with EU law, given that the entities entrusted with the type-approval process were at the same time active in the telecommunications market.

---

[66] However, it is interesting to note that the general tendency of directives to be increasingly precise is often imposed by the members of the Council themselves in order to limit distortions on competition arising from differences in the implementation of the directive in national law (JP Jacqué (6th edn, Dalloz 2010) 521).

[67] Joined Cases C-271/90, C-281/90, and C-289/90 *Telecommunications Services* [1992] ECR I-5864, para 17.

[68] Joined Cases C-271/90, C-281/90, and C-289/90 *Telecommunications Services* [1992] ECR I-5865, para 22.

[69] M Kerf, 'The Policy of the Commission of the EEC Toward National Monopolies. An Analysis of the Measures Adopted on the Basis of Article 90(3) of the EEC Treaty' (1993) 17(1) World Competition 90.

[70] C Hocepied, 'Les directives Article 90, paragraphe 3. Une espèce juridique en voie de disparition?' [1994] ii RAE 56.

[71] Joined Cases C-48/90 and C-66/90 *Dutch PTT* [1992] ECR I-565, para 28; Case C-107/95 P *Expert Accountants (appeal)* [1996] ECR I-947, para 23.

[72] Article 288 TFEU, para 3.

[73] Joined Cases C-46/90 and C-93/91 *Procureur du Roi v Jean-Marie Lagauche and others (Lagauche)* [1993] ECR I-5267; Case C-69/91 *Criminal proceedings against Francine Gillon, née Decoster (Decoster)* [1993] ECR I-5335; Case C-92/91 *Criminal proceedings against Annick Neny, née Taillandier (Taillandier)* [1993] ECR I-5383.

The Court proceeded to examine whether this situation was compatible with Articles 106(1) and 102 TFEU (for the period prior to the coming into force of Article 6 of the directive, 1 July 1989) and with Article 6 of the directive (for the period after Article 6 came into force).

20.35 It is clear that the Court wished to differentiate between two standards: while a degree of independence between the regulator and the operator is a general requirement directly derived from Articles 106(1) and 102, the level of independence required is much higher as regards Article 6 of the directive. Thus, the Court appeared to suggest that where a public undertaking were given the functions of *monitoring* and *type-approval*, this would not be incompatible with Articles 106(1) and 102 as long as the specifications concerned were *fixed* by the public authority.[74] It should be recalled that in the field of Article 6 of the directive, the attribution of any regulatory functions to an operator, whether these relate to drawing up specifications, type-approval, or simply monitoring activities, is prohibited. From this it appears clear that the function attributed to directives under Article 106(3) to specify the Treaty obligations implies the power to specify those means that Member States have to employ to fulfil their obligations. The obligations of Member States become more precise than they were before the directive as a consequence of the directive.

Directives under Article 106(3) are not a repressive instrument of specific infringements

20.36 If Article 106(3) confers on the Commission the power to repress specific infringements, this power can only be exercised through individual decisions and not through directives. Thus, even in the context of Article 106(3), directives are regulatory not repressive instruments. As the ECJ recognized in *Telecommunications Terminal Equipment*, a directive under Article 106(3) cannot be used to declare the existence of specific infringements and require their elimination:[75]

> Article 90(3) [now Article 106(3)] of the Treaty empowers the Commission to specify in general terms the obligations arising under Article 90(1) [now Article 106(1)] by adopting directives. The Commission exercises that power where, *without taking into consideration the particular situation existing in the various Member States*, it defines in concrete terms the obligations imposed on them under the Treaty. *In view of its very nature, such a power cannot be used to make a finding that a Member States has failed to fulfil a particular obligation under the Treaty.* (emphasis added)

Accordingly, there are no grounds for interpreting Article 106(3) directives as 'bundles' of decisions under Article 106(3). The reasoning used to justify directives under Article 106(3) is both abstract and general. This would, in many cases, provide an inadequate basis on which to found a declaration that a specific infringement has been committed by a Member State.[76] A directive under Article 106(3) is therefore not a particular application of the Treaty to a given case, but rather a rule-making act which specifies the scope of the Treaty in a general and abstract way.

The principles of 'necessity' and 'proportionality'

20.37 In addition, Article 106(3) directives, in their preventive guise, can impose obligations on Member States which do not directly derive from the Treaty, but which are necessary for the Commission to be able to fulfil its role as guardian of the Treaty. For example, obligations of accounting transparency do not directly derive from the Treaty, but they are necessary to

---

[74] In this regard *Lagauche* clearly modifies the rule established in *RTT* (para 26) despite the claims of the Court that the two judgments are consistent. See L Hancher, 'Judgments of the Court Lagauche, Decoster and Taillandier' (1994) xxxi CML Rev 857.

[75] Case C-202/88 *Telecommunications Terminal Equipment* [1991] ECR I-1264, para 17.

[76] Opinion of AG Tesauro in Case C-202/88 *Telecommunications Terminal Equipment* [1991] ECR I-1250, paras 32–40.

enable the Commission to ensure that Articles 107 and 108 TFEU, regarding State aids to public undertakings and undertakings entrusted with special or exclusive rights and/or providing services of general economic interest for which they are compensated by the State, are respected. In the Transparency Directive, the Commission did not specify the scope of the pre-existing Treaty rules. Instead, it created fresh obligations which were necessary for the fulfilment of the guardian role conferred on it by Article 106(3).

> It is not sufficient for an obligation to be 'useful' for the fulfilment of the task of overseeing: it must be 'necessary'. Nevertheless, the ECJ has recognized that the Commission has some discretion when judging which measures are necessary. Only the establishment of obligations that are clearly disproportionate will be considered to be a breach of the inherent limits contained in Article [106(3)] of the Treaty. The proportionality principle therefore constitutes a limit on the rule-making actions of the Commission in the context of Article [106(3)] of the Treaty.[77]

Form of directives under Article 106(3)

20.38 The general principle of legal certainty requires that all acts destined to produce legal effects expressly indicate the legal basis that authorizes their adoption and the legal form that they take. The legal effects of 'specifying the Treaty rules' or of 'creating preventive rules' can only be achieved validly through acts which take the legal form of directives or decisions and which expressly invoke the legal basis of Article 106(3) TFEU. This question was debated in 1991, when the Commission adopted a communication concerning the application of the rules of State aid contained in the Treaty and the application of the Transparency Directive in relation to public undertakings in the manufacturing sector.[78] The communication presented, on the one hand, the Commission's interpretation of the case law of the Court concerning public undertakings, as well as the approach which it intended to adopt on the question of the control of State aids. The communication then went on to point out that Article 5 of the Transparency Directive obliged Member States to maintain certain accountancy information for five years and to present such information to the Commission should they request it. This information would allow financial flows between the different undertakings and public authorities to be identified. The communication concluded by 'inviting' Member States to present in advance to the Commission an annual declaration as regards undertakings which exceeded a given volume of business and that included an amount of information which was not expressly provided for in the directive. The French government appealed against the communication, arguing that its aim was to create new obligations (filing of annual reports, additional information) without respecting the formalities of Article 106(3).

20.39 In *Transparency Communication*, the ECJ, following the Opinion of AG Tesauro, found in favour of the French government and annulled the Commission communication. The Court held that the object of the communication was to produce, in a general and abstract mode, its own legal effects distinct from those of Article 5 of the Transparency Directive. For this reason, it effectively purported to be an amendment of that directive and as such an amendment could only be properly affected through the adoption of another directive under Article 106(3), the communication was annulled.[79] As a result of this judgment, in 1993

---

[77] LM Pais Antunes, 'L'Article 86 du Traité CEE—Obligations des Etats Membres et pouvoirs de la Commission' (1991) ii RTDE 203; F Melin-Soucramanien 'Les pouvoirs spéciaux conférés à la Commission en matière de concurrence par l'article 90.3 du Traité de Rome' (1994) 382 RMCUE 606.
[78] Commission Communication to the Member States on the application of Articles 92–93 [now Arts 107 and 108] of the EEC Treaty [now TFEU] and of Article 5 of Commission Directive 80/723 (EEC) to public undertakings in the manufacturing sector [1991] OJ C273/2.
[79] Case C-325/91 *France v Commission (Transparency Communication)* [1993] ECR I-3283–3313.

the Commission adopted a directive under Article 106(3) which amended the Transparency Directive, introducing the obligations contained in the annulled communication.[80] No action was brought against this new directive. Accordingly, the use of communications and other instruments of 'soft law' is limited to cases where the intention is not to create new obligations for Member States.[81]

Reasons for adopting directives under Article 106(3)

20.40 By virtue of Article 296 TFEU, the reasons for adopting directives under Article 106(3) must be expressed. The Commission must explain sufficiently clearly its interpretation of the Treaty rules and/or the reasons that it considers the measures contained in the directive to be necessary. It should be recalled, however, that the reasons in a directive must be general and abstract, with no intention of showing the existence of specific infringements. The ECJ annulled two of the articles contained in the Terminals and Services Directives for failure to contain sufficient reasoning. In both cases the Commission was criticized for having required the abolition of special rights without previously having differentiated this category with respect to exclusive rights, and without having explained why special rights breached the Treaty.[82] The reasons concerning exclusive rights were considered, by contrast, to be sufficiently clear.[83]

Publication and entering into force of directives under Article 106(3)

20.41 Article 297(2) TFEU[84] provides that directives which are addressed to all Member States are to be published in the OJ and 'shall enter into force on the date specified in them or, in the absence thereof, on the twentieth day following that of their publication'. This provision also applies to directives adopted under Article 106(3) TFEU. Initially, however, some authors doubted that directives under Article 106(3) could 'enter into force'. These doubts were based on a misconception of such directives being 'bundles' of decisions which were limited to declaring infringements of the Treaty rules, rules which had been in force since the entering into force of the Treaty itself. This approach probably explains the fact that in the 1988 Terminals and 1990 Services Directives, the expression 'entering into force' was not used, but instead Member States were required to notify the Commission of the measures they had taken before the dates established in the directives. Subsequently, the ECJ has repeatedly confirmed that Article 106(3) directives can have their own legal effect, distinct from that of the Treaty rules on which they are based. It is therefore quite correct to use the expression 'entering into force', and this wording has been used in all the recent Article 106(3) directives. Nevertheless, to the extent that the content of the directive corresponds with the content of obligations derived from the Treaty, the entering into force of the directive will not affect the existing legal situation, and it will therefore be superfluous.[85]

---

[80] Commission Directive (EEC) 93/84 amending Directive (EEC) 80/723 on the transparency of financial relations between Member States and public undertakings [1993] OJ L254/16.

[81] A Papaioannou, 'Case C-325/91, France v Commission (Transparency communication)' (1994) xxxi CML Rev 161.

[82] Case C-202/88 *Telecommunications Terminal Equipment* [1991] ECR I-1270, paras 45–7; Joined Cases C-271/90, C-281/90, and C-289/90 *Telecommunications Services* [1992] ECR I-5866, paras 28–31. It is interesting to note that, years later, the ECJ ended up endorsing the approach, considering 'exclusive rights' and 'special rights' as synonyms in Case C-475/99 *Ambulanz Glöckner* [2001] ECR I-8089, para 24. This convergence can also be noted in Commission Directive (EC) 2002/77 [2002] OJ L249/21 on competition in the markets for electronic communications networks and services.

[83] Case C-202/88 *Telecommunications Terminal Equipment* [1991] ECR I-1272, para 61.

[84] The text of the current Art 297(2) of the Treaty was introduced by Art G point 63 of the TEU. Previously, Art 254 did not require publication of directives (although the usual practice was to publish them), did not speak of 'coming into force', and provided that they took effect from the moment of notification.

[85] See the Opinion of AG Tesauro in Case C-69/91 *Decoster* [1993] ECR I-5364, n 13.

Binding nature of directives under Article 106(3)

Once in force, directives adopted under Article 106(3) will bind Member States in accord- **20.42**
ance with Article 288 TFEU, para 3. It is important to emphasize that directives under Article
106(3) have *their own legally binding, independent effect* from those Treaty rules whose scope
they determined or whose observation they help to ensure.[86] If a Member State does not
respect a directive, this could in itself lead to infringement proceedings, regardless of whether
this failure to fulfil an obligation is, in many cases, also an infringement of the Treaty rules.[87]

Direct effect of Article 106(3) directives

In principle, directives are not directly applicable, but instead need to be transposed through **20.43**
acts of national law. However, the ECJ has recognized that provisions contained in directives,
as long as they are sufficiently precise and unconditional, can have a degree of direct effect. In
order for direct effect to exist, the time limit within which Member States must take measures
to transpose them into national law must have expired or the measures taken by the Member
States must be inconsistent with the directive.[88] Thus, in these cases, the case law recognizes the
'vertical' direct effect of directives: the right of individuals to invoke *against Member States* in
the national courts provisions of a directive. This right can be invoked to oppose the application
of national rules which contravene the directive or to require the State to fulfil the obligations
which the directive imposes on it. While the ECJ has recognized the 'vertical' direct effect
of directives, it has refused to admit the possibility of directives having so-called 'horizontal'
direct effect. This is the right of individuals to invoke *against another individual* in the national
courts provisions of a directive in force which have not been transposed (or which have been
incorrectly transposed) by the Member State. From this it can be deduced that before being
transposed, a directive in force can bind the authorities of a Member State, but it cannot bind
individuals.[89] The absence of direct horizontal effect must be qualified, however, in the light of
the wide interpretation that the ECJ gave to the concept of 'authority of a Member State'. For
the purposes of delimiting the entities which are obliged to respect a directive even before it
has been transposed into national law, all entities subject to the control or influence of public
authorities or that possess exorbitant powers have to be included in this category.[90] This means

---

[86] D Edward and M Hoskins, 'Article 90: Deregulation and EC Law. Reflections arising from the XVI FIDE Conference' (1995) xxxii CML Rev 184.

[87] LM Pais Antunes, 'L'Article 86 du Traité CEE—Obligations des Etats Membres et pouvoirs de la Commission' [1991] RTDE ii 203. This is fully consistent with the idea that the function of Article 106 Directives is to 'specify' the obligations contained in the Treaty. However, it is not always true that a breach of a directive—or a horizontal decision under Article 106(3)—would automatically involve a breach of the Treaty. Consider in this regard the situation that exists when a Member State fails to comply with appropriate documentation of transactions with public undertakings. This will lead to an infringement of the Transparency Directive, but would this automatically lead to a direct infringement of Arts 106 and/or 107 TFEU?

[88] JV Louis, 'Le rôle de la Commission dans la procédure en manquement selon la jurisprudence de la Cour de justice' in Various, (Nomos Verlagsgesellschaft 1987) 505; G Isaac, *Droit communautaire général* (4th edn, Edition Masson 1994) 128. See Case C-129/96 *Inter-Environnement Wallonie ASBL v Région wallonne* [1997] ECR I-7411, whose para 50 states that 'The second paragraph of Article 5 and the third paragraph of Article 189 of the EEC Treaty, and Directive 91/156, require the Member States to which that directive is addressed to refrain, during the period laid down therein for its implementation, from adopting measures liable seriously to compromise the result prescribed.' For cases in which the directive 'specifies' a general principle of EU Law and, thus, it can be invoked before the delay of transposition has elapsed, see Case C-144/04 *Mangold* [2005] ECR I-9981, as well as Case C-555/07 *Kücükdeveci* [2010] ECR I-365.

[89] However, it is possible to identify a kind of 'indirect' horizontal effect of directives when the direct effect of directives is invoked against the Member State (see Case C-201/02 *Wells* [2004] ECR I-723) or when applying the 'principle of consistent interpretation' (see Case C-106/89 *Marleasing* [1990] ECR I-4135, as well as Cases C-379–403/01 *Pfeiffer v Deutsche Rote Kreuz* [2004] ECR I-8835).

[90] Case 152/84 *MH Marshall v Southampton and South-West Hampshire Area Health Authority (Teaching)* *(Marshall)* [1986] ECR 723 et seq; Case C-188/89 *A Foster and others v British Gas plc (Foster)* [1990] ECR I-3313, para 18. See also JV Louis, 'Le rôle de la Commission dans la procédure en manquement selon la

that not only public authorities but also public undertakings and private undertakings that enjoy exclusive or special rights will be subject to the 'vertical' direct effect of directives.[91]

20.44   As far as specific directives under Article 106(3) are concerned, there is no doubt that once the time limit for transposing the directive has expired, individuals can invoke the direct effect of its provisions before the national courts. This they can do not only against Member States,[92] but also against public undertakings and private undertakings which enjoy exclusive or special rights. For example, if a directive obliged a Member State to abolish a particular exclusive right, an individual could begin to operate the activity in question legally once the period for transposing the directive had expired. If the individual were faced with legal action for breach of the exclusive right, he could invoke the incompatibility of such exclusive rights with the directive in question before the national courts. The direct effect of directives under Article 106(3) has been recognized on various occasions by the ECJ. The question arose in various criminal proceedings already mentioned, which were brought against undertakings having imported into France and Belgium telephones which had not been approved in accordance with the legislation of those countries. The accused parties alleged that the legislation in question empowered the respective State telecommunications undertakings with approving the terminals, and these undertakings were also importers of such products. This situation created a conflict of interests and was incompatible with Article 6 of the Terminals Directive, which required that the regulatory and type-approval functions be carried out by entities independent from the State telecommunications undertakings.

20.45   The question of the direct effect of Article 6 of the Terminals Directive was examined by AGs Lenz and Tesauro. Both accepted that in principle Article 106(3) was capable of having direct effect; however they differed in their Opinions as to whether Article 6 in particular had direct effect. AG Lenz considered that Article 6 was not sufficiently specific to have direct effect.[93] Against this, AG Tesauro recognized 'without any hesitation' the existence of direct effect; his view was that Article 6 specified the precise nature of Treaty rules which had already been recognized as having direct effect and it was a 'clear, precise and unconditional prohibition'.[94] The ECJ favoured AG Tesauro's approach, and in all the cases examined held that this provision had direct effect.[95] It is submitted that, contrary to what AG Tesauro suggested, the direct effect of directives under Article 106(3) should not be limited to cases where the directive provides precise detail of the meaning of Treaty rules which themselves have direct effect. Indeed, if a Treaty rule lacks direct effect, this may be due precisely to its lack of precision. If this is the case, the intervention of the Commission under Article 106(3) can remedy the lack of precision of the provision in question, thus giving it direct effect.[96] The doubts concerning the limits to the direct effect of Article 106(3) directives do not apply to Article 106(3) decisions. Decisions are normally considered as having direct effect.[97] This effect does not depend on whether they are addressed to one Member State or all of them.[98]

---

jurisprudence de la Cour de justice' in Various, (Nomos Verlagsgesellschaft 1987) 509; D Curtin, '(1990) 15(3) ELR 195; M Hecquart-Theron, '[1990] xxvi (iv) RTDE 693.

[91]   As explained in JL Buendía Sierra, *Exclusive Rights and State Monopolies in EC Law* (Oxford University Press 1999) ch 6, para 229, one of the legal effects of Art 106 TFEU is to subject public and privileged undertakings to certain obligations that EU law imposes on Member States.

[92]   N Emiliou, 'Treading a Slippery Slope: The Commission's Original Legislative Powers' (1993) 18(4) ELR 311.

[93]   Opinion of AG Lenz in Joined Cases C-46/90 and C-93/91 *Lagauche* [1993] ECR I-5317, paras 13–19.

[94]   Opinion of AG Tesauro in Case C-69/91 *Decoster* [1993] ECR I-5363.

[95]   Lagauche, Decoster, and Taillandier; Case C-314/93 *Criminal proceedings against François Rouffeteau and Robert Badia (Rouffeteau)* [1994] ECR I-3257; Case C-91/94 *Criminal Proceedings against Thierry Tranchant and Telephone Store SARL, Party Liable In Civil Law (Tranchart)* [1995] ECR I-3911.

[96]   This position is fully supported by M Kerf, 'The Policy of the Commission of the EEC Toward National Monopolies. An Analysis of the Measures Adopted on the Basis of Article 90(3) of the EEC Treaty' (1993) 17(1) World Competition 89.

[97]   Case C-156/91 *Hansa Fleisch* [1992] ECR I-5567; Case C-249/85 *Albako* [1987] ECR I-2345, paras 17–18.

[98]   Cf JP Jacqué, *Droit institutionnel de l'Union européenne* (6th edn, Dalloz 2010) 571.

3. Relations between directives under Article 106(3) TFEU and harmonization directives

One of the main arguments against directives under Article 106(3) was that the rules con- **20.46**
tained in them could have been adopted by the Council on other legal bases. The rules of the
Transparency Directive could probably have been the object of a Council regulation based on
Article 109. In the same way, the rules relating to the liberalization of telecommunications
contained in the Terminals and Services Directives could probably have been adopted by the
Council on the basis of Articles 103 and/or 114 TFEU. In the opinion of the Member States
who have brought proceedings on this ground, the existence of legal bases such as Articles 103,
109, and 114, which recognize the competence of the Council to regulate an area, exclude the
competence of the Commission to adopt directives under Article 106 concerning the same
subject. According to this view, the rule-making power which Article 106(3) recognized the
Commission as having would, in any event, be merely residual with respect to the legislative competence of the Council. In the *Transparency Directive, Telecommunications Terminal
Equipment*, and *Telecommunications Services* cases, the ECJ totally rejected this argument.
According to the Court, the fact that the provisions of a directive adopted under Article 106(3)
could have been adopted by the Council on other legal bases such as Articles 103, 109, or 114
TFEU in no way affected the legitimacy of using Article 106(3), given the different objects of
these provisions.[99] Thus, Article 106(3) has a different and more specific object than that of
the other Articles mentioned. The object of Article 103 is the adoption of appropriate regulations or directives to give effect to the principles contained in Articles 101 and 102, that is, the
competition rules applicable to all undertakings.[100] Article 109 forms part of a group of provisions which regulate the field of State aid, irrespective of the forms and recipients of such aid.[101]
Article 114 refers to the adoption of measures concerning the harmonization of the legal, regulatory, and administrative provisions of the Member States whose object is the establishment
and functioning of the internal market.[102] The competence of the Commission under Article
106(3) is limited to taking the necessary measures for the effective fulfilment of the guardian
role with regard to public and privileged undertakings which this provision imposes on it.

It should be added that, to the extent that directives under Article 106(3) substantially coincide **20.47**
with obligations under the Treaty that are directly applicable, their object cannot, in theory, coincide with the object of harmonization directives. Thus, by definition, harmonization only occurs
with respect to measures which, despite being *compatible* with the Treaty, produce difficulties for
the internal market.[103] On the contrary, directives under Article 106(3), to the extent that they
specify the obligations under the Treaty, only eliminate measures which are *incompatible* with the
Treaty. As a result, theoretically, there should be no overlapping between the object of the two sets
of directives.[104] Of course, in practice things are not that simple, and harmonization directives
are employed in certain cases to liberalize exclusive rights whose compatibility with the Treaty
is, at the very least, doubtful (at the same time allowing for exceptions and transitional periods

---

[99] Joined Cases 188–190/80 *Transparency Directive* [1982] ECR 2575, paras 11–14; Case C-202/88
Telecommunications Terminal Equipment [1991] ECR I-1265, paras 23–6; Joined Cases C-271/90, C-281/90,
and C-289/90 *Telecommunications Services* [1992] ECR I-5863, para 14.
[100] Case C-202/88 *Telecommunications Terminal Equipment* [1991] ECR I-1266, para 24.
[101] Cases 188–190/80 *Transparency Directive* [1982] ECR 2575, para 12.
[102] Case C-202/88 *Telecommunications Terminal Equipment* [1991] ECR I-1265, para 24.
[103] PJ Slot, 'Harmonisation' [1996] xxi ELR 379–80.
[104] A Abate, 'Droit Communautaire, privatisations, déréglementations—rapport com-munautaire' in
Various, *Le processus de libéralisation d'activités économiques et de privatisation d'entreprises face au Droit de la concurrence*, XVI Congrès de la FIDE [1994] FIDE Rome iii 82 (text also published in [1994] iii RMUE 11–73).

not provided for in the Treaty).[105] Regardless of the possible legal actions against such provisions, the truth is that in practice there is some overlapping between the liberalization directives under Article 106(3) and the harmonization directives. As well as differences of object, there are also differences in the conditions necessary for the employment of the two types of directives. As the Court stated in the *Transparency Directive* case, while Article 109 permits the Council to adopt all regulations which are useful for the application of Articles 107 and 108, Article 106(3) only allows the Commission to adopt the 'necessary' measures.[106] Although the Court has not emphasized this point in subsequent judgments, it appears clear that the room for manoeuvre which the EU legislator enjoys by virtue of Articles 103, 109, and 114 is greater than that enjoyed by the Commission under Article 106(3). The legislator 'creates' rules and therefore the scope of his decision-making is largely conditioned by considerations of opportunity, whereas the Commission has to limit itself to specifying what the existing law is, and therefore the limits on its discretion are much greater.

20.48   On the basis of these differences in the object and the conditions of application, the ECJ reached the following conclusion:[107]

> It follows that the Commission's power to issue the contested directive depends on the needs inherent in its duty of surveillance provided for in Article 90 [now 106] and that the possibility that rules might be laid down by the Council, by virtue of its general power under Article 94 [now 109], containing provisions impinging upon the specific sphere of aids granted to public undertakings does not preclude the exercise of that power by the Commission.

The rule-making competence that the Commission has under Article 106(3) is therefore *concurrent* with the legislative competences of the Council. In other words, the Court recognizes that there is a certain degree of overlapping between the object of Article 106(3) and the legislative competences of the Council. Certain areas can be regulated by both a directive of the Commission or of the Council. This concurrent nature of the competences of the Commission and the Council also means that a directive adopted by the Commission under Article 106(3) could modify, within its own field of competence, the provisions of a directive previously adopted by the Council.[108] This overlapping between the competences of the Council and the Commission is found primarily in questions of liberalization. Thus, when the Commission considers that it is necessary to tackle the question of liberalization in a given sector, it will be faced with a delicate question: whether to opt for adopting a directive itself based on Article 106(3) or to propose to the Council a draft directive on a different legal basis. From a strictly legal point of view, the decision to choose one or other instrument rests with the Commission, since the Council cannot adopt any legislation which has not been first proposed by the Commission. Nevertheless, it would be totally unrealistic to ignore the political context in which such decisions are taken.

20.49   An essential aspect of this question is the participation of the European Parliament in the legislative process. Thus, Article 114 TFEU gives to the European Parliament a prominent role in the legislative process. Following the Maastricht Treaty, the Parliament can even reject, by simple majority, a proposed directive based on Article 114. Thus, directives under Article 114 enjoy reinforced democratic legitimacy which directives adopted under Article 106(3) do not have.[109]

---

[105] See, *inter alia*, the authorization system established in Reg (EC) 1073/2009 of the European Parliament and of the Council of 21 October 2009 on common rules for access to the international market for coach and bus services [2009] OJ L300/88.

[106] Joined Cases 188–190/80 *Transparency Directive* [1982] ECR 2575, para 13.

[107] Joined Cases 188–190/80 *Transparency Directive* [1982] ECR 2575, para 14; Case C-202/88 *Telecommunications Terminal Equipment* [1991] ECR I-1266, para 26; Joined Cases C-271/90, C-281/90, and C-289/90 *Telecommunications Services* [1992] ECR I-5863, para 14.

[108] C Hocepied, 'Les directives articles 90, paragraphe 3. Une espèce juridique en voie de disparition?' [1994] ii RAE 54.

[109] C Hocepied, 'Les directives articles 90, paragraphe 3. Une espèce juridique en voie de disparition?' [1994] ii RAE 60.

As would be expected, the European Parliament exerts political pressure on the Commission in the hope that it will choose to act, whenever possible, under Article 114 instead of Article 106(3), given that the latter provision does not provide for the intervention of Parliament.[110] It is clear that in such a context, the room for manoeuvre which the Commission theoretically enjoys when choosing which legal basis to proceed under is, from a political point of view, in fact very limited. This explains the fact that despite enjoying the power to adopt directives under Article 106(3), the Commission has used this power very sparingly. Leaving on one side the Transparency Directive and its amendments, applicable to all sectors although of a very limited scope, all the other directives adopted under Article 106(3) relate to the telecommunications sector, a sector where there is almost complete agreement in favour of liberalization. In other monopolized sectors, where unanimity in favour of liberalization is a long way off, the Commission has in general opted for proposing directives under Article 114 (or other legal bases under which the Council has competence), despite in many cases considering it possible to take action through adopting directives under Article 106(3).[111] The prudence of the Commission is seen by many to be clearly excessive.[112] Apart from the telecommunications sector, the majority of liberalization programmes have been carried out on the basis of directives or regulations adopted by the Council and, in some cases, also by the European Parliament. This has been the case with air transport,[113] airport ground handling services,[114] rail transport,[115] exploration and operation activities concerning hydrocarbons,[116] electricity,[117] gas,[118] and postal services.[119]

---

[110] This fact probably helps explain the Commission's common practice of consulting the European Parliament informally before adopting directives under Art 106(3).

[111] This was declared by the Commission in relation to energy in its document 'The internal market in energy' COM (90) 124 final, 12–13. As regards airport assistance services, see XXI Report on Competition Policy (1992), para 519.

[112] C Hocepied, 'Les directives articles 90, paragraphe 3. Une espèce juridique en voie de disparition?' [1994] ii RAE 60.

[113] Council Reg (EEC) 92/2407 on licensing of air carriers [1992] OJ L240/1; Council Reg (EEC) 2408/92 on access of Community air carriers to intra-Community air routes [1992] OJ L240/8. Both of them were repealed by Reg (EC) 1008/2008 of the European Parliament and of the Council of 24 September 2008 on common rules for the operation of air services in the Community [2008] OJ L293/3.

[114] Council Directive (EC) 96/67 on access to the groundhandling market at Community airports [1996] OJ L272/36.

[115] Council Directive (EC) 95/18 on the licensing of railway undertakings [1995] OJ L143/70; Council Directive (EC) 95/19 on the allocation of railway infrastructure capacity and the charging of infrastructure fees [1995] OJ L143/75, modified by Directive 2001/13/EC of the European Parliament and of the Council of 26 February 2001 amending Council Directive 95/18/EC on the licensing of railway undertakings [2001] OJ L75/26, as well as by Directive 2004/49/EC of the European Parliament and of the Council of 29 April 2004 on safety on the Community's railways and amending Council Directive 95/18/EC on the licensing of railway undertakings and Directive 2001/14/EC on the allocation of railway infrastructure capacity and the levying of charges for the use of railway infrastructure and safety certification (Railway Safety Directive) [2004] OJ L164/44.

[116] European Parliament and Council Directive (EC) 94/22 on the conditions for granting and using authorizations for the prospection, exploration and production of hydrocarbons [1994] OJ L164/3.

[117] European Parliament and Council Directive (EC) 96/92 concerning common rules for the internal market in electricity [1996] OJ L27/20. This directive has been repealed by Directive 2003/54/EC of the European Parliament and of the Council concerning common rules for the internal market in electricity [2003] OJ L176/37. In its turn, Directive 2003/54 has been repealed by Directive 2009/72/EC of the European Parliament and of the Council of 13 July 2009 concerning common rules for the internal market in electricity and repealing Directive 2003/54/EC [2009] OJ L211/55.

[118] Directive of the European Parliament and the Council (EC) 98/30 concerning common rules for the internal market in natural gas [1998] OJ L204/1. Repealed by Directive 2003/55/EC of the European Parliament and of the Council of 26 June 2003 concerning common rules for the internal market in natural gas and repealing Directive 98/30/EC [2003] OJ L176/57. In its turn, this Directive was repealed by Directive 2009/73/EC of the European Parliament and of the Council of 13 July 2009 concerning common rules for the internal market in natural gas and repealing Directive 2003/55/EC, [2009] OJ L211/94.

[119] Directive of the European Parliament and the Council (EC) 97/67 on common rules for the development of the internal market in Community postal services and the improvement of quality of service [1998] OJ L15/14, as well as Directive 2008/6/EC of the European Parliament and of the Council of

20.50 If these facts appear to qualify the role of directives under Article 106(3) as instruments of liberalization, it would be wrong to think that such rule-making powers play no part outside the telecommunications sector. Nothing could be further from the truth. The simple fact that within the Commission's armoury is the *possibility* of adopting a directive under Article 106(3) without doubt influences the attitude of the different actors in the legal process. The mere existence of Article 106(3) is enough to prevent Member States and the Parliament from blocking *sine die* draft directives presented by the Commission on the basis of Article 114.[120] In the context of long and difficult negotiations concerning the liberalization of the electricity and postal service, as well as the professional services sectors, the Commission has evoked, on various occasions, the possibility of having recourse to Article 106(3) if the situation remained locked in a stalemate. Probably partly because of these timely reminders, it has been possible to conclude both processes with specific results.

20.51 In this way, Article 106(3) plays a 'dissuasive' role against excessive resistance to liberalization found in certain sectors. While it is necessary for the liberalization process to enjoy broad support, it must not be forgotten that the choice of a system of free competition is part of the basic principles of the EU legal system.[121] In this respect, unlike the situation pertaining in other legal systems, the abolition of exclusive rights is not a question which is simply left to the legislator of the moment. Rather, it is a fundamental choice, deeply rooted in the core of internal market rules, which has been largely carried out by the signatory States to the Treaty of Rome, agreed to by new Member States and ratified whenever the treaties have been revised. It is submitted that the system of concurrent rule-making powers currently provided for in the Treaty allows the fundamental choices enshrined in the Treaty to co-exist reasonably with the position of the legislator of the moment.

20.52 The EU legislator enjoys great discretion in reaching decisions and therefore can take into account a wider range of considerations. However, it should not be forgotten that he is also limited to some extent by the need to respect the Treaty provisions, which play a similar role to the constitution in national legal systems. Given that the EU is a '[Union] based on the rule of Law',[122] the EU legislator is obliged to respect, in the exercise of his legislative powers, the limits set out in the Treaty. The substantive content of EU legislation cannot ignore the substantive rules derived from the Treaties.[123] In principle, a Council directive should not, therefore, come into direct conflict with the principle of non-distorted competition derived from the Treaty.[124] Faced with such a case, the ECJ could, in theory, declare the directive to be incompatible with the Treaty.

---

20 February 2008 amending Directive 97/67/EC with regard to the full accomplishment of the internal market of Community postal services [2008] OJ L52/3.

[120] M Kerf, 'The Policy of the Commission of the EEC Toward National Monopolies. An Analysis of the Measures Adopted on the Basis of Article 90(3) of the EEC Treaty' (1993) 17(1) World Competition 111.

[121] Albeit the removal of Art 3(1)(g) of the EC Treaty see Protocol n 27 attached to the TFEU, which inseparably links internal market and competition rules. See JL Buendía Sierra 'Writing Straight with Crooked Lines: Competition Policy and Services of General Economic Interest in the Treaty of Lisbon' in A Biondi and P Eeckhout (eds), (Oxford University Press 2011).

[122] Case 294/83 *Parti écologiste 'Les Verts' v European Parliament* [1986] ECR-1339, para 23.

[123] G Isaac, *Droit communautaire général* (4th edn, Edition Masson 1994) 130.

[124] G Marenco in 'Le Traité CEE interdit-il aux Etats membres de restreindre la concurrence?' [1986] CDE année XXII, iii–iv, 285–6, n 2, interprets the Court's case law in this way, although without being in favour of the Court's approach. See Case 114/76 *Bela-Mühle Josef Bergmann KG v Grows-Farm GmbH & CO KG (Bela-Mühle)* [1977] ECR 1211; Case 139/79 *Maizena GmbH v Council (Maizena)* [1980] ECR 3393, paras 22–3; Case 172/82 *Syndicat national des fabricants raffineurs d'huile de graissage and others v Groupement d'intérêt économique 'Inter-Huiles' and others (Used Oils)* [1983] ECR 565, paras 9 and 15; Case 66/86 *Ahmed Saeed* [1989] ECR 852, para 51. See the Opinion of AG Rozes in Case 172/82 *Used Oils* [1983] ECR 571.

C. Regulations under Article 14 TFEU

The application of EU rules to services of general economic interest has always been a **20.53** politically sensitive matter. The issue is a recurring subject for discussion at the successive Intergovernmental Conferences on the amendment of the Treaties, in which the position of certain Member States in this regard provided a good example of perseverance. Initially, the Treaty of Amsterdam introduced Article 16 of the EC Treaty (broadly corresponding to current Article 14 TFEU), a declaration of intent that did not involve any significant change, since it reiterated what was already provided by Article 106(2) TFEU.[125] The original wording of Article 16 EC read as follows:

> [W]ithout prejudice to Articles 73, 86 and 87 [currently Articles 93, 106, and 107 TFEU] and given the place occupied by services of general economic interest in the shared values of the Union as well as their role in promoting social and territorial cohesion, the Community and the Member States, each within their respective powers and within the scope of application of this Treaty, shall take care that such services operate on the basis of principles and conditions which enable them to fulfil their missions.

The debate on the relationship between EU law and services of general economic interest was also affected by the evolution of ECJ case law and, in particular, its landmark 2003 *Altmark* judgment.[126] Following this judgment the Commission returned to the fray and in 2005 adopted the post-*Altmark* package,[127] which included a block exemption for small services of general economic interest on the basis of Article 86(3) EC Treaty [now Article 106(3) TFEU]. The adoption of this package by the Commission showed that the treaties in force at the time provided sufficient legal basis from which to clarify the rules concerning services of general economic interest.[128]

On the other side of the debate, the supporters of a Treaty modification, while avoiding an open **20.54** debate on the issue, managed to slip in a modification of Article 16 EC, strangely tabled at the very last minute of the works of the European Convention.[129] The change was introduced in Article III-122 of the Draft Constitutional Treaty and provided an additional legal basis for establishing principles and conditions for the provisions of services of general economic interest.[130]

---

[125] See JL Buendia Sierra, in A Biondi and P Eeckhout (eds), (Oxford University Press 2011); T Prosser, (Oxford University Press 2009); T Prosser, '*The Limits of Competition Law Markets and Public Services* in C Graham and F Smiths (eds), (Hart Publishing 2004); L Flynn, in D O'Keefe and P Twomey (eds), (Hart Publishing 1999); W Sauter, 'Services of General Economic Interest and Universal Service in EU Law' (2008) 17 TILEC Discussion Paper; M Ross 'Article 16 EC and the Services of General Interest: From Derogation to Obligation?' [2000] European Law Review 38; cf N Fiedziuk [2011] European Law Review 36; M Ross '[2000] European Law Review 38.

[126] This judgment clarifies the conditions under which financial compensation granted to the operator of a SGEI is not State aid. See Case C-280/00 *Altmark* [2003] ECR I-7747.

[127] Decision 2005/842/EC on the application of Article 86(2) of the EC Treaty to State Aid in the form of public service compensation granted to certain undertakings entrusted with the operation of services of general economic interest [2005] OJ L312/67; Community framework for State aid in the form of public service compensation [2005] OJ C294/4; Directive 2005/81/EC amending Directive 80/723/EEC on the transparency of financial relationships between Member States and public undertakings as well as on financial transparency within certain undertakings [2005] OJ L312/47.

[128] See JL Buendía Sierra 'Finding the Right Balance: State Aid and Services of General Economic Interest' in *EC State Aid Law: Liber Amicorum Francisco Santaolalla* (Kluwer 2008), ch 10, 221–2.

[129] See the minutes of the penultimate plenary session of the European Convention held in Brussels on 4 July 2003, CONV 849/03, according to which the initiative for the adoption of this provision came from the Presidium of the Convention. In the last session, certain members of the Convention voiced their disagreement with the introduction of this amendment, on the basis that it was not of technical nature. See the minutes of the last plenary session of the European Convention held in Brussels on 9 and 10 July 2003, CONV 853/03.

[130] The Article read as follows: 'Without prejudice to Articles I-5, III-167 and III-238, and given the place occupied by services of general economic interest as services to which all in the Union attribute value as well

20.55 Albeit the provision was one of the casualties of the rejection of the Draft Constitutional Treaty by the French and Dutch voters, its content was recycled into what is now Article 14 TFEU. This Article now goes beyond the rather rhetorical formulation of former Article 16 EC by including a new legal basis. The text of the new provision is as follows (the words in italic indicate the changes compared to the wording of Article 16 EC Treaty):

> [W]ithout prejudice to *Article 4 of the Treaty on the European Union or to* Articles 93, 106 and 107 of this Treaty and given the place occupied by services of general economic interest in the shared values of the Union as well as their role in promoting social and territorial cohesion, The *Union* and the Member States, each within their respective powers *on the basis of principles and conditions, particularly economic and financial conditions, which enable them to fulfil their missions. The European Parliament and the Council, acting by means of regulations in accordance with the ordinary legislative procedure, shall establish these principles and set these conditions without prejudice to the competence of Member States, in compliance with the Treaties, to provide, to commission and to fund such services.*

On its substantive side, the Article should be read jointly with Article 1 of the Protocol on Services of General Interest, that describes the common values of the EU in relation to them, insisting on the discretion enjoyed by the national, regional, and local authorities to design the provision of such services. Article 2 of the said Protocol specifies that the competence of Member States to provide, entrust, and organize services of general interest of a non-economic nature is not affected by the Treaty.

20.56 Article 14 is not at all easy to interpret. Its convoluted grammar suggests a Herculean struggle to combine references to services of general economic interest with the autonomy that Member States have in this area and with the respect for previously existing provisions of the Treaties, like Articles 106 and 107 TFEU. It is hard to predict what the outcome of such conflicting elements will be.

20.57 The current regulation of services of general economic interest in the Treaty is, therefore, undoubtedly paradoxical. At first sight, it could be argued that the values of solidarity that underlie services of general economic interest should lead to strengthened integration at the European level, and not to a closing of national borders. However, the idea of a positive competence in this area—including solidarity elements between citizens of different Member States—is totally excluded. The concept of European public services simply does not exist; instead the debate is entirely about protecting national public services from EU interference.

20.58 Given this context, it is paradoxical that in this area, there is an EU legal basis for services of general economic interest, but no EU competence on it, not even one that is shared with Member States. What purpose, then, does this legal basis serve, if any? One can only imagine the kind of purpose the proponents of this legal basis had in mind. Perhaps they wanted a legal basis enabling the adoption of rules, a framework 'directive' that would establish a type of 'protective shield' around operators of services of general economic interest in an attempt to protect them from the application of competition rules, and particularly, the provisions of the Treaty on State aid. The key point is that such a legal instrument can be adopted by qualified majority, whereas changes to the Treaties require unanimity.

20.59 If this were the point of the proposal, it would seem very difficult to achieve from a purely legal point of view. Indeed, if one wants to restrict the scope of a Treaty provision (namely Article 107 and/or 106(2) TFEU) the only legal way to do this is to amend it in accordance with the procedures for amendment of the Treaties. Secondary legislation can never modify primary law. Even if, for the sake of argument, a secondary law instrument could modify the Treaty, it is clear that a legal basis that starts with the words 'without prejudice to

Articles… 106 and 107 of this Treaty' would not be the ideal instrument to use for amending the scope of those Articles. Given the accumulation of contradictory caveats in its wording, it seems much easier to identify what cannot be done with Article 14 TFEU (amend the scope of competition or State aid rules, change the allocation of competences between EU and Member States…) than what can be done with it.

Ultimately, it may well be that the actual impact of this new legal basis is limited. The Treaties **20.60** have other provisions that have so far never been used.[131] Indeed, in November 2007, the European Commission refused to exercise its power to initiate legislation to propose this framework directive, arguing that the new protocol would be sufficient.[132] At the time of writing, the Commission has presented its new package on services of general economic interest. The package consists of:

(i) a Commission Communication on the application of the EU State aid rules to compensation granted for the provision of services of general economic interest;[133]
(ii) a decision on the application of Article 106(2) of the TFEU to State aid in the form of public service compensation granted to certain undertakings entrusted with the operation of services of general economic interest —adopted under the basis of Article 106(3) TFEU;[134]
(iii) a Communication from the Commission with the EU framework for State aid in the form of public service compensation;[135] and
(iv) a Commission Regulation on the application of Articles 107 and 108 of the TFEU to *de minimis* aid granted to undertakings providing services of general economic interest[136] —adopted under the basis of Regulation (EC) 994/98.[137]

None of the norms of the package is a proposal of the Commission on a Regulation to be issued under Article 14 TFEU.

1. Generalities on regulations adopted under Article 14 TFEU

Giving their—at this stage—purely speculative nature it is only possible to hypothesize on **20.61** the characteristics that regulations issued under Article 14 TFEU may have. At least, Article 14 provides that the regulations referred to it should be adopted by the European Parliament and the Council according to the ordinary legislative procedure. This legislative procedure may entail three successive readings by the Parliament and the Council, but an agreement can be achieved in the first or second reading without the need to cover all the procedures

---

as their role in promoting its social and territorial cohesion, the Union and the Member States, each within their respective competences and within the scope of application of the Constitution, shall take care that such services operate on the basis of principles and conditions, in particular economic and financial conditions which enable them to fulfil their missions. European laws shall establish these principles and set the conditions without prejudice to the competence of the Member States, in compliance with the Constitution, to provide, to commission and to fund such services.'

[131] For instance, Arts 116 and 117 TFEU.

[132] Communication of the Commission to the European Parliament, the Council, the European Economic and Social Committee and the Committee of the Regions, accompanying the Communication 'A single market for the 21st Century Europe', Services of general interest, including social services of general interest: a new European commitment [COM (2007)724final] Brussels, 20 November 2007.

[133] [2012] OJ C8/4.

[134] [2012] OJ C7/3.

[135] [2012] OJ C8/15.

[136] [2012] OJ C114/8.

[137] Council Reg (EC) 994/98 of 7 May 1998 on the application of Articles 92 and 93 of the Treaty establishing the European Community to certain categories of horizontal State aid [1998] OJ L142/1.

foreseen in Article 294 TFEU. However, it is worth noting that the ordinary legislative procedure entails a restriction of the role of the Commission vis-à-vis its traditional position within
the different legislative procedures. Indeed, the Parliament and the Council have ample powers to modify the Commission's legislative proposal in the conciliation phase and they can
largely modify it as long as they remain within the scope of the proposal.[138] This fact could—
at least partially—explain the reluctance of the Commission to make use of Article 14 when
modifying the post-*Altmark* package.

20.62   The fact that proponents of Article 14 could consider it as a suitable base for framework
'directives' does not alter the fact that regulations under Article 14 are norms belonging to
the defined legal category of regulations adopted by the institutions of the EU and, as such,
do have direct effect *ex* Article 288 TFEU. What the consequences of this fact could be would
largely depend on the content of such hypothetical regulations.

20.63   Relationships between hypothetical regulations issued under Article 14 TFEU and secondary
law giving effect to Articles 106 and 107 threaten to be complex. The wording of Article 14
itself when introducing the Article, 'without prejudice to Articles 93, 106 and 107', suggests
that there is a prevalence of the content of those Articles over Article 14 TFEU. On these
bases, it can be inferred that EU secondary legislation issued to give effect to Articles 106
and 107 [decisions or directives issued under Article 106(3) and/or regulations issued under
Articles 108(4) and 109 TFEU] would also prevail over the legislation issued to give effect to
Article 14. However, at the present stage this controversy remains purely hypothetical.

---

[138] Case C-408/95 *Eurotunnel* [1997] ECR I-6315. On the ordinary legislative procedure and the powers of the Commission within it see JP Jacqué, *Droit institutionnel de l'Union européenne* (6th edn, Dalloz
2010) 407.

PART IV

STATE AID
(ARTICLES 107 AND 108 TFEU)

21

GENERAL QUESTIONS ON PROCEDURE. CONTROL OF STATE AID COMPATIBILITY. COUNCIL'S DECISION-MAKING POWER

Jean Paul Keppenne and Carlos Urraca Caviedes

I. Introduction

Article 108 of the Treaty on the Functioning of the European Union ('TFEU') provides for a **21.01** special control system to check on the compatibility of aid. This comes largely under the control of the Commission, which not only decides beforehand on the compatibility of new aid (Article 108(2) and (3)), but also permanently reviews existing aid schemes (Article 108(1) and (2)). As part of this latter role, the Commission, in cooperation with Member States, decides whether or not the smooth running of the Internal market calls for these schemes to be altered or abolished. If so, the Commission has to follow the procedure laid down in paragraphs 1 and 2 of Article 108 TFEU when ordering the Member State(s) concerned to alter or abolish their schemes, with future effect. As regards new aid, the Commission is empowered to rule directly on its compatibility. To enable the Commission to carry out this task, Member States are bound to notify it of their aid plans before putting them into effect. Aid declared to be incompatible with the internal market by the Commission cannot be granted; if it has already been paid unlawfully, the Commission will ask the Member State in question to recover it from the undertaking that has benefited from it. National courts, moreover, have the power to enforce the obligation to notify new aid.

21.02 Article 108 TFEU lays down the fundamental rules governing the procedure for the control of State aid. The detailed terms of these rules were progressively fleshed out by the Court of Justice ('ECJ') and finally set out in Council Regulation (EC) 659/1999 of 22 March 1999, laying down detailed rules for the application of Article 93 of the EC Treaty (hereinafter the 'Procedural Regulation').[1] As well as systematizing the practice to date, the Regulation also introduced some new rules: the concept of 'existing aid' was extended to include measures that become aid due to the evolution of the common market, a limitation period was established for the recovery of unlawful aid, etc. The provisions of the Regulation deal successively with notified aid, unlawful aid, misuse of aid, existing aid, and monitoring methods. Although it did introduce some new features, this Regulation did not fundamentally change the aid review procedure. Its principal merit resides in its binding legal nature, thereby confirming and clarifying the rules established in the case law of the ECJ and from the texts and practice of the Commission. Also worthy of note is the fact that the Commission and Council have confirmed the traditional approach according to which the control of State aid is part and parcel of a bilateral dialogue between the Commission and the Member State concerned. Certain complementary arrangements were established in a subsequent Commission Regulation.[2]

21.03 The Regulation came into force on 16 April 1999. Its provisions are procedural in nature and as such are applicable, unless a transitional provision expressly states otherwise, to all administrative State aid procedures that were pending before the Commission at the time the Regulation came into force.[3]

II. Classification of Measures as State Aid

21.04 Article 108 TFEU, which deals with the procedure for checking on the compatibility of State aid, says nothing about the procedure to follow for ascertaining whether or not a given measure falls within the scope of Article 107(1) TFEU and, if so, whether it is new or existing aid.[4] But this has been shown in practice to be potentially a contentious issue.

21.05 The competence for determining measures as State aid, and also for ascertaining whether it is new or existing in character, is shared between the Commission and the national authorities, especially the judicial authorities.

---

[1] [1999] OJ L83/1. On 13 July 2012, the Commission invited comments on the application of procedural rules in State aid investigations, as it proposes to clarify and simplify the current regime, in particular with regard to the handling of complaints and the collection of market information. The Commission considers it should be able to set priorities for handling complaints and should have efficient tools to obtain the necessary information from market participants in good time. In light of the comments received, the Commission proposed reforms to the State Aid Enabling Regulation and Procedural Regulation: Commission Press Release IP/12/316 'State Aid: Commission proposes to reform state aid procedures and exempt certain categories of aid from prior notification', Commission MEMO/12/936 and MEMO/12/942, 5 December 2012.

[2] Commission Reg (EC) 794/2004 of 21 April 2004 implementing Council Reg (EC) 659/1999 laying down detailed rules for the application of Art 93 of the EC Treaty [2004] OJ L140/1, as last amended by Commission Reg (EC) 1125/2009 of 23 November 2009 OJ L308/5. The Commission has also issued a Notice on a Simplified procedure for the treatment of certain types of State aid ([2009] OJ C136/3, with a corrigendum [2009] OJ C157/20) and a Notice on a Best Practices Code on the conduct of State aid control proceedings ([2009] OJ C136/13).

[3] Case T-274/01 *Valmont Nederland v Commission* [2004] ECR II-3145, para 56.

[4] On this second question see also Ch 24, 'Control of Existing Aid Schemes'.

A. Powers of the Commission

1. Characteristics

Principle

Endowed with exclusive[5] powers for deciding on the compatibility of State aid with the inter- **21.06**
nal market, the Commission should also be considered as empowered to determine beforehand whether the measures under examination really do constitute State aid under Article
107(1) TFEU.[6] This power is not exclusive, however, since it is also enjoyed by national
courts.[7]

Discretionary power

In cases of application of Article 107(1) TFEU involving complex questions of an economic **21.07**
or legal nature that have to be implemented in a EU context, there would be some grounds
for considering the Commission to have some discretionary power,[8] which would amount to
a limited jurisdictional control. For instance, where the Commission needs to apply the test
of a prudent private investor's normal conduct when deciding whether or not a measure constitutes aid, this normally entails a complex economic appraisal.[9] On the other hand, given
that aid is an objective concept, defining a measure as State aid cannot in principle justify
the Commission having a broad discretion, except in particular circumstances owing to the
complex nature of the State intervention in question.[10]

Any discretionary power exercised by the Commission in deciding whether or not a measure **21.08**
constitutes aid is thus qualitatively different[11] from—and more reduced than—the broad
discretionary power it has when reviewing the compatibility of aid.[12]

Obligation to give reasoned decisions

The Commission must explain its grounds for considering that the measure in question **21.09**
comes within Article 107(1) TFEU.[13] It does not have to give its opinion on all submissions
made by the interested parties; its remit extends only to setting out the facts of the case and

---

[5] Subject to certain exceptions and reductions (see para 21.32 et seq).
[6] Case 323/82 *Intermills v Commission* [1984] ECR 3809, para 32 and Case C-301/87 *France v Commission*
[1990] ECR I-307, para 13.
[7] See Ch 26, 'Role of National Courts'. The fact that the Commission does not have exclusive powers for
deciding on the existence of aid does not exempt it from the obligation of dealing with all measures submitted
to it within a reasonable time.
[8] Case C-409/00 *Spain v Commission* [2003] ECR I-1487, para 69.
[9] In particular, Case C-56/93 *Belgium v Commission* [1996] ECR I-723, para 11 and Case T-358/94 *Air
France v Commission* [1996] ECR II-2109, paras 71–2.
[10] Case T-67/94 *Ladbroke v Commission* [1998] ECR II-1, para 52.
[11] The GC clearly pointed to this difference in Case T-95/94 *Sytraval v Commission* [1995] ECR II-2651,
para 54 and Case T-67/94 *Ladbroke v Commission* [1998] ECR II-1, para 52. It has, however, sometimes
employed the term 'a discretion' in speaking of the Commission's finding of the existence of aid (Case
T-358/94 *Air France v Commission* [1996] ECR II-2109, para 72).
[12] Besides, the procedure under Art 108 TFEU must never produce a result which is contrary to the specific
provisions of the Treaty. Accordingly, State aid, certain conditions of which contravene other provisions of
the Treaty, cannot be declared by the Commission to be compatible with the internal market. Similarly, State
aid, certain of the conditions of which contravene the general principles of Union law, such as the principle
of equal treatment, cannot be declared by the Commission to be compatible with the internal market (Case
C-390/06 *Nuova Agricast* [2008] ECR I-2577, paras 50–1).
[13] Case T-16/96 *Cityflyer Express v Commission* [1998] ECR II-757, para 66; Joined Cases T-228/99 and
T-233/99 *WestLB and others v Commission* [2003] ECR II-435, para 281; and Case T-109/01 *Fleuren Compost
v Commission* [2004] ECR II-127, para 120.

the legal considerations upon which the decision was largely based.[14] In particular, it is not bound to state its position on an aspect which is as manifestly immaterial to the classification of the contested measures as State aid.[15]

21.10 The Commission's obligation to give grounds for its decisions is less strict when it is able to base its case on facts that have not been contested by the Member State involved (for example when the Member State concerned formally acknowledges that the measure under examination does come within Article 107(1) TFEU).

2. Terms

21.11 The TFEU does not provide any particular procedure for classifying a measure as State aid. It takes it for granted that this previous stage, before compatibility is examined, will be carried out without problems.

Procedure for examining the nature of a measure

21.12 In view of the Treaty's silence, the Commission has considered that the set of procedures for checking the compatibility of new and existing aid, as laid down in Article 108 TFEU, could be used for ascertaining whether or not the disputed measures do actually come within the scope of Article 107(1) TFEU. As regards 'new measures', the Commission adheres to the procedure laid down in Article 108(2) TFEU to verify whether a State measure constitutes State aid. To deal with 'existing measures' (by analogy with existing aid), the Commission likewise makes use of the procedure laid down in paragraphs 1 and 2 of Article 108 TFEU. This practice has been borne out by the EU Courts. Certain subsequent developments concerning the Commission's examination of aid compatibility hence apply *mutatis mutandis* to the procedure followed by the Commission for classifying a measure as State aid—witness in particular the developments concerning the nature of the examination procedure, the interlocutors of the Commission, and the internal operation of the latter.

21.13 Whereas the Commission is bound to cooperate on an ongoing basis with Member States in vetting the compatibility of existing aid, the same cooperation obligation is not incumbent upon it when ascertaining whether a measure can be classified as aid. In theory it could forge its own completely independent method of evaluation, subject to the control of the EU Courts.[16] In practice, however, the Commission takes care to obtain the Member States' backing, or at least present its evaluation to them beforehand.

Prior notification

21.14 The Commission sought to extend the Member States' notification obligations by informing them that they must still notify even when they deem that the measure in question does not have all the characteristics of Article 107(1) TFEU.[17] According to this approach, the notification obligation would extend to measures 'which may involve aid within the meaning

---

[14] Case T-214/95 *Vlaams Gewest v Commission* [1998] ECR II-717, para 63 and Case T-16/96 *Cityflyer Express v Commission*, para 65.

[15] Case C-5/01 *Belgium v Commission* [2002] ECR I-11991, para 71.

[16] However, in view of the legal consequences of a decision to initiate the procedure provided for in Art 108(2) TFEU, provisionally classifying the measures concerned as new aid, even though the Member State concerned is unlikely to subscribe to that classification, the Commission must first broach the subject of the measures in question with the Member State concerned, so that the latter has an opportunity, if appropriate, to inform the Commission that, in its view, those measures do not constitute aid or constitute existing aid (Case C-400/99 *Italy v Commission* [2001] ECR I-7303, para 48; Case T-211/05 *Italy v Commission* [2009] ECR II-2777, para 37).

[17] Commission Communication [1983] OJ C318/3, or *Competition Law in the European Communities*, Vol IIA (1999) 59.

of Article [107](1) of the Treaty' and the scope of Article 108(3) would to some extent be broader than that of Article 107(1). It would nonetheless seem more correct to consider the notification obligation to be applicable at the very most when the Member State is not sure that all the criteria of Article 107(1) are in fact met.

The Commission has likewise sought to make sure that it has all the information necessary **21.15** by making use of its power under Article 106(3) to force Member States to provide it with certain information about their financial relations with their public undertakings.[18]

External expertise

The Commission has sometimes resorted to outside help from consultants in deciding **21.16** whether or not it is dealing with a case of State aid. The EU Courts have held that the Commission is entitled but not bound to avail itself of outside help, but it is not thereby exempted from the duty of appraising their work.[19]

3. Quasi-regulations of the Commission

The Commission has approved texts of a general nature relating to the scope of Article 107(1) **21.17** TFEU. These deal with the classification of certain financial transactions vis-à-vis Article 107(1) TFEU, and lay down the criteria for the Commission's evaluation of capital investments, State guarantees, and other types of financial transfers in favour of undertakings. These texts represent a sort of systemization of the Commission's action, backed up as need be by certain case law decisions.

The ECJ has accepted that the Commission is entitled to take the view, in the notices and **21.18** guidelines it draws up, that certain aid does not come within Article 107 TFEU, but it can do so only 'in accordance with the Treaty'.[20] These texts, which, being an internal measure adopted by the administration, cannot be regarded as a rule of law; nevertheless they form rules of practice from which the administration may not depart in an individual case without giving reasons which are compatible with the principle of equal treatment.[21] Therefore, they express an interpretation of Article 107(1) TFEU that is valid only as long as it is in accordance with the Treaty and that is always, in the last resort, subject to judicial control. Moreover, the Commission does not have the exclusive right to interpret Article 107(1) TFEU.

4. Transparency Directive

The sheer complexity of the financial relations of the national public authorities with **21.19** public undertakings is enough to jeopardize the Commission's task of reviewing aid. The Commission therefore obliges Member States to ensure the transparency of their financial relations with public undertakings through its Directive 2006/111/EC of 16 November 2006.[22] Member States must keep a record of certain financial information and produce this to the Commission when so requested; they must also supply annually certain information on each public undertaking operating in the manufacturing sector. There is also an obligation on certain undertakings to keep separate accounts: separate accounts must be kept by

---

[18] See the Transparency Directive mentioned at para 21.19.
[19] Case T-106/95 *FFSA and others v Commission* [1997] ECR II-229, para 102, and Case T-274/01 *Valmont Nederland v Commission* [2004] ECR II-3145, para 72.
[20] Case C-409/00 *Spain v Commission* [2003] ECR I-1487, para 69.
[21] Joined Cases C-465/09 P to C-470/09 P *Diputación Foral de Vizcaya and Others v Commission* [2011] ECR I-83, para 120; and Joined Cases C-106/09 P and C-107/09 P *Commission v Government of Gibraltar* [2011] ECR I-59, para 128.
[22] On the transparency of financial relations between Member States and public undertakings as well as on financial transparency within certain undertakings [2006] OJ L318/17, and repealing Directive 80/723/EEC of 25 June 1980 [1980] OJ L195/35 ('Transparency Directive').

public and private undertakings which have been granted special or exclusive rights by an EU State or which are responsible for operating a service of general economic interest and which receive public service compensation in any form whatsoever in relation to such service and at the same time perform other activities.

21.20 The ECJ has confirmed the validity of this approach after having in particular ruled that the financial relations obtaining between public undertakings and the public authorities are of a particular type, very different from those existing between public authorities and private undertakings.[23]

B. Powers of the National Courts

21.21 Following the procedure of the Commission, a national court may have cause to pronounce on the application of Article 107(1) TFEU and on the new or existing nature of the aid in question. This subject is dealt with in more detail in Chapter 26.

III. Control of State Aid Compatibility

A. Introduction

21.22 The procedure for controlling the compatibility of State aid is regulated by Article 108 TFEU, the Procedural Regulation of the Council, the case law of the EU Courts, and the practice of the Commission.[24] Many informal texts of the Commission on certain procedural questions have been declared obsolete since April 2004.[25] Moreover, many particular procedural rules only apply to certain aid categories or economic sectors (reinforced notification obligations, accelerated examination procedures, specific notification forms, etc).

B. General Principles

21.23 Article 108 TFEU lays down a special procedure for the constant review and control of State aid by the Commission.[26] The competent authority is in principle the Commission, which exerts its control in the context of a special administrative procedure, the main interlocutor being the Member State concerned.

1. Exclusive powers of the Commission

Exclusivity principle

21.24 **Competence of the Commission** The Treaty establishes certain derogations from the general principle that aid is prohibited. It is therefore necessary to establish which authority is invested

---

[23] Joined Cases 188/80 to 190/80 *French Republic and others v Commission* [1982] ECR 2545. See also para 7 of the Opinion of AG Reischl in this case.

[24] See the Notice on a Simplified procedure for the treatment of certain types of State aid ([2009] OJ C136/3, with a corrigendum [2009] OJ C157/20) and the Notice on a Best Practices Code on the conduct of State aid control proceedings ([2009] OJ C136/13).

[25] See in particular Commission Communication concerning the obsolescence of certain State aid policy documents [2004] OJ C115/1.

[26] Case C-367/95 P *Commission v Sytraval* [1998] ECR I-1719, para 35.

with this competence: the Treaty provides that the Commission is responsible for implementing the aid control procedure.[27]

This competence of the Commission extends first and foremost to new aid that Member States **21.25** wish to grant and which has to be previously authorized before it can be granted, pursuant to paragraphs 2 and 3 of Article 108 TFEU. It then extends to existing aid, which the Commission is bound to keep under constant review and, where necessary, alter or abolish it.[28]

Exclusivity   The Commission's competence, subject to certain exceptions and reductions, is **21.26** 'exclusive'.[29] To ensure the consistency of the aid authorization policy, the Treaty has in effect given the Commission the sole responsibility for pronouncing on the compatibility of aid.

Control obligation   The Commission's remit is to ensure that no aid that conflicts with **21.27** the common interest is granted. As a result of the exclusive and obligatory character of the Commission's authorization, it is bound to carry out its remit fully.[30] In other words, in the absence of any other authority entitled to pronounce on the compatibility of an aid project, the Commission has to pronounce on each case that comes to its notice,[31] and is also bound to act within a reasonable time period.[32] Unlike the situation under Articles 101 and 102 TFEU, therefore, it would seem difficult to argue that it is entitled to waive its responsibility in the absence of any 'Union interest'.[33]

This obligation to review the compatibility of aid takes the following forms: **21.28**

- Vis-à-vis the Member State granting the aid and the beneficiary thereof in the case of new aid: if it is established that the measure in question does indeed come within the scope of Article 107 TFEU, the Commission is the only authority that can validate the grant of aid. In other words, in default of Commission control, the aid in question cannot lawfully be granted and its status will remain challengeable. The Commission's responsibility is onerous, therefore, since it must carefully examine and determine its position as regards all new aid that comes to its notice.
- Vis-à-vis the competitors of the beneficiary in the case of unlawful aid.

---

[27] Case 78/76 *Steinike and Weinlig* [1977] ECR 595, para 9; Case C-301/87 *France v Commission* [1990] ECR I-307, para 16; Case C-354/90 *French Salmon* [1991] ECR I-5505, para 9; and Case C-387/92 *Banco Exterior de España* [1994] ECR I-877, para 16.

[28] The distinction between existing aid and new aid is equally valid for State aid granted to undertakings under Art 106(2) TFEU (Case C-387/92 *Banco Exterior de España*, para 18).

[29] Case C-354/90 *French Salmon* [1991] ECR I-5505, para 14; Case C-44/93 *Namur-Les assurances du crédit* [1994] ECR I-3829, para 17; Case T-95/94 *Sytraval and others v Commission* [1995] ECR II-2651, para 54; and Case T-95/96 *Gestevisión Telecinco v Commission* [1998] ECR II-3407, para 54.

[30] See Arts 4(2) and 10(1) of the Procedural Regulation. According to the ECJ, 'for its part, the Commission is bound to ensure respect for the provisions of [Art 108 TFEU], and is required, in cooperation with Member States, to keep under constant review existing systems of aids' (Case 6/64 *Costa* [1964] ECR 585, paras 6–64). According to Attorney-General ('AG') Tesauro, 'in aid matters the Commission has the obligation to rule on the compatibility of any aid as soon as the granting thereof comes to its notice (by means of a notification, a complaint or by any other means)' (Opinion in Case C-198/91 *William Cook v Commission* [1993] ECR I-2487, para 32).

[31] Case T-95/96 *Gestevisión Telecinco v Commission* [1998] ECR II-3407, paras 54–5 and 71 et seq. Furthermore, Art 10(1) and the first sentence of Art 20(2) of Reg 659/1999 grant to a person concerned the right to set in motion the preliminary examination stage provided for in Art 108(3) TFEU, by sending information regarding any allegedly unlawful aid to the Commission, which it is then obliged to examine, without delay, the possible existence of aid and its compatibility with the internal market (Case C-521/06 P *Athinaïki Techniki v Commission* [2008] ECR I-5829, para 37).

[32] Case T-182/98 *UPS Europe v Commission* [1999] ECR II-2857, para 46; and Joined Cases C-471/09 P to C-473/09 P *Territorio Histórico de Vizcaya v Commission* [2011], para 20.

[33] See in this regard Opinion of AG Tesauro in Case C-142/87 *Belgium v Commission* [1990] ECR I-59, para 20.

21.29 In this regard, after an interested party has set in motion the preliminary examination stage provided for in Article 108(3) TFEU, by sending information regarding allegedly unlawful aid to the Commission, Article 13(1) of the Procedural Regulation obliges the Commission to close the preliminary examination stage by adopting a decision pursuant to Article 4(2), (3), or (4) of that regulation, that is to say, a decision stating that aid does not exist, raising no objections, or initiating the formal investigation procedure. Thus, once the preliminary examination stage has been completed the Commission is bound either to initiate a procedure against the subject of the complaint, or to adopt a definitive decision rejecting the complaint.[34]

21.30 As for existing aid, although the Commission's responsibility might appear at first sight to be just as important, its binding character is less immediate. In effect, any failure by the Commission in exercising its permanent power of review does not prevent Member States from granting aid in application of their existing schemes. It is rather in the interests of the beneficiaries' competitor undertakings to ensure that the Commission enforces the compatibility requisites on existing schemes. The vetting power over existing schemes is therefore exercised more broadly at the Commission's discretion.

21.31 **Control of the EU Courts** The Commission exercises its powers subject to the control of the EU Courts. Its action can be censored by the ECJ or the GC. These courts, however, are not entitled to replace the Commission's assessment with their own, whether in terms of the determination of the existence of aid or its compatibility with the internal market.

Attenuations of the exclusivity principle

21.32 **Role of the Council and Member States** In exercising its power of control over the compatibility of State aid, the Commission has to liaise mainly with the Council on the one hand and Member States on the other.

21.33 The Council is invested with several powers. First and foremost it possesses powers of a regulatory nature.[35] Under Article 107(3)(e) TFEU, it is entitled to determine the supplementary categories of aid that can be considered to be compatible by the Commission. Article 109 TFEU also authorizes it to make any appropriate regulations for application of Articles 107 and 108 TFEU, in particular to determine the conditions under which Article 108(3) TFEU shall apply and the categories of aid exempted from this procedure. Thus, in authorizing the Council to lay down the general derogations from the prior aid-notification obligation, Article 109 TFEU allows it to remove these categories of aid from the control of the Commission. This might involve a significant limitation on the Commission's exclusive control powers.

21.34 Besides its regulatory powers, in certain cases the Council, instead of the Commission, is also entitled to pronounce directly on the compatibility of particular aid. This power is conferred on it under the third and fourth subparagraphs of Article 108(2) TFEU. This provision allows the Commission's normal powers on new aid to be, to some extent, short-circuited, each Member State being entitled to request the Council for a ruling on whether an aid project 'should' be considered to be compatible.[36]

21.35 *A priori*, the Member States hardly seem eligible for taking part in the aid control procedure, since it is their own measures that are under review.[37] They do, however, play an important role in the field of aid control. Article 108 TFEU does indeed impose on Member States

---

[34] Case C-521/06 P *Athinaïki Techniki v Commission* [2008] ECR I-5829, paras 33–46.

[35] The Council has specific powers in the farming and transport sectors.

[36] This power of the Council is examined in more detail below, paras 21.100–21.114.

[37] See, however, the proposal for a procedural regulation, which provided for the setting up of an independent control authority in each Member State. This idea was not taken up by the Council in the final version of the regulation.

'clear-cut obligations designed to facilitate the task of the Commission and to prevent the latter from being confronted with a fait accompli'.[38]

First, the Commission is bound to cooperate closely with Member States in its constant **21.36** review of existing aid under Article 108(1) TFEU. Secondly they are also the Commission's main interlocutors in the control of new aid; each Member State notifies it of its aid plans, cooperates with it in providing all appropriate information, and the Member States are also the only addressees of all decisions adopted.[39] An Advisory Committee on State Aid has also been set up by the Procedural Regulation (Article 28) to involve Member States in the procedure for adopting the implementing provisions of this Regulation.

The cooperation of Member States is therefore essential in the aid control procedure, for the **21.37** Commission itself has hardly any direct investigative authority over the undertakings concerned,[40] and its only official interlocutors are the Member States. This apparent weakness in the Commission's position is hardly a handicap, however, since if the Member State concerned does not cooperate, the Commission is authorized to exercise its powers on the basis of the information to hand. It is hence possible to say that Member States have a real 'duty to cooperate' with the Commission, so that they must supply the Commission with all the information it needs to check that the conditions of the derogation claimed are in fact met.[41] This duty to cooperate is a by-product of Member States' general duty to cooperate fully with the Commission as laid down in Article 4(3) of the Treaty on European Union ('TEU').[42]

2. Nature of the examination procedure

The examination procedure is special and administrative in nature

Special nature of the aid examination procedure   Article 108 TFEU lays down a 'special **21.38** procedure'[43] for reviewing the compatibility of State aid; this procedure is different from the general procedures designed to ensure respect for EU law. According to the ECJ:

> the intention of the Treaty, in providing for a permanent aid vetting procedure by the Commission in Article [108 TFEU], is that the finding that an aid may be incompatible with the [internal] market is to be determined, subject to review by the Court, by means of an appropriate procedure that it is the Commission's responsibility to set in motion.[44]

The Commission's 'specific duty of supervision'[45] therefore implies a particular procedure, albeit as part and parcel of the Commission's general mission as 'guardian of the Treaty' under Article 17(1) TEU.

This particular procedure bears witness to the singular nature of State aid supervision as laid **21.39** down in the Treaty. First and foremost it exists to 'ensure the efficacy' of aid prohibition.[46]

---

[38] Case 171/83 R *Commission v France* [1983] ECR 2621, para 10.

[39] Member States are in particular bound to indicate the compatibility criterion serving as grounds for their claim, failing which the Commission cannot be held liable for having failed to examine it (Case C-382/99 *Netherlands v Commission* [2002] ECR I-5163, para 84). The same applies as regards justification of the selective character of a measure based on the nature or overall structure of the tax system (Joined Cases C-106/09 P and C-107/09 P *Commission v Government of Gibraltar* [2011] ECR I-59, paras 145–6).

[40] See, however, the onsite monitoring provision contained in Art 22 of the Procedural Regulation.

[41] Case C-364/90 *Italy v Commission* [1993] ECR I-2097, para 20 and Case C-372/97 *Italy v Commission* [2004] ECR I-3679, para 81.

[42] Case C-382/99 *Netherlands v Commission* [2002] ECR I-5163, para 48.

[43] Case C-256/97 *DM Transport* [1999] ECR I-3913, para 14.

[44] Case 74/76 *Iannelli* [1977] ECR 557, para 12; Case C-354/90 *French Salmon* [1991] ECR I-5505, para 9 and Case C-256/97 *DM Transport* [1999] ECR I-3913, para 16.

[45] Case 171/83 R *Commission v France* [1983] ECR 2621, para 10.

[46] Case C-404/00 *Commission v Spain* [2003] ECR I-6695, para 20.

Secondly it aims to reconcile, on the one hand 'the general interest of the [EU]' at work, particularly in the context of the preliminary aid examination procedure laid down in Article 108(3) TFEU, and, on the other, 'the interests of the private parties concerned', assured in the context of the formal examination procedure of Article 108(2) TFEU.[47] Indeed, the procedure laid down in Article 108(2) TFEU grants to the interested parties guarantees that go well beyond those granted by the infringement procedure laid down in Article 258 TFEU, involving the participation only of the Commission and the Member State concerned.[48] The existence of this special procedure implies that the Commission is duty bound to use it to supervise the aid granted by the Member States and may not replace it by a simple action for failure to fulfil an obligation except under certain particular circumstances.

21.40 When implementing this procedure, the Commission is essentially bound to make a diligent and impartial examination of the facts. This obligation is associated with the right to sound administration, which is one of the general principles that are observed in a State governed by the rule of law and are common to the constitutional traditions of the different Member States.[49]

21.41 **Derogations**   This special procedure constitutes the general rule from which derogations may be laid down by the Council, on the basis of Article 109 TFEU or any other Treaty provision. Thus:

- First and foremost—and this is the most important derogation—the Council regulation on block exemptions derogates from the normal application of the control mechanisms of Article 108 TFEU.
- Second, in the agricultural sector, Articles 107 and 108 TFEU are applicable only by virtue of secondary legislation and sometimes in derogation from the normal application of the control procedure. Thus, only the provisions of Article 108(1) and (3) TFEU, first sentence, are applicable to State aid granted in favour of the production and marketing of agricultural products for which no common organization of the markets has been adopted.
- Third, in other sectors, like road, rail or navigable waterway transport, some Council regulations have also limited the application of Article 108 TFEU.

21.42 **Administrative nature of the examination procedure**   The assessment procedure laid down in Article 108 TFEU is administrative in nature, rather than judicial, penal, etc. It culminates in decisions that authorize or prohibit State aid, on a provisional or definitive basis, but involving no penalties against the States or undertakings concerned.

3. The Member State concerned as the Commission's main interlocutor

Principle

21.43 **Member State as the addressee of the decision**   State aid decisions adopted by the Commission are addressed to the Member State concerned.[50]

21.44 **Bilateral dialogue**   In principle, the Member State granting the aid is the Commission's sole interlocutor, the only party with whom a truly *inter partes* procedure exists. It is the

---

[47] On these two aspects see Joined Cases 91/83 and 127/83 *Heineken Brouwerijen* [1984] ECR 3435, para 14. As regards the taking into account of the general interest of the EU, see also Case C-301/87 *France v Commission* [1990] ECR I-307, para 17 and, para 19 of the Opinion of AG Tesauro in Case C-142/87 [1990] ECR I-959.

[48] Case 290/83 *Commission v France* [1985] ECR 439, para 17.

[49] Joined Cases T-228/99 and T-233/99 *WestLB and others v Commission* [2003] ECR II-435, para 167.

[50] Case C-367/95 P *Commission v Sytraval and Brink's France* [1998] ECR I-1719, para 45 and Case T-82/96 *ARAP and others v Commission* [1999] ECR II-1889, para 28. With the same purport see Art 25 of the Procedural Reg.

Member State that informs the Commission of the aid project; it is the Member State the Commission contacts to obtain information; and it is the Member State that is the addressee of the decision adopted. The supervision of aid should therefore always take the form of a series of bilateral dialogues between the Commission and each Member State. The procedure for reviewing State aid is, in view of its general scheme, a procedure initiated in respect of the Member State responsible under its EU obligations for granting the aid.[51]

This idea, as set out in the Treaty, is based on the premise that the control of State aid is **21.45** pre-emptive in the sense that Member States cannot grant the aid before receiving authorization from the Commission. The control procedure at EU level therefore precedes in principle the effective implementation of aid at national level and is independent thereof. In this context, neither the situation of the designated aid recipient nor that of its competitors would seem to be directly influenced by the particular dialogue between the Member State and the Commission, for at the time that this dialogue takes place the recipient has not yet, in principle, acquired any rights vis-à-vis the Member State. Normally, it is only after the Commission's authorization has been given that any binding legal relationships are likely to be formed between the Member State and the recipient of the aid.

The particular situation of infra-State entities   The general trend towards regionalization **21.46** and decentralization in Member States has generated new aid-supervision problems. In the EU system, the central government authorities of the Member States are the only direct interlocutors with the European institutions. It is they, through their Permanent Representation in the EU, to whom the institutions' acts are addressed. This general rule also applies to State aid supervision matters. The control procedure therefore does not vary according to the government level of the national body effectively granting the aid, whether it be the central State, a region, a district, a municipality, etc. It is therefore up to the national authorities to organize themselves: should the central government of a Member State fail to meet its prior-notification obligations, for example, to the detriment of an aid-paying territorial group, this is an internal problem for the Member State involved and cannot be blamed on the Commission.

Reduction of the Member State's role as main interlocutor

Even though Member States remain the sole addressees of the Commission's decisions, their **21.47** role as its main interlocutor, under the terms of the Treaty, has been reduced over time both by the actual practice of the Commission and the case law of the EU Courts. The other parties involved are essentially three in number: beneficiary undertakings; competitor undertakings; and associations of undertakings.

Role of beneficiary undertakings   In practice, the undertakings benefiting from the aid **21.48** that is controlled by the Commission play a role that goes beyond that of a mere third party. They are obviously in a position to be able to furnish useful information for assessing the compatibility of the measures examined. They can therefore play an important role vis-à-vis the Commission during the examination of the measures in question; they can directly furnish information and could take part in working meetings with the services of the Commission, etc. Moreover, they benefit from privileged treatment in terms of access to the EU Courts. Formally, however, they are not in a different procedural situation from that of competitor undertakings.[52]

---

[51] Case T-198/01 *TGI v Commission*, para 191.
[52] As only the Member States are under the obligation to notify, this obligation can thus not be regarded as satisfied by notification by the undertaking receiving the aid. The machinery for reviewing and examining State aid established by Art 108 TFEU does not impose any specific obligation on the recipient of aid. First,

21.49 **Role of competitor undertakings**   Directly interested in the content of the Commission's decisions, those undertakings that are in competition with a beneficiary of State aid have progressively come to have a role as private interlocutors vis-à-vis the Commission. They often play the role of complainants, reporting the existence of unlawful aid, and are in contact with the Commission in its initial investigations. They are also authorized to put forward their observations in the formal examination procedure of Article 108(2) TFEU and also, under certain conditions, to contest the Commission's decisions before the EU Courts.

21.50 **Role of associations of undertakings**   Associations of undertakings have come to play a twofold role, firstly as interlocutors with the Commission in the examination of the compatibility of national measures, and, secondly, as claimants before EU jurisdictions. They are also closely associated with the process of drawing up the general aid-compatibility criteria, laid down by the Commission.

Dealing with complaints

21.51 **Status of complainant**   The Commission's State aid decisions are addressed to the Member States concerned in each case. This applies equally to cases where the Commission, acting on a complaint about State measures claimed to be State aid in breach of the Treaty, declines to open the procedure laid down in Article 108(2) TFEU, either because it deems the reported measures not to be State aid within the meaning of Article 107 TFEU, or because they are considered to be compatible with the internal market.[53] If the Commission adopts such decisions and, in due accordance with the duty of good administration, informs the complainants of this, any action for annulment which the complainant wishes to bring must be against the Decision addressed to the Member State, rather than the letter addressed to the latter informing it of the Commission's decision.[54]

21.52 The complainant therefore plays a restricted role in the procedure for controlling State aid.[55] As a person concerned, the complainant has the right to set in motion the preliminary examination stage provided for in Article 108(3) TFEU by sending information regarding any allegedly unlawful aid to the Commission, which it is then obliged to examine, without delay, for the possible existence of aid and its compatibility with the internal market.[56]

21.53 **Procedural rights of complainants**   It thus follows that complainants have only the same procedural rights as any other interested party in the examination of a measure by the Commission. There are no grounds for imposing on the Commission an obligation to engage in adversarial proceedings with the complainant.[57] The Commission therefore has no obligation to hear the complainants during the preliminary phase for the examination of aid under Article 108(3) TFEU. Moreover, after the formal phase of Article 108(2) TFEU, the

---

the notification requirement and the prior prohibition on implementing planned aid are directed to the Member State. Second, the Member State is also the addressee of the decision by which the Commission finds that aid is incompatible with the internal market and requests the Member State to abolish the aid within the period determined by the Commission (Joined Cases C-442/03 P and C-471/03 P *P&O European Ferries (Vizcaya) and Diputación Foral de Vizcaya v Commission* [2006] ECR I-4845, para 103).

[53] Article 13(1) of Reg 659/1999 obliges the Commission to close the preliminary examination stage by adopting a decision pursuant to Art 4(2), (3), or (4) of that regulation, that is to say, a decision stating that aid does not exist, raising no objections, or initiating the formal investigation procedure (Case C-521/06 P *Athinaïki Techniki v Commission* [2008] ECR I-5829, para 40).

[54] Case C-367/95 P *Commission v Sytraval* [1998] ECR I-1719, paras 44 and 45 and Case T-82/96 *ARAP and others v Commission* [1999] ECR II-1889, para 28; Case T-182/98 *UPS Europe v Commission* [1999] ECR II-2857, paras 37 and 38.

[55] Case C-367/95 P *Commission v Sytraval* [1998] ECR I-1719 and Case T-188/95 *Waterleiding v Commission* [1998] ECR II-3713, para 144.

[56] Case C-521/06 P *Athinaïki Techniki v Commission* [2008] ECR I-5829, para 37.

[57] Procedural Reg, Art 20(2).

Commission is only obliged to serve notice on the interested parties, including the complainants, to present their observations.[58]

Neither is the Commission under any obligation to examine of its own motion objections **21.54** that the complainant would undoubtedly have lodged if it had been given the opportunity to become fully aware of the information obtained by the Commission in the course of its enquiry. According to the ECJ, this criterion, which requires the Commission to place itself in the complainant's shoes, is not an appropriate criterion for defining the scope of the Commission's obligation of investigation.[59]

In practice, despite this case law, the Commission does in fact often liaise closely with certain **21.55** complainants, both in the preliminary examination procedures and the formal examination procedures. Moreover, the existence of a complaint obliges the Commission to examine the matter and also impinges on its obligation to give reasons for its decisions.

Form for the submission of complaints The Commission has published in all twenty-two **21.56** EU languages a 'Form for the submission of complaints concerning alleged unlawful State aid', which indicates what information it needs to be able to look into a complaint.[60]

Power of investigation

Under Article 108 TFEU, the Commission does not have a power of investigation in its own **21.57** right for controlling State aid; it needs to fall back on the information given by Member States and, as the case may be, by third parties.[61] On the other hand, Member States are duty bound, under Article 4(3) TEU, to cooperate with the Commission. The confidential nature of the economic, accounting, or other information of the undertakings concerned cannot be invoked as grounds for not supplying this information to the Commission, since the latter is bound by an obligation of professional secrecy under Article 339 TFEU.[62] Moreover, as regards notified aid, the Commission is entitled to refrain from giving its approval until such time as it is in possession of all necessary information; as far as unlawful aid is concerned, it is even authorized to base its decision on the only information to hand if the Member State does not fully fulfil its duty to cooperate and fails to furnish all necessary information.

Article 22 of the Procedural Regulation has in any case invested the Commission with the **21.58** power to make 'on-site monitoring visits' in the undertakings.[63]

4. Internal workings of the Commission

Each year, the Commission is responsible for making declarations on the compatibility of **21.59** hundreds of aid or aid-scheme files. This requires a great deal in terms of human and technical resources and internal organization.

---

[58] Case C-367/95 P *Commission v Sytraval* [1998] ECR I-1719, paras 58 and 59.

[59] Case C-367/95 P *Commission v Sytraval* [1998] ECR I-1719, paras 60 and 61.

[60] [2003] OJ C116/3. On 13 July 2012, the Commission has invited comments on the application of procedural rules in State aid investigations and in particular with regard to the handling of complaints, with a view to proposing a revised Procedural Regulation (see Commission Press Release IP/12/783).

[61] See especially the Opinion of AG Darmon in Joined Cases C-324/90 and C-342/90 *Germany and Pleuger Worthington v Commission* [1994] ECR I-1173, paras 31 and 35.

[62] Case T-86/96 R *Arbeitsgemeinschaft Deutscher Luftfahrt-Unternehmen and others v Commission* [1998] ECR II-641, para 69.

[63] On 13 July 2012, the Commission has invited comments on the application of procedural rules in State aid investigations and in particular with regard to the collection of market information, with a view to proposing a revised Procedural Regulation (see Commission Press Release IP/12/783 'State aid: Commission consults on reform of procedures' of 13 July 2012).

The principle of collegiality

21.60 The Commission in the strict sense, ie the College of Commissioners, is bound to adopt all decisions itself, subject to the possibility of delegating certain matters. Indeed, the operation of the Commission is governed by the principle of collegiality,[64] which means that the members of the Commission are all equally entitled to take part in the decision-making process. It also means, even more importantly, not only that all decisions should be deliberated in common, but also that all college members are to be held collectively liable, in political terms, for the whole series of decisions taken. The delegation procedure is hence compatible with the collegiality principle only as regards the adoption of managerial or administrative measures.[65]

21.61 In view of the broad discretionary power at play in the State aid control procedure, the College should in principle adopt all decisions itself.[66] This is also clear from the judgment of the GC in *Italgrani*, where a State aid supervision decision made solely on the basis of a limited check to see that the conditions of a former decision of the Commission to approve the corresponding aid scheme was in fact being observed in the case of this individual aid does not necessarily constitute a management or administrative measure.[67] This collegiality principle is also essential in terms of giving reasons for decisions; these reasons cannot therefore be tagged on afterwards.[68] Only in cases of simple administrative acts would it be possible for the Commission's services to speak on behalf of the latter.

Commission limited to dealing only with current business

21.62 According to the General Court ('GC'), where the Commission can only deal with the management of current business, in the sense of Article 234 TFEU, paragraph 2, second sentence, it is authorized to adopt individual decisions only if, in doing so, it restricts itself to implementing a legal system composed of long-standing rules and principles.[69]

Internal organization

21.63 It is the Commissioner with special responsibility for competition who presents his/her proposals to the College. The service he or she is in charge of (the Directorate-General for Competition, 'DG COMP') is in charge of the files in this area, except as regards aid files that concern some common EU policies, namely agriculture and fisheries. These files are the direct responsibility of the respective Commissioners.

21.64 The same distribution of tasks is found at the level of Commission services. DG COMP deals with State aid files, except for the sectors of agriculture and fisheries. All proposals brought before the College are subjected to a preliminary consultation procedure to elicit the opinion of the main services concerned, notably the Legal Service, which issues an opinion on each file.

---

[64] This also implies that the Commission has to be properly constituted (for the decisions adopted during the 'leave of absence' of Mr Bangemann see Case C-334/99 *Germany v Commission* [2003] ECR I-1139, paras 17–28 and Joined Cases T-227/99 and T-134/00 *Kvaerner Warnow Werft v Commission* [2002] ECR II-1205, para 57 et seq).

[65] Case 5/85 *AKZO Chemie v Commission* [1986] ECR 2585; Case C-137/92 P *Commission v BASF and others (PVC)* [1994] ECR I-2555; and Case T-435/93 *ASPEC and others v Commission* [1995] ECR II-1281, paras 101 and 102.

[66] Decision to initiate the formal investigation procedure, decision to raise no objection, final decision (see Case T-435/93 *ASPEC and others v Commission* [1995] ECR II-1281, paras 118–124), suspension injunction, etc.

[67] Case T-435/93 *ASPEC and others v Commission* [1995] ECR II-1281, paras 105–14.

[68] Joined Cases T-371/94 and T-394/94 *British Airways and others v Commission* [1998] ECR II-2405, paras 117 and 279, and Case T-157/01 *Danske Busvognmænd v Commission* [2004] ECR II-917, para 115.

[69] Joined Cases T-228/99 and T-233/99 *WestLB and others v Commission* [2003] ECR II-435, paras 94–105; for information on the caretaker Santer Commission that dealt with current business, see Case T-219/99 *British Airways v Commission* [2003] ECR II-5917, paras 46–57.

C. Regulatory Framework

The regulatory framework of the State aid control procedure is governed by a diversity of texts. **21.65**
For a long time, the matter was governed only by Commission texts of a quasi-regulatory scope,
plus some Council regulations of a limited scope. For some years now, the Council has been
making proper use of its own regulatory powers.

1. Quasi-regulations of the Commission

Due to the lack of Council intervention, the Commission was forced to draw up a regula- **21.66**
tory framework. It soon became aware that a case-by-case treatment of the files had serious
drawbacks: it took too long, given the sheer number of cases to be dealt with, it ran the risk of
introducing discrimination into the treatment of the files, and it generated a lack of legal certainty. The Commission has therefore progressively fleshed out a varied and complex range of
guidelines that aim to help it, first of all, to decide when a measure constitutes State aid, when
such aid would be declared to be compatible with the internal market, and, finally, to lay down
the procedure to be followed for that purpose.

The Court has endorsed the Commission's right to produce these guidelines.[70] These docu- **21.67**
ments contain indicative rules that cannot derogate from the Treaty provisions.[71]

The Commission is bound by the guidelines or notices that it adopts in the field of State **21.68**
aid control and may not go outside them in individual cases,[72] unless there is good reason
for doing so; otherwise it will be in breach of the principle of equal treatment.[73] When the
Commission adopts guidelines which are consistent with the Treaty and are designed to
specify the criteria it intends to apply in the exercise of its discretion, the Commission itself
limits that discretion, in that it must comply with the indicative rules which it has imposed
upon itself.[74] The parties concerned are therefore entitled to rely on these self-imposed rules
and the Court will check to see whether the Commission has abided by them in adopting
the contested decision.[75]

In the absence of a clear legal base, these texts have mushroomed in a disorderly fashion.[76]   **21.69**

---

[70] Case C-382/99 *Netherlands v Commission* [2002] ECR I-5163, para 24 and Case C-242/00 *Germany v Commission* [2002] ECR I-5603, para 27.

[71] Case 310/85 *Deufil v Commission* [1987] ECR 901, para 22; Case T-214/95 *Vlaams Gewest v Commission* [1998] ECR II-717, para 79; Case T-110/97 *Kneissl Dachstein Sportartikel v Commission* [1999] ECR II-2881, para 51, and Case C-382/99 *Netherlands v Commission* [2002] ECR I-5163, para 24.

[72] Case C-313/90 *CIRFS and others v Commission* [1993] ECR I-1125, para 44; Case C-351/98 *Spain v Commission* [2002] ECR I-8031, para 53; and Case C-409/00 *Spain v Commission* [2003] ECR I-1487, para 95.

[73] Joined Cases C-465/09 P to C-407/09 P *Territorio Histórico de Vizcaya* [2011] ECR I-83, para 120. For more general information on Commission communications, see the Opinion of AG Ruiz-Jarabo in Case C-387/97 *Commission v Greece* [2000] ECR I-5047, paras 12 and 100, and AG Jacobs in Case C-91/01 *Italy v Commission* [2004] ECR I-4355, para 38.

[74] Joined Cases C-75/05 P and C-80/05 P *Germany and Others v Kronofrance* [2008] ECR I-6619, paras 59–60; and Case C-464/09 P *Holland Malt v Commission* [2010] ECR I-12443, paras 46–7; and Case T-27/02 *Kronofrance v Commission* [2004] ECR II-4177, para 79.

[75] Case T-35/99 *Keller and Keller Meccanica v Commission* [2002] ECR II-261, paras 74 and 77 and Case T-176/01 *Ferriere Nord v Commission* [2004] ECR II-3931, para 134.

[76] The sheer diversity of the vocabulary used is in itself an indication of this disorderliness: communication, guidelines, framework, disciplines, letters, circulars, working documents, etc. The dissemination of
these texts is also very variable: publication in the Official Journal of the European Union ('OJ'), in the
Commission reports, or in a simple letter to the Member States. On its website, DG COMP offers the possibility of consulting and downloading a single file containing the EU State aid rules in force.

Legal certainty and equal treatment

21.70   The adoption of general rules for deciding on the compatibility of aid helps to ensure that the principles of legal certainty and equal treatment are complied with. In terms of legal certainty, the Commission endeavours to adopt rules that allow Member States and the beneficiaries of aid to predict its decisions with sufficient certainty, even when aid plans are being examined on a case-by-case basis.[77] Rules of a general scope also help to ensure equal treatment throughout the whole of the EU, at least in so far as the Commission ensures that its rules apply both to notified aid and existing aid schemes through appropriate measures.

21.71   These texts published by the Commission have a special status, which varies according to the measures they refer to. The rules they lay down have a twofold purpose, first vis-à-vis new aid and secondly vis-à-vis existing aid:

> They constitute first and foremost "appropriate measures" within the meaning of Article [108], paragraph 1 and secondly they follow from the specific exercising [of] [the Commission's] power of discretion under Article [107], paragraph 3.[78]

Assessment criteria for new aid

21.72   As regards new aid dealt with in Article 108(3) TFEU, the notices or guidelines in force contain the criteria on the basis of which the Commission takes its individual decisions about the compatibility or incompatibility of the aid. Although they lack any legal value in their own right vis-à-vis the Member States and parties concerned, these texts nonetheless do acquire such a validity in so far as the Member States are bound to abide by them as a formal condition of the Commission's decisions to approve a given aid or scheme. By way of example, when a Member State notifies the Commission of a new regional aid scheme, the Commission makes sure in principle that the State concerned expressly accepts that, once the scheme has been put into effect, it will be bound to observe not only the general regional aid criteria, but also any other existing rules for governing certain individual cases of application of the scheme (for example stricter rules pertaining to certain sectors). If it does not obtain the express commitment of the Member State, the Commission will then resort to the Article 108(2) TFEU procedure for enforcing such rules by way of formal conditions laid down in the final decision.[79]

21.73   The EU Courts have often had to take into account these quasi regulations of the Commission. The GC has ruled in particular that the power to make all appropriate regulations conferred on the Council under Article 108 TFEU is in no way called into question by the fact that the Commission uses such 'pre-established operational criteria'.[80] Quite on the contrary, the court decisions have sometimes even seemed to make the adoption of such general criteria a prior condition of the exercising of the Commission's control power.[81] The Commission

---

[77] As regards the old multi-sectoral framework, see eg the Communication concerning Germany's refusal to accept the introduction of this framework [1998] OJ C171/4.

[78] Paragraph 15 of the Opinion of AG Lenz in Case C-311/94 *IJssel-Vliet Combinatie* [1996] ECR I-5023.

[79] Cf para 49 of the Opinion of AG Lenz in Case C-311/94 *IJssel-Vliet Combinatie* [1996] ECR I-5023, according to which, by accepting the appropriate measures, the Member State also accepts them for all future new aid. The Commission would hence not be bound to expressly impose the obligation to observe these rules after the approval of each individual aid or each scheme. This opinion has not been supported by others. See for assessment of regional aid scheme: Commission Communication, Guidelines on regional state aid for 2014–2020, C(2013) 3769 final, 28 June 2013.

[80] Joined Cases T-132/96 and T-143/96 *Freistaat Sachsen and others v Commission* [1999] ECR II-3663, para 241.

[81] In Joined Cases C-278/92 to C-280/92 *Spain v Commission* [1994] ECR I-4103, the ECJ declared, with respect to a 'loophole' in the rules adopted by the Commission, that the latter is bound 'beforehand [ie before adopting the case of application] to specify the criteria according to which it considers aid *ad hoc* to have exceptionally a regional character' (para 49).

is therefore entitled to impose guidance rules on itself for exercising its discretion, in the form of guidelines or notices, in so far as they contain rules indicating the course to be followed by the Commission and do not stray from the rules of the Treaty.[82] According to the GC, the adoption by the Commission of such guidelines is an example of the exercising of its discretion and requires only a self-imposed limitation of that power in the examination of aid to which these guidelines apply, in accordance with the principle of equal treatment. By assessing specific aid in the light of such guidelines, which it has previously adopted, the Commission cannot be said to have overstepped the limits of its discretion or waived its right thereto. On the one hand, it reserves the right to repeal or amend the guidelines if circumstances so dictate. On the other, the guidelines concern a specific sector and are based on the desire to follow a policy determined by the Commission itself.[83]

Appropriate measures vis-à-vis existing aid

21.74 The general texts adopted by the Commission also represent a regular and periodical cooperation arrangement whereby the Commission permanently reviews existing aid schemes together with the Member States.[84] Indeed these schemes are generally approved by the Commission for long periods of time, so whenever it decides to make stricter its criteria for authorizing new aid, it also has to make sure that no new individual cases of application of existing schemes now slip through the more rigorous net that it has seen fit to introduce.[85] To keep track of this situation, the Commission, whenever it adopts new guidelines that are stricter than the previous ones, addresses them in principle by way of 'appropriate measures' to all the Member States and asks them to confirm that all their existing aid schemes will henceforth abide by the content of the new text. After these appropriate measures have been sent out, two scenarios are possible with regard to each Member State. In the first scenario, the Member State accepts them and expresses its conformity within the deadline for doing so;[86] in this case the procedure stops with regard to this Member State, on which the appropriate measures now have a binding effect, and it is hence bound to make sure the implementation conditions of its aid schemes are brought into line with the appropriate measures it has accepted. In the second scenario the State refuses to accept them, whereupon the Commission normally initiates the formal examination procedure vis-à-vis all the existing schemes in that Member State and enforces these new rules by means of a final decision that is binding on the addressee Member State.

21.75 In principle all Commission texts making its previous practice stricter should be addressed to Member States in the form of appropriate measures, since they might well be applicable to existing schemes and contain new rules that render these schemes incompatible. Indeed, without the appropriate measures, the Commission would create a situation where there

---

[82] Case C-313/90 *CIRFS and others v Commission*, paras 34 and 36; Case T-380/94 *AIUF-FASS and AKT v Commission* [1996] ECR II-2169, para 57; Case T-149/95 *Établissement R. Ducros v Commission* [1997] ECR II-2031, para 61; Case T-214/95 *Vlaams Gewest v Commission* [1998] ECR II-717, para 79; and Case T-16/96 *Cityflyer Express v Commission* [1998] ECR II-757, para 57. Obviously it is a question only of 'clarifications given to the Member States and not an invitation to grant such aid' (answer to the written question P-3945/97 [1998] OJ C187/187).

[83] Case T-214/95 *Vlaams Gewest v Commission* [1998] ECR II-717, para 89.

[84] Case C-242/00 *Germany v Commission* [2002] ECR I-5603, para 28.

[85] It is a question of implementing a general rule whereby, in due accordance with the principle of non-discrimination, 'a new rule applies immediately to the future effects of a situation which arose under the earlier rules' (in particular Case 278/84 *Germany v Commission* [1987] ECR 1, para 36; Joined Cases C-465/09 P to C-407/09 P *Territorio Histórico de Vizcaya* [2011] ECR I-83, para 120; and Case T-176/01 *Ferriere Nord v Commission* [2004] ECR II-3931, para 138 et seq).

[86] This is the most frequent situation, since the Commission endeavours to prepare its communications in agreement with the Member States.

would be discrimination between the operators of different Member States, whereby some of them would only be able to benefit from aid conforming to the new, stricter criteria laid down by the Commission, while others would be entitled to more generous aid on the basis of an existing scheme.[87]

Horizontal and sectoral regulations

21.76 An overall distinction can be made between two types of rules in the communications, notices, and guidelines adopted by the Commission: on the one hand, the regulations of a horizontal type that examine the compatibility of certain types of aid regardless of the sectors concerned; and on the other, sectoral regulations which determine the compatibility of aid in terms of the particular characteristics of the sector in question. The cumulative application of several communications might therefore give rise to conflicting rules, which are usually solved in an ad hoc manner.

2. Regulations of the Council

21.77 The draftspersons of the Treaty of Rome allowed the basic provisions of Articles 107 and 108 TFEU to be developed by secondary regulations. To this end a very generally worded provision, Article 109 TFEU, has been added to the essential principles laid down in Articles 107 and 108, allowing the Council to legislate in this field. It stipulates that the Council:

> may make any appropriate regulations for the application of Articles 107 and 108 and may in particular determine the conditions in which Article 108(3) shall apply and the categories of aid exempted from this procedure.

This power offered by the Treaty was hardly used for some time. Barring a Commission proposal for a regulation in 1966, which came to nothing,[88] only certain specific rules of a very limited scope were adopted on the basis of Article 109 pertaining to particular economic sectors, namely transport and shipbuilding. Otherwise, the legislative loophole persisted for over forty years.

21.78 The sheer number of files to be dealt with and the rapid proliferation of litigation finally convinced the Council of the need to make use of the potential of Article 109 TFEU. The Council thus exercised its power in adopting, first of all, the regulation on block exemptions (the enabling regulation),[89] the Procedural Regulation. and also certain procedural rules applicable to particular sectors (for example the coal industry).[90]

Regulation 994/98

21.79 Council Regulation (EC) 994/98 on the application of Articles 92 and 93 of the Treaty establishing the European Community to certain categories of horizontal State aid was adopted on 7 May 1998.[91] It marked a turning point in the way the control of State aid was dealt with. The essential provisions of the Regulation are twofold. First, it authorizes the Commission to decide, by means of a Regulation, that aid not exceeding a certain fixed amount per undertaking does not meet all the criteria of Article 107(1) TFEU and are hence exempted from

---

[87] Instead of proposing to the Member States that they directly modify their existing schemes, the Commission has sometimes established a transition period of several years, during which it reviews all existing schemes in each Member State, demanding that the new rules be phased in while this review is being carried out. Sometimes the Commission approves the national schemes only for the duration of the temporal scope of application of the notices or guidelines in question.

[88] COM(66) 95 definition of 30 March 1966 (amended by COM(66) 457 of 10 November 1966).

[89] See paras 21.82 and 21.83.

[90] Regulation 1407/2002, now replaced by Council Decision of 10 December 2010 on State aid to facilitate the closure of uncompetitive coal mines (OJ L336/24).

[91] [1998] OJ L142/1.

the notification procedure (Article 2—the *de minimis* provision). Secondly, the Commission may also declare that certain categories of aid, if they meet certain criteria, are automatically compatible with the internal market and, by derogation from Article 108(3) TFEU, are also exempt from the notification requirement (Article 1).

The Regulation constitutes a solid base for shoring up the Commission's compatibility crite- **21.80** ria, clearing up some of the uncertainties about the legal scope of its guidelines and notices. It also takes a heavy workload off the Commission, which is transferred to national courts as regards aid not involving any undue risk of distorting the free play of competition. The Regulation is implemented through Commission regulations.

The de minimis *rule*

Article 2 of the Council Regulation entitles the Commission, by means of a regulation, **21.81** to decide that, having regard to the development and functioning of the internal market, certain aid does not meet all of the Article 107(1) TFEU criteria and that they are therefore exempted from the notification procedure contained in Article 108(3) TFEU, provided that aid granted to the same undertaking over a given period of time does not exceed a certain fixed amount.

As regards the *de minimis* rule, Article 2 seeks to give a more solid legal base than was provided **21.82** by the Commission's previous practice. This practice was in fact beset by certain doubts; there was no provision expressly authorizing the Commission to exclude certain aid from the scope of Article 107(1) TFEU. This official recognition of a *de minimis* aid category aimed above all to release the Commission services from the obligation of examining aid of lesser amounts. The content of the Commission's *de minimis* regulation is very similar to the Commission's previous communication on the same subject.

Paradoxically, the Commission's *de minimis*[92] regulations and its exemption regulations work **21.83** in opposite directions: the latter's effect is to increase the powers of the national courts (which now have certain power, albeit limited, for monitoring compatibility), whereas the former restricts these powers. Beforehand, indeed, the competence for establishing whether or not a measure came within the scope of Article 107(1) TFEU belonged both to the Commission and the national courts, each dealing with a different part. Thus, the Commission had to decide whether or not a measure constituted aid under this provision before being able to assess its compatibility. For their part, the national courts, before penalizing any infringement of the previous notification obligation contained in the last sentence of Article 108(3) TFEU, had to ensure that the measure in dispute effectively came under Article 107(1) TFEU. But the *de minimis* regulation has increased the powers of the Commission at the expense of the national courts. The latter are indeed bound by the Regulation due to the supremacy of EU law,[93] and are entitled only to verify that the measure in dispute comes within its scope. If it does, they must then take note of this and recognize the non-application of Article

---

[92] Commission Reg (EC) 1998/2006, which applies until 31 December 2013. It establishes a ceiling of EUR 200,000 as the total that can be granted to the same undertaking in any three-year period. Certain sectors, as well as certain categories of aid, are excluded (Art 1). Article 3 of the Regulation lays down the monitoring arrangements that Member States have to make to ensure observance of the *de minimis* ceiling when granting such aid. Commission Reg (EC) 1535/2007 on the *de minimis* aid in the sector of agriculture production sector and Commission Reg (EC) 875/2007 on the *de minimis* aid in the fisheries sector lay down stricter conditions. See also Commission Regulation (EU) 360/2012 of 25 April 2012 on the application of Articles 107 and 108 TFEU to *de minimis* aid granted to undertakings providing services of general economic interest. On 20 March 2013, the Commission published a draft of a new, revised State aid *de minimis* Regulation that would apply from 1 January 2014 until 31 December 2020 (the draft and the Commission's explanatory note are both available at DG COMP's consultation page).

[93] Subject to referral to the ECJ for a preliminary ruling on validity.

107(1) TFEU and *ipso facto* the absence of any infringement of the last sentence of Article 108(3) TFEU.

Exemption by category of certain horizontal aid

21.84 Article 1 of the Regulation authorizes the Commission, through regulations, to declare certain categories of aid to be compatible with the internal market and hence exempt from the notification obligation laid down in Article 108(3) TFEU. The categories concerned are:

- aid in favour of small and medium-sized undertakings, research and development, protection of the environment, employment and training; and
- aid that complies with the map approved by the Commission for each Member State for the grant of regional aid.

21.85 As regards the material scope of the authorization, it applies only to certain categories of 'horizontal' (as opposed to 'sectoral') aid.[94] The Regulation does not refer specifically to paragraph 3 of Article 107 TFEU when it enumerates the categories of horizontal aid eligible to be declared compatible by the Commission regulation. These categories, however, would seem to be inferable only through those mentioned in paragraph 3, to the exclusion of the very specific categories of paragraph 2.[95]

21.86 The scope of the authorization conferred on the Commission is very broad: within the various categories identified by the Regulation, the Commission has carte blanche for determining the compatibility criteria that make aid eligible for exemption from the preliminary notification obligation. The Commission already had such a *de facto* power, since it exercised its control powers in the absence of all legislation in this field. The Regulation has nonetheless changed the scope of these powers by permitting the Commission to authorize exemptions from the previous notification obligation laid down in Article 108(3) TFEU. Such an authority would seem to be in keeping with the idea of the Commission's 'exclusive' powers in aid compatibility assessment, as laid down in the Treaty.

21.87 As for the rest, the Regulation is characterized by an absence of any radical change of the ground rules; the aid categories mentioned were already well known and had already been dealt with in Commission guidelines or notices.

21.88 By allowing the adoption of exemption regulations for certain aid categories, the Regulation profoundly alters the aid control procedure: Article 1 stipulates that the aid categories determined by the Commission are not subject to the notification obligation laid down in Article 108(3) TFEU. It is therefore no longer necessary for the measure to pass through the Commission beforehand.

21.89 As regards the schemes that Member States will implement directly on the basis of a Commission exemption regulation, without being subject to previous approval by the Commission, Article 4(1) of the Council Regulation states that they are exempt 'for the period of validity of that regulation [of exemption]'. Each time the Commission alters or abolishes an exemption regulation, all existing schemes which were exempted by it are therefore directly affected.[96]

---

[94] 'Sectoral aid' means aid paid to undertakings operating in sectors covered by specific Commission regulations.
[95] In this sense, see Art 3(1) of the old Reg 1/2004.
[96] The exemption regulations sometimes provide that aid schemes exempted thereunder shall remain exempt for a six-month adjustment period after the exemption regulation itself has run its term (Art 20(3) of the old Reg 1/2004).

The Commission in principle expressly states that aid granted before the entry into force of **21.90** an exemption regulation is nonetheless covered by the said exemption.[97]

The Commission's exemption regulations have only a 'positive direct effect' and not a 'nega- **21.91** tive direct effect'. This means that the effect of the regulations is to automatically confer compatibility on national aid meeting the criteria they lay down and exempting them from the Commission's preliminary control procedure, but they cannot, on the other hand, serve as the basis for automatically establishing the incompatibility of State aid coming within their scope and not meeting the criteria laid down therein. The Commission's exemption regulations are therefore not exhaustive, in the sense that horizontal aid coming within the scope of one of these regulations is not automatically incompatible on the sole grounds that it does not meet the criteria laid down in that regulation. This limit restricts the scope of the group exemption regulation. Indeed the Commission always remains exclusively responsible for examining the compatibility of all aid brought to its knowledge and not covered by an exemption regulation. This means that it cannot merely refer any complaint to the national court, but must continue to examine all complaints with due diligence, just as in the past. Moreover, in principle, the exemption regulations do not prevent the Member States from notifying aid coming under these regulations if they so wish.[98]

The essential provision of the Regulation is that the Commission is not bound to carry out **21.92** a preliminary review of new aid (individual aid and aid schemes) that meets the criteria laid down by the exemption regulations. The latter have a direct effect that allows Member States themselves to review the compatibility of their aid plans, under the control of national courts. The Regulation thus enshrines a power that was envisaged by the ECJ as early as 1973.[99]

This development has led to a change in the distribution of powers between the Commission **21.93** and the national courts: when a case is brought before them by a disgruntled competitor, the national courts may now check directly whether the aid meets the compatibility criteria laid down by the Commission and can thus be granted without previous notification to the latter. This new competence of the national courts remains limited, however, in terms of the examination of the compatibility. They can find that the aid meets the conditions laid down by one of the Commission's exemption regulations[100] and can therefore be granted directly; in this case, however, it is always the lawfulness of the aid grant that is the central object of the control; observance of the compatibility conditions is only a prerequisite, and the national court has no discretionary power in this context. If, on the other hand, a court finds that aid paid out directly does not satisfy the compatibility conditions laid down by the Commission, it cannot declare the aid to be incompatible (absence of negative direct effect) and is entitled only to penalize the unlawful nature of its granting (non-compliance with the Commission's previous notification obligation). Outside the scope of the group exemption regulations, the distribution of powers is the traditional situation of the Commission monitoring compat-ibility and the national courts monitoring lawfulness.

Diverse provisions of the regulation

As regards the arrangements for drawing up the Commission regulations, the Council **21.94** Regulation makes provision, on the one hand, for the publication of the draft regulation to enable all interested parties to submit their comments on it (Article 6) and, on the other, for

---

[97] See Art 44(1) of the General Block Exemption Regulation (Reg 800/2008).
[98] See preamble Recital (7) of Reg 800/2008.
[99] Case 77/72 *Capolongo* [1973] ECR 611, para 6.
[100] To ensure a more efficient monitoring, the Commission decided in 2008 to replace the various Block Exemption Regulations by a single simplified Regulation (the General Block Exemption Regulation, [2008] OJ L214/3). In September 2012, the Commission published new guidance on the practical application of the

previous liaison of the Commission with an Advisory Committee on State Aid made up of representatives of the Member States (Article 8).

21.95 Article 3 of the Regulation contains numerous publication and transparency rules, with the aim of obtaining information similar to that which is currently obtained by the preliminary control procedure. The information is addressed as the case may be to the Commission (paragraph 3), to the Member States (paragraph 4), or to all interested parties (paragraph 2).

21.96 In default of any transitory provision in the Regulation itself, the Commission's guidelines and notices remain applicable until otherwise decided.

IV. Council's Decision-Making Power

A. Principles

21.97 The third and fourth subparagraphs of Article 108(2) TFEU state as follows:

> On application by a Member State, the Council may, acting unanimously, decide that aid which that State is granting or intends to grant shall be considered to be compatible with the internal market, in derogation from the provisions of Article 107 or from the regulations provided for in Article 109, if such a decision is justified by exceptional circumstances. If, as regards the aid in question, the Commission has already initiated the procedure provided for in the first subparagraph of this paragraph, the fact that the State concerned has made its application to the Council shall have the effect of suspending that procedure until the Council has made its attitude known.
>
> If, however, the Council has not made its attitude known within three months of the said application being made, the Commission shall give its decision on the case.

This is, therefore, a derogation procedure under which, in exceptional circumstances, the Council can replace the Commission's assessment of aid compatibility with its own. This procedure represents a sort of 'safety valve',[101] an 'exceptional and particular case',[102] with the object of allowing Member States to override the Commission's point of view, for political reasons.

21.98 The decisions that the Council can adopt on this basis have an individual rather than a regulatory character. Unlike the powers conferred on the Council under Article 107(3)(e) and Article 109 TFEU, which aim to set up general measures, this is a power enabling the specific authorization of a special aid measure in a particular case.[103] These Council decisions deal with the compatibility of aid as laid down in Article 107(1) TFEU. It does not seem possible, however, for the Council to use this power, as the Commission does regularly to decide that a measure does not come under Article 107(1) TFEU.

21.99 Furthermore, the place where this provision is inserted suggests that this power of the Council under the third and fourth subparagraph of Article 108(2) TFEU to make its own declaration on the compatibility of certain aid in exceptional circumstances can be exercised not only in

---

General Block Exemption Regulation (see General Block Exemption Regulation (GBER)—Frequently Asked Questions, available on DG COMP's website).

[101] According to the expression used by AG Cosmas in his Opinion in the Case C-122/94 *Commission v EU Council* [1996] ECR I-881, para 62.

[102] Case 156/77 *Commission v Belgium* [1978] ECR 1881, para 16 and Case C-110/02 *Commission v EU Council* [2004] ECR I-6333, para 30.

[103] Opinion of AG Cosmas in Case C-122/94 *Commission v EU Council* [1996] ECR I-881, para 58.

relation to new aid but also in relation to existing aid.[104] It is therefore possible to imagine a case in which a Member State that has rejected the appropriate measures proposed by the Commission against one of its existing schemes then turns to the Council on the day the Commission initiates the procedure, seeking confirmation of the compatibility of its scheme.[105]

Article 108(2)(3) TFEU is used on a discrete basis by the Council. The decisions are mainly **21.100** related to the agricultural sector. This power of the Council is bound by no condition whatsoever as regards the form of its decisions. It adopts simple decisions of principle, the content of which is then immediately sent on to the Member State concerned in the form of a simple letter. The Commission is also informed by post to avoid the possibility of its conducting its own examination of the compatibility of the aid concerned.

Previously there was no system for publishing the Council's decisions in the OJ.[106] The **21.101** Procedural Regulation only partly plugged this loophole by providing that the Council may decide to publish its decisions in the OJ.[107]

B. Scope of the Council's Power

The power conferred on the Council is clearly exceptional in character.[108] Nonetheless the **21.102** Council does have a wide margin of discretion in terms of assessing the appropriateness of taking certain measures ('the Council...may decide').[109] This textual interpretation is borne out by the case law of the ECJ, according to which the Council is invested with 'extensive power' or a 'wide discretion' in terms of accepting State aid by derogation from the general prohibition laid down in Article 107(1) TFEU.[110] In a 1996 judgment, concerning the assessment of a complex economic situation to do with the Council's implementation of the Community's agricultural policy, the Court even came to the conclusion that the Council's discretion extends not only to the nature and scope of the measures to be taken, but also, to some extent, to the finding of the basic facts.[111]

In the case of aid to the wine sector, which concerned agriculture,[112] the Commission brought **21.103** an action before the ECJ for annulment of a Council decision declaring wine-sector aid paid by France and Italy to be compatible.[113] The Commission argued that when the Council

---

[104] The first sentence of the third subparagraph of Art 108(2) TFEU speaks of 'aid which that State is granting or intends to grant'.

[105] In the same sense, see the Opinion of AG Mayras in Case 70/72 *Commission v Germany* [1973] ECR 813.

[106] If the Commission has already initiated the formal examination procedure, it nonetheless makes mention of the Council's intervention in the termination of the procedure adopted consecutively by the Commission, which is then published in Series C of the OJ (see eg the termination in [1999] OJ C120/16).

[107] Article 26(5).

[108] Case C-110/02 *Commission v EU Council* [2004] ECR I-6333, para 31.

[109] See the Opinion of AG Cosmas in Case C-122/94 *Commission v EU Council* [1996] ECR I-881, para 75. An action for failure to comply with its obligations cannot in principle, therefore, be lodged against the Council if it decides to take no measures.

[110] See, respectively, Case 74/76 *Iannelli* [1977] ECR 557, para 11; Case 78/76 *Steinike & Weinlig* [1977] ECR 595, para 8; and Case C-225/91 *Matra v Commission* [1993] ECR I-3203, para 41.

[111] Case C-122/94 *Commission v EU Council* [1996] ECR I-881, paras 18 and 19.

[112] Case C-122/94 *Commission v EU Council* [1996] ECR I-881.

[113] The considerations made by the Court on this occasion should nonetheless be treated with some caution, given the very specific nature of the case being dealt with. Indeed, Art 108 TFEU is applicable only by virtue of secondary EU legislation, namely the Council Regulation on the common organization of the market concerned. It cannot therefore be ruled out that this particular regulatory framework influenced the Court, given the predominance of common agricultural policy objectives over those of competition policy.

makes use of its powers under the third subparagraph of Article 108(2) TFEU, it can derogate only from the provisions of Article 107 TFEU or regulations provided for by Article 109
TFEU and not from other rules of EU law. In this particular case, it considered the Council
to have derogated from the agricultural legislation. After brief reflection, the ECJ rejected this
line of argument on the following grounds: under Article 42 TFEU, the Council had made
Articles 107 to 109 TFEU applicable to the production of and trade in wines and musts;
it followed that the power conferred on the Council by the third subparagraph of Article
108(2) TFEU is to apply in the wine sector, within the limits indicated by that provision,
namely the existence of exceptional circumstances.[114] Since these exceptional circumstances
in fact existed, the Council was entitled in its individual decisions to derogate from the rules of
common organization of the sector in question.[115]

C. Existence of Exceptional Circumstances

21.104   The Council's powers apply only if it can establish the existence of 'exceptional circumstances'.
According to AG Cosmas, this term has to be understood as:

> the idea of the extraordinary, the unforeseen or, at least, the non-permanent, non-continuous
> and, obviously, something that strays beyond the boundaries of the normal.[116]

According to the AG, 'exceptional circumstances' are facts or situations that might depend on a
particular sector or the economy in general, but which, assessed in each particular case in a reasonable manner, within the context of a specific Member State and specific sector, show that an
alteration of such magnitude has occurred, viewed in relation to situations hitherto considered
to be normal, or at least non-extraordinary, that it becomes obvious that the situations existing
up to that moment have changed, that new situations have been created, and that it was also
necessary to take corrective measures, the adoption of which is not provided for by the existing
regulations governing the sector concerned.[117]

21.105   The ECJ checks whether the exceptional circumstances in fact exist in each particular case. This
is therefore a binding limit to be met by the Council. In the light of the political nature of the
Council's intervention, however, the Court has been careful in fact to set a wide margin to this
limit. It has therefore ruled that, even if the situation of the market concerned was similar to
that of previous years, this does not preclude the Council from considering the situation as
exceptional.[118]

21.106   On the other hand, in the *GAEC de la Ségaude* case, AG Slynn concluded that a Council decision authorizing aid with the goal of offsetting the loss of revenue suffered by German farmers
as a result of the phasing out of the system of monetary compensatory amounts represented an
exceeding of its powers in so far as it had not demonstrated that the action was justified on the
grounds of the existence of exceptional circumstances.[119] The ECJ did not have the occasion to
examine this point.

---

[114] Case C-122/94 *Commission v EU Council* [1996] ECR I-881, paras 12 and 13.
[115] Along the same lines, see the Opinion of AG Slynn in Case 253/84 *GAEC de la Ségaude v EU Council and Commission* [1987] ECR I-123.
[116] Opinion in Case C-122/94 *Commission v EU Council* [1996] ECR I-881, para 83.
[117] Case C-122/94 *Commission v EU Council* [1996] ECR I-881, para 85.
[118] Case C-122/94 *Commission v EU Council* [1996] ECR I-881, para 21.
[119] Opinion in Case 253/84 *GAEC de la Ségaude v Council and Commission* [1987] ECR I-123.

D. Procedure

Application to the Council by a Member State suspends the examination underway in the **21.107** Commission for up to three months. Once this deadline has passed without the Council having defined its position, the Commission can make its own ruling and the Council is no longer competent to adopt a decision. The taking of decisions which contradict each other is thereby avoided.[120] The Court has also judged the Council to be no longer competent if the Member State concerned has made no application to the Council before the Commission declares the aid in question to be incompatible.[121]

The Council is not empowered to rule on an aid measure whose aim is to allocate to ben- **21.108** eficiaries of the illegal aid previously declared incompatible by a Commission decision an amount designed to compensate for the repayments which they are obliged to make pursuant to that decision. Accepting such a competence would indeed be tantamount to undermining the effectiveness of the decisions taken by the Commission. The aid granted in the second instance is in effect so indissolubly linked to that previously found by the Commission to be incompatible with the internal market that it appears largely artificial to claim to make a distinction between those aids for the purposes of applying Article 108(2) TFEU.[122]

The fact that the aid has already been implemented does not seem to prevent the case from **21.109** being brought before the Council. Where the aid has been granted unlawfully, however, there is some doubt about the effect of the Council's involvement on the unlawful character of the aid's implementation. The procedure initiated by the Commission is certainly suspended, but the last sentence of Article 108(3) TFEU continues to apply, so the aid should still be considered for all intents and purposes as unlawful. A competitor could still bring the mat- ter before a national court, therefore, despite the application made to the Council by the Member State.

Finally, the Council's declaration of an aid scheme's compatibility no doubt rules out any **21.110** immediate attempt by the Commission to initiate a procedure of appropriate measures under Article 108(1) TFEU, where the latter has doubts about the compatibility of this scheme. Such a possibility would not be precluded in the medium term, however, if there is any change in the circumstances upon which the Council's decision was based.

---

[120] Case C-110/02 *Commission v EU Council* [2004] ECR I-6333, para 32.
[121] Case C-110/02 *Commission v EU Council* [2004] ECR I-6333, para 33 and Case C-399/03 *Commission v EU Council* [2006] ECR I-5629, para 24. According to AG Mayras, if an application could be made to the Council after the Commission had produced its final decision, the intervention of the Council, 'essentially a question of opportuneness', could not then be reconciled with the Commission's acknowledged right of applying to the Court for an action for failure to fulfil an obligation (Opinion in Case 70/72 *Commission v Germany* [1973] ECR 813). In the case of an aid scheme, however, it is not at all clear whether a Member State could invite the Council to deal with a file even if the Commission has already adopted a decision, by hypothesis negative. In such a case, the Council could declare the scheme to be compatible, if only with future effect, to avoid directly contradicting the Commission's decision (See the Opinion of AG Mayras in Case 156/77 *Commission v Belgium* [1978] ECR 1881, who seems to accept that the effect of a negative decision by the Commission could 'be called into question for the future... by a new act of the Commission or Council').
[122] Case C-110/02 *Commission v EU Council* [2004] ECR I-6333, para 37 et seq and Case C-399/03 *Commission v EU Council* [2006] ECR I-5629, para 24 et seq.

22

PRIOR CONTROL OF NEW NOTIFIED AID

Jean Paul Keppenne and Carlos Urraca Caviedes

A 'preventive' control procedure has been set up to deal with any new aid (and alterations to existing aid) that the Member States might intend to grant. Only after having been reviewed under this procedure can the aid be considered to have been lawfully granted.[1] **22.01**

Section A of this chapter defines what is meant by 'new aid'. The scope of the Member States' previous notification obligation is examined in Section B, while the subsequent stages of the procedure are dealt with in Sections C (preliminary procedure) and D (formal procedure). Section E deals with the final decision that closes the whole procedure. **22.02**

A. Concept of New Aid

Article 1(c) of the Procedural Regulation[2] defines new aid as 'all aid that is not existing aid, including alterations to existing aid'. All measures to grant or alter aid must therefore be **22.03**

---

[1] Case C-44/93 *Namur-Les assurances de crédit* [1994] ECR I-3829, para 12, and Case C-367/95 P *Commission v Sytraval* [1998] ECR I-1719, para 35.
[2] Council Regulation (EC) 659/1999 of 22 March 1999, laying down detailed rules for the application of Article 93 of the EC Treaty [1999] OJ L83/1.

considered to be new aid,[3] and their compatibility with the internal market should be checked by the Commission before they can be granted.[4]

22.04 New aid has to be notified to the Commission before being granted (notified aid). Should the public authorities grant the aid before having received authorization from the Commission, the aid is then unlawful (or unlawfully granted).

22.05 The Member States are also bound to submit any 'plans to alter aid' for a preliminary review by the Commission. This concept of the alteration of existing aid is not defined in the Treaty. Its scope has to be interpreted in functional terms and is determined in accordance with the object of the Commission's control procedure.[5]

22.06 According to Article 4 of Regulation 794/2004:[6]

> an alteration to existing aid shall mean any change, other than alterations of a purely formal or administrative nature which cannot affect the evaluation of the compatibility of the aid measure with the [internal] market. However an increase in the original budget of an existing aid scheme by up to 20% shall not be considered an alteration to existing aid.[7]

22.07 Thus, the fact that the legal basis of an aid scheme is altered, without changing the characteristics of the aid itself, should not be construed as an alteration of aid.[8] On the other hand, an extension of time for a measure that was approved for a set period does constitute an alteration, and it therefore has to be approved by the Commission.[9] This is particularly so when the temporary character of the measure was apparently an essential factor in the Commission's decision to declare it compatible; in such a case, the extension is tantamount to a substantial alteration of the aid.[10]

---

[3] Case C-44/93 *Namur-Les assurances du crédit* [1994] ECR I-3829, para 13. The fact alone that a measure which has been found not to constitute aid continues to be implemented, in some cases following an extension of the legal act which introduced it, cannot convert it into State aid (Case C-194/09 P *Alcoa v Commission* [2011], para 110).

[4] As Advocate-General ('AG') Lenz pointed out, 'The expression "grant or alteration of aid" refers to . . . an event that, by virtue of its potential effects on the [internal] market, needs to be looked at systematically to check whether the advantage afforded to the undertaking is compatible with the principles set out in Article [107](1)' (Opinion in Case C-44/93 *Namur-Les Assurances du Crédit* [1994] ECR I-3829, para 59).

[5] AG Warner called for a strict interpretation of this concept, otherwise the object of Art 108(3) TFEU may be frustrated. He admits, however, under the legal principle of *de minimis non curat lex*, that any amendment that may justly be defined as negligible can be ignored (Opinion in Case 177/78).

[6] Commission Reg (EC) 794/2004 of 21 April 2004 implementing Council Reg (EC) 659/1999 laying down detailed rules for the application of Art 93 of the EC Treaty [2004] OJ L140/1.

[7] Thus in Case C-138/09 *Todaro Nunziatina* [2010] ECR I-4561, para 47, the ECJ considered that by providing both for an increase in the budget allocated to the aid scheme in an amount exceeding 50 per cent and for a two-year extension of the period during which the conditions for grant of that aid were applicable, the Member State created new aid.

[8] See, however, the strict and somewhat formal stance taken by the ECJ in Case 169/82 *Commission v Italy* [1984] ECR 1603, paras 9 and 10, where it declared that Art [108(3) TFEU] applies to laws that are merely a 'single simplifying procedure connected with the establishment of the budget by means of the substantial renewal of existing provisions which are well known and are not contested at Community level'.

[9] See Case 70/72 *Commission v Germany* [1973] ECR 813, in which the ECJ considered in para 3 that Germany, under the terms of Art [108](3) TFEU, had to notify a two-year extension of an aid-establishing law originally approved by the Commission. Similarly, transitional rules, which are intended to preserve the effects of a new scheme which was not notified and which the Commission has already declared to be incompatible, constitute new aid which must be notified (Case C-297/01 *Sicilcassa and Others* [2003] ECR I-7849, para 45). Even the amendments of a non notified aid measure, when the original measure is under a Commission's investigation and the amendments aim at putting the measure in line with the Commission's concerns, constitute new aid subject to the notification requirement (Joined Cases C-442/03 P and C-471/03 P *P&O European Ferries (Vizcaya) and Diputación Foral de Vizcaya v Commission* [2006] ECR I-4845, paras 93–4).

[10] Opinion of AG Mayras in Case 70/72 *Commission v Germany* [1973] ECR 813. See eg the communication on a toll exemption system on the Tauern motorway for undertakings set up in the district of Lungau [1998] OJ C198/6, para 20.

If an alteration affects the very substance of an existing scheme, the whole scheme becomes a new **22.08** aid scheme. Conversely, if the new feature is clearly severable from the initial scheme (for example the extension to new categories of measures or beneficiaries), the procedure can be initiated only to deal with the alteration properly speaking.[11]

The definition of what is an alteration to aid is important, for this will determine when there is **22.09** a need for a new notification to be made to the Commission, pursuant to Article 108(3) of the Treaty on the Functioning of the European Union ('TFEU').[12]

With respect to a 'pre-accession' existing aid scheme, the ECJ has declared that, by applica- **22.10** tion of paragraphs 1 and 3 of Article 108 TFEU, the emergence of new aid or the alteration of existing aid cannot be assessed according to the scale of the aid or, in particular, its amount in financial terms at any moment in the life of the undertaking concerned when the aid is provided under earlier statutory provisions that remain unaltered. According to the Court, the aid can be qualified as new or an alteration to existing aid only in reference to the provisions providing for it, the arrangements and limits thereof.[13] Nonetheless, this judgment should not be construed as meaning that Member States can freely vary the budgets of all of their existing aid schemes.[14]

In principle, when an aid scheme has been approved by the Commission, this approval covers **22.11** future applications of that scheme, which do not therefore have to be examined afresh by the Commission[15] (except, in cases of doubt, to verify that they in fact comply with the conditions under which the scheme was approved). In its scheme approval decision, however, the Commission is entitled to make an exception to that rule and expressly lay down that certain cases of application should still be notified individually on the basis of Article 108(3) TFEU. The cases of application in question might concern certain sectors where specific guidelines have been adopted, cases of application exceeding a threshold, or even, sometimes, all cases of application of the scheme without distinction.

This prior notification obligation with respect to certain individual cases should be consid- **22.12** ered as a reservation to the scheme approval.[16] This implies that these cases of application are

---

[11] Joined Cases T-195/01 and T-207/01 *Gibraltar v Commission* [2002] ECR II-2309, paras 111–15. In this regard, the GC has observed that a measure that merely extends an existing aid scheme to new beneficiaries, without making a substantive alteration to the existing scheme, is severable from the initial scheme and constitutes new aid which is subject to the obligation to notify (Joined Cases T-254/00, T-270/00, and T-277/00 *Hotel Cipriani and Others v Commission* [2008] ECR II-3269, para 162).

[12] Note, however, that the alterations of existing schemes are in principle for notification by the simplified procedure (see Art 4(2) of the aforementioned Regulation 794/2004).

[13] Case C-44/93 *Namur-Les assurances du crédit* [1994] ECR I-3829, para 28.

[14] In this case the Court was dealing with a pre-accession scheme and could not ascertain which characteristics of the scheme would have had decisive importance compatibility-wise in the Commission's eyes. It is therefore logical for it to have chosen to define existing pre-accession aid in terms of the only legal provisions that have established it and defined the scope thereof. The situation is different for aid that the Commission would have approved in the light, in particular, of its budget (see Case T-3/09 *Italy v Commission*, not yet reported, paras 32–46). See also Commission Press Release, IP/13/565 'State aid: Commission approves changes to restructuring plan of Croatian shipyard 3.Mai', 19 June 2013, giving the Commission's approval of the privatization of the company prior to the country's accession to the EU on 1 July 2013. See also Judgment of the ECJ of 29 November 2012 in Case C-262/11 *Kremitovtzi AD v Bulgarian Minister and Deputy Minister of economy, energy and tourism* involving a preliminary reference from a Bulgarian court concerning the legal basis for assessing and ordering the recovering of state aid implemented and completed before Bulgaria's accession to the EU.

[15] Case C-47/91 *Italy v Commission* [1994] ECR I-4635, para 21.

[16] Joined Cases T-447/93, T-448/93, and T-449/93, *AITEC and others v Commission* [1996] ECR II-1631, para 129.

in principle wholly submitted to the new-aid control procedure, despite the scheme being originally approved in principle.[17] In such a case the Commission cannot limit itself to checking that the individual aid in question meets the terms laid down in the scheme approval decision, which would be only a partial examination, but is bound to conduct a complete examination of its compatibility with the terms of Article 107 TFEU.[18]

B. Prior Notification Obligation for New Aid[19]

1. Prior notification obligation

22.13 According to Article 108(3) TFEU, the Commission has to be informed of any plans to grant or alter aid in sufficient time to enable it to present its comments.[20] This obligation affects Member States, which are bound to notify their aid projects before putting them into practice, and cannot be regarded as satisfied by notification by the undertaking receiving the aid.[21] This prior notification obligation is the key to the Treaty's whole system of supervision, for it enables the Commission to carry out a pre-emptive examination of all aid plans.[22]

Scope of the notification obligation

22.14 Although the wording of Article 108(3) TFEU is not very clear on this matter, the Procedural Regulation has confirmed that the notification obligation applies only to aid fulfilling all of the conditions of Article 107(1) TFEU.[23] Member States are therefore not systematically bound to notify the Commission of the numerous cases of State support that do not fall within the scope of this provision (this covers in particular the numerous subsidies of lesser amounts granted to small, local, and handicraft undertakings).[24] *De minimis* aid in particular is exempted from the prior notification obligation. Neither the complexity of the aid measure nor its periodic nature can release the Member State from its obligation to notify or give rise to any legitimate expectation on the part of the company receiving the aid.[25]

Notification in case of doubt?

22.15 It is a moot point whether Member States can themselves determine whether the conditions of Article 107(1) TFEU are complied with or whether they must necessarily notify all measures where they have any doubts about them. The Commission has sometimes advocated the

---

[17] In the *AITEC* case, the GC considered that this principle applied equally to a case of application of a scheme predating the Commission's approval of the scheme (Joined Cases T-447/93, T-448/93, and T-449/93 *AITEC and others v Commission* [1996] ECR II-1631, para 130).

[18] Joined Cases T-447/93, T-448/93, and T-449/93 *AITEC and others v Commission* [1996] ECR II-1631, paras 135 and 137.

[19] See Arts 2 et seq of the Procedural Regulation.

[20] The Commission shall inform the Member State concerned without delay of the receipt of a notification (see Art 2 of the Procedural Regulation).

[21] Joined Cases C-442/03 P and C-471/03 P *P&O European Ferries (Vizcaya) and Diputación Foral de Vizcaya v Commission* [2006] ECR I-4845, paras 102–5.

[22] The Commission drew Member States' attention to this obligation (see the communications published in [1980] OJ C252/2, and [1983] OJ C318/3).

[23] See Arts 1(a) and 2(1) of the Procedural Regulation and Joined Cases 91 and 127/83 *Heineken Brouwerijen* [1984] ECR 3435, para 11, according to which individuals may invoke a breach of Art 108(3) before a national court 'only if the national measures in question constitute aid within the meaning of Article [107]', and Case C-345/02 *Pearle* [2004] ECR I-7139, para 31.

[24] Cf AG Slynn, who claimed that the scope of Art 108 TFEU is broader than that of Art 107(1) TFEU in that the former would not limit the scope of the notification obligation to aid that distorts or threatens to distort the free play of competition and affects trade between Member States. Those are matters to be examined by the Commission during its review of the aid plan (Opinion in Joined Cases 67, 68, and 70/85 *Van der Kooy v Commission* [1988] ECR 219).

[25] Case C-81/10 P *France Télécom v Commission* [2011], para 62.

latter approach,[26] which would seem reasonable[27] and in keeping with the philosophy of a system based on *a priori* control.

The Member State's obligation will, however, largely depend on the facts of the particular **22.16** case. Thus, according to the ECJ, if the Commission has previously decided that a certain type of measure does constitute aid, a new measure of the same type can only be put into effect if it is clear that it does not constitute aid.[28] In any case, notification of a measure which is capable of granting an advantage to a company is the means provided for by the Treaty for a Member State to obtain legal certainty about that measure.[29]

Notification in cases of presumption of aid

The Commission also considers that, when certain conditions are met, notification is required **22.17** in the case of a 'presumption of aid' pertaining to those circumstances. Such is the case, for example, in any sale of land by a Member State that was not concluded on the basis of an open and unconditional tendering procedure or without any independent expert valuation.[30]

As regards public authorities' holdings with characteristics that give rise to a presumption of **22.18** aid, the Commission asks the Member States to send it 'preliminary information' and reserves the right to decide within fifteen days whether or not there are grounds for considering this information to be a notification within the meaning of Article 108(3) TFEU.[31]

It should be noted, finally, that the obligation notification also applies to aid likely to benefit **22.19** from an authorization under Article 107(2) TFEU, for the Commission has to check that it meets the requisite conditions; also worthy of note is that fact that, to reinforce its control, the Commission permanently vets transfers from public funds to undertakings in the public or private sector.[32]

Notification of an individual case of application of aid schemes

Once a general aid scheme has been approved by the Commission, the individual cases **22.20** of application represent the implementation of an existing scheme and do not have to be

---

[26] See the Communication published in [1983] OJ C318/3: 'As there is no provision for any exception concerning the obligation to inform the Commission "in sufficient time", Member States cannot evade this obligation, even if they consider that the measures they plan do not have all the characteristics described in Article [107](1).' Along the same lines, see para 13 of Case C-301/87 *France v Commission* [1990] ECR I-307, according to which 'the provisions of Articles [107], [108] and [109] lay down procedures which imply that the Commission is in a position to determine, on the basis of the material at its disposal, whether the disputed financial assistance constitutes aid within the meaning of those Articles'.

[27] According to AG Lenz, 'The very wording of Article [108](3) sentence 1 [TFEU]...as well as the object and goal of this provision plead in favour of a wide-ranging information obligation incumbent on the Member States, since it is desirable as far as possible to head off any differences of opinion between the Commission and the Member States on the lawfulness of aid. The information obligation laid down in Article [108(3) TFEU] thus concerns not only the aid cases where it suffices to vet the compatibility with the [FEU] Treaty but also the measures whose classification as aid might appear doubtful' (Opinion in Case 40/85 *Belgium v Commission* [1986] ECR 2321).

[28] Joined Cases 67, 68, and 70/85 R *Van der Kooy v Commission* [1985] ECR 1315, para 43.

[29] Joined Cases T-427/04 and T-17/05 *French Republic and France Télécom v Commission* [2009] ECR II-4315, para 266.

[30] Communication on State aid elements in sales of land and buildings by public authorities [1997] OJ C209/3, para 3.

[31] Section 4.4 of the Communication on the application of Articles 92 and 93 of the EEC Treaty to public authorities' holdings, EC Bull, 9, 1984.

[32] 'Transparency Directive' 2006/111/EC of 16 November 2006 (OJ L318/17) and Communication on the application of Articles 92 and 93 of the EEC Treaty to public authorities' holdings, EC Bull, 9, 1984 (by virtue of this text, Member States are in particular bound to furnish *a posteriori* annual reports on certain public authority holdings).

notified unless a reservation to this effect was made by the Commission in its approval decision. Indeed, since the individual grants of aid are merely measures implementing the general
aid scheme, the factors to be taken into account by the Commission in its assessment would
be the same as those applied in the examination of the scheme. In principle, therefore, there
is no need to submit individual grants of aid for examination by the Commission.[33]

Purpose, contents, and arrangements of the notification

22.21 The purpose of the notification is to give the Commission the chance to exert its control over all
plans to grant or alter aid, doing so in the appropriate time and in the general interest of the EU.[34]

22.22 The content of the notification is important because it is on this basis that any necessary
clarification of the scope of the Commission's decision will be made.[35]

22.23 The notification therefore needs to be sufficiently clear and complete to enable the
Commission to reach a decision. As pointed out by Advocate-General ('AG') Jacobs:

> the obligation to notify proposed aids is of such manifest importance for the functioning
> of the [internal] market that, in the absence of any Council regulations on the matter, it is
> plain that the obligation must be rigorously observed both as to content and as to form, and
> it is essential, in particular, that the notification should make it clear beyond doubt that its
> purpose is to enable the Commission to submit its comments under Article [108](3) and if
> necessary to initiate the procedure provided for in Article [108](2) before the proposed aid
> is implemented.[36]

22.24 The notification has to be complete.[37] The notification is 'considered as complete' if the
Commission does not ask for further information within a given time period.[38] For a notification to be regarded as complete, it is thus sufficient if the Commission has at its disposal,
during the preliminary examination phase, all such information as will enable it to conclude,
without any extensive review being called for, whether a given State measure is compatible
with the Treaty or raises doubt as to its compatibility.[39] A request for additional information,
by which the Commission requests further information on the scope of an aid scheme notified by a Member State, as well as the reply by the national authorities to that request, must
be considered to be an indivisible part of the notified aid scheme.[40]

22.25 If the notification of proposed aid is an essential requirement of the control of that aid,
it is nevertheless only a procedural obligation. It cannot therefore have the effect of setting the legal framework applicable to the aid notified. Consequently, the notification by a
Member State does not give rise to a definitively established legal situation which requires
the Commission to rule on their compatibility with the internal market by applying the
rules in force at the date on which that notification took place. On the contrary, it is for the
Commission to apply the rules in force at the time when it gives its decision.[41]

---

[33] Case C-47/91 *Italy v Commission* [1994] ECR I-4635, para 21 and Case T-20/03 *Kahla Thüringen
Porzellan v Commission* [2008] ECR II-2305, para 92.

[34] Case C-301/87 *France v Commission* [1990] ECR I-307, para 17, and Joined Cases T-126/96 and
T-127/97 *Breda Fucine Meridionali and others v Commission* [1998] ECR II-3437, para 46.

[35] The ECJ has ruled, on the basis of a notification by Germany, that the Commission's decision has
neither the purpose nor the effect of rejecting an additional request of that Member State (Case C-242/00
Germany v Commission [2002] ECR I-5603).

[36] Opinion in Case C-301/87 *France v Commission* [1990] ECR I-307, para 19.

[37] See Art 2(2) of the Procedural Regulation.

[38] Article 4(5) of the Procedural Regulation.

[39] Case C-99/98 *Austria v Commission* [2001] ECR I-1101, para 54.

[40] Case C-537/08 P *Kahla Thüringen Porzellan v Commission* [2010] ECR I-12917, para 45.

[41] Case C-334/07 P *Commission v Freistaat Sachsen* [2008] ECR I-9465, paras 50–3.

The State is bound in particular to indicate the compatibility criterion serving as grounds for **22.26** its claim, failing which the Commission cannot be held liable for having failed to examine it.[42]

The Commission has indicated to Member States the information that needs to be included **22.27** in their notification for it to be considered as complete and provided for a compulsory notification form.[43] The notification forms and other rules have been updated by Regulations 271/2008,[44] 1147/2008,[45] and 1125/2009.[46]

When the aid financing method is an integral part of the measure, the notification must also **22.28** cover this financing method so that the Commission can conduct its examination on the basis of all the facts.[47]

Subsequent alterations

If subsequent alterations are made to an initial aid plan, these alterations also have to be **22.29** brought to the Commission's notice:

- If the Commission has not yet ruled on the initial notification, such information may be supplied to the Commission in the course of the consultations which take place between the Commission and the Member State concerned following the initial notification.[48]
- On the contrary, if these alterations take place after the Commission's decision, a new notification has to be made under the terms of Article 108(3) TFEU. In particular no Member State will be entitled to unilaterally extend the scope of an initial aid-scheme authorization by means of a post-authorization alteration thereof.[49]

The General Court ('GC') seems to have confirmed the Commission's requirement to the **22.30** effect that, for a notification to be accepted as valid, a communication from the national authorities to the Commission must make an express reference to Article 108(3) TFEU and be presented to the Commission's Secretariat-General.[50]

---

[42] Case C-382/99 *Netherlands v Commission* [2002] ECR I-5163, para 84. The same applies as regards justification of the selective character of a measure based on the nature or overall structure of the tax system (Joined Cases T-127/99, T-129/99, and T-148/99 *Diputación Foral de Álava v Commission* [2002] ECR II-1275, para 250).

[43] Regulation 794/2004.

[44] EU Commission Regulation (EC) No 271/2008 of 30 January 2008 amending Regulation (EC) No 794/2004 implementing Council Regulation (EC) No 659/1999 laying down detailed rules for the application of Article 93 of the EC Treaty [2008] OJ L82/1.

[45] EU Commission Regulation (EC) No 1147/2008 of 31 October 2008 amending Regulation (EC) No 794/2004 implementing Council Regulation (EC) No 659/1999 laying down detailed rules for the application of Article 93 of the EC Treaty, as regards Part III.10 of its Annex 1 [2008] OJ L313/1.

[46] EU Commission Regulation (EC) No 1125/2009 of 23 November 2009 amending Regulation (EC) No 794/2004 implementing Council Regulation (EC) No 659/1999 laying down detailed rules for the application of Article 93 of the EC Treaty, as regards Part III.2, Part III.3, and Part III.7 of its Annex I [2009] OJ L308.

[47] Case C-345/02 *Pearle* [2004] ECR I-7139, para 30 and Case C-174/02 *Streekgewest* [2005] ECR I-85, para 26.

[48] Joined Cases 91/83 and 127/83 *Heineken Brouwerijen* [1984] ECR 3435, para 17. These alterations to an aid plan notified during the investigation phase do not therefore have to be formally notified to the Commission by means of a new and separate notification (see, however, the ambiguously worded last sentence of para 13 of Case C-44/93 *Namur-Les assurances du crédit* [1994] ECR I-3829, which would seem to call for a formal notification of the said alterations).

[49] Case T-109/01 *Fleuren Compost v Commission* [2004] ECR II-127, para 80.

[50] Joined Cases T-126/96 and T-127/96 *Breda Fucine Meridionali and others v Commission* [1998] ECR II-3437, para 47. See also Joined Cases T-116/01 and T-118/01 *P&O European Ferries (Vizcaya) and Diputación Foral de Vizcaya v Commission* [2003] ECR II-2957, para 64. However, it cannot be excluded that, under certain circumstances, notification of a national allocation plan under Directive 2003/87 might also constitute notification for the purposes of Article 108(3) TFEU, or might even have to be regarded as such (Case T-387/04 *EnBW Energie Baden-Württemberg v Commission* [2007] ECR II-1195, para 132).

Publicizing the notification

22.31   The notification of an aid plan made to the Commission by a Member State does not have to be brought to the notice of all interested parties, whether by the notifying State or the Commission, unless the Commission decides to open the procedure under Article 108(2) TFEU.[51] However, concerning cases following the simplified procedure,[52] the Commission publishes on its website a summary of the notification.[53]

Withdrawal of the notification

22.32   Should the Member State decide not to grant the aid after having notified the Commission, it is entitled to withdraw its notification.[54] Similarly, the notification shall be deemed to be withdrawn if the information requested by the Commission is not provided within the prescribed period. If the notification is deemed to be withdrawn, the Commission shall inform the Member State thereof.[55]

Exemption from the notification obligation

22.33   The Council is authorized under Article 109 TFEU to exempt certain categories of aid from the previous notification obligation. It has made use of this authority in the block exemption regulations.[56]

Simplified notification

22.34   Article 4 of Reg 794/2004 provides for a simplified notification form for the notification of certain alterations to existing aid. The Commission uses its best endeavours to take a decision on any aid notified on the simplified notification form within a period of one month.[57]

2. Suspension obligation

22.35   According to the last sentence of Article 108(3) TFEU, the Member State concerned cannot put the planned measures into effect until the procedure has run its course. The Member State is hence bound to suspend the implementation of the aid until such time as the Commission has pronounced on its compatibility with the internal market, failing which it is unlawful to grant the aid. This standstill arrangement for new aid is intended to ensure that the aid measures do not come into effect before the Commission has had a reasonable time to examine the aid plan in detail and, if need be, initiate the formal examination procedure.[58] The standstill

---

[51] Joined Cases 91/83 and 127/83 *Heineken Brouwerijen* [1984] ECR 3435, para 15.

[52] Notice from the Commission on a simplified procedure for treatment of certain types of State Aid [2009] OJ C136/3.

[53] Notice from the Commission on a simplified procedure for treatment of certain types of State Aid [2009] OJ C136/3, para 20.

[54] Article 8 of the Procedural Regulation.

[55] Article 5 of the Procedural Regulation.

[56] See Ch 21, 'General Questions on Procedure. Control of State Aid Compatibility. Council's Decision-Making Power', para 21.82 et seq. The Commission also adopted a decision based on Art 106(3) TFEU providing for an exemption from the notification obligation as regards aid granted for financing services of general economic interest (Commission Decision of 20 December 2011 on the application of Art 106(2) TFEU to State aid in the form of public service compensation granted to certain undertakings entrusted with the operation of services of general economic interest [2012] OJ L7/3). Besides, Member States are not required to notify an increase in the budget of an authorized aid scheme if the increase does not exceed 20 per cent of the original amount, provided that the other conditions of the aid scheme remain unchanged (Art 4(1) of Reg 794/2004).

[57] The simplified notification provided for by Art 4 of Reg 794/2004 should not be confused with the Notice from the Commission on a simplified procedure for treatment of certain types of State aid (see paras 22.41–22.43).

[58] Joined Cases 91/83 and 127/83 *Heineken Brouwerijen* [1984] ECR 3435, para 20; Case C-301/87 *France v Commission* [1990] ECR I-307, para 17; and Case C-138/09 *Todaro Nunziatina & C* [2010] ECR I-4561, para 61.

lasts throughout the preliminary phase, during which the Member State concerned cannot implement the aid plan.[59] Should the examination procedure provided for in Article 108(2) TFEU be initiated, this standstill will last until such time as the Commission gives its final decision.[60] Compliance with this standstill obligation, which has direct effect, determines the lawfulness of the aid being implemented.

According to the ECJ, the final sentence of Article 108 TFEU is the means of safeguarding **22.36** the review machinery laid down by that Article, which, in turn, is essential for ensuring the proper functioning of the internal market. It therefore follows that, even if the Member State deems the aid measure to be compatible with the internal market, this does not entitle it to defy the clear provisions of Article 108 TFEU.[61]

Should a Member State make any alterations to a previously approved aid scheme without **22.37** informing the Commission, the Court has held that the final sentence of Article 108(3) TFEU precludes the implementation of the aid scheme in its entirety, unless the alteration in question is in fact a different aid measure that should be assessed separately and therefore does not impinge on the Commission's initial assessment of the plan.[62]

Concept of putting aid into effect

To ascertain the scope of the standstill obligation incumbent on Member States, it is neces- **22.38** sary first of all to determine what is to be understood by the 'putting into effect' or implementation of aid. In principle, aid is considered to have been implemented from the moment that a responsible authority has entered into a legally binding agreement to that effect.[63] The Commission thus refers to the act of implementing or instituting the aid at a legislative level and according to the constitutional rules of the Member State concerned. Aid is therefore deemed to have been put into effect as soon as the legislative machinery enabling it to be granted, without the need for any further formalities, has been set up.[64] A Member State fails to fulfil its obligations under Article 108(3) TFEU by failing to notify measures introducing aid schemes until after they have been enacted as legislation. Aid can therefore be considered to have been put into effect, even if the actual money has not yet been granted to the beneficiary. A Member State will therefore be in breach of its obligations under Article 108(3) TFEU if it fails to notify the Commission of any draft legislation instituting aid schemes until after they have been passed as legislation.[65]

---

[59] In particular Joined Cases C-278/92, C-279/92, and C-280/92 *Spain v Commission* [1994] ECR I-41031 para 14.
[60] Case 120/73 *Lorenz* [1973] ECR 1471, para 4; Case 171/83 R *Commission v France* [1983] ECR 2621, para 13; Case 310/85 *Deufil v Commission* [1987] ECR 901, para 24 and Case C-367/95 P *Commission v Sytraval* [1998] ECR I-1719, para 37. Aid implemented after a Commission's positive decision is presumed lawful until the EU Court decides to annul that decision. Subsequently, on the latter decision, the aid in question is deemed not to have been declared compatible by the annulled decision, with the result that its implementation must be regarded as unlawful (Case C-199/06 *CELF and Ministre de la Culture et de la Communication* [2008] ECR I-469, para 63).
[61] Joined Cases 31/77 R and 53/77 R *Commission v UK* [1977] ECR 921 and Case 171/83 R *Commission v France* [1983] ECR 2621, para 12.
[62] Joined Cases 91/83 and 127/83 *Heineken Brouwerijen* [1984] ECR 3435, para 21.
[63] Case T-109/01 *Fleuren Compost v Commission* [2004] ECR II-127, para 74; Joined Cases T-362/05 and T-363/05 *Nuova Agricast v Commission* [2008] ECR II-297, para 80.
[64] Letter to Member States SG (89) D/5521 of 27 April 1989 at <http://ec.europa.eu/competition/state_aid/legislation/archive_docs/d5521_en.html>.
[65] Case 169/82 *Commission v Italy* [1984] ECR 1603, para 11; and Case T-62/08 *ThyssenKrupp Acciai Speciali Terni v Commission* [2010] ECR II-3229, paras 234–6.

22.39 This definition implies that aid measures should be notified to the Commission when they are still at the draft stage, ie before being put into effect and while they can still be modified in line with any observations the Commission might like to make. Given that Article 108(3) TFEU contains no formal criteria, the onus is on each Member State to determine at which stage of the procedure, legislative or otherwise, it should submit the plan for the Commission's examination, always on condition that the plan is not put into effect before the Commission has pronounced on its compatibility with the internal market.[66]

22.40 When a decision in principle to grant aid has been made subject to a reservation (standstill clause) linked with the Commission's declaration of compatibility, the latter considers that the aid in question has not been put into effect nor has it been granted unlawfully. Conversely, once the aid has effectively been paid out to its beneficiary, there is automatically a breach of the final sentence of Article 108(3) TFEU, and it is not then possible to remedy this breach simply by providing for a revision clause to bring it into line with the EU rules or any similar sort of clause. In other words, such clauses do not cancel the unlawful character of the aid, for the aid has already produced its economic effects.

3. The Notice from the Commission on a simplified procedure

22.41 In 2009, the Commission adopted the Notice on a simplified procedure for treatment of certain types of State aid.[67] This Notice sets out a new simplified procedure under which the Commission intends, in close cooperation with the Member State concerned, to examine within an accelerated time frame certain types of State support measures which only require the Commission to verify that the measure is in accordance with existing rules and practices without exercising any discretionary powers. When all the conditions set out in the Notice are met, the Commission will use its best endeavours to adopt a short-form decision that the notified measure does not constitute aid or not to raise objections within twenty working days of the date of notification.

22.42 The Notice provides three categories of aid measures which are in principle suitable for treatment under the simplified procedure: (i) measures falling within the 'standard assessment' sections of existing frameworks or guidelines; (ii) measures corresponding to well-established Commission decision-making practice; and (iii) prolongation or extension of existing schemes. Unlawful aids are excluded. The simplified procedure does not apply either to aid favouring activities in the fishery and aquaculture sectors, activities in the primary production of agricultural products, or activities in the processing or marketing of agricultural products. Where the notification form is not complete or contains misleading or incorrect information, the Commission will not apply the simplified procedure. In addition, to the extent that the notification involves novel legal issues of a general interest, the Commission will not normally apply the simplified procedure. Besides, the Commission may revert to the normal procedure at any time.

22.43 The assessment of a State support measure under the simplified procedure is conditional upon the Member State holding pre-notification contacts with the Commission. Within two weeks from the receipt of the draft notification form, the Commission services organize a first pre-notification contact. Within five working days after the last pre-notification contact, the Commission services inform the Member State concerned whether the case qualifies *prima facie* for treatment under the simplified procedure, which information still needs to be provided for the measure to qualify for treatment under that procedure, or whether the case will remain

---

[66] Case T-188/95 *Waterleiding v Commission* [1998] ECR II-3713, para 118; and Case T-62/08 *ThyssenKrupp Acciai Speciali Terni v Commission* [2010] ECR II-3229, paras 234–6.
[67] [2009] OJ C136/3, with a corrigendum [2009] OJ C157/20.

subject to the normal procedure. The Member State must notify the aid measure(s) concerned no later than two months after it is informed by the Commission services that the measure qualifies *prima facie* for treatment under the simplified procedure. The Commission publishes on its website a summary of the notification, based on the information provided by the Member State, in the standard form set out in the Annex to the Notice. Interested parties then have ten working days to submit observations. If the Commission is satisfied that the notified measure fulfils the criteria for the simplified procedure, it issues a short-form decision. The Commission will use its best endeavours to adopt a decision that the notified measure does not constitute aid or a decision not to raise objections within twenty working days from the date of notification. The Commission publishes a summary notice of the decision in the Official Journal of the European Union ('OJ'). The short-form decision is made available on the Commission's website.

4. The Code of Best Practice

22.44 The Code of Best Practice for the conduct of State aid control procedures[68] sets out day-to-day best practices to contribute to speedier, more transparent, and more predictable State aid procedures at each step of the investigation of a notified or non-notified case or a complaint, without, however, creating or altering any rights or obligations as set out in the Treaty and secondary legislation.

22.45 The Code formalizes the pre-notification contacts, which offer the possibility of discussing and providing guidance to the Member State concerned about the scope of the information to be submitted in the notification form to ensure it is complete as from the date of notification. As a general rule, pre-notification contacts, which are held in strict confidence, should last no longer than two months and should be followed by a complete notification. The Commission recommends that beneficiaries of individual aid be involved in the pre-notification contacts. The Commission services endeavour to provide the Member State concerned with an informal preliminary assessment of the pre-notification phase. In cases which are particularly novel, technically complex, or otherwise sensitive, or which have to be examined as a matter of absolute urgency, the Commission services offer mutually agreed planning to the Member State, including the priority treatment of the case, the information to be provided by the Member State and/or the beneficiary, and the likely form and duration of the assessment of the case, once notified.

C. Preliminary Examination Procedure for Notified Aid

22.46 At the end of a common preliminary procedure, the procedure then followed by the Commission for pronouncing on aid compatibility can take two different paths: sometimes the aid can be declared to be compatible straightaway, by means of a 'decision not to raise objections'; on other occasions, the Commission resorts to the more complex arrangements of the formal examination procedure contained in Article 108(2) TFEU.

22.47 As regards the procedure laid down in Article 108 TFEU, a distinction has to be made between the preliminary examination phase and the formal examination procedure. The preliminary examination phase laid down in Article 108(3) TFEU has the sole object of allowing the Commission to form a *prima facie* opinion on the partial or total conformity of the aid in question (and, previously, on whether it does in fact qualify as aid).[69] The purpose of the

---

[68] [2009] OJ C136/13.
[69] Case 84/82 *Germany v Commission* [1984] ECR 1451, para 11 and Case C-198/91 *Cook v Commission* [1993] ECR I-2487, para 22. See also the Judgment of the ECJ of 24 January 2013 in C-646/11 P *Falles Fagligt Forbund (3F) v Commission*, para 32 stating that the long duration of the Commission's preliminary examination would not, of itself, be sufficient to lead to the conclusion that the Commission should have initiated a formal investigation.

formal examination procedure of Article 108(2) TFEU is to allow the Commission to be fully informed of all the facts of the case.[70]

1. Preliminary examination procedure

22.48 When the Commission learns of any new aid plan, it must carry out immediately a preliminary evaluation of its compatibility. The Member State cannot put the measure into effect before having notified the Commission; this prohibition is effective throughout the whole of the preliminary stage.[71]

22.49 The preliminary examination is in substance a dialogue between the Commission and the Member State concerned. Interested parties, including the beneficiary of the aid, do not play a formal role in it. The fact that it is a preliminary examination does not, however, prevent the Commission from carrying out enquiries in this period and gathering supplementary information. It is not necessarily bound to limit itself to examining the notified aid plan.[72] The notifying Member State and the Commission must work together in good faith in order to enable the Commission to overcome any difficulties that it may encounter when examining a notified aid plan.[73]

22.50 In the case of an aid scheme, the Commission may confine itself to examining the general characteristics of the scheme in question without being required to examine each particular case in which it applies,[74] even if the aid scheme in question has ceased to apply,[75] and even where the aid scheme has been applied only once.[76] In order for an aid scheme to be considered compatible with the internal market, it is not sufficient that the required conditions be fulfilled in certain cases where the scheme could, potentially, be applied. It is necessary for the aid granted on the basis of that scheme to fulfil those conditions in all such cases.[77]

2. Commission examination deadline

'Lorenz' time limit

22.51 The Commission has an initial time period of two months for reacting to the notification made by the Member State. By setting this time limit in its Article 4, the Procedural Regulation has endorsed the so-called *Lorenz* time limit, the name 'Lorenz' being taken from the case of that name. In 1973, the Court ruled that in stating that the Commission shall be informed of plans to grant new or alter existing aid 'in sufficient time to enable it to submit its comments', the intention of the Treaty was to provide this institution with sufficient time for consideration and investigation to form a *prima facie* opinion on the partial or complete conformity with the Treaty of the plans notified to it. It is only after being put in a position to form this opinion that the Commission is bound, if it considers the plan incompatible with the internal market, to initiate without delay the formal examination procedure.[78] The Commission must act with due expedition in order to take account of the Member States' interest in obtaining

---

[70] Case C-198/91 *Cook v Commission* [1993] ECR I-2487, para 22; Case C-225/91 *Matra v Commission* [1993] ECR I-3203, para 16 and Case C-367/95 P *Commission v Sytraval* [1998] ECR I-1719, para 38.
[71] Case 84/82 *Germany v Commission* [1984] ECR 1451, para 11.
[72] See the Opinion of AG Slynn in Case 84/82 *Germany v Commission* [1984] ECR 1451.
[73] Case C-349/93 *Commission v Italy* [1995] ECR I-343, para 13.
[74] Case C-66/02 *Italy v Commission* [2005] ECR I-10901, para 91.
[75] Case C-278/00 *Greece v Commission* [2004] ECR I-3997, para 24.
[76] Joined Cases T-239/04 and T-323/04 *Italy and Brandt Italia v Commission* [2007] ECR II-3265, para 142.
[77] Joined Cases T-239/04 and T-323/04 *Italy and Brandt Italia v Commission* [2007] ECR II-3265, para 94.
[78] Case 120/73 *Lorenz* [1973] ECR 1471, para 3.

clarification in cases in which there may be an urgent need to take action.[79] It therefore has a time limit for carrying out this preliminary examination, a time limit set by the Court at two months, in keeping with Articles 263 and 265 TFEU.[80] This is a mandatory time limit[81] which is binding on all the parties to the preliminary examination procedure. The Member State concerned is not, therefore, entitled to release itself from that obligation by invoking urgency.[82]

If the Commission fails to come to a decision or has not asked for any further information **22.52** from the Member State concerned by the end of this two-month time period, this Member State can then make the necessary arrangements to implement its aid plan. It must, however, first notify the Commission,[83] if need be simply by fax.[84] The Commission then has an additional period of fifteen days to take a decision[85] and notify the Member State;[86] once this period has ended, the aid becomes existing aid.

Consequences of inaction by the Commission

When the aid has been put into effect at the end of the *Lorenz* time limit without any ruling **22.53** from the Commission, this cannot be construed to mean that the aid is in fact compatible with the Treaty. At most it becomes existing aid. In principle it is then governed by the provisions of Article 108(1) and (3) TFEU[87] (but aid granted as a lump sum cannot then be made the object of appropriate measures).

Extension of the Lorenz time limit

In practice, the two-month time limit is often extended by mutual agreement; this is not pos- **22.54** sible without the State's express consent.[88] Nonetheless, a long extension might be a sign that the Commission has run into difficulties which should have prompted it to initiate the formal examination procedure.[89]

This two-month time limit does not start to run until the Commission is in possession of a **22.55** complete notification.

3. Decision not to raise objections

At the end of its preliminary examination of the aid, the Commission can either adopt a deci- **22.56** sion not to raise objections or alternatively decide to open the formal examination procedure of

---

[79] Case 84/82 *Germany v Commission* [1984] ECR 1451, para 11.

[80] Case 171/83 R *Commission v France* [1983] ECR 2621, para 13.

[81] Case C-334/99 *Germany v Commission* [2003] ECR I-1139, para 49.

[82] Joined Cases T-239/04 and T-323/04 *Italy and Brandt Italia v Commission* [2007] ECR II-3265, para 89.

[83] On this matter the Procedural Regulation has confirmed the case law of the ECJ, whereby the demands of legal certainty mean that the Member State, after the two-month period has run its course, should give previous notice to the Commission before putting its aid plans into effect (Case 171/83 R *Commission v France* [1983] ECR 2621, para 14 and Case 120/73 *Lorenz* [1973] ECR 1471, para 4; Case 84/82 *Germany v Commission* [1984] ECR 1451, para 11 and Case C-312/90 *Spain v Commission* [1992] ECR I-4117, para 18).

[84] Case C-398/00 *Spain v Commission* [2002] ECR I-5643, para 23.

[85] Article 4(6) of the Procedural Regulation.

[86] According to the strict interpretation of Case C-398/00 *Spain v Commission* [2002] ECR I-5643, para 32.

[87] Case 120/73 *Lorenz* [1973] ECR 1471, para 5. The silence of the Commission should not, therefore, be seen as a legitimate way of approving notified aid. In view of the Commission's examination obligation, it would be anomalous for potentially incompatible aid to become existing aid due to an oversight of the Commission.

[88] Article 4(5) of the Procedural Regulation. Case C-334/99 *Germany v Commission* [2003] ECR I-1139, para 50.

[89] See Case 84/82 *Germany v Commission* [1984] ECR 1451, para 15, in which the Court ruled that a sixteen-month time period from the initial notification to the decision not to raise objections 'well exceeds the period normally required for a preliminary examination under Article [108](3).'

Article 108(2) TFEU. The decision not to raise objections brings the procedure to an end and authorizes the aid to be put into effect.

Content

22.57 'Decision not to raise objections' means the Commission's decision addressed to the Member State in question declaring without further ado either that the measure in question does not constitute aid or that it constitutes aid that is compatible with the Treaty (Article 4 of the Procedural Regulation).⁹⁰ In particular, if the Commission declares that the aid is compatible, then the aid in question, granted after the Commission's approval, becomes 'existing aid' and is subject to the permanent review laid down in Article 108(1) TFEU. In practice, the Commission can also reach the conclusion that it is an individual application of an existing aid scheme. The Commission has no power to impose conditions in a decision not to raise objections. However, following discussion with the Commission, the Member State may offer certain commitments in order to remove any doubts concerning the compatibility of the aid. These commitments become an integral part of the notification and the Commission takes note of them in the text of the decision.⁹¹

Decisions not to classify the measure as aid

22.58 Even though the Treaty only lays down the review procedure with reference to the compatibility of measures, it follows from the practice of the Commission, case law, and the Procedural Regulation (Article 4(2)) that decisions not to raise objections can also have the object of deciding that a measure cannot be classified as aid.

22.59 To declassify a measure as aid, the Commission often issues comfort letters to the requesting Member States, setting forth its point of view on the basis of the information that the Member State has furnished.

Procedural arrangements

22.60 One of the main traits distinguishing the formal examination procedure of Article 108(2) from the preliminary phase of Article 108(3) TFEU is that the Commission is under no obligation whatsoever at the preliminary stage to give notice to the parties concerned to submit their comments before taking its decision.⁹² In the preliminary phase, third parties are therefore in principle excluded from the examination procedure.⁹³ However, the Commission is required to examine all the facts and points of law brought to its notice by persons, undertakings, and associations whose interests may be affected by the granting of the aid. It is therefore in the light of both the information notified by the State concerned and that provided by any complainants that the institution must make its assessment in the context of the preliminary examination.⁹⁴

---

⁹⁰ The scope of a decision by which the Commission raises no objections to an aid scheme notified by a Member State must be determined not only by reference to the actual wording of that decision, only a summary of which is published in the OJ, but also by taking account of the aid scheme notified by the Member State concerned (Case C-537/08 P *Kahla Thüringen Porzellan v Commission* [2010] ECR I-12917, para 44; and Case C-67/09 P *Nuova Agricast v Commission* [2010] ECR I-9811, para 64).

⁹¹ See para 76 of the Notice from the Commission—Towards an effective implementation of Commission decisions ordering Member States to recover unlawful and incompatible State aid [2007] OJ C272/4).

⁹² Case 84/82 *Germany v Commission* [1984] ECR 1451, para 13; Case C-198/91 *Cook v Commission* [1993] ECR I-2487, para 22; Case C-225/91 *Matra v Commission* [1993] ECR I-3203, para 53; and Case T-266/94 *Skibsværfsforeningen and others v Commission* [1996] ECR II-1399, para 257.

⁹³ With the exception of the simplified procedure (see para 21 of the Notice on a simplified procedure).

⁹⁴ Case C-204/97 *Portugal v Commission* [2001] ECR I-3175, para 35.

Conditions

The Commission may restrict itself to the preliminary examination under Article 108(3) TFEU **22.61** when taking a decision in favour of a plan to grant aid only if it is convinced after the preliminary examination that the plan is compatible with the Treaty.[95] If it has any doubts, however, it must initiate the formal examination procedure.

It is for the Commission to decide, on the basis of the factual and legal circumstances of the case, **22.62** whether the difficulties involved in assessing the compatibility of the aid require the initiation of that procedure. That decision must satisfy three requirements. First, under Article 108 TFEU the Commission's power to find aid to be compatible with the internal market upon the conclusion of the preliminary examination procedure is restricted to aid measures that raise no serious difficulties. That criterion is thus an exclusive one. The Commission may not, therefore, decline to initiate the formal investigation procedure in reliance upon other circumstances, such as third party interests, considerations of economy of procedure, or any other ground of administrative or political convenience. Secondly, where it encounters serious difficulties, the Commission must initiate the formal procedure, having no discretion in this regard. Thirdly, the notion of serious difficulties is an objective one. Whether or not such difficulties exist requires investigation of both the circumstances under which the contested measure was adopted and its content. That investigation must be conducted objectively, comparing the grounds of the decision with the information available to the Commission when it took a decision on the compatibility of the disputed aid with the internal market.[96] The mere fact that discussions took place between the Commission and the Member State concerned during the preliminary examination stage and that, in that context, the Commission asked for additional information about the measures submitted for its review, cannot in itself be regarded as evidence that the Commission was confronted with serious difficulties of assessment.[97]

Appeal procedures

A decision not to raise objections is in principle favourable to the Member State concerned, **22.63** so it should in principle give rise to no appeal by the latter or the beneficiary undertaking.[98] Third parties, for their part, are in principle excluded from the preliminary procedure, so their only possibility of contesting the decision is to assert before the EU Court that the Commission has made a mistake or should have initiated the formal examination procedure. The ECJ has therefore recognized that such a decision by the Commission was an adversely affecting act against which it is possible to bring an action for annulment.

Publication

Summaries of decisions not to raise objections are published in the OJ series C. This publica- **22.64** tion takes the form of an 'information box', which sums up the main characteristics of the aid

---

[95] Case 84/82 *Germany v Commission* [1984] ECR 1451, para 13.
[96] Case T-73/98 *Prayon-Rupel v Commission* [2001] ECR II-867, paras 42–7 and Case T-388/03 *Deutsche Post AG and DHL International v Commission* [2009] ECR II-867, paras 86–95. Consideration of whether serious difficulties exist is not aimed at establishing whether the Commission applied Art 107 TFEU correctly, but whether, at the time of its adoption of the contested decision, there was sufficiently comprehensive information available to it to enable it to assess the compatibility of the disputed measure with the internal market (Case T-36/06 *Bundesverband deutscher Banken v Commission* [2010], ECR II-537 para 129).
[97] Case C-225/91 *Matra v Commission* [1993] ECR I-3203, para 38; and Case T-30/03 RENV *3F v Commission* [2011], para 71.
[98] Nevertheless, a decision based on Art 107(1) and (3) TFEU which, while classifying the measure in question as State aid, declares it compatible with the internal market, must be regarded as a challengeable act under Art 263 TFEU (Case C-279/08 P *Commission v Netherlands (NOx)* [2011], paras 35–42). See also Case T-301/01 *Alitalia v Commission* [2008] ECR II-1753, paras 377–88.

(amount, beneficiaries, etc). This publication, however, does not always provide details of the scope of the Commission's decisions.[99]

D. Formal Examination Procedure for Notified Aid[100]

22.65   If the Commission is not in a position to decide outright to raise no objection to the aid, it has to resort to the formal examination procedure laid down in Article 108(2) TFEU.

1. Opening of the procedure

Doubts about the compatibility of the aid (Article 4 of the Procedural Regulation)

22.66   As soon as the Commission encounters difficulties in deciding whether an aid plan is compatible with the internal market, it is bound to initiate the formal examination procedure laid down in Article 108(2) TFEU.[101] Indeed, if the preliminary phase has convinced the Commission that the aid is incompatible, or has not (objectively[102]) enabled it to overcome all the difficulties raised by the assessment of the compatibility of the State measure in question with the internal market, it is duty bound to obtain all necessary opinions.[103]

Doubts about the existence of aid

22.67   Although neither Article 108 TFEU nor the Procedural Regulation makes any express provision on this point, it is generally accepted that the formal examination procedure can and, if need be, must be opened to solve any doubts about whether a measure does in fact constitute aid coming within the scope of Article 107(1) TFEU.[104] In this case, however, according to the GC, the Commission is only bound to initiate the procedure when its initial examination has not enabled it to overcome all doubts about whether the measure concerned, assuming that this measure does in fact constitute aid, is in any case compatible with the internal market.[105] This implies, in principle, that the State cannot put the measure into effect until the Commission has closed the procedure. The Commission brings this procedure to an end in classic fashion, by adopting a final decision.

Control

22.68   The need to initiate the procedure has to be determined by the Commission, subject to the control of the EU Courts, depending on the factual and legal circumstances involved in the case.[106] The existence of any difficulties is evaluated by the EU Courts in an objective manner, comparing the grounds of the decision with the information available to the Commission

---

[99] Article 26(1) of the Procedural Regulation. In the Best Practice Code, the Commission endeavours to publish its decision to open the formal investigation procedure, including the meaningful summaries, within two months of the date of adoption of that decision (para 32).

[100] Besides the case of notified aid, the formal examination procedure can be opened to cover three other situations, namely the examination of any unlawful aid (see para 23.14), misuse of aid (see para 25.13), and when a Member State rejects the appropriate measures proposed by the Commission concerning an existing aid scheme (see para 24.45).

[101] Case 194/09 P *Alcoa v Commission* [2011], para 60.

[102] Case T-114/00 *ARE v Commission* [2002] ECR II-5121, para 48.

[103] Case 84/82 *Germany v Commission* [1984] ECR 1451, para 13; Case C-198/91 *Cook v Commission* [1993] ECR I-2487, para 29; Case C-225/91 *Matra v Commission* [1993] ECR I-3203, para 33; Case T-49/93 *SIDE v Commission* [1995] ECR II-2501, para 58.

[104] See, implicitly, Case T-95/94 *Sytraval v Commission* [1995] ECR II-2651, para 79 *in fine*, and, explicitly, Case T-11/95 *BP Chemicals v Commission* [1998] ECR II-3235, para 166.

[105] Case T-11/95 *BP Chemicals v Commission* [1998] ECR II-3235, para 166, Joined Cases T-269/99, T-271/99, and T-272/99 *Territorio Histórico de Guipúzcoa and others v Commission* [2002] ECR II-4217, para 45, and Joined Cases T-346/99, T-347/99, and T-348/99 *Territorio Histórico de Álava and others v Commission* [2002] ECR II-4259, para 41.

[106] Case C-198/91 *Cook v Commission* [1993] ECR I-2487, para 30.

when it took a decision on the compatibility of the disputed aid with the internal market.[107] Judicial review by the Court of the existence of serious difficulties will, by nature, go beyond consideration of whether or not there has been a manifest error of assessment.[108] If the examination carried out by the Commission during the preliminary examination procedure is insufficient or incomplete, this constitutes evidence of the existence of serious difficulties.[109] Other signs of the fact that the Commission should initiate the procedure are the length of its discussions with the Member State and the fact that the initial plan has to be altered to be able to be declared compatible,[110] the link that exists between the measure under examination and other measures for which a procedure has been initiated,[111] the Commission's inability to produce the clear calculations made at the time of the preliminary examination,[112] etc.

On the other hand, any review by that Court of the legality of a decision to initiate the **22.69** formal investigation procedure must necessarily be limited. In an action against such a decision, where the applicants challenge the Commission's assessment classifying the disputed measure as State aid, review by the EU judicature is limited to ascertaining whether or not the Commission has made a manifest error of assessment.[113] The obligation to initiate the procedure does not depend on the aid's implementation conditions (notified aid or unlawful aid) or the provision of Article 107 TFEU that is applied.[114] Moreover, the amount of the investment or aid in question cannot in itself constitute a serious difficulty, as otherwise the Commission would be obliged to initiate the procedure under Article 108(2) TFEU whenever the investment or aid exceeded a certain level, which would moreover have to be defined.[115] Likewise, supplementation of the original scheme by the Member State with additional information and detail cannot be considered to be significant alterations complying with the conditions laid down by the Commission and justifying the initiation of the procedure. Finally, the obligation imposed on the Member State to produce an annual assessment report cannot be considered to be proof of the existence of serious assessment difficulties.[116]

Purpose of the formal examination procedure
The goal of this procedure is twofold: first, to oblige the Commission to ensure that all per- **22.70** sons who may be concerned, including other Member States, are given an opportunity of putting forward their arguments;[117] and secondly, it enables the Commission to obtain all necessary opinions and become completely clear about all the facts of the case before taking its definitive decision on whether the measure can be classified as aid and, if so, if it is compatible with the internal market.[118]

---

[107] Case T-49/93 *SIDE v Commission* [1995] ECR II-2501, para 60.
[108] Case T-388/03 *Deutsche Post AG and DHL International v Commission* [2009] ECR II-867, para 92; and Case T-359/04 *British Aggregates v Commission* [2010] ECR II-4227, para 56.
[109] Case C-204/97 *Portugal v Commission* [2001] ECR I-3175, paras 46–9; and Case T-359/04 *British Aggregates v Commission* [2010] ECR II-4227, para 57.
[110] Case 84/82 *Germany v Commission* [1984] ECR 1451, paras 14–17.
[111] Case T-11/95 *BP Chemicals v Commission* [1998] ECR II-3235, para 170 et seq.
[112] Case T-11/95 *BP Chemicals v Commission* [1998] ECR II-3235, para 193.
[113] Case C-194/09 P *Alcoa v Commission* [2011], para 61.
[114] Case C-198/91 *Cook v Commission* [1993] ECR I-2487, para 30.
[115] Case C-225/91 *Matra v Commission* [1993] ECR I-3203, para 36.
[116] Case C-225/91 *Matra v Commission* [1993] ECR I-3203, para 38.
[117] Case 323/82 *Intermills v Commission* [1984] ECR 3809, para 17. In the particular case of an aid beneficiary concerned in the initiation of the procedure, the Commission in principle asks the Member State to inform it of the opening of the procedure as soon as possible.
[118] Case 84/82 *Germany v Commission* [1984] ECR 1451, para 13; Case T-266/94 *Skibsværftsforeningen and others v Commission* [1996] ECR II-1399, para 256; Joined Cases T-371/94 and T-394/94 *British Airways and others v Commission* [1998] ECR 11-2405, para 58; and Joined Cases T-269/99, T-271/99, and T-272/99 *Territorio Histórico de Guipúzcoa and others v Commission* [2002] ECR II-4217, paras 47 and 93.

Contents and scope of the decision to initiate the procedure

22.71 The formal examination procedure can be initiated only by a 'decision' within the meaning of Article 288(4) TFEU.[119] According to Article 6 of the Procedural Regulation, the decision to initiate the procedure summarizes the relevant issues of fact and law, including a 'preliminary assessment' of the measure, and also gives the grounds for any doubts about its compatibility.[120] The nature of the information to be furnished is determined by the need to allow the interested parties to participate effectively in the procedure. The Commission cannot be required to present a complete analysis on the aid in question in its notice of intention to initiate that procedure, but must define sufficiently the framework of its investigation so as not to render meaningless the right of interested parties to put forward their comments.[121] For that purpose, it is sufficient for the parties concerned to be aware of the reasoning which has led the Commission to conclude provisionally that the measure in issue might constitute new aid incompatible with the internal market.[122] The formal investigation procedure enables a more in-depth examination and clarification of the questions raised in the decision to initiate the procedure, so that any difference between that decision and the final decision cannot be regarded in itself as constituting a defect rendering the final decision unlawful.[123] Indeed, the Commission cannot be prevented, in its final decision, at the end of the formal investigation procedure, from supplementing its 'preliminary' assessment by adopting the point of view expressed by those interested parties.[124] The identification of the beneficiary of the aid is necessarily one of the relevant issues of fact and law which must be contained in the decision to open the procedure, if that is possible at that stage of the procedure, since it is on the basis of that identification that the Commission will be able to adopt the recovery decision.[125]

Assessment of the nature of the aid

22.72 Given that the decision to initiate the procedure represents only a 'preliminary assessment' of the nature of the aid, the GC considers that the classification of the measure as State aid does not have a definitive character: this decision is necessarily provisional, as is the assessment of its compatibility with the internal market.[126] According to the GC, the fact that the Commission does not expressly state any doubts in the decision to initiate the procedure about the classification of the measure in dispute as State aid does not in any way show that this classification is not provisional; it considers in effect that, in a decision to initiate the procedure, the Commission is only bound to state expressly its doubts about the compatibility of the measure with the internal market.[127]

[119] Joined Cases T-195/01 and T-207/01 *Government of Gibraltar v Commission*, para 74.

[120] Case 194/09 P *Alcoa v Commission* [2011], para 58.

[121] Case T-354/99 *Kuwait Petroleum v Commission* [2006] ECR II-1475, para 85 and Joined Cases T-273/06 and T-297/06 *ISD Polska and Others v Commission* [2009] ECR II-2185, para 126.

[122] Case T-211/05 *Italy v Commission* [2009] ECR II-2777, para 54.

[123] Case T-211/05 *Italy v Commission* [2009] ECR II-2777, para 55.

[124] Joined Cases C-106/09 P and C-107/09 P *Commission and Spain v Gibraltar and UK* [2011], para 165.

[125] Case T-34/02 *Le Levant 001 v Commission* [2006] ECR II-267, para 82.

[126] Joined Cases T-269/99, T-271/99, and T-272/99 *Territorio Histórico de Guipúzcoa and others v Commission* [2002] ECR II-4217, paras 47 and 82; Joined Cases T-346/99, T-347/99, and T-348/99 *Territorio Histórico de Álava and others v Commission* [2002] ECR II-4259, paras 43, 75, and 78 ; and Case T-190/00 *Regione Siciliana v Commission* [2003] ECR II-5015, reported para 48.

[127] Joined Cases T-269/99, T-271/99, and T-272/99 *Territorio Histórico de Guipúzcoa and others v Commission* [2002] ECR II-4217, para 84 and Joined Cases T-346/99, T-347/99, and T-348/99 *Territorio Histórico de Álava and others v Commission* [2002] ECR II-4259, para 77 and Case T-87/09 *Jørgen Andersen v Commission*, para 55.

Assessment of the nature of new aid

The initiation of the procedure also has the effect of confirming the Commission's classification **22.73** as new aid (or misuse of existing aid) of the measure under examination, which is thenceforth subjected to the standstill effect contained in the last sentence of Article 108(3) TFEU. The classification of the measure as new aid is equally provisional, limited in time until the conclusion of the formal procedure.[128] Despite its preparatory nature, an initiation decision can be a contestable act, if it produces legal effects independent of the final decision.[129] In order to avoid confusion between the administrative and judicial proceedings, and to preserve the division of powers between the Commission and the EU Courts, any review by the GC of the legality of a decision to initiate the formal investigation procedure must necessarily be limited. The EU Courts must in fact avoid giving a final ruling on questions on which the Commission has merely formed a provisional view. Thus, review by the EU Courts is limited to ascertaining whether or not the Commission has made a manifest error of assessment in forming the view that it was unable to resolve all the difficulties on that point during its initial examination of the measure concerned.[130]

Assessment of compatibility

The Commission can only set forth its 'doubts', which does not prejudice its final decision.   **22.74**

Penalizing the failure to initiate the procedure

Wrongful omission by the Commission to initiate the formal examination procedure before **22.75** ruling on the existence and compatibility of aid constitutes an essential procedural infringement which, in the event of litigation, automatically renders null and void the decision not to raise objections.[131] Indeed, in so acting, the Commission infringes the procedural rights of the applicant as a party concerned within the meaning of Article 108(2) TFEU.[132]

Cases in which the Commission is not empowered to initiate the procedure

For certain aid in favour of agriculture, the Commission, even if it judges the aid to be incompat- **22.76** ible with the internal market, is not entitled to initiate the procedure laid down in Article 108(2) TFEU, but only to give its recommendations.

2. Extension of the procedure

The Commission will extend the procedure when new facts come to light after the initiation of **22.77** the procedure and these new facts might affect the final decision, to make sure that the final decision is not based on grounds on which the Member State and the interested parties were unable to make known their comments.[133] These facts are usually either ones that the Commission discovers during the procedure or alterations to the aid under examination, proposed by the State concerned to facilitate the Commission's approval. On the contrary, when any alterations do not change the main elements of the aid and therefore seem unlikely to affect the contents of the final decision, the Commission is not required to extend the procedure, so as not to lengthen

---

[128] Case T-190/00 *Regione Siciliana v Commission* [2003] ECR II-5015, para 46.
[129] Case C-312/90 *Spain v Commission* [1992] ECR I-4117, paras 17–24; Case C-400/99 *Italy v Commission* [2001] ECR I-7303, paras 57–65; and Case T-332/06 *Alcoa Trasformazione v Commission* [2009] ECR II 29, paras 35–6.
[130] Case T-332/06 *Alcoa Trasformazione v Commission* [2009] ECR II-29, paras 60–2.
[131] Case 84/82 *Germany v Commission* [1984] ECR 1451, para 19.
[132] Case T-11/95 *BP Chemicals v Commission* [1998] ECR II-3235, para 200.
[133] Case T-176/01 *Ferriere Nord v Commission* [2004] ECR II-3931, paras 80–1. In *KG Holding* (Joined Cases T-81/07–T-83/07 *KG Holding v Commission* [2009] ECR II-2411, paras 115–38), the GC annulled a decision that took position on a measure that was not included in the opening decision.

the examination of the file unduly. The Commission is thus not obliged to reopen the formal investigation when, during the formal examination of a restructuring aid project, the Member State makes some amendments to the restructuring plan.[134]

22.78 A particular case arises when, during the examination of aid that is to be granted to an undertaking, the Commission is informed of the existence of other aid, whether notified or unlawful, in favour of the same beneficiary, which was not taken into account at the time of initiating the procedure. In this case the Commission will either deal with the aid in separate procedures or in an overall manner, particularly when they mutually affect each other, in extending the initial procedure to aid that has subsequently come to light. The danger of this second approach, when public authorities proceed to pay out aid regularly to an undertaking in breach of Article 108(3) TFEU, is that it might postpone the adoption of a final decision almost indefinitely.

3. Suspensive effect

22.79 The initiation of the formal examination procedure has the effect of extending the standstill situation arising under Article 108(3) TFEU, last sentence.[135] As far as new aid is concerned, this standstill effect associated with the initiation of the procedure cannot be broken unless the Member State obtains an approval decision from the Council on the basis of the third subparagraph of Article 108(2) TFEU,[136] or when the Member State has lodged an action for annulment against the decision to initiate the procedure on the grounds, for example, that the measure manifestly cannot be classified as aid and it requests and obtains provisional measures from the ECJ.[137]

4. Procedural arrangements

Burden of proof

22.80 When the Commission decides to open the formal procedure, the onus is on the Member State and the potential recipient of aid to put forward the arguments in which they seek to show that the planned aid corresponds to the exceptions provided for in the application of the Treaty. Although the Commission is required to express its doubts clearly, the fact remains that it is for the aid applicant to dispel those doubts.[138]

Participation of the Member State concerned

22.81 The procedure laid down by Article 108(2) TFEU takes place primarily between the Commission and the Member State concerned. Indeed, by virtue of its very structure, the administrative procedure is opened only against the Member State concerned.[139] It is also the Member State that is the addressee of the Commission's final decision. All this justifies the

---

[134] Case T-301/01 *Alitalia v Commission* [2008] ECR II-1753, para 143. See also Case T-424/05 *Italy v Commission* [2009] ECR II-23, para 6 and Joined Cases T-231/06 and T-237/06 *Netherlands v Commission* [2008] ECR II-5993, para 50.

[135] Case 120/73 *Lorenz* [1973] ECR 1471, para 8.

[136] For more information on this procedure see Ch 21, 'General Questions on Procedure. Control of State Aid Compatibility. Council's Decision-Making Power', para 21.100.

[137] See the Opinion of AG Mayras in Case 156/77 *Commission v Belgium* [1978] ECR 1881.

[138] Case T-176/01 *Ferriere Nord v Commission* [2004] ECR II-3931, paras 93–4. This also entails the need to show that there is no cumulative effect of the new aid and earlier unlawful aid that was incompatible with the internal market and that has not been repaid (Case T-25/07 *Iride and Iride Energia v Commission* [2009] ECR II-245, para 104).

[139] Joined Cases T-228/99 and T-233/99 *WestLB and others v Commission* [2003] ECR II-435, para 122; Case T-109/01 *Fleuren Compost v Commission* [2004] ECR II-127, para 42; and Case T-198/01 *TGI v Commission* [2004] ECR II-2717, para 191.

Member States' privileged status in terms of contacts with the Commission[140] and in particular their rights to a fair defence.[141]

According to settled case law, the right to be heard is, in all proceedings initiated against a **22.82** person that are liable to culminate in a measure adversely affecting that person, a fundamental principle of EU law.[142] This principle means that the Member State involved in the process has to be allowed to effectively make known its point of view on the observations made by third parties pursuant to Article 108(2) TFEU, upon which the Commission intends to base its decision. The Commission's decision may therefore be based only on information that the Member State was previously afforded the opportunity of commenting on.[143]

Penalty for failure to give a Member State a proper hearing Should the Commission base **22.83** its decision on documents to which the Member State has not been afforded access, the EU Courts do not take a dogmatic stance, but rather examine the importance of access to those documents in the context of the administrative procedure as a whole, analysing whether this has prevented the Member State from effectively making known its point of view on the situation, and the pertinence of the facts, grievances, and circumstances alleged by the Commission.[144]

In practice As a general rule, the Commission services' consultations with the Member **22.84** State concerned are made in successive stages. First of all, the Member State reacts to the Commission's letter on the initiating of the procedure, addressed to the former and informing it of the measures in dispute.[145] At this point, the Commission often chooses to initiate the procedure as a means of requesting from the Member State certain information or documents it deems to be essential for carrying out its examination properly. The Member State then receives a copy of any third-party comments received by the Commission and is given the opportunity to make its own comments on these texts, doing so within a set time limit that does not normally exceed one month (Article 6(2) of the Procedural Regulation). The contacts made thereafter with the Member State vary according to the particular case. Meetings are frequently held between the Commission services and the State representatives to clarify their respective positions. The discussions between the Member State and the Commission are necessarily more thorough than those conducted with the interested parties in terms of such factors as the details of the aid plan, the economic, financial, and competitive situation of the beneficiary undertaking, and its internal operation.[146]

The Commission expects the Member State to take responsibility for its submissions made **22.85** during the procedure, since the final decision is based on these submissions, which, if they turn out to be incorrect, could throw the decision itself into doubt.

---

[140] Case T-198/01 *TGI v Commission* [2004] ECR II-2717, para 61. On this matter see Art 6(?) of the Procedural Regulation.

[141] Case T-176/01 *Ferriere Nord v Commission* [2004] ECR II-3931, para 74.

[142] Joined Cases T-228/99 and T-233/99 *WestLB and others v Commission* [2003] ECR II-435, para 121.

[143] Case 234/84 *Belgium v Commission* [1986] ECR 2263, para 30; Case 40/85 *Belgium v Commission* [1986] ECR 2321, para 30; Case 259/85 *France v Commission* [1987] ECR 4393, para 12; Case C-142/87 *Belgium v Commission* [1990] ECR I-959, paras 46 and 47; and Joined Cases C-106/09 P and C-107/09 P *Commission and Spain v Gibraltar and UK* [2011], para 165.

[144] Joined Cases T-228/99 and T-233/99 *WestLB and others v Commission* [2003] ECR II-435, para 150 et seq.

[145] Case T-323/99 *INMA and Itainvest v Commission* [2002] ECR II-545, para 91.

[146] Joined Cases T-371/94 and T-394/94 *British Airways and others v Commission* [1998] ECR II-2405, para 62.

Consultation with the parties concerned

22.86 When the procedure is initiated, the Commission is required to give notice to the parties concerned to present their comments.[147]

22.87 **The notion of 'parties concerned** 'The parties concerned represent an indeterminate group of persons to whom notice must be given.[148] This concept covers not only the undertaking(s) receiving aid,[149] but equally the persons, undertakings, or associations whose interests might be affected by the granting of the State aid concerned.[150] According to the GC, to be considered as a 'party concerned', it is necessary to be able to show a 'legitimate interest' in whether or not the aid measures in dispute are actually put into effect or maintained when they have already been agreed.[151]

22.88 Besides the recipients of the aid, the notion of 'parties concerned' covers the following:

- Competitor undertakings[152] and trade associations.[153] As regards undertakings, the GC has ruled in many judgments that any undertaking other than the aid beneficiary needs to show that its competitive position is affected by the granting of the aid before it can be considered as a party concerned.[154] In the case of an association, it is necessary in principle that it has been set up to promote the collective interest of its members and that at least some of the latter can themselves be considered to be parties concerned, or that it claims a specific legal interest in bringing proceedings because its negotiating position is affected by the contested decision.[155]
- Infra-State regional entities granting the aid.[156]
- Member States other than the State concerned.
- Workers' representative bodies of the aid-receiving undertaking, in so far as they are concerned parties within the meaning of Article 108(2) TFEU, may be entitled to present to the Commission their observations on matters of a social order that might, in the context, be taken into consideration by the latter.[157]
- The purchasers or suppliers of the aid-receiving undertaking.[158]
- Undertakings which are not direct competitors of the aid beneficiary, but which are active in an upstream or downstream market where their competitive position may be affected by the aid.[159]

---

[147] Joined Cases T-228/99 and T-233/99 *WestLB and others v Commission* [2003] ECR II-435, para 123.

[148] Case 323/82 *Intermills v Commission* [1984] ECR 3809, para 16 and Case T-189/97 *Comité d'entreprise de la Société française de production and others v Commission* [1998] ECR II-335, para 42.

[149] Joined Cases T-228/99 and T-233/99 [2003] ECR II-435 *WestLB and others v Commission* [2003] ECR II-435, para 122.

[150] Case T-41/01 *Rafael Pérez Escolar v Commission* [2003] ECR II-2157, para 34.

[151] Case T-41/01 *Rafael Pérez Escolar v Commission* [2003] ECR II-2157, para 35.

[152] Their legitimate interest consists in the safeguarding of their competitive position in the market (Case T-41/01 *Rafael Pérez Escolar v Commission* [2003] ECR II-2157, para 35).

[153] See Art 1(h) of the Procedural Regulation Case 323/82 *Intermills v Commission* [1984] ECR 3809, para 16; Case C-198/91 *Cook v Commission* [1993] ECR I-2487, paras 24–6; Case C-225/91 *Matra v Commission* [1993] ECR I-3203, para 18 ; and Case T-189/97 *Comité d'entreprise de la Société française de production and others v Commission* [1998] ECR II-335, para 42.

[154] Case T-188/95 *Waterleiding Maatschappij v Commission* [1998] ECR II-3713, para 62; and Case T-114/00 *ARE v Commission* [2002] ECR II-5121, para 51.

[155] Case T-114/00 *ARE v Commission* [2002] ECR II-5121, paras 53 and 65.

[156] Joined Cases T-228/99 and T-233/99 *WestLB and others v Commission* [2003] ECR II-435, para 122.

[157] Case T-189/97 *Comité d'entreprise de la Société française de production and others v Commission* [1998] ECR II-335, para 41.

[158] Opinion of AG Verloren van Themaat in Case 323/82 *Intermills v Commission* [1984] ECR I-3809, para 2.1.

[159] Case T-388/02 *Kronoply and Kronotex v Commission* [2008] ECR II-305, para 74; and Case C-83/09 P *Commission v Kronoply and Kronotex* [2011], paras 63–71.

Although the group of 'parties concerned' is indeterminate, this does not mean that it is **22.89**
infinite. Thus, according to the GC, it is not enough to have a purely general or indirect
interest.[160] In particular the notion of 'parties concerned' cannot be construed to mean that
any taxpayer is a party concerned within the meaning of Article 108(2) TFEU in relation to
aid financed through the general tax resources of a Member State.[161]

The notion of 'parties concerned' is ambiguous because it serves a twofold purpose: **22.90**

• it determines the persons who are entitled to take part in the formal examination procedure;
• it is used in the *Cook* and *Matra* case law for determining which persons are entitled to lodge
  an action for annulment against a Commission decision not to initiate the formal examination procedure, claiming an infringement of their procedural rights. Case law has shown this
  second question to be the most important because it involves the determination of whether a
  person is a party concerned.[162]

Consultations with the parties concerned aim only to obtain from them all the necessary **22.91**
information, so that the Commission can base its future decision on all relevant facts.[163]
The essential role of the parties concerned for the Commission is therefore one of 'sources
of information'.[164] It follows, therefore, that they can lay claim to no right to be heard in
the procedure, an entitlement recognized for persons against whom the procedure has been
initiated;[165] their only right is to be associated with the administrative procedure as far as is
necessary for the particular circumstances of the case in hand.[166] This latter right is respected
in so far as the concerned parties are able to put forward their arguments in presenting their
opinion in writing, in the supporting documents, and to discuss aspects of the case at meetings with representatives of the Commission, etc.[167]

According to the GC, the EU Court cannot, on the basis of general legal principles such **22.92**
as those of the right to due process, the right to be heard, sound administration, or equal

---

[160] Case T-41/01 *Rafael Pérez Escolar v Commission* [2003] ECR II-2157, para 36.
[161] Case T-188/95 *Waterleiding v Commission* [1998] ECR II-3713, para 68. In this respect, the situation
of a person who finances an aid-implementing parafiscal charge is without any doubt specific.
[162] Indeed, the GC quickly realized in applying the *Cook* judgment that using the concept of 'concerned
party' in its widest sense might well deprive of all legal sense the concept of 'person individually concerned'
within the meaning of the fourth subparagraph of Art 263 TFEU (Case T-398/94 *Kahn Scheepvaart v
Commission* [1996] ECR II-477, para 50 and Case T-188/95 *Waterleiding v Commission* [1998] ECR II-3713,
para 68). To avoid this danger, it diverged down two different paths. First, in an isolated judgment, *Kahn
Scheepvaart*, it purely and simply rejected *Cook* and considered that the simple fact of being a 'party concerned' in the sense of Art 108(2) TFEU was not enough to be individually concerned. Later, the GC moved
the goalposts again and instead of rejecting *Cook* interpreted the notion of 'concerned party' more restrictively
to bring it within subparagraph 4 of Art 263 TFEU (Case T-188/95 *Waterleiding v Commission* [1998] ECR
II-3713 and Case T-41/01 *Rafael Pérez Escolar v Commission* [2003] ECR II-2157, para 36).
[163] Case 70/72 *Commission v Germany* [1973] ECR 813, para 19; Joined Cases T-371/94 and T-394/94
British Airways and others v Commission [1998] ECR II-2405, para 59; and Case T-109/01 *Fleuren Compost v
Commission* [2004] ECR II-127, para 41.
[164] Case T-266/94 *Skibsværftsforeningen and others v Commission* [1996] ECR II-1399, para 256; Joined
Cases T-371/94 and T-394/94 *British Airways and others v Commission* [1998] ECR II-2405, para 59; Joined
Cases T-228/99 and T-233/99 *WestLB and others v Commission* [2003] ECR II-435, para 125; and Case
T-198/01 *TGI v Commission* [2004] ECR II-2717, para 192.
[165] Case T-176/01 *Ferriere Nord v Commission* [2004] ECR II-3931, para 74. In particular, they can claim
no right to debate the issues with the Commission (Case T-198/01 *TGI v Commission* [2004] ECR II-2717,
para 192).
[166] Joined Cases T-371/94 and T-394/94 *British Airways and others v Commission* [1998] ECR II-2405,
para 60; Joined Cases T-228/99 and T-233/99 *WestLB and others v Commission* [2003] ECR II-435, para 125;
and Case T-301/01 *Alitalia v Commission* [2008] ECR II-1753, paras 169–72.
[167] Joined Cases T-228/99 and T-233/99 *WestLB and others v Commission* [2003] ECR II-435, para 129
and Case T-354/99 *Kuwait Petroleum (Nederland) v Commission* [2006] ECR II-1475, paras 83–5.

treatment, extend the procedural rights conferred on interested parties in State aid review procedures by the Treaty and secondary legislation.[168] The Article 108(2) TFEU procedure is therefore an *inter partes* procedure only in relation to the Member State concerned and not in relation to the parties concerned.[169] Nonetheless, there is a certain tendency in some case law decisions to extend the right of an *inter partes* procedure in particular to the aid recipient.[170] The restricted nature of the concerned parties' rights impinges on the content of the information they have to be furnished with.[171] Finally, it should be noted that the restricted nature of the concerned parties' rights does not affect the Commission's duty of giving sufficient grounds for its final decision.[172]

22.93 **Status of the aid recipient** None of the provisions on the procedure for reviewing State aid reserves a special role, among the interested parties, for the aid recipient. Moreover, this procedure is not a procedure initiated 'against the aid recipient' that gives rise to rights on which it may rely and which are as extensive as the rights to a fair defence as such.[173]

22.94 **Status of the Member States other than the granter of the aid** The Member States other than the Member State concerned have no particular rights vis-à-vis the other concerned parties. They are therefore only entitled to put forward their comments. In particular, the Commission is not bound to pass on to them the observations it has received from the government of the Member State seeking authorization to grant the aid. The other Member States are therefore involved in a specific case of aid only where, in application of subparagraph three of Article 108(2) TFEU, that case has, at the request of the Member State concerned, been submitted to the Council.[174]

22.95 **Method of giving information to parties concerned** Article 108(2) TFEU does not require individual notice to be given to particular persons.[175] Its sole purpose is to oblige the Commission to take steps to ensure that all persons who may be concerned are notified and given an opportunity of putting forward their arguments. Under those circumstances, the publication of a notice in the OJ series C is an appropriate means of informing all the parties concerned that a procedure has been initiated.[176] Since the entry into force of the Procedural

---

[168] Case T-198/01 *TGI v Commission* [2004] ECR II-2717, para 194.

[169] Joined Cases T-228/99 and T-233/99 *WestLB and others v Commission* [2003] ECR II-435, para 168; Case T-109/01 *Fleuren Compost v Commission* [2004] ECR II-127, para 43 ; and Case T-198/01 *TGI v Commission* [2004] ECR II-2717, para 61.

[170] See Case T-198/01 R *TGI v Commission* [2002] ECR II-2153, para 85, in which the President of the GC obliged the Commission to pass on to the aid recipient a comment containing the specific observations it had expressly requested from a competitor in answer to the comments initially lodged by the aid recipient. On appeal, the President of the ECJ was somewhat loath to accept this approach, declaring that such a procedural obligation on the Commission was not contained either in the regulations or the case law (Case C-232/02 P(R) *Commission v TGI* [2002] ECR I-8977, para 76).

[171] See para 22.87.

[172] Joined Cases T-228/99 and T-233/99 *WestLB and others v Commission* [2003] ECR II-435, para 132. For more information on the obligation to give the grounds for decisions, see para 22.116.

[173] Case T-109/01 *Fleuren Compost v Commission* [2004] ECR II-127, para 44 and Case T-198/01 *TGI v Commission* [2004] ECR II-2717, para 193.

[174] Joined Cases T-371/94 and T-394/94 *British Airways and others v Commission* [1998] ECR II-2405, para 76. For more information on Council intervention, see Ch 21, 'General Questions on Procedure. Control of State Aid Compatibility. Council's Decision-Making Power', para 21.100.

[175] A beneficiary of an aid measure may not plead infringement of the principle of sound administration on the ground that the Commission did not specifically solicit its comments regarding the aid investigation procedure (Case T-354/99 *Kuwait Petroleum v Commission* [2006] ECR II-1475, para 82).

[176] Case 323/82 *Intermills v Commission* [1984] ECR 3809, para 17; Joined Cases T-371/94 and T-394/94 *British Airways and others v Commission* [1998] ECR II-2405, para 59; Joined Cases T-228/99 and T-233/99 *WestLB and others v Commission* [2003] ECR II-435, para 124; and Case T-109/01 *Fleuren Compost v Commission* [2004] ECR II-127, para 41.

Regulation, only a summary of the procedure initiated is published in all EU languages, with the entire text being made available in the authentic language version.[177] Under no circumstances may the Commission be held liable for any omission by the Member State concerned in notifying the aid recipient of the letter communicating the initiation of the procedure.[178]

Information to be communicated to the parties concerned[179]

The content of the information to be included in the decision to initiate the formal inves-   **22.96**
tigation procedure should be determined on a case-by-case basis. The information given to the parties concerned should in the first place be sufficient to allow them to realize that they are involved in the enquiry as addressees or as competitors of the addressees.[180] It should then allow them to effectively put forward their arguments on the aspects about which the Commission entertains doubts. The notice does not, therefore, have to mention matters about which the Commission entertains no doubts.[181] On the other hand, if the Commission intends to base its decision on new principles or assessment criteria, not mentioned in the initiation decision, it should ask the concerned parties for their observations on this matter.[182] It suffices for the concerned parties to know the grounds that have led the Commission to consider provisionally that the measure in question constitutes new aid that is incompatible with the internal market.[183]

According to the case law, there may be two reasons for restricting the extent of the concerned   **22.97**
parties' right to be given information during this procedure:

- On the one hand, after having carried out a thorough discussion with the Member State concerned, the Commission is entitled to limit its notice in the OJ to the points of the aid plan that it still entertains doubts about.
- On the other, the Commission is bound under Article 339 TFEU not to furnish concerned parties with information of the kind covered by the obligation of professional secrecy.[184] To meet this obligation, the Commission asks the Member State concerned to inform it, by way of a reasoned request, which information in the letter communicating the initiation decision it considers to be confidential, doing so within fifteen days of receiving the said

---

[177] See Art 26(2) of the Procedural Regulation. The Commission is entitled to send the decision to open the formal investigation to identified third parties (Case T-198/01 *TGI v Commission* [2004] ECR II-2717, para 195; Joined Cases C-74/00 P and C-75/00 P *Falck Spa and others v Commission* [2002] ECR I-7869, para 83). In the Best Practice Code, the Commission announces that its services may send a copy of the decision to initiate the formal investigation procedure to identified interested parties, including trade or business associations, and invite them to comment on specific aspects of the case. Interested parties' cooperation in this context is purely voluntary. In order to ensure equal treatment between interested parties the Commission will send the same invitation to comment to the aid beneficiary (para 34).

[178] Case T-109/01 *Fleuren Compost v Commission* [2004] ECR II-127, para 47.

[179] See Art 6(1) of the Procedural Regulation.

[180] Case 323/82 *Intermills v Commission* [1984] ECR 3809, para 18.

[181] This incomplete character of the communication does not however prevent the concerned parties from arguing before the EU Court that the Commission's final decision is insufficiently reasoned or contains manifest errors of assessment or law in regard to these matters, even if they have not been mentioned in the communication (Joined Cases T-371/94 and T-394/94 *British Airways and others v Commission* [1998] ECR II-2405, paras 66 and 67).

[182] Case T-176/01 *Ferriere Nord v Commission* [2004] ECR II-3931, paras 75 and 80.

[183] Joined Cases T-269/99, T-271/99, and T-272/99 *Territorio Histórico de Guipúzcoa and others v Commission* [2002] ECR II-4217, para 105 and Joined Cases T-346/99, T-347/99, and T-348/99 *Territorio Histórico de Álava and others v Commission* [2002] ECR II-4259, para 100.

[184] Joined Cases T-371/94 and T-394/94 *British Airways and others v Commission* [1998] ECR II-2405, paras 61–3. See also Art 24 of the Procedural Regulation.

letter, so that this confidential information can then be omitted from the publication in the OJ.[185]

22.98 The sufficient character of the information contained in the notice of initiation should also be assessed in the light of the Member State's degree of cooperation with the Commission. Thus the aid recipient cannot criticize the Commission for the vague and imprecise character of the information contained in the notice of the initiation of the procedure, if this is the result of the national authorities' failure to furnish the Commission with the information asked for; moreover, as the aid recipient itself, it can hardly have been unaware of the State aid it has received over previous years.[186]

22.99 The information communicated does not need to be limited to a simple description of the measure. The Commission is fully entitled to make known its reservations about the plan that has come to its attention, so as to notify all the parties concerned of its initial reaction and thus permit the undertakings concerned to ensure that their interests are defended.[187] The information, however, can have no other effect than to make known the initiation of the formal examination procedure[188] and not to give any definitive ruling on certain elements of the file before the adoption of the final decision.[189] In so far as the Commission is not under an obligation to conduct an exchange of views and arguments with the complainants, it is not required to indicate to them the legal basis on which it intends to base its decision.[190]

Access to documents

22.100 The Procedural Regulation and, in particular, Article 20 thereof, do not lay down any right of access to documents in the Commission's administrative file for interested parties in the context of the review procedure opened in accordance with Article 108(2) TFEU. If those interested parties were able to obtain access, on the basis of Regulation 1049/2001,[191] to the documents in the Commission's administrative file, the system for the review of State aid would be called into question. Therefore, for the purposes of interpreting the exception laid down in Article 4(2), third indent, of Regulation 1049/2001, based on protection of the purposes of inspections, investigations, and audits, there exists a general presumption that disclosure of documents in the administrative file in principle undermines the protection of the objectives of investigation activities. That general presumption does not exclude the right of those interested parties to demonstrate that a given document, disclosure of which has been requested, is not covered by that presumption, or that there is a higher public interest

---

[185] If the Commission does not receive any reasoned request before the deadline, it considers the Member State to be in agreement with the publication of the notice of initiation in its entirety.

[186] Joined Cases T-126/96 and T-127/96 *Breda Fucine Meridionali and others v Commission* [1998] ECR II-3437, paras 48–53.

[187] Case 323/82 *Intermills v Commission* [1984] ECR 3809, para 21.

[188] Case 323/82 *Intermills v Commission* [1984] ECR 3809, para 21.

[189] Case T-87/09 *Jørgen Andersen v Commission*, para 55. However, nothing prevents the Commission from adopting in one single act a decision to initiate the procedure against certain elements of aid *and* a decision not to raise objections with regard to other measures in favour of the same recipient(s).

[190] Case T-95/03 *Asociación de Estaciones de Servicio de Madrid and Federación Catalana de Estaciones de Servicio v Commission* [2006] ECR II-4739, para 140.

[191] European Parliament and Council Regulation (EC) No 1049/2001 of 30 May 2001 regarding public access to European Parliament, Council and Commission documents [2001] OJ L145/43. This Regulation is designed to confer on the public as wide a right of access as possible to documents of the institutions. That right of access is nevertheless subject to certain limits based on reasons of public or private interest. It is, in principle, open to the EU institution to base its decisions in that regard on general presumptions which apply to certain categories of documents.

justifying the disclosure of the document concerned by virtue of Article 4(2) of Regulation 1049/2001.[192]

Processing the information received: the time limit for presenting observations

The Commission sets a time limit, usually one month, within which the parties concerned **22.101** can make their observations; this time period usually runs from the date of publication of the initiation of the procedure in the OJ.[193] It enforces this deadline fairly strictly,[194] and seems to consider that it is not authorized to take into consideration any information that is submitted late.[195] The Commission does not violate the principle of legitimate expectations, nor that of sound administration in refusing to take into account unsolicited supplementary information sent by a third party after the deadline provided.[196]

The Commission is bound to take due consideration of the information received and give **22.102** grounds for its decision accordingly. The absence of such observations, however, does not prohibit it from concluding that the aid is incompatible. Moreover, the Commission cannot be held to blame for not having taken into consideration any issues of fact or law that could have been but were not in fact presented during the administrative procedure, since the Commission is not bound to examine *ex officio* and on the basis of supposition the information that might have been submitted.[197]

When the Commission draws up its decisions, it is not in principle either obliged to turn **22.103** to external experts[198] or prohibited from doing so,[199] but it is not exempted from assessing their work.[200] The Commission is not obliged to hear the views of third parties on the expert report.[201]

Deadline for the formal examination procedure

Before the entry into force of the Procedural Regulation, the Commission was not bound **22.104** to adopt its final decision within a given deadline, whether minimum or maximum; no text stated that State aid decisions adopted under Article 108(2) TFEU had to adhere to a fixed deadline.[202] According to the ECJ, when the Commission decided to initiate a procedure

---

[192] Case 139/07 P *Commission v Technische Glaswerke Ilmenau* [2010] ECR I-5885, paras 51–62. The general presumption covers internal Commission documents (Joined Cases T-494/08 to T-500/08 and T-509/08 *Ryanair v Commission* [2010] ECR II-5723, para 74). See also Joined Cases T-109/05 and T-444/05 *Navigazione Libera del Golfo v Commission* [2011] ECR II-2479 concerning the application, after the adoption of the final decision, of the exception laid down in Art 4(2), first indent, of Reg 1049/2001, based on commercial interests of a natural or legal person.
[193] Article 6(1) of the Procedural Regulation.
[194] In the Best Practice Code the Commission indicates that this deadline will in general not be extended (para 33).
[195] Case C-290/07 P *Commission v Scott* [2010] ECR I-7763, para 95.
[196] Joined Cases T-230/01 and T-267/01–T-269/01 *Diputación Foral de Álava and Others v Commission* [2009] ECR II-139, paras 273–9.
[197] Case T-109/01 *Fleuren Compost v Commission* [2004] ECR II-127, paras 48–9.
[198] Joined Cases T-371/94 and T-394/94 *British Airways and others v Commission* [1998] ECR II-2405, para 72.
[199] Case T-106/95 *FFSA and others v Commission* [1997] ECR II-229, para 102.
[200] Case T-274/01 *Valmont v Commission* [2004] ECR II-3145, para 72 and Case T-369/06 *Holland Malt v Commission* [2009] ECR II-3313, para 112.
[201] Case T-301/01 *Alitalia v Commission* [2008] ECR II-1753, para 175.
[202] Joined Cases T-371/94 and T-394/94 *British Airways and others v Commission* [1998] ECR II-2405, para 71 (in this case the Commission had been criticized for taking its decision too quickly given the complexity of the disputed aid plan. The GC rejected this argument, without ruling out the possibility that any undue haste by the Commission might involve a breach of specific procedural rules or the duty to give reasons, or of the internal legality of the disputed decision).

under Article 108 TFEU, it then had a reasonable time limit to see this procedure through.[203] The specification of this reasonable time limit depended on the particular case in question. If the Commission took too long to give its decision and indefinitely thwarting the action of the Member State concerned, an action for failure to comply with its obligations could not be ruled out. For its part, the Commission endeavoured to end the procedure within six months.[204]

22.105 Currently, the Procedural Regulation suggests a time limit of eighteen months, extendable by common agreement.[205] This is not a mandatory time limit.[206] When this time limit has run its course, the Member State in question can request the Commission to adopt a decision within a final time period of two months (Article 7(6) and (7)).[207]

22.106 The Commission is not bound to inform the Member State concerned that the adoption of a decision is imminent, for this would allow it to submit new information, a process that would be liable to create procedural delays preventing the Commission from closing the administrative procedure under way.[208]

22.107 According to the case law, when the conditions justifying the initiation of the procedure are met, no alternative procedure can be pursued. It would therefore not suffice for the Commission to enter into consultations with the Member States in the form of bilateral meetings,[209] nor for it to engage in a simple *inter partes* dialogue with any complainant in the context of the preliminary phase laid down in Article 108(3) TFEU.[210]

E. Final Decision

22.108 At the end of the examination procedure, the Commission adopts in principle a final decision on the existence of aid and its compatibility or incompatibility with the internal market.

1. General considerations

Form and effect

22.109 The final decision is a decision as defined in subparagraph 4 of Article 288 TFEU, 'binding in its entirety on those to whom it is addressed',[211] namely, the Member State concerned. This means that the Member State has the obligation to abide by a negative decision, which corresponds in essence to a ban on putting the aid into effect. A positive decision, on the other hand, constitutes a simple authorization that is in no way binding on the addressee State, which remains at liberty to decide in the end not to put the aid into effect.[212] The final decision adopted by the Commission also has direct effect.

Content

22.110 The Procedural Regulation provides for four types of final decisions (Article 7):

---

[203] Case 59/79 *Producteurs de vins de table and vins de pays v Commission* [1979] ECR 2425.
[204] See s 42 of the Guide to the Procedures Applicable to State aid (obsolete).
[205] See Art 7(6) of the Procedural Regulation.
[206] Case T-190/00 *Regione Siciliana v Commission* [2003] ECR II-5015, para 139 and Case T-176/01 *Ferriere Nord v Commission* [2004] ECR II-3931, para 69.
[207] Note that the Commission's proposal refrains from laying down a maximum time limit at the end of which it must adopt its final decision.
[208] Case T-198/01 *TGI v Commission* [2004] ECR II-2717, para 156.
[209] Case 84/82 *Germany v Commission* [1984] ECR 1451, para 18.
[210] Case C-367/95 P *Commission v Sytraval and others* [1998] ECR I-1719, para 59.
[211] Case 156/77 *Commission v Belgium* [1978] ECR 1881, para 18.
[212] See paras 38–9 of the Opinion in Case C-6/99 *Greenpeace France* [2000] ECR I-1651.

- The Commission can first of all decide that the measure in question 'does not constitute aid', ie that it does not meet all the conditions of Article 107(1) TFEU. Apart from the lack of any selective advantage involved in the measure, the Commission can also come to that decision on the grounds that the measure is not directly or indirectly funded by State resources, that it does not affect trade, or that it is not likely to impinge on competition. Moreover, nothing prevents the Commission from finally deciding that the measure in question in fact constitutes existing aid.[213]
- Secondly, the Commission can adopt a 'positive decision'.[214] The Procedural Regulation provides that the decision must mention which exception under the Treaty is being applied. This stands to reason, and, in fact, the Commission's obligations to give grounds go further than this essential point.[215]
- The Commission can also adopt a 'conditional decision'. The Regulation expressly provides that the Commission is entitled to subject its decision on the compatibility of aid to certain conditions. It certainly does not give any precise idea of the nature of these 'conditions' that can be imposed by the Commission. The Commission sometimes seeks to obtain any concession under the form of voluntary 'commitments' by the Member State if it is unable to impose it as a condition.
- The Commission can finally adopt a 'negative decision' declaring the aid to be incompatible and impossible to grant.

The Commission may alter the assessment made in the decision to initiate the procedure.[216] On the contrary, it must be careful not to adopt decisions that lie beyond the powers conferred upon it, for example by requiring a State to extend its aid to other recipients.[217] **22.111**

The question whether aid is State aid within the meaning of the Treaty must be determined **22.112** on the basis of objective elements, which must be appraised on the date on which the Commission takes its decision. Accordingly, it is the appraisal of the situation carried out by the Commission on that date which is to be reviewed by the EU Courts. In addition, the rules, principles, and criteria of assessment of the compatibility of State aid in force at the date on which the Commission takes its decision may, as a rule, be regarded as better adapted to the context of competition.[218]

Withdrawal

If a Member State decides not to grant the aid under examination and withdraws its notifica- **22.113** tion (or, in the case of unlawful aid, if the State recovers the whole sum on its own initiative), the Commission adopts a non-objection decision recording the withdrawal of the notification or the disappearance of the aid.[219] Article 8 of the Procedural Regulation formally authorizes Member States to withdraw a notification before the Commission has adopted a decision. The Commission's competence is in effect always linked either to the existence of unlawfully granted aid or a notification made in the correct form. Notification of withdrawal usually occurs because the Member State concerned decides not to grant the notified aid, either due to difficulties

---

[213] Case T-190/00 *Regione Siciliana v Commission* [2003] ECR II-5015, para 48.

[214] These are decisions that were previously adopted in the form of a simple letter.

[215] See para 22.116.

[216] Case T-190/00 *Regione Siciliana v Commission* [2003] ECR II-5015, para 51.

[217] Case T-107/96 *Pantochim v Commission* [1998] ECR II-311, para 52. On the other hand, it is entitled to take note of the transformation of aid into a general measure in view of its extension to all potential recipients.

[218] Case C-334/07 P *Commission v Freistaat Sachsen* [2008] ECR I-9465, paras 50–1.

[219] It would seem that the Commission, acting prudently, sometimes makes sure that the aid plan has actually been revoked under the national procedures before closing the examination procedure.

encountered with the Commission or for independent reasons. There is, however, a risk of this withdrawal procedure being used illegally by Member States.[220]

Information

22.114 As soon as the decision has been taken, the Commission's Secretariat-General informs the Permanent Representation of the Member State concerned of the decision in a brief letter, which precedes the sending of the full text of the decision.[221] On the other hand, the Commission is not required to inform the Member State concerned of its position before adopting its decision.[222]

22.115 Moreover, Article 20(1) of the Procedural Regulation provides that any interested party that has submitted comments during the formal examination procedure and any beneficiary of individual aid shall be sent a copy of the final decision.

Reasons for the decision

22.116 The decision is subject to Article 296 TFEU. The requirement to give reasoned decisions implies that the Commission should state the essential considerations upon which its decision is based.[223] The requirements to be satisfied by the statement of reasons depend in particular on the need for information of the undertakings to whom the measure is addressed or of other parties to whom it is of direct and individual concern within the meaning of Article 263 TFEU,[224] in particular when they have played an active role in the procedure prior to the adoption of the contested measure and knew the reasons of fact and law which led the Commission to take its decision.[225] The requirement to provide reasons for a decision taken in regard to State aid thus cannot be determined solely on the basis of the interest which the addressee Member State may have in obtaining information.[226] A final aid-authorizing decision must contain sufficient reasons that address all the essential complaints which parties directly and individually concerned by that decision have made either on their own initiative or as a result of information supplied by the Commission. Thus, even on the assumption that the Commission may, in a particular case, validly prefer to use other sources of information and thereby reduce the significance of the participation of interested parties, it is not thereby released from its obligation to include an adequate statement of reasons in its decision.[227]

22.117 However, the Commission's duty to give reasons for its decisions in rejecting an argument brought by a concerned party during the administrative procedure cannot be understood to

---

[220] When the Commission opens the formal examination procedure on an aid plan, for example, it has sometimes happened in the past that the Member State withdraws its notification and simultaneously notifies an amended plan within the meaning required by the Commission. Such a manoeuvre deprives the aid approval procedure of all transparency, for the positive decision is then a decision 'not to raise objections' which is only subject to an extremely summary publication, whereas the formal examination procedure is closed by a simple letter of termination; the parties concerned do not even realize that the aid plan has been withdrawn with one hand, only to be reintroduced with another.

[221] See Art 26(3) of the Procedural Regulation. The Member State has the opportunity to indicate the information which it considers to be covered by the obligation of professional secrecy, and that should thus be omitted from the text of the decision before it is sent to the other parties or published.

[222] Joined Case T-198/01 *TGI v Commission* [2004] ECR II-2717, para 198.

[223] Joined Cases T-228/99 and T-233/99 *WestLB and others v Commission* [2003] ECR II-435, para 402.

[224] Joined Cases 296/82 and 318/82 *Netherlands and Leeuwarder Papierwarenfabriek v Commission* [1985] ECR 809, para 19 and Joined Cases T-371/94 and T-394/94 *British Airways and others v Commission* [1998] ECR II-2405, para 90.

[225] Joined Cases T-132/96 and T-143/96 *Freistaat Sachsen and others v Commission* [1999] ECR II-3663, para 268.

[226] Joined Cases T-371/94 and T-394/94 *British Airways and others v Commission* [1998] ECR II-2405, para 92.

[227] Joined Cases T-371/94 and T-394/94 *British Airways and others v Commission* [1998] ECR II-2405, paras 64 and 96.

be as extensive as its requirement to give reasons to the addressee Member State whose arguments it has rejected.[228]

The obligation to give grounds may be less in certain cases. First, the requirement to give **22.118** reasons for a final decision has to be weighed up not only in terms of its wording but also its context and the whole set of legal rules governing the issue concerned. Any former decisions should therefore be taken into account, as well as the content of the notification of the formal initiation of the examination procedure.[229] Secondly, the Commission is not bound to respond to all issues of law or fact raised by the concerned parties, as long as it gives due consideration to all the relevant factors and circumstances of the particular case.[230] Lastly, the reasons for a decision must appear in the actual body of the decision and, save in exceptional circumstances, explanations given *ex post facto* cannot be taken into account; it follows that the decision must be self-sufficient and that the reasons on which it is based may not be stated in written or oral explanations given subsequently when the decision in question is already the subject of proceedings brought before the EU judicature.[231]

Publication

The final decisions adopted by the Commission are published in the OJ[232] series L.[233] In the case **22.119** of individual decisions, pursuant to Article 297(2) TFEU, the publication of final decisions is not a *sine qua non* of their entry into force. They come into force upon receipt by the addressee.

Confidential information

The Commission can exclude from publication in the OJ such information as it deems to be **22.120** covered by the obligation of professional secrecy, pursuant to Article 339 TFEU.[234] A defect in form as regards the giving of reasons vis-à-vis the addressee cannot, therefore, be justified by the obligation laid down in Article 339 TFEU to safeguard professional secrecy, and especially the commercial secrecy of the undertaking concerned.

Revocation of decisions

A formal procedure for revoking Commission decisions is laid down in Article 9 of the **22.121** Procedural Regulation. This allows the Commission to 'revoke' a decision not to raise objections or a final positive or conditional decision when this decision was based on incorrect information furnished during the procedure, and this inaccuracy had a significant effect on the decision handed down. The Commission is bound to open a formal examination procedure before adopting a new final decision. The Commission's right to revoke a decision is not restricted solely to the situation referred to in Article 9 of the Procedural Regulation, since such a withdrawal may always be carried out provided that the institution which adopted the act complies with the conditions relating to reasonable time limits and the legitimate expectations of beneficiaries of the act who have been entitled to rely on its lawfulness.[235]

---

[228] Case T-198/01 *TGI v Commission* [2004] ECR II-2717, para 64.

[229] Case C-56/93 *Belgium v Commission* [1996] ECR I-723, para 86; and Case T-238/09 *Sniace v Commission* [2011], para 81.

[230] Joined Cases T-132/96 and T-143/96 *Freistaat Sachsen and others v Commission* [1999] ECR II-3663, para 268.

[231] Case T-349/03 *Corsica Ferries France v Commission* [2005] ECR II-2197, para 287.

[232] See Art 26(3) of the Procedural Regulation.

[233] Formerly, the positive decisions were adopted in the form of simple letters of termination addressed to the Member State and published in the OJ series C.

[234] Joined Cases 296/82 and 318/82 *Netherlands and Leeuwarder Papierwarenfabriek v Commission* [1985] ECR 809, para 28.

[235] Case T-25/04 *González y Díez v Commission* [2007] ECR II-3121, para 97; and Joined Cases T-267/08 and T-279/08 *Région Nord-Pas de Calais v Commission* [2011], paras 189–90.

2. Decision ruling out the existence of aid

22.122   A final decision may first conclude that the notified measure does not constitute aid within the meaning of Article 107 TFEU, the Commission hence finding that there is no State aid involved in the case. Decisions concluding that Article 107(1) TFEU does not apply to a notified measure may, for example, be based on the finding that the measure affords no advantage to the undertaking concerned, because it is justifiable on the basis of the market-economy private-investor principle.

3. Positive final decision

22.123   The Commission:

- either adopts a decision that rules definitively and positively on the compatibility of the aid with the internal market. In principle, the aid can then be granted; or
- could also conclude that the measure constitutes an individual application of an existing scheme.

4. Conditional final decision

Conditional authorization

22.124   The Commission may declare the aid to be compatible while making this decision dependent on certain conditions or reservations that are added to the notification arrangements and the commitments agreed to by the Member State.[236] The usefulness of such conditions is that, if the recipient undertaking were to fail to observe the authorization conditions, it would be for the Member State to make sure that the decision was properly carried out and, failing that, for the Commission to assess whether it was appropriate to demand that the aid be repaid.[237] If the Member State fails to enforce the Commission's aid-approval conditions, the Commission is also entitled under the second subparagraph of Article 108(2) TFEU, in derogation from the provisions of Articles 258 and 259 TFEU, to refer the matter directly to the ECJ.[238]

22.125   In an action for annulment, a mere statement that one of the conditions on which a decision authorising the grant of aid was based will not be complied with cannot cast doubt on the legality of the decision.[239] Only those complaints alleging that the conditions of authorization were inherently and manifestly inappropriate, and, in particular, legally inadequate in scope, may be capable of justifying the annulment of the contested decision.[240]

5. (Partially) negative final decision

22.126   In a negative final decision the Commission declares the aid under examination to be totally or partially incompatible with the internal market. In this case, the Member State cannot

---

[236] For examples of the possibility of the Commission's making its decision subject to conditions or reservations, see in particular Joined Cases T-244/93 and T-486/93 *TWD v Commission* [1995] ECR II-2265, para 55; Joined Cases T-371/94 and T-394/94 *British Airways and others v Commission* [1998] ECR II-2405, para 288; and Case C-321/99 P *ARAP and others v Commission* [2002] ECR I-4287, para 72.

[237] Case T-380/94 *AIUFFASS and AKT v Commission* [1996] ECR II-2169, para 128 and Joined Cases T-371/94 and T-394/94 *British Airways and others v Commission* [1998] ECR II-2405, para 290.

[238] Case C-294/90 *British Aerospace and Rover v Commission* [1994] ECR I-5423, para 11 and Joined Cases T-371/94 and T-394/94 *British Airways and others v Commission* [1998] ECR II-2405, paras 290 and 348.

[239] Case T-380/94 *AIUFFASS and AKT v Commission* [1996] ECR II-2169, para 128 and Joined Cases T-371/94 and T-394/94 *British Airways and others v Commission* [1998] ECR II-2405, para 291.

[240] Joined Cases T-371/94 and T-394/94 *British Airways and others v Commission* [1998] ECR II-2405, para 293.

put part or all of the aid into effect. An example of partially incompatible aid is where aid is declared to be incompatible only once its intensity exceeds a maximum allowable threshold.

6. Implementation of final decision

In principle, the execution of final decisions on aid not yet granted raises no particular prob- **22.127** lem, the Member State being bound simply not to put the planned measures into effect. For this reason, the principles governing the execution of negative final decisions are examined exclusively in Chapter 23 on unlawful aid, which is more problematic from this point of view.

The remedies to hand in the event of any breach of a Commission decision are dealt with in **22.128** Chapter 25.

23

UNLAWFUL AID

Jean Paul Keppenne and Carlos Urraca Caviedes

I. General Matters

Aid is considered to be unlawful (or unlawfully granted) when it is put into effect without **23.01** first having been notified to the Commission, or when it has been notified but then put into effect before the Commission has made a decision within the given time limit.[1] Its

---

[1] The prohibition laid down by Art 108(3) TFEU is designed to ensure that an aid scheme cannot become operational before the Commission has had a reasonable period in which to study the proposed measures in detail and, if necessary, to initiate the procedure provided for in Art 108(2) TFEU (Case C-301/87 *France v Commission ('Boussac Saint Frères')* [1990] ECR I-307, para 17 and Case C-199/06 *CELF and Ministre de la Culture et de la Communication* [2008] ECR I-469, para 36).

unlawfulness derives from an infringement of the last sentence of Article 108(3) of the Treaty on the Functioning of the European Union ('TFEU').

23.02 The existence of unlawful aid represents a 'pathological' situation in relation to the procedure laid down by the Treaty, thus explaining why it is not dealt with as such therein. The particular features of the unlawful aid control procedure have therefore had to be established on the basis of the Commission's practice, the case law of the Court of Justice ('ECJ'), and the Council's Procedural Regulation.[2] The general principle is one of parallelism with the review of notified aid, unless otherwise specified. Thus, the notion of existing aid serves to determine whether or not it is a case of unlawful aid. As for the procedure to be followed by the Commission in controlling unlawful aid, it also ensues from the stages laid down for the notified aid review procedure, namely the preliminary examination procedure and, if need be, the formal procedure, leading in principle to the adoption of a final decision. Three different principles, examined later, nonetheless characterize the unlawful aid control procedure: the *Lorenz* two-month time limit does not apply; the Commission can use its powers to impose injunctions; finally, if the aid is declared to be incompatible, the Commission has to demand its recovery.

23.03 It is possible for initially notified aid to become subsequently unlawful if the Member State puts it into effect without waiting for the Commission's final decision. This means that the rules for dealing with notified aid, laid down in Chapter II of the Procedural Regulation, may immediately become those of Chapter III, on unlawful aid, for dealing with the measure in question.

A. Consequences of the Unlawful Implementation of Aid

1. Direct effect of the final sentence of Article 108(3) TFEU

23.04 The status of unlawfully granted aid is challengeable. The prohibition laid down in the final sentence of Article 108(3) TFEU, which is formulated 'in unequivocal terms'[3] has direct effect; this means that the infringement can be brought before a national court.[4]

2. Obligation to examine the compatibility of unlawful aid

23.05 Some jurists originally argued that, in the event of the unlawful granting of aid, the Commission should prosecute the infringing Member State under Article 258 TFEU to obtain the annulment of the national measure, and hence could no longer follow the Article 108 TFEU procedure.[5] The ECJ did not reach the same conclusion. On the contrary, it established a strict separation between the unlawfulness of the aid, arising from a breach of the procedural obligation of the final sentence of Article 108(3) TFEU, and the incompatibility of the aid with the internal market, pursuant to Article 107 TFEU. It deduced from this that the Commission is not entitled to prohibit the aid for irregularities of form, since this aid could turn out to be compatible with the internal market.[6] The irregularity arising from the implementation of the aid before the end of the procedure laid down in Article 108(3) TFEU renders the aid in question unlawful, but does not make the examination of its compatibility superfluous,[7] which is always the responsibility of the Commission.[8]

---

[2] Council Regulation (EC) 659/1999 of 22 March 1999, laying down detailed rules for the application of Article 93 of the EC Treaty [1999] OJ L83/1.

[3] Case 171/83 R *Commission v France* [1983] ECR 2621, para 11.

[4] This question is examined more in detail in Ch 26, 'Role of National Courts'.

[5] See the Opinion of AG Warner in Case 173/73 *Italy v Commission* [1974] ECR 709.

[6] Case C-301/87 *France v Commission* [1990] ECR I-307.

[7] Case C-142/87 *Belgium v Commission* [1990] ECR I-959, para 20 and Case C-91/01 *Italy v Commission* [2004] ECR I-4355, para 44.

[8] Case C-409/00 *Spain v Commission* [2003] ECR I-1487, para 94.

3. Obligation to deal with complaints of unlawful aid

According to Article 10(1) of the Procedural Regulation, where the Commission has in its **23.06** possession information from any source regarding alleged unlawful aid, it must examine that information immediately.[9] Since the Commission has exclusive competence for pronouncing on the compatibility of aid, it is bound to conduct a diligent and impartial examination of all complaints received[10] (which may make it necessary for it to examine matters not expressly raised by the complainant[11]), otherwise it would run the risk of an action for failure to comply with its obligations being lodged against it.[12] Unlike the competition rules laid down in Articles 101 TFEU and 102 TFEU, in relation to which the lodging of a complaint is regulated by Regulations 1/2003 and 773/2004, in the case of State aid no specific formal requirement attaches to the lodging of a complaint. As the use of the standard form[13] is not required by any rule of EU law, it cannot be set up as a condition of 'admissibility' for lodging a complaint concerning State aid.[14]

Article 10(1) and the first sentence of Article 20(2) of the Procedural Regulation grant to a **23.07** person concerned the right to set in motion the preliminary examination stage provided for in Article 108(3) TFEU, by sending information regarding any allegedly unlawful aid to the Commission, which it is then obliged to examine, without delay, for the possible existence of aid and its compatibility with the internal market. Where the Commission informs the interested parties that there are insufficient grounds for taking a view on the case, it is required to allow the interested parties to submit additional comments within a reasonable period. Once those comments have been lodged, or the reasonable period has expired, Article 13(1) of the Procedural Regulation obliges the Commission to close the preliminary examination stage by adopting a decision stating that aid does not exist, raising no objections, or initiating the formal investigation procedure. The Commission is not, therefore, authorized to persist in its failure to act during the preliminary examination stage.[15] Once that stage in the procedure has been completed, it is bound either to initiate the next stage of the examination procedure, or to adopt a definitive decision to take no further action, and, where the Commission takes such a decision on the basis of information supplied by an interested party, it must send that party a copy of the decision.[16]

---

[9] See Case T-351/02 *Deutsche Bahn v Commission* [2006] ECR II-1047, paras 40–1.

[10] Joined Cases T-30/01 to T-32/01 and T-86/02 to T-88/02 *Territorio Histórico de Álava v Commission* [2009] ECR II-2919, para 260.

[11] Case C-367/95 P *Commission v Sytraval and Brink's France* [1998] ECR I-1719, para 62.

[12] Case T-95/96 *Gestevisión Telecinco v Commission* [1998] ECR II-3407, paras 57–70, and Case T-17/96 *TF1 v Commission* [1999] ECR II-1757, paras 26–36.

[13] In 2008, the Commission published on the Internet a standard form for submitting complaints, which indicates the information needed by the Commission to examine a complaint.

[14] Case T-442/07 *Ryanair v Commission* [2011], paras 33–4. However, on 13 July 2012, the Commission invited comments on the application of procedural rules in State aid investigations and in particular with regard to the handling of complaints, with a view to proposing a revised Procedural Regulation (see Commission Press Release IP/12/783 'State aid: Commission consults on reform of procedures' of 13 July 2012).

[15] The Commission is not required, however, to define its position on matters which are manifestly irrelevant or insignificant, or plainly of secondary importance (Case C-367/95 P *Commission v Sytraval* [1998] ECR I-1719, paras 62 and 64).

[16] Case C-521/06 P *Athinaïki Techniki v Commission* [2008] ECR I-5829, paras 37–40 and Case C-362/09 P *Athinaïki Techniki v Commission* [2010] ECR I-13275, para 63. If the Commission were entitled to withdraw a decision to take no further action on a complaint regarding alleged unlawful aid, it could perpetuate a state of inaction during the preliminary examination stage, contrary to its obligations under Arts 13(1) and 20(2) of the Procedural Regulation, and avoid any judicial review. The Commission may only withdraw such a decision in order to remedy illegality affecting that decision and cannot, after such withdrawal, pick up the procedure again at a stage earlier than the exact point at which the illegality found had occurred (*Athinaïki Techniki v Commission* [2010], paras 68–70). For a decision of the European Ombudsman on a complaint alleging maladministration by the Commission in its handling of a complaint, see 'Decision of the European Ombudsman closing his inquiry into complaint 1708/2011/JF against the European Commission', 14 February 2013.

B. Examination Procedures for Unlawful Aid

1. Preliminary examination procedure

23.08 The Commission has first of all to come to a preliminary opinion on the compatibility of the measure, on the basis of which it then adopts either a decision not to raise objections (as aid does not exist or is compatible) or a decision to initiate the formal examination procedure. In the case of unlawful aid, which it may learn of in various ways (late notification, a complaint, the press, etc), the two-month time limit is not applicable.[17] Silence by the Commission of more than two months does not therefore have the effect of giving the unlawful aid the status of existing aid,[18] and does not prevent the Commission from initiating a formal examination procedure as regards this aid.[19]

Action within a reasonable time period

23.09 The Commission is nonetheless bound to carry out its investigation with all due diligence,[20] in particular when dealing with complaints,[21] otherwise it again runs the risk of being appealed against for failure to act. The fundamental requirement of legal certainty in itself demands that the Commission should not be allowed to drag out the exercising of its powers indefinitely.[22] The question of whether or not the conduct of the procedure is characterized by excessive delay or lack of due diligence most certainly has to be ascertained, not in terms of the time elapsed since the unlawful aid was granted, but rather the date on which the Commission became aware that the aid had been granted. From that moment on the Commission is bound, under Article 10 of the Procedural Regulation, to examine the information in its possession 'without delay'.[23] The Commission is entitled to give differing degrees of priority to the complaints brought before it.[24]

---

[17] Case C-39/94 *SFEI and others* [1996] ECR I-3547, paras 46–8 and Case T-95/96 *Gestevisión Telecinco v Commission* [1998] ECR II-3407, paras 77–8, and Art 13(2) of the Procedural Regulation.

[18] Joined Cases T-30/01 to T-32/01 and T-86/02 to T-88/02 *Territorio Histórico de Álava v Commission* [2009] ECR 2919, para 153 and Joined Cases T-195/01 and T-207/01 *Government of Gibraltar v Commission* [2002] ECR II-2309, para 129. See also the Opinion of AG Slynn in Joined Cases 296 and 318/82 *Netherlands and Leeuwarder Papierwarenfabriek v Commission* [1985] ECR 809.

[19] See, in particular, Case C-305/89 *Italy v Commission* [1991] ECR I-1603, para 30.

[20] Joined Cases T-30/01 to T-32/01 and T-86/02 to T-88/02 *Territorio Histórico de Álava v Commission* [2009] ECR II-2919, para 260. According to AG Slynn, even in the case of unlawful aid, the Commission is not entitled to drag out the case indefinitely. He argued that, by analogy with the *Lorenz* decision in relation to notified aid (see Ch 22, 'Prior Control of New Notified Aid', para 22.51), the Commission must come to a preliminary conclusion with due diligence, in a time period that should not normally exceed two months (Opinion in Case 223/85 *RSV v Commission* [1987] ECR 4617).

[21] Joined Cases T-297/01 and T-298/01 *SIC v Commission* [2004] ECR II-743, para 56. According to the Code of Best Practice (see Ch 22, 'Prior Control of New Notified Aid', paras 22.44–22.45), the Commission will use its best endeavours to investigate a complaint within an indicative time frame of twelve months from its receipt (para 47). In the case of unsubstantiated complaints, the Commission services will inform the complainant within two months from receipt of the complaint that there are insufficient grounds for taking a view on the case, and that the complaint will be deemed to be withdrawn if further substantive comments are not provided within one month. As regards complaints which refer to approved aid, the Commission services will also endeavour to reply to the complainant within two months of receipt of the complaint (para 49).

[22] Case C-521/06 P *Athinaïki Techniki v Commission* [2008] ECR I-5829, para 40 and Case T-109/01 *Fleuren Compost v Commission* [2004] ECR II-127, para 145.

[23] The appropriate time limit for carrying out the examination of a complaint depends, *inter alia*, on the complexity of the case. Cases which are new and display a certain novelty may require more time in order to be investigated. In any case, the Commission should be able to prove that it did not remain inactive after receiving the complaint (Case T-395/04 *Air One v Commission* [2006] ECR II-1343, paras 63–7).

[24] Case T-475/04 *Bouygues and Bouygues Télécom v Commission* [2007] ECR II-2097 and Joined Cases T-30/01 to T-32/01 and T-86/02 to T-88/02 *Territorio Histórico de Álava—Diputación Foral de Álava and Others v Commission* [2009] ECR II-2919, para 274. See also para 48 of the Code of Best Practice.

Request for information

Article 10(2) of the Procedural Regulation provides that: **23.10**

> If necessary [the Commission] shall request information from the Member State concerned. Article 2(2) [State's obligation to provide all necessary information] and Article 5(1) and (2) [Commission's obligation to send a reminder to a State that fails to come up with the information first time], shall apply *mutatis mutandis*.

This provision imposes an immediate obligation on the Member State concerned to provide all necessary information following a request from the Commission. This is a particular application of the general obligation of loyal cooperation laid down in Article 4(3) of the Treaty on European Union ('TEU').[25]

In view of the legal consequences of a decision to initiate the procedure provided for in Article   **23.11**
108(2) TFEU, classifying the measures concerned as new aid, even though the Member State concerned is unlikely to subscribe to that classification, the Commission must first broach the subject of the measures in question with the Member State concerned so that the latter has an opportunity, if appropriate, to inform the Commission that, in its view, those measures do not constitute aid or else constitute existing aid.[26]

Information of third parties

The Commission is not under a duty to warn potentially interested persons, including the   **23.12**
beneficiary of the aid, of the measures it is taking in respect of unlawful aid before it initiates the formal examination procedure.

Voluntary recovery of unlawful aid

Should a Member State change its mind after having granted unlawful aid and then wishes   **23.13**
to prevent a formal decision thereon from the Commission, it has to prove that the aid, including any interest, has been totally recovered and that its effects no longer obtain. For the Commission to conclude that aid no longer exists after such a voluntary recovery procedure by the national authorities, it is necessary for the latter to furnish material proof of the effective recovery of the updated amount of the aid initially paid out. The updating has to cover the period running from the date of actual payment of the aid until its effective repayment.

2. Formal examination procedure

The procedure is similar to that used for notified aid. Since it is a case of unlawful aid, the   **23.14**
Commission's decision to initiate the formal examination procedure gives some indication of the precarious character of the aid and the consequences deriving therefrom.[27]

When the Commission has initiated the formal examination procedure in respect of an aid   **23.15**
scheme which has already been implemented, it cannot be required to extend that procedure when the Member State concerned modifies the scheme in question. If the opposite were the case, the State would in fact be able to draw out the procedure for as long as it pleased, and thus postpone the adoption of a final decision.[28]

---

[25] The Member State is not entitled to refuse to furnish the information on the grounds that, in its opinion, it is not relevant.

[26] Case T-211/05 *Italy v Commission* [2009] ECR II-2777, para 37 and Case C-400/99 *Italy v Commission* [2001] ECR I-7303 ('the interlocutory judgment'), paras 59 and 60.

[27] Case C-400/99 *Italy v Commission* [2001] ECR I-7303, para 59.

[28] Joined Cases C-15/98 and C-105/99 *Italy and Sardegna Lines v Commission* [2000] ECR I-8855, para 43.

23.16 The Procedural Regulation does not establish a limit for the duration of the formal investigation.[29] The Commission must in any case act within a reasonable time.

3. Applicable rules *ratione temporis*

23.17 In so far as the Commission adopts frameworks, guidelines, and similar instruments when it wishes to bind itself to apply certain compatibility criteria, it is entitled to determine in each case how they should apply in time. A Member State that has not notified an aid scheme cannot expect that the Commission rules on its compatibility by applying the rules in force at the date on which the aid scheme was adopted.[30]

C. Final Decision

23.18 At the end of its examination procedure the Commission adopts a final decision on the compatibility of the measure.[31]

1. Positive decision

23.19 If the measure does not constitute aid or if the aid is declared to be compatible, the Commission approves it. Although the compatibility decision does not provide a remedy for any infringement of Article 108(3) TFEU, the Commission is not then entitled to demand the recovery thereof on those grounds alone. Furthermore, the Procedural Regulation contains no provision allowing the Commission to penalize Member States for unlawful payment of aid declared thereafter to be compatible.[32]

2. Negative or conditional decision

23.20 If the aid is declared to be incompatible, the Commission requires it to be recovered or altered in the formal decision it adopts. It is then up to the Member State concerned to enforce this decision.[33] Indeed, the Member States are bound to comply with the final decisions addressed to them, by virtue of their duty of loyal cooperation under Article 4(3) TEU and also the supremacy of EU law. Since it is a case of aid declared to be incompatible, the role of the national authorities is merely to give effect to the Commission's decision. The authorities do not, therefore, have any discretion regarding the revocation of a decision granting aid.[34]

23.21 In order to obtain approval of new or modified aid by way of derogation from the Treaty rules, the Member State concerned must, in order to fulfil its duty to cooperate with the

---

[29] If the Commission adopts a decision requiring the Member State provisionally to recover any unlawful aid until the Commission has taken a decision on the compatibility of the aid, after the aid has been effectively recovered the Commission shall take a decision within the time limits applicable to notified aid (Art 11.2 of the Procedural Regulation).

[30] Joined Cases C-465/09 P to C-470/09 P *Diputación Foral de Vizcaya and Others v Commission*, paras 123–7.

[31] The wording of Art 13(1) of the Procedural Regulation seems to render the adoption of a decision necessary, so the Commission could not abstain to act for lack of 'Union interest'.

[32] It would be possible to imagine, for example, that the Commission would be authorized, in the case of compatible but unlawful aid, to impose the payment of interest covering the period running from the payment of the aid to the Commission's final decision on the compatibility (see the Opinion of AG Tesauro in Case C-142/87 *Belgium v Commission* [1990] ECR I-959 and of AG Cosmas in Joined Cases C-329/93, C-62/95, and C-63/95 *Germany, Hanseatische Industrie-Beteiligungen and Bremer Vulkan Verbund v Commission* [1996] ECR I-2633).

[33] Joined Cases T-228/99 and T-233/99 *WestLB and others v Commission* [2003] ECR II-435, para 140.

[34] Case C-24/95 *Alcan Deutschland* [1997] ECR I-1591, para 34.

Commission, provide all the information necessary to enable that institution to verify that the conditions for the derogation from which it seeks to benefit are satisfied.[35] The Commission is empowered to adopt a decision on the basis of the information available when it is faced with a Member State which fails to comply with its obligation of cooperation towards that institution to provide information requested from it either for the purpose of assessing the compatibility of new or modified aid with the internal market or of verifying whether aid previously approved has been properly applied. Before taking such a decision, however, the Commission must order the Member State to provide it, within the time limit it lays down, with all the documentation, information, and data necessary to carry out its review.[36] It is only if the Member State, notwithstanding the Commission's order, fails to provide the information requested, that the Commission is empowered to terminate the procedure and make a decision on the basis of the information available to it.[37] The possibility granted to the Commission of adopting a decision on whether or not the aid is compatible with the internal market on the basis of the information available, where it is faced with a Member State which does not fulfil its duty to cooperate and has not provided the Commission with the information requested, cannot be interpreted as releasing that institution entirely from the obligation to base its decisions on reliable and coherent evidence to support the conclusions which it arrives at.[38]

Should a Member State fail to observe with all due diligence a negative or conditional deci- **23.22** sion reached by the Commission, the latter or any other Member State concerned will be entitled, under Article 108(2)(2) TFEU to bring the matter directly before the ECJ by derogation from Articles 258 and 259 TFEU.

Time limit

No legal time limit for execution is laid down within the framework of the exceptional rules **23.23** for bringing an action for failure to comply, based on the second subparagraph of Article 108(2) TFEU.[39] Unlike in the case of existing aid, when adopting a negative decision on unlawful aid the Commission is not bound to grant a time limit to the Member State for implementing its decision, since the measure concerned should not have been put into effect.[40] The ECJ has insisted that the execution of the Commission's decision has to be immediate.[41]

If the decision lays down a given deadline for implementing its obligations, the Member **23.24** State must abide by this deadline. In the past, the Commission's recovery decisions specified a single time limit of two months, within which the Member State concerned was required to communicate to the Commission the measures it had taken to comply with a given decision. The ECJ acknowledged that this deadline is to be regarded as the deadline for the execution of the Commission decision itself.[42] The ECJ further concluded that contacts and negotiations between the Commission and the Member State, in the context of the execution

---

[35] Case C-364/90 *Italy v Commission* [1993] ECR I-2097, para 20; and Case T-17/03 *Schmitz-Gotha Fahrzeugwerke v Commission* [2006] ECR II-1139, para 48.

[36] When, despite an information injunction, the Commission considers the information received to be insufficient and bases its negative decision on the only information to hand, it is bound to put that fact on record (Case T-126/99 *Graphischer Maschinenbau v Commission* [2002] ECR II-2427, para 95).

[37] Case C-301/87 *France v Commission ('Boussac')* [1990] ECR I-307, para 22 and Joined Cases T-415/05, T-416/05, and T-423/05 *Greece and Others v Commission* [2010] ECR II-4749, para 226.

[38] Case C-520/07 P *Commission v MTU* [2009] ECR I-8555, paras 54–5.

[39] Case C-499/99 *Spain v Commission* [2002] ECR I-6031, para 42.

[40] Article 14(3) of the Procedural Regulation states that recovery shall be effected without delay.

[41] Case C-232/05 *Commission v France* [2006] ECR I-10071, paras 49–50.

[42] Case C-207/05 *Commission v Italy* [2006] ECR I-70, paras 31–6.

of the Commission decision, could not relieve the Member State from the duty to take all necessary measures to execute the decision within the prescribed time limit.[43] In its Recovery Notice,[44] the Commission recognized that the two-month deadline for the execution of the Commission decisions is too short in the majority of cases. Therefore, it decided to prolong to four months the deadline for the execution of the recovery decisions. From that moment on, the Commission specifies two time limits in its decisions: a first time limit of two months following the entry into force of the decision, within which the Member State must inform the Commission of the measures planned or taken; and a second time limit of four months following the entry into force of the decision, within which the Commission decision must have been executed. If a Member State encounters serious difficulties that prevent it from respecting either one of these deadlines, it must inform the Commission of these difficulties, providing an appropriate justification. The Commission may then prolong the deadline in accordance with the principle of loyal cooperation.[45]

Abolition of aid

23.25 When a State is obliged to abolish aid declared to be incompatible, it has to do so fully. This means in particular that, if the Commission has identified an aid scheme in reference to a legal act providing for same, the State infringes its obligations if it repeals that act, but maintains the measure by adopting a different act.[46] Moreover, it is not enough for the State simply to stop paying the aid involved in a scheme declared to be incompatible. It is also bound in principle to formally repeal the provisions declared to be incompatible.[47]

II. Recovery of Incompatible Aid Unlawfully put into Effect

A. Recovery Principle

1. Principle

23.26 The principle of recovering incompatible aid unlawfully put into effect is laid down in Article 14 of the Procedural Regulation, which provides that, in the case of a negative decision, the Commission 'shall decide' that the aid must be recovered. The words 'shall decide' shows that it is an obligation for the Commission, once unlawful aid has been declared to be incompatible.

---

[43] Case C-5/86 *Commission v Belgium* [1987] ECR 1773.

[44] Notice from the Commission—Towards an effective implementation of Commission decisions ordering Member States to recover unlawful and incompatible State aid [2007] OJ 2007 C272/4.

[45] See Notice from the Commission—Towards an effective implementation of Commission decisions ordering Member States to recover unlawful and incompatible State aid [2007] OJ 2007 C272/4, paras 40–3.

[46] See Case 203/82 *Commission v Italy* [1983] ECR 2633, in which the Court ruled against Italy for having extended by successive decree-laws an aid that the Commission had demanded be abolished on the grounds of its original decree-law. As AG Rozès pointed out: 'true it is that the provision that the Commission's final decision required the Italian government to abolish no longer formally exists because decree law 503...has been repealed, but the substance thereof has been reproduced without any break in the subsequent texts' (Opinion in Case 203/82, para V).

[47] Case 130/83 *Commission v Italy* [1984] ECR 2849, para 7. This formal repeal obligation is logical since it is the formal adoption of the regulation that is considered to constitute the institution of the aid under Art 108(3) TFEU.

This provision bears out previous case law.[48] Indeed, faced with a relatively high number of **23.27** cases in which aid had been paid out to its recipient before being approved, the Commission had previously demanded the recovery thereof, in cases where such aid had been declared incompatible, and the Court had approved this practice.[49]

According to the ECJ, since the Commission is empowered under Article 108(2) TFEU to **23.28** decide whether the State should abolish or alter incompatible aid, this abolition or alteration, to be of practical effect, may involve an obligation placed on the Member State to demand repayment of the aid granted in breach of the Treaty.[50]

The recovery of unlawfully granted State aid aims to restore the situation existing prior to **23.29** the payment of such aid.[51] This cannot be considered, in principle, to be a measure disproportionate to the Treaty's objectives as regards State aid.[52] The recovery of unlawful and incompatible aid is not a penalty either.[53] Quite on the contrary, 'the abolition of unlawful aid by way of recovery is the logical consequence of the finding that it is illegal'.[54] The Court has in particular refused to take into consideration any damage the recovery might cause to third parties, for example creditors.[55]

2. Recovery and form of the aid

The possibility of requiring the recovery of aid cannot be made to depend on the form in which **23.30** it was granted.[56] Member States could otherwise evade the applicable State-aid rules by giving the aid a particular form.[57]

The ECJ does not provide that any particular grounds must be given for justifying a deci- **23.31** sion requiring the recovery of aid, since its incompatibility with the internal market has been established.[58] Neither is the Commission bound to establish that the aid has actually been

---

[48] Case C-404/00 *Commission v Spain* [2003] ECR I-6695, para 23. The ECJ confirmed for the first time that the Commission has the power to order the recovery of unlawful and incompatible State aid in Case 70/72 *Commission v Germany* [1973] ECR 813, para 13.

[49] As AG Jacobs pointed out: 'The most important point to bear in mind is that the question of recovery would never arise if Member States complied with their obligation to inform the Commission, in advance, of any plans to grant or alter aid, in accordance with the first sentence of Article [108(3)] of the Treaty, and with their obligation to refrain from implementing plans to grant aid until the Commission has given its final decision, as required by the last sentence of Article [108(3)].' Opinion in Joined Cases C-278/92, C-279/92 and C-280/92 *Spain v Commission* [1994] ECR I-4103, para 63.

[50] Case 70/72 *Commission v Germany* [1973] ECR 813, para 13; Case 310/85 *Deufil v Commission* [1987] ECR 901, para 24; Case C-24/95 *Alcan Deutschland* [1997] ECR I-1591, para 22; Case C-209/00 *Commission v Germany* [2002] ECR I-11695, para 30; and Case C-404/00 *Commission v Spain* [2003] ECR I-6695, para 20.

[51] Case C-348/93 *Commission v Italy* [1995] ECR I-673, para 26; Case C-350/93 [1995] ECR I-699, para 21; Case C-24/95 *Alcan Deutschland* [1997] ECR I-1591, para 23; Case C-298/00 P *Italy v Commission* [2004] ECR I-4087, para 76; and Case T-198/01 *TGI v Commission* [2004] ECR II-2717, para 132.

[52] Case C-142/87 *Belgium v Commission* [1990] ECR I-959, para 66; Joined Cases C-278/92, C-279/92 and C-280/92 *Spain v Commission* [1994] ECR I-4103, para 75; Case C-298/00 P *Italy v Commission* [2004] ECR I-4087, para 75, and Case T-198/01 *TGI v Commission* [2004] ECR II-2717, para 133.

[53] Case C-75/97 *Belgium v Commission* [1999] ECR I-3671, para 65.

[54] Case C-142/87 *Belgium v Commission* [1990] ECR I-959, para 66; Case C-305/89 *Italy v Commission* [1991] ECR I-1603, para 41; Case C-169/95 *Spain v Commission* [1997] ECR I-135, para 47; Case C-404/00 *Commission v Spain* [2003] ECR I-6695, para 44; Case C-99/02 *Commission v Italy* [2004] ECR I-3353, para 15.

[55] Case C-142/87 *Belgium v Commission* [1990] ECR I-959, paras 65 and 66.

[56] Case C-183/91 *Commission v Greece* [1993] ECR I-3131, para 16; and Case C-99/02 *Commission v Italy* [2004] ECR I-3353, para 15. The fact that the aid was granted under a private law contract, for example, is deemed to have no relevance (Case C-278/00 *Greece v Commission* [2004] ECR I-3997, para 113).

[57] Case C-278/00 *Greece v Commission* [2004] ECR I-3997, para 113.

[58] Case C-303/88 *Italy v Commission* [1991] ECR I-1433, para 54 and Joined Cases C-278/92, C-279/92, and C-280/92 *Spain v Commission* [1994] ECR I-4103, para 78. See, in this sense, the observations of AG

granted before requiring the recovery thereof; in the absence of any guarantee to this effect, the Commission cannot be criticized for clearly setting out the practical consequences of its decision with the intention of creating greater legal certainty.[59]

23.32   The ECJ has, however, imposed an important limit on the Commission's power to order the recovery of aid: such a recovery can be the consequence only of the aid's incompatibility with the internal market and represents the means of restoring the pre-aid situation. The Commission therefore has to establish the incompatible character of aid, by definition unlawfully granted, before being able to order its recovery.[60]

3. Practice

Evolution of the Commission's practice

23.33   The recovery of incompatible aid was originally a simple power that the Commission used in an uneven manner. However, it soon decided to do so in a systematic way, barring justified exceptions. In a Communication of 1983, it informed

> potential recipients of State aid of the risk attached to any aid granted to them unlawfully, inasmuch as all recipients of unlawfully granted aid, i.e. without the Commission having reached a definitive solution on its compatibility, might be called upon to refund the aid.[61]

The Procedural Regulation has since borne out the systematic character of aid recovery (Article 14). Further implementing provisions on recovery were included in the Implementing Regulation (Regulation 794/2004). In 2007, the Commission explained its policy towards the implementation of recovery decisions in the Recovery Notice.[62]

Difficulties in enforcing aid recovery decisions

23.34   If, when executing a recovery decision, the addressee Member State encounters unforeseen or unforeseeable difficulties or perceives consequences overlooked by the Commission, it must submit those problems to the Commission for consideration, together with proposals for suitable amendments of the decision in question. In such a case the Commission and the Member State concerned must respect the principle underlying Article 4(3) TEU, which imposes a duty of genuine cooperation on the Member States and EU institutions; accordingly, they must work together in good faith with a view to overcoming difficulties, whilst fully observing the Treaty provisions, and in particular the provisions on aid.[63]

Darmon in Joined Cases C-324/90 and C-342/90 *Germany and Pleuger Worthington v Commission* [1994] ECR I-1173, paras 106–19; he rules in particular that a requirement of a statement of specific reasons for the repayment of aid would favour those States that, in breach of Art 108(3) TFEU, did not previously notify their aid, since there is no such requirement when the Commission objects to aid which has not yet been granted.

[59] Case C-364/90 *Italy v Commission* [1993] ECR I-2097, paras 48 and 49. The Commission therefore can claim the repayment of 'any aid already paid'.

[60] Case C-301/87 *France v Commission* [1990] ECR I-307, para 11; Case T-49/93 *SIDE v Commission* [1995] ECR II-2501, para 84; and Case C-39/94 *SFEI and others* [1996] ECR I-3547, para 43.

[61] [1983] OJ C318/3. The Court based its arguments on the existence of this Communication to dismiss the claim of a principle of legitimate expectations on behalf of the recipients of unlawful aid (Case C-5/89 *Commission v Germany* [1990] ECR I-3437, para 15).

[62] Notice from the Commission—Towards an effective implementation of Commission decisions ordering Member States to recover unlawful and incompatible State aid [2007] OJ C272/4; for a recent example, see Commission Press Release IP/13/566 'State aid: Terrestrial digital platform operators in Spain must pay back incompatible subsidies', 19 June 2013.

[63] Case 52/84 *Commission v Belgium* [1986] ECR 89, para 16; Case 94/87 *Commission v Germany* [1989] ECR 175, para 9; Case C-99/02 *Commission v Italy* [2004] ECR I-3353, para 17; and Case C-278/00 *Greece v Commission* [2004] ECR I-3997, para 114.

The Member State cannot, therefore, take the passive attitude of merely informing the **23.35** Commission of the practical, political, or legal difficulties involved in implementing the decision. It is bound to take all due steps to recover the aid from the undertaking in question and propose to the Commission any alternative arrangements that might allow those difficulties to be overcome,[64] in the interests of finding 'common ground' with the Commission.[65] Nonetheless, the State's commitment to enter into negotiations with the Commission will not be understood to exempt it from the obligation of taking all necessary measures for complying with the Commission's decision in the time limit laid down for doing so.[66] Moreover, no procedural or other difficulties in regard to the implementation of the contested measure can have any influence on the lawfulness thereof.[67]

The application of national procedures is subject to the condition that those procedures **23.36** allow the immediate and effective execution of the Commission's decision, a condition which reflects the requirements of the principle of effectiveness. The application of national procedures should not, therefore, impede the restoration of effective competition by preventing the immediate and effective execution of the Commission's decision. To achieve this result, Member States should take all necessary measures ensuring the effectiveness of that decision.[68]

In the absence of sufficient details in the decision itself, the implementation obligation is not **23.37** then incumbent on the Member State until such time as the Commission is in a position to specify with the necessary precision exactly what its obligations are.[69]

B. Exceptions to Recovery

What are the exceptions to the recovery of incompatible aid? **23.38**

1. Recovery time limit

Limitation period for the recovery of unlawful aid

Formerly there was no time limit laid down in legislation for the recovery of unlawful aid. In **23.39** order to fulfil their function of ensuring legal certainty, limitation periods must be fixed in advance; the fixing of their duration and the detailed rules for their application come within the powers of the EU legislature. It followed from these two factors that the Commission was not subject to any limitation period as regards the unlawfulness or incompatibility of aid.[70]

Aid that had been paid out for several years or even several decades before it came to the **23.40** Commission's notice could therefore always be examined and, as the case may be, declared incompatible and made subject to recovery. The Commission in effect considered that the effects of aid granted in the past persisted and therefore justified action on its part. It was only

---

[64] Case 94/87 *Commission v Germany* [1989] ECR 175, para 10; Case C-183/91 *Commission v Greece* [1993] ECR I-3131, para 19; Case C 280/95 *Commission v Italy* [1998] ECR I-259, para 14; Case C-499/99 *Commission v Spain* [2002] ECR I-6031, para 25; and Case C-99/02 *Commission v Italy* [2004] ECR I-3353, para 18.

[65] Case C-499/99 *Commission v Spain* [2002] ECR I-6031, para 27.

[66] Case 5/86 *Commission v Belgium* [1987] ECR 1773, especially paras 7 and 11.

[67] Case C-142/87 *Belgium v Commission* [1990] ECR I-959, para 63.

[68] In this regard, the ECJ found that the French rule providing for the suspensory effect of actions brought against demands for payment should therefore have been left unapplied (Case C-232/05 *Commission v France* [2006] ECR I-10071, paras 49–53).

[69] Case 70/72 *Commission v Germany* [1973] ECR 813, para 23.

[70] Joined Cases T-126/96 and T-127/96 *Breda Fucine Meridionali v Commission* [1998] ECR II-3437, para 67; and Case C-298/00 P *Italy v Commission* [2004] ECR I-4087, para 89.

in exceptional circumstances, therefore, for example when the beneficiary undertaking had definitively ceased to exist, that it sometimes chose not to examine the incompatibility of the aid or not to demand its refund.

Article 15 of the Procedural Regulation

23.41 This situation changed with the introduction of a limitation period in Article 15 of the Procedural Regulation. Article 15(1) provides that '[t]he Commission's powers to recover aid shall be subject to a limitation period of ten years'. The limitation period does not in any way express a general principle whereby new aid is transformed into existing aid, but merely precludes recovery of aid established more than ten years before the Commission first intervened.[71] It is a single limitation period that applies in the same way to the Member State concerned, the aid recipient, and third parties. The fact that the recipient or a third party was not aware of the existence of measures interrupting the limitation period is, therefore, irrelevant.

23.42 According to Article 15(2) of the Procedural Regulation:

> The limitation period shall begin on the day on which the unlawful aid is awarded to the beneficiary either as individual aid or as aid under an aid scheme. Any action taken by the Commission or by a Member State, acting at the request of the Commission, with regard to the unlawful aid shall interrupt the limitation period. Each interruption shall start time running afresh. The limitation period shall be suspended for as long as the decision of the Commission is the subject of proceedings pending before the ECJ of the European Communities.

The General Court ('GC') has considered that the limitation period starts to run on the day when the aid can be considered as being granted. When the aid depends on the adoption of legally binding acts, it starts to run on the date of adoption of those acts. When the presence of aid can only be established on an annual basis, the limitation period cannot start running on the date on which the aid scheme was first introduced.[72] The measures interrupting the limitation period may be adopted by the Commission or the Member State acting at the Commission's behest.

Transitional provisions

23.43 Article 15 contains no transitional provision as regards its application in time, and hence applies to any definitive action ordering recovery of aid taken after the date on which the regulation entered into force, including aid granted before that date. Aid granted before the entry into force of the Regulation can therefore benefit from the limitation period. As a corollary, however, a request for information made by the Commission before the entry into force of the Regulation, even though it did not 'then' have the effect of interrupting the limitation period, acquires such an effect in some way thereafter, thereby enabling the Commission to recover the aid after the entry into force of the Regulation.

2. Disappearance of the distortion of competition

23.44 The Commission sometimes declines to demand the recovery of aid when the distortion-of-competition effects have disappeared, thereby terminating the infringement of Article 107(1) TFEU. This might occur when the aided undertaking has definitively ceased

---

[71] Joined Cases T-195/01 and T-207/01 *Government of Gibraltar v Commission* [2002] ECR II-2309, para 130. This finding appears difficult to reconcile with the text of Arts 1(b)(iv) and 15(3) of the Procedural Regulation.
[72] Joined Cases T-427/04 and T-17/05 *French Republic and France Télécom v Commission* [2009] ECR II-4315, paras 321–5.

trading before the adoption of the Commission's final decision and the benefit of the aid has not been transferred to another company.

3. General principles of law preventing the recovery of aid

Principle

Exceptional circumstances may sometimes mean that the recovery of the aid is not demanded. **23.45** The exceptional circumstances invoked often involve the legitimate expectations of the recipient or of the State. The Procedural Regulation confirms that the Commission will not require recovery of the aid if this would be against a general principle of EU law (Article 14). On the contrary, the simple existence of internal difficulties would not be sufficient justification.[73]

Legitimate expectations

The general principle of law most often invoked against the recovery of aid is that of legiti- **23.46** mate expectations, either of the Member State or the aid recipient. Except where there are 'exceptional circumstances',[74] such a claim will not succeed.

The right to rely on the principle of the protection of legitimate expectations extends to any **23.47** person in a situation where the EU authority has, by giving him precise assurances, caused him to entertain expectations which are justified. If a prudent and alert economic operator could have foreseen the adoption of a measure likely to affect his interests, he cannot plead that principle if the measure is adopted. The assurances given must, in addition, be in accordance with the applicable rules.[75] In view of the mandatory nature of the review of State aid by the Commission under Article 108 TFEU, undertakings to which aid has been granted may not, in principle, entertain a legitimate expectation that the aid is lawful unless it has been granted in compliance with the procedure laid down therein. A diligent businessman should normally be able to determine whether that procedure has been followed.[76] It follows that until such time as the Commission has taken an approval decision, and even until such time as the deadline for lodging appeals against that decision has expired,[77] the recipient cannot be certain about the lawfulness of the proposed aid, which certainty alone is capable of giving rise to a legitimate expectation on its part.[78]

Consequently, the legitimate expectations of the recipients of unlawful aid cannot in princi- **23.48** ple be invoked as grounds for annulment by the EU Courts of the Commission's decision to demand recovery of the aid or a refusal by the national courts to order the effective restitution in execution of that decision.

In view of their privileged negotiating position with the Commission, the national authorities **23.49** are less able than the recipients of aid to claim that their legitimate expectations have been prejudiced.[79] As for recipients, they cannot argue on the grounds of their small size that they were not obliged to be aware of EU law, otherwise the effectiveness of this law would be undermined.[80] Any apparent failure to act by the Commission is equally irrelevant when an aid

---

[73] Case C-298/00 P *Italy v Commission* [2004] ECR I-4087, para 78.
[74] Joined Cases C-183/02 P and C-187/02 P *Demesa v Commission* [2004] ECR I-10609, para 51.
[75] Case C-369/09 P *ISD Polska v Commission* [2011], para 23; and Case C-67/09 P *Nuova Agricast v Commission* [2010] ECR I-9811, para 71.
[76] Case C-5/89 *Commission v Germany* [1990] ECR I-3437, para 17; Case C-169/95 *Spain v Commission* [1997] ECR I-135, para 51; Joined Cases C-183/02 P and C-187/02 P *Demesa v Commission* [2004] ECR I-10609, para 44; and Case C-81/10 P *France Télécom v Commission* [2011], para 59.
[77] Joined Cases T-116/01 and T-118/01 *P & O European Ferries (Vizcaya) and Diputación Foral de Vizcaya v Commission* [2003] ECR II-2957, para 205.
[78] Case C-91/01 *Italy v Commission* [2004] ECR I-4355, para 66; and Case C-1/09 *CELF* [2010] ECR I-2099, para 53.
[79] Case C-334/99 *Germany v Commission* [2003] ECR I-1139, para 45.
[80] Case C-298/00 P *Italy v Commission* [2004] ECR I-4087, para 88.

scheme has not been notified.[81] The fact that they have not been informed by their national authorities of the progress of the administrative procedure cannot be deemed to be an exceptional circumstance serving as grounds for their legitimate expectation. The only possibly valid grounds would therefore be when the Commission had given them precise assurances of such a nature as to engender well-founded expectations of the lawfulness of the aid concerned.[82]

23.50 The mere passing of time cannot be deemed to create such a legitimate expectation if it did not exist originally.[83] The practice of the Commission is to limit the legitimate expectations until the date of the publication of the decision to initiate the formal investigation procedure under Article 108(2) TFEU.[84]

C. Implementation

1. Obligations of the Member State

23.51 Under Article 288 TFEU, the Member State to which a decision ordering the recovery of unlawful aid is addressed must take all necessary measures to ensure the implementation of the said decision.[85] This must result in the actual recovery of the sums owed.[86] A Member State fulfils its obligations as regards recovery if the measures it takes are conducive to the re-establishment of the normal conditions of competition which were distorted by the grant of the illegal aid and are consistent with the relevant provisions of EU law.[87] The refunding of aid therefore implies that the recipient no longer has effective enjoyment of it, or, in other words, that it is deprived of any illicit competitive advantage deriving from it.[88] The Member State is free to choose the means by which it will execute this obligation, provided that the measures chosen do not adversely affect the scope and effectiveness of EU law.[89]

23.52 The ECJ and the Commission sometimes rule that, in order to implement a recovery-ordering decision, the Member State is required to act like a 'private creditor'.[90] The Member State must thus exhaust all the legal instruments available under its own legal system, such as those used to combat fraud against creditors in the form of acts carried out by the firm in liquidation during

---

[81] Joined Cases C-183/02 P and C-187/02 P *Demesa v Commission* [2004] ECR I-10609, para 52; and Case C-81/10 P *France Télécom v Commission* [2011], para 60.

[82] Case T-109/01 *Fleuren Compost v Commission* [2004] ECR II-127, paras 140–2.

[83] Joined Cases T-126/96 and T-127/96 *Breda Fucine Meridionali and others v Commission* [1998] ECR II-3437, paras 69 and 70.

[84] Commission Decision of 7 February 2007 concerning the exemption from excise duty on mineral oils used as fuel for alumina production in Gardanne, in the Shannon region and in Sardinia implemented by France, Ireland, and Italy [2007] OJ L190/13, 55, and Commission Decision of 24 June 2003 on the aid scheme implemented by Belgium—Tax ruling system for United States foreign sales corporations [2004] OJ L23/14, 79.

[85] Case C-209/00 *Commission v Germany* [2002] ECR I-11695, para 31; and Case C-404/00 *Commission v Spain* [2003] ECR I-6695, para 21.

[86] Case C-232/05 *Commission v France* [2006] ECR I-10071, para 42; and Case C-331/09 *Commission v Poland* [2011] ECR I-2933 para 55. See also on the possibility of imposing fines (including coercive penalties) on a Member State for its failure to recover illegal State aid, Case C-610/10 *Commission v Kingdom of Spain* [2013] OJ C38/5 dealing with Spain's failure to recover aid from the Magefesa group.

[87] Case C-209/00 *Commission v Germany* [2002] ECR I-11695, para 35.

[88] A simple provision in an undertaking's balance sheet in anticipation of a future recovery is therefore not the same as repaying the aid in question (Joined Cases T-244/93 and T-486/93 *TWD v Commission* [1995] ECR II-2265, para 84).

[89] Case C-209/00 *Commission v Germany* [2002] ECR I-11695, para 34; Case C-404/00 *Commission v Spain* [2003] ECR I-6695, para 24; and Case C-210/09 *Scott and Kimberly Clark* [2010] ECR I-4613, para 21. Therefore, the application of national procedures is subject to the condition that those procedures allow the immediate and effective execution of the Commission's decision, a condition which reflects the requirements of the principle of effectiveness (Case C-232/05 *Commission v France* [2006] ECR I-10071, paras 49–53).

[90] Joined Cases C-328/99 and C-399/00 *Italy and others v Commission* [2003] ECR I-4035, para 68.

the suspect period prior to the bankruptcy, which would allow such acts to be declared invalid.[91] The ECJ has recalled that a Commission decision addressed to a Member State is binding on all the organs of that State, including its Courts.[92] EU law does not prescribe which organ of the Member State should be in charge of the practical implementation of a recovery decision. It is for the domestic legal system of each Member State to designate the bodies that will be responsible for the implementation of the recovery decision.

Alternative means of recovery

Instead of a 'transfer of funds', the Member State may make arrangements for returning the **23.53** aid by other measures, providing these measures have an identical, unconditional effect and are applicable without delay. When a Member State chooses to recover unlawful aid by any means other than a cash payment, it must ensure that the measures it chooses are sufficiently transparent and that it furnishes the Commission with all due information, allowing it to verify that the method chosen is in fact an alternative way of achieving the decision's purpose.[93]

Liquidation of the recipient undertaking

In cases in which the aid has to be recovered from undertakings which are bankrupt or subject **23.54** to bankruptcy proceedings whose purpose is to realize the assets and clear the liabilities, it is settled case law that the fact that undertakings are in difficulties or bankrupt does not affect the obligation of recovery.[94] To ensure that the Commission decision is implemented correctly, the Member State is required to recover the aid without delay, using all the legal means at its disposal, including seizure of the firm's assets and, where necessary, its liquidation if it is unable to repay the amounts in question.[95] If the national authorities are not able to recover the full amount of the aid, the recovery obligation is only satisfied if the beneficiary is liquidated, and has thus definitively and completely ceased its activity.[96] Accordingly, the Commission's objective in abolishing the aid, could likewise be achieved from the competition point of view, in the absence of an effective recovery, by winding up the company and including the aid recovery as a creditor to be satisfied in the list of claims in the liquidation of the assets.[97] This procedure frees the market segment previously held by the wound-up undertaking, allows public creditors to enforce their claims against the assets or acquire them and reallocate them more effectively. In the absence of recoverable assets, this procedure is the only way of showing the absolute impossibility of recovering the aid.[98] The fact that insolvency proceedings have been brought against the undertaking after the adoption of the Commission's decision ordering the recovery of the aid can in any case cast no doubts on the lawfulness of the decision.[99]

2. Recovery Procedure

Procedural arrangements

The sole addressee of a Commission decision ordering the recovery of aid is the Member State **23.55** concerned and it generates no direct payment obligation vis-à-vis the undertaking that has

---

[91] Joined Cases C-328/99 and C-399/00 *Italy and others v Commission* [2003] ECR I-4035, para 69.
[92] Case 249/85 *Albako v BALM* [1987] ECR 2345.
[93] Case C-209/00 *Commission v Germany* [2002] ECR I-11695, paras 40–4 and 57–8.
[94] Case C-280/05 *Commission v Italy* [2007] ECR I-181, para 28.
[95] Joined Cases C-328/99 and C-399/00 *Italy and others v Commission* [2003] ECR I-4035, para 69.
[96] Case C-454/09 *Commission v Italy* [2011], para 36.
[97] Case 52/84 *Commission v Belgium* [1986] ECR 89, para 14; Case C-499/99 *Spain v Commission* [2002] ECR I-6031, para 38, Case C-277/00 *Germany v Commission* [2004] ECR I-3925, para 85; and Case C-331/09 *Commission v Poland* [2011], ECR I-2933, para 60.
[98] Case C-499/99 *Spain v Commission* [2002] ECR I-6031, para 37; and Joined Cases C-328/99 and C-399/00 *Italy and others v Commission* [2003] ECR I-4035, para 69.
[99] Joined Cases C-278/92, C-279/92, and C-280/92 *Spain v Commission* [1994] ECR I-4103, para 80; and Case C-42/93 [1994] ECR I-4175, para 33.

benefited from the aid.[100] EU law does not, therefore, require that it be enforceable in the relevant national legal system.

23.56 According to the Procedural Regulation, the recovery is effected in accordance with the procedures under the national law of the Member State concerned, but only 'provided that they allow the immediate and effective execution of the Commission's decision'. The aim of this provision is to remedy the drawn-out process and obstacles that the recovery procedure currently runs into.[101]

23.57 The actions undertaken by the Member State must result in the actual recovery of the sums owed by the beneficiary.[102] National procedures which do not fulfil the conditions laid down in Article 14(3) of the Procedural Regulation should be left unapplied.[103]

Referral to national law

23.58 Since there are no EU provisions on the procedure to be followed, the aid must, in principle, be recovered in accordance with the relevant procedural provisions of national law.[104]

23.59 The Commission's decisions merely order the recovery of the aid without laying down the actual procedures to be followed. Providing that the provisions of the Procedural Regulation are observed, the recovery of the aid can be effected in accordance with the relevant procedural provisions of national law,[105] by virtue of the principle of 'procedural autonomy'. In their arrangements to recover the aid, national authorities have to make use of the most appropriate internal legal instruments to hand, with due consideration being paid to the nature of the instrument by which the aid was granted, the identity of the direct aid-paying authority, etc. The possibility of recovering aid, however, cannot be made to depend on the form in which the aid in question was granted.[106]

23.60 When aid was granted by way of an administrative decision, which is in fact the most frequent case, the national authorities generally adopt a revocation and recovery decision on the basis of the national procedure for the revocation of unlawful administrative acts.

Limits on the referral to national law

23.61 The Member States' procedural autonomy, both administrative and jurisdictional, for recovering State aid declared to be incompatible is not limitless.

23.62 **Administrative procedure** No action for annulment having been lodged against the Commission's decision, the competent authorities of the addressee Member States cannot themselves refuse to execute the decision on grounds taken from their internal law. Their role is merely to give effect to the Commission's decision and they are not entitled

---

[100] See the Commission's explanations in para 19 of Case 310/85 R *Deufil v Commission* [1986] ECR 537.

[101] The Council, on the contrary, refused to endorse the Commission's proposal, according to which the recourses offered by national law could no longer have a suspensive effect.

[102] Case C-415/03 *Commission v Greece* [2005] ECR I-3875, para 44 and Case C-207/05 *Commission v Italy* [2006] ECR I-70, paras 36–7.

[103] Case C-232/05 *Commission v France* [2006] ECR I-10071, para 42.

[104] Case C-404/00 *Commission v Spain* [2003] ECR I-6695, para 22.

[105] Case T-459/93 *Siemens v Commission* [1995] ECR II-1675, para 82; Case C-24/95 *Alcan Deutschland* [1997] ECR I-1591, para 24; and Case C-209/00 *Commission v Germany* [2002] ECR I-11695, para 32.

[106] For this reason the Court rejected the Greek government's arguments that the recovery of a tax exemption was impossible because it would necessarily have to take the form of a retrospective tax, which would be incompatible with the Greek Constitution and the general principles of law (Case C-183/91 *Commission v Greece* [1993] ECR I-3131, para 17).

to reach any other finding.[107] Only the undertaking receiving aid is entitled to adopt such an attitude.[108]

Jurisdictional procedure   The Court accepts that the recovery of unlawful aid should in principle be carried out in accordance with the pertinent provisions of national law, but these provisions must be applied subject to the following two conditions: first, in such a way as to ensure that the recovery required by EU law is not rendered practically impossible and the interests of the EU are taken fully into consideration in the application of provisions that require the various interests involved to be weighed up before a defective administrative measure is withdrawn; and, secondly, in a non-discriminatory way in relation to comparable cases governed only by national law.[109] Here again we come across the traditional principles of 'effectiveness' and 'equivalence'.[110]   **23.63**

In this respect, although the EU legal system cannot override national legislation that ensures respect for legitimate expectations and legal certainty in the recovery process, the Court has nonetheless ruled that, in view of the mandatory nature of the supervision of State aid by the Commission under Article 108 TFEU, undertakings to which aid has been granted may not, in principle, have a legitimate expectation that the aid is lawful unless it has been granted in compliance with the procedure laid down in that Article. Indeed, any diligent business-men should normally be able to ensure that this procedure is observed.[111] It is therefore only in 'exceptional circumstances' that the recipient of unlawful aid may properly rely on legitimate expectation of the lawful character of that aid to challenge the recovery order. In such a case, it is for the national court, if the case comes before it, to assess the circumstances in question, if necessary after submitting to the ECJ questions for a preliminary ruling on interpretation.[112]   **23.64**

The ECJ has emphasized the need to avoid rendering the recovery required under EU law practically impossible. As regards the aid-recipient's legitimate expectations and the principle of legal certainty, the Court has thus declared that, from the moment the recipient is informed of the Commission's decision declaring the aid to be incompatible and demanding the recovery thereof, the recipient is no longer in a position of legal uncertainty, in view of the obligation of the national authorities to implement this decision without having any discretionary power in regard thereto.[113] It cannot therefore claim that it does not know   **23.65**

---

[107]   Case C-24/95 *Alcan Deutschland* [1997] ECR I-1591, para 34.

[108]   Case C-5/89 *Commission v Germany* [1990] ECR I-3437, para 17.

[109]   Case 94/87 *Commission v Germany* [1989] ECR 175, para 12; Case C-382/99 *Netherlands v Commission* [2003] ECR I-4035, para 90; and Case C-404/00 *Commission v Spain* [2003] ECR I-6695, para 51.

[110]   In this regard, Art 14(3) of the Procedural Regulation does not preclude, when the aid has already been recovered, annulment by the national court of assessments issued in order to recover the unlawful State aid on grounds of there being a procedural defect, where it is possible to rectify that procedural defect under national law. That provision does, however, preclude those amounts from being paid once again, even provisionally, to the beneficiary of that aid (Case C-210/09 *Scott and Kimberly Clark* [2010] ECR I-4613, para 31).

[111]   Case 310/85 *Deufil v Commission* [1987] ECR 901, paras 20–5; Case C-5/89 *Commission v Germany* [1990] ECR I-3437, para 14; Joined Cases T-244/93 and T-486/93 *TWD v Commission* [1995] ECR II-2265, para 69; and Case C-24/95 *Alcan Deutschland* [1997] ECR I-1591, para 25.

[112]   Case C-5/89 *Commission v Germany* [1990] ECR I-3437, para 16 and Joined Cases T-244/93 and T-486/93 *TWD v Commission* [1995] ECR II-2265, para 69.

[113]   In reality, already the adoption of a decision to initiate the procedure under Art 108(2) TFEU in relation to a measure in the course of implementation and classified as new aid necessarily alters the legal position of the measure under consideration and that of the undertakings which are its beneficiaries, particularly as regards the pursuit of its implementation. Whereas, until the adoption of such a decision, the Member State, the beneficiary undertakings, and other economic operators may think that the measure does not constitute

whether the competent authorities are going to reach a decision and will not be able to set the principle of legal certainty against the recovery of the aid on the grounds that the national authorities have taken too long to comply with the recovery decision.[114] Moreover, even if it is the authority that is responsible for the illegality of the aid decision to such a degree that revocation appears to be a breach of good faith towards the recipient, this cannot be construed as grounds for giving the recipient legitimate expectations as to the lawfulness of the aid.[115] Finally, the aid recipient cannot base its case on the fact that the benefit (of the aid) no longer exists, even in the absence of bad faith on its part.[116]

23.66   Such a restrictive account of the arguments that could be legitimately put forward before a national court would seem to be even more justified in the case where the aid-benefiting undertaking had already had the chance to submit an action for annulment directly to the GC against the Commission's decision and to bring up the question of legitimate expectations, which forms part of the fundamental rights underpinning the EU legal order.[117] It cannot be totally ruled out, however, that the recipient could claim before the national courts that it had acquired a legitimate expectation after the adoption of the Commission's decision, for example because of the behaviour of the latter.

23.67   Furthermore, EU law does not prevent national courts from deferring a preliminary question to the Court under Article 267 TFEU or ordering a stay of execution of the recovery requirement proceedings while the basic issue is being dealt with in the EU Court.[118] Suspension interim measures may be granted by national courts provided that certain conditions are met, namely where: the national court entertains serious doubts as to the validity of the EU measure and the validity of the contested measure is not already in issue before the ECJ, that court itself refers the question to the Court; there is urgency, in that the interim relief is necessary to avoid serious and irreparable damage being caused to the party seeking the relief; the national court takes due account of the interests of the EU; in its assessment of all those conditions, the national court complies with any decisions of the EU Courts ruling on the lawfulness of the EU measure or on an application for provisional measures seeking similar interim relief at EU level. Besides, the national court cannot restrict itself to referring the question on validity to the Court for a preliminary ruling, but must, when making the interim order, set out the reasons for which it considers that the Court should find the EU measure to be invalid. These requirements are also applicable to any action seeking a stay of the appeal proceedings in which the national measure for recovery of the unlawful aid is challenged.[119]

---

aid or constitutes existing aid, after its adoption there is at the very least a significant element of doubt as to the legality of that measure which is capable of leading the undertakings that are beneficiaries of the measure to refuse new payments in any event, or to hold the necessary sums as provision for possible subsequent repayments (see Case C- 400/99 *Italy v Commission* [2001] ECR I-7303, para 59).

[114] Case C-24/95 *Alcan Deutschland* [1997] ECR I-1591, paras 27–38. Only delay caused by the Commission, therefore, could be taken into consideration.

[115] Case C-24/95 *Alcan Deutschland* [1997] ECR I-1591, paras 39–43.

[116] Case C-24/95 *Alcan Deutschland* [1997] ECR I-1591, paras 44–54. This is so because, first, it has no legitimate expectations regarding the lawfulness of the aid, and, secondly, it continues in principle to reap the advantages of the aid, in terms of the retention of its place on the market, reputation, and goodwill, even if the benefit resulting from the grant of State aid no longer appears in its balance sheet.

[117] As the undertaking Deufil has done eg in Case 310/85 *Deufil v Commission* [1987] ECR I-537, paras 20–5. See also para 22 of the Opinion of AG Darmon in Case C-5/89 *Commission v Germany* [1990] ECR I-3437. See, however, Case T-459/93 *Siemens v Commission* [1995] ECR II-1675, para 104.

[118] Case T-181/02 R *Neue Erba Lautex v Commission* [2002] ECR II-5081, para 108.

[119] Case C-304/09 *Commission v Italy* [2010] ECR I-13903, paras 45–7; and Case C-243/10 *Commission v Italy* [2012], para 49.

3. Determination of the person bound to return the aid

The aid is to be recovered from the aid recipients, ie the persons who have actually benefited **23.68** from it.[120] The implementation of this rule is not always straightforward, especially in the event of the sale of the undertaking or the part of the undertaking concerned between the moment of granting the aid and the moment the Commission's decision was taken. The implementation arrangements must always take into account that the main purpose of the reimbursement is to eliminate the distortion of competition.[121] Therefore, if, at the stage of the implementation, it appears that the aid was transferred to other entities, recovery may have to be extended to encompass all effective beneficiaries to ensure that the recovery obligation is not circumvented. The obligation to recover aid paid to a company in difficulty may thus be extended to a new company to which the company in question has transferred part of its assets, where that transfer permits the conclusion that there is an economic continuity between the two companies. For a finding of the existence of an economic continuity, the following factors may be taken into consideration: the subject matter of the transfer (assets and liabilities, maintenance of the workforce, grouped assets); the price of the transfer; the identity of the shareholders or the owners of the undertaking which takes over and of the initial undertaking; the time at which the transfer takes place (after the beginning of the investigation, the opening of the procedure or the final decision); or the economic logic of the operation.[122]

Recovery from third party undertakings

In certain decisions the Commission has ordered incompatible aid to be recovered not only **23.69** from the direct recipient thereof, but also other undertakings in whose benefit there has been a transfer of shares ('share deal') or assets ('asset deal') from the direct recipient, in particular when it suspects that this transfer had been carried out to undermine the effects of the Commission's decision.

In the case of a 'share deal', the aid-receiving undertaking continues to exist; only the own- **23.70** ership thereof has changed. The recovery obligation is hence still incumbent on it, the aid following the undertaking. The Court has held that where an undertaking that has benefited from unlawful State aid is bought at the market price, that is to say at the highest price which a private investor acting under normal competitive conditions was ready to pay for that company in the situation it was in, in particular after having enjoyed State aid, the aid element was assessed at the market price and included in the purchase price. In such circumstances, the buyer cannot be regarded as having benefited from an advantage in relation to other market operators.[123]

In the case of an 'asset deal', the Court concentrates on the financial conditions of these transac- **23.71** tions. When there is a sale at a market price, it considers that the aid element has been assessed

---

[120] Case C-303/88 *Italy v Commission* [1991] ECR I-1433, para 57; Joined Cases C-328/99 and C-399/00 *Italy and others v Commission* [2003] ECR I-4035, para 65; and Case C-277/00 *Germany v Commission* [2004] ECR I-3925, para 75.

[121] Case C-277/00 *Germany v Commission* [2004] ECR I-3925, para 76.

[122] Joined Cases C-328/99 and C-399/00 *Italy and others v Commission* [2003] ECR I-4035, paras 77–8; Joined Cases T-415/05, T-416/05, and T-423/05 *Greece and Others v Commission* [2010] ECR I-4749, para 135; and Case T-123/09 *Ryanair v Commission* [2012], para 155. See also Commission Decision N 321/2008, N 322/2008, N 323/2008 Olympic Airlines [2010] OJ C18/9; Commission Decision N 510/2008 Vente des actifs d'Alitalia [2009] OJ C46/6; Commission Decision SA.34547 Analyse de la continuité économique dans le cadre de la reprise des actifs de Sernam [2012] OJ C305/10.

[123] Case C-277/00 *Germany v Commission* [2004] ECR I-3925, paras 80–1 (see, by contrast, para 78 of the judgment of 20 September 2001 in Case C-390/98 *Banks* [2001] ECR I-6117, in which the Court

at market price and included in the purchase price, and therefore the purchaser of the assets cannot in principle be considered to have benefited from a competitive market advantage.[124]

23.72 The ECJ acknowledges that certain circumstances can undermine the effectiveness of the recovery decision, especially when, after the Commission's enquiry or decision, the undertaking's assets and liabilities are transferred to another company (for example, a shell company[125]), controlled by the same persons at below-market prices or by way of procedures that lack transparency; the purpose of such a transaction may be to safeguard the assets from the decision and allow the economic activity in question to be continued indefinitely.[126] It then accepts that the recovery should not be restricted to the original firm, but should also be extended to the firm that continues the activity of the original firm, using the transferred means of production, in cases where certain elements of the transfer point to economic continuity between the two firms. The factors that have to be taken into account are the purpose of the transfer, the identity of the shareholders or owners of the acquiring firm and of the original firm, the moment at which the transfer was carried out, the economic logic, and, above all, the transfer price. The Commission has to be able to establish that the assignment price has been influenced (downwards) by the purchaser's risk of having to return the aid in due course; if not, the Court considers that it is the original undertaking or its shareholders that have kept the benefit of the aid received from the sale of its shares at market price.[127] In other words, in the case of a repurchase of assets at market price, the aid element would have been included in the purchase price and the purchaser cannot be regarded as having benefited from an advantage in relation to other market operators.[128]

4. Determination of the body through which the aid-repayment operation is to be effected

23.73 Unless specifically indicated by the Commission, in principle it is sufficient for the recipient to repay the aid through the body from which it had originally received it. True, it cannot be ruled out that such an allocation of funds to this body could in turn be considered as new aid. But such aid is not covered by the Commission's original negative decision and it cannot therefore demand that the aid be returned into the coffers of the public authorities in the strict sense,[129] at least in the absence of any explicit indication to that effect in the decision.

5. Calculation of the sum to be recovered

23.74 No provision requires the Commission, when ordering the recovery of aid declared incompatible with the internal market, to fix the exact amount of the aid to be recovered. It is sufficient for the Commission's decision to include information enabling the recipient to work out that amount itself, without too much difficulty.[130] The obligation on a Member State to calculate

asserted that 'when a company which has benefited from aid has been sold at the market price, the purchase price reflects the consequences of the previous aid, and it is the seller of that company that keeps the benefit of the aid').

[124] Case C-390/98 *Banks* [2001] ECR I-6117, para 77 and Case C-277/00 *Germany v Commission* [2004] ECR I-3925, para 80.
[125] Case C-277/00 *Germany v Commission* [2004] ECR I-3925, para 86.
[126] Joined Cases C-328/99 and C-399/00 *Italy and others v Commission* [2003] ECR I-4035, para 69.
[127] Joined Cases C-328/99 and C-399/00 *Italy and others v Commission* [2003] ECR I-4035, paras 77–85.
[128] Case C-390/98 *Banks* [2001] ECR I-6117, para 77 and Case C-277/00 *Germany v Commission* [2004] ECR I-3925, para 80.
[129] Case C-348/93 *Commission v Italy* [1995] ECR I-673, paras 28–9 and Case C-350/93 *Commission v Italy* [1995] ECR I-699, paras 23–4.
[130] Case 102/87 *France v Commission* [1988] ECR 4067, para 33; Case C-415/03 *Commission v Greece* [2005] ECR I-3875, para 39; Case C-441/06 *Commission v France* [2007] ECR I-8887, para 29; and Case T-177/07 *Mediaset v Commission* [2010] ECR II-2341, para 181.

the exact amount of aid to be recovered—particularly where that calculation is dependent on information which that Member State has not provided to the Commission—forms part of the more general reciprocal obligation to cooperate in good faith in the implementation of Treaty rules concerning State aids imposed on the Commission and the Member States.[131]

In particular, in so far as the calculation of the amount of aid to be recovered may call for **23.75** consideration of tax regimes where the basis of assessment, the rates, and the rules governing recovery are fixed directly by the relevant domestic legislation, the Commission is entitled merely to make a general statement that the recipient is obliged to repay the aid in question and to leave it up to the national authorities to calculate the exact amount of aid to be recovered.[132] The Commission is not obliged to determine the incidence of tax on the amount of aid to be recovered, since that calculation falls within the scope of national law; it is merely required to indicate the gross sum to be recovered. The restoration of the previous situation, which would have prevailed if the operations in question had been carried out without the tax reduction, accordingly calls for the recovery from the beneficiaries of the difference between the standard tax and the reduced tax resulting from the measure at issue.[133] That does not imply reconstructing past events differently on the basis of hypothetical elements, such as the choices, often numerous, which could have been made by the operators concerned, since the choices actually made with the aid might prove to be irreversible. Re-establishing the status quo ante merely enables account to be taken, at the stage of recovery of the aid by the national authorities, of tax treatment which may be more favourable than the ordinary treatment which, in the absence of unlawful aid and in accordance with domestic rules which are compatible with EU law, would have been granted on the basis of the operation actually carried out.[134]

Interest on the sum to be repaid

The sums to be reimbursed shall include interest calculated from the moment the aid was **23.76** granted to the moment of its effective repayment.[135] This addition of interest, applied by initiative of the Commission and then approved by the EU Courts, was finally enshrined as an official rule in the Procedural Regulation (Article 14(2)).[136] The restoration of the situation that obtained before payment of the unlawful aid indeed entails the elimination of all financial advantages resulting from the aid and adversely affecting competition within the internal market. It follows that a Commission decision ordering the recovery of unlawful aid pursuant to Article 108(2) TFEU will also require interest to be recovered on the sums granted in order to eliminate any financial advantages incidental to such aid. This interest represents the equivalent of the financial advantage accruing from the free provision of the capital in question for a certain period. The absence of any claim to interest on the unlawfully granted sums at the time of their recovery would amount to maintaining incidental financial advantages, consisting of the grant of an interest-free loan, for the undertaking concerned; this would in itself represent the granting of aid that would distort or jeopardize competition.[137]

---

[131] Case C-382/99 *Netherlands v Commission* [2002] ECR I-5163, para 91. For a practical example of a partial recovery ordered by the Commission, IP/13/253 'State aid: Commission orders partial recovery of state aid granted to short-term export-credit insurance companies Ducroire of Belgium and SACE BT of Italy', 20 March 2013.

[132] Case T-67/94 *Ladbroke Racing v Commission* [1998] ECR II-1, para 188 and Case C-480/98 *Spain v Commission* [2000] ECR I-8717, para 26.

[133] Case T-445/05 *Fineco v Commission* [2009] ECR II-289, para 201.

[134] Case C-148/04 *Unicredito Italiano* [2005] ECR I-11137, paras 117–19.

[135] See, initially the letter of 4 March 1991 at <http://ec.europa.eu/competition/state_aid/legislation/archive_docs/d4577_en.html>.

[136] The Court often spoke of 'default interest' (Case C-480/98 *Spain v Commission* [2000] ECR I-8717, para 35).

[137] Case T-459/93 *Siemens v Commission* [1995] ECR II-1675, paras 97–102 and Case C-480/98 *Spain v Commission* [2000] ECR I-8717, para 35.

Exception to the charging of interest

23.77 According to the ECJ, the Commission ought to accept any provisions under national legislation whereby interest ceases to accrue on the debts of undertakings that have been declared insolvent with effect from the date of the relevant declaration. The Court based its position on the following factors: the objective sought by this legislation (the common interest of the creditors not to impose new obligations on the assets of the bankrupt undertaking, likely only to worsen its situation); the absence of any discrimination in its application; and the fact that it applies only to interest falling due after the declaration of insolvency on aid unlawfully received before that declaration, concluding that the legislation cannot be regarded as contrary to the principle of effectiveness.[138]

Calculation of interest

23.78 To determine the interest rate to be applied, the Commission at first merely deferred to national legislation on default interest on State debts. This method soon proved unsatisfactory, so it decided to fix the interest rate. The method for fixing the interest rate is now laid down in Article 9 of Regulation 794/2004.[139] The interest period runs from the date on which the aid was actually made available until the date of its effective repayment.[140]

III. Interim Measures and the Commission's Power to Grant Injunctions

A. Principle

23.79 Although the Treaty is silent on the point, the ECJ has accepted in practice that the Commission should be able to grant certain interim measures to alleviate any infringement by a Member State of its standstill obligation on new aid.[141] It considers that the Treaty's *a priori* control system, if it is to be effective, presupposes that measures may be taken to counteract any infringement of the rules laid down in Article 108(3) TFEU and that such measures may, with a view to protecting the legitimate interests of the Member States, form the subject matter of an action.[142] Conversely, any precautionary measures that might be taken by the Commission seek only to obviate any infringement of the rules of Article 108(3) TFEU, so any interim measure that does not seek such an end will be regarded as unlawful.[143]

23.80 Three types of measures are envisaged, namely decisions ordering the Member State to suspend payment of aid, its provisional recovery, or the provision of information.[144]

---

[138] Case C-480/98 *Spain v Commission* [2000] ECR I-8717, para 37.

[139] As amended by Regulation (EC) 271/2008 of 30 January 2008 [2008] OJ L82/1). See Commission notice on State aid recovery interest rates and reference/discount rates for all 27 EU Member States applicable from 1 June 2013, [2013] OJ C144/7.

[140] Case T-459/93 *Siemens v Commission* [1995] ECR II-1675, para 103 and Case C-169/95 *Spain v Commission* [1997] ECR I-135, para 47. The interest application method is also dealt with in Art 11 of Reg 794/2004.

[141] This possibility of taking 'immediate interim' measures if need be, within the context of Art 108(3) TFEU, was first acknowledged in Case 70/72 *Commission v Germany* [1973] ECR 813, para 20.

[142] Case C-301/87 *France v Commission* [1990] ECR I-307, para 18.

[143] Case T-107/96 R *Pantochim v Commission* [1996] ECR II-1361, paras 40 and 41.

[144] The 'Boussac' suspension injunction as presented in Court judgments usually includes a requirement of information from the State, but such a requirement does not seem to be necessarily bound up with the adoption of a suspension injunction. These two types of injunction are dealt with separately in the sections that follow.

B. 'Boussac' Suspension Injunction

1. Object

This injunction is dealt with in Article 11(1) of the Procedural Regulation. When the **23.81** Commission finds that aid has been set up or altered without preliminary notification, it can carry out the examination to assess the compatibility of this measure with the internal market, but it is also empowered, after having afforded the Member State concerned the opportunity to make its comments, to issue an interim decision requiring it to suspend immediately the payment of the aid pending the result of the aid examination procedure (the so-called 'Boussac' injunction). The Commission has the same power in cases where it has been notified of aid but the Member State in question, instead of awaiting the outcome of the procedure provided for under Article 108(2) and (3) TFEU, has instead proceeded to put the aid into effect, contrary to the prohibition contained in Article 108(3) TFEU.[145]

Such a suspension can be effective only if the aid concerned has not already been entirely **23.82** paid. It would hence seem to be a suitable measure for 'freezing' the implementation of unlawful aid schemes, rather than combating the unlawful payment of individual aid.[146]

When a Member State has complied in full with the Commission's order, the Commission is **23.83** obliged to examine the compatibility of the aid with the internal market, in accordance with the procedure laid down in Article 108(2) and (3) TFEU.[147] Conversely, if the Member State fails to suspend payment of the aid, the ECJ has recognized the Commission's right, while carrying out the substantive examination of the matter, to bring the matter directly before the Court by applying for a declaration that such payment amounts to an infringement of the Treaty. According to the Court, such a referral is justified on the grounds of urgency because there has been a decision embodying an order, taken after the Member State in question has been given an opportunity to submit its comments and thus at the conclusion of a preliminary procedure in which it has been allowed to put forward its arguments, as in the case of the means of redress provided under the second subparagraph of Article 108(2) TFEU.[148]

2. Form

The Commission has sometimes adopted suspension injunctions in the form of a formal deci- **23.84** sion published in the Official Journal of the European Union ('OJ') series L[149] and sometimes in the form of a simple communication, often at the same time as the start of the procedure.[150]

---

[145] Case C-301/87 *France v Commission* [1990] ECR I-307, paras 19 and 20 and Case C-303/88 *Italy v Commission* [1991] ECR I-1433, para 46.

[146] See para 39 of the Opinion of AG Jacobs in Case C-42/93 *Spain v Commission* [1994] ECR I-4175.

[147] Case C-301/87 *France v Commission* [1990] ECR I-307, para 21 and Case C-303/88 *Italy v Commission* [1991] ECR I-1433, para 47.

[148] Case C-301/87 *France v Commission* [1990] ECR I-307, para 23 and Case C-303/88 *Italy v Commission* [1991] ECR I-1433, para 48.

[149] See the Decision of 11 June 1991 requiring the French government to suspend the implementation of the aid described below in favour of PMU and introduced in breach of Art 93(3) [1992] OJ L14/35; and Decision of 30 April 1997 requiring the Portuguese government to suspend the aid in the form of a State guarantee granted to the undertaking EPAC [1997] OJ L186/25.

[150] See, eg the Communication on guidelines introduced by the Burgenland authorities on holdings in companies *in fine* [1998] OJ C154/7; Commission Decision in case C37/2005 *A tax-exempt reserve fund for certain companies in Greece* [2006] OJ C20/6; Commission Decision in Case C41/2007 *Privatisation of Tractorul* [2007] OJ C249/21; and Commission Decision in Case C46/2007 *Privatisation of Automobile Craiova* [2007] OJ C248/25. Even if the opening of the formal investigation already has the legal effect of triggering the standstill obligation, non-compliance with a suspension injunction allows the Commission to refer the matter directly to the ECJ (Art 12 of the Procedural Regulation).

3. Preliminary procedure

23.85 Before adopting a suspension injunction, the Commission is bound to give the Member State concerned an opportunity to submit its comments. This preliminary letter from the Commission requires the State to suspend implementation of the aid and inform the Commission of the measures taken to meet this obligation. The Commission then gives it in principle a thirty-day period to respond. This letter is often enclosed with the letter communicating the initiation of the formal examination procedure.[151] The injunction properly speaking is then adopted if the Member State declines or fails to respond.

4. Simple enabling power

23.86 The Commission is simply empowered to resort to this procedure but is by no means required automatically to order the Member State concerned to suspend the payment of aid that has not been duly notified.[152] The Commission is hence invested with a discretionary power and would not be bound to give grounds to a disgruntled competitor for its decision not to make use of this suspension procedure.

C. Provisional Recovery Injunction

23.87 According to Article 11(2) of the Procedural Regulation, the Commission may, after giving the Member State concerned the opportunity to submit its comments, adopt a decision requiring the Member State provisionally to recover any unlawful aid until the Commission has taken a decision on the compatibility of the aid with the internal market.[153] It lays down strict eligibility conditions for resorting to this recovery injunction; there must be no doubts about the aid character of the measure concerned; there must be an urgency to act and a serious risk of substantial and irreparable damage to a competitor. The burden of proof is on the Commission, so this procedure is difficult to resort to and hence rarely used.

23.88 After the aid has been effectively recovered, the Commission shall take a decision within the time limits applicable to notified aid. The Commission may authorize the Member State to couple the refunding of the aid with the payment of rescue aid to the firm concerned. This type of injunction may be applicable only to unlawful aid implemented after the entry into force of the Procedural Regulation. Non-compliance with a recovery injunction allows

---

[151] See eg the Communication on the guidelines of the Wirtschaftsservice Burgen-land Aktiengesellschaft on holdings in companies [1998] OJ C154/7, 11.

[152] Case T-49/93 *SIDE v Commission* [1995] ECR II-2501, para 83.

[153] On the basis of the *Boussac* judgment, the Commission had previously regarded itself as also empowered to take decisions requiring Member States to provisionally recover aid paid out in breach of the last sentence of Art 108(3) TFEU, to counter this breach, this entitlement lasting until the final decision on the compatibility of the measure (Communication to Member States [1995] OJ C156/5). The compatibility of such an injunction with the case law of the Court was not certain, however: AG Jacobs had requested a solution of this type in 1994 (Opinion in Case C-42/93 *Spain v Commission* [1994] ECR I-4175, para 39), but the Court, in para 45 of the judgment of 11 July 1996 in Case C-39/94 *SFEI and others* [1996] ECR I-3547, declared that 'the Commission can do no more than order further payments to be suspended so long as it has not adopted its final decision on the substance of the matter'. The Commission itself seemed resigned to not being able to order a provisional recovery pending the Council regulation (see the position expressed by this institution in para 26 of the Order of 21 October 1996 in Case T-107/96 R *Pantochim v Commission* [1996] ECR II-1361). It is no doubt for this reason that the Commission has seen fit since to waive the use of this power that it had thought itself entitled to.

the Commission to refer the matter directly to the ECJ for a declaration that the failure to comply constitutes an infringement of the Treaty.

D. Information Injunction

The information injunction contained in Article 10(2) and (3) of the Procedural Regulation **23.89** is an instrument at the disposal of the Commission when faced with a Member State that does not comply with its duty to cooperate with the Commission and fails to furnish the information requested. The failure to furnish the Commission with sufficient information hardly raises any problem when the Member State has complied with its duty of not paying the aid before receiving the Commission's approval; indeed, the Commission can refrain from authorizing the implementation of the aid until it has received all necessary information. It is therefore not necessary to resort to an information injunction. However, the same cannot be said of unlawful aid, for in this case it is in the interests of the internal market for the Commission to be able to alleviate the effects of any incompatibility of the measure as soon as possible.

To guarantee the effectiveness of the system, the ECJ decided that, failing the cooperation **23.90** of the Member State concerned, the Commission was empowered to base its decision on the only information to hand. The Member State's silence hence played against it. In view of the exorbitant nature of this power granted to the Commission, however, the ECJ ruled that, before taking a decision, the Commission had to require the Member State to furnish all necessary information. This is therefore a procedural stage introduced by the Court in an attempt to reconcile the States' right to a defence and the need to deal with unlawful aid cases swiftly and efficiently.[154]

Such an injunction is not systematically made use of; it is only when the Commission consid- **23.91** ers that it is not in possession of all the necessary information that it requires the Member State concerned to furnish it. It is perfectly entitled to adopt a final decision directly without doing so, on the understanding that when it has not made use of its powers to require the Member State concerned to furnish it with information, it cannot then justify its decision on the grounds of the fragmentary nature of the information to hand.[155] The possibility granted to the Commission of adopting a decision on whether or not the aid is compatible with the internal market on the basis of the information available, where it is faced with a Member State which does not fulfil its duty to cooperate and has not provided the Commission with the information requested, cannot be interpreted as releasing that institution entirely from the obligation to base its decisions on reliable and coherent evidence to support the conclusions which it arrives at.[156]

---

[154] An information injunction is intended to produce binding legal effects and therefore constitutes an act open to challenge for the purposes of Art 263 TFEU (Joined Cases C-463/10 P and C-475/10 P *Deutsche Post and Germany v Commission* [2011], para 45).

[155] Case T-274/01 *Valmont Nederland v Commission* [2004] ECR II-3145, paras 58 and 60. On 13 July 2012, the Commission invited comments on the application of procedural rules in State aid investigations and in particular with regard to the collection of market information, with a view to proposing a revised Procedural Regulation (see Commission Press Release IP/12/783 'State aid: Commission consults on reform of procedures' of 13 July 2012). It is yet to be seen whether any new powers granted to the Commission will have consequences as regards the current possibility of basing its decision on the information to hand.

[156] Case C-520/07 P *Commission v MTU* [2002] ECR I-8555, paras 54–5.

23.92 The Procedural Regulation envisages the information injunction as part of the unlawful aid control procedure and obliges the Commission to address a first request for information to the State concerned (Article 10(2) and (3)) and then, if need be, a reminder. Two situations are possible depending on whether the purpose of the injunction is to allow the Commission to open the examination procedure with standstill effect (*Italgrani* injunction) or to enable it to adopt a final decision (*Pleuger* injunction).

1. *Italgrani* injunction

23.93 The first case covers those situations in which individual aid or an aid scheme has been approved by the Commission and therefore constitutes in principle an existing aid, but the Commission suspects that the existing aid has been applied in an improper fashion (breaching the approval decision), or that, under cover of existing aid, entirely new aid has in fact been paid out. In such a case the Commission might be bound to send a previous information injunction to the Member State before being able to open the formal examination procedure and come to the conclusion that it in fact consists of new aid or an improper use of existing aid. This injunction, called the *Italgrani* injunction, is part of the wider picture of the vetting of existing aid and is dealt with in more detail in Chapter 24, 'Control of Existing Aid Schemes', at paragraph 24.27.

2. *Pleuger* injunction

23.94 The other situation arises when the Commission is conducting an enquiry into unlawfully granted aid and the Member State fails to furnish the Commission with certain information on the aid, either due to deliberate evasion or lack of organization. In this case, the Commission formally asks it to furnish the information required. and it is only if the Member State still fails to come up with the information sought, despite the Commission's order, that the latter is entitled to put an end to the procedure and base its final decision on the information to hand.[157] Thus, in the *Pleuger* case, the Court held that in order for the Commission to be able to deal with the whole set of individual aid as a scheme or programme, as it appeared solely from the information to hand (thus permitting it to establish the application of Article 107 TFEU globally and not in relation to each individual aid) when the Member State has denied the existence of such a scheme, the Commission must first require the Member State by way of an interim decision to furnish it with all relevant information on the whole set of aid concerned.[158] In this case, the Commission's injunction is normally adopted after or concurrently with the opening of a procedure under Article 108(2) TFEU and before the final decision (unlike an *Italgrani* injunction, which has to be adopted before the initiation of the procedure). The *Pleuger* injunction probably does not constitute a contestable act. Such an injunction can be adopted at the same time as a *Boussac* injunction for suspension of the part of the aid not yet granted.

23.95 A variant of this procedure concerns aid that the Commission suspects is being misused and in relation to which it has already opened the examination procedure.

---

[157] Case C-301/87 *France v Commission* [1990] ECR I-307, para 22; Case C-303/88 *Italy v Commission* [1991] ECR I-1433, para 47; Joined Cases C-324/90 and C-342/90 *Germany and Pleuger Worthington v Commission* [1994] ECR I-1173, para 26; and Case T-274/01 *Valmont Nederland v Commission* [2004] ECR II-3145, para 55.

[158] Joined Cases C-324/90 and C-342/90 *Germany and Pleuger Worthington v Commission* [1994] ECR I-1173.

24

CONTROL OF EXISTING AID SCHEMES

Jean Paul Keppenne and Carlos Urraca Caviedes

The existing aid schemes in the various Member States are permanently reviewed by the **24.01** Commission under Article 108(1) of the Treaty on the Functioning of the European Union ('TFEU'). It can propose or demand that these schemes be altered or abolished when it considers that their compatibility with the internal market is not clear.

The notion of 'existing aid' is examined in Part I of this chapter and the determina- **24.02** tion of whether aid can be considered to be existing aid is examined in Part II. Part III deals with the procedural arrangements for the permanent review system exercised by the Commission in cooperation with Member States.

I. Concept of Existing Aid Scheme

The category of existing aid takes in the whole set of aid that can be or has been granted **24.03** by Member States. The notion of existing aid aims to ensure legal certainty for Member States and recipient undertakings by guaranteeing the legality of the aid concerned.

Existing aid can therefore continue to be paid as long as the Commission has not found it to be incompatible with the internal market.[1]

A. Distinction between an Existing Aid Scheme and Existing Individual Aid

24.04 The control of existing aid, properly speaking, concerns only aid schemes and not individual aid. When an aid scheme is said to be 'existing', this means that the individual aid can be paid to recipients in application of this scheme (individual case of application) without the Commission needing in principle to carry out a new preliminary review. In so far as such a scheme allows the granting of a host of individual aid during a period that might be unlimited, therefore, it is important that there be a system in place for regularly reviewing and reassessing its compatibility with the internal market in line with ongoing economic and regulatory trends. This is not the case, however, with existing individual aid, which has been approved on the basis of its own characteristics and can hence be paid to its recipient without being called into question any longer.

24.05 The permanent review procedure for existing aid contained in paragraphs 1 and 2 of Article 108 TFEU concerns in principle, therefore, only aid schemes. Indeed, in so far as it is a procedure that has only future effects, it makes sense only in relation to measures that have not yet been paid to their recipients.

B. Categories of Existing Aid

24.06 The TFEU does not contain a definition of existing aid. It merely refers to it in Article 108(1) TFEU, which provides that the Commission shall, in cooperation with Member States, keep under constant review all systems of aid existing in those States and shall propose to the latter any appropriate measures required by the progressive development or by the functioning of the internal market. The notion of existing aid can initially be traced through the case law of the European Court of Justice ('ECJ') and was finally codified in the Procedural Regulation,[2] where existing aid is grouped into five categories; three main ones,[3] namely approved aid, 'pre-accession' aid, and *Lorenz* aid; and two subsidiary categories, aid benefiting from the recovery limitation period and measures that become aid after coming into force, which were added by the Procedural Regulation.[4]

1. Approved aid[5]

24.07 First of all, existing aid is considered to be aid that has already been approved by an express decision from the Commission declaring it to be compatible with the internal market[6] (or, as the case may be, by the Council on the basis of Article 108(2)(3) TFEU). This is the most

---

[1] Case C-387/92 *Banco Exterior de España* [1994] ECR I-877, para 20.
[2] Council Regulation (EC) 659/1999 of 22 March 1999, laying down detailed rules for the application of Article 93 of the EC Treaty [1999] OJ L83/1.
[3] Case C-44/93 *Namur-Les assurances du crédit* [1994] ECR I-3829, para 13.
[4] See also alterations to existing aid (Ch 22, 'Prior Control of New Notified Aid', para 22.05 et seq).
[5] See Art 1(b)(ii) of the Procedural Regulation.
[6] See in this regard Joined Cases C-465/09 P to C-470/09 P *Diputación Foral de Vizcaya and Others v Commission* [2011] ECR I-83, paras 91–103.

important category; most of the aid granted by Member States is deemed to be in application of aid schemes whose particular arrangements have been approved by the Commission.

To qualify as existing aid, it is necessary for the individual application of an approved scheme to observe completely not only the particular arrangements of the scheme as they have been notified to the Commission, but also any conditions or restrictions, sectoral or otherwise, that might have been imposed by the Commission at the moment of approving the scheme. In other words, it must be aid that represents the strict and foreseeable application of the conditions laid down in the decision approving the general aid scheme.[7] **24.08**

2. Pre-accession aid

Secondly, all aid that already 'existed' on the day a given Member State joined the EU is, in principle, considered to be existing aid. This obviously takes in all the individual aid that had been granted to undertakings before accession, but also aid schemes in force on the day of accession. The individual cases of application of these schemes can therefore continue to be legally granted after accession.[8] **24.09**

Given that 'pre-accession' aid may turn out to be incompatible with existing legislation or the Commission's practice, provision needs to be made for bringing it into line with EU interests. This can be done either at the moment the new Member State joins the EU, by inserting specific provisions in the Act of Accession, or later by following the classic *ex nunc* aid-altering procedure as laid down in paragraphs 1 and 2 of Article 108 TFEU. **24.10**

In the case of Austria, Finland, and Sweden, consideration was given to the fact that an EFTA (European Free Trade Association) aid control system already existed. Article 172 of the Act of Accession made provision for a transmission of powers from the EFTA Surveillance Authority ('ESA') to the Commission. In particular, it stipulated that all decisions taken by the ESA before the date of accession remain valid in regard to Article 107 TFEU, but that aid granted in 1994 by the new Member States in breach of the control procedure laid down in the EEA agreement is not considered to be existing aid within the meaning of Article 108(1) TFEU.[9] **24.11**

Accessions in 2004, 2007, and 2013

Some specific provisions have been made in the most recent Acts of Accession.[10] A specific procedure has in particular been set up allowing the Commission to assess the compatibility of aid already approved by the public-aid review authority of the new Member State. Some one-off interim derogations have also been agreed to for certain new Member States. **24.12**

3. 'Lorenz' aid

To lessen the impact of any failing by the Commission, the ECJ had set up another category of existing aid, subsequently endorsed in the Procedural Regulation: when a Member State **24.13**

---

[7] Case C-321/99 P *ARAP and Others v Commission* [2002] ECR I-4287, para 83; Case T-20/03 *Kahla Thüringen Porzellan v Commission* [2008] ECR II-2305, para 93; and Joined Cases T-102/07 and T-120/07 *Freistaat Sachsen v Commission* [2010] ECR II-585, para 60. By contrast, where aid alleged to have been granted in pursuance of a previously authorized scheme of aid does not comply with the conditions laid down in the Commission decision approving the scheme and is therefore not covered by it, that aid must be regarded as new aid (Case C-36/00 *Spain v Commission* [2002] ECR I-3243, para 24).
[8] See Case C-387/92 *Banco Exterior de España* [1994] ECR I-877, para 19, discussed at para 24.03.
[9] Acts of Accession [1994] OJ C241/1. In the agricultural sector see Art 144 of the Act of Accession.
[10] Annex IV (List referred to in Art 22 of the Act of Accession), s 3 (Competition Policy) [2003] OJ L236/797; Annex V (List referred to in Art 18 of the Protocol: other permanent provisions), s 2 (Competition Policy) [2005] OJ L157/93; and Annex IV (List referred to in Article 16 of the Act of Accession: other permanent provisions), s 2 (Competition Policy) [2012] OJ L112/60.

notifies new aid to the Commission, but the Commission then fails to react to this notification within two months, the Member State is then authorized to pay the aid to the recipient, after having informed the Commission thereof. This aid then comes under the system of existing aid.[11] This is a category of aid where its compatibility with the internal market may be problematic, but which Member States are nonetheless entitled to grant to make up for any failing by the Commission.[12]

4. Aid benefiting from the recovery limitation period

24.14 The Procedural Regulation has introduced a category of aid granted unlawfully but then benefiting from the ten-year time limit, after which a recovery order can no longer be made.[13]

5. Measures that become aid after coming into force

24.15 The Procedural Regulation has introduced a category of aid which is deemed to be existing aid because it can be established that it did not constitute aid at the time it was implemented, but subsequently became aid due to the 'evolution of the common market' and without itself being altered.[14] That concept of 'evolution of the common market' can be understood as a change in the economic and legal framework of the sector concerned by the measure in question. Such a change can, in particular, be the result of the liberalization of a market initially closed to competition.

24.16 The concept of 'evolution of the common market' does not cover the situation where the Commission alters its appraisal on the basis only of a more rigorous application of the Treaty rules on State aid. It follows that the mere finding that there has been a development of State aid policy is not, in itself, sufficient to constitute an 'evolution of the common market'.[15]

II. Determination of whether Aid can be Considered to be Existing Aid

24.17 As in the classification of a measure as aid, deciding whether aid is new or existing cannot be allowed to depend on a subjective assessment by the Commission; instead, it must be determined quite independently of any previous administrative practice.[16] It is sometimes difficult to decide whether or not aid should be defined as existing. This might especially be the case when a Member State wishes to pay aid to a private undertaking in application of an existing aid scheme in which it is difficult to decide whether, in this particular case, the compatibility

---

[11] Case 120/73 *Lorenz* [1973] ECR 1971, para 4 and Case C-312/90 *Spain v Commission* [1992] ECR I-4117, para 18.

[12] The *Lorenz* procedure is dealt with in Ch 22, 'Prior Control of New Notified Aid', para 22.51 et seq.

[13] See Ch 23, 'Unlawful Aid', para 23.41.

[14] Procedural Regulation, Art 1(b)(v).

[15] Joined Cases C-182/03 and C-217/03 *Belgium and Forum 187 v Commission* [2006] ECR I-5479, para 71; Case C-89/08 P *Commission v Ireland* [2009] ECR I-11245, para 71; and Joined Cases T-30/01 to T-32/01 and T-86/02 to T-88/02 *Territorio Histórico de Álava and Others v Commission* [2009] ECR II-2919, paras 174 and 186. The fact that an aid was introduced at a time when the markets were, in any event, albeit almost certainly to differing degrees, open to competition, leads to the conclusion that the aid cannot be regarded as falling within Art 1(b)(v) of the Procedural Regulation (Case T-189/03 ASM *Brescia SpA v Commission* [2009] ECR II-1831, para 109).

[16] Case C-295/97 *Piaggio* [1999] ECR I-3735, paras 45–8; Joined Cases T-195/01 and T-207/01 *Government of Gibraltar v Commission* [2002] ECR II-2309, para 121; and Joined Cases T-269/99, T-271/99, and T-272/99 *Territorio Histórico de Guipúzcoa and others v Commission* [2002] ECR II-4217, para 80.

conditions under which the aid was granted are still being met. This might also occur in the case of individual aid when there are doubts about whether the Member State is complying with the conditions subject to which aid was approved.

There are two types of eligibility conditions to be met for aid to be able to be granted as existing aid: **24.18**

- The national rules governing the scheme or the individual aid arrangements, such as they are recorded in the notification to the Commission.
- The supplementary conditions imposed by the Commission at the time of approving the scheme or the aid. These might be specific conditions pertaining to the approved aid, or general obligations arising from quasi regulatory texts adopted by the Commission. The aim of the latter, in principle, is to ensure that the aid approval provisions are met when the aid scheme is subsequently put into effect.

A. Importance of the Question

Deciding whether aid can be regarded as existing aid is crucial because only then can it be granted directly to the beneficiary undertaking without a new notification and control procedure. In the particular case of aid agreed under a scheme already approved by the Commission, the latter is entitled in principle only to verify that the aforementioned scheme conditions are still being met; if so, there will be no need for a subsequent examination of the compatibility of the aid with the Treaty. **24.19**

B. Procedure

There is no regulation laying down how, where there is doubt, it should be decided whether State aid is existing aid. The question arises when aid has already been granted and the Member State concerned claims that it is a particular application of an approved scheme or is being applied in a normal fashion as approved by the Commission, while the Commission itself contests this claim and believes that it might be a case of unlawful aid.[17] **24.20**

1. Individual case of application of an existing scheme

The decision 'albeit on a provisional basis' on whether or not aid should be considered as new or existing aid has to be taken before opening the formal examination procedure.[18] When the Commission has before it a specific grant of aid alleged to be made in pursuance of a previously authorized scheme, it cannot at the outset examine it directly in relation to the Treaty. Prior to the initiation of any procedure, it must first examine whether the aid is covered by the general scheme and satisfies the conditions laid down in the decision approving it. If it did not do so, the Commission could, whenever it examined individual aid, go back on its decision approving the aid scheme which already involved an examination in the light of Article 107 TFEU. This would jeopardize the principles of the protection of legitimate expectations and legal certainty from the point of view of both the Member States and traders, **24.21**

---

[17] On the other hand, if the Member State accepts that the aid constitutes new aid or an alteration of existing aid, the Commission may immediately treat it as such and is then *a priori* justified in initiating the formal examination procedure under the regime applicable to new aid (Case T-190/00 *Regione Siciliana v Commission* [2003] ECR II-5015, para 65).

[18] Joined Cases T-297/01 and T-298/01 *SIC v Commission* [2004] ECR II-743, para 49.

since individual aid in strict conformity with the decision approving the aid scheme could at any time be called into question anew by the Commission.[19]

24.22 Should the Commission find, after an examination in the aforementioned limited sense, that individual aid abides by the aid-scheme approval decision, this aid should then be treated as authorized aid and *ipso facto* as existing aid. The Commission cannot then suspend such aid, because Article 108(3) TFEU empowers it to do so only in relation to new aid. Conversely, should the Commission find that the individual aid is not covered by its aid-scheme approval decision, the aid should then be considered to be new aid.[20]

24.23 However, this case law can be properly invoked only when the national authorities have clearly asserted that the aid comes under an approved scheme and not:

- when they first claimed that the aid in question was existing aid only after the initiation of the formal examination procedure;[21] or
- when they themselves notified the measure to the Commission as new aid in application of Article 108(3) TFEU.[22]

24.24 When the Commission has already opened the formal examination procedure laid down in Article 108(2) TFEU against aid it considers to be new, and then, while the procedure is underway, the Member State concerned proposes some amendments to the project to bring it into line with a general aid-scheme approval decision, the Commission should first assess whether such amendments really do bring the project into line with the aid-scheme approval decision. If so, it no longer has the right to assess the aid project's compatibility with Article 107 TFEU, since this assessment has already been made in the context of the procedure culminating in the decision approving the general scheme.[23]

2. Application of individual aid (ad hoc aid)

24.25 The same reasoning applies when a Member State claims that individual aid has been implemented in due accordance with the Commission decision that approved it. The Commission should first check whether the aid has been properly applied in a normal fashion and can benefit from the initial approval before, if need be, opening a formal examination procedure if it considers there to be a misuse of aid.

3. Procedure to be followed for carrying out this preliminary check: the *Italgrani* case

24.26 If the Commission already has enough evidence to hand to cast doubts on the measure's right to be qualified as existing aid, it can immediately open the examination procedure laid down in Article 108(2) TFEU.[24] However, in view of the legal consequences of a decision to initiate the procedure provided for in Article 108(2) TFEU, classifying the measures concerned as new aid even though the Member State concerned is unlikely to subscribe to that classification, the Commission must first broach the subject of the measures in question with the

---

[19] Case C-47/91 *Italy v Commission* [1994] ECR I-4635, para 24; Case C-400/99 *Italy v Commission* [2005] ECR I-3657, para 57; and Case T-176/01 *Ferriere Nord v Commission* [2004] ECR II-3931, para 51.

[20] Case C-47/91 *Italy v Commission* [1994] ECR I-4635, paras 25 and 26; and Joined Cases T-30/01 to T-32/01 and T-86/02 to T-88/02 *Territorio Histórico de Álava and Others v Commission* [2009] ECR 2919, para 197.

[21] Case T-190/00 *Regione Siciliana v Commission* [2003] ECR II-5015, para 78.

[22] Case T-176/01 *Ferriere Nord v Commission* [2004] ECR II-3931, paras 54–6.

[23] Case T-435/93 *ASPEC and others v Commission* [1995] ECR II-1281, para 105 and Case T-442/93 *AAC and others v Commission* [1995] ECR II-1329, para 86.

[24] Case C-47/91 *Italy v Commission* [1994] ECR I-4635, para 31.

Member State concerned so that the latter has an opportunity, if appropriate, to inform the Commission that, in its view, those measures do not constitute aid or else constitute existing aid.[25] The effect of opening this procedure is then to treat the aid as new aid or misuse of aid; this implies that the aid is considered to be unlawful and the payment thereof should be suspended.

On the other hand, if the Commission only entertains doubts about whether individual aid **24.27** is compatible with its scheme-approval decision, it should first of all ask the Member State concerned to furnish it with all necessary information and documentation for deciding on the conformity of the aid in question with the scheme and its scheme approval decision (the so-called '*Italgrani* injunction'), within the time period laid down by the Commission.[26] It is only if the Commission finds after this examination that the individual aid is not covered by the scheme as approved that the aid in question can be considered to be new aid and treated as such. Should the Member State fail to come up with the required information, despite the Commission's injunction, the Commission will then be entitled to order the suspension of the aid and directly assess its conformity with the Treaty as though it were a case of new aid.[27] By definition, therefore, the *Italgrani* injunction is adopted before initiating the formal procedure of Article 108(2) TFEU.

A variant of this situation occurs when the Commission thinks that its initial approval deci- **24.28** sion has been tainted by false information given by the Member State and wishes to reopen the file. If the Member State contests the Commission's interpretation, it would seem that the Commission is bound, in the event of doubt, to ask the Member State to provide it with all information it needs to reach a decision before being able to initiate the examination procedure for abuse of aid, which procedure suspends the implementation of the aid.

The deadline given to the Member State to provide the information required is usually short, **24.29** being only a few weeks.

4. Consequences of an error of assessment

Should the Commission realize at any stage of the procedure that it has made a mistake in its **24.30** assessment of the new or existing character of aid, it should try as far as possible to obviate the consequences of this error. Nothing prevents the Commission, after initially determining in the decision to open the formal investigation procedure that the measure in question constitutes new aid, from deciding in the decision concluding the procedure that the measure constitutes existing aid.[28]

5. Interpretation of the scope of an existing scheme

The attempt to ascertain whether individual aid is an application of an existing scheme might **24.31** raise some questions of interpretation about the scope of the scheme in question. In such cases, it is necessary to interpret the national provisions concerning an authorized regime in light of the EU rules on the matter, namely, the Commission's decision to approve this scheme and the relevant provisions of the Treaty.[29]

---

[25] Case T-211/05 *Italy v Commission* [2009] ECR II-2777, para 37 and Case C-400/99 *Italy v Commission* [2001] ECR I-7303 ('the interlocutory judgment'), paras 59 and 60.

[26] Case C-47/91 *Italy v Commission* [1994] ECR I-4635, para 34.

[27] Case C-47/91 *Italy v Commission* [1994] ECR I-4635, para 35.

[28] Case T-190/00 *Regione Siciliana v Commission* [2003] ECR II-5015, para 48. Similarly, the Commission should be able to classify the measures under examination as new aid and open the formal investigation procedure after having initially opted for the cooperation procedure provided for in Art 108(1) TFEU.

[29] Case T-459/93 *Siemens v Commission* [1995] ECR II-1675, para 45 and Case C-278/95 P *Siemens v Commission* [1997] ECR I-2507, paras 31–3.

24.32 The Commission has considered that aid granted on the basis of an aid scheme but before this scheme has been authorized by the Commission cannot be considered to be covered by such a scheme.[30]

III. Permanent Review of the Compatibility of Existing Aid

24.33 In view of the fact that an aid scheme might remain in force for a long time, or even indefinitely, the Treaty has made provision for a permanent review procedure whereby the Commission can prohibit or alter existing aid, doing so with future effect.

24.34 This procedure involves permanent cooperation between the Commission and the Member States. If Member States fail to meet their obligations in this regard, the Commission can alter or abolish aid as it sees fit.

A. Permanent Cooperation with Member States

24.35 To ensure the control of existing aid, the Treaty has laid down a permanent cooperation procedure between the Commission and Member States. More specifically, the ECJ considers that Article 108(1) TFEU involves an obligation of regular, periodic cooperation on the part of the Commission and Member States, from which neither the Commission nor a Member State can release itself for an indefinite period of its own volition.[31] Apart from specific obligations, the Court refers to a 'spirit of regular, periodic cooperation'[32] that has to preside over the application of Article 108(1) TFEU. The procedure involves three phases, dealt with in the sections that follow: information to be presented by the Member State concerned; proposal of appropriate measures addressed to the said Member State; and finally either acceptance of these measures by the Member State or the initiation of the formal examination procedure and adoption of a final decision.

1. Exchange of information

24.36 The Commission and the Member States regularly exchange views on a bilateral basis and also in the form of 'multilateral' meetings organized by the Commission. The Commission also makes sure that it is kept informed by Member States of all their existing aid schemes so that it can permanently review them; this is done by means of annual reports.[33]

2. Appropriate measures

Proposal of appropriate measures

24.37 Article 17(1) of the Procedural Regulation provides that the Commission shall obtain from the Member State concerned all necessary information for the review, in cooperation with

---

[30] Decision of 21 December 2000 on the State aid granted by the Federal Republic of Germany to Zeuro Möbelwerk GmbH, Thüringen [2002] OJ L82/1 s 39.

[31] Case C-135/93 *Spain v Commission* [1995] ECR I-1651, para 24 and Case C-311/94 *IJssel-Vliet* [1998] ECR II-1129, para 36.

[32] Case C-311/94 *IJssel-Vliet* [1998] ECR II-1129, para 37.

[33] Article 21 of the Procedural Regulation requires Member States to submit annual reports to the Commission on all existing aid schemes or individual aid granted outside an approved aid scheme in respect of which no specific reporting obligations have been imposed in a conditional decision (see Art 5 of Reg 794/2004).

that Member State, of existing aid schemes, pursuant to Article 108(1) TFEU. Article 17(2) of the Procedural Regulation further provides that, where the Commission considers that an existing aid scheme is not, or is no longer, compatible with the internal market, it shall inform the Member State concerned of its preliminary view and give it the opportunity to submit its comments within a period of one month (which can be extended in duly justified cases). This letter may contain initial indications concerning the modifications that the Member State could introduce to the existing aid in order to render it compatible with the internal market.[34] If the Member State modifies the scheme in line with such indications (without waiting for a formal proposal for appropriate measures) then the Commission usually closes the existing aid procedure by informing the Member State concerned that, after the modifications introduced, the existing aid scheme is compatible with the internal market and that the existing aid procedure is closed.[35]

According to Article 18 of the Procedural Regulation, where the Commission, in the light of **24.38** the information submitted by the Member State pursuant to Article 17, considers that the existing aid scheme does not meet the current compatibility criteria, it sends the Member State concerned a proposal of appropriate measures, in accordance with Article 108(1) TFEU. This is not a binding act producing its own legal effects, but rather a simple recommendation within the meaning of Article 288 TFEU, and the Member State is not obliged to abide by it.[36] It is therefore not an act against which an action for annulment can be brought.

Pursuant to Article 19 of the Procedural Regulation, where the Member State accepts the **24.39** proposed measures and informs the Commission thereof, the Commission shall record that finding[37] and inform the Member State thereof.[38] The consequence of the Member State expressing its consent is that the measures are then binding upon it.[39] The Member State undertakes to alter with future effect the terms for the granting of its existing schemes, in line with the provisions laid down in the proposal of appropriate measures.[40] The arrangement is hence of a quasi-contractual nature, committing both the Member State concerned and the Commission. The scheme's individual cases of application granted by the Member State before accepting the appropriate measures remain valid and are in no way affected by the alteration of the scheme. If, on the contrary, the Member State refuses to accept the appropriate measures proposed by the Commission or fails to give its express consent, the

---

[34] For an example, see Case T-354/05 *TF1 v Commission* [2009] ECR I-471, paras 38–40.

[35] Article 19 of the Procedural Regulation is thus applied by analogy. The GC has endorsed this approach (Case T-354/05 *TF1 v Commission* [2009] ECR I-471, para 43).

[36] Case T-330/94 *Salt Union v Commission* [1996] ECR II-1475, para 35 and Case T-354/05 *TF1 v Commission* [2009] ECR I-471, para 65.

[37] Case T-354/05 *TF1 v Commission* [2009] ECR I-471, paras 45–6.

[38] However, once guidelines have been adopted in the form of appropriate measures, these guidelines containing specific provisions regarding cooperation with Member States, it is then these provisions that govern relationships with Member States, providing these provisions abide by the basic principles of Art 108(1) TFEU. Thus, if the first appropriate measures make due provision for the same, the agreement of the Member States is not necessary when the Commission is merely extending guidelines for a given period without making any alteration thereto (in particular, the *a contrario* interpretation of para 30 of Case C-292/95 *Spain v Commission* [1997] ECR I-1931).

[39] Case C-311/94 *IJssel-Vliet Combinatie* [1998] ECR II-1129, para 42; Case C-242/00 *Germany v Commission* [2002] ECR I-5603, para 28; and Case T-354/05 *TF1 v Commission* [2009] ECR I-471, para 73. This decision can produce binding legal effects capable of affecting the interests of competitors of the aid beneficiary and therefore can constitute a measure which may be the subject of an action for annulment under Art 263 TFEU (Case T-354/05 *TF1 v Commission* [2009] ECR I-471, paras 79–81).

[40] Non-compliance with the appropriate measures will result in the aid being classified as new aid as from the date fixed for the implementation of the appropriate measures (Case C-313/90 *CIRFS and Others v Commission* [1993] ECR I-1125, para 35).

Commission can then follow the procedure laid down in Article 108(2) TFEU to bind the Member State to enforce them.

24.40 Apart from the straightforward abolition of the scheme, the appropriate measures may also deal with the aid compatibility criteria (lowering of maximum intensities, limitation of activities eligible for grants, etc) or the aid-scheme control procedure arrangements (for example, by requiring that certain individual cases of application of existing schemes have to be notified in the future and individually approved before being granted, or by requiring that specific information on the application of existing schemes be sent to the Commission).

Lack of direct effect

24.41 The provisions of Article 108(1) and (2) TFEU governing the control of existing aid schemes do not have direct effect and cannot therefore be invoked before national courts unless they have been put into specific form by acts having general application provided for by Article 109 TFEU or by decisions in particular cases envisaged by Article 108(2) TFEU.[41]

Categories of appropriate measures

24.42 In practice, the appropriate measures proposed by the Commission can be broken down into two different categories depending on their addressees and purpose:

- Sometimes the appropriate measures concern a particular aid scheme that has to be brought into line with the EU rules governing the type of aid concerned.
- On other occasions the appropriate measures are directed at the whole set of existing schemes in one or several Member States and aim to implement a change in the Commission's policy. The appropriate measures then serve to apply the Commission's new guidelines or notices to all existing schemes and comprise rules of general application. If, for example, the Commission intends to bring in stricter rules for aid granted to recipients trading in a certain economic sector (textile, automobile sector, etc), it will propose to Member States that they alter the conditions for granting aid with respect to all their existing schemes affecting the sector in question. In this last case, the alterations proposed by the Commission might come into force at different times in different Member States: in some Member States, from the moment of their acceptance, and in others, those that have rejected the appropriate measures, only from the moment of the adoption of a final decision. To avoid this disparity of treatment, the Commission endeavours, in its appropriate measures, to establish an entry-into-force date for the new rules that is far enough ahead to be valid for all Member States.[42]

24.43 The initiative as to how to operate the control procedure thus belongs to the Commission.[43] It is a case of discretionary power,[44] hedged in by no time limit, which the Commission is not bound to use.[45] It follows that a refusal to issue appropriate measures following a complaint

---

[41] Case 77/72 *Capolongo* [1973] ECR 611, para 6.

[42] Thus, the Commission proposed to Member States that the multi-sectoral guidelines should apply as from 1 September 1998. Germany rejected these appropriate measures, so the Commission had time to initiate the examination procedure in relation to all existing schemes in Germany ([1998] OJ C171/4) and then adopt a final decision that could be notified to Germany before 1 September 1998; these guidelines therefore came into force simultaneously in all Member States on 1 September 1998.

[43] Case C-44/93 *Namur-Les assurances du crédit* [1994] ECR I-3829, para 11.

[44] Case T-354/05 *TF1 v Commission* [2009] ECR I-471, para 188.

[45] As opposed to the situation with new aid, when the Commission is bound to lay down a reasonable time limit from learning of the existence of the aid in question, after a notification, complaint, etc.

cannot be the object of an action for annulment,[46] nor can the Commission's inaction on such a complaint be sanctioned through an action for failure to act.

Duration of the appropriate measures

The obligation of regular periodic cooperation under Article 108(1) TFEU precludes existing **24.44** systems of aid from being examined according to rules established or agreed for an indefinite period depending on the unilateral will of either the Commission or the Member States.[47] It follows that the appropriate measures proposed by the Commission for altering existing schemes of the Member States can have only a limited duration, and their content must be confirmed or altered regularly, in accordance with the procedure laid down in Article 108(1) TFEU.

B. Formal Examination Procedure

If the Member State concerned refuses to accept the appropriate measures proposed by the **24.45** Commission, the Procedural Regulation states that the Articles on new aid shall then apply, *mutatis mutandis*. The Commission, after having examined the arguments put forward by the Member State, can then initiate the formal procedure laid down in paragraph 2 of Article 108 TFEU to bind the Member State to alter its scheme(s). It then invites the Member State concerned and all other parties concerned to make their observations. The procedure initiated must deal with the same aid as that involved in the appropriate measures and have the same object. Thus, if the appropriate measures required alteration of all the existing schemes of a Member State, the procedure as initiated must also deal with the whole set of these schemes.

Unlike the consequences when a Member State notifies new aid, there is no question of a **24.46** standstill effect here as in the examination procedure of Article 108(2) TFEU. Its implementation does not aim to freeze the normal application of existing aid schemes. The Member State concerned can therefore continue to pay its aid on the basis of the existing scheme throughout the whole procedure.[48]

Except for the standstill effect, the arrangements of the formal examination procedure are the **24.47** same as those used for the examination of new aid, as described previously.[49]

Should the Member State voluntarily decide to accept the Commission's appropriate meas- **24.48** ures after initiation of the procedure, the Commission makes an official note thereof and closes the examination procedure,[50] otherwise the procedure follows its course and leads in principle to the adoption of a final decision.

---

[46] Case T-330/94 *Salt Union v Commission* [1996] ECR II-1475, paras 34–5. The Commission's recommendation proposing appropriate measures to the Member State concerned pursuant to Art 18 of the Procedural Regulation is not, taken in isolation, a challengeable act (Case T-354/05 *TF1 v Commission* [2009] ECR I-471, para 65).

[47] Case C-135/93 *Spain v Commission*, para 38 and Case C-311/94 *IJssel-Vliet* [1998] ECR II-1129, para 36.

[48] Case C-312/90 *Spain v Commission* [1992] ECR I-4117, para 17; Case C-47/91 *Italy v Commission* [1992] ECR I-4145, para 25; and Case C-400/99 *Italy v Commission* [2001] ECR I-7303, para 48.

[49] See in particular the comments on the consultation of the parties concerned (see Ch 22, 'Prior Control of New Notified Aid', para 22.86 et seq) and of the Member State concerned (see para 22.81 et seq). On the other hand, since it is a question of existing aid, the Commission does not seem bound to bring the procedure to an end within any deadline.

[50] See, eg the termination of the procedure started against Sweden for enforcing the Community guidelines on State aid to the motor vehicle industry [1998] OJ C122/4.

C. Final Decision

24.49 After the State's refusal to accept the appropriate measures and the initiation of the formal examination procedure, the Commission can adopt a final decision that imposes the alterations or abolitions it considers appropriate.[51] In the course of the examination procedure of existing aid, this final decision is the first act with binding effect.[52] Its effect is only forward looking and therefore, as a general principle of law, it cannot have a retrospective effect. Such a decision hence has a constitutive rather than declaratory effect. It is as a result of the decision and the decision alone that the abolition of the aid or the obligation to alter it, as the case may be, arises.[53]

24.50 It is therefore only as of the date of the Commission's decision, which date must be later than its adoption date, that the aid concerned loses its status of existing aid. Individual aid can continue to be lawfully paid in application of the existing scheme throughout the whole procedure for the re-examination of the scheme, whether this be after the sending of the appropriate measures or after the initiation of the examination procedure.

24.51 According to Article 108(2) TFEU, the Commission's decision can oblige the Member State to abolish or alter the aid 'within a period of time to be determined by the Commission'. According to the ECJ, the idea of cooperation underpinning Article 108 TFEU, in terms of the permanent review of existing aid, obliges the Commission to allow the Member State concerned a period of time within which to comply with the decision taken.[54] It is a moot point whether this means that a fixed deadline should be laid down in the decision.[55] According to Advocate-General ('AG') Mayras, the Commission has to bear in mind the internal procedures necessary for implementing its decision; it could, however, merely require the Member State concerned to act 'without delay.'[56] If the deadline is reached and the Member State has not complied with the decision, any further implementation of the scheme constitutes new and unlawful aid.

24.52 After adopting a decision, the Commission is then bound to ensure that it is entirely and fully put into effect. To do so, it sometimes requires the Member State to send it regular reports on the execution of its decision. The Member States are also bound to send the Commission annual reports on the application of their existing schemes.[57]

[51] Case 70/72 *Commission v Germany* [1973] ECR 813, para 20.
[52] Case T-330/94 *Salt Union v Commission* [1996] ECR II-1475, para 35.
[53] See the Opinion of AG Mayras in Case 70/72 *Commission v Germany* [1973] ECR 813.
[54] Case 173/73 *Italy v Commission* [1974] ECR 709. Along the same lines, Joined Cases C-182/03 R and C-217/03 R *Belgium and Forum 187 v Commission* [2003] ECR I-6887, para 124.
[55] If the Commission has not specified a deadline, but has nevertheless requested the Member State to inform it of the action taken to comply with the decision by a certain date, that date is deemed to constitute the deadline by which the measure must be implemented (Case 213/85 *Commission v Netherlands* [1988] ECR 281, para 19).
[56] See the Opinion of AG Mayras in Case 70/72 *Commission v Germany* [1973] ECR 813.
[57] Articles 5–7 of Reg 794/2004.

25

IMPLEMENTATION OF THE COMMISSION'S DECISIONS

Jean Paul Keppenne and Carlos Urraca Caviedes

I. *A Posteriori* Control by the Commission

A. Annual Reports

Article 21 of the Procedural Regulation[1] requires Member States to submit to the Commission annual reports on all existing aid schemes with regard to which no specific reporting obligations have been imposed in a conditional decision.[2] Where, despite a reminder, the Member State concerned fails to submit an annual report, the Commission may propose appropriate measures with regard to the aid scheme in question. **25.01**

---

[1] Council Regulation (EC) 659/1999 of 22 March 1999, laying down detailed rules for the application of Article 93 of the EC Treaty [1999] OJ L83/1.

[2] Article 5 of Reg 794/2004 details the form and content of the annual reports. The Commission may ask Member States to provide additional data for selected topics, which have to be discussed in advance with the Member States. The annual report must be submitted to the Commission not later than 30 June of the year following the year to which the report relates. Each year the Commission publishes a State aid synopsis containing a synthesis of the information provided in the annual reports (Art 6 of Reg 794/2004). The transmission of annual reports shall not be considered to constitute compliance with the obligation to notify aid measures before they are put into effect, nor shall such transmission in any way prejudice the outcome of any investigation into allegedly unlawful aid (Art 7 of Reg 794/2004).

B. On-site Monitoring

25.02 Breaking with precedent,[3] the Procedural Regulation lays down the principle of 'on-site monitoring' (Article 22). Previously, the Commission used to impose certain control conditions addressed directly to the State: it was the latter that was bound to furnish the Commission, where applicable with the assistance of the undertaking concerned, with sufficient information for checking on compliance with its decision. If the Commission did not receive the necessary information (where necessary after having served an information injunction), it opened the examination procedure for misuse of aid and could finally adopt a negative decision on the basis of the only information to hand. It was hence conducive to the interests of the State and, indirectly, the recipient undertaking to cooperate with the Commission.

25.03 The Procedural Regulation on the other hand lays down direct rights of the Commission services vis-à-vis undertakings. This development seems to be fraught with consequences. While it is true that it facilitates enforcement of the Commission's decisions, it is arguable whether the Commission could henceforth limit its proceedings to simply questioning the Member State concerned before taking a negative decision, or whether it is not always bound to use fully the powers invested in it by the Regulation.[4] It could be argued, moreover, that the Regulation should not be construed as having direct effects against the undertakings concerned; it is rather a case of proceedings to be adopted by Member States with binding character as regards the undertakings concerned (Article 22(6)).[5]

II. Remedies if any of the Commission's Decisions are Breached

25.04 There are several options open to the Commission when it finds that one of its decisions has not been fully complied with. It can first of all bring the matter directly before the European Court of Justice ('ECJ') by applying for a declaration that such payment amounts to an infringement committed by the State. It may also initiate the formal examination procedure to examine the misuse of aid by the Member State. And finally, it may decide to block all new aid to a given undertaking on the grounds of past failures to recover incompatible aid from the same undertaking.

A. Bringing the Matter before the European Court of Justice[6]

25.05 If the Member State does not comply with a Commission decision finding proposed aid to be incompatible or does not meet the conditions placed by the Commission on an aid approval decision, under the second subparagraph of Article 108(2) of the Treaty on the Functioning

---

[3] On-site monitoring by the Commission had already been established in certain particular cases, however. See old Council Reg 1013/97 of 2 June 1997, Art 2 of which stated as follows: 'The programme of monitoring shall include on site monitoring by the Commission.'

[4] See in this regard Joined Cases T-111/01 and T-133/01 *Saxonia Edelmetalle v Commission* [2005] ECR II-1579, paras 99 and 100, where it is considered that the Commission was not under any obligation to carry out an on-site monitoring visit because, in light of the information provided by the national authorities, it could no longer have serious doubts as to whether the aid had not been used in accordance with the decision approving the aid.

[5] In this regard, it should be recalled that on 13 July 2012, the Commission invited comments on the application of procedural rules in State aid investigations and in particular with regard to the collection of market information, with a view to proposing a revised Procedural Regulation (see Commission Press Release IP/12/783 'State aid: Commission consults on reform of procedures' of 13 July 2012).

[6] See Ch 27, 'State Aid Litigation before the EU Courts', para 27.94 et seq.

of the European Union ('TFEU'), both the Commission and any other Member State concerned are entitled to bring the matter directly before the Court by derogation from Articles 258 and 259 TFEU.[7] This option is simply a variant of the action for a failure to comply with obligations, as adapted to the specific internal-market competition problems caused by State aid (or 'the maintenance of State aid declared to be illegal'[8]).[9]

This possibility of direct referral to the Court is part and parcel of the Commission's wider remit of enforcing compliance with its decisions by the Member States. The Commission's monitoring powers over Member States that do not comply with its decisions within the prescribed period mean that the Commission has a wide margin of discretion. The Commission is not, therefore, under any obligation to commence the proceedings provided for in that provision. On the contrary, its wide discretion prevents any individual from requiring it to adopt a specific position.[10] Third parties, therefore, have no procedural rights in the context of monitoring the execution of a decision under the second subparagraph of Article 108(2) TFEU.[11]   **25.06**

In practice, the Commission tends to resort to this option only when a Member State fails to execute a completely negative decision (ordering the abolition or recovery of aid). In cases where a State has failed to abide fully by a conditional decision, it generally tends to initiate a new formal procedure for misuse of aid,[12] because this procedure, unlike direct referral to the Court, allows it to order recovery of the aid for breach of the conditions attached to the declaration of compatibility.   **25.07**

It follows from the wording of the second subparagraph of Article 108(2) TFEU[13] that this possibility of direct referral to the Court is limited to cases in which the Commission has adopted a final decision at the end of a formal examination procedure, on the basis of Article 108(2) TFEU.[14]   **25.08**

B. Procedure in the Event of Abusive Application of Existing Aid

Just as it can initiate a formal procedure against new aid where it has doubts about its compatibility, the Commission may also initiate a formal examination procedure pursuant to Article 108(2) TFEU to ascertain whether aid has been misused.[15]   **25.09**

---

[7] See Art 23 of the Procedural Regulation and Case C-294/90 *British Aerospace and Rover v Commission* [1994] ECR I-5423, para 11, and Case T-277/94 *AITEC v Commission* [1996] ECR II-351, para 65. The Commission can also open a classic procedure for failure to comply with obligations under Art 258 TFEU (Case C-209/00 *Commission v Germany* [2002] ECR I-11695, para 37 and Case C-404/00 *Commission v Spain* [2003] ECR I-6695, para 25).

[8] Case C-209/00 *Commission v Germany* [2002] ECR I-11695, para 37.

[9] Case C-301/87 *France v Commission* [1990] ECR I 307, para 23 and Case T-358/94 *Air France v Commission* [1996] ECR II-2109, para 60.

[10] Case T-277/94 *AITEC v Commission* [1996] ECR II-351, paras 65 and 66.

[11] Case T-277/94 *AITEC v Commission* [1996] ECR II-351, para 54 *in fine*. In particular, private individuals are not entitled to bring proceedings against a refusal by the Commission to institute or continue proceedings against a Member State for failure to fulfil its obligations (para 55).

[12] See para 25.09 et seq.

[13] See also Art 23 of the Procedural Regulation.

[14] The problem is not posed in principle by a decision not to raise objections, adopted at the end of the preliminary examination procedure, for such a decision is by definition a positive decision and is therefore not breachable as such. If a Member State breaches the commitments it made and of which notice was taken in a decision not to raise objections, the Commission may initiate the formal examination procedure to examine the misuse of aid by the Member State.

[15] See Art 16 of the Procedural Regulation.

25.10 Subject to the caveats laid down in paragraphs 25.11 et seq, a misuse of existing aid is dealt with by means of the same procedure as that used in a formal procedure on new unlawful aid. The Commission can therefore initiate the formal examination procedure and adopt a final decision; it can require recovery of aid that has been misused; it can adopt interim measures forcing the State to suspend the improper application of the aid, etc.

25.11 The Procedural Regulation, however, gives a restrictive definition of the notion of misuse of aid, while at the same time laying down an unprecedented 'revocation' procedure. It restricts the concept of misuse of aid to those cases of misuse 'by the beneficiary' (Article 1(g)).[16] It is in principle for the Commission to establish that all or part of the aid previously authorized by it in an earlier decision has been misused by the beneficiary.[17] However, where a Member State fails to comply with an order to provide information, the Commission can close the formal investigation procedure on the basis of the information available, finding that the aid in question has been misused.[18]

25.12 One of the classic conditions placed on the declaration of aid compatibility is the prohibition of granting new aid to the same undertaking, in principle over a set period. Such a prohibition is in particular imposed on undertakings in difficulty.

25.13 According to the ECJ, if this condition is not observed and the undertaking receives new aid, the Commission has to choose from the two following procedures:[19]

- Either it considers it to be a breach of the condition attached to the first decision, in which case it can refer the matter directly to the ECJ, under the second subparagraph of Article 108(2) TFEU.[20]
- Or it can deem it to be new aid that has not been examined under the procedure culminating in the first decision, in which case it initiates a formal examination procedure. If the Member State submits no new information during the formal examination procedure, the Commission is entitled to base its decision on the assessments it made in its previous decision and on the failure to comply with the condition it had imposed therein.[21] In this case it does not, therefore, have to initiate a new detailed examination, provided, however, that it takes its decision at the end of a new procedure under Article 108(2) TFEU.

25.14 There is also a third option, which consists in initiating the procedure in relation to the whole set of aid, so as to examine at the same time the misuse of the first aid and the compatibility of the new aid. The investigation will result in a new decision in which the Commission gives its findings concerning both the previously approved aid and the unnotified payments and in which, if appropriate, it may demand recovery of all aid (both previously approved and subsequently discovered) which it finds to be incompatible with the internal market in the light of the new information.[22]

---

[16] See also Art 9 of the Procedural Regulation. The GC has held that it is not possible for the Commission to adopt, on the basis of this provision, a decision approving the alteration of aid already granted and authorized (Case T-162/06 *Kronoply v Commission* [2009] ECR II-1, para 41).

[17] Joined Cases T-111/01 and T-133/01 *Saxonia Edelmetalle and Zemag v Commission* [2005] ECR II-1579, para 86 and Case T-68/03 *Olympiaki Aeroporia Ypiresies v Commission* [2007] ECR II-2911, para 34.

[18] Joined Cases T-111/01 and T-133/01 *Saxonia Edelmetalle and Zemag v Commission* [2005] ECR II-1579, para 86.

[19] Case C-294/90 *British Aerospace and Rover v Commission* [1992] ECR I-493, paras 12 and 13.

[20] See Case C-36/00 *Spain v Commission* [2002] ECR I-3243, para 25.

[21] Case C-261/89 *Italy v Commission* [1991] ECR I-4437, para 23.

[22] This possibility had already been pointed out by AG Van Gerven in his Opinion in Case C-294/90 *British Aerospace Public and Rover v Commission* [1992] ECR I-5423, para 11.

C. Taking into Account the Non-recovery of Unlawful Aid in the Consideration of New Aid

The Commission found it to be by no means a straightforward matter to get Member States **25.15** to expedite the recovery of unlawful aid declared to be incompatible and sought ways to remedy this situation. In two decisions concerning the undertaking TWD Deggendorf, it expressly declared for the first time that notified aid in favour of an undertaking could not be declared compatible and the granting of the aid should be suspended until such time as certain aid previously paid to the same undertaking and since declared to be incompatible should be recovered.

The General Court ('GC'), followed by the ECJ, has borne out this practice by handing **25.16** down decisions in the sense that new aid considered in itself to be compatible with the internal market may not be authorized until the cumulative effect of the old aid has been eliminated.[23] The Commission can act in this way, on the grounds that the main objective sought is to ensure that competition in the internal market is not distorted by the cumulative effect of the aid in question, provided that the formal examination procedure contained in Article 108(2) TFEU is followed. EU law does not require the Commission, before so acting, to await the outcome of national litigation dealing with the recovery of the old aid. This conclusion is based on three factors: first, the fact that the old aid was not granted in accordance with the procedure laid down in Article 108(3) TFEU; secondly, on the fact that the legitimate expectations upon which the undertaking relies in the national proceedings may be acknowledged only in exceptional circumstances; and thirdly, the fact that the national court has not made a reference to the ECJ in order to obtain a preliminary ruling on whether such exceptional circumstances exist in the present case.[24]

At first the Commission did not resort to this option systematically. It has since made increas- **25.17** ing use of it[25] in a progressively stricter sense.[26]

The suspension of new aid payment, as in the *Deggendorf* case, has been analysed by the EU **25.18** Courts as an integral part of the normal analysis of aid compatibility. This suggests that the Commission is, in principle, bound to take account of this aspect when analysing the compatibility of aid and give grounds, if need be, for its assessments in this sense.

---

[23] Joined Cases T-244/93 and T-486/93 *TWD v Commission* [1995] ECR II-2265, para 51; Case C-355/95 P *TWD v Commission* [1997] ECR I-2549, para 22; Order in Case C-150/09 P *Iride and Iride Energia v Commission* [2010] ECR I-5, para 70; and Case C-480/09 P *AceaElectrabel v Commission* [2010] ECR I-3355, paras 96–7. The need to prevent the cumulative effect of the aid which has not been repaid and of the aid which is planned remains the same, whether the aid concerned is individual aid or aid granted under an aid scheme (Case T-25/07 *Iride v Commission* [2009] ECR II-245, para 88; and Order in Case C-150/09 P *Iride and Iride Energia v Commission* [2010] ECR I-5, paras 49–50).

[24] Joined Cases T-244/93 and T-486/93 *TWD v Commission*, paras 70 and 71.

[25] For example, the Decision of 12 March 2002 on aid in favour of Neue Erba Lautex GmbH and Erba Lautex GmbH [2002] OJ L282/48, paras 57–59.

[26] See para 23 of the 2004 Community guidelines on State aid for rescuing and restructuring firms in difficulty [2004] OJ C244/2.

26

ROLE OF NATIONAL COURTS

Jean Paul Keppenne and Carlos Urraca Caviedes

I. The Enforcement of the Obligation not to Grant Unauthorized Aid

The concept of the 'lawfulness' of aid involves compliance with the procedural obligation laid **26.01** down in Article 108(3) of the Treaty on the Functioning of the European Union ('TFEU'), ie the obligation incumbent on Member States not to grant any aid before it is approved by the Commission. According to the European Court of Justice ('ECJ'), in the Treaty system it is, in principle, the national courts that are responsible for enforcing this obligation, in cooperation with the EU institutions.[1]

A. Role of the National Judge

1. Direct effect of Article 108(3) TFEU, last sentence

The clear and unconditional prohibition laid down in the final sentence of Article 108(3) **26.02** TFEU has direct effect,[2] for it establishes procedural criteria that national courts can appraise.[3]

---

[1] The Council Regulation (EC) 659/1999 of 22 March 1999, laying down detailed rules for the application of Article 93 of the EC Treaty [1999] OJ L83/1 ('Procedural Regulation') does not contain any provision relating to the powers and obligations of the national courts, which continue to be governed by the provisions of the Treaty as interpreted by the Court (Case C-368/04 *Transalpine Ölleitung in Österreich* [2006] ECR I-9957, para 35). The Commission has issued a Notice on the enforcement of State aid law by national courts ([2009] OJ C85/1) to inform national courts and third parties about the remedies available in the event of a breach of State aid rules and to provide them with guidance as to the practical application of those rules.

[2] Case 6/64 *Costa* [1964] ECR 585.

[3] Case 77/72 *Capolongo* [1973] ECR 611, para 6.

The direct effect of that prohibition extends to all aid that has been implemented without being notified and, in the event of notification, operates during the preliminary period, and where the Commission sets in motion the contentious procedure, up to the final decision.[4]

2. Powers of the national courts

26.03 The involvement of national courts is the result of the direct effect that the last sentence of Article 108(3) TFEU is acknowledged to have.[5] This provision creates rights in favour of individuals, which national courts are bound to protect.[6] The standstill obligation incumbent on Member States can be invoked before national courts, and, moreover, in many different types of case. The most obvious example is when a competitor of the aid-receiving undertaking appeals to the competent court for annulment of the aid granted, and the refunding thereof. The commonest case, in practice, is when a taxpayer seeks to avoid payment of a tax resulting from an aid payment. Many other hypothetical cases might be mentioned.[7]

26.04 An examination is made in the next section of the obligations incumbent on the national court when it is called upon to deal with an action based on the direct effect of the last sentence of Article 108(3) TFEU.

Determination of the existence of a breach of Article 108(3) TFEU, last sentence

26.05 The national court has to ascertain whether the State measure in dispute was set up without taking into account the preliminary control procedure of Article 108(3) TFEU, and then if it should be subject thereto. Indeed the national court can intervene only:

> if the national measures in question constitute aid within the meaning of Article [107] and if the procedure for review provided for in Article [108](3) has not been complied with.[8]

To do so the national court must follow this procedure:

- It first of all has to ascertain whether the measure in dispute does indeed come under Article 107(1) TFEU,[9] which might oblige it to interpret and apply the notion of aid as laid down in Article 107 TFEU.[10]

---

[4] Case 120/73 *Lorenz* [1973] ECR 1471, para 8; Case C-354/90 *French Salmon* [1991] ECR I-5505, para 11; Case C-39/94 *SFEI and others* [1996] ECR I-3547, para 39; and Case T-182/98 *UPS Europe v Commission* [1999] ECR II-2857, para 48.

[5] Case C-354/90 *French Salmon* [1991] ECR I-5505, para 11; Case C-44/93 *Namur-Les assurances du crédit* [1994] ECR I-3829, para 16; and C-39/94 *SFEI and others* [1996] ECR I-3547, para 39.

[6] Case 120/73 *Lorenz* [1973] ECR 1471, para 8.

[7] Thus in the *Sloman Neptun* case, a Seafarers' Committee objected to the employment on more favourable terms of sailors with no fixed abode in Germany, on the grounds that the German legislation allowing such a hiring arrangement constituted a State aid. After the Seafarers' Committee's refusal to give its consent to the employment of the persons in question, the undertaking concerned applied to the competent national court to do so in lieu of the Seafarers' Committee. The national court took the view that it needed an interpretation of the concept of aid as laid down in Art 107 TFEU to ascertain whether or not the German legislation in dispute, set up without giving any consideration to the preliminary control procedure of Art 108(3) TFEU, should in fact be subjected thereto (Joined Cases C-72/91 and C-73/91 *Sloman Neptun* [1993] ECR I-887).

[8] Joined Cases 91/83 and 127/83 *Heineken Brouwerijen* [1984] ECR 3435, para 11. See on the necessary measures to be taken by the national authorities, especially national courts, to guarantee compliance with the obligation of suspension, Opinion of AG Mengozzi of 27 June 2013 in Case-284/12 *Deutsche Lufthansa AG v Flughafen Frankfurt Hahn GmbH*, para 46.

[9] Case 78/76 *Steinike and Weinlig* [1977] ECR 595, para 14 and Case C-189/91 *Kirsammer-Hack* [1993] ECR I-6185, para 14.

[10] Case C-354/90 *French Salmon* [1991] ECR I-5505, para 10; Case C-44/93 *Namur-Les assurances du crédit* [1994] ECR I-3829, para 16; Case C-39/94 *SFEI and others* [1996] ECR I-3547, para 49; and Case C-368/04 *Transalpine Ölleitung in Österreich* [2006] ECR I-9957, para 39. As will be examined later, where doubts exist as to the qualification of State aid, national courts may ask for a Commission opinion. This is without prejudice to the possibility or the obligation for a national court to refer the matter to the ECJ for a preliminary ruling.

- When a national court has to deal with an individual application of a rule that it deems to constitute an unlawful aid scheme, it is debatable whether the national court should take a position on the law as such or only the individual case in regard to Article 107(1) TFEU. The Court has stressed the assessment of the individual case.[11]
- Then, if it does turn out to be aid, the national court has to determine whether it has been granted in breach of Article 108(3) TFEU, which might oblige it, if necessary, to examine whether it is a case of new aid or existing aid.[12]
- Where necessary, the national court has to check whether the aid comes under a block exemption regulation or an existing or approved aid scheme,[13] in which case there would be no infringement of the last sentence of Article 108(3) TFEU.

If decisions have already been adopted by the Commission, the national court is bound to take them into consideration, under the principle of the supremacy of EU law. Thus, where a formal examination procedure has been initiated to deal with the measure in question, from which examination it transpires that the Commission does not rule out the possibility of it being new aid, the national court is bound by this classification.[14] Likewise a final decision whereby the Commission confirms the aid character of the measure or, as the case may be, the unlawful nature of its granting,[15] binds the national court in its assessment of the existence of a breach of the final sentence of Article 108(3) TFEU. **26.06**

Consequences flowing from the unlawful character of aid

General matters   If the national court finds that there has indeed been a breach of the standstill obligation incumbent on the State, it has to determine the consequences of this for the case in hand. After initially giving national authorities a certain leeway,[16] the ECJ then chose to specify the nature of these consequences in more detail. According to the consecrated formula, national courts must offer to individuals in a position to rely on such a **26.07**

---

[11] Case C-200/97 *Ecotrade* [1998] ECR I-7907. In his opinion in this case, Advocate-General ('AG') Fennelly argued that the national court could base its case on the general characteristics of the rule to ascertain whether or not in principle it constitutes aid, but that this conclusion should be open to refutation in any given case, where the undertaking in question is in a position to demonstrate to the satisfaction of the competent court that the one-off application of the rule in its favour does not constitute aid (para 31).

[12] In this sense see Case C-44/93 *Namur-Les assurances du crédit* [1994] ECR I-3829, in particular para 18.

[13] See Ch 21, 'General Questions on Procedure. Control of State Aid Compatibility. Council's Decision-Making Power', para 21.82 et seq. Where the applicability of a block exemption regulation or existing or approved aid scheme is at stake, the national court can only assess whether all the conditions of the Regulation or scheme are met. It cannot assess the compatibility of an aid measure where this is not the case, since that assessment is the exclusive responsibility of the Commission (Case C-199/06 *CELF I* [2008] ECR I-469, para 38). The national court may ask the Commission for an opinion if it has doubts concerning the applicability of a block exemption regulation or an existing or approved aid scheme.

[14] See, in this sense, para 23 of Case C-312/90 *Spain v Commission* [1992] ECR I-4117, which acts as the link between the *French Salmon* judgment and the Commission's classification of a measure as new aid. See also para 59 of Case C-400/99 *Italy v Commission* [2001] ECR I-7303, according to which an initiation decision could be invoked before a national court called upon to establish all the consequences arising from the infringement of the last sentence of Art 108(3) TFEU.

[15] Indeed, if the Commission cannot declare aid to be incompatible for the sole fact that it has been granted unlawfully, this does not prevent it, however, from formally recording this unlawfulness in its decision ruling on the compatibility of the aid with the internal market (in this sense, see the Opinion of AG Cosmas in Joined Cases C-329/93, C-62/95, and C-63/95 *Germany, Hanseatische Industrie-Beteiligungen and Bremer Vulkan Verbund v Commission* [1996] ECR I-5151, para 96). Moreover, this is the constant practice of the Commission.

[16] In *Lorenz* the referring national court asked for a ruling on whether the unlawful character of an aid scheme brought in by legislation rendered the said legislation void. The Court replied that national courts are bound to apply the prohibition laid down in the last sentence of Art 108(3) TFEU but it was for the internal legal system of every Member State to determine the legal procedure leading to this result (Case 120/73 *Lorenz* [1973] ECR 1471, para 9).

breach the certain prospect that all the necessary inferences will be drawn, in accordance with their national law, as regards the validity of measures giving effect to the aid, the recovery of financial support granted in disregard of that provision, and possible interim measures.[17] In this sense, the role of the national court goes beyond that of a judge ruling on an application for interim relief. The national court is under a duty to provide protection in the final judgment it gives in such a case against the consequences of unlawful implementation of aid.[18]

26.08 The intervention of the national court is particularly important, since it is the only authority that can directly penalize the unlawfulness of the aid, without detriment to such interim measures as the Commission may adopt against the unlawful aid (*Boussac* injunction, etc).[19] It should be noted, however, that the possibility of remedying an infringement of Article 108(3) TFEU at a national level is limited by a series of factors (lack of transparency in the granting of aid, differences between the various national legal systems, difficulties for national courts in obtaining the necessary information, etc).[20] In practice, therefore, only a tiny fraction of unlawful aid is actually blocked by national courts.

26.09 The main consequences that may flow from the unlawful character of aid are set out in the paragraphs that follow.

26.10 **Implementation of the aid is rendered void** First and foremost the 'validity' of the measures leading to the implementation of the aid is affected by the national authority's disregard of the last sentence of Article 108(3) TFEU.

26.11 **Preventing the payment of unlawful aid** National courts must draw all appropriate legal consequences, in accordance with national law, where an infringement of Article 108(3) TFEU has occurred.[21] The national courts' obligations are not limited to unlawful aid already disbursed. They also extend to cases where an unlawful payment is about to be made. As part of their duties under Article 108(3) TFEU, national courts must safeguard the rights of individuals against possible disregard of those rights.[22] Where unlawful aid is about to be disbursed, the national court is therefore obliged to prevent this payment from taking place.[23]

26.12 **Reimbursement of aid** A finding that aid has been granted in breach of the last sentence of Article 108(3) TFEU must, in principle, lead to its repayment in accordance with the procedural rules of domestic law.[24] Indeed, the logical consequence of a finding that aid is unlawful is to remove it by means of recovery in order to restore the situation previously obtaining.[25]

---

[17] Case C-354/90 *French Salmon* [1991] ECR I-5505, para 12 and Case C-39/94 *SFEI and others* [1996] ECR I-3547, para 40.

[18] Case C-39/94 *SFEI and others* [1996] ECR I-3547, para 67.

[19] As explained at para 26.25 et seq, the Commission's own powers to protect competitors and other third parties against unlawful aid are limited. In particular, the Commission cannot adopt a final decision ordering recovery merely because the aid was not notified in accordance with Art 108(3) TFEU (Case C-301/87 *France v Commission* ('*Boussac*') [1990] ECR I-307 and Case C-142/87 *Belgium v Commission* ('*Tubemeuse*') [1990] ECR I-959), and must therefore conduct a full compatibility assessment, regardless of whether the standstill obligation has been respected or not.

[20] In this regard, see para 8 of the Opinion of AG Tesauro in Case C-142/87 *Belgium v Commission* [1987] ECR I-2589.

[21] Case C-354/90 *French Salmon* [1991] ECR I-5505, para 12; Case C-199/06 *CELF I* [2008] ECR I-469, para 41; and Case C-275/10 *Residex Capital IV* [2011], para 29.

[22] Case C-368/04 *Transalpine Ölleitung in Österreich* [2006] ECR I-9957, paras 38 and 44 and Case C-295/97 *Piaggio* [1999] ECR I-3735, para 31.

[23] See section 2.2.1 of the Commission Notice on the enforcement of State aid law by national courts [2009] OJ C85/1).

[24] Case C-39/94 *SFEI and others* [1996] ECR I-3547, para 68 and Case C-71/04 *Xunta de Galicia* [2005] ECR I-7419, para 49.

[25] Case C-403/10 P *Mediaset v Commission* [2011], para 122 and Case C-275/10 *Residex Capital IV* [2011], para 33.

A national court requested to order the repayment of aid must thus grant that application,[26] unless, because of exceptional circumstances, repayment is inappropriate.[27] The recovery obligation of the national court is thus not dependent on the compatibility of the aid measure with Article 107(2) or (3) TFEU. A national court before which an application has been brought, on the basis of Article 108(3) TFEU, for repayment of unlawful State aid, may not stay the adoption of its decision on that application until the Commission has ruled on the compatibility of the aid with the internal market.[28]

The legal standard as to the exceptional circumstances in which the recovery of unlawful State **26.13** aid would not be appropriate should be similar to the one applicable under Articles 14 and 15 of the Procedural Regulation.[29] Therefore, circumstances which would not stand in the way of a recovery order by the Commission cannot justify a national court refraining from ordering full recovery under Article 108(3) TFEU.[30]

The national court's obligation to order full recovery of unlawful State aid ceases if, by the time **26.14** the national court renders its judgment, the Commission has already decided that the aid is compatible with the internal market. Since the purpose of the standstill obligation is to ensure that only compatible aid can be implemented, this purpose can no longer be frustrated where the Commission has already confirmed compatibility. The national court's obligation to protect individual rights under Article 108(3) TFEU remains unaffected where the Commission has not yet taken a decision, regardless of whether a Commission procedure is pending or not.[31] While after a positive Commission decision the national court is no longer under an EU law obligation to order full recovery, a recovery obligation may exist under national law.[32]

Recovery of interests The need to recover the financial advantage resulting from premature **26.15** implementation of the aid (the 'illegality interest') is part of the national courts' obligation

---

[26] Thus, for instance, national courts have jurisdiction to cancel a guarantee in a situation in which unlawful aid was implemented by means of a guarantee provided by a public authority in order to cover a loan granted by a finance company to an undertaking which would not have been able to secure such financing under normal market conditions. When exercising that jurisdiction, those courts are required to ensure that the aid is recovered and, to that end, they can cancel the guarantee, in particular where, in the absence of less onerous procedural measures, that cancellation is such as to lead to or facilitate the restoration of the competitive situation which existed before that guarantee was provided (Case C-275/10 *Residex Capital IV* [2011], para 49).

[27] Case C-5/89 *Commission v Germany* [1990] ECR I-3437, para 16; Case C-39/94 *SFEI and others* [1996] ECR I-3547, para 71; and Case C-275/10 *Residex Capital IV* [2011], para 35. In particular, when the Commission has already adopted a negative final decision, a recipient of illegally granted aid is not precluded from relying on exceptional circumstances on the basis of which it had legitimately assumed the aid to be lawful and thus declining to refund that aid. If such a case is brought before a national court, it is for that court to assess the circumstances of the case, if necessary after obtaining a preliminary ruling on interpretation from the ECJ (Case C-5/89 *Commission v Germany* [1990] ECR I-3437, para 16 and Case C-199/06 *CELFI* [2008] ECR I-469, para 43).

[28] Case C-1/09 *CELF II* [2010] ECR I-2099, para 40.

[29] See para 32 of the Commission Notice on the enforcement of State aid law by national courts [2009] OJ C85/1). See also paras 73–5 of AG Jacobs' Opinion in Case C-39/94 *SFEI and others* [1996] ECR I-3547.

[30] For instance, the adoption by the Commission of three successive decisions declaring aid to be compatible with the internal market, which were subsequently annulled by the EU judicature, is not, in itself, capable of constituting an exceptional circumstance such as to justify a limitation of the recipient's obligation to repay that aid, in the case where that aid was implemented contrary to Art 108(3) TFEU (Case C-1/09 *CELF II* [2010] ECR I-2099, para 55).

[31] Case C-199/06 *CELF I* [2008] ECR I-469, paras 41–55.

[32] Case C-199/06 *CELF I* [2008] ECR I-469, paras 53 and 55 and Case C-384/07 *Wienstrom* [2008] ECR I-10393, para 28. Therefore, in a situation where the unlawful putting into effect of aid is followed by a positive Commission decision, EU law does not appear to preclude the recipient from, on the one hand, demanding the disbursement of aid payable for the future and, on the other hand, keeping aid received that was granted prior to the positive decision (*Wienstrom*, para 30).

under Article 108(3) TFEU. This obligation can arise in two different settings. First, where the national court must order full recovery of unlawful aid, illegality interest needs to be added to the original aid amount when determining the total recovery amount. Secondly, when there is no obligation to order full recovery, the national court's obligation to order recovery of illegality interest remains in place even after a positive Commission decision.[33]

26.16 Liability of the Member State A breach of the final sentence of Article 108(3) TFEU may in certain cases be considered to be a sufficiently serious breach for the Member State to be held liable for any damage caused to private individuals, applying the principles contained in *Francovich* and *Brasserie du Pêcheur*.[34] The possibility of claiming damages is, in principle, independent of any parallel Commission investigation concerning the same aid measure. Such an ongoing investigation does not release the national court from its obligation to safeguard individual rights under Article 108(3) TFEU. Since the claimant may be able to demonstrate that he suffered loss due to the premature implementation of the aid, and, more specifically, as a result of the beneficiary's illegal time advantage, successful damages claims are also not ruled out where the Commission has already approved the aid by the time the national court decides.[35]

26.17 Damages claims against the beneficiary As Article 108(3) TFEU does not impose any direct obligations on the beneficiary, there is no sufficient EU law basis for direct damages actions against the beneficiary under EU law. However, this does not in any way prejudice the possibility of a successful damages action against the beneficiary on the basis of substantive national law.[36]

26.18 Provisional jurisdictional protection Where there is likely to be some delay before final judgment can be given, a national court should consider whether it is appropriate to order interim measures, such as suspension of payment of the aid, in accordance with the applicable national procedural rules, in order to safeguard the interests of the parties.[37]

26.19 Particular cases: tax-financed aid When national taxes are used to finance unlawful aid, should the national court order the repayment of the taxes to guarantee the full effect of the last sentence of Article 108(3) TFEU? In the *van Calster* case,[38] the Court declared that the consequences ensuing from a breach of the obligation of notifying aid plans applies equally to their mode of financing. Therefore, where an aid measure of which the method of financing

---

[33] Case C-199/06 *CELF I* [2008] ECR I-469, paras 50–5 and Case C-384/07 *Wienstrom* [2008] ECR I-10393, paras 26–31. The Commission has clarified the principles to be applied by national courts when calculating the interest amount in para 41 of the Commission Notice on the enforcement of State aid law by national courts [2009] OJ C85/1).

[34] Joined Cases C-6/90 and C-9/90 *Francovich and others* [1991] ECR I-5357 and Joined Cases C-46/93 and C-48/93 *Brasserie du Pêcheur and Factortame* [1996] ECR I-1029. See para 77 of the Opinion of AG Jacobs in Case C-39/94 *SFEI* [1996] ECR I-3547. According to this jurisprudence, Member States are required to compensate for loss and damage caused to individuals as a result of breaches of EU law for which the State is responsible where (i) the rule of law infringed is intended to confer rights on individuals; (ii) the breach is sufficiently serious; and (iii) there is a direct causal link between the breach of the Member State's obligation and the damage suffered by the injured parties. The Commission has clarified the application of these requirements in paras 46–9 of the Commission Notice on the enforcement of State aid law by national courts [2009] OJ C85/1).

[35] Case C-199/06 *CELF I* [2008] ECR I-469, paras 53 and 55.

[36] Case C-39/94 *SFEI and others* [1996] ECR I-3547, paras 72–5; Case C-199/06 *CELF I* [2008] ECR I-469, paras 53 and 55; and Case C-384/07 *Wienstrom* [2008] ECR I-10393, para 29.

[37] Case C-354/90 *French Salmon* [1991] ECR I-5505, para 12; Case C-39/94 *SFEI and others* [1996] ECR I-3547, para 52; and Case C-368/04 *Transalpine Ölleitung in Österreich* [2006] ECR I-9957, para 46. See paras 57–62 of the Commission Notice on the enforcement of State aid law by national courts [2009] OJ C85/1.

[38] Joined Cases C-261/01 and C-262/01 *van Calster* [2003] ECR I-12249, paras 44 and 54.

is an integral part has been implemented in breach of the obligation to notify, national courts must in principle order reimbursement of charges or contributions levied specifically for the purpose of financing that aid. In *Laboratoires Boiron*,[39] the Court considered that an economic operator liable to pay a charge is entitled to plead that such charge is unlawful for the purposes of applying for reimbursement, on the grounds that it amounts to an aid measure.

Extension of aid?   According to the ECJ, persons liable to pay an obligatory contribu-   **26.20** tion cannot rely on the argument that the exemption enjoyed by other persons constitutes unlawful State aid in order to avoid payment of that contribution.[40] It follows that, even if the exemption constitutes aid, the fact that the aid may be unlawful does not affect the legality of the tax itself. An extension of the circle of potential recipients to other undertakings would not make it possible to eliminate the effects of aid granted in breach of Article 108(3) TFEU, but would rather, on the contrary, lead to an increase in the effects of that aid.[41] However, it would be otherwise if the tax and the envisaged exemption were an integral part of an aid measure.[42] In this regard, when giving its decision, the national court must preserve the interests of individuals, but has also to take fully into consideration the interests of the EU. Therefore, the national court should have available to it all the facts enabling it to assess whether the measure which it proposes to adopt ensures that the rights of individuals are safeguarded by neutralizing the effects of the aid on competitors of the recipient undertakings, while taking EU law fully into consideration and avoiding adoption of a measure which would have the sole effect of extending the circle of recipients of that aid.[43]

Influence of the Commission's decisions on the obligations of the national judge   The   **26.21** national court is bound by the Commission's assessment of the existence of aid or its character of new or existing aid. On the other hand, its role cannot be made to depend on the state of the Commission's examination of the matter. Thus the opening by the Commission of a preliminary examination procedure under Article 108(3) TFEU or the formal examination procedure laid down in Article 108(2) TFEU cannot be held to exempt national courts from their obligation to safeguard the rights of individuals in the event of any breach of the previous notification obligation.[44]

The consequences of a final decision from the Commission ruling on the compatibility of   **26.22** the aid have been progressively clarified in the case law. In *French Salmon*, the Court stated that the Commission's final decision on the compatibility of the aid does not have the effect of regularizing *ex post facto* the implementing measures which were invalid because they had been taken in breach of the prohibition laid down by the last sentence of Article 108(3) TFEU, since otherwise the direct effect of that prohibition would be impaired and the interests of individuals, which, as stated earlier, are to be protected by national courts, would be disregarded.[45] It follows that, even when the Commission's final decision declares the aid

---

[39] Case C-526/04 *Laboratoires Boiron* [2006] ECR I-7529, paras 27–48.
[40] Case C-390/98 *Banks* [2001] ECR I-6117, para 80 and Joined Cases C-430/99 and C-431/99 *Sea-Land Service and Nedlloyd Lijnen* [2002] ECR I-5235, para 47.
[41] Joined Cases C-393/04 and C-41/05 *Air Liquide* [2006] ECR I-5293, paras 43 and 45.
[42] Joined Cases C-393/04 and C-41/05 *Air Liquide* [2006] ECR I-5293, para 46. For a tax to be regarded as forming an integral part of an aid measure, it must be hypothecated to the aid measure under the relevant national rules, in the sense that the revenue from the tax is necessarily allocated for the financing of the aid and has a direct impact on the amount thereof and, consequently, on the assessment of the compatibility of that aid with the internal market (Case C-174/02 *Streekgewest* [2005] ECR I-85, para 26; Joined Cases C-266/04 to C-270/04, C-276/04, and C-321/04 to C-325/04 *Casino France and Others* [2005] ECR I-9481, para 40; and Case C-333/07 *Régie Networks* [2008] ECR I-10807, para 99).
[43] Case C-368/04 *Transalpine Ölleitung in Österreich* [2006] ECR I-9957, paras 48–53.
[44] Case C-39/94 *SFEI and others* [1996] ECR I-3547, para 44.
[45] Case C-354/90 *French Salmon* [1991] ECR I-5505, para 16.

to be compatible with the internal market, national courts may still be called on to declare invalid the implementing measures adopted by Member State authorities that are in breach of the last sentence of Article 108(3) TFEU.[46]

26.23   In the *CELF I* judgment, the Court held that the national court's obligation to order full recovery of unlawful State aid ceases if, by the time the national court renders its judgment, the Commission has already decided that the aid is compatible with the internal market. Since the purpose of the standstill obligation is to ensure that only compatible aid can be implemented, this purpose can no longer be frustrated where the Commission has already confirmed compatibility. Therefore, the national court's obligation to protect individual rights under Article 108(3) TFEU remains unaffected where the Commission has not yet taken a decision, regardless of whether a Commission procedure is pending or not.[47]

Cumulative infringement of the last sentence of Article 108(3) TFEU and of another provision of EU law

26.24   In its examination of the lawfulness of a national measure, the national court has to give due consideration not only to any Commission decision on the compatibility of aid or an infringement of the last sentence of Article 108(3) TFEU, but also the possible direct effect of any other provision of EU law that might equally be breached by the measure under examination. In order to fully observe the principles of direct effect and the primacy of EU law, it is in principle bound to annul the measure in dispute as soon as any infringement of the three tenets mentioned earlier has been proven. The Court, however, has mitigated the full effect of this principle in the following circumstances:

- When a national court is dealing with aid in which only one of the constituent elements which is not necessary for attaining the objective of the aid represents an infringement of a EU provision with direct effect, this circumstance does not entitle national courts to make a declaration to the effect that the aid scheme is incompatible 'as a whole' with the Treaty.[48]
- The Court has ruled that the procedure under Article 108 TFEU, dealt with by the Commission, must be used when an infringement of any other EU law provision concerns constituent elements of the aid so indissolubly linked to the object thereof that it would be impossible to evaluate them separately.[49] In such a case the national court cannot therefore itself establish all the consequences of the breach of the provision concerned.

3. Distinction between the role of the national judge and the role of the Commission

26.25   Under Article 108 TFEU, 'the Commission and the national courts have different powers and responsibilities'.[50] In other words, they play complementary and different roles.[51]

26.26   According to the ECJ, the principal and exclusive role conferred on the Commission by Articles 107 and 108 TFEU, namely to hold aid to be incompatible with the internal market where this

---

[46] Case T-49/93 *SIDE v Commission* [1995] ECR II-2501, para 86 and Order of 30 September 1999 in Case T-182/98 *UPS Europe v Commission* [1999] ECR II-2857, para 48.

[47] Case C-199/06 *CELF I* [2008] ECR I-469, paras 49–55 and Case C-384/07 *Wienstrom* [2008] ECR I-10393, para 28.

[48] Case 74/76 *Iannelli/Meroni* [1977] ECR 557, para 16 (concerning the existence within a system of aid of a measure having an effect equivalent to a quantitative restriction).

[49] Case 74/76 *Iannelli/Meroni* [1977] ECR 557, para 14 and Case C-225/91 *Matra v Commission* [1993] ECR I-3203, para 41.

[50] Case C-44/93 *Namur-Les assurances du crédit* [1994] ECR I-3829, para 14.

[51] Case C-39/94 *SFEI and others* [1996] ECR I-3547, para 41 and Case C-368/04 *Transalpine Ölleitung in Österreich* [2006] ECR I-9957, para 37.

is appropriate, is fundamentally different from the role of national courts in safeguarding rights that individuals enjoy as a result of the direct effect of the prohibition laid down in the last sentence of Article 108(3) TFEU. Whilst the Commission must examine the compatibility of the proposed aid with the internal market, even where the Member State has acted in breach of the prohibition on giving effect to aid, national courts do no more than preserve, until the final decision of the Commission, the rights of individuals faced with a possible breach by Member State authorities of the prohibition laid down by the last sentence of Article 108(3) TFEU. When those courts make a ruling on such a matter, they do not thereby decide on the compatibility of the aid with the internal market; the final determination of that matter is the exclusive responsibility of the Commission, subject to the supervision of the EU Courts.[52]

Individuals therefore cannot, on the basis of Article 107 TFEU alone, challenge the compatibility of aid with EU law before the national courts or ask them to decide as to any incompatibility that may be the main issue in actions before them or may arise as a subsidiary issue.[53] **26.27**

This traditional dichotomy between the Commission (monitoring of compatibility) and national court (monitoring of lawfulness) has one exception, due to the Regulation on block exemptions: the national court and the Commission may be brought to effect the same monitoring procedure, ie to check whether the aid in question comes under a particular exemption regulation and could hence be paid without previous notification to the Commission. **26.28**

B. Cooperation with the European Court of Justice and the Commission

1. Cooperation with the European Court of Justice

Within the context of the control of the lawfulness of aid, the national court cooperates with the ECJ in the form of a reference for a preliminary ruling: **26.29**

- A national court may have cause to interpret and apply the concept of aid contained in Article 107 TFEU in order to determine whether State aid introduced without observance of the preliminary examination procedure provided for in Article 108(3) TFEU ought to have been subject to this procedure. In this context, a national court may have cause to refer a question concerning the interpretation of Article 107 TFEU to the ECJ if it considers that a decision thereon is necessary to enable it to pass judgment.[54]
- A national court may question the ECJ about certain aspects of the procedure under Article 108(3) TFEU to ascertain whether or not the aid involved in the main action has been lawfully granted.[55]
- A national court may examine the validity of a Commission decision declaring aid to be compatible with the internal market. Since the power to hold an EU measure invalid is

---

[52] Case C-354/90 *French Salmon* [1991] ECR I-5505, para 14 and Case C-44/93 *Namur-Les assurances du crédit* [1994] ECR I-3829, paras 16 and 17.

[53] Case 74/76 *Iannelli and Volpi* [1977] ECR 557; Case 78/76 *Steinike and Weinlig* [1977] ECR 595; and Joined Cases C-78/90 to C-83/90 *Compagnie commerciale de l'Ouest* [1992] ECR I-1847, para 33.

[54] Case 78/76 *Steinike & Weinlig* [1977] ECR 595, paras 14–15; Joined Cases C-72/91 and C-73/91 *Sloman Neptun* [1993] ECR I-887, para 12; Case C-189/91 *Kirsammer-Hack* [1993] ECR I-6185, para 14; Case C-39/94 *SFEI and others* [1996] ECR I-3547, para 51; and Case C-256/97 *DM Transport* [1999] ECR I-3913, para 15.

[55] See, eg the pre-litigation questions on the scope of Art 108(3) TFEU, which are answered in Joined Cases 91/83 and 127/83 *Heineken Brouwerijen* [1984] ECR 3435.

reserved to the ECJ, a national court that considers the decision in question to be invalid is required to refer a question to the ECJ for a preliminary ruling.[56]

- On the other hand, the ECJ has no jurisdiction to respond to a referral for a preliminary ruling on the compatibility of aid with the Treaty, since such an assessment would in principle be the exclusive responsibility of the Commission.[57]

2. Cooperation with the Commission

26.30 The national court may be called upon to cooperate with the Commission.[58] According to the ECJ, where the national court has doubts as to whether the measures at issue should be categorized as State aid, it may seek clarification from the Commission. As a consequence of the duty of loyal cooperation between the Community institutions and the Member States under Article 4(3) of the Treaty on European Union ('TEU'), the Commission must respond as quickly as possible to such requests from national courts.[59]

26.31 In order notably to encourage national courts to address questions to it, the Commission has issued a general notice on the enforcement of State aid law by national courts which deals in particular with the cooperation between national courts and the Commission in the field of State aid, along the lines of what it had already done in terms of the implementation of Articles 101 and 102 TFEU.[60] The notice provides that Commission support to national courts can take two different forms: (i) the national court may ask the Commission to transmit to it relevant information in its possession;[61] (ii) the national court may ask the Commission for an opinion concerning the application of the State aid rules.[62]

II. Other Litigation before the National Courts

26.32 Apart from the monitoring of the legality of the granting of aid, which is linked to the direct effect of the final sentence of Article 108(3) TFEU with regard to the application of Commission decisions, it must be stressed that the Commission's State aid decisions in principle have a direct effect. They can be invoked in national litigation of all types, whether civil, administrative, or criminal procedures, etc.

26.33 The Commission's positive aid decisions are binding on national courts, unless they have made a submission to the ECJ for a preliminary ruling on validity. The existence of such a

---

[56] Case T-188/95 *Waterleiding v Commission* [1998] ECR II-3713, para 147.

[57] Case C-256/97 *DM Transport* [1999] ECR I-3913, para 16.

[58] It was AG Lenz who first sketched out the main lines of this cooperation procedure in his Opinion in Case C-44/93 *Namur-Les Assurances du Crédit* [1994] ECR I-3829, paras 104–8. In his view, it is useful in such cases for the national court to know the criteria which the Commission has employed or contemplates employing. Moreover, account must be taken of the fact that proceedings under Art 108(3) TFEU before the national court have the remit of safeguarding the Commission's prerogatives and therefore should be concluded as quickly as possible. This is why, in his opinion, it would seem to be out of the question to propose the suspension of proceedings until the Commission has taken a decision.

[59] Case C-39/94 *SFEI and others* [1996] ECR I-3547, para 50.

[60] Commission Notice on the enforcement of State aid law by national courts [2009] OJ C85/1, which replaces the 1995 Notice on cooperation between national courts and the Commission in the State aid field [1995] OJ C312/8.

[61] See section 3.1 of the Commission Notice on the enforcement of State aid law by national courts [2009] OJ C85/1.

[62] See section 3.2 of the Commission Notice on the enforcement of State aid law by national courts [2009] OJ C85/1.

decision, however, does not *a posteriori* remedy the unlawfulness of any national aid-granting act adopted in breach of the last sentence of Article 108(3) TFEU.[63]

National courts may be appealed to by public authorities seeking to recover aid declared to be incompatible. They may also be appealed to by a competitor trying to annul the granting of aid for the same reason. Indeed, it is up to national courts to uphold the rights of those concerned, by drawing all the inferences, in accordance with their national law, as regards the validity of measures implementing the aid in question and the recovery of the financial support granted, where the Commission finds by a decision adopted under Article 108(2) TFEU that a measure granting aid is incompatible with the internal market.[64] **26.34**

The most critical case obviously concerns the situation where public authorities seek to obtain the recovery of aid that had been paid out unlawfully, after a Commission decision declaring the aid to be incompatible and ordering them to recover it. **26.35**

Further, when a national court is called upon to take a Commission decision into consideration to deal with a case brought before it, it may come up against problems of interpretation of this decision or entertain doubts about its validity. In these circumstances it can (or must, as the case may be) ask the ECJ for a preliminary ruling on interpretation or validity, pursuant to Article 267 TFEU. **26.36**

As regards negative Commission decisions, the case law of the ECJ has been careful to interpret restrictively the preliminary ruling procedure to reduce the possibility of that decision being indefinitely called into question.[65] **26.37**

A. Challenging the Validity of a National Recovery Order

According to Article 14(3) of the Procedural Regulation, Member States must implement recovery decisions without delay. Recovery takes place according to the procedures available under national law, provided they allow for immediate and effective execution of the recovery decision. Where a national procedural rule prevents immediate and/or effective recovery, the national court must leave this provision unapplied.[66] **26.38**

National court actions cannot challenge the validity of the underlying Commission decision where the claimant could have challenged this decision directly before the EU courts.[67] Where a challenge under Article 263 TFEU would have been possible, the national court may not suspend the execution of the recovery decision on grounds linked to the validity of the Commission decision.[68] **26.39**

Where it is not clear that the claimant can bring an annulment action under Article 263 TFEU, the national court must offer legal protection.[69] However, even in those circumstances, the national judge must request a preliminary ruling under Article 267 TFEU where the legal action concerns the validity and lawfulness of the Commission decision.[70] **26.40**

---

[63] Case C-199/06 *CELF I* [2008] ECR I-469, para 40.
[64] Case C-17/91 *Lornoy* [1992] ECR I-6523, para 31, referring to Case 78/76 *Steinike and Weinlig* [1977] ECR 595.
[65] Case C-188/92 *TWD Textilwerke Deggendorf* [1994] ECR I-833, para 29.
[66] Case C-232/05 *Commission v France ('Scott')* [2006] ECR I-10071, paras 49–53.
[67] Case C-232/05 *Commission v France ('Scott')* [2006] ECR I-10071, para 59.
[68] Case C-232/05 *Commission v France ('Scott')* [2006] ECR I-10071, paras 59–60.
[69] See Art 19(1)2 TEU.
[70] Case C-119/05 *Lucchini* [2007] ECR I-6199, para 53.

26.41 Granting interim relief is subject to the very strict legal requirements defined in the *Zuckerfabrik*[71] and *Atlanta*[72] jurisprudence: a national court may only suspend recovery orders under the following conditions:

(i) the national court has serious doubts regarding the validity of the EU act. If the validity of the contested act is not already in issue before the EU Courts, it must itself refer the question to the ECJ;

(ii) there must be urgency in the sense that the interim relief is necessary to avoid serious and irreparable damage to the party seeking relief; and

(iii) the national court has to take due account of the EU interest.

In its assessment of all those conditions, the national court must respect any ruling by the EU courts on the lawfulness of the Commission decision or on an application for interim relief at EU level.

---

[71] Joined Cases C-143/88 and C-92/89 *Zuckerfabrik Süderdithmarschen and Zuckerfabrik Soest* [1991] ECR I-415, para 33.

[72] Case C-465/93 *Atlanta Fruchthandelsgesellschaft and Others (I)* [1995] ECR I-3761, para 51.

27

STATE AID LITIGATION BEFORE THE EUROPEAN UNION COURTS

Jean Paul Keppenne and Carlos Urraca Caviedes

State aid litigation before EU Courts can take the most varied forms. The contending parties **27.01** may be Member States and EU institutions, or EU institutions and private persons, usually undertakings and associations of undertakings. As for the types of procedures, the vast majority of cases involve actions for annulment or for failure to fulfil an obligation, to which may be added some proceedings for failure to act or non-contractual liability.

The main questions raised by this litigation involve the admissibility of the appeal, due to **27.02** uncertainties about determining the contestable acts, on the one hand, and the *locus standi* of the persons concerned, on the other.

27.03 According to Article 40 of the Statute of the Court of Justice, Member States and institutions of the EU may intervene in cases before the Court. The same right is open to any other person establishing an interest in the result of any case submitted to the Court.[1] This means that it has to establish a direct, existing interest in the grant of the order as sought by one of the parties, and not a mere interest in the pleas in law put forward.[2]

27.04 No interest in intervening will exist when the applicant shows only an indirect interest in the solution of the case on the grounds of similarity between its own situation and that of one of the parties.[3]

I. Procedures against the Commission

A. Scope of the Judicial Review

27.05 Considerations of two types might limit the scope of the judicial review of the merits of the Commission's decisions.

27.06 First of all a decision has to be made on whether or not the Commission has any discretion: the EU judicature is in principle bound to exert a complete control over the question of deciding whether or not a measure falls within the field of application of Article 107(1) of the Treaty on the Functioning of the European Union ('TFEU'), paying due consideration to the specific elements of the case submitted to it and the technical or complex character of the appraisals made by the Commission;[4] on the other hand it is equally bound not to encroach on the Commission's wide discretion in deciding on the compatibility of aid under Article 107(3) TFEU: its control on this point is therefore not as 'comprehensive' as it is under Article 107(1) TFEU.[5]

---

[1] Natural or legal persons cannot intervene in cases between Member States, between institutions of the EU, or between Member States and institutions of the EU.

[2] The aid beneficiary undertaking may be given leave to intervene in support of the Commission: Case T-443/93 *Casillo Grani v Commission* [1995] ECR II-1375, para 2. Beneficiary undertakings may intervene in support of another beneficiary undertaking: Case 323/82 *Intermills v Commission* [1984] ECR 3809, para 2. The competitors of a beneficiary undertaking may intervene in support of the Commission or of an applicant demanding the annulment of a positive decision: Joined Cases 296/82 and 318/82 *Netherlands and Leeuwarder Papierwarenfabriek v Commission* [1985] ECR 809, para 11 and Case T-442/93 *AAC and others v Commission* [1995] ECR II-1329, para 30. The authority in charge of the defence of the interests of a region may also be given leave to intervene when the economic situation of the region is likely to be directly affected by the aid in question: Order of 6 March 2003 in Case C-186/02 P *Ramondín and others v Commission* [2003] ECR I-2415, para 9.

[3] Take the example of a region of a Member State that claims that the legal questions brought up in a case are equally likely to be applicable to aid it has paid out or wishes to grant (Order of 6 March 2003 in Case C-186/02 P *Ramondín and others v Commission* [2003] ECR I-2415, paras 15–18).

[4] State aid is a legal concept which must be interpreted on the basis of objective factors. For that reason, the EU judicature must, in principle, and having regard both to the specific features of the case before it and to the technical or complex nature of the Commission's assessments, carry out a comprehensive review as to whether a measure falls within the scope of Art 107(1) TFEU (Case C-83/98 P *France v Ladbroke Racing and Commission* [2000] ECR I-3271, para 25; Case C-452/10 P *BNP Paribas v Commission* [2012], para 100; and Case T-196/04 *Ryanair v Commission* [2008] ECR II-3643, para 40).

[5] Case C-372/97 *Italy v Commission* [2004] ECR I-3679, para 83 and Joined Cases T-228/99 and T-233/99 *WestLB and others v Commission* [2003] ECR II-435, para 282. Thus, for instance, the General Court ('GC') has found that, when appraising the Commission's assessment of a plan designed to restructure an undertaking in economic and financial difficulties, 'it is only in cases where the Commission has committed a particularly manifest and serious error when assessing such a plan that the Court may rule against

Secondly, given that the Commission's decisions in State aid control matters are usually based **27.07** on complex judgments of an economic and social order, the judicial review is restricted, in the sense that the court limits itself, in principle, to verifying:

(i) observance of the rules of procedure and giving reasoned decisions;
(ii) the material exactness of the facts upon which the contested decision is based;
(iii) the absence of any manifest error in the appraisal of the facts; and
(iv) the absence of manifest error of assessment or misuse of power.

Not only must the European EU judicature, *inter alia*, establish whether the evidence relied on is factually accurate, reliable, and consistent, but also whether that evidence contains all the relevant information that must be taken into account in order to assess a complex situation and whether it is capable of substantiating the conclusions drawn from it.[6]

The preceding paragraphs refer to both the Commission's assessments on the existence of **27.08** aid[7] and the compatibility of aid.[8] In particular the Court of Justice ('ECJ') is not entitled to substitute its own assessment, especially in the economic sphere, for that of the author of the decision.[9]

The limited scope of the judicial review reinforces the burden of proof on the applicant **27.09** contesting the Commission's interpretation.[10] The applicant has to prove to the EU Courts, beyond any reasonable doubt, that the Commission made errors that undermine the conclusions it finally came to.[11]

In contrast to the limited character of the EU Court's review of the Commission's substantive **27.10** interpretations, the EU Court exerts a strict control over the procedural rules, in so far as these rules represent the concerned parties' main guarantee of being associated with the Commission's decisions.[12] The Commission's discretion thus goes hand in hand with the obligation to observe

---

the authorisation of State aid intended to finance such restructuring' (Joined Cases T-371/94 and T-394/94 *British Airways and others v Commission* [1998] ECR II-2405, para 447).

   [6] Case C-290/07 P *Commission v Scott* [2010] ECR I-7763, paras 65–6.
   [7] Case C-56/93 *Belgium v Commission* [1996] ECR I-723, para 11; Case C-487/06 P *British Aggregates v Commission* [2008] ECR I-10515, para 114; and Case C-452/10 P *BNP Paribas v Commission* [2012], para 103.
   [8] Joined Cases T-244/93 and T-486/93 *TWD v Commission* [1995] ECR II-2265, para 82; Case T-152/99 *HAMSA v Commission* [2002] ECR II-3049, para 48; and Case C-409/00 *Spain v Commission* [2003] ECR I-1487, para 93.
   [9] Case C-225/91 *Matra v Commission* [1993] ECR I-3203, para 23; Case C-169/95 *Spain v Commission* [1997] ECR I-135, para 34; Case C-372/97 *Italy v Commission* [2004] ECR I-3679, para 83; Case C-323/00 P *DSG v Commission* [2002] ECR I-3919, para 43; and Case T-196/04 *Ryanair v Commission* [2008] ECR II-3643, para 41. As regards interim measures, Case T-107/96 R *Pantochim v Commission* [1996] ECR II-1361, para 44. For a case of manifest misuse of powers by the EU Court, see Case T-126/99 *Graphischer Maschinenbau v Commission* [2002] ECR II-2427 from para 50 onwards.
   [10] Case T-266/94 *Skibsværftsforeningen and others v Commission* [1996] ECR II-1399, para 176.
   [11] See the Opinion of AG Fennelly in Case C-56/93 *Belgium v Commission* [1996] ECR I-723, para 29. The applicant is notably bound to adduce factual evidence 'sufficient to cast serious doubt' on the elements contained in the contested decision (Case T-266/94 *Skibsværftsforeningen and others v Commission* [1996] ECR II-1399, para 195) or advance figures that are 'fundamentally' different from the data taken into account by the Commission (Case T-123/97 *Salomon v Commission* [1999] ECR II-2925, para 89). Nonetheless the Commission is bound to furnish all possible assistance to the EU Court (Opinion of AG Fennelly in Case C-56/93 *Belgium v Commission* [1996] ECR I-723, para 309). The ECJ may also decide to obtain the assistance of independent economic experts (see Case C-169/84 *Cofaz v Commission* [1990] ECR I-3083).
   [12] According to the settled case law of the ECJ, respect for the rights guaranteed by the EU legal order in administrative procedures is of even more fundamental importance where the EU institutions have a power of appraisal (Case C-269/90 *Technische Universität München* [1991] ECR I-5469, para 14 and Case C-525/04 P *Spain v Lenzing* [2007] ECR I-9947, para 58).

scrupulously the procedural rules within which its decision was taken and to examine with due care and impartiality all the relevant facts of the case in hand, all of which reflects on its obligation to state the reasons for its decisions.[13]

27.11   In principle, an infringement of the procedural rules by the Commission is not, however, grounds for annulling the contested decision if it is established that the decision would have been no different even in the absence of the alleged breach. In other words, in order for such an infringement to result in annulment, it must be established that, had it not been for such an irregularity, the outcome of the procedure might have been different.[14]

27.12   The lawfulness of the Commission's approach has to be interpreted:

   (i) in terms of the issues of fact and law existing at the time the measure was adopted.[15] It cannot be made to depend on retrospective considerations of its effectiveness,[16] nor on arguments relating to the detailed rules for implementation of the decision, claiming that they have not been or will not be completely observed;[17]

   (ii) strictly in light of the information to hand, either potentially or actually when the Commission reached its decision.[18] Thus an applicant cannot rely on factual arguments which were unknown to the Commission and which it had not notified to the latter during the examination procedure.[19] This applies first and foremost to Member States, which will not be entitled to complain of the Commission's failure to take certain evidence into account if at no stage in the administrative procedure did they submit that evidence to the Commission, thereby refusing to cooperate fairly therewith.[20] This is also *a fortiori* the case where the Member State has refused to reply to an express request for information from the Commission.[21] In the case of an appeal brought by the State to which the decision was addressed, the ECJ has rejected certain legal pleas for the simple reason that the applicant did not make them in sufficient time, having previously

---

[13] Joined Cases T-371/94 and T-394/94 *British Airways and others v Commission* [1998] ECR II-2405, para 95.

[14] Case T-198/01 *TGI v Commission* [2004] ECR II-2717, para 201. As regards an infringement of the Member State's defence rights, established as such, but without having any effect on the content of the contested decision, see Case 234/84 *Belgium v Commission* [1986] ECR 2263, para 30; Case 40/85, para 30; Case 259/85 *France v Commission* [1987] ECR 4393, para 13; and Case T-211/05 *Italy v Commission* [2009] ECR II-2777, para 45. As regards the failure by the Member State concerned to produce certain documents within the time limit for doing so, see Case T-266/94 *Skibsværftsforeningen and others v Commission* [1996] ECR II-1399, paras 197 and 243.

[15] Cases 15/76 and 16/76 *France v Commission* [1979] ECR 321, para 7; Case T-109/01 *Fleuren Compost v Commission* [2004] ECR II-127, para 50; and Case T-11/07 *Frucona Košice a.s. v Commission* [2010] ECR II-4353, para 48.

[16] As regards decisions on State aid matters, see Joined Cases T-371/94 and T-394/94 *British Airways and others v Commission* [1998] ECR II-2405, para 81 and Case T-123/97 *Salomon v Commission* [1999] ECR II-2925, paras 49 and 115.

[17] Case T-380/94 *AIUFFASS and AKT v Commission* [1996] ECR II-2169, para 128 and Case T-67/94 *Ladbroke Racing v Commission* [1998] ECR II-1, para 190.

[18] As regards decisions on State aid matters, see Case 234/84 *Belgium v Commission* [1986] ECR 2263, para 16; Case C-241/94 *France v Commission* [1996] ECR 4551, para 33; Case C-276/02 *Spain v Commission* [2004] ECR I-8091, para 31; and Case T-274/01 *Valmont Nederland v Commission* [2004] ECR II-3145, para 38. Nevertheless, the Commission might still be placed under the obligation of endeavouring to obtain more information.

[19] Case T-110/97 *Kneissl Dachstein Sportartikel v Commission* [1999] ECR II-2881, para 102 and Case T-176/01 *Ferriere Nord v Commission* [2004] ECR II-3931, para 154.

[20] Case 102/87 *France v Commission* [1988] ECR 4067, para 27; Joined Cases C-278/92, C-279/92, and C-280/92 *Spain v Commission* [1994] ECR I-4103, para 31; Case C-382/99 *Netherlands v Commission* [2002] ECR I-5163, paras 49 and 76; Case T-109/01 *Fleuren Compost v Commission* [2004] ECR II-127, para 51; and Case C-277/00 *Germany v Commission* [2004] ECR I-3925, para 39.

[21] Case C-382/99 *Netherlands v Commission* [2002] ECR I-5163, para 76.

refrained from contesting a Commission decision that had foreshadowed the later one. The same goes for a beneficiary undertaking that has failed to present information or documents during the administrative phase.[22] This only applies to factual matters, however. Nothing prevents the interested party from raising against the final decision a legal argument that was not made during the administrative procedure.[23]

B. Action for Annulment

1. General principles

Contestable act

An action for annulment can be brought against measures producing legal effects which are bind- **27.13**
ing on and capable of affecting the interests of the applicant by having a significant effect on its legal position.[24] It is necessary to look to the actual substance of an act in order to classify it. The form in which an act or decision is adopted is, in principle, irrelevant to the right to challenge such acts or decisions by way of an action for annulment. It is therefore, in principle, irrelevant for the classification of the act in question whether or not it satisfies certain formal requirements, namely, in particular, that it is duly identified by its author and that it mentions the provisions providing the legal basis for it. It is irrelevant, too, that the act may not be described as a 'decision' or that it does not refer to Article 4(2), (3), or (4) of the Procedural Regulation.[25] It is also of no importance that the Member State concerned was not notified of the act at issue by the Commission, infringing Article 25 of the Procedural Regulation, as such an error is not capable of altering the substance of that act. Furthermore, it is, in principle, those measures that definitively determine the position of the Commission upon the conclusion of an administrative procedure, and which are intended to have legal effects capable of affecting the interests of the complainant, that constitute acts open to challenge, and not intermediate measures whose purpose is to prepare for the final decision, which do not have those effects.[26]

One difficulty of annulment proceedings in State aid matters may thus be to determine the **27.14**
act of which the annulment is sought. Some cases are fairly straightforward, for example when the action for annulment is brought against the decision to initiate the formal examination procedure or against a final decision adopted at the end of a formal examination procedure.[27] But other actions may be brought against Commission letters or its services, involving acts not specifically defined as such in the official rules: refusal to initiate the formal examination procedure; refusal to address the appropriate measures; decision to consider aid to be compatible with the conditions of an existing scheme, etc. The same act can sometimes be construed as implicitly encapsulating different decisions.

---

[22] Joined Cases T-126/96 and T-127/96 *Breda Fucine Meridionali and others v Commission* [1998] ECR II-3437, para 88 and Case T-176/01 *Ferriere Nord v Commission* [2004] ECR II-3931, paras 123 and 154.

[23] Case T-123/97 *Salomon v Commission* [1999] ECR II-2925, para 55 and Joined Cases T-81/07 to T-83/07 *KG Holding and Others v Commission* [2009] ECR II-2411, para 195.

[24] In particular, in State aid matters, Case C-521/06 P *Athinaïki Techniki v Commission* [2008] ECR I-5829, para 29.

[25] Council Regulation (EC) 659/1999 of 22 March 1999, laying down detailed rules for the application of Article 93 of the EC Treaty [1999] OJ L83/1.

[26] Case C-521/06 P *Athinaïki Techniki v Commission*, paras 42–4; Case C-322/09 P *NDSHT v Commission* [2010], paras 46–8; and Order of 13 April 2010 in Joined Cases T-529/08 to T-531/08 *Diputación Foral de Álava and Others v Commission* [2010], paras 28–9.

[27] An information injunction (taken pursuant to Art 10(3) of the Procedural Regulation) is intended to produce binding legal effects and therefore constitutes an act open to challenge for the purposes of Art 263 TFEU (Joined Cases C-463/10 P and C-475/10 P *Deutsche Post and Germany v Commission* [2011], para 45).

27.15 The act against which an action for annulment is being brought by a third party has sometimes to be ascertained in terms of the previous correspondence between that third party and the Commission and in particular the requests made therein. This seems to be paradoxical, since the Commission's decisions are always supposed to be addressed only to the Member State concerned and not the third party.[28]

27.16 An ostensibly single decision might, as the case may be, have to be analysed as a bundle of different decisions (for example decisions on different items of aid granted to the same undertaking by different public entities).[29]

27.17 The letters addressed directly to third parties, in particular to complainants, have to be considered as sent for information purposes and hence do not constitute acts that may be challenged in annulment actions.[30] These letters may, however, reflect the content of a decision, even if it has not effectively been sent to the Member State concerned.[31] When the Commission addresses a letter to a third party informing it of the contents of a decision it has adopted on a State measure, this third party's action for annulment against the letter will not necessarily be inadmissible: the EU Courts have admitted the action if the Commission had adopted a decision in the contested letter addressed in fact to the Member State concerned, even if that decision had not effectively been sent to said State.[32] In general, where the Commission adopts a decision not to initiate the procedure under Art 108(2) TFEU and, in accordance with its duty of sound administration, proceeds to inform the complainants thereof, it is the decision addressed to the Member State which must form the subject matter of any action for annulment which the complainant may bring, and not the letter to that complainant.[33]

27.18 Should the Commission fail to adopt a position on certain measures included in the complaint, without expressly rejecting the complaint in this respect and while opening the formal examination procedure to deal with other measures included in the complaint, this circumstance does not affect the lawfulness of the Commission's decision. If the complainant wishes to obtain a decision on the complaint as a whole, it behoves it to call upon the Commission to do so in accordance with Article 265 TFEU.[34] In sum, purely informative letters not in any way constituting a decision are not acts open to challenge.[35]

---

[28] Thus, in the examination of a decision establishing the absence of aid, addressed to France, the GC found that the Commission had acted correctly in restricting its examination to certain measures and not others, inasmuch as it might reasonably have assumed that the complainants against the original decision had abandoned their complaints in relation to these other measures (Case T-106/95 *FFSA and others v Commission* [1997] ECR II-229, para 38).

[29] Joined Cases T-127/99, T-129/99, and T-148/99 *Territorio Histórico de Álava and others v Commission* [2002] ECR II-1275, para 56.

[30] See Case C-198/91 *Cook v Commission* [1993] ECR I-2487, para 14 (as Attorney-General ('AG') Tesauro observed in his Opinion in Case C-198/91 *Cook v Commission* [1993] ECR I-2487, para 32, 'in the framework of the procedure laid down in Art [108 TFEU], unlike the procedures followed by application of Art [101 and 102 TFEU], the only decision the Commission can make is to rule on the compatibility of aid. An autonomous and different decision involving the rejection of a complaint brought by a competitor undertaking of the beneficiary undertaking is therefore not conceivable').

[31] Case T-182/98 *UPS Europe v Commission* [1999] ECR II-2857, para 38.

[32] Case T-182/98 *UPS Europe v Commission* [1999] ECR II-2857, paras 38 and 41.

[33] Case C-367/95 P *Commission v Sytraval and Brink's France* [1998] ECR I-1719; Case C-521/06 P *Athinaïki Techniki v Commission*, para 30; and Case T-82/96 *ARAP and others v Commission* [1999] ECR II-1889, paras 29 and 30.

[34] Case T-67/94 *Ladbroke Racing v Commission* [1998] ECR II-1, para 92.

[35] Case T-82/96 *ARAP and others v Commission* [1999] ECR II-1889, para 30. When the Commission, upon examining new aid, replies to an argument or a request put forward by a complainant in respect of different aid already approved, that circumstance does not in itself demonstrate that the latter has been the subject of a fresh examination by the Commission: Case T-188/95 *Waterleiding v Commission* [1998] ECR II-3713, para 128.

The principle of EU legality implies the obligation of recognizing the full efficacy of EU acts   **27.19**
as long as they have not been declared to be invalid (presumption of legality). Moreover,
under the terms of Article 278 TFEU, actions brought before the EU Courts do not have a
suspensory effect. Unless an interim measure is obtained from the judge responsible for dealing with such applications, the challenged decisions have to be put into effect even if their
annulment has meanwhile been sought.[36] Failing that, the Commission is entitled to bring
an action for failure to fulfil an obligation before the ECJ, which is examined independently
of the action for annulment brought against the decision whose breach prompted this action
for failure to fulfil an obligation.[37]

Likewise, the fact that an action for annulment has been lodged against a negative decision   **27.20**
by the Commission does not, in principle, prevent it from adopting other negative decisions
with regard to supplementary aid granted to the same beneficiary.[38]

Locus standi

The Member State concerned is, in principle, the addressee of the Commission's decisions.   **27.21**
Moreover, the Member States and the EU institutions benefit in all circumstances from a
privileged access to the EU Courts, by virtue of the second paragraph of Article 263 TFEU.
As regards the Member States' *locus standi*, the ECJ has ruled that, even when a Member
State has infringed the provisions of Article 108 TFEU, it may not be deprived of the right to
challenge before the Court the legality of a Commission decision adversely affecting it, under
Articles 263 TFEU et seq in particular.[39]

The Commission's State aid decisions are addressed to the Member State granting the aid   **27.22**
dealt with in the decision, whether it is a matter of a decision ruling on the absence of aid,[40]
a decision ruling on the existing character of aid,[41] a decision ruling on the compatibility of
aid,[42] or a decision to refuse to initiate the formal examination procedure adopted after the
lodging of a complaint.[43]

The admissibility of actions brought by persons other than the addressee Member State is there-   **27.23**
fore a thorny issue. It is necessary to establish, on the one hand, an interest in bringing proceedings; on the other, a direct and individual concern, or merely direct concern if the action is
instituted against a regulatory act which does not entail implementing measures (Article 263
TFEU, fourth paragraph).[44]

---

[36] See Case 310/85 R *Deufil v Commission* [1986] ECR 537, para 13 and Case 63/87 *Commission v Greece*
[1988] ECR 2875, paras 10–12.
[37] Case C-177/06 *Commission v Spain* [2007] ECR I-7689, para 37. In the past, the ECJ tended to deal
with these two types of actions in parallel (see eg Joined Cases 67, 68, and 70/85 *Van der Kooy v Commission*
[1988] ECR 219; Case 213/85 *Commission v Netherlands* [1988] ECR 281; Case 57/86 *Greece v Commission*
[1988] ECR 2855; and Case 63/87 *Commission v Greece* [2000] ECR I-5047).
[38] Case C-399/95 R *Germany v Commission* [1996] ECR I-2441, paras 71–3.
[39] Joined Cases 67, 68, and 70/85 R *Van der Kooy v Commission* [1988] ECR 1315, para 37. As AG Slynn
pointed out, the Commission cannot challenge the admissibility of the procedure on the grounds of the
unlawful granting of the aid, since it has a wide range of powers dealing with the illegal implementation of
aid (Opinion in Cases 67, 68, and 70/85).
[40] See Case T-178/94 *ATM v Commission* [1997] ECR II-2529, para 51.
[41] See Case C-313/90 *CIRFS and others v Commission* [1993] ECR I-1125, para 28.
[42] See Case T-189/97 *Comité d'entreprise de la Société française de production and others v Commission*
[1998] ECR II-335, para 31.
[43] Case T-188/95 *Waterleiding v Commission* [1998] ECR II-3713, para 127.
[44] The last part of the fourth paragraph of Art 263 TFEU has been introduced in the Treaty of Lisbon.
The EU courts have once interpreted it in State aid cases. The GC has observed that a final negative decision
with recovery cannot be described as an act not entailing implementing measures, by reason of the existence
of recovery measures. Moreover, the measures implementing the decision are not confined to the recovery

27.24   The person concerned has to prove a legally protected and existing interest, or, failing that, a future and certain interest. In order for such an interest to be present, the annulment of the measure must of itself be capable of having legal consequences, or, in other words, the action must be liable, if successful, to procure an advantage for the party who has brought it.[45] That interest must be determined at the time when the application is lodged.[46] It cannot be assessed in the light of a future and uncertain occurrence. In particular, if the interest which an applicant claims concerns a future legal situation, he must demonstrate that the prejudice to that situation is already certain.[47]

27.25   The interest in bringing an action is usually present in the case of actions brought by the undertakings benefiting from the aid concerned or the competitors thereof (or the associations representing the latter). The ECJ has ruled that a third party who is not in competition with the aid beneficiary or does not represent persons in competition therewith, cannot be considered to be concerned by the contested decision, the confirmation or annulment thereof in no way affecting its interests.[48]

27.26   The interest in bringing an action may likewise not exist when the applicant requires annulment of certain parts of a decision whose operative part is favourable to it. Nevertheless, a decision based on Article 107(1) and (3) TFEU which, while classifying the measure in question as State aid, declares it compatible with the internal market, must be regarded as a challengeable act under Article 263 TFEU.[49] If the beneficiary is not subject to any obligation to repay the aid, the annulment of the contested decision would not procure any advantage for the applicant in that regard and thus has no standing to bring proceedings.[50] However, the interest in bringing proceedings can result from a genuine 'risk' that the applicant's legal position will be affected by legal proceedings, or where the 'risk' of legal proceedings was vested and present at the date on which the action was brought before the EU judicature.[51]

27.27   The concept of direct and individual interest has to be examined on a case-by-case basis, in view of the nature of the contested act and the *locus standi* of the applicant. The main

---

measures, but include also all the measures for implementing the incompatibility decision, including, *inter alia*, the measure rejecting an application for the tax advantage at issue, a rejection which the applicant may also challenge before the national court. This conclusion rendered unnecessary a ruling on whether that decision is a regulatory act (Case T-221/10 *Iberdrola v Commission* [2012], paras 46–8).

[45] Case T-188/07 *Fastweb v Commission* [2008], para 21.

[46] Joined Cases C-373/06 P, C-379/06 P, and C-382/06 P *Flaherty and Others v Commission* [2008] ECR I-2649, para 25 and Case T-16/96 *Cityflyer Express v Commission* [1998] ECR II-757, para 30.

[47] Case T-138/89 *NBV and NVB v Commission* [1992] ECR II-2181, para 33 and Joined Cases T-228/00 and others *Gruppo ormeggiatori del porto di Venezia and Others v Commission* [2005] ECR II-787, para 23.

[48] Case C-295/92 *Landbouwschap v Commission* [1992] ECR I-5003, para 12. The case concerned an association representing undertakings that were not in competition with the aid beneficiaries, but wished to benefit themselves from the contested aid. The GC adopted the same approach in relation to an action brought by the mutual provident association of an undertaking objecting to State aid allegedly awarded to that undertaking, ruling that the confirmation or annulment of the Commission's decision was in no way liable to affect the interests of that association or its members (Case T-178/94 *ATM v Commission* [1997] ECR II-2529).

[49] Case C-279/08 P *Commission v Netherlands (NOx)* [2011], paras 35–42. See also Case T-301/01 *Alitalia v Commission* [2008] ECR II-1753, paras 377–88. See, however, Case T-212/00 *Nuove Industrie Molisane v Commission* [2002] ECR II-347; Case T-141/03 *Sniace v Commission* [2005] ECR II-1197; and Case T-136/05 *Salvat père & fils and Others v Commission* [2007] ECR II-4063, paras 34–48.

[50] Orders of the GC of 19 March 2009 in Case T-96/07 *Telecom Italia Media v Commission* [2009], paras 22–4; of 25 November 2008 in Case T-188/07 *Fastweb v Commission* [2008], paras 26–8; and of 20 September 2005 in Case T-258/99 *Makro Cash & Carry v Commission* [2005] ECR II-14, paras 43–5; and Case T-354/99 *Kuwait Petroleum v Commission* [2006] ECR II-1475, paras 34–5.

[51] Joined Cases T-309/04, T-317/04, T-329/04, and T-336/04 *TV 2/Danmark v Commission* [2008] ECR II-2935, paras 78–82. See also Joined Cases T-425/04, T-444/04, T-450/04, and T-456/04 *France v Commission* [2010] ECR II-2099, para 122.

problems concern the individual interest, in particular when decisions on aid schemes are being dealt with.

One issue here is to ascertain whether other public authorities or groups besides the central **27.28** authorities of the State concerned, such as regional or local authorities, etc, are also entitled to bring actions against the Commission's aid decisions, in so far as they are the grantors of such aid. The EU Courts have generally found such actions to be admissible, on the grounds that said public authorities, even if they cannot be considered to be the addressees of the Commission's decisions, were directly and individually concerned by such decisions and could lay claim to their own interests. The individual interest may arise from a set of circumstances, in particular the fact that the contested decision affects acts of which they are the authors, when it prevents them from exercising, as they see fit, their own powers, which they enjoy directly under national law, or that it has the effect of obliging them to engage in the administrative aid recovery procedure, etc.[52] The direct interest arises from the fact that, even when the contested decision is addressed to the Member State, the national authorities in principle exercise no discretion in communicating it to the infra-State authority.[53] The rightful interest of these authorities ensues from the autonomy they are granted under their national law.[54]

Locus standi is ruled out when the regional authority is not the grantor of the aid and lays **27.29** claim only to the socio-economic knock-on effects of the contested act on its territory,[55] or when there is no rightful or special interest to act against the Commission's decision because this interest is not clearly distinguishable from the Member State's.[56]

The EU Courts are in principle in favour of collective action brought by associations for this **27.30** has the procedural advantage of obviating the need for numerous separate actions against the same decision.[57] Actions brought by associations are admissible in certain situations: where the association represents the interests of undertakings which themselves have *locus standi*; where the association is differentiated by reason of the impact on its own interests as an association, in particular because its position as a negotiator has been affected by the measure of which annulment is sought; and where a legal provision expressly confers on it a number of rights of a procedural nature.[58] The defence of general interests is not sufficient to establish the admissibility

---

[52] See Joined Cases 62/87 and 72/87 *Exécutif Régional Wallon v Commission* [1988] ECR 1573; Case T-214/95 *Vlaams Gewest v Commission* [1998] ECR II-717, para 28; Joined Cases T-127/99, T-129/99, and T-148/99 *Territorio Histórico de Álava and others v Commission* [2002] ECR II-1275, para 50; Joined Cases T-269/99, T-271/99, and T-272/99 *Territorio Histórico de Guipúzcoa and others v Commission* [2002] ECR II-4217, para 41; and Joined Cases T-346/99, T-347/99, and T-348/99 *Territorio Histórico de Álava and others v Commission* [2002] ECR II-4259, para 37.

[53] Joined Cases T-132/96 and T-143/96 *Freistaat Sachsen and others v Commission* [1999] ECR II-3663, paras 89–90.

[54] Joined Cases T-132/96 and T-143/96 *Freistaat Sachsen and others v Commission* [1999] ECR II-3663, para 91.

[55] Case T-238/97 *Comunidad Autónoma de Cantabria v Council* [1998] ECR II-2271.

[56] Case 282/85 *DEFI v Commission* [1986] ECR 2469, para 18. Some Member States have established procedures to assure the regional governments that Member States can take action to defend their interests before EU Courts where exclusive regional powers are at stake, and there have been cases in which Member States represented interests of regions before the EU Courts (Case C-88/03 *Portugal v Commission* [2006] ECR I-7115).

[57] Joined Cases T-447/93 to T-449/93 *AITEC and others v Commission* [1996] ECR II-1631, para 60.

[58] Case T-292/02 *Confservizi v Commission* [2009] ECR II-1659, para 52. An association cannot represent the interests of those of its members that are already representing their own interests (Case T-292/02 *Confservizi v Commission*, para 55 and Order of the GC in Case T-236/10 *Asociación Española de Banca v Commission* [2012], para 24).

of an action for annulment brought by an association.[59] It is not excluded that a trade union may be regarded as 'concerned' within the meaning of Article 108(2) TFEU (and thus have *locus standi*) if it shows that its interests or those of its members might be affected by the granting of aid. The trade union must, however, show to the requisite legal standard that the aid is likely to have a real effect on its situation or that of its members. This is possible for it to do by showing that it is in fact in a competitive position in relation to other trade unions operating in the same market.[60]

27.31 When several applicants seek annulment of the same Commission decision, it may turn out that only some of them are judged to have *locus standi*. In such a case, if they have brought separate actions, the EU Court checks the admissibility of each one and may declare certain of them to be inadmissible, even if all the cases are joined for judgment purposes.[61] On the other hand, when a single action is involved, it is admitted if at least one of the applications is eligible for bringing it.[62]

Admissible legal pleas

27.32 As regards pleas based on illegal procedures, an applicant is in principle not entitled to object to an illegality that has not directly had an adverse effect on it. An infringement of the rights of the defence results in annulment only if, had it not been for such an irregularity, the outcome of the procedure might have been different.[63]

27.33 As regards pleas dealing with the merits of a case, a plea put forward by a complainant is not inadmissible on the grounds that it has not been previously brought before the Commission. This principle was first applied to a situation where the adoption of the Commission's decision had not been preceded by the initiation of the formal examination procedure, declaring that there did not have to be strict consistency between the complaint and the action.[64] It has subsequently been applied to cases where the Commission has initiated the formal examination procedure, laying it down that 'no provision in the field of State aid makes the right for a person directly and individually concerned to challenge a measure addressed to a third party conditional upon all the complaints set out in the application having been raised during the administrative procedure'.[65]

27.34 Likewise, an applicant is not prevented from putting forward certain pleas against a final decision on the grounds that it has not previously raised them when objecting to the decision to initiate proceedings.[66] The applicant therefore has the right to bring an action for the annulment of the decision in its entirety, including the classification of aid as new aid,

[59] Joined Cases T-227/01 to T-229/01, T-265/01, T-266/01, and T-270/01 *Diputación Foral de Álava and Others v Commission* [2009] ECR II-3029, para 107.
[60] Case C-319/07 P *3F v Commission* [2009] ECR I-5963, paras 33–59.
[61] Joined Cases 67, 68, and 70/85 *Van der Kooy v Commission* [1988] ECR 219, para 16.
[62] Case C-313/90 *CIRFS and others v Commission* [1993] ECR I-1125, para 31; Joined Cases T-127/99, T-129/99, and T-148/99 *Territorio Histórico de Álava and others v Commission* [2002] ECR II-1275, para 52; and Joined Cases T-227/01 to T-229/01, T-265/01, T-266/01, and T-270/01 *Diputación Foral de Álava and Others v Commission* [2009] ECR II-3029, para 77.
[63] Case C-142/87 *Belgium v Commission* [1990] ECR I-959, para 48; Case C-288/96 *Germany v Commission* [2000] ECR I-8237, para 101; and Joined Cases C-106//09 P and C-107/09 P *Commission and Spain v Gibraltar and UK* [2011], para 179.
[64] Case T-49/93 *SIDE v Commission* [1995] ECR II-2501, para 73.
[65] Case T-380/94 *AIUFFASS and AKT* [1996] ECR II-2169, para 64 and Case T-16/96 *Cityflyer Express v Commission* [1998] ECR II-757, para 39. Along the same lines, Case T-110/97 *Kneissl Dachstein Sportartikel v Commission* [1999] ECR II-2881, para 102 and Case T-442/03 *SIC v Commission* [2008] ECR II-1161, para 141.
[66] Joined Cases T-126/96 and T-127/96 *Breda Fucine Meridionali and others v Commission* [1998] ECR II-3437, para 43.

irrespective of whether or not it challenged that aspect of the decision to start the formal investigation procedure in respect of the aid in question.[67] It is, in principle, entitled to invoke any illegality that might vitiate the preparatory acts for the final decision.[68]

The plea of legitimate expectations is often put forward: the Commission, in following the **27.35** State aid examination procedure, is bound to take account of the legitimate expectations which the parties concerned may entertain as a result of what was said in the decision opening the procedure and, consequently, not to base its final decision on the absence of elements which, in light of those indications, the parties concerned could not consider that they were bound to furnish.[69] There is also the question of whether a Member State applying for the annulment of a negative Commission decision is entitled to invoke the legitimate expectations of the beneficiaries when the State authorities have granted aid in breach of the procedural rules laid down in Article 108 TFEU. Case law on this point changed over time. The Court at first seemed to simply transpose its case law on actions for failure to fulfil an obligation brought by the Commission against the failure to execute its decisions. This implied that the State could not put forward such a plea in support of an action for annulment brought against the Commission's decision.[70] Subsequently, however, the ECJ admitted that there is a difference according to whether such a plea is put forward by the State as defendant wishing to avoid the obligation entailed in the Commission's decision, or as an appellant challenging the validity of that decision. When dealing with an action for annulment, it first examines whether the claim of the beneficiary's legitimate expectations was well founded before dismissing it when looking at the substantive issues of the case.[71]

Pleas claiming that insufficient reasons were given for the decision are often put forward, and **27.36** often with a degree of success.

A Commission decision based on factual errors or an arbitrary approach is prone to be **27.37** annulled, without the EU Courts, thereby prejudging the result that would have been obtained in the absence of this factual error.[72]

Burden of proof

Acts of the EU institutions are presumed to be valid. It therefore behoves parties seeking their **27.38** annulment to rebut that presumption by producing convincing evidence to cast doubt on the assessments made by the Commission.[73]

---

[67] Case T-190/00 *Regione Siciliana v Commission* [2003] ECR II-5015, para 49. As the GC rightly pointed out in this judgment, a contrary interpretation would amount to admitting that a ruling by the EU judicature at a preliminary stage of the procedure on preparatory measures such as the decision to initiate a formal investigation procedure, and in particular on the classification of aid as new aid, would prevent the parties concerned from challenging the final decision, where the Commission may alter the assessment made in the initiating decision (para 51).

[68] Case T-182/98 *UPS Europe v Commission* [1999] ECR II-2857, para 47.

[69] Case T-176/01 *Ferriere Nord v Commission* [2004] ECR II-3931, para 88. Any inaction by the Commission with regard to a national measure cannot be taken as a precise assurance by the Commission that a similar measure does not constitute State aid (Joined Cases T-346/99, T-347/99, and T-348/99 *Territorio Histórico de Álava and others v Commission* [2002] ECR II-4259, para 95).

[70] Joined Cases C-278/92, C-279/92, and C-280/92 *Spain v Commission* [1994] ECR I-4103, para 76.

[71] Case C-169/95 *Spain v Commission* [1997] ECR I-135, paras 49 and 50. See also Joined Cases C-465/09 P to C-470/09 P *Diputación Foral de Vizcaya* [2011], paras 150–3.

[72] For examples in the aid field see Joined Cases T-127/99, T-129/99, and T-148/99 *Territorio Histórico de Álava and others v Commission* [2002] ECR II-1275, para 90 and Case C-276/02 *Spain v Commission* [2004] ECR I-8091, para 31 et seq.

[73] Case T-110/97 *Kneiss Dachstein Sportartikel v Commission* [1999] ECR II-2881, para 45.

Time limit for bringing the action

27.39 The interested parties have to make sure they exercise their appeal rights within the requisite time limits, which are public policy provisions. Failing that, not only is the annulment no longer possible,[74] but they also risk forfeiting the right to challenge the legality of the decision in any later collateral proceeding. Thus, a Member State that has received a negative decision will not be able to call into question the validity of this decision in any action for failure to fulfil an obligation brought against it by the Commission for having failed to execute it. Likewise, any beneficiary undertaking of individual aid that could have brought an action for annulment against a negative Commission decision cannot later invoke the unlawfulness of this decision, whether before the national court[75] or before the EU Courts.[76]

27.40 For the addressee to whom the decision is notified (in principle the Member State), time starts to run from the date of the notification. For others, it is the date of publication in the Official Journal of the European Union ('OJ') that is taken into account. The criterion based on the moment that the contested act came to the knowledge of the applicant is subsidiary to the other criteria of notification or publication. For decisions that are normally published in the OJ, therefore, it is the date of publication that marks the start of the time limit, whether the applicant is a Member State (except for the addressee to whom the decision is notified) or an interested third party, even if the latter learned of it earlier.[77] The fact that the Commission gives third parties full access to the text of a decision placed on its website, combined with publication of a summary notice in the OJ enabling interested parties to identify the decision in question and notifying them of this possibility of access via the internet, must be considered as publication for the purposes of Article 263 TFEU, sixth paragraph.[78]

2. Appeal against a decision not to raise objections/a refusal to initiate the formal examination procedure

Contestable act

27.41 The Commission may decide not to raise any objection to a measure after a preliminary examination thereof. This category of decisions takes in, on the one hand, decisions concluding that the measure concerned does not constitute aid,[79] and, on the other, decisions concluding that new aid, notified or otherwise, is compatible. Such decisions also imply a refusal, implied or express (in the case of a complaint), to initiate the formal examination procedure of the measure, for the Commission cannot declare aid to be incompatible without having previously initiated that procedure.[80] These are contestable acts. It does not matter

---

[74] For cases of inadmissibility due to late application, see Order of 24 August 2002 in Case T-21/02 *Atzeni and others v Commission*.

[75] Case C-188/92 *TWD* [1994] ECR I-883 and Joined Cases T-254/00, T-270/00, and T-277/00 *Hotel Cipriani v Commission* [2008] ECR II-3269, para 90.

[76] Joined Cases T-244/93 and T-486/93 *TWD v Commission* [1995] ECR II-2265, para 103.

[77] Case T-11/95 *BP Chemicals v Commission* [1998] ECR II-3235, para 47; Case T-110/97 *Kneissl Dachstein Sportartikel v Commission* [1999] ECR II-2881, paras 40–3; Case T-123/97 *Salomon v Commission* [1999] ECR II-2925, paras 42–4; Case T-296/97 *Alitalia v Commission* [2000] ECR II-3871, para 61; Case T-190/00 *Regione Siciliana v Commission* [2003] ECR II-5015, para 30; and Case T-17/02 *Olsen v Commission* [2005] ECR II-2031, para 77.

[78] Case T-17/02 *Olsen v Commission* [2005] ECR II-2031, para 80; Orders of the Court of First Instance in Case T-321/04 *Air Bourbon v Commission* [2005] ECR II-3469, para 34, and in Case T-426/04 *Tramarin v Commission* [2005] ECR II-4765, para 53, and Case T-388/02 *Kronoply v Commission* [2008] ECR II-305, paras 29–34.

[79] See, eg Case T-11/95 *BP Chemicals v Commission* [1998] ECR II-3235, para 84 et seq.

[80] Case T-398/94 *Kahn Scheepvaart v Commission* [1996] ECR II-477, para 47 and Case T-11/95 *BP Chemicals v Commission* [1998] ECR II-3235, para 88.

whether they have been adopted after notification by the Member State or after a third-party complaint.

Locus standi

The refusal to initiate the formal examination procedure deprives the parties concerned (in the sense of the first subparagraph of Article 108(2) TFEU) of their right to make their submissions to the Commission. In *Cook*, the ECJ held that the persons intending to benefit from the procedural guarantees of Article 108(2) TFEU may secure compliance therewith only if they are able to challenge that decision by the Commission before the EU Courts. To be able to challenge such a decision, therefore, it suffices to fulfil a twofold condition: namely, to be a concerned party as defined in Article 108(2) TFEU, and to be seeking to safeguard the procedural rights laid down in that provision.[81] This is sufficient to be considered as directly and individually concerned within the meaning of the fourth paragraph of Article 263 TFEU. The specific status of 'interested party' within the meaning of Article 1(h) of the Procedural Regulation, in conjunction with the specific subject matter of the action, is sufficient to distinguish individually, for the purposes of the fourth paragraph of Article 263 TFEU, the applicant contesting a decision not to raise objections.[82] This principle applies both when the ground on which the decision is taken is that the Commission regards the aid as compatible with the internal market, and when, in its view, the very existence of aid must be discounted.[83] **27.42**

The principle established in *Cook*, based on the safeguarding of procedural rights, is wider than that laid down in *Cofaz*,[84] which concerns the admissibility of an action for annulment of a final decision taken at the end of the formal examination procedure.[85] **27.43**

The concerned parties are any persons, undertakings, or associations whose interests might have been affected by the granting of the aid, in particular the beneficiary undertakings.[86] This concept, mainly dealt with in the Treaty in the context of the administrative procedure carried out before the Commission, finally turns out, therefore, to be actually more important with respect to court proceedings.[87] **27.44**

As well as being a concerned party, the applicant also has to contest specifically the Commission's refusal to initiate the formal examination procedure. In other words the applicant must be seeking in its action to safeguard the procedural rights laid down in Article **27.45**

---

[81] Case C-198/91 *Cook v Commission* [1993] ECR I-2487, paras 23 and 24; Case C-225/91 *Matra v Commission* [1993] ECR I-3203, paras 17 and 18; Case C-78/03 P *Commission v Aktionsgemeinschaft Recht und Eigentum* [2005] ECR I-10737, para 35; Joined Cases C-75/05 P and C-80/05 P *Germany and Others v Kronofrance* [2008] ECR I-6619, para 38; and Case C-487/06 P *British Aggregates v Commission* [2008] ECR I-10515, para 28.

[82] Case C-83/09 P *Commission v Kronoply and Kronotex* [2011] ECR I-4441, para 48.

[83] Case T-11/95 *BP Chemicals v Commission* [1998] ECR II-3235, paras 89 and 165.

[84] Case 169/84 *Cofaz v Commission* [1986] ECR 391; see para 27.62.

[85] This greater flexibility for action taken against decisions adopted without initiating the procedure is justified on two grounds: first, it would seem normal for competitors not to be obliged to prove a 'substantial detriment' when they challenge a decision not to raise objections, in so far as in such a case they are usually in possession only of the information on the aid communicated by the Commission or gleaned from the summary publication in the OJ; secondly, it is also reasonable not to require competitors to have participated in the preliminary procedure, in so far as they might have been completely ignorant of the fact that this procedure had been initiated (see paras 41 and 43 of the Opinion of AG Tesauro in Case C-198/91 *Cook v Commission* [1993] ECR I-2487).

[86] Case C-367/95 P *Commission v Sytraval and Brink's France* [1998] ECR I-1719, para 41; Case C-78/03 P *Commission v Aktionsgemeinschaft Recht und Eigentum* [2005] ECR I-10737, para 36; and Case C-487/06 P *British Aggregates v Commission* [2008] ECR I-10505, para 29. See also Art 1(h) of the Procedural Regulation.

[87] See Ch 22, 'Prior Control of New Notified Aid', para 22.87 et seq.

108(2) TFEU.[88] However, it matters little whether the application initiating proceedings states that it is seeking the annulment of a decision not to raise objections or of a decision not to initiate the formal investigation procedure, since the Commission takes a position on both aspects of the question by means of a single decision.[89] As for the pleas that may be put forward, once a party has challenged the decision not to initiate the procedure in defence of its procedural rights, it may then put forward any plea for annulment, without being limited to relying on infringement of its procedural rights.[90] Indeed, it is not for the EU court to interpret an action challenging exclusively the merits of an aid assessment decision, as such, as seeking, in reality, to ensure the respect of the procedural rights available to the applicant under Article 108(2) TFEU, where the applicant has not expressly raised a plea to that effect. In such circumstances, the interpretation of the plea would be tantamount to re-defining the subject matter of the action. That limit on its jurisdiction to construe pleas in law does not have the effect of preventing it from examining arguments which the applicant has put forward regarding the substance, in order to ascertain whether strands of those arguments additionally support a plea, also raised by the applicant, which expressly alleges the existence of serious difficulties justifying initiation of the procedure under Article 108(2) TFEU.[91]

27.46   If the applicant limits itself to challenging the aid approval decisions as such, putting forward pleas based on the merits of the case but without claiming infringement of its procedural rights, the simple fact of its being eligible for consideration as a 'concerned' party within the meaning of Article 108(2) TFEU will not be sufficient to guarantee the admissibility of the action. Here, the *Cofaz* case law[92] is applied and the applicant is bound to prove that it is in a particular situation distinguishing it individually from all other businessmen.[93] An undertaking must therefore prove that its competitive position could be substantially affected by the granting of the disputed aid.[94] The action brought by an association is therefore admissible in so far as it is acting as an agent for its members, some of whom have *locus standi* by virtue of the effect on their competitive position.[95]

27.47   As for decisions to raise no objection against aid schemes, the same principles apply.[96]

---

[88] See Case C-78/03 P *Commission v Aktionsgemeinschaft Recht und Eigentum* [2005] ECR I-10737, paras 44–5, in which the ECJ held that the GC was wrong to consider that the applicant had implicitly put forward a plea alleging failure by the Commission to fulfil its obligation to initiate the formal review procedure provided for in Article 108(2) TFEU. See also Joined Cases C-75/05 P and C-80/05 P *Germany and Others v Kronofrance* [2008] ECR I-6619. In this case, the Court did not follow the suggestion of Advocate General ('AG') Bot to apply the *Cook* case law to all actions brought against decisions adopted on the basis of Art 108(3) TFEU, in the sense that where a person contests the merits of the Commission's assessment, adopted at the end of the preliminary examination, it would necessarily call in question the failure to initiate the formal investigation procedure and would therefore seek to obtain protection of its procedural rights (paras 109–13).

[89] Case C-83/09 P *Commission v Kronoply and Kronotex* [2011] ECR I-4441, para 52.

[90] Case T-157/01 *Danske Busvognmænd v Commission* [2004] ECR II-917, para 41.

[91] Case C-83/09 P *Commission v Kronoply and Kronotex* [2011] ECR I-4441, paras 55–6.

[92] See para 27.62.

[93] Case T-193/06 *TF1 v Commission* [2010] ECR II-4967, paras 74–6 and Case T-188/95 *Waterleiding Maatschappij v Commission* [1998] ECR II-3713, para 54.

[94] Case C-106/98 P *Comité d'entreprise de la Société française de production and Others v Commission* [2000] ECR I-3659, paras 40 and 41; Case C-525/04 P *Spain v Commission* [2007] ECR I-9947, para 33; and Case T-117/04 *Werkgroep Commerciële Jachthavens Zuidelijke Randmeren and Others v Commission* [2006] ECR II-3861, para 53.

[95] Case C-487/06 P *British Aggregates v Commission* [2008] ECR I-10505, para 39; Case T-266/94 *Skibsværftsforeningen and others v Commission* [1996] ECR II-1399, para 50; and Case T-157/01 *Danske Busvognmænd v Commission* [2004] ECR II-917, para 40.

[96] Case C-78/03 P *Commission v Aktionsgemeinschaft* [2008] ECR I-10737, para 31 and Case T-193/06 *TF1 v Commission* [2010] ECR II-4967, para 73.

Effects of an annulment

If the ECJ annuls a decision not to raise objections, this normally means that the Commission **27.48** is bound to initiate the formal examination procedure.[97] It is nonetheless conceivable that a decision annulled due to a technical defect (failure to give reasons or infringement of the principle of collegiality in the Commission, for example) could simply be adopted anew under the form of a decision not to raise objections.

3. Appeal against a decision considering aid to constitute existing aid

Contestable act

Without initiating the formal procedure, the Commission can adopt a decision concluding **27.49** that aid is existing aid on the grounds that it constitutes an individual case of application of an existing aid scheme (hence the ensuing decision not to initiate the formal examination procedure). This type of decision is usually taken in response to a complaint. This category also takes in decisions concluding that there is no misuse of existing individual aid (hence the ensuing decision not to initiate the formal examination procedure).

The contestable character of such acts depends on the particular circumstances. When the **27.50** applicant has previously contested a disputed measure's character of existing aid in a complaint to the Commission, then the Commission's decision rejecting the complaints represents a 'statement of position' and *ipso facto* a contestable act, in so far as the refusal to initiate the formal examination procedure has a definitive character.[98] On the contrary, if the applicant has previously only asked the Commission for information without calling upon it to take any decision and without claiming that the disputed measure was covered by an existing scheme, then the Commission's letter indicating that the disputed measure was individual aid covered by an existing scheme is not a contestable act.[99] In such a case the Commission would only 'formally record' the fact that the measures at issue were in the nature of existing aid.[100]

Locus standi

The principles governing *locus standi* in actions for annulment against a decision not to raise **27.51** objections or a refusal to open the formal examination procedure can be extrapolated to the present case, in which the decision considering the measure to be existing aid is also adopted without initiating the procedure.[101]

Effects of annulment

If a Commission decision considering aid to be existing aid is annulled, this would normally **27.52** be because the aid in fact constitutes new aid, subjected to the previous notification obligation. After such a judgment, therefore, the Commission will, in principle, be bound to treat the aid as new aid and will have to take a decision on it after the due preliminary examination or after having opened the formal examination procedure to deal with it.

---

[97] Case C-313/90 R *CIRFS and others v Commission* [1991] ECR I-2557, para 21.

[98] Case C-313/90 R *CIRFS and others v Commission* [1993] ECR I-1125, para 26; Case C-321/99 P *ARAP and others v Commission* [2002] ECR I-4287, para 61; and Case C-322/09 P *NDSHT v Commission* [2010] ECR I-1911, para 53.

[99] Case T-154/94 *CSF and CSME v Commission* [1996] ECR II-1377, paras 38–45.

[100] Case C-321/99 P *ARAP and others v Commission* [2002] ECR I-4287, para 61.

[101] Where it receives a complaint relating to allegedly unlawful aid, the Commission, in classifying the measure as existing aid, subjects it to the procedure provided for by Art 108(1) TFEU and thus refuses by implication to initiate the procedure provided for by Art 108(2) TFEU (Case C-322/09 P *NDSHT v Commission* [2010], paras 52–6).

4. Appeal against a final decision

Contestable act

27.53 A final Commission decision constitutes a contestable act under Article 263 TFEU. Whether it is positive, negative, modifying, or conditional, it normally has binding legal effects that are likely to affect the interests of the concerned parties, for it brings the procedure at issue to a close and gives a definitive ruling on the nature and/or compatibility of the measure examined.

Eligibility for bringing the action

27.54 As well as Member States and other institutions the other parties that could have *locus standi* for bringing an action for annulment are the beneficiary undertakings of the aid in question, the competitor firms of these beneficiaries, and the associations representing these two categories of undertakings.

Beneficiaries

27.55 The beneficiary is bound to prove that it is in a particular situation distinguishing it individually in the sense of *Plaumann*.[102] This will be easy in the case of ad-hoc aid, in which the applicant would be the only beneficiary of the aid. Indeed, as the aid recipient, it is in fact distinguished, as in the case of the addressee of the decision.[103]

27.56 Individual concern is more complex if the applicant is an individual beneficiary of an aid scheme. As a general rule, an undertaking cannot bring an action for the annulment of a Commission decision prohibiting an aid scheme if it is concerned by that decision solely by virtue of the fact that it belongs to the sector in question and is a potential beneficiary of the scheme.[104] The applicant has to show that it is an actual recipient of individual aid granted under the aid scheme, recovery of which has been ordered by the Commission.[105] Individualization results from the specific adverse effect of the recovery order on the interests of the members of the closed class of actual beneficiaries of an aid scheme, particularly affected by the obligation to recover the aid paid out imposed by the Commission on the Member State concerned.[106]

27.57 Direct concern is clear in the case of a negative decision with recovery, as the national authorities are required by the contested decision to nullify the aid declared incompatible with the internal market and to recover any such aid which has been unlawfully granted. The national

---

[102] Case 25/62 *Plaumann v Commission* [1963] ECR 95.

[103] See Case 730/79 *Philip Morris v Commission* [1980] ECR 2671, para 5; Joined Cases 296/82 and 318/82 *Netherlands and Leeuwarder Papierwarenfabriek v Commission* [1985] ECR 809, para 13; Case C-188/92 *TWD Textilwerke Deggendorf* [1994] ECR I-833, para 14; and Case T-358/94 *Air France v Commission* [1996] ECR II-2109, para 31.

[104] For this reason, a beneficiary of a notified aid scheme (not put into effect) will not be individually concerned by the final negative Commission decision.

[105] Cases C-15/98 and C-105/99 *Italy and Sardegna Lines v Commission* [2000] ECR I-8855, paras 34–5; Case C-298/00 P *Italy v Commission* [2004] ECR I-4087, paras 38–9; Case T-445/05 *Associazione italiana del risparmio gestito and Fineco Asset Management v Commission* [2009] ECR II-289, para 49; Joined Cases T-227/01 to T-229/01, T-265/01, T-266/01, and T-270/01 *Diputación Foral de Álava and Others v Commission* [2009] ECR II-3029, paras 112–13; and Case T-221/10 *Iberdrola v Commission* [2012], paras 26–7.

[106] Joined Cases T-254/00, T-270/00, and T-277/00 *Hotel Cipriani v Commission* [2008] ECR II-3269, para 84. The ECJ has confirmed that actual beneficiaries of individual aids granted under a system of aids of which the Commission has ordered recovery are, by that fact, individually concerned, in that they are exposed, as from the time of the adoption of the contested decision, to the risk that the advantages which they have received will be recovered (Joined Cases C-71/09 P, C-73/09 P, and C-76/09 P *Comitato 'Venezia vuole vivere'* [2011] ECR I-4727, paras 53–6). See also Case T-292/02 *Confservizi v Commission* [2009] ECR II-1659, para 54.

authorities have no discretion when it comes to implementing the contested decision.[107] Similarly, in the case of notified aid, the decision prevents the beneficiary from receiving the aid it had been assured of.[108]

If the beneficiary is not affected by the obligation to recover the aid, the GC has considered **27.58** that it has no legal interest in bringing proceedings.[109] However, the GC has also considered that the interest in bringing proceedings can result from a genuine 'risk' that the applicant's legal position will be affected by legal proceedings, or where the 'risk' of legal proceedings was vested and present at the date on which the action was brought before the EU judicature.[110]

Concerning the last part of the fourth paragraph of Article 263 TFEU (introduced by the **27.59** Treaty of Lisbon) according to which any natural or legal person may institute proceedings against a regulatory act which is of direct concern to them and does not entail implementing measures, the GC has found that a final negative decision with recovery cannot be described as an act not entailing implementing measures, by reason of the existence of recovery measures. Moreover, the measures implementing the decision are not confined to the recovery measures, but also include all the measures for implementing the incompatibility decision, including, *inter alia*, the measure rejecting an application for the tax advantage at issue, a rejection which the applicant may also challenge before the national court.[111]

Competitors

Any of the beneficiary's competitor firms that are not satisfied with a final Commission deci- **27.60** sion are entitled to request its annulment if they are directly and individually concerned by the act. The contested decision would in principle be a positive or conditional decision.

Their direct concern can, in principle, be established in either of the following two circum- **27.61** stances: first, when the aid has already been granted (or the engagement to do so made), in which case the contested decision, which allows the conservation of the aid, directly affects the competitor applying for its abolition;[112] and secondly, when the aid has not yet been granted at the moment of adopting the contested decision, but there is no doubt about the public authorities' will to make use of the authorization and pay out the aid.[113] A decision declaring a measure not to constitute aid likewise has direct effects vis-à-vis all concerned parties.[114]

---

[107] Joined Cases T-254/00, T-270/00, and T-277/00 *Hotel Cipriani v Commission* [2008] ECR II-3269, para 69.
[108] See, first of all, Case 730/79 *Philip Morris v Commission* [1980] ECR 2671, para 5. See also Case 323/82 *Intermills v Commission* [1984] ECR 3809, para 5.
[109] Orders of the GC of 10 March 2005 in Joined Cases T-228/00 and others *Gruppo ormeggiatori del porto di Venezia and Others v Commission* [2005] ECR II-787, paras 33–5; of 19 March 2009 in Case T-96/07 *Telecom Italia Media v Commission*, paras 22–4; of 25 November 2008 in Case T-188/07 *Fastweb v Commission* [2008], paras 26–8; and of 20 September 2005 in Case T-258/99 *Makro Cash & Carry v Commission* [2005] ECR II-14, paras 43–5. See also Case T-354/99 *Kuwait Petroleum v Commission* [2006] ECR II-1475, paras 34–5.
[110] Joined Cases T-309/04, T-317/04, T-329/04, and T-336/04 *TV 2/Danmark v Commission* [2008] ECR II-2935, paras 78–82. See also Joined Cases T-425/04, T-444/04, T-450/04, and T-456/04 *France v Commission* [2010] ECR II-2099, para 122.
[111] Case T-221/10 *Iberdrola v Commission* [2012], paras 46–8. That conclusion rendered it unnecessary to rule on whether that decision is a regulatory act.
[112] Case 169/84 *Cofaz v Commission* [1986] ECR 391, para 30; Joined Cases T-447/93, T-448/93, and T-449/93 *AITEC and others v Commission* [1995] ECR II-1971, para 41; Case T-149/95 *Ducros v Commission* [1997] ECR II-2031, para 32; and Case T-11/95 *BP Chemicals v Commission* [1998] ECR II-3235, para 70. See Judgment of the ECJ of 13 June 2013 in Case C287/12 P *Ryanair Ltd v Commission*, paras 54–62 where the Court dismissed Ryanair's claim that the GC erred in its assessment of the admissibility of its action by failing to examine whether its competitive position was significantly affected.
[113] Case T-435/93 *ASPEC and others v Commission* [1995] ECR II-1281, para 60; Case T-442/93 *AAC and others v Commission* [1995] ECR II-1329, para 45; and Case T-266/94 *Skibsværftsforeningen and others v Commission* [1996] ECR II-1399, para 49.
[114] Case T-358/02 *Deutsche Post and DHL International v Commission* [2004] ECR II-1565, para 32.

27.62 It is somewhat harder to demonstrate individual concern. Indeed, the fact that the applicant is a party concerned within the meaning of Article 108(2) TFEU is not sufficient in itself to distinguish it as in the case of the addressee of the decision.[115] Once the formal investigation procedure has been open, competitors cannot base their admissibility in the *Cook* and *Matra* case law, as the normal *Plaumann* test applies.[116] The ECJ clarified this test in *Cofaz*,[117] establishing that an undertaking's individual interest meant fulfilling a dual condition: first that it has played a role in the procedure laid down in Article 108 TFEU; and, secondly, that its market position is substantially affected by the aid measure dealt with in the contested decision. Subsequent case law has removed the condition that the applicant must have participated in the administrative proceedings.[118] Participation in the administrative procedure is thus neither a necessary nor a sufficient[119] condition for the finding that a decision is of individual concern to an undertaking.[120]

27.63 As regards the substantial effect on the applicant's market position, the mere fact that a measure may exercise an influence on the competitive relationships that exist on the relevant market and that the undertaking concerned was in a competitive relationship with the addressee of that measure, cannot in any event suffice for that undertaking to be regarded as individually concerned by that measure.[121] Therefore, an undertaking cannot rely solely on its status as a competitor of the undertaking which benefits from the measure in question, but must additionally demonstrate the magnitude of the prejudice to its position on the market.[122] It does not follow from the case law that a particular position of this kind has to be inferred from factors such as a significant decline in turnover, appreciable financial losses, or a significant reduction in market share following the grant of the aid in question. An adverse effect on the competitive situation of an operator can result in the loss of an opportunity to make a profit or a less favourable development than would have been the case without such aid. The seriousness of such an effect may vary according to a large number of factors, such as, in particular, the structure of the market concerned or the nature of the aid in question. The applicant will have to rely on a number of factors, such as the number of competitors, the situation of production overcapacity, the significance of the distortion

---

[115] Case T-11/95 *BP Chemicals v Commission* [1998] ECR II-3235, para 73.

[116] According to this case law, persons other than those to whom a decision is addressed may claim to be individually concerned only if that decision affects them by reason of certain attributes which are peculiar to them or by reason of circumstances in which they are differentiated from all other persons and by virtue of those factors distinguishes them individually just as in the case of the person addressed (Case 25/62 *Plaumann v Commission* [1963] ECR 95).

[117] Case 169/84 *Cofaz v Commission* [1986] ECR 391, para 23 et seq.

[118] Case C-47/91 *Italy v Commission* [1994] ECR I-4635; Case C-260/05 P *Sniace v Commission* [2007] ECR I-10005, para 57; Case C-367/04 P *Deutsche Post v Commission* [2006] ECR I-26, para 12; Case T-435/93 *ASPEC and Others v Commission* [1995] ECR II-1281, para 64 ; and Case T-11/95 *BP Chemicals v Commission* [1998] ECR II-3235, paras 72–7.

[119] Case T-54/07 *Vtesse Networks v Commission* [2011] ECR II-6, paras 92–3.

[120] Similarly, the fact of being subject to a parafiscal charge meant to finance the aid or having lodged a complaint with the Commission against the aid is not material (Order of 27 August 2008 in Case T-315/05 *Adomex International v Commission*, paras 27–30).

[121] Joined Cases 10/68 and 18/68 *Eridania and Others v Commission* [1969] ECR 459, para 7; Case C-260/05 P *Sniace v Commission* [2007] ECR I-10005, para 32; and Order of 21 February 2006 in Case C-367/04 P *Deutsche Post v Commission* [2006] ECR I-26, para 40.

[122] Case C-106/98 P *Comité d'entreprise de la Société française de production and Others v Commission* [2000] ECR I-3659, paras 40 and 41; Case C-525/04 P *Spain v Commission* [2007] ECR I-9947, para 33; and Case T-117/04 *Werkgroep Commerciële Jachthavens Zuidelijke Randmeren and Others v Commission* [2006] ECR II-3861, para 53.

created by the grant of the aid in question, and the effect of that aid on the prices of the beneficiary.[123]

The general scope of a decision, which results from the fact that it is designed to authorize aid schemes which apply to a category of operators defined in a general and abstract manner, is not such as to constitute a barrier to the application of this case law.[124]

27.64

In the case of a negative decision with recovery, it would seem difficult for a competitor to prove an interest in bringing proceedings, as the annulment of the measure would not be liable to procure an advantage to him. In the case of a negative decision without recovery, the *Cofaz* case law would apply.

27.65

Associations

A professional association which is responsible for protecting the collective interests of its applicant members, is entitled to bring an action for the annulment of a final decision of the Commission on State aid only in two sets of circumstances: first, where the undertakings which it represents or some of those undertakings themselves have *locus standi*; and, second, if it can prove an interest of its own, in particular because its position as a negotiator has been affected by the measure of which annulment is sought.[125] An association can also claim to be affected by the Commission's final decision as the negotiator of aid schemes in the interests of its members, when it is one of the signatories of an agreement whereby the contested scheme was set up and it has been obliged to undertake new negotiations and reach a new agreement to implement the final decision. In such circumstances it is entitled to bring annulment proceedings against a final decision on an aid scheme.[126] It is therefore conceivable that associations could lay claim to have *locus standi* on the basis of different considerations.[127]

27.66

Effects of an annulment

If the ECJ or the GC annuls a final Commission decision, neither of them is entitled to substitute its own assessment for the Commission's. The Commission therefore has to adopt a new decision in light of the findings made by the EU Courts.

27.67

The question of whether the Commission is bound to repeat the whole aid examination process, or whether it can simply and immediately adopt a new decision, depends on the reasons for the annulment, as the procedure for replacing an annulled measure may be resumed at the very point at which the illegality occurred. Annulment of a measure does not necessarily affect the preparatory acts. Where, in spite of the fact that investigation measures have been taken allowing an exhaustive analysis to be made of the compatibility of the aid, the analysis carried out by the Commission is incomplete, thus making the decision unlawful,

27.68

---

[123] Case C-525/04 P *Spain v Commission* [2007] ECR I-9947, paras 34–8 (see also the opinion of AG Kokott in the same case, paras 44–6) and Case C-487/06 P *British Aggregates v Commission* [2008] ECR I-10505, paras 42–56.

[124] Case C-487/06 P *British Aggregates v Commission* [2008] ECR I-10505, para 31 and Case T-193/06 *TF1 v Commission* [2010] ECR II-4967, para 73.

[125] Joined Cases C-182/03 and C-217/03 *Belgium and Forum 187 v Commission* [2006] ECR II-5479, para 56; Joined Cases T-227/01 to T-229/01, T-265/01, T-266/01, and T-270/01 *Diputación Foral de Álava and Others v Commission* [2009] ECR II-3029, para 108; and Order of the GC in Case T-236/10 *Asociación Española de Banca v Commission* [2012], para 19.

[126] Joined Cases 67, 68, and 70/85 *Van der Kooy v Commission* [1985] ECR 219, paras 20–4. See also Case C-313/90 *CIRFS and others v Commission* [1993] ECR I-1125, para 30.

[127] The judge responsible for hearing applications for interim measures has thus not flatly ruled out the idea that an association whose *raison d'être* is affected by the decision might be able to claim a rightful interest in calling for the annulment (Joined Cases C-182/03 R and C-217/03 R *Belgium and Forum 187 v Commission* [2003] ECR I-6887, para 103).

the procedure for replacing that decision can be resumed at that point by means of a fresh analysis of the investigation measures.[128] When the ECJ annuls a decision due to manifest errors of appraisal, the Commission is obliged to initiate the procedure anew if it bases its new analysis on information which it did not have at the time of the adoption of the first decision, so that the Member State concerned and the interested parties can take a position on that information.[129] In cases where the final decisions have been annulled due to a failure to give sufficient reasons for the decision, the Commission has been able to immediately adopt a new final decision that sets forth the reasons upon which it is based, without having to renew the preparatory procedure.[130]

Appeal against a decision to propose appropriate measures or a refusal to adopt such a decision

27.69 According to the GC, neither a decision to propose appropriate measures to one or several Member States, nor a refusal to adopt such a decision, is an act against which an action for annulment may be brought. Appropriate measures are simple propositions, which are not binding on the addressee State.[131]

Appeal against a refusal to bring an action for failure to fulfil an obligation pursuant to subparagraph 2 of Article 108(2) TFEU

27.70 If a Member State fails to enforce correctly a Commission decision, interested third parties have hardly any means of asserting their rights. Indeed, private individuals are not entitled to bring proceedings against a refusal by the Commission to institute proceedings against a Member State for failure to fulfil its obligations, on the basis of the second subparagraph of Article 108(2) TFEU, which concerns failures to enforce a final decision.[132]

C. Action for Failure to Act

1. General principles

27.71 Pursuant to Article 265 TFEU, should the Commission fail to act, in infringement of the Treaty, then an action may be brought before the ECJ to have this infringement established. This action may be brought by Member States and by other EU institutions, or, under certain conditions, by any natural or legal person. The ECJ has ruled that, just as the fourth paragraph of Article 263 TFEU allows individuals to bring an action for annulment against a measure of an institution not addressed to them, provided that the measure is of direct and individual concern to them, the third paragraph of Article 265 TFEU must be interpreted as also entitling them to bring an action for failure to act against an institution which they claim has failed to adopt a measure that would have concerned them in the same way.[133] All the questions of interpretation that crop up in the context of actions for annulment, concerning

---

[128] Case T-301/01 *Alitalia v Commission* [2008] ECR II-1753, paras 100–3.

[129] Case C-415/96 *Spain v Commission* [1998] ECR I-6993, para 40.

[130] See Case C-415/96 *Spain v Commission* [1998] ECR I-6993 and the Opinion of AG Jacobs. See the decision on aid to *Air France* [1999] OJ L63/66, adopted one month after Joined Cases T-371/94 and T-394/94 *British Airways and others v Commission* [1998] ECR II-2405, which had annulled the first decision due to a failure to give sufficient reasons.

[131] Case T-330/94 *Salt Union v Commission* [1996] ECR II-1475, paras 33–7. It is unclear whether or not the same applies with regard to the Commission's record of the Member State's acceptance of the appropriate measures.

[132] Case T-277/94 *AITEC v Commission* [1996] ECR II-351, paras 55 and 56.

[133] Case C-68/95 *T Port* [1996] ECR I-6065, para 59 ; Case T-395/04 *Air One v Commission* [2006] ECR II-1343, para 25 ; and Joined Cases T-30/01 to T-32/01 and T-86/02 to T-88/02 *Diputación Foral de Álava and Others v Commission* [2009] ECR II-2919, para 154.

the direct and individual interest and, in particular, the notion of 'concerned party', also apply, *mutatis mutandis*, in the context of an action for failure to act.[134] Article 265 TFEU refers to a failure to act, not the adoption of a measure different from that desired by the applicant.[135] As long as the Commission defines its position, this will suffice.[136]

2. Appeal against a failure to adopt a decision not to raise objections

A Member State that has notified aid plans to the Commission is entitled to grant the aid at **27.72** the end of the two-month *Lorenz* time limit. It would therefore be unlikely to bring an action for failure to act against the Commission if it does not react within that time limit. Such a possibility cannot be completely ruled out, however. The Commission is, in principle, bound to rule on all aid that comes to its knowledge, and the Member State might rightfully wish to obtain certainty from the Commission about the compatibility of its aid. The same might apply to the beneficiary/ies of the aid concerned.

3. Appeal against a failure to rule on a complaint and/or to initiate the formal examination procedure

A Member State or a third party competitor can bring an action for failure to act against **27.73** the Commission if it refrains from initiating the formal examination procedure on unlawful aid.[137] This entitlement is a useful means of forcing the Commission to deal with complaints that are brought before it. In this case, the failure to act is ended by either a decision to initiate the formal examination procedure or a refusal to initiate that procedure. This refusal will normally be adopted at the same time as a decision not to raise objections.[138]

4. Appeal against a failure to bring an action for failure to fulfil an obligation under the second subparagraph of Article 108(2) TFEU

An action for failure to act brought by a third party following the Commission's failure to **27.74** institute an action for failure to fulfil an obligation under the second subparagraph of Article 108(2) TFEU is not possible; in no case would the act sought be of direct concern to the applicant and the Commission has a wide margin of discretion in terms of deciding whether or not to bring a matter directly before the ECJ.[139]

---

[134] For a ruling on the inadmissibility of an action for failure to act on the grounds that the applicant does not qualify as a 'concerned party' within the meaning of Art 108(2) TFEU, see Case T-41/01 *Rafael Pérez Escolar v Commission* [2003] ECR II-2157.

[135] Case T-26/01 *Fiocchi* [2003] ECR II-3951, para 82.

[136] Case T-26/01 *Fiocchi* [2003] ECR II-3951, paras 90–2.

[137] The Commission is not authorized to persist in its failure to act during the preliminary examination stage. Once that stage in the procedure has been completed, it is bound either to initiate the next stage of the examination procedure, or to adopt a definitive decision rejecting the complaint (Case C-521/06 P *Athinaïki Techniki v Commission* [2008] ECR I-5829, para 40 and Case C-362/09 P *Athinaïki Techniki v Commission* [2010] ECR I-13275, para 64). See Judgment of the ECJ of 16 May 2013 in Case C-615/11 P *Commission v Ryanair Ltd*, where the ECJ upheld the GC's finding that the Commission had failed to fulfil its obligation to adopt a decision in breach of Article 265 TFEU.

[138] See the actions for failure to act that gave rise to Joined Cases 166/86 and 220/86 *Irish Cement* [1988] ECR 6473; Case T-95/96 *Gestevisión Telecinco v Commission* [1998] ECR II-3407; and Case T-41/01 *Rafael Pérez Escolar v Commission* [2003] ECR II-2157.

[139] Case T-277/94 *AITEC v Commission* [1996] ECR II-351, paras 63 and 65–8. Note that paras 58–60 of this judgment, based on the premise that it is necessary to be the potential addressee of an act to be eligible for bringing the action for failure to act, are no longer relevant after Case C-68/95 *T Port*, whereby the ECJ has interpreted Art 265(3) TFEU as entitling private individuals to bring an action for failure to act against an institution that they claim has failed to adopt a measure which would have concerned them, even if they are not the addressees thereof.

5. **Appeal against a failure to take the measures involved in the execution of a judgment of the ECJ or the GC**

27.75 The examination of such an appeal implies determining the execution measures involved in the judgment upon which the appeal is based.[140]

D. Action for Non-Contractual Liability

27.76 Under the second paragraph of Article 340 TFEU, dealing with non-contractual liability, the EU shall, in accordance with the general principles common to the laws of the Member States, 'make good any damage caused by its institutions or by its servants in the performance of their duties'.

27.77 Such actions are conceivable in the field of State aid, in particular when a complainant has suffered a loss as a result of an infringement by the Commission of the reasonable time period for adopting measures involved in the execution of a previous judgment.[141] To date, however, there have been few actions of this type,[142] and only one has ended in the granting of damages.[143]

E. Application for Interim Measures

1. General principles

27.78 Under Articles 278 and 279 TFEU, the EU Courts may order the application of a contested act to be suspended or prescribe any necessary interim measures if the requisite conditions (urgency, *prima facie* good case, and balance of interests) are met.

27.79 This procedure is possible in the field of State aid. In general, however, the judge dealing with the case will be reluctant to grant the measures sought if his intervention is likely to encroach on the Commission's wide margin of discretion in deciding on the compatibility of State aid. Such an intervention would effectively undermine the Commission's role in protecting competition as laid down in Articles 107 and 108 TFEU.[144]

27.80 The Courts may grant the interim measures even before the observations of the opposite party have been submitted.[145]

2. Interim measures and stay of execution of a decision to initiate the formal examination procedure

27.81 It is conceivable that a Member State or aid beneficiary may seek a stay of execution of a Commission decision to open the formal examination procedure. Conversely, a competitor

---

[140] Joined Cases T-297/01 and T-298/01 *SIC v Commission* [2004] ECR II-743, para 32.

[141] Joined Cases T-297/01 and T-298/01 *SIC v Commission* [2004] ECR II-743, para 58.

[142] Case 40/75 *Société des produits Bertand v Commission* [1976] ECR 1; Case 114/83 *Société d'initiative et de coopération agricoles v Commission* [1984] ECR 2589; Case 289/83 *GAARM and others v Commission* [1984] ECR 4295; Case T–107/96 *Pantochin v Commission* [1998] ECR II-311; Case T-176/01 *Ferriere Nord v Commission* [2004] ECR II-3931; Case T-344/04 *Bouychou v Commission* [2007] ECR II-91; Case T-360/04 *FG Marine v Commission* [2007] ECR II-92; and Joined Cases T-362/05 and T-363/05 *Nuova Agricast v Commission* [2008] ECR II-297.

[143] Case T-88/09 *Idromacchine v Commission* [2011].

[144] See in particular Case T-86/96 R *Arbeitsgemeinschaft Deutscher Luftfahrt-Unternehmen and others v Commission* [1998] ECR II-641, para 74.

[145] See eg Order of 17 February 2011 in Case T-486/10 R *Iberdrola v Commission*, para 22.

undertaking of an aid beneficiary will not, in principle, be entitled to seek an order directing the Commission to require the Member State concerned to extend the aid to benefit it as well, not even on an interim basis.[146] A particularly serious *prima facie* case and manifest urgency have been required as regards the initiation of the State aid procedure in the case of a non-notified and already implemented measure.[147]

3. Interim measures and stay of execution of a decision to amend or abolish an existing aid scheme

When a Commission decision orders the amendment or abolition of an existing aid scheme **27.82** against which an action for annulment has been brought, a stay of execution of the decision may be sought until the validity of the decision has been definitively settled.

4. Interim measures and stay of execution of a negative decision

Negative decision on notified aid

When the Commission prohibits the grant of new aid by a State, a simple stay of execution **27.83** is pointless. Even if the negative decision is suspended, the aid still cannot be granted until it has been expressly approved by the Commission. Moreover, it is not at all certain that the applicant could persuade the judge dealing with the application to authorize the granting of the aid on an interim basis, for such a measure could be seen as exceeding the object of the main claim and encroaching on the Commission's exclusive responsibility for approving aid.

Negative decision on unlawful aid

It is often the case that a stay of execution is requested on a Commission decision declaring **27.84** aid or an aid scheme to be incompatible and calling for the recovery or interruption thereof. This application can be made by the aid-granting State, the aid beneficiary, or even the public authority or body that has granted the aid. They can, in fact, challenge the decision under the fourth paragraph of Article 263 TFEU and seek at the same time a suspension of implementation of the decision.[148]

The ECJ has held that, even if a Member State has infringed the provisions of Article 108 **27.85** TFEU, it may not be deprived of the right to challenge before the court, by means of Articles 263 TFEU et seq, in particular, the legality of a Commission decision adversely affecting it, and consequently it must be entitled to apply for the suspension of the operation of that decision in accordance with Article 279 TFEU.[149] The same goes, *a fortiori*, for the beneficiary of unlawful aid.[150] The EU Courts have confirmed, in particular, that the beneficiary does not have to wait for the engagement of the recovery procedure by the national authorities, then using the internal appeal procedures that are open to it for challenging this recovery, but is entitled to address the EU judge for dealing with applications for interim measures directly; the admissibility of an application for the stay of execution of the act of a EU institution is subordinated only to the condition that the applicant has already contested this act in an action before the EU Courts.[151] Any infringement of Article 108(3) TFEU is, however, taken into

---

[146] Case T-107/96 R *Pantochim v Commission* [1996] ECR II-1361.
[147] Joined Cases T-195/01 R and T-207/01 R *Gibraltar v Commission* [2001] ECR II-3915, para 115.
[148] Case T-155/96 R *Ville de Mayence v Commission* [1996] ECR II-1655 and Case T-238/09 R *Sniace v Commission* [2009] ECR II-125.
[149] Joined Cases 67, 68, and 70/85 R *Van der Kooy v Commission* [1985] ECR 1315, para 37.
[150] See Case C-232/02 P(R) *Commission v TGI* [2002] ECR I-8977, paras 30–6. Earlier, the *locus standi* of the beneficiary undertaking had not been contested in Case 310/85 R *Deufil v Commission* [1986] ECR 537.
[151] Case C-232/02 P(R) *Commission v TGI* [2002] ECR I-8977, paras 30–6 and Case T-181/02 R *Neue Erba Lautex v Commission* [2002] ECR II-5081, para 39.

consideration as an unfavourable element in weighing up the interests involved and deciding whether or not to grant the requested stay of execution.[152]

27.86 When assessing the existence of serious damage to the undertaking concerned, the EU Courts take a number of factors into account. The first is the likelihood of the alleged damage actually occurring. In accordance with normal rules, the imminence of the damage does not have to be established with absolute certainty; it suffices for it to be foreseeable with a sufficient degree of probability.[153] However, the applicant is required to prove the facts forming the basis of its claim that serious and irreparable damage is likely.[154] Secondly, the serious and irreparable nature of the damage. It is up to the undertaking concerned to establish the circumstances on the basis of precise, individual, and well-founded indications.[155] In this regard, an adverse effect on the rights of the persons considered to be the recipients of State aid which is incompatible with the internal market forms an integral part of any Commission decision requiring the recovery of such aid and cannot be regarded as constituting in itself serious and irreparable damage.[156] Damage must be personal to the (private) applicant.[157] Moreover, damage of a pecuniary nature cannot, save in exceptional circumstances, be regarded as irreparable, or even as being reparable only with difficulty, since it can ultimately be the subject of financial compensation.[158] An interim measure is justified only if it appears that, without that measure, the undertaking would be in a position that could imperil its existence before final judgment in the main action.[159] The applicant undertaking therefore has to establish to the requisite legal standard that the implementation of the contested decision would inevitably cause it to go into liquidation and disappear from the market before a ruling is given in the main action.[160] Such an assessment must, however, be carried out on a case-by-case basis, having regard to the facts of each case and the legal issues involved.[161]

---

[152] Joined Cases 67, 68, and 70/85 R *Van der Kooy v Commission* [1985] ECR 1315, para 44.

[153] Damage may not be certain enough if further action by national authorities is necessary for damage to materialize (Case T-34/02 R *B v Commission* [2002] ECR II-2803, para 89; Case T-423/05 R *Olympiki Aeroporia v Commission* [2007] ECR II-6, paras 69 and 74–111). The contention that the applicant ought to have waited for the national authorities to bring proceedings for recovery of the disputed aid in the domestic courts and then have availed itself of all the remedies available before the national courts was rejected by the ECJ (Case C-232/02 P(R) *Commission v TGI* [2002] ECR I-8977, paras 30–5). See, however, Case T-440/07 R *Huta Buczek v Commission* [2008] ECR II-39, para 68; and Case T-238/09 R *Sniace v Commission* [2009] ECR II-125, para 27.

[154] Case T-181/02 R *Neue Erba Lautex v Commission* [2002] ECR II-5081, para 83 and Case T-207/07 R *Eurallumina SpA v Commission* [2011] ECR II-171, para 23.

[155] Case T-86/96 R *Arbeitsgemeinschaft Deutscher Luftfahrt-Unternehmen and others v Commission* [1998] ECR II-641, para 64 et seq.

[156] Case T-237/99 R *BP Nederland and others v Commission* [2000] ECR II-3849, para 52; Case T-34/02 R *B v Commission* [2002] ECR II-2803, para 97, and Case T-316/04 R *Wam v Commission* [2004] ECR II-3917, para 33.

[157] Thus, the judge hearing an application for interim measures lodged by a private applicant may not take into account damage to future employees in a new capacity if the State aid was authorized, as such damage is not caused to the interests of the party seeking interim relief, ie it does not affect him or her personally (Case T-455/05 R *Componenta v Commission* [2006] ECR II-38, para 41).

[158] In particular, in the field of aid, Case T-91/02 R *Klausner Nordic Timber v Commission*, para 30.

[159] State of insolvency may not mean disappearance of the market if applicant may still be in the market and avoid liquidation (Case T-440/07 R *Huta Buczek v Commission* [2008] ECR II-39, para 72).

[160] Case T-181/02 R *Neue Erba Lautex v Commission* [2002] ECR II-5081, paras 85 and 86. In the context of the examination of the applicant's financial viability, its material situation may be assessed by taking into account in particular the characteristics of the group to which it belongs by virtue of its shareholding (Case T-111/01 R *Saxonia Edelmetalle v Commission* [2001] ECR II-2335, paras 25–7; Case T-181/02 R *Neue Erba Lautex v Commission* [2002] ECR II-5081, paras 92–104). The fact that the group has decided not to help is irrelevant (Case T-468/08 R *AES-Tisza Erömü v Commission* [2008] ECR II-46, paras 36–45).

[161] Case T-468/08 R *AES-Tisza Erömü v Commission* [2008] ECR II-46, para 89.

To assess the existence of serious and irreparable damage to a Member State, the damage **27.87** suffered by the undertakings concerned has sometimes been taken into account as such.[162] A Member State may nonetheless invoke the risk to its national economy in general due to the bankruptcy of the undertakings involved in the recovery procedure and its knock-on effects.[163]

If the applicant is able to establish the urgency (serious and irreparable damage) and the **27.88** existence of a *prima facie* good case, the judge hearing the application for interim relief then has to weigh up, on the one hand, the applicant's interest in obtaining the interim measures sought and, on the other, the public interest in the execution of decisions taken in the framework of State-aid control. Case law on this matter has established that, in connection with an application for interim measures seeking the suspension of the obligation imposed by the Commission to repay aid which it has declared to be incompatible with the internal market, the interest of the EU must normally, if not always, take precedence over the interest of the aid recipient in avoiding enforcement of the obligation to repay it before judgment is given in the main proceedings. Therefore, suspension of recovery of State aids can only be granted in exceptional circumstances.[164]

5. Interim measures and stay of execution of a positive decision

A Member State might try to block the Commission's approval of aid notified by another **27.89** Member State. A competitor undertaking seeking annulment of a Commission decision declaring a measure not to constitute aid[165] or to be compatible aid[166] can likewise seek a stay of execution of this decision. Even a beneficiary can ask for interim measures.[167]

II. Procedures against Member States

Member States are often brought before the EU Courts by the Commission in an attempt to **27.90** establish the infringement of their State aid obligations.

---

[162] Case 57/86 R *Greece v Commission* [1986] ECR 1497, para 12.

[163] Case 303/88 R *Italy v Commission* [1989] ECR 801. The Court has rejected the Commission's argument that, in the case of a decision ordering the recovery of restructuring aid, there is always urgency, because of the aid beneficiary's insolvency problems, so that it is necessary to apply particularly strict criteria for acknowledging that there is a *prima facie* case. The President of the ECJ, after recalling that undertakings have been unable to establish the condition of urgency in support of applications for suspension of decisions ordering recovery of State aid, including restructuring aid, considered that the Commission's approach could not be accepted without reservations, because it might reduce interim judicial protection to an excessive extent and limit the broad discretion which the judge hearing an application for interim relief must have in order to exercise the powers conferred on him (Case C-232/02 P(R) *Commission v TGI* [2002] ECR I-8977, paras 54–9).

[164] Case T-198/01 R *TGI v Commission* [2002] ECR II-2153, paras 113–16; Case T-440/07 R *Huta Buczek v Commission* [2008], paras 75–8; Case T-352/08 R *Panon Höerömü v Commission* [2009] ECR II-9, paras 58–60; and Case T-238/09 R *Sniace v Commission* [2009] ECR II-125, paras 30–2.

[165] Case T-79/10 R *Colt Télécommunications France v Commission* [2010] ECR II-107.

[166] Case T-520/10 R *Comunidad Autónoma de Galicia v Commission* [2011] ECR II-27 and Case T-533/10 R *DTS Distribuidora de Televisión Digital v Commission* [2011] ECR II-168.

[167] Case T-484/10 R *Gas Natural Fenosa v Commission*; Case T-486/10 R *Iberdrola v Commission*; Case T-490/10 R *Endesa v Commission*.

A. Distinction between the Administrative Aid-Control Procedure and the Infringement Procedure

27.91 When the Commission considers that a State has infringed the provisions of Article 107 TFEU by granting incompatible aid, it necessarily has to follow the procedure laid down in Article 108(2) TFEU if it wishes to establish the incompatibility of a measure, as aid, with the internal market. The procedure laid down in Article 108(2) TFEU provides all the parties concerned with guarantees which are specifically adapted to the special problems created by State aid with regard to competition in the internal market and which go much further than those provided in the preliminary procedure laid down in Article 258 TFEU in which only the Commission and the Member State concerned participate. The Commission cannot, therefore, directly bring an action for failure to fulfil an obligation on the grounds of infringement of Article 107 TFEU without first having followed the procedure laid down in Article 108 TFEU, even if the aid in question has been established by a law.[168]

27.92 On the other hand, the Commission can follow the procedure laid down in Article 258 TFEU to ascertain whether the Member State has failed to meet any of its procedural obligations under Article 108(3) TFEU.[169] In such a case, the EU Court, in order to admit the action, has to verify that the measures concerned are aid within the meaning of Article 107 TFEU and should have been previously notified under Article 108(3) TFEU. The Commission could accompany such an action with an application for interim relief with a view to obtaining the recovery or suspension of the measure.

27.93 Direct recourse to the procedure of Article 258 TFEU is also possible when the Commission intends to establish the infringement of other EU law provisions rather than those of Article 107 TFEU.[170] In particular, in the agricultural sector, when the Commission believes that a State has granted aid in breach of the provisions of a common organization of the markets ('COM'), it can bring an action for failure to fulfil an obligation, even if Articles 107 and 108 TFEU have been made applicable by the provisions of the COM. Likewise, when a parafiscal tax is likely to represent an infringement of either Article 110 TFEU or the aid prohibition, the Commission is entitled to bring an action for failure to fulfil an obligation on the grounds of infringement of Article 110 TFEU.[171] It is only when the aspect related to Article 107 TFEU is inseparable from another infringement of EU law that the Commission is bound to follow the procedure contained in Article 108 TFEU.

B. Direct Referral to the ECJ

1. General principles

27.94 Pursuant to the second subparagraph of Article 108(2) TFEU, should a State fail to comply, within the prescribed time, with a final Commission decision adopted at the end of a formal

---

[168] Case 290/83 *Commission v France* [1985] ECR 439, para 17 and Joined Cases C-356/90 and C-180/91 *Belgium v Commission* [1993] ECR I-2323, para 18.

[169] See the action for failure to fulfil an obligation in Case 171/83, which was withdrawn (Order of 20 September 1983, Case 171/83 R *Commission v France* [1983] ECR 2621, para 1) and also Case 169/82 *Commission v Italy* [1984] ECR 1603; Case C-35/88 *Commission v Greece* [1990] ECR I-3125, para 34; and Case C-61/90 *Commission v Greece* [1992] ECR 1-2407, para 25.

[170] Case 290/83 *Commission v France* [1985] ECR 439, para 17.

[171] See, eg Case 277/83 *Commission v Italy* [1985] ECR 2049, para 16.

examination procedure, then the Commission or any other interested Member State may, in derogation from Articles 258 and 259 TFEU, refer the matter directly to the ECJ.

Direct referral of a matter to the ECJ is justified on the grounds that the Commission has already **27.95** given notice to the Member State concerned to submit its comments. The *inter partes* nature of the preliminary procedure has therefore been respected.[172] Moreover all the rules governing the standard action for failure to fulfil an obligation are applicable.[173]

As regards the reference date to be taken into account, Article 108(2) TFEU subparagraph 2 **27.96** does not provide for a pre-litigation phase in which the Commission allows the Member States a certain period within which to comply with its decision, so the reference period can only be that provided for in the decision whose implementation is being contested or, where appropriate, that subsequently fixed by the Commission.[174]

In the past, the Commission's decisions specified a single time limit of two months, within which **27.97** the Member State concerned was required to communicate to the Commission the measures it had taken to comply with a given decision.[175] In 2007, the Commission recognized that the two-month deadline for the execution of the decisions was too short in the majority of cases.[176] Therefore, it decided to prolong to four months the deadline for the execution of the recovery decisions. Since then, the Commission specifies two time limits in its decisions: a first time limit of two months following the entry into force of the decision, within which the Member State must inform the Commission of the measures planned or taken; and a second time limit of four months following the entry into force of the decision, within which the Commission decision must have been executed. If a Member State encounters serious difficulties that prevent it from respecting either one of these deadlines, it must inform the Commission of these difficulties, providing an appropriate justification. The Commission may then prolong the deadline in accordance with the principle of loyal cooperation.[177]

The existence of this direct referral under subparagraph 2 of Article 108(2) TFEU does not **27.98** prevent the Commission or a State from also resorting to the procedures under Articles 258 or 259 TFEU.[178]

If the ECJ finds in favour of the Commission, the Member State is then bound to take such **27.99** measures as may be laid down in the judgment of the ECJ. Failing that, the Commission would be entitled to apply to the ECJ anew on the basis of Article 260 TFEU for it to impose on the State concerned a lump-sum fine or penalty payment.[179]

---

[172] See the Opinion of AG Mayras in Case 70/72 *Commission v Germany* [1973] ECR 813.

[173] For example, the burden of proof incumbent on the Commission (Case C-404/00 *Commission v Spain* [2003] ECR I-6695, para 26).

[174] Case C-99/02 *Commission v Italy* [2004] ECR I-3353, para 24.

[175] The ECJ acknowledged that this deadline is to be regarded as the deadline for the execution of the Commission decision itself (Case C 207/05 *Commission v Italy* [2006] ECR I-70, paras 31–6 and Case C-378/98 *Commission v Belgium* [2001] ECR I-5107, para 28). Contacts and negotiations between the Commission and the Member State, in the context of the execution of the Commission decision, could not relieve the Member State from the duty to take all necessary measures to execute the decision within the prescribed time limit (Case C-5/86 *Commission v Belgium* [1987] ECR 1773).

[176] See paras 40–3 of the Commission Notice Towards an effective implementation of Commission decisions ordering Member States to recover unlawful and incompatible State aid [2007] OJ C 272/4.

[177] Case C-207/05 *Commission v Italy* [2006] ECR I-70.

[178] Case 70/72 *Commission v Germany* [1973] ECR 813, para 13; Case C-209/00 *Commission v Germany* [2002] ECR I-11695, para 37; and Case C-404/00 *Commission v Spain* [2003] ECR I-6695, para 25.

[179] See Case C-369/07 *Commission v Greece* [2009] ECR I-5703 and Case C-496/09 *Commission v Italy* [2011]. The ECJ has indicated that the Member State cannot be required, for the purpose of calculating the penalty payment and where bankrupt undertakings or undertakings involved in bankruptcy proceedings are concerned, to prove not only the registration of the liabilities against them but also the sale of their assets

2. Grounds of defence that may be put forward by the Member State

Invalid grounds

27.100 **Prohibition of invoking the illegality of the decision**   Once a Member State has allowed the mandatory time limit for bringing an action for annulment against a Commission decision to expire, it will no longer be able to call into question that decision by means of Article 277 TFEU when an action for failure to fulfil an obligation is lodged by the Commission for failure to execute the said decision.[180] Such a solution would indeed be impossible to reconcile with the principles governing the legal remedies established by the Treaty and would jeopardize the stability of that system and the principle of legal certainty upon which it is based, by allowing EU acts having legal effects to be indefinitely called into question.[181] The position could be different if the measure in question contained such particularly serious and manifest defects that it could be deemed non-existent.[182]

27.101 **Prohibition of invoking the legitimate expectations of the beneficiary**   A Member State whose authorities have granted aid contrary to the procedural rules laid down in Article 108 TFEU may not rely on the legitimate expectations of recipients in order to justify a failure to comply with the obligation to take the steps necessary to implement a Commission decision instructing it to recover the aid. If it could do so, Articles 107 and 108 TFEU would be redundant, since national authorities would thus be able to rely on their own unlawful conduct in order to deprive decisions taken by the Commission under these provisions of their effectiveness.[183]

27.102 **Prohibition on invoking the existence of a parallel action for annulment**   As already seen, the existence of an action for annulment against the disputed decision will not be grounds for exempting the Member State from the duty of executing it, unless it has obtained an interim measure to this effect from the EU Courts.[184]

Valid grounds

27.103 **Indeterminate character of the obligation laid down in the decision**   The Member State can, however, claim that the obligation imposed on it by the Commission's decision is indeterminate, if it has been couched in vague and obscure terms.[185]

27.104 **Absolute impossibility of implementing the decision**   If the Commission's decision imposes a clear obligation on the Member State, the only grounds for defence that the Member State could put forward against an action for failure to fulfil an obligation is that it

---

under market conditions. The sums which have not yet been recovered from undertakings in bankruptcy, but which the State has made its best efforts to recover, should not be taken into account for the purpose of allowing the Commission's application relating to the payment of the penalty payments (para 75).

[180] Case 156/77 *Commission v Belgium* [1978] ECR 1881, para 21; Case 52/83 *Commission v France* [1983] ECR 3707, para 10; Case C-183/91 *Commission v Greece* [1993] ECR I-3131, para 10; Case C-188/92 *TWD Textilwerke Deggendorf* [1994] ECR I-833, para 15; and Case C-404/00 *Commission v Spain* [2003] ECR I-6695, para 40. This applies in an action for failure to fulfil obligations based either on Articles 258 or 259 TFEU or on the second subparagraph of Art 108(2) TFEU (Case C-177/06 *Commission v Spain* [2007] ECR I-7689, para 30–2).

[181] Case 156/77 *Commission v Belgium* [1978] ECR 1881, para 24 and Case C-188/92 *TWD Textilwerke Deggendorf* [1994] ECR I-883, para 16.

[182] Case C-404/00 *Commission v Spain* [2003] ECR I-6695, para 41.

[183] Case C-5/89 *Commission v Germany* [1990] ECR I-3437, para 17 and Case C-183/91 *Commission v Greece* [1993] ECR I-3131, para 18; and Case C-99/02 *Commission v Italy* [2004] ECR I-3353, para 21.

[184] See para 27.19.

[185] Case 70/72 *Commission v Germany* [1973] ECR 813, paras 21–3.

was absolutely impossible to implement the decision properly.[186] This impossibility may refer to the object of the decision or the timeframe for implementing it.[187] The ECJ interprets this concept in a restrictive way.

In the event of unforeseen and unforeseeable difficulties or consequences, the ECJ invites the **27.105** Member State to come to some arrangement with the Commission. However, the condition that it be absolutely impossible to implement a decision is not fulfilled where the Member State merely informs the Commission of the legal, political, or practical difficulties involved in implementing the decision, without taking any real steps to recover the aid from the undertakings concerned, and without proposing to the Commission any alternative arrangements for implementing the decision which could have enabled the difficulties to be overcome.[188] The fact that the Member State in question finds it necessary to verify the individual situation of each company concerned, to conduct a screening to identify persons in receipt of benefits covered by the Commission's decision, cannot justify non-implementation of that decision.[189]

It is up to the Member State concerned to prove that the necessary measures could not **27.106** have been implemented within the deadline laid down in the Commission's decision.[190] It therefore has to back up such a plea with specific arguments demonstrating that the alleged absolute impossibility actually existed.[191]

C. Applications for the Adoption of Interim Measures

An action for failure to fulfil an obligation brought against a Member State could be accom- **27.107** panied with an application for interim measures.

III. Procedure for Action against Council Decisions Adopted on the Basis of the Third Subparagraph of Article 108(2) TFEU

Two actions are conceivable against the Council when it exercises the powers conferred **27.108** on it under the third subparagraph of Article 108(2) TFEU. In particular Council decisions can be appealed against by actions for annulment,[192] or liability questions can be

---

[186] Case 52/84 *Commission v Belgium* [1986] ECR 89, para 14; Case C-99/02 *Commission v Italy* [2004] ECR I-3353, para 16; Case C-177/06 *Commission v Spain* [2007] ECR I-7689, para 46, and Case C-214/07 *Commission v France* [2008] ECR I-8357, para 44.

[187] Opinion of AG Slynn in Case 63/87 *Commission v Greece* [2000] ECR I-5047.

[188] Case C-499/99 *Commission v Spain* [2002] ECR I-6031, para 25; Case C-404/00 *Commission v Spain* [2003] ECR I-6695, para 47; Joined Cases C-485/03 to C-490/03 *Commission v Spain* [2006] ECR I-11887, para 74; and Case C-214/07 *Commission v France* [2008] ECR I-8357, para 46.

[189] Case C-99/02 *Commission v Italy* [2004] ECR I-3353, para 23; Case C-305/09 *Commission v Italy* [2011] ECR I-3225, para 37; and Case C-354/10 *Commission v Greece* [2012], para 73.

[190] Case 213/85 *Commission v Netherlands* [1988] ECR 281, para 24.

[191] Case 63/87 *Commission v Greece* [2000] ECR I-5047, para 14.

[192] See the actions for annulment brought by the Commission in Joined Cases C-122/94 *Commission v Council* [1996] ECR I-881, C-309/95 *Commission v Council* [1998] ECR I-655, and C-399/03 *Commission v Council* [2006] ECR I-5629.

raised.[193] The questions of admissibility and *locus standi* raised by an action for annulment are essentially the same as those raised by an appeal against a Commission decision.

IV. Reference for a Preliminary Ruling

27.109 The ECJ does not have jurisdiction to rule upon the compatibility of a national measure with EU law. Nor does the Court have jurisdiction to rule on the compatibility of State aid or of an aid scheme with the internal market, since that assessment falls within the exclusive competence of the Commission, subject to review by the Court. The Court also has no jurisdiction to give a ruling on the facts in an individual case or to apply the EU law rules which it has interpreted to national measures or situations, since those questions are matters for the exclusive jurisdiction of the national court. However, the Court does have jurisdiction to give the national court full guidance on the interpretation of EU law in order to enable it to determine the issue of compatibility of a national measure with that law for the purposes of deciding the case before it. In the area of State aid, the Court has jurisdiction, *inter alia*, to give the national court guidance on interpretation in order to enable it to determine whether a national measure may be classified as State aid under European EU law.[194]

---

[193] See the action brought by GAEC in Case 253/84 *GAEC de la Ségaude v Council and Commission* [1987] ECR I-123, claiming compensation for the damage it alleges to have sustained as a result of a Council decision authorizing certain aid. The ECJ rejected the appeal after finding that the damage and its causal link to the disputed decision had not been proven.

[194] Case C-140/99 *Fallimento Traghetti del Mediterraneo* [2010] ECR I-5243, paras 22–4. In Case C-333/07 *Régie Networks* [2008] ECR I-10807, paras 121–8, after declaring that the Commission decision is invalid, the Court determined that the effects of that declaration would be suspended pending the adoption of a new decision by the Commission under Art 108 TFEU.

PART V

COMPETITION LAW AND PROCEDURE IN THE EUROPEAN ECONOMIC AREA

28

EUROPEAN ECONOMIC AREA COMPETITION PROCEDURE

Kieron Beal

I. Introduction to the Agreement on the European Economic Area

28.01 This chapter seeks to set out the general structure of the competition provisions and procedure, together with an overview of the rules on State aid, applicable under the Agreement on the European Economic Area ('EEA Agreement'). It will briefly set out the background to the EEA Agreement, before describing its substantive competition rules, the procedure to be followed in their application, and the allocation of jurisdiction between the EU Commission and the European Free Trade Association ('EFTA') Surveillance Authority ('ESA') in that application. The EEA provisions corresponding to EU merger control and State monopolies will be identified. A separate section will briefly explore EEA rules on State aids (equivalent to Articles 107 to 109 on the Treaty on the Functioning of the European Union, 'TFEU'). In practical terms, the scope of application of the EEA provisions is relatively limited. Nonetheless, undertakings situated in Iceland, Liechtenstein, and Norway, or undertakings doing business with those countries, will need to take heed of the EEA provisions. This chapter is therefore intended to provide only a brief overview of some of the key procedural aspects and differences in EEA competition law. Practitioners in this area are referred to more detailed practitioners' texts for further information.[1]

A. Formation and General Institutional Framework

28.02 The European Free Trade Association ('EFTA') was established in 1960 by Austria, Denmark, Norway, Portugal, Sweden, Switzerland, and the United Kingdom. Its goal was to reduce or remove import duties, quotas, and other obstacles to trade in Western Europe and to uphold liberal, non-discriminatory practices in world trade. Iceland joined EFTA in 1970, while Finland became an associate member in 1961 and a full member in 1986. Liechtenstein became a member in 1991. Six members have since left EFTA to join the European Union ('EU'): the United Kingdom and Denmark in 1973; Portugal in 1986; and Austria, Finland, and Sweden in 1995. Norway completed negotiations for accession to the EU, but decided against membership in a referendum in November 1994. The present members of EFTA are therefore Iceland, Liechtenstein, Norway, and Switzerland.[2] EFTA membership served as a platform for EFTA members to negotiate a specific agreement with Member States of the European Community for an extension of the internal market to those countries.

---

[1] See, *inter alia*, S Norberg, K Hökborg, M Johansson, D Eliasson, and L Dedichen, *The European Economic Area, EEA Law: A Commentary on the EEA Agreement* (Kluwer, 1993) and T Blanchet, R Piipponen, and M Westman-Clément, *The Agreement on the European Economic Area (EEA). A Guide to the Free Movement of Goods and Competition Rules* (Clarendon Press, 1994).

[2] See the summary found on EFTA's website at <http://www.eftasurv.int/about-the-authority/the-authority-at-a-glance-/> and EFTA's own publication 'This is EFTA 2012' at <http://www.efta.int/~/media/Files/Publications/this-is-efta/this-is-EFTA-2012.pdf>.

The resultant EEA Agreement came into force on 1 January 1994.[3] It was first signed on 2 May 1992 at Oporto, Portugal, between the European Community, its then twelve Member States, and the seven other countries[4] of EFTA. Since that date, Austria, Finland, and Sweden have joined the EU. Switzerland is no longer a contracting party to the EEA Agreement.[5] Liechtenstein became a full member of the EEA on 1 May 1995.[6] Further, the enlargement of the EU on 1 May 2004 has been reflected in the EEA Agreement.[7] In December 2002, the ten countries acceding to the EU applied for EEA membership. Negotiations for their admission were successful. The EEA Enlargement Agreement was signed on 14 October 2003.[8] There was, therefore, a parallel enlargement of the EEA and EU on 1 May 2004.[9] Provisions were also made for the accession of Bulgaria and Romania to the EU and the EEA in 2007.[10] Thus, after various modifications,[11] the EEA now encompasses the newly enlarged EU with its twenty-seven Member States, together with Iceland, Liechtenstein, and Norway. Further arrangements will be put in place to address Croatia's accession to the EU with effect from 1 July 2013.

---

[3] See Decision 94/1/ECSC, EC of the Council and Commission of 13 December 1993 on the conclusion of the Agreement on the European Economic Area, together with the Final Act [1994] OJ L1/1; and Decision 94/2/ECSC, EC of the Council and Commission of 13 December 1993 on the conclusion of the Protocol adjusting the Agreement on the European Economic Area,[1994] OJ L1/571. A special edition of the *Common Market Law Reports* contains the original EEA Treaty and ESA, together with the relevant Notices and Guidelines. See [1994] 5 CMLR Parts 2 and 3. An updated version of the EEA Agreement is available on the EFTA secretariat website at <http://www.efta.int/~/media/Documents/legal-texts/eea/the-eea-agreement/Main%20Text%20of%20the%20Agreement/EEAagreement.pdf>. See also H Charlton, 'EC Competition Law: The New Regime under the EEA Agreement' (1994) 15(2)ECLR 55; A Diem, 'EEA Competition Law' (1994) 15(5) ECLR 263; M Broberg, 'The Delimitation of Jurisdiction with regard to Concentration Control under the EEA Agreement' (1995) 16(1)ECLR 30.

[4] Austria, Finland, Iceland, Liechtenstein, Norway, Sweden, and Switzerland.

[5] In a referendum on 6 December 1992, a majority of both the Cantons and citizens voted against membership. A Protocol to the Agreement was signed on 17 March 1993, recognizing this change. Switzerland remains a party to the EFTA Convention, originally signed in 1960 in Stockholm. The original Stockholm Convention was replaced and updated in Vaduz in 2001. Article 18 of the Vaduz Convention (ie the updated EFTA Convention) requires Member States to recognize that conduct equivalent to that prohibited by Arts 101 and 102 TFEU is incompatible with the Convention.

[6] Liechtenstein was obliged initially to wait for an EEA Council resolution confirming that its customs union with Switzerland would not adversely affect the functioning of the EEA before fully taking part.

[7] Article 128 of the EEA Agreement provides that any European country becoming a member of the 'Community' (now the EU) shall also apply for membership of the EEA. Applications are submitted to the EEA Council and subject to ratification by all parties to the EEA Agreement.

[8] The Agreement on the participation of the Czech Republic, the Republic of Estonia, the Republic of Cyprus, the Republic of Latvia, the Republic of Lithuania, the Republic of Hungary, the Republic of Malta, the Republic of Poland, the Republic of Slovenia and the Slovak Republic in the European Economic Area signed on 14 October 2003 in Luxembourg [2004] OJ L130/3. See also Decision of the EEA Joint Committee No 68/2004 of 4 May 2004 extending the application of certain Decisions of the EEA Joint Committee to the New Contracting Parties and amending certain Annexes to the EEA Agreement following the enlargement of the European Union [2004] OJ L277/187.

[9] The national parliaments of all twenty-eight contracting parties to the EEA Enlargement Agreement were expected to ratify the Instruments by the end of 2004. In the meantime, the EEA/EFTA States and the EU signed an agreement (constituted by an exchange of letters) that permitted the EEA Enlargement Agreement to enter into force provisionally on 1 May 2004. See [2004] OJ L130/1.

[10] Agreement on the participation of Bulgaria and Romania in the European Economic Area of 25 July 2007 [2007] OJ L221/15, applicable from 1 August 2007.

[11] Some of these, as mentioned earlier, were brought about by the political process. For example, the EEA Agreement was amended by the Agreement between the European Union, Iceland, Lichtenstein and Norway on an EEA Financial Mechanism for the period 2009–2014 [2010] OJ L291/4. Others, such as changes to the institutional structure, came as a response to an opinion of the Court of Justice ('ECJ'), Opinion 1/91 of 14 December 1991 [1991] ECR I-6079, which held that the judicial system as initially established by the EEA Agreement was incompatible with the Treaty of Rome. An amended Agreement received the blessing of the ECJ in Opinion 1/92 [1992] ECR I-282 and was signed in its revised form by the parties on 2 May 1992.

28.03   The EEA Agreement is an international treaty that is considered to be *sui generis* and which contains a distinct legal order of its own.[12] The Agreement, whilst falling short of a customs union, has created the world's largest integrated economic area.[13] The EEA countries now represent a single market in services, capital, and manufactured goods for over 500 million people. The EEA Agreement reiterates the *acquis communautaire* in seeking to establish the 'four freedoms' of the TFEU in the EEA territory, as well as covering a wide range of areas linked to the achievement of the four freedoms, such as social policy, consumer protection, the environment, and competition.[14] The EEA 2004 and 2007 Enlargement Agreements each consist of a main agreement listing the amendments to be made to the previous text of the EEA Agreement. The Protocols and Annexes to the EEA Agreement have also been amended to take into account the changes made to the EU *acquis* by the EU Treaties of Accession for new Member States in 2003 and 2005. This has been done by a simple cross-referencing technique.[15] A consolidated version of the EEA Agreement can be found on the EFTA Secretariat website.[16]

28.04   The EEA Agreement is founded on a 'two-pillar' approach, with each 'pillar', the EU side and the EFTA[17] side, responsible for its own share of the work. The Agreement sets up several joint institutions.[18] The EEA Council is the highest political body. The EEA Joint Parliamentary Committee and the EEA Consultative Committee are intended to coordinate at a political level with their EU counterparts. The EEA Joint Committee takes decisions and administers the Agreement. All decisions made by these institutions must meet with unanimous agreement from the relevant EU institutions. The EFTA States, through two Agreements signed on 2 May 1992,[19] have created three additional institutions to ensure the proper functioning of the EEA Agreement, which are of particular relevance to the EEA competition provisions:

---

[12] See the Advisory Opinion of the EFTA Court of 10 December 1998, Case E-9/97 *Erla María Sveinbjörnsdóttir v Iceland* [1999] 1 CMLR 884, para 59.

[13] See the Advisory Opinion of the EFTA Court in Case E-2/97 *Mag Instrument Inc v California Trading Company Norway* [1997] EFTA Court Report 127, para 25.

[14] For general information on the EEA Competition provisions, see the website of the ESA at <http://www.eftasurv.int/> and the overview provided on the European Commission's website at <http://ec.europa.eu/competition/international/multilateral/eea.html/>.

[15] See eg [2004] OJ L130/3 and EEA Supplement [2004] OJ 23/1. Article 3 of the 2004 EEA Enlargement Agreement states that all amendments made to the Community *acquis* by the EU Act of Accession of 2003 are hereby 'incorporated into and made part' of the EEA Agreement. Annex A to the Enlargement Agreement lists all the acts referred to in the Annexes of the EEA Agreement that have been amended by the EU 2003 Act of Accession and indicates where these acts are to be found in the EEA Agreement. A similar legislative technique was adopted by Art 3 of the 2007 Enlargement Agreement by reference to the Act of Accession of 25 April 2005. The list of amendments was set out in Annex B to the 2007 EEA Enlargement Agreement.

[16] <http://www.efta.int/~/media/Documents/legal-texts/eea/the-eea-agreement/Main%20Text%20of%20the%20Agreement/EEAagreement.pdf>.

[17] The term EFTA is used here, even though, as has been seen, only three participating countries are 'true' EFTA States for the purposes of the EEA Agreement. This terminology is sanctioned by the Protocol adjusting the Agreement on the European Economic Area [1994] OJ L1/571.

[18] See generally C Reymond, 'Institutions, Decision-making Procedure and Settlement of Disputes in the European Economic Area' (1993) 30 CML Rev 449.

[19] First, the Agreement between the EFTA States on the Establishment of a Surveillance Authority and a Court of Justice [1994] OJ L344/1 ('Surveillance and Court Agreement'), adjusted by the Protocol Adjusting the Agreement between the EFTA States on the Establishment of a Surveillance Authority and a Court of Justice signed in Brussels on 17 March 1993 and subsequently by the Agreement Adjusting certain Agreements between the EFTA States signed in Brussels on 29 December 1994. The Surveillance and Court Agreement has been amended on numerous occasions between 1994 and 2009. A consolidated version can be found on the EFTA secretariat website at <http://www.efta.int/~/media/documents/legal-texts/the-surveillance-and-court-agreement/agreement-annexes-and-protocols/surveillance-and-court-agreement-consolidated.ashx>. Secondly, the Agreement on a Standing Committee of the EFTA States, amended by the Protocol Adjusting the Agreement on a Standing Committee of the EFTA States signed in Brussels on 17 March 1993, by

- First, the EFTA Surveillance Authority ('ESA'),[20] an independent body with powers similar to those of the EU Commission, which is in charge of ensuring that the EFTA States fulfil their obligations. It is also responsible for ensuring the application of the competition rules. Based in Brussels, the ESA is led by a College of three Members, one from each EFTA State participating in the EEA.[21] College Members are appointed by common agreement of the governments of the EFTA/EEA States for a period of four years. A President is appointed from among the College Members for a period of two years. The College is completely independent of other institutions, as well as of the EFTA States. It takes decisions according to the majority vote of its Members. Its working language is English.

- Secondly, the EFTA Court[22] which mainly deals with: (i) infringement actions brought by the ESA against an EFTA State with regard to the implementation, application or interpretation of an EEA rule; (ii) the settlement of disputes between two or more EFTA States; (iii) appeals concerning decisions taken by the ESA; and (iv) giving advisory opinions to courts in EFTA States on the interpretation of EEA rules. It only has jurisdiction with regard to EFTA States which are parties to the EEA Agreement. The EFTA Court consists of three judges, one nominated by each of the EFTA States party to the EEA Agreement. The judges are appointed by common accord of the Governments for a period of six years. The judges elect their president for a term of three years.[23] All proceedings are in English except in cases where an advisory opinion is sought by a national court of an EFTA State party to the EEA, where the opinion of the Court will be both in English and in the national language of the requesting court.[24]

- Thirdly, the EFTA Standing Committee, composed of the EFTA States' representatives.[25] The Committee provides a forum in which the EEA/EFTA States may consult one another and arrive at a common position before meeting with the EU side in the EEA Joint Committee.[26] It consists of representatives from Iceland, Liechtenstein, and Norway, and observers from Switzerland and the ESA. Chairmanship of the Committee rotates between the EEA/EFTA States. The EFTA Standing Committee formally liaises with the EU Commission under the auspices of the EEA Joint Committee. The main function of the EEA Joint Committee is to adopt decisions extending Community Regulations and Directives to the EEA/EFTA States. The EEA is thus managed on a day-to-day basis by the EEA Joint Committee, with political direction given by the EEA Council. The EEA Council meets twice a year at ministerial level and twice a month at the level of heads of the permanent national delegations.

---

the Decision No 2/94/SC of the Standing Committee of the EFTA States of 10 January 1994 [1994] OJ L85/76, and EEA Supplement No 1, 30 March 1994, 14, and subsequently by the Agreement Adjusting certain Agreements between the EFTA States signed in Brussels on 29 December 1994 ('Standing Committee Agreement').

[20] See Art 108(1) of the EEA Agreement.

[21] The current College members are: Oda Helen Sletnes, President; Sabine Monauni-Tömördy; and Sverrir Haukur Gunnlaugsson. The College heads a Competition and State Aid Directorate.

[22] See Art 108(2) of the EEA Agreement.

[23] The current full-time judges are Carl Baudenbacher (Liechtenstein), President; Páll Hreinsson (Iceland); and Per Christiansen (Norway). A system of ad hoc judges has also been created in case one of the full-time judges is unable to sit.

[24] Guidance on references to the EFTA Court for advisory opinions is contained in [1999] 3 CMLR 525. Guidance for Counsel in written and oral proceedings is at [1999] 2 CMLR 883.

[25] Andreas Diem notes that 'while the EFTA institutions apply EEA law only, the Commission, the ECJ and the CFI will act partly as EC institutions and partly as EEA institutions and will apply different law in each case.' A Diem, 'EEA Competition Law' (1994) 15(5) ECLR 263, 264. However, he also notes that, given the substantial similarity between EEA and EU provisions and the duty to interpret in the same way, any differences will have little significance.

[26] As to the nature of the EEA Joint Committee, see Case E-6/01 *CIBA Speciality Chemicals Water Treatment Ltd v Norway*, judgment of the EFTA Court dated 9 October 2002, paras 32–3.

28.05 The institutional structure is represented in tabular form as follows:[27]

EEA bodies	Joint bodies	EU bodies
Iceland, Liechtenstein, and Norway	*EEA Council*	EU Council
	Ministers of EU and EFTA/ EEA States	
EFTA Standing Committee	*EEA Joint Committee*	European Commission
	Commission and EU and EFTA	
EFTA Secretariat	Government Representatives	Commission Services
EFTA Surveillance Authority	-	
EFTA Court	-	Court of Justice of the European Union
Committee of MPs of the EFTA States	*EEA Joint Parliamentary Committee* MPs from the EFTA Parliaments and MEPs	European Parliament EP Secretariat
EFTA Secretariat	*EEA Consultative Committee*	Economic and Social Committee ('ECOSOC')
EFTA Consultative Committee EFTA Secretariat		ECOSOC Secretariat

B. An Overview of the Competition Provisions of the EEA Agreement

28.06 The general aim of the EEA Agreement, as laid down in Article 1(1) EEA, is to promote a continuous and balanced strengthening of trade and economic relations between the contracting parties with equal conditions of competition and the respect of the same rules, with a view to creating a homogenous European Economic Area.[28] To this end, Article 1(2)(e) EEA provides for the creation and maintenance of a system ensuring that competition is not distorted and that the corresponding rules are equally respected. The EEA competition rules may be found in Articles 53 to 60, Annex XIV, and Protocols 21 to 24 of the Agreement. To all intents and purposes, these provisions adapt in their entirety the substantive rules on competition found in the original EC Treaty. They also include identical provisions to the Merger Control Regulation,[29] most of the block exemptions, and many of the Commission notices applicable to competition policy. Article 59 contains rules governing public undertakings or those undertakings granted special or exclusive rights by EFTA States. Chapter 2 of the EEA

---

[27] Information for this table was derived from a website formerly maintained by the Principality of Liechtenstein.

[28] See also the fourth and fifteenth recitals to the Preamble of the Agreement and Case E-9/97 *Erla María Sveinbjörnsdóttir v Iceland* [1998] EFTA Court Report 95, paras 47–51.

[29] Council Regulation (EC) 139/2004 of 20 January 2004 on the control of concentrations between undertakings [2004] OJ L24/1 ('Merger Control Regulation').

Agreement, incorporating Articles 61 to 64, together with Annex XV to the Agreement, set out comparable rules on State aid to those found in EU law.

One important difference relates to the range of products falling within the scope of the **28.07** competition provisions. Article 8(3) of the EEA Agreement defines the products covered by the rules of the EEA by reference to the Harmonized Commodity Description and Coding System. The EEA provisions do not apply to products described in Chapters 1 to 24 of that System, save to the extent that they are brought within the remit of the Agreement by Tables I and II attached to Protocol 3 to the Agreement. In practical terms, the EEA competition provisions will not generally apply to agricultural and fisheries products, except for a limited number of processed agricultural products. The following list provides a brief overview of the main provisions of the EEA competition rules:

- Article 53 EEA contains a general prohibition on anticompetitive agreements and practices.
- Article 54 EEA prohibits the abuse of a dominant position by undertakings.
- Article 57 EEA governs large mergers and other concentrations of undertakings.
- Article 59 EEA lays down provisions on anticompetitive behaviour by public undertakings.
- Articles 61 to 64 EEA set out comparable provisions on State aid.
- Protocol 21 to the EEA Agreement deals with the implementation of competition rules applicable to undertakings.
- Protocol 22 concerns the definition of undertaking and turnover.[30]
- Protocol 23 addresses the cooperation between the surveillance authorities (based also on Article 58 EEA).
- Protocol 24 contains rules on cooperation in the field of control of concentrations.
- Protocol 26 stipulates that the ESA is entrusted with equivalent powers and similar functions to those of the European Commission in the field of State aid.
- Protocol 27 lays down the principles according to which the ESA and the Commission shall cooperate in order to ensure a uniform application of the State aid rules.
- Annex XIV to the EEA Agreement incorporates by reference the EU *acquis* in the competition field, subject to certain sectoral adaptations.
- Annex XV to the Agreement incorporates by reference the EU *acquis* in the field of State aid, subject to certain sectoral adaptations.
- Finally, the procedural rules relevant to the application of the EEA competition rules can be found in Chapter II, Part I of Protocol 4 to the Surveillance and Court Agreement. Protocol 3 to the Surveillance and Court Agreement contains procedural rules relating to the implementation of the provisions on State aid.

The introduction or amendment of secondary EU legislation applicable in the competition **28.08** field has, over the years, been given equivalent effect under the EEA Agreement through decisions of the EEA Joint Committee.[31] The EEA Joint Committee is obliged to ensure the effective implementation and operation of the EEA Agreement. Its decisions insert new pieces of EU legislation into the EEA Agreement through the amendment of the twenty-two Annexes to the EEA Agreement.[32] In this way, the parallel application of EU and EEA law in parallel fields is maintained, achieving the homogeneity across the entire EEA that the

---

[30] See also the judgment of the EFTA Court in Joined Cases E-4/10, E-6/10, and E-7/10 *Principality of Lichtenstein v ESA* [2011] EFTA Court Report 16, paras 53–5.

[31] In accordance with the provisions of Chapter II, Part VII of the EEA Agreement, which sets out the decision-making procedure. If no decision is taken to transpose the EU legislation, the general structure of the EEA Agreement cannot be relied upon to fill the gap. See Case E-1/97 *Jan and Kristian Jaegar AS v Opel Norge AS* [1999] 4 CMLR 147, para 30.

[32] Article 7 EEA establishes the legally binding nature of secondary EU legislation incorporated into the EEA Agreement in this manner.

EEA Agreement mandates. It should be noted, however, that if the EU legislation is not expressly adopted by the EEA legislature, the principle of 'homogeneity' cannot be used to fill the gap.[33] New pieces of EU legislation with relevance to the EEA countries are marked 'text with EEA relevance' in any Official Journal ('OJ') publication. Non-binding acts in the competition area, such as notices adopted by the EC Commission, have been promulgated for the EFTA/EEA States by the ESA.

28.09   Under Article 6 of the EEA Treaty, the provisions of the EEA Agreement shall, in so far as they are identical in substance to corresponding provisions of the EC Treaty, be interpreted in conformity with the relevant rulings of the Court of Justice ('ECJ') given prior to the date of signature of the EEA Agreement. Article 3(2) of the Surveillance and Court Agreement[34] also provides that 'due account' shall be paid to the relevant rulings of the ECJ given after the date of signature of the EEA Agreement. Where the EEA substantive rules are identical to the Community/EU law rules from which they are drawn, the legal result should in practice be the same regardless of which set of rules is applied to the given facts.[35] Subject to the process of decentralization of enforcement of competition law, the competition rules in the EEA will be enforced by the EU Commission and the ESA.[36] However in accordance with a 'one-stop-shop' principle, cases are attributed either to the EU Commission or the ESA. In cases falling within the responsibility of the EU Commission,[37] the implementation of the EEA competition rules will be based on the existing EU competences, supplemented by the provisions contained in the EEA Agreement.

II. The Substantive Competition Rules of the EEA Agreement: A Brief Description

A. The Basic Rules

1. Article 53 EEA (Article 101 TFEU)

28.10   The substantive EEA competition rules are essentially identical to the corresponding EU competition rules. The only major difference is in their geographical scope. This is widened in the EEA rules to include the EFTA States. Thus Article 53(1) EEA prohibits, as incompatible with the functioning of the EEA Agreement, agreements between undertakings, decisions by associations of undertakings, and concerted practices which have as their object or effect the prevention, restriction, or distortion of competition within the territory 'covered by this Agreement': in other words, within the territory of the contracting parties to the EEA. This provision is the exact counterpart to Article 101 TFEU, except that trade between the EU and one or more EFTA

---

[33] Case E-3/97 *Jan and Kristian Jaeger v Opel Norge AS* [1998] EFTA Court Reports 1, para 30.

[34] [1994] OJ L344/3, as amended on a number of occasions. A consolidated version of the text with amendments up to 7 March 2012 is available at <http://www.efta.int/legal-texts/>.

[35] See Case E-N8/00 *Landsorganisasjonen i Norge v Norsk Kommuneforbund* [2002] 5 CMLR 5, para 39. Articles 111 et seq of the EEA Agreement sets up a dispute settlement procedure for differences in interpretation of the EEA rules between EU and EFTA institutions. The dispute is first referred by either side to the EEA Joint Committee, which attempts to reconcile the conflicting interpretations. If the provision in dispute is identical in substance to an EU provision, the question may, after three months, be referred with the consent of both sides to the ECJ for a definitive ruling.

[36] EEA, Art 55(1).

[37] For details of how jurisdiction is allocated between the EU Commission and the ESA, see para 28.27 et seq.

States or between EFTA States must be affected, if the prohibition is to apply. Article 53(1) lists five paradigmatic practices which are caught by the prohibition. Articles 53(2) and 53(3) follow Articles 101(2) TFEU and 101(3) TFEU word for word.[38]

2. Article 54 EEA (Article 82 EC)

Similarly, Article 54 EEA prohibits, as incompatible with the functioning of the EEA Agreement, **28.11** any abuse by undertakings of a dominant position within the territory covered by the Agreement or a substantial part of it. As with Article 53, the only major divergence from Article 102 TFEU is that trade between the EU and one or more EFTA States or between EFTA States must be affected. A list of the main abusive practices specified in Article 102 TFEU is repeated in Article 54.

3. Article 57 EEA (The Merger Control Regulation)

Article 57(1) EEA renders incompatible with the EEA Agreement, concentrations which create **28.12** or strengthen a dominant position as a result of which effective competition would be significantly impeded within the territory covered by the EEA Agreement or a substantial part of it. The original Merger Control Regulation[39] was applied to EEA law (with appropriate modifications) by Article 57(2) EEA, Annex XIV, and Protocol 24 to the EEA Agreement. The original Merger Control Regulation was replaced with a new Merger Control Regulation at Community level in early 2004, following a comprehensive review of merger control.[40] While the wording of Article 57(2) has not been updated, two EEA Joint Committee decisions now set out the applicability of the Merger Control Regulation to the entire EEA area.[41] The new text of Protocol 24, when read with Article 57 EEA and Article 1 of the Merger Control Regulation establishes that the EU Commission retains sole competence to rule on concentrations with a 'Community dimension'. The ESA only has competence to deal with applications to approve mergers if there is no Community dimension and an EFTA dimension is established.[42] No concentrations falling within its competence have yet been notified to the ESA, but it has dealt with many mixed merger cases in conjunction with the EU Commission.

4. Article 59 EEA (cf Article 102 TFEU)

Article 59 EEA requires EFTA States to ensure that no anticompetitive measures are either **28.13** enacted or maintained in force for public undertakings or for undertakings to which they have granted special or exclusive rights. This provision principally affects State monopolies having a commercial character.[43] A derogation is provided under Article 59(2) for such

---

[38] The EFTA Court has also interpreted the principle of 'nullity' pursuant to Art 53(2) in a way that is consistent with the case law on Art 101(2) TFEU. See Case E-7/01 *Hegelstad Eiendomsselskap Arvid B. Hegelstad v Hydro Texaco AS* [2002] EFTA Court Report 310, para 43.

[39] Council Regulation (EEC) 4064/89 of 21 December 1989 on the Control of Concentrations between Undertakings [1989] OJ L395/1—as amended by [1990] OJ L257/13.

[40] Council Regulation (EC) 139/2004 of 20 January 2004 on the control of concentrations between undertakings [2004] OJ L24/1 ('Merger Control Regulation'). The Merger Control Regulation is accompanied by Commission Regulation (EC) 802/2004 of 7 April 2004 implementing Council Regulation (EC) 139/2004 on the control of concentrations between undertakings OJ L279/3 ('Implementing Regulation').

[41] The EEA Joint Committee adopted Decision No 78/2004 [2004] OJ L219/1 and Decision No 79/2004 [2004] OJ L219/24 on 8 June 2004. The first decision, 78/2004, entered into force on 9 June 2004. The entry into force of the second decision, 79/2004, was delayed pending notification under Art 103(1) EEA from Iceland and Norway. It finally entered into force on 1 July 2005. Decision 78/2004 established a new Protocol 24 to the EEA Agreement, which takes into account the promulgation of the Merger Control Regulation and the Implementing Regulation.

[42] The tests for establishing an EFTA dimension are set out at para 28.40 et seq.

[43] See eg Case E-1/94 *Ravintoloitsijain Liiton Kustannus Oy Restamark* [1995] EFTA Court Report 15, para 48, where the EFTA Court considered a State monopoly on the importation of alcohol under the free

entities which provide services in the general economic interest or which have the character of a revenue-producing monopoly. The competition rules continue to apply to such entities, but only in so far as the application of the rules does 'not obstruct the performance, in law or in fact, of the particular tasks assigned to them'. The derogation is itself subject to the proviso that the 'development of trade must not be affected to such an extent as would be contrary to the interests of the Contracting Parties'.

28.14 The EEA Agreement also requires EFTA States, under Article 16 EEA, to adjust any State monopoly of a commercial character so that no discrimination exists between EEA nationals regarding the conditions under which goods are procured and marketed. The ESA delivered reasoned opinions to Norway in December 1994, and to Iceland in February 1995 concerning State monopolies in the importation and wholesale of alcoholic products. Both countries subsequently amended their legislation, leading to the termination of exclusive rights for the State alcohol monopolies in those countries. Annex XIV to the EEA Agreement has also incorporated (with appropriate modifications) relevant EU measures which apply to public undertakings. In particular, the *acquis* incorporated into EEA law includes Commission Directive 2008/63/EC of 20 June 2008 on competition in the markets in telecommunications terminal equipment;[44] and Commission Directive 2002/77/EC of 16 September 2002 on competition in the markets for electronic communications networks and services.[45]

5. Article 3 EEA (cf Article 10 EC)

28.15 Finally, Article 3 of the EEA Agreement corresponds to Article 4(3) of the Treaty on European Union ('TEU') and imposes a duty on the contracting parties to take appropriate measures to ensure the fulfilment of obligations arising from the Agreement.[46]

B. 'Acts' Giving Effect to the Basic Rules

1. Block exemptions

28.16 The implementation of Article 53 is also subject to various block exemptions, which were either in force when the EEA Agreement was signed, or as have been updated from time to time.[47] New block exemption regulations have to be implemented under the rather

---

movement provisions of the EEA Agreement, but recognized that these fell to be interpreted in light of competition considerations as well. See also Case E-6/96 *Tore Wilhelmsen AS v Oslo kommune* [1997] EFTA Court Report 53; and Case E-9/00 *EFTA Surveillance Authority v Norway* [2002] EFTA Court Report 72; [2002] 2 CMLR 17, which concerned in part the Norwegian State monopoly on the retail of alcoholic beverages.

[44] [2008] OJ L162/20.

[45] [2002] OJ L249/21.

[46] See also Case E-13/11 *Granville Establishment v Volker Anhalt*, judgment of the EFTA Court dated 25 April 2012, not yet reported, at para 52, concerning the obligation imposed on EFTA States to give full effect to the EEA Agreement.

[47] EEA Agreement, Art 60 and Annex XIV, s B– F and J. The block exemptions listed in Annex XIV to the EEA Agreement are currently:

- Commission Regulation (EU) No 330/2010 of 20 April 2010 on the application of Article 101(3) of the Treaty on the Functioning of the European Union to categories of vertical agreements and concerted practices [2010] OJ L102/1, also known as the Vertical Agreements Block Exemption.
- Commission Regulation (EU) No 461/2010 of 27 May 2010 on the application of Article 101(3) of the Treaty on the Functioning of the European Union to categories of vertical agreements and concerted practices in the motor vehicle sector [2010] OJ L129/52, also known as the Motor Vehicle Block Exemption.
- Commission Regulation (EC) 772/2004 of 27 April 2004 on the application of Art 81(3) of the Treaty to categories of technology transfer agreements—the Technology Transfer Block Exemption [2004] OJ L123/11, as corrected by [2004] OJ L127/158.

complicated scheme contained in Articles 102 to 104 of the EEA Agreement. Annex XIV to the EEA Agreement also transposes into an EEA context a Council Regulation applying the competition rules to the transport sector.[48]

The block exemptions have been supplemented and modified by the provisions of Protocol 1 to the EEA Agreement ('horizontal adaptations') and by Annex XIV of the EEA Agreement ('sectoral and specific adaptations'). The original text of the EU block exemptions must therefore be read subject to these adaptations. The block exemptions thus adapted will be automatically applied by the EU Commission and the ESA when dealing with EEA competition cases within their respective jurisdictions. They will also fall to be applied directly by national courts and national competition authorities ('NCAs') acting in accordance with the Modernisation Regulation (Regulation 1/2003)[49] as implemented in EEA law. **28.17**

Two important differences should be noted. First, the scope for withdrawing the benefit of the exemption is expanded. Both the Commission and the ESA may now withdraw the exemption not only on their own initiative or at the request of a State or of a natural or legal person claiming a legitimate interest, but furthermore at the request of the other surveillance authority. Secondly, the provisions in any given block exemption are applied in an EEA context only through the prism of specific provisions in Protocol 21 to the EEA Agreement.[50] **28.18**

2. Commission Notices and Guidelines

The Commission and the ESA are obliged, when applying the EEA competition rules, to take into account pertinent, existing Commission Notices and Guidelines. The list of notices to be taken into account is set out in Annex XIV.[51] These Notices and Guidelines have not **28.19**

- Commission Regulation (EU) No 1218/2010 of 14 December 2010 on the application of Article 101(3) of the Treaty on the Functioning of the European Union to certain categories of specialisation agreements [2010] OJ L33/43, also known as the Specialisation Agreements Block Exemption.
- Commission Regulation (EU) 1217/2010 of 14 December 2010 on the application of Article 101(3) of the Treaty on the Functioning of the European Union to certain categories of research and development agreements, also known as the Research and Development Block Exemption.
- Commission Regulation (EC) 906/2009 of 28 September 2009 on the application of Art 81(3) of the Treaty to certain categories of agreements, decisions and concerted practices between liner shipping companies (consortia)—the Liner companies block exemption [2009] OJ L256/31.
- Commission Regulation (EU) 267/2010 of 24 March 2010 on the application of Art 101(3) of the Treaty on the Functioning of the European Union to certain categories of agreements, decisions and concerted practices in the insurance sector [2010] OJ L83/1, also known as the Insurance agreements block exemption.

[48] Council Regulation (EC) No 169/2009 of 26 February 2009 applying rules of competition to transport by rail, road and inland waterway [2009] OJ L61/1.

[49] Council Regulation (EC) 1/2003 of 16 December 2002 on the implementation of the rules on competition laid down in Articles 81 and 82 of the Treaty [2003] OJ L1/1, as amended by Council Regulation (EC) 411/2004 amending Regulation (EC) 1/2003 [2004] OJ L68/1 and Council Regulation (EC) No 1419/2006 of 25 September 2006 [2006] OJ L269/1.

[50] Protocol 21 on the implementation of competition rules applicable to undertakings. See Part IV Section B of this chapter.

[51] The Notices and Guidelines listed in Annex XIV are:

- Commission Notice regarding restrictions ancillary to concentrations [1990] OJ C203/5.
- Commission Notice regarding the concentrative and co-operative operations under Council Regulation (EEC) 4064/89 of 21 December 1989 on the control of concentrations between undertakings [1990] C203/10.
- Commission Notice concerning Commission Regulation (EEC) 1983/83 and (EEC) 1984/83 of 22 June 1983 on the application of Article 85(3) of the Treaty to categories of exclusive distribution and exclusive purchasing agreements [1984] OJ C101/2.

been adapted for EEA purposes. Instead the ESA is simply obliged to take due account of the principles and rules contained in them, when applying Articles 53 to 60 of the Agreement.[52] The existing Notices and Guidelines are read in light of their *effet utile* for the application of the EEA competition provisions. It is worth noting, therefore, that a number of notices are included in the list which relate to Community measures that are no longer in force. These notices will be of largely historical interest only. They represent measures adopted by the EC Commission up to 31 July 1991.

28.20 More modern notices are not included in an amended version of Annex XIV but are instead adopted by the ESA under its own competence. From the date of entry into force of the EEA Agreement, acts corresponding to measures taken by the EU Commission are adopted by the ESA under Articles 5(2)(b) and 25 of the Surveillance and Court Agreement. They are published in accordance with the exchange of letters on publication of EEA relevant information.[53] Thus, for example, a series of ten Annexes to a Decision of the ESA adopted in January 1994 contained the equivalent text of ten Commission Notices and Guidelines to be applied by the ESA in an EEA context.[54] Both surveillance authorities shall take due account of these measures in cases where they have jurisdiction under the EEA Agreement.[55] The scope for divergence in application is further reduced by the obligation imposed on the EU Commission to ensure that equal conditions of competition are met in the EEA as in the EU itself. The ESA has not issued interpretative guidelines or notices in the field of merger control. Instead, it has simply indicated that it will apply the principles set out in relevant notices issued by the EU Commission.

- Commission Notice concerning Regulation (EEC) 123/85 of 12 December 1984 on the application of Article 85(3) of the Treaty to certain categories of motor vehicle distribution and servicing agreements [1985] OJ C17/4.
- Commission Notice on exclusive dealing contracts with commercial agents [1962] OJ 139/2921/62.
- Commission Notice concerning agreements, decisions and concerted practices in the field of cooperation between enterprises [1968] OJ C75/3, as corrected by [1968] OJ C84/14.
- Commission Notice concerning imports into the Community of Japanese goods falling within the scope of the Rome Treaty [1972] OJ C111/13.
- Commission Notice of 18 December 1978 concerning its assessment of certain subcontracting agreements in relation to Article 85(1) of the EEC Treaty [1979] OJ C1/2.
- Commission Notice on agreements of minor importance which do not fall under Art 85(1) of the Treaty establishing the European Economic Community [1986] OJ C231/2.
- Guidelines on the application of EEC competition rules in the telecommunication sector [1991] OJ C233/2.

[52] See Preamble to the section headed 'Acts of which the EC Commission and the EFTA Surveillance Authority shall take due account' in Annex XIV to the Agreement.

[53] The acts adopted by the Commission will not be integrated into Annex XIV, but a reference to their publication in the Official Journal of the European Union ('OJ') will be made in the EEA Supplement to the OJ. The corresponding acts adopted by the ESA are to be published in the EEA Supplement to, and the EEA Section of, the OJ.

[54] Decision of the EFTA Surveillance Authority No 3/94/COL of 12 January 1994 on the issuing of 10 notices and guidelines in the field of competition [1994] OJ L153/1.

[55] Examples of such measures include Notice on Cooperation between the EFTA Surveillance Authority and the courts of the EFTA States in the application of Arts 53 and 54 of the EEA Agreement [2006] OJ C305/19; EFTA Surveillance Authority Notice on cooperation within the EFTA Network of Competition Authorities [2006] OJ C227/10; EFTA Surveillance Authority Guidelines on the applicability of Art 53 of the EEA Agreement to Horizontal Cooperation Agreements, 23 May 2012, not yet published in the OJ; and EFTA Surveillance Authority Guidelines on Vertical Restraints, 15 December 2010, not published in the OJ but available on the ESA website. Supplementary guidelines on the motor vehicle block exemption were also adopted on 25 May 2011, but again, are as yet only available on the ESA website.

III. The Procedure for the Application of the EEA Competition Rules

A. The Modernization of EU Competition Law

Article 55 of the EEA Agreement entrusts the enforcement of the EEA Competition pro- **28.21** visions to both the EU Commission and the ESA. Article 55(1) requires the 'competent surveillance authority' to investigate cases of suspected infringement of the EEA competition rules and to take appropriate measures to bring them to an end. It may launch an investigation of its own initiative, on the application of an EEA State within its respective territory, or on the application of the other surveillance authority. Investigations are required to be carried out in cooperation with the national authorities in the respective territory and with the other surveillance authority. Article 55 imposes an obligation on a surveillance authority to assist its counterpart in accordance with its own internal rules. Under Article 55(2), findings in relation to infringements must be set out in a reasoned decision, which may be published. The competent surveillance authority is also empowered to authorize States within its territory to 'take the measures, the conditions and details of which it shall determine, needed to remedy the situation'. It may also request the other surveillance authority to authorize States within the other respective territory to take such measures.

While the terms of Article 55 EEA are silent as to the detailed measures needed to ensure the **28.22** enforcement of the EEA competition rules, the implicit emphasis is upon a system of centralized enforcement by the competent surveillance authorities. But such an emphasis is misplaced. The EU reformed the centralized system of enforcement provided for by Regulation 17/62 and by reference to which the original terms of Article 55 were drafted. The EU has implemented a system of decentralized enforcement of the competition provisions, leaving the EU Commission free to focus its resources on a limited number of significant cases. The 'Modernisation Regulation'—Council Regulation 1/2003—was adopted on 16 December 2002 and entered into force on 1 May 2004.[56] It brought with it a radical shake up of the enforcement of the competition rules in the EU. Its scope and effect are examined in detail in the main body of this work. The Modernisation Regulation has been accompanied by a Commission Regulation ('Implementing Regulation') that sets out the provisions governing the exercise by the Commission of its powers in the wake of the decentralization of enforcement of EC competition law.[57]

The cross application of the Modernisation Regulation to undertakings established in, or **28.23** conducting business with, the EEA/EFTA States was effected by two EEA Joint Committee Decisions. By EEA Joint Committee Decision 130/2004, the text of the Modernisation Regulation has been formally applied to the EEA competition regime with effect from 19 May 2005. Further, by EEA Joint Committee Decision 178/2004, the Implementing Regulation No 773/2004 was also brought within the scope of the EEA rules with effect from 1 July 2005. Necessary amendments have been made to Annex XIV and Protocols 21

---

[56] Council Regulation (EC) 1/2003 of 16 December 2002 on the implementation of the rules on competition laid down in Articles 81 and 82 of the Treaty [2003] OJ L1/1, as amended by Council Regulation (EC) 411/2004 amending Regulation (EC) 1/2003 [2004] OJ L68/1 and Council Regulation (EC) No 1419/2006 of 25 September 2006 [2006] OJ L269/1.

[57] Commission Regulation (EC) 773/2004 of 7 April 2004 relating to the conduct of proceedings by the Commission pursuant to Article 81 and 82 of the EC Treaty [2004] OJ L123/18, as amended by Commission Regulation (EC) No 1792/2006 of 23 October 2006 [2006] OJ L362/1; and Commission Regulation (EC) No 622/2008 of 30 June 2008 [2008] OJ L171/3.

and 23 of the EEA Agreement. Indeed, the implementation of Joint Decisions 130/2004 and 178/2004 has seen Protocol 23 replaced in its entirety. In addition, changes have been made to Protocol 4 to the Surveillance and Court Agreement, which contains the procedural rules applied by the ESA for the purposes of implementing Articles 53 and 54 EEA. These changes incorporate the terms of the Modernisation Regulation in Chapter II to Protocol 4 and the Implementing Regulation in Chapter III to Protocol 4. The ESA has adopted a number of notices equivalent to those adopted by the EU Commission as part of the modernization package. Notices adopted to date include Informal Guidance to be provided by the Authority concerning the application of Articles 53 and 54 EEA;[58] the Effect on Trade Concept contained in Articles 53 and 54 EEA;[59] a Notice on immunity from fines and reduction of fines in cartel cases;[60] a Notice on the definition of the relevant market;[61] and the Application of Article 53(3) EEA.[62]

28.24   The Joint Committee decision 130/2004 was adopted on 24 September 2004 and entered into force with effect from 20 May 2005.[63] Decision 178/2004 was adopted on 3 December 2004 and entered into force on 20 May 2005.[64] The entry into force of both measures was delayed pending notification from Iceland under Article 103 of the EEA Agreement. Nonetheless, the modernization regime provisionally applied to EEA competition law with effect from 24 March 2005. This is because Article 103(2) of the EEA Agreement provides that, if, upon the expiry of a period of six months after the decision of the EEA Joint Committee, relevant notification under Article 103 has not taken place, the decision of the EEA Joint Committee shall be applied provisionally pending the fulfilment of the constitutional requirements. This is the case unless a contracting party notifies that such a provisional application cannot take place. As no such reservation was lodged by Iceland, the modernization regime in fact took effect from March 2005.

28.25   Chapter II and Chapter III of the Protocol to the Surveillance and Court Agreement set out the procedural rules implementing Articles 53 and 54 of the EEA Agreement and gave the ESA the same powers as those the EU Commission enjoys under Regulation 1/2003 and Commission Regulation 773/2004. The ESA no longer receives notifications concerning the application of Articles 53 and 54 EEA. Instead, it focuses upon investigations conducted of its own initiative and complaints made to it by members of the public. The ESA nonetheless retains enforcement powers equivalent to those of the EU Commission. It is therefore able to:

• issue decisions finding that an agreement or practice does not infringe Articles 53 or 54 EEA;
• close proceedings subject to commitments assumed by undertakings which will be binding upon them;
• impose structural remedies to deal with competition concerns;
• enjoy increased powers while on inspections; and
• impose higher fines when procedural rules have not been complied with.[65]

---

[58] [2006] OJ C305/34.
[59] [2006] OJ C291/46.
[60] [2009] OJ C294/7.
[61] [1998] OJ C200/46.
[62] [2007] OJ C208/1.
[63] [2005] OJ L64/57.
[64] [2005] OJ L133/35.
[65] ESA, *Annual Report* (2003) 46, available on the ESA website at <http://www.eftasurv.int/press--publications/annual-reports/>.

In keeping with the spirit of the Modernisation Regulation, the ESA indicated from the **28.26** inception of the new regime that it would seek to give priority (in terms of its in-depth investigations) to cases where one or more of the following conditions are met:

- The ESA has sole jurisdiction (notably in competition cases involving the potential application of Article 59 EEA to an EFTA State).
- Articles 53 and 54 may resolve a competition concern where national rules differ from EEA provisions to such an extent that they could not achieve a similar result.
- A hardcore infringement of the EEA competition rules can be established.
- The economic impact of a violation is significant in the relevant market.
- A case raises new points of law which will benefit from clarification.[66]

B. Division of Responsibility between the EC Commission and the EFTA Surveillance Authority

The ESA has been granted equivalent powers and similar functions to those of the **28.27** Commission, to enable it to carry out the implementation of the EEA competition rules. It applies procedural rules similar to those applied in the EU itself.[67] The EU Commission continues to use its own procedural rules even when dealing with EEA cases. But the EU is obliged, under Article 1 of Protocol 21 to the EEA Agreement, to adopt any necessary provisions to ensure that the Commission is granted the necessary powers to enforce EEA competition rules under the EU pillar. This position is maintained over time by virtue of Article 2 of Protocol 21. This requires corresponding amendments to be made to the ESA's powers so that it is 'entrusted simultaneously with equivalent powers and similar functions to those of the EC Commission.' The EEA Agreement envisages close cooperation between the EU Commission and the ESA in order to achieve a uniform application of the competition rules throughout the EEA. The two authorities are obliged to exchange information and consult one another on general policy issues and in connection with individual cases.[68] A high degree of cooperation has been achieved in practice.[69]

Given the dual enforcement policy, it is essential that some method of allocating cases to the **28.28** respective authorities is established. This has been achieved through Articles 56 and 57 of the EEA Agreement. These provisions remain unchanged by the Modernisation Regulation. Article 56 caters for allocation of cases concerning restrictive agreements and abuses of dominant positions. Article 57 deals with allocation for merger control cases. Whilst the EEA competition system is based on 'two pillars', a 'one-stop shop' approach has been adopted for the convenience of undertakings involved.[70] This means that undertakings should deal

---

[66] ESA, *Annual Report* (2003) 55.

[67] See generally Arts 1 and 2 of Protocol 21. The powers and functions of the EU Commission for the application of the EU competition rules are reflected in the acts which are listed in Art 3 of Protocol 21 to the EEA Agreement. This refers principally to the Modernisation Regulation and the Implementing Regulation, but also refers back to the various acts listed in Annex XIV (mentioned earlier). Cross-references are also made to other procedural regulations in the field of merger control, transport, and coal and steel.

[68] See Art 1 of Protocol 23 to the EEA Agreement.

[69] See the *Annual Reports* prepared by the ESA for the years 2001–2011, available on its website at <http://www.eftasurv.int/press--publications/annual-reports/>. These show the level of involvement of the ESA in 'mixed cases' in both competition and merger cases.

[70] Article 55 of the EEA Agreement mandates the 'competent surveillance authority' to ensure the application of Arts 53 and 54. On the application of the 'one stop shop' principle, see also Joined Cases T-67/00, T-68/00, T-71/00, and T-78/00 *JFE Engineering Corp and others v EC Commission* [2004] ECR II-2501, paras 489 and 490, where the Court nonetheless observed that the EEA Agreement cannot deprive the

either solely with the Commission or solely with the ESA in relation to any given agreement or practice.

28.29 The following rules are important in practice, as they represent the only significant point of departure from the otherwise very similar substantive and procedural rules already found in EU competition law.

C. Allocation of Cases[71]

1. Article 53 cases

28.30 Where a case raises issues of agreements, decisions, or concerted practices caught by Article 53, Article 56 of the Agreement attributes competence between the EU Commission and the ESA as described in the paragraphs that follow.

EU pure cases

28.31 These cases involve only trade between EU Member States. They are decided by the EU Commission on the basis of Article 101 TFEU. As a matter of law, these cases do not fall within the ambit of the EEA Competition rules at all.

EFTA pure cases

28.32 Where only trade between EFTA States is implicated, the case is dealt with by the ESA. Article 53 of the EEA Agreement is then the controlling, substantive provision.[72]

Mixed cases

28.33 So-called 'mixed cases' involve two situations which must be distinguished if the rules on attribution of competence are to be understood. 'Mixed cases' in the broad sense are those cases where trade between the EU and one or more EFTA States is affected by the Agreement or practice in question, regardless of whether trade between the EU Member States themselves is also affected. In addition there is a sub-category of 'mixed cases' which has been referred to as '1 + 1 cases'.[73] These are cases where trade between EU Member States is not affected, only trade between the EU and one or more EFTA States. The first question to ask, therefore, when considering the rules governing the attribution of cases between the two authorities, is whether or not trade between EU Member States is affected. Mixed cases where both trade between EU Member States and trade between the EU and one or more EFTA/ EEA States is involved will almost always be handled by the Commission.[74] An exception

---

Commission of its power to investigate anticompetitive conduct affecting trade between Member States of the EU. An appeal to the ECJ in Case C-403/04 P did not address this point.

[71] For a commentary on the origin of the allocation provisions, together with an explanation of their resulting nature and reasons why they are quite complicated, see T Blanchet, R Piipponen, and M Westman-Clément, *The Agreement on the European Economic Area (EEA). A Guide to the Free Movement of Goods and Competition Rules* (Clarendon Press 1994) 184–6. See also Bellamy and Child, *European Community Law of Competition* (5th edn, Sweet & Maxwell 2001) para 12-164ff.

[72] See Art 56(1)(a) EEA.

[73] The phrase and definition comes from T Blanchet, R Piipponen, and M Westman-Clément, *The Agreement on the European Economic Area (EEA). A Guide to the Free Movement of Goods and Competition Rules* (Clarendon Press 1994) 186 et seq.

[74] EEA, Art 56(1)(c). See eg Case T-44/00 *Mannesmanröhren-Werke AG v EC Commission* [2004] ECR II-2223, GCEU, para 5. The fact that the ESA may already have commenced an investigation does not operate as a bar to the Commission exercising its own powers in relation to the same agreements or practices. See Joined Cases T-67/00, T-68/00, T-71/00, and T-78/00 *JFE Engineering Corp and others v EC Commission* [2004] ECR II-2501, paras 459–93.

is where the agreements or practices concerned, whilst formally affecting inter-EU trade or competition within the internal market, do so only to a limited extent. That is, if the effect on trade between EU Member States or on competition within the EU is not appreciable, the ESA assumes jurisdiction. It has been accepted by the contracting parties to the Agreement that for these purposes, the phrase 'appreciable' shall correlate to the definition of *de minimis* agreements found already in EU Competition law.[75] The allocation of '1 + 1 cases', where trade between EU Member States is not affected, is slightly more complicated. In such cases, jurisdiction is determined by a threshold criterion. Article 56(1)(b) of the EEA Agreement provides that if the turnover of the undertakings concerned in EFTA territories is equal to or greater than 33 per cent of their turnover in the EEA as a whole, then the ESA will handle the matter.[76] The Commission decides on all other cases where the threshold criterion is not met, regardless of the existence of any effect on competition in the EU or not. The fact that the undertakings achieve 67 per cent of their turnover within the EU will be sufficient to ground the Commission's jurisdiction. In practice, though, the ESA will decide the case if the effect on competition[77] within the EU is not an appreciable one, under Article 56(3). Two particular situations deserve clarification:

- Article 56(1)(c) refers only to an effect on *trade* between EU Member States, not on *competition* more generally within the EU. Provided, therefore, that the matter qualifies as a '1 + 1 case' (trade between EU Member States not being affected) and the turnover threshold is met, the ESA will handle the case even if competition in the EU is affected to an appreciable extent.
- The ESA will also have jurisdiction over cases where the undertakings involved generate less than 33 per cent of their turnover in EFTA States, but the effect on either trade or competition within the EU is not appreciable.[78]

The allocation of jurisdiction in 'mixed cases' can therefore be seen to be based essentially **28.34** on a two-step test; a determination of whether trade between EU Member States is affected and a threshold determination of turnover, both subject to a residual 'appreciable effect' consideration. As a rough guide, it would seem that the Commission will deal with a case if either greater than two-thirds of the undertakings' turnover is achieved in the EU, or if trade between Member States or competition generally in the EU is affected to an appreciable extent. The overall process is demonstrated in Figure 28.1.

2. Article 54 cases

Article 56(2) provides that '[i]ndividual cases falling under Article 54 shall be decided upon **28.35** by the surveillance authority in the territory of which a dominant position is found to exist'. The only exception is where a dominant position exists within the territories of both the EU Member States and the EFTA States. Then identical rules to those for Article 53 cases apply.

---

[75] Article 56(3) of the Agreement. See also the Notice of the ESA on agreements of minor importance which do not appreciably restrict competition under Art 53(1) of the EEA Agreement (*de minimis*) [2003] OJ C67/20.

[76] This would technically encompass mixed cases generally and not just '1 + 1 cases'. Article 56(1)(b) is, however, expressed to be without prejudice to sub-para (c). Therefore, even if this threshold is met, the EU Commission retains an element of 'residual' competence. Provided that trade between EU Member States is affected to some extent, then the Commission assumes jurisdiction, relinquishing it only if the effect is not appreciable pursuant to Art 56(3). This is, in reality, simply the application of the mixed case attribution just described.

[77] The effect must be on competition, not trade, since *ex hypothesi*, in a '1 + 1 case', trade between Member States is not affected.

[78] See Art 56(3) EEA.

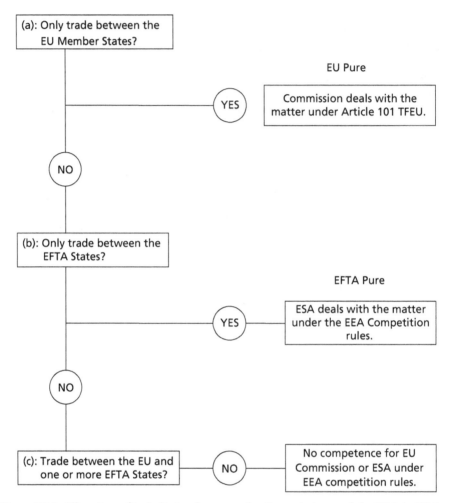

Figure 28.1 Allocation of jurisdiction between the Commission and the ESA in EEA competition cases falling under Article 53

That is, the relevant case will be attributed to the ESA where: (i) either trade or competition within the EU is not affected to an appreciable extent; or (ii) there being no effect on trade between EU Member States and the turnover of the undertaking(s) concerned in the territory of the EFTA States equals 33 per cent or more of its (their) turnover in the territory of the EEA, even if there is an appreciable effect on competition within the EU. The Commission is competent for all other cases.

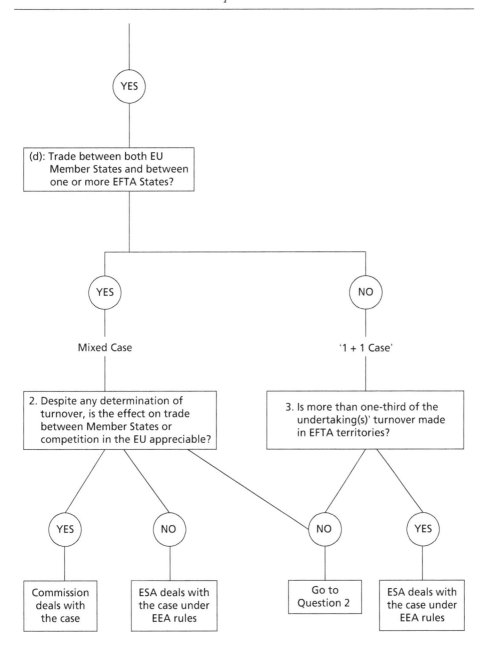

The overall process can be seen in Figure 28.2.   **28.36**

The appreciable effect criterion used in both Articles 53 and 54 cases, may be equated with the   **28.37**
notion of *de minimis* thresholds already encountered in EU Competition law. The ESA's Notice
on agreements of minor importance which do not appreciably restrict competition under
Article 53(1) of the EEA Agreement (*de minimis*)[79] quantifies, with the help of market share

---

[79] [2003] OJ C67/20; and EEA Supplement No 15, p 11, 20 March 2003. The ESA's Notice follows the
terms of the Commission Notice on agreements of minor importance which do not appreciably restrict competition under Art 81(1) of the Treaty establishing the European Community (*de minimis*) [2001] OJ C368/13.

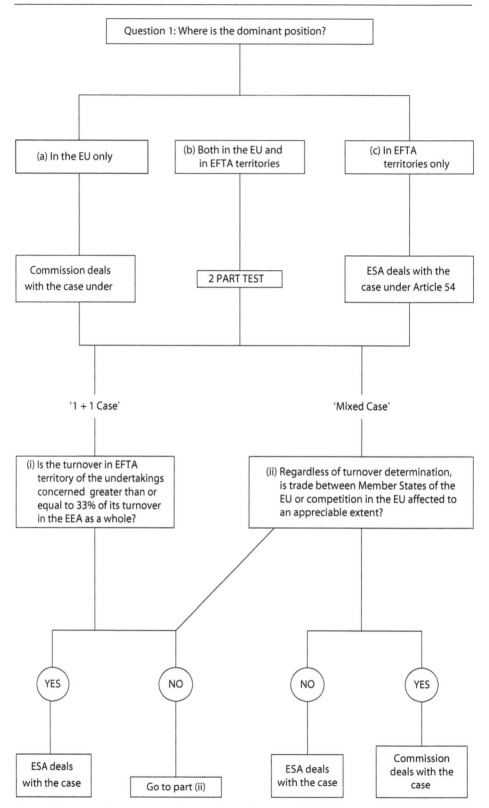

Figure 28.2 The allocation of jurisdiction in Article 54 cases

thresholds, a negative test for determining what is not an appreciable restriction of competition for the purposes of Article 53 EEA. Paragraph 7 of the Notice sets out the ESA's view that agreements between undertakings[80] which affect trade between the contracting parties to the EEA Agreement do not appreciably restrict competition within the meaning of Article 53(1) EEA:

 (i) if the aggregate market share held by the parties to the agreement does not exceed 10 per cent on any of the relevant markets affected by the agreement, where the agreement is made between undertakings which are actual or potential competitors on any of these markets (agreements between competitors);
 (ii) if the market share held by each of the parties to the agreement does not exceed 15 per cent on any of the relevant markets affected by the agreement, where the agreement is made between undertakings which are not actual or potential competitors on any of these markets (agreements between non-competitors).

In cases where it is difficult to classify the agreement as either an agreement between competitors **28.38** or an agreement between non-competitors, the 10 per cent threshold is applicable. Paragraph 9 permits undertakings a 'leeway' to exceed these thresholds by 2 per cent, limited to a duration of two successive calendar years. Definitions of the terms 'undertaking' and 'turnover' are contained in Protocol 22 to the EEA Agreement.[81] Turnover calculation is restricted by Article 2 to the territory covered by the EEA Agreement. The threshold classification is subject to a number of qualifications. First, there is a saving in respect of the foreclosure effect of parallel networks of agreements having similar effects on the market. Where market foreclosure is established, the relevant thresholds set out previously are reduced in each case to 5 per cent. The reasoning is that it is assumed that individual suppliers or distributors with market shares of less than 5 per cent do not contribute significantly to the cumulative foreclosure effect of a network of similar agreements. The ESA has indicated that a foreclosure effect is unlikely to be found if the effect of parallel networks of agreements covers less than 30 per cent of the market.[82] Secondly, paragraph 11 sets out a number of 'hardcore restrictions' whose presence in an agreement between undertakings will preclude the application of the *de minimis* provisions.

The ESA has indicated that it will not institute proceedings (either upon application or on **28.39** its own initiative) against undertakings falling within the *de minimis* Notice. Further, where undertakings assume in good faith that they fall within its terms, the ESA will not impose fines in the event of a finding of an infringement of Articles 53 or 54 EEA. Paragraph 3 to the Notice makes clear that agreements may in addition not fall under Article 53(1) EEA because they are not capable of appreciably affecting trade between the contracting parties to the EEA Agreement. The *de minimis* Notice does not deal with this issue. It does not quantify what amounts to 'an appreciable effect on trade'. The ESA has, however, acknowledged that agreements between small and medium-sized undertakings[83] are rarely capable of appreciably affecting trade between the contracting parties to the EEA Agreement. Small

---

[80] An undertaking is defined in Art 1 of Protocol 22 as 'any entity carrying out activities of a commercial or economic nature.'

[81] Specific rules will be used for the banking and insurance sectors (Art 3 of Protocol 22) as well as for distribution and supply arrangements and transfers of technology (Art 4 of Protocol 22). Specific rules are also included to calculate the turnover of ECSC undertakings for a mixture of ECSC and EEC products (Art 5 of Protocol 22).

[82] See para 8 of the *de minimis* Notice.

[83] As defined in the EFTA Surveillance Authority Decision No 112/96/COL of 11 September 1996 [1996] OJ L42/33, and EEA Supplement No 7, 1, 13 February 1997. This decision corresponds to European Commission Recommendation 96/280/EC [1996] OJ L107/4. That recommendation has been superseded by Commission Recommendation 2003/361/EC of 6 May 2003 concerning the definition of micro, small, and medium-sized enterprises [2003] OJ L124/36, which provides an amended definition of 'SMEs' as those undertakings that employ fewer than 250 persons and which have an annual turnover not exceeding EUR 50 million, and/or an annual balance sheet total not exceeding EUR 43 million.

and medium-sized undertakings are defined by the ESA as undertakings which have fewer than 250 employees and have either an annual turnover not exceeding EUR 40 million or an annual balance-sheet total not exceeding EUR 27 million.[84]

3. Merger cases

28.40   The decision as to whether a merger case is allocated to the EU Commission or to the ESA depends on whether or not the merger creates an 'EFTA dimension'. Article 57(2) EEA provides that the control of concentrations falling within Article 57(1) EEA shall be carried out by the EU Commission in cases falling under the Merger Control Regulation, in which case the control shall be conducted under the Merger Control Regulation and in accordance with Protocols 21 and 24 and Annex XIV to the EEA Agreement. In contrast, the ESA has jurisdiction in any other cases where the relevant thresholds set out in Annex XIV are fulfilled in the territory of the EFTA States, in accordance with Protocols 21 and 24 and Annex XIV to the EEA Agreement. However, that jurisdiction is expressed to be without prejudice to the competence of the EU Member States.

28.41   The result of these provisions is that the EU Commission will have sole competence to rule on concentrations with a 'Community dimension', as defined in Article 1 of the Merger Control Regulation (Regulation (EC) 139/2004). As set out in the main body of this work, the existence of a Community dimension depends on a number of thresholds being met within the EU as regards the turnover of the parties to the concentration. A 'Community dimension' will not, however, be established if each undertaking concerned achieves more than two-thirds of its aggregate EU-wide turnover within one and the same Member State of the EU. Articles 6(5) and 13 of Protocol 24 to the EEA Agreement and Article 4(5) of the Merger Control Regulation provide that where a concentration is capable of being reviewed under the national competition laws of at least three EU Member States and at least one EFTA State, the parties to the concentration can, by way of a reasoned submission, request the EU Commission to examine the concentration. If the competent Member States do not express their disagreement, the concentration will be deemed to have a 'Community dimension'. Should one of the competent EFTA States express its disagreement, the competent EFTA States shall retain their competence to examine the concentration.

28.42   In contrast, an EFTA dimension is established if the turnover thresholds set out in the Merger Control Regulation are met within the EFTA pillar; ie, the combined aggregate worldwide turnover of all the undertakings involved is more than EUR 5 billion and the aggregate EFTA-wide turnover of each of at least two of the undertakings is greater than EUR 250 million. If, however, all the undertakings involved achieve more than two-thirds of their turnover within one and the same EFTA State, the requisite EFTA dimension would be lacking. The proposed merger would then be dealt with at a national level. Alternatively, a concentration which does not meet these thresholds will still have an EFTA dimension where:

(i)   the combined aggregate worldwide turnover of all of the undertakings concerned is more than EUR 2.5 billion;
(ii) in each of at least three EFTA States, the combined aggregate turnover of all of the undertakings concerned is more than EUR 100 million euros;

---

[84] The ESA Notice anticipates that the European Commission will revise its recommendation to increase the annual turnover threshold from EUR 40 million to EUR 50 million, and the annual balance-sheet total threshold from EUR 27 million to EUR 43 million. It is likely that the ESA will apply the terms of Recommendation 2003/161/EC to like effect.

(iii) in each of at least three EFTA States included for the purpose of point (ii), the aggregate turnover of each of at least two of the undertakings concerned is more than EUR 25 million; and

(iv) the aggregate EFTA-wide turnover of each of at least two of the undertakings concerned is more than EUR 100 million.

This is subject to the same exception for each of the undertakings achieving more than two-thirds of its aggregate EFTA-wide turnover in one and the same EFTA State.[85]

4. Public undertakings

Article 59 EEA reproduces most of the text of Article 106 TFEU (ex Article 86 EC) con- **28.43** cerning the application of the competition rules to public undertakings or undertakings that have been granted special or exclusive rights. The difference lies in Article 59(3) EEA. This provides that responsibility for the application of the provisions of Article 59(1) and (2) EEA shall be allocated to either the EU Commission or the ESA, based on their 'respective competence'. Within its own sphere of competence, therefore, the ESA will be responsible for addressing 'appropriate measures' to States falling within its territory. This is to be contrasted with the more specific power granted to the EU Commission, under Article 106(3) TFEU, to address decisions or directives to Member States.

D. Cooperation between the EC Commission and the ESA

Article 58 states that through the functioning of the EEA Agreement, it is intended to develop **28.44** and maintain a uniform surveillance on competition throughout the EEA and 'to promote a homogeneous implementation, application and interpretation of the relevant rules'.[86] To this end, the Article further stipulates that 'the competent authorities shall cooperate in accordance with the provisions...[of] Protocols 23 and 24'.[87] The cooperation extends to general policy issues as well as involvement in particular cases.[88] The aim is to coordinate the method of and the policy behind the application of EEA Competition rules for both the Commission and the ESA. Thus, for example, the ESA participated in discussions with the Commission concerning the review of competition rules relating to vertical restraints; the review of leniency policy; the re-drafting of the *de minimis* Notice; and, more recently, the need for modernization of the EU competition regime, to name but a few.

The duty of cooperation between the surveillance authorities applies, as regards Articles 53 **28.45** and 54 of the EEA Agreement, only in 'mixed cases'. In such cases, both surveillance authorities have historically supplied one another with copies of notifications, complaints, and information about the opening of *ex officio* procedures. For Article 53 and 54 cases, the key aspects of cooperation are as follows:

• The EU Commission and the ESA regularly consult and inform each other at different stages of proceedings.[89] Each of the surveillance authorities and the States within the respective territories are entitled to attend any hearings or Advisory Committees held by their counterparts. Furthermore, each surveillance authority may, before the other surveillance

---

[85] See Art 57(1) and (2); Annex XIV, Section A, Merger Control; and Protocols 21 and 24 to the Agreement.
[86] See also Case E-1/94 *Ravintoloitsijain Liiton Kustannus Oy Restamark* [1994–1995] EFTA Court Report 15, paras 32–5.
[87] Protocol 23 applies to Art 53 and 54 cases and Protocol 24 relates to merger cases.
[88] See Art 109(2) EEA and Art 1 of Protocol 23 to the EEA Agreement.
[89] See para 28.67.

authority takes a final decision, make any observations it considers appropriate. To this end, each surveillance authority is entitled to see copies of the important documents held by the other.

• In addition to this exchange of information, the Commission and ESA grant each other more tangible, administrative assistance,[90] if the need arises in individual cases. For instance, each competent surveillance authority may request the other surveillance authority to undertake investigations within its territory, and may take an active part in such investigations. Thus in 1994, the ESA asked the EU Commission to carry out investigations at the premises of a number of EU undertakings as part of the ESA investigation into the supply of steel tubes to the Norwegian offshore industry.[91] Conversely, in 1998, the ESA carried out investigations at the Commission's request into undertakings in its territory operating in the zinc phosphate industry. Parallel investigations have also occurred, for example, into the telecommunications sector.[92] In practice, cooperation has tended to involve the ESA assisting the EC Commission with the latter's case load. Between 1994 and 2001, the ESA was involved in assisting with or commenting on over 400 cases managed by the EU Commission. During the same period, the ESA took only two formal decisions finding infringements in competition matters.[93]

28.46 A detailed system of cooperation is also provided for in merger cases by virtue of Protocol 24. If a notification or complaint is not properly addressed to the competent authority, it will be transferred between the EC Commission and the ESA so as to reach the authority which has competence. Article 1(2) of Protocol 24 provides that the EC Commission and the ESA shall cooperate in those cases where the EC Commission has sole competence in relation to the merger, by virtue of Article 57(2)(a) of the EEA Agreement. In other words, where the EU Commission has competence in a 'mixed case', the ESA is still obliged to participate in the decision-making process. Article 2 further specifies that cooperation shall take place in one of five circumstances:

• the combined turnover of the undertakings concerned in the territory of the EFTA States equals 25 per cent or more of their total turnover within the territory covered by the Agreement;
• each of at least two of the undertakings concerned has a turnover exceeding EUR 250 million in the territory of the EFTA States;
• the concentration is liable to impede significantly effective competition in the territories of the EFTA States, or a substantial part thereof, in particular as a result of the creation or strengthening of a dominant position;
• the concentration fulfils the criteria for referral to the competent body of an EFTA State, under Article 6 of Protocol 24;
• an EFTA State wishes to take protective measures with regard to one of its legitimate interests, under Article 7 of Protocol 24.

28.47 Article 3 of Protocol 24 imposes a tight requirement on the Commission to transmit copies of the notifications to the ESA within a period of three days, but only in two situations: in

---

[90] For further details, see para 28.67 et seq.
[91] This culminated in the Commission's decision challenged in Joined Cases T-67/00, T-68/00, T-71/00, and T-78/00 *JFE Engineering Corp and others v Commission* [2004] ECR II-2501, upheld on appeal in Case C-403/04 *Sumitomo Metal Industries* [2007] ECR I-729, ECJ.
[92] Commission Press Release IP/99/786; ESA Press Release PR(99)19.
[93] Both concerning the markets for round wood in Norway. See the summary given by the ESA on its website.

cases where the 25 per cent turnover criterion is met; or where the concentration fulfils the criteria for an Article 6 referral to an EFTA State. In those two scenarios, the ESA also has a right to be represented at the hearings of the undertakings concerned, pursuant to Article 4 of Protocol 24. Close cooperation will take place with the relevant authority of the EFTA State in the case of an Article 6 referral. An Article 6 referral may take place where the concentration threatens to significantly affect competition in a market within a particular EFTA State, which presents all the characteristics of a distinct market. It may alternatively be referred where there is a lesser anticompetitive effect on such a distinct market, but that market does not constitute a substantial part of the territory covered by the Agreement.

In all other cases, the obligation on the Commission is merely to maintain 'close and con-   **28.48** stant liaison' with the ESA. The ESA is obliged to provide the EU Commission with administrative assistance in order to enable it to discharge its functions under Article 57 of the EEA Agreement.[94] The ESA and EFTA States are entitled to be present at meetings of the EU Advisory Committee on Concentrations and to express their views. They are not, however, given any voting rights.[95] The ESA is informed in advance of any interview by the EU Commission of a natural or legal person in the ESA's territory. The ESA has a right to attend such interviews.[96]

There has not yet been a merger case with an EFTA dimension dealt with solely by the ESA.[97]   **28.49** In 2004, the ESA was involved in fourteen merger cases handled by the EU Commission. The new referral procedures contained in Article 6 of Protocol 24 were used for the first time in the *CVC Group/ANI Printing Inks* case.[98] This was a referral to the Commission from Norway and eight Member States after a reasoned submission from the parties to the merger. The ESA acted in a liaison capacity between the EU Commission and the Norwegian NCAs. However, by 2011 the level of merger activity had diminished. The ESA was only involved in assisting in two merger cases in 2011: the acquisition by Seagate Technology of Samsung's hard disk business and the acquisition by Western Digital of Vivital Technologies.

E. Judicial Review

The General Court of the European Union ('GC') and the ECJ hear applications for annul-   **28.50** ment and appeals concerning decisions taken by the EU Commission in the competition field. The EFTA Court entertains challenges to competition decisions adopted by the ESA.[99] For example, in Case E-15/10 *Posten Norge AS v the EFTA Surveillance Authority*,[100] the EFTA Court dismissed a challenge brought by Norway Post against a decision of the ESA, finding that the company had abused its dominant position in the business to consumer parcel market in Norway.[101] The two court systems operate in parallel and exchange information with each other on the development of their case law.

---

[94] Article 8 of Protocol 24 to the EEA Agreement.
[95] Article 5(3) of Protocol 24.
[96] Article 8(3) of Protocol 24.
[97] Indeed, the ESA recognizes at p 46 of its Annual Report 2011 that in practice the EU Commission is the competent authority to deal with mergers under the EEA Agreement.
[98] Case M.3564, leading to a clearance decision: see Press Release IP/04/1326 of 29 October 2004.
[99] See A Diem, 'EEA Competition Law' [1994] ECLR 263, 270, n 3.
[100] Judgment of the EFTA Court of 18 April 2012 in Case E-15/10 *Posten Norge AS v the EFTA Surveillance Authority*.
[101] The EFTA Court noted at para 87 that it had the power under Art 36 of the Surveillance and Court Agreement to annul contested competition decisions of the ESA. It accordingly found that although the ESA was not an independent tribunal when it imposed fines in competition cases, the full merits review conducted

F. Rights of Lawyers

28.51   Individuals and undertakings have the right to be represented, before the GC and ECJ as well as before the EFTA Court, by lawyers entitled to practice either before the EU or EFTA national courts. Lawyers of EU Member States and EFTA/EEA States further enjoy rights as to legal privilege, whether the proceeding is conducted by the EU Commission or the ESA, meaning that special protection is granted as regards their relationship with their clients.[102]

IV. Practical Procedural Aspects in Articles 53 and 54 Cases

A. The Former System of Notifications, Applications, and Complaints

28.52   Formerly, undertakings that wished to obtain a negative clearance or an individual exemption or partake in the 'opposition procedure' under various block exemption regulations had to notify their agreements or practices to the competent surveillance authority.[103] The ESA would be required to examine a case where an agreement was notified to it, an application was made for an individual exemption, or where a complaint was received from another undertaking. It might also decide to investigate a matter on its own initiative. In fact, the ESA found that the majority of its cases were opened either as a result of complaints received or on the authority's own initiative. The ESA on average opened between ten and twelve new competition cases a year between 1994 and 2003. By the end of 2003, it had twenty-five pending cases awaiting resolution. Of these, eighteen had arisen from complaints.[104] By the end of 2004, the figure for pending cases handled by the ESA had dropped to nineteen, and the number of mixed antitrust cases handled by the EU Commission had risen to thirty-one.[105] There have been low levels of new cases addressed by the ESA under the 'modernized' regime in the period from 2007 to 2011.[106]

B. The Decentralized Enforcement of the EEA Competition Rules

28.53   Neither Article 101(3) TFEU nor Article 53(3) EEA State who should (or could) grant exemptions from the provisions of Articles 101(1) and 53(1) respectively. The former regime[107] provided that only the competent surveillance authority, be it the Commission or

---

by the EFTA Court was sufficient to ensure compatibility with the right to a fair hearing in accordance with general principles of EEA law (reflecting Art 6 of the Convention for the Protection of Human Rights and Fundamental Freedoms (European Convention on Human Rights, 'ECHR'). See paras 91, 92, and 100 of the judgment.

   [102]   The right to legal privilege is, however, circumscribed in the case of in-house counsel: Case C-550/07 P *Akzo Nobel Chemicals Ltd and Akcros Chemicals Limited v. European Commission* [2010] ECR I-8301, ECJ, confirming the approach taken in Case 155/79 *A M & S Europe Ltd v Commission* [1982] ECR 1575.

   [103]   The relevant rules were contained in the previous version of Protocol 23 to the EEA Agreement.

   [104]   See the Annual Report for 2003 available on the ESA's website; 88 per cent of the ESA's cases between 1994 and 2003 related to Norway.

   [105]   See the Annual Report for 2004, available on the ESA's website.

   [106]   See the Annual Report for 2011 at section 6, which reveals only a handful of new cases opened by the ESA over this period.

   [107]   Under Reg 17/62 as transposed to the EEA context.

the ESA, could grant individual exemptions. By 2003, however, it was considered that the centralized scheme no longer secured a proper balance between effective supervision of the competition provisions and, as far as possible, a simplified administration. The centralized scheme for enforcement was felt to hamper the application of competition law by the courts and NCAs of the Member States. Further, the administrative burden of the notification scheme prevented the Commission from concentrating its resources on the most serious infringements. The EU therefore decided to decentralize the enforcement of competition law. It put in place a directly applicable 'exception system'. This permits both the national authorities and the courts of the Member States to consider Article 53 in its entirety and grant exemptions where they consider the relevant conditions are met. The system of notifications and applications for negative clearance and/or exemption has now been swept away.

C. The Main Features of the Decentralized Regime

The key features of the 'modernized' regime are as follows: **28.54**

- The enforcement of Articles 53 and 54 in their entirety is now permitted by the NCAs and national courts of the EFTA/EEA States. Indeed, NCAs and national courts are obliged to apply these provisions to cases before them which may affect trade between EEA States when they apply national competition law. Further, they should also apply Article 54 EEA whenever they apply national competition law to any abuse prohibited by that Article. In order to ensure a level playing field, national competition law can no longer prohibit agreements, decisions, or concerted practices which are not also prohibited by the EEA competition rules. Nonetheless, EFTA/EEA States will not be prevented from applying on their own territory stricter national laws which prohibit or sanction unilateral conduct engaged in by undertakings. Nor will EFTA/EEA States be precluded by these provisions from applying national laws which predominantly pursue an objective different from that of Articles 53 or 54 EEA.[108]
- Despite this decentralization, the Commission and the ESA retain a key role in the enforcement of the competition provisions. They are each empowered to make a finding that there has been an infringement of the competition provisions. They may then take steps to terminate that infringement. The competent surveillance authorities are empowered to impose both structural and behavioural remedies where they find an infringement. Each is also empowered to impose interim measures and to accept binding commitments from an undertaking to cease its infringing behaviour.[109] In addition, where the public interest so requires it, the ESA may, acting on its own initiative, make a finding that Articles 53 and/or 54 EEA are inapplicable to an agreement, decision, and concerted practice or to the actions or omissions of an undertaking in a dominant position.[110]
- The Commission, ESA, and NCAs of the EFTA/EEA States form a network of public authorities applying the EU and EEA competition rules. This provides for close cooperation between the different bodies and for the exchange of information. The Modernisation

---

[108] See Art 3 of the Modernisation Regulation, read together with Recitals (6)–(9) of the Preamble to the Reg; and Art 3 of Chapter II, Part I of Protocol 4 to the Surveillance and Court Agreement.

[109] The ESA accepted commitments provided in relation to the restructuring of the telecommunications market in Lichtenstein in ESA Decision 605/08/COL of 17 September 2008, [2009] OJ C138/8. The commitments were given by Liechtensteinische Kraftwerke Anstalt and Telecom Liechtenstein AG.

[110] See Arts 7–10 of the Modernisation Regulation, read together with Recitals (10)–(14) of the Preamble; and Arts 7–10 of Chapter II, Protocol 4.

Regulation makes provision for the Commission to assume sole responsibility for the proceedings in a given case. Equivalent powers have been granted to the ESA. Provision is also made for determining which NCA should deal with a case where two or more are interested. The Advisory Committee on Restrictive Practices and Dominant Positions is retained. A network of cooperation also operates between different national courts.[111]

- The Commission and ESA are permitted to carry out investigations into sectors of the economy or to specific types of agreement.[112] This enables them to investigate suspicious pricing structures across the board in a market or industry. It frees the surveillance authorities from the need to concentrate on one particular undertaking. This is a particularly valuable tool in newly liberalized sectors of the economy and emerging markets. It has been used effectively in the telecommunications sector, for example, the examination into international mobile phone roaming rates. A sector inquiry may lead to individual enforcement action in due course. The ESA retains powers to require undertakings to supply them with all necessary information. In addition, the surveillance authorities are empowered to take statements from the personnel of undertakings, carry out inspections, and seek assistance from NCAs. This now expressly encompasses a power to carry out a search in the private homes of directors, subject to prior sanction from a national judicial authority. Officials from the competent surveillance authority may also assist with investigations conducted by NCAs.[113]

- The ESA has the power to impose fines for breach of procedural requirements and for infringements of the substantive provisions of Articles 53 and 54 EEA.[114] It is also authorized to impose periodic penalty payments on defaulters.[115]

- Provision is made for limitation periods governing both the powers exercised by the competent surveillance authority and the imposition of penalties under the Modernisation Regulation or pursuant to Section VI of Chapter II to Protocol 4 of the Surveillance and Court Agreement.[116]

- The Modernisation Regulation and Protocol 4 also provide for the rights of the defence in hearings involving parties, complainants, and others. Protection is afforded for documents that are covered by obligations of professional secrecy.[117]

- The Recitals to the Preamble of the Modernisation Regulation envisage the use of guidance letters by the competent surveillance authorities to ease uncertainty; and the application to the competition field of the principles contained in the Charter of Fundamental Rights of the European Union.[118]

---

[111] See Arts 11–16 of the Modernisation Regulation and Recitals (15)–(22) of the Preamble; and Arts 11–16 of Chapter II, Protocol 4.

[112] Under Art 17 of Chapter II, Protocol 4, the ESA may decide to conduct an inquiry into a particular sector of the economy or into particular types of agreements across various sectors. This will be done where the trend of trade between the EEA States, the rigidity of prices or other circumstances suggest that competition may be restricted or distorted within the territory covered by the EEA Agreement. The ESA conducted two sectoral enquiries in 2008, one into retail banking and one into business insurance.

[113] See Arts 17–22 and Recitals (23)–(28) to the Preamble; and Arts 17–22 of Chapter II, Protocol 4.

[114] The ESA imposed a fine of EUR 18.8 million on Color Line, AS, the Norwegian ferry operator, by Decision in Case No 59120 *Color Line*, dated 14 December 2011. The fine was imposed for infringements of Articles 53 and 54 EEA in the period from 1999 to 2005.

[115] Articles 23 and 24 of the Modernisation Regulation and Recitals (29) and (30) to the Preamble; Arts 23 and 24 of Chapter II, Protocol 4.

[116] Article 25 and 26 and Recital (31) to the Preamble; Arts 25 and 26 of Chapter II, Protocol 4.

[117] Articles 27 and 28 of the Modernisation Regulation and Recital (32); Arts 27 and 28 of Chapter II, Protocol 4; and Arts 10–16 of Chapter III, Protocol 4.

[118] Recitals (38) and (37) respectively.

D. Powers of the Competition Authorities and National Courts of EFTA/EEA States

The EEA Joint Committee Decision 130/2004 requires Articles 53 and 54 EEA to be applied, **28.55** consistently with the decentralized regime found in the Modernisation Regulation, by both the NCAs of the EFTA/EEA States and by their national courts.

The power to give effect to Articles 53 and 54 is conferred on the EFTA states domestic **28.56** courts and competition authorities by virtue of Articles 5 and 6 of Chapter II to Protocol 4. Such domestic bodies are entitled to rule on whether or not agreements, decisions, or concerted practices of undertakings or associations of undertakings which otherwise fall within Article 53(1) may nonetheless be saved by the application of Article 53(3). This is not a case of the national competition authority or national court granting the undertaking in question an individual exemption. Instead, the national body will simply apply Article 53 as a whole. This change to the procedure from the former regime brought about various consequences. First, undertakings no longer have the security blanket of an individual exemption for a particular agreement for a period of time. Parties are expected to place greater reliance on the block exemption regulations. There is also a greater risk of multiple challenges to offending agreements, possibly across different jurisdictions. Secondly, the national competition authorities now have power to require that an infringement of Article 53 be brought to an end without waiting for a notification to the ESA to be dealt with. They also have greater powers for ordering interim measures, accepting commitments and imposing fines, periodic penalty payments and other penalties provided for under national law.

It is doubtful, however, that Articles 53 or 54 EEA are directly applicable under EEA law. **28.57** The principle of direct effect appeared initially to be recognized in the EFTA Court case law, in the sense that Protocol 35 of the EEA Agreement was observed to require the EFTA States to ensure, if necessary by domestic legislation, that in the event of a conflict between domestic law and the EEA rules, the EEA rules shall prevail.[119] Nonetheless, subsequent developments in the case law,[120] culminating in *Karlsson*[121] establish that no doctrine of direct effect applies in EEA law.[122] Nonetheless, national courts are obliged to construe domestic law in conformity, so far as possible, with EEA law and an EFTA State can be held liable for the non-implementation of EEA law if certain conditions are met.[123] Thus, an EFTA state might decide to legislate to recognize the direct application of EEA rules under its national legal order. Or, if it does not do so, and that State fails to implement the requirements of a Directive, then the initial remedy lies in recourse to the principle of conforming

---

[119] See Case E-1/94 *Ravintoloitsijain Liiton Kustannus Oy Restamark* [1995] EFTA Court Report 15, paras 77–8.

[120] In Case E-9/97 *Sveinbjörnsdóttir* [1998] EFTA Court Report 95, at paras 62 and 63, the EFTA Court held that, while the EEA Agreement does not entail a transfer of legislative powers, the principle of State liability for loss caused to individuals by an infringement of EEA law was an integral part of the EEA Agreement. A failure to implement a directive could give rise to State liability if certain conditions (akin to the *Francovich* test found in Joined Cases C-6/90 and C-9/90 *Francovich and Others* [1991] ECR I-5357) were met.

[121] Case E-4/01 *Karlsson* [2002] EFTA Case Report 240. The EFTA Court held at para 28 that EEA law does not require that individuals and economic operators can rely directly on non-implemented EEA rules before national courts.

[122] In Case E-1/07 *Criminal proceedings against A* [2007] EFTA Court Report 246, the EFTA Court noted that the EEA Agreement did not require recognition of the principles of supremacy of EEA law or direct effect.

[123] See para 43 of the judgment in Case E-1/07 *Criminal proceedings against A* [2007] EFTA Court Report 246.

interpretation. If the application of that principle does not secure the desired result then, if the conditions are met, recourse may be had to the principle of State liability.

28.58 Both NCAs and national courts have to pay heed to the notices issued by the ESA. Such notices give guidance equivalent to that found in, among others, the following notices issued by the Commission:[124]

- Commission Notice on cooperation within the Network of Competition Authorities.[125] A separate notice has been issued in relation to cooperation within the EFTA Network of Competition Authorities.[126]
- Commission Notice on the cooperation between the Commission and the courts of the EU Member States in the application of Articles 81 and 82 EC.[127] The Notice on Cooperation with the Courts of the EFTA States was issued in 2006.[128]
- Commission Notice—Guidelines on the effect on trade concept contained in Articles 81 and 82 of the Treaty.[129] The equivalent guidance from the ESA was also issued in 2006.[130]
- Communication from the Commission—Notice—Guidelines on the application of Article 81(3) of the Treaty.[131] The ESA's Notice gives guidance on the application of Article 53(3).[132]

E. Powers of the ESA as a Competent Surveillance Authority under the Modernized Regime

28.59 The ESA retains a major role in the enforcement of the competition rules in the EFTA/EEA States. This section will briefly examine the procedure adopted by the ESA during the course of a competition case under the modernized regime. These following procedural steps will be considered in turn:

(1) the opening of the case file;
(2) cooperation between the ESA and the Commission in the conduct of the proceedings;
(3) investigations and inquiries conducted by the ESA;
(4) a formal or informal decision being taken by the ESA;
(5) the nature and extent of any remedies adopted by way of subsequent action.

1. The opening of the case file

28.60 The case will be opened by the ESA upon receipt of a complaint, by the ESA of its own initiative or upon the case being transmitted to it by the EU Commission. Historically, the majority of the cases before the ESA have arisen as a result of complaints. From 2003, the ESA has also put in place a leniency regime, in the form of an ESA Notice on immunity from fines and reduction of fines in cartel cases.[133] The leniency regime has not yet generated the

---

[124] By virtue of the provisions of Art 2 to Protocol 21 to the EEA Agreement.
[125] [2004] OJ C101/1; [2004] OJ C101/43.
[126] [2006] OJ C227/10 and EEA Supplement [2006] OJ 47/1.
[127] [2004] OJ C101/4; [2004] OJ C101/54.
[128] [2006] OJ C305/19 and EEA Supplement [2006] OJ 62/21.
[129] [2004] OJ C101/81.
[130] [2006] OJ C291/46 and EEA Supplement [2006] OJ 59/18.
[131] [2004] OJ C101/97.
[132] [2007] OJ C208/1 and EEA Supplement [2007] OJ 42/1.
[133] See Notice on Immunity from fines and reduction of fines in cartel cases [2003] OJ C10/13, and EEA Supplement to [2003] OJ 3/1. The current (2009) version of the Leniency Notice can be found at [2009] OJ C294/7 and EEA Supplement [2009] OJ 64/1.

discovery of hidden cartel behaviour in the EFTA States, akin to that seen with the implementation of the EU Commission's equivalent leniency regime.

Complaints

Complaints may be lodged by either natural or legal persons who can show a legitimate **28.61** interest, or by one of the EEA/EFTA States (or Member States of the EU).[134] Article 11 of Protocol 23 provides that complaints may be made to either competent surveillance authority. A transfer system operates between the Commission and ESA so that any complaint should end up in the right hands, even if it is technically addressed to the wrong authority.[135] A complaint may be rejected by the ESA without it formally initiating proceedings.[136]

Complaints should usually be made on the appropriate Form C provided by the competent **28.62** surveillance authorities. They have to be submitted in one of the official languages of the EU or one of the official languages of the EFTA States.[137] This principle also applies as regards proceedings which are opened upon the ESA's own initiative.[138] In order to ensure a rapid and efficient procedure, undertakings have traditionally been encouraged to use one of the official or working languages of the respective surveillance authority that is responsible.[139] The address of the ESA for such complaints is 'EFTA Surveillance Authority, Competition Directorate, Rue Belliard 35, B-1040 Brussels, Belgium' and its email address is competition@eftasurv.int. The ESA has published guidance on how it will handle complaints.[140]

Cases opened on the ESA's own initiative

The ESA may decide to initiate proceedings with a view to adopting one of the various deci- **28.63** sions open to it under Section III of Chapter II of Protocol 4 to the Surveillance and Court Agreement. Such proceedings may be initiated at any stage, but no later than the earliest of the dates on which it:[141]

(i) issues a preliminary assessment, pursuant to Article 9(1) of Chapter II to Part II of Protocol 4;
(ii) issues a statement of objections; or
(iii) publishes a notice under Article 27(4) of Chapter II to Protocol 4.

Each of these stages might be considered to be already part of the 'procedure' opened by the **28.64** ESA. Nonetheless, Article 2(3) of Chapter III of Part II to Protocol 4 expressly provides that the ESA may exercise its powers of investigation prior to initiating formal proceedings as such. Accordingly, formal proceedings are initiated when the ESA forms a view that it might adopt one of the decisions set out in Section III of Chapter II to Part II of Protocol 4 (ie a finding of an infringement, an interim measure, an acceptance of a commitment, or a finding

---

[134] See Art 7(2) of the Modernisation Regulation; Art 5(1) of the Implementing Regulation; and Arts 5–7 of Chapter III to Protocol 4.
[135] See section IV.E.(1)(c) of this chapter.
[136] Article 2(4) of Chapter III to Protocol 4.
[137] See Art 5(3) of Chapter III to Protocol 4 and Art 12 of Protocol 23 to the EEA Agreement.
[138] Article 12 of Protocol 23 provides that this choice of language 'shall also cover all instances of a proceeding, whether it be opened following a complaint or *ex officio* by the competent surveillance authority.'
[139] It should be noted that English (an official language of the EU) is the working language of the ESA, in addition to one of the official languages of the EFTA States. In practice, therefore, it may be easier for undertakings, if not to choose English as the language of the proceedings, then at least to submit a translation of all documentation into English, which satisfies the requirements of both the Commission and the ESA.
[140] EFTA Surveillance Authority Notice on the handling of complaints by the Authority under Articles 53 and 54 of the EEA Agreement [2007] OJ C287/12.
[141] Article 2(1) of Chapter III to Part II of Protocol 4.

of inapplicability). The ESA is required to inform the parties concerned that it has initiated proceedings and may then make the initiation public in an appropriate way.[142]

Transfer of cases

28.65 If a complaint is addressed to a surveillance authority that is not competent to decide on a given case under Article 56 EEA, then it must be transferred without delay to the other competent surveillance authority.[143] Similarly, if during the course of the Commission's investigation it becomes apparent that the case should properly be with the ESA, it will also be transferred.[144] In order to avoid cases being transferred several times between the authorities, such individual cases may not be re-transmitted to the initial surveillance authority once a transfer of the file has taken place.[145] Further, once a case has reached a certain point, it cannot be transferred between the two competent authorities. This cut-off arises when either:

(i) the statement of objections has been sent to the undertaking(s) or association(s) of undertakings concerned;

(ii) a letter has been sent to the complainant informing him that there are insufficient grounds for pursuing the complaint;

(iii) the publication of the intention to adopt a decision declaring Article 53 or 54 not applicable; or

(iv) the publication of the intention to adopt a decision making commitments offered by the undertaking(s) binding on the undertaking(s).

28.66 New or transferred proceedings before the EU Commission (instigated either on the basis of complaints or on the Commission's own initiative) will take into account the EEA competition provisions where appropriate. In either event, the decision should refer to the relevant provisions.

2. Cooperation between the ESA and the Commission in the conduct of the proceedings

28.67 In order to make the cooperation between the surveillance authorities effective, exchange of information and consultation between the surveillance authorities takes place at different stages of the proceeding.[146] A task force consisting of representatives from the Commission and from the ESA has prepared pro-forma letters which are used in this consultation process, and this should ensure an uncomplicated implementation of the cooperation procedure. The surveillance authority with initial responsibility for the conduct of the case first examines whether the case appears to have a 'mixed' nature, ie, whether it is likely to produce effects both within the internal market and within the EFTA territory.[147] Each surveillance authority generally only has a right to be consulted or informed in 'mixed cases'. In practice, however, the two authorities liaise very closely with each other all the time. In relation to 'mixed cases', the ESA will inform the Commission both when it decides to open an *ex officio* procedure on its own initiative and where it receives a complaint where it is not clear that it has also been received by the Commission.[148] It will also let the Commission know when formal investigative measures have been started by one of the NCAs within the ESA's territory. The Commission may present comments within thirty days of receipt of the information. This facilitates the operation of the transfer mechanism described earlier. In practice, this also

---

[142] Article 2(2) of Chapter III to Part II of Protocol 4.
[143] Article 11(1) of Protocol 23.
[144] Article 11(2) of Protocol 23.
[145] See Art 11(3) of Protocol 23.
[146] See Art 58 of the EEA Agreement and Protocol 23 attached thereto.
[147] A practical indication to be considered is, in particular, whether turnover is apparent in both territories.
[148] Article 2 of Protocol 23 to the EEA Agreement.

means that the ESA will refrain from taking any definitive measures[149] within those thirty days which might pre-empt any observations that are received. Further consultation takes place when a competent surveillance authority is:[150]

- addressing to undertakings a statement of objections;
- publishing its intention to adopt a decision declaring Article 53 or 54 of the Agreement not applicable; or
- publishing its intention to adopt a decision making commitments offered by the undertakings binding on the undertakings.

The surveillance authority which is consulted makes its comments within the time frame **28.68** as set out in the publication or in the statement of objections. Observations received from the undertakings involved or comments received from third parties as a result of the communications mentioned earlier are similarly transmitted between the two authorities.[151] The surveillance authorities inform each other if an individual case is settled by a formal decision. Transmission of copies of the administrative letters by which a file is closed or a complaint is rejected is also provided for.[152] More generally, in 'mixed cases', the surveillance authority not in charge of the matter may request at any stage of proceedings copies of the most important documents lodged and filed with their counterpart.[153] The authorities may also, at any stage before a final decision is made, submit any observations it considers appropriate. For the purpose of applying Articles 53 and 54 of the EEA Agreement, the ESA and the EU Commission have the power to provide one another with any matter of fact or of law, including confidential information.[154] Nonetheless, such information may only be used in evidence by the receiving surveillance authority for the purpose of procedures under Articles 53 and 54 EEA and in respect of the subject matter for which it was collected.[155] Detailed rules govern evidence obtained under the application of a leniency programme, by which information received as a result of the application of the other surveillance authority's leniency process cannot be used as the basis for starting a fresh investigation in the other jurisdiction.[156] Information may also be passed on to NCAs.[157]

The provisions guaranteeing professional secrecy and ensuring restricted use of information **28.69** apply both to information received by the surveillance authorities on the basis of their own internal rules and to the information that is received in the context of cooperation and administrative assistance between the surveillance authorities and NCAs. Neither the surveillance authorities nor the competent authorities of Member States and EFTA States may disclose any information covered by the obligation of professional secrecy and obtained in the course of EEA competition procedures. This limitation applies equally to officials and employees of any such authority.[158] These rules (and any national rules protecting professional secrecy) will not, however, prevent the exchange of information envisaged by the Protocol itself.[159]

---

[149] Conversely, this means that urgent or provisional measures could be taken.
[150] See Art 3 to Protocol 23.
[151] Article 3(2) and (2) of Protocol 23.
[152] See Art 4 of Protocol 23.
[153] See Art 7 of Protocol 23.
[154] Article 9(1) of Protocol 23.
[155] Article 9(2) of Protocol 23.
[156] Article 9(3) to (5) of Protocol 23; and Arts 11A and 11B of Chapter II to Protocol 4 to the Surveillance and Court Agreement.
[157] Article 10(1) of Protocol 23.
[158] See Reg 28 of the Modernisation Regulation and Art 10(2) of Protocol 23.
[159] Article 10(3) of Protocol 23.

28.70 Further, when the competent surveillance authority either requests or, by decision, requires an undertaking or association of undertakings located within the territory of the other surveillance authority to supply information, it shall at the same time forward a copy of the request or decision to the other surveillance authority.[160] Cooperation between the two authorities also takes place with regard to investigations and inspections[161] and hearings[162] (both addressed later in this chapter). Protocol 23 to the EEA Agreement establishes a procedure for cooperation in the context of the Advisory Committee on Restrictive Practices and Dominant Positions. Whenever an Advisory Committee is to be convened before a final decision is taken by one of the surveillance authorities, the latter is obliged to inform the other authority of the date of the Advisory Committee meeting and transmit any relevant documentation.[163] The other surveillance authority, as well as representatives of the States of its territory, have the right to attend the meetings and to express their views at it. There is, however, no attendant right to vote at such meetings.[164] The consultation process may be conducted as a written procedure unless a request is made for an oral hearing by the non-competent surveillance authority.[165]

3. Investigations and inquiries conducted by the ESA

28.71 As indicated previously, the EU Commission and the ESA will follow the same procedural rules,[166] namely those which are in use in the EU (listed in Article 3 of Protocol 21 to the EEA Agreement and as supplemented by guidance adopted by the ESA since the conclusion of the EEA Agreement). In the context of the EEA Agreement, some more particular aspects should be observed. The ESA will be able to investigate not only simply individual agreements or abuses, but also particular sectors of the economy or particular types of agreement.[167] It is open to the ESA in such circumstances to publish a report of its inquiry and simultaneously to take action against individual infringements. In the course of its inquiry, the ESA may request that undertakings supply it with all information necessary to give effect to Articles 53 and 54 EEA. It may also carry out inspections for that purpose.

28.72 The ESA also has more general powers to obtain information from undertakings.[168] First, the ESA may, by simple request or by decision, require undertakings to provide all necessary information to it.[169] Whichever course is adopted, the request or decision must identify the information to be provided and the time limit within which the information is to be produced. The communication should also set out the penalties which might be levied under Article 23 of Chapter II in the event that the ESA is supplied with incorrect or misleading information. If a formal decision is taken requiring information to be supplied, the decision should additionally set out the periodic penalty payments which can be charged under Article 24 in the event that no correct information is forthcoming. The final amount of the periodic penalty payments may, where necessary, be fixed at a later date.

28.73 Secondly, the ESA may interview any natural or legal person who consents to be interviewed for the purpose of collecting information relating to the subject matter of an investigation.[170]

---

[160] Article 8(1) of Protocol 23.
[161] Article 8(2) to (6) of Protocol 23.
[162] Article 5 of Protocol 23.
[163] See Art 6(1) of Protocol 23; and Art 14 of Chapter II to Protocol 4.
[164] See Art 6(2) and (3) of Protocol 23.
[165] Article 6(4) of Protocol 23.
[166] See Art 1 of Protocol 21. Chapters II and III to Part II of Protocol 4 to the Surveillance and Court Agreement reproduce (with adaptations for the EEA context) the procedural rules applied by the Commission in competition cases.
[167] Art 17 of Chapter II to Protocol 4.
[168] Articles 18–22 of Chapter II to Protocol 4.
[169] See Art 18(1) of Chapter II to Protocol 4.
[170] Article 19 of Chapter II to Protocol 4.

This may be carried out in cooperation with the authorities of the EEA/EFTA State in whose territory the interview takes place. The ESA may also interview a consenting natural or legal person in the Commission's territory. If it does so, it must inform the Commission. Both the Commission and officials from the NCA of the Member State concerned are entitled to be present.[171] The interviewer must state the legal basis for the interview at its inception. He or she must also reiterate its voluntary nature and inform the interviewee that a record of the interview will be taken.[172]

Thirdly, the ESA may conduct inspections of undertakings.[173] Inspections may take place of **28.74** premises, land, or means of transport. Written authorization for inspections must be obtained from the ESA. The authorization stipulates the subject matter and purpose of the inspection. The ESA may adopt a formal decision requiring an undertaking to submit to an inspection. This is adopted only after consultation by the ESA with the competition authority of the EEA/EFTA State in whose territory the inspection is to take place. The ESA may call on the assistance of the competition and police authorities of that EEA/EFTA State, if necessary with prior judicial approval from the State in question. This allows the ESA to make unannounced 'dawn raids' if there is a danger that evidence will be tampered with otherwise. Inspections may also be carried out at the premises of other third parties, such as directors, managers, and other members of staff of the undertaking concerned. This can include the homes of the persons concerned. There must be a reasonable suspicion that business books or records may be found there (which may prove a serious violation of Articles 53 and 54 EEA) before such an inspection will be permitted.[174] Furthermore, an additional safeguard is that prior authorization from the national judicial authority of the EFTA/EEA State concerned must be obtained.[175] Officials and other accompanying persons authorized by the ESA to conduct an inspection are empowered to:[176]

(i)   enter the undertaking's premises;
(ii) examine the books and records of the undertaking, in whatever medium they may be stored;
(iii) take or obtain copies of the business records;
(iv) seal the business premises and records for the period necessary for the inspection;
(v)   ask questions of representatives of the undertaking (or members of its staff) seeking explanations for any fact or document relating to the subject matter and purpose of the inspection and to record the answers.

Each surveillance authority informs the other of the fact that inspections have taken place and will receive upon request a note of the outcome of these investigations.[177]

Fourthly, the ESA may consider that inspections in the territory of the Commission (as the **28.75** other surveillance authority) are necessary. If a request is made to this effect, an inspection must be organized and carried out by the Commission. The inspection will be conducted in accordance with the Commission's own internal rules, but the ESA will be entitled to be present.[178] Finally, the ESA may enlist the administrative assistance of the NCAs of the EEA/EFTA States to carry out their own inspections or fact-finding missions on behalf of the ESA or the Commission.[179] Indeed, it is relatively common for coordinated inspections to be

---

[171] Article 8(6) of Protocol 23.
[172] Article 3(1) of Chapter III to Protocol 4.
[173] Article 20 of Chapter II to Protocol 4.
[174] Article 21 of Chapter II to Protocol 4.
[175] Article 21(3) of Chapter II to Protocol 4.
[176] Article 20(2) of Chapter II to Protocol 4 and Articles 3 and 4 of Chapter III to Part II of Protocol 4.
[177] See Art 8(5) of Protocol 23 to the EEA Agreement.
[178] See Art 8(2) and (3) of Protocol 23.
[179] Article 22 of Chapter II to Protocol 4.

instigated simultaneously in both the EU and EFTA territories, involving close cooperation between the Commission, the ESA, and NCAs.

28.76 Undertakings involved in competition procedures have the right to be heard in a certain number of instances, including the right to make written observations.[180] Such written observations—as well as observations from third parties—shall be transmitted to the other surveillance authority for information. Where an oral hearing is organized in a 'mixed case', the competent surveillance authority must invite its counterpart to be represented and extend the invitation to representatives of States of the other territory, which both have the right to attend such hearings.[181] Ordinarily the right to be heard will be accompanied by a right to have access to the ESA's file of documents.[182] This ensures equality of arms. Nonetheless, when the ESA grants access to the file to recipients of a statement of objections, the right does not extend to internal documents of the Commission or of the competition authorities of the EU Member States and the EFTA States involved. Nor does the right of access to the file extend to correspondence between the surveillance authorities, between a surveillance authority and the competition authorities of the EU Member States or EFTA States, or between the competition authorities of the EC Member States or EFTA States where such correspondence is contained in the file of the competent surveillance authority.[183] The EEA has made similar provision for the appointment of a Hearing Officer to that found in EU law.[184] The main task of the Hearing Officer is to ensure that the procedural rights of the parties involved in competition proceedings are respected.[185] He or she will determine any dispute about access to the file and ensure that business secrets and professional confidentiality are maintained.[186]

28.77 In order to encourage undertakings to blow the whistle on anticompetitive practices and agreements, the ESA has adopted a leniency programme in similar terms to that adopted by the Commission.[187] The adoption of a formal programme was a response to two developments. First, the desire of the EU Commission and the ESA to concentrate their efforts on hard-core cartels that have a significant impact on competition. Secondly, the need to fight against increasingly sophisticated methods adopted by cartelists in the coordination of their behaviour. The ESA will accordingly grant total immunity from fines to the first company to submit evidence on a cartel unknown to, or unproved by, the ESA where it is competent to handle the case. This takes two forms. First, total immunity will be granted to the first member of a cartel to provide sufficient information to allow the ESA to launch an inspection on the premises of the suspected cartelists. Secondly, in cases where the existence of the cartel has already been discovered, such immunity will alternatively be afforded to the first member

---

[180] See generally Art 27 of Chapter II to Protocol 4; and Arts 10 to 14 of Chapter III.

[181] See Art 5 of Protocol 23.

[182] See Arts 15 and 16 of Chapter III to Protocol 4.

[183] Article 10A of Protocol 23.

[184] ESA Decision 442/12/Col on the function and terms of reference of the hearing officer in certain competition proceedings.

[185] ESA Decision 177/12/COL of 30 October 2002 set out the terms of reference of Hearing Officers in certain competition proceedings. Decision 177l\2lCOL was revised by Decision 792l08lCOL of 17 December 2008 delegating certain powers in the field of competition to the Hearing Officers. Those decisions have now been amalgamated and replaced in Decision 442/12/COL.

[186] See Art 122 EEA which imposes an obligation on both EFTA States and officials acting under the EEA Agreement not to disclose information of a kind covered by the obligation of professional secrecy or business sensitive information.

[187] The leniency programme was initially established by the Notice on Immunity from fines and reduction of fines in cartel cases [2003] OJ C10/13, and EEA Supplement [2003] OJ 3/1. The current (2009) version of the Leniency Notice can be found at [2009] OJ C294/7 and EEA Supplement [2009] OJ 64/1.

of a cartel to provide evidence which enables the ESA to establish an infringement of Article 53 EEA. This alternative immunity only applies where no member of the cartel has benefited from the first type of immunity. The ESA expects full and continuous cooperation if immunity is to be awarded. The ESA also operates a rewards system falling short of full immunity. Fines may be reduced in respect of undertakings whose evidence provides 'significant added value' to the prosecution of an infringement. A tiered approach to reductions is adopted, so that the first in time to provide such evidence will be given a reduction of 30 to 50 per cent of the fine imposed, with reductions tapering down for subsequent informants. Any decision will be confirmed in a formal letter.

4. Formal and informal decisions taken by the ESA

There are a number of formal decisions which the ESA may take in respect of agreements or abuses that fall within its jurisdiction: **28.78**

- The ESA may address to undertakings or associations of undertakings decisions which bring to an end any infringement of Articles 53 or 54 EEA.[188] If a legitimate interest is served by it, the ESA may also adopt a decision finding that an infringement of the competition provisions occurred in the past. This is so even if the ESA does not proceed to impose any fines on the undertakings concerned.[189]
- The ESA is also empowered to adopt interim measures in cases of urgency. The urgency must stem from the risk of serious and irreparable damage to competition. In addition, the ESA must show that there is a *prima facie* finding of an infringement.[190]
- The ESA may also adopt a decision making commitments offered by the parties binding on those parties.[191]
- In exceptional circumstances, where the public interest of the Community requires it, the ESA may also make a finding of non-applicability. This consists in a declaration from the ESA that the provisions of Article 53 and/or 54 do not apply. The purpose behind this is to clarify the law and ensure the consistent application of the competition provisions throughout the EFTA territory.[192] The recital to the Modernisation Regulation envisages that this will be of particular use in relation to new agreements, for which existing case law and administrative practice may provide an uncertain guide.
- Finally, the ESA may withdraw the benefit of a block exemption where the agreement, decision or concerted practice in question produces effects that are incompatible with Article 53(3) EEA.[193] This power is exercised by the ESA either on the basis of complaints made to it; or on its own initiative.

An obligation is imposed on the ESA by Article 30 of Chapter II to Part II of Protocol 4 to the Surveillance and Court Agreement to publish any such formal decisions which it takes. In addition, the ESA may decide that, on the basis of the information in its possession, there are insufficient grounds for acting on a complaint.[194] If so, the ESA is required to inform the **28.79**

---

[188] Articles 4 and 7(1) of Chapter II to Part II of Protocol 4 to the Surveillance and Court Agreement.
[189] See Recital (11) to the Modernisation Regulation and Art 7(1); Art 7(1) of Chapter II of Part II to Protocol 4.
[190] Recital (11) and Art 8 of the Modernisation Regulation; Art 8 of Chapter II.
[191] Article 9 of Chapter II to Protocol 4. The ESA accepted commitments provided in relation to the restructuring of the telecommunications market in Lichtenstein in ESA Decision 605/08/COL of 17 September 2008, [2009] OJ C138/8.
[192] Recital (14) and Art 10 of the Modernisation Regulation; Art 10 of Chapter II to Part II of Protocol 4.
[193] Article 29 of Chapter II.
[194] See Art 7 of Chapter III to Part II of Protocol 4.

complainant of the reasons for its decision.[195] It must also set a time limit within which the complainant must set out its views in writing. If the further views provided do not persuade the ESA to change its proposed course of action, a decision rejecting the complaint must be taken. If no views are made known within that period, the complaint is deemed to have been withdrawn.[196] The ESA will no longer provide 'comfort' or 'discomfort' letters to undertakings within its territory. A notice equivalent to the Commission's Notice on informal guidance relating to novel questions concerning Articles 81 and 82 of the EC Treaty that arise in individual cases (guidance letters)[197] has, however, been adopted by the ESA on 18 May 2005.[198] The ESA may issue guidance letters to concerned undertakings.

5. The nature and extent of any remedies adopted by way of subsequent action

28.80 Once the ESA has made a finding of an infringement of Articles 53 and/or 54, it may take various steps to ensure that the infringement is effectively terminated. The power to adopt remedies is subject, however, to the requirement that any remedy proposed should be proportionate.[199] The Modernisation Regulation and the equivalent provisions in Protocol 4 for the first time envisage the use by the competent competition authorities of structural as well as behavioural remedies. This is permissible only where there is no equally effective behavioural remedy or where any equally effective behavioural remedy would in fact be more burdensome on the undertaking than the structural remedy initially proposed.[200] The relevant provisions make clear that changes to the structure of the undertaking will only be proportionate where there is a substantial risk of a lasting or repeated infringement of the competition provisions that derives from the very structure of the undertaking itself. The ESA may also accept commitments offered by undertakings which meet its concerns. Protocol 4 makes provision for these commitments to be binding on the undertakings which have given them.[201] Decisions as to commitments may be stipulated to last for a specified period. The decision must also state that there are no longer any grounds for action by the ESA. Nonetheless, the ESA may re-open their proceedings despite commitments having been given in three situations:

(i) where there has been a material change in the facts underpinning the decision;
(ii) where the undertaking has acted contrary to its commitments given; or
(iii) where the initial decision was based on incomplete, incorrect or misleading information given by the parties.

Nevertheless, the adoption of a binding commitments decision does not preclude the competition authorities or courts of the EFTA/EEA States from making their own finding of an infringement of Articles 53 and/or 54 EEA.[202]

28.81 In respect of failures by undertakings to comply properly or at all with requests for information or disclosure of business records or for breaking seals affixed by ESA officials, the ESA

---

[195] The EFTA Court has confirmed that the statement of reasons must be 'clear and unequivocal' and sufficient to enable a party to understand why a decision has been taken and whether there are grounds to seek judicial review in respect of it. See Case E14/10 *Konkurrenten.no AS v ESA* [2011] EFTA Court Report 266, paras 41–2.
[196] Article 7(3) of Chapter III.
[197] [2004] OJ C101/78.
[198] EFTA Surveillance Authority Notice on informal guidance relating to novel questions concerning Articles 53 and 54 of the EEA Agreement that arise in individual cases (guidance letters) [2006] OJ C305/34 and EEA Supplement [2006] OJ 62/17.
[199] Article 7(1) of Chapter II to Protocol 4.
[200] Recital (12) to and Art 7(1) of the Modernisation Regulation; Art 7(1) of Chapter II to Protocol 4.
[201] See Recital (13) to the Modernisation Regulation and Art 9; Art 9 of Chapter II to Protocol 4.
[202] See Recital (13) to the Modernisation Regulation.

has power to impose fines of up to 1 per cent of the total turnover of the undertakings concerned for the preceding business year.[203] Fines of up to 10 per cent of such turnover may be imposed for substantive infringements of the competition provisions or a failure to comply with binding commitments.[204] Periodic penalty payments may also be levied in respect of continued failures to bring infringements to an end; to comply with decisions ordering interim measures; to comply with commitments; to supply complete and correct information; or to submit to an inspection ordered by decision.[205] There is a limitation period of three years for imposing procedural penalties and a limit of five years for the imposition of fines for substantive infringements.[206] The ESA has published guidance on its approach to setting fines.[207]

V. Practical Procedural Aspects in Merger Cases

A. The Adoption of the Revised Merger Control Regulation

Procedural rules governing the control of mergers under the EEA Agreement are to be found **28.82** in the amended versions of Annex XIV and Protocol 24 to the EEA Agreement, and in Part III of Protocol 4 to the Surveillance and Court Agreement. Part III to Protocol 4 contains two separate chapters: Chapter IV contains rules relating to the control of concentrations between undertakings; Chapter V contains rules on the notifications, time limits, and hearings in the field of the control of concentrations.

The changes introduced to the EEA Agreement in June 2004 give effect to the revised Merger **28.83** Control Regulation and the Implementing Regulation. The amended legislation clarifies the substantive test applied in challenging a concentration. In keeping with the changes to EU merger control, it moves the analysis from an examination solely of dominance to an examination of whether a concentration would significantly impede competition in the relevant market (albeit within which analysis dominance will continue to be highly relevant). It also elaborates on the pre-existing 'one-stop shop' principle behind merger control through the adoption of a more streamlined referral system in certain circumstances. Where a merger raises an EFTA dimension and is to be dealt with by the ESA, the application of national merger provisions is precluded.[208]

---

[203] Article 23(1) of the Modernisation Regulation; Art 23(1) of Chapter II to Protocol 4.

[204] Article 23(2) of Chapter II to Protocol 4.

[205] Article 24(1) of Chapter II to Protocol 4.

[206] Article 25 of Chapter II to Protocol 4. Time starts to run on the later of: (i) the day on which the infringement is committed; and (ii) the day on which a repeated or continuing infringement ceases. Provision is also made for the interruption of the limitation period, but with a longstop limitation date based on twice the underlying limitation period in question.

[207] Guidelines on the method of setting fines imposed pursuant to Article 23(2)(A) of Chapter II of Protocol 4 to the Surveillance and Court Agreement [2006] OJ C314/84 and EEA Supplement [2006] OJ 63/44.

[208] Article 21 of Chapter IV, Part III, Protocol 4 to the Surveillance and Court Agreement.

B. Pre-Notification Procedures

28.84 As with the Merger Control Regulation, certain pre-notification procedures are available to the parties to a concentration. The procedures are slightly different, depending on whether or not the concentration has an EFTA dimension.

28.85 Prior to the notification of a concentration with an EFTA dimension, the parties can send a reasoned submission requesting that their concentration be looked at in whole or in part by an EFTA State. In order to benefit from the referral, certain criteria must be met.[209] These are that the concentration must significantly affect competition in a market within an EFTA State which presents all the characteristics of a distinct market and which should therefore be examined, in whole or in part, by that EFTA State. The ESA transmits the reasoned submission to all the EFTA States. The EFTA State that is the subject matter of the request then has a period of fifteen days within which to confirm its agreement or disagreement with the proposed referral. A failure to reply constitutes a deemed acceptance. Unless the EFTA State disagrees, the ESA must consider whether or not the criteria are met. If they are, the case can be transferred in whole or in part to the NCAs of the EFTA State. The ESA has a time limit of twenty-five days in which to make its assessment from date of receipt of the reasoned submission. A failure to respond leads to a deemed decision to refer. If a referral is made, no notification is needed and the matter is dealt with by the relevant NCAs. An equivalent procedure is also available to the EU Commission (who may refer the case to an EFTA State) in a concentration in a mixed case, pursuant to Article 6(4) of Protocol 24 to the EEA Agreement.

28.86 If the concentration does not have an EFTA dimension, the parties may nonetheless request that it be treated as if it did have an EFTA dimension and ask for it to be assessed by the ESA if certain criteria are met.[210] The concentration must be capable of being reviewed under the national competition laws of at least three EFTA States. The request is made by means of a reasoned submission and is transmitted to the EFTA States. The onus is then on any EFTA State within fifteen days to lodge its disagreement to the proposed transfer of competence. If disagreement is expressed, the case is not transferred. Otherwise the case is deemed to have an EFTA dimension and will be dealt with by the ESA. Again, an equivalent power is bestowed upon the Commission in a mixed case, under Article 6(5) of Protocol 24. The difference is that the merger must be capable of being reviewed under the national competition laws of at least three EU Member States and one EFTA State. This was the procedure adopted in the *CVC Group/ANI Printing Inks* case referred to earlier.

C. Notifications of Concentrations

28.87 Notification of a concentration with an EFTA dimension is mandatory. With certain limited exceptions, it cannot be implemented before its notification or until after it has been declared compatible with the EEA Agreement.[211] Notification is now possible on the basis of a good-faith intent to merge, without the need for a formal, binding agreement.

---

[209] Article 4(4) of Part III, Chapter IV to Protocol 4 to the Surveillance and Court Agreement.
[210] Article 4(5) of Chapter IV, Part III to Protocol 4.
[211] Article 7, Part III, Chapter IV to Protocol 4. The exceptions relate to the implementation of a public bid or a series of transactions in securities, subject to conditions laid down in Art 7.

The procedure for notifying a concentration is virtually identical to that found in EU law. A Form **28.88**
CO is used.[212] Certain information and documents are required to be provided.[213] Notifications
may be in an official language either of the EFTA States or of the EU.[214] Nonetheless, if a language is used which is not an official language of the EFTA States or the working language of
the ESA (ie any EU language other than English), a translation into one of the official languages
or into the working language of all documents must be provided. The standard requirements
for documentation apply, subject to any dispensation that may be granted by the ESA.[215] The
effective date of notification is the date of receipt by the ESA.[216] Copies of any notification and
the important documents will be transmitted to the competent authorities of the EFTA States
within three working days.

D. Procedure Once Notified

The ESA is obliged to consider the notification as soon as it is received.[217] It may take one of the **28.89**
following decisions:

- make a finding (in a formal decision) that the concentration does not fall within the scope of
the Merger Control Regulation as applied under EEA law;
- make a decision not to oppose the concentration and to declare it compatible with the
EEA Agreement;[218]
- initiate proceedings (ie move to Phase 2) if it considers that the concentration falls within
the scope of the relevant provisions and there are serious doubts as to its compatibility with
the EEA Agreement;
- if a concentration is modified to the ESA's satisfaction, it is open to the ESA to make a
subsequent declaration of compatibility.[219]

The ESA has the power in Phase 2 of the procedure to declare a concentration compatible **28.90**
with the EEA agreement if the relevant substantive criteria are fulfilled. The relevant substantive criteria are found in Article 2(2) of the Merger Control Regulation and, in certain other
cases, the criteria contained in Article 53(3) EEA.[220] The ESA has power to attach conditions
to a concentration or require commitments to be given before clearing it.[221] A decision declaring the concentration compatible with the EEA Agreement can be made once the original
concentration has been modified to the ESA's satisfaction.[222] It also has the power to declare
the concentration incompatible with the EEA Agreement. If the ESA finds that an incompatible concentration has been implemented or that a condition has not been complied with, a
wide range of remedial powers are available to it.[223] These mirror the powers available to the
EU Commission. They include the power to require the merger to be dissolved, restorative

---

[212] Article 3 of Chapter V, Part III to Protocol 4 to the Surveillance and Court Agreement.
[213] Articles 3–4 of Chapter V.
[214] See also Art 12 of Protocol 24 to the EEA Agreement.
[215] Article 4 of Chapter V, Part III to Protocol 4.
[216] Article 5 of Chapter V, Part III to Protocol 4; and Arts 10 and 11 of Protocol 24.
[217] Article 6(1) of Part III, Chapter IV to Protocol 4 of the Surveillance and Court Agreement.
[218] These first two types of decision are revocable if they were based on incorrect information. See Art 6(3)
of Part III, Chapter IV.
[219] Article 6(2) of Part III, Chapter IV.
[220] Article 8(1) of Chapter IV, Part III to Protocol 4.
[221] Article 8(2) of Chapter IV and Arts 19 and 20 of Chapter V to Protocol 4.
[222] Article 8(2) of Chapter IV.
[223] Article 8(4) of Chapter IV.

measures to be taken, and/or any other appropriate measure. They also include the power to take appropriate interim measures.[224]

28.91 Decisions are taken after consultation with the Advisory Committee on Concentrations and in liaison with the competent authorities of the EFTA States.[225] They are published in the EEA Section of the OJ. There are strict time limits for Phase 1 decisions and more relaxed time limits for Phase 2 decisions, in keeping with the EU approach.[226] Time limits may be suspended in certain circumstances.[227]

28.92 In addition, certain other referral procedures are available following notification of a concentration:

- After notification of a concentration without a Community dimension, an EFTA State may join a request made by one or more EU States requesting that the Commission examine the concentration.
- After notification of a concentration with an EFTA dimension, an EFTA State may request a transfer to its NCA. The ESA may refer a notified concentration, in whole or in part, to an EFTA State in which the concentration threatens significantly to affect competition in a market within that EFTA State, which has the characteristics of a distinct market. The same procedure is also available where the concentration affects competition in a market within that EFTA State, which presents the characteristics of a distinct market and which does not constitute a substantial part of the territory of the EFTA States.[228] An equivalent power is open to the EC Commission under Article 6 of Protocol 24 to the EEA Agreement.
- After notification of a concentration, or otherwise when a concentration is made known to an EFTA State, that State may request the ESA to examine a concentration that does not have an EFTA dimension.[229] Any such request must be made within fifteen days of the concentration coming to the EFTA State's attention. It will be transmitted to the other EFTA States, who may join in the request. The ESA may decide to examine the concentration if it affects trade between EFTA States and threatens significantly to affect competition within the territory of the EFTA State or States making the request. The ESA has ten days to decide whether or not to take the case over.

E. Powers Available to the ESA in Dealing with Merger Cases

28.93 The ESA has been granted the usual range of powers to enable it to discharge its functions, including the ability to make requests for information,[230] conduct interviews,[231] organize inspections to be carried out by the NCAs of the EFTA States, or conduct its own inspections,[232] and impose fines and periodic penalty payments in an equivalent range of circumstances to that found under EU law.[233] Similar provision is also made for protecting

---

[224] Article 8(5) of Chapter IV.
[225] Article 19 of Chapter IV.
[226] Article 10 of Chapter IV.
[227] See eg Arts 8(7) and 10(4) of Chapter IV.
[228] Article 9(2) of Chapter IV to Protocol 4;
[229] Article 22 of Chapter IV to Protocol 4.
[230] Article 11 of Chapter IV, Part III of Protocol 4 to the Surveillance and Court Agreement.
[231] Article 11(7) of Chapter IV.
[232] Articles 12 and 13 of Chapter IV.
[233] Articles 14 and 15 of Chapter IV.

professional secrecy,[234] and for the conduct of any hearings involving the merging parties and any third parties.[235]

VI. An Overview of the EEA Provisions on State Aid

A. Introduction

The EEA Agreement follows the TFEU in establishing a general prohibition on measures **28.94** taken by contracting parties that are likely to distort competition by favouring certain industries or enterprises. This prohibition is subject to exemption if certain conditions are met. A wide definition is given to State aid. It encompasses not merely old-style subsidies to national industries, but other forms of State intervention or assistance, such as preferential tax treatment,[236] favourable loans,[237] or trading guarantees provided by public bodies. The ESA is required to approve any new State aid measures. It also supervises and proposes appropriate measures against existing aid.[238]

B. The Basic Provisions

The substantive provisions on State aid under the EEA Agreement are contained in Articles **28.95** 61 to 63 EEA. Article 61 EEA states that any aid granted by EU Member States, EFTA States, or through State resources in any form whatsoever which distorts or threatens to distort competition by favouring certain undertakings or the production of certain goods, is, in principle, incompatible with the functioning of the EEA Agreement in so far as it affects trade between contracting parties. Article 61(2) provides a list of compatible aids, which is mandatory in its terms. Three types of aid must be declared compatible by the ESA:

- aid having a social character, granted to individual consumers, provided that such aid is granted without discrimination related to the origin of the products concerned;
- aid granted to make good damage caused by natural disasters or exceptional occurrences;
- aid granted to the economy of certain areas of the Federal Republic of Germany affected by the division of Germany, in so far as such aid is required in order to compensate for the economic disadvantages caused by that division.

In contrast, Article 61(3) sets out the types of aid which may, in the discretion of the ESA, be **28.96** considered to be compatible with the EEA Agreement. The four categories are:

- aid to promote the economic development of areas where the standard of living is abnormally low or where there is serious underemployment;
- aid to promote the execution of an important project of common European interest or to remedy a serious disturbance in the economy of an EU Member State or an EFTA State;

---

[234] Article 17 of Chapter IV; Arts 17–18 of Chapter V.
[235] Article 18 of Chapter IV; Arts 11 to 16 of Chapter V.
[236] See eg Case E-6/98 *Norway v ESA* [1998] EFTA Court Report 242, [1999] 2 CMLR 1033; and Joined Cases E-4/10, E-6/10, and E-7/10 *Principality of Lichtenstein v ESA* [2011] EFTA Court Report 16, paras 69–70.
[237] See eg Case E-4/97 *Norwegian Bankers' Association v ESA (No 2)* [1999] 4 CMLR 1292.
[238] See, in particular, the website maintained by the ESA <http://www.eftasurv.int/>.

- aid to facilitate the development of certain economic activities or of certain economic areas, where such aid does not adversely affect trading conditions to an extent contrary to the common interest;
- such other categories of aid as may be specified by the EEA Joint Committee in accordance with Part VII.

28.97 Article 62 also requires the ESA to conduct a constant review of existing measures of aid found in EFTA States and to assess their compatibility with Article 61 EEA. For this purpose, Article 62 confers on the ESA the powers and functions described in Protocol 26. Further, Article 62(2) provides for cooperation between the EU Commission and the ESA on matters relating to State aid, in accordance with the provisions of Protocol 27.

28.98 The rules on State aid in an EEA context have used a similar mechanism to that adopted in the competition context to ensure homogeneity between the EU and EFTA pillars. Article 63 thus provides that Annex XV to the EEA Agreement contains specific provisions on State aid. Annex XV then sets out a detailed list of measures which form the basis of the *acquis communautaire* for State aid. Annex XV also incorporates by reference the sectoral adaptations found in the mainstream competition provisions. The procedural rules are generally found in Protocol 3 to the Surveillance and Court Agreement.[239] The ESA has published very detailed guidelines on its State aid practice and procedure. Specific provisions are also laid down for the transport sector and for coal and steel.[240]

C. Powers and Functions of the ESA

28.99 Protocol 26 confers on the ESA 'equivalent powers and similar functions' to those afforded to the EC Commission under the EU State aid regime. Protocol 26 is not very forthcoming about the specific powers conferred on the ESA. That task is left to Protocol 3 to the Surveillance and Court Agreement.

1. Examination of new aid

28.100 Article 2 of Part II of Protocol 3[241] requires any EFTA State which is planning to make an award of new State aid to notify the ESA in sufficient time. The notification must contain sufficient detail and documentation to enable the ESA to make a decision. If a notification does not contain full and complete notification, any subsequent decision based on it may be revoked.[242] An EFTA State is not permitted to give effect to a new measure of State aid without the prior approval of the ESA.[243] The ESA upon receipt of the notification will carry out a preliminary investigation.[244] Unless a notification is withdrawn under Article 8 to Protocol

---

[239] The purpose of Protocol 3 is to examine and keep under constant review aid granted by the EFTA States or through State resources. See Joined Cases E-4/10, E-6/10, and E-7/10 *Principality of Lichtenstein v ESA* [2011] EFTA Court Report 16, para 112.

[240] See Parts III and IV of Protocol 3 to the Surveillance and Court Agreement.

[241] See also Art 1(2) and 1(3) of Part I of Protocol 3.

[242] Article 9 of Part II to Protocol 3. See also the ESA Decision 195/04/COL dated 14 July 2004 on the Implementing Provisions referred to under Art 27 in Part II of Protocol 3 to the EEA Agreement, which provides, *inter alia*, for a simplified notification procedure in relation to certain alterations to existing aid.

[243] Article 3 of Part II to Protocol 3.

[244] Article 4 of Part II to Protocol 3. In Case E-2/02 *Technologien Bau—und Wirtschaftsberatung GmbH and Bellona Foundation v EFTA Surveillance Authority* [2003] EFTA Court Report 52, para 44, the EFTA Court stressed the preliminary nature of this investigation, in contrast to the more detailed procedure described at para 28-100. See also Case E-5/07 *Private BArnehagers Landsforbund v ESA* [2008] EFTA Court Report 62, para 74.

3, it must then take one of several decisions within a period of two months from the date of receipt of the notification:

- It can decide that the proposed measure does not constitute aid for the purposes of EEA law.[245]
- It can decide not to raise any objections to the aid and take a formal decision confirming that the proposed measure is compatible with the EEA Agreement. The decision must record which of the exceptions contained in Article 61 EEA is satisfied.[246]
- If, after a preliminary examination, it finds that doubts[247] are raised as to the compatibility with the functioning of the EEA Agreement of a notified measure, it shall decide to initiate the formal investigation procedure.[248]

If the ESA feels that it has insufficient information to reach one of these formal decisions, it may request further information from the EFTA State concerned. If the relevant information is not provided, the notification is deemed to be withdrawn.[249] **28.101**

The formal investigation procedure commences with the ESA producing a summary of all relevant issues of fact and law, together with a preliminary assessment of the nature of the aid granted by the proposed measure. The ESA shall also spell out its doubts as to compatibility.[250] The EFTA State is then invited to comment on this document. Unless the notification is withdrawn by the EFTA State, the ESA then reaches one of the following decisions to bring the procedure to an end. A non-binding time limit of eighteen months is provided for such decisions.[251] **28.102**

- It can decide, if appropriate after necessary modifications from the EFTA State concerned, that the measure does not constitute aid.[252]
- It can decide, if appropriate after necessary modifications from the EFTA State, to take a 'positive decision', ie, to find that the aid is compatible with the EEA Agreement. The exception relied upon must be specified.[253]
- It can take a positive decision, but impose conditions to be met by the EFTA State.[254]
- It can take a 'negative decision' that the aid in question should not be implemented.[255]

2. Powers of the ESA to deal with unlawful State aid

Wide powers are available to the ESA to deal with unlawful State aid which has not been notified to the ESA in a proper fashion. The ESA is required to examine any such situation as **28.103**

---

[245] Article 4(2) of Part II to Protocol 3.
[246] Article 4(3) of Part II to Protocol 3.
[247] The notion of 'doubts' is an objective one, requiring an investigation of the content of the contested aid scheme and the circumstances under which it was adopted or implemented: Joined Cases E-4/10, E-6/10, and E-7/10 *Principality of Lichtenstein v ESA* [2011] EFTA Court Report 16, paragraph 76; and Case E-9/04 *The Bankers' and Securities' Dealers Association of Iceland v ESA* [2006] EFTA Court Reports 42, para 64, where the EFTA Court considered the doubts in relation to the scheme in question justified a formal investigation procedure.
[248] Article 4(4) of Part II to Protocol 3.
[249] Article 5 of Part II to Protocol 3.
[250] Article 6 of Part II to Protocol 3.
[251] Article 7(6) of Part II to Protocol 3. Once that eighteen-month period has expired, an EFTA State may request that the ESA take a decision on the basis of the information then available to it within a further period of two months. If the ESA cannot resolve its doubts on compatibility, it shall take a negative decision.
[252] Article 7(2) of Part II to Protocol 3.
[253] Article 7(3) of Part II to Protocol 3.
[254] Article 7(4) of Part II to Protocol 3.
[255] Article 7(5) of Part II to Protocol 3.

soon as it is brought to its attention.[256] It can then take a decision to suspend or provisionally recover the aid, before it proceeds to adopt the preliminary investigation and, if necessary, the formal investigation procedures referred to previously.[257] The ESA is not, however, bound by any time limits where the aid was not notified to it. Non-compliance with any ESA injunctions against an EFTA State either to provide information or to recover aid can lead to infraction proceedings before the EFTA Court.[258]

28.104 Where negative decisions are taken in cases of unlawful aid, the ESA must issue a formal decision that the EFTA State concerned shall take all necessary measures to recover the aid from the beneficiary, referred to as a 'recovery decision', unless to do so would be contrary to a general principle of EEA law.[259] The aid to be recovered pursuant to a recovery decision shall include interest at an appropriate rate fixed by the ESA. Interest is payable from the date on which the unlawful aid was at the disposal of the beneficiary until the date of its recovery. An obligation is imposed on EFTA States to effect recovery without delay and in accordance with the procedures under the national law of the EFTA State concerned, provided that they allow the immediate and effective execution of the ESA's decision. EFTA States may be required to take interim or provisional measures where appropriate. Recovery of aid is subject to an overall limitation period of ten years.[260]

3. Review of existing aid

28.105 The ESA is obliged to liaise with EFTA States to conduct a review of their existing aid schemes.[261] Where the ESA considers that an existing aid scheme is not, or is no longer, compatible with the functioning of the EEA Agreement, it shall inform the EFTA State concerned of its preliminary view and give the EFTA State concerned the opportunity to submit its comments within a period of one month. If the ESA considers that the aid is not, or is no longer, compatible with the EEA Agreement, it shall issue a recommendation of proposed measures. This recommendation may suggest:

- the substantive amendment of the aid scheme;
- the introduction of procedural requirements; or
- the abolition of the scheme.

28.106 If the EFTA State accepts the recommendation, the ESA issues a binding decision to that effect. If the recommendation is not accepted, the ESA must initiate the preliminary investigation and, if necessary, the formal investigation procedures referred to earlier.[262]

D. Complaints

28.107 A complaint that a measure from an EFTA State is unlawful State aid may be lodged by both individuals and undertakings, or their legal representatives.[263] The ESA's State Aid Guidelines

---

[256] Article 10 of Part II to Protocol 3.

[257] Articles 11–13 of Part II to Protocol 3. See also Case E14/10 *Konkurrenten.no AS v ESA* [2011] EFTA Court Report 266, para 78.

[258] Article 12 of Part II to Protocol 3. See also Art 23 of Part II to Protocol 3.

[259] Article 14 of Part II to Protocol 3. The 'recovery' of the aid is the logical consequence of a finding that it is unlawful. See Joined Cases E-4/10, E-6/10 and E-7/10 *Principality of Lichtenstein v ESA* [2011] EFTA Court Report 16, para 141.

[260] Article 15 of Part II to Protocol 3. The limitation period may be suspended in certain circumstances.

[261] Article 17 of Part II to Protocol 3.

[262] Article 19 of Part II to Protocol 3.

[263] See Art 20 of Part II to Protocol 3.

provide information about the submission of a complaint.[264] To lodge a complaint, a complaint form is sent to the ESA's Competition and State Aid Directorate. Upon receipt of a complaint, the ESA will conduct a preliminary assessment. If the ESA considers the complaint to be unfounded or outside its competence, it will inform the complainant that it intends to close the file without further action. Otherwise, the ESA informs the EFTA State of the complaint and initiates the procedures set out earlier.[265] The complainant may be asked to supply further information to the ESA and will be informed of the outcome of the investigation. Article 24 to Protocol 3 requires the ESA and its officials to respect professional secrecy. In addition, the identity of complainants is protected unless they agree to having their names divulged. While individuals and economic operators are entitled to address the ESA in any of the official languages of the EFTA States or of the EU, they are in practice encouraged to use English to avoid delay in the handling of a complaint.

E. Cooperation between the EU Commission and the ESA

Protocol 27 provides that, in order to ensure a uniform implementation, application, and interpretation of the rules on State aid throughout the territory of the contracting parties, the EU Commission and ESA would cooperate in a number of different ways. These include: **28.108**

- exchange of information and views on general policy issues;
- exchange of periodic surveys on State aid in their respective territories;
- informing one another of salient decisions;
- exchange of information and views on a case-by-case basis.

Article 64 EEA provides for a dispute resolution mechanism where one of the surveillance authorities considers that the other's implementation of the State aid provisions is not maintaining equal conditions of competition in their respective territories. **28.109**

VII. Adaptation Periods

A. Article 53

Articles 8 and 10 to 13 of Protocol 21 to the EEA Agreement continue to provide for certain transitional arrangements to apply to agreements, decisions, and concerted practices in existence at the date of entry into force of the EEA Agreement.[266] **28.110**

1. New agreements

The EEA Agreement does not provide for transition periods for agreements between enterprises which are concluded after its entry into force.[267] **28.111**

---

[264] <http://www.eftasurv.int/media/state-aid-guidelines/State-aid-Guidelines.pdf>.

[265] Depending on the level of involvement of the complainant and its status, it may have standing to challenge any subsequent decision taken before the EFTA Court: see Case E-2/02 *Technologien Bau- und Wirtschaftsberatung GmbH and Bellona Foundation v EFTA Surveillance Authority* [2003] EFTA Court Report 52.

[266] See Case E-7/01 *Hegelstad Eiendomsselskap Arvid B Hegelstad v Hydro Texaco A/S* [2003] 4 CMLR 6, para 17.

[267] This was formerly addressed under Art 4 of Protocol 21. The amendment of Protocol 21 by Decision 130/2004 has removed that provision. The proposition is now only shown by the absence of any saving provision for new agreements in the terms of Protocol 21 or in Part V, Chapter VIII to Protocol 4 to the Surveillance and Court Agreement.

2. Existing agreements

28.112 An adaptation period was provided for existing agreements which, by virtue of the entry into force of the EEA Agreement, fell under the prohibition contained in Article 53(1).[268]

General

28.113 Undertakings were allowed a period of six months as from the entry into force of the EEA Agreement to adapt such arrangements to or take any other steps necessary to bring them into line with the new provisions of the EEA. This period has now well passed. Undertakings should either have:

- modified their agreements or practices so that they now comply with existing block exemptions, taking into account the ESA dimension;[269]
- obtained an individual exemption from the Commission which has not yet expired and in respect of which the Commission has not yet decided that it should be discontinued. Agreements which, at the date of entry into force of the EEA Agreement, already enjoyed a formal individual exemption granted by the EU Commission will continue to benefit from this, even in relation to EEA aspects for the duration stipulated in the exemption decision, unless the Commission decides to withdraw the exemption;[270]
- modified them in such a way that they are no longer caught by the prohibition of Article 53(1) of the EEA Agreement.[271]

28.114 It remains advisable for undertakings which have not verified their agreements but suspect that Article 53 may be applicable to them, to carry out compliance programmes to ensure that their agreements are not at risk. Agreements already the subject of an administrative letter from the Commission before the entry into force of the EEA Agreement should have been brought into conformity with the EEA provisions. Article 35 of Chapter II to Part II of Protocol 4 to the Surveillance and Court Agreement states that applications and notifications made under the former procedural regime (prior to modernization) shall lapse. However, certain other procedural steps which have been taken may continue to have effect. Specific provision is made under Article 39 to Chapter II of Protocol 4 for the duration and revocation of decisions taken by the ESA under Article 53(3) EEA.

B. Article 54

28.115 No specific transitional provisions are envisaged in respect of Article 54 EEA.

C. The Merger Control Regulation

28.116 Article 14 of Protocol 24 to the EEA Agreement provides that Article 57 EEA shall not apply to any concentration which was the subject of an agreement or announcement or where

---

[268] However, aside from reliance on the transitional provisions, the fact that an agreement was concluded prior to the entry into force of the EEA Agreement does not preclude the application of Art 53(1) EEA. See Case E-7/01 *Hegelstad Eiendomsselskap Arvid B. Hegelstad v Hydro Texaco AS* [2002] EFTA Court Report 310, para 17.
[269] See Art 11 of Protocol 21 and Art 7 of Chapter VIII to Protocol 4 to the Surveillance and Court Agreement. The corresponding rules in the EU context are contained in different block exemptions.
[270] See Art 13 of Protocol 21 and Art 9 of Chapter VIII, Protocol 4.
[271] See Art 12 of Protocol 21 and Art 8 of Chapter VIII, Protocol 4.

control was acquired before the date of entry into force of the EEA Agreement. Nor shall it apply to a concentration where proceedings were initiated before that date by an NCA.[272]

VIII. Conclusion

The substantive EEA competition rules should not pose any particular problems for undertak-   **28.117** ings already used to the enforcement of competition policy in the EU. The substantive provisions are, to all intents and purposes, identical. The EFTA Court has shown itself willing to apply the long-established case law of the ECJ in competition matters.[273] The two most significant differences are to be found in the wider geographical scope of the rules and the system of attribution of cases and cooperation between the two surveillance authorities. In terms of the enforcement of those provisions, the message is mixed. First, the Modernisation Regulation regime had a delayed entry into force, leaving EEA competition law for some time in a curious limbo. This was not an ideal start. In Case E-4/01 *Karl Karlsson hf v The Icelandic State*,[274] the EFTA Court held that unimplemented EEA provisions would be of persuasive, not binding, authority:

> It follows from Article 7 EEA and Protocol 35 to the EEA Agreement that EEA law does not entail a transfer of legislative powers. Therefore, EEA law does not require that individuals and economic operators can rely directly on non-implemented EEA rules before national courts. At the same time, it is inherent in the general objective of the EEA Agreement of establishing a dynamic and homogeneous market, in the ensuing emphasis on the judicial defence and enforcement of the rights of individuals, as well as in the public international law principle of effectiveness, that national courts will consider any relevant element of EEA law, whether implemented or not, when interpreting national law.

Now that the initial teething problems have been overcome, it remains to be seen whether   **28.118** there will be an increased level of domestic enforcement of EEA competition law. Currently competition complaints to the ESA are few. Decided competition cases are even fewer. It remains to be seen whether the trend towards an increasing number of domestic competition actions in the EU will find an echo in domestic actions based on Articles 53 and 54 EEA. It should also be remembered that the domestic application of EU competition law has also been slow to find its feet. Secondly, experience has shown that the ESA has adopted a subsidiary, but nonetheless important, enforcement role to that exercised by the EU Commission. It would be fair to say that the EU Commission has led the way in most of the joint EEA/EU investigations into anticompetitive behaviour. In the residual areas where primary enforcement of the competition rules falls to the competent surveillance authority, there is no reason why this trend should not continue.

Finally, the centralized system of enforcement permitted close and constant cooperation   **28.119** between the EC Commission and the ESA. Further, the judicial control exercised, as appropriate, by the GC, the ECJ, and the EFTA Court (following the jurisprudence set down by the ECJ) largely led to the 'homogeneous application' of the EEA competition rules throughout the area, as envisaged by the EEA Agreement. It remains to be seen whether the same degree of homogeneity can be maintained in an era of decentralized enforcement across the thirty States which now comprise the EEA territory (shortly to be 31 States with the accession of Croatia to the EU on 1 July 2013).

---

[272] See also Art 10 of Chapter VIII, Part V, Protocol 4.
[273] See eg Case E-1/97 *Jan and Kristian Jaegar AS v Opel Norge AS* [1999] 4 CMLR 147.
[274] Judgment of the EFTA Court dated 30 May 2002, para 28.

PART VI

ARBITRATION

29

EU COMPETITION ARBITRATION

Gordon Blanke

I. Introduction

This chapter endeavours to provide an overview of the role of arbitration as an alternative **29.01** means of dispute resolution in the private enforcement of EU competition law. In doing so, it focuses exclusively on the use of arbitration within the context of EU competition law and does not delve into the wider realms of antitrust arbitration in relation to the private enforcement of, for example, various Member State competition laws[1] or indeed US antitrust law,[2] which is widely recognized as being at the origin of antitrust arbitration internationally.[3] That said, deliberate recourse to national competition or antitrust law regimes may be had for illustrative purposes or to draw instructive analogies to facilitate a practical understanding of EU competition arbitration in context.

A. General Scope of EU Competition Arbitration

29.02 Competition arbitration is of some relevance to a number of areas of EU competition law. In particular, it has come to play a role in:

- the private enforcement of the EU competition law provisions, ie Articles 101 and 102 TFEU;[4]
- the private enforcement of behavioural commitments in EU merger control, under commitment decisions adopted pursuant to Article 9 of Regulation 1/2003 and under former exemption decisions pursuant to Article 81(3) EC, now Article 101(3) TFEU;[5] and
- the private adjudication of select questions of the EU State aid regime under Article 107 TFEU, as well as public undertakings and exclusive or special rights within the meaning of Article 106 TFEU.

Each of these areas of EU competition arbitration will be discussed in further detail later in this chapter.

29.03 For the avoidance of doubt, this chapter will primarily discuss the practical procedural aspects of EU competition arbitration and seek to highlight relevant discrepancies with the procedural practice prevailing before the Member State courts. Before doing so, it will provide a brief introduction to arbitration as a private dispute resolution mechanism commonly used as an alternative to litigation. This will assist in a proper understanding of the practical utility of arbitration for private enforcement in the context of EU competition law.

29.04 Finally, the considerations made in this chapter apply to EU competition arbitration in the European Economic Area ('EEA') *mutatis mutandis*, unless expressly stated otherwise.

---

[1] For further discussions, see the 'Arbitration and ADR' section of the various country reports in G Blanke and R Nazzini (eds), *International Competition Litigation: A Multi-jurisdictional Handbook* (Kluwer Law International 2012).

[2] For a detailed treatment of US antitrust law in arbitration, see Part III in G Blanke and P Landolt (eds), *EU and US Antitrust Arbitration: A Handbook for Practitioners* (Kluwer Law International 2011) 1293–760.

[3] See the famous *Mitsubishi* decision of the US Supreme Court, *Mitsubishi Motors Corp v Soler Chrysler-Plymouth, Inc*, 473 US 614 (1985), which is considered the *fons origo* of modern antitrust arbitrability, even though there are selective examples of competition arbitration in Europe long before then, see eg arbitration practice in Germany. For further detail on antitrust arbitrability, see paras 29.19–29.42.

[4] Also referred to as 'ordinary competition arbitrations', see paras 29.13–29.14.

[5] Also referred to as 'commitment arbitrations', see paras 29.15–29.16.

B. What is Arbitration?[6]

Arbitration is a private dispute resolution mechanism based on a contractual agreement between **29.05** the parties, ie the arbitration agreement.[7] Usually, apart from being private, arbitration proceedings are strictly confidential, thus protecting arbitrating parties from adverse publicity, which—in competition arbitration more specifically—may prevent an adverse impact on consumer behaviour and hence an unforeseen distortion of existing trade patterns. Depending on the parties' agreement, the proceedings may be institutional[8] or ad hoc.[9]

Most subject matters of the law can be arbitrated and are hence 'arbitrable'.[10] Depending on the **29.06** subject matter of the arbitration, the parties are free to choose an arbitrator or an arbitration tribunal with the requisite expertise and relevant experience in the industry sector concerned. This may be of particular importance in EU competition arbitration to the extent that an accurate definition of the product and geographic markets as well as the evaluation of economic evidence may require some form of pre-experience.

Arbitration tribunals are generally understood to be delocalized, ie they do not possess a forum. **29.07** Accordingly, in the *conduct* of the proceedings, arbitration tribunals are only bound by the relevant arbitration laws of the seat of the arbitration (to the extent that these do not conflict with the chosen arbitration rules) as well as mandatory provisions of law that are of transnational application, including various competition or antitrust law provisions.[11]

Arbitration tribunals render arbitral awards, ie private judgments that are enforceable in more **29.08** than 140 countries worldwide[12] in accordance with the terms of the New York Convention.[13, 14] Awards cannot be appealed on the merits and can only be refused enforcement or set aside on grounds of undue process, including violations of mandatory laws and/or public policy.[15] Tribunals are widely recognized to be subject to a best efforts commitment to render an enforceable award, which may include compliance with certain competition law provisions.[16] This also applies to so-called consent awards, whereby an arbitrator gives effect to a settlement between the parties by way of a final award.

---

[6] For major arbitration works providing exhaustive guidance on the subject matter, see GB Born, *International Commercial Arbitration* (Kluwer Law International 2009); J-F Poudret and S Besson, *Comparative Law of International Arbitration* (Sweet & Maxwell 2007); and JDM Lew, LA Mistelis, and SM Kröll, *Comparative International Commercial Arbitration* (Kluwer Law International 2003).

[7] Or the submission agreement, provided the parties decide to resort to arbitration *ex post*, after a dispute has arisen between them.

[8] ie governed by arbitration rules ordained by a previously agreed and designated arbitration body, such as eg the International Chamber of Commerce ('ICC'), International Court of Arbitration, or the London Court of International Arbitration ('LCIA').

[9] ie take place outside any preordained institutional framework. Even then, the UNCITRAL Rules of Arbitration may provide a full set of ad hoc rules for procedural guidance in the conduct of the proceedings.

[10] On the arbitrability of EU competition law more specifically, see para 29.19 et seq.

[11] In the EU competition law context more specifically, see para 29.83.

[12] Including the current twenty-eight EU Member States and other leading industrial nations in the world. For a full list of membership, see <http://www.uncitral.org/uncitral/en/uncitral_texts/arbitration/NYConvention.html>.

[13] Convention on the Recognition and Enforcement of foreign arbitral awards, done at New York, on 10 June 1958.

[14] Or other bi-lateral or multi-lateral enforcement instruments, such as the so-called Geneva Convention, none of them, however, as wide in scope and as influential as the New York Convention.

[15] On supervisory court practice where faced with awards that violate EU competition law, see paras 29.82–29.89.

[16] See eg Art 35 of the International Chamber of Commerce ('ICC') International Court of Arbitration Rules of Arbitration ('ICC Rules').

29.09 The speed, procedural flexibility, and confidentiality of arbitration are generally recognized as the main advantages of this form of dispute resolution that weigh in favour of competition *arbitration*.

C. Modernization and EU Competition Arbitration

29.10 The environment of private enforcement created by the modernization of EU competition law[17] through the adoption of Regulation 1/2003 has also produced a positive impact on EU competition arbitration.[18] The decentralization of the enforcement of EU competition law away from the public authorities to private actors implies by definition a more pronounced role for arbitration in the private enforcement of EU competition law. This was expressly recognized by the competition law establishment as a motivating factor behind modernization prior to the adoption of Regulation 1/2003[19] and has since been confirmed by arbitration practice.[20]

II. Some Ontological Preliminaries

29.11 To start, it is important to appreciate some ontological preliminaries that provide the overall framework of competition arbitration, ie:

(i) the context within which the arbitration of competition law generally arises;
(ii) the basic presumption of the arbitrability of EU competition law; and
(iii) the scope and construction of the underlying arbitration agreement, which in turn determines the base ambit of the arbitrator's mandate in each individual case; as well as
(iv) its enforceability.

A. Context

29.12 EU competition arbitrations may arise in various contexts either:

- in the form of 'ordinary competition arbitrations' in relation to Articles 101 and 102 TFEU; or
- in the form of 'commitment arbitrations' for purposes of monitoring the competition-compliant implementation of behavioural commitments in EU merger control or under Article 9 commitment decisions[21] and former Article 81(3) EC exemption decisions.

---

[17] See Ch 1 'Institutional Framework', para 1.07 et seq; Ch 2 'The Role of National Judicial Authorities', para 2.17 et seq.

[18] Despite the fact that Reg 1/2003 does not expressly provide for the arbitration of EU competition law. For a further discussion, see para 29.79.

[19] Prof C-D Ehlermann in C-D Ehlermann and I Atanasiu (eds), *European Competition Law Annual 2001: Effective Private Enforcement of EC Antitrust Law* (Hart Publishing 2003) 303 ('in future, the European Commission will have to take a more positive stand towards arbitration, as this is a pre-condition for the success of the modernisation exercise').

[20] AP Komninos, 'Arbitration and EU Competition Law in the Post-Modernization Era' in G Blanke and P Landolt (eds), *EU and US Antitrust Arbitration: A Handbook for Practitioners* (Kluwer Law International 2011) 433; and A Mourre, 'Arbitrability of Antitrust Law from the European and US Perspectives' in G Blanke and P Landolt (eds), *EU and US Antitrust Arbitration: A Handbook for Practitioners* (Kluwer Law International 2011) 3, paras 1-123 and 1-146.

[21] There is no reason to believe why the practice of the Commission's use of arbitration in the context of Art 9 commitments may not also be extended *mutatis mutandis* to the enforcement of remedies accorded under Art 7 of Reg 1/2003. For confirmation, see G Blanke, 'International Arbitration and ADR in Remedy Scenarios Arising under Articles 101 and 102 TFEU' in G Blanke and P Landolt (eds), *EU and US Antitrust Arbitration: A Handbook for Practitioners* (Kluwer Law International 2011) 1053, paras 30-242–30-243.

There exists a residual category of EU competition-related arbitrations that deals with discrete aspects of the EU State aid regime as well as public undertakings under EU law.

1. Ordinary EU competition arbitrations

Ordinary EU competition arbitrations are arbitrations that deal with Articles 101 and 102 **29.13** TFEU. These can arise either as a principal claim or by way of defence. In the former scenario, a party that wishes to terminate an existing contractual relationship will commonly argue that an agreement it has concluded with a contracting partner is null and void *ab initio* under Article 101(1) TFEU and should hence be set aside under Article 101(2) TFEU. Alternatively, a party may argue that a contracting partner has abused a dominant position in violation of Article 102 TFEU in the way and manner it has performed obligations in the existing agreement between them. In the latter scenario, a party will make the same arguments, but by way of defence a defendant will hence raise the nullity under Article 101 TFEU or the abusive performance of an agreement under Article 102 TFEU in order to defeat claims brought by a contracting partner for breach of contract. This latter scenario is commonly referred to as the 'Euro-defence'.[22]

Importantly, EU competition arbitrations are dependent on the existence of an arbitration **29.14** agreement between the contracting parties in the main contractual relationship between them. This is invariably the case in international trade more generally: distribution and supply agreements, licence agreements, joint ventures, and cooperation agreements hence commonly provide for dispute resolution by arbitration. Alternatively, the disputing parties may enter into a so-called submission agreement whereby they submit an already existing dispute between them to arbitration *ex post facto*. In the light of the tortious nature of EU competition claims under Article 102 TFEU, a claim for an abuse of dominance is only rarely based on the performance of a pre-existing agreement with a contracting partner: it is thus less likely that an arbitration agreement is already in place where a party seeks to bring a claim for abuse of dominance, and it is therefore necessary to agree to the submission of the dispute to arbitration with the tortfeasor.[23]

2. EU commitment arbitrations

EU commitment arbitrations arise in relation to the deficient implementation of behavioural **29.15** commitments[24] in EU competition law and EU merger control. Essentially, these arbitrations deal with disputes that arise either from commercial agreements that serve the implementation of

---

Given that there have been no practical instances to date in which the Commission has deployed arbitration mechanisms under Art 7, the remainder of this chapter is confined to references to arbitration in the context of Art 9 only, without prejudice, however, to the corresponding potential relevance of arbitration in the context of Art 7. See also G Blanke and L Ortiz Blanco, 'El arbitraje en el ambito del Derecho de la competencia europeo' (2012) Arbitraje V(3) 9.

[22] See in particular ICC practice, G Blanke, 'Antitrust Arbitration under the ICC Rules' in G Blanke and P Landolt (eds), *EU and US Antitrust Arbitration: A Handbook for Practitioners* (Kluwer Law International 2011) 1763, paras 49-058 and 49-070.

[23] See L Idot, 'Arbitration and the Reform of Regulation 17/62' in C-D Ehlermann and I Atanasiu (eds), *European Competition Law Annual 2001: Effective Private Enforcement of EC Antitrust Law* (Hart Publishing 2003) 307 et seq, at 310–11.

[24] Note that there are isolated examples of EU commitment arbitrations in relation to structural remedies, in particular in the EU merger control context. See Commission Decision of 8 May 2000 in Case Comp/M.2268 *Pernod Ricard/Diageo/Seagram Spirits* [2002] OJ C16/13); Commission Decision of 3 May 2000 in Case Comp/M.1671 *Dow Chemical/Union Carbide* [2001] OJ C245 1; Commission Decision of 30 June 2008 in Case Comp/M.4835 *Hexion/Huntsman* (not yet published); and G Blanke, *The Use and Utility of International Arbitration in EU Commission Merger Remedies: A Supranational Paradigm in the Making?* (Europa Law Publishing 2006) 59–60.

those behavioural commitments or alternatively from the absence of such agreements (ie where the parties concerned have failed to agree upon the terms and conditions that such agreements should take). Such agreements are commonly referred to as 'implementation agreements' and invariably seek to provide fair and non-discriminatory access for third-party competitors (beneficiaries) to key infrastructure or technology controlled by a merged entity or the party that is subject to the Article 9 commitment decision. In this sense, the majority of commitments concerned here are access commitments that are implemented through access agreements, including in particular some form of access to technology (ie an essential facility) or infrastructure, the establishment and maintenance of supply and purchasing relationships, the termination of exclusive or long-term contractual arrangements, or the termination of anticompetitive distribution agreements.[25] Many of these access agreements are, in turn, implemented in a variety of industry sectors, including most prominently the airline industry.[26]

29.16 Historically speaking, predecessors of this type of arbitration existed under a number of individual exemptions pursuant to former Article 81(3) EC (now Article 101(3) TFEU)[27] as well as a number of block exemption regulations.[28] Some of these, however, have more appropriately been qualified as instances of cartel arbitration or '*Kartellschiedsgerichtsbarkeit*'.[29] Given that the majority of these exemption decisions and block exemption regulations have expired at the time of writing, they are not further discussed in this chapter.[30]

3. EU competition-related arbitrations

29.17 The EU State aid regime may give rise to EU competition-related arbitrations to the extent that an arbitrator may have to address the question as to whether certain measures may constitute State aid within the meaning of Article 107(1) TFEU and to determine whether they may fall within the

---

[25] G Blanke, *The Use and Utility of International Arbitration in EU Commission Merger Remedies: A Supranational Paradigm in the Making?* (Europa Law Publishing 2006) and G Blanke, 'International Arbitration and ADR in Conditional EU Merger Clearance Decisions' in G Blanke and P Landolt (eds), *EU and US Antitrust Arbitration: A Handbook for Practitioners* (Kluwer Law International 2011) 1605, paras 46-019–46-020.

[26] In relation to EU commitments in EU merger control: eg Commission Decision of 11 February 2004 in Case Comp./M.3280 *Air France/KLM* [2004] OJ 060/5); Commission Decision of 20 July 1995 in Case IV/M.616 *Swissair/Sabena II* [1995] OJ C200/10); Commission Decision of 4 July 2005 in Case Comp./M.3770 *Lufthansa/Swiss* [2005] OJ C204/3); Commission Decision of 22 December 2005 in Case Comp./M.3940 *Lufthansa/Eurowings* [2006] OJ C18/22); Commission Decision of 22 June 2009 in Case Comp./M.5335 *Lufthansa/SNAH* (not yet published); Commission Decision of 9 January 2009 in Case Comp./M.5364 *Iberia/Vueling/Clickair* (not yet published); Commission Decision of 28 August 2009 in Case Comp./M.5440 *Lufthansa/Austrian Airlines* (not yet published); and Commission Decision of 30 March 2012 in Case Comp./M.6447 *IAG/BMI* (not yet published). In relation to commitments under Art 9 of Reg 1/2003: Commission Decision of 14 July 2010 in Case COMP/39.596 *BA/AA/IB*.

[27] For a comprehensive tabular overview, see G Blanke, 'Annex I: Table on Commission's Experience of Arbitration in Exemption Decisions Under Article 81(3) EC (Article 101(3) TFEU)' in G Blanke and P Landolt (eds), *EU and US Antitrust Arbitration: A Handbook for Practitioners* (Kluwer Law International 2011) 1901.

[28] For an exhaustive analysis, see G Blanke, 'The Use of International Arbitration under Article 81(3) of the EC Treaty and Article 9 of Regulation 1/2003' [2008] SchiedsVZ 243; and G Blanke, 'International Arbitration and ADR in Remedy Scenarios Arising under Articles 101 and 102 TFEU' in G Blanke and P Landolt (eds), *EU and US Antitrust Arbitration: A Handbook for Practitioners* (Kluwer Law International 2011) 1053.

[29] G Blanke, 'International Arbitration and ADR in Remedy Scenarios Arising under Articles 101 and 102 TFEU' in G Blanke and P Landolt (eds), *EU and US Antitrust Arbitration: A Handbook for Practitioners* (Kluwer Law International 2011) 1053, para 30-032.

[30] For an exhaustive treatment, see G Blanke, 'International Arbitration and ADR in Remedy Scenarios Arising under Articles 101 and 102 TFEU' in G Blanke and P Landolt (eds), *EU and US Antitrust Arbitration: A Handbook for Practitioners* (Kluwer Law International 2011) 1053, paras 30-053–30-148.

General Block Exemption Regulation.[31] This would usually be the case in investment arbitrations involving an EU Member State and a foreign individual investor or in disputes between lenders and borrowers in relation to products or product rates potentially affected by EU State aid.[32]

Alternatively, an arbitrator may be required to assess the special or exclusive nature of rights of **29.18** undertakings that provide services of general public interest in order to ascertain whether they are validly exempted from compliance with the EU competition law rules on a case-by-case basis.[33]

B. Antitrust Arbitrability

For a long time, antitrust issues were regarded as non-arbitrable. This was essentially because **29.19** antitrust law was considered to pursue public policy objectives which naturally fall outside adjudication by a private individual and hence outside arbitration as a private dispute resolution mechanism. The *status quo ante* dramatically changed with the adoption by the US Supreme Court of the *Mitsubishi* decision,[34] which set the stage for the arbitrability of antitrust issues in the US. This was shortly followed by the ruling of the Court of Justice ('ECJ') in *Eco Swiss*,[35] which has since set the standard for competition arbitrability in the EU Member States. Hence, nowadays, subject to minor exceptions,[36] the arbitrability of competition law is a *fait accompli* in most European jurisdictions.[37]

As a general rule, only those aspects of EU competition law that fall within the exclusive **29.20** competence of the Commission or a national competition authority ('NCA') or a Member State court are non-arbitrable. For example, any criminal liability that may result from a violation of EU competition law before a Member State court cannot be arbitrated. However, in matters of EU competition law, an arbitrator's jurisdiction is, generally speaking, co-extensive with the jurisdiction of the Member State courts, ie provided a matter of EU competition law is admissible to the jurisdiction of the courts, then it also can be arbitrated.

The practice of the International Chamber of Commerce ('ICC') International Court of **29.21** Arbitration confirms the arbitrability of Articles 101 and 102 TFEU.[38] More recently, some

---

[31] Commission Regulation (EC) No 800/2008 of 6 August 2008, declaring certain categories of aid compatible with the common market in application of Articles 87 and 88 of the Treaty [now Articles 107 and 108 TFEU] [2008] OJ L241/3.

[32] L Hancher, 'Arbitrating EU State Aid Issues' in G Blanke and P Landolt (eds), *EU and US Antitrust Arbitration: A Handbook for Practitioners* (Kluwer Law International 2011) 965.

[33] PJ Slot, 'Arbitrating Competition-Law-Related Issues under Articles 3(1)(b) TFEU, 4(3) TEU and 106 TFEU' in G Blanke and P Landolt (eds), *EU and US Antitrust Arbitration: A Handbook for Practitioners* (Kluwer Law International 2011) 1017.

[34] *Mitsubishi Motors Corp v Soler Chrysler-Plymouth, Inc,* 473 US 614 (1985), in which the US Supreme Court held that US antitrust laws were arbitrable.

[35] Judgment of the ECJ of 1 June 1999 in Case C-126/97 *Eco Swiss China Ltd and Benetton International NV* [1999] ECR I-3055.

[36] See eg Lithuania, whose arbitration law originally excluded the private adjudication of competition law disputes; see Art 11(1) of the Lithuanian Law of Arbitration of 2 April 1996. For most recent reform, competition law now being capable of submission to arbitration in Lithuania, see Arts 11 and 12 of the Lithuanian Law on Commercial Arbitration of 30 June 2012.

[37] See A Mourre, 'Arbitrability of Antitrust Law from the European and US Perspectives' in G Blanke and P Landolt (eds), *EU and US Antitrust Arbitration: A Handbook for Practitioners* (Kluwer Law International 2011) 3, para 1-037 et seq.

[38] G Blanke, 'Antitrust Arbitration under the ICC Rules' in G Blanke and P Landolt (eds), *EU and US Antitrust Arbitration: A Handbook for Practitioners* (Kluwer Law International 2011)1763, para 49-067. For a comprehensive tabular overview, see G Blanke, 'Annex III: Table on ICC Arbitration Awards Involving Antitrust Issues over the Period 1964–2010' in G Blanke and P Landolt (eds), *EU and US Antitrust Arbitration: A Handbook for Practitioners* (Kluwer Law International 2011) 2063.

EU Member State jurisdictions have even actively sought the promotion of the private enforcement of competition law claims, including those of EU law provenance, through arbitration.[39]

1. Arbitrability of Article 101 TFEU

29.22 Given that claims for nullity under Article 101 TFEU presume the prior existence of a contract and given that arbitration requires a contractual basis, which is often found in such pre-existing contracts,[40] the arbitrability of Article 101 TFEU lies at the heart of EU competition arbitration. The question of whether and, if so, to what extent Article 101 TFEU is arbitrable was controversial for a while, but has now settled in favour of the *full* arbitrability of Article 101 TFEU.

Article 101 TFEU

29.23 In the mid-twentieth century, most arbitrators—subject to minor exceptions[41]—used to be reticent to apply EU competition law, and in particular Article 101 TFEU in its former incarnation as Article 81 EC or Article 85 EEC, and would instead only refer to it to the extent that they could find that EU competition law was eventually not applicable to the dispute before them.[42] This reticence was largely motivated by the public policy character of EU competition law enforcement and the widespread assumption that arbitrators did not have competence to find the illegality of an agreement under the corresponding equivalents of Articles 81(2) EC or Article 85 EEC, and that such finding was ultimately reserved to the jurisdiction of the Commission.

29.24 In hindsight, the arbitrator's former reticence was only partly justified in that the application of the individual exemption provision under Article 81(3) EC or Article 85(3) EEC was then in fact a prerogative of the Commission. However, the remaining provisions of Article 81 EC and Article 85 EEC were not and could be applied by Member State courts and arbitrators alike.[43] This meant that any competition law analysis had to be bifurcated between the nullity assessment, which could be carried out through private enforcement, ie before an arbitration tribunal or a Member State court, and the application of the exemption provision, which was the exclusive preserve of the Commission.

29.25 The ECJ's judgment in *Eco Swiss*[44] of 1996 finally dispersed any doubts as to and indirectly confirmed the arbitrability of then Article 81 EC, to the exclusion of the individual exemption

---

[39] See eg the UK, where the Office of Fair Trading ('OFT') and other relevant stakeholders in the competition discourse have been noted to make particular efforts in this respect: More specifically, see the OFT's 'Quick guide to private litigation in competition cases', March 2010, available at <http://www.oft.gov.uk/business-advice/competing/private-litigation> as well as the UK Department for Business Innovation and Skills ('BIS'), 'Private Actions in Competition Law: A Consultation on Options for Reform' (April 2012), and the UK Government's response, both available at <https://www.gov.uk/government/consultations/private-actions-in-competition-law-a-consultation-on-options-for-reform>. In this context, also note the interest expressed at the wider international level by the Organisation for Economic Co-operation and Development ('OECD') in Paris, which has recently—through Working Party No 3 of its Competition Committee—issued a hearing report on Arbitration and Competition dated 13 December 2011, including the desirability of private enforcement of EU competition law, following a hearing with experts held on 26 October 2010: DAF/COMP(2010)40, available at <http://search.oecd.org/officialdocuments/displaydocumentpdf/?cote=DAF/COMP(2010)40&docLanguage=En>.

[40] Cf para 29.14.

[41] Note in this context the more familiar application of EU competition law by German arbitrators even before the arbitration of EU competition law had become more generally acceptable in other European jurisdictions, eg Judgment of the German Federal Supreme Court of 20 May 1966 in *Eiskonfekt* GRUR 1966, Heft 10, 576–82.

[42] eg ICC Award of 16 March 1964 Rev arb (1964) pp 171 et seq; and ICC Award No 6106.

[43] eg ICC Award No 6503.

[44] Judgment of the ECJ of 1 June 1999 in Case C-126/97 *Eco Swiss China Ltd and Benetton International NV* [1999] ECR I-3055.

provision under subparagraph (3). The ECJ's judgment in this case was based on the *presumption* that Article 81 EC was arbitrable and did not even discuss the question of competition arbitrability as such,[45] focusing instead on the qualification of Article 81 EC as forming part of the concept of public policy within the meaning of the New York Convention.[46] Following *Eco Swiss*, other Member State jurisdictions followed suit, confirming the arbitrability of the present Article 101 TFEU.[47] Emblematic of the ubiquitous recognition of competition arbitrability by the EU Member State courts is the English High Court's ruling in *ET Plus*,[48] which—dealing with alleged infringements of EC (now EU) competition law—concluded that 'there is no realistic doubt that such "competition" or "antitrust" claims are arbitrable'.[49]

Article 101(3) TFEU

Whereas initially, under Regulation 17 of 1962, the individual exemption provision of former **29.26** Article 101 TFEU fell within the sole jurisdiction of the Commission,[50] since modernization and the adoption of the self-assessment regime under Regulation 1/2003, Article 101 TFEU is now fully arbitrable, including the legal exception under Article 101(3) TFEU.[51] This is so even though Regulation 1/2003 remains entirely silent on arbitration and refers to the Member State courts' competence to apply Article 101(3) TFEU only.[52] Otherwise, arbitration would be placed under a significant, unjustifiable procedural disadvantage as compared to litigation, in that an arbitrator seized of an EU competition law reference would have to refer matters in relation to the application of Article 101(3) TFEU to a competent Member State court.[53] This would, no doubt, be procedurally impractical and significantly slow down the arbitration process. In addition, the frequently encountered argument that arbitrators are not sufficiently equipped, or are less well equipped than the courts, to apply the grounds for legal exception under Article 101(3) TFEU is—in light of the high degree of specialism of a number of arbitrators in the field—controversial and rather unconvincing, to say the least.

---

[45] See Mustill and Boyd, *Commercial Arbitration* (Sweet & Maxwell 1989).

[46] On which see further para 29.83.

[47] See C Liebscher, 'EU Member State Court Application of *Eco Swiss*: Review of the Case Law and Future Prospects' in G Blanke and P Landolt (eds), *EU and US Antitrust Arbitration: A Handbook for Practitioners* (Kluwer Law International 2011) 785.

[48] *ET Plus SA v Welters* [2005] EWHC 2115 (Comm). For comment, see G Blanke, 'Arbitrating Competition Disputes: The English High Court has Confirmed that EC Competition Law Claims are Arbitrable in Principle' (November 2005) 29 Competition Law Insight 5; and R Merkin (April 2006) 6(4) Arbitration Law Monthly 1.

[49] G Blanke, 'The Application of EU Law to Arbitration in England' in J Lew, H Bor, G Fullelove, and J Greenaway (eds), *Arbitration in England* (forthcoming 2013); and G Blanke, R Nazzini, A Nikpay, and V Smith, 'England and Wales' in G Blanke and R Nazzini (eds), *International Competition Litigation: A Multi-jurisdictional Handbook* (Kluwer Law International 2012).

[50] Article 9 of Council Regulation (EEC) No 17: First Regulation implementing Articles 85 and 86 of the Treaty [1962] OJ 13/205–11 (English version to be found in the English special edition of the OJ, Series I Chapter 1959–1962, 81 et seq) ('Regulation 17/62').

[51] See A Mourre, 'Arbitrability of Antitrust Law from the European and US Perspectives' in G Blanke and P Landolt (eds), *EU and US Antitrust Arbitration: A Handbook for Practitioners* (Kluwer Law International 2011) 3, paras 1-123 and 1-145.

[52] See AP Komninos, 'Arbitration and EU Competition Law in the Post-Modernization Era' in G Blanke and P Landolt (eds), *EU and US Antitrust Arbitration: A Handbook for Practitioners* (Kluwer Law International 2011) 433, para 12-113 et seq, according to whom the silence was not intended to exclude arbitration from the application of the individual exception provision, but was instead motivated by the Commission's desire to avoid further (unnecessary) controversies in the overall modernization exercise. Also AP Komninos, 'Arbitration and the Modernisation of European Competition Law Enforcement' (2001) 24(2) World Competition 211.

[53] See L Idot, 'Arbitration and the Reform of Regulation 17/62' in C-D Ehlermann and I Atanasiu (eds), *European Competition Law Annual 2001: Effective Private Enforcement of EC Antitrust Law* (Hart Publishing 2003) 307, at 317.

29.27   In any event, in recognition of arbitral competence in this subject area, the Commission itself has so far raised no objections to the arbitrability of Article 101(3) TFEU. On the contrary, a number of Commission officials have expressly endorsed it.[54] Any other view would be counterproductive and in particular run counter to the spirit of EU private enforcement introduced by the Modernisation Regulation.

2. Arbitrability of Article 102 TFEU

29.28   By analogy to the development in relation to Article 101 TFEU, Article 102 TFEU and its predecessors, Articles 82 EC and 86 EEC, have equally been found to be arbitrable. This is so despite the general tortious nature of claims in relation to abuse of dominance.[55] Again, emblematic of the ubiquitous recognition of competition arbitrability by the EU Member State courts, including in relation to claims for abuse of dominance, is the wide wording adopted by the English High Court's ruling in *ET Plus*.[56]

29.29   Furthermore, neither the Commission nor any other European institution is known ever to have in any form objected to the arbitrability of Article 102 TFEU or its predecessors, Articles 82 EC and 86 EEC.

3. Arbitrability of behavioural commitments under Articles 101 and 102 TFEU and in EU merger control

29.30   The arbitrability of behavioural commitments under the EU competition law provisions and in EU merger control is largely uncontroversial. Despite initial doubts as to the Commission's power to delegate the monitoring of commitments to a private third party, ie an arbitrator,[57] the Commission's own practice in this area would tend to confirm that there is no improper delegation of competences between the Commission and the arbitrator. On the contrary, both under the Merger Control Regulation and under Regulation 1/2003, the Commission ultimately remains responsible and in control of the competition-compliant implementation of the commitments concerned.

29.31   For the avoidance of doubt, the ruling of the Court of First Instance ('CFI') (and now of the General Court, 'GC') in *Microsoft*[58] does not change this conclusion.[59] That ruling, whereby the CFI set aside a Commission decision that sought to outsource the implementation of a set of behavioural commitments entirely to a monitoring trustee under Regulation 17 of 1962,[60]

---

[54] See eg J Lübking, 'The European Commission's View of Arbitrating Competition Law Issues' in G Blanke, 'Arbitrating Competition Law Issues: A European and a US Perspective' (2008) 19(1) EBLR (Special Edition) 76. By contrast, see, however, de Keyser in D de Groot, 'Arbitration and the Modernisation of EC Competition Law' in G Blanke, 'Arbitrating Competition Law Issues: A European and a US Perspective' (2008) 19(1) EBLR (Special Edition) 175, at 187. For a critical assessment of de Keyser's view, however, see G Blanke, 'EC Competition Law Claims in International Arbitration' in C Klausegger et al (eds), *Austrian Arbitration Yearbook 2009* (Manz/Stämpfli/Beck 2009) 3, at 30–2; and de Groot, 'Arbitration and the Modernisation of EC Competition Law', 187.

[55] See A Komninos and M Burianski, 'Arbitration and Damages Actions Post-White Paper: Four Common Misconceptions' (2009) 2(1) GCLR 16.

[56] *ET Plus SA v Welters* [2005] EWHC 2115 (Comm). See para 29.25.

[57] In the context of EU merger control more specifically, see L Idot, 'Une Innovation Surprenante: L'Introduction de l'Arbitrage dans le Contrôle Communautaire des Concentrations' (2000) Rev arb 591, whose considerations arguably apply *mutatis mutandis* to the arbitrability of commitments under Reg 1/2003.

[58] Judgment of the European CFI of 17 September 2007 in Case T-201/04 *Microsoft v Commission*.

[59] To this effect, see also 'Arbitration and Competition', note by Prof L Idot in OECD Report on Competition and Arbitration, DAF/COMP(2010)40, available at <http://search.oecd.org/officialdocuments/displaydocumentpdf/?cote=DAF/COMP(2010)40&docLanguage=En>, 51 at 82.

[60] Cf also in this context the ancillary role played by monitoring trustees in arbitration mandates in EU merger control, see G Blanke, 'International Arbitration and ADR in Conditional EU Merger Clearance Decisions' in G Blanke and P Landolt (eds), *EU and US Antitrust Arbitration: A Handbook for Practitioners* (Kluwer Law International 2011) 1605, para 46-033 et seq.

has to be distinguished from the situation where an arbitrator is mandated to monitor the implementation of commitments under the Merger Control Regulation or under Regulation 1/2003 on several counts. Essentially, unlike in the case in *Microsoft*, in EU commitment arbitrations, the Commission does not delegate its own supervisory functions to a private third-party individual without the affected parties' consent; nor does it in fact delegate any of its powers in relation to the proper implementation of the conditions and obligations of the original commitments, ie the first-order obligations, which remain within the exclusive jurisdiction of the Commission; on the contrary, in EU commitment arbitrations, arbitrators are only mandated to deal with second-order obligations, ie the terms and conditions of the implementation agreement, which in turn are based on the original commitments.[61]

Nevertheless, to the extent that the arbitration of behavioural commitments arises from implementation agreements, which are essentially ordinary commercial agreements, their arbitrability cannot be in doubt. The only difference to the arbitration of ordinary commercial agreements is that the arbitration of behavioural commitments have to take into account the original objectives of the underlying commitments and hence be competition-compliant. Precisely for this reason, these EU commitment arbitrations constitute EU competition arbitrations. **29.32**

Finally, it should be noted that the arbitrability of behavioural commitments is not affected by the 'without privity' nature of the underlying arbitration commitment.[62] This is particularly so given that the arbitration commitment, which is only binding on the merging entity or the party benefiting from the Article 7 or Article 9 commitment decisions, as the case may be, forms the basis of and blueprint for a separate arbitration agreement[63] to be concluded between that party and the third-party beneficiary as per the terms of the underlying commitment decision. That arbitration agreement, in turn, will be binding on both parties and hence create the missing privity between them. That said, however, even if no such arbitration agreement is adopted between the parties, the third-party beneficiary may rely upon the original arbitration commitment to trigger an 'arbitration without privity'.[64] **29.33**

Behavioural commitments under Articles 101 and 102 TFEU

Equally, the Commission has accepted a number of arbitration commitments in the context of Article 9 commitment decisions in order to allay initial competition concerns pursuant to Articles 101 and 102 TFEU, as well as their predecessors Articles 81 and 82 EC.[65] It has been argued that arbitration commitments could equally be used in the adoption by the Commission **29.34**

---

[61] On the distinction between first- and second-order obligations in this context, see paras 29.95–29.96. In relation to the Merger Control Regulation, see G Blanke, 'International Arbitration and ADR in Conditional EU Merger Clearance Decisions' in G Blanke and P Landolt (eds), *EU and US Antitrust Arbitration: A Handbook for Practitioners* (Kluwer Law International 2011) 1605, para 46-034; and in relation to Reg 1/2003, see G Blanke, 'International Arbitration and ADR in Remedy Scenarios Arising under Articles 101 and 102 TFEU' in Blanke and Landolt (eds), *EU and US Antitrust Arbitration* 1053, para 30-273 et seq and, in particular, para 30-276.

[62] See para 29.93.

[63] Or arbitration clause, which forms in turn part of the implementation agreement.

[64] See para 29.97.

[65] See eg Commission Decision of 19 January 2005 in Case COMP/C-2/37.214 *Joint selling of the media rights to the German Bundesliga*; Commission Decisions of 13 September 2007 in Case COMP/E-2/39.140 *DaimlerChrysler* and Case COMP/E-2/39.142 *Toyota* and COMP/E-2/39.143 *Opel*; Commission Decision of 14 July 2010 in Case COMP/39.596 *BA/AA/IB*; and Commission Decision of 13 December 2011 in Case COMP/C-3/39692 *IBM Maintenance Services*. See G Blanke, 'International Arbitration and ADR in Remedy Scenarios Arising under Articles 101 and 102 TFEU' in G Blanke and P Landolt (eds), *EU and US Antitrust Arbitration: A Handbook for Practitioners* (Kluwer Law International 2011) 1053.

of a prohibition decision pursuant to Article 7 of Regulation 1/2003.[66] The Commission's accept-ance of such arbitration commitments must, in and of itself, be reflective of the arbitrability of behavioural commitments in this context.

Behavioural commitments in EU merger control

29.35 The Commission has—since the early 1990s—accepted a number of arbitration commitments in the context of conditional merger clearance decisions.[67] This practice, in and of itself, is indica-tive of the admissibility of behavioural merger control commitments to arbitration. In addi-tion, in obvious recognition of the arbitrability of behavioural commitments in this context, the

---

[66] G Blanke, 'International Arbitration and ADR in Remedy Scenarios Arising under Articles 101 and 102 TFEU' in G Blanke and P Landolt (eds), *EU and US Antitrust Arbitration: A Handbook for Practitioners* (Kluwer Law International 2011) 1053, paras 30-242–30-243.

[67] See eg Commission Decision of 21 March 2000 in Case IV/JV.37 *BskyB/Kirch Pay TV* [2000] OJ C110/45); Commission Decision of 30 September 1992 in Case IV/M.214 *Du Pont/ICI* [1993] OJ L7/13); Commission Decision of 4 September 1992 in Case IV/M.235 *Elf Aquitaine-Thyssen/Minol* [1992] OJ C232/5; Commission Decision of 27 November 1992 in Case IV/M.259 *British Airways/TAT* [1992] OJ C326/10; Commission Decision of 20 July 1995 in Case IV/M.616 *Swissair/Sabena II* [1995] OJ C200/10; Commission Decision of 16 January 1996 in Case IV/M.623 *Kimberley-Clerk/Scott* [1996] OJ L183/1; Commission Decision of 30 July 1997 in Case IV/M.877 *Boeing/McDonnell Douglas* [1997] OJ L336/16; Commission Decision of 15 October 1997 in Case IV/M.938 *Guinness/Grand Metropolitan* [1997] (OJ L288/24; Commission Decision of 27 May 1998 in Case IV/M.993 *Bertelsmann/Kirch/Premiere* [1998] OJ L53/1; Commission Decision of 27 May 1998 in Case IV/M.1027 *Deutsche Telekom/BetaResearch* [1998] OJ L53/1; Commission Decision of 4 June 1998 in Case IV/M.1185 *Alcatel Thomson CSF-SCS* [1998] OJ C272/5; Commission Decision of 28 April 1999 in Case IV/M.1309 *Matra/Aérospatiale* [1999] OJ C109/4; Commission Decision of 9 March 1999 in Case IV/M.1313 *Danish Crown/Vesjyske Slagterier* [1999] OJ L201/1; Commission Decision of 1 January in Case IV/M.1578 *Sanitec/Sphinx* [1999] OJ C294/1; Commission Decision of 1 December 1999 in Case Comp./M. 1601 *Allied Signal/Honeywell* [1999] OJ L152/1; Commission Decision of 3 May 2000 in Case Comp./M.1671 *Dow Chemical/Union Carbide* [2000] OJ L245/1; Commission Decision of 25 January 2000 in Case Comp./M.1684 *Carrefour/Promodès* [2000] OJ C164/5; Commission Decision of 29 March 2000 in Case Comp./M.1751 *Shell/BASF/JV-Project Nicole* [2000] OJ C142/35; Commission Decision of 12 April 2000 in Case Comp./M.1795 *Vodafone Airtouch/Mannesmann* [2000] OJ C141/19; Commission Decision of 12 July 2000 in Case Comp./M.1813 *Industri Kapital/(Norden)/Dyno* [2001] OJ L154/41; Commission Decision of 8 May 2000 in Case Comp./M.1846 *Glaxo Wellcome/Smithkline Beecham* [2000] OJ C170/6; Commission Decision of 13 October 2000 in Case Comp./M.2050 *Vivendi/Canal+/Seagram* [2000] OJ C311/3; Commission Decision of 3 July 2001 in Case Comp./M.2220 *GE/Honeywell* (not yet published) (unofficial version only); Commission Decision of 8 May 2001 in Case Comp./M.2268 *Pernod Ricard/Diageo/Seagram Spirits* [2001] OJ C16/13; Commission Decision of 20 December in Case Comp./M.2389 *Shell/DEA* [2003] OJ C15/35; Commission Decision of 13 January 2003 in Case Comp./M.2416 *Tetra Laval/Sidel* [2004] OJ L43/13; Commission Decision of 20 December 2001 in Case Comp./M. 2530 *Südzucker/Saint Louis Sucre* [2003] OJ L103/1; Commission Decision of 20 December 2001 in Case Comp./M.2533 *BP/E.ON* [2002] OJ C276/31; Commission Decision of 8 January 2002 in Case Comp./M.2621 *SEB/Moulinex* [2002] OJ C49/8; Commission Decision of 10 July 2002 in Case Comp/M.2803 *Telia/Sonera* [2002] OJ C201/19; Commission Decision of 2 April 2003 in Case Comp./M.2876 *Newscorp/Telepiù* [2004] OJ L110/73; Commission Decision of 30 April 2003 in Case Comp./M.2903 *Daimler-Chrysler/Deutsche Telekom/JV* [2003] OJ L300/62; Commission Decision of 2 September 2003 in Case Comp./M.3083 *GE/Instrumentarium* [2004] OJ L109/1; Commission Decision of 29 Spetember 2003 in Case Comp./M.3225 *Alcan/Péchiney (II)* [2003] OJ C299/19; Commission Decision of 11 February 2004 in Case Comp./M.3280 *Air France/KLM* [2004] OJ 060/5; Commission Decision of 22 November in Case Comp./M.3570 *Piaggio/Aprilia* [2005] OJ C7/5; Commission Decision of 28 April 2005 in Case Comp./M.3680 *Alcatel/Finmeccanica/Alcatel Alenia Space & Telespazio* [2005] OJ C139/37; Commission Decision of 30 March 2005 in Case Comp./M.3686 *Honeywell/Novar* [2005] OJ C104/20; Commission Decision of 25 August 2005 in Case Comp./M.3687 *Johnson&Johnson/Guidant* (not yet pub-lished) (unofficial version only); Commission Decision of 23 May 2005 in Case Comp./M.3770 *Reuters/Telerate* [2005] OJ C154/10; Commission Decision of 4 July 2005 in Case Comp./M.3770 *Lufthansa/Swiss* [2005] OJ C204/3; Commission Decision of 26 April 2006 in Case Comp./M.3916 *T-Mobile Austria/Tele.ring* (not yet published); Commission Decision of 22 December 2005 in Case Comp./M.3940 *Lufthansa/Eurowings* [2006] OJ C18/22; Commission Decision of 19 May 2006 in Case Comp./M.3998 *Axalto/Gemplus* (not yet published); Commission Decision of 14 November 2006 in Case Comp./M.4180 *Gaz*

Commission has expressly provided for the availability of arbitration commitments for monitoring purposes in its revised Notice on Remedies.[68] In the terms of that Notice:

> In order to render them effective, those [ie non-structural] commitments have to contain the procedural requirements necessary for monitoring them, such as the requirement of separate accounts for the infrastructure in order to allow a review of the costs involved, and suitable monitoring devices. Normally, such monitoring has to be done by the market participants themselves, eg by those undertakings wishing to benefit from the commitments. Measures allowing third parties themselves to enforce the commitments *are in particular access to a fast dispute resolution mechanism via arbitration proceedings (together with trustees) or via arbitration proceedings involving national regulatory authorities* if existing for the markets concerned. If the Commission can conclude that the mechanisms foreseen in the commitments will allow the market participants themselves to effectively enforce them in a timely manner, no permanent monitoring of the commitments by the Commission is required. In those cases, an intervention by the Commission would only be necessary in cases *where the parties do not comply with the solutions found by those dispute resolution mechanisms.*[69]

Apart from the Commission, the EU Courts in Luxembourg—both in their official[70] and **29.36** their unofficial capacity[71]—appear to have approved of the use of arbitration commitments

---

de France/Suez (not yet published); Commission Decision of 11 December 2006 in Case Comp./M.4314 *Johnson&Johnson/Pfizer Consumer Healthcare* (not yet published); Commission Decision of 10 May 2007 in Case Comp./M.4381 *JCI/VB/Fiamm* (not yet published); Commission Decision of 8 February 2007 in Case Comp./M.4475 *Schneider Electric/APC* (not yet published); Commission Decision of 20 February 2007 in Case Comp./M.4494 *Evraz/Highfeld* (not yet published); Commission Decision of 18 July 2007 in Case Comp./M.4504 *SFR/Télé 2 France* (not yet published); Commission Decision of 11 November 2007 in Case Comp./M.4691 *Schering-Plough/Organon Biosciences* (not yet published); Commission Decision of 21 September 2007 in Case Comp./M.4730 *Yara/Kemira Growhow* (not yet published); Commission Decision of 6 November 2007 in Case Comp./M.4746 *Deutsche Bahn/English Welsh & Scottish Railway Holdings (EWS)* (not yet published); Commission Decision of 13 December 2007 in Case Comp./M.4779 *Akzo Nobel/ICI* (not yet published); Commission Decision of 30 June 2008 in Case Comp./M/4835 *Hexion/ Huntsman* (not yet published); Commission Decision of 31 October 2007 in Case Comp./M.4842 *Danone/ Numico* (not yet published); Commission Decision of 17 December 2008 in Case Comp./M.5046 *Friesland Foods/Campina* (not yet published); Commission Decision of 9 January 2009 in Case Comp./M.5153 *Arsenal/DSP* (not yet published); Commission Decision of 22 June 2009 in Case Comp./M.5335 *Lufthansa/ SNAH* (not yet published); Commission Decision of 9 January 2009 in Case Comp./M.5364 *Iberia/Vueling/ Clickair* (not yet published); Commission Decision of 28 August 2009 in Case Comp./M.5440 *Lufthansa/ Austrian Airlines* (not yet published); Commission Decision of 22 January 2010 in Case Comp./M.5579 *TLP/ERMEWA* (not yet published); Commission Decision of 17 June 2010 in Case Comp./M.5756 *DFDS/ Norfolk* (not yet published); Commission Decision of 26 January 2011 in Case Comp./M.5984 *INTEL/ McAfee* (not yet published); Commission Decision of 2 March 2011 in Case Comp./M.6095 *Ericsson/Nortel Group (MSS & Global Services)* (not yet published); and Commission Decision of 30 March 2012 in Case Comp./M.6447 *IAG/BMI* (not yet published). For a comprehensive tabular overview covering all relevant Commission decisions up to end of August 2009, see G Blanke, 'Annex II: Table on Conditional EU Merger Clearance Decisions Incorporating Arbitration Commitments over the Period 1992–2009' in G Blanke and P Landolt (eds), *EU and US Antitrust Arbitration: A Handbook for Practitioners* (Kluwer Law International 2011) 1925.

[68] Commission Notice on remedies acceptable under Council Regulation (EC) No 139/2004 and under Commission Regulation (EC) No 802/2004 [2008] OJ C267/1.

[69] Paragraph 66 of the revised Notice on Remedies (emphasis added; original footnotes omitted).

[70] See Judgment of the CFI of 30 September 2003 in Case T-158/00 *ARD v Commission*; and Judgment of the CFI of 4 July 2006 in Case T-177/04 *easyJet Airline Co Ltd v European Commission*.

[71] See the comments by Judge Forwood of the GC, made in his private capacity, in N Forwood, 'Foreword' in G Blanke and P Landolt (eds), *EU and US Antitrust Arbitration: A Handbook for Practitioners* (Kluwer Law International 2011) cvii: 'reliance on regulators alone to enforce competition law rules will never be sufficient. The "private enforcement" of the anti-trust rules has long been the primary enforcement mechanism in the United States, and it is now becoming increasingly crucial in the European Union. Ordinary courts may sometimes provide an effective forum in competition cases where the facts are simple, the remedies sought are conventional, and where the existence of an infringement has been previously determined by the

in the context of EU merger control. Approval has also been received from the Organisation for Economic Co-operation and Development ('OECD') in Paris.[72]

29.37 For the sake of completeness, it should be noted that there are some isolated examples of the Commission's use of arbitration for the monitoring of structural commitments in EU merger control.[73] For the same reasons as behavioural commitments, structural commitments are in this context arbitrable.

4. Arbitrability of questions relating to EU State aids and public undertakings

29.38 Those aspects of questions relating to EU State aids and public undertakings and exclusive or special rights that do not fall within the exclusive prerogative of the Commission have been recognized to be arbitrable.

Questions relating to EU State aids under Articles 107 and 108 TFEU[74]

29.39 Given its directly effective nature, there can be little doubt that Articles 107 and 108 TFEU are arbitrable. On the same basis, an arbitration tribunal is equally competent to apply the Commission Block Exemption Decision on State Aid[75] and the General Block Exemption Regulation declaring certain categories of aid compatible with the internal market.[76]

29.40 Nevertheless, the arbitrability of Articles 107 and 108 TFEU is subject to the Commission's exclusive power to declare the compatibility of individual State aid measures with the EU competition law rules.[77]

---

regulator. But in many situations, in both the EU and the US, arbitrating competition law disputes offers real advantages. It enables the parties to select arbitrators experienced in the law and economics of competition and anti-trust—still regrettably an exception for many national judges. It allows greater procedural flexibility, as well as a less public forum for resolving matters that can be of the greatest commercial sensitivity. Competition law also has as one of its main distinguishing characteristics the fact that the issues requiring resolution frequently concern the present and the future, rather than the past. This is particularly the case when the issues to be resolved arise in the field of merger control, when recourse to arbitration is increasingly considered as a key component of the monitoring mechanisms of non-structural remedies imposed on the merging entities.'

[72] See Report on Remedies in Merger Cases issued by the OECD Competition Committee on 30 July 2012, DAF/COMP(2011)13, available at <http://www.oecd.org/daf/competition/RemediesinMergerCases2011.pdf>, especially at 13 and 25 et seq.

[73] See eg Commission Decision of 8 May 2001 in Case Comp./M.2268 *Pernod Ricard/Diageo/Seagram Spirits* [2002] OJ C16/13; Case Comp./M.1671 *Dow Chemical/Union Carbide*, Commission decision of 3 May 2000 [2001] OJ L245/1); and Case Comp./M/4835 *Hexion/Huntsman*, Commission decision of 30 June 2008 (not yet published). See also G Blanke, *The Use and Utility of International Arbitration in EU Commission Merger Remedies: A Supranational Paradigm in the Making?* (Europa Law Publishing 2006) 59–60.

[74] L Hancher, 'Arbitrating EU State Aid Issues' in G Blanke and P Landolt (eds), *EU and US Antitrust Arbitration: A Handbook for Practitioners* (Kluwer Law International 2011) 965.

[75] Exemption Decision on the application of notifications of Article 86(2) EC [now Article 106(3) TFEU] to state aid in the form of public service compensation.

[76] Commission Regulation (EC) No 800/2008 of 6 August 2008 declaring certain categories of aid compatible with the common market in application of Arts 87 and 88 of the Treaty [now Arts 107 and 108 TFEU] [2008] OJ L241/3. See L Hancher, 'Arbitrating EU State Aid Issues' in G Blanke and P Landolt (eds), *EU and US Antitrust Arbitration: A Handbook for Practitioners* (Kluwer Law International 2011) 965, paras 28-027 and 28-067.

[77] L Hancher, 'Arbitrating EU State Aid Issues' in G Blanke and P Landolt (eds), *EU and US Antitrust Arbitration: A Handbook for Practitioners* (Kluwer Law International 2011) 965, paras 28-028, 28-067, and 28-072.

Questions relating to public undertakings under Article 106 TFEU[78]

In light of its direct effect, Article 106 TFEU may be applied by arbitration tribunals.[79] **29.41**
Questions in relation to Article 106 TFEU will in particular arise as a defence advanced by
a State entity in response to claims for violation of the EU competition law rules. More specifically, it is arguable that the concept of 'public undertaking' within the meaning of Article
106 TFEU has to date been sufficiently developed to allow its application by arbitrators.[80]
Equally, the principles developed by the ECJ in *Altmark*[81] and relevant regulations[82] can be
applied by arbitrators.[83] The State compulsion defence may also be pleaded before an arbitration tribunal.[84]

In addition, ancillary legal arguments under Articles 3(1)(b) TFEU and 4(3) TEU may argu- **29.42**
ably be heard by arbitrators, again enough content having been given to these Treaty provisions over the years to render their application in arbitration proceedings sufficiently precise.[85]

C. The Arbitration Agreement

The arbitration agreement forms the basis of any arbitration procedure: without an arbitra- **29.43**
tion agreement, there can be no arbitration. The scope and construction of this agreement—
provided one does exist—and its enforceability are hence key to the operation of arbitration
generally as well as in the context of EU competition law.

1. Scope and construction

Whether in an individual reference a matter is properly subject to arbitration also depends **29.44**
on the personal scope (*ratione personae*) and the substantive or subject matter scope (*ratione
materiae*) of the underlying arbitration agreement. This, in turn, is dependent on how the
arbitration agreement may be construed literally and in context. The importance of the construction of arbitration agreements in the competition context more specifically has been confirmed by the English High Court in *ET Plus*[86] in the following terms: '[T]here is no realistic

---

[78] PJ Slot, 'Arbitrating Competition-Law-Related Issues under Articles 3(1)(b) TFEU, 4(3) TEU and
106 TFEU' in G Blanke and P Landolt (eds), *EU and US Antitrust Arbitration: A Handbook for Practitioners*
(Kluwer Law International 2011) 1017, paras 29-003 and 29-103.
[79] PJ Slot, 'Arbitrating Competition-Law-Related Issues under Articles 3(1)(b) TFEU, 4(3) TEU and
106 TFEU' in G Blanke and P Landolt (eds), *EU and US Antitrust Arbitration: A Handbook for Practitioners*
(Kluwer Law International 2011) 1017, paras 29-083–29-085, including a discussion about potential reservations about but ultimately confirming the arbitrability of Article 106(2) TFEU.
[80] PJ Slot, 'Arbitrating Competition-Law-Related Issues under Articles 3(1)(b) TFEU, 4(3) TEU and
106 TFEU' in G Blanke and P Landolt (eds), *EU and US Antitrust Arbitration: A Handbook for Practitioners*
(Kluwer Law International 2011) 1017, para 29-019.
[81] Case C-280/00 *Altmark Trans v Regierungspräsidium Magdeburg* [2003] ECR I-7747.
[82] For further details, see Part III of this book.
[83] PJ Slot, 'Arbitrating Competition-Law-Related Issues under Articles 3(1)(b) TFEU, 4(3) TEU and
106 TFEU' in G Blanke and P Landolt (eds), *EU and US Antitrust Arbitration: A Handbook for Practitioners*
(Kluwer Law International 2011) 1017, para 29-068.
[84] PJ Slot, 'Arbitrating Competition-Law-Related Issues under Articles 3(1)(b) TFEU, 4(3) TEU and
106 TFEU' in G Blanke and P Landolt (eds), *EU and US Antitrust Arbitration: A Handbook for Practitioners*
(Kluwer Law International 2011) 1017, para 29-098.
[85] PJ Slot, 'Arbitrating Competition-Law-Related Issues under Articles 3(1)(b) TFEU, 4(3) TEU and
106 TFEU' in G Blanke and P Landolt (eds), *EU and US Antitrust Arbitration: A Handbook for Practitioners*
(Kluwer Law International 2011) 1017, para 29-037.
[86] *ET Plus SA v Welters* [2005] EWHC 2115 (Comm). For comment, see G Blanke, 'Arbitrating
Competition Disputes: The English High Court has Confirmed that EC Competition Law Claims are
Arbitrable in Principle' (November 2005) 29 Competition Law Insight 5; and R Merkin (April 2006) 6(4)
Arbitration Law Monthly 1.

doubt that such "competition" or "antitrust" claims are arbitrable: the matter is whether they come within the scope of the arbitration clause, as a matter of its true construction.'[87]

29.45 *Ratione personae*, only parties to an arbitration agreement can usually be made subject to arbitration. This also generally applies to ordinary EU competition arbitrations. As regards EU commitment arbitrations, however, these usually contain *erga omnes* offers to arbitrate, which are unilaterally binding on the merged entity or on the party subject to an Article 9 commitment decision only and can optionally be accepted by the third-party beneficiary. To the extent that the third-party beneficiary is not subject to an arbitration *obligation* and is at liberty to exercise an arbitration *option*, EU commitment arbitrations constitute 'arbitration without privity'. However, the third-party beneficiary may become properly bound by an arbitration agreement in a variety of ways which will be discussed further later in this chapter.[88]

29.46 *Ratione materiae*, arbitration agreements are nowadays interpreted to be sufficiently wide in scope to cover both contractual and tortious causes of action.[89] Thus, standard arbitration agreements whereby 'any dispute relating to/arising from this agreement shall be referred to arbitration' are generally regarded as wide enough to accommodate tortious claims that are closely related to the underlying main agreement and hence any contractual claim that may be articulated in relation to it.[90]

29.47 Finally, arbitration agreements are generally considered separable from the underlying main agreement.[91] This allows the arbitrator to retain jurisdiction to determine the illegality *vel non* of the main agreement pursuant to Article 101 TFEU, for example.[92]

2. Enforceability

29.48 In order to ensure the enforcement of arbitration agreements, some jurisdictions offer so-called anti-suit injunctions to estop a party from bringing an action before the courts that—pursuant to the terms of a pre-existing arbitration clause—should be brought before an arbitration tribunal. Importantly, since the ECJ's ruling in *West Tankers*,[93] such anti-suit injunctions are no longer available from EU Member State courts against other Member State courts first seized within the meaning of the Brussels Regulation.[94] In other words, where EU competition claims are brought by a party before a Member State court in violation of an

---

[87] *ET Plus SA v Welters* [2005] EWHC 2115 (Comm), at para 51.

[88] See para 29.94.

[89] For an outmoded approach to the reading of the genuine scope of arbitration clauses, drawing artificial distinctions between disputes 'concerning', 'relating to', 'arising out of' etc, with some permitting contractual and others contractual and tortious claims, see J-F Poudret and S Besson, *Comparative Law of International Arbitration* (Sweet & Maxwell 2007) paras 306–7. For recent developments in English law in favour of the wider reading of arbitration clauses, see G Blanke, R Nazzini, A Nikpay, and V Smith, 'England and Wales' in G Blanke and R Nazzini (eds), *International Competition Litigation: A Multi-jurisdictional Handbook* (Kluwer Law International 2012).

[90] G Blanke, 'EC Competition Law Claims in International Arbitration' in C Klausegger et al (eds), *Austrian Arbitration Yearbook 2009* (Manz/Stämpfli/Beck 2009) 3, at 24 et seq.

[91] See eg ICC Award No 6503; and ICC Award No 7097.

[92] See G Blanke, 'EC Competition Law Claims in International Arbitration' in C Klausegger et al (eds), *Austrian Arbitration Yearbook 2009* (Manz/Stämpfli/Beck 2009) 3, at 26.

[93] Judgment of the ECJ of 10 February 2009 in Case C-185/07 *Allianz SpA (formerly Riunione Adriatica Di Sicurta SpA) and Others v West Tankers Inc* [2009] ECR I-663.

[94] Council Regulation (EC) No 44/2001 of 22 December 2000 on jurisdiction and the recognition and enforcement of judgments in civil and commercial matters [2001] OJ L12/1 (formerly the Brussels Convention, ie the Convention of 27 September 1968 on Jurisdiction and the Enforcement of Judgments in Civil and Commercial Matters), which is applicable to all EU Member States (following subsequent amendments to reflect the accession of Denmark and the enlargement of the EU to twenty-eight Member States). See in particular the impact on the English courts that had developed a reputation for granting anti-suit

arbitration agreement, the opposing party will no longer be able to rely upon the existence of that arbitration agreement in order to obtain an anti-suit injunction.[95] Other remedies, however, may be available in the alternative, such as a request for an anti-suit injunction to be granted by the arbitration tribunal itself.[96]

In the context of EU commitment arbitrations more specifically, it is worth emphasizing   **29.49** that a Member State court first seized within the meaning of the Brussels Regulation will have to pay deference to the direct effect and hence binding nature of the underlying EU merger clearance decision or the commitment decision before the court and give precedence to the arbitration commitment[97] at the risk of incurring State liability in the event of non-compliance.[98] That said, the arbitration commitment in any event qualifies as an 'obligation',[99] which is enforceable before the Commission on pain of the usual fines and penalties and the possible dismantlement of an already-consumed merger under the Merger Control Regulation[100] or the withdrawal and subsequent substitution of an Article 9 with an Article 7 commitment decision under Regulation 1/2003. For the avoidance of doubt, prior to resorting to any of the more draconian measures, the Commission will—in the first instance—be likely to engage in its own investigations as to whether a party has defaulted on the arbitration commitment.

Finally, arbitration provisions that are in and of themselves in violation of EU competition   **29.50** law, eg that seek the enforcement of a cartel in violation of Article 101 TFEU, will be unenforceable before the EU Member State courts.[101] In this context, it is important to note that contracting parties may not contract out of the application of otherwise applicable EU competition laws. As a result, an arbitration clause whereby the contracting parties seek to exclude the application of EU competition law from the resolution of a dispute between them will per se be null and void *ab initio* and as such unenforceable, unless the carve-out is intended to provide, to the extent possible, for the resolution of any competition law issues before an alternative forum, such as an EU Member State court or a mediator.[102]

III. Ordinary EU Competition Arbitrations[103]

As stated previously, 'ordinary EU competition arbitrations' are those arbitrations that arise   **29.51** from a *principal* claim of illegality or abuse of dominance under Articles 101 or 102 TFEU

---

injunctions in like circumstances: G Blanke, 'The Application of EU Law to Arbitration in England' in J Lew, H Bor, G Fullelove, and J Greenaway, *Arbitration in England* (forthcoming 2013).

[95] See also R Nazzini, 'Parallel Proceedings before the Tribunal and the Courts/Competition Authorities' in G Blanke and P Landolt (eds), *EU and US Antitrust Arbitration: A Handbook for Practitioners* (Kluwer Law International 2011) 881, paras 25-027–25.029.

[96] For a range of alternatives available within the context of (EU competition) arbitration in the UK, see G Blanke, 'The Application of EU Law to Arbitration in England' in J Lew, H Bor, G Fullelove, and J Greenaway, *Arbitration in England* (forthcoming 2013).

[97] On the direct effectiveness of the arbitration commitment, see para 29.93.

[98] On which see paras 29.90–29.91.

[99] Within the meaning of para 12 of the Notice on Remedies (now para 19 of the revised Notice on Remedies).

[100] See Ch 2 'The Role of National Judicial Authorities', para 2.17 et seq.

[101] G Blanke, 'Antitrust Arbitration under the ICC Rules' in G Blanke and P Landolt (eds), *EU and US Antitrust Arbitration: A Handbook for Practitioners* (Kluwer Law International 2011) pp 1763–898, paras 49-071 and 49-096.

[102] See G Blanke and R Nazzini, 'Arbitration and ADR of Global Antitrust Disputes: Taking Stock (Part I)' (2008) 1(1) GCLR 46.

[103] For the main specialist texts, see P Landolt, *Modernised EC Competition Law in International Arbitration* (Kluwer Law International 2006); K Hilbig, *Das gemeinschaftsrechtliche Kartellverbot im internationalen*

or that arise *incidentally* (as a defence or otherwise) from claims of breach of contract in a(n) (international) commercial arbitration.

A. Scope of Ordinary EU Competition Arbitrations

29.52 The scope of EU competition arbitrations depends on the breadth *ratione materiae* of the underlying arbitration clause. Provided that the arbitration clause adopts standard wording, it will usually be wide enough to cover both contractual claims under Article 101 TFEU and tortious claims for abuse of dominance under Article 102 TFEU. This has been discussed in detail elsewhere in this chapter[104] and will be further discussed in some further detail later.[105] Suffice it to add here that many of the claims brought—whether principal or incidental— arise from joint venture, technology licensing, supply, and distribution agreements.

B. The Arbitrator's Mandate

29.53 The arbitrator's mandate together with the arbitration clause lies at the heart of any arbitration procedure. Taken together, they form the contractual basis for the arbitrator's services and set out more specifically the ambit of the arbitrator's jurisdiction and his/her procedural powers in the individual reference before him/her. Importantly, in the competition law context more specifically, to the extent that the arbitrator's mandate expressly excises from the arbitrator's jurisdiction the consideration of certain EU competition law issues which—if properly considered—would result in a declaration of voidness and hence the nullification of the underlying main agreement, that mandate may be affected by illegality in violation of Article 101 TFEU in and of itself and thus be void *ab initio*. Whether this is truly so in practice depends, of course, on whether in the individual reference, the contracting parties have chosen an alternative forum for the determination of the EU competition law issues and whether these are genuinely separable from those issues that have properly been submitted for determination by the arbitrator. If not, failure to submit these may invalidate the arbitrator's mandate and in fact the entire reference.[106]

29.54 It should be noted that by analogy to the jurisdiction of the EU Member State courts, it is the arbitrator's mandate to draw the civil law consequences from a party's infringement of relevant EU competition law provisions. By contrast, the Commission is responsible for the sanctioning of the infringing party by reference to the available public law remedies. In this sense, the arbitrator's and the Commission's mandates in EU competition law are complementary.

1. Basis for the application of EU competition law

29.55 There are a variety of grounds for the application of EU competition law in arbitration. Most commonly, an arbitrator will be able to rely upon the principles of direct effect and

---

Handelsschiedsverfahren: Anwendung und gerichtliche Kontrolle (Beck 2006); T Zuberbühler and C Oetiker (eds), *Practical Aspects of Arbitrating EC Competition Law* (Schulthess 2007); G Blanke (ed), 'Arbitrating Competition Law Issues: A European and a US Perspective' (2008) 19(1) EBLR Special Edition; and G Blanke and P Landolt (eds), *EU and US Antitrust Arbitration: A Handbook for Practitioners*, Vols 1 & 2 (Kluwer Law International 2011). For an insight into EU competition arbitration from a global perspective, see the various country reports in G Blanke and R Nazzini (eds), *International Competition Litigation: A Multi-jurisdictional Handbook* (Kluwer Law International 2012).

[104] See para 29.44 et seq.
[105] See para 29.63 et seq.
[106] G Blanke and R Nazzini, 'Arbitration and ADR of Global Antitrust Disputes: Taking Stock (Part I)' (2008) 1(1) GCLR 46.

supremacy, the combined effect of which makes Articles 101 and 102 TFEU, as well as a number of block exemption regulations,[107] directly applicable as part of the law of the land in any EU Member State. In other words, where the *lex contractus*, ie the law on the merits or the law governing the main agreement, is the law of one of the EU Member States, EU competition law may be invoked by the arbitrator or any of the parties merely by reference to that law. This is supplemented by the extraterritorial application of EU competition law and, more specifically, the effects doctrine, whereby the application of EU competition law is motivated by the effects produced by an infringing agreement or violating behaviour within the internal market from outside. On occasion, tribunals may also invoke some conflicts of laws rules to ground the application of EU competition law, although recourse to classical conflicts of laws rules is by definition rare in international arbitration due to its delocalized nature: To date, this has mostly been the case in arbitration references governed by Swiss law with a seat in Switzerland.[108] Finally, tribunals may rely upon their widely recognized best-efforts commitment to render an enforceable award as well as the public policy nature of EU competition law as grounds for the application of the EU competition law rules in references before them.[109] Last but not least, all these grounds may apply cumulatively.[110]

Nevertheless, the actual application of EU competition law in an individual reference ultimately depends on whether the individual threshold criteria of the applicability of EU competition law have been met on a case-by-case basis. **29.56**

2. Investigations by the arbitrator

Generally speaking, arbitrators base their awards on the pleadings—both oral and written—made by the parties over the course of an arbitration. This also implies that the burden of education rests on the arbitrating parties. The arbitrator is hence not permitted to substitute any of the parties in identifying legal arguments that have not been advanced by and may support either of the parties' cases. **29.57**

That said, under some arbitration laws, arbitrators are expressly entitled to engage in fact-finding activities.[111] Such entitlement may in particular serve an arbitrator's *ex officio* duty to raise and decide EU competition law issues in references before him/her. In other words, an arbitrator may use investigative powers invested in him/her by the applicable arbitration laws in order to seek clarification of the facts pleaded by the parties with a view to ascertaining the need to raise with them questions of illegality and voidness or an abuse of dominance under Articles 101 and 102 TFEU. **29.58**

In the final analysis, the extent of an arbitrator's *ex officio* investigations will depend on the applicable arbitration law and on the intensity of supervisory court review at the place of arbitration (where the resultant award may be challenged by the debtor party) or at the prospective place of enforcement.[112] **29.59**

---

[107] See eg ICC Award No 7181; ICC Award No 8626; and ICC Award No 10246.

[108] eg ICC Award No 6858.

[109] For further detail, see para 29.70.

[110] For ICC practice, see G Blanke, 'Antitrust Arbitration under the ICC Rules' in G Blanke and P Landolt (eds), *EU and US Antitrust Arbitration: A Handbook for Practitioners* (Kluwer Law International 2011) 1763, paras 49-065–49-088. For alternative (further) grounds, see also 'Arbitration and Competition Law: The Position of the Courts and of Arbitrators', note by Prof L Radicati di Brozolo in OECD Report on Competition and Arbitration, DAF/COMP(2010)40, available at <http://search.oecd.org/officialdocuments/displaydocumentpdf/?cote=DAF/COMP(2010)40&docLanguage=En>, 31 at 44 et seq.

[111] For the English example in particular, see section 34 of the Arbitration Act 1996.

[112] See G Blanke, 'EC Competition Law Claims in International Arbitration' in C Klausegger et al (eds), *Austrian Arbitration Yearbook 2009* (Manz/Stämpfli/Beck 2009) 3, 74.

3. Production of evidence

29.60 In EU competition arbitration—as is the case in competition law disputes more generally—each party has the burden of proving its own case. This is clearly so in accordance with the terms of Regulation 1/2003,[113] which—being directly effective—arguably have to be applied in material part by arbitration tribunals in references before them.[114]

29.61 As is the case in litigation, it is commonplace in EU competition arbitration that all evidence to prove discrete competition infringements is in the possession of the perpetrator. To compensate for such evidentiary imbalance between the parties, arbitration has developed a number of mechanisms that seek to redress that imbalance in favour of the purported victim of an EU competition law infringement. These include mechanisms like the *prima facie* evidence rule[115] and the reversal of the burden of proof. In addition, under the widely used International Bar Association ('IBA') Rules on the Taking of Evidence in International Arbitration,[116] an arbitrator remains free to draw adverse inferences from the non-production of a document that has clearly been found to be or that must be in the possession of the opposing party. In a final instance, an arbitration tribunal may also rely for disclosure upon the supportive functions of the EU Member State courts under the prevailing arbitration laws at the place of arbitration.[117]

4. The arbitrator's decision-making powers

29.62 The arbitrator's decision-making powers in ordinary EU competition arbitrations include powers to award declaratory relief and powers to award other civil law remedies. For the avoidance of doubt, an arbitrator lacks powers to award public law remedies, such as fines and penalties, which are the exclusive preserve of the Commission or the Member State NCAs, as the case may be.

Powers to award declaratory relief

29.63 In light of the principle of *kompetenz-kompetenz*, which empowers an arbitral tribunal to decide upon its own jurisdiction in accordance with the governing arbitration law, an arbitrator seized of an EU competition law issue will be entitled to determine as a preliminary matter whether that issue falls within his/her proper jurisdiction. This, in turn, is essentially a question of the scope and construction of the underlying arbitration agreement, which has been discussed in detail at Part II Section C.1 of this chapter.

29.64 Provided the EU competition issue falls within his/her proper jurisdiction, the arbitrator has the power to award various forms of declaratory relief depending on whether the claims before him/her are for illegality for breach of contract under Article 101 TFEU or for abuse of dominance under Article 102 TFEU. As regards claims for illegality under Article 101 TFEU, the arbitrator has, in particular, a power to declare:

- that the main contract is null and void pursuant to Article 101(2) TFEU;
- that the purportedly infringing main contract does not in fact violate Article 101(1) TFEU at all and is hence not null and void under Article 101(2) TFEU;
- that the agreement subject to the arbitration is block-exempted; or

---

[113] See Art 2 of Reg 1/2003 on the allocation of burden of proof in EU competition cases.

[114] See G Blanke, 'EC Competition Law Claims in International Arbitration' in C Klausegger et al (eds), *Austrian Arbitration Yearbook 2009* (Manz/Stämpfli/Beck 2009) 3, 74.

[115] M Blessing, *Arbitrating Antitrust and Merger Control Issues* (Helbing & Lichtenhahn 2003).

[116] Article 9(5) of the IBA Rules in their latest version, which entered into effect on 29 May 2010.

[117] See eg the potential assistance of the English courts pursuant to section 44 of the Arbitration Act 1996; and G Blanke, 'Antitrust Arbitration under the Arbitration Act 1996: A Commentary' (2011) 22(2) EBLR 119, at 145.

- that the legal exception applies pursuant to Article 101(3) TFEU and that the agreement subject to the arbitration is hence not null and void within the meaning of Article 102(2) TFEU.[118]

As regards claims for abuse of dominance under Article 102 TFEU, the arbitrator has, in particular, a power to declare that a party has a dominant position and that an abuse of dominance has occurred.[119]

Powers to award other civil law remedies

In addition to the various powers to award declaratory relief, the arbitrator is empowered to **29.65** award other civil law remedies, including, in particular, the following:[120]

- *Specific performance*—The arbitrator may order specific performance of the main agreement once he/she has found against an infringement of Article 101 TFEU or that entry into the agreement does not constitute an abuse of dominance within the meaning of Article 102 TFEU.
- *Amendments/modifications to the main agreement*—The arbitrator may propose amendments and modifications to the purportedly infringing agreement to make it compliant with Article 101(1) TFEU or with the legal exception criteria set out in Article 101(3) TFEU.
- *Compensatory damages*—The arbitrator may award damages caused by a competition law infringement under the doctrine developed by the ECJ in *Courage*[121] and *Manfredi*;[122] issues of causation and the measure of damages, however, are determined by reference to the applicable substantive law, subject to the principles of equivalence and effectiveness (together referred to as the principle of procedural autonomy) within the meaning of the ECJ's jurisprudence in *Courage* and *Manfredi*. This said, the claimant's contributory negligence and unjust enrichment will be taken into account in the calculation of the overall damages recoverable by the claimant, depending—*inter alia*—on the claimant's individual commercial power and the respondent's commercial standing. Finally, arbitrators—unlike a number of EU Member State courts[123]—are prone to award compound interest.[124]
- *Extra-compensatory damages*—By analogy to the award of compensatory damages, the arbitrator may award extra-compensatory damages for EU competition law infringements, again subject to the principle of procedural autonomy as applied in the ECJ's ruling in *Manfredi*. As a result, the exact level of extra-compensatory damages recoverable at the national level may vary from EU Member State to EU Member State depending on their specific nature.

---

[118] G Blanke, 'EC Competition Law Claims in International Arbitration' in C Klausegger et al (eds), *Austrian Arbitration Yearbook 2009* (Manz/Stämpfli/Beck 2009) 3, 67–8.

[119] G Blanke, 'EC Competition Law Claims in International Arbitration' in C Klausegger et al (eds), *Austrian Arbitration Yearbook 2009* (Manz/Stämpfli/Beck 2009) 3, 67–8.

[120] G Blanke, 'EC Competition Law Claims in International Arbitration' in C Klausegger et al (eds), *Austrian Arbitration Yearbook 2009* (Manz/Stämpfli/Beck 2009) 3, 68 et seq; and P Landolt, 'Remedies in Arbitration for EU Competition Law Violations' in G Blanke and P Landolt (eds), *EU and US Antitrust Arbitration: A Handbook for Practitioners* (Kluwer Law International 2011) pp 627–48.

[121] Judgment of the ECJ of 20 September 2001 in Case C-453/99 *Courage Ltd v Bernard Crehan* [2001] ECR I-6297.

[122] Judgment of the ECJ of 13 July 2006 in Joined Cases C-295/04 to C-298/04 *Vincenzo Manfredi v Lloyd Adriatico Assicurazioni SpA, Antonio Cannito v Fondiaria Sai SpA, and Nicolò Tricarico, Pasqualina Murgolo v Assitalia SpA* [2006] ECR I-6619.

[123] For the English example, see G Blanke, 'Antitrust Arbitration under the Arbitration Act 1996: A Commentary' (2011) 22(2) EBLR 119, at 142.

[124] G Blanke, 'EC Competition Law Claims in International Arbitration' in C Klausegger et al (eds), *Austrian Arbitration Yearbook 2009* (Manz/Stämpfli/Beck 2009) 3, 71.

- *Injunctions*—The arbitrator may also pronounce various forms of injunctions, whether mandatory or prohibitory, to the extent that such measures of relief are available means of redress under the applicable substantive law.[125]

5. The arbitrator's potential liability

29.66 To the extent that the arbitrator ignores relevant EU competition law issues which—if properly considered—would result in a declaration of voidness and the nullification of the underlying main agreement, an arbitrator might exceptionally become liable for breach of Article 101 TFEU. This is because the arbitrator might be found to constitute an 'undertaking' within the meaning of EU competition law. This may particularly be the case where the arbitrator has consciously (and possibly willingly) contributed to and thus become complicit in the enforcement of a cartel in conspicuous violation of the EU competition law rules. Even though there has, to date, been no precedent of a finding of liability by the Commission to that effect, instructive analogies can be drawn from the *Treuhand* case,[126] in which the Commission found that the Swiss consultancy company AC Treuhand played a key role in the cartel, organizing meetings, often in Zurich, producing papers with the agreed market shares which could not be taken outside AC Treuhand's premises, and reimbursing the travel expenses of participants to avoid leaving any traces about the illegal meetings. As a consequence, AC Treuhand was found to have infringed then Article 81 EC (now 101 TFEU).[127]

29.67 In addition, in similar terms, an arbitrator's criminal liability might arguably be engaged for breach of EU competition law under relevant applicable Member State laws.[128]

29.68 To avoid any form of liability, once aware of the EU competition law issues and the parties' reluctance to submit these to the reference before him/her, an arbitrator may withdraw from his/her mandate[129] or alternatively render an award that contains a provision to the effect that the award will become only final and binding once the parties have advised the tribunal of the outcome of either court or other proceedings on the identified EU competition law issues subject to a reservation by the Tribunal to amend the award taking account of that outcome.[130]

C. Procedural Conduct of EU Competition Arbitrations

29.69 In the light of the special features of the arbitrator's mandate in EU competition arbitration as already outlined, the conduct of EU competition arbitrations is subject to a number of

---

[125] For an English example, see *LauritzenCool AB v Lady Navigation Inc* [2004] EWHC 2607 (Comm), affirmed by *LauritzenCool AB v Lady Navigation Inc* [2995] EWCA Civ 579; and G Blanke, 'Antitrust Arbitration under the Arbitration Act 1996: A Commentary' (2011) 22(2) EBLR 119, at 145–6.

[126] The Commission only imposed a token fine of EUR 1,000 on the company in question because of the novelty of the approach. See Case COMP/E-2/37.857– *Organic Peroxides* [2005] OJ L110/44, affirmed by the Judgment of the CFI of 8 July 2008 in Case T-99/04 *AC-Treuhand AG v Commission of the European Communities*.

[127] G Blanke and R Nazzini, 'Arbitration and ADR of Global Antitrust Disputes: Taking Stock (Part III)' (2008) 1(3) GCLR 133–5.

[128] For the situation in England under the Enterprise Act 2002, see G Blanke, 'The Application of EU Law to Arbitration in England' in J Lew, H Bor, G Fullelove, and J Greenaway, *Arbitration in England* (forthcoming 2013). Also P Heitzmann, 'Arbitration and Criminal Liability for Competition Law Violations in Europe' in G Blanke and P Landolt (eds), *EU and US Antitrust Arbitration: A Handbook for Practitioners* (Kluwer Law International 2011) 1251–92.

[129] For the situation in England under the Arbitration Act 1996, see G Blanke, 'Antitrust Arbitration under the Arbitration Act 1996: A Commentary' (2011) 22(2) EBLR 119, at 137–8.

[130] R von Mehren, 'The Eco-Swiss Case and International Arbitration' (2003) 19 Arb Int 464, 465. See also G Blanke, 'EC Competition Law Claims in International Arbitration' in C Klausegger et al (eds), *Austrian Arbitration Yearbook 2009* (Manz/Stämpfli/Beck 2009) 3, 55–6.

procedural requirements that diverge from the procedural standards applicable to ordinary commercial arbitration.

1. The arbitrator's *ex officio* duty to raise competition law issues[131]

It has been demonstrated that in EU competition arbitration, the arbitrator is under an **29.70** implicit duty to raise EU competition law issues *ex officio* in order to ensure the enforceability of the resultant award.[132] Such duty is based on the arbitrator's widely recognized best efforts commitment to render an enforceable award[133] and on the recognition of the EU competition rules as forming part of the public policy concept under the New York Convention.[134] Importantly, before deciding on any EU competition law matters on which the arbitrator believes that the parties before him/her have remained silent, he/she will have to submit these for comments to the parties in accordance with overarching rules of due process and, in particular, the parties' right to a fair hearing as well as to avoid challenges of a resultant award on grounds of being *extra petita* under Article V(1)(c) of the New York Convention.[135] Importantly, a requirement to resolve a dispute *ex aequo et bono*, ie on the basis of equity or without being bound by the application of any (particular) laws, does not absolve the arbitrator[136] from his/her obligation to consider the application of EU competition law.[137]

The arbitrator's *ex officio* duty to raise EU competition law issues is also well established in **29.71** ICC practice.[138]

2. The status of previous EU Commission or NCA decisions[139]

The status of previous EU Commission and NCA decisions is of particular importance in **29.72** 'follow-on' arbitrations, ie arbitrations that deal with follow-on damages.[140] Even though there is no legislative text that binds a tribunal to accept a previous decision on liability on the same subject matter between the same parties in a claim for damages before it, the tribunal will take that previous decision into account as a matter of evidence. In light of the fact that EU Member State courts—in their supervisory capacity in enforcement and setting aside proceedings—are bound by the *Masterfoods*[141] decision and hence have to give priority to any previous Commission decision on an identical subject matter between the same

---

[131] D de Groot, 'The Ex Officio Application of European Competition Law by Arbitrators' in G Blanke and P Landolt (eds), *EU and US Antitrust Arbitration: A Handbook for Practitioners* (Kluwer Law International 2011) 567–625; and G Blanke and R Nazzini, 'Arbitration and ADR of Global Antitrust Disputes: Taking Stock (Part II)' (2008) 1(2) GCLR 78–89.

[132] G Blanke, 'The Role of EC Competition Law in International Arbitration: A Plaidoyer' (2005) 16(1) EBLR 169–80.

[133] See eg Art 35 of the ICC Rules.

[134] On which see para 29.83.

[135] G Blanke, 'EC Competition Law Claims in International Arbitration' in C Klausegger et al (eds), *Austrian Arbitration Yearbook 2009* (Manz/Stämpfli/Beck 2009) 3, at 42–3.

[136] Nor the parties.

[137] Judgment of the ECJ of 27 April 1994 in Case C-393/92 *Municipality of Almelo v Energiebedriff-Jellemij* [1994] ECR I-1477.

[138] eg ICC Award No 7539. See G Blanke, 'Antitrust Arbitration under the ICC Rules' in G Blanke and P Landolt (eds), *EU and US Antitrust Arbitration: A Handbook for Practitioners* (Kluwer Law International 2011) 1763, paras 49-089–49-091; and K Hilbig, *Das gemeinschaftsrechtliche Kartellverbot im internationalen Handelsschiedsverfahren: Anwendung und gerichtliche Kontrolle* (Beck 2006) 137 et seq.

[139] R Nazzini, *Concurrent Proceedings in Competition Law: Procedure, Evidence and Remedies* (Oxford University Press 2004); and R Nazzini, 'Authority and Influence in Arbitrations of Previous Decisions on EU Competition Law' in G Blanke and P Landolt (eds), *EU and US Antitrust Arbitration: A Handbook for Practitioners* (Kluwer Law International 2011) 699.

[140] On follow-on damages actions in EU context more specifically, see Ch 2 'National Judicial Authorities', para 2.08. See also G Blanke, 'EC Competition Law Claims in International Arbitration' in C Klausegger et al (eds), *Austrian Arbitration Yearbook 2009* (Manz/Stämpfli/Beck 2009) 3, at 57–9.

[141] Case C-344/98 *Masterfoods Ltd v H.B. Ice Cream Ltd* [2000] ECR I-11369, para 52.

parties over any contrary arbitration award (that does not comply with the terms of that Commission decision), a tribunal will have to give full effect to it in the evidentiary process in order to ensure the enforceability of its award. Like an EU Member State court, unless new facts that have not previously (and could have) been pleaded come to light that may change the outcome of the case, in follow-on arbitrations, a tribunal will rely on the liability found by the Commission in its decision as a proven point and only hear evidence on the necessary causal link between the established competition infringement and the damages claimed as well as quantum.

29.73   The same is, of course, equally true outside the context of strict follow-on arbitrations where a previous Commission decision has compelling evidentiary value on the basis of its factual similarities with the reference to arbitration and may therefore strongly influence the decision-making of an EU Member State supervisory court in enforcement proceedings.[142] By virtue of the principles of direct effect, supremacy, and loyal (or sincere) cooperation, a Member State court is arguably estopped from enforcing an award that runs counter to a previous Commission decision.[143]

29.74   Analogical considerations apply in the context of previous NCA decisions,[144] subject to the precise legal status of the relevant NCA decisions under consideration.[145]

3. The status of parallel proceedings[146]

29.75   Parallel proceedings in EU competition law are generally permissible to the extent that they are complementary. This is in particular the case where proceedings before the competent competition authorities, including the Commission and relevant NCAs, are complemented by private enforcement actions before an arbitration tribunal or a competent EU Member State court.

29.76   Nevertheless, where the same EU competition law claims between the same parties are brought before competing jurisdictions, such as an arbitration tribunal and a Member State court, the question arises as to whether either the court or the tribunal should stay their proceedings whilst the action before the competing jurisdiction is pending.[147] As discussed previously, anti-suit injunctions in favour of arbitration proceedings are nowadays of limited

---

[142]   For an example, see *Repsol/Arco*.

[143]   G Blanke, 'EC Competition Law Claims in International Arbitration' in C Klausegger et al (eds), *Austrian Arbitration Yearbook 2009* (Manz/Stämpfli/Beck 2009) 3, 59.

[144]   For the English example, see G Blanke, 'The Application of EU Law to Arbitration in England' in J Lew, H Bor, G Fullelove, and J Greenaway, *Arbitration in England* (forthcoming 2013). For a full typology of decisions adopted by Member State competition authorities and their impact on concurrent or subsequent arbitration proceedings, see R Nazzini, 'Authority and Influence in Arbitrations of Previous Decisions on EU Competition Law' in G Blanke and P Landolt (eds), *EU and US Antitrust Arbitration: A Handbook for Practitioners* (Kluwer Law International 2011) 699.

[145]   For further detail, see Laurence Idot, according to whom, for example, decisions of the French Competition Authority are not legally binding on the French courts and therefore can only have persuasive evidentiary force: 'Arbitration and Competition', note by Prof L Idot in OECD Report on Competition and Arbitration, DAF/COMP(2010)40, available at <http://search.oecd.org/officialdocuments/displaydocumentpdf/?cote=DAF/COMP(2010)40&docLanguage=En>, 51, at 71.

[146]   R Nazzini, *Concurrent Proceedings in Competition Law: Procedure, Evidence and Remedies* (Oxford University Press 2004); and R Nazzini, 'Parallel Proceedings before the Tribunal and the Courts/Competition Authorities' in G Blanke and P Landolt (eds), *EU and US Antitrust Arbitration: A Handbook for Practitioners* (Kluwer Law International 2011) 881.

[147]   For an instructive example, see the English High Court's approach in *ET Plus SA v Welters* [2005] EWHC 2115 (Comm), where it stayed proceedings in favour of an ICC arbitration in relation to the same EU competition law claims. See G Blanke, 'The Application of EU Law to Arbitration in England' in J Lew, H Bor, G Fullelove, and J Greenaway, *Arbitration in England* (forthcoming 2013); and G Blanke, R Nazzini, A Nikpay, and V Smith, 'England and Wales' in G Blanke and R Nazzini (eds), *International Competition Litigation: A Multi-jurisdictional Handbook* (Kluwer Law International 2012).

availability.[148] Accordingly, the parties will have to rely upon alternative mechanisms to ensure the proper enforcement of a promise to arbitrate.[149]

In addition, in order to ensure the enforceability of a prospective award, a stay of arbitration **29.77** proceedings may be desirable to await the outcome of a Commission decision on the same or similar subject matter,[150] unless the situation is one of '*acte clair*'.[151]

Analogical considerations arguably apply in the context of parallel proceedings before an NCA.[152] **29.78**

4. The arbitrator's cooperation with the EU Commission and/or the competent NCA

It is common ground that arbitration tribunals are not authorized to make preliminary refer- **29.79** ences to the ECJ pursuant to Article 267 TFEU.[153] This means that in complex, unresolved legal questions of EU competition law that require interpretation by the ECJ, tribunals may not avail themselves of the preliminary reference procedure. Equally, given their silence on the subject matter, the formal mechanisms of cooperation between the Commission and the EU Member State courts provided for under Regulation 1/2003 and the National Courts Cooperation Notice[154] are not officially applicable to the cooperation between tribunals and the Commission.[155]

With this in mind, in EU competition arbitration more specifically, tribunals have identified **29.80** viable alternatives to compensate for the inaccessibility of the ECJ and the unavailability of formal means of cooperation. Apart from indirect preliminary references, which may be of assistance in some EU jurisdictions,[156] requests for interpretation by the EU Commission and possibly other competent authorities, such as NCAs, in relation to discrete EU competition law issues may be available. Other means of cooperation, such as requests for information

---

[148] Para 29.48.

[149] G Blanke, R Nazzini, A Nikpay, and V Smith, 'England and Wales' in G Blanke and R Nazzini (eds), *International Competition Litigation: A Multi-jurisdictional Handbook* (Kluwer Law International 2012).

[150] See eg the English High Court's approach in its *obiter dictum* in *LauritzenCool AB v Lady Navigation Inc* [2004] EWHC 2607 (Comm). See G Blanke, 'The Application of EU Law to Arbitration in England' in J Lew, H Bor, G Fullelove, and J Greenaway, *Arbitration in England* (forthcoming 2013).

[151] G Blanke, 'EC Competition Law Claims in International Arbitration' in C Klausegger et al (eds), *Austrian Arbitration Yearbook 2009* (Manz/Stämpfli/Beck 2009) 3, at 61.

[152] On parallel proceedings before the OFT and the Competition Appeal Tribunal ('CAT'), see G Blanke, 'The Application of EU Law to Arbitration in England' in J Lew, H Bor, G Fullelove, and J Greenaway, *Arbitration in England* (forthcoming 2013); G Blanke, R Nazzini, A Nikpay, and V Smith, 'England and Wales' in G Blanke and R Nazzini (eds), *International Competition Litigation: A Multi-jurisdictional Handbook* (Kluwer Law International 2012); and R Nazzini, 'Parallel Proceedings before the Tribunal and the Courts/ Competition Authorities' in G Blanke and P Landolt (eds), *EU and US Antitrust Arbitration: A Handbook for Practitioners* (Kluwer Law International 2011) 881–916.

[153] Judgment of the ECJ of 23 March 1981 in Case 102/81 *Nordsee Deutsche Hochseefischerei GmbH v Reederei Mond Hochseefischerei Nordstern AG & Co KG and Reederei Friedrich Busse Hochseefischerei Nordstern AG & Co KG* [1982] ECR 1095, where the ECJ did not consider arbitrators as 'a court or tribunal of a Member State' within the meaning of Art 234 EC (now Art 267 TFEU) and as a consequence found them incapable of making a preliminary reference to the EC (now EU) judiciary. To the same effect, see also most recently Judgment of the ECJ of 27 January 2005 in Case C-125/04 *Denuit v Transorient* [2005] ECR I-923. Cf, however, the availability of indirect preliminary references in a number of EU Member State jurisdictions, eg England, *Bulk Oil Ltd v Sun International Ltd* [1984] 1 All ER 386; see G Blanke, 'Antitrust Arbitration under the Arbitration Act 1996: A Commentary' (2011) 22(2) EBLR 119, at 156.

[154] Commission Notice on the cooperation between the Commission and the courts of the EU Member States in the application of Articles 81 and 82 EC [2004] OJ C101.

[155] AP Komninos, 'Arbitration and EU Competition Law in the Post-Modernization Era' in G Blanke and P Landolt (eds), *EU and US Antitrust Arbitration: A Handbook for Practitioners* (Kluwer Law International 2011) 433–87.

[156] For the English example, see para 29.79.

from the Commission or competent NCAs to obtain relevant market information for market definition purposes, for example, may also support the individual tribunal in rendering an enforceable award. Importantly, the Commission has not, in principle, objected to any such involvement to date and some attempts at cooperation have been made in the past.[157] Further, tentative best practice guidelines on the role of the Commission as *amicus arbitri* in EU competition arbitration[158] have been developed and debated[159] within the former ICC Task Force for Arbitrating Competition Law Issues.[160]

29.81 In any event, any cooperation between a tribunal and the Commission or a competent NCA should only take place with the approval and the involvement of the arbitrating parties given that the arbitral process is subject to strict requirements of party autonomy and due process.

D. Supervisory Court Review of EU Competition Law Awards[161]

29.82 The extent to which arbitral awards are enforceable or to which they may be set aside depends on the intensity of supervisory court review. Bearing in mind the well-established prohibition of appeals on the merits in international arbitration practice, supervisory court review is particularly sensitive in areas of law that command the public interest. Antitrust law, and in particular EU competition law is, no doubt, one such area of law and hence requires particular scrutiny in enforcement or annulment proceedings.

1. Supervisory court review in Europe

29.83 In the EU competition law context more specifically, the supervisory court review performed by EU Member State courts essentially constitutes a public policy review of the award subject to an application for enforcement or an action for annulment. This is particularly so following the ECJ's ruling in *Eco Swiss*,[162] in which the Court elevated former Article 85 EEC (now Article 101 TFEU) to the status of public policy within the meaning of the New York Convention. In the terms of that ruling:

> 36. ... according to Article 3(g) of the EEC Treaty [after amendment, Article 3(1)(g) EC[163] and now Article 3(1)(b) TFEU[164]], Article 85 of the Treaty [now Article 101 TFEU]

---

[157] eg ICC Award No 7146.

[158] C Nisser and G Blanke, 'ICC Draft Best Practice Note on the European Commission Acting as *Amicus Curiae* in International Arbitration Proceedings—The Text' in G Blanke (ed), *Arbitrating Competition Law Issues* (EBLR Special Edition 2008)198.

[159] For criticism, see A Mourre, 'Dissenting Opinion on a Dangerous Project' in G Blanke (ed), *Arbitrating Competition Law Issues* (EBLR Special Edition 2008) 219; and 'Arbitration and Competition', note by Prof L Idot in OECD Report on Competition and Arbitration, DAF/COMP(2010)40, available at <http://search.oecd.org/officialdocuments/displaydocumentpdf/?cote=DAF/COMP(2010)40&docLanguage=En> 51, at 68 et seq.

[160] G Blanke, 'Antitrust Arbitration under the ICC Rules' in G Blanke and P Landolt (eds), *EU and US Antitrust Arbitration: A Handbook for Practitioners* (Kluwer Law International 2011) 1763–898, para 49-015.

[161] For a most recent treatment of the subject matter, see L G Radicati di Brozolo, 'Court Review of Competition Law Awards in Setting Aside and Enforcement Proceedings' in G Blanke and P Landolt (eds), *EU and US Antitrust Arbitration: A Handbook for Practitioners* (Kluwer Law International 2011) 755.

[162] Judgment of the ECJ of 1 June 1999 Case C-126/97 *Eco Swiss China Ltd and Benetton International NV* [1999] ECR I-3055.

[163] Article 3(1)(g) of the EC Treaty provides as follows: 'For the purposes of Article 2, the activities of the Community shall include, as provided in this Treaty and in accordance with the timetable set out therein: ... (g) a system ensuring that competition in the internal market is not distorted' (author's footnote).

[164] Following adoption of the Lisbon Treaty, Art 3(1)(g) EC has been in substance replaced by Art 3(1)(b) TFEU, which bestows upon the EU exclusive powers in 'the establishing of the competition rules necessary for the functioning of the internal market'. Also in this context note Art 119 TFEU, according to which EU

constitutes a fundamental provision which is essential for the accomplishment of the tasks entrusted to the Community and, in particular, for the functioning of the internal market. The importance of such a provision led the framers of the Treaty to provide expressly, in Article 85(2) [now Article 101(2) TFEU] of the Treaty that any agreements or decisions prohibited pursuant to that article are to be automatically void…[T]he provisions of Article 85 [now Article 101 TFEU] of the Treaty may be regarded as a matter of public policy within the meaning of the New York Convention.

37. … where its domestic rules for procedure require a national court to grant an application for annulment of an arbitration award where such an arbitration is founded on a failure to observe national rules of public policy, it must also grant such an application where it is founded on a failure to comply with the prohibition laid down in Article 85(1) EEC [now Article 101(1) TFEU] … [Therefore,] a national court to which application is made for annulment of an arbitration award must grant that application if it considers that the award in question is, in fact, contrary to Article 85(1) EEC [now Article 101(1) TFEU], where its domestic rules of procedure require it to grant an application for annulment founded on failure to observe national rules of public policy.

…

39. For the reasons stated in paragraph 36 above, the provisions of Article 85 of the Treaty [now Art. 101 TFEU] may be regarded as a matter of public policy within the meaning of the New York Convention.

Further, in the light of the ECJ's later ruling in *Manfredi*,[165] it has also been found that Article 82 EC (now Article 102 TFEU) qualifies for a public policy review under the New York Convention.[166]

29.84 As a result, an EU Member State court seized of the enforcement or setting aside of an arbitration award is under an obligation to scrutinize compliance of that award with the relevant EU competition law provisions under Articles 101 and 102 TFEU with a view to avoiding a violation of the public policy concept under the New York Convention. This may not be the case where enforcement is sought outside the EU.[167]

29.85 Nevertheless, the standard and the procedure for the enforcement or setting aside of an award before the EU Member State courts are subject to the principle of procedural autonomy (ie equivalence and effectiveness).[168] This means that in some Member States, specific domestic procedural requirements, such as the principle of legal certainty, may prevail over the non-enforcement or the setting aside of an award that does not comply with applicable EU competition law provisions. This will, of course, be subject to the proviso that those prevailing national procedural

---

and Member State economic policies are to be 'conducted in accordance with the principle of an open market economy and free competition', as well as the Protocol on the Internal Market and Competition annexed to the TEU, according to which 'the internal market as set out in Article 3 of the Treaty on European Union includes a system ensuring that competition is not distorted' (author's footnote).

[165] Judgment of the ECJ of 13 July 2006 in Joined Cases C-295/04 to C-298/04 *Vincenzo Manfredi v Lloyd Adriatico Assicurazioni SpA, Antonio Cannito v Fondiaria Sai SpA, and Nicolò Tricarico, Pasqualina Murgolo v Assitalia SpA* [2006] ECR I-6619.

[166] P Landolt, 'Limits on Court Review of International Arbitration Awards Assessed in Light of States' Interests and in Particular in Light of EU Law Requirements' (2007) 23(1) Arb Int 63, at n 48: 'This reference to EU Member State courts having automatically to apply Arts 81 EC and 82 EC [101 and 102 TFEU] looks like clarification, in so far as one was needed, that *Eco Swiss* requires that these provisions be applied even *ex officio*. The fact that EU Member State courts must raise at least certain elements of Community [now EU] law of their own motion underscores how demanding the requirements on them must be to ensure that arbitral awards conform to Community [now EU] law.' (italics in the original)

[167] For the Swiss example, see P Landolt, 'The Application of EU Competition Law in International Arbitration in Switzerland' in G Blanke and P Landolt (eds), *EU and US Antitrust Arbitration: A Handbook for Practitioners* (Kluwer Law International 2011) 545–65, para 15-015 et seq.

[168] G Blanke, 'EC Competition Law Claims in International Arbitration' in C Klausegger et al (eds), *Austrian Arbitration Yearbook 2009* (Manz/Stämpfli/Beck 2009) 3, 87–8.

requirements equally apply in the domestic context and that, despite their applicability, the application of EU competition law is not made impossible or exceedingly difficult.[169]

2. The 'minimalist' and 'maximalist' schools of review[170]

29.86 The intensity of supervisory court review of arbitration awards involving EU competition law varies from Member State to Member State, depending on the individual Member State court's perception and understanding of its own jurisdictional duties under EU competition law. Some of them adopt a more stringent, others a more lax definition of their obligation to review arbitration awards to ensure their compliance with EU competition law. Hence, some EU Member State courts perform a detailed substantive review of the reasoning as well as the dispositive part of the underlying award in order to ascertain the absence of any violation of the EU competition law rules,[171] whereas others confine their review to an examination of the dispositive part only.[172] It should be cautioned that there is no common standard of supervisory court review across the EU:[173] By way of illustration, some awards raising EU competition law concerns have been enforced and set aside in parallel proceedings before different EU Member State courts on the basis of clearly divergent standards of review;[174] on occasion, different supervisory courts in even one and the same Member State have adopted

---

[169] See eg Judgment of the ECJ of 14 December 1995 in Case C-312/93 *Peterbroeck, Van Campenhout & Cie SCS v Belgian State* [1995] ECR I-4599 (sixty-day time limit for award to become final and hence *res iudicata* deemed acceptable); Judgment of the ECJ of 14 December 1995 in Joined Cases C-430-431/93 *Van Schijndel and van Veen v Stichting Pensioensfonds voor Fysiotherapeuten* [1995] ECR I-4705 (rule of passivity of the national judiciary not in violation of EU law); Judgment of the ECJ of 1 June 1999 in Case C-126/97 *Eco Swiss China Ltd and Benetton International NV* (three-month time limit for challenging an award before it becomes *res iudicata* deemed not excessive); and Judgment of the ECJ of 6 October 2009 in Case C-40/08 *Asturcom Telecomunicaciones SL v. Cristina Rodríguez Nogeuira* (two-month time limit for award to become final and hence *res iudicata* deemed acceptable). It should be noted in this context that a complete absence of Member State supervisory court review of an arbitration award for compliance with EU competition law may qualify as a failure to comply with a Member State's obligations under the principle of effectiveness.

[170] G Blanke, 'EC Competition Law Claims in International Arbitration' in C Klausegger et al (eds), *Austrian Arbitration Yearbook 2009* (Manz/Stämpfli/Beck 2009) 3, 78–85; and G Blanke, 'The "Minimalist" and "Maximalist" Approach to Reviewing Competition Law Awards—A Never-Ending Saga' (2007) 2 SIAR 51–78.

[171] Deutsche Bundesgerichtshof (German Federal Supreme Court), Judgment of 25 October 1966, Bghz 46, 365; *Sesam v Betoncentrale*, Hof Amsterdam, 12 October 2000, (2002) Nederlandse Jurisprudentie (NJ), Case no 111; OLG Düsseldorf, Judgment of 15 July 2002, Az I-6 Sch 5/02; *Marketing Displays International Inc v VR Van Raalte Reclame BV*, Judgment of the Court of Appeal of The Hague of 24 March 2005; OLG Dresden, Judgment of 20 April 2005; and *La SNF SAS c/La Cytec Industries*, Judgment of the Tribunal de Première Instance de Bruxelles of 8 March 2007, RG 2005/7721/A No 53 71ième Chambre, although subsequently set aside: RG No 2007/AR/1742, *Cytec Industries BV c/SNF SAS*, Cour d'appel de Bruxelles, 17ème chambre, 22 June 2009 (on grounds unrelated to the intensity of the CFI's supervisory review; see G Blanke and R Nazzini, (2009) 2(3) GCLR R-42).

[172] Decision of the Paris Court of Appeal of 18 November 2004 in *Thalès v Euromissile*; Judgment of the Paris Court of Appeal of 23 March 2006 in *SNF SAS c/Cytec Industries BV*, as recently affirmed by the French Supreme Court in Arrêt no 680, Cour de Cassation, 4 June 2008; Judgment of the Court of Appeal of Florence of 21 March 2006 in *Nuovo Pignone Spa c Schlumberger SA*; Judgment of the Court of Appeal in Milan of 15 July 2006 in *Terrarmata v Tensacciai*; OLG Thüringen, Judgment of 8 August 2007, Az 4 Sch 03/06; Judgment of the Paris Court of Appeal of 20 March 2008 in *Jean-Louis Jacquetin c La Société Intercaves SA*, Cour d'Appel de Paris (1ère Ch, SC) RG 06/06860; see G Blanke and R Nazzini, (2008) 1(3) GCLR R-67–R-68; and *La Société Linde Aktiengesellschaft et al c La Société Halyvourgiki—AE*, Cour d'appel de Paris, Pôle 1 Chambre 1, Judgment of the Paris Court of Appeal of 22 October 2009, RG no 2008/21022, see G Blanke and R Nazzini (2010) 3(1) GCLR R-1–R-2.

[173] See 'Arbitration and Competition', note by Prof L Idot in OECD Report on Competition and Arbitration, DAF/COMP(2010)40, available at <http://search.oecd.org/officialdocuments/displaydocumentpdf/?cote=DAF/COMP(2010)40&docLanguage=En> 51, at 72 et seq.

[174] eg Judgment of the Tribunal de Première Instance de Bruxelles of 8 March 2007 in *La SNF SAS c/La Cytec Industries* RG 2005/7721/A No 53 71ième Chambre; and Judgment of the Paris Court of Appeal of 23 March 2006 in *SNF SAS c/Cytec Industries BV*.

contradictory standards of review.[175] Accordingly, some courts, in particular the French, will only set aside an award on the basis of a violation of EU competition law provided that violation is manifest, ie readily discernible on the face, that is the operative part of the award.[176]

The extreme opposing ends of the spectrum of supervisory court review are occupied by the **29.87** so-called 'maximalists'[177] and 'minimalists'.[178] Whereas the minimalists insist on the final and binding nature of an award to justify their *pro forma* review of the dispositive part of the award, the maximalists endeavour to put in place some form of *effective* review system that allows for a *genuine* second look at the arbitrator's assessment of his or her omission to assess relevant EU competition law issues.[179] In principle, according to the maximalists, a stricter review is a logical consequence of the expansion of the concept of arbitrability to include competition law disputes; by this token, an effective review is designed to ensure the Member States' trust in conceding some of their sovereign powers in the competition law context and thereby their continued approval of the permission and promotion of antitrust arbitrability.[180] Further, it has also recently been argued that on a literal reading, *Eco Swiss* itself requires a substantive review of the award

---

[175] See eg the ruling of the OLG Düsseldorf of 21 July 2004, Vi-Sch (Kart) 1/02 and the previous ruling of the Kartellsenat (the German Cartel Court) in the same matter. See also Judgment of the Tribunal de Première Instance de Bruxelles of 8 March 2007 in *La SNF SAS c/La Cytec Industries* RG 2005/7721/A No 53 71ième Chambre; and Judgment of the Brussels Court of Appeal of 22 June 2009 in *Cytec Industries v SNF* (although it should be noted that in this case, the Brussels' Court of Appeal did not query the intensity of the CFI's supervisory review).

[176] eg Decision of the Paris Court of Appeal of 18 November 2004 in *Thalès v Euromissile*.

[177] For maximalist tendencies, see in particular A Mourre and L Radicati di Brozolo, 'SNF c/Cytec' (2007) 2 Rev arb 303; and, most recently, on the Brussels Court's decision in *Cytec* in (2007) Rev Arb 318–39; L Radicati di Brozolo, 'Antitrust: A Paradigm of the Relations between Mandatory Rules and Arbitration—A Fresh Look at the "Second Look"' (2004) 1 Int ALR 23; C Liebscher, 'Arbitration and EC Competition Law—The New Competition Regulation: Back to Square One?' (2003) 3 Int ALR 84–9. For a critical assessment of the Brussels Court's decision in *Cytec*, mentioned earlier, see also P Heitzmann and J Grierson, '*SNF v Cytec Industrie*: National Courts within the EC Apply Different Standards to Review International Awards Allegedly Contrary to Art. 81 EC' (2007) 2 SIAR 39–49. Most vociferously in support of the 'minimalist' view more generally, see also A Mourre and L Radicati di Brozolo, 'Towards Finality of Arbitral Awards: Two Steps Forward and One Step Back' (2006) 23(2) J of Int A 171–88; A Mourre, 'Le libre arbitre, ou l'aveuglement de Zaleucus: Variations sur l'arbitrage, l'ordre public et le droit communautaire' in F Bohnet and P Wessner (eds), *Mélanges en l'Honneur de François Knoepfler* (Helbing Lichtenhahn 2005) 283–323; and most recently, A Mourre, case note on *SAS SNF c/Cytec Industries BV*, JDI n. 4/2008, 1107–134; LR di Brozolo, 'Arbitration and Competition Law: The Position of the Courts and of Arbitrators' (2011) 1 Arb Int 1–26; and 'Arbitration and Competition Law: The Position of the Courts and of Arbitrators', note by Prof L Radicati di Brozolo in OECD Report on Competition and Arbitration, DAF/COMP(2010)40, available at <http://search.oecd.org/officialdocuments/displaydocumentpdf/?cote=DAF/COMP(2010)40&docLanguage=En> 31, at 33 et seq.

[178] For maximalist tendencies, see eg G Blanke, 'The "Minimalist" and "Maximalist" Approach to Reviewing Competition Law Awards—A Never-Ending Saga' (2007) 2 SIAR 51–79; C Seraglini, *Lois de police et justice arbitrale internationale* (Dalloz 2001); C Seraglini, 'L'intensité du contrôle du respect par l'arbitre de l'ordre public: Note—Cour d'appel de Paris (1re Ch C) 14 juin 2001' (2001) 4 Rev arb 781–804; P Landolt, 'Limits on Court Review of International Arbitration Awards Assessed in Light of States' Interests and in Particular in Light of EU Law Requirements' (2007) 23(1) Arb Int 63; and W Abdelgawad, *Arbitrage et Droit de la Concurrence: Contribution à l'Etude des Rapports entre Ordre Spontané et Ordre Organisé* (2001). Most recently, see also P Mayer, 'L'étendue du contrôle, par le juge étatique, de la conformité des sentences arbitrales aux lois de police' in [2008] Mélanges Gaudemet Tallon 459; C Seraglini, 'Le contrôle de la sentence au regard de l'ordre public international par le juge étatique: mythes et réalités' (2009) 1 Cahiers de l'arbitrage 5; and B Hanotiau and O Capresse, 'Introductory Report' in E Gaillard, *The Review of International Arbitral Awards* (Juris 2010) 1, in particular at 74 et seq. It should be noted that in reality, most of these authors are trying to identify a workable balance between the 'minimalist' and the 'maximalist' approach.

[179] eg D de Groot, 'Observations' (2005) 2 SIAR 209–16, arguing for the need for an 'effective review'. See also most recently the ruling of the Tribunal Superior de Justicia del País Vasco, Sala de lo Civil y Penal, of 19 April 2012, rec 5/2011 and the commentary by G Blanke (2012) 5(3) GCLR.

[180] P Landolt, 'Limits on Court Review of International Arbitration Awards Assessed in Light of States' Interests and in Particular in Light of EU Law Requirements' (2007) 23(1) Arb Int 63.

in question and prescribes the annulment or setting aside of an award that is incompatible with relevant EU competition law provisions, irrespective of the type or degree of the infringement.[181]

29.88 In actual practice, the difference between the maximalists and minimalists may be more imagined than real. It has been argued that there may well be a 'middle way' that allows a practical combination of the two schools of review, creating a workable balance between the principle of finality of arbitration awards on the one hand and the need for an effective review of EU competition law awards on the other.[182] Adopting the middle way, a supervisory court will essentially confine its review to an examination of the reasoning and the dispositive part of the award in light of the facts as presented and interpreted by the tribunal in the text of the award, without re-opening the proceedings or for that matter re-assessing the facts.[183]

29.89 That said, for as long as there is no consensus among EU Member State courts as to the required intensity of review of arbitration awards for compliance with EU competition law, arbitrating parties as well as arbitrators are advised to tread carefully and take EU competition law concerns seriously in order to avoid the nullification of a resultant award at the enforcement stage.

3. Consequences of non-compliance

29.90 Irrespective of the varying approaches taken by EU Member State courts to the supervisory review of EU competition law awards, a Member State courts' failure to comply with the EU competition law rules by giving effect to an award that violates those rules may engage the enforcing State's responsibility under the State liability doctrines developed by the ECJ in *Francovich*[184] and *Köbler*.[185]

29.91 More specifically, according to the ECJ's ruling in *Francovich*, it is a principle of EU law that a Member State—including its courts which qualify as an emanation of the state—has an obligation to make good loss and damage caused to individuals by breaches of EU law for which it can be held responsible. In application of the *Köbler* doctrine, an injured party would, in turn, be entitled to claim reparation for damages caused to it by the enforcement of an arbitral award that infringes the EU competition law rules, provided that the conditions for State liability enumerated at paragraph 51 of the ECJ's ruling are met in the individual case:

---

[181] G Blanke, 'The "Minimalist" and "Maximalist" Approach to Reviewing Competition Law Awards—A Never-Ending Saga' (2007) 2 SIAR 51, at 61 et seq.

[182] G Blanke, 'EC Competition Law Claims in International Arbitration' in C Klausegger et al (eds), *Austrian Arbitration Yearbook 2009* (Manz/Stämpfli/Beck 2009) 3, 78–85; also confirmed by T Eilmansberger, 'Die Bedeutung der Art. 81 und 82 EG für Schiedsverfahren' (2006) 4 SchiedsVZ. Most recently, see G Blanke, 'The "Minimalist" and "Maximalist" Approach to Reviewing Competition Law Awards—A Never-Ending Saga Revisited or the Middle Way at Last?' in D Bray and H Bray (eds), *Post-Hearing Issues in International Arbitration* (forthcoming 2013) 169–227.

[183] For an example of this approach, see Judgment of the Tribunal de Première Instance de Bruxelles of 8 March 2007 in *La SNF SAS c/La Cytec Industries* RG 2005/7721/A No 53 71ième Chambre; and most recently Tribunal Superior de Justicia del Pais Vasco, Sala de lo Civil y Penal, Auto de 19 Abr. 2012, rec 5/2011.

[184] Judgment of the ECJ of 19 November 1991 in Cases C-6 and C-9/90 *Francovich v Italy* [1991] ECR I-5357.

[185] Judgment of the ECJ of 30 September 2003 in Case C-224/01 *Gerhard Köbler v Republik Österreich* [2003] ECR I-10239. G Blanke, 'EC Competition Law Claims in International Arbitration' in C Klausegger et al (eds), *Austrian Arbitration Yearbook 2009* (Manz/Stämpfli/Beck 2009) 3, 91; and M Barbier de La Serre and C Nourissat, 'Contrôle des sentences arbitrales à l'aune du droit de la concurrence: à la recherche du bon équilibre…' (février 2005/avril 2005) 2 Revue Lamy de la Concurrence 68.

- the rule of law violated in the individual instance must be intended to confer rights on individuals (which clearly is the case in the context of EU competition law and in particular Articles 101 and 102 TFEU);
- the violation must be sufficiently serious (which again would be the case with respect to a violation of EU competition law through enforcement of an arbitral award, depending on the kind and gravity of the violation in each individual case);[186] and
- there must be a causal link between the violation of the obligation incumbent on the State and the loss or damage sustained by the injured party (the causal link between the infringing award and the supervisory court's failure to annul or set aside the award being manifest).

IV. EU Commitment Arbitrations[187]

As stated previously, EU commitment arbitrations are those arbitrations that arise from the **29.92** deficient implementation of or the failure to implement behavioural commitments under Article 9 of Regulation 1/2003 or under the Merger Control Regulation. This will usually mean that the parties failed to agree upon the terms and conditions of a suitable implementation agreement, or that, despite the adoption of such an agreement, its terms and conditions have not been properly implemented.

Typically, the arbitration mechanism deployed in EU commitment arbitrations is based on **29.93** an arbitration commitment that contains a unilateral *erga omnes* offer to arbitrate, which—as to its effects—only binds the merged entity or the party subject to the Article 9 commitment decision. Conversely, the third-party beneficiary, who benefits from the implementation of the commitments (eg by being provided access to the merged entity's key technology or infrastructure on fair and non-discriminatory terms) is under no obligation to go to arbitration and remains free to resort to the courts or lodge a complaint with the Commission for failure to comply with the underlying conditional merger clearance or commitment decision instead. In other words, the third-party beneficiary has an option, yet no obligation, to arbitrate. In this sense, EU commitment arbitrations are a form of 'arbitration without privity'.[188] The third-party beneficiary may exercise his/her arbitration option in a number of ways, either in reliance on the original arbitration commitment, which is directly effective,[189] or by reference to the arbitration clause modeled on the original arbitration commitment and contained in the implementation agreement.

---

[186] There being no EU definition, the degree of seriousness of the violation required is subject to interpretation by individual EU Member State courts. See eg the ruling of the English High Court in *Stephen Cooper v HM Attorney-General* [2008] EWHC 2285, in which it held that claims based on the *Köbler* cause of action were to be reserved to exceptional cases involving errors that were manifest. It would thus appear that cartel violations would definitely qualify.

[187] For the main specialist texts, see nn 191 and 193 in this chapter.

[188] J Paulsson, 'Arbitration without Privity' (1995) 10(2) ICSID Review 232; G Blanke and B Sabahi, 'The New World of Unilateral Offers to Arbitrate: Investment Arbitration and EC Merger Control' (2008) 74(3) Arbitration 211–24.

[189] Given that it (i) is sufficiently precise (which most of the arbitration commitments are, their wording being sufficiently clear to enable the commencement and conduct of entire arbitration proceedings); (ii) does not require any national implementing measures (*idem*); and (iii) confers a right upon an individual (most arbitration commitments entitle third-party beneficiaries to enforce the substantive rights they derive from a commitment decision before an arbitration tribunal).

29.94   The third-party beneficiary's option to arbitrate may turn into an obligation under a number of circumstances, including in particular where the implementation agreement—rather than just replicating verbatim the original unilateral offer to arbitrate contained in the arbitration commitment—features a wider arbitration provision that is binding upon both contracting parties, ie including the third-party beneficiary.

A. Scope of EU Commitment Arbitrations

29.95   Importantly, EU commitment arbitrations focus on the implementation of so-called second-order obligations, ie the terms and conditions of the underlying implementation agreement. Second-order obligations, in turn, are based on so-called first-order obligations, ie the conditions and obligations of the underlying merger or Article 9 commitment. Essentially, the second-order obligations transpose the first-order obligations from the public to the private sphere, making the conditions and obligations of the individual commitments binding on the third-party beneficiary as second-order obligations, ie as terms and conditions of a private law agreement, which is the implementation agreement it concludes with the merged entity or the party subject to the Article 9 commitment decision. In simplified terms, whereas the arbitrator's jurisdiction is confined to the competition-compliant implementation of the second-order obligations, the compliance with the first-order obligations is the prerogative of the Commission. These latter are only relevant to the arbitrator's mandate to the extent that they impart the competition objectives which the Commission had in mind when adopting the original commitment and which the arbitrator has to take into account in order to ensure the enforceability of the resultant award. Given that supervisory Member State courts are bound by a previous commitment decision,[190] non-compliance of the award with the competition objectives of the original commitment decision may result in the nullification of the award at the enforcement stage.

29.96   In line with the conceptual distinction between first- and second-order obligations, the scope of EU commitment arbitrations is confined to the recovery of private law relief, whereas it is for the Commission to provide public law remedies, such as fines, penalty payments, the dismantling of an already consumed merger, or the substitution of an Article 9 with an Article 7 commitment decision.

1. Commitment arbitrations in EU merger control[191]

29.97   Commitment arbitrations in EU merger control primarily focus on the question as to whether a behavioural commitment, typically an access commitment, offered in return for the clearance by the Commission of a proposed concentration, has been correctly implemented by the merged entity post merger. The question of the correct implementation of such a commitment in turn focuses on whether fair and non-discriminatory access has been provided by the merged entity to an intended third-party beneficiary. This, in turn, may either be a legal or a technical question:

---

[190] Due to the principles of direct effect and supremacy in EU law.

[191] For the main specialist texts, see M Blessing, *Arbitrating Antitrust and Merger Control Issues* (Helbing & Lichtenhahn 2003); M Blessing, 'Arbitration and EU Merger Control' in G Kaufmann-Kohler and A Johnson (eds), *Arbitration of Merger and Acquisition Disputes*, (May 2005) ASA Special Series No 24 99; F Heukamp, *Schiedszusagen in der Europäischen Fusionskontrolle* (Heymanns Verlag 2006); G Blanke, *The Use and Utility of International Arbitration in EU Commission Merger Remedies: A Supranational Paradigm in the Making?* (Europa Law Publishing 2006); and G Blanke, 'International Arbitration and ADR in Conditional EU Merger Clearance Decisions' in G Blanke and P Landolt (eds), *EU and US Antitrust Arbitration: A Handbook for Practitioners* (Kluwer Law International 2011) 1605.

(i) legal to the extent that the arbitrator will have to determine whether the parties have agreed on the terms and conditions of an implementation agreement to provide fair and non-discriminatory access, and if so, whether the terms and conditions of that agreement can work in practice in order to achieve the intended competition objectives of the underlying commitment read together with the conditional merger clearance decision;

(ii) technical to the extent that the arbitrator will have to determine whether the access provided by the underlying implementation agreement is in fact fair and non-discriminatory and complies with the competition objectives which the underlying commitment seeks to achieve.[192]

In a given reference, the arbitrator may thus have to determine the terms and conditions of a suitable implementation agreement or adjust those of an already existing one. For the relevant competition analysis, ie to determine whether the implementation agreement is competition-compliant, the arbitrator will have to rely on the conditions and obligations of the underlying conditional merger clearance decision and relevant provisions of EU competition law as well as the Merger Control Regulation.

The arbitrator may also be requested to determine a number of preliminary issues, such as **29.98** (i) whether the third-party beneficiary bringing the action has proper standing, ie is a 'party with sufficient interest'; and (ii) whether any prescribed alternative dispute resolution ('ADR') regime has been exhausted prior to the commencement of the arbitration proceedings. The arbitrator may further be requested to make a preliminary ruling on the merits, ordering, for example, specific performance of (specific provisions of) the implementation agreement (eg hence granting the required access) or injuncting the merged entity from apparent violations of the commitments whilst the arbitration proceedings and the final award (and the final redress pronounced therein) are pending. Such a preliminary ruling would be intended to operate as a form of interim relief and to prevent the third-party beneficiary's premature exit from the market.

In terms of relief sought, the arbitrator will typically have to consider a request from the **29.99** third-party beneficiary for specific performance of the implementation agreement together with damages for the merged entity's past failure to perform (ie refusal to grant access to the third-party beneficiary). For the avoidance of doubt, the arbitrator is only competent to award private law remedies, any public law redress being the prerogative of the Commission under the Merger Control Regulation (eg the payment of fines and/or penalties and/or the dismantlement of an already-consumed merger).

2. Commitment arbitrations under Article 9 of Regulation 1/2003[193]

Similarly, commitment arbitrations under Article 9 of Regulation 1/2003 primarily focus on **29.100** the correct implementation of access agreements. The considerations made in the preceding paragraph apply here *mutatis mutandis*. That said, however, Article 9 commitment arbitrations require the arbitrator to determine in particular whether the implementation of the commitments complies with the requirements of Articles 101 and 102 TFEU, depending on

---

[192] Note that to the extent that the behavioural commitment forms part of a set of other behavioural commitments or of a mixed remedy package, including both structural and behavioural remedies, the technical analysis required from the arbitrator may become exponentially more complex.

[193] For the main specialist texts, see G Blanke, 'The Use of International Arbitration under Article 81(3) of the EC Treaty and Article 9 of Regulation 1/2003' [2008] SchiedsVZ 243; and G Blanke, 'International Arbitration and ADR in Remedy Scenarios Arising under Articles 101 and 102 TFEU' in G Blanke and P Landolt (eds), *EU and US Antitrust Arbitration: A Handbook for Practitioners* (Kluwer Law International 2011) 1053.

whether the underlying commitments were originally accepted by the Commission to allay concerns of a potential violation of Article 101 or Article 102 TFEU.

29.101 In terms of relief sought, it is worth emphasizing that again, the arbitrator's competence will be strictly confined to the award of private law remedies (eg an order for specific performance of the underlying implementation agreement and/or an award for damages to compensate for past non-performance) as opposed to the Commission's exclusive prerogative to provide public law redress (eg the substitution of a previous Article 9 by an Article 7 prohibition decision).

B. Procedural Conduct of EU Commitment Arbitrations

29.102 EU commitment arbitrations impose a number of procedural requirements that go beyond what is usually expected of international commercial arbitrations or even ordinary EU competition arbitrations. These requirements have, in the past, justified reference to EU commitment arbitrations as a form of 'supranational arbitration'.[194] Supranational arbitration is a form of arbitration *à l'européenne*, which requires the parties and the arbitrator to take into account the constitutional idiosyncrasies of the EU legal order as a separate and autonomous legal order *sui generis*.[195] These include, for present purposes, in particular the principles of direct effect and supremacy and the principle of loyal (or sincere) cooperation.[196] Correctly applied, these principles require supervisory Member State courts to take into account a previous conditional merger clearance decision or an Article 9 commitment decision in the enforcement of awards resulting from an EU commitment arbitration arising from those decisions. A supervisory Member State court will thus be prevented from enforcing an award that does not comply with the conditions and obligations of the original commitment decision and violates, for example, the competition-compliant objectives of the commitments underlying those decisions.

29.103 In order to ensure the enforceability of awards resulting from EU commitment arbitrations, the underlying arbitration commitments typically provide for a number of procedural safeguards. These include:

- some form of coordinated cooperation between the Commission and the arbitrator and in particular:
  (i) requests for information from the arbitrator to the Commission, especially to assist in the accurate definition of geographic and product markets; and
  (ii) requests for interpretation from the arbitrator to the Commission in relation to the correct interpretation of the intended objectives and effects behind individual commitments in order to ensure that the arbitrator have an accurate understanding of the intended competition-compliant operation of the commitments;
- the Commission's role as *amicus arbitri*, including in particular the Commission's entitlement:
  (i) to receive the main submissions and procedural documentation issued over the course of the arbitration procedure;
  (ii) to make submissions to the arbitrator at all stages of the arbitration procedure; and

---

[194] For this terminology in the EU merger control context, see G Blanke, *The Use and Utility of International Arbitration in EU Commission Merger Remedies: A Supranational Paradigm in the Making?* (Europa Law Publishing 2006).

[195] Cf Judgment of the ECJ of 5 February 1963 in Case 26/62 *Van Gend en Loos v Administratie der Belastingen* Rec 1963 [1963] ECR 1.

[196] See para 29.73.

(iii) to participate in the main evidentiary hearing as observer, expert witness or otherwise (including an entitlement to ask questions);[197] and

- a general reporting requirement, whereby the arbitrator is required to report procedural developments in the arbitration to the Commission at regular, specified intervals.[198]

Further procedural safeguards put in place to cater for the particular nature of EU commitment arbitrations are:

- the *prima facie* evidence rule, whereby in the event that the merged entity or the party subject to an Article 9 commitment decision fails to refute a *prima facie* case made against it by a third-party beneficiary, the arbitrator will have to find in the latter's favour, or even a reversal of the burden of proof in favour of the third-party beneficiary; and
- the fast-track nature of the arbitration proceedings to ensure that any access problems be resolved in real time and to prevent any third-party beneficiary from being forced to exit the market prematurely (ie prior to the issuance of a final award).[199]

As all these safeguards are expressly provided for in the underlying arbitration commitment, **29.104** and given that a third-party beneficiary will have consented to these once he/she has triggered his/her arbitration option in compliance with the arbitration commitment (or a corresponding arbitration clause in the event that a suitable implementation agreement has been put in place), they firmly form part of the underlying arbitration reference and hence the arbitrator's mandate. There can therefore be little controversy about the propriety of such procedural safeguards in the context of EU commitment arbitration.[200]

V. Other EU Competition-Related Arbitrations

As discussed previously, other EU competition-related issues may become subject to arbitration. **29.105** Given the very special nature of such questions, actual arbitration practice in the area is notably sparse. Therefore, practical guidance remains, as of date the time of writing, limited.

---

[197] C Nisser and G Blanke, 'ICC Draft Best Practice Note on the European Commission Acting as *Amicus Curiae* in International Arbitration Proceedings—The Text' in G Blanke (ed), *Arbitrating Competition Law Issues* (EBLR Special Edition 2008)198. For a background note, see C Nisser and G Blanke, 'ICC Draft Best Practice Note on the European Commission Acting as *Amicus Curiae* in International Arbitration Proceedings—An Explanatory Note' in G Blanke (ed), *Arbitrating Competition Law Issues* (EBLR Special Edition 2008) 193–7. Alternatively, see C Nisser and G Blanke, 'Projet de lignes directrices sur la Commission européenne intervenant en tant qu'*amicus curiae* dans les procédures d'arbitrage international' (juillet/septembre 2007) Revue Lamy de la Concurrence 148–58. For further commentary, see C Nisser and G Blanke, 'Reflections on the Role of the European Commission as Amicus Curiae in International Arbitration Proceedings' (2006) 4 ECLR 174–83.

[198] See G Blanke, *The Use and Utility of International Arbitration in EU Commission Merger Remedies: A Supranational Paradigm in the Making?* (Europa Law Publishing 2006); and M Blessing, *Arbitrating Antitrust and Merger Control Issues* (Helbing & Lichtenhahn 2003).

[199] G Blanke, *The Use and Utility of International Arbitration in EU Commission Merger Remedies: A Supranational Paradigm in the Making?* (Europa Law Publishing 2006); and M Blessing, *Arbitrating Antitrust and Merger Control Issues* (Helbing & Lichtenhahn 2003).

[200] Cf, however, the staunch criticism voiced by A Mourre, 'Dissenting Opinion on a Dangerous Project' in G Blanke (ed), *Arbitrating Competition Law Issues* (EBLR Special Edition 2008)219; and AP Komninos, 'Assistance by the European Commission and Member State Authorities in Arbitrations' in G Blanke and P Landolt (eds), *EU and US Antitrust Arbitration: A Handbook for Practitioners* (Kluwer Law International 2011) 727–53. For the reasons mentioned earlier, this criticism is misplaced. See also in favour, 'Arbitration and Competition', note by Prof L Idot in OECD Report on Competition and Arbitration, DAF/COMP(2010)40, available at <http://search.oecd.org/officialdocuments/displaydocumentpdf/?cote=DAF/COMP(2010)40&docLanguage=En> 51, at 84 et seq.

A. Arbitration of Questions Relating to the EU State Aid Regime[201]

29.106   Questions in relation to the EU State aid regime usually arise incidentally and not as a main claim in arbitration proceedings. More specifically, an allegation that a company has received State aid within the meaning of Article 107(1) TFEU may be raised in a number of various ways. For instance, in an investment arbitration between an investor and an EU Member State, the Member State party may rely upon the EU State aid regime as a defence to a claim brought by the investor for a purported breach of contract by the Member State, for example by failing to give effect to a loan or a guarantee or to transfer assets and/or land at a particularly advantageous, pre-agreed price.[202] Alternatively, the EU State aid rules may play a role in ordinary commercial arbitrations relating to, for example, the enforceability of a loan granted by a lender to a borrower on market uncompetitive rates.[203] Finally, an arbitration tribunal may be requested to address the issue as to whether a claim for damages or compensation against an EU Member State may, in and of itself, constitute an illegal form of State aid in violation of the EU State aid provisions, including in particular where there may be a previous instance of illegal aid.[204]

29.107   Even though generally rare,[205] there have been a number of isolated instances in which questions in relation to EU State aids have, in actual fact, arisen in an arbitration.[206] In this context, the ECJ has approved of a finding by arbitrators that the recovery of illegal aid could be set off against an outstanding debt in the form of compensation in a related matter.[207] Further, in another case it has been found that the compensation awarded by an UNCITRAL tribunal with seat in Sweden did not, on the basis of the evidence before the Svea Court of Appeal, violate the EU State aid rules.[208] Equally, a Dutch district court refused the annulment of an award rendered under the Netherlands Arbitration Institution Rules on the basis that compensation granted by the Tribunal did not conflict with a previous Commission decision on a related subject matter.[209] There have also been a number of investment arbitrations bearing on the subject matter, including in particular in relation to the compatibility of a compensation award with a previous negative EU State aid decision rendered by the Commission.[210]

---

[201]   See in particular L Hancher, 'Arbitrating EU State Aid Issues' in G Blanke and P Landolt (eds), *EU and US Antitrust Arbitration: A Handbook for Practitioners* (Kluwer Law International 2011) 965.

[202]   L Hancher, 'Arbitrating EU State Aid Issues' in G Blanke and P Landolt (eds), *EU and US Antitrust Arbitration: A Handbook for Practitioners* (Kluwer Law International 2011) 965, para 28-004.

[203]   L Hancher, 'Arbitrating EU State Aid Issues' in G Blanke and P Landolt (eds), *EU and US Antitrust Arbitration: A Handbook for Practitioners* (Kluwer Law International 2011) 965, para 28-005.

[204]   L Hancher, 'Arbitrating EU State Aid Issues' in G Blanke and P Landolt (eds), *EU and US Antitrust Arbitration: A Handbook for Practitioners* (Kluwer Law International 2011) 965, para 28-093.

[205]   L Hancher, 'Arbitrating EU State Aid Issues' in G Blanke and P Landolt (eds), *EU and US Antitrust Arbitration: A Handbook for Practitioners* (Kluwer Law International 2011) 965, para 28-111.

[206]   L Hancher, 'Arbitrating EU State Aid Issues' in G Blanke and P Landolt (eds), *EU and US Antitrust Arbitration: A Handbook for Practitioners* (Kluwer Law International 2011) 965, paras 28-094–28-028-110.

[207]   Ruling of the ECJ of 7 July 2009 in Case C-369/07 *Commission v Greece* [2009] ECR I-5703; also L Hancher, 'Arbitrating EU State Aid Issues' in G Blanke and P Landolt (eds), *EU and US Antitrust Arbitration: A Handbook for Practitioners* (Kluwer Law International 2011) 965, paras 28-024–28-096.

[208]   Case T-5730-03, 2005, Svea Court of Appeal; see also L Hancher, 'Arbitrating EU State Aid Issues' in G Blanke and P Landolt (eds), *EU and US Antitrust Arbitration: A Handbook for Practitioners* (2011) 965, paras 28-101–28-102.

[209]   Decision of the District Court of The Hague of 1 August 2007 in *Dutch State v BV Nederlands Elektriciteit Administratie Kantoor*. See also L Hancher, 'Arbitrating EU State Aid Issues' in G Blanke and P Landolt (eds), *EU and US Antitrust Arbitration: A Handbook for Practitioners* (Kluwer Law International 2011) 965, paras 28-103–28-104; and D de Groot (2008) 1(3) GCLR R-69–R-70.

[210]   L Hancher, 'Arbitrating EU State Aid Issues' in G Blanke and P Landolt (eds), *EU and US Antitrust Arbitration: A Handbook for Practitioners* (Kluwer Law International 2011) 965, paras 28-105–28-110; and T Eilmansberger, 'Bilateral Investment Treaties and EU Law' (2009) 46 CMLR 383–429.

In arbitrations involving EU State aid issues, an arbitrator—by analogy to the powers given to the EU Member State courts—will be empowered to: **29.108**

(i) declare whether a particular State measure requires notification to the Commission under the EU State aid rules;

(ii) declare whether a particular State measure constitutes existing or new aid within the meaning of Article 107(1) TFEU;

(iii) decide whether the General Block Exemption Regulation or the Commission Decision on State aids apply to the individual reference, rendering a notification to the Commission unnecessary;

(iv) decide—in application of the criteria pronounced by the ECJ in *Altmark*[211]—that state financing received for the performance of a particular service is compensation that does not constitute State aid;

(v) decide whether State aid that has been notified to and authorized by the Commission has been misused, ie used for purposes other than those for which it had been originally granted; and

(vi) award an appropriate level of compensation for the damage caused by an unlawful State aid measure.[212]

A tribunal may also have to decide whether compensation claimed from an EU Member State may in and of itself violate the EU State aid rules.[213] For the avoidance of doubt, as stated previously,[214] an arbitration tribunal is not authorized to declare State aid compatible with the EU State aid rules; this remains a prerogative of the Commission.

As regards the appropriate procedural conduct of arbitrations involving questions of EU State aids, it is arguable that to ensure the enforceability of a resultant award, an arbitration tribunal will have to explore and apply *mutatis mutandis* the same procedural techniques that have been discussed in relation to ordinary EU antitrust arbitrations previously.[215] It is notable that the Commission has repeatedly acted as 'an expert in EU law' in a number of investment arbitrations involving EU State aid issues to date, highlighting in particular a risk of conflict between compensation awarded by the arbitration tribunal and a previous negative State aid decision by the Commission.[216] In terms of EU supervisory court review, it should be noted that the District Court of The Hague performed an in-depth review to ensure compliance of the tribunal's award with a previous Commission decision declaring the State aid measure concerned compatible with the internal market.[217] Against this background, EU Member State supervisory courts are likely to regard EU State aids as a matter of public policy within the meaning of the New York Convention.[218] **29.109**

---

[211] Case C-280/00 *Altmark Trans v Regierungspräsidium Magdeburg* [2003] ECR I-7747.

[212] L Hancher, 'Arbitrating EU State Aid Issues' in G Blanke and P Landolt (eds), *EU and US Antitrust Arbitration: A Handbook for Practitioners* (Kluwer Law International 2011) 965, paras 28-024, 28-027, 28-043, and 28-067.

[213] L Hancher, 'Arbitrating EU State Aid Issues' in G Blanke and P Landolt (eds), *EU and US Antitrust Arbitration: A Handbook for Practitioners* (Kluwer Law International 2011) 965, para 28-093 et seq.

[214] Para 29.40.

[215] Para 29.70 et seq.

[216] L Hancher, 'Arbitrating EU State Aid Issues' in G Blanke and P Landolt (eds), *EU and US Antitrust Arbitration: A Handbook for Practitioners* (Kluwer Law International 2011) 965, para 28-107.

[217] Decision of the District Court of The Hague of 1 August 2007 in *Dutch State v BV Nederlands Elektriciteit Administratie Kantoor*; L Hancher, 'Arbitrating EU State Aid Issues' in G Blanke and P Landolt (eds), *EU and US Antitrust Arbitration: A Handbook for Practitioners* (Kluwer Law International 2011) 965, para 28-103.

[218] L Hancher, 'Arbitrating EU State Aid Issues' in G Blanke and P Landolt (eds), *EU and US Antitrust Arbitration: A Handbook for Practitioners* (Kluwer Law International 2011) 965, paras 28-102 and 28-104.

B. Arbitration of Questions Relating to Public Undertakings and Exclusive or Special Rights[219]

29.110 Questions in relation to public undertakings and exclusive or special rights may well arise in arbitration proceedings to which such undertakings are a party. Often, these undertakings provide services of a general economic interest, such as pension and sickness funds or hospitals, and may benefit from the provisions of Article 106 TFEU in the event that they are accused of anticompetitive behaviour in the performance of their general commercial relationships, which in turn frequently provide for dispute resolution by arbitration.

29.111 Nevertheless, reliance on Articles 3(1)(b) TFEU and 4(3) TEU may:

    (i) exonerate conduct otherwise prohibited under Articles 101 and 102 TFEU,

   (ii) be raised to challenge government actions that restrict competition, or

  (iii) neutralize the State compulsion exemption.[220]

29.112 As regards the appropriate procedural conduct of arbitrations involving questions in relation to public undertakings and exclusive or special rights, it is arguable that to ensure the enforceability of a resultant award, an arbitration tribunal will have to explore and apply *mutatis mutandis* the same procedural techniques that have previously been discussed in relation to ordinary EU antitrust arbitrations.[221] Importantly, where an arbitrator wrongly accords an exemption under Article 106(2) TFEU, it is arguable that the Commission will be entitled to re-examine the situation by virtue of Article 106(3) TFEU.[222]

VI. Conclusion

29.113 As this chapter has demonstrated, arbitration has come to play an increasingly important role in the private enforcement of the EU competition law rules over the past two decades, and in particular since the adoption and entry into force of Regulation 1/2003. Even though the special procedural requirements of EU competition arbitrations may not yet have been fully settled and remain in a state of flux at the time of writing, there can be little doubt that, taken together, such requirements arguably give rise to the development of a distinctly supranational form of arbitration that serves the prerequisites of the EU constitutional order and the establishment of the internal market. It is to be hoped that, going forward, the increasing familiarity of international conglomerates with the advantages of EU competition arbitration and the usefulness of arbitration as a monitoring tool in Article 9 commitment decisions and EU conditional merger clearance decisions will further encourage the future use of arbitration in this field.

---

[219] See in particular PJ Slot, 'Arbitrating Competition-Law-Related Issues under Articles 3(1)(b) TFEU, 4(3) TEU and 106 TFEU' in G Blanke and P Landolt (eds), *EU and US Antitrust Arbitration: A Handbook for Practitioners* (Kluwer Law International 2011) 1017.

[220] PJ Slot, 'Arbitrating Competition-Law-Related Issues under Articles 3(1)(b) TFEU, 4(3) TEU and 106 TFEU' in G Blanke and P Landolt (eds), *EU and US Antitrust Arbitration: A Handbook for Practitioners* (Kluwer Law International 2011) 1017, para 29-003.

[221] Para 29.70 et seq.

[222] PJ Slot, 'Arbitrating Competition-Law-Related Issues under Articles 3(1)(b) TFEU, 4(3) TEU and 106 TFEU' in G Blanke and P Landolt (eds), *EU and US Antitrust Arbitration: A Handbook for Practitioners* (Kluwer Law International 2011) 1017, para 29-087.

INDEX